The RV Rating Book
Best of Used Motor Homes

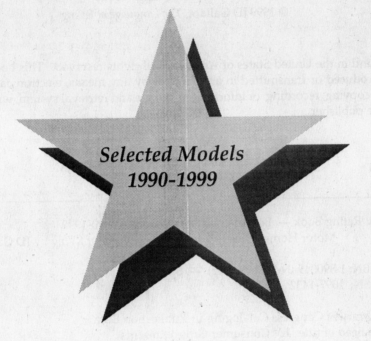

Selected Models
1990-1999

with

Motor Homes Glossary from *The Language of RVing*

by JD Gallant

RV Consumer Group
Quilcene, Washington 98376
U.S.A.

The RV Rating Book
Best of Used Motor Homes
Selected Models 1990-1999

RV Consumer Group
PO Box 520 • Quilcene, WA 98376   U.S.A.

The RV Rating Book — Best of Used Motor Homes 1990-1999
Motor Homes Glossary from *The Language of RVing* by JD Gallant.

ISBN: 1-890049-09-3 (softcover) — Special Edition
ISSN: 1097-1432

Library of Congress Cataloging-in-Publication Data:
At head of title: RV Consumer Group presents
1. Recreational vehicles—Purchasing. 2. Recreational vehicles—Dictionaries.
I. Gallant, JD   II. RV Consumer Group.
TL298.R87 1999
629.226'029'6-DC20

NOTICE

Printed in the United States of America

Acknowledgements

I wish to thank the staff and members of RV Consumer Group for gathering and researching the voluminous data required to bring you this special edition covering ten years of the best rated used motor homes.

As always, I am especially grateful to my wife Connie Gallant, editor and chief administrator of RV Consumer Group, for handling the daily activities with the staff, the membership, and all publications, to allow me the time to focus on special research projects.

JD Gallant

Table of Contents

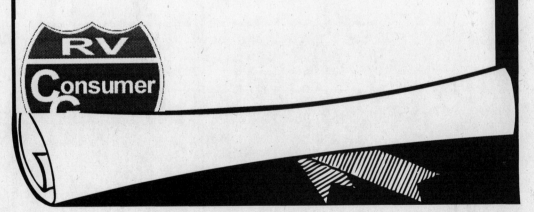

About...

RV Consumer Group is a nonprofit organization. Our primary objective is to promote RV safety through our ratings, publications, and website. Our financial support comes from membership dues, book sales, tax deductible contributions, and grants. We are not aligned or affiliated with the RV industry.

RV Consumer Group
PO Box 520
Quilcene, WA 98376 U.S.A.

360-765-3846
email: rvgroup@rv.org
Website address: www.rv.org

About...
JD Gallant

Through seminars, workshops, and books, JD Gallant has guided thousands of RVers on the right path to selecting and purchasing their RVs with safety first in mind.

As an advocate of RV consumer programs, he continues to raise the awareness level of both the RV consumer and the RV manufacturers. He is slowly, but surely, making a difference in an industry prone to ignoring the safety and quality of vehicles built to carry families on America's highways.

JD has been an RV enthusiast and RV trekker for over 30 years. Besides loving the fun and adventures of RVing, he has actively worked as a technical writer, teacher, auto and RV salesperson, and RV technical advisor for many years. JD is president of RV Consumer Group. He currently serves as vice chair of the Factory Assembled Structures Advisory Board as appointed by Governor Gary Locke of Washington State.

JD's other consumer books include:

The Green Book—RVs Rated
The Language of RVing
How to Buy an RV Without Getting Ripped Off
How to Outwit Any Auto, Truck, or RV Dealer Every Time — A Guide
    to Auto and RV Buying.

He resides in the state of Washington where he continues to be an advocate of RV consumer programs emphasizing safety.

The RV Rating Book
Best of Used
Motor Homes
1990-1999

This book is designed to help you buy a good, used motor home. Because it spans 10 years, it has been limited to those brands that have received a good or better rating in durability without substantial questions relating to structural integrity. The data has been accumulated over a decade and has been constantly updated as new information became available. The information is unique because it compares RV brands and gives detailed ratings on each model. It reflects the results of data collection and input, used RV appraisals, and user satisfaction polls. It is as complete as we can present it in this format. You will find more details on our website at *www.rv.org*.

This book is designed as a guide - not an exact science. Because it is maintained by a staff of specially-trained technicians, I have confidence that it will lead you to motor homes that will reduce your risk of financial loss, structural failure, and travel-related accidents. For these reasons, you should always take this book with you when you go RV shopping.

This book presents ratings for thousands of motor home models based on computerized, standard formulas. These formulas are not new to the RV industry. To the contrary, all the formulas are based on general standards used by major RV manufacturers since 1970 but never formally standardized. In the interest of RV consumerism, *The RV Rating Book* is formalizing these standards.

A very special notice: Some **brands** are not in this book. About 50% of the brands you will be looking at will not be listed here. You might even be shocked to find that many brands you may have considered quality motor homes are not included. When we designed this edition, we realized that we had to give our readers the most complete information we had available within the limits of 500 pages. We had to be without bias and coldhearted — but we are also human. We have a conscience. We determined at the offset that we would not list any brand that we would not recommend to our relatives and friends. If a brand, for any reason, was not on our list of brands worth considering, we would not list them here.

You will find some **models** of acceptable brands listed without even one star. You might even ask why we should list models that we do not recommend. The "best of used" is a list of those brands that have received good ratings in durability — not in highway safety. Some of our supporters do not agree with our assessment of what constitutes highway safety. Some think that our parameters are too strict. Some think that our highway control factors should not apply to them because they are safe drivers and the chances of them getting in an accident are extremely rare. Therefore, those brands listed in this book must have a good rating based upon satisfaction polls, staff appraisals of used motor homes, and the evaluation of new motor homes. Structural integrity is included in the durability rating whenever the results of an accident tell us that a specific brand may not be built well enough to protect the occupants during a rollover or frontal impact at 30 miles per hour. Below, I explain why some brands were excluded.

I personally accept the responsibility of excluding any brand that has questions of structural integrity, inconsistent quality of design, or any other build characteristic that relates to highway safety. Although the staff generally concurs with my decision, in the end it was my decision to do so based upon the information available to me — and when close to the line, gut feeling. Following are some of my reasonings for these exclusions.

Fleetwood, the world's largest RV manufacturer, has been a major concern for me. When I first started writing about RV manufacturers in the early nineties, I was very positive about Fleetwood. I thought they were doing a good job at building middle-quality RVs. The engineering was generally good and customer satisfaction appeared to be in the good to very good range. I still think I was pretty much right on about their durability in general. However, when we formed RV Consumer Group, we started collecting information that went beyond satisfaction polls and general appraisals. By the mid-nineties we were specialists at collecting hard facts about structural integrity and overall highway safety. My eyes were beginning to open. I could see things that were once hidden. Owner comments about handling and accident reports began giving me enough information to change my opinion about Fleetwood. From the limited amount of information I have at this time, I believe that Southwind, Pace Arrow,

Bounder, Flair and some other Fleetwood class-A brands are not structurally sound enough to withstand a reasonable rollover or a frontal impact at 30 miles-per-hour without the structure disintegrating. We have not collected enough information on the Discovery and American series to justify my considering those brands as unsound. Because the Pace Arrow Vision is being built at the same plant as the Discovery and the American Series, I will also include that brand in this book.

Gulf Stream is another major manufacturer that I think is very inconsistent in building RVs. Sometimes the quality appears good, but too often the quality of workmanship is substandard. Gulf Stream brands consistently have satisfaction polls all over the board with an average generally in the fair range. Appraisals and evaluations are about the same. This keeps the durability ratings out of the good range and out of this book.

Damon's biggest problem has been quality control. Customer satisfaction and dealer satisfaction have been too low to even consider their brands. Damon could have a good future in the RV arena if the management gets quality under control. Having worked in that area, I know it can be done. Not one of the Damon brands have received high enough ratings to be included in this book.

Some Thor brands are included in this book while others are not. As an investment company, Thor has a different way of looking at RV manufacturing. It is primarily concerned with the profit margin at plant level. This philosophy has developed sufficiently to allow each plant some latitude for controlling quality and design. As a result, you might find a Thor brand with ratings in the good range while another brand may be barely acceptable.

Coachmen is not doing well overall. The satisfaction polls and appraisals are telling me that some of the Coachmen brands are not even acceptable. The workmanship on the Santara brand, for example, has been so bad that RV Consumer Group uses that brand as a training test for our volunteer appraisers. I am not satisfied with Coachmen's engineering skills. All in all, I do not recommend this brand unless you accept the risk of about a 50% chance of developing some very frustrating failures.

Although you'll find most brands of Winnebago, National, Rexhall, Tiffin, Georgie Boy, Triple E, and some other motor home manufacturers in this book, you'll need to watch the durability ratings and compare them carefully with the other ratings of the same brand. If you're an RV Consumer Group member, you'll want to visit the member library and read the comments about the brand in which you are interested. There will be some instructions in Section 1 of this book on how to evaluate, and even extrapolate, enough information to arrive at an acceptable highway-safety determination.

Even with so many brands excluded, there are still over 5,000 models listed that have good durability ratings. There are over 2,000 listed with three or more stars. This means that if you are careful with your analysis of the ratings, the chance of getting a good one will be much higher than by guessing. If you decide to ignore some of the safety ratings, that will be your choice. However, I don't recommend that you do so.

Thank you for purchasing this book and supporting our efforts to help you select a good motor home. I hope you join us at RV Consumer Group and other RVers in being an advocate of good RV consumer information. If you decide you want more information on brands listed or not listed here, I invite you to visit our website at www.rv.org and look at the membership benefits offered by our nonprofit organization.

JD Gallant

DISCLAIMER

All rating data is based upon manufacturers' specifications when they are available. We use Gross Vehicle Weight Ratings, Wheelbase, and Unloaded Vehicle Weight or Gross Dry Weight as primary data. Gross Dry Weight is considered as the total vehicle weight with standard equipment only and all tanks empty. Unloaded Vehicle Weight is defined as being weighed with all factory-installed equipment plus a full tank of fuel. If weights are not available, we will estimate it from brands of similar build and size. Average Curb Weight and Payload are computer-generated based upon full fuel tanks and fresh water tanks plus average option weights based upon size, type, and use classification of the RV.

Although we attempt to make the results as accurate as possible, RV Consumer Group, its members, and staff do not assume any responsibility for any damages due to the use of this information. All deliberations for purchase and use should be made with this as a consideration. We reserve the right to estimate any specifications or make adjustments to data that we consider inaccurate. We also reserve the right to adjust our calculating formula as we deem necessary and without notice.

Motor Home Types

Class A — built on a stripped chassis.

Class B — built on a van chassis.

Class C — built on a cutaway chassis.

How to use this book

There are techniques, and even "secret" techniques, for buying a used motor home. Because the industry — especially the dealerships — would like to keep you ignorant, you'll have to dig deep and be smart to become skilled enough to buy right. You'll find, however, that being smart has its drawbacks. Smart RV consumers wouldn't even consider most of the motor homes on the average sales lot. You'll reject many motor homes for safety reasons; and when you learn to look closely for flaws, you will probably find few that will pass your initial inspection. It's the inspection that takes skill. If you are interested in developing skills for used motor home inspection, you should visit www.basecamps.org to see what our Base Camps Rangers are doing to put together a pictorial walk-around and walk-through for RV buyers. You really need to see lots of pictures to understand what to look for. Between learning to make a good inspection and having this book, you should greatly reduce the risk when buying a used motor home.

We tried to make this book as concise, precise, and clear as possible without losing valuable information. There isn't enough room to give you everything we have, but I think the staff of RV Consumer Group has done a good job at an almost impossible task. Let's begin with various columns and headings which are listed in the same order as the table columns in Section 2. They will help you navigate and understand the abbreviations and information provided in the tables.

Brand — The brand name is usually the largest identifying mark on the RV. Sometimes it is the same as the manufacturer's name. The brand usually refers to a complete line of similarly built RVs in varying lengths and floor plans. Some brands have a series of models that vary slightly from the primary brand. We usually list this series after the brand name. Sometimes, however, we list the series in the model column. In this book, brands are listed in alphabetical order. (See Brand Directory, Section 4.)

It is important for you to realize that even generally well-built brands can have models with an unacceptable highway safety rating or a lower-than-average value rating. Many factors are involved in these ratings.

Type — The type is shown by letter designation. MHA is for class A motor homes which are built on a stripped chassis; MHB is for modified vans or class B motor homes; MHC is for class C (often called mini) motor homes which are built on a cutaway chassis. For more details, see Section 3 under each type.

Length — Length is listed by feet. Motor homes are measured from bumper to bumper. Unfortunately, many manufacturers do not show accurate overall lengths in their brochures. From the information given, our computer will round off the measurement to the nearest foot.

Model — Models are designated by manufacturers with numbers, names, or a combination of each. Lowercase letters after models are our additions showing changes during the model year or slideout additions to the model. For example, when you see the lowercase designation of "opsl" after a model name or number, this is our addition for a model with an optional slideout room; "myc" stands for midyear change; and "opch" stands for optional chassis. When you see these lowercase designations, you might also notice a difference in weight factors — which sometimes adversely affects the highway safety rating of models. Optional chassis, optional slideouts, and midyear changes can often be considered as cautionary flags to the buyer. For example, an RV should never be built that allows for an optional slideout because optional slideouts change the weight and balance factors dramatically. They should be engineered into each model. These types of modifications often reveal poor engineering techniques on the part of the manufacturer.

Chassis — The two upper case letters following motor home model designation indicate the chassis manufacturer: CH=Chevrolet, FO=Ford, OS=Oshkosh, SP=Spartan, FR=Freightliner, RO=Roadmaster, DY=DynoMax, MA=Magnum, GI=Gillig, WO=Workhorse, etc. After the chassis designations, you will see engine size and fuel type.

Engine — This designation is taken from manufacturers' brochures. You might find some inconsistency at times because each manufacturer has different ideas on how to list the engine displacement or horsepower. Many times optional engines are available, so you need to be sure whether the engine has been downgraded or upgraded from the standard engine.

Fuel Type — At this time, there are two fuel types available in motor homes: diesel and gas. We show these with the designations "D" or "G." There have been some brands using diesel engines as a standard or optional front engine (puller). Don't automatically assume that class A's with diesel engines are pushers.

Average Price Per Linear Foot — This is a quick reference guide to help you determine what the average price of the brand sold for when it was new. Although this is not meant to be a guide for buying used, as a quick reference it can give you a general idea of the market price at specific ages. For example, we know that the average motor home depreciates about 40% of the fair-market value during the first five years then about 5% for each year to 10 years. After 10 years, depreciation depends pretty much on condition. Because our computer looks at the average price of all models of the brand, in some cases the price may vary quite a bit. Use this number strictly as a quick reference budget guide. As a negotiating guide, you should use my book, *How to Buy an RV Without Getting Ripped Off.*

Adjusted Wheelbase — It is very important that you understand how to measure wheelbase and the safety issues relating to wheelbase and wheelbase-to-length ratio. In Section 3 there is good information on wheelbase and wheelbase-to-length ratio. Study it closely. If you know approximately what length you are looking for in a motor home, make notes of the various lengths with minimum wheelbases you will require. A few minutes here might save your life.

The adjusted wheelbase takes into consideration adjustments for tag axles. Our computer automatically adds a maximum of 24 inches to the standard wheelbase whenever a manufacturer indicates that a model has a tag axle. Manufacturers often add as much as 48 inches to the wheelbase for tag axles. We do not consider measurement to the center of the tag axle as being a good basis for increasing effective wheelbase — although it may add somewhat to the payload carrying capacity of the chassis.

Even though a tag axle may increase the highway safety rating, we do not recommend tag axles for off-highway use because multiple axles resist the turning of the vehicle. This condition may be dangerous on gravel or slippery road surfaces. We prefer a better chassis rather than the addition of a tag axle. However, with the advent of large slideout rooms, tag axles can be effective at reducing front axle overload while maintaining a good wheelbase-to-length ratio. The addition of slideout rooms to motor homes has brought a sensitive balancing act to the RV arena.

The wheelbase-to-length ratio, as shown on the second line, is the ratio of the length of the wheelbase (measured from the center of the front axle to the center of the rear axle) to the length of the motor home. We consider 54 percent as a minimum wheelbase-to-length ratio for safe highway travel. The categories for wheelbase-to-length ratio are as follows:

❏ below 50% is considered dangerous at any speed on any road.

❏ 50%-53% is considered fatiguing to drive because it will probably not maintain a straight and steady course under normal highway driving conditions with side winds or heavy truck traffic. Wheelbases in this category are not forgiving to adverse highway or driving conditions.

❑ 54%-57% is considered generally good when the motor home is well balanced. For reasons noted below, these are the percentages that most motor home engineers should work with to acquire optimum balance and highway control.

❑ 58% and above is excellent. Any wheelbase in this category should maintain a straight and steady course under most adverse driving conditions. Long wheelbases, however, have a tendency to overload the front axle with front engine motor homes or the addition of slideout rooms. Although long wheelbases are very effective at keeping the vehicle under control, engineers should never compromise by overloading front axles to acquire long wheelbases. Because we have an almost impossible task of trying to collect front axle curb weights, we must leave it up to you to determine if there is a compromise. Check out www.basecamps.org for weighing techniques.

Wheelbase-to-length ratio is discussed extensively in RV Consumer Group's Letters Library at www.rv.org. This information is available to RVCG members. Also read the Glossary in Section 3.

Approximate Towing Capacity: The towing capacity is the maximum amount of weight a motor home can efficiently pull on a mountain grade of 5 to 8 percent. The towing capacity is generally established by the chassis manufacturer and is indicated through a gross combined weight rating (GCWR). This is determined by such factors as engine, transmission, and rear axle ratio. The tow capacity is the amount of trailer or dinghy weight your motor home should be able to pull without taking an excessive beating. Our database determines the tow capacity by subtracting the gross vehicle weight rating (GVWR) from the GCWR.

If the GCWR is not listed in the brochures or if the manufacturer does not respond to our requests for data, our computer automatically defaults to a 1500 pound tow capacity. However, if the GCWR is not shown in the brochures, you should always consider the towing capacity of the motor home to be no more than the GVWR — which means you should not pull any vehicle until the GCWR is verified. See Section 3 for a complete definition of these terms.

Average Curb Weight: The curb weight is the amount the motor home should weigh when ready to take on a trip before people and personal supplies are loaded. Curb weight includes a full tank of engine fuel, propane, full fresh water tanks, batteries, and optional equipment added to the RV by the manufacturer and dealer. It is important to understand, however, that it all begins with the dry weight of the vehicle with standard equipment or the unloaded vehicle weight (UVW) as provided by the manufacturer. If these weight figures are not available from the manufacturer, our computer will calculate the curb weight based upon RV type, chassis, size, and use classification as matched with similar motor homes. If there is any question about weight or payload, you should weigh the RV to be sure the curb weight allows for sufficient payload. (Note: If you find the curb weight shown in a brochure, it will probably not mean the same as defined here. Some manufacturers define curb weight as dry weight plus fuel.)

When you weigh the motor home, be sure you weigh the front and rear axles separately. If you don't think you know how to do this, go to www.basecamps.org and see if the Base Camps Rangers have finished their production of a guide about weighing RVs. This pictorial guide will help you determine if there are any danger signs relating to weight in the motor home you are getting ready to purchase.

Approximate Net Payload Pounds: The net payload pounds is the GVWR less the curb weight. Problems show up in this area because some manufacturers are using too light a chassis or are weighing their RVs inaccurately. If you question the personal payload (net payload) rating as shown in this book, you should weigh the RV completely empty of persons, personal equipment, and supplies, but include the total amount of liquids in the fuel and fresh water tanks. Then send us the weight ticket with the GVWR and a list of the added options. You will receive a free analysis based on your weights.

If you find a discrepancy between the manufacturer's payload figures and our figures, it's probably because most manufacturers do not compute water, propane, auxiliary fuel, and average dealer installed options into their numbers. Their net-carrying-capacity (NCC) is usually computed from a dry weight plus engine fuel and factory installed optional equipment instead of a wet weight that includes full fuel, fresh water, and all optional equipment. There is little consistency among manufacturers in getting the right figures to the consumer.

Some RV manufacturers justify leaving specifications out of brochures by saying that they are showing UVW inside of the RV itself. They will say that somewhere in a closet or cabinet is a label that shows the weight of the RV with standard and optional equipment plus fuel. Generally, this label does not show the true wet or curb weight. Because weight labeling is a voluntary program established by the Recreational Vehicle Industry Association (RVIA), a dues-paying association within the industry, I can't imagine uninformed consumers getting what they need from this program.

Because some RV manufacturers are hiding true weight figures, we have decided to build an estimating program into our database. This estimating program is used when weight figures are missing from manufacturers' brochures or considered inaccurate by our technicians. You must keep in mind that estimated weight calculations are based on the top of a scale of average weights of similar RV types. If we eliminated the estimating — as manufacturers want us to do — we would be forcing the consumer to call the manufacturer for weight figures. Although our estimated figures are generally close enough to be a guide, we ask every buyer to weigh the RV before purchase.

You should also realize that too much payload may give the RV a "stiff" ride which will affect the durability of the RV and cause fatigue on both driver and passengers. For this reason excessive payload depreciates the highway safety rating. Our optimums for payload are 20 percent of the GVWR for motor homes. RV manufacturers should be able to design RVs with payloads within 5 percent of these optimums. A minimum net payload should be 10% of the GVWR. This doesn't allow enough for serious RVing, but it will work for some uses with careful loading. Below 5% we consider deficient. You always need at least 5% left over as a tolerance (or forgiveness) factor. It's never safe to drive a vehicle of any type to its maximum capacity, or "on the axles".

There is a very special problem with motor home payload. This problem is serious because overloading a motor home chassis is dangerous to the driver and passengers and to others on the road. There have been many accidents with motor homes because of inadequate braking or loss of control. Many manufacturers are trying hard to hide their responsibility for chassis inadequacies related to wheelbase and payload carrying capacity. They know they are collectively responsible for thousands of accidents, yet they do not have the will to correct this situation. I am adamant that many RV accidents are caused by deficiencies in the design of the RV.

RV Consumer Group takes chassis inadequacies seriously. We want every model of every brand to have complete specifications with a listed dry weight in the brochures. The process is simple: The manufacturer weighs the first built of each model with standard equipment, then they publish this weight and the weight of each option in their brochure. They can also show an average unloaded vehicle weight for each model. With this information — which should be in the brochure — any consumer armed with a calculator can figure the personal payload of any model after they have added desired options and liquids. When a specific model is considered, the informed buyer can check the numbers from the brochure with the weight figures in the cabinet of the motor home. Any discrepancy can be resolved with a trip to the local weigh station. To us, this would be doing it the right way.

The question has come up regarding payloads for motor homes with GVWRs ranging from 36,000 to 48,000 pounds. Should they not have a different scale for payload-to-capacity percentages? You might think that a payload of 8,000 pounds would be excessive for a motor home weighing 32,000 pounds with a 40,000 pound GVWR (20% optimum). Consider that a motor home with 40,000 pounds GVWR would normally have an unloaded vehicle weight (UVW) of 32,000 pounds. Because the stopping distance is gauged by the GVWR, every pound added to payload increases the stopping distance. We know these 40,000 GVWR motor homes should stop easily when weighing 32,000 pounds. They are designed to stop well at a total weight of 36,000 pounds. We can only hope that they will stop at their maximum GVWR of 40,000 pounds within a safe distance on a 7 percent downgrade in an emergency situation even after there has been some wear on the brakes. However, if you think a 40,000-pound GVWR motor home that has an actual weight of 40,000 pounds will stop easily at 60 miles per hour on a 7 percent downgrade, you need to think about it a bit longer. I believe that a motor home with a 40,000-pound GVWR should not weigh over 32,000 pounds unloaded at the curb. Thus, for this motor home, an 8,000-pound net payload would not be excessive because at least 5% of the GVWR (4,000 pounds) should be left in reserve as a safety tolerance against malfunction or normal wear. RV manufacturers will undoubtedly disagree.

Livability Code: The livability code should help you determine whether the size, construction features, and interior equipment will satisfy your needs for temperature control and homelike qualities. This designation is determined by the quality of the standard equipment and features as shown in the brochure — not the optional equipment and features. As an example, roof venting to satisfy live-in qualities requires that serious venting fans have been included as standard equipment in every model of a brand. Good roof venting, quality countertops, home-quality shower stalls, and hardwood cabinet doors are all examples of interior equipment required for our fulltiming classification. For a complete list of live-in features for motor homes, check the *basecamps.org* website.

The two letters preceding the numbers will indicate the use classification as follows:

WE stands for weekending. A weekending RV is considered good for short, camping-type stays. Weekending RVs are class B motor homes and other small RVs not adequate for longer stays because living amenities are limited. These RVs generally work best in temperatures ranging from 40-80 degrees Fahrenheit (5-25 degrees Celsius).

VA stands for vacationing. The vacationing classification is reserved for RVs generally designed for stays from 2 days to 2 weeks at a time for up to a total of 60 days a year. A motor home designed for this purpose may have vinyl wrapped cabinet doors and cabinet framing. It does not require a backsplash or endcaps on the galley (kitchen) counter. It should have a good combination of slider and torque windows to allow plenty of air circulation while keeping out blowing rain. Even though a vacationing motor home does not need a full wraparound shower stall, it should have a good shower and solid tub.

There is a wide range in the quality of vacation-class motor homes. Some come very close to satisfying snowbirding or fulltiming requirements while others appear as if they won't make it through the first year. Vacation-class motor homes are generally comfortable for the occupants in temperatures from 30-90 degrees Fahrenheit (0-30 degrees Celsius).

RT stands for RV trekking — or getting in where most people fear to go. If you want an RV that will take a beating on the back roads and as a camp home, you will want to look at the RT classifications. An RV trekking motor home will have a tough exterior, a heavy-duty chassis, and a well built interior. Because RV trekkers generally keep their RVs for decades, it is important that such vehicles have well designed houses made with high-quality materials and consistently good workmanship. We look at RV trekking motor homes as being close to the quality of fulltiming motor homes but smaller in size.

An RV trekking motor home should have an efficient heating system and stove-top pilot controls. It should have natural wood in all the cabinetry. Any vinyl wrapping must be of the highest quality. It must have good windows and roof venting. The shower stall must be close to live-in quality. The floor must be built of high quality material and protected from water spills or plumbing leaks. The roof should be covered with good fiberglass or thick EPDM rubber. Although segmented or special aluminum for a roof covering may be acceptable, one-piece thin aluminum is not. An RV trekking motor home must have a heavy-duty chassis. Because RV trekking motor homes are often used by adventurers who travel to places with extreme temperatures, they should have insulation and temperature control equipment to satisfy temperatures from below freezing to Death Valley hot. With all this said about RV trekking, we have a tough time finding motor home brands that satisfy this use classification.

SB stands for snowbirding. RVs for snowbirds are designed for live-in situations up to 6 months a year in temperatures from 30-90 degrees Fahrenheit (0-30 degrees Celsius). Snowbird use is primarily determined, however, by the design of the interior. If our analysis shows that a motor home has an interior designed with standard equipment to sustain live-in use for 6 months a year without substantial deterioration, it will receive a snowbirding classification.

FT stands for fulltiming. Fulltiming RVs must have the interior designed for live-in use on a full-time basis. We consider things like good galley design, proper environment controls, well built baths, good bathroom venting, good appliances, and quality upholstery and furniture as standard for the brand. Optional equipment does not count. A buyer may upgrade a snowbirding RV to a fulltiming RV by choosing optional upgrades. These choices will be discussed extensively in the *www.basecamps.org* website.

The temperature comfort zone of a motor home is important to a fulltimer. If you always go south during the winter and north during the summer, the insulation factors will not be very important. But if you think you would like to spend some time where water turns to ice, you will need to consider insulation, wall structure, window size, interior venting, heating equipment, cooling equipment, and window venting. See Section 3 for more explanation about fulltiming.

Highway Safety Penalties: These penalties are given to brands that we consider to have design deficiencies relating to RV safety. Below is a list of items and the year that we have initiated, or will initiate, the penalty program for those items.

- ❏ chassis problems — 1998
- ❏ too short of a wheelbase — 1998
- ❏ payload capacity below acceptable limits — 1998
- ❏ reputation or suspicion that the house structure is not capable of sustaining a rollover — 1999
- ❏ cabinets without positive latches — 1999
- ❏ slideout rooms that do not lock into the wall — 2000
- ❏ slideout room appliances, furniture, cabinets, and other appendages not sufficiently attached to slideout walls — 2000
- ❏ overhead television in cockpit — especially over the occupants — 2000
- ❏ furniture that is not fastened to floor or wall — 2000
- ❏ the absence of low-speed collision protection — 2000

The penalty number represents the total number of points for deficiencies found in all categories that are deducted from the highway safety rating.

We get many requests for listing staff penalties on each model. The extra line it would take would add another 100 pages to this book. Although we are planning on some sort of a coded system in the near future, our computer programmers did not get it together quickly enough for this edition.

We list the deficiencies on the computer as soon as they are discovered. With hundreds of brands and never enough workers or funds, we are always behind where we would like to be. For this reason, we think you should be cognizant of any item listed as a potential safety hazard. We are compiling images for a publication on the *www.basecamps.org* website to guide our researchers through the process of analyzing for highway safety. You may wish to visit the website to look for this and other publications relating to safe RV travel.

Value Rating: The value rating is based on a 1 to 100 scale. Our computer looks at the many factors that influence value in the long haul. As an example, vacation-class RVs tend to deteriorate faster when they exceed 26 feet in length and slower when the RV is shorter than 26 feet. Another factor is depreciation. A depreciation factor is figured by calculating data of each brand from appraisal books commonly used in the RV industry. Length and depreciation are, however, only two of many factors that our computer uses to determine a value rating.

Durability Rating: The durability rating is based on a 1 to 100 scale. It is computer-generated from appraisals of used vehicles, evaluations of new models, and an analysis of owner satisfaction polls. In essence, the durability rating represents the percentage of the brand that will reach 10 years of age without serious problems or deterioration. When our appraisers go into the field, they primarily look for RVs that are between 5 and 10 years old to get an idea of how the brand is holding together overall. The appraisers use checklists that allow for easy data entry, and camcorders to record problem areas. For instance, a water stain on the ceiling indicates a problem. Water stains in 30 percent of a specific brand's model will indicate serious problems with design or build techniques. This system helps minimize the opinion factor. Used RV appraisals, evaluations of new models, and input from letters, claims, and commentaries from owners determine 50 percent of the durability rating, while the result of owner satisfaction polls determine the other 50 percent. To be included in this book, a brand must have a durability rating of at least 70.

Highway Control Rating: The highway control rating is based on a 1 to 100 scale that gives a representation of the ability of the motor home to cling to the highway and be controlled by the driver — especially under adverse road and accident avoidance conditions. Specifically, this is the rating of the RV's ability to respond to your commands. Wheelbase and payload are primary factors for motor homes.

If we discover that a specific model shows a propensity for poor balance caused by the location of holding tanks, large storage areas, or slideout rooms, we will make certain data adjustments to that particular model. Such adjustments, however, often require the cooperation of the RV manufacturer — which is not always easy to obtain. We are always hoping for more verified data from RVCG members who weigh the motor home before they buy it.

If the basic information needed is not available in the brochures and specifications, we will send a fax to the manufacturer requesting the information. The information returned from the manufacturer is scrutinized closer than the data given in published brochures or specification sheets. Through our notices and bulletins to manufacturers, we attempt to impress the importance of giving correct information.

Another major problem is that manufacturers often change the specifications after initial production of new models and brochures. For example, manufacturers introduce their new models during July. By October or November, a manufacturer may have made some changes which differ greatly from their initial production. This, of course, upsets the apple cart. If we get this new information, we enter it as a midyear change, indicated by "myc" in the model field. If we do not get the change but the dealer does, you might think that our information is inaccurate and accept the dealer's data as accurate. The danger here is that the manufacturer has produced some models with earlier specifications — which you may not want. To double-check specifications, use a 50-foot measuring tape to determine the motor home length and wheelbase. Finding the ID tag to get the GVWR is always a smart thing to do when buying a new or used motor home. After that, all you have to do is weigh the motor home at front and rear axles to complete the specifications required for good analysis.

Highway Safety Rating: This rating is the same as the highway control rating minus highway safety penalties. Thus, you may wish to disregard these penalties and base your decisions on the ability of the motor home to be controlled by the driver. To ignore the highway safety rating, however, means you are likewise ignoring the possibility of a collision or rollover accident.

Star Award: This 5-star designation is another quick reference feature of *The RV Rating Book*. One to five stars are awarded to those models that have achieved across-the-board ratings of 50 or higher, using the lowest of the ratings as the basis for the star awards. The higher the overall ratings, the more stars are awarded. However, you should never use stars by themselves for the selection process. They should be used in conjunction with the four primary ratings of value, durability, highway control, and highway safety. The stars are meant to be a quick-reference visual guide. Generally, the stars indicate the following:

★ Star — You should expect overall performance to be "barely acceptable" for a motor home with a 1-star rating. If you like a floor plan in a model with a 1-star rating, you should be very careful that you study the individual ratings so that you understand the risks involved in potential financial losses, frustration from excessive problems, or personal safety of yourself and your passengers. Scale for 1 star: 50-59.

★★ Stars — Overall performance is "fair" with any model that has only 2 stars. Unfortunately, there are too many models in this range. If the model has a high value and durability rating but the highway control and highway safety ratings are below 70, you might want to study the numbers closely to see if there has been any change in the wheelbase or GVWR as shown. Scale for 2 stars: 60-69.

★★★ Stars — A 3-star rating indicates a "good" record of overall performance. However, there might be some weaknesses that will be indicated by the individual ratings. Be careful when studying the numbers themselves because a 3-star rating has a wide range between 70 and 79 on our number scale. A 70 is close to a 2-star rating and a 79 is close to a 4-star rating. This should make a difference in your choice. Scale for 3 stars: 70-79.

★★★★ Stars — A 4-star rating means the brand overall has no serious complaints registered with us through owner satisfaction polls, our used-appraisal program, or new model evaluations. We consider 4-stars as "very good" overall for performance in value, durability, and safety. This year we are very conservative in awarding 4-star ratings. We hope that in the near future we will be able to give at least 10 percent of all RV models a 4-star rating. Scale for 4 stars: 80-89.

★★★★★ Stars — To get a 5-star rating a brand needs to have an exemplary record of performance in value, durability, and safety that is indicated by all ratings being 90 or higher. Performance will include the manufacturer's willingness to stand behind their product. Any serious problem recorded with us could drop a model or an entire brand from a 5-star rating. This rating has little bearing on price range or use designation. It is based strictly on performance. You will find very few 5-star models in this edition, but by studying the numbers of 3-star and 4-star models, you should be able to get an indication of which models and brands will be climbing the "starcase" towards the greatest award we can give an RV manufacturer. Let's hope that someday we will have at least 5 percent of all models in the 5-star range. Scale for 5 stars: 90-100.

Although the stars make an excellent guide, again I must stress that you need to study the ratings carefully and double-check the specifications as listed in the book. Manufacturers may send us incorrect specifications or make a change that we did not catch, and there is always a possibility of an inputting error. There is about a 3% chance that the wheelbase or GVWR as shown in the book will not be exactly the same as on the motor home. Be especially careful to check these two items.

You can help yourself, us, and RV consumers everywhere by complaining to every manufacturer who does not provide accurate data. Many manufacturers will not respond to consumer requests for information. Some manufacturers will give weight information over the phone to consumers, but this should always be taken with skepticism. Some give their dealers specification sheets that show basic weights, but they are usually incomplete. They will always give a reason for not showing complete weight figures in the brochures, but that reason never holds water with us. Manufacturers who do not provide complete and accurately written specifications cannot be trusted with your life. If you find a brand listed that indicates "accurate specs n/a," I recommend you do not place that brand on your list of RVs worth considering until you investigate further. In some cases, you will find these manufacturers hiding information because there is something to hide. To help you locate RV manufacturers, we have included a brand directory in Section 4.

The Ratings

Section 2: The Ratings

Brand	Year	Type	Length	Model	Chassis	Engine	Fuel Type	Average Price per Linear Foot When New	Adjusted Wheel-base	Approx. Towing Capacity	Gross Vehicle Weight Rating	Average Curb Weight
Admiral	**1999**	MHA	30	29W	FO	6.8L	G	$2300	190	5,000	18,000	14,600

Livability Code: SB 30-90   Wheelbase-to-length ratio of 53% is considered ○ dangerous ◉ fatiguing ○ good ○ excellent *

The approximate net payload of 3400 pounds at 19% of GVWR on this model is ○ deficient ○ excessive ○ cautionary ○ good ◉ excellent *

Total highway safety penalties are: 2 *   Value: **7 7**   Durability: **7 0**   Highway Control Rating: **7 7**   Highway Safety: **7 5**   ★★★

| **Admiral** | **1999** | MHA | 33 | 32C | FO | 6.8L | G | $2300 | 208 | 5,000 | 18,000 | 15,356 |

Livability Code: SB 30-90   Wheelbase-to-length ratio of 53% is considered ○ dangerous ◉ fatiguing ○ good ○ excellent *

The approximate net payload of 2644 pounds at 15% of GVWR on this model is ○ deficient ○ excessive ○ cautionary ◉ good ○ excellent *

Total highway safety penalties are: 2 *   Value: **7 7**   Durability: **7 0**   Highway Control Rating: **7 3**   Highway Safety: **7 1**   ★★★

| **Admiral** | **1999** | MHA | 33 | 32S | FO | 6.8L | G | $2300 | 208 | 5,500 | 20,500 | 16,756 |

Livability Code: SB 30-90   Wheelbase-to-length ratio of 53% is considered ○ dangerous ◉ fatiguing ○ good ○ excellent *

The approximate net payload of 3744 pounds at 18% of GVWR on this model is ○ deficient ○ excessive ○ cautionary ○ good ◉ excellent *

Total highway safety penalties are: 12 *   Value: **7 2**   Durability: **7 0**   Highway Control Rating: **7 7**   Highway Safety: **6 5**   ★★

| **Admiral** | **1999** | MHA | 35 | 34F | FO | 6.8L | G | $2300 | 228 | 5,500 | 20,500 | 17,350 |

Livability Code: SB 30-90   Wheelbase-to-length ratio of 54% is considered ○ dangerous ○ fatiguing ◉ good ○ excellent *

The approximate net payload of 3150 pounds at 15% of GVWR on this model is ○ deficient ○ excessive ○ cautionary ◉ good ○ excellent *

Total highway safety penalties are: 12 *   Value: **7 2**   Durability: **7 0**   Highway Control Rating: **8 3**   Highway Safety: **7 1**   ★★★

| **Admiral** | **1999** | MHA | 35 | 34S | FO | 6.8L | G | $2300 | 228 | 5,500 | 20,500 | 17,350 |

Livability Code: SB 30-90   Wheelbase-to-length ratio of 54% is considered ○ dangerous ○ fatiguing ◉ good ○ excellent *

The approximate net payload of 3150 pounds at 15% of GVWR on this model is ○ deficient ○ excessive ○ cautionary ◉ good ○ excellent *

Total highway safety penalties are: 12 *   Value: **7 2**   Durability: **7 0**   Highway Control Rating: **8 3**   Highway Safety: **7 1**   ★★★

| **Admiral** | **1999** | MHA | 37 | 36G | FO | 6.8L | G | $2200 | 228 | 5,500 | 20,500 | 17,782 |

Livability Code: SB 30-90   Wheelbase-to-length ratio of 52% is considered ○ dangerous ◉ fatiguing ○ good ○ excellent *

The approximate net payload of 2718 pounds at 13% of GVWR on this model is ○ deficient ○ excessive ○ cautionary ◉ good ○ excellent *

Total highway safety penalties are: 12 *   Value: **7 2**   Durability: **7 0**   Highway Control Rating: **6 1**   Highway Safety: **4 9**

| **Adventurer** | **1992** | MHA | 32 | 32 RQ | CH | 7.4L | G | $1700 | 208 | 4,000 | 16,000 | 13,280 |

Livability Code: SB 30-90   Wheelbase-to-length ratio of 54% is considered ○ dangerous ○ fatiguing ◉ good ○ excellent *

The approximate net payload of 2720 pounds at 17% of GVWR on this model is ○ deficient ○ excessive ○ cautionary ○ good ◉ excellent *

Total highway safety penalties are: 6 *   Value: **8 3**   Durability: **7 8**   Highway Control Rating: **8 3**   Highway Safety: **7 7**   ★★★

| **Adventurer** | **1992** | MHA | 32 | 32 RQ | FO | 7.5L | G | $1700 | 208 | 8,000 | 17,000 | 13,780 |

Livability Code: SB 30-90   Wheelbase-to-length ratio of 54% is considered ○ dangerous ○ fatiguing ◉ good ○ excellent *

The approximate net payload of 3220 pounds at 19% of GVWR on this model is ○ deficient ○ excessive ○ cautionary ○ good ◉ excellent *

Total highway safety penalties are: 2 *   Value: **8 5**   Durability: **7 8**   Highway Control Rating: **8 5**   Highway Safety: **8 3**   ★★★

| **Adventurer** | **1992** | MHA | 34 | 34RQ | CH | 7.4L | G | $1700 | 228 | 4,000 | 16,000 | 13,760 |

Livability Code: SB 30-90   Wheelbase-to-length ratio of 56% is considered ○ dangerous ○ fatiguing ◉ good ○ excellent *

The approximate net payload of 2240 pounds at 14% of GVWR on this model is ○ deficient ○ excessive ○ cautionary ◉ good ○ excellent *

Total highway safety penalties are: 7 *   Value: **8 3**   Durability: **7 8**   Highway Control Rating: **9 2**   Highway Safety: **8 5**   ★★★

| **Adventurer** | **1992** | MHA | 34 | 34RA | CH | 7.4L | G | $1700 | 228 | 4,000 | 16,000 | 13,760 |

Livability Code: SB 30-90   Wheelbase-to-length ratio of 56% is considered ○ dangerous ○ fatiguing ◉ good ○ excellent *

The approximate net payload of 2240 pounds at 14% of GVWR on this model is ○ deficient ○ excessive ○ cautionary ◉ good ○ excellent *

Total highway safety penalties are: 7 *   Value: **8 3**   Durability: **7 8**   Highway Control Rating: **9 2**   Highway Safety: **8 5**   ★★★

| **Adventurer** | **1992** | MHA | 34 | 34RQ | FO | 7.5L | G | $1700 | 228 | 8,000 | 17,000 | 14,260 |

Livability Code: SB 30-90   Wheelbase-to-length ratio of 56% is considered ○ dangerous ○ fatiguing ◉ good ○ excellent *

The approximate net payload of 2740 pounds at 16% of GVWR on this model is ○ deficient ○ excessive ○ cautionary ○ good ◉ excellent *

Total highway safety penalties are: 2 *   Value: **8 5**   Durability: **7 8**   Highway Control Rating: **9 6**   Highway Safety: **9 4**   ★★★

| **Adventurer** | **1992** | MHA | 34 | 34 RA | FO | 7.5L | G | $1700 | 228 | 8,000 | 17,000 | 14,260 |

Livability Code: SB 30-90   Wheelbase-to-length ratio of 56% is considered ○ dangerous ○ fatiguing ◉ good ○ excellent *

The approximate net payload of 2740 pounds at 16% of GVWR on this model is ○ deficient ○ excessive ○ cautionary ○ good ◉ excellent *

Total highway safety penalties are: 2 *   Value: **8 5**   Durability: **7 8**   Highway Control Rating: **9 6**   Highway Safety: **9 4**   ★★★

Note: Safety ratings are based on the assumption that the engineering of the RV has allowed for proper balance by placing fresh, gray, and black holding tanks in a location so as not to change the balance of the RV when the tanks are empty or full. **Always double-check wheelbase, GVWR, and weights at front and rear axles.**

*See Section 1 for details on how conclusions are reached.

Section 2: The Ratings

Brand	Year	Type	Length	Model	Chassis	Engine	Fuel Type	Average Price per Linear Foot When New	Adjusted Wheelbase	Approx. Towing Capacity	Gross Vehicle Weight Rating	Average Curb Weight
Adventurer	1992	MHA	34	34RQ-P	OS	CU190	D	$2500	228	1,500	18,000	14,960

Livability Code: SB 30-90
Wheelbase-to-length ratio of 56% is considered ○ dangerous ○ fatiguing ◉ good ○ excellent *
The approximate net payload of 3040 pounds at 17% of GVWR on this model is ○ deficient ○ excessive ○ cautionary ○ good ◉ excellent *
Total highway safety penalties are: 2 *   Value: 8 5   Durability: 7 8   Highway Control Rating: 9 7   Highway Safety: 9 5   ★★★

Brand	Year	Type	Length	Model	Chassis	Engine	Fuel Type	Average Price per Linear Foot When New	Adjusted Wheelbase	Approx. Towing Capacity	Gross Vehicle Weight Rating	Average Curb Weight
Adventurer	1993	MHA	32	32 RQ	CH	7.4L	G	$1700	208	4,000	16,000	13,280

Livability Code: SB 30-90
Wheelbase-to-length ratio of 54% is considered ○ dangerous ○ fatiguing ◉ good ○ excellent *
The approximate net payload of 2720 pounds at 17% of GVWR on this model is ○ deficient ○ excessive ○ cautionary ○ good ◉ excellent *
Total highway safety penalties are: 6 *   Value: 8 3   Durability: 7 8   Highway Control Rating: 8 3   Highway Safety: 7 7   ★★★

Brand	Year	Type	Length	Model	Chassis	Engine	Fuel Type	Average Price per Linear Foot When New	Adjusted Wheelbase	Approx. Towing Capacity	Gross Vehicle Weight Rating	Average Curb Weight
Adventurer	1993	MHA	32	32 RQ	FO	7.5L	G	$1700	208	8,000	17,000	13,780

Livability Code: SB 30-90
Wheelbase-to-length ratio of 54% is considered ○ dangerous ○ fatiguing ◉ good ○ excellent *
The approximate net payload of 3220 pounds at 19% of GVWR on this model is ○ deficient ○ excessive ○ cautionary ○ good ◉ excellent *
Total highway safety penalties are: 2 *   Value: 8 5   Durability: 7 8   Highway Control Rating: 8 5   Highway Safety: 8 3   ★★★

Brand	Year	Type	Length	Model	Chassis	Engine	Fuel Type	Average Price per Linear Foot When New	Adjusted Wheelbase	Approx. Towing Capacity	Gross Vehicle Weight Rating	Average Curb Weight
Adventurer	1993	MHA	34	34 RQ	CH	7.4L	G	$1700	228	4,000	16,000	13,760

Livability Code: SB 30-90
Wheelbase-to-length ratio of 56% is considered ○ dangerous ○ fatiguing ◉ good ○ excellent *
The approximate net payload of 2240 pounds at 14% of GVWR on this model is ○ deficient ○ excessive ○ cautionary ◉ good ○ excellent *
Total highway safety penalties are: 7 *   Value: 8 3   Durability: 7 8   Highway Control Rating: 9 2   Highway Safety: 8 5   ★★★

Brand	Year	Type	Length	Model	Chassis	Engine	Fuel Type	Average Price per Linear Foot When New	Adjusted Wheelbase	Approx. Towing Capacity	Gross Vehicle Weight Rating	Average Curb Weight
Adventurer	1993	MHA	34	34 RA	CH	7.4L	G	$1700	228	4,000	16,000	13,760

Livability Code: SB 30-90
Wheelbase-to-length ratio of 56% is considered ○ dangerous ○ fatiguing ◉ good ○ excellent *
The approximate net payload of 2240 pounds at 14% of GVWR on this model is ○ deficient ○ excessive ○ cautionary ◉ good ○ excellent *
Total highway safety penalties are: 7 *   Value: 8 3   Durability: 7 8   Highway Control Rating: 9 2   Highway Safety: 8 5   ★★★

Brand	Year	Type	Length	Model	Chassis	Engine	Fuel Type	Average Price per Linear Foot When New	Adjusted Wheelbase	Approx. Towing Capacity	Gross Vehicle Weight Rating	Average Curb Weight
Adventurer	1993	MHA	34	34 RQ	FO	7.5L	G	$1700	228	8,000	17,000	14,260

Livability Code: SB 30-90
Wheelbase-to-length ratio of 56% is considered ○ dangerous ○ fatiguing ◉ good ○ excellent *
The approximate net payload of 2740 pounds at 16% of GVWR on this model is ○ deficient ○ excessive ○ cautionary ○ good ◉ excellent *
Total highway safety penalties are: 2 *   Value: 8 5   Durability: 7 8   Highway Control Rating: 9 6   Highway Safety: 9 4   ★★★

Brand	Year	Type	Length	Model	Chassis	Engine	Fuel Type	Average Price per Linear Foot When New	Adjusted Wheelbase	Approx. Towing Capacity	Gross Vehicle Weight Rating	Average Curb Weight
Adventurer	1993	MHA	34	34 RA	FO	7.5L	G	$1700	228	8,000	17,000	14,260

Livability Code: SB 30-90
Wheelbase-to-length ratio of 56% is considered ○ dangerous ○ fatiguing ◉ good ○ excellent *
The approximate net payload of 2740 pounds at 16% of GVWR on this model is ○ deficient ○ excessive ○ cautionary ○ good ◉ excellent *
Total highway safety penalties are: 2 *   Value: 8 5   Durability: 7 8   Highway Control Rating: 9 6   Highway Safety: 9 4   ★★★

Brand	Year	Type	Length	Model	Chassis	Engine	Fuel Type	Average Price per Linear Foot When New	Adjusted Wheelbase	Approx. Towing Capacity	Gross Vehicle Weight Rating	Average Curb Weight
Adventurer	1993	MHA	34	34 RQ-P	OS	CU190	D	$2500	228	1,500	18,000	14,960

Livability Code: SB 30-90
Wheelbase-to-length ratio of 56% is considered ○ dangerous ○ fatiguing ◉ good ○ excellent *
The approximate net payload of 3040 pounds at 17% of GVWR on this model is ○ deficient ○ excessive ○ cautionary ○ good ◉ excellent *
Total highway safety penalties are: 2 *   Value: 8 5   Durability: 7 8   Highway Control Rating: 9 7   Highway Safety: 9 5   ★★★

Brand	Year	Type	Length	Model	Chassis	Engine	Fuel Type	Average Price per Linear Foot When New	Adjusted Wheelbase	Approx. Towing Capacity	Gross Vehicle Weight Rating	Average Curb Weight
Adventurer	1993	MHA	37	37 RW	CH	7.4L	G	$1700	252 T	1,500	18,000	15,476

Livability Code: SB 30-90
Wheelbase-to-length ratio of 56% is considered ○ dangerous ○ fatiguing ◉ good ○ excellent *
The approximate net payload of 2524 pounds at 14% of GVWR on this model is ○ deficient ○ excessive ○ cautionary ○ good ○ excellent *
Total highway safety penalties are: 11 *   Value: 8 1   Durability: 7 8   Highway Control Rating: 9 3   Highway Safety: 8 2   ★★★

Brand	Year	Type	Length	Model	Chassis	Engine	Fuel Type	Average Price per Linear Foot When New	Adjusted Wheelbase	Approx. Towing Capacity	Gross Vehicle Weight Rating	Average Curb Weight
Adventurer	1993	MHA	37	37 RW	FO	7.5L	G	$1700	252 T	7,000	18,000	15,476

Livability Code: SB 30-90
Wheelbase-to-length ratio of 56% is considered ○ dangerous ○ fatiguing ◉ good ○ excellent *
The approximate net payload of 2524 pounds at 14% of GVWR on this model is ○ deficient ○ excessive ○ cautionary ○ good ○ excellent *
Total highway safety penalties are: 4 *   Value: 8 4   Durability: 7 8   Highway Control Rating: 9 3   Highway Safety: 8 9   ★★★

Brand	Year	Type	Length	Model	Chassis	Engine	Fuel Type	Average Price per Linear Foot When New	Adjusted Wheelbase	Approx. Towing Capacity	Gross Vehicle Weight Rating	Average Curb Weight
Adventurer	1994	MHA	30	29RQ	CH	7.4L	G	$1900	178	4,200	14,800	12,700

Livability Code: SB 30-90
Wheelbase-to-length ratio of 49% is considered ◉ dangerous ○ fatiguing ○ good ○ excellent *
The approximate net payload of 2100 pounds at 14% of GVWR on this model is ○ deficient ○ excessive ○ cautionary ○ good ○ excellent *
Total highway safety penalties are: 5 *   Value: 8 4   Durability: 7 8   Highway Control Rating: 3 9   Highway Safety: 3 4

Brand	Year	Type	Length	Model	Chassis	Engine	Fuel Type	Average Price per Linear Foot When New	Adjusted Wheelbase	Approx. Towing Capacity	Gross Vehicle Weight Rating	Average Curb Weight
Adventurer	1994	MHA	30	29RQ	FO	7.5L	G	$1900	178	3,800	15,200	13,100

Livability Code: SB 30-90
Wheelbase-to-length ratio of 49% is considered ◉ dangerous ○ fatiguing ○ good ○ excellent *
The approximate net payload of 2100 pounds at 14% of GVWR on this model is ○ deficient ○ excessive ○ cautionary ○ good ○ excellent *
Total highway safety penalties are: 2 *   Value: 8 5   Durability: 7 8   Highway Control Rating: 3 9   Highway Safety: 3 7

Note: Safety ratings are based on the assumption that the engineering of the RV has allowed for proper balance by placing fresh, gray, and black holding tanks in a location so as not to change the balance of the RV when the tanks are empty or full. **Always double-check wheelbase, GVWR, and weights at front and rear axles.**

*See Section 1 for details on how conclusions are reached.

Section 2: The Ratings

Brand	Year	Type	Length	Model	Chassis	Engine	Fuel Type	Average Price per Linear Foot When New	Adjusted Wheelbase	Approx. Towing Capacity	Gross Vehicle Weight Rating	Average Curb Weight
Adventurer	1994	MHA	32	32RQ	CH	7.4L	G	$1800	208	3,000	16,000	13,280

Livability Code: SB 30-90
Wheelbase-to-length ratio of 54% is considered ○ dangerous ○ fatiguing ● good ○ excellent *
The approximate net payload of 2720 pounds at 17% of GVWR on this model is ○ deficient ○ excessive ○ cautionary ○ good ● excellent *
Total highway safety penalties are: 6 *   Value: 8 3   Durability: 7 8   Highway Control Rating: 8 3   Highway Safety: 7 7   ★★★

Brand	Year	Type	Length	Model	Chassis	Engine	Fuel Type	Avg Price/Ft	Adj WB	Towing	GVWR	Curb Wt
Adventurer	1994	MHA	32	32RQ	FO	7.5L	G	$1800	208	8,000	17,000	13,780

Livability Code: SB 30-90
Wheelbase-to-length ratio of 54% is considered ○ dangerous ○ fatiguing ● good ○ excellent *
The approximate net payload of 3220 pounds at 19% of GVWR on this model is ○ deficient ○ excessive ○ cautionary ○ good ● excellent *
Total highway safety penalties are: 2 *   Value: 8 5   Durability: 7 8   Highway Control Rating: 8 5   Highway Safety: 8 3   ★★★

Adventurer	1994	MHA	34	34RQ	CH	7.4L	G	$2100	228	5,000	16,000	13,760

Livability Code: SB 30-90
Wheelbase-to-length ratio of 56% is considered ○ dangerous ○ fatiguing ● good ○ excellent *
The approximate net payload of 2240 pounds at 14% of GVWR on this model is ○ deficient ○ excessive ○ cautionary ● good ○ excellent *
Total highway safety penalties are: 7 *   Value: 8 3   Durability: 7 8   Highway Control Rating: 9 2   Highway Safety: 8 5   ★★★

Adventurer	1994	MHA	34	34RA	CH	7.4L	G	$1800	228	3,000	16,000	13,760

Livability Code: SB 30-90
Wheelbase-to-length ratio of 56% is considered ○ dangerous ○ fatiguing ● good ○ excellent *
The approximate net payload of 2240 pounds at 14% of GVWR on this model is ○ deficient ○ excessive ○ cautionary ● good ○ excellent *
Total highway safety penalties are: 7 *   Value: 8 3   Durability: 7 8   Highway Control Rating: 9 2   Highway Safety: 8 5   ★★★

Adventurer	1994	MHA	34	34RQ	FO	7.5L	G	$2100	228	8,000	17,000	14,260

Livability Code: SB 30-90
Wheelbase-to-length ratio of 56% is considered ○ dangerous ○ fatiguing ● good ○ excellent *
The approximate net payload of 2740 pounds at 16% of GVWR on this model is ○ deficient ○ excessive ○ cautionary ○ good ● excellent *
Total highway safety penalties are: 2 *   Value: 8 5   Durability: 7 8   Highway Control Rating: 9 6   Highway Safety: 9 4   ★★★

Adventurer	1994	MHA	34	34RA	FO	7.5L	G	$1800	228	8,000	17,000	14,260

Livability Code: SB 30-90
Wheelbase-to-length ratio of 56% is considered ○ dangerous ○ fatiguing ● good ○ excellent *
The approximate net payload of 2740 pounds at 16% of GVWR on this model is ○ deficient ○ excessive ○ cautionary ○ good ● excellent *
Total highway safety penalties are: 2 *   Value: 8 5   Durability: 7 8   Highway Control Rating: 9 6   Highway Safety: 9 4   ★★★

Adventurer	1994	MHA	34	34RQ-P	OS	CU190	D	$2800	228	5,000	19,840	15,760

Livability Code: SB 30-90
Wheelbase-to-length ratio of 56% is considered ○ dangerous ○ fatiguing ● good ○ excellent *
The approximate net payload of 4080 pounds at 21% of GVWR on this model is ○ deficient ○ excessive ○ cautionary ○ good ● excellent *
Total highway safety penalties are: 2 *   Value: 8 5   Durability: 7 8   Highway Control Rating: 9 9   Highway Safety: 9 7   ★★★

Adventurer	1994	MHA	37	37RW	CH	7.4L	G	$1900	252 T	3,000	18,000	15,476

Livability Code: SB 30-90
Wheelbase-to-length ratio of 56% is considered ○ dangerous ○ fatiguing ● good ○ excellent *
The approximate net payload of 2524 pounds at 14% of GVWR on this model is ○ deficient ○ excessive ○ cautionary ● good ○ excellent *
Total highway safety penalties are: 11 *   Value: 8 1   Durability: 7 8   Highway Control Rating: 9 3   Highway Safety: 8 2   ★★★

Adventurer	1994	MHA	37	37RW	FO	7.5L	G	$1900	252 T	6,000	19,000	15,776

Livability Code: SB 30-90
Wheelbase-to-length ratio of 56% is considered ○ dangerous ○ fatiguing ● good ○ excellent *
The approximate net payload of 3224 pounds at 17% of GVWR on this model is ○ deficient ○ excessive ○ cautionary ● good ○ excellent *
Total highway safety penalties are: 4 *   Value: 8 4   Durability: 7 8   Highway Control Rating: 9 8   Highway Safety: 9 4   ★★★

Adventurer	1995	MHA	30	30WQ	FO	7.5L	G	$2000	178	9,800	15,200	13,550

Livability Code: SB 30-90
Wheelbase-to-length ratio of 49% is considered ● dangerous ○ fatiguing ○ good ○ excellent *
The approximate net payload of 1650 pounds at 11% of GVWR on this model is ○ deficient ○ excessive ○ cautionary ○ good ● excellent *
Total highway safety penalties are: 2 *   Value: 8 5   Durability: 7 8   Highway Control Rating: 3 3   Highway Safety: 3 1

Adventurer	1995	MHA	32	32WQ	CH	7.4L	G	$2100	208	4,500	16,500	13,911

Livability Code: SB 30-90
Wheelbase-to-length ratio of 54% is considered ○ dangerous ○ fatiguing ● good ○ excellent *
The approximate net payload of 2589 pounds at 16% of GVWR on this model is ○ deficient ○ excessive ○ cautionary ○ good ● excellent *
Total highway safety penalties are: 6 *   Value: 8 3   Durability: 7 8   Highway Control Rating: 8 1   Highway Safety: 7 5   ★★★

Adventurer	1995	MHA	32	32WQ	FO	7.5L	G	$2100	208	8,000	17,000	14,311

Livability Code: SB 30-90
Wheelbase-to-length ratio of 54% is considered ○ dangerous ○ fatiguing ● good ○ excellent *
The approximate net payload of 2689 pounds at 16% of GVWR on this model is ○ deficient ○ excessive ○ cautionary ○ good ● excellent *
Total highway safety penalties are: 2 *   Value: 8 5   Durability: 7 8   Highway Control Rating: 8 1   Highway Safety: 7 9   ★★★

Note: Safety ratings are based on the assumption that the engineering of the RV has allowed for proper balance by placing fresh, gray, and black holding tanks in a location so as not to change the balance of the RV when the tanks are empty or full. **Always double-check wheelbase, GVWR, and weights at front and rear axles.**

*See Section 1 for details on how conclusions are reached.

Brand	Year	Type	Length	Model	Chassis	Engine	Fuel Type	Average Price per Linear Foot When New	Adjusted Wheelbase	Approx. Towing Capacity	Gross Vehicle Weight Rating	Average Curb Weight
Adventurer	1995	MHA	34	34WQ	CH	7.4L	G	$2100	228	2,500	16,500	14,421

Livability Code: SB 30-90 — Wheelbase-to-length ratio of 56% is considered ○ dangerous ○ fatiguing ◉ good ○ excellent *
The approximate net payload of 2079 pounds at 13% of GVWR on this model is ○ deficient ○ excessive ○ cautionary ◉ good ○ excellent *
Total highway safety penalties are: 7 * — Value: **8 3** — Durability: **7 8** — Highway Control Rating: **8 8** — Highway Safety: **8 1** — ★★★

Brand	Year	Type	Length	Model	Chassis	Engine	Fuel Type	Average Price per Linear Foot When New	Adjusted Wheelbase	Approx. Towing Capacity	Gross Vehicle Weight Rating	Average Curb Weight
Adventurer	1995	MHA	34	34WA	CH	7.4L	G	$1900	228	2,500	16,500	14,421

Livability Code: SB 30-90 — Wheelbase-to-length ratio of 56% is considered ○ dangerous ○ fatiguing ◉ good ○ excellent *
The approximate net payload of 2079 pounds at 13% of GVWR on this model is ○ deficient ○ excessive ○ cautionary ◉ good ○ excellent *
Total highway safety penalties are: 7 * — Value: **8 3** — Durability: **7 8** — Highway Control Rating: **8 8** — Highway Safety: **8 1** — ★★★

Brand	Year	Type	Length	Model	Chassis	Engine	Fuel Type	Average Price per Linear Foot When New	Adjusted Wheelbase	Approx. Towing Capacity	Gross Vehicle Weight Rating	Average Curb Weight
Adventurer	1995	MHA	34	34WQ	FO	7.5L	G	$2100	228	8,000	17,000	14,821

Livability Code: SB 30-90 — Wheelbase-to-length ratio of 56% is considered ○ dangerous ○ fatiguing ◉ good ○ excellent *
The approximate net payload of 2179 pounds at 13% of GVWR on this model is ○ deficient ○ excessive ○ cautionary ◉ good ○ excellent *
Total highway safety penalties are: 2 * — Value: **8 5** — Durability: **7 8** — Highway Control Rating: **8 8** — Highway Safety: **8 6** — ★★★

Brand	Year	Type	Length	Model	Chassis	Engine	Fuel Type	Average Price per Linear Foot When New	Adjusted Wheelbase	Approx. Towing Capacity	Gross Vehicle Weight Rating	Average Curb Weight
Adventurer	1995	MHA	34	34WA	FO	7.5L	G	$1900	228	8,000	17,000	14,821

Livability Code: SB 30-90 — Wheelbase-to-length ratio of 56% is considered ○ dangerous ○ fatiguing ◉ good ○ excellent *
The approximate net payload of 2179 pounds at 13% of GVWR on this model is ○ deficient ○ excessive ○ cautionary ◉ good ○ excellent *
Total highway safety penalties are: 2 * — Value: **8 5** — Durability: **7 8** — Highway Control Rating: **8 8** — Highway Safety: **8 6** — ★★★

Brand	Year	Type	Length	Model	Chassis	Engine	Fuel Type	Average Price per Linear Foot When New	Adjusted Wheelbase	Approx. Towing Capacity	Gross Vehicle Weight Rating	Average Curb Weight
Adventurer	1995	MHA	34	34WQ-P	OS	CU230	D	$3000	228	1,500	19,840	16,321

Livability Code: SB 30-90 — Wheelbase-to-length ratio of 56% is considered ○ dangerous ○ fatiguing ◉ good ○ excellent *
The approximate net payload of 3519 pounds at 18% of GVWR on this model is ○ deficient ○ excessive ○ cautionary ○ good ◉ excellent *
Total highway safety penalties are: 2 * — Value: **8 5** — Durability: **7 8** — Highway Control Rating: **9 6** — Highway Safety: **9 4** — ★★★

Brand	Year	Type	Length	Model	Chassis	Engine	Fuel Type	Average Price per Linear Foot When New	Adjusted Wheelbase	Approx. Towing Capacity	Gross Vehicle Weight Rating	Average Curb Weight
Adventurer	1996	MHA	30	30WQ	CH	7.4L	G	$2000	178	4,200	14,800	13,201

Livability Code: SB 30-90 — Wheelbase-to-length ratio of 49% is considered ◉ dangerous ○ fatiguing ○ good ○ excellent *
The approximate net payload of 1599 pounds at 11% of GVWR on this model is ○ deficient ○ excessive ○ cautionary ◉ good ○ excellent *
Total highway safety penalties are: 5 * — Value: **8 4** — Durability: **7 8** — Highway Control Rating: **3 1** — Highway Safety: **2 6**

Brand	Year	Type	Length	Model	Chassis	Engine	Fuel Type	Average Price per Linear Foot When New	Adjusted Wheelbase	Approx. Towing Capacity	Gross Vehicle Weight Rating	Average Curb Weight
Adventurer	1996	MHA	30	30WQ	CH	GM6.5	D	$2100	178	4,200	14,800	13,201

Livability Code: SB 30-90 — Wheelbase-to-length ratio of 49% is considered ◉ dangerous ○ fatiguing ○ good ○ excellent *
The approximate net payload of 1599 pounds at 11% of GVWR on this model is ○ deficient ○ excessive ○ cautionary ◉ good ○ excellent *
Total highway safety penalties are: 5 * — Value: **8 4** — Durability: **7 8** — Highway Control Rating: **3 1** — Highway Safety: **2 6**

Brand	Year	Type	Length	Model	Chassis	Engine	Fuel Type	Average Price per Linear Foot When New	Adjusted Wheelbase	Approx. Towing Capacity	Gross Vehicle Weight Rating	Average Curb Weight
Adventurer	1996	MHA	30	30WQ	FO	7.5L	G	$2000	178	9,800	15,200	13,601

Livability Code: SB 30-90 — Wheelbase-to-length ratio of 49% is considered ◉ dangerous ○ fatiguing ○ good ○ excellent *
The approximate net payload of 1599 pounds at 11% of GVWR on this model is ○ deficient ○ excessive ○ cautionary ◉ good ○ excellent *
Total highway safety penalties are: 2 * — Value: **8 5** — Durability: **7 8** — Highway Control Rating: **3 1** — Highway Safety: **2 9**

Brand	Year	Type	Length	Model	Chassis	Engine	Fuel Type	Average Price per Linear Foot When New	Adjusted Wheelbase	Approx. Towing Capacity	Gross Vehicle Weight Rating	Average Curb Weight
Adventurer	1996	MHA	32	32WQ	CH	7.4L	G	$1900	208	4,500	16,500	13,937

Livability Code: SB 30-90 — Wheelbase-to-length ratio of 54% is considered ○ dangerous ○ fatiguing ◉ good ○ excellent *
The approximate net payload of 2564 pounds at 16% of GVWR on this model is ○ deficient ○ excessive ○ cautionary ○ good ◉ excellent *
Total highway safety penalties are: 6 * — Value: **8 3** — Durability: **7 8** — Highway Control Rating: **8 0** — Highway Safety: **7 4** — ★★★

Brand	Year	Type	Length	Model	Chassis	Engine	Fuel Type	Average Price per Linear Foot When New	Adjusted Wheelbase	Approx. Towing Capacity	Gross Vehicle Weight Rating	Average Curb Weight
Adventurer	1996	MHA	32	32WQ	FO	7.5L	G	$1900	208	8,000	17,000	14,337

Livability Code: SB 30-90 — Wheelbase-to-length ratio of 54% is considered ○ dangerous ○ fatiguing ◉ good ○ excellent *
The approximate net payload of 2664 pounds at 16% of GVWR on this model is ○ deficient ○ excessive ○ cautionary ○ good ◉ excellent *
Total highway safety penalties are: 2 * — Value: **8 5** — Durability: **7 8** — Highway Control Rating: **8 0** — Highway Safety: **7 8** — ★★★

Brand	Year	Type	Length	Model	Chassis	Engine	Fuel Type	Average Price per Linear Foot When New	Adjusted Wheelbase	Approx. Towing Capacity	Gross Vehicle Weight Rating	Average Curb Weight
Adventurer	1996	MHA	34	34WQ	CH	7.4L	G	$2100	228	2,500	16,500	14,447

Livability Code: SB 30-90 — Wheelbase-to-length ratio of 55% is considered ○ dangerous ○ fatiguing ◉ good ○ excellent *
The approximate net payload of 2054 pounds at 12% of GVWR on this model is ○ deficient ○ excessive ○ cautionary ◉ good ○ excellent *
Total highway safety penalties are: 7 * — Value: **8 3** — Durability: **7 8** — Highway Control Rating: **8 6** — Highway Safety: **7 9** — ★★★

Brand	Year	Type	Length	Model	Chassis	Engine	Fuel Type	Average Price per Linear Foot When New	Adjusted Wheelbase	Approx. Towing Capacity	Gross Vehicle Weight Rating	Average Curb Weight
Adventurer	1996	MHA	34	34WK	CH	7.4L	G	$1900	228	4,500	16,500	14,447

Livability Code: SB 30-90 — Wheelbase-to-length ratio of 55% is considered ○ dangerous ○ fatiguing ◉ good ○ excellent *
The approximate net payload of 2054 pounds at 12% of GVWR on this model is ○ deficient ○ excessive ○ cautionary ◉ good ○ excellent *
Total highway safety penalties are: 7 * — Value: **8 3** — Durability: **7 8** — Highway Control Rating: **8 6** — Highway Safety: **7 9** — ★★★

Note: Safety ratings are based on the assumption that the engineering of the RV has allowed for proper balance by placing fresh, gray, and black holding tanks in a location so as not to change the balance of the RV when the tanks are empty or full. **Always double-check wheelbase, GVWR, and weights at front and rear axles.**

*See Section 1 for details on how conclusions are reached.

Brand	Year	Type	Length	Model	Chassis	Engine	Fuel Type	Average Price per Linear Foot When New	Adjusted Wheelbase	Approx. Towing Capacity	Gross Vehicle Weight Rating	Average Curb Weight
Adventurer	1996	MHA	34	34WA	CH	7.4L	G	$1900	228	2,500	16,500	14,447

Livability Code: SB 30-90
Wheelbase-to-length ratio of 55% is considered ○ dangerous ○ fatiguing ◉ good ○ excellent *
The approximate net payload of 2054 pounds at 12% of GVWR on this model is ○ deficient ○ excessive ○ cautionary ◉ good ○ excellent *
Total highway safety penalties are: 7 *   Value: 8 3   Durability: 7 8   Highway Control Rating: 8 6   Highway Safety: 7 9   ★★★

Brand	Year	Type	Length	Model	Chassis	Engine	Fuel Type		Adjusted Wheelbase	Approx. Towing Capacity	Gross Vehicle Weight Rating	Average Curb Weight
Adventurer	1996	MHA	34	34RQ	CH	7.4L	G	$2100	228	4,500	16,500	14,907

Livability Code: SB 30-90
Wheelbase-to-length ratio of 55% is considered ○ dangerous ○ fatiguing ◉ good ○ excellent *
The approximate net payload of 1593 pounds at 10% of GVWR on this model is ○ deficient ○ excessive ○ cautionary ◉ good ○ excellent *
Total highway safety penalties are: 13 *   Value: 8 0   Durability: 7 8   Highway Control Rating: 8 8   Highway Safety: 7 5   ★★★

Adventurer	1996	MHA	34	34WQ	FO	7.5L	G	$2100	228	8,000	17,000	14,847

Livability Code: SB 30-90
Wheelbase-to-length ratio of 55% is considered ○ dangerous ○ fatiguing ◉ good ○ excellent *
The approximate net payload of 2154 pounds at 13% of GVWR on this model is ○ deficient ○ excessive ○ cautionary ◉ good ○ excellent *
Total highway safety penalties are: 2 *   Value: 8 5   Durability: 7 8   Highway Control Rating: 8 8   Highway Safety: 8 6   ★★★

Adventurer	1996	MHA	34	34WK	FO	7.5L	G	$1900	228	8,000	17,000	14,847

Livability Code: SB 30-90
Wheelbase-to-length ratio of 55% is considered ○ dangerous ○ fatiguing ◉ good ○ excellent *
The approximate net payload of 2154 pounds at 13% of GVWR on this model is ○ deficient ○ excessive ○ cautionary ◉ good ○ excellent *
Total highway safety penalties are: 2 *   Value: 8 5   Durability: 7 8   Highway Control Rating: 8 8   Highway Safety: 8 6   ★★★

Adventurer	1996	MHA	34	34WA	FO	7.5L	G	$1900	228	8,000	17,000	14,847

Livability Code: SB 30-90
Wheelbase-to-length ratio of 55% is considered ○ dangerous ○ fatiguing ◉ good ○ excellent *
The approximate net payload of 2154 pounds at 13% of GVWR on this model is ○ deficient ○ excessive ○ cautionary ◉ good ○ excellent *
Total highway safety penalties are: 2 *   Value: 8 5   Durability: 7 8   Highway Control Rating: 8 8   Highway Safety: 8 6   ★★★

Adventurer	1996	MHA	34	34RQ	FO	7.5L	G	$2100	228	8,000	17,000	15,307

Livability Code: SB 30-90
Wheelbase-to-length ratio of 55% is considered ○ dangerous ○ fatiguing ◉ good ○ excellent *
The approximate net payload of 1693 pounds at 10% of GVWR on this model is ○ deficient ○ excessive ○ cautionary ◉ good ○ excellent *
Total highway safety penalties are: 8 *   Value: 8 2   Durability: 7 8   Highway Control Rating: 8 8   Highway Safety: 8 0   ★★★

Adventurer	1996	MHA	34	34WQ-P	FR	CU230	D	$2800	228	5,160	19,840	16,447

Livability Code: SB 30-90
Wheelbase-to-length ratio of 55% is considered ○ dangerous ○ fatiguing ◉ good ○ excellent *
The approximate net payload of 3394 pounds at 17% of GVWR on this model is ○ deficient ○ excessive ○ cautionary ○ good ◉ excellent *
Total highway safety penalties are: 2 *   Value: 8 5   Durability: 7 8   Highway Control Rating: 9 5   Highway Safety: 9 3   ★★★

Adventurer	1996	MHA	34	34WK-P	FR	CU230	D	$2800	228	5,160	19,840	16,447

Livability Code: SB 30-90
Wheelbase-to-length ratio of 55% is considered ○ dangerous ○ fatiguing ◉ good ○ excellent *
The approximate net payload of 3394 pounds at 17% of GVWR on this model is ○ deficient ○ excessive ○ cautionary ○ good ◉ excellent *
Total highway safety penalties are: 2 *   Value: 8 5   Durability: 7 8   Highway Control Rating: 9 5   Highway Safety: 9 3   ★★★

Adventurer	1996	MHA	34	34RQ-P	FR	CU230	D	$3000	228	4,160	19,840	16,907

Livability Code: SB 30-90
Wheelbase-to-length ratio of 55% is considered ○ dangerous ○ fatiguing ◉ good ○ excellent *
The approximate net payload of 2933 pounds at 15% of GVWR on this model is ○ deficient ○ excessive ○ cautionary ◉ good ○ excellent *
Total highway safety penalties are: 8 *   Value: 8 2   Durability: 7 8   Highway Control Rating: 9 2   Highway Safety: 8 4   ★★★

Adventurer	1996	MHA	37	37RW	FO	7.5L	G	$2100	252 T	5,000	20,000	16,735

Livability Code: SB 30-90
Wheelbase-to-length ratio of 58% is considered ○ dangerous ○ fatiguing ○ good ◉ excellent *
The approximate net payload of 3265 pounds at 16% of GVWR on this model is ○ deficient ○ excessive ○ cautionary ○ good ◉ excellent *
Total highway safety penalties are: 10 *   Value: 8 1   Durability: 7 8   Highway Control Rating: 1 0 0   Highway Safety: 9 0   ★★★

Adventurer	1996	MHA	37	36WQ-P	FR	CU230	D	$2700	252	5,160	19,840	17,008

Livability Code: SB 30-90
Wheelbase-to-length ratio of 58% is considered ○ dangerous ○ fatiguing ○ good ◉ excellent *
The approximate net payload of 2833 pounds at 14% of GVWR on this model is ○ deficient ○ excessive ○ cautionary ◉ good ○ excellent *
Total highway safety penalties are: 2 *   Value: 8 5   Durability: 7 8   Highway Control Rating: 9 8   Highway Safety: 9 6   ★★★

Adventurer	1997	MHA	30	30WQ	CH	7.4L	G	$2100	178	4,200	14,800	13,084

Livability Code: SB 30-90
Wheelbase-to-length ratio of 49% is considered ◉ dangerous ○ fatiguing ○ good ○ excellent *
The approximate net payload of 1716 pounds at 12% of GVWR on this model is ○ deficient · ○ excessive ○ cautionary ◉ good ○ excellent *
Total highway safety penalties are: 5 *   Value: 8 4   Durability: 7 8   Highway Control Rating: 3 3   Highway Safety: 2 8

Note: Safety ratings are based on the assumption that the engineering of the RV has allowed for proper balance by placing fresh, gray, and black holding tanks in a location so as not to change the balance of the RV when the tanks are empty or full. **Always double-check wheelbase, GVWR, and weights at front and rear axles.**

*See Section 1 for details on how conclusions are reached.

Section 2: The Ratings

Brand	Year	Type	Length	Model	Chassis	Engine	Fuel Type	Average Price per Linear Foot When New	Adjusted Wheelbase	Approx. Towing Capacity	Gross Vehicle Weight Rating	Average Curb Weight
Adventurer	1997	MHA	30	30WQ	FO	7.5L	G	$2100	178	9,800	15,200	13,511

Livability Code: SB 30-90 Wheelbase-to-length ratio of 49% is considered ◉ dangerous ○ fatiguing ○ good ○ excellent*
The approximate net payload of 1689 pounds at 11% of GVWR on this model is ○ deficient ○ excessive ○ cautionary ◉ good ○ excellent*
Total highway safety penalties are: 2*   Value: 85   Durability: 78   Highway Control Rating: 32   Highway Safety: 30

Brand	Year	Type	Length	Model	Chassis	Engine	Fuel Type	Avg Price/Lin Ft	Adj Wheelbase	Towing	GVWR	Avg Curb Wt
Adventurer	1997	MHA	32	32WQ	CH	7.4L	G	$2000	208	3,500	16,500	13,554

Livability Code: SB 30-90 Wheelbase-to-length ratio of 54% is considered ○ dangerous ○ fatiguing ◉ good ○ excellent*
The approximate net payload of 2947 pounds at 18% of GVWR on this model is ○ deficient ○ excessive ○ cautionary ○ good ◉ excellent*
Total highway safety penalties are: 6*   Value: 83   Durability: 78   Highway Control Rating: 82   Highway Safety: 76   ★★★

Adventurer	1997	MHA	32	32WQ	FO	7.5L	G	$2000	208	8,000	17,000	14,188

Livability Code: SB 30-90 Wheelbase-to-length ratio of 54% is considered ○ dangerous ○ fatiguing ◉ good ○ excellent*
The approximate net payload of 2812 pounds at 17% of GVWR on this model is ○ deficient ○ excessive ○ cautionary ○ good ◉ excellent*
Total highway safety penalties are: 2*   Value: 85   Durability: 78   Highway Control Rating: 81   Highway Safety: 79   ★★★

Adventurer	1997	MHA	34	34WK	CH	7.4L	G	$2000	228	3,500	16,500	14,081

Livability Code: SB 30-90 Wheelbase-to-length ratio of 55% is considered ○ dangerous ○ fatiguing ◉ good ○ excellent*
The approximate net payload of 2419 pounds at 15% of GVWR on this model is ○ deficient ○ excessive ○ cautionary ◉ good ○ excellent*
Total highway safety penalties are: 7*   Value: 83   Durability: 78   Highway Control Rating: 92   Highway Safety: 85   ★★★

Adventurer	1997	MHA	34	34WA	CH	7.4L	G	$2000	228	3,500	16,500	14,025

Livability Code: SB 30-90 Wheelbase-to-length ratio of 55% is considered ○ dangerous ○ fatiguing ◉ good ○ excellent*
The approximate net payload of 2475 pounds at 15% of GVWR on this model is ○ deficient ○ excessive ○ cautionary ◉ good ○ excellent*
Total highway safety penalties are: 7*   Value: 83   Durability: 78   Highway Control Rating: 92   Highway Safety: 85   ★★★

Adventurer	1997	MHA	34	34RQ	CH	7.4L	G	$2200	216	3,500	16,500	14,874

Livability Code: SB 30-90 Wheelbase-to-length ratio of 52% is considered ○ dangerous ◉ fatiguing ○ good ○ excellent*
The approximate net payload of 1626 pounds at 10% of GVWR on this model is ○ deficient ○ excessive ○ cautionary ◉ good ○ excellent*
Total highway safety penalties are: 13*   Value: 80   Durability: 78   Highway Control Rating: 49   Highway Safety: 36

Adventurer	1997	MHA	34	34DQ	CH	7.4L	G	$2500	216	3,500	16,500	15,624

Livability Code: SB 30-90 Wheelbase-to-length ratio of 52% is considered ○ dangerous ◉ fatiguing ○ good ○ excellent*
The approximate net payload of 876 pounds at 5% of GVWR on this model is ◉ deficient ○ excessive ○ cautionary ○ good ○ excellent*
Total highway safety penalties are: 13*   Value: 80   Durability: 78   Highway Control Rating: 25   Highway Safety: 12

Adventurer	1997	MHA	34	34WK	FO	7.5L	G	$2000	228	8,000	17,000	14,764

Livability Code: SB 30-90 Wheelbase-to-length ratio of 55% is considered ○ dangerous ○ fatiguing ◉ good ○ excellent*
The approximate net payload of 2236 pounds at 13% of GVWR on this model is ○ deficient ○ excessive ○ cautionary ◉ good ○ excellent*
Total highway safety penalties are: 2*   Value: 85   Durability: 78   Highway Control Rating: 88   Highway Safety: 86   ★★★

Adventurer	1997	MHA	34	34WA	FO	7.5L	G	$2000	228	8,000	17,000	14,701

Livability Code: SB 30-90 Wheelbase-to-length ratio of 55% is considered ○ dangerous ○ fatiguing ◉ good ○ excellent*
The approximate net payload of 2299 pounds at 14% of GVWR on this model is ○ deficient ○ excessive ○ cautionary ◉ good ○ excellent*
Total highway safety penalties are: 2*   Value: 85   Durability: 78   Highway Control Rating: 90   Highway Safety: 88   ★★★

Adventurer	1997	MHA	34	34RQ	FO	7.5L	G	$2200	216	8,000	17,000	15,236

Livability Code: SB 30-90 Wheelbase-to-length ratio of 52% is considered ○ dangerous ◉ fatiguing ○ good ○ excellent*
The approximate net payload of 1764 pounds at 10% of GVWR on this model is ○ deficient ○ excessive ○ cautionary ◉ good ○ excellent*
Total highway safety penalties are: 8*   Value: 82   Durability: 78   Highway Control Rating: 49   Highway Safety: 41

Adventurer	1997	MHA	34	34DQ	FO	7.5L	G	$2500	216	8,000	17,000	16,168

Livability Code: SB 30-90 Wheelbase-to-length ratio of 52% is considered ○ dangerous ◉ fatiguing ○ good ○ excellent*
The approximate net payload of 832 pounds at 5% of GVWR on this model is ◉ deficient ○ excessive ○ cautionary ○ good ○ excellent*
Total highway safety penalties are: 8*   Value: 82   Durability: 78   Highway Control Rating: 25   Highway Safety: 17

Adventurer	1997	MHA	34	34WK-P	FR	CU230	D	$3200	228	5,000	20,700	18,689

Livability Code: SB 30-90 Wheelbase-to-length ratio of 55% is considered ○ dangerous ○ fatiguing ◉ good ○ excellent*
The approximate net payload of 2011 pounds at 10% of GVWR on this model is ○ deficient ○ excessive ○ cautionary ◉ good ○ excellent*
Total highway safety penalties are: 8*   Value: 82   Durability: 78   Highway Control Rating: 88   Highway Safety: 80   ★★★

Note: Safety ratings are based on the assumption that the engineering of the RV has allowed for proper balance by placing fresh, gray, and black holding tanks in a location so as not to change the balance of the RV when the tanks are empty or full. **Always double-check wheelbase, GVWR, and weights at front and rear axles.**

*See Section 1 for details on how conclusions are reached.

Section 2: The Ratings

Brand	Year	Type	Length	Model	Chassis	Engine	Fuel Type	Average Price per Linear Foot When New	Adjusted Wheelbase	Approx. Towing Capacity	Gross Vehicle Weight Rating	Average Curb Weight
Adventurer	1997	MHA	36	35WQ	CH	7.4L	G	$2000	228	2,500	16,500	14,880

Livability Code: SB 30-90
Wheelbase-to-length ratio of 53% is considered ○ dangerous ◉ fatiguing ○ good ○ excellent *
The approximate net payload of 1620 pounds at 10% of GVWR on this model is ○ deficient ○ excessive ○ cautionary ◉ good ○ excellent *
Total highway safety penalties are: 8 *　Value: **8 2**　Durability: **7 8**　Highway Control Rating: **5 8**　Highway Safety: **5 0**　★

Brand	Year	Type	Length	Model	Chassis	Engine	Fuel Type	Price/LF	Wheelbase	Towing	GVWR	Curb Wt
Adventurer	1997	MHA	36	35WQ slide	CH	7.4L	G	$2400	228	2,500	16,500	15,405

Livability Code: SB 30-90
Wheelbase-to-length ratio of 53% is considered ○ dangerous ◉ fatiguing ○ good ○ excellent *
The approximate net payload of 1095 pounds at 7% of GVWR on this model is ○ deficient ○ excessive ◉ cautionary ○ good ○ excellent *
Total highway safety penalties are: 11 *　Value: **8 1**　Durability: **7 8**　Highway Control Rating: **4 0**　Highway Safety: **2 9**

Adventurer	1997	MHA	36	35WQ	FO	7.5L	G	$2000	228	8,000	17,000	14,808

Livability Code: SB 30-90
Wheelbase-to-length ratio of 53% is considered ○ dangerous ◉ fatiguing ○ good ○ excellent *
The approximate net payload of 2192 pounds at 13% of GVWR on this model is ○ deficient ○ excessive ○ cautionary ◉ good ○ excellent *
Total highway safety penalties are: 2 *　Value: **8 5**　Durability: **7 8**　Highway Control Rating: **6 4**　Highway Safety: **6 2**　★★

Adventurer	1997	MHA	36	35WQ slide	FO	7.5L	G	$2000	228	8,000	17,000	15,358

Livability Code: SB 30-90
Wheelbase-to-length ratio of 53% is considered ○ dangerous ◉ fatiguing ○ good ○ excellent *
The approximate net payload of 1642 pounds at 10% of GVWR on this model is ○ deficient ○ excessive ○ cautionary ◉ good ○ excellent *
Total highway safety penalties are: 5 *　Value: **8 4**　Durability: **7 8**　Highway Control Rating: **5 7**　Highway Safety: **5 2**　★

Adventurer	1997	MHA	38	37RW	FO	7.5L	G	$2100	252 T	5,000	20,000	17,093

Livability Code: SB 30-90
Wheelbase-to-length ratio of 56% is considered ○ dangerous ○ fatiguing ◉ good ○ excellent *
The approximate net payload of 2907 pounds at 15% of GVWR on this model is ○ deficient ○ excessive ○ cautionary ◉ good ○ excellent *
Total highway safety penalties are: 10 *　Value: **8 1**　Durability: **7 8**　Highway Control Rating: **9 3**　Highway Safety: **8 3**　★★★

Adventurer	1998	MHA	31	30WQ	CH	7.4L	G	$2100	190	4,500	16,500	13,650

Livability Code: SB 30-90
Wheelbase-to-length ratio of 51% is considered ○ dangerous ◉ fatiguing ○ good ○ excellent *
The approximate net payload of 2850 pounds at 17% of GVWR on this model is ○ deficient ○ excessive ○ cautionary ○ good ◉ excellent *
Total highway safety penalties are: 5 *　Value: **8 4**　Durability: **7 8**　Highway Control Rating: **5 0**　Highway Safety: **4 5**

Adventurer	1998	MHA	31	30WQ	FO	7.5L	G	$2100	190	8,000	17,000	14,043

Livability Code: SB 30-90
Wheelbase-to-length ratio of 51% is considered ○ dangerous ◉ fatiguing ○ good ○ excellent *
The approximate net payload of 2957 pounds at 17% of GVWR on this model is ○ deficient ○ excessive ○ cautionary ○ good ◉ excellent *
Total highway safety penalties are: 2 *　Value: **8 5**　Durability: **7 8**　Highway Control Rating: **5 0**　Highway Safety: **4 8**

Adventurer	1998	MHA	31	30WQ myc	FO	6.8L	G	$2000	190	8,000	18,000	14,380

Livability Code: SB 30-90
Wheelbase-to-length ratio of 51% is considered ○ dangerous ◉ fatiguing ○ good ○ excellent *
The approximate net payload of 3621 pounds at 20% of GVWR on this model is ○ deficient ○ excessive ○ cautionary ○ good ◉ excellent *
Total highway safety penalties are: 2 *　Value: **8 5**　Durability: **7 8**　Highway Control Rating: **5 3**　Highway Safety: **5 1**　★

Adventurer	1998	MHA	32	32WQ	CH	7.4L	G	$2100	208	4,500	16,500	13,887

Livability Code: SB 30-90
Wheelbase-to-length ratio of 53% is considered ○ dangerous ◉ fatiguing ○ good ○ excellent *
The approximate net payload of 2613 pounds at 16% of GVWR on this model is ○ deficient ○ excessive ○ cautionary ○ good ◉ excellent *
Total highway safety penalties are: 6 *　Value: **8 3**　Durability: **7 8**　Highway Control Rating: **7 2**　Highway Safety: **6 6**　★★

Adventurer	1998	MHA	32	32WQ	FO	7.5L	G	$2100	208	8,000	17,000	14,289

Livability Code: SB 30-90
Wheelbase-to-length ratio of 53% is considered ○ dangerous ◉ fatiguing ○ good ○ excellent *
The approximate net payload of 2711 pounds at 16% of GVWR on this model is ○ deficient ○ excessive ○ cautionary ○ good ◉ excellent *
Total highway safety penalties are: 2 *　Value: **8 5**　Durability: **7 8**　Highway Control Rating: **7 2**　Highway Safety: **7 0**　★★★

Adventurer	1998	MHA	32	32WQ myc	FO	6.8L	G	$2100	208	8,000	18,000	14,762

Livability Code: SB 30-90
Wheelbase-to-length ratio of 53% is considered ○ dangerous ◉ fatiguing ○ good ○ excellent *
The approximate net payload of 3238 pounds at 18% of GVWR on this model is ○ deficient ○ excessive ○ cautionary ○ good ◉ excellent *
Total highway safety penalties are: 2 *　Value: **8 5**　Durability: **7 8**　Highway Control Rating: **7 4**　Highway Safety: **7 2**　★★★

Adventurer	1998	MHA	34	33WQ	FO	7.5L	G	$2200	216	8,000	17,000	15,324

Livability Code: SB 30-90
Wheelbase-to-length ratio of 54% is considered ○ dangerous ○ fatiguing ◉ good ○ excellent *
The approximate net payload of 1676 pounds at 10% of GVWR on this model is ○ deficient ○ excessive ○ cautionary ◉ good ○ excellent *
Total highway safety penalties are: 12 *　Value: **8 0**　Durability: **7 8**　Highway Control Rating: **7 4**　Highway Safety: **6 2**　★★

Note: Safety ratings are based on the assumption that the engineering of the RV has allowed for proper balance by placing fresh, gray, and black holding tanks in a location so as not to change the balance of the RV when the tanks are empty or full. **Always double-check wheelbase, GVWR, and weights at front and rear axles.**

*See Section 1 for details on how conclusions are reached.

Brand	Year	Type	Length	Model	Chassis	Engine	Fuel Type	Average Price per Linear Foot When New	Adjusted Wheelbase	Approx. Towing Capacity	Gross Vehicle Weight Rating	Average Curb Weight
Adventurer	1998	MHA	34	33WQ myc	FO	6.8L	G	$2100	216	5,500	20,500	16,468

Livability Code: SB 30-90

Wheelbase-to-length ratio of 54% is considered ○ dangerous ○ fatiguing ◉ good ○ excellent *

The approximate net payload of 4032 pounds at 20% of GVWR on this model is ○ deficient ○ excessive ○ cautionary ○ good ◉ excellent *

Total highway safety penalties are: 12 *   Value: **8 0**   Durability: **7 8**   Highway Control Rating: **8 4**   Highway Safety: **7 2**   ★★★

Brand	Year	Type	Length	Model	Chassis	Engine	Fuel Type	Price/Ft	Wheelbase	Towing	GVWR	Curb Wt
Adventurer	1998	MHA	34	34WQ-P	FR	CU230	D	$2900	228	5,000	20,700	18,635

Livability Code: SB 30-90

Wheelbase-to-length ratio of 55% is considered ○ dangerous ○ fatiguing ◉ good ○ excellent *

The approximate net payload of 2065 pounds at 10% of GVWR on this model is ○ deficient ○ excessive ○ cautionary ◉ good ○ excellent *

Total highway safety penalties are: 8 *   Value: **8 2**   Durability: **7 8**   Highway Control Rating: **8 8**   Highway Safety: **8 0**   ★★★

Brand	Year	Type	Length	Model	Chassis	Engine	Fuel Type	Price/Ft	Wheelbase	Towing	GVWR	Curb Wt
Adventurer	1998	MHA	35	34WA	CH	7.4L	G	$2000	228	4,500	16,500	14,309

Livability Code: SB 30-90

Wheelbase-to-length ratio of 54% is considered ○ dangerous ○ fatiguing ◉ good ○ excellent *

The approximate net payload of 2191 pounds at 13% of GVWR on this model is ○ deficient ○ excessive ○ cautionary ◉ good ○ excellent *

Total highway safety penalties are: 7 *   Value: **8 3**   Durability: **7 8**   Highway Control Rating: **8 0**   Highway Safety: **7 3**   ★★★

Brand	Year	Type	Length	Model	Chassis	Engine	Fuel Type	Price/Ft	Wheelbase	Towing	GVWR	Curb Wt
Adventurer	1998	MHA	35	35WP	CH	7.4L	G	$2000	216	4,500	16,500	14,463

Livability Code: SB 30-90

Wheelbase-to-length ratio of 51% is considered ○ dangerous ◉ fatiguing ○ good ○ excellent *

The approximate net payload of 2037 pounds at 12% of GVWR on this model is ○ deficient ○ excessive ○ cautionary ◉ good ○ excellent *

Total highway safety penalties are: 7 *   Value: **8 3**   Durability: **7 8**   Highway Control Rating: **4 2**   Highway Safety: **3 5**

Brand	Year	Type	Length	Model	Chassis	Engine	Fuel Type	Price/Ft	Wheelbase	Towing	GVWR	Curb Wt
Adventurer	1998	MHA	35	34WA opch	FO	7.5L	G	$2000	228	8,000	17,000	14,768

Livability Code: SB 30-90

Wheelbase-to-length ratio of 54% is considered ○ dangerous ○ fatiguing ◉ good ○ excellent *

The approximate net payload of 2232 pounds at 13% of GVWR on this model is ○ deficient ○ excessive ○ cautionary ◉ good ○ excellent *

Total highway safety penalties are: 2 *   Value: **8 5**   Durability: **7 8**   Highway Control Rating: **8 0**   Highway Safety: **7 8**   ★★★

Brand	Year	Type	Length	Model	Chassis	Engine	Fuel Type	Price/Ft	Wheelbase	Towing	GVWR	Curb Wt
Adventurer	1998	MHA	35	35WP opch	FO	7.5L	G	$2000	216	8,000	17,000	14,796

Livability Code: SB 30-90

Wheelbase-to-length ratio of 51% is considered ○ dangerous ◉ fatiguing ○ good ○ excellent *

The approximate net payload of 2204 pounds at 13% of GVWR on this model is ○ deficient ○ excessive ○ cautionary ◉ good ○ excellent *

Total highway safety penalties are: 2 *   Value: **8 5**   Durability: **7 8**   Highway Control Rating: **4 4**   Highway Safety: **4 2**

Brand	Year	Type	Length	Model	Chassis	Engine	Fuel Type	Price/Ft	Wheelbase	Towing	GVWR	Curb Wt
Adventurer	1998	MHA	35	35WP slide	FO	7.5L	G	$2100	216	8,000	17,000	15,386

Livability Code: SB 30-90

Wheelbase-to-length ratio of 51% is considered ○ dangerous ◉ fatiguing ○ good ○ excellent *

The approximate net payload of 1614 pounds at 9% of GVWR on this model is ○ deficient ○ excessive ◉ cautionary ○ good ○ excellent *

Total highway safety penalties are: 8 *   Value: **8 2**   Durability: **7 8**   Highway Control Rating: **3 3**   Highway Safety: **2 5**

Brand	Year	Type	Length	Model	Chassis	Engine	Fuel Type	Price/Ft	Wheelbase	Towing	GVWR	Curb Wt
Adventurer	1998	MHA	35	34WA opch myc	FO	6.8L	G	$2200	228	5,500	20,500	15,925

Livability Code: SB 30-90

Wheelbase-to-length ratio of 54% is considered ○ dangerous ○ fatiguing ◉ good ○ excellent *

The approximate net payload of 4575 pounds at 22% of GVWR on this model is ○ deficient ○ excessive ○ cautionary ○ good ◉ excellent *

Total highway safety penalties are: 2 *   Value: **8 5**   Durability: **7 8**   Highway Control Rating: **8 4**   Highway Safety: **8 2**   ★★★

Brand	Year	Type	Length	Model	Chassis	Engine	Fuel Type	Price/Ft	Wheelbase	Towing	GVWR	Curb Wt
Adventurer	1998	MHA	35	35WP opch myc	FO	6.8L	G	$2000	216	5,500	20,500	15,925

Livability Code: SB 30-90

Wheelbase-to-length ratio of 51% is considered ○ dangerous ◉ fatiguing ○ good ○ excellent *

The approximate net payload of 4575 pounds at 22% of GVWR on this model is ○ deficient ○ excessive ○ cautionary ○ good ◉ excellent *

Total highway safety penalties are: 2 *   Value: **8 5**   Durability: **7 8**   Highway Control Rating: **5 1**   Highway Safety: **4 9**

Brand	Year	Type	Length	Model	Chassis	Engine	Fuel Type	Price/Ft	Wheelbase	Towing	GVWR	Curb Wt
Adventurer	1998	MHA	35	35WP slide myc	FO	6.8L	G	$2100	216	5,500	20,500	16,900

Livability Code: SB 30-90

Wheelbase-to-length ratio of 51% is considered ○ dangerous ◉ fatiguing ○ good ○ excellent *

The approximate net payload of 3600 pounds at 18% of GVWR on this model is ○ deficient ○ excessive ○ cautionary ○ good ◉ excellent *

Total highway safety penalties are: 8 *   Value: **8 2**   Durability: **7 8**   Highway Control Rating: **5 1**   Highway Safety: **4 3**

Brand	Year	Type	Length	Model	Chassis	Engine	Fuel Type	Price/Ft	Wheelbase	Towing	GVWR	Curb Wt
Adventurer	1998	MHA	38	37WW	FO	7.5L	G	$2100	252 T	5,000	20,000	16,988

Livability Code: SB 30-90

Wheelbase-to-length ratio of 56% is considered ○ dangerous ○ fatiguing ◉ good ○ excellent *

The approximate net payload of 3012 pounds at 15% of GVWR on this model is ○ deficient ○ excessive ○ cautionary ◉ good ○ excellent *

Total highway safety penalties are: 10 *   Value: **8 1**   Durability: **7 8**   Highway Control Rating: **9 3**   Highway Safety: **8 3**   ★★★

Brand	Year	Type	Length	Model	Chassis	Engine	Fuel Type	Price/Ft	Wheelbase	Towing	GVWR	Curb Wt
Adventurer	1999	MHA	31	30A	CH	7.4L	G	$2400	190	4,500	16,500	13,945

Livability Code: SB 30-90

Wheelbase-to-length ratio of 51% is considered ○ dangerous ◉ fatiguing ○ good ○ excellent *

The approximate net payload of 2555 pounds at 15% of GVWR on this model is ○ deficient ○ excessive ○ cautionary ◉ good ○ excellent *

Total highway safety penalties are: 5 *   Value: **8 4**   Durability: **7 8**   Highway Control Rating: **5 8**   Highway Safety: **5 3**   ★

Note: Safety ratings are based on the assumption that the engineering of the RV has allowed for proper balance by placing fresh, gray, and black holding tanks in a location so as not to change the balance of the RV when the tanks are empty or full. **Always double-check wheelbase, GVWR, and weights at front and rear axles.**

*See Section 1 for details on how conclusions are reached.

Section 2: The Ratings

Brand	Year	Type	Length	Model	Chassis	Engine	Fuel Type	Average Price per Linear Foot When New	Adjusted Wheelbase	Approx. Towing Capacity	Gross Vehicle Weight Rating	Average Curb Weight
Adventurer	1999	MHA	31	30A	FO	6.8L	G	$2500	190	8,000	18,000	14,741
Adventurer	1999	MHA	32	32T	CH	7.4L	G	$2400	208	4,500	16,500	14,489
Adventurer	1999	MHA	32	32T	FO	6.8L	G	$2500	208	8,000	18,000	15,343
Adventurer	1999	MHA	34	33B	CH	7.4L	G	$2300	216	4,500	16,500	15,561
Adventurer	1999	MHA	34	33B	FO	6.8L	G	$2300	216	5,500	20,500	16,325
Adventurer	1999	MHA	34	34V-P	FR	CU275	D	$3100	228	5,000	23,600	19,350
Adventurer	1999	MHA	35	34H	CH	7.4L	G	$2200	228	4,500	16,500	15,087
Adventurer	1999	MHA	35	35C	CH	7.4L	G	$2200	220	4,500	16,500	15,184
Adventurer	1999	MHA	35	35C slide	CH	7.4L	G	$2200	220	4,500	16,500	15,984
Adventurer	1999	MHA	35	34H	FO	6.8L	G	$2200	228	5,500	20,500	15,861
Adventurer	1999	MHA	35	35C	FO	6.8L	G	$2200	228	5,500	20,500	16,108
Adventurer	1999	MHA	35	35C slide	FO	6.8L	G	$2300	228	5,500	20,500	16,908

Adventurer 1999 MHA 31 30A
Livability Code: SB 30-90
Wheelbase-to-length ratio of 51% is considered ○ dangerous ◉ fatiguing ○ good ○ excellent *
The approximate net payload of 3259 pounds at 18% of GVWR on this model is ○ deficient ○ excessive ○ cautionary ○ good ◉ excellent *
Total highway safety penalties are: 2 *   Value: 85   Durability: 78   Highway Control Rating: 61   Highway Safety: 59   ★

Adventurer 1999 MHA 32 32T (CH)
Livability Code: SB 30-90
Wheelbase-to-length ratio of 53% is considered ○ dangerous ◉ fatiguing ○ good ○ excellent *
The approximate net payload of 2011 pounds at 12% of GVWR on this model is ○ deficient ○ excessive ○ cautionary ◉ good ○ excellent *
Total highway safety penalties are: 6 *   Value: 83   Durability: 78   Highway Control Rating: 69   Highway Safety: 63   ★★

Adventurer 1999 MHA 32 32T (FO)
Livability Code: SB 30-90
Wheelbase-to-length ratio of 53% is considered ○ dangerous ◉ fatiguing ○ good ○ excellent *
The approximate net payload of 2657 pounds at 15% of GVWR on this model is ○ deficient ○ excessive ○ cautionary ◉ good ○ excellent *
Total highway safety penalties are: 2 *   Value: 85   Durability: 78   Highway Control Rating: 75   Highway Safety: 73   ★★★

Adventurer 1999 MHA 34 33B (CH)
Livability Code: SB 30-90
Wheelbase-to-length ratio of 54% is considered ○ dangerous ○ fatiguing ◉ good ○ excellent *
The approximate net payload of 939 pounds at 6% of GVWR on this model is ◉ deficient ○ excessive ○ cautionary ○ good ○ excellent *
Total highway safety penalties are: 17 *   Value: 78   Durability: 78   Highway Control Rating: 47   Highway Safety: 30

Adventurer 1999 MHA 34 33B (FO)
Livability Code: SB 30-90
Wheelbase-to-length ratio of 54% is considered ○ dangerous ○ fatiguing ◉ good ○ excellent *
The approximate net payload of 4175 pounds at 20% of GVWR on this model is ○ deficient ○ excessive ○ cautionary ○ good ◉ excellent *
Total highway safety penalties are: 12 *   Value: 80   Durability: 78   Highway Control Rating: 86   Highway Safety: 74   ★★★

Adventurer 1999 MHA 34 34V-P
Livability Code: SB 30-90
Wheelbase-to-length ratio of 55% is considered ○ dangerous ○ fatiguing ◉ good ○ excellent *
The approximate net payload of 4250 pounds at 18% of GVWR on this model is ○ deficient ○ excessive ○ cautionary ○ good ◉ excellent *
Total highway safety penalties are: 8 *   Value: 82   Durability: 78   Highway Control Rating: 96   Highway Safety: 88   ★★★

Adventurer 1999 MHA 35 34H (CH)
Livability Code: SB 30-90
Wheelbase-to-length ratio of 54% is considered ○ dangerous ○ fatiguing ◉ good ○ excellent *
The approximate net payload of 1413 pounds at 9% of GVWR on this model is ○ deficient ○ excessive ◉ cautionary ○ good ○ excellent *
Total highway safety penalties are: 7 *   Value: 83   Durability: 78   Highway Control Rating: 68   Highway Safety: 61   ★★

Adventurer 1999 MHA 35 35C (CH)
Livability Code: SB 30-90
Wheelbase-to-length ratio of 52% is considered ○ dangerous ◉ fatiguing ○ good ○ excellent *
The approximate net payload of 1316 pounds at 8% of GVWR on this model is ○ deficient ○ excessive ◉ cautionary ○ good ○ excellent *
Total highway safety penalties are: 7 *   Value: 83   Durability: 78   Highway Control Rating: 45   Highway Safety: 38

Adventurer 1999 MHA 35 35C slide (CH)
Livability Code: SB 30-90
Wheelbase-to-length ratio of 52% is considered ○ dangerous ◉ fatiguing ○ good ○ excellent *
The approximate net payload of 516 pounds at 3% of GVWR on this model is ◉ deficient ○ excessive ○ cautionary ○ good ○ excellent *
Total highway safety penalties are: 12 *   Value: 80   Durability: 78   Highway Control Rating: 30   Highway Safety: 18

Adventurer 1999 MHA 35 34H (FO)
Livability Code: SB 30-90
Wheelbase-to-length ratio of 54% is considered ○ dangerous ○ fatiguing ◉ good ○ excellent *
The approximate net payload of 4639 pounds at 23% of GVWR on this model is ○ deficient ○ excessive ○ cautionary ○ good ◉ excellent *
Total highway safety penalties are: 2 *   Value: 85   Durability: 78   Highway Control Rating: 86   Highway Safety: 84   ★★★

Adventurer 1999 MHA 35 35C (FO)
Livability Code: SB 30-90
Wheelbase-to-length ratio of 54% is considered ○ dangerous ○ fatiguing ◉ good ○ excellent *
The approximate net payload of 4392 pounds at 21% of GVWR on this model is ○ deficient ○ excessive ○ cautionary ○ good ◉ excellent *
Total highway safety penalties are: 2 *   Value: 85   Durability: 78   Highway Control Rating: 88   Highway Safety: 86   ★★★

Adventurer 1999 MHA 35 35C slide (FO)
Livability Code: SB 30-90
Wheelbase-to-length ratio of 54% is considered ○ dangerous ○ fatiguing ◉ good ○ excellent *
The approximate net payload of 3592 pounds at 18% of GVWR on this model is ○ deficient ○ excessive ○ cautionary ○ good ◉ excellent *
Total highway safety penalties are: 7 *   Value: 83   Durability: 78   Highway Control Rating: 87   Highway Safety: 80   ★★★

Note: Safety ratings are based on the assumption that the engineering of the RV has allowed for proper balance by placing fresh, gray, and black holding tanks in a location so as not to change the balance of the RV when the tanks are empty or full. **Always double-check wheelbase, GVWR, and weights at front and rear axles.**

*See Section 1 for details on how conclusions are reached.

Brand	Year	Type	Length	Model	Chassis	Engine	Fuel Type	Average Price per Linear Foot When New	Adjusted Wheelbase	Approx. Towing Capacity	Gross Vehicle Weight Rating	Average Curb Weight
Adventurer	**1999**	MHA	38	37G	FO	6.8L	G	$2200	248	5,500	20,500	17,928

Livability Code: SB 30-90 Wheelbase-to-length ratio of 55% is considered ○ dangerous ○ fatiguing ◉ good ○ excellent *

The approximate net payload of 2572 pounds at 13% of GVWR on this model is ○ deficient ○ excessive ○ cautionary ◉ good ○ excellent *

Total highway safety penalties are: 8 * Value: **8 2** Durability: **7 8** Highway Control Rating: **8 5** Highway Safety: **7 7** ★★★

Brand	Year	Type	Length	Model	Chassis	Engine	Fuel Type		Adjusted Wheelbase	Approx. Towing Capacity	Gross Vehicle Weight Rating	Average Curb Weight
Aerbus	**1991**	MHA	27	S526	CH	7.4L	G	$1700	190	2,500	14,500	12,631

Livability Code: SB 30-90 Wheelbase-to-length ratio of 59% is considered ○ dangerous ○ fatiguing ○ good ◉ excellent *

The approximate net payload of 1869 pounds at 13% of GVWR on this model is ○ deficient ○ excessive ○ cautionary ◉ good ○ excellent *

Total highway safety penalties are: 3 * Value: **8 3** Durability: **7 4** Highway Control Rating: **1 0 0** Highway Safety: **9 7** ★★★

Aerbus	**1991**	MHA	27	S526	FO	7.5L	G	$1700	190	8,000	17,000	13,331

Livability Code: SB 30-90 Wheelbase-to-length ratio of 59% is considered ○ dangerous ○ fatiguing ○ good ◉ excellent *

The approximate net payload of 3669 pounds at 22% of GVWR on this model is ○ deficient ○ excessive ○ cautionary ○ good ◉ excellent *

Total highway safety penalties are: 2 * Value: **8 4** Durability: **7 4** Highway Control Rating: **1 0 0** Highway Safety: **9 8** ★★★

Aerbus	**1991**	MHA	28	S527	CH	7.4L	G	$1700	190	2,500	14,500	12,846

Livability Code: SB 30-90 Wheelbase-to-length ratio of 57% is considered ○ dangerous ○ fatiguing ◉ good ○ excellent *

The approximate net payload of 1654 pounds at 11% of GVWR on this model is ○ deficient ○ excessive ○ cautionary ◉ good ○ excellent *

Total highway safety penalties are: 3 * Value: **8 3** Durability: **7 4** Highway Control Rating: **9 1** Highway Safety: **8 8** ★★★

Aerbus	**1991**	MHA	28	S528	CH	7.4L	G	$1700	190	2,500	14,500	12,846

Livability Code: SB 30-90 Wheelbase-to-length ratio of 57% is considered ○ dangerous ○ fatiguing ◉ good ○ excellent *

The approximate net payload of 1654 pounds at 11% of GVWR on this model is ○ deficient ○ excessive ○ cautionary ◉ good ○ excellent *

Total highway safety penalties are: 3 * Value: **8 3** Durability: **7 4** Highway Control Rating: **9 1** Highway Safety: **8 8** ★★★

Aerbus	**1991**	MHA	28	S527	FO	7.5L	G	$1700	190	8,000	17,000	13,546

Livability Code: SB 30-90 Wheelbase-to-length ratio of 57% is considered ○ dangerous ○ fatiguing ◉ good ○ excellent *

The approximate net payload of 3454 pounds at 20% of GVWR on this model is ○ deficient ○ excessive ○ cautionary ○ good ◉ excellent *

Total highway safety penalties are: 2 * Value: **8 4** Durability: **7 4** Highway Control Rating: **1 0 0** Highway Safety: **9 8** ★★★

Aerbus	**1991**	MHA	28	S528	FO	7.5L	G	$1700	190	8,000	17,000	13,546

Livability Code: SB 30-90 Wheelbase-to-length ratio of 57% is considered ○ dangerous ○ fatiguing ◉ good ○ excellent *

The approximate net payload of 3454 pounds at 20% of GVWR on this model is ○ deficient ○ excessive ○ cautionary ○ good ◉ excellent *

Total highway safety penalties are: 2 * Value: **8 4** Durability: **7 4** Highway Control Rating: **1 0 0** Highway Safety: **9 8** ★★★

Aerbus	**1991**	MHA	30	S530	CH	7.4L	G	$1700	208	2,500	14,500	13,491

Livability Code: SB 30-90 Wheelbase-to-length ratio of 58% is considered ○ dangerous ○ fatiguing ○ good ◉ excellent *

The approximate net payload of 1009 pounds at 7% of GVWR on this model is ○ deficient ○ excessive ◉ cautionary ○ good ○ excellent *

Total highway safety penalties are: 5 * Value: **8 2** Durability: **7 4** Highway Control Rating: **7 3** Highway Safety: **6 8** ★★

Aerbus	**1991**	MHA	30	S530	FO	7.5L	G	$1700	208	8,000	17,000	14,191

Livability Code: SB 30-90 Wheelbase-to-length ratio of 58% is considered ○ dangerous ○ fatiguing ○ good ◉ excellent *

The approximate net payload of 2809 pounds at 17% of GVWR on this model is ○ deficient ○ excessive ○ cautionary ○ good ◉ excellent *

Total highway safety penalties are: 2 * Value: **8 4** Durability: **7 4** Highway Control Rating: **1 0 0** Highway Safety: **9 8** ★★★

Aerbus	**1991**	MHA	32	S531	CH	7.4L	G	$1600	208	2,500	14,500	13,867

Livability Code: SB 30-90 Wheelbase-to-length ratio of 55% is considered ○ dangerous ○ fatiguing ◉ good ○ excellent *

The approximate net payload of 633 pounds at 4% of GVWR on this model is ◉ deficient ○ excessive ○ cautionary ○ good ○ excellent *

Total highway safety penalties are: 5 * Value: **8 2** Durability: **7 4** Highway Control Rating: **5 6** Highway Safety: **5 1** ★

Aerbus	**1991**	MHA	32	S531	FO	7.5L	G	$1600	208	8,000	17,000	14,567

Livability Code: SB 30-90 Wheelbase-to-length ratio of 55% is considered ○ dangerous ○ fatiguing ◉ good ○ excellent *

The approximate net payload of 2433 pounds at 14% of GVWR on this model is ○ deficient ○ excessive ○ cautionary ◉ good ○ excellent *

Total highway safety penalties are: 2 * Value: **8 4** Durability: **7 4** Highway Control Rating: **8 9** Highway Safety: **8 7** ★★★

Aerbus	**1991**	MHA	34	S534	FO	7.5L	G	$1700	232 T	8,000	17,000	15,239

Livability Code: SB 30-90 Wheelbase-to-length ratio of 57% is considered ○ dangerous ○ fatiguing ◉ good ○ excellent *

The approximate net payload of 1761 pounds at 10% of GVWR on this model is ○ deficient ○ excessive ○ cautionary ◉ good ○ excellent *

Total highway safety penalties are: 4 * Value: **8 2** Durability: **7 4** Highway Control Rating: **8 8** Highway Safety: **8 4** ★★★

Note: Safety ratings are based on the assumption that the engineering of the RV has allowed for proper balance by placing fresh, gray, and black holding tanks in a location so as not to change the balance of the RV when the tanks are empty or full. **Always double-check wheelbase, GVWR, and weights at front and rear axles.**

*See Section 1 for details on how conclusions are reached.

Brand	Year	Type	Length	Model	Chassis	Engine	Fuel Type	Average Price per Linear Foot When New	Adjusted Wheelbase	Approx. Towing Capacity	Gross Vehicle Weight Rating	Average Curb Weight
Aerbus	1991	MHA	35	S534	CH	7.4L	G	$1600	252 T	1,500	17,500	15,600

Livability Code: SB 30-90
Wheelbase-to-length ratio of 61% is considered ○ dangerous ○ fatiguing ○ good ● excellent *
The approximate net payload of 1900 pounds at 11% of GVWR on this model is ○ deficient ○ excessive ○ cautionary ● good ○ excellent *
Total highway safety penalties are: 9 *   Value: 80   Durability: 74   Highway Control Rating: 100   Highway Safety: 91   ★★★

Brand	Year	Type	Length	Model	Chassis	Engine	Fuel Type	Avg Price/Lin Ft	Adj Wheelbase	Towing Cap	GVWR	Avg Curb Wt
Aerbus	1991	MHA	36	S535	FO	7.5L	G	$1600	232 T	8,000	17,000	15,723

Livability Code: SB 30-90
Wheelbase-to-length ratio of 54% is considered ○ dangerous ○ fatiguing ● good ○ excellent *
The approximate net payload of 1277 pounds at 8% of GVWR on this model is ○ deficient ○ excessive ● cautionary ○ good ○ excellent *
Total highway safety penalties are: 4 *   Value: 82   Durability: 74   Highway Control Rating: 58   Highway Safety: 54   ★

Aerbus	1991	MHA	39	S538	FO	7.5L	G	$1600	252 T	8,000	17,000	16,529

Livability Code: SB 30-90
Wheelbase-to-length ratio of 54% is considered ○ dangerous ○ fatiguing ● good ○ excellent *
The approximate net payload of 471 pounds at 3% of GVWR on this model is ● deficient ○ excessive ○ cautionary ○ good ○ excellent *
Total highway safety penalties are: 4 *   Value: 82   Durability: 74   Highway Control Rating: 44   Highway Safety: 40

Aerbus	1994	MHA	27	S626	CH	7.4L	G	$2200	190	1,500 e	14,800	12,758

Livability Code: SB 30-90
Wheelbase-to-length ratio of 59% is considered ○ dangerous ○ fatiguing ○ good ● excellent *
The approximate net payload of 2042 pounds at 14% of GVWR on this model is ○ deficient ○ excessive ○ cautionary ● good ○ excellent *
Total highway safety penalties are: 3 *   Value: 84   Durability: 77   Highway Control Rating: 100   Highway Safety: 97   ★★★

Aerbus	1994	MHA	27	S626	FO	7.5L	G	$2200	190	1,500 e	15,200	13,158

Livability Code: SB 30-90
Wheelbase-to-length ratio of 59% is considered ○ dangerous ○ fatiguing ○ good ● excellent *
The approximate net payload of 2042 pounds at 13% of GVWR on this model is ○ deficient ○ excessive ○ cautionary ● good ○ excellent *
Total highway safety penalties are: 2 *   Value: 85   Durability: 77   Highway Control Rating: 100   Highway Safety: 98   ★★★

Aerbus	1994	MHA	28	S528	CH	7.4L	G	$2100	190	1,500 e	14,800	12,946

Livability Code: SB 30-90
Wheelbase-to-length ratio of 57% is considered ○ dangerous ○ fatiguing ● good ○ excellent *
The approximate net payload of 1854 pounds at 13% of GVWR on this model is ○ deficient ○ excessive ○ cautionary ● good ○ excellent *
Total highway safety penalties are: 3 *   Value: 84   Durability: 77   Highway Control Rating: 94   Highway Safety: 91   ★★★

Aerbus	1994	MHA	28	S528	FO	7.5L	G	$2100	190	1,500 e	15,200	13,346

Livability Code: SB 30-90
Wheelbase-to-length ratio of 57% is considered ○ dangerous ○ fatiguing ● good ○ excellent *
The approximate net payload of 1854 pounds at 12% of GVWR on this model is ○ deficient ○ excessive ○ cautionary ● good ○ excellent *
Total highway safety penalties are: 2 *   Value: 85   Durability: 77   Highway Control Rating: 93   Highway Safety: 91   ★★★

Aerbus	1994	MHA	29	XL2800	CH	7.4L	G	$2100	190	4,000	16,000	13,904

Livability Code: SB 30-90
Wheelbase-to-length ratio of 55% is considered ○ dangerous ○ fatiguing ○ good ● excellent *
The approximate net payload of 2096 pounds at 13% of GVWR on this model is ○ deficient ○ excessive ○ cautionary ● good ○ excellent *
Total highway safety penalties are: 4 *   Value: 84   Durability: 77   Highway Control Rating: 86   Highway Safety: 82   ★★★

Aerbus	1994	MHA	29	XL2800	FO	7.5L	G	$2100	190	8,000	17,000	14,444

Livability Code: SB 30-90
Wheelbase-to-length ratio of 55% is considered ○ dangerous ○ fatiguing ○ good ● excellent *
The approximate net payload of 2556 pounds at 15% of GVWR on this model is ○ deficient ○ excessive ○ cautionary ● good ○ excellent *
Total highway safety penalties are: 2 *   Value: 85   Durability: 77   Highway Control Rating: 90   Highway Safety: 88   ★★★

Aerbus	1994	MHA	30	S630	CH	7.4L	G	$2000	208	1,500 e	16,000	13,691

Livability Code: SB 30-90
Wheelbase-to-length ratio of 58% is considered ○ dangerous ○ fatiguing ○ good ● excellent *
The approximate net payload of 2309 pounds at 14% of GVWR on this model is ○ deficient ○ excessive ○ cautionary ● good ○ excellent *
Total highway safety penalties are: 5 *   Value: 84   Durability: 77   Highway Control Rating: 98   Highway Safety: 93   ★★★

Aerbus	1994	MHA	30	S630	FO	7.5L	G	$2000	208	1,500 e	17,000	14,191

Livability Code: SB 30-90
Wheelbase-to-length ratio of 58% is considered ○ dangerous ○ fatiguing ○ good ● excellent *
The approximate net payload of 2809 pounds at 17% of GVWR on this model is ○ deficient ○ excessive ○ cautionary ● good ○ excellent *
Total highway safety penalties are: 2 *   Value: 85   Durability: 77   Highway Control Rating: 100   Highway Safety: 98   ★★★

Aerbus	1994	MHA	30	XL2900	CH	7.4L	G	$2000	208	4,000	16,000	14,254

Livability Code: SB 30-90
Wheelbase-to-length ratio of 57% is considered ○ dangerous ○ fatiguing ○ good ● excellent *
The approximate net payload of 1746 pounds at 11% of GVWR on this model is ○ deficient ○ excessive ○ cautionary ● good ○ excellent *
Total highway safety penalties are: 5 *   Value: 83   Durability: 77   Highway Control Rating: 90   Highway Safety: 85   ★★★

Note: Safety ratings are based on the assumption that the engineering of the RV has allowed for proper balance by placing fresh, gray, and black holding tanks in a location so as not to change the balance of the RV when the tanks are empty or full. **Always double-check wheelbase, GVWR, and weights at front and rear axles.**

*See Section 1 for details on how conclusions are reached.

Section 2: The Ratings

Brand	Year	Type	Length	Model	Chassis	Engine	Fuel Type	Average Price per Linear Foot When New	Adjusted Wheelbase	Approx. Towing Capacity	Gross Vehicle Weight Rating	Average Curb Weight
Aerbus	**1994**	MHA	30	S629	CH	7.4L	G	$2000	208	1,500 e	16,000	13,745

Livability Code: SB 30-90   Wheelbase-to-length ratio of 57% is considered ○ dangerous ○ fatiguing ◉ good ○ excellent *

The approximate net payload of 2255 pounds at 14% of GVWR on this model is ○ deficient ○ excessive ○ cautionary ◉ good ○ excellent *

Total highway safety penalties are: 5 *   Value: **83**   Durability: **77**   Highway Control Rating: **97**   Highway Safety: **92**   ★★★

Brand	Year	Type	Length	Model	Chassis	Engine	Fuel Type	Avg Price/Ft	Wheelbase	Towing	GVWR	Curb Weight
Aerbus	**1994**	MHA	30	XL2900	FO	7.5L	G	$2000	208	8,000	17,000	14,796

Livability Code: SB 30-90   Wheelbase-to-length ratio of 57% is considered ○ dangerous ○ fatiguing ◉ good ○ excellent *

The approximate net payload of 2204 pounds at 13% of GVWR on this model is ○ deficient ○ excessive ○ cautionary ◉ good ○ excellent *

Total highway safety penalties are: 2 *   Value: **85**   Durability: **77**   Highway Control Rating: **94**   Highway Safety: **92**   ★★★

Aerbus	**1994**	MHA	30	S629	FO	7.5L	G	$2000	208	1,500 e	17,000	14,245

Livability Code: SB 30-90   Wheelbase-to-length ratio of 57% is considered ○ dangerous ○ fatiguing ◉ good ○ excellent *

The approximate net payload of 2755 pounds at 16% of GVWR on this model is ○ deficient ○ excessive ○ cautionary ○ good ◉ excellent *

Total highway safety penalties are: 2 *   Value: **85**   Durability: **77**   Highway Control Rating: **100**   Highway Safety: **98**   ★★★

Aerbus	**1994**	MHA	31	XL3000	CH	7.4L	G	$2000	208	4,000	16,000	14,465

Livability Code: SB 30-90   Wheelbase-to-length ratio of 56% is considered ○ dangerous ○ fatiguing ◉ good ○ excellent *

The approximate net payload of 1535 pounds at 10% of GVWR on this model is ○ deficient ○ excessive ○ cautionary ◉ good ○ excellent *

Total highway safety penalties are: 5 *   Value: **83**   Durability: **77**   Highway Control Rating: **89**   Highway Safety: **84**   ★★★

Aerbus	**1994**	MHA	31	XL3000	FO	7.5L	G	$2000	208	8,000	17,000	15,070

Livability Code: SB 30-90   Wheelbase-to-length ratio of 56% is considered ○ dangerous ○ fatiguing ◉ good ○ excellent *

The approximate net payload of 1930 pounds at 11% of GVWR on this model is ○ deficient ○ excessive ○ cautionary ◉ good ○ excellent *

Total highway safety penalties are: 2 *   Value: **85**   Durability: **77**   Highway Control Rating: **86**   Highway Safety: **84**   ★★★

Aerbus	**1994**	MHA	32	S631	CH	7.4L	G	$1900	208	1,500 e	16,000	14,067

Livability Code: SB 30-90   Wheelbase-to-length ratio of 55% is considered ○ dangerous ○ fatiguing ◉ good ○ excellent *

The approximate net payload of 1933 pounds at 12% of GVWR on this model is ○ deficient ○ excessive ○ cautionary ◉ good ○ excellent *

Total highway safety penalties are: 5 *   Value: **83**   Durability: **77**   Highway Control Rating: **85**   Highway Safety: **80**   ★★★

Aerbus	**1994**	MHA	32	S631	FO	7.5L	G	$1900	208	1,500 e	17,000	14,567

Livability Code: SB 30-90   Wheelbase-to-length ratio of 55% is considered ○ dangerous ○ fatiguing ◉ good ○ excellent *

The approximate net payload of 2433 pounds at 14% of GVWR on this model is ○ deficient ○ excessive ○ cautionary ◉ good ○ excellent *

Total highway safety penalties are: 2 *   Value: **85**   Durability: **77**   Highway Control Rating: **89**   Highway Safety: **87**   ★★★

Aerbus	**1994**	MHA	32	XL3200 opch	OS	CU190	D	$2400	190	1,500	20,500	18,010

Livability Code: SB 30-90   Wheelbase-to-length ratio of 50% is considered ◉ dangerous ○ fatiguing ○ good ○ excellent *

The approximate net payload of 2490 pounds at 12% of GVWR on this model is ○ deficient ○ excessive ○ cautionary ◉ good ○ excellent *

Total highway safety penalties are: 2 *   Value: **85**   Durability: **77**   Highway Control Rating: **36**   Highway Safety: **34**

Aerbus	**1994**	MHA	32	XL3200	CH	7.4L	G	$2000	208	4,000	16,000	14,663

Livability Code: SB 30-90   Wheelbase-to-length ratio of 54% is considered ○ dangerous ○ fatiguing ◉ good ○ excellent *

The approximate net payload of 1337 pounds at 8% of GVWR on this model is ○ deficient ○ excessive ◉ cautionary ○ good ○ excellent *

Total highway safety penalties are: 6 *   Value: **83**   Durability: **77**   Highway Control Rating: **60**   Highway Safety: **54**   ★

Aerbus	**1994**	MHA	32	XL3200	FO	7.5L	G	$2000	208	8,000	17,000	15,268

Livability Code: SB 30-90   Wheelbase-to-length ratio of 54% is considered ○ dangerous ○ fatiguing ◉ good ○ excellent *

The approximate net payload of 1732 pounds at 10% of GVWR on this model is ○ deficient ○ excessive ○ cautionary ◉ good ○ excellent *

Total highway safety penalties are: 2 *   Value: **85**   Durability: **77**   Highway Control Rating: **76**   Highway Safety: **74**   ★★★

Aerbus	**1994**	MHA	33	XL3300	FO	7.5L	G	$2000	228	8,000	17,000	15,670

Livability Code: SB 30-90   Wheelbase-to-length ratio of 57% is considered ○ dangerous ○ fatiguing ◉ good ○ excellent *

The approximate net payload of 1330 pounds at 8% of GVWR on this model is ○ deficient ○ excessive ◉ cautionary ○ good ○ excellent *

Total highway safety penalties are: 2 *   Value: **85**   Durability: **77**   Highway Control Rating: **76**   Highway Safety: **74**   ★★★

Aerbus	**1994**	MHA	34	XL3300	CH	7.4L	G	$2000	228	4,000	16,000	15,069

Livability Code: SB 30-90   Wheelbase-to-length ratio of 57% is considered ○ dangerous ○ fatiguing ◉ good ○ excellent *

The approximate net payload of 931 pounds at 6% of GVWR on this model is ◉ deficient ○ excessive ○ cautionary ○ good ○ excellent *

Total highway safety penalties are: 6 *   Value: **83**   Durability: **77**   Highway Control Rating: **64**   Highway Safety: **58**   ★

Note: Safety ratings are based on the assumption that the engineering of the RV has allowed for proper balance by placing fresh, gray, and black holding tanks in a location so as not to change the balance of the RV when the tanks are empty or full. **Always double-check wheelbase, GVWR, and weights at front and rear axles.**

*See Section 1 for details on how conclusions are reached.

Brand	Year	Type	Length	Model	Chassis	Engine	Fuel Type	Average Price per Linear Foot When New	Adjusted Wheelbase	Approx. Towing Capacity	Gross Vehicle Weight Rating	Average Curb Weight
Aerbus	1994	MHA	34	S633	CH	7.4L	G	$2000	232 T	1,500 e	19,000	15,505

Livability Code: SB 30-90

Wheelbase-to-length ratio of 58% is considered ○ dangerous ○ fatiguing ○ good ● excellent *

The approximate net payload of 3495 pounds at 18% of GVWR on this model is ○ deficient ○ excessive ○ cautionary ○ good ● excellent *

Total highway safety penalties are: 9 *   Value: **81**   Durability: **77**   Highway Control Rating: **100**   Highway Safety: **91**   ★★★

Brand	Year	Type	Length	Model	Chassis	Engine	Fuel Type	Price/Ft	Wheelbase	Towing	GVWR	Curb Wt
Aerbus	1994	MHA	34	S633	FO	7.5L	G	$2000	228	1,500 e	17,000	15,105

Livability Code: SB 30-90

Wheelbase-to-length ratio of 57% is considered ○ dangerous ○ fatiguing ● good ○ excellent *

The approximate net payload of 1895 pounds at 11% of GVWR on this model is ○ deficient ○ excessive ○ cautionary ● good ○ excellent *

Total highway safety penalties are: 2 *   Value: **85**   Durability: **77**   Highway Control Rating: **89**   Highway Safety: **87**   ★★★

Brand	Year	Type	Length	Model	Chassis	Engine	Fuel Type	Price/Ft	Wheelbase	Towing	GVWR	Curb Wt
Aerbus	1994	MHA	34	XL3400	CH	7.4L	G	$2000	232 T	1,000	19,000	15,973

Livability Code: SB 30-90

Wheelbase-to-length ratio of 57% is considered ○ dangerous ○ fatiguing ○ good ○ excellent *

The approximate net payload of 3027 pounds at 16% of GVWR on this model is ○ deficient ○ excessive ○ cautionary ○ good ● excellent *

Total highway safety penalties are: 9 *   Value: **81**   Durability: **77**   Highway Control Rating: **99**   Highway Safety: **90**   ★★★

Brand	Year	Type	Length	Model	Chassis	Engine	Fuel Type	Price/Ft	Wheelbase	Towing	GVWR	Curb Wt
Aerbus	1994	MHA	34	XL3400	FO	7.5L	G	$2000	232 T	5,000	20,000	16,618

Livability Code: SB 30-90

Wheelbase-to-length ratio of 57% is considered ○ dangerous ○ fatiguing ○ good ● excellent *

The approximate net payload of 3382 pounds at 17% of GVWR on this model is ○ deficient ○ excessive ○ cautionary ○ good ● excellent *

Total highway safety penalties are: 4 *   Value: **84**   Durability: **77**   Highway Control Rating: **100**   Highway Safety: **96**   ★★★

Brand	Year	Type	Length	Model	Chassis	Engine	Fuel Type	Price/Ft	Wheelbase	Towing	GVWR	Curb Wt
Aerbus	1994	MHA	36	XL3600	CH	7.4L	G	$1900	252 T	1,000	19,000	16,782

Livability Code: SB 30-90

Wheelbase-to-length ratio of 58% is considered ○ dangerous ○ fatiguing ○ good ● excellent *

The approximate net payload of 2218 pounds at 12% of GVWR on this model is ○ deficient ○ excessive ○ cautionary ● good ○ excellent *

Total highway safety penalties are: 10 *   Value: **81**   Durability: **77**   Highway Control Rating: **96**   Highway Safety: **86**   ★★★

Brand	Year	Type	Length	Model	Chassis	Engine	Fuel Type	Price/Ft	Wheelbase	Towing	GVWR	Curb Wt
Aerbus	1994	MHA	36	XL3600	FO	7.5L	G	$1900	252 T	5,000	20,000	17,044

Livability Code: SB 30-90

Wheelbase-to-length ratio of 58% is considered ○ dangerous ○ fatiguing ○ good ● excellent *

The approximate net payload of 2956 pounds at 15% of GVWR on this model is ○ deficient ○ excessive ○ cautionary ● good ○ excellent *

Total highway safety penalties are: 4 *   Value: **84**   Durability: **77**   Highway Control Rating: **100**   Highway Safety: **96**   ★★★

Brand	Year	Type	Length	Model	Chassis	Engine	Fuel Type	Price/Ft	Wheelbase	Towing	GVWR	Curb Wt
Aerbus	1994	MHA	38	S638	FO	7.5L	G	$1800	228	1,500 e	20,000	17,295

Livability Code: SB 30-90

Wheelbase-to-length ratio of 50% is considered ● dangerous ○ fatiguing ○ good ○ excellent *

The approximate net payload of 2705 pounds at 14% of GVWR on this model is ○ deficient ○ excessive ○ cautionary ● good ○ excellent *

Total highway safety penalties are: 2 *   Value: **85**   Durability: **77**   Highway Control Rating: **39**   Highway Safety: **37**

Brand	Year	Type	Length	Model	Chassis	Engine	Fuel Type	Price/Ft	Wheelbase	Towing	GVWR	Curb Wt
Aerbus	1995	MHA	29	XL2800	CH	7.4L	G	$2200	190	3,500	16,500	13,984

Livability Code: SB 30-90

Wheelbase-to-length ratio of 54% is considered ○ dangerous ○ fatiguing ● good ○ excellent *

The approximate net payload of 2516 pounds at 15% of GVWR on this model is ○ deficient ○ excessive ○ cautionary ● good ○ excellent *

Total highway safety penalties are: 4 *   Value: **83**   Durability: **74**   Highway Control Rating: **82**   Highway Safety: **78**   ★★★

Brand	Year	Type	Length	Model	Chassis	Engine	Fuel Type	Price/Ft	Wheelbase	Towing	GVWR	Curb Wt
Aerbus	1995	MHA	29	XL2800	FO	7.5L	G	$2200	190	8,000	17,000	14,474

Livability Code: SB 30-90

Wheelbase-to-length ratio of 54% is considered ○ dangerous ○ fatiguing ● good ○ excellent *

The approximate net payload of 2526 pounds at 15% of GVWR on this model is ○ deficient ○ excessive ○ cautionary ● good ○ excellent *

Total highway safety penalties are: 2 *   Value: **84**   Durability: **74**   Highway Control Rating: **82**   Highway Safety: **80**   ★★★

Brand	Year	Type	Length	Model	Chassis	Engine	Fuel Type	Price/Ft	Wheelbase	Towing	GVWR	Curb Wt
Aerbus	1995	MHA	31	XL2900	CH	7.4L	G	$2100	208	3,500	16,500	14,300

Livability Code: SB 30-90

Wheelbase-to-length ratio of 56% is considered ○ dangerous ○ fatiguing ● good ○ excellent *

The approximate net payload of 2200 pounds at 13% of GVWR on this model is ○ deficient ○ excessive ○ cautionary ● good ○ excellent *

Total highway safety penalties are: 5 *   Value: **82**   Durability: **74**   Highway Control Rating: **95**   Highway Safety: **90**   ★★★

Brand	Year	Type	Length	Model	Chassis	Engine	Fuel Type	Price/Ft	Wheelbase	Towing	GVWR	Curb Wt
Aerbus	1995	MHA	31	XL2900	FO	7.5L	G	$2100	208	8,000	17,000	15,005

Livability Code: SB 30-90

Wheelbase-to-length ratio of 56% is considered ○ dangerous ○ fatiguing ● good ○ excellent *

The approximate net payload of 1995 pounds at 12% of GVWR on this model is ○ deficient ○ excessive ○ cautionary ● good ○ excellent *

Total highway safety penalties are: 2 *   Value: **84**   Durability: **74**   Highway Control Rating: **94**   Highway Safety: **92**   ★★★

Brand	Year	Type	Length	Model	Chassis	Engine	Fuel Type	Price/Ft	Wheelbase	Towing	GVWR	Curb Wt
Aerbus	1995	MHA	32	XL3000	CH	7.4L	G	$2000	208	3,500	16,500	14,574

Livability Code: SB 30-90

Wheelbase-to-length ratio of 55% is considered ○ dangerous ○ fatiguing ● good ○ excellent *

The approximate net payload of 1926 pounds at 12% of GVWR on this model is ○ deficient ○ excessive ○ cautionary ● good ○ excellent *

Total highway safety penalties are: 5 *   Value: **82**   Durability: **74**   Highway Control Rating: **88**   Highway Safety: **83**   ★★★

Note: Safety ratings are based on the assumption that the engineering of the RV has allowed for proper balance by placing fresh, gray, and black holding tanks in a location so as not to change the balance of the RV when the tanks are empty or full. **Always double-check wheelbase, GVWR, and weights at front and rear axles.**

*See Section 1 for details on how conclusions are reached.

Brand	Year	Type	Length	Model	Chassis	Engine	Fuel Type	Average Price per Linear Foot When New	Adjusted Wheel-base	Approx. Towing Capacity	Gross Vehicle Weight Rating	Average Curb Weight
Aerbus	1995	MHA	32	XL3000	FO	7.5L	G	$2000	208	8,000	17,000	15,129

Livability Code: SB 30-90 Wheelbase-to-length ratio of 55% is considered ○ dangerous ○ fatiguing ◉ good ○ excellent *

The approximate net payload of 1871 pounds at 11% of GVWR on this model is ○ deficient ○ excessive ○ cautionary ◉ good ○ excellent *

Total highway safety penalties are: 2 *   Value: **8 4** Durability: **7 4** Highway Control Rating: **8 8**   Highway Safety: **8 6**   ★★★

Brand	Year	Type	Length	Model	Chassis	Engine	Fuel Type	Price/Ft	Wheelbase	Towing	GVWR	Curb Weight
Aerbus	1995	MHA	32	XL3200	CH	7.4L	G	$2100	208	3,500	16,500	14,742

Livability Code: SB 30-90 Wheelbase-to-length ratio of 54% is considered ○ dangerous ○ fatiguing ◉ good ○ excellent *

The approximate net payload of 1758 pounds at 11% of GVWR on this model is ○ deficient ○ excessive ○ cautionary ◉ good ○ excellent *

Total highway safety penalties are: 6 *   Value: **8 2** Durability: **7 4** Highway Control Rating: **7 6**   Highway Safety: **7 0**   ★★★

Aerbus	1995	MHA	32	XL3250 sl	CH	7.4L	G	$2300	208	3,500	16,500	15,796

Livability Code: SB 30-90 Wheelbase-to-length ratio of 54% is considered ○ dangerous ○ fatiguing ◉ good ○ excellent *

The approximate net payload of 704 pounds at 4% of GVWR on this model is ◉ deficient ○ excessive ○ cautionary ○ good ○ excellent *

Total highway safety penalties are: 11 *   Value: **7 9** Durability: **7 4** Highway Control Rating: **4 4**   Highway Safety: **3 3**

Aerbus	1995	MHA	32	XL3100	CH	7.4L	G	$2200	208	3,500	16,500	14,896

Livability Code: SB 30-90 Wheelbase-to-length ratio of 54% is considered ○ dangerous ○ fatiguing ◉ good ○ excellent *

The approximate net payload of 1604 pounds at 10% of GVWR on this model is ○ deficient ○ excessive ○ cautionary ◉ good ○ excellent *

Total highway safety penalties are: 6 *   Value: **8 2** Durability: **7 4** Highway Control Rating: **7 5**   Highway Safety: **6 9**   ★★

Aerbus	1995	MHA	32	XL3200	FO	7.5L	G	$2100	208	8,000	17,000	15,297

Livability Code: SB 30-90 Wheelbase-to-length ratio of 54% is considered ○ dangerous ○ fatiguing ◉ good ○ excellent *

The approximate net payload of 1703 pounds at 10% of GVWR on this model is ○ deficient ○ excessive ○ cautionary ◉ good ○ excellent *

Total highway safety penalties are: 2 *   Value: **8 4** Durability: **7 4** Highway Control Rating: **7 5**   Highway Safety: **7 3**   ★★★

Aerbus	1995	MHA	32	XL3100	FO	7.5L	G	$2200	208	8,000	17,000	15,296

Livability Code: SB 30-90 Wheelbase-to-length ratio of 54% is considered ○ dangerous ○ fatiguing ◉ good ○ excellent *

The approximate net payload of 1704 pounds at 10% of GVWR on this model is ○ deficient ○ excessive ○ cautionary ◉ good ○ excellent *

Total highway safety penalties are: 2 *   Value: **8 4** Durability: **7 4** Highway Control Rating: **7 5**   Highway Safety: **7 3**   ★★★

Aerbus	1995	MHA	32	XL3250 sl	FO	7.5L	G	$2300	208	8,000	17,000	16,196

Livability Code: SB 30-90 Wheelbase-to-length ratio of 54% is considered ○ dangerous ○ fatiguing ◉ good ○ excellent *

The approximate net payload of 804 pounds at 5% of GVWR on this model is ◉ deficient ○ excessive ○ cautionary ○ good ○ excellent *

Total highway safety penalties are: 7 *   Value: **8 1** Durability: **7 4** Highway Control Rating: **4 5**   Highway Safety: **3 8**

Aerbus	1995	MHA	32	XL3200 opch	OS	CU230	D	$3400	190	4,500	20,500	17,396

Livability Code: SB 30-90 Wheelbase-to-length ratio of 49% is considered ◉ dangerous ○ fatiguing ○ good ○ excellent *

The approximate net payload of 3104 pounds at 15% of GVWR on this model is ○ deficient ○ excessive ○ cautionary ◉ good ○ excellent *

Total highway safety penalties are: 2 *   Value: **8 4** Durability: **7 4** Highway Control Rating: **4 0**   Highway Safety: **3 8**

Aerbus	1995	MHA	32	XL3100 opch	OS	CU230	D	$3400	208	4,500	20,500	17,396

Livability Code: SB 30-90 Wheelbase-to-length ratio of 54% is considered ○ dangerous ○ fatiguing ◉ good ○ excellent *

The approximate net payload of 3104 pounds at 15% of GVWR on this model is ○ deficient ○ excessive ○ cautionary ◉ good ○ excellent *

Total highway safety penalties are: 2 *   Value: **8 4** Durability: **7 4** Highway Control Rating: **7 9**   Highway Safety: **7 7**   ★★★

Aerbus	1995	MHA	34	XL3300	CH	7.4L	G	$2000	228	3,500	16,500	15,178

Livability Code: SB 30-90 Wheelbase-to-length ratio of 56% is considered ○ dangerous ○ fatiguing ◉ good ○ excellent *

The approximate net payload of 1322 pounds at 8% of GVWR on this model is ○ deficient ○ excessive ◉ cautionary ○ good ○ excellent *

Total highway safety penalties are: 6 *   Value: **8 1** Durability: **7 4** Highway Control Rating: **7 3**   Highway Safety: **6 7**   ★★

Aerbus	1995	MHA	34	XL3300	FO	7.5L	G	$2000	228	8,000	17,000	15,743

Livability Code: SB 30-90 Wheelbase-to-length ratio of 56% is considered ○ dangerous ○ fatiguing ◉ good ○ excellent *

The approximate net payload of 1257 pounds at 7% of GVWR on this model is ○ deficient ○ excessive ◉ cautionary ○ good ○ excellent *

Total highway safety penalties are: 2 *   Value: **8 4** Durability: **7 4** Highway Control Rating: **6 8**   Highway Safety: **6 6**   ★★

Aerbus	1995	MHA	34	XL3300 opch	OS	CU230	D	$3200	208	4,500	20,500	17,882

Livability Code: SB 30-90 Wheelbase-to-length ratio of 51% is considered ○ dangerous ◉ fatiguing ○ good ○ excellent *

The approximate net payload of 2618 pounds at 13% of GVWR on this model is ○ deficient ○ excessive ○ cautionary ◉ good ○ excellent *

Total highway safety penalties are: 2 *   Value: **8 4** Durability: **7 4** Highway Control Rating: **4 3**   Highway Safety: **4 1**

Note: Safety ratings are based on the assumption that the engineering of the RV has allowed for proper balance by placing fresh, gray, and black holding tanks in a location so as not to change the balance of the RV when the tanks are empty or full. **Always double-check wheelbase, GVWR, and weights at front and rear axles.**

*See Section 1 for details on how conclusions are reached.

Brand	Year	Type	Length	Model	Chassis	Engine	Fuel Type	Average Price per Linear Foot When New	Adjusted Wheelbase	Approx. Towing Capacity	Gross Vehicle Weight Rating	Average Curb Weight
Aerbus	1995	MHA	34	XL3400	CH	7.4L	G	$2000	232 T	1,000	19,000	16,003

Livability Code: SB 30-90
Wheelbase-to-length ratio of 57% is considered ○ dangerous ○ fatiguing ◉ good ○ excellent *
The approximate net payload of 2997 pounds at 16% of GVWR on this model is ○ deficient ○ excessive ○ cautionary ○ good ◉ excellent *
Total highway safety penalties are: 9 *   Value: 8 0   Durability: 7 4   Highway Control Rating: 9 8   Highway Safety: 8 9   ★★★

| Aerbus | 1995 | MHA | 34 | XL3400 | FO | 7.5L | G | $2000 | 232 T | 5,000 | 20,000 | 16,648 |

Livability Code: SB 30-90
Wheelbase-to-length ratio of 57% is considered ○ dangerous ○ fatiguing ◉ good ○ excellent *
The approximate net payload of 3352 pounds at 17% of GVWR on this model is ○ deficient ○ excessive ○ cautionary ○ good ◉ excellent *
Total highway safety penalties are: 4 *   Value: 8 2   Durability: 7 4   Highway Control Rating: 9 9   Highway Safety: 9 5   ★★★

| Aerbus | 1995 | MHA | 34 | XL3400 opch | OS | CU230 | D | $3200 | 208 | 4,500 | 20,500 | 17,968 |

Livability Code: SB 30-90
Wheelbase-to-length ratio of 51% is considered ○ dangerous ◉ fatiguing ○ good ○ excellent *
The approximate net payload of 2532 pounds at 12% of GVWR on this model is ○ deficient ○ excessive ○ cautionary ○ good ○ excellent *
Total highway safety penalties are: 2 *   Value: 8 4   Durability: 7 4   Highway Control Rating: 4 0   Highway Safety: 3 8

| Aerbus | 1995 | MHA | 36 | XL3500 | CH | 7.4L | G | $2000 | 252 T | 1,000 | 19,000 | 16,254 |

Livability Code: SB 30-90
Wheelbase-to-length ratio of 59% is considered ○ dangerous ○ fatiguing ○ good ◉ excellent *
The approximate net payload of 2746 pounds at 14% of GVWR on this model is ○ deficient ○ excessive ○ cautionary ◉ good ○ excellent *
Total highway safety penalties are: 10 *   Value: 8 0   Durability: 7 4   Highway Control Rating: 1 0 0   Highway Safety: 9 0   ★★★

| Aerbus | 1995 | MHA | 36 | XL3550 sl | CH | 7.4L | G | $2100 | 252 T | 1,000 | 19,000 | 17,446 |

Livability Code: SB 30-90
Wheelbase-to-length ratio of 59% is considered ○ dangerous ○ fatiguing ○ good ◉ excellent *
The approximate net payload of 1554 pounds at 8% of GVWR on this model is ○ deficient ○ excessive ◉ cautionary ○ good ○ excellent *
Total highway safety penalties are: 14 *   Value: 7 7   Durability: 7 4   Highway Control Rating: 8 3   Highway Safety: 6 9   ★★

| Aerbus | 1995 | MHA | 36 | XL3500 | FO | 7.5L | G | $2000 | 252 T | 5,000 | 20,000 | 16,849 |

Livability Code: SB 30-90
Wheelbase-to-length ratio of 59% is considered ○ dangerous ○ fatiguing ○ good ◉ excellent *
The approximate net payload of 3151 pounds at 16% of GVWR on this model is ○ deficient ○ excessive ○ cautionary ○ good ◉ excellent *
Total highway safety penalties are: 4 *   Value: 8 2   Durability: 7 4   Highway Control Rating: 1 0 0   Highway Safety: 9 6   ★★★

| Aerbus | 1995 | MHA | 36 | XL3550 sl | FO | 7.5L | G | $1900 | 252 T | 5,000 | 20,000 | 17,946 |

Livability Code: SB 30-90
Wheelbase-to-length ratio of 59% is considered ○ dangerous ○ fatiguing ○ good ◉ excellent *
The approximate net payload of 2054 pounds at 10% of GVWR on this model is ○ deficient ○ excessive ○ cautionary ◉ good ○ excellent *
Total highway safety penalties are: 9 *   Value: 8 0   Durability: 7 4   Highway Control Rating: 9 5   Highway Safety: 8 6   ★★★

| Aerbus | 1995 | MHA | 36 | XL3500 opch | OS | CU230 | D | $3000 | 228 | 4,500 | 20,500 | 18,396 |

Livability Code: SB 30-90
Wheelbase-to-length ratio of 53% is considered ○ dangerous ◉ fatiguing ○ good ○ excellent *
The approximate net payload of 2104 pounds at 10% of GVWR on this model is ○ deficient ○ excessive ○ cautionary ◉ good ○ excellent *
Total highway safety penalties are: 2 *   Value: 8 4   Durability: 7 4   Highway Control Rating: 6 0   Highway Safety: 5 8   ★

| Aerbus | 1995 | MHA | 36 | XL3550 opch sl | OS | CU230 | D | $3000 | 228 | 4,500 | 20,500 | 19,296 |

Livability Code: SB 30-90
Wheelbase-to-length ratio of 53% is considered ○ dangerous ◉ fatiguing ○ good ○ excellent *
The approximate net payload of 1204 pounds at 6% of GVWR on this model is ◉ deficient ○ excessive ○ cautionary ○ good ○ excellent *
Total highway safety penalties are: 7 *   Value: 8 1   Durability: 7 4   Highway Control Rating: 3 6   Highway Safety: 2 9

| Aerbus | 1995 | MHA | 36 | XL3600 | CH | 7.4L | G | $2000 | 252 T | 1,000 | 19,000 | 16,518 |

Livability Code: SB 30-90
Wheelbase-to-length ratio of 58% is considered ○ dangerous ○ fatiguing ○ good ◉ excellent *
The approximate net payload of 2482 pounds at 13% of GVWR on this model is ○ deficient ○ excessive ○ cautionary ◉ good ○ excellent *
Total highway safety penalties are: 10 *   Value: 8 0   Durability: 7 4   Highway Control Rating: 1 0 0   Highway Safety: 9 0   ★★★

| Aerbus | 1995 | MHA | 36 | XL3600 | CH | 7.4L | G | $2000 | 252 T | 1,000 | 19,000 | 16,498 |

Livability Code: SB 30-90
Wheelbase-to-length ratio of 58% is considered ○ dangerous ○ fatiguing ○ good ◉ excellent *
The approximate net payload of 2502 pounds at 13% of GVWR on this model is ○ deficient ○ excessive ○ cautionary ◉ good ○ excellent *
Total highway safety penalties are: 10 *   Value: 8 0   Durability: 7 4   Highway Control Rating: 9 8   Highway Safety: 8 8   ★★★

| Aerbus | 1995 | MHA | 36 | XL3650 sl | CH | 7.4L | G | $2000 | 252 T | 1,000 | 19,000 | 17,889 |

Livability Code: SB 30-90
Wheelbase-to-length ratio of 58% is considered ○ dangerous ○ fatiguing ○ good ◉ excellent *
The approximate net payload of 1111 pounds at 6% of GVWR on this model is ◉ deficient ○ excessive ○ cautionary ○ good ○ excellent *
Total highway safety penalties are: 16 *   Value: 7 6   Durability: 7 4   Highway Control Rating: 6 8   Highway Safety: 5 2   ★

Note: Safety ratings are based on the assumption that the engineering of the RV has allowed for proper balance by placing fresh, gray, and black holding tanks in a location so as not to change the balance of the RV when the tanks are empty or full. **Always double-check wheelbase, GVWR, and weights at front and rear axles.**

*See Section 1 for details on how conclusions are reached.

Brand	Year	Type	Length	Model	Chassis	Engine	Fuel Type	Average Price per Linear Foot When New	Adjusted Wheelbase	Approx. Towing Capacity	Gross Vehicle Weight Rating	Average Curb Weight
Aerbus	**1995**	MHA	36	XL3600	FO	7.5L	G	$2000	252 T	5,000	20,000	17,073

Livability Code: SB 30-90

Wheelbase-to-length ratio of 58% is considered ○ dangerous ○ fatiguing ○ good ◉ excellent *

The approximate net payload of 2927 pounds at 15% of GVWR on this model is ○ deficient ○ excessive ○ cautionary ◉ good ○ excellent *

Total highway safety penalties are: 4 *   Value: **8 2**   Durability: **7 4**   Highway Control Rating: **1 0 0**   Highway Safety: **9 6**   ★★★

| **Aerbus** | **1995** | MHA | 36 | XL3600 | FO | 7.5L | G | $2000 | 252 T | 5,000 | 20,000 | 17,339 |

Livability Code: SB 30-90

Wheelbase-to-length ratio of 58% is considered ○ dangerous ○ fatiguing ○ good ◉ excellent *

The approximate net payload of 2661 pounds at 13% of GVWR on this model is ○ deficient ○ excessive ○ cautionary ◉ good ○ excellent *

Total highway safety penalties are: 4 *   Value: **8 2**   Durability: **7 4**   Highway Control Rating: **9 8**   Highway Safety: **9 4**   ★★★

| **Aerbus** | **1995** | MHA | 36 | XL3650 sl | FO | 7.5L | G | $2100 | 252 T | 5,000 | 20,000 | 18,389 |

Livability Code: SB 30-90

Wheelbase-to-length ratio of 58% is considered ○ dangerous ○ fatiguing ○ good ◉ excellent *

The approximate net payload of 1611 pounds at 8% of GVWR on this model is ○ deficient ○ excessive ◉ cautionary ○ good ○ excellent *

Total highway safety penalties are: 11 *   Value: **7 9**   Durability: **7 4**   Highway Control Rating: **8 0**   Highway Safety: **6 9**   ★★

| **Aerbus** | **1995** | MHA | 36 | XL3600 opch | OS | CU230 | D | $3000 | 228 | 4,500 | 20,500 | 18,539 |

Livability Code: SB 30-90

Wheelbase-to-length ratio of 52% is considered ○ dangerous ◉ fatiguing ○ good ○ excellent *

The approximate net payload of 1961 pounds at 10% of GVWR on this model is ○ deficient ○ excessive ○ cautionary ◉ good ○ excellent *

Total highway safety penalties are: 2 *   Value: **8 4**   Durability: **7 4**   Highway Control Rating: **4 9**   Highway Safety: **4 7**

| **Aerbus** | **1995** | MHA | 36 | XL3650 opch sl | OS | CU230 | D | $3000 | 228 | 4,500 | 20,500 | 19,589 |

Livability Code: SB 30-90

Wheelbase-to-length ratio of 52% is considered ○ dangerous ◉ fatiguing ○ good ○ excellent *

The approximate net payload of 911 pounds at 4% of GVWR on this model is ◉ deficient ○ excessive ○ cautionary ○ good ○ excellent *

Total highway safety penalties are: 8 *   Value: **8 0**   Durability: **7 4**   Highway Control Rating: **2 5**   Highway Safety: **1 7**

| **Aerbus** | **1995** | MHA | 39 | XL3800 | FO | 7.5L | G | $1900 | 252 T | 5,000 | 20,000 | 18,053 |

Livability Code: SB 30-90

Wheelbase-to-length ratio of 54% is considered ○ dangerous ○ fatiguing ◉ good ○ excellent *

The approximate net payload of 1947 pounds at 10% of GVWR on this model is ○ deficient ○ excessive ○ cautionary ◉ good ○ excellent *

Total highway safety penalties are: 4 *   Value: **8 2**   Durability: **7 4**   Highway Control Rating: **7 6**   Highway Safety: **7 2**   ★★★

| **Aerbus** | **1996** | MHA | 29 | XL2800 | CH | 7.4L | G | $2200 | 190 | 3,500 | 16,500 | 13,984 |

Livability Code: SB 30-90

Wheelbase-to-length ratio of 54% is considered ○ dangerous ○ fatiguing ◉ good ○ excellent *

The approximate net payload of 2516 pounds at 15% of GVWR on this model is ○ deficient ○ excessive ○ cautionary ◉ good ○ excellent *

Total highway safety penalties are: 4 *   Value: **8 3**   Durability: **7 4**   Highway Control Rating: **8 1**   Highway Safety: **7 7**   ★★★

| **Aerbus** | **1996** | MHA | 29 | XL2800 | FO | 7.5L | G | $2200 | 190 | 8,000 | 17,000 | 14,474 |

Livability Code: SB 30-90

Wheelbase-to-length ratio of 54% is considered ○ dangerous ○ fatiguing ◉ good ○ excellent *

The approximate net payload of 2526 pounds at 15% of GVWR on this model is ○ deficient ○ excessive ○ cautionary ◉ good ○ excellent *

Total highway safety penalties are: 2 *   Value: **8 4**   Durability: **7 4**   Highway Control Rating: **8 1**   Highway Safety: **7 9**   ★★★

| **Aerbus** | **1996** | MHA | 31 | XL2900 | CH | 7.4L | G | $2100 | 208 | 3,500 | 16,500 | 14,300 |

Livability Code: SB 30-90

Wheelbase-to-length ratio of 56% is considered ○ dangerous ○ fatiguing ◉ good ○ excellent *

The approximate net payload of 2200 pounds at 13% of GVWR on this model is ○ deficient ○ excessive ○ cautionary ◉ good ○ excellent *

Total highway safety penalties are: 5 *   Value: **8 2**   Durability: **7 4**   Highway Control Rating: **9 2**   Highway Safety: **8 7**   ★★★

| **Aerbus** | **1996** | MHA | 31 | XL2900 | FO | 7.5L | G | $2100 | 208 | 8,000 | 17,000 | 15,005 |

Livability Code: SB 30-90

Wheelbase-to-length ratio of 56% is considered ○ dangerous ○ fatiguing ◉ good ○ excellent *

The approximate net payload of 1995 pounds at 12% of GVWR on this model is ○ deficient ○ excessive ○ cautionary ◉ good ○ excellent *

Total highway safety penalties are: 2 *   Value: **8 4**   Durability: **7 4**   Highway Control Rating: **9 0**   Highway Safety: **8 8**   ★★★

| **Aerbus** | **1996** | MHA | 32 | XL3000 | CH | 7.4L | G | $2000 | 208 | 3,500 | 16,500 | 14,574 |

Livability Code: SB 30-90

Wheelbase-to-length ratio of 55% is considered ○ dangerous ○ fatiguing ◉ good ○ excellent *

The approximate net payload of 1926 pounds at 12% of GVWR on this model is ○ deficient ○ excessive ○ cautionary ◉ good ○ excellent *

Total highway safety penalties are: 5 *   Value: **8 2**   Durability: **7 4**   Highway Control Rating: **8 8**   Highway Safety: **8 3**   ★★★

| **Aerbus** | **1996** | MHA | 32 | XL3000 | FO | 7.5L | G | $2000 | 208 | 8,000 | 17,000 | 15,129 |

Livability Code: SB 30-90

Wheelbase-to-length ratio of 55% is considered ○ dangerous ○ fatiguing ◉ good ○ excellent *

The approximate net payload of 1871 pounds at 11% of GVWR on this model is ○ deficient ○ excessive ○ cautionary ◉ good ○ excellent *

Total highway safety penalties are: 2 *   Value: **8 4**   Durability: **7 4**   Highway Control Rating: **8 8**   Highway Safety: **8 6**   ★★★

Note: Safety ratings are based on the assumption that the engineering of the RV has allowed for proper balance by placing fresh, gray, and black holding tanks in a location so as not to change the balance of the RV when the tanks are empty or full. **Always double-check wheelbase, GVWR, and weights at front and rear axles.**

*See Section 1 for details on how conclusions are reached.

Brand	Year	Type	Length	Model	Chassis	Engine	Fuel Type	Average Price per Linear Foot When New	Adjusted Wheel-base	Approx. Towing Capacity	Gross Vehicle Weight Rating	Average Curb Weight
Aerbus	1996	MHA	32	XL3200	CH	7.4L	G	$2100	208	3,500	16,500	14,742

Livability Code: SB 30-90
Wheelbase-to-length ratio of 54% is considered ○ dangerous ○ fatiguing ◉ good ○ excellent *
The approximate net payload of 1758 pounds at 11% of GVWR on this model is ○ deficient ○ excessive ○ cautionary ◉ good ○ excellent *
Total highway safety penalties are: 6 * Value: 8 2 Durability: 7 4 Highway Control Rating: 7 6 Highway Safety: 7 0 ★★★

Brand	Year	Type	Length	Model	Chassis	Engine	Fuel Type	Price/Ft	Wheelbase	Towing	GVWR	Curb
Aerbus	1996	MHA	32	XL3250 sl	CH	7.4L	G	$2300	208	3,500	16,500	15,507

Livability Code: SB 30-90
Wheelbase-to-length ratio of 54% is considered ○ dangerous ○ fatiguing ◉ good ○ excellent *
The approximate net payload of 993 pounds at 6% of GVWR on this model is ◉ deficient ○ excessive ○ cautionary ○ good ○ excellent *
Total highway safety penalties are: 11 * Value: 7 9 Durability: 7 4 Highway Control Rating: 4 6 Highway Safety: 3 5

Brand	Year	Type	Length	Model	Chassis	Engine	Fuel Type	Price/Ft	Wheelbase	Towing	GVWR	Curb
Aerbus	1996	MHA	32	XL3100	CH	7.4L	G	$2200	208	3,500	16,500	14,896

Livability Code: SB 30-90
Wheelbase-to-length ratio of 54% is considered ○ dangerous ○ fatiguing ◉ good ○ excellent *
The approximate net payload of 1604 pounds at 10% of GVWR on this model is ○ deficient ○ excessive ○ cautionary ◉ good ○ excellent *
Total highway safety penalties are: 6 * Value: 8 2 Durability: 7 4 Highway Control Rating: 7 5 Highway Safety: 6 9 ★★

Brand	Year	Type	Length	Model	Chassis	Engine	Fuel Type	Price/Ft	Wheelbase	Towing	GVWR	Curb
Aerbus	1996	MHA	32	XL3200	FO	7.5L	G	$2100	208	8,000	17,000	15,172

Livability Code: SB 30-90
Wheelbase-to-length ratio of 54% is considered ○ dangerous ○ fatiguing ◉ good ○ excellent *
The approximate net payload of 1828 pounds at 11% of GVWR on this model is ○ deficient ○ excessive ○ cautionary ◉ good ○ excellent *
Total highway safety penalties are: 2 * Value: 8 4 Durability: 7 4 Highway Control Rating: 7 6 Highway Safety: 7 4 ★★★

Brand	Year	Type	Length	Model	Chassis	Engine	Fuel Type	Price/Ft	Wheelbase	Towing	GVWR	Curb
Aerbus	1996	MHA	32	XL3100	FO	7.5L	G	$2200	208	8,000	17,000	15,296

Livability Code: SB 30-90
Wheelbase-to-length ratio of 54% is considered ○ dangerous ○ fatiguing ◉ good ○ excellent *
The approximate net payload of 1704 pounds at 10% of GVWR on this model is ○ deficient ○ excessive ○ cautionary ◉ good ○ excellent *
Total highway safety penalties are: 2 * Value: 8 4 Durability: 7 4 Highway Control Rating: 7 5 Highway Safety: 7 3 ★★★

Brand	Year	Type	Length	Model	Chassis	Engine	Fuel Type	Price/Ft	Wheelbase	Towing	GVWR	Curb
Aerbus	1996	MHA	32	XL3250 sl	FO	7.5L	G	$2300	208	8,000	17,000	15,622

Livability Code: SB 30-90
Wheelbase-to-length ratio of 54% is considered ○ dangerous ○ fatiguing ◉ good ○ excellent *
The approximate net payload of 1378 pounds at 8% of GVWR on this model is ○ deficient ○ excessive ◉ cautionary ○ good ○ excellent *
Total highway safety penalties are: 7 * Value: 8 1 Durability: 7 4 Highway Control Rating: 5 8 Highway Safety: 5 1 ★

Brand	Year	Type	Length	Model	Chassis	Engine	Fuel Type	Price/Ft	Wheelbase	Towing	GVWR	Curb
Aerbus	1996	MHA	32	XL3100	FO	7.5L	G	$2200	208	8,000	17,000	15,296

Livability Code: SB 30-90
Wheelbase-to-length ratio of 54% is considered ○ dangerous ○ fatiguing ◉ good ○ excellent *
The approximate net payload of 1704 pounds at 10% of GVWR on this model is ○ deficient ○ excessive ○ cautionary ◉ good ○ excellent *
Total highway safety penalties are: 2 * Value: 8 4 Durability: 7 4 Highway Control Rating: 7 5 Highway Safety: 7 3 ★★★

Brand	Year	Type	Length	Model	Chassis	Engine	Fuel Type	Price/Ft	Wheelbase	Towing	GVWR	Curb
Aerbus	1996	MHA	32	XL3250 op tag	FO	7.5L	G	$2400	214 T	5,000	20,000	17,096

Livability Code: SB 30-90
Wheelbase-to-length ratio of 55% is considered ○ dangerous ○ fatiguing ◉ good ○ excellent *
The approximate net payload of 2904 pounds at 15% of GVWR on this model is ○ deficient ○ excessive ○ cautionary ◉ good ○ excellent *
Total highway safety penalties are: 10 * Value: 8 0 Durability: 7 4 Highway Control Rating: 9 1 Highway Safety: 8 1 ★★★

Brand	Year	Type	Length	Model	Chassis	Engine	Fuel Type	Price/Ft	Wheelbase	Towing	GVWR	Curb
Aerbus	1996	MHA	32	XL3200 opch	OS	CU230	D	$3100	190	4,500	20,500	18,093

Livability Code: SB 30-90
Wheelbase-to-length ratio of 49% is considered ◉ dangerous ○ fatiguing ○ good ○ excellent *
The approximate net payload of 2407 pounds at 12% of GVWR on this model is ○ deficient ○ excessive ○ cautionary ◉ good ○ excellent *
Total highway safety penalties are: 2 * Value: 8 4 Durability: 7 4 Highway Control Rating: 3 4 Highway Safety: 3 2

Brand	Year	Type	Length	Model	Chassis	Engine	Fuel Type	Price/Ft	Wheelbase	Towing	GVWR	Curb
Aerbus	1996	MHA	34	XL3300	CH	7.4L	G	$2000	228	3,500	16,500	15,178

Livability Code: SB 30-90
Wheelbase-to-length ratio of 56% is considered ○ dangerous ○ fatiguing ◉ good ○ excellent *
The approximate net payload of 1322 pounds at 8% of GVWR on this model is ○ deficient ○ excessive ◉ cautionary ○ good ○ excellent *
Total highway safety penalties are: 6 * Value: 8 1 Durability: 7 4 Highway Control Rating: 7 3 Highway Safety: 6 7 ★★

Brand	Year	Type	Length	Model	Chassis	Engine	Fuel Type	Price/Ft	Wheelbase	Towing	GVWR	Curb
Aerbus	1996	MHA	34	XL3300	FO	7.5L	G	$2000	228	8,000	17,000	15,583

Livability Code: SB 30-90
Wheelbase-to-length ratio of 56% is considered ○ dangerous ○ fatiguing ◉ good ○ excellent *
The approximate net payload of 1417 pounds at 8% of GVWR on this model is ○ deficient ○ excessive ◉ cautionary ○ good ○ excellent *
Total highway safety penalties are: 2 * Value: 8 4 Durability: 7 4 Highway Control Rating: 7 4 Highway Safety: 7 2 ★★★

Brand	Year	Type	Length	Model	Chassis	Engine	Fuel Type	Price/Ft	Wheelbase	Towing	GVWR	Curb
Aerbus	1996	MHA	34	XL3300 opch	OS	CU230	D	$2900	208	4,500	20,500	18,561

Livability Code: SB 30-90
Wheelbase-to-length ratio of 51% is considered ○ dangerous ◉ fatiguing ○ good ○ excellent *
The approximate net payload of 1939 pounds at 9% of GVWR on this model is ○ deficient ○ excessive ◉ cautionary ○ good ○ excellent *
Total highway safety penalties are: 2 * Value: 8 4 Durability: 7 4 Highway Control Rating: 3 2 Highway Safety: 3 0

Note: Safety ratings are based on the assumption that the engineering of the RV has allowed for proper balance by placing fresh, gray, and black holding tanks in a location so as not to change the balance of the RV when the tanks are empty or full. **Always double-check wheelbase, GVWR, and weights at front and rear axles.**

*See Section 1 for details on how conclusions are reached.

Brand	Year	Type	Length	Model	Chassis	Engine	Fuel Type	Average Price per Linear Foot When New	Adjusted Wheelbase	Approx. Towing Capacity	Gross Vehicle Weight Rating	Average Curb Weight
Aerbus	1996	MHA	34	XL3400	CH	7.4L	G	$2000	232 T	1,000	19,000	16,003

Livability Code: SB 30-90 — Wheelbase-to-length ratio of 57% is considered ○ dangerous ○ fatiguing ◉ good ○ excellent *
The approximate net payload of 2997 pounds at 16% of GVWR on this model is ○ deficient ○ excessive ○ cautionary ○ good ◉ excellent *
Total highway safety penalties are: 9 * — Value: 80 — Durability: 74 — Highway Control Rating: 98 — Highway Safety: 89 — ★★★

Brand	Year	Type	Length	Model	Chassis	Engine	Fuel Type		Adjusted Wheelbase	Approx. Towing Capacity	GVWR	Curb Weight
Aerbus	1996	MHA	34	XL3400	FO	7.5L	G	$2000	232 T	5,000	20,000	16,628

Livability Code: SB 30-90 — Wheelbase-to-length ratio of 57% is considered ○ dangerous ○ fatiguing ◉ good ○ excellent *
The approximate net payload of 3372 pounds at 17% of GVWR on this model is ○ deficient ○ excessive ○ cautionary ○ good ◉ excellent *
Total highway safety penalties are: 4 * — Value: 82 — Durability: 74 — Highway Control Rating: 99 — Highway Safety: 95 — ★★★

Aerbus	1996	MHA	34	XL3400 opch	OS	CU230	D	$2900	208	4,500	20,500	18,644

Livability Code: SB 30-90 — Wheelbase-to-length ratio of 51% is considered ○ dangerous ◉ fatiguing ○ good ○ excellent *
The approximate net payload of 1856 pounds at 9% of GVWR on this model is ○ deficient ○ excessive ◉ cautionary ○ good ○ excellent *
Total highway safety penalties are: 2 * — Value: 84 — Durability: 74 — Highway Control Rating: 30 — Highway Safety: 28

Aerbus	1996	MHA	36	XL3550 sl	CH	7.4L	G	$2100	252 T	1,000	19,000	17,446

Livability Code: SB 30-90 — Wheelbase-to-length ratio of 59% is considered ○ dangerous ○ fatiguing ○ good ◉ excellent *
The approximate net payload of 1554 pounds at 8% of GVWR on this model is ○ deficient ○ excessive ◉ cautionary ○ good ○ excellent *
Total highway safety penalties are: 14 * — Value: 77 — Durability: 74 — Highway Control Rating: 83 — Highway Safety: 69 — ★★

Aerbus	1996	MHA	36	XL3500	CH	7.4L	G	$2000	252 T	1,000	19,000	16,254

Livability Code: SB 30-90 — Wheelbase-to-length ratio of 59% is considered ○ dangerous ○ fatiguing ○ good ◉ excellent *
The approximate net payload of 2746 pounds at 14% of GVWR on this model is ○ deficient ○ excessive ○ cautionary ○ good ◉ excellent *
Total highway safety penalties are: 10 * — Value: 80 — Durability: 74 — Highway Control Rating: 100 — Highway Safety: 90 — ★★★

Aerbus	1996	MHA	36	XL3550 sl	FO	7.5L	G	$1900	252 T	5,000	20,000	17,946

Livability Code: SB 30-90 — Wheelbase-to-length ratio of 59% is considered ○ dangerous ○ fatiguing ○ good ◉ excellent *
The approximate net payload of 2054 pounds at 10% of GVWR on this model is ○ deficient ○ excessive ○ cautionary ◉ good ○ excellent *
Total highway safety penalties are: 9 * — Value: 80 — Durability: 74 — Highway Control Rating: 95 — Highway Safety: 86 — ★★★

Aerbus	1996	MHA	36	XL3500	FO	7.4L	G	$2000	252 T	5,000	20,000	16,754

Livability Code: SB 30-90 — Wheelbase-to-length ratio of 59% is considered ○ dangerous ○ fatiguing ○ good ◉ excellent *
The approximate net payload of 3246 pounds at 16% of GVWR on this model is ○ deficient ○ excessive ○ cautionary ○ good ◉ excellent *
Total highway safety penalties are: 4 * — Value: 82 — Durability: 74 — Highway Control Rating: 100 — Highway Safety: 96 — ★★★

Aerbus	1996	MHA	36	XL3500 opch	OS	CU230	D	$2800	228	4,500	20,500	19,057

Livability Code: SB 30-90 — Wheelbase-to-length ratio of 53% is considered ○ dangerous ◉ fatiguing ○ good ○ excellent *
The approximate net payload of 1443 pounds at 7% of GVWR on this model is ○ deficient ○ excessive ◉ cautionary ○ good ○ excellent *
Total highway safety penalties are: 2 * — Value: 84 — Durability: 74 — Highway Control Rating: 42 — Highway Safety: 40

Aerbus	1996	MHA	36	XL3650 sl	CH	7.4L	G	$2000	252 T	1,000	19,000	17,889

Livability Code: SB 30-90 — Wheelbase-to-length ratio of 58% is considered ○ dangerous ○ fatiguing ○ good ◉ excellent *
The approximate net payload of 1111 pounds at 6% of GVWR on this model is ◉ deficient ○ excessive ○ cautionary ○ good ○ excellent *
Total highway safety penalties are: 16 * — Value: 76 — Durability: 74 — Highway Control Rating: 68 — Highway Safety: 52 — ★

Aerbus	1996	MHA	36	XL3600	FO	7.5L	G	$2000	252 T	5,000	20,000	17,339

Livability Code: SB 30-90 — Wheelbase-to-length ratio of 58% is considered ○ dangerous ○ fatiguing ○ good ◉ excellent *
The approximate net payload of 2661 pounds at 13% of GVWR on this model is ○ deficient ○ excessive ○ cautionary ◉ good ○ excellent *
Total highway safety penalties are: 4 * — Value: 82 — Durability: 74 — Highway Control Rating: 98 — Highway Safety: 94 — ★★★

Aerbus	1996	MHA	36	XL3650 sl	FO	7.5L	G	$2100	252 T	5,000	20,000	18,389

Livability Code: SB 30-90 — Wheelbase-to-length ratio of 58% is considered ○ dangerous ○ fatiguing ○ good ◉ excellent *
The approximate net payload of 1611 pounds at 8% of GVWR on this model is ○ deficient ○ excessive ◉ cautionary ○ good ○ excellent *
Total highway safety penalties are: 11 * — Value: 79 — Durability: 74 — Highway Control Rating: 80 — Highway Safety: 69 — ★★

Aerbus	1996	MHA	36	XL3650 opch sl	OS	CU230	D	$2800	228	4,500	20,500	20,244

Livability Code: SB 30-90 — Wheelbase-to-length ratio of 52% is considered ○ dangerous ◉ fatiguing ○ good ○ excellent *
The approximate net payload of 256 pounds at 1% of GVWR on this model is ◉ deficient ○ excessive ○ cautionary ○ good ○ excellent *
Total highway safety penalties are: 8 * — Value: 80 — Durability: 74 — Highway Control Rating: 21 — Highway Safety: 13

Note: Safety ratings are based on the assumption that the engineering of the RV has allowed for proper balance by placing fresh, gray, and black holding tanks in a location so as not to change the balance of the RV when the tanks are empty or full. **Always double-check wheelbase, GVWR, and weights at front and rear axles.**

*See Section 1 for details on how conclusions are reached.

Section 2: The Ratings

Brand	Year	Type	Length	Model	Chassis	Engine	Fuel Type	Average Price per Linear Foot When New	Adjusted Wheelbase	Approx. Towing Capacity	Gross Vehicle Weight Rating	Average Curb Weight
Aerbus	1996	MHA	39	XL3800	FO	7.5L	G	$1900	252 T	5,000	20,000	18,053

Livability Code: SB 30-90
Wheelbase-to-length ratio of 54% is considered ○ dangerous ○ fatiguing ◉ good ○ excellent *
The approximate net payload of 1947 pounds at 10% of GVWR on this model is ○ deficient ○ excessive ○ cautionary ◉ good ○ excellent *
Total highway safety penalties are: 4 * Value: 8 2 Durability: 7 4 Highway Control Rating: 7 6 Highway Safety: 7 2 ★★★

Brand	Year	Type	Length	Model	Chassis	Engine	Fuel Type	Average Price per Linear Foot When New	Adjusted Wheelbase	Approx. Towing Capacity	Gross Vehicle Weight Rating	Average Curb Weight
Aerbus	1997	MHA	29	XL2800	CH	7.4L	G	$2200	190	3,500	16,500	14,011

Livability Code: SB 30-90
Wheelbase-to-length ratio of 54% is considered ○ dangerous ○ fatiguing ◉ good ○ excellent *
The approximate net payload of 2489 pounds at 15% of GVWR on this model is ○ deficient ○ excessive ○ cautionary ◉ good ○ excellent *
Total highway safety penalties are: 4 * Value: 8 3 Durability: 7 4 Highway Control Rating: 8 1 Highway Safety: 7 7 ★★★

Brand	Year	Type	Length	Model	Chassis	Engine	Fuel Type	Average Price per Linear Foot When New	Adjusted Wheelbase	Approx. Towing Capacity	Gross Vehicle Weight Rating	Average Curb Weight
Aerbus	1997	MHA	29	XL2800	FO	7.5L	G	$2200	190	8,000	17,000	14,411

Livability Code: SB 30-90
Wheelbase-to-length ratio of 54% is considered ○ dangerous ○ fatiguing ◉ good ○ excellent *
The approximate net payload of 2589 pounds at 15% of GVWR on this model is ○ deficient ○ excessive ○ cautionary ◉ good ○ excellent *
Total highway safety penalties are: 2 * Value: 8 4 Durability: 7 4 Highway Control Rating: 8 1 Highway Safety: 7 9 ★★★

Brand	Year	Type	Length	Model	Chassis	Engine	Fuel Type	Average Price per Linear Foot When New	Adjusted Wheelbase	Approx. Towing Capacity	Gross Vehicle Weight Rating	Average Curb Weight
Aerbus	1997	MHA	31	XL2900	CH	7.4L	G	$2100	208	3,500	16,500	14,468

Livability Code: SB 30-90
Wheelbase-to-length ratio of 56% is considered ○ dangerous ○ fatiguing ◉ good ○ excellent *
The approximate net payload of 2032 pounds at 12% of GVWR on this model is ○ deficient ○ excessive ○ cautionary ◉ good ○ excellent *
Total highway safety penalties are: 5 * Value: 8 2 Durability: 7 4 Highway Control Rating: 9 0 Highway Safety: 8 5 ★★★

Brand	Year	Type	Length	Model	Chassis	Engine	Fuel Type	Average Price per Linear Foot When New	Adjusted Wheelbase	Approx. Towing Capacity	Gross Vehicle Weight Rating	Average Curb Weight
Aerbus	1997	MHA	31	XL2900	FO	7.5L	G	$2100	208	8,000	17,000	14,868

Livability Code: SB 30-90
Wheelbase-to-length ratio of 56% is considered ○ dangerous ○ fatiguing ◉ good ○ excellent *
The approximate net payload of 2132 pounds at 13% of GVWR on this model is ○ deficient ○ excessive ○ cautionary ◉ good ○ excellent *
Total highway safety penalties are: 2 * Value: 8 4 Durability: 7 4 Highway Control Rating: 9 1 Highway Safety: 8 9 ★★★

Brand	Year	Type	Length	Model	Chassis	Engine	Fuel Type	Average Price per Linear Foot When New	Adjusted Wheelbase	Approx. Towing Capacity	Gross Vehicle Weight Rating	Average Curb Weight
Aerbus	1997	MHA	32	XL3000	CH	7.4L	G	$2000	208	3,500	16,500	14,696

Livability Code: SB 30-90
Wheelbase-to-length ratio of 55% is considered ○ dangerous ○ fatiguing ◉ good ○ excellent *
The approximate net payload of 1804 pounds at 11% of GVWR on this model is ○ deficient ○ excessive ○ cautionary ◉ good ○ excellent *
Total highway safety penalties are: 5 * Value: 8 2 Durability: 7 4 Highway Control Rating: 8 8 Highway Safety: 8 3 ★★★

Brand	Year	Type	Length	Model	Chassis	Engine	Fuel Type	Average Price per Linear Foot When New	Adjusted Wheelbase	Approx. Towing Capacity	Gross Vehicle Weight Rating	Average Curb Weight
Aerbus	1997	MHA	32	XL3000	FO	7.5L	G	$2000	208	8,000	17,000	15,096

Livability Code: SB 30-90
Wheelbase-to-length ratio of 55% is considered ○ dangerous ○ fatiguing ◉ good ○ excellent *
The approximate net payload of 1904 pounds at 11% of GVWR on this model is ○ deficient ○ excessive ○ cautionary ◉ good ○ excellent *
Total highway safety penalties are: 2 * Value: 8 4 Durability: 7 4 Highway Control Rating: 8 8 Highway Safety: 8 6 ★★★

Brand	Year	Type	Length	Model	Chassis	Engine	Fuel Type	Average Price per Linear Foot When New	Adjusted Wheelbase	Approx. Towing Capacity	Gross Vehicle Weight Rating	Average Curb Weight
Aerbus	1997	MHA	32	XL3100	CH	7.4L	G	$2200	208	3,500	16,500	14,896

Livability Code: SB 30-90
Wheelbase-to-length ratio of 54% is considered ○ dangerous ○ fatiguing ◉ good ○ excellent *
The approximate net payload of 1604 pounds at 10% of GVWR on this model is ○ deficient ○ excessive ○ cautionary ◉ good ○ excellent *
Total highway safety penalties are: 6 * Value: 8 2 Durability: 7 4 Highway Control Rating: 7 5 Highway Safety: 6 9 ★★

Brand	Year	Type	Length	Model	Chassis	Engine	Fuel Type	Average Price per Linear Foot When New	Adjusted Wheelbase	Approx. Towing Capacity	Gross Vehicle Weight Rating	Average Curb Weight
Aerbus	1997	MHA	32	XL3200	CH	7.4L	G	$2100	208	3,500	16,500	14,896

Livability Code: SB 30-90
Wheelbase-to-length ratio of 54% is considered ○ dangerous ○ fatiguing ◉ good ○ excellent *
The approximate net payload of 1604 pounds at 10% of GVWR on this model is ○ deficient ○ excessive ○ cautionary ◉ good ○ excellent *
Total highway safety penalties are: 6 * Value: 8 2 Durability: 7 4 Highway Control Rating: 7 5 Highway Safety: 6 9 ★★

Brand	Year	Type	Length	Model	Chassis	Engine	Fuel Type	Average Price per Linear Foot When New	Adjusted Wheelbase	Approx. Towing Capacity	Gross Vehicle Weight Rating	Average Curb Weight
Aerbus	1997	MHA	32	XL3250	CH	7.4L	G	$2100	208	3,500	16,500	15,796

Livability Code: SB 30-90
Wheelbase-to-length ratio of 54% is considered ○ dangerous ○ fatiguing ◉ good ○ excellent *
The approximate net payload of 704 pounds at 4% of GVWR on this model is ◉ deficient ○ excessive ○ cautionary ○ good ○ excellent *
Total highway safety penalties are: 11 * Value: 7 9 Durability: 7 4 Highway Control Rating: 4 4 Highway Safety: 3 3

Brand	Year	Type	Length	Model	Chassis	Engine	Fuel Type	Average Price per Linear Foot When New	Adjusted Wheelbase	Approx. Towing Capacity	Gross Vehicle Weight Rating	Average Curb Weight
Aerbus	1997	MHA	32	XL3100	FO	7.5L	G	$2300	208	8,000	17,000	15,296

Livability Code: SB 30-90
Wheelbase-to-length ratio of 54% is considered ○ dangerous ○ fatiguing ◉ good ○ excellent *
The approximate net payload of 1704 pounds at 10% of GVWR on this model is ○ deficient ○ excessive ○ cautionary ◉ good ○ excellent *
Total highway safety penalties are: 2 * Value: 8 4 Durability: 7 4 Highway Control Rating: 7 5 Highway Safety: 7 3 ★★★

Brand	Year	Type	Length	Model	Chassis	Engine	Fuel Type	Average Price per Linear Foot When New	Adjusted Wheelbase	Approx. Towing Capacity	Gross Vehicle Weight Rating	Average Curb Weight
Aerbus	1997	MHA	32	XL3200	FO	7.5L	G	$2100	208	8,000	17,000	15,296

Livability Code: SB 30-90
Wheelbase-to-length ratio of 54% is considered ○ dangerous ○ fatiguing ◉ good ○ excellent *
The approximate net payload of 1704 pounds at 10% of GVWR on this model is ○ deficient ○ excessive ○ cautionary ◉ good ○ excellent *
Total highway safety penalties are: 2 * Value: 8 4 Durability: 7 4 Highway Control Rating: 7 5 Highway Safety: 7 3 ★★★

Note: Safety ratings are based on the assumption that the engineering of the RV has allowed for proper balance by placing fresh, gray, and black holding tanks in a location so as not to change the balance of the RV when the tanks are empty or full. **Always double-check wheelbase, GVWR, and weights at front and rear axles.**

*See Section 1 for details on how conclusions are reached.

Brand	Year	Type	Length	Model	Chassis	Engine	Fuel Type	Average Price per Linear Foot When New	Adjusted Wheelbase	Approx. Towing Capacity	Gross Vehicle Weight Rating	Average Curb Weight
Aerbus	**1997**	MHA	32	XL3250	FO	7.5L	G	$2300	208	8,000	17,000	16,196

Livability Code: SB 30-90

Wheelbase-to-length ratio of 54% is considered ○ dangerous ○ fatiguing ● good ○ excellent *

The approximate net payload of 804 pounds at 5% of GVWR on this model is ● deficient ○ excessive ○ cautionary ○ good ○ excellent *

Total highway safety penalties are: 7 *   Value: 8 1   Durability: 7 4   Highway Control Rating: 4 5   Highway Safety: 3 8

Brand	Year	Type	Length	Model	Chassis	Engine	Fuel Type	Price/Ft	Wheelbase	Towing	GVWR	Curb Weight
Aerbus	**1997**	MHA	32	XL3100	FR	Cu230	D	$3400	190	4,500	20,500	17,396

Livability Code: SB 30-90

Wheelbase-to-length ratio of 49% is considered ● dangerous ○ fatiguing ○ good ○ excellent *

The approximate net payload of 3104 pounds at 15% of GVWR on this model is ○ deficient ○ excessive ○ cautionary ● good ○ excellent *

Total highway safety penalties are: 2 *   Value: 8 4   Durability: 7 4   Highway Control Rating: 4 0   Highway Safety: 3 8

Brand	Year	Type	Length	Model	Chassis	Engine	Fuel Type	Price/Ft	Wheelbase	Towing	GVWR	Curb Weight
Aerbus	**1997**	MHA	32	XL3200	FR	Cu230	D	$3400	190	4,500	20,500	17,396

Livability Code: SB 30-90

Wheelbase-to-length ratio of 49% is considered ● dangerous ○ fatiguing ○ good ○ excellent *

The approximate net payload of 3104 pounds at 15% of GVWR on this model is ○ deficient ○ excessive ○ cautionary ● good ○ excellent *

Total highway safety penalties are: 2 *   Value: 8 4   Durability: 7 4   Highway Control Rating: 4 0   Highway Safety: 3 8

Brand	Year	Type	Length	Model	Chassis	Engine	Fuel Type	Price/Ft	Wheelbase	Towing	GVWR	Curb Weight
Aerbus	**1997**	MHA	32	XL3250	FR	Cu230	D	$3400	190	4,500	20,500	18,296

Livability Code: SB 30-90

Wheelbase-to-length ratio of 49% is considered ● dangerous ○ fatiguing ○ good ○ excellent *

The approximate net payload of 2204 pounds at 11% of GVWR on this model is ○ deficient ○ excessive ○ cautionary ● good ○ excellent *

Total highway safety penalties are: 7 *   Value: 8 1   Durability: 7 4   Highway Control Rating: 3 2   Highway Safety: 2 5

Brand	Year	Type	Length	Model	Chassis	Engine	Fuel Type	Price/Ft	Wheelbase	Towing	GVWR	Curb Weight
Aerbus	**1997**	MHA	32	XL3100	SP	Cu230	D	$3400	190	1,000	24,000	20,539

Livability Code: SB 30-90

Wheelbase-to-length ratio of 49% is considered ● dangerous ○ fatiguing ○ good ○ excellent *

The approximate net payload of 3461 pounds at 14% of GVWR on this model is ○ deficient ○ excessive ○ cautionary ● good ○ excellent *

Total highway safety penalties are: 2 *   Value: 8 4   Durability: 7 4   Highway Control Rating: 3 8   Highway Safety: 3 6

Brand	Year	Type	Length	Model	Chassis	Engine	Fuel Type	Price/Ft	Wheelbase	Towing	GVWR	Curb Weight
Aerbus	**1997**	MHA	32	XL3200	SP	Cu230	D	$3400	190	1,000	24,000	20,539

Livability Code: SB 30-90

Wheelbase-to-length ratio of 49% is considered ● dangerous ○ fatiguing ○ good ○ excellent *

The approximate net payload of 3461 pounds at 14% of GVWR on this model is ○ deficient ○ excessive ○ cautionary ● good ○ excellent *

Total highway safety penalties are: 2 *   Value: 8 4   Durability: 7 4   Highway Control Rating: 3 8   Highway Safety: 3 6

Brand	Year	Type	Length	Model	Chassis	Engine	Fuel Type	Price/Ft	Wheelbase	Towing	GVWR	Curb Weight
Aerbus	**1997**	MHA	32	XL3250	SP	Cu230	D	$3400	190	1,000	24,000	21,439

Livability Code: SB 30-90

Wheelbase-to-length ratio of 49% is considered ● dangerous ○ fatiguing ○ good ○ excellent *

The approximate net payload of 2561 pounds at 11% of GVWR on this model is ○ deficient ○ excessive ○ cautionary ● good ○ excellent *

Total highway safety penalties are: 7 *   Value: 8 1   Durability: 7 4   Highway Control Rating: 3 1   Highway Safety: 2 4

Brand	Year	Type	Length	Model	Chassis	Engine	Fuel Type	Price/Ft	Wheelbase	Towing	GVWR	Curb Weight
Aerbus	**1997**	MHA	34	XL3300	CH	7.4L	G	$2100	228	3,500	16,500	15,382

Livability Code: SB 30-90

Wheelbase-to-length ratio of 56% is considered ○ dangerous ○ fatiguing ● good ○ excellent *

The approximate net payload of 1118 pounds at 7% of GVWR on this model is ○ deficient ○ excessive ● cautionary ○ good ○ excellent *

Total highway safety penalties are: 6 *   Value: 8 1   Durability: 7 4   Highway Control Rating: 6 7   Highway Safety: 6 1   ★★

Brand	Year	Type	Length	Model	Chassis	Engine	Fuel Type	Price/Ft	Wheelbase	Towing	GVWR	Curb Weight
Aerbus	**1997**	MHA	34	XL3300	FO	7.5L	G	$2100	228	8,000	17,000	15,601

Livability Code: SB 30-90

Wheelbase-to-length ratio of 56% is considered ○ dangerous ○ fatiguing ● good ○ excellent *

The approximate net payload of 1399 pounds at 8% of GVWR on this model is ○ deficient ○ excessive ● cautionary ○ good ○ excellent *

Total highway safety penalties are: 2 *   Value: 8 4   Durability: 7 4   Highway Control Rating: 7 4   Highway Safety: 7 2   ★★★

Brand	Year	Type	Length	Model	Chassis	Engine	Fuel Type	Price/Ft	Wheelbase	Towing	GVWR	Curb Weight
Aerbus	**1997**	MHA	34	XL3300	FR	Cu230	D	$3200	208	4,500	20,500	17,882

Livability Code: SB 30-90

Wheelbase-to-length ratio of 51% is considered ○ dangerous ● fatiguing ○ good ○ excellent *

The approximate net payload of 2618 pounds at 13% of GVWR on this model is ○ deficient ○ excessive ○ cautionary ● good ○ excellent *

Total highway safety penalties are: 2 *   Value: 8 4   Durability: 7 4   Highway Control Rating: 4 3   Highway Safety: 4 1

Brand	Year	Type	Length	Model	Chassis	Engine	Fuel Type	Price/Ft	Wheelbase	Towing	GVWR	Curb Weight
Aerbus	**1997**	MHA	34	XL3300	SP	Cu230	D	$3200	208	1,000	24,000	20,990

Livability Code: SB 30-90

Wheelbase-to-length ratio of 51% is considered ○ dangerous ● fatiguing ○ good ○ excellent *

The approximate net payload of 3010 pounds at 13% of GVWR on this model is ○ deficient ○ excessive ○ cautionary ● good ○ excellent *

Total highway safety penalties are: 2 *   Value: 8 4   Durability: 7 4   Highway Control Rating: 4 2   Highway Safety: 4 0

Brand	Year	Type	Length	Model	Chassis	Engine	Fuel Type	Price/Ft	Wheelbase	Towing	GVWR	Curb Weight
Aerbus	**1997**	MHA	34	XL3400	CH	7.4L	G	$2100	232 T	1,000	19,500	16,368

Livability Code: SB 30-90

Wheelbase-to-length ratio of 57% is considered ○ dangerous ○ fatiguing ● good ○ excellent *

The approximate net payload of 3132 pounds at 16% of GVWR on this model is ○ deficient ○ excessive ○ cautionary ○ good ● excellent *

Total highway safety penalties are: 9 *   Value: 8 0   Durability: 7 4   Highway Control Rating: 9 8   Highway Safety: 8 9   ★★★

Note: Safety ratings are based on the assumption that the engineering of the RV has allowed for proper balance by placing fresh, gray, and black holding tanks in a location so as not to change the balance of the RV when the tanks are empty or full. **Always double-check wheelbase, GVWR, and weights at front and rear axles.**

*See Section 1 for details on how conclusions are reached.

Brand	Year	Type	Length	Model	Chassis	Engine	Fuel Type	Average Price per Linear Foot When New	Adjusted Wheelbase	Approx. Towing Capacity	Gross Vehicle Weight Rating	Average Curb Weight
Aerbus	1997	MHA	34	XL3400	FO	7.5L	G	$2100	232 T	5,000	20,000	16,768

Livability Code: SB 30-90
Wheelbase-to-length ratio of 57% is considered ○ dangerous ○ fatiguing ◉ good ○ excellent *
The approximate net payload of 3232 pounds at 16% of GVWR on this model is ○ deficient ○ excessive ○ cautionary ○ good ◉ excellent *
Total highway safety penalties are: 4 *   Value: 8 2   Durability: 7 4   Highway Control Rating: 9 8   Highway Safety: 9 4   ★★★

Brand	Year	Type	Length	Model	Chassis	Engine	Fuel Type	Avg Price/Ft	Adj Wheelbase	Towing	GVWR	Curb Weight
Aerbus	1997	MHA	34	XL3400	FR	Cu230	D	$3200	208	4,500	20,500	17,968

Livability Code: SB 30-90
Wheelbase-to-length ratio of 51% is considered ○ dangerous ◉ fatiguing ○ good ○ excellent *
The approximate net payload of 2532 pounds at 12% of GVWR on this model is ○ deficient ○ excessive ○ cautionary ◉ good ○ excellent *
Total highway safety penalties are: 2 *   Value: 8 4   Durability: 7 4   Highway Control Rating: 4 0   Highway Safety: 3 8

Aerbus	1997	MHA	34	XL3400	SP	Cu230	D	$3200	208	1,000	24,000	21,070

Livability Code: SB 30-90
Wheelbase-to-length ratio of 51% is considered ○ dangerous ◉ fatiguing ○ good ○ excellent *
The approximate net payload of 2930 pounds at 12% of GVWR on this model is ○ deficient ○ excessive ○ cautionary ◉ good ○ excellent *
Total highway safety penalties are: 2 *   Value: 8 4   Durability: 7 4   Highway Control Rating: 3 9   Highway Safety: 3 7

Aerbus	1997	MHA	36	XL3500	CH	7.4L	G	$2000	252 T	1,000	19,500	16,796

Livability Code: SB 30-90
Wheelbase-to-length ratio of 59% is considered ○ dangerous ○ fatiguing ○ good ◉ excellent *
The approximate net payload of 2704 pounds at 14% of GVWR on this model is ○ deficient ○ excessive ○ cautionary ◉ good ○ excellent *
Total highway safety penalties are: 10 *   Value: 8 0   Durability: 7 4   Highway Control Rating: 1 0 0   Highway Safety: 9 0   ★★★

Aerbus	1997	MHA	36	XL3550	CH	7.4L	G	$2100	252 T	1,000	19,500	17,546

Livability Code: SB 30-90
Wheelbase-to-length ratio of 59% is considered ○ dangerous ○ fatiguing ○ good ◉ excellent *
The approximate net payload of 1954 pounds at 10% of GVWR on this model is ○ deficient ○ excessive ○ cautionary ◉ good ○ excellent *
Total highway safety penalties are: 14 *   Value: 7 7   Durability: 7 4   Highway Control Rating: 9 4   Highway Safety: 8 0   ★★★

Aerbus	1997	MHA	36	XL3500	FO	7.5L	G	$2000	252 T	5,000	20,000	17,196

Livability Code: SB 30-90
Wheelbase-to-length ratio of 59% is considered ○ dangerous ○ fatiguing ○ good ◉ excellent *
The approximate net payload of 2804 pounds at 14% of GVWR on this model is ○ deficient ○ excessive ○ cautionary ◉ good ○ excellent *
Total highway safety penalties are: 4 *   Value: 8 2   Durability: 7 4   Highway Control Rating: 1 0 0   Highway Safety: 9 6   ★★★

Aerbus	1997	MHA	36	XL3550	FO	7.5L	G	$2100	252 T	5,000	20,000	18,096

Livability Code: SB 30-90
Wheelbase-to-length ratio of 59% is considered ○ dangerous ○ fatiguing ○ good ◉ excellent *
The approximate net payload of 1904 pounds at 10% of GVWR on this model is ○ deficient ○ excessive ○ cautionary ◉ good ○ excellent *
Total highway safety penalties are: 10 *   Value: 8 0   Durability: 7 4   Highway Control Rating: 9 4   Highway Safety: 8 4   ★★★

Aerbus	1997	MHA	36	XL3500	FR	Cu230	D	$3100	228	4,500	20,500	18,396

Livability Code: SB 30-90
Wheelbase-to-length ratio of 53% is considered ○ dangerous ◉ fatiguing ○ good ○ excellent *
The approximate net payload of 2104 pounds at 10% of GVWR on this model is ○ deficient ○ excessive ○ cautionary ◉ good ○ excellent *
Total highway safety penalties are: 2 *   Value: 8 4   Durability: 7 4   Highway Control Rating: 6 0   Highway Safety: 5 8   ★

Aerbus	1997	MHA	36	XL3550	FR	Cu230	D	$3100	228	4,500	20,500	19,146

Livability Code: SB 30-90
Wheelbase-to-length ratio of 53% is considered ○ dangerous ◉ fatiguing ○ good ○ excellent *
The approximate net payload of 1354 pounds at 7% of GVWR on this model is ○ deficient ○ excessive ◉ cautionary ○ good ○ excellent *
Total highway safety penalties are: 7 *   Value: 8 1   Durability: 7 4   Highway Control Rating: 4 2   Highway Safety: 3 5

Aerbus	1997	MHA	36	XL3500	SP	Cu230	D	$3100	228	1,000	24,000	21,468

Livability Code: SB 30-90
Wheelbase-to-length ratio of 53% is considered ○ dangerous ◉ fatiguing ○ good ○ excellent *
The approximate net payload of 2532 pounds at 11% of GVWR on this model is ○ deficient ○ excessive ○ cautionary ◉ good ○ excellent *
Total highway safety penalties are: 2 *   Value: 8 4   Durability: 7 4   Highway Control Rating: 6 1   Highway Safety: 5 9   ★

Aerbus	1997	MHA	36	XL3550	SP	Cu230	D	$3100	228	2,000	24,000	22,218

Livability Code: SB 30-90
Wheelbase-to-length ratio of 53% is considered ○ dangerous ◉ fatiguing ○ good ○ excellent *
The approximate net payload of 1782 pounds at 7% of GVWR on this model is ○ deficient ○ excessive ◉ cautionary ○ good ○ excellent *
Total highway safety penalties are: 7 *   Value: 8 1   Durability: 7 4   Highway Control Rating: 4 3   Highway Safety: 3 6

Aerbus	1997	MHA	36	XL3600	CH	7.4L	G	$2000	252 T	1,000	19,500	16,939

Livability Code: SB 30-90
Wheelbase-to-length ratio of 58% is considered ○ dangerous ○ fatiguing ○ good ◉ excellent *
The approximate net payload of 2561 pounds at 13% of GVWR on this model is ○ deficient ○ excessive ○ cautionary ◉ good ○ excellent *
Total highway safety penalties are: 10 *   Value: 8 0   Durability: 7 4   Highway Control Rating: 9 7   Highway Safety: 8 7   ★★★

Note: Safety ratings are based on the assumption that the engineering of the RV has allowed for proper balance by placing fresh, gray, and black holding tanks in a location so as not to change the balance of the RV when the tanks are empty or full. **Always double-check wheelbase, GVWR, and weights at front and rear axles.**

*See Section 1 for details on how conclusions are reached.

Section 2: The Ratings

Brand	Year	Type	Length	Model	Chassis	Engine	Fuel Type	Average Price per Linear Foot When New	Adjusted Wheelbase	Approx. Towing Capacity	Gross Vehicle Weight Rating	Average Curb Weight

Aerbus 1997 MHA 36 XL3650 CH 7.4L G $2100 252 T 1,000 19,500 17,989
Livability Code: SB 30-90
Wheelbase-to-length ratio of 58% is considered ○ dangerous ○ fatiguing ○ good ◉ excellent *
The approximate net payload of 1511 pounds at 8% of GVWR on this model is ○ deficient ○ excessive ◉ cautionary ○ good ○ excellent *
Total highway safety penalties are: 16 *   Value: **7 6** Durability: **7 4** Highway Control Rating: **8 0** Highway Safety: **6 4** ★★

Aerbus 1997 MHA 36 XL3600 FO 7.5L G $2000 252 T 5,000 20,000 17,339
Livability Code: SB 30-90
Wheelbase-to-length ratio of 58% is considered ○ dangerous ○ fatiguing ○ good ◉ excellent *
The approximate net payload of 2661 pounds at 13% of GVWR on this model is ○ deficient ○ excessive ○ cautionary ◉ good ○ excellent *
Total highway safety penalties are: 4 *   Value: **8 2** Durability: **7 4** Highway Control Rating: **9 8** Highway Safety: **9 4** ★★★

Aerbus 1997 MHA 36 XL3650 FO 7.5L G $2100 252 T 5,000 20,000 18,389
Livability Code: SB 30-90
Wheelbase-to-length ratio of 58% is considered ○ dangerous ○ fatiguing ○ good ◉ excellent *
The approximate net payload of 1611 pounds at 8% of GVWR on this model is ○ deficient ○ excessive ◉ cautionary ○ good ○ excellent *
Total highway safety penalties are: 11 *   Value: **7 9** Durability: **7 4** Highway Control Rating: **8 0** Highway Safety: **6 9** ★★

Aerbus 1997 MHA 36 XL3600 FR Cu230 D $3100 228 4,500 20,500 18,539
Livability Code: SB 30-90
Wheelbase-to-length ratio of 52% is considered ○ dangerous ◉ fatiguing ○ good ○ excellent *
The approximate net payload of 1961 pounds at 10% of GVWR on this model is ○ deficient ○ excessive ○ cautionary ◉ good ○ excellent *
Total highway safety penalties are: 2 *   Value: **8 4** Durability: **7 4** Highway Control Rating: **4 9** Highway Safety: **4 7**

Aerbus 1997 MHA 36 XL3650 FR Cu230 D $3100 228 4,500 20,500 19,589
Livability Code: SB 30-90
Wheelbase-to-length ratio of 52% is considered ○ dangerous ◉ fatiguing ○ good ○ excellent *
The approximate net payload of 911 pounds at 4% of GVWR on this model is ◉ deficient ○ excessive ○ cautionary ○ good ○ excellent *
Total highway safety penalties are: 8 *   Value: **8 0** Durability: **7 4** Highway Control Rating: **2 5** Highway Safety: **1 7**

Aerbus 1997 MHA 36 XL3600 SP Cu230 D $3100 228 2,000 24,000 21,600
Livability Code: SB 30-90
Wheelbase-to-length ratio of 52% is considered ○ dangerous ◉ fatiguing ○ good ○ excellent *
The approximate net payload of 2400 pounds at 10% of GVWR on this model is ○ deficient ○ excessive ○ cautionary ◉ good ○ excellent *
Total highway safety penalties are: 2 *   Value: **8 4** Durability: **7 4** Highway Control Rating: **4 9** Highway Safety: **4 7**

Aerbus 1997 MHA 36 XL3650 SP Cu230 D $3100 228 2,000 24,000 22,650
Livability Code: SB 30-90
Wheelbase-to-length ratio of 52% is considered ○ dangerous ◉ fatiguing ○ good ○ excellent *
The approximate net payload of 1350 pounds at 6% of GVWR on this model is ◉ deficient ○ excessive ○ cautionary ○ good ○ excellent *
Total highway safety penalties are: 8 *   Value: **8 0** Durability: **7 4** Highway Control Rating: **2 6** Highway Safety: **1 8**

Aerbus 1997 MHA 39 XL3800 FO 7.5L G $1900 252 T 5,000 20,000 18,053
Livability Code: SB 30-90
Wheelbase-to-length ratio of 54% is considered ○ dangerous ○ fatiguing ◉ good ○ excellent *
The approximate net payload of 1947 pounds at 10% of GVWR on this model is ○ deficient ○ excessive ○ cautionary ◉ good ○ excellent *
Total highway safety penalties are: 4 *   Value: **8 2** Durability: **7 4** Highway Control Rating: **7 6** Highway Safety: **7 2** ★★★

Aerbus 1998 MHA 29 XL2800 CH 7.4L G $2400 190 1,500 16,500 14,011
Livability Code: SB 30-90
Wheelbase-to-length ratio of 54% is considered ○ dangerous ○ fatiguing ◉ good ○ excellent *
The approximate net payload of 2489 pounds at 15% of GVWR on this model is ○ deficient ○ excessive ○ cautionary ◉ good ○ excellent *
Total highway safety penalties are: 4 *   Value: **8 4** Durability: **7 7** Highway Control Rating: **8 1** Highway Safety: **7 7** ★★★

Aerbus 1998 MHA 29 XL2800 FO 7.5L G $2600 190 1,500 17,000 14,411
Livability Code: SB 30-90
Wheelbase-to-length ratio of 54% is considered ○ dangerous ○ fatiguing ◉ good ○ excellent *
The approximate net payload of 2589 pounds at 15% of GVWR on this model is ○ deficient ○ excessive ○ cautionary ◉ good ○ excellent *
Total highway safety penalties are: 2 *   Value: **8 5** Durability: **7 7** Highway Control Rating: **8 1** Highway Safety: **7 9** ★★★

Aerbus 1998 MHA 31 XL2900DS CH 7.4L G $2300 190 1,500 16,500 14,411
Livability Code: SB 30-90
Wheelbase-to-length ratio of 52% is considered ○ dangerous ◉ fatiguing ○ good ○ excellent *
The approximate net payload of 2089 pounds at 13% of GVWR on this model is ○ deficient ○ excessive ○ cautionary ◉ good ○ excellent *
Total highway safety penalties are: 5 *   Value: **8 3** Durability: **7 7** Highway Control Rating: **5 3** Highway Safety: **4 8**

Aerbus 1998 MHA 31 XL2900DS FO 7.5L G $2400 190 1,500 17,000 14,811
Livability Code: SB 30-90
Wheelbase-to-length ratio of 52% is considered ○ dangerous ◉ fatiguing ○ good ○ excellent *
The approximate net payload of 2189 pounds at 13% of GVWR on this model is ○ deficient ○ excessive ○ cautionary ◉ good ○ excellent *
Total highway safety penalties are: 2 *   Value: **8 5** Durability: **7 7** Highway Control Rating: **5 3** Highway Safety: **5 1** ★

Note: Safety ratings are based on the assumption that the engineering of the RV has allowed for proper balance by placing fresh, gray, and black holding tanks in a location so as not to change the balance of the RV when the tanks are empty or full. **Always double-check wheelbase, GVWR, and weights at front and rear axles.**

*See Section 1 for details on how conclusions are reached.

Brand	Year	Type	Length	Model	Chassis	Engine	Fuel Type	Average Price per Linear Foot When New	Adjusted Wheelbase	Approx. Towing Capacity	Gross Vehicle Weight Rating	Average Curb Weight
Aerbus	1998	MHA	31	XL2900	CH	7.4L	G	$2300	208	1,500	16,500	14,468

Livability Code: SB 30-90
Wheelbase-to-length ratio of 56% is considered ○ dangerous ○ fatiguing ◉ good ○ excellent *
The approximate net payload of 2032 pounds at 12% of GVWR on this model is ○ deficient ○ excessive ○ cautionary ◉ good ○ excellent *
Total highway safety penalties are: 5 *   Value: 8 3   Durability: 7 7   Highway Control Rating: 9 0   Highway Safety: 8 5   ★★★

Brand	Year	Type	Length	Model	Chassis	Engine	Fuel Type	Avg Price/Ft	Adj Wheelbase	Towing	GVWR	Curb Weight
Aerbus	1998	MHA	31	XL2900	FO	7.5L	G	$2400	208	1,500	17,000	14,868

Livability Code: SB 30-90
Wheelbase-to-length ratio of 56% is considered ○ dangerous ○ fatiguing ◉ good ○ excellent *
The approximate net payload of 2132 pounds at 13% of GVWR on this model is ○ deficient ○ excessive ○ cautionary ◉ good ○ excellent *
Total highway safety penalties are: 2 *   Value: 8 5   Durability: 7 7   Highway Control Rating: 9 1   Highway Safety: 8 9   ★★★

Brand	Year	Type	Length	Model	Chassis	Engine	Fuel Type	Avg Price/Ft	Adj Wheelbase	Towing	GVWR	Curb Weight
Aerbus	1998	MHA	31	XL2900FB	CH	7.4L	G	$2300	208	1,500	16,500	14,554

Livability Code: SB 30-90
Wheelbase-to-length ratio of 56% is considered ○ dangerous ○ fatiguing ◉ good ○ excellent *
The approximate net payload of 1946 pounds at 12% of GVWR on this model is ○ deficient ○ excessive ○ cautionary ◉ good ○ excellent *
Total highway safety penalties are: 5 *   Value: 8 3   Durability: 7 7   Highway Control Rating: 8 8   Highway Safety: 8 3   ★★★

Brand	Year	Type	Length	Model	Chassis	Engine	Fuel Type	Avg Price/Ft	Adj Wheelbase	Towing	GVWR	Curb Weight
Aerbus	1998	MHA	31	XL2900FB	FO	7.5L	G	$2400	208	1,500	17,000	14,954

Livability Code: SB 30-90
Wheelbase-to-length ratio of 56% is considered ○ dangerous ○ fatiguing ◉ good ○ excellent *
The approximate net payload of 2046 pounds at 12% of GVWR on this model is ○ deficient ○ excessive ○ cautionary ◉ good ○ excellent *
Total highway safety penalties are: 2 *   Value: 8 5   Durability: 7 7   Highway Control Rating: 8 8   Highway Safety: 8 6   ★★★

Brand	Year	Type	Length	Model	Chassis	Engine	Fuel Type	Avg Price/Ft	Adj Wheelbase	Towing	GVWR	Curb Weight
Aerbus	1998	MHA	32	XL3000	CH	7.4L	G	$2300	208	1,500	16,500	14,696

Livability Code: SB 30-90
Wheelbase-to-length ratio of 55% is considered ○ dangerous ○ fatiguing ◉ good ○ excellent *
The approximate net payload of 1804 pounds at 11% of GVWR on this model is ○ deficient ○ excessive ○ cautionary ◉ good ○ excellent *
Total highway safety penalties are: 5 *   Value: 8 3   Durability: 7 7   Highway Control Rating: 8 8   Highway Safety: 8 3   ★★★

Brand	Year	Type	Length	Model	Chassis	Engine	Fuel Type	Avg Price/Ft	Adj Wheelbase	Towing	GVWR	Curb Weight
Aerbus	1998	MHA	32	XL3000	FO	7.5L	G	$2300	208	1,500	17,000	15,096

Livability Code: SB 30-90
Wheelbase-to-length ratio of 55% is considered ○ dangerous ○ fatiguing ◉ good ○ excellent *
The approximate net payload of 1904 pounds at 11% of GVWR on this model is ○ deficient ○ excessive ○ cautionary ◉ good ○ excellent *
Total highway safety penalties are: 2 *   Value: 8 5   Durability: 7 7   Highway Control Rating: 8 8   Highway Safety: 8 6   ★★★

Brand	Year	Type	Length	Model	Chassis	Engine	Fuel Type	Avg Price/Ft	Adj Wheelbase	Towing	GVWR	Curb Weight
Aerbus	1998	MHA	32	XL3100	CH	7.4L	G	$2300	208	1,500	16,500	14,896

Livability Code: SB 30-90
Wheelbase-to-length ratio of 54% is considered ○ dangerous ○ fatiguing ◉ good ○ excellent *
The approximate net payload of 1604 pounds at 10% of GVWR on this model is ○ deficient ○ excessive ○ cautionary ◉ good ○ excellent *
Total highway safety penalties are: 6 *   Value: 8 3   Durability: 7 7   Highway Control Rating: 7 5   Highway Safety: 6 9   ★★

Brand	Year	Type	Length	Model	Chassis	Engine	Fuel Type	Avg Price/Ft	Adj Wheelbase	Towing	GVWR	Curb Weight
Aerbus	1998	MHA	32	XL3200	CH	7.4L	G	$2300	208	1,500	16,500	14,896

Livability Code: SB 30-90
Wheelbase-to-length ratio of 54% is considered ○ dangerous ○ fatiguing ◉ good ○ excellent *
The approximate net payload of 1604 pounds at 10% of GVWR on this model is ○ deficient ○ excessive ○ cautionary ◉ good ○ excellent *
Total highway safety penalties are: 6 *   Value: 8 3   Durability: 7 7   Highway Control Rating: 7 5   Highway Safety: 6 9   ★★

Brand	Year	Type	Length	Model	Chassis	Engine	Fuel Type	Avg Price/Ft	Adj Wheelbase	Towing	GVWR	Curb Weight
Aerbus	1998	MHA	32	XL3250	CH	7.4L	G	$2300	208	1,500	16,500	15,796

Livability Code: SB 30-90
Wheelbase-to-length ratio of 54% is considered ○ dangerous ○ fatiguing ◉ good ○ excellent *
The approximate net payload of 704 pounds at 4% of GVWR on this model is ◉ deficient ○ excessive ○ cautionary ○ good ○ excellent *
Total highway safety penalties are: 11 *   Value: 8 0   Durability: 7 7   Highway Control Rating: 4 4   Highway Safety: 3 3

Brand	Year	Type	Length	Model	Chassis	Engine	Fuel Type	Avg Price/Ft	Adj Wheelbase	Towing	GVWR	Curb Weight
Aerbus	1998	MHA	32	XL3100	FO	7.5L	G	$2300	208	1,500	17,000	15,296

Livability Code: SB 30-90
Wheelbase-to-length ratio of 54% is considered ○ dangerous ○ fatiguing ◉ good ○ excellent *
The approximate net payload of 1704 pounds at 10% of GVWR on this model is ○ deficient ○ excessive ○ cautionary ◉ good ○ excellent *
Total highway safety penalties are: 2 *   Value: 8 5   Durability: 7 7   Highway Control Rating: 7 5   Highway Safety: 7 3   ★★★

Brand	Year	Type	Length	Model	Chassis	Engine	Fuel Type	Avg Price/Ft	Adj Wheelbase	Towing	GVWR	Curb Weight
Aerbus	1998	MHA	32	XL3200	FO	7.5L	G	$2300	208	1,500	17,000	15,296

Livability Code: SB 30-90
Wheelbase-to-length ratio of 54% is considered ○ dangerous ○ fatiguing ◉ good ○ excellent *
The approximate net payload of 1704 pounds at 10% of GVWR on this model is ○ deficient ○ excessive ○ cautionary ◉ good ○ excellent *
Total highway safety penalties are: 2 *   Value: 8 5   Durability: 7 7   Highway Control Rating: 7 5   Highway Safety: 7 3   ★★★

Brand	Year	Type	Length	Model	Chassis	Engine	Fuel Type	Avg Price/Ft	Adj Wheelbase	Towing	GVWR	Curb Weight
Aerbus	1998	MHA	32	XL3250	FO	7.5L	G	$2300	208	1,500	17,000	16,196

Livability Code: SB 30-90
Wheelbase-to-length ratio of 54% is considered ○ dangerous ○ fatiguing ◉ good ○ excellent *
The approximate net payload of 804 pounds at 5% of GVWR on this model is ◉ deficient ○ excessive ○ cautionary ○ good ○ excellent *
Total highway safety penalties are: 7 *   Value: 8 2   Durability: 7 7   Highway Control Rating: 4 5   Highway Safety: 3 8

Note: Safety ratings are based on the assumption that the engineering of the RV has allowed for proper balance by placing fresh, gray, and black holding tanks in a location so as not to change the balance of the RV when the tanks are empty or full. **Always double-check wheelbase, GVWR, and weights at front and rear axles.**

*See Section 1 for details on how conclusions are reached.

Brand	Year	Type	Length	Model	Chassis	Engine	Fuel Type	Average Price per Linear Foot When New	Adjusted Wheelbase	Approx. Towing Capacity	Gross Vehicle Weight Rating	Average Curb Weight

Aerbus 1998 MHA 34 XL3300 CH 7.4L G $2200 228 1,500 16,500 15,382
Livability Code: SB 30-90
Wheelbase-to-length ratio of 56% is considered ○ dangerous ○ fatiguing ● good ○ excellent *
The approximate net payload of 1118 pounds at 7% of GVWR on this model is ○ deficient ○ excessive ● cautionary ○ good ○ excellent *
Total highway safety penalties are: 6 *   Value: 83   Durability: 77   Highway Control Rating: 67   Highway Safety: 61   ★★

Aerbus 1998 MHA 34 XL3300S CH 7.4L G $2200 228 1,500 16,500 15,382
Livability Code: SB 30-90
Wheelbase-to-length ratio of 56% is considered ○ dangerous ○ fatiguing ● good ○ excellent *
The approximate net payload of 1118 pounds at 7% of GVWR on this model is ○ deficient ○ excessive ● cautionary ○ good ○ excellent *
Total highway safety penalties are: 6 *   Value: 83   Durability: 77   Highway Control Rating: 67   Highway Safety: 61   ★★

Aerbus 1998 MHA 34 XL3300 FO 7.5L G $2200 228 1,500 17,000 15,782
Livability Code: SB 30-90
Wheelbase-to-length ratio of 56% is considered ○ dangerous ○ fatiguing ● good ○ excellent *
The approximate net payload of 1218 pounds at 7% of GVWR on this model is ○ deficient ○ excessive ● cautionary ○ good ○ excellent *
Total highway safety penalties are: 2 *   Value: 85   Durability: 77   Highway Control Rating: 68   Highway Safety: 66   ★★

Aerbus 1998 MHA 34 XL3300S FO 7.5L G $2200 228 1,500 17,000 15,782
Livability Code: SB 30-90
Wheelbase-to-length ratio of 56% is considered ○ dangerous ○ fatiguing ● good ○ excellent *
The approximate net payload of 1218 pounds at 7% of GVWR on this model is ○ deficient ○ excessive ● cautionary ○ good ○ excellent *
Total highway safety penalties are: 2 *   Value: 85   Durability: 77   Highway Control Rating: 68   Highway Safety: 66   ★★

Aerbus 1998 MHA 34 XL3400 CH 7.4L G $2200 232 T 1,500 19,500 16,368
Livability Code: SB 30-90
Wheelbase-to-length ratio of 57% is considered ○ dangerous ○ fatiguing ● good ○ excellent *
The approximate net payload of 3132 pounds at 16% of GVWR on this model is ○ deficient ○ excessive ○ cautionary ○ good ● excellent *
Total highway safety penalties are: 9 *   Value: 81   Durability: 77   Highway Control Rating: 98   Highway Safety: 89   ★★★

Aerbus 1998 MHA 34 XL3450 CH 7.4L G $2200 232 T 1,500 19,500 17,418
Livability Code: SB 30-90
Wheelbase-to-length ratio of 57% is considered ○ dangerous ○ fatiguing ● good ○ excellent *
The approximate net payload of 2082 pounds at 11% of GVWR on this model is ○ deficient ○ excessive ○ cautionary ● good ○ excellent *
Total highway safety penalties are: 15 *   Value: 78   Durability: 77   Highway Control Rating: 88   Highway Safety: 73   ★★★

Aerbus 1998 MHA 34 XL3400 FO 7.5L G $2200 232 T 1,500 20,000 16,768
Livability Code: SB 30-90
Wheelbase-to-length ratio of 57% is considered ○ dangerous ○ fatiguing ● good ○ excellent *
The approximate net payload of 3232 pounds at 16% of GVWR on this model is ○ deficient ○ excessive ○ cautionary ○ good ● excellent *
Total highway safety penalties are: 4 *   Value: 84   Durability: 77   Highway Control Rating: 98   Highway Safety: 94   ★★★

Aerbus 1998 MHA 34 XL3450 FO 7.5L G $2200 232 T 1,500 20,000 17,818
Livability Code: SB 30-90
Wheelbase-to-length ratio of 57% is considered ○ dangerous ○ fatiguing ● good ○ excellent *
The approximate net payload of 2182 pounds at 11% of GVWR on this model is ○ deficient ○ excessive ○ cautionary ● good ○ excellent *
Total highway safety penalties are: 11 *   Value: 80   Durability: 77   Highway Control Rating: 88   Highway Safety: 77   ★★★

Aerbus 1998 MHA 36 XL3500 CH 7.4L G $2100 252 T 1,500 19,500 16,796
Livability Code: SB 30-90
Wheelbase-to-length ratio of 59% is considered ○ dangerous ○ fatiguing ○ good ● excellent *
The approximate net payload of 2704 pounds at 14% of GVWR on this model is ○ deficient ○ excessive ○ cautionary ● good ○ excellent *
Total highway safety penalties are: 10 *   Value: 81   Durability: 77   Highway Control Rating: 100   Highway Safety: 90   ★★★

Aerbus 1998 MHA 36 XL3550D CH 7.4L G $2100 252 T 1,500 19,500 17,546
Livability Code: SB 30-90
Wheelbase-to-length ratio of 59% is considered ○ dangerous ○ fatiguing ○ good ● excellent *
The approximate net payload of 1954 pounds at 10% of GVWR on this model is ○ deficient ○ excessive ○ cautionary ● good ○ excellent *
Total highway safety penalties are: 14 *   Value: 79   Durability: 77   Highway Control Rating: 94   Highway Safety: 80   ★★★

Aerbus 1998 MHA 36 XL3500 FO 7.5L G $2100 252 T 1,500 20,000 17,196
Livability Code: SB 30-90
Wheelbase-to-length ratio of 59% is considered ○ dangerous ○ fatiguing ○ good ● excellent *
The approximate net payload of 2804 pounds at 14% of GVWR on this model is ○ deficient ○ excessive ○ cautionary ● good ○ excellent *
Total highway safety penalties are: 4 *   Value: 84   Durability: 77   Highway Control Rating: 100   Highway Safety: 96   ★★★

Aerbus 1998 MHA 36 XL3550D FO 7.5L G $2100 252 T 1,500 20,000 17,946
Livability Code: SB 30-90
Wheelbase-to-length ratio of 59% is considered ○ dangerous ○ fatiguing ○ good ● excellent *
The approximate net payload of 2054 pounds at 10% of GVWR on this model is ○ deficient ○ excessive ○ cautionary ● good ○ excellent *
Total highway safety penalties are: 9 *   Value: 81   Durability: 77   Highway Control Rating: 95   Highway Safety: 86   ★★★

Note: Safety ratings are based on the assumption that the engineering of the RV has allowed for proper balance by placing fresh, gray, and black holding tanks in a location so as not to change the balance of the RV when the tanks are empty or full. **Always double-check wheelbase, GVWR, and weights at front and rear axles.**

*See Section 1 for details on how conclusions are reached.

Section 2: The Ratings

Brand	Year	Type	Length	Model	Chassis	Engine	Fuel Type	Average Price per Linear Foot When New	Adjusted Wheelbase	Approx. Towing Capacity	Gross Vehicle Weight Rating	Average Curb Weight
Aerbus	1998	MHA	36	XL3600S	FO	7.5L	G	$2100	252 T	1,500	20,000	17,339

Livability Code: SB 30-90 — Wheelbase-to-length ratio of 58% is considered ○ dangerous ○ fatiguing ○ good ◉ excellent *

The approximate net payload of 2661 pounds at 13% of GVWR on this model is ○ deficient ○ excessive ○ cautionary ◉ good ○ excellent *

Total highway safety penalties are: 4 * Value: 8 4 Durability: 7 7 Highway Control Rating: 9 8 Highway Safety: 9 4 ★★★

Brand	Year	Type	Length	Model	Chassis	Engine	Fuel Type	Price/Ft	Wheelbase	Towing	GVWR	Curb Weight
Aerbus	1998	MHA	36	XL3650	FO	7.5L	G	$2100	252 T	1,500	20,000	18,239

Livability Code: SB 30-90 — Wheelbase-to-length ratio of 58% is considered ○ dangerous ○ fatiguing ○ good ◉ excellent *

The approximate net payload of 1761 pounds at 9% of GVWR on this model is ○ deficient ○ excessive ◉ cautionary ○ good ○ excellent *

Total highway safety penalties are: 10 * Value: 8 1 Durability: 7 7 Highway Control Rating: 8 6 Highway Safety: 7 6 ★★★

Brand	Year	Type	Length	Model	Chassis	Engine	Fuel Type	Price/Ft	Wheelbase	Towing	GVWR	Curb Weight
Aerbus	1998	MHA	39	XL3800	FO	7.5L	G	$2000	252 T	1,500	20,000	18,053

Livability Code: SB 30-90 — Wheelbase-to-length ratio of 54% is considered ○ dangerous ○ fatiguing ◉ good ○ excellent *

The approximate net payload of 1947 pounds at 10% of GVWR on this model is ○ deficient ○ excessive ○ cautionary ◉ good ○ excellent *

Total highway safety penalties are: 4 * Value: 8 4 Durability: 7 7 Highway Control Rating: 7 6 Highway Safety: 7 2 ★★★

Brand	Year	Type	Length	Model	Chassis	Engine	Fuel Type	Price/Ft	Wheelbase	Towing	GVWR	Curb Weight
Aerbus	1999	MHA	26	XL2500	CH	7.4L	G	$2300	158	4,500	16,500	13,108

Livability Code: SB 30-90 — Wheelbase-to-length ratio of 51% is considered ○ dangerous ◉ fatiguing ○ good ○ excellent *

The approximate net payload of 3392 pounds at 21% of GVWR on this model is ○ deficient ○ excessive ○ cautionary ○ good ◉ excellent *

Total highway safety penalties are: 2 * Value: 8 5 Durability: 7 7 Highway Control Rating: 6 2 Highway Safety: 6 0 ★★

Brand	Year	Type	Length	Model	Chassis	Engine	Fuel Type	Price/Ft	Wheelbase	Towing	GVWR	Curb Weight
Aerbus	1999	MHA	26	XL2500	FO	6.8L	G	$2500	158	10,300	15,700	13,808

Livability Code: SB 30-90 — Wheelbase-to-length ratio of 51% is considered ○ dangerous ◉ fatiguing ○ good ○ excellent *

The approximate net payload of 1892 pounds at 12% of GVWR on this model is ○ deficient ○ excessive ○ cautionary ◉ good ○ excellent *

Total highway safety penalties are: 2 * Value: 8 5 Durability: 7 7 Highway Control Rating: 5 0 Highway Safety: 4 8

Brand	Year	Type	Length	Model	Chassis	Engine	Fuel Type	Price/Ft	Wheelbase	Towing	GVWR	Curb Weight
Aerbus	1999	MHA	29	XL2800	CH	7.4L	G	$2200	190	4,500	16,500	13,981

Livability Code: SB 30-90 — Wheelbase-to-length ratio of 55% is considered ○ dangerous ○ fatiguing ◉ good ○ excellent *

The approximate net payload of 2519 pounds at 15% of GVWR on this model is ○ deficient ○ excessive ○ cautionary ◉ good ○ excellent *

Total highway safety penalties are: 4 * Value: 8 4 Durability: 7 7 Highway Control Rating: 9 0 Highway Safety: 8 6 ★★★

Brand	Year	Type	Length	Model	Chassis	Engine	Fuel Type	Price/Ft	Wheelbase	Towing	GVWR	Curb Weight
Aerbus	1999	MHA	29	XL2800	FO	6.8L	G	$2400	190	8,000	18,000	14,688

Livability Code: SB 30-90 — Wheelbase-to-length ratio of 55% is considered ○ dangerous ○ fatiguing ◉ good ○ excellent *

The approximate net payload of 3312 pounds at 18% of GVWR on this model is ○ deficient ○ excessive ○ cautionary ○ good ◉ excellent *

Total highway safety penalties are: 2 * Value: 8 5 Durability: 7 7 Highway Control Rating: 9 4 Highway Safety: 9 2 ★★★

Brand	Year	Type	Length	Model	Chassis	Engine	Fuel Type	Price/Ft	Wheelbase	Towing	GVWR	Curb Weight
Aerbus	1999	MHA	31	XL2900	FO	6.8L	G	$2300	208	8,000	18,000	15,028

Livability Code: SB 30-90 — Wheelbase-to-length ratio of 56% is considered ○ dangerous ○ fatiguing ◉ good ○ excellent *

The approximate net payload of 2972 pounds at 17% of GVWR on this model is ○ deficient ○ excessive ○ cautionary ○ good ◉ excellent *

Total highway safety penalties are: 2 * Value: 8 5 Durability: 7 7 Highway Control Rating: 9 6 Highway Safety: 9 4 ★★★

Brand	Year	Type	Length	Model	Chassis	Engine	Fuel Type	Price/Ft	Wheelbase	Towing	GVWR	Curb Weight
Aerbus	1999	MHA	31	XL2900-D	FO	6.8L	G	$2300	208	8,000	18,000	15,088

Livability Code: SB 30-90 — Wheelbase-to-length ratio of 56% is considered ○ dangerous ○ fatiguing ◉ good ○ excellent *

The approximate net payload of 2912 pounds at 16% of GVWR on this model is ○ deficient ○ excessive ○ cautionary ○ good ◉ excellent *

Total highway safety penalties are: 2 * Value: 8 5 Durability: 7 7 Highway Control Rating: 9 6 Highway Safety: 9 4 ★★★

Brand	Year	Type	Length	Model	Chassis	Engine	Fuel Type	Price/Ft	Wheelbase	Towing	GVWR	Curb Weight
Aerbus	1999	MHA	31	XL2900FBGT	FO	6.8L	G	$2300	208	8,000	18,000	15,288

Livability Code: SB 30-90 — Wheelbase-to-length ratio of 56% is considered ○ dangerous ○ fatiguing ◉ good ○ excellent *

The approximate net payload of 2712 pounds at 15% of GVWR on this model is ○ deficient ○ excessive ○ cautionary ◉ good ○ excellent *

Total highway safety penalties are: 2 * Value: 8 5 Durability: 7 7 Highway Control Rating: 9 4 Highway Safety: 9 2 ★★★

Brand	Year	Type	Length	Model	Chassis	Engine	Fuel Type	Price/Ft	Wheelbase	Towing	GVWR	Curb Weight
Aerbus	1999	MHA	31	XL3000	FO	6.8L	G	$2300	208	8,000	18,000	15,288

Livability Code: SB 30-90 — Wheelbase-to-length ratio of 56% is considered ○ dangerous ○ fatiguing ◉ good ○ excellent *

The approximate net payload of 2712 pounds at 15% of GVWR on this model is ○ deficient ○ excessive ○ cautionary ◉ good ○ excellent *

Total highway safety penalties are: 2 * Value: 8 5 Durability: 7 7 Highway Control Rating: 9 3 Highway Safety: 9 1 ★★★

Brand	Year	Type	Length	Model	Chassis	Engine	Fuel Type	Price/Ft	Wheelbase	Towing	GVWR	Curb Weight
Aerbus	1999	MHA	31	XL2900-FB	FO	6.8L	G	$2300	208	8,000	18,000	15,248

Livability Code: SB 30-90 — Wheelbase-to-length ratio of 56% is considered ○ dangerous ○ fatiguing ◉ good ○ excellent *

The approximate net payload of 2752 pounds at 15% of GVWR on this model is ○ deficient ○ excessive ○ cautionary ◉ good ○ excellent *

Total highway safety penalties are: 2 * Value: 8 5 Durability: 7 7 Highway Control Rating: 9 3 Highway Safety: 9 1 ★★★

Note: Safety ratings are based on the assumption that the engineering of the RV has allowed for proper balance by placing fresh, gray, and black holding tanks in a location so as not to change the balance of the RV when the tanks are empty or full. **Always double-check wheelbase, GVWR, and weights at front and rear axles.**

*See Section 1 for details on how conclusions are reached.

Section 2: The Ratings

Brand	Year	Type	Length	Model	Chassis	Engine	Fuel Type	Average Price per Linear Foot When New	Adjusted Wheel-base	Approx. Towing Capacity	Gross Vehicle Weight Rating	Average Curb Weight
Aerbus	1999	MHA	32	XL3100	CH	7.4L	G	$2300	208	5,000	21,000	16,124

Livability Code: SB 30-90

Wheelbase-to-length ratio of 54% is considered ○ dangerous ○ fatiguing ◉ good ○ excellent*

The approximate net payload of 4876 pounds at 23% of GVWR on this model is ○ deficient ○ excessive ○ cautionary ○ good ◉ excellent*

Total highway safety penalties are: 6* Value: 8 3 Durability: 7 7 Highway Control Rating: 8 5 Highway Safety: 7 9 ★★★

Brand	Year	Type	Length	Model	Chassis	Engine	Fuel Type	Price/Ft	Wheelbase	Towing	GVWR	Curb Weight
Aerbus	1999	MHA	32	XL3100	FO	6.8L	G	$2200	208	8,000	18,000	15,548

Livability Code: SB 30-90

Wheelbase-to-length ratio of 54% is considered ○ dangerous ○ fatiguing ◉ good ○ excellent*

The approximate net payload of 2452 pounds at 14% of GVWR on this model is ○ deficient ○ excessive ○ cautionary ◉ good ○ excellent*

Total highway safety penalties are: 2* Value: 8 5 Durability: 7 7 Highway Control Rating: 8 0 Highway Safety: 7 8 ★★★

Aerbus	1999	MHA	32	XL3250BLS	FO	6.8L	G	$2200	208	5,500	20,500	17,608

Livability Code: SB 30-90

Wheelbase-to-length ratio of 54% is considered ○ dangerous ○ fatiguing ◉ good ○ excellent*

The approximate net payload of 2892 pounds at 14% of GVWR on this model is ○ deficient ○ excessive ○ cautionary ◉ good ○ excellent*

Total highway safety penalties are: 10* Value: 8 1 Durability: 7 7 Highway Control Rating: 8 1 Highway Safety: 7 1 ★★★

Aerbus	1999	MHA	32	XL3250	CH	7.4L	G	$2300	208	5,000	21,000	17,648

Livability Code: SB 30-90

Wheelbase-to-length ratio of 54% is considered ○ dangerous ○ fatiguing ◉ good ○ excellent*

The approximate net payload of 3352 pounds at 16% of GVWR on this model is ○ deficient ○ excessive ○ cautionary ○ good ◉ excellent*

Total highway safety penalties are: 11* Value: 8 0 Durability: 7 7 Highway Control Rating: 8 4 Highway Safety: 7 3 ★★★

Aerbus	1999	MHA	32	XL3250	FO	6.8L	G	$2200	208	8,000	18,000	16,728

Livability Code: SB 30-90

Wheelbase-to-length ratio of 54% is considered ○ dangerous ○ fatiguing ◉ good ○ excellent*

The approximate net payload of 1272 pounds at 7% of GVWR on this model is ○ deficient ○ excessive ◉ cautionary ○ good ○ excellent*

Total highway safety penalties are: 7* Value: 8 2 Durability: 7 7 Highway Control Rating: 5 5 Highway Safety: 4 8

Aerbus	1999	MHA	33	XL3350BGT	FO	6.8L	G	$2200	208	5,500	20,500	18,028

Livability Code: SB 30-90

Wheelbase-to-length ratio of 53% is considered ○ dangerous ◉ fatiguing ○ good ○ excellent*

The approximate net payload of 2472 pounds at 12% of GVWR on this model is ○ deficient ○ excessive ○ cautionary ◉ good ○ excellent*

Total highway safety penalties are: 15* Value: 7 8 Durability: 7 7 Highway Control Rating: 6 7 Highway Safety: 5 2 ★

Aerbus	1999	MHA	34	XL3300S	CH	7.4L	G	$2200	228	5,000	21,000	16,381

Livability Code: SB 30-90

Wheelbase-to-length ratio of 56% is considered ○ dangerous ○ fatiguing ◉ good ○ excellent*

The approximate net payload of 4619 pounds at 22% of GVWR on this model is ○ deficient ○ excessive ○ cautionary ○ good ◉ excellent*

Total highway safety penalties are: 6* Value: 8 3 Durability: 7 7 Highway Control Rating: 9 9 Highway Safety: 9 3 ★★★

Aerbus	1999	MHA	34	XL3300S opch	FO	6.8L	G	$2200	228	5,500	20,500	16,008

Livability Code: SB 30-90

Wheelbase-to-length ratio of 56% is considered ○ dangerous ○ fatiguing ◉ good ○ excellent*

The approximate net payload of 4492 pounds at 22% of GVWR on this model is ○ deficient ○ excessive ○ cautionary ○ good ◉ excellent*

Total highway safety penalties are: 2* Value: 8 5 Durability: 7 7 Highway Control Rating: 9 9 Highway Safety: 9 7 ★★★

Aerbus	1999	MHA	34	XL3300S myc	FO	6.8L	G	$2200	228	8,000	18,000	16,081

Livability Code: SB 30-90

Wheelbase-to-length ratio of 56% is considered ○ dangerous ○ fatiguing ◉ good ○ excellent*

The approximate net payload of 1919 pounds at 11% of GVWR on this model is ○ deficient ○ excessive ○ cautionary ◉ good ○ excellent*

Total highway safety penalties are: 2* Value: 8 5 Durability: 7 7 Highway Control Rating: 8 7 Highway Safety: 8 5 ★★★

Aerbus	1999	MHA	34	XL3400	FO	6.8L	G	$2200	228	8,000	18,000	16,208

Livability Code: SB 30-90

Wheelbase-to-length ratio of 56% is considered ○ dangerous ○ fatiguing ◉ good ○ excellent*

The approximate net payload of 1792 pounds at 10% of GVWR on this model is ○ deficient ○ excessive ○ cautionary ◉ good ○ excellent*

Total highway safety penalties are: 2* Value: 8 5 Durability: 7 7 Highway Control Rating: 8 4 Highway Safety: 8 2 ★★★

Aerbus	1999	MHA	35	XL3450	CH	7.4L	G	$2100	228	5,000	21,000	17,977

Livability Code: SB 30-90

Wheelbase-to-length ratio of 54% is considered ○ dangerous ○ fatiguing ◉ good ○ excellent*

The approximate net payload of 3023 pounds at 14% of GVWR on this model is ○ deficient ○ excessive ○ cautionary ◉ good ○ excellent*

Total highway safety penalties are: 13* Value: 7 9 Durability: 7 7 Highway Control Rating: 8 1 Highway Safety: 6 8 ★★

Aerbus	1999	MHA	35	XL3450GT	FO	6.8L	G	$2200	228	5,500	20,500	17,408

Livability Code: SB 30-90

Wheelbase-to-length ratio of 54% is considered ○ dangerous ○ fatiguing ◉ good ○ excellent*

The approximate net payload of 3092 pounds at 15% of GVWR on this model is ○ deficient ○ excessive ○ cautionary ◉ good ○ excellent*

Total highway safety penalties are: 13* Value: 7 9 Durability: 7 7 Highway Control Rating: 8 3 Highway Safety: 7 0 ★★★

Note: Safety ratings are based on the assumption that the engineering of the RV has allowed for proper balance by placing fresh, gray, and black holding tanks in a location so as not to change the balance of the RV when the tanks are empty or full. **Always double-check wheelbase, GVWR, and weights at front and rear axles.**

*See Section 1 for details on how conclusions are reached.

Section 2: The Ratings

Brand	Year	Type	Length	Model	Chassis	Engine	Fuel Type	Average Price per Linear Foot When New	Adjusted Wheelbase	Approx. Towing Capacity	Gross Vehicle Weight Rating	Average Curb Weight
Aerbus	1999	MHA	35	XL3400	SP	CU8.3L	D	$3100	208	10,000	24,000	20,692

Livability Code: SB 30-90
Wheelbase-to-length ratio of 49% is considered ◉ dangerous ○ fatiguing ○ good ○ excellent *
The approximate net payload of 3308 pounds at 14% of GVWR on this model is ○ deficient ○ excessive ○ cautionary ◉ good ○ excellent *
Total highway safety penalties are: 2 * Value: 8 5 Durability: 7 7 Highway Control Rating: 4 8 Highway Safety: 4 6

Brand	Year	Type	Length	Model	Chassis	Engine	Fuel Type	Price/Ft	Wheelbase	Towing	GVWR	Curb Wt
Aerbus	1999	MHA	35	XL3450	SP	CU8.3L	D	$3100	208	10,000	24,000	21,987

Livability Code: SB 30-90
Wheelbase-to-length ratio of 49% is considered ◉ dangerous ○ fatiguing ○ good ○ excellent *
The approximate net payload of 2013 pounds at 8% of GVWR on this model is ○ deficient ○ excessive ◉ cautionary ○ good ○ excellent *
Total highway safety penalties are: 13 * Value: 7 9 Durability: 7 7 Highway Control Rating: 2 9 Highway Safety: 1 6

Brand	Year	Type	Length	Model	Chassis	Engine	Fuel Type	Price/Ft	Wheelbase	Towing	GVWR	Curb Wt
Aerbus	1999	MHA	35	XL3500	FO	6.8L	G	$2200	242	8,000	18,000	16,088

Livability Code: SB 30-90
Wheelbase-to-length ratio of 57% is considered ○ dangerous ○ fatiguing ◉ good ○ excellent *
The approximate net payload of 1912 pounds at 11% of GVWR on this model is ○ deficient ○ excessive ○ cautionary ◉ good ○ excellent *
Total highway safety penalties are: 2 * Value: 8 5 Durability: 7 7 Highway Control Rating: 9 0 Highway Safety: 8 8 ★★★

Brand	Year	Type	Length	Model	Chassis	Engine	Fuel Type	Price/Ft	Wheelbase	Towing	GVWR	Curb Wt
Aerbus	1999	MHA	36	XL3550BSL	FO	6.8L	G	$2200	242	5,500	20,500	18,468

Livability Code: SB 30-90
Wheelbase-to-length ratio of 57% is considered ○ dangerous ○ fatiguing ◉ good ○ excellent *
The approximate net payload of 2032 pounds at 10% of GVWR on this model is ○ deficient ○ excessive ○ cautionary ◉ good ○ excellent *
Total highway safety penalties are: 10 * Value: 8 1 Durability: 7 7 Highway Control Rating: 8 6 Highway Safety: 7 6 ★★★

Brand	Year	Type	Length	Model	Chassis	Engine	Fuel Type	Price/Ft	Wheelbase	Towing	GVWR	Curb Wt
Aerbus	1999	MHA	36	XL3550-D	FO	6.8L	G	$2200	242	5,500	20,500	17,448

Livability Code: SB 30-90
Wheelbase-to-length ratio of 57% is considered ○ dangerous ○ fatiguing ◉ good ○ excellent *
The approximate net payload of 3052 pounds at 15% of GVWR on this model is ○ deficient ○ excessive ○ cautionary ◉ good ○ excellent *
Total highway safety penalties are: 7 * Value: 8 3 Durability: 7 7 Highway Control Rating: 9 6 Highway Safety: 8 9 ★★★

Brand	Year	Type	Length	Model	Chassis	Engine	Fuel Type	Price/Ft	Wheelbase	Towing	GVWR	Curb Wt
Aerbus	1999	MHA	36	XL3650LG	FO	6.8L	G	$2200	242	5,500	20,500	17,768

Livability Code: SB 30-90
Wheelbase-to-length ratio of 56% is considered ○ dangerous ○ fatiguing ◉ good ○ excellent *
The approximate net payload of 2732 pounds at 13% of GVWR on this model is ○ deficient ○ excessive ○ cautionary ◉ good ○ excellent *
Total highway safety penalties are: 12 * Value: 8 0 Durability: 7 7 Highway Control Rating: 9 1 Highway Safety: 7 9 ★★★

Brand	Year	Type	Length	Model	Chassis	Engine	Fuel Type	Price/Ft	Wheelbase	Towing	GVWR	Curb Wt
Aerbus	1999	MHA	36	XL3650BSL	FO	6.8L	G	$2200	242	5,500	20,500	18,668

Livability Code: SB 30-90
Wheelbase-to-length ratio of 56% is considered ○ dangerous ○ fatiguing ◉ good ○ excellent *
The approximate net payload of 1832 pounds at 9% of GVWR on this model is ○ deficient ○ excessive ◉ cautionary ○ good ○ excellent *
Total highway safety penalties are: 10 * Value: 8 1 Durability: 7 7 Highway Control Rating: 7 9 Highway Safety: 6 9 ★★

Brand	Year	Type	Length	Model	Chassis	Engine	Fuel Type	Price/Ft	Wheelbase	Towing	GVWR	Curb Wt
Aerbus	1999	MHA	36	XL3650-GT	FO	6.8L	G	$2200	242	5,500	20,500	18,328

Livability Code: SB 30-90
Wheelbase-to-length ratio of 56% is considered ○ dangerous ○ fatiguing ◉ good ○ excellent *
The approximate net payload of 2172 pounds at 11% of GVWR on this model is ○ deficient ○ excessive ○ cautionary ◉ good ○ excellent *
Total highway safety penalties are: 12 * Value: 8 0 Durability: 7 7 Highway Control Rating: 8 6 Highway Safety: 7 4 ★★★

Brand	Year	Type	Length	Model	Chassis	Engine	Fuel Type	Price/Ft	Wheelbase	Towing	GVWR	Curb Wt
Aerbus	1999	MHA	37	XL3550D	SP	CU8.3L	D	$3000	228	10,000	24,000	21,955

Livability Code: SB 30-90
Wheelbase-to-length ratio of 51% is considered ○ dangerous ◉ fatiguing ○ good ○ excellent *
The approximate net payload of 2045 pounds at 9% of GVWR on this model is ○ deficient ○ excessive ◉ cautionary ○ good ○ excellent *
Total highway safety penalties are: 7 * Value: 8 3 Durability: 7 7 Highway Control Rating: 4 2 Highway Safety: 3 5

Brand	Year	Type	Length	Model	Chassis	Engine	Fuel Type	Price/Ft	Wheelbase	Towing	GVWR	Curb Wt
Aerbus	1999	MHA	37	XL3600	SP	CU8.3L	D	$3000	228	10,000	24,000	21,590

Livability Code: SB 30-90
Wheelbase-to-length ratio of 51% is considered ○ dangerous ◉ fatiguing ○ good ○ excellent *
The approximate net payload of 2410 pounds at 10% of GVWR on this model is ○ deficient ○ excessive ○ cautionary ◉ good ○ excellent *
Total highway safety penalties are: 2 * Value: 8 5 Durability: 7 7 Highway Control Rating: 4 8 Highway Safety: 4 6

Brand	Year	Type	Length	Model	Chassis	Engine	Fuel Type	Price/Ft	Wheelbase	Towing	GVWR	Curb Wt
Aerbus	1999	MHA	37	XL3650LG	SP	CU8.3L	D	$3000	228	10,000	24,000	22,310

Livability Code: SB 30-90
Wheelbase-to-length ratio of 51% is considered ○ dangerous ◉ fatiguing ○ good ○ excellent *
The approximate net payload of 1690 pounds at 7% of GVWR on this model is ○ deficient ○ excessive ◉ cautionary ○ good ○ excellent *
Total highway safety penalties are: 12 * Value: 8 0 Durability: 7 7 Highway Control Rating: 3 1 Highway Safety: 1 9

Brand	Year	Type	Length	Model	Chassis	Engine	Fuel Type	Price/Ft	Wheelbase	Towing	GVWR	Curb Wt
Aerbus	1999	MHA	37	XL3650-GT	SP	CU8.3L	D	$3000	228	10,000	24,000	22,430

Livability Code: SB 30-90
Wheelbase-to-length ratio of 51% is considered ○ dangerous ◉ fatiguing ○ good ○ excellent *
The approximate net payload of 1570 pounds at 7% of GVWR on this model is ○ deficient ○ excessive ◉ cautionary ○ good ○ excellent *
Total highway safety penalties are: 12 * Value: 8 0 Durability: 7 7 Highway Control Rating: 3 0 Highway Safety: 1 8

Note: Safety ratings are based on the assumption that the engineering of the RV has allowed for proper balance by placing fresh, gray, and black holding tanks in a location so as not to change the balance of the RV when the tanks are empty or full. **Always double-check wheelbase, GVWR, and weights at front and rear axles.**

*See Section 1 for details on how conclusions are reached.

Brand	Year	Type	Length	Model	Chassis	Engine	Fuel Type	Average Price per Linear Foot When New	Adjusted Wheelbase	Approx. Towing Capacity	Gross Vehicle Weight Rating	Average Curb Weight
Affinity	1991	MHA	37	37	GI	CA300	D	$7700	228	1,500	31,680	28,966

Livability Code: FT 30-90
Wheelbase-to-length ratio of 51% is considered ○ dangerous ● fatiguing ○ good ○ excellent *
The approximate net payload of 2714 pounds at 9% of GVWR on this model is ○ deficient ○ excessive ● cautionary ○ good ○ excellent *
Total highway safety penalties are: 2 *   Value: 85   Durability: 90   Highway Control Rating: 32   Highway Safety: 30

Brand	Year	Type	Length	Model	Chassis	Engine	Fuel Type	Average Price per Linear Foot When New	Adjusted Wheelbase	Approx. Towing Capacity	Gross Vehicle Weight Rating	Average Curb Weight
Affinity	1991	MHA	40	40	GI	CA325	D	$7100	262	1,500	36,220	31,166

Livability Code: FT 30-90
Wheelbase-to-length ratio of 55% is considered ○ dangerous ○ fatiguing ● good ○ excellent *
The approximate net payload of 5054 pounds at 14% of GVWR on this model is ○ deficient ○ excessive ○ cautionary ● good ○ excellent *
Total highway safety penalties are: 2 *   Value: 85   Durability: 90   Highway Control Rating: 87   Highway Safety: 85   ★★★★

Brand	Year	Type	Length	Model	Chassis	Engine	Fuel Type	Average Price per Linear Foot When New	Adjusted Wheelbase	Approx. Towing Capacity	Gross Vehicle Weight Rating	Average Curb Weight
Affinity	1992	MHA	40	40	GI	De 6V	D	$7100	262	1,500	36,220	31,701

Livability Code: FT 30-90
Wheelbase-to-length ratio of 55% is considered ○ dangerous ○ fatiguing ● good ○ excellent *
The approximate net payload of 4519 pounds at 12% of GVWR on this model is ○ deficient ○ excessive ○ cautionary ● good ○ excellent *
Total highway safety penalties are: 2 *   Value: 85   Durability: 90   Highway Control Rating: 88   Highway Safety: 86   ★★★★

Brand	Year	Type	Length	Model	Chassis	Engine	Fuel Type	Average Price per Linear Foot When New	Adjusted Wheelbase	Approx. Towing Capacity	Gross Vehicle Weight Rating	Average Curb Weight
Affinity	1994	MHA	38	38	GI	CA325	D	$8400	254	1,500	35,700	30,253

Livability Code: FT 30-90
Wheelbase-to-length ratio of 56% is considered ○ dangerous ○ fatiguing ● good ○ excellent *
The approximate net payload of 5447 pounds at 15% of GVWR on this model is ○ deficient ○ excessive ○ cautionary ● good ○ excellent *
Total highway safety penalties are: 2 *   Value: 85   Durability: 90   Highway Control Rating: 93   Highway Safety: 91   ★★★★

Brand	Year	Type	Length	Model	Chassis	Engine	Fuel Type	Average Price per Linear Foot When New	Adjusted Wheelbase	Approx. Towing Capacity	Gross Vehicle Weight Rating	Average Curb Weight
Affinity	1995	MHA	38	38	GI	DE350	D	$8900	254	1,500	35,720	30,263

Livability Code: FT 30-90
Wheelbase-to-length ratio of 56% is considered ○ dangerous ○ fatiguing ● good ○ excellent *
The approximate net payload of 5457 pounds at 15% of GVWR on this model is ○ deficient ○ excessive ○ cautionary ● good ○ excellent *
Total highway safety penalties are: 2 *   Value: 85   Durability: 90   Highway Control Rating: 93   Highway Safety: 91   ★★★★

Brand	Year	Type	Length	Model	Chassis	Engine	Fuel Type	Average Price per Linear Foot When New	Adjusted Wheelbase	Approx. Towing Capacity	Gross Vehicle Weight Rating	Average Curb Weight
Affinity	1995	MHA	40	40	GI	DE350	D	$8800	278	1,500	35,720	30,916

Livability Code: FT 30-90
Wheelbase-to-length ratio of 58% is considered ○ dangerous ○ fatiguing ○ good ● excellent *
The approximate net payload of 4804 pounds at 13% of GVWR on this model is ○ deficient ○ excessive ○ cautionary ● good ○ excellent *
Total highway safety penalties are: 2 *   Value: 85   Durability: 90   Highway Control Rating: 97   Highway Safety: 95   ★★★★

Brand	Year	Type	Length	Model	Chassis	Engine	Fuel Type	Average Price per Linear Foot When New	Adjusted Wheelbase	Approx. Towing Capacity	Gross Vehicle Weight Rating	Average Curb Weight
Affinity	1996	MHA	38	38	GI	DE350	D	$8700	254	1,500	35,720	30,263

Livability Code: FT 30-90
Wheelbase-to-length ratio of 56% is considered ○ dangerous ○ fatiguing ● good ○ excellent *
The approximate net payload of 5457 pounds at 15% of GVWR on this model is ○ deficient ○ excessive ○ cautionary ● good ○ excellent *
Total highway safety penalties are: 2 *   Value: 85   Durability: 90   Highway Control Rating: 93   Highway Safety: 91   ★★★★

Brand	Year	Type	Length	Model	Chassis	Engine	Fuel Type	Average Price per Linear Foot When New	Adjusted Wheelbase	Approx. Towing Capacity	Gross Vehicle Weight Rating	Average Curb Weight
Affinity	1996	MHA	40	40	GI	DE350	D	$8600	278	1,500	35,720	30,916

Livability Code: FT 30-90
Wheelbase-to-length ratio of 58% is considered ○ dangerous ○ fatiguing ○ good ● excellent *
The approximate net payload of 4804 pounds at 13% of GVWR on this model is ○ deficient ○ excessive ○ cautionary ● good ○ excellent *
Total highway safety penalties are: 2 *   Value: 85   Durability: 90   Highway Control Rating: 97   Highway Safety: 95   ★★★★

Brand	Year	Type	Length	Model	Chassis	Engine	Fuel Type	Average Price per Linear Foot When New	Adjusted Wheelbase	Approx. Towing Capacity	Gross Vehicle Weight Rating	Average Curb Weight
Affinity	1997	MHA	38	38	GI	CA350	D	$9000	254	5,000	35,700	30,253

Livability Code: FT 30-90
Wheelbase-to-length ratio of 56% is considered ○ dangerous ○ fatiguing ● good ○ excellent *
The approximate net payload of 5447 pounds at 15% of GVWR on this model is ○ deficient ○ excessive ○ cautionary ● good ○ excellent *
Total highway safety penalties are: 2 *   Value: 85   Durability: 90   Highway Control Rating: 93   Highway Safety: 91   ★★★★

Brand	Year	Type	Length	Model	Chassis	Engine	Fuel Type	Average Price per Linear Foot When New	Adjusted Wheelbase	Approx. Towing Capacity	Gross Vehicle Weight Rating	Average Curb Weight
Affinity	1997	MHA	40	40	GI	CA350	D	$8800	278	5,000	35,700	30,906

Livability Code: FT 30-90
Wheelbase-to-length ratio of 58% is considered ○ dangerous ○ fatiguing ○ good ● excellent *
The approximate net payload of 4794 pounds at 13% of GVWR on this model is ○ deficient ○ excessive ○ cautionary ● good ○ excellent *
Total highway safety penalties are: 2 *   Value: 85   Durability: 90   Highway Control Rating: 97   Highway Safety: 95   ★★★★

Brand	Year	Type	Length	Model	Chassis	Engine	Fuel Type	Average Price per Linear Foot When New	Adjusted Wheelbase	Approx. Towing Capacity	Gross Vehicle Weight Rating	Average Curb Weight
Affinity	1998	MHA	38	38	GI	CA425	D	$9100	254	7,000	35,700	30,877

Livability Code: FT 30-90
Wheelbase-to-length ratio of 56% is considered ○ dangerous ○ fatiguing ● good ○ excellent *
The approximate net payload of 4823 pounds at 14% of GVWR on this model is ○ deficient ○ excessive ○ cautionary ● good ○ excellent *
Total highway safety penalties are: 2 *   Value: 90   Durability: 90   Highway Control Rating: 91   Highway Safety: 89   ★★★★

Brand	Year	Type	Length	Model	Chassis	Engine	Fuel Type	Average Price per Linear Foot When New	Adjusted Wheelbase	Approx. Towing Capacity	Gross Vehicle Weight Rating	Average Curb Weight
Affinity	1998	MHA	40	40	GI	CA425	D	$8900	278	7,000	35,700	31,803

Livability Code: FT 30-90
Wheelbase-to-length ratio of 58% is considered ○ dangerous ○ fatiguing ○ good ● excellent *
The approximate net payload of 3897 pounds at 11% of GVWR on this model is ○ deficient ○ excessive ○ cautionary ● good ○ excellent *
Total highway safety penalties are: 2 *   Value: 90   Durability: 90   Highway Control Rating: 93   Highway Safety: 91   ★★★★★

Note: Safety ratings are based on the assumption that the engineering of the RV has allowed for proper balance by placing fresh, gray, and black holding tanks in a location so as not to change the balance of the RV when the tanks are empty or full. **Always double-check wheelbase, GVWR, and weights at front and rear axles.**

*See Section 1 for details on how conclusions are reached.

Section 2: The Ratings

Brand	Year	Type	Length	Model	Chassis	Engine	Fuel Type	Average Price per Linear Foot When New	Adjusted Wheel-base	Approx. Towing Capacity	Gross Vehicle Weight Rating	Average Curb Weight
Affinity	1998	MHA	40	40 Galley Slide	GI	CA425	D	$9300	278	7,000	35,700	33,303

Livability Code: FT 30-90
Wheelbase-to-length ratio of 58% is considered ○ dangerous ○ fatiguing ○ good ◉ excellent *
The approximate net payload of 2397 pounds at 7% of GVWR on this model is ○ deficient ○ excessive ◉ cautionary ○ good ○ excellent *
Total highway safety penalties are: 12 * Value: 8 0 Durability: 9 0 Highway Control Rating: 7 4 Highway Safety: 6 2 ★★

| Affinity | 1999 | MHA | 38 | Celebrity | DY | CA455 | D | $9200 | 254 | 7,000 | 35,700 | 30,253 |

Livability Code: FT 30-90
Wheelbase-to-length ratio of 56% is considered ○ dangerous ○ fatiguing ◉ good ○ excellent *
The approximate net payload of 5447 pounds at 15% of GVWR on this model is ○ deficient ○ excessive ○ cautionary ◉ good ○ excellent *
Total highway safety penalties are: 2 * Value: 9 6 Durability: 9 3 Highway Control Rating: 9 3 Highway Safety: 9 1 ★★★★★

| Affinity | 1999 | MHA | 38 | Spirit (discon.) | DY | CA455 | D | $9200 | 254 | 7,000 | 39,000 | 31,903 |

Livability Code: FT 30-90
Wheelbase-to-length ratio of 56% is considered ○ dangerous ○ fatiguing ◉ good ○ excellent *
The approximate net payload of 7097 pounds at 18% of GVWR on this model is ○ deficient ○ excessive ○ cautionary ○ good ◉ excellent *
Total highway safety penalties are: 2 * Value: 9 6 Durability: 9 3 Highway Control Rating: 9 7 Highway Safety: 9 5 ★★★★★

| Affinity | 1999 | MHA | 38 | Celebrity myc | DY | CA455 | D | $9200 | 254 | 3,700 | 39,000 | 32,192 |

Livability Code: FT 30-90
Wheelbase-to-length ratio of 56% is considered ○ dangerous ○ fatiguing ◉ good ○ excellent *
The approximate net payload of 6808 pounds at 17% of GVWR on this model is ○ deficient ○ excessive ○ cautionary ○ good ◉ excellent *
Total highway safety penalties are: 2 * Value: 9 6 Durability: 9 3 Highway Control Rating: 9 6 Highway Safety: 9 4 ★★★★★

| Affinity | 1999 | MHA | 40 | Grande Chalet | DY | CA455 | D | $8800 | 278 | 7,000 | 36,300 | 32,181 |

Livability Code: FT 30-90
Wheelbase-to-length ratio of 58% is considered ○ dangerous ○ fatiguing ○ good ◉ excellent *
The approximate net payload of 4119 pounds at 11% of GVWR on this model is ○ deficient ○ excessive ○ cautionary ◉ good ○ excellent *
Total highway safety penalties are: 8 * Value: 9 3 Durability: 9 3 Highway Control Rating: 9 3 Highway Safety: 8 5 ★★★★

| Affinity | 1999 | MHA | 40 | Captiva | DY | CA455 | D | $8800 | 278 | 7,000 | 35,700 | 30,906 |

Livability Code: FT 30-90
Wheelbase-to-length ratio of 58% is considered ○ dangerous ○ fatiguing ○ good ◉ excellent *
The approximate net payload of 4794 pounds at 13% of GVWR on this model is ○ deficient ○ excessive ○ cautionary ◉ good ○ excellent *
Total highway safety penalties are: 2 * Value: 9 6 Durability: 9 3 Highway Control Rating: 9 7 Highway Safety: 9 5 ★★★★★

| Affinity | 1999 | MHA | 40 | Legacy | DY | CA455 | D | $8800 | 278 | 7,000 | 35,700 | 30,906 |

Livability Code: FT 30-90
Wheelbase-to-length ratio of 58% is considered ○ dangerous ○ fatiguing ○ good ◉ excellent *
The approximate net payload of 4794 pounds at 13% of GVWR on this model is ○ deficient ○ excessive ○ cautionary ◉ good ○ excellent *
Total highway safety penalties are: 2 * Value: 9 6 Durability: 9 3 Highway Control Rating: 9 7 Highway Safety: 9 5 ★★★★★

| Affinity | 1999 | MHA | 40 | American Pride (disc.) | DY | CA455 | D | $8800 | 278 | 7,000 | 39,000 | 32,556 |

Livability Code: FT 30-90
Wheelbase-to-length ratio of 58% is considered ○ dangerous ○ fatiguing ○ good ◉ excellent *
The approximate net payload of 6444 pounds at 17% of GVWR on this model is ○ deficient ○ excessive ○ cautionary ○ good ◉ excellent *
Total highway safety penalties are: 2 * Value: 9 6 Durability: 9 3 Highway Control Rating: 1 0 0 Highway Safety: 9 8 ★★★★★

| Affinity | 1999 | MHA | 40 | Optima | DY | CA455 | D | $8800 | 278 | 7,000 | 35,700 | 30,906 |

Livability Code: FT 30-90
Wheelbase-to-length ratio of 58% is considered ○ dangerous ○ fatiguing ○ good ◉ excellent *
The approximate net payload of 4794 pounds at 13% of GVWR on this model is ○ deficient ○ excessive ○ cautionary ◉ good ○ excellent *
Total highway safety penalties are: 2 * Value: 9 6 Durability: 9 3 Highway Control Rating: 9 7 Highway Safety: 9 5 ★★★★★

| Affinity | 1999 | MHA | 40 | Tropicana (discon.) | DY | CA455 | D | $8800 | 278 | 7,000 | 39,000 | 32,556 |

Livability Code: FT 30-90
Wheelbase-to-length ratio of 58% is considered ○ dangerous ○ fatiguing ○ good ◉ excellent *
The approximate net payload of 6444 pounds at 17% of GVWR on this model is ○ deficient ○ excessive ○ cautionary ○ good ◉ excellent *
Total highway safety penalties are: 2 * Value: 9 6 Durability: 9 3 Highway Control Rating: 1 0 0 Highway Safety: 9 8 ★★★★★

| Affinity | 1999 | MHA | 40 | Grande Chalet myc | DY | CA455 | D | $8800 | 278 | 7,000 | 39,000 | 33,611 |

Livability Code: FT 30-90
Wheelbase-to-length ratio of 58% is considered ○ dangerous ○ fatiguing ○ good ◉ excellent *
The approximate net payload of 5390 pounds at 14% of GVWR on this model is ○ deficient ○ excessive ○ cautionary ◉ good ○ excellent *
Total highway safety penalties are: 8 * Value: 9 3 Durability: 9 3 Highway Control Rating: 9 9 Highway Safety: 9 1 ★★★★★

| Affinity | 1999 | MHA | 40 | Captiva myc | DY | CA455 | D | $8800 | 278 | 7,000 | 39,000 | 32,277 |

Livability Code: FT 30-90
Wheelbase-to-length ratio of 58% is considered ○ dangerous ○ fatiguing ○ good ◉ excellent *
The approximate net payload of 6723 pounds at 17% of GVWR on this model is ○ deficient ○ excessive ○ cautionary ○ good ◉ excellent *
Total highway safety penalties are: 2 * Value: 9 6 Durability: 9 3 Highway Control Rating: 1 0 0 Highway Safety: 9 8 ★★★★★

Note: Safety ratings are based on the assumption that the engineering of the RV has allowed for proper balance by placing fresh, gray, and black holding tanks in a location so as not to change the balance of the RV when the tanks are empty or full. **Always double-check wheelbase, GVWR, and weights at front and rear axles.**

*See Section 1 for details on how conclusions are reached.

Brand	Year	Type	Length	Model	Chassis	Engine	Fuel Type	Average Price per Linear Foot When New	Adjusted Wheel-base	Approx. Towing Capacity	Gross Vehicle Weight Rating	Average Curb Weight
Affinity	1999	MHA	40	Legacy myc	DY	CA455	D	$8800	278	7,000	39,000	33,335

Livability Code: FT 30-90 — Wheelbase-to-length ratio of 58% is considered ○ dangerous ○ fatiguing ○ good ◉ excellent *
The approximate net payload of 5665 pounds at 15% of GVWR on this model is ○ deficient ○ excessive ○ cautionary ◉ good ○ excellent *
Total highway safety penalties are: 2 * Value: 96 Durability: 93 Highway Control Rating: 100 Highway Safety: 98 ★★★★

Brand	Year	Type	Length	Model	Chassis	Engine	Fuel Type	Price/Ft	Wheelbase	Towing	GVWR	Curb Weight
Affinity	1999	MHA	40	Optima myc	DY	CA455	D	$8800	278	7,000	39,000	31,800

Livability Code: FT 30-90 — Wheelbase-to-length ratio of 58% is considered ○ dangerous ○ fatiguing ○ good ◉ excellent *
The approximate net payload of 7201 pounds at 18% of GVWR on this model is ○ deficient ○ excessive ○ cautionary ○ good ◉ excellent *
Total highway safety penalties are: 2 * Value: 96 Durability: 93 Highway Control Rating: 100 Highway Safety: 98 ★★★★

Affinity	1999	MHA	42	Dinner Party	DY	CA455	D	$8300	294 T	7,000	47,000	38,184

Livability Code: FT 30-90 — Wheelbase-to-length ratio of 58% is considered ○ dangerous ○ fatiguing ○ good ◉ excellent *
The approximate net payload of 8816 pounds at 19% of GVWR on this model is ○ deficient ○ excessive ○ cautionary ○ good ◉ excellent *
Total highway safety penalties are: 15 * Value: 90 Durability: 93 Highway Control Rating: 100 Highway Safety: 85 ★★★

Affinity	1999	MHA	42	Bed & Breakfast	DY	CA455	D	$8300	294 T	7,000	47,000	38,709

Livability Code: FT 30-90 — Wheelbase-to-length ratio of 58% is considered ○ dangerous ○ fatiguing ○ good ◉ excellent *
The approximate net payload of 8291 pounds at 18% of GVWR on this model is ○ deficient ○ excessive ○ cautionary ○ good ◉ excellent *
Total highway safety penalties are: 18 * Value: 88 Durability: 93 Highway Control Rating: 100 Highway Safety: 82 ★★★

Airstream Classic	1991	MHA	36	35	CH	7.4L	G	$3700	232 T	1,500	17,800	16,560

Livability Code: SB 30-80 — Wheelbase-to-length ratio of 54% is considered ○ dangerous ○ fatiguing ◉ good ○ excellent *
The approximate net payload of 1240 pounds at 7% of GVWR on this model is ○ deficient ○ excessive ◉ cautionary ○ good ○ excellent *
Total highway safety penalties are: 10 * Value: 76 Durability: 77 Highway Control Rating: 51 Highway Safety: 41

Airstream Classic	1995	MHA	36	360	CH	7.4L	G	$3400	232 T	1,500	18,000	16,817

Livability Code: SB 30-90 — Wheelbase-to-length ratio of 54% is considered ○ dangerous ○ fatiguing ◉ good ○ excellent *
The approximate net payload of 1184 pounds at 7% of GVWR on this model is ○ deficient ○ excessive ◉ cautionary ○ good ○ excellent *
Total highway safety penalties are: 10 * Value: 76 Durability: 77 Highway Control Rating: 51 Highway Safety: 41

Airstream Classic	1995	MHA	36	36-DP	SP	CU230	D	$4400	228	1,500	20,000	17,967

Livability Code: SB 30-90 — Wheelbase-to-length ratio of 53% is considered ○ dangerous ◉ fatiguing ○ good ○ excellent *
The approximate net payload of 2034 pounds at 10% of GVWR on this model is ○ deficient ○ excessive ○ cautionary ◉ good ○ excellent *
Total highway safety penalties are: 2 * Value: 80 Durability: 77 Highway Control Rating: 58 Highway Safety: 56 ★

Airstream LE	1990	MHA	35	345	CH	7.4L	G	$3500	228 T	1,500	19,500	16,289

Livability Code: SB 30-90 — Wheelbase-to-length ratio of 55% is considered ○ dangerous ○ fatiguing ◉ good ○ excellent *
The approximate net payload of 3212 pounds at 16% of GVWR on this model is ○ deficient ○ excessive ○ cautionary ◉ good ○ excellent *
Total highway safety penalties are: 9 * Value: 73 Durability: 70 Highway Control Rating: 93 Highway Safety: 84 ★★★

Airstream Legacy	1993	MHA	34	34CB	CH	7.4L	G	$1900	208	1,500	16,000	15,148

Livability Code: SB 30-90 — Wheelbase-to-length ratio of 51% is considered ○ dangerous ◉ fatiguing ○ good ○ excellent *
The approximate net payload of 853 pounds at 5% of GVWR on this model is ◉ deficient ○ excessive ○ cautionary ○ good ○ excellent *
Total highway safety penalties are: 7 * Value: 75 Durability: 70 Highway Control Rating: 13 Highway Safety: 6

Allegro	1990	MHA	32	31 SB	CH	7.4L	G	$1700	178	1,500	16,000	13,564

Livability Code: SB 30-90 — Wheelbase-to-length ratio of 46% is considered ◉ dangerous ○ fatiguing ○ good ○ excellent *
The approximate net payload of 2436 pounds at 15% of GVWR on this model is ○ deficient ○ excessive ○ cautionary ◉ good ○ excellent *
Total highway safety penalties are: 6 * Value: 84 Durability: 74 Highway Control Rating: 30 Highway Safety: 24

Allegro	1991	MHA	28	26 SB	CH	5.7L	G	$1700	176	1,500	12,800	11,700

Livability Code: SB 30-90 — Wheelbase-to-length ratio of 53% is considered ○ dangerous ◉ fatiguing ○ good ○ excellent *
The approximate net payload of 1100 pounds at 9% of GVWR on this model is ○ deficient ○ excessive ◉ cautionary ○ good ○ excellent *
Total highway safety penalties are: 3 * Value: 85 Durability: 74 Highway Control Rating: 54 Highway Safety: 51 ★

Allegro	1991	MHA	33	31SB	FO	7.5L	G	$1500	190	1,500	17,000	14,238

Livability Code: SB 30-90 — Wheelbase-to-length ratio of 48% is considered ◉ dangerous ○ fatiguing ○ good ○ excellent *
The approximate net payload of 2763 pounds at 16% of GVWR on this model is ○ deficient ○ excessive ○ cautionary ○ good ◉ excellent *
Total highway safety penalties are: 2 * Value: 86 Durability: 74 Highway Control Rating: 39 Highway Safety: 37

Note: Safety ratings are based on the assumption that the engineering of the RV has allowed for proper balance by placing fresh, gray, and black holding tanks in a location so as not to change the balance of the RV when the tanks are empty or full. **Always double-check wheelbase, GVWR, and weights at front and rear axles.**

*See Section 1 for details on how conclusions are reached.

Brand	Year	Type	Length	Model	Chassis	Engine	Fuel Type	Average Price per Linear Foot When New	Adjusted Wheelbase	Approx. Towing Capacity	Gross Vehicle Weight Rating	Average Curb Weight
Allegro	1995	MHA	33	31	FO	7.5L	G	$1500	190	3,800	15,200	13,820

Livability Code: SB 30-90
Wheelbase-to-length ratio of 48% is considered ● dangerous ○ fatiguing ○ good ○ excellent *
The approximate net payload of 1380 pounds at 9% of GVWR on this model is ○ deficient ○ excessive ● cautionary ○ good ○ excellent *
Total highway safety penalties are: 2 *   Value: 8 6   Durability: 7 4   Highway Control Rating: 2 1   Highway Safety: 1 9

Brand	Year	Type	Length	Model	Chassis	Engine	Fuel Type	Price/Ft	Wheelbase	Towing	GVWR	Curb Weight
Allegro	1995	MHA	34	33	FO	7.5L	G	$1500	208	3,800	15,200	14,156

Livability Code: SB 30-90
Wheelbase-to-length ratio of 50% is considered ● dangerous ○ fatiguing ○ good ○ excellent *
The approximate net payload of 1044 pounds at 7% of GVWR on this model is ○ deficient ○ excessive ● cautionary ○ good ○ excellent *
Total highway safety penalties are: 2 *   Value: 8 6   Durability: 7 4   Highway Control Rating: 1 7   Highway Safety: 1 5

Allegro	1996	MHA	25	25	CH	7.4L	G	$1900	138	4,700	12,300	11,040

Livability Code: SB 30-90
Wheelbase-to-length ratio of 46% is considered ● dangerous ○ fatiguing ○ good ○ excellent *
The approximate net payload of 1260 pounds at 10% of GVWR on this model is ○ deficient ○ excessive ○ cautionary ● good ○ excellent *
Total highway safety penalties are: 2 *   Value: 8 6   Durability: 7 4   Highway Control Rating: 1 9   Highway Safety: 1 7

Allegro	1996	MHA	25	25 myc	CH	7.4L	G	$1900	158	4,700	12,300	11,040

Livability Code: SB 30-90
Wheelbase-to-length ratio of 53% is considered ○ dangerous ● fatiguing ○ good ○ excellent *
The approximate net payload of 1260 pounds at 10% of GVWR on this model is ○ deficient ○ excessive ● cautionary ○ good ○ excellent *
Total highway safety penalties are: 2 *   Value: 8 6   Durability: 7 4   Highway Control Rating: 5 8   Highway Safety: 5 6   ★

Allegro	1996	MHA	29	28	CH	7.4L	G	$1800	158	4,200	14,800	12,180

Livability Code: SB 30-90
Wheelbase-to-length ratio of 45% is considered ● dangerous ○ fatiguing ○ good ○ excellent *
The approximate net payload of 2620 pounds at 18% of GVWR on this model is ○ deficient ○ excessive ○ cautionary ○ good ● excellent *
Total highway safety penalties are: 4 *   Value: 8 5   Durability: 7 4   Highway Control Rating: 3 0   Highway Safety: 2 6

Allegro	1996	MHA	29	28 myc	CH	7.4L	G	$1800	178	4,200	14,800	12,180

Livability Code: SB 30-90
Wheelbase-to-length ratio of 51% is considered ○ dangerous ● fatiguing ○ good ○ excellent *
The approximate net payload of 2620 pounds at 18% of GVWR on this model is ○ deficient ○ excessive ○ cautionary ○ good ● excellent *
Total highway safety penalties are: 4 *   Value: 8 5   Durability: 7 4   Highway Control Rating: 5 0   Highway Safety: 4 6

Allegro	1996	MHA	32	31	CH	7.4L	G	$1800	190	4,200	14,800	13,180

Livability Code: SB 30-90
Wheelbase-to-length ratio of 49% is considered ● dangerous ○ fatiguing ○ good ○ excellent *
The approximate net payload of 1620 pounds at 11% of GVWR on this model is ○ deficient ○ excessive ○ cautionary ● good ○ excellent *
Total highway safety penalties are: 6 *   Value: 8 4   Durability: 7 4   Highway Control Rating: 3 3   Highway Safety: 2 7

Allegro	1996	MHA	32	31 myc	CH	7.4L	G	$1800	208	4,200	14,800	13,370

Livability Code: SB 30-90
Wheelbase-to-length ratio of 54% is considered ○ dangerous ○ fatiguing ● good ○ excellent *
The approximate net payload of 1430 pounds at 10% of GVWR on this model is ○ deficient ○ excessive ○ cautionary ● good ○ excellent *
Total highway safety penalties are: 6 *   Value: 8 4   Durability: 7 4   Highway Control Rating: 7 6   Highway Safety: 7 0   ★★★

Allegro	1996	MHA	32	31	FO	7.5L	G	$1800	190	8,000	17,000	13,660

Livability Code: SB 30-90
Wheelbase-to-length ratio of 49% is considered ● dangerous ○ fatiguing ○ good ○ excellent *
The approximate net payload of 3340 pounds at 20% of GVWR on this model is ○ deficient ○ excessive ○ cautionary ○ good ● excellent *
Total highway safety penalties are: 2 *   Value: 8 6   Durability: 7 4   Highway Control Rating: 4 6   Highway Safety: 4 4

Allegro	1996	MHA	32	31 myc	FO	7.5L	G	$1800	208	8,000	17,000	13,660

Livability Code: SB 30-90
Wheelbase-to-length ratio of 54% is considered ○ dangerous ○ fatiguing ● good ○ excellent *
The approximate net payload of 3340 pounds at 20% of GVWR on this model is ○ deficient ○ excessive ○ cautionary ○ good ● excellent *
Total highway safety penalties are: 2 *   Value: 8 6   Durability: 7 4   Highway Control Rating: 8 6   Highway Safety: 8 4   ★★★

Allegro	1996	MHA	34	33	CH	7.4L	G	$1700	208	3,500	16,500	13,780

Livability Code: SB 30-90
Wheelbase-to-length ratio of 52% is considered ○ dangerous ● fatiguing ○ good ○ excellent *
The approximate net payload of 2720 pounds at 16% of GVWR on this model is ○ deficient ○ excessive ○ cautionary ○ good ● excellent *
Total highway safety penalties are: 6 *   Value: 8 3   Durability: 7 4   Highway Control Rating: 5 8   Highway Safety: 5 2   ★

Allegro	1996	MHA	34	33 myc	CH	7.4L	G	$1700	228	3,500	16,500	13,780

Livability Code: SB 30-90
Wheelbase-to-length ratio of 57% is considered ○ dangerous ○ fatiguing ● good ○ excellent *
The approximate net payload of 2720 pounds at 16% of GVWR on this model is ○ deficient ○ excessive ○ cautionary ○ good ● excellent *
Total highway safety penalties are: 6 *   Value: 8 3   Durability: 7 4   Highway Control Rating: 9 9   Highway Safety: 9 3   ★★★

Note: Safety ratings are based on the assumption that the engineering of the RV has allowed for proper balance by placing fresh, gray, and black holding tanks in a location so as not to change the balance of the RV when the tanks are empty or full. **Always double-check wheelbase, GVWR, and weights at front and rear axles.**

*See Section 1 for details on how conclusions are reached.

Section 2: The Ratings

Brand	Year	Type	Length	Model	Chassis	Engine	Fuel Type	Average Price per Linear Foot When New	Adjusted Wheelbase	Approx. Towing Capacity	Gross Vehicle Weight Rating	Average Curb Weight

Allegro — 1996 — MHA — 34 — Model 33 — Chassis FO — Engine 7.5L — Fuel Type G — $1700 — Wheelbase 208 — Towing 8,000 — GVWR 17,000 — Curb 14,350

Livability Code: SB 30-90
Wheelbase-to-length ratio of 52% is considered ○ dangerous ● fatiguing ○ good ○ excellent *
The approximate net payload of 2650 pounds at 16% of GVWR on this model is ○ deficient ○ excessive ○ cautionary ○ good ● excellent *
Total highway safety penalties are: 2 *   Value: 8 6   Durability: 7 4   Highway Control Rating: 5 7   Highway Safety: 5 5   ★

Allegro — 1996 — MHA — 34 — Model 33 myc — Chassis FO — Engine 7.5L — Fuel Type G — $1700 — Wheelbase 228 — Towing 8,000 — GVWR 17,000 — Curb 14,350

Livability Code: SB 30-90
Wheelbase-to-length ratio of 57% is considered ○ dangerous ○ fatiguing ● good ○ excellent *
The approximate net payload of 2650 pounds at 16% of GVWR on this model is ○ deficient ○ excessive ○ cautionary ○ good ● excellent *
Total highway safety penalties are: 2 *   Value: 8 6   Durability: 7 4   Highway Control Rating: 9 8   Highway Safety: 9 6   ★★★

Allegro — 1997 — MHA — 26 — Model 25 — Chassis CH — Engine 7.4L — Fuel Type G — $1900 — Wheelbase 158 — Towing 6,700 — GVWR 12,300 — Curb 11,250

Livability Code: SB 30-90
Wheelbase-to-length ratio of 52% is considered ○ dangerous ● fatiguing ○ good ○ excellent *
The approximate net payload of 1050 pounds at 9% of GVWR on this model is ○ deficient ○ excessive ● cautionary ○ good ○ excellent *
Total highway safety penalties are: 2 *   Value: 8 5   Durability: 7 4   Highway Control Rating: 4 1   Highway Safety: 3 9

Allegro — 1997 — MHA — 30 — Model 28 — Chassis CH — Engine 7.4L — Fuel Type G — $1800 — Wheelbase 178 — Towing 4,200 — GVWR 14,800 — Curb 12,480

Livability Code: SB 30-90
Wheelbase-to-length ratio of 50% is considered ● dangerous ○ fatiguing ○ good ○ excellent *
The approximate net payload of 2320 pounds at 16% of GVWR on this model is ○ deficient ○ excessive ○ cautionary ○ good ● excellent *
Total highway safety penalties are: 4 *   Value: 8 4   Durability: 7 4   Highway Control Rating: 4 5   Highway Safety: 4 1

Allegro — 1997 — MHA — 30 — Model 28 — Chassis FO — Engine 7.5L — Fuel Type G — $1800 — Wheelbase 178 — Towing 9,800 — GVWR 15,200 — Curb 12,980

Livability Code: SB 30-90
Wheelbase-to-length ratio of 50% is considered ● dangerous ○ fatiguing ○ good ○ excellent *
The approximate net payload of 2220 pounds at 15% of GVWR on this model is ○ deficient ○ excessive ○ cautionary ● good ○ excellent *
Total highway safety penalties are: 2 *   Value: 8 6   Durability: 7 4   Highway Control Rating: 4 3   Highway Safety: 4 1

Allegro — 1997 — MHA — 32 — Model 31 — Chassis CH — Engine 7.4L — Fuel Type G — $1800 — Wheelbase 208 — Towing 4,200 — GVWR 14,800 — Curb 13,570

Livability Code: SB 30-90
Wheelbase-to-length ratio of 54% is considered ○ dangerous ○ fatiguing ● good ○ excellent *
The approximate net payload of 1230 pounds at 8% of GVWR on this model is ○ deficient ○ excessive ● cautionary ○ good ○ excellent *
Total highway safety penalties are: 6 *   Value: 8 4   Durability: 7 4   Highway Control Rating: 5 9   Highway Safety: 5 3   ★

Allegro — 1997 — MHA — 32 — Model 31 — Chassis FO — Engine 7.5L — Fuel Type G — $1800 — Wheelbase 208 — Towing 8,000 — GVWR 17,000 — Curb 13,860

Livability Code: SB 30-90
Wheelbase-to-length ratio of 54% is considered ○ dangerous ○ fatiguing ● good ○ excellent *
The approximate net payload of 3140 pounds at 18% of GVWR on this model is ○ deficient ○ excessive ○ cautionary ○ good ● excellent *
Total highway safety penalties are: 2 *   Value: 8 6   Durability: 7 4   Highway Control Rating: 8 5   Highway Safety: 8 3   ★★★

Allegro — 1997 — MHA — 34 — Model 33 — Chassis CH — Engine 7.4L — Fuel Type G — $1800 — Wheelbase 228 — Towing 3,500 — GVWR 16,500 — Curb 13,980

Livability Code: SB 30-90
Wheelbase-to-length ratio of 57% is considered ○ dangerous ○ fatiguing ● good ○ excellent *
The approximate net payload of 2520 pounds at 15% of GVWR on this model is ○ deficient ○ excessive ○ cautionary ● good ○ excellent *
Total highway safety penalties are: 6 *   Value: 8 3   Durability: 7 4   Highway Control Rating: 9 6   Highway Safety: 9 0   ★★★

Allegro — 1997 — MHA — 34 — Model 33 — Chassis FO — Engine 7.5L — Fuel Type G — $1800 — Wheelbase 228 — Towing 8,000 — GVWR 17,000 — Curb 14,470

Livability Code: SB 30-90
Wheelbase-to-length ratio of 57% is considered ○ dangerous ○ fatiguing ● good ○ excellent *
The approximate net payload of 2530 pounds at 15% of GVWR on this model is ○ deficient ○ excessive ○ cautionary ● good ○ excellent *
Total highway safety penalties are: 2 *   Value: 8 6   Durability: 7 4   Highway Control Rating: 9 6   Highway Safety: 9 4   ★★★

Allegro — 1998 — MHA — 26 — Model 25 side bath — Chassis CH — Engine 7.4L — Fuel Type G — $1800 — Wheelbase 158 — Towing 6,700 — GVWR 12,300 — Curb 11,250

Livability Code: SB 30-90
Wheelbase-to-length ratio of 52% is considered ○ dangerous ● fatiguing ○ good ○ excellent *
The approximate net payload of 1050 pounds at 9% of GVWR on this model is ○ deficient ○ excessive ● cautionary ○ good ○ excellent *
Total highway safety penalties are: 2 *   Value: 7 8   Durability: 7 4   Highway Control Rating: 4 1   Highway Safety: 3 9

Allegro — 1998 — MHA — 30 — Model 28 split bath — Chassis CH — Engine 7.4L — Fuel Type G — $1700 — Wheelbase 178 — Towing 4,200 — GVWR 14,800 — Curb 12,480

Livability Code: SB 30-90
Wheelbase-to-length ratio of 50% is considered ● dangerous ○ fatiguing ○ good ○ excellent *
The approximate net payload of 2320 pounds at 16% of GVWR on this model is ○ deficient ○ excessive ○ cautionary ○ good ● excellent *
Total highway safety penalties are: 4 *   Value: 7 7   Durability: 7 4   Highway Control Rating: 4 5   Highway Safety: 4 1

Allegro — 1998 — MHA — 30 — Model 28 split bath — Chassis FO — Engine 7.5L — Fuel Type G — $1700 — Wheelbase 178 — Towing 7,800 — GVWR 15,200 — Curb 12,980

Livability Code: SB 30-90
Wheelbase-to-length ratio of 50% is considered ● dangerous ○ fatiguing ○ good ○ excellent *
The approximate net payload of 2220 pounds at 15% of GVWR on this model is ○ deficient ○ excessive ○ cautionary ● good ○ excellent *
Total highway safety penalties are: 2 *   Value: 7 9   Durability: 7 4   Highway Control Rating: 4 3   Highway Safety: 4 1

Note: Safety ratings are based on the assumption that the engineering of the RV has allowed for proper balance by placing fresh, gray, and black holding tanks in a location so as not to change the balance of the RV when the tanks are empty or full. **Always double-check wheelbase, GVWR, and weights at front and rear axles.**

*See Section 1 for details on how conclusions are reached.

Brand	Year	Type	Length	Model	Chassis	Engine	Fuel Type	Average Price per Linear Foot When New	Adjusted Wheelbase	Approx. Towing Capacity	Gross Vehicle Weight Rating	Average Curb Weight
Allegro	1998	MHA	32	31 side bath	CH	7.4L	G	$1700	208	4,200	14,800	13,570

Livability Code: SB 30-90
Wheelbase-to-length ratio of 54% is considered ○ dangerous ○ fatiguing ◉ good ○ excellent *
The approximate net payload of 1230 pounds at 8% of GVWR on this model is ○ deficient ○ excessive ◉ cautionary ○ good ○ excellent *
Total highway safety penalties are: 6 *   Value: 7 7   Durability: 7 4   Highway Control Rating: 5 9   Highway Safety: 5 3   ★

Brand	Year	Type	Length	Model	Chassis	Engine	Fuel Type	Price/LF	Adj Wheelbase	Towing	GVWR	Curb Wt
Allegro	1998	MHA	32	31 split bath	CH	7.4L	G	$1700	208	4,200	14,800	13,570

Livability Code: SB 30-90
Wheelbase-to-length ratio of 54% is considered ○ dangerous ○ fatiguing ◉ good ○ excellent *
The approximate net payload of 1230 pounds at 8% of GVWR on this model is ○ deficient ○ excessive ◉ cautionary ○ good ○ excellent *
Total highway safety penalties are: 6 *   Value: 7 7   Durability: 7 4   Highway Control Rating: 5 9   Highway Safety: 5 3   ★

Brand	Year	Type	Length	Model	Chassis	Engine	Fuel Type	Price/LF	Adj Wheelbase	Towing	GVWR	Curb Wt
Allegro	1998	MHA	32	31 side bath	FO	7.5L	G	$1700	208	8,000	17,000	13,860

Livability Code: SB 30-90
Wheelbase-to-length ratio of 54% is considered ○ dangerous ○ fatiguing ◉ good ○ excellent *
The approximate net payload of 3140 pounds at 18% of GVWR on this model is ○ deficient ○ excessive ○ cautionary ○ good ◉ excellent *
Total highway safety penalties are: 2 *   Value: 7 9   Durability: 7 4   Highway Control Rating: 8 5   Highway Safety: 8 3   ★★★

Brand	Year	Type	Length	Model	Chassis	Engine	Fuel Type	Price/LF	Adj Wheelbase	Towing	GVWR	Curb Wt
Allegro	1998	MHA	32	31 split bath	FO	7.5L	G	$1700	208	8,000	17,000	13,860

Livability Code: SB 30-90
Wheelbase-to-length ratio of 54% is considered ○ dangerous ○ fatiguing ◉ good ○ excellent *
The approximate net payload of 3140 pounds at 18% of GVWR on this model is ○ deficient ○ excessive ○ cautionary ○ good ◉ excellent *
Total highway safety penalties are: 2 *   Value: 7 9   Durability: 7 4   Highway Control Rating: 8 5   Highway Safety: 8 3   ★★★

Brand	Year	Type	Length	Model	Chassis	Engine	Fuel Type	Price/LF	Adj Wheelbase	Towing	GVWR	Curb Wt
Allegro	1998	MHA	34	33 split bath	CH	7.4L	G	$1700	228	4,500	16,500	13,980

Livability Code: SB 30-90
Wheelbase-to-length ratio of 57% is considered ○ dangerous ○ fatiguing ◉ good ○ excellent *
The approximate net payload of 2520 pounds at 15% of GVWR on this model is ○ deficient ○ excessive ○ cautionary ◉ good ○ excellent *
Total highway safety penalties are: 6 *   Value: 7 6   Durability: 7 4   Highway Control Rating: 9 6   Highway Safety: 9 0   ★★★

Brand	Year	Type	Length	Model	Chassis	Engine	Fuel Type	Price/LF	Adj Wheelbase	Towing	GVWR	Curb Wt
Allegro	1998	MHA	34	33 split bath opsl	CH	7.4L	G	$1800	228	4,500	16,500	14,780

Livability Code: SB 30-90
Wheelbase-to-length ratio of 57% is considered ○ dangerous ○ fatiguing ◉ good ○ excellent *
The approximate net payload of 1720 pounds at 10% of GVWR on this model is ○ deficient ○ excessive ○ cautionary ◉ good ○ excellent *
Total highway safety penalties are: 12 *   Value: 7 4   Durability: 7 4   Highway Control Rating: 8 7   Highway Safety: 7 5   ★★★

Brand	Year	Type	Length	Model	Chassis	Engine	Fuel Type	Price/LF	Adj Wheelbase	Towing	GVWR	Curb Wt
Allegro	1998	MHA	34	33 split bath	FO	7.5L	G	$1600	228	8,000	17,000	14,470

Livability Code: SB 30-90
Wheelbase-to-length ratio of 57% is considered ○ dangerous ○ fatiguing ◉ good ○ excellent *
The approximate net payload of 2530 pounds at 15% of GVWR on this model is ○ deficient ○ excessive ○ cautionary ◉ good ○ excellent *
Total highway safety penalties are: 2 *   Value: 7 9   Durability: 7 4   Highway Control Rating: 9 6   Highway Safety: 9 4   ★★★

Brand	Year	Type	Length	Model	Chassis	Engine	Fuel Type	Price/LF	Adj Wheelbase	Towing	GVWR	Curb Wt
Allegro	1998	MHA	34	33 split bath opsl	FO	7.5L	G	$1800	228	8,000	17,000	15,270

Livability Code: SB 30-90
Wheelbase-to-length ratio of 57% is considered ○ dangerous ○ fatiguing ◉ good ○ excellent *
The approximate net payload of 1730 pounds at 10% of GVWR on this model is ○ deficient ○ excessive ○ cautionary ◉ good ○ excellent *
Total highway safety penalties are: 7 *   Value: 7 6   Durability: 7 4   Highway Control Rating: 8 6   Highway Safety: 7 9   ★★★

Brand	Year	Type	Length	Model	Chassis	Engine	Fuel Type	Price/LF	Adj Wheelbase	Towing	GVWR	Curb Wt
Allegro	1999	MHA	30	28	CH	7.4L	G	$2000	178	4,200	14,800	12,480

Livability Code: SB 30-90
Wheelbase-to-length ratio of 50% is considered ◉ dangerous ○ fatiguing ○ good ○ excellent *
The approximate net payload of 2320 pounds at 16% of GVWR on this model is ○ deficient ○ excessive ○ cautionary ○ good ◉ excellent *
Total highway safety penalties are: 4 *   Value: 8 2   Durability: 7 4   Highway Control Rating: 5 5   Highway Safety: 5 1

Brand	Year	Type	Length	Model	Chassis	Engine	Fuel Type	Price/LF	Adj Wheelbase	Towing	GVWR	Curb Wt
Allegro	1999	MHA	30	28	FO	6.8L	G	$2000	178	8,000	18,000	14,160

Livability Code: SB 30-90
Wheelbase-to-length ratio of 50% is considered ◉ dangerous ○ fatiguing ○ good ○ excellent *
The approximate net payload of 3840 pounds at 21% of GVWR on this model is ○ deficient ○ excessive ○ cautionary ○ good ◉ excellent *
Total highway safety penalties are: 2 *   Value: 8 4   Durability: 7 4   Highway Control Rating: 5 8   Highway Safety: 5 6

Brand	Year	Type	Length	Model	Chassis	Engine	Fuel Type	Price/LF	Adj Wheelbase	Towing	GVWR	Curb Wt
Allegro	1999	MHA	32	31	CH	7.4L	G	$1900	208	4,500	16,500	13,570

Livability Code: SB 30-90
Wheelbase-to-length ratio of 54% is considered ○ dangerous ○ fatiguing ◉ good ○ excellent *
The approximate net payload of 2930 pounds at 18% of GVWR on this model is ○ deficient ○ excessive ○ cautionary ○ good ◉ excellent *
Total highway safety penalties are: 6 *   Value: 8 2   Durability: 7 4   Highway Control Rating: 8 6   Highway Safety: 8 0   ★★★

Brand	Year	Type	Length	Model	Chassis	Engine	Fuel Type	Price/LF	Adj Wheelbase	Towing	GVWR	Curb Wt
Allegro	1999	MHA	32	31 opsl	CH	7.4L	G	$1900	208	4,500	16,500	14,370

Livability Code: SB 30-90
Wheelbase-to-length ratio of 54% is considered ○ dangerous ○ fatiguing ◉ good ○ excellent *
The approximate net payload of 2130 pounds at 13% of GVWR on this model is ○ deficient ○ excessive ○ cautionary ◉ good ○ excellent *
Total highway safety penalties are: 16 *   Value: 7 7   Durability: 7 4   Highway Control Rating: 7 9   Highway Safety: 6 3   ★★

Note: Safety ratings are based on the assumption that the engineering of the RV has allowed for proper balance by placing fresh, gray, and black holding tanks in a location so as not to change the balance of the RV when the tanks are empty or full. **Always double-check wheelbase, GVWR, and weights at front and rear axles.**

*See Section 1 for details on how conclusions are reached.

Brand	Year	Type	Length	Model	Chassis	Engine	Fuel Type	Average Price per Linear Foot When New	Adjusted Wheelbase	Approx. Towing Capacity	Gross Vehicle Weight Rating	Average Curb Weight
Allegro	1999	MHA	32	31	FO	6.8L	G	$1900	208	8,000	18,000	14,360

Livability Code: SB 30-90
Wheelbase-to-length ratio of 54% is considered ○ dangerous ○ fatiguing ◉ good ○ excellent *
The approximate net payload of 3640 pounds at 20% of GVWR on this model is ○ deficient ○ excessive ○ cautionary ○ good ◉ excellent *
Total highway safety penalties are: 2 *   Value: 8 4   Durability: 7 4   Highway Control Rating: 8 8   Highway Safety: 8 6   ★★★

Brand	Year	Type	Length	Model	Chassis	Engine	Fuel Type	Avg Price/Linear Foot	Adj. Wheelbase	Towing Cap.	GVWR	Curb Weight
Allegro	1999	MHA	32	31 opsl	FO	6.8L	G	$1900	208	8,000	18,000	15,160

Livability Code: SB 30-90
Wheelbase-to-length ratio of 54% is considered ○ dangerous ○ fatiguing ◉ good ○ excellent *
The approximate net payload of 2840 pounds at 16% of GVWR on this model is ○ deficient ○ excessive ○ cautionary ○ good ◉ excellent *
Total highway safety penalties are: 12 *   Value: 7 8   Durability: 7 4   Highway Control Rating: 8 4   Highway Safety: 7 2   ★★★

Allegro	1999	MHA	34	33	CH	7.4L	G	$1800	228	4,500	16,500	13,980

Livability Code: SB 30-90
Wheelbase-to-length ratio of 57% is considered ○ dangerous ○ fatiguing ◉ good ○ excellent *
The approximate net payload of 2520 pounds at 15% of GVWR on this model is ○ deficient ○ excessive ○ cautionary ◉ good ○ excellent *
Total highway safety penalties are: 6 *   Value: 8 1   Durability: 7 4   Highway Control Rating: 9 6   Highway Safety: 9 0   ★★★

Allegro	1999	MHA	34	33 opsl	CH	7.4L	G	$1800	228	4,500	16,500	14,780

Livability Code: SB 30-90
Wheelbase-to-length ratio of 57% is considered ○ dangerous ○ fatiguing ◉ good ○ excellent *
The approximate net payload of 1720 pounds at 10% of GVWR on this model is ○ deficient ○ excessive ○ cautionary ◉ good ○ excellent *
Total highway safety penalties are: 17 *   Value: 7 6   Durability: 7 4   Highway Control Rating: 8 7   Highway Safety: 7 0   ★★★

Allegro	1999	MHA	34	33	FO	6.8L	G	$1800	228	8,000	18,000	15,160

Livability Code: SB 30-90
Wheelbase-to-length ratio of 57% is considered ○ dangerous ○ fatiguing ◉ good ○ excellent *
The approximate net payload of 2840 pounds at 16% of GVWR on this model is ○ deficient ○ excessive ○ cautionary ○ good ◉ excellent *
Total highway safety penalties are: 2 *   Value: 8 4   Durability: 7 4   Highway Control Rating: 9 8   Highway Safety: 9 6   ★★★

Allegro	1999	MHA	34	33 opsl	FO	6.8L	G	$1800	228	8,000	18,000	15,960

Livability Code: SB 30-90
Wheelbase-to-length ratio of 57% is considered ○ dangerous ○ fatiguing ◉ good ○ excellent *
The approximate net payload of 2040 pounds at 11% of GVWR on this model is ○ deficient ○ excessive ○ cautionary ◉ good ○ excellent *
Total highway safety penalties are: 12 *   Value: 7 8   Durability: 7 4   Highway Control Rating: 8 8   Highway Safety: 7 6   ★★★

Allegro Bay	1991	MHA	32	R8-D32	OS	7.5L	G	$2400	190	1,500	18,000	15,094

Livability Code: SB 30-90
Wheelbase-to-length ratio of 49% is considered ◉ dangerous ○ fatiguing ○ good ○ excellent *
The approximate net payload of 2906 pounds at 16% of GVWR on this model is ○ deficient ○ excessive ○ cautionary ○ good ◉ excellent *
Total highway safety penalties are: 2 *   Value: 8 6   Durability: 7 4   Highway Control Rating: 4 3   Highway Safety: 4 1

Allegro Bay	1991	MHA	34	34SB	CH	7.4L	G	$1800	208	1,500	16,000	14,516

Livability Code: SB 30-90
Wheelbase-to-length ratio of 50% is considered ◉ dangerous ○ fatiguing ○ good ○ excellent *
The approximate net payload of 1484 pounds at 9% of GVWR on this model is ○ deficient ○ excessive ◉ cautionary ○ good ○ excellent *
Total highway safety penalties are: 7 *   Value: 8 3   Durability: 7 4   Highway Control Rating: 2 9   Highway Safety: 2 2

Allegro Bay	1993	MHA	31	30	CH	7.4L	G	$1800	178	1,500	16,000	13,635

Livability Code: SB 30-90
Wheelbase-to-length ratio of 48% is considered ◉ dangerous ○ fatiguing ○ good ○ excellent *
The approximate net payload of 2365 pounds at 15% of GVWR on this model is ○ deficient ○ excessive ○ cautionary ◉ good ○ excellent *
Total highway safety penalties are: 5 *   Value: 8 4   Durability: 7 4   Highway Control Rating: 3 5   Highway Safety: 3 0

Allegro Bay	1993	MHA	31	30	FO	7.5L	G	$1800	178	8,000	17,000	14,135

Livability Code: SB 30-90
Wheelbase-to-length ratio of 48% is considered ◉ dangerous ○ fatiguing ○ good ○ excellent *
The approximate net payload of 2865 pounds at 17% of GVWR on this model is ○ deficient ○ excessive ○ cautionary ○ good ◉ excellent *
Total highway safety penalties are: 2 *   Value: 8 6   Durability: 7 4   Highway Control Rating: 3 8   Highway Safety: 3 6

Allegro Bay	1993	MHA	31	30-190	OS	CU190	D	$2200	178	1,500	16,000	14,135

Livability Code: SB 30-90
Wheelbase-to-length ratio of 48% is considered ◉ dangerous ○ fatiguing ○ good ○ excellent *
The approximate net payload of 1865 pounds at 12% of GVWR on this model is ○ deficient ○ excessive ○ cautionary ◉ good ○ excellent *
Total highway safety penalties are: 2 *   Value: 8 6   Durability: 7 4   Highway Control Rating: 2 9   Highway Safety: 2 7

Allegro Bay	1993	MHA	33	32	CH	7.4L	G	$1800	190	1,500	16,000	14,154

Livability Code: SB 30-90
Wheelbase-to-length ratio of 48% is considered ◉ dangerous ○ fatiguing ○ good ○ excellent *
The approximate net payload of 1846 pounds at 12% of GVWR on this model is ○ deficient ○ excessive ○ cautionary ◉ good ○ excellent *
Total highway safety penalties are: 6 *   Value: 8 4   Durability: 7 4   Highway Control Rating: 2 9   Highway Safety: 2 3

Note: Safety ratings are based on the assumption that the engineering of the RV has allowed for proper balance by placing fresh, gray, and black holding tanks in a location so as not to change the balance of the RV when the tanks are empty or full. **Always double-check wheelbase, GVWR, and weights at front and rear axles.**

*See Section 1 for details on how conclusions are reached.

Section 2: The Ratings

Brand	Year	Type	Length	Model	Chassis	Engine	Fuel Type	Average Price per Linear Foot When New	Adjusted Wheelbase	Approx. Towing Capacity	Gross Vehicle Weight Rating	Average Curb Weight
Allegro Bay	**1993**	MHA	33	32	FO	7.5L	G	$1800	190	8,000	17,000	14,654

Livability Code: SB 30-90
Wheelbase-to-length ratio of 48% is considered ⦿ dangerous ○ fatiguing ○ good ○ excellent *
The approximate net payload of 2346 pounds at 14% of GVWR on this model is ○ deficient ○ excessive ○ cautionary ⦿ good ○ excellent *
Total highway safety penalties are: 2 * Value: **86** Durability: **74** Highway Control Rating: **33** Highway Safety: **31**

| **Allegro Bay** | **1993** | MHA | 33 | 32-190 | OS | CU190 | D | $2300 | 190 | 1,500 | 16,000 | 14,654 |

Livability Code: SB 30-90
Wheelbase-to-length ratio of 48% is considered ⦿ dangerous ○ fatiguing ○ good ○ excellent *
The approximate net payload of 1346 pounds at 8% of GVWR on this model is ○ deficient ○ excessive ⦿ cautionary ○ good ○ excellent *
Total highway safety penalties are: 2 * Value: **86** Durability: **74** Highway Control Rating: **15** Highway Safety: **13**

| **Allegro Bay** | **1993** | MHA | 33 | 32 DP | OS | Cu5.9L | D | $2600 | 208 | 1,500 | 17,400 | 15,554 |

Livability Code: SB 30-90
Wheelbase-to-length ratio of 53% is considered ○ dangerous ⦿ fatiguing ○ good ○ excellent *
The approximate net payload of 1846 pounds at 11% of GVWR on this model is ○ deficient ○ excessive ○ cautionary ⦿ good ○ excellent *
Total highway safety penalties are: 2 * Value: **86** Durability: **74** Highway Control Rating: **58** Highway Safety: **56** ★

| **Allegro Bay** | **1993** | MHA | 34 | 34 | CH | 7.4L | G | $1800 | 208 | 1,500 | 16,000 | 14,516 |

Livability Code: SB 30-90
Wheelbase-to-length ratio of 50% is considered ⦿ dangerous ○ fatiguing ○ good ○ excellent *
The approximate net payload of 1484 pounds at 9% of GVWR on this model is ○ deficient ○ excessive ⦿ cautionary ○ good ○ excellent *
Total highway safety penalties are: 7 * Value: **83** Durability: **74** Highway Control Rating: **29** Highway Safety: **22**

| **Allegro Bay** | **1993** | MHA | 34 | 34 | FO | 7.5L | G | $1800 | 208 | 8,000 | 17,000 | 15,016 |

Livability Code: SB 30-90
Wheelbase-to-length ratio of 50% is considered ⦿ dangerous ○ fatiguing ○ good ○ excellent *
The approximate net payload of 1984 pounds at 12% of GVWR on this model is ○ deficient ○ excessive ○ cautionary ⦿ good ○ excellent *
Total highway safety penalties are: 2 * Value: **86** Durability: **74** Highway Control Rating: **38** Highway Safety: **36**

| **Allegro Bay** | **1993** | MHA | 34 | 34-190 | OS | CU190 | D | $2200 | 208 | 1,500 | 16,000 | 15,016 |

Livability Code: SB 30-90
Wheelbase-to-length ratio of 50% is considered ⦿ dangerous ○ fatiguing ○ good ○ excellent *
The approximate net payload of 984 pounds at 6% of GVWR on this model is ⦿ deficient ○ excessive ○ cautionary ○ good ○ excellent *
Total highway safety penalties are: 2 * Value: **86** Durability: **74** Highway Control Rating: **11** Highway Safety: **9**

| **Allegro Bay** | **1993** | MHA | 35 | 34 DP | OS | Cu5.9L | D | $2400 | 228 | 1,500 | 17,400 | 16,020 |

Livability Code: SB 30-90
Wheelbase-to-length ratio of 55% is considered ○ dangerous ○ fatiguing ⦿ good ○ excellent *
The approximate net payload of 1380 pounds at 8% of GVWR on this model is ○ deficient ○ excessive ⦿ cautionary ○ good ○ excellent *
Total highway safety penalties are: 2 * Value: **86** Durability: **74** Highway Control Rating: **68** Highway Safety: **66** ★★

| **Allegro Bay** | **1993** | MHA | 37 | 36 DP | OS | Cu5.9L | D | $2500 | 252 | 1,500 | 18,400 | 16,839 |

Livability Code: SB 30-90
Wheelbase-to-length ratio of 57% is considered ○ dangerous ○ fatiguing ⦿ good ○ excellent *
The approximate net payload of 1561 pounds at 8% of GVWR on this model is ○ deficient ○ excessive ⦿ cautionary ○ good ○ excellent *
Total highway safety penalties are: 2 * Value: **86** Durability: **74** Highway Control Rating: **77** Highway Safety: **75** ★★★

| **Allegro Bay** | **1993** | MHA | 37 | 37 | CH | 7.4L | G | $1800 | 232 T | 1,500 | 19,500 | 16,294 |

Livability Code: SB 30-90
Wheelbase-to-length ratio of 52% is considered ○ dangerous ⦿ fatiguing ○ good ○ excellent *
The approximate net payload of 3206 pounds at 16% of GVWR on this model is ○ deficient ○ excessive ○ cautionary ○ good ⦿ excellent *
Total highway safety penalties are: 11 * Value: **81** Durability: **74** Highway Control Rating: **59** Highway Safety: **48**

| **Allegro Bay** | **1993** | MHA | 37 | 37 | FO | 7.5L | G | $1800 | 232 T | 4,500 | 20,500 | 17,094 |

Livability Code: SB 30-90
Wheelbase-to-length ratio of 52% is considered ○ dangerous ⦿ fatiguing ○ good ○ excellent *
The approximate net payload of 3406 pounds at 17% of GVWR on this model is ○ deficient ○ excessive ○ cautionary ○ good ⦿ excellent *
Total highway safety penalties are: 4 * Value: **84** Durability: **74** Highway Control Rating: **59** Highway Safety: **55** ★

| **Allegro Bay** | **1993** | MHA | 37 | 37-190 | OS | CU190 | D | $2700 | 208 | 0 | 19,300 | 17,294 |

Livability Code: SB 30-90
Wheelbase-to-length ratio of 46% is considered ⦿ dangerous ○ fatiguing ○ good ○ excellent *
The approximate net payload of 2006 pounds at 10% of GVWR on this model is ○ deficient ○ excessive ○ cautionary ⦿ good ○ excellent *
Total highway safety penalties are: 2 * Value: **86** Durability: **74** Highway Control Rating: **20** Highway Safety: **18**

| **Allegro Bay** | **1994** | MHA | 31 | 30 | CH | 7.4L | G | $1600 | 178 | 1,500 | 16,000 | 13,635 |

Livability Code: SB 30-90
Wheelbase-to-length ratio of 48% is considered ⦿ dangerous ○ fatiguing ○ good ○ excellent *
The approximate net payload of 2365 pounds at 15% of GVWR on this model is ○ deficient ○ excessive ○ cautionary ⦿ good ○ excellent *
Total highway safety penalties are: 5 * Value: **84** Durability: **74** Highway Control Rating: **35** Highway Safety: **30**

Note: Safety ratings are based on the assumption that the engineering of the RV has allowed for proper balance by placing fresh, gray, and black holding tanks in a location so as not to change the balance of the RV when the tanks are empty or full. **Always double-check wheelbase, GVWR, and weights at front and rear axles.**

*See Section 1 for details on how conclusions are reached.

Brand	Year	Type	Length	Model	Chassis	Engine	Fuel Type	Average Price per Linear Foot When New	Adjusted Wheelbase	Approx. Towing Capacity	Gross Vehicle Weight Rating	Average Curb Weight
Allegro Bay	1994	MHA	31	30	FO	7.5L	G	$1600	178	8,000	17,000	14,135

Livability Code: SB 30-90 Wheelbase-to-length ratio of 48% is considered ◉ dangerous ○ fatiguing ○ good ○ excellent *

The approximate net payload of 2865 pounds at 17% of GVWR on this model is ○ deficient ○ excessive ○ cautionary ○ good ◉ excellent *

Total highway safety penalties are: 2 *   Value: 8 6   Durability: 7 4   Highway Control Rating: 3 8   Highway Safety: 3 6

Brand	Year	Type	Length	Model	Chassis	Engine	Fuel Type	Avg Price/Ft	Wheelbase	Towing	GVWR	Curb Weight
Allegro Bay	1994	MHA	33	32	CH	7.4L	G	$1700	190	1,500	16,000	14,154

Livability Code: SB 30-90 Wheelbase-to-length ratio of 48% is considered ◉ dangerous ○ fatiguing ○ good ○ excellent *

The approximate net payload of 1846 pounds at 12% of GVWR on this model is ○ deficient ○ excessive ○ cautionary ◉ good ○ excellent *

Total highway safety penalties are: 6 *   Value: 8 4   Durability: 7 4   Highway Control Rating: 2 9   Highway Safety: 2 3

Allegro Bay	1994	MHA	33	32	FO	7.5L	G	$1700	190	8,000	17,000	14,654

Livability Code: SB 30-90 Wheelbase-to-length ratio of 48% is considered ◉ dangerous ○ fatiguing ○ good ○ excellent *

The approximate net payload of 2346 pounds at 14% of GVWR on this model is ○ deficient ○ excessive ○ cautionary ◉ good ○ excellent *

Total highway safety penalties are: 2 *   Value: 8 6   Durability: 7 4   Highway Control Rating: 3 3   Highway Safety: 3 1

Allegro Bay	1994	MHA	33	32	OS	CU190	D	$2300	208	1,500	18,000	15,354

Livability Code: SB 30-90 Wheelbase-to-length ratio of 53% is considered ○ dangerous ◉ fatiguing ○ good ○ excellent *

The approximate net payload of 2646 pounds at 15% of GVWR on this model is ○ deficient ○ excessive ○ cautionary ◉ good ○ excellent *

Total highway safety penalties are: 2 *   Value: 8 6   Durability: 7 4   Highway Control Rating: 6 6   Highway Safety: 6 4   ★★

Allegro Bay	1994	MHA	33	32	OS	CU230	D	$2600	208	4,500	20,500	16,754

Livability Code: SB 30-90 Wheelbase-to-length ratio of 53% is considered ○ dangerous ◉ fatiguing ○ good ○ excellent *

The approximate net payload of 3746 pounds at 18% of GVWR on this model is ○ deficient ○ excessive ○ cautionary ○ good ◉ excellent *

Total highway safety penalties are: 2 *   Value: 8 6   Durability: 7 4   Highway Control Rating: 7 1   Highway Safety: 6 9   ★★

Allegro Bay	1994	MHA	34	34	CH	7.4L	G	$1700	208	1,500	16,000	14,516

Livability Code: SB 30-90 Wheelbase-to-length ratio of 50% is considered ◉ dangerous ○ fatiguing ○ good ○ excellent *

The approximate net payload of 1484 pounds at 9% of GVWR on this model is ○ deficient ○ excessive ◉ cautionary ○ good ○ excellent *

Total highway safety penalties are: 7 *   Value: 8 3   Durability: 7 4   Highway Control Rating: 2 9   Highway Safety: 2 2

Allegro Bay	1994	MHA	34	34S	CH	7.4L	G	$1800	208	1,000	16,000	15,416

Livability Code: SB 30-90 Wheelbase-to-length ratio of 50% is considered ◉ dangerous ○ fatiguing ○ good ○ excellent *

The approximate net payload of 584 pounds at 4% of GVWR on this model is ◉ deficient ○ excessive ○ cautionary ○ good ○ excellent *

Total highway safety penalties are: 12 *   Value: 8 1   Durability: 7 4   Highway Control Rating: 9   Highway Safety: - 3

Allegro Bay	1994	MHA	34	34	FO	7.5L	G	$1900	208	8,000	17,000	15,016

Livability Code: SB 30-90 Wheelbase-to-length ratio of 50% is considered ◉ dangerous ○ fatiguing ○ good ○ excellent *

The approximate net payload of 1984 pounds at 12% of GVWR on this model is ○ deficient ○ excessive ○ cautionary ◉ good ○ excellent *

Total highway safety penalties are: 2 *   Value: 8 6   Durability: 7 4   Highway Control Rating: 3 8   Highway Safety: 3 6

Allegro Bay	1994	MHA	34	34S	FO	7.5L	G	$2100	208	8,000	17,000	15,916

Livability Code: SB 30-90 Wheelbase-to-length ratio of 50% is considered ◉ dangerous ○ fatiguing ○ good ○ excellent *

The approximate net payload of 1084 pounds at 6% of GVWR on this model is ◉ deficient ○ excessive ○ cautionary ○ good ◉ excellent *

Total highway safety penalties are: 7 *   Value: 8 3   Durability: 7 4   Highway Control Rating: 1 2   Highway Safety: 5

Allegro Bay	1994	MHA	35	34	OS	CU190	D	$2200	228	1,500	18,000	15,820

Livability Code: SB 30-90 Wheelbase-to-length ratio of 55% is considered ○ dangerous ○ fatiguing ◉ good ○ excellent *

The approximate net payload of 2180 pounds at 12% of GVWR on this model is ○ deficient ○ excessive ○ cautionary ◉ good ○ excellent *

Total highway safety penalties are: 2 *   Value: 8 6   Durability: 7 4   Highway Control Rating: 8 7   Highway Safety: 8 5   ★★★

Allegro Bay	1994	MHA	35	34	OS	CU230	D	$2400	228	4,500	20,500	17,220

Livability Code: SB 30-90 Wheelbase-to-length ratio of 55% is considered ○ dangerous ○ fatiguing ◉ good ○ excellent *

The approximate net payload of 3280 pounds at 16% of GVWR on this model is ○ deficient ○ excessive ○ cautionary ○ good ◉ excellent *

Total highway safety penalties are: 2 *   Value: 8 6   Durability: 7 4   Highway Control Rating: 9 1   Highway Safety: 8 9   ★★★

Allegro Bay	1994	MHA	35	34	OS	Cu230	D	$2600	228	4,500	20,500	17,220

Livability Code: SB 30-90 Wheelbase-to-length ratio of 55% is considered ○ dangerous ○ fatiguing ◉ good ○ excellent *

The approximate net payload of 3280 pounds at 16% of GVWR on this model is ○ deficient ○ excessive ○ cautionary ○ good ◉ excellent *

Total highway safety penalties are: 2 *   Value: 8 6   Durability: 7 4   Highway Control Rating: 9 1   Highway Safety: 8 9   ★★★

Note: Safety ratings are based on the assumption that the engineering of the RV has allowed for proper balance by placing fresh, gray, and black holding tanks in a location so as not to change the balance of the RV when the tanks are empty or full. **Always double-check wheelbase, GVWR, and weights at front and rear axles.**

*See Section 1 for details on how conclusions are reached.

Section 2: The Ratings

Brand	Year	Type	Length	Model	Chassis	Engine	Fuel Type	Average Price per Linear Foot When New	Adjusted Wheelbase	Approx. Towing Capacity	Gross Vehicle Weight Rating	Average Curb Weight
Allegro Bay	1994	MHA	35	34S	OS	CU190	D	$2300	228	1,500	18,000	16,720

Livability Code: SB 30-90
Wheelbase-to-length ratio of 55% is considered ○ dangerous ○ fatiguing ● good ○ excellent*
The approximate net payload of 1280 pounds at 7% of GVWR on this model is ○ deficient ○ excessive ● cautionary ○ good ○ excellent*
Total highway safety penalties are: 7* Value: 83 Durability: 74 Highway Control Rating: 62 Highway Safety: 55 ★

Brand	Year	Type	Length	Model	Chassis	Engine	Fuel Type	Average Price per Linear Foot When New	Adjusted Wheelbase	Approx. Towing Capacity	Gross Vehicle Weight Rating	Average Curb Weight
Allegro Bay	1994	MHA	37	36	OS	CU190	D	$2300	252	6,600	18,400	16,787

Livability Code: SB 30-90
Wheelbase-to-length ratio of 57% is considered ○ dangerous ○ fatiguing ● good ○ excellent*
The approximate net payload of 1613 pounds at 9% of GVWR on this model is ○ deficient ○ excessive ● cautionary ○ good ○ excellent*
Total highway safety penalties are: 2* Value: 86 Durability: 74 Highway Control Rating: 84 Highway Safety: 82 ★★★

Brand	Year	Type	Length	Model	Chassis	Engine	Fuel Type	Average Price per Linear Foot When New	Adjusted Wheelbase	Approx. Towing Capacity	Gross Vehicle Weight Rating	Average Curb Weight
Allegro Bay	1994	MHA	37	36	OS	CU230	D	$2200	258	4,500	20,500	17,739

Livability Code: SB 30-90
Wheelbase-to-length ratio of 58% is considered ○ dangerous ○ fatiguing ○ good ● excellent*
The approximate net payload of 2761 pounds at 13% of GVWR on this model is ○ deficient ○ excessive ○ cautionary ● good ○ excellent*
Total highway safety penalties are: 2* Value: 86 Durability: 74 Highway Control Rating: 99 Highway Safety: 97 ★★★

Brand	Year	Type	Length	Model	Chassis	Engine	Fuel Type	Average Price per Linear Foot When New	Adjusted Wheelbase	Approx. Towing Capacity	Gross Vehicle Weight Rating	Average Curb Weight
Allegro Bay	1994	MHA	37	36S	OS	CU190	D	$2400	252	6,600	18,400	17,739

Livability Code: SB 30-90
Wheelbase-to-length ratio of 57% is considered ○ dangerous ○ fatiguing ● good ○ excellent*
The approximate net payload of 661 pounds at 4% of GVWR on this model is ● deficient ○ excessive ○ cautionary ○ good ○ excellent*
Total highway safety penalties are: 7* Value: 83 Durability: 74 Highway Control Rating: 63 Highway Safety: 56 ★

Brand	Year	Type	Length	Model	Chassis	Engine	Fuel Type	Average Price per Linear Foot When New	Adjusted Wheelbase	Approx. Towing Capacity	Gross Vehicle Weight Rating	Average Curb Weight
Allegro Bay	1994	MHA	37	36S	OS	CU230	D	$2400	258	4,500	20,500	18,639

Livability Code: SB 30-90
Wheelbase-to-length ratio of 58% is considered ○ dangerous ○ fatiguing ○ good ● excellent*
The approximate net payload of 1861 pounds at 9% of GVWR on this model is ○ deficient ○ excessive ● cautionary ○ good ○ excellent*
Total highway safety penalties are: 7* Value: 83 Durability: 74 Highway Control Rating: 88 Highway Safety: 81 ★★★

Brand	Year	Type	Length	Model	Chassis	Engine	Fuel Type	Average Price per Linear Foot When New	Adjusted Wheelbase	Approx. Towing Capacity	Gross Vehicle Weight Rating	Average Curb Weight
Allegro Bay	1994	MHA	37	37	CH	7.4L	G	$1700	232 T	1,500	19,500	16,294

Livability Code: SB 30-90
Wheelbase-to-length ratio of 52% is considered ○ dangerous ● fatiguing ○ good ○ excellent*
The approximate net payload of 3206 pounds at 16% of GVWR on this model is ○ deficient ○ excessive ○ cautionary ○ good ● excellent*
Total highway safety penalties are: 11* Value: 81 Durability: 74 Highway Control Rating: 59 Highway Safety: 48

Brand	Year	Type	Length	Model	Chassis	Engine	Fuel Type	Average Price per Linear Foot When New	Adjusted Wheelbase	Approx. Towing Capacity	Gross Vehicle Weight Rating	Average Curb Weight
Allegro Bay	1994	MHA	38	37S	CH	7.4L	G	$1800	232 T	1,500	19,500	17,272

Livability Code: SB 30-90
Wheelbase-to-length ratio of 51% is considered ○ dangerous ● fatiguing ○ good ○ excellent*
The approximate net payload of 2228 pounds at 11% of GVWR on this model is ○ deficient ○ excessive ○ cautionary ● good ○ excellent*
Total highway safety penalties are: 16* Value: 79 Durability: 74 Highway Control Rating: 40 Highway Safety: 24

Brand	Year	Type	Length	Model	Chassis	Engine	Fuel Type	Average Price per Linear Foot When New	Adjusted Wheelbase	Approx. Towing Capacity	Gross Vehicle Weight Rating	Average Curb Weight
Allegro Bay	1994	MHA	38	37	FO	7.5L	G	$1800	232 T	4,500	20,500	17,172

Livability Code: SB 30-90
Wheelbase-to-length ratio of 51% is considered ○ dangerous ● fatiguing ○ good ○ excellent*
The approximate net payload of 3328 pounds at 16% of GVWR on this model is ○ deficient ○ excessive ○ cautionary ○ good ● excellent*
Total highway safety penalties are: 4* Value: 84 Durability: 74 Highway Control Rating: 49 Highway Safety: 45

Brand	Year	Type	Length	Model	Chassis	Engine	Fuel Type	Average Price per Linear Foot When New	Adjusted Wheelbase	Approx. Towing Capacity	Gross Vehicle Weight Rating	Average Curb Weight
Allegro Bay	1994	MHA	38	37S	FO	7.5L	G	$1900	232 T	4,500	20,500	18,072

Livability Code: SB 30-90
Wheelbase-to-length ratio of 51% is considered ○ dangerous ● fatiguing ○ good ○ excellent*
The approximate net payload of 2428 pounds at 12% of GVWR on this model is ○ deficient ○ excessive ○ cautionary ● good ○ excellent*
Total highway safety penalties are: 10* Value: 82 Durability: 74 Highway Control Rating: 41 Highway Safety: 31

Brand	Year	Type	Length	Model	Chassis	Engine	Fuel Type	Average Price per Linear Foot When New	Adjusted Wheelbase	Approx. Towing Capacity	Gross Vehicle Weight Rating	Average Curb Weight
Allegro Bay	1995	MHA	33	32 sl	CH	7.4L	G	$1700	190	1,500	16,000	15,054

Livability Code: SB 30-90
Wheelbase-to-length ratio of 48% is considered ● dangerous ○ fatiguing ○ good ○ excellent*
The approximate net payload of 946 pounds at 6% of GVWR on this model is ● deficient ○ excessive ○ cautionary ○ good ○ excellent*
Total highway safety penalties are: 11* Value: 81 Durability: 74 Highway Control Rating: 2 Highway Safety: -9

Brand	Year	Type	Length	Model	Chassis	Engine	Fuel Type	Average Price per Linear Foot When New	Adjusted Wheelbase	Approx. Towing Capacity	Gross Vehicle Weight Rating	Average Curb Weight
Allegro Bay	1995	MHA	33	32	CH	7.4L	G	$1800	190	1,500 e	16,000	14,154

Livability Code: SB 30-90
Wheelbase-to-length ratio of 48% is considered ● dangerous ○ fatiguing ○ good ○ excellent*
The approximate net payload of 1846 pounds at 12% of GVWR on this model is ○ deficient ○ excessive ○ cautionary ● good ○ excellent*
Total highway safety penalties are: 6* Value: 82 Durability: 74 Highway Control Rating: 29 Highway Safety: 23

Brand	Year	Type	Length	Model	Chassis	Engine	Fuel Type	Average Price per Linear Foot When New	Adjusted Wheelbase	Approx. Towing Capacity	Gross Vehicle Weight Rating	Average Curb Weight
Allegro Bay	1995	MHA	33	32	FO	7.5L	G	$1700	190	8,000	17,000	14,654

Livability Code: SB 30-90
Wheelbase-to-length ratio of 48% is considered ● dangerous ○ fatiguing ○ good ○ excellent*
The approximate net payload of 2346 pounds at 14% of GVWR on this model is ○ deficient ○ excessive ○ cautionary ● good ○ excellent*
Total highway safety penalties are: 2* Value: 86 Durability: 74 Highway Control Rating: 33 Highway Safety: 31

Note: Safety ratings are based on the assumption that the engineering of the RV has allowed for proper balance by placing fresh, gray, and black holding tanks in a location so as not to change the balance of the RV when the tanks are empty or full. **Always double-check wheelbase, GVWR, and weights at front and rear axles.**

*See Section 1 for details on how conclusions are reached.

Brand	Year	Type	Length	Model	Chassis	Engine	Fuel Type	Average Price per Linear Foot When New	Adjusted Wheelbase	Approx. Towing Capacity	Gross Vehicle Weight Rating	Average Curb Weight
Allegro Bay	1995	MHA	33	32 sl	FO	7.5L	G	$1800	190	8,000	17,000	15,554

Livability Code: SB 30-90   Wheelbase-to-length ratio of 48% is considered ● dangerous ○ fatiguing ○ good ○ excellent *
The approximate net payload of 1446 pounds at 9% of GVWR on this model is ○ deficient ○ excessive ● cautionary ○ good ○ excellent *
Total highway safety penalties are: 7 *   Value: 81   Durability: 74   Highway Control Rating: 20   Highway Safety: 13

Brand	Year	Type	Length	Model	Chassis	Engine	Fuel Type	Avg Price/LF	Adj Wheelbase	Towing	GVWR	Curb Wt
Allegro Bay	1995	MHA	33	32	OS	CU230	D	$2500	208	1,500	20,000	17,054

Livability Code: SB 30-90   Wheelbase-to-length ratio of 53% is considered ○ dangerous ● fatiguing ○ good ○ excellent *
The approximate net payload of 2946 pounds at 15% of GVWR on this model is ○ deficient ○ excessive ○ cautionary ● good ○ excellent *
Total highway safety penalties are: 7 *   Value: 83   Durability: 74   Highway Control Rating: 66   Highway Safety: 59   ★

Allegro Bay	1995	MHA	33	32 sl	OS	CU230	D	$2600	208	1,500	20,000	17,054

Livability Code: SB 30-90   Wheelbase-to-length ratio of 53% is considered ○ dangerous ● fatiguing ○ good ○ excellent *
The approximate net payload of 2946 pounds at 15% of GVWR on this model is ○ deficient ○ excessive ○ cautionary ● good ○ excellent *
Total highway safety penalties are: 7 *   Value: 83   Durability: 74   Highway Control Rating: 66   Highway Safety: 59   ★

Allegro Bay	1995	MHA	34	34 sl	CH	7.4L	G	$1800	208	1,500	16,000	15,416

Livability Code: SB 30-90   Wheelbase-to-length ratio of 50% is considered ● dangerous ○ fatiguing ○ good ○ excellent *
The approximate net payload of 584 pounds at 4% of GVWR on this model is ● deficient ○ excessive ○ cautionary ○ good ○ excellent *
Total highway safety penalties are: 12 *   Value: 81   Durability: 74   Highway Control Rating: 9   Highway Safety: -3

Allegro Bay	1995	MHA	34	34 BSMT	CH	7.4L	G	$1700	208	1,500	16,000	14,516

Livability Code: SB 30-90   Wheelbase-to-length ratio of 50% is considered ● dangerous ○ fatiguing ○ good ○ excellent *
The approximate net payload of 1484 pounds at 9% of GVWR on this model is ○ deficient ○ excessive ● cautionary ○ good ○ excellent *
Total highway safety penalties are: 7 *   Value: 83   Durability: 74   Highway Control Rating: 29   Highway Safety: 22

Allegro Bay	1995	MHA	34	34 sl	FO	7.5L	G	$1800	208	8,000	17,000	15,916

Livability Code: SB 30-90   Wheelbase-to-length ratio of 50% is considered ● dangerous ○ fatiguing ○ good ○ excellent *
The approximate net payload of 1084 pounds at 6% of GVWR on this model is ● deficient ○ excessive ○ cautionary ○ good ○ excellent *
Total highway safety penalties are: 7 *   Value: 83   Durability: 74   Highway Control Rating: 12   Highway Safety: 5

Allegro Bay	1995	MHA	34	34 BSMT	FO	7.5L	G	$1700	208	8,000	17,000	15,016

Livability Code: SB 30-90   Wheelbase-to-length ratio of 50% is considered ● dangerous ○ fatiguing ○ good ○ excellent *
The approximate net payload of 1984 pounds at 12% of GVWR on this model is ○ deficient ○ excessive ○ cautionary ● good ○ excellent *
Total highway safety penalties are: 2 *   Value: 86   Durability: 74   Highway Control Rating: 38   Highway Safety: 36

Allegro Bay	1995	MHA	35	34 sl	OS	CU230	D	$2400	228	1,500	17,000	16,720

Livability Code: SB 30-90   Wheelbase-to-length ratio of 55% is considered ○ dangerous ○ fatiguing ● good ○ excellent *
The approximate net payload of 280 pounds at 2% of GVWR on this model is ● deficient ○ excessive ○ cautionary ○ good ○ excellent *
Total highway safety penalties are: 7 *   Value: 83   Durability: 74   Highway Control Rating: 52   Highway Safety: 45

Allegro Bay	1995	MHA	37	36	OS	CU230	D	$2400	252	1,500	17,000	16,339

Livability Code: SB 30-90   Wheelbase-to-length ratio of 57% is considered ○ dangerous ○ fatiguing ● good ○ excellent *
The approximate net payload of 661 pounds at 4% of GVWR on this model is ● deficient ○ excessive ○ cautionary ○ good ○ excellent *
Total highway safety penalties are: 2 *   Value: 86   Durability: 74   Highway Control Rating: 63   Highway Safety: 61   ★

Allegro Bay	1995	MHA	37	36 sl	OS	CU230	D	$2600	258	1,500	20,000	18,039

Livability Code: SB 30-90   Wheelbase-to-length ratio of 58% is considered ○ dangerous ○ fatiguing ○ good ● excellent *
The approximate net payload of 1961 pounds at 10% of GVWR on this model is ○ deficient ○ excessive ○ cautionary ● good ○ excellent *
Total highway safety penalties are: 7 *   Value: 83   Durability: 74   Highway Control Rating: 93   Highway Safety: 86   ★★★

Allegro Bay	1995	MHA	38	37 sl	CH	7.4L	G	$1800	232 T	1,500	19,500	17,272

Livability Code: SB 30-90   Wheelbase-to-length ratio of 51% is considered ○ dangerous ● fatiguing ○ good ○ excellent *
The approximate net payload of 2228 pounds at 11% of GVWR on this model is ○ deficient ○ excessive ○ cautionary ● good ○ excellent *
Total highway safety penalties are: 16 *   Value: 79   Durability: 74   Highway Control Rating: 40   Highway Safety: 24

Allegro Bay	1995	MHA	38	37 BSMT	CH	7.4L	G	$1700	232 T	1,500	19,500	16,372

Livability Code: SB 30-90   Wheelbase-to-length ratio of 51% is considered ○ dangerous ● fatiguing ○ good ○ excellent *
The approximate net payload of 3128 pounds at 16% of GVWR on this model is ○ deficient ○ excessive ○ cautionary ○ good ● excellent *
Total highway safety penalties are: 11 *   Value: 81   Durability: 74   Highway Control Rating: 49   Highway Safety: 38

Note: Safety ratings are based on the assumption that the engineering of the RV has allowed for proper balance by placing fresh, gray, and black holding tanks in a location so as not to change the balance of the RV when the tanks are empty or full. **Always double-check wheelbase, GVWR, and weights at front and rear axles.**

*See Section 1 for details on how conclusions are reached.

Brand	Year	Type	Length	Model	Chassis	Engine	Fuel Type	Average Price per Linear Foot When New	Adjusted Wheelbase	Approx. Towing Capacity	Gross Vehicle Weight Rating	Average Curb Weight
Allegro Bay	1995	MHA	38	37 sl	FO	7.5L	G	$1800	232 T	4,500	20,500	18,072

Livability Code: SB 30-90
Wheelbase-to-length ratio of 51% is considered ○ dangerous ● fatiguing ○ good ○ excellent *
The approximate net payload of 2428 pounds at 12% of GVWR on this model is ○ deficient ○ excessive ○ cautionary ● good ○ excellent *
Total highway safety penalties are: 10 *   Value: 82   Durability: 74   Highway Control Rating: 41   Highway Safety: 31

Brand	Year	Type	Length	Model	Chassis	Engine	Fuel Type	Price/LF	Wheelbase	Towing	GVWR	Curb Wt
Allegro Bay	1995	MHA	38	37 BSMT	FO	7.5L	G	$1700	232 T	4,500	20,500	17,172

Livability Code: SB 30-90
Wheelbase-to-length ratio of 51% is considered ○ dangerous ● fatiguing ○ good ○ excellent *
The approximate net payload of 3328 pounds at 16% of GVWR on this model is ○ deficient ○ excessive ○ cautionary ○ good ● excellent *
Total highway safety penalties are: 4 *   Value: 84   Durability: 74   Highway Control Rating: 49   Highway Safety: 45

Brand	Year	Type	Length	Model	Chassis	Engine	Fuel Type	Price/LF	Wheelbase	Towing	GVWR	Curb Wt
Allegro Bay	1995	MHA	38	37	OS	CU230	D	$2800	228	1,500	21,500	18,672

Livability Code: SB 30-90
Wheelbase-to-length ratio of 50% is considered ● dangerous ○ fatiguing ○ good ○ excellent *
The approximate net payload of 2828 pounds at 13% of GVWR on this model is ○ deficient ○ excessive ○ cautionary ● good ○ excellent *
Total highway safety penalties are: 2 *   Value: 86   Durability: 74   Highway Control Rating: 40   Highway Safety: 38

Brand	Year	Type	Length	Model	Chassis	Engine	Fuel Type	Price/LF	Wheelbase	Towing	GVWR	Curb Wt
Allegro Bay	1995	MHA	38	37 sl	OS	CU250	D	$2900	252	1,500	24,500	19,872

Livability Code: SB 30-90
Wheelbase-to-length ratio of 56% is considered ○ dangerous ○ fatiguing ● good ○ excellent *
The approximate net payload of 4628 pounds at 19% of GVWR on this model is ○ deficient ○ excessive ○ cautionary ○ good ● excellent *
Total highway safety penalties are: 7 *   Value: 83   Durability: 74   Highway Control Rating: 98   Highway Safety: 91   ★★★

Brand	Year	Type	Length	Model	Chassis	Engine	Fuel Type	Price/LF	Wheelbase	Towing	GVWR	Curb Wt
Allegro Bay	1996	MHA	33	32	CH	7.4L	G	$2000	190	2,500	16,500	14,220

Livability Code: SB 30-90
Wheelbase-to-length ratio of 48% is considered ● dangerous ○ fatiguing ○ good ○ excellent *
The approximate net payload of 2280 pounds at 14% of GVWR on this model is ○ deficient ○ excessive ○ cautionary ● good ○ excellent *
Total highway safety penalties are: 6 *   Value: 82   Durability: 74   Highway Control Rating: 34   Highway Safety: 28

Brand	Year	Type	Length	Model	Chassis	Engine	Fuel Type	Price/LF	Wheelbase	Towing	GVWR	Curb Wt
Allegro Bay	1996	MHA	33	32 ops	CH	7.4L	G	$1900	190	2,500	16,500	15,020

Livability Code: SB 30-90
Wheelbase-to-length ratio of 48% is considered ● dangerous ○ fatiguing ○ good ○ excellent *
The approximate net payload of 1480 pounds at 9% of GVWR on this model is ○ deficient ○ excessive ● cautionary ○ good ○ excellent *
Total highway safety penalties are: 11 *   Value: 81   Durability: 74   Highway Control Rating: 21   Highway Safety: 10

Brand	Year	Type	Length	Model	Chassis	Engine	Fuel Type	Price/LF	Wheelbase	Towing	GVWR	Curb Wt
Allegro Bay	1996	MHA	33	32	FO	7.5L	G	$2000	190	8,000	17,000	14,710

Livability Code: SB 30-90
Wheelbase-to-length ratio of 48% is considered ● dangerous ○ fatiguing ○ good ○ excellent *
The approximate net payload of 2290 pounds at 13% of GVWR on this model is ○ deficient ○ excessive ○ cautionary ● good ○ excellent *
Total highway safety penalties are: 2 *   Value: 86   Durability: 74   Highway Control Rating: 32   Highway Safety: 30

Brand	Year	Type	Length	Model	Chassis	Engine	Fuel Type	Price/LF	Wheelbase	Towing	GVWR	Curb Wt
Allegro Bay	1996	MHA	33	32 ops	FO	7.5L	G	$1900	190	8,000	17,000	15,510

Livability Code: SB 30-90
Wheelbase-to-length ratio of 48% is considered ● dangerous ○ fatiguing ○ good ○ excellent *
The approximate net payload of 1490 pounds at 9% of GVWR on this model is ○ deficient ○ excessive ● cautionary ○ good ○ excellent *
Total highway safety penalties are: 7 *   Value: 83   Durability: 74   Highway Control Rating: 21   Highway Safety: 14

Brand	Year	Type	Length	Model	Chassis	Engine	Fuel Type	Price/LF	Wheelbase	Towing	GVWR	Curb Wt
Allegro Bay	1996	MHA	33	32	OS	Cum	D	$2000	190	5,160	19,840	15,910

Livability Code: SB 30-90
Wheelbase-to-length ratio of 48% is considered ● dangerous ○ fatiguing ○ good ○ excellent *
The approximate net payload of 3930 pounds at 20% of GVWR on this model is ○ deficient ○ excessive ○ cautionary ○ good ● excellent *
Total highway safety penalties are: 2 *   Value: 86   Durability: 74   Highway Control Rating: 41   Highway Safety: 39

Brand	Year	Type	Length	Model	Chassis	Engine	Fuel Type	Price/LF	Wheelbase	Towing	GVWR	Curb Wt
Allegro Bay	1996	MHA	34	34	CH	7.4L	G	$2000	208	3,500	16,500	14,585

Livability Code: SB 30-90
Wheelbase-to-length ratio of 51% is considered ○ dangerous ● fatiguing ○ good ○ excellent **
The approximate net payload of 1915 pounds at 12% of GVWR on this model is ○ deficient ○ excessive ○ cautionary ● good ○ excellent *
Total highway safety penalties are: 7 *   Value: 83   Durability: 74   Highway Control Rating: 38   Highway Safety: 31

Brand	Year	Type	Length	Model	Chassis	Engine	Fuel Type	Price/LF	Wheelbase	Towing	GVWR	Curb Wt
Allegro Bay	1996	MHA	34	34 ops	CH	7.4L	G	$2000	208	3,500	16,500	15,385

Livability Code: SB 30-90
Wheelbase-to-length ratio of 51% is considered ○ dangerous ● fatiguing ○ good ○ excellent *
The approximate net payload of 1115 pounds at 7% of GVWR on this model is ○ deficient ○ excessive ● cautionary ○ good ○ excellent *
Total highway safety penalties are: 12 *   Value: 81   Durability: 74   Highway Control Rating: 17   Highway Safety: 5

Brand	Year	Type	Length	Model	Chassis	Engine	Fuel Type	Price/LF	Wheelbase	Towing	GVWR	Curb Wt
Allegro Bay	1996	MHA	34	34	FO	7.5L	G	$2000	208	8,000	17,000	15,340

Livability Code: SB 30-90
Wheelbase-to-length ratio of 51% is considered ○ dangerous ● fatiguing ○ good ○ excellent *
The approximate net payload of 1660 pounds at 10% of GVWR on this model is ○ deficient ○ excessive ○ cautionary ● good ○ excellent *
Total highway safety penalties are: 2 *   Value: 86   Durability: 74   Highway Control Rating: 34   Highway Safety: 32

Note: Safety ratings are based on the assumption that the engineering of the RV has allowed for proper balance by placing fresh, gray, and black holding tanks in a location so as not to change the balance of the RV when the tanks are empty or full. **Always double-check wheelbase, GVWR, and weights at front and rear axles.**

*See Section 1 for details on how conclusions are reached.

Brand	Year	Type	Length	Model	Chassis	Engine	Fuel Type	Average Price per Linear Foot When New	Adjusted Wheelbase	Approx. Towing Capacity	Gross Vehicle Weight Rating	Average Curb Weight
Allegro Bay	**1996**	MHA	34	34 ops	FO	7.5L	G	$2000	208	8,000	17,000	16,140

Livability Code: SB 30-90 — Wheelbase-to-length ratio of 51% is considered ○ dangerous ◉ fatiguing ○ good ○ excellent *
The approximate net payload of 860 pounds at 5% of GVWR on this model is ◉ deficient ○ excessive ○ cautionary ○ good ○ excellent *
Total highway safety penalties are: 7 *   Value: 8 3   Durability: 7 4   Highway Control Rating: 1 1   Highway Safety: 4

Brand	Year	Type	Length	Model	Chassis	Engine	Fuel Type	Avg. Price/Lin Ft	Adj. Wheelbase	Towing Cap.	GVWR	Avg. Curb Wt
Allegro Bay	**1996**	MHA	35	34 ops	FR	Cum	D	$2800	208	5,160	19,840	17,620

Livability Code: SB 30-90 — Wheelbase-to-length ratio of 50% is considered ◉ dangerous ○ fatiguing ○ good ○ excellent *
The approximate net payload of 2220 pounds at 11% of GVWR on this model is ○ deficient ○ excessive ○ cautionary ◉ good ○ excellent *
Total highway safety penalties are: 7 *   Value: 8 3   Durability: 7 4   Highway Control Rating: 3 4   Highway Safety: 2 7

Brand	Year	Type	Length	Model	Chassis	Engine	Fuel Type	Avg. Price/Lin Ft	Adj. Wheelbase	Towing Cap.	GVWR	Avg. Curb Wt
Allegro Bay	**1996**	MHA	35	34 ops myc	FR	Cum	D	$2800	228	5,160	19,840	17,620

Livability Code: SB 30-90 — Wheelbase-to-length ratio of 55% is considered ○ dangerous ○ fatiguing ◉ good ○ excellent *
The approximate net payload of 2220 pounds at 11% of GVWR on this model is ○ deficient ○ excessive ○ cautionary ◉ good ○ excellent *
Total highway safety penalties are: 7 *   Value: 8 3   Durability: 7 4   Highway Control Rating: 8 6   Highway Safety: 7 9   ★★★

Brand	Year	Type	Length	Model	Chassis	Engine	Fuel Type	Avg. Price/Lin Ft	Adj. Wheelbase	Towing Cap.	GVWR	Avg. Curb Wt
Allegro Bay	**1996**	MHA	35	34 myc	FR	Cum	D	$2700	228	5,160	19,840	16,720

Livability Code: SB 30-90 — Wheelbase-to-length ratio of 55% is considered ○ dangerous ○ fatiguing ◉ good ○ excellent *
The approximate net payload of 3120 pounds at 16% of GVWR on this model is ○ deficient ○ excessive ○ cautionary ○ good ◉ excellent *
Total highway safety penalties are: 2 *   Value: 8 6   Durability: 7 4   Highway Control Rating: 9 1   Highway Safety: 8 9   ★★★

Brand	Year	Type	Length	Model	Chassis	Engine	Fuel Type	Avg. Price/Lin Ft	Adj. Wheelbase	Towing Cap.	GVWR	Avg. Curb Wt
Allegro Bay	**1996**	MHA	35	34	OS	Cum	D	$2700	208	5,160	19,840	17,010

Livability Code: SB 30-90 — Wheelbase-to-length ratio of 50% is considered ◉ dangerous ○ fatiguing ○ good ○ excellent *
The approximate net payload of 2830 pounds at 14% of GVWR on this model is ○ deficient ○ excessive ○ cautionary ◉ good ○ excellent *
Total highway safety penalties are: 2 *   Value: 8 6   Durability: 7 4   Highway Control Rating: 4 0   Highway Safety: 3 8

Brand	Year	Type	Length	Model	Chassis	Engine	Fuel Type	Avg. Price/Lin Ft	Adj. Wheelbase	Towing Cap.	GVWR	Avg. Curb Wt
Allegro Bay	**1996**	MHA	36	35	CH	7.4L	G	$2000	228	3,500	16,500	15,100

Livability Code: SB 30-90 — Wheelbase-to-length ratio of 53% is considered ○ dangerous ◉ fatiguing ○ good ○ excellent *
The approximate net payload of 1400 pounds at 8% of GVWR on this model is ○ deficient ○ excessive ◉ cautionary ○ good ○ excellent *
Total highway safety penalties are: 8 *   Value: 8 3   Durability: 7 4   Highway Control Rating: 4 7   Highway Safety: 3 9

Brand	Year	Type	Length	Model	Chassis	Engine	Fuel Type	Avg. Price/Lin Ft	Adj. Wheelbase	Towing Cap.	GVWR	Avg. Curb Wt
Allegro Bay	**1996**	MHA	36	35	FO	7.5L	G	$2000	228	8,000	17,000	15,560

Livability Code: SB 30-90 — Wheelbase-to-length ratio of 53% is considered ○ dangerous ◉ fatiguing ○ good ○ excellent *
The approximate net payload of 1440 pounds at 8% of GVWR on this model is ○ deficient ○ excessive ◉ cautionary ○ good ○ excellent *
Total highway safety penalties are: 2 *   Value: 8 6   Durability: 7 4   Highway Control Rating: 4 7   Highway Safety: 4 5

Brand	Year	Type	Length	Model	Chassis	Engine	Fuel Type	Avg. Price/Lin Ft	Adj. Wheelbase	Towing Cap.	GVWR	Avg. Curb Wt
Allegro Bay	**1996**	MHA	38	37	CH	7.4L	G	$2000	232 T	2,000	19,500	16,950

Livability Code: SB 30-90 — Wheelbase-to-length ratio of 51% is considered ○ dangerous ◉ fatiguing ○ good ○ excellent *
The approximate net payload of 2550 pounds at 13% of GVWR on this model is ○ deficient ○ excessive ○ cautionary ◉ good ○ excellent *
Total highway safety penalties are: 11 *   Value: 8 1   Durability: 7 4   Highway Control Rating: 4 1   Highway Safety: 3 0

Brand	Year	Type	Length	Model	Chassis	Engine	Fuel Type	Avg. Price/Lin Ft	Adj. Wheelbase	Towing Cap.	GVWR	Avg. Curb Wt
Allegro Bay	**1996**	MHA	38	37 ops	CH	7.4L	G	$2100	232 T	2,000	19,500	17,750

Livability Code: SB 30-90 — Wheelbase-to-length ratio of 51% is considered ○ dangerous ◉ fatiguing ○ good ○ excellent *
The approximate net payload of 1750 pounds at 9% of GVWR on this model is ○ deficient ○ excessive ○ cautionary ○ good ○ excellent *
Total highway safety penalties are: 16 *   Value: 7 8   Durability: 7 4   Highway Control Rating: 3 0   Highway Safety: 1 4

Brand	Year	Type	Length	Model	Chassis	Engine	Fuel Type	Avg. Price/Lin Ft	Adj. Wheelbase	Towing Cap.	GVWR	Avg. Curb Wt
Allegro Bay	**1996**	MHA	38	37	FO	7.5L	G	$2000	232 T	5,000	20,000	17,460

Livability Code: SB 30-90 — Wheelbase-to-length ratio of 51% is considered ○ dangerous ◉ fatiguing ○ good ○ excellent *
The approximate net payload of 2540 pounds at 13% of GVWR on this model is ○ deficient ○ excessive ○ cautionary ◉ good ○ excellent *
Total highway safety penalties are: 4 *   Value: 8 4   Durability: 7 4   Highway Control Rating: 4 1   Highway Safety: 3 7

Brand	Year	Type	Length	Model	Chassis	Engine	Fuel Type	Avg. Price/Lin Ft	Adj. Wheelbase	Towing Cap.	GVWR	Avg. Curb Wt
Allegro Bay	**1996**	MHA	38	37 ops	FO	7.5L	G	$2100	232 T	5,000	20,000	18,260

Livability Code: SB 30-90 — Wheelbase-to-length ratio of 51% is considered ○ dangerous ◉ fatiguing ○ good ○ excellent *
The approximate net payload of 1740 pounds at 9% of GVWR on this model is ○ deficient ○ excessive ◉ cautionary ○ good ○ excellent *
Total highway safety penalties are: 10 *   Value: 8 2   Durability: 7 4   Highway Control Rating: 3 0   Highway Safety: 2 0

Brand	Year	Type	Length	Model	Chassis	Engine	Fuel Type	Avg. Price/Lin Ft	Adj. Wheelbase	Towing Cap.	GVWR	Avg. Curb Wt
Allegro Bay	**1997**	MHA	25	24.5	CH	7.4L	G	$2000	138	6,700	12,300	11,000

Livability Code: SB 30-90 — Wheelbase-to-length ratio of 46% is considered ◉ dangerous ○ fatiguing ○ good ○ excellent *
The approximate net payload of 1300 pounds at 11% of GVWR on this model is ○ deficient ○ excessive ○ cautionary ◉ good ○ excellent *
Total highway safety penalties are: 2 *   Value: 8 6   Durability: 7 4   Highway Control Rating: 2 0   Highway Safety: 1 8

Note: Safety ratings are based on the assumption that the engineering of the RV has allowed for proper balance by placing fresh, gray, and black holding tanks in a location so as not to change the balance of the RV when the tanks are empty or full. **Always double-check wheelbase, GVWR, and weights at front and rear axles.**

*See Section 1 for details on how conclusions are reached.

Brand	Year	Type	Length	Model	Chassis	Engine	Fuel Type	Average Price per Linear Foot When New	Adjusted Wheelbase	Approx. Towing Capacity	Gross Vehicle Weight Rating	Average Curb Weight
Allegro Bay	1997	MHA	29	28	CH	7.4L	G	$1900	158	4,200	14,800	12,080

Livability Code: SB 30-90
Wheelbase-to-length ratio of 45% is considered ◉ dangerous ○ fatiguing ○ good ○ excellent *
The approximate net payload of 2720 pounds at 18% of GVWR on this model is ○ deficient ○ excessive ○ cautionary ○ good ◉ excellent *
Total highway safety penalties are: 4 *　　Value: 8 5　Durability: 7 4　Highway Control Rating: 3 1　Highway Safety: 2 7

Brand	Year	Type	Length	Model	Chassis	Engine	Fuel Type	Price/Ft	Wheelbase	Towing	GVWR	Curb Wt
Allegro Bay	1997	MHA	32	31	CH	7.4L	G	$2000	190	4,200	14,800	13,350

Livability Code: SB 30-90
Wheelbase-to-length ratio of 49% is considered ◉ dangerous ○ fatiguing ○ good ○ excellent *
The approximate net payload of 1450 pounds at 10% of GVWR on this model is ○ deficient ○ excessive ○ cautionary ◉ good ○ excellent *
Total highway safety penalties are: 6 *　　Value: 8 4　Durability: 7 4　Highway Control Rating: 3 1　Highway Safety: 2 5

Brand	Year	Type	Length	Model	Chassis	Engine	Fuel Type	Price/Ft	Wheelbase	Towing	GVWR	Curb Wt
Allegro Bay	1997	MHA	32	31	FO	7.5L	G	$2000	190	8,000	17,000	13,850

Livability Code: SB 30-90
Wheelbase-to-length ratio of 49% is considered ◉ dangerous ○ fatiguing ○ good ○ excellent *
The approximate net payload of 3150 pounds at 19% of GVWR on this model is ○ deficient ○ excessive ○ cautionary ○ good ◉ excellent *
Total highway safety penalties are: 2 *　　Value: 8 6　Durability: 7 4　Highway Control Rating: 4 5　Highway Safety: 4 3

Brand	Year	Type	Length	Model	Chassis	Engine	Fuel Type	Price/Ft	Wheelbase	Towing	GVWR	Curb Wt
Allegro Bay	1997	MHA	33	32	CH	7.4L	G	$2000	190	3,500	16,500	15,240

Livability Code: SB 30-90
Wheelbase-to-length ratio of 48% is considered ◉ dangerous ○ fatiguing ○ good ○ excellent *
The approximate net payload of 1260 pounds at 8% of GVWR on this model is ○ deficient ○ excessive ◉ cautionary ○ good ○ excellent *
Total highway safety penalties are: 10 *　　Value: 8 1　Durability: 7 4　Highway Control Rating: 1 5　Highway Safety: 5

Brand	Year	Type	Length	Model	Chassis	Engine	Fuel Type	Price/Ft	Wheelbase	Towing	GVWR	Curb Wt
Allegro Bay	1997	MHA	33	32	FO	7.5L	G	$2000	190	8,000	17,000	15,730

Livability Code: SB 30-90
Wheelbase-to-length ratio of 48% is considered ◉ dangerous ○ fatiguing ○ good ○ excellent *
The approximate net payload of 1270 pounds at 7% of GVWR on this model is ○ deficient ○ excessive ◉ cautionary ○ good ○ excellent *
Total highway safety penalties are: 7 *　　Value: 8 3　Durability: 7 4　Highway Control Rating: 1 0　Highway Safety: 3

Brand	Year	Type	Length	Model	Chassis	Engine	Fuel Type	Price/Ft	Wheelbase	Towing	GVWR	Curb Wt
Allegro Bay	1997	MHA	33	32	FR	230HP	D	$2400	208	5,160	19,840	16,930

Livability Code: SB 30-90
Wheelbase-to-length ratio of 53% is considered ○ dangerous ◉ fatiguing ○ good ○ excellent *
The approximate net payload of 2910 pounds at 15% of GVWR on this model is ○ deficient ○ excessive ○ cautionary ◉ good ○ excellent *
Total highway safety penalties are: 7 *　　Value: 8 3　Durability: 7 4　Highway Control Rating: 6 6　Highway Safety: 5 9　★

Brand	Year	Type	Length	Model	Chassis	Engine	Fuel Type	Price/Ft	Wheelbase	Towing	GVWR	Curb Wt
Allegro Bay	1997	MHA	34	34	CH	7.4L	G	$2000	228	3,500	16,500	15,605

Livability Code: SB 30-90
Wheelbase-to-length ratio of 55% is considered ○ dangerous ○ fatiguing ◉ good ○ excellent *
The approximate net payload of 895 pounds at 5% of GVWR on this model is ◉ deficient ○ excessive ○ cautionary ○ good ○ excellent *
Total highway safety penalties are: 11 *　　Value: 8 1　Durability: 7 4　Highway Control Rating: 5 8　Highway Safety: 4 7

Brand	Year	Type	Length	Model	Chassis	Engine	Fuel Type	Price/Ft	Wheelbase	Towing	GVWR	Curb Wt
Allegro Bay	1997	MHA	34	34	FO	7.5L	G	$2000	208	8,000	17,000	16,360

Livability Code: SB 30-90
Wheelbase-to-length ratio of 51% is considered ○ dangerous ◉ fatiguing ○ good ○ excellent *
The approximate net payload of 640 pounds at 4% of GVWR on this model is ◉ deficient ○ excessive ○ cautionary ○ good ○ excellent *
Total highway safety penalties are: 7 *　　Value: 8 3　Durability: 7 4　Highway Control Rating: 9　Highway Safety: 2

Brand	Year	Type	Length	Model	Chassis	Engine	Fuel Type	Price/Ft	Wheelbase	Towing	GVWR	Curb Wt
Allegro Bay	1997	MHA	35	34	FR	230HP	D	$2600	228	5,160	19,840	18,030

Livability Code: SB 30-90
Wheelbase-to-length ratio of 55% is considered ○ dangerous ○ fatiguing ◉ good ○ excellent *
The approximate net payload of 1810 pounds at 9% of GVWR on this model is ○ deficient ○ excessive ◉ cautionary ○ good ○ excellent *
Total highway safety penalties are: 7 *　　Value: 8 3　Durability: 7 4　Highway Control Rating: 7 4　Highway Safety: 6 7　★★

Brand	Year	Type	Length	Model	Chassis	Engine	Fuel Type	Price/Ft	Wheelbase	Towing	GVWR	Curb Wt
Allegro Bay	1997	MHA	36	35	CH	7.4L	G	$2100	228	3,500	16,500	15,420

Livability Code: SB 30-90
Wheelbase-to-length ratio of 53% is considered ○ dangerous ◉ fatiguing ○ good ○ excellent *
The approximate net payload of 1080 pounds at 7% of GVWR on this model is ○ deficient ○ excessive ◉ cautionary ○ good ○ excellent *
Total highway safety penalties are: 8 *　　Value: 8 3　Durability: 7 4　Highway Control Rating: 4 0　Highway Safety: 3 2

Brand	Year	Type	Length	Model	Chassis	Engine	Fuel Type	Price/Ft	Wheelbase	Towing	GVWR	Curb Wt
Allegro Bay	1997	MHA	36	35	FO	7.5L	G	$2100	228	8,000	17,000	15,880

Livability Code: SB 30-90
Wheelbase-to-length ratio of 53% is considered ○ dangerous ◉ fatiguing ○ good ○ excellent *
The approximate net payload of 1120 pounds at 7% of GVWR on this model is ○ deficient ○ excessive ◉ cautionary ○ good ○ excellent *
Total highway safety penalties are: 2 *　　Value: 8 6　Durability: 7 4　Highway Control Rating: 4 0　Highway Safety: 3 8

Brand	Year	Type	Length	Model	Chassis	Engine	Fuel Type	Price/Ft	Wheelbase	Towing	GVWR	Curb Wt
Allegro Bay	1997	MHA	38	37	CH	7.4L	G	$2100	232 T	1,500	20,000	17,970

Livability Code: SB 30-90
Wheelbase-to-length ratio of 51% is considered ○ dangerous ◉ fatiguing ○ good ○ excellent *
The approximate net payload of 2030 pounds at 10% of GVWR on this model is ○ deficient ○ excessive ○ cautionary ◉ good ○ excellent *
Total highway safety penalties are: 16 *　　Value: 7 9　Durability: 7 4　Highway Control Rating: 3 5　Highway Safety: 1 9

Note: Safety ratings are based on the assumption that the engineering of the RV has allowed for proper balance by placing fresh, gray, and black holding tanks in a location so as not to change the balance of the RV when the tanks are empty or full. **Always double-check wheelbase, GVWR, and weights at front and rear axles.**

*See Section 1 for details on how conclusions are reached.

Brand	Year	Type	Length	Model	Chassis	Engine	Fuel Type	Average Price per Linear Foot When New	Adjusted Wheelbase	Approx. Towing Capacity	Gross Vehicle Weight Rating	Average Curb Weight
Allegro Bay	1997	MHA	38	37	FO	7.5L	G	$2100	232 T	5,000	20,000	18,480

Livability Code: SB 30-90   Wheelbase-to-length ratio of 51% is considered ○ dangerous ⦿ fatiguing ○ good ○ excellent *

The approximate net payload of 1520 pounds at 8% of GVWR on this model is ○ deficient ○ excessive ⦿ cautionary ○ good ○ excellent *

Total highway safety penalties are: 9 *   Value: 8 2 Durability: 7 4 Highway Control Rating: 2 4   Highway Safety: 1 5

Brand	Year	Type	Length	Model	Chassis	Engine	Fuel Type	Avg Price/Lin Ft	Wheelbase	Towing	GVWR	Curb Weight
Allegro Bay	1998	MHA	33	32 side bath	FO	7.5L	G	$1900	190	8,000	17,000	14,880

Livability Code: SB 30-90   Wheelbase-to-length ratio of 48% is considered ⦿ dangerous ○ fatiguing ○ good ○ excellent *

The approximate net payload of 2120 pounds at 12% of GVWR on this model is ○ deficient ○ excessive ○ cautionary ⦿ good ○ excellent *

Total highway safety penalties are: 2 *   Value: 8 4 Durability: 7 4 Highway Control Rating: 3 2   Highway Safety: 3 0

Allegro Bay	1998	MHA	33	32 side bath	CH	7.4L	G	$2000	190	4,500	16,500	14,180

Livability Code: SB 30-90   Wheelbase-to-length ratio of 48% is considered ⦿ dangerous ○ fatiguing ○ good ○ excellent *

The approximate net payload of 2320 pounds at 14% of GVWR on this model is ○ deficient ○ excessive ○ cautionary ⦿ good ○ excellent *

Total highway safety penalties are: 6 *   Value: 8 2 Durability: 7 4 Highway Control Rating: 3 5   Highway Safety: 2 9

Allegro Bay	1998	MHA	34	34 side bath	CH	7.4L	G	$2000	208	4,500	16,500	14,905

Livability Code: SB 30-90   Wheelbase-to-length ratio of 51% is considered ○ dangerous ⦿ fatiguing ○ good ○ excellent *

The approximate net payload of 1595 pounds at 10% of GVWR on this model is ○ deficient ○ excessive ○ cautionary ⦿ good ○ excellent *

Total highway safety penalties are: 7 *   Value: 8 1 Durability: 7 4 Highway Control Rating: 3 4   Highway Safety: 2 7

Allegro Bay	1998	MHA	34	34 side bath opsl	CH	7.4L	G	$2100	208	4,500	16,500	15,705

Livability Code: SB 30-90   Wheelbase-to-length ratio of 51% is considered ○ dangerous ⦿ fatiguing ○ good ○ excellent *

The approximate net payload of 795 pounds at 5% of GVWR on this model is ⦿ deficient ○ excessive ○ cautionary ○ good ○ excellent *

Total highway safety penalties are: 12 *   Value: 7 9 Durability: 7 4 Highway Control Rating: 1 1   Highway Safety: - 1

Allegro Bay	1998	MHA	34	34 side bath	FO	7.5L	G	$1900	208	8,000	17,000	15,660

Livability Code: SB 30-90   Wheelbase-to-length ratio of 51% is considered ○ dangerous ⦿ fatiguing ○ good ○ excellent *

The approximate net payload of 1340 pounds at 8% of GVWR on this model is ○ deficient ○ excessive ⦿ cautionary ○ good ○ excellent *

Total highway safety penalties are: 2 *   Value: 8 4 Durability: 7 4 Highway Control Rating: 2 4   Highway Safety: 2 2

Allegro Bay	1998	MHA	34	34 side bath opsl	FO	7.5L	G	$2100	208	8,000	17,000	16,460

Livability Code: SB 30-90   Wheelbase-to-length ratio of 51% is considered ○ dangerous ⦿ fatiguing ○ good ○ excellent *

The approximate net payload of 540 pounds at 3% of GVWR on this model is ⦿ deficient ○ excessive ○ cautionary ○ good ○ excellent *

Total highway safety penalties are: 7 *   Value: 8 1 Durability: 7 4 Highway Control Rating: 9   Highway Safety: 2

Allegro Bay	1998	MHA	36	36 side bath	CH	7.4L	G	$2100	232 T	2,000	19,500	17,270

Livability Code: SB 30-90   Wheelbase-to-length ratio of 54% is considered ○ dangerous ○ fatiguing ⦿ good ○ excellent *

The approximate net payload of 2230 pounds at 11% of GVWR on this model is ○ deficient ○ excessive ○ cautionary ⦿ good ○ excellent *

Total highway safety penalties are: 10 *   Value: 8 0 Durability: 7 4 Highway Control Rating: 7 6   Highway Safety: 6 6   ★★

Allegro Bay	1998	MHA	36	36 side bath opsl	CH	7.4L	G	$2200	232 T	2,000	19,500	18,070

Livability Code: SB 30-90   Wheelbase-to-length ratio of 54% is considered ○ dangerous ○ fatiguing ⦿ good ○ excellent *

The approximate net payload of 1430 pounds at 7% of GVWR on this model is ○ deficient ○ excessive ⦿ cautionary ○ good ○ excellent *

Total highway safety penalties are: 15 *   Value: 7 7 Durability: 7 4 Highway Control Rating: 5 2   Highway Safety: 3 7

Allegro Bay	1998	MHA	36	36 side aisle	CH	7.4L	G	$2100	232 T	2,000	19,500	17,270

Livability Code: SB 30-90   Wheelbase-to-length ratio of 54% is considered ○ dangerous ○ fatiguing ⦿ good ○ excellent *

The approximate net payload of 2230 pounds at 11% of GVWR on this model is ○ deficient ○ excessive ○ cautionary ⦿ good ○ excellent *

Total highway safety penalties are: 15 *   Value: 7 7 Durability: 7 4 Highway Control Rating: 7 6   Highway Safety: 6 1   ★★

Allegro Bay	1998	MHA	36	36 side aisle opsl	CH	7.4L	G	$2200	232 T	2,000	19,500	18,070

Livability Code: SB 30-90   Wheelbase-to-length ratio of 54% is considered ○ dangerous ○ fatiguing ⦿ good ○ excellent *

The approximate net payload of 1430 pounds at 7% of GVWR on this model is ○ deficient ○ excessive ⦿ cautionary ○ good ○ excellent *

Total highway safety penalties are: 15 *   Value: 7 7 Durability: 7 4 Highway Control Rating: 5 2   Highway Safety: 3 7

Allegro Bay	1998	MHA	36	36 side bath	FO	7.5L	G	$2000	232 T	5,000	20,000	17,780

Livability Code: SB 30-90   Wheelbase-to-length ratio of 54% is considered ○ dangerous ○ fatiguing ⦿ good ○ excellent *

The approximate net payload of 2220 pounds at 11% of GVWR on this model is ○ deficient ○ excessive ○ cautionary ⦿ good ○ excellent *

Total highway safety penalties are: 4 *   Value: 8 2 Durability: 7 4 Highway Control Rating: 7 6   Highway Safety: 7 2   ★★★

Note: Safety ratings are based on the assumption that the engineering of the RV has allowed for proper balance by placing fresh, gray, and black holding tanks in a location so as not to change the balance of the RV when the tanks are empty or full. **Always double-check wheelbase, GVWR, and weights at front and rear axles.**

*See Section 1 for details on how conclusions are reached.

Section 2: The Ratings

Brand	Year	Type	Length	Model	Chassis	Engine	Fuel Type	Average Price per Linear Foot When New	Adjusted Wheelbase	Approx. Towing Capacity	Gross Vehicle Weight Rating	Average Curb Weight
Allegro Bay	**1998**	MHA	36	36 side bath opsl	FO	7.5L	G	$2100	232 T	5,000	20,000	18,580

Livability Code: SB 30-90
Wheelbase-to-length ratio of **54%** is considered ○ dangerous ○ fatiguing ◉ good ○ excellent *
The approximate net payload of **1420** pounds at **7%** of GVWR on this model is ○ deficient ○ excessive ◉ cautionary ○ good ○ excellent *
Total highway safety penalties are: **10** *   Value: **8 0**   Durability: **7 4**   Highway Control Rating: **5 2**   Highway Safety: **4 2**

Brand	Year	Type	Length	Model	Chassis	Engine	Fuel Type		Adjusted Wheelbase	Approx. Towing Capacity	Gross Vehicle Weight Rating	Average Curb Weight
Allegro Bay	**1998**	MHA	36	36 side aisle	FO	7.5L	G	$2000	232 T	5,000	20,000	17,780

Livability Code: SB 30-90
Wheelbase-to-length ratio of **54%** is considered ○ dangerous ○ fatiguing ◉ good ○ excellent *
The approximate net payload of **2220** pounds at **11%** of GVWR on this model is ○ deficient ○ excessive ○ cautionary ◉ good ○ excellent *
Total highway safety penalties are: **10** *   Value: **8 0**   Durability: **7 4**   Highway Control Rating: **7 6**   Highway Safety: **6 6**   ★★

Brand	Year	Type	Length	Model	Chassis	Engine	Fuel Type		Adjusted Wheelbase	Approx. Towing Capacity	Gross Vehicle Weight Rating	Average Curb Weight
Allegro Bay	**1998**	MHA	36	36 side aisle opsl	FO	7.5L	G	$2100	232 T	5,000	20,000	18,580

Livability Code: SB 30-90
Wheelbase-to-length ratio of **54%** is considered ○ dangerous ○ fatiguing ◉ good ○ excellent *
The approximate net payload of **1420** pounds at **7%** of GVWR on this model is ○ deficient ○ excessive ◉ cautionary ○ good ○ excellent *
Total highway safety penalties are: **10** *   Value: **8 0**   Durability: **7 4**   Highway Control Rating: **5 2**   Highway Safety: **4 2**

Brand	Year	Type	Length	Model	Chassis	Engine	Fuel Type		Adjusted Wheelbase	Approx. Towing Capacity	Gross Vehicle Weight Rating	Average Curb Weight
Allegro Bay	**1999**	MHA	33	32	FO	6.8L	G	$2100	190	8,000	18,000	14,880

Livability Code: SB 30-90
Wheelbase-to-length ratio of **48%** is considered ◉ dangerous ○ fatiguing ○ good ○ excellent *
The approximate net payload of **3120** pounds at **17%** of GVWR on this model is ○ deficient ○ excessive ○ cautionary ○ good ◉ excellent *
Total highway safety penalties are: **2** *   Value: **8 4**   Durability: **7 4**   Highway Control Rating: **5 0**   Highway Safety: **4 8**

Brand	Year	Type	Length	Model	Chassis	Engine	Fuel Type		Adjusted Wheelbase	Approx. Towing Capacity	Gross Vehicle Weight Rating	Average Curb Weight
Allegro Bay	**1999**	MHA	33	32 opsl	FO	6.8L	G	$2100	190	8,000	18,000	15,680

Livability Code: SB 30-90
Wheelbase-to-length ratio of **48%** is considered ◉ dangerous ○ fatiguing ○ good ○ excellent *
The approximate net payload of **2320** pounds at **13%** of GVWR on this model is ○ deficient ○ excessive ○ cautionary ◉ good ○ excellent *
Total highway safety penalties are: **12** *   Value: **7 8**   Durability: **7 4**   Highway Control Rating: **4 3**   Highway Safety: **3 1**

Brand	Year	Type	Length	Model	Chassis	Engine	Fuel Type		Adjusted Wheelbase	Approx. Towing Capacity	Gross Vehicle Weight Rating	Average Curb Weight
Allegro Bay	**1999**	MHA	34	34 opsl	FO	6.8L	G	$2100	208	8,000	18,000	16,460

Livability Code: SB 30-90
Wheelbase-to-length ratio of **51%** is considered ○ dangerous ◉ fatiguing ○ good ○ excellent *
The approximate net payload of **1540** pounds at **9%** of GVWR on this model is ○ deficient ○ excessive ◉ cautionary ○ good ○ excellent *
Total highway safety penalties are: **7** *   Value: **8 1**   Durability: **7 4**   Highway Control Rating: **3 9**   Highway Safety: **3 2**

Brand	Year	Type	Length	Model	Chassis	Engine	Fuel Type		Adjusted Wheelbase	Approx. Towing Capacity	Gross Vehicle Weight Rating	Average Curb Weight
Allegro Bay	**1999**	MHA	34	34	FO	6.8L	G	$2100	208	8,000	18,000	15,660

Livability Code: SB 30-90
Wheelbase-to-length ratio of **51%** is considered ○ dangerous ◉ fatiguing ○ good ○ excellent *
The approximate net payload of **2340** pounds at **13%** of GVWR on this model is ○ deficient ○ excessive ○ cautionary ◉ good ○ excellent *
Total highway safety penalties are: **2** *   Value: **8 4**   Durability: **7 4**   Highway Control Rating: **5 1**   Highway Safety: **4 9**

Brand	Year	Type	Length	Model	Chassis	Engine	Fuel Type		Adjusted Wheelbase	Approx. Towing Capacity	Gross Vehicle Weight Rating	Average Curb Weight
Allegro Bay	**1999**	MHA	36	36 opsl	FO	6.8L	G	$1900	228	5,500	20,500	18,580

Livability Code: SB 30-90
Wheelbase-to-length ratio of **53%** is considered ○ dangerous ◉ fatiguing ○ good ○ excellent *
The approximate net payload of **1920** pounds at **9%** of GVWR on this model is ○ deficient ○ excessive ◉ cautionary ○ good ○ excellent *
Total highway safety penalties are: **7** *   Value: **8 1**   Durability: **7 4**   Highway Control Rating: **5 8**   Highway Safety: **5 1**   ★

Brand	Year	Type	Length	Model	Chassis	Engine	Fuel Type		Adjusted Wheelbase	Approx. Towing Capacity	Gross Vehicle Weight Rating	Average Curb Weight
Allegro Bay	**1999**	MHA	36	36	FO	6.8L	G	$1900	228	5,500	20,500	17,780

Livability Code: SB 30-90
Wheelbase-to-length ratio of **53%** is considered ○ dangerous ◉ fatiguing ○ good ○ excellent *
The approximate net payload of **2720** pounds at **13%** of GVWR on this model is ○ deficient ○ excessive ○ cautionary ◉ good ○ excellent *
Total highway safety penalties are: **2** *   Value: **8 4**   Durability: **7 4**   Highway Control Rating: **6 9**   Highway Safety: **6 7**   ★★

Brand	Year	Type	Length	Model	Chassis	Engine	Fuel Type		Adjusted Wheelbase	Approx. Towing Capacity	Gross Vehicle Weight Rating	Average Curb Weight
Allegro Bay	**1999**	MHA	37	37 slide	FR	CU	D	$2000	228	5,000	25,910	21,120

Livability Code: SB 30-90
Wheelbase-to-length ratio of **51%** is considered ○ dangerous ◉ fatiguing ○ good ○ excellent *
The approximate net payload of **4790** pounds at **18%** of GVWR on this model is ○ deficient ○ excessive ○ cautionary ○ good ◉ excellent *
Total highway safety penalties are: **7** *   Value: **8 1**   Durability: **7 4**   Highway Control Rating: **6 0**   Highway Safety: **5 3**   ★

Brand	Year	Type	Length	Model	Chassis	Engine	Fuel Type		Adjusted Wheelbase	Approx. Towing Capacity	Gross Vehicle Weight Rating	Average Curb Weight
Allegro Bay Conventional	**1995**	MHA	33	31	FO	7.5L	G	$1500	190	8,000	17,000	14,654

Livability Code: SB 30-90
Wheelbase-to-length ratio of **48%** is considered ◉ dangerous ○ fatiguing ○ good ○ excellent *
The approximate net payload of **2346** pounds at **14%** of GVWR on this model is ○ deficient ○ excessive ○ cautionary ◉ good ○ excellent *
Total highway safety penalties are: **2** *   Value: **8 6**   Durability: **7 4**   Highway Control Rating: **3 3**   Highway Safety: **3 1**

Brand	Year	Type	Length	Model	Chassis	Engine	Fuel Type		Adjusted Wheelbase	Approx. Towing Capacity	Gross Vehicle Weight Rating	Average Curb Weight
Allegro Bay Conventional	**1995**	MHA	34	33	FO	7.5L	G	$1500	208	8,000	17,000	15,016

Livability Code: SB 30-90
Wheelbase-to-length ratio of **50%** is considered ◉ dangerous ○ fatiguing ○ good ○ excellent *
The approximate net payload of **1984** pounds at **12%** of GVWR on this model is ○ deficient ○ excessive ○ cautionary ◉ good ○ excellent *
Total highway safety penalties are: **2** *   Value: **8 6**   Durability: **7 4**   Highway Control Rating: **3 8**   Highway Safety: **3 6**

Note: Safety ratings are based on the assumption that the engineering of the RV has allowed for proper balance by placing fresh, gray, and black holding tanks in a location so as not to change the balance of the RV when the tanks are empty or full. **Always double-check wheelbase, GVWR, and weights at front and rear axles.**

*See Section 1 for details on how conclusions are reached.

Section 2: The Ratings

Brand	Year	Type	Length	Model	Chassis	Engine	Fuel Type	Average Price per Linear Foot When New	Adjusted Wheelbase	Approx. Towing Capacity	Gross Vehicle Weight Rating	Average Curb Weight

Allegro Bay Mini   1994   MHC   23   23 RB   FO   7.5L   G $1900   146   1,500   10,500   9,399

Livability Code: VA 30-90

Wheelbase-to-length ratio of 53% is considered ○ dangerous ● fatiguing ○ good ○ excellent *

The approximate net payload of 1101 pounds at 10% of GVWR on this model is ○ deficient ○ excessive ○ cautionary ● good ○ excellent *

Total highway safety penalties are: 2 *   Value: 8 6   Durability: 7 4   Highway Control Rating: 6 6   Highway Safety: 6 4   ★★

Allegro Bay Mini   1994   MHC   27   27SB   FO   7.5L   G $1700   188   1,500   10,500   10,268

Livability Code: VA 30-90

Wheelbase-to-length ratio of 58% is considered ○ dangerous ○ fatiguing ○ good ● excellent *

The approximate net payload of 232 pounds at 2% of GVWR on this model is ● deficient ○ excessive ○ cautionary ○ good ○ excellent *

Total highway safety penalties are: 2 *   Value: 8 6   Durability: 7 4   Highway Control Rating: 6 5   Highway Safety: 6 3   ★

Allegro Bay Mini   1994   MHC   28   27.5 SB   FO   7.5L   G $1700   192   1,500   12,800   10,677

Livability Code: VA 30-90

Wheelbase-to-length ratio of 58% is considered ○ dangerous ○ fatiguing ○ good ● excellent *

The approximate net payload of 2123 pounds at 17% of GVWR on this model is ○ deficient ○ excessive ○ cautionary ○ good ● excellent *

Total highway safety penalties are: 2 *   Value: 8 6   Durability: 7 4   Highway Control Rating: 1 0 0   Highway Safety: 9 8   ★★★

Allegro Bus   1995   MHA   33   32-SB   CH   7.4L   G $1800   208   1,500   16,500   15,070

Livability Code: SB 30-90

Wheelbase-to-length ratio of 53% is considered ○ dangerous ● fatiguing ○ good ○ excellent *

The approximate net payload of 1430 pounds at 9% of GVWR on this model is ○ deficient ○ excessive ● cautionary ○ good ○ excellent *

Total highway safety penalties are: 6 *   Value: 8 4   Durability: 7 4   Highway Control Rating: 5 1   Highway Safety: 4 5

Allegro Bus   1995   MHA   33   32-SB   FO   7.5L   G $1800   208   1,500   17,000   15,530

Livability Code: SB 30-90

Wheelbase-to-length ratio of 53% is considered ○ dangerous ● fatiguing ○ good ○ excellent *

The approximate net payload of 1470 pounds at 9% of GVWR on this model is ○ deficient ○ excessive ● cautionary ○ good ○ excellent *

Total highway safety penalties are: 2 *   Value: 8 6   Durability: 7 4   Highway Control Rating: 5 1   Highway Safety: 4 9

Allegro Bus   1995   MHA   33   32-SB   OS   230HP   D $3000   208   1,500   18,000   15,690

Livability Code: SB 30-90

Wheelbase-to-length ratio of 53% is considered ○ dangerous ● fatiguing ○ good ○ excellent *

The approximate net payload of 2310 pounds at 13% of GVWR on this model is ○ deficient ○ excessive ○ cautionary ● good ○ excellent *

Total highway safety penalties are: 2 *   Value: 8 6   Durability: 7 4   Highway Control Rating: 6 3   Highway Safety: 6 1   ★★

Allegro Bus   1995   MHA   35   34-SB   OS   230HP   D $2900   228   1,500   20,000   16,710

Livability Code: SB 30-90

Wheelbase-to-length ratio of 54% is considered ○ dangerous ○ fatiguing ● good ○ excellent *

The approximate net payload of 3290 pounds at 16% of GVWR on this model is ○ deficient ○ excessive ○ cautionary ○ good ● excellent *

Total highway safety penalties are: 2 *   Value: 8 6   Durability: 7 4   Highway Control Rating: 8 3   Highway Safety: 8 1   ★★★

Allegro Bus   1995   MHA   35   34-SB FLR   OS   230HP   D $2900   228   1,500   20,000   16,710

Livability Code: SB 30-90

Wheelbase-to-length ratio of 54% is considered ○ dangerous ○ fatiguing ● good ○ excellent *

The approximate net payload of 3290 pounds at 16% of GVWR on this model is ○ deficient ○ excessive ○ cautionary ○ good ● excellent *

Total highway safety penalties are: 2 *   Value: 8 6   Durability: 7 4   Highway Control Rating: 8 3   Highway Safety: 8 1   ★★★

Allegro Bus   1995   MHA   35   34-SB sl   OS   230HP   D $2900   228   1,500   20,000   17,510

Livability Code: SB 30-90

Wheelbase-to-length ratio of 54% is considered ○ dangerous ○ fatiguing ● good ○ excellent *

The approximate net payload of 2490 pounds at 12% of GVWR on this model is ○ deficient ○ excessive ○ cautionary ● good ○ excellent *

Total highway safety penalties are: 7 *   Value: 8 3   Durability: 7 4   Highway Control Rating: 7 9   Highway Safety: 7 2   ★★★

Allegro Bus   1995   MHA   36   35-SB   CH   7.4L   G $1900   232 T   1,500   19,500   18,600

Livability Code: SB 30-90

Wheelbase-to-length ratio of 54% is considered ○ dangerous ○ fatiguing ● good ○ excellent *

The approximate net payload of 900 pounds at 5% of GVWR on this model is ● deficient ○ excessive ○ cautionary ○ good ○ excellent *

Total highway safety penalties are: 10 *   Value: 8 2   Durability: 7 4   Highway Control Rating: 4 4   Highway Safety: 3 4

Allegro Bus   1995   MHA   36   35-FLR   CH   7.4L   G $1900   232 T   1,500   19,500   18,600

Livability Code: SB 30-90

Wheelbase-to-length ratio of 54% is considered ○ dangerous ○ fatiguing ● good ○ excellent *

The approximate net payload of 900 pounds at 5% of GVWR on this model is ● deficient ○ excessive ○ cautionary ○ good ○ excellent *

Total highway safety penalties are: 10 *   Value: 8 2   Durability: 7 4   Highway Control Rating: 4 4   Highway Safety: 3 4

Allegro Bus   1995   MHA   36   35-SB   FO   7.5L   G $1900   232 T   1,500   20,000   18,560

Livability Code: SB 30-90

Wheelbase-to-length ratio of 54% is considered ○ dangerous ○ fatiguing ● good ○ excellent *

The approximate net payload of 1440 pounds at 7% of GVWR on this model is ○ deficient ○ excessive ● cautionary ○ good ○ excellent *

Total highway safety penalties are: 4 *   Value: 8 4   Durability: 7 4   Highway Control Rating: 5 2   Highway Safety: 4 8

Note: Safety ratings are based on the assumption that the engineering of the RV has allowed for proper balance by placing fresh, gray, and black holding tanks in a location so as not to change the balance of the RV when the tanks are empty or full. **Always double-check wheelbase, GVWR, and weights at front and rear axles.**

Section 2: The Ratings

Brand	Year	Type	Length	Model	Chassis	Engine	Fuel Type	Average Price per Linear Foot When New	Adjusted Wheelbase	Approx. Towing Capacity	Gross Vehicle Weight Rating	Average Curb Weight
Allegro Bus	1995	MHA	36	35-FLR	FO	7.5L	G	$1900	232 T	1,500	20,000	18,560

Livability Code: SB 30-90
Wheelbase-to-length ratio of 54% is considered ○ dangerous ○ fatiguing ◉ good ○ excellent *
The approximate net payload of 1440 pounds at 7% of GVWR on this model is ○ deficient ○ excessive ◉ cautionary ○ good ○ excellent *
Total highway safety penalties are: 4 *   Value: 8 4   Durability: 7 4   Highway Control Rating: 5 2   Highway Safety: 4 8

Brand	Year	Type	Length	Model	Chassis	Engine	Fuel Type	Price/ft	Wheelbase	Towing	GVWR	Curb Weight
Allegro Bus	1995	MHA	38	37-SB	OS	250HP	D	$2900	228	1,500	24,500	19,820

Livability Code: SB 30-90
Wheelbase-to-length ratio of 50% is considered ◉ dangerous ○ fatiguing ○ good ○ excellent *
The approximate net payload of 4680 pounds at 19% of GVWR on this model is ○ deficient ○ excessive ○ cautionary ○ good ◉ excellent *
Total highway safety penalties are: 2 *   Value: 8 6   Durability: 7 4   Highway Control Rating: 4 8   Highway Safety: 4 6

Brand	Year	Type	Length	Model	Chassis	Engine	Fuel Type	Price/ft	Wheelbase	Towing	GVWR	Curb Weight
Allegro Bus	1995	MHA	38	37-SB sl	OS	250HP	D	$3000	228	1,500	24,500	20,620

Livability Code: SB 30-90
Wheelbase-to-length ratio of 50% is considered ◉ dangerous ○ fatiguing ○ good ○ excellent *
The approximate net payload of 3880 pounds at 16% of GVWR on this model is ○ deficient ○ excessive ○ cautionary ○ good ◉ excellent *
Total highway safety penalties are: 7 *   Value: 8 3   Durability: 7 4   Highway Control Rating: 4 5   Highway Safety: 3 8

Brand	Year	Type	Length	Model	Chassis	Engine	Fuel Type	Price/ft	Wheelbase	Towing	GVWR	Curb Weight
Allegro Bus	1995	MHA	40	39-SB	OS	300HP	D	$3000	252	1,500	26,000	22,040

Livability Code: SB 30-90
Wheelbase-to-length ratio of 53% is considered ○ dangerous ◉ fatiguing ○ good ○ excellent *
The approximate net payload of 3960 pounds at 15% of GVWR on this model is ○ deficient ○ excessive ○ cautionary ◉ good ○ excellent *
Total highway safety penalties are: 2 *   Value: 8 6   Durability: 7 4   Highway Control Rating: 6 7   Highway Safety: 6 5   ★★

Brand	Year	Type	Length	Model	Chassis	Engine	Fuel Type	Price/ft	Wheelbase	Towing	GVWR	Curb Weight
Allegro Bus	1995	MHA	40	39-SB sl	OS	300HP	D	$3100	252	1,500	26,000	22,840

Livability Code: SB 30-90
Wheelbase-to-length ratio of 53% is considered ○ dangerous ◉ fatiguing ○ good ○ excellent *
The approximate net payload of 3160 pounds at 12% of GVWR on this model is ○ deficient ○ excessive ○ cautionary ◉ good ○ excellent *
Total highway safety penalties are: 7 *   Value: 8 3   Durability: 7 4   Highway Control Rating: 6 1   Highway Safety: 5 4   ★

Brand	Year	Type	Length	Model	Chassis	Engine	Fuel Type	Price/ft	Wheelbase	Towing	GVWR	Curb Weight
Allegro Bus	1996	MHA	33	32	CH	7.4L	G	$3000	208	3,500	16,500	14,993

Livability Code: SB 30-90
Wheelbase-to-length ratio of 53% is considered ○ dangerous ◉ fatiguing ○ good ○ excellent *
The approximate net payload of 1507 pounds at 9% of GVWR on this model is ○ deficient ○ excessive ◉ cautionary ○ good ○ excellent *
Total highway safety penalties are: 6 *   Value: 8 4   Durability: 7 4   Highway Control Rating: 5 2   Highway Safety: 4 6

Brand	Year	Type	Length	Model	Chassis	Engine	Fuel Type	Price/ft	Wheelbase	Towing	GVWR	Curb Weight
Allegro Bus	1996	MHA	33	32	FO	7.5L	G	$2200	208	8,000	17,000	15,460

Livability Code: SB 30-90
Wheelbase-to-length ratio of 53% is considered ○ dangerous ◉ fatiguing ○ good ○ excellent *
The approximate net payload of 1540 pounds at 9% of GVWR on this model is ○ deficient ○ excessive ◉ cautionary ○ good ○ excellent *
Total highway safety penalties are: 2 *   Value: 8 6   Durability: 7 4   Highway Control Rating: 5 2   Highway Safety: 5 0   ★

Brand	Year	Type	Length	Model	Chassis	Engine	Fuel Type	Price/ft	Wheelbase	Towing	GVWR	Curb Weight
Allegro Bus	1996	MHA	33	32	FR	CU230	D	$3300	190	5,160	19,840	17,060

Livability Code: SB 30-90
Wheelbase-to-length ratio of 48% is considered ◉ dangerous ○ fatiguing ○ good ○ excellent *
The approximate net payload of 2780 pounds at 14% of GVWR on this model is ○ deficient ○ excessive ○ cautionary ◉ good ○ excellent *
Total highway safety penalties are: 2 *   Value: 8 6   Durability: 7 4   Highway Control Rating: 3 3   Highway Safety: 3 1

Brand	Year	Type	Length	Model	Chassis	Engine	Fuel Type	Price/ft	Wheelbase	Towing	GVWR	Curb Weight
Allegro Bus	1996	MHA	33	32 myc	FR	CU230	D	$3300	190	5,160	19,840	17,060

Livability Code: SB 30-90
Wheelbase-to-length ratio of 48% is considered ◉ dangerous ○ fatiguing ○ good ○ excellent *
The approximate net payload of 2780 pounds at 14% of GVWR on this model is ○ deficient ○ excessive ○ cautionary ◉ good ○ excellent *
Total highway safety penalties are: 2 *   Value: 8 6   Durability: 7 4   Highway Control Rating: 3 3   Highway Safety: 3 1

Brand	Year	Type	Length	Model	Chassis	Engine	Fuel Type	Price/ft	Wheelbase	Towing	GVWR	Curb Weight
Allegro Bus	1996	MHA	35	34	FR	CU230	D	$2800	208	5,160	19,840	17,710

Livability Code: SB 30-90
Wheelbase-to-length ratio of 50% is considered ◉ dangerous ○ fatiguing ○ good ○ excellent *
The approximate net payload of 2130 pounds at 11% of GVWR on this model is ○ deficient ○ excessive ○ cautionary ◉ good ○ excellent *
Total highway safety penalties are: 2 *   Value: 8 6   Durability: 7 4   Highway Control Rating: 3 4   Highway Safety: 3 2

Brand	Year	Type	Length	Model	Chassis	Engine	Fuel Type	Price/ft	Wheelbase	Towing	GVWR	Curb Weight
Allegro Bus	1996	MHA	35	34 opsl	FR	CU230	D	$3300	208	5,160	19,840	18,510

Livability Code: SB 30-90
Wheelbase-to-length ratio of 50% is considered ◉ dangerous ○ fatiguing ○ good ○ excellent *
The approximate net payload of 1330 pounds at 7% of GVWR on this model is ○ deficient ○ excessive ◉ cautionary ○ good ○ excellent *
Total highway safety penalties are: 7 *   Value: 8 3   Durability: 7 4   Highway Control Rating: 1 5   Highway Safety: 8

Brand	Year	Type	Length	Model	Chassis	Engine	Fuel Type	Price/ft	Wheelbase	Towing	GVWR	Curb Weight
Allegro Bus	1996	MHA	35	35	CH	7.4L	G	$2500	232 T	2,000	19,500	17,200

Livability Code: SB 30-90
Wheelbase-to-length ratio of 55% is considered ○ dangerous ○ fatiguing ◉ good ○ excellent *
The approximate net payload of 2300 pounds at 12% of GVWR on this model is ○ deficient ○ excessive ○ cautionary ◉ good ○ excellent *
Total highway safety penalties are: 9 *   Value: 8 2   Durability: 7 4   Highway Control Rating: 8 5   Highway Safety: 7 6   ★★★

Note: Safety ratings are based on the assumption that the engineering of the RV has allowed for proper balance by placing fresh, gray, and black holding tanks in a location so as not to change the balance of the RV when the tanks are empty or full. **Always double-check wheelbase, GVWR, and weights at front and rear axles.**

*See Section 1 for details on how conclusions are reached.

Section 2: The Ratings

Brand	Year	Type	Length	Model	Chassis	Engine	Fuel Type	Average Price per Linear Foot When New	Adjusted Wheelbase	Approx. Towing Capacity	Gross Vehicle Weight Rating	Average Curb Weight
Allegro Bus	1996	MHA	35	35	FO	7.5L	G	$2500	232 T	1,500	20,000	17,720

Livability Code: SB 30-90 — Wheelbase-to-length ratio of 55% is considered ○ dangerous ○ fatiguing ◉ good ○ excellent *
The approximate net payload of 2280 pounds at 11% of GVWR on this model is ○ deficient ○ excessive ○ cautionary ◉ good ○ excellent *
Total highway safety penalties are: 4 * — Value: **8 4** — Durability: **7 4** — Highway Control Rating: **8 9** — Highway Safety: **8 5** — ★★★

Brand	Year	Type	Length	Model	Chassis	Engine	Fuel Type		Adjusted Wheelbase	Approx. Towing Capacity	Gross Vehicle Weight Rating	Average Curb Weight
Allegro Bus	1996	MHA	36	35	FR	CU230	D	$3400	208	5,000	23,000	19,610

Livability Code: SB 30-90 — Wheelbase-to-length ratio of 48% is considered ◉ dangerous ○ fatiguing ○ good ○ excellent *
The approximate net payload of 3390 pounds at 15% of GVWR on this model is ○ deficient ○ excessive ○ cautionary ◉ good ○ excellent *
Total highway safety penalties are: 2 * — Value: **8 6** — Durability: **7 4** — Highway Control Rating: **3 6** — Highway Safety: **3 4**

Allegro Bus	1996	MHA	36	35 opsl	FR	CU230	D	$3500	208	5,000	23,000	20,410

Livability Code: SB 30-90 — Wheelbase-to-length ratio of 48% is considered ◉ dangerous ○ fatiguing ○ good ○ excellent *
The approximate net payload of 2590 pounds at 11% of GVWR on this model is ○ deficient ○ excessive ○ cautionary ◉ good ○ excellent *
Total highway safety penalties are: 7 * — Value: **8 3** — Durability: **7 4** — Highway Control Rating: **2 8** — Highway Safety: **2 1**

Allegro Bus	1996	MHA	38	37	FR	CU250	D	$3500	228	3,500	24,500	21,220

Livability Code: SB 30-90 — Wheelbase-to-length ratio of 50% is considered ◉ dangerous ○ fatiguing ○ good ○ excellent *
The approximate net payload of 3280 pounds at 13% of GVWR on this model is ○ deficient ○ excessive ○ cautionary ◉ good ○ excellent *
Total highway safety penalties are: 2 * — Value: **8 6** — Durability: **7 4** — Highway Control Rating: **4 0** — Highway Safety: **3 8**

Allegro Bus	1996	MHA	38	37 opsl	FR	CU250	D	$3600	228	4,500	24,500	22,020

Livability Code: SB 30-90 — Wheelbase-to-length ratio of 50% is considered ◉ dangerous ○ fatiguing ○ good ○ excellent *
The approximate net payload of 2480 pounds at 10% of GVWR on this model is ○ deficient ○ excessive ○ cautionary ◉ good ○ excellent *
Total highway safety penalties are: 7 * — Value: **8 3** — Durability: **7 4** — Highway Control Rating: **3 3** — Highway Safety: **2 6**

Allegro Bus	1996	MHA	40	39	FR	CU250	D	$3600	252	5,000	26,000	22,910

Livability Code: SB 30-90 — Wheelbase-to-length ratio of 53% is considered ○ dangerous ◉ fatiguing ○ good ○ excellent *
The approximate net payload of 3090 pounds at 12% of GVWR on this model is ○ deficient ○ excessive ○ cautionary ◉ good ○ excellent *
Total highway safety penalties are: 2 * — Value: **8 6** — Durability: **7 4** — Highway Control Rating: **6 1** — Highway Safety: **5 9** — ★

Allegro Bus	1996	MHA	40	39 opsl	FR	CU250	D	$3700	252	5,000	26,000	23,810

Livability Code: SB 30-90 — Wheelbase-to-length ratio of 53% is considered ○ dangerous ◉ fatiguing ○ good ○ excellent *
The approximate net payload of 2190 pounds at 8% of GVWR on this model is ○ deficient ○ excessive ◉ cautionary ○ good ○ excellent *
Total highway safety penalties are: 8 * — Value: **8 2** — Durability: **7 4** — Highway Control Rating: **4 7** — Highway Safety: **3 9**

Allegro Bus	1997	MHA	33	32	CH	7.4L	G	$2400	208	4,500	16,500	15,313

Livability Code: SB 30-90 — Wheelbase-to-length ratio of 53% is considered ○ dangerous ◉ fatiguing ○ good ○ excellent *
The approximate net payload of 1187 pounds at 7% of GVWR on this model is ○ deficient ○ excessive ◉ cautionary ○ good ○ excellent *
Total highway safety penalties are: 6 * — Value: **8 4** — Durability: **7 4** — Highway Control Rating: **4 0** — Highway Safety: **3 4**

Allegro Bus	1997	MHA	33	32	FO	7.5L	G	$2400	208	8,000	17,000	15,780

Livability Code: SB 30-90 — Wheelbase-to-length ratio of 53% is considered ○ dangerous ◉ fatiguing ○ good ○ excellent *
The approximate net payload of 1220 pounds at 7% of GVWR on this model is ○ deficient ○ excessive ◉ cautionary ○ good ○ excellent *
Total highway safety penalties are: 2 * — Value: **8 6** — Durability: **7 4** — Highway Control Rating: **4 0** — Highway Safety: **3 8**

Allegro Bus	1997	MHA	33	32	FR	230HP	D	$3300	208	5,160	19,840	17,380

Livability Code: SB 30-90 — Wheelbase-to-length ratio of 53% is considered ○ dangerous ◉ fatiguing ○ good ○ excellent *
The approximate net payload of 2460 pounds at 12% of GVWR on this model is ○ deficient ○ excessive ○ cautionary ◉ good ○ excellent *
Total highway safety penalties are: 2 * — Value: **8 6** — Durability: **7 4** — Highway Control Rating: **6 1** — Highway Safety: **5 9** — ★

Allegro Bus	1997	MHA	34	34	FR	230HP	D	$2300	228	5,000	21,500	18,030

Livability Code: SB 30-90 — Wheelbase-to-length ratio of 55% is considered ○ dangerous ○ fatiguing ◉ good ○ excellent *
The approximate net payload of 3470 pounds at 16% of GVWR on this model is ○ deficient ○ excessive ○ cautionary ○ good ◉ excellent *
Total highway safety penalties are: 2 * — Value: **8 6** — Durability: **7 4** — Highway Control Rating: **9 4** — Highway Safety: **9 2** — ★★★

Allegro Bus	1997	MHA	35	35	FR	230HP	D	$3500	208	5,600	24,250	19,930

Livability Code: SB 30-90 — Wheelbase-to-length ratio of 49% is considered ◉ dangerous ○ fatiguing ○ good ○ excellent *
The approximate net payload of 4320 pounds at 18% of GVWR on this model is ○ deficient ○ excessive ○ cautionary ○ good ◉ excellent *
Total highway safety penalties are: 2 * — Value: **8 6** — Durability: **7 4** — Highway Control Rating: **4 3** — Highway Safety: **4 1**

Note: Safety ratings are based on the assumption that the engineering of the RV has allowed for proper balance by placing fresh, gray, and black holding tanks in a location so as not to change the balance of the RV when the tanks are empty or full. **Always double-check wheelbase, GVWR, and weights at front and rear axles.**

*See Section 1 for details on how conclusions are reached.

Brand	Year	Type	Length	Model	Chassis	Engine	Fuel Type	Average Price per Linear Foot When New	Adjusted Wheelbase	Approx. Towing Capacity	Gross Vehicle Weight Rating	Average Curb Weight
Allegro Bus	1997	MHA	35	35 op eng	FR	275HP	D	$3500	208	5,600	24,250	20,430

Livability Code: SB 30-90
Wheelbase-to-length ratio of 49% is considered ● dangerous ○ fatiguing ○ good ○ excellent *
The approximate net payload of 3820 pounds at 16% of GVWR on this model is ○ deficient ○ excessive ○ cautionary ○ good ● excellent *
Total highway safety penalties are: 2 *   Value: 7 9   Durability: 7 4   Highway Control Rating: 4 1   Highway Safety: 3 9

Brand	Year	Type	Length	Model	Chassis	Engine	Fuel Type		Adjusted Wheelbase	Approx. Towing Capacity	Gross Vehicle Weight Rating	Average Curb Weight
Allegro Bus	1997	MHA	37	37	CH	7.4L	G	$2400	232 T	1,500	20,000	17,520

Livability Code: SB 30-90
Wheelbase-to-length ratio of 52% is considered ○ dangerous ● fatiguing ○ good ○ excellent *
The approximate net payload of 2480 pounds at 12% of GVWR on this model is ○ deficient ○ excessive ○ cautionary ● good ○ excellent *
Total highway safety penalties are: 10 *   Value: 8 1   Durability: 7 4   Highway Control Rating: 5 3   Highway Safety: 4 3

Allegro Bus	1997	MHA	37	37	FO	7.5L	G	$2400	232 T	5,000	20,000	18,640

Livability Code: SB 30-90
Wheelbase-to-length ratio of 52% is considered ○ dangerous ● fatiguing ○ good ○ excellent *
The approximate net payload of 1360 pounds at 7% of GVWR on this model is ○ deficient ○ excessive ● cautionary ○ good ○ excellent *
Total highway safety penalties are: 4 *   Value: 8 4   Durability: 7 4   Highway Control Rating: 3 1   Highway Safety: 2 7

Allegro Bus	1997	MHA	37	37	FR	275HP	D	$3600	228	5,000	25,500	21,680

Livability Code: SB 30-90
Wheelbase-to-length ratio of 51% is considered ○ dangerous ● fatiguing ○ good ○ excellent *
The approximate net payload of 3820 pounds at 15% of GVWR on this model is ○ deficient ○ excessive ○ cautionary ● good ○ excellent *
Total highway safety penalties are: 2 *   Value: 8 6   Durability: 7 4   Highway Control Rating: 4 6   Highway Safety: 4 4

Allegro Bus	1997	MHA	37	37 opsl	FR	CA275	D	$3800	228	5,000	25,500	22,580

Livability Code: SB 30-90
Wheelbase-to-length ratio of 51% is considered ○ dangerous ● fatiguing ○ good ○ excellent *
The approximate net payload of 2920 pounds at 11% of GVWR on this model is ○ deficient ○ excessive ○ cautionary ● good ○ excellent *
Total highway safety penalties are: 8 *   Value: 8 0   Durability: 7 4   Highway Control Rating: 4 9   Highway Safety: 4 1

Allegro Bus	1997	MHA	40	39	FR	325HP	D	$3700	252	5,000	26,000	23,180

Livability Code: SB 30-90
Wheelbase-to-length ratio of 53% is considered ○ dangerous ○ fatiguing ● good ○ excellent *
The approximate net payload of 2820 pounds at 11% of GVWR on this model is ○ deficient ○ excessive ○ cautionary ● good ○ excellent *
Total highway safety penalties are: 2 *   Value: 8 6   Durability: 7 4   Highway Control Rating: 5 9   Highway Safety: 5 7   ★

Allegro Bus	1998	MHA	33	32 Side Bath	CH	7.4L	G	$2200	208	4,500	16,500	15,313

Livability Code: SB 30-90
Wheelbase-to-length ratio of 53% is considered ○ dangerous ● fatiguing ○ good ○ excellent *
The approximate net payload of 1187 pounds at 7% of GVWR on this model is ○ deficient ○ excessive ● cautionary ○ good ○ excellent *
Total highway safety penalties are: 6 *   Value: 7 7   Durability: 7 4   Highway Control Rating: 4 0   Highway Safety: 3 4

Allegro Bus	1998	MHA	33	32 Side Bath opsl	CH	7.4L	G	$2300	208	4,500	16,500	16,063

Livability Code: SB 30-90
Wheelbase-to-length ratio of 53% is considered ○ dangerous ● fatiguing ○ good ○ excellent *
The approximate net payload of 437 pounds at 3% of GVWR on this model is ● deficient ○ excessive ○ cautionary ○ good ○ excellent *
Total highway safety penalties are: 16 *   Value: 7 2   Durability: 7 4   Highway Control Rating: 3 0   Highway Safety: 1 4

Allegro Bus	1998	MHA	33	32 Side Bath	FO	7.5L	G	$2100	208	8,000	17,000	15,780

Livability Code: SB 30-90
Wheelbase-to-length ratio of 53% is considered ○ dangerous ● fatiguing ○ good ○ excellent *
The approximate net payload of 1220 pounds at 7% of GVWR on this model is ○ deficient ○ excessive ● cautionary ○ good ○ excellent *
Total highway safety penalties are: 2 *   Value: 8 4   Durability: 7 4   Highway Control Rating: 4 0   Highway Safety: 3 8

Allegro Bus	1998	MHA	33	32 Side Bath opsl	FO	7.5L	G	$2300	208	8,000	17,000	16,530

Livability Code: SB 30-90
Wheelbase-to-length ratio of 53% is considered ○ dangerous ● fatiguing ○ good ○ excellent *
The approximate net payload of 470 pounds at 3% of GVWR on this model is ● deficient ○ excessive ○ cautionary ○ good ○ excellent *
Total highway safety penalties are: 12 *   Value: 7 9   Durability: 7 4   Highway Control Rating: 3 1   Highway Safety: 1 9

Allegro Bus	1998	MHA	33	32 Side Bath	FR	CU275	D	$3300	190	5,000	24,850	19,680

Livability Code: SB 30-90
Wheelbase-to-length ratio of 48% is considered ● dangerous ○ fatiguing ○ good ○ excellent *
The approximate net payload of 5170 pounds at 21% of GVWR on this model is ○ deficient ○ excessive ○ cautionary ○ good ● excellent *
Total highway safety penalties are: 2 *   Value: 8 4   Durability: 7 4   Highway Control Rating: 4 1   Highway Safety: 3 9

Allegro Bus	1998	MHA	33	32 Side Bath opsl	FR	CU275	D	$3400	190	5,000	24,850	20,480

Livability Code: SB 30-90
Wheelbase-to-length ratio of 48% is considered ● dangerous ○ fatiguing ○ good ○ excellent *
The approximate net payload of 4370 pounds at 18% of GVWR on this model is ○ deficient ○ excessive ○ cautionary ○ good ● excellent *
Total highway safety penalties are: 7 *   Value: 8 1   Durability: 7 4   Highway Control Rating: 3 9   Highway Safety: 3 2

Note: Safety ratings are based on the assumption that the engineering of the RV has allowed for proper balance by placing fresh, gray, and black holding tanks in a location so as not to change the balance of the RV when the tanks are empty or full. **Always double-check wheelbase, GVWR, and weights at front and rear axles.**

*See Section 1 for details on how conclusions are reached.

Section 2: The Ratings

Brand	Year	Type	Length	Model	Chassis	Engine	Fuel Type	Average Price per Linear Foot When New	Adjusted Wheelbase	Approx. Towing Capacity	Gross Vehicle Weight Rating	Average Curb Weight
Allegro Bus	1998	MHA	35	35 Side Bath	FR	CU275	D	$3100	208	5,000	24,850	19,930

Livability Code: SB 30-90
Wheelbase-to-length ratio of 49% is considered ◉ dangerous ○ fatiguing ○ good ○ excellent *
The approximate net payload of 4920 pounds at 20% of GVWR on this model is ○ deficient ○ excessive ○ cautionary ○ good ◉ excellent *
Total highway safety penalties are: 2 *   Value: **8 4**   Durability: **7 4**   Highway Control Rating: **4 5**   Highway Safety: **4 3**

| **Allegro Bus** | 1998 | MHA | 35 | 35 Side Bath opsl | FR | CU275 | D | $3300 | 208 | 5,000 | 24,850 | 20,780 |

Livability Code: SB 30-90
Wheelbase-to-length ratio of 49% is considered ◉ dangerous ○ fatiguing ○ good ○ excellent *
The approximate net payload of 4070 pounds at 16% of GVWR on this model is ○ deficient ○ excessive ○ cautionary ○ good ◉ excellent *
Total highway safety penalties are: 8 *   Value: **8 1**   Durability: **7 4**   Highway Control Rating: **4 2**   Highway Safety: **3 4**

| **Allegro Bus** | 1998 | MHA | 35 | 35 Open Bath | FR | CU275 | D | $3100 | 208 | 5,000 | 24,850 | 19,930 |

Livability Code: SB 30-90
Wheelbase-to-length ratio of 49% is considered ◉ dangerous ○ fatiguing ○ good ○ excellent *
The approximate net payload of 4920 pounds at 20% of GVWR on this model is ○ deficient ○ excessive ○ cautionary ○ good ◉ excellent *
Total highway safety penalties are: 2 *   Value: **8 4**   Durability: **7 4**   Highway Control Rating: **4 5**   Highway Safety: **4 3**

| **Allegro Bus** | 1998 | MHA | 35 | 35 Open Bath opsl | FR | CU275 | D | $3300 | 208 | 5,000 | 24,850 | 20,780 |

Livability Code: SB 30-90
Wheelbase-to-length ratio of 49% is considered ◉ dangerous ○ fatiguing ○ good ○ excellent *
The approximate net payload of 4070 pounds at 16% of GVWR on this model is ○ deficient ○ excessive ○ cautionary ○ good ◉ excellent *
Total highway safety penalties are: 8 *   Value: **8 1**   Durability: **7 4**   Highway Control Rating: **4 2**   Highway Safety: **3 4**

| **Allegro Bus** | 1998 | MHA | 37 | 37 Side Bath | CH | 7.4L | G | $2200 | 232 T | 2,000 | 19,500 | 17,520 |

Livability Code: SB 30-90
Wheelbase-to-length ratio of 52% is considered ○ dangerous ◉ fatiguing ○ good ○ excellent *
The approximate net payload of 1980 pounds at 10% of GVWR on this model is ○ deficient ○ excessive ○ cautionary ◉ good ○ excellent *
Total highway safety penalties are: 10 *   Value: **7 9**   Durability: **7 4**   Highway Control Rating: **4 8**   Highway Safety: **3 8**

| **Allegro Bus** | 1998 | MHA | 37 | 37 Side Bath | FO | 7.5L | G | $2200 | 232 T | 5,000 | 20,000 | 18,040 |

Livability Code: SB 30-90
Wheelbase-to-length ratio of 52% is considered ○ dangerous ◉ fatiguing ○ good ○ excellent *
The approximate net payload of 1960 pounds at 10% of GVWR on this model is ○ deficient ○ excessive ○ cautionary ◉ good ○ excellent *
Total highway safety penalties are: 4 *   Value: **8 2**   Durability: **7 4**   Highway Control Rating: **4 8**   Highway Safety: **4 4**

| **Allegro Bus** | 1998 | MHA | 37 | 37 Side Bath | FR | CA300 | D | $3200 | 228 | 5,000 | 25,910 | 21,680 |

Livability Code: SB 30-90
Wheelbase-to-length ratio of 51% is considered ○ dangerous ◉ fatiguing ○ good ○ excellent *
The approximate net payload of 4230 pounds at 16% of GVWR on this model is ○ deficient ○ excessive ○ cautionary ○ good ◉ excellent *
Total highway safety penalties are: 2 *   Value: **8 4**   Durability: **7 4**   Highway Control Rating: **4 8**   Highway Safety: **4 6**

| **Allegro Bus** | 1998 | MHA | 37 | 37 Side Bath opsl | FR | CA300 | D | $3300 | 228 | 5,000 | 25,910 | 22,530 |

Livability Code: SB 30-90
Wheelbase-to-length ratio of 51% is considered ○ dangerous ◉ fatiguing ○ good ○ excellent *
The approximate net payload of 3380 pounds at 13% of GVWR on this model is ○ deficient ○ excessive ○ cautionary ◉ good ○ excellent *
Total highway safety penalties are: 8 *   Value: **8 1**   Durability: **7 4**   Highway Control Rating: **4 2**   Highway Safety: **3 4**

| **Allegro Bus** | 1998 | MHA | 40 | 39 Open Bath | FR | CU 325 | D | $3100 | 252 | 5,000 | 27,410 | 23,180 |

Livability Code: SB 30-90
Wheelbase-to-length ratio of 53% is considered ○ dangerous ◉ fatiguing ○ good ○ excellent *
The approximate net payload of 4230 pounds at 15% of GVWR on this model is ○ deficient ○ excessive ○ cautionary ◉ good ○ excellent *
Total highway safety penalties are: 2 *   Value: **8 4**   Durability: **7 4**   Highway Control Rating: **6 7**   Highway Safety: **6 5**   ★★

| **Allegro Bus** | 1998 | MHA | 40 | 39 Open Bath opsl | FR | CU 325 | D | $3300 | 252 | 5,000 | 27,410 | 24,080 |

Livability Code: SB 30-90
Wheelbase-to-length ratio of 53% is considered ○ dangerous ◉ fatiguing ○ good ○ excellent *
The approximate net payload of 3330 pounds at 12% of GVWR on this model is ○ deficient ○ excessive ○ cautionary ◉ good ○ excellent *
Total highway safety penalties are: 13 *   Value: **7 8**   Durability: **7 4**   Highway Control Rating: **6 1**   Highway Safety: **4 8**

| **Allegro Bus** | 1998 | MHA | 40 | 39 Side Bath | FR | CU 325 | D | $3100 | 252 | 5,000 | 27,410 | 23,180 |

Livability Code: SB 30-90
Wheelbase-to-length ratio of 53% is considered ○ dangerous ◉ fatiguing ○ good ○ excellent *
The approximate net payload of 4230 pounds at 15% of GVWR on this model is ○ deficient ○ excessive ○ cautionary ◉ good ○ excellent *
Total highway safety penalties are: 2 *   Value: **8 4**   Durability: **7 4**   Highway Control Rating: **6 7**   Highway Safety: **6 5**   ★★

| **Allegro Bus** | 1998 | MHA | 40 | 39 Side Bath opsl | FR | CU 325 | D | $3300 | 252 | 5,000 | 27,410 | 24,080 |

Livability Code: SB 30-90
Wheelbase-to-length ratio of 53% is considered ○ dangerous ◉ fatiguing ○ good ○ excellent *
The approximate net payload of 3330 pounds at 12% of GVWR on this model is ○ deficient ○ excessive ○ cautionary ◉ good ○ excellent *
Total highway safety penalties are: 8 *   Value: **8 0**   Durability: **7 4**   Highway Control Rating: **6 1**   Highway Safety: **5 3**   ★

Note: Safety ratings are based on the assumption that the engineering of the RV has allowed for proper balance by placing fresh, gray, and black holding tanks in a location so as not to change the balance of the RV when the tanks are empty or full. **Always double-check wheelbase, GVWR, and weights at front and rear axles.**

See Section 1 for details on how conclusions are reached.

Section 2: The Ratings

Brand	Year	Type	Length	Model	Chassis	Engine	Fuel Type	Average Price per Linear Foot When New	Adjusted Wheel-base	Approx. Towing Capacity	Gross Vehicle Weight Rating	Average Curb Weight
Allegro Bus	1998	MHA	40	39 Split Bath	FR	CU 325	D	$3100	252	5,000	27,410	23,180

Livability Code: SB 30-90
Wheelbase-to-length ratio of 53% is considered ○ dangerous ● fatiguing ○ good ○ excellent *
The approximate net payload of 4230 pounds at 15% of GVWR on this model is ○ deficient ○ excessive ○ cautionary ● good ○ excellent *
Total highway safety penalties are: 2 *   Value: **8 4**   Durability: **7 4**   Highway Control Rating: **6 7**   Highway Safety: **6 5**   ★★

Brand	Year	Type	Length	Model	Chassis	Engine	Fuel Type	Price/Ft	Wheelbase	Towing	GVWR	Curb Wt
Allegro Bus	1998	MHA	40	39 Split Bath opsl	FR	CU 325	D	$3300	252	5,000	27,410	24,080

Livability Code: SB 30-90
Wheelbase-to-length ratio of 53% is considered ○ dangerous ● fatiguing ○ good ○ excellent *
The approximate net payload of 3330 pounds at 12% of GVWR on this model is ○ deficient ○ excessive ○ cautionary ● good ○ excellent *
Total highway safety penalties are: 8 *   Value: **8 0**   Durability: **7 4**   Highway Control Rating: **6 1**   Highway Safety: **5 3**   ★

Brand	Year	Type	Length	Model	Chassis	Engine	Fuel Type	Price/Ft	Wheelbase	Towing	GVWR	Curb Wt
Allegro Bus	1999	MHA	33	32	FO	6.8L	G	$2400	208	8,000	18,000	16,302

Livability Code: SB 30-90
Wheelbase-to-length ratio of 53% is considered ○ dangerous ● fatiguing ○ good ○ excellent *
The approximate net payload of 1698 pounds at 9% of GVWR on this model is ○ deficient ○ excessive ● cautionary ○ good ○ excellent *
Total highway safety penalties are: 12 *   Value: **7 8**   Durability: **7 4**   Highway Control Rating: **5 7**   Highway Safety: **4 5**

Brand	Year	Type	Length	Model	Chassis	Engine	Fuel Type	Price/Ft	Wheelbase	Towing	GVWR	Curb Wt
Allegro Bus	1999	MHA	33	32	FO	6.8L	G	$2400	208	8,000	18,000	16,816

Livability Code: SB 30-90
Wheelbase-to-length ratio of 53% is considered ○ dangerous ● fatiguing ○ good ○ excellent *
The approximate net payload of 1184 pounds at 7% of GVWR on this model is ○ deficient ○ excessive ● cautionary ○ good ○ excellent *
Total highway safety penalties are: 12 *   Value: **7 8**   Durability: **7 4**   Highway Control Rating: **4 4**   Highway Safety: **3 2**

Brand	Year	Type	Length	Model	Chassis	Engine	Fuel Type	Price/Ft	Wheelbase	Towing	GVWR	Curb Wt
Allegro Bus	1999	MHA	33	32 Diesel	FR	CU275	D	$3900	190	5,000	24,850	20,102

Livability Code: SB 30-90
Wheelbase-to-length ratio of 48% is considered ● dangerous ○ fatiguing ○ good ○ excellent *
The approximate net payload of 4748 pounds at 19% of GVWR on this model is ○ deficient ○ excessive ○ cautionary ○ good ● excellent *
Total highway safety penalties are: 7 *   Value: **8 1**   Durability: **7 4**   Highway Control Rating: **5 1**   Highway Safety: **4 4**

Brand	Year	Type	Length	Model	Chassis	Engine	Fuel Type	Price/Ft	Wheelbase	Towing	GVWR	Curb Wt
Allegro Bus	1999	MHA	33	32 Diesel slide	FR	CU275	D	$3900	190	5,000	24,850	20,378

Livability Code: SB 30-90
Wheelbase-to-length ratio of 48% is considered ● dangerous ○ fatiguing ○ good ○ excellent *
The approximate net payload of 4472 pounds at 18% of GVWR on this model is ○ deficient ○ excessive ○ cautionary ○ good ● excellent *
Total highway safety penalties are: 7 *   Value: **8 1**   Durability: **7 4**   Highway Control Rating: **4 9**   Highway Safety: **4 2**

Brand	Year	Type	Length	Model	Chassis	Engine	Fuel Type	Price/Ft	Wheelbase	Towing	GVWR	Curb Wt
Allegro Bus	1999	MHA	35	35 Diesel	FR	CU275	D	$3700	208	3,500	26,350	20,556

Livability Code: SB 30-90
Wheelbase-to-length ratio of 49% is considered ● dangerous ○ fatiguing ○ good ○ excellent *
The approximate net payload of 5794 pounds at 22% of GVWR on this model is ○ deficient ○ excessive ○ cautionary ○ good ● excellent *
Total highway safety penalties are: 12 *   Value: **7 8**   Durability: **7 4**   Highway Control Rating: **5 3**   Highway Safety: **4 1**

Brand	Year	Type	Length	Model	Chassis	Engine	Fuel Type	Price/Ft	Wheelbase	Towing	GVWR	Curb Wt
Allegro Bus	1999	MHA	35	35 Diesel slide	FR	CU275	D	$3700	208	3,500	26,350	21,103

Livability Code: SB 30-90
Wheelbase-to-length ratio of 49% is considered ● dangerous ○ fatiguing ○ good ○ excellent *
The approximate net payload of 5247 pounds at 20% of GVWR on this model is ○ deficient ○ excessive ○ cautionary ○ good ● excellent *
Total highway safety penalties are: 12 *   Value: **7 8**   Durability: **7 4**   Highway Control Rating: **5 5**   Highway Safety: **4 3**

Brand	Year	Type	Length	Model	Chassis	Engine	Fuel Type	Price/Ft	Wheelbase	Towing	GVWR	Curb Wt
Allegro Bus	1999	MHA	36	36	CH	7.4L	G	$2200	228	5,000	21,000	18,331

Livability Code: SB 30-90
Wheelbase-to-length ratio of 53% is considered ○ dangerous ● fatiguing ○ good ○ excellent *
The approximate net payload of 2669 pounds at 13% of GVWR on this model is ○ deficient ○ excessive ○ cautionary ● good ○ excellent *
Total highway safety penalties are: 13 *   Value: **7 8**   Durability: **7 4**   Highway Control Rating: **6 8**   Highway Safety: **5 5**   ★

Brand	Year	Type	Length	Model	Chassis	Engine	Fuel Type	Price/Ft	Wheelbase	Towing	GVWR	Curb Wt
Allegro Bus	1999	MHA	36	36 slide	CH	7.4L	G	$2200	228	5,000	21,000	18,902

Livability Code: SB 30-90
Wheelbase-to-length ratio of 53% is considered ○ dangerous ● fatiguing ○ good ○ excellent *
The approximate net payload of 2098 pounds at 10% of GVWR on this model is ○ deficient ○ excessive ○ cautionary ● good ○ excellent *
Total highway safety penalties are: 13 *   Value: **7 8**   Durability: **7 4**   Highway Control Rating: **6 3**   Highway Safety: **5 0**   ★

Brand	Year	Type	Length	Model	Chassis	Engine	Fuel Type	Price/Ft	Wheelbase	Towing	GVWR	Curb Wt
Allegro Bus	1999	MHA	36	36	FO	6.8L	G	$2200	228	5,500	20,500	17,881

Livability Code: SB 30-90
Wheelbase-to-length ratio of 53% is considered ○ dangerous ● fatiguing ○ good ○ excellent *
The approximate net payload of 2619 pounds at 13% of GVWR on this model is ○ deficient ○ excessive ○ cautionary ● good ○ excellent *
Total highway safety penalties are: 7 *   Value: **8 1**   Durability: **7 4**   Highway Control Rating: **6 8**   Highway Safety: **6 1**   ★★

Brand	Year	Type	Length	Model	Chassis	Engine	Fuel Type	Price/Ft	Wheelbase	Towing	GVWR	Curb Wt
Allegro Bus	1999	MHA	36	36 slide	FO	6.8L	G	$2200	228	5,500	20,500	18,519

Livability Code: SB 30-90
Wheelbase-to-length ratio of 53% is considered ○ dangerous ● fatiguing ○ good ○ excellent *
The approximate net payload of 1981 pounds at 10% of GVWR on this model is ○ deficient ○ excessive ○ cautionary ● good ○ excellent *
Total highway safety penalties are: 7 *   Value: **8 1**   Durability: **7 4**   Highway Control Rating: **6 2**   Highway Safety: **5 5**   ★

Note: Safety ratings are based on the assumption that the engineering of the RV has allowed for proper balance by placing fresh, gray, and black holding tanks in a location so as not to change the balance of the RV when the tanks are empty or full. **Always double-check wheelbase, GVWR, and weights at front and rear axles.**

*See Section 1 for details on how conclusions are reached.

Brand	Year	Type	Length	Model	Chassis	Engine	Fuel Type	Average Price per Linear Foot When New	Adjusted Wheel-base	Approx. Towing Capacity	Gross Vehicle Weight Rating	Average Curb Weight
Allegro Bus	1999	MHA	37	37	FR	CA300	D	$3500	228	5,000	25,910	21,416

Livability Code: SB 30-90 Wheelbase-to-length ratio of 51% is considered ○ dangerous ◉ fatiguing ○ good ○ excellent *

The approximate net payload of 4494 pounds at 17% of GVWR on this model is ○ deficient ○ excessive ○ cautionary ○ good ◉ excellent *

Total highway safety penalties are: 7 *   Value: 8 1   Durability: 7 4   Highway Control Rating: 5 9   Highway Safety: 5 2   ★

| **Allegro Bus** | 1999 | MHA | 37 | 37 slide | FR | CA300 | D | $3500 | 228 | 5,000 | 25,910 | 21,753 |

Livability Code: SB 30-90 Wheelbase-to-length ratio of 51% is considered ○ dangerous ◉ fatiguing ○ good ○ excellent *

The approximate net payload of 4157 pounds at 16% of GVWR on this model is ○ deficient ○ excessive ○ cautionary ○ good ◉ excellent *

Total highway safety penalties are: 7 *   Value: 8 1   Durability: 7 4   Highway Control Rating: 5 8   Highway Safety: 5 1   ★

| **Allegro Bus** | 1999 | MHA | 40 | 39 | FR | CU325 | D | $3500 | 252 | 5,000 | 27,410 | 23,772 |

Livability Code: SB 30-90 Wheelbase-to-length ratio of 53% is considered ○ dangerous ◉ fatiguing ○ good ○ excellent *

The approximate net payload of 3638 pounds at 13% of GVWR on this model is ○ deficient ○ excessive ○ cautionary ◉ good ○ excellent *

Total highway safety penalties are: 12 *   Value: 7 8   Durability: 7 4   Highway Control Rating: 6 8   Highway Safety: 5 6   ★

| **Allegro Bus** | 1999 | MHA | 40 | 39 slide | FR | CU325 | D | $3500 | 252 | 5,000 | 27,410 | 23,775 |

Livability Code: SB 30-90 Wheelbase-to-length ratio of 53% is considered ○ dangerous ◉ fatiguing ○ good ○ excellent *

The approximate net payload of 3635 pounds at 13% of GVWR on this model is ○ deficient ○ excessive ○ cautionary ◉ good ○ excellent *

Total highway safety penalties are: 12 *   Value: 7 8   Durability: 7 4   Highway Control Rating: 6 8   Highway Safety: 5 6   ★

| **Allegro Mini** | 1990 | MHC | 24 | 23RBR | CH | 7.4L | G | $1900 | 146 | 1,500 | 12,800 | 10,521 |

Livability Code: VA 30-90 Wheelbase-to-length ratio of 52% is considered ○ dangerous ◉ fatiguing ○ good ○ excellent *

The approximate net payload of 2279 pounds at 18% of GVWR on this model is ○ deficient ○ excessive ○ cautionary ○ good ◉ excellent *

Total highway safety penalties are: 2 *   Value: 8 6   Durability: 7 4   Highway Control Rating: 7 1   Highway Safety: 6 9   ★★

| **Allegro Star** | 1997 | MHA | 25 | 24.5 | CH | 7.4L | G | $1900 | 138 | 6,700 | 12,300 | 10,840 |

Livability Code: SB 30-90 Wheelbase-to-length ratio of 46% is considered ◉ dangerous ○ fatiguing ○ good ○ excellent *

The approximate net payload of 1460 pounds at 12% of GVWR on this model is ○ deficient ○ excessive ○ cautionary ◉ good ○ excellent *

Total highway safety penalties are: 2 *   Value: 8 6   Durability: 7 4   Highway Control Rating: 2 2   Highway Safety: 2 0

| **Allegro Star** | 1997 | MHA | 29 | 28 | CH | 7.4L | G | $1700 | 158 | 4,200 | 14,800 | 11,980 |

Livability Code: SB 30-90 Wheelbase-to-length ratio of 45% is considered ◉ dangerous ○ fatiguing ○ good ○ excellent *

The approximate net payload of 2820 pounds at 19% of GVWR on this model is ○ deficient ○ excessive ○ cautionary ○ good ◉ excellent *

Total highway safety penalties are: 4 *   Value: 8 5   Durability: 7 4   Highway Control Rating: 3 1   Highway Safety: 2 7

| **Allegro Star** | 1997 | MHA | 32 | 31 | CH | 7.4L | G | $1700 | 190 | 4,200 | 14,800 | 13,270 |

Livability Code: SB 30-90 Wheelbase-to-length ratio of 49% is considered ◉ dangerous ○ fatiguing ○ good ○ excellent *

The approximate net payload of 1530 pounds at 10% of GVWR on this model is ○ deficient ○ excessive ○ cautionary ◉ good ○ excellent *

Total highway safety penalties are: 6 *   Value: 8 4   Durability: 7 4   Highway Control Rating: 3 1   Highway Safety: 2 5

| **Allegro Star** | 1997 | MHA | 32 | 31 | FO | 7.5L | G | $1700 | 190 | 9,800 | 15,200 | 13,560 |

Livability Code: SB 30-90 Wheelbase-to-length ratio of 49% is considered ◉ dangerous ○ fatiguing ○ good ○ excellent *

The approximate net payload of 1640 pounds at 11% of GVWR on this model is ○ deficient ○ excessive ○ cautionary ◉ good ○ excellent *

Total highway safety penalties are: 2 *   Value: 8 6   Durability: 7 4   Highway Control Rating: 3 3   Highway Safety: 3 1

| **Allegro Star** | 1998 | MHA | 25 | 24.5 Split Bath | CH | 7.4L | G | $2000 | 138 | 6,700 | 12,300 | 10,840 |

Livability Code: SB 30-90 Wheelbase-to-length ratio of 46% is considered ◉ dangerous ○ fatiguing ○ good ○ excellent *

The approximate net payload of 1460 pounds at 12% of GVWR on this model is ○ deficient ○ excessive ○ cautionary ◉ good ○ excellent *

Total highway safety penalties are: 2 *   Value: 8 4   Durability: 7 4   Highway Control Rating: 2 2   Highway Safety: 2 0

| **Allegro Star** | 1998 | MHA | 29 | 28 Split Bath | CH | 7.4L | G | $1700 | 158 | 4,200 | 14,800 | 11,980 |

Livability Code: SB 30-90 Wheelbase-to-length ratio of 45% is considered ◉ dangerous ○ fatiguing ○ good ○ excellent *

The approximate net payload of 2820 pounds at 19% of GVWR on this model is ○ deficient ○ excessive ○ cautionary ○ good ◉ excellent *

Total highway safety penalties are: 4 *   Value: 7 8   Durability: 7 4   Highway Control Rating: 3 1   Highway Safety: 2 7

| **Allegro Star** | 1998 | MHA | 32 | 31 Split Bath | CH | 7.4L | G | $1600 | 190 | 4,200 | 14,800 | 13,270 |

Livability Code: SB 30-90 Wheelbase-to-length ratio of 49% is considered ◉ dangerous ○ fatiguing ○ good ○ excellent *

The approximate net payload of 1530 pounds at 10% of GVWR on this model is ○ deficient ○ excessive ○ cautionary ◉ good ○ excellent *

Total highway safety penalties are: 6 *   Value: 7 7   Durability: 7 4   Highway Control Rating: 3 1   Highway Safety: 2 5

Note: Safety ratings are based on the assumption that the engineering of the RV has allowed for proper balance by placing fresh, gray, and black holding tanks in a location so as not to change the balance of the RV when the tanks are empty or full. **Always double-check wheelbase, GVWR, and weights at front and rear axles.**

*See Section 1 for details on how conclusions are reached.

Section 2: The Ratings

Brand	Year	Type	Length	Model	Chassis	Engine	Fuel Type	Average Price per Linear Foot When New	Adjusted Wheelbase	Approx. Towing Capacity	Gross Vehicle Weight Rating	Average Curb Weight
Allegro Star	1998	MHA	32	31 Split Bath	FO	7.5L	G	$1600	190	9,800	15,200	13,560

Livability Code: SB 30-90   Wheelbase-to-length ratio of 49% is considered ◉dangerous ○fatiguing ○good ○excellent *

The approximate net payload of 1640 pounds at 11% of GVWR on this model is ○deficient ○excessive ○cautionary ◉good ○excellent *

Total highway safety penalties are: 2 *   Value: 7 9   Durability: 7 4   Highway Control Rating: 3 3   Highway Safety: 3 1

Brand	Year	Type	Length	Model	Chassis	Engine	Fuel Type	Price/Lin Ft	Wheelbase	Towing	GVWR	Curb Wt
Allure	1996	MHA	32	Amitage	DY	CU250	D	$4900	195	1,500	25,000	22,292

Livability Code: FT 30-90   Wheelbase-to-length ratio of 51% is considered ○dangerous ◉fatiguing ○good ○excellent *

The approximate net payload of 2708 pounds at 11% of GVWR on this model is ○deficient ○excessive ○cautionary ◉good ○excellent *

Total highway safety penalties are: 2 *   Value: 8 5   Durability: 9 0   Highway Control Rating: 3 7   Highway Safety: 3 5

Allure	1996	MHA	36	Cascadia	DY	CU250	D	$4500	243	1,500	27,000	24,727

Livability Code: FT 30-90   Wheelbase-to-length ratio of 56% is considered ○dangerous ○fatiguing ◉good ○excellent *

The approximate net payload of 2274 pounds at 8% of GVWR on this model is ○deficient ○excessive ◉cautionary ○good ○excellent *

Total highway safety penalties are: 2 *   Value: 8 5   Durability: 9 0   Highway Control Rating: 7 5   Highway Safety: 7 3   ★★★

Allure	1996	MHA	36	Klamath	DY	CU250	D	$4500	243	1,500	27,000	24,516

Livability Code: FT 30-90   Wheelbase-to-length ratio of 56% is considered ○dangerous ○fatiguing ◉good ○excellent *

The approximate net payload of 2484 pounds at 9% of GVWR on this model is ○deficient ○excessive ◉cautionary ○good ○excellent *

Total highway safety penalties are: 2 *   Value: 8 5   Durability: 9 0   Highway Control Rating: 8 0   Highway Safety: 7 8   ★★★

Allure	1996	MHA	36	Rogue	DY	CU250	D	$4900	243	1,500	27,000	25,935

Livability Code: FT 30-90   Wheelbase-to-length ratio of 56% is considered ○dangerous ○fatiguing ◉good ○excellent *

The approximate net payload of 1066 pounds at 4% of GVWR on this model is ◉deficient ○excessive ○cautionary ○good ○excellent *

Total highway safety penalties are: 7 *   Value: 8 2   Durability: 9 0   Highway Control Rating: 6 0   Highway Safety: 5 3   ★

Allure	1997	MHA	32	Armitage	DY	CU275	D	$5100	195	6,000	30,000	24,792

Livability Code: FT 30-90   Wheelbase-to-length ratio of 51% is considered ○dangerous ◉fatiguing ○good ○excellent *

The approximate net payload of 5208 pounds at 17% of GVWR on this model is ○deficient ○excessive ○cautionary ○good ◉excellent *

Total highway safety penalties are: 2 *   Value: 8 5   Durability: 9 0   Highway Control Rating: 4 9   Highway Safety: 4 7

Allure	1997	MHA	36	Cascadia	DY	CU275	D	$5300	243	6,000	30,000	26,016

Livability Code: FT 30-90   Wheelbase-to-length ratio of 56% is considered ○dangerous ○fatiguing ◉good ○excellent *

The approximate net payload of 3984 pounds at 13% of GVWR on this model is ○deficient ○excessive ○cautionary ◉good ○excellent *

Total highway safety penalties are: 2 *   Value: 8 5   Durability: 9 0   Highway Control Rating: 9 1   Highway Safety: 8 9   ★★★★

Allure	1997	MHA	36	Rogue Great Room	DY	CU275	D	$5700	243	6,000	30,000	26,916

Livability Code: FT 30-90   Wheelbase-to-length ratio of 56% is considered ○dangerous ○fatiguing ◉good ○excellent *

The approximate net payload of 3084 pounds at 10% of GVWR on this model is ○deficient ○excessive ○cautionary ◉good ○excellent *

Total highway safety penalties are: 7 *   Value: 8 2   Durability: 9 0   Highway Control Rating: 8 5   Highway Safety: 7 8   ★★★

Allure	1997	MHA	36	Klamath	DY	CU275	D	$5300	243	6,000	30,000	26,016

Livability Code: FT 30-90   Wheelbase-to-length ratio of 56% is considered ○dangerous ○fatiguing ◉good ○excellent *

The approximate net payload of 3984 pounds at 13% of GVWR on this model is ○deficient ○excessive ○cautionary ◉good ○excellent *

Total highway safety penalties are: 2 *   Value: 8 5   Durability: 9 0   Highway Control Rating: 9 1   Highway Safety: 8 9   ★★★★

Allure	1997	MHA	40	Bandon	DY	CU275	D	$5000	281	6,000	30,000	27,240

Livability Code: FT 30-90   Wheelbase-to-length ratio of 59% is considered ○dangerous ○fatiguing ○good ◉excellent *

The approximate net payload of 2760 pounds at 9% of GVWR on this model is ○deficient ○excessive ◉cautionary ○good ○excellent *

Total highway safety penalties are: 2 *   Value: 8 5   Durability: 9 0   Highway Control Rating: 8 8   Highway Safety: 8 6   ★★★★

Allure	1997	MHA	40	Seneca Great Room	DY	CU275	D	$5300	281	6,000	30,000	28,140

Livability Code: FT 30-90   Wheelbase-to-length ratio of 59% is considered ○dangerous ○fatiguing ○good ◉excellent *

The approximate net payload of 1860 pounds at 6% of GVWR on this model is ◉deficient ○excessive ○cautionary ○good ○excellent *

Total highway safety penalties are: 7 *   Value: 8 2   Durability: 9 0   Highway Control Rating: 7 1   Highway Safety: 6 4   ★

Allure	1998	MHA	32	32	DY	CU275	D	$4900	195	6,000	30,000	24,271

Livability Code: FT 30-90   Wheelbase-to-length ratio of 51% is considered ○dangerous ◉fatiguing ○good ○excellent *

The approximate net payload of 5729 pounds at 19% of GVWR on this model is ○deficient ○excessive ○cautionary ○good ◉excellent *

Total highway safety penalties are: 2 *   Value: 8 5   Durability: 9 0   Highway Control Rating: 5 1   Highway Safety: 4 9

Note: Safety ratings are based on the assumption that the engineering of the RV has allowed for proper balance by placing fresh, gray, and black holding tanks in a location so as not to change the balance of the RV when the tanks are empty or full. **Always double-check wheelbase, GVWR, and weights at front and rear axles.**

*See Section 1 for details on how conclusions are reached.

Brand	Year	Type	Length	Model	Chassis	Engine	Fuel Type	Average Price per Linear Foot When New	Adjusted Wheelbase	Approx. Towing Capacity	Gross Vehicle Weight Rating	Average Curb Weight
Allure	1998	MHA	36	36	DY	CU275	D	$4600	243	6,000	30,000	25,308

Livability Code: FT 30-90   Wheelbase-to-length ratio of 56% is considered ○ dangerous ○ fatiguing ◉ good ○ excellent *

The approximate net payload of 4692 pounds at 16% of GVWR on this model is ○ deficient ○ excessive ○ cautionary ○ good ◉ excellent *

Total highway safety penalties are: 2 *   Value: 90   Durability: 90   Highway Control Rating: 97   Highway Safety: 95   ★★★★★

| Allure | 1998 | MHA | 36 | 36 Great Room | DY | CU275 | D | $4900 | 243 | 6,000 | 30,000 | 26,508 |

Livability Code: FT 30-90   Wheelbase-to-length ratio of 56% is considered ○ dangerous ○ fatiguing ◉ good ○ excellent *

The approximate net payload of 3492 pounds at 12% of GVWR on this model is ○ deficient ○ excessive ○ cautionary ◉ good ○ excellent *

Total highway safety penalties are: 7 *   Value: 82   Durability: 90   Highway Control Rating: 89   Highway Safety: 82   ★★★★

| Allure | 1998 | MHA | 40 | 40 | DY | CU275 | D | $4200 | 281 | 6,000 | 30,000 | 26,170 |

Livability Code: FT 30-90   Wheelbase-to-length ratio of 59% is considered ○ dangerous ○ fatiguing ○ good ◉ excellent *

The approximate net payload of 3830 pounds at 13% of GVWR on this model is ○ deficient ○ excessive ○ cautionary ◉ good ○ excellent *

Total highway safety penalties are: 2 *   Value: 90   Durability: 90   Highway Control Rating: 99   Highway Safety: 97   ★★★★★

| Allure | 1998 | MHA | 40 | 40 Great Room | DY | CU275 | D | $4500 | 281 | 6,000 | 30,000 | 27,570 |

Livability Code: FT 30-90   Wheelbase-to-length ratio of 59% is considered ○ dangerous ○ fatiguing ○ good ◉ excellent *

The approximate net payload of 2430 pounds at 8% of GVWR on this model is ○ deficient ○ excessive ◉ cautionary ○ good ○ excellent *

Total highway safety penalties are: 7 *   Value: 87   Durability: 90   Highway Control Rating: 82   Highway Safety: 75   ★★★

| Allure | 1999 | MHA | 32 | Armitage | DY | CU275 | D | $5600 | 195 | 6,000 | 32,200 | 24,537 |

Livability Code: FT 30-90   Wheelbase-to-length ratio of 51% is considered ○ dangerous ◉ fatiguing ○ good ○ excellent *

The approximate net payload of 7664 pounds at 24% of GVWR on this model is ○ deficient ○ excessive ○ cautionary ○ good ◉ excellent *

Total highway safety penalties are: 2 *   Value: 96   Durability: 93   Highway Control Rating: 58   Highway Safety: 56   ★

| Allure | 1999 | MHA | 36 | Rogue | DY | CU275 | D | $5000 | 243 | 6,000 | 32,200 | 26,840 |

Livability Code: FT 30-90   Wheelbase-to-length ratio of 56% is considered ○ dangerous ○ fatiguing ◉ good ○ excellent *

The approximate net payload of 5361 pounds at 17% of GVWR on this model is ○ deficient ○ excessive ○ cautionary ○ good ◉ excellent *

Total highway safety penalties are: 8 *   Value: 93   Durability: 93   Highway Control Rating: 98   Highway Safety: 90   ★★★★★

| Allure | 1999 | MHA | 36 | Klamath | DY | CU275 | D | $5000 | 243 | 6,000 | 32,200 | 25,570 |

Livability Code: FT 30-90   Wheelbase-to-length ratio of 56% is considered ○ dangerous ○ fatiguing ◉ good ○ excellent *

The approximate net payload of 6630 pounds at 21% of GVWR on this model is ○ deficient ○ excessive ○ cautionary ○ good ◉ excellent *

Total highway safety penalties are: 2 *   Value: 96   Durability: 93   Highway Control Rating: 100   Highway Safety: 98   ★★★★★

| Allure | 1999 | MHA | 36 | Deschutes | DY | CU275 | D | $5000 | 243 | 6,000 | 32,200 | 26,903 |

Livability Code: FT 30-90   Wheelbase-to-length ratio of 56% is considered ○ dangerous ○ fatiguing ◉ good ○ excellent *

The approximate net payload of 5298 pounds at 16% of GVWR on this model is ○ deficient ○ excessive ○ cautionary ○ good ◉ excellent *

Total highway safety penalties are: 13 *   Value: 91   Durability: 93   Highway Control Rating: 97   Highway Safety: 84   ★★★★

| Allure | 1999 | MHA | 40 | Bandon | DY | CU275 | D | $4500 | 281 | 6,000 | 32,200 | 26,434 |

Livability Code: FT 30-90   Wheelbase-to-length ratio of 59% is considered ○ dangerous ○ fatiguing ○ good ◉ excellent *

The approximate net payload of 5767 pounds at 18% of GVWR on this model is ○ deficient ○ excessive ○ cautionary ○ good ◉ excellent *

Total highway safety penalties are: 2 *   Value: 96   Durability: 93   Highway Control Rating: 100   Highway Safety: 98   ★★★★★

| Allure | 1999 | MHA | 40 | LaPine | DY | CU275 | D | $4500 | 281 | 6,000 | 32,200 | 28,032 |

Livability Code: FT 30-90   Wheelbase-to-length ratio of 59% is considered ○ dangerous ○ fatiguing ○ good ◉ excellent *

The approximate net payload of 4169 pounds at 13% of GVWR on this model is ○ deficient ○ excessive ○ cautionary ◉ good ○ excellent *

Total highway safety penalties are: 13 *   Value: 91   Durability: 93   Highway Control Rating: 99   Highway Safety: 86   ★★★★

| Allure | 1999 | MHA | 40 | Seneca | DY | CU275 | D | $4500 | 281 | 6,000 | 32,200 | 28,035 |

Livability Code: FT 30-90   Wheelbase-to-length ratio of 59% is considered ○ dangerous ○ fatiguing ○ good ◉ excellent *

The approximate net payload of 4165 pounds at 13% of GVWR on this model is ○ deficient ○ excessive ○ cautionary ◉ good ○ excellent *

Total highway safety penalties are: 8 *   Value: 93   Durability: 93   Highway Control Rating: 99   Highway Safety: 91   ★★★★★

| Alpine Coach | 1999 | MHA | 37 | 36FDS | WE | CU275 | D | $4300 | 252 | 5,000 | 28,000 | 24,853 |

Livability Code: SB 30-90   Wheelbase-to-length ratio of 57% is considered ○ dangerous ○ fatiguing ◉ good ○ excellent *

The approximate net payload of 3147 pounds at 11% of GVWR on this model is ○ deficient ○ excessive ○ cautionary ◉ good ○ excellent *

Total highway safety penalties are: 12 *   Value: 72   Durability: 78   Highway Control Rating: 89   Highway Safety: 77   ★★★

Note: Safety ratings are based on the assumption that the engineering of the RV has allowed for proper balance by placing fresh, gray, and black holding tanks in a location so as not to change the balance of the RV when the tanks are empty or full. **Always double-check wheelbase, GVWR, and weights at front and rear axles.**

*See Section 1 for details on how conclusions are reached.

Brand	Year	Type	Length	Model	Chassis	Engine	Fuel Type	Average Price per Linear Foot When New	Adjusted Wheel-base	Approx. Towing Capacity	Gross Vehicle Weight Rating	Average Curb Weight
Alpine Coach	**1999**	MHA	37	36SDS	WE	CU275	D	$4300	252	5,000	28,000	24,853

Livability Code: SB 30-90
Wheelbase-to-length ratio of 57% is considered ○ dangerous ○ fatiguing ◉ good ○ excellent *
The approximate net payload of 3147 pounds at 11% of GVWR on this model is ○ deficient ○ excessive ○ cautionary ◉ good ○ excellent *
Total highway safety penalties are: 12 * Value: **7 2** Durability: **7 8** Highway Control Rating: **8 9** Highway Safety: **7 7** ★★★

Brand	Year	Type	Length	Model	Chassis	Engine	Fuel Type	Price/ft	Wheelbase	Towing	GVWR	Curb
Alpine Coach	**1999**	MHA	37	36FDS op eng	WE	CU330	D	$4300	252	5,000	28,000	25,383

Livability Code: SB 30-90
Wheelbase-to-length ratio of 57% is considered ○ dangerous ○ fatiguing ◉ good ○ excellent *
The approximate net payload of 2617 pounds at 9% of GVWR on this model is ○ deficient ○ excessive ◉ cautionary ○ good ○ excellent *
Total highway safety penalties are: 12 * Value: **7 2** Durability: **7 8** Highway Control Rating: **8 2** Highway Safety: **7 0** ★★★

Alpine Coach	**1999**	MHA	37	36SDS op eng	WE	CU330	D	$4300	252	5,000	28,000	25,383

Livability Code: SB 30-90
Wheelbase-to-length ratio of 57% is considered ○ dangerous ○ fatiguing ◉ good ○ excellent *
The approximate net payload of 2617 pounds at 9% of GVWR on this model is ○ deficient ○ excessive ◉ cautionary ○ good ○ excellent *
Total highway safety penalties are: 12 * Value: **7 2** Durability: **7 8** Highway Control Rating: **8 2** Highway Safety: **7 0** ★★★

Alpine Coach	**1999**	MHA	37	36FD	WE	CU275	D	$4300	252	5,000	28,000	24,403

Livability Code: SB 30-90
Wheelbase-to-length ratio of 57% is considered ○ dangerous ○ fatiguing ◉ good ○ excellent *
The approximate net payload of 3597 pounds at 13% of GVWR on this model is ○ deficient ○ excessive ○ cautionary ◉ good ○ excellent *
Total highway safety penalties are: 2 * Value: **7 7** Durability: **7 8** Highway Control Rating: **9 3** Highway Safety: **9 1** ★★★

Alpine Coach	**1999**	MHA	37	36FD op eng	WE	CU330	D	$4300	252	5,000	28,000	24,933

Livability Code: SB 30-90
Wheelbase-to-length ratio of 57% is considered ○ dangerous ○ fatiguing ◉ good ○ excellent *
The approximate net payload of 3067 pounds at 11% of GVWR on this model is ○ deficient ○ excessive ○ cautionary ◉ good ○ excellent *
Total highway safety penalties are: 2 * Value: **7 7** Durability: **7 8** Highway Control Rating: **8 9** Highway Safety: **8 7** ★★★

Alpine Coach	**1999**	MHA	40	40FDS	WE	CU330	D	$4000	278	5,000	31,000	26,946

Livability Code: SB 30-90
Wheelbase-to-length ratio of 58% is considered ○ dangerous ○ fatiguing ○ good ◉ excellent *
The approximate net payload of 4054 pounds at 13% of GVWR on this model is ○ deficient ○ excessive ○ cautionary ◉ good ○ excellent *
Total highway safety penalties are: 12 * Value: **8 0** Durability: **7 8** Highway Control Rating: **9 7** Highway Safety: **8 5** ★★★

Alpine Coach	**1999**	MHA	40	40FDS op eng	WE	CU350	D	$4000	278	5,000	31,000	27,476

Livability Code: SB 30-90
Wheelbase-to-length ratio of 58% is considered ○ dangerous ○ fatiguing ○ good ◉ excellent *
The approximate net payload of 3524 pounds at 11% of GVWR on this model is ○ deficient ○ excessive ○ cautionary ◉ good ○ excellent *
Total highway safety penalties are: 12 * Value: **8 0** Durability: **7 8** Highway Control Rating: **9 3** Highway Safety: **8 1** ★★★

Aluma-Lite	**1989**	MHA	26	25WB	FO	7.5L	G	$1300	158	7,500	11,500	10,122

Livability Code: SB 30-90
Wheelbase-to-length ratio of 50% is considered ◉ dangerous ○ fatiguing ○ good ○ excellent *
The approximate net payload of 1378 pounds at 12% of GVWR on this model is ○ deficient ○ excessive ○ cautionary ◉ good ○ excellent *
Total highway safety penalties are: 2 * Value: **7 8** Durability: **7 2** Highway Control Rating: **4 2** Highway Safety: **4 0**

Aluma-Lite	**1989**	MHA	28	27WB/XS	CH	7.4L	G	$1600	158	3,500	14,500	11,557

Livability Code: SB 30-90
Wheelbase-to-length ratio of 47% is considered ◉ dangerous ○ fatiguing ○ good ○ excellent *
The approximate net payload of 2943 pounds at 20% of GVWR on this model is ○ deficient ○ excessive ○ cautionary ○ good ◉ excellent *
Total highway safety penalties are: 4 * Value: **7 7** Durability: **7 2** Highway Control Rating: **3 8** Highway Safety: **3 4**

Aluma-Lite	**1989**	MHA	29	28LK	CH	7.4L	G	$1500	158	3,500	14,500	11,659

Livability Code: SB 30-90
Wheelbase-to-length ratio of 46% is considered ◉ dangerous ○ fatiguing ○ good ○ excellent *
The approximate net payload of 2841 pounds at 20% of GVWR on this model is ○ deficient ○ excessive ○ cautionary ○ good ◉ excellent *
Total highway safety penalties are: 4 * Value: **7 7** Durability: **7 2** Highway Control Rating: **3 5** Highway Safety: **3 1**

Aluma-Lite	**1989**	MHA	30	30RB	CH	7.4L	G	$1600	178	3,500	14,500	12,073

Livability Code: SB 30-90
Wheelbase-to-length ratio of 49% is considered ◉ dangerous ○ fatiguing ○ good ○ excellent *
The approximate net payload of 2427 pounds at 17% of GVWR on this model is ○ deficient ○ excessive ○ cautionary ○ good ◉ excellent *
Total highway safety penalties are: 5 * Value: **7 6** Durability: **7 2** Highway Control Rating: **4 1** Highway Safety: **3 6**

Aluma-Lite	**1989**	MHA	32	31WB/XS	CH	7.4L	G	$1700	182 T	3,500	16,500	13,137

Livability Code: SB 30-90
Wheelbase-to-length ratio of 48% is considered ◉ dangerous ○ fatiguing ○ good ○ excellent *
The approximate net payload of 3363 pounds at 20% of GVWR on this model is ○ deficient ○ excessive ○ cautionary ○ good ◉ excellent *
Total highway safety penalties are: 8 * Value: **7 5** Durability: **7 2** Highway Control Rating: **4 1** Highway Safety: **3 3**

Note: Safety ratings are based on the assumption that the engineering of the RV has allowed for proper balance by placing fresh, gray, and black holding tanks in a location so as not to change the balance of the RV when the tanks are empty or full. **Always double-check wheelbase, GVWR, and weights at front and rear axles.**

*See Section 1 for details on how conclusions are reached.

Section 2: The Ratings

Brand	Year	Type	Length	Model	Chassis	Engine	Fuel Type	Average Price per Linear Foot When New	Adjusted Wheelbase	Approx. Towing Capacity	Gross Vehicle Weight Rating	Average Curb Weight
Aluma-Lite	1990	MHA	26	25WB	FO	7.5L	G	$1600	158	7,500	11,500	10,371

Livability Code: SB 30-90 Wheelbase-to-length ratio of 50% is considered ●dangerous ○fatiguing ○good ○excellent *
The approximate net payload of 1129 pounds at 10% of GVWR on this model is ○deficient ○excessive ○cautionary ●good ○excellent *
Total highway safety penalties are: 3 * Value: 7 8 Durability: 7 2 Highway Control Rating: 3 4 Highway Safety: 3 1

Brand	Year	Type	Length	Model	Chassis	Engine	Fuel Type	Price/Ft	Wheelbase	Towing	GVWR	Curb Wt
Aluma-Lite	1990	MHA	28	27 WBXS	CH	7.5L	G	$1800	158	4,500	14,500	11,870

Livability Code: SB 30-90 Wheelbase-to-length ratio of 47% is considered ●dangerous ○fatiguing ○good ○excellent *
The approximate net payload of 2630 pounds at 18% of GVWR on this model is ○deficient ○excessive ○cautionary ○good ●excellent *
Total highway safety penalties are: 4 * Value: 7 7 Durability: 7 2 Highway Control Rating: 3 6 Highway Safety: 3 2

Brand	Year	Type	Length	Model	Chassis	Engine	Fuel Type	Price/Ft	Wheelbase	Towing	GVWR	Curb Wt
Aluma-Lite	1990	MHA	28	28 WB	CH	7.5L	G	$1800	158	4,500	14,500	11,791

Livability Code: SB 30-90 Wheelbase-to-length ratio of 46% is considered ●dangerous ○fatiguing ○good ○excellent *
The approximate net payload of 2709 pounds at 19% of GVWR on this model is ○deficient ○excessive ○cautionary ○good ●excellent *
Total highway safety penalties are: 4 * Value: 7 7 Durability: 7 2 Highway Control Rating: 3 4 Highway Safety: 3 0

Brand	Year	Type	Length	Model	Chassis	Engine	Fuel Type	Price/Ft	Wheelbase	Towing	GVWR	Curb Wt
Aluma-Lite	1990	MHA	30	29 WBXS	CH	7.5L	G	$1800	178	4,500	14,500	12,254

Livability Code: SB 30-90 Wheelbase-to-length ratio of 50% is considered ●dangerous ○fatiguing ○good ○excellent *
The approximate net payload of 2246 pounds at 15% of GVWR on this model is ○deficient ○excessive ○cautionary ●good ○excellent *
Total highway safety penalties are: 4 * Value: 7 7 Durability: 7 2 Highway Control Rating: 4 3 Highway Safety: 3 9

Brand	Year	Type	Length	Model	Chassis	Engine	Fuel Type	Price/Ft	Wheelbase	Towing	GVWR	Curb Wt
Aluma-Lite	1990	MHA	32	31 WBXS	CH	7.5L	G	$1900	182 T	4,500	16,500	13,664

Livability Code: SB 30-90 Wheelbase-to-length ratio of 48% is considered ●dangerous ○fatiguing ○good ○excellent *
The approximate net payload of 2836 pounds at 17% of GVWR on this model is ○deficient ○excessive ○cautionary ○good ●excellent *
Total highway safety penalties are: 8 * Value: 7 5 Durability: 7 2 Highway Control Rating: 3 8 Highway Safety: 3 0

Brand	Year	Type	Length	Model	Chassis	Engine	Fuel Type	Price/Ft	Wheelbase	Towing	GVWR	Curb Wt
Aluma-Lite	1990	MHA	33	33 CSXS	CH	7.5L	G	$1900	202 T	4,500	16,500	14,128

Livability Code: SB 30-90 Wheelbase-to-length ratio of 51% is considered ○dangerous ●fatiguing ○good ○excellent *
The approximate net payload of 2372 pounds at 14% of GVWR on this model is ○deficient ○excessive ○cautionary ●good ○excellent *
Total highway safety penalties are: 9 * Value: 7 5 Durability: 7 2 Highway Control Rating: 4 3 Highway Safety: 3 4

Brand	Year	Type	Length	Model	Chassis	Engine	Fuel Type	Price/Ft	Wheelbase	Towing	GVWR	Curb Wt
Aluma-Lite	1990	MHA	34	33 CS	CH	7.5L	G	$1800	202 T	4,500	16,500	14,015

Livability Code: SB 30-90 Wheelbase-to-length ratio of 49% is considered ●dangerous ○fatiguing ○good ○excellent *
The approximate net payload of 2485 pounds at 15% of GVWR on this model is ○deficient ○excessive ○cautionary ●good ○excellent *
Total highway safety penalties are: 9 * Value: 7 4 Durability: 7 2 Highway Control Rating: 4 0 Highway Safety: 3 1

Brand	Year	Type	Length	Model	Chassis	Engine	Fuel Type	Price/Ft	Wheelbase	Towing	GVWR	Curb Wt
Aluma-Lite	1990	MHA	35	34 WB	CH	7.5L	G	$1700	202 T	4,500	16,500	14,050

Livability Code: SB 30-90 Wheelbase-to-length ratio of 48% is considered ●dangerous ○fatiguing ○good ○excellent *
The approximate net payload of 2451 pounds at 15% of GVWR on this model is ○deficient ○excessive ○cautionary ●good ○excellent *
Total highway safety penalties are: 9 * Value: 7 4 Durability: 7 2 Highway Control Rating: 3 6 Highway Safety: 2 7

Brand	Year	Type	Length	Model	Chassis	Engine	Fuel Type	Price/Ft	Wheelbase	Towing	GVWR	Curb Wt
Aluma-Lite	1990	MHA	35	34 CS	CH	7.5L	G	$1700	202 T	4,500	16,500	14,025

Livability Code: SB 30-90 Wheelbase-to-length ratio of 48% is considered ●dangerous ○fatiguing ○good ○excellent *
The approximate net payload of 2476 pounds at 15% of GVWR on this model is ○deficient ○excessive ○cautionary ●good ○excellent *
Total highway safety penalties are: 9 * Value: 7 4 Durability: 7 2 Highway Control Rating: 3 6 Highway Safety: 2 7

Brand	Year	Type	Length	Model	Chassis	Engine	Fuel Type	Price/Ft	Wheelbase	Towing	GVWR	Curb Wt
Aluma-Lite	1990	MHA	35	35 CSXS	CH	7.5L	G	$1900	202 T	7,800	17,200	14,356

Livability Code: SB 30-90 Wheelbase-to-length ratio of 48% is considered ●dangerous ○fatiguing ○good ○excellent *
The approximate net payload of 2845 pounds at 17% of GVWR on this model is ○deficient ○excessive ○cautionary ○good ●excellent *
Total highway safety penalties are: 9 * Value: 7 4 Durability: 7 2 Highway Control Rating: 3 8 Highway Safety: 2 9

Brand	Year	Type	Length	Model	Chassis	Engine	Fuel Type	Price/Ft	Wheelbase	Towing	GVWR	Curb Wt
Aluma-Lite	1992	MHA	26	25 WB	FO	7.5L	G	$1900	158	7,500	11,500	10,568

Livability Code: SB 30-90 Wheelbase-to-length ratio of 50% is considered ●dangerous ○fatiguing ○good ○excellent *
The approximate net payload of 932 pounds at 8% of GVWR on this model is ○deficient ○excessive ●cautionary ○good ○excellent *
Total highway safety penalties are: 2 * Value: 7 8 Durability: 7 2 Highway Control Rating: 2 3 Highway Safety: 2 1

Brand	Year	Type	Length	Model	Chassis	Engine	Fuel Type	Price/Ft	Wheelbase	Towing	GVWR	Curb Wt
Aluma-Lite	1992	MHA	28	27 WBXS	CH	7.4L	G	$2000	158	4,200	14,800	11,832

Livability Code: SB 30-90 Wheelbase-to-length ratio of 47% is considered ●dangerous ○fatiguing ○good ○excellent *
The approximate net payload of 2969 pounds at 20% of GVWR on this model is ○deficient ○excessive ○cautionary ○good ●excellent *
Total highway safety penalties are: 4 * Value: 7 7 Durability: 7 2 Highway Control Rating: 3 8 Highway Safety: 3 4

Note: Safety ratings are based on the assumption that the engineering of the RV has allowed for proper balance by placing fresh, gray, and black holding tanks in a location so as not to change the balance of the RV when the tanks are empty or full. **Always double-check wheelbase, GVWR, and weights at front and rear axles.**

*See Section 1 for details on how conclusions are reached.

Brand	Year	Type	Length	Model	Chassis	Engine	Fuel Type	Average Price per Linear Foot When New	Adjusted Wheelbase	Approx. Towing Capacity	Gross Vehicle Weight Rating	Average Curb Weight
Aluma-Lite	1992	MHA	30	29 WBXS	CH	7.4L	G	$2000	178	4,200	14,800	12,503

Livability Code: SB 30-90
Wheelbase-to-length ratio of 50% is considered ● dangerous ○ fatiguing ○ good ○ excellent *
The approximate net payload of 2297 pounds at 16% of GVWR on this model is ○ deficient ○ excessive ○ cautionary ○ good ● excellent *
Total highway safety penalties are: 4 * Value: 7 7 Durability: 7 2 Highway Control Rating: 4 4 Highway Safety: 4 0

Brand	Year	Type	Length	Model	Chassis	Engine	Fuel Type	Price/ft	Wheelbase	Towing	GVWR	Curb Weight
Aluma-Lite	1992	MHA	30	29 WBXS	FO	7.5L	G	$2000	178	8,000	17,000	13,075

Livability Code: SB 30-90
Wheelbase-to-length ratio of 50% is considered ● dangerous ○ fatiguing ○ good ○ excellent *
The approximate net payload of 3925 pounds at 23% of GVWR on this model is ○ deficient ○ excessive ○ cautionary ○ good ● excellent *
Total highway safety penalties are: 2 * Value: 7 8 Durability: 7 2 Highway Control Rating: 4 5 Highway Safety: 4 3

Brand	Year	Type	Length	Model	Chassis	Engine	Fuel Type	Price/ft	Wheelbase	Towing	GVWR	Curb Weight
Aluma-Lite	1992	MHA	32	31 CBXS	CH	7.4L	G	$2000	190	4,000	16,000	13,078

Livability Code: SB 30-90
Wheelbase-to-length ratio of 50% is considered ● dangerous ○ fatiguing ○ good ○ excellent *
The approximate net payload of 2922 pounds at 18% of GVWR on this model is ○ deficient ○ excessive ○ cautionary ○ good ● excellent *
Total highway safety penalties are: 5 * Value: 7 6 Durability: 7 2 Highway Control Rating: 4 7 Highway Safety: 4 2

Brand	Year	Type	Length	Model	Chassis	Engine	Fuel Type	Price/ft	Wheelbase	Towing	GVWR	Curb Weight
Aluma-Lite	1992	MHA	32	31 CSXS	CH	7.4L	G	$1900	190	4,000	16,000	13,078

Livability Code: SB 30-90
Wheelbase-to-length ratio of 50% is considered ● dangerous ○ fatiguing ○ good ○ excellent *
The approximate net payload of 2922 pounds at 18% of GVWR on this model is ○ deficient ○ excessive ○ cautionary ○ good ● excellent *
Total highway safety penalties are: 5 * Value: 7 6 Durability: 7 2 Highway Control Rating: 4 7 Highway Safety: 4 2

Brand	Year	Type	Length	Model	Chassis	Engine	Fuel Type	Price/ft	Wheelbase	Towing	GVWR	Curb Weight
Aluma-Lite	1992	MHA	32	31 CBXS	FO	7.5L	G	$2000	178	2,000	17,000	13,608

Livability Code: SB 30-90
Wheelbase-to-length ratio of 47% is considered ● dangerous ○ fatiguing ○ good ○ excellent *
The approximate net payload of 3392 pounds at 20% of GVWR on this model is ○ deficient ○ excessive ○ cautionary ○ good ○ excellent *
Total highway safety penalties are: 2 * Value: 7 8 Durability: 7 2 Highway Control Rating: 3 7 Highway Safety: 3 5

Brand	Year	Type	Length	Model	Chassis	Engine	Fuel Type	Price/ft	Wheelbase	Towing	GVWR	Curb Weight
Aluma-Lite	1992	MHA	32	31 CSXS	FO	7.5L	G	$1900	178	2,000	17,000	13,608

Livability Code: SB 30-90
Wheelbase-to-length ratio of 47% is considered ● dangerous ○ fatiguing ○ good ○ excellent *
The approximate net payload of 3392 pounds at 20% of GVWR on this model is ○ deficient ○ excessive ○ cautionary ○ good ○ excellent *
Total highway safety penalties are: 2 * Value: 7 8 Durability: 7 2 Highway Control Rating: 3 7 Highway Safety: 3 5

Brand	Year	Type	Length	Model	Chassis	Engine	Fuel Type	Price/ft	Wheelbase	Towing	GVWR	Curb Weight
Aluma-Lite	1992	MHA	33	33 CSXS	CH	7.4L	G	$2100	202 T	1,500	17,500	14,179

Livability Code: SB 30-90
Wheelbase-to-length ratio of 51% is considered ○ dangerous ● fatiguing ○ good ○ excellent *
The approximate net payload of 3321 pounds at 19% of GVWR on this model is ○ deficient ○ excessive ○ cautionary ○ good ● excellent *
Total highway safety penalties are: 9 * Value: 7 5 Durability: 7 2 Highway Control Rating: 5 0 Highway Safety: 4 1

Brand	Year	Type	Length	Model	Chassis	Engine	Fuel Type	Price/ft	Wheelbase	Towing	GVWR	Curb Weight
Aluma-Lite	1992	MHA	33	33 CSXS	FO	7.5L	G	$2100	202 T	7,000	18,000	14,467

Livability Code: SB 30-90
Wheelbase-to-length ratio of 51% is considered ○ dangerous ● fatiguing ○ good ○ excellent *
The approximate net payload of 3533 pounds at 20% of GVWR on this model is ○ deficient ○ excessive ○ cautionary ○ good ● excellent *
Total highway safety penalties are: 4 * Value: 7 7 Durability: 7 2 Highway Control Rating: 5 0 Highway Safety: 4 6

Brand	Year	Type	Length	Model	Chassis	Engine	Fuel Type	Price/ft	Wheelbase	Towing	GVWR	Curb Weight
Aluma-Lite	1992	MHA	35	34 CS	CH	7.4L	G	$1900	202 T	1,500	17,500	14,432

Livability Code: SB 30-90
Wheelbase-to-length ratio of 48% is considered ● dangerous ○ fatiguing ○ good ○ excellent *
The approximate net payload of 3068 pounds at 18% of GVWR on this model is ○ deficient ○ excessive ○ cautionary ○ good ● excellent *
Total highway safety penalties are: 9 * Value: 7 4 Durability: 7 2 Highway Control Rating: 3 9 Highway Safety: 3 0

Brand	Year	Type	Length	Model	Chassis	Engine	Fuel Type	Price/ft	Wheelbase	Towing	GVWR	Curb Weight
Aluma-Lite	1992	MHA	35	34 CS	FO	7.5L	G	$1900	202 T	7,000	18,000	14,555

Livability Code: SB 30-90
Wheelbase-to-length ratio of 48% is considered ● dangerous ○ fatiguing ○ good ○ excellent *
The approximate net payload of 3445 pounds at 19% of GVWR on this model is ○ deficient ○ excessive ○ cautionary ○ good ● excellent *
Total highway safety penalties are: 4 * Value: 7 7 Durability: 7 2 Highway Control Rating: 4 1 Highway Safety: 3 7

Brand	Year	Type	Length	Model	Chassis	Engine	Fuel Type	Price/ft	Wheelbase	Towing	GVWR	Curb Weight
Aluma-Lite	1993	MHA	31	30CB	CH	7.4L	G	$2200	178	3,000	16,000	13,635

Livability Code: SB 30-90
Wheelbase-to-length ratio of 48% is considered ● dangerous ○ fatiguing ○ good ○ excellent *
The approximate net payload of 2365 pounds at 15% of GVWR on this model is ○ deficient ○ excessive ○ cautionary ● good ○ excellent *
Total highway safety penalties are: 5 * Value: 7 6 Durability: 7 2 Highway Control Rating: 3 5 Highway Safety: 3 0

Brand	Year	Type	Length	Model	Chassis	Engine	Fuel Type	Price/ft	Wheelbase	Towing	GVWR	Curb Weight
Aluma-Lite	1993	MHA	31	30CB	FO	7.5L	G	$2200	178	8,000	17,000	14,135

Livability Code: SB 30-90
Wheelbase-to-length ratio of 48% is considered ● dangerous ○ fatiguing ○ good ○ excellent *
The approximate net payload of 2865 pounds at 17% of GVWR on this model is ○ deficient ○ excessive ○ cautionary ○ good ● excellent *
Total highway safety penalties are: 2 * Value: 7 8 Durability: 7 2 Highway Control Rating: 3 8 Highway Safety: 3 6

Note: Safety ratings are based on the assumption that the engineering of the RV has allowed for proper balance by placing fresh, gray, and black holding tanks in a location so as not to change the balance of the RV when the tanks are empty or full. **Always double-check wheelbase, GVWR, and weights at front and rear axles.**

*See Section 1 for details on how conclusions are reached.

Section 2: The Ratings

Brand	Year	Type	Length	Model	Chassis	Engine	Fuel Type	Average Price per Linear Foot When New	Adjusted Wheelbase	Approx. Towing Capacity	Gross Vehicle Weight Rating	Average Curb Weight
Aluma-Lite	1993	MHA	33	32CB	CH	7.4L	G	$2300	190	3,000	16,000	14,076

Livability Code: SB 30-90 — Wheelbase-to-length ratio of 48% is considered ◉ dangerous ○ fatiguing ○ good ○ excellent *

The approximate net payload of 1924 pounds at 12% of GVWR on this model is ○ deficient ○ excessive ○ cautionary ◉ good ○ excellent *

Total highway safety penalties are: 6 * — Value: 7 6 Durability: 7 2 Highway Control Rating: 3 1 Highway Safety: 2 5

Brand	Year	Type	Length	Model	Chassis	Engine	Fuel Type	Price/Ft	Wheelbase	Towing	GVWR	Curb Weight
Aluma-Lite	1993	MHA	33	32CB	FO	7.5L	G	$2300	190	8,000	17,000	14,576

Livability Code: SB 30-90 — Wheelbase-to-length ratio of 48% is considered ◉ dangerous ○ fatiguing ○ good ○ excellent *

The approximate net payload of 2424 pounds at 14% of GVWR on this model is ○ deficient ○ excessive ○ cautionary ◉ good ○ excellent *

Total highway safety penalties are: 2 * — Value: 7 8 Durability: 7 2 Highway Control Rating: 3 5 Highway Safety: 3 3

Brand	Year	Type	Length	Model	Chassis	Engine	Fuel Type	Price/Ft	Wheelbase	Towing	GVWR	Curb Weight
Aluma-Lite	1993	MHA	34	34CBT	CH	7.4L	G	$2400	214 T	1,000	18,000	15,416

Livability Code: SB 30-90 — Wheelbase-to-length ratio of 52% is considered ○ dangerous ◉ fatiguing ○ good ○ excellent *

The approximate net payload of 2584 pounds at 14% of GVWR on this model is ○ deficient ○ excessive ○ cautionary ◉ good ○ excellent *

Total highway safety penalties are: 9 * — Value: 7 4 Durability: 7 2 Highway Control Rating: 5 5 Highway Safety: 4 6

Brand	Year	Type	Length	Model	Chassis	Engine	Fuel Type	Price/Ft	Wheelbase	Towing	GVWR	Curb Weight
Aluma-Lite	1993	MHA	34	34CB	FO	7.5L	G	$2200	208	8,000	17,000	15,016

Livability Code: SB 30-90 — Wheelbase-to-length ratio of 50% is considered ◉ dangerous ○ fatiguing ○ good ○ excellent *

The approximate net payload of 1984 pounds at 12% of GVWR on this model is ○ deficient ○ excessive ○ cautionary ◉ good ○ excellent *

Total highway safety penalties are: 2 * — Value: 7 8 Durability: 7 2 Highway Control Rating: 3 8 Highway Safety: 3 6

Brand	Year	Type	Length	Model	Chassis	Engine	Fuel Type	Price/Ft	Wheelbase	Towing	GVWR	Curb Weight
Aluma-Lite	1993	MHA	34	34CBT	FO	7.5L	G	$2400	214 T	5,600	19,400	15,916

Livability Code: SB 30-90 — Wheelbase-to-length ratio of 52% is considered ○ dangerous ◉ fatiguing ○ good ○ excellent *

The approximate net payload of 3484 pounds at 18% of GVWR on this model is ○ deficient ○ excessive ○ cautionary ○ good ◉ excellent *

Total highway safety penalties are: 4 * — Value: 7 7 Durability: 7 2 Highway Control Rating: 6 1 Highway Safety: 5 7 ★

Brand	Year	Type	Length	Model	Chassis	Engine	Fuel Type	Price/Ft	Wheelbase	Towing	GVWR	Curb Weight
Aluma-Lite	1993	MHA	37	36SA	FO	7.5L	G	$2200	214 T	5,600	19,400	16,564

Livability Code: SB 30-90 — Wheelbase-to-length ratio of 48% is considered ◉ dangerous ○ fatiguing ○ good ○ excellent *

The approximate net payload of 2836 pounds at 15% of GVWR on this model is ○ deficient ○ excessive ○ cautionary ◉ good ○ excellent *

Total highway safety penalties are: 4 * — Value: 7 7 Durability: 7 2 Highway Control Rating: 3 6 Highway Safety: 3 2

Brand	Year	Type	Length	Model	Chassis	Engine	Fuel Type	Price/Ft	Wheelbase	Towing	GVWR	Curb Weight
Aluma-Lite	1993	MHA	37	36SA	CH	7.4L	G	$2200	214 T	1,000	18,000	16,090

Livability Code: SB 30-90 — Wheelbase-to-length ratio of 48% is considered ◉ dangerous ○ fatiguing ○ good ○ excellent *

The approximate net payload of 1910 pounds at 11% of GVWR on this model is ○ deficient ○ excessive ○ cautionary ◉ good ○ excellent *

Total highway safety penalties are: 10 * — Value: 7 4 Durability: 7 2 Highway Control Rating: 2 8 Highway Safety: 1 8

Brand	Year	Type	Length	Model	Chassis	Engine	Fuel Type	Price/Ft	Wheelbase	Towing	GVWR	Curb Weight
Aluma-Lite	1993	MHA	37	36CB	CH	7.4L	G	$2200	214 T	1,000	18,000	16,090

Livability Code: SB 30-90 — Wheelbase-to-length ratio of 48% is considered ◉ dangerous ○ fatiguing ○ good ○ excellent *

The approximate net payload of 1910 pounds at 11% of GVWR on this model is ○ deficient ○ excessive ○ cautionary ◉ good ○ excellent *

Total highway safety penalties are: 10 * — Value: 7 4 Durability: 7 2 Highway Control Rating: 2 8 Highway Safety: 1 8

Brand	Year	Type	Length	Model	Chassis	Engine	Fuel Type	Price/Ft	Wheelbase	Towing	GVWR	Curb Weight
Aluma-Lite	1993	MHA	37	36CB	FO	7.5L	G	$2200	214 T	5,600	19,400	16,590

Livability Code: SB 30-90 — Wheelbase-to-length ratio of 48% is considered ◉ dangerous ○ fatiguing ○ good ○ excellent *

The approximate net payload of 2810 pounds at 14% of GVWR on this model is ○ deficient ○ excessive ○ cautionary ◉ good ○ excellent *

Total highway safety penalties are: 4 * — Value: 7 7 Durability: 7 2 Highway Control Rating: 3 5 Highway Safety: 3 1

Brand	Year	Type	Length	Model	Chassis	Engine	Fuel Type	Price/Ft	Wheelbase	Towing	GVWR	Curb Weight
Aluma-Lite	1994	MHA	31	30CB	CH	7.4L	G	$2200	178	3,000	16,000	13,635

Livability Code: SB 30-90 — Wheelbase-to-length ratio of 48% is considered ◉ dangerous ○ fatiguing ○ good ○ excellent *

The approximate net payload of 2365 pounds at 15% of GVWR on this model is ○ deficient ○ excessive ○ cautionary ◉ good ○ excellent *

Total highway safety penalties are: 5 * — Value: 7 6 Durability: 7 2 Highway Control Rating: 3 5 Highway Safety: 3 0

Brand	Year	Type	Length	Model	Chassis	Engine	Fuel Type	Price/Ft	Wheelbase	Towing	GVWR	Curb Weight
Aluma-Lite	1994	MHA	31	30CB	FO	7.5L	G	$2200	178	8,000	17,000	14,135

Livability Code: SB 30-90 — Wheelbase-to-length ratio of 48% is considered ◉ dangerous ○ fatiguing ○ good ○ excellent *

The approximate net payload of 2865 pounds at 17% of GVWR on this model is ○ deficient ○ excessive ○ cautionary ○ good ◉ excellent *

Total highway safety penalties are: 2 * — Value: 7 8 Durability: 7 2 Highway Control Rating: 3 8 Highway Safety: 3 6

Brand	Year	Type	Length	Model	Chassis	Engine	Fuel Type	Price/Ft	Wheelbase	Towing	GVWR	Curb Weight
Aluma-Lite	1994	MHA	33	32CB	CH	7.4L	G	$2100	190	3,000	16,000	14,076

Livability Code: SB 30-90 — Wheelbase-to-length ratio of 48% is considered ◉ dangerous ○ fatiguing ○ good ○ excellent *

The approximate net payload of 1924 pounds at 12% of GVWR on this model is ○ deficient ○ excessive ○ cautionary ◉ good ○ excellent *

Total highway safety penalties are: 6 * — Value: 7 6 Durability: 7 2 Highway Control Rating: 3 1 Highway Safety: 2 5

Note: Safety ratings are based on the assumption that the engineering of the RV has allowed for proper balance by placing fresh, gray, and black holding tanks in a location so as not to change the balance of the RV when the tanks are empty or full. **Always double-check wheelbase, GVWR, and weights at front and rear axles.**

*See Section 1 for details on how conclusions are reached.

Brand	Year	Type	Length	Model	Chassis	Engine	Fuel Type	Average Price per Linear Foot When New	Adjusted Wheelbase	Approx. Towing Capacity	Gross Vehicle Weight Rating	Average Curb Weight
Aluma-Lite	**1994**	MHA	33	32CB	FO	7.5L	G	$2100	190	8,000	17,000	14,576

Livability Code: SB 30-90   Wheelbase-to-length ratio of 48% is considered ● dangerous ○ fatiguing ○ good ○ excellent *

The approximate net payload of 2424 pounds at 14% of GVWR on this model is ○ deficient ○ excessive ○ cautionary ● good ○ excellent *

Total highway safety penalties are: 2 *   Value: **7 8**   Durability: **7 2**   Highway Control Rating: **3 5**   Highway Safety: **3 3**

Brand	Year	Type	Length	Model	Chassis	Engine	Fuel Type	Avg Price/Lin Ft	Adj Wheelbase	Towing Cap	GVWR	Avg Curb Weight
Aluma-Lite	**1994**	MHA	34	34CBT	CH	7.4L	G	$2200	214 T	1,000	18,000	15,416

Livability Code: SB 30-90   Wheelbase-to-length ratio of 52% is considered ○ dangerous ● fatiguing ○ good ○ excellent *

The approximate net payload of 2584 pounds at 14% of GVWR on this model is ○ deficient ○ excessive ○ cautionary ● good ○ excellent *

Total highway safety penalties are: 9 *   Value: **7 4**   Durability: **7 2**   Highway Control Rating: **5 5**   Highway Safety: **4 6**

Brand	Year	Type	Length	Model	Chassis	Engine	Fuel Type	Avg Price/Lin Ft	Adj Wheelbase	Towing Cap	GVWR	Avg Curb Weight
Aluma-Lite	**1994**	MHA	34	34CB	FO	7.5L	G	$2100	208	8,000	17,000	15,016

Livability Code: SB 30-90   Wheelbase-to-length ratio of 50% is considered ● dangerous ○ fatiguing ○ good ○ excellent *

The approximate net payload of 1984 pounds at 12% of GVWR on this model is ○ deficient ○ excessive ○ cautionary ● good ○ excellent *

Total highway safety penalties are: 2 *   Value: **7 8**   Durability: **7 2**   Highway Control Rating: **3 8**   Highway Safety: **3 6**

Brand	Year	Type	Length	Model	Chassis	Engine	Fuel Type	Avg Price/Lin Ft	Adj Wheelbase	Towing Cap	GVWR	Avg Curb Weight
Aluma-Lite	**1994**	MHA	34	34CBT	FO	7.5L	G	$2200	214 T	5,600	19,400	15,916

Livability Code: SB 30-90   Wheelbase-to-length ratio of 52% is considered ○ dangerous ● fatiguing ○ good ○ excellent *

The approximate net payload of 3484 pounds at 18% of GVWR on this model is ○ deficient ○ excessive ○ cautionary ○ good ● excellent *

Total highway safety penalties are: 4 *   Value: **7 7**   Durability: **7 2**   Highway Control Rating: **6 1**   Highway Safety: **5 7**   ★

Brand	Year	Type	Length	Model	Chassis	Engine	Fuel Type	Avg Price/Lin Ft	Adj Wheelbase	Towing Cap	GVWR	Avg Curb Weight
Aluma-Lite	**1994**	MHA	35	35D	SP	230HP	D	$2900	208	2,000	20,000	16,698

Livability Code: SB 30-90   Wheelbase-to-length ratio of 49% is considered ● dangerous ○ fatiguing ○ good ○ excellent *

The approximate net payload of 3302 pounds at 17% of GVWR on this model is ○ deficient ○ excessive ● cautionary ○ good ○ excellent *

Total highway safety penalties are: 2 *   Value: **7 8**   Durability: **7 2**   Highway Control Rating: **4 3**   Highway Safety: **4 1**

Brand	Year	Type	Length	Model	Chassis	Engine	Fuel Type	Avg Price/Lin Ft	Adj Wheelbase	Towing Cap	GVWR	Avg Curb Weight
Aluma-Lite	**1994**	MHA	37	36SA	FO	7.5L	G	$2100	214 T	5,600	19,400	16,564

Livability Code: SB 30-90   Wheelbase-to-length ratio of 48% is considered ● dangerous ○ fatiguing ○ good ○ excellent *

The approximate net payload of 2836 pounds at 15% of GVWR on this model is ○ deficient ○ excessive ○ cautionary ● good ○ excellent *

Total highway safety penalties are: 4 *   Value: **7 7**   Durability: **7 2**   Highway Control Rating: **3 6**   Highway Safety: **3 2**

Brand	Year	Type	Length	Model	Chassis	Engine	Fuel Type	Avg Price/Lin Ft	Adj Wheelbase	Towing Cap	GVWR	Avg Curb Weight
Aluma-Lite	**1994**	MHA	37	36SA	CH	7.4L	G	$2100	214 T	1,000	18,000	16,090

Livability Code: SB 30-90   Wheelbase-to-length ratio of 48% is considered ● dangerous ○ fatiguing ○ good ○ excellent *

The approximate net payload of 1910 pounds at 11% of GVWR on this model is ○ deficient ○ excessive ○ cautionary ● good ○ excellent *

Total highway safety penalties are: 10 *   Value: **7 4**   Durability: **7 2**   Highway Control Rating: **2 8**   Highway Safety: **1 8**

Brand	Year	Type	Length	Model	Chassis	Engine	Fuel Type	Avg Price/Lin Ft	Adj Wheelbase	Towing Cap	GVWR	Avg Curb Weight
Aluma-Lite	**1994**	MHA	37	36CB	CH	7.4L	G	$1900	214 T	1,000	18,000	16,090

Livability Code: SB 30-90   Wheelbase-to-length ratio of 48% is considered ● dangerous ○ fatiguing ○ good ○ excellent *

The approximate net payload of 1910 pounds at 11% of GVWR on this model is ○ deficient ○ excessive ○ cautionary ● good ○ excellent *

Total highway safety penalties are: 10 *   Value: **7 4**   Durability: **7 2**   Highway Control Rating: **2 8**   Highway Safety: **1 8**

Brand	Year	Type	Length	Model	Chassis	Engine	Fuel Type	Avg Price/Lin Ft	Adj Wheelbase	Towing Cap	GVWR	Avg Curb Weight
Aluma-Lite	**1994**	MHA	37	36CB	FO	7.5L	G	$2100	214 T	5,600	19,400	16,590

Livability Code: SB 30-90   Wheelbase-to-length ratio of 48% is considered ● dangerous ○ fatiguing ○ good ○ excellent *

The approximate net payload of 2810 pounds at 14% of GVWR on this model is ○ deficient ○ excessive ○ cautionary ● good ○ excellent *

Total highway safety penalties are: 4 *   Value: **7 7**   Durability: **7 2**   Highway Control Rating: **3 5**   Highway Safety: **3 1**

Brand	Year	Type	Length	Model	Chassis	Engine	Fuel Type	Avg Price/Lin Ft	Adj Wheelbase	Towing Cap	GVWR	Avg Curb Weight
Aluma-Lite Mini	**1989**	MHC	26	25RB	FO	5.8L	G	$1300	158	1,500	11,500	10,421

Livability Code: VA 30-90   Wheelbase-to-length ratio of 51% is considered ○ dangerous ● fatiguing ○ good ○ excellent *

The approximate net payload of 1079 pounds at 9% of GVWR on this model is ○ deficient ○ excessive ● cautionary ○ good ○ excellent *

Total highway safety penalties are: 2 *   Value: **7 8**   Durability: **7 2**   Highway Control Rating: **4 8**   Highway Safety: **4 6**

Brand	Year	Type	Length	Model	Chassis	Engine	Fuel Type	Avg Price/Lin Ft	Adj Wheelbase	Towing Cap	GVWR	Avg Curb Weight
Aluma-Lite Mini	**1989**	MHC	28	27SB	FO	7.5L	G	$1700	182 T	1,500	14,000	11,651

Livability Code: VA 30-90   Wheelbase-to-length ratio of 54% is considered ○ dangerous ○ fatiguing ● good ○ excellent *

The approximate net payload of 2349 pounds at 17% of GVWR on this model is ○ deficient ○ excessive ○ cautionary ○ good ● excellent *

Total highway safety penalties are: 4 *   Value: **7 7**   Durability: **7 2**   Highway Control Rating: **8 7**   Highway Safety: **8 3**   ★★★

Brand	Year	Type	Length	Model	Chassis	Engine	Fuel Type	Avg Price/Lin Ft	Adj Wheelbase	Towing Cap	GVWR	Avg Curb Weight
Aluma-Lite Mini	**1990**	MHC	25	24 RB	FO	5.8L	G	$1600	158	1,500	11,000	9,863

Livability Code: VA 30-90   Wheelbase-to-length ratio of 54% is considered ○ dangerous ○ fatiguing ● good ○ excellent *

The approximate net payload of 1137 pounds at 10% of GVWR on this model is ○ deficient ○ excessive ○ cautionary ● good ○ excellent *

Total highway safety penalties are: 2 *   Value: **7 8**   Durability: **7 2**   Highway Control Rating: **7 9**   Highway Safety: **7 7**   ★★★

Note: Safety ratings are based on the assumption that the engineering of the RV has allowed for proper balance by placing fresh, gray, and black holding tanks in a location so as not to change the balance of the RV when the tanks are empty or full. **Always double-check wheelbase, GVWR, and weights at front and rear axles.**

*See Section 1 for details on how conclusions are reached.

Brand	Year	Type	Length	Model	Chassis	Engine	Fuel Type	Average Price per Linear Foot When New	Adjusted Wheel-base	Approx. Towing Capacity	Gross Vehicle Weight Rating	Average Curb Weight
Aluma-Lite Mini	1990	MHC	27	26 RB	FO	7.5L	G	$1600	176	1,500	11,000	10,721

Livability Code: VA 30-90
Wheelbase-to-length ratio of 54% is considered ○ dangerous ○ fatiguing ◉ good ○ excellent *
The approximate net payload of 279 pounds at 3% of GVWR on this model is ◉ deficient ○ excessive ○ cautionary ○ good ○ excellent *
Total highway safety penalties are: 2 *   Value: **7 8**   Durability: **7 2**   Highway Control Rating: **4 8**   Highway Safety: **4 6**

Brand	Year	Type	Length	Model	Chassis	Engine	Fuel Type	Price/ft	Wheelbase	Towing	GVWR	Curb Wt
Aluma-Lite Mini	1990	MHC	27	26 SB	FO	7.5L	G	$1600	176	1,500	11,000	10,409

Livability Code: VA 30-90
Wheelbase-to-length ratio of 54% is considered ○ dangerous ○ fatiguing ◉ good ○ excellent *
The approximate net payload of 591 pounds at 5% of GVWR on this model is ◉ deficient ○ excessive ○ cautionary ○ good ○ excellent *
Total highway safety penalties are: 2 *   Value: **7 8**   Durability: **7 2**   Highway Control Rating: **5 1**   Highway Safety: **4 9**

Brand	Year	Type	Length	Model	Chassis	Engine	Fuel Type	Price/ft	Wheelbase	Towing	GVWR	Curb Wt
Aluma-Lite Mini	1990	MHC	28	27 WBLK	FO	7.5L	G	$1600	176	1,500	11,000	10,905

Livability Code: VA 30-90
Wheelbase-to-length ratio of 53% is considered ○ dangerous ◉ fatiguing ○ good ○ excellent *
The approximate net payload of 95 pounds at 1% of GVWR on this model is ◉ deficient ○ excessive ○ cautionary ○ good ○ excellent *
Total highway safety penalties are: 2 *   Value: **7 8**   Durability: **7 2**   Highway Control Rating: **3 7**   Highway Safety: **3 5**

Brand	Year	Type	Length	Model	Chassis	Engine	Fuel Type	Price/ft	Wheelbase	Towing	GVWR	Curb Wt
Aluma-Lite Mini	1990	MHC	28	27 SB	FO	7.5L	G	$1700	182 T	1,500	14,000	11,354

Livability Code: VA 30-90
Wheelbase-to-length ratio of 54% is considered ○ dangerous ○ fatiguing ◉ good ○ excellent *
The approximate net payload of 2646 pounds at 19% of GVWR on this model is ○ deficient ○ excessive ○ cautionary ○ good ◉ excellent *
Total highway safety penalties are: 4 *   Value: **7 7**   Durability: **7 2**   Highway Control Rating: **8 9**   Highway Safety: **8 5**   ★★★

Brand	Year	Type	Length	Model	Chassis	Engine	Fuel Type	Price/ft	Wheelbase	Towing	GVWR	Curb Wt
Aluma-Lite Mini	1990	MHC	28	27 WB	FO	7.5L	G	$1700	182 T	1,500	14,000	11,457

Livability Code: VA 30-90
Wheelbase-to-length ratio of 54% is considered ○ dangerous ○ fatiguing ◉ good ○ excellent *
The approximate net payload of 2543 pounds at 18% of GVWR on this model is ○ deficient ○ excessive ○ cautionary ○ good ◉ excellent *
Total highway safety penalties are: 4 *   Value: **7 7**   Durability: **7 2**   Highway Control Rating: **8 8**   Highway Safety: **8 4**   ★★★

Brand	Year	Type	Length	Model	Chassis	Engine	Fuel Type	Price/ft	Wheelbase	Towing	GVWR	Curb Wt
Aluma-Lite Mini	1990	MHC	28	XL27WB	FO	7.5L	G	$1700	182 T	1,500	14,000	11,553

Livability Code: VA 30-90
Wheelbase-to-length ratio of 54% is considered ○ dangerous ○ fatiguing ◉ good ○ excellent *
The approximate net payload of 2447 pounds at 17% of GVWR on this model is ○ deficient ○ excessive ○ cautionary ○ good ◉ excellent *
Total highway safety penalties are: 4 *   Value: **7 7**   Durability: **7 2**   Highway Control Rating: **8 7**   Highway Safety: **8 3**   ★★★

Brand	Year	Type	Length	Model	Chassis	Engine	Fuel Type	Price/ft	Wheelbase	Towing	GVWR	Curb Wt
Aluma-Lite Mini	1991	MHC	28	27 WBXS	FO	7.5L	G	$1700	182 T	1,500	14,000	11,920

Livability Code: VA 30-90
Wheelbase-to-length ratio of 54% is considered ○ dangerous ○ fatiguing ◉ good ○ excellent *
The approximate net payload of 2080 pounds at 15% of GVWR on this model is ○ deficient ○ excessive ○ cautionary ○ good ◉ excellent *
Total highway safety penalties are: 4 *   Value: **7 7**   Durability: **7 2**   Highway Control Rating: **8 4**   Highway Safety: **8 0**   ★★★

Brand	Year	Type	Length	Model	Chassis	Engine	Fuel Type	Price/ft	Wheelbase	Towing	GVWR	Curb Wt
Aluma-Lite Mini	1992	MHC	23	22 SBRK	FO	7.5L	G	$1900	158	7,000	11,500	9,663

Livability Code: VA 30-90
Wheelbase-to-length ratio of 57% is considered ○ dangerous ○ fatiguing ◉ good ○ excellent *
The approximate net payload of 1837 pounds at 16% of GVWR on this model is ○ deficient ○ excessive ○ cautionary ○ good ◉ excellent *
Total highway safety penalties are: 2 *   Value: **7 8**   Durability: **7 2**   Highway Control Rating: **1 0 0**   Highway Safety: **9 8**   ★★★

Brand	Year	Type	Length	Model	Chassis	Engine	Fuel Type	Price/ft	Wheelbase	Towing	GVWR	Curb Wt
Aluma-Lite Mini	1992	MHC	24	24 RB	FO	7.5L	G	$1900	158	7,000	11,500	9,861

Livability Code: VA 30-90
Wheelbase-to-length ratio of 54% is considered ○ dangerous ○ fatiguing ◉ good ○ excellent *
The approximate net payload of 1639 pounds at 14% of GVWR on this model is ○ deficient ○ excessive ○ cautionary ◉ good ○ excellent *
Total highway safety penalties are: 2 *   Value: **7 8**   Durability: **7 2**   Highway Control Rating: **8 1**   Highway Safety: **7 9**   ★★★

Brand	Year	Type	Length	Model	Chassis	Engine	Fuel Type	Price/ft	Wheelbase	Towing	GVWR	Curb Wt
Aluma-Lite Mini	1992	MHC	28	27 WBLK	FO	7.5L	G	$1800	176	6,700	11,800	11,060

Livability Code: VA 30-90
Wheelbase-to-length ratio of 53% is considered ○ dangerous ◉ fatiguing ○ good ○ excellent *
The approximate net payload of 740 pounds at 6% of GVWR on this model is ◉ deficient ○ excessive ○ cautionary ○ good ○ excellent *
Total highway safety penalties are: 2 *   Value: **7 8**   Durability: **7 2**   Highway Control Rating: **4 2**   Highway Safety: **4 0**

Brand	Year	Type	Length	Model	Chassis	Engine	Fuel Type	Price/ft	Wheelbase	Towing	GVWR	Curb Wt
Aluma-Lite Mini	1992	MHC	28	27 WB	FO	7.5L	G	$1800	182 T	4,500	14,000	11,009

Livability Code: VA 30-90
Wheelbase-to-length ratio of 54% is considered ○ dangerous ○ fatiguing ◉ good ○ excellent *
The approximate net payload of 2992 pounds at 21% of GVWR on this model is ○ deficient ○ excessive ○ cautionary ○ good ◉ excellent *
Total highway safety penalties are: 4 *   Value: **7 7**   Durability: **7 2**   Highway Control Rating: **8 8**   Highway Safety: **8 4**   ★★★

Brand	Year	Type	Length	Model	Chassis	Engine	Fuel Type	Price/ft	Wheelbase	Towing	GVWR	Curb Wt
Aluma-Lite XL	1991	MHA	30	29 WBXS	CH	7.4L	G	$1800	202 T	2,500	14,500	12,564

Livability Code: SB 30-90
Wheelbase-to-length ratio of 57% is considered ○ dangerous ○ fatiguing ◉ good ○ excellent *
The approximate net payload of 1936 pounds at 13% of GVWR on this model is ○ deficient ○ excessive ○ cautionary ◉ good ○ excellent *
Total highway safety penalties are: 7 *   Value: **7 5**   Durability: **7 2**   Highway Control Rating: **9 3**   Highway Safety: **8 6**   ★★★

Note: Safety ratings are based on the assumption that the engineering of the RV has allowed for proper balance by placing fresh, gray, and black holding tanks in a location so as not to change the balance of the RV when the tanks are empty or full. **Always double-check wheelbase, GVWR, and weights at front and rear axles.**

*See Section 1 for details on how conclusions are reached.

Section 2: The Ratings

Brand	Year	Type	Length	Model	Chassis	Engine	Fuel Type	Average Price per Linear Foot When New	Adjusted Wheelbase	Approx. Towing Capacity	Gross Vehicle Weight Rating	Average Curb Weight
Ambassador	1993	MHA	33	330Q	CH	7.4L	G	$2000	208	1,500	16,000	13,994

Livability Code: SB 30-90
Wheelbase-to-length ratio of 53% is considered ○ dangerous ● fatiguing ○ good ○ excellent *
The approximate net payload of 2006 pounds at 13% of GVWR on this model is ○ deficient ○ excessive ○ cautionary ● good ○ excellent *
Total highway safety penalties are: 6 *   Value: 7 5   Durability: 7 1   Highway Control Rating: 6 2   Highway Safety: 5 6   ★

Brand	Year	Type	Length	Model	Chassis	Engine	Fuel Type	Price	Wheelbase	Towing	GVWR	Curb Weight
Ambassador	1995	MHA	32	310	CH	7.4L	G	$2300	190	1,500	16,000	13,736

Livability Code: SB 30-90
Wheelbase-to-length ratio of 50% is considered ● dangerous ○ fatiguing ○ good ○ excellent *
The approximate net payload of 2264 pounds at 14% of GVWR on this model is ○ deficient ○ excessive ○ cautionary ● good ○ excellent *
Total highway safety penalties are: 5 *   Value: 7 6   Durability: 7 1   Highway Control Rating: 4 1   Highway Safety: 3 6

Brand	Year	Type	Length	Model	Chassis	Engine	Fuel Type	Price	Wheelbase	Towing	GVWR	Curb Weight
Ambassador	1995	MHA	32	310	FO	7.5L	G	$2300	190	8,000	17,000	14,186

Livability Code: SB 30-90
Wheelbase-to-length ratio of 50% is considered ● dangerous ○ fatiguing ○ good ○ excellent *
The approximate net payload of 2814 pounds at 17% of GVWR on this model is ○ deficient ○ excessive ○ cautionary ○ good ● excellent *
Total highway safety penalties are: 2 *   Value: 7 7   Durability: 7 1   Highway Control Rating: 4 6   Highway Safety: 4 4

Brand	Year	Type	Length	Model	Chassis	Engine	Fuel Type	Price	Wheelbase	Towing	GVWR	Curb Weight
Ambassador	1995	MHA	33	330	CH	7.4L	G	$2300	208	1,500	16,000	14,078

Livability Code: SB 30-90
Wheelbase-to-length ratio of 53% is considered ○ dangerous ● fatiguing ○ good ○ excellent *
The approximate net payload of 1922 pounds at 12% of GVWR on this model is ○ deficient ○ excessive ○ cautionary ● good ○ excellent *
Total highway safety penalties are: 6 *   Value: 7 5   Durability: 7 1   Highway Control Rating: 6 1   Highway Safety: 5 5   ★

Brand	Year	Type	Length	Model	Chassis	Engine	Fuel Type	Price	Wheelbase	Towing	GVWR	Curb Weight
Ambassador	1995	MHA	33	330	FO	7.5L	G	$2300	208	8,000	17,000	14,528

Livability Code: SB 30-90
Wheelbase-to-length ratio of 53% is considered ○ dangerous ● fatiguing ○ good ○ excellent *
The approximate net payload of 2472 pounds at 15% of GVWR on this model is ○ deficient ○ excessive ○ cautionary ● good ○ excellent *
Total highway safety penalties are: 2 *   Value: 7 7   Durability: 7 1   Highway Control Rating: 6 6   Highway Safety: 6 4   ★★

Brand	Year	Type	Length	Model	Chassis	Engine	Fuel Type	Price	Wheelbase	Towing	GVWR	Curb Weight
Ambassador	1995	MHA	34	335-190	OS	Cu5.9L	D	$3300	228	1,500	18,000	16,752

Livability Code: SB 30-90
Wheelbase-to-length ratio of 56% is considered ○ dangerous ○ fatiguing ● good ○ excellent *
The approximate net payload of 1248 pounds at 7% of GVWR on this model is ○ deficient ○ excessive ● cautionary ○ good ○ excellent *
Total highway safety penalties are: 2 *   Value: 7 7   Durability: 7 1   Highway Control Rating: 6 7   Highway Safety: 6 5   ★★

Brand	Year	Type	Length	Model	Chassis	Engine	Fuel Type	Price	Wheelbase	Towing	GVWR	Curb Weight
Ambassador	1995	MHA	36	360-190	OS	Cu5.9L	D	$3300	252	1,500	19,840	18,128

Livability Code: SB 30-90
Wheelbase-to-length ratio of 58% is considered ○ dangerous ○ fatiguing ○ good ● excellent *
The approximate net payload of 1712 pounds at 9% of GVWR on this model is ○ deficient ○ excessive ● cautionary ○ good ○ excellent *
Total highway safety penalties are: 2 *   Value: 7 7   Durability: 7 1   Highway Control Rating: 8 7   Highway Safety: 8 5   ★★★

Brand	Year	Type	Length	Model	Chassis	Engine	Fuel Type	Price	Wheelbase	Towing	GVWR	Curb Weight
American	1990	MHC	28	TB-275	FO	7.5L	G	$1300	194	1,500	11,000	9,916

Livability Code: SB 30-90
Wheelbase-to-length ratio of 59% is considered ○ dangerous ○ fatiguing ○ good ● excellent *
The approximate net payload of 1084 pounds at 10% of GVWR on this model is ○ deficient ○ excessive ○ cautionary ● good ○ excellent *
Total highway safety penalties are: 2 *   Value: 8 0   Durability: 7 8   Highway Control Rating: 9 3   Highway Safety: 9 1   ★★★

Brand	Year	Type	Length	Model	Chassis	Engine	Fuel Type	Price	Wheelbase	Towing	GVWR	Curb Weight
American Clipper	1998	MHA	24	C-23	CH	7.4L	G	$3100	158	1,500	14,800	11,569

Livability Code: SB 30-90
Wheelbase-to-length ratio of 55% is considered ○ dangerous ○ fatiguing ● good ○ excellent *
The approximate net payload of 3231 pounds at 22% of GVWR on this model is ○ deficient ○ excessive ○ cautionary ○ good ● excellent *
Total highway safety penalties are: 1 *   Value: 8 5   Durability: 7 7   Highway Control Rating: 9 6   Highway Safety: 9 5   ★★★

Brand	Year	Type	Length	Model	Chassis	Engine	Fuel Type	Price	Wheelbase	Towing	GVWR	Curb Weight
American Clipper	1998	MHA	26	C-25	FO	7.5L	G	$2900	158	1,500	15,200	12,479

Livability Code: SB 30-90
Wheelbase-to-length ratio of 51% is considered ○ dangerous ● fatiguing ○ good ○ excellent *
The approximate net payload of 2721 pounds at 18% of GVWR on this model is ○ deficient ○ excessive ○ cautionary ○ good ● excellent *
Total highway safety penalties are: 2 *   Value: 8 5   Durability: 7 7   Highway Control Rating: 5 0   Highway Safety: 4 8

Brand	Year	Type	Length	Model	Chassis	Engine	Fuel Type	Price	Wheelbase	Towing	GVWR	Curb Weight
American Clipper	1998	MHA	26	C-25 myc	FO	7.5L	G	$2900	158	1,500	15,500	13,034

Livability Code: SB 30-90
Wheelbase-to-length ratio of 51% is considered ○ dangerous ● fatiguing ○ good ○ excellent *
The approximate net payload of 2467 pounds at 16% of GVWR on this model is ○ deficient ○ excessive ○ cautionary ○ good ● excellent *
Total highway safety penalties are: 2 *   Value: 8 5   Durability: 7 7   Highway Control Rating: 5 8   Highway Safety: 5 6   ★

Brand	Year	Type	Length	Model	Chassis	Engine	Fuel Type	Price	Wheelbase	Towing	GVWR	Curb Weight
American Clipper	1998	MHA	28	C-27	FO	7.5L	G	$2700	178	1,500	15,200	12,989

Livability Code: SB 30-90
Wheelbase-to-length ratio of 53% is considered ○ dangerous ● fatiguing ○ good ○ excellent *
The approximate net payload of 2211 pounds at 15% of GVWR on this model is ○ deficient ○ excessive ○ cautionary ● good ○ excellent *
Total highway safety penalties are: 2 *   Value: 8 5   Durability: 7 7   Highway Control Rating: 6 9   Highway Safety: 6 7   ★★

Note: Safety ratings are based on the assumption that the engineering of the RV has allowed for proper balance by placing fresh, gray, and black holding tanks in a location so as not to change the balance of the RV when the tanks are empty or full. **Always double-check wheelbase, GVWR, and weights at front and rear axles.**

*See Section 1 for details on how conclusions are reached.

Brand	Year	Type	Length	Model	Chassis	Engine	Fuel Type	Average Price per Linear Foot When New	Adjusted Wheelbase	Approx. Towing Capacity	Gross Vehicle Weight Rating	Average Curb Weight
American Clipper	1998	MHA	28	C-27 myc	FO	7.5L	G	$2700	178	1,500	15,500	13,459

Livability Code: SB 30-90
Wheelbase-to-length ratio of 53% is considered ○ dangerous ● fatiguing ○ good ○ excellent *
The approximate net payload of 2042 pounds at 13% of GVWR on this model is ○ deficient ○ excessive ○ cautionary ● good ○ excellent *
Total highway safety penalties are: 2 *   Value: 8 5   Durability: 7 7   Highway Control Rating: 7 1   Highway Safety: 6 9   ★★

Brand	Year	Type	Length	Model	Chassis	Engine	Fuel Type	Price/Lin Ft	Wheelbase	Towing	GVWR	Curb Wt
American Clipper	1998	MHA	30	C-29	FO	7.5L	G	$2500	190	1,500	15,200	13,550

Livability Code: SB 30-90
Wheelbase-to-length ratio of 53% is considered ○ dangerous ● fatiguing ○ good ○ excellent *
The approximate net payload of 1650 pounds at 11% of GVWR on this model is ○ deficient ○ excessive ○ cautionary ● good ○ excellent *
Total highway safety penalties are: 2 *   Value: 8 5   Durability: 7 7   Highway Control Rating: 6 0   Highway Safety: 5 8   ★

American Clipper	1998	MHA	34	C-34	FO	7.5L	G	$2200	228	1,500	17,000	14,770

Livability Code: SB 30-90
Wheelbase-to-length ratio of 56% is considered ○ dangerous ○ fatiguing ● good ○ excellent *
The approximate net payload of 2230 pounds at 13% of GVWR on this model is ○ deficient ○ excessive ○ cautionary ● good ○ excellent *
Total highway safety penalties are: 2 *   Value: 8 5   Durability: 7 7   Highway Control Rating: 9 0   Highway Safety: 8 8   ★★★

American Clipper	1999	MHA	24	C-23	CH	7.4L	G	$3100	158	1,500	14,800	11,579

Livability Code: SB 30-90
Wheelbase-to-length ratio of 55% is considered ○ dangerous ○ fatiguing ● good ○ excellent *
The approximate net payload of 3222 pounds at 22% of GVWR on this model is ○ deficient ○ excessive ○ cautionary ○ good ● excellent *
Total highway safety penalties are: 1 *   Value: 8 5   Durability: 7 7   Highway Control Rating: 9 6   Highway Safety: 9 5   ★★★

American Clipper	1999	MHA	26	C-25	CH	7.4L	G	$2900	158	4,500 e	16,500	12,284

Livability Code: SB 30-90
Wheelbase-to-length ratio of 51% is considered ○ dangerous ● fatiguing ○ good ○ excellent *
The approximate net payload of 4217 pounds at 26% of GVWR on this model is ○ deficient ○ excessive ○ cautionary ● good ○ excellent *
Total highway safety penalties are: 2 *   Value: 8 5   Durability: 7 7   Highway Control Rating: 5 7   Highway Safety: 5 5   ★

American Clipper	1999	MHA	26	C-25	FO	6.8L	G	$2900	158	10,300	15,700	13,034

Livability Code: SB 30-90
Wheelbase-to-length ratio of 51% is considered ○ dangerous ● fatiguing ○ good ○ excellent *
The approximate net payload of 2667 pounds at 17% of GVWR on this model is ○ deficient ○ excessive ○ cautionary ○ good ● excellent *
Total highway safety penalties are: 2 *   Value: 8 5   Durability: 7 7   Highway Control Rating: 5 9   Highway Safety: 5 7   ★

American Clipper	1999	MHA	28	C-27	FO	6.8L	G	$2700	178	10,300	15,700	13,459

Livability Code: SB 30-90
Wheelbase-to-length ratio of 53% is considered ○ dangerous ● fatiguing ○ good ○ excellent *
The approximate net payload of 2242 pounds at 14% of GVWR on this model is ○ deficient ○ excessive ○ cautionary ● good ○ excellent *
Total highway safety penalties are: 2 *   Value: 8 5   Durability: 7 7   Highway Control Rating: 7 3   Highway Safety: 7 1   ★★★

American Clipper	1999	MHA	30	C-29	FO	6.8L	G	$2500	190	10,300	15,700	13,979

Livability Code: SB 30-90
Wheelbase-to-length ratio of 53% is considered ○ dangerous ● fatiguing ○ good ○ excellent *
The approximate net payload of 1721 pounds at 11% of GVWR on this model is ○ deficient ○ excessive ○ cautionary ● good ○ excellent *
Total highway safety penalties are: 2 *   Value: 8 5   Durability: 7 7   Highway Control Rating: 6 5   Highway Safety: 6 3   ★★

American Cruiser	1999	MHB	20	RE2000	DO	5.2L	G	$3000	138	1,500	8,700	8,064

Livability Code: SB 30-80
Wheelbase-to-length ratio of 56% is considered ○ dangerous ○ fatiguing ● good ○ excellent *
The approximate net payload of 636 pounds at 7% of GVWR on this model is ○ deficient ○ excessive ● cautionary ○ good ○ excellent *
Total highway safety penalties are: 2 *   Value: 7 9   Durability: 7 5   Highway Control Rating: 6 9   Highway Safety: 6 7   ★★

American Cruiser	1999	MHB	20	RE2000 op eng	DO	5.9L	G	$3000	138	1,500	8,700	8,064

Livability Code: SB 30-80
Wheelbase-to-length ratio of 56% is considered ○ dangerous ○ fatiguing ● good ○ excellent *
The approximate net payload of 636 pounds at 7% of GVWR on this model is ○ deficient ○ excessive ● cautionary ○ good ○ excellent *
Total highway safety penalties are: 2 *   Value: 7 9   Durability: 7 5   Highway Control Rating: 6 9   Highway Safety: 6 7   ★★

American Dream	1995	MHA	39	39WA	SP	CU300	D	$5100	258	5,000	29,400	25,594

Livability Code: SB 30-90
Wheelbase-to-length ratio of 55% is considered ○ dangerous ○ fatiguing ● good ○ excellent *
The approximate net payload of 3806 pounds at 13% of GVWR on this model is ○ deficient ○ excessive ○ cautionary ● good ○ excellent *
Total highway safety penalties are: 2 *   Value: 8 5   Durability: 7 8   Highway Control Rating: 8 6   Highway Safety: 8 4   ★★★

American Dream	1995	MHA	39	39DAF	SP	CU300	D	$5100	258	5,000	29,400	25,594

Livability Code: SB 30-90
Wheelbase-to-length ratio of 55% is considered ○ dangerous ○ fatiguing ● good ○ excellent *
The approximate net payload of 3806 pounds at 13% of GVWR on this model is ○ deficient ○ excessive ○ cautionary ● good ○ excellent *
Total highway safety penalties are: 2 *   Value: 8 5   Durability: 7 8   Highway Control Rating: 8 6   Highway Safety: 8 4   ★★★

Note: Safety ratings are based on the assumption that the engineering of the RV has allowed for proper balance by placing fresh, gray, and black holding tanks in a location so as not to change the balance of the RV when the tanks are empty or full. **Always double-check wheelbase, GVWR, and weights at front and rear axles.**

*See Section 1 for details on how conclusions are reached.

Brand	Year	Type	Length	Model	Chassis	Engine	Fuel Type	Average Price per Linear Foot When New	Adjusted Wheelbase	Approx. Towing Capacity	Gross Vehicle Weight Rating	Average Curb Weight
American Dream	1995	MHA	39	39WJ	SP	CU300	D	$5100	258	5,000	29,400	25,794

American Dream — 1995 — MHA — 39 — 39WJ
Livability Code: SB 30-90
Wheelbase-to-length ratio of 55% is considered ○ dangerous ○ fatiguing ◉ good ○ excellent *
The approximate net payload of 3606 pounds at 12% of GVWR on this model is ○ deficient ○ excessive ○ cautionary ◉ good ○ excellent *
Total highway safety penalties are: 2 *   Value: 8 5   Durability: 7 8   Highway Control Rating: 8 8   Highway Safety: 8 6   ★★★

American Dream — 1995 — MHA — 39 — 39DJF — SP — CU300 — D — $5100 — 258 — 5,000 — 29,400 — 25,794
Livability Code: SB 30-90
Wheelbase-to-length ratio of 55% is considered ○ dangerous ○ fatiguing ◉ good ○ excellent *
The approximate net payload of 3606 pounds at 12% of GVWR on this model is ○ deficient ○ excessive ○ cautionary ◉ good ○ excellent *
Total highway safety penalties are: 2 *   Value: 8 5   Durability: 7 8   Highway Control Rating: 8 8   Highway Safety: 8 6   ★★★

American Dream — 1996 — MHA — 39 — 39DAF — SP — CU300 — D — $5100 — 258 — 5,000 — 31,000 — 26,049
Livability Code: SB 30-90
Wheelbase-to-length ratio of 55% is considered ○ dangerous ○ fatiguing ◉ good ○ excellent *
The approximate net payload of 4951 pounds at 16% of GVWR on this model is ○ deficient ○ excessive ○ cautionary ○ good ◉ excellent *
Total highway safety penalties are: 2 *   Value: 8 5   Durability: 7 8   Highway Control Rating: 9 2   Highway Safety: 9 0   ★★★

American Dream — 1996 — MHA — 39 — 36WA — SP — CU300 — D — $5100 — 258 — 5,000 — 31,000 — 26,049
Livability Code: SB 30-90
Wheelbase-to-length ratio of 55% is considered ○ dangerous ○ fatiguing ◉ good ○ excellent *
The approximate net payload of 4951 pounds at 16% of GVWR on this model is ○ deficient ○ excessive ○ cautionary ○ good ◉ excellent *
Total highway safety penalties are: 2 *   Value: 8 5   Durability: 7 8   Highway Control Rating: 9 2   Highway Safety: 9 0   ★★★

American Dream — 1996 — MHA — 39 — 39WJ — SP — CU300 — D — $5100 — 258 — 5,000 — 31,000 — 26,049
Livability Code: SB 30-90
Wheelbase-to-length ratio of 55% is considered ○ dangerous ○ fatiguing ◉ good ○ excellent *
The approximate net payload of 4951 pounds at 16% of GVWR on this model is ○ deficient ○ excessive ○ cautionary ○ good ◉ excellent *
Total highway safety penalties are: 2 *   Value: 8 5   Durability: 7 8   Highway Control Rating: 9 2   Highway Safety: 9 0   ★★★

American Dream — 1996 — MHA — 39 — 39JF — SP — CU300 — D — $5100 — 258 — 5,000 — 31,000 — 26,049
Livability Code: SB 30-90
Wheelbase-to-length ratio of 55% is considered ○ dangerous ○ fatiguing ◉ good ○ excellent *
The approximate net payload of 4951 pounds at 16% of GVWR on this model is ○ deficient ○ excessive ○ cautionary ○ good ◉ excellent *
Total highway safety penalties are: 2 *   Value: 8 5   Durability: 7 8   Highway Control Rating: 9 2   Highway Safety: 9 0   ★★★

American Dream — 1996 — MHA — 40 — 40VF — SP — CU300 — D — $5300 — 266 — 5,000 — 31,000 — 26,891
Livability Code: SB 30-90
Wheelbase-to-length ratio of 55% is considered ○ dangerous ○ fatiguing ◉ good ○ excellent *
The approximate net payload of 4109 pounds at 13% of GVWR on this model is ○ deficient ○ excessive ○ cautionary ◉ good ○ excellent *
Total highway safety penalties are: 2 *   Value: 8 5   Durability: 7 8   Highway Control Rating: 8 7   Highway Safety: 8 5   ★★★

American Dream — 1997 — MHA — 36 — 36DWF — SP — CU300 — D — $5600 — 225 — 5,000 — 29,400 — 23,830
Livability Code: SB 30-90
Wheelbase-to-length ratio of 52% is considered ○ dangerous ◉ fatiguing ○ good ○ excellent *
The approximate net payload of 5570 pounds at 19% of GVWR on this model is ○ deficient ○ excessive ○ cautionary ○ good ◉ excellent *
Total highway safety penalties are: 2 *   Value: 8 5   Durability: 7 8   Highway Control Rating: 6 3   Highway Safety: 6 1   ★★

American Dream — 1997 — MHA — 39 — 39DAF — SP — CU300 — D — $5100 — 258 — 5,000 — 31,000 — 26,050
Livability Code: SB 30-90
Wheelbase-to-length ratio of 55% is considered ○ dangerous ○ fatiguing ◉ good ○ excellent *
The approximate net payload of 4950 pounds at 16% of GVWR on this model is ○ deficient ○ excessive ○ cautionary ○ good ◉ excellent *
Total highway safety penalties are: 2 *   Value: 8 5   Durability: 7 8   Highway Control Rating: 9 2   Highway Safety: 9 0   ★★★

American Dream — 1998 — MHA — 36 — 36DWF — SP — CU300 — D — $5600 — 225 — 10,000 — 29,400 — 23,880
Livability Code: SB 30-90
Wheelbase-to-length ratio of 52% is considered ○ dangerous ◉ fatiguing ○ good ○ excellent *
The approximate net payload of 5520 pounds at 19% of GVWR on this model is ○ deficient ○ excessive ○ cautionary ○ good ◉ excellent *
Total highway safety penalties are: 2 *   Value: 8 5   Durability: 7 8   Highway Control Rating: 6 2   Highway Safety: 6 0   ★★

American Dream — 1998 — MHA — 39 — 39DAF — SP — CU325 — D — $5100 — 258 — 10,000 — 31,000 — 25,300
Livability Code: SB 30-90
Wheelbase-to-length ratio of 55% is considered ○ dangerous ○ fatiguing ◉ good ○ excellent *
The approximate net payload of 5700 pounds at 18% of GVWR on this model is ○ deficient ○ excessive ○ cautionary ○ good ◉ excellent *
Total highway safety penalties are: 2 *   Value: 8 6   Durability: 8 0   Highway Control Rating: 9 4   Highway Safety: 9 2   ★★★★

American Dream — 1998 — MHA — 40 — 40DVS — SP — CU325 — D — $5000 — 266 — 10,000 — 31,000 — 26,400
Livability Code: SB 30-90
Wheelbase-to-length ratio of 55% is considered ○ dangerous ○ fatiguing ◉ good ○ excellent *
The approximate net payload of 4600 pounds at 15% of GVWR on this model is ○ deficient ○ excessive ○ cautionary ◉ good ○ excellent *
Total highway safety penalties are: 12 *   Value: 8 0   Durability: 7 8   Highway Control Rating: 9 1   Highway Safety: 7 9   ★★★

Note: Safety ratings are based on the assumption that the engineering of the RV has allowed for proper balance by placing fresh, gray, and black holding tanks in a location so as not to change the balance of the RV when the tanks are empty or full. **Always double-check wheelbase, GVWR, and weights at front and rear axles.**

*See Section 1 for details on how conclusions are reached.

Section 2: The Ratings

Brand	Year	Type	Length	Model	Chassis	Engine	Fuel Type	Average Price per Linear Foot When New	Adjusted Wheelbase	Approx. Towing Capacity	Gross Vehicle Weight Rating	Average Curb Weight
American Dream	1999	MHA	39	39DAF	SP	CU330	D	$5100	258	10,000	31,000	25,300

Livability Code: SB 30-90 — Wheelbase-to-length ratio of 55% is considered ○ dangerous ○ fatiguing ◉ good ○ excellent *
The approximate net payload of 5700 pounds at 18% of GVWR on this model is ○ deficient ○ excessive ○ cautionary ○ good ◉ excellent *
Total highway safety penalties are: 2 * Value: 8 5 Durability: 7 8 Highway Control Rating: 9 4 Highway Safety: 9 2 ★★★

Brand	Year	Type	Length	Model	Chassis	Engine	Fuel Type	Price/Ft	Wheelbase	Towing	GVWR	Curb Weight
American Dream	1999	MHA	40	40DVS	SP	CU330	D	$5000	266	10,000	31,000	26,400

Livability Code: SB 30-90 — Wheelbase-to-length ratio of 55% is considered ○ dangerous ○ fatiguing ◉ good ○ excellent *
The approximate net payload of 4600 pounds at 15% of GVWR on this model is ○ deficient ○ excessive ○ cautionary ◉ good ○ excellent *
Total highway safety penalties are: 13 * Value: 8 0 Durability: 7 8 Highway Control Rating: 9 1 Highway Safety: 7 8 ★★★

Brand	Year	Type	Length	Model	Chassis	Engine	Fuel Type	Price/Ft	Wheelbase	Towing	GVWR	Curb Weight
American Eagle	1991	MHA	38	38J	SP	CU300	D	$4700	258	1,500	26,000	23,510

Livability Code: FT 30-90 — Wheelbase-to-length ratio of 56% is considered ○ dangerous ○ fatiguing ◉ good ○ excellent *
The approximate net payload of 2490 pounds at 10% of GVWR on this model is ○ deficient ○ excessive ○ cautionary ◉ good ○ excellent *
Total highway safety penalties are: 2 * Value: 8 8 Durability: 8 5 Highway Control Rating: 8 5 Highway Safety: 8 3 ★★★★

Brand	Year	Type	Length	Model	Chassis	Engine	Fuel Type	Price/Ft	Wheelbase	Towing	GVWR	Curb Weight
American Eagle	1994	MHA	38	38J	SP	CU300	D	$5400	258	5,000	29,400	25,500

Livability Code: FT 30-90 — Wheelbase-to-length ratio of 56% is considered ○ dangerous ○ fatiguing ◉ good ○ excellent *
The approximate net payload of 3900 pounds at 13% of GVWR on this model is ○ deficient ○ excessive ○ cautionary ◉ good ○ excellent *
Total highway safety penalties are: 2 * Value: 8 8 Durability: 8 5 Highway Control Rating: 9 1 Highway Safety: 8 9 ★★★★

Brand	Year	Type	Length	Model	Chassis	Engine	Fuel Type	Price/Ft	Wheelbase	Towing	GVWR	Curb Weight
American Eagle	1994	MHA	38	38A	SP	CU300	D	$5400	258	5,000	29,400	25,500

Livability Code: FT 30-90 — Wheelbase-to-length ratio of 56% is considered ○ dangerous ○ fatiguing ◉ good ○ excellent *
The approximate net payload of 3900 pounds at 13% of GVWR on this model is ○ deficient ○ excessive ○ cautionary ◉ good ○ excellent *
Total highway safety penalties are: 2 * Value: 8 8 Durability: 8 5 Highway Control Rating: 9 1 Highway Safety: 8 9 ★★★★

Brand	Year	Type	Length	Model	Chassis	Engine	Fuel Type	Price/Ft	Wheelbase	Towing	GVWR	Curb Weight
American Eagle	1995	MHA	40	39WA opch	Gl	CU300	D	$5700	258	1,500	31,000	28,358

Livability Code: FT 30-90 — Wheelbase-to-length ratio of 54% is considered ○ dangerous ○ fatiguing ◉ good ○ excellent *
The approximate net payload of 2642 pounds at 9% of GVWR on this model is ○ deficient ○ excessive ◉ cautionary ○ good ○ excellent *
Total highway safety penalties are: 2 * Value: 8 8 Durability: 8 5 Highway Control Rating: 6 4 Highway Safety: 6 2 ★★

Brand	Year	Type	Length	Model	Chassis	Engine	Fuel Type	Price/Ft	Wheelbase	Towing	GVWR	Curb Weight
American Eagle	1995	MHA	40	39AF opch	Gl	CU300	D	$5700	258	1,500	31,000	28,358

Livability Code: FT 30-90 — Wheelbase-to-length ratio of 54% is considered ○ dangerous ○ fatiguing ◉ good ○ excellent *
The approximate net payload of 2642 pounds at 9% of GVWR on this model is ○ deficient ○ excessive ◉ cautionary ○ good ○ excellent *
Total highway safety penalties are: 2 * Value: 8 8 Durability: 8 5 Highway Control Rating: 6 4 Highway Safety: 6 2 ★★

Brand	Year	Type	Length	Model	Chassis	Engine	Fuel Type	Price/Ft	Wheelbase	Towing	GVWR	Curb Weight
American Eagle	1995	MHA	40	39AF opch	Gl	CU300	D	$5700	258	1,500	31,000	28,358

Livability Code: FT 30-90 — Wheelbase-to-length ratio of 54% is considered ○ dangerous ○ fatiguing ◉ good ○ excellent *
The approximate net payload of 2642 pounds at 9% of GVWR on this model is ○ deficient ○ excessive ◉ cautionary ○ good ○ excellent *
Total highway safety penalties are: 2 * Value: 8 8 Durability: 8 5 Highway Control Rating: 6 4 Highway Safety: 6 2 ★★

Brand	Year	Type	Length	Model	Chassis	Engine	Fuel Type	Price/Ft	Wheelbase	Towing	GVWR	Curb Weight
American Eagle	1995	MHA	40	39WA	SP	CU300	D	$5600	258	5,000	29,400	26,705

Livability Code: FT 30-90 — Wheelbase-to-length ratio of 54% is considered ○ dangerous ○ fatiguing ◉ good ○ excellent *
The approximate net payload of 2695 pounds at 9% of GVWR on this model is ○ deficient ○ excessive ◉ cautionary ○ good ○ excellent *
Total highway safety penalties are: 2 * Value: 8 8 Durability: 8 5 Highway Control Rating: 6 4 Highway Safety: 6 2 ★★

Brand	Year	Type	Length	Model	Chassis	Engine	Fuel Type	Price/Ft	Wheelbase	Towing	GVWR	Curb Weight
American Eagle	1995	MHA	40	39AF	SP	CU300	D	$5700	258	5,000	29,400	26,858

Livability Code: FT 30-90 — Wheelbase-to-length ratio of 54% is considered ○ dangerous ○ fatiguing ◉ good ○ excellent *
The approximate net payload of 2542 pounds at 9% of GVWR on this model is ○ deficient ○ excessive ◉ cautionary ○ good ○ excellent *
Total highway safety penalties are: 2 * Value: 8 8 Durability: 8 5 Highway Control Rating: 6 4 Highway Safety: 6 2 ★★

Brand	Year	Type	Length	Model	Chassis	Engine	Fuel Type	Price/Ft	Wheelbase	Towing	GVWR	Curb Weight
American Eagle	1996	MHA	39	39 All opch	Gl	CU300	D	$5600	258	5,000	31,000	26,650

Livability Code: FT 30-90 — Wheelbase-to-length ratio of 55% is considered ○ dangerous ○ fatiguing ◉ good ○ excellent *
The approximate net payload of 4350 pounds at 14% of GVWR on this model is ○ deficient ○ excessive ○ cautionary ◉ good ○ excellent *
Total highway safety penalties are: 2 * Value: 8 8 Durability: 8 5 Highway Control Rating: 8 8 Highway Safety: 8 6 ★★★★

Brand	Year	Type	Length	Model	Chassis	Engine	Fuel Type	Price/Ft	Wheelbase	Towing	GVWR	Curb Weight
American Eagle	1996	MHA	39	39 All	SP	CU300	D	$5600	258	5,000	31,000	26,650

Livability Code: FT 30-90 — Wheelbase-to-length ratio of 55% is considered ○ dangerous ○ fatiguing ◉ good ○ excellent *
The approximate net payload of 4350 pounds at 14% of GVWR on this model is ○ deficient ○ excessive ○ cautionary ◉ good ○ excellent *
Total highway safety penalties are: 2 * Value: 8 8 Durability: 8 5 Highway Control Rating: 8 8 Highway Safety: 8 6 ★★★★

Note: Safety ratings are based on the assumption that the engineering of the RV has allowed for proper balance by placing fresh, gray, and black holding tanks in a location so as not to change the balance of the RV when the tanks are empty or full. **Always double-check wheelbase, GVWR, and weights at front and rear axles.**

*See Section 1 for details on how conclusions are reached.

Brand	Year	Type	Length	Model	Chassis	Engine	Fuel Type	Average Price per Linear Foot When New	Adjusted Wheel-base	Approx. Towing Capacity	Gross Vehicle Weight Rating	Average Curb Weight
American Eagle	1996	MHA	40	40VF opch	GI	CU300	D	$5500	266	5,000	31,000	27,491

Livability Code: FT 30-90   Wheelbase-to-length ratio of 55% is considered ○ dangerous ○ fatiguing ● good ○ excellent *
The approximate net payload of 3509 pounds at 11% of GVWR on this model is ○ deficient ○ excessive ○ cautionary ● good ○ excellent *
Total highway safety penalties are: 2 *   Value: 8 8   Durability: 8 5   Highway Control Rating: 8 8   Highway Safety: 8 6   ★★★★

Brand	Year	Type	Length	Model	Chassis	Engine	Fuel Type	Avg Price/Ft	Wheelbase	Towing	GVWR	Curb Wt
American Eagle	1996	MHA	40	40VF	SP	CU300	D	$6000	266	5,000	31,000	27,491

Livability Code: FT 30-90   Wheelbase-to-length ratio of 55% is considered ○ dangerous ○ fatiguing ● good ○ excellent *
The approximate net payload of 3509 pounds at 11% of GVWR on this model is ○ deficient ○ excessive ○ cautionary ● good ○ excellent *
Total highway safety penalties are: 2 *   Value: 8 8   Durability: 8 5   Highway Control Rating: 8 8   Highway Safety: 8 6   ★★★★

American Eagle	1997	MHA	39	39 EAF	SP	CU300	D	$5100	258	4,000	32,000	26,650

Livability Code: FT 30-90   Wheelbase-to-length ratio of 55% is considered ○ dangerous ○ fatiguing ● good ○ excellent *
The approximate net payload of 5350 pounds at 17% of GVWR on this model is ○ deficient ○ excessive ○ cautionary ○ good ● excellent *
Total highway safety penalties are: 2 *   Value: 8 8   Durability: 8 5   Highway Control Rating: 9 3   Highway Safety: 9 1   ★★★★

American Eagle	1997	MHA	40	40 EVF	SP	CU300	D	$6200	266	4,000	32,000	27,491

Livability Code: FT 30-90   Wheelbase-to-length ratio of 55% is considered ○ dangerous ○ fatiguing ● good ○ excellent *
The approximate net payload of 4509 pounds at 14% of GVWR on this model is ○ deficient ○ excessive ○ cautionary ● good ○ excellent *
Total highway safety penalties are: 2 *   Value: 8 8   Durability: 8 5   Highway Control Rating: 8 9   Highway Safety: 8 7   ★★★★

American Eagle	1997	MHA	40	40 EVS	SP	CU300	D	$6400	266	4,000	32,000	27,900

Livability Code: FT 30-90   Wheelbase-to-length ratio of 55% is considered ○ dangerous ○ fatiguing ● good ○ excellent *
The approximate net payload of 4100 pounds at 13% of GVWR on this model is ○ deficient ○ excessive ○ cautionary ● good ○ excellent *
Total highway safety penalties are: 7 *   Value: 8 5   Durability: 8 5   Highway Control Rating: 8 7   Highway Safety: 8 0   ★★★★

American Eagle	1998	MHA	39	39EAF	SP	CU325	D	$5600	258	10,000	31,000	26,650

Livability Code: FT 30-90   Wheelbase-to-length ratio of 55% is considered ○ dangerous ○ fatiguing ● good ○ excellent *
The approximate net payload of 4350 pounds at 14% of GVWR on this model is ○ deficient ○ excessive ○ cautionary ● good ○ excellent *
Total highway safety penalties are: 2 *   Value: 8 8   Durability: 8 5   Highway Control Rating: 8 8   Highway Safety: 8 6   ★★★★

American Eagle	1998	MHA	40	40EVF	SP	CU325	D	$5500	266	10,000	31,000	26,800

Livability Code: FT 30-90   Wheelbase-to-length ratio of 55% is considered ○ dangerous ○ fatiguing ● good ○ excellent *
The approximate net payload of 4200 pounds at 14% of GVWR on this model is ○ deficient ○ excessive ○ cautionary ● good ○ excellent *
Total highway safety penalties are: 2 *   Value: 8 8   Durability: 8 5   Highway Control Rating: 8 9   Highway Safety: 8 7   ★★★★

American Eagle	1998	MHA	40	40EVS	SP	CU325	D	$5500	266	10,000	31,000	27,400

Livability Code: FT 30-90   Wheelbase-to-length ratio of 55% is considered ○ dangerous ○ fatiguing ● good ○ excellent *
The approximate net payload of 3600 pounds at 12% of GVWR on this model is ○ deficient ○ excessive ○ cautionary ● good ○ excellent *
Total highway safety penalties are: 12 *   Value: 8 3   Durability: 8 5   Highway Control Rating: 8 5   Highway Safety: 7 3   ★★★

American Eagle	1999	MHA	40	40ENS	SP	CU350	D	$5500	266	10,000	31,000	27,400

Livability Code: FT 30-90   Wheelbase-to-length ratio of 55% is considered ○ dangerous ○ fatiguing ● good ○ excellent *
The approximate net payload of 3600 pounds at 12% of GVWR on this model is ○ deficient ○ excessive ○ cautionary ● good ○ excellent *
Total highway safety penalties are: 13 *   Value: 8 2   Durability: 8 5   Highway Control Rating: 8 5   Highway Safety: 7 2   ★★★

American Eagle	1999	MHA	40	40EVF	SP	CU350	D	$5500	266	10,000	31,000	26,800

Livability Code: FT 30-90   Wheelbase-to-length ratio of 55% is considered ○ dangerous ○ fatiguing ● good ○ excellent *
The approximate net payload of 4200 pounds at 14% of GVWR on this model is ○ deficient ○ excessive ○ cautionary ● good ○ excellent *
Total highway safety penalties are: 2 *   Value: 8 8   Durability: 8 5   Highway Control Rating: 8 9   Highway Safety: 8 7   ★★★★

American Eagle	1999	MHA	40	40EVS	SP	CU350	D	$5500	266	10,000	31,000	27,400

Livability Code: FT 30-90   Wheelbase-to-length ratio of 55% is considered ○ dangerous ○ fatiguing ● good ○ excellent *
The approximate net payload of 3600 pounds at 12% of GVWR on this model is ○ deficient ○ excessive ○ cautionary ● good ○ excellent *
Total highway safety penalties are: 13 *   Value: 8 2   Durability: 8 5   Highway Control Rating: 8 5   Highway Safety: 7 2   ★★★

American Tradition	1996	MHA	38	37 T/TF	SP	Cu8.3L	D	$4300	228	5,000	26,500	23,400

Livability Code: SB 30-90   Wheelbase-to-length ratio of 50% is considered ● dangerous ○ fatiguing ○ good ○ excellent *
The approximate net payload of 3100 pounds at 12% of GVWR on this model is ○ deficient ○ excessive ○ cautionary ● good ○ excellent *
Total highway safety penalties are: 2 *   Value: 8 5   Durability: 7 8   Highway Control Rating: 3 6   Highway Safety: 3 4

Note: Safety ratings are based on the assumption that the engineering of the RV has allowed for proper balance by placing fresh, gray, and black holding tanks in a location so as not to change the balance of the RV when the tanks are empty or full. **Always double-check wheelbase, GVWR, and weights at front and rear axles.**

*See Section 1 for details on how conclusions are reached.

Brand	Year	Type	Length	Model	Chassis	Engine	Fuel Type	Average Price per Linear Foot When New	Adjusted Wheelbase	Approx. Towing Capacity	Gross Vehicle Weight Rating	Average Curb Weight

American Tradition 1997 MHA 38 38 TT SP Cu8.3L D $4400 237 5,000 28,000 24,100
Livability Code: SB 30-90
Wheelbase-to-length ratio of 52% is considered ○ dangerous ◉ fatiguing ○ good ○ excellent *
The approximate net payload of 3900 pounds at 14% of GVWR on this model is ○ deficient ○ excessive ○ cautionary ◉ good ○ excellent *
Total highway safety penalties are: 2 * Value: 8 5 Durability: 7 8 Highway Control Rating: 5 5 Highway Safety: 5 3 ★

American Tradition 1997 MHA 38 38 TT F SP Cu8.3L D $4400 237 5,000 28,000 24,100
Livability Code: SB 30-90
Wheelbase-to-length ratio of 52% is considered ○ dangerous ◉ fatiguing ○ good ○ excellent *
The approximate net payload of 3900 pounds at 14% of GVWR on this model is ○ deficient ○ excessive ○ cautionary ◉ good ○ excellent *
Total highway safety penalties are: 2 * Value: 8 5 Durability: 7 8 Highway Control Rating: 5 5 Highway Safety: 5 3 ★

American Tradition 1998 MHA 38 38TT SP CU275 D $4200 237 10,000 29,400 23,500
Livability Code: SB 30-90
Wheelbase-to-length ratio of 52% is considered ○ dangerous ◉ fatiguing ○ good ○ excellent *
The approximate net payload of 5900 pounds at 20% of GVWR on this model is ○ deficient ○ excessive ○ cautionary ○ good ◉ excellent *
Total highway safety penalties are: 2 * Value: 8 5 Durability: 7 8 Highway Control Rating: 6 3 Highway Safety: 6 1 ★★

American Tradition 1998 MHA 38 38TT op eng SP CU300 D $4200 237 10,000 29,400 24,000
Livability Code: SB 30-90
Wheelbase-to-length ratio of 52% is considered ○ dangerous ◉ fatiguing ○ good ○ excellent *
The approximate net payload of 5400 pounds at 18% of GVWR on this model is ○ deficient ○ excessive ○ cautionary ○ good ◉ excellent *
Total highway safety penalties are: 2 * Value: 8 5 Durability: 7 8 Highway Control Rating: 6 2 Highway Safety: 6 0 ★★

American Tradition 1998 MHA 38 38TTF SP CU275 D $4200 237 10,000 29,400 23,400
Livability Code: SB 30-90
Wheelbase-to-length ratio of 52% is considered ○ dangerous ◉ fatiguing ○ good ○ excellent *
The approximate net payload of 6000 pounds at 20% of GVWR on this model is ○ deficient ○ excessive ○ cautionary ○ good ◉ excellent *
Total highway safety penalties are: 2 * Value: 8 5 Durability: 7 8 Highway Control Rating: 6 3 Highway Safety: 6 1 ★★

American Tradition 1998 MHA 38 38TTF op eng SP CU300 D $4200 237 10,000 29,400 23,900
Livability Code: SB 30-90
Wheelbase-to-length ratio of 52% is considered ○ dangerous ◉ fatiguing ○ good ○ excellent *
The approximate net payload of 5500 pounds at 19% of GVWR on this model is ○ deficient ○ excessive ○ cautionary ○ good ◉ excellent *
Total highway safety penalties are: 2 * Value: 8 5 Durability: 7 8 Highway Control Rating: 6 2 Highway Safety: 6 0 ★★

American Tradition 1998 MHA 41 40TVS SP CU275 D $3900 266 10,000 29,400 25,400
Livability Code: SB 30-90
Wheelbase-to-length ratio of 54% is considered ○ dangerous ○ fatiguing ◉ good ○ excellent *
The approximate net payload of 4000 pounds at 14% of GVWR on this model is ○ deficient ○ excessive ○ cautionary ◉ good ○ excellent *
Total highway safety penalties are: 12 * Value: 8 0 Durability: 7 8 Highway Control Rating: 7 8 Highway Safety: 6 6 ★★

American Tradition 1998 MHA 41 40TVS op eng SP CU300 D $3900 266 10,000 29,400 25,900
Livability Code: SB 30-90
Wheelbase-to-length ratio of 54% is considered ○ dangerous ○ fatiguing ◉ good ○ excellent *
The approximate net payload of 3500 pounds at 12% of GVWR on this model is ○ deficient ○ excessive ○ cautionary ◉ good ○ excellent *
Total highway safety penalties are: 12 * Value: 8 0 Durability: 7 8 Highway Control Rating: 7 9 Highway Safety: 6 7 ★★

American Tradition 1999 MHA 38 38TTF SP CU300 D $4200 237 10,000 29,400 23,400
Livability Code: SB 30-90
Wheelbase-to-length ratio of 52% is considered ○ dangerous ◉ fatiguing ○ good ○ excellent *
The approximate net payload of 6000 pounds at 20% of GVWR on this model is ○ deficient ○ excessive ○ cautionary ○ good ◉ excellent *
Total highway safety penalties are: 2 * Value: 8 5 Durability: 7 8 Highway Control Rating: 7 0 Highway Safety: 6 8 ★★

American Tradition 1999 MHA 41 40TVS SP CU300 D $3900 266 10,000 31,000 25,400
Livability Code: SB 30-90
Wheelbase-to-length ratio of 54% is considered ○ dangerous ○ fatiguing ◉ good ○ excellent *
The approximate net payload of 5600 pounds at 18% of GVWR on this model is ○ deficient ○ excessive ○ cautionary ○ good ◉ excellent *
Total highway safety penalties are: 12 * Value: 8 0 Durability: 7 8 Highway Control Rating: 8 8 Highway Safety: 7 6 ★★★

Anthem 1998 MHA 32 A3250 CH 7.4L G $4100 208 1,500 e 21,000 17,596
Livability Code: SB 30-90
Wheelbase-to-length ratio of 54% is considered ○ dangerous ○ fatiguing ◉ good ○ excellent *
The approximate net payload of 3404 pounds at 16% of GVWR on this model is ○ deficient ○ excessive ○ cautionary ○ good ◉ excellent *
Total highway safety penalties are: 11 * Value: 8 0 Durability: 7 7 Highway Control Rating: 8 1 Highway Safety: 7 0 ★★★

Anthem 1998 MHA 33 A3100 SP CU210 D $3900 190 1,500 e 20,000 16,878
Livability Code: SB 30-90
Wheelbase-to-length ratio of 48% is considered ◉ dangerous ○ fatiguing ○ good ○ excellent *
The approximate net payload of 3122 pounds at 16% of GVWR on this model is ○ deficient ○ excessive ○ cautionary ○ good ◉ excellent *
Total highway safety penalties are: 2 * Value: 8 5 Durability: 7 7 Highway Control Rating: 3 7 Highway Safety: 3 5

Note: Safety ratings are based on the assumption that the engineering of the RV has allowed for proper balance by placing fresh, gray, and black holding tanks in a location so as not to change the balance of the RV when the tanks are empty or full. **Always double-check wheelbase, GVWR, and weights at front and rear axles.**

*See Section 1 for details on how conclusions are reached.

Brand	Year	Type	Length	Model	Chassis	Engine	Fuel Type	Average Price per Linear Foot When New	Adjusted Wheel-base	Approx. Towing Capacity	Gross Vehicle Weight Rating	Average Curb Weight
Anthem	1998	MHA	33	A3250	SP	CU210	D	$3900	190	1,500 e	20,000	17,778

Livability Code: SB 30-90
Wheelbase-to-length ratio of 48% is considered ◉ dangerous ○ fatiguing ○ good ○ excellent *
The approximate net payload of 2222 pounds at 11% of GVWR on this model is ○ deficient ○ excessive ○ cautionary ◉ good ○ excellent *
Total highway safety penalties are: 7 *   Value: 8 2   Durability: 7 7   Highway Control Rating: 2 8   Highway Safety: 2 1

Brand	Year	Type	Length	Model	Chassis	Engine	Fuel Type	Avg Price/Linear Foot	Adj. Wheelbase	Approx. Towing	GVWR	Avg Curb Weight
Anthem	1998	MHA	33	A3300	CH	7.4L	G	$3900	228	1,500 e	21,000	16,953

Livability Code: SB 30-90
Wheelbase-to-length ratio of 57% is considered ○ dangerous ○ fatiguing ◉ good ○ excellent *
The approximate net payload of 4047 pounds at 19% of GVWR on this model is ○ deficient ○ excessive ○ cautionary ○ good ◉ excellent *
Total highway safety penalties are: 6 *   Value: 8 3   Durability: 7 7   Highway Control Rating: 1 0 0   Highway Safety: 9 4   ★★★

Anthem	1998	MHA	34	A3300	SP	CU210	D	$3800	208	1,500	20,000	17,221

Livability Code: SB 30-90
Wheelbase-to-length ratio of 50% is considered ◉ dangerous ○ fatiguing ○ good ○ excellent *
The approximate net payload of 2779 pounds at 14% of GVWR on this model is ○ deficient ○ excessive ○ cautionary ◉ good ○ excellent *
Total highway safety penalties are: 2 *   Value: 8 5   Durability: 7 7   Highway Control Rating: 4 2   Highway Safety: 4 0

Anthem	1999	MHA	32	3100	CH	7.4L	G	$2800	208	5,000	21,000	16,628

Livability Code: SB 30-90
Wheelbase-to-length ratio of 54% is considered ○ dangerous ○ fatiguing ◉ good ○ excellent *
The approximate net payload of 4372 pounds at 21% of GVWR on this model is ○ deficient ○ excessive ○ cautionary ○ good ◉ excellent *
Total highway safety penalties are: 6 *   Value: 8 3   Durability: 7 7   Highway Control Rating: 8 7   Highway Safety: 8 1   ★★★

Anthem	1999	MHA	32	XL3100GT	CH	7.4L	G	$2800	208	5,000	21,000	16,748

Livability Code: SB 30-90
Wheelbase-to-length ratio of 54% is considered ○ dangerous ○ fatiguing ◉ good ○ excellent *
The approximate net payload of 4252 pounds at 20% of GVWR on this model is ○ deficient ○ excessive ○ cautionary ○ good ◉ excellent *
Total highway safety penalties are: 6 *   Value: 8 3   Durability: 7 7   Highway Control Rating: 8 8   Highway Safety: 8 2   ★★★

Anthem	1999	MHA	32	3250	CH	7.4L	G	$2800	208	5,000	21,000	17,818

Livability Code: SB 30-90
Wheelbase-to-length ratio of 53% is considered ○ dangerous ◉ fatiguing ○ good ○ excellent *
The approximate net payload of 3182 pounds at 15% of GVWR on this model is ○ deficient ○ excessive ○ cautionary ◉ good ○ excellent *
Total highway safety penalties are: 11 *   Value: 8 0   Durability: 7 7   Highway Control Rating: 7 5   Highway Safety: 6 4   ★★

Anthem	1999	MHA	33	3250	FO	6.8L	G	$2700	208	5,500	20,500	17,200

Livability Code: SB 30-90
Wheelbase-to-length ratio of 53% is considered ○ dangerous ◉ fatiguing ○ good ○ excellent *
The approximate net payload of 3300 pounds at 16% of GVWR on this model is ○ deficient ○ excessive ○ cautionary ○ good ◉ excellent *
Total highway safety penalties are: 7 *   Value: 8 2   Durability: 7 7   Highway Control Rating: 7 6   Highway Safety: 6 9   ★★

Anthem	1999	MHA	33	3100	SP	CU210	D	$3900	190	5,000	20,000	16,927

Livability Code: SB 30-90
Wheelbase-to-length ratio of 48% is considered ◉ dangerous ○ fatiguing ○ good ○ excellent *
The approximate net payload of 3073 pounds at 15% of GVWR on this model is ○ deficient ○ excessive ○ cautionary ◉ good ○ excellent *
Total highway safety penalties are: 2 *   Value: 8 5   Durability: 7 7   Highway Control Rating: 4 5   Highway Safety: 4 3

Anthem	1999	MHA	33	3250	SP	CU210	D	$3900	190	5,000	20,000	17,827

Livability Code: SB 30-90
Wheelbase-to-length ratio of 48% is considered ◉ dangerous ○ fatiguing ○ good ○ excellent *
The approximate net payload of 2173 pounds at 11% of GVWR on this model is ○ deficient ○ excessive ○ cautionary ◉ good ○ excellent *
Total highway safety penalties are: 7 *   Value: 8 2   Durability: 7 7   Highway Control Rating: 3 6   Highway Safety: 2 9

Anthem	1999	MHA	34	3300S	CH	7.4L	G	$2600	228	5,000	21,000	16,888

Livability Code: SB 30-90
Wheelbase-to-length ratio of 56% is considered ○ dangerous ○ fatiguing ◉ good ○ excellent *
The approximate net payload of 4112 pounds at 20% of GVWR on this model is ○ deficient ○ excessive ○ cautionary ○ good ◉ excellent *
Total highway safety penalties are: 7 *   Value: 8 3   Durability: 7 7   Highway Control Rating: 9 9   Highway Safety: 9 2   ★★★

Anthem	1999	MHA	35	3300	SP	CU210	D	$3700	208	5,000	20,000	17,344

Livability Code: SB 30-90
Wheelbase-to-length ratio of 50% is considered ◉ dangerous ○ fatiguing ○ good ○ excellent *
The approximate net payload of 2656 pounds at 13% of GVWR on this model is ○ deficient ○ excessive ○ cautionary ◉ good ○ excellent *
Total highway safety penalties are: 2 *   Value: 8 5   Durability: 7 7   Highway Control Rating: 4 8   Highway Safety: 4 6

Anthem	1999	MHA	35	3300L	SP	CU210	D	$3700	208	5,000	20,000	17,344

Livability Code: SB 30-90
Wheelbase-to-length ratio of 50% is considered ◉ dangerous ○ fatiguing ○ good ○ excellent *
The approximate net payload of 2656 pounds at 13% of GVWR on this model is ○ deficient ○ excessive ○ cautionary ◉ good ○ excellent *
Total highway safety penalties are: 2 *   Value: 8 5   Durability: 7 7   Highway Control Rating: 4 8   Highway Safety: 4 6

Note: Safety ratings are based on the assumption that the engineering of the RV has allowed for proper balance by placing fresh, gray, and black holding tanks in a location so as not to change the balance of the RV when the tanks are empty or full. **Always double-check wheelbase, GVWR, and weights at front and rear axles.**

*See Section 1 for details on how conclusions are reached.

Brand	Year	Type	Length	Model	Chassis	Engine	Fuel Type	Average Price per Linear Foot When New	Adjusted Wheel-base	Approx. Towing Capacity	Gross Vehicle Weight Rating	Average Curb Weight
Baronet	1991	MHA	36	Windsor 35	GI	Cat	D	$4700	216	1,500	28,980	24,071

Livability Code: FT 30-90

Wheelbase-to-length ratio of 51% is considered ○ dangerous ◉ fatiguing ○ good ○ excellent *

The approximate net payload of 4909 pounds at 17% of GVWR on this model is ○ deficient ○ excessive ○ cautionary ○ good ◉ excellent *

Total highway safety penalties are: 2 * Value: **81** Durability: **80** Highway Control Rating: **48** Highway Safety: **46**

Brand	Year	Type	Length	Model	Chassis	Engine	Fuel Type	Price/LF	Wheelbase	Towing	GVWR	Curb Wt
Baronet	1991	MHA	36	Windsor 36	GI	De311	D	$4700	216	1,500	28,980	24,071

Livability Code: FT 30-90

Wheelbase-to-length ratio of 51% is considered ○ dangerous ◉ fatiguing ○ good ○ excellent *

The approximate net payload of 4909 pounds at 17% of GVWR on this model is ○ deficient ○ excessive ○ cautionary ○ good ◉ excellent *

Total highway safety penalties are: 2 * Value: **81** Durability: **80** Highway Control Rating: **48** Highway Safety: **46**

Brand	Year	Type	Length	Model	Chassis	Engine	Fuel Type	Price/LF	Wheelbase	Towing	GVWR	Curb Wt
Baronet	1992	MHA	36	35	GI	Cat	D	$4900	216	5,000	24,980	22,407

Livability Code: FT 30-90

Wheelbase-to-length ratio of 51% is considered ○ dangerous ◉ fatiguing ○ good ○ excellent *

The approximate net payload of 2573 pounds at 10% of GVWR on this model is ○ deficient ○ excessive ○ cautionary ◉ good ○ excellent *

Total highway safety penalties are: 2 * Value: **81** Durability: **80** Highway Control Rating: **35** Highway Safety: **33**

Brand	Year	Type	Length	Model	Chassis	Engine	Fuel Type	Price/LF	Wheelbase	Towing	GVWR	Curb Wt
Barth	1998	MHA	29	29	FO	7.5L	G	$3100	178	1,500	17,000	14,077

Livability Code: SB 30-90

Wheelbase-to-length ratio of 50% is considered ◉ dangerous ○ fatiguing ○ good ○ excellent *

The approximate net payload of 2924 pounds at 17% of GVWR on this model is ○ deficient ○ excessive ○ cautionary ○ good ◉ excellent *

Total highway safety penalties are: 2 * Value: **79** Durability: **75** Highway Control Rating: **47** Highway Safety: **45**

Brand	Year	Type	Length	Model	Chassis	Engine	Fuel Type	Price/LF	Wheelbase	Towing	GVWR	Curb Wt
Barth	1998	MHA	32	32	FO	7.5L	G	$2900	202 T	1,500	22,000	16,819

Livability Code: SB 30-90

Wheelbase-to-length ratio of 52% is considered ○ dangerous ◉ fatiguing ○ good ○ excellent *

The approximate net payload of 5181 pounds at 24% of GVWR on this model is ○ deficient ○ excessive ○ cautionary ○ good ◉ excellent *

Total highway safety penalties are: 4 * Value: **78** Durability: **75** Highway Control Rating: **60** Highway Safety: **56** ★

Brand	Year	Type	Length	Model	Chassis	Engine	Fuel Type	Price/LF	Wheelbase	Towing	GVWR	Curb Wt
Barth	1998	MHA	34	XL34	SP	CU275	D	$4200	208	1,500	26,000	23,098

Livability Code: SB 30-90

Wheelbase-to-length ratio of 51% is considered ○ dangerous ◉ fatiguing ○ good ○ excellent *

The approximate net payload of 2902 pounds at 11% of GVWR on this model is ○ deficient ○ excessive ○ cautionary ◉ good ○ excellent *

Total highway safety penalties are: 2 * Value: **79** Durability: **75** Highway Control Rating: **38** Highway Safety: **36**

Brand	Year	Type	Length	Model	Chassis	Engine	Fuel Type	Price/LF	Wheelbase	Towing	GVWR	Curb Wt
Barth	1998	MHA	37	XL36	SP	CU325	D	$4200	238	1,500	29,000	25,370

Livability Code: SB 30-90

Wheelbase-to-length ratio of 54% is considered ○ dangerous ○ fatiguing ◉ good ○ excellent *

The approximate net payload of 3630 pounds at 13% of GVWR on this model is ○ deficient ○ excessive ○ cautionary ◉ good ○ excellent *

Total highway safety penalties are: 2 * Value: **79** Durability: **75** Highway Control Rating: **79** Highway Safety: **77** ★★★

Brand	Year	Type	Length	Model	Chassis	Engine	Fuel Type	Price/LF	Wheelbase	Towing	GVWR	Curb Wt
Barth	1998	MHA	38	XL38	SP	CU325	D	$4300	257	1,500	33,000	27,816

Livability Code: SB 30-90

Wheelbase-to-length ratio of 56% is considered ○ dangerous ○ fatiguing ◉ good ○ excellent *

The approximate net payload of 5184 pounds at 16% of GVWR on this model is ○ deficient ○ excessive ○ cautionary ○ good ◉ excellent *

Total highway safety penalties are: 2 * Value: **79** Durability: **75** Highway Control Rating: **97** Highway Safety: **95** ★★★

Brand	Year	Type	Length	Model	Chassis	Engine	Fuel Type	Price/LF	Wheelbase	Towing	GVWR	Curb Wt
Barth	1998	MHA	40	XL40	SP	CU400	D	$4500	267	1,500	36,200	29,980

Livability Code: SB 30-90

Wheelbase-to-length ratio of 56% is considered ○ dangerous ○ fatiguing ◉ good ○ excellent *

The approximate net payload of 6220 pounds at 17% of GVWR on this model is ○ deficient ○ excessive ○ cautionary ○ good ◉ excellent *

Total highway safety penalties are: 2 * Value: **79** Durability: **75** Highway Control Rating: **96** Highway Safety: **94** ★★★

Brand	Year	Type	Length	Model	Chassis	Engine	Fuel Type	Price/LF	Wheelbase	Towing	GVWR	Curb Wt
Bigfoot	1995	MHC	20	C20	FO		G	$2500	138	3,500	10,500	9,267

Livability Code: VA 30-90

Wheelbase-to-length ratio of 58% is considered ○ dangerous ○ fatiguing ○ good ◉ excellent *

The approximate net payload of 1233 pounds at 12% of GVWR on this model is ○ deficient ○ excessive ○ cautionary ◉ good ○ excellent *

Total highway safety penalties are: 2 * Value: **86** Durability: **80** Highway Control Rating: **93** Highway Safety: **91** ★★★★

Brand	Year	Type	Length	Model	Chassis	Engine	Fuel Type	Price/LF	Wheelbase	Towing	GVWR	Curb Wt
Bigfoot	1995	MHC	29	C28	FO		G	$1800	176	2,500	11,500	10,317

Livability Code: VA 30-90

Wheelbase-to-length ratio of 51% is considered ○ dangerous ◉ fatiguing ○ good ○ excellent *

The approximate net payload of 1183 pounds at 10% of GVWR on this model is ○ deficient ○ excessive ○ cautionary ◉ good ○ excellent *

Total highway safety penalties are: 2 * Value: **86** Durability: **80** Highway Control Rating: **53** Highway Safety: **51** ★

Brand	Year	Type	Length	Model	Chassis	Engine	Fuel Type	Price/LF	Wheelbase	Towing	GVWR	Curb Wt
Bigfoot	1996	MHC	20	C20	FO		G	$2500	138	1,500	11,300	9,328

Livability Code: VA 30-90

Wheelbase-to-length ratio of 58% is considered ○ dangerous ○ fatiguing ○ good ◉ excellent *

The approximate net payload of 1972 pounds at 17% of GVWR on this model is ○ deficient ○ excessive ○ cautionary ○ good ◉ excellent *

Total highway safety penalties are: 2 * Value: **86** Durability: **80** Highway Control Rating: **100** Highway Safety: **98** ★★★★

Note: Safety ratings are based on the assumption that the engineering of the RV has allowed for proper balance by placing fresh, gray, and black holding tanks in a location so as not to change the balance of the RV when the tanks are empty or full. **Always double-check wheelbase, GVWR, and weights at front and rear axles.**

*See Section 1 for details on how conclusions are reached.

Brand	Year	Type	Length	Model	Chassis	Engine	Fuel Type	Average Price per Linear Foot When New	Adjusted Wheelbase	Approx. Towing Capacity	Gross Vehicle Weight Rating	Average Curb Weight
Bigfoot	1996	MHC	25	C26	FO		G	$2100	158	1,500	12,600	9,419

Livability Code: VA 30-90

Wheelbase-to-length ratio of 54% is considered ○ dangerous ○ fatiguing ● good ○ excellent *

The approximate net payload of 3181 pounds at 25% of GVWR on this model is ○ deficient ○ excessive ○ cautionary ● good ○ excellent *

Total highway safety penalties are: 2 *   Value: 86   Durability: 80   Highway Control Rating: 82   Highway Safety: 80   ★★★★

| Bigfoot | 1996 | MHC | 27 | C26 | FO | | G | $2000 | 176 | 1,400 | 12,600 | 10,072 |

Livability Code: VA 30-90

Wheelbase-to-length ratio of 55% is considered ○ dangerous ○ fatiguing ● good ○ excellent *

The approximate net payload of 2528 pounds at 20% of GVWR on this model is ○ deficient ○ excessive ○ cautionary ○ good ● excellent *

Total highway safety penalties are: 2 *   Value: 86   Durability: 80   Highway Control Rating: 95   Highway Safety: 93   ★★★★

| Bigfoot | 1996 | MHC | 29 | C28 | FO | | G | $1800 | 176 | 1,400 | 12,600 | 10,455 |

Livability Code: VA 30-90

Wheelbase-to-length ratio of 51% is considered ○ dangerous ● fatiguing ○ good ○ excellent *

The approximate net payload of 2145 pounds at 17% of GVWR on this model is ○ deficient ○ excessive ○ cautionary ○ good ● excellent *

Total highway safety penalties are: 2 *   Value: 86   Durability: 80   Highway Control Rating: 65   Highway Safety: 63   ★★

| Bigfoot | 1999 | MHC | 30 | C29 garage | FO | 6.8L | G | $1800 | 200 | 1,500 e | 14,050 | 12,698 |

Livability Code: WE30-80

Wheelbase-to-length ratio of 56% is considered ○ dangerous ○ fatiguing ● good ○ excellent *

The approximate net payload of 1352 pounds at 10% of GVWR on this model is ○ deficient ○ excessive ○ cautionary ● good ○ excellent *

Total highway safety penalties are: 2 *   Value: 86   Durability: 80   Highway Control Rating: 84   Highway Safety: 82   ★★★★

| Born Free | 1990 | MHC | 26 | President FT26 | FO | 5.8L | G | $1900 | 176 | 1,500 | 11,500 | 10,843 |

Livability Code: RT 30-90

Wheelbase-to-length ratio of 56% is considered ○ dangerous ○ fatiguing ● good ○ excellent *

The approximate net payload of 657 pounds at 6% of GVWR on this model is ● deficient ○ excessive ○ cautionary ○ good ○ excellent *

Total highway safety penalties are: 2 *   Value: 93   Durability: 84   Highway Control Rating: 62   Highway Safety: 60   ★

| Born Free | 1992 | MHC | 26 | President 26 | FO | 7.5L | G | $2000 | 176 | 1,500 | 14,050 | 11,690 |

Livability Code: RT 30-90

Wheelbase-to-length ratio of 56% is considered ○ dangerous ○ fatiguing ● good ○ excellent *

The approximate net payload of 2360 pounds at 17% of GVWR on this model is ○ deficient ○ excessive ○ cautionary ○ good ● excellent *

Total highway safety penalties are: 2 *   Value: 93   Durability: 84   Highway Control Rating: 98   Highway Safety: 96   ★★★★

| Born Free | 1995 | MHC | 21 | 21 President | FO | 7.5L | G | $2800 | 158 | 1,500 | 11,500 | 9,742 |

Livability Code: RT 30-90

Wheelbase-to-length ratio of 63% is considered ○ dangerous ○ fatiguing ○ good ● excellent *

The approximate net payload of 1758 pounds at 15% of GVWR on this model is ○ deficient ○ excessive ○ cautionary ● good ○ excellent *

Total highway safety penalties are: 2 *   Value: 93   Durability: 84   Highway Control Rating: 100   Highway Safety: 98   ★★★★

| Born Free | 1995 | MHC | 21 | 21 President Dsl | FO | 7.3L | D | $3000 | 158 | 1,500 | 11,500 | 9,742 |

Livability Code: RT 30-90

Wheelbase-to-length ratio of 63% is considered ○ dangerous ○ fatiguing ○ good ● excellent *

The approximate net payload of 1758 pounds at 15% of GVWR on this model is ○ deficient ○ excessive ○ cautionary ● good ○ excellent *

Total highway safety penalties are: 2 *   Value: 93   Durability: 84   Highway Control Rating: 100   Highway Safety: 98   ★★★★

| Born Free | 1995 | MHC | 21 | 21 BFT | FO | 7.5L | G | $2600 | 158 | 1,500 | 11,500 | 9,173 |

Livability Code: RT 30-90

Wheelbase-to-length ratio of 63% is considered ○ dangerous ○ fatiguing ○ good ● excellent *

The approximate net payload of 2328 pounds at 20% of GVWR on this model is ○ deficient ○ excessive ○ cautionary ○ good ● excellent *

Total highway safety penalties are: 2 *   Value: 93   Durability: 84   Highway Control Rating: 100   Highway Safety: 98   ★★★★

| Born Free | 1995 | MHC | 21 | 21 BFT Dsl | FO | 7.3L | D | $2900 | 158 | 1,500 | 11,500 | 9,173 |

Livability Code: RT 30-90

Wheelbase-to-length ratio of 63% is considered ○ dangerous ○ fatiguing ○ good ● excellent *

The approximate net payload of 2328 pounds at 20% of GVWR on this model is ○ deficient ○ excessive ○ cautionary ○ good ● excellent *

Total highway safety penalties are: 2 *   Value: 93   Durability: 84   Highway Control Rating: 100   Highway Safety: 98   ★★★★

| Born Free | 1995 | MHC | 23 | 23 BFT | FO | 7.5L | G | $2500 | 158 | 2,500 | 11,500 | 9,618 |

Livability Code: RT 30-90

Wheelbase-to-length ratio of 57% is considered ○ dangerous ○ fatiguing ● good ○ excellent *

The approximate net payload of 1883 pounds at 16% of GVWR on this model is ○ deficient ○ excessive ○ cautionary ○ good ● excellent *

Total highway safety penalties are: 2 *   Value: 93   Durability: 84   Highway Control Rating: 100   Highway Safety: 98   ★★★★

| Born Free | 1995 | MHC | 23 | 23 BFT Dsl | FO | 7.3L | D | $2700 | 158 | 1,500 | 11,500 | 9,618 |

Livability Code: RT 30-90

Wheelbase-to-length ratio of 57% is considered ○ dangerous ○ fatiguing ● good ○ excellent *

The approximate net payload of 1883 pounds at 16% of GVWR on this model is ○ deficient ○ excessive ○ cautionary ○ good ● excellent *

Total highway safety penalties are: 2 *   Value: 93   Durability: 84   Highway Control Rating: 100   Highway Safety: 98   ★★★★

Note: Safety ratings are based on the assumption that the engineering of the RV has allowed for proper balance by placing fresh, gray, and black holding tanks in a location so as not to change the balance of the RV when the tanks are empty or full. **Always double-check wheelbase, GVWR, and weights at front and rear axles.**

*See Section 1 for details on how conclusions are reached.

Brand	Year	Type	Length	Model	Chassis	Engine	Fuel Type	Average Price per Linear Foot When New	Adjusted Wheelbase	Approx. Towing Capacity	Gross Vehicle Weight Rating	Average Curb Weight

Born Free 1995 MHC 24 24 President FO 7.5L G $2500 158 2,500 11,500 10,465
Livability Code: RT 30-90
Wheelbase-to-length ratio of 55% is considered ○ dangerous ○ fatiguing ◉ good ○ excellent *
The approximate net payload of 1035 pounds at 9% of GVWR on this model is ○ deficient ○ excessive ◉ cautionary ○ good ○ excellent *
Total highway safety penalties are: 2 *   Value: 9 3   Durability: 8 4   Highway Control Rating: 7 6   Highway Safety: 7 4   ★★★

Born Free 1995 MHC 24 24 President Dsl FO 7.3L D $2800 158 1,500 11,500 10,465
Livability Code: RT 30-90
Wheelbase-to-length ratio of 55% is considered ○ dangerous ○ fatiguing ◉ good ○ excellent *
The approximate net payload of 1035 pounds at 9% of GVWR on this model is ○ deficient ○ excessive ◉ cautionary ○ good ○ excellent *
Total highway safety penalties are: 2 *   Value: 9 3   Durability: 8 4   Highway Control Rating: 7 6   Highway Safety: 7 4   ★★★

Born Free 1995 MHC 26 26 President FO 7.5L G $2600 176 3,500 11,500 10,990
Livability Code: RT 30-90
Wheelbase-to-length ratio of 56% is considered ○ dangerous ○ fatiguing ◉ good ○ excellent *
The approximate net payload of 510 pounds at 4% of GVWR on this model is ◉ deficient ○ excessive ○ cautionary ○ good ○ excellent *
Total highway safety penalties are: 2 *   Value: 9 3   Durability: 8 4   Highway Control Rating: 6 1   Highway Safety: 5 9   ★

Born Free 1995 MHC 26 26 President Dsl FO 7.3L D $2800 176 1,500 11,500 10,990
Livability Code: RT 30-90
Wheelbase-to-length ratio of 56% is considered ○ dangerous ○ fatiguing ◉ good ○ excellent *
The approximate net payload of 510 pounds at 4% of GVWR on this model is ◉ deficient ○ excessive ○ cautionary ○ good ○ excellent *
Total highway safety penalties are: 2 *   Value: 9 3   Durability: 8 4   Highway Control Rating: 6 1   Highway Safety: 5 9   ★

Born Free 1996 MHC   accurate specs n/a   ?
Livability Code: RT 30-90
Wheelbase-to-length ratio of   ? is considered ○ dangerous ○ fatiguing ○ good ○ excellent *
The approximate net payload of   pounds at   of GVWR on this model is ○ deficient ○ excessive ○ cautionary ○ good ○ excellent *
Total highway safety penalties are: 0 *   Value: 0   Durability: 8 4   Highway Control Rating: 0   Highway Safety: 0

Born Free 1997 MHC 21 President 21 FO 5.4L G $2600 158 1,500 11,500 9,742
Livability Code: RT 30-90
Wheelbase-to-length ratio of 63% is considered ○ dangerous ○ fatiguing ○ good ◉ excellent *
The approximate net payload of 1758 pounds at 15% of GVWR on this model is ○ deficient ○ excessive ○ cautionary ◉ good ○ excellent *
Total highway safety penalties are: 2 *   Value: 9 3   Durability: 8 4   Highway Control Rating: 1 0 0   Highway Safety: 9 8   ★★★★

Born Free 1997 MHC 21 President 21 FO 7.3L D $2900 158 1,500 11,500 9,742
Livability Code: RT 30-90
Wheelbase-to-length ratio of 63% is considered ○ dangerous ○ fatiguing ○ good ◉ excellent *
The approximate net payload of 1758 pounds at 15% of GVWR on this model is ○ deficient ○ excessive ○ cautionary ◉ good ○ excellent *
Total highway safety penalties are: 2 *   Value: 9 3   Durability: 8 4   Highway Control Rating: 1 0 0   Highway Safety: 9 8   ★★★★

Born Free 1997 MHC 23 BFT 23 FO 5.4L G $2500 158 1,500 11,500 10,020
Livability Code: RT 30-90
Wheelbase-to-length ratio of 57% is considered ○ dangerous ○ fatiguing ◉ good ○ excellent *
The approximate net payload of 1480 pounds at 13% of GVWR on this model is ○ deficient ○ excessive ○ cautionary ◉ good ○ excellent *
Total highway safety penalties are: 2 *   Value: 9 3   Durability: 8 4   Highway Control Rating: 9 4   Highway Safety: 9 2   ★★★★

Born Free 1997 MHC 23 President 23 FO 7.3L D $2700 158 1,500 11,500 10,241
Livability Code: RT 30-90
Wheelbase-to-length ratio of 57% is considered ○ dangerous ○ fatiguing ◉ good ○ excellent *
The approximate net payload of 1259 pounds at 11% of GVWR on this model is ○ deficient ○ excessive ○ cautionary ◉ good ○ excellent *
Total highway safety penalties are: 2 *   Value: 9 3   Durability: 8 4   Highway Control Rating: 9 1   Highway Safety: 8 9   ★★★★

Born Free 1997 MHC 24 President 24 FO 7.3L D $2800 158 1,500 11,500 10,490
Livability Code: RT 30-90
Wheelbase-to-length ratio of 55% is considered ○ dangerous ○ fatiguing ◉ good ○ excellent *
The approximate net payload of 1010 pounds at 9% of GVWR on this model is ○ deficient ○ excessive ◉ cautionary ○ good ○ excellent *
Total highway safety penalties are: 2 *   Value: 9 3   Durability: 8 4   Highway Control Rating: 7 5   Highway Safety: 7 3   ★★★

Born Free 1997 MHC 25 President 24 FO 5.4L G $2500 158 1,500 11,500 10,715
Livability Code: RT 30-90
Wheelbase-to-length ratio of 53% is considered ○ dangerous ◉ fatiguing ○ good ○ excellent *
The approximate net payload of 785 pounds at 7% of GVWR on this model is ○ deficient ○ excessive ◉ cautionary ○ good ○ excellent *
Total highway safety penalties are: 2 *   Value: 9 3   Durability: 8 4   Highway Control Rating: 4 8   Highway Safety: 4 6

Born Free 1997 MHC 26 President 26 FO 5.4L G $2600 176 1,500 11,500 10,990
Livability Code: RT 30-90
Wheelbase-to-length ratio of 56% is considered ○ dangerous ○ fatiguing ◉ good ○ excellent *
The approximate net payload of 510 pounds at 4% of GVWR on this model is ◉ deficient ○ excessive ○ cautionary ○ good ○ excellent *
Total highway safety penalties are: 2 *   Value: 9 3   Durability: 8 4   Highway Control Rating: 6 1   Highway Safety: 5 9   ★

Note: Safety ratings are based on the assumption that the engineering of the RV has allowed for proper balance by placing fresh, gray, and black holding tanks in a location so as not to change the balance of the RV when the tanks are empty or full. **Always double-check wheelbase, GVWR, and weights at front and rear axles.**

*See Section 1 for details on how conclusions are reached.

Brand	Year	Type	Length	Model	Chassis	Engine	Fuel Type	Average Price per Linear Foot When New	Adjusted Wheelbase	Approx. Towing Capacity	Gross Vehicle Weight Rating	Average Curb Weight
Born Free	1997	MHC	26	President 26	FO	7.3L	D	$2800	176	1,500	11,500	10,990

Livability Code: RT 30-90
Wheelbase-to-length ratio of 56% is considered ○ dangerous ○ fatiguing ◉ good ○ excellent *
The approximate net payload of 510 pounds at 4% of GVWR on this model is ◉ deficient ○ excessive ○ cautionary ○ good ○ excellent *
Total highway safety penalties are: 2 *   Value: 9 3   Durability: 8 4   Highway Control Rating: 6 1   Highway Safety: 5 9   ★

Born Free	1998	MHC	22	Cub 21	FO	5.4L	G	$3000	138	1,500 e	10,500	9,305

Livability Code: RT 30-90
Wheelbase-to-length ratio of 53% is considered ○ dangerous ◉ fatiguing ○ good ○ excellent *
The approximate net payload of 1195 pounds at 11% of GVWR on this model is ○ deficient ○ excessive ○ cautionary ◉ good ○ excellent *
Total highway safety penalties are: 2 *   Value: 9 3   Durability: 8 4   Highway Control Rating: 6 7   Highway Safety: 6 5   ★★

Born Free	1998	MHC	22	Cub 21 op eng	FO	7.3L	D	$3000	138	1,500 e	10,500	9,805

Livability Code: RT 30-90
Wheelbase-to-length ratio of 53% is considered ○ dangerous ◉ fatiguing ○ good ○ excellent *
The approximate net payload of 695 pounds at 7% of GVWR on this model is ○ deficient ○ excessive ◉ cautionary ○ good ○ excellent *
Total highway safety penalties are: 2 *   Value: 9 3   Durability: 8 4   Highway Control Rating: 4 8   Highway Safety: 4 6

Born Free	1998	MHC	22	BFT 21	FO	5.4L	G	$3000	158	8,500	11,500	9,360

Livability Code: RT 30-90
Wheelbase-to-length ratio of 60% is considered ○ dangerous ○ fatiguing ○ good ◉ excellent *
The approximate net payload of 2140 pounds at 19% of GVWR on this model is ○ deficient ○ excessive ○ cautionary ○ good ◉ excellent *
Total highway safety penalties are: 2 *   Value: 9 3   Durability: 8 4   Highway Control Rating: 1 0 0   Highway Safety: 9 8   ★★★★

Born Free	1998	MHC	22	BFT 21 op eng	FO	7.3L	D	$3000	158	8,500	11,500	10,060

Livability Code: RT 30-90
Wheelbase-to-length ratio of 60% is considered ○ dangerous ○ fatiguing ○ good ◉ excellent *
The approximate net payload of 1440 pounds at 13% of GVWR on this model is ○ deficient ○ excessive ○ cautionary ◉ good ○ excellent *
Total highway safety penalties are: 2 *   Value: 9 3   Durability: 8 4   Highway Control Rating: 1 0 0   Highway Safety: 9 8   ★★★★

Born Free	1998	MHC	22	President 21	FO	5.4L	G	$3000	158	8,500	11,500	9,856

Livability Code: RT 30-90
Wheelbase-to-length ratio of 60% is considered ○ dangerous ○ fatiguing ○ good ◉ excellent *
The approximate net payload of 1644 pounds at 14% of GVWR on this model is ○ deficient ○ excessive ○ cautionary ○ good ◉ excellent *
Total highway safety penalties are: 2 *   Value: 9 3   Durability: 8 4   Highway Control Rating: 1 0 0   Highway Safety: 9 8   ★★★★

Born Free	1998	MHC	22	President 21 op eng	FO	7.3L	D	$3000	158	8,500	11,500	10,556

Livability Code: RT 30-90
Wheelbase-to-length ratio of 60% is considered ○ dangerous ○ fatiguing ○ good ◉ excellent *
The approximate net payload of 944 pounds at 8% of GVWR on this model is ○ deficient ○ excessive ◉ cautionary ○ good ○ excellent *
Total highway safety penalties are: 2 *   Value: 9 3   Durability: 8 4   Highway Control Rating: 8 6   Highway Safety: 8 4   ★★★★

Born Free	1998	MHC	24	BFT 23	FO	5.4L	G	$2800	158	8,500	11,500	10,129

Livability Code: RT 30-90
Wheelbase-to-length ratio of 56% is considered ○ dangerous ○ fatiguing ◉ good ○ excellent *
The approximate net payload of 1371 pounds at 12% of GVWR on this model is ○ deficient ○ excessive ○ cautionary ◉ good ○ excellent *
Total highway safety penalties are: 2 *   Value: 9 3   Durability: 8 4   Highway Control Rating: 8 7   Highway Safety: 8 5   ★★★★

Born Free	1998	MHC	24	BFT 23 op eng	FO	7.3L	D	$2800	158	8,500	11,500	10,829

Livability Code: RT 30-90
Wheelbase-to-length ratio of 56% is considered ○ dangerous ○ fatiguing ◉ good ○ excellent *
The approximate net payload of 671 pounds at 6% of GVWR on this model is ◉ deficient ○ excessive ○ cautionary ○ good ○ excellent *
Total highway safety penalties are: 2 *   Value: 9 3   Durability: 8 4   Highway Control Rating: 5 9   Highway Safety: 5 7   ★

Born Free	1998	MHC	25	President 24	FO	5.4L	G	$2600	158	8,500	11,500	10,432

Livability Code: RT 30-90
Wheelbase-to-length ratio of 53% is considered ○ dangerous ◉ fatiguing ○ good ○ excellent *
The approximate net payload of 1068 pounds at 9% of GVWR on this model is ○ deficient ○ excessive ◉ cautionary ○ good ○ excellent *
Total highway safety penalties are: 2 *   Value: 9 3   Durability: 8 4   Highway Control Rating: 6 0   Highway Safety: 5 8   ★

Born Free	1998	MHC	25	President 24 op eng	FO	7.3L	D	$2600	158	8,500	11,500	11,132

Livability Code: RT 30-90
Wheelbase-to-length ratio of 53% is considered ○ dangerous ◉ fatiguing ○ good ○ excellent *
The approximate net payload of 368 pounds at 3% of GVWR on this model is ◉ deficient ○ excessive ○ cautionary ○ good ○ excellent *
Total highway safety penalties are: 2 *   Value: 9 3   Durability: 8 4   Highway Control Rating: 3 9   Highway Safety: 3 7

Born Free	1998	MHC	25	President 24 opch	FO	5.4L	G	$2600	158	5,950	14,050	10,782

Livability Code: RT 30-90
Wheelbase-to-length ratio of 53% is considered ○ dangerous ◉ fatiguing ○ good ○ excellent *
The approximate net payload of 3268 pounds at 23% of GVWR on this model is ○ deficient ○ excessive ○ cautionary ○ good ◉ excellent *
Total highway safety penalties are: 2 *   Value: 9 3   Durability: 8 4   Highway Control Rating: 7 7   Highway Safety: 7 5   ★★★

Note: Safety ratings are based on the assumption that the engineering of the RV has allowed for proper balance by placing fresh, gray, and black holding tanks in a location so as not to change the balance of the RV when the tanks are empty or full. **Always double-check wheelbase, GVWR, and weights at front and rear axles.**

*See Section 1 for details on how conclusions are reached.

Brand	Year	Type	Length	Model	Chassis	Engine	Fuel Type	Average Price per Linear Foot When New	Adjusted Wheelbase	Approx. Towing Capacity	Gross Vehicle Weight Rating	Average Curb Weight
Born Free	**1998**	MHC	25	President 24	FO	7.3L	D	$2600	158	5,950	14,050	10,982

Livability Code: RT 30-90   Wheelbase-to-length ratio of 53% is considered ○ dangerous ● fatiguing ○ good ○ excellent *

The approximate net payload of 3068 pounds at 22% of GVWR on this model is ○ deficient ○ excessive ○ cautionary ○ good ● excellent *

Total highway safety penalties are: 2 *   Value: 9 3   Durability: 8 4   Highway Control Rating: 7 9   Highway Safety: 7 7   ★★★

Brand	Year	Type	Length	Model	Chassis	Engine	Fuel Type	Avg Price/Ft	Wheelbase	Towing	GVWR	Curb Wt
Born Free	**1998**	MHC	27	President 26	FO	5.4L	G	$2400	176	5,950	14,050	11,617

Livability Code: RT 30-90   Wheelbase-to-length ratio of 55% is considered ○ dangerous ○ fatiguing ● good ○ excellent *

The approximate net payload of 2433 pounds at 17% of GVWR on this model is ○ deficient ○ excessive ○ cautionary ○ good ● excellent *

Total highway safety penalties are: 2 *   Value: 9 3   Durability: 8 4   Highway Control Rating: 9 3   Highway Safety: 9 1   ★★★★

Brand	Year	Type	Length	Model	Chassis	Engine	Fuel Type	Avg Price/Ft	Wheelbase	Towing	GVWR	Curb Wt
Born Free	**1998**	MHC	27	President 26 op eng	FO	7.3L	D	$2400	176	5,950	14,050	12,317

Livability Code: RT 30-90   Wheelbase-to-length ratio of 55% is considered ○ dangerous ○ fatiguing ● good ○ excellent *

The approximate net payload of 1733 pounds at 12% of GVWR on this model is ○ deficient ○ excessive ○ cautionary ● good ○ excellent *

Total highway safety penalties are: 2 *   Value: 9 3   Durability: 8 4   Highway Control Rating: 8 4   Highway Safety: 8 2   ★★★★

Brand	Year	Type	Length	Model	Chassis	Engine	Fuel Type	Avg Price/Ft	Wheelbase	Towing	GVWR	Curb Wt
Born Free	**1999**	MHC	22	21 BFT	FO	6.8L	G	$3000	138	9,500	10,500	9,042

Livability Code: RT 30-90   Wheelbase-to-length ratio of 53% is considered ○ dangerous ● fatiguing ○ good ○ excellent *

The approximate net payload of 1458 pounds at 14% of GVWR on this model is ○ deficient ○ excessive ○ cautionary ● good ○ excellent *

Total highway safety penalties are: 2 *   Value: 9 3   Durability: 8 4   Highway Control Rating: 7 2   Highway Safety: 7 0   ★★★

Brand	Year	Type	Length	Model	Chassis	Engine	Fuel Type	Avg Price/Ft	Wheelbase	Towing	GVWR	Curb Wt
Born Free	**1999**	MHC	23	22 President RB	FO	6.8L	G	$2900	158	8,500	11,500	10,004

Livability Code: RT 30-90   Wheelbase-to-length ratio of 58% is considered ○ dangerous ○ fatiguing ○ good ● excellent *

The approximate net payload of 1496 pounds at 13% of GVWR on this model is ○ deficient ○ excessive ○ cautionary ● good ○ excellent *

Total highway safety penalties are: 2 *   Value: 9 3   Durability: 8 4   Highway Control Rating: 9 6   Highway Safety: 9 4   ★★★★

Brand	Year	Type	Length	Model	Chassis	Engine	Fuel Type	Avg Price/Ft	Wheelbase	Towing	GVWR	Curb Wt
Born Free	**1999**	MHC	23	22 President RD	FO	6.8L	G	$2900	158	8,500	11,500	10,066

Livability Code: RT 30-90   Wheelbase-to-length ratio of 57% is considered ○ dangerous ○ fatiguing ● good ○ excellent *

The approximate net payload of 1434 pounds at 12% of GVWR on this model is ○ deficient ○ excessive ○ cautionary ● good ○ excellent *

Total highway safety penalties are: 2 *   Value: 9 3   Durability: 8 4   Highway Control Rating: 9 3   Highway Safety: 9 1   ★★★★

Brand	Year	Type	Length	Model	Chassis	Engine	Fuel Type	Avg Price/Ft	Wheelbase	Towing	GVWR	Curb Wt
Born Free	**1999**	MHC	24	23 President RK	FO	6.8L	G	$2800	158	8,500	11,500	10,208

Livability Code: RT 30-90   Wheelbase-to-length ratio of 56% is considered ○ dangerous ○ fatiguing ● good ○ excellent *

The approximate net payload of 1292 pounds at 11% of GVWR on this model is ○ deficient ○ excessive ○ cautionary ● good ○ excellent *

Total highway safety penalties are: 2 *   Value: 9 3   Durability: 8 4   Highway Control Rating: 8 5   Highway Safety: 8 3   ★★★★

Brand	Year	Type	Length	Model	Chassis	Engine	Fuel Type	Avg Price/Ft	Wheelbase	Towing	GVWR	Curb Wt
Born Free	**1999**	MHC	24	23 President RK opch	FO	6.8L	G	$2800	158	5,950	14,050	10,748

Livability Code: RT 30-90   Wheelbase-to-length ratio of 56% is considered ○ dangerous ○ fatiguing ● good ○ excellent *

The approximate net payload of 3302 pounds at 24% of GVWR on this model is ○ deficient ○ excessive ○ cautionary ○ good ● excellent *

Total highway safety penalties are: 2 *   Value: 9 3   Durability: 8 4   Highway Control Rating: 9 5   Highway Safety: 9 3   ★★★★

Brand	Year	Type	Length	Model	Chassis	Engine	Fuel Type	Avg Price/Ft	Wheelbase	Towing	GVWR	Curb Wt
Born Free	**1999**	MHC	25	24 President RB	FO	6.8L	G	$2600	158	8,500	11,500	10,408

Livability Code: RT 30-90   Wheelbase-to-length ratio of 53% is considered ○ dangerous ● fatiguing ○ good ○ excellent *

The approximate net payload of 1092 pounds at 9% of GVWR on this model is ○ deficient ○ excessive ● cautionary ○ good ○ excellent *

Total highway safety penalties are: 2 *   Value: 9 3   Durability: 8 4   Highway Control Rating: 6 0   Highway Safety: 5 8   ★

Brand	Year	Type	Length	Model	Chassis	Engine	Fuel Type	Avg Price/Ft	Wheelbase	Towing	GVWR	Curb Wt
Born Free	**1999**	MHC	25	24 President RB opch	FO	6.8L	G	$2600	158	5,950	14,050	10,948

Livability Code: RT 30-90   Wheelbase-to-length ratio of 53% is considered ○ dangerous ● fatiguing ○ good ○ excellent *

The approximate net payload of 3102 pounds at 22% of GVWR on this model is ○ deficient ○ excessive ○ cautionary ○ good ● excellent *

Total highway safety penalties are: 2 *   Value: 9 3   Durability: 8 4   Highway Control Rating: 7 9   Highway Safety: 7 7   ★★★

Brand	Year	Type	Length	Model	Chassis	Engine	Fuel Type	Avg Price/Ft	Wheelbase	Towing	GVWR	Curb Wt
Born Free	**1999**	MHC	25	24 President RSB	FO	6.8L	G	$2600	158	8,500	11,500	10,686

Livability Code: RT 30-90   Wheelbase-to-length ratio of 53% is considered ○ dangerous ● fatiguing ○ good ○ excellent *

The approximate net payload of 814 pounds at 7% of GVWR on this model is ○ deficient ○ excessive ● cautionary ○ good ○ excellent *

Total highway safety penalties are: 2 *   Value: 9 3   Durability: 8 4   Highway Control Rating: 4 8   Highway Safety: 4 6

Brand	Year	Type	Length	Model	Chassis	Engine	Fuel Type	Avg Price/Ft	Wheelbase	Towing	GVWR	Curb Wt
Born Free	**1999**	MHC	25	24 Pres RSB opch	FO	6.8L	G	$2600	158	5,950	14,050	11,226

Livability Code: RT 30-90   Wheelbase-to-length ratio of 53% is considered ○ dangerous ● fatiguing ○ good ○ excellent *

The approximate net payload of 2824 pounds at 20% of GVWR on this model is ○ deficient ○ excessive ○ cautionary ○ good ● excellent *

Total highway safety penalties are: 2 *   Value: 9 3   Durability: 8 4   Highway Control Rating: 8 1   Highway Safety: 7 9   ★★★

Note: Safety ratings are based on the assumption that the engineering of the RV has allowed for proper balance by placing fresh, gray, and black holding tanks in a location so as not to change the balance of the RV when the tanks are empty or full. **Always double-check wheelbase, GVWR, and weights at front and rear axles.**

*See Section 1 for details on how conclusions are reached.

Section 2: The Ratings

Brand	Year	Type	Length	Model	Chassis	Engine	Fuel Type	Average Price per Linear Foot When New	Adjusted Wheelbase	Approx. Towing Capacity	Gross Vehicle Weight Rating	Average Curb Weight
Born Free	1999	MHC	27	26 President RB	FO	6.8L	G	$2400	176	5,950	14,050	11,611

Livability Code: RT 30-90
Wheelbase-to-length ratio of 55% is considered ○ dangerous ○ fatiguing ◉ good ○ excellent*
The approximate net payload of 2439 pounds at 17% of GVWR on this model is ○ deficient ○ excessive ○ cautionary ○ good ◉ excellent*
Total highway safety penalties are: 2*　Value: 9 3　Durability: 8 4　Highway Control Rating: 9 3　Highway Safety: 9 1　★★★★

Brand	Year	Type	Length	Model	Chassis	Engine	Fuel Type	Avg Price/Ln Ft	Adj Wheelbase	Towing Cap	GVWR	Avg Curb Wt
Born Free	1999	MHC	27	26 President RSB	FO	6.8L	G	$2400	176	5,950	14,050	11,618

Livability Code: RT 30-90
Wheelbase-to-length ratio of 55% is considered ○ dangerous ○ fatiguing ◉ good ○ excellent*
The approximate net payload of 2432 pounds at 17% of GVWR on this model is ○ deficient ○ excessive ○ cautionary ○ good ◉ excellent*
Total highway safety penalties are: 2*　Value: 9 3　Durability: 8 4　Highway Control Rating: 9 3　Highway Safety: 9 1　★★★★

Brave	1992	MHA	23	23RC opch,op eng	CH	GM6.5	D	$1800	137	1,500	12,300	10,430

Livability Code: VA 30-90
Wheelbase-to-length ratio of 50% is considered ◉ dangerous ○ fatiguing ○ good ○ excellent*
The approximate net payload of 1870 pounds at 15% of GVWR on this model is ○ deficient ○ excessive ○ cautionary ◉ good ○ excellent*
Total highway safety penalties are: 1*　Value: 8 5　Durability: 7 5　Highway Control Rating: 4 4　Highway Safety: 4 3

Brave	1992	MHA	23	23RC	CH	7.4L	G	$1700	137	4,200	11,800	9,830

Livability Code: VA 30-90
Wheelbase-to-length ratio of 50% is considered ◉ dangerous ○ fatiguing ○ good ○ excellent*
The approximate net payload of 1970 pounds at 17% of GVWR on this model is ○ deficient ○ excessive ○ cautionary ○ good ◉ excellent*
Total highway safety penalties are: 1*　Value: 8 5　Durability: 7 5　Highway Control Rating: 4 6　Highway Safety: 4 5

Brave	1992	MHA	23	23RC	CH	7.4L	G	$1700	137	4,200	11,800	9,830

Livability Code: VA 30-90
Wheelbase-to-length ratio of 50% is considered ◉ dangerous ○ fatiguing ○ good ○ excellent*
The approximate net payload of 1970 pounds at 17% of GVWR on this model is ○ deficient ○ excessive ○ cautionary ○ good ◉ excellent*
Total highway safety penalties are: 1*　Value: 8 5　Durability: 7 5　Highway Control Rating: 4 6　Highway Safety: 4 5

Brave	1992	MHA	27	27RC	CH	7.4L	G	$1600	158	1,500	12,300	10,921

Livability Code: SB 30-90
Wheelbase-to-length ratio of 49% is considered ◉ dangerous ○ fatiguing ○ good ○ excellent*
The approximate net payload of 1379 pounds at 11% of GVWR on this model is ○ deficient ○ excessive ○ cautionary ◉ good ○ excellent*
Total highway safety penalties are: 3*　Value: 8 4　Durability: 7 5　Highway Control Rating: 3 1　Highway Safety: 2 8

Brave	1992	MHA	27	27 RCopch,op eng	CH	GM6.5	D	$1700	158	1,500	12,300	11,421

Livability Code: SB 30-90
Wheelbase-to-length ratio of 49% is considered ◉ dangerous ○ fatiguing ○ good ○ excellent*
The approximate net payload of 879 pounds at 7% of GVWR on this model is ○ deficient ○ excessive ◉ cautionary ○ good ○ excellent*
Total highway safety penalties are: 3*　Value: 8 4　Durability: 7 5　Highway Control Rating: 1 2　Highway Safety: 9

Brave	1992	MHA	30	30RU	CH	7.4L	G	$1600	178	2,200	14,800	12,504

Livability Code: SB 30-90
Wheelbase-to-length ratio of 49% is considered ◉ dangerous ○ fatiguing ○ good ○ excellent*
The approximate net payload of 2296 pounds at 16% of GVWR on this model is ○ deficient ○ excessive ○ cautionary ○ good ◉ excellent*
Total highway safety penalties are: 5*　Value: 8 3　Durability: 7 5　Highway Control Rating: 4 0　Highway Safety: 3 5

Brave	1992	MHA	31	30RU	FO	7.5L	G	$1500	178	8,000	17,000	13,335

Livability Code: SB 30-90
Wheelbase-to-length ratio of 47% is considered ◉ dangerous ○ fatiguing ○ good ○ excellent*
The approximate net payload of 3665 pounds at 22% of GVWR on this model is ○ deficient ○ excessive ○ cautionary ○ good ◉ excellent*
Total highway safety penalties are: 2*　Value: 8 4　Durability: 7 5　Highway Control Rating: 3 7　Highway Safety: 3 5

Brave	1993	MHA	23	23RC	CH	7.4L	G	$1800	137	4,200	11,800	9,899

Livability Code: VA 30-90
Wheelbase-to-length ratio of 50% is considered ◉ dangerous ○ fatiguing ○ good ○ excellent*
The approximate net payload of 1901 pounds at 16% of GVWR on this model is ○ deficient ○ excessive ○ cautionary ○ good ◉ excellent*
Total highway safety penalties are: 1*　Value: 8 5　Durability: 7 5　Highway Control Rating: 4 3　Highway Safety: 4 2

Brave	1993	MHA	23	23RCopch,op eng	CH	GM6.2	D	$1900	137	1,500	12,300	10,499

Livability Code: VA 30-90
Wheelbase-to-length ratio of 50% is considered ◉ dangerous ○ fatiguing ○ good ○ excellent*
The approximate net payload of 1801 pounds at 15% of GVWR on this model is ○ deficient ○ excessive ○ cautionary ◉ good ○ excellent*
Total highway safety penalties are: 1*　Value: 8 5　Durability: 7 5　Highway Control Rating: 4 1　Highway Safety: 4 0

Brave	1993	MHA	27	27RC	CH	7.4L	G	$1700	158	3,700	12,300	10,921

Livability Code: SB 30-90
Wheelbase-to-length ratio of 49% is considered ◉ dangerous ○ fatiguing ○ good ○ excellent*
The approximate net payload of 1379 pounds at 11% of GVWR on this model is ○ deficient ○ excessive ○ cautionary ◉ good ○ excellent*
Total highway safety penalties are: 3*　Value: 8 4　Durability: 7 5　Highway Control Rating: 3 1　Highway Safety: 2 8

Note: Safety ratings are based on the assumption that the engineering of the RV has allowed for proper balance by placing fresh, gray, and black holding tanks in a location so as not to change the balance of the RV when the tanks are empty or full. **Always double-check wheelbase, GVWR, and weights at front and rear axles.**

*See Section 1 for details on how conclusions are reached.

Section 2: The Ratings

Brand	Year	Type	Length	Model	Chassis	Engine	Fuel Type	Average Price per Linear Foot When New	Adjusted Wheelbase	Approx. Towing Capacity	Gross Vehicle Weight Rating	Average Curb Weight
Brave	1993	MHA	27	27RQ	CH	7.4L	G	$1700	158	3,700	12,300	10,921

Livability Code: SB 30-90 — Wheelbase-to-length ratio of 49% is considered ◉ dangerous ○ fatiguing ○ good ○ excellent *
The approximate net payload of 1379 pounds at 11% of GVWR on this model is ○ deficient ○ excessive ○ cautionary ◉ good ○ excellent *
Total highway safety penalties are: 3 * Value: 8 4 Durability: 7 5 Highway Control Rating: 3 1 Highway Safety: 2 8

Brand	Year	Type	Length	Model	Chassis	Engine	Fuel Type	Avg Price/Lin Ft	Adj Wheelbase	Approx Towing	GVWR	Avg Curb Wt
Brave	1993	MHA	27	27RCopch,op eng	CH	GM6.2	D	$1800	158	2,500	14,500	12,121

Livability Code: SB 30-90 — Wheelbase-to-length ratio of 49% is considered ◉ dangerous ○ fatiguing ○ good ○ excellent *
The approximate net payload of 2379 pounds at 16% of GVWR on this model is ○ deficient ○ excessive ○ cautionary ○ good ◉ excellent *
Total highway safety penalties are: 3 * Value: 8 4 Durability: 7 5 Highway Control Rating: 4 1 Highway Safety: 3 8

| **Brave** | 1993 | MHA | 27 | 27RQopch,op eng | CH | GM6.2 | D | $1800 | 158 | 2,500 | 14,500 | 12,121 |

Livability Code: SB 30-90 — Wheelbase-to-length ratio of 49% is considered ◉ dangerous ○ fatiguing ○ good ○ excellent *
The approximate net payload of 2379 pounds at 16% of GVWR on this model is ○ deficient ○ excessive ○ cautionary ○ good ◉ excellent *
Total highway safety penalties are: 3 * Value: 8 4 Durability: 7 5 Highway Control Rating: 4 1 Highway Safety: 3 8

| **Brave** | 1993 | MHA | 31 | 31RQ | CH | 7.4L | G | $1600 | 190 | 2,200 | 14,800 | 12,735 |

Livability Code: SB 30-90 — Wheelbase-to-length ratio of 50% is considered ◉ dangerous ○ fatiguing ○ good ○ excellent *
The approximate net payload of 2065 pounds at 14% of GVWR on this model is ○ deficient ○ excessive ○ cautionary ◉ good ○ excellent *
Total highway safety penalties are: 5 * Value: 8 2 Durability: 7 5 Highway Control Rating: 4 2 Highway Safety: 3 7

| **Brave** | 1993 | MHA | 31 | 31RQ | FO | 7.5L | G | $1700 | 190 | 8,000 | 17,000 | 13,335 |

Livability Code: SB 30-90 — Wheelbase-to-length ratio of 50% is considered ◉ dangerous ○ fatiguing ○ good ○ excellent *
The approximate net payload of 3665 pounds at 22% of GVWR on this model is ○ deficient ○ excessive ○ cautionary ○ good ◉ excellent *
Total highway safety penalties are: 2 * Value: 8 4 Durability: 7 5 Highway Control Rating: 4 9 Highway Safety: 4 7

| **Brave** | 1993 | MHA | 34 | 33RQ | CH | 7.4L | G | $1500 | 208 | 2,200 | 14,800 | 13,264 |

Livability Code: SB 30-90 — Wheelbase-to-length ratio of 51% is considered ○ dangerous ◉ fatiguing ○ good ○ excellent *
The approximate net payload of 1536 pounds at 10% of GVWR on this model is ○ deficient ○ excessive ○ cautionary ◉ good ○ excellent *
Total highway safety penalties are: 6 * Value: 8 2 Durability: 7 5 Highway Control Rating: 3 8 Highway Safety: 3 2

| **Brave** | 1993 | MHA | 34 | 33 RQ opch | CH | 7.4L | G | $1500 | 208 | 1,500 e | 16,000 | 13,364 |

Livability Code: SB 30-90 — Wheelbase-to-length ratio of 51% is considered ○ dangerous ◉ fatiguing ○ good ○ excellent *
The approximate net payload of 2636 pounds at 16% of GVWR on this model is ○ deficient ○ excessive ○ cautionary ○ good ◉ excellent *
Total highway safety penalties are: 6 * Value: 8 2 Durability: 7 5 Highway Control Rating: 6 0 Highway Safety: 5 4 ★

| **Brave** | 1993 | MHA | 34 | 33RQ | FO | 7.5L | G | $1600 | 208 | 8,000 | 17,000 | 13,864 |

Livability Code: SB 30-90 — Wheelbase-to-length ratio of 51% is considered ○ dangerous ◉ fatiguing ○ good ○ excellent *
The approximate net payload of 3136 pounds at 18% of GVWR on this model is ○ deficient ○ excessive ○ cautionary ○ good ◉ excellent *
Total highway safety penalties are: 2 * Value: 8 4 Durability: 7 5 Highway Control Rating: 5 2 Highway Safety: 5 0 ★

| **Brave** | 1994 | MHA | 23 | 23RC | CH | 7.4L | G | $1900 | 137 | 4,200 | 11,800 | 9,899 |

Livability Code: VA 30-90 — Wheelbase-to-length ratio of 50% is considered ◉ dangerous ○ fatiguing ○ good ○ excellent *
The approximate net payload of 1901 pounds at 16% of GVWR on this model is ○ deficient ○ excessive ○ cautionary ○ good ◉ excellent *
Total highway safety penalties are: 1 * Value: 8 5 Durability: 7 5 Highway Control Rating: 4 3 Highway Safety: 4 2

| **Brave** | 1994 | MHA | 23 | 23RC op eng | CH | GM6.2 | D | $2000 | 137 | 1,500 | 12,300 | 10,499 |

Livability Code: VA 30-90 — Wheelbase-to-length ratio of 50% is considered ◉ dangerous ○ fatiguing ○ good ○ excellent *
The approximate net payload of 1801 pounds at 15% of GVWR on this model is ○ deficient ○ excessive ○ cautionary ◉ good ○ excellent *
Total highway safety penalties are: 1 * Value: 8 5 Durability: 7 5 Highway Control Rating: 4 1 Highway Safety: 4 0

| **Brave** | 1994 | MHA | 27 | 27RC | CH | 7.4L | G | $1800 | 158 | 3,700 | 12,300 | 10,921 |

Livability Code: SB 30-90 — Wheelbase-to-length ratio of 49% is considered ◉ dangerous ○ fatiguing ○ good ○ excellent *
The approximate net payload of 1379 pounds at 11% of GVWR on this model is ○ deficient ○ excessive ○ cautionary ◉ good ○ excellent *
Total highway safety penalties are: 3 * Value: 8 4 Durability: 7 5 Highway Control Rating: 3 1 Highway Safety: 2 8

| **Brave** | 1994 | MHA | 27 | 27RQ | CH | 7.4L | G | $1900 | 158 | 3,700 | 12,300 | 10,921 |

Livability Code: SB 30-90 — Wheelbase-to-length ratio of 49% is considered ◉ dangerous ○ fatiguing ○ good ○ excellent *
The approximate net payload of 1379 pounds at 11% of GVWR on this model is ○ deficient ○ excessive ○ cautionary ◉ good ○ excellent *
Total highway safety penalties are: 3 * Value: 8 4 Durability: 7 5 Highway Control Rating: 3 1 Highway Safety: 2 8

Note: Safety ratings are based on the assumption that the engineering of the RV has allowed for proper balance by placing fresh, gray, and black holding tanks in a location **so as not to change the balance of the RV when the tanks are empty or full. Always double-check wheelbase, GVWR, and weights at front and rear axles.**

*See Section 1 for details on how conclusions are reached.

Section 2: The Ratings

Brand	Year	Type	Length	Model	Chassis	Engine	Fuel Type	Average Price per Linear Foot When New	Adjusted Wheelbase	Approx. Towing Capacity	Gross Vehicle Weight Rating	Average Curb Weight
Brave	1994	MHA	27	27RC op eng	CH	GM6.2	D	$1900	158	2,500	14,500	12,121

Livability Code: SB 30-90

Wheelbase-to-length ratio of 49% is considered ◉ dangerous ○ fatiguing ○ good ○ excellent *

The approximate net payload of 2379 pounds at 16% of GVWR on this model is ○ deficient ○ excessive ○ cautionary ○ good ◉ excellent *

Total highway safety penalties are: 3 *　Value: 8 4　Durability: 7 5　Highway Control Rating: 4 1　Highway Safety: 3 8

Brand	Year	Type	Length	Model	Chassis	Engine	Fuel Type	Price/Ft	Wheelbase	Towing	GVWR	Curb Wt
Brave	1994	MHA	27	27RQ op eng	CH	GM6.2	D	$2000	158	2,500	14,500	12,121

Livability Code: SB 30-90

Wheelbase-to-length ratio of 49% is considered ◉ dangerous ○ fatiguing ○ good ○ excellent *

The approximate net payload of 2379 pounds at 16% of GVWR on this model is ○ deficient ○ excessive ○ cautionary ○ good ◉ excellent *

Total highway safety penalties are: 3 *　Value: 8 4　Durability: 7 5　Highway Control Rating: 4 1　Highway Safety: 3 8

Brand	Year	Type	Length	Model	Chassis	Engine	Fuel Type	Price/Ft	Wheelbase	Towing	GVWR	Curb Wt
Brave	1994	MHA	30	29RQ	CH	7.4L	G	$1800	178	4,200	14,800	12,343

Livability Code: SB 30-90

Wheelbase-to-length ratio of 50% is considered ◉ dangerous ○ fatiguing ○ good ○ excellent *

The approximate net payload of 2457 pounds at 17% of GVWR on this model is ○ deficient ○ excessive ○ cautionary ○ good ◉ excellent *

Total highway safety penalties are: 4 *　Value: 8 3　Durability: 7 5　Highway Control Rating: 4 5　Highway Safety: 4 1

Brand	Year	Type	Length	Model	Chassis	Engine	Fuel Type	Price/Ft	Wheelbase	Towing	GVWR	Curb Wt
Brave	1994	MHA	30	29RQ op eng	CH	GM6.2	D	$1900	178	2,500	14,500	12,743

Livability Code: SB 30-90

Wheelbase-to-length ratio of 50% is considered ◉ dangerous ○ fatiguing ○ good ○ excellent *

The approximate net payload of 1757 pounds at 12% of GVWR on this model is ○ deficient ○ excessive ○ cautionary ◉ good ○ excellent *

Total highway safety penalties are: 4 *　Value: 8 3　Durability: 7 5　Highway Control Rating: 3 7　Highway Safety: 3 3

Brand	Year	Type	Length	Model	Chassis	Engine	Fuel Type	Price/Ft	Wheelbase	Towing	GVWR	Curb Wt
Brave	1994	MHA	30	29RQ	FO	7.5L	G	$1800	178	3,800	15,200	12,743

Livability Code: SB 30-90

Wheelbase-to-length ratio of 50% is considered ◉ dangerous ○ fatiguing ○ good ○ excellent *

The approximate net payload of 2457 pounds at 16% of GVWR on this model is ○ deficient ○ excessive ○ cautionary ○ good ◉ excellent *

Total highway safety penalties are: 2 *　Value: 8 4　Durability: 7 5　Highway Control Rating: 4 5　Highway Safety: 4 3

Brand	Year	Type	Length	Model	Chassis	Engine	Fuel Type	Price/Ft	Wheelbase	Towing	GVWR	Curb Wt
Brave	1994	MHA	32	31RQ	CH	7.4L	G	$1800	190	4,200	14,800	12,758

Livability Code: SB 30-90

Wheelbase-to-length ratio of 50% is considered ◉ dangerous ○ fatiguing ○ good ○ excellent *

The approximate net payload of 2042 pounds at 14% of GVWR on this model is ○ deficient ○ excessive ○ cautionary ◉ good ○ excellent *

Total highway safety penalties are: 5 *　Value: 8 2　Durability: 7 5　Highway Control Rating: 4 1　Highway Safety: 3 6

Brand	Year	Type	Length	Model	Chassis	Engine	Fuel Type	Price/Ft	Wheelbase	Towing	GVWR	Curb Wt
Brave	1994	MHA	32	31RQ op eng	CH	GM6.2	D	$1800	190	2,500	14,500	13,158

Livability Code: SB 30-90

Wheelbase-to-length ratio of 50% is considered ◉ dangerous ○ fatiguing ○ good ○ excellent *

The approximate net payload of 1342 pounds at 9% of GVWR on this model is ○ deficient ○ excessive ◉ cautionary ○ good ○ excellent *

Total highway safety penalties are: 5 *　Value: 8 2　Durability: 7 5　Highway Control Rating: 2 9　Highway Safety: 2 4

Brand	Year	Type	Length	Model	Chassis	Engine	Fuel Type	Price/Ft	Wheelbase	Towing	GVWR	Curb Wt
Brave	1994	MHA	32	31RQ	FO	7.5L	G	$1800	190	3,800	15,200	13,158

Livability Code: SB 30-90

Wheelbase-to-length ratio of 50% is considered ◉ dangerous ○ fatiguing ○ good ○ excellent *

The approximate net payload of 2042 pounds at 13% of GVWR on this model is ○ deficient ○ excessive ○ cautionary ◉ good ○ excellent *

Total highway safety penalties are: 2 *　Value: 8 4　Durability: 7 5　Highway Control Rating: 4 0　Highway Safety: 3 8

Brand	Year	Type	Length	Model	Chassis	Engine	Fuel Type	Price/Ft	Wheelbase	Towing	GVWR	Curb Wt
Brave	1994	MHA	34	33RQ	CH	7.4L	G	$1800	208	4,200	14,800	13,334

Livability Code: SB 30-90

Wheelbase-to-length ratio of 51% is considered ○ dangerous ◉ fatiguing ○ good ○ excellent *

The approximate net payload of 1466 pounds at 10% of GVWR on this model is ○ deficient ○ excessive ○ cautionary ◉ good ○ excellent *

Total highway safety penalties are: 7 *　Value: 8 2　Durability: 7 5　Highway Control Rating: 3 6　Highway Safety: 2 9

Brand	Year	Type	Length	Model	Chassis	Engine	Fuel Type	Price/Ft	Wheelbase	Towing	GVWR	Curb Wt
Brave	1994	MHA	34	33RQ opch	CH	7.4L	G	$1800	208	1,500 e	16,000	13,434

Livability Code: SB 30-90

Wheelbase-to-length ratio of 51% is considered ○ dangerous ◉ fatiguing ○ good ○ excellent *

The approximate net payload of 2566 pounds at 16% of GVWR on this model is ○ deficient ○ excessive ○ cautionary ○ good ◉ excellent *

Total highway safety penalties are: 7 *　Value: 8 2　Durability: 7 5　Highway Control Rating: 5 8　Highway Safety: 5 1　★

Brand	Year	Type	Length	Model	Chassis	Engine	Fuel Type	Price/Ft	Wheelbase	Towing	GVWR	Curb Wt
Brave	1994	MHA	34	33RQ	FO	7.5L	G	$1800	208	8,000	17,000	13,934

Livability Code: SB 30-90

Wheelbase-to-length ratio of 51% is considered ○ dangerous ◉ fatiguing ○ good ○ excellent *

The approximate net payload of 3066 pounds at 18% of GVWR on this model is ○ deficient ○ excessive ○ cautionary ○ good ◉ excellent *

Total highway safety penalties are: 2 *　Value: 8 4　Durability: 7 5　Highway Control Rating: 5 0　Highway Safety: 4 8

Brand	Year	Type	Length	Model	Chassis	Engine	Fuel Type	Price/Ft	Wheelbase	Towing	GVWR	Curb Wt
Brave	1995	MHA	23	23RC	CH	7.4L	G	$1900	137	3,700	12,300	9,999

Livability Code: VA 30-90

Wheelbase-to-length ratio of 50% is considered ◉ dangerous ○ fatiguing ○ good ○ excellent *

The approximate net payload of 2301 pounds at 19% of GVWR on this model is ○ deficient ○ excessive ○ cautionary ○ good ◉ excellent *

Total highway safety penalties are: 1 *　Value: 8 5　Durability: 7 5　Highway Control Rating: 4 6　Highway Safety: 4 5

Note: Safety ratings are based on the assumption that the engineering of the RV has allowed for proper balance by placing fresh, gray, and black holding tanks in a location so as not to change the balance of the RV when the tanks are empty or full. **Always double-check wheelbase, GVWR, and weights at front and rear axles.**

*See Section 1 for details on how conclusions are reached.

Brand	Year	Type	Length	Model	Chassis	Engine	Fuel Type	Average Price per Linear Foot When New	Adjusted Wheelbase	Approx. Towing Capacity	Gross Vehicle Weight Rating	Average Curb Weight
Brave	1995	MHA	23	23RC op eng	CH	GM6.5	D	$2000	137	4,700	12,300	10,499

Livability Code: VA 30-90
Wheelbase-to-length ratio of 50% is considered ◉ dangerous ○ fatiguing ○ good ○ excellent *
The approximate net payload of 1801 pounds at 15% of GVWR on this model is ○ deficient ○ excessive ○ cautionary ◉ good ○ excellent *
Total highway safety penalties are: 1 *   Value: 8 5   Durability: 7 5   Highway Control Rating: 4 1   Highway Safety: 4 0

| Brave | 1995 | MHA | 27 | 27RQ | CH | 7.4L | G | $1800 | 158 | 3,700 | 12,300 | 10,921 |

Livability Code: SB 30-90
Wheelbase-to-length ratio of 49% is considered ◉ dangerous ○ fatiguing ○ good ○ excellent *
The approximate net payload of 1379 pounds at 11% of GVWR on this model is ○ deficient ○ excessive ○ cautionary ◉ good ○ excellent *
Total highway safety penalties are: 3 *   Value: 8 4   Durability: 7 5   Highway Control Rating: 3 1   Highway Safety: 2 8

| Brave | 1995 | MHA | 27 | 27RQ op eng | CH | GM6.5 | D | $1900 | 158 | 4,200 | 14,800 | 12,221 |

Livability Code: SB 30-90
Wheelbase-to-length ratio of 49% is considered ◉ dangerous ○ fatiguing ○ good ○ excellent *
The approximate net payload of 2579 pounds at 17% of GVWR on this model is ○ deficient ○ excessive ○ cautionary ○ good ◉ excellent *
Total highway safety penalties are: 3 *   Value: 8 4   Durability: 7 5   Highway Control Rating: 4 2   Highway Safety: 3 9

| Brave | 1995 | MHA | 28 | 28RC | CH | 7.4L | G | $1900 | 158 | 4,200 | 14,800 | 11,951 |

Livability Code: SB 30-90
Wheelbase-to-length ratio of 47% is considered ◉ dangerous ○ fatiguing ○ good ○ excellent *
The approximate net payload of 2849 pounds at 19% of GVWR on this model is ○ deficient ○ excessive ○ cautionary ○ good ◉ excellent *
Total highway safety penalties are: 4 *   Value: 8 3   Durability: 7 5   Highway Control Rating: 3 7   Highway Safety: 3 3

| Brave | 1995 | MHA | 28 | 28RC op eng | CH | GM6.5 | D | $2000 | 158 | 4,200 | 14,800 | 12,451 |

Livability Code: SB 30-90
Wheelbase-to-length ratio of 47% is considered ◉ dangerous ○ fatiguing ○ good ○ excellent *
The approximate net payload of 2349 pounds at 16% of GVWR on this model is ○ deficient ○ excessive ○ cautionary ○ good ◉ excellent *
Total highway safety penalties are: 4 *   Value: 8 3   Durability: 7 5   Highway Control Rating: 3 4   Highway Safety: 3 0

| Brave | 1995 | MHA | 30 | 29RQ | CH | 7.4L | G | $1800 | 178 | 4,200 | 14,800 | 12,343 |

Livability Code: SB 30-90
Wheelbase-to-length ratio of 50% is considered ◉ dangerous ○ fatiguing ○ good ○ excellent *
The approximate net payload of 2457 pounds at 17% of GVWR on this model is ○ deficient ○ excessive ○ cautionary ◉ good ○ excellent *
Total highway safety penalties are: 4 *   Value: 8 3   Durability: 7 5   Highway Control Rating: 4 5   Highway Safety: 4 1

| Brave | 1995 | MHA | 30 | 29RQ op eng | CH | GM6.5 | D | $1900 | 178 | 4,200 | 14,800 | 12,843 |

Livability Code: SB 30-90
Wheelbase-to-length ratio of 50% is considered ◉ dangerous ○ fatiguing ○ good ○ excellent *
The approximate net payload of 1957 pounds at 13% of GVWR on this model is ○ deficient ○ excessive ○ cautionary ◉ good ○ excellent *
Total highway safety penalties are: 4 *   Value: 8 3   Durability: 7 5   Highway Control Rating: 3 9   Highway Safety: 3 5

| Brave | 1995 | MHA | 30 | 29RQ | FO | 7.5L | G | $1900 | 178 | 3,800 | 15,200 | 12,743 |

Livability Code: SB 30-90
Wheelbase-to-length ratio of 50% is considered ◉ dangerous ○ fatiguing ○ good ○ excellent *
The approximate net payload of 2457 pounds at 16% of GVWR on this model is ○ deficient ○ excessive ○ cautionary ○ good ◉ excellent *
Total highway safety penalties are: 2 *   Value: 8 4   Durability: 7 5   Highway Control Rating: 4 5   Highway Safety: 4 3

| Brave | 1995 | MHA | 32 | 31RQ | CH | 7.4L | G | $1800 | 190 | 4,200 | 14,800 | 12,758 |

Livability Code: SB 30-90
Wheelbase-to-length ratio of 50% is considered ◉ dangerous ○ fatiguing ○ good ○ excellent *
The approximate net payload of 2042 pounds at 14% of GVWR on this model is ○ deficient ○ excessive ○ cautionary ◉ good ○ excellent *
Total highway safety penalties are: 5 *   Value: 8 2   Durability: 7 5   Highway Control Rating: 4 3   Highway Safety: 3 8

| Brave | 1995 | MHA | 32 | 31RQ | FO | 7.5L | G | $1800 | 190 | 3,800 | 15,200 | 13,158 |

Livability Code: SB 30-90
Wheelbase-to-length ratio of 50% is considered ◉ dangerous ○ fatiguing ○ good ○ excellent *
The approximate net payload of 2042 pounds at 13% of GVWR on this model is ○ deficient ○ excessive ○ cautionary ◉ good ○ excellent *
Total highway safety penalties are: 2 *   Value: 8 4   Durability: 7 5   Highway Control Rating: 4 0   Highway Safety: 3 8

| Brave | 1995 | MHA | 33 | 32RQ-P | OS | CU190 | D | $1800 | 178 | 1,500 | 17,000 | 14,403 |

Livability Code: SB 30-90
Wheelbase-to-length ratio of 45% is considered ◉ dangerous ○ fatiguing ○ good ○ excellent *
The approximate net payload of 2597 pounds at 15% of GVWR on this model is ○ deficient ○ excessive ○ cautionary ◉ good ○ excellent *
Total highway safety penalties are: 2 *   Value: 8 4   Durability: 7 5   Highway Control Rating: 2 5   Highway Safety: 2 3

| Brave | 1995 | MHA | 34 | 33RQ | CH | 7.4L | G | $1800 | 208 | 4,200 | 14,800 | 13,334 |

Livability Code: SB 30-90
Wheelbase-to-length ratio of 51% is considered ○ dangerous ◉ fatiguing ○ good ○ excellent *
The approximate net payload of 1466 pounds at 10% of GVWR on this model is ○ deficient ○ excessive ○ cautionary ◉ good ○ excellent *
Total highway safety penalties are: 7 *   Value: 8 2   Durability: 7 5   Highway Control Rating: 3 6   Highway Safety: 2 9

Note: Safety ratings are based on the assumption that the engineering of the RV has allowed for proper balance by placing fresh, gray, and black holding tanks in a location so as not to change the balance of the RV when the tanks are empty or full. **Always double-check wheelbase, GVWR, and weights at front and rear axles.**

*See Section 1 for details on how conclusions are reached.

Brand	Year	Type	Length	Model	Chassis	Engine	Fuel Type	Average Price per Linear Foot When New	Adjusted Wheelbase	Approx. Towing Capacity	Gross Vehicle Weight Rating	Average Curb Weight
Brave	1995	MHA	34	33RQ	FO	7.5L	G	$1800	208	8,000	17,000	13,934

Livability Code: SB 30-90
Wheelbase-to-length ratio of 51% is considered ○ dangerous ◉ fatiguing ○ good ○ excellent *
The approximate net payload of 3066 pounds at 18% of GVWR on this model is ○ deficient ○ excessive ○ cautionary ○ good ◉ excellent *
Total highway safety penalties are: 2 *   Value: **8 4** Durability: **7 5** Highway Control Rating: **5 0** Highway Safety: **4 8**

Brand	Year	Type	Length	Model	Chassis	Engine	Fuel Type	Price/Lin Ft	Adj Wheelbase	Towing	GVWR	Curb Wt
Brave	1996	MHA	25	25RC	CH	7.4L	G	$1900	158	3,700	12,300	10,552

Livability Code: SB 30-90
Wheelbase-to-length ratio of 52% is considered ○ dangerous ◉ fatiguing ○ good ○ excellent *
The approximate net payload of 1748 pounds at 14% of GVWR on this model is ○ deficient ○ excessive ○ cautionary ◉ good ○ excellent *
Total highway safety penalties are: 2 *   Value: **8 4** Durability: **7 5** Highway Control Rating: **5 5** Highway Safety: **5 3**   ★

Brand	Year	Type	Length	Model	Chassis	Engine	Fuel Type	Price/Lin Ft	Adj Wheelbase	Towing	GVWR	Curb Wt
Brave	1996	MHA	25	25RC op eng	CH	GM6.5	D	$2100	158	3,700	12,300	11,052

Livability Code: SB 30-90
Wheelbase-to-length ratio of 52% is considered ○ dangerous ◉ fatiguing ○ good ○ excellent *
The approximate net payload of 1248 pounds at 10% of GVWR on this model is ○ deficient ○ excessive ○ cautionary ◉ good ○ excellent *
Total highway safety penalties are: 2 *   Value: **8 4** Durability: **7 5** Highway Control Rating: **4 7** Highway Safety: **4 5**

Brand	Year	Type	Length	Model	Chassis	Engine	Fuel Type	Price/Lin Ft	Adj Wheelbase	Towing	GVWR	Curb Wt
Brave	1996	MHA	25	25RC opch	CH	7.4L	G	$2000	158	1,200	14,800	11,352

Livability Code: SB 30-90
Wheelbase-to-length ratio of 52% is considered ○ dangerous ◉ fatiguing ○ good ○ excellent *
The approximate net payload of 3448 pounds at 23% of GVWR on this model is ○ deficient ○ excessive ○ cautionary ○ good ◉ excellent *
Total highway safety penalties are: 2 *   Value: **8 4** Durability: **7 5** Highway Control Rating: **5 9** Highway Safety: **5 7**   ★

Brand	Year	Type	Length	Model	Chassis	Engine	Fuel Type	Price/Lin Ft	Adj Wheelbase	Towing	GVWR	Curb Wt
Brave	1996	MHA	28	28RC	CH	7.4L	G	$1900	158	4,200	14,800	11,951

Livability Code: SB 30-90
Wheelbase-to-length ratio of 47% is considered ◉ dangerous ○ fatiguing ○ good ○ excellent *
The approximate net payload of 2849 pounds at 19% of GVWR on this model is ○ deficient ○ excessive ○ cautionary ○ good ○ excellent *
Total highway safety penalties are: 4 *   Value: **8 3** Durability: **7 5** Highway Control Rating: **3 7** Highway Safety: **3 3**

Brand	Year	Type	Length	Model	Chassis	Engine	Fuel Type	Price/Lin Ft	Adj Wheelbase	Towing	GVWR	Curb Wt
Brave	1996	MHA	28	28RC op eng	CH	GM6.5	D	$2000	158	4,200	14,800	12,451

Livability Code: SB 30-90
Wheelbase-to-length ratio of 47% is considered ◉ dangerous ○ fatiguing ○ good ○ excellent *
The approximate net payload of 2349 pounds at 16% of GVWR on this model is ○ deficient ○ excessive ○ cautionary ○ good ◉ excellent *
Total highway safety penalties are: 4 *   Value: **8 3** Durability: **7 5** Highway Control Rating: **3 4** Highway Safety: **3 0**

Brand	Year	Type	Length	Model	Chassis	Engine	Fuel Type	Price/Lin Ft	Adj Wheelbase	Towing	GVWR	Curb Wt
Brave	1996	MHA	30	29RQ	CH	7.4L	G	$1800	178	4,200	14,800	12,343

Livability Code: SB 30-90
Wheelbase-to-length ratio of 50% is considered ◉ dangerous ○ fatiguing ○ good ○ excellent *
The approximate net payload of 2457 pounds at 17% of GVWR on this model is ○ deficient ○ excessive ○ cautionary ○ good ◉ excellent *
Total highway safety penalties are: 4 *   Value: **8 3** Durability: **7 5** Highway Control Rating: **4 5** Highway Safety: **4 1**

Brand	Year	Type	Length	Model	Chassis	Engine	Fuel Type	Price/Lin Ft	Adj Wheelbase	Towing	GVWR	Curb Wt
Brave	1996	MHA	30	29RQ op eng	CH	GM6.5	D	$1900	178	4,200	14,800	12,843

Livability Code: SB 30-90
Wheelbase-to-length ratio of 50% is considered ◉ dangerous ○ fatiguing ○ good ○ excellent *
The approximate net payload of 1957 pounds at 13% of GVWR on this model is ○ deficient ○ excessive ○ cautionary ◉ good ○ excellent *
Total highway safety penalties are: 4 *   Value: **8 3** Durability: **7 5** Highway Control Rating: **3 9** Highway Safety: **3 5**

Brand	Year	Type	Length	Model	Chassis	Engine	Fuel Type	Price/Lin Ft	Adj Wheelbase	Towing	GVWR	Curb Wt
Brave	1996	MHA	30	29RQ	FO	7.5L	G	$1800	178	9,800	15,200	12,743

Livability Code: SB 30-90
Wheelbase-to-length ratio of 50% is considered ◉ dangerous ○ fatiguing ○ good ○ excellent *
The approximate net payload of 2457 pounds at 16% of GVWR on this model is ○ deficient ○ excessive ○ cautionary ○ good ◉ excellent *
Total highway safety penalties are: 2 *   Value: **8 4** Durability: **7 5** Highway Control Rating: **4 5** Highway Safety: **4 3**

Brand	Year	Type	Length	Model	Chassis	Engine	Fuel Type	Price/Lin Ft	Adj Wheelbase	Towing	GVWR	Curb Wt
Brave	1996	MHA	32	31RQ	CH	7.4L	G	$1800	190	4,200	14,800	12,758

Livability Code: SB 30-90
Wheelbase-to-length ratio of 50% is considered ◉ dangerous ○ fatiguing ○ good ○ excellent *
The approximate net payload of 2042 pounds at 14% of GVWR on this model is ○ deficient ○ excessive ○ cautionary ◉ good ○ excellent *
Total highway safety penalties are: 5 *   Value: **8 2** Durability: **7 5** Highway Control Rating: **4 1** Highway Safety: **3 6**

Brand	Year	Type	Length	Model	Chassis	Engine	Fuel Type	Price/Lin Ft	Adj Wheelbase	Towing	GVWR	Curb Wt
Brave	1996	MHA	32	31RQ op eng	CH	GM6.5	D	$1800	190	4,200	14,800	13,258

Livability Code: SB 30-90
Wheelbase-to-length ratio of 50% is considered ◉ dangerous ○ fatiguing ○ good ○ excellent *
The approximate net payload of 1542 pounds at 10% of GVWR on this model is ○ deficient ○ excessive ○ cautionary ◉ good ○ excellent *
Total highway safety penalties are: 5 *   Value: **8 2** Durability: **7 5** Highway Control Rating: **3 4** Highway Safety: **2 9**

Brand	Year	Type	Length	Model	Chassis	Engine	Fuel Type	Price/Lin Ft	Adj Wheelbase	Towing	GVWR	Curb Wt
Brave	1996	MHA	32	31RQ	FO	7.5L	G	$1800	190	9,800	15,200	13,158

Livability Code: SB 30-90
Wheelbase-to-length ratio of 50% is considered ◉ dangerous ○ fatiguing ○ good ○ excellent *
The approximate net payload of 2042 pounds at 13% of GVWR on this model is ○ deficient ○ excessive ○ cautionary ◉ good ○ excellent *
Total highway safety penalties are: 2 *   Value: **8 4** Durability: **7 5** Highway Control Rating: **4 0** Highway Safety: **3 8**

Note: Safety ratings are based on the assumption that the engineering of the RV has allowed for proper balance by placing fresh, gray, and black holding tanks in a location so as not to change the balance of the RV when the tanks are empty or full. **Always double-check wheelbase, GVWR, and weights at front and rear axles.**

*See Section 1 for details on how conclusions are reached.

Brand	Year	Type	Length	Model	Chassis	Engine	Fuel Type	Average Price per Linear Foot When New	Adjusted Wheelbase	Approx. Towing Capacity	Gross Vehicle Weight Rating	Average Curb Weight
Brave	**1996**	MHA	34	33RQ	CH	7.4L	G	$1700	208	4,200	14,800	13,288

Livability Code: SB 30-90 — Wheelbase-to-length ratio of 51% is considered ⚪ dangerous ⚫ fatiguing ⚪ good ⚪ excellent *

The approximate net payload of 1512 pounds at 10% of GVWR on this model is ⚪ deficient ⚪ excessive ⚪ cautionary ⚫ good ⚪ excellent *

Total highway safety penalties are: 6 * — Value: **8 2** Durability: **7 5** Highway Control Rating: **3 8** Highway Safety: **3 2**

Brand	Year	Type	Length	Model	Chassis	Engine	Fuel Type	Price/LF	Wheelbase	Towing	GVWR	Curb Wt
Brave	**1996**	MHA	34	33RQ opch	CH	7.4L	G	$1700	208	3,500	16,500	13,488

Livability Code: SB 30-90 — Wheelbase-to-length ratio of 51% is considered ⚪ dangerous ⚫ fatiguing ⚪ good ⚪ excellent *

The approximate net payload of 3012 pounds at 18% of GVWR on this model is ⚪ deficient ⚪ excessive ⚪ cautionary ⚪ good ⚫ excellent *

Total highway safety penalties are: 6 * — Value: **8 2** Durability: **7 5** Highway Control Rating: **5 1** Highway Safety: **4 5**

Brand	Year	Type	Length	Model	Chassis	Engine	Fuel Type	Price/LF	Wheelbase	Towing	GVWR	Curb Wt
Brave	**1996**	MHA	34	33RQ	FO	7.5L	G	$1700	208	8,000	17,000	13,888

Livability Code: SB 30-90 — Wheelbase-to-length ratio of 51% is considered ⚪ dangerous ⚫ fatiguing ⚪ good ⚪ excellent *

The approximate net payload of 3112 pounds at 18% of GVWR on this model is ⚪ deficient ⚪ excessive ⚪ cautionary ⚪ good ⚫ excellent *

Total highway safety penalties are: 2 * — Value: **8 4** Durability: **7 5** Highway Control Rating: **5 2** Highway Safety: **5 0** ★

Brand	Year	Type	Length	Model	Chassis	Engine	Fuel Type	Price/LF	Wheelbase	Towing	GVWR	Curb Wt
Brave	**1997**	MHA	25	25RC	CH	7.4L	G	$2100	158	3,700	12,300	10,768

Livability Code: SB 30-90 — Wheelbase-to-length ratio of 52% is considered ⚪ dangerous ⚫ fatiguing ⚪ good ⚪ excellent *

The approximate net payload of 1532 pounds at 12% of GVWR on this model is ⚪ deficient ⚪ excessive ⚪ cautionary ⚫ good ⚪ excellent *

Total highway safety penalties are: 2 * — Value: **8 4** Durability: **7 5** Highway Control Rating: **5 3** Highway Safety: **5 1** ★

Brand	Year	Type	Length	Model	Chassis	Engine	Fuel Type	Price/LF	Wheelbase	Towing	GVWR	Curb Wt
Brave	**1997**	MHA	25	25RC opch (Ca.)	CH	7.4L	G	$2100	158	4,200	14,800	11,077

Livability Code: SB 30-90 — Wheelbase-to-length ratio of 52% is considered ⚪ dangerous ⚫ fatiguing ⚪ good ⚪ excellent *

The approximate net payload of 3723 pounds at 25% of GVWR on this model is ⚪ deficient ⚪ excessive ⚪ cautionary ⚫ good ⚪ excellent *

Total highway safety penalties are: 2 * — Value: **8 4** Durability: **7 5** Highway Control Rating: **6 0** Highway Safety: **5 8** ★

Brand	Year	Type	Length	Model	Chassis	Engine	Fuel Type	Price/LF	Wheelbase	Towing	GVWR	Curb Wt
Brave	**1997**	MHA	28	28RC	CH	7.4L	G	$2000	158	4,200	14,800	12,096

Livability Code: SB 30-90 — Wheelbase-to-length ratio of 48% is considered ⚫ dangerous ⚪ fatiguing ⚪ good ⚪ excellent *

The approximate net payload of 2704 pounds at 18% of GVWR on this model is ⚪ deficient ⚪ excessive ⚪ cautionary ⚪ good ⚫ excellent *

Total highway safety penalties are: 3 * — Value: **8 3** Durability: **7 5** Highway Control Rating: **3 8** Highway Safety: **3 5**

Brand	Year	Type	Length	Model	Chassis	Engine	Fuel Type	Price/LF	Wheelbase	Towing	GVWR	Curb Wt
Brave	**1997**	MHA	29	29RQ	CH	7.4L	G	$2000	178	4,200	14,800	12,110

Livability Code: SB 30-90 — Wheelbase-to-length ratio of 50% is considered ⚫ dangerous ⚪ fatiguing ⚪ good ⚪ excellent *

The approximate net payload of 2690 pounds at 18% of GVWR on this model is ⚪ deficient ⚪ excessive ⚪ cautionary ⚪ good ⚫ excellent *

Total highway safety penalties are: 4 * — Value: **8 3** Durability: **7 5** Highway Control Rating: **4 8** Highway Safety: **4 4**

Brand	Year	Type	Length	Model	Chassis	Engine	Fuel Type	Price/LF	Wheelbase	Towing	GVWR	Curb Wt
Brave	**1997**	MHA	29	29RQ	FO	7.5L	G	$2000	178	9,800	15,200	12,694

Livability Code: SB 30-90 — Wheelbase-to-length ratio of 50% is considered ⚫ dangerous ⚪ fatiguing ⚪ good ⚪ excellent *

The approximate net payload of 2506 pounds at 16% of GVWR on this model is ⚪ deficient ⚪ excessive ⚪ cautionary ⚪ good ⚫ excellent *

Total highway safety penalties are: 2 * — Value: **8 4** Durability: **7 5** Highway Control Rating: **4 7** Highway Safety: **4 5**

Brand	Year	Type	Length	Model	Chassis	Engine	Fuel Type	Price/LF	Wheelbase	Towing	GVWR	Curb Wt
Brave	**1997**	MHA	31	31RQ	CH	7.4L	G	$1900	190	4,200	14,800	12,519

Livability Code: SB 30-90 — Wheelbase-to-length ratio of 51% is considered ⚪ dangerous ⚫ fatiguing ⚪ good ⚪ excellent *

The approximate net payload of 2281 pounds at 15% of GVWR on this model is ⚪ deficient ⚪ excessive ⚪ cautionary ⚫ good ⚪ excellent *

Total highway safety penalties are: 5 * — Value: **8 2** Durability: **7 5** Highway Control Rating: **4 5** Highway Safety: **4 0**

Brand	Year	Type	Length	Model	Chassis	Engine	Fuel Type	Price/LF	Wheelbase	Towing	GVWR	Curb Wt
Brave	**1997**	MHA	31	31RQ	FO	7.5L	G	$1900	190	9,800	15,200	13,196

Livability Code: SB 30-90 — Wheelbase-to-length ratio of 51% is considered ⚪ dangerous ⚫ fatiguing ⚪ good ⚪ excellent *

The approximate net payload of 2004 pounds at 13% of GVWR on this model is ⚪ deficient ⚪ excessive ⚪ cautionary ⚫ good ⚪ excellent *

Total highway safety penalties are: 2 * — Value: **8 4** Durability: **7 5** Highway Control Rating: **4 1** Highway Safety: **3 9**

Brand	Year	Type	Length	Model	Chassis	Engine	Fuel Type	Price/LF	Wheelbase	Towing	GVWR	Curb Wt
Brave	**1997**	MHA	33	33RQ	CH	7.4L	G	$1900	216	4,200	14,800	13,109

Livability Code: SB 30-90 — Wheelbase-to-length ratio of 55% is considered ⚪ dangerous ⚪ fatiguing ⚫ good ⚪ excellent *

The approximate net payload of 1691 pounds at 11% of GVWR on this model is ⚪ deficient ⚪ excessive ⚪ cautionary ⚫ good ⚪ excellent *

Total highway safety penalties are: 6 * — Value: **8 2** Durability: **7 5** Highway Control Rating: **8 8** Highway Safety: **8 2** ★★★

Brand	Year	Type	Length	Model	Chassis	Engine	Fuel Type	Price/LF	Wheelbase	Towing	GVWR	Curb Wt
Brave	**1997**	MHA	33	33RQ opch	CH	7.4L	G	$1900	216	3,500	16,500	12,838

Livability Code: SB 30-90 — Wheelbase-to-length ratio of 55% is considered ⚪ dangerous ⚪ fatiguing ⚫ good ⚪ excellent *

The approximate net payload of 3662 pounds at 22% of GVWR on this model is ⚪ deficient ⚪ excessive ⚪ cautionary ⚪ good ⚫ excellent *

Total highway safety penalties are: 6 * — Value: **8 2** Durability: **7 5** Highway Control Rating: **9 4** Highway Safety: **8 8** ★★★

Note: Safety ratings are based on the assumption that the engineering of the RV has allowed for proper balance by placing fresh, gray, and black holding tanks in a location so as not to change the balance of the RV when the tanks are empty or full. **Always double-check wheelbase, GVWR, and weights at front and rear axles.**

*See Section 1 for details on how conclusions are reached.

Section 2: The Ratings

Brand	Year	Type	Length	Model	Chassis	Engine	Fuel Type	Average Price per Linear Foot When New	Adjusted Wheelbase	Approx. Towing Capacity	Gross Vehicle Weight Rating	Average Curb Weight
Brave	1997	MHA	33	33RQ opsl	CH	7.4L	G	$1800	216	3,500	16,500	13,694

Livability Code: SB 30-90
Wheelbase-to-length ratio of 55% is considered ○ dangerous ○ fatiguing ◉ good ○ excellent*
The approximate net payload of 2806 pounds at 17% of GVWR on this model is ○ deficient ○ excessive ○ cautionary ○ good ◉ excellent*
Total highway safety penalties are: 9* Value: 8 0 Durability: 7 5 Highway Control Rating: 9 4 Highway Safety: 8 5 ★★★

Brand	Year	Type	Length	Model	Chassis	Engine	Fuel Type	Price/LF	Wheelbase	Towing	GVWR	Curb Wt
Brave	1997	MHA	33	33RQ	FO	7.5L	G	$1900	216	8,000	17,000	13,521

Livability Code: SB 30-90
Wheelbase-to-length ratio of 55% is considered ○ dangerous ○ fatiguing ◉ good ○ excellent*
The approximate net payload of 3479 pounds at 20% of GVWR on this model is ○ deficient ○ excessive ○ cautionary ○ good ◉ excellent*
Total highway safety penalties are: 2* Value: 8 4 Durability: 7 5 Highway Control Rating: 9 6 Highway Safety: 9 4 ★★★

Brand	Year	Type	Length	Model	Chassis	Engine	Fuel Type	Price/LF	Wheelbase	Towing	GVWR	Curb Wt
Brave	1997	MHA	33	33RQ opsl	FO	7.5L	G	$1800	216	8,000	17,000	14,121

Livability Code: SB 30-90
Wheelbase-to-length ratio of 55% is considered ○ dangerous ○ fatiguing ◉ good ○ excellent*
The approximate net payload of 2879 pounds at 17% of GVWR on this model is ○ deficient ○ excessive ○ cautionary ○ good ◉ excellent*
Total highway safety penalties are: 6* Value: 8 2 Durability: 7 5 Highway Control Rating: 9 4 Highway Safety: 8 8 ★★★

Brand	Year	Type	Length	Model	Chassis	Engine	Fuel Type	Price/LF	Wheelbase	Towing	GVWR	Curb Wt
Brave	1998	MHA	26	SE26WU	CH	7.4L	G	$2000	159	3,700	12,300	10,944

Livability Code: SB 30-90
Wheelbase-to-length ratio of 51% is considered ○ dangerous ◉ fatiguing ○ good ○ excellent*
The approximate net payload of 1356 pounds at 11% of GVWR on this model is ○ deficient ○ excessive ○ cautionary ◉ good ○ excellent*
Total highway safety penalties are: 3* Value: 8 4 Durability: 7 5 Highway Control Rating: 3 7 Highway Safety: 3 4

Brand	Year	Type	Length	Model	Chassis	Engine	Fuel Type	Price/LF	Wheelbase	Towing	GVWR	Curb Wt
Brave	1998	MHA	26	SE26WU opch (Ca)	CH	7.4L	G	$2000	159	4,200	14,800	11,343

Livability Code: SB 30-90
Wheelbase-to-length ratio of 51% is considered ○ dangerous ◉ fatiguing ○ good ○ excellent*
The approximate net payload of 3457 pounds at 23% of GVWR on this model is ○ deficient ○ excessive ○ cautionary ○ good ◉ excellent*
Total highway safety penalties are: 3* Value: 8 4 Durability: 7 5 Highway Control Rating: 4 7 Highway Safety: 4 4

Brand	Year	Type	Length	Model	Chassis	Engine	Fuel Type	Price/LF	Wheelbase	Towing	GVWR	Curb Wt
Brave	1998	MHA	30	SE29WQ opch	CH	7.4L	G	$2000	178	4,500	16,500	12,928

Livability Code: SB 30-90
Wheelbase-to-length ratio of 50% is considered ◉ dangerous ○ fatiguing ○ good ○ excellent*
The approximate net payload of 3572 pounds at 22% of GVWR on this model is ○ deficient ○ excessive ○ cautionary ○ good ◉ excellent*
Total highway safety penalties are: 4* Value: 8 3 Durability: 7 5 Highway Control Rating: 4 6 Highway Safety: 4 2

Brand	Year	Type	Length	Model	Chassis	Engine	Fuel Type	Price/LF	Wheelbase	Towing	GVWR	Curb Wt
Brave	1998	MHA	30	SE29WQ	FO	7.5L	G	$1900	178	9,800	15,200	13,222

Livability Code: SB 30-90
Wheelbase-to-length ratio of 50% is considered ◉ dangerous ○ fatiguing ○ good ○ excellent*
The approximate net payload of 1978 pounds at 13% of GVWR on this model is ○ deficient ○ excessive ○ cautionary ◉ good ○ excellent*
Total highway safety penalties are: 2* Value: 8 4 Durability: 7 5 Highway Control Rating: 3 7 Highway Safety: 3 5

Brand	Year	Type	Length	Model	Chassis	Engine	Fuel Type	Price/LF	Wheelbase	Towing	GVWR	Curb Wt
Brave	1998	MHA	31	30WQ opch	CH	7.4L	G	$2000	190	4,500	16,500	13,475

Livability Code: SB 30-90
Wheelbase-to-length ratio of 51% is considered ○ dangerous ◉ fatiguing ○ good ○ excellent*
The approximate net payload of 3025 pounds at 18% of GVWR on this model is ○ deficient ○ excessive ○ cautionary ○ good ◉ excellent*
Total highway safety penalties are: 5* Value: 8 3 Durability: 7 5 Highway Control Rating: 5 1 Highway Safety: 4 6

Brand	Year	Type	Length	Model	Chassis	Engine	Fuel Type	Price/LF	Wheelbase	Towing	GVWR	Curb Wt
Brave	1998	MHA	31	30WQ	FO	7.5L	G	$1900	190	9,800	15,200	13,715

Livability Code: SB 30-90
Wheelbase-to-length ratio of 51% is considered ○ dangerous ◉ fatiguing ○ good ○ excellent*
The approximate net payload of 1485 pounds at 10% of GVWR on this model is ○ deficient ○ excessive ○ cautionary ◉ good ○ excellent*
Total highway safety penalties are: 2* Value: 8 4 Durability: 7 5 Highway Control Rating: 3 6 Highway Safety: 3 4

Brand	Year	Type	Length	Model	Chassis	Engine	Fuel Type	Price/LF	Wheelbase	Towing	GVWR	Curb Wt
Brave	1998	MHA	31	30WQ opch	FO	7.5L	G	$1900	190	8,000	17,000	14,299

Livability Code: SB 30-90
Wheelbase-to-length ratio of 51% is considered ○ dangerous ◉ fatiguing ○ good ○ excellent*
The approximate net payload of 2701 pounds at 16% of GVWR on this model is ○ deficient ○ excessive ○ cautionary ○ good ◉ excellent*
Total highway safety penalties are: 2* Value: 8 4 Durability: 7 5 Highway Control Rating: 4 8 Highway Safety: 4 6

Brand	Year	Type	Length	Model	Chassis	Engine	Fuel Type	Price/LF	Wheelbase	Towing	GVWR	Curb Wt
Brave	1998	MHA	32	SE31WQ opch	CH	7.4L	G	$1900	190	4,500	16,500	13,249

Livability Code: SB 30-90
Wheelbase-to-length ratio of 50% is considered ◉ dangerous ○ fatiguing ○ good ○ excellent*
The approximate net payload of 3251 pounds at 20% of GVWR on this model is ○ deficient ○ excessive ○ cautionary ○ good ◉ excellent*
Total highway safety penalties are: 5* Value: 8 2 Durability: 7 5 Highway Control Rating: 4 8 Highway Safety: 4 3

Brand	Year	Type	Length	Model	Chassis	Engine	Fuel Type	Price/LF	Wheelbase	Towing	GVWR	Curb Wt
Brave	1998	MHA	32	DL31DQ	CH	7.4L	G	$2000	190	4,500	16,500	13,329

Livability Code: SB 30-90
Wheelbase-to-length ratio of 50% is considered ◉ dangerous ○ fatiguing ○ good ○ excellent*
The approximate net payload of 3171 pounds at 19% of GVWR on this model is ○ deficient ○ excessive ○ cautionary ○ good ◉ excellent*
Total highway safety penalties are: 5* Value: 8 2 Durability: 7 5 Highway Control Rating: 4 7 Highway Safety: 4 2

Note: Safety ratings are based on the assumption that the engineering of the RV has allowed for proper balance by placing fresh, gray, and black holding tanks in a location so as not to change the balance of the RV when the tanks are empty or full. **Always double-check wheelbase, GVWR, and weights at front and rear axles.**

*See Section 1 for details on how conclusions are reached.

Section 2: The Ratings

Brand	Year	Type	Length	Model	Chassis	Engine	Fuel Type	Average Price per Linear Foot When New	Adjusted Wheelbase	Approx. Towing Capacity	Gross Vehicle Weight Rating	Average Curb Weight
Brave	1998	MHA	32	SE31WQ	FO	7.5L	G	$1800	190	9,800	15,200	13,409

Livability Code: SB 30-90
Wheelbase-to-length ratio of 50% is considered ⦿ dangerous ○ fatiguing ○ good ○ excellent *
The approximate net payload of 1791 pounds at 12% of GVWR on this model is ○ deficient ○ excessive ○ cautionary ⦿ good ○ excellent *
Total highway safety penalties are: 2 * Value: **8 4** Durability: **7 5** Highway Control Rating: **3 6** Highway Safety: **3 4**

Brand	Year	Type	Length	Model	Chassis	Engine	Fuel Type	Avg Price/LF	Adj. Wheelbase	Towing Cap	GVWR	Curb Wt
Brave	1998	MHA	32	SE31WQ opch	FO	7.5L	G	$1800	190	8,000	17,000	13,629

Livability Code: SB 30-90
Wheelbase-to-length ratio of 50% is considered ⦿ dangerous ○ fatiguing ○ good ○ excellent *
The approximate net payload of 3371 pounds at 20% of GVWR on this model is ○ deficient ○ excessive ○ cautionary ○ good ⦿ excellent *
Total highway safety penalties are: 2 * Value: **8 4** Durability: **7 5** Highway Control Rating: **4 8** Highway Safety: **4 6**

Brand	Year	Type	Length	Model	Chassis	Engine	Fuel Type	Avg Price/LF	Adj. Wheelbase	Towing Cap	GVWR	Curb Wt
Brave	1998	MHA	32	DL31DQ opch	FO	7.5L	G	$2000	190	8,000	17,000	13,790

Livability Code: SB 30-90
Wheelbase-to-length ratio of 50% is considered ⦿ dangerous ○ fatiguing ○ good ○ excellent *
The approximate net payload of 3210 pounds at 19% of GVWR on this model is ○ deficient ○ excessive ○ cautionary ○ good ⦿ excellent *
Total highway safety penalties are: 2 * Value: **8 4** Durability: **7 5** Highway Control Rating: **4 7** Highway Safety: **4 5**

Brand	Year	Type	Length	Model	Chassis	Engine	Fuel Type	Avg Price/LF	Adj. Wheelbase	Towing Cap	GVWR	Curb Wt
Brave	1998	MHA	32	32WQ	CH	7.4L	G	$2000	208	4,500	16,500	13,731

Livability Code: SB 30-90
Wheelbase-to-length ratio of 54% is considered ○ dangerous ○ fatiguing ⦿ good ○ excellent *
The approximate net payload of 2769 pounds at 17% of GVWR on this model is ○ deficient ○ excessive ○ cautionary ○ good ⦿ excellent *
Total highway safety penalties are: 16 * Value: **7 7** Durability: **7 5** Highway Control Rating: **8 2** Highway Safety: **6 6** ★★

Brand	Year	Type	Length	Model	Chassis	Engine	Fuel Type	Avg Price/LF	Adj. Wheelbase	Towing Cap	GVWR	Curb Wt
Brave	1998	MHA	32	32WQ	FO	7.5L	G	$1900	208	8,000	17,000	14,215

Livability Code: SB 30-90
Wheelbase-to-length ratio of 54% is considered ○ dangerous ○ fatiguing ⦿ good ○ excellent *
The approximate net payload of 2785 pounds at 16% of GVWR on this model is ○ deficient ○ excessive ○ cautionary ○ good ⦿ excellent *
Total highway safety penalties are: 12 * Value: **7 9** Durability: **7 5** Highway Control Rating: **8 1** Highway Safety: **6 9** ★★

Brand	Year	Type	Length	Model	Chassis	Engine	Fuel Type	Avg Price/LF	Adj. Wheelbase	Towing Cap	GVWR	Curb Wt
Brave	1998	MHA	33	DL33DQ	FO	7.5L	G	$2000	216	8,000	17,000	14,127

Livability Code: SB 30-90
Wheelbase-to-length ratio of 55% is considered ○ dangerous ○ fatiguing ⦿ good ○ excellent *
The approximate net payload of 2873 pounds at 17% of GVWR on this model is ○ deficient ○ excessive ○ cautionary ○ good ⦿ excellent *
Total highway safety penalties are: 2 * Value: **8 4** Durability: **7 5** Highway Control Rating: **9 2** Highway Safety: **9 0** ★★★

Brand	Year	Type	Length	Model	Chassis	Engine	Fuel Type	Avg Price/LF	Adj. Wheelbase	Towing Cap	GVWR	Curb Wt
Brave	1998	MHA	35	34WA myc	CH	7.4L	G	$1900	228	4,500	16,500	14,197

Livability Code: SB 30-90
Wheelbase-to-length ratio of 54% is considered ○ dangerous ○ fatiguing ⦿ good ○ excellent *
The approximate net payload of 2303 pounds at 14% of GVWR on this model is ○ deficient ○ excessive ○ cautionary ⦿ good ○ excellent *
Total highway safety penalties are: 7 * Value: **8 2** Durability: **7 5** Highway Control Rating: **7 8** Highway Safety: **7 1** ★★★

Brand	Year	Type	Length	Model	Chassis	Engine	Fuel Type	Avg Price/LF	Adj. Wheelbase	Towing Cap	GVWR	Curb Wt
Brave	1998	MHA	35	35WP	CH	7.4L	G	$1900	216	4,500	16,500	14,311

Livability Code: SB 30-90
Wheelbase-to-length ratio of 51% is considered ○ dangerous ⦿ fatiguing ○ good ○ excellent *
The approximate net payload of 2189 pounds at 13% of GVWR on this model is ○ deficient ○ excessive ○ cautionary ⦿ good ○ excellent *
Total highway safety penalties are: 7 * Value: **8 2** Durability: **7 5** Highway Control Rating: **4 4** Highway Safety: **3 7**

Brand	Year	Type	Length	Model	Chassis	Engine	Fuel Type	Avg Price/LF	Adj. Wheelbase	Towing Cap	GVWR	Curb Wt
Brave	1998	MHA	35	35WP	FO	7.5L	G	$1900	216	8,000	17,000	14,777

Livability Code: SB 30-90
Wheelbase-to-length ratio of 51% is considered ○ dangerous ⦿ fatiguing ○ good ○ excellent *
The approximate net payload of 2223 pounds at 13% of GVWR on this model is ○ deficient ○ excessive ○ cautionary ⦿ good ○ excellent *
Total highway safety penalties are: 2 * Value: **8 4** Durability: **7 5** Highway Control Rating: **4 4** Highway Safety: **4 2**

Brand	Year	Type	Length	Model	Chassis	Engine	Fuel Type	Avg Price/LF	Adj. Wheelbase	Towing Cap	GVWR	Curb Wt
Brave	1998	MHA	35	35WP slide	FO	7.5L	G	$2100	216	8,000	17,000	15,367

Livability Code: SB 30-90
Wheelbase-to-length ratio of 51% is considered ○ dangerous ⦿ fatiguing ○ good ○ excellent *
The approximate net payload of 1633 pounds at 10% of GVWR on this model is ○ deficient ○ excessive ○ cautionary ⦿ good ○ excellent *
Total highway safety penalties are: 7 * Value: **8 1** Durability: **7 5** Highway Control Rating: **3 7** Highway Safety: **3 0**

Brand	Year	Type	Length	Model	Chassis	Engine	Fuel Type	Avg Price/LF	Adj. Wheelbase	Towing Cap	GVWR	Curb Wt
Brave	1999	MHA	26	26P	CH	7.4L	G	$2200	159	3,700	12,300	11,211

Livability Code: SB 30-90
Wheelbase-to-length ratio of 50% is considered ⦿ dangerous ○ fatiguing ○ good ○ excellent *
The approximate net payload of 1089 pounds at 9% of GVWR on this model is ○ deficient ○ excessive ⦿ cautionary ○ good ○ excellent *
Total highway safety penalties are: 3 * Value: **8 4** Durability: **7 5** Highway Control Rating: **3 9** Highway Safety: **3 6**

Brand	Year	Type	Length	Model	Chassis	Engine	Fuel Type	Avg Price/LF	Adj. Wheelbase	Towing Cap	GVWR	Curb Wt
Brave	1999	MHA	26	26P opch	CH	7.4L	G	$2200	159	4,200	14,800	11,552

Livability Code: SB 30-90
Wheelbase-to-length ratio of 50% is considered ⦿ dangerous ○ fatiguing ○ good ○ excellent *
The approximate net payload of 3248 pounds at 22% of GVWR on this model is ○ deficient ○ excessive ○ cautionary ○ good ⦿ excellent *
Total highway safety penalties are: 3 * Value: **8 4** Durability: **7 5** Highway Control Rating: **5 8** Highway Safety: **5 5**

Note: Safety ratings are based on the assumption that the engineering of the RV has allowed for proper balance by placing fresh, gray, and black holding tanks in a location so as not to change the balance of the RV when the tanks are empty or full. **Always double-check wheelbase, GVWR, and weights at front and rear axles.**

Brand	Year	Type	Length	Model	Chassis	Engine	Fuel Type	Average Price per Linear Foot When New	Adjusted Wheelbase	Approx. Towing Capacity	Gross Vehicle Weight Rating	Average Curb Weight

Brave — 1999 — MHA — 30 — 29A — CH — 7.4L — G — $1900 — 178 — 4,200 — 14,800 — 12,993
Livability Code: SB 30-90
Wheelbase-to-length ratio of 50% is considered ◉ dangerous ○ fatiguing ○ good ○ excellent *
The approximate net payload of 1807 pounds at 12% of GVWR on this model is ○ deficient ○ excessive ○ cautionary ◉ good ○ excellent *
Total highway safety penalties are: 4 *   Value: 8 3   Durability: 7 5   Highway Control Rating: 4 6   Highway Safety: 4 2

Brave — 1999 — MHA — 30 — 29A — FO — 6.8L — G — $1900 — 178 — 10,300 — 15,700 — 13,652
Livability Code: SB 30-90
Wheelbase-to-length ratio of 50% is considered ◉ dangerous ○ fatiguing ○ good ○ excellent *
The approximate net payload of 2048 pounds at 13% of GVWR on this model is ○ deficient ○ excessive ○ cautionary ◉ good ○ excellent *
Total highway safety penalties are: 2 *   Value: 8 4   Durability: 7 5   Highway Control Rating: 4 7   Highway Safety: 4 5

Brave — 1999 — MHA — 31 — 30A — CH — 7.4L — G — $1800 — 190 — 4,200 — 14,800 — 13,373
Livability Code: SB 30-90
Wheelbase-to-length ratio of 51% is considered ○ dangerous ◉ fatiguing ○ good ○ excellent *
The approximate net payload of 1427 pounds at 10% of GVWR on this model is ○ deficient ○ excessive ○ cautionary ◉ good ○ excellent *
Total highway safety penalties are: 5 *   Value: 8 3   Durability: 7 5   Highway Control Rating: 4 7   Highway Safety: 4 2

Brave — 1999 — MHA — 31 — 30A — FO — 6.8L — G — $1800 — 190 — 10,300 — 15,700 — 14,107
Livability Code: SB 30-90
Wheelbase-to-length ratio of 51% is considered ○ dangerous ◉ fatiguing ○ good ○ excellent *
The approximate net payload of 1593 pounds at 10% of GVWR on this model is ○ deficient ○ excessive ○ cautionary ◉ good ○ excellent *
Total highway safety penalties are: 2 *   Value: 8 4   Durability: 7 5   Highway Control Rating: 4 8   Highway Safety: 4 6

Brave — 1999 — MHA — 31 — 30A opch — FO — 6.8L — G — $1800 — 190 — 8,000 — 18,000 — 14,230
Livability Code: SB 30-90
Wheelbase-to-length ratio of 51% is considered ○ dangerous ◉ fatiguing ○ good ○ excellent *
The approximate net payload of 3770 pounds at 21% of GVWR on this model is ○ deficient ○ excessive ○ cautionary ◉ good ◉ excellent *
Total highway safety penalties are: 2 *   Value: 8 4   Durability: 7 5   Highway Control Rating: 6 3   Highway Safety: 6 1   ★★

Brave — 1999 — MHA — 32 — 31B — FO — 6.8L — G — $1800 — 190 — 10,300 — 15,700 — 14,017
Livability Code: SB 30-90
Wheelbase-to-length ratio of 50% is considered ◉ dangerous ○ fatiguing ○ good ○ excellent *
The approximate net payload of 1683 pounds at 11% of GVWR on this model is ○ deficient ○ excessive ○ cautionary ◉ good ○ excellent *
Total highway safety penalties are: 2 *   Value: 8 4   Durability: 7 5   Highway Control Rating: 4 4   Highway Safety: 4 2

Brave — 1999 — MHA — 32 — 31B opch — FO — 6.8L — G — $1800 — 190 — 8,000 — 18,000 — 14,069
Livability Code: SB 30-90
Wheelbase-to-length ratio of 50% is considered ◉ dangerous ○ fatiguing ○ good ○ excellent *
The approximate net payload of 3931 pounds at 22% of GVWR on this model is ○ deficient ○ excessive ○ cautionary ○ good ◉ excellent *
Total highway safety penalties are: 2 *   Value: 8 4   Durability: 7 5   Highway Control Rating: 5 6   Highway Safety: 5 4

Brave — 1999 — MHA — 32 — 32T — CH — 7.4L — G — $1800 — 208 — 4,500 — 16,500 — 13,680
Livability Code: SB 30-90
Wheelbase-to-length ratio of 54% is considered ○ dangerous ○ fatiguing ◉ good ○ excellent *
The approximate net payload of 2820 pounds at 17% of GVWR on this model is ○ deficient ○ excessive ○ cautionary ○ good ◉ excellent *
Total highway safety penalties are: 6 *   Value: 8 2   Durability: 7 5   Highway Control Rating: 8 4   Highway Safety: 7 8   ★★★

Brave — 1999 — MHA — 32 — 32T — FO — 6.8L — G — $1800 — 208 — 8,000 — 18,000 — 14,446
Livability Code: SB 30-90
Wheelbase-to-length ratio of 54% is considered ○ dangerous ○ fatiguing ○ good ○ excellent *
The approximate net payload of 3554 pounds at 20% of GVWR on this model is ○ deficient ○ excessive ○ cautionary ○ good ◉ excellent *
Total highway safety penalties are: 2 *   Value: 8 4   Durability: 7 5   Highway Control Rating: 8 7   Highway Safety: 8 5   ★★★

Brave — 1999 — MHA — 35 — 35C — CH — 7.4L — G — $1600 — 220 — 4,500 — 16,500 — 14,507
Livability Code: SB 30-90
Wheelbase-to-length ratio of 52% is considered ○ dangerous ◉ fatiguing ○ good ○ excellent *
The approximate net payload of 1993 pounds at 12% of GVWR on this model is ○ deficient ○ excessive ○ cautionary ◉ good ○ excellent *
Total highway safety penalties are: 7 *   Value: 8 2   Durability: 7 5   Highway Control Rating: 6 0   Highway Safety: 5 3   ★

Brave — 1999 — MHA — 35 — 35C slide — CH — 7.4L — G — $1600 — 220 — 4,500 — 16,500 — 15,307
Livability Code: SB 30-90
Wheelbase-to-length ratio of 52% is considered ○ dangerous ◉ fatiguing ○ good ○ excellent *
The approximate net payload of 1193 pounds at 7% of GVWR on this model is ○ deficient ○ excessive ◉ cautionary ○ good ○ excellent *
Total highway safety penalties are: 12 *   Value: 7 9   Durability: 7 5   Highway Control Rating: 4 0   Highway Safety: 2 8

Brave — 1999 — MHA — 35 — 35C — FO — 6.8L — G — $1600 — 228 — 5,500 — 20,500 — 15,394
Livability Code: SB 30-90
Wheelbase-to-length ratio of 54% is considered ○ dangerous ○ fatiguing ◉ good ○ excellent *
The approximate net payload of 5106 pounds at 25% of GVWR on this model is ○ deficient ○ excessive ○ cautionary ◉ good ○ excellent *
Total highway safety penalties are: 2 *   Value: 8 4   Durability: 7 5   Highway Control Rating: 8 4   Highway Safety: 8 2   ★★★

Note: Safety ratings are based on the assumption that the engineering of the RV has allowed for proper balance by placing fresh, gray, and black holding tanks in a location so as not to change the balance of the RV when the tanks are empty or full. **Always double-check wheelbase, GVWR, and weights at front and rear axles.**

*See Section 1 for details on how conclusions are reached.

Brand	Year	Type	Length	Model	Chassis	Engine	Fuel Type	Average Price per Linear Foot When New	Adjusted Wheelbase	Approx. Towing Capacity	Gross Vehicle Weight Rating	Average Curb Weight
Brave	1999	MHA	35	35C slide	FO	6.8L	G	$1600	228	5,500	20,500	16,194

Livability Code: SB 30-90   Wheelbase-to-length ratio of 54% is considered ○ dangerous ○ fatiguing ◉ good ○ excellent *

The approximate net payload of 4306 pounds at 21% of GVWR on this model is ○ deficient ○ excessive ○ cautionary ○ good ◉ excellent *

Total highway safety penalties are: 7 *   Value: **8 1**   Durability: **7 5**   Highway Control Rating: **8 8**   Highway Safety: **8 1**   ★★★

Brand	Year	Type	Length	Model	Chassis	Engine	Fuel Type		Adjusted Wheelbase	Approx. Towing Capacity	Gross Vehicle Weight Rating	Average Curb Weight
Cabaret	1990	MHA	29	CB285 DB	CH	7.4L	G	$1400	178	1,500	12,700	10,865

Livability Code: SB 30-90   Wheelbase-to-length ratio of 52% is considered ○ dangerous ◉ fatiguing ○ good ○ excellent *

The approximate net payload of 1835 pounds at 14% of GVWR on this model is ○ deficient ○ excessive ○ cautionary ◉ good ○ excellent *

Total highway safety penalties are: 4 *   Value: **7 6**   Durability: **7 0**   Highway Control Rating: **5 4**   Highway Safety: **5 0**   ★

Cabaret	1991	MHA	29	CB-285 -DB	CH	7.4L	G	$1500	178	1,500	12,700	12,216

Livability Code: SB 30-90   Wheelbase-to-length ratio of 52% is considered ○ dangerous ◉ fatiguing ○ good ○ excellent *

The approximate net payload of 484 pounds at 4% of GVWR on this model is ◉ deficient ○ excessive ○ cautionary ○ good ○ excellent *

Total highway safety penalties are: 4 *   Value: **7 6**   Durability: **7 0**   Highway Control Rating: **2 1**   Highway Safety: **1 7**

Callista	1991	MHC	27	260	FO	7.5L	G	$2100	176	1,500	11,500	10,861

Livability Code: RT 30-90   Wheelbase-to-length ratio of 55% is considered ○ dangerous ○ fatiguing ◉ good ○ excellent *

The approximate net payload of 639 pounds at 6% of GVWR on this model is ◉ deficient ○ excessive ○ cautionary ○ good ○ excellent *

Total highway safety penalties are: 2 *   Value: **8 7**   Durability: **8 2**   Highway Control Rating: **5 8**   Highway Safety: **5 6**   ★

Callista	1992	MHC	24	2350	FO	7.5L	G	$2400	158	2,500	11,500	10,536

Livability Code: RT 30-90   Wheelbase-to-length ratio of 54% is considered ○ dangerous ○ fatiguing ◉ good ○ excellent *

The approximate net payload of 964 pounds at 8% of GVWR on this model is ○ deficient ○ excessive ◉ cautionary ○ good ○ excellent *

Total highway safety penalties are: 2 *   Value: **8 7**   Durability: **8 2**   Highway Control Rating: **6 4**   Highway Safety: **6 2**   ★★

Callista	1992	MHC	27	2550	FO	7.5L	G	$2200	176	2,500	11,500	10,867

Livability Code: RT 30-90   Wheelbase-to-length ratio of 55% is considered ○ dangerous ○ fatiguing ◉ good ○ excellent *

The approximate net payload of 633 pounds at 6% of GVWR on this model is ◉ deficient ○ excessive ○ cautionary ○ good ○ excellent *

Total highway safety penalties are: 2 *   Value: **8 7**   Durability: **8 2**   Highway Control Rating: **5 8**   Highway Safety: **5 6**   ★

Callista	1992	MHC	27	2551	FO	7.5L	G	$2200	176	2,500	11,500	10,867

Livability Code: RT 30-90   Wheelbase-to-length ratio of 55% is considered ○ dangerous ○ fatiguing ◉ good ○ excellent *

The approximate net payload of 633 pounds at 6% of GVWR on this model is ◉ deficient ○ excessive ○ cautionary ○ good ○ excellent *

Total highway safety penalties are: 2 *   Value: **8 7**   Durability: **8 2**   Highway Control Rating: **5 8**   Highway Safety: **5 6**   ★

Callista	1992	MHC	27	2552	FO	7.5L	G	$2200	176	2,500	11,500	10,867

Livability Code: RT 30-90   Wheelbase-to-length ratio of 55% is considered ○ dangerous ○ fatiguing ◉ good ○ excellent *

The approximate net payload of 633 pounds at 6% of GVWR on this model is ◉ deficient ○ excessive ○ cautionary ○ good ○ excellent *

Total highway safety penalties are: 2 *   Value: **8 7**   Durability: **8 2**   Highway Control Rating: **5 8**   Highway Safety: **5 6**   ★

Callista	1992	MHC	29	2750	FO	7.5L	G	$2100	194	2,500	11,500	11,089

Livability Code: RT 30-90   Wheelbase-to-length ratio of 56% is considered ○ dangerous ○ fatiguing ◉ good ○ excellent *

The approximate net payload of 411 pounds at 4% of GVWR on this model is ◉ deficient ○ excessive ○ cautionary ○ good ○ excellent *

Total highway safety penalties are: 2 *   Value: **8 7**   Durability: **8 2**   Highway Control Rating: **6 0**   Highway Safety: **5 8**   ★

Callista	1992	MHC	29	2751	FO	7.5L	G	$2100	194	2,500	11,500	11,089

Livability Code: RT 30-90   Wheelbase-to-length ratio of 56% is considered ○ dangerous ○ fatiguing ◉ good ○ excellent *

The approximate net payload of 411 pounds at 4% of GVWR on this model is ◉ deficient ○ excessive ○ cautionary ○ good ○ excellent *

Total highway safety penalties are: 2 *   Value: **8 7**   Durability: **8 2**   Highway Control Rating: **6 0**   Highway Safety: **5 8**   ★

Callista	1992	MHC	29	2752	FO	7.5L	G	$2100	194	2,500	11,500	11,089

Livability Code: RT 30-90   Wheelbase-to-length ratio of 56% is considered ○ dangerous ○ fatiguing ◉ good ○ excellent *

The approximate net payload of 411 pounds at 4% of GVWR on this model is ◉ deficient ○ excessive ○ cautionary ○ good ○ excellent *

Total highway safety penalties are: 2 *   Value: **8 7**   Durability: **8 2**   Highway Control Rating: **6 0**   Highway Safety: **5 8**   ★

Callista	1992	MHC	29	2753	FO	7.5L	G	$2100	194	2,500	11,500	11,089

Livability Code: RT 30-90   Wheelbase-to-length ratio of 56% is considered ○ dangerous ○ fatiguing ◉ good ○ excellent *

The approximate net payload of 411 pounds at 4% of GVWR on this model is ◉ deficient ○ excessive ○ cautionary ○ good ○ excellent *

Total highway safety penalties are: 2 *   Value: **8 7**   Durability: **8 2**   Highway Control Rating: **6 0**   Highway Safety: **5 8**   ★

Note: Safety ratings are based on the assumption that the engineering of the RV has allowed for proper balance by placing fresh, gray, and black holding tanks in a location so as not to change the balance of the RV when the tanks are empty or full. **Always double-check wheelbase, GVWR, and weights at front and rear axles.**

Section 2: The Ratings

Brand	Year	Type	Length	Model	Chassis	Engine	Fuel Type	Average Price per Linear Foot When New	Adjusted Wheelbase	Approx. Towing Capacity	Gross Vehicle Weight Rating	Average Curb Weight
Callista	1994	MHC	24	2350-1	FO	7.5L	G	$2500	158	2,500	11,500	10,430

Livability Code: RT 30-90
Wheelbase-to-length ratio of 55% is considered ○ dangerous ○ fatiguing ◉ good ○ excellent*
The approximate net payload of 1070 pounds at 9% of GVWR on this model is ○ deficient ○ excessive ◉ cautionary ○ good ○ excellent*
Total highway safety penalties are: 2*   Value: 8 7   Durability: 8 2   Highway Control Rating: 7 5   Highway Safety: 7 3   ★★★

Brand	Year	Type	Length	Model	Chassis	Engine	Fuel Type	Price/Ft	Wheelbase	Towing	GVWR	Curb Wt
Callista	1994	MHC	27	2551-2-3	FO	7.5L	G	$2300	176	2,500	11,500	10,755

Livability Code: RT 30-90
Wheelbase-to-length ratio of 55% is considered ○ dangerous ○ fatiguing ◉ good ○ excellent*
The approximate net payload of 745 pounds at 6% of GVWR on this model is ◉ deficient ○ excessive ○ cautionary ○ good ○ excellent*
Total highway safety penalties are: 2*   Value: 8 7   Durability: 8 2   Highway Control Rating: 5 9   Highway Safety: 5 7   ★

Callista	1994	MHC	29	2754-5-6-7	FO	7.5L	G	$2200	194	2,500	11,500	10,977

Livability Code: RT 30-90
Wheelbase-to-length ratio of 56% is considered ○ dangerous ○ fatiguing ◉ good ○ excellent*
The approximate net payload of 523 pounds at 5% of GVWR on this model is ◉ deficient ○ excessive ○ cautionary ○ good ○ excellent*
Total highway safety penalties are: 2*   Value: 8 7   Durability: 8 2   Highway Control Rating: 6 1   Highway Safety: 5 9   ★

Callista	1995	MHC	24	2350-1	FO	7.5L	G	$2600	158	740	13,260	10,837

Livability Code: RT 30-90
Wheelbase-to-length ratio of 55% is considered ○ dangerous ○ fatiguing ◉ good ○ excellent*
The approximate net payload of 2423 pounds at 18% of GVWR on this model is ○ deficient ○ excessive ○ cautionary ○ good ◉ excellent*
Total highway safety penalties are: 2*   Value: 8 7   Durability: 8 2   Highway Control Rating: 9 4   Highway Safety: 9 2   ★★★★

Callista	1995	MHC	27	2652	FO	7.5L	G	$2300	176	740	13,260	11,250

Livability Code: RT 30-90
Wheelbase-to-length ratio of 54% is considered ○ dangerous ○ fatiguing ◉ good ○ excellent*
The approximate net payload of 2010 pounds at 15% of GVWR on this model is ○ deficient ○ excessive ○ cautionary ◉ good ○ excellent*
Total highway safety penalties are: 2*   Value: 8 7   Durability: 8 2   Highway Control Rating: 8 5   Highway Safety: 8 3   ★★★★

Callista	1995	MHC	29	2854-5-6-7	FO	7.5L	G	$2200	194	740	13,260	11,642

Livability Code: RT 30-90
Wheelbase-to-length ratio of 56% is considered ○ dangerous ○ fatiguing ◉ good ○ excellent*
The approximate net payload of 1618 pounds at 12% of GVWR on this model is ○ deficient ○ excessive ○ cautionary ◉ good ○ excellent*
Total highway safety penalties are: 2*   Value: 8 7   Durability: 8 2   Highway Control Rating: 8 7   Highway Safety: 8 5   ★★★★

Callista	1996	MHC	27	2662	FO	7.5L	G	$2400	176	1,500	12,600	10,627

Livability Code: RT 30-90
Wheelbase-to-length ratio of 54% is considered ○ dangerous ○ fatiguing ◉ good ○ excellent*
The approximate net payload of 1973 pounds at 16% of GVWR on this model is ○ deficient ○ excessive ○ cautionary ○ good ◉ excellent*
Total highway safety penalties are: 2*   Value: 8 7   Durability: 8 2   Highway Control Rating: 8 3   Highway Safety: 8 1   ★★★★

Callista	1996	MHC	27	2663	FO	7.5L	G	$2400	176	1,500	12,600	10,627

Livability Code: RT 30-90
Wheelbase-to-length ratio of 54% is considered ○ dangerous ○ fatiguing ◉ good ○ excellent*
The approximate net payload of 1973 pounds at 16% of GVWR on this model is ○ deficient ○ excessive ○ cautionary ○ good ◉ excellent*
Total highway safety penalties are: 2*   Value: 8 7   Durability: 8 2   Highway Control Rating: 8 3   Highway Safety: 8 1   ★★★★

Callista	1996	MHC	27	2662D	FO	7.3L	D	$2600	176	1,500	12,600	11,013

Livability Code: RT30-90
Wheelbase-to-length ratio of 54% is considered ○ dangerous ○ fatiguing ◉ good ○ excellent*
The approximate net payload of 1587 pounds at 13% of GVWR on this model is ○ deficient ○ excessive ○ cautionary ◉ good ○ excellent*
Total highway safety penalties are: 2*   Value: 8 7   Durability: 8 2   Highway Control Rating: 7 7   Highway Safety: 7 5   ★★★

Callista	1996	MHC	27	2663D	FO	7.3L	D	$2600	176	1,500	12,600	11,013

Livability Code: RT30-90
Wheelbase-to-length ratio of 54% is considered ○ dangerous ○ fatiguing ◉ good ○ excellent*
The approximate net payload of 1587 pounds at 13% of GVWR on this model is ○ deficient ○ excessive ○ cautionary ◉ good ○ excellent*
Total highway safety penalties are: 2*   Value: 8 7   Durability: 8 2   Highway Control Rating: 7 7   Highway Safety: 7 5   ★★★

Callista	1996	MHC	29	2864	FO	7.5L	G	$2200	194	1,500	12,600	10,980

Livability Code: RT30-90
Wheelbase-to-length ratio of 55% is considered ○ dangerous ○ fatiguing ◉ good ○ excellent*
The approximate net payload of 1620 pounds at 13% of GVWR on this model is ○ deficient ○ excessive ○ cautionary ◉ good ○ excellent*
Total highway safety penalties are: 2*   Value: 8 7   Durability: 8 2   Highway Control Rating: 8 8   Highway Safety: 8 6   ★★★★

Callista	1996	MHC	29	2865	FO	7.5L	G	$2200	194	1,500	12,600	10,980

Livability Code: RT30-90
Wheelbase-to-length ratio of 55% is considered ○ dangerous ○ fatiguing ◉ good ○ excellent*
The approximate net payload of 1620 pounds at 13% of GVWR on this model is ○ deficient ○ excessive ○ cautionary ◉ good ○ excellent*
Total highway safety penalties are: 2*   Value: 8 7   Durability: 8 2   Highway Control Rating: 8 8   Highway Safety: 8 6   ★★★★

Note: Safety ratings are based on the assumption that the engineering of the RV has allowed for proper balance by placing fresh, gray, and black holding tanks in a location so as not to change the balance of the RV when the tanks are empty or full. **Always double-check wheelbase, GVWR, and weights at front and rear axles.**

*See Section 1 for details on how conclusions are reached.

Brand	Year	Type	Length	Model	Chassis	Engine	Fuel Type	Average Price per Linear Foot When New	Adjusted Wheel-base	Approx. Towing Capacity	Gross Vehicle Weight Rating	Average Curb Weight
Callista	**1996**	MHC	29	2867	FO	7.5L	G	$2300	194	1,500	12,600	10,970

Livability Code: RT30-90
Wheelbase-to-length ratio of 55% is considered ○ dangerous ○ fatiguing ◉ good ○ excellent *
The approximate net payload of 1630 pounds at 13% of GVWR on this model is ○ deficient ○ excessive ○ cautionary ◉ good ○ excellent *
Total highway safety penalties are: 2 *   Value: 8 7   Durability: 8 2   Highway Control Rating: 8 8   Highway Safety: 8 6   ★★★★

Brand	Year	Type	Length	Model	Chassis	Engine	Fuel Type	Avg Price	Wheelbase	Towing	GVWR	Curb
Callista	**1996**	MHC	29	2864D	FO	7.3L	D	$2300	194	1,500	12,600	11,428

Livability Code: RT30-90
Wheelbase-to-length ratio of 55% is considered ○ dangerous ○ fatiguing ◉ good ○ excellent *
The approximate net payload of 1172 pounds at 9% of GVWR on this model is ○ deficient ○ excessive ◉ cautionary ○ good ○ excellent *
Total highway safety penalties are: 2 *   Value: 8 7   Durability: 8 2   Highway Control Rating: 7 7   Highway Safety: 7 5   ★★★

Brand	Year	Type	Length	Model	Chassis	Engine	Fuel	Avg Price	WB	Towing	GVWR	Curb
Callista	**1996**	MHC	29	2865D	FO	7.3L	D	$2400	194	1,500	12,600	11,428

Livability Code: RT30-90
Wheelbase-to-length ratio of 55% is considered ○ dangerous ○ fatiguing ◉ good ○ excellent *
The approximate net payload of 1172 pounds at 9% of GVWR on this model is ○ deficient ○ excessive ◉ cautionary ○ good ○ excellent *
Total highway safety penalties are: 2 *   Value: 8 7   Durability: 8 2   Highway Control Rating: 7 7   Highway Safety: 7 5   ★★★

Brand	Year	Type	Length	Model	Chassis	Engine	Fuel	Avg Price	WB	Towing	GVWR	Curb
Callista	**1996**	MHC	29	2867D	FO	7.3L	D	$2400	194	1,500	12,600	11,428

Livability Code: RT30-90
Wheelbase-to-length ratio of 55% is considered ○ dangerous ○ fatiguing ◉ good ○ excellent *
The approximate net payload of 1172 pounds at 9% of GVWR on this model is ○ deficient ○ excessive ◉ cautionary ○ good ○ excellent *
Total highway safety penalties are: 2 *   Value: 8 7   Durability: 8 2   Highway Control Rating: 7 7   Highway Safety: 7 5   ★★★

Brand	Year	Type	Length	Model	Chassis	Engine	Fuel	Avg Price	WB	Towing	GVWR	Curb
Callista Cove	**1990**	MHC	26	2502CB	FO	5.8L	G	$1500	176	1,500	11,000	9,552

Livability Code: VA 30-90
Wheelbase-to-length ratio of 56% is considered ○ dangerous ○ fatiguing ◉ good ○ excellent *
The approximate net payload of 1448 pounds at 13% of GVWR on this model is ○ deficient ○ excessive ○ cautionary ◉ good ○ excellent *
Total highway safety penalties are: 2 *   Value: 8 6   Durability: 7 9   Highway Control Rating: 9 2   Highway Safety: 9 0   ★★★

Brand	Year	Type	Length	Model	Chassis	Engine	Fuel	Avg Price	WB	Towing	GVWR	Curb
Callista Cove	**1991**	MHC	28	280	FO	5.8L	G	$1500	194	1,500	11,500	10,176

Livability Code: VA 30-90
Wheelbase-to-length ratio of 58% is considered ○ dangerous ○ fatiguing ○ good ◉ excellent *
The approximate net payload of 1324 pounds at 12% of GVWR on this model is ○ deficient ○ excessive ○ cautionary ◉ good ○ excellent *
Total highway safety penalties are: 2 *   Value: 8 6   Durability: 7 9   Highway Control Rating: 9 4   Highway Safety: 9 2   ★★★

Brand	Year	Type	Length	Model	Chassis	Engine	Fuel	Avg Price	WB	Towing	GVWR	Curb
Callista Cove	**1992**	MHC	23	2200	FO	5.8L	G	$1700	158	1,500	11,500	8,978

Livability Code: VA 30-90
Wheelbase-to-length ratio of 58% is considered ○ dangerous ○ fatiguing ○ good ◉ excellent *
The approximate net payload of 2522 pounds at 22% of GVWR on this model is ○ deficient ○ excessive ○ cautionary ○ good ◉ excellent *
Total highway safety penalties are: 2 *   Value: 8 6   Durability: 7 9   Highway Control Rating: 1 0 0   Highway Safety: 9 8   ★★★

Brand	Year	Type	Length	Model	Chassis	Engine	Fuel	Avg Price	WB	Towing	GVWR	Curb
Callista Cove	**1992**	MHC	23	2201	FO	5.8L	G	$1700	158	1,500	11,500	8,978

Livability Code: VA 30-90
Wheelbase-to-length ratio of 58% is considered ○ dangerous ○ fatiguing ○ good ◉ excellent *
The approximate net payload of 2522 pounds at 22% of GVWR on this model is ○ deficient ○ excessive ○ cautionary ○ good ◉ excellent *
Total highway safety penalties are: 2 *   Value: 8 6   Durability: 7 9   Highway Control Rating: 1 0 0   Highway Safety: 9 8   ★★★

Brand	Year	Type	Length	Model	Chassis	Engine	Fuel	Avg Price	WB	Towing	GVWR	Curb
Callista Cove	**1992**	MHC	26	2500	FO	5.8L	G	$1600	176	1,500	11,500	9,582

Livability Code: VA 30-90
Wheelbase-to-length ratio of 56% is considered ○ dangerous ○ fatiguing ◉ good ○ excellent *
The approximate net payload of 1918 pounds at 17% of GVWR on this model is ○ deficient ○ excessive ○ cautionary ○ good ◉ excellent *
Total highway safety penalties are: 2 *   Value: 8 6   Durability: 7 9   Highway Control Rating: 9 8   Highway Safety: 9 6   ★★★

Brand	Year	Type	Length	Model	Chassis	Engine	Fuel	Avg Price	WB	Towing	GVWR	Curb
Callista Cove	**1992**	MHC	26	2501	FO	5.8L	G	$1600	176	1,500	11,500	9,582

Livability Code: VA 30-90
Wheelbase-to-length ratio of 56% is considered ○ dangerous ○ fatiguing ◉ good ○ excellent *
The approximate net payload of 1918 pounds at 17% of GVWR on this model is ○ deficient ○ excessive ○ cautionary ○ good ◉ excellent *
Total highway safety penalties are: 2 *   Value: 8 6   Durability: 7 9   Highway Control Rating: 9 8   Highway Safety: 9 6   ★★★

Brand	Year	Type	Length	Model	Chassis	Engine	Fuel	Avg Price	WB	Towing	GVWR	Curb
Callista Cove	**1992**	MHC	26	2502	FO	5.8L	G	$1600	176	1,500	11,500	9,582

Livability Code: VA 30-90
Wheelbase-to-length ratio of 56% is considered ○ dangerous ○ fatiguing ◉ good ○ excellent *
The approximate net payload of 1918 pounds at 17% of GVWR on this model is ○ deficient ○ excessive ○ cautionary ○ good ◉ excellent *
Total highway safety penalties are: 2 *   Value: 8 6   Durability: 7 9   Highway Control Rating: 9 8   Highway Safety: 9 6   ★★★

Brand	Year	Type	Length	Model	Chassis	Engine	Fuel	Avg Price	WB	Towing	GVWR	Curb
Callista Cove	**1992**	MHC	26	2503	FO	5.8L	G	$1600	176	1,500	11,500	9,582

Livability Code: VA 30-90
Wheelbase-to-length ratio of 56% is considered ○ dangerous ○ fatiguing ◉ good ○ excellent *
The approximate net payload of 1918 pounds at 17% of GVWR on this model is ○ deficient ○ excessive ○ cautionary ○ good ◉ excellent *
Total highway safety penalties are: 2 *   Value: 8 6   Durability: 7 9   Highway Control Rating: 9 8   Highway Safety: 9 6   ★★★

Note: Safety ratings are based on the assumption that the engineering of the RV has allowed for proper balance by placing fresh, gray, and black holding tanks in a location so as not to change the balance of the RV when the tanks are empty or full. **Always double-check wheelbase, GVWR, and weights at front and rear axles.**

Brand	Year	Type	Length	Model	Chassis	Engine	Fuel Type	Average Price per Linear Foot When New	Adjusted Wheelbase	Approx. Towing Capacity	Gross Vehicle Weight Rating	Average Curb Weight
Callista Cove	1992	MHC	26	2704	FO	5.8L	G	$1700	194	1,500	11,500	10,162

Livability Code: VA 30-90
Wheelbase-to-length ratio of 62% is considered ○ dangerous ○ fatiguing ○ good ◉ excellent *
The approximate net payload of 1338 pounds at 12% of GVWR on this model is ○ deficient ○ excessive ○ cautionary ◉ good ○ excellent *
Total highway safety penalties are: 2 *   Value: 86   Durability: 79   Highway Control Rating: 100   Highway Safety: 98   ★★★

Brand	Year	Type	Length	Model	Chassis	Engine	Fuel Type	Avg Price/Linear Foot	Adj Wheelbase	Approx Towing	GVWR	Avg Curb Weight
Callista Cove	1994	MHC	24	2300-1	FO	5.8L	G	$1900	158	1,500	11,500	8,960

Livability Code: VA 30-90
Wheelbase-to-length ratio of 55% is considered ○ dangerous ○ fatiguing ◉ good ○ excellent *
The approximate net payload of 2540 pounds at 22% of GVWR on this model is ○ deficient ○ excessive ○ cautionary ○ good ◉ excellent *
Total highway safety penalties are: 2 *   Value: 86   Durability: 79   Highway Control Rating: 94   Highway Safety: 92   ★★★

Callista Cove	1994	MHC	26	2501-3	FO	5.8L	G	$1800	176	1,500	11,500	9,550

Livability Code: VA 30-90
Wheelbase-to-length ratio of 56% is considered ○ dangerous ○ fatiguing ◉ good ○ excellent *
The approximate net payload of 1950 pounds at 17% of GVWR on this model is ○ deficient ○ excessive ○ cautionary ○ good ◉ excellent *
Total highway safety penalties are: 2 *   Value: 86   Durability: 79   Highway Control Rating: 99   Highway Safety: 97   ★★★

Callista Cove	1994	MHC	27	2600	FO	5.8L	G	$1700	176	1,500	11,500	9,840

Livability Code: VA 30-90
Wheelbase-to-length ratio of 54% is considered ○ dangerous ○ fatiguing ◉ good ○ excellent *
The approximate net payload of 1660 pounds at 14% of GVWR on this model is ○ deficient ○ excessive ○ cautionary ◉ good ○ excellent *
Total highway safety penalties are: 2 *   Value: 86   Durability: 79   Highway Control Rating: 83   Highway Safety: 81   ★★★

Callista Cove	1994	MHC	28	2704-8	FO	5.8L	G	$1700	194	1,500	11,500	10,150

Livability Code: VA 30-90
Wheelbase-to-length ratio of 58% is considered ○ dangerous ○ fatiguing ○ good ◉ excellent *
The approximate net payload of 1350 pounds at 12% of GVWR on this model is ○ deficient ○ excessive ○ cautionary ◉ good ○ excellent *
Total highway safety penalties are: 2 *   Value: 86   Durability: 79   Highway Control Rating: 94   Highway Safety: 92   ★★★

Callista Cove	1994	MHC	28	2709 LTD	FO	5.8L	G	$2000	194	1,500	11,500	10,150

Livability Code: VA 30-90
Wheelbase-to-length ratio of 58% is considered ○ dangerous ○ fatiguing ○ good ◉ excellent *
The approximate net payload of 1350 pounds at 12% of GVWR on this model is ○ deficient ○ excessive ○ cautionary ◉ good ○ excellent *
Total highway safety penalties are: 2 *   Value: 86   Durability: 79   Highway Control Rating: 94   Highway Safety: 92   ★★★

Callista Cove	1995	MHC	22	2100	FO	5.8L	G	$2000	138	1,500	13,260	9,630

Livability Code: VA 30-90
Wheelbase-to-length ratio of 52% is considered ○ dangerous ◉ fatiguing ○ good ○ excellent *
The approximate net payload of 3630 pounds at 27% of GVWR on this model is ○ deficient ○ excessive ○ cautionary ◉ good ○ excellent *
Total highway safety penalties are: 2 *   Value: 86   Durability: 79   Highway Control Rating: 68   Highway Safety: 66   ★★

Callista Cove	1995	MHC	24	2300-1	FO	5.8L	G	$1900	158	1,500	13,260	9,930

Livability Code: VA 30-90
Wheelbase-to-length ratio of 55% is considered ○ dangerous ○ fatiguing ◉ good ○ excellent *
The approximate net payload of 3330 pounds at 25% of GVWR on this model is ○ deficient ○ excessive ○ cautionary ◉ good ○ excellent *
Total highway safety penalties are: 2 *   Value: 86   Durability: 79   Highway Control Rating: 91   Highway Safety: 89   ★★★

Callista Cove	1995	MHC	27	2602	FO	5.8L	G	$1700	176	1,500	13,260	10,522

Livability Code: VA 30-90
Wheelbase-to-length ratio of 54% is considered ○ dangerous ○ fatiguing ◉ good ○ excellent *
The approximate net payload of 2738 pounds at 21% of GVWR on this model is ○ deficient ○ excessive ○ cautionary ○ good ◉ excellent *
Total highway safety penalties are: 2 *   Value: 86   Durability: 79   Highway Control Rating: 90   Highway Safety: 88   ★★★

Callista Cove	1995	MHC	28	2700	FO	5.8L	G	$1700	176	1,500	13,260	10,682

Livability Code: VA 30-90
Wheelbase-to-length ratio of 52% is considered ○ dangerous ◉ fatiguing ○ good ○ excellent *
The approximate net payload of 2578 pounds at 19% of GVWR on this model is ○ deficient ○ excessive ○ cautionary ○ good ◉ excellent *
Total highway safety penalties are: 2 *   Value: 86   Durability: 79   Highway Control Rating: 75   Highway Safety: 73   ★★★

Callista Cove	1995	MHC	29	2804-9	FO	5.8L	G	$1700	194	1,500	13,260	10,830

Livability Code: VA 30-90
Wheelbase-to-length ratio of 56% is considered ○ dangerous ○ fatiguing ◉ good ○ excellent *
The approximate net payload of 2430 pounds at 18% of GVWR on this model is ○ deficient ○ excessive ○ cautionary ○ good ◉ excellent *
Total highway safety penalties are: 2 *   Value: 86   Durability: 79   Highway Control Rating: 98   Highway Safety: 96   ★★★

Callista Cove	1996	MHC	25	2340	FO	5.8L	G	$1900	170	1,500	12,600	9,785

Livability Code: VA 30-90
Wheelbase-to-length ratio of 57% is considered ○ dangerous ○ fatiguing ◉ good ○ excellent *
The approximate net payload of 2815 pounds at 22% of GVWR on this model is ○ deficient ○ excessive ○ cautionary ○ good ◉ excellent *
Total highway safety penalties are: 2 *   Value: 86   Durability: 79   Highway Control Rating: 100   Highway Safety: 98   ★★★

Note: Safety ratings are based on the assumption that the engineering of the RV has allowed for proper balance by placing fresh, gray, and black holding tanks in a location so as not to change the balance of the RV when the tanks are empty or full. **Always double-check wheelbase, GVWR, and weights at front and rear axles.**

*See Section 1 for details on how conclusions are reached.

Brand	Year	Type	Length	Model	Chassis	Engine	Fuel Type	Average Price per Linear Foot When New	Adjusted Wheelbase	Approx. Towing Capacity	Gross Vehicle Weight Rating	Average Curb Weight
Callista Cove	**1996**	MHC	25	2340	FO	7.5L	G	$1900	170	1,500	12,600	9,785

Livability Code: VA 30-90 Wheelbase-to-length ratio of 57% is considered ○ dangerous ○ fatiguing ◉ good ○ excellent *
The approximate net payload of 2815 pounds at 22% of GVWR on this model is ○ deficient ○ excessive ○ cautionary ○ good ◉ excellent *
Total highway safety penalties are: 2 *   Value: 86   Durability: 79   Highway Control Rating: 100   Highway Safety: 98   ★★★

Brand	Year	Type	Length	Model	Chassis	Engine	Fuel Type	Avg. Price/Linear Foot	Adjusted Wheelbase	Approx. Towing Capacity	GVWR	Avg. Curb Weight
Callista Cove	**1996**	MHC	25	2340D	FO	7.3L	D	$2100	170	1,500	12,600	9,917

Livability Code: VA 30-90 Wheelbase-to-length ratio of 57% is considered ○ dangerous ○ fatiguing ◉ good ○ excellent *
The approximate net payload of 2683 pounds at 21% of GVWR on this model is ○ deficient ○ excessive ○ cautionary ○ good ◉ excellent *
Total highway safety penalties are: 2 *   Value: 86   Durability: 79   Highway Control Rating: 100   Highway Safety: 98   ★★★

Callista Cove	**1996**	MHC	25	2341	FO	5.8L	G	$1900	170	1,500	12,600	9,785

Livability Code: VA 30-90 Wheelbase-to-length ratio of 57% is considered ○ dangerous ○ fatiguing ◉ good ○ excellent *
The approximate net payload of 2815 pounds at 22% of GVWR on this model is ○ deficient ○ excessive ○ cautionary ○ good ◉ excellent *
Total highway safety penalties are: 2 *   Value: 86   Durability: 79   Highway Control Rating: 100   Highway Safety: 98   ★★★

Callista Cove	**1996**	MHC	25	2341	FO	7.5L	G	$1900	170	1,500	12,600	9,785

Livability Code: VA 30-90 Wheelbase-to-length ratio of 57% is considered ○ dangerous ○ fatiguing ◉ good ○ excellent *
The approximate net payload of 2815 pounds at 22% of GVWR on this model is ○ deficient ○ excessive ○ cautionary ○ good ◉ excellent *
Total highway safety penalties are: 2 *   Value: 86   Durability: 79   Highway Control Rating: 100   Highway Safety: 98   ★★★

Callista Cove	**1996**	MHC	25	2341D	FO	7.3L	D	$2100	170	1,500	12,600	9,917

Livability Code: VA 30-90 Wheelbase-to-length ratio of 57% is considered ○ dangerous ○ fatiguing ◉ good ○ excellent *
The approximate net payload of 2683 pounds at 21% of GVWR on this model is ○ deficient ○ excessive ○ cautionary ○ good ◉ excellent *
Total highway safety penalties are: 2 *   Value: 86   Durability: 79   Highway Control Rating: 100   Highway Safety: 98   ★★★

Callista Cove	**1996**	MHC	27	2642	FO	5.8L	G	$1800	178	1,500	12,600	10,273

Livability Code: VA 30-90 Wheelbase-to-length ratio of 55% is considered ○ dangerous ○ fatiguing ◉ good ○ excellent *
The approximate net payload of 2327 pounds at 18% of GVWR on this model is ○ deficient ○ excessive ○ cautionary ○ good ◉ excellent *
Total highway safety penalties are: 2 *   Value: 86   Durability: 79   Highway Control Rating: 95   Highway Safety: 93   ★★★

Callista Cove	**1996**	MHC	27	2642	FO	7.5L	G	$1800	178	1,500	12,600	10,273

Livability Code: VA 30-90 Wheelbase-to-length ratio of 55% is considered ○ dangerous ○ fatiguing ◉ good ○ excellent *
The approximate net payload of 2327 pounds at 18% of GVWR on this model is ○ deficient ○ excessive ○ cautionary ○ good ◉ excellent *
Total highway safety penalties are: 2 *   Value: 86   Durability: 79   Highway Control Rating: 95   Highway Safety: 93   ★★★

Callista Cove	**1996**	MHC	27	2642D	FO	7.3L	D	$2000	178	1,500	12,600	10,402

Livability Code: VA 30-90 Wheelbase-to-length ratio of 55% is considered ○ dangerous ○ fatiguing ◉ good ○ excellent *
The approximate net payload of 2198 pounds at 17% of GVWR on this model is ○ deficient ○ excessive ○ cautionary ○ good ◉ excellent *
Total highway safety penalties are: 2 *   Value: 86   Durability: 79   Highway Control Rating: 94   Highway Safety: 92   ★★★

Callista Cove	**1996**	MHC	27	2643	FO	5.8L	G	$1800	178	1,500	12,600	10,273

Livability Code: VA 30-90 Wheelbase-to-length ratio of 55% is considered ○ dangerous ○ fatiguing ◉ good ○ excellent *
The approximate net payload of 2327 pounds at 18% of GVWR on this model is ○ deficient ○ excessive ○ cautionary ○ good ◉ excellent *
Total highway safety penalties are: 2 *   Value: 86   Durability: 79   Highway Control Rating: 95   Highway Safety: 93   ★★★

Callista Cove	**1996**	MHC	27	2643	FO	7.5L	G	$1900	178	1,500	12,600	10,273

Livability Code: VA 30-90 Wheelbase-to-length ratio of 55% is considered ○ dangerous ○ fatiguing ◉ good ○ excellent *
The approximate net payload of 2327 pounds at 18% of GVWR on this model is ○ deficient ○ excessive ○ cautionary ○ good ◉ excellent *
Total highway safety penalties are: 2 *   Value: 86   Durability: 79   Highway Control Rating: 95   Highway Safety: 93   ★★★

Callista Cove	**1996**	MHC	27	2643D	FO	7.3L	D	$2000	178	1,500	12,600	10,402

Livability Code: VA 30-90 Wheelbase-to-length ratio of 55% is considered ○ dangerous ○ fatiguing ◉ good ○ excellent *
The approximate net payload of 2198 pounds at 17% of GVWR on this model is ○ deficient ○ excessive ○ cautionary ○ good ◉ excellent *
Total highway safety penalties are: 2 *   Value: 86   Durability: 79   Highway Control Rating: 94   Highway Safety: 92   ★★★

Callista Cove	**1996**	MHC	29	2844	FO	5.8L	G	$1700	194	1,500	12,600	10,577

Livability Code: VA 30-90 Wheelbase-to-length ratio of 56% is considered ○ dangerous ○ fatiguing ◉ good ○ excellent *
The approximate net payload of 2023 pounds at 16% of GVWR on this model is ○ deficient ○ excessive ○ cautionary ○ good ◉ excellent *
Total highway safety penalties are: 2 *   Value: 86   Durability: 79   Highway Control Rating: 96   Highway Safety: 94   ★★★

Note: Safety ratings are based on the assumption that the engineering of the RV has allowed for proper balance by placing fresh, gray, and black holding tanks in a location so as not to change the balance of the RV when the tanks are empty or full. **Always double-check wheelbase, GVWR, and weights at front and rear axles.**

*See Section 1 for details on how conclusions are reached.

Brand	Year	Type	Length	Model	Chassis	Engine	Fuel Type	Average Price per Linear Foot When New	Adjusted Wheelbase	Approx. Towing Capacity	Gross Vehicle Weight Rating	Average Curb Weight
Callista Cove	1996	MHC	29	2844	FO	7.5L	G	$1800	194	1,500	12,600	10,577

Livability Code: VA 30-90
Wheelbase-to-length ratio of 56% is considered ○ dangerous ○ fatiguing ◉ good ○ excellent*
The approximate net payload of 2023 pounds at 16% of GVWR on this model is ○ deficient ○ excessive ○ cautionary ○ good ◉ excellent*
Total highway safety penalties are: 2*   Value: 8 6   Durability: 7 9   Highway Control Rating: 9 6   Highway Safety: 9 4   ★★★

Brand	Year	Type	Length	Model	Chassis	Engine	Fuel Type					Curb Weight
Callista Cove	1996	MHC	29	2844D	FO	7.3L	D	$1900	194	1,500	12,600	10,804

Livability Code: VA 30-90
Wheelbase-to-length ratio of 56% is considered ○ dangerous ○ fatiguing ◉ good ○ excellent*
The approximate net payload of 1796 pounds at 14% of GVWR on this model is ○ deficient ○ excessive ○ cautionary ◉ good ○ excellent*
Total highway safety penalties are: 2*   Value: 8 6   Durability: 7 9   Highway Control Rating: 9 2   Highway Safety: 9 0   ★★★

| **Callista Cove** | 1996 | MHC | 29 | 2845 | FO | 5.8L | G | $1700 | 194 | 1,500 | 12,600 | 10,577 |

Livability Code: VA 30-90
Wheelbase-to-length ratio of 56% is considered ○ dangerous ○ fatiguing ◉ good ○ excellent*
The approximate net payload of 2023 pounds at 16% of GVWR on this model is ○ deficient ○ excessive ○ cautionary ○ good ◉ excellent*
Total highway safety penalties are: 2*   Value: 8 6   Durability: 7 9   Highway Control Rating: 9 6   Highway Safety: 9 4   ★★★

| **Callista Cove** | 1996 | MHC | 29 | 2845 | FO | 7.5L | G | $1800 | 194 | 1,500 | 12,600 | 10,577 |

Livability Code: VA 30-90
Wheelbase-to-length ratio of 56% is considered ○ dangerous ○ fatiguing ◉ good ○ excellent*
The approximate net payload of 2023 pounds at 16% of GVWR on this model is ○ deficient ○ excessive ○ cautionary ○ good ◉ excellent*
Total highway safety penalties are: 2*   Value: 8 6   Durability: 7 9   Highway Control Rating: 9 6   Highway Safety: 9 4   ★★★

| **Callista Cove** | 1996 | MHC | 29 | 2845D | FO | 7.3L | D | $1900 | 194 | 1,500 | 12,600 | 10,804 |

Livability Code: VA 30-90
Wheelbase-to-length ratio of 56% is considered ○ dangerous ○ fatiguing ◉ good ○ excellent*
The approximate net payload of 1796 pounds at 14% of GVWR on this model is ○ deficient ○ excessive ○ cautionary ◉ good ○ excellent*
Total highway safety penalties are: 2*   Value: 8 6   Durability: 7 9   Highway Control Rating: 9 2   Highway Safety: 9 0   ★★★

| **Callista Cove** | 1996 | MHC | 29 | 2846 | FO | 5.8L | G | $1700 | 194 | 1,500 | 12,600 | 10,462 |

Livability Code: VA 30-90
Wheelbase-to-length ratio of 56% is considered ○ dangerous ○ fatiguing ◉ good ○ excellent*
The approximate net payload of 2138 pounds at 17% of GVWR on this model is ○ deficient ○ excessive ○ cautionary ○ good ◉ excellent*
Total highway safety penalties are: 2*   Value: 8 6   Durability: 7 9   Highway Control Rating: 9 7   Highway Safety: 9 5   ★★★

| **Callista Cove** | 1996 | MHC | 29 | 2846 | FO | 7.5L | G | $1800 | 194 | 1,500 | 12,600 | 10,462 |

Livability Code: VA 30-90
Wheelbase-to-length ratio of 56% is considered ○ dangerous ○ fatiguing ◉ good ○ excellent*
The approximate net payload of 2138 pounds at 17% of GVWR on this model is ○ deficient ○ excessive ○ cautionary ○ good ◉ excellent*
Total highway safety penalties are: 2*   Value: 8 6   Durability: 7 9   Highway Control Rating: 9 7   Highway Safety: 9 5   ★★★

| **Callista Cove** | 1996 | MHC | 29 | 2846D | FO | 7.3L | D | $1900 | 194 | 1,500 | 12,600 | 10,804 |

Livability Code: VA 30-90
Wheelbase-to-length ratio of 56% is considered ○ dangerous ○ fatiguing ◉ good ○ excellent*
The approximate net payload of 1796 pounds at 14% of GVWR on this model is ○ deficient ○ excessive ○ cautionary ◉ good ○ excellent*
Total highway safety penalties are: 2*   Value: 8 6   Durability: 7 9   Highway Control Rating: 9 2   Highway Safety: 9 0   ★★★

| **Callista Cove** | 1996 | MHC | 29 | 2847 | FO | 5.8L | G | $1700 | 194 | 1,500 | 12,600 | 10,567 |

Livability Code: VA 30-90
Wheelbase-to-length ratio of 56% is considered ○ dangerous ○ fatiguing ◉ good ○ excellent*
The approximate net payload of 2033 pounds at 16% of GVWR on this model is ○ deficient ○ excessive ○ cautionary ○ good ◉ excellent*
Total highway safety penalties are: 2*   Value: 8 6   Durability: 7 9   Highway Control Rating: 9 6   Highway Safety: 9 4   ★★★

| **Callista Cove** | 1996 | MHC | 29 | 2847 | FO | 7.5L | G | $1800 | 194 | 1,500 | 12,600 | 10,567 |

Livability Code: VA 30-90
Wheelbase-to-length ratio of 56% is considered ○ dangerous ○ fatiguing ◉ good ○ excellent*
The approximate net payload of 2033 pounds at 16% of GVWR on this model is ○ deficient ○ excessive ○ cautionary ○ good ◉ excellent*
Total highway safety penalties are: 2*   Value: 8 6   Durability: 7 9   Highway Control Rating: 9 6   Highway Safety: 9 4   ★★★

| **Callista Cove** | 1996 | MHC | 29 | 2847D | FO | 7.3L | D | $1900 | 194 | 1,500 | 12,600 | 10,804 |

Livability Code: VA 30-90
Wheelbase-to-length ratio of 56% is considered ○ dangerous ○ fatiguing ◉ good ○ excellent*
The approximate net payload of 1796 pounds at 14% of GVWR on this model is ○ deficient ○ excessive ○ cautionary ◉ good ○ excellent*
Total highway safety penalties are: 2*   Value: 8 6   Durability: 7 9   Highway Control Rating: 9 2   Highway Safety: 9 0   ★★★

| **Callista Cove** | 1996 | MHC | 29 | 2849 | FO | 5.8L | G | $1900 | 194 | 1,500 | 12,600 | 10,567 |

Livability Code: VA 30-90
Wheelbase-to-length ratio of 56% is considered ○ dangerous ○ fatiguing ◉ good ○ excellent*
The approximate net payload of 2033 pounds at 16% of GVWR on this model is ○ deficient ○ excessive ○ cautionary ○ good ◉ excellent*
Total highway safety penalties are: 2*   Value: 8 6   Durability: 7 9   Highway Control Rating: 9 6   Highway Safety: 9 4   ★★★

Note: Safety ratings are based on the assumption that the engineering of the RV has allowed for proper balance by placing fresh, gray, and black holding tanks in a location so as not to change the balance of the RV when the tanks are empty or full. **Always double-check wheelbase, GVWR, and weights at front and rear axles.**

*See Section 1 for details on how conclusions are reached.

Brand	Year	Type	Length	Model	Chassis	Engine	Fuel Type	Average Price per Linear Foot When New	Adjusted Wheelbase	Approx. Towing Capacity	Gross Vehicle Weight Rating	Average Curb Weight
Callista Cove	1996	MHC	29	2849	FO	7.5L	G	$1900	194	1,500	12,600	10,567

Livability Code: VA 30-90
Wheelbase-to-length ratio of 56% is considered ○ dangerous ○ fatiguing ◉ good ○ excellent *
The approximate net payload of 2033 pounds at 16% of GVWR on this model is ○ deficient ○ excessive ○ cautionary ○ good ◉ excellent *
Total highway safety penalties are: 2 * Value: 8 6 Durability: 7 9 Highway Control Rating: 9 6 Highway Safety: 9 4 ★★★

Brand	Year	Type	Length	Model	Chassis	Engine	Fuel Type		Adjusted Wheelbase	Approx. Towing Capacity	Gross Vehicle Weight Rating	Average Curb Weight
Callista Cove	1996	MHC	29	2849D	FO	7.3L	D	$2100	194	1,500	12,600	10,804

Livability Code: VA 30-90
Wheelbase-to-length ratio of 56% is considered ○ dangerous ○ fatiguing ◉ good ○ excellent *
The approximate net payload of 1796 pounds at 14% of GVWR on this model is ○ deficient ○ excessive ○ cautionary ○ good ◉ excellent *
Total highway safety penalties are: 2 * Value: 8 6 Durability: 7 9 Highway Control Rating: 9 2 Highway Safety: 9 0 ★★★

Callista Cruiser	1994	MHC	24	2330	FO	5.8L	G	$1700	158	1,500	11,500	8,960

Livability Code: VA 30-90
Wheelbase-to-length ratio of 55% is considered ○ dangerous ○ fatiguing ◉ good ○ excellent *
The approximate net payload of 2540 pounds at 22% of GVWR on this model is ○ deficient ○ excessive ○ cautionary ○ good ◉ excellent *
Total highway safety penalties are: 2 * Value: 8 6 Durability: 7 9 Highway Control Rating: 9 4 Highway Safety: 9 2 ★★★

Callista Cruiser	1994	MHC	26	2532	FO	5.8L	G	$1600	176	1,500	11,500	9,550

Livability Code: VA 30-90
Wheelbase-to-length ratio of 56% is considered ○ dangerous ○ fatiguing ◉ good ○ excellent *
The approximate net payload of 1950 pounds at 17% of GVWR on this model is ○ deficient ○ excessive ○ cautionary ○ good ◉ excellent *
Total highway safety penalties are: 2 * Value: 8 6 Durability: 7 9 Highway Control Rating: 9 9 Highway Safety: 9 7 ★★★

Callista Cruiser	1994	MHC	28	2734-7	FO	5.8L	G	$1500	194	1,500	11,500	10,150

Livability Code: VA 30-90
Wheelbase-to-length ratio of 58% is considered ○ dangerous ○ fatiguing ○ good ◉ excellent *
The approximate net payload of 1350 pounds at 12% of GVWR on this model is ○ deficient ○ excessive ○ cautionary ○ good ◉ excellent *
Total highway safety penalties are: 2 * Value: 8 6 Durability: 7 9 Highway Control Rating: 9 4 Highway Safety: 9 2 ★★★

Callista Cruiser	1995	MHC	22	2130	FO	5.8L	G	$1800	138	1,500	13,260	9,425

Livability Code: VA 30-90
Wheelbase-to-length ratio of 52% is considered ○ dangerous ◉ fatiguing ○ good ○ excellent *
The approximate net payload of 3835 pounds at 29% of GVWR on this model is ○ deficient ○ excessive ○ cautionary ◉ good ○ excellent *
Total highway safety penalties are: 2 * Value: 8 6 Durability: 7 9 Highway Control Rating: 6 7 Highway Safety: 6 5 ★★

Callista Cruiser	1995	MHC	24	2330	FO	5.8L	G	$1700	158	1,500	13,260	9,728

Livability Code: VA 30-90
Wheelbase-to-length ratio of 55% is considered ○ dangerous ○ fatiguing ◉ good ○ excellent *
The approximate net payload of 3532 pounds at 27% of GVWR on this model is ○ deficient ○ excessive ○ cautionary ◉ good ○ excellent *
Total highway safety penalties are: 2 * Value: 8 6 Durability: 7 9 Highway Control Rating: 8 9 Highway Safety: 8 7 ★★★

Callista Cruiser	1995	MHC	27	2632	FO	5.8L	G	$1500	176	1,500	13,260	10,332

Livability Code: VA 30-90
Wheelbase-to-length ratio of 54% is considered ○ dangerous ○ fatiguing ◉ good ○ excellent *
The approximate net payload of 2928 pounds at 22% of GVWR on this model is ○ deficient ○ excessive ○ cautionary ○ good ◉ excellent *
Total highway safety penalties are: 2 * Value: 8 6 Durability: 7 9 Highway Control Rating: 8 8 Highway Safety: 8 6 ★★★

Callista Cruiser	1995	MHC	28	2730	FO	5.8L	G	$1500	176	1,500	13,260	10,482

Livability Code: VA 30-90
Wheelbase-to-length ratio of 52% is considered ○ dangerous ◉ fatiguing ○ good ○ excellent *
The approximate net payload of 2778 pounds at 21% of GVWR on this model is ○ deficient ○ excessive ○ cautionary ○ good ◉ excellent *
Total highway safety penalties are: 2 * Value: 8 6 Durability: 7 9 Highway Control Rating: 7 5 Highway Safety: 7 3 ★★★

Callista Cruiser	1995	MHC	29	2834-9	FO	5.8L	G	$1500	194	1,500	13,260	10,632

Livability Code: VA 30-90
Wheelbase-to-length ratio of 56% is considered ○ dangerous ○ fatiguing ◉ good ○ excellent *
The approximate net payload of 2628 pounds at 20% of GVWR on this model is ○ deficient ○ excessive ○ cautionary ○ good ◉ excellent *
Total highway safety penalties are: 2 * Value: 8 6 Durability: 7 9 Highway Control Rating: 9 9 Highway Safety: 9 7 ★★★

Callista Cruiser	1996	MHC	25	2320	FO	5.8L	G	$1700	170	1,500	12,600	9,785

Livability Code: VA 30-90
Wheelbase-to-length ratio of 57% is considered ○ dangerous ○ fatiguing ◉ good ○ excellent *
The approximate net payload of 2815 pounds at 22% of GVWR on this model is ○ deficient ○ excessive ○ cautionary ○ good ◉ excellent *
Total highway safety penalties are: 2 * Value: 8 6 Durability: 7 9 Highway Control Rating: 1 0 0 Highway Safety: 9 8 ★★★

Callista Cruiser	1996	MHC	25	2320	FO	7.5L	G	$1700	170	1,500	12,600	9,785

Livability Code: VA 30-90
Wheelbase-to-length ratio of 57% is considered ○ dangerous ○ fatiguing ◉ good ○ excellent *
The approximate net payload of 2815 pounds at 22% of GVWR on this model is ○ deficient ○ excessive ○ cautionary ○ good ◉ excellent *
Total highway safety penalties are: 2 * Value: 8 6 Durability: 7 9 Highway Control Rating: 1 0 0 Highway Safety: 9 8 ★★★

Note: Safety ratings are based on the assumption that the engineering of the RV has allowed for proper balance by placing fresh, gray, and black holding tanks in a location so as not to change the balance of the RV when the tanks are empty or full. **Always double-check wheelbase, GVWR, and weights at front and rear axles.**

*See Section 1 for details on how conclusions are reached.

Section 2: The Ratings

Brand	Year	Type	Length	Model	Chassis	Engine	Fuel Type	Average Price per Linear Foot When New	Adjusted Wheelbase	Approx. Towing Capacity	Gross Vehicle Weight Rating	Average Curb Weight
Callista Cruiser	1996	MHC	25	2320D	FO	7.3L	D	$1800	170	1,500	12,600	9,680

Livability Code: VA 30-90
Wheelbase-to-length ratio of 57% is considered ○ dangerous ○ fatiguing ◉ good ○ excellent *
The approximate net payload of 2920 pounds at 23% of GVWR on this model is ○ deficient ○ excessive ○ cautionary ○ good ◉ excellent *
Total highway safety penalties are: 2 * Value: 86 Durability: 79 Highway Control Rating: 100 Highway Safety: 98 ★★★

Brand	Year	Type	Length	Model	Chassis	Engine	Fuel Type	Price/Ft	Wheelbase	Towing	GVWR	Curb Weight
Callista Cruiser	1996	MHC	25	2321	FO	5.8L	G	$1700	170	1,500	12,600	9,788

Livability Code: VA 30-90
Wheelbase-to-length ratio of 57% is considered ○ dangerous ○ fatiguing ◉ good ○ excellent *
The approximate net payload of 2812 pounds at 22% of GVWR on this model is ○ deficient ○ excessive ○ cautionary ○ good ◉ excellent *
Total highway safety penalties are: 2 * Value: 86 Durability: 79 Highway Control Rating: 100 Highway Safety: 98 ★★★

Brand	Year	Type	Length	Model	Chassis	Engine	Fuel Type	Price/Ft	Wheelbase	Towing	GVWR	Curb Weight
Callista Cruiser	1996	MHC	25	2321	FO	7.5L	G	$1700	170	1,500	12,600	9,788

Livability Code: VA 30-90
Wheelbase-to-length ratio of 57% is considered ○ dangerous ○ fatiguing ◉ good ○ excellent *
The approximate net payload of 2812 pounds at 22% of GVWR on this model is ○ deficient ○ excessive ○ cautionary ○ good ◉ excellent *
Total highway safety penalties are: 2 * Value: 86 Durability: 79 Highway Control Rating: 100 Highway Safety: 98 ★★★

Brand	Year	Type	Length	Model	Chassis	Engine	Fuel Type	Price/Ft	Wheelbase	Towing	GVWR	Curb Weight
Callista Cruiser	1996	MHC	25	2321D	FO	7.3L	D	$1900	170	1,500	12,600	9,740

Livability Code: VA 30-90
Wheelbase-to-length ratio of 57% is considered ○ dangerous ○ fatiguing ◉ good ○ excellent *
The approximate net payload of 2860 pounds at 23% of GVWR on this model is ○ deficient ○ excessive ○ cautionary ○ good ◉ excellent *
Total highway safety penalties are: 2 * Value: 86 Durability: 79 Highway Control Rating: 100 Highway Safety: 98 ★★★

Brand	Year	Type	Length	Model	Chassis	Engine	Fuel Type	Price/Ft	Wheelbase	Towing	GVWR	Curb Weight
Callista Cruiser	1996	MHC	28	2622	FO	5.8L	G	$1600	178	1,500	12,600	10,279

Livability Code: VA 30-90
Wheelbase-to-length ratio of 54% is considered ○ dangerous ○ fatiguing ◉ good ○ excellent *
The approximate net payload of 2321 pounds at 18% of GVWR on this model is ○ deficient ○ excessive ○ cautionary ○ good ◉ excellent *
Total highway safety penalties are: 2 * Value: 86 Durability: 79 Highway Control Rating: 87 Highway Safety: 85 ★★★

Brand	Year	Type	Length	Model	Chassis	Engine	Fuel Type	Price/Ft	Wheelbase	Towing	GVWR	Curb Weight
Callista Cruiser	1996	MHC	28	2622	FO	7.5L	G	$1600	178	1,500	12,600	10,279

Livability Code: VA 30-90
Wheelbase-to-length ratio of 54% is considered ○ dangerous ○ fatiguing ◉ good ○ excellent *
The approximate net payload of 2321 pounds at 18% of GVWR on this model is ○ deficient ○ excessive ○ cautionary ○ good ◉ excellent *
Total highway safety penalties are: 2 * Value: 86 Durability: 79 Highway Control Rating: 87 Highway Safety: 85 ★★★

Brand	Year	Type	Length	Model	Chassis	Engine	Fuel Type	Price/Ft	Wheelbase	Towing	GVWR	Curb Weight
Callista Cruiser	1996	MHC	28	2622D	FO	7.3L	D	$1700	178	1,500	12,600	10,264

Livability Code: VA 30-90
Wheelbase-to-length ratio of 54% is considered ○ dangerous ○ fatiguing ◉ good ○ excellent *
The approximate net payload of 2336 pounds at 19% of GVWR on this model is ○ deficient ○ excessive ○ cautionary ○ good ◉ excellent *
Total highway safety penalties are: 2 * Value: 86 Durability: 79 Highway Control Rating: 87 Highway Safety: 85 ★★★

Brand	Year	Type	Length	Model	Chassis	Engine	Fuel Type	Price/Ft	Wheelbase	Towing	GVWR	Curb Weight
Callista Cruiser	1996	MHC	28	2623	FO	5.8L	G	$1600	178	1,500	12,600	10,289

Livability Code: VA 30-90
Wheelbase-to-length ratio of 54% is considered ○ dangerous ○ fatiguing ◉ good ○ excellent *
The approximate net payload of 2311 pounds at 18% of GVWR on this model is ○ deficient ○ excessive ○ cautionary ○ good ◉ excellent *
Total highway safety penalties are: 2 * Value: 86 Durability: 79 Highway Control Rating: 87 Highway Safety: 85 ★★★

Brand	Year	Type	Length	Model	Chassis	Engine	Fuel Type	Price/Ft	Wheelbase	Towing	GVWR	Curb Weight
Callista Cruiser	1996	MHC	28	2623D	FO	7.3L	D	$1700	178	1,500	12,600	10,264

Livability Code: VA 30-90
Wheelbase-to-length ratio of 54% is considered ○ dangerous ○ fatiguing ◉ good ○ excellent *
The approximate net payload of 2336 pounds at 19% of GVWR on this model is ○ deficient ○ excessive ○ cautionary ○ good ◉ excellent *
Total highway safety penalties are: 2 * Value: 86 Durability: 79 Highway Control Rating: 87 Highway Safety: 85 ★★★

Brand	Year	Type	Length	Model	Chassis	Engine	Fuel Type	Price/Ft	Wheelbase	Towing	GVWR	Curb Weight
Callista Cruiser	1996	MHC	28	2623	FO	7.5L	G	$1600	178	1,500	12,600	10,289

Livability Code: VA 30-90
Wheelbase-to-length ratio of 54% is considered ○ dangerous ○ fatiguing ◉ good ○ excellent *
The approximate net payload of 2311 pounds at 18% of GVWR on this model is ○ deficient ○ excessive ○ cautionary ○ good ◉ excellent *
Total highway safety penalties are: 2 * Value: 86 Durability: 79 Highway Control Rating: 87 Highway Safety: 85 ★★★

Brand	Year	Type	Length	Model	Chassis	Engine	Fuel Type	Price/Ft	Wheelbase	Towing	GVWR	Curb Weight
Callista Cruiser	1996	MHC	29	2824	FO	5.8L	G	$1500	194	1,500	12,600	10,580

Livability Code: VA 30-90
Wheelbase-to-length ratio of 55% is considered ○ dangerous ○ fatiguing ◉ good ○ excellent *
The approximate net payload of 2020 pounds at 16% of GVWR on this model is ○ deficient ○ excessive ○ cautionary ○ good ◉ excellent *
Total highway safety penalties are: 2 * Value: 86 Durability: 79 Highway Control Rating: 94 Highway Safety: 92 ★★★

Brand	Year	Type	Length	Model	Chassis	Engine	Fuel Type	Price/Ft	Wheelbase	Towing	GVWR	Curb Weight
Callista Cruiser	1996	MHC	29	2824	FO	7.5L	G	$1500	194	1,500	12,600	10,580

Livability Code: VA 30-90
Wheelbase-to-length ratio of 55% is considered ○ dangerous ○ fatiguing ◉ good ○ excellent *
The approximate net payload of 2020 pounds at 16% of GVWR on this model is ○ deficient ○ excessive ○ cautionary ○ good ◉ excellent *
Total highway safety penalties are: 2 * Value: 86 Durability: 79 Highway Control Rating: 94 Highway Safety: 92 ★★★

Note: Safety ratings are based on the assumption that the engineering of the RV has allowed for proper balance by placing fresh, gray, and black holding tanks in a location so as not to change the balance of the RV when the tanks are empty or full. **Always double-check wheelbase, GVWR, and weights at front and rear axles.**

*See Section 1 for details on how conclusions are reached.

Brand	Year	Type	Length	Model	Chassis	Engine	Fuel Type	Average Price per Linear Foot When New	Adjusted Wheelbase	Approx. Towing Capacity	Gross Vehicle Weight Rating	Average Curb Weight
Callista Cruiser	1996	MHC	29	2824D	FO	7.3L	D	$1600	194	1,500	12,600	10,587

Livability Code: VA 30-90

Wheelbase-to-length ratio of 55% is considered ○ dangerous ○ fatiguing ◉ good ○ excellent *

The approximate net payload of 2013 pounds at 16% of GVWR on this model is ○ deficient ○ excessive ○ cautionary ○ good ◉ excellent *

Total highway safety penalties are: 2 *   Value: 8 6   Durability: 7 9   Highway Control Rating: 9 4   Highway Safety: 9 2   ★★★

Brand	Year	Type	Length	Model	Chassis	Engine	Fuel Type	Price/Ft	Wheelbase	Towing	GVWR	Curb Wt
Callista Cruiser	1996	MHC	29	2825	FO	5.8L	G	$1600	194	1,500	12,600	10,580

Livability Code: VA 30-90

Wheelbase-to-length ratio of 55% is considered ○ dangerous ○ fatiguing ◉ good ○ excellent *

The approximate net payload of 2020 pounds at 16% of GVWR on this model is ○ deficient ○ excessive ○ cautionary ○ good ◉ excellent *

Total highway safety penalties are: 2 *   Value: 8 6   Durability: 7 9   Highway Control Rating: 9 4   Highway Safety: 9 2   ★★★

Callista Cruiser	1996	MHC	29	2825	FO	7.5L	G	$1600	194	1,500	12,600	10,580

Livability Code: VA 30-90

Wheelbase-to-length ratio of 55% is considered ○ dangerous ○ fatiguing ◉ good ○ excellent *

The approximate net payload of 2020 pounds at 16% of GVWR on this model is ○ deficient ○ excessive ○ cautionary ○ good ◉ excellent *

Total highway safety penalties are: 2 *   Value: 8 6   Durability: 7 9   Highway Control Rating: 9 4   Highway Safety: 9 2   ★★★

Callista Cruiser	1996	MHC	29	2825D	FO	7.3L	D	$1700	194	1,500	12,600	10,587

Livability Code: VA 30-90

Wheelbase-to-length ratio of 55% is considered ○ dangerous ○ fatiguing ◉ good ○ excellent *

The approximate net payload of 2013 pounds at 16% of GVWR on this model is ○ deficient ○ excessive ○ cautionary ○ good ◉ excellent *

Total highway safety penalties are: 2 *   Value: 8 6   Durability: 7 9   Highway Control Rating: 9 4   Highway Safety: 9 2   ★★★

Callista Cruiser	1996	MHC	29	2826	FO	5.8L	G	$1600	194	1,500	12,600	10,465

Livability Code: VA 30-90

Wheelbase-to-length ratio of 55% is considered ○ dangerous ○ fatiguing ◉ good ○ excellent *

The approximate net payload of 2135 pounds at 17% of GVWR on this model is ○ deficient ○ excessive ○ cautionary ○ good ◉ excellent *

Total highway safety penalties are: 2 *   Value: 8 6   Durability: 7 9   Highway Control Rating: 9 5   Highway Safety: 9 3   ★★★

Callista Cruiser	1996	MHC	29	2826D	FO	7.3L	D	$1700	194	1,500	12,600	10,587

Livability Code: VA 30-90

Wheelbase-to-length ratio of 55% is considered ○ dangerous ○ fatiguing ◉ good ○ excellent *

The approximate net payload of 2013 pounds at 16% of GVWR on this model is ○ deficient ○ excessive ○ cautionary ○ good ◉ excellent *

Total highway safety penalties are: 2 *   Value: 8 6   Durability: 7 9   Highway Control Rating: 9 4   Highway Safety: 9 2   ★★★

Callista Cruiser	1996	MHC	29	2826	FO	7.5L	G	$1600	194	1,500	12,600	10,465

Livability Code: VA 30-90

Wheelbase-to-length ratio of 55% is considered ○ dangerous ○ fatiguing ◉ good ○ excellent *

The approximate net payload of 2135 pounds at 17% of GVWR on this model is ○ deficient ○ excessive ○ cautionary ○ good ◉ excellent *

Total highway safety penalties are: 2 *   Value: 8 6   Durability: 7 9   Highway Control Rating: 9 5   Highway Safety: 9 3   ★★★

Callista Cruiser	1996	MHC	29	2827	FO	5.8L	G	$1600	194	1,500	12,600	10,570

Livability Code: VA 30-90

Wheelbase-to-length ratio of 55% is considered ○ dangerous ○ fatiguing ◉ good ○ excellent *

The approximate net payload of 2030 pounds at 16% of GVWR on this model is ○ deficient ○ excessive ○ cautionary ○ good ◉ excellent *

Total highway safety penalties are: 2 *   Value: 8 6   Durability: 7 9   Highway Control Rating: 9 4   Highway Safety: 9 2   ★★★

Callista Cruiser	1996	MHC	29	2827	FO	7.5L	G	$1600	194	1,500	12,600	10,570

Livability Code: VA 30-90

Wheelbase-to-length ratio of 55% is considered ○ dangerous ○ fatiguing ◉ good ○ excellent *

The approximate net payload of 2030 pounds at 16% of GVWR on this model is ○ deficient ○ excessive ○ cautionary ○ good ◉ excellent *

Total highway safety penalties are: 2 *   Value: 8 6   Durability: 7 9   Highway Control Rating: 9 4   Highway Safety: 9 2   ★★★

Callista Cruiser	1996	MHC	29	2827D	FO	7.3L	D	$1700	194	1,500	12,600	10,587

Livability Code: VA 30-90

Wheelbase-to-length ratio of 55% is considered ○ dangerous ○ fatiguing ◉ good ○ excellent *

The approximate net payload of 2013 pounds at 16% of GVWR on this model is ○ deficient ○ excessive ○ cautionary ○ good ◉ excellent *

Total highway safety penalties are: 2 *   Value: 8 6   Durability: 7 9   Highway Control Rating: 9 4   Highway Safety: 9 2   ★★★

Callista Cruiser	1996	MHC	29	2829	FO	5.8L	G	$1600	194	1,500	12,600	10,435

Livability Code: VA 30-90

Wheelbase-to-length ratio of 55% is considered ○ dangerous ○ fatiguing ◉ good ○ excellent *

The approximate net payload of 2165 pounds at 17% of GVWR on this model is ○ deficient ○ excessive ○ cautionary ○ good ◉ excellent *

Total highway safety penalties are: 2 *   Value: 8 6   Durability: 7 9   Highway Control Rating: 9 5   Highway Safety: 9 3   ★★★

Callista Cruiser	1996	MHC	29	2829	FO	7.5L	G	$1600	194	1,500	12,600	10,435

Livability Code: VA 30-90

Wheelbase-to-length ratio of 55% is considered ○ dangerous ○ fatiguing ◉ good ○ excellent *

The approximate net payload of 2165 pounds at 17% of GVWR on this model is ○ deficient ○ excessive ○ cautionary ○ good ◉ excellent *

Total highway safety penalties are: 2 *   Value: 8 6   Durability: 7 9   Highway Control Rating: 9 5   Highway Safety: 9 3   ★★★

Note: Safety ratings are based on the assumption that the engineering of the RV has allowed for proper balance by placing fresh, gray, and black holding tanks in a location so as not to change the balance of the RV when the tanks are empty or full. **Always double-check wheelbase, GVWR, and weights at front and rear axles.**

*See Section 1 for details on how conclusions are reached.

Section 2: The Ratings

Brand	Year	Type	Length	Model	Chassis	Engine	Fuel Type	Average Price per Linear Foot When New	Adjusted Wheelbase	Approx. Towing Capacity	Gross Vehicle Weight Rating	Average Curb Weight
Callista Cruiser	1996	MHC	29	2829D	FO	7.3L	D	$1700	194	1,500	12,600	10,587

Livability Code: VA 30-90
Wheelbase-to-length ratio of 55% is considered ○ dangerous ○ fatiguing ◉ good ○ excellent*
The approximate net payload of 2013 pounds at 16% of GVWR on this model is ○ deficient ○ excessive ○ cautionary ○ good ◉ excellent*
Total highway safety penalties are: 2*   Value: 8 6   Durability: 7 9   Highway Control Rating: 9 4   Highway Safety: 9 2   ★★★

Brand	Year	Type	Length	Model	Chassis	Engine	Fuel Type	Price/ft	Wheelbase	Towing	GVWR	Curb Wt
Chieftain	1991	MHA	32	32 RQ	CH	7.4L	G	$1800	200	1,500	16,000	13,672

Livability Code: SB 30-90
Wheelbase-to-length ratio of 52% is considered ○ dangerous ◉ fatiguing ○ good ○ excellent*
The approximate net payload of 2328 pounds at 15% of GVWR on this model is ○ deficient ○ excessive ○ cautionary ◉ good ○ excellent*
Total highway safety penalties are: 6*   Value: 8 3   Durability: 7 6   Highway Control Rating: 5 7   Highway Safety: 5 1   ★

Chieftain	1993	MHA	28	28 RT	CH	7.4L	G	$2100	168	2,200	14,800	12,589

Livability Code: SB 30-90
Wheelbase-to-length ratio of 49% is considered ◉ dangerous ○ fatiguing ○ good ○ excellent*
The approximate net payload of 2211 pounds at 15% of GVWR on this model is ○ deficient ○ excessive ○ cautionary ◉ good ○ excellent*
Total highway safety penalties are: 4*   Value: 8 4   Durability: 7 6   Highway Control Rating: 4 0   Highway Safety: 3 6

Chieftain	1993	MHA	31	30 RT	CH	7.4L	G	$2000	178	2,200	14,800	13,288

Livability Code: SB 30-90
Wheelbase-to-length ratio of 48% is considered ◉ dangerous ○ fatiguing ○ good ○ excellent*
The approximate net payload of 1512 pounds at 10% of GVWR on this model is ○ deficient ○ excessive ○ cautionary ◉ good ○ excellent*
Total highway safety penalties are: 5*   Value: 8 3   Durability: 7 6   Highway Control Rating: 2 4   Highway Safety: 1 9

Chieftain	1993	MHA	31	30 RT	FO	7.5L	G	$2000	178	8,000	17,000	13,888

Livability Code: SB 30-90
Wheelbase-to-length ratio of 48% is considered ◉ dangerous ○ fatiguing ○ good ○ excellent*
The approximate net payload of 3112 pounds at 18% of GVWR on this model is ○ deficient ○ excessive ○ cautionary ○ good ◉ excellent*
Total highway safety penalties are: 2*   Value: 8 4   Durability: 7 6   Highway Control Rating: 3 8   Highway Safety: 3 6

Chieftain	1993	MHA	33	32 RQ	CH	7.4L	G	$1900	200	1,500	16,000	13,837

Livability Code: SB 30-90
Wheelbase-to-length ratio of 51% is considered ○ dangerous ◉ fatiguing ○ good ○ excellent*
The approximate net payload of 2163 pounds at 14% of GVWR on this model is ○ deficient ○ excessive ○ cautionary ◉ good ○ excellent*
Total highway safety penalties are: 6*   Value: 8 2   Durability: 7 6   Highway Control Rating: 4 2   Highway Safety: 3 6

Chieftain	1993	MHA	33	32 RQ	FO	7.5L	G	$1900	200	8,000	17,000	14,337

Livability Code: SB 30-90
Wheelbase-to-length ratio of 51% is considered ○ dangerous ◉ fatiguing ○ good ○ excellent*
The approximate net payload of 2663 pounds at 16% of GVWR on this model is ○ deficient ○ excessive ○ cautionary ○ good ◉ excellent*
Total highway safety penalties are: 2*   Value: 8 4   Durability: 7 6   Highway Control Rating: 4 6   Highway Safety: 4 4

Chieftain	1993	MHA	35	34 RQ	CH	7.4L	G	$1900	228	1,500	16,000	14,411

Livability Code: SB 30-90
Wheelbase-to-length ratio of 54% is considered ○ dangerous ○ fatiguing ◉ good ○ excellent*
The approximate net payload of 1589 pounds at 10% of GVWR on this model is ○ deficient ○ excessive ○ cautionary ◉ good ○ excellent*
Total highway safety penalties are: 7*   Value: 8 2   Durability: 7 6   Highway Control Rating: 7 5   Highway Safety: 6 8   ★★

Chieftain	1993	MHA	35	34 RQ	FO	7.5L	G	$1900	228	8,000	17,000	14,911

Livability Code: SB 30-90
Wheelbase-to-length ratio of 54% is considered ○ dangerous ○ fatiguing ◉ good ○ excellent*
The approximate net payload of 2089 pounds at 12% of GVWR on this model is ○ deficient ○ excessive ○ cautionary ◉ good ○ excellent*
Total highway safety penalties are: 2*   Value: 8 4   Durability: 7 6   Highway Control Rating: 7 7   Highway Safety: 7 5   ★★★

Chieftain	1998	MHA	34	33WB	FO	7.5L	G	$2800	216	8,000	17,000	15,999

Livability Code: SB 30-90
Wheelbase-to-length ratio of 53% is considered ○ dangerous ◉ fatiguing ○ good ○ excellent*
The approximate net payload of 1001 pounds at 6% of GVWR on this model is ◉ deficient ○ excessive ○ cautionary ○ good ○ excellent*
Total highway safety penalties are: 12*   Value: 8 1   Durability: 8 0   Highway Control Rating: 3 6   Highway Safety: 2 4

Chieftain	1998	MHA	35	34WY myc	FO	6.8L	G	$2700	228	5,500	20,500	17,378

Livability Code: SB 30-90
Wheelbase-to-length ratio of 55% is considered ○ dangerous ○ fatiguing ◉ good ○ excellent*
The approximate net payload of 3122 pounds at 15% of GVWR on this model is ○ deficient ○ excessive ○ cautionary ◉ good ○ excellent*
Total highway safety penalties are: 16*   Value: 7 9   Durability: 8 0   Highway Control Rating: 9 0   Highway Safety: 7 4   ★★★

Chieftain	1998	MHA	36	35WH	CH	7.4L	G	$2300	228	4,500	16,500	14,988

Livability Code: SB 30-90
Wheelbase-to-length ratio of 53% is considered ○ dangerous ◉ fatiguing ○ good ○ excellent*
The approximate net payload of 1512 pounds at 9% of GVWR on this model is ○ deficient ○ excessive ◉ cautionary ○ good ○ excellent*
Total highway safety penalties are: 7*   Value: 8 3   Durability: 8 0   Highway Control Rating: 5 3   Highway Safety: 4 6

Note: Safety ratings are based on the assumption that the engineering of the RV has allowed for proper balance by placing fresh, gray, and black holding tanks in a location so as not to change the balance of the RV when the tanks are empty or full. **Always double-check wheelbase, GVWR, and weights at front and rear axles.**

*See Section 1 for details on how conclusions are reached.

Brand	Year	Type	Length	Model	Chassis	Engine	Fuel Type	Average Price per Linear Foot When New	Adjusted Wheelbase	Approx. Towing Capacity	Gross Vehicle Weight Rating	Average Curb Weight
Chieftain	1998	MHA	36	35WH opch	FO	7.5L	G	$2600	228	8,000	17,000	15,373

Livability Code: SB 30-90
Wheelbase-to-length ratio of 53% is considered ○ dangerous ● fatiguing ○ good ○ excellent *
The approximate net payload of 1627 pounds at 10% of GVWR on this model is ○ deficient ○ excessive ○ cautionary ● good ○ excellent *
Total highway safety penalties are: 2 *   Value: 86   Durability: 80   Highway Control Rating: 58   Highway Safety: 56   ★

Brand	Year	Type	Length	Model	Chassis	Engine	Fuel Type	Price/ft	Wheelbase	Towing	GVWR	Curb Wt
Chieftain	1998	MHA	36	36WL myc	CH	7.4L	G	$2700	233	5,000	21,000	18,008

Livability Code: SB 30-90
Wheelbase-to-length ratio of 54% is considered ○ dangerous ○ fatiguing ● good ○ excellent *
The approximate net payload of 2992 pounds at 14% of GVWR on this model is ○ deficient ○ excessive ○ cautionary ● good ○ excellent *
Total highway safety penalties are: 19 *   Value: 78   Durability: 80   Highway Control Rating: 78   Highway Safety: 59   ★

Chieftain	1998	MHA	36	36WL-P	FR	CU275	D	$3500	228	5,000	24,850	20,251

Livability Code: SB 30-90
Wheelbase-to-length ratio of 53% is considered ○ dangerous ● fatiguing ○ good ○ excellent *
The approximate net payload of 4599 pounds at 19% of GVWR on this model is ○ deficient ○ excessive ○ cautionary ○ good ● excellent *
Total highway safety penalties are: 13 *   Value: 80   Durability: 80   Highway Control Rating: 72   Highway Safety: 59   ★

Chieftain	1998	MHA	36	36WL-P myc	FR	CU275	D	$3500	242	5,000	24,850	19,951

Livability Code: SB 30-90
Wheelbase-to-length ratio of 56% is considered ○ dangerous ○ fatiguing ● good ○ excellent *
The approximate net payload of 4899 pounds at 20% of GVWR on this model is ○ deficient ○ excessive ○ cautionary ○ good ● excellent *
Total highway safety penalties are: 13 *   Value: 80   Durability: 80   Highway Control Rating: 100   Highway Safety: 87   ★★★★

Chieftain	1999	MHA	34	33B	FO	6.8L	G	$2900	216	5,500	20,500	16,769

Livability Code: SB 30-90
Wheelbase-to-length ratio of 53% is considered ○ dangerous ● fatiguing ○ good ○ excellent *
The approximate net payload of 3731 pounds at 18% of GVWR on this model is ○ deficient ○ excessive ○ cautionary ○ good ● excellent *
Total highway safety penalties are: 12 *   Value: 81   Durability: 80   Highway Control Rating: 78   Highway Safety: 66   ★★

Chieftain	1999	MHA	35	34Y	CH	7.4L	G	$2900	219	5,000	21,000	18,028

Livability Code: SB 30-90
Wheelbase-to-length ratio of 52% is considered ○ dangerous ● fatiguing ○ good ○ excellent *
The approximate net payload of 2972 pounds at 14% of GVWR on this model is ○ deficient ○ excessive ○ cautionary ● good ○ excellent *
Total highway safety penalties are: 20 *   Value: 77   Durability: 80   Highway Control Rating: 64   Highway Safety: 44

Chieftain	1999	MHA	35	34Y	FO	6.8L	G	$2900	228	5,500	20,500	17,421

Livability Code: SB 30-90
Wheelbase-to-length ratio of 54% is considered ○ dangerous ○ fatiguing ● good ○ excellent *
The approximate net payload of 3079 pounds at 15% of GVWR on this model is ○ deficient ○ excessive ○ cautionary ● good ○ excellent *
Total highway safety penalties are: 15 *   Value: 79   Durability: 80   Highway Control Rating: 84   Highway Safety: 69   ★★

Chieftain	1999	MHA	35	35C	CH	7.4L	G	$2900	219	5,000	21,000	17,646

Livability Code: SB 30-90
Wheelbase-to-length ratio of 52% is considered ○ dangerous ● fatiguing ○ good ○ excellent *
The approximate net payload of 3354 pounds at 16% of GVWR on this model is ○ deficient ○ excessive ○ cautionary ○ good ● excellent *
Total highway safety penalties are: 13 *   Value: 81   Durability: 80   Highway Control Rating: 65   Highway Safety: 52   ★

Chieftain	1999	MHA	35	35U	CH	7.4L	G	$2900	233	5,000	21,000	18,239

Livability Code: SB 30-90
Wheelbase-to-length ratio of 55% is considered ○ dangerous ○ fatiguing ● good ○ excellent *
The approximate net payload of 2761 pounds at 13% of GVWR on this model is ○ deficient ○ excessive ○ cautionary ● good ○ excellent *
Total highway safety penalties are: 18 *   Value: 78   Durability: 80   Highway Control Rating: 86   Highway Safety: 68   ★★

Chieftain	1999	MHA	35	35C	FO	6.8L	G	$2900	228	5,500	20,500	17,149

Livability Code: SB 30-90
Wheelbase-to-length ratio of 54% is considered ○ dangerous ○ fatiguing ● good ○ excellent *
The approximate net payload of 3351 pounds at 16% of GVWR on this model is ○ deficient ○ excessive ○ cautionary ○ good ● excellent *
Total highway safety penalties are: 7 *   Value: 83   Durability: 80   Highway Control Rating: 83   Highway Safety: 76   ★★★

Chieftain	1999	MHA	35	35U	FO	6.8L	G	$2900	228	5,500	20,500	17,855

Livability Code: SB 30-90
Wheelbase-to-length ratio of 54% is considered ○ dangerous ○ fatiguing ● good ○ excellent *
The approximate net payload of 2645 pounds at 13% of GVWR on this model is ○ deficient ○ excessive ○ cautionary ● good ○ excellent *
Total highway safety penalties are: 13 *   Value: 81   Durability: 80   Highway Control Rating: 77   Highway Safety: 64   ★★

Chieftain	1999	MHA	36	36L	CH	7.4L	G	$2800	233	5,000	21,000	17,949

Livability Code: SB 30-90
Wheelbase-to-length ratio of 54% is considered ○ dangerous ○ fatiguing ● good ○ excellent *
The approximate net payload of 3051 pounds at 15% of GVWR on this model is ○ deficient ○ excessive ○ cautionary ● good ○ excellent *
Total highway safety penalties are: 18 *   Value: 78   Durability: 80   Highway Control Rating: 81   Highway Safety: 63   ★★

Note: Safety ratings are based on the assumption that the engineering of the RV has allowed for proper balance by placing fresh, gray, and black holding tanks in a location so as not to change the balance of the RV when the tanks are empty or full. **Always double-check wheelbase, GVWR, and weights at front and rear axles.**

*See Section 1 for details on how conclusions are reached.

Section 2: The Ratings

Brand	Year	Type	Length	Model	Chassis	Engine	Fuel Type	Average Price per Linear Foot When New	Adjusted Wheelbase	Approx. Towing Capacity	Gross Vehicle Weight Rating	Average Curb Weight
Chieftain	1999	MHA	36	36L	FO	6.8L	G	$2800	242	5,500	20,500	17,671

Livability Code: SB 30-90
Wheelbase-to-length ratio of 56% is considered ○ dangerous ○ fatiguing ● good ○ excellent*
The approximate net payload of 2829 pounds at 14% of GVWR on this model is ○ deficient ○ excessive ○ cautionary ● good ○ excellent*
Total highway safety penalties are: 12* — Value: **81** Durability: **80** Highway Control Rating: **92** Highway Safety: **80** ★★★★

Brand	Year	Type	Length	Model	Chassis	Engine	Fuel Type	Avg Price/LF	Adj WB	Towing	GVWR	Curb Wt
Chieftain	1999	MHA	36	36L-P	FR	CU275	D	$3400	242	5,000	24,850	19,976

Livability Code: SB 30-90
Wheelbase-to-length ratio of 56% is considered ○ dangerous ○ fatiguing ● good ○ excellent*
The approximate net payload of 4874 pounds at 20% of GVWR on this model is ○ deficient ○ excessive ○ cautionary ○ good ● excellent*
Total highway safety penalties are: 12* — Value: **81** Durability: **80** Highway Control Rating: **100** Highway Safety: **88** ★★★★

Brand	Year	Type	Length	Model	Chassis	Engine	Fuel Type	Avg Price/LF	Adj WB	Towing	GVWR	Curb Wt
Chieftain Super Chief	1991	MHA	34	34 RA	CH	7.4L	G	$1700	228	1,500	16,000	14,286

Livability Code: SB 30-90
Wheelbase-to-length ratio of 56% is considered ○ dangerous ○ fatiguing ● good ○ excellent*
The approximate net payload of 1714 pounds at 11% of GVWR on this model is ○ deficient ○ excessive ○ cautionary ● good ○ excellent*
Total highway safety penalties are: 6* — Value: **82** Durability: **76** Highway Control Rating: **87** Highway Safety: **81** ★★★

Brand	Year	Type	Length	Model	Chassis	Engine	Fuel Type	Avg Price/LF	Adj WB	Towing	GVWR	Curb Wt
Chieftain SuperChief	1990	MHA	28	27RQ	CH	7.4L	G	$1800	158	2,500	14,500	12,314

Livability Code: SB 30-90
Wheelbase-to-length ratio of 48% is considered ● dangerous ○ fatiguing ○ good ○ excellent*
The approximate net payload of 2186 pounds at 15% of GVWR on this model is ○ deficient ○ excessive ○ cautionary ● good ○ excellent*
Total highway safety penalties are: 3* — Value: **84** Durability: **76** Highway Control Rating: **34** Highway Safety: **31**

Brand	Year	Type	Length	Model	Chassis	Engine	Fuel Type	Avg Price/LF	Adj WB	Towing	GVWR	Curb Wt
Chieftain SuperChief	1990	MHA	32	31 RQ	FO	7.5L	G	$1700	190	5,000	16,000	13,587

Livability Code: SB 30-90
Wheelbase-to-length ratio of 49% is considered ● dangerous ○ fatiguing ○ good ○ excellent*
The approximate net payload of 2413 pounds at 15% of GVWR on this model is ○ deficient ○ excessive ○ cautionary ● good ○ excellent*
Total highway safety penalties are: 2* — Value: **84** Durability: **76** Highway Control Rating: **41** Highway Safety: **39**

Brand	Year	Type	Length	Model	Chassis	Engine	Fuel Type	Avg Price/LF	Adj WB	Towing	GVWR	Curb Wt
Chieftain SuperChief	1990	MHA	33	31 RQ	CH	7.4L	G	$1700	190	4,500	15,000	13,575

Livability Code: SB 30-90
Wheelbase-to-length ratio of 48% is considered ● dangerous ○ fatiguing ○ good ○ excellent*
The approximate net payload of 1425 pounds at 9% of GVWR on this model is ○ deficient ○ excessive ● cautionary ○ good ○ excellent*
Total highway safety penalties are: 6* — Value: **82** Durability: **76** Highway Control Rating: **21** Highway Safety: **15**

Brand	Year	Type	Length	Model	Chassis	Engine	Fuel Type	Avg Price/LF	Adj WB	Towing	GVWR	Curb Wt
Chieftain SuperChief	1990	MHA	34	34 RA	FO	7.5L	G	$1600	228	5,000	16,000	13,818

Livability Code: SB 30-90
Wheelbase-to-length ratio of 56% is considered ○ dangerous ○ fatiguing ● good ○ excellent*
The approximate net payload of 2182 pounds at 14% of GVWR on this model is ○ deficient ○ excessive ○ cautionary ● good ○ excellent*
Total highway safety penalties are: 2* — Value: **84** Durability: **76** Highway Control Rating: **93** Highway Safety: **91** ★★★

Brand	Year	Type	Length	Model	Chassis	Engine	Fuel Type	Avg Price/LF	Adj WB	Towing	GVWR	Curb Wt
Chieftain SuperChief	1990	MHA	34	34 RA	CH	7.4L	G	$1700	228	4,500	15,000	13,936

Livability Code: SB 30-90
Wheelbase-to-length ratio of 56% is considered ○ dangerous ○ fatiguing ● good ○ excellent*
The approximate net payload of 1064 pounds at 7% of GVWR on this model is ○ deficient ○ excessive ● cautionary ○ good ○ excellent*
Total highway safety penalties are: 6* — Value: **82** Durability: **76** Highway Control Rating: **68** Highway Safety: **62** ★★

Brand	Year	Type	Length	Model	Chassis	Engine	Fuel Type	Avg Price/LF	Adj WB	Towing	GVWR	Curb Wt
Chieftain SuperChief	1990	MHA	40	40 RQ	OS	7.5L	G	$2000	236 T	6,500	18,500	17,584

Livability Code: SB 30-90
Wheelbase-to-length ratio of 49% is considered ● dangerous ○ fatiguing ○ good ○ excellent*
The approximate net payload of 916 pounds at 5% of GVWR on this model is ● deficient ○ excessive ○ cautionary ○ good ○ excellent*
Total highway safety penalties are: 4* — Value: **83** Durability: **76** Highway Control Rating: **6** Highway Safety: **2**

Brand	Year	Type	Length	Model	Chassis	Engine	Fuel Type	Avg Price/LF	Adj WB	Towing	GVWR	Curb Wt
Chinook	1989	MHC	21	Concourse 18 Plus	FO	350	G	$2200	138	3,400	10,600	9,314

Livability Code: VA 30-90
Wheelbase-to-length ratio of 55% is considered ○ dangerous ○ fatiguing ● good ○ excellent*
The approximate net payload of 1286 pounds at 12% of GVWR on this model is ○ deficient ○ excessive ○ cautionary ● good ○ excellent*
Total highway safety penalties are: 2* — Value: **81** Durability: **81** Highway Control Rating: **84** Highway Safety: **82** ★★★★

Brand	Year	Type	Length	Model	Chassis	Engine	Fuel Type	Avg Price/LF	Adj WB	Towing	GVWR	Curb Wt
Chinook	1990	MHC	21	Concourse	FO	5.8L	G	$2200	138	1,500	10,500	8,742

Livability Code: VA 30-90
Wheelbase-to-length ratio of 55% is considered ○ dangerous ○ fatiguing ● good ○ excellent*
The approximate net payload of 1758 pounds at 17% of GVWR on this model is ○ deficient ○ excessive ○ cautionary ○ good ● excellent*
Total highway safety penalties are: 2* — Value: **81** Durability: **81** Highway Control Rating: **92** Highway Safety: **90** ★★★★

Brand	Year	Type	Length	Model	Chassis	Engine	Fuel Type	Avg Price/LF	Adj WB	Towing	GVWR	Curb Wt
Chinook	1991	MHB	19	Voyager II	CH	5.7L	G	$1900	125	1,500	8,600	7,325

Livability Code: VA 30-90
Wheelbase-to-length ratio of 55% is considered ○ dangerous ○ fatiguing ● good ○ excellent*
The approximate net payload of 1275 pounds at 15% of GVWR on this model is ○ deficient ○ excessive ○ cautionary ● good ○ excellent*
Total highway safety penalties are: 2* — Value: **81** Durability: **81** Highway Control Rating: **90** Highway Safety: **88** ★★★★

Note: Safety ratings are based on the assumption that the engineering of the RV has allowed for proper balance by placing fresh, gray, and black holding tanks in a location so as not to change the balance of the RV when the tanks are empty or full. **Always double-check wheelbase, GVWR, and weights at front and rear axles.**

*See Section 1 for details on how conclusions are reached.

Brand	Year	Type	Length	Model	Chassis	Engine	Fuel Type	Average Price per Linear Foot When New	Adjusted Wheelbase	Approx. Towing Capacity	Gross Vehicle Weight Rating	Average Curb Weight
Chinook	1991	MHC	21	Concourse 18 T	FO	7.5L	G	$2300	138	3,500	10,500	9,314

Livability Code: VA 30-90

Wheelbase-to-length ratio of 55% is considered ○ dangerous ○ fatiguing ◉ good ○ excellent *

The approximate net payload of 1186 pounds at 11% of GVWR on this model is ○ deficient ○ excessive ○ cautionary ◉ good ○ excellent *

Total highway safety penalties are: 2 *   Value: 8 1   Durability: 8 1   Highway Control Rating: 8 2   Highway Safety: 8 0   ★★★★

Brand	Year	Type	Length	Model	Chassis	Engine	Fuel Type	Price/ft	Wheelbase	Towing	GVWR	Curb Wt
Chinook	1994	MHC	21	Premier 21	FO	7.5L		$2300	138	8,000	10,500	9,125

Livability Code: VA 30-90

Wheelbase-to-length ratio of 55% is considered ○ dangerous ○ fatiguing ◉ good ○ excellent *

The approximate net payload of 1375 pounds at 13% of GVWR on this model is ○ deficient ○ excessive ○ cautionary ◉ good ○ excellent *

Total highway safety penalties are: 2 *   Value: 8 1   Durability: 8 1   Highway Control Rating: 8 6   Highway Safety: 8 4   ★★★★

Chinook	1994	MHC	22	Concourse XL 21	FO	7.5L	G	$2600	138	3,500	10,500	9,548

Livability Code: VA 30-90

Wheelbase-to-length ratio of 52% is considered ○ dangerous ◉ fatiguing ○ good ○ excellent *

The approximate net payload of 952 pounds at 9% of GVWR on this model is ○ deficient ○ excessive ◉ cautionary ○ good ○ excellent *

Total highway safety penalties are: 2 *   Value: 8 1   Durability: 8 1   Highway Control Rating: 5 5   Highway Safety: 5 3   ★

Chinook	1995	MHC	21	Concourse XL	FO	7.5L	G	$2700	138	3,500	10,500	9,314

Livability Code: VA 30-90

Wheelbase-to-length ratio of 55% is considered ○ dangerous ○ fatiguing ◉ good ○ excellent *

The approximate net payload of 1186 pounds at 11% of GVWR on this model is ○ deficient ○ excessive ○ cautionary ◉ good ○ excellent *

Total highway safety penalties are: 2 *   Value: 8 1   Durability: 8 1   Highway Control Rating: 8 2   Highway Safety: 8 0   ★★★★

Chinook	1995	MHC	21	Concourse	FO	7.5L	G	$2500	138	3,500	10,500	9,314

Livability Code: VA 30-90

Wheelbase-to-length ratio of 55% is considered ○ dangerous ○ fatiguing ◉ good ○ excellent *

The approximate net payload of 1186 pounds at 11% of GVWR on this model is ○ deficient ○ excessive ○ cautionary ◉ good ○ excellent *

Total highway safety penalties are: 2 *   Value: 8 1   Durability: 8 1   Highway Control Rating: 8 2   Highway Safety: 8 0   ★★★★

Chinook	1995	MHC	21	Premier	FO	7.5L	G	$2300	138	3,500	10,500	9,125

Livability Code: VA 30-90

Wheelbase-to-length ratio of 55% is considered ○ dangerous ○ fatiguing ◉ good ○ excellent *

The approximate net payload of 1375 pounds at 13% of GVWR on this model is ○ deficient ○ excessive ○ cautionary ◉ good ○ excellent *

Total highway safety penalties are: 2 *   Value: 8 1   Durability: 8 1   Highway Control Rating: 8 6   Highway Safety: 8 4   ★★★★

Chinook	1995	MHC	21	Premier XLT	FO	7.5L	G	$2800	138	3,500	10,500	9,125

Livability Code: VA 30-90

Wheelbase-to-length ratio of 55% is considered ○ dangerous ○ fatiguing ◉ good ○ excellent *

The approximate net payload of 1375 pounds at 13% of GVWR on this model is ○ deficient ○ excessive ○ cautionary ◉ good ○ excellent *

Total highway safety penalties are: 2 *   Value: 8 1   Durability: 8 1   Highway Control Rating: 8 6   Highway Safety: 8 4   ★★★★

Chinook	1997	MHC	21	Concourse	FO	7.5L	G	$3000	138	8,000	10,500	9,190

Livability Code: VA 30-90

Wheelbase-to-length ratio of 55% is considered ○ dangerous ○ fatiguing ◉ good ○ excellent *

The approximate net payload of 1310 pounds at 12% of GVWR on this model is ○ deficient ○ excessive ○ cautionary ◉ good ○ excellent *

Total highway safety penalties are: 2 *   Value: 8 1   Durability: 8 1   Highway Control Rating: 8 4   Highway Safety: 8 2   ★★★★

Chinook	1997	MHC	21	Premier	FO	7.5L	G	$2500	138	8,000	10,500	9,190

Livability Code: VA 30-90

Wheelbase-to-length ratio of 55% is considered ○ dangerous ○ fatiguing ◉ good ○ excellent *

The approximate net payload of 1310 pounds at 12% of GVWR on this model is ○ deficient ○ excessive ○ cautionary ◉ good ○ excellent *

Total highway safety penalties are: 2 *   Value: 8 1   Durability: 8 1   Highway Control Rating: 8 4   Highway Safety: 8 2   ★★★★

Chinook	1997	MHC	21	Concourse XL	FO	7.5L	G	$3400	138	8,000	10,500	9,190

Livability Code: VA 30-90

Wheelbase-to-length ratio of 55% is considered ○ dangerous ○ fatiguing ◉ good ○ excellent *

The approximate net payload of 1310 pounds at 12% of GVWR on this model is ○ deficient ○ excessive ○ cautionary ◉ good ○ excellent *

Total highway safety penalties are: 2 *   Value: 8 1   Durability: 8 1   Highway Control Rating: 8 4   Highway Safety: 8 2   ★★★★

Chinook	1998	MHC	21	Concourse	FO	6.8L	G	$3100	138	8,000	10,500	9,366

Livability Code: VA 30-90

Wheelbase-to-length ratio of 55% is considered ○ dangerous ○ fatiguing ◉ good ○ excellent *

The approximate net payload of 1134 pounds at 11% of GVWR on this model is ○ deficient ○ excessive ○ cautionary ◉ good ○ excellent *

Total highway safety penalties are: 2 *   Value: 8 1   Durability: 8 1   Highway Control Rating: 8 2   Highway Safety: 8 0   ★★★★

Chinook	1998	MHC	21	Premiere	FO	6.8L	G	$3100	138	8,000	10,500	8,966

Livability Code: VA 30-90

Wheelbase-to-length ratio of 55% is considered ○ dangerous ○ fatiguing ◉ good ○ excellent *

The approximate net payload of 1534 pounds at 15% of GVWR on this model is ○ deficient ○ excessive ○ cautionary ◉ good ○ excellent *

Total highway safety penalties are: 2 *   Value: 8 1   Durability: 8 1   Highway Control Rating: 8 9   Highway Safety: 8 7   ★★★★

Note: Safety ratings are based on the assumption that the engineering of the RV has allowed for proper balance by placing fresh, gray, and black holding tanks in a location so as not to change the balance of the RV when the tanks are empty or full. **Always double-check wheelbase, GVWR, and weights at front and rear axles.**

*See Section 1 for details on how conclusions are reached.

Brand	Year	Type	Length	Model	Chassis	Engine	Fuel Type	Average Price per Linear Foot When New	Adjusted Wheelbase	Approx. Towing Capacity	Gross Vehicle Weight Rating	Average Curb Weight
Chinook	1998	MHC	21	Concourse SE	FO	6.8L	G	$3100	138	8,000	10,500	9,366

Livability Code: VA 30-90
Wheelbase-to-length ratio of 55% is considered ○ dangerous ○ fatiguing ◉ good ○ excellent *
The approximate net payload of 1134 pounds at 11% of GVWR on this model is ○ deficient ○ excessive ○ cautionary ◉ good ○ excellent *
Total highway safety penalties are: 2 *   Value: **8 1**   Durability: **8 1**   Highway Control Rating: **8 2**   Highway Safety: **8 0**   ★★★★

Brand	Year	Type	Length	Model	Chassis	Engine	Fuel Type	Price/ft	Wheelbase	Towing	GVWR	Curb Weight
Chinook	1999	MHC	21	Concourse	FO	6.8L	G	$3100	138	8,000	10,700	9,366

Livability Code: VA 30-90
Wheelbase-to-length ratio of 55% is considered ○ dangerous ○ fatiguing ◉ good ○ excellent *
The approximate net payload of 1334 pounds at 12% of GVWR on this model is ○ deficient ○ excessive ○ cautionary ◉ good ○ excellent *
Total highway safety penalties are: 2 *   Value: **8 1**   Durability: **8 1**   Highway Control Rating: **8 4**   Highway Safety: **8 2**   ★★★★

Brand	Year	Type	Length	Model	Chassis	Engine	Fuel Type	Price/ft	Wheelbase	Towing	GVWR	Curb Weight
Chinook	1999	MHC	21	Premier	FO	6.8L	G	$3100	138	8,000	10,700	8,966

Livability Code: VA 30-90
Wheelbase-to-length ratio of 55% is considered ○ dangerous ○ fatiguing ◉ good ○ excellent *
The approximate net payload of 1734 pounds at 16% of GVWR on this model is ○ deficient ○ excessive ○ cautionary ○ good ◉ excellent *
Total highway safety penalties are: 2 *   Value: **8 1**   Durability: **8 1**   Highway Control Rating: **9 2**   Highway Safety: **9 0**   ★★★★

Brand	Year	Type	Length	Model	Chassis	Engine	Fuel Type	Price/ft	Wheelbase	Towing	GVWR	Curb Weight
Claraion	1991	MHA	23	Clarion 23	CL	Fo 5.8L	G	$2200	155	1,500	10,200	8,654

Livability Code: FT 30-90
Wheelbase-to-length ratio of 56% is considered ○ dangerous ○ fatiguing ◉ good ○ excellent *
The approximate net payload of 1546 pounds at 15% of GVWR on this model is ○ deficient ○ excessive ○ cautionary ◉ good ○ excellent *
Total highway safety penalties are: 2 *   Value: **8 1**   Durability: **8 0**   Highway Control Rating: **9 4**   Highway Safety: **9 2**   ★★★★

Brand	Year	Type	Length	Model	Chassis	Engine	Fuel Type	Price/ft	Wheelbase	Towing	GVWR	Curb Weight
Coach House	1990	MHB	20	193TB	DO	5.2L	G	$1700	127	1,500	7,500	6,754

Livability Code: WE 40-80
Wheelbase-to-length ratio of 54% is considered ○ dangerous ○ fatiguing ◉ good ○ excellent *
The approximate net payload of 746 pounds at 10% of GVWR on this model is ○ deficient ○ excessive ○ cautionary ◉ good ○ excellent *
Total highway safety penalties are: 2 *   Value: **8 1**   Durability: **8 0**   Highway Control Rating: **7 4**   Highway Safety: **7 2**   ★★★

Brand	Year	Type	Length	Model	Chassis	Engine	Fuel Type	Price/ft	Wheelbase	Towing	GVWR	Curb Weight
Coach House	1991	MHB	19	19	DO	5,9L	G	$1800	127	1,500	7,500	6,647

Livability Code: WE 40-80
Wheelbase-to-length ratio of 56% is considered ○ dangerous ○ fatiguing ◉ good ○ excellent *
The approximate net payload of 854 pounds at 11% of GVWR on this model is ○ deficient ○ excessive ○ cautionary ◉ good ○ excellent *
Total highway safety penalties are: 2 *   Value: **8 1**   Durability: **8 0**   Highway Control Rating: **8 8**   Highway Safety: **8 6**   ★★★★

Brand	Year	Type	Length	Model	Chassis	Engine	Fuel Type	Price/ft	Wheelbase	Towing	GVWR	Curb Weight
Coach House	1995	MHB	19	193RD		7.4L	G	$2400	146	1,500	8,600	7,261

Livability Code: WE 40-80
Wheelbase-to-length ratio of 63% is considered ○ dangerous ○ fatiguing ○ good ◉ excellent *
The approximate net payload of 1339 pounds at 16% of GVWR on this model is ○ deficient ○ excessive ○ cautionary ○ good ◉ excellent *
Total highway safety penalties are: 2 *   Value: **8 1**   Durability: **8 0**   Highway Control Rating: **1 0 0**   Highway Safety: **9 8**   ★★★★

Brand	Year	Type	Length	Model	Chassis	Engine	Fuel Type	Price/ft	Wheelbase	Towing	GVWR	Curb Weight
Coach House	1995	MHB	19	193CTB		7.4L	G	$2400	146	1,500	8,600	7,261

Livability Code: WE 40-80
Wheelbase-to-length ratio of 63% is considered ○ dangerous ○ fatiguing ○ good ◉ excellent *
The approximate net payload of 1339 pounds at 16% of GVWR on this model is ○ deficient ○ excessive ○ cautionary ○ good ◉ excellent *
Total highway safety penalties are: 2 *   Value: **8 1**   Durability: **8 0**   Highway Control Rating: **1 0 0**   Highway Safety: **9 8**   ★★★★

Brand	Year	Type	Length	Model	Chassis	Engine	Fuel Type	Price/ft	Wheelbase	Towing	GVWR	Curb Weight
Coach House	1995	MHB	19	194RD		7.4L	G	$2400	146	1,500	8,600	7,261

Livability Code: WE 40-80
Wheelbase-to-length ratio of 63% is considered ○ dangerous ○ fatiguing ○ good ◉ excellent *
The approximate net payload of 1339 pounds at 16% of GVWR on this model is ○ deficient ○ excessive ○ cautionary ○ good ◉ excellent *
Total highway safety penalties are: 2 *   Value: **8 1**   Durability: **8 0**   Highway Control Rating: **1 0 0**   Highway Safety: **9 8**   ★★★★

Brand	Year	Type	Length	Model	Chassis	Engine	Fuel Type	Price/ft	Wheelbase	Towing	GVWR	Curb Weight
Coach House	1995	MHB	19	192SD	CH	7.4L	G	$2400	146	1,500	8,600	7,261

Livability Code: WE 40-80
Wheelbase-to-length ratio of 63% is considered ○ dangerous ○ fatiguing ○ good ◉ excellent *
The approximate net payload of 1339 pounds at 16% of GVWR on this model is ○ deficient ○ excessive ○ cautionary ○ good ◉ excellent *
Total highway safety penalties are: 2 *   Value: **8 1**   Durability: **8 0**   Highway Control Rating: **1 0 0**   Highway Safety: **9 8**   ★★★★

Brand	Year	Type	Length	Model	Chassis	Engine	Fuel Type	Price/ft	Wheelbase	Towing	GVWR	Curb Weight
Coach House	1995	MHB	19	192RL	FO	7.5L	G	$2400	138	1,500	9,300	7,509

Livability Code: WE 40-80
Wheelbase-to-length ratio of 60% is considered ○ dangerous ○ fatiguing ○ good ◉ excellent *
The approximate net payload of 1791 pounds at 19% of GVWR on this model is ○ deficient ○ excessive ○ cautionary ○ good ◉ excellent *
Total highway safety penalties are: 2 *   Value: **8 1**   Durability: **8 0**   Highway Control Rating: **1 0 0**   Highway Safety: **9 8**   ★★★★

Brand	Year	Type	Length	Model	Chassis	Engine	Fuel Type	Price/ft	Wheelbase	Towing	GVWR	Curb Weight
Coach House	1995	MHB	19	193RL	FO	7.5L	G	$2400	138	1,500	9,300	7,509

Livability Code: WE 40-80
Wheelbase-to-length ratio of 60% is considered ○ dangerous ○ fatiguing ○ good ◉ excellent *
The approximate net payload of 1791 pounds at 19% of GVWR on this model is ○ deficient ○ excessive ○ cautionary ○ good ◉ excellent *
Total highway safety penalties are: 2 *   Value: **8 1**   Durability: **8 0**   Highway Control Rating: **1 0 0**   Highway Safety: **9 8**   ★★★★

Note: Safety ratings are based on the assumption that the engineering of the RV has allowed for proper balance by placing fresh, gray, and black holding tanks in a location so as not to change the balance of the RV when the tanks are empty or full. **Always double-check wheelbase, GVWR, and weights at front and rear axles.**

*See Section 1 for details on how conclusions are reached.

Brand	Year	Type	Length	Model	Chassis	Engine	Fuel Type	Average Price per Linear Foot When New	Adjusted Wheelbase	Approx. Towing Capacity	Gross Vehicle Weight Rating	Average Curb Weight
Coach House	1995	MHB	19	192SD	FO	7.5L	G	$2400	138	1,500	9,300	7,509

Livability Code: WE 40-80 Wheelbase-to-length ratio of 60% is considered ○ dangerous ○ fatiguing ○ good ◉ excellent*
The approximate net payload of 1791 pounds at 19% of GVWR on this model is ○ deficient ○ excessive ○ cautionary ○ good ◉ excellent*
Total highway safety penalties are: 2*   Value: 81   Durability: 80   Highway Control Rating: 100   Highway Safety: 98   ★★★★

Brand	Year	Type	Length	Model	Chassis	Engine	Fuel Type	Average Price per Linear Foot When New	Adjusted Wheelbase	Approx. Towing Capacity	Gross Vehicle Weight Rating	Average Curb Weight
Coach House	1995	MHB	20	192RL	DO	5.9L	G	$2300	128	1,500	8,510	7,221

Livability Code: WE 40-80 Wheelbase-to-length ratio of 54% is considered ○ dangerous ○ fatiguing ◉ good ○ excellent*
The approximate net payload of 1290 pounds at 15% of GVWR on this model is ○ deficient ○ excessive ○ cautionary ◉ good ○ excellent*
Total highway safety penalties are: 2*   Value: 81   Durability: 80   Highway Control Rating: 86   Highway Safety: 84   ★★★★

Brand	Year	Type	Length	Model	Chassis	Engine	Fuel Type	Average Price per Linear Foot When New	Adjusted Wheelbase	Approx. Towing Capacity	Gross Vehicle Weight Rating	Average Curb Weight
Coach House	1995	MHB	20	193RL	DO	5.9L	G	$2300	128	1,500	8,510	7,221

Livability Code: WE 40-80 Wheelbase-to-length ratio of 54% is considered ○ dangerous ○ fatiguing ◉ good ○ excellent*
The approximate net payload of 1290 pounds at 15% of GVWR on this model is ○ deficient ○ excessive ○ cautionary ◉ good ○ excellent*
Total highway safety penalties are: 2*   Value: 81   Durability: 80   Highway Control Rating: 86   Highway Safety: 84   ★★★★

Brand	Year	Type	Length	Model	Chassis	Engine	Fuel Type	Average Price per Linear Foot When New	Adjusted Wheelbase	Approx. Towing Capacity	Gross Vehicle Weight Rating	Average Curb Weight
Coach House	1995	MHB	20	194RD	DO	5.9L	G	$2300	128	1,500	8,510	7,221

Livability Code: WE 40-80 Wheelbase-to-length ratio of 54% is considered ○ dangerous ○ fatiguing ◉ good ○ excellent*
The approximate net payload of 1290 pounds at 15% of GVWR on this model is ○ deficient ○ excessive ○ cautionary ◉ good ○ excellent*
Total highway safety penalties are: 2*   Value: 81   Durability: 80   Highway Control Rating: 86   Highway Safety: 84   ★★★★

Brand	Year	Type	Length	Model	Chassis	Engine	Fuel Type	Average Price per Linear Foot When New	Adjusted Wheelbase	Approx. Towing Capacity	Gross Vehicle Weight Rating	Average Curb Weight
Coach House	1996	MHB	19	193CTB	CH	7.4L	G	$2400	146	1,500	8,600	7,261

Livability Code: WE 40-80 Wheelbase-to-length ratio of 63% is considered ○ dangerous ○ fatiguing ○ good ◉ excellent*
The approximate net payload of 1339 pounds at 16% of GVWR on this model is ○ deficient ○ excessive ○ cautionary ○ good ◉ excellent*
Total highway safety penalties are: 2*   Value: 81   Durability: 80   Highway Control Rating: 100   Highway Safety: 98   ★★★★

Brand	Year	Type	Length	Model	Chassis	Engine	Fuel Type	Average Price per Linear Foot When New	Adjusted Wheelbase	Approx. Towing Capacity	Gross Vehicle Weight Rating	Average Curb Weight
Coach House	1996	MHB	19	194RD	CH	7.4L	G	$2400	146	1,500	8,600	7,261

Livability Code: WE 40-80 Wheelbase-to-length ratio of 63% is considered ○ dangerous ○ fatiguing ○ good ◉ excellent*
The approximate net payload of 1339 pounds at 16% of GVWR on this model is ○ deficient ○ excessive ○ cautionary ○ good ◉ excellent*
Total highway safety penalties are: 2*   Value: 81   Durability: 80   Highway Control Rating: 100   Highway Safety: 98   ★★★★

Brand	Year	Type	Length	Model	Chassis	Engine	Fuel Type	Average Price per Linear Foot When New	Adjusted Wheelbase	Approx. Towing Capacity	Gross Vehicle Weight Rating	Average Curb Weight
Coach House	1996	MHB	19	193RD	CH	7.4L	G	$2400	146	1,500	8,600	7,261

Livability Code: WE 40-80 Wheelbase-to-length ratio of 63% is considered ○ dangerous ○ fatiguing ○ good ◉ excellent*
The approximate net payload of 1339 pounds at 16% of GVWR on this model is ○ deficient ○ excessive ○ cautionary ○ good ◉ excellent*
Total highway safety penalties are: 2*   Value: 81   Durability: 80   Highway Control Rating: 100   Highway Safety: 98   ★★★★

Brand	Year	Type	Length	Model	Chassis	Engine	Fuel Type	Average Price per Linear Foot When New	Adjusted Wheelbase	Approx. Towing Capacity	Gross Vehicle Weight Rating	Average Curb Weight
Coach House	1996	MHB	19	192SD	FO	7.5L	G	$2400	138	1,500	9,300	7,509

Livability Code: WE 40-80 Wheelbase-to-length ratio of 60% is considered ○ dangerous ○ fatiguing ○ good ◉ excellent*
The approximate net payload of 1791 pounds at 19% of GVWR on this model is ○ deficient ○ excessive ○ cautionary ○ good ◉ excellent*
Total highway safety penalties are: 2*   Value: 81   Durability: 80   Highway Control Rating: 100   Highway Safety: 98   ★★★★

Brand	Year	Type	Length	Model	Chassis	Engine	Fuel Type	Average Price per Linear Foot When New	Adjusted Wheelbase	Approx. Towing Capacity	Gross Vehicle Weight Rating	Average Curb Weight
Coach House	1996	MHB	20	192RL	DO	5.9L	G	$2300	128	1,500	8,510	7,221

Livability Code: WE 40-80 Wheelbase-to-length ratio of 54% is considered ○ dangerous ○ fatiguing ◉ good ○ excellent*
The approximate net payload of 1290 pounds at 15% of GVWR on this model is ○ deficient ○ excessive ○ cautionary ◉ good ○ excellent*
Total highway safety penalties are: 2*   Value: 81   Durability: 80   Highway Control Rating: 86   Highway Safety: 84   ★★★★

Brand	Year	Type	Length	Model	Chassis	Engine	Fuel Type	Average Price per Linear Foot When New	Adjusted Wheelbase	Approx. Towing Capacity	Gross Vehicle Weight Rating	Average Curb Weight
Coach House	1996	MHB	20	193RL	DO	5.9L	G	$2300	128	1,500	8,510	7,221

Livability Code: WE 40-80 Wheelbase-to-length ratio of 54% is considered ○ dangerous ○ fatiguing ◉ good ○ excellent*
The approximate net payload of 1290 pounds at 15% of GVWR on this model is ○ deficient ○ excessive ○ cautionary ◉ good ○ excellent*
Total highway safety penalties are: 2*   Value: 81   Durability: 80   Highway Control Rating: 86   Highway Safety: 84   ★★★★

Brand	Year	Type	Length	Model	Chassis	Engine	Fuel Type	Average Price per Linear Foot When New	Adjusted Wheelbase	Approx. Towing Capacity	Gross Vehicle Weight Rating	Average Curb Weight
Coach House	1997	MHB	19	192 TB	GM	7.4L	G	$2400	146	1,500	8,600	7,308

Livability Code: WE 40-80 Wheelbase-to-length ratio of 64% is considered ○ dangerous ○ fatiguing ○ good ◉ excellent*
The approximate net payload of 1292 pounds at 15% of GVWR on this model is ○ deficient ○ excessive ○ cautionary ◉ good ○ excellent*
Total highway safety penalties are: 2*   Value: 81   Durability: 80   Highway Control Rating: 100   Highway Safety: 98   ★★★★

Brand	Year	Type	Length	Model	Chassis	Engine	Fuel Type	Average Price per Linear Foot When New	Adjusted Wheelbase	Approx. Towing Capacity	Gross Vehicle Weight Rating	Average Curb Weight
Coach House	1997	MHB	19	192 RL	GM	7.4L	G	$2400	146	1,500	8,600	7,308

Livability Code: WE 40-80 Wheelbase-to-length ratio of 64% is considered ○ dangerous ○ fatiguing ○ good ◉ excellent*
The approximate net payload of 1292 pounds at 15% of GVWR on this model is ○ deficient ○ excessive ○ cautionary ◉ good ○ excellent*
Total highway safety penalties are: 2*   Value: 81   Durability: 80   Highway Control Rating: 100   Highway Safety: 98   ★★★★

Note: Safety ratings are based on the assumption that the engineering of the RV has allowed for proper balance by placing fresh, gray, and black holding tanks in a location so as not to change the balance of the RV when the tanks are empty or full. **Always double-check wheelbase, GVWR, and weights at front and rear axles.**

*See Section 1 for details on how conclusions are reached.

Brand	Year	Type	Length	Model	Chassis	Engine	Fuel Type	Average Price per Linear Foot When New	Adjusted Wheelbase	Approx. Towing Capacity	Gross Vehicle Weight Rating	Average Curb Weight
Coach House	1997	MHB	19	192 SD	GM	7.4L	G	$2400	146	1,500	8,600	7,308

Livability Code: WE 40-80

Wheelbase-to-length ratio of 64% is considered ○ dangerous ○ fatiguing ○ good ◉ excellent*

The approximate net payload of 1292 pounds at 15% of GVWR on this model is ○ deficient ○ excessive ○ cautionary ◉ good ○ excellent*

Total highway safety penalties are: 2*   Value: 81   Durability: 80   Highway Control Rating: 100   Highway Safety: 98   ★★★★

Brand	Year	Type	Length	Model	Chassis	Engine	Fuel Type		Adj. WB	Tow	GVWR	Curb
Coach House	1997	MHB	19	192 RD	GM	7.4L	G	$2400	146	1,500	8,600	7,308

Livability Code: WE 40-80

Wheelbase-to-length ratio of 64% is considered ○ dangerous ○ fatiguing ○ good ◉ excellent*

The approximate net payload of 1292 pounds at 15% of GVWR on this model is ○ deficient ○ excessive ○ cautionary ◉ good ○ excellent*

Total highway safety penalties are: 2*   Value: 81   Durability: 80   Highway Control Rating: 100   Highway Safety: 98   ★★★★

Coach House	1997	MHB	19	193 TB	GM	7.4L	G	$2400	146	1,500	8,600	7,308

Livability Code: WE 40-80

Wheelbase-to-length ratio of 64% is considered ○ dangerous ○ fatiguing ○ good ◉ excellent*

The approximate net payload of 1292 pounds at 15% of GVWR on this model is ○ deficient ○ excessive ○ cautionary ◉ good ○ excellent*

Total highway safety penalties are: 2*   Value: 81   Durability: 80   Highway Control Rating: 100   Highway Safety: 98   ★★★★

Coach House	1997	MHB	19	193 RL	GM	7.4L	G	$2400	146	1,500	8,600	7,308

Livability Code: WE 40-80

Wheelbase-to-length ratio of 64% is considered ○ dangerous ○ fatiguing ○ good ◉ excellent*

The approximate net payload of 1292 pounds at 15% of GVWR on this model is ○ deficient ○ excessive ○ cautionary ◉ good ○ excellent*

Total highway safety penalties are: 2*   Value: 81   Durability: 80   Highway Control Rating: 100   Highway Safety: 98   ★★★★

Coach House	1997	MHB	19	193SD	GM	7.4L	G	$2400	146	1,500	8,600	7,308

Livability Code: WE 40-80

Wheelbase-to-length ratio of 64% is considered ○ dangerous ○ fatiguing ○ good ◉ excellent*

The approximate net payload of 1292 pounds at 15% of GVWR on this model is ○ deficient ○ excessive ○ cautionary ◉ good ○ excellent*

Total highway safety penalties are: 2*   Value: 81   Durability: 80   Highway Control Rating: 100   Highway Safety: 98   ★★★★

Coach House	1997	MHB	19	193 RD	GM	7.4L	G	$2400	146	1,500	8,600	7,308

Livability Code: WE 40-80

Wheelbase-to-length ratio of 64% is considered ○ dangerous ○ fatiguing ○ good ◉ excellent*

The approximate net payload of 1292 pounds at 15% of GVWR on this model is ○ deficient ○ excessive ○ cautionary ◉ good ○ excellent*

Total highway safety penalties are: 2*   Value: 81   Durability: 80   Highway Control Rating: 100   Highway Safety: 98   ★★★★

Coach House	1997	MHB	19	192 TB	FO	5.8L	G	$2400	138	1,500	8,550	7,370

Livability Code: WE 40-80

Wheelbase-to-length ratio of 59% is considered ○ dangerous ○ fatiguing ○ good ◉ excellent*

The approximate net payload of 1180 pounds at 14% of GVWR on this model is ○ deficient ○ excessive ○ cautionary ◉ good ○ excellent*

Total highway safety penalties are: 2*   Value: 81   Durability: 80   Highway Control Rating: 100   Highway Safety: 98   ★★★★

Coach House	1997	MHB	19	192 RL	FO	5.8L	G	$2400	138	1,500	8,550	7,370

Livability Code: WE 40-80

Wheelbase-to-length ratio of 59% is considered ○ dangerous ○ fatiguing ○ good ◉ excellent*

The approximate net payload of 1180 pounds at 14% of GVWR on this model is ○ deficient ○ excessive ○ cautionary ◉ good ○ excellent*

Total highway safety penalties are: 2*   Value: 81   Durability: 80   Highway Control Rating: 100   Highway Safety: 98   ★★★★

Coach House	1997	MHB	19	192 SD	FO	5.8L	G	$2400	138	1,500	8,550	7,370

Livability Code: WE 40-80

Wheelbase-to-length ratio of 59% is considered ○ dangerous ○ fatiguing ○ good ◉ excellent*

The approximate net payload of 1180 pounds at 14% of GVWR on this model is ○ deficient ○ excessive ○ cautionary ◉ good ○ excellent*

Total highway safety penalties are: 2*   Value: 81   Durability: 80   Highway Control Rating: 100   Highway Safety: 98   ★★★★

Coach House	1997	MHB	19	192 RD	FO	5.8L	G	$2400	138	1,500	8,550	7,370

Livability Code: WE 40-80

Wheelbase-to-length ratio of 59% is considered ○ dangerous ○ fatiguing ○ good ◉ excellent*

The approximate net payload of 1180 pounds at 14% of GVWR on this model is ○ deficient ○ excessive ○ cautionary ◉ good ○ excellent*

Total highway safety penalties are: 2*   Value: 81   Durability: 80   Highway Control Rating: 100   Highway Safety: 98   ★★★★

Coach House	1997	MHB	19	193 TB	FO	5.8L	G	$2400	138	1,500	8,550	7,370

Livability Code: WE 40-80

Wheelbase-to-length ratio of 59% is considered ○ dangerous ○ fatiguing ○ good ◉ excellent*

The approximate net payload of 1180 pounds at 14% of GVWR on this model is ○ deficient ○ excessive ○ cautionary ◉ good ○ excellent*

Total highway safety penalties are: 2*   Value: 81   Durability: 80   Highway Control Rating: 100   Highway Safety: 98   ★★★★

Coach House	1997	MHB	19	193 RL	FO	5.8L	G	$2400	138	1,500	8,550	7,370

Livability Code: WE 40-80

Wheelbase-to-length ratio of 59% is considered ○ dangerous ○ fatiguing ○ good ◉ excellent*

The approximate net payload of 1180 pounds at 14% of GVWR on this model is ○ deficient ○ excessive ○ cautionary ◉ good ○ excellent*

Total highway safety penalties are: 2*   Value: 81   Durability: 80   Highway Control Rating: 100   Highway Safety: 98   ★★★★

Note: Safety ratings are based on the assumption that the engineering of the RV has allowed for proper balance by placing fresh, gray, and black holding tanks in a location so as not to change the balance of the RV when the tanks are empty or full. **Always double-check wheelbase, GVWR, and weights at front and rear axles.**

*See Section 1 for details on how conclusions are reached.

Brand	Year	Type	Length	Model	Chassis	Engine	Fuel Type	Average Price per Linear Foot When New	Adjusted Wheel-base	Approx. Towing Capacity	Gross Vehicle Weight Rating	Average Curb Weight
Coach House	1997	MHB	19	193 SD	FO	5.8L	G	$2400	138	1,500	8,550	7,370

Livability Code: WE 40-80
Wheelbase-to-length ratio of 59% is considered ○ dangerous ○ fatiguing ○ good ● excellent *
The approximate net payload of 1180 pounds at 14% of GVWR on this model is ○ deficient ○ excessive ○ cautionary ● good ○ excellent *
Total highway safety penalties are: 2 *   Value: 81   Durability: 80   Highway Control Rating: 100   Highway Safety: 98   ★★★★

| Coach House | 1997 | MHB | 19 | 193 RD | FO | 5.8L | G | $2400 | 138 | 1,500 | 8,550 | 7,370 |

Livability Code: WE 40-80
Wheelbase-to-length ratio of 59% is considered ○ dangerous ○ fatiguing ○ good ● excellent *
The approximate net payload of 1180 pounds at 14% of GVWR on this model is ○ deficient ○ excessive ○ cautionary ● good ○ excellent *
Total highway safety penalties are: 2 *   Value: 81   Durability: 80   Highway Control Rating: 100   Highway Safety: 98   ★★★★

| Coach House | 1997 | MHB | 20 | 192 TB | DO | 5.9L | G | $2300 | 128 | 1,500 | 8,510 | 7,341 |

Livability Code: WE 40-80
Wheelbase-to-length ratio of 54% is considered ○ dangerous ○ fatiguing ● good ○ excellent *
The approximate net payload of 1169 pounds at 14% of GVWR on this model is ○ deficient ○ excessive ○ cautionary ● good ○ excellent *
Total highway safety penalties are: 2 *   Value: 81   Durability: 80   Highway Control Rating: 81   Highway Safety: 79   ★★★

| Coach House | 1997 | MHB | 20 | 192 RL | DO | 5.9L | G | $2300 | 128 | 1,500 | 8,510 | 7,341 |

Livability Code: WE 40-80
Wheelbase-to-length ratio of 54% is considered ○ dangerous ○ fatiguing ● good ○ excellent *
The approximate net payload of 1169 pounds at 14% of GVWR on this model is ○ deficient ○ excessive ○ cautionary ● good ○ excellent *
Total highway safety penalties are: 2 *   Value: 81   Durability: 80   Highway Control Rating: 81   Highway Safety: 79   ★★★

| Coach House | 1997 | MHB | 20 | 192 SD | DO | 5.9L | G | $2300 | 128 | 1,500 | 8,510 | 7,341 |

Livability Code: WE 40-80
Wheelbase-to-length ratio of 54% is considered ○ dangerous ○ fatiguing ● good ○ excellent *
The approximate net payload of 1169 pounds at 14% of GVWR on this model is ○ deficient ○ excessive ○ cautionary ● good ○ excellent *
Total highway safety penalties are: 2 *   Value: 81   Durability: 80   Highway Control Rating: 81   Highway Safety: 79   ★★★

| Coach House | 1997 | MHB | 20 | 192 RD | DO | 5.9L | G | $2300 | 128 | 1,500 | 8,510 | 7,341 |

Livability Code: WE 40-80
Wheelbase-to-length ratio of 54% is considered ○ dangerous ○ fatiguing ● good ○ excellent *
The approximate net payload of 1169 pounds at 14% of GVWR on this model is ○ deficient ○ excessive ○ cautionary ● good ○ excellent *
Total highway safety penalties are: 2 *   Value: 81   Durability: 80   Highway Control Rating: 81   Highway Safety: 79   ★★★

| Coach House | 1997 | MHB | 20 | 193 TB | DO | 5.9L | G | $2300 | 128 | 1,500 | 8,510 | 7,341 |

Livability Code: WE 40-80
Wheelbase-to-length ratio of 54% is considered ○ dangerous ○ fatiguing ● good ○ excellent *
The approximate net payload of 1169 pounds at 14% of GVWR on this model is ○ deficient ○ excessive ○ cautionary ● good ○ excellent *
Total highway safety penalties are: 2 *   Value: 81   Durability: 80   Highway Control Rating: 81   Highway Safety: 79   ★★★

| Coach House | 1997 | MHB | 20 | 193 RL | DO | 5.9L | G | $2300 | 128 | 1,500 | 8,510 | 7,341 |

Livability Code: WE 40-80
Wheelbase-to-length ratio of 54% is considered ○ dangerous ○ fatiguing ● good ○ excellent *
The approximate net payload of 1169 pounds at 14% of GVWR on this model is ○ deficient ○ excessive ○ cautionary ● good ○ excellent *
Total highway safety penalties are: 2 *   Value: 81   Durability: 80   Highway Control Rating: 81   Highway Safety: 79   ★★★

| Coach House | 1997 | MHB | 20 | 193 SD | DO | 5.9L | G | $2300 | 128 | 1,500 | 8,510 | 7,341 |

Livability Code: WE 40-80
Wheelbase-to-length ratio of 54% is considered ○ dangerous ○ fatiguing ● good ○ excellent *
The approximate net payload of 1169 pounds at 14% of GVWR on this model is ○ deficient ○ excessive ○ cautionary ● good ○ excellent *
Total highway safety penalties are: 2 *   Value: 81   Durability: 80   Highway Control Rating: 81   Highway Safety: 79   ★★★

| Coach House | 1997 | MHB | 20 | 193 RD | DO | 5.9L | G | $2300 | 128 | 1,500 | 8,510 | 7,341 |

Livability Code: WE 40-80
Wheelbase-to-length ratio of 54% is considered ○ dangerous ○ fatiguing ● good ○ excellent *
The approximate net payload of 1169 pounds at 14% of GVWR on this model is ○ deficient ○ excessive ○ cautionary ● good ○ excellent *
Total highway safety penalties are: 2 *   Value: 81   Durability: 80   Highway Control Rating: 81   Highway Safety: 79   ★★★

| Coach House | 1997 | MHB | 20 | 194 RD | DO | 5.9L | G | $2300 | 128 | 1,500 | 8,510 | 7,341 |

Livability Code: WE 40-80
Wheelbase-to-length ratio of 54% is considered ○ dangerous ○ fatiguing ● good ○ excellent *
The approximate net payload of 1169 pounds at 14% of GVWR on this model is ○ deficient ○ excessive ○ cautionary ● good ○ excellent *
Total highway safety penalties are: 2 *   Value: 81   Durability: 80   Highway Control Rating: 81   Highway Safety: 79   ★★★

| Coach House | 1997 | MHB | 20 | 194 RL | DO | 5.9L | G | $2300 | 128 | 1,500 | 8,510 | 7,341 |

Livability Code: WE 40-80
Wheelbase-to-length ratio of 54% is considered ○ dangerous ○ fatiguing ● good ○ excellent *
The approximate net payload of 1169 pounds at 14% of GVWR on this model is ○ deficient ○ excessive ○ cautionary ● good ○ excellent *
Total highway safety penalties are: 2 *   Value: 81   Durability: 80   Highway Control Rating: 81   Highway Safety: 79   ★★★

Note: Safety ratings are based on the assumption that the engineering of the RV has allowed for proper balance by placing fresh, gray, and black holding tanks in a location so as not to change the balance of the RV when the tanks are empty or full. **Always double-check wheelbase, GVWR, and weights at front and rear axles.**

*See Section 1 for details on how conclusions are reached.

Brand	Year	Type	Length	Model	Chassis	Engine	Fuel Type	Average Price per Linear Foot When New	Adjusted Wheelbase	Approx. Towing Capacity	Gross Vehicle Weight Rating	Average Curb Weight
Coach House	1998	MHB	20	192 std	DO	5.9L	G	$2500	128	4,990	8,510	7,394

Livability Code: WE 40-80
Wheelbase-to-length ratio of 54% is considered ○ dangerous ○ fatiguing ◉ good ○ excellent *
The approximate net payload of 1116 pounds at 13% of GVWR on this model is ○ deficient ○ excessive ○ cautionary ◉ good ○ excellent *
Total highway safety penalties are: 2 *   Value: 81   Durability: 80   Highway Control Rating: 79   Highway Safety: 77   ★★★

Coach House	1998	MHB	20	193 std	DO	5.9L	G	$2500	128	4,990	8,510	7,394

Livability Code: WE 40-80
Wheelbase-to-length ratio of 54% is considered ○ dangerous ○ fatiguing ◉ good ○ excellent *
The approximate net payload of 1116 pounds at 13% of GVWR on this model is ○ deficient ○ excessive ○ cautionary ◉ good ○ excellent *
Total highway safety penalties are: 2 *   Value: 81   Durability: 80   Highway Control Rating: 79   Highway Safety: 77   ★★★

Coach House	1998	MHB	20	194 std	DO	5.9L	G	$2500	128	4,990	8,510	7,394

Livability Code: WE 40-80
Wheelbase-to-length ratio of 54% is considered ○ dangerous ○ fatiguing ◉ good ○ excellent *
The approximate net payload of 1116 pounds at 13% of GVWR on this model is ○ deficient ○ excessive ○ cautionary ◉ good ○ excellent *
Total highway safety penalties are: 2 *   Value: 81   Durability: 80   Highway Control Rating: 79   Highway Safety: 77   ★★★

Coach House	1998	MHB	20	192 wb	DO	5.9L	G	$2500	128	4,990	8,510	7,805

Livability Code: WE 40-80
Wheelbase-to-length ratio of 53% is considered ○ dangerous ◉ fatiguing ○ good ○ excellent *
The approximate net payload of 705 pounds at 8% of GVWR on this model is ○ deficient ○ excessive ◉ cautionary ○ good ○ excellent *
Total highway safety penalties are: 2 *   Value: 81   Durability: 80   Highway Control Rating: 58   Highway Safety: 56   ★

Coach House	1998	MHB	20	193 wb	DO	5.9L	G	$2500	128	4,990	8,510	7,805

Livability Code: WE 40-80
Wheelbase-to-length ratio of 53% is considered ○ dangerous ◉ fatiguing ○ good ○ excellent *
The approximate net payload of 705 pounds at 8% of GVWR on this model is ○ deficient ○ excessive ◉ cautionary ○ good ○ excellent *
Total highway safety penalties are: 2 *   Value: 81   Durability: 80   Highway Control Rating: 58   Highway Safety: 56   ★

Coach House	1998	MHB	20	194 wb	DO	5.9L	G	$2500	128	4,990	8,510	7,805

Livability Code: WE 40-80
Wheelbase-to-length ratio of 53% is considered ○ dangerous ◉ fatiguing ○ good ○ excellent *
The approximate net payload of 705 pounds at 8% of GVWR on this model is ○ deficient ○ excessive ◉ cautionary ○ good ○ excellent *
Total highway safety penalties are: 2 *   Value: 81   Durability: 80   Highway Control Rating: 58   Highway Safety: 56   ★

Coach House	1998	MHB	20	192 std	FO	5.4L	G	$2500	138	4,400	8,600	7,608

Livability Code: WE 40-80
Wheelbase-to-length ratio of 57% is considered ○ dangerous ○ fatiguing ◉ good ○ excellent *
The approximate net payload of 993 pounds at 12% of GVWR on this model is ○ deficient ○ excessive ○ cautionary ◉ good ○ excellent *
Total highway safety penalties are: 2 *   Value: 81   Durability: 80   Highway Control Rating: 92   Highway Safety: 90   ★★★★

Coach House	1998	MHB	20	192 std	FO	7.3L	D	$2500	138	1,500	9,400	7,780

Livability Code: WE 40-80
Wheelbase-to-length ratio of 57% is considered ○ dangerous ○ fatiguing ◉ good ○ excellent *
The approximate net payload of 1620 pounds at 17% of GVWR on this model is ○ deficient ○ excessive ○ cautionary ○ good ◉ excellent *
Total highway safety penalties are: 2 *   Value: 81   Durability: 80   Highway Control Rating: 100   Highway Safety: 98   ★★★★

Coach House	1999	MHB	20	192RL	DO	5.9L	G	$2500	128	4,990	8,510	7,404

Livability Code: WE 40-80
Wheelbase-to-length ratio of 53% is considered ○ dangerous ◉ fatiguing ○ good ○ excellent *
The approximate net payload of 1106 pounds at 13% of GVWR on this model is ○ deficient ○ excessive ○ cautionary ◉ good ○ excellent *
Total highway safety penalties are: 2 *   Value: 92   Durability: 80   Highway Control Rating: 75   Highway Safety: 73   ★★★

Coach House	1999	MHB	20	193RL	DO	5.9L	G	$2500	128	4,990	8,510	7,404

Livability Code: WE 40-80
Wheelbase-to-length ratio of 53% is considered ○ dangerous ◉ fatiguing ○ good ○ excellent *
The approximate net payload of 1106 pounds at 13% of GVWR on this model is ○ deficient ○ excessive ○ cautionary ◉ good ○ excellent *
Total highway safety penalties are: 2 *   Value: 92   Durability: 80   Highway Control Rating: 75   Highway Safety: 73   ★★★

Coach House	1999	MHB	20	192SD	DO	5.9L	G	$2500	128	4,990	8,510	7,404

Livability Code: WE 40-80
Wheelbase-to-length ratio of 53% is considered ○ dangerous ◉ fatiguing ○ good ○ excellent *
The approximate net payload of 1106 pounds at 13% of GVWR on this model is ○ deficient ○ excessive ○ cautionary ◉ good ○ excellent *
Total highway safety penalties are: 2 *   Value: 92   Durability: 80   Highway Control Rating: 75   Highway Safety: 73   ★★★

Coach House	1999	MHB	20	193SD	DO	5.9L	G	$2500	128	4,990	8,510	7,404

Livability Code: WE 40-80
Wheelbase-to-length ratio of 53% is considered ○ dangerous ◉ fatiguing ○ good ○ excellent *
The approximate net payload of 1106 pounds at 13% of GVWR on this model is ○ deficient ○ excessive ○ cautionary ◉ good ○ excellent *
Total highway safety penalties are: 2 *   Value: 92   Durability: 80   Highway Control Rating: 75   Highway Safety: 73   ★★★

Note: Safety ratings are based on the assumption that the engineering of the RV has allowed for proper balance by placing fresh, gray, and black holding tanks in a location so as not to change the balance of the RV when the tanks are empty or full. **Always double-check wheelbase, GVWR, and weights at front and rear axles.**

*See Section 1 for details on how conclusions are reached.

Brand	Year	Type	Length	Model	Chassis	Engine	Fuel Type	Average Price per Linear Foot When New	Adjusted Wheelbase	Approx. Towing Capacity	Gross Vehicle Weight Rating	Average Curb Weight
Coach House	1999	MHB	20	192TB	DO	5.9L	G	$2500	128	4,990	8,510	7,404

Livability Code: WE 40-80

Wheelbase-to-length ratio of 53% is considered ○ dangerous ● fatiguing ○ good ○ excellent *

The approximate net payload of 1106 pounds at 13% of GVWR on this model is ○ deficient ○ excessive ○ cautionary ● good ○ excellent *

Total highway safety penalties are: 2 *   Value: 92   Durability: 80   Highway Control Rating: 75   Highway Safety: 73   ★★★

| Coach House | 1999 | MHB | 20 | 193TB | DO | 5.9L | G | $2500 | 128 | 4,990 | 8,510 | 7,404 |

Livability Code: WE 40-80

Wheelbase-to-length ratio of 53% is considered ○ dangerous ● fatiguing ○ good ○ excellent *

The approximate net payload of 1106 pounds at 13% of GVWR on this model is ○ deficient ○ excessive ○ cautionary ● good ○ excellent *

Total highway safety penalties are: 2 *   Value: 92   Durability: 80   Highway Control Rating: 75   Highway Safety: 73   ★★★

| Coach House | 1999 | MHB | 20 | 194RD | DO | 5.9L | G | $2500 | 128 | 4,990 | 8,510 | 7,404 |

Livability Code: WE 40-80

Wheelbase-to-length ratio of 53% is considered ○ dangerous ● fatiguing ○ good ○ excellent *

The approximate net payload of 1106 pounds at 13% of GVWR on this model is ○ deficient ○ excessive ○ cautionary ● good ○ excellent *

Total highway safety penalties are: 2 *   Value: 92   Durability: 80   Highway Control Rating: 75   Highway Safety: 73   ★★★

| Coach House | 1999 | MHB | 20 | 194RL | DO | 5.9L | G | $2500 | 128 | 4,990 | 8,510 | 7,404 |

Livability Code: WE 40-80

Wheelbase-to-length ratio of 53% is considered ○ dangerous ● fatiguing ○ good ○ excellent *

The approximate net payload of 1106 pounds at 13% of GVWR on this model is ○ deficient ○ excessive ○ cautionary ● good ○ excellent *

Total highway safety penalties are: 2 *   Value: 92   Durability: 80   Highway Control Rating: 75   Highway Safety: 73   ★★★

| Coach House | 1999 | MHB | 20 | 194RS (WB) | DO | 5.9L | G | $2500 | 128 | 4,990 | 8,510 | 7,805 |

Livability Code: WE 40-80

Wheelbase-to-length ratio of 53% is considered ○ dangerous ● fatiguing ○ good ○ excellent *

The approximate net payload of 705 pounds at 8% of GVWR on this model is ○ deficient ○ excessive ● cautionary ○ good ○ excellent *

Total highway safety penalties are: 2 *   Value: 92   Durability: 80   Highway Control Rating: 57   Highway Safety: 55   ★

| Coach House | 1999 | MHB | 20 | 192KS (WB) | DO | 5.9L | G | $2500 | 128 | 4,990 | 8,510 | 7,805 |

Livability Code: WE 40-80

Wheelbase-to-length ratio of 53% is considered ○ dangerous ● fatiguing ○ good ○ excellent *

The approximate net payload of 705 pounds at 8% of GVWR on this model is ○ deficient ○ excessive ● cautionary ○ good ○ excellent *

Total highway safety penalties are: 2 *   Value: 92   Durability: 80   Highway Control Rating: 57   Highway Safety: 55   ★

| Coach House | 1999 | MHB | 20 | 193KS (WB) | DO | 5.9L | G | $2500 | 128 | 4,990 | 8,510 | 7,805 |

Livability Code: WE 40-80

Wheelbase-to-length ratio of 53% is considered ○ dangerous ● fatiguing ○ good ○ excellent *

The approximate net payload of 705 pounds at 8% of GVWR on this model is ○ deficient ○ excessive ● cautionary ○ good ○ excellent *

Total highway safety penalties are: 2 *   Value: 92   Durability: 80   Highway Control Rating: 57   Highway Safety: 55   ★

| Coach House | 1999 | MHB | 20 | 192SD (WB) | DO | 5.9L | G | $2500 | 128 | 4,990 | 8,510 | 7,805 |

Livability Code: WE 40-80

Wheelbase-to-length ratio of 53% is considered ○ dangerous ● fatiguing ○ good ○ excellent *

The approximate net payload of 705 pounds at 8% of GVWR on this model is ○ deficient ○ excessive ● cautionary ○ good ○ excellent *

Total highway safety penalties are: 2 *   Value: 92   Durability: 80   Highway Control Rating: 57   Highway Safety: 55   ★

| Coach House | 1999 | MHB | 20 | 193SD (WB) | DO | 5.9L | G | $2500 | 128 | 4,990 | 8,510 | 7,805 |

Livability Code: WE 40-80

Wheelbase-to-length ratio of 53% is considered ○ dangerous ● fatiguing ○ good ○ excellent *

The approximate net payload of 705 pounds at 8% of GVWR on this model is ○ deficient ○ excessive ● cautionary ○ good ○ excellent *

Total highway safety penalties are: 2 *   Value: 92   Durability: 80   Highway Control Rating: 57   Highway Safety: 55   ★

| Coach House | 1999 | MHB | 20 | 192TB (WB) | DO | 5.9L | G | $2500 | 128 | 4,990 | 8,510 | 7,805 |

Livability Code: WE 40-80

Wheelbase-to-length ratio of 53% is considered ○ dangerous ● fatiguing ○ good ○ excellent *

The approximate net payload of 705 pounds at 8% of GVWR on this model is ○ deficient ○ excessive ● cautionary ○ good ○ excellent *

Total highway safety penalties are: 2 *   Value: 92   Durability: 80   Highway Control Rating: 57   Highway Safety: 55   ★

| Coach House | 1999 | MHB | 20 | 193TB (WB) | DO | 5.9L | G | $2500 | 128 | 4,990 | 8,510 | 7,805 |

Livability Code: WE 40-80

Wheelbase-to-length ratio of 53% is considered ○ dangerous ● fatiguing ○ good ○ excellent *

The approximate net payload of 705 pounds at 8% of GVWR on this model is ○ deficient ○ excessive ● cautionary ○ good ○ excellent *

Total highway safety penalties are: 2 *   Value: 92   Durability: 80   Highway Control Rating: 57   Highway Safety: 55   ★

| Coach House | 1999 | MHB | 20 | 192RL opch | FO | 5.4L | G | $2500 | 138 | 4,400 | 8,600 | 7,595 |

Livability Code: WE 40-80

Wheelbase-to-length ratio of 57% is considered ○ dangerous ○ fatiguing ● good ○ excellent *

The approximate net payload of 1005 pounds at 12% of GVWR on this model is ○ deficient ○ excessive ○ cautionary ● good ○ excellent *

Total highway safety penalties are: 2 *   Value: 92   Durability: 80   Highway Control Rating: 92   Highway Safety: 90   ★★★★

Note: Safety ratings are based on the assumption that the engineering of the RV has allowed for proper balance by placing fresh, gray, and black holding tanks in a location so as not to change the balance of the RV when the tanks are empty or full. **Always double-check wheelbase, GVWR, and weights at front and rear axles.**

*See Section 1 for details on how conclusions are reached.

Section 2: The Ratings

Brand	Year	Type	Length	Model	Chassis	Engine	Fuel Type	Average Price per Linear Foot When New	Adjusted Wheelbase	Approx. Towing Capacity	Gross Vehicle Weight Rating	Average Curb Weight
Coach House	1999	MHB	20	192SD opch	FO	5.4L	G	$2500	138	4,400	8,600	7,595

Livability Code: WE 40-80
Wheelbase-to-length ratio of 57% is considered ○ dangerous ○ fatiguing ◉ good ○ excellent*
The approximate net payload of 1005 pounds at 12% of GVWR on this model is ○ deficient ○ excessive ○ cautionary ◉ good ○ excellent*
Total highway safety penalties are: 2* Value: 9 2 Durability: 8 0 Highway Control Rating: 9 2 Highway Safety: 9 0 ★★★★

Brand	Year	Type	Length	Model	Chassis	Engine	Fuel Type					
Coach House	1999	MHB	20	192TB opch	FO	5.4L	G	$2500	138	4,400	8,600	7,595

Livability Code: WE 40-80
Wheelbase-to-length ratio of 57% is considered ○ dangerous ○ fatiguing ◉ good ○ excellent*
The approximate net payload of 1005 pounds at 12% of GVWR on this model is ○ deficient ○ excessive ○ cautionary ◉ good ○ excellent*
Total highway safety penalties are: 2* Value: 9 2 Durability: 8 0 Highway Control Rating: 9 2 Highway Safety: 9 0 ★★★★

Brand	Year	Type	Length	Model	Chassis	Engine	Fuel Type					
Coach House	1999	MHB	20	192RL op eng	FO	6.8L	G	$2500	138	3,600	9,400	7,755

Livability Code: WE 40-80
Wheelbase-to-length ratio of 57% is considered ○ dangerous ○ fatiguing ◉ good ○ excellent*
The approximate net payload of 1645 pounds at 18% of GVWR on this model is ○ deficient ○ excessive ○ cautionary ○ good ◉ excellent*
Total highway safety penalties are: 2* Value: 9 2 Durability: 8 0 Highway Control Rating: 1 0 0 Highway Safety: 9 8 ★★★★

Brand	Year	Type	Length	Model	Chassis	Engine	Fuel Type					
Coach House	1999	MHB	20	192SD op eng	FO	6.8L	G	$2500	138	3,600	9,400	7,755

Livability Code: WE 40-80
Wheelbase-to-length ratio of 57% is considered ○ dangerous ○ fatiguing ◉ good ○ excellent*
The approximate net payload of 1645 pounds at 18% of GVWR on this model is ○ deficient ○ excessive ○ cautionary ○ good ◉ excellent*
Total highway safety penalties are: 2* Value: 9 2 Durability: 8 0 Highway Control Rating: 1 0 0 Highway Safety: 9 8 ★★★★

Brand	Year	Type	Length	Model	Chassis	Engine	Fuel Type					
Coach House	1999	MHB	20	192RL op eng	FO	6.8L	G	$2500	138	3,600	9,400	7,755

Livability Code: WE 40-80
Wheelbase-to-length ratio of 57% is considered ○ dangerous ○ fatiguing ◉ good ○ excellent*
The approximate net payload of 1645 pounds at 18% of GVWR on this model is ○ deficient ○ excessive ○ cautionary ○ good ◉ excellent*
Total highway safety penalties are: 2* Value: 9 2 Durability: 8 0 Highway Control Rating: 1 0 0 Highway Safety: 9 8 ★★★★

Brand	Year	Type	Length	Model	Chassis	Engine	Fuel Type					
Coach House	1999	MHB	20	192RL op eng	FO	7.3L	D	$2500	138	3,600	9,400	8,255

Livability Code: WE 40-80
Wheelbase-to-length ratio of 57% is considered ○ dangerous ○ fatiguing ◉ good ○ excellent*
The approximate net payload of 1145 pounds at 12% of GVWR on this model is ○ deficient ○ excessive ○ cautionary ◉ good ○ excellent*
Total highway safety penalties are: 2* Value: 9 2 Durability: 8 0 Highway Control Rating: 9 3 Highway Safety: 9 1 ★★★★

Brand	Year	Type	Length	Model	Chassis	Engine	Fuel Type					
Coach House	1999	MHB	20	192SD op eng	FO	7.3L	D	$2500	138	3,600	9,400	8,255

Livability Code: WE 40-80
Wheelbase-to-length ratio of 57% is considered ○ dangerous ○ fatiguing ◉ good ○ excellent*
The approximate net payload of 1145 pounds at 12% of GVWR on this model is ○ deficient ○ excessive ○ cautionary ◉ good ○ excellent*
Total highway safety penalties are: 2* Value: 9 2 Durability: 8 0 Highway Control Rating: 9 3 Highway Safety: 9 1 ★★★★

Brand	Year	Type	Length	Model	Chassis	Engine	Fuel Type					
Coach House	1999	MHB	20	192TB op eng	FO	7.3L	D	$2500	138	3,600	9,400	8,255

Livability Code: WE 40-80
Wheelbase-to-length ratio of 57% is considered ○ dangerous ○ fatiguing ◉ good ○ excellent*
The approximate net payload of 1145 pounds at 12% of GVWR on this model is ○ deficient ○ excessive ○ cautionary ◉ good ○ excellent*
Total highway safety penalties are: 2* Value: 9 2 Durability: 8 0 Highway Control Rating: 9 3 Highway Safety: 9 1 ★★★★

Brand	Year	Type	Length	Model	Chassis	Engine	Fuel Type					
Columbus	1994	MHA	23	230	CH	7.4L	G	$2500	137	4,200	11,800	10,460

Livability Code: SB 30-90
Wheelbase-to-length ratio of 50% is considered ◉ dangerous ○ fatiguing ○ good ○ excellent*
The approximate net payload of 1340 pounds at 11% of GVWR on this model is ○ deficient ○ excessive ○ cautionary ◉ good ○ excellent*
Total highway safety penalties are: 1* Value: 7 8 Durability: 7 1 Highway Control Rating: 3 4 Highway Safety: 3 3

Brand	Year	Type	Length	Model	Chassis	Engine	Fuel Type					
Columbus	1994	MHA	27	270	CH	7.4L	G	$1700	158	1,500	12,300	11,605

Livability Code: SB 30-90
Wheelbase-to-length ratio of 49% is considered ◉ dangerous ○ fatiguing ○ good ○ excellent*
The approximate net payload of 695 pounds at 6% of GVWR on this model is ◉ deficient ○ excessive ○ cautionary ○ good ○ excellent*
Total highway safety penalties are: 3* Value: 7 7 Durability: 7 1 Highway Control Rating: 4 Highway Safety: 1

Brand	Year	Type	Length	Model	Chassis	Engine	Fuel Type					
Columbus	1994	MHA	30	295	CH	7.4L	G	$1700	190	2,200	14,800	13,169

Livability Code: SB 30-90
Wheelbase-to-length ratio of 53% is considered ○ dangerous ◉ fatiguing ○ good ○ excellent*
The approximate net payload of 1631 pounds at 11% of GVWR on this model is ○ deficient ○ excessive ○ cautionary ◉ good ○ excellent*
Total highway safety penalties are: 5* Value: 7 6 Durability: 7 1 Highway Control Rating: 5 9 Highway Safety: 5 4 ★

Brand	Year	Type	Length	Model	Chassis	Engine	Fuel Type					
Columbus	1994	MHA	33	325	CH	7.4L	G	$1600	208	2,200	14,800	13,832

Livability Code: SB 30-90
Wheelbase-to-length ratio of 53% is considered ○ dangerous ◉ fatiguing ○ good ○ excellent*
The approximate net payload of 968 pounds at 7% of GVWR on this model is ○ deficient ○ excessive ◉ cautionary ○ good ○ excellent*
Total highway safety penalties are: 6* Value: 7 5 Durability: 7 1 Highway Control Rating: 4 1 Highway Safety: 3 5

Note: Safety ratings are based on the assumption that the engineering of the RV has allowed for proper balance by placing fresh, gray, and black holding tanks in a location so as not to change the balance of the RV when the tanks are empty or full. **Always double-check wheelbase, GVWR, and weights at front and rear axles.**

*See Section 1 for details on how conclusions are reached.

Brand	Year	Type	Length	Model	Chassis	Engine	Fuel Type	Average Price per Linear Foot When New	Adjusted Wheelbase	Approx. Towing Capacity	Gross Vehicle Weight Rating	Average Curb Weight
Columbus	1995	MHA	27	270	CH	7.4L	G	$2000	158	1,500	12,700	11,863

Livability Code: SB 30-90
Wheelbase-to-length ratio of 49% is considered ●dangerous ○fatiguing ○good ○excellent*
The approximate net payload of 837 pounds at 7% of GVWR on this model is ○deficient ○excessive ●cautionary ○good ○excellent*
Total highway safety penalties are: 3* Value: 77 Durability: 71 Highway Control Rating: 10 Highway Safety: 7

Columbus	1995	MHA	30	295	CH	7.4L	G	$1900	190	4,200	14,800	13,053

Livability Code: SB 30-90
Wheelbase-to-length ratio of 53% is considered ○dangerous ●fatiguing ○good ○excellent*
The approximate net payload of 1747 pounds at 12% of GVWR on this model is ○deficient ○excessive ○cautionary ●good ○excellent*
Total highway safety penalties are: 5* Value: 76 Durability: 71 Highway Control Rating: 61 Highway Safety: 56 ★

Columbus	1995	MHA	33	325QB	CH	7.4L	G	$1800	208	3,500	16,500	13,872

Livability Code: SB 30-90
Wheelbase-to-length ratio of 53% is considered ○dangerous ●fatiguing ○good ○excellent*
The approximate net payload of 2628 pounds at 16% of GVWR on this model is ○deficient ○excessive ○cautionary ○good ●excellent*
Total highway safety penalties are: 6* Value: 75 Durability: 71 Highway Control Rating: 70 Highway Safety: 64 ★★

Columbus	1995	MHA	33	325LX	CH	7.4L	G	$1800	208	3,500	16,500	13,922

Livability Code: SB 30-90
Wheelbase-to-length ratio of 53% is considered ○dangerous ●fatiguing ○good ○excellent*
The approximate net payload of 2578 pounds at 16% of GVWR on this model is ○deficient ○excessive ○cautionary ○good ●excellent*
Total highway safety penalties are: 6* Value: 75 Durability: 71 Highway Control Rating: 70 Highway Safety: 64 ★★

Columbus	1995	MHA	35	345	CH	7.4L	G	$1800	228	3,500	16,500	14,654

Livability Code: SB 30-90
Wheelbase-to-length ratio of 55% is considered ○dangerous ○fatiguing ●good ○excellent*
The approximate net payload of 1846 pounds at 11% of GVWR on this model is ○deficient ○excessive ○cautionary ●good ○excellent*
Total highway safety penalties are: 7* Value: 75 Durability: 71 Highway Control Rating: 87 Highway Safety: 80 ★★★

Columbus	1995	MHA	35	345	FO	7.5L	G	$1800	228	8,000	17,000	14,916

Livability Code: SB 30-90
Wheelbase-to-length ratio of 55% is considered ○dangerous ○fatiguing ●good ○excellent*
The approximate net payload of 2084 pounds at 12% of GVWR on this model is ○deficient ○excessive ○cautionary ●good ○excellent*
Total highway safety penalties are: 2* Value: 77 Durability: 71 Highway Control Rating: 85 Highway Safety: 83 ★★★

Columbus	1996	MHA	33	325LX	CH	7.4L	G	$1900	208	3,500	16,500	13,922

Livability Code: SB 30-90
Wheelbase-to-length ratio of 53% is considered ○dangerous ●fatiguing ○good ○excellent*
The approximate net payload of 2578 pounds at 16% of GVWR on this model is ○deficient ○excessive ○cautionary ○good ●excellent*
Total highway safety penalties are: 6* Value: 75 Durability: 71 Highway Control Rating: 70 Highway Safety: 64 ★★

Concept	1995	MHA	36	36	GI	DE350	D	$10900	220	1,500	37,400	30,450

Livability Code: FT 30-90
Wheelbase-to-length ratio of 51% is considered ○dangerous ●fatiguing ○good ○excellent*
The approximate net payload of 6950 pounds at 19% of GVWR on this model is ○deficient ○excessive ○cautionary ○good ●excellent*
Total highway safety penalties are: 2* Value: 85 Durability: 90 Highway Control Rating: 51 Highway Safety: 49

Concept	1995	MHA	40	40	GI	DE350	D	$10400	262	1,500	37,400	31,756

Livability Code: FT 30-90
Wheelbase-to-length ratio of 55% is considered ○dangerous ○fatiguing ●good ○excellent*
The approximate net payload of 5644 pounds at 15% of GVWR on this model is ○deficient ○excessive ○cautionary ●good ○excellent*
Total highway safety penalties are: 2* Value: 85 Durability: 90 Highway Control Rating: 89 Highway Safety: 87 ★★★★

Concept	1995	MHA	40	40	GI	DE450	D	$10800	262	1,500	37,400	31,756

Livability Code: FT 30-90
Wheelbase-to-length ratio of 55% is considered ○dangerous ○fatiguing ●good ○excellent*
The approximate net payload of 5644 pounds at 15% of GVWR on this model is ○deficient ○excessive ○cautionary ●good ○excellent*
Total highway safety penalties are: 2* Value: 85 Durability: 90 Highway Control Rating: 89 Highway Safety: 87 ★★★★

Concept	1997	MHA	45	45 Omega	GI	DE500	D	$12300	310 T	5,000	45,100	37,238

Livability Code: FT 30-90
Wheelbase-to-length ratio of 57% is considered ○dangerous ○fatiguing ●good ○excellent*
The approximate net payload of 7862 pounds at 17% of GVWR on this model is ○deficient ○excessive ○cautionary ○good ●excellent*
Total highway safety penalties are: 4* Value: 84 Durability: 90 Highway Control Rating: 100 Highway Safety: 96 ★★★★

Concept	1998	MHA	40	40 Alpha	GI	DE500	D	$13100	240	7,000	46,500	39,159

Livability Code: FT 30-90
Wheelbase-to-length ratio of 50% is considered ●dangerous ○fatiguing ○good ○excellent*
The approximate net payload of 7341 pounds at 16% of GVWR on this model is ○deficient ○excessive ○cautionary ○good ●excellent*
Total highway safety penalties are: 2* Value: 85 Durability: 90 Highway Control Rating: 44 Highway Safety: 42

Note: Safety ratings are based on the assumption that the engineering of the RV has allowed for proper balance by placing fresh, gray, and black holding tanks in a location so as not to change the balance of the RV when the tanks are empty or full. **Always double-check wheelbase, GVWR, and weights at front and rear axles.**

*See Section 1 for details on how conclusions are reached.

Section 2: The Ratings

Brand	Year	Type	Length	Model	Chassis	Engine	Fuel Type	Average Price per Linear Foot When New	Adjusted Wheelbase	Approx. Towing Capacity	Gross Vehicle Weight Rating	Average Curb Weight
Concept	1998	MHA	45	45 Omega	Gl	DE500	D	$12300	286	7,000	46,500	40,825

Livability Code: FT 30-90
Wheelbase-to-length ratio of 53% is considered ○ dangerous ◉ fatiguing ○ good ○ excellent *
The approximate net payload of 5675 pounds at 12% of GVWR on this model is ○ deficient ○ excessive ○ cautionary ◉ good ○ excellent *
Total highway safety penalties are: 2 *   Value: 85   Durability: 90   Highway Control Rating: 63   Highway Safety: 61   ★★

Brand	Year	Type	Length	Model	Chassis	Engine	Fuel Type	Price/Ft	Wheelbase	Towing	GVWR	Curb
Concept	1999	MHA	40	Alpha	DY	DE500	D	$13800	264 T	7,000	46,500	36,306

Livability Code: FT 30-90
Wheelbase-to-length ratio of 55% is considered ○ dangerous ○ fatiguing ◉ good ○ excellent *
The approximate net payload of 10194 pounds at 22% of GVWR on this model is ○ deficient ○ excessive ○ cautionary ○ good ◉ excellent *
Total highway safety penalties are: 4 *   Value: 95   Durability: 93   Highway Control Rating: 95   Highway Safety: 91   ★★★★

Concept	1999	MHA	40	Alpha myc	DY	DE500	D	$13800	264 T	7,000	48,500	38,745

Livability Code: FT 30-90
Wheelbase-to-length ratio of 55% is considered ○ dangerous ○ fatiguing ◉ good ○ excellent *
The approximate net payload of 9756 pounds at 20% of GVWR on this model is ○ deficient ○ excessive ○ cautionary ○ good ◉ excellent *
Total highway safety penalties are: 4 *   Value: 95   Durability: 93   Highway Control Rating: 96   Highway Safety: 92   ★★★★

Concept	1999	MHA	45	Omega	DY	DE500	D	$12200	310 T	7,000	46,500	37,938

Livability Code: FT 30-90
Wheelbase-to-length ratio of 57% is considered ○ dangerous ○ fatiguing ◉ good ○ excellent *
The approximate net payload of 8562 pounds at 18% of GVWR on this model is ○ deficient ○ excessive ○ cautionary ○ good ◉ excellent *
Total highway safety penalties are: 4 *   Value: 95   Durability: 93   Highway Control Rating: 100   Highway Safety: 96   ★★★★

Concept	1999	MHA	45	Omega myc	DY	DE500	D	$12200	310 T	7,000	48,500	40,572

Livability Code: FT 30-90
Wheelbase-to-length ratio of 57% is considered ○ dangerous ○ fatiguing ◉ good ○ excellent *
The approximate net payload of 7929 pounds at 16% of GVWR on this model is ○ deficient ○ excessive ○ cautionary ○ good ◉ excellent *
Total highway safety penalties are: 4 *   Value: 95   Durability: 93   Highway Control Rating: 100   Highway Safety: 96   ★★★★

Contessa	1990	MHA	34	Falcon 34	Gl	Cat	D	$5400	200	1,500	25,000	17,085

Livability Code: FT 30-90
Wheelbase-to-length ratio of 49% is considered ◉ dangerous ○ fatiguing ○ good ○ excellent *
The approximate net payload of 7915 pounds at 32% of GVWR on this model is ○ deficient ○ excessive ◉ cautionary ○ good ○ excellent *
Total highway safety penalties are: 2 *   Value: 81   Durability: 80   Highway Control Rating: 33   Highway Safety: 31

Contessa	1990	MHA	37	Tiara 36	Gl	Ca320	D	$5300	228	1,500	25,600	20,534

Livability Code: FT 30-90
Wheelbase-to-length ratio of 52% is considered ○ dangerous ◉ fatiguing ○ good ○ excellent *
The approximate net payload of 5066 pounds at 20% of GVWR on this model is ○ deficient ○ excessive ○ cautionary ○ good ◉ excellent *
Total highway safety penalties are: 2 *   Value: 81   Durability: 80   Highway Control Rating: 63   Highway Safety: 61   ★★

Contessa	1991	MHA	37	36	Gl	Cat	D	$6400	228	3,000	28,910	21,378

Livability Code: FT 30-90
Wheelbase-to-length ratio of 52% is considered ○ dangerous ◉ fatiguing ○ good ○ excellent *
The approximate net payload of 7532 pounds at 26% of GVWR on this model is ○ deficient ○ excessive ○ cautionary ◉ good ○ excellent *
Total highway safety penalties are: 2 *   Value: 81   Durability: 80   Highway Control Rating: 57   Highway Safety: 55   ★

Contessa	1991	MHA	39	38	Gl	Cat	D	$5400	252	190	31,720	22,995

Livability Code: FT 30-90
Wheelbase-to-length ratio of 54% is considered ○ dangerous ○ fatiguing ◉ good ○ excellent *
The approximate net payload of 8725 pounds at 28% of GVWR on this model is ○ deficient ○ excessive ○ cautionary ◉ good ○ excellent *
Total highway safety penalties are: 2 *   Value: 81   Durability: 80   Highway Control Rating: 79   Highway Safety: 77   ★★★

Contessa	1991	MHA	39	38	Gl	Cat	D	$5200	252	1,500	29,810	22,842

Livability Code: FT 30-90
Wheelbase-to-length ratio of 54% is considered ○ dangerous ○ fatiguing ◉ good ○ excellent *
The approximate net payload of 6968 pounds at 23% of GVWR on this model is ○ deficient ○ excessive ○ cautionary ○ good ◉ excellent *
Total highway safety penalties are: 2 *   Value: 81   Durability: 80   Highway Control Rating: 84   Highway Safety: 82   ★★★★

Contessa	1992	MHA	37	36	Gl	Cat	D	$6700	228	5,000	28,910	22,069

Livability Code: FT 30-90
Wheelbase-to-length ratio of 52% is considered ○ dangerous ◉ fatiguing ○ good ○ excellent *
The approximate net payload of 6841 pounds at 24% of GVWR on this model is ○ deficient ○ excessive ○ cautionary ○ good ◉ excellent *
Total highway safety penalties are: 2 *   Value: 81   Durability: 80   Highway Control Rating: 59   Highway Safety: 57   ★

Contessa	1992	MHA	39	38	Gl	Cat	D	$7300	252	5,000	31,720	23,699

Livability Code: FT 30-90
Wheelbase-to-length ratio of 54% is considered ○ dangerous ○ fatiguing ◉ good ○ excellent *
The approximate net payload of 8021 pounds at 25% of GVWR on this model is ○ deficient ○ excessive ○ cautionary ◉ good ○ excellent *
Total highway safety penalties are: 2 *   Value: 81   Durability: 80   Highway Control Rating: 82   Highway Safety: 80   ★★★★

Note: Safety ratings are based on the assumption that the engineering of the RV has allowed for proper balance by placing fresh, gray, and black holding tanks in a location so as not to change the balance of the RV when the tanks are empty or full. **Always double-check wheelbase, GVWR, and weights at front and rear axles.**

*See Section 1 for details on how conclusions are reached.

Brand	Year	Type	Length	Model	Chassis	Engine	Fuel Type	Average Price per Linear Foot When New	Adjusted Wheelbase	Approx. Towing Capacity	Gross Vehicle Weight Rating	Average Curb Weight
Contessa	1993	MHA	37	36	GI	Cu8.3L	D	$7300	228	5,000	28,910	22,122

Livability Code: FT 30-90
Wheelbase-to-length ratio of 52% is considered ○ dangerous ◉ fatiguing ○ good ○ excellent *
The approximate net payload of 6788 pounds at 23% of GVWR on this model is ○ deficient ○ excessive ○ cautionary ○ good ◉ excellent *
Total highway safety penalties are: 2 *   Value: 8 1   Durability: 8 0   Highway Control Rating: 6 0   Highway Safety: 5 8   ★

Brand	Year	Type	Length	Model	Chassis	Engine	Fuel Type		Adjusted Wheelbase	Approx. Towing Capacity	Gross Vehicle Weight Rating	Average Curb Weight
Contessa	1993	MHA	39	38	GI	Cu8.3L	D	$7100	252	5,000	31,720	23,699

Livability Code: FT 30-90
Wheelbase-to-length ratio of 54% is considered ○ dangerous ○ fatiguing ◉ good ○ excellent *
The approximate net payload of 8021 pounds at 25% of GVWR on this model is ○ deficient ○ excessive ○ cautionary ◉ good ○ excellent *
Total highway safety penalties are: 2 *   Value: 8 1   Durability: 8 0   Highway Control Rating: 8 2   Highway Safety: 8 0   ★★★★

Contessa	1993	MHA	40	40	GI	Cu8.3L	D	$7400	262	5,000	31,720	24,523

Livability Code: FT 30-90
Wheelbase-to-length ratio of 55% is considered ○ dangerous ○ fatiguing ◉ good ○ excellent *
The approximate net payload of 7197 pounds at 23% of GVWR on this model is ○ deficient ○ excessive ○ cautionary ○ good ◉ excellent *
Total highway safety penalties are: 2 *   Value: 8 1   Durability: 8 0   Highway Control Rating: 9 2   Highway Safety: 9 0   ★★★★

Contessa	1999	MHA	39	San Marco 38	MA	CA330	D	$14100	231	5,000	28,000	25,994

Livability Code: FT 30-90
Wheelbase-to-length ratio of 49% is considered ◉ dangerous ○ fatiguing ○ good ○ excellent *
The approximate net payload of 2006 pounds at 7% of GVWR on this model is ○ deficient ○ excessive ◉ cautionary ○ good ○ excellent *
Total highway safety penalties are: 12 *   Value: 8 0   Durability: 7 7   Highway Control Rating: 2 4   Highway Safety: 1 2

Contessa	1999	MHA	41	Viano 40	MA	CA330	D	$13400	266	5,000	28,000	25,733

Livability Code: FT 30-90
Wheelbase-to-length ratio of 54% is considered ○ dangerous ○ fatiguing ◉ good ○ excellent *
The approximate net payload of 2267 pounds at 8% of GVWR on this model is ○ deficient ○ excessive ◉ cautionary ○ good ○ excellent *
Total highway safety penalties are: 2 *   Value: 8 5   Durability: 7 7   Highway Control Rating: 6 2   Highway Safety: 6 0   ★★

Contessa	1999	MHA	41	Naples 40	MA	CA330	D	$13400	266	5,000	28,000	26,633

Livability Code: FT 30-90
Wheelbase-to-length ratio of 54% is considered ○ dangerous ○ fatiguing ◉ good ○ excellent *
The approximate net payload of 1367 pounds at 5% of GVWR on this model is ◉ deficient ○ excessive ○ cautionary ○ good ○ excellent *
Total highway safety penalties are: 12 *   Value: 8 0   Durability: 7 7   Highway Control Rating: 4 9   Highway Safety: 3 7

Continental	1993	MHA	38	3730	OS	Cu8.3L	D	$4400	252	7,500	22,500	22,141

Livability Code: FT 30-90
Wheelbase-to-length ratio of 55% is considered ○ dangerous ○ fatiguing ○ good ○ excellent *
The approximate net payload of 359 pounds at 2% of GVWR on this model is ◉ deficient ○ excessive ○ cautionary ○ good ○ excellent *
Total highway safety penalties are: 2 *   Value: 8 1   Durability: 8 1   Highway Control Rating: 5 4   Highway Safety: 5 2   ★

Continental	1993	MHA	38	3730 opch	OS	Cu8.3L	D	$4400	252	5,500	24,500	22,741

Livability Code: FT 30-90
Wheelbase-to-length ratio of 55% is considered ○ dangerous ○ fatiguing ◉ good ○ excellent *
The approximate net payload of 1759 pounds at 7% of GVWR on this model is ○ deficient ○ excessive ◉ cautionary ○ good ○ excellent *
Total highway safety penalties are: 2 *   Value: 8 1   Durability: 8 1   Highway Control Rating: 6 5   Highway Safety: 6 3   ★★

Continental	1993	MHA	40	4030	OS	Cu8.3L	D	$4600	278	4,600	25,400	23,748

Livability Code: FT 30-90
Wheelbase-to-length ratio of 58% is considered ○ dangerous ○ fatiguing ○ good ◉ excellent *
The approximate net payload of 1652 pounds at 7% of GVWR on this model is ○ deficient ○ excessive ◉ cautionary ○ good ○ excellent *
Total highway safety penalties are: 2 *   Value: 8 1   Durability: 8 1   Highway Control Rating: 7 4   Highway Safety: 7 2   ★★★

Continental	1995	MHA	38	3730	MA	Cu8.3L	D	$5200	252	4,100	25,900	22,701

Livability Code: FT 30-90
Wheelbase-to-length ratio of 55% is considered ○ dangerous ○ fatiguing ◉ good ○ excellent *
The approximate net payload of 3199 pounds at 12% of GVWR on this model is ○ deficient ○ excessive ○ cautionary ◉ good ○ excellent *
Total highway safety penalties are: 2 *   Value: 8 1   Durability: 8 1   Highway Control Rating: 8 6   Highway Safety: 8 4   ★★★★

Continental	1995	MHA	38	3750	MA	Cu8.3L	D	$5200	252	4,100	25,900	22,701

Livability Code: FT 30-90
Wheelbase-to-length ratio of 55% is considered ○ dangerous ○ fatiguing ◉ good ○ excellent *
The approximate net payload of 3199 pounds at 12% of GVWR on this model is ○ deficient ○ excessive ○ cautionary ◉ good ○ excellent *
Total highway safety penalties are: 2 *   Value: 8 1   Durability: 8 1   Highway Control Rating: 8 6   Highway Safety: 8 4   ★★★★

Continental	1995	MHA	38	3760	MA	Cu8.3L	D	$5200	252	4,100	25,900	22,701

Livability Code: FT 30-90
Wheelbase-to-length ratio of 55% is considered ○ dangerous ○ fatiguing ◉ good ○ excellent *
The approximate net payload of 3199 pounds at 12% of GVWR on this model is ○ deficient ○ excessive ○ cautionary ◉ good ○ excellent *
Total highway safety penalties are: 2 *   Value: 8 1   Durability: 8 1   Highway Control Rating: 8 6   Highway Safety: 8 4   ★★★★

Note: Safety ratings are based on the assumption that the engineering of the RV has allowed for proper balance by placing fresh, gray, and black holding tanks in a location so as not to change the balance of the RV when the tanks are empty or full. **Always double-check wheelbase, GVWR, and weights at front and rear axles.**

Brand	Year	Type	Length	Model	Chassis	Engine	Fuel Type	Average Price per Linear Foot When New	Adjusted Wheelbase	Approx. Towing Capacity	Gross Vehicle Weight Rating	Average Curb Weight
Continental	1995	MHA	40	4030	MA	Cu8.3L	D	$5100	278	4,100	25,900	23,553

Livability Code: FT 30-90
Wheelbase-to-length ratio of 57% is considered ○ dangerous ○ fatiguing ◉ good ○ excellent *
The approximate net payload of 2347 pounds at 9% of GVWR on this model is ○ deficient ○ excessive ◉ cautionary ○ good ○ excellent *
Total highway safety penalties are: 2 * Value: **8 1** Durability: **8 1** Highway Control Rating: **8 5** Highway Safety: **8 3** ★★★★

Brand	Year	Type	Length	Model	Chassis	Engine	Fuel Type	Avg Price/Linear Foot	Adjusted Wheelbase	Towing Cap.	GVWR	Avg Curb Weight
Continental	1995	MHA	40	4050	MA	Cu8.3L	D	$5100	278	4,100	25,900	23,553

Livability Code: FT 30-90
Wheelbase-to-length ratio of 57% is considered ○ dangerous ○ fatiguing ◉ good ○ excellent *
The approximate net payload of 2347 pounds at 9% of GVWR on this model is ○ deficient ○ excessive ◉ cautionary ○ good ○ excellent *
Total highway safety penalties are: 2 * Value: **8 1** Durability: **8 1** Highway Control Rating: **8 5** Highway Safety: **8 3** ★★★★

Continental	1995	MHA	40	4088	MA	Cu8.3L	D	$5200	278	4,100	25,900	23,553

Livability Code: FT 30-90
Wheelbase-to-length ratio of 57% is considered ○ dangerous ○ fatiguing ◉ good ○ excellent *
The approximate net payload of 2347 pounds at 9% of GVWR on this model is ○ deficient ○ excessive ◉ cautionary ○ good ○ excellent *
Total highway safety penalties are: 2 * Value: **8 1** Durability: **8 1** Highway Control Rating: **8 5** Highway Safety: **8 3** ★★★★

Continental	1995	MHA	40	4090	MA	Cu8.3L	D	$5200	278	4,100	25,900	23,553

Livability Code: FT 30-90
Wheelbase-to-length ratio of 57% is considered ○ dangerous ○ fatiguing ◉ good ○ excellent *
The approximate net payload of 2347 pounds at 9% of GVWR on this model is ○ deficient ○ excessive ◉ cautionary ○ good ○ excellent *
Total highway safety penalties are: 2 * Value: **8 1** Durability: **8 1** Highway Control Rating: **8 5** Highway Safety: **8 3** ★★★★

Continental	1996	MHA	38	3730-300	MA	Cu8.3L	D	$5200	252	4,100	25,900	22,701

Livability Code: FT 30-90
Wheelbase-to-length ratio of 55% is considered ○ dangerous ○ fatiguing ◉ good ○ excellent *
The approximate net payload of 3199 pounds at 12% of GVWR on this model is ○ deficient ○ excessive ○ cautionary ◉ good ○ excellent *
Total highway safety penalties are: 2 * Value: **8 1** Durability: **8 1** Highway Control Rating: **8 6** Highway Safety: **8 4** ★★★★

Continental	1996	MHA	38	3750-300	MA	Cu8.3L	D	$5200	252	4,100	25,900	22,701

Livability Code: FT 30-90
Wheelbase-to-length ratio of 55% is considered ○ dangerous ○ fatiguing ◉ good ○ excellent *
The approximate net payload of 3199 pounds at 12% of GVWR on this model is ○ deficient ○ excessive ○ cautionary ◉ good ○ excellent *
Total highway safety penalties are: 2 * Value: **8 1** Durability: **8 1** Highway Control Rating: **8 6** Highway Safety: **8 4** ★★★★

Continental	1996	MHA	38	3760-300	MA	Cu8.3L	D	$5200	252	4,100	25,900	22,701

Livability Code: FT 30-90
Wheelbase-to-length ratio of 55% is considered ○ dangerous ○ fatiguing ◉ good ○ excellent *
The approximate net payload of 3199 pounds at 12% of GVWR on this model is ○ deficient ○ excessive ○ cautionary ◉ good ○ excellent *
Total highway safety penalties are: 2 * Value: **8 1** Durability: **8 1** Highway Control Rating: **8 6** Highway Safety: **8 4** ★★★★

Continental	1996	MHA	38	3740-300	MA	Cu8.3L	D	$5200	252	4,100	25,900	22,701

Livability Code: FT 30-90
Wheelbase-to-length ratio of 55% is considered ○ dangerous ○ fatiguing ◉ good ○ excellent *
The approximate net payload of 3199 pounds at 12% of GVWR on this model is ○ deficient ○ excessive ○ cautionary ◉ good ○ excellent *
Total highway safety penalties are: 2 * Value: **8 1** Durability: **8 1** Highway Control Rating: **8 6** Highway Safety: **8 4** ★★★★

Continental	1996	MHA	40	4030-300	MA	Cu8.3L	D	$5100	278	4,100	25,900	23,553

Livability Code: FT 30-90
Wheelbase-to-length ratio of 57% is considered ○ dangerous ○ fatiguing ◉ good ○ excellent *
The approximate net payload of 2347 pounds at 9% of GVWR on this model is ○ deficient ○ excessive ◉ cautionary ○ good ○ excellent *
Total highway safety penalties are: 2 * Value: **8 1** Durability: **8 1** Highway Control Rating: **8 5** Highway Safety: **8 3** ★★★★

Continental	1996	MHA	40	4050-300	MA	Cu8.3L	D	$5100	278	4,100	25,900	23,553

Livability Code: FT 30-90
Wheelbase-to-length ratio of 57% is considered ○ dangerous ○ fatiguing ◉ good ○ excellent *
The approximate net payload of 2347 pounds at 9% of GVWR on this model is ○ deficient ○ excessive ◉ cautionary ○ good ○ excellent *
Total highway safety penalties are: 2 * Value: **8 1** Durability: **8 1** Highway Control Rating: **8 5** Highway Safety: **8 3** ★★★★

Continental	1996	MHA	40	4088-300	MA	Cu8.3L	D	$5200	278	4,100	25,900	23,553

Livability Code: FT 30-90
Wheelbase-to-length ratio of 57% is considered ○ dangerous ○ fatiguing ◉ good ○ excellent *
The approximate net payload of 2347 pounds at 9% of GVWR on this model is ○ deficient ○ excessive ◉ cautionary ○ good ○ excellent *
Total highway safety penalties are: 2 * Value: **8 1** Durability: **8 1** Highway Control Rating: **8 5** Highway Safety: **8 3** ★★★★

Continental	1996	MHA	40	4090-300	MA	Cu8.3L	D	$5200	278	4,100	25,900	23,553

Livability Code: FT 30-90
Wheelbase-to-length ratio of 57% is considered ○ dangerous ○ fatiguing ◉ good ○ excellent *
The approximate net payload of 2347 pounds at 9% of GVWR on this model is ○ deficient ○ excessive ◉ cautionary ○ good ○ excellent *
Total highway safety penalties are: 2 * Value: **8 1** Durability: **8 1** Highway Control Rating: **8 5** Highway Safety: **8 3** ★★★★

Note: Safety ratings are based on the assumption that the engineering of the RV has allowed for proper balance by placing fresh, gray, and black holding tanks in a location so as not to change the balance of the RV when the tanks are empty or full. **Always double-check wheelbase, GVWR, and weights at front and rear axles.**

*See Section 1 for details on how conclusions are reached.

Brand	Year	Type	Length	Model	Chassis	Engine	Fuel Type	Average Price per Linear Foot When New	Adjusted Wheelbase	Approx. Towing Capacity	Gross Vehicle Weight Rating	Average Curb Weight
Continental	1996	MHA	40	4040-300	MA	Cu8.3L	D	$5100	278	4,100	25,900	23,553

Livability Code: FT 30-90
Wheelbase-to-length ratio of 57% is considered ○ dangerous ○ fatiguing ◉ good ○ excellent*
The approximate net payload of 2347 pounds at 9% of GVWR on this model is ○ deficient ○ excessive ◉ cautionary ○ good ○ excellent*
Total highway safety penalties are: 2*   Value: **81**   Durability: **81**   Highway Control Rating: **85**   Highway Safety: **83**   ★★★★

Brand	Year	Type	Length	Model	Chassis	Engine	Fuel Type	Avg Price/Linear Foot	Adj Wheelbase	Approx Towing	GVWR	Avg Curb Weight
Continental	1997	MHA	38	3730	MA	Cu330	D	$5300	252	4,000	29,000	25,353

Livability Code: FT 30-90
Wheelbase-to-length ratio of 55% is considered ○ dangerous ○ fatiguing ◉ good ○ excellent*
The approximate net payload of 3647 pounds at 13% of GVWR on this model is ○ deficient ○ excessive ○ cautionary ◉ good ○ excellent*
Total highway safety penalties are: 2*   Value: **81**   Durability: **81**   Highway Control Rating: **87**   Highway Safety: **85**   ★★★★

Continental	1997	MHA	38	3740	MA	Cu330	D	$5200	252	4,000	29,000	25,353

Livability Code: FT 30-90
Wheelbase-to-length ratio of 55% is considered ○ dangerous ○ fatiguing ◉ good ○ excellent*
The approximate net payload of 3647 pounds at 13% of GVWR on this model is ○ deficient ○ excessive ○ cautionary ◉ good ○ excellent*
Total highway safety penalties are: 2*   Value: **81**   Durability: **81**   Highway Control Rating: **87**   Highway Safety: **85**   ★★★★

Continental	1997	MHA	38	3750	MA	Cu330	D	$5200	252	4,000	29,000	25,353

Livability Code: FT 30-90
Wheelbase-to-length ratio of 55% is considered ○ dangerous ○ fatiguing ◉ good ○ excellent*
The approximate net payload of 3647 pounds at 13% of GVWR on this model is ○ deficient ○ excessive ○ cautionary ◉ good ○ excellent*
Total highway safety penalties are: 2*   Value: **81**   Durability: **81**   Highway Control Rating: **87**   Highway Safety: **85**   ★★★★

Continental	1997	MHA	40	4030	MA	Cu330	D	$5100	276	4,000	29,000	25,924

Livability Code: FT 30-90
Wheelbase-to-length ratio of 58% is considered ○ dangerous ○ fatiguing ○ good ◉ excellent*
The approximate net payload of 3076 pounds at 11% of GVWR on this model is ○ deficient ○ excessive ○ cautionary ◉ good ○ excellent*
Total highway safety penalties are: 2*   Value: **81**   Durability: **81**   Highway Control Rating: **91**   Highway Safety: **89**   ★★★★

Continental	1997	MHA	40	4040	MA	Cu330	D	$5200	276	4,000	29,000	25,924

Livability Code: FT 30-90
Wheelbase-to-length ratio of 58% is considered ○ dangerous ○ fatiguing ○ good ◉ excellent*
The approximate net payload of 3076 pounds at 11% of GVWR on this model is ○ deficient ○ excessive ○ cautionary ◉ good ○ excellent*
Total highway safety penalties are: 2*   Value: **81**   Durability: **81**   Highway Control Rating: **91**   Highway Safety: **89**   ★★★★

Continental	1997	MHA	40	4050	MA	Cu330	D	$5100	276	4,000	29,000	25,924

Livability Code: FT 30-90
Wheelbase-to-length ratio of 58% is considered ○ dangerous ○ fatiguing ○ good ◉ excellent*
The approximate net payload of 3076 pounds at 11% of GVWR on this model is ○ deficient ○ excessive ○ cautionary ◉ good ○ excellent*
Total highway safety penalties are: 2*   Value: **81**   Durability: **81**   Highway Control Rating: **91**   Highway Safety: **89**   ★★★★

Continental	1997	MHA	40	4088	MA	Cu330	D	$5100	276	4,000	29,000	25,924

Livability Code: FT 30-90
Wheelbase-to-length ratio of 58% is considered ○ dangerous ○ fatiguing ○ good ◉ excellent*
The approximate net payload of 3076 pounds at 11% of GVWR on this model is ○ deficient ○ excessive ○ cautionary ◉ good ○ excellent*
Total highway safety penalties are: 2*   Value: **81**   Durability: **81**   Highway Control Rating: **91**   Highway Safety: **89**   ★★★★

Continental	1998	MHA	37	3706	MA	CA330	D	$5400	252	5,000	30,000	26,467

Livability Code: FT 30-90
Wheelbase-to-length ratio of 57% is considered ○ dangerous ○ fatiguing ◉ good ○ excellent*
The approximate net payload of 3533 pounds at 12% of GVWR on this model is ○ deficient ○ excessive ○ cautionary ◉ good ○ excellent*
Total highway safety penalties are: 12*   Value: **76**   Durability: **81**   Highway Control Rating: **91**   Highway Safety: **79**   ★★★

Continental	1998	MHA	37	3740	MA	CA330	D	$5400	252	5,000	30,000	25,074

Livability Code: FT 30-90
Wheelbase-to-length ratio of 57% is considered ○ dangerous ○ fatiguing ◉ good ○ excellent*
The approximate net payload of 4926 pounds at 16% of GVWR on this model is ○ deficient ○ excessive ○ cautionary ○ good ◉ excellent*
Total highway safety penalties are: 2*   Value: **86**   Durability: **81**   Highway Control Rating: **99**   Highway Safety: **97**   ★★★★

Continental	1998	MHA	37	3750	MA	CA330	D	$5400	252	5,000	30,000	25,074

Livability Code: FT 30-90
Wheelbase-to-length ratio of 57% is considered ○ dangerous ○ fatiguing ◉ good ○ excellent*
The approximate net payload of 4926 pounds at 16% of GVWR on this model is ○ deficient ○ excessive ○ cautionary ○ good ◉ excellent*
Total highway safety penalties are: 2*   Value: **86**   Durability: **81**   Highway Control Rating: **99**   Highway Safety: **97**   ★★★★

Continental	1998	MHA	40	4006	MA	CA330	D	$5000	276	5,000	30,000	27,324

Livability Code: FT 30-90
Wheelbase-to-length ratio of 58% is considered ○ dangerous ○ fatiguing ○ good ◉ excellent*
The approximate net payload of 2676 pounds at 9% of GVWR on this model is ○ deficient ○ excessive ◉ cautionary ○ good ○ excellent*
Total highway safety penalties are: 12*   Value: **76**   Durability: **81**   Highway Control Rating: **84**   Highway Safety: **72**   ★★★

Note: Safety ratings are based on the assumption that the engineering of the RV has allowed for proper balance by placing fresh, gray, and black holding tanks in a location so as not to change the balance of the RV when the tanks are empty or full. **Always double-check wheelbase, GVWR, and weights at front and rear axles.**

*See Section 1 for details on how conclusions are reached.

Section 2: The Ratings

Brand	Year	Type	Length	Model	Chassis	Engine	Fuel Type	Average Price per Linear Foot When New	Adjusted Wheelbase	Approx. Towing Capacity	Gross Vehicle Weight Rating	Average Curb Weight

Continental 1998 MHA 40 4040 MA CA330 D $5000 276 5,000 30,000 26,032
Livability Code: FT 30-90
Wheelbase-to-length ratio of 58% is considered ○ dangerous ○ fatiguing ○ good ◉ excellent*
The approximate net payload of 3968 pounds at 13% of GVWR on this model is ○ deficient ○ excessive ○ cautionary ◉ good ○ excellent*
Total highway safety penalties are: 2* Value: **8 6** Durability: **8 1** Highway Control Rating: **9 6** Highway Safety: **9 4** ★★★★

Continental 1998 MHA 40 4050 MA CA330 D $5000 276 5,000 30,000 26,032
Livability Code: FT 30-90
Wheelbase-to-length ratio of 58% is considered ○ dangerous ○ fatiguing ○ good ◉ excellent*
The approximate net payload of 3968 pounds at 13% of GVWR on this model is ○ deficient ○ excessive ○ cautionary ◉ good ○ excellent*
Total highway safety penalties are: 2* Value: **8 6** Durability: **8 1** Highway Control Rating: **9 6** Highway Safety: **9 4** ★★★★

Continental 1998 MHA 40 4060 MA CA330 D $5000 276 5,000 30,000 26,032
Livability Code: FT 30-90
Wheelbase-to-length ratio of 58% is considered ○ dangerous ○ fatiguing ○ good ◉ excellent*
The approximate net payload of 3968 pounds at 13% of GVWR on this model is ○ deficient ○ excessive ○ cautionary ◉ good ○ excellent*
Total highway safety penalties are: 2* Value: **7 6** Durability: **8 1** Highway Control Rating: **9 6** Highway Safety: **9 4** ★★★★

Continental 1998 MHA 40 4066 MA CA330 D $5000 276 5,000 30,000 27,324
Livability Code: FT 30-90
Wheelbase-to-length ratio of 58% is considered ○ dangerous ○ fatiguing ○ good ◉ excellent*
The approximate net payload of 2676 pounds at 9% of GVWR on this model is ○ deficient ○ excessive ◉ cautionary ○ good ○ excellent*
Total highway safety penalties are: 12* Value: **7 6** Durability: **8 1** Highway Control Rating: **8 4** Highway Safety: **7 2** ★★★

Continental 1998 MHA 40 4006 opch MA CA425 D $5000 272 5,000 31,000 27,824
Livability Code: FT 30-90
Wheelbase-to-length ratio of 57% is considered ○ dangerous ○ fatiguing ◉ good ○ excellent*
The approximate net payload of 3176 pounds at 10% of GVWR on this model is ○ deficient ○ excessive ○ cautionary ◉ good ○ excellent*
Total highway safety penalties are: 12* Value: **7 6** Durability: **8 1** Highway Control Rating: **8 7** Highway Safety: **7 5** ★★★

Continental 1998 MHA 40 4040 opch MA CA425 D $5000 272 5,000 31,000 27,310
Livability Code: FT 30-90
Wheelbase-to-length ratio of 57% is considered ○ dangerous ○ fatiguing ◉ good ○ excellent*
The approximate net payload of 3690 pounds at 12% of GVWR on this model is ○ deficient ○ excessive ○ cautionary ◉ good ○ excellent*
Total highway safety penalties are: 2* Value: **8 6** Durability: **8 1** Highway Control Rating: **9 0** Highway Safety: **8 8** ★★★★

Continental 1998 MHA 40 4050 opch MA CA425 D $5000 272 5,000 31,000 27,310
Livability Code: FT 30-90
Wheelbase-to-length ratio of 57% is considered ○ dangerous ○ fatiguing ◉ good ○ excellent*
The approximate net payload of 3690 pounds at 12% of GVWR on this model is ○ deficient ○ excessive ○ cautionary ◉ good ○ excellent*
Total highway safety penalties are: 2* Value: **8 6** Durability: **8 1** Highway Control Rating: **9 0** Highway Safety: **8 8** ★★★★

Continental 1998 MHA 40 4060 opch MA CA425 D $5000 272 5,000 31,000 27,310
Livability Code: FT 30-90
Wheelbase-to-length ratio of 57% is considered ○ dangerous ○ fatiguing ◉ good ○ excellent*
The approximate net payload of 3690 pounds at 12% of GVWR on this model is ○ deficient ○ excessive ○ cautionary ◉ good ○ excellent*
Total highway safety penalties are: 2* Value: **8 6** Durability: **8 1** Highway Control Rating: **9 0** Highway Safety: **8 8** ★★★★

Continental 1998 MHA 40 4066 opch MA CA425 D $5000 272 5,000 31,000 27,824
Livability Code: FT 30-90
Wheelbase-to-length ratio of 57% is considered ○ dangerous ○ fatiguing ◉ good ○ excellent*
The approximate net payload of 3176 pounds at 10% of GVWR on this model is ○ deficient ○ excessive ○ cautionary ◉ good ○ excellent*
Total highway safety penalties are: 12* Value: **7 6** Durability: **8 1** Highway Control Rating: **8 7** Highway Safety: **7 5** ★★★

Continental 1999 MHA 39 3706 slide MA CA330 D $5100 232 5,000 30,000 27,336
Livability Code: FT 30-90
Wheelbase-to-length ratio of 50% is considered ◉ dangerous ○ fatiguing ○ good ○ excellent*
The approximate net payload of 2664 pounds at 9% of GVWR on this model is ○ deficient ○ excessive ◉ cautionary ○ good ○ excellent*
Total highway safety penalties are: 13* Value: **8 0** Durability: **7 9** Highway Control Rating: **3 7** Highway Safety: **2 4**

Continental 1999 MHA 39 3706 no slide MA CA330 D $5100 232 5,000 30,000 26,349
Livability Code: FT 30-90
Wheelbase-to-length ratio of 50% is considered ◉ dangerous ○ fatiguing ○ good ○ excellent*
The approximate net payload of 3651 pounds at 12% of GVWR on this model is ○ deficient ○ excessive ○ cautionary ◉ good ○ excellent*
Total highway safety penalties are: 2* Value: **8 6** Durability: **7 9** Highway Control Rating: **4 6** Highway Safety: **4 4**

Continental 1999 MHA 41 4006 slide MA CA330 D $4900 266 5,000 30,000 28,263
Livability Code: FT 30-90
Wheelbase-to-length ratio of 54% is considered ○ dangerous ○ fatiguing ◉ good ○ excellent*
The approximate net payload of 1737 pounds at 6% of GVWR on this model is ◉ deficient ○ excessive ○ cautionary ○ good ○ excellent*
Total highway safety penalties are: 14* Value: **8 0** Durability: **7 9** Highway Control Rating: **4 9** Highway Safety: **3 5**

Note: Safety ratings are based on the assumption that the engineering of the RV has allowed for proper balance by placing fresh, gray, and black holding tanks in a location so as not to change the balance of the RV when the tanks are empty or full. **Always double-check wheelbase, GVWR, and weights at front and rear axles.**

*See Section 1 for details on how conclusions are reached.

Brand	Year	Type	Length	Model	Chassis	Engine	Fuel Type	Average Price per Linear Foot When New	Adjusted Wheelbase	Approx. Towing Capacity	Gross Vehicle Weight Rating	Average Curb Weight
Continental	1999	MHA	41	4066 slide	MA	CA330	D	$4900	266	5,000	30,000	28,263

Livability Code: FT 30-90
Wheelbase-to-length ratio of 54% is considered ○ dangerous ○ fatiguing ◉ good ○ excellent *
The approximate net payload of 1737 pounds at 6% of GVWR on this model is ◉ deficient ○ excessive ○ cautionary ○ good ○ excellent *
Total highway safety penalties are: 14 *   Value: 80   Durability: 79   Highway Control Rating: 49   Highway Safety: 35

Brand	Year	Type	Length	Model	Chassis	Engine	Fuel Type	Price/Ft	Wheelbase	Towing	GVWR	Curb Weight
Continental	1999	MHA	41	Panther 4006 slide	MA	CA425	D	$4900	272	5,000	31,000	28,791

Livability Code: FT 30-90
Wheelbase-to-length ratio of 55% is considered ○ dangerous ○ fatiguing ◉ good ○ excellent *
The approximate net payload of 2209 pounds at 7% of GVWR on this model is ○ deficient ○ excessive ◉ cautionary ○ good ○ excellent *
Total highway safety penalties are: 14 *   Value: 80   Durability: 79   Highway Control Rating: 64   Highway Safety: 50   ★

Continental	1999	MHA	41	Panther 4066 slide	MA	CA425	D	$4900	272	5,000	31,000	28,791

Livability Code: FT 30-90
Wheelbase-to-length ratio of 55% is considered ○ dangerous ○ fatiguing ◉ good ○ excellent *
The approximate net payload of 2209 pounds at 7% of GVWR on this model is ○ deficient ○ excessive ◉ cautionary ○ good ○ excellent *
Total highway safety penalties are: 14 *   Value: 80   Durability: 79   Highway Control Rating: 64   Highway Safety: 50   ★

Continental	1999	MHA	41	4006 no slide	MA	CA330	D	$4900	266	5,000	30,000	27,200

Livability Code: FT 30-90
Wheelbase-to-length ratio of 54% is considered ○ dangerous ○ fatiguing ◉ good ○ excellent *
The approximate net payload of 2800 pounds at 9% of GVWR on this model is ○ deficient ○ excessive ◉ cautionary ○ good ○ excellent *
Total highway safety penalties are: 2 *   Value: 86   Durability: 79   Highway Control Rating: 67   Highway Safety: 65   ★★

Continental	1999	MHA	41	4066 no slide	MA	CA330	D	$4900	266	5,000	30,000	27,200

Livability Code: FT 30-90
Wheelbase-to-length ratio of 54% is considered ○ dangerous ○ fatiguing ◉ good ○ excellent *
The approximate net payload of 2800 pounds at 9% of GVWR on this model is ○ deficient ○ excessive ◉ cautionary ○ good ○ excellent *
Total highway safety penalties are: 2 *   Value: 86   Durability: 79   Highway Control Rating: 67   Highway Safety: 65   ★★

Continental	1999	MHA	41	Panther 4006 no slide	MA	CA425	D	$4900	272	5,000	31,000	27,728

Livability Code: FT 30-90
Wheelbase-to-length ratio of 55% is considered ○ dangerous ○ fatiguing ◉ good ○ excellent *
The approximate net payload of 3272 pounds at 11% of GVWR on this model is ○ deficient ○ excessive ○ cautionary ◉ good ○ excellent *
Total highway safety penalties are: 2 *   Value: 86   Durability: 79   Highway Control Rating: 83   Highway Safety: 81   ★★★

Continental	1999	MHA	41	Panther 4066 no slide	MA	CA425	D	$4900	272	5,000	31,000	27,728

Livability Code: FT 30-90
Wheelbase-to-length ratio of 55% is considered ○ dangerous ○ fatiguing ◉ good ○ excellent *
The approximate net payload of 3272 pounds at 11% of GVWR on this model is ○ deficient ○ excessive ○ cautionary ◉ good ○ excellent *
Total highway safety penalties are: 2 *   Value: 86   Durability: 79   Highway Control Rating: 83   Highway Safety: 81   ★★★

Country Coach	1987	MHA	38	38 LTD	GI	CA300	D	$5700	252	1,500	29,640	26,586

Livability Code: FT 30-90
Wheelbase-to-length ratio of 55% is considered ○ dangerous ○ fatiguing ◉ good ○ excellent *
The approximate net payload of 3054 pounds at 10% of GVWR on this model is ○ deficient ○ excessive ○ cautionary ◉ good ○ excellent *
Total highway safety penalties are: 2 *   Value: 82   Durability: 82   Highway Control Rating: 86   Highway Safety: 84   ★★★★

Country Coach	1990	MHA	38	Savannah 38	GI	Cat	D	$5700	238	1,500	29,640	27,729

Livability Code: FT 30-90
Wheelbase-to-length ratio of 52% is considered ○ dangerous ◉ fatiguing ○ good ○ excellent *
The approximate net payload of 1911 pounds at 6% of GVWR on this model is ◉ deficient ○ excessive ○ cautionary ○ good ○ excellent *
Total highway safety penalties are: 2 *   Value: 82   Durability: 82   Highway Control Rating: 26   Highway Safety: 24

Country Coach	1990	MHA	40	Polaris 40	GI	Det 6V	D	$8600	262	1,500	37,400	33,716

Livability Code: FT 30-90
Wheelbase-to-length ratio of 55% is considered ○ dangerous ○ fatiguing ◉ good ○ excellent *
The approximate net payload of 3684 pounds at 10% of GVWR on this model is ○ deficient ○ excessive ○ cautionary ◉ good ○ excellent *
Total highway safety penalties are: 2 *   Value: 82   Durability: 82   Highway Control Rating: 85   Highway Safety: 83   ★★★★

Country Coach	1990	MHA	40	Winnepeg 40	PR	Det 8V	D	$10900	304 T	1,500	42,000	34,056

Livability Code: FT 30-90
Wheelbase-to-length ratio of 63% is considered ○ dangerous ○ fatiguing ○ good ◉ excellent *
The approximate net payload of 7944 pounds at 19% of GVWR on this model is ○ deficient ○ excessive ○ cautionary ○ good ◉ excellent *
Total highway safety penalties are: 4 *   Value: 81   Durability: 82   Highway Control Rating: 100   Highway Safety: 96   ★★★★

Country Coach	1991	MHA	40	40	GI	Det	D	$9500	262	1,500	37,400	33,846

Livability Code: FT 30-90
Wheelbase-to-length ratio of 55% is considered ○ dangerous ○ fatiguing ◉ good ○ excellent *
The approximate net payload of 3554 pounds at 10% of GVWR on this model is ○ deficient ○ excessive ○ cautionary ◉ good ○ excellent *
Total highway safety penalties are: 2 *   Value: 82   Durability: 82   Highway Control Rating: 85   Highway Safety: 83   ★★★★

Note: Safety ratings are based on the assumption that the engineering of the RV has allowed for proper balance by placing fresh, gray, and black holding tanks in a location so as not to change the balance of the RV when the tanks are empty or full. **Always double-check wheelbase, GVWR, and weights at front and rear axles.**

Section 2: The Ratings

Brand	Year	Type	Length	Model	Chassis	Engine	Fuel Type	Average Price per Linear Foot When New	Adjusted Wheelbase	Approx. Towing Capacity	Gross Vehicle Weight Rating	Average Curb Weight
Country Coach	1991	MHA	40	XL Conversion	PR		D	$11100	280	1,500	42,000	34,056

Livability Code: FT 30-90
Wheelbase-to-length ratio of 58% is considered ○ dangerous ○ fatiguing ○ good ◉ excellent *
The approximate net payload of 7944 pounds at 19% of GVWR on this model is ○ deficient ○ excessive ○ cautionary ○ good ◉ excellent *
Total highway safety penalties are: 2 *   Value: **8 2**   Durability: **8 2**   Highway Control Rating: **1 0 0**   Highway Safety: **9 8**   ★★★★

Brand	Year	Type	Length	Model	Chassis	Engine	Fuel Type	Price/Ft	Adj Wheelbase	Towing	GVWR	Curb Wt
Country Coach	1993	MHA	40	Winnepeg 40 XL	PR	DE500	D	$13900	304 T	1,500	42,000	34,056

Livability Code: FT 30-90
Wheelbase-to-length ratio of 63% is considered ○ dangerous ○ fatiguing ○ good ◉ excellent *
The approximate net payload of 7944 pounds at 19% of GVWR on this model is ○ deficient ○ excessive ○ cautionary ○ good ◉ excellent *
Total highway safety penalties are: 4 *   Value: **8 1**   Durability: **8 2**   Highway Control Rating: **1 0 0**   Highway Safety: **9 6**   ★★★★

Brand	Year	Type	Length	Model	Chassis	Engine	Fuel Type	Price/Ft	Adj Wheelbase	Towing	GVWR	Curb Wt
Crown Imperial	1989	MHA	35	35CS XS	CH	7.4L	G	$3000	202 T	1,500	17,200	16,466

Livability Code: FT 30-90
Wheelbase-to-length ratio of 48% is considered ◉ dangerous ○ fatiguing ○ good ○ excellent *
The approximate net payload of 734 pounds at 4% of GVWR on this model is ◉ deficient ○ excessive ○ cautionary ○ good ○ excellent *
Total highway safety penalties are: 10 *   Value: **7 8**   Durability: **8 3**   Highway Control Rating: **1**   Highway Safety: **- 9**

Brand	Year	Type	Length	Model	Chassis	Engine	Fuel Type	Price/Ft	Adj Wheelbase	Towing	GVWR	Curb Wt
Crown Imperial	1990	MHA	35	35 CSXS	CH	7.4L	G	$3000	202 T	1,500	17,200	16,400

Livability Code: SB 30-90
Wheelbase-to-length ratio of 48% is considered ◉ dangerous ○ fatiguing ○ good ○ excellent *
The approximate net payload of 800 pounds at 5% of GVWR on this model is ◉ deficient ○ excessive ○ cautionary ○ good ○ excellent *
Total highway safety penalties are: 10 *   Value: **7 8**   Durability: **8 3**   Highway Control Rating: **1**   Highway Safety: **- 9**

Brand	Year	Type	Length	Model	Chassis	Engine	Fuel Type	Price/Ft	Adj Wheelbase	Towing	GVWR	Curb Wt
Crown Royale	1990	MHA	37	36	RO	Cum	D	$5400	238	1,500	28,000	25,946

Livability Code: FT 30-90
Wheelbase-to-length ratio of 54% is considered ○ dangerous ○ fatiguing ◉ good ○ excellent *
The approximate net payload of 2054 pounds at 7% of GVWR on this model is ○ deficient ○ excessive ◉ cautionary ○ good ○ excellent *
Total highway safety penalties are: 2 *   Value: **7 9**   Durability: **7 5**   Highway Control Rating: **5 4**   Highway Safety: **5 2**   ★

Brand	Year	Type	Length	Model	Chassis	Engine	Fuel Type	Price/Ft	Adj Wheelbase	Towing	GVWR	Curb Wt
Crown Royale	1991	MHA	37	36 Bishop	RO	Cu8.3L	D	$5600	238	1,500	28,000	26,227

Livability Code: FT 30-90
Wheelbase-to-length ratio of 54% is considered ○ dangerous ○ fatiguing ◉ good ○ excellent *
The approximate net payload of 1773 pounds at 6% of GVWR on this model is ◉ deficient ○ excessive ○ cautionary ○ good ○ excellent *
Total highway safety penalties are: 2 *   Value: **7 9**   Durability: **7 5**   Highway Control Rating: **4 8**   Highway Safety: **4 6**

Brand	Year	Type	Length	Model	Chassis	Engine	Fuel Type	Price/Ft	Adj Wheelbase	Towing	GVWR	Curb Wt
Crown Royale	1993	MHA	40	Monarch 40	RO	Cu8.3L	D	$7200	270	1,500	35,000	30,556

Livability Code: FT 30-90
Wheelbase-to-length ratio of 56% is considered ○ dangerous ○ fatiguing ○ good ◉ excellent *
The approximate net payload of 4444 pounds at 13% of GVWR on this model is ○ deficient ○ excessive ○ cautionary ◉ good ○ excellent *
Total highway safety penalties are: 2 *   Value: **7 9**   Durability: **7 5**   Highway Control Rating: **9 1**   Highway Safety: **8 9**   ★★★

Brand	Year	Type	Length	Model	Chassis	Engine	Fuel Type	Price/Ft	Adj Wheelbase	Towing	GVWR	Curb Wt
Cruise Air	1990	MHA	35	3491	OS	7.5L	G	$1600	208	1,500	16,000	14,489

Livability Code: SB 30-90
Wheelbase-to-length ratio of 50% is considered ◉ dangerous ○ fatiguing ○ good ○ excellent *
The approximate net payload of 1511 pounds at 9% of GVWR on this model is ○ deficient ○ excessive ◉ cautionary ○ good ○ excellent *
Total highway safety penalties are: 2 *   Value: **7 9**   Durability: **7 4**   Highway Control Rating: **2 9**   Highway Safety: **2 7**

Brand	Year	Type	Length	Model	Chassis	Engine	Fuel Type	Price/Ft	Adj Wheelbase	Towing	GVWR	Curb Wt
Cruise Air	1991	MHA	35	3490	FO	7.5L	G	$1600	208	8,000	17,000	14,711

Livability Code: SB 30-90
Wheelbase-to-length ratio of 50% is considered ◉ dangerous ○ fatiguing ○ good ○ excellent *
The approximate net payload of 2289 pounds at 13% of GVWR on this model is ○ deficient ○ excessive ○ cautionary ◉ good ○ excellent *
Total highway safety penalties are: 2 *   Value: **7 9**   Durability: **7 4**   Highway Control Rating: **3 8**   Highway Safety: **3 6**

Brand	Year	Type	Length	Model	Chassis	Engine	Fuel Type	Price/Ft	Adj Wheelbase	Towing	GVWR	Curb Wt
Cruise Air	1992	MHA	30	3090	CH	7.4L	G	$1800	178	1,500	16,000	13,010

Livability Code: SB 30-90
Wheelbase-to-length ratio of 49% is considered ◉ dangerous ○ fatiguing ○ good ○ excellent *
The approximate net payload of 2990 pounds at 19% of GVWR on this model is ○ deficient ○ excessive ○ cautionary ○ good ◉ excellent *
Total highway safety penalties are: 5 *   Value: **7 7**   Durability: **7 4**   Highway Control Rating: **4 5**   Highway Safety: **4 0**

Brand	Year	Type	Length	Model	Chassis	Engine	Fuel Type	Price/Ft	Adj Wheelbase	Towing	GVWR	Curb Wt
Cruise Air	1992	MHA	30	3095	CH	7.4L	G	$1800	178	1,500	16,000	13,010

Livability Code: SB 30-90
Wheelbase-to-length ratio of 49% is considered ◉ dangerous ○ fatiguing ○ good ○ excellent *
The approximate net payload of 2990 pounds at 19% of GVWR on this model is ○ deficient ○ excessive ○ cautionary ○ good ◉ excellent *
Total highway safety penalties are: 5 *   Value: **7 7**   Durability: **7 4**   Highway Control Rating: **4 5**   Highway Safety: **4 0**

Brand	Year	Type	Length	Model	Chassis	Engine	Fuel Type	Price/Ft	Adj Wheelbase	Towing	GVWR	Curb Wt
Cruise Air	1992	MHA	30	3090	FO	7.5L	G	$1800	178	8,000	17,000	13,510

Livability Code: SB 30-90
Wheelbase-to-length ratio of 49% is considered ◉ dangerous ○ fatiguing ○ good ○ excellent *
The approximate net payload of 3490 pounds at 21% of GVWR on this model is ○ deficient ○ excessive ○ cautionary ○ good ◉ excellent *
Total highway safety penalties are: 2 *   Value: **7 9**   Durability: **7 4**   Highway Control Rating: **4 6**   Highway Safety: **4 4**

Note: Safety ratings are based on the assumption that the engineering of the RV has allowed for proper balance by placing fresh, gray, and black holding tanks in a location so as not to change the balance of the RV when the tanks are empty or full. **Always double-check wheelbase, GVWR, and weights at front and rear axles.**

*See Section 1 for details on how conclusions are reached.

Brand	Year	Type	Length	Model	Chassis	Engine	Fuel Type	Average Price per Linear Foot When New	Adjusted Wheelbase	Approx. Towing Capacity	Gross Vehicle Weight Rating	Average Curb Weight
Cruise Air	1992	MHA	30	3095	FO	7.5L	G	$1800	178	8,000	17,000	13,510

Livability Code: SB 30-90   Wheelbase-to-length ratio of 49% is considered ◉ dangerous ○ fatiguing ○ good ○ excellent *
The approximate net payload of 3490 pounds at 21% of GVWR on this model is ○ deficient ○ excessive ○ cautionary ○ good ◉ excellent *
Total highway safety penalties are: 2 *   Value: **7 9**   Durability: **7 4**   Highway Control Rating: **4 6**   Highway Safety: **4 4**

Brand	Year	Type	Length	Model	Chassis	Engine	Fuel Type	Price/Ft	Wheelbase	Towing	GVWR	Curb Wt
Cruise Air	1992	MHA	30	3090	OS		D	$2200	178	1,500	15,600	13,810

Livability Code: SB 30-90   Wheelbase-to-length ratio of 49% is considered ◉ dangerous ○ fatiguing ○ good ○ excellent *
The approximate net payload of 1790 pounds at 11% of GVWR on this model is ○ deficient ○ excessive ○ cautionary ◉ good ○ excellent *
Total highway safety penalties are: 2 *   Value: **7 9**   Durability: **7 4**   Highway Control Rating: **3 3**   Highway Safety: **3 1**

Brand	Year	Type	Length	Model	Chassis	Engine	Fuel Type	Price/Ft	Wheelbase	Towing	GVWR	Curb Wt
Cruise Air	1992	MHA	30	3095	OS		D	$2200	178	1,500	15,600	13,810

Livability Code: SB 30-90   Wheelbase-to-length ratio of 49% is considered ◉ dangerous ○ fatiguing ○ good ○ excellent *
The approximate net payload of 1790 pounds at 11% of GVWR on this model is ○ deficient ○ excessive ○ cautionary ◉ good ○ excellent *
Total highway safety penalties are: 2 *   Value: **7 9**   Durability: **7 4**   Highway Control Rating: **3 3**   Highway Safety: **3 1**

Brand	Year	Type	Length	Model	Chassis	Engine	Fuel Type	Price/Ft	Wheelbase	Towing	GVWR	Curb Wt
Cruise Air	1992	MHA	32	3290	CH	7.4L	G	$1700	190	1,500	16,000	13,504

Livability Code: SB 30-90   Wheelbase-to-length ratio of 49% is considered ◉ dangerous ○ fatiguing ○ good ○ excellent *
The approximate net payload of 2496 pounds at 16% of GVWR on this model is ○ deficient ○ excessive ○ cautionary ○ good ◉ excellent *
Total highway safety penalties are: 6 *   Value: **7 7**   Durability: **7 4**   Highway Control Rating: **4 2**   Highway Safety: **3 6**

Brand	Year	Type	Length	Model	Chassis	Engine	Fuel Type	Price/Ft	Wheelbase	Towing	GVWR	Curb Wt
Cruise Air	1992	MHA	32	3290	FO	7.5L	G	$1700	190	8,000	17,000	14,004

Livability Code: SB 30-90   Wheelbase-to-length ratio of 49% is considered ◉ dangerous ○ fatiguing ○ good ○ excellent *
The approximate net payload of 2996 pounds at 18% of GVWR on this model is ○ deficient ○ excessive ○ cautionary ○ good ◉ excellent *
Total highway safety penalties are: 2 *   Value: **7 9**   Durability: **7 4**   Highway Control Rating: **4 4**   Highway Safety: **4 2**

Brand	Year	Type	Length	Model	Chassis	Engine	Fuel Type	Price/Ft	Wheelbase	Towing	GVWR	Curb Wt
Cruise Air	1992	MHA	32	3290	OS		D	$2100	190	1,500	15,600	14,304

Livability Code: SB 30-90   Wheelbase-to-length ratio of 49% is considered ◉ dangerous ○ fatiguing ○ good ○ excellent *
The approximate net payload of 1296 pounds at 8% of GVWR on this model is ○ deficient ○ excessive ◉ cautionary ○ good ○ excellent *
Total highway safety penalties are: 2 *   Value: **7 9**   Durability: **7 4**   Highway Control Rating: **2 0**   Highway Safety: **1 8**

Brand	Year	Type	Length	Model	Chassis	Engine	Fuel Type	Price/Ft	Wheelbase	Towing	GVWR	Curb Wt
Cruise Air	1992	MHA	34	3490	CH	7.4L	G	$1700	208	1,500	16,000	13,998

Livability Code: SB 30-90   Wheelbase-to-length ratio of 51% is considered ○ dangerous ◉ fatiguing ○ good ○ excellent *
The approximate net payload of 2002 pounds at 13% of GVWR on this model is ○ deficient ○ excessive ○ cautionary ◉ good ○ excellent *
Total highway safety penalties are: 7 *   Value: **7 6**   Durability: **7 4**   Highway Control Rating: **4 2**   Highway Safety: **3 5**

Brand	Year	Type	Length	Model	Chassis	Engine	Fuel Type	Price/Ft	Wheelbase	Towing	GVWR	Curb Wt
Cruise Air	1992	MHA	34	3491	CH	7.4L	G	$1700	208	1,500	16,000	13,998

Livability Code: SB 30-90   Wheelbase-to-length ratio of 51% is considered ○ dangerous ◉ fatiguing ○ good ○ excellent *
The approximate net payload of 2002 pounds at 13% of GVWR on this model is ○ deficient ○ excessive ○ cautionary ◉ good ○ excellent *
Total highway safety penalties are: 7 *   Value: **7 6**   Durability: **7 4**   Highway Control Rating: **4 2**   Highway Safety: **3 5**

Brand	Year	Type	Length	Model	Chassis	Engine	Fuel Type	Price/Ft	Wheelbase	Towing	GVWR	Curb Wt
Cruise Air	1992	MHA	34	3496	CH	7.4L	G	$1700	208	1,500	16,000	13,998

Livability Code: SB 30-90   Wheelbase-to-length ratio of 51% is considered ○ dangerous ◉ fatiguing ○ good ○ excellent *
The approximate net payload of 2002 pounds at 13% of GVWR on this model is ○ deficient ○ excessive ○ cautionary ◉ good ○ excellent *
Total highway safety penalties are: 7 *   Value: **7 6**   Durability: **7 4**   Highway Control Rating: **4 2**   Highway Safety: **3 5**

Brand	Year	Type	Length	Model	Chassis	Engine	Fuel Type	Price/Ft	Wheelbase	Towing	GVWR	Curb Wt
Cruise Air	1992	MHA	34	3490	FO	7.5L	G	$1700	208	8,000	17,000	14,498

Livability Code: SB 30-90   Wheelbase-to-length ratio of 51% is considered ○ dangerous ◉ fatiguing ○ good ○ excellent *
The approximate net payload of 2502 pounds at 15% of GVWR on this model is ○ deficient ○ excessive ○ cautionary ◉ good ○ excellent *
Total highway safety penalties are: 2 *   Value: **7 9**   Durability: **7 4**   Highway Control Rating: **4 6**   Highway Safety: **4 4**

Brand	Year	Type	Length	Model	Chassis	Engine	Fuel Type	Price/Ft	Wheelbase	Towing	GVWR	Curb Wt
Cruise Air	1992	MHA	34	3491	FO	7.5L	G	$1700	208	8,000	17,000	14,498

Livability Code: SB 30-90   Wheelbase-to-length ratio of 51% is considered ○ dangerous ◉ fatiguing ○ good ○ excellent *
The approximate net payload of 2502 pounds at 15% of GVWR on this model is ○ deficient ○ excessive ○ cautionary ◉ good ○ excellent *
Total highway safety penalties are: 2 *   Value: **7 9**   Durability: **7 4**   Highway Control Rating: **4 6**   Highway Safety: **4 4**

Brand	Year	Type	Length	Model	Chassis	Engine	Fuel Type	Price/Ft	Wheelbase	Towing	GVWR	Curb Wt
Cruise Air	1992	MHA	34	3496	FO	7.5L	G	$1700	208	8,000	17,000	14,498

Livability Code: SB 30-90   Wheelbase-to-length ratio of 51% is considered ○ dangerous ◉ fatiguing ○ good ○ excellent *
The approximate net payload of 2502 pounds at 15% of GVWR on this model is ○ deficient ○ excessive ○ cautionary ◉ good ○ excellent *
Total highway safety penalties are: 2 *   Value: **7 9**   Durability: **7 4**   Highway Control Rating: **4 6**   Highway Safety: **4 4**

Note: Safety ratings are based on the assumption that the engineering of the RV has allowed for proper balance by placing fresh, gray, and black holding tanks in a location so as not to change the balance of the RV when the tanks are empty or full. **Always double-check wheelbase, GVWR, and weights at front and rear axles.**

*See Section 1 for details on how conclusions are reached.

Section 2: The Ratings

Brand	Year	Type	Length	Model	Chassis	Engine	Fuel Type	Average Price per Linear Foot When New	Adjusted Wheelbase	Approx. Towing Capacity	Gross Vehicle Weight Rating	Average Curb Weight

Cruise Air   **1992**   MHA   34   3490   OS   D $2000   208   1,500   16,000   14,498

Livability Code: SB 30-90   Wheelbase-to-length ratio of 51% is considered ○ dangerous ◉ fatiguing ○ good ○ excellent *

The approximate net payload of 1502 pounds at 9% of GVWR on this model is ○ deficient ○ excessive ◉ cautionary ○ good ○ excellent *

Total highway safety penalties are: 2 *   Value: 79   Durability: 74   Highway Control Rating: 32   Highway Safety: 30

Cruise Air   **1992**   MHA   34   3491   OS   D $2000   208   1,500   16,000   14,498

Livability Code: SB 30-90   Wheelbase-to-length ratio of 51% is considered ○ dangerous ◉ fatiguing ○ good ○ excellent *

The approximate net payload of 1502 pounds at 9% of GVWR on this model is ○ deficient ○ excessive ◉ cautionary ○ good ○ excellent *

Total highway safety penalties are: 2 *   Value: 79   Durability: 74   Highway Control Rating: 32   Highway Safety: 30

Cruise Air   **1992**   MHA   34   3496   OS   D $2000   208   1,500   16,000   14,498

Livability Code: SB 30-90   Wheelbase-to-length ratio of 51% is considered ○ dangerous ◉ fatiguing ○ good ○ excellent *

The approximate net payload of 1502 pounds at 9% of GVWR on this model is ○ deficient ○ excessive ◉ cautionary ○ good ○ excellent *

Total highway safety penalties are: 2 *   Value: 79   Durability: 74   Highway Control Rating: 32   Highway Safety: 30

Cruise Air   **1992**   MHA   36   3696   OS   CU190   D $1800   228   1,500   18,000   15,692

Livability Code: SB 30-90   Wheelbase-to-length ratio of 53% is considered ○ dangerous ◉ fatiguing ○ good ○ excellent *

The approximate net payload of 2308 pounds at 13% of GVWR on this model is ○ deficient ○ excessive ○ cautionary ◉ good ○ excellent *

Total highway safety penalties are: 8 *   Value: 76   Durability: 74   Highway Control Rating: 63   Highway Safety: 55   ★

Cruise Air   **1994**   MHA   32   3210   CH   7.4L   G $1900   208   1,500   16,000   13,504

Livability Code: SB 30-90   Wheelbase-to-length ratio of 54% is considered ○ dangerous ○ fatiguing ◉ good ○ excellent *

The approximate net payload of 2496 pounds at 16% of GVWR on this model is ○ deficient ○ excessive ○ cautionary ○ good ◉ excellent *

Total highway safety penalties are: 6 *   Value: 77   Durability: 74   Highway Control Rating: 82   Highway Safety: 76   ★★★

Cruise Air   **1994**   MHA   33   3210   FO   7.5L   G $1800   208   8,000   17,000   14,202

Livability Code: SB 30-90   Wheelbase-to-length ratio of 53% is considered ○ dangerous ◉ fatiguing ○ good ○ excellent *

The approximate net payload of 2798 pounds at 16% of GVWR on this model is ○ deficient ○ excessive ○ cautionary ○ good ◉ excellent *

Total highway safety penalties are: 2 *   Value: 79   Durability: 74   Highway Control Rating: 70   Highway Safety: 68   ★★

Cruise Air   **1994**   MHA   34   3400   CH   7.4L   G $1800   228   1,500   16,000   14,023

Livability Code: SB 30-90   Wheelbase-to-length ratio of 56% is considered ○ dangerous ○ fatiguing ◉ good ○ excellent *

The approximate net payload of 1977 pounds at 12% of GVWR on this model is ○ deficient ○ excessive ○ cautionary ◉ good ○ excellent *

Total highway safety penalties are: 7 *   Value: 76   Durability: 74   Highway Control Rating: 88   Highway Safety: 81   ★★★

Cruise Air   **1994**   MHA   34   3401   CH   7.4L   G $1800   228   1,500   16,000   14,023

Livability Code: SB 30-90   Wheelbase-to-length ratio of 56% is considered ○ dangerous ○ fatiguing ◉ good ○ excellent *

The approximate net payload of 1977 pounds at 12% of GVWR on this model is ○ deficient ○ excessive ○ cautionary ◉ good ○ excellent *

Total highway safety penalties are: 7 *   Value: 76   Durability: 74   Highway Control Rating: 88   Highway Safety: 81   ★★★

Cruise Air   **1994**   MHA   34   3405   CH   7.4L   G $1800   228   1,500   16,000   14,023

Livability Code: SB 30-90   Wheelbase-to-length ratio of 56% is considered ○ dangerous ○ fatiguing ◉ good ○ excellent *

The approximate net payload of 1977 pounds at 12% of GVWR on this model is ○ deficient ○ excessive ○ cautionary ◉ good ○ excellent *

Total highway safety penalties are: 7 *   Value: 76   Durability: 74   Highway Control Rating: 88   Highway Safety: 81   ★★★

Cruise Air   **1994**   MHA   34   3400   FO   7.5L   G $1800   228   8,000   17,000   14,523

Livability Code: SB 30-90   Wheelbase-to-length ratio of 56% is considered ○ dangerous ○ fatiguing ◉ good ○ excellent *

The approximate net payload of 2477 pounds at 15% of GVWR on this model is ○ deficient ○ excessive ○ cautionary ○ good ◉ excellent *

Total highway safety penalties are: 2 *   Value: 79   Durability: 74   Highway Control Rating: 93   Highway Safety: 91   ★★★

Cruise Air   **1994**   MHA   34   3401   FO   7.5L   G $1800   228   8,000   17,000   14,523

Livability Code: SB 30-90   Wheelbase-to-length ratio of 56% is considered ○ dangerous ○ fatiguing ◉ good ○ excellent *

The approximate net payload of 2477 pounds at 15% of GVWR on this model is ○ deficient ○ excessive ○ cautionary ○ good ◉ excellent *

Total highway safety penalties are: 2 *   Value: 79   Durability: 74   Highway Control Rating: 93   Highway Safety: 91   ★★★

Cruise Air   **1994**   MHA   34   3405   FO   7.5L   G $1800   228   8,000   17,000   14,523

Livability Code: SB 30-90   Wheelbase-to-length ratio of 56% is considered ○ dangerous ○ fatiguing ◉ good ○ excellent *

The approximate net payload of 2477 pounds at 15% of GVWR on this model is ○ deficient ○ excessive ○ cautionary ◉ good ○ excellent *

Total highway safety penalties are: 2 *   Value: 79   Durability: 74   Highway Control Rating: 93   Highway Safety: 91   ★★★

Note: Safety ratings are based on the assumption that the engineering of the RV has allowed for proper balance by placing fresh, gray, and black holding tanks in a location so as not to change the balance of the RV when the tanks are empty or full. **Always double-check wheelbase, GVWR, and weights at front and rear axles.**

*See Section 1 for details on how conclusions are reached.

Brand	Year	Type	Length	Model	Chassis	Engine	Fuel Type	Average Price per Linear Foot When New	Adjusted Wheelbase	Approx. Towing Capacity	Gross Vehicle Weight Rating	Average Curb Weight
Cruise Air	1994	MHA	34	3400	SP	Cu230	D	$2600	208	1,500	18,000	14,923

Livability Code: SB 30-90   Wheelbase-to-length ratio of 51% is considered ○ dangerous ● fatiguing ○ good ○ excellent *

The approximate net payload of 3077 pounds at 17% of GVWR on this model is ○ deficient ○ excessive ○ cautionary ○ good ● excellent *

Total highway safety penalties are: 2 *   Value: 7 9   Durability: 7 4   Highway Control Rating: 4 9   Highway Safety: 4 7

Brand	Year	Type	Length	Model	Chassis	Engine	Fuel Type		Adjusted Wheelbase	Approx. Towing Capacity	Gross Vehicle Weight Rating	Average Curb Weight
Cruise Air	1994	MHA	35	3691	FO	7.5L	G	$1800	208	8,000	17,000	14,770

Livability Code: SB 30-90   Wheelbase-to-length ratio of 49% is considered ● dangerous ○ fatiguing ○ good ○ excellent *

The approximate net payload of 2230 pounds at 13% of GVWR on this model is ○ deficient ● excessive ○ cautionary ● good ○ excellent *

Total highway safety penalties are: 2 *   Value: 7 9   Durability: 7 4   Highway Control Rating: 3 7   Highway Safety: 3 5

Cruise Air	1994	MHA	35	3692	CH	7.4L	G	$2000	232 T	1,500	18,000	15,194

Livability Code: SB 30-90   Wheelbase-to-length ratio of 55% is considered ○ dangerous ○ fatiguing ● good ○ excellent *

The approximate net payload of 2806 pounds at 16% of GVWR on this model is ○ deficient ○ excessive ○ cautionary ○ good ● excellent *

Total highway safety penalties are: 10 *   Value: 7 5   Durability: 7 4   Highway Control Rating: 9 2   Highway Safety: 8 2   ★★★

Cruise Air	1995	MHA	34	3405	CH	7.4L	G	$2300	228	1,500	16,000	14,023

Livability Code: SB 30-90   Wheelbase-to-length ratio of 56% is considered ○ dangerous ○ fatiguing ● good ○ excellent *

The approximate net payload of 1977 pounds at 12% of GVWR on this model is ○ deficient ○ excessive ○ cautionary ● good ○ excellent *

Total highway safety penalties are: 7 *   Value: 7 6   Durability: 7 4   Highway Control Rating: 8 8   Highway Safety: 8 1   ★★★

Cruise Air	1995	MHA	34	3405	FO	7.5L	G	$2200	228	8,000	17,000	14,966

Livability Code: SB 30-90   Wheelbase-to-length ratio of 56% is considered ○ dangerous ○ fatiguing ● good ○ excellent *

The approximate net payload of 2034 pounds at 12% of GVWR on this model is ○ deficient ○ excessive ○ cautionary ● good ○ excellent *

Total highway safety penalties are: 2 *   Value: 7 9   Durability: 7 4   Highway Control Rating: 8 7   Highway Safety: 8 5   ★★★

Cruise Air	1995	MHA	34	3405 slide	FO	7.5L	G	$2400	228	8,000	17,000	15,423

Livability Code: SB 30-90   Wheelbase-to-length ratio of 56% is considered ○ dangerous ○ fatiguing ● good ○ excellent *

The approximate net payload of 1577 pounds at 9% of GVWR on this model is ○ deficient ○ excessive ● cautionary ○ good ○ excellent *

Total highway safety penalties are: 7 *   Value: 7 6   Durability: 7 4   Highway Control Rating: 7 8   Highway Safety: 7 1   ★★★

Cruise Air	1995	MHA	34	3405	SP	CU230	D	$3200	208	1,500	18,000	14,923

Livability Code: SB 30-90   Wheelbase-to-length ratio of 51% is considered ○ dangerous ● fatiguing ○ good ○ excellent *

The approximate net payload of 3077 pounds at 17% of GVWR on this model is ○ deficient ○ excessive ○ cautionary ○ good ● excellent *

Total highway safety penalties are: 2 *   Value: 7 9   Durability: 7 4   Highway Control Rating: 4 9   Highway Safety: 4 7

Cruise Air	1995	MHA	35	3595	CH	7.4L	G	$2200	228	1,500	16,000	14,245

Livability Code: SB 30-90   Wheelbase-to-length ratio of 54% is considered ○ dangerous ○ fatiguing ● good ○ excellent *

The approximate net payload of 1755 pounds at 11% of GVWR on this model is ○ deficient ○ excessive ○ cautionary ● good ○ excellent *

Total highway safety penalties are: 7 *   Value: 7 6   Durability: 7 4   Highway Control Rating: 7 8   Highway Safety: 7 1   ★★★

Cruise Air	1995	MHA	35	3595	FO	7.5L	G	$2200	228	8,000	17,000	14,745

Livability Code: SB 30-90   Wheelbase-to-length ratio of 54% is considered ○ dangerous ○ fatiguing ● good ○ excellent *

The approximate net payload of 2255 pounds at 13% of GVWR on this model is ○ deficient ○ excessive ○ cautionary ● good ○ excellent *

Total highway safety penalties are: 2 *   Value: 7 9   Durability: 7 4   Highway Control Rating: 8 0   Highway Safety: 7 8   ★★★

Cruise Air	1995	MHA	36	3605	SP	CU230	D	$3100	228	1,500	18,000	15,392

Livability Code: SB 30-90   Wheelbase-to-length ratio of 53% is considered ○ dangerous ● fatiguing ○ good ○ excellent *

The approximate net payload of 2608 pounds at 14% of GVWR on this model is ○ deficient ○ excessive ○ cautionary ● good ○ excellent *

Total highway safety penalties are: 2 *   Value: 7 9   Durability: 7 4   Highway Control Rating: 6 6   Highway Safety: 6 4   ★★

Cruise Air	1995	MHA	36	3605 slide	SP	CU230	D	$3200	228	1,500	18,000	16,292

Livability Code: SB 30-90   Wheelbase-to-length ratio of 53% is considered ○ dangerous ● fatiguing ○ good ○ excellent *

The approximate net payload of 1708 pounds at 9% of GVWR on this model is ○ deficient ○ excessive ● cautionary ○ good ○ excellent *

Total highway safety penalties are: 7 *   Value: 7 6   Durability: 7 4   Highway Control Rating: 5 3   Highway Safety: 4 6

Cruise Air	1996	MHA	33	3290W	CH	7.4L	G	$2300	228	1,500	16,500	14,384

Livability Code: SB 30-90   Wheelbase-to-length ratio of 57% is considered ○ dangerous ○ fatiguing ● good ○ excellent *

The approximate net payload of 2116 pounds at 13% of GVWR on this model is ○ deficient ○ excessive ○ cautionary ● good ○ excellent *

Total highway safety penalties are: 6 *   Value: 7 7   Durability: 7 4   Highway Control Rating: 9 3   Highway Safety: 8 7   ★★★

Note: Safety ratings are based on the assumption that the engineering of the RV has allowed for proper balance by placing fresh, gray, and black holding tanks in a location so as not to change the balance of the RV when the tanks are empty or full. **Always double-check wheelbase, GVWR, and weights at front and rear axles.**

Section 2: The Ratings

Brand	Year	Type	Length	Model	Chassis	Engine	Fuel Type	Average Price per Linear Foot When New	Adjusted Wheelbase	Approx. Towing Capacity	Gross Vehicle Weight Rating	Average Curb Weight
Cruise Air	1996	MHA	33	3290W	FO	7.5L	G	$2300	228	8,000	17,000	14,784

Livability Code: SB 30-90
Wheelbase-to-length ratio of 57% is considered ○ dangerous ○ fatiguing ● good ○ excellent *
The approximate net payload of 2216 pounds at 13% of GVWR on this model is ○ deficient ○ excessive ○ cautionary ● good ○ excellent *
Total highway safety penalties are: 2 *   Value: **7 9**   Durability: **7 4**   Highway Control Rating: **9 3**   Highway Safety: **9 1**   ★★★

Brand	Year	Type	Length	Model	Chassis	Engine	Fuel Type	Price/Ft	Wheelbase	Towing	GVWR	Curb Wt
Cruise Air	1996	MHA	35	3405	CH	7.4L	G	$2200	228	1,500	16,500	14,670

Livability Code: SB 30-90
Wheelbase-to-length ratio of 55% is considered ○ dangerous ○ fatiguing ● good ○ excellent *
The approximate net payload of 1830 pounds at 11% of GVWR on this model is ○ deficient ○ excessive ○ cautionary ● good ○ excellent *
Total highway safety penalties are: 7 *   Value: **7 6**   Durability: **7 4**   Highway Control Rating: **8 8**   Highway Safety: **8 1**   ★★★

Brand	Year	Type	Length	Model	Chassis	Engine	Fuel Type	Price/Ft	Wheelbase	Towing	GVWR	Curb Wt
Cruise Air	1996	MHA	35	3405-sl	CH	7.4L	G	$2300	228	1,500	16,500	15,570

Livability Code: SB 30-90
Wheelbase-to-length ratio of 55% is considered ○ dangerous ○ fatiguing ● good ○ excellent *
The approximate net payload of 930 pounds at 6% of GVWR on this model is ● deficient ○ excessive ○ cautionary ○ good ○ excellent *
Total highway safety penalties are: 12 *   Value: **7 4**   Durability: **7 4**   Highway Control Rating: **5 8**   Highway Safety: **4 6**

Brand	Year	Type	Length	Model	Chassis	Engine	Fuel Type	Price/Ft	Wheelbase	Towing	GVWR	Curb Wt
Cruise Air	1996	MHA	35	3405	FO	7.5L	G	$2200	228	8,000	17,000	15,070

Livability Code: SB 30-90
Wheelbase-to-length ratio of 55% is considered ○ dangerous ○ fatiguing ● good ○ excellent *
The approximate net payload of 1930 pounds at 11% of GVWR on this model is ○ deficient ○ excessive ○ cautionary ● good ○ excellent *
Total highway safety penalties are: 2 *   Value: **7 9**   Durability: **7 4**   Highway Control Rating: **8 8**   Highway Safety: **8 6**   ★★★

Brand	Year	Type	Length	Model	Chassis	Engine	Fuel Type	Price/Ft	Wheelbase	Towing	GVWR	Curb Wt
Cruise Air	1996	MHA	35	3405-sl	FO	7.5L	G	$2300	228	8,000	17,000	15,970

Livability Code: SB 30-90
Wheelbase-to-length ratio of 55% is considered ○ dangerous ○ fatiguing ● good ○ excellent *
The approximate net payload of 1030 pounds at 6% of GVWR on this model is ● deficient ○ excessive ○ cautionary ○ good ○ excellent *
Total highway safety penalties are: 7 *   Value: **7 6**   Durability: **7 4**   Highway Control Rating: **5 8**   Highway Safety: **5 1**   ★

Brand	Year	Type	Length	Model	Chassis	Engine	Fuel Type	Price/Ft	Wheelbase	Towing	GVWR	Curb Wt
Cruise Air	1996	MHA	35	3485W	CH	7.4L	G	$2200	228	1,500	16,500	14,748

Livability Code: SB 30-90
Wheelbase-to-length ratio of 55% is considered ○ dangerous ○ fatiguing ● good ○ excellent *
The approximate net payload of 1752 pounds at 11% of GVWR on this model is ○ deficient ○ excessive ○ cautionary ● good ○ excellent *
Total highway safety penalties are: 7 *   Value: **7 6**   Durability: **7 4**   Highway Control Rating: **8 6**   Highway Safety: **7 9**   ★★★

Brand	Year	Type	Length	Model	Chassis	Engine	Fuel Type	Price/Ft	Wheelbase	Towing	GVWR	Curb Wt
Cruise Air	1996	MHA	35	3485W	FO	7.5L	G	$2200	228	8,000	17,000	15,148

Livability Code: SB 30-90
Wheelbase-to-length ratio of 55% is considered ○ dangerous ○ fatiguing ● good ○ excellent *
The approximate net payload of 1852 pounds at 11% of GVWR on this model is ○ deficient ○ excessive ○ cautionary ● good ○ excellent *
Total highway safety penalties are: 2 *   Value: **7 9**   Durability: **7 4**   Highway Control Rating: **8 6**   Highway Safety: **8 4**   ★★★

Brand	Year	Type	Length	Model	Chassis	Engine	Fuel Type	Price/Ft	Wheelbase	Towing	GVWR	Curb Wt
Cruise Air	1996	MHA	35	3595	CH	7.4L	G	$2200	228	1,500	16,500	14,904

Livability Code: SB 30-90
Wheelbase-to-length ratio of 54% is considered ○ dangerous ○ fatiguing ● good ○ excellent *
The approximate net payload of 1596 pounds at 10% of GVWR on this model is ○ deficient ○ excessive ○ cautionary ● good ○ excellent *
Total highway safety penalties are: 7 *   Value: **7 6**   Durability: **7 4**   Highway Control Rating: **7 4**   Highway Safety: **6 7**   ★★

Brand	Year	Type	Length	Model	Chassis	Engine	Fuel Type	Price/Ft	Wheelbase	Towing	GVWR	Curb Wt
Cruise Air	1996	MHA	35	3595	FO	7.5L	G	$2200	228	8,000	17,000	15,304

Livability Code: SB 30-90
Wheelbase-to-length ratio of 54% is considered ○ dangerous ○ fatiguing ● good ○ excellent *
The approximate net payload of 1696 pounds at 10% of GVWR on this model is ○ deficient ○ excessive ○ cautionary ● good ○ excellent *
Total highway safety penalties are: 2 *   Value: **7 9**   Durability: **7 4**   Highway Control Rating: **7 4**   Highway Safety: **7 2**   ★★★

Brand	Year	Type	Length	Model	Chassis	Engine	Fuel Type	Price/Ft	Wheelbase	Towing	GVWR	Curb Wt
Cruise Air	1997	MHA	33	3211W	CH	7.4L	G	$2400	218	1,500	16,500	14,663

Livability Code: SB 30-90
Wheelbase-to-length ratio of 55% is considered ○ dangerous ○ fatiguing ● good ○ excellent *
The approximate net payload of 1837 pounds at 11% of GVWR on this model is ○ deficient ○ excessive ○ cautionary ● good ○ excellent *
Total highway safety penalties are: 6 *   Value: **7 7**   Durability: **7 4**   Highway Control Rating: **8 6**   Highway Safety: **8 0**   ★★★

Brand	Year	Type	Length	Model	Chassis	Engine	Fuel Type	Price/Ft	Wheelbase	Towing	GVWR	Curb Wt
Cruise Air	1997	MHA	33	3211W slide	CH	7.4L	G	$2300	218	1,500	16,500	14,888

Livability Code: SB 30-90
Wheelbase-to-length ratio of 55% is considered ○ dangerous ○ fatiguing ● good ○ excellent *
The approximate net payload of 1612 pounds at 10% of GVWR on this model is ○ deficient ○ excessive ○ cautionary ● good ○ excellent *
Total highway safety penalties are: 9 *   Value: **7 5**   Durability: **7 4**   Highway Control Rating: **8 5**   Highway Safety: **7 6**   ★★★

Brand	Year	Type	Length	Model	Chassis	Engine	Fuel Type	Price/Ft	Wheelbase	Towing	GVWR	Curb Wt
Cruise Air	1997	MHA	33	3211W	FO	7.5L	G	$2400	218	1,500	17,000	14,921

Livability Code: SB 30-90
Wheelbase-to-length ratio of 55% is considered ○ dangerous ○ fatiguing ● good ○ excellent *
The approximate net payload of 2079 pounds at 12% of GVWR on this model is ○ deficient ○ excessive ○ cautionary ● good ○ excellent *
Total highway safety penalties are: 2 *   Value: **7 9**   Durability: **7 4**   Highway Control Rating: **8 7**   Highway Safety: **8 5**   ★★★

Note: Safety ratings are based on the assumption that the engineering of the RV has allowed for proper balance by placing fresh, gray, and black holding tanks in a location so as not to change the balance of the RV when the tanks are empty or full. **Always double-check wheelbase, GVWR, and weights at front and rear axles.**

*See Section 1 for details on how conclusions are reached.

Brand	Year	Type	Length	Model	Chassis	Engine	Fuel Type	Average Price per Linear Foot When New	Adjusted Wheelbase	Approx. Towing Capacity	Gross Vehicle Weight Rating	Average Curb Weight
Cruise Air	1997	MHA	33	3211W slide	FO	7.5L	G	$2400	218	1,500	17,000	15,146

Livability Code: SB 30-90
Wheelbase-to-length ratio of 55% is considered ○ dangerous ○ fatiguing ◉ good ○ excellent *
The approximate net payload of 1854 pounds at 11% of GVWR on this model is ○ deficient ○ excessive ○ cautionary ◉ good ○ excellent *
Total highway safety penalties are: 5 *   Value: **7 7**   Durability: **7 4**   Highway Control Rating: **8 6**   Highway Safety: **8 1**   ★★★

Brand	Year	Type	Length	Model	Chassis	Engine	Fuel Type	Price	Wheelbase	Towing	GVWR	Curb
Cruise Air	1997	MHA	35	3405W	CH	7.4L	G	$2300	246 T	1,500	19,000	16,578

Livability Code: SB 30-90
Wheelbase-to-length ratio of 58% is considered ○ dangerous ○ fatiguing ○ good ◉ excellent *
The approximate net payload of 2422 pounds at 13% of GVWR on this model is ○ deficient ○ excessive ○ cautionary ◉ good ○ excellent *
Total highway safety penalties are: 15 *   Value: **7 2**   Durability: **7 4**   Highway Control Rating: **9 7**   Highway Safety: **8 2**   ★★★

Cruise Air	1997	MHA	35	3413W	CH	7.4L	G	$2300	228	1,500	16,500	15,054

Livability Code: SB 30-90
Wheelbase-to-length ratio of 54% is considered ○ dangerous ○ fatiguing ◉ good ○ excellent *
The approximate net payload of 1446 pounds at 9% of GVWR on this model is ○ deficient ○ excessive ◉ cautionary ○ good ○ excellent *
Total highway safety penalties are: 7 *   Value: **7 6**   Durability: **7 4**   Highway Control Rating: **6 4**   Highway Safety: **5 7**   ★

Cruise Air	1997	MHA	35	3415W	CH	7.4L	G	$2300	220	1,500	16,500	15,015

Livability Code: SB 30-90
Wheelbase-to-length ratio of 52% is considered ○ dangerous ◉ fatiguing ○ good ○ excellent *
The approximate net payload of 1486 pounds at 9% of GVWR on this model is ○ deficient ○ excessive ◉ cautionary ○ good ○ excellent *
Total highway safety penalties are: 7 *   Value: **7 6**   Durability: **7 4**   Highway Control Rating: **4 2**   Highway Safety: **3 5**

Cruise Air	1997	MHA	35	3415W slide	CH	7.4L	G	$2300	220	1,500	16,500	15,465

Livability Code: SB 30-90
Wheelbase-to-length ratio of 52% is considered ○ dangerous ◉ fatiguing ○ good ○ excellent *
The approximate net payload of 1036 pounds at 6% of GVWR on this model is ◉ deficient ○ excessive ○ cautionary ○ good ○ excellent *
Total highway safety penalties are: 13 *   Value: **7 3**   Durability: **7 4**   Highway Control Rating: **2 4**   Highway Safety: **1 1**

Cruise Air	1997	MHA	35	3413W	FO	7.5L	G	$2300	228	1,500	17,000	15,411

Livability Code: SB 30-90
Wheelbase-to-length ratio of 54% is considered ○ dangerous ○ fatiguing ◉ good ○ excellent *
The approximate net payload of 1589 pounds at 9% of GVWR on this model is ○ deficient ○ excessive ◉ cautionary ○ good ○ excellent *
Total highway safety penalties are: 2 *   Value: **7 9**   Durability: **7 4**   Highway Control Rating: **6 4**   Highway Safety: **6 2**   ★★

Cruise Air	1997	MHA	35	3415W	FO	7.5L	G	$2300	220	1,500	17,000	15,466

Livability Code: SB 30-90
Wheelbase-to-length ratio of 52% is considered ○ dangerous ◉ fatiguing ○ good ○ excellent *
The approximate net payload of 1535 pounds at 9% of GVWR on this model is ○ deficient ○ excessive ◉ cautionary ○ good ○ excellent *
Total highway safety penalties are: 2 *   Value: **7 9**   Durability: **7 4**   Highway Control Rating: **4 2**   Highway Safety: **4 0**

Cruise Air	1997	MHA	35	3415W slide	FO	7.5L	G	$2300	220	1,500	17,000	15,916

Livability Code: SB 30-90
Wheelbase-to-length ratio of 52% is considered ○ dangerous ◉ fatiguing ○ good ○ excellent *
The approximate net payload of 1085 pounds at 6% of GVWR on this model is ◉ deficient ○ excessive ○ cautionary ○ good ○ excellent *
Total highway safety penalties are: 7 *   Value: **7 6**   Durability: **7 4**   Highway Control Rating: **2 5**   Highway Safety: **1 8**

Cruise Air	1998	MHA	33	3311	CH	7.4L	G	$2600	212	4,500	16,500	14,459

Livability Code: SB 30-90
Wheelbase-to-length ratio of 53% is considered ○ dangerous ◉ fatiguing ○ good ○ excellent *
The approximate net payload of 2041 pounds at 12% of GVWR on this model is ○ deficient ○ excessive ○ cautionary ◉ good ○ excellent *
Total highway safety penalties are: 6 *   Value: **7 7**   Durability: **7 6**   Highway Control Rating: **6 3**   Highway Safety: **5 7**   ★

Cruise Air	1998	MHA	33	3311 slide	CH	7.4L	G	$2600	212	4,500	16,500	14,889

Livability Code: SB 30-90
Wheelbase-to-length ratio of 53% is considered ○ dangerous ◉ fatiguing ○ good ○ excellent *
The approximate net payload of 1611 pounds at 10% of GVWR on this model is ○ deficient ○ excessive ○ cautionary ◉ good ○ excellent *
Total highway safety penalties are: 9 *   Value: **7 6**   Durability: **7 6**   Highway Control Rating: **5 8**   Highway Safety: **4 9**

Cruise Air	1998	MHA	33	3311	FO	7.5L	G	$2600	212	8,000	17,000	14,804

Livability Code: SB 30-90
Wheelbase-to-length ratio of 53% is considered ○ dangerous ◉ fatiguing ○ good ○ excellent *
The approximate net payload of 2196 pounds at 13% of GVWR on this model is ○ deficient ○ excessive ○ cautionary ◉ good ○ excellent *
Total highway safety penalties are: 2 *   Value: **7 9**   Durability: **7 6**   Highway Control Rating: **6 5**   Highway Safety: **6 3**   ★★

Cruise Air	1998	MHA	33	3311 slide	FO	7.5L	G	$2600	212	8,000	17,000	15,159

Livability Code: SB 30-90
Wheelbase-to-length ratio of 53% is considered ○ dangerous ◉ fatiguing ○ good ○ excellent *
The approximate net payload of 1841 pounds at 11% of GVWR on this model is ○ deficient ○ excessive ○ cautionary ◉ good ○ excellent *
Total highway safety penalties are: 5 *   Value: **7 8**   Durability: **7 6**   Highway Control Rating: **6 0**   Highway Safety: **5 5**   ★

Note: Safety ratings are based on the assumption that the engineering of the RV has allowed for proper balance by placing fresh, gray, and black holding tanks in a location so as not to change the balance of the RV when the tanks are empty or full. **Always double-check wheelbase, GVWR, and weights at front and rear axles.**

*See Section 1 for details on how conclusions are reached.

Section 2: The Ratings

Brand	Year	Type	Length	Model	Chassis	Engine	Fuel Type	Average Price per Linear Foot When New	Adjusted Wheelbase	Approx. Towing Capacity	Gross Vehicle Weight Rating	Average Curb Weight
Cruise Air	1998	MHA	35	3505	CH	7.4L	G	$2400	246 T	1,500	19,500	16,363

Livability Code: SB 30-90
Wheelbase-to-length ratio of 58% is considered ○ dangerous ○ fatiguing ○ good ◉ excellent *
The approximate net payload of 3137 pounds at 16% of GVWR on this model is ○ deficient ○ excessive ○ cautionary ○ good ◉ excellent *
Total highway safety penalties are: 15 *   Value: 73   Durability: 76   Highway Control Rating: 100   Highway Safety: 85   ★★★

Brand	Year	Type	Length	Model	Chassis	Engine	Fuel Type	Price/Ft	Wheelbase	Towing	GVWR	Curb Wt
Cruise Air	1998	MHA	35	3513	CH	7.4L	G	$2400	228	4,500	16,500	14,758

Livability Code: SB 30-90
Wheelbase-to-length ratio of 54% is considered ○ dangerous ○ fatiguing ◉ good ○ excellent *
The approximate net payload of 1742 pounds at 11% of GVWR on this model is ○ deficient ○ excessive ○ cautionary ◉ good ○ excellent *
Total highway safety penalties are: 7 *   Value: 77   Durability: 76   Highway Control Rating: 75   Highway Safety: 68   ★★

Brand	Year	Type	Length	Model	Chassis	Engine	Fuel Type	Price/Ft	Wheelbase	Towing	GVWR	Curb Wt
Cruise Air	1998	MHA	35	3513	FO	7.5L	G	$2400	228	8,000	17,000	15,133

Livability Code: SB 30-90
Wheelbase-to-length ratio of 54% is considered ○ dangerous ○ fatiguing ◉ good ○ excellent *
The approximate net payload of 1867 pounds at 11% of GVWR on this model is ○ deficient ○ excessive ○ cautionary ◉ good ○ excellent *
Total highway safety penalties are: 2 *   Value: 79   Durability: 76   Highway Control Rating: 76   Highway Safety: 74   ★★★

Brand	Year	Type	Length	Model	Chassis	Engine	Fuel Type	Price/Ft	Wheelbase	Towing	GVWR	Curb Wt
Cruise Air	1998	MHA	35	3515	FO	7.5L	G	$2400	220	8,000	17,000	15,446

Livability Code: SB 30-90
Wheelbase-to-length ratio of 52% is considered ○ dangerous ◉ fatiguing ○ good ○ excellent *
The approximate net payload of 1554 pounds at 9% of GVWR on this model is ○ deficient ○ excessive ◉ cautionary ○ good ○ excellent *
Total highway safety penalties are: 2 *   Value: 79   Durability: 76   Highway Control Rating: 42   Highway Safety: 40

Brand	Year	Type	Length	Model	Chassis	Engine	Fuel Type	Price/Ft	Wheelbase	Towing	GVWR	Curb Wt
Cruise Air	1998	MHA	35	3515 slide	FO	7.5L	G	$2400	228	8,000	17,000	16,000

Livability Code: SB 30-90
Wheelbase-to-length ratio of 54% is considered ○ dangerous ○ fatiguing ◉ good ○ excellent *
The approximate net payload of 1000 pounds at 6% of GVWR on this model is ◉ deficient ○ excessive ○ cautionary ○ good ○ excellent *
Total highway safety penalties are: 7 *   Value: 77   Durability: 76   Highway Control Rating: 46   Highway Safety: 39

Brand	Year	Type	Length	Model	Chassis	Engine	Fuel Type	Price/Ft	Wheelbase	Towing	GVWR	Curb Wt
Cruise Air	1998	MHA	38	3815	FO	7.5L	G	$2200	252 T	5,000	20,000	16,750

Livability Code: SB 30-90
Wheelbase-to-length ratio of 56% is considered ○ dangerous ○ fatiguing ◉ good ○ excellent *
The approximate net payload of 3250 pounds at 16% of GVWR on this model is ○ deficient ○ excessive ○ cautionary ○ good ◉ excellent *
Total highway safety penalties are: 4 *   Value: 78   Durability: 76   Highway Control Rating: 96   Highway Safety: 92   ★★★

Brand	Year	Type	Length	Model	Chassis	Engine	Fuel Type	Price/Ft	Wheelbase	Towing	GVWR	Curb Wt
Cruise Air	1998	MHA	38	3815 slide	FO	7.5L	G	$2200	252 T	5,000	20,000	17,525

Livability Code: SB 30-90
Wheelbase-to-length ratio of 56% is considered ○ dangerous ○ fatiguing ◉ good ○ excellent *
The approximate net payload of 2475 pounds at 12% of GVWR on this model is ○ deficient ○ excessive ○ cautionary ◉ good ○ excellent *
Total highway safety penalties are: 11 *   Value: 75   Durability: 76   Highway Control Rating: 88   Highway Safety: 77   ★★★

Brand	Year	Type	Length	Model	Chassis	Engine	Fuel Type	Price/Ft	Wheelbase	Towing	GVWR	Curb Wt
Cruise Air	1999	MHA		accurate specs n/a								?

Livability Code: SB 30-90
Wheelbase-to-length ratio of   ? is considered ○ dangerous ○ fatiguing ○ good ○ excellent *
The approximate net payload of   pounds at   of GVWR on this model is ○ deficient ○ excessive ○ cautionary ○ good ○ excellent *
Total highway safety penalties are: 0 *   Value: 0   Durability: 76   Highway Control Rating: 0   Highway Safety: 0

Brand	Year	Type	Length	Model	Chassis	Engine	Fuel Type	Price/Ft	Wheelbase	Towing	GVWR	Curb Wt
Cruise Master	1990	MHA	30	3095	CH	7.4L	G	$1500	178	1,500	16,000	12,670

Livability Code: SB 30-90
Wheelbase-to-length ratio of 49% is considered ◉ dangerous ○ fatiguing ○ good ○ excellent *
The approximate net payload of 3330 pounds at 21% of GVWR on this model is ○ deficient ○ excessive ○ cautionary ○ good ◉ excellent *
Total highway safety penalties are: 5 *   Value: 83   Durability: 76   Highway Control Rating: 44   Highway Safety: 39

Brand	Year	Type	Length	Model	Chassis	Engine	Fuel Type	Price/Ft	Wheelbase	Towing	GVWR	Curb Wt
Cruise Master	1991	MHA	30	3095	FO	7.5L	G	$1600	178	8,000	17,000	13,322

Livability Code: SB 30-90
Wheelbase-to-length ratio of 49% is considered ◉ dangerous ○ fatiguing ○ good ○ excellent *
The approximate net payload of 3678 pounds at 22% of GVWR on this model is ○ deficient ○ excessive ○ cautionary ○ good ◉ excellent *
Total highway safety penalties are: 2 *   Value: 84   Durability: 76   Highway Control Rating: 43   Highway Safety: 41

Brand	Year	Type	Length	Model	Chassis	Engine	Fuel Type	Price/Ft	Wheelbase	Towing	GVWR	Curb Wt
Cruise Master	1992	MHA	28	2810	CH	7.4L	G	$1700	158	2,200	14,800	12,150

Livability Code: SB 30-90
Wheelbase-to-length ratio of 47% is considered ◉ dangerous ○ fatiguing ○ good ○ excellent *
The approximate net payload of 2650 pounds at 18% of GVWR on this model is ○ deficient ○ excessive ○ cautionary ○ good ◉ excellent *
Total highway safety penalties are: 4 *   Value: 84   Durability: 76   Highway Control Rating: 36   Highway Safety: 32

Brand	Year	Type	Length	Model	Chassis	Engine	Fuel Type	Price/Ft	Wheelbase	Towing	GVWR	Curb Wt
Cruise Master	1992	MHA	28	2850	CH	7.4L	G	$1700	158	2,200	14,800	12,150

Livability Code: SB 30-90
Wheelbase-to-length ratio of 47% is considered ◉ dangerous ○ fatiguing ○ good ○ excellent *
The approximate net payload of 2650 pounds at 18% of GVWR on this model is ○ deficient ○ excessive ○ cautionary ○ good ◉ excellent *
Total highway safety penalties are: 4 *   Value: 84   Durability: 76   Highway Control Rating: 36   Highway Safety: 32

Note: Safety ratings are based on the assumption that the engineering of the RV has allowed for proper balance by placing fresh, gray, and black holding tanks in a location so as not to change the balance of the RV when the tanks are empty or full. **Always double-check wheelbase, GVWR, and weights at front and rear axles.**

*See Section 1 for details on how conclusions are reached.

Brand	Year	Type	Length	Model	Chassis	Engine	Fuel Type	Average Price per Linear Foot When New	Adjusted Wheelbase	Approx. Towing Capacity	Gross Vehicle Weight Rating	Average Curb Weight

Cruise Master 1992 MHA 28 2890 CH 7.4L G $1700 158 2,200 14,800 12,150
Livability Code: SB 30-90
Wheelbase-to-length ratio of 47% is considered ● dangerous ○ fatiguing ○ good ○ excellent *
The approximate net payload of 2650 pounds at 18% of GVWR on this model is ○ deficient ○ excessive ○ cautionary ○ good ● excellent *
Total highway safety penalties are: 4 *   Value: 8 4   Durability: 7 6   Highway Control Rating: 3 6   Highway Safety: 3 2

Cruise Master 1992 MHA 30 3090 CH 7.4L G $1600 178 2,200 14,800 12,625
Livability Code: SB 30-90
Wheelbase-to-length ratio of 49% is considered ● dangerous ○ fatiguing ○ good ○ excellent *
The approximate net payload of 2175 pounds at 15% of GVWR on this model is ○ deficient ○ excessive ○ cautionary ● good ○ excellent *
Total highway safety penalties are: 5 *   Value: 8 3   Durability: 7 6   Highway Control Rating: 4 0   Highway Safety: 3 5

Cruise Master 1992 MHA 30 3095 CH 7.4L G $1600 178 2,200 14,800 12,625
Livability Code: SB 30-90
Wheelbase-to-length ratio of 49% is considered ● dangerous ○ fatiguing ○ good ○ excellent *
The approximate net payload of 2175 pounds at 15% of GVWR on this model is ○ deficient ○ excessive ○ cautionary ● good ○ excellent *
Total highway safety penalties are: 5 *   Value: 8 3   Durability: 7 6   Highway Control Rating: 4 0   Highway Safety: 3 5

Cruise Master 1992 MHA 30 3090 FO 7.5L G $1600 178 8,000 17,000 13,225
Livability Code: SB 30-90
Wheelbase-to-length ratio of 49% is considered ● dangerous ○ fatiguing ○ good ○ excellent *
The approximate net payload of 3775 pounds at 22% of GVWR on this model is ○ deficient ○ excessive ○ cautionary ○ good ● excellent *
Total highway safety penalties are: 2 *   Value: 8 4   Durability: 7 6   Highway Control Rating: 4 4   Highway Safety: 4 2

Cruise Master 1992 MHA 30 3095 FO 7.5L G $1600 178 8,000 17,000 13,225
Livability Code: SB 30-90
Wheelbase-to-length ratio of 49% is considered ● dangerous ○ fatiguing ○ good ○ excellent *
The approximate net payload of 3775 pounds at 22% of GVWR on this model is ○ deficient ○ excessive ○ cautionary ○ good ● excellent *
Total highway safety penalties are: 2 *   Value: 8 4   Durability: 7 6   Highway Control Rating: 4 4   Highway Safety: 4 2

Cruise Master 1992 MHA 30 3090 OS G $2300 178 1,500 15,600 13,525
Livability Code: SB 30-90
Wheelbase-to-length ratio of 49% is considered ● dangerous ○ fatiguing ○ good ○ excellent *
The approximate net payload of 2075 pounds at 13% of GVWR on this model is ○ deficient ○ excessive ○ cautionary ● good ○ excellent *
Total highway safety penalties are: 2 *   Value: 8 4   Durability: 7 6   Highway Control Rating: 3 7   Highway Safety: 3 5

Cruise Master 1992 MHA 30 3095 OS G $2300 178 1,500 15,600 13,525
Livability Code: SB 30-90
Wheelbase-to-length ratio of 49% is considered ● dangerous ○ fatiguing ○ good ○ excellent *
The approximate net payload of 2075 pounds at 13% of GVWR on this model is ○ deficient ○ excessive ○ cautionary ● good ○ excellent *
Total highway safety penalties are: 2 *   Value: 8 4   Durability: 7 6   Highway Control Rating: 3 7   Highway Safety: 3 5

Cruise Master 1992 MHA 32 3290 CH 7.4L G $1600 190 2,200 14,800 13,100
Livability Code: SB 30-90
Wheelbase-to-length ratio of 49% is considered ● dangerous ○ fatiguing ○ good ○ excellent *
The approximate net payload of 1700 pounds at 11% of GVWR on this model is ○ deficient ○ excessive ○ cautionary ● good ○ excellent *
Total highway safety penalties are: 6 *   Value: 8 3   Durability: 7 6   Highway Control Rating: 3 3   Highway Safety: 2 7

Cruise Master 1992 MHA 32 3290 FO 7.5L G $1600 190 8,000 17,000 13,700
Livability Code: SB 30-90
Wheelbase-to-length ratio of 49% is considered ● dangerous ○ fatiguing ○ good ○ excellent *
The approximate net payload of 3300 pounds at 19% of GVWR on this model is ○ deficient ○ excessive ○ cautionary ○ good ● excellent *
Total highway safety penalties are: 2 *   Value: 8 4   Durability: 7 6   Highway Control Rating: 4 6   Highway Safety: 4 4

Cruise Master 1992 MHA 32 3290 OS G $4100 190 1,500 15,600 14,000
Livability Code: SB 30-90
Wheelbase-to-length ratio of 49% is considered ● dangerous ○ fatiguing ○ good ○ excellent *
The approximate net payload of 1600 pounds at 10% of GVWR on this model is ○ deficient ○ excessive ○ cautionary ● good ○ excellent *
Total highway safety penalties are: 2 *   Value: 8 4   Durability: 7 6   Highway Control Rating: 3 1   Highway Safety: 2 9

Cruise Master 1992 MHA 34 3490 CH 7.4L G $1500 208 2,200 14,800 13,575
Livability Code: SB 30-90
Wheelbase-to-length ratio of 51% is considered ○ dangerous ● fatiguing ○ good ○ excellent *
The approximate net payload of 1225 pounds at 8% of GVWR on this model is ○ deficient ○ excessive ● cautionary ○ good ○ excellent *
Total highway safety penalties are: 7 *   Value: 8 2   Durability: 7 6   Highway Control Rating: 2 6   Highway Safety: 1 9

Cruise Master 1992 MHA 34 3491 CH 7.4L G $1500 208 2,200 14,800 13,575
Livability Code: SB 30-90
Wheelbase-to-length ratio of 51% is considered ○ dangerous ● fatiguing ○ good ○ excellent *
The approximate net payload of 1225 pounds at 8% of GVWR on this model is ○ deficient ○ excessive ● cautionary ○ good ○ excellent *
Total highway safety penalties are: 7 *   Value: 8 2   Durability: 7 6   Highway Control Rating: 2 6   Highway Safety: 1 9

Note: Safety ratings are based on the assumption that the engineering of the RV has allowed for proper balance by placing fresh, gray, and black holding tanks in a location so as not to change the balance of the RV when the tanks are empty or full. **Always double-check wheelbase, GVWR, and weights at front and rear axles.**

*See Section 1 for details on how conclusions are reached.

Section 2: The Ratings

Brand	Year	Type	Length	Model	Chassis	Engine	Fuel Type	Average Price per Linear Foot When New	Adjusted Wheelbase	Approx. Towing Capacity	Gross Vehicle Weight Rating	Average Curb Weight
Cruise Master	1992	MHA	34	3490	FO	7.5L	G	$1500	208	8,000	17,000	14,175

Livability Code: SB 30-90 — Wheelbase-to-length ratio of 51% is considered ○ dangerous ◉ fatiguing ○ good ○ excellent *
The approximate net payload of 2825 pounds at 17% of GVWR on this model is ○ deficient ○ excessive ○ cautionary ○ good ◉ excellent *
Total highway safety penalties are: 2 * — Value: 8 4 — Durability: 7 6 — Highway Control Rating: 4 9 — Highway Safety: 4 7

Brand	Year	Type	Length	Model	Chassis	Engine	Fuel Type	Price/Ft	Wheelbase	Towing	GVWR	Curb Weight
Cruise Master	1992	MHA	34	3491	FO	7.5L	G	$1500	208	8,000	17,000	14,175

Livability Code: SB 30-90 — Wheelbase-to-length ratio of 51% is considered ○ dangerous ◉ fatiguing ○ good ○ excellent *
The approximate net payload of 2825 pounds at 17% of GVWR on this model is ○ deficient ○ excessive ○ cautionary ○ good ◉ excellent *
Total highway safety penalties are: 2 * — Value: 8 4 — Durability: 7 6 — Highway Control Rating: 4 9 — Highway Safety: 4 7

Brand	Year	Type	Length	Model	Chassis	Engine	Fuel Type	Price/Ft	Wheelbase	Towing	GVWR	Curb Weight
Cruise Master	1992	MHA	34	3490	OS		G	$2100	208	1,500	16,000	14,175

Livability Code: SB 30-90 — Wheelbase-to-length ratio of 51% is considered ○ dangerous ◉ fatiguing ○ good ○ excellent *
The approximate net payload of 1825 pounds at 11% of GVWR on this model is ○ deficient ○ excessive ○ cautionary ◉ good ○ excellent *
Total highway safety penalties are: 2 * — Value: 8 4 — Durability: 7 6 — Highway Control Rating: 3 9 — Highway Safety: 3 7

Brand	Year	Type	Length	Model	Chassis	Engine	Fuel Type	Price/Ft	Wheelbase	Towing	GVWR	Curb Weight
Cruise Master	1992	MHA	34	3491	OS		G	$2100	208	1,500	15,600	14,475

Livability Code: SB 30-90 — Wheelbase-to-length ratio of 51% is considered ○ dangerous ◉ fatiguing ○ good ○ excellent *
The approximate net payload of 1125 pounds at 7% of GVWR on this model is ○ deficient ○ excessive ◉ cautionary ○ good ○ excellent *
Total highway safety penalties are: 2 * — Value: 8 4 — Durability: 7 6 — Highway Control Rating: 1 9 — Highway Safety: 1 7

Brand	Year	Type	Length	Model	Chassis	Engine	Fuel Type	Price/Ft	Wheelbase	Towing	GVWR	Curb Weight
Cruise Master	1993	MHA	28	2800	CH	7.4L	G	$1700	178	1,500	12,300	11,350

Livability Code: SB 30-90 — Wheelbase-to-length ratio of 53% is considered ○ dangerous ◉ fatiguing ○ good ○ excellent *
The approximate net payload of 950 pounds at 8% of GVWR on this model is ○ deficient ○ excessive ◉ cautionary ○ good ○ excellent *
Total highway safety penalties are: 4 * — Value: 8 4 — Durability: 7 6 — Highway Control Rating: 4 7 — Highway Safety: 4 3

Brand	Year	Type	Length	Model	Chassis	Engine	Fuel Type	Price/Ft	Wheelbase	Towing	GVWR	Curb Weight
Cruise Master	1993	MHA	30	3001	CH	7.4L	G	$1700	190	2,200	14,800	12,625

Livability Code: SB 30-90 — Wheelbase-to-length ratio of 53% is considered ○ dangerous ◉ fatiguing ○ good ○ excellent *
The approximate net payload of 2175 pounds at 15% of GVWR on this model is ○ deficient ○ excessive ○ cautionary ◉ good ○ excellent *
Total highway safety penalties are: 5 * — Value: 8 3 — Durability: 7 6 — Highway Control Rating: 6 7 — Highway Safety: 6 2 — ★★

Brand	Year	Type	Length	Model	Chassis	Engine	Fuel Type	Price/Ft	Wheelbase	Towing	GVWR	Curb Weight
Cruise Master	1993	MHA	32	3210	CH	7.4L	G	$1600	208	2,200	14,800	13,100

Livability Code: SB 30-90 — Wheelbase-to-length ratio of 54% is considered ○ dangerous ○ fatiguing ◉ good ○ excellent *
The approximate net payload of 1700 pounds at 11% of GVWR on this model is ○ deficient ○ excessive ○ cautionary ◉ good ○ excellent *
Total highway safety penalties are: 6 * — Value: 8 3 — Durability: 7 6 — Highway Control Rating: 7 8 — Highway Safety: 7 2 — ★★★

Brand	Year	Type	Length	Model	Chassis	Engine	Fuel Type	Price/Ft	Wheelbase	Towing	GVWR	Curb Weight
Cruise Master	1993	MHA	34	3404	CH	7.4L	G	$1600	228	2,200	14,800	13,575

Livability Code: SB 30-90 — Wheelbase-to-length ratio of 56% is considered ○ dangerous ○ fatiguing ◉ good ○ excellent *
The approximate net payload of 1225 pounds at 8% of GVWR on this model is ○ deficient ○ excessive ◉ cautionary ○ good ○ excellent *
Total highway safety penalties are: 7 * — Value: 8 2 — Durability: 7 6 — Highway Control Rating: 7 3 — Highway Safety: 6 6 — ★★

Brand	Year	Type	Length	Model	Chassis	Engine	Fuel Type	Price/Ft	Wheelbase	Towing	GVWR	Curb Weight
Cruise Master	1994	MHA	29	2708	CH	7.4L	G	$2100	178	2,200	14,800	12,316

Livability Code: SB 30-90 — Wheelbase-to-length ratio of 52% is considered ○ dangerous ◉ fatiguing ○ good ○ excellent *
The approximate net payload of 2484 pounds at 17% of GVWR on this model is ○ deficient ○ excessive ○ cautionary ○ good ◉ excellent *
Total highway safety penalties are: 4 * — Value: 8 3 — Durability: 7 6 — Highway Control Rating: 5 9 — Highway Safety: 5 5 — ★

Brand	Year	Type	Length	Model	Chassis	Engine	Fuel Type	Price/Ft	Wheelbase	Towing	GVWR	Curb Weight
Cruise Master	1994	MHA	31	2995	CH	7.4L	G	$1900	190	2,200	14,800	12,791

Livability Code: SB 30-90 — Wheelbase-to-length ratio of 52% is considered ○ dangerous ◉ fatiguing ○ good ○ excellent *
The approximate net payload of 2009 pounds at 14% of GVWR on this model is ○ deficient ○ excessive ○ cautionary ◉ good ○ excellent *
Total highway safety penalties are: 5 * — Value: 8 3 — Durability: 7 6 — Highway Control Rating: 5 3 — Highway Safety: 4 8

Brand	Year	Type	Length	Model	Chassis	Engine	Fuel Type	Price/Ft	Wheelbase	Towing	GVWR	Curb Weight
Cruise Master	1994	MHA	31	3190	CH	7.4L	G	$1900	218	2,200	14,800	12,791

Livability Code: SB 30-90 — Wheelbase-to-length ratio of 59% is considered ○ dangerous ○ fatiguing ○ good ◉ excellent *
The approximate net payload of 2009 pounds at 14% of GVWR on this model is ○ deficient ○ excessive ○ cautionary ◉ good ○ excellent *
Total highway safety penalties are: 5 * — Value: 8 3 — Durability: 7 6 — Highway Control Rating: 1 0 0 — Highway Safety: 9 5 — ★★★

Brand	Year	Type	Length	Model	Chassis	Engine	Fuel Type	Price/Ft	Wheelbase	Towing	GVWR	Curb Weight
Cruise Master	1994	MHA	31	2995	FO	7.5L	G	$1900	190	3,800	15,200	13,191

Livability Code: SB 30-90 — Wheelbase-to-length ratio of 52% is considered ○ dangerous ◉ fatiguing ○ good ○ excellent *
The approximate net payload of 2009 pounds at 13% of GVWR on this model is ○ deficient ○ excessive ○ cautionary ◉ good ○ excellent *
Total highway safety penalties are: 2 * — Value: 8 4 — Durability: 7 6 — Highway Control Rating: 5 2 — Highway Safety: 5 0 — ★

Note: Safety ratings are based on the assumption that the engineering of the RV has allowed for proper balance by placing fresh, gray, and black holding tanks in a location so as not to change the balance of the RV when the tanks are empty or full. **Always double-check wheelbase, GVWR, and weights at front and rear axles.**

*See Section 1 for details on how conclusions are reached.

Section 2: The Ratings

Brand	Year	Type	Length	Model	Chassis	Engine	Fuel Type	Average Price per Linear Foot When New	Adjusted Wheelbase	Approx. Towing Capacity	Gross Vehicle Weight Rating	Average Curb Weight
Cruise Master	1994	MHA	33	3190	FO	7.5L	G	$1800	218	8,000	17,000	13,866

Livability Code: SB 30-90   Wheelbase-to-length ratio of 56% is considered ○ dangerous ○ fatiguing ◉ good ○ excellent *

The approximate net payload of 3134 pounds at 18% of GVWR on this model is ○ deficient ○ excessive ○ cautionary ○ good ◉ excellent *

Total highway safety penalties are: 2 *   Value: 84   Durability: 76   Highway Control Rating: 97   Highway Safety: 95   ★★★

| **Cruise Master** | 1994 | MHA | 33 | 3190 | SP | GM190 | D | $3000 | 208 | 1,500 | 16,000 | 14,266 |

Livability Code: SB 30-90   Wheelbase-to-length ratio of 53% is considered ○ dangerous ◉ fatiguing ○ good ○ excellent *

The approximate net payload of 1734 pounds at 11% of GVWR on this model is ○ deficient ○ excessive ○ cautionary ◉ good ○ excellent *

Total highway safety penalties are: 2 *   Value: 84   Durability: 76   Highway Control Rating: 60   Highway Safety: 58   ★

| **Cruise Master** | 1994 | MHA | 34 | 3410 | CH | 7.4L | G | $1800 | 228 | 2,200 | 14,800 | 13,623 |

Livability Code: SB 30-90   Wheelbase-to-length ratio of 56% is considered ○ dangerous ○ fatiguing ◉ good ○ excellent *

The approximate net payload of 1178 pounds at 8% of GVWR on this model is ○ deficient ○ excessive ◉ cautionary ○ good ○ excellent *

Total highway safety penalties are: 7 *   Value: 82   Durability: 76   Highway Control Rating: 72   Highway Safety: 65   ★★

| **Cruise Master** | 1994 | MHA | 34 | 3410 | FO | 7.5L | G | $1800 | 228 | 8,000 | 17,000 | 14,223 |

Livability Code: SB 30-90   Wheelbase-to-length ratio of 56% is considered ○ dangerous ○ fatiguing ◉ good ○ excellent *

The approximate net payload of 2778 pounds at 16% of GVWR on this model is ○ deficient ○ excessive ○ cautionary ○ good ◉ excellent *

Total highway safety penalties are: 2 *   Value: 84   Durability: 76   Highway Control Rating: 95   Highway Safety: 93   ★★★

| **Cruise Master** | 1994 | MHA | 34 | 3406 | CH | 7.4L | G | $1800 | 228 | 2,200 | 14,800 | 13,670 |

Livability Code: SB 30-90   Wheelbase-to-length ratio of 55% is considered ○ dangerous ○ fatiguing ◉ good ○ excellent *

The approximate net payload of 1130 pounds at 8% of GVWR on this model is ○ deficient ○ excessive ◉ cautionary ○ good ○ excellent *

Total highway safety penalties are: 7 *   Value: 82   Durability: 76   Highway Control Rating: 70   Highway Safety: 63   ★★

| **Cruise Master** | 1994 | MHA | 34 | 3406 | FO | 7.5L | G | $1800 | 228 | 8,000 | 17,000 | 14,270 |

Livability Code: SB 30-90   Wheelbase-to-length ratio of 55% is considered ○ dangerous ○ fatiguing ◉ good ○ excellent *

The approximate net payload of 2730 pounds at 16% of GVWR on this model is ○ deficient ○ excessive ○ cautionary ○ good ◉ excellent *

Total highway safety penalties are: 2 *   Value: 84   Durability: 76   Highway Control Rating: 93   Highway Safety: 91   ★★★

| **Cruise Master** | 1995 | MHA | 29 | 2708 | CH | 7.4L | G | $2000 | 178 | 4,200 | 14,800 | 12,256 |

Livability Code: SB 30-90   Wheelbase-to-length ratio of 52% is considered ○ dangerous ◉ fatiguing ○ good ○ excellent *

The approximate net payload of 2544 pounds at 17% of GVWR on this model is ○ deficient ○ excessive ○ cautionary ○ good ◉ excellent *

Total highway safety penalties are: 4 *   Value: 83   Durability: 76   Highway Control Rating: 59   Highway Safety: 55   ★

| **Cruise Master** | 1995 | MHA | 29 | 2708 | FO | 7.5L | G | $2000 | 178 | 3,800 | 15,200 | 12,716 |

Livability Code: SB 30-90   Wheelbase-to-length ratio of 52% is considered ○ dangerous ◉ fatiguing ○ good ○ excellent *

The approximate net payload of 2484 pounds at 16% of GVWR on this model is ○ deficient ○ excessive ○ cautionary ○ good ◉ excellent *

Total highway safety penalties are: 2 *   Value: 84   Durability: 76   Highway Control Rating: 59   Highway Safety: 57   ★

| **Cruise Master** | 1995 | MHA | 31 | 2995 | CH | 7.4L | G | $1900 | 190 | 4,200 | 14,800 | 12,817 |

Livability Code: SB 30-90   Wheelbase-to-length ratio of 52% is considered ○ dangerous ◉ fatiguing ○ good ○ excellent *

The approximate net payload of 1983 pounds at 13% of GVWR on this model is ○ deficient ○ excessive ○ cautionary ◉ good ○ excellent *

Total highway safety penalties are: 5 *   Value: 83   Durability: 76   Highway Control Rating: 52   Highway Safety: 47

| **Cruise Master** | 1995 | MHA | 31 | 2995 | FO | 7.5L | G | $1900 | 190 | 3,800 | 15,200 | 13,191 |

Livability Code: SB 30-90   Wheelbase-to-length ratio of 52% is considered ○ dangerous ◉ fatiguing ○ good ○ excellent *

The approximate net payload of 2009 pounds at 13% of GVWR on this model is ○ deficient ○ excessive ○ cautionary ◉ good ○ excellent *

Total highway safety penalties are: 2 *   Value: 84   Durability: 76   Highway Control Rating: 52   Highway Safety: 50   ★

| **Cruise Master** | 1995 | MHA | 33 | 3190 | CH | 7.4L | G | $1800 | 218 | 4,200 | 14,800 | 13,182 |

Livability Code: SB 30-90   Wheelbase-to-length ratio of 56% is considered ○ dangerous ○ fatiguing ◉ good ○ excellent *

The approximate net payload of 1618 pounds at 11% of GVWR on this model is ○ deficient ○ excessive ○ cautionary ◉ good ○ excellent *

Total highway safety penalties are: 6 *   Value: 82   Durability: 76   Highway Control Rating: 85   Highway Safety: 79   ★★★

| **Cruise Master** | 1995 | MHA | 33 | 3190 | FO | 7.5L | G | $1800 | 218 | 8,000 | 17,000 | 13,866 |

Livability Code: SB 30-90   Wheelbase-to-length ratio of 56% is considered ○ dangerous ○ fatiguing ◉ good ○ excellent *

The approximate net payload of 3134 pounds at 18% of GVWR on this model is ○ deficient ○ excessive ○ cautionary ○ good ◉ excellent *

Total highway safety penalties are: 2 *   Value: 84   Durability: 76   Highway Control Rating: 97   Highway Safety: 95   ★★★

Note: Safety ratings are based on the assumption that the engineering of the RV has allowed for proper balance by placing fresh, gray, and black holding tanks in a location so as not to change the balance of the RV when the tanks are empty or full. **Always double-check wheelbase, GVWR, and weights at front and rear axles.**

*See Section 1 for details on how conclusions are reached.

Section 2: The Ratings

Brand	Year	Type	Length	Model	Chassis	Engine	Fuel Type	Average Price per Linear Foot When New	Adjusted Wheelbase	Approx. Towing Capacity	Gross Vehicle Weight Rating	Average Curb Weight

Cruise Master — 1995 — MHA — 33 — 3295 — CH — 7.4L — G — $1800 — 218 — 4,200 — 14,800 — 13,302
Livability Code: SB 30-90
Wheelbase-to-length ratio of 55% is considered ○ dangerous ○ fatiguing ◉ good ○ excellent *
The approximate net payload of 1498 pounds at 10% of GVWR on this model is ○ deficient ○ excessive ○ cautionary ◉ good ○ excellent *
Total highway safety penalties are: 6 *   Value: 8 2   Durability: 7 6   Highway Control Rating: 8 7   Highway Safety: 8 1   ★★★

Cruise Master — 1995 — MHA — 33 — 3295 — FO — 7.5L — G — $1900 — 218 — 8,000 — 17,000 — 13,938
Livability Code: SB 30-90
Wheelbase-to-length ratio of 55% is considered ○ dangerous ○ fatiguing ◉ good ○ excellent *
The approximate net payload of 3063 pounds at 18% of GVWR on this model is ○ deficient ○ excessive ○ cautionary ○ good ◉ excellent *
Total highway safety penalties are: 2 *   Value: 8 4   Durability: 7 6   Highway Control Rating: 9 5   Highway Safety: 9 3   ★★★

Cruise Master — 1995 — MHA — 35 — 3411 — CH — 7.4L — G — $1800 — 228 — 1,500 — 16,000 — 13,763
Livability Code: SB 30-90
Wheelbase-to-length ratio of 54% is considered ○ dangerous ○ fatiguing ◉ good ○ excellent *
The approximate net payload of 2237 pounds at 14% of GVWR on this model is ○ deficient ○ excessive ○ cautionary ◉ good ○ excellent *
Total highway safety penalties are: 7 *   Value: 8 2   Durability: 7 6   Highway Control Rating: 7 8   Highway Safety: 7 1   ★★★

Cruise Master — 1995 — MHA — 35 — 3412 — CH — 7.4L — G — $1800 — 228 — 1,500 — 16,000 — 13,798
Livability Code: SB 30-90
Wheelbase-to-length ratio of 54% is considered ○ dangerous ○ fatiguing ◉ good ○ excellent *
The approximate net payload of 2202 pounds at 14% of GVWR on this model is ○ deficient ○ excessive ○ cautionary ◉ good ○ excellent *
Total highway safety penalties are: 7 *   Value: 8 2   Durability: 7 6   Highway Control Rating: 7 8   Highway Safety: 7 1   ★★★

Cruise Master — 1995 — MHA — 35 — 3411 — FO — 7.5L — G — $1800 — 228 — 8,000 — 17,000 — 14,436
Livability Code: SB 30-90
Wheelbase-to-length ratio of 54% is considered ○ dangerous ○ fatiguing ◉ good ○ excellent *
The approximate net payload of 2564 pounds at 15% of GVWR on this model is ○ deficient ○ excessive ○ cautionary ○ good ○ excellent *
Total highway safety penalties are: 2 *   Value: 8 4   Durability: 7 6   Highway Control Rating: 8 0   Highway Safety: 7 8   ★★★

Cruise Master — 1995 — MHA — 35 — 3412 — FO — 7.5L — G — $1800 — 228 — 8,000 — 17,000 — 14,436
Livability Code: SB 30-90
Wheelbase-to-length ratio of 54% is considered ○ dangerous ○ fatiguing ○ good ○ excellent *
The approximate net payload of 2564 pounds at 15% of GVWR on this model is ○ deficient ○ excessive ○ cautionary ○ good ○ excellent *
Total highway safety penalties are: 2 *   Value: 8 4   Durability: 7 6   Highway Control Rating: 8 0   Highway Safety: 7 8   ★★★

Cruise Master — 1995 — MHA — 36 — 3595 — CH — 7.4L — G — $1700 — 228 — 1,500 — 16,000 — 13,975
Livability Code: SB 30-90
Wheelbase-to-length ratio of 53% is considered ○ dangerous ◉ fatiguing ○ good ○ excellent *
The approximate net payload of 2026 pounds at 13% of GVWR on this model is ○ deficient ○ excessive ○ cautionary ◉ good ○ excellent *
Total highway safety penalties are: 8 *   Value: 8 2   Durability: 7 6   Highway Control Rating: 6 3   Highway Safety: 5 5   ★

Cruise Master — 1995 — MHA — 36 — 3595 — FO — 7.5L — G — $1700 — 228 — 8,000 — 17,000 — 14,650
Livability Code: SB 30-90
Wheelbase-to-length ratio of 53% is considered ○ dangerous ◉ fatiguing ○ good ○ excellent *
The approximate net payload of 2350 pounds at 14% of GVWR on this model is ○ deficient ○ excessive ○ cautionary ◉ good ○ excellent *
Total highway safety penalties are: 2 *   Value: 8 4   Durability: 7 6   Highway Control Rating: 6 5   Highway Safety: 6 3   ★★

Cruise Master — 1996 — MHA — 30 — 2808W — CH — 7.4L — G — $1900 — 178 — 2,200 — 14,800 — 12,910
Livability Code: SB 30-90
Wheelbase-to-length ratio of 50% is considered ◉ dangerous ○ fatiguing ○ good ○ excellent *
The approximate net payload of 1890 pounds at 13% of GVWR on this model is ○ deficient ○ excessive ○ cautionary ◉ good ○ excellent *
Total highway safety penalties are: 4 *   Value: 8 3   Durability: 7 6   Highway Control Rating: 3 8   Highway Safety: 3 4

Cruise Master — 1996 — MHA — 30 — 2808W -sl — CH — 7.4L — G — $2000 — 178 — 1,500 — 16,500 — 13,575
Livability Code: SB 30-90
Wheelbase-to-length ratio of 50% is considered ◉ dangerous ○ fatiguing ○ good ○ excellent *
The approximate net payload of 2925 pounds at 18% of GVWR on this model is ○ deficient ○ excessive ○ cautionary ○ good ◉ excellent *
Total highway safety penalties are: 7 *   Value: 8 2   Durability: 7 6   Highway Control Rating: 4 6   Highway Safety: 3 9

Cruise Master — 1996 — MHA — 30 — 2808W — FO — 7.5L — G — $1900 — 178 — 3,800 — 15,200 — 13,325
Livability Code: SB 30-90
Wheelbase-to-length ratio of 50% is considered ◉ dangerous ○ fatiguing ○ good ○ excellent *
The approximate net payload of 1875 pounds at 12% of GVWR on this model is ○ deficient ○ excessive ○ cautionary ◉ good ○ excellent *
Total highway safety penalties are: 2 *   Value: 8 4   Durability: 7 6   Highway Control Rating: 3 7   Highway Safety: 3 5

Cruise Master — 1996 — MHA — 30 — 2808W -sl — FO — 7.5L — G — $2000 — 178 — 8,000 — 17,000 — 13,975
Livability Code: SB 30-90
Wheelbase-to-length ratio of 50% is considered ◉ dangerous ○ fatiguing ○ good ○ excellent *
The approximate net payload of 3025 pounds at 18% of GVWR on this model is ○ deficient ○ excessive ○ cautionary ○ good ◉ excellent *
Total highway safety penalties are: 5 *   Value: 8 3   Durability: 7 6   Highway Control Rating: 4 6   Highway Safety: 4 1

Note: Safety ratings are based on the assumption that the engineering of the RV has allowed for proper balance by placing fresh, gray, and black holding tanks in a location so as not to change the balance of the RV when the tanks are empty or full. **Always double-check wheelbase, GVWR, and weights at front and rear axles.**

*See Section 1 for details on how conclusions are reached.

Brand	Year	Type	Length	Model	Chassis	Engine	Fuel Type	Average Price per Linear Foot When New	Adjusted Wheel-base	Approx. Towing Capacity	Gross Vehicle Weight Rating	Average Curb Weight
Cruise Master	1996	MHA	32	2995W	CH	7.4L	G	$1800	190	2,200	14,800	13,258

Livability Code: SB 30-90
Wheelbase-to-length ratio of 50% is considered ● dangerous ○ fatiguing ○ good ○ excellent *
The approximate net payload of 1543 pounds at 10% of GVWR on this model is ○ deficient ○ excessive ○ cautionary ● good ○ excellent *
Total highway safety penalties are: 5 *   Value: 8 3   Durability: 7 6   Highway Control Rating: 3 3   Highway Safety: 2 8

Brand	Year	Type	Length	Model	Chassis	Engine	Fuel Type	Price/LF	Wheelbase	Towing	GVWR	Curb Weight
Cruise Master	1996	MHA	32	2995W -sl	CH	7.4L	G	$1900	190	1,500	16,500	14,075

Livability Code: SB 30-90
Wheelbase-to-length ratio of 50% is considered ● dangerous ○ fatiguing ○ good ○ excellent *
The approximate net payload of 2425 pounds at 15% of GVWR on this model is ○ deficient ○ excessive ○ cautionary ● good ○ excellent *
Total highway safety penalties are: 8 *   Value: 8 1   Durability: 7 6   Highway Control Rating: 4 2   Highway Safety: 3 4

Cruise Master	1996	MHA	32	2995W	FO	7.5L	G	$1800	190	3,800	15,200	13,825

Livability Code: SB 30-90
Wheelbase-to-length ratio of 50% is considered ● dangerous ○ fatiguing ○ good ○ excellent *
The approximate net payload of 1375 pounds at 9% of GVWR on this model is ○ deficient ○ excessive ● cautionary ○ good ○ excellent *
Total highway safety penalties are: 2 *   Value: 8 4   Durability: 7 6   Highway Control Rating: 2 8   Highway Safety: 2 6

Cruise Master	1996	MHA	32	2995W -sl	FO	7.5L	G	$1900	190	8,000	17,000	14,475

Livability Code: SB 30-90
Wheelbase-to-length ratio of 50% is considered ● dangerous ○ fatiguing ○ good ○ excellent *
The approximate net payload of 2525 pounds at 15% of GVWR on this model is ○ deficient ○ excessive ○ cautionary ● good ○ excellent *
Total highway safety penalties are: 5 *   Value: 8 3   Durability: 7 6   Highway Control Rating: 4 2   Highway Safety: 3 7

Cruise Master	1996	MHA	34	3190W	CH	7.4L	G	$1800	212	1,500	16,500	13,970

Livability Code: SB 30-90
Wheelbase-to-length ratio of 52% is considered ○ dangerous ● fatiguing ○ good ○ excellent *
The approximate net payload of 2530 pounds at 15% of GVWR on this model is ○ deficient ○ excessive ○ cautionary ● good ○ excellent *
Total highway safety penalties are: 6 *   Value: 8 2   Durability: 7 6   Highway Control Rating: 5 9   Highway Safety: 5 3   ★

Cruise Master	1996	MHA	34	3190W -sl	CH	7.4L	G	$1900	212	1,500	16,500	14,575

Livability Code: SB 30-90
Wheelbase-to-length ratio of 52% is considered ○ dangerous ● fatiguing ○ good ○ excellent *
The approximate net payload of 1925 pounds at 12% of GVWR on this model is ○ deficient ○ excessive ○ cautionary ● good ○ excellent *
Total highway safety penalties are: 9 *   Value: 8 1   Durability: 7 6   Highway Control Rating: 5 3   Highway Safety: 4 4

Cruise Master	1996	MHA	34	3190W	FO	7.5L	G	$1800	212	8,000	17,000	14,525

Livability Code: SB 30-90
Wheelbase-to-length ratio of 52% is considered ○ dangerous ● fatiguing ○ good ○ excellent *
The approximate net payload of 2475 pounds at 15% of GVWR on this model is ○ deficient ○ excessive ○ cautionary ● good ○ excellent *
Total highway safety penalties are: 2 *   Value: 8 4   Durability: 7 6   Highway Control Rating: 5 8   Highway Safety: 5 6   ★

Cruise Master	1996	MHA	34	3190W -sl	FO	7.5L	G	$1900	212	8,000	17,000	14,975

Livability Code: SB 30-90
Wheelbase-to-length ratio of 52% is considered ○ dangerous ● fatiguing ○ good ○ excellent *
The approximate net payload of 2025 pounds at 12% of GVWR on this model is ○ deficient ○ excessive ○ cautionary ● good ○ excellent *
Total highway safety penalties are: 5 *   Value: 8 3   Durability: 7 6   Highway Control Rating: 5 3   Highway Safety: 4 8

Cruise Master	1996	MHA	34	3190W	SP	CU210	D	$2900	190	1,500	18,000	15,050

Livability Code: SB 30-90
Wheelbase-to-length ratio of 46% is considered ● dangerous ○ fatiguing ○ good ○ excellent *
The approximate net payload of 2950 pounds at 16% of GVWR on this model is ○ deficient ○ excessive ○ cautionary ○ good ● excellent *
Total highway safety penalties are: 2 *   Value: 8 4   Durability: 7 6   Highway Control Rating: 3 2   Highway Safety: 3 0

Cruise Master	1996	MHA	35	3300W	CH	7.4L	G	$1800	220	1,500	16,500	14,368

Livability Code: SB 30-90
Wheelbase-to-length ratio of 52% is considered ○ dangerous ● fatiguing ○ good ○ excellent *
The approximate net payload of 2133 pounds at 13% of GVWR on this model is ○ deficient ○ excessive ○ cautionary ● good ○ excellent *
Total highway safety penalties are: 7 *   Value: 8 2   Durability: 7 6   Highway Control Rating: 5 4   Highway Safety: 4 7

Cruise Master	1996	MHA	35	3300W -sl	CH	7.4L	G	$1800	220	1,500	16,500	14,950

Livability Code: SB 30-90
Wheelbase-to-length ratio of 52% is considered ○ dangerous ● fatiguing ○ good ○ excellent *
The approximate net payload of 1550 pounds at 9% of GVWR on this model is ○ deficient ○ excessive ● cautionary ○ good ○ excellent *
Total highway safety penalties are: 10 *   Value: 8 1   Durability: 7 6   Highway Control Rating: 4 3   Highway Safety: 3 3

Cruise Master	1996	MHA	35	3300W	FO	7.5L	G	$1800	220	8,000	17,000	14,900

Livability Code: SB 30-90
Wheelbase-to-length ratio of 52% is considered ○ dangerous ● fatiguing ○ good ○ excellent *
The approximate net payload of 2100 pounds at 12% of GVWR on this model is ○ deficient ○ excessive ○ cautionary ● good ○ excellent *
Total highway safety penalties are: 2 *   Value: 8 4   Durability: 7 6   Highway Control Rating: 5 2   Highway Safety: 5 0   ★

Note: Safety ratings are based on the assumption that the engineering of the RV has allowed for proper balance by placing fresh, gray, and black holding tanks in a location so as not to change the balance of the RV when the tanks are empty or full. **Always double-check wheelbase, GVWR, and weights at front and rear axles.**

*See Section 1 for details on how conclusions are reached.

Section 2: The Ratings

Brand	Year	Type	Length	Model	Chassis	Engine	Fuel Type	Average Price per Linear Foot When New	Adjusted Wheelbase	Approx. Towing Capacity	Gross Vehicle Weight Rating	Average Curb Weight
Cruise Master	1996	MHA	35	3412W	CH	7.4L	G	$1800	228	1,500	16,500	14,518

Livability Code: SB 30-90
Wheelbase-to-length ratio of 54% is considered ○ dangerous ○ fatiguing ◉ good ○ excellent *
The approximate net payload of 1983 pounds at 12% of GVWR on this model is ○ deficient ○ excessive ○ cautionary ◉ good ○ excellent *
Total highway safety penalties are: 7 *   Value: 8 2   Durability: 7 6   Highway Control Rating: 7 7   Highway Safety: 7 0   ★★★

Brand	Year	Type	Length	Model	Chassis	Engine	Fuel Type	Average Price per Linear Foot When New	Adjusted Wheelbase	Approx. Towing Capacity	Gross Vehicle Weight Rating	Average Curb Weight
Cruise Master	1996	MHA	35	3412W -sl	CH	7.4L	G	$1800	220	1,500	16,500	15,425

Livability Code: SB 30-90
Wheelbase-to-length ratio of 52% is considered ○ dangerous ◉ fatiguing ○ good ○ excellent *
The approximate net payload of 1075 pounds at 7% of GVWR on this model is ○ deficient ○ excessive ◉ cautionary ○ good ○ excellent *
Total highway safety penalties are: 13 *   Value: 7 9   Durability: 7 6   Highway Control Rating: 3 0   Highway Safety: 1 7

Brand	Year	Type	Length	Model	Chassis	Engine	Fuel Type	Average Price per Linear Foot When New	Adjusted Wheelbase	Approx. Towing Capacity	Gross Vehicle Weight Rating	Average Curb Weight
Cruise Master	1996	MHA	35	3412W	FO	7.5L	G	$1800	228	8,000	17,000	14,925

Livability Code: SB 30-90
Wheelbase-to-length ratio of 54% is considered ○ dangerous ○ fatiguing ◉ good ○ excellent *
The approximate net payload of 2075 pounds at 12% of GVWR on this model is ○ deficient ○ excessive ○ cautionary ◉ good ○ excellent *
Total highway safety penalties are: 2 *   Value: 8 4   Durability: 7 6   Highway Control Rating: 7 7   Highway Safety: 7 5   ★★★

Brand	Year	Type	Length	Model	Chassis	Engine	Fuel Type	Average Price per Linear Foot When New	Adjusted Wheelbase	Approx. Towing Capacity	Gross Vehicle Weight Rating	Average Curb Weight
Cruise Master	1996	MHA	35	3412W -sl	FO	7.5L	G	$1800	220	8,000	17,000	15,825

Livability Code: SB 30-90
Wheelbase-to-length ratio of 52% is considered ○ dangerous ◉ fatiguing ○ good ○ excellent *
The approximate net payload of 1175 pounds at 7% of GVWR on this model is ○ deficient ○ excessive ◉ cautionary ○ good ○ excellent *
Total highway safety penalties are: 7 *   Value: 8 2   Durability: 7 6   Highway Control Rating: 3 0   Highway Safety: 2 3

Brand	Year	Type	Length	Model	Chassis	Engine	Fuel Type	Average Price per Linear Foot When New	Adjusted Wheelbase	Approx. Towing Capacity	Gross Vehicle Weight Rating	Average Curb Weight
Cruise Master	1996	MHA	36	3411W	CH	7.4L	G	$1800	228	1,500	16,500	14,505

Livability Code: SB 30-90
Wheelbase-to-length ratio of 53% is considered ○ dangerous ◉ fatiguing ○ good ○ excellent *
The approximate net payload of 1995 pounds at 12% of GVWR on this model is ○ deficient ○ excessive ○ cautionary ◉ good ○ excellent *
Total highway safety penalties are: 7 *   Value: 8 2   Durability: 7 6   Highway Control Rating: 6 4   Highway Safety: 5 7   ★

Brand	Year	Type	Length	Model	Chassis	Engine	Fuel Type	Average Price per Linear Foot When New	Adjusted Wheelbase	Approx. Towing Capacity	Gross Vehicle Weight Rating	Average Curb Weight
Cruise Master	1996	MHA	36	3411W -sl	CH	7.4L	G	$1800	228	1,500	16,500	15,050

Livability Code: SB 30-90
Wheelbase-to-length ratio of 53% is considered ○ dangerous ◉ fatiguing ○ good ○ excellent *
The approximate net payload of 1450 pounds at 9% of GVWR on this model is ○ deficient ○ excessive ◉ cautionary ○ good ○ excellent *
Total highway safety penalties are: 10 *   Value: 8 0   Durability: 7 6   Highway Control Rating: 5 5   Highway Safety: 4 5

Brand	Year	Type	Length	Model	Chassis	Engine	Fuel Type	Average Price per Linear Foot When New	Adjusted Wheelbase	Approx. Towing Capacity	Gross Vehicle Weight Rating	Average Curb Weight
Cruise Master	1996	MHA	36	3411W	FO	7.5L	G	$1800	228	8,000	17,000	15,000

Livability Code: SB 30-90
Wheelbase-to-length ratio of 53% is considered ○ dangerous ◉ fatiguing ○ good ○ excellent *
The approximate net payload of 2000 pounds at 12% of GVWR on this model is ○ deficient ○ excessive ○ cautionary ◉ good ○ excellent *
Total highway safety penalties are: 2 *   Value: 8 4   Durability: 7 6   Highway Control Rating: 6 4   Highway Safety: 6 2   ★★

Brand	Year	Type	Length	Model	Chassis	Engine	Fuel Type	Average Price per Linear Foot When New	Adjusted Wheelbase	Approx. Towing Capacity	Gross Vehicle Weight Rating	Average Curb Weight
Cruise Master	1996	MHA	36	3411W -sl	FO	7.5L	G	$1800	228	8,000	17,000	15,450

Livability Code: SB 30-90
Wheelbase-to-length ratio of 53% is considered ○ dangerous ◉ fatiguing ○ good ○ excellent *
The approximate net payload of 1550 pounds at 9% of GVWR on this model is ○ deficient ○ excessive ◉ cautionary ○ good ○ excellent *
Total highway safety penalties are: 5 *   Value: 8 3   Durability: 7 6   Highway Control Rating: 5 5   Highway Safety: 5 0   ★

Brand	Year	Type	Length	Model	Chassis	Engine	Fuel Type	Average Price per Linear Foot When New	Adjusted Wheelbase	Approx. Towing Capacity	Gross Vehicle Weight Rating	Average Curb Weight
Cruise Master	1996	MHA	36	3412W	SP	CU210	D	$2800	208	1,500	18,000	15,400

Livability Code: SB 30-90
Wheelbase-to-length ratio of 49% is considered ◉ dangerous ○ fatiguing ○ good ○ excellent *
The approximate net payload of 2600 pounds at 14% of GVWR on this model is ○ deficient ○ excessive ○ cautionary ◉ good ○ excellent *
Total highway safety penalties are: 2 *   Value: 8 4   Durability: 7 6   Highway Control Rating: 3 6   Highway Safety: 3 4

Brand	Year	Type	Length	Model	Chassis	Engine	Fuel Type	Average Price per Linear Foot When New	Adjusted Wheelbase	Approx. Towing Capacity	Gross Vehicle Weight Rating	Average Curb Weight
Cruise Master	1996	MHA	36	3595W	CH	7.4L	G	$1700	228	1,500	16,500	14,668

Livability Code: SB 30-90
Wheelbase-to-length ratio of 53% is considered ○ dangerous ◉ fatiguing ○ good ○ excellent *
The approximate net payload of 1833 pounds at 11% of GVWR on this model is ○ deficient ○ excessive ○ cautionary ◉ good ○ excellent *
Total highway safety penalties are: 8 *   Value: 8 2   Durability: 7 6   Highway Control Rating: 5 9   Highway Safety: 5 1   ★

Brand	Year	Type	Length	Model	Chassis	Engine	Fuel Type	Average Price per Linear Foot When New	Adjusted Wheelbase	Approx. Towing Capacity	Gross Vehicle Weight Rating	Average Curb Weight
Cruise Master	1996	MHA	36	3595W -sl	CH	7.4L	G	$1800	228	1,500	16,500	15,175

Livability Code: SB 30-90
Wheelbase-to-length ratio of 53% is considered ○ dangerous ◉ fatiguing ○ good ○ excellent *
The approximate net payload of 1325 pounds at 8% of GVWR on this model is ○ deficient ○ excessive ◉ cautionary ○ good ○ excellent *
Total highway safety penalties are: 10 *   Value: 8 0   Durability: 7 6   Highway Control Rating: 4 6   Highway Safety: 3 6

Brand	Year	Type	Length	Model	Chassis	Engine	Fuel Type	Average Price per Linear Foot When New	Adjusted Wheelbase	Approx. Towing Capacity	Gross Vehicle Weight Rating	Average Curb Weight
Cruise Master	1996	MHA	36	3595W	FO	7.5L	G	$1700	228	8,000	17,000	15,125

Livability Code: SB 30-90
Wheelbase-to-length ratio of 53% is considered ○ dangerous ◉ fatiguing ○ good ○ excellent *
The approximate net payload of 1875 pounds at 11% of GVWR on this model is ○ deficient ○ excessive ○ cautionary ◉ good ○ excellent *
Total highway safety penalties are: 2 *   Value: 8 4   Durability: 7 6   Highway Control Rating: 5 9   Highway Safety: 5 7   ★

Note: Safety ratings are based on the assumption that the engineering of the RV has allowed for proper balance by placing fresh, gray, and black holding tanks in a location so as not to change the balance of the RV when the tanks are empty or full. **Always double-check wheelbase, GVWR, and weights at front and rear axles.**

*See Section 1 for details on how conclusions are reached.

Brand	Year	Type	Length	Model	Chassis	Engine	Fuel Type	Average Price per Linear Foot When New	Adjusted Wheelbase	Approx. Towing Capacity	Gross Vehicle Weight Rating	Average Curb Weight

Cruise Master 1996 MHA 36 3595W -sl FO 7.5L G $1800 228 8,000 17,000 15,575
Livability Code: SB 30-90
Wheelbase-to-length ratio of 53% is considered ○ dangerous ● fatiguing ○ good ○ excellent *
The approximate net payload of 1425 pounds at 8% of GVWR on this model is ○ deficient ○ excessive ● cautionary ○ good ○ excellent *
Total highway safety penalties are: 5 * Value: 8 3 Durability: 7 6 Highway Control Rating: 4 7 Highway Safety: 4 2

Cruise Master 1997 MHA 30 2808W CH 7.4L G $1900 178 1,500 14,800 12,910
Livability Code: SB 30-90
Wheelbase-to-length ratio of 50% is considered ● dangerous ○ fatiguing ○ good ○ excellent *
The approximate net payload of 1890 pounds at 13% of GVWR on this model is ○ deficient ○ excessive ○ cautionary ● good ○ excellent *
Total highway safety penalties are: 4 * Value: 8 3 Durability: 7 6 Highway Control Rating: 3 8 Highway Safety: 3 4

Cruise Master 1997 MHA 30 2808W opsl CH 7.4L G $2000 178 1,500 16,500 13,485
Livability Code: SB 30-90
Wheelbase-to-length ratio of 50% is considered ● dangerous ○ fatiguing ○ good ○ excellent *
The approximate net payload of 3015 pounds at 18% of GVWR on this model is ○ deficient ○ excessive ○ cautionary ○ good ● excellent *
Total highway safety penalties are: 7 * Value: 8 2 Durability: 7 6 Highway Control Rating: 4 7 Highway Safety: 4 0

Cruise Master 1997 MHA 30 2808W FO 7.5L G $1900 178 1,500 15,200 13,325
Livability Code: SB 30-90
Wheelbase-to-length ratio of 50% is considered ● dangerous ○ fatiguing ○ good ○ excellent *
The approximate net payload of 1875 pounds at 12% of GVWR on this model is ○ deficient ○ excessive ○ cautionary ● good ○ excellent *
Total highway safety penalties are: 2 * Value: 8 4 Durability: 7 6 Highway Control Rating: 3 7 Highway Safety: 3 5

Cruise Master 1997 MHA 30 2808W opsl FO 7.5L G $2000 178 1,500 17,000 13,975
Livability Code: SB 30-90
Wheelbase-to-length ratio of 50% is considered ● dangerous ○ fatiguing ○ good ○ excellent *
The approximate net payload of 3025 pounds at 18% of GVWR on this model is ○ deficient ○ excessive ○ cautionary ○ good ● excellent *
Total highway safety penalties are: 5 * Value: 8 3 Durability: 7 6 Highway Control Rating: 4 6 Highway Safety: 4 1

Cruise Master 1997 MHA 32 2995W CH 7.4L G $1800 190 1,500 14,800 13,258
Livability Code: SB 30-90
Wheelbase-to-length ratio of 50% is considered ● dangerous ○ fatiguing ○ good ○ excellent *
The approximate net payload of 1543 pounds at 10% of GVWR on this model is ○ deficient ○ excessive ○ cautionary ● good ○ excellent *
Total highway safety penalties are: 5 * Value: 8 3 Durability: 7 6 Highway Control Rating: 3 3 Highway Safety: 2 8

Cruise Master 1997 MHA 32 2995W opsl CH 7.4L G $1900 190 1,500 16,500 13,833
Livability Code: SB 30-90
Wheelbase-to-length ratio of 50% is considered ● dangerous ○ fatiguing ○ good ○ excellent *
The approximate net payload of 2668 pounds at 16% of GVWR on this model is ○ deficient ○ excessive ○ cautionary ○ good ● excellent *
Total highway safety penalties are: 8 * Value: 8 1 Durability: 7 6 Highway Control Rating: 4 5 Highway Safety: 3 7

Cruise Master 1997 MHA 32 2995W FO 7.5L G $1800 190 1,500 15,200 13,825
Livability Code: SB 30-90
Wheelbase-to-length ratio of 50% is considered ● dangerous ○ fatiguing ○ good ○ excellent *
The approximate net payload of 1375 pounds at 9% of GVWR on this model is ○ deficient ○ excessive ● cautionary ○ good ○ excellent *
Total highway safety penalties are: 2 * Value: 8 4 Durability: 7 6 Highway Control Rating: 2 8 Highway Safety: 2 6

Cruise Master 1997 MHA 32 2995W opsl FO 7.5L G $1900 190 1,500 17,000 14,475
Livability Code: SB 30-90
Wheelbase-to-length ratio of 50% is considered ● dangerous ○ fatiguing ○ good ○ excellent *
The approximate net payload of 2525 pounds at 15% of GVWR on this model is ○ deficient ○ excessive ○ cautionary ● good ○ excellent *
Total highway safety penalties are: 5 * Value: 8 3 Durability: 7 6 Highway Control Rating: 4 2 Highway Safety: 3 7

Cruise Master 1997 MHA 34 3190w CH 7.4L G $1800 212 1,500 14,800 13,870
Livability Code: SB 30-90
Wheelbase-to-length ratio of 52% is considered ○ dangerous ● fatiguing ○ good ○ excellent *
The approximate net payload of 930 pounds at 6% of GVWR on this model is ● deficient ○ excessive ○ cautionary ○ good ○ excellent *
Total highway safety penalties are: 6 * Value: 8 2 Durability: 7 6 Highway Control Rating: 2 6 Highway Safety: 2 0

Cruise Master 1997 MHA 34 3190W opsl CH 7.4L G $1900 212 1,500 16,500 14,445
Livability Code: SB 30-90
Wheelbase-to-length ratio of 52% is considered ○ dangerous ● fatiguing ○ good ○ excellent *
The approximate net payload of 2055 pounds at 12% of GVWR on this model is ○ deficient ○ excessive ○ cautionary ● good ○ excellent *
Total highway safety penalties are: 9 * Value: 8 1 Durability: 7 6 Highway Control Rating: 5 3 Highway Safety: 4 4

Cruise Master 1997 MHA 34 3190W FO 7.5L G $1800 212 1,500 17,000 14,525
Livability Code: SB 30-90
Wheelbase-to-length ratio of 52% is considered ○ dangerous ● fatiguing ○ good ○ excellent *
The approximate net payload of 2475 pounds at 15% of GVWR on this model is ○ deficient ○ excessive ○ cautionary ● good ○ excellent *
Total highway safety penalties are: 2 * Value: 8 4 Durability: 7 6 Highway Control Rating: 5 8 Highway Safety: 5 6 ★

Note: Safety ratings are based on the assumption that the engineering of the RV has allowed for proper balance by placing fresh, gray, and black holding tanks in a location so as not to change the balance of the RV when the tanks are empty or full. **Always double-check wheelbase, GVWR, and weights at front and rear axles.**

*See Section 1 for details on how conclusions are reached.

Section 2: The Ratings

Brand	Year	Type	Length	Model	Chassis	Engine	Fuel Type	Average Price per Linear Foot When New	Adjusted Wheelbase	Approx. Towing Capacity	Gross Vehicle Weight Rating	Average Curb Weight
Cruise Master	1997	MHA	34	3190W opsl	FO	7.5L	G	$1900	212	1,500	17,000	14,975

Livability Code: SB 30-90
Wheelbase-to-length ratio of 52% is considered ○ dangerous ◉ fatiguing ○ good ○ excellent*
The approximate net payload of 2025 pounds at 12% of GVWR on this model is ○ deficient ○ excessive ○ cautionary ◉ good ○ excellent*
Total highway safety penalties are: 5*   Value: 83 Durability: 76 Highway Control Rating: 53 Highway Safety: 48

Brand	Year	Type	Length	Model	Chassis	Engine	Fuel Type	Avg Price/ft	Adj Wheelbase	Towing	GVWR	Curb Wt
Cruise Master	1997	MHA	34	3190W	SP	CU210	D	$2900	190	1,500	18,000	15,050

Livability Code: SB 30-90
Wheelbase-to-length ratio of 46% is considered ◉ dangerous ○ fatiguing ○ good ○ excellent*
The approximate net payload of 2950 pounds at 16% of GVWR on this model is ○ deficient ○ excessive ○ cautionary ○ good ◉ excellent*
Total highway safety penalties are: 2*   Value: 84 Durability: 76 Highway Control Rating: 32 Highway Safety: 30

Brand	Year	Type	Length	Model	Chassis	Engine	Fuel Type	Avg Price/ft	Adj Wheelbase	Towing	GVWR	Curb Wt
Cruise Master	1997	MHA	34	3190W opsl	SP	CU210	D	$2900	190	1,500	18,000	15,500

Livability Code: SB 30-90
Wheelbase-to-length ratio of 46% is considered ◉ dangerous ○ fatiguing ○ good ○ excellent*
The approximate net payload of 2500 pounds at 14% of GVWR on this model is ○ deficient ○ excessive ○ cautionary ◉ good ○ excellent*
Total highway safety penalties are: 5*   Value: 83 Durability: 76 Highway Control Rating: 27 Highway Safety: 22

Brand	Year	Type	Length	Model	Chassis	Engine	Fuel Type	Avg Price/ft	Adj Wheelbase	Towing	GVWR	Curb Wt
Cruise Master	1997	MHA	35	3412W	CH	7.4L	G	$1800	228	1,500	16,500	14,455

Livability Code: SB 30-90
Wheelbase-to-length ratio of 54% is considered ○ dangerous ○ fatiguing ◉ good ○ excellent*
The approximate net payload of 2045 pounds at 12% of GVWR on this model is ○ deficient ○ excessive ○ cautionary ◉ good ○ excellent*
Total highway safety penalties are: 7*   Value: 82 Durability: 76 Highway Control Rating: 77 Highway Safety: 70 ★★★

Brand	Year	Type	Length	Model	Chassis	Engine	Fuel Type	Avg Price/ft	Adj Wheelbase	Towing	GVWR	Curb Wt
Cruise Master	1997	MHA	35	3412W opsl	CH	7.4L	G	$1800	220	1,500	16,500	15,189

Livability Code: SB 30-90
Wheelbase-to-length ratio of 52% is considered ○ dangerous ◉ fatiguing ○ good ○ excellent*
The approximate net payload of 1312 pounds at 8% of GVWR on this model is ○ deficient ○ excessive ◉ cautionary ○ good ○ excellent*
Total highway safety penalties are: 13*   Value: 79 Durability: 76 Highway Control Rating: 36 Highway Safety: 23

Brand	Year	Type	Length	Model	Chassis	Engine	Fuel Type	Avg Price/ft	Adj Wheelbase	Towing	GVWR	Curb Wt
Cruise Master	1997	MHA	35	3412W	FO	7.5L	G	$1800	228	1,500	17,000	14,925

Livability Code: SB 30-90
Wheelbase-to-length ratio of 54% is considered ○ dangerous ○ fatiguing ◉ good ○ excellent*
The approximate net payload of 2075 pounds at 12% of GVWR on this model is ○ deficient ○ excessive ○ cautionary ◉ good ○ excellent*
Total highway safety penalties are: 2*   Value: 84 Durability: 76 Highway Control Rating: 77 Highway Safety: 75 ★★★

Brand	Year	Type	Length	Model	Chassis	Engine	Fuel Type	Avg Price/ft	Adj Wheelbase	Towing	GVWR	Curb Wt
Cruise Master	1997	MHA	35	3412W opsl	FO	7.5L	G	$1800	220	1,500	17,000	15,825

Livability Code: SB 30-90
Wheelbase-to-length ratio of 52% is considered ○ dangerous ◉ fatiguing ○ good ○ excellent*
The approximate net payload of 1175 pounds at 7% of GVWR on this model is ○ deficient ○ excessive ◉ cautionary ○ good ○ excellent*
Total highway safety penalties are: 7*   Value: 82 Durability: 76 Highway Control Rating: 30 Highway Safety: 23

Brand	Year	Type	Length	Model	Chassis	Engine	Fuel Type	Avg Price/ft	Adj Wheelbase	Towing	GVWR	Curb Wt
Cruise Master	1997	MHA	35	3415W	CH	7.4L	G	$1800	228	1,500	16,500	14,673

Livability Code: SB 30-90
Wheelbase-to-length ratio of 54% is considered ○ dangerous ○ fatiguing ◉ good ○ excellent*
The approximate net payload of 1827 pounds at 11% of GVWR on this model is ○ deficient ○ excessive ○ cautionary ◉ good ○ excellent*
Total highway safety penalties are: 7*   Value: 82 Durability: 76 Highway Control Rating: 75 Highway Safety: 68 ★★

Brand	Year	Type	Length	Model	Chassis	Engine	Fuel Type	Avg Price/ft	Adj Wheelbase	Towing	GVWR	Curb Wt
Cruise Master	1997	MHA	35	3415W opsl	CH	7.4L	G	$1800	220	1,500	16,500	15,455

Livability Code: SB 30-90
Wheelbase-to-length ratio of 52% is considered ○ dangerous ◉ fatiguing ○ good ○ excellent*
The approximate net payload of 1045 pounds at 6% of GVWR on this model is ◉ deficient ○ excessive ○ cautionary ○ good ○ excellent*
Total highway safety penalties are: 13*   Value: 79 Durability: 76 Highway Control Rating: 24 Highway Safety: 11

Brand	Year	Type	Length	Model	Chassis	Engine	Fuel Type	Avg Price/ft	Adj Wheelbase	Towing	GVWR	Curb Wt
Cruise Master	1997	MHA	35	3415W	FO	7.5L	G	$1800	228	1,500	17,000	14,950

Livability Code: SB 30-90
Wheelbase-to-length ratio of 54% is considered ○ dangerous ○ fatiguing ◉ good ○ excellent*
The approximate net payload of 2050 pounds at 12% of GVWR on this model is ○ deficient ○ excessive ○ cautionary ◉ good ○ excellent*
Total highway safety penalties are: 2*   Value: 84 Durability: 76 Highway Control Rating: 76 Highway Safety: 74 ★★★

Brand	Year	Type	Length	Model	Chassis	Engine	Fuel Type	Avg Price/ft	Adj Wheelbase	Towing	GVWR	Curb Wt
Cruise Master	1997	MHA	35	3415W opsl	FO	7.5L	G	$1800	220	1,500	17,000	15,850

Livability Code: SB 30-90
Wheelbase-to-length ratio of 52% is considered ○ dangerous ◉ fatiguing ○ good ○ excellent*
The approximate net payload of 1150 pounds at 7% of GVWR on this model is ○ deficient ○ excessive ◉ cautionary ○ good ○ excellent*
Total highway safety penalties are: 7*   Value: 82 Durability: 76 Highway Control Rating: 29 Highway Safety: 22

Brand	Year	Type	Length	Model	Chassis	Engine	Fuel Type	Avg Price/ft	Adj Wheelbase	Towing	GVWR	Curb Wt
Cruise Master	1997	MHA	36	3595W	CH	7.4L	G	$1700	228	1,500	16,500	14,668

Livability Code: SB 30-90
Wheelbase-to-length ratio of 53% is considered ○ dangerous ◉ fatiguing ○ good ○ excellent*
The approximate net payload of 1833 pounds at 11% of GVWR on this model is ○ deficient ○ excessive ○ cautionary ◉ good ○ excellent*
Total highway safety penalties are: 8*   Value: 82 Durability: 76 Highway Control Rating: 59 Highway Safety: 51 ★

Note: Safety ratings are based on the assumption that the engineering of the RV has allowed for proper balance by placing fresh, gray, and black holding tanks in a location so as not to change the balance of the RV when the tanks are empty or full. **Always double-check wheelbase, GVWR, and weights at front and rear axles.**

*See Section 1 for details on how conclusions are reached.

Brand	Year	Type	Length	Model	Chassis	Engine	Fuel Type	Average Price per Linear Foot When New	Adjusted Wheelbase	Approx. Towing Capacity	Gross Vehicle Weight Rating	Average Curb Weight
Cruise Master	1997	MHA	36	3595 W opsl	CH	7.4L	G	$1800	228	1,500	16,500	15,137

Livability Code: SB 30-90
Wheelbase-to-length ratio of 53% is considered ○ dangerous ◉ fatiguing ○ good ○ excellent *
The approximate net payload of 1363 pounds at 8% of GVWR on this model is ○ deficient ○ excessive ◉ cautionary ○ good ○ excellent *
Total highway safety penalties are: 11 * Value: 8 0 Durability: 7 6 Highway Control Rating: 4 6 Highway Safety: 3 5

Brand	Year	Type	Length	Model	Chassis	Engine	Fuel Type	Avg Price/Ft	Wheelbase	Towing	GVWR	Curb Weight
Cruise Master	1997	MHA	36	3595W	FO	7.5L	G	$1700	228	1,500	17,000	15,125

Livability Code: SB 30-90
Wheelbase-to-length ratio of 53% is considered ○ dangerous ◉ fatiguing ○ good ○ excellent *
The approximate net payload of 1875 pounds at 11% of GVWR on this model is ○ deficient ○ excessive ○ cautionary ◉ good ○ excellent *
Total highway safety penalties are: 2 * Value: 8 4 Durability: 7 6 Highway Control Rating: 5 9 Highway Safety: 5 7 ★

Brand	Year	Type	Length	Model	Chassis	Engine	Fuel Type	Avg Price/Ft	Wheelbase	Towing	GVWR	Curb Weight
Cruise Master	1997	MHA	36	3595W opsl	FO	7.5L	G	$1800	228	1,500	17,000	15,650

Livability Code: SB 30-90
Wheelbase-to-length ratio of 53% is considered ○ dangerous ◉ fatiguing ○ good ○ excellent *
The approximate net payload of 1350 pounds at 8% of GVWR on this model is ○ deficient ○ excessive ◉ cautionary ○ good ○ excellent *
Total highway safety penalties are: 5 * Value: 8 3 Durability: 7 6 Highway Control Rating: 4 6 Highway Safety: 4 1

Brand	Year	Type	Length	Model	Chassis	Engine	Fuel Type	Avg Price/Ft	Wheelbase	Towing	GVWR	Curb Weight
Cruise Master	1998	MHA	30	2908	CH	7.4L	G	$2000	178	4,200	14,800	12,623

Livability Code: SB 30-90
Wheelbase-to-length ratio of 50% is considered ◉ dangerous ○ fatiguing ○ good ○ excellent *
The approximate net payload of 2177 pounds at 15% of GVWR on this model is ○ deficient ○ excessive ○ cautionary ◉ good ○ excellent *
Total highway safety penalties are: 4 * Value: 8 3 Durability: 7 6 Highway Control Rating: 4 3 Highway Safety: 3 9

Brand	Year	Type	Length	Model	Chassis	Engine	Fuel Type	Avg Price/Ft	Wheelbase	Towing	GVWR	Curb Weight
Cruise Master	1998	MHA	30	2908 slide	CH	7.4L	G	$2000	178	4,500	16,500	13,563

Livability Code: SB 30-90
Wheelbase-to-length ratio of 50% is considered ◉ dangerous ○ fatiguing ○ good ○ excellent *
The approximate net payload of 2937 pounds at 18% of GVWR on this model is ○ deficient ○ excessive ○ cautionary ○ good ◉ excellent *
Total highway safety penalties are: 10 * Value: 8 1 Durability: 7 6 Highway Control Rating: 4 7 Highway Safety: 3 7

Brand	Year	Type	Length	Model	Chassis	Engine	Fuel Type	Avg Price/Ft	Wheelbase	Towing	GVWR	Curb Weight
Cruise Master	1998	MHA	30	2908	FO	7.5L	G	$2000	178	9,800	15,200	13,206

Livability Code: SB 30-90
Wheelbase-to-length ratio of 50% is considered ◉ dangerous ○ fatiguing ○ good ○ excellent *
The approximate net payload of 1995 pounds at 13% of GVWR on this model is ○ deficient ○ excessive ○ cautionary ◉ good ○ excellent *
Total highway safety penalties are: 2 * Value: 8 4 Durability: 7 6 Highway Control Rating: 4 0 Highway Safety: 3 8

Brand	Year	Type	Length	Model	Chassis	Engine	Fuel Type	Avg Price/Ft	Wheelbase	Towing	GVWR	Curb Weight
Cruise Master	1998	MHA	30	2908 slide	FO	7.5L	G	$2000	178	8,000	17,000	13,986

Livability Code: SB 30-90
Wheelbase-to-length ratio of 50% is considered ◉ dangerous ○ fatiguing ○ good ○ excellent *
The approximate net payload of 3015 pounds at 18% of GVWR on this model is ○ deficient ○ excessive ○ cautionary ○ good ◉ excellent *
Total highway safety penalties are: 7 * Value: 8 2 Durability: 7 6 Highway Control Rating: 4 7 Highway Safety: 4 0

Brand	Year	Type	Length	Model	Chassis	Engine	Fuel Type	Avg Price/Ft	Wheelbase	Towing	GVWR	Curb Weight
Cruise Master	1998	MHA	32	3195	CH	7.4L	G	$1900	190	4,200	14,800	13,213

Livability Code: SB 30-90
Wheelbase-to-length ratio of 50% is considered ◉ dangerous ○ fatiguing ○ good ○ excellent *
The approximate net payload of 1587 pounds at 11% of GVWR on this model is ○ deficient ○ excessive ○ cautionary ◉ good ○ excellent *
Total highway safety penalties are: 5 * Value: 8 3 Durability: 7 6 Highway Control Rating: 3 5 Highway Safety: 3 0

Brand	Year	Type	Length	Model	Chassis	Engine	Fuel Type	Avg Price/Ft	Wheelbase	Towing	GVWR	Curb Weight
Cruise Master	1998	MHA	32	3195 slide	CH	7.4L	G	$1900	190	4,500	16,500	14,153

Livability Code: SB 30-90
Wheelbase-to-length ratio of 50% is considered ◉ dangerous ○ fatiguing ○ good ○ excellent *
The approximate net payload of 2347 pounds at 14% of GVWR on this model is ○ deficient ○ excessive ○ cautionary ◉ good ○ excellent *
Total highway safety penalties are: 11 * Value: 8 0 Durability: 7 6 Highway Control Rating: 4 1 Highway Safety: 3 0

Brand	Year	Type	Length	Model	Chassis	Engine	Fuel Type	Avg Price/Ft	Wheelbase	Towing	GVWR	Curb Weight
Cruise Master	1998	MHA	32	3195	FO	7.5L	G	$1900	190	9,800	15,200	13,828

Livability Code: SB 30-90
Wheelbase-to-length ratio of 50% is considered ◉ dangerous ○ fatiguing ○ good ○ excellent *
The approximate net payload of 1372 pounds at 9% of GVWR on this model is ○ deficient ○ excessive ◉ cautionary ○ good ○ excellent *
Total highway safety penalties are: 2 * Value: 8 4 Durability: 7 6 Highway Control Rating: 2 8 Highway Safety: 2 6

Brand	Year	Type	Length	Model	Chassis	Engine	Fuel Type	Avg Price/Ft	Wheelbase	Towing	GVWR	Curb Weight
Cruise Master	1998	MHA	32	3195 slide	FO	7.5L	G	$1900	190	8,000	17,000	14,648

Livability Code: SB 30-90
Wheelbase-to-length ratio of 50% is considered ◉ dangerous ○ fatiguing ○ good ○ excellent *
The approximate net payload of 2352 pounds at 14% of GVWR on this model is ○ deficient ○ excessive ○ cautionary ◉ good ○ excellent *
Total highway safety penalties are: 7 * Value: 8 2 Durability: 7 6 Highway Control Rating: 4 1 Highway Safety: 3 4

Brand	Year	Type	Length	Model	Chassis	Engine	Fuel Type	Avg Price/Ft	Wheelbase	Towing	GVWR	Curb Weight
Cruise Master	1998	MHA	34	3390	CH	7.4L	G	$1800	212	4,200	14,800	13,718

Livability Code: SB 30-90
Wheelbase-to-length ratio of 53% is considered ○ dangerous ◉ fatiguing ○ good ○ excellent *
The approximate net payload of 1082 pounds at 7% of GVWR on this model is ○ deficient ○ excessive ◉ cautionary ○ good ○ excellent *
Total highway safety penalties are: 6 * Value: 8 2 Durability: 7 6 Highway Control Rating: 4 0 Highway Safety: 3 4

Note: Safety ratings are based on the assumption that the engineering of the RV has allowed for proper balance by placing fresh, gray, and black holding tanks in a location so as not to change the balance of the RV when the tanks are empty or full. **Always double-check wheelbase, GVWR, and weights at front and rear axles.**

*See Section 1 for details on how conclusions are reached.

Section 2: The Ratings

Brand	Year	Type	Length	Model	Chassis	Engine	Fuel Type	Average Price per Linear Foot When New	Adjusted Wheelbase	Approx. Towing Capacity	Gross Vehicle Weight Rating	Average Curb Weight
Cruise Master	1998	MHA	34	3390 slide	CH	7.4L	G	$1800	212	4,500	16,500	14,433

Livability Code: SB 30-90 — Wheelbase-to-length ratio of 53% is considered ○ dangerous ◉ fatiguing ○ good ○ excellent *
The approximate net payload of 2067 pounds at 13% of GVWR on this model is ○ deficient ○ excessive ○ cautionary ◉ good ○ excellent *
Total highway safety penalties are: 9 * — Value: 8 1 — Durability: 7 6 — Highway Control Rating: 6 2 — Highway Safety: 5 3 — ★

Brand	Year	Type	Length	Model	Chassis	Engine	Fuel Type	Avg Price/Lin Ft	Adj Wheelbase	Towing Cap	GVWR	Avg Curb Wt
Cruise Master	1998	MHA	34	3390	FO	7.5L	G	$1800	212	8,000	17,000	14,408

Livability Code: SB 30-90 — Wheelbase-to-length ratio of 53% is considered ○ dangerous ◉ fatiguing ○ good ○ excellent *
The approximate net payload of 2592 pounds at 15% of GVWR on this model is ○ deficient ○ excessive ○ cautionary ◉ good ○ excellent *
Total highway safety penalties are: 2 * — Value: 8 4 — Durability: 7 6 — Highway Control Rating: 6 7 — Highway Safety: 6 5 — ★★

Brand	Year	Type	Length	Model	Chassis	Engine	Fuel Type	Avg Price/Lin Ft	Adj Wheelbase	Towing Cap	GVWR	Avg Curb Wt
Cruise Master	1998	MHA	34	3390 slide	FO	7.5L	G	$1800	212	8,000	17,000	15,078

Livability Code: SB 30-90 — Wheelbase-to-length ratio of 53% is considered ○ dangerous ◉ fatiguing ○ good ○ excellent *
The approximate net payload of 1922 pounds at 11% of GVWR on this model is ○ deficient ○ excessive ○ cautionary ◉ good ○ excellent *
Total highway safety penalties are: 7 * — Value: 8 2 — Durability: 7 6 — Highway Control Rating: 5 9 — Highway Safety: 5 2 — ★

Brand	Year	Type	Length	Model	Chassis	Engine	Fuel Type	Avg Price/Lin Ft	Adj Wheelbase	Towing Cap	GVWR	Avg Curb Wt
Cruise Master	1998	MHA	35	3590	FR	CU230	D	$2900	190	5,000	20,500	16,843

Livability Code: SB 30-90 — Wheelbase-to-length ratio of 46% is considered ◉ dangerous ○ fatiguing ○ good ○ excellent *
The approximate net payload of 3658 pounds at 18% of GVWR on this model is ○ deficient ○ excessive ○ cautionary ○ good ◉ excellent *
Total highway safety penalties are: 2 * — Value: 8 4 — Durability: 7 6 — Highway Control Rating: 3 1 — Highway Safety: 2 9

Brand	Year	Type	Length	Model	Chassis	Engine	Fuel Type	Avg Price/Lin Ft	Adj Wheelbase	Towing Cap	GVWR	Avg Curb Wt
Cruise Master	1998	MHA	35	3512	CH	7.4L	G	$1700	228	4,500	16,500	14,503

Livability Code: SB 30-90 — Wheelbase-to-length ratio of 54% is considered ○ dangerous ○ fatiguing ◉ good ○ excellent *
The approximate net payload of 1997 pounds at 12% of GVWR on this model is ○ deficient ○ excessive ○ cautionary ◉ good ○ excellent *
Total highway safety penalties are: 7 * — Value: 8 2 — Durability: 7 6 — Highway Control Rating: 7 6 — Highway Safety: 6 9 — ★★

Brand	Year	Type	Length	Model	Chassis	Engine	Fuel Type	Avg Price/Lin Ft	Adj Wheelbase	Towing Cap	GVWR	Avg Curb Wt
Cruise Master	1998	MHA	35	3512 slide	CH	7.4L	G	$1700	220	4,500	16,500	15,288

Livability Code: SB 30-90 — Wheelbase-to-length ratio of 52% is considered ○ dangerous ◉ fatiguing ○ good ○ excellent *
The approximate net payload of 1212 pounds at 7% of GVWR on this model is ○ deficient ○ excessive ◉ cautionary ○ good ○ excellent *
Total highway safety penalties are: 13 * — Value: 7 9 — Durability: 7 6 — Highway Control Rating: 3 0 — Highway Safety: 1 7

Brand	Year	Type	Length	Model	Chassis	Engine	Fuel Type	Avg Price/Lin Ft	Adj Wheelbase	Towing Cap	GVWR	Avg Curb Wt
Cruise Master	1998	MHA	35	3515	CH	7.4L	G	$1700	228	4,500	16,500	14,620

Livability Code: SB 30-90 — Wheelbase-to-length ratio of 54% is considered ○ dangerous ○ fatiguing ◉ good ○ excellent *
The approximate net payload of 1880 pounds at 11% of GVWR on this model is ○ deficient ○ excessive ○ cautionary ◉ good ○ excellent *
Total highway safety penalties are: 7 * — Value: 8 2 — Durability: 7 6 — Highway Control Rating: 7 6 — Highway Safety: 6 9 — ★★

Brand	Year	Type	Length	Model	Chassis	Engine	Fuel Type	Avg Price/Lin Ft	Adj Wheelbase	Towing Cap	GVWR	Avg Curb Wt
Cruise Master	1998	MHA	35	3515 slide	CH	7.4L	G	$1700	220	4,500	16,500	15,308

Livability Code: SB 30-90 — Wheelbase-to-length ratio of 52% is considered ○ dangerous ◉ fatiguing ○ good ○ excellent *
The approximate net payload of 1193 pounds at 7% of GVWR on this model is ○ deficient ○ excessive ◉ cautionary ○ good ○ excellent *
Total highway safety penalties are: 13 * — Value: 7 9 — Durability: 7 6 — Highway Control Rating: 3 0 — Highway Safety: 1 7

Brand	Year	Type	Length	Model	Chassis	Engine	Fuel Type	Avg Price/Lin Ft	Adj Wheelbase	Towing Cap	GVWR	Avg Curb Wt
Cruise Master	1998	MHA	35	3512	FO	7.5L	G	$1700	228	8,000	17,000	14,891

Livability Code: SB 30-90 — Wheelbase-to-length ratio of 54% is considered ○ dangerous ○ fatiguing ◉ good ○ excellent *
The approximate net payload of 2110 pounds at 12% of GVWR on this model is ○ deficient ○ excessive ○ cautionary ◉ good ○ excellent *
Total highway safety penalties are: 2 * — Value: 8 4 — Durability: 7 6 — Highway Control Rating: 7 7 — Highway Safety: 7 5 — ★★★

Brand	Year	Type	Length	Model	Chassis	Engine	Fuel Type	Avg Price/Lin Ft	Adj Wheelbase	Towing Cap	GVWR	Avg Curb Wt
Cruise Master	1998	MHA	35	3512 slide	FO	7.5L	G	$1700	220	8,000	17,000	15,666

Livability Code: SB 30-90 — Wheelbase-to-length ratio of 52% is considered ○ dangerous ◉ fatiguing ○ good ○ excellent *
The approximate net payload of 1335 pounds at 8% of GVWR on this model is ○ deficient ○ excessive ◉ cautionary ○ good ○ excellent *
Total highway safety penalties are: 7 * — Value: 8 2 — Durability: 7 6 — Highway Control Rating: 3 6 — Highway Safety: 2 9

Brand	Year	Type	Length	Model	Chassis	Engine	Fuel Type	Avg Price/Lin Ft	Adj Wheelbase	Towing Cap	GVWR	Avg Curb Wt
Cruise Master	1998	MHA	35	3515	FO	7.5L	G	$1700	228	8,000	17,000	14,880

Livability Code: SB 30-90 — Wheelbase-to-length ratio of 54% is considered ○ dangerous ○ fatiguing ◉ good ○ excellent *
The approximate net payload of 2120 pounds at 12% of GVWR on this model is ○ deficient ○ excessive ○ cautionary ◉ good ○ excellent *
Total highway safety penalties are: 2 * — Value: 8 4 — Durability: 7 6 — Highway Control Rating: 7 7 — Highway Safety: 7 5 — ★★★

Brand	Year	Type	Length	Model	Chassis	Engine	Fuel Type	Avg Price/Lin Ft	Adj Wheelbase	Towing Cap	GVWR	Avg Curb Wt
Cruise Master	1998	MHA	35	3515 slide	FO	7.5L	G	$1700	220	8,000	17,000	15,780

Livability Code: SB 30-90 — Wheelbase-to-length ratio of 52% is considered ○ dangerous ◉ fatiguing ○ good ○ excellent *
The approximate net payload of 1220 pounds at 7% of GVWR on this model is ○ deficient ○ excessive ◉ cautionary ○ good ○ excellent *
Total highway safety penalties are: 7 * — Value: 8 2 — Durability: 7 6 — Highway Control Rating: 3 0 — Highway Safety: 2 3

Note: Safety ratings are based on the assumption that the engineering of the RV has allowed for proper balance by placing fresh, gray, and black holding tanks in a location so as not to change the balance of the RV when the tanks are empty or full. **Always double-check wheelbase, GVWR, and weights at front and rear axles.**

*See Section 1 for details on how conclusions are reached.

Brand	Year	Type	Length	Model	Chassis	Engine	Fuel Type	Average Price per Linear Foot When New	Adjusted Wheelbase	Approx. Towing Capacity	Gross Vehicle Weight Rating	Average Curb Weight
Cruise Master	1999	MHA	33	3190 slide	CH	7.4L	G	$1800	212	4,500	16,500	14,758

Livability Code: SB 30-90
Wheelbase-to-length ratio of 53% is considered ○ dangerous ◉ fatiguing ○ good ○ excellent *
The approximate net payload of 1742 pounds at 11% of GVWR on this model is ○ deficient ○ excessive ○ cautionary ◉ good ○ excellent *
Total highway safety penalties are: 17 *   Value: 7 7   Durability: 7 6   Highway Control Rating: 6 5   Highway Safety: 4 8

| Cruise Master | 1999 | MHA | 33 | 3190 | CH | 7.4L | G | $1800 | 212 | 4,200 | 14,800 | 13,526 |

Livability Code: SB 30-90
Wheelbase-to-length ratio of 53% is considered ○ dangerous ◉ fatiguing ○ good ○ excellent *
The approximate net payload of 1274 pounds at 9% of GVWR on this model is ○ deficient ○ excessive ◉ cautionary ○ good ○ excellent *
Total highway safety penalties are: 6 *   Value: 8 2   Durability: 7 6   Highway Control Rating: 5 8   Highway Safety: 5 2   ★

| Cruise Master | 1999 | MHA | 33 | 3190 | FO | 6.8L | G | $1800 | 212 | 8,000 | 18,000 | 14,965 |

Livability Code: SB 30-90
Wheelbase-to-length ratio of 53% is considered ○ dangerous ◉ fatiguing ○ good ○ excellent *
The approximate net payload of 3035 pounds at 17% of GVWR on this model is ○ deficient ○ excessive ○ cautionary ○ good ◉ excellent *
Total highway safety penalties are: 2 *   Value: 8 4   Durability: 7 6   Highway Control Rating: 7 6   Highway Safety: 7 4   ★★★

| Cruise Master | 1999 | MHA | 33 | 3190 slide | FO | 6.8L | G | $1800 | 212 | 8,000 | 18,000 | 15,836 |

Livability Code: SB 30-90
Wheelbase-to-length ratio of 53% is considered ○ dangerous ◉ fatiguing ○ good ○ excellent *
The approximate net payload of 2164 pounds at 12% of GVWR on this model is ○ deficient ○ excessive ○ cautionary ◉ good ○ excellent *
Total highway safety penalties are: 6 *   Value: 8 3   Durability: 7 6   Highway Control Rating: 6 7   Highway Safety: 6 1   ★★

| Cruise Master | 1999 | MHA | 34 | 3215 | CH | 7.4L | G | $1800 | 212 | 4,500 | 16,500 | 14,758 |

Livability Code: SB 30-90
Wheelbase-to-length ratio of 53% is considered ○ dangerous ◉ fatiguing ○ good ○ excellent *
The approximate net payload of 1742 pounds at 11% of GVWR on this model is ○ deficient ○ excessive ○ cautionary ◉ good ○ excellent *
Total highway safety penalties are: 6 *   Value: 8 2   Durability: 7 6   Highway Control Rating: 6 4   Highway Safety: 5 8   ★

| Cruise Master | 1999 | MHA | 34 | 3215 | FO | 6.8L | G | $1800 | 212 | 8,000 | 18,000 | 15,836 |

Livability Code: SB 30-90
Wheelbase-to-length ratio of 53% is considered ○ dangerous ◉ fatiguing ○ good ○ excellent *
The approximate net payload of 2164 pounds at 12% of GVWR on this model is ○ deficient ○ excessive ○ cautionary ◉ good ○ excellent *
Total highway safety penalties are: 2 *   Value: 8 4   Durability: 7 6   Highway Control Rating: 6 7   Highway Safety: 6 5   ★★

| Cruise Master | 1999 | MHA | 34 | 3410 | FO | 6.8L | G | $1800 | 220 | 8,000 | 18,000 | 15,836 |

Livability Code: SB 30-90
Wheelbase-to-length ratio of 53% is considered ○ dangerous ◉ fatiguing ○ good ○ excellent *
The approximate net payload of 2164 pounds at 12% of GVWR on this model is ○ deficient ○ excessive ○ cautionary ◉ good ○ excellent *
Total highway safety penalties are: 12 *   Value: 7 9   Durability: 7 6   Highway Control Rating: 6 9   Highway Safety: 5 7   ★

| Cruise Master | 1999 | MHA | 35 | 3590 | FR | 275HP | D | $2900 | 190 | 5,000 | 24,850 | 18,875 |

Livability Code: SB 30-90
Wheelbase-to-length ratio of 46% is considered ◉ dangerous ○ fatiguing ○ good ○ excellent *
The approximate net payload of 5975 pounds at 24% of GVWR on this model is ○ deficient ○ excessive ○ cautionary ○ good ◉ excellent *
Total highway safety penalties are: 2 *   Value: 8 4   Durability: 7 6   Highway Control Rating: 3 9   Highway Safety: 3 7

| Cruise Master | 1999 | MHA | 36 | 3515 | CH | 7.4L | G | $1700 | 228 | 4,500 | 16,500 | 14,640 |

Livability Code: SB 30-90
Wheelbase-to-length ratio of 54% is considered ○ dangerous ○ fatiguing ◉ good ○ excellent *
The approximate net payload of 1860 pounds at 11% of GVWR on this model is ○ deficient ○ excessive ○ cautionary ◉ good ○ excellent *
Total highway safety penalties are: 7 *   Value: 8 2   Durability: 7 6   Highway Control Rating: 7 8   Highway Safety: 7 1   ★★★

| Cruise Master | 1999 | MHA | 36 | 3515 | FO | 6.8L | G | $1700 | 228 | 8,000 | 18,000 | 15,673 |

Livability Code: SB 30-90
Wheelbase-to-length ratio of 54% is considered ○ dangerous ○ fatiguing ◉ good ○ excellent *
The approximate net payload of 2327 pounds at 13% of GVWR on this model is ○ deficient ○ excessive ○ cautionary ◉ good ○ excellent *
Total highway safety penalties are: 2 *   Value: 8 4   Durability: 7 6   Highway Control Rating: 7 6   Highway Safety: 7 4   ★★★

| Cruise Master | 1999 | MHA | 36 | 3515 slide | FO | 6.8L | G | $1700 | 228 | 8,000 | 18,000 | 15,673 |

Livability Code: SB 30-90
Wheelbase-to-length ratio of 54% is considered ○ dangerous ○ fatiguing ◉ good ○ excellent *
The approximate net payload of 2327 pounds at 13% of GVWR on this model is ○ deficient ○ excessive ○ cautionary ◉ good ○ excellent *
Total highway safety penalties are: 12 *   Value: 7 9   Durability: 7 6   Highway Control Rating: 7 6   Highway Safety: 6 4   ★★

| Cruise Master | 1999 | MHA | 36 | 3610 | FR | 275HP | D | $2800 | 208 | 5,000 | 24,850 | 20,000 |

Livability Code: SB 30-90
Wheelbase-to-length ratio of 49% is considered ◉ dangerous ○ fatiguing ○ good ○ excellent *
The approximate net payload of 4850 pounds at 20% of GVWR on this model is ○ deficient ○ excessive ○ cautionary ○ good ◉ excellent *
Total highway safety penalties are: 12 *   Value: 7 9   Durability: 7 6   Highway Control Rating: 5 3   Highway Safety: 4 1

Note: Safety ratings are based on the assumption that the engineering of the RV has allowed for proper balance by placing fresh, gray, and black holding tanks in a location so as not to change the balance of the RV when the tanks are empty or full. **Always double-check wheelbase, GVWR, and weights at front and rear axles.**

*See Section 1 for details on how conclusions are reached.

Section 2: The Ratings

Brand	Year	Type	Length	Model	Chassis	Engine	Fuel Type	Average Price per Linear Foot When New	Adjusted Wheelbase	Approx. Towing Capacity	Gross Vehicle Weight Rating	Average Curb Weight
Cruise Master	1999	MHA	36	3510	FO	6.8L	G	$1700	228	8,000	18,000	15,860

Livability Code: SB 30-90
Wheelbase-to-length ratio of 53% is considered ○ dangerous ◉ fatiguing ○ good ○ excellent *
The approximate net payload of 2140 pounds at 12% of GVWR on this model is ○ deficient ○ excessive ○ cautionary ◉ good ○ excellent *
Total highway safety penalties are: 2 * Value: 8 4 Durability: 7 6 Highway Control Rating: 6 7 Highway Safety: 6 5 ★★

Brand	Year	Type	Length	Model	Chassis	Engine	Fuel Type	Price/Ft	Wheelbase	Towing	GVWR	Curb Wt
Cruise Master	1999	MHA	37	3620	CH	7.4L	G	$1600	228	4,500	16,500	14,825

Livability Code: SB 30-90
Wheelbase-to-length ratio of 52% is considered ○ dangerous ◉ fatiguing ○ good ○ excellent *
The approximate net payload of 1675 pounds at 10% of GVWR on this model is ○ deficient ○ excessive ○ cautionary ◉ good ○ excellent *
Total highway safety penalties are: 8 * Value: 8 2 Durability: 7 6 Highway Control Rating: 5 5 Highway Safety: 4 7

Brand	Year	Type	Length	Model	Chassis	Engine	Fuel Type	Price/Ft	Wheelbase	Towing	GVWR	Curb Wt
Cruise Master	1999	MHA	37	3620	FO	6.8L	G	$1600	228	8,000	18,000	15,756

Livability Code: SB 30-90
Wheelbase-to-length ratio of 52% is considered ○ dangerous ◉ fatiguing ○ good ○ excellent *
The approximate net payload of 2244 pounds at 12% of GVWR on this model is ○ deficient ○ excessive ○ cautionary ◉ good ○ excellent *
Total highway safety penalties are: 2 * Value: 8 4 Durability: 7 6 Highway Control Rating: 6 0 Highway Safety: 5 8 ★

Brand	Year	Type	Length	Model	Chassis	Engine	Fuel Type	Price/Ft	Wheelbase	Towing	GVWR	Curb Wt
Custom	1997	MHA	25	2501	CH	7.4L	G	$2100	158	4,700	12,300	10,766

Livability Code: SB 30-90
Wheelbase-to-length ratio of 53% is considered ○ dangerous ◉ fatiguing ○ good ○ excellent *
The approximate net payload of 1534 pounds at 12% of GVWR on this model is ○ deficient ○ excessive ○ cautionary ◉ good ○ excellent *
Total highway safety penalties are: 2 * Value: 7 9 Durability: 7 5 Highway Control Rating: 6 2 Highway Safety: 6 0 ★★

Brand	Year	Type	Length	Model	Chassis	Engine	Fuel Type	Price/Ft	Wheelbase	Towing	GVWR	Curb Wt
Custom	1997	MHA	28	2808	CH	7.4L	G	$2000	178	4,200	14,800	11,873

Livability Code: SB 30-90
Wheelbase-to-length ratio of 53% is considered ○ dangerous ◉ fatiguing ○ good ○ excellent *
The approximate net payload of 2928 pounds at 20% of GVWR on this model is ○ deficient ○ excessive ○ cautionary ○ good ◉ excellent *
Total highway safety penalties are: 4 * Value: 7 8 Durability: 7 5 Highway Control Rating: 7 4 Highway Safety: 7 0 ★★★

Brand	Year	Type	Length	Model	Chassis	Engine	Fuel Type	Price/Ft	Wheelbase	Towing	GVWR	Curb Wt
Custom	1997	MHA	28	2808	FO	7.5L	G	$2000	178	9,800	15,200	12,493

Livability Code: SB 30-90
Wheelbase-to-length ratio of 53% is considered ○ dangerous ◉ fatiguing ○ good ○ excellent *
The approximate net payload of 2707 pounds at 18% of GVWR on this model is ○ deficient ○ excessive ○ cautionary ○ good ◉ excellent *
Total highway safety penalties are: 2 * Value: 7 9 Durability: 7 5 Highway Control Rating: 7 2 Highway Safety: 7 0 ★★★

Brand	Year	Type	Length	Model	Chassis	Engine	Fuel Type	Price/Ft	Wheelbase	Towing	GVWR	Curb Wt
Custom	1997	MHA	29	2901	CH	7.4L	G	$1900	190	4,200	14,800	12,288

Livability Code: SB 30-90
Wheelbase-to-length ratio of 55% is considered ○ dangerous ○ fatiguing ◉ good ○ excellent *
The approximate net payload of 2512 pounds at 17% of GVWR on this model is ○ deficient ○ excessive ○ cautionary ○ good ◉ excellent *
Total highway safety penalties are: 4 * Value: 7 8 Durability: 7 5 Highway Control Rating: 9 2 Highway Safety: 8 8 ★★★

Brand	Year	Type	Length	Model	Chassis	Engine	Fuel Type	Price/Ft	Wheelbase	Towing	GVWR	Curb Wt
Custom	1997	MHA	29	2901	FO	7.5L	G	$1900	190	9,800	15,200	12,852

Livability Code: SB 30-90
Wheelbase-to-length ratio of 55% is considered ○ dangerous ○ fatiguing ◉ good ○ excellent *
The approximate net payload of 2348 pounds at 15% of GVWR on this model is ○ deficient ○ excessive ○ cautionary ○ good ◉ excellent *
Total highway safety penalties are: 2 * Value: 7 9 Durability: 7 5 Highway Control Rating: 9 0 Highway Safety: 8 8 ★★★

Brand	Year	Type	Length	Model	Chassis	Engine	Fuel Type	Price/Ft	Wheelbase	Towing	GVWR	Curb Wt
Custom	1997	MHA	32	3200	FO	7.5L	G	$1800	208	4,200	14,800	12,804

Livability Code: SB 30-90
Wheelbase-to-length ratio of 55% is considered ○ dangerous ○ fatiguing ◉ good ○ excellent *
The approximate net payload of 1996 pounds at 13% of GVWR on this model is ○ deficient ○ excessive ○ cautionary ◉ good ○ excellent *
Total highway safety penalties are: 2 * Value: 7 9 Durability: 7 5 Highway Control Rating: 8 5 Highway Safety: 8 3 ★★★

Brand	Year	Type	Length	Model	Chassis	Engine	Fuel Type	Price/Ft	Wheelbase	Towing	GVWR	Curb Wt
Custom	1997	MHA	32	3200	FO	7.5L	G	$1800	208	9,800	15,200	13,316

Livability Code: SB 30-90
Wheelbase-to-length ratio of 55% is considered ○ dangerous ○ fatiguing ◉ good ○ excellent *
The approximate net payload of 1884 pounds at 12% of GVWR on this model is ○ deficient ○ excessive ○ cautionary ◉ good ○ excellent *
Total highway safety penalties are: 2 * Value: 7 9 Durability: 7 5 Highway Control Rating: 8 7 Highway Safety: 8 5 ★★★

Brand	Year	Type	Length	Model	Chassis	Engine	Fuel Type	Price/Ft	Wheelbase	Towing	GVWR	Curb Wt
Custom	1997	MHA	32	3150	CH	7.4L	G	$1800	212	4,200	14,800	12,971

Livability Code: SB 30-90
Wheelbase-to-length ratio of 55% is considered ○ dangerous ○ fatiguing ◉ good ○ excellent *
The approximate net payload of 1829 pounds at 12% of GVWR on this model is ○ deficient ○ excessive ○ cautionary ◉ good ○ excellent *
Total highway safety penalties are: 6 * Value: 7 7 Durability: 7 5 Highway Control Rating: 8 6 Highway Safety: 8 0 ★★★

Brand	Year	Type	Length	Model	Chassis	Engine	Fuel Type	Price/Ft	Wheelbase	Towing	GVWR	Curb Wt
Custom	1997	MHA	32	3150	FO	7.5L	G	$1800	212	9,800	15,200	13,481

Livability Code: SB 30-90
Wheelbase-to-length ratio of 55% is considered ○ dangerous ○ fatiguing ◉ good ○ excellent *
The approximate net payload of 1719 pounds at 11% of GVWR on this model is ○ deficient ○ excessive ○ cautionary ◉ good ○ excellent *
Total highway safety penalties are: 2 * Value: 7 9 Durability: 7 5 Highway Control Rating: 8 9 Highway Safety: 8 7 ★★★

Note: Safety ratings are based on the assumption that the engineering of the RV has allowed for proper balance by placing fresh, gray, and black holding tanks in a location so as not to change the balance of the RV when the tanks are empty or full. **Always double-check wheelbase, GVWR, and weights at front and rear axles.**

*See Section 1 for details on how conclusions are reached.

Brand	Year	Type	Length	Model	Chassis	Engine	Fuel Type	Average Price per Linear Foot When New	Adjusted Wheelbase	Approx. Towing Capacity	Gross Vehicle Weight Rating	Average Curb Weight

Diplomat — 1999 MHA 37 — Model 36B Slide — Chassis RO — Engine CU275 — Fuel Type D — $3800 — Wheelbase 216 — Towing 5,000 — GVWR 29,000 — Curb 26,350
Livability Code: SB 30-90
Wheelbase-to-length ratio of 49% is considered ● dangerous ○ fatiguing ○ good ○ excellent *
The approximate net payload of 2650 pounds at 9% of GVWR on this model is ○ deficient ○ excessive ● cautionary ○ good ○ excellent *
Total highway safety penalties are: 12 * Value: 7 3 Durability: 7 3 Highway Control Rating: 3 5 Highway Safety: 2 3

Diplomat — 1999 MHA 39 — Model 38C — Chassis RO — Engine CU275 — Fuel Type D — $3600 — Wheelbase 242 — Towing 5,000 — GVWR 29,000 — Curb 26,050
Livability Code: SB 30-90
Wheelbase-to-length ratio of 52% is considered ○ dangerous ● fatiguing ○ good ○ excellent *
The approximate net payload of 2950 pounds at 10% of GVWR on this model is ○ deficient ○ excessive ○ cautionary ● good ○ excellent *
Total highway safety penalties are: 2 * Value: 7 8 Durability: 7 3 Highway Control Rating: 5 6 Highway Safety: 5 4 ★

Diplomat — 1999 MHA 39 — Model 38A Slide — Chassis RO — Engine CU275 — Fuel Type D — $3600 — Wheelbase 242 — Towing 5,000 — GVWR 29,000 — Curb 26,950
Livability Code: SB 30-90
Wheelbase-to-length ratio of 52% is considered ○ dangerous ● fatiguing ○ good ○ excellent *
The approximate net payload of 2050 pounds at 7% of GVWR on this model is ○ deficient ○ excessive ● cautionary ○ good ○ excellent *
Total highway safety penalties are: 12 * Value: 7 3 Durability: 7 3 Highway Control Rating: 3 9 Highway Safety: 2 7

Discovery — 1997 MHA 37 — Model 36R — Chassis FR — Engine Cu230 — Fuel Type D — $2800 — Wheelbase 228 — Towing 5,000 — GVWR 24,850 — Curb 20,922
Livability Code: SB 30-90
Wheelbase-to-length ratio of 51% is considered ○ dangerous ● fatiguing ○ good ○ excellent *
The approximate net payload of 3928 pounds at 16% of GVWR on this model is ○ deficient ○ excessive ○ cautionary ○ good ● excellent *
Total highway safety penalties are: 2 * Value: 7 7 Durability: 7 0 Highway Control Rating: 5 9 Highway Safety: 5 7 ★

Discovery — 1997 MHA 37 — Model 36RS — Chassis FR — Engine Cu230 — Fuel Type D — $2800 — Wheelbase 228 — Towing 5,000 — GVWR 24,850 — Curb 21,822
Livability Code: SB 30-90
Wheelbase-to-length ratio of 51% is considered ○ dangerous ● fatiguing ○ good ○ excellent *
The approximate net payload of 3028 pounds at 12% of GVWR on this model is ○ deficient ○ excessive ○ cautionary ● good ○ excellent *
Total highway safety penalties are: 7 * Value: 7 4 Durability: 7 0 Highway Control Rating: 5 2 Highway Safety: 4 5

Discovery — 1998 MHA 35 — Model 34Q — Chassis FR — Engine Cu275 — Fuel Type D — $3000 — Wheelbase 208 — Towing 5,000 — GVWR 24,850 — Curb 20,893
Livability Code: SB 30-90
Wheelbase-to-length ratio of 50% is considered ● dangerous ○ fatiguing ○ good ○ excellent *
The approximate net payload of 3957 pounds at 16% of GVWR on this model is ○ deficient ○ excessive ○ cautionary ○ good ● excellent *
Total highway safety penalties are: 12 * Value: 7 5 Durability: 7 9 Highway Control Rating: 5 4 Highway Safety: 4 2

Discovery — 1998 MHA 36 — Model 36A — Chassis FR — Engine Cu275 — Fuel Type D — $2900 — Wheelbase 228 — Towing 5,000 — GVWR 24,850 — Curb 20,665
Livability Code: SB 30-90
Wheelbase-to-length ratio of 52% is considered ○ dangerous ● fatiguing ○ good ○ excellent *
The approximate net payload of 4185 pounds at 17% of GVWR on this model is ○ deficient ○ excessive ○ cautionary ○ good ● excellent *
Total highway safety penalties are: 2 * Value: 8 1 Durability: 7 9 Highway Control Rating: 6 9 Highway Safety: 6 7 ★★

Discovery — 1998 MHA 36 — Model 36R — Chassis FR — Engine Cu275 — Fuel Type D — $2900 — Wheelbase 228 — Towing 5,000 — GVWR 24,850 — Curb 20,670
Livability Code: SB 30-90
Wheelbase-to-length ratio of 52% is considered ○ dangerous ● fatiguing ○ good ○ excellent *
The approximate net payload of 4180 pounds at 17% of GVWR on this model is ○ deficient ○ excessive ○ cautionary ○ good ● excellent *
Total highway safety penalties are: 2 * Value: 8 1 Durability: 7.9 Highway Control Rating: 6 9 Highway Safety: 6 7 ★★

Discovery — 1998 MHA 36 — Model 36T — Chassis FR — Engine Cu275 — Fuel Type D — $2900 — Wheelbase 228 — Towing 5,000 — GVWR 24,850 — Curb 21,505
Livability Code: SB 30-90
Wheelbase-to-length ratio of 52% is considered ○ dangerous ● fatiguing ○ good ○ excellent *
The approximate net payload of 3345 pounds at 13% of GVWR on this model is ○ deficient ○ excessive ○ cautionary ● good ○ excellent *
Total highway safety penalties are: 7 * Value: 7 8 Durability: 7 9 Highway Control Rating: 6 3 Highway Safety: 5 6

Discovery — 1998 MHA 37 — Model 36A — Chassis FR — Engine Cu230 — Fuel Type D — $2800 — Wheelbase 228 — Towing 5,000 — GVWR 24,850 — Curb 20,922
Livability Code: SB 30-90
Wheelbase-to-length ratio of 51% is considered ○ dangerous ● fatiguing ○ good ○ excellent *
The approximate net payload of 3928 pounds at 16% of GVWR on this model is ○ deficient ○ excessive ○ cautionary ○ good ● excellent *
Total highway safety penalties are: 2 * Value: 7 7 Durability: 7 0 Highway Control Rating: 5 9 Highway Safety: 5 7

Discovery — 1999 MHA 35 — Model 34Q — Chassis FR — Engine CU275 — Fuel Type D — $3400 — Wheelbase 208 — Towing 5,000 — GVWR 24,850 — Curb 20,935
Livability Code: SB 30-90
Wheelbase-to-length ratio of 50% is considered ● dangerous ○ fatiguing ○ good ○ excellent *
The approximate net payload of 3915 pounds at 16% of GVWR on this model is ○ deficient ○ excessive ○ cautionary ○ good ● excellent *
Total highway safety penalties are: 13 * Value: 8 0 Durability: 7 9 Highway Control Rating: 5 4 Highway Safety: 4 1

Discovery — 1999 MHA 36 — Model 36A — Chassis FR — Engine CU275 — Fuel Type D — $3300 — Wheelbase 228 — Towing 5,000 — GVWR 24,850 — Curb 20,689
Livability Code: SB 30-90
Wheelbase-to-length ratio of 52% is considered ○ dangerous ● fatiguing ○ good ○ excellent *
The approximate net payload of 4161 pounds at 17% of GVWR on this model is ○ deficient ○ excessive ○ cautionary ○ good ● excellent *
Total highway safety penalties are: 2 * Value: 8 6 Durability: 7 9 Highway Control Rating: 6 9 Highway Safety: 6 7 ★★

Note: Safety ratings are based on the assumption that the engineering of the RV has allowed for proper balance by placing fresh, gray, and black holding tanks in a location so as not to change the balance of the RV when the tanks are empty or full. **Always double-check wheelbase, GVWR, and weights at front and rear axles.**

*See Section 1 for details on how conclusions are reached.

Brand	Year	Type	Length	Model	Chassis	Engine	Fuel Type	Average Price per Linear Foot When New	Adjusted Wheelbase	Approx. Towing Capacity	Gross Vehicle Weight Rating	Average Curb Weight
Discovery	**1999**	MHA	36	36R	FR	CU275	D	$3300	228	5,000	24,850	20,694

Livability Code: SB 30-90
Wheelbase-to-length ratio of 52% is considered ○ dangerous ◉ fatiguing ○ good ○ excellent *
The approximate net payload of 4156 pounds at 17% of GVWR on this model is ○ deficient ○ excessive ○ cautionary ○ good ◉ excellent *
Total highway safety penalties are: 2 * Value: **8 6** Durability: **7 9** Highway Control Rating: **6 9** Highway Safety: **6 7** ★★

Brand	Year	Type	Length	Model	Chassis	Engine	Fuel Type		Adj. WB	Tow	GVWR	Curb Wt
Discovery	**1999**	MHA	36	36T	FR	CU275	D	$3300	228	5,000	24,850	21,548

Livability Code: SB 30-90
Wheelbase-to-length ratio of 52% is considered ○ dangerous ◉ fatiguing ○ good ○ excellent *
The approximate net payload of 3302 pounds at 13% of GVWR on this model is ○ deficient ○ excessive ○ cautionary ◉ good ○ excellent *
Total highway safety penalties are: 8 * Value: **8 3** Durability: **7 9** Highway Control Rating: **6 2** Highway Safety: **5 4** ★

Brand	Year	Type	Length	Model	Chassis	Engine	Fuel Type		Adj. WB	Tow	GVWR	Curb Wt
Discovery	**1999**	MHA	38	37V	FR	CU275	D	$3200	242	5,000	24,850	22,324

Livability Code: SB 30-90
Wheelbase-to-length ratio of 54% is considered ○ dangerous ○ fatiguing ◉ good ○ excellent *
The approximate net payload of 2526 pounds at 10% of GVWR on this model is ○ deficient ○ excessive ○ cautionary ◉ good ○ excellent *
Total highway safety penalties are: 9 * Value: **8 2** Durability: **7 9** Highway Control Rating: **7 7** Highway Safety: **6 8** ★★

Brand	Year	Type	Length	Model	Chassis	Engine	Fuel Type		Adj. WB	Tow	GVWR	Curb Wt
Dolphin	**1990**	MHA	27	2740	CH	7.4L	G	$2100	178	2,500	14,500	12,658

Livability Code: SB 30-90
Wheelbase-to-length ratio of 55% is considered ○ dangerous ○ fatiguing ◉ good ○ excellent *
The approximate net payload of 1842 pounds at 13% of GVWR on this model is ○ deficient ○ excessive ○ cautionary ◉ good ○ excellent *
Total highway safety penalties are: 3 * Value: **9 0** Durability: **9 0** Highway Control Rating: **8 6** Highway Safety: **8 3** ★★★★

Brand	Year	Type	Length	Model	Chassis	Engine	Fuel Type		Adj. WB	Tow	GVWR	Curb Wt
Dolphin	**1990**	MHA	27	2750	CH	7.4L	G	$2100	178	2,500	14,500	12,658

Livability Code: SB 30-90
Wheelbase-to-length ratio of 55% is considered ○ dangerous ○ fatiguing ◉ good ○ excellent *
The approximate net payload of 1842 pounds at 13% of GVWR on this model is ○ deficient ○ excessive ○ cautionary ◉ good ○ excellent *
Total highway safety penalties are: 3 * Value: **9 0** Durability: **9 0** Highway Control Rating: **8 6** Highway Safety: **8 3** ★★★★

Brand	Year	Type	Length	Model	Chassis	Engine	Fuel Type		Adj. WB	Tow	GVWR	Curb Wt
Dolphin	**1990**	MHA	27	2760	CH	7.4L	G	$2100	178	2,500	14,500	12,658

Livability Code: SB 30-90
Wheelbase-to-length ratio of 55% is considered ○ dangerous ○ fatiguing ◉ good ○ excellent *
The approximate net payload of 1842 pounds at 13% of GVWR on this model is ○ deficient ○ excessive ○ cautionary ◉ good ○ excellent *
Total highway safety penalties are: 3 * Value: **9 0** Durability: **9 0** Highway Control Rating: **8 6** Highway Safety: **8 3** ★★★★

Brand	Year	Type	Length	Model	Chassis	Engine	Fuel Type		Adj. WB	Tow	GVWR	Curb Wt
Dolphin	**1990**	MHA	31	3140	CH	7.4L	G	$2000	208	1,500	16,000	13,933

Livability Code: SB 30-90
Wheelbase-to-length ratio of 56% is considered ○ dangerous ○ fatiguing ◉ good ○ excellent *
The approximate net payload of 2067 pounds at 13% of GVWR on this model is ○ deficient ○ excessive ○ cautionary ◉ good ○ excellent *
Total highway safety penalties are: 5 * Value: **8 9** Durability: **9 0** Highway Control Rating: **9 0** Highway Safety: **8 5** ★★★★

Brand	Year	Type	Length	Model	Chassis	Engine	Fuel Type		Adj. WB	Tow	GVWR	Curb Wt
Dolphin	**1990**	MHA	31	3150	CH	7.4L	G	$2000	208	1,500	16,000	13,933

Livability Code: SB 30-90
Wheelbase-to-length ratio of 56% is considered ○ dangerous ○ fatiguing ◉ good ○ excellent *
The approximate net payload of 2067 pounds at 13% of GVWR on this model is ○ deficient ○ excessive ○ cautionary ◉ good ○ excellent *
Total highway safety penalties are: 5 * Value: **8 9** Durability: **9 0** Highway Control Rating: **9 0** Highway Safety: **8 5** ★★★★

Brand	Year	Type	Length	Model	Chassis	Engine	Fuel Type		Adj. WB	Tow	GVWR	Curb Wt
Dolphin	**1990**	MHA	31	3150	FO	7.5L	G	$2000	208	5,000	17,000	14,433

Livability Code: SB 30-90
Wheelbase-to-length ratio of 56% is considered ○ dangerous ○ fatiguing ◉ good ○ excellent *
The approximate net payload of 2567 pounds at 15% of GVWR on this model is ○ deficient ○ excessive ○ cautionary ◉ good ○ excellent *
Total highway safety penalties are: 2 * Value: **9 0** Durability: **9 0** Highway Control Rating: **9 4** Highway Safety: **9 2** ★★★★★

Brand	Year	Type	Length	Model	Chassis	Engine	Fuel Type		Adj. WB	Tow	GVWR	Curb Wt
Dolphin	**1990**	MHA	31	3140	FO	7.5L	G	$2000	208	5,000	17,000	14,433

Livability Code: SB 30-90
Wheelbase-to-length ratio of 56% is considered ○ dangerous ○ fatiguing ◉ good ○ excellent *
The approximate net payload of 2567 pounds at 15% of GVWR on this model is ○ deficient ○ excessive ○ cautionary ◉ good ○ excellent *
Total highway safety penalties are: 2 * Value: **9 0** Durability: **9 0** Highway Control Rating: **9 4** Highway Safety: **9 2** ★★★★★

Brand	Year	Type	Length	Model	Chassis	Engine	Fuel Type		Adj. WB	Tow	GVWR	Curb Wt
Dolphin	**1990**	MHA	34	3400	CH	7.4L	G	$1900	228	1,500	16,000	14,739

Livability Code: SB 30-90
Wheelbase-to-length ratio of 56% is considered ○ dangerous ○ fatiguing ◉ good ○ excellent *
The approximate net payload of 1261 pounds at 8% of GVWR on this model is ○ deficient ○ excessive ◉ cautionary ○ good ○ excellent *
Total highway safety penalties are: 7 * Value: **8 8** Durability: **9 0** Highway Control Rating: **7 3** Highway Safety: **6 6** ★★

Brand	Year	Type	Length	Model	Chassis	Engine	Fuel Type		Adj. WB	Tow	GVWR	Curb Wt
Dolphin	**1990**	MHA	34	3450	CH	7.4L	G	$1900	228	1,500	16,000	14,739

Livability Code: SB 30-90
Wheelbase-to-length ratio of 56% is considered ○ dangerous ○ fatiguing ◉ good ○ excellent *
The approximate net payload of 1261 pounds at 8% of GVWR on this model is ○ deficient ○ excessive ◉ cautionary ○ good ○ excellent *
Total highway safety penalties are: 7 * Value: **8 8** Durability: **9 0** Highway Control Rating: **7 3** Highway Safety: **6 6** ★★

Note: Safety ratings are based on the assumption that the engineering of the RV has allowed for proper balance by placing fresh, gray, and black holding tanks in a location so as not to change the balance of the RV when the tanks are empty or full. **Always double-check wheelbase, GVWR, and weights at front and rear axles.**

*See Section 1 for details on how conclusions are reached.

Brand	Year	Type	Length	Model	Chassis	Engine	Fuel Type	Average Price per Linear Foot When New	Adjusted Wheel-base	Approx. Towing Capacity	Gross Vehicle Weight Rating	Average Curb Weight
Dolphin	**1990**	MHA	34	3400	FO	7.5L	G	$1900	228	5,000	17,000	15,239

Livability Code: SB 30-90
Wheelbase-to-length ratio of 56% is considered ○ dangerous ○ fatiguing ◉ good ○ excellent *
The approximate net payload of 1761 pounds at 10% of GVWR on this model is ○ deficient ○ excessive ○ cautionary ◉ good ○ excellent *
Total highway safety penalties are: 2 *   Value: **9 0**   Durability: **9 0**   Highway Control Rating: **9 0**   Highway Safety: **8 8**   ★★★★

Brand	Year	Type	Length	Model	Chassis	Engine	Fuel Type	Average Price per Linear Foot When New	Adjusted Wheel-base	Approx. Towing Capacity	Gross Vehicle Weight Rating	Average Curb Weight
Dolphin	**1990**	MHA	34	3450	FO	7.5L	G	$1900	228	5,000	17,000	15,239

Livability Code: SB 30-90
Wheelbase-to-length ratio of 56% is considered ○ dangerous ○ fatiguing ◉ good ○ excellent *
The approximate net payload of 1761 pounds at 10% of GVWR on this model is ○ deficient ○ excessive ○ cautionary ◉ good ○ excellent *
Total highway safety penalties are: 2 *   Value: **9 0**   Durability: **9 0**   Highway Control Rating: **9 0**   Highway Safety: **8 8**   ★★★★

Brand	Year	Type	Length	Model	Chassis	Engine	Fuel Type	Average Price per Linear Foot When New	Adjusted Wheel-base	Approx. Towing Capacity	Gross Vehicle Weight Rating	Average Curb Weight
Dolphin	**1990**	MMH	22	900	TO	3.0L	G	$1800	137	1,500 e	6,000	5,489

Livability Code: SB 30-90
Wheelbase-to-length ratio of 53% is considered ○ dangerous ◉ fatiguing ○ good ○ excellent *
The approximate net payload of 511 pounds at 9% of GVWR on this model is ○ deficient ○ excessive ◉ cautionary ○ good ○ excellent *
Total highway safety penalties are: 2 *   Value: **9 0**   Durability: **9 0**   Highway Control Rating: **5 2**   Highway Safety: **5 0**   ★

Brand	Year	Type	Length	Model	Chassis	Engine	Fuel Type	Average Price per Linear Foot When New	Adjusted Wheel-base	Approx. Towing Capacity	Gross Vehicle Weight Rating	Average Curb Weight
Dolphin	**1991**	MHA	32	3100	FO	7.5L	G	$1900	208	1,500	17,000	14,041

Livability Code: SB 30-90
Wheelbase-to-length ratio of 55% is considered ○ dangerous ○ fatiguing ◉ good ○ excellent *
The approximate net payload of 2959 pounds at 17% of GVWR on this model is ○ deficient ○ excessive ○ cautionary ○ good ◉ excellent *
Total highway safety penalties are: 5 *   Value: **8 8**   Durability: **9 0**   Highway Control Rating: **9 3**   Highway Safety: **8 8**   ★★★★

Brand	Year	Type	Length	Model	Chassis	Engine	Fuel Type	Average Price per Linear Foot When New	Adjusted Wheel-base	Approx. Towing Capacity	Gross Vehicle Weight Rating	Average Curb Weight
Dolphin	**1994**	MHA	32	432	FO	7.5L	G	$1700	208	8,000	17,000	14,792

Livability Code: SB 30-90
Wheelbase-to-length ratio of 55% is considered ○ dangerous ○ fatiguing ◉ good ○ excellent *
The approximate net payload of 2208 pounds at 13% of GVWR on this model is ○ deficient ○ excessive ○ cautionary ◉ good ○ excellent *
Total highway safety penalties are: 2 *   Value: **9 0**   Durability: **9 0**   Highway Control Rating: **8 5**   Highway Safety: **8 3**   ★★★★

Brand	Year	Type	Length	Model	Chassis	Engine	Fuel Type	Average Price per Linear Foot When New	Adjusted Wheel-base	Approx. Towing Capacity	Gross Vehicle Weight Rating	Average Curb Weight
Dolphin	**1994**	MHA	32	432	CH	7.4L	G	$2000	208	3,000	16,000	14,335

Livability Code: SB 30-90
Wheelbase-to-length ratio of 54% is considered ○ dangerous ○ fatiguing ◉ good ○ excellent *
The approximate net payload of 1665 pounds at 10% of GVWR on this model is ○ deficient ○ excessive ○ cautionary ◉ good ○ excellent *
Total highway safety penalties are: 5 *   Value: **8 8**   Durability: **9 0**   Highway Control Rating: **7 7**   Highway Safety: **7 2**   ★★★

Brand	Year	Type	Length	Model	Chassis	Engine	Fuel Type	Average Price per Linear Foot When New	Adjusted Wheel-base	Approx. Towing Capacity	Gross Vehicle Weight Rating	Average Curb Weight
Dolphin	**1994**	MHA	34	32D	OS	CU190	D	$2800	190	3,660	18,340	16,212

Livability Code: SB 30-90
Wheelbase-to-length ratio of 47% is considered ◉ dangerous ○ fatiguing ○ good ○ excellent *
The approximate net payload of 2128 pounds at 12% of GVWR on this model is ○ deficient ○ excessive ○ cautionary ◉ good ○ excellent *
Total highway safety penalties are: 2 *   Value: **9 0**   Durability: **9 0**   Highway Control Rating: **2 6**   Highway Safety: **2 4**

Brand	Year	Type	Length	Model	Chassis	Engine	Fuel Type	Average Price per Linear Foot When New	Adjusted Wheel-base	Approx. Towing Capacity	Gross Vehicle Weight Rating	Average Curb Weight
Dolphin	**1994**	MHA	34	32D	OS	CU190	D	$2800	190	4,000	19,000	16,662

Livability Code: SB 30-90
Wheelbase-to-length ratio of 47% is considered ◉ dangerous ○ fatiguing ○ good ○ excellent *
The approximate net payload of 1338 pounds at 7% of GVWR on this model is ○ deficient ○ excessive ◉ cautionary ○ good ○ excellent *
Total highway safety penalties are: 2 *   Value: **9 0**   Durability: **9 0**   Highway Control Rating: **6**   Highway Safety: **4**

Brand	Year	Type	Length	Model	Chassis	Engine	Fuel Type	Average Price per Linear Foot When New	Adjusted Wheel-base	Approx. Towing Capacity	Gross Vehicle Weight Rating	Average Curb Weight
Dolphin	**1994**	MHA	35	434	CH	7.4L	G	$1900	228	3,000	16,000	14,890

Livability Code: SB 30-90
Wheelbase-to-length ratio of 55% is considered ○ dangerous ○ fatiguing ◉ good ○ excellent *
The approximate net payload of 1110 pounds at 7% of GVWR on this model is ○ deficient ○ excessive ◉ cautionary ○ good ○ excellent *
Total highway safety penalties are: 7 *   Value: **8 8**   Durability: **9 0**   Highway Control Rating: **6 3**   Highway Safety: **5 6**   ★

Brand	Year	Type	Length	Model	Chassis	Engine	Fuel Type	Average Price per Linear Foot When New	Adjusted Wheel-base	Approx. Towing Capacity	Gross Vehicle Weight Rating	Average Curb Weight
Dolphin	**1994**	MHA	35	434	FO	7.5L	G	$1600	228	8,000	17,000	15,480

Livability Code: SB 30-90
Wheelbase-to-length ratio of 55% is considered ○ dangerous ○ fatiguing ◉ good ○ excellent *
The approximate net payload of 1520 pounds at 9% of GVWR on this model is ○ deficient ○ excessive ◉ cautionary ○ good ○ excellent *
Total highway safety penalties are: 2 *   Value: **9 0**   Durability: **9 0**   Highway Control Rating: **7 5**   Highway Safety: **7 3**   ★★★

Brand	Year	Type	Length	Model	Chassis	Engine	Fuel Type	Average Price per Linear Foot When New	Adjusted Wheel-base	Approx. Towing Capacity	Gross Vehicle Weight Rating	Average Curb Weight
Dolphin	**1994**	MHA	35	34D	OS	CU190	D	$2700	208	4,000	19,000	16,895

Livability Code: SB 30-90
Wheelbase-to-length ratio of 50% is considered ◉ dangerous ○ fatiguing ○ good ○ excellent *
The approximate net payload of 2105 pounds at 11% of GVWR on this model is ○ deficient ○ excessive ○ cautionary ◉ good ○ excellent *
Total highway safety penalties are: 2 *   Value: **9 0**   Durability: **9 0**   Highway Control Rating: **3 4**   Highway Safety: **3 2**

Brand	Year	Type	Length	Model	Chassis	Engine	Fuel Type	Average Price per Linear Foot When New	Adjusted Wheel-base	Approx. Towing Capacity	Gross Vehicle Weight Rating	Average Curb Weight
Dolphin	**1994**	MHA	35	34D	OS	CU230	D	$2900	208	4,500	20,500	17,615

Livability Code: SB 30-90
Wheelbase-to-length ratio of 50% is considered ◉ dangerous ○ fatiguing ○ good ○ excellent *
The approximate net payload of 2885 pounds at 14% of GVWR on this model is ○ deficient ○ excessive ○ cautionary ◉ good ○ excellent *
Total highway safety penalties are: 2 *   Value: **9 0**   Durability: **9 0**   Highway Control Rating: **4 0**   Highway Safety: **3 8**

Note: Safety ratings are based on the assumption that the engineering of the RV has allowed for proper balance by placing fresh, gray, and black holding tanks in a location so as not to change the balance of the RV when the tanks are empty or full. **Always double-check wheelbase, GVWR, and weights at front and rear axles.**

*See Section 1 for details on how conclusions are reached.

Section 2: The Ratings

Brand	Year	Type	Length	Model	Chassis	Engine	Fuel Type	Average Price per Linear Foot When New	Adjusted Wheelbase	Approx. Towing Capacity	Gross Vehicle Weight Rating	Average Curb Weight
Dolphin	1995	MHA	32	432	CH	7.5L	G	$2000	208	3,500	16,500	14,385

Livability Code: SB 30-90 Wheelbase-to-length ratio of 54% is considered ○ dangerous ○ fatiguing ◉ good ○ excellent *
The approximate net payload of 2115 pounds at 13% of GVWR on this model is ○ deficient ○ excessive ○ cautionary ◉ good ○ excellent *
Total highway safety penalties are: 5 * Value: 8 8 Durability: 9 0 Highway Control Rating: 8 0 Highway Safety: 7 5 ★★★

Brand	Year	Type	Length	Model	Chassis	Engine	Fuel Type	Price/LF	Wheelbase	Towing	GVWR	Curb
Dolphin	1995	MHA	32	432	FO	7.5L	G	$2000	208	8,000	17,000	14,820

Livability Code: SB 30-90 Wheelbase-to-length ratio of 54% is considered ○ dangerous ○ fatiguing ◉ good ○ excellent *
The approximate net payload of 2180 pounds at 13% of GVWR on this model is ○ deficient ○ excessive ○ cautionary ◉ good ○ excellent *
Total highway safety penalties are: 2 * Value: 9 0 Durability: 9 0 Highway Control Rating: 8 0 Highway Safety: 7 8 ★★★

Dolphin	1995	MHA	32	531	FO	7.5L	G	$2100	208	8,000	17,000	15,328

Livability Code: SB 30-90 Wheelbase-to-length ratio of 54% is considered ○ dangerous ○ fatiguing ◉ good ○ excellent *
The approximate net payload of 1672 pounds at 10% of GVWR on this model is ○ deficient ○ excessive ○ cautionary ◉ good ○ excellent *
Total highway safety penalties are: 2 * Value: 9 0 Durability: 9 0 Highway Control Rating: 7 6 Highway Safety: 7 4 ★★★

Dolphin	1995	MHA	34	632	OS	CU190	D	$2900	190	4,660	18,340	16,913

Livability Code: SB 30-90 Wheelbase-to-length ratio of 47% is considered ◉ dangerous ○ fatiguing ○ good ○ excellent *
The approximate net payload of 1427 pounds at 8% of GVWR on this model is ○ deficient ○ excessive ◉ cautionary ○ good ○ excellent *
Total highway safety penalties are: 2 * Value: 9 0 Durability: 9 0 Highway Control Rating: 1 1 Highway Safety: 9

Dolphin	1995	MHA	34	533	FO	7.5L	G	$2000	228	8,000	17,000	15,958

Livability Code: SB 30-90 Wheelbase-to-length ratio of 56% is considered ○ dangerous ○ fatiguing ◉ good ○ excellent *
The approximate net payload of 1042 pounds at 6% of GVWR on this model is ◉ deficient ○ excessive ○ cautionary ○ good ○ excellent *
Total highway safety penalties are: 2 * Value: 9 0 Durability: 9 0 Highway Control Rating: 6 2 Highway Safety: 6 0 ★

Dolphin	1995	MHA	35	434	CH	7.5L	G	$1900	228	3,500	16,500	14,940

Livability Code: SB 30-90 Wheelbase-to-length ratio of 55% is considered ○ dangerous ○ fatiguing ◉ good ○ excellent *
The approximate net payload of 1560 pounds at 9% of GVWR on this model is ○ deficient ○ excessive ◉ cautionary ○ good ○ excellent *
Total highway safety penalties are: 7 * Value: 8 8 Durability: 9 0 Highway Control Rating: 7 5 Highway Safety: 6 8 ★★

Dolphin	1995	MHA	35	434	FO	7.5L	G	$1900	228	8,000	17,000	15,480

Livability Code: SB 30-90 Wheelbase-to-length ratio of 55% is considered ○ dangerous ○ fatiguing ◉ good ○ excellent *
The approximate net payload of 1520 pounds at 9% of GVWR on this model is ○ deficient ○ excessive ◉ cautionary ○ good ○ excellent *
Total highway safety penalties are: 2 * Value: 9 0 Durability: 9 0 Highway Control Rating: 7 5 Highway Safety: 7 3 ★★★

Dolphin	1995	MHA	35	634	OS	CU190	D	$3000	208	4,000	20,500	17,626

Livability Code: SB 30-90 Wheelbase-to-length ratio of 50% is considered ◉ dangerous ○ fatiguing ○ good ○ excellent *
The approximate net payload of 2874 pounds at 14% of GVWR on this model is ○ deficient ○ excessive ○ cautionary ◉ good ○ excellent *
Total highway safety penalties are: 2 * Value: 9 0 Durability: 9 0 Highway Control Rating: 3 9 Highway Safety: 3 7

Dolphin	1995	MHA	35	535-S	FO	7.5L	G	$2000	232 T	5,000	20,000	17,393

Livability Code: SB 30-90 Wheelbase-to-length ratio of 55% is considered ○ dangerous ○ fatiguing ◉ good ○ excellent *
The approximate net payload of 2607 pounds at 13% of GVWR on this model is ○ deficient ○ excessive ○ cautionary ◉ good ○ excellent *
Total highway safety penalties are: 4 * Value: 8 9 Durability: 9 0 Highway Control Rating: 8 6 Highway Safety: 8 2 ★★★★

Dolphin	1996	MHA	34	533A	FO	7.5L	G	$1900	228	8,000	17,000	15,762

Livability Code: SB 30-90 Wheelbase-to-length ratio of 55% is considered ○ dangerous ○ fatiguing ◉ good ○ excellent *
The approximate net payload of 1238 pounds at 7% of GVWR on this model is ○ deficient ○ excessive ◉ cautionary ○ good ○ excellent *
Total highway safety penalties are: 2 * Value: 9 0 Durability: 9 0 Highway Control Rating: 6 5 Highway Safety: 6 3 ★★

Dolphin	1996	MHA	34	533L	FO	7.5L	G	$1900	228	8,000	17,000	15,762

Livability Code: SB 30-90 Wheelbase-to-length ratio of 55% is considered ○ dangerous ○ fatiguing ◉ good ○ excellent *
The approximate net payload of 1238 pounds at 7% of GVWR on this model is ○ deficient ○ excessive ◉ cautionary ○ good ○ excellent *
Total highway safety penalties are: 2 * Value: 9 0 Durability: 9 0 Highway Control Rating: 6 5 Highway Safety: 6 3 ★★

Dolphin	1996	MHA	35	635-S	FR	CU230	D	$3000	208	5,000	20,000	19,020

Livability Code: SB 30-90 Wheelbase-to-length ratio of 49% is considered ◉ dangerous ○ fatiguing ○ good ○ excellent *
The approximate net payload of 980 pounds at 5% of GVWR on this model is ◉ deficient ○ excessive ○ cautionary ○ good ○ excellent *
Total highway safety penalties are: 7 * Value: 8 7 Durability: 9 0 Highway Control Rating: 5 Highway Safety: - 2

Note: Safety ratings are based on the assumption that the engineering of the RV has allowed for proper balance by placing fresh, gray, and black holding tanks in a location so as not to change the balance of the RV when the tanks are empty or full. **Always double-check wheelbase, GVWR, and weights at front and rear axles.**

*See Section 1 for details on how conclusions are reached.

Section 2: The Ratings

Brand	Year	Type	Length	Model	Chassis	Engine	Fuel Type	Average Price per Linear Foot When New	Adjusted Wheel-base	Approx. Towing Capacity	Gross Vehicle Weight Rating	Average Curb Weight
Dolphin	1996	MHA	36	534G	FO	7.5L	G	$1800	228	8,000	17,000	16,244

Livability Code: SB 30-90   Wheelbase-to-length ratio of 52% is considered ○ dangerous ● fatiguing ○ good ○ excellent*
The approximate net payload of 756 pounds at 4% of GVWR on this model is ● deficient ○ excessive ○ cautionary ○ good ○ excellent*
Total highway safety penalties are: 2*   Value: **9 0** Durability: **9 0** Highway Control Rating: **2 5**   Highway Safety: **2 3**

Brand	Year	Type	Length	Model	Chassis	Engine	Fuel Type	Price/Lin.Ft	Adj. Wheelbase	Tow Cap.	GVWR	Curb Wt
Dolphin	1996	MHA	37	535-S	CH	7.5L	G	$1900	232 T	0	19,500	17,651

Livability Code: SB 30-90   Wheelbase-to-length ratio of 53% is considered ○ dangerous ● fatiguing ○ good ○ excellent*
The approximate net payload of 1849 pounds at 9% of GVWR on this model is ○ deficient ○ excessive ● cautionary ○ good ○ excellent*
Total highway safety penalties are: 16*   Value: **8 3** Durability: **9 0** Highway Control Rating: **5 3**   Highway Safety: **3 7**

Dolphin	1996	MHA	37	535-S	FO	7.5L	G	$1900	232 T	5,000	20,000	18,151

Livability Code: SB 30-90   Wheelbase-to-length ratio of 53% is considered ○ dangerous ● fatiguing ○ good ○ excellent*
The approximate net payload of 1849 pounds at 9% of GVWR on this model is ○ deficient ○ excessive ● cautionary ○ good ○ excellent*
Total highway safety penalties are: 10*   Value: **8 6** Durability: **9 0** Highway Control Rating: **5 3**   Highway Safety: **4 3**

Dolphin	1997	MHA	34	533S	FO	7.5L	G	$2300	208	8,000	17,000	16,596

Livability Code: SB 30-90   Wheelbase-to-length ratio of 52% is considered ○ dangerous ● fatiguing ○ good ○ excellent*
The approximate net payload of 404 pounds at 2% of GVWR on this model is ● deficient ○ excessive ○ cautionary ○ good ○ excellent*
Total highway safety penalties are: 7*   Value: **8 7** Durability: **9 0** Highway Control Rating: **1 9**   Highway Safety: **1 2**

Dolphin	1997	MHA	34	532	FO	7.5L	G	$2200	228	8,000	17,000	15,722

Livability Code: SB 30-90   Wheelbase-to-length ratio of 55% is considered ○ dangerous ○ fatiguing ● good ○ excellent*
The approximate net payload of 1278 pounds at 8% of GVWR on this model is ○ deficient ○ excessive ● cautionary ○ good ○ excellent*
Total highway safety penalties are: 2*   Value: **9 0** Durability: **9 0** Highway Control Rating: **7 0**   Highway Safety: **6 8**   ★★

Dolphin	1997	MHA	36	534	FO	7.5L	G	$2100	228	8,000	17,000	16,017

Livability Code: SB 30-90   Wheelbase-to-length ratio of 53% is considered ○ dangerous ● fatiguing ○ good ○ excellent*
The approximate net payload of 983 pounds at 6% of GVWR on this model is ● deficient ○ excessive ○ cautionary ○ good ○ excellent*
Total highway safety penalties are: 2*   Value: **9 0** Durability: **9 0** Highway Control Rating: **3 5**   Highway Safety: **3 3**

Dolphin	1997	MHA	36	535S	CH	7.4L	G	$2400	232 T	1,500	19,500	17,796

Livability Code: SB 30-90   Wheelbase-to-length ratio of 54% is considered ○ dangerous ○ fatiguing ● good ○ excellent*
The approximate net payload of 1704 pounds at 9% of GVWR on this model is ○ deficient ○ excessive ● cautionary ○ good ○ excellent*
Total highway safety penalties are: 15*   Value: **8 3** Durability: **9 0** Highway Control Rating: **6 3**   Highway Safety: **4 8**

Dolphin	1997	MHA	36	536S	CH	7.4L	G	$2500	232 T	1,500	19,500	17,566

Livability Code: SB 30-90   Wheelbase-to-length ratio of 54% is considered ○ dangerous ○ fatiguing ● good ○ excellent*
The approximate net payload of 1934 pounds at 10% of GVWR on this model is ○ deficient ○ excessive ○ cautionary ● good ○ excellent*
Total highway safety penalties are: 15*   Value: **8 3** Durability: **9 0** Highway Control Rating: **7 4**   Highway Safety: **5 9**   ★

Dolphin	1997	MHA	36	535S	FO	7.5L	G	$2400	232 T	5,000	20,000	18,096

Livability Code: SB 30-90   Wheelbase-to-length ratio of 54% is considered ○ dangerous ○ fatiguing ● good ○ excellent*
The approximate net payload of 1904 pounds at 10% of GVWR on this model is ○ deficient ○ excessive ○ cautionary ● good ○ excellent*
Total highway safety penalties are: 10*   Value: **8 6** Durability: **9 0** Highway Control Rating: **7 4**   Highway Safety: **6 4**   ★★

Dolphin	1997	MHA	36	536S	FO	7.5L	G	$2400	232 T	5,000	20,000	18,171

Livability Code: SB 30-90   Wheelbase-to-length ratio of 54% is considered ○ dangerous ○ fatiguing ● good ○ excellent*
The approximate net payload of 1829 pounds at 9% of GVWR on this model is ○ deficient ○ excessive ● cautionary ○ good ○ excellent*
Total highway safety penalties are: 10*   Value: **8 6** Durability: **9 0** Highway Control Rating: **6 4**   Highway Safety: **5 4**   ★

Dolphin	1998	MHA	34	5330	FO	7.5L	G	$2500	208	5,000	17,000	16,060

Livability Code: SB 30-90   Wheelbase-to-length ratio of 52% is considered ○ dangerous ● fatiguing ○ good ○ excellent*
The approximate net payload of 940 pounds at 6% of GVWR on this model is ● deficient ○ excessive ○ cautionary ○ good ○ excellent*
Total highway safety penalties are: 7*   Value: **9 2** Durability: **9 0** Highway Control Rating: **2 2**   Highway Safety: **1 5**

Dolphin	1998	MHA	36	5340	FO	7.5L	G	$2200	228	5,000	17,000	15,680

Livability Code: SB 30-90   Wheelbase-to-length ratio of 53% is considered ○ dangerous ● fatiguing ○ good ○ excellent*
The approximate net payload of 1320 pounds at 8% of GVWR on this model is ○ deficient ○ excessive ● cautionary ○ good ○ excellent*
Total highway safety penalties are: 2*   Value: **9 5** Durability: **9 0** Highway Control Rating: **4 7**   Highway Safety: **4 5**

Note: Safety ratings are based on the assumption that the engineering of the RV has allowed for proper balance by placing fresh, gray, and black holding tanks in a location so as not to change the balance of the RV when the tanks are empty or full. **Always double-check wheelbase, GVWR, and weights at front and rear axles.**

*See Section 1 for details on how conclusions are reached.

Brand	Year	Type	Length	Model	Chassis	Engine	Fuel Type	Average Price per Linear Foot When New	Adjusted Wheelbase	Approx. Towing Capacity	Gross Vehicle Weight Rating	Average Curb Weight
Dolphin	1998	MHA	36	5350	CH	7.4L	G	$2500	232 T	1,500	19,500	17,810

Livability Code: SB 30-90
Wheelbase-to-length ratio of 54% is considered ○ dangerous ○ fatiguing ◉ good ○ excellent *
The approximate net payload of 1690 pounds at 9% of GVWR on this model is ○ deficient ○ excessive ◉ cautionary ○ good ○ excellent *
Total highway safety penalties are: 15 * Value: 8 8 Durability: 9 0 Highway Control Rating: 6 3 Highway Safety: 4 8

Brand	Year	Type	Length	Model	Chassis	Engine	Fuel Type	Price/Linear Foot	Adjusted Wheelbase	Towing Capacity	GVWR	Avg Curb Weight
Dolphin	1998	MHA	36	5360	CH	7.4L	G	$2500	232 T	1,500	19,500	18,100

Livability Code: SB 30-90
Wheelbase-to-length ratio of 54% is considered ○ dangerous ○ fatiguing ◉ good ○ excellent *
The approximate net payload of 1400 pounds at 7% of GVWR on this model is ○ deficient ○ excessive ◉ cautionary ○ good ○ excellent *
Total highway safety penalties are: 15 * Value: 8 8 Durability: 9 0 Highway Control Rating: 5 2 Highway Safety: 3 7

Brand	Year	Type	Length	Model	Chassis	Engine	Fuel Type	Price/Linear Foot	Adjusted Wheelbase	Towing Capacity	GVWR	Avg Curb Weight
Dolphin	1998	MHA	36	5350	FO	7.5L	G	$2500	232 T	5,000	20,000	18,010

Livability Code: SB 30-90
Wheelbase-to-length ratio of 54% is considered ○ dangerous ○ fatiguing ◉ good ○ excellent *
The approximate net payload of 1990 pounds at 10% of GVWR on this model is ○ deficient ○ excessive ○ cautionary ◉ good ○ excellent *
Total highway safety penalties are: 10 * Value: 9 1 Durability: 9 0 Highway Control Rating: 7 4 Highway Safety: 6 4 ★★

Brand	Year	Type	Length	Model	Chassis	Engine	Fuel Type	Price/Linear Foot	Adjusted Wheelbase	Towing Capacity	GVWR	Avg Curb Weight
Dolphin	1998	MHA	36	5360	FO	7.5L	G	$2500	232 T	5,000	20,000	18,160

Livability Code: SB 30-90
Wheelbase-to-length ratio of 54% is considered ○ dangerous ○ fatiguing ◉ good ○ excellent *
The approximate net payload of 1840 pounds at 9% of GVWR on this model is ○ deficient ○ excessive ◉ cautionary ○ good ○ excellent *
Total highway safety penalties are: 10 * Value: 9 1 Durability: 9 0 Highway Control Rating: 6 4 Highway Safety: 5 4 ★

Brand	Year	Type	Length	Model	Chassis	Engine	Fuel Type	Price/Linear Foot	Adjusted Wheelbase	Towing Capacity	GVWR	Avg Curb Weight
Dolphin	1999	MHA	34	5330	FO	6.8L	G	$2600	208	5,000	18,000	16,285

Livability Code: SB 30-90
Wheelbase-to-length ratio of 52% is considered ○ dangerous ◉ fatiguing ○ good ○ excellent *
The approximate net payload of 1715 pounds at 10% of GVWR on this model is ○ deficient ○ excessive ○ cautionary ◉ good ○ excellent *
Total highway safety penalties are: 7 * Value: 9 2 Durability: 9 0 Highway Control Rating: 5 3 Highway Safety: 4 6

Brand	Year	Type	Length	Model	Chassis	Engine	Fuel Type	Price/Linear Foot	Adjusted Wheelbase	Towing Capacity	GVWR	Avg Curb Weight
Dolphin	1999	MHA	36	5340	FO	6.8L	G	$2500	228	5,000	18,000	15,905

Livability Code: SB 30-90
Wheelbase-to-length ratio of 53% is considered ○ dangerous ◉ fatiguing ○ good ○ excellent *
The approximate net payload of 2095 pounds at 12% of GVWR on this model is ○ deficient ○ excessive ○ cautionary ◉ good ○ excellent *
Total highway safety penalties are: 2 * Value: 9 5 Durability: 9 0 Highway Control Rating: 6 7 Highway Safety: 6 5 ★★

Brand	Year	Type	Length	Model	Chassis	Engine	Fuel Type	Price/Linear Foot	Adjusted Wheelbase	Towing Capacity	GVWR	Avg Curb Weight
Dolphin	1999	MHA	36	5350	CH	7.4L	G	$2500	232 T	1,500	19,500	17,810

Livability Code: SB 30-90
Wheelbase-to-length ratio of 54% is considered ○ dangerous ○ fatiguing ◉ good ○ excellent *
The approximate net payload of 1690 pounds at 9% of GVWR on this model is ○ deficient ○ excessive ◉ cautionary ○ good ○ excellent *
Total highway safety penalties are: 15 * Value: 8 8 Durability: 9 0 Highway Control Rating: 6 6 Highway Safety: 5 1 ★

Brand	Year	Type	Length	Model	Chassis	Engine	Fuel Type	Price/Linear Foot	Adjusted Wheelbase	Towing Capacity	GVWR	Avg Curb Weight
Dolphin	1999	MHA	36	5360	CH	7.4L	G	$2500	232 T	1,500	19,500	18,100

Livability Code: SB 30-90
Wheelbase-to-length ratio of 54% is considered ○ dangerous ○ fatiguing ◉ good ○ excellent *
The approximate net payload of 1400 pounds at 7% of GVWR on this model is ○ deficient ○ excessive ◉ cautionary ○ good ○ excellent *
Total highway safety penalties are: 15 * Value: 8 8 Durability: 9 0 Highway Control Rating: 5 4 Highway Safety: 3 9

Brand	Year	Type	Length	Model	Chassis	Engine	Fuel Type	Price/Linear Foot	Adjusted Wheelbase	Towing Capacity	GVWR	Avg Curb Weight
Dolphin	1999	MHA	36	5350	FO	6.8L	G	$2500	232 T	5,000	20,500	18,450

Livability Code: SB 30-90
Wheelbase-to-length ratio of 54% is considered ○ dangerous ○ fatiguing ◉ good ○ excellent *
The approximate net payload of 2050 pounds at 10% of GVWR on this model is ○ deficient ○ excessive ○ cautionary ◉ good ○ excellent *
Total highway safety penalties are: 10 * Value: 9 1 Durability: 9 0 Highway Control Rating: 7 7 Highway Safety: 6 7 ★★

Brand	Year	Type	Length	Model	Chassis	Engine	Fuel Type	Price/Linear Foot	Adjusted Wheelbase	Towing Capacity	GVWR	Avg Curb Weight
Dolphin	1999	MHA	36	5360	FO	6.8L	G	$2500	232 T	5,000	20,500	18,600

Livability Code: SB 30-90
Wheelbase-to-length ratio of 54% is considered ○ dangerous ○ fatiguing ◉ good ○ excellent *
The approximate net payload of 1900 pounds at 9% of GVWR on this model is ○ deficient ○ excessive ◉ cautionary ○ good ○ excellent *
Total highway safety penalties are: 10 * Value: 9 1 Durability: 9 0 Highway Control Rating: 6 6 Highway Safety: 5 6 ★

Brand	Year	Type	Length	Model	Chassis	Engine	Fuel Type	Price/Linear Foot	Adjusted Wheelbase	Towing Capacity	GVWR	Avg Curb Weight
Dolphin	1999	MHA	37	5370 myc	FO	6.8L	G	$2400	252 T	5,000	20,500	18,460

Livability Code: SB 30-90
Wheelbase-to-length ratio of 57% is considered ○ dangerous ○ fatiguing ◉ good ○ excellent *
The approximate net payload of 2040 pounds at 10% of GVWR on this model is ○ deficient ○ excessive ○ cautionary ◉ good ○ excellent *
Total highway safety penalties are: 15 * Value: 8 9 Durability: 9 0 Highway Control Rating: 8 7 Highway Safety: 7 2 ★★★

Brand	Year	Type	Length	Model	Chassis	Engine	Fuel Type	Price/Linear Foot	Adjusted Wheelbase	Towing Capacity	GVWR	Avg Curb Weight
Dolphin 900	1991	MMH	22	21	TO	3.0L	G	$1300	137	1,500	6,000	5,336

Livability Code: VA 30-90
Wheelbase-to-length ratio of 52% is considered ○ dangerous ◉ fatiguing ○ good ○ excellent *
The approximate net payload of 664 pounds at 11% of GVWR on this model is ○ deficient ○ excessive ○ cautionary ◉ good ○ excellent *
Total highway safety penalties are: 2 * Value: 9 0 Durability: 9 0 Highway Control Rating: 4 8 Highway Safety: 4 6

Note: Safety ratings are based on the assumption that the engineering of the RV has allowed for proper balance by placing fresh, gray, and black holding tanks in a location so as not to change the balance of the RV when the tanks are empty or full. **Always double-check wheelbase, GVWR, and weights at front and rear axles.**

*See Section 1 for details on how conclusions are reached.

Brand	Year	Type	Length	Model	Chassis	Engine	Fuel Type	Average Price per Linear Foot When New	Adjusted Wheelbase	Approx. Towing Capacity	Gross Vehicle Weight Rating	Average Curb Weight
Dutch Star	1991	MHA	28	27 CB	FO	7.5L	G	$1300	158	1,500	11,000	10,684

Livability Code: VA 30-90 Wheelbase-to-length ratio of 47% is considered ● dangerous ○ fatiguing ○ good ○ excellent *

The approximate net payload of 316 pounds at 3% of GVWR on this model is ● deficient ○ excessive ○ cautionary ○ good ○ excellent *

Total highway safety penalties are: 2 * Value: 8 0 Durability: 7 8 Highway Control Rating: 1 Highway Safety: - 1

Brand	Year	Type	Length	Model	Chassis	Engine	Fuel Type	Price/Ft	Wheelbase	Towing	GVWR	Curb Weight
Dutch Star	1991	MHA	33	31 CBD	CH	7.4L	G	$1400	178	1,500	16,000	13,111

Livability Code: SB 30-90 Wheelbase-to-length ratio of 46% is considered ● dangerous ○ fatiguing ○ good ○ excellent *

The approximate net payload of 2889 pounds at 18% of GVWR on this model is ○ deficient ○ excessive ○ cautionary ○ good ● excellent *

Total highway safety penalties are: 6 * Value: 7 8 Durability: 7 8 Highway Control Rating: 3 1 Highway Safety: 2 5

Brand	Year	Type	Length	Model	Chassis	Engine	Fuel Type	Price/Ft	Wheelbase	Towing	GVWR	Curb Weight
Dutch Star	1994	MHA	28	27 WCB	CH	7.4L	G	$2000	178	4,000	16,000	12,272

Livability Code: SB 30-90 Wheelbase-to-length ratio of 53% is considered ○ dangerous ● fatiguing ○ good ○ excellent *

The approximate net payload of 3728 pounds at 23% of GVWR on this model is ○ deficient ○ excessive ○ cautionary ○ good ● excellent *

Total highway safety penalties are: 3 * Value: 8 0 Durability: 7 8 Highway Control Rating: 7 2 Highway Safety: 6 9 ★★

Brand	Year	Type	Length	Model	Chassis	Engine	Fuel Type	Price/Ft	Wheelbase	Towing	GVWR	Curb Weight
Dutch Star	1994	MHA	28	27 WCB	FO	7.5L	G	$2000	178	8,000	17,000	12,772

Livability Code: SB 30-90 Wheelbase-to-length ratio of 53% is considered ○ dangerous ● fatiguing ○ good ○ excellent *

The approximate net payload of 4228 pounds at 25% of GVWR on this model is ○ deficient ○ excessive ○ cautionary ● good ○ excellent *

Total highway safety penalties are: 2 * Value: 8 0 Durability: 7 8 Highway Control Rating: 7 1 Highway Safety: 6 9 ★★

Brand	Year	Type	Length	Model	Chassis	Engine	Fuel Type	Price/Ft	Wheelbase	Towing	GVWR	Curb Weight
Dutch Star	1994	MHA	32	31 WCB	CH	7.4L	G	$1800	220	4,000	16,000	13,280

Livability Code: SB 30-90 Wheelbase-to-length ratio of 57% is considered ○ dangerous ○ fatiguing ○ good ○ excellent *

The approximate net payload of 2720 pounds at 17% of GVWR on this model is ○ deficient ○ excessive ○ cautionary ○ good ● excellent *

Total highway safety penalties are: 6 * Value: 7 8 Durability: 7 8 Highway Control Rating: 1 0 0 Highway Safety: 9 4 ★★★

Brand	Year	Type	Length	Model	Chassis	Engine	Fuel Type	Price/Ft	Wheelbase	Towing	GVWR	Curb Weight
Dutch Star	1994	MHA	32	31 WCB	FO	7.5L	G	$1800	220	8,000	17,000	13,780

Livability Code: SB 30-90 Wheelbase-to-length ratio of 57% is considered ○ dangerous ○ fatiguing ● good ○ excellent *

The approximate net payload of 3220 pounds at 19% of GVWR on this model is ○ deficient ○ excessive ○ cautionary ○ good ● excellent *

Total highway safety penalties are: 2 * Value: 8 0 Durability: 7 8 Highway Control Rating: 1 0 0 Highway Safety: 9 8 ★★★

Brand	Year	Type	Length	Model	Chassis	Engine	Fuel Type	Price/Ft	Wheelbase	Towing	GVWR	Curb Weight
Dutch Star	1994	MHA	33	32 WCB-sl	FO	7.5L	G	$1900	203	8,000	17,000	14,920

Livability Code: SB 30-90 Wheelbase-to-length ratio of 51% is considered ○ dangerous ● fatiguing ○ good ○ excellent *

The approximate net payload of 2080 pounds at 12% of GVWR on this model is ○ deficient ○ excessive ○ cautionary ● good ○ excellent *

Total highway safety penalties are: 5 * Value: 7 9 Durability: 7 8 Highway Control Rating: 4 1 Highway Safety: 3 6

Brand	Year	Type	Length	Model	Chassis	Engine	Fuel Type	Price/Ft	Wheelbase	Towing	GVWR	Curb Weight
Dutch Star	1994	MHA	35	34 SACB	CH	7.4L	G	$1700	228	4,000	16,000	13,928

Livability Code: SB 30-90 Wheelbase-to-length ratio of 55% is considered ○ dangerous ○ fatiguing ● good ○ excellent *

The approximate net payload of 2072 pounds at 13% of GVWR on this model is ○ deficient ○ excessive ○ cautionary ● good ○ excellent *

Total highway safety penalties are: 7 * Value: 7 8 Durability: 7 8 Highway Control Rating: 8 6 Highway Safety: 7 9 ★★★

Brand	Year	Type	Length	Model	Chassis	Engine	Fuel Type	Price/Ft	Wheelbase	Towing	GVWR	Curb Weight
Dutch Star	1994	MHA	35	34 WCB1	CH	7.4L	G	$1700	228	4,000	16,000	13,928

Livability Code: SB 30-90 Wheelbase-to-length ratio of 55% is considered ○ dangerous ○ fatiguing ● good ○ excellent *

The approximate net payload of 2072 pounds at 13% of GVWR on this model is ○ deficient ○ excessive ○ cautionary ● good ○ excellent *

Total highway safety penalties are: 7 * Value: 7 8 Durability: 7 8 Highway Control Rating: 8 6 Highway Safety: 7 9 ★★★

Brand	Year	Type	Length	Model	Chassis	Engine	Fuel Type	Price/Ft	Wheelbase	Towing	GVWR	Curb Weight
Dutch Star	1994	MHA	35	34 CBD2-sl	FO	7.5L	G	$1800	216	8,000	17,000	15,328

Livability Code: SB 30-90 Wheelbase-to-length ratio of 52% is considered ○ dangerous ● fatiguing ○ good ○ excellent *

The approximate net payload of 1672 pounds at 10% of GVWR on this model is ○ deficient ○ excessive ○ cautionary ● good ○ excellent *

Total highway safety penalties are: 5 * Value: 7 9 Durability: 7 8 Highway Control Rating: 4 7 Highway Safety: 4 2

Brand	Year	Type	Length	Model	Chassis	Engine	Fuel Type	Price/Ft	Wheelbase	Towing	GVWR	Curb Weight
Dutch Star	1994	MHA	35	34 SACB	FO	7.5L	G	$1700	228	8,000	17,000	14,428

Livability Code: SB 30-90 Wheelbase-to-length ratio of 55% is considered ○ dangerous ○ fatiguing ● good ○ excellent *

The approximate net payload of 2572 pounds at 15% of GVWR on this model is ○ deficient ○ excessive ○ cautionary ● good ○ excellent *

Total highway safety penalties are: 2 * Value: 8 0 Durability: 7 8 Highway Control Rating: 9 0 Highway Safety: 8 8 ★★★

Brand	Year	Type	Length	Model	Chassis	Engine	Fuel Type	Price/Ft	Wheelbase	Towing	GVWR	Curb Weight
Dutch Star	1994	MHA	35	34 WCB1	FO	7.5L	G	$1700	228	8,000	17,000	14,428

Livability Code: SB 30-90 Wheelbase-to-length ratio of 55% is considered ○ dangerous ○ fatiguing ● good ○ excellent *

The approximate net payload of 2572 pounds at 15% of GVWR on this model is ○ deficient ○ excessive ○ cautionary ● good ○ excellent *

Total highway safety penalties are: 2 * Value: 8 0 Durability: 7 8 Highway Control Rating: 9 0 Highway Safety: 8 8 ★★★

Note: Safety ratings are based on the assumption that the engineering of the RV has allowed for proper balance by placing fresh, gray, and black holding tanks in a location so as not to change the balance of the RV when the tanks are empty or full. **Always double-check wheelbase, GVWR, and weights at front and rear axles.**

*See Section 1 for details on how conclusions are reached.

Section 2: The Ratings

Brand	Year	Type	Length	Model	Chassis	Engine	Fuel Type	Average Price per Linear Foot When New	Adjusted Wheelbase	Approx. Towing Capacity	Gross Vehicle Weight Rating	Average Curb Weight
Dutch Star	1994	MHA	35	34 WCB2-sl	FO	7.5L	G	$1800	216	8,000	17,000	15,328

Livability Code: SB 30-90
Wheelbase-to-length ratio of 52% is considered ○ dangerous ◉ fatiguing ○ good ○ excellent *
The approximate net payload of 1672 pounds at 10% of GVWR on this model is ○ deficient ○ excessive ○ cautionary ◉ good ○ excellent *
Total highway safety penalties are: 5 *   Value: 7 9   Durability: 7 8   Highway Control Rating: 4 7   Highway Safety: 4 2

Brand	Year	Type	Length	Model	Chassis	Engine	Fuel Type	Avg Price/Lin Ft	Adj Wheelbase	Approx Towing	GVWR	Avg Curb Wt
Dutch Star	1994	MHA	35	34 CBS-sl	SP	Cum	D	$2900	212	4,000	20,000	17,287

Livability Code: SB 30-90
Wheelbase-to-length ratio of 51% is considered ○ dangerous ◉ fatiguing ○ good ○ excellent *
The approximate net payload of 2713 pounds at 14% of GVWR on this model is ○ deficient ○ excessive ○ cautionary ◉ good ○ excellent *
Total highway safety penalties are: 5 *   Value: 7 9   Durability: 7 8   Highway Control Rating: 4 3   Highway Safety: 3 8

Dutch Star	1994	MHA	35	34 WBS2-sl	SP	Cum	D	$2900	212	4,000	20,000	17,287

Livability Code: SB 30-90
Wheelbase-to-length ratio of 51% is considered ○ dangerous ◉ fatiguing ○ good ○ excellent *
The approximate net payload of 2713 pounds at 14% of GVWR on this model is ○ deficient ○ excessive ○ cautionary ◉ good ○ excellent *
Total highway safety penalties are: 5 *   Value: 7 9   Durability: 7 8   Highway Control Rating: 4 3   Highway Safety: 3 8

Dutch Star	1995	MHA	28	DA 2705	FO	7.5L	G	$2000	178	8,000	17,000	12,772

Livability Code: SB 30-90
Wheelbase-to-length ratio of 53% is considered ○ dangerous ◉ fatiguing ○ good ○ excellent *
The approximate net payload of 4228 pounds at 25% of GVWR on this model is ○ deficient ○ excessive ○ cautionary ◉ good ○ excellent *
Total highway safety penalties are: 2 *   Value: 8 0   Durability: 7 8   Highway Control Rating: 7 1   Highway Safety: 6 9   ★★

Dutch Star	1995	MHA	32	DA 3105	FO	7.5L	G	$1800	220	8,000	17,000	13,780

Livability Code: SB 30-90
Wheelbase-to-length ratio of 57% is considered ○ dangerous ○ fatiguing ◉ good ○ excellent *
The approximate net payload of 3220 pounds at 19% of GVWR on this model is ○ deficient ○ excessive ○ cautionary ○ good ◉ excellent *
Total highway safety penalties are: 2 *   Value: 8 0   Durability: 7 8   Highway Control Rating: 1 0 0   Highway Safety: 9 8   ★★★

Dutch Star	1995	MHA	33	DA 3255-sl	FO	7.5L	G	$1900	203	8,000	17,000	14,920

Livability Code: SB 30-90
Wheelbase-to-length ratio of 51% is considered ○ dangerous ◉ fatiguing ○ good ○ excellent *
The approximate net payload of 2080 pounds at 12% of GVWR on this model is ○ deficient ○ excessive ○ cautionary ◉ good ○ excellent *
Total highway safety penalties are: 5 *   Value: 7 9   Durability: 7 8   Highway Control Rating: 4 1   Highway Safety: 3 6

Dutch Star	1995	MHA	35	DA 3400	FO	7.5L	G	$1700	228	8,000	17,000	14,428

Livability Code: SB 30-90
Wheelbase-to-length ratio of 55% is considered ○ dangerous ○ fatiguing ◉ good ○ excellent *
The approximate net payload of 2572 pounds at 15% of GVWR on this model is ○ deficient ○ excessive ○ cautionary ◉ good ○ excellent *
Total highway safety penalties are: 2 *   Value: 8 0   Durability: 7 8   Highway Control Rating: 9 0   Highway Safety: 8 8   ★★★

Dutch Star	1995	MHA	35	DA 3450-sl	FO	7.5L	G	$1900	216	8,000	17,000	15,328

Livability Code: SB 30-90
Wheelbase-to-length ratio of 52% is considered ○ dangerous ◉ fatiguing ○ good ○ excellent *
The approximate net payload of 1672 pounds at 10% of GVWR on this model is ○ deficient ○ excessive ○ cautionary ◉ good ○ excellent *
Total highway safety penalties are: 5 *   Value: 7 9   Durability: 7 8   Highway Control Rating: 4 7   Highway Safety: 4 2

Dutch Star	1995	MHA	35	DP 3450-sl	SP	250HP	D	$3300	212	5,000	26,000	20,887

Livability Code: SB 30-90
Wheelbase-to-length ratio of 51% is considered ○ dangerous ◉ fatiguing ○ good ○ excellent *
The approximate net payload of 5113 pounds at 20% of GVWR on this model is ○ deficient ○ excessive ○ cautionary ○ good ◉ excellent *
Total highway safety penalties are: 5 *   Value: 7 9   Durability: 7 8   Highway Control Rating: 5 1   Highway Safety: 4 6

Dutch Star	1995	MHA	35	DP 3455-sl	SP	250HP	D	$3300	212	5,000	26,000	20,887

Livability Code: SB 30-90
Wheelbase-to-length ratio of 51% is considered ○ dangerous ◉ fatiguing ○ good ○ excellent *
The approximate net payload of 5113 pounds at 20% of GVWR on this model is ○ deficient ○ excessive ○ cautionary ○ good ◉ excellent *
Total highway safety penalties are: 5 *   Value: 7 9   Durability: 7 8   Highway Control Rating: 5 1   Highway Safety: 4 6

Dutch Star	1995	MHA	37	DP 3655-sl	SP	250HP	D	$3200	236	5,000	26,000	21,367

Livability Code: SB 30-90
Wheelbase-to-length ratio of 54% is considered ○ dangerous ○ fatiguing ◉ good ○ excellent *
The approximate net payload of 4633 pounds at 18% of GVWR on this model is ○ deficient ○ excessive ○ cautionary ○ good ◉ excellent *
Total highway safety penalties are: 5 *   Value: 7 9   Durability: 7 8   Highway Control Rating: 8 2   Highway Safety: 7 7   ★★★

Dutch Star	1996	MHA	32	DA 3106	CH	7.4L	G	$1800	200	3,500	16,500	13,687

Livability Code: SB 30-90
Wheelbase-to-length ratio of 52% is considered ○ dangerous ◉ fatiguing ○ good ○ excellent *
The approximate net payload of 2813 pounds at 17% of GVWR on this model is ○ deficient ○ excessive ○ cautionary ○ good ◉ excellent *
Total highway safety penalties are: 6 *   Value: 7 8   Durability: 7 8   Highway Control Rating: 6 1   Highway Safety: 5 5   ★

Note: Safety ratings are based on the assumption that the engineering of the RV has allowed for proper balance by placing fresh, gray, and black holding tanks in a location so as not to change the balance of the RV when the tanks are empty or full. **Always double-check wheelbase, GVWR, and weights at front and rear axles.**

*See Section 1 for details on how conclusions are reached.

Section 2: The Ratings

Brand	Year	Type	Length	Model	Chassis	Engine	Fuel Type	Average Price per Linear Foot When New	Adjusted Wheelbase	Approx. Towing Capacity	Gross Vehicle Weight Rating	Average Curb Weight

Dutch Star | 1996 | MHA | 32 | DA 3106 | FO | 7.5L | G | $1800 | 200 | 8,000 | 17,000 | 14,087
Livability Code: SB 30-90
Wheelbase-to-length ratio of 52% is considered ○ dangerous ● fatiguing ○ good ○ excellent*
The approximate net payload of 2913 pounds at 17% of GVWR on this model is ○ deficient ○ excessive ○ cautionary ○ good ● excellent*
Total highway safety penalties are: 2*   Value: 80   Durability: 78   Highway Control Rating: 61   Highway Safety: 59   ★

Dutch Star | 1996 | MHA | 33 | DA 3255 | CH | 7.4L | G | $1800 | 203 | 3,500 | 16,500 | 14,837
Livability Code: SB 30-90
Wheelbase-to-length ratio of 51% is considered ○ dangerous ● fatiguing ○ good ○ excellent*
The approximate net payload of 1663 pounds at 10% of GVWR on this model is ○ deficient ○ excessive ○ cautionary ● good ○ excellent*
Total highway safety penalties are: 9*   Value: 77   Durability: 78   Highway Control Rating: 37   Highway Safety: 28

Dutch Star | 1996 | MHA | 33 | DA 3255 | FO | 7.5L | G | $1800 | 203 | 8,000 | 17,000 | 15,237
Livability Code: SB 30-90
Wheelbase-to-length ratio of 51% is considered ○ dangerous ● fatiguing ○ good ○ excellent*
The approximate net payload of 1763 pounds at 10% of GVWR on this model is ○ deficient ○ excessive ○ cautionary ● good ○ excellent*
Total highway safety penalties are: 5*   Value: 79   Durability: 78   Highway Control Rating: 38   Highway Safety: 33

Dutch Star | 1996 | MHA | 34 | DA 3401 | CH | 7.4L | G | $1700 | 208 | 3,500 | 16,500 | 14,186
Livability Code: SB 30-90
Wheelbase-to-length ratio of 51% is considered ○ dangerous ● fatiguing ○ good ○ excellent*
The approximate net payload of 2314 pounds at 14% of GVWR on this model is ○ deficient ○ excessive ○ cautionary ● good ○ excellent*
Total highway safety penalties are: 7*   Value: 78   Durability: 78   Highway Control Rating: 44   Highway Safety: 37

Dutch Star | 1996 | MHA | 35 | DP 3450-sl | SP | Cu | D | $3300 | 212 | 17,000 | 23,000 | 20,086
Livability Code: SB 30-90
Wheelbase-to-length ratio of 51% is considered ○ dangerous ● fatiguing ○ good ○ excellent*
The approximate net payload of 2914 pounds at 13% of GVWR on this model is ○ deficient ○ excessive ○ cautionary ● good ○ excellent*
Total highway safety penalties are: 5*   Value: 79   Durability: 78   Highway Control Rating: 42   Highway Safety: 37

Dutch Star | 1996 | MHA | 35 | DP 3455-sl | SP | Cu | D | $3300 | 212 | 17,000 | 23,000 | 20,086
Livability Code: SB 30-90
Wheelbase-to-length ratio of 51% is considered ○ dangerous ● fatiguing ○ good ○ excellent*
The approximate net payload of 2914 pounds at 13% of GVWR on this model is ○ deficient ○ excessive ○ cautionary ● good ○ excellent*
Total highway safety penalties are: 5*   Value: 79   Durability: 78   Highway Control Rating: 42   Highway Safety: 37

Dutch Star | 1996 | MHA | 35 | DA 3412 | CH | 7.4L | G | $1700 | 208 | 3,500 | 16,500 | 14,436
Livability Code: SB 30-90
Wheelbase-to-length ratio of 50% is considered ● dangerous ○ fatiguing ○ good ○ excellent*
The approximate net payload of 2064 pounds at 13% of GVWR on this model is ○ deficient ○ excessive ○ cautionary ● good ○ excellent*
Total highway safety penalties are: 7*   Value: 78   Durability: 78   Highway Control Rating: 37   Highway Safety: 30

Dutch Star | 1996 | MHA | 35 | DA 3450-sl | CH | 7.4L | G | $1700 | 208 | 3,500 | 16,500 | 15,336
Livability Code: SB 30-90
Wheelbase-to-length ratio of 50% is considered ● dangerous ○ fatiguing ○ good ○ excellent*
The approximate net payload of 1164 pounds at 7% of GVWR on this model is ○ deficient ○ excessive ● cautionary ○ good ○ excellent*
Total highway safety penalties are: 10*   Value: 76   Durability: 78   Highway Control Rating: 14   Highway Safety: 4

Dutch Star | 1996 | MHA | 35 | DA 3455-sl | CH | 7.4L | G | $1700 | 208 | 3,500 | 16,500 | 15,336
Livability Code: SB 30-90
Wheelbase-to-length ratio of 50% is considered ● dangerous ○ fatiguing ○ good ○ excellent*
The approximate net payload of 1164 pounds at 7% of GVWR on this model is ○ deficient ○ excessive ● cautionary ○ good ○ excellent*
Total highway safety penalties are: 10*   Value: 76   Durability: 78   Highway Control Rating: 14   Highway Safety: 4

Dutch Star | 1996 | MHA | 35 | DA 3401 | FO | 7.5L | G | $1700 | 208 | 8,000 | 17,000 | 14,836
Livability Code: SB 30-90
Wheelbase-to-length ratio of 50% is considered ● dangerous ○ fatiguing ○ good ○ excellent*
The approximate net payload of 2164 pounds at 13% of GVWR on this model is ○ deficient ○ excessive ○ cautionary ● good ○ excellent*
Total highway safety penalties are: 2*   Value: 80   Durability: 78   Highway Control Rating: 37   Highway Safety: 35

Dutch Star | 1996 | MHA | 35 | DA 3412 | FO | 7.5L | G | $1700 | 208 | 8,000 | 17,000 | 14,836
Livability Code: SB 30-90
Wheelbase-to-length ratio of 50% is considered ● dangerous ○ fatiguing ○ good ○ excellent*
The approximate net payload of 2164 pounds at 13% of GVWR on this model is ○ deficient ○ excessive ○ cautionary ● good ○ excellent*
Total highway safety penalties are: 2*   Value: 80   Durability: 78   Highway Control Rating: 37   Highway Safety: 35

Dutch Star | 1996 | MHA | 35 | DA 3455-sl | FO | 7.5L | G | $1700 | 208 | 8,000 | 17,000 | 15,736
Livability Code: SB 30-90
Wheelbase-to-length ratio of 50% is considered ● dangerous ○ fatiguing ○ good ○ excellent*
The approximate net payload of 1264 pounds at 7% of GVWR on this model is ○ deficient ○ excessive ● cautionary ○ good ○ excellent*
Total highway safety penalties are: 5*   Value: 79   Durability: 78   Highway Control Rating: 15   Highway Safety: 10

Note: Safety ratings are based on the assumption that the engineering of the RV has allowed for proper balance by placing fresh, gray, and black holding tanks in a location so as not to change the balance of the RV when the tanks are empty or full. **Always double-check wheelbase, GVWR, and weights at front and rear axles.**

*See Section 1 for details on how conclusions are reached.

Brand	Year	Type	Length	Model	Chassis	Engine	Fuel Type	Average Price per Linear Foot When New	Adjusted Wheelbase	Approx. Towing Capacity	Gross Vehicle Weight Rating	Average Curb Weight
Dutch Star	**1996**	MHA	35	DA 3455 -sl	FO	7.5L	G	$1700	208	8,000	17,000	15,736

Livability Code: SB 30-90
Wheelbase-to-length ratio of 50% is considered ● dangerous ○ fatiguing ○ good ○ excellent *
The approximate net payload of 1264 pounds at 7% of GVWR on this model is ○ deficient ○ excessive ● cautionary ○ good ○ excellent *
Total highway safety penalties are: 5 *   Value: **7 9**   Durability: **7 8**   Highway Control Rating: **1 5**   Highway Safety: **1 0**

Brand	Year	Type	Length	Model	Chassis	Engine	Fuel Type	Average Price per Linear Foot When New	Adjusted Wheelbase	Approx. Towing Capacity	Gross Vehicle Weight Rating	Average Curb Weight
Dutch Star	**1996**	MHA	37	DA 3658-sl	CH	7.4L	G	$1600	238 T	1,500	18,500	16,635

Livability Code: SB 30-90
Wheelbase-to-length ratio of 54% is considered ○ dangerous ○ fatiguing ● good ○ excellent *
The approximate net payload of 1865 pounds at 10% of GVWR on this model is ○ deficient ○ excessive ○ cautionary ● good ○ excellent *
Total highway safety penalties are: 13 *   Value: **7 5**   Durability: **7 8**   Highway Control Rating: **7 4**   Highway Safety: **6 1**   ★★

Brand	Year	Type	Length	Model	Chassis	Engine	Fuel Type	Average Price per Linear Foot When New	Adjusted Wheelbase	Approx. Towing Capacity	Gross Vehicle Weight Rating	Average Curb Weight
Dutch Star	**1996**	MHA	37	DA 3658-sl	FO	7.5L	G	$1600	238 T	5,000	20,000	17,135

Livability Code: SB 30-90
Wheelbase-to-length ratio of 54% is considered ○ dangerous ○ fatiguing ● good ○ excellent *
The approximate net payload of 2865 pounds at 14% of GVWR on this model is ○ deficient ○ excessive ○ cautionary ● good ○ excellent *
Total highway safety penalties are: 7 *   Value: **7 8**   Durability: **7 8**   Highway Control Rating: **7 8**   Highway Safety: **7 1**   ★★★

Brand	Year	Type	Length	Model	Chassis	Engine	Fuel Type	Average Price per Linear Foot When New	Adjusted Wheelbase	Approx. Towing Capacity	Gross Vehicle Weight Rating	Average Curb Weight
Dutch Star	**1996**	MHA	37	DP 3730	SP	Cu	D	$3200	240	16,000	26,000	20,916

Livability Code: SB 30-90
Wheelbase-to-length ratio of 54% is considered ○ dangerous ○ fatiguing ● good ○ excellent *
The approximate net payload of 5084 pounds at 20% of GVWR on this model is ○ deficient ○ excessive ○ cautionary ○ good ● excellent *
Total highway safety penalties are: 2 *   Value: **8 0**   Durability: **7 8**   Highway Control Rating: **8 5**   Highway Safety: **8 3**   ★★★

Brand	Year	Type	Length	Model	Chassis	Engine	Fuel Type	Average Price per Linear Foot When New	Adjusted Wheelbase	Approx. Towing Capacity	Gross Vehicle Weight Rating	Average Curb Weight
Dutch Star	**1996**	MHA	37	DP 3757-sl	SP	Cu	D	$3300	240	16,000	26,000	21,816

Livability Code: SB 30-90
Wheelbase-to-length ratio of 54% is considered ○ dangerous ○ fatiguing ● good ○ excellent *
The approximate net payload of 4184 pounds at 16% of GVWR on this model is ○ deficient ○ excessive ○ cautionary ○ good ● excellent *
Total highway safety penalties are: 5 *   Value: **7 9**   Durability: **7 8**   Highway Control Rating: **8 2**   Highway Safety: **7 7**   ★★★

Brand	Year	Type	Length	Model	Chassis	Engine	Fuel Type	Average Price per Linear Foot When New	Adjusted Wheelbase	Approx. Towing Capacity	Gross Vehicle Weight Rating	Average Curb Weight
Dutch Star	**1996**	MHA	37	DP 3762-sl	SP	Cu	D	$3300	240	16,000	26,000	21,816

Livability Code: SB 30-90
Wheelbase-to-length ratio of 54% is considered ○ dangerous ○ fatiguing ● good ○ excellent *
The approximate net payload of 4184 pounds at 16% of GVWR on this model is ○ deficient ○ excessive ○ cautionary ○ good ● excellent *
Total highway safety penalties are: 5 *   Value: **7 9**   Durability: **7 8**   Highway Control Rating: **8 2**   Highway Safety: **7 7**   ★★★

Brand	Year	Type	Length	Model	Chassis	Engine	Fuel Type	Average Price per Linear Foot When New	Adjusted Wheelbase	Approx. Towing Capacity	Gross Vehicle Weight Rating	Average Curb Weight
Dutch Star	**1997**	MHA	32	DA3106	CH	7.4L	G	$1800	200	4,500	16,500	13,994

Livability Code: SB 30-90
Wheelbase-to-length ratio of 52% is considered ○ dangerous ● fatiguing ○ good ○ excellent *
The approximate net payload of 2506 pounds at 15% of GVWR on this model is ○ deficient ○ excessive ○ cautionary ● good ○ excellent *
Total highway safety penalties are: 6 *   Value: **7 8**   Durability: **7 8**   Highway Control Rating: **5 8**   Highway Safety: **5 2**   ★

Brand	Year	Type	Length	Model	Chassis	Engine	Fuel Type	Average Price per Linear Foot When New	Adjusted Wheelbase	Approx. Towing Capacity	Gross Vehicle Weight Rating	Average Curb Weight
Dutch Star	**1997**	MHA	32	DA3106	FO	7.5L	G	$1800	200	8,000	17,000	14,394

Livability Code: SB 30-90
Wheelbase-to-length ratio of 52% is considered ○ dangerous ● fatiguing ○ good ○ excellent *
The approximate net payload of 2606 pounds at 15% of GVWR on this model is ○ deficient ○ excessive ○ cautionary ● good ○ excellent *
Total highway safety penalties are: 2 *   Value: **8 0**   Durability: **7 8**   Highway Control Rating: **5 8**   Highway Safety: **5 6**   ★

Brand	Year	Type	Length	Model	Chassis	Engine	Fuel Type	Average Price per Linear Foot When New	Adjusted Wheelbase	Approx. Towing Capacity	Gross Vehicle Weight Rating	Average Curb Weight
Dutch Star	**1997**	MHA	32	DA3106 fr.dsl	FR	Cu210	D	$2500	200	5,000	20,500	15,494

Livability Code: SB 30-90
Wheelbase-to-length ratio of 52% is considered ○ dangerous ● fatiguing ○ good ○ excellent *
The approximate net payload of 5006 pounds at 24% of GVWR on this model is ○ deficient ○ excessive ○ cautionary ○ good ● excellent *
Total highway safety penalties are: 2 *   Value: **8 0**   Durability: **7 8**   Highway Control Rating: **5 9**   Highway Safety: **5 7**   ★

Brand	Year	Type	Length	Model	Chassis	Engine	Fuel Type	Average Price per Linear Foot When New	Adjusted Wheelbase	Approx. Towing Capacity	Gross Vehicle Weight Rating	Average Curb Weight
Dutch Star	**1997**	MHA	33	DA3256	CH	7.4L	G	$2000	200	4,500	16,500	15,154

Livability Code: SB 30-90
Wheelbase-to-length ratio of 51% is considered ○ dangerous ● fatiguing ○ good ○ excellent *
The approximate net payload of 1346 pounds at 8% of GVWR on this model is ○ deficient ○ excessive ● cautionary ○ good\ ○ excellent *
Total highway safety penalties are: 9 *   Value: **7 7**   Durability: **7 8**   Highway Control Rating: **2 4**   Highway Safety: **1 5**

Brand	Year	Type	Length	Model	Chassis	Engine	Fuel Type	Average Price per Linear Foot When New	Adjusted Wheelbase	Approx. Towing Capacity	Gross Vehicle Weight Rating	Average Curb Weight
Dutch Star	**1997**	MHA	33	DA3256	FO	7.5L	G	$2000	200	8,000	17,000	15,554

Livability Code: SB 30-90
Wheelbase-to-length ratio of 51% is considered ○ dangerous ● fatiguing ○ good ○ excellent *
The approximate net payload of 1446 pounds at 9% of GVWR on this model is ○ deficient ○ excessive ● cautionary ○ good ○ excellent *
Total highway safety penalties are: 5 *   Value: **7 9**   Durability: **7 8**   Highway Control Rating: **2 9**   Highway Safety: **2 4**

Brand	Year	Type	Length	Model	Chassis	Engine	Fuel Type	Average Price per Linear Foot When New	Adjusted Wheelbase	Approx. Towing Capacity	Gross Vehicle Weight Rating	Average Curb Weight
Dutch Star	**1997**	MHA	33	DA3256 fr.dsl	FR	Cu210	D	$2400	200	5,000	20,500	16,654

Livability Code: SB 30-90
Wheelbase-to-length ratio of 51% is considered ○ dangerous ● fatiguing ○ good ○ excellent *
The approximate net payload of 3846 pounds at 19% of GVWR on this model is ○ deficient ○ excessive ○ cautionary ○ good ● excellent *
Total highway safety penalties are: 5 *   Value: **7 9**   Durability: **7 8**   Highway Control Rating: **4 9**   Highway Safety: **4 4**

Note: Safety ratings are based on the assumption that the engineering of the RV has allowed for proper balance by placing fresh, gray, and black holding tanks in a location so as not to change the balance of the RV when the tanks are empty or full. **Always double-check wheelbase, GVWR, and weights at front and rear axles.**

*See Section 1 for details on how conclusions are reached.

Brand	Year	Type	Length	Model	Chassis	Engine	Fuel Type	Average Price per Linear Foot When New	Adjusted Wheelbase	Approx. Towing Capacity	Gross Vehicle Weight Rating	Average Curb Weight
Dutch Star	1997	MHA	35	DP3456 pusher	SP	Cu250	D	$3600	212	5,000	26,000	21,535

Livability Code: SB 30-90   Wheelbase-to-length ratio of 51% is considered ○ dangerous ● fatiguing ○ good ○ excellent *

The approximate net payload of 4465 pounds at 17% of GVWR on this model is ○ deficient ○ excessive ○ cautionary ○ good ● excellent *

Total highway safety penalties are: 5 *   Value: 79   Durability: 78   Highway Control Rating: 50   Highway Safety: 45

| Dutch Star | 1997 | MHA | 35 | DA3450 | CH | 7.4L | G | $1900 | 208 | 4,500 | 16,500 | 15,672 |

Livability Code: SB 30-90   Wheelbase-to-length ratio of 50% is considered ● dangerous ○ fatiguing ○ good ○ excellent *

The approximate net payload of 828 pounds at 5% of GVWR on this model is ● deficient ○ excessive ○ cautionary ○ good ○ excellent *

Total highway safety penalties are: 10 *   Value: 76   Durability: 78   Highway Control Rating: 7   Highway Safety: -3

| Dutch Star | 1997 | MHA | 35 | DA3455 | CH | 7.4L | G | $1900 | 208 | 4,500 | 16,500 | 15,672 |

Livability Code: SB 30-90   Wheelbase-to-length ratio of 50% is considered ● dangerous ○ fatiguing ○ good ○ excellent *

The approximate net payload of 828 pounds at 5% of GVWR on this model is ● deficient ○ excessive ○ cautionary ○ good ○ excellent *

Total highway safety penalties are: 10 *   Value: 76   Durability: 78   Highway Control Rating: 7   Highway Safety: -3

| Dutch Star | 1997 | MHA | 35 | DA3401 | FO | 7.5L | G | $1700 | 228 | 8,000 | 17,000 | 15,172 |

Livability Code: SB 30-90   Wheelbase-to-length ratio of 54% is considered ○ dangerous ○ fatiguing ● good ○ excellent *

The approximate net payload of 1828 pounds at 11% of GVWR on this model is ○ deficient ○ excessive ○ cautionary ● good ○ excellent *

Total highway safety penalties are: 2 *   Value: 80   Durability: 78   Highway Control Rating: 77   Highway Safety: 75   ★★★

| Dutch Star | 1997 | MHA | 35 | DA3450 | FO | 7.5L | G | $1900 | 208 | 8,000 | 17,000 | 16,072 |

Livability Code: SB 30-90   Wheelbase-to-length ratio of 50% is considered ● dangerous ○ fatiguing ○ good ○ excellent *

The approximate net payload of 928 pounds at 5% of GVWR on this model is ● deficient ○ excessive ○ cautionary ○ good ○ excellent *

Total highway safety penalties are: 5 *   Value: 79   Durability: 78   Highway Control Rating: 8   Highway Safety: 3

| Dutch Star | 1997 | MHA | 35 | DA3455 | FO | 7.5L | G | $1900 | 208 | 8,000 | 17,000 | 16,072 |

Livability Code: SB 30-90   Wheelbase-to-length ratio of 50% is considered ● dangerous ○ fatiguing ○ good ○ excellent *

The approximate net payload of 928 pounds at 5% of GVWR on this model is ● deficient ○ excessive ○ cautionary ○ good ○ excellent *

Total highway safety penalties are: 5 *   Value: 79   Durability: 78   Highway Control Rating: 8   Highway Safety: 3

| Dutch Star | 1997 | MHA | 35 | DA3401 fr.dsl | FR | Cu210 | D | $2300 | 228 | 5,000 | 20,500 | 16,272 |

Livability Code: SB 30-90   Wheelbase-to-length ratio of 54% is considered ○ dangerous ○ fatiguing ● good ○ excellent *

The approximate net payload of 4228 pounds at 21% of GVWR on this model is ○ deficient ○ excessive ○ cautionary ○ good ● excellent *

Total highway safety penalties are: 2 *   Value: 80   Durability: 78   Highway Control Rating: 86   Highway Safety: 84   ★★★

| Dutch Star | 1997 | MHA | 35 | DA3450 fr.dsl | FR | Cu210 | D | $2300 | 208 | 5,000 | 20,500 | 17,247 |

Livability Code: SB 30-90   Wheelbase-to-length ratio of 50% is considered ● dangerous ○ fatiguing ○ good ○ excellent *

The approximate net payload of 3253 pounds at 16% of GVWR on this model is ○ deficient ○ excessive ○ cautionary ○ good ● excellent *

Total highway safety penalties are: 5 *   Value: 79   Durability: 78   Highway Control Rating: 43   Highway Safety: 38

| Dutch Star | 1997 | MHA | 35 | DA3455 fr.dsl | FR | Cu210 | D | $2300 | 208 | 5,000 | 20,500 | 17,172 |

Livability Code: SB 30-90   Wheelbase-to-length ratio of 50% is considered ● dangerous ○ fatiguing ○ good ○ excellent *

The approximate net payload of 3328 pounds at 16% of GVWR on this model is ○ deficient ○ excessive ○ cautionary ○ good ● excellent *

Total highway safety penalties are: 5 *   Value: 79   Durability: 78   Highway Control Rating: 43   Highway Safety: 38

| Dutch Star | 1997 | MHA | 37 | DA3658 | FO | 7.5L | G | $2000 | 238 T | 5,000 | 20,000 | 17,565 |

Livability Code: SB 30-90   Wheelbase-to-length ratio of 54% is considered ○ dangerous ○ fatiguing ● good ○ excellent *

The approximate net payload of 2435 pounds at 12% of GVWR on this model is ○ deficient ○ excessive ○ cautionary ● good ○ excellent *

Total highway safety penalties are: 8 *   Value: 77   Durability: 78   Highway Control Rating: 76   Highway Safety: 68   ★★

| Dutch Star | 1997 | MHA | 37 | DA3682 | FO | 7.5L | G | $2000 | 238 T | 5,000 | 20,000 | 17,490 |

Livability Code: SB 30-90   Wheelbase-to-length ratio of 54% is considered ○ dangerous ○ fatiguing ● good ○ excellent *

The approximate net payload of 2510 pounds at 13% of GVWR on this model is ○ deficient ○ excessive ○ cautionary ● good ○ excellent *

Total highway safety penalties are: 7 *   Value: 78   Durability: 78   Highway Control Rating: 77   Highway Safety: 70   ★★★

| Dutch Star | 1997 | MHA | 37 | DA3658 fr.dsl | FR | Cu210 | D | $2200 | 228 | 5,000 | 20,500 | 17,765 |

Livability Code: SB 30-90   Wheelbase-to-length ratio of 51% is considered ○ dangerous ● fatiguing ○ good ○ excellent *

The approximate net payload of 2735 pounds at 13% of GVWR on this model is ○ deficient ○ excessive ○ cautionary ● good ○ excellent *

Total highway safety penalties are: 5 *   Value: 79   Durability: 78   Highway Control Rating: 44   Highway Safety: 39

Note: Safety ratings are based on the assumption that the engineering of the RV has allowed for proper balance by placing fresh, gray, and black holding tanks in a location so as not to change the balance of the RV when the tanks are empty or full. **Always double-check wheelbase, GVWR, and weights at front and rear axles.**

*See Section 1 for details on how conclusions are reached.

Brand	Year	Type	Length	Model	Chassis	Engine	Fuel Type	Average Price per Linear Foot When New	Adjusted Wheelbase	Approx. Towing Capacity	Gross Vehicle Weight Rating	Average Curb Weight

Dutch Star 1997 MHA 37 DA3682 fr.dsl FR Cu210 D $2200 228 5,000 20,500 17,765
Livability Code: SB 30-90
Wheelbase-to-length ratio of 51% is considered ○ dangerous ◉ fatiguing ○ good ○ excellent *
The approximate net payload of 2735 pounds at 13% of GVWR on this model is ○ deficient ○ excessive ○ cautionary ◉ good ○ excellent *
Total highway safety penalties are: 5 *   Value: 7 9   Durability: 7 8   Highway Control Rating: 4 4   Highway Safety: 3 9

Dutch Star 1997 MHA 37 DP3757 pusher SP Cu250 D $3400 240 5,000 26,000 22,190
Livability Code: SB 30-90
Wheelbase-to-length ratio of 54% is considered ○ dangerous ○ fatiguing ◉ good ○ excellent *
The approximate net payload of 3810 pounds at 15% of GVWR on this model is ○ deficient ○ excessive ○ cautionary ◉ good ○ excellent *
Total highway safety penalties are: 5 *   Value: 7 9   Durability: 7 8   Highway Control Rating: 7 9   Highway Safety: 7 4   ★★★

Dutch Star 1997 MHA 37 DP3758 pusher SP Cu250 D $3400 240 5,000 26,000 22,190
Livability Code: SB 30-90
Wheelbase-to-length ratio of 54% is considered ○ dangerous ○ fatiguing ◉ good ○ excellent *
The approximate net payload of 3810 pounds at 15% of GVWR on this model is ○ deficient ○ excessive ○ cautionary ◉ good ○ excellent *
Total highway safety penalties are: 5 *   Value: 7 9   Durability: 7 8   Highway Control Rating: 7 9   Highway Safety: 7 4   ★★★

Dutch Star 1997 MHA 38 DP3860 pusher SP Cu250 D $3300 252 5,000 26,000 22,463
Livability Code: SB 30-90
Wheelbase-to-length ratio of 55% is considered ○ dangerous ○ fatiguing ◉ good ○ excellent *
The approximate net payload of 3537 pounds at 14% of GVWR on this model is ○ deficient ○ excessive ○ cautionary ◉ good ○ excellent *
Total highway safety penalties are: 5 *   Value: 7 9   Durability: 7 8   Highway Control Rating: 8 9   Highway Safety: 8 4   ★★★

Dutch Star 1998 MHA 33 DA3205 opch CH 7.4L G $2400 200 4,500 16,500 14,570
Livability Code: SB 30-90
Wheelbase-to-length ratio of 51% is considered ○ dangerous ◉ fatiguing ○ good ○ excellent *
The approximate net payload of 1930 pounds at 12% of GVWR on this model is ○ deficient ○ excessive ○ cautionary ◉ good ○ excellent *
Total highway safety penalties are: 6 *   Value: 7 8   Durability: 7 8   Highway Control Rating: 3 8   Highway Safety: 3 2

Dutch Star 1998 MHA 33 DA3256 opch CH 7.4L G $2400 200 4,500 16,500 15,470
Livability Code: SB 30-90
Wheelbase-to-length ratio of 51% is considered ○ dangerous ◉ fatiguing ○ good ○ excellent *
The approximate net payload of 1030 pounds at 6% of GVWR on this model is ◉ deficient ○ excessive ○ cautionary ○ good ○ excellent *
Total highway safety penalties are: 9 *   Value: 7 7   Durability: 7 8   Highway Control Rating: 1 2   Highway Safety: 3

Dutch Star 1998 MHA 33 DA3205 FO 7.5L G $2400 200 8,000 17,000 14,970
Livability Code: SB 30-90
Wheelbase-to-length ratio of 51% is considered ○ dangerous ◉ fatiguing ○ good ○ excellent *
The approximate net payload of 2030 pounds at 12% of GVWR on this model is ○ deficient ○ excessive ○ cautionary ◉ good ○ excellent *
Total highway safety penalties are: 2 *   Value: 8 0   Durability: 7 8   Highway Control Rating: 3 8   Highway Safety: 3 6

Dutch Star 1998 MHA 33 DA3256 FO 7.5L G $2400 200 8,000 17,000 15,870
Livability Code: SB 30-90
Wheelbase-to-length ratio of 51% is considered ○ dangerous ◉ fatiguing ○ good ○ excellent *
The approximate net payload of 1130 pounds at 7% of GVWR on this model is ○ deficient ○ excessive ◉ cautionary ○ good ○ excellent *
Total highway safety penalties are: 5 *   Value: 7 9   Durability: 7 8   Highway Control Rating: 1 7   Highway Safety: 1 2

Dutch Star 1998 MHA 33 DA3205 fr.dsl FR 210HP D $3000 200 5,000 20,500 16,070
Livability Code: SB 30-90
Wheelbase-to-length ratio of 51% is considered ○ dangerous ◉ fatiguing ○ good ○ excellent *
The approximate net payload of 4430 pounds at 22% of GVWR on this model is ○ deficient ○ excessive ○ cautionary ○ good ◉ excellent *
Total highway safety penalties are: 2 *   Value: 8 0   Durability: 7 8   Highway Control Rating: 4 9   Highway Safety: 4 7

Dutch Star 1998 MHA 33 DA3256 fr.dsl FR 210HP D $3000 200 5,000 20,500 16,970
Livability Code: SB 30-90
Wheelbase-to-length ratio of 51% is considered ○ dangerous ◉ fatiguing ○ good ○ excellent *
The approximate net payload of 3530 pounds at 17% of GVWR on this model is ○ deficient ○ excessive ○ cautionary ○ good ◉ excellent *
Total highway safety penalties are: 5 *   Value: 7 9   Durability: 7 8   Highway Control Rating: 4 8   Highway Safety: 4 3

Dutch Star 1998 MHA 35 DA3450 opch CH 7.4L G $2300 208 4,500 16,500 16,008
Livability Code: SB 30-90
Wheelbase-to-length ratio of 50% is considered ◉ dangerous ○ fatiguing ○ good ○ excellent *
The approximate net payload of 492 pounds at 3% of GVWR on this model is ◉ deficient ○ excessive ○ cautionary ○ good ○ excellent *
Total highway safety penalties are: 10 *   Value: 7 6   Durability: 7 8   Highway Control Rating: 5   Highway Safety: - 5

Dutch Star 1998 MHA 35 DA3451 opch CH 7.4L G $2300 208 4,500 16,500 16,008
Livability Code: SB 30-90
Wheelbase-to-length ratio of 50% is considered ◉ dangerous ○ fatiguing ○ good ○ excellent *
The approximate net payload of 492 pounds at 3% of GVWR on this model is ◉ deficient ○ excessive ○ cautionary ○ good ○ excellent *
Total highway safety penalties are: 10 *   Value: 7 6   Durability: 7 8   Highway Control Rating: 5   Highway Safety: - 5

Note: Safety ratings are based on the assumption that the engineering of the RV has allowed for proper balance by placing fresh, gray, and black holding tanks in a location so as not to change the balance of the RV when the tanks are empty or full. **Always double-check wheelbase, GVWR, and weights at front and rear axles.**

*See Section 1 for details on how conclusions are reached.

Section 2: The Ratings

Brand	Year	Type	Length	Model	Chassis	Engine	Fuel Type	Average Price per Linear Foot When New	Adjusted Wheelbase	Approx. Towing Capacity	Gross Vehicle Weight Rating	Average Curb Weight
Dutch Star	1998	MHA	35	DA3455 opch	CH	7.4L	G	$2300	208	4,500	16,500	16,008

Livability Code: SB 30-90
Wheelbase-to-length ratio of 50% is considered ◉ dangerous ○ fatiguing ○ good ○ excellent *
The approximate net payload of 492 pounds at 3% of GVWR on this model is ◉ deficient ○ excessive ○ cautionary ○ good ○ excellent *
Total highway safety penalties are: 10 * Value: 7 6 Durability: 7 8 Highway Control Rating: 5 Highway Safety: - 5

Brand	Year	Type	Length	Model	Chassis	Engine	Fuel Type	Price/Ft	Wheelbase	Towing	GVWR	Curb Weight
Dutch Star	1998	MHA	35	DA3401	FO	7.5L	G	$2300	216	8,000	17,000	15,508

Livability Code: SB 30-90
Wheelbase-to-length ratio of 51% is considered ○ dangerous ◉ fatiguing ○ good ○ excellent *
The approximate net payload of 1492 pounds at 9% of GVWR on this model is ○ deficient ○ excessive ◉ cautionary ○ good ○ excellent *
Total highway safety penalties are: 2 * Value: 8 0 Durability: 7 8 Highway Control Rating: 3 3 Highway Safety: 3 1

Brand	Year	Type	Length	Model	Chassis	Engine	Fuel Type	Price/Ft	Wheelbase	Towing	GVWR	Curb Weight
Dutch Star	1998	MHA	35	DA3450	FO	7.5L	G	$2300	208	8,000	17,000	16,408

Livability Code: SB 30-90
Wheelbase-to-length ratio of 50% is considered ◉ dangerous ○ fatiguing ○ good ○ excellent *
The approximate net payload of 592 pounds at 3% of GVWR on this model is ◉ deficient ○ excessive ○ cautionary ○ good ○ excellent *
Total highway safety penalties are: 5 * Value: 7 9 Durability: 7 8 Highway Control Rating: 6 Highway Safety: 1

Brand	Year	Type	Length	Model	Chassis	Engine	Fuel Type	Price/Ft	Wheelbase	Towing	GVWR	Curb Weight
Dutch Star	1998	MHA	35	DA3451	FO	7.5L	G	$2300	208	8,000	17,000	16,408

Livability Code: SB 30-90
Wheelbase-to-length ratio of 50% is considered ◉ dangerous ○ fatiguing ○ good ○ excellent *
The approximate net payload of 592 pounds at 3% of GVWR on this model is ◉ deficient ○ excessive ○ cautionary ○ good ○ excellent *
Total highway safety penalties are: 5 * Value: 7 9 Durability: 7 8 Highway Control Rating: 6 Highway Safety: 1

Brand	Year	Type	Length	Model	Chassis	Engine	Fuel Type	Price/Ft	Wheelbase	Towing	GVWR	Curb Weight
Dutch Star	1998	MHA	35	DA3455	FO	7.5L	G	$2300	208	8,000	17,000	16,408

Livability Code: SB 30-90
Wheelbase-to-length ratio of 50% is considered ◉ dangerous ○ fatiguing ○ good ○ excellent *
The approximate net payload of 592 pounds at 3% of GVWR on this model is ◉ deficient ○ excessive ○ cautionary ○ good ○ excellent *
Total highway safety penalties are: 5 * Value: 7 9 Durability: 7 8 Highway Control Rating: 6 Highway Safety: 1

Brand	Year	Type	Length	Model	Chassis	Engine	Fuel Type	Price/Ft	Wheelbase	Towing	GVWR	Curb Weight
Dutch Star	1998	MHA	35	DA3401 fr.dsl	FR	210HP	D	$2900	216	5,000	20,500	16,608

Livability Code: SB 30-90
Wheelbase-to-length ratio of 51% is considered ○ dangerous ◉ fatiguing ○ good ○ excellent *
The approximate net payload of 3892 pounds at 19% of GVWR on this model is ○ deficient ○ excessive ○ cautionary ○ good ◉ excellent *
Total highway safety penalties are: 2 * Value: 8 0 Durability: 7 8 Highway Control Rating: 5 3 Highway Safety: 5 1 ★

Brand	Year	Type	Length	Model	Chassis	Engine	Fuel Type	Price/Ft	Wheelbase	Towing	GVWR	Curb Weight
Dutch Star	1998	MHA	35	DA3450 fr.dsl	FR	210HP	D	$2900	208	5,000	20,500	17,508

Livability Code: SB 30-90
Wheelbase-to-length ratio of 50% is considered ◉ dangerous ○ fatiguing ○ good ○ excellent *
The approximate net payload of 2992 pounds at 15% of GVWR on this model is ○ deficient ○ excessive ○ cautionary ◉ good ○ excellent *
Total highway safety penalties are: 5 * Value: 7 9 Durability: 7 8 Highway Control Rating: 4 1 Highway Safety: 3 6

Brand	Year	Type	Length	Model	Chassis	Engine	Fuel Type	Price/Ft	Wheelbase	Towing	GVWR	Curb Weight
Dutch Star	1998	MHA	35	DA3451 fr.dsl	FR	210HP	D	$2900	208	5,000	20,500	17,508

Livability Code: SB 30-90
Wheelbase-to-length ratio of 50% is considered ◉ dangerous ○ fatiguing ○ good ○ excellent *
The approximate net payload of 2992 pounds at 15% of GVWR on this model is ○ deficient ○ excessive ○ cautionary ◉ good ○ excellent *
Total highway safety penalties are: 5 * Value: 7 9 Durability: 7 8 Highway Control Rating: 4 1 Highway Safety: 3 6

Brand	Year	Type	Length	Model	Chassis	Engine	Fuel Type	Price/Ft	Wheelbase	Towing	GVWR	Curb Weight
Dutch Star	1998	MHA	35	DA3455 fr.dsl	FR	210HP	D	$2900	208	5,000	20,500	17,508

Livability Code: SB 30-90
Wheelbase-to-length ratio of 50% is considered ◉ dangerous ○ fatiguing ○ good ○ excellent *
The approximate net payload of 2992 pounds at 15% of GVWR on this model is ○ deficient ○ excessive ○ cautionary ◉ good ○ excellent *
Total highway safety penalties are: 5 * Value: 7 9 Durability: 7 8 Highway Control Rating: 4 1 Highway Safety: 3 6

Brand	Year	Type	Length	Model	Chassis	Engine	Fuel Type	Price/Ft	Wheelbase	Towing	GVWR	Curb Weight
Dutch Star	1998	MHA	35	DP3558 opch	FR	CA300	D	$3600	216	5,000	26,000	21,698

Livability Code: SB 30-90
Wheelbase-to-length ratio of 51% is considered ○ dangerous ◉ fatiguing ○ good ○ excellent *
The approximate net payload of 4302 pounds at 17% of GVWR on this model is ○ deficient ○ excessive ○ cautionary ○ good ◉ excellent *
Total highway safety penalties are: 5 * Value: 7 9 Durability: 7 8 Highway Control Rating: 5 0 Highway Safety: 4 5

Brand	Year	Type	Length	Model	Chassis	Engine	Fuel Type	Price/Ft	Wheelbase	Towing	GVWR	Curb Weight
Dutch Star	1998	MHA	35	DP3558	SP	CU300	D	$3600	216	10,000	26,000	21,998

Livability Code: SB 30-90
Wheelbase-to-length ratio of 51% is considered ○ dangerous ◉ fatiguing ○ good ○ excellent *
The approximate net payload of 4002 pounds at 15% of GVWR on this model is ○ deficient ○ excessive ○ cautionary ◉ good ○ excellent *
Total highway safety penalties are: 5 * Value: 7 9 Durability: 7 8 Highway Control Rating: 4 8 Highway Safety: 4 3

Brand	Year	Type	Length	Model	Chassis	Engine	Fuel Type	Price/Ft	Wheelbase	Towing	GVWR	Curb Weight
Dutch Star	1998	MHA	37	DA3656	FO	7.5L	G	$2200	238 T	5,000	20,000	17,846

Livability Code: SB 30-90
Wheelbase-to-length ratio of 54% is considered ○ dangerous ○ fatiguing ◉ good ○ excellent *
The approximate net payload of 2154 pounds at 11% of GVWR on this model is ○ deficient ○ excessive ○ cautionary ◉ good ○ excellent *
Total highway safety penalties are: 7 * Value: 7 8 Durability: 7 8 Highway Control Rating: 7 5 Highway Safety: 6 8 ★★

Note: Safety ratings are based on the assumption that the engineering of the RV has allowed for proper balance by placing fresh, gray, and black holding tanks in a location so as not to change the balance of the RV when the tanks are empty or full. **Always double-check wheelbase, GVWR, and weights at front and rear axles.**

The RV Rating Book

*See Section 1 for details on how conclusions are reached.

Section 2: The Ratings

Brand	Year	Type	Length	Model	Chassis	Engine	Fuel Type	Average Price per Linear Foot When New	Adjusted Wheelbase	Approx. Towing Capacity	Gross Vehicle Weight Rating	Average Curb Weight
Dutch Star	1998	MHA	37	DA3658	FO	7.5L	G	$2200	238 T	5,000	20,000	17,846

Dutch Star — 1998 — MHA 37 — DA3658
Livability Code: SB 30-90
Wheelbase-to-length ratio of 54% is considered ○ dangerous ○ fatiguing ◉ good ○ excellent*
The approximate net payload of 2154 pounds at 11% of GVWR on this model is ○ deficient ○ excessive ○ cautionary ◉ good ○ excellent*
Total highway safety penalties are: 7*   Value: **7 8**   Durability: **7 8**   Highway Control Rating: **7 5**   Highway Safety: **6 8**   ★★

| Dutch Star | 1998 | MHA | 37 | DA3656 fr.dsl | FR | 210HP | D | $3400 | 228 | 5,000 | 20,500 | 18,046 |

Dutch Star — 1998 — MHA 37 — DA3656 fr.dsl
Livability Code: SB 30-90
Wheelbase-to-length ratio of 51% is considered ○ dangerous ◉ fatiguing ○ good ○ excellent*
The approximate net payload of 2454 pounds at 12% of GVWR on this model is ○ deficient ○ excessive ○ cautionary ◉ good ○ excellent*
Total highway safety penalties are: 5*   Value: **7 9**   Durability: **7 8**   Highway Control Rating: **4 2**   Highway Safety: **3 7**

| Dutch Star | 1998 | MHA | 37 | DA3658 fr.dsl | FR | 210HP | D | $3400 | 228 | 5,000 | 20,500 | 18,046 |

Dutch Star — 1998 — MHA 37 — DA3658 fr.dsl
Livability Code: SB 30-90
Wheelbase-to-length ratio of 51% is considered ○ dangerous ◉ fatiguing ○ good ○ excellent*
The approximate net payload of 2454 pounds at 12% of GVWR on this model is ○ deficient ○ excessive ○ cautionary ◉ good ○ excellent*
Total highway safety penalties are: 5*   Value: **7 9**   Durability: **7 8**   Highway Control Rating: **4 2**   Highway Safety: **3 7**

| Dutch Star | 1998 | MHA | 38 | DP3857 opch | FR | CA300 | D | $3300 | 252 | 5,000 | 27,400 | 23,746 |

Dutch Star — 1998 — MHA 38 — DP3857 opch
Livability Code: SB 30-90
Wheelbase-to-length ratio of 55% is considered ○ dangerous ○ fatiguing ◉ good ○ excellent*
The approximate net payload of 3654 pounds at 13% of GVWR on this model is ○ deficient ○ excessive ○ cautionary ◉ good ○ excellent*
Total highway safety penalties are: 5*   Value: **7 9**   Durability: **7 8**   Highway Control Rating: **8 8**   Highway Safety: **8 3**   ★★★

| Dutch Star | 1998 | MHA | 38 | DP3858 opch | FR | CA300 | D | $3300 | 252 | 5,000 | 27,400 | 23,746 |

Dutch Star — 1998 — MHA 38 — DP3858 opch
Livability Code: SB 30-90
Wheelbase-to-length ratio of 55% is considered ○ dangerous ○ fatiguing ◉ good ○ excellent*
The approximate net payload of 3654 pounds at 13% of GVWR on this model is ○ deficient ○ excessive ○ cautionary ◉ good ○ excellent*
Total highway safety penalties are: 5*   Value: **7 9**   Durability: **7 8**   Highway Control Rating: **8 8**   Highway Safety: **8 3**   ★★★

| Dutch Star | 1998 | MHA | 38 | DP3860 opch | FR | CA300 | D | $3300 | 252 | 5,000 | 27,400 | 23,746 |

Dutch Star — 1998 — MHA 38 — DP3860 opch
Livability Code: SB 30-90
Wheelbase-to-length ratio of 55% is considered ○ dangerous ○ fatiguing ◉ good ○ excellent*
The approximate net payload of 3654 pounds at 13% of GVWR on this model is ○ deficient ○ excessive ○ cautionary ◉ good ○ excellent*
Total highway safety penalties are: 5*   Value: **7 9**   Durability: **7 8**   Highway Control Rating: **8 8**   Highway Safety: **8 3**   ★★★

| Dutch Star | 1998 | MHA | 38 | DP3865 opch | FR | CA300 | D | $3300 | 252 | 5,000 | 27,400 | 23,746 |

Dutch Star — 1998 — MHA 38 — DP3865 opch
Livability Code: SB 30-90
Wheelbase-to-length ratio of 55% is considered ○ dangerous ○ fatiguing ◉ good ○ excellent*
The approximate net payload of 3654 pounds at 13% of GVWR on this model is ○ deficient ○ excessive ○ cautionary ◉ good ○ excellent*
Total highway safety penalties are: 10*   Value: **7 6**   Durability: **7 8**   Highway Control Rating: **8 8**   Highway Safety: **7 8**   ★★★

| Dutch Star | 1998 | MHA | 38 | DP3866 opch | FR | CA300 | D | $3300 | 252 | 5,000 | 27,400 | 23,746 |

Dutch Star — 1998 — MHA 38 — DP3866 opch
Livability Code: SB 30-90
Wheelbase-to-length ratio of 55% is considered ○ dangerous ○ fatiguing ◉ good ○ excellent*
The approximate net payload of 3654 pounds at 13% of GVWR on this model is ○ deficient ○ excessive ○ cautionary ◉ good ○ excellent*
Total highway safety penalties are: 10*   Value: **7 6**   Durability: **7 8**   Highway Control Rating: **8 8**   Highway Safety: **7 8**   ★★★

| Dutch Star | 1998 | MHA | 38 | DP3883 opch | FR | CA300 | D | $3300 | 252 | 5,000 | 27,400 | 23,746 |

Dutch Star — 1998 — MHA 38 — DP3883 opch
Livability Code: SB 30-90
Wheelbase-to-length ratio of 55% is considered ○ dangerous ○ fatiguing ◉ good ○ excellent*
The approximate net payload of 3654 pounds at 13% of GVWR on this model is ○ deficient ○ excessive ○ cautionary ◉ good ○ excellent*
Total highway safety penalties are: 5*   Value: **7 9**   Durability: **7 8**   Highway Control Rating: **8 8**   Highway Safety: **8 3**   ★★★

| Dutch Star | 1998 | MHA | 38 | DP3866 opch | FR | CA300 | D | $3300 | 252 | 5,000 | 27,400 | 23,746 |

Dutch Star — 1998 — MHA 38 — DP3866 opch
Livability Code: SB 30-90
Wheelbase-to-length ratio of 55% is considered ○ dangerous ○ fatiguing ◉ good ○ excellent*
The approximate net payload of 3654 pounds at 13% of GVWR on this model is ○ deficient ○ excessive ○ cautionary ◉ good ○ excellent*
Total highway safety penalties are: 10*   Value: **7 6**   Durability: **7 8**   Highway Control Rating: **8 8**   Highway Safety: **7 8**   ★★★

| Dutch Star | 1998 | MHA | 38 | DP3857 | SP | CU300 | D | $3300 | 252 | 10,000 | 27,400 | 23,846 |

Dutch Star — 1998 — MHA 38 — DP3857
Livability Code: SB 30-90
Wheelbase-to-length ratio of 55% is considered ○ dangerous ○ fatiguing ◉ good ○ excellent*
The approximate net payload of 3554 pounds at 13% of GVWR on this model is ○ deficient ○ excessive ○ cautionary ◉ good ○ excellent*
Total highway safety penalties are: 5*   Value: **7 9**   Durability: **7 8**   Highway Control Rating: **8 7**   Highway Safety: **8 2**   ★★★

| Dutch Star | 1998 | MHA | 38 | DP3858 | SP | CU300 | D | $3300 | 252 | 10,000 | 27,400 | 23,846 |

Dutch Star — 1998 — MHA 38 — DP3858
Livability Code: SB 30-90
Wheelbase-to-length ratio of 55% is considered ○ dangerous ○ fatiguing ◉ good ○ excellent*
The approximate net payload of 3554 pounds at 13% of GVWR on this model is ○ deficient ○ excessive ○ cautionary ◉ good ○ excellent*
Total highway safety penalties are: 5*   Value: **7 9**   Durability: **7 8**   Highway Control Rating: **8 7**   Highway Safety: **8 2**   ★★★

Note: Safety ratings are based on the assumption that the engineering of the RV has allowed for proper balance by placing fresh, gray, and black holding tanks in a location so as not to change the balance of the RV when the tanks are empty or full. **Always double-check wheelbase, GVWR, and weights at front and rear axles.**

*See Section 1 for details on how conclusions are reached.

Section 2: The Ratings

Brand	Year	Type	Length	Model	Chassis	Engine	Fuel Type	Average Price per Linear Foot When New	Adjusted Wheelbase	Approx. Towing Capacity	Gross Vehicle Weight Rating	Average Curb Weight
Dutch Star	1998	MHA	38	DP3860	SP	CU300	D	$3300	252	10,000	27,400	23,846

Livability Code: SB 30-90
Wheelbase-to-length ratio of 55% is considered ○ dangerous ○ fatiguing ◉ good ○ excellent *
The approximate net payload of 3554 pounds at 13% of GVWR on this model is ○ deficient ○ excessive ○ cautionary ◉ good ○ excellent *
Total highway safety penalties are: 5 *   Value: 7 9   Durability: 7 8   Highway Control Rating: 8 7   Highway Safety: 8 2   ★★★

Brand	Year	Type	Length	Model	Chassis	Engine	Fuel Type	Average Price per Linear Foot When New	Adjusted Wheelbase	Approx. Towing Capacity	Gross Vehicle Weight Rating	Average Curb Weight
Dutch Star	1998	MHA	38	DP3865	SP	CU300	D	$3300	252	10,000	27,400	23,846

Livability Code: SB 30-90
Wheelbase-to-length ratio of 55% is considered ○ dangerous ○ fatiguing ◉ good ○ excellent *
The approximate net payload of 3554 pounds at 13% of GVWR on this model is ○ deficient ○ excessive ○ cautionary ◉ good ○ excellent *
Total highway safety penalties are: 10 *   Value: 7 6   Durability: 7 8   Highway Control Rating: 8 7   Highway Safety: 7 7   ★★★

Brand	Year	Type	Length	Model	Chassis	Engine	Fuel Type	Average Price per Linear Foot When New	Adjusted Wheelbase	Approx. Towing Capacity	Gross Vehicle Weight Rating	Average Curb Weight
Dutch Star	1998	MHA	38	DP3866	SP	CU300	D	$3300	252	10,000	27,400	23,846

Livability Code: SB 30-90
Wheelbase-to-length ratio of 55% is considered ○ dangerous ○ fatiguing ◉ good ○ excellent *
The approximate net payload of 3554 pounds at 13% of GVWR on this model is ○ deficient ○ excessive ○ cautionary ◉ good ○ excellent *
Total highway safety penalties are: 10 *   Value: 7 6   Durability: 7 8   Highway Control Rating: 8 7   Highway Safety: 7 7   ★★★

Brand	Year	Type	Length	Model	Chassis	Engine	Fuel Type	Average Price per Linear Foot When New	Adjusted Wheelbase	Approx. Towing Capacity	Gross Vehicle Weight Rating	Average Curb Weight
Dutch Star	1998	MHA	38	DP3883	SP	CU300	D	$3300	252	10,000	27,400	23,846

Livability Code: SB 30-90
Wheelbase-to-length ratio of 55% is considered ○ dangerous ○ fatiguing ◉ good ○ excellent *
The approximate net payload of 3554 pounds at 13% of GVWR on this model is ○ deficient ○ excessive ○ cautionary ◉ good ○ excellent *
Total highway safety penalties are: 5 *   Value: 7 9   Durability: 7 8   Highway Control Rating: 8 7   Highway Safety: 8 2   ★★★

Brand	Year	Type	Length	Model	Chassis	Engine	Fuel Type	Average Price per Linear Foot When New	Adjusted Wheelbase	Approx. Towing Capacity	Gross Vehicle Weight Rating	Average Curb Weight
Dutch Star	1999	MHA	30	DA2957	FO	6.8L	G	$2800	172	8,000	18,000	15,875

Livability Code: SB 30-90
Wheelbase-to-length ratio of 48% is considered ◉ dangerous ○ fatiguing ○ good ○ excellent *
The approximate net payload of 2125 pounds at 12% of GVWR on this model is ○ deficient ○ excessive ○ cautionary ◉ good ○ excellent *
Total highway safety penalties are: 5 *   Value: 8 4   Durability: 7 8   Highway Control Rating: 3 9   Highway Safety: 3 4

Brand	Year	Type	Length	Model	Chassis	Engine	Fuel Type	Average Price per Linear Foot When New	Adjusted Wheelbase	Approx. Towing Capacity	Gross Vehicle Weight Rating	Average Curb Weight
Dutch Star	1999	MHA	30	DA2957 fr.dsl	FR	CU210	D	$4300	172	5,000	20,500	16,575

Livability Code: SB 30-90
Wheelbase-to-length ratio of 48% is considered ◉ dangerous ○ fatiguing ○ good ○ excellent *
The approximate net payload of 3925 pounds at 19% of GVWR on this model is ○ deficient ○ excessive ○ cautionary ○ good ◉ excellent *
Total highway safety penalties are: 5 *   Value: 8 4   Durability: 7 8   Highway Control Rating: 5 0   Highway Safety: 4 5

Brand	Year	Type	Length	Model	Chassis	Engine	Fuel Type	Average Price per Linear Foot When New	Adjusted Wheelbase	Approx. Towing Capacity	Gross Vehicle Weight Rating	Average Curb Weight
Dutch Star	1999	MHA	33	DA3205	FO	6.8L	G	$2600	200	8,000	18,000	15,740

Livability Code: SB 30-90
Wheelbase-to-length ratio of 51% is considered ○ dangerous ◉ fatiguing ○ good ○ excellent *
The approximate net payload of 2260 pounds at 13% of GVWR on this model is ○ deficient ○ excessive ○ cautionary ◉ good ○ excellent *
Total highway safety penalties are: 2 *   Value: 8 5   Durability: 7 8   Highway Control Rating: 5 0   Highway Safety: 4 8

Brand	Year	Type	Length	Model	Chassis	Engine	Fuel Type	Average Price per Linear Foot When New	Adjusted Wheelbase	Approx. Towing Capacity	Gross Vehicle Weight Rating	Average Curb Weight
Dutch Star	1999	MHA	33	DA3256	FO	6.8L	G	$2600	200	8,000	18,000	16,640

Livability Code: SB 30-90
Wheelbase-to-length ratio of 51% is considered ○ dangerous ◉ fatiguing ○ good ○ excellent *
The approximate net payload of 1360 pounds at 8% of GVWR on this model is ○ deficient ○ excessive ◉ cautionary ○ good ○ excellent *
Total highway safety penalties are: 5 *   Value: 8 4   Durability: 7 8   Highway Control Rating: 3 3   Highway Safety: 2 8

Brand	Year	Type	Length	Model	Chassis	Engine	Fuel Type	Average Price per Linear Foot When New	Adjusted Wheelbase	Approx. Towing Capacity	Gross Vehicle Weight Rating	Average Curb Weight
Dutch Star	1999	MHA	33	DA3205 fr.dsl	FR	CU210	D	$3900	200	5,000	20,500	16,440

Livability Code: SB 30-90
Wheelbase-to-length ratio of 51% is considered ○ dangerous ◉ fatiguing ○ good ○ excellent *
The approximate net payload of 4060 pounds at 20% of GVWR on this model is ○ deficient ○ excessive ○ cautionary ○ good ◉ excellent *
Total highway safety penalties are: 2 *   Value: 8 5   Durability: 7 8   Highway Control Rating: 6 0   Highway Safety: 5 8   ★

Brand	Year	Type	Length	Model	Chassis	Engine	Fuel Type	Average Price per Linear Foot When New	Adjusted Wheelbase	Approx. Towing Capacity	Gross Vehicle Weight Rating	Average Curb Weight
Dutch Star	1999	MHA	33	DA3256 fr.dsl	FR	CU210	D	$3900	200	5,000	20,500	17,340

Livability Code: SB 30-90
Wheelbase-to-length ratio of 51% is considered ○ dangerous ◉ fatiguing ○ good ○ excellent *
The approximate net payload of 3160 pounds at 15% of GVWR on this model is ○ deficient ○ excessive ○ cautionary ◉ good ○ excellent *
Total highway safety penalties are: 5 *   Value: 8 4   Durability: 7 8   Highway Control Rating: 5 5   Highway Safety: 5 0   ★

Brand	Year	Type	Length	Model	Chassis	Engine	Fuel Type	Average Price per Linear Foot When New	Adjusted Wheelbase	Approx. Towing Capacity	Gross Vehicle Weight Rating	Average Curb Weight
Dutch Star	1999	MHA	35	DA3401	FO	6.8L	G	$2400	216	8,000	18,000	16,300

Livability Code: SB 30-90
Wheelbase-to-length ratio of 51% is considered ○ dangerous ◉ fatiguing ○ good ○ excellent *
The approximate net payload of 1700 pounds at 9% of GVWR on this model is ○ deficient ○ excessive ◉ cautionary ○ good ○ excellent *
Total highway safety penalties are: 2 *   Value: 8 5   Durability: 7 8   Highway Control Rating: 4 3   Highway Safety: 4 1

Brand	Year	Type	Length	Model	Chassis	Engine	Fuel Type	Average Price per Linear Foot When New	Adjusted Wheelbase	Approx. Towing Capacity	Gross Vehicle Weight Rating	Average Curb Weight
Dutch Star	1999	MHA	35	DA3450	FO	6.8L	G	$2400	208	8,000	18,000	17,200

Livability Code: SB 30-90
Wheelbase-to-length ratio of 50% is considered ◉ dangerous ○ fatiguing ○ good ○ excellent *
The approximate net payload of 800 pounds at 4% of GVWR on this model is ◉ deficient ○ excessive ○ cautionary ○ good ○ excellent *
Total highway safety penalties are: 5 *   Value: 8 4   Durability: 7 8   Highway Control Rating: 1 7   Highway Safety: 1 2

Note: Safety ratings are based on the assumption that the engineering of the RV has allowed for proper balance by placing fresh, gray, and black holding tanks in a location so as not to change the balance of the RV when the tanks are empty or full. **Always double-check wheelbase, GVWR, and weights at front and rear axles.**

The RV Rating Book

*See Section 1 for details on how conclusions are reached.

Brand	Year	Type	Length	Model	Chassis	Engine	Fuel Type	Average Price per Linear Foot When New	Adjusted Wheelbase	Approx. Towing Capacity	Gross Vehicle Weight Rating	Average Curb Weight
Dutch Star	1999	MHA	35	DA3451	FO	6.8L	G	$2400	208	8,000	18,000	17,200

Livability Code: SB 30-90

Wheelbase-to-length ratio of 50% is considered ● dangerous ○ fatiguing ○ good ○ excellent *

The approximate net payload of 800 pounds at 4% of GVWR on this model is ● deficient ○ excessive ○ cautionary ○ good ○ excellent *

Total highway safety penalties are: 5 *   Value: **8 4**   Durability: **7 8**   Highway Control Rating: **1 7**   Highway Safety: **1 2**

Brand	Year	Type	Length	Model	Chassis	Engine	Fuel Type	Avg Price/Lin Ft	Adj Wheelbase	Approx Towing	GVWR	Avg Curb Weight
Dutch Star	1999	MHA	35	DA3455	FO	6.8L	G	$2400	208	8,000	18,000	17,200

Livability Code: SB 30-90

Wheelbase-to-length ratio of 50% is considered ● dangerous ○ fatiguing ○ good ○ excellent *

The approximate net payload of 800 pounds at 4% of GVWR on this model is ● deficient ○ excessive ○ cautionary ○ good ○ excellent *

Total highway safety penalties are: 5 *   Value: **8 4**   Durability: **7 8**   Highway Control Rating: **1 7**   Highway Safety: **1 2**

Brand	Year	Type	Length	Model	Chassis	Engine	Fuel Type	Avg Price/Lin Ft	Adj Wheelbase	Approx Towing	GVWR	Avg Curb Weight
Dutch Star	1999	MHA	35	DA3401 fr.dsl	FR	CU210	D	$3700	216	5,000	20,500	17,000

Livability Code: SB 30-90

Wheelbase-to-length ratio of 51% is considered ○ dangerous ● fatiguing ○ good ○ excellent *

The approximate net payload of 3500 pounds at 17% of GVWR on this model is ○ deficient ○ excessive ○ cautionary ○ good ● excellent *

Total highway safety penalties are: 2 *   Value: **8 5**   Durability: **7 8**   Highway Control Rating: **6 1**   Highway Safety: **5 9**   ★

Brand	Year	Type	Length	Model	Chassis	Engine	Fuel Type	Avg Price/Lin Ft	Adj Wheelbase	Approx Towing	GVWR	Avg Curb Weight
Dutch Star	1999	MHA	35	DA3450 fr.dsl	FR	CU210	D	$3700	208	5,000	20,500	17,900

Livability Code: SB 30-90

Wheelbase-to-length ratio of 50% is considered ● dangerous ○ fatiguing ○ good ○ excellent *

The approximate net payload of 2600 pounds at 13% of GVWR on this model is ○ deficient ○ excessive ○ cautionary ● good ○ excellent *

Total highway safety penalties are: 5 *   Value: **8 4**   Durability: **7 8**   Highway Control Rating: **4 7**   Highway Safety: **4 2**

Brand	Year	Type	Length	Model	Chassis	Engine	Fuel Type	Avg Price/Lin Ft	Adj Wheelbase	Approx Towing	GVWR	Avg Curb Weight
Dutch Star	1999	MHA	35	DA3451 fr.dsl	FR	CU210	D	$3700	208	5,000	20,500	17,900

Livability Code: SB 30-90

Wheelbase-to-length ratio of 50% is considered ● dangerous ○ fatiguing ○ good ○ excellent *

The approximate net payload of 2600 pounds at 13% of GVWR on this model is ○ deficient ○ excessive ○ cautionary ● good ○ excellent *

Total highway safety penalties are: 5 *   Value: **8 4**   Durability: **7 8**   Highway Control Rating: **4 7**   Highway Safety: **4 2**

Brand	Year	Type	Length	Model	Chassis	Engine	Fuel Type	Avg Price/Lin Ft	Adj Wheelbase	Approx Towing	GVWR	Avg Curb Weight
Dutch Star	1999	MHA	35	DA3455 fr.dsl	FR	CU210	D	$3700	208	5,000	20,500	17,900

Livability Code: SB 30-90

Wheelbase-to-length ratio of 50% is considered ● dangerous ○ fatiguing ○ good ○ excellent *

The approximate net payload of 2600 pounds at 13% of GVWR on this model is ○ deficient ○ excessive ○ cautionary ● good ○ excellent *

Total highway safety penalties are: 5 *   Value: **8 4**   Durability: **7 8**   Highway Control Rating: **4 7**   Highway Safety: **4 2**

Brand	Year	Type	Length	Model	Chassis	Engine	Fuel Type	Avg Price/Lin Ft	Adj Wheelbase	Approx Towing	GVWR	Avg Curb Weight
Dutch Star	1999	MHA	37	DA3656	FO	6.8L	G	$2300	228	5,500	20,500	18,260

Livability Code: SB 30-90

Wheelbase-to-length ratio of 51% is considered ○ dangerous ● fatiguing ○ good ○ excellent *

The approximate net payload of 2240 pounds at 11% of GVWR on this model is ○ deficient ○ excessive ○ cautionary ● good ○ excellent *

Total highway safety penalties are: 5 *   Value: **8 4**   Durability: **7 8**   Highway Control Rating: **4 9**   Highway Safety: **4 4**

Brand	Year	Type	Length	Model	Chassis	Engine	Fuel Type	Avg Price/Lin Ft	Adj Wheelbase	Approx Towing	GVWR	Avg Curb Weight
Dutch Star	1999	MHA	37	DA3656 fr.dsl	FR	CU210	D	$3500	228	5,000	20,500	18,460

Livability Code: SB 30-90

Wheelbase-to-length ratio of 51% is considered ○ dangerous ● fatiguing ○ good ○ excellent *

The approximate net payload of 2040 pounds at 10% of GVWR on this model is ○ deficient ○ excessive ○ cautionary ● good ○ excellent *

Total highway safety penalties are: 5 *   Value: **8 4**   Durability: **7 8**   Highway Control Rating: **4 8**   Highway Safety: **4 3**

Brand	Year	Type	Length	Model	Chassis	Engine	Fuel Type	Avg Price/Lin Ft	Adj Wheelbase	Approx Towing	GVWR	Avg Curb Weight
Dutch Star	1999	MHA	38	DP3858	FR	CA300	D	$3400	252	5,000	27,400	24,514

Livability Code: SB 30-90

Wheelbase-to-length ratio of 55% is considered ○ dangerous ○ fatiguing ● good ○ excellent *

The approximate net payload of 2886 pounds at 11% of GVWR on this model is ○ deficient ○ excessive ○ cautionary ● good ○ excellent *

Total highway safety penalties are: 5 *   Value: **8 4**   Durability: **7 8**   Highway Control Rating: **8 3**   Highway Safety: **7 8**   ★★★

Brand	Year	Type	Length	Model	Chassis	Engine	Fuel Type	Avg Price/Lin Ft	Adj Wheelbase	Approx Towing	GVWR	Avg Curb Weight
Dutch Star	1999	MHA	38	DP3862	FR	CA300	D	$3400	252	5,000	27,400	23,746

Livability Code: SB 30-90

Wheelbase-to-length ratio of 55% is considered ○ dangerous ○ fatiguing ● good ○ excellent *

The approximate net payload of 3654 pounds at 13% of GVWR on this model is ○ deficient ○ excessive ○ cautionary ● good ○ excellent *

Total highway safety penalties are: 5 *   Value: **8 4**   Durability: **7 8**   Highway Control Rating: **8 8**   Highway Safety: **8 3**   ★★★

Brand	Year	Type	Length	Model	Chassis	Engine	Fuel Type	Avg Price/Lin Ft	Adj Wheelbase	Approx Towing	GVWR	Avg Curb Weight
Dutch Star	1999	MHA	38	DP3865	FR	CA300	D	$3400	252	5,000	27,400	23,746

Livability Code: SB 30-90

Wheelbase-to-length ratio of 55% is considered ○ dangerous ○ fatiguing ● good ○ excellent *

The approximate net payload of 3654 pounds at 13% of GVWR on this model is ○ deficient ○ excessive ○ cautionary ● good ○ excellent *

Total highway safety penalties are: 10 *   Value: **8 1**   Durability: **7 8**   Highway Control Rating: **8 8**   Highway Safety: **7 8**   ★★★

Brand	Year	Type	Length	Model	Chassis	Engine	Fuel Type	Avg Price/Lin Ft	Adj Wheelbase	Approx Towing	GVWR	Avg Curb Weight
Dutch Star	1999	MHA	38	DP3884	FR	CA300	D	$3400	252	5,000	27,400	23,746

Livability Code: SB 30-90

Wheelbase-to-length ratio of 55% is considered ○ dangerous ○ fatiguing ● good ○ excellent *

The approximate net payload of 3654 pounds at 13% of GVWR on this model is ○ deficient ○ excessive ○ cautionary ● good ○ excellent *

Total highway safety penalties are: 5 *   Value: **8 4**   Durability: **7 8**   Highway Control Rating: **8 8**   Highway Safety: **8 3**   ★★★

Note: Safety ratings are based on the assumption that the engineering of the RV has allowed for proper balance by placing fresh, gray, and black holding tanks in a location so as not to change the balance of the RV when the tanks are empty or full. **Always double-check wheelbase, GVWR, and weights at front and rear axles.**

*See Section 1 for details on how conclusions are reached.

Brand	Year	Type	Length	Model	Chassis	Engine	Fuel Type	Average Price per Linear Foot When New	Adjusted Wheelbase	Approx. Towing Capacity	Gross Vehicle Weight Rating	Average Curb Weight
Dutch Star	1999	MHA	38	DP3858 opch	SP	CU300	D	$3400	252	10,000	27,400	23,846

Livability Code: SB 30-90 — Wheelbase-to-length ratio of 55% is considered ○ dangerous ○ fatiguing ◉ good ○ excellent *

The approximate net payload of 3554 pounds at 13% of GVWR on this model is ○ deficient ○ excessive ○ cautionary ◉ good ○ excellent *

Total highway safety penalties are: 5 * Value: 8 4 Durability: 7 8 Highway Control Rating: 8 7 Highway Safety: 8 2 ★★★

Brand	Year	Type	Length	Model	Chassis	Engine	Fuel Type	Price/LF	Adj WB	Tow	GVWR	Curb Wt
Dutch Star	1999	MHA	38	DP3862 opch	SP	CU300	D	$3400	252	10,000	27,400	23,846

Livability Code: SB 30-90 — Wheelbase-to-length ratio of 55% is considered ○ dangerous ○ fatiguing ◉ good ○ excellent *

The approximate net payload of 3554 pounds at 13% of GVWR on this model is ○ deficient ○ excessive ○ cautionary ◉ good ○ excellent *

Total highway safety penalties are: 5 * Value: 8 4 Durability: 7 8 Highway Control Rating: 8 7 Highway Safety: 8 2 ★★★

Brand	Year	Type	Length	Model	Chassis	Engine	Fuel Type	Price/LF	Adj WB	Tow	GVWR	Curb Wt
Dutch Star	1999	MHA	38	DP3865 opch	SP	CU300	D	$3400	252	10,000	27,400	23,846

Livability Code: SB 30-90 — Wheelbase-to-length ratio of 55% is considered ○ dangerous ○ fatiguing ◉ good ○ excellent *

The approximate net payload of 3554 pounds at 13% of GVWR on this model is ○ deficient ○ excessive ○ cautionary ◉ good ○ excellent *

Total highway safety penalties are: 10 * Value: 8 1 Durability: 7 8 Highway Control Rating: 8 7 Highway Safety: 7 7 ★★★

Brand	Year	Type	Length	Model	Chassis	Engine	Fuel Type	Price/LF	Adj WB	Tow	GVWR	Curb Wt
Dutch Star	1999	MHA	38	DP3884 opch	SP	CU300	D	$3400	252	10,000	27,400	23,846

Livability Code: SB 30-90 — Wheelbase-to-length ratio of 55% is considered ○ dangerous ○ fatiguing ◉ good ○ excellent *

The approximate net payload of 3554 pounds at 13% of GVWR on this model is ○ deficient ○ excessive ○ cautionary ◉ good ○ excellent *

Total highway safety penalties are: 5 * Value: 8 4 Durability: 7 8 Highway Control Rating: 8 7 Highway Safety: 8 2 ★★★

Brand	Year	Type	Length	Model	Chassis	Engine	Fuel Type	Price/LF	Adj WB	Tow	GVWR	Curb Wt
Dynasty	1991	MHA	36	Duke 36	RO	CU250	D	$4300	228	1,500	28,000	25,750

Livability Code: FT 30-90 — Wheelbase-to-length ratio of 53% is considered ○ dangerous ◉ fatiguing ○ good ○ excellent *

The approximate net payload of 2250 pounds at 8% of GVWR on this model is ○ deficient ○ excessive ◉ cautionary ○ good ○ excellent *

Total highway safety penalties are: 2 * Value: 7 9 Durability: 7 5 Highway Control Rating: 4 7 Highway Safety: 4 5

Brand	Year	Type	Length	Model	Chassis	Engine	Fuel Type	Price/LF	Adj WB	Tow	GVWR	Curb Wt
Dynasty	1991	MHA	36	Duke 36	RO	CU300	D	$4500	228	1,500	28,000	25,750

Livability Code: FT 30-90 — Wheelbase-to-length ratio of 53% is considered ○ dangerous ◉ fatiguing ○ good ○ excellent *

The approximate net payload of 2250 pounds at 8% of GVWR on this model is ○ deficient ○ excessive ◉ cautionary ○ good ○ excellent *

Total highway safety penalties are: 2 * Value: 7 9 Durability: 7 5 Highway Control Rating: 4 7 Highway Safety: 4 5

Brand	Year	Type	Length	Model	Chassis	Engine	Fuel Type	Price/LF	Adj WB	Tow	GVWR	Curb Wt
Dynasty	1991	MHA	37	36 Commodore	RO	Cu8.3L	D	$3900	228	1,500	28,000	25,323

Livability Code: FT 30-90 — Wheelbase-to-length ratio of 52% is considered ○ dangerous ◉ fatiguing ○ good ○ excellent *

The approximate net payload of 2677 pounds at 10% of GVWR on this model is ○ deficient ○ excessive ○ cautionary ◉ good ○ excellent *

Total highway safety penalties are: 2 * Value: 7 9 Durability: 7 5 Highway Control Rating: 4 7 Highway Safety: 4 5

Brand	Year	Type	Length	Model	Chassis	Engine	Fuel Type	Price/LF	Adj WB	Tow	GVWR	Curb Wt
Dynasty	1992	MHA	30	30	RO	Cu5.9L	D	$3600	178	1,500	22,500	20,911

Livability Code: FT 30-90 — Wheelbase-to-length ratio of 49% is considered ◉ dangerous ○ fatiguing ○ good ○ excellent *

The approximate net payload of 1589 pounds at 7% of GVWR on this model is ○ deficient ○ excessive ◉ cautionary ○ good ○ excellent *

Total highway safety penalties are: 2 * Value: 7 9 Durability: 7 5 Highway Control Rating: 1 4 Highway Safety: 1 2

Brand	Year	Type	Length	Model	Chassis	Engine	Fuel Type	Price/LF	Adj WB	Tow	GVWR	Curb Wt
Dynasty	1992	MHA	31	Knight 31	RO	Cu5.9L	D	$4300	194	1,500	28,000	24,118

Livability Code: FT 30-90 — Wheelbase-to-length ratio of 52% is considered ○ dangerous ◉ fatiguing ○ good ○ excellent *

The approximate net payload of 3882 pounds at 14% of GVWR on this model is ○ deficient ○ excessive ○ cautionary ◉ good ○ excellent *

Total highway safety penalties are: 2 * Value: 7 9 Durability: 7 5 Highway Control Rating: 5 6 Highway Safety: 5 4 ★

Brand	Year	Type	Length	Model	Chassis	Engine	Fuel Type	Price/LF	Adj WB	Tow	GVWR	Curb Wt
Dynasty	1992	MHA	34	Prince 34	RO	Cu5.9L	D	$4300	204	1,500	28,000	25,098

Livability Code: FT 30-90 — Wheelbase-to-length ratio of 50% is considered ◉ dangerous ○ fatiguing ○ good ○ excellent *

The approximate net payload of 2902 pounds at 10% of GVWR on this model is ○ deficient ○ excessive ○ cautionary ◉ good ○ excellent *

Total highway safety penalties are: 2 * Value: 7 9 Durability: 7 5 Highway Control Rating: 3 3 Highway Safety: 3 1

Brand	Year	Type	Length	Model	Chassis	Engine	Fuel Type	Price/LF	Adj WB	Tow	GVWR	Curb Wt
Dynasty	1992	MHA	36	Duke 36	RO	Cu8.3L	D	$4200	228	1,500	28,000	25,750

Livability Code: FT 30-90 — Wheelbase-to-length ratio of 53% is considered ○ dangerous ◉ fatiguing ○ good ○ excellent *

The approximate net payload of 2250 pounds at 8% of GVWR on this model is ○ deficient ○ excessive ◉ cautionary ○ good ○ excellent *

Total highway safety penalties are: 2 * Value: 7 9 Durability: 7 5 Highway Control Rating: 4 7 Highway Safety: 4 5

Brand	Year	Type	Length	Model	Chassis	Engine	Fuel Type	Price/LF	Adj WB	Tow	GVWR	Curb Wt
Dynasty	1994	MHA	30	30	RO	Cu5.9L	D	$4300	178	1,500	29,000	24,292

Livability Code: FT 30-90 — Wheelbase-to-length ratio of 49% is considered ◉ dangerous ○ fatiguing ○ good ○ excellent *

The approximate net payload of 4708 pounds at 16% of GVWR on this model is ○ deficient ○ excessive ○ cautionary ○ good ◉ excellent *

Total highway safety penalties are: 2 * Value: 7 9 Durability: 7 5 Highway Control Rating: 4 3 Highway Safety: 4 1

Note: Safety ratings are based on the assumption that the engineering of the RV has allowed for proper balance by placing fresh, gray, and black holding tanks in a location so as not to change the balance of the RV when the tanks are empty or full. **Always double-check wheelbase, GVWR, and weights at front and rear axles.**

The RV Rating Book

*See Section 1 for details on how conclusions are reached.

Brand	Year	Type	Length	Model	Chassis	Engine	Fuel Type	Average Price per Linear Foot When New	Adjusted Wheelbase	Approx. Towing Capacity	Gross Vehicle Weight Rating	Average Curb Weight
Dynasty	1994	MHA	32	32	RO	Cu5.9L	D	$4800	198	1,500	29,000	24,945

Livability Code: FT 30-90
Wheelbase-to-length ratio of 52% is considered ○ dangerous ● fatiguing ○ good ○ excellent *
The approximate net payload of 4055 pounds at 14% of GVWR on this model is ○ deficient ○ excessive ○ cautionary ● good ○ excellent *
Total highway safety penalties are: 2 *   Value: 79   Durability: 75   Highway Control Rating: 56   Highway Safety: 54   ★

Brand	Year	Type	Length	Model	Chassis	Engine	Fuel Type					
Dynasty	1994	MHA	34	34	RO	Cu5.9L	D	$4700	204	1,500	29,000	25,598

Livability Code: FT 30-90
Wheelbase-to-length ratio of 50% is considered ● dangerous ○ fatiguing ○ good ○ excellent *
The approximate net payload of 3402 pounds at 12% of GVWR on this model is ○ deficient ○ excessive ○ cautionary ● good ○ excellent *
Total highway safety penalties are: 2 *   Value: 79   Durability: 75   Highway Control Rating: 40   Highway Safety: 38

Dynasty	1994	MHA	36	36	RO	Cu8.3L	D	$4600	228	1,500	29,000	26,250

Livability Code: FT 30-90
Wheelbase-to-length ratio of 53% is considered ○ dangerous ● fatiguing ○ good ○ excellent *
The approximate net payload of 2750 pounds at 9% of GVWR on this model is ○ deficient ○ excessive ● cautionary ○ good ○ excellent *
Total highway safety penalties are: 2 *   Value: 79   Durability: 75   Highway Control Rating: 53   Highway Safety: 51   ★

Dynasty	1994	MHA	38	38	RO	Cu8.3L	D	$4600	252	1,500	29,000	26,903

Livability Code: FT 30-90
Wheelbase-to-length ratio of 55% is considered ○ dangerous ○ fatiguing ● good ○ excellent *
The approximate net payload of 2097 pounds at 7% of GVWR on this model is ○ deficient ○ excessive ● cautionary ○ good ○ excellent *
Total highway safety penalties are: 2 *   Value: 79   Durability: 75   Highway Control Rating: 65   Highway Safety: 63   ★★

Dynasty	1995	MHA	32	32	RO	CU230	D	$4800	198	10,000	29,500	24,628

Livability Code: FT 30-90
Wheelbase-to-length ratio of 52% is considered ○ dangerous ● fatiguing ○ good ○ excellent *
The approximate net payload of 4872 pounds at 17% of GVWR on this model is ○ deficient ○ excessive ○ cautionary ○ good ● excellent *
Total highway safety penalties are: 2 *   Value: 79   Durability: 75   Highway Control Rating: 58   Highway Safety: 56   ★

Dynasty	1995	MHA	34	34	RO	CU230	D	$4700	204	10,000	29,500	25,652

Livability Code: FT 30-90
Wheelbase-to-length ratio of 50% is considered ● dangerous ○ fatiguing ○ good ○ excellent *
The approximate net payload of 3848 pounds at 13% of GVWR on this model is ○ deficient ○ excessive ○ cautionary ● good ○ excellent *
Total highway safety penalties are: 2 *   Value: 79   Durability: 75   Highway Control Rating: 42   Highway Safety: 40

Dynasty	1995	MHA	34	34	RO	CU250	D	$4800	204	10,000	29,500	25,902

Livability Code: FT 30-90
Wheelbase-to-length ratio of 50% is considered ● dangerous ○ fatiguing ○ good ○ excellent *
The approximate net payload of 3598 pounds at 12% of GVWR on this model is ○ deficient ○ excessive ○ cautionary ● good ○ excellent *
Total highway safety penalties are: 2 *   Value: 79   Durability: 75   Highway Control Rating: 37   Highway Safety: 35

Dynasty	1995	MHA	34	34	RO	CU300	D	$5000	204	10,000	29,500	25,902

Livability Code: FT 30-90
Wheelbase-to-length ratio of 50% is considered ● dangerous ○ fatiguing ○ good ○ excellent *
The approximate net payload of 3598 pounds at 12% of GVWR on this model is ○ deficient ○ excessive ○ cautionary ● good ○ excellent *
Total highway safety penalties are: 2 *   Value: 79   Durability: 75   Highway Control Rating: 37   Highway Safety: 35

Dynasty	1995	MHA	36	36	RO	CU250	D	$4700	228	10,000	29,500	26,279

Livability Code: FT 30-90
Wheelbase-to-length ratio of 53% is considered ○ dangerous ● fatiguing ○ good ○ excellent *
The approximate net payload of 3221 pounds at 11% of GVWR on this model is ○ deficient ○ excessive ○ cautionary ● good ○ excellent *
Total highway safety penalties are: 2 *   Value: 79   Durability: 75   Highway Control Rating: 65   Highway Safety: 63   ★★

Dynasty	1995	MHA	36	36	RO	CU300	D	$4900	228	10,000	29,500	26,279

Livability Code: FT 30-90
Wheelbase-to-length ratio of 53% is considered ○ dangerous ● fatiguing ○ good ○ excellent *
The approximate net payload of 3221 pounds at 11% of GVWR on this model is ○ deficient ○ excessive ○ cautionary ● good ○ excellent *
Total highway safety penalties are: 2 *   Value: 79   Durability: 75   Highway Control Rating: 60   Highway Safety: 58   ★

Dynasty	1995	MHA	38	38	RO	CU250	D	$4600	252	12,000	29,500	27,010

Livability Code: FT 30-90
Wheelbase-to-length ratio of 55% is considered ○ dangerous ○ fatiguing ● good ○ excellent *
The approximate net payload of 2490 pounds at 8% of GVWR on this model is ○ deficient ○ excessive ● cautionary ○ good ○ excellent *
Total highway safety penalties are: 2 *   Value: 79   Durability: 75   Highway Control Rating: 71   Highway Safety: 69   ★★

Dynasty	1995	MHA	38	38	RO	CU300	D	$4800	252	12,000	29,500	27,010

Livability Code: FT 30-90
Wheelbase-to-length ratio of 55% is considered ○ dangerous ○ fatiguing ● good ○ excellent *
The approximate net payload of 2490 pounds at 8% of GVWR on this model is ○ deficient ○ excessive ● cautionary ○ good ○ excellent *
Total highway safety penalties are: 2 *   Value: 79   Durability: 75   Highway Control Rating: 71   Highway Safety: 69   ★★

Note: Safety ratings are based on the assumption that the engineering of the RV has allowed for proper balance by placing fresh, gray, and black holding tanks in a location so as not to change the balance of the RV when the tanks are empty or full. **Always double-check wheelbase, GVWR, and weights at front and rear axles.**

*See Section 1 for details on how conclusions are reached.

Brand	Year	Type	Length	Model	Chassis	Engine	Fuel Type	Average Price per Linear Foot When New	Adjusted Wheel-base	Approx. Towing Capacity	Gross Vehicle Weight Rating	Average Curb Weight
Dynasty	**1995**	MHA	40	40	RO	CU250	D	$4600	270	12,000	29,500	28,102

Livability Code: FT 30-90   Wheelbase-to-length ratio of 56% is considered ○ dangerous ○ fatiguing ◉ good ○ excellent *

The approximate net payload of 1398 pounds at 5% of GVWR on this model is ◉ deficient ○ excessive ○ cautionary ○ good ○ excellent *

Total highway safety penalties are: 2 *   Value: **7 9**   Durability: **7 5**   Highway Control Rating: **6 1**   Highway Safety: **5 9**   ★

Brand	Year	Type	Length	Model	Chassis	Engine	Fuel Type	Price/Ft	Wheelbase	Towing	GVWR	Curb Weight
Dynasty	**1995**	MHA	40	40	RO	CU300	D	$4800	270	12,000	29,500	28,102

Livability Code: FT 30-90   Wheelbase-to-length ratio of 56% is considered ○ dangerous ○ fatiguing ◉ good ○ excellent *

The approximate net payload of 1398 pounds at 5% of GVWR on this model is ◉ deficient ○ excessive ○ cautionary ○ good ○ excellent *

Total highway safety penalties are: 2 *   Value: **7 9**   Durability: **7 5**   Highway Control Rating: **6 1**   Highway Safety: **5 9**   ★

Brand	Year	Type	Length	Model	Chassis	Engine	Fuel Type	Price/Ft	Wheelbase	Towing	GVWR	Curb Weight
Dynasty	**1996**	MHA	32	32	RO	CU300	D	$6000	191	10,000	29,500	24,580

Livability Code: FT 30-90   Wheelbase-to-length ratio of 50% is considered ◉ dangerous ○ fatiguing ○ good ○ excellent *

The approximate net payload of 4920 pounds at 17% of GVWR on this model is ○ deficient ○ excessive ○ cautionary ○ good ◉ excellent *

Total highway safety penalties are: 2 *   Value: **7 9**   Durability: **7 5**   Highway Control Rating: **4 4**   Highway Safety: **4 2**

Brand	Year	Type	Length	Model	Chassis	Engine	Fuel Type	Price/Ft	Wheelbase	Towing	GVWR	Curb Weight
Dynasty	**1996**	MHA	34	34	RO	CU300	D	$5500	204	10,000	29,500	25,659

Livability Code: FT 30-90   Wheelbase-to-length ratio of 50% is considered ◉ dangerous ○ fatiguing ○ good ○ excellent *

The approximate net payload of 3841 pounds at 13% of GVWR on this model is ○ deficient ○ excessive ○ cautionary ◉ good ○ excellent *

Total highway safety penalties are: 2 *   Value: **7 9**   Durability: **7 5**   Highway Control Rating: **3 9**   Highway Safety: **3 7**

Brand	Year	Type	Length	Model	Chassis	Engine	Fuel Type	Price/Ft	Wheelbase	Towing	GVWR	Curb Weight
Dynasty	**1996**	MHA	36	36	RO	CU300	D	$5400	204	10,000	29,500	25,987

Livability Code: FT 30-90   Wheelbase-to-length ratio of 47% is considered ◉ dangerous ○ fatiguing ○ good ○ excellent *

The approximate net payload of 3513 pounds at 12% of GVWR on this model is ○ deficient ○ excessive ○ cautionary ◉ good ○ excellent *

Total highway safety penalties are: 2 *   Value: **7 9**   Durability: **7 5**   Highway Control Rating: **2 7**   Highway Safety: **2 5**

Brand	Year	Type	Length	Model	Chassis	Engine	Fuel Type	Price/Ft	Wheelbase	Towing	GVWR	Curb Weight
Dynasty	**1996**	MHA	38	38	RO	CU300	D	$5300	252	10,000	31,500	28,258

Livability Code: FT 30-90   Wheelbase-to-length ratio of 55% is considered ○ dangerous ○ fatiguing ◉ good ○ excellent *

The approximate net payload of 3242 pounds at 10% of GVWR on this model is ○ deficient ○ excessive ○ cautionary ◉ good ○ excellent *

Total highway safety penalties are: 2 *   Value: **7 9**   Durability: **7 5**   Highway Control Rating: **8 8**   Highway Safety: **8 6**   ★★★

Brand	Year	Type	Length	Model	Chassis	Engine	Fuel Type	Price/Ft	Wheelbase	Towing	GVWR	Curb Weight
Dynasty	**1996**	MHA	40	40	RO	CU300	D	$5200	270	10,000	31,500	28,735

Livability Code: FT 30-90   Wheelbase-to-length ratio of 56% is considered ○ dangerous ○ fatiguing ◉ good ○ excellent *

The approximate net payload of 2765 pounds at 9% of GVWR on this model is ○ deficient ○ excessive ◉ cautionary ○ good ○ excellent *

Total highway safety penalties are: 2 *   Value: **7 9**   Durability: **7 5**   Highway Control Rating: **8 0**   Highway Safety: **7 8**   ★★★

Brand	Year	Type	Length	Model	Chassis	Engine	Fuel Type	Price/Ft	Wheelbase	Towing	GVWR	Curb Weight
Dynasty	**1997**	MHA	32	32	RO	CU300	D	$6000	191	10,000	29,500	25,195

Livability Code: FT 30-90   Wheelbase-to-length ratio of 50% is considered ◉ dangerous ○ fatiguing ○ good ○ excellent *

The approximate net payload of 4305 pounds at 15% of GVWR on this model is ○ deficient ○ excessive ○ cautionary ◉ good ○ excellent *

Total highway safety penalties are: 2 *   Value: **7 9**   Durability: **7 5**   Highway Control Rating: **4 1**   Highway Safety: **3 9**

Brand	Year	Type	Length	Model	Chassis	Engine	Fuel Type	Price/Ft	Wheelbase	Towing	GVWR	Curb Weight
Dynasty	**1997**	MHA	34	34	RO	CU300	D	$5800	204	10,000	29,500	25,848

Livability Code: FT 30-90   Wheelbase-to-length ratio of 50% is considered ◉ dangerous ○ fatiguing ○ good ○ excellent *

The approximate net payload of 3652 pounds at 12% of GVWR on this model is ○ deficient ○ excessive ○ cautionary ◉ good ○ excellent *

Total highway safety penalties are: 2 *   Value: **7 9**   Durability: **7 5**   Highway Control Rating: **3 7**   Highway Safety: **3 5**

Brand	Year	Type	Length	Model	Chassis	Engine	Fuel Type	Price/Ft	Wheelbase	Towing	GVWR	Curb Weight
Dynasty	**1997**	MHA	36	36	RO	CU300	D	$5600	228	10,000	29,500	26,500

Livability Code: FT 30-90   Wheelbase-to-length ratio of 53% is considered ○ dangerous ◉ fatiguing ○ good ○ excellent *

The approximate net payload of 3000 pounds at 10% of GVWR on this model is ○ deficient ○ excessive ○ cautionary ◉ good ○ excellent *

Total highway safety penalties are: 2 *   Value: **7 9**   Durability: **7 5**   Highway Control Rating: **5 8**   Highway Safety: **5 6**   ★

Brand	Year	Type	Length	Model	Chassis	Engine	Fuel Type	Price/Ft	Wheelbase	Towing	GVWR	Curb Weight
Dynasty	**1997**	MHA	38	38	RO	CU300	D	$5500	252	10,000	31,500	28,153

Livability Code: FT 30-90   Wheelbase-to-length ratio of 55% is considered ○ dangerous ○ fatiguing ◉ good ○ excellent *

The approximate net payload of 3347 pounds at 11% of GVWR on this model is ○ deficient ○ excessive ○ cautionary ◉ good ○ excellent *

Total highway safety penalties are: 2 *   Value: **7 9**   Durability: **7 5**   Highway Control Rating: **8 8**   Highway Safety: **8 6**   ★★★

Brand	Year	Type	Length	Model	Chassis	Engine	Fuel Type	Price/Ft	Wheelbase	Towing	GVWR	Curb Weight
Dynasty	**1997**	MHA	38	38 slide	RO	CU300	D	$5700	252	10,000	31,500	29,053

Livability Code: FT 30-90   Wheelbase-to-length ratio of 55% is considered ○ dangerous ○ fatiguing ◉ good ○ excellent *

The approximate net payload of 2447 pounds at 8% of GVWR on this model is ○ deficient ○ excessive ◉ cautionary ○ good ○ excellent *

Total highway safety penalties are: 7 *   Value: **7 6**   Durability: **7 5**   Highway Control Rating: **7 0**   Highway Safety: **6 3**   ★★

Note: Safety ratings are based on the assumption that the engineering of the RV has allowed for proper balance by placing fresh, gray, and black holding tanks in a location so as not to change the balance of the RV when the tanks are empty or full. **Always double-check wheelbase, GVWR, and weights at front and rear axles.**

*See Section 1 for details on how conclusions are reached.

Brand	Year	Type	Length	Model	Chassis	Engine	Fuel Type	Average Price per Linear Foot When New	Adjusted Wheelbase	Approx. Towing Capacity	Gross Vehicle Weight Rating	Average Curb Weight
Dynasty	1997	MHA	40	40	RO	CU300	D	$5400	270	10,000	31,500	28,806

Livability Code: FT 30-90

Wheelbase-to-length ratio of 56% is considered ○ dangerous ○ fatiguing ● good ○ excellent *

The approximate net payload of 2694 pounds at 9% of GVWR on this model is ○ deficient ○ excessive ● cautionary ○ good ○ excellent *

Total highway safety penalties are: 2 *   Value: **7 9**   Durability: **7 5**   Highway Control Rating: **8 0**   Highway Safety: **7 8**   ★★★

Brand	Year	Type	Length	Model	Chassis	Engine	Fuel Type	Average Price per Linear Foot When New	Adjusted Wheelbase	Approx. Towing Capacity	Gross Vehicle Weight Rating	Average Curb Weight
Dynasty	1997	MHA	40	40 slide	RO	CU300	D	$5600	270	10,000	31,500	29,706

Livability Code: FT 30-90

Wheelbase-to-length ratio of 56% is considered ○ dangerous ○ fatiguing ● good ○ excellent *

The approximate net payload of 1794 pounds at 6% of GVWR on this model is ● deficient ○ excessive ○ cautionary ○ good ○ excellent *

Total highway safety penalties are: 7 *   Value: **7 6**   Durability: **7 5**   Highway Control Rating: **6 2**   Highway Safety: **5 5**   ★

Brand	Year	Type	Length	Model	Chassis	Engine	Fuel Type	Average Price per Linear Foot When New	Adjusted Wheelbase	Approx. Towing Capacity	Gross Vehicle Weight Rating	Average Curb Weight
Dynasty	1998	MHA	33	32 Duchess	RO	CU325	D	$5900	191	10,000	29,500	25,746

Livability Code: FT 30-90

Wheelbase-to-length ratio of 48% is considered ● dangerous ○ fatiguing ○ good ○ excellent *

The approximate net payload of 3754 pounds at 13% of GVWR on this model is ○ deficient ○ excessive ○ cautionary ● good ○ excellent *

Total highway safety penalties are: 2 *   Value: **7 9**   Durability: **7 5**   Highway Control Rating: **3 2**   Highway Safety: **3 0**

Brand	Year	Type	Length	Model	Chassis	Engine	Fuel Type	Average Price per Linear Foot When New	Adjusted Wheelbase	Approx. Towing Capacity	Gross Vehicle Weight Rating	Average Curb Weight
Dynasty	1998	MHA	35	34 Baron II	RO	CU325	D	$5700	204	10,000	29,500	26,397

Livability Code: FT 30-90

Wheelbase-to-length ratio of 49% is considered ● dangerous ○ fatiguing ○ good ○ excellent *

The approximate net payload of 3103 pounds at 11% of GVWR on this model is ○ deficient ○ excessive ○ cautionary ● good ○ excellent *

Total highway safety penalties are: 2 *   Value: **7 9**   Durability: **7 5**   Highway Control Rating: **2 9**   Highway Safety: **2 7**

Brand	Year	Type	Length	Model	Chassis	Engine	Fuel Type	Average Price per Linear Foot When New	Adjusted Wheelbase	Approx. Towing Capacity	Gross Vehicle Weight Rating	Average Curb Weight
Dynasty	1998	MHA	35	34 Knight	RO	CU325	D	$5700	204	10,000	29,500	26,397

Livability Code: FT 30-90

Wheelbase-to-length ratio of 49% is considered ● dangerous ○ fatiguing ○ good ○ excellent *

The approximate net payload of 3103 pounds at 11% of GVWR on this model is ○ deficient ○ excessive ○ cautionary ● good ○ excellent *

Total highway safety penalties are: 2 *   Value: **7 9**   Durability: **7 5**   Highway Control Rating: **2 9**   Highway Safety: **2 7**

Brand	Year	Type	Length	Model	Chassis	Engine	Fuel Type	Average Price per Linear Foot When New	Adjusted Wheelbase	Approx. Towing Capacity	Gross Vehicle Weight Rating	Average Curb Weight
Dynasty	1998	MHA	37	36 Baron	RO	CU325	D	$5500	228	10,000	29,500	27,068

Livability Code: FT 30-90

Wheelbase-to-length ratio of 51% is considered ○ dangerous ● fatiguing ○ good ○ excellent *

The approximate net payload of 2432 pounds at 8% of GVWR on this model is ○ deficient ○ excessive ● cautionary ○ good ○ excellent *

Total highway safety penalties are: 2 *   Value: **7 9**   Durability: **7 5**   Highway Control Rating: **2 7**   Highway Safety: **2 5**

Brand	Year	Type	Length	Model	Chassis	Engine	Fuel Type	Average Price per Linear Foot When New	Adjusted Wheelbase	Approx. Towing Capacity	Gross Vehicle Weight Rating	Average Curb Weight
Dynasty	1998	MHA	37	36 Count	RO	CU325	D	$5500	228	10,000	29,500	27,068

Livability Code: FT 30-90

Wheelbase-to-length ratio of 51% is considered ○ dangerous ● fatiguing ○ good ○ excellent *

The approximate net payload of 2432 pounds at 8% of GVWR on this model is ○ deficient ○ excessive ● cautionary ○ good ○ excellent *

Total highway safety penalties are: 2 *   Value: **7 9**   Durability: **7 5**   Highway Control Rating: **2 7**   Highway Safety: **2 5**

Brand	Year	Type	Length	Model	Chassis	Engine	Fuel Type	Average Price per Linear Foot When New	Adjusted Wheelbase	Approx. Towing Capacity	Gross Vehicle Weight Rating	Average Curb Weight
Dynasty	1998	MHA	37	36 Suite Slide	RO	CU325	D	$5700	228	10,000	31,500	28,018

Livability Code: FT 30-90

Wheelbase-to-length ratio of 51% is considered ○ dangerous ● fatiguing ○ good ○ excellent *

The approximate net payload of 3482 pounds at 11% of GVWR on this model is ○ deficient ○ excessive ○ cautionary ● good ○ excellent *

Total highway safety penalties are: 12 *   Value: **7 4**   Durability: **7 5**   Highway Control Rating: **4 0**   Highway Safety: **2 8**

Brand	Year	Type	Length	Model	Chassis	Engine	Fuel Type	Average Price per Linear Foot When New	Adjusted Wheelbase	Approx. Towing Capacity	Gross Vehicle Weight Rating	Average Curb Weight
Dynasty	1998	MHA	39	38 Baron III	RO	CU325	D	$5400	252	10,000	31,500	28,455

Livability Code: FT 30-90

Wheelbase-to-length ratio of 54% is considered ○ dangerous ○ fatiguing ● good ○ excellent *

The approximate net payload of 3045 pounds at 10% of GVWR on this model is ○ deficient ○ excessive ○ cautionary ● good ○ excellent *

Total highway safety penalties are: 2 *   Value: **7 9**   Durability: **7 5**   Highway Control Rating: **7 5**   Highway Safety: **7 3**   ★★★

Brand	Year	Type	Length	Model	Chassis	Engine	Fuel Type	Average Price per Linear Foot When New	Adjusted Wheelbase	Approx. Towing Capacity	Gross Vehicle Weight Rating	Average Curb Weight
Dynasty	1998	MHA	39	38 Duke	RO	CU325	D	$5400	252	10,000	31,500	28,270

Livability Code: FT 30-90

Wheelbase-to-length ratio of 54% is considered ○ dangerous ○ fatiguing ● good ○ excellent *

The approximate net payload of 3230 pounds at 10% of GVWR on this model is ○ deficient ○ excessive ○ cautionary ● good ○ excellent *

Total highway safety penalties are: 2 *   Value: **7 9**   Durability: **7 5**   Highway Control Rating: **7 5**   Highway Safety: **7 3**   ★★★

Brand	Year	Type	Length	Model	Chassis	Engine	Fuel Type	Average Price per Linear Foot When New	Adjusted Wheelbase	Approx. Towing Capacity	Gross Vehicle Weight Rating	Average Curb Weight
Dynasty	1998	MHA	39	38 Suite Slide	RO	CU325	D	$5600	252	10,000	31,500	29,380

Livability Code: FT 30-90

Wheelbase-to-length ratio of 54% is considered ○ dangerous ○ fatiguing ● good ○ excellent *

The approximate net payload of 2120 pounds at 7% of GVWR on this model is ○ deficient ○ excessive ● cautionary ○ good ○ excellent *

Total highway safety penalties are: 12 *   Value: **7 4**   Durability: **7 5**   Highway Control Rating: **5 2**   Highway Safety: **4 0**

Brand	Year	Type	Length	Model	Chassis	Engine	Fuel Type	Average Price per Linear Foot When New	Adjusted Wheelbase	Approx. Towing Capacity	Gross Vehicle Weight Rating	Average Curb Weight
Dynasty	1998	MHA	39	38 PBS Suite Slide	RO	CU325	D	$5600	252	10,000	31,500	28,770

Livability Code: FT 30-90

Wheelbase-to-length ratio of 54% is considered ○ dangerous ○ fatiguing ● good ○ excellent *

The approximate net payload of 2730 pounds at 9% of GVWR on this model is ○ deficient ○ excessive ● cautionary ○ good ○ excellent *

Total highway safety penalties are: 12 *   Value: **7 4**   Durability: **7 5**   Highway Control Rating: **6 4**   Highway Safety: **5 2**   ★

Note: Safety ratings are based on the assumption that the engineering of the RV has allowed for proper balance by placing fresh, gray, and black holding tanks in a location so as not to change the balance of the RV when the tanks are empty or full. **Always double-check wheelbase, GVWR, and weights at front and rear axles.**

*See Section 1 for details on how conclusions are reached.

Brand	Year	Type	Length	Model	Chassis	Engine	Fuel Type	Average Price per Linear Foot When New	Adjusted Wheelbase	Approx. Towing Capacity	Gross Vehicle Weight Rating	Average Curb Weight
Dynasty	1998	MHA	40	40 Baron IV	RO	CU325	D	$5500	270	10,000	31,500	28,708

Livability Code: FT 30-90   Wheelbase-to-length ratio of 56% is considered ○ dangerous ○ fatiguing ◉ good ○ excellent *
The approximate net payload of 2792 pounds at 9% of GVWR on this model is ○ deficient ○ excessive ◉ cautionary ○ good ○ excellent *
Total highway safety penalties are: 2 *   Value: **7 9**   Durability: **7 5**   Highway Control Rating: **7 8**   Highway Safety: **7 6**   ★★★

Brand	Year	Type	Length	Model	Chassis	Engine	Fuel Type	Price/LF	Wheelbase	Towing	GVWR	Curb Weight
Dynasty	1998	MHA	40	40 Duke	RO	CU325	D	$5500	270	10,000	31,500	28,708

Livability Code: FT 30-90   Wheelbase-to-length ratio of 56% is considered ○ dangerous ○ fatiguing ◉ good ○ excellent *
The approximate net payload of 2792 pounds at 9% of GVWR on this model is ○ deficient ○ excessive ◉ cautionary ○ good ○ excellent *
Total highway safety penalties are: 2 *   Value: **7 9**   Durability: **7 5**   Highway Control Rating: **7 8**   Highway Safety: **7 6**   ★★★

Dynasty	1998	MHA	40	40 Princess	RO	CU325	D	$5500	270	10,000	31,500	28,708

Livability Code: FT 30-90   Wheelbase-to-length ratio of 56% is considered ○ dangerous ○ fatiguing ◉ good ○ excellent *
The approximate net payload of 2792 pounds at 9% of GVWR on this model is ○ deficient ○ excessive ◉ cautionary ○ good ○ excellent *
Total highway safety penalties are: 2 *   Value: **7 9**   Durability: **7 5**   Highway Control Rating: **7 8**   Highway Safety: **7 6**   ★★★

Dynasty	1998	MHA	40	40 PBS Suite Slide	RO	CU325	D	$5700	270	10,000	31,500	29,736

Livability Code: FT 30-90   Wheelbase-to-length ratio of 56% is considered ○ dangerous ○ fatiguing ◉ good ○ excellent *
The approximate net payload of 1764 pounds at 6% of GVWR on this model is ◉ deficient ○ excessive ○ cautionary ○ good ○ excellent *
Total highway safety penalties are: 12 *   Value: **7 4**   Durability: **7 5**   Highway Control Rating: **6 0**   Highway Safety: **4 8**

Dynasty	1999	MHA	33	32 Duchess FD	RO	CU330	D	$7100	191	10,000	32,300	26,921

Livability Code: FT 30-90   Wheelbase-to-length ratio of 48% is considered ◉ dangerous ○ fatiguing ○ good ○ excellent *
The approximate net payload of 5379 pounds at 17% of GVWR on this model is ○ deficient ○ excessive ○ cautionary ○ good ◉ excellent *
Total highway safety penalties are: 2 *   Value: **7 9**   Durability: **7 5**   Highway Control Rating: **4 9**   Highway Safety: **4 7**

Dynasty	1999	MHA	33	32 Duchess FD op	RO	CU350	D	$7100	191	10,000	32,300	27,421

Livability Code: FT 30-90   Wheelbase-to-length ratio of 48% is considered ◉ dangerous ○ fatiguing ○ good ○ excellent *
The approximate net payload of 4879 pounds at 15% of GVWR on this model is ○ deficient ○ excessive ○ cautionary ◉ good ○ excellent *
Total highway safety penalties are: 2 *   Value: **7 9**   Durability: **7 5**   Highway Control Rating: **4 6**   Highway Safety: **4 4**

Dynasty	1999	MHA	35	34 Baron II FD	RO	CU330	D	$6700	204	10,000	32,300	27,574

Livability Code: FT 30-90   Wheelbase-to-length ratio of 49% is considered ◉ dangerous ○ fatiguing ○ good ○ excellent *
The approximate net payload of 4726 pounds at 15% of GVWR on this model is ○ deficient ○ excessive ○ cautionary ◉ good ○ excellent *
Total highway safety penalties are: 2 *   Value: **7 9**   Durability: **7 5**   Highway Control Rating: **4 7**   Highway Safety: **4 5**

Dynasty	1999	MHA	35	34 Baron II FD op eng	RO	CU350	D	$6700	204	10,000	32,300	28,074

Livability Code: FT 30-90   Wheelbase-to-length ratio of 49% is considered ◉ dangerous ○ fatiguing ○ good ○ excellent *
The approximate net payload of 4226 pounds at 13% of GVWR on this model is ○ deficient ○ excessive ○ cautionary ◉ good ○ excellent *
Total highway safety penalties are: 2 *   Value: **7 9**   Durability: **7 5**   Highway Control Rating: **4 4**   Highway Safety: **4 2**

Dynasty	1999	MHA	37	36 Duke	RO	CU330	D	$6400	228	10,000	32,300	28,227

Livability Code: FT 30-90   Wheelbase-to-length ratio of 51% is considered ○ dangerous ◉ fatiguing ○ good ○ excellent *
The approximate net payload of 4073 pounds at 13% of GVWR on this model is ○ deficient ○ excessive ○ cautionary ◉ good ○ excellent *
Total highway safety penalties are: 2 *   Value: **7 9**   Durability: **7 5**   Highway Control Rating: **5 3**   Highway Safety: **5 1**   ★

Dynasty	1999	MHA	37	36 Suite Slide FD	RO	CU330	D	$6400	228	10,000	32,300	29,127

Livability Code: FT 30-90   Wheelbase-to-length ratio of 51% is considered ○ dangerous ◉ fatiguing ○ good ○ excellent *
The approximate net payload of 3173 pounds at 10% of GVWR on this model is ○ deficient ○ excessive ○ cautionary ◉ good ○ excellent *
Total highway safety penalties are: 12 *   Value: **7 4**   Durability: **7 5**   Highway Control Rating: **4 7**   Highway Safety: **3 5**

Dynasty	1999	MHA	37	36 Duke op eng	RO	CU350	D	$6400	228	10,000	32,300	28,727

Livability Code: FT 30-90   Wheelbase-to-length ratio of 51% is considered ○ dangerous ◉ fatiguing ○ good ○ excellent *
The approximate net payload of 3573 pounds at 11% of GVWR on this model is ○ deficient ○ excessive ○ cautionary ◉ good ○ excellent *
Total highway safety penalties are: 2 *   Value: **7 9**   Durability: **7 5**   Highway Control Rating: **5 0**   Highway Safety: **4 8**

Dynasty	1999	MHA	37	36 Suite Slide FD op	RO	CU350	D	$6400	228	10,000	32,300	29,627

Livability Code: FT 30-90   Wheelbase-to-length ratio of 51% is considered ○ dangerous ◉ fatiguing ○ good ○ excellent *
The approximate net payload of 2673 pounds at 8% of GVWR on this model is ○ deficient ○ excessive ◉ cautionary ○ good ○ excellent *
Total highway safety penalties are: 12 *   Value: **7 4**   Durability: **7 5**   Highway Control Rating: **3 7**   Highway Safety: **2 5**

Note: Safety ratings are based on the assumption that the engineering of the RV has allowed for proper balance by placing fresh, gray, and black holding tanks in a location so as not to change the balance of the RV when the tanks are empty or full. **Always double-check wheelbase, GVWR, and weights at front and rear axles.**

Section 2: The Ratings

Brand	Year	Type	Length	Model	Chassis	Engine	Fuel Type	Average Price per Linear Foot When New	Adjusted Wheelbase	Approx. Towing Capacity	Gross Vehicle Weight Rating	Average Curb Weight

Dynasty — 1999 — MHA — 39 — 38 Baron III FD — RO — CU330 — D — $6000 — 252 — 10,000 — 32,300 — 28,880
Livability Code: FT 30-90
Wheelbase-to-length ratio of 54% is considered ○ dangerous ○ fatiguing ◉ good ○ excellent *
The approximate net payload of 3420 pounds at 11% of GVWR on this model is ○ deficient ○ excessive ○ cautionary ◉ good ○ excellent *
Total highway safety penalties are: 2 *   Value: 7 9   Durability: 7 5   Highway Control Rating: 7 8   Highway Safety: 7 6   ★★★

Dynasty — 1999 — MHA — 39 — 38 Duke FD — RO — CU330 — D — $6000 — 252 — 10,000 — 32,300 — 28,880
Livability Code: FT 30-90
Wheelbase-to-length ratio of 54% is considered ○ dangerous ○ fatiguing ◉ good ○ excellent *
The approximate net payload of 3420 pounds at 11% of GVWR on this model is ○ deficient ○ excessive ○ cautionary ◉ good ○ excellent *
Total highway safety penalties are: 2 *   Value: 7 9   Durability: 7 5   Highway Control Rating: 7 8   Highway Safety: 7 6   ★★★

Dynasty — 1999 — MHA — 39 — 38 PBS Suite SlideFD — RO — CU330 — D — $6000 — 252 — 10,000 — 32,300 — 29,780
Livability Code: FT 30-90
Wheelbase-to-length ratio of 54% is considered ○ dangerous ○ fatiguing ◉ good ○ excellent *
The approximate net payload of 2520 pounds at 8% of GVWR on this model is ○ deficient ○ excessive ◉ cautionary ○ good ○ excellent *
Total highway safety penalties are: 12 *   Value: 7 4   Durability: 7 5   Highway Control Rating: 6 0   Highway Safety: 4 8

Dynasty — 1999 — MHA — 39 — 38 Baron SD — RO — CU330 — D — $6000 — 252 — 10,000 — 32,300 — 28,880
Livability Code: FT 30-90
Wheelbase-to-length ratio of 54% is considered ○ dangerous ○ fatiguing ◉ good ○ excellent *
The approximate net payload of 3420 pounds at 11% of GVWR on this model is ○ deficient ○ excessive ○ cautionary ◉ good ○ excellent *
Total highway safety penalties are: 2 *   Value: 7 9   Durability: 7 5   Highway Control Rating: 7 8   Highway Safety: 7 6   ★★★

Dynasty — 1999 — MHA — 39 — 38 Baron III FD op eng — RO — CU350 — D — $6000 — 252 — 10,000 — 32,300 — 29,380
Livability Code: FT 30-90
Wheelbase-to-length ratio of 54% is considered ○ dangerous ○ fatiguing ◉ good ○ excellent *
The approximate net payload of 2920 pounds at 9% of GVWR on this model is ○ deficient ○ excessive ◉ cautionary ○ good ○ excellent *
Total highway safety penalties are: 2 *   Value: 7 9   Durability: 7 5   Highway Control Rating: 6 7   Highway Safety: 6 5   ★★

Dynasty — 1999 — MHA — 39 — 38 Duke FD op eng — RO — CU350 — D — $6000 — 252 — 10,000 — 32,300 — 29,380
Livability Code: FT 30-90
Wheelbase-to-length ratio of 54% is considered ○ dangerous ○ fatiguing ◉ good ○ excellent *
The approximate net payload of 2920 pounds at 9% of GVWR on this model is ○ deficient ○ excessive ◉ cautionary ○ good ○ excellent *
Total highway safety penalties are: 2 *   Value: 7 9   Durability: 7 5   Highway Control Rating: 6 7   Highway Safety: 6 5   ★★

Dynasty — 1999 — MHA — 39 — 38 PBS Suite op eng — RO — CU350 — D — $6000 — 252 — 10,000 — 32,300 — 30,280
Livability Code: FT 30-90
Wheelbase-to-length ratio of 54% is considered ○ dangerous ○ fatiguing ◉ good ○ excellent *
The approximate net payload of 2020 pounds at 6% of GVWR on this model is ◉ deficient ○ excessive ○ cautionary ○ good ○ excellent *
Total highway safety penalties are: 12 *   Value: 7 4   Durability: 7 5   Highway Control Rating: 4 9   Highway Safety: 3 7

Dynasty — 1999 — MHA — 39 — 38 Baron SD — RO — CU350 — D — $6000 — 252 — 10,000 — 32,300 — 28,880
Livability Code: FT 30-90
Wheelbase-to-length ratio of 54% is considered ○ dangerous ○ fatiguing ◉ good ○ excellent *
The approximate net payload of 3420 pounds at 11% of GVWR on this model is ○ deficient ○ excessive ○ cautionary ◉ good ○ excellent *
Total highway safety penalties are: 2 *   Value: 7 9   Durability: 7 5   Highway Control Rating: 7 8   Highway Safety: 7 6   ★★★

Dynasty — 1999 — MHA — 40 — 40 PBS SS FD — RO — CU330 — D — $5900 — 270 — 10,000 — 32,300 — 30,106
Livability Code: FT 30-90
Wheelbase-to-length ratio of 56% is considered ○ dangerous ○ fatiguing ◉ good ○ excellent *
The approximate net payload of 2194 pounds at 7% of GVWR on this model is ○ deficient ○ excessive ◉ cautionary ○ good ○ excellent *
Total highway safety penalties are: 12 *   Value: 7 4   Durability: 7 5   Highway Control Rating: 6 8   Highway Safety: 5 6   ★

Dynasty — 1999 — MHA — 40 — 40 PBS SS FD op eng — RO — CU350 — D — $5900 — 270 — 10,000 — 32,300 — 30,606
Livability Code: FT 30-90
Wheelbase-to-length ratio of 56% is considered ○ dangerous ○ fatiguing ◉ good ○ excellent *
The approximate net payload of 1694 pounds at 5% of GVWR on this model is ◉ deficient ○ excessive ○ cautionary ○ good ○ excellent *
Total highway safety penalties are: 12 *   Value: 7 4   Durability: 7 5   Highway Control Rating: 6 1   Highway Safety: 4 9

Dynasty — 1999 — MHA — 40 — 40 Baron IV FD — RO — CU330 — D — $5900 — 270 — 10,000 — 32,300 — 29,337
Livability Code: FT 30-90
Wheelbase-to-length ratio of 56% is considered ○ dangerous ○ fatiguing ◉ good ○ excellent *
The approximate net payload of 2963 pounds at 9% of GVWR on this model is ○ deficient ○ excessive ◉ cautionary ○ good ○ excellent *
Total highway safety penalties are: 2 *   Value: 7 9   Durability: 7 5   Highway Control Rating: 7 8   Highway Safety: 7 6   ★★★

Dynasty — 1999 — MHA — 40 — 40 Duke FD — RO — CU330 — D — $5900 — 270 — 10,000 — 32,300 — 29,337
Livability Code: FT 30-90
Wheelbase-to-length ratio of 56% is considered ○ dangerous ○ fatiguing ◉ good ○ excellent *
The approximate net payload of 2963 pounds at 9% of GVWR on this model is ○ deficient ○ excessive ◉ cautionary ○ good ○ excellent *
Total highway safety penalties are: 2 *   Value: 7 9   Durability: 7 5   Highway Control Rating: 7 8   Highway Safety: 7 6   ★★★

Note: Safety ratings are based on the assumption that the engineering of the RV has allowed for proper balance by placing fresh, gray, and black holding tanks in a location so as not to change the balance of the RV when the tanks are empty or full. **Always double-check wheelbase, GVWR, and weights at front and rear axles.**

*See Section 1 for details on how conclusions are reached.

Section 2: The Ratings

Brand	Year	Type	Length	Model	Chassis	Engine	Fuel Type	Average Price per Linear Foot When New	Adjusted Wheelbase	Approx. Towing Capacity	Gross Vehicle Weight Rating	Average Curb Weight
Dynasty	1999	MHA	40	40 Princess FD	RO	CU330	D	$5900	270	10,000	32,300	29,337

Livability Code: FT 30-90   Wheelbase-to-length ratio of 56% is considered ○ dangerous ○ fatiguing ◉ good ○ excellent *

The approximate net payload of 2963 pounds at 9% of GVWR on this model is ○ deficient ○ excessive ◉ cautionary ○ good ○ excellent *

Total highway safety penalties are: 2 *   Value: **7 9**   Durability: **7 5**   Highway Control Rating: **7 8**   Highway Safety: **7 6**   ★★★

Brand	Year	Type	Length	Model	Chassis	Engine	Fuel Type	Price/Ft	Wheelbase	Towing	GVWR	Curb Wt
Dynasty	1999	MHA	40	40 Tycoon SD	RO	CU330	D	$5900	270	10,000	32,300	29,337

Livability Code: FT 30-90   Wheelbase-to-length ratio of 56% is considered ○ dangerous ○ fatiguing ◉ good ○ excellent *

The approximate net payload of 2963 pounds at 9% of GVWR on this model is ○ deficient ○ excessive ◉ cautionary ○ good ○ excellent *

Total highway safety penalties are: 2 *   Value: **7 9**   Durability: **7 5**   Highway Control Rating: **7 8**   Highway Safety: **7 6**   ★★★

Brand	Year	Type	Length	Model	Chassis	Engine	Fuel Type	Price/Ft	Wheelbase	Towing	GVWR	Curb Wt
Dynasty	1999	MHA	40	40 Baron IV FD op eng	RO	CU350	D	$5900	270	10,000	32,300	29,837

Livability Code: FT 30-90   Wheelbase-to-length ratio of 56% is considered ○ dangerous ○ fatiguing ◉ good ○ excellent *

The approximate net payload of 2463 pounds at 8% of GVWR on this model is ○ deficient ○ excessive ◉ cautionary ○ good ○ excellent *

Total highway safety penalties are: 2 *   Value: **7 9**   Durability: **7 5**   Highway Control Rating: **7 2**   Highway Safety: **7 0**   ★★★

Brand	Year	Type	Length	Model	Chassis	Engine	Fuel Type	Price/Ft	Wheelbase	Towing	GVWR	Curb Wt
Dynasty	1999	MHA	40	40 Duke FD	RO	CU350	D	$5900	270	10,000	32,300	29,337

Livability Code: FT 30-90   Wheelbase-to-length ratio of 56% is considered ○ dangerous ○ fatiguing ◉ good ○ excellent *

The approximate net payload of 2963 pounds at 9% of GVWR on this model is ○ deficient ○ excessive ◉ cautionary ○ good ○ excellent *

Total highway safety penalties are: 2 *   Value: **7 9**   Durability: **7 5**   Highway Control Rating: **7 8**   Highway Safety: **7 6**   ★★★

Brand	Year	Type	Length	Model	Chassis	Engine	Fuel Type	Price/Ft	Wheelbase	Towing	GVWR	Curb Wt
Dynasty	1999	MHA	40	40 Princess FD	RO	CU350	D	$5900	270	10,000	32,300	29,337

Livability Code: FT 30-90   Wheelbase-to-length ratio of 56% is considered ○ dangerous ○ fatiguing ◉ good ○ excellent *

The approximate net payload of 2963 pounds at 9% of GVWR on this model is ○ deficient ○ excessive ◉ cautionary ○ good ○ excellent *

Total highway safety penalties are: 2 *   Value: **7 9**   Durability: **7 5**   Highway Control Rating: **7 8**   Highway Safety: **7 6**   ★★★

Brand	Year	Type	Length	Model	Chassis	Engine	Fuel Type	Price/Ft	Wheelbase	Towing	GVWR	Curb Wt
Dynasty	1999	MHA	40	40 Tycoon SD	RO	CU350	D	$5900	270	10,000	32,300	29,337

Livability Code: FT 30-90   Wheelbase-to-length ratio of 56% is considered ○ dangerous ○ fatiguing ◉ good ○ excellent *

The approximate net payload of 2963 pounds at 9% of GVWR on this model is ○ deficient ○ excessive ◉ cautionary ○ good ○ excellent *

Total highway safety penalties are: 2 *   Value: **7 9**   Durability: **7 5**   Highway Control Rating: **7 8**   Highway Safety: **7 6**   ★★★

Brand	Year	Type	Length	Model	Chassis	Engine	Fuel Type	Price/Ft	Wheelbase	Towing	GVWR	Curb Wt
Dynasty	1999	MHA	40	40 SD King	RO	CU330	D	$5900	270	10,000	32,300	30,237

Livability Code: FT 30-90   Wheelbase-to-length ratio of 56% is considered ○ dangerous ○ fatiguing ◉ good ○ excellent *

The approximate net payload of 2063 pounds at 6% of GVWR on this model is ◉ deficient ○ excessive ○ cautionary ○ good ○ excellent *

Total highway safety penalties are: 12 *   Value: **7 4**   Durability: **7 5**   Highway Control Rating: **6 1**   Highway Safety: **4 9**

Brand	Year	Type	Length	Model	Chassis	Engine	Fuel Type	Price/Ft	Wheelbase	Towing	GVWR	Curb Wt
Dynasty	1999	MHA	40	40 SD King op eng	RO	CU350	D	$5900	270	10,000	32,300	30,737

Livability Code: FT 30-90   Wheelbase-to-length ratio of 56% is considered ○ dangerous ○ fatiguing ◉ good ○ excellent *

The approximate net payload of 1563 pounds at 5% of GVWR on this model is ◉ deficient ○ excessive ○ cautionary ○ good ○ excellent *

Total highway safety penalties are: 12 *   Value: **7 4**   Durability: **7 5**   Highway Control Rating: **5 9**   Highway Safety: **4 7**

Brand	Year	Type	Length	Model	Chassis	Engine	Fuel Type	Price/Ft	Wheelbase	Towing	GVWR	Curb Wt
Elandan	1990	MHA	37	37RQ	CH	7.4L	G	$1900	232 T	1,500	18,000	15,785

Livability Code: SB 30-90   Wheelbase-to-length ratio of 52% is considered ○ dangerous ◉ fatiguing ○ good ○ excellent *

The approximate net payload of 2215 pounds at 12% of GVWR on this model is ○ deficient ○ excessive ○ cautionary ◉ good ○ excellent *

Total highway safety penalties are: 11 *   Value: **7 8**   Durability: **7 0**   Highway Control Rating: **5 2**   Highway Safety: **4 1**

Brand	Year	Type	Length	Model	Chassis	Engine	Fuel Type	Price/Ft	Wheelbase	Towing	GVWR	Curb Wt
Elandan	1991	MHA	38	37RQ	CH	7.4L	G	$2000	232 T	1,500	18,000	15,846

Livability Code: SB 30-90   Wheelbase-to-length ratio of 51% is considered ○ dangerous ◉ fatiguing ○ good ○ excellent *

The approximate net payload of 2154 pounds at 12% of GVWR on this model is ○ deficient ○ excessive ○ cautionary ◉ good ○ excellent *

Total highway safety penalties are: 11 *   Value: **7 8**   Durability: **7 0**   Highway Control Rating: **4 0**   Highway Safety: **2 9**

Brand	Year	Type	Length	Model	Chassis	Engine	Fuel Type	Price/Ft	Wheelbase	Towing	GVWR	Curb Wt
Elante'	1993	MHA	34	33RQ	FO	7.5L	G	$2300	200	8,000	17,000	14,498

Livability Code: SB 30-90   Wheelbase-to-length ratio of 49% is considered ◉ dangerous ○ fatiguing ○ good ○ excellent *

The approximate net payload of 2502 pounds at 15% of GVWR on this model is ○ deficient ○ excessive ○ cautionary ◉ good ○ excellent *

Total highway safety penalties are: 2 *   Value: **8 2**   Durability: **7 0**   Highway Control Rating: **3 9**   Highway Safety: **3 7**

Brand	Year	Type	Length	Model	Chassis	Engine	Fuel Type	Price/Ft	Wheelbase	Towing	GVWR	Curb Wt
Elante'	1993	MHA	38	37RQ	FO	7.5L	G	$2300	252 T	6,000	19,000	16,063

Livability Code: SB 30-90   Wheelbase-to-length ratio of 56% is considered ○ dangerous ○ fatiguing ◉ good ○ excellent *

The approximate net payload of 2938 pounds at 15% of GVWR on this model is ○ deficient ○ excessive ○ cautionary ◉ good ○ excellent *

Total highway safety penalties are: 4 *   Value: **8 1**   Durability: **7 0**   Highway Control Rating: **9 5**   Highway Safety: **9 1**   ★★★

Note: Safety ratings are based on the assumption that the engineering of the RV has allowed for proper balance by placing fresh, gray, and black holding tanks in a location so as not to change the balance of the RV when the tanks are empty or full. **Always double-check wheelbase, GVWR, and weights at front and rear axles.**

*See Section 1 for details on how conclusions are reached.

Brand	Year	Type	Length	Model	Chassis	Engine	Fuel Type	Average Price per Linear Foot When New	Adjusted Wheelbase	Approx. Towing Capacity	Gross Vehicle Weight Rating	Average Curb Weight
Elante'	1994	MHA	34	33RQ	CH	7.4L	G	$2400	200	3,000	16,000	13,998

Livability Code: SB 30-90
Wheelbase-to-length ratio of 49% is considered ● dangerous ○ fatiguing ○ good ○ excellent *
The approximate net payload of 2002 pounds at 13% of GVWR on this model is ○ deficient ○ excessive ○ cautionary ● good ○ excellent *
Total highway safety penalties are: 7 *   Value: 8 0   Durability: 7 0   Highway Control Rating: 3 5   Highway Safety: 2 8

Brand	Year	Type	Length	Model	Chassis	Engine	Fuel Type	Avg Price/Linear Foot	Adj Wheelbase	Approx Towing	GVWR	Avg Curb Weight
Elante'	1994	MHA	34	33RQ	FO	7.5L	G	$2400	200	8,000	17,000	14,498

Livability Code: SB 30-90
Wheelbase-to-length ratio of 49% is considered ● dangerous ○ fatiguing ○ good ○ excellent *
The approximate net payload of 2502 pounds at 15% of GVWR on this model is ○ deficient ○ excessive ○ cautionary ● good ○ excellent *
Total highway safety penalties are: 2 *   Value: 8 2   Durability: 7 0   Highway Control Rating: 3 9   Highway Safety: 3 7

| Elante' | 1994 | MHA | 38 | 37RQ | CH | 7.4L | G | $2400 | 232 T | 1,000 | 18,000 | 15,763 |

Livability Code: SB 30-90
Wheelbase-to-length ratio of 52% is considered ○ dangerous ● fatiguing ○ good ○ excellent *
The approximate net payload of 2238 pounds at 12% of GVWR on this model is ○ deficient ○ excessive ○ cautionary ● good ○ excellent *
Total highway safety penalties are: 11 *   Value: 7 8   Durability: 7 0   Highway Control Rating: 5 0   Highway Safety: 3 9

| Elante' | 1994 | MHA | 38 | 37RQ | FO | 7.5L | G | $2400 | 252 T | 6,000 | 19,000 | 16,063 |

Livability Code: SB 30-90
Wheelbase-to-length ratio of 56% is considered ○ dangerous ○ fatiguing ● good ○ excellent *
The approximate net payload of 2938 pounds at 15% of GVWR on this model is ○ deficient ○ excessive ○ cautionary ● good ○ excellent *
Total highway safety penalties are: 4 *   Value: 8 1   Durability: 7 0   Highway Control Rating: 9 5   Highway Safety: 9 1   ★★★

| Encounter | 1990 | MHA | 37 | 3691 | OS | 7.5L | G | $2000 | 228 | 7,000 | 18,000 | 16,082 |

Livability Code: SB 30-90
Wheelbase-to-length ratio of 51% is considered ○ dangerous ● fatiguing ○ good ○ excellent *
The approximate net payload of 1918 pounds at 11% of GVWR on this model is ○ deficient ○ excessive ○ cautionary ● good ○ excellent *
Total highway safety penalties are: 2 *   Value: 7 9   Durability: 7 4   Highway Control Rating: 3 9   Highway Safety: 3 7

| Encounter | 1991 | MHA | 36 | 3691 | FO | 7.5L | G | $1900 | 228 | 8,000 | 17,000 | 15,607 |

Livability Code: SB 30-90
Wheelbase-to-length ratio of 53% is considered ○ dangerous ● fatiguing ○ good ○ excellent *
The approximate net payload of 1393 pounds at 8% of GVWR on this model is ○ deficient ○ excessive ● cautionary ○ good ○ excellent *
Total highway safety penalties are: 2 *   Value: 7 9   Durability: 7 4   Highway Control Rating: 4 6   Highway Safety: 4 4

| Encounter | 1992 | MHA | 32 | 3290 | CH | 7.4L | G | $2000 | 190 | 1,500 | 16,000 | 14,112 |

Livability Code: SB 30-90
Wheelbase-to-length ratio of 49% is considered ● dangerous ○ fatiguing ○ good ○ excellent *
The approximate net payload of 1888 pounds at 12% of GVWR on this model is ○ deficient ○ excessive ○ cautionary ● good ○ excellent *
Total highway safety penalties are: 6 *   Value: 7 7   Durability: 7 4   Highway Control Rating: 3 5   Highway Safety: 2 9

| Encounter | 1992 | MHA | 32 | 3290 | FO | 7.5L | G | $1900 | 190 | 8,000 | 17,000 | 14,612 |

Livability Code: SB 30-90
Wheelbase-to-length ratio of 49% is considered ● dangerous ○ fatiguing ○ good ○ excellent *
The approximate net payload of 2388 pounds at 14% of GVWR on this model is ○ deficient ○ excessive ○ cautionary ● good ○ excellent *
Total highway safety penalties are: 2 *   Value: 7 9   Durability: 7 4   Highway Control Rating: 3 9   Highway Safety: 3 7

| Encounter | 1992 | MHA | 32 | 3290 | OS | 7.5L | G | $2300 | 190 | 9,400 | 15,600 | 14,912 |

Livability Code: SB 30-90
Wheelbase-to-length ratio of 49% is considered ● dangerous ○ fatiguing ○ good ○ excellent *
The approximate net payload of 688 pounds at 4% of GVWR on this model is ● deficient ○ excessive ○ cautionary ○ good ○ excellent *
Total highway safety penalties are: 2 *   Value: 7 9   Durability: 7 4   Highway Control Rating: 6   Highway Safety: 4

| Encounter | 1992 | MHA | 34 | 3490 | FO | 7.5L | G | $1900 | 208 | 8,000 | 17,000 | 15,144 |

Livability Code: SB 30-90
Wheelbase-to-length ratio of 51% is considered ○ dangerous ● fatiguing ○ good ○ excellent *
The approximate net payload of 1856 pounds at 11% of GVWR on this model is ○ deficient ○ excessive ○ cautionary ● good ○ excellent *
Total highway safety penalties are: 2 *   Value: 7 9   Durability: 7 4   Highway Control Rating: 3 8   Highway Safety: 3 6

| Encounter | 1992 | MHA | 34 | 3496 | FO | 7.5L | G | $1900 | 208 | 8,000 | 17,000 | 15,144 |

Livability Code: SB 30-90
Wheelbase-to-length ratio of 51% is considered ○ dangerous ● fatiguing ○ good ○ excellent *
The approximate net payload of 1856 pounds at 11% of GVWR on this model is ○ deficient ○ excessive ○ cautionary ● good ○ excellent *
Total highway safety penalties are: 2 *   Value: 7 9   Durability: 7 4   Highway Control Rating: 3 8   Highway Safety: 3 6

| Encounter | 1992 | MHA | 34 | 3490 | OS | 7.5L | G | $2000 | 208 | 7,000 | 18,000 | 15,844 |

Livability Code: SB 30-90
Wheelbase-to-length ratio of 51% is considered ○ dangerous ● fatiguing ○ good ○ excellent *
The approximate net payload of 2156 pounds at 12% of GVWR on this model is ○ deficient ○ excessive ○ cautionary ● good ○ excellent *
Total highway safety penalties are: 2 *   Value: 7 9   Durability: 7 4   Highway Control Rating: 4 0   Highway Safety: 3 8

Note: Safety ratings are based on the assumption that the engineering of the RV has allowed for proper balance by placing fresh, gray, and black holding tanks in a location so as not to change the balance of the RV when the tanks are empty or full. **Always double-check wheelbase, GVWR, and weights at front and rear axles.**

*See Section 1 for details on how conclusions are reached.

Brand	Year	Type	Length	Model	Chassis	Engine	Fuel Type	Average Price per Linear Foot When New	Adjusted Wheelbase	Approx. Towing Capacity	Gross Vehicle Weight Rating	Average Curb Weight
Encounter	**1992**	MHA	34	3496	OS	7.5L	G	$2000	208	7,000	18,000	15,844

Livability Code: SB 30-90 — Wheelbase-to-length ratio of 51% is considered ○ dangerous ◉ fatiguing ○ good ○ excellent*

The approximate net payload of 2156 pounds at 12% of GVWR on this model is ○ deficient ○ excessive ○ cautionary ◉ good ○ excellent*

Total highway safety penalties are: 2*   Value: **7 9**   Durability: **7 4**   Highway Control Rating: **4 0**   Highway Safety: **3 8**

Brand	Year	Type	Length	Model	Chassis	Engine	Fuel Type	Price/Ft	Wheelbase	Towing	GVWR	Curb Wt
Encounter	**1992**	MHA	36	3691	FO	7.5L	G	$1900	228	8,000	17,000	15,676

Livability Code: SB 30-90 — Wheelbase-to-length ratio of 53% is considered ○ dangerous ◉ fatiguing ○ good ○ excellent*

The approximate net payload of 1324 pounds at 8% of GVWR on this model is ○ deficient ○ excessive ◉ cautionary ○ good ○ excellent*

Total highway safety penalties are: 2*   Value: **7 9**   Durability: **7 4**   Highway Control Rating: **4 6**   Highway Safety: **4 4**

Encounter	**1992**	MHA	36	3696	FO	7.5L	G	$1900	228	8,000	17,000	15,676

Livability Code: SB 30-90 — Wheelbase-to-length ratio of 53% is considered ○ dangerous ◉ fatiguing ○ good ○ excellent*

The approximate net payload of 1324 pounds at 8% of GVWR on this model is ○ deficient ○ excessive ◉ cautionary ○ good ○ excellent*

Total highway safety penalties are: 2*   Value: **7 9**   Durability: **7 4**   Highway Control Rating: **4 6**   Highway Safety: **4 4**

Encounter	**1992**	MHA	36	3691	OS	7.5L	G	$1900	228	7,000	18,000	16,376

Livability Code: SB 30-90 — Wheelbase-to-length ratio of 53% is considered ○ dangerous ◉ fatiguing ○ good ○ excellent*

The approximate net payload of 1624 pounds at 9% of GVWR on this model is ○ deficient ○ excessive ◉ cautionary ○ good ○ excellent*

Total highway safety penalties are: 2*   Value: **7 9**   Durability: **7 4**   Highway Control Rating: **5 3**   Highway Safety: **5 1**   ★

Encounter	**1992**	MHA	36	3692	OS	7.5L	G	$1900	232 T	7,000	18,000	16,376

Livability Code: SB 30-90 — Wheelbase-to-length ratio of 54% is considered ○ dangerous ○ fatiguing ◉ good ○ excellent*

The approximate net payload of 1624 pounds at 9% of GVWR on this model is ○ deficient ○ excessive ◉ cautionary ○ good ○ excellent*

Total highway safety penalties are: 4*   Value: **7 7**   Durability: **7 4**   Highway Control Rating: **6 4**   Highway Safety: **6 0**   ★★

Encounter	**1992**	MHA	36	3696	OS	7.5L	G	$1900	228	7,000	18,000	16,376

Livability Code: SB 30-90 — Wheelbase-to-length ratio of 53% is considered ○ dangerous ◉ fatiguing ○ good ○ excellent*

The approximate net payload of 1624 pounds at 9% of GVWR on this model is ○ deficient ○ excessive ◉ cautionary ○ good ○ excellent*

Total highway safety penalties are: 2*   Value: **7 9**   Durability: **7 4**   Highway Control Rating: **5 3**   Highway Safety: **5 1**   ★

Encounter	**1994**	MHA	34	3210	CH	7.4L	G	$1800	208	1,500	16,000	14,591

Livability Code: SB 30-90 — Wheelbase-to-length ratio of 51% is considered ○ dangerous ◉ fatiguing ○ good ○ excellent*

The approximate net payload of 1409 pounds at 9% of GVWR on this model is ○ deficient ○ excessive ◉ cautionary ○ good ○ excellent*

Total highway safety penalties are: 6*   Value: **7 6**   Durability: **7 4**   Highway Control Rating: **3 2**   Highway Safety: **2 6**

Encounter	**1994**	MHA	34	3210	FO	7.5L	G	$1800	228	8,000	17,000	15,091

Livability Code: SB 30-90 — Wheelbase-to-length ratio of 56% is considered ○ dangerous ○ fatiguing ◉ good ○ excellent*

The approximate net payload of 1909 pounds at 11% of GVWR on this model is ○ deficient ○ excessive ○ cautionary ◉ good ○ excellent*

Total highway safety penalties are: 2*   Value: **7 9**   Durability: **7 4**   Highway Control Rating: **8 7**   Highway Safety: **8 5**   ★★★

Encounter	**1994**	MHA	36	3400	FO	7.5L	G	$1800	228	8,000	17,000	15,596

Livability Code: SB 30-90 — Wheelbase-to-length ratio of 53% is considered ○ dangerous ◉ fatiguing ○ good ○ excellent*

The approximate net payload of 1404 pounds at 8% of GVWR on this model is ○ deficient ○ excessive ◉ cautionary ○ good ○ excellent*

Total highway safety penalties are: 2*   Value: **7 9**   Durability: **7 4**   Highway Control Rating: **4 9**   Highway Safety: **4 7**

Encounter	**1994**	MHA	36	3405	FO	7.5L	G	$1800	228	8,000	17,000	15,596

Livability Code: SB 30-90 — Wheelbase-to-length ratio of 53% is considered ○ dangerous ◉ fatiguing ○ good ○ excellent*

The approximate net payload of 1404 pounds at 8% of GVWR on this model is ○ deficient ○ excessive ◉ cautionary ○ good ○ excellent*

Total highway safety penalties are: 2*   Value: **7 9**   Durability: **7 4**   Highway Control Rating: **4 9**   Highway Safety: **4 7**

Encounter	**1994**	MHA	36	3401	FO	7.5L	G	$1800	228	8,000	17,000	15,676

Livability Code: SB 30-90 — Wheelbase-to-length ratio of 53% is considered ○ dangerous ◉ fatiguing ○ good ○ excellent*

The approximate net payload of 1324 pounds at 8% of GVWR on this model is ○ deficient ○ excessive ◉ cautionary ○ good ○ excellent*

Total highway safety penalties are: 2*   Value: **7 9**   Durability: **7 4**   Highway Control Rating: **4 6**   Highway Safety: **4 4**

Encounter	**1994**	MHA	37	3692	CH	7.4L	G	$1900	232 T	1,500	18,000	16,236

Livability Code: SB 30-90 — Wheelbase-to-length ratio of 53% is considered ○ dangerous ◉ fatiguing ○ good ○ excellent*

The approximate net payload of 1764 pounds at 10% of GVWR on this model is ○ deficient ○ excessive ○ cautionary ◉ good ○ excellent*

Total highway safety penalties are: 10*   Value: **7 5**   Durability: **7 4**   Highway Control Rating: **5 8**   Highway Safety: **4 8**

Note: Safety ratings are based on the assumption that the engineering of the RV has allowed for proper balance by placing fresh, gray, and black holding tanks in a location so as not to change the balance of the RV when the tanks are empty or full. **Always double-check wheelbase, GVWR, and weights at front and rear axles.**

*See Section 1 for details on how conclusions are reached.

Brand	Year	Type	Length	Model	Chassis	Engine	Fuel Type	Average Price per Linear Foot When New	Adjusted Wheelbase	Approx. Towing Capacity	Gross Vehicle Weight Rating	Average Curb Weight
Encounter	1994	MHA	37	3691	FO	7.5L	G	$1800	228	8,000	17,000	15,836

Livability Code: SB 30-90
Wheelbase-to-length ratio of 52% is considered ○ dangerous ● fatiguing ○ good ○ excellent *
The approximate net payload of 1164 pounds at 7% of GVWR on this model is ○ deficient ○ excessive ● cautionary ○ good ○ excellent *
Total highway safety penalties are: 2 * Value: 79 Durability: 74 Highway Control Rating: 30 Highway Safety: 28

| Encounter | 1995 | MHA | 36 | 3405 | CH | 7.4L | G | $2200 | 228 | 3,000 | 16,000 | 15,063 |

Livability Code: SB 30-90
Wheelbase-to-length ratio of 54% is considered ○ dangerous ○ fatiguing ● good ○ excellent *
The approximate net payload of 937 pounds at 6% of GVWR on this model is ● deficient ○ excessive ○ cautionary ○ good ○ excellent *
Total highway safety penalties are: 7 * Value: 76 Durability: 74 Highway Control Rating: 45 Highway Safety: 38

| Encounter | 1995 | MHA | 36 | 3405 | FO | 7.5L | G | $2100 | 228 | 8,000 | 17,000 | 15,543 |

Livability Code: SB 30-90
Wheelbase-to-length ratio of 54% is considered ○ dangerous ○ fatiguing ● good ○ excellent *
The approximate net payload of 1457 pounds at 9% of GVWR on this model is ○ deficient ○ excessive ● cautionary ○ good ○ excellent *
Total highway safety penalties are: 2 * Value: 79 Durability: 74 Highway Control Rating: 62 Highway Safety: 60 ★★

| Encounter | 1995 | MHA | 36 | 3595 | CH | 7.4L | G | $2200 | 228 | 3,000 | 16,000 | 15,300 |

Livability Code: SB 30-90
Wheelbase-to-length ratio of 52% is considered ○ dangerous ● fatiguing ○ good ○ excellent *
The approximate net payload of 700 pounds at 4% of GVWR on this model is ● deficient ○ excessive ○ cautionary ○ good ○ excellent *
Total highway safety penalties are: 8 * Value: 76 Durability: 74 Highway Control Rating: 25 Highway Safety: 17

| Encounter | 1995 | MHA | 36 | 3595 | FO | 7.5L | G | $2100 | 228 | 8,000 | 17,000 | 15,729 |

Livability Code: SB 30-90
Wheelbase-to-length ratio of 52% is considered ○ dangerous ● fatiguing ○ good ○ excellent *
The approximate net payload of 1271 pounds at 7% of GVWR on this model is ○ deficient ○ excessive ● cautionary ○ good ○ excellent *
Total highway safety penalties are: 2 * Value: 79 Durability: 74 Highway Control Rating: 33 Highway Safety: 31

| Encounter | 1995 | MHA | 37 | 3605 | FO | 7.5L | G | $1800 | 228 | 8,000 | 17,000 | 15,915 |

Livability Code: SB 30-90
Wheelbase-to-length ratio of 51% is considered ○ dangerous ● fatiguing ○ good ○ excellent *
The approximate net payload of 1085 pounds at 6% of GVWR on this model is ● deficient ○ excessive ○ cautionary ○ good ○ excellent *
Total highway safety penalties are: 2 * Value: 79 Durability: 74 Highway Control Rating: 15 Highway Safety: 13

| Encounter | 1997 | MHA | 36 | 3405 | FR | CA250 | D | $3100 | 208 | 1,500 | 24,850 | 19,140 |

Livability Code: SB 30-90
Wheelbase-to-length ratio of 49% is considered ● dangerous ○ fatiguing ○ good ○ excellent *
The approximate net payload of 5710 pounds at 23% of GVWR on this model is ○ deficient ○ excessive ○ cautionary ○ good ● excellent *
Total highway safety penalties are: 2 * Value: 79 Durability: 74 Highway Control Rating: 41 Highway Safety: 39

| Encounter | 1997 | MHA | 38 | 3701 | FR | CA275 | D | $3900 | 228 | 1,500 | 24,850 | 19,610 |

Livability Code: SB 30-90
Wheelbase-to-length ratio of 50% is considered ● dangerous ○ fatiguing ○ good ○ excellent *
The approximate net payload of 5240 pounds at 21% of GVWR on this model is ○ deficient ○ excessive ○ cautionary ○ good ● excellent *
Total highway safety penalties are: 2 * Value: 79 Durability: 74 Highway Control Rating: 49 Highway Safety: 47

| Encounter | 1997 | MHA | 38 | 3701 slide | FR | CA275 | D | $3900 | 228 | 1,500 | 24,850 | 20,360 |

Livability Code: SB 30-90
Wheelbase-to-length ratio of 50% is considered ● dangerous ○ fatiguing ○ good ○ excellent *
The approximate net payload of 4490 pounds at 18% of GVWR on this model is ○ deficient ○ excessive ○ cautionary ○ good ● excellent *
Total highway safety penalties are: 7 * Value: 76 Durability: 74 Highway Control Rating: 48 Highway Safety: 41

| Encounter | 1997 | MHA | 38 | 3702 | FR | CA275 | D | $3900 | 228 | 1,500 | 24,850 | 19,610 |

Livability Code: SB 30-90
Wheelbase-to-length ratio of 50% is considered ● dangerous ○ fatiguing ○ good ○ excellent *
The approximate net payload of 5240 pounds at 21% of GVWR on this model is ○ deficient ○ excessive ○ cautionary ○ good ● excellent *
Total highway safety penalties are: 2 * Value: 79 Durability: 74 Highway Control Rating: 49 Highway Safety: 47

| Encounter | 1997 | MHA | 38 | 3702 slide | FR | CA275 | D | $3900 | 228 | 1,500 | 24,850 | 20,360 |

Livability Code: SB 30-90
Wheelbase-to-length ratio of 50% is considered ● dangerous ○ fatiguing ○ good ○ excellent *
The approximate net payload of 4490 pounds at 18% of GVWR on this model is ○ deficient ○ excessive ○ cautionary ○ good ● excellent *
Total highway safety penalties are: 7 * Value: 76 Durability: 74 Highway Control Rating: 48 Highway Safety: 41

| Encounter | 1998 | MHA | 36 | 3505 | FR | CA300 | D | $4200 | 208 | 5,000 | 24,850 | 19,734 |

Livability Code: SB 30-90
Wheelbase-to-length ratio of 49% is considered ● dangerous ○ fatiguing ○ good ○ excellent *
The approximate net payload of 5116 pounds at 21% of GVWR on this model is ○ deficient ○ excessive ○ cautionary ○ good ● excellent *
Total highway safety penalties are: 2 * Value: 79 Durability: 74 Highway Control Rating: 43 Highway Safety: 41

Note: Safety ratings are based on the assumption that the engineering of the RV has allowed for proper balance by placing fresh, gray, and black holding tanks in a location so as not to change the balance of the RV when the tanks are empty or full. **Always double-check wheelbase, GVWR, and weights at front and rear axles.**

*See Section 1 for details on how conclusions are reached.

Section 2: The Ratings

Brand	Year	Type	Length	Model	Chassis	Engine	Fuel Type	Average Price per Linear Foot When New	Adjusted Wheelbase	Approx. Towing Capacity	Gross Vehicle Weight Rating	Average Curb Weight
Encounter	1998	MHA	36	3505 slide	FR	CA300	D	$4200	208	5,000	24,850	20,584

Livability Code: SB 30-90
Wheelbase-to-length ratio of 49% is considered ● dangerous ○ fatiguing ○ good ○ excellent *
The approximate net payload of 4266 pounds at 17% of GVWR on this model is ○ deficient ○ excessive ○ cautionary ○ good ● excellent *
Total highway safety penalties are: 7 *   Value: 7 6   Durability: 7 4   Highway Control Rating: 4 1   Highway Safety: 3 4

Brand	Year	Type	Length	Model	Chassis	Engine	Fuel Type	Price/Ft	Wheelbase	Towing	GVWR	Curb Wt
Encounter	1998	MHA	37	3701	FR	CA300	D	$4100	228	5,000	24,850	20,210

Livability Code: SB 30-90
Wheelbase-to-length ratio of 51% is considered ○ dangerous ● fatiguing ○ good ○ excellent *
The approximate net payload of 4641 pounds at 19% of GVWR on this model is ○ deficient ○ excessive ○ cautionary ○ good ● excellent *
Total highway safety penalties are: 2 *   Value: 7 9   Durability: 7 4   Highway Control Rating: 5 0   Highway Safety: 4 8

Brand	Year	Type	Length	Model	Chassis	Engine	Fuel Type	Price/Ft	Wheelbase	Towing	GVWR	Curb Wt
Encounter	1998	MHA	37	3701 slide	FR	CA300	D	$4100	208	5,000	24,850	21,047

Livability Code: SB 30-90
Wheelbase-to-length ratio of 46% is considered ● dangerous ○ fatiguing ○ good ○ excellent *
The approximate net payload of 3803 pounds at 15% of GVWR on this model is ○ deficient ○ excessive ○ cautionary ● good ○ excellent *
Total highway safety penalties are: 7 *   Value: 7 6   Durability: 7 4   Highway Control Rating: 3 0   Highway Safety: 2 3

Brand	Year	Type	Length	Model	Chassis	Engine	Fuel Type	Price/Ft	Wheelbase	Towing	GVWR	Curb Wt
Encounter	1998	MHA	37	3702	FR	CA300	D	$4100	228	5,000	24,850	20,297

Livability Code: SB 30-90
Wheelbase-to-length ratio of 51% is considered ○ dangerous ● fatiguing ○ good ○ excellent *
The approximate net payload of 4553 pounds at 18% of GVWR on this model is ○ deficient ○ excessive ○ cautionary ○ good ● excellent *
Total highway safety penalties are: 2 *   Value: 7 9   Durability: 7 4   Highway Control Rating: 5 0   Highway Safety: 4 8

Brand	Year	Type	Length	Model	Chassis	Engine	Fuel Type	Price/Ft	Wheelbase	Towing	GVWR	Curb Wt
Encounter	1998	MHA	37	3702 slide	FR	CA300	D	$4100	228	5,000	24,850	21,122

Livability Code: SB 30-90
Wheelbase-to-length ratio of 51% is considered ○ dangerous ● fatiguing ○ good ○ excellent *
The approximate net payload of 3728 pounds at 15% of GVWR on this model is ○ deficient ○ excessive ○ cautionary ● good ○ excellent *
Total highway safety penalties are: 7 *   Value: 7 6   Durability: 7 4   Highway Control Rating: 4 6   Highway Safety: 3 9

Brand	Year	Type	Length	Model	Chassis	Engine	Fuel Type	Price/Ft	Wheelbase	Towing	GVWR	Curb Wt
Encounter	1998	MHA	38	3816	FR	CA300	D	$3900	228	5,000	24,850	21,206

Livability Code: SB 30-90
Wheelbase-to-length ratio of 50% is considered ● dangerous ○ fatiguing ○ good ○ excellent *
The approximate net payload of 3644 pounds at 15% of GVWR on this model is ○ deficient ○ excessive ○ cautionary ○ good ● excellent *
Total highway safety penalties are: 7 *   Value: 7 6   Durability: 7 4   Highway Control Rating: 4 2   Highway Safety: 3 5

Brand	Year	Type	Length	Model	Chassis	Engine	Fuel Type	Price/Ft	Wheelbase	Towing	GVWR	Curb Wt
Endeavor	1993	MHA	33	33D	OS	CU230	D	$2900	208	5,160	19,840	17,104

Livability Code: SB 30-90
Wheelbase-to-length ratio of 53% is considered ○ dangerous ● fatiguing ○ good ○ excellent *
The approximate net payload of 2736 pounds at 14% of GVWR on this model is ○ deficient ○ excessive ○ cautionary ● good ○ excellent *
Total highway safety penalties are: 2 *   Value: 8 5   Durability: 7 8   Highway Control Rating: 6 5   Highway Safety: 6 3   ★★

Brand	Year	Type	Length	Model	Chassis	Engine	Fuel Type	Price/Ft	Wheelbase	Towing	GVWR	Curb Wt
Endeavor	1993	MHA	35	35D	OS	CU230	D	$2800	228	5,160	19,840	17,565

Livability Code: SB 30-90
Wheelbase-to-length ratio of 55% is considered ○ dangerous ○ fatiguing ● good ○ excellent *
The approximate net payload of 2275 pounds at 11% of GVWR on this model is ○ deficient ○ excessive ○ cautionary ● good ○ excellent *
Total highway safety penalties are: 2 *   Value: 8 5   Durability: 7 8   Highway Control Rating: 8 8   Highway Safety: 8 6   ★★★

Brand	Year	Type	Length	Model	Chassis	Engine	Fuel Type	Price/Ft	Wheelbase	Towing	GVWR	Curb Wt
Endeavor	1994	MHA	31	30CB	FO	7.5L	G	$1900	178	8,000	17,000	15,207

Livability Code: SB 30-90
Wheelbase-to-length ratio of 48% is considered ● dangerous ○ fatiguing ○ good ○ excellent *
The approximate net payload of 1793 pounds at 11% of GVWR on this model is ○ deficient ○ excessive ○ cautionary ● good ○ excellent *
Total highway safety penalties are: 2 *   Value: 8 5   Durability: 7 8   Highway Control Rating: 3 2   Highway Safety: 3 0

Brand	Year	Type	Length	Model	Chassis	Engine	Fuel Type	Price/Ft	Wheelbase	Towing	GVWR	Curb Wt
Endeavor	1994	MHA	33	32CB	CH	7.5L	G	$1900	190	4,000	16,000	15,326

Livability Code: SB 30-90
Wheelbase-to-length ratio of 48% is considered ● dangerous ○ fatiguing ○ good ○ excellent *
The approximate net payload of 674 pounds at 4% of GVWR on this model is ● deficient ○ excessive ○ cautionary ○ good ○ excellent *
Total highway safety penalties are: 6 *   Value: 8 3   Durability: 7 8   Highway Control Rating: 1   Highway Safety: - 5

Brand	Year	Type	Length	Model	Chassis	Engine	Fuel Type	Price/Ft	Wheelbase	Towing	GVWR	Curb Wt
Endeavor	1994	MHA	33	32CB	FO	7.5L	G	$1900	190	8,000	17,000	15,994

Livability Code: SB 30-90
Wheelbase-to-length ratio of 48% is considered ● dangerous ○ fatiguing ○ good ○ excellent *
The approximate net payload of 1007 pounds at 6% of GVWR on this model is ● deficient ○ excessive ○ cautionary ○ good ○ excellent *
Total highway safety penalties are: 2 *   Value: 8 5   Durability: 7 8   Highway Control Rating: 2   Highway Safety: 0

Brand	Year	Type	Length	Model	Chassis	Engine	Fuel Type	Price/Ft	Wheelbase	Towing	GVWR	Curb Wt
Endeavor	1994	MHA	33	33D	OS	CU230	D	$2800	208	5,160	19,840	17,182

Livability Code: SB 30-90
Wheelbase-to-length ratio of 53% is considered ○ dangerous ● fatiguing ○ good ○ excellent *
The approximate net payload of 2659 pounds at 13% of GVWR on this model is ○ deficient ○ excessive ○ cautionary ● good ○ excellent *
Total highway safety penalties are: 2 *   Value: 8 5   Durability: 7 8   Highway Control Rating: 6 6   Highway Safety: 6 4   ★★

Note: Safety ratings are based on the assumption that the engineering of the RV has allowed for proper balance by placing fresh, gray, and black holding tanks in a location so as not to change the balance of the RV when the tanks are empty or full. **Always double-check wheelbase, GVWR, and weights at front and rear axles.**

*See Section 1 for details on how conclusions are reached.

Brand	Year	Type	Length	Model	Chassis	Engine	Fuel Type	Average Price per Linear Foot When New	Adjusted Wheel-base	Approx. Towing Capacity	Gross Vehicle Weight Rating	Average Curb Weight

Endeavor 1994 MHA 35 35D OS CU230 D $2600 228 5,160 19,840 17,565
Livability Code: SB 30-90
Wheelbase-to-length ratio of 55% is considered ○ dangerous ○ fatiguing ◉ good ○ excellent *
The approximate net payload of 2275 pounds at 11% of GVWR on this model is ○ deficient ○ excessive ○ cautionary ◉ good ○ excellent *
Total highway safety penalties are: 2 *   Value: 8 5   Durability: 7 8   Highway Control Rating: 8 8   Highway Safety: 8 6   ★★★

Endeavor 1994 MHA 35 34CB CH 7.4L G $1900 214 T 2,000 18,000 16,580
Livability Code: SB 30-90
Wheelbase-to-length ratio of 51% is considered ○ dangerous ◉ fatiguing ○ good ○ excellent *
The approximate net payload of 1420 pounds at 8% of GVWR on this model is ○ deficient ○ excessive ◉ cautionary ○ good ○ excellent *
Total highway safety penalties are: 9 *   Value: 8 2   Durability: 7 8   Highway Control Rating: 2 5   Highway Safety: 1 6

Endeavor 1994 MHA 35 34CB FO 7.5L G $1900 214 T 5,600 19,400 17,080
Livability Code: SB 30-90
Wheelbase-to-length ratio of 51% is considered ○ dangerous ◉ fatiguing ○ good ○ excellent *
The approximate net payload of 2320 pounds at 12% of GVWR on this model is ○ deficient ○ excessive ○ cautionary ◉ good ○ excellent *
Total highway safety penalties are: 4 *   Value: 8 4   Durability: 7 8   Highway Control Rating: 4 4   Highway Safety: 4 0

Endeavor 1994 MHA 37 36WB FO 7.5L G $1800 214 T 5,600 19,400 17,627
Livability Code: SB 30-90
Wheelbase-to-length ratio of 48% is considered ◉ dangerous ○ fatiguing ○ good ○ excellent *
The approximate net payload of 1773 pounds at 9% of GVWR on this model is ○ deficient ○ excessive ○ cautionary ◉ good ○ excellent *
Total highway safety penalties are: 4 *   Value: 8 4   Durability: 7 8   Highway Control Rating: 2 2   Highway Safety: 1 8

Endeavor 1995 MHA 31 30CB FO 7.5L G $2000 178 8,000 17,000 14,907
Livability Code: SB 30-90
Wheelbase-to-length ratio of 48% is considered ◉ dangerous ○ fatiguing ○ good ○ excellent *
The approximate net payload of 2093 pounds at 12% of GVWR on this model is ○ deficient ○ excessive ○ cautionary ◉ good ○ excellent *
Total highway safety penalties are: 2 *   Value: 8 5   Durability: 7 8   Highway Control Rating: 2 9   Highway Safety: 2 7

Endeavor 1995 MHA 31 LE 30CB FO 7.5L G $2200 178 8,000 17,000 15,156
Livability Code: SB 30-90
Wheelbase-to-length ratio of 48% is considered ◉ dangerous ○ fatiguing ○ good ○ excellent *
The approximate net payload of 1844 pounds at 11% of GVWR on this model is ○ deficient ○ excessive ○ cautionary ◉ good ○ excellent *
Total highway safety penalties are: 2 *   Value: 8 5   Durability: 7 8   Highway Control Rating: 2 7   Highway Safety: 2 5

Endeavor 1995 MHA 33 32CB CH 7.4L G $1900 190 3,000 16,000 15,119
Livability Code: SB 30-90
Wheelbase-to-length ratio of 48% is considered ◉ dangerous ○ fatiguing ○ good ○ excellent *
The approximate net payload of 881 pounds at 6% of GVWR on this model is ◉ deficient ○ excessive ○ cautionary ○ good ○ excellent *
Total highway safety penalties are: 6 *   Value: 8 3   Durability: 7 8   Highway Control Rating: 2   Highway Safety: - 4

Endeavor 1995 MHA 33 32CB FO 7.5L G $1900 190 8,000 17,000 15,519
Livability Code: SB 30-90
Wheelbase-to-length ratio of 48% is considered ◉ dangerous ○ fatiguing ○ good ○ excellent *
The approximate net payload of 1481 pounds at 9% of GVWR on this model is ○ deficient ○ excessive ◉ cautionary ○ good ○ excellent *
Total highway safety penalties are: 2 *   Value: 8 5   Durability: 7 8   Highway Control Rating: 2 0   Highway Safety: 1 8

Endeavor 1995 MHA 33 LE 32CB FO 7.5L G $2100 190 8,000 17,000 15,777
Livability Code: SB 30-90
Wheelbase-to-length ratio of 48% is considered ◉ dangerous ○ fatiguing ○ good ○ excellent *
The approximate net payload of 1223 pounds at 7% of GVWR on this model is ○ deficient ○ excessive ◉ cautionary ○ good ○ excellent *
Total highway safety penalties are: 2 *   Value: 8 5   Durability: 7 8   Highway Control Rating: 9   Highway Safety: 7

Endeavor 1995 MHA 33 33D OS CU230 D $2800 208 3,500 19,840 17,176
Livability Code: SB 30-90
Wheelbase-to-length ratio of 53% is considered ○ dangerous ◉ fatiguing ○ good ○ excellent *
The approximate net payload of 2665 pounds at 13% of GVWR on this model is ○ deficient ○ excessive ○ cautionary ◉ good ○ excellent *
Total highway safety penalties are: 2 *   Value: 8 5   Durability: 7 8   Highway Control Rating: 6 3   Highway Safety: 6 1   ★★

Endeavor 1995 MHA 33 LE 33D OS CU230 D $2900 208 3,500 19,840 17,434
Livability Code: SB 30-90
Wheelbase-to-length ratio of 53% is considered ○ dangerous ◉ fatiguing ○ good ○ excellent *
The approximate net payload of 2406 pounds at 12% of GVWR on this model is ○ deficient ○ excessive ○ cautionary ◉ good ○ excellent *
Total highway safety penalties are: 2 *   Value: 8 5   Durability: 7 8   Highway Control Rating: 6 1   Highway Safety: 5 9   ★

Endeavor 1995 MHA 35 35D OS CU230 D $2700 228 3,500 19,840 17,598
Livability Code: SB 30-90
Wheelbase-to-length ratio of 55% is considered ○ dangerous ○ fatiguing ◉ good ○ excellent *
The approximate net payload of 2242 pounds at 11% of GVWR on this model is ○ deficient ○ excessive ○ cautionary ◉ good ○ excellent *
Total highway safety penalties are: 2 *   Value: 8 5   Durability: 7 8   Highway Control Rating: 8 8   Highway Safety: 8 6   ★★★

Note: Safety ratings are based on the assumption that the engineering of the RV has allowed for proper balance by placing fresh, gray, and black holding tanks in a location so as not to change the balance of the RV when the tanks are empty or full. **Always double-check wheelbase, GVWR, and weights at front and rear axles.**

*See Section 1 for details on how conclusions are reached.

Brand	Year	Type	Length	Model	Chassis	Engine	Fuel Type	Average Price per Linear Foot When New	Adjusted Wheelbase	Approx. Towing Capacity	Gross Vehicle Weight Rating	Average Curb Weight
Endeavor	1995	MHA	35	LE 35D	OS	CU230	D	$2700	228	3,500	19,840	17,864

Livability Code: SB 30-90
Wheelbase-to-length ratio of 55% is considered ○ dangerous ○ fatiguing ◉ good ○ excellent *
The approximate net payload of 1976 pounds at 10% of GVWR on this model is ○ deficient ○ excessive ○ cautionary ◉ good ○ excellent *
Total highway safety penalties are: 2 *   Value: 85   Durability: 78   Highway Control Rating: 86   Highway Safety: 84   ★★★

Brand	Year	Type	Length	Model	Chassis	Engine	Fuel Type	Average Price	Adjusted Wheelbase	Approx. Towing Capacity	GVWR	Average Curb Weight
Endeavor	1995	MHA	35	34CB	CH	7.4L	G	$2000	214 T	1,000	18,000	16,532

Livability Code: SB 30-90
Wheelbase-to-length ratio of 51% is considered ○ dangerous ◉ fatiguing ○ good ○ excellent *
The approximate net payload of 1469 pounds at 8% of GVWR on this model is ○ deficient ○ excessive ◉ cautionary ○ good ○ excellent *
Total highway safety penalties are: 9 *   Value: 82   Durability: 78   Highway Control Rating: 25   Highway Safety: 16

Endeavor	1995	MHA	35	34CB	FO	7.5L	G	$2000	214 T	5,600	19,400	16,975

Livability Code: SB 30-90
Wheelbase-to-length ratio of 51% is considered ○ dangerous ◉ fatiguing ○ good ○ excellent *
The approximate net payload of 2426 pounds at 13% of GVWR on this model is ○ deficient ○ excessive ○ cautionary ◉ good ○ excellent *
Total highway safety penalties are: 4 *   Value: 84   Durability: 78   Highway Control Rating: 42   Highway Safety: 38

Endeavor	1995	MHA	35	LE 34CB	FO	7.5L	G	$2100	214 T	5,600	19,400	17,243

Livability Code: SB 30-90
Wheelbase-to-length ratio of 51% is considered ○ dangerous ◉ fatiguing ○ good ○ excellent *
The approximate net payload of 2158 pounds at 11% of GVWR on this model is ○ deficient ○ excessive ○ cautionary ◉ good ○ excellent *
Total highway safety penalties are: 4 *   Value: 84   Durability: 78   Highway Control Rating: 38   Highway Safety: 34

Endeavor	1995	MHA	37	36WB	FO	7.5L	G	$1900	232 T	5,600	19,400	17,582

Livability Code: SB 30-90
Wheelbase-to-length ratio of 52% is considered ○ dangerous ◉ fatiguing ○ good ○ excellent *
The approximate net payload of 1818 pounds at 9% of GVWR on this model is ○ deficient ○ excessive ◉ cautionary ○ good ○ excellent *
Total highway safety penalties are: 4 *   Value: 84   Durability: 78   Highway Control Rating: 44   Highway Safety: 40

Endeavor	1995	MHA	37	LE 36WB	FO	7.5L	G	$2000	232 T	5,600	19,400	17,859

Livability Code: SB 30-90
Wheelbase-to-length ratio of 52% is considered ○ dangerous ◉ fatiguing ○ good ○ excellent *
The approximate net payload of 1541 pounds at 8% of GVWR on this model is ○ deficient ○ excessive ◉ cautionary ○ good ○ excellent *
Total highway safety penalties are: 4 *   Value: 84   Durability: 78   Highway Control Rating: 38   Highway Safety: 34

Endeavor	1996	MHA	30	LE 30CB	FO	7.5L	G	$2300	178	8,000	17,000	15,318

Livability Code: SB 30-90
Wheelbase-to-length ratio of 49% is considered ◉ dangerous ○ fatiguing ○ good ○ excellent *
The approximate net payload of 1682 pounds at 10% of GVWR on this model is ○ deficient ○ excessive ○ cautionary ◉ good ○ excellent *
Total highway safety penalties are: 2 *   Value: 85   Durability: 78   Highway Control Rating: 31   Highway Safety: 29

Endeavor	1996	MHA	31	30CB	FO	7.5L	G	$2000	178	8,000	17,000	15,233

Livability Code: SB 30-90
Wheelbase-to-length ratio of 48% is considered ◉ dangerous ○ fatiguing ○ good ○ excellent *
The approximate net payload of 1767 pounds at 10% of GVWR on this model is ○ deficient ○ excessive ○ cautionary ◉ good ○ excellent *
Total highway safety penalties are: 2 *   Value: 85   Durability: 78   Highway Control Rating: 25   Highway Safety: 23

Endeavor	1996	MHA	33	32CB	CH	7.4L	G	$1900	190	2,500	16,500	15,092

Livability Code: SB 30-90
Wheelbase-to-length ratio of 48% is considered ◉ dangerous ○ fatiguing ○ good ○ excellent *
The approximate net payload of 1409 pounds at 9% of GVWR on this model is ○ deficient ○ excessive ◉ cautionary ○ good ○ excellent *
Total highway safety penalties are: 6 *   Value: 83   Durability: 78   Highway Control Rating: 20   Highway Safety: 14

Endeavor	1996	MHA	33	32CB	FO	7.5L	G	$1900	190	8,000	17,000	15,507

Livability Code: SB 30-90
Wheelbase-to-length ratio of 48% is considered ◉ dangerous ○ fatiguing ○ good ○ excellent *
The approximate net payload of 1493 pounds at 9% of GVWR on this model is ○ deficient ○ excessive ◉ cautionary ○ good ○ excellent *
Total highway safety penalties are: 2 *   Value: 85   Durability: 78   Highway Control Rating: 20   Highway Safety: 18

Endeavor	1996	MHA	33	LE 32CB	FO	7.5L	G	$1900	190	8,000	17,000	15,755

Livability Code: SB 30-90
Wheelbase-to-length ratio of 48% is considered ◉ dangerous ○ fatiguing ○ good ○ excellent *
The approximate net payload of 1245 pounds at 7% of GVWR on this model is ○ deficient ○ excessive ◉ cautionary ○ good ○ excellent *
Total highway safety penalties are: 2 *   Value: 85   Durability: 78   Highway Control Rating: 9   Highway Safety: 7

Endeavor	1996	MHA	35	34CB	CH	7.4L	G	$2000	214 T	1,000	18,000	16,687

Livability Code: SB 30-90
Wheelbase-to-length ratio of 51% is considered ○ dangerous ◉ fatiguing ○ good ○ excellent *
The approximate net payload of 1314 pounds at 7% of GVWR on this model is ○ deficient ○ excessive ◉ cautionary ○ good ○ excellent *
Total highway safety penalties are: 9 *   Value: 82   Durability: 78   Highway Control Rating: 19   Highway Safety: 10

Note: Safety ratings are based on the assumption that the engineering of the RV has allowed for proper balance by placing fresh, gray, and black holding tanks in a location so as not to change the balance of the RV when the tanks are empty or full. **Always double-check wheelbase, GVWR, and weights at front and rear axles.**

*See Section 1 for details on how conclusions are reached.

Brand	Year	Type	Length	Model	Chassis	Engine	Fuel Type	Average Price per Linear Foot When New	Adjusted Wheel-base	Approx. Towing Capacity	Gross Vehicle Weight Rating	Average Curb Weight
Endeavor	1996	MHA	35	34CB	FO	7.5L	G	$2000	214 T	3,500	19,400	17,227

Livability Code: SB 30-90
Wheelbase-to-length ratio of 51% is considered ○ dangerous ● fatiguing ○ good ○ excellent*
The approximate net payload of 2174 pounds at 11% of GVWR on this model is ○ deficient ○ excessive ○ cautionary ● good ○ excellent*
Total highway safety penalties are: 4*   Value: **8 4**   Durability: **7 8**   Highway Control Rating: **3 8**   Highway Safety: **3 4**

Brand	Year	Type	Length	Model	Chassis	Engine	Fuel Type	Avg Price/Linear Foot	Wheelbase	Towing	GVWR	Curb Weight
Endeavor	1996	MHA	35	LE 34CB	FO	7.5L	G	$2000	214 T	3,500	19,400	17,505

Livability Code: SB 30-90
Wheelbase-to-length ratio of 51% is considered ○ dangerous ● fatiguing ○ good ○ excellent*
The approximate net payload of 1896 pounds at 10% of GVWR on this model is ○ deficient ○ excessive ○ cautionary ● good ○ excellent*
Total highway safety penalties are: 4*   Value: **8 4**   Durability: **7 8**   Highway Control Rating: **3 6**   Highway Safety: **3 2**

Brand	Year	Type	Length	Model	Chassis	Engine	Fuel Type	Avg Price/Linear Foot	Wheelbase	Towing	GVWR	Curb Weight
Endeavor	1996	MHA	36	35CD	FR	CU230	D	$2700	218	3,500	24,000	20,616

Livability Code: SB 30-90
Wheelbase-to-length ratio of 50% is considered ● dangerous ○ fatiguing ○ good ○ excellent*
The approximate net payload of 3384 pounds at 14% of GVWR on this model is ○ deficient ○ excessive ○ cautionary ● good ○ excellent*
Total highway safety penalties are: 2*   Value: **8 5**   Durability: **7 8**   Highway Control Rating: **4 2**   Highway Safety: **4 0**

Brand	Year	Type	Length	Model	Chassis	Engine	Fuel Type	Avg Price/Linear Foot	Wheelbase	Towing	GVWR	Curb Weight
Endeavor	1996	MHA	36	35CDS	FR	CU230	D	$2700	218	3,500	24,000	21,666

Livability Code: SB 30-90
Wheelbase-to-length ratio of 50% is considered ● dangerous ○ fatiguing ○ good ○ excellent*
The approximate net payload of 2334 pounds at 10% of GVWR on this model is ○ deficient ○ excessive ○ cautionary ● good ○ excellent*
Total highway safety penalties are: 13*   Value: **8 0**   Durability: **7 8**   Highway Control Rating: **3 4**   Highway Safety: **2 1**

Brand	Year	Type	Length	Model	Chassis	Engine	Fuel Type	Avg Price/Linear Foot	Wheelbase	Towing	GVWR	Curb Weight
Endeavor	1996	MHA	37	36WB	FO	7.5L	G	$1900	232 T	3,500	19,400	17,876

Livability Code: SB 30-90
Wheelbase-to-length ratio of 52% is considered ○ dangerous ● fatiguing ○ good ○ excellent*
The approximate net payload of 1524 pounds at 8% of GVWR on this model is ○ deficient ○ excessive ● cautionary ○ good ○ excellent*
Total highway safety penalties are: 4*   Value: **8 4**   Durability: **7 8**   Highway Control Rating: **3 7**   Highway Safety: **3 3**

Brand	Year	Type	Length	Model	Chassis	Engine	Fuel Type	Avg Price/Linear Foot	Wheelbase	Towing	GVWR	Curb Weight
Endeavor	1996	MHA	37	LE 36WB	FO	7.5L	G	$1900	232 T	3,500	19,400	18,164

Livability Code: SB 30-90
Wheelbase-to-length ratio of 52% is considered ○ dangerous ● fatiguing ○ good ○ excellent*
The approximate net payload of 1236 pounds at 6% of GVWR on this model is ● deficient ○ excessive ○ cautionary ○ good ○ excellent*
Total highway safety penalties are: 4*   Value: **8 4**   Durability: **7 8**   Highway Control Rating: **2 6**   Highway Safety: **2 2**

Brand	Year	Type	Length	Model	Chassis	Engine	Fuel Type	Avg Price/Linear Foot	Wheelbase	Towing	GVWR	Curb Weight
Endeavor	1996	MHA	38	37WD	FR	CU230	D	$2600	242	3,500	24,000	21,228

Livability Code: SB 30-90
Wheelbase-to-length ratio of 53% is considered ○ dangerous ● fatiguing ○ good ○ excellent*
The approximate net payload of 2772 pounds at 12% of GVWR on this model is ○ deficient ○ excessive ○ cautionary ● good ○ excellent*
Total highway safety penalties are: 2*   Value: **8 5**   Durability: **7 8**   Highway Control Rating: **6 2**   Highway Safety: **6 0**   ★★

Brand	Year	Type	Length	Model	Chassis	Engine	Fuel Type	Avg Price/Linear Foot	Wheelbase	Towing	GVWR	Curb Weight
Endeavor	1996	MHA	38	37WDS	FR	CU230	D	$2700	242	3,500	24,000	22,428

Livability Code: SB 30-90
Wheelbase-to-length ratio of 53% is considered ○ dangerous ● fatiguing ○ good ○ excellent*
The approximate net payload of 1572 pounds at 7% of GVWR on this model is ○ deficient ○ excessive ● cautionary ○ good ○ excellent*
Total highway safety penalties are: 14*   Value: **7 9**   Durability: **7 8**   Highway Control Rating: **4 1**   Highway Safety: **2 7**

Brand	Year	Type	Length	Model	Chassis	Engine	Fuel Type	Avg Price/Linear Foot	Wheelbase	Towing	GVWR	Curb Weight
Endeavor	1996	MHA	38	37CD	FR	CU230	D	$2700	242	3,500	24,000	21,228

Livability Code: SB 30-90
Wheelbase-to-length ratio of 53% is considered ○ dangerous ● fatiguing ○ good ○ excellent*
The approximate net payload of 2772 pounds at 12% of GVWR on this model is ○ deficient ○ excessive ○ cautionary ● good ○ excellent*
Total highway safety penalties are: 2*   Value: **8 5**   Durability: **7 8**   Highway Control Rating: **6 2**   Highway Safety: **6 0**   ★★

Brand	Year	Type	Length	Model	Chassis	Engine	Fuel Type	Avg Price/Linear Foot	Wheelbase	Towing	GVWR	Curb Weight
Endeavor	1996	MHA	38	37CDS	FR	CU230	D	$2800	242	3,500	24,000	22,278

Livability Code: SB 30-90
Wheelbase-to-length ratio of 53% is considered ○ dangerous ● fatiguing ○ good ○ excellent*
The approximate net payload of 1722 pounds at 7% of GVWR on this model is ○ deficient ○ excessive ● cautionary ○ good ○ excellent*
Total highway safety penalties are: 13*   Value: **8 0**   Durability: **7 8**   Highway Control Rating: **4 2**   Highway Safety: **2 9**

Brand	Year	Type	Length	Model	Chassis	Engine	Fuel Type	Avg Price/Linear Foot	Wheelbase	Towing	GVWR	Curb Weight
Endeavor	1997	MHA	35	34CB	CH	7.4L	G	$2000	214 T	3,000	18,000	16,580

Livability Code: SB 30-90
Wheelbase-to-length ratio of 51% is considered ○ dangerous ● fatiguing ○ good ○ excellent*
The approximate net payload of 1420 pounds at 8% of GVWR on this model is ○ deficient ○ excessive ● cautionary ○ good ○ excellent*
Total highway safety penalties are: 9*   Value: **8 2**   Durability: **7 8**   Highway Control Rating: **2 5**   Highway Safety: **1 6**

Brand	Year	Type	Length	Model	Chassis	Engine	Fuel Type	Avg Price/Linear Foot	Wheelbase	Towing	GVWR	Curb Weight
Endeavor	1997	MHA	35	34CB	FO	7.5L	G	$2000	214 T	3,500	19,400	17,080

Livability Code: SB 30-90
Wheelbase-to-length ratio of 51% is considered ○ dangerous ● fatiguing ○ good ○ excellent*
The approximate net payload of 2320 pounds at 12% of GVWR on this model is ○ deficient ○ excessive ○ cautionary ● good ○ excellent*
Total highway safety penalties are: 4*   Value: **8 4**   Durability: **7 8**   Highway Control Rating: **4 0**   Highway Safety: **3 6**

Note: Safety ratings are based on the assumption that the engineering of the RV has allowed for proper balance by placing fresh, gray, and black holding tanks in a location so as not to change the balance of the RV when the tanks are empty or full. **Always double-check wheelbase, GVWR, and weights at front and rear axles.**

*See Section 1 for details on how conclusions are reached.

Brand	Year	Type	Length	Model	Chassis	Engine	Fuel Type	Average Price per Linear Foot When New	Adjusted Wheelbase	Approx. Towing Capacity	Gross Vehicle Weight Rating	Average Curb Weight

Endeavor 1997 MHA 35 34WGS FO 7.5L G $2100 214 T 3,500 19,400 18,009
Livability Code: SB 30-90   Wheelbase-to-length ratio of 51% is considered ○ dangerous ◉ fatiguing ○ good ○ excellent *
The approximate net payload of 1391 pounds at 7% of GVWR on this model is ○ deficient ○ excessive ◉ cautionary ○ good ○ excellent *
Total highway safety penalties are: 10 *   Value: 8 1   Durability: 7 8   Highway Control Rating: 1 9   Highway Safety: 9

Endeavor 1997 MHA 36 35CD FR CU230 D $3400 218 4,000 24,850 21,216
Livability Code: SB 30-90   Wheelbase-to-length ratio of 50% is considered ◉ dangerous ○ fatiguing ○ good ○ excellent *
The approximate net payload of 3634 pounds at 15% of GVWR on this model is ○ deficient ○ excessive ○ cautionary ◉ good ○ excellent *
Total highway safety penalties are: 2 *   Value: 8 5   Durability: 7 8   Highway Control Rating: 4 4   Highway Safety: 4 2

Endeavor 1997 MHA 36 35CDS FR CU230 D $3500 218 4,000 24,850 22,266
Livability Code: SB 30-90   Wheelbase-to-length ratio of 50% is considered ◉ dangerous ○ fatiguing ○ good ○ excellent *
The approximate net payload of 2584 pounds at 10% of GVWR on this model is ○ deficient ○ excessive ○ cautionary ◉ good ○ excellent *
Total highway safety penalties are: 13 *   Value: 8 0   Durability: 7 8   Highway Control Rating: 3 5   Highway Safety: 2 2

Endeavor 1997 MHA 37 36WB FO 7.5L G $1900 232 T 3,500 19,400 17,656
Livability Code: SB 30-90   Wheelbase-to-length ratio of 52% is considered ○ dangerous ◉ fatiguing ○ good ○ excellent *
The approximate net payload of 1744 pounds at 9% of GVWR on this model is ○ deficient ○ excessive ◉ cautionary ○ good ○ excellent *
Total highway safety penalties are: 4 *   Value: 8 4   Durability: 7 8   Highway Control Rating: 4 3   Highway Safety: 3 9

Endeavor 1997 MHA 38 37WD FR CU230 D $3300 242 4,000 24,850 21,828
Livability Code: SB 30-90   Wheelbase-to-length ratio of 53% is considered ○ dangerous ◉ fatiguing ○ good ○ excellent *
The approximate net payload of 3022 pounds at 12% of GVWR on this model is ○ deficient ○ excessive ○ cautionary ◉ good ○ excellent *
Total highway safety penalties are: 2 *   Value: 8 5   Durability: 7 8   Highway Control Rating: 6 3   Highway Safety: 6 1   ★★

Endeavor 1997 MHA 38 37WDS FR CU230 D $3400 242 4,000 24,850 23,028
Livability Code: SB 30-90   Wheelbase-to-length ratio of 53% is considered ○ dangerous ◉ fatiguing ○ good ○ excellent *
The approximate net payload of 1822 pounds at 7% of GVWR on this model is ○ deficient ○ excessive ◉ cautionary ○ good ○ excellent *
Total highway safety penalties are: 14 *   Value: 7 9   Durability: 7 8   Highway Control Rating: 4 2   Highway Safety: 2 8

Endeavor 1997 MHA 38 37CD FR CU230 D $3300 242 4,000 24,850 21,828
Livability Code: SB 30-90   Wheelbase-to-length ratio of 53% is considered ○ dangerous ◉ fatiguing ○ good ○ excellent *
The approximate net payload of 3022 pounds at 12% of GVWR on this model is ○ deficient ○ excessive ○ cautionary ◉ good ○ excellent *
Total highway safety penalties are: 2 *   Value: 8 5   Durability: 7 8   Highway Control Rating: 6 3   Highway Safety: 6 1   ★★

Endeavor 1997 MHA 38 37CDS FR CU230 D $3400 242 4,000 24,850 22,878
Livability Code: SB 30-90   Wheelbase-to-length ratio of 53% is considered ○ dangerous ◉ fatiguing ○ good ○ excellent *
The approximate net payload of 1972 pounds at 8% of GVWR on this model is ○ deficient ○ excessive ◉ cautionary ○ good ○ excellent *
Total highway safety penalties are: 13 *   Value: 8 0   Durability: 7 8   Highway Control Rating: 4 8   Highway Safety: 3 5

Endeavor 1998 MHA 34 34CG CH 7.4L G $2100 228 3,500 16,500 15,960
Livability Code: SB 30-90   Wheelbase-to-length ratio of 56% is considered ○ dangerous ○ fatiguing ◉ good ○ excellent *
The approximate net payload of 540 pounds at 3% of GVWR on this model is ◉ deficient ○ excessive ○ cautionary ○ good ○ excellent *
Total highway safety penalties are: 7 *   Value: 8 3   Durability: 7 8   Highway Control Rating: 5 7   Highway Safety: 5 0   ★

Endeavor 1998 MHA 34 34CG FO 7.5L G $2500 228 3,500 17,000 16,360
Livability Code: SB 30-90   Wheelbase-to-length ratio of 56% is considered ○ dangerous ○ fatiguing ◉ good ○ excellent *
The approximate net payload of 640 pounds at 4% of GVWR on this model is ◉ deficient ○ excessive ○ cautionary ○ good ○ excellent *
Total highway safety penalties are: 2 *   Value: 8 5   Durability: 7 8   Highway Control Rating: 5 7   Highway Safety: 5 5   ★

Endeavor 1998 MHA 35 35WG FO 7.5L G $2400 232 T 3,500 19,400 17,500
Livability Code: SB 30-90   Wheelbase-to-length ratio of 55% is considered ○ dangerous ○ fatiguing ◉ good ○ excellent *
The approximate net payload of 1900 pounds at 10% of GVWR on this model is ○ deficient ○ excessive ○ cautionary ◉ good ○ excellent *
Total highway safety penalties are: 4 *   Value: 8 4   Durability: 7 8   Highway Control Rating: 8 7   Highway Safety: 8 3   ★★★

Endeavor 1998 MHA 35 35WGS FO 7.5L G $2400 232 T 3,500 19,400 18,400
Livability Code: SB 30-90   Wheelbase-to-length ratio of 55% is considered ○ dangerous ○ fatiguing ◉ good ○ excellent *
The approximate net payload of 1000 pounds at 5% of GVWR on this model is ◉ deficient ○ excessive ○ cautionary ○ good ○ excellent *
Total highway safety penalties are: 15 *   Value: 7 9   Durability: 7 8   Highway Control Rating: 5 8   Highway Safety: 4 3

Note: Safety ratings are based on the assumption that the engineering of the RV has allowed for proper balance by placing fresh, gray, and black holding tanks in a location so as not to change the balance of the RV when the tanks are empty or full. **Always double-check wheelbase, GVWR, and weights at front and rear axles.**

*See Section 1 for details on how conclusions are reached.

Section 2: The Ratings

Brand	Year	Type	Length	Model	Chassis	Engine	Fuel Type	Average Price per Linear Foot When New	Adjusted Wheelbase	Approx. Towing Capacity	Gross Vehicle Weight Rating	Average Curb Weight
Endeavor	1998	MHA	35	34WDS	FR	CU275	D	$3700	208	5,000	24,850	21,810

Livability Code: SB 30-90
Wheelbase-to-length ratio of 50% is considered ◉ dangerous ○ fatiguing ○ good ○ excellent *
The approximate net payload of 3040 pounds at 12% of GVWR on this model is ○ deficient ○ excessive ○ cautionary ◉ good ○ excellent *
Total highway safety penalties are: 12 *   Value: 80 Durability: 78 Highway Control Rating: 35   Highway Safety: 23

Endeavor	1998	MHA	35	34WD	FR	CU275	D	$3700	208	5,000	24,850	20,910

Livability Code: SB 30-90
Wheelbase-to-length ratio of 50% is considered ◉ dangerous ○ fatiguing ○ good ○ excellent *
The approximate net payload of 3940 pounds at 16% of GVWR on this model is ○ deficient ○ excessive ○ cautionary ○ good ◉ excellent *
Total highway safety penalties are: 2 *   Value: 85 Durability: 78 Highway Control Rating: 43   Highway Safety: 41

Endeavor	1998	MHA	36	36SG	FO	7.5L	G	$2400	232 T	3,500	19,400	17,800

Livability Code: SB 30-90
Wheelbase-to-length ratio of 54% is considered ○ dangerous ○ fatiguing ◉ good ○ excellent *
The approximate net payload of 1600 pounds at 8% of GVWR on this model is ○ deficient ○ excessive ◉ cautionary ○ good ○ excellent *
Total highway safety penalties are: 4 *   Value: 84 Durability: 78 Highway Control Rating: 58   Highway Safety: 54   ★

Endeavor	1998	MHA	36	36SGS	FO	7.5L	G	$2400	232 T	3,500	19,400	18,700

Livability Code: SB 30-90
Wheelbase-to-length ratio of 54% is considered ○ dangerous ○ fatiguing ◉ good ○ excellent *
The approximate net payload of 700 pounds at 4% of GVWR on this model is ◉ deficient ○ excessive ○ cautionary ○ good ○ excellent *
Total highway safety penalties are: 15 *   Value: 79 Durability: 78 Highway Control Rating: 43   Highway Safety: 28

Endeavor	1998	MHA	36	36WG	FO	7.5L	G	$2400	232 T	3,500	19,400	17,800

Livability Code: SB 30-90
Wheelbase-to-length ratio of 54% is considered ○ dangerous ○ fatiguing ◉ good ○ excellent *
The approximate net payload of 1600 pounds at 8% of GVWR on this model is ○ deficient ○ excessive ◉ cautionary ○ good ○ excellent *
Total highway safety penalties are: 4 *   Value: 84 Durability: 78 Highway Control Rating: 58   Highway Safety: 54   ★

Endeavor	1998	MHA	36	36WGS	FO	7.5L	G	$2400	232 T	3,500	19,400	18,700

Livability Code: SB 30-90
Wheelbase-to-length ratio of 54% is considered ○ dangerous ○ fatiguing ◉ good ○ excellent *
The approximate net payload of 700 pounds at 4% of GVWR on this model is ◉ deficient ○ excessive ○ cautionary ○ good ○ excellent *
Total highway safety penalties are: 15 *   Value: 79 Durability: 78 Highway Control Rating: 43   Highway Safety: 28

Endeavor	1998	MHA	36	35WDS	FR	CU275	D	$3600	218	5,000	24,850	22,116

Livability Code: SB 30-90
Wheelbase-to-length ratio of 50% is considered ◉ dangerous ○ fatiguing ○ good ○ excellent *
The approximate net payload of 2734 pounds at 11% of GVWR on this model is ○ deficient ○ excessive ○ cautionary ○ good ○ excellent *
Total highway safety penalties are: 12 *   Value: 80 Durability: 78 Highway Control Rating: 36   Highway Safety: 24

Endeavor	1998	MHA	36	35WD	FR	CU275	D	$3600	218	5,000	24,850	21,216

Livability Code: SB 30-90
Wheelbase-to-length ratio of 50% is considered ◉ dangerous ○ fatiguing ○ good ○ excellent *
The approximate net payload of 3634 pounds at 15% of GVWR on this model is ○ deficient ○ excessive ○ cautionary ◉ good ○ excellent *
Total highway safety penalties are: 2 *   Value: 85 Durability: 78 Highway Control Rating: 44   Highway Safety: 42

Endeavor	1998	MHA	38	37WDS	FR	CU275	D	$3400	242	5,000	24,850	22,636

Livability Code: SB 30-90
Wheelbase-to-length ratio of 53% is considered ○ dangerous ◉ fatiguing ○ good ○ excellent *
The approximate net payload of 2214 pounds at 9% of GVWR on this model is ○ deficient ○ excessive ◉ cautionary ○ good ○ excellent *
Total highway safety penalties are: 12 *   Value: 80 Durability: 78 Highway Control Rating: 55   Highway Safety: 43

Endeavor	1998	MHA	38	37CDS	FR	CU275	D	$3400	242	5,000	24,850	22,636

Livability Code: SB 30-90
Wheelbase-to-length ratio of 53% is considered ○ dangerous ◉ fatiguing ○ good ○ excellent *
The approximate net payload of 2214 pounds at 9% of GVWR on this model is ○ deficient ○ excessive ◉ cautionary ○ good ○ excellent *
Total highway safety penalties are: 12 *   Value: 80 Durability: 78 Highway Control Rating: 55   Highway Safety: 43

Endeavor	1998	MHA	38	37CDM	FR	CU275	D	$3400	242	5,000	24,850	22,636

Livability Code: SB 30-90
Wheelbase-to-length ratio of 53% is considered ○ dangerous ◉ fatiguing ○ good ○ excellent *
The approximate net payload of 2214 pounds at 9% of GVWR on this model is ○ deficient ○ excessive ◉ cautionary ○ good ○ excellent *
Total highway safety penalties are: 12 *   Value: 80 Durability: 78 Highway Control Rating: 55   Highway Safety: 43

Endeavor	1998	MHA	38	37WDM	FR	CU275	D	$3400	242	5,000	24,850	22,636

Livability Code: SB 30-90
Wheelbase-to-length ratio of 53% is considered ○ dangerous ◉ fatiguing ○ good ○ excellent *
The approximate net payload of 2214 pounds at 9% of GVWR on this model is ○ deficient ○ excessive ◉ cautionary ○ good ○ excellent *
Total highway safety penalties are: 12 *   Value: 80 Durability: 78 Highway Control Rating: 55   Highway Safety: 43

Note: Safety ratings are based on the assumption that the engineering of the RV has allowed for proper balance by placing fresh, gray, and black holding tanks in a location so as not to change the balance of the RV when the tanks are empty or full. **Always double-check wheelbase, GVWR, and weights at front and rear axles.**

*See Section 1 for details on how conclusions are reached.

Brand	Year	Type	Length	Model	Chassis	Engine	Fuel Type	Average Price per Linear Foot When New	Adjusted Wheelbase	Approx. Towing Capacity	Gross Vehicle Weight Rating	Average Curb Weight
Endeavor	1998	MHA	38	37CD	FR	CU275	D	$3400	242	5,000	24,850	21,736

Livability Code: SB 30-90 — Wheelbase-to-length ratio of 53% is considered ○ dangerous ◉ fatiguing ○ good ○ excellent *

The approximate net payload of 3114 pounds at 13% of GVWR on this model is ○ deficient ○ excessive ○ cautionary ◉ good ○ excellent *

Total highway safety penalties are: 2 *   Value: 85   Durability: 78   Highway Control Rating: 66   Highway Safety: 64   ★★

Brand	Year	Type	Length	Model	Chassis	Engine	Fuel Type	Price/LF	Wheelbase	Towing	GVWR	Curb Weight
Endeavor	1998	MHA	38	37WD	FR	CU275	D	$3400	242	5,000	24,850	21,736

Livability Code: SB 30-90 — Wheelbase-to-length ratio of 53% is considered ○ dangerous ◉ fatiguing ○ good ○ excellent *

The approximate net payload of 3114 pounds at 13% of GVWR on this model is ○ deficient ○ excessive ○ cautionary ◉ good ○ excellent *

Total highway safety penalties are: 2 *   Value: 85   Durability: 78   Highway Control Rating: 66   Highway Safety: 64   ★★

Endeavor	1998	MHA	38	37WM	FR	CU275	D	$3400	242	5,000	24,850	21,736

Livability Code: SB 30-90 — Wheelbase-to-length ratio of 53% is considered ○ dangerous ◉ fatiguing ○ good ○ excellent *

The approximate net payload of 3114 pounds at 13% of GVWR on this model is ○ deficient ○ excessive ○ cautionary ◉ good ○ excellent *

Total highway safety penalties are: 2 *   Value: 85   Durability: 78   Highway Control Rating: 66   Highway Safety: 64   ★★

Endeavor	1998	MHA	38	37CM	FR	CU275	D	$3400	242	5,000	24,850	21,736

Livability Code: SB 30-90 — Wheelbase-to-length ratio of 53% is considered ○ dangerous ◉ fatiguing ○ good ○ excellent *

The approximate net payload of 3114 pounds at 13% of GVWR on this model is ○ deficient ○ excessive ○ cautionary ◉ good ○ excellent *

Total highway safety penalties are: 2 *   Value: 85   Durability: 78   Highway Control Rating: 66   Highway Safety: 64   ★★

Endeavor	1999	MHA	34	34CG	FO	6.8L	G	$2600	228	5,000	20,500	17,260

Livability Code: SB 30-90 — Wheelbase-to-length ratio of 56% is considered ○ dangerous ○ fatiguing ◉ good ○ excellent *

The approximate net payload of 3240 pounds at 16% of GVWR on this model is ○ deficient ○ excessive ○ cautionary ◉ good ○ excellent *

Total highway safety penalties are: 2 *   Value: 85   Durability: 78   Highway Control Rating: 94   Highway Safety: 92   ★★★

Endeavor	1999	MHA	35	35WGS	FO	6.8L	G	$2600	228	5,000	20,500	18,400

Livability Code: SB 30-90 — Wheelbase-to-length ratio of 54% is considered ○ dangerous ○ fatiguing ◉ good ○ excellent *

The approximate net payload of 2100 pounds at 10% of GVWR on this model is ○ deficient ○ excessive ○ cautionary ◉ good ○ excellent *

Total highway safety penalties are: 12 *   Value: 80   Durability: 78   Highway Control Rating: 79   Highway Safety: 67   ★★

Endeavor	1999	MHA	35	34WD	FR	CU275	D	$3400	218	3,650	24,850	20,910

Livability Code: SB 30-90 — Wheelbase-to-length ratio of 52% is considered ○ dangerous ◉ fatiguing ○ good ○ excellent *

The approximate net payload of 3940 pounds at 16% of GVWR on this model is ○ deficient ○ excessive ○ cautionary ◉ good ○ excellent *

Total highway safety penalties are: 2 *   Value: 85   Durability: 78   Highway Control Rating: 66   Highway Safety: 64   ★★

Endeavor	1999	MHA	35	34WDS	FR	CU275	D	$3400	218	3,650	24,850	21,810

Livability Code: SB 30-90 — Wheelbase-to-length ratio of 52% is considered ○ dangerous ◉ fatiguing ○ good ○ excellent *

The approximate net payload of 3040 pounds at 12% of GVWR on this model is ○ deficient ○ excessive ○ cautionary ◉ good ○ excellent *

Total highway safety penalties are: 12 *   Value: 80   Durability: 78   Highway Control Rating: 59   Highway Safety: 47

Endeavor	1999	MHA	36	36SGS	FO	6.8L	G	$2500	228	5,000	20,500	18,700

Livability Code: SB 30-90 — Wheelbase-to-length ratio of 53% is considered ○ dangerous ◉ fatiguing ○ good ○ excellent *

The approximate net payload of 1800 pounds at 9% of GVWR on this model is ○ deficient ○ excessive ◉ cautionary ○ good ○ excellent *

Total highway safety penalties are: 12 *   Value: 80   Durability: 78   Highway Control Rating: 57   Highway Safety: 45

Endeavor	1999	MHA	36	36WGS	FO	6.8L	G	$2500	228	5,000	20,500	18,700

Livability Code: SB 30-90 — Wheelbase-to-length ratio of 53% is considered ○ dangerous ◉ fatiguing ○ good ○ excellent *

The approximate net payload of 1800 pounds at 9% of GVWR on this model is ○ deficient ○ excessive ◉ cautionary ○ good ○ excellent *

Total highway safety penalties are: 12 *   Value: 80   Durability: 78   Highway Control Rating: 57   Highway Safety: 45

Endeavor	1999	MHA	36	35WDS	FR	CU275	D	$3300	218	3,650	24,850	22,116

Livability Code: SB 30-90 — Wheelbase-to-length ratio of 50% is considered ◉ dangerous ○ fatiguing ○ good ○ excellent *

The approximate net payload of 2734 pounds at 11% of GVWR on this model is ○ deficient ○ excessive ○ cautionary ◉ good ○ excellent *

Total highway safety penalties are: 12 *   Value: 80   Durability: 78   Highway Control Rating: 46   Highway Safety: 34

Endeavor	1999	MHA	38	37WD	FR	CU275	D	$3200	242	3,650	24,850	21,828

Livability Code: SB 30-90 — Wheelbase-to-length ratio of 53% is considered ○ dangerous ◉ fatiguing ○ good ○ excellent *

The approximate net payload of 3022 pounds at 12% of GVWR on this model is ○ deficient ○ excessive ○ cautionary ◉ good ○ excellent *

Total highway safety penalties are: 2 *   Value: 85   Durability: 78   Highway Control Rating: 68   Highway Safety: 66   ★★

Note: Safety ratings are based on the assumption that the engineering of the RV has allowed for proper balance by placing fresh, gray, and black holding tanks in a location so as not to change the balance of the RV when the tanks are empty or full. **Always double-check wheelbase, GVWR, and weights at front and rear axles.**

*See Section 1 for details on how conclusions are reached.

Section 2: The Ratings

Brand	Year	Type	Length	Model	Chassis	Engine	Fuel Type	Average Price per Linear Foot When New	Adjusted Wheelbase	Approx. Towing Capacity	Gross Vehicle Weight Rating	Average Curb Weight
Endeavor	1999	MHA	38	37WDS	FR	CU275	D	$3200	242	3,650	24,850	22,728

Livability Code: SB 30-90 — Wheelbase-to-length ratio of 53% is considered ○ dangerous ◉ fatiguing ○ good ○ excellent *
The approximate net payload of 2122 pounds at 9% of GVWR on this model is ○ deficient ○ excessive ◉ cautionary ○ good ○ excellent *
Total highway safety penalties are: 12 * Value: 8 0 Durability: 7 8 Highway Control Rating: 5 8 Highway Safety: 4 6

Brand	Year	Type	Length	Model	Chassis	Engine	Fuel Type					
Endeavor	1999	MHA	38	37WDS4	FR	CU275	D	$3200	242	3,650	24,850	22,728

Livability Code: SB 30-90 — Wheelbase-to-length ratio of 53% is considered ○ dangerous ◉ fatiguing ○ good ○ excellent *
The approximate net payload of 2122 pounds at 9% of GVWR on this model is ○ deficient ○ excessive ◉ cautionary ○ good ○ excellent *
Total highway safety penalties are: 12 * Value: 8 0 Durability: 7 8 Highway Control Rating: 5 8 Highway Safety: 4 6

Brand	Year	Type	Length	Model	Chassis	Engine	Fuel Type					
Endeavor	1999	MHA	38	37CDS	FR	CU275	D	$3200	242	3,650	24,850	22,728

Livability Code: SB 30-90 — Wheelbase-to-length ratio of 53% is considered ○ dangerous ◉ fatiguing ○ good ○ excellent *
The approximate net payload of 2122 pounds at 9% of GVWR on this model is ○ deficient ○ excessive ◉ cautionary ○ good ○ excellent *
Total highway safety penalties are: 12 * Value: 8 0 Durability: 7 8 Highway Control Rating: 5 8 Highway Safety: 4 6

Brand	Year	Type	Length	Model	Chassis	Engine	Fuel Type					
Endeavor	1999	MHA	38	37CDS4	FR	CU275	D	$3200	242	3,650	24,850	22,728

Livability Code: SB 30-90 — Wheelbase-to-length ratio of 53% is considered ○ dangerous ◉ fatiguing ○ good ○ excellent *
The approximate net payload of 2122 pounds at 9% of GVWR on this model is ○ deficient ○ excessive ◉ cautionary ○ good ○ excellent *
Total highway safety penalties are: 12 * Value: 8 0 Durability: 7 8 Highway Control Rating: 5 8 Highway Safety: 4 6

Brand	Year	Type	Length	Model	Chassis	Engine	Fuel Type					
Endeavor	1999	MHA	38	37CDM	FR	CU275	D	$3200	242	3,650	24,850	22,728

Livability Code: SB 30-90 — Wheelbase-to-length ratio of 53% is considered ○ dangerous ◉ fatiguing ○ good ○ excellent *
The approximate net payload of 2122 pounds at 9% of GVWR on this model is ○ deficient ○ excessive ◉ cautionary ○ good ○ excellent *
Total highway safety penalties are: 12 * Value: 8 0 Durability: 7 8 Highway Control Rating: 5 8 Highway Safety: 4 6

Brand	Year	Type	Length	Model	Chassis	Engine	Fuel Type					
Endeavor	1999	MHA	38	37WDM	FR	CU275	D	$3200	242	3,650	24,850	22,728

Livability Code: SB 30-90 — Wheelbase-to-length ratio of 53% is considered ○ dangerous ◉ fatiguing ○ good ○ excellent *
The approximate net payload of 2122 pounds at 9% of GVWR on this model is ○ deficient ○ excessive ◉ cautionary ○ good ○ excellent *
Total highway safety penalties are: 12 * Value: 8 0 Durability: 7 8 Highway Control Rating: 5 8 Highway Safety: 4 6

Brand	Year	Type	Length	Model	Chassis	Engine	Fuel Type					
Europa	1994	MHA	23	23	DO	5.7L	G	$2100	155	1,500	10,100	8,216

Livability Code: SB 30-90 — Wheelbase-to-length ratio of 56% is considered ○ dangerous ○ fatiguing ○ good ◉ excellent *
The approximate net payload of 1884 pounds at 19% of GVWR on this model is ○ deficient ○ excessive ○ cautionary ○ good ◉ excellent *
Total highway safety penalties are: 2 * Value: 8 6 Durability: 8 0 Highway Control Rating: 9 8 Highway Safety: 9 6 ★★★★

Brand	Year	Type	Length	Model	Chassis	Engine	Fuel Type					
Europa	1996	MHA	23	230	CH	5.7L	G	$2100	157	2,500	11,000	9,484

Livability Code: SB 30-90 — Wheelbase-to-length ratio of 56% is considered ○ dangerous ○ fatiguing ◉ good ○ excellent *
The approximate net payload of 1516 pounds at 14% of GVWR on this model is ○ deficient ○ excessive ○ cautionary ◉ good ○ excellent *
Total highway safety penalties are: 1 * Value: 8 6 Durability: 8 0 Highway Control Rating: 9 3 Highway Safety: 9 2 ★★★★

Brand	Year	Type	Length	Model	Chassis	Engine	Fuel Type					
Europa	1996	MHA	27	270	CH	5.7L	G	$1900	190	1,700	11,800	10,475

Livability Code: SB 30-90 — Wheelbase-to-length ratio of 58% is considered ○ dangerous ○ fatiguing ○ good ◉ excellent *
The approximate net payload of 1325 pounds at 11% of GVWR on this model is ○ deficient ○ excessive ○ cautionary ◉ good ○ excellent *
Total highway safety penalties are: 3 * Value: 8 5 Durability: 8 0 Highway Control Rating: 9 4 Highway Safety: 9 1 ★★★★

Brand	Year	Type	Length	Model	Chassis	Engine	Fuel Type					
Europa	1996	MHA	27	272	CH	5.7L	G	$1900	190	1,700	11,800	10,475

Livability Code: SB 30-90 — Wheelbase-to-length ratio of 58% is considered ○ dangerous ○ fatiguing ○ good ◉ excellent *
The approximate net payload of 1325 pounds at 11% of GVWR on this model is ○ deficient ○ excessive ○ cautionary ◉ good ○ excellent *
Total highway safety penalties are: 3 * Value: 8 5 Durability: 8 0 Highway Control Rating: 9 4 Highway Safety: 9 1 ★★★★

Brand	Year	Type	Length	Model	Chassis	Engine	Fuel Type					
Europa	1997	MHA	23	230	CH	5.7L	G	$2300	157	2,500	11,000	9,492

Livability Code: SB 30-90 — Wheelbase-to-length ratio of 56% is considered ○ dangerous ○ fatiguing ◉ good ○ excellent *
The approximate net payload of 1508 pounds at 14% of GVWR on this model is ○ deficient ○ excessive ○ cautionary ◉ good ○ excellent *
Total highway safety penalties are: 1 * Value: 8 6 Durability: 8 0 Highway Control Rating: 9 3 Highway Safety: 9 2 ★★★★

Brand	Year	Type	Length	Model	Chassis	Engine	Fuel Type					
Europa	1997	MHA	23	230	CH	GM6.5	D	$2300	157	2,500	11,000	9,492

Livability Code: SB 30-90 — Wheelbase-to-length ratio of 56% is considered ○ dangerous ○ fatiguing ◉ good ○ excellent *
The approximate net payload of 1508 pounds at 14% of GVWR on this model is ○ deficient ○ excessive ○ cautionary ◉ good ○ excellent *
Total highway safety penalties are: 1 * Value: 8 6 Durability: 8 0 Highway Control Rating: 9 3 Highway Safety: 9 2 ★★★★

Note: Safety ratings are based on the assumption that the engineering of the RV has allowed for proper balance by placing fresh, gray, and black holding tanks in a location so as not to change the balance of the RV when the tanks are empty or full. **Always double-check wheelbase, GVWR, and weights at front and rear axles.**

*See Section 1 for details on how conclusions are reached.

Brand	Year	Type	Length	Model	Chassis	Engine	Fuel Type	Average Price per Linear Foot When New	Adjusted Wheelbase	Approx. Towing Capacity	Gross Vehicle Weight Rating	Average Curb Weight
Europa	1997	MHA	28	280	CH	5.7L	G	$2000	190	1,700	11,800	10,691

Livability Code: SB 30-90 Wheelbase-to-length ratio of 56% is considered ○ dangerous ○ fatiguing ◉ good ○ excellent*

The approximate net payload of 1109 pounds at 9% of GVWR on this model is ○ deficient ○ excessive ◉ cautionary ○ good ○ excellent*

Total highway safety penalties are: 4*   Value: 8 5 Durability: 8 0 Highway Control Rating: 8 0 Highway Safety: 7 6 ★★★

Brand	Year	Type	Length	Model	Chassis	Engine	Fuel Type	Price	Wheelbase	Towing	GVWR	Curb Weight
Europa	1997	MHA	28	280	CH	GM6.5	D	$2000	190	1,700	11,800	10,691

Livability Code: SB 30-90 Wheelbase-to-length ratio of 56% is considered ○ dangerous ○ fatiguing ◉ good ○ excellent*

The approximate net payload of 1109 pounds at 9% of GVWR on this model is ○ deficient ○ excessive ◉ cautionary ○ good ○ excellent*

Total highway safety penalties are: 4*   Value: 8 5 Durability: 8 0 Highway Control Rating: 8 0 Highway Safety: 7 6 ★★★

Brand	Year	Type	Length	Model	Chassis	Engine	Fuel Type	Price	Wheelbase	Towing	GVWR	Curb Weight
Europa	1997	MHA	28	282	CH	5.7L	G	$2100	190	1,700	11,800	10,691

Livability Code: SB 30-90 Wheelbase-to-length ratio of 56% is considered ○ dangerous ○ fatiguing ◉ good ○ excellent*

The approximate net payload of 1109 pounds at 9% of GVWR on this model is ○ deficient ○ excessive ◉ cautionary ○ good ○ excellent*

Total highway safety penalties are: 4*   Value: 8 5 Durability: 8 0 Highway Control Rating: 8 0 Highway Safety: 7 6 ★★★

Brand	Year	Type	Length	Model	Chassis	Engine	Fuel Type	Price	Wheelbase	Towing	GVWR	Curb Weight
Europa	1997	MHA	28	282	CH	GM6.5	D	$2100	190	1,700	11,800	10,691

Livability Code: SB 30-90 Wheelbase-to-length ratio of 56% is considered ○ dangerous ○ fatiguing ◉ good ○ excellent*

The approximate net payload of 1109 pounds at 9% of GVWR on this model is ○ deficient ○ excessive ◉ cautionary ○ good ○ excellent*

Total highway safety penalties are: 4*   Value: 8 5 Durability: 8 0 Highway Control Rating: 8 0 Highway Safety: 7 6 ★★★

Brand	Year	Type	Length	Model	Chassis	Engine	Fuel Type	Price	Wheelbase	Towing	GVWR	Curb Weight
EuroVan	1995	MHB	17	16	VW	2.5L	G	$1800	131	1,500 e	5,995	5,254

Livability Code: WE 40-80 Wheelbase-to-length ratio of 64% is considered ○ dangerous ○ fatiguing ○ good ◉ excellent*

The approximate net payload of 741 pounds at 12% of GVWR on this model is ○ deficient ○ excessive ○ cautionary ○ good ◉ excellent*

Total highway safety penalties are: 2*   Value: 7 7 Durability: 7 0 Highway Control Rating: 1 0 0 Highway Safety: 9 8 ★★★

Brand	Year	Type	Length	Model	Chassis	Engine	Fuel Type	Price	Wheelbase	Towing	GVWR	Curb Weight
Executive	1990	MHA	40	40 LTD	GI	De 6V	D	$6600	262	1,500	36,000	30,320

Livability Code: FT 30-90 Wheelbase-to-length ratio of 55% is considered ○ dangerous ○ fatiguing ◉ good ○ excellent*

The approximate net payload of 5680 pounds at 16% of GVWR on this model is ○ deficient ○ excessive ○ cautionary ○ good ◉ excellent*

Total highway safety penalties are: 2*   Value: 8 5 Durability: 7 8 Highway Control Rating: 9 1 Highway Safety: 8 9 ★★★

Brand	Year	Type	Length	Model	Chassis	Engine	Fuel Type	Price	Wheelbase	Towing	GVWR	Curb Weight
Executive	1992	MHA	36	36-250	RO	Cu8.3L	D	$6000	222	1,500	31,220	28,462

Livability Code: FT 30-90 Wheelbase-to-length ratio of 51% is considered ○ dangerous ◉ fatiguing ○ good ○ excellent*

The approximate net payload of 2758 pounds at 9% of GVWR on this model is ○ deficient ○ excessive ◉ cautionary ○ good ○ excellent*

Total highway safety penalties are: 2*   Value: 8 5 Durability: 7 8 Highway Control Rating: 3 3 Highway Safety: 3 1

Brand	Year	Type	Length	Model	Chassis	Engine	Fuel Type	Price	Wheelbase	Towing	GVWR	Curb Weight
Executive	1992	MHA	36	36-300	RO	Cu8.3L	D	$6300	222	1,500	31,220	28,462

Livability Code: FT 30-90 Wheelbase-to-length ratio of 51% is considered ○ dangerous ◉ fatiguing ○ good ○ excellent*

The approximate net payload of 2758 pounds at 9% of GVWR on this model is ○ deficient ○ excessive ◉ cautionary ○ good ○ excellent*

Total highway safety penalties are: 2*   Value: 8 5 Durability: 7 8 Highway Control Rating: 3 3 Highway Safety: 3 1

Brand	Year	Type	Length	Model	Chassis	Engine	Fuel Type	Price	Wheelbase	Towing	GVWR	Curb Weight
Executive	1992	MHA	38	38-250	RO	Cu8.3L	D	$6100	246	1,500	31,220	29,176

Livability Code: FT 30-90 Wheelbase-to-length ratio of 54% is considered ○ dangerous ○ fatiguing ◉ good ○ excellent*

The approximate net payload of 2044 pounds at 7% of GVWR on this model is ○ deficient ○ excessive ◉ cautionary ○ good ○ excellent*

Total highway safety penalties are: 2*   Value: 8 5 Durability: 7 8 Highway Control Rating: 5 2 Highway Safety: 5 0 ★

Brand	Year	Type	Length	Model	Chassis	Engine	Fuel Type	Price	Wheelbase	Towing	GVWR	Curb Weight
Executive	1992	MHA	38	38-300	RO	Cu8.3L	D	$6300	246	1,500	31,220	29,176

Livability Code: FT 30-90 Wheelbase-to-length ratio of 54% is considered ○ dangerous ○ fatiguing ◉ good ○ excellent*

The approximate net payload of 2044 pounds at 7% of GVWR on this model is ○ deficient ○ excessive ◉ cautionary ○ good ○ excellent*

Total highway safety penalties are: 2*   Value: 8 5 Durability: 7 8 Highway Control Rating: 5 2 Highway Safety: 5 0 ★

Brand	Year	Type	Length	Model	Chassis	Engine	Fuel Type	Price	Wheelbase	Towing	GVWR	Curb Weight
Executive	1992	MHA	38	38-L10	RO	Cu8.3L	D	$6800	246	1,500	31,220	29,176

Livability Code: FT 30-90 Wheelbase-to-length ratio of 54% is considered ○ dangerous ○ fatiguing ◉ good ○ excellent*

The approximate net payload of 2044 pounds at 7% of GVWR on this model is ○ deficient ○ excessive ◉ cautionary ○ good ○ excellent*

Total highway safety penalties are: 2*   Value: 8 5 Durability: 7 8 Highway Control Rating: 5 2 Highway Safety: 5 0 ★

Brand	Year	Type	Length	Model	Chassis	Engine	Fuel Type	Price	Wheelbase	Towing	GVWR	Curb Weight
Executive	1992	MHA	40	40-300	RO	Cu8.3L	D	$6300	270	1,500	31,220	29,890

Livability Code: FT 30-90 Wheelbase-to-length ratio of 56% is considered ○ dangerous ○ fatiguing ◉ good ○ excellent*

The approximate net payload of 1330 pounds at 4% of GVWR on this model is ◉ deficient ○ excessive ○ cautionary ○ good ○ excellent*

Total highway safety penalties are: 2*   Value: 8 5 Durability: 7 8 Highway Control Rating: 6 0 Highway Safety: 5 8 ★

Note: Safety ratings are based on the assumption that the engineering of the RV has allowed for proper balance by placing fresh, gray, and black holding tanks in a location so as not to change the balance of the RV when the tanks are empty or full. **Always double-check wheelbase, GVWR, and weights at front and rear axles.**

*See Section 1 for details on how conclusions are reached.

Section 2: The Ratings

Brand	Year	Type	Length	Model	Chassis	Engine	Fuel Type	Average Price per Linear Foot When New	Adjusted Wheelbase	Approx. Towing Capacity	Gross Vehicle Weight Rating	Average Curb Weight
Executive	1992	MHA	40	40-L10	RO	Cu8.3L	D	$6800	270	1,500	31,220	29,890

Livability Code: FT 30-90
Wheelbase-to-length ratio of 56% is considered ○ dangerous ○ fatiguing ◉ good ○ excellent *
The approximate net payload of 1330 pounds at 4% of GVWR on this model is ◉ deficient ○ excessive ○ cautionary ○ good ○ excellent *
Total highway safety penalties are: 2 *   Value: 8 5   Durability: 7 8   Highway Control Rating: 6 0   Highway Safety: 5 8   ★

Brand	Year	Type	Length	Model	Chassis	Engine	Fuel Type					
Executive	1995	MHA	36	36SB-300	RO	Cu8.3L	D	$6400	222	10,000	35,000	30,210

Livability Code: FT 30-90
Wheelbase-to-length ratio of 51% is considered ○ dangerous ◉ fatiguing ○ good ○ excellent *
The approximate net payload of 4790 pounds at 14% of GVWR on this model is ○ deficient ○ excessive ○ cautionary ◉ good ○ excellent *
Total highway safety penalties are: 2 *   Value: 8 5   Durability: 7 8   Highway Control Rating: 4 5   Highway Safety: 4 3

Executive	1995	MHA	36	36SB-400	RO	Cu8.3L	D	$7000	222	10,000	35,000	30,684

Livability Code: FT 30-90
Wheelbase-to-length ratio of 51% is considered ○ dangerous ◉ fatiguing ○ good ○ excellent *
The approximate net payload of 4316 pounds at 12% of GVWR on this model is ○ deficient ○ excessive ○ cautionary ◉ good ○ excellent *
Total highway safety penalties are: 2 *   Value: 8 5   Durability: 7 8   Highway Control Rating: 4 2   Highway Safety: 4 0

Executive	1995	MHA	38	38SB-300	RO	Cu8.3L	D	$6200	246	10,000	35,000	31,437

Livability Code: FT 30-90
Wheelbase-to-length ratio of 54% is considered ○ dangerous ○ fatiguing ◉ good ○ excellent *
The approximate net payload of 3563 pounds at 10% of GVWR on this model is ○ deficient ○ excessive ○ cautionary ◉ good ○ excellent *
Total highway safety penalties are: 2 *   Value: 8 5   Durability: 7 8   Highway Control Rating: 7 6   Highway Safety: 7 4   ★★★

Executive	1995	MHA	38	38SB-400	RO	Cu8.3L	D	$6800	246	10,000	35,000	31,911

Livability Code: FT 30-90
Wheelbase-to-length ratio of 54% is considered ○ dangerous ○ fatiguing ◉ good ○ excellent *
The approximate net payload of 3089 pounds at 9% of GVWR on this model is ○ deficient ○ excessive ◉ cautionary ○ good ○ excellent *
Total highway safety penalties are: 2 *   Value: 8 5   Durability: 7 8   Highway Control Rating: 6 4   Highway Safety: 6 2   ★★

Executive	1995	MHA	40	40PB-300	RO	Cu8.3L	D	$6100	270	10,000	35,000	31,988

Livability Code: FT 30-90
Wheelbase-to-length ratio of 56% is considered ○ dangerous ○ fatiguing ◉ good ○ excellent *
The approximate net payload of 3012 pounds at 9% of GVWR on this model is ○ deficient ○ excessive ◉ cautionary ○ good ○ excellent *
Total highway safety penalties are: 2 *   Value: 8 5   Durability: 7 8   Highway Control Rating: 8 0   Highway Safety: 7 8   ★★★

Executive	1995	MHA	40	40PB-400	RO	Cu8.3L	D	$6700	270	10,000	35,000	32,438

Livability Code: FT 30-90
Wheelbase-to-length ratio of 56% is considered ○ dangerous ○ fatiguing ◉ good ○ excellent *
The approximate net payload of 2562 pounds at 7% of GVWR on this model is ○ deficient ○ excessive ◉ cautionary ○ good ○ excellent *
Total highway safety penalties are: 2 *   Value: 8 5   Durability: 7 8   Highway Control Rating: 6 8   Highway Safety: 6 6   ★★

Executive	1996	MHA	36	36SB - 300	RO	Cu300	D	$6700	222	10,000	35,000	30,352

Livability Code: FT 30-90
Wheelbase-to-length ratio of 51% is considered ○ dangerous ◉ fatiguing ○ good ○ excellent *
The approximate net payload of 4648 pounds at 13% of GVWR on this model is ○ deficient ○ excessive ○ cautionary ◉ good ○ excellent *
Total highway safety penalties are: 2 *   Value: 8 5   Durability: 7 8   Highway Control Rating: 4 4   Highway Safety: 4 2

Executive	1996	MHA	36	36SB - 400	RO	Cu300	D	$7300	222	10,000	35,000	30,352

Livability Code: FT 30-90
Wheelbase-to-length ratio of 51% is considered ○ dangerous ◉ fatiguing ○ good ○ excellent *
The approximate net payload of 4648 pounds at 13% of GVWR on this model is ○ deficient ○ excessive ○ cautionary ◉ good ○ excellent *
Total highway safety penalties are: 2 *   Value: 8 5   Durability: 7 8   Highway Control Rating: 4 4   Highway Safety: 4 2

Executive	1996	MHA	38	38PBFD - 300	RO	Cu300	D	$6500	246	10,000	35,000	31,066

Livability Code: FT 30-90
Wheelbase-to-length ratio of 54% is considered ○ dangerous ○ fatiguing ◉ good ○ excellent *
The approximate net payload of 3934 pounds at 11% of GVWR on this model is ○ deficient ○ excessive ○ cautionary ◉ good ○ excellent *
Total highway safety penalties are: 2 *   Value: 8 5   Durability: 7 8   Highway Control Rating: 7 7   Highway Safety: 7 5   ★★★

Executive	1996	MHA	38	38PBFD - 400	RO	Cu300	D	$7100	246	10,000	35,000	31,066

Livability Code: FT 30-90
Wheelbase-to-length ratio of 54% is considered ○ dangerous ○ fatiguing ◉ good ○ excellent *
The approximate net payload of 3934 pounds at 11% of GVWR on this model is ○ deficient ○ excessive ○ cautionary ◉ good ○ excellent *
Total highway safety penalties are: 2 *   Value: 8 5   Durability: 7 8   Highway Control Rating: 7 7   Highway Safety: 7 5   ★★★

Executive	1996	MHA	40	40CAFD - 300	RO	Cu300	D	$6400	270	10,000	35,000	31,780

Livability Code: FT 30-90
Wheelbase-to-length ratio of 56% is considered ○ dangerous ○ fatiguing ◉ good ○ excellent *
The approximate net payload of 3220 pounds at 9% of GVWR on this model is ○ deficient ○ excessive ◉ cautionary ○ good ○ excellent *
Total highway safety penalties are: 2 *   Value: 8 5   Durability: 7 8   Highway Control Rating: 8 0   Highway Safety: 7 8   ★★★

Note: Safety ratings are based on the assumption that the engineering of the RV has allowed for proper balance by placing fresh, gray, and black holding tanks in a location so as not to change the balance of the RV when the tanks are empty or full. **Always double-check wheelbase, GVWR, and weights at front and rear axles.**

*See Section 1 for details on how conclusions are reached.

Brand	Year	Type	Length	Model	Chassis	Engine	Fuel Type	Average Price per Linear Foot When New	Adjusted Wheelbase	Approx. Towing Capacity	Gross Vehicle Weight Rating	Average Curb Weight
Executive	1996	MHA	40	40CAFD - 400	RO	Cu300	D	$7000	270	10,000	35,000	31,780

Livability Code: FT 30-90   Wheelbase-to-length ratio of 56% is considered ○ dangerous ○ fatiguing ◉ good ○ excellent *

The approximate net payload of 3220 pounds at 9% of GVWR on this model is ○ deficient ○ excessive ◉ cautionary ○ good ○ excellent *

Total highway safety penalties are: 2 *   Value: 8 5   Durability: 7 8   Highway Control Rating: 8 0   Highway Safety: 7 8   ★★★

Brand	Year	Type	Length	Model	Chassis	Engine	Fuel Type		Adjusted Wheelbase	Approx. Towing Capacity	Gross Vehicle Weight Rating	Average Curb Weight
Executive	1997	MHA	36	36 SBFD	RO	Cu325	D	$6800	222	10,000	35,000	30,352

Livability Code: FT 30-90   Wheelbase-to-length ratio of 51% is considered ○ dangerous ◉ fatiguing ○ good ○ excellent *

The approximate net payload of 4648 pounds at 13% of GVWR on this model is ○ deficient ○ excessive ○ cautionary ◉ good ○ excellent *

Total highway safety penalties are: 2 *   Value: 8 5   Durability: 7 8   Highway Control Rating: 4 4   Highway Safety: 4 2

| Executive | 1997 | MHA | 38 | 38 PBFD | RO | Cu325 | D | $6600 | 246 | 10,000 | 35,000 | 31,066 |

Livability Code: FT 30-90   Wheelbase-to-length ratio of 54% is considered ○ dangerous ○ fatiguing ◉ good ○ excellent *

The approximate net payload of 3934 pounds at 11% of GVWR on this model is ○ deficient ○ excessive ○ cautionary ◉ good ○ excellent *

Total highway safety penalties are: 2 *   Value: 8 5   Durability: 7 8   Highway Control Rating: 7 7   Highway Safety: 7 5   ★★★

| Executive | 1997 | MHA | 38 | 38 SBFD | RO | Cu325 | D | $6600 | 246 | 10,000 | 35,000 | 31,066 |

Livability Code: FT 30-90   Wheelbase-to-length ratio of 54% is considered ○ dangerous ○ fatiguing ◉ good ○ excellent *

The approximate net payload of 3934 pounds at 11% of GVWR on this model is ○ deficient ○ excessive ○ cautionary ◉ good ○ excellent *

Total highway safety penalties are: 2 *   Value: 8 5   Durability: 7 8   Highway Control Rating: 7 7   Highway Safety: 7 5   ★★★

| Executive | 1997 | MHA | 38 | 38 DBFD | RO | Cu325 | D | $6600 | 246 | 10,000 | 35,000 | 31,066 |

Livability Code: FT 30-90   Wheelbase-to-length ratio of 54% is considered ○ dangerous ○ fatiguing ◉ good ○ excellent *

The approximate net payload of 3934 pounds at 11% of GVWR on this model is ○ deficient ○ excessive ○ cautionary ◉ good ○ excellent *

Total highway safety penalties are: 2 *   Value: 8 5   Durability: 7 8   Highway Control Rating: 7 7   Highway Safety: 7 5   ★★★

| Executive | 1997 | MHA | 38 | 38 SO | RO | Cu325 | D | $6600 | 246 | 10,000 | 35,000 | 31,966 |

Livability Code: FT 30-90   Wheelbase-to-length ratio of 54% is considered ○ dangerous ○ fatiguing ◉ good ○ excellent *

The approximate net payload of 3034 pounds at 9% of GVWR on this model is ○ deficient ○ excessive ◉ cautionary ○ good ○ excellent *

Total highway safety penalties are: 7 *   Value: 8 3   Durability: 7 8   Highway Control Rating: 6 4   Highway Safety: 5 7   ★

| Executive | 1997 | MHA | 40 | 40 CAFD | RO | Cu325 | D | $6600 | 270 | 10,000 | 35,000 | 31,780 |

Livability Code: FT 30-90   Wheelbase-to-length ratio of 56% is considered ○ dangerous ○ fatiguing ◉ good ○ excellent *

The approximate net payload of 3220 pounds at 9% of GVWR on this model is ○ deficient ○ excessive ◉ cautionary ○ good ○ excellent *

Total highway safety penalties are: 2 *   Value: 8 5   Durability: 7 8   Highway Control Rating: 8 0   Highway Safety: 7 8   ★★★

| Executive | 1997 | MHA | 40 | 40 CBFD | RO | Cu325 | D | $6600 | 270 | 10,000 | 35,000 | 31,780 |

Livability Code: FT 30-90   Wheelbase-to-length ratio of 56% is considered ○ dangerous ○ fatiguing ◉ good ○ excellent *

The approximate net payload of 3220 pounds at 9% of GVWR on this model is ○ deficient ○ excessive ◉ cautionary ○ good ○ excellent *

Total highway safety penalties are: 2 *   Value: 8 5   Durability: 7 8   Highway Control Rating: 8 0   Highway Safety: 7 8   ★★★

| Executive | 1997 | MHA | 40 | 40 PBFD | RO | Cu325 | D | $6600 | 270 | 10,000 | 35,000 | 31,780 |

Livability Code: FT 30-90   Wheelbase-to-length ratio of 56% is considered ○ dangerous ○ fatiguing ◉ good ○ excellent *

The approximate net payload of 3220 pounds at 9% of GVWR on this model is ○ deficient ○ excessive ◉ cautionary ○ good ○ excellent *

Total highway safety penalties are: 2 *   Value: 8 5   Durability: 7 8   Highway Control Rating: 8 0   Highway Safety: 7 8   ★★★

| Executive | 1997 | MHA | 40 | 40 CAPBFD | RO | Cu325 | D | $6600 | 270 | 10,000 | 35,000 | 31,780 |

Livability Code: FT 30-90   Wheelbase-to-length ratio of 56% is considered ○ dangerous ○ fatiguing ◉ good ○ excellent *

The approximate net payload of 3220 pounds at 9% of GVWR on this model is ○ deficient ○ excessive ◉ cautionary ○ good ○ excellent *

Total highway safety penalties are: 2 *   Value: 8 5   Durability: 7 8   Highway Control Rating: 8 0   Highway Safety: 7 8   ★★★

| Executive | 1997 | MHA | 40 | 40 SO | RO | Cu325 | D | $6600 | 270 | 10,000 | 35,000 | 32,680 |

Livability Code: FT 30-90   Wheelbase-to-length ratio of 56% is considered ○ dangerous ○ fatiguing ◉ good ○ excellent *

The approximate net payload of 2320 pounds at 7% of GVWR on this model is ○ deficient ○ excessive ◉ cautionary ○ good ○ excellent *

Total highway safety penalties are: 7 *   Value: 8 3   Durability: 7 8   Highway Control Rating: 6 8   Highway Safety: 6 1   ★★

| Executive | 1998 | MHA | 36 | 36 No Slide | RO | CU325 | D | $6900 | 222 | 10,000 | 35,000 | 30,352 |

Livability Code: FT 30-90   Wheelbase-to-length ratio of 51% is considered ○ dangerous ◉ fatiguing ○ good ○ excellent *

The approximate net payload of 4648 pounds at 13% of GVWR on this model is ○ deficient ○ excessive ○ cautionary ◉ good ○ excellent *

Total highway safety penalties are: 2 *   Value: 8 5   Durability: 7 8   Highway Control Rating: 4 4   Highway Safety: 4 2

Note: Safety ratings are based on the assumption that the engineering of the RV has allowed for proper balance by placing fresh, gray, and black holding tanks in a location so as not to change the balance of the RV when the tanks are empty or full. **Always double-check wheelbase, GVWR, and weights at front and rear axles.**

*See Section 1 for details on how conclusions are reached.

Brand	Year	Type	Length	Model	Chassis	Engine	Fuel Type	Average Price per Linear Foot When New	Adjusted Wheelbase	Approx. Towing Capacity	Gross Vehicle Weight Rating	Average Curb Weight
Executive	1998	MHA	38	38 No Slide	RO	CU325	D	$6700	246	10,000	35,000	31,066

Livability Code: FT 30-90
Wheelbase-to-length ratio of 54% is considered ○ dangerous ○ fatiguing ◉ good ○ excellent*
The approximate net payload of 3934 pounds at 11% of GVWR on this model is ○ deficient ○ excessive ○ cautionary ◉ good ○ excellent*
Total highway safety penalties are: 2* Value: **8 5** Durability: **7 8** Highway Control Rating: **7 7** Highway Safety: **7 5** ★★★

Brand	Year	Type	Length	Model	Chassis	Engine	Fuel Type	Price/Lin Ft	Wheelbase	Towing	GVWR	Curb Wt
Executive	1998	MHA	38	38 Slide	RO	CU325	D	$6900	246	10,000	35,000	31,966

Livability Code: FT 30-90
Wheelbase-to-length ratio of 54% is considered ○ dangerous ○ fatiguing ◉ good ○ excellent*
The approximate net payload of 3034 pounds at 9% of GVWR on this model is ○ deficient ○ excessive ◉ cautionary ○ good ○ excellent*
Total highway safety penalties are: 12* Value: **8 0** Durability: **7 8** Highway Control Rating: **6 4** Highway Safety: **5 2** ★

Brand	Year	Type	Length	Model	Chassis	Engine	Fuel Type	Price/Lin Ft	Wheelbase	Towing	GVWR	Curb Wt
Executive	1998	MHA	40	40 No Slide	RO	CU325	D	$6600	270	10,000	35,000	31,780

Livability Code: FT 30-90
Wheelbase-to-length ratio of 56% is considered ○ dangerous ○ fatiguing ◉ good ○ excellent*
The approximate net payload of 3220 pounds at 9% of GVWR on this model is ○ deficient ○ excessive ◉ cautionary ○ good ○ excellent*
Total highway safety penalties are: 2* Value: **8 5** Durability: **7 8** Highway Control Rating: **8 0** Highway Safety: **7 8** ★★★

Brand	Year	Type	Length	Model	Chassis	Engine	Fuel Type	Price/Lin Ft	Wheelbase	Towing	GVWR	Curb Wt
Executive	1998	MHA	40	40 Slide	RO	CU325	D	$6800	270	10,000	35,000	32,680

Livability Code: FT 30-90
Wheelbase-to-length ratio of 56% is considered ○ dangerous ○ fatiguing ◉ good ○ excellent*
The approximate net payload of 2320 pounds at 7% of GVWR on this model is ○ deficient ○ excessive ◉ cautionary ○ good ○ excellent*
Total highway safety penalties are: 12* Value: **8 0** Durability: **7 8** Highway Control Rating: **6 8** Highway Safety: **5 6** ★

Brand	Year	Type	Length	Model	Chassis	Engine	Fuel Type	Price/Lin Ft	Wheelbase	Towing	GVWR	Curb Wt
Executive	1999	MHA	38	38DB FD	RO	CU350	D	$7200	246	10,000	35,000	31,066

Livability Code: FT 30-90
Wheelbase-to-length ratio of 54% is considered ○ dangerous ○ fatiguing ◉ good ○ excellent*
The approximate net payload of 3934 pounds at 11% of GVWR on this model is ○ deficient ○ excessive ○ cautionary ◉ good ○ excellent*
Total highway safety penalties are: 2* Value: **8 5** Durability: **7 8** Highway Control Rating: **7 9** Highway Safety: **7 7** ★★★

Brand	Year	Type	Length	Model	Chassis	Engine	Fuel Type	Price/Lin Ft	Wheelbase	Towing	GVWR	Curb Wt
Executive	1999	MHA	38	38PB FD	RO	CU350	D	$7200	246	10,000	35,000	31,066

Livability Code: FT 30-90
Wheelbase-to-length ratio of 54% is considered ○ dangerous ○ fatiguing ◉ good ○ excellent*
The approximate net payload of 3934 pounds at 11% of GVWR on this model is ○ deficient ○ excessive ○ cautionary ◉ good ○ excellent*
Total highway safety penalties are: 2* Value: **8 5** Durability: **7 8** Highway Control Rating: **7 9** Highway Safety: **7 7** ★★★

Brand	Year	Type	Length	Model	Chassis	Engine	Fuel Type	Price/Lin Ft	Wheelbase	Towing	GVWR	Curb Wt
Executive	1999	MHA	38	38SB FD	RO	CU350	D	$7200	246	10,000	35,000	31,066

Livability Code: FT 30-90
Wheelbase-to-length ratio of 54% is considered ○ dangerous ○ fatiguing ◉ good ○ excellent*
The approximate net payload of 3934 pounds at 11% of GVWR on this model is ○ deficient ○ excessive ○ cautionary ◉ good ○ excellent*
Total highway safety penalties are: 2* Value: **8 5** Durability: **7 8** Highway Control Rating: **7 9** Highway Safety: **7 7** ★★★

Brand	Year	Type	Length	Model	Chassis	Engine	Fuel Type	Price/Lin Ft	Wheelbase	Towing	GVWR	Curb Wt
Executive	1999	MHA	38	38PBS FD	RO	CU350	D	$7200	246	10,000	35,000	31,966

Livability Code: FT 30-90
Wheelbase-to-length ratio of 54% is considered ○ dangerous ○ fatiguing ◉ good ○ excellent*
The approximate net payload of 3034 pounds at 9% of GVWR on this model is ○ deficient ○ excessive ◉ cautionary ○ good ○ excellent*
Total highway safety penalties are: 12* Value: **8 0** Durability: **7 8** Highway Control Rating: **6 7** Highway Safety: **5 5** ★

Brand	Year	Type	Length	Model	Chassis	Engine	Fuel Type	Price/Lin Ft	Wheelbase	Towing	GVWR	Curb Wt
Executive	1999	MHA	38	38DB FD op eng	RO	CU450	D	$7200	246	10,000	35,000	31,566

Livability Code: FT 30-90
Wheelbase-to-length ratio of 54% is considered ○ dangerous ○ fatiguing ◉ good ○ excellent*
The approximate net payload of 3434 pounds at 10% of GVWR on this model is ○ deficient ○ excessive ○ cautionary ◉ good ○ excellent*
Total highway safety penalties are: 2* Value: **8 5** Durability: **7 8** Highway Control Rating: **7 8** Highway Safety: **7 6** ★★★

Brand	Year	Type	Length	Model	Chassis	Engine	Fuel Type	Price/Lin Ft	Wheelbase	Towing	GVWR	Curb Wt
Executive	1999	MHA	38	38PB FD op eng	RO	CU450	D	$7200	246	10,000	35,000	31,566

Livability Code: FT 30-90
Wheelbase-to-length ratio of 54% is considered ○ dangerous ○ fatiguing ◉ good ○ excellent*
The approximate net payload of 3434 pounds at 10% of GVWR on this model is ○ deficient ○ excessive ○ cautionary ◉ good ○ excellent*
Total highway safety penalties are: 2* Value: **8 5** Durability: **7 8** Highway Control Rating: **7 8** Highway Safety: **7 6** ★★★

Brand	Year	Type	Length	Model	Chassis	Engine	Fuel Type	Price/Lin Ft	Wheelbase	Towing	GVWR	Curb Wt
Executive	1999	MHA	38	38SB FD op eng	RO	CU450	D	$7200	246	10,000	35,000	31,566

Livability Code: FT 30-90
Wheelbase-to-length ratio of 54% is considered ○ dangerous ○ fatiguing ◉ good ○ excellent*
The approximate net payload of 3434 pounds at 10% of GVWR on this model is ○ deficient ○ excessive ○ cautionary ◉ good ○ excellent*
Total highway safety penalties are: 2* Value: **8 5** Durability: **7 8** Highway Control Rating: **7 8** Highway Safety: **7 6** ★★★

Brand	Year	Type	Length	Model	Chassis	Engine	Fuel Type	Price/Lin Ft	Wheelbase	Towing	GVWR	Curb Wt
Executive	1999	MHA	38	38PBS FD op eng	RO	CU450	D	$7200	246	10,000	35,000	32,466

Livability Code: FT 30-90
Wheelbase-to-length ratio of 54% is considered ○ dangerous ○ fatiguing ◉ good ○ excellent*
The approximate net payload of 2534 pounds at 7% of GVWR on this model is ○ deficient ○ excessive ◉ cautionary ○ good ○ excellent*
Total highway safety penalties are: 12* Value: **8 0** Durability: **7 8** Highway Control Rating: **5 5** Highway Safety: **4 3**

Note: Safety ratings are based on the assumption that the engineering of the RV has allowed for proper balance by placing fresh, gray, and black holding tanks in a location so as not to change the balance of the RV when the tanks are empty or full. **Always double-check wheelbase, GVWR, and weights at front and rear axles.**

*See Section 1 for details on how conclusions are reached.

Brand	Year	Type	Length	Model	Chassis	Engine	Fuel Type	Average Price per Linear Foot When New	Adjusted Wheelbase	Approx. Towing Capacity	Gross Vehicle Weight Rating	Average Curb Weight
Executive	1999	MHA	40	40CB FD	RO	CU350	D	$6900	270	10,000	35,000	31,780

Livability Code: FT 30-90 Wheelbase-to-length ratio of 56% is considered ○ dangerous ○ fatiguing ◉ good ○ excellent *
The approximate net payload of 3220 pounds at 9% of GVWR on this model is ○ deficient ○ excessive ◉ cautionary ○ good ○ excellent *
Total highway safety penalties are: 2 * Value: 8 5 Durability: 7 8 Highway Control Rating: 8 0 Highway Safety: 7 8 ★★★

Brand	Year	Type	Length	Model	Chassis	Engine	Fuel Type	Average Price per Linear Foot When New	Adjusted Wheelbase	Approx. Towing Capacity	Gross Vehicle Weight Rating	Average Curb Weight
Executive	1999	MHA	40	40CAPB FD	RO	CU350	D	$6900	270	10,000	35,000	31,440

Livability Code: FT 30-90 Wheelbase-to-length ratio of 56% is considered ○ dangerous ○ fatiguing ◉ good ○ excellent *
The approximate net payload of 3560 pounds at 10% of GVWR on this model is ○ deficient ○ excessive ○ cautionary ◉ good ○ excellent *
Total highway safety penalties are: 2 * Value: 8 5 Durability: 7 8 Highway Control Rating: 8 5 Highway Safety: 8 3 ★★★

Brand	Year	Type	Length	Model	Chassis	Engine	Fuel Type	Average Price per Linear Foot When New	Adjusted Wheelbase	Approx. Towing Capacity	Gross Vehicle Weight Rating	Average Curb Weight
Executive	1999	MHA	40	40 Suite Slide FD	RO	CU350	D	$6900	270	10,000	35,000	31,890

Livability Code: FT 30-90 Wheelbase-to-length ratio of 56% is considered ○ dangerous ○ fatiguing ◉ good ○ excellent *
The approximate net payload of 3110 pounds at 9% of GVWR on this model is ○ deficient ○ excessive ◉ cautionary ○ good ○ excellent *
Total highway safety penalties are: 12 * Value: 8 0 Durability: 7 8 Highway Control Rating: 8 0 Highway Safety: 6 8 ★★

Brand	Year	Type	Length	Model	Chassis	Engine	Fuel Type	Average Price per Linear Foot When New	Adjusted Wheelbase	Approx. Towing Capacity	Gross Vehicle Weight Rating	Average Curb Weight
Executive	1999	MHA	40	40PB FD	RO	CU350	D	$6900	270	10,000	35,000	31,780

Livability Code: FT 30-90 Wheelbase-to-length ratio of 56% is considered ○ dangerous ○ fatiguing ◉ good ○ excellent *
The approximate net payload of 3220 pounds at 9% of GVWR on this model is ○ deficient ○ excessive ◉ cautionary ○ good ○ excellent *
Total highway safety penalties are: 2 * Value: 8 5 Durability: 7 8 Highway Control Rating: 8 0 Highway Safety: 7 8 ★★★

Brand	Year	Type	Length	Model	Chassis	Engine	Fuel Type	Average Price per Linear Foot When New	Adjusted Wheelbase	Approx. Towing Capacity	Gross Vehicle Weight Rating	Average Curb Weight
Executive	1999	MHA	40	40CB FD op eng	RO	CU450	D	$6900	270	10,000	35,000	32,280

Livability Code: FT 30-90 Wheelbase-to-length ratio of 56% is considered ○ dangerous ○ fatiguing ◉ good ○ excellent *
The approximate net payload of 2720 pounds at 8% of GVWR on this model is ○ deficient ○ excessive ◉ cautionary ○ good ○ excellent *
Total highway safety penalties are: 2 * Value: 8 5 Durability: 7 8 Highway Control Rating: 7 4 Highway Safety: 7 2 ★★★

Brand	Year	Type	Length	Model	Chassis	Engine	Fuel Type	Average Price per Linear Foot When New	Adjusted Wheelbase	Approx. Towing Capacity	Gross Vehicle Weight Rating	Average Curb Weight
Executive	1999	MHA	40	40CAPB FD op eng	RO	CU450	D	$6900	270	10,000	35,000	32,280

Livability Code: FT 30-90 Wheelbase-to-length ratio of 56% is considered ○ dangerous ○ fatiguing ◉ good ○ excellent *
The approximate net payload of 2720 pounds at 8% of GVWR on this model is ○ deficient ○ excessive ◉ cautionary ○ good ○ excellent *
Total highway safety penalties are: 2 * Value: 8 5 Durability: 7 8 Highway Control Rating: 7 4 Highway Safety: 7 2 ★★★

Brand	Year	Type	Length	Model	Chassis	Engine	Fuel Type	Average Price per Linear Foot When New	Adjusted Wheelbase	Approx. Towing Capacity	Gross Vehicle Weight Rating	Average Curb Weight
Executive	1999	MHA	40	40 Suite Slide FD op	RO	CU450	D	$6900	270	10,000	35,000	33,180

Livability Code: FT 30-90 Wheelbase-to-length ratio of 56% is considered ○ dangerous ○ fatiguing ◉ good ○ excellent *
The approximate net payload of 1820 pounds at 5% of GVWR on this model is ◉ deficient ○ excessive ○ cautionary ○ good ○ excellent *
Total highway safety penalties are: 12 * Value: 8 0 Durability: 7 8 Highway Control Rating: 6 1 Highway Safety: 4 9

Brand	Year	Type	Length	Model	Chassis	Engine	Fuel Type	Average Price per Linear Foot When New	Adjusted Wheelbase	Approx. Towing Capacity	Gross Vehicle Weight Rating	Average Curb Weight
Executive	1999	MHA	40	40PB FD op eng	RO	CU450	D	$6900	270	10,000	35,000	32,280

Livability Code: FT 30-90 Wheelbase-to-length ratio of 56% is considered ○ dangerous ○ fatiguing ◉ good ○ excellent *
The approximate net payload of 2720 pounds at 8% of GVWR on this model is ○ deficient ○ excessive ◉ cautionary ○ good ○ excellent *
Total highway safety penalties are: 2 * Value: 8 5 Durability: 7 8 Highway Control Rating: 7 4 Highway Safety: 7 2 ★★★

Brand	Year	Type	Length	Model	Chassis	Engine	Fuel Type	Average Price per Linear Foot When New	Adjusted Wheelbase	Approx. Towing Capacity	Gross Vehicle Weight Rating	Average Curb Weight
Executive	1999	MHA	42	42 Suite Slide PLS	RO	CU450	D	$6500	285 T	10,000	45,000	38,501

Livability Code: FT 30-90 Wheelbase-to-length ratio of 56% is considered ○ dangerous ○ fatiguing ◉ good ○ excellent *
The approximate net payload of 6499 pounds at 14% of GVWR on this model is ○ deficient ○ excessive ○ cautionary ◉ good ○ excellent *
Total highway safety penalties are: 15 * Value: 7 9 Durability: 7 8 Highway Control Rating: 9 3 Highway Safety: 7 8 ★★★

Brand	Year	Type	Length	Model	Chassis	Engine	Fuel Type	Average Price per Linear Foot When New	Adjusted Wheelbase	Approx. Towing Capacity	Gross Vehicle Weight Rating	Average Curb Weight
Executive	1999	MHA	42	42PL	RO	CU450	D	$6500	285 T	10,000	45,000	37,601

Livability Code: FT 30-90 Wheelbase-to-length ratio of 56% is considered ○ dangerous ○ fatiguing ◉ good ○ excellent *
The approximate net payload of 7399 pounds at 16% of GVWR on this model is ○ deficient ○ excessive ○ cautionary ○ good ◉ excellent *
Total highway safety penalties are: 4 * Value: 8 4 Durability: 7 8 Highway Control Rating: 9 7 Highway Safety: 9 3 ★★★

Brand	Year	Type	Length	Model	Chassis	Engine	Fuel Type	Average Price per Linear Foot When New	Adjusted Wheelbase	Approx. Towing Capacity	Gross Vehicle Weight Rating	Average Curb Weight
Falcon	1990	MHB	19	190TBF	CH	5.7L	G	$2400	146	1,500	8,600	7,245

Livability Code: WE 40-80 Wheelbase-to-length ratio of 64% is considered ○ dangerous ○ fatiguing ○ good ◉ excellent *
The approximate net payload of 1355 pounds at 16% of GVWR on this model is ○ deficient ○ excessive ○ cautionary ○ good ◉ excellent *
Total highway safety penalties are: 2 * Value: 8 1 Durability: 7 9 Highway Control Rating: 1 0 0 Highway Safety: 9 8 ★★★

Brand	Year	Type	Length	Model	Chassis	Engine	Fuel Type	Average Price per Linear Foot When New	Adjusted Wheelbase	Approx. Towing Capacity	Gross Vehicle Weight Rating	Average Curb Weight
Falcon	1990	MHC	27	XT27SBF	FO	7.5L	G	$1500	176	1,500	11,000	10,586

Livability Code: WE 40-80 Wheelbase-to-length ratio of 54% is considered ○ dangerous ○ fatiguing ◉ good ○ excellent *
The approximate net payload of 414 pounds at 4% of GVWR on this model is ◉ deficient ○ excessive ○ cautionary ○ good ○ excellent *
Total highway safety penalties are: 2 * Value: 8 1 Durability: 7 9 Highway Control Rating: 4 9 Highway Safety: 4 7

Note: Safety ratings are based on the assumption that the engineering of the RV has allowed for proper balance by placing fresh, gray, and black holding tanks in a location so as not to change the balance of the RV when the tanks are empty or full. **Always double-check wheelbase, GVWR, and weights at front and rear axles.**

*See Section 1 for details on how conclusions are reached.

Brand	Year	Type	Length	Model	Chassis	Engine	Fuel Type	Average Price per Linear Foot When New	Adjusted Wheelbase	Approx. Towing Capacity	Gross Vehicle Weight Rating	Average Curb Weight

Falcon & Horizon — 1996 — MHB — 19 — 17 Chevrolet — CH — 5.7L — G — $1800 — 125 — 1,500 — 7,400 — 6,672
Livability Code: WE 40-80
Wheelbase-to-length ratio of 56% is considered ○ dangerous ○ fatiguing ◉ good ○ excellent *
The approximate net payload of 728 pounds at 10% of GVWR on this model is ○ deficient ○ excessive ○ cautionary ◉ good ○ excellent *
Total highway safety penalties are: 2 *   Value: **81**   Durability: **79**   Highway Control Rating: **84**   Highway Safety: **82**   ★★★

Falcon & Horizon — 1996 — MHB — 19 — 17 Dodge — DO — 5.9L — G — $1800 — 127 — 1,500 — 7,500 — 6,730
Livability Code: WE 40-80
Wheelbase-to-length ratio of 57% is considered ○ dangerous ○ fatiguing ◉ good ○ excellent *
The approximate net payload of 771 pounds at 10% of GVWR on this model is ○ deficient ○ excessive ○ cautionary ◉ good ○ excellent *
Total highway safety penalties are: 2 *   Value: **81**   Durability: **79**   Highway Control Rating: **88**   Highway Safety: **86**   ★★★

Falcon & Horizon — 1996 — MHB — 19 — 17 Ford — FO — 5.8L — G — $1800 — 138 — 1,500 — 7,500 — 6,942
Livability Code: WE 40-80
Wheelbase-to-length ratio of 62% is considered ○ dangerous ○ fatiguing ○ good ◉ excellent *
The approximate net payload of 558 pounds at 7% of GVWR on this model is ○ deficient ○ excessive ◉ cautionary ○ good ○ excellent *
Total highway safety penalties are: 2 *   Value: **81**   Durability: **79**   Highway Control Rating: **88**   Highway Safety: **86**   ★★★

Falcon & Horizon — 1996 — MHB — 20 — 19 Chevrolet — CH — 5.7L — G — $2000 — 146 — 1,500 — 8,600 — 7,563
Livability Code: WE 40-80
Wheelbase-to-length ratio of 61% is considered ○ dangerous ○ fatiguing ○ good ◉ excellent *
The approximate net payload of 1038 pounds at 12% of GVWR on this model is ○ deficient ○ excessive ○ cautionary ◉ good ○ excellent *
Total highway safety penalties are: 2 *   Value: **81**   Durability: **79**   Highway Control Rating: **100**   Highway Safety: **98**   ★★★

Falcon & Horizon — 1996 — MHB — 20 — 19 Dodge — DO — 5.9L — G — $2000 — 127 — 1,500 — 8,510 — 7,320
Livability Code: WE 40-80
Wheelbase-to-length ratio of 53% is considered ○ dangerous ◉ fatiguing ○ good ○ excellent *
The approximate net payload of 1191 pounds at 14% of GVWR on this model is ○ deficient ○ excessive ○ cautionary ◉ good ○ excellent *
Total highway safety penalties are: 2 *   Value: **81**   Durability: **79**   Highway Control Rating: **76**   Highway Safety: **74**   ★★★

Falcon & Horizon — 1996 — MHB — 20 — 19 Ford — FO — 5.8L — G — $2000 — 138 — 1,500 — 8,550 — 7,578
Livability Code: WE 40-80
Wheelbase-to-length ratio of 58% is considered ○ dangerous ○ fatiguing ○ good ◉ excellent *
The approximate net payload of 973 pounds at 11% of GVWR on this model is ○ deficient ○ excessive ○ cautionary ◉ good ○ excellent *
Total highway safety penalties are: 2 *   Value: **81**   Durability: **79**   Highway Control Rating: **92**   Highway Safety: **90**   ★★★

Falcon Ultra — 1990 — MHB — 19 — 190SLF — FO — 5.8L — G — $1700 — 138 — 1,500 — 8,100 — 7,157
Livability Code: WE 40-80
Wheelbase-to-length ratio of 61% is considered ○ dangerous ○ fatiguing ○ good ◉ excellent *
The approximate net payload of 943 pounds at 12% of GVWR on this model is ○ deficient ○ excessive ○ cautionary ◉ good ○ excellent *
Total highway safety penalties are: 2 *   Value: **81**   Durability: **79**   Highway Control Rating: **100**   Highway Safety: **98**   ★★★

Foretravel — 1990 — MHA — 36 — 3600 U280 SBID — UN — Ca — D — $7000 — 228 — 1,500 e — 28,000 — 23,331
Livability Code: FT 30-90
Wheelbase-to-length ratio of 53% is considered ○ dangerous ◉ fatiguing ○ good ○ excellent *
The approximate net payload of 4669 pounds at 17% of GVWR on this model is ○ deficient ○ excessive ○ cautionary ○ good ◉ excellent *
Total highway safety penalties are: 2 *   Value: **86**   Durability: **81**   Highway Control Rating: **70**   Highway Safety: **68**   ★★

Foretravel — 1990 — MHA — 36 — 3600 SBID — OS — De — D — $4300 — 228 — 1,500 e — 20,500 — 19,069
Livability Code: FT 30-90
Wheelbase-to-length ratio of 52% is considered ○ dangerous ◉ fatiguing ○ good ○ excellent *
The approximate net payload of 1431 pounds at 7% of GVWR on this model is ○ deficient ○ excessive ◉ cautionary ○ good ○ excellent *
Total highway safety penalties are: 2 *   Value: **86**   Durability: **81**   Highway Control Rating: **32**   Highway Safety: **30**

Foretravel — 1990 — MHA — 40 — 4000 U300 SAI — UN — De — D — $7600 — 276 — 1,500 e — 30,000 — 25,660
Livability Code: FT 30-90
Wheelbase-to-length ratio of 58% is considered ○ dangerous ○ fatiguing ○ good ◉ excellent *
The approximate net payload of 4341 pounds at 14% of GVWR on this model is ○ deficient ○ excessive ○ cautionary ◉ good ○ excellent *
Total highway safety penalties are: 2 *   Value: **86**   Durability: **81**   Highway Control Rating: **98**   Highway Safety: **96**   ★★★★

Foretravel — 1991 — MHA — 36 — 3600 U-300 SAI — UN — Det — D — $8200 — 228 — 1,500 e — 30,000 — 24,331
Livability Code: FT 30-90
Wheelbase-to-length ratio of 53% is considered ○ dangerous ◉ fatiguing ○ good ○ excellent *
The approximate net payload of 5669 pounds at 19% of GVWR on this model is ○ deficient ○ excessive ○ cautionary ○ good ◉ excellent *
Total highway safety penalties are: 2 *   Value: **86**   Durability: **81**   Highway Control Rating: **72**   Highway Safety: **70**   ★★★

Foretravel — 1991 — MHA — 36 — 3600 U-300 SBI — UN — Det — D — $8200 — 228 — 1,500 e — 30,000 — 24,331
Livability Code: FT 30-90
Wheelbase-to-length ratio of 53% is considered ○ dangerous ◉ fatiguing ○ good ○ excellent *
The approximate net payload of 5669 pounds at 19% of GVWR on this model is ○ deficient ○ excessive ○ cautionary ○ good ◉ excellent *
Total highway safety penalties are: 2 *   Value: **86**   Durability: **81**   Highway Control Rating: **72**   Highway Safety: **70**   ★★★

Note: Safety ratings are based on the assumption that the engineering of the RV has allowed for proper balance by placing fresh, gray, and black holding tanks in a location so as not to change the balance of the RV when the tanks are empty or full. **Always double-check wheelbase, GVWR, and weights at front and rear axles.**

*See Section 1 for details on how conclusions are reached.

Brand	Year	Type	Length	Model	Chassis	Engine	Fuel Type	Average Price per Linear Foot When New	Adjusted Wheelbase	Approx. Towing Capacity	Gross Vehicle Weight Rating	Average Curb Weight
Foretravel	1991	MHA	36	3600 U-300 SBID	UN	Det	D	$8200	228	1,500 e	30,000	24,331

Livability Code: FT 30-90
Wheelbase-to-length ratio of 53% is considered ○ dangerous ◉ fatiguing ○ good ○ excellent *
The approximate net payload of 5669 pounds at 19% of GVWR on this model is ○ deficient ○ excessive ○ cautionary ○ good ◉ excellent *
Total highway safety penalties are: 2 * Value: **8 6** Durability: **8 1** Highway Control Rating: **7 2** Highway Safety: **7 0** ★★★

Brand	Year	Type	Length	Model	Chassis	Engine	Fuel Type	Price/ft	Wheelbase	Towing	GVWR	Curb Weight
Foretravel	1991	MHA	36	3600 U-280 SAI	UN	Ca	D	$7100	228	1,500 e	28,000	23,331

Livability Code: FT 30-90
Wheelbase-to-length ratio of 53% is considered ○ dangerous ◉ fatiguing ○ good ○ excellent *
The approximate net payload of 4669 pounds at 17% of GVWR on this model is ○ deficient ○ excessive ○ cautionary ○ good ◉ excellent *
Total highway safety penalties are: 2 * Value: **8 6** Durability: **8 1** Highway Control Rating: **7 0** Highway Safety: **6 8** ★★

Foretravel	1991	MHA	36	3600 U-280 SBI	UN	Ca	D	$7100	228	1,500 e	28,000	23,331

Livability Code: FT 30-90
Wheelbase-to-length ratio of 53% is considered ○ dangerous ◉ fatiguing ○ good ○ excellent *
The approximate net payload of 4669 pounds at 17% of GVWR on this model is ○ deficient ○ excessive ○ cautionary ○ good ◉ excellent *
Total highway safety penalties are: 2 * Value: **8 6** Durability: **8 1** Highway Control Rating: **7 0** Highway Safety: **6 8** ★★

Foretravel	1991	MHA	36	3600 U-280 SBID	UN	Ca	D	$7100	228	1,500 e	28,000	23,331

Livability Code: FT 30-90
Wheelbase-to-length ratio of 53% is considered ○ dangerous ◉ fatiguing ○ good ○ excellent *
The approximate net payload of 4669 pounds at 17% of GVWR on this model is ○ deficient ○ excessive ○ cautionary ○ good ◉ excellent *
Total highway safety penalties are: 2 * Value: **8 6** Durability: **8 1** Highway Control Rating: **7 0** Highway Safety: **6 8** ★★

Foretravel	1991	MHA	36	3600 U-240 SB	UN	Ca	D	$5000	228	1,500 e	24,000	21,331

Livability Code: FT 30-90
Wheelbase-to-length ratio of 53% is considered ○ dangerous ◉ fatiguing ○ good ○ excellent *
The approximate net payload of 2669 pounds at 11% of GVWR on this model is ○ deficient ○ excessive ○ cautionary ◉ good ○ excellent *
Total highway safety penalties are: 2 * Value: **8 6** Durability: **8 1** Highway Control Rating: **6 0** Highway Safety: **5 8** ★

Foretravel	1991	MHA	36	3600 U-240 SBI	UN	Cat320	D	$5000	228	1,500 e	24,000	21,331

Livability Code: FT 30-90
Wheelbase-to-length ratio of 53% is considered ○ dangerous ◉ fatiguing ○ good ○ excellent *
The approximate net payload of 2669 pounds at 11% of GVWR on this model is ○ deficient ○ excessive ○ cautionary ◉ good ○ excellent *
Total highway safety penalties are: 2 * Value: **8 6** Durability: **8 1** Highway Control Rating: **6 0** Highway Safety: **5 8** ★

Foretravel	1991	MHA	36	3600 U-240 SBID	UN	Ca	D	$5000	228	1,500 e	24,000	21,331

Livability Code: FT 30-90
Wheelbase-to-length ratio of 53% is considered ○ dangerous ◉ fatiguing ○ good ○ excellent *
The approximate net payload of 2669 pounds at 11% of GVWR on this model is ○ deficient ○ excessive ○ cautionary ◉ good ○ excellent *
Total highway safety penalties are: 2 * Value: **8 6** Durability: **8 1** Highway Control Rating: **6 0** Highway Safety: **5 8** ★

Foretravel	1991	MHA	36	3600 SBID	OS	Cum	D	$4100	228	1,500 e	22,500	20,384

Livability Code: FT 30-90
Wheelbase-to-length ratio of 52% is considered ○ dangerous ◉ fatiguing ○ good ○ excellent *
The approximate net payload of 2116 pounds at 9% of GVWR on this model is ○ deficient ○ excessive ◉ cautionary ○ good ○ excellent *
Total highway safety penalties are: 2 * Value: **8 6** Durability: **8 1** Highway Control Rating: **4 4** Highway Safety: **4 2**

Foretravel	1991	MHA	36	3600 U225 SBI	UN	Cu5.9L	D	$4900	228	1,500 e	22,500	20,226

Livability Code: FT 30-90
Wheelbase-to-length ratio of 52% is considered ○ dangerous ◉ fatiguing ○ good ○ excellent *
The approximate net payload of 2274 pounds at 10% of GVWR on this model is ○ deficient ○ excessive ○ cautionary ◉ good ○ excellent *
Total highway safety penalties are: 2 * Value: **8 6** Durability: **8 1** Highway Control Rating: **4 9** Highway Safety: **4 7**

Foretravel	1991	MHA	40	4000 U-300 SAI	UN	Det	D	$7800	276	1,500 e	30,000	25,660

Livability Code: FT 30-90
Wheelbase-to-length ratio of 58% is considered ○ dangerous ○ fatiguing ○ good ◉ excellent *
The approximate net payload of 4341 pounds at 14% of GVWR on this model is ○ deficient ○ excessive ○ cautionary ◉ good ○ excellent *
Total highway safety penalties are: 2 * Value: **8 6** Durability: **8 1** Highway Control Rating: **9 8** Highway Safety: **9 6** ★★★★

Foretravel	1991	MHA	40	4000 U-300 SBID	UN	Det	D	$7800	276	1,500 e	30,000	25,368

Livability Code: FT 30-90
Wheelbase-to-length ratio of 58% is considered ○ dangerous ○ fatiguing ○ good ◉ excellent *
The approximate net payload of 4632 pounds at 15% of GVWR on this model is ○ deficient ○ excessive ○ cautionary ◉ good ○ excellent *
Total highway safety penalties are: 2 * Value: **8 6** Durability: **8 1** Highway Control Rating: **1 0 0** Highway Safety: **9 8** ★★★★

Foretravel	1991	MHA	40	4000 U-280 SBID	UN	Ca	D	$7000	276	1,500 e	28,000	24,368

Livability Code: FT 30-90
Wheelbase-to-length ratio of 58% is considered ○ dangerous ○ fatiguing ○ good ◉ excellent *
The approximate net payload of 3632 pounds at 13% of GVWR on this model is ○ deficient ○ excessive ○ cautionary ◉ good ○ excellent *
Total highway safety penalties are: 2 * Value: **8 6** Durability: **8 1** Highway Control Rating: **9 5** Highway Safety: **9 3** ★★★★

Note: Safety ratings are based on the assumption that the engineering of the RV has allowed for proper balance by placing fresh, gray, and black holding tanks in a location so as not to change the balance of the RV when the tanks are empty or full. **Always double-check wheelbase, GVWR, and weights at front and rear axles.**

*See Section 1 for details on how conclusions are reached.

Section 2: The Ratings

Brand	Year	Type	Length	Model	Chassis	Engine	Fuel Type	Average Price per Linear Foot When New	Adjusted Wheelbase	Approx. Towing Capacity	Gross Vehicle Weight Rating	Average Curb Weight
Foretravel	1991	MHA	40	4000 U-280 SAI	UN	Ca	D	$7000	276	1,500 e	28,000	24,368

Livability Code: FT 30-90
Wheelbase-to-length ratio of 58% is considered ○ dangerous ○ fatiguing ○ good ◉ excellent *
The approximate net payload of 3632 pounds at 13% of GVWR on this model is ○ deficient ○ excessive ○ cautionary ◉ good ○ excellent *
Total highway safety penalties are: 2 * Value: 8 6 Durability: 8 1 Highway Control Rating: 9 5 Highway Safety: 9 3 ★★★★

| Foretravel | 1992 | MHA | 29 | 2900 SBI Gas | OS | 7.5L | G | $3800 | 190 | 9,000 | 16,000 | 15,517 |

Livability Code: FT 30-90
Wheelbase-to-length ratio of 55% is considered ○ dangerous ○ fatiguing ◉ good ○ excellent *
The approximate net payload of 483 pounds at 3% of GVWR on this model is ◉ deficient ○ excessive ○ cautionary ○ good ○ excellent *
Total highway safety penalties are: 2 * Value: 8 6 Durability: 8 1 Highway Control Rating: 5 3 Highway Safety: 5 1 ★

| Foretravel | 1992 | MHA | 29 | 2900 RB Gas | OS | 7.5L | G | $3800 | 190 | 9,000 | 16,000 | 15,517 |

Livability Code: FT 30-90
Wheelbase-to-length ratio of 55% is considered ○ dangerous ○ fatiguing ◉ good ○ excellent *
The approximate net payload of 483 pounds at 3% of GVWR on this model is ◉ deficient ○ excessive ○ cautionary ○ good ○ excellent *
Total highway safety penalties are: 2 * Value: 8 6 Durability: 8 1 Highway Control Rating: 5 3 Highway Safety: 5 1 ★

| Foretravel | 1992 | MHA | 29 | 2900 SBI Desl | OS | Cu5.9L | D | $4000 | 190 | 2,000 | 18,000 | 16,517 |

Livability Code: FT 30-90
Wheelbase-to-length ratio of 55% is considered ○ dangerous ○ fatiguing ◉ good ○ excellent *
The approximate net payload of 1483 pounds at 8% of GVWR on this model is ○ deficient ○ excessive ◉ cautionary ○ good ○ excellent *
Total highway safety penalties are: 2 * Value: 8 6 Durability: 8 1 Highway Control Rating: 6 8 Highway Safety: 6 6 ★★

| Foretravel | 1992 | MHA | 29 | 2900 RB Desl | OS | Cu5.9L | D | $4000 | 190 | 2,000 | 18,000 | 16,517 |

Livability Code: FT 30-90
Wheelbase-to-length ratio of 55% is considered ○ dangerous ○ fatiguing ◉ good ○ excellent *
The approximate net payload of 1483 pounds at 8% of GVWR on this model is ○ deficient ○ excessive ◉ cautionary ○ good ○ excellent *
Total highway safety penalties are: 2 * Value: 8 6 Durability: 8 1 Highway Control Rating: 6 8 Highway Safety: 6 6 ★★

| Foretravel | 1992 | MHA | 30 | 3000 SB Gas | OS | 7.5L | G | $3700 | 190 | 9,000 | 16,000 | 15,776 |

Livability Code: FT 30-90
Wheelbase-to-length ratio of 53% is considered ○ dangerous ◉ fatiguing ○ good ○ excellent *
The approximate net payload of 224 pounds at 1% of GVWR on this model is ◉ deficient ○ excessive ○ cautionary ○ good ○ excellent *
Total highway safety penalties are: 2 * Value: 8 6 Durability: 8 1 Highway Control Rating: 3 0 Highway Safety: 2 8

| Foretravel | 1992 | MHA | 30 | 3000 SB Desl | OS | Cu5.9L | D | $3900 | 190 | 2,000 | 18,000 | 16,776 |

Livability Code: FT 30-90
Wheelbase-to-length ratio of 53% is considered ○ dangerous ◉ fatiguing ○ good ○ excellent *
The approximate net payload of 1224 pounds at 7% of GVWR on this model is ○ deficient ○ excessive ◉ cautionary ○ good ○ excellent *
Total highway safety penalties are: 2 * Value: 8 6 Durability: 8 1 Highway Control Rating: 4 1 Highway Safety: 3 9

| Foretravel | 1992 | MHA | 33 | 3300 SBI Gas | OS | 7.5L | G | $3800 | 208 | 7,000 | 18,000 | 17,554 |

Livability Code: FT 30-90
Wheelbase-to-length ratio of 53% is considered ○ dangerous ◉ fatiguing ○ good ○ excellent *
The approximate net payload of 446 pounds at 2% of GVWR on this model is ◉ deficient ○ excessive ○ cautionary ○ good ○ excellent *
Total highway safety penalties are: 2 * Value: 8 6 Durability: 8 1 Highway Control Rating: 3 0 Highway Safety: 2 8

| Foretravel | 1992 | MHA | 33 | 3300 RB Gas | OS | 7.5L | G | $3800 | 208 | 7,000 | 18,000 | 17,554 |

Livability Code: FT 30-90
Wheelbase-to-length ratio of 53% is considered ○ dangerous ◉ fatiguing ○ good ○ excellent *
The approximate net payload of 446 pounds at 2% of GVWR on this model is ◉ deficient ○ excessive ○ cautionary ○ good ○ excellent *
Total highway safety penalties are: 2 * Value: 8 6 Durability: 8 1 Highway Control Rating: 3 0 Highway Safety: 2 8

| Foretravel | 1992 | MHA | 33 | 3300 SBI Desl | OS | Cu5.9L | D | $4000 | 208 | 2,000 | 18,000 | 17,554 |

Livability Code: FT 30-90
Wheelbase-to-length ratio of 53% is considered ○ dangerous ◉ fatiguing ○ good ○ excellent *
The approximate net payload of 446 pounds at 2% of GVWR on this model is ◉ deficient ○ excessive ○ cautionary ○ good ○ excellent *
Total highway safety penalties are: 2 * Value: 8 6 Durability: 8 1 Highway Control Rating: 3 0 Highway Safety: 2 8

| Foretravel | 1992 | MHA | 33 | 3300 RB Desl | OS | Cu5.9L | D | $4000 | 208 | 2,000 | 18,000 | 17,554 |

Livability Code: FT 30-90
Wheelbase-to-length ratio of 53% is considered ○ dangerous ◉ fatiguing ○ good ○ excellent *
The approximate net payload of 446 pounds at 2% of GVWR on this model is ◉ deficient ○ excessive ○ cautionary ○ good ○ excellent *
Total highway safety penalties are: 2 * Value: 8 6 Durability: 8 1 Highway Control Rating: 3 0 Highway Safety: 2 8

| Foretravel | 1992 | MHA | 34 | 3400 SBI | OS | Cu8.3L | D | $4900 | 204 | 4,000 | 22,500 | 20,063 |

Livability Code: FT 30-90
Wheelbase-to-length ratio of 50% is considered ◉ dangerous ○ fatiguing ○ good ○ excellent *
The approximate net payload of 2437 pounds at 11% of GVWR on this model is ○ deficient ○ excessive ○ cautionary ◉ good ○ excellent *
Total highway safety penalties are: 2 * Value: 8 6 Durability: 8 1 Highway Control Rating: 3 5 Highway Safety: 3 3

Note: Safety ratings are based on the assumption that the engineering of the RV has allowed for proper balance by placing fresh, gray, and black holding tanks in a location so as not to change the balance of the RV when the tanks are empty or full. **Always double-check wheelbase, GVWR, and weights at front and rear axles.**

*See Section 1 for details on how conclusions are reached.

Brand	Year	Type	Length	Model	Chassis	Engine	Fuel Type	Average Price per Linear Foot When New	Adjusted Wheelbase	Approx. Towing Capacity	Gross Vehicle Weight Rating	Average Curb Weight
Foretravel	1992	MHA	36	3600 SBID	OS	Cu8.3L	D	$4600	228	4,000	22,500	20,581

Livability Code: FT 30-90   Wheelbase-to-length ratio of 53% is considered ○ dangerous ● fatiguing ○ good ○ excellent *

The approximate net payload of 1919 pounds at 9% of GVWR on this model is ○ deficient ○ excessive ● cautionary ○ good ○ excellent *

Total highway safety penalties are: 2 *   Value: 86   Durability: 81   Highway Control Rating: 52   Highway Safety: 50   ★

Brand	Year	Type	Length	Model	Chassis	Engine	Fuel Type					
Foretravel	1992	MHA	36	3600 SBI	OS	Cu8.3L	D	$4600	228	4,000	22,500	20,581

Livability Code: FT 30-90   Wheelbase-to-length ratio of 53% is considered ○ dangerous ● fatiguing ○ good ○ excellent *

The approximate net payload of 1919 pounds at 9% of GVWR on this model is ○ deficient ○ excessive ● cautionary ○ good ○ excellent *

Total highway safety penalties are: 2 *   Value: 86   Durability: 81   Highway Control Rating: 52   Highway Safety: 50   ★

Foretravel	1992	MHA	36	3600 U225 SBID	UN	Cu5.9L	D	$5100	228	1,500	22,500	20,581

Livability Code: FT 30-90   Wheelbase-to-length ratio of 53% is considered ○ dangerous ● fatiguing ○ good ○ excellent *

The approximate net payload of 1919 pounds at 9% of GVWR on this model is ○ deficient ○ excessive ● cautionary ○ good ○ excellent *

Total highway safety penalties are: 2 *   Value: 86   Durability: 81   Highway Control Rating: 52   Highway Safety: 50   ★

Foretravel	1992	MHA	36	3600 U225 SBI	UN	Cu5.9L	D	$5100	228	1,500	22,500	20,581

Livability Code: FT 30-90   Wheelbase-to-length ratio of 53% is considered ○ dangerous ● fatiguing ○ good ○ excellent *

The approximate net payload of 1919 pounds at 9% of GVWR on this model is ○ deficient ○ excessive ● cautionary ○ good ○ excellent *

Total highway safety penalties are: 2 *   Value: 86   Durability: 81   Highway Control Rating: 52   Highway Safety: 50   ★

Foretravel	1992	MHA	36	3600 U240 SBID	UN	Ca	D	$5400	228	2,500	24,000	21,331

Livability Code: FT 30-90   Wheelbase-to-length ratio of 53% is considered ○ dangerous ● fatiguing ○ good ○ excellent *

The approximate net payload of 2669 pounds at 11% of GVWR on this model is ○ deficient ○ excessive ○ cautionary ● good ○ excellent *

Total highway safety penalties are: 2 *   Value: 86   Durability: 81   Highway Control Rating: 60   Highway Safety: 58   ★

Foretravel	1992	MHA	36	3600 U240 SBI	UN	Ca	D	$5400	228	2,500	24,000	21,331

Livability Code: FT 30-90   Wheelbase-to-length ratio of 53% is considered ○ dangerous ● fatiguing ○ good ○ excellent *

The approximate net payload of 2669 pounds at 11% of GVWR on this model is ○ deficient ○ excessive ○ cautionary ● good ○ excellent *

Total highway safety penalties are: 2 *   Value: 86   Durability: 81   Highway Control Rating: 60   Highway Safety: 58   ★

Foretravel	1992	MHA	36	3600 U300 SBI	UN	De	D	$8300	228	6,000	30,000	24,331

Livability Code: FT 30-90   Wheelbase-to-length ratio of 53% is considered ○ dangerous ● fatiguing ○ good ○ excellent *

The approximate net payload of 5669 pounds at 19% of GVWR on this model is ○ deficient ○ excessive ○ cautionary ○ good ● excellent *

Total highway safety penalties are: 2 *   Value: 86   Durability: 81   Highway Control Rating: 72   Highway Safety: 70   ★★★

Foretravel	1992	MHA	36	3600 U280 SBI	UN	Cu8.3L	D	$7200	228	1,500 e	28,000	23,331

Livability Code: FT 30-90   Wheelbase-to-length ratio of 53% is considered ○ dangerous ● fatiguing ○ good ○ excellent *

The approximate net payload of 4669 pounds at 17% of GVWR on this model is ○ deficient ○ excessive ○ cautionary ○ good ● excellent *

Total highway safety penalties are: 2 *   Value: 86   Durability: 81   Highway Control Rating: 70   Highway Safety: 68   ★★

Foretravel	1992	MHA	38	3800 U300 SBI	UN	De	D	$8100	252	6,000	30,000	24,850

Livability Code: FT 30-90   Wheelbase-to-length ratio of 55% is considered ○ dangerous ○ fatiguing ● good ○ excellent *

The approximate net payload of 5150 pounds at 17% of GVWR on this model is ○ deficient ○ excessive ○ cautionary ○ good ● excellent *

Total highway safety penalties are: 2 *   Value: 86   Durability: 81   Highway Control Rating: 95   Highway Safety: 93   ★★★★

Foretravel	1992	MHA	38	3800 U280 SBI	UN	Cu8.3L	D	$7100	252	1,500 e	28,000	23,850

Livability Code: FT 30-90   Wheelbase-to-length ratio of 55% is considered ○ dangerous ○ fatiguing ● good ○ excellent *

The approximate net payload of 4150 pounds at 15% of GVWR on this model is ○ deficient ○ excessive ○ cautionary ● good ○ excellent *

Total highway safety penalties are: 2 *   Value: 86   Durability: 81   Highway Control Rating: 91   Highway Safety: 89   ★★★★

Foretravel	1992	MHA	40	4000 U300 WTBI	UN	De	D	$7900	276	6,000	30,000	25,368

Livability Code: FT 30-90   Wheelbase-to-length ratio of 58% is considered ○ dangerous ○ fatiguing ○ good ● excellent *

The approximate net payload of 4632 pounds at 15% of GVWR on this model is ○ deficient ○ excessive ○ cautionary ○ good ● excellent *

Total highway safety penalties are: 2 *   Value: 86   Durability: 81   Highway Control Rating: 100   Highway Safety: 98   ★★★★

Foretravel	1992	MHA	40	4000 U300 SBI	UN	De	D	$7900	276	6,000	30,000	25,368

Livability Code: FT 30-90   Wheelbase-to-length ratio of 58% is considered ○ dangerous ○ fatiguing ○ good ● excellent *

The approximate net payload of 4632 pounds at 15% of GVWR on this model is ○ deficient ○ excessive ○ cautionary ○ good ● excellent *

Total highway safety penalties are: 2 *   Value: 86   Durability: 81   Highway Control Rating: 100   Highway Safety: 98   ★★★★

Note: Safety ratings are based on the assumption that the engineering of the RV has allowed for proper balance by placing fresh, gray, and black holding tanks in a location so as not to change the balance of the RV when the tanks are empty or full. **Always double-check wheelbase, GVWR, and weights at front and rear axles.**

*See Section 1 for details on how conclusions are reached.

Section 2: The Ratings

Brand	Year	Type	Length	Model	Chassis	Engine	Fuel Type	Average Price per Linear Foot When New	Adjusted Wheelbase	Approx. Towing Capacity	Gross Vehicle Weight Rating	Average Curb Weight

Foretravel **1992** MHA 40 4000 U300 SBID UN De D $7900 276 6,000 30,000 25,368
Livability Code: FT 30-90   Wheelbase-to-length ratio of 58% is considered ○ dangerous ○ fatiguing ○ good ◉ excellent *
The approximate net payload of 4632 pounds at 15% of GVWR on this model is ○ deficient ○ excessive ○ cautionary ◉ good ○ excellent *
Total highway safety penalties are: 2 *   Value: 86   Durability: 81   Highway Control Rating: 100   Highway Safety: 98   ★★★★

Foretravel **1992** MHA 40 4000 U300 SAI UN De D $7900 276 6,000 30,000 25,368
Livability Code: FT 30-90   Wheelbase-to-length ratio of 58% is considered ○ dangerous ○ fatiguing ○ good ◉ excellent *
The approximate net payload of 4632 pounds at 15% of GVWR on this model is ○ deficient ○ excessive ○ cautionary ◉ good ○ excellent *
Total highway safety penalties are: 2 *   Value: 86   Durability: 81   Highway Control Rating: 100   Highway Safety: 98   ★★★★

Foretravel **1992** MHA 40 4000 U280 WTBI UN Cu8.3L D $7100 276 1,500 e 28,000 24,368
Livability Code: FT 30-90   Wheelbase-to-length ratio of 58% is considered ○ dangerous ○ fatiguing ○ good ◉ excellent *
The approximate net payload of 3632 pounds at 13% of GVWR on this model is ○ deficient ○ excessive ○ cautionary ◉ good ○ excellent *
Total highway safety penalties are: 2 *   Value: 86   Durability: 81   Highway Control Rating: 95   Highway Safety: 93   ★★★★

Foretravel **1992** MHA 40 4000 U280 SBI UN Cu8.3L D $7100 276 1,500 e 28,000 24,368
Livability Code: FT 30-90   Wheelbase-to-length ratio of 58% is considered ○ dangerous ○ fatiguing ○ good ◉ excellent *
The approximate net payload of 3632 pounds at 13% of GVWR on this model is ○ deficient ○ excessive ○ cautionary ◉ good ○ excellent *
Total highway safety penalties are: 2 *   Value: 86   Durability: 81   Highway Control Rating: 95   Highway Safety: 93   ★★★★

Foretravel **1992** MHA 40 4000 U280 SBID UN Cu8.3L D $7100 276 1,500 e 28,000 24,368
Livability Code: FT 30-90   Wheelbase-to-length ratio of 58% is considered ○ dangerous ○ fatiguing ○ good ◉ excellent *
The approximate net payload of 3632 pounds at 13% of GVWR on this model is ○ deficient ○ excessive ○ cautionary ◉ good ○ excellent *
Total highway safety penalties are: 2 *   Value: 86   Durability: 81   Highway Control Rating: 95   Highway Safety: 93   ★★★★

Foretravel **1992** MHA 40 4000 U280 SAI UN Cu8.3L D $7100 276 1,500 e 28,000 24,368
Livability Code: FT 30-90   Wheelbase-to-length ratio of 58% is considered ○ dangerous ○ fatiguing ○ good ◉ excellent *
The approximate net payload of 3632 pounds at 13% of GVWR on this model is ○ deficient ○ excessive ○ cautionary ◉ good ○ excellent *
Total highway safety penalties are: 2 *   Value: 86   Durability: 81   Highway Control Rating: 95   Highway Safety: 93   ★★★★

Foretravel **1994** MHA 36 3600 U225 SBID UN Cu5.9L D $5400 228 1,500 22,500 21,532
Livability Code: FT 30-90   Wheelbase-to-length ratio of 53% is considered ○ dangerous ◉ fatiguing ○ good ○ excellent *
The approximate net payload of 968 pounds at 4% of GVWR on this model is ◉ deficient ○ excessive ○ cautionary ○ good ○ excellent *
Total highway safety penalties are: 2 *   Value: 86   Durability: 81   Highway Control Rating: 33   Highway Safety: 31

Foretravel **1994** MHA 36 3600 U225 SBI UN Cu5.9L D $5400 228 1,500 22,500 21,532
Livability Code: FT 30-90   Wheelbase-to-length ratio of 53% is considered ○ dangerous ◉ fatiguing ○ good ○ excellent *
The approximate net payload of 968 pounds at 4% of GVWR on this model is ◉ deficient ○ excessive ○ cautionary ○ good ○ excellent *
Total highway safety penalties are: 2 *   Value: 86   Durability: 81   Highway Control Rating: 33   Highway Safety: 31

Foretravel **1994** MHA 36 3600 U225 WTBI UN Cu5.9L D $5400 228 1,500 22,500 21,532
Livability Code: FT 30-90   Wheelbase-to-length ratio of 53% is considered ○ dangerous ◉ fatiguing ○ good ○ excellent *
The approximate net payload of 968 pounds at 4% of GVWR on this model is ◉ deficient ○ excessive ○ cautionary ○ good ○ excellent *
Total highway safety penalties are: 2 *   Value: 86   Durability: 81   Highway Control Rating: 33   Highway Safety: 31

Foretravel **1994** MHA 36 3600 U240 SBID UN Cat D $5700 228 2,500 24,000 22,282
Livability Code: FT 30-90   Wheelbase-to-length ratio of 53% is considered ○ dangerous ◉ fatiguing ○ good ○ excellent *
The approximate net payload of 1718 pounds at 7% of GVWR on this model is ○ deficient ○ excessive ◉ cautionary ○ good ○ excellent *
Total highway safety penalties are: 2 *   Value: 86   Durability: 81   Highway Control Rating: 41   Highway Safety: 39

Foretravel **1994** MHA 36 3600 U240 SBI UN Cat D $5700 228 2,500 24,000 22,282
Livability Code: FT 30-90   Wheelbase-to-length ratio of 53% is considered ○ dangerous ◉ fatiguing ○ good ○ excellent *
The approximate net payload of 1718 pounds at 7% of GVWR on this model is ○ deficient ○ excessive ◉ cautionary ○ good ○ excellent *
Total highway safety penalties are: 2 *   Value: 86   Durability: 81   Highway Control Rating: 41   Highway Safety: 39

Foretravel **1994** MHA 36 3600 U240 WTBI UN Cat D $5700 228 2,500 24,000 22,282
Livability Code: FT 30-90   Wheelbase-to-length ratio of 53% is considered ○ dangerous ◉ fatiguing ○ good ○ excellent *
The approximate net payload of 1718 pounds at 7% of GVWR on this model is ○ deficient ○ excessive ◉ cautionary ○ good ○ excellent *
Total highway safety penalties are: 2 *   Value: 86   Durability: 81   Highway Control Rating: 41   Highway Safety: 39

Note: Safety ratings are based on the assumption that the engineering of the RV has allowed for proper balance by placing fresh, gray, and black holding tanks in a location so as not to change the balance of the RV when the tanks are empty or full. **Always double-check wheelbase, GVWR, and weights at front and rear axles.**

*See Section 1 for details on how conclusions are reached.

Brand	Year	Type	Length	Model	Chassis	Engine	Fuel Type	Average Price per Linear Foot When New	Adjusted Wheel-base	Approx. Towing Capacity	Gross Vehicle Weight Rating	Average Curb Weight

Foretravel 1994 MHA 36 3600 U280 SBID UN Cum D $7700 228 1,500 e 28,000 24,282
Livability Code: FT 30-90
Wheelbase-to-length ratio of 53% is considered ○ dangerous ◉ fatiguing ○ good ○ excellent*
The approximate net payload of 3718 pounds at 13% of GVWR on this model is ○ deficient ○ excessive ○ cautionary ◉ good ○ excellent*
Total highway safety penalties are: 2* Value: 8 6 Durability: 8 1 Highway Control Rating: 6 4 Highway Safety: 6 2 ★★

Foretravel 1994 MHA 36 3600 U280 WTBI UN Cum D $7700 228 1,500 e 28,000 24,282
Livability Code: FT 30-90
Wheelbase-to-length ratio of 53% is considered ○ dangerous ◉ fatiguing ○ good ○ excellent*
The approximate net payload of 3718 pounds at 13% of GVWR on this model is ○ deficient ○ excessive ○ cautionary ◉ good ○ excellent*
Total highway safety penalties are: 2* Value: 8 6 Durability: 8 1 Highway Control Rating: 6 4 Highway Safety: 6 2 ★★

Foretravel 1994 MHA 36 3600 U280 SBI UN Cum D $7700 228 1,500 e 28,000 24,282
Livability Code: FT 30-90
Wheelbase-to-length ratio of 53% is considered ○ dangerous ◉ fatiguing ○ good ○ excellent*
The approximate net payload of 3718 pounds at 13% of GVWR on this model is ○ deficient ○ excessive ○ cautionary ◉ good ○ excellent*
Total highway safety penalties are: 2* Value: 8 6 Durability: 8 1 Highway Control Rating: 6 4 Highway Safety: 6 2 ★★

Foretravel 1994 MHA 36 3600 U300W SBID UN Det D $8800 228 6,000 30,000 25,282
Livability Code: FT 30-90
Wheelbase-to-length ratio of 53% is considered ○ dangerous ◉ fatiguing ○ good ○ excellent*
The approximate net payload of 4718 pounds at 16% of GVWR on this model is ○ deficient ○ excessive ○ cautionary ○ good ◉ excellent*
Total highway safety penalties are: 2* Value: 8 6 Durability: 8 1 Highway Control Rating: 6 9 Highway Safety: 6 7 ★★

Foretravel 1994 MHA 36 3600 U300W WTBI UN Det D $8800 228 6,000 30,000 25,282
Livability Code: FT 30-90
Wheelbase-to-length ratio of 53% is considered ○ dangerous ◉ fatiguing ○ good ○ excellent*
The approximate net payload of 4718 pounds at 16% of GVWR on this model is ○ deficient ○ excessive ○ cautionary ○ good ◉ excellent*
Total highway safety penalties are: 2* Value: 8 6 Durability: 8 1 Highway Control Rating: 6 9 Highway Safety: 6 7 ★★

Foretravel 1994 MHA 36 3600 U300W SBI UN Det D $8800 228 6,000 30,000 25,282
Livability Code: FT 30-90
Wheelbase-to-length ratio of 53% is considered ○ dangerous ◉ fatiguing ○ good ○ excellent*
The approximate net payload of 4718 pounds at 16% of GVWR on this model is ○ deficient ○ excessive ○ cautionary ○ good ◉ excellent*
Total highway safety penalties are: 2* Value: 8 6 Durability: 8 1 Highway Control Rating: 6 9 Highway Safety: 6 7 ★★

Foretravel 1994 MHA 40 4000 U280 SBI UN Cum D $7500 276 1,500 e 28,000 25,424
Livability Code: FT 30-90
Wheelbase-to-length ratio of 58% is considered ○ dangerous ○ fatiguing ○ good ◉ excellent*
The approximate net payload of 2576 pounds at 9% of GVWR on this model is ○ deficient ○ excessive ◉ cautionary ○ good ○ excellent*
Total highway safety penalties are: 2* Value: 8 6 Durability: 8 1 Highway Control Rating: 8 5 Highway Safety: 8 3 ★★★★

Foretravel 1994 MHA 40 4000 U280 SAI UN Cum D $7500 276 1,500 e 28,000 25,424
Livability Code: FT 30-90
Wheelbase-to-length ratio of 58% is considered ○ dangerous ○ fatiguing ○ good ◉ excellent*
The approximate net payload of 2576 pounds at 9% of GVWR on this model is ○ deficient ○ excessive ◉ cautionary ○ good ○ excellent*
Total highway safety penalties are: 2* Value: 8 6 Durability: 8 1 Highway Control Rating: 8 5 Highway Safety: 8 3 ★★★★

Foretravel 1994 MHA 40 4000 U280 WTB UN Cum D $7500 276 1,500 e 28,000 25,424
Livability Code: FT 30-90
Wheelbase-to-length ratio of 58% is considered ○ dangerous ○ fatiguing ○ good ○ excellent*
The approximate net payload of 2576 pounds at 9% of GVWR on this model is ○ deficient ○ excessive ○ cautionary ○ good ○ excellent*
Total highway safety penalties are: 2* Value: 8 6 Durability: 8 1 Highway Control Rating: 8 5 Highway Safety: 8 3 ★★★★

Foretravel 1994 MHA 40 4000 U300W SBI UN Det D $8300 276 6,000 30,000 26,424
Livability Code: FT 30-90
Wheelbase-to-length ratio of 58% is considered ○ dangerous ○ fatiguing ○ good ◉ excellent*
The approximate net payload of 3576 pounds at 12% of GVWR on this model is ○ deficient ○ excessive ○ cautionary ◉ good ○ excellent*
Total highway safety penalties are: 2* Value: 8 6 Durability: 8 1 Highway Control Rating: 9 3 Highway Safety: 9 1 ★★★★

Foretravel 1994 MHA 40 4000 U300W SAI UN Det D $8300 276 6,000 30,000 26,424
Livability Code: FT 30-90
Wheelbase-to-length ratio of 58% is considered ○ dangerous ○ fatiguing ○ good ◉ excellent*
The approximate net payload of 3576 pounds at 12% of GVWR on this model is ○ deficient ○ excessive ○ cautionary ◉ good ○ excellent*
Total highway safety penalties are: 2* Value: 8 6 Durability: 8 1 Highway Control Rating: 9 3 Highway Safety: 9 1 ★★★★

Foretravel 1994 MHA 40 4000 U300W WTB UN Det D $8300 276 6,000 30,000 26,424
Livability Code: FT 30-90
Wheelbase-to-length ratio of 58% is considered ○ dangerous ○ fatiguing ○ good ◉ excellent*
The approximate net payload of 3576 pounds at 12% of GVWR on this model is ○ deficient ○ excessive ○ cautionary ◉ good ○ excellent*
Total highway safety penalties are: 2* Value: 8 6 Durability: 8 1 Highway Control Rating: 9 3 Highway Safety: 9 1 ★★★★

Note: Safety ratings are based on the assumption that the engineering of the RV has allowed for proper balance by placing fresh, gray, and black holding tanks in a location so as not to change the balance of the RV when the tanks are empty or full. **Always double-check wheelbase, GVWR, and weights at front and rear axles.**

*See Section 1 for details on how conclusions are reached.

Section 2: The Ratings

Brand	Year	Type	Length	Model	Chassis	Engine	Fuel Type	Average Price per Linear Foot When New	Adjusted Wheelbase	Approx. Towing Capacity	Gross Vehicle Weight Rating	Average Curb Weight

Foretravel 1994 MHA 40 4000 U300W WTBS UN Det D $8600 276 6,000 30,000 26,424
Livability Code: FT 30-90
Wheelbase-to-length ratio of 58% is considered ○ dangerous ○ fatiguing ○ good ● excellent *
The approximate net payload of 3576 pounds at 12% of GVWR on this model is ○ deficient ○ excessive ○ cautionary ● good ○ excellent *
Total highway safety penalties are: 2 *   Value: 8 6   Durability: 8 1   Highway Control Rating: 9 3   Highway Safety: 9 1   ★★★★

Foretravel 1994 MHA 40 4000-U280 WTBS UN Det D $7500 276 6,000 30,000 26,424
Livability Code: FT 30-90
Wheelbase-to-length ratio of 58% is considered ○ dangerous ○ fatiguing ○ good ● excellent *
The approximate net payload of 3576 pounds at 12% of GVWR on this model is ○ deficient ○ excessive ○ cautionary ● good ○ excellent *
Total highway safety penalties are: 2 *   Value: 8 6   Durability: 8 1   Highway Control Rating: 9 3   Highway Safety: 9 1   ★★★★

Foretravel 1995 MHA 36 3600-U240 SBDI UN Ca250 D $5900 228 2,500 24,000 22,649
Livability Code: FT 30-90
Wheelbase-to-length ratio of 53% is considered ○ dangerous ● fatiguing ○ good ○ excellent *
The approximate net payload of 1351 pounds at 6% of GVWR on this model is ● deficient ○ excessive ○ cautionary ○ good ○ excellent *
Total highway safety penalties are: 2 *   Value: 8 6   Durability: 8 1   Highway Control Rating: 3 4   Highway Safety: 3 2

Foretravel 1995 MHA 36 3600-U240 SBI UN Ca250 D $5900 228 2,500 24,000 22,594
Livability Code: FT 30-90
Wheelbase-to-length ratio of 53% is considered ○ dangerous ● fatiguing ○ good ○ excellent *
The approximate net payload of 1406 pounds at 6% of GVWR on this model is ● deficient ○ excessive ○ cautionary ○ good ○ excellent *
Total highway safety penalties are: 2 *   Value: 8 6   Durability: 8 1   Highway Control Rating: 3 5   Highway Safety: 3 3

Foretravel 1995 MHA 36 3600-U240 WTBI UN Ca250 D $5900 228 2,500 24,000 22,649
Livability Code: FT 30-90
Wheelbase-to-length ratio of 53% is considered ○ dangerous ● fatiguing ○ good ○ excellent *
The approximate net payload of 1351 pounds at 6% of GVWR on this model is ● deficient ○ excessive ○ cautionary ○ good ○ excellent *
Total highway safety penalties are: 2 *   Value: 8 6   Durability: 8 1   Highway Control Rating: 3 4   Highway Safety: 3 2

Foretravel 1995 MHA 36 3600-U280W SBID UN Cu300 D $8000 228 1,500 e 28,000 24,649
Livability Code: FT 30-90
Wheelbase-to-length ratio of 53% is considered ○ dangerous ● fatiguing ○ good ○ excellent *
The approximate net payload of 3351 pounds at 12% of GVWR on this model is ○ deficient ○ excessive ○ cautionary ● good ○ excellent *
Total highway safety penalties are: 2 *   Value: 8 6   Durability: 8 1   Highway Control Rating: 6 2   Highway Safety: 6 0   ★★

Foretravel 1995 MHA 36 3600-U280W WTBI UN Cu300 D $8000 228 1,500 e 28,000 24,649
Livability Code: FT 30-90
Wheelbase-to-length ratio of 53% is considered ○ dangerous ● fatiguing ○ good ○ excellent *
The approximate net payload of 3351 pounds at 12% of GVWR on this model is ○ deficient ○ excessive ○ cautionary ● good ○ excellent *
Total highway safety penalties are: 2 *   Value: 8 6   Durability: 8 1   Highway Control Rating: 6 2   Highway Safety: 6 0   ★★

Foretravel 1995 MHA 36 3600-U280W SBI UN Cu8.3L D $8000 228 1,500 e 28,000 24,649
Livability Code: FT 30-90
Wheelbase-to-length ratio of 53% is considered ○ dangerous ● fatiguing ○ good ○ excellent *
The approximate net payload of 3351 pounds at 12% of GVWR on this model is ○ deficient ○ excessive ○ cautionary ● good ○ excellent *
Total highway safety penalties are: 2 *   Value: 8 6   Durability: 8 1   Highway Control Rating: 6 2   Highway Safety: 6 0   ★★

Foretravel 1995 MHA 36 3600-U300W SBID UN Ca350 D $9100 228 1,500 e 30,000 25,649
Livability Code: FT 30-90
Wheelbase-to-length ratio of 53% is considered ○ dangerous ● fatiguing ○ good ○ excellent *
The approximate net payload of 4351 pounds at 15% of GVWR on this model is ○ deficient ○ excessive ○ cautionary ● good ○ excellent *
Total highway safety penalties are: 2 *   Value: 8 6   Durability: 8 1   Highway Control Rating: 6 7   Highway Safety: 6 5   ★★

Foretravel 1995 MHA 36 3600-U300W WTBI UN Ca350 D $9100 228 1,500 e 30,000 25,649
Livability Code: FT 30-90
Wheelbase-to-length ratio of 53% is considered ○ dangerous ● fatiguing ○ good ○ excellent *
The approximate net payload of 4351 pounds at 15% of GVWR on this model is ○ deficient ○ excessive ○ cautionary ● good ○ excellent *
Total highway safety penalties are: 2 *   Value: 8 6   Durability: 8 1   Highway Control Rating: 6 7   Highway Safety: 6 5   ★★

Foretravel 1995 MHA 36 3600-U300W SBI UN Ca350 D $9100 228 1,500 e 30,000 25,649
Livability Code: FT 30-90
Wheelbase-to-length ratio of 53% is considered ○ dangerous ● fatiguing ○ good ○ excellent *
The approximate net payload of 4351 pounds at 15% of GVWR on this model is ○ deficient ○ excessive ○ cautionary ● good ○ excellent *
Total highway safety penalties are: 2 *   Value: 8 6   Durability: 8 1   Highway Control Rating: 6 7   Highway Safety: 6 5   ★★

Foretravel 1995 MHA 40 4000 U280W SBI UN Cu300 D $7800 276 1,500 e 28,000 25,832
Livability Code: FT 30-90
Wheelbase-to-length ratio of 58% is considered ○ dangerous ○ fatiguing ○ good ● excellent *
The approximate net payload of 2168 pounds at 8% of GVWR on this model is ○ deficient ○ excessive ● cautionary ○ good ○ excellent *
Total highway safety penalties are: 2 *   Value: 8 6   Durability: 8 1   Highway Control Rating: 7 8   Highway Safety: 7 6   ★★★

Note: Safety ratings are based on the assumption that the engineering of the RV has allowed for proper balance by placing fresh, gray, and black holding tanks in a location so as not to change the balance of the RV when the tanks are empty or full. **Always double-check wheelbase, GVWR, and weights at front and rear axles.**

*See Section 1 for details on how conclusions are reached.

Brand	Year	Type	Length	Model	Chassis	Engine	Fuel Type	Average Price per Linear Foot When New	Adjusted Wheelbase	Approx. Towing Capacity	Gross Vehicle Weight Rating	Average Curb Weight
Foretravel	1995	MHA	40	4000 U280W SAI	UN	Cu300	D	$7800	276	1,500 e	28,000	25,832

Livability Code: FT 30-90   Wheelbase-to-length ratio of 58% is considered ○ dangerous ○ fatiguing ○ good ◉ excellent *

The approximate net payload of 2168 pounds at 8% of GVWR on this model is ○ deficient ○ excessive ◉ cautionary ○ good ○ excellent *

Total highway safety penalties are: 2 *   Value: 8 6   Durability: 8 1   Highway Control Rating: 7 8   Highway Safety: 7 6   ★★★

| Foretravel | 1995 | MHA | 40 | 4000 U280W WTBI | UN | Cu300 | D | $7800 | 276 | 1,500 e | 28,000 | 25,832 |

Livability Code: FT 30-90   Wheelbase-to-length ratio of 58% is considered ○ dangerous ○ fatiguing ○ good ◉ excellent *

The approximate net payload of 2168 pounds at 8% of GVWR on this model is ○ deficient ○ excessive ◉ cautionary ○ good ○ excellent *

Total highway safety penalties are: 2 *   Value: 8 6   Durability: 8 1   Highway Control Rating: 7 8   Highway Safety: 7 6   ★★★

| Foretravel | 1995 | MHA | 40 | 4000 U300W SBI | UN | Ca350 | D | $8600 | 276 | 1,500 e | 30,000 | 26,832 |

Livability Code: FT 30-90   Wheelbase-to-length ratio of 58% is considered ○ dangerous ○ fatiguing ○ good ◉ excellent *

The approximate net payload of 3168 pounds at 11% of GVWR on this model is ○ deficient ○ excessive ○ cautionary ◉ good ○ excellent *

Total highway safety penalties are: 2 *   Value: 8 6   Durability: 8 1   Highway Control Rating: 9 1   Highway Safety: 8 9   ★★★★

| Foretravel | 1995 | MHA | 40 | 4000 U300W SAI | UN | Ca350 | D | $8600 | 276 | 1,500 e | 30,000 | 26,832 |

Livability Code: FT 30-90   Wheelbase-to-length ratio of 58% is considered ○ dangerous ○ fatiguing ○ good ◉ excellent *

The approximate net payload of 3168 pounds at 11% of GVWR on this model is ○ deficient ○ excessive ○ cautionary ◉ good ○ excellent *

Total highway safety penalties are: 2 *   Value: 8 6   Durability: 8 1   Highway Control Rating: 9 1   Highway Safety: 8 9   ★★★★

| Foretravel | 1995 | MHA | 40 | 4000 U300W WTBI | UN | Ca350 | D | $8600 | 276 | 1,500 e | 30,000 | 26,832 |

Livability Code: FT 30-90   Wheelbase-to-length ratio of 58% is considered ○ dangerous ○ fatiguing ○ good ◉ excellent *

The approximate net payload of 3168 pounds at 11% of GVWR on this model is ○ deficient ○ excessive ○ cautionary ◉ good ○ excellent *

Total highway safety penalties are: 2 *   Value: 8 6   Durability: 8 1   Highway Control Rating: 9 1   Highway Safety: 8 9   ★★★★

| Foretravel | 1995 | MHA | 40 | 4000 U280 SE | UN | Cu8.3L | D | $8000 | 276 | 1,500 e | 28,000 | 25,832 |

Livability Code: FT 30-90   Wheelbase-to-length ratio of 58% is considered ○ dangerous ○ fatiguing ○ good ◉ excellent *

The approximate net payload of 2168 pounds at 8% of GVWR on this model is ○ deficient ○ excessive ◉ cautionary ○ good ○ excellent *

Total highway safety penalties are: 2 *   Value: 8 6   Durability: 8 1   Highway Control Rating: 7 8   Highway Safety: 7 6   ★★★

| Foretravel | 1995 | MHA | 40 | 4000 U300 SE | UN | Ca350 | D | $8800 | 276 | 1,500 e | 30,000 | 26,832 |

Livability Code: FT 30-90   Wheelbase-to-length ratio of 58% is considered ○ dangerous ○ fatiguing ○ good ◉ excellent *

The approximate net payload of 3168 pounds at 11% of GVWR on this model is ○ deficient ○ excessive ○ cautionary ◉ good ○ excellent *

Total highway safety penalties are: 2 *   Value: 8 6   Durability: 8 1   Highway Control Rating: 9 1   Highway Safety: 8 9   ★★★★

| Foretravel | 1995 | MHA | 40 | 4000 U320C W TBI | UN | Ca370 | D | $9200 | 276 | 6,000 | 32,000 | 27,832 |

Livability Code: FT 30-90   Wheelbase-to-length ratio of 58% is considered ○ dangerous ○ fatiguing ○ good ◉ excellent *

The approximate net payload of 4168 pounds at 13% of GVWR on this model is ○ deficient ○ excessive ○ cautionary ◉ good ○ excellent *

Total highway safety penalties are: 2 *   Value: 8 6   Durability: 8 1   Highway Control Rating: 9 6   Highway Safety: 9 4   ★★★★

| Foretravel | 1995 | MHA | 40 | 4000 U320C CAI | UN | Ca370 | D | $9200 | 276 | 6,000 | 32,000 | 27,832 |

Livability Code: FT 30-90   Wheelbase-to-length ratio of 58% is considered ○ dangerous ○ fatiguing ○ good ◉ excellent *

The approximate net payload of 4168 pounds at 13% of GVWR on this model is ○ deficient ○ excessive ○ cautionary ◉ good ○ excellent *

Total highway safety penalties are: 2 *   Value: 8 6   Durability: 8 1   Highway Control Rating: 9 6   Highway Safety: 9 4   ★★★★

| Foretravel | 1995 | MHA | 40 | 4000 U320C SE | UN | Ca370 | D | $9500 | 276 | 6,000 | 32,000 | 27,832 |

Livability Code: FT 30-90   Wheelbase-to-length ratio of 58% is considered ○ dangerous ○ fatiguing ○ good ◉ excellent *

The approximate net payload of 4168 pounds at 13% of GVWR on this model is ○ deficient ○ excessive ○ cautionary ◉ good ○ excellent *

Total highway safety penalties are: 2 *   Value: 8 6   Durability: 8 1   Highway Control Rating: 9 6   Highway Safety: 9 4   ★★★★

| Foretravel | 1996 | MHA | 36 | 3600 - U270 WTBI | UN | Cu8.3 | D | $6200 | 228 | 6,000 | 30,000 | 26,078 |

Livability Code: FT 30-90   Wheelbase-to-length ratio of 53% is considered ○ dangerous ◉ fatiguing ○ good ○ excellent *

The approximate net payload of 3922 pounds at 13% of GVWR on this model is ○ deficient ○ excessive ○ cautionary ◉ good ○ excellent *

Total highway safety penalties are: 2 *   Value: 8 6   Durability: 8 1   Highway Control Rating: 6 4   Highway Safety: 6 2   ★★

| Foretravel | 1996 | MHA | 36 | 3600 - U270 CSGI | UN | Cu8.3 | D | $6200 | 228 | 6,000 | 30,000 | 26,078 |

Livability Code: FT 30-90   Wheelbase-to-length ratio of 53% is considered ○ dangerous ◉ fatiguing ○ good ○ excellent *

The approximate net payload of 3922 pounds at 13% of GVWR on this model is ○ deficient ○ excessive ○ cautionary ◉ good ○ excellent *

Total highway safety penalties are: 2 *   Value: 8 6   Durability: 8 1   Highway Control Rating: 6 4   Highway Safety: 6 2   ★★

Note: Safety ratings are based on the assumption that the engineering of the RV has allowed for proper balance by placing fresh, gray, and black holding tanks in a location so as not to change the balance of the RV when the tanks are empty or full. **Always double-check wheelbase, GVWR, and weights at front and rear axles.**

The RV Rating Book

*See Section 1 for details on how conclusions are reached.

Brand	Year	Type	Length	Model	Chassis	Engine	Fuel Type	Average Price per Linear Foot When New	Adjusted Wheelbase	Approx. Towing Capacity	Gross Vehicle Weight Rating	Average Curb Weight
Foretravel	1996	MHA	36	3600 - U295 WTBI	UN	Cu8.3	D	$8100	228	6,000	30,000	26,078

Livability Code: FT 30-90
Wheelbase-to-length ratio of 53% is considered ○ dangerous ● fatiguing ○ good ○ excellent *
The approximate net payload of 3922 pounds at 13% of GVWR on this model is ○ deficient ○ excessive ○ cautionary ● good ○ excellent *
Total highway safety penalties are: 2 *   Value: 86   Durability: 81   Highway Control Rating: 64   Highway Safety: 62   ★★

Brand	Year	Type	Length	Model	Chassis	Engine	Fuel Type	Avg Price/Lin Ft	Adj Wheelbase	Approx Towing	GVWR	Avg Curb Wt
Foretravel	1996	MHA	36	3600 - U295 CAI	UN	Cu8.3	D	$8100	228	6,000	30,000	26,418

Livability Code: FT 30-90
Wheelbase-to-length ratio of 53% is considered ○ dangerous ● fatiguing ○ good ○ excellent *
The approximate net payload of 3582 pounds at 12% of GVWR on this model is ○ deficient ○ excessive ○ cautionary ● good ○ excellent *
Total highway safety penalties are: 2 *   Value: 86   Durability: 81   Highway Control Rating: 62   Highway Safety: 60   ★★

Foretravel	1996	MHA	36	3600 - U295 SBID	UN	Cu8.3	D	$8100	228	6,000	30,000	26,418

Livability Code: FT 30-90
Wheelbase-to-length ratio of 53% is considered ○ dangerous ● fatiguing ○ good ○ excellent *
The approximate net payload of 3582 pounds at 12% of GVWR on this model is ○ deficient ○ excessive ○ cautionary ● good ○ excellent *
Total highway safety penalties are: 2 *   Value: 86   Durability: 81   Highway Control Rating: 62   Highway Safety: 60   ★★

Foretravel	1996	MHA	36	3600 - U280 WTB	UN	Cu8.3	D	$7600	228	6,000	30,000	26,147

Livability Code: FT 30-90
Wheelbase-to-length ratio of 52% is considered ○ dangerous ● fatiguing ○ good ○ excellent *
The approximate net payload of 3853 pounds at 13% of GVWR on this model is ○ deficient ○ excessive ○ cautionary ● good ○ excellent *
Total highway safety penalties are: 2 *   Value: 86   Durability: 81   Highway Control Rating: 54   Highway Safety: 52   ★

Foretravel	1996	MHA	36	3600 - U280 SBID	UN	Cu8.3	D	$7600	228	6,000	30,000	26,147

Livability Code: FT 30-90
Wheelbase-to-length ratio of 52% is considered ○ dangerous ● fatiguing ○ good ○ excellent *
The approximate net payload of 3853 pounds at 13% of GVWR on this model is ○ deficient ○ excessive ○ cautionary ● good ○ excellent *
Total highway safety penalties are: 2 *   Value: 86   Durability: 81   Highway Control Rating: 54   Highway Safety: 52   ★

Foretravel	1996	MHA	40	4000 - U295 WTBI	UN	Cu8.3	D	$8000	276	6,000	30,000	27,660

Livability Code: FT 30-90
Wheelbase-to-length ratio of 58% is considered ○ dangerous ○ fatiguing ○ good ● excellent *
The approximate net payload of 2340 pounds at 8% of GVWR on this model is ○ deficient ○ excessive ● cautionary ○ good ○ excellent *
Total highway safety penalties are: 2 *   Value: 86   Durability: 81   Highway Control Rating: 78   Highway Safety: 76   ★★★

Foretravel	1996	MHA	40	4000 - U295 CAI	UN	Cu8.3	D	$8000	276	6,000	30,000	27,660

Livability Code: FT 30-90
Wheelbase-to-length ratio of 58% is considered ○ dangerous ○ fatiguing ○ good ● excellent *
The approximate net payload of 2340 pounds at 8% of GVWR on this model is ○ deficient ○ excessive ● cautionary ○ good ○ excellent *
Total highway safety penalties are: 2 *   Value: 86   Durability: 81   Highway Control Rating: 78   Highway Safety: 76   ★★★

Foretravel	1996	MHA	40	4000 -U320 WTBI	UN	Cu11L	D	$9300	276	6,000	32,000	28,830

Livability Code: FT 30-90
Wheelbase-to-length ratio of 58% is considered ○ dangerous ○ fatiguing ○ good ● excellent *
The approximate net payload of 3171 pounds at 10% of GVWR on this model is ○ deficient ○ excessive ○ cautionary ● good ○ excellent *
Total highway safety penalties are: 2 *   Value: 86   Durability: 81   Highway Control Rating: 89   Highway Safety: 87   ★★★★

Foretravel	1996	MHA	40	4000 -U320 CAI	UN	Cu11L	D	$9300	276	6,000	32,000	28,830

Livability Code: FT 30-90
Wheelbase-to-length ratio of 58% is considered ○ dangerous ○ fatiguing ○ good ● excellent *
The approximate net payload of 3171 pounds at 10% of GVWR on this model is ○ deficient ○ excessive ○ cautionary ● good ○ excellent *
Total highway safety penalties are: 2 *   Value: 86   Durability: 81   Highway Control Rating: 89   Highway Safety: 87   ★★★★

Foretravel	1996	MHA	40	4000 - U280 WTBI	UN	Cu8.3	D	$7600	276	6,000	30,000	27,454

Livability Code: FT 30-90
Wheelbase-to-length ratio of 57% is considered ○ dangerous ○ fatiguing ● good ○ excellent *
The approximate net payload of 2546 pounds at 8% of GVWR on this model is ○ deficient ○ excessive ● cautionary ○ good ○ excellent *
Total highway safety penalties are: 2 *   Value: 86   Durability: 81   Highway Control Rating: 78   Highway Safety: 76   ★★★

Foretravel	1996	MHA	40	4000 - U280 SAI	UN	Cu8.3	D	$7600	276	6,000	30,000	27,454

Livability Code: FT 30-90
Wheelbase-to-length ratio of 57% is considered ○ dangerous ○ fatiguing ● good ○ excellent *
The approximate net payload of 2546 pounds at 8% of GVWR on this model is ○ deficient ○ excessive ● cautionary ○ good ○ excellent *
Total highway safety penalties are: 2 *   Value: 86   Durability: 81   Highway Control Rating: 78   Highway Safety: 76   ★★★

Foretravel	1996	MHA	40	4000 - U300 WTBI	UN	Cu11L	D	$8800	276	6,000	32,000	28,078

Livability Code: FT 30-90
Wheelbase-to-length ratio of 57% is considered ○ dangerous ○ fatiguing ● good ○ excellent *
The approximate net payload of 3922 pounds at 12% of GVWR on this model is ○ deficient ○ excessive ○ cautionary ● good ○ excellent *
Total highway safety penalties are: 2 *   Value: 86   Durability: 81   Highway Control Rating: 92   Highway Safety: 90   ★★★★

Note: Safety ratings are based on the assumption that the engineering of the RV has allowed for proper balance by placing fresh, gray, and black holding tanks in a location so as not to change the balance of the RV when the tanks are empty or full. **Always double-check wheelbase, GVWR, and weights at front and rear axles.**

*See Section 1 for details on how conclusions are reached.

Brand	Year	Type	Length	Model	Chassis	Engine	Fuel Type	Average Price per Linear Foot When New	Adjusted Wheelbase	Approx. Towing Capacity	Gross Vehicle Weight Rating	Average Curb Weight
Foretravel	1996	MHA	40	4000 - U300 SAI	UN	Cu11L	D	$8800	276	6,000	32,000	28,078

Livability Code: FT 30-90
Wheelbase-to-length ratio of 57% is considered ○ dangerous ○ fatiguing ◉ good ○ excellent *
The approximate net payload of 3922 pounds at 12% of GVWR on this model is ○ deficient ○ excessive ○ cautionary ◉ good ○ excellent *
Total highway safety penalties are: 2 * Value: 86 Durability: 81 Highway Control Rating: 92 Highway Safety: 90 ★★★★

Brand	Year	Type	Length	Model	Chassis	Engine	Fuel Type	Price/Ft	Wheelbase	Towing	GVWR	Curb Weight
Foretravel	1997	MHA	34	U270	UN	Cu325	D	$7000	228	8,000	30,000	25,404

Livability Code: FT 30-90
Wheelbase-to-length ratio of 56% is considered ○ dangerous ○ fatiguing ◉ good ○ excellent *
The approximate net payload of 4596 pounds at 15% of GVWR on this model is ○ deficient ○ excessive ○ cautionary ◉ good ○ excellent *
Total highway safety penalties are: 2 * Value: 86 Durability: 81 Highway Control Rating: 94 Highway Safety: 92 ★★★★

Brand	Year	Type	Length	Model	Chassis	Engine	Fuel Type	Price/Ft	Wheelbase	Towing	GVWR	Curb Weight
Foretravel	1997	MHA	36	3600 U270 WTBI	UN	Cu325	D	$6600	228	6,000	30,000	26,016

Livability Code: FT 30-90
Wheelbase-to-length ratio of 53% is considered ○ dangerous ◉ fatiguing ○ good ○ excellent *
The approximate net payload of 3984 pounds at 13% of GVWR on this model is ○ deficient ○ excessive ○ cautionary ◉ good ○ excellent *
Total highway safety penalties are: 2 * Value: 86 Durability: 81 Highway Control Rating: 64 Highway Safety: 62 ★★

Brand	Year	Type	Length	Model	Chassis	Engine	Fuel Type	Price/Ft	Wheelbase	Towing	GVWR	Curb Weight
Foretravel	1997	MHA	36	3600 U270 CSGI	UN	Cu325	D	$6600	228	6,000	30,000	26,016

Livability Code: FT 30-90
Wheelbase-to-length ratio of 53% is considered ○ dangerous ◉ fatiguing ○ good ○ excellent *
The approximate net payload of 3984 pounds at 13% of GVWR on this model is ○ deficient ○ excessive ○ cautionary ◉ good ○ excellent *
Total highway safety penalties are: 2 * Value: 86 Durability: 81 Highway Control Rating: 64 Highway Safety: 62 ★★

Brand	Year	Type	Length	Model	Chassis	Engine	Fuel Type	Price/Ft	Wheelbase	Towing	GVWR	Curb Weight
Foretravel	1997	MHA	36	3600 U295 WTBI	UN	Cu325	D	$8500	228	6,000	30,000	26,016

Livability Code: FT 30-90
Wheelbase-to-length ratio of 53% is considered ○ dangerous ◉ fatiguing ○ good ○ excellent *
The approximate net payload of 3984 pounds at 13% of GVWR on this model is ○ deficient ○ excessive ○ cautionary ◉ good ○ excellent *
Total highway safety penalties are: 2 * Value: 86 Durability: 81 Highway Control Rating: 64 Highway Safety: 62 ★★

Brand	Year	Type	Length	Model	Chassis	Engine	Fuel Type	Price/Ft	Wheelbase	Towing	GVWR	Curb Weight
Foretravel	1997	MHA	36	3600 U295 CAI	UN	Cu325	D	$8500	228	6,000	30,000	26,016

Livability Code: FT 30-90
Wheelbase-to-length ratio of 53% is considered ○ dangerous ◉ fatiguing ○ good ○ excellent *
The approximate net payload of 3984 pounds at 13% of GVWR on this model is ○ deficient ○ excessive ○ cautionary ◉ good ○ excellent *
Total highway safety penalties are: 2 * Value: 86 Durability: 81 Highway Control Rating: 64 Highway Safety: 62 ★★

Brand	Year	Type	Length	Model	Chassis	Engine	Fuel Type	Price/Ft	Wheelbase	Towing	GVWR	Curb Weight
Foretravel	1997	MHA	36	3600 U295 SBID	UN	Cu325	D	$8500	228	6,000	30,000	26,016

Livability Code: FT 30-90
Wheelbase-to-length ratio of 53% is considered ○ dangerous ◉ fatiguing ○ good ○ excellent *
The approximate net payload of 3984 pounds at 13% of GVWR on this model is ○ deficient ○ excessive ○ cautionary ◉ good ○ excellent *
Total highway safety penalties are: 2 * Value: 86 Durability: 81 Highway Control Rating: 64 Highway Safety: 62 ★★

Brand	Year	Type	Length	Model	Chassis	Engine	Fuel Type	Price/Ft	Wheelbase	Towing	GVWR	Curb Weight
Foretravel	1997	MHA	36	U320	UN	Cu450	D	$10800	228	6,000	32,000	27,016

Livability Code: FT 30-90
Wheelbase-to-length ratio of 53% is considered ○ dangerous ◉ fatiguing ○ good ○ excellent *
The approximate net payload of 4984 pounds at 16% of GVWR on this model is ○ deficient ○ excessive ○ cautionary ○ good ◉ excellent *
Total highway safety penalties are: 2 * Value: 86 Durability: 81 Highway Control Rating: 69 Highway Safety: 67 ★★

Brand	Year	Type	Length	Model	Chassis	Engine	Fuel Type	Price/Ft	Wheelbase	Towing	GVWR	Curb Weight
Foretravel	1997	MHA	40	4000 U295 WTBI	UN	Cu325	D	$8400	276	6,000	30,000	27,240

Livability Code: FT 30-90
Wheelbase-to-length ratio of 58% is considered ○ dangerous ○ fatiguing ○ good ◉ excellent *
The approximate net payload of 2760 pounds at 9% of GVWR on this model is ○ deficient ○ excessive ◉ cautionary ○ good ○ excellent *
Total highway safety penalties are: 2 * Value: 86 Durability: 81 Highway Control Rating: 85 Highway Safety: 83 ★★★★

Brand	Year	Type	Length	Model	Chassis	Engine	Fuel Type	Price/Ft	Wheelbase	Towing	GVWR	Curb Weight
Foretravel	1997	MHA	40	4000 U295 CAI	UN	Cu325	D	$8400	276	6,000	30,000	27,240

Livability Code: FT 30-90
Wheelbase-to-length ratio of 58% is considered ○ dangerous ○ fatiguing ○ good ◉ excellent *
The approximate net payload of 2760 pounds at 9% of GVWR on this model is ○ deficient ○ excessive ◉ cautionary ○ good ○ excellent *
Total highway safety penalties are: 2 * Value: 86 Durability: 81 Highway Control Rating: 85 Highway Safety: 83 ★★★★

Brand	Year	Type	Length	Model	Chassis	Engine	Fuel Type	Price/Ft	Wheelbase	Towing	GVWR	Curb Weight
Foretravel	1997	MHA	40	4000 U300 WTBI	UN	Cu450	D	$9700	276	6,000	32,000	28,240

Livability Code: FT 30-90
Wheelbase-to-length ratio of 58% is considered ○ dangerous ○ fatiguing ○ good ◉ excellent *
The approximate net payload of 3760 pounds at 12% of GVWR on this model is ○ deficient ○ excessive ○ cautionary ◉ good ○ excellent *
Total highway safety penalties are: 2 * Value: 86 Durability: 81 Highway Control Rating: 93 Highway Safety: 91 ★★★★

Brand	Year	Type	Length	Model	Chassis	Engine	Fuel Type	Price/Ft	Wheelbase	Towing	GVWR	Curb Weight
Foretravel	1997	MHA	40	4000 U300 SAI	UN	Cu450	D	$9700	276	6,000	32,000	28,240

Livability Code: FT 30-90
Wheelbase-to-length ratio of 58% is considered ○ dangerous ○ fatiguing ○ good ◉ excellent *
The approximate net payload of 3760 pounds at 12% of GVWR on this model is ○ deficient ○ excessive ○ cautionary ◉ good ○ excellent *
Total highway safety penalties are: 2 * Value: 86 Durability: 81 Highway Control Rating: 93 Highway Safety: 91 ★★★★

Note: Safety ratings are based on the assumption that the engineering of the RV has allowed for proper balance by placing fresh, gray, and black holding tanks in a location so as not to change the balance of the RV when the tanks are empty or full. **Always double-check wheelbase, GVWR, and weights at front and rear axles.**

*See Section 1 for details on how conclusions are reached.

Brand	Year	Type	Length	Model	Chassis	Engine	Fuel Type	Average Price per Linear Foot When New	Adjusted Wheelbase	Approx. Towing Capacity	Gross Vehicle Weight Rating	Average Curb Weight
Foretravel	1997	MHA	40	4000 U320 CSGI	UN	Cu450	D	$9700	276	6,000	32,000	28,240

Livability Code: FT 30-90
Wheelbase-to-length ratio of 58% is considered ○ dangerous ○ fatiguing ○ good ◉ excellent *
The approximate net payload of 3760 pounds at 12% of GVWR on this model is ○ deficient ○ excessive ○ cautionary ◉ good ○ excellent *
Total highway safety penalties are: 2 *   Value: 86   Durability: 81   Highway Control Rating: 93   Highway Safety: 91   ★★★★

Brand	Year	Type	Length	Model	Chassis	Engine	Fuel Type	Price/LF	Wheelbase	Towing	GVWR	Curb Weight
Foretravel	1997	MHA	40	4000 U320 WTBI	UN	CUu50	D	$9700	276	6,000	32,000	28,240

Livability Code: FT 30-90
Wheelbase-to-length ratio of 58% is considered ○ dangerous ○ fatiguing ○ good ◉ excellent *
The approximate net payload of 3760 pounds at 12% of GVWR on this model is ○ deficient ○ excessive ○ cautionary ◉ good ○ excellent *
Total highway safety penalties are: 2 *   Value: 86   Durability: 81   Highway Control Rating: 93   Highway Safety: 91   ★★★★

Foretravel	1998	MHA	34	U270WTFE	UN	CU325	D	$7500	204	5,000	31,000	25,893

Livability Code: FT 30-90
Wheelbase-to-length ratio of 50% is considered ◉ dangerous ○ fatiguing ○ good ○ excellent *
The approximate net payload of 5108 pounds at 16% of GVWR on this model is ○ deficient ○ excessive ○ cautionary ○ good ◉ excellent *
Total highway safety penalties are: 2 *   Value: 86   Durability: 81   Highway Control Rating: 45   Highway Safety: 43

Foretravel	1998	MHA	36	U270CSGI	UN	CU325	D	$7200	228	5,000	31,000	26,469

Livability Code: FT 30-90
Wheelbase-to-length ratio of 53% is considered ○ dangerous ◉ fatiguing ○ good ○ excellent *
The approximate net payload of 4532 pounds at 15% of GVWR on this model is ○ deficient ○ excessive ○ cautionary ◉ good ○ excellent *
Total highway safety penalties are: 2 *   Value: 86   Durability: 81   Highway Control Rating: 67   Highway Safety: 65   ★★

Foretravel	1998	MHA	36	U295CAI	UN	CU325	D	$9000	228	5,000	31,000	27,079

Livability Code: FT 30-90
Wheelbase-to-length ratio of 53% is considered ○ dangerous ◉ fatiguing ○ good ○ excellent *
The approximate net payload of 3922 pounds at 13% of GVWR on this model is ○ deficient ○ excessive ○ cautionary ◉ good ○ excellent *
Total highway safety penalties are: 2 *   Value: 86   Durability: 81   Highway Control Rating: 63   Highway Safety: 61   ★★

Foretravel	1998	MHA	36	U295WTFE	UN	CU325	D	$9000	228	5,000	31,000	27,049

Livability Code: FT 30-90
Wheelbase-to-length ratio of 53% is considered ○ dangerous ◉ fatiguing ○ good ○ excellent *
The approximate net payload of 3952 pounds at 13% of GVWR on this model is ○ deficient ○ excessive ○ cautionary ◉ good ○ excellent *
Total highway safety penalties are: 2 *   Value: 86   Durability: 81   Highway Control Rating: 63   Highway Safety: 61   ★★

Foretravel	1998	MHA	36	U295WYME	UN	CU325	D	$9000	228	5,000	31,000	27,239

Livability Code: FT 30-90
Wheelbase-to-length ratio of 53% is considered ○ dangerous ◉ fatiguing ○ good ○ excellent *
The approximate net payload of 3762 pounds at 12% of GVWR on this model is ○ deficient ○ excessive ○ cautionary ◉ good ○ excellent *
Total highway safety penalties are: 2 *   Value: 86   Durability: 81   Highway Control Rating: 62   Highway Safety: 60   ★★

Foretravel	1998	MHA	36	U320CAI	UN	CU450	D	$10400	228	5,650	32,350	28,296

Livability Code: FT 30-90
Wheelbase-to-length ratio of 53% is considered ○ dangerous ◉ fatiguing ○ good ○ excellent *
The approximate net payload of 4055 pounds at 13% of GVWR on this model is ○ deficient ○ excessive ○ cautionary ◉ good ○ excellent *
Total highway safety penalties are: 2 *   Value: 86   Durability: 81   Highway Control Rating: 63   Highway Safety: 61   ★★

Foretravel	1998	MHA	36	U320WTFE	UN	CU450	D	$10400	228	5,650	32,350	28,266

Livability Code: FT 30-90
Wheelbase-to-length ratio of 53% is considered ○ dangerous ◉ fatiguing ○ good ○ excellent *
The approximate net payload of 4085 pounds at 13% of GVWR on this model is ○ deficient ○ excessive ○ cautionary ◉ good ○ excellent *
Total highway safety penalties are: 2 *   Value: 86   Durability: 81   Highway Control Rating: 63   Highway Safety: 61   ★★

Foretravel	1998	MHA	36	U320WTME	UN	CU450	D	$10400	228	5,650	32,350	28,236

Livability Code: FT 30-90
Wheelbase-to-length ratio of 53% is considered ○ dangerous ◉ fatiguing ○ good ○ excellent *
The approximate net payload of 4115 pounds at 13% of GVWR on this model is ○ deficient ○ excessive ○ cautionary ◉ good ○ excellent *
Total highway safety penalties are: 2 *   Value: 86   Durability: 81   Highway Control Rating: 63   Highway Safety: 61   ★★

Foretravel	1998	MHA	36	U270WTFE	UN	CU325	D	$7200	228	5,000	31,000	26,419

Livability Code: FT 30-90
Wheelbase-to-length ratio of 53% is considered ○ dangerous ◉ fatiguing ○ good ○ excellent *
The approximate net payload of 4582 pounds at 15% of GVWR on this model is ○ deficient ○ excessive ○ cautionary ◉ good ○ excellent *
Total highway safety penalties are: 2 *   Value: 86   Durability: 81   Highway Control Rating: 67   Highway Safety: 65   ★★

Foretravel	1998	MHA	40	U295CAI	UN	CU325	D	$8100	276	5,000	31,000	28,291

Livability Code: FT 30-90
Wheelbase-to-length ratio of 58% is considered ○ dangerous ○ fatiguing ○ good ◉ excellent *
The approximate net payload of 2710 pounds at 9% of GVWR on this model is ○ deficient ○ excessive ◉ cautionary ○ good ○ excellent *
Total highway safety penalties are: 2 *   Value: 86   Durability: 81   Highway Control Rating: 84   Highway Safety: 82   ★★★★

Note: Safety ratings are based on the assumption that the engineering of the RV has allowed for proper balance by placing fresh, gray, and black holding tanks in a location so as not to change the balance of the RV when the tanks are empty or full. **Always double-check wheelbase, GVWR, and weights at front and rear axles.**

*See Section 1 for details on how conclusions are reached.

Brand	Year	Type	Length	Model	Chassis	Engine	Fuel Type	Average Price per Linear Foot When New	Adjusted Wheelbase	Approx. Towing Capacity	Gross Vehicle Weight Rating	Average Curb Weight
Foretravel	1998	MHA	40	U295WTFE	UN	CU325	D	$8800	276	5,000	31,000	28,371

Livability Code: FT 30-90   Wheelbase-to-length ratio of 58% is considered ○ dangerous ○ fatiguing ○ good ◉ excellent *

The approximate net payload of 2630 pounds at 8% of GVWR on this model is ○ deficient ○ excessive ◉ cautionary ○ good ○ excellent *

Total highway safety penalties are: 2 *   Value: 8 6   Durability: 8 1   Highway Control Rating: 7 9   Highway Safety: 7 7   ★★★

Brand	Year	Type	Length	Model	Chassis	Engine	Fuel	Price/LF	Wheelbase	Towing	GVWR	Curb Wt
Foretravel	1998	MHA	40	U295WTME	UN	CU325	D	$8800	276	5,000	31,000	28,271

Livability Code: FT 30-90   Wheelbase-to-length ratio of 58% is considered ○ dangerous ○ fatiguing ○ good ◉ excellent *

The approximate net payload of 2730 pounds at 9% of GVWR on this model is ○ deficient ○ excessive ◉ cautionary ○ good ○ excellent *

Total highway safety penalties are: 2 *   Value: 8 6   Durability: 8 1   Highway Control Rating: 8 4   Highway Safety: 8 2   ★★★★

Foretravel	1998	MHA	40	U320CAI	UN	CU450	D	$10100	276	5,650	32,350	29,738

Livability Code: FT 30-90   Wheelbase-to-length ratio of 58% is considered ○ dangerous ○ fatiguing ○ good ◉ excellent *

The approximate net payload of 2613 pounds at 8% of GVWR on this model is ○ deficient ○ excessive ◉ cautionary ○ good ○ excellent *

Total highway safety penalties are: 2 *   Value: 8 6   Durability: 8 1   Highway Control Rating: 7 9   Highway Safety: 7 7   ★★★

Foretravel	1998	MHA	40	U320WTFE	UN	CU450	D	$10100	276	5,650	32,350	29,668

Livability Code: FT 30-90   Wheelbase-to-length ratio of 58% is considered ○ dangerous ○ fatiguing ○ good ◉ excellent *

The approximate net payload of 2683 pounds at 8% of GVWR on this model is ○ deficient ○ excessive ◉ cautionary ○ good ○ excellent *

Total highway safety penalties are: 2 *   Value: 8 6   Durability: 8 1   Highway Control Rating: 7 9   Highway Safety: 7 7   ★★★

Foretravel	1998	MHA	40	U320WTME	UN	CU450	D	$10100	276	5,650	32,350	29,558

Livability Code: FT 30-90   Wheelbase-to-length ratio of 58% is considered ○ dangerous ○ fatiguing ○ good ◉ excellent *

The approximate net payload of 2793 pounds at 9% of GVWR on this model is ○ deficient ○ excessive ◉ cautionary ○ good ○ excellent *

Total highway safety penalties are: 2 *   Value: 8 6   Durability: 8 1   Highway Control Rating: 8 4   Highway Safety: 8 2   ★★★★

Foretravel	1998	MHA	42	U320RCFE	UN	CU450	D	$10900	300 T	6,000	42,000	33,786

Livability Code: FT 30-90   Wheelbase-to-length ratio of 60% is considered ○ dangerous ○ fatiguing ○ good ◉ excellent *

The approximate net payload of 8214 pounds at 20% of GVWR on this model is ○ deficient ○ excessive ○ cautionary ○ good ◉ excellent *

Total highway safety penalties are: 4 *   Value: 8 5   Durability: 8 1   Highway Control Rating: 1 0 0   Highway Safety: 9 6   ★★★★

Foretravel	1998	MHA	42	U320DGFE	UN	CU450	D	$10900	300 T	6,000	42,000	33,616

Livability Code: FT 30-90   Wheelbase-to-length ratio of 60% is considered ○ dangerous ○ fatiguing ○ good ◉ excellent *

The approximate net payload of 8384 pounds at 20% of GVWR on this model is ○ deficient ○ excessive ○ cautionary ○ good ◉ excellent *

Total highway safety penalties are: 4 *   Value: 8 5   Durability: 8 1   Highway Control Rating: 1 0 0   Highway Safety: 9 6   ★★★★

Foretravel	1999	MHA	34	U270 3402 WTFE	UN	CU350	D	$12600	204	10,000	31,000	25,695

Livability Code: FT 30-90   Wheelbase-to-length ratio of 50% is considered ◉ dangerous ○ fatiguing ○ good ○ excellent *

The approximate net payload of 5305 pounds at 17% of GVWR on this model is ○ deficient ○ excessive ○ cautionary ○ good ◉ excellent *

Total highway safety penalties are: 2 *   Value: 8 6   Durability: 8 1   Highway Control Rating: 5 6   Highway Safety: 5 4

Foretravel	1999	MHA	36	U270 3602 WTFE	UN	CU350	D	$11900	228	10,000	31,000	26,191

Livability Code: FT 30-90   Wheelbase-to-length ratio of 53% is considered ○ dangerous ◉ fatiguing ○ good ○ excellent *

The approximate net payload of 4809 pounds at 16% of GVWR on this model is ○ deficient ○ excessive ○ cautionary ○ good ◉ excellent *

Total highway safety penalties are: 2 *   Value: 8 6   Durability: 8 1   Highway Control Rating: 7 4   Highway Safety: 7 2   ★★★

Foretravel	1999	MHA	36	U295 3600 CAI	UN	CU350	D	$11900	228	10,000	33,000	27,331

Livability Code: FT 30-90   Wheelbase-to-length ratio of 53% is considered ○ dangerous ◉ fatiguing ○ good ○ excellent *

The approximate net payload of 5669 pounds at 17% of GVWR on this model is ○ deficient ○ excessive ○ cautionary ○ good ◉ excellent *

Total highway safety penalties are: 2 *   Value: 8 6   Durability: 8 1   Highway Control Rating: 7 6   Highway Safety: 7 4   ★★★

Foretravel	1999	MHA	36	U295 3600 WTFE	UN	CU350	D	$11900	228	10,000	33,000	27,251

Livability Code: FT 30-90   Wheelbase-to-length ratio of 53% is considered ○ dangerous ◉ fatiguing ○ good ○ excellent *

The approximate net payload of 5749 pounds at 17% of GVWR on this model is ○ deficient ○ excessive ○ cautionary ○ good ◉ excellent *

Total highway safety penalties are: 2 *   Value: 8 6   Durability: 8 1   Highway Control Rating: 7 6   Highway Safety: 7 4   ★★★

Foretravel	1999	MHA	36	U320 3600 CAI	UN	CU450	D	$11900	228	10,000	34,880	28,624

Livability Code: FT 30-90   Wheelbase-to-length ratio of 53% is considered ○ dangerous ◉ fatiguing ○ good ○ excellent *

The approximate net payload of 6257 pounds at 18% of GVWR on this model is ○ deficient ○ excessive ○ cautionary ○ good ◉ excellent *

Total highway safety penalties are: 2 *   Value: 8 6   Durability: 8 1   Highway Control Rating: 7 7   Highway Safety: 7 5   ★★★

Note: Safety ratings are based on the assumption that the engineering of the RV has allowed for proper balance by placing fresh, gray, and black holding tanks in a location so as not to change the balance of the RV when the tanks are empty or full. **Always double-check wheelbase, GVWR, and weights at front and rear axles.**

Brand	Year	Type	Length	Model	Chassis	Engine	Fuel Type	Average Price per Linear Foot When New	Adjusted Wheelbase	Approx. Towing Capacity	Gross Vehicle Weight Rating	Average Curb Weight
Foretravel	1999	MHA	36	U320 3600 WTFE	UN	CU450	D	$11900	228	10,000	34,880	28,584

Livability Code: FT 30-90
Wheelbase-to-length ratio of 53% is considered ○ dangerous ● fatiguing ○ good ○ excellent *
The approximate net payload of 6297 pounds at 18% of GVWR on this model is ○ deficient ○ excessive ○ cautionary ○ good ● excellent *
Total highway safety penalties are: 2 * Value: 8 6 Durability: 8 1 Highway Control Rating: 7 7 Highway Safety: 7 5 ★★★

Brand	Year	Type	Length	Model	Chassis	Engine	Fuel Type	Price/ft	Wheelbase	Towing	GVWR	Curb Weight
Foretravel	1999	MHA	40	U270 4002 CAI	UN	CU350	D	$11000	276	10,000	31,000	27,563

Livability Code: FT 30-90
Wheelbase-to-length ratio of 58% is considered ○ dangerous ○ fatiguing ○ good ● excellent *
The approximate net payload of 3437 pounds at 11% of GVWR on this model is ○ deficient ○ excessive ○ cautionary ● good ○ excellent *
Total highway safety penalties are: 2 * Value: 8 6 Durability: 8 1 Highway Control Rating: 9 2 Highway Safety: 9 0 ★★★★

Foretravel	1999	MHA	40	U295 4000 CAI	UN	CU350	D	$11000	276	10,000	33,000	28,513

Livability Code: FT 30-90
Wheelbase-to-length ratio of 58% is considered ○ dangerous ○ fatiguing ○ good ● excellent *
The approximate net payload of 4487 pounds at 14% of GVWR on this model is ○ deficient ○ excessive ○ cautionary ● good ○ excellent *
Total highway safety penalties are: 2 * Value: 8 6 Durability: 8 1 Highway Control Rating: 9 7 Highway Safety: 9 5 ★★★★

Foretravel	1999	MHA	40	U295 4000 WTFE	UN	CU350	D	$11000	276	10,000	33,000	28,593

Livability Code: FT 30-90
Wheelbase-to-length ratio of 58% is considered ○ dangerous ○ fatiguing ○ good ● excellent *
The approximate net payload of 4407 pounds at 13% of GVWR on this model is ○ deficient ○ excessive ○ cautionary ● good ○ excellent *
Total highway safety penalties are: 2 * Value: 8 6 Durability: 8 1 Highway Control Rating: 9 6 Highway Safety: 9 4 ★★★★

Foretravel	1999	MHA	40	U295 4000 DGFE	UN	CU350	D	$11000	276	10,000	33,000	28,633

Livability Code: FT 30-90
Wheelbase-to-length ratio of 58% is considered ○ dangerous ○ fatiguing ○ good ● excellent *
The approximate net payload of 4367 pounds at 13% of GVWR on this model is ○ deficient ○ excessive ○ cautionary ● good ○ excellent *
Total highway safety penalties are: 2 * Value: 8 6 Durability: 8 1 Highway Control Rating: 9 6 Highway Safety: 9 4 ★★★★

Foretravel	1999	MHA	40	U320 4000 CAI	UN	CU450	D	$11000	276	10,000	34,880	29,956

Livability Code: FT 30-90
Wheelbase-to-length ratio of 58% is considered ○ dangerous ○ fatiguing ○ good ● excellent *
The approximate net payload of 4925 pounds at 14% of GVWR on this model is ○ deficient ○ excessive ○ cautionary ● good ○ excellent *
Total highway safety penalties are: 2 * Value: 8 6 Durability: 8 1 Highway Control Rating: 9 8 Highway Safety: 9 6 ★★★★

Foretravel	1999	MHA	40	U320 4000 WTFE	UN	CU450	D	$11000	276	10,000	34,880	29,826

Livability Code: FT 30-90
Wheelbase-to-length ratio of 58% is considered ○ dangerous ○ fatiguing ○ good ● excellent *
The approximate net payload of 5055 pounds at 14% of GVWR on this model is ○ deficient ○ excessive ○ cautionary ● good ○ excellent *
Total highway safety penalties are: 2 * Value: 8 6 Durability: 8 1 Highway Control Rating: 9 8 Highway Safety: 9 6 ★★★★

Foretravel	1999	MHA	40	U320 4000 DGFE	UN	CU450	D	$11000	276	10,000	34,880	30,269

Livability Code: FT 30-90
Wheelbase-to-length ratio of 58% is considered ○ dangerous ○ fatiguing ○ good ● excellent *
The approximate net payload of 4611 pounds at 13% of GVWR on this model is ○ deficient ○ excessive ○ cautionary ● good ○ excellent *
Total highway safety penalties are: 2 * Value: 8 6 Durability: 8 1 Highway Control Rating: 9 6 Highway Safety: 9 4 ★★★★

Foretravel	1999	MHA	42	U320 4200 RCFE	UN	CU450	D	$10500	300 T	10,000	42,000	33,002

Livability Code: FT 30-90
Wheelbase-to-length ratio of 60% is considered ○ dangerous ○ fatiguing ○ good ● excellent *
The approximate net payload of 8999 pounds at 21% of GVWR on this model is ○ deficient ○ excessive ○ cautionary ○ good ● excellent *
Total highway safety penalties are: 4 * Value: 8 5 Durability: 8 1 Highway Control Rating: 1 0 0 Highway Safety: 9 6 ★★★★

Foretravel	1999	MHA	42	U320 4200 DGFE	UN	CU450	D	$10500	300 T	10,000	42,000	33,432

Livability Code: FT 30-90
Wheelbase-to-length ratio of 60% is considered ○ dangerous ○ fatiguing ○ good ● excellent *
The approximate net payload of 8569 pounds at 20% of GVWR on this model is ○ deficient ○ excessive ○ cautionary ○ good ● excellent *
Total highway safety penalties are: 4 * Value: 8 5 Durability: 8 1 Highway Control Rating: 1 0 0 Highway Safety: 9 6 ★★★★

Holiday Rambler 1000	1992	MHA	30	29 WBXS	CH	7.4L	G	$1900	178	4,200	14,800	12,481

Livability Code: SB 30-90
Wheelbase-to-length ratio of 49% is considered ● dangerous ○ fatiguing ○ good ○ excellent *
The approximate net payload of 2319 pounds at 16% of GVWR on this model is ○ deficient ○ excessive ○ cautionary ○ good ● excellent *
Total highway safety penalties are: 5 * Value: 8 0 Durability: 8 0 Highway Control Rating: 4 2 Highway Safety: 3 7

Holiday Rambler 1000	1992	MHA	30	29 WBXS	FO	7.5L	G	$1900	178	8,000	17,000	12,914

Livability Code: SB 30-90
Wheelbase-to-length ratio of 49% is considered ● dangerous ○ fatiguing ○ good ○ excellent *
The approximate net payload of 4086 pounds at 24% of GVWR on this model is ○ deficient ○ excessive ○ cautionary ○ good ● excellent *
Total highway safety penalties are: 2 * Value: 8 1 Durability: 8 0 Highway Control Rating: 4 2 Highway Safety: 4 0

Note: Safety ratings are based on the assumption that the engineering of the RV has allowed for proper balance by placing fresh, gray, and black holding tanks in a location so as not to change the balance of the RV when the tanks are empty or full. **Always double-check wheelbase, GVWR, and weights at front and rear axles.**

*See Section 1 for details on how conclusions are reached.

Brand	Year	Type	Length	Model	Chassis	Engine	Fuel Type	Average Price per Linear Foot When New	Adjusted Wheelbase	Approx. Towing Capacity	Gross Vehicle Weight Rating	Average Curb Weight
Holiday Rambler 1000	1992	MHA	32	31 CBXS	CH	7.4L	G	$1800	190	4,000	16,000	13,228

Livability Code: SB 30-90 · Wheelbase-to-length ratio of 49% is considered ●dangerous ○fatiguing ○good ○excellent *
The approximate net payload of 2772 pounds at 17% of GVWR on this model is ○deficient ○excessive ○cautionary ○good ●excellent *
Total highway safety penalties are: 6 * · Value: 7 9 · Durability: 8 0 · Highway Control Rating: 4 4 · Highway Safety: 3 8

Brand	Year	Type	Length	Model	Chassis	Engine	Fuel Type	Price/Ft	Wheelbase	Towing	GVWR	Curb Wt
Holiday Rambler 1000	1992	MHA	32	31 CSXS	CH	7.4L	G	$1800	190	4,000	16,000	13,228

Livability Code: SB 30-90 · Wheelbase-to-length ratio of 49% is considered ●dangerous ○fatiguing ○good ○excellent *
The approximate net payload of 2772 pounds at 17% of GVWR on this model is ○deficient ○excessive ○cautionary ○good ●excellent *
Total highway safety penalties are: 6 * · Value: 7 9 · Durability: 8 0 · Highway Control Rating: 4 4 · Highway Safety: 3 8

Brand	Year	Type	Length	Model	Chassis	Engine	Fuel Type	Price/Ft	Wheelbase	Towing	GVWR	Curb Wt
Holiday Rambler 1000	1992	MHA	32	31 CBXS	FO	7.5L	G	$1800	178	2,000	17,000	13,409

Livability Code: SB 30-90 · Wheelbase-to-length ratio of 46% is considered ●dangerous ○fatiguing ○good ○excellent *
The approximate net payload of 3591 pounds at 21% of GVWR on this model is ○deficient ○excessive ○cautionary ○good ●excellent *
Total highway safety penalties are: 2 * · Value: 8 1 · Durability: 8 0 · Highway Control Rating: 3 4 · Highway Safety: 3 2

Brand	Year	Type	Length	Model	Chassis	Engine	Fuel Type	Price/Ft	Wheelbase	Towing	GVWR	Curb Wt
Holiday Rambler 1000	1992	MHA	32	31 CSXS	FO	7.5L	G	$1800	178	2,000	17,000	13,409

Livability Code: SB 30-90 · Wheelbase-to-length ratio of 46% is considered ●dangerous ○fatiguing ○good ○excellent *
The approximate net payload of 3591 pounds at 21% of GVWR on this model is ○deficient ○excessive ○cautionary ○good ●excellent *
Total highway safety penalties are: 2 * · Value: 8 1 · Durability: 8 0 · Highway Control Rating: 3 4 · Highway Safety: 3 2

Brand	Year	Type	Length	Model	Chassis	Engine	Fuel Type	Price/Ft	Wheelbase	Towing	GVWR	Curb Wt
Holiday Rambler 1000	1992	MHA	34	33 CSXS	CH	7.4L	G	$1800	202 T	1,500	17,500	14,187

Livability Code: SB 30-90 · Wheelbase-to-length ratio of 50% is considered ●dangerous ○fatiguing ○good ○excellent *
The approximate net payload of 3313 pounds at 19% of GVWR on this model is ○deficient ○excessive ○cautionary ○good ●excellent *
Total highway safety penalties are: 9 * · Value: 7 8 · Durability: 8 0 · Highway Control Rating: 4 6 · Highway Safety: 3 7

Brand	Year	Type	Length	Model	Chassis	Engine	Fuel Type	Price/Ft	Wheelbase	Towing	GVWR	Curb Wt
Holiday Rambler 1000	1992	MHA	34	33 CSXS	FO	7.5L	G	$1800	208	8,000	17,000	14,059

Livability Code: SB 30-90 · Wheelbase-to-length ratio of 51% is considered ○dangerous ●fatiguing ○good ○excellent *
The approximate net payload of 2941 pounds at 17% of GVWR on this model is ○deficient ○excessive ○cautionary ○good ●excellent *
Total highway safety penalties are: 2 * · Value: 8 1 · Durability: 8 0 · Highway Control Rating: 5 0 · Highway Safety: 4 8

Brand	Year	Type	Length	Model	Chassis	Engine	Fuel Type	Price/Ft	Wheelbase	Towing	GVWR	Curb Wt
Holiday Rambler 1000	1992	MHA	35	35 CSXS	CH	7.4L	G	$1800	202 T	1,500	17,500	14,510

Livability Code: SB 30-90 · Wheelbase-to-length ratio of 48% is considered ●dangerous ○fatiguing ○good ○excellent *
The approximate net payload of 2990 pounds at 17% of GVWR on this model is ○deficient ○excessive ○cautionary ○good ●excellent *
Total highway safety penalties are: 10 * · Value: 7 7 · Durability: 8 0 · Highway Control Rating: 3 7 · Highway Safety: 2 7

Brand	Year	Type	Length	Model	Chassis	Engine	Fuel Type	Price/Ft	Wheelbase	Towing	GVWR	Curb Wt
Holiday Rambler 1000	1992	MHA	35	35 CSXS	FO	7.5L	G	$1800	208	8,000	17,000	14,433

Livability Code: SB 30-90 · Wheelbase-to-length ratio of 49% is considered ●dangerous ○fatiguing ○good ○excellent *
The approximate net payload of 2567 pounds at 15% of GVWR on this model is ○deficient ○excessive ○cautionary ●good ○excellent *
Total highway safety penalties are: 2 * · Value: 8 1 · Durability: 8 0 · Highway Control Rating: 3 9 · Highway Safety: 3 7

Brand	Year	Type	Length	Model	Chassis	Engine	Fuel Type	Price/Ft	Wheelbase	Towing	GVWR	Curb Wt
Holiday Rambler 1000	1993	MHA	30	29 WBXS	CH	7.4L	G	$2000	178	4,200	14,800	12,481

Livability Code: SB 30-90 · Wheelbase-to-length ratio of 49% is considered ●dangerous ○fatiguing ○good ○excellent *
The approximate net payload of 2319 pounds at 16% of GVWR on this model is ○deficient ○excessive ○cautionary ○good ●excellent *
Total highway safety penalties are: 5 * · Value: 8 0 · Durability: 8 0 · Highway Control Rating: 4 2 · Highway Safety: 3 7

Brand	Year	Type	Length	Model	Chassis	Engine	Fuel Type	Price/Ft	Wheelbase	Towing	GVWR	Curb Wt
Holiday Rambler 1000	1993	MHA	30	29 WBXS	FO	7.5L	G	$2000	178	8,000	17,000	12,914

Livability Code: SB 30-90 · Wheelbase-to-length ratio of 49% is considered ●dangerous ○fatiguing ○good ○excellent *
The approximate net payload of 4086 pounds at 24% of GVWR on this model is ○deficient ○excessive ○cautionary ○good ●excellent *
Total highway safety penalties are: 2 * · Value: 8 1 · Durability: 8 0 · Highway Control Rating: 4 2 · Highway Safety: 4 0

Brand	Year	Type	Length	Model	Chassis	Engine	Fuel Type	Price/Ft	Wheelbase	Towing	GVWR	Curb Wt
Holiday Rambler 1000	1993	MHA	32	31 CBXS	CH	7.4L	G	$1900	190	3,000	16,000	13,228

Livability Code: SB 30-90 · Wheelbase-to-length ratio of 49% is considered ●dangerous ○fatiguing ○good ○excellent *
The approximate net payload of 2772 pounds at 17% of GVWR on this model is ○deficient ○excessive ○cautionary ○good ●excellent *
Total highway safety penalties are: 6 * · Value: 7 9 · Durability: 8 0 · Highway Control Rating: 4 4 · Highway Safety: 3 8

Brand	Year	Type	Length	Model	Chassis	Engine	Fuel Type	Price/Ft	Wheelbase	Towing	GVWR	Curb Wt
Holiday Rambler 1000	1993	MHA	32	31 CSXS	CH	7.4L	G	$1900	190	3,000	16,000	13,228

Livability Code: SB 30-90 · Wheelbase-to-length ratio of 49% is considered ●dangerous ○fatiguing ○good ○excellent *
The approximate net payload of 2772 pounds at 17% of GVWR on this model is ○deficient ○excessive ○cautionary ○good ●excellent *
Total highway safety penalties are: 6 * · Value: 7 9 · Durability: 8 0 · Highway Control Rating: 4 4 · Highway Safety: 3 8

Note: Safety ratings are based on the assumption that the engineering of the RV has allowed for proper balance by placing fresh, gray, and black holding tanks in a location so as not to change the balance of the RV when the tanks are empty or full. **Always double-check wheelbase, GVWR, and weights at front and rear axles.**

*See Section 1 for details on how conclusions are reached.

Brand	Year	Type	Length	Model	Chassis	Engine	Fuel Type	Average Price per Linear Foot When New	Adjusted Wheelbase	Approx. Towing Capacity	Gross Vehicle Weight Rating	Average Curb Weight
Holiday Rambler 1000	**1993**	MHA	32	31 CBXS	FO	7.5L	G	$1900	190	8,000	17,000	13,409

Livability Code: SB 30-90
Wheelbase-to-length ratio of 49% is considered ◉ dangerous ○ fatiguing ○ good ○ excellent *
The approximate net payload of 3591 pounds at 21% of GVWR on this model is ○ deficient ○ excessive ○ cautionary ○ good ◉ excellent *
Total highway safety penalties are: 2 *   Value: **8 1**   Durability: **8 0**   Highway Control Rating: **4 5**   Highway Safety: **4 3**

Brand	Year	Type	Length	Model	Chassis	Engine	Fuel Type	Average Price per Linear Foot When New	Adjusted Wheelbase	Approx. Towing Capacity	Gross Vehicle Weight Rating	Average Curb Weight
Holiday Rambler 1000	**1993**	MHA	32	31 CSXS	FO	7.5L	G	$1900	190	8,000	17,000	13,409

Livability Code: SB 30-90
Wheelbase-to-length ratio of 49% is considered ◉ dangerous ○ fatiguing ○ good ○ excellent *
The approximate net payload of 3591 pounds at 21% of GVWR on this model is ○ deficient ○ excessive ○ cautionary ○ good ◉ excellent *
Total highway safety penalties are: 2 *   Value: **8 1**   Durability: **8 0**   Highway Control Rating: **4 5**   Highway Safety: **4 3**

Brand	Year	Type	Length	Model	Chassis	Engine	Fuel Type	Average Price per Linear Foot When New	Adjusted Wheelbase	Approx. Towing Capacity	Gross Vehicle Weight Rating	Average Curb Weight
Holiday Rambler 1000	**1993**	MHA	34	33 CST	CH	7.4L	G	$2000	202 T	1,500	18,000	14,451

Livability Code: SB 30-90
Wheelbase-to-length ratio of 50% is considered ◉ dangerous ○ fatiguing ○ good ○ excellent *
The approximate net payload of 3549 pounds at 20% of GVWR on this model is ○ deficient ○ excessive ○ cautionary ○ good ◉ excellent *
Total highway safety penalties are: 9 *   Value: **7 8**   Durability: **8 0**   Highway Control Rating: **4 7**   Highway Safety: **3 8**

Brand	Year	Type	Length	Model	Chassis	Engine	Fuel Type	Average Price per Linear Foot When New	Adjusted Wheelbase	Approx. Towing Capacity	Gross Vehicle Weight Rating	Average Curb Weight
Holiday Rambler 1000	**1993**	MHA	34	33 CSXS	FO	7.5L	G	$1900	208	8,000	17,000	14,059

Livability Code: SB 30-90
Wheelbase-to-length ratio of 51% is considered ○ dangerous ◉ fatiguing ○ good ○ excellent *
The approximate net payload of 2941 pounds at 17% of GVWR on this model is ○ deficient ○ excessive ○ cautionary ○ good ◉ excellent *
Total highway safety penalties are: 2 *   Value: **8 1**   Durability: **8 0**   Highway Control Rating: **5 0**   Highway Safety: **4 8**

Brand	Year	Type	Length	Model	Chassis	Engine	Fuel Type	Average Price per Linear Foot When New	Adjusted Wheelbase	Approx. Towing Capacity	Gross Vehicle Weight Rating	Average Curb Weight
Holiday Rambler 1000	**1993**	MHA	34	33 CST	FO	7.5L	G	$2000	202 T	5,600	19,400	14,381

Livability Code: SB 30-90
Wheelbase-to-length ratio of 50% is considered ◉ dangerous ○ fatiguing ○ good ○ excellent *
The approximate net payload of 5019 pounds at 26% of GVWR on this model is ○ deficient ○ excessive ○ cautionary ◉ good ○ excellent *
Total highway safety penalties are: 4 *   Value: **8 0**   Durability: **8 0**   Highway Control Rating: **4 2**   Highway Safety: **3 8**

Brand	Year	Type	Length	Model	Chassis	Engine	Fuel Type	Average Price per Linear Foot When New	Adjusted Wheelbase	Approx. Towing Capacity	Gross Vehicle Weight Rating	Average Curb Weight
Holiday Rambler 1000	**1993**	MHA	35	35 CST	CH	7.4L	G	$2000	202 T	1,500	18,000	14,772

Livability Code: SB 30-90
Wheelbase-to-length ratio of 48% is considered ◉ dangerous ○ fatiguing ○ good ○ excellent *
The approximate net payload of 3228 pounds at 18% of GVWR on this model is ○ deficient ○ excessive ○ cautionary ○ good ◉ excellent *
Total highway safety penalties are: 10 *   Value: **7 7**   Durability: **8 0**   Highway Control Rating: **3 8**   Highway Safety: **2 8**

Brand	Year	Type	Length	Model	Chassis	Engine	Fuel Type	Average Price per Linear Foot When New	Adjusted Wheelbase	Approx. Towing Capacity	Gross Vehicle Weight Rating	Average Curb Weight
Holiday Rambler 1000	**1993**	MHA	35	35 CSXS	FO	7.5L	G	$1900	228	8,000	17,000	14,433

Livability Code: SB 30-90
Wheelbase-to-length ratio of 54% is considered ○ dangerous ○ fatiguing ◉ good ○ excellent *
The approximate net payload of 2567 pounds at 15% of GVWR on this model is ○ deficient ○ excessive ○ cautionary ○ good ○ excellent *
Total highway safety penalties are: 2 *   Value: **8 1**   Durability: **8 0**   Highway Control Rating: **7 8**   Highway Safety: **7 6**   ★★★

Brand	Year	Type	Length	Model	Chassis	Engine	Fuel Type	Average Price per Linear Foot When New	Adjusted Wheelbase	Approx. Towing Capacity	Gross Vehicle Weight Rating	Average Curb Weight
Holiday Rambler 1000	**1993**	MHA	35	35 CST	FO	7.5L	G	$2000	202 T	5,600	19,400	14,674

Livability Code: SB 30-90
Wheelbase-to-length ratio of 48% is considered ◉ dangerous ○ fatiguing ○ good ○ excellent *
The approximate net payload of 4726 pounds at 24% of GVWR on this model is ○ deficient ○ excessive ○ cautionary ○ good ◉ excellent *
Total highway safety penalties are: 4 *   Value: **8 0**   Durability: **8 0**   Highway Control Rating: **3 6**   Highway Safety: **3 2**

Brand	Year	Type	Length	Model	Chassis	Engine	Fuel Type	Average Price per Linear Foot When New	Adjusted Wheelbase	Approx. Towing Capacity	Gross Vehicle Weight Rating	Average Curb Weight
HRC Limited	**1990**	MHA	40	40 CB	GI	Cat	D	$5500	262	1,500	29,640	25,059

Livability Code: SB 30-90
Wheelbase-to-length ratio of 55% is considered ○ dangerous ○ fatiguing ◉ good ○ excellent *
The approximate net payload of 4581 pounds at 15% of GVWR on this model is ○ deficient ○ excessive ○ cautionary ◉ good ○ excellent *
Total highway safety penalties are: 2 *   Value: **8 1**   Durability: **8 0**   Highway Control Rating: **9 0**   Highway Safety: **8 8**   ★★★★

Brand	Year	Type	Length	Model	Chassis	Engine	Fuel Type	Average Price per Linear Foot When New	Adjusted Wheelbase	Approx. Towing Capacity	Gross Vehicle Weight Rating	Average Curb Weight
Imperial	**1987**	MHA	40	40	GI	Cat	D	$4500	262	1,500	25,800	21,791

Livability Code: FT 30-90
Wheelbase-to-length ratio of 55% is considered ○ dangerous ○ fatiguing ◉ good ○ excellent *
The approximate net payload of 4009 pounds at 16% of GVWR on this model is ○ deficient ○ excessive ○ cautionary ○ good ◉ excellent *
Total highway safety penalties are: 2 *   Value: **8 2**   Durability: **8 3**   Highway Control Rating: **9 1**   Highway Safety: **8 9**   ★★★★

Brand	Year	Type	Length	Model	Chassis	Engine	Fuel Type	Average Price per Linear Foot When New	Adjusted Wheelbase	Approx. Towing Capacity	Gross Vehicle Weight Rating	Average Curb Weight
Imperial	**1990**	MHA	33	33 CSXS	CH	7.4L	G	$2500	202 T	1,500	16,500	15,084

Livability Code: SB 30-90
Wheelbase-to-length ratio of 50% is considered ◉ dangerous ○ fatiguing ○ good ○ excellent *
The approximate net payload of 1416 pounds at 9% of GVWR on this model is ○ deficient ○ excessive ◉ cautionary ○ good ○ excellent *
Total highway safety penalties are: 9 *   Value: **7 9**   Durability: **8 3**   Highway Control Rating: **2 9**   Highway Safety: **2 0**

Brand	Year	Type	Length	Model	Chassis	Engine	Fuel Type	Average Price per Linear Foot When New	Adjusted Wheelbase	Approx. Towing Capacity	Gross Vehicle Weight Rating	Average Curb Weight
Imperial	**1990**	MHC	28	27SB	FO	7.5L	G	$2000	158	1,500	14,000	12,805

Livability Code: FT 30-90
Wheelbase-to-length ratio of 47% is considered ◉ dangerous ○ fatiguing ○ good ○ excellent *
The approximate net payload of 1196 pounds at 9% of GVWR on this model is ○ deficient ○ excessive ◉ cautionary ○ good ○ excellent *
Total highway safety penalties are: 2 *   Value: **8 1**   Durability: **8 0**   Highway Control Rating: **3 2**   Highway Safety: **3 0**

Note: Safety ratings are based on the assumption that the engineering of the RV has allowed for proper balance by placing fresh, gray, and black holding tanks in a location so as not to change the balance of the RV when the tanks are empty or full. **Always double-check wheelbase, GVWR, and weights at front and rear axles.**

*See Section 1 for details on how conclusions are reached.

Brand	Year	Type	Length	Model	Chassis	Engine	Fuel Type	Average Price per Linear Foot When New	Adjusted Wheel-base	Approx. Towing Capacity	Gross Vehicle Weight Rating	Average Curb Weight
Imperial	1991	MHA	35	34 CS	CH	7.4L	G	$2500	202 T	1,500	17,200	15,658

Livability Code: SB 30-90   Wheelbase-to-length ratio of 48% is considered ◉ dangerous ○ fatiguing ○ good ○ excellent *

The approximate net payload of 1543 pounds at 9% of GVWR on this model is ○ deficient ◉ excessive ◉ cautionary ○ good ○ excellent *

Total highway safety penalties are: 9 *   Value: 79 Durability: 83 Highway Control Rating: 21   Highway Safety: 12

| Imperial | 1991 | MHC | 29 | 28 CB | FO | 7.5L | G | $2000 | 176 | 1,500 | 14,000 | 13,494 |

Livability Code: VA 30-90   Wheelbase-to-length ratio of 51% is considered ○ dangerous ◉ fatiguing ○ good ○ excellent *

The approximate net payload of 506 pounds at 4% of GVWR on this model is ◉ deficient ○ excessive ○ cautionary ○ good ○ excellent *

Total highway safety penalties are: 2 *   Value: 82 Durability: 83 Highway Control Rating: 26   Highway Safety: 24

| Imperial | 1994 | MHA | 34 | 33CS | CH | 7.4L | G | $3200 | 202 T | 1,000 | 18,000 | 16,900 |

Livability Code: FT 30-90   Wheelbase-to-length ratio of 50% is considered ◉ dangerous ○ fatiguing ○ good ○ excellent *

The approximate net payload of 1100 pounds at 6% of GVWR on this model is ◉ deficient ○ excessive ○ cautionary ○ good ○ excellent *

Total highway safety penalties are: 9 *   Value: 79 Durability: 83 Highway Control Rating: 11   Highway Safety: 2

| Imperial | 1994 | MHA | 34 | 33CS | FO | 7.5L | G | $3200 | 202 T | 5,600 | 19,400 | 17,235 |

Livability Code: FT 30-90   Wheelbase-to-length ratio of 50% is considered ◉ dangerous ○ fatiguing ○ good ○ excellent *

The approximate net payload of 2165 pounds at 11% of GVWR on this model is ○ deficient ○ excessive ○ cautionary ◉ good ○ excellent *

Total highway safety penalties are: 4 *   Value: 81 Durability: 83 Highway Control Rating: 36   Highway Safety: 32

| Imperial | 1994 | MHA | 35 | 35CS | CH | 7.4L | G | $3100 | 202 T | 1,000 | 18,000 | 17,301 |

Livability Code: FT 30-90   Wheelbase-to-length ratio of 48% is considered ◉ dangerous ○ fatiguing ○ good ○ excellent *

The approximate net payload of 699 pounds at 4% of GVWR on this model is ◉ deficient ○ excessive ○ cautionary ○ good ○ excellent *

Total highway safety penalties are: 9 *   Value: 78 Durability: 83 Highway Control Rating: 1   Highway Safety: - 8

| Imperial | 1994 | MHA | 35 | 35CS | FO | 7.5L | G | $3100 | 202 T | 5,600 | 19,400 | 17,774 |

Livability Code: FT 30-90   Wheelbase-to-length ratio of 48% is considered ◉ dangerous ○ fatiguing ○ good ○ excellent *

The approximate net payload of 1626 pounds at 8% of GVWR on this model is ○ deficient ○ excessive ◉ cautionary ○ good ○ excellent *

Total highway safety penalties are: 4 *   Value: 81 Durability: 83 Highway Control Rating: 15   Highway Safety: 11

| Imperial | 1994 | MHA | 36 | 36SA | CH | 7.4L | G | $3100 | 214 T | 1,000 | 18,000 | 17,547 |

Livability Code: FT 30-90   Wheelbase-to-length ratio of 49% is considered ◉ dangerous ○ fatiguing ○ good ○ excellent *

The approximate net payload of 453 pounds at 3% of GVWR on this model is ◉ deficient ○ excessive ○ cautionary ○ good ○ excellent *

Total highway safety penalties are: 10 *   Value: 78 Durability: 83 Highway Control Rating: 4   Highway Safety: - 6

| Imperial | 1994 | MHA | 36 | 36SA | FO | 7.5L | G | $3100 | 214 T | 5,600 | 19,400 | 18,116 |

Livability Code: FT 30-90   Wheelbase-to-length ratio of 49% is considered ◉ dangerous ○ fatiguing ○ good ○ excellent *

The approximate net payload of 1284 pounds at 7% of GVWR on this model is ○ deficient ○ excessive ◉ cautionary ○ good ○ excellent *

Total highway safety penalties are: 4 *   Value: 81 Durability: 83 Highway Control Rating: 13   Highway Safety: 9

| Imperial | 1994 | MHA | 36 | 36W | SP | CU250 | D | $4300 | 252 | 5,000 | 26,000 | 22,382 |

Livability Code: FT 30-90   Wheelbase-to-length ratio of 58% is considered ○ dangerous ○ fatiguing ○ good ◉ excellent *

The approximate net payload of 3618 pounds at 14% of GVWR on this model is ○ deficient ○ excessive ○ cautionary ◉ good ○ excellent *

Total highway safety penalties are: 2 *   Value: 82 Durability: 83 Highway Control Rating: 98   Highway Safety: 96   ★★★★

| Imperial | 1994 | MHA | 36 | 36S | SP | CU250 | D | $4200 | 252 | 5,000 | 26,000 | 22,732 |

Livability Code: FT 30-90   Wheelbase-to-length ratio of 58% is considered ○ dangerous ○ fatiguing ○ good ◉ excellent *

The approximate net payload of 3268 pounds at 13% of GVWR on this model is ○ deficient ○ excessive ○ cautionary ◉ good ○ excellent *

Total highway safety penalties are: 2 *   Value: 82 Durability: 83 Highway Control Rating: 96   Highway Safety: 94   ★★★★

| Imperial | 1994 | MHA | 38 | 37CB | FO | 7.5L | G | $2900 | 232 T | 5,600 | 19,400 | 19,018 |

Livability Code: FT 30-90   Wheelbase-to-length ratio of 51% is considered ○ dangerous ◉ fatiguing ○ good ○ excellent *

The approximate net payload of 382 pounds at 2% of GVWR on this model is ◉ deficient ○ excessive ○ cautionary ○ good ○ excellent *

Total highway safety penalties are: 4 *   Value: 81 Durability: 83 Highway Control Rating: 9   Highway Safety: 5

| Imperial | 1995 | MHA | 37 | 36WD | SP | CU250 | D | $4100 | 246 | 3,500 | 29,000 | 23,463 |

Livability Code: FT 30-90   Wheelbase-to-length ratio of 56% is considered ○ dangerous ○ fatiguing ◉ good ○ excellent *

The approximate net payload of 5537 pounds at 19% of GVWR on this model is ○ deficient ○ excessive ○ cautionary ○ good ◉ excellent *

Total highway safety penalties are: 2 *   Value: 81 Durability: 80 Highway Control Rating: 98   Highway Safety: 96   ★★★★

Note: Safety ratings are based on the assumption that the engineering of the RV has allowed for proper balance by placing fresh, gray, and black holding tanks in a location so as not to change the balance of the RV when the tanks are empty or full. **Always double-check wheelbase, GVWR, and weights at front and rear axles.**

The RV Rating Book

*See Section 1 for details on how conclusions are reached.

Brand	Year	Type	Length	Model	Chassis	Engine	Fuel Type	Average Price per Linear Foot When New	Adjusted Wheelbase	Approx. Towing Capacity	Gross Vehicle Weight Rating	Average Curb Weight
Imperial	1995	MHA	38	37SD	SP	CU250	D	$4300	262	3,500	29,000	24,477

Livability Code: FT 30-90
Wheelbase-to-length ratio of 58% is considered ○ dangerous ○ fatiguing ○ good ◉ excellent *
The approximate net payload of 4523 pounds at 16% of GVWR on this model is ○ deficient ○ excessive ○ cautionary ○ good ◉ excellent *
Total highway safety penalties are: 2 *   Value: **82** Durability: **83** Highway Control Rating: **100** Highway Safety: **98** ★★★★

| Imperial | 1995 | MHA | 38 | 37WDS-sl | SP | CU250 | D | $4400 | 262 | 3,500 | 29,000 | 25,221 |

Livability Code: FT 30-90
Wheelbase-to-length ratio of 58% is considered ○ dangerous ○ fatiguing ○ good ◉ excellent *
The approximate net payload of 3779 pounds at 13% of GVWR on this model is ○ deficient ○ excessive ○ cautionary ◉ good ○ excellent *
Total highway safety penalties are: 7 *   Value: **80** Durability: **83** Highway Control Rating: **96** Highway Safety: **89** ★★★★

| Imperial | 1995 | MHA | 38 | 37SDS-sl | SP | CU250 | D | $4400 | 262 | 3,500 | 29,000 | 25,109 |

Livability Code: FT 30-90
Wheelbase-to-length ratio of 58% is considered ○ dangerous ○ fatiguing ○ good ◉ excellent *
The approximate net payload of 3891 pounds at 13% of GVWR on this model is ○ deficient ○ excessive ○ cautionary ◉ good ○ excellent *
Total highway safety penalties are: 7 *   Value: **80** Durability: **83** Highway Control Rating: **96** Highway Safety: **89** ★★★★

| Imperial | 1995 | MHA | 39 | 39WD | SP | CU250 | D | $4200 | 246 | 3,500 | 29,000 | 24,423 |

Livability Code: FT 30-90
Wheelbase-to-length ratio of 52% is considered ○ dangerous ◉ fatiguing ○ good ○ excellent *
The approximate net payload of 4577 pounds at 16% of GVWR on this model is ○ deficient ○ excessive ○ cautionary ○ good ◉ excellent *
Total highway safety penalties are: 2 *   Value: **82** Durability: **83** Highway Control Rating: **60** Highway Safety: **58** ★

| Imperial | 1996 | MHA | 37 | 36WD | SP | CU250 | D | $4500 | 246 | 4,000 | 29,000 | 23,463 |

Livability Code: FT 30-90
Wheelbase-to-length ratio of 56% is considered ○ dangerous ○ fatiguing ◉ good ○ excellent *
The approximate net payload of 5537 pounds at 19% of GVWR on this model is ○ deficient ○ excessive ○ cautionary ○ good ◉ excellent *
Total highway safety penalties are: 2 *   Value: **82** Durability: **83** Highway Control Rating: **98** Highway Safety: **96** ★★★★

| Imperial | 1996 | MHA | 38 | 37SD | SP | CU250 | D | $4400 | 262 | 4,000 | 29,000 | 24,477 |

Livability Code: FT 30-90
Wheelbase-to-length ratio of 58% is considered ○ dangerous ○ fatiguing ○ good ◉ excellent *
The approximate net payload of 4523 pounds at 16% of GVWR on this model is ○ deficient ○ excessive ○ cautionary ○ good ◉ excellent *
Total highway safety penalties are: 2 *   Value: **82** Durability: **83** Highway Control Rating: **100** Highway Safety: **98** ★★★★

| Imperial | 1996 | MHA | 38 | 37WDS-sl | SP | CU250 | D | $4500 | 262 | 4,000 | 29,000 | 25,221 |

Livability Code: FT 30-90
Wheelbase-to-length ratio of 58% is considered ○ dangerous ○ fatiguing ○ good ◉ excellent *
The approximate net payload of 3779 pounds at 13% of GVWR on this model is ○ deficient ○ excessive ○ cautionary ◉ good ○ excellent *
Total highway safety penalties are: 7 *   Value: **80** Durability: **83** Highway Control Rating: **96** Highway Safety: **89** ★★★★

| Imperial | 1996 | MHA | 38 | 37SDS-sl | SP | CU250 | D | $4500 | 262 | 4,000 | 29,000 | 25,109 |

Livability Code: FT 30-90
Wheelbase-to-length ratio of 58% is considered ○ dangerous ○ fatiguing ○ good ◉ excellent *
The approximate net payload of 3891 pounds at 13% of GVWR on this model is ○ deficient ○ excessive ○ cautionary ◉ good ○ excellent *
Total highway safety penalties are: 7 *   Value: **80** Durability: **83** Highway Control Rating: **96** Highway Safety: **89** ★★★★

| Imperial | 1996 | MHA | 39 | 39WD | SP | CU250 | D | $4600 | 246 | 4,000 | 29,000 | 24,823 |

Livability Code: FT 30-90
Wheelbase-to-length ratio of 52% is considered ○ dangerous ◉ fatiguing ○ good ○ excellent *
The approximate net payload of 4177 pounds at 14% of GVWR on this model is ○ deficient ○ excessive ○ cautionary ◉ good ○ excellent *
Total highway safety penalties are: 2 *   Value: **82** Durability: **83** Highway Control Rating: **56** Highway Safety: **54** ★

| Imperial | 1996 | MHA | 39 | 39WDS-sl | SP | CU250 | D | $4600 | 246 | 4,000 | 29,000 | 26,141 |

Livability Code: FT 30-90
Wheelbase-to-length ratio of 52% is considered ○ dangerous ◉ fatiguing ○ good ○ excellent *
The approximate net payload of 2859 pounds at 10% of GVWR on this model is ○ deficient ○ excessive ○ cautionary ◉ good ○ excellent *
Total highway safety penalties are: 7 *   Value: **80** Durability: **83** Highway Control Rating: **48** Highway Safety: **41**

| Imperial | 1997 | MHA | 37 | 36WD | SP | CU300 | D | $4600 | 220 | 4,000 | 29,000 | 24,054 |

Livability Code: FT 30-90
Wheelbase-to-length ratio of 50% is considered ◉ dangerous ○ fatiguing ○ good ○ excellent *
The approximate net payload of 4946 pounds at 17% of GVWR on this model is ○ deficient ○ excessive ○ cautionary ○ good ◉ excellent *
Total highway safety penalties are: 2 *   Value: **82** Durability: **83** Highway Control Rating: **44** Highway Safety: **42**

| Imperial | 1997 | MHA | 38 | 37WDS | SP | CU300 | D | $4600 | 228 | 4,000 | 29,000 | 25,306 |

Livability Code: FT 30-90
Wheelbase-to-length ratio of 51% is considered ○ dangerous ◉ fatiguing ○ good ○ excellent *
The approximate net payload of 3694 pounds at 13% of GVWR on this model is ○ deficient ○ excessive ○ cautionary ◉ good ○ excellent *
Total highway safety penalties are: 8 *   Value: **79** Durability: **83** Highway Control Rating: **40** Highway Safety: **32**

Note: Safety ratings are based on the assumption that the engineering of the RV has allowed for proper balance by placing fresh, gray, and black holding tanks in a location so as not to change the balance of the RV when the tanks are empty or full. **Always double-check wheelbase, GVWR, and weights at front and rear axles.**

*See Section 1 for details on how conclusions are reached.

Brand	Year	Type	Length	Model	Chassis	Engine	Fuel Type	Average Price per Linear Foot When New	Adjusted Wheel-base	Approx. Towing Capacity	Gross Vehicle Weight Rating	Average Curb Weight
Imperial	1997	MHA	39	38CDS	SP	CU300	D	$4600	242	4,000	29,000	25,744

Livability Code: FT 30-90   Wheelbase-to-length ratio of 52% is considered ○ dangerous ● fatiguing ○ good ○ excellent*
The approximate net payload of 3256 pounds at 11% of GVWR on this model is ○ deficient ○ excessive ○ cautionary ● good ○ excellent*
Total highway safety penalties are: 13*   Value: 7 7   Durability: 8 3   Highway Control Rating: 4 9   Highway Safety: 3 6

Brand	Year	Type	Length	Model	Chassis	Engine	Fuel Type	Avg Price/LF	Wheelbase	Towing	GVWR	Curb Weight
Imperial	1997	MHA	39	38CD	SP	CU300	D	$4600	242	4,000	29,000	24,694

Livability Code: FT 30-90   Wheelbase-to-length ratio of 52% is considered ○ dangerous ● fatiguing ○ good ○ excellent*
The approximate net payload of 4306 pounds at 15% of GVWR on this model is ○ deficient ○ excessive ○ cautionary ● good ○ excellent*
Total highway safety penalties are: 2*   Value: 8 2   Durability: 8 3   Highway Control Rating: 5 7   Highway Safety: 5 5   ★

| Imperial | 1997 | MHA | 39 | 38WDS | SP | CU300 | D | $4600 | 242 | 4,000 | 29,000 | 25,744 |

Livability Code: FT 30-90   Wheelbase-to-length ratio of 52% is considered ○ dangerous ● fatiguing ○ good ○ excellent*
The approximate net payload of 3256 pounds at 11% of GVWR on this model is ○ deficient ○ excessive ○ cautionary ● good ○ excellent*
Total highway safety penalties are: 13*   Value: 7 7   Durability: 8 3   Highway Control Rating: 4 9   Highway Safety: 3 6

| Imperial | 1997 | MHA | 40 | 40WD | SP | CU300 | D | $4700 | 262 | 4,000 | 29,000 | 25,199 |

Livability Code: FT 30-90   Wheelbase-to-length ratio of 54% is considered ○ dangerous ○ fatiguing ● good ○ excellent*
The approximate net payload of 3801 pounds at 13% of GVWR on this model is ○ deficient ○ excessive ○ cautionary ● good ○ excellent*
Total highway safety penalties are: 2*   Value: 8 2   Durability: 8 3   Highway Control Rating: 7 9   Highway Safety: 7 7   ★★★

| Imperial | 1997 | MHA | 40 | 40WDS | SP | CU300 | D | $4800 | 262 | 4,000 | 29,000 | 26,249 |

Livability Code: FT 30-90   Wheelbase-to-length ratio of 54% is considered ○ dangerous ○ fatiguing ● good ○ excellent*
The approximate net payload of 2751 pounds at 9% of GVWR on this model is ○ deficient ○ excessive ● cautionary ○ good ○ excellent*
Total highway safety penalties are: 13*   Value: 7 7   Durability: 8 3   Highway Control Rating: 6 5   Highway Safety: 5 2   ★

| Imperial | 1998 | MHA | 38 | 37KDS | RO | CU325 | D | $4700 | 234 | 10,000 | 31,000 | 25,988 |

Livability Code: FT 30-90   Wheelbase-to-length ratio of 52% is considered ○ dangerous ● fatiguing ○ good ○ excellent*
The approximate net payload of 5012 pounds at 16% of GVWR on this model is ○ deficient ○ excessive ○ cautionary ○ good ● excellent*
Total highway safety penalties are: 12*   Value: 7 6   Durability: 8 0   Highway Control Rating: 5 9   Highway Safety: 4 7

| Imperial | 1998 | MHA | 39 | 38CD | RO | CU325 | D | $4600 | 248 | 10,000 | 31,000 | 25,420 |

Livability Code: FT 30-90   Wheelbase-to-length ratio of 53% is considered ○ dangerous ● fatiguing ○ good ○ excellent*
The approximate net payload of 5581 pounds at 18% of GVWR on this model is ○ deficient ○ excessive ○ cautionary ○ good ● excellent*
Total highway safety penalties are: 2*   Value: 8 1   Durability: 8 0   Highway Control Rating: 7 3   Highway Safety: 7 1   ★★★

| Imperial | 1998 | MHA | 39 | 38CDS | RO | CU325 | D | $4600 | 248 | 10,000 | 31,000 | 26,320 |

Livability Code: FT 30-90   Wheelbase-to-length ratio of 53% is considered ○ dangerous ● fatiguing ○ good ○ excellent*
The approximate net payload of 4681 pounds at 15% of GVWR on this model is ○ deficient ○ excessive ○ cautionary ● good ○ excellent*
Total highway safety penalties are: 12*   Value: 7 6   Durability: 8 0   Highway Control Rating: 6 9   Highway Safety: 5 7   ★

| Imperial | 1998 | MHA | 39 | 38WDS | RO | CU325 | D | $4600 | 248 | 10,000 | 31,000 | 26,320 |

Livability Code: FT 30-90   Wheelbase-to-length ratio of 53% is considered ○ dangerous ● fatiguing ○ good ○ excellent*
The approximate net payload of 4681 pounds at 15% of GVWR on this model is ○ deficient ○ excessive ○ cautionary ● good ○ excellent*
Total highway safety penalties are: 12*   Value: 7 6   Durability: 8 0   Highway Control Rating: 6 9   Highway Safety: 5 7   ★

| Imperial | 1998 | MHA | 40 | 40WD | RO | CU325 | D | $4500 | 268 | 10,000 | 31,000 | 25,802 |

Livability Code: FT 30-90   Wheelbase-to-length ratio of 55% is considered ○ dangerous ○ fatiguing ● good ○ excellent*
The approximate net payload of 5198 pounds at 17% of GVWR on this model is ○ deficient ○ excessive ○ cautionary ○ good ● excellent*
Total highway safety penalties are: 2*   Value: 8 1   Durability: 8 0   Highway Control Rating: 9 4   Highway Safety: 9 2   ★★★★

| Imperial | 1998 | MHA | 40 | 40WDS | RO | CU325 | D | $4500 | 268 | 10,000 | 31,000 | 26,702 |

Livability Code: FT 30-90   Wheelbase-to-length ratio of 55% is considered ○ dangerous ○ fatiguing ● good ○ excellent*
The approximate net payload of 4298 pounds at 14% of GVWR on this model is ○ deficient ○ excessive ○ cautionary ● good ○ excellent*
Total highway safety penalties are: 12*   Value: 7 6   Durability: 8 0   Highway Control Rating: 8 9   Highway Safety: 7 7   ★★★

| Imperial | 1999 | MHA | 39 | 38 CDS | RO | CU330 | D | $4600 | 248 | 5,000 | 31,000 | 27,510 |

Livability Code: FT 30-90   Wheelbase-to-length ratio of 53% is considered ○ dangerous ● fatiguing ○ good ○ excellent*
The approximate net payload of 3490 pounds at 11% of GVWR on this model is ○ deficient ○ excessive ○ cautionary ● good ○ excellent*
Total highway safety penalties are: 12*   Value: 8 1   Durability: 8 0   Highway Control Rating: 6 6   Highway Safety: 5 4   ★

Note: Safety ratings are based on the assumption that the engineering of the RV has allowed for proper balance by placing fresh, gray, and black holding tanks in a location so as not to change the balance of the RV when the tanks are empty or full. **Always double-check wheelbase, GVWR, and weights at front and rear axles.**

*See Section 1 for details on how conclusions are reached.

Brand	Year	Type	Length	Model	Chassis	Engine	Fuel Type	Average Price per Linear Foot When New	Adjusted Wheelbase	Approx. Towing Capacity	Gross Vehicle Weight Rating	Average Curb Weight

Imperial — 1999 — MHA — 39 — 38 WDS — RO — CU330 — D — $4600 — 248 — 5,000 — 31,000 — 27,510
Livability Code: FT 30-90
Wheelbase-to-length ratio of 53% is considered ○ dangerous ◉ fatiguing ○ good ○ excellent*
The approximate net payload of 3490 pounds at 11% of GVWR on this model is ○ deficient ○ excessive ○ cautionary ◉ good ○ excellent*
Total highway safety penalties are: 12*   Value: 8 1   Durability: 8 0   Highway Control Rating: 6 6   Highway Safety: 5 4   ★

Imperial — 1999 — MHA — 39 — 38 CD op eng — RO — CU350 — D — $4600 — 248 — 5,000 — 31,000 — 27,110
Livability Code: FT 30-90
Wheelbase-to-length ratio of 53% is considered ○ dangerous ◉ fatiguing ○ good ○ excellent*
The approximate net payload of 3890 pounds at 13% of GVWR on this model is ○ deficient ○ excessive ○ cautionary ◉ good ○ excellent*
Total highway safety penalties are: 2*   Value: 8 6   Durability: 8 0   Highway Control Rating: 6 9   Highway Safety: 6 7   ★★

Imperial — 1999 — MHA — 39 — 38 CDS op eng — RO — CU350 — D — $4600 — 248 — 5,000 — 31,000 — 28,010
Livability Code: FT 30-90
Wheelbase-to-length ratio of 53% is considered ○ dangerous ◉ fatiguing ○ good ○ excellent*
The approximate net payload of 2990 pounds at 10% of GVWR on this model is ○ deficient ○ excessive ○ cautionary ◉ good ○ excellent*
Total highway safety penalties are: 12*   Value: 8 1   Durability: 8 0   Highway Control Rating: 6 4   Highway Safety: 5 2   ★

Imperial — 1999 — MHA — 39 — 38 WDS op eng — RO — CU350 — D — $4600 — 248 — 5,000 — 31,000 — 28,010
Livability Code: FT 30-90
Wheelbase-to-length ratio of 53% is considered ○ dangerous ◉ fatiguing ○ good ○ excellent*
The approximate net payload of 2990 pounds at 10% of GVWR on this model is ○ deficient ○ excessive ○ cautionary ◉ good ○ excellent*
Total highway safety penalties are: 12*   Value: 8 1   Durability: 8 0   Highway Control Rating: 6 4   Highway Safety: 5 2   ★

Imperial — 1999 — MHA — 39 — 38 CD — RO — CU330 — D — $4600 — 248 — 5,000 — 31,000 — 26,610
Livability Code: FT 30-90
Wheelbase-to-length ratio of 53% is considered ○ dangerous ◉ fatiguing ○ good ○ excellent*
The approximate net payload of 4390 pounds at 14% of GVWR on this model is ○ deficient ○ excessive ○ cautionary ◉ good ○ excellent*
Total highway safety penalties are: 2*   Value: 8 6   Durability: 8 0   Highway Control Rating: 7 2   Highway Safety: 7 0   ★★★

Imperial — 1999 — MHA — 40 — 40 PBS — RO — CU330 — D — $4500 — 268 — 5,000 — 31,000 — 27,938
Livability Code: FT 30-90
Wheelbase-to-length ratio of 55% is considered ○ dangerous ○ fatiguing ◉ good ○ excellent*
The approximate net payload of 3062 pounds at 10% of GVWR on this model is ○ deficient ○ excessive ○ cautionary ◉ good ○ excellent*
Total highway safety penalties are: 12*   Value: 8 1   Durability: 8 0   Highway Control Rating: 8 1   Highway Safety: 6 9   ★★

Imperial — 1999 — MHA — 40 — 40 CDS — RO — CU330 — D — $4500 — 268 — 5,000 — 31,000 — 27,938
Livability Code: FT 30-90
Wheelbase-to-length ratio of 55% is considered ○ dangerous ○ fatiguing ◉ good ○ excellent*
The approximate net payload of 3062 pounds at 10% of GVWR on this model is ○ deficient ○ excessive ○ cautionary ◉ good ○ excellent*
Total highway safety penalties are: 12*   Value: 8 1   Durability: 8 0   Highway Control Rating: 8 1   Highway Safety: 6 9   ★★

Imperial — 1999 — MHA — 40 — 40 WDS — RO — CU330 — D — $4500 — 268 — 5,000 — 31,000 — 27,938
Livability Code: FT 30-90
Wheelbase-to-length ratio of 55% is considered ○ dangerous ○ fatiguing ◉ good ○ excellent*
The approximate net payload of 3062 pounds at 10% of GVWR on this model is ○ deficient ○ excessive ○ cautionary ◉ good ○ excellent*
Total highway safety penalties are: 12*   Value: 8 1   Durability: 8 0   Highway Control Rating: 8 1   Highway Safety: 6 9   ★★

Imperial — 1999 — MHA — 40 — 40 PBS op eng — RO — CU350 — D — $4500 — 268 — 5,000 — 31,000 — 28,438
Livability Code: FT 30-90
Wheelbase-to-length ratio of 55% is considered ○ dangerous ○ fatiguing ◉ good ○ excellent*
The approximate net payload of 2562 pounds at 8% of GVWR on this model is ○ deficient ○ excessive ◉ cautionary ○ good ○ excellent*
Total highway safety penalties are: 12*   Value: 8 1   Durability: 8 0   Highway Control Rating: 7 1   Highway Safety: 5 9   ★

Imperial — 1999 — MHA — 40 — 40 CDS op eng — RO — CU350 — D — $4500 — 268 — 5,000 — 31,000 — 28,438
Livability Code: FT 30-90
Wheelbase-to-length ratio of 55% is considered ○ dangerous ○ fatiguing ◉ good ○ excellent*
The approximate net payload of 2562 pounds at 8% of GVWR on this model is ○ deficient ○ excessive ◉ cautionary ○ good ○ excellent*
Total highway safety penalties are: 12*   Value: 8 1   Durability: 8 0   Highway Control Rating: 7 1   Highway Safety: 5 9   ★

Imperial — 1999 — MHA — 40 — 40 WDS op eng — RO — CU350 — D — $4500 — 268 — 5,000 — 31,000 — 28,438
Livability Code: FT 30-90
Wheelbase-to-length ratio of 55% is considered ○ dangerous ○ fatiguing ◉ good ○ excellent*
The approximate net payload of 2562 pounds at 8% of GVWR on this model is ○ deficient ○ excessive ◉ cautionary ○ good ○ excellent*
Total highway safety penalties are: 12*   Value: 8 1   Durability: 8 0   Highway Control Rating: 7 1   Highway Safety: 5 9   ★

Impulse — 1990 — MHB — 18 — Impulse III — DO — 5.2L — G — $2500 — 138 — 1,500 — 5,270 — 4,967
Livability Code: SB 30-90
Wheelbase-to-length ratio of 63% is considered ○ dangerous ○ fatiguing ○ good ◉ excellent*
The approximate net payload of 303 pounds at 6% of GVWR on this model is ◉ deficient ○ excessive ○ cautionary ○ good ○ excellent*
Total highway safety penalties are: 2*   Value: 7 7   Durability: 7 0   Highway Control Rating: 8 5   Highway Safety: 8 3   ★★

Note: Safety ratings are based on the assumption that the engineering of the RV has allowed for proper balance by placing fresh, gray, and black holding tanks in a location so as not to change the balance of the RV when the tanks are empty or full. **Always double-check wheelbase, GVWR, and weights at front and rear axles.**

*See Section 1 for details on how conclusions are reached.

Brand	Year	Type	Length	Model	Chassis	Engine	Fuel Type	Average Price per Linear Foot When New	Adjusted Wheelbase	Approx. Towing Capacity	Gross Vehicle Weight Rating	Average Curb Weight
Impulse	**1991**	MHA	31	3290	FO	7.5L	G	$1800	190	8,000	17,000	13,748

Livability Code: SB 30-90
Wheelbase-to-length ratio of 51% is considered ○ dangerous ◉ fatiguing ○ good ○ excellent *
The approximate net payload of 3252 pounds at 19% of GVWR on this model is ○ deficient ○ excessive ○ cautionary ○ good ◉ excellent *
Total highway safety penalties are: 2 * Value: 7 7 Durability: 7 0 Highway Control Rating: 5 2 Highway Safety: 5 0 ★

Brand	Year	Type	Length	Model	Chassis	Engine	Fuel Type	Price/LF	Wheelbase	Towing	GVWR	Curb Weight
Intrigue	**1995**	MHA	32	32	GI	CU250	D	$5400	192	1,500	26,500	23,042

Livability Code: FT 30-90
Wheelbase-to-length ratio of 50% is considered ◉ dangerous ○ fatiguing ○ good ○ excellent *
The approximate net payload of 3458 pounds at 13% of GVWR on this model is ○ deficient ○ excessive ○ cautionary ◉ good ○ excellent *
Total highway safety penalties are: 2 * Value: 9 0 Durability: 9 0 Highway Control Rating: 3 9 Highway Safety: 3 7

Intrigue	**1995**	MHA	36	36	GI	CU250	D	$5000	240	1,500	27,910	24,971

Livability Code: FT 30-90
Wheelbase-to-length ratio of 56% is considered ○ dangerous ○ fatiguing ◉ good ○ excellent *
The approximate net payload of 2939 pounds at 11% of GVWR on this model is ○ deficient ○ excessive ○ cautionary ◉ good ○ excellent *
Total highway safety penalties are: 2 * Value: 9 0 Durability: 9 0 Highway Control Rating: 8 9 Highway Safety: 8 7 ★★★★

Intrigue	**1995**	MHA	40	40	GI	CU250	D	$4700	278	7,000	29,410	26,945

Livability Code: FT 30-90
Wheelbase-to-length ratio of 58% is considered ○ dangerous ○ fatiguing ○ good ◉ excellent *
The approximate net payload of 2465 pounds at 8% of GVWR on this model is ○ deficient ○ excessive ◉ cautionary ○ good ○ excellent *
Total highway safety penalties are: 2 * Value: 9 0 Durability: 9 0 Highway Control Rating: 8 0 Highway Safety: 7 8 ★★★

Intrigue	**1996**	MHA	32	32	GI	CU250	D	$5400	192	1,500	26,500	23,042

Livability Code: FT 30-90
Wheelbase-to-length ratio of 50% is considered ◉ dangerous ○ fatiguing ○ good ○ excellent *
The approximate net payload of 3458 pounds at 13% of GVWR on this model is ○ deficient ○ excessive ○ cautionary ◉ good ○ excellent *
Total highway safety penalties are: 2 * Value: 9 0 Durability: 9 0 Highway Control Rating: 3 9 Highway Safety: 3 7

Intrigue	**1996**	MHA	36	36	GI	CU250	D	$5000	240	1,500	27,910	24,971

Livability Code: FT 30-90
Wheelbase-to-length ratio of 56% is considered ○ dangerous ○ fatiguing ◉ good ○ excellent *
The approximate net payload of 2939 pounds at 11% of GVWR on this model is ○ deficient ○ excessive ○ cautionary ◉ good ○ excellent *
Total highway safety penalties are: 2 * Value: 9 0 Durability: 9 0 Highway Control Rating: 8 9 Highway Safety: 8 7 ★★★★

Intrigue	**1996**	MHA	36	36 Great Room	GI	CU250	D	$5400	240	1,500	27,910	25,871

Livability Code: FT 30-90
Wheelbase-to-length ratio of 56% is considered ○ dangerous ○ fatiguing ◉ good ○ excellent *
The approximate net payload of 2039 pounds at 7% of GVWR on this model is ○ deficient ○ excessive ◉ cautionary ○ good ○ excellent *
Total highway safety penalties are: 7 * Value: 8 7 Durability: 9 0 Highway Control Rating: 6 6 Highway Safety: 5 9 ★

Intrigue	**1996**	MHA	40	40	GI	CU250	D	$4700	278	7,000	29,410	26,945

Livability Code: FT 30-90
Wheelbase-to-length ratio of 58% is considered ○ dangerous ○ fatiguing ○ good ◉ excellent *
The approximate net payload of 2465 pounds at 8% of GVWR on this model is ○ deficient ○ excessive ◉ cautionary ○ good ○ excellent *
Total highway safety penalties are: 2 * Value: 9 0 Durability: 9 0 Highway Control Rating: 8 0 Highway Safety: 7 8 ★★★

Intrigue	**1996**	MHA	40	40 Great Room	GI	CU250	D	$5100	278	7,000	29,410	27,845

Livability Code: FT 30-90
Wheelbase-to-length ratio of 58% is considered ○ dangerous ○ fatiguing ○ good ◉ excellent *
The approximate net payload of 1565 pounds at 5% of GVWR on this model is ◉ deficient ○ excessive ○ cautionary ○ good ○ excellent *
Total highway safety penalties are: 7 * Value: 8 7 Durability: 9 0 Highway Control Rating: 6 7 Highway Safety: 6 0 ★

Intrigue	**1997**	MHA	32	32	DY	CU300	D	$5800	195	6,000	30,000	24,792

Livability Code: FT 30-90
Wheelbase-to-length ratio of 51% is considered ○ dangerous ◉ fatiguing ○ good ○ excellent *
The approximate net payload of 5208 pounds at 17% of GVWR on this model is ○ deficient ○ excessive ○ cautionary ○ good ◉ excellent *
Total highway safety penalties are: 2 * Value: 9 0 Durability: 9 0 Highway Control Rating: 4 9 Highway Safety: 4 7

Intrigue	**1997**	MHA	32	32	GI	CU300	D	$5800	192	9,500	26,500	23,042

Livability Code: FT 30-90
Wheelbase-to-length ratio of 50% is considered ◉ dangerous ○ fatiguing ○ good ○ excellent *
The approximate net payload of 3458 pounds at 13% of GVWR on this model is ○ deficient ○ excessive ○ cautionary ◉ good ○ excellent *
Total highway safety penalties are: 2 * Value: 9 0 Durability: 9 0 Highway Control Rating: 3 9 Highway Safety: 3 7

Intrigue	**1997**	MHA	36	36	DY	CU300	D	$5300	243	6,000	30,000	26,016

Livability Code: FT 30-90
Wheelbase-to-length ratio of 56% is considered ○ dangerous ○ fatiguing ◉ good ○ excellent *
The approximate net payload of 3984 pounds at 13% of GVWR on this model is ○ deficient ○ excessive ○ cautionary ◉ good ○ excellent *
Total highway safety penalties are: 2 * Value: 9 0 Durability: 9 0 Highway Control Rating: 9 1 Highway Safety: 8 9 ★★★★

Note: Safety ratings are based on the assumption that the engineering of the RV has allowed for proper balance by placing fresh, gray, and black holding tanks in a location so as not to change the balance of the RV when the tanks are empty or full. **Always double-check wheelbase, GVWR, and weights at front and rear axles.**

*See Section 1 for details on how conclusions are reached.

Section 2: The Ratings

Brand	Year	Type	Length	Model	Chassis	Engine	Fuel Type	Average Price per Linear Foot When New	Adjusted Wheelbase	Approx. Towing Capacity	Gross Vehicle Weight Rating	Average Curb Weight

Intrigue 1997 MHA 36 36 slide DY CU300 D $5700 243 6,000 30,000 26,916
Livability Code: FT 30-90
Wheelbase-to-length ratio of 56% is considered ◯ dangerous ◯ fatiguing ◉ good ◯ excellent *
The approximate net payload of 3084 pounds at 10% of GVWR on this model is ◯ deficient ◯ excessive ◯ cautionary ◉ good ◯ excellent *
Total highway safety penalties are: 7 *   Value: 8 7   Durability: 9 0   Highway Control Rating: 8 5   Highway Safety: 7 8   ★★★

Intrigue 1997 MHA 36 36 GI CU300 D $5300 240 8,090 27,910 24,971
Livability Code: FT 30-90
Wheelbase-to-length ratio of 56% is considered ◯ dangerous ◯ fatiguing ◉ good ◯ excellent *
The approximate net payload of 2939 pounds at 11% of GVWR on this model is ◯ deficient ◯ excessive ◯ cautionary ◉ good ◯ excellent *
Total highway safety penalties are: 2 *   Value: 9 0   Durability: 9 0   Highway Control Rating: 8 9   Highway Safety: 8 7   ★★★★

Intrigue 1997 MHA 36 36 Great Room GI CU300 D $5700 240 6,590 29,410 26,621
Livability Code: FT 30-90
Wheelbase-to-length ratio of 56% is considered ◯ dangerous ◯ fatiguing ◉ good ◯ excellent *
The approximate net payload of 2789 pounds at 9% of GVWR on this model is ◯ deficient ◯ excessive ◉ cautionary ◯ good ◯ excellent *
Total highway safety penalties are: 7 *   Value: 8 7   Durability: 9 0   Highway Control Rating: 7 8   Highway Safety: 7 1   ★★★

Intrigue 1997 MHA 40 40 DY CU300 D $5000 281 6,000 30,000 27,240
Livability Code: FT 30-90
Wheelbase-to-length ratio of 59% is considered ◯ dangerous ◯ fatiguing ◯ good ◉ excellent *
The approximate net payload of 2760 pounds at 9% of GVWR on this model is ◯ deficient ◯ excessive ◉ cautionary ◯ good ◯ excellent *
Total highway safety penalties are: 2 *   Value: 9 0   Durability: 9 0   Highway Control Rating: 8 8   Highway Safety: 8 6   ★★★★

Intrigue 1997 MHA 40 40 slide DY CU300 D $5300 281 6,000 30,000 28,140
Livability Code: FT 30-90
Wheelbase-to-length ratio of 59% is considered ◯ dangerous ◯ fatiguing ◯ good ◉ excellent *
The approximate net payload of 1860 pounds at 6% of GVWR on this model is ◉ deficient ◯ excessive ◯ cautionary ◯ good ◯ excellent *
Total highway safety penalties are: 7 *   Value: 8 7   Durability: 9 0   Highway Control Rating: 7 1   Highway Safety: 6 4   ★

Intrigue 1997 MHA 40 40 GI CU300 D $4900 278 6,590 29,410 26,945
Livability Code: FT 30-90
Wheelbase-to-length ratio of 58% is considered ◯ dangerous ◯ fatiguing ◯ good ◉ excellent *
The approximate net payload of 2465 pounds at 8% of GVWR on this model is ◯ deficient ◯ excessive ◉ cautionary ◯ good ◯ excellent *
Total highway safety penalties are: 2 *   Value: 9 0   Durability: 9 0   Highway Control Rating: 8 0   Highway Safety: 7 8   ★★★

Intrigue 1997 MHA 40 40 Great Room GI CU300 D $5400 278 6,590 29,410 27,845
Livability Code: FT 30-90
Wheelbase-to-length ratio of 58% is considered ◯ dangerous ◯ fatiguing ◯ good ◉ excellent *
The approximate net payload of 1565 pounds at 5% of GVWR on this model is ◉ deficient ◯ excessive ◯ cautionary ◯ good ◯ excellent *
Total highway safety penalties are: 7 *   Value: 8 7   Durability: 9 0   Highway Control Rating: 6 7   Highway Safety: 6 0   ★

Intrigue 1998 MHA 32 32 DY CU300 D $5800 195 6,000 30,000 24,446
Livability Code: FT 30-90
Wheelbase-to-length ratio of 51% is considered ◯ dangerous ◉ fatiguing ◯ good ◯ excellent *
The approximate net payload of 5554 pounds at 19% of GVWR on this model is ◯ deficient ◯ excessive ◯ cautionary ◯ good ◉ excellent *
Total highway safety penalties are: 2 *   Value: 9 0   Durability: 9 0   Highway Control Rating: 5 0   Highway Safety: 4 8

Intrigue 1998 MHA 36 36 DY CU300 D $5300 243 6,000 30,000 25,308
Livability Code: FT 30-90
Wheelbase-to-length ratio of 56% is considered ◯ dangerous ◯ fatiguing ◉ good ◯ excellent *
The approximate net payload of 4692 pounds at 16% of GVWR on this model is ◯ deficient ◯ excessive ◯ cautionary ◯ good ◉ excellent *
Total highway safety penalties are: 2 *   Value: 9 0   Durability: 9 0   Highway Control Rating: 9 7   Highway Safety: 9 5   ★★★★★

Intrigue 1998 MHA 36 36 Great Room DY CU300 D $5700 243 6,000 30,000 26,708
Livability Code: FT 30-90
Wheelbase-to-length ratio of 56% is considered ◯ dangerous ◯ fatiguing ◉ good ◯ excellent *
The approximate net payload of 3292 pounds at 11% of GVWR on this model is ◯ deficient ◯ excessive ◯ cautionary ◉ good ◯ excellent *
Total highway safety penalties are: 7 *   Value: 8 7   Durability: 9 0   Highway Control Rating: 8 7   Highway Safety: 8 0   ★★★★

Intrigue 1998 MHA 40 40 DY CU300 D $5000 281 6,000 30,000 26,470
Livability Code: FT 30-90
Wheelbase-to-length ratio of 59% is considered ◯ dangerous ◯ fatiguing ◯ good ◉ excellent *
The approximate net payload of 3530 pounds at 12% of GVWR on this model is ◯ deficient ◯ excessive ◯ cautionary ◉ good ◯ excellent *
Total highway safety penalties are: 2 *   Value: 9 0   Durability: 9 0   Highway Control Rating: 9 7   Highway Safety: 9 5   ★★★★★

Intrigue 1998 MHA 40 40 Great Room DY CU300 D $5300 281 6,000 30,000 27,770
Livability Code: FT 30-90
Wheelbase-to-length ratio of 59% is considered ◯ dangerous ◯ fatiguing ◯ good ◉ excellent *
The approximate net payload of 2230 pounds at 7% of GVWR on this model is ◯ deficient ◯ excessive ◉ cautionary ◯ good ◯ excellent *
Total highway safety penalties are: 7 *   Value: 8 7   Durability: 9 0   Highway Control Rating: 7 7   Highway Safety: 7 0   ★★★

Note: Safety ratings are based on the assumption that the engineering of the RV has allowed for proper balance by placing fresh, gray, and black holding tanks in a location so as not to change the balance of the RV when the tanks are empty or full. **Always double-check wheelbase, GVWR, and weights at front and rear axles.**

*See Section 1 for details on how conclusions are reached.

Brand	Year	Type	Length	Model	Chassis	Engine	Fuel Type	Average Price per Linear Foot When New	Adjusted Wheelbase	Approx. Towing Capacity	Gross Vehicle Weight Rating	Average Curb Weight
Intrigue	1999	MHA	32	32 Garnet	DY	CU330	D	$6700	192	6,000	32,200	24,652

Livability Code: FT 30-90
Wheelbase-to-length ratio of 50% is considered ● dangerous ○ fatiguing ○ good ○ excellent *
The approximate net payload of 7549 pounds at 23% of GVWR on this model is ○ deficient ○ excessive ○ cautionary ○ good ● excellent *
Total highway safety penalties are: 2 *　Value: 9 6　Durability: 9 3　Highway Control Rating: 5 5　Highway Safety: 5 3

Brand	Year	Type	Length	Model	Chassis	Engine	Fuel Type	Avg Price/LF	Adj WB	Tow Cap	GVWR	Curb Wt
Intrigue	1999	MHA	36	36 Montage	DY	CU330	D	$5900	240	6,000	32,200	25,737

Livability Code: FT 30-90
Wheelbase-to-length ratio of 56% is considered ○ dangerous ○ fatiguing ● good ○ excellent *
The approximate net payload of 6463 pounds at 20% of GVWR on this model is ○ deficient ○ excessive ○ cautionary ○ good ● excellent *
Total highway safety penalties are: 2 *　Value: 9 6　Durability: 9 3　Highway Control Rating: 9 8　Highway Safety: 9 6　★★★★★

Brand	Year	Type	Length	Model	Chassis	Engine	Fuel Type	Avg Price/LF	Adj WB	Tow Cap	GVWR	Curb Wt
Intrigue	1999	MHA	36	36 Tiara	DY	CU330	D	$5900	240	6,000	32,200	25,695

Livability Code: FT 30-90
Wheelbase-to-length ratio of 56% is considered ○ dangerous ○ fatiguing ● good ○ excellent *
The approximate net payload of 6506 pounds at 20% of GVWR on this model is ○ deficient ○ excessive ○ cautionary ○ good ● excellent *
Total highway safety penalties are: 2 *　Value: 9 6　Durability: 9 3　Highway Control Rating: 9 8　Highway Safety: 9 6　★★★★★

Brand	Year	Type	Length	Model	Chassis	Engine	Fuel Type	Avg Price/LF	Adj WB	Tow Cap	GVWR	Curb Wt
Intrigue	1999	MHA	36	36 Horizon	DY	CU330	D	$5900	240	6,000	32,200	26,684

Livability Code: FT 30-90
Wheelbase-to-length ratio of 56% is considered ○ dangerous ○ fatiguing ● good ○ excellent *
The approximate net payload of 5517 pounds at 17% of GVWR on this model is ○ deficient ○ excessive ○ cautionary ○ good ● excellent *
Total highway safety penalties are: 7 *　Value: 9 4　Durability: 9 3　Highway Control Rating: 9 6　Highway Safety: 8 9　★★★★

Brand	Year	Type	Length	Model	Chassis	Engine	Fuel Type	Avg Price/LF	Adj WB	Tow Cap	GVWR	Curb Wt
Intrigue	1999	MHA	36	36 Galley's Open	DY	CU330	D	$5900	240	6,000	32,200	27,121

Livability Code: FT 30-90
Wheelbase-to-length ratio of 56% is considered ○ dangerous ○ fatiguing ● good ○ excellent *
The approximate net payload of 5079 pounds at 16% of GVWR on this model is ○ deficient ○ excessive ○ cautionary ○ good ● excellent *
Total highway safety penalties are: 13 *　Value: 9 1　Durability: 9 3　Highway Control Rating: 9 4　Highway Safety: 8 1　★★★★

Brand	Year	Type	Length	Model	Chassis	Engine	Fuel Type	Avg Price/LF	Adj WB	Tow Cap	GVWR	Curb Wt
Intrigue	1999	MHA	36	36 Cook's Nook	DY	CU330	D	$5900	240	6,000	32,200	27,089

Livability Code: FT 30-90
Wheelbase-to-length ratio of 56% is considered ○ dangerous ○ fatiguing ● good ○ excellent *
The approximate net payload of 5112 pounds at 16% of GVWR on this model is ○ deficient ○ excessive ○ cautionary ○ good ● excellent *
Total highway safety penalties are: 13 *　Value: 9 1　Durability: 9 3　Highway Control Rating: 9 4　Highway Safety: 8 1　★★★★

Brand	Year	Type	Length	Model	Chassis	Engine	Fuel Type	Avg Price/LF	Adj WB	Tow Cap	GVWR	Curb Wt
Intrigue	1999	MHA	40	40 Amadeus	DY	CU330	D	$5400	278	6,000	32,200	26,646

Livability Code: FT 30-90
Wheelbase-to-length ratio of 58% is considered ○ dangerous ○ fatiguing ○ good ● excellent *
The approximate net payload of 5554 pounds at 17% of GVWR on this model is ○ deficient ○ excessive ○ cautionary ○ good ● excellent *
Total highway safety penalties are: 2 *　Value: 9 6　Durability: 9 3　Highway Control Rating: 1 0 0　Highway Safety: 9 8　★★★★★

Brand	Year	Type	Length	Model	Chassis	Engine	Fuel Type	Avg Price/LF	Adj WB	Tow Cap	GVWR	Curb Wt
Intrigue	1999	MHA	40	40 Wisteria	DY	CU330	D	$5400	278	6,000	32,200	26,981

Livability Code: FT 30-90
Wheelbase-to-length ratio of 58% is considered ○ dangerous ○ fatiguing ○ good ● excellent *
The approximate net payload of 5219 pounds at 16% of GVWR on this model is ○ deficient ○ excessive ○ cautionary ○ good ● excellent *
Total highway safety penalties are: 2 *　Value: 9 6　Durability: 9 3　Highway Control Rating: 1 0 0　Highway Safety: 9 8　★★★★★

Brand	Year	Type	Length	Model	Chassis	Engine	Fuel Type	Avg Price/LF	Adj WB	Tow Cap	GVWR	Curb Wt
Intrigue	1999	MHA	40	40 Prism	DY	CU330	D	$5400	278	6,000	32,200	26,779

Livability Code: FT 30-90
Wheelbase-to-length ratio of 58% is considered ○ dangerous ○ fatiguing ○ good ● excellent *
The approximate net payload of 5421 pounds at 17% of GVWR on this model is ○ deficient ○ excessive ○ cautionary ○ good ● excellent *
Total highway safety penalties are: 2 *　Value: 9 6　Durability: 9 3　Highway Control Rating: 1 0 0　Highway Safety: 9 8　★★★★★

Brand	Year	Type	Length	Model	Chassis	Engine	Fuel Type	Avg Price/LF	Adj WB	Tow Cap	GVWR	Curb Wt
Intrigue	1999	MHA	40	40 Vista	DY	CU330	D	$5400	278	6,000	32,200	27,904

Livability Code: FT 30-90
Wheelbase-to-length ratio of 58% is considered ○ dangerous ○ fatiguing ○ good ● excellent *
The approximate net payload of 4296 pounds at 13% of GVWR on this model is ○ deficient ○ excessive ○ cautionary ● good ○ excellent *
Total highway safety penalties are: 7 *　Value: 9 4　Durability: 9 3　Highway Control Rating: 9 7　Highway Safety: 9 0　★★★★★

Brand	Year	Type	Length	Model	Chassis	Engine	Fuel Type	Avg Price/LF	Adj WB	Tow Cap	GVWR	Curb Wt
Intrigue	1999	MHA	40	40 Grandview	DY	CU330	D	$5400	278	6,000	32,200	28,062

Livability Code: FT 30-90
Wheelbase-to-length ratio of 58% is considered ○ dangerous ○ fatiguing ○ good ● excellent *
The approximate net payload of 4138 pounds at 13% of GVWR on this model is ○ deficient ○ excessive ○ cautionary ● good ○ excellent *
Total highway safety penalties are: 7 *　Value: 9 4　Durability: 9 3　Highway Control Rating: 9 7　Highway Safety: 9 0　★★★★★

Brand	Year	Type	Length	Model	Chassis	Engine	Fuel Type	Avg Price/LF	Adj WB	Tow Cap	GVWR	Curb Wt
Intrigue	1999	MHA	40	40 Cook's Delight	DY	CU330	D	$5400	278	6,000	32,200	28,266

Livability Code: FT 30-90
Wheelbase-to-length ratio of 58% is considered ○ dangerous ○ fatiguing ○ good ● excellent *
The approximate net payload of 3935 pounds at 12% of GVWR on this model is ○ deficient ○ excessive ○ cautionary ● good ○ excellent *
Total highway safety penalties are: 13 *　Value: 9 1　Durability: 9 3　Highway Control Rating: 9 5　Highway Safety: 8 2　★★★★

Note: Safety ratings are based on the assumption that the engineering of the RV has allowed for proper balance by placing fresh, gray, and black holding tanks in a location so as not to change the balance of the RV when the tanks are empty or full. **Always double-check wheelbase, GVWR, and weights at front and rear axles.**

*See Section 1 for details on how conclusions are reached.

Brand	Year	Type	Length	Model	Chassis	Engine	Fuel Type	Average Price per Linear Foot When New	Adjusted Wheelbase	Approx. Towing Capacity	Gross Vehicle Weight Rating	Average Curb Weight
Intrigue	1999	MHA	40	40 Gourmet on Road	DY	CU330	D	$5400	278	6,000	32,200	28,332

Livability Code: FT 30-90   Wheelbase-to-length ratio of 58% is considered ○ dangerous ○ fatiguing ○ good ● excellent *

The approximate net payload of 3868 pounds at 12% of GVWR on this model is ○ deficient ○ excessive ○ cautionary ● good ○ excellent *

Total highway safety penalties are: 8 *   Value: 9 3   Durability: 9 3   Highway Control Rating: 9 5   Highway Safety: 8 7   ★★★★

Brand	Year	Type	Length	Model	Chassis	Engine	Fuel Type					
Isata	1998	MHA		accurate specs n/a								?

Livability Code: SB 30-90   Wheelbase-to-length ratio of ? is considered ○ dangerous ○ fatiguing ○ good ○ excellent *

The approximate net payload of pounds at of GVWR on this model is ○ deficient ○ excessive ○ cautionary ○ good ○ excellent *

Total highway safety penalties are: 0 *   Value: 0   Durability: 7 7   Highway Control Rating: 0   Highway Safety: 0

Brand	Year	Type	Length	Model	Chassis	Engine	Fuel Type	Price/ft	Wheelbase	Towing	GVWR	Curb Wt
Isata	1999	MHA	24	230	GM	5.7L	G	$3300	157	2,500	11,000	9,448

Livability Code: SB 30-90   Wheelbase-to-length ratio of 55% is considered ○ dangerous ○ fatiguing ● good ○ excellent *

The approximate net payload of 1552 pounds at 14% of GVWR on this model is ○ deficient ○ excessive ○ cautionary ● good ○ excellent *

Total highway safety penalties are: 0 *   Value: 8 6   Durability: 7 7   Highway Control Rating: 9 0   Highway Safety: 9 0   ★★★

Isata	1999	MHA	24	232RB	GM	5.7L	G	$3300	157	2,500	11,000	9,420

Livability Code: SB 30-90   Wheelbase-to-length ratio of 55% is considered ○ dangerous ○ fatiguing ● good ○ excellent *

The approximate net payload of 1580 pounds at 14% of GVWR on this model is ○ deficient ○ excessive ○ cautionary ● good ○ excellent *

Total highway safety penalties are: 0 *   Value: 8 6   Durability: 7 7   Highway Control Rating: 9 1   Highway Safety: 9 1   ★★★

Isata	1999	MHA	29	280	GM	5.7L	G	$2800	190	1,500	12,000	10,205

Livability Code: SB 30-90   Wheelbase-to-length ratio of 55% is considered ○ dangerous ○ fatiguing ● good ○ excellent *

The approximate net payload of 1795 pounds at 15% of GVWR on this model is ○ deficient ○ excessive ○ cautionary ● good ○ excellent *

Total highway safety penalties are: 0 *   Value: 8 6   Durability: 7 7   Highway Control Rating: 9 2   Highway Safety: 9 2   ★★★

Isata	1999	MHA	29	282	GM	5.7L	G	$2800	190	1,500	12,000	10,221

Livability Code: SB 30-90   Wheelbase-to-length ratio of 55% is considered ○ dangerous ○ fatiguing ● good ○ excellent *

The approximate net payload of 1779 pounds at 15% of GVWR on this model is ○ deficient ○ excessive ○ cautionary ● good ○ excellent *

Total highway safety penalties are: 0 *   Value: 8 6   Durability: 7 7   Highway Control Rating: 9 2   Highway Safety: 9 2   ★★★

Isata	1999	MHA	29	282RB	GM	5.7L	G	$2800	190	1,500	12,000	10,540

Livability Code: SB 30-90   Wheelbase-to-length ratio of 55% is considered ○ dangerous ○ fatiguing ● good ○ excellent *

The approximate net payload of 1460 pounds at 12% of GVWR on this model is ○ deficient ○ excessive ○ cautionary ● good ○ excellent *

Total highway safety penalties are: 0 *   Value: 8 6   Durability: 7 7   Highway Control Rating: 8 6   Highway Safety: 8 6   ★★★

Isata	1999	MHA	32	310	GM	5.7L	G	$2500	202 T	0 e	13,500	11,612

Livability Code: SB 30-90   Wheelbase-to-length ratio of 53% is considered ○ dangerous ● fatiguing ○ good ○ excellent *

The approximate net payload of 1888 pounds at 14% of GVWR on this model is ○ deficient ○ excessive ○ cautionary ● good ○ excellent *

Total highway safety penalties are: 2 *   Value: 8 5   Durability: 7 7   Highway Control Rating: 7 2   Highway Safety: 7 0   ★★★

Isata	1999	MHA	32	312	GM	5.7L	G	$2500	202 T	0 e	13,500	11,612

Livability Code: SB 30-90   Wheelbase-to-length ratio of 53% is considered ○ dangerous ● fatiguing ○ good ○ excellent *

The approximate net payload of 1888 pounds at 14% of GVWR on this model is ○ deficient ○ excessive ○ cautionary ● good ○ excellent *

Total highway safety penalties are: 2 *   Value: 8 5   Durability: 7 7   Highway Control Rating: 7 2   Highway Safety: 7 0   ★★★

Itasca Micro	1991	MHC	21	320 RB	TO	3.0L	G	$1300	137	1,500	6,000	5,319

Livability Code: VA 30-90   Wheelbase-to-length ratio of 55% is considered ○ dangerous ○ fatiguing ● good ○ excellent *

The approximate net payload of 681 pounds at 11% of GVWR on this model is ○ deficient ○ excessive ○ cautionary ● good ○ excellent *

Total highway safety penalties are: 2 *   Value: 8 4   Durability: 7 4   Highway Control Rating: 8 4   Highway Safety: 8 2   ★★★

Itasca Micro	1991	MHC	22	321 RB	TO	3.0L	G	$1300	137	1,500	6,000	5,455

Livability Code: VA 30-90   Wheelbase-to-length ratio of 53% is considered ○ dangerous ● fatiguing ○ good ○ excellent *

The approximate net payload of 545 pounds at 9% of GVWR on this model is ○ deficient ○ excessive ● cautionary ○ good ○ excellent *

Total highway safety penalties are: 2 *   Value: 8 4   Durability: 7 4   Highway Control Rating: 6 1   Highway Safety: 5 9   ★

Ivory	1995	MHA	36	3530	MA	Cu8.3L	D	$4400	228	4,100	25,900	21,461

Livability Code: SB 30-90   Wheelbase-to-length ratio of 54% is considered ○ dangerous ○ fatiguing ● good ○ excellent *

The approximate net payload of 4439 pounds at 17% of GVWR on this model is ○ deficient ○ excessive ○ cautionary ○ good ● excellent *

Total highway safety penalties are: 2 *   Value: 7 3   Durability: 7 2   Highway Control Rating: 8 1   Highway Safety: 7 9   ★★★

Note: Safety ratings are based on the assumption that the engineering of the RV has allowed for proper balance by placing fresh, gray, and black holding tanks in a location so as not to change the balance of the RV when the tanks are empty or full. **Always double-check wheelbase, GVWR, and weights at front and rear axles.**

*See Section 1 for details on how conclusions are reached.

Brand	Year	Type	Length	Model	Chassis	Engine	Fuel Type	Average Price per Linear Foot When New	Adjusted Wheelbase	Approx. Towing Capacity	Gross Vehicle Weight Rating	Average Curb Weight
Ivory	1995	MHA	36	3550	MA	Cu8.3L	D	$4400	228	4,100	25,900	21,461

Livability Code: SB 30-90 Wheelbase-to-length ratio of 54% is considered ○ dangerous ○ fatiguing ◉ good ○ excellent *

The approximate net payload of 4439 pounds at 17% of GVWR on this model is ○ deficient ○ excessive ○ cautionary ○ good ◉ excellent *

Total highway safety penalties are: 2 * Value: 7 3 Durability: 7 2 Highway Control Rating: 8 1 Highway Safety: 7 9 ★★★

Brand	Year	Type	Length	Model	Chassis	Engine	Fuel Type	Price/Ft	Wheelbase	Towing	GVWR	Curb Wt
Ivory	1995	MHA	36	3560	MA	Cu8.3L	D	$4400	228	4,100	25,900	21,461

Livability Code: SB 30-90 Wheelbase-to-length ratio of 54% is considered ○ dangerous ○ fatiguing ◉ good ○ excellent *

The approximate net payload of 4439 pounds at 17% of GVWR on this model is ○ deficient ○ excessive ○ cautionary ○ good ◉ excellent *

Total highway safety penalties are: 2 * Value: 7 3 Durability: 7 2 Highway Control Rating: 8 1 Highway Safety: 7 9 ★★★

Ivory	1995	MHA	38	3730	MA	Cu8.3L	D	$4500	252	4,100	25,900	22,318

Livability Code: SB 30-90 Wheelbase-to-length ratio of 55% is considered ○ dangerous ○ fatiguing ◉ good ○ excellent *

The approximate net payload of 3582 pounds at 14% of GVWR on this model is ○ deficient ○ excessive ○ cautionary ◉ good ○ excellent *

Total highway safety penalties are: 2 * Value: 7 3 Durability: 7 2 Highway Control Rating: 8 9 Highway Safety: 8 7 ★★★

Ivory	1995	MHA	38	3750	MA	Cu8.3L	D	$4500	252	4,100	25,900	22,318

Livability Code: SB 30-90 Wheelbase-to-length ratio of 55% is considered ○ dangerous ○ fatiguing ◉ good ○ excellent *

The approximate net payload of 3582 pounds at 14% of GVWR on this model is ○ deficient ○ excessive ○ cautionary ◉ good ○ excellent *

Total highway safety penalties are: 2 * Value: 7 3 Durability: 7 2 Highway Control Rating: 8 9 Highway Safety: 8 7 ★★★

Ivory	1995	MHA	38	3760	MA	Cu8.3L	D	$4500	252	4,100	25,900	22,318

Livability Code: SB 30-90 Wheelbase-to-length ratio of 55% is considered ○ dangerous ○ fatiguing ◉ good ○ excellent *

The approximate net payload of 3582 pounds at 14% of GVWR on this model is ○ deficient ○ excessive ○ cautionary ◉ good ○ excellent *

Total highway safety penalties are: 2 * Value: 7 3 Durability: 7 2 Highway Control Rating: 8 9 Highway Safety: 8 7 ★★★

Ivory	1995	MHA	40	4030	MA	Cu8.3L	D	$4400	278	4,100	25,900	23,146

Livability Code: SB 30-90 Wheelbase-to-length ratio of 57% is considered ○ dangerous ○ fatiguing ◉ good ○ excellent *

The approximate net payload of 2754 pounds at 11% of GVWR on this model is ○ deficient ○ excessive ○ cautionary ◉ good ○ excellent *

Total highway safety penalties are: 2 * Value: 7 3 Durability: 7 2 Highway Control Rating: 9 1 Highway Safety: 8 9 ★★★

Ivory	1995	MHA	40	4050	MA	Cu8.3L	D	$4400	278	4,100	25,900	23,146

Livability Code: SB 30-90 Wheelbase-to-length ratio of 57% is considered ○ dangerous ○ fatiguing ◉ good ○ excellent *

The approximate net payload of 2754 pounds at 11% of GVWR on this model is ○ deficient ○ excessive ○ cautionary ◉ good ○ excellent *

Total highway safety penalties are: 2 * Value: 7 3 Durability: 7 2 Highway Control Rating: 9 1 Highway Safety: 8 9 ★★★

Ivory	1996	MHA	34	3334	MA	Ca300	D	$4800	208	5,000	28,000	23,281

Livability Code: SB 30-90 Wheelbase-to-length ratio of 51% is considered ○ dangerous ◉ fatiguing ○ good ○ excellent *

The approximate net payload of 4719 pounds at 17% of GVWR on this model is ○ deficient ○ excessive ○ cautionary ○ good ◉ excellent *

Total highway safety penalties are: 2 * Value: 7 3 Durability: 7 2 Highway Control Rating: 5 1 Highway Safety: 4 9

Ivory	1996	MHA	34	3354	MA	Ca300	D	$4800	208	5,000	28,000	23,281

Livability Code: SB 30-90 Wheelbase-to-length ratio of 51% is considered ○ dangerous ◉ fatiguing ○ good ○ excellent *

The approximate net payload of 4719 pounds at 17% of GVWR on this model is ○ deficient ○ excessive ○ cautionary ○ good ◉ excellent *

Total highway safety penalties are: 2 * Value: 7 3 Durability: 7 2 Highway Control Rating: 5 1 Highway Safety: 4 9

Ivory	1996	MHA	34	3390	MA	Ca300	D	$4800	208	5,000	28,000	23,281

Livability Code: SB 30-90 Wheelbase-to-length ratio of 51% is considered ○ dangerous ◉ fatiguing ○ good ○ excellent *

The approximate net payload of 4719 pounds at 17% of GVWR on this model is ○ deficient ○ excessive ○ cautionary ○ good ◉ excellent *

Total highway safety penalties are: 2 * Value: 7 3 Durability: 7 2 Highway Control Rating: 5 1 Highway Safety: 4 9

Ivory	1996	MHA	36	3530	MA	Ca300	D	$4600	228	5,000	28,000	23,777

Livability Code: SB 30-90 Wheelbase-to-length ratio of 54% is considered ○ dangerous ○ fatiguing ◉ good ○ excellent *

The approximate net payload of 4223 pounds at 15% of GVWR on this model is ○ deficient ○ excessive ○ cautionary ◉ good ○ excellent *

Total highway safety penalties are: 2 * Value: 7 3 Durability: 7 2 Highway Control Rating: 7 8 Highway Safety: 7 6 ★★★

Ivory	1996	MHA	36	3550	MA	Ca300	D	$4600	228	5,000	28,000	23,777

Livability Code: SB 30-90 Wheelbase-to-length ratio of 54% is considered ○ dangerous ○ fatiguing ◉ good ○ excellent *

The approximate net payload of 4223 pounds at 15% of GVWR on this model is ○ deficient ○ excessive ○ cautionary ◉ good ○ excellent *

Total highway safety penalties are: 2 * Value: 7 3 Durability: 7 2 Highway Control Rating: 7 8 Highway Safety: 7 6 ★★★

Note: Safety ratings are based on the assumption that the engineering of the RV has allowed for proper balance by placing fresh, gray, and black holding tanks in a location so as not to change the balance of the RV when the tanks are empty or full. **Always double-check wheelbase, GVWR, and weights at front and rear axles.**

*See Section 1 for details on how conclusions are reached.

Brand	Year	Type	Length	Model	Chassis	Engine	Fuel Type	Average Price per Linear Foot When New	Adjusted Wheelbase	Approx. Towing Capacity	Gross Vehicle Weight Rating	Average Curb Weight
Ivory	**1996**	MHA	36	3590	MA	Ca300	D	$4600	228	5,000	28,000	23,777

Livability Code: SB 30-90

Wheelbase-to-length ratio of 54% is considered ○ dangerous ○ fatiguing ◉ good ○ excellent *

The approximate net payload of 4223 pounds at 15% of GVWR on this model is ○ deficient ○ excessive ○ cautionary ◉ good ○ excellent *

Total highway safety penalties are: 2 *   Value: **7 3**   Durability: **7 2**   Highway Control Rating: **7 8**   Highway Safety: **7 6**   ★★★

Brand	Year	Type	Length	Model	Chassis	Engine	Fuel Type	Price/LF	Wheelbase	Towing	GVWR	Curb Weight
Ivory	**1996**	MHA	37	3730	MA	Ca300	D	$4700	252	5,000	28,000	24,190

Livability Code: SB 30-90

Wheelbase-to-length ratio of 57% is considered ○ dangerous ○ fatiguing ◉ good ○ excellent *

The approximate net payload of 3810 pounds at 14% of GVWR on this model is ○ deficient ○ excessive ○ cautionary ◉ good ○ excellent *

Total highway safety penalties are: 2 *   Value: **7 3**   Durability: **7 2**   Highway Control Rating: **9 4**   Highway Safety: **9 2**   ★★★

Ivory	**1996**	MHA	38	3740	MA	Ca300	D	$4600	252	5,000	28,000	24,465

Livability Code: SB 30-90

Wheelbase-to-length ratio of 55% is considered ○ dangerous ○ fatiguing ◉ good ○ excellent *

The approximate net payload of 3535 pounds at 13% of GVWR on this model is ○ deficient ○ excessive ○ cautionary ◉ good ○ excellent *

Total highway safety penalties are: 2 *   Value: **7 3**   Durability: **7 2**   Highway Control Rating: **8 7**   Highway Safety: **8 5**   ★★★

Ivory	**1996**	MHA	38	3750	MA	Ca300	D	$4600	252	5,000	28,000	24,465

Livability Code: SB 30-90

Wheelbase-to-length ratio of 55% is considered ○ dangerous ○ fatiguing ◉ good ○ excellent *

The approximate net payload of 3535 pounds at 13% of GVWR on this model is ○ deficient ○ excessive ○ cautionary ◉ good ○ excellent *

Total highway safety penalties are: 2 *   Value: **7 3**   Durability: **7 2**   Highway Control Rating: **8 7**   Highway Safety: **8 5**   ★★★

Ivory	**1996**	MHA	38	3790	MA	Ca300	D	$4600	252	5,000	28,000	24,465

Livability Code: SB 30-90

Wheelbase-to-length ratio of 55% is considered ○ dangerous ○ fatiguing ◉ good ○ excellent *

The approximate net payload of 3535 pounds at 13% of GVWR on this model is ○ deficient ○ excessive ○ cautionary ◉ good ○ excellent *

Total highway safety penalties are: 2 *   Value: **7 3**   Durability: **7 2**   Highway Control Rating: **8 7**   Highway Safety: **8 5**   ★★★

Ivory	**1996**	MHA	40	4030	MA	Ca300	D	$4600	278	5,000	28,000	25,099

Livability Code: SB 30-90

Wheelbase-to-length ratio of 57% is considered ○ dangerous ○ fatiguing ◉ good ○ excellent *

The approximate net payload of 2901 pounds at 10% of GVWR on this model is ○ deficient ○ excessive ○ cautionary ◉ good ○ excellent *

Total highway safety penalties are: 2 *   Value: **7 3**   Durability: **7 2**   Highway Control Rating: **9 0**   Highway Safety: **8 8**   ★★★

Ivory	**1996**	MHA	40	4050	MA	Ca300	D	$4600	278	5,000	28,000	25,099

Livability Code: SB 30-90

Wheelbase-to-length ratio of 57% is considered ○ dangerous ○ fatiguing ◉ good ○ excellent *

The approximate net payload of 2901 pounds at 10% of GVWR on this model is ○ deficient ○ excessive ○ cautionary ◉ good ○ excellent *

Total highway safety penalties are: 2 *   Value: **7 3**   Durability: **7 2**   Highway Control Rating: **9 0**   Highway Safety: **8 8**   ★★★

Ivory	**1996**	MHA	40	4088	MA	Ca300	D	$4600	278	5,000	28,000	25,099

Livability Code: SB 30-90

Wheelbase-to-length ratio of 57% is considered ○ dangerous ○ fatiguing ◉ good ○ excellent *

The approximate net payload of 2901 pounds at 10% of GVWR on this model is ○ deficient ○ excessive ○ cautionary ◉ good ○ excellent *

Total highway safety penalties are: 2 *   Value: **7 3**   Durability: **7 2**   Highway Control Rating: **9 0**   Highway Safety: **8 8**   ★★★

Ivory	**1996**	MHA	40	4090	MA	Ca300	D	$4600	278	5,000	28,000	25,099

Livability Code: SB 30-90

Wheelbase-to-length ratio of 57% is considered ○ dangerous ○ fatiguing ◉ good ○ excellent *

The approximate net payload of 2901 pounds at 10% of GVWR on this model is ○ deficient ○ excessive ○ cautionary ◉ good ○ excellent *

Total highway safety penalties are: 2 *   Value: **7 3**   Durability: **7 2**   Highway Control Rating: **9 0**   Highway Safety: **8 8**   ★★★

Ivory	**1997**	MHA	33	3334	MA	Ca300	D	$5100	208	5,000	28,000	23,088

Livability Code: SB 30-90

Wheelbase-to-length ratio of 53% is considered ○ dangerous ◉ fatiguing ○ good ○ excellent *

The approximate net payload of 4912 pounds at 18% of GVWR on this model is ○ deficient ○ excessive ○ cautionary ○ good ◉ excellent *

Total highway safety penalties are: 2 *   Value: **7 3**   Durability: **7 2**   Highway Control Rating: **7 0**   Highway Safety: **6 8**   ★★

Ivory	**1997**	MHA	33	3354	MA	Ca300	D	$5100	208	5,000	28,000	23,088

Livability Code: SB 30-90

Wheelbase-to-length ratio of 53% is considered ○ dangerous ◉ fatiguing ○ good ○ excellent *

The approximate net payload of 4912 pounds at 18% of GVWR on this model is ○ deficient ○ excessive ○ cautionary ○ good ◉ excellent *

Total highway safety penalties are: 2 *   Value: **7 3**   Durability: **7 2**   Highway Control Rating: **7 0**   Highway Safety: **6 8**   ★★

Ivory	**1997**	MHA	35	3530	MA	Ca300	D	$4900	228	5,000	28,000	23,639

Livability Code: SB 30-90

Wheelbase-to-length ratio of 54% is considered ○ dangerous ○ fatiguing ◉ good ○ excellent *

The approximate net payload of 4361 pounds at 16% of GVWR on this model is ○ deficient ○ excessive ○ cautionary ○ good ◉ excellent *

Total highway safety penalties are: 2 *   Value: **7 3**   Durability: **7 2**   Highway Control Rating: **8 2**   Highway Safety: **8 0**   ★★★

Note: Safety ratings are based on the assumption that the engineering of the RV has allowed for proper balance by placing fresh, gray, and black holding tanks in a location so as not to change the balance of the RV when the tanks are empty or full. **Always double-check wheelbase, GVWR, and weights at front and rear axles.**

*See Section 1 for details on how conclusions are reached.

Brand	Year	Type	Length	Model	Chassis	Engine	Fuel Type	Average Price per Linear Foot When New	Adjusted Wheelbase	Approx. Towing Capacity	Gross Vehicle Weight Rating	Average Curb Weight
Ivory	**1997**	MHA	35	3540	MA	Ca300	D	$4900	228	5,000	28,000	23,639

Livability Code: SB 30-90
Wheelbase-to-length ratio of 54% is considered ○ dangerous ○ fatiguing ◉ good ○ excellent *
The approximate net payload of 4361 pounds at 16% of GVWR on this model is ○ deficient ○ excessive ○ cautionary ○ good ◉ excellent *
Total highway safety penalties are: 2 *   Value: **7 3**   Durability: **7 2**   Highway Control Rating: **8 2**   Highway Safety: **8 0**   ★★★

Brand	Year	Type	Length	Model	Chassis	Engine	Fuel Type	Avg Price/Linear Foot	Adj Wheelbase	Towing	GVWR	Curb Wt
Ivory	**1997**	MHA	35	3550	MA	Ca300	D	$5000	228	5,000	28,000	23,639

Livability Code: SB 30-90
Wheelbase-to-length ratio of 54% is considered ○ dangerous ○ fatiguing ◉ good ○ excellent *
The approximate net payload of 4361 pounds at 16% of GVWR on this model is ○ deficient ○ excessive ○ cautionary ○ good ◉ excellent *
Total highway safety penalties are: 2 *   Value: **7 3**   Durability: **7 2**   Highway Control Rating: **8 2**   Highway Safety: **8 0**   ★★★

Ivory	**1997**	MHA	37	3730	MA	Ca300	D	$4800	252	5,000	28,000	24,190

Livability Code: SB 30-90
Wheelbase-to-length ratio of 57% is considered ○ dangerous ○ fatiguing ◉ good ○ excellent *
The approximate net payload of 3810 pounds at 14% of GVWR on this model is ○ deficient ○ excessive ○ cautionary ◉ good ○ excellent *
Total highway safety penalties are: 2 *   Value: **7 3**   Durability: **7 2**   Highway Control Rating: **9 4**   Highway Safety: **9 2**   ★★★

Ivory	**1997**	MHA	37	3740	MA	Ca300	D	$4900	252	5,000	28,000	24,190

Livability Code: SB 30-90
Wheelbase-to-length ratio of 57% is considered ○ dangerous ○ fatiguing ◉ good ○ excellent *
The approximate net payload of 3810 pounds at 14% of GVWR on this model is ○ deficient ○ excessive ○ cautionary ◉ good ○ excellent *
Total highway safety penalties are: 2 *   Value: **7 3**   Durability: **7 2**   Highway Control Rating: **9 4**   Highway Safety: **9 2**   ★★★

Ivory	**1997**	MHA	37	3750	MA	Ca300	D	$4900	252	5,000	28,000	24,190

Livability Code: SB 30-90
Wheelbase-to-length ratio of 57% is considered ○ dangerous ○ fatiguing ◉ good ○ excellent *
The approximate net payload of 3810 pounds at 14% of GVWR on this model is ○ deficient ○ excessive ○ cautionary ◉ good ○ excellent *
Total highway safety penalties are: 2 *   Value: **7 3**   Durability: **7 2**   Highway Control Rating: **9 4**   Highway Safety: **9 2**   ★★★

Ivory	**1997**	MHA	40	4030	MA	Ca300	D	$4800	276	5,000	28,000	25,016

Livability Code: SB 30-90
Wheelbase-to-length ratio of 58% is considered ○ dangerous ○ fatiguing ○ good ◉ excellent *
The approximate net payload of 2984 pounds at 11% of GVWR on this model is ○ deficient ○ excessive ○ cautionary ◉ good ○ excellent *
Total highway safety penalties are: 2 *   Value: **7 3**   Durability: **7 2**   Highway Control Rating: **9 1**   Highway Safety: **8 9**   ★★★

Ivory	**1997**	MHA	40	4050	MA	Ca300	D	$4800	276	5,000	28,000	25,016

Livability Code: SB 30-90
Wheelbase-to-length ratio of 58% is considered ○ dangerous ○ fatiguing ○ good ◉ excellent *
The approximate net payload of 2984 pounds at 11% of GVWR on this model is ○ deficient ○ excessive ○ cautionary ◉ good ○ excellent *
Total highway safety penalties are: 2 *   Value: **7 3**   Durability: **7 2**   Highway Control Rating: **9 1**   Highway Safety: **8 9**   ★★★

Ivory	**1997**	MHA	40	4040	MA	Ca300	D	$4800	276	5,000	28,000	25,016

Livability Code: SB 30-90
Wheelbase-to-length ratio of 58% is considered ○ dangerous ○ fatiguing ○ good ◉ excellent *
The approximate net payload of 2984 pounds at 11% of GVWR on this model is ○ deficient ○ excessive ○ cautionary ◉ good ○ excellent *
Total highway safety penalties are: 2 *   Value: **7 3**   Durability: **7 2**   Highway Control Rating: **9 1**   Highway Safety: **8 9**   ★★★

Ivory	**1999**	MHA	39	3726 slide	MA	CA300	D	$4600	252	5,000	30,000	25,944

Livability Code: SB 30-90
Wheelbase-to-length ratio of 54% is considered ○ dangerous ○ fatiguing ◉ good ○ excellent *
The approximate net payload of 4056 pounds at 14% of GVWR on this model is ○ deficient ○ excessive ○ cautionary ◉ good ○ excellent *
Total highway safety penalties are: 13 *   Value: **6 7**   Durability: **7 0**   Highway Control Rating: **8 0**   Highway Safety: **6 7**   ★★

Ivory	**1999**	MHA	39	3706 no slide	MA	CA300	D	$4600	252	5,000	30,000	25,082

Livability Code: SB 30-90
Wheelbase-to-length ratio of 54% is considered ○ dangerous ○ fatiguing ◉ good ○ excellent *
The approximate net payload of 4918 pounds at 16% of GVWR on this model is ○ deficient ○ excessive ○ cautionary ○ good ◉ excellent *
Total highway safety penalties are: 2 *   Value: **7 2**   Durability: **7 0**   Highway Control Rating: **8 5**   Highway Safety: **8 3**   ★★★

Ivory	**1999**	MHA	39	3726 no slide	MA	CA300	D	$4600	252	5,000	30,000	25,082

Livability Code: SB 30-90
Wheelbase-to-length ratio of 54% is considered ○ dangerous ○ fatiguing ◉ good ○ excellent *
The approximate net payload of 4918 pounds at 16% of GVWR on this model is ○ deficient ○ excessive ○ cautionary ○ good ◉ excellent *
Total highway safety penalties are: 2 *   Value: **7 2**   Durability: **7 0**   Highway Control Rating: **8 5**   Highway Safety: **8 3**   ★★★

Ivory	**1999**	MHA	39	3706 slide opch	MA	CA300	D	$4600	232	5,000	30,000	26,444

Livability Code: SB 30-90
Wheelbase-to-length ratio of 50% is considered ◉ dangerous ○ fatiguing ○ good ○ excellent *
The approximate net payload of 3556 pounds at 12% of GVWR on this model is ○ deficient ○ excessive ○ cautionary ◉ good ○ excellent *
Total highway safety penalties are: 13 *   Value: **6 7**   Durability: **7 0**   Highway Control Rating: **4 6**   Highway Safety: **3 3**

Note: Safety ratings are based on the assumption that the engineering of the RV has allowed for proper balance by placing fresh, gray, and black holding tanks in a location so as not to change the balance of the RV when the tanks are empty or full. **Always double-check wheelbase, GVWR, and weights at front and rear axles.**

*See Section 1 for details on how conclusions are reached.

Brand	Year	Type	Length	Model	Chassis	Engine	Fuel Type	Average Price per Linear Foot When New	Adjusted Wheelbase	Approx. Towing Capacity	Gross Vehicle Weight Rating	Average Curb Weight
Ivory	1999	MHA	39	3706 no sl opch	MA	CA300	D	$4600	232	5,000	30,000	25,582

Livability Code: SB 30-90
Wheelbase-to-length ratio of 50% is considered ◉ dangerous ○ fatiguing ○ good ○ excellent *
The approximate net payload of 4418 pounds at 15% of GVWR on this model is ○ deficient ○ excessive ○ cautionary ◉ good ○ excellent *
Total highway safety penalties are: 2 *   Value: 7 2   Durability: 7 0   Highway Control Rating: 5 2   Highway Safety: 5 0

| Ivory | 1999 | MHA | 39 | 3706 slide | MA | CA300 | D | $4600 | 252 | 5,000 | 30,000 | 25,944 |

Livability Code: SB 30-90
Wheelbase-to-length ratio of 54% is considered ○ dangerous ○ fatiguing ◉ good ○ excellent *
The approximate net payload of 4056 pounds at 14% of GVWR on this model is ○ deficient ○ excessive ○ cautionary ◉ good ○ excellent *
Total highway safety penalties are: 13 *   Value: 6 7   Durability: 7 0   Highway Control Rating: 8 0   Highway Safety: 6 7   ★★

| Ivory | 1999 | MHA | 41 | 4006 slide | MA | CA300 | D | $4400 | 276 | 5,000 | 30,000 | 26,347 |

Livability Code: SB 30-90
Wheelbase-to-length ratio of 56% is considered ○ dangerous ○ fatiguing ◉ good ○ excellent *
The approximate net payload of 3653 pounds at 12% of GVWR on this model is ○ deficient ○ excessive ○ cautionary ◉ good ○ excellent *
Total highway safety penalties are: 14 *   Value: 6 6   Durability: 7 0   Highway Control Rating: 8 8   Highway Safety: 7 4   ★★

| Ivory | 1999 | MHA | 41 | 4066 slide | MA | CA300 | D | $4400 | 276 | 5,000 | 30,000 | 26,347 |

Livability Code: SB 30-90
Wheelbase-to-length ratio of 56% is considered ○ dangerous ○ fatiguing ◉ good ○ excellent *
The approximate net payload of 3653 pounds at 12% of GVWR on this model is ○ deficient ○ excessive ○ cautionary ◉ good ○ excellent *
Total highway safety penalties are: 14 *   Value: 6 6   Durability: 7 0   Highway Control Rating: 8 8   Highway Safety: 7 4   ★★

| Ivory | 1999 | MHA | 41 | 4006 no slide | MA | CA300 | D | $4400 | 276 | 5,000 | 30,000 | 25,410 |

Livability Code: SB 30-90
Wheelbase-to-length ratio of 56% is considered ○ dangerous ○ fatiguing ◉ good ○ excellent *
The approximate net payload of 4590 pounds at 15% of GVWR on this model is ○ deficient ○ excessive ○ cautionary ◉ good ○ excellent *
Total highway safety penalties are: 2 *   Value: 7 2   Durability: 7 0   Highway Control Rating: 9 4   Highway Safety: 9 2   ★★★

| Ivory | 1999 | MHA | 41 | 4066 no slide | MA | CA300 | D | $4400 | 276 | 5,000 | 30,000 | 25,410 |

Livability Code: SB 30-90
Wheelbase-to-length ratio of 56% is considered ○ dangerous ○ fatiguing ◉ good ○ excellent *
The approximate net payload of 4590 pounds at 15% of GVWR on this model is ○ deficient ○ excessive ○ cautionary ◉ good ○ excellent *
Total highway safety penalties are: 2 *   Value: 7 2   Durability: 7 0   Highway Control Rating: 9 4   Highway Safety: 9 2   ★★★

| Ivory | 1999 | MHA | 41 | 4006 slide opch | MA | CA300 | D | $4400 | 266 | 5,000 | 30,000 | 26,847 |

Livability Code: SB 30-90
Wheelbase-to-length ratio of 54% is considered ○ dangerous ○ fatiguing ◉ good ○ excellent *
The approximate net payload of 3153 pounds at 11% of GVWR on this model is ○ deficient ○ excessive ○ cautionary ◉ good ○ excellent *
Total highway safety penalties are: 14 *   Value: 6 6   Durability: 7 0   Highway Control Rating: 7 8   Highway Safety: 6 4   ★★

| Ivory | 1999 | MHA | 41 | 4066 slide opch | MA | CA300 | D | $4400 | 266 | 5,000 | 30,000 | 26,847 |

Livability Code: SB 30-90
Wheelbase-to-length ratio of 54% is considered ○ dangerous ○ fatiguing ◉ good ○ excellent *
The approximate net payload of 3153 pounds at 11% of GVWR on this model is ○ deficient ○ excessive ○ cautionary ◉ good ○ excellent *
Total highway safety penalties are: 14 *   Value: 6 6   Durability: 7 0   Highway Control Rating: 7 8   Highway Safety: 6 4   ★★

| Ivory | 1999 | MHA | 41 | 4006 no sl opch | MA | CA300 | D | $4400 | 266 | 5,000 | 30,000 | 25,910 |

Livability Code: SB 30-90
Wheelbase-to-length ratio of 54% is considered ○ dangerous ○ fatiguing ◉ good ○ excellent *
The approximate net payload of 4090 pounds at 14% of GVWR on this model is ○ deficient ○ excessive ○ cautionary ◉ good ○ excellent *
Total highway safety penalties are: 2 *   Value: 7 2   Durability: 7 0   Highway Control Rating: 7 9   Highway Safety: 7 7   ★★★

| Ivory | 1999 | MHA | 41 | 4066 no sl opch | MA | CA300 | D | $4400 | 266 | 5,000 | 30,000 | 25,910 |

Livability Code: SB 30-90
Wheelbase-to-length ratio of 54% is considered ○ dangerous ○ fatiguing ◉ good ○ excellent *
The approximate net payload of 4090 pounds at 14% of GVWR on this model is ○ deficient ○ excessive ○ cautionary ◉ good ○ excellent *
Total highway safety penalties are: 2 *   Value: 7 2   Durability: 7 0   Highway Control Rating: 7 9   Highway Safety: 7 7   ★★★

| Jamboree | 1989 | MHC | 24 | D24 | FO | 7.5L | G | $1700 | 146 | 4,500 | 10,500 | 9,693 |

Livability Code: VA 30-90
Wheelbase-to-length ratio of 50% is considered ◉ dangerous ○ fatiguing ○ good ○ excellent *
The approximate net payload of 807 pounds at 8% of GVWR on this model is ○ deficient ○ excessive ◉ cautionary ○ good ○ excellent *
Total highway safety penalties are: 2 *   Value: 7 9   Durability: 7 4   Highway Control Rating: 3 8   Highway Safety: 3 6

| Jamboree | 1989 | MHC | 25 | D24 | FO | 7.5L | G | $1700 | 158 | 4,000 | 11,000 | 9,970 |

Livability Code: VA 30-90
Wheelbase-to-length ratio of 53% is considered ○ dangerous ◉ fatiguing ○ good ○ excellent *
The approximate net payload of 1030 pounds at 9% of GVWR on this model is ○ deficient ○ excessive ◉ cautionary ○ good ○ excellent *
Total highway safety penalties are: 2 *   Value: 7 9   Durability: 7 4   Highway Control Rating: 6 2   Highway Safety: 6 0   ★★

Note: Safety ratings are based on the assumption that the engineering of the RV has allowed for proper balance by placing fresh, gray, and black holding tanks in a location so as not to change the balance of the RV when the tanks are empty or full. **Always double-check wheelbase, GVWR, and weights at front and rear axles.**

*See Section 1 for details on how conclusions are reached.

Brand	Year	Type	Length	Model	Chassis	Engine	Fuel Type	Average Price per Linear Foot When New	Adjusted Wheelbase	Approx. Towing Capacity	Gross Vehicle Weight Rating	Average Curb Weight
Jamboree	1989	MHC	27	F26	FO	7.5L	G	$1600	176	3,800	11,200	10,470

Livability Code: VA 30-90 — Wheelbase-to-length ratio of 54% is considered ○ dangerous ○ fatiguing ◉ good ○ excellent*

The approximate net payload of 730 pounds at 7% of GVWR on this model is ○ deficient ○ excessive ◉ cautionary ○ good ○ excellent*

Total highway safety penalties are: 2* Value: 7 9 Durability: 7 4 Highway Control Rating: 5 7 Highway Safety: 5 5 ★

Brand	Year	Type	Length	Model	Chassis	Engine	Fuel Type		Adjusted Wheelbase	Approx. Towing Capacity	Gross Vehicle Weight Rating	Average Curb Weight
Jamboree	1989	MHC	27	S26	FO	7.5L	G	$1600	176	3,800	11,200	10,470

Livability Code: VA 30-90 — Wheelbase-to-length ratio of 54% is considered ○ dangerous ○ fatiguing ◉ good ○ excellent*

The approximate net payload of 730 pounds at 7% of GVWR on this model is ○ deficient ○ excessive ◉ cautionary ○ good ○ excellent*

Total highway safety penalties are: 2* Value: 7 9 Durability: 7 4 Highway Control Rating: 5 7 Highway Safety: 5 5 ★

Jamboree	1989	MHC	27	T26	FO	7.5L	G	$1600	176	3,800	11,200	10,470

Livability Code: VA 30-90 — Wheelbase-to-length ratio of 54% is considered ○ dangerous ○ fatiguing ◉ good ○ excellent*

The approximate net payload of 730 pounds at 7% of GVWR on this model is ○ deficient ○ excessive ◉ cautionary ○ good ○ excellent*

Total highway safety penalties are: 2* Value: 7 9 Durability: 7 4 Highway Control Rating: 5 7 Highway Safety: 5 5 ★

Jamboree	1990	MHC	25	D24	CH	5.7L	G	$1700	146	1,500	10,500	9,735

Livability Code: VA 30-90 — Wheelbase-to-length ratio of 49% is considered ◉ dangerous ○ fatiguing ○ good ○ excellent*

The approximate net payload of 765 pounds at 7% of GVWR on this model is ○ deficient ○ excessive ◉ cautionary ○ good ○ excellent*

Total highway safety penalties are: 2* Value: 7 9 Durability: 7 4 Highway Control Rating: 2 9 Highway Safety: 2 7

Jamboree	1991	MHC	27	F26	FO	7.5L	G	$1700	176	3,500	11,500	10,545

Livability Code: VA 30-90 — Wheelbase-to-length ratio of 54% is considered ○ dangerous ○ fatiguing ◉ good ○ excellent*

The approximate net payload of 955 pounds at 8% of GVWR on this model is ○ deficient ○ excessive ◉ cautionary ○ good ○ excellent*

Total highway safety penalties are: 2* Value: 7 9 Durability: 7 4 Highway Control Rating: 6 4 Highway Safety: 6 2 ★★

Jamboree	1991	MHC	27	S26	FO	7.5L	G	$1700	176	3,500	11,500	10,558

Livability Code: VA 30-90 — Wheelbase-to-length ratio of 54% is considered ○ dangerous ○ fatiguing ◉ good ○ excellent*

The approximate net payload of 942 pounds at 8% of GVWR on this model is ○ deficient ○ excessive ◉ cautionary ○ good ○ excellent*

Total highway safety penalties are: 2* Value: 7 9 Durability: 7 4 Highway Control Rating: 6 4 Highway Safety: 6 2 ★★

Jamboree	1991	MHC	27	T26	FO	7.5L	G	$1700	176	3,500	11,500	10,623

Livability Code: VA 30-90 — Wheelbase-to-length ratio of 54% is considered ○ dangerous ○ fatiguing ◉ good ○ excellent*

The approximate net payload of 877 pounds at 8% of GVWR on this model is ○ deficient ○ excessive ◉ cautionary ○ good ○ excellent*

Total highway safety penalties are: 2* Value: 7 9 Durability: 7 4 Highway Control Rating: 6 3 Highway Safety: 6 1 ★★

Jamboree	1992	MHC	27	S26	FO	7.5L	G	$1700	176	3,500	11,500	10,558

Livability Code: VA 30-90 — Wheelbase-to-length ratio of 54% is considered ○ dangerous ○ fatiguing ◉ good ○ excellent*

The approximate net payload of 942 pounds at 8% of GVWR on this model is ○ deficient ○ excessive ◉ cautionary ○ good ○ excellent*

Total highway safety penalties are: 2* Value: 7 9 Durability: 7 4 Highway Control Rating: 6 4 Highway Safety: 6 2 ★★

Jamboree	1992	MHC	28	F28	FO	7.5L	G	$1700	176	3,500	11,500	10,637

Livability Code: VA 30-90 — Wheelbase-to-length ratio of 52% is considered ○ dangerous ◉ fatiguing ○ good ○ excellent*

The approximate net payload of 863 pounds at 8% of GVWR on this model is ○ deficient ○ excessive ◉ cautionary ○ good ○ excellent*

Total highway safety penalties are: 2* Value: 7 9 Durability: 7 4 Highway Control Rating: 4 7 Highway Safety: 4 5

Jamboree	1992	MHC	28	Y28	FO	7.5L	G	$1700	176	3,500	11,500	10,768

Livability Code: VA 30-90 — Wheelbase-to-length ratio of 52% is considered ○ dangerous ◉ fatiguing ○ good ○ excellent*

The approximate net payload of 732 pounds at 6% of GVWR on this model is ◉ deficient ○ excessive ○ cautionary ○ good ○ excellent*

Total highway safety penalties are: 2* Value: 7 9 Durability: 7 4 Highway Control Rating: 3 6 Highway Safety: 3 4

Jamboree	1994	MHC	24	23D	FO	7.5L	G	$1600	158	3,500	12,400	10,114

Livability Code: VA 30-90 — Wheelbase-to-length ratio of 55% is considered ○ dangerous ○ fatiguing ◉ good ○ excellent*

The approximate net payload of 2286 pounds at 18% of GVWR on this model is ○ deficient ○ excessive ○ cautionary ○ good ◉ excellent*

Total highway safety penalties are: 2* Value: 7 9 Durability: 7 4 Highway Control Rating: 9 4 Highway Safety: 9 2 ★★★

Jamboree	1994	MHC	29	28V	FO	7.5L	G	$1700	190	3,500	12,400	11,175

Livability Code: VA 30-90 — Wheelbase-to-length ratio of 55% is considered ○ dangerous ○ fatiguing ◉ good ○ excellent*

The approximate net payload of 1225 pounds at 10% of GVWR on this model is ○ deficient ○ excessive ○ cautionary ◉ good ○ excellent*

Total highway safety penalties are: 2* Value: 7 9 Durability: 7 4 Highway Control Rating: 8 1 Highway Safety: 7 9 ★★★

Note: Safety ratings are based on the assumption that the engineering of the RV has allowed for proper balance by placing fresh, gray, and black holding tanks in a location so as not to change the balance of the RV when the tanks are empty or full. **Always double-check wheelbase, GVWR, and weights at front and rear axles.**

*See Section 1 for details on how conclusions are reached.

Section 2: The Ratings

Brand	Year	Type	Length	Model	Chassis	Engine	Fuel Type	Average Price per Linear Foot When New	Adjusted Wheelbase	Approx. Towing Capacity	Gross Vehicle Weight Rating	Average Curb Weight
Jamboree	1994	MHC	29	28V	FO	7.5L	G	$1700	190	3,500	12,400	11,175

Livability Code: VA 30-90
Wheelbase-to-length ratio of 55% is considered ○ dangerous ○ fatiguing ◉ good ○ excellent *
The approximate net payload of 1225 pounds at 10% of GVWR on this model is ○ deficient ○ excessive ○ cautionary ◉ good ○ excellent *
Total highway safety penalties are: 2 *   Value: 79   Durability: 74   Highway Control Rating: 81   Highway Safety: 79   ★★★

Brand	Year	Type	Length	Model	Chassis	Engine	Fuel Type	Price/Ft	Wheelbase	Towing	GVWR	Curb Weight
Jamboree	1998	MHC	20	19A	FO	6.8L	G	$2700	138	3,500	10,500	8,912

Livability Code: VA 30-90
Wheelbase-to-length ratio of 58% is considered ○ dangerous ○ fatiguing ○ good ◉ excellent *
The approximate net payload of 1588 pounds at 15% of GVWR on this model is ○ deficient ○ excessive ○ cautionary ◉ good ○ excellent *
Total highway safety penalties are: 2 *   Value: 80   Durability: 77   Highway Control Rating: 100   Highway Safety: 98   ★★★

Brand	Year	Type	Length	Model	Chassis	Engine	Fuel Type	Price/Ft	Wheelbase	Towing	GVWR	Curb Weight
Jamboree	1998	MHC	23	22C	FO	6.8L	G	$2300	138	3,500	10,500	9,476

Livability Code: VA 30-90
Wheelbase-to-length ratio of 51% is considered ○ dangerous ◉ fatiguing ○ good ○ excellent *
The approximate net payload of 1024 pounds at 10% of GVWR on this model is ○ deficient ○ excessive ○ cautionary ◉ good ○ excellent *
Total highway safety penalties are: 2 *   Value: 80   Durability: 77   Highway Control Rating: 51   Highway Safety: 49

Brand	Year	Type	Length	Model	Chassis	Engine	Fuel Type	Price/Ft	Wheelbase	Towing	GVWR	Curb Weight
Jamboree	1998	MHC	23	22E	FO	6.8L	G	$2300	138	3,500	10,500	9,589

Livability Code: VA 30-90
Wheelbase-to-length ratio of 50% is considered ◉ dangerous ○ fatiguing ○ good ○ excellent *
The approximate net payload of 911 pounds at 9% of GVWR on this model is ○ deficient ○ excessive ◉ cautionary ○ good ○ excellent *
Total highway safety penalties are: 2 *   Value: 80   Durability: 77   Highway Control Rating: 42   Highway Safety: 40

Brand	Year	Type	Length	Model	Chassis	Engine	Fuel Type	Price/Ft	Wheelbase	Towing	GVWR	Curb Weight
Jamboree	1998	MHC	25	24D	FO	6.8L	G	$2100	158	4,500	10,500	10,245

Livability Code: VA 30-90
Wheelbase-to-length ratio of 54% is considered ○ dangerous ○ fatiguing ◉ good ○ excellent *
The approximate net payload of 255 pounds at 2% of GVWR on this model is ◉ deficient ○ excessive ○ cautionary ○ good ○ excellent *
Total highway safety penalties are: 2 *   Value: 80   Durability: 77   Highway Control Rating: 45   Highway Safety: 43

Brand	Year	Type	Length	Model	Chassis	Engine	Fuel Type	Price/Ft	Wheelbase	Towing	GVWR	Curb Weight
Jamboree	1998	MHC	25	24D	CH	7.4L	G	$2100	159	2,700	12,300	10,640

Livability Code: VA 30-90
Wheelbase-to-length ratio of 53% is considered ○ dangerous ◉ fatiguing ○ good ○ excellent *
The approximate net payload of 1660 pounds at 13% of GVWR on this model is ○ deficient ○ excessive ○ cautionary ◉ good ○ excellent *
Total highway safety penalties are: 2 *   Value: 80   Durability: 77   Highway Control Rating: 72   Highway Safety: 70   ★★★

Brand	Year	Type	Length	Model	Chassis	Engine	Fuel Type	Price/Ft	Wheelbase	Towing	GVWR	Curb Weight
Jamboree	1998	MHC	27	26F	FO	6.8L	G	$2000	176	3,500	14,050	11,544

Livability Code: VA 30-90
Wheelbase-to-length ratio of 55% is considered ○ dangerous ○ fatiguing ◉ good ○ excellent *
The approximate net payload of 2506 pounds at 18% of GVWR on this model is ○ deficient ○ excessive ○ cautionary ◉ good ○ excellent *
Total highway safety penalties are: 2 *   Value: 80   Durability: 77   Highway Control Rating: 94   Highway Safety: 92   ★★★

Brand	Year	Type	Length	Model	Chassis	Engine	Fuel Type	Price/Ft	Wheelbase	Towing	GVWR	Curb Weight
Jamboree	1998	MHC	29	29Z	FO	6.8L	G	$1800	190	3,500	14,050	12,162

Livability Code: VA 30-90
Wheelbase-to-length ratio of 54% is considered ○ dangerous ○ fatiguing ◉ good ○ excellent *
The approximate net payload of 1888 pounds at 13% of GVWR on this model is ○ deficient ○ excessive ○ cautionary ◉ good ○ excellent *
Total highway safety penalties are: 2 *   Value: 80   Durability: 77   Highway Control Rating: 80   Highway Safety: 78   ★★★

Brand	Year	Type	Length	Model	Chassis	Engine	Fuel Type	Price/Ft	Wheelbase	Towing	GVWR	Curb Weight
Jamboree	1998	MHC	30	GT 29H	FO	6.8L	G	$1800	214	3,500	14,050	12,328

Livability Code: VA 30-90
Wheelbase-to-length ratio of 59% is considered ○ dangerous ○ fatiguing ○ good ◉ excellent *
The approximate net payload of 1722 pounds at 12% of GVWR on this model is ○ deficient ○ excessive ○ cautionary ◉ good ○ excellent *
Total highway safety penalties are: 2 *   Value: 80   Durability: 77   Highway Control Rating: 100   Highway Safety: 98   ★★★

Brand	Year	Type	Length	Model	Chassis	Engine	Fuel Type	Price/Ft	Wheelbase	Towing	GVWR	Curb Weight
Jamboree	1998	MHC	31	GT 31K	FO	6.8L	G	$1700	214	3,500	14,050	12,661

Livability Code: VA 30-90
Wheelbase-to-length ratio of 57% is considered ○ dangerous ○ fatiguing ◉ good ○ excellent *
The approximate net payload of 1389 pounds at 10% of GVWR on this model is ○ deficient ○ excessive ○ cautionary ◉ good ○ excellent *
Total highway safety penalties are: 2 *   Value: 80   Durability: 77   Highway Control Rating: 87   Highway Safety: 85   ★★★

Brand	Year	Type	Length	Model	Chassis	Engine	Fuel Type	Price/Ft	Wheelbase	Towing	GVWR	Curb Weight
Jamboree	1998	MHC	31	GT 31W	FO	6.8L	G	$1700	214	3,500	14,050	13,561

Livability Code: VA 30-90
Wheelbase-to-length ratio of 57% is considered ○ dangerous ○ fatiguing ◉ good ○ excellent *
The approximate net payload of 489 pounds at 3% of GVWR on this model is ◉ deficient ○ excessive ○ cautionary ○ good ○ excellent *
Total highway safety penalties are: 7 *   Value: 77   Durability: 77   Highway Control Rating: 62   Highway Safety: 55   ★

Brand	Year	Type	Length	Model	Chassis	Engine	Fuel Type	Price/Ft	Wheelbase	Towing	GVWR	Curb Weight
Jamboree	1999	MHC	23	22C	FO	6.8L	G	$2300	138	3,500	10,500	9,746

Livability Code: VA 30-90
Wheelbase-to-length ratio of 51% is considered ○ dangerous ◉ fatiguing ○ good ○ excellent *
The approximate net payload of 754 pounds at 7% of GVWR on this model is ○ deficient ○ excessive ◉ cautionary ○ good ○ excellent *
Total highway safety penalties are: 2 *   Value: 78   Durability: 72   Highway Control Rating: 35   Highway Safety: 33

Note: Safety ratings are based on the assumption that the engineering of the RV has allowed for proper balance by placing fresh, gray, and black holding tanks in a location so as not to change the balance of the RV when the tanks are empty or full. **Always double-check wheelbase, GVWR, and weights at front and rear axles.**

*See Section 1 for details on how conclusions are reached.

Brand	Year	Type	Length	Model	Chassis	Engine	Fuel Type	Average Price per Linear Foot When New	Adjusted Wheelbase	Approx. Towing Capacity	Gross Vehicle Weight Rating	Average Curb Weight
Jamboree	1999	MHC	23	22 C	CH	7.4L	G	$2300	139	3,500	12,300	10,165

Livability Code: VA 30-90 — Wheelbase-to-length ratio of 50% is considered ⦿ dangerous ○ fatiguing ○ good ○ excellent *
The approximate net payload of 2135 pounds at 17% of GVWR on this model is ○ deficient ○ excessive ○ cautionary ○ good ⦿ excellent *
Total highway safety penalties are: 2 * — Value: 7 8 Durability: 7 2 Highway Control Rating: 6 2 Highway Safety: 6 0

| Jamboree | 1999 | MHC | 24 | 23B | FO | 6.8L | G | $2200 | 158 | 3,500 | 11,500 | 10,155 |

Livability Code: VA 30-90 — Wheelbase-to-length ratio of 55% is considered ○ dangerous ○ fatiguing ⦿ good ○ excellent *
The approximate net payload of 1345 pounds at 12% of GVWR on this model is ○ deficient ○ excessive ○ cautionary ⦿ good ○ excellent *
Total highway safety penalties are: 2 * — Value: 7 8 Durability: 7 2 Highway Control Rating: 8 5 Highway Safety: 8 3 ★★★

| Jamboree | 1999 | MHC | 24 | 23 B | CH | 7.4L | G | $2200 | 159 | 3,500 | 12,300 | 10,426 |

Livability Code: VA 30-90 — Wheelbase-to-length ratio of 55% is considered ○ dangerous ○ fatiguing ⦿ good ○ excellent *
The approximate net payload of 1874 pounds at 15% of GVWR on this model is ○ deficient ○ excessive ○ cautionary ⦿ good ○ excellent *
Total highway safety penalties are: 2 * — Value: 7 8 Durability: 7 2 Highway Control Rating: 9 1 Highway Safety: 8 9 ★★★

| Jamboree | 1999 | MHC | 25 | 24D | FO | 6.8L | G | $2100 | 158 | 3,500 | 11,500 | 10,345 |

Livability Code: VA 30-90 — Wheelbase-to-length ratio of 54% is considered ○ dangerous ○ fatiguing ⦿ good ○ excellent *
The approximate net payload of 1155 pounds at 10% of GVWR on this model is ○ deficient ○ excessive ○ cautionary ⦿ good ○ excellent *
Total highway safety penalties are: 2 * — Value: 7 8 Durability: 7 2 Highway Control Rating: 7 8 Highway Safety: 7 6 ★★★

| Jamboree | 1999 | MHC | 25 | 24D 4x4 | FO | 6.8L | G | $2100 | 158 | 1,500 e | 14,050 | 11,245 |

Livability Code: VA 30-90 · — Wheelbase-to-length ratio of 54% is considered ○ dangerous ○ fatiguing ⦿ good ○ excellent *
The approximate net payload of 2805 pounds at 20% of GVWR on this model is ○ deficient ○ excessive ○ cautionary ⦿ good ○ excellent *
Total highway safety penalties are: 2 * — Value: 7 8 Durability: 7 2 Highway Control Rating: 8 7 Highway Safety: 8 5 ★★★

| Jamboree | 1999 | MHC | 25 | 24D | CH | 7.4L | G | $2100 | 159 | 3,500 | 12,300 | 10,640 |

Livability Code: VA 30-90 — Wheelbase-to-length ratio of 53% is considered ○ dangerous ⦿ fatiguing ○ good ○ excellent *
The approximate net payload of 1660 pounds at 13% of GVWR on this model is ○ deficient ○ excessive ○ cautionary ⦿ good ○ excellent *
Total highway safety penalties are: 2 * — Value: 7 8 Durability: 7 2 Highway Control Rating: 7 2 Highway Safety: 7 0 ★★★

| Jamboree | 1999 | MHC | 27 | 26F | FO | 6.8L | G | $2000 | 176 | 3,500 | 14,050 | 11,280 |

Livability Code: VA 30-90 — Wheelbase-to-length ratio of 55% is considered ○ dangerous ○ fatiguing ⦿ good ○ excellent *
The approximate net payload of 2770 pounds at 20% of GVWR on this model is ○ deficient ○ excessive ○ cautionary ○ good ⦿ excellent *
Total highway safety penalties are: 2 * — Value: 7 8 Durability: 7 2 Highway Control Rating: 9 6 Highway Safety: 9 4 ★★★

| Jamboree | 1999 | MHC | 29 | 29L | FO | 6.8L | G | $1800 | 190 | 3,500 | 14,050 | 12,912 |

Livability Code: VA 30-90 — Wheelbase-to-length ratio of 54% is considered ○ dangerous ○ fatiguing ⦿ good ○ excellent *
The approximate net payload of 1138 pounds at 8% of GVWR on this model is ○ deficient ○ excessive ⦿ cautionary ○ good ○ excellent *
Total highway safety penalties are: 12 * — Value: 7 3 Durability: 7 2 Highway Control Rating: 6 3 Highway Safety: 5 1 ★

| Jamboree | 1999 | MHC | 29 | 29V | FO | 6.8L | G | $1800 | 190 | 3,500 | 14,050 | 12,162 |

Livability Code: VA 30-90 — Wheelbase-to-length ratio of 54% is considered ○ dangerous ○ fatiguing ⦿ good ○ excellent *
The approximate net payload of 1888 pounds at 13% of GVWR on this model is ○ deficient ○ excessive ○ cautionary ⦿ good ○ excellent *
Total highway safety penalties are: 2 * — Value: 7 8 Durability: 7 2 Highway Control Rating: 8 0 Highway Safety: 7 8 ★★★

| Jamboree | 1999 | MHC | 30 | 29H | FO | 6.8L | G | $1800 | 214 | 3,500 | 14,050 | 12,328 |

Livability Code: VA 30-90 — Wheelbase-to-length ratio of 59% is considered ○ dangerous ○ fatiguing ⦿ good ○ excellent *
The approximate net payload of 1722 pounds at 12% of GVWR on this model is ○ deficient ○ excessive ○ cautionary ⦿ good ○ excellent *
Total highway safety penalties are: 2 * — Value: 7 8 Durability: 7 2 Highway Control Rating: 1 0 0 Highway Safety: 9 8 ★★★

| Jamboree | 1999 | MHC | 31 | 31K | FO | 6.8L | G | $1700 | 214 | 3,500 | 14,050 | 12,661 |

Livability Code: VA 30-90 — Wheelbase-to-length ratio of 57% is considered ○ dangerous ○ fatiguing ⦿ good ○ excellent *
The approximate net payload of 1389 pounds at 10% of GVWR on this model is ○ deficient ○ excessive ○ cautionary ⦿ good ○ excellent *
Total highway safety penalties are: 2 * — Value: 7 8 Durability: 7 2 Highway Control Rating: 8 7 Highway Safety: 8 5 ★★★

| Jamboree | 1999 | MHC | 31 | 31 W | FO | 6.8L | G | $1700 | 214 | 3,500 | 14,050 | 13,561 |

Livability Code: VA 30-90 — Wheelbase-to-length ratio of 57% is considered ○ dangerous ○ fatiguing ⦿ good ○ excellent *
The approximate net payload of 489 pounds at 3% of GVWR on this model is ⦿ deficient ○ excessive ○ cautionary ○ good ○ excellent *
Total highway safety penalties are: 7 * — Value: 7 5 Durability: 7 2 Highway Control Rating: 6 2 Highway Safety: 5 5 ★

Note: Safety ratings are based on the assumption that the engineering of the RV has allowed for proper balance by placing fresh, gray, and black holding tanks in a location so as not to change the balance of the RV when the tanks are empty or full. **Always double-check wheelbase, GVWR, and weights at front and rear axles.**

*See Section 1 for details on how conclusions are reached.

Brand	Year	Type	Length	Model	Chassis	Engine	Fuel Type	Average Price per Linear Foot When New	Adjusted Wheelbase	Approx. Towing Capacity	Gross Vehicle Weight Rating	Average Curb Weight
Jamboree C Sport	1995	MHC	22	21C	FO	7.5L	G	$1800	138	3,500	10,500	9,221

Livability Code: VA 30-90

Wheelbase-to-length ratio of 52% is considered ○ dangerous ◉ fatiguing ○ good ○ excellent*

The approximate net payload of 1279 pounds at 12% of GVWR on this model is ○ deficient ○ excessive ○ cautionary ◉ good ○ excellent*

Total highway safety penalties are: 2*   Value: 79   Durability: 74   Highway Control Rating: 61   Highway Safety: 59   ★

| Jamboree C Sport | 1995 | MHC | 25 | 24D | FO | 7.5L | G | $1700 | 158 | 3,500 | 12,400 | 10,083 |

Livability Code: VA 30-90

Wheelbase-to-length ratio of 53% is considered ○ dangerous ◉ fatiguing ○ good ○ excellent*

The approximate net payload of 2317 pounds at 19% of GVWR on this model is ○ deficient ○ excessive ○ cautionary ○ good ◉ excellent*

Total highway safety penalties are: 2*   Value: 79   Durability: 74   Highway Control Rating: 80   Highway Safety: 78   ★★★

| Jamboree C Sport | 1995 | MHC | 30 | 29V | FO | 7.5L | G | $1500 | 190 | 3,500 | 12,400 | 11,186 |

Livability Code: VA 30-90

Wheelbase-to-length ratio of 53% is considered ○ dangerous ◉ fatiguing ○ good ○ excellent*

The approximate net payload of 1214 pounds at 10% of GVWR on this model is ○ deficient ○ excessive ○ cautionary ◉ good ○ excellent*

Total highway safety penalties are: 2*   Value: 79   Durability: 74   Highway Control Rating: 65   Highway Safety: 63   ★★

| Jamboree C Sport | 1995 | MHC | 30 | 29Z | FO | 7.5L | G | $1500 | 190 | 3,500 | 12,400 | 11,186 |

Livability Code: VA 30-90

Wheelbase-to-length ratio of 53% is considered ○ dangerous ◉ fatiguing ○ good ○ excellent*

The approximate net payload of 1214 pounds at 10% of GVWR on this model is ○ deficient ○ excessive ○ cautionary ◉ good ○ excellent*

Total highway safety penalties are: 2*   Value: 79   Durability: 74   Highway Control Rating: 65   Highway Safety: 63   ★★

| Jamboree C Sport | 1996 | MHC | 20 | 19A-460 | FO | 7.5L | G | $2200 | 138 | 3,500 | 10,500 | 8,638 |

Livability Code: VA 30-90

Wheelbase-to-length ratio of 59% is considered ○ dangerous ○ fatiguing ○ good ◉ excellent*

The approximate net payload of 1862 pounds at 18% of GVWR on this model is ○ deficient ○ excessive ○ cautionary ○ good ◉ excellent*

Total highway safety penalties are: 2*   Value: 79   Durability: 74   Highway Control Rating: 100   Highway Safety: 98   ★★★

| Jamboree C Sport | 1996 | MHC | 20 | 19A-351 | FO | 5.8L | G | $2200 | 138 | 1,000 | 10,500 | 8,638 |

Livability Code: VA 30-90

Wheelbase-to-length ratio of 59% is considered ○ dangerous ○ fatiguing ○ good ◉ excellent*

The approximate net payload of 1862 pounds at 18% of GVWR on this model is ○ deficient ○ excessive ○ cautionary ○ good ◉ excellent*

Total highway safety penalties are: 2*   Value: 79   Durability: 74   Highway Control Rating: 100   Highway Safety: 98   ★★★

| Jamboree C Sport | 1996 | MHC | 22 | 21C-460 | FO | 7.5L | G | $2000 | 138 | 3,500 | 10,500 | 9,156 |

Livability Code: VA 30-90

Wheelbase-to-length ratio of 52% is considered ○ dangerous ◉ fatiguing ○ good ○ excellent*

The approximate net payload of 1344 pounds at 13% of GVWR on this model is ○ deficient ○ excessive ○ cautionary ◉ good ○ excellent*

Total highway safety penalties are: 2*   Value: 79   Durability: 74   Highway Control Rating: 65   Highway Safety: 63   ★★

| Jamboree C Sport | 1996 | MHC | 22 | 21C-351 | FO | 5.8L | G | $2100 | 138 | 1,000 | 10,500 | 9,156 |

Livability Code: VA 30-90

Wheelbase-to-length ratio of 52% is considered ○ dangerous ◉ fatiguing ○ good ○ excellent*

The approximate net payload of 1344 pounds at 13% of GVWR on this model is ○ deficient ○ excessive ○ cautionary ◉ good ○ excellent*

Total highway safety penalties are: 2*   Value: 79   Durability: 74   Highway Control Rating: 65   Highway Safety: 63   ★★

| Jamboree C Sport | 1996 | MHC | 25 | 23D-460 | FO | 7.5L | G | $1800 | 158 | 1,600 | 12,400 | 10,019 |

Livability Code: VA 30-90

Wheelbase-to-length ratio of 54% is considered ○ dangerous ○ fatiguing ◉ good ○ excellent*

The approximate net payload of 2381 pounds at 19% of GVWR on this model is ○ deficient ○ excessive ○ cautionary ○ good ◉ excellent*

Total highway safety penalties are: 2*   Value: 79   Durability: 74   Highway Control Rating: 87   Highway Safety: 85   ★★★

| Jamboree C Sport | 1996 | MHC | 25 | 23D-351 | FO | 5.8L | G | $1800 | 158 | 1,500 | 12,400 | 10,019 |

Livability Code: VA 30-90

Wheelbase-to-length ratio of 54% is considered ○ dangerous ○ fatiguing ◉ good ○ excellent*

The approximate net payload of 2381 pounds at 19% of GVWR on this model is ○ deficient ○ excessive ○ cautionary ○ good ◉ excellent*

Total highway safety penalties are: 2*   Value: 79   Durability: 74   Highway Control Rating: 87   Highway Safety: 85   ★★★

| Jamboree C Sport | 1996 | MHC | 29 | 29Z-460 | FO | 7.5L | G | $1700 | 190 | 1,600 | 12,400 | 10,970 |

Livability Code: VA 30-90

Wheelbase-to-length ratio of 55% is considered ○ dangerous ○ fatiguing ◉ good ○ excellent*

The approximate net payload of 1430 pounds at 12% of GVWR on this model is ○ deficient ○ excessive ○ cautionary ◉ good ○ excellent*

Total highway safety penalties are: 2*   Value: 79   Durability: 74   Highway Control Rating: 83   Highway Safety: 81   ★★★

| Jamboree C Sport | 1996 | MHC | 29 | 29Z-351 | FO | 5.8L | G | $1700 | 190 | 1,500 | 12,400 | 10,970 |

Livability Code: VA 30-90

Wheelbase-to-length ratio of 55% is considered ○ dangerous ○ fatiguing ◉ good ○ excellent*

The approximate net payload of 1430 pounds at 12% of GVWR on this model is ○ deficient ○ excessive ○ cautionary ◉ good ○ excellent*

Total highway safety penalties are: 2*   Value: 79   Durability: 74   Highway Control Rating: 83   Highway Safety: 81   ★★★

Note: Safety ratings are based on the assumption that the engineering of the RV has allowed for proper balance by placing fresh, gray, and black holding tanks in a location so as not to change the balance of the RV when the tanks are empty or full. **Always double-check wheelbase, GVWR, and weights at front and rear axles.**

*See Section 1 for details on how conclusions are reached.

Section 2: The Ratings

Brand	Year	Type	Length	Model	Chassis	Engine	Fuel Type	Average Price per Linear Foot When New	Adjusted Wheelbase	Approx. Towing Capacity	Gross Vehicle Weight Rating	Average Curb Weight
Jamboree C Sport	**1997**	MHC	20	19 A	FO	6.8L	G	$2300	138	3,500	10,500	8,724

Livability Code: VA 30-90   Wheelbase-to-length ratio of 58% is considered ○ dangerous ○ fatiguing ○ good ◉ excellent *

The approximate net payload of 1776 pounds at 17% of GVWR on this model is ○ deficient ○ excessive ○ cautionary ○ good ◉ excellent *

Total highway safety penalties are: 2 *   Value: **7 9**   Durability: **7 4**   Highway Control Rating: **1 0 0**   Highway Safety: **9 8**   ★★★

Brand	Year	Type	Length	Model	Chassis	Engine	Fuel Type	Price/ft	Wheelbase	Towing	GVWR	Curb Wt
Jamboree C Sport	**1997**	MHC	23	22 C	FO	6.8L	G	$2000	138	3,500	10,500	9,265

Livability Code: VA 30-90   Wheelbase-to-length ratio of 51% is considered ○ dangerous ◉ fatiguing ○ good ○ excellent *

The approximate net payload of 1236 pounds at 12% of GVWR on this model is ○ deficient ◉ excessive ○ cautionary ○ good ○ excellent *

Total highway safety penalties are: 2 *   Value: **7 9**   Durability: **7 4**   Highway Control Rating: **5 5**   Highway Safety: **5 3**   ★

Brand	Year	Type	Length	Model	Chassis	Engine	Fuel Type	Price/ft	Wheelbase	Towing	GVWR	Curb Wt
Jamboree C Sport	**1997**	MHC	23	22 E	FO	6.8L	G	$2000	138	3,500	10,500	9,373

Livability Code: VA 30-90   Wheelbase-to-length ratio of 50% is considered ◉ dangerous ○ fatiguing ○ good ○ excellent *

The approximate net payload of 1127 pounds at 11% of GVWR on this model is ○ deficient ○ excessive ○ cautionary ◉ good ○ excellent *

Total highway safety penalties are: 2 *   Value: **7 9**   Durability: **7 4**   Highway Control Rating: **4 9**   Highway Safety: **4 7**

Brand	Year	Type	Length	Model	Chassis	Engine	Fuel Type	Price/ft	Wheelbase	Towing	GVWR	Curb Wt
Jamboree C Sport	**1997**	MHC	25	24 D	FO	6.8L	G	$1900	158	3,500	11,500	9,905

Livability Code: VA 30-90   Wheelbase-to-length ratio of 53% is considered ○ dangerous ◉ fatiguing ○ good ○ excellent *

The approximate net payload of 1595 pounds at 14% of GVWR on this model is ○ deficient ○ excessive ○ cautionary ◉ good ○ excellent *

Total highway safety penalties are: 2 *   Value: **7 9**   Durability: **7 4**   Highway Control Rating: **7 3**   Highway Safety: **7 1**   ★★★

Brand	Year	Type	Length	Model	Chassis	Engine	Fuel Type	Price/ft	Wheelbase	Towing	GVWR	Curb Wt
Jamboree C Sport	**1997**	MHC	29	26 F	FO	6.8L	G	$1600	176	3,500	14,050	11,405

Livability Code: VA 30-90   Wheelbase-to-length ratio of 51% is considered ○ dangerous ◉ fatiguing ○ good ○ excellent *

The approximate net payload of 2645 pounds at 19% of GVWR on this model is ○ deficient ○ excessive ○ cautionary ○ good ◉ excellent *

Total highway safety penalties are: 2 *   Value: **7 9**   Durability: **7 4**   Highway Control Rating: **6 6**   Highway Safety: **6 4**   ★★

Brand	Year	Type	Length	Model	Chassis	Engine	Fuel Type	Price/ft	Wheelbase	Towing	GVWR	Curb Wt
Jamboree C Sport	**1997**	MHC	29	29 Z	FO	6.8L	G	$1700	190	3,500	14,050	11,535

Livability Code: VA 30-90   Wheelbase-to-length ratio of 54% is considered ○ dangerous ○ fatiguing ◉ good ○ excellent *

The approximate net payload of 2515 pounds at 18% of GVWR on this model is ○ deficient ○ excessive ○ cautionary ○ good ◉ excellent *

Total highway safety penalties are: 2 *   Value: **7 9**   Durability: **7 4**   Highway Control Rating: **8 7**   Highway Safety: **8 5**   ★★★

Brand	Year	Type	Length	Model	Chassis	Engine	Fuel Type	Price/ft	Wheelbase	Towing	GVWR	Curb Wt
Jamboree Rallye	**1989**	MHC	22	C21	CH	5.7L	G	$1600	125	3,500	10,200	8,801

Livability Code: SB 30-80   Wheelbase-to-length ratio of 48% is considered ◉ dangerous ○ fatiguing ○ good ○ excellent *

The approximate net payload of 1399 pounds at 14% of GVWR on this model is ○ deficient ○ excessive ○ cautionary ◉ good ○ excellent *

Total highway safety penalties are: 2 *   Value: **7 9**   Durability: **7 5**   Highway Control Rating: **5 0**   Highway Safety: **4 8**

Brand	Year	Type	Length	Model	Chassis	Engine	Fuel Type	Price/ft	Wheelbase	Towing	GVWR	Curb Wt
Jamboree Rallye	**1989**	MHC	22	C21	FO	5.7L	G	$1600	138	5,000	10,500	9,010

Livability Code: SB 30-80   Wheelbase-to-length ratio of 52% is considered ○ dangerous ◉ fatiguing ○ good ○ excellent *

The approximate net payload of 1490 pounds at 14% of GVWR on this model is ○ deficient ○ excessive ○ cautionary ◉ good ○ excellent *

Total highway safety penalties are: 2 *   Value: **7 9**   Durability: **7 5**   Highway Control Rating: **6 8**   Highway Safety: **6 6**   ★★

Brand	Year	Type	Length	Model	Chassis	Engine	Fuel Type	Price/ft	Wheelbase	Towing	GVWR	Curb Wt
Jamboree Rallye	**1989**	MHC	24	D23	CH	5.7L	G	$1500	146	3,200	10,500	9,372

Livability Code: SB 30-80   Wheelbase-to-length ratio of 51% is considered ○ dangerous ◉ fatiguing ○ good ○ excellent *

The approximate net payload of 1128 pounds at 11% of GVWR on this model is ○ deficient ○ excessive ○ cautionary ◉ good ○ excellent *

Total highway safety penalties are: 2 *   Value: **7 9**   Durability: **7 5**   Highway Control Rating: **5 2**   Highway Safety: **5 0**   ★

Brand	Year	Type	Length	Model	Chassis	Engine	Fuel Type	Price/ft	Wheelbase	Towing	GVWR	Curb Wt
Jamboree Rallye	**1989**	MHC	25	D23	FO	7.5L	G	$1500	158	4,000	11,000	9,765

Livability Code: SB 30-80   Wheelbase-to-length ratio of 53% is considered ○ dangerous ◉ fatiguing ○ good ○ excellent *

The approximate net payload of 1235 pounds at 11% of GVWR on this model is ○ deficient ○ excessive ○ cautionary ◉ good ○ excellent *

Total highway safety penalties are: 2 *   Value: **7 9**   Durability: **7 5**   Highway Control Rating: **6 9**   Highway Safety: **6 7**   ★★

Brand	Year	Type	Length	Model	Chassis	Engine	Fuel Type	Price/ft	Wheelbase	Towing	GVWR	Curb Wt
Jamboree Rallye	**1989**	MHC	26	F26	FO	7.5L	G	$1500	176	3,800	11,200	10,063

Livability Code: SB 30-80   Wheelbase-to-length ratio of 56% is considered ○ dangerous ○ fatiguing ◉ good ○ excellent *

The approximate net payload of 1137 pounds at 10% of GVWR on this model is ○ deficient ○ excessive ○ cautionary ◉ good ○ excellent *

Total highway safety penalties are: 2 *   Value: **7 9**   Durability: **7 5**   Highway Control Rating: **8 4**   Highway Safety: **8 2**   ★★★

Brand	Year	Type	Length	Model	Chassis	Engine	Fuel Type	Price/ft	Wheelbase	Towing	GVWR	Curb Wt
Jamboree Rallye	**1989**	MHC	26	R26	FO	7.5L	G	$1500	176	3,800	11,200	10,083

Livability Code: SB 30-80   Wheelbase-to-length ratio of 56% is considered ○ dangerous ○ fatiguing ◉ good ○ excellent *

The approximate net payload of 1117 pounds at 10% of GVWR on this model is ○ deficient ○ excessive ○ cautionary ◉ good ○ excellent *

Total highway safety penalties are: 2 *   Value: **7 9**   Durability: **7 5**   Highway Control Rating: **8 3**   Highway Safety: **8 1**   ★★★

Note: Safety ratings are based on the assumption that the engineering of the RV has allowed for proper balance by placing fresh, gray, and black holding tanks in a location so as not to change the balance of the RV when the tanks are empty or full. **Always double-check wheelbase, GVWR, and weights at front and rear axles.**

*See Section 1 for details on how conclusions are reached.

Section 2: The Ratings

Brand	Year	Type	Length	Model	Chassis	Engine	Fuel Type	Average Price per Linear Foot When New	Adjusted Wheelbase	Approx. Towing Capacity	Gross Vehicle Weight Rating	Average Curb Weight
Jamboree Rallye	1989	MHC	26	S26	FO	7.5L	G	$1500	176	3,800	11,200	10,063

Livability Code: SB 30-80
Wheelbase-to-length ratio of 56% is considered ○ dangerous ○ fatiguing ◉ good ○ excellent *
The approximate net payload of 1137 pounds at 10% of GVWR on this model is ○ deficient ○ excessive ○ cautionary ◉ good ○ excellent *
Total highway safety penalties are: 2 *   Value: 7 9   Durability: 7 5   Highway Control Rating: 8 4   Highway Safety: 8 2   ★★★

Brand	Year	Type	Length	Model	Chassis	Engine	Fuel Type	Price	Wheelbase	Towing	GVWR	Curb Weight
Jamboree Rallye	1989	MHC	27	Y27	FO	7.5L	G	$1500	176	3,800	11,200	10,278

Livability Code: SB 30-80
Wheelbase-to-length ratio of 54% is considered ○ dangerous ○ fatiguing ◉ good ○ excellent *
The approximate net payload of 922 pounds at 8% of GVWR on this model is ○ deficient ○ excessive ◉ cautionary ○ good ○ excellent *
Total highway safety penalties are: 2 *   Value: 7 9   Durability: 7 5   Highway Control Rating: 6 1   Highway Safety: 5 9   ★

Brand	Year	Type	Length	Model	Chassis	Engine	Fuel Type	Price	Wheelbase	Towing	GVWR	Curb Weight
Jamboree Rallye	1990	MHC	27	Y27	FO	7.5L	G	$1500	176	1,500	11,200	10,346

Livability Code: SB 30-80
Wheelbase-to-length ratio of 54% is considered ○ dangerous ○ fatiguing ◉ good ○ excellent *
The approximate net payload of 854 pounds at 8% of GVWR on this model is ○ deficient ○ excessive ◉ cautionary ○ good ○ excellent *
Total highway safety penalties are: 2 *   Value: 7 9   Durability: 7 5   Highway Control Rating: 6 0   Highway Safety: 5 8   ★

Brand	Year	Type	Length	Model	Chassis	Engine	Fuel Type	Price	Wheelbase	Towing	GVWR	Curb Weight
Jamboree Rallye	1991	MHC	24	P23	CH	7.4L	G	$1600	146	3,200	10,500	9,552

Livability Code: SB 30-80
Wheelbase-to-length ratio of 51% is considered ○ dangerous ◉ fatiguing ○ good ○ excellent *
The approximate net payload of 948 pounds at 9% of GVWR on this model is ○ deficient ○ excessive ◉ cautionary ○ good ○ excellent *
Total highway safety penalties are: 2 *   Value: 7 9   Durability: 7 5   Highway Control Rating: 4 5   Highway Safety: 4 3

Brand	Year	Type	Length	Model	Chassis	Engine	Fuel Type	Price	Wheelbase	Towing	GVWR	Curb Weight
Jamboree Rallye	1991	MHC	24	P23	FO	7.5L	G	$1600	158	4,000	11,500	9,781

Livability Code: SB 30-80
Wheelbase-to-length ratio of 55% is considered ○ dangerous ○ fatiguing ◉ good ○ excellent *
The approximate net payload of 1719 pounds at 15% of GVWR on this model is ○ deficient ○ excessive ○ cautionary ◉ good ○ excellent *
Total highway safety penalties are: 2 *   Value: 7 9   Durability: 7 5   Highway Control Rating: 9 0   Highway Safety: 8 8   ★★★

Brand	Year	Type	Length	Model	Chassis	Engine	Fuel Type	Price	Wheelbase	Towing	GVWR	Curb Weight
Jamboree Rallye	1991	MHC	26	S26	FO	7.5L	G	$1500	176	4,000	11,500	10,242

Livability Code: SB 30-80
Wheelbase-to-length ratio of 56% is considered ○ dangerous ○ fatiguing ◉ good ○ excellent *
The approximate net payload of 1258 pounds at 11% of GVWR on this model is ○ deficient ○ excessive ○ cautionary ◉ good ○ excellent *
Total highway safety penalties are: 2 *   Value: 7 9   Durability: 7 5   Highway Control Rating: 8 5   Highway Safety: 8 3   ★★★

Brand	Year	Type	Length	Model	Chassis	Engine	Fuel Type	Price	Wheelbase	Towing	GVWR	Curb Weight
Jamboree Rallye	1991	MHC	27	Y27	FO	7.5L	G	$1500	176	4,000	11,500	10,504

Livability Code: SB 30-80
Wheelbase-to-length ratio of 54% is considered ○ dangerous ○ fatiguing ◉ good ○ excellent *
The approximate net payload of 996 pounds at 9% of GVWR on this model is ○ deficient ○ excessive ◉ cautionary ○ good ○ excellent *
Total highway safety penalties are: 2 *   Value: 7 9   Durability: 7 5   Highway Control Rating: 6 6   Highway Safety: 6 4   ★★

Brand	Year	Type	Length	Model	Chassis	Engine	Fuel Type	Price	Wheelbase	Towing	GVWR	Curb Weight
Jamboree Rallye	1992	MHC	24	P23	CH	7.4L	G	$1700	146	3,500	10,500	9,622

Livability Code: SB 30-80
Wheelbase-to-length ratio of 51% is considered ○ dangerous ◉ fatiguing ○ good ○ excellent *
The approximate net payload of 878 pounds at 8% of GVWR on this model is ○ deficient ○ excessive ◉ cautionary ○ good ○ excellent *
Total highway safety penalties are: 2 *   Value: 7 9   Durability: 7 5   Highway Control Rating: 4 0   Highway Safety: 3 8

Brand	Year	Type	Length	Model	Chassis	Engine	Fuel Type	Price	Wheelbase	Towing	GVWR	Curb Weight
Jamboree Rallye	1992	MHC	24	P23	FO	7.5L	G	$1700	158	3,500	11,500	9,704

Livability Code: SB 30-80
Wheelbase-to-length ratio of 55% is considered ○ dangerous ○ fatiguing ◉ good ○ excellent *
The approximate net payload of 1796 pounds at 16% of GVWR on this model is ○ deficient ○ excessive ○ cautionary ○ good ◉ excellent *
Total highway safety penalties are: 2 *   Value: 7 9   Durability: 7 5   Highway Control Rating: 9 2   Highway Safety: 9 0   ★★★

Brand	Year	Type	Length	Model	Chassis	Engine	Fuel Type	Price	Wheelbase	Towing	GVWR	Curb Weight
Jamboree Rallye	1992	MHC	26	S26	FO	7.5L	G	$1600	176	3,500	11,500	10,242

Livability Code: SB 30-80
Wheelbase-to-length ratio of 56% is considered ○ dangerous ○ fatiguing ◉ good ○ excellent *
The approximate net payload of 1258 pounds at 11% of GVWR on this model is ○ deficient ○ excessive ○ cautionary ◉ good ○ excellent *
Total highway safety penalties are: 2 *   Value: 7 9   Durability: 7 5   Highway Control Rating: 8 5   Highway Safety: 8 3   ★★★

Brand	Year	Type	Length	Model	Chassis	Engine	Fuel Type	Price	Wheelbase	Towing	GVWR	Curb Weight
Jamboree Rallye	1992	MHC	27	F27	FO	7.5L	G	$1600	176	3,500	11,500	10,371

Livability Code: SB 30-80
Wheelbase-to-length ratio of 54% is considered ○ dangerous ○ fatiguing ◉ good ○ excellent *
The approximate net payload of 1129 pounds at 10% of GVWR on this model is ○ deficient ○ excessive ○ cautionary ◉ good ○ excellent *
Total highway safety penalties are: 2 *   Value: 7 9   Durability: 7 5   Highway Control Rating: 7 7   Highway Safety: 7 5   ★★★

Brand	Year	Type	Length	Model	Chassis	Engine	Fuel Type	Price	Wheelbase	Towing	GVWR	Curb Weight
Jamboree Rallye	1992	MHC	27	Y27	FO	7.5L	G	$1600	176	3,500	11,500	10,498

Livability Code: SB 30-80
Wheelbase-to-length ratio of 54% is considered ○ dangerous ○ fatiguing ◉ good ○ excellent *
The approximate net payload of 1002 pounds at 9% of GVWR on this model is ○ deficient ○ excessive ◉ cautionary ○ good ○ excellent *
Total highway safety penalties are: 2 *   Value: 7 9   Durability: 7 5   Highway Control Rating: 6 6   Highway Safety: 6 4   ★★

Note: Safety ratings are based on the assumption that the engineering of the RV has allowed for proper balance by placing fresh, gray, and black holding tanks in a location so as not to change the balance of the RV when the tanks are empty or full. **Always double-check wheelbase, GVWR, and weights at front and rear axles.**

*See Section 1 for details on how conclusions are reached.

Brand	Year	Type	Length	Model	Chassis	Engine	Fuel Type	Average Price per Linear Foot When New	Adjusted Wheelbase	Approx. Towing Capacity	Gross Vehicle Weight Rating	Average Curb Weight
Jamboree Rallye	1994	MHC	31	31T	FO	7.5L	G	$1500	214	3,500	12,400	11,489

Livability Code: SB 30-80   Wheelbase-to-length ratio of 57% is considered ○ dangerous ◉ fatiguing ○ good ○ excellent *

The approximate net payload of 911 pounds at 7% of GVWR on this model is ○ deficient ○ excessive ◉ cautionary ○ good ○ excellent *

Total highway safety penalties are: 2 *   Value: 7 9   Durability: 7 5   Highway Control Rating: 7 0   Highway Safety: 6 8   ★★

Brand	Year	Type	Length	Model	Chassis	Engine	Fuel Type	Price/ft	Wheelbase	Towing	GVWR	Curb Wt
Jamboree Rallye	1995	MHC	22	21C	FO	7.5L	G	$1700	138	3,500	10,500	9,156

Livability Code: SB 30-80   Wheelbase-to-length ratio of 52% is considered ○ dangerous ◉ fatiguing ○ good ○ excellent *

The approximate net payload of 1344 pounds at 13% of GVWR on this model is ○ deficient ○ excessive ○ cautionary ◉ good ○ excellent *

Total highway safety penalties are: 2 *   Value: 7 9   Durability: 7 5   Highway Control Rating: 6 5   Highway Safety: 6 3   ★★

Jamboree Rallye	1995	MHC	23	22B	FO	7.5L	G	$1700	138	3,500	10,500	9,308

Livability Code: SB 30-80   Wheelbase-to-length ratio of 51% is considered ○ dangerous ◉ fatiguing ○ good ○ excellent *

The approximate net payload of 1192 pounds at 11% of GVWR on this model is ○ deficient ○ excessive ○ cautionary ◉ good ○ excellent *

Total highway safety penalties are: 2 *   Value: 7 9   Durability: 7 5   Highway Control Rating: 5 2   Highway Safety: 5 0   ★

Jamboree Rallye	1995	MHC	25	23D	FO	7.5L	G	$1600	158	3,500	12,400	10,019

Livability Code: SB 30-80   Wheelbase-to-length ratio of 54% is considered ○ dangerous ○ fatiguing ◉ good ○ excellent *

The approximate net payload of 2381 pounds at 19% of GVWR on this model is ○ deficient ○ excessive ○ cautionary ○ good ◉ excellent *

Total highway safety penalties are: 2 *   Value: 7 9   Durability: 7 5   Highway Control Rating: 8 7   Highway Safety: 8 5   ★★★

Jamboree Rallye	1995	MHC	25	23P	FO	7.5L	G	$1600	158	3,500	12,400	10,019

Livability Code: SB 30-80   Wheelbase-to-length ratio of 54% is considered ○ dangerous ○ fatiguing ◉ good ○ excellent *

The approximate net payload of 2381 pounds at 19% of GVWR on this model is ○ deficient ○ excessive ○ cautionary ○ good ◉ excellent *

Total highway safety penalties are: 2 *   Value: 7 9   Durability: 7 5   Highway Control Rating: 8 7   Highway Safety: 8 5   ★★★

Jamboree Rallye	1995	MHC	28	27V	FO	7.5L	G	$1500	190	3,500	12,400	10,732

Livability Code: SB 30-80   Wheelbase-to-length ratio of 57% is considered ○ dangerous ○ fatiguing ◉ good ○ excellent *

The approximate net payload of 1668 pounds at 13% of GVWR on this model is ○ deficient ○ excessive ○ cautionary ◉ good ○ excellent *

Total highway safety penalties are: 2 *   Value: 7 9   Durability: 7 5   Highway Control Rating: 9 3   Highway Safety: 9 1   ★★★

Jamboree Rallye	1995	MHC	30	29H	FO	7.5L	G	$1600	214	3,500	12,400	11,600

Livability Code: SB 30-80   Wheelbase-to-length ratio of 59% is considered ○ dangerous ○ fatiguing ○ good ◉ excellent *

The approximate net payload of 800 pounds at 6% of GVWR on this model is ◉ deficient ○ excessive ○ cautionary ○ good ○ excellent *

Total highway safety penalties are: 2 *   Value: 7 9   Durability: 7 5   Highway Control Rating: 7 4   Highway Safety: 7 2   ★★

Jamboree Rallye	1995	MHC	31	31N	FO	7.5L	G	$1600	214	3,500	12,400	11,922

Livability Code: SB 30-80   Wheelbase-to-length ratio of 57% is considered ○ dangerous ○ fatiguing ◉ good ○ excellent *

The approximate net payload of 478 pounds at 4% of GVWR on this model is ◉ deficient ○ excessive ○ cautionary ○ good ○ excellent *

Total highway safety penalties are: 2 *   Value: 7 9   Durability: 7 5   Highway Control Rating: 6 2   Highway Safety: 6 0   ★

Jamboree Rallye	1995	MHC	31	31T	FO	7.5L	G	$1600	214	3,500	12,400	11,922

Livability Code: SB 30-80   Wheelbase-to-length ratio of 57% is considered ○ dangerous ○ fatiguing ◉ good ○ excellent *

The approximate net payload of 478 pounds at 4% of GVWR on this model is ◉ deficient ○ excessive ○ cautionary ○ good ○ excellent *

Total highway safety penalties are: 2 *   Value: 7 9   Durability: 7 5   Highway Control Rating: 6 2   Highway Safety: 6 0   ★

Jamboree Rallye	1996	MHC	30	29G	FO	7.5L	G	$1800	214	3,500	12,400	11,600

Livability Code: SB 30-80   Wheelbase-to-length ratio of 59% is considered ○ dangerous ○ fatiguing ○ good ◉ excellent *

The approximate net payload of 800 pounds at 6% of GVWR on this model is ◉ deficient ○ excessive ○ cautionary ○ good ○ excellent *

Total highway safety penalties are: 2 *   Value: 7 9   Durability: 7 5   Highway Control Rating: 7 4   Highway Safety: 7 2   ★★

Jamboree Rallye	1996	MHC	30	29H	FO	7.5L	G	$1800	214	3,500	12,400	11,600

Livability Code: SB 30-80   Wheelbase-to-length ratio of 59% is considered ○ dangerous ○ fatiguing ○ good ◉ excellent *

The approximate net payload of 800 pounds at 6% of GVWR on this model is ◉ deficient ○ excessive ○ cautionary ○ good ○ excellent *

Total highway safety penalties are: 2 *   Value: 7 9   Durability: 7 5   Highway Control Rating: 7 4   Highway Safety: 7 2   ★★

Jamboree Rallye	1996	MHC	30	29K	FO	7.5L	G	$1800	214	3,500	12,400	11,600

Livability Code: SB 30-80   Wheelbase-to-length ratio of 59% is considered ○ dangerous ○ fatiguing ○ good ◉ excellent *

The approximate net payload of 800 pounds at 6% of GVWR on this model is ◉ deficient ○ excessive ○ cautionary ○ good ○ excellent *

Total highway safety penalties are: 2 *   Value: 7 9   Durability: 7 5   Highway Control Rating: 7 4   Highway Safety: 7 2   ★★

Note: Safety ratings are based on the assumption that the engineering of the RV has allowed for proper balance by placing fresh, gray, and black holding tanks in a location so as not to change the balance of the RV when the tanks are empty or full. **Always double-check wheelbase, GVWR, and weights at front and rear axles.**

*See Section 1 for details on how conclusions are reached.

Section 2: The Ratings

Brand	Year	Type	Length	Model	Chassis	Engine	Fuel Type	Average Price per Linear Foot When New	Adjusted Wheelbase	Approx. Towing Capacity	Gross Vehicle Weight Rating	Average Curb Weight
Jamboree Rallye	1996	MHC	31	31N	CH	7.4L	G	$1800	208	4,500	14,500	12,622

Livability Code: SB 30-80

Wheelbase-to-length ratio of 55% is considered ○ dangerous ○ fatiguing ◉ good ○ excellent*

The approximate net payload of 1878 pounds at 13% of GVWR on this model is ○ deficient ○ excessive ○ cautionary ◉ good ○ excellent*

Total highway safety penalties are: 2*   Value: 7 9   Durability: 7 5   Highway Control Rating: 8 7   Highway Safety: 8 5   ★★★

Brand	Year	Type	Length	Model	Chassis	Engine	Fuel Type	Price/Ft	Wheelbase	Towing	GVWR	Curb Weight
Jamboree Rallye	1996	MHC	31	31T	CH	7.4L	G	$1800	208	4,500	14,500	12,622

Livability Code: SB 30-80

Wheelbase-to-length ratio of 55% is considered ○ dangerous ○ fatiguing ◉ good ○ excellent*

The approximate net payload of 1878 pounds at 13% of GVWR on this model is ○ deficient ○ excessive ○ cautionary ◉ good ○ excellent*

Total highway safety penalties are: 2*   Value: 7 9   Durability: 7 5   Highway Control Rating: 8 7   Highway Safety: 8 5   ★★★

Jamboree Rallye	1997	MHC	30	29 H	FO	6.8L	G	$1900	214	3,500	14,050	11,826

Livability Code: SB 30-80

Wheelbase-to-length ratio of 59% is considered ○ dangerous ○ fatiguing ○ good ◉ excellent*

The approximate net payload of 2224 pounds at 16% of GVWR on this model is ○ deficient ○ excessive ○ cautionary ○ good ◉ excellent*

Total highway safety penalties are: 2*   Value: 7 9   Durability: 7 5   Highway Control Rating: 1 0 0   Highway Safety: 9 8   ★★★

Jamboree Rallye	1997	MHC	31	31 K	FO	6.8L	G	$1900	214	3,500	14,050	12,003

Livability Code: SB 30-80

Wheelbase-to-length ratio of 57% is considered ○ dangerous ○ fatiguing ◉ good ○ excellent*

The approximate net payload of 2047 pounds at 15% of GVWR on this model is ○ deficient ○ excessive ○ cautionary ○ good ○ excellent*

Total highway safety penalties are: 2*   Value: 7 9   Durability: 7 5   Highway Control Rating: 9 7   Highway Safety: 9 5   ★★★

Jamboree Rallye	1997	MHC	31	31 N	FO	6.8L	G	$1900	214	3,500	14,050	11,966

Livability Code: SB 30-80

Wheelbase-to-length ratio of 57% is considered ○ dangerous ○ fatiguing ◉ good ○ excellent*

The approximate net payload of 2084 pounds at 15% of GVWR on this model is ○ deficient ○ excessive ○ cautionary ◉ good ○ excellent*

Total highway safety penalties are: 2*   Value: 7 9   Durability: 7 5   Highway Control Rating: 9 7   Highway Safety: 9 5   ★★★

Jamboree Rallye	1997	MHC	31	31 T	FO	6.8L	G	$1900	214	3,500	14,050	11,966

Livability Code: SB 30-80

Wheelbase-to-length ratio of 57% is considered ○ dangerous ○ fatiguing ◉ good ○ excellent*

The approximate net payload of 2084 pounds at 15% of GVWR on this model is ○ deficient ○ excessive ○ cautionary ◉ good ○ excellent*

Total highway safety penalties are: 2*   Value: 7 9   Durability: 7 5   Highway Control Rating: 9 7   Highway Safety: 9 5   ★★★

Jamboree Searcher	1989	MHC	22	C21	CH	5.7L	G	$1400	125	3,500	10,200	8,700

Livability Code: VA 30-90

Wheelbase-to-length ratio of 48% is considered ◉ dangerous ○ fatiguing ○ good ○ excellent*

The approximate net payload of 1500 pounds at 15% of GVWR on this model is ○ deficient ○ excessive ○ cautionary ○ good ○ excellent*

Total highway safety penalties are: 2*   Value: 7 8   Durability: 7 3   Highway Control Rating: 5 2   Highway Safety: 5 0

Jamboree Searcher	1989	MHC	22	C21	FO	5.7L	G	$1500	138	5,000	10,500	8,906

Livability Code: VA 30-90

Wheelbase-to-length ratio of 52% is considered ○ dangerous ◉ fatiguing ○ good ○ excellent*

The approximate net payload of 1594 pounds at 15% of GVWR on this model is ○ deficient ○ excessive ○ cautionary ○ good ○ excellent*

Total highway safety penalties are: 2*   Value: 7 8   Durability: 7 3   Highway Control Rating: 7 0   Highway Safety: 6 8   ★★

Jamboree Searcher	1989	MHC	24	D23	CH	5.7L	G	$1400	146	3,200	10,500	9,260

Livability Code: VA 30-90

Wheelbase-to-length ratio of 51% is considered ○ dangerous ◉ fatiguing ○ good ○ excellent*

The approximate net payload of 1240 pounds at 12% of GVWR on this model is ○ deficient ○ excessive ○ cautionary ○ good ○ excellent*

Total highway safety penalties are: 2*   Value: 7 8   Durability: 7 3   Highway Control Rating: 5 4   Highway Safety: 5 2   ★

Jamboree Searcher	1989	MHC	25	D23	FO	7.5L	G	$1300	158	4,000	11,000	9,648

Livability Code: VA 30-90

Wheelbase-to-length ratio of 53% is considered ○ dangerous ◉ fatiguing ○ good ○ excellent*

The approximate net payload of 1352 pounds at 12% of GVWR on this model is ○ deficient ○ excessive ○ cautionary ○ good ○ excellent*

Total highway safety penalties are: 2*   Value: 7 8   Durability: 7 3   Highway Control Rating: 7 1   Highway Safety: 6 9   ★★

Jamboree Searcher	1989	MHC	26	S26	FO	7.5L	G	$1300	176	3,800	11,200	9,939

Livability Code: VA 30-90

Wheelbase-to-length ratio of 56% is considered ○ dangerous ○ fatiguing ◉ good ○ excellent*

The approximate net payload of 1261 pounds at 11% of GVWR on this model is ○ deficient ○ excessive ○ cautionary ◉ good ○ excellent*

Total highway safety penalties are: 2*   Value: 7 8   Durability: 7 3   Highway Control Rating: 8 6   Highway Safety: 8 4   ★★★

Jamboree Searcher	1989	MHC	27	Y27	FO	7.5L	G	$1300	176	3,800	11,200	10,149

Livability Code: VA 30-90

Wheelbase-to-length ratio of 54% is considered ○ dangerous ○ fatiguing ◉ good ○ excellent*

The approximate net payload of 1051 pounds at 9% of GVWR on this model is ○ deficient ○ excessive ◉ cautionary ○ good ○ excellent*

Total highway safety penalties are: 2*   Value: 7 8   Durability: 7 3   Highway Control Rating: 6 7   Highway Safety: 6 5   ★★

Note: Safety ratings are based on the assumption that the engineering of the RV has allowed for proper balance by placing fresh, gray, and black holding tanks in a location so as not to change the balance of the RV when the tanks are empty or full. **Always double-check wheelbase, GVWR, and weights at front and rear axles.**

*See Section 1 for details on how conclusions are reached.

Brand	Year	Type	Length	Model	Chassis	Engine	Fuel Type	Average Price per Linear Foot When New	Adjusted Wheel-base	Approx. Towing Capacity	Gross Vehicle Weight Rating	Average Curb Weight
Jamboree Searcher	1990	MHC	24	D23	CH	5.7L	G	$1300	146	1,500	10,500	9,287

Livability Code: VA 30-90   Wheelbase-to-length ratio of 51% is considered ○ dangerous ● fatiguing ○ good ○ excellent *

The approximate net payload of 1213 pounds at 12% of GVWR on this model is ○ deficient ○ excessive ○ cautionary ● good ○ excellent *

Total highway safety penalties are: 2 *   Value: 7 8   Durability: 7 3   Highway Control Rating: 5 5   Highway Safety: 5 3   ★

Brand	Year	Type	Length	Model	Chassis	Engine	Fuel Type	Price/Ft	Wheelbase	Towing	GVWR	Curb Weight
Jamboree Searcher	1991	MHC	19	A18	CH	7.4L	G	$1700	125	3,500	10,200	8,608

Livability Code: VA 30-90   Wheelbase-to-length ratio of 55% is considered ○ dangerous ○ fatiguing ● good ○ excellent *

The approximate net payload of 1592 pounds at 16% of GVWR on this model is ○ deficient ○ excessive ○ cautionary ○ good ● excellent *

Total highway safety penalties are: 2 *   Value: 7 8   Durability: 7 3   Highway Control Rating: 9 3   Highway Safety: 9 1   ★★★

Jamboree Searcher	1991	MHC	19	A18	FO	7.5L	G	$1600	138	5,000	10,500	8,768

Livability Code: VA 30-90   Wheelbase-to-length ratio of 61% is considered ○ dangerous ○ fatiguing ○ good ● excellent *

The approximate net payload of 1732 pounds at 16% of GVWR on this model is ○ deficient ○ excessive ○ cautionary ○ good ● excellent *

Total highway safety penalties are: 2 *   Value: 7 8   Durability: 7 3   Highway Control Rating: 1 0 0   Highway Safety: 9 8   ★★★

Jamboree Searcher	1991	MHC	22	C21	CH	7.4L	G	$1500	125	3,500	10,200	8,898

Livability Code: VA 30-90   Wheelbase-to-length ratio of 48% is considered ● dangerous ○ fatiguing ○ good ○ excellent *

The approximate net payload of 1302 pounds at 13% of GVWR on this model is ○ deficient ○ excessive ○ cautionary ● good ○ excellent *

Total highway safety penalties are: 2 *   Value: 7 8   Durability: 7 3   Highway Control Rating: 4 8   Highway Safety: 4 6

Jamboree Searcher	1991	MHC	22	C21	FO	7.5L	G	$1500	138	5,000	10,500	9,063

Livability Code: VA 30-90   Wheelbase-to-length ratio of 53% is considered ○ dangerous ● fatiguing ○ good ○ excellent *

The approximate net payload of 1437 pounds at 14% of GVWR on this model is ○ deficient ○ excessive ○ cautionary ● good ○ excellent *

Total highway safety penalties are: 2 *   Value: 7 8   Durability: 7 3   Highway Control Rating: 7 5   Highway Safety: 7 3   ★★★

Jamboree Searcher	1991	MHC	24	D23	CH	7.4L	G	$1400	146	3,200	10,500	9,490

Livability Code: VA 30-90   Wheelbase-to-length ratio of 51% is considered ○ dangerous ● fatiguing ○ good ○ excellent *

The approximate net payload of 1010 pounds at 10% of GVWR on this model is ○ deficient ○ excessive ○ cautionary ● good ○ excellent *

Total highway safety penalties are: 2 *   Value: 7 8   Durability: 7 3   Highway Control Rating: 5 0   Highway Safety: 4 8

Jamboree Searcher	1991	MHC	24	D23	FO	7.5L	G	$1400	158	4,000	11,500	9,665

Livability Code: VA 30-90   Wheelbase-to-length ratio of 55% is considered ○ dangerous ○ fatiguing ● good ○ excellent *

The approximate net payload of 1835 pounds at 16% of GVWR on this model is ○ deficient ○ excessive ○ cautionary ○ good ● excellent *

Total highway safety penalties are: 2 *   Value: 7 8   Durability: 7 3   Highway Control Rating: 9 2   Highway Safety: 9 0   ★★★

Jamboree Searcher	1995	MHC	22	21C	FO	5.8L	G	$1700	138	1,000	10,500	9,156

Livability Code: VA 30-90   Wheelbase-to-length ratio of 52% is considered ○ dangerous ● fatiguing ○ good ○ excellent *

The approximate net payload of 1344 pounds at 13% of GVWR on this model is ○ deficient ○ excessive ○ cautionary ● good ○ excellent *

Total highway safety penalties are: 2 *   Value: 7 8   Durability: 7 3   Highway Control Rating: 6 5   Highway Safety: 6 3   ★★

Jamboree Searcher	1995	MHC	23	22B	FO	5.8L	G	$1600	138	1,000	10,500	9,308

Livability Code: VA 30-90   Wheelbase-to-length ratio of 51% is considered ○ dangerous ● fatiguing ○ good ○ excellent *

The approximate net payload of 1192 pounds at 11% of GVWR on this model is ○ deficient ○ excessive ○ cautionary ● good ○ excellent *

Total highway safety penalties are: 2 *   Value: 7 8   Durability: 7 3   Highway Control Rating: 5 2   Highway Safety: 5 0   ★

Jamboree Searcher	1995	MHC	25	23D	FO	5.8L	G	$1600	158	1,500	12,400	10,019

Livability Code: VA 30-90   Wheelbase-to-length ratio of 54% is considered ○ dangerous ○ fatiguing ● good ○ excellent *

The approximate net payload of 2381 pounds at 19% of GVWR on this model is ○ deficient ○ excessive ○ cautionary ○ good ● excellent *

Total highway safety penalties are: 2 *   Value: 7 8   Durability: 7 3   Highway Control Rating: 8 7   Highway Safety: 8 5   ★★★

Jamboree Searcher	1995	MHC	25	23P	FO	5.8L	G	$1600	158	1,500	12,400	10,019

Livability Code: VA 30-90   Wheelbase-to-length ratio of 54% is considered ○ dangerous ○ fatiguing ● good ○ excellent *

The approximate net payload of 2381 pounds at 19% of GVWR on this model is ○ deficient ○ excessive ○ cautionary ○ good ● excellent *

Total highway safety penalties are: 2 *   Value: 7 8   Durability: 7 3   Highway Control Rating: 8 7   Highway Safety: 8 5   ★★★

Jamboree Searcher	1995	MHC	29	29Z	FO	7.5L	G	$1500	190	3,500	12,400	10,970

Livability Code: VA 30-90   Wheelbase-to-length ratio of 55% is considered ○ dangerous ○ fatiguing ● good ○ excellent *

The approximate net payload of 1430 pounds at 12% of GVWR on this model is ○ deficient ○ excessive ○ cautionary ● good ○ excellent *

Total highway safety penalties are: 2 *   Value: 7 8   Durability: 7 3   Highway Control Rating: 8 3   Highway Safety: 8 1   ★★★

Note: Safety ratings are based on the assumption that the engineering of the RV has allowed for proper balance by placing fresh, gray, and black holding tanks in a location so as not to change the balance of the RV when the tanks are empty or full. **Always double-check wheelbase, GVWR, and weights at front and rear axles.**

*See Section 1 for details on how conclusions are reached.

Section 2: The Ratings

Brand	Year	Type	Length	Model	Chassis	Engine	Fuel Type	Average Price per Linear Foot When New	Adjusted Wheelbase	Approx. Towing Capacity	Gross Vehicle Weight Rating	Average Curb Weight
Jamboree Searcher	1996	MHC	22	21C-460	FO	7.5L	G	$2000	138	3,500	10,500	9,460

Livability Code: VA 30-90
Wheelbase-to-length ratio of 52% is considered ○ dangerous ◉ fatiguing ○ good ○ excellent *
The approximate net payload of 1040 pounds at 10% of GVWR on this model is ○ deficient ○ excessive ○ cautionary ◉ good ○ excellent *
Total highway safety penalties are: 2 *   Value: 7 8   Durability: 7 3   Highway Control Rating: 6 0   Highway Safety: 5 8   ★

Brand	Year	Type	Length	Model	Chassis	Engine	Fuel Type	Price/Ft	Wheelbase	Towing	GVWR	Curb Wt
Jamboree Searcher	1996	MHC	22	21C-351	FO	5.8L	G	$2000	138	1,000	10,500	9,460

Livability Code: VA 30-90
Wheelbase-to-length ratio of 52% is considered ○ dangerous ◉ fatiguing ○ good ○ excellent *
The approximate net payload of 1040 pounds at 10% of GVWR on this model is ○ deficient ○ excessive ○ cautionary ◉ good ○ excellent *
Total highway safety penalties are: 2 *   Value: 7 8   Durability: 7 3   Highway Control Rating: 6 0   Highway Safety: 5 8   ★

Jamboree Searcher	1996	MHC	23	22B-460	FO	7.5L	G	$2000	138	1,600	12,400	9,921

Livability Code: VA 30-90
Wheelbase-to-length ratio of 51% is considered ○ dangerous ◉ fatiguing ○ good ○ excellent *
The approximate net payload of 2479 pounds at 20% of GVWR on this model is ○ deficient ○ excessive ○ cautionary ○ good ◉ excellent *
Total highway safety penalties are: 2 *   Value: 7 8   Durability: 7 3   Highway Control Rating: 6 6   Highway Safety: 6 4   ★★

Jamboree Searcher	1996	MHC	23	22B-351	FO	5.8L	G	$2000	138	1,500	12,400	9,921

Livability Code: VA 30-90
Wheelbase-to-length ratio of 51% is considered ○ dangerous ◉ fatiguing ○ good ○ excellent *
The approximate net payload of 2479 pounds at 20% of GVWR on this model is ○ deficient ○ excessive ○ cautionary ○ good ◉ excellent *
Total highway safety penalties are: 2 *   Value: 7 8   Durability: 7 3   Highway Control Rating: 6 6   Highway Safety: 6 4   ★★

Jamboree Searcher	1996	MHC	25	23D-460	FO	7.5L	G	$1800	158	3,500	12,400	10,358

Livability Code: VA 30-90
Wheelbase-to-length ratio of 54% is considered ○ dangerous ○ fatiguing ◉ good ○ excellent *
The approximate net payload of 2042 pounds at 16% of GVWR on this model is ○ deficient ○ excessive ○ cautionary ○ good ◉ excellent *
Total highway safety penalties are: 2 *   Value: 7 8   Durability: 7 3   Highway Control Rating: 8 4   Highway Safety: 8 2   ★★★

Jamboree Searcher	1996	MHC	25	23D-351	FO	5.8L	G	$1800	158	1,000	12,400	10,358

Livability Code: VA 30-90
Wheelbase-to-length ratio of 54% is considered ○ dangerous ○ fatiguing ◉ good ○ excellent *
The approximate net payload of 2042 pounds at 16% of GVWR on this model is ○ deficient ○ excessive ○ cautionary ○ good ◉ excellent *
Total highway safety penalties are: 2 *   Value: 7 8   Durability: 7 3   Highway Control Rating: 8 4   Highway Safety: 8 2   ★★★

Jamboree Searcher	1996	MHC	25	23P-460	FO	7.5L	G	$1900	158	3,500	12,400	10,358

Livability Code: VA 30-90
Wheelbase-to-length ratio of 54% is considered ○ dangerous ○ fatiguing ◉ good ○ excellent *
The approximate net payload of 2042 pounds at 16% of GVWR on this model is ○ deficient ○ excessive ○ cautionary ○ good ◉ excellent *
Total highway safety penalties are: 2 *   Value: 7 8   Durability: 7 3   Highway Control Rating: 8 4   Highway Safety: 8 2   ★★★

Jamboree Searcher	1996	MHC	25	23P-351	FO	5.8L	G	$1900	158	1,000	12,400	10,358

Livability Code: VA 30-90
Wheelbase-to-length ratio of 54% is considered ○ dangerous ○ fatiguing ◉ good ○ excellent *
The approximate net payload of 2042 pounds at 16% of GVWR on this model is ○ deficient ○ excessive ○ cautionary ○ good ◉ excellent *
Total highway safety penalties are: 2 *   Value: 7 8   Durability: 7 3   Highway Control Rating: 8 4   Highway Safety: 8 2   ★★★

Jamboree Searcher	1996	MHC	29	29M-460	FO	7.5L	G	$1700	190	3,500	12,400	11,370

Livability Code: VA 30-90
Wheelbase-to-length ratio of 55% is considered ○ dangerous ○ fatiguing ◉ good ○ excellent *
The approximate net payload of 1030 pounds at 8% of GVWR on this model is ○ deficient ○ excessive ◉ cautionary ○ good ○ excellent *
Total highway safety penalties are: 2 *   Value: 7 8   Durability: 7 3   Highway Control Rating: 6 9   Highway Safety: 6 7   ★★

Jamboree Searcher	1996	MHC	29	29M-351	FO	5.8L	G	$1700	190	1,000	12,400	11,370

Livability Code: VA 30-90
Wheelbase-to-length ratio of 55% is considered ○ dangerous ○ fatiguing ◉ good ○ excellent *
The approximate net payload of 1030 pounds at 8% of GVWR on this model is ○ deficient ○ excessive ◉ cautionary ○ good ○ excellent *
Total highway safety penalties are: 2 *   Value: 7 8   Durability: 7 3   Highway Control Rating: 6 9   Highway Safety: 6 7   ★★

Jamboree Searcher	1996	MHC	29	29Z-460	FO	7.5L	G	$1700	190	3,500	12,400	11,370

Livability Code: VA 30-90
Wheelbase-to-length ratio of 55% is considered ○ dangerous ○ fatiguing ◉ good ○ excellent *
The approximate net payload of 1030 pounds at 8% of GVWR on this model is ○ deficient ○ excessive ◉ cautionary ○ good ○ excellent *
Total highway safety penalties are: 2 *   Value: 7 8   Durability: 7 3   Highway Control Rating: 6 9   Highway Safety: 6 7   ★★

Jamboree Searcher	1996	MHC	29	29Z-351	FO	5.8L	G	$1700	190	1,000	12,400	11,370

Livability Code: VA 30-90
Wheelbase-to-length ratio of 55% is considered ○ dangerous ○ fatiguing ◉ good ○ excellent *
The approximate net payload of 1030 pounds at 8% of GVWR on this model is ○ deficient ○ excessive ◉ cautionary ○ good ○ excellent *
Total highway safety penalties are: 2 *   Value: 7 8   Durability: 7 3   Highway Control Rating: 6 9   Highway Safety: 6 7   ★★

Note: Safety ratings are based on the assumption that the engineering of the RV has allowed for proper balance by placing fresh, gray, and black holding tanks in a location so as not to change the balance of the RV when the tanks are empty or full. **Always double-check wheelbase, GVWR, and weights at front and rear axles.**

*See Section 1 for details on how conclusions are reached.

Brand	Year	Type	Length	Model	Chassis	Engine	Fuel Type	Average Price per Linear Foot When New	Adjusted Wheelbase	Approx. Towing Capacity	Gross Vehicle Weight Rating	Average Curb Weight
Jamboree Searcher	1997	MHC	23	22 C	FO	6.8L	G	$2000	138	3,500	10,500	9,343

Livability Code: VA 30-90 Wheelbase-to-length ratio of 51% is considered ○ dangerous ◉ fatiguing ○ good ○ excellent *
The approximate net payload of 1157 pounds at 11% of GVWR on this model is ○ deficient ○ excessive ○ cautionary ◉ good ○ excellent *
Total highway safety penalties are: 2 *   Value: **7 8** Durability: **7 3** Highway Control Rating: **5 4** Highway Safety: **5 2**   ★

Jamboree Searcher	1997	MHC	23	22 B	FO	6.8L	G	$2000	138	3,500	10,500	9,498

Livability Code: VA 30-90 Wheelbase-to-length ratio of 50% is considered ◉ dangerous ○ fatiguing ○ good ○ excellent *
The approximate net payload of 1002 pounds at 10% of GVWR on this model is ○ deficient ○ excessive ○ cautionary ◉ good ○ excellent *
Total highway safety penalties are: 2 *   Value: **7 8** Durability: **7 3** Highway Control Rating: **4 7** Highway Safety: **4 5**

Jamboree Searcher	1997	MHC	25	24 D	FO	6.8L	G	$1900	158	3,500	11,500	9,909

Livability Code: VA 30-90 Wheelbase-to-length ratio of 53% is considered ○ dangerous ◉ fatiguing ○ good ○ excellent *
The approximate net payload of 1591 pounds at 14% of GVWR on this model is ○ deficient ○ excessive ○ cautionary ◉ good ○ excellent *
Total highway safety penalties are: 2 *   Value: **7 8** Durability: **7 3** Highway Control Rating: **7 3** Highway Safety: **7 1**   ★★★

Jamboree Searcher	1997	MHC	25	24 D dsl	FO	7.3L	D	$2000	158	3,500	11,500	10,265

Livability Code: VA 30-90 Wheelbase-to-length ratio of 53% is considered ○ dangerous ◉ fatiguing ○ good ○ excellent *
The approximate net payload of 1235 pounds at 11% of GVWR on this model is ○ deficient ○ excessive ○ cautionary ◉ good ○ excellent *
Total highway safety penalties are: 2 *   Value: **7 8** Durability: **7 3** Highway Control Rating: **6 7** Highway Safety: **6 5**   ★★

Jamboree Searcher	1997	MHC	25	24 P	FO	6.8L	G	$1900	158	3,500	11,500	10,005

Livability Code: VA 30-90 Wheelbase-to-length ratio of 53% is considered ○ dangerous ◉ fatiguing ○ good ○ excellent *
The approximate net payload of 1495 pounds at 13% of GVWR on this model is ○ deficient ○ excessive ○ cautionary ◉ good ○ excellent *
Total highway safety penalties are: 2 *   Value: **7 8** Durability: **7 3** Highway Control Rating: **7 1** Highway Safety: **6 9**   ★★

Jamboree Searcher	1997	MHC	27	26 F	FO	6.8L	G	$1800	176	3,500	14,050	11,280

Livability Code: VA 30-90 Wheelbase-to-length ratio of 55% is considered ○ dangerous ○ fatiguing ○ good ○ excellent *
The approximate net payload of 2770 pounds at 20% of GVWR on this model is ○ deficient ○ excessive ○ cautionary ○ good ◉ excellent *
Total highway safety penalties are: 2 *   Value: **7 8** Durability: **7 3** Highway Control Rating: **9 6** Highway Safety: **9 4**   ★★★

Jamboree Searcher	1997	MHC	29	29 Z	FO	6.8L	G	$1700	190	3,500	14,050	11,618

Livability Code: VA 30-90 Wheelbase-to-length ratio of 54% is considered ○ dangerous ○ fatiguing ◉ good ○ excellent *
The approximate net payload of 2432 pounds at 17% of GVWR on this model is ○ deficient ○ excessive ○ cautionary ○ good ◉ excellent *
Total highway safety penalties are: 2 *   Value: **7 8** Durability: **7 3** Highway Control Rating: **8 7** Highway Safety: **8 5**   ★★★

Jayco Designer	1999	MHC	28	2730W	FO	6.8L	G	$1700	182	1,500	14,050	11,920

Livability Code: VA 30-90 Wheelbase-to-length ratio of 54% is considered ○ dangerous ○ fatiguing ◉ good ○ excellent *
The approximate net payload of 2130 pounds at 15% of GVWR on this model is ○ deficient ○ excessive ○ cautionary ◉ good ○ excellent *
Total highway safety penalties are: 2 *   Value: **7 7** Durability: **7 0** Highway Control Rating: **8 4** Highway Safety: **8 2**   ★★★

Jayco Designer	1999	MHC	29	2830G	FO	6.8L	G	$1700	185	1,500	14,050	12,088

Livability Code: VA 30-90 Wheelbase-to-length ratio of 54% is considered ○ dangerous ○ fatiguing ◉ good ○ excellent *
The approximate net payload of 1962 pounds at 14% of GVWR on this model is ○ deficient ○ excessive ○ cautionary ◉ good ○ excellent *
Total highway safety penalties are: 2 *   Value: **7 7** Durability: **7 0** Highway Control Rating: **8 0** Highway Safety: **7 8**   ★★★

Jayco Designer	1999	MHC	31	3130H	FO	6.8L	G	$1500	218	1,500	14,050	12,664

Livability Code: VA 30-90 Wheelbase-to-length ratio of 58% is considered ○ dangerous ○ fatiguing ○ good ◉ excellent *
The approximate net payload of 1386 pounds at 10% of GVWR on this model is ○ deficient ○ excessive ○ cautionary ◉ good ○ excellent *
Total highway safety penalties are: 2 *   Value: **7 7** Durability: **7 0** Highway Control Rating: **9 3** Highway Safety: **9 1**   ★★★

Jayco Designer	1999	MHC	33	3230K	FO	6.8L	G	$1500	218	1,500 e	14,050	13,648

Livability Code: VA 30-90 Wheelbase-to-length ratio of 56% is considered ○ dangerous ○ fatiguing ○ good ○ excellent *
The approximate net payload of 402 pounds at 3% of GVWR on this model is ◉ deficient ○ excessive ○ cautionary ○ good ○ excellent *
Total highway safety penalties are: 6 *   Value: **7 5** Durability: **7 0** Highway Control Rating: **5 7** Highway Safety: **5 1**   ★

Jayco Designer	1999	MHC	33	3240P	FO	6.8L	G	$1500	218	1,500	14,050	13,048

Livability Code: VA 30-90 Wheelbase-to-length ratio of 56% is considered ○ dangerous ○ fatiguing ◉ good ○ excellent *
The approximate net payload of 1002 pounds at 7% of GVWR on this model is ○ deficient ○ excessive ◉ cautionary ○ good ○ excellent *
Total highway safety penalties are: 2 *   Value: **7 7** Durability: **7 0** Highway Control Rating: **6 6** Highway Safety: **6 4**   ★★

Note: Safety ratings are based on the assumption that the engineering of the RV has allowed for proper balance by placing fresh, gray, and black holding tanks in a location so as not to change the balance of the RV when the tanks are empty or full. **Always double-check wheelbase, GVWR, and weights at front and rear axles.**

*See Section 1 for details on how conclusions are reached.

Brand	Year	Type	Length	Model	Chassis	Engine	Fuel Type	Average Price per Linear Foot When New	Adjusted Wheelbase	Approx. Towing Capacity	Gross Vehicle Weight Rating	Average Curb Weight
Jayco Eagle	1999	MHC	23	232 U	CH	7.4L	G	$2100	159	1,500	12,300	10,059

Livability Code: VA 30-90
Wheelbase-to-length ratio of 57% is considered ○ dangerous ○ fatiguing ◉ good ○ excellent*
The approximate net payload of 2241 pounds at 18% of GVWR on this model is ○ deficient ○ excessive ○ cautionary ○ good ◉ excellent*
Total highway safety penalties are: 2*   Value: 77   Durability: 70   Highway Control Rating: 100   Highway Safety: 98   ★★★

Brand	Year	Type	Length	Model	Chassis	Engine	Fuel Type	Avg Price/Ft	Adj. Wheelbase	Towing	GVWR	Curb Weight
Jayco Eagle	1999	MHC	24	232 U opch	FO	6.8L	G	$2000	158	1,500	11,500	9,974

Livability Code: VA 30-90
Wheelbase-to-length ratio of 55% is considered ○ dangerous ○ fatiguing ◉ good ○ excellent*
The approximate net payload of 1526 pounds at 13% of GVWR on this model is ○ deficient ○ excessive ○ cautionary ◉ good ○ excellent*
Total highway safety penalties are: 2*   Value: 77   Durability: 70   Highway Control Rating: 88   Highway Safety: 86   ★★★

Brand	Year	Type	Length	Model	Chassis	Engine	Fuel Type	Avg Price/Ft	Adj. Wheelbase	Towing	GVWR	Curb Weight
Jayco Eagle	1999	MHC	24	241 M opch	FO	6.8L	G	$2000	158	1,500	11,500	10,020

Livability Code: VA 30-90
Wheelbase-to-length ratio of 55% is considered ○ dangerous ○ fatiguing ◉ good ○ excellent*
The approximate net payload of 1480 pounds at 13% of GVWR on this model is ○ deficient ○ excessive ○ cautionary ◉ good ○ excellent*
Total highway safety penalties are: 2*   Value: 77   Durability: 70   Highway Control Rating: 86   Highway Safety: 84   ★★★

Brand	Year	Type	Length	Model	Chassis	Engine	Fuel Type	Avg Price/Ft	Adj. Wheelbase	Towing	GVWR	Curb Weight
Jayco Eagle	1999	MHC	25	241 M	CH	7.4L	G	$1900	159	1,500	12,300	10,335

Livability Code: VA 30-90
Wheelbase-to-length ratio of 54% is considered ○ dangerous ○ fatiguing ◉ good ○ excellent*
The approximate net payload of 1965 pounds at 16% of GVWR on this model is ○ deficient ○ excessive ○ cautionary ○ good ◉ excellent*
Total highway safety penalties are: 2*   Value: 77   Durability: 70   Highway Control Rating: 85   Highway Safety: 83   ★★★

Brand	Year	Type	Length	Model	Chassis	Engine	Fuel Type	Avg Price/Ft	Adj. Wheelbase	Towing	GVWR	Curb Weight
Jayco Eagle	1999	MHC	27	267 F opch	FO	6.8L	G	$1800	176	1,500	11,500	10,710

Livability Code: VA 30-90
Wheelbase-to-length ratio of 54% is considered ○ dangerous ○ fatiguing ◉ good ○ excellent*
The approximate net payload of 790 pounds at 7% of GVWR on this model is ○ deficient ○ excessive ◉ cautionary ○ good ○ excellent*
Total highway safety penalties are: 2*   Value: 77   Durability: 70   Highway Control Rating: 57   Highway Safety: 55   ★

Brand	Year	Type	Length	Model	Chassis	Engine	Fuel Type	Avg Price/Ft	Adj. Wheelbase	Towing	GVWR	Curb Weight
Jayco Eagle	1999	MHC	27	267 F	CH	7.4L	G	$1800	177	1,500	12,300	10,979

Livability Code: VA 30-90
Wheelbase-to-length ratio of 54% is considered ○ dangerous ○ fatiguing ◉ good ○ excellent*
The approximate net payload of 1321 pounds at 11% of GVWR on this model is ○ deficient ○ excessive ○ cautionary ◉ good ○ excellent*
Total highway safety penalties are: 2*   Value: 77   Durability: 70   Highway Control Rating: 75   Highway Safety: 73   ★★★

Brand	Year	Type	Length	Model	Chassis	Engine	Fuel Type	Avg Price/Ft	Adj. Wheelbase	Towing	GVWR	Curb Weight
Jayco Eagle	1999	MHC	29	283 G	FO	6.8L	G	$1700	185	1,500	14,050	11,801

Livability Code: VA 30-90
Wheelbase-to-length ratio of 54% is considered ○ dangerous ○ fatiguing ◉ good ○ excellent*
The approximate net payload of 2249 pounds at 16% of GVWR on this model is ○ deficient ○ excessive ○ cautionary ○ good ◉ excellent*
Total highway safety penalties are: 2*   Value: 77   Durability: 70   Highway Control Rating: 84   Highway Safety: 82   ★★★

Brand	Year	Type	Length	Model	Chassis	Engine	Fuel Type	Avg Price/Ft	Adj. Wheelbase	Towing	GVWR	Curb Weight
Jayco Eagle	1999	MHC	30	294 R	FO	6.8L	G	$1600	199	1,500	14,050	12,077

Livability Code: VA 30-90
Wheelbase-to-length ratio of 55% is considered ○ dangerous ○ fatiguing ◉ good ○ excellent*
The approximate net payload of 1973 pounds at 14% of GVWR on this model is ○ deficient ○ excessive ○ cautionary ◉ good ○ excellent*
Total highway safety penalties are: 2*   Value: 77   Durability: 70   Highway Control Rating: 90   Highway Safety: 88   ★★★

Brand	Year	Type	Length	Model	Chassis	Engine	Fuel Type	Avg Price/Ft	Adj. Wheelbase	Towing	GVWR	Curb Weight
Jayco Eagle	1999	MHC	31	313 H	FO	6.8L	G	$1500	218	1,500	14,050	12,353

Livability Code: VA 30-90
Wheelbase-to-length ratio of 58% is considered ○ dangerous ○ fatiguing ○ good ◉ excellent*
The approximate net payload of 1697 pounds at 12% of GVWR on this model is ○ deficient ○ excessive ○ cautionary ◉ good ○ excellent*
Total highway safety penalties are: 2*   Value: 77   Durability: 70   Highway Control Rating: 97   Highway Safety: 95   ★★★

Brand	Year	Type	Length	Model	Chassis	Engine	Fuel Type	Avg Price/Ft	Adj. Wheelbase	Towing	GVWR	Curb Weight
Jayco Eagle	1999	MHC	33	323 K	FO	6.8L	G	$1500	218	1,500 e	14,050	13,321

Livability Code: VA 30-90
Wheelbase-to-length ratio of 56% is considered ○ dangerous ○ fatiguing ◉ good ○ excellent*
The approximate net payload of 729 pounds at 5% of GVWR on this model is ◉ deficient ○ excessive ○ cautionary ○ good ○ excellent*
Total highway safety penalties are: 6*   Value: 75   Durability: 70   Highway Control Rating: 59   Highway Safety: 53   ★

Brand	Year	Type	Length	Model	Chassis	Engine	Fuel Type	Avg Price/Ft	Adj. Wheelbase	Towing	GVWR	Curb Weight
Kalahari	1994	MHA	31	3040-190	MA	GM6.5	D	$2600	178	2,500	16,000	14,696

Livability Code: SB 30-90
Wheelbase-to-length ratio of 49% is considered ◉ dangerous ○ fatiguing ○ good ○ excellent*
The approximate net payload of 1304 pounds at 8% of GVWR on this model is ○ deficient ○ excessive ◉ cautionary ○ good ○ excellent*
Total highway safety penalties are: 2*   Value: 74   Durability: 75   Highway Control Rating: 17   Highway Safety: 15

Brand	Year	Type	Length	Model	Chassis	Engine	Fuel Type	Avg Price/Ft	Adj. Wheelbase	Towing	GVWR	Curb Weight
Kalahari	1994	MHA	31	3040-230	MA	GM6.5	D	$3200	178	2,500	16,000	14,696

Livability Code: SB 30-90
Wheelbase-to-length ratio of 49% is considered ◉ dangerous ○ fatiguing ○ good ○ excellent*
The approximate net payload of 1304 pounds at 8% of GVWR on this model is ○ deficient ○ excessive ◉ cautionary ○ good ○ excellent*
Total highway safety penalties are: 2*   Value: 74   Durability: 75   Highway Control Rating: 17   Highway Safety: 15

Note: Safety ratings are based on the assumption that the engineering of the RV has allowed for proper balance by placing fresh, gray, and black holding tanks in a location so as not to change the balance of the RV when the tanks are empty or full. **Always double-check wheelbase, GVWR, and weights at front and rear axles.**

*See Section 1 for details on how conclusions are reached.

Brand	Year	Type	Length	Model	Chassis	Engine	Fuel Type	Average Price per Linear Foot When New	Adjusted Wheel-base	Approx. Towing Capacity	Gross Vehicle Weight Rating	Average Curb Weight
Kalahari	1994	MHA	33	3330	MA	GM6.5	D	$2600	210	2,500	16,000	15,383

Livability Code: SB 30-90
Wheelbase-to-length ratio of 53% is considered ○ dangerous ◉ fatiguing ○ good ○ excellent *
The approximate net payload of 617 pounds at 4% of GVWR on this model is ◉ deficient ○ excessive ○ cautionary ○ good ○ excellent *
Total highway safety penalties are: 2 *   Value: **7 4**   Durability: **7 5**   Highway Control Rating: **3 2**   Highway Safety: **3 0**

Brand	Year	Type	Length	Model	Chassis	Engine	Fuel Type	Price/Ft	Wheelbase	Towing	GVWR	Curb Wt
Kalahari	1994	MHA	33	3352	MA	GM6.5	D	$2600	210	2,500	16,000	15,383

Livability Code: SB 30-90
Wheelbase-to-length ratio of 53% is considered ○ dangerous ◉ fatiguing ○ good ○ excellent *
The approximate net payload of 617 pounds at 4% of GVWR on this model is ◉ deficient ○ excessive ○ cautionary ○ good ○ excellent *
Total highway safety penalties are: 2 *   Value: **7 4**   Durability: **7 5**   Highway Control Rating: **3 2**   Highway Safety: **3 0**

Brand	Year	Type	Length	Model	Chassis	Engine	Fuel Type	Price/Ft	Wheelbase	Towing	GVWR	Curb Wt
Kalahari	1994	MHA	35	3430-190	MA	Cu5.9L	D	$2600	252	4,000	18,000	16,239

Livability Code: SB 30-90
Wheelbase-to-length ratio of 61% is considered ○ dangerous ○ fatiguing ○ good ◉ excellent *
The approximate net payload of 1761 pounds at 10% of GVWR on this model is ○ deficient ○ excessive ○ cautionary ◉ good ○ excellent *
Total highway safety penalties are: 2 *   Value: **7 4**   Durability: **7 5**   Highway Control Rating: **1 0 0**   Highway Safety: **9 8**   ★★★

Brand	Year	Type	Length	Model	Chassis	Engine	Fuel Type	Price/Ft	Wheelbase	Towing	GVWR	Curb Wt
Kalahari	1994	MHA	35	3430-230	MA	Cu5.9L	D	$2900	252	4,000	18,000	16,239

Livability Code: SB 30-90
Wheelbase-to-length ratio of 61% is considered ○ dangerous ○ fatiguing ○ good ◉ excellent *
The approximate net payload of 1761 pounds at 10% of GVWR on this model is ○ deficient ○ excessive ○ cautionary ◉ good ○ excellent *
Total highway safety penalties are: 2 *   Value: **7 4**   Durability: **7 5**   Highway Control Rating: **1 0 0**   Highway Safety: **9 8**   ★★★

Brand	Year	Type	Length	Model	Chassis	Engine	Fuel Type	Price/Ft	Wheelbase	Towing	GVWR	Curb Wt
Kalahari	1994	MHA	35	3452-190	MA	Cu5.9L	D	$2600	252	4,000	18,000	16,239

Livability Code: SB 30-90
Wheelbase-to-length ratio of 61% is considered ○ dangerous ○ fatiguing ○ good ◉ excellent *
The approximate net payload of 1761 pounds at 10% of GVWR on this model is ○ deficient ○ excessive ○ cautionary ◉ good ○ excellent *
Total highway safety penalties are: 2 *   Value: **7 4**   Durability: **7 5**   Highway Control Rating: **1 0 0**   Highway Safety: **9 8**   ★★★

Brand	Year	Type	Length	Model	Chassis	Engine	Fuel Type	Price/Ft	Wheelbase	Towing	GVWR	Curb Wt
Kalahari	1994	MHA	35	3452-230	MA	Cu5.9L	D	$2900	252	4,000	18,000	16,239

Livability Code: SB 30-90
Wheelbase-to-length ratio of 61% is considered ○ dangerous ○ fatiguing ○ good ◉ excellent *
The approximate net payload of 1761 pounds at 10% of GVWR on this model is ○ deficient ○ excessive ○ cautionary ◉ good ○ excellent *
Total highway safety penalties are: 2 *   Value: **7 4**   Durability: **7 5**   Highway Control Rating: **1 0 0**   Highway Safety: **9 8**   ★★★

Brand	Year	Type	Length	Model	Chassis	Engine	Fuel Type	Price/Ft	Wheelbase	Towing	GVWR	Curb Wt
Kountry Aire	1990	MHA	29	28WCB	FO	7.5L	G	$2000	182 T	1,500	15,000	12,669

Livability Code: SB 30-90
Wheelbase-to-length ratio of 52% is considered ○ dangerous ◉ fatiguing ○ good ○ excellent *
The approximate net payload of 2332 pounds at 16% of GVWR on this model is ○ deficient ○ excessive ○ cautionary ○ good ◉ excellent *
Total highway safety penalties are: 4 *   Value: **7 9**   Durability: **7 8**   Highway Control Rating: **5 9**   Highway Safety: **5 5**   ★

Brand	Year	Type	Length	Model	Chassis	Engine	Fuel Type	Price/Ft	Wheelbase	Towing	GVWR	Curb Wt
Kountry Aire	1990	MHA	38	37 SACB SS	CH	7.4L	G	$2100	224 T	1,500	18,000	15,335

Livability Code: SB 30-90
Wheelbase-to-length ratio of 49% is considered ◉ dangerous ○ fatiguing ○ good ○ excellent *
The approximate net payload of 2665 pounds at 15% of GVWR on this model is ○ deficient ○ excessive ○ cautionary ◉ good ○ excellent *
Total highway safety penalties are: 11 *   Value: **7 6**   Durability: **7 8**   Highway Control Rating: **3 9**   Highway Safety: **2 8**

Brand	Year	Type	Length	Model	Chassis	Engine	Fuel Type	Price/Ft	Wheelbase	Towing	GVWR	Curb Wt
Kountry Aire	1991	MHA	28	27 WCB	FO	7.5L	G	$2500	158	1,500	11,000	10,907

Livability Code: VA 30-90
Wheelbase-to-length ratio of 47% is considered ◉ dangerous ○ fatiguing ○ good ○ excellent *
The approximate net payload of 93 pounds at 1% of GVWR on this model is ◉ deficient ○ excessive ○ cautionary ○ good ○ excellent *
Total highway safety penalties are: 2 *   Value: **8 0**   Durability: **7 8**   Highway Control Rating: **1**   Highway Safety: **- 1**

Brand	Year	Type	Length	Model	Chassis	Engine	Fuel Type	Price/Ft	Wheelbase	Towing	GVWR	Curb Wt
Kountry Aire	1991	MHA	38	37 SACBSS	CH	7.4L	G	$2600	202 T	1,500	18,500	16,609

Livability Code: SB 30-90
Wheelbase-to-length ratio of 44% is considered ◉ dangerous ○ fatiguing ○ good ○ excellent *
The approximate net payload of 1892 pounds at 10% of GVWR on this model is ○ deficient ○ excessive ○ cautionary ◉ good ○ excellent *
Total highway safety penalties are: 11 *   Value: **7 6**   Durability: **7 8**   Highway Control Rating: **1 3**   Highway Safety: **2**

Brand	Year	Type	Length	Model	Chassis	Engine	Fuel Type	Price/Ft	Wheelbase	Towing	GVWR	Curb Wt
Kountry Aire	1994	MHA	33	32CBD-sl	FO	7.5L	G	$3100	200	8,000	17,000	15,911

Livability Code: SB 30-90
Wheelbase-to-length ratio of 51% is considered ○ dangerous ◉ fatiguing ○ good ○ excellent *
The approximate net payload of 1089 pounds at 6% of GVWR on this model is ◉ deficient ○ excessive ○ cautionary ○ good ○ excellent *
Total highway safety penalties are: 5 *   Value: **7 9**   Durability: **7 8**   Highway Control Rating: **1 4**   Highway Safety: **9**

Brand	Year	Type	Length	Model	Chassis	Engine	Fuel Type	Price/Ft	Wheelbase	Towing	GVWR	Curb Wt
Kountry Aire	1994	MHA	35	34CBD-sl	CH	7.4L	G	$3100	202 T	1,500	18,500	16,835

Livability Code: SB 30-90
Wheelbase-to-length ratio of 49% is considered ◉ dangerous ○ fatiguing ○ good ○ excellent *
The approximate net payload of 1665 pounds at 9% of GVWR on this model is ○ deficient ○ excessive ◉ cautionary ○ good ○ excellent *
Total highway safety penalties are: 12 *   Value: **7 5**   Durability: **7 8**   Highway Control Rating: **2 2**   Highway Safety: **1 0**

Note: Safety ratings are based on the assumption that the engineering of the RV has allowed for proper balance by placing fresh, gray, and black holding tanks in a location so as not to change the balance of the RV when the tanks are empty or full. **Always double-check wheelbase, GVWR, and weights at front and rear axles.**

The RV Rating Book

*See Section 1 for details on how conclusions are reached.

Brand	Year	Type	Length	Model	Chassis	Engine	Fuel Type	Average Price per Linear Foot When New	Adjusted Wheelbase	Approx. Towing Capacity	Gross Vehicle Weight Rating	Average Curb Weight
Kountry Aire	1994	MHA	35	34CBDS-sl	CH	7.4L	G	$3100	202 T	1,500	18,500	16,850

Livability Code: SB 30-90

Wheelbase-to-length ratio of 49% is considered ◉ dangerous ○ fatiguing ○ good ○ excellent*

The approximate net payload of 1650 pounds at 9% of GVWR on this model is ○ deficient ○ excessive ◉ cautionary ○ good ○ excellent*

Total highway safety penalties are: 12*   Value: 7 5   Durability: 7 8   Highway Control Rating: 2 2   Highway Safety: 1 0

Brand	Year	Type	Length	Model	Chassis	Engine	Fuel Type	Price/Ft	Wheelbase	Towing	GVWR	Curb Wt
Kountry Aire	1994	MHA	35	34WCB	CH	7.4L	G	$3000	202 T	1,500	18,500	15,885

Livability Code: SB 30-90

Wheelbase-to-length ratio of 49% is considered ◉ dangerous ○ fatiguing ○ good ○ excellent*

The approximate net payload of 2615 pounds at 14% of GVWR on this model is ○ deficient ○ excessive ○ cautionary ◉ good ○ excellent*

Total highway safety penalties are: 9*   Value: 7 7   Durability: 7 8   Highway Control Rating: 3 6   Highway Safety: 2 7

Brand	Year	Type	Length	Model	Chassis	Engine	Fuel Type	Price/Ft	Wheelbase	Towing	GVWR	Curb Wt
Kountry Aire	1994	MHA	35	34WCBS-sl	CH	7.4L	G	$3100	202 T	1,500	18,500	16,850

Livability Code: SB 30-90

Wheelbase-to-length ratio of 49% is considered ◉ dangerous ○ fatiguing ○ good ○ excellent*

The approximate net payload of 1650 pounds at 9% of GVWR on this model is ○ deficient ○ excessive ◉ cautionary ○ good ○ excellent*

Total highway safety penalties are: 12*   Value: 7 5   Durability: 7 8   Highway Control Rating: 2 2   Highway Safety: 1 0

Brand	Year	Type	Length	Model	Chassis	Engine	Fuel Type	Price/Ft	Wheelbase	Towing	GVWR	Curb Wt
Kountry Aire	1994	MHA	35	34CBD-sl	FO	7.5L	G	$3100	202 T	5,500	19,500	17,273

Livability Code: SB 30-90

Wheelbase-to-length ratio of 49% is considered ◉ dangerous ○ fatiguing ○ good ○ excellent*

The approximate net payload of 2227 pounds at 11% of GVWR on this model is ○ deficient ○ excessive ○ cautionary ◉ good ○ excellent*

Total highway safety penalties are: 7*   Value: 7 8   Durability: 7 8   Highway Control Rating: 3 0   Highway Safety: 2 3

Brand	Year	Type	Length	Model	Chassis	Engine	Fuel Type	Price/Ft	Wheelbase	Towing	GVWR	Curb Wt
Kountry Aire	1994	MHA	35	34CBDS-sl	FO	7.5L	G	$3100	202 T	5,500	19,500	17,285

Livability Code: SB 30-90

Wheelbase-to-length ratio of 49% is considered ◉ dangerous ○ fatiguing ○ good ○ excellent*

The approximate net payload of 2215 pounds at 11% of GVWR on this model is ○ deficient ○ excessive ○ cautionary ◉ good ○ excellent*

Total highway safety penalties are: 7*   Value: 7 8   Durability: 7 8   Highway Control Rating: 3 0   Highway Safety: 2 3

Brand	Year	Type	Length	Model	Chassis	Engine	Fuel Type	Price/Ft	Wheelbase	Towing	GVWR	Curb Wt
Kountry Aire	1994	MHA	35	34WCB	FO	7.5L	G	$3000	202 T	5,500	19,500	16,323

Livability Code: SB 30-90

Wheelbase-to-length ratio of 49% is considered ◉ dangerous ○ fatiguing ○ good ○ excellent*

The approximate net payload of 3177 pounds at 16% of GVWR on this model is ○ deficient ○ excessive ○ cautionary ○ good ◉ excellent*

Total highway safety penalties are: 4*   Value: 7 9   Durability: 7 8   Highway Control Rating: 4 0   Highway Safety: 3 6

Brand	Year	Type	Length	Model	Chassis	Engine	Fuel Type	Price/Ft	Wheelbase	Towing	GVWR	Curb Wt
Kountry Aire	1994	MHA	35	34WCBS-sl	FO	7.5L	G	$3100	202 T	5,500	19,500	17,273

Livability Code: SB 30-90

Wheelbase-to-length ratio of 49% is considered ◉ dangerous ○ fatiguing ○ good ○ excellent*

The approximate net payload of 2227 pounds at 11% of GVWR on this model is ○ deficient ○ excessive ○ cautionary ◉ good ○ excellent*

Total highway safety penalties are: 7*   Value: 7 8   Durability: 7 8   Highway Control Rating: 3 0   Highway Safety: 2 3

Brand	Year	Type	Length	Model	Chassis	Engine	Fuel Type	Price/Ft	Wheelbase	Towing	GVWR	Curb Wt
Kountry Aire	1994	MHA	38	37CBSA-sl	FO	7.5L	G	$2800	224 T	5,500	19,500	18,016

Livability Code: SB 30-90

Wheelbase-to-length ratio of 49% is considered ◉ dangerous ○ fatiguing ○ good ○ excellent*

The approximate net payload of 1484 pounds at 8% of GVWR on this model is ○ deficient ○ excessive ◉ cautionary ○ good ○ excellent*

Total highway safety penalties are: 7*   Value: 7 8   Durability: 7 8   Highway Control Rating: 1 8   Highway Safety: 1 1

Brand	Year	Type	Length	Model	Chassis	Engine	Fuel Type	Price/Ft	Wheelbase	Towing	GVWR	Curb Wt
Kountry Aire	1994	MHA	38	37WDSK-sl	FO	7.5L	G	$2800	224 T	5,500	19,500	18,159

Livability Code: SB 30-90

Wheelbase-to-length ratio of 49% is considered ◉ dangerous ○ fatiguing ○ good ○ excellent*

The approximate net payload of 1341 pounds at 7% of GVWR on this model is ○ deficient ○ excessive ◉ cautionary ○ good ○ excellent*

Total highway safety penalties are: 7*   Value: 7 8   Durability: 7 8   Highway Control Rating: 1 3   Highway Safety: 6

Brand	Year	Type	Length	Model	Chassis	Engine	Fuel Type	Price/Ft	Wheelbase	Towing	GVWR	Curb Wt
Kountry Aire	1995	MHA	33	KA 3200	FO	7.5L	G	$3000	200	8,000	17,000	14,890

Livability Code: SB 30-90

Wheelbase-to-length ratio of 51% is considered ○ dangerous ◉ fatiguing ○ good ○ excellent*

The approximate net payload of 2110 pounds at 12% of GVWR on this model is ○ deficient ○ excessive ○ cautionary ◉ good ○ excellent*

Total highway safety penalties are: 2*   Value: 8 0   Durability: 7 8   Highway Control Rating: 4 1   Highway Safety: 3 9

Brand	Year	Type	Length	Model	Chassis	Engine	Fuel Type	Price/Ft	Wheelbase	Towing	GVWR	Curb Wt
Kountry Aire	1995	MHA	35	KA 3410	FO	7.5L	G	$3000	202 T	5,500	19,500	16,327

Livability Code: SB 30-90

Wheelbase-to-length ratio of 49% is considered ◉ dangerous ○ fatiguing ○ good ○ excellent*

The approximate net payload of 3173 pounds at 16% of GVWR on this model is ○ deficient ○ excessive ○ cautionary ○ good ◉ excellent*

Total highway safety penalties are: 4*   Value: 7 9   Durability: 7 8   Highway Control Rating: 4 0   Highway Safety: 3 6

Brand	Year	Type	Length	Model	Chassis	Engine	Fuel Type	Price/Ft	Wheelbase	Towing	GVWR	Curb Wt
Kountry Aire	1995	MHA	35	KA 3450-sl	FO	7.5L	G	$3100	202 T	5,000	20,000	17,227

Livability Code: SB 30-90

Wheelbase-to-length ratio of 49% is considered ◉ dangerous ○ fatiguing ○ good ○ excellent*

The approximate net payload of 2773 pounds at 14% of GVWR on this model is ○ deficient ○ excessive ○ cautionary ◉ good ○ excellent*

Total highway safety penalties are: 7*   Value: 7 8   Durability: 7 8   Highway Control Rating: 3 5   Highway Safety: 2 8

Note: Safety ratings are based on the assumption that the engineering of the RV has allowed for proper balance by placing fresh, gray, and black holding tanks in a location so as not to change the balance of the RV when the tanks are empty or full. **Always double-check wheelbase, GVWR, and weights at front and rear axles.**

*See Section 1 for details on how conclusions are reached.

Brand	Year	Type	Length	Model	Chassis	Engine	Fuel Type	Average Price per Linear Foot When New	Adjusted Wheelbase	Approx. Towing Capacity	Gross Vehicle Weight Rating	Average Curb Weight
Kountry Aire	**1995**	MHA	35	KA 3451-sl	FO	7.5L	G	$3100	202 T	5,000	20,000	17,227

Livability Code: SB 30-90
Wheelbase-to-length ratio of 49% is considered ◉ dangerous ○ fatiguing ○ good ○ excellent *
The approximate net payload of 2773 pounds at 14% of GVWR on this model is ○ deficient ○ excessive ○ cautionary ◉ good ○ excellent *
Total highway safety penalties are: 7 *　Value: **7 8**　Durability: **7 8**　Highway Control Rating: **3 5**　Highway Safety: **2 8**

Brand	Year	Type	Length	Model	Chassis	Engine	Fuel Type	Avg Price/LF	Adj Wheelbase	Tow Cap	GVWR	Curb Wt
Kountry Aire	**1995**	MHA	35	KA 3455-sl	FO	7.5L	G	$3100	202 T	5,000	20,000	17,227

Livability Code: SB 30-90
Wheelbase-to-length ratio of 49% is considered ◉ dangerous ○ fatiguing ○ good ○ excellent *
The approximate net payload of 2773 pounds at 14% of GVWR on this model is ○ deficient ○ excessive ○ cautionary ◉ good ○ excellent *
Total highway safety penalties are: 7 *　Value: **7 8**　Durability: **7 8**　Highway Control Rating: **3 5**　Highway Safety: **2 8**

Kountry Aire	**1995**	MHA	38	KA 3710	FO	7.5L	G	$2900	224 T	5,500	19,500	17,214

Livability Code: SB 30-90
Wheelbase-to-length ratio of 49% is considered ◉ dangerous ○ fatiguing ○ good ○ excellent *
The approximate net payload of 2286 pounds at 12% of GVWR on this model is ○ deficient ○ excessive ○ cautionary ◉ good ○ excellent *
Total highway safety penalties are: 4 *　Value: **7 9**　Durability: **7 8**　Highway Control Rating: **3 3**　Highway Safety: **2 9**

Kountry Aire	**1995**	MHA	38	KA 3755-sl	FO	7.5L	G	$2900	224 T	5,000	20,000	18,114

Livability Code: SB 30-90
Wheelbase-to-length ratio of 49% is considered ◉ dangerous ○ fatiguing ○ good ○ excellent *
The approximate net payload of 1886 pounds at 9% of GVWR on this model is ○ deficient ○ excessive ◉ cautionary ○ good ○ excellent *
Total highway safety penalties are: 7 *　Value: **7 8**　Durability: **7 8**　Highway Control Rating: **2 5**　Highway Safety: **1 8**

Kountry Aire	**1995**	MHA	38	KA 3756-sl	FO	7.5L	G	$2900	224 T	5,000	20,000	18,114

Livability Code: SB 30-90
Wheelbase-to-length ratio of 49% is considered ◉ dangerous ○ fatiguing ○ good ○ excellent *
The approximate net payload of 1886 pounds at 9% of GVWR on this model is ○ deficient ○ excessive ◉ cautionary ○ good ○ excellent *
Total highway safety penalties are: 7 *　Value: **7 8**　Durability: **7 8**　Highway Control Rating: **2 5**　Highway Safety: **1 8**

Kountry Aire	**1995**	MHA	38	KA 3760-sl	FO	7.5L	G	$2900	224 T	5,000	20,000	18,114

Livability Code: SB 30-90
Wheelbase-to-length ratio of 49% is considered ◉ dangerous ○ fatiguing ○ good ○ excellent *
The approximate net payload of 1886 pounds at 9% of GVWR on this model is ○ deficient ○ excessive ◉ cautionary ○ good ○ excellent *
Total highway safety penalties are: 7 *　Value: **7 8**　Durability: **7 8**　Highway Control Rating: **2 5**　Highway Safety: **1 8**

Kountry Aire	**1996**	MHA	33	KA 3255-sl	FO	7.5L	G	$3000	200	8,000	17,000	15,870

Livability Code: SB 30-90
Wheelbase-to-length ratio of 51% is considered ○ dangerous ◉ fatiguing ○ good ○ excellent *
The approximate net payload of 1130 pounds at 7% of GVWR on this model is ○ deficient ○ excessive ◉ cautionary ○ good ○ excellent *
Total highway safety penalties are: 5 *　Value: **7 9**　Durability: **7 8**　Highway Control Rating: **1 7**　Highway Safety: **1 2**

Kountry Aire	**1996**	MHA	35	KA 3410	CH	7.4L	G	$3000	202 T	1,500	18,500	15,908

Livability Code: SB 30-90
Wheelbase-to-length ratio of 48% is considered ◉ dangerous ○ fatiguing ○ good ○ excellent *
The approximate net payload of 2592 pounds at 14% of GVWR on this model is ○ deficient ○ excessive ○ cautionary ◉ good ○ excellent *
Total highway safety penalties are: 9 *　Value: **7 7**　Durability: **7 8**　Highway Control Rating: **3 4**　Highway Safety: **2 5**

Kountry Aire	**1996**	MHA	35	KA 3450-sl	CH	7.4L	G	$3100	202 T	1,500	18,500	16,808

Livability Code: SB 30-90
Wheelbase-to-length ratio of 48% is considered ◉ dangerous ○ fatiguing ○ good ○ excellent *
The approximate net payload of 1692 pounds at 9% of GVWR on this model is ○ deficient ○ excessive ◉ cautionary ○ good ○ excellent *
Total highway safety penalties are: 12 *　Value: **7 5**　Durability: **7 8**　Highway Control Rating: **2 1**　Highway Safety: **9**

Kountry Aire	**1996**	MHA	35	KA 3451-sl	CH	7.4L	G	$3100	202 T	1,500	18,500	16,808

Livability Code: SB 30-90
Wheelbase-to-length ratio of 48% is considered ◉ dangerous ○ fatiguing ○ good ○ excellent *
The approximate net payload of 1692 pounds at 9% of GVWR on this model is ○ deficient ○ excessive ◉ cautionary ○ good ○ excellent *
Total highway safety penalties are: 12 *　Value: **7 5**　Durability: **7 8**　Highway Control Rating: **2 1**　Highway Safety: **9**

Kountry Aire	**1996**	MHA	35	KA 3455-sl	CH	7.4L	G	$3100	202 T	1,500	18,500	16,808

Livability Code: SB 30-90
Wheelbase-to-length ratio of 48% is considered ◉ dangerous ○ fatiguing ○ good ○ excellent *
The approximate net payload of 1692 pounds at 9% of GVWR on this model is ○ deficient ○ excessive ◉ cautionary ○ good ○ excellent *
Total highway safety penalties are: 12 *　Value: **7 5**　Durability: **7 8**　Highway Control Rating: **2 1**　Highway Safety: **9**

Kountry Aire	**1996**	MHA	35	KA 3458-sl	CH	7.4L	G	$3100	202 T	1,500	18,500	16,808

Livability Code: SB 30-90
Wheelbase-to-length ratio of 48% is considered ◉ dangerous ○ fatiguing ○ good ○ excellent *
The approximate net payload of 1692 pounds at 9% of GVWR on this model is ○ deficient ○ excessive ◉ cautionary ○ good ○ excellent *
Total highway safety penalties are: 12 *　Value: **7 5**　Durability: **7 8**　Highway Control Rating: **2 1**　Highway Safety: **9**

Note: Safety ratings are based on the assumption that the engineering of the RV has allowed for proper balance by placing fresh, gray, and black holding tanks in a location so as not to change the balance of the RV when the tanks are empty or full. **Always double-check wheelbase, GVWR, and weights at front and rear axles.**

*See Section 1 for details on how conclusions are reached.

Brand	Year	Type	Length	Model	Chassis	Engine	Fuel Type	Average Price per Linear Foot When New	Adjusted Wheelbase	Approx. Towing Capacity	Gross Vehicle Weight Rating	Average Curb Weight
Kountry Aire	1996	MHA	35	KA 3410	FO	7.5L	G	$3000	202 T	5,000	20,000	16,408

Livability Code: SB 30-90
Wheelbase-to-length ratio of 48% is considered ◉ dangerous ○ fatiguing ○ good ○ excellent *
The approximate net payload of 3592 pounds at 18% of GVWR on this model is ○ deficient ○ excessive ○ cautionary ○ good ◉ excellent *
Total highway safety penalties are: 4 *   Value: **7 9**   Durability: **7 8**   Highway Control Rating: **4 0**   Highway Safety: **3 6**

Brand	Year	Type	Length	Model	Chassis	Engine	Fuel Type	Average Price per Linear Foot When New	Adjusted Wheelbase	Approx. Towing Capacity	Gross Vehicle Weight Rating	Average Curb Weight
Kountry Aire	1996	MHA	35	KA 3450-sl	FO	7.5L	G	$3100	202 T	5,000	20,000	17,308

Livability Code: SB 30-90
Wheelbase-to-length ratio of 48% is considered ◉ dangerous ○ fatiguing ○ good ○ excellent *
The approximate net payload of 2692 pounds at 13% of GVWR on this model is ○ deficient ○ excessive ○ cautionary ◉ good ○ excellent *
Total highway safety penalties are: 7 *   Value: **7 8**   Durability: **7 8**   Highway Control Rating: **3 2**   Highway Safety: **2 5**

Brand	Year	Type	Length	Model	Chassis	Engine	Fuel Type	Average Price per Linear Foot When New	Adjusted Wheelbase	Approx. Towing Capacity	Gross Vehicle Weight Rating	Average Curb Weight
Kountry Aire	1996	MHA	35	KA 3451-sl	FO	7.5L	G	$3100	202 T	5,000	20,000	17,308

Livability Code: SB 30-90
Wheelbase-to-length ratio of 48% is considered ◉ dangerous ○ fatiguing ○ good ○ excellent *
The approximate net payload of 2692 pounds at 13% of GVWR on this model is ○ deficient ○ excessive ○ cautionary ◉ good ○ excellent *
Total highway safety penalties are: 7 *   Value: **7 8**   Durability: **7 8**   Highway Control Rating: **3 2**   Highway Safety: **2 5**

Brand	Year	Type	Length	Model	Chassis	Engine	Fuel Type	Average Price per Linear Foot When New	Adjusted Wheelbase	Approx. Towing Capacity	Gross Vehicle Weight Rating	Average Curb Weight
Kountry Aire	1996	MHA	35	KA 3455-sl	FO	7.5L	G	$3100	202 T	5,000	20,000	17,308

Livability Code: SB 30-90
Wheelbase-to-length ratio of 48% is considered ◉ dangerous ○ fatiguing ○ good ○ excellent *
The approximate net payload of 2692 pounds at 13% of GVWR on this model is ○ deficient ○ excessive ○ cautionary ◉ good ○ excellent *
Total highway safety penalties are: 7 *   Value: **7 8**   Durability: **7 8**   Highway Control Rating: **3 2**   Highway Safety: **2 5**

Brand	Year	Type	Length	Model	Chassis	Engine	Fuel Type	Average Price per Linear Foot When New	Adjusted Wheelbase	Approx. Towing Capacity	Gross Vehicle Weight Rating	Average Curb Weight
Kountry Aire	1996	MHA	35	KA 3458-sl	FO	7.5L	G	$3100	202 T	5,000	20,000	17,308

Livability Code: SB 30-90
Wheelbase-to-length ratio of 48% is considered ◉ dangerous ○ fatiguing ○ good ○ excellent *
The approximate net payload of 2692 pounds at 13% of GVWR on this model is ○ deficient ○ excessive ○ cautionary ◉ good ○ excellent *
Total highway safety penalties are: 7 *   Value: **7 8**   Durability: **7 8**   Highway Control Rating: **3 2**   Highway Safety: **2 5**

Brand	Year	Type	Length	Model	Chassis	Engine	Fuel Type	Average Price per Linear Foot When New	Adjusted Wheelbase	Approx. Towing Capacity	Gross Vehicle Weight Rating	Average Curb Weight
Kountry Aire	1996	MHA	38	KA 3710	FO	7.5L	G	$2900	224 T	5,000	20,000	17,214

Livability Code: SB 30-90
Wheelbase-to-length ratio of 49% is considered ◉ dangerous ○ fatiguing ○ good ○ excellent *
The approximate net payload of 2786 pounds at 14% of GVWR on this model is ○ deficient ○ excessive ○ cautionary ◉ good ○ excellent *
Total highway safety penalties are: 4 *   Value: **7 9**   Durability: **7 8**   Highway Control Rating: **3 8**   Highway Safety: **3 4**

Brand	Year	Type	Length	Model	Chassis	Engine	Fuel Type	Average Price per Linear Foot When New	Adjusted Wheelbase	Approx. Towing Capacity	Gross Vehicle Weight Rating	Average Curb Weight
Kountry Aire	1996	MHA	38	KA 3755-sl	FO	7.5L	G	$2900	224 T	5,000	20,000	18,114

Livability Code: SB 30-90
Wheelbase-to-length ratio of 49% is considered ◉ dangerous ○ fatiguing ○ good ○ excellent *
The approximate net payload of 1886 pounds at 9% of GVWR on this model is ○ deficient ○ excessive ◉ cautionary ○ good ○ excellent *
Total highway safety penalties are: 7 *   Value: **7 8**   Durability: **7 8**   Highway Control Rating: **2 5**   Highway Safety: **1 8**

Brand	Year	Type	Length	Model	Chassis	Engine	Fuel Type	Average Price per Linear Foot When New	Adjusted Wheelbase	Approx. Towing Capacity	Gross Vehicle Weight Rating	Average Curb Weight
Kountry Aire	1996	MHA	38	KA 3756-sl	FO	7.5L	G	$2900	224 T	5,000	20,000	18,114

Livability Code: SB 30-90
Wheelbase-to-length ratio of 49% is considered ◉ dangerous ○ fatiguing ○ good ○ excellent *
The approximate net payload of 1886 pounds at 9% of GVWR on this model is ○ deficient ○ excessive ◉ cautionary ○ good ○ excellent *
Total highway safety penalties are: 7 *   Value: **7 8**   Durability: **7 8**   Highway Control Rating: **2 5**   Highway Safety: **1 8**

Brand	Year	Type	Length	Model	Chassis	Engine	Fuel Type	Average Price per Linear Foot When New	Adjusted Wheelbase	Approx. Towing Capacity	Gross Vehicle Weight Rating	Average Curb Weight
Kountry Aire	1996	MHA	38	KA 3757-sl	FO	7.5L	G	$2900	224 T	5,000	20,000	18,114

Livability Code: SB 30-90
Wheelbase-to-length ratio of 49% is considered ◉ dangerous ○ fatiguing ○ good ○ excellent *
The approximate net payload of 1886 pounds at 9% of GVWR on this model is ○ deficient ○ excessive ◉ cautionary ○ good ○ excellent *
Total highway safety penalties are: 7 *   Value: **7 8**   Durability: **7 8**   Highway Control Rating: **2 5**   Highway Safety: **1 8**

Brand	Year	Type	Length	Model	Chassis	Engine	Fuel Type	Average Price per Linear Foot When New	Adjusted Wheelbase	Approx. Towing Capacity	Gross Vehicle Weight Rating	Average Curb Weight
Kountry Aire	1996	MHA	38	KA 3760-sl	FO	7.5L	G	$2900	224 T	5,000	20,000	18,114

Livability Code: SB 30-90
Wheelbase-to-length ratio of 49% is considered ◉ dangerous ○ fatiguing ○ good ○ excellent *
The approximate net payload of 1886 pounds at 9% of GVWR on this model is ○ deficient ○ excessive ◉ cautionary ○ good ○ excellent *
Total highway safety penalties are: 7 *   Value: **7 8**   Durability: **7 8**   Highway Control Rating: **2 5**   Highway Safety: **1 8**

Brand	Year	Type	Length	Model	Chassis	Engine	Fuel Type	Average Price per Linear Foot When New	Adjusted Wheelbase	Approx. Towing Capacity	Gross Vehicle Weight Rating	Average Curb Weight
Kountry Aire	1997	MHA	35	KA3458 opch	CH	7.4L	G	$3200	214 T	2,000	19,000	17,144

Livability Code: SB 30-90
Wheelbase-to-length ratio of 51% is considered ○ dangerous ◉ fatiguing ○ good ○ excellent *
The approximate net payload of 1856 pounds at 10% of GVWR on this model is ○ deficient ○ excessive ○ cautionary ◉ good ○ excellent *
Total highway safety penalties are: 12 *   Value: **7 5**   Durability: **7 8**   Highway Control Rating: **3 6**   Highway Safety: **2 4**

Brand	Year	Type	Length	Model	Chassis	Engine	Fuel Type	Average Price per Linear Foot When New	Adjusted Wheelbase	Approx. Towing Capacity	Gross Vehicle Weight Rating	Average Curb Weight
Kountry Aire	1997	MHA	35	KA3481 opch	CH	7.4L	G	$3300	214 T	2,000	19,000	17,144

Livability Code: SB 30-90
Wheelbase-to-length ratio of 51% is considered ○ dangerous ◉ fatiguing ○ good ○ excellent *
The approximate net payload of 1856 pounds at 10% of GVWR on this model is ○ deficient ○ excessive ○ cautionary ◉ good ○ excellent *
Total highway safety penalties are: 12 *   Value: **7 5**   Durability: **7 8**   Highway Control Rating: **3 6**   Highway Safety: **2 4**

Note: Safety ratings are based on the assumption that the engineering of the RV has allowed for proper balance by placing fresh, gray, and black holding tanks in a location so as not to change the balance of the RV when the tanks are empty or full. **Always double-check wheelbase, GVWR, and weights at front and rear axles.**

*See Section 1 for details on how conclusions are reached.

Brand	Year	Type	Length	Model	Chassis	Engine	Fuel Type	Average Price per Linear Foot When New	Adjusted Wheelbase	Approx. Towing Capacity	Gross Vehicle Weight Rating	Average Curb Weight

Kountry Aire — 1997 — MHA — 35 — KA 3458 — FO — 7.5L — G — $3200 — 214 T — 5,000 — 20,000 — 17,644
Livability Code: SB 30-90   Wheelbase-to-length ratio of 51% is considered ○ dangerous ● fatiguing ○ good ○ excellent *
The approximate net payload of 2356 pounds at 12% of GVWR on this model is ○ deficient ○ excessive ○ cautionary ● good ○ excellent *
Total highway safety penalties are: 7 *   Value: 7 8   Durability: 7 8   Highway Control Rating: 4 0   Highway Safety: 3 3

Kountry Aire — 1997 — MHA — 35 — KA 3481 — FO — 7.5L — G — $3300 — 214 T — 5,000 — 20,000 — 17,644
Livability Code: SB 30-90   Wheelbase-to-length ratio of 51% is considered ○ dangerous ● fatiguing ○ good ○ excellent *
The approximate net payload of 2356 pounds at 12% of GVWR on this model is ○ deficient ○ excessive ○ cautionary ● good ○ excellent *
Total highway safety penalties are: 7 *   Value: 7 8   Durability: 7 8   Highway Control Rating: 4 0   Highway Safety: 3 3

Kountry Aire — 1997 — MHA — 35 — KA 3356 fr.dsl — FR — Cu210 — D — $4300 — 200 — 4,500 — 20,500 — 17,844
Livability Code: SB 30-90   Wheelbase-to-length ratio of 48% is considered ● dangerous ○ fatiguing ○ good ○ excellent *
The approximate net payload of 2656 pounds at 13% of GVWR on this model is ○ deficient ○ excessive ○ cautionary ● good ○ excellent *
Total highway safety penalties are: 5 *   Value: 7 9   Durability: 7 8   Highway Control Rating: 3 0   Highway Safety: 2 5

Kountry Aire — 1997 — MHA — 35 — KA3458 fr.dsl — FR — Cu210 — D — $4300 — 216 — 4,500 — 20,500 — 17,844
Livability Code: SB 30-90   Wheelbase-to-length ratio of 51% is considered ○ dangerous ● fatiguing ○ good ○ excellent *
The approximate net payload of 2656 pounds at 13% of GVWR on this model is ○ deficient ○ excessive ○ cautionary ● good ○ excellent *
Total highway safety penalties are: 5 *   Value: 7 9   Durability: 7 8   Highway Control Rating: 4 4   Highway Safety: 3 9

Kountry Aire — 1997 — MHA — 35 — KA3481 fr.dsl — FR — Cu210 — D — $4300 — 216 — 4,500 — 20,500 — 17,844
Livability Code: SB 30-90   Wheelbase-to-length ratio of 51% is considered ○ dangerous ● fatiguing ○ good ○ excellent *
The approximate net payload of 2656 pounds at 13% of GVWR on this model is ○ deficient ○ excessive ○ cautionary ● good ○ excellent *
Total highway safety penalties are: 5 *   Value: 7 9   Durability: 7 8   Highway Control Rating: 4 4   Highway Safety: 3 9

Kountry Aire — 1997 — MHA — 36 — KP3481 opch pusher — FR — Cu300 — D — $4200 — 212 — 5,000 — 26,000 — 21,683
Livability Code: SB 30-90   Wheelbase-to-length ratio of 50% is considered ● dangerous ○ fatiguing ○ good ○ excellent *
The approximate net payload of 4317 pounds at 17% of GVWR on this model is ○ deficient ○ excessive ○ cautionary ○ good ● excellent *
Total highway safety penalties are: 5 *   Value: 7 9   Durability: 7 8   Highway Control Rating: 4 4   Highway Safety: 3 9

Kountry Aire — 1997 — MHA — 36 — KP3481 pusher — SP — Cu300 — D — $4200 — 212 — 5,000 — 26,000 — 21,983
Livability Code: SB 30-90   Wheelbase-to-length ratio of 50% is considered ● dangerous ○ fatiguing ○ good ○ excellent *
The approximate net payload of 4017 pounds at 15% of GVWR on this model is ○ deficient ○ excessive ○ cautionary ● good ○ excellent *
Total highway safety penalties are: 5 *   Value: 7 9   Durability: 7 8   Highway Control Rating: 4 2   Highway Safety: 3 7

Kountry Aire — 1997 — MHA — 38 — KA 3757 — FO — 7.5L — G — $3100 — 236 T — 5,000 — 20,000 — 18,479
Livability Code: SB 30-90   Wheelbase-to-length ratio of 52% is considered ○ dangerous ● fatiguing ○ good ○ excellent *
The approximate net payload of 1521 pounds at 8% of GVWR on this model is ○ deficient ○ excessive ● cautionary ○ good ○ excellent *
Total highway safety penalties are: 7 *   Value: 7 8   Durability: 7 8   Highway Control Rating: 3 5   Highway Safety: 2 8

Kountry Aire — 1997 — MHA — 38 — KA 3760 — FO — 7.5L — G — $3100 — 236 T — 5,000 — 20,000 — 18,479
Livability Code: SB 30-90   Wheelbase-to-length ratio of 52% is considered ○ dangerous ● fatiguing ○ good ○ excellent *
The approximate net payload of 1521 pounds at 8% of GVWR on this model is ○ deficient ○ excessive ● cautionary ○ good ○ excellent *
Total highway safety penalties are: 7 *   Value: 7 8   Durability: 7 8   Highway Control Rating: 3 5   Highway Safety: 2 8

Kountry Aire — 1997 — MHA — 38 — KA 3780 — FO — 7.5L — G — $3100 — 236 T — 5,000 — 20,000 — 18,479
Livability Code: SB 30-90   Wheelbase-to-length ratio of 52% is considered ○ dangerous ● fatiguing ○ good ○ excellent *
The approximate net payload of 1521 pounds at 8% of GVWR on this model is ○ deficient ○ excessive ● cautionary ○ good ○ excellent *
Total highway safety penalties are: 7 *   Value: 7 8   Durability: 7 8   Highway Control Rating: 3 5   Highway Safety: 2 8

Kountry Aire — 1997 — MHA — 38 — KA3757 fr.dsl — FR — Cu210 — D — $3900 — 228 — 4,500 — 20,500 — 18,679
Livability Code: SB 30-90   Wheelbase-to-length ratio of 50% is considered ● dangerous ○ fatiguing ○ good ○ excellent *
The approximate net payload of 1821 pounds at 9% of GVWR on this model is ○ deficient ○ excessive ● cautionary ○ good ○ excellent *
Total highway safety penalties are: 5 *   Value: 7 9   Durability: 7 8   Highway Control Rating: 2 8   Highway Safety: 2 3

Kountry Aire — 1997 — MHA — 38 — KA3760 fr.dsl — FR — Cu210 — D — $3900 — 228 — 4,500 — 20,500 — 18,679
Livability Code: SB 30-90   Wheelbase-to-length ratio of 50% is considered ● dangerous ○ fatiguing ○ good ○ excellent *
The approximate net payload of 1821 pounds at 9% of GVWR on this model is ○ deficient ○ excessive ● cautionary ○ good ○ excellent *
Total highway safety penalties are: 5 *   Value: 7 9   Durability: 7 8   Highway Control Rating: 2 8   Highway Safety: 2 3

Note: Safety ratings are based on the assumption that the engineering of the RV has allowed for proper balance by placing fresh, gray, and black holding tanks in a location so as not to change the balance of the RV when the tanks are empty or full. **Always double-check wheelbase, GVWR, and weights at front and rear axles.**

*See Section 1 for details on how conclusions are reached.

Section 2: The Ratings

Brand	Year	Type	Length	Model	Chassis	Engine	Fuel Type	Average Price per Linear Foot When New	Adjusted Wheelbase	Approx. Towing Capacity	Gross Vehicle Weight Rating	Average Curb Weight
Kountry Aire	1997	MHA	38	KA3780 fr.dsl	FR	Cu210	D	$3900	228	4,500	20,500	18,679

Livability Code: SB 30-90

Wheelbase-to-length ratio of 50% is considered ◉ dangerous ○ fatiguing ○ good ○ excellent*

The approximate net payload of 1821 pounds at 9% of GVWR on this model is ○ deficient ○ excessive ◉ cautionary ○ good ○ excellent*

Total highway safety penalties are: 5*   Value: **7 9**   Durability: **7 8**   Highway Control Rating: **2 8**   Highway Safety: **2 3**

Brand	Year	Type	Length	Model	Chassis	Engine	Fuel Type	Avg Price/Lin Ft	Adj Wheelbase	Towing	GVWR	Curb Wt
Kountry Aire	1997	MHA	39	KP3860 opch	FR	Cu300	D	$3800	252	5,000	27,400	23,802

Livability Code: SB 30-90

Wheelbase-to-length ratio of 54% is considered ○ dangerous ○ fatiguing ◉ good ○ excellent*

The approximate net payload of 3598 pounds at 13% of GVWR on this model is ○ deficient ○ excessive ○ cautionary ◉ good ○ excellent*

Total highway safety penalties are: 5*   Value: **7 9**   Durability: **7 8**   Highway Control Rating: **7 9**   Highway Safety: **7 4**   ★★★

Brand	Year	Type	Length	Model	Chassis	Engine	Fuel Type	Avg Price/Lin Ft	Adj Wheelbase	Towing	GVWR	Curb Wt
Kountry Aire	1997	MHA	39	KP3880 opch	FR	Cu300	D	$3800	252	5,000	27,400	23,802

Livability Code: SB 30-90

Wheelbase-to-length ratio of 54% is considered ○ dangerous ○ fatiguing ◉ good ○ excellent*

The approximate net payload of 3598 pounds at 13% of GVWR on this model is ○ deficient ○ excessive ○ cautionary ◉ good ○ excellent*

Total highway safety penalties are: 5*   Value: **7 9**   Durability: **7 8**   Highway Control Rating: **7 9**   Highway Safety: **7 4**   ★★★

Brand	Year	Type	Length	Model	Chassis	Engine	Fuel Type	Avg Price/Lin Ft	Adj Wheelbase	Towing	GVWR	Curb Wt
Kountry Aire	1997	MHA	39	KP3860 pusher	SP	Cu300	D	$3800	252	5,000	27,400	23,902

Livability Code: SB 30-90

Wheelbase-to-length ratio of 54% is considered ○ dangerous ○ fatiguing ◉ good ○ excellent*

The approximate net payload of 3498 pounds at 13% of GVWR on this model is ○ deficient ○ excessive ○ cautionary ◉ good ○ excellent*

Total highway safety penalties are: 5*   Value: **7 9**   Durability: **7 8**   Highway Control Rating: **7 9**   Highway Safety: **7 4**   ★★★

Brand	Year	Type	Length	Model	Chassis	Engine	Fuel Type	Avg Price/Lin Ft	Adj Wheelbase	Towing	GVWR	Curb Wt
Kountry Aire	1997	MHA	39	KP3880 pusher	SP	Cu300	D	$3800	252	5,000	27,400	23,902

Livability Code: SB 30-90

Wheelbase-to-length ratio of 54% is considered ○ dangerous ○ fatiguing ◉ good ○ excellent*

The approximate net payload of 3498 pounds at 13% of GVWR on this model is ○ deficient ○ excessive ○ cautionary ◉ good ○ excellent*

Total highway safety penalties are: 5*   Value: **7 9**   Durability: **7 8**   Highway Control Rating: **7 9**   Highway Safety: **7 4**   ★★★

Brand	Year	Type	Length	Model	Chassis	Engine	Fuel Type	Avg Price/Lin Ft	Adj Wheelbase	Towing	GVWR	Curb Wt
Kountry Aire	1997	MHA	41	KP4057 opch	FR	Cu300	D	$3700	276	5,000	31,000	24,659

Livability Code: SB 30-90

Wheelbase-to-length ratio of 56% is considered ○ dangerous ○ fatiguing ◉ good ○ excellent*

The approximate net payload of 6341 pounds at 20% of GVWR on this model is ○ deficient ○ excessive ○ cautionary ○ good ◉ excellent*

Total highway safety penalties are: 5*   Value: **7 9**   Durability: **7 8**   Highway Control Rating: **1 0 0**   Highway Safety: **9 5**   ★★★

Brand	Year	Type	Length	Model	Chassis	Engine	Fuel Type	Avg Price/Lin Ft	Adj Wheelbase	Towing	GVWR	Curb Wt
Kountry Aire	1997	MHA	41	KP4060 opch	FR	Cu300	D	$3700	276	5,000	31,000	24,659

Livability Code: SB 30-90

Wheelbase-to-length ratio of 56% is considered ○ dangerous ○ fatiguing ◉ good ○ excellent*

The approximate net payload of 6341 pounds at 20% of GVWR on this model is ○ deficient ○ excessive ○ cautionary ○ good ◉ excellent*

Total highway safety penalties are: 5*   Value: **7 9**   Durability: **7 8**   Highway Control Rating: **1 0 0**   Highway Safety: **9 5**   ★★★

Brand	Year	Type	Length	Model	Chassis	Engine	Fuel Type	Avg Price/Lin Ft	Adj Wheelbase	Towing	GVWR	Curb Wt
Kountry Aire	1997	MHA	41	KP4080 opch pusher	FR	Cu300	D	$3700	276	5,000	31,000	24,659

Livability Code: SB 30-90

Wheelbase-to-length ratio of 56% is considered ○ dangerous ○ fatiguing ◉ good ○ excellent*

The approximate net payload of 6341 pounds at 20% of GVWR on this model is ○ deficient ○ excessive ○ cautionary ○ good ◉ excellent*

Total highway safety penalties are: 5*   Value: **7 9**   Durability: **7 8**   Highway Control Rating: **1 0 0**   Highway Safety: **9 5**   ★★★

Brand	Year	Type	Length	Model	Chassis	Engine	Fuel Type	Avg Price/Lin Ft	Adj Wheelbase	Towing	GVWR	Curb Wt
Kountry Aire	1997	MHA	41	KP4057 pusher	SP	Cu300	D	$3700	276	5,000	31,000	24,759

Livability Code: SB 30-90

Wheelbase-to-length ratio of 56% is considered ○ dangerous ○ fatiguing ◉ good ○ excellent*

The approximate net payload of 6241 pounds at 20% of GVWR on this model is ○ deficient ○ excessive ○ cautionary ○ good ◉ excellent*

Total highway safety penalties are: 5*   Value: **7 9**   Durability: **7 8**   Highway Control Rating: **1 0 0**   Highway Safety: **9 5**   ★★★

Brand	Year	Type	Length	Model	Chassis	Engine	Fuel Type	Avg Price/Lin Ft	Adj Wheelbase	Towing	GVWR	Curb Wt
Kountry Aire	1997	MHA	41	KP4060 pusher	SP	Cu300	D	$3700	276	5,000	31,000	24,759

Livability Code: SB 30-90

Wheelbase-to-length ratio of 56% is considered ○ dangerous ○ fatiguing ◉ good ○ excellent*

The approximate net payload of 6241 pounds at 20% of GVWR on this model is ○ deficient ○ excessive ○ cautionary ○ good ◉ excellent*

Total highway safety penalties are: 5*   Value: **7 9**   Durability: **7 8**   Highway Control Rating: **1 0 0**   Highway Safety: **9 5**   ★★★

Brand	Year	Type	Length	Model	Chassis	Engine	Fuel Type	Avg Price/Lin Ft	Adj Wheelbase	Towing	GVWR	Curb Wt
Kountry Aire	1997	MHA	41	KP4080 pusher	SP	Cu300	D	$3700	276	5,000	31,000	24,759

Livability Code: SB 30-90

Wheelbase-to-length ratio of 56% is considered ○ dangerous ○ fatiguing ◉ good ○ excellent*

The approximate net payload of 6241 pounds at 20% of GVWR on this model is ○ deficient ○ excessive ○ cautionary ○ good ◉ excellent*

Total highway safety penalties are: 5*   Value: **7 9**   Durability: **7 8**   Highway Control Rating: **1 0 0**   Highway Safety: **9 5**   ★★★

Brand	Year	Type	Length	Model	Chassis	Engine	Fuel Type	Avg Price/Lin Ft	Adj Wheelbase	Towing	GVWR	Curb Wt
Kountry Aire	1998	MHA	34	KA3356 fr.dsl	FR	CU210	D	$4100	200	5,000	20,500	18,218

Livability Code: SB 30-90

Wheelbase-to-length ratio of 49% is considered ◉ dangerous ○ fatiguing ○ good ○ excellent*

The approximate net payload of 2282 pounds at 11% of GVWR on this model is ○ deficient ○ excessive ○ cautionary ◉ good ○ excellent*

Total highway safety penalties are: 5*   Value: **8 5**   Durability: **8 0**   Highway Control Rating: **3 1**   Highway Safety: **2 6**

Note: Safety ratings are based on the assumption that the engineering of the RV has allowed for proper balance by placing fresh, gray, and black holding tanks in a location so as not to change the balance of the RV when the tanks are empty or full. **Always double-check wheelbase, GVWR, and weights at front and rear axles.**

*See Section 1 for details on how conclusions are reached.

Brand	Year	Type	Length	Model	Chassis	Engine	Fuel Type	Average Price per Linear Foot When New	Adjusted Wheelbase	Approx. Towing Capacity	Gross Vehicle Weight Rating	Average Curb Weight
Kountry Aire	1998	MHA	35	KA3481	FO	7.5L	G	$2600	214 T	5,000	20,000	18,316

Livability Code: SB 30-90
Wheelbase-to-length ratio of 51% is considered ○ dangerous ◉ fatiguing ○ good ○ excellent *
The approximate net payload of 1684 pounds at 8% of GVWR on this model is ○ deficient ○ excessive ◉ cautionary ○ good ○ excellent *
Total highway safety penalties are: 7 *   Value: 83   Durability: 80   Highway Control Rating: 26   Highway Safety: 19

Brand	Year	Type	Length	Model	Chassis	Engine	Fuel Type	Price	Wheelbase	Towing	GVWR	Curb Wt
Kountry Aire	1998	MHA	35	KA3481 opch fr.dsl	FR	CU210	D	$4000	216	5,000	20,500	18,516

Livability Code: SB 30-90
Wheelbase-to-length ratio of 51% is considered ○ dangerous ◉ fatiguing ○ good ○ excellent *
The approximate net payload of 1984 pounds at 10% of GVWR on this model is ○ deficient ○ excessive ○ cautionary ◉ good ○ excellent *
Total highway safety penalties are: 5 *   Value: 85   Durability: 80   Highway Control Rating: 38   Highway Safety: 33

Brand	Year	Type	Length	Model	Chassis	Engine	Fuel Type	Price	Wheelbase	Towing	GVWR	Curb Wt
Kountry Aire	1998	MHA	36	KA3535	FO	7.5L	G	$2500	214 T	5,000	20,000	17,714

Livability Code: SB 30-90
Wheelbase-to-length ratio of 50% is considered ◉ dangerous ○ fatiguing ○ good ○ excellent *
The approximate net payload of 2286 pounds at 11% of GVWR on this model is ○ deficient ○ excessive ○ cautionary ◉ good ○ excellent *
Total highway safety penalties are: 4 *   Value: 85   Durability: 80   Highway Control Rating: 34   Highway Safety: 30

Brand	Year	Type	Length	Model	Chassis	Engine	Fuel Type	Price	Wheelbase	Towing	GVWR	Curb Wt
Kountry Aire	1998	MHA	36	KA3535 opch fr.dsl	FR	CU210	D	$3900	216	5,000	20,500	17,914

Livability Code: SB 30-90
Wheelbase-to-length ratio of 50% is considered ◉ dangerous ○ fatiguing ○ good ○ excellent *
The approximate net payload of 2586 pounds at 13% of GVWR on this model is ○ deficient ○ excessive ○ cautionary ◉ good ○ excellent *
Total highway safety penalties are: 8 *   Value: 83   Durability: 80   Highway Control Rating: 38   Highway Safety: 30

Brand	Year	Type	Length	Model	Chassis	Engine	Fuel Type	Price	Wheelbase	Towing	GVWR	Curb Wt
Kountry Aire	1998	MHA	38	KA3761	FO	7.5L	G	$2400	236 T	5,000	20,000	19,209

Livability Code: SB 30-90
Wheelbase-to-length ratio of 52% is considered ○ dangerous ◉ fatiguing ○ good ○ excellent *
The approximate net payload of 791 pounds at 4% of GVWR on this model is ◉ deficient ○ excessive ○ cautionary ○ good ○ excellent *
Total highway safety penalties are: 7 *   Value: 83   Durability: 80   Highway Control Rating: 22   Highway Safety: 15

Brand	Year	Type	Length	Model	Chassis	Engine	Fuel Type	Price	Wheelbase	Towing	GVWR	Curb Wt
Kountry Aire	1998	MHA	38	KA3780	FO	7.5L	G	$2400	236 T	5,000	20,000	19,209

Livability Code: SB 30-90
Wheelbase-to-length ratio of 52% is considered ○ dangerous ◉ fatiguing ○ good ○ excellent *
The approximate net payload of 791 pounds at 4% of GVWR on this model is ◉ deficient ○ excessive ○ cautionary ○ good ○ excellent *
Total highway safety penalties are: 7 *   Value: 83   Durability: 80   Highway Control Rating: 22   Highway Safety: 15

Brand	Year	Type	Length	Model	Chassis	Engine	Fuel Type	Price	Wheelbase	Towing	GVWR	Curb Wt
Kountry Aire	1998	MHA	38	KA3796	FO	7.5L	G	$2400	236 T	5,000	20,000	19,209

Livability Code: SB 30-90
Wheelbase-to-length ratio of 52% is considered ○ dangerous ◉ fatiguing ○ good ○ excellent *
The approximate net payload of 791 pounds at 4% of GVWR on this model is ◉ deficient ○ excessive ○ cautionary ○ good ○ excellent *
Total highway safety penalties are: 7 *   Value: 83   Durability: 80   Highway Control Rating: 22   Highway Safety: 15

Brand	Year	Type	Length	Model	Chassis	Engine	Fuel Type	Price	Wheelbase	Towing	GVWR	Curb Wt
Kountry Aire	1998	MHA	38	KA3797	FO	7.5L	G	$2400	236 T	5,000	20,000	19,209

Livability Code: SB 30-90
Wheelbase-to-length ratio of 52% is considered ○ dangerous ◉ fatiguing ○ good ○ excellent *
The approximate net payload of 791 pounds at 4% of GVWR on this model is ◉ deficient ○ excessive ○ cautionary ○ good ○ excellent *
Total highway safety penalties are: 7 *   Value: 83   Durability: 80   Highway Control Rating: 22   Highway Safety: 15

Brand	Year	Type	Length	Model	Chassis	Engine	Fuel Type	Price	Wheelbase	Towing	GVWR	Curb Wt
Kountry Aire	1998	MHA	38	KA3761 opch fr.dsl	FR	CU210	D	$3700	228	5,000	20,500	19,409

Livability Code: SB 30-90
Wheelbase-to-length ratio of 50% is considered ◉ dangerous ○ fatiguing ○ good ○ excellent *
The approximate net payload of 1091 pounds at 5% of GVWR on this model is ◉ deficient ○ excessive ○ cautionary ○ good ○ excellent *
Total highway safety penalties are: 5 *   Value: 85   Durability: 80   Highway Control Rating: 9   Highway Safety: 4

Brand	Year	Type	Length	Model	Chassis	Engine	Fuel Type	Price	Wheelbase	Towing	GVWR	Curb Wt
Kountry Aire	1998	MHA	38	KA3780 opch fr.dsl	FR	CU210	D	$3700	228	5,000	20,500	19,409

Livability Code: SB 30-90
Wheelbase-to-length ratio of 50% is considered ◉ dangerous ○ fatiguing ○ good ○ excellent *
The approximate net payload of 1091 pounds at 5% of GVWR on this model is ◉ deficient ○ excessive ○ cautionary ○ good ○ excellent *
Total highway safety penalties are: 5 *   Value: 85   Durability: 80   Highway Control Rating: 9   Highway Safety: 4

Brand	Year	Type	Length	Model	Chassis	Engine	Fuel Type	Price	Wheelbase	Towing	GVWR	Curb Wt
Kountry Aire	1998	MHA	38	KA3796 opch fr.dsl	FR	CU210	D	$3700	228	5,000	20,500	19,409

Livability Code: SB 30-90
Wheelbase-to-length ratio of 50% is considered ◉ dangerous ○ fatiguing ○ good ○ excellent *
The approximate net payload of 1091 pounds at 5% of GVWR on this model is ◉ deficient ○ excessive ○ cautionary ○ good ○ excellent *
Total highway safety penalties are: 5 *   Value: 85   Durability: 80   Highway Control Rating: 9   Highway Safety: 4

Brand	Year	Type	Length	Model	Chassis	Engine	Fuel Type	Price	Wheelbase	Towing	GVWR	Curb Wt
Kountry Aire	1998	MHA	38	KA3797 opch fr.dsl	FR	CU210	D	$3700	228	5,000	20,500	19,409

Livability Code: SB 30-90
Wheelbase-to-length ratio of 50% is considered ◉ dangerous ○ fatiguing ○ good ○ excellent *
The approximate net payload of 1091 pounds at 5% of GVWR on this model is ◉ deficient ○ excessive ○ cautionary ○ good ○ excellent *
Total highway safety penalties are: 5 *   Value: 85   Durability: 80   Highway Control Rating: 9   Highway Safety: 4

Note: Safety ratings are based on the assumption that the engineering of the RV has allowed for proper balance by placing fresh, gray, and black holding tanks in a location so as not to change the balance of the RV when the tanks are empty or full. **Always double-check wheelbase, GVWR, and weights at front and rear axles.**

*See Section 1 for details on how conclusions are reached.

Section 2: The Ratings

Brand	Year	Type	Length	Model	Chassis	Engine	Fuel Type	Average Price per Linear Foot When New	Adjusted Wheelbase	Approx. Towing Capacity	Gross Vehicle Weight Rating	Average Curb Weight

Kountry Aire — 1998 — MHA — 41 — KP4031 opch — FR — CA330 — D — $3400 — 276 — 5,000 — 31,000 — 24,542
Livability Code: SB 30-90
Wheelbase-to-length ratio of 56% is considered ○ dangerous ○ fatiguing ◉ good ○ excellent*
The approximate net payload of 6458 pounds at 21% of GVWR on this model is ○ deficient ○ excessive ○ cautionary ○ good ◉ excellent*
Total highway safety penalties are: 2*   Value: 86   Durability: 80   Highway Control Rating: 100   Highway Safety: 98   ★★★★

Kountry Aire — 1998 — MHA — 41 — KP4057 opch — FR — CA330 — D — $3400 — 276 — 5,000 — 31,000 — 25,442
Livability Code: SB 30-90
Wheelbase-to-length ratio of 56% is considered ○ dangerous ○ fatiguing ◉ good ○ excellent*
The approximate net payload of 5558 pounds at 18% of GVWR on this model is ○ deficient ○ excessive ○ cautionary ○ good ◉ excellent*
Total highway safety penalties are: 5*   Value: 85   Durability: 80   Highway Control Rating: 99   Highway Safety: 94   ★★★★

Kountry Aire — 1998 — MHA — 41 — KP4060 opch — FR — CA330 — D — $3400 — 276 — 5,000 — 31,000 — 25,442
Livability Code: SB 30-90
Wheelbase-to-length ratio of 56% is considered ○ dangerous ○ fatiguing ◉ good ○ excellent*
The approximate net payload of 5558 pounds at 18% of GVWR on this model is ○ deficient ○ excessive ○ cautionary ○ good ◉ excellent*
Total highway safety penalties are: 5*   Value: 85   Durability: 80   Highway Control Rating: 99   Highway Safety: 94   ★★★★

Kountry Aire — 1998 — MHA — 41 — KP4081 opch — FR — CA330 — D — $3400 — 276 — 5,000 — 31,000 — 25,442
Livability Code: SB 30-90
Wheelbase-to-length ratio of 56% is considered ○ dangerous ○ fatiguing ◉ good ○ excellent*
The approximate net payload of 5558 pounds at 18% of GVWR on this model is ○ deficient ○ excessive ○ cautionary ○ good ◉ excellent*
Total highway safety penalties are: 5*   Value: 85   Durability: 80   Highway Control Rating: 99   Highway Safety: 94   ★★★★

Kountry Aire — 1998 — MHA — 41 — KP4087 opch — FR — CA330 — D — $3400 — 276 — 5,000 — 31,000 — 25,442
Livability Code: SB 30-90
Wheelbase-to-length ratio of 56% is considered ○ dangerous ○ fatiguing ◉ good ○ excellent*
The approximate net payload of 5558 pounds at 18% of GVWR on this model is ○ deficient ○ excessive ○ cautionary ○ good ◉ excellent*
Total highway safety penalties are: 5*   Value: 85   Durability: 80   Highway Control Rating: 99   Highway Safety: 94   ★★★★

Kountry Aire — 1998 — MHA — 41 — KP4031 — SP — CU325 — D — $3400 — 276 — 10,000 — 31,000 — 24,642
Livability Code: SB 30-90
Wheelbase-to-length ratio of 56% is considered ○ dangerous ○ fatiguing ◉ good ○ excellent*
The approximate net payload of 6358 pounds at 21% of GVWR on this model is ○ deficient ○ excessive ○ cautionary ○ good ◉ excellent*
Total highway safety penalties are: 2*   Value: 86   Durability: 80   Highway Control Rating: 100   Highway Safety: 98   ★★★★

Kountry Aire — 1998 — MHA — 41 — KP4057 — SP — CU325 — D — $3400 — 276 — 10,000 — 31,000 — 25,542
Livability Code: SB 30-90
Wheelbase-to-length ratio of 56% is considered ○ dangerous ○ fatiguing ◉ good ○ excellent*
The approximate net payload of 5458 pounds at 18% of GVWR on this model is ○ deficient ○ excessive ○ cautionary ○ good ◉ excellent*
Total highway safety penalties are: 5*   Value: 85   Durability: 80   Highway Control Rating: 99   Highway Safety: 94   ★★★★

Kountry Aire — 1998 — MHA — 41 — KP4060 — SP — CU325 — D — $3400 — 276 — 10,000 — 31,000 — 25,542
Livability Code: SB 30-90
Wheelbase-to-length ratio of 56% is considered ○ dangerous ○ fatiguing ◉ good ○ excellent*
The approximate net payload of 5458 pounds at 18% of GVWR on this model is ○ deficient ○ excessive ○ cautionary ○ good ◉ excellent*
Total highway safety penalties are: 5*   Value: 85   Durability: 80   Highway Control Rating: 99   Highway Safety: 94   ★★★★

Kountry Aire — 1998 — MHA — 41 — KP4081 — SP — CU325 — D — $3400 — 276 — 10,000 — 31,000 — 25,542
Livability Code: SB 30-90
Wheelbase-to-length ratio of 56% is considered ○ dangerous ○ fatiguing ◉ good ○ excellent*
The approximate net payload of 5458 pounds at 18% of GVWR on this model is ○ deficient ○ excessive ○ cautionary ○ good ◉ excellent*
Total highway safety penalties are: 5*   Value: 85   Durability: 80   Highway Control Rating: 99   Highway Safety: 94   ★★★★

Kountry Aire — 1998 — MHA — 41 — KP4087 — SP — CU325 — D — $3400 — 276 — 10,000 — 31,000 — 25,542
Livability Code: SB 30-90
Wheelbase-to-length ratio of 56% is considered ○ dangerous ○ fatiguing ◉ good ○ excellent*
The approximate net payload of 5458 pounds at 18% of GVWR on this model is ○ deficient ○ excessive ○ cautionary ○ good ◉ excellent*
Total highway safety penalties are: 5*   Value: 85   Durability: 80   Highway Control Rating: 99   Highway Safety: 94   ★★★★

Kountry Star — 1990 — MHA — 28 — 26WCBA — FO — 7.5L — G — $1600 — 158 — 1,500 — 11,000 — 10,808
Livability Code: SB 30-90
Wheelbase-to-length ratio of 47% is considered ◉ dangerous ○ fatiguing ○ good ○ excellent*
The approximate net payload of 192 pounds at 2% of GVWR on this model is ◉ deficient ○ excessive ○ cautionary ○ good ○ excellent*
Total highway safety penalties are: 2*   Value: 85   Durability: 78   Highway Control Rating: 1   Highway Safety: -1

Kountry Star — 1990 — MHA — 37 — 36 CBD SS — CH — 7.4L — G — $1700 — 202 T — 1,500 — 18,000 — 14,847
Livability Code: SB 30-90
Wheelbase-to-length ratio of 45% is considered ◉ dangerous ○ fatiguing ○ good ○ excellent*
The approximate net payload of 3153 pounds at 18% of GVWR on this model is ○ deficient ○ excessive ○ cautionary ○ good ◉ excellent*
Total highway safety penalties are: 10*   Value: 81   Durability: 78   Highway Control Rating: 30   Highway Safety: 20

Note: Safety ratings are based on the assumption that the engineering of the RV has allowed for proper balance by placing fresh, gray, and black holding tanks in a location so as not to change the balance of the RV when the tanks are empty or full. **Always double-check wheelbase, GVWR, and weights at front and rear axles.**

*See Section 1 for details on how conclusions are reached.

Brand	Year	Type	Length	Model	Chassis	Engine	Fuel Type	Average Price per Linear Foot When New	Adjusted Wheel-base	Approx. Towing Capacity	Gross Vehicle Weight Rating	Average Curb Weight
Kountry Star	1991	MHA	28	27 WCB	FO	7.5L	G	$1900	158	1,500	11,000	9,739

Livability Code: SB 30-90
Wheelbase-to-length ratio of 47% is considered ◉ dangerous ○ fatiguing ○ good ○ excellent *
The approximate net payload of 1261 pounds at 11% of GVWR on this model is ○ deficient ○ excessive ○ cautionary ◉ good ○ excellent *
Total highway safety penalties are: 2 *   Value: 8 5   Durability: 7 8   Highway Control Rating: 2 4   Highway Safety: 2 2

Brand	Year	Type	Length	Model	Chassis	Engine	Fuel Type	Price	Wheelbase	Towing	GVWR	Curb Weight
Kountry Star	1991	MHA	35	33 CBDSS	CH	7.4L	G	$2200	202 T	1,500	18,500	14,874

Livability Code: SB 30-90
Wheelbase-to-length ratio of 49% is considered ◉ dangerous ○ fatiguing ○ good ○ excellent *
The approximate net payload of 3626 pounds at 20% of GVWR on this model is ○ deficient ○ excessive ○ cautionary ○ good ◉ excellent *
Total highway safety penalties are: 9 *   Value: 8 2   Durability: 7 8   Highway Control Rating: 4 3   Highway Safety: 3 4

Brand	Year	Type	Length	Model	Chassis	Engine	Fuel Type	Price	Wheelbase	Towing	GVWR	Curb Weight
Kountry Star	1992	MHA	34	33 CBDSS	CH	7.4L	G	$1800	202 T	1,500	18,500	14,156

Livability Code: SB 30-90
Wheelbase-to-length ratio of 49% is considered ◉ dangerous ○ fatiguing ○ good ○ excellent *
The approximate net payload of 4344 pounds at 23% of GVWR on this model is ○ deficient ○ excessive ○ cautionary ○ good ◉ excellent *
Total highway safety penalties are: 9 *   Value: 8 2   Durability: 7 8   Highway Control Rating: 4 2   Highway Safety: 3 3

Brand	Year	Type	Length	Model	Chassis	Engine	Fuel Type	Price	Wheelbase	Towing	GVWR	Curb Weight
Kountry Star	1994	MHA	30	29WCB	CH	7.4L	G	$2600	178	4,000	16,000	13,406

Livability Code: SB 30-90
Wheelbase-to-length ratio of 49% is considered ◉ dangerous ○ fatiguing ○ good ○ excellent *
The approximate net payload of 2595 pounds at 16% of GVWR on this model is ○ deficient ○ excessive ○ cautionary ○ good ◉ excellent *
Total highway safety penalties are: 5 *   Value: 8 4   Durability: 7 8   Highway Control Rating: 4 3   Highway Safety: 3 8

Brand	Year	Type	Length	Model	Chassis	Engine	Fuel Type	Price	Wheelbase	Towing	GVWR	Curb Weight
Kountry Star	1994	MHA	30	29WCB	FO	7.5L	G	$2600	178	8,000	17,000	13,841

Livability Code: SB 30-90
Wheelbase-to-length ratio of 49% is considered ◉ dangerous ○ fatiguing ○ good ○ excellent *
The approximate net payload of 3160 pounds at 19% of GVWR on this model is ○ deficient ○ excessive ○ cautionary ○ good ◉ excellent *
Total highway safety penalties are: 2 *   Value: 8 5   Durability: 7 8   Highway Control Rating: 4 5   Highway Safety: 4 3

Brand	Year	Type	Length	Model	Chassis	Engine	Fuel Type	Price	Wheelbase	Towing	GVWR	Curb Weight
Kountry Star	1994	MHA	33	32CBD-sl	FO	7.5L	G	$2600	200	8,000	17,000	15,497

Livability Code: SB 30-90
Wheelbase-to-length ratio of 51% is considered ○ dangerous ◉ fatiguing ○ good ○ excellent *
The approximate net payload of 1503 pounds at 9% of GVWR on this model is ○ deficient ○ excessive ◉ cautionary ○ good ○ excellent *
Total highway safety penalties are: 5 *   Value: 8 4   Durability: 7 8   Highway Control Rating: 3 1   Highway Safety: 2 6

Brand	Year	Type	Length	Model	Chassis	Engine	Fuel Type	Price	Wheelbase	Towing	GVWR	Curb Weight
Kountry Star	1994	MHA	35	34CBD-sl	CH	7.4L	G	$2600	202 T	1,500	18,500	16,402

Livability Code: SB 30-90
Wheelbase-to-length ratio of 49% is considered ◉ dangerous ○ fatiguing ○ good ○ excellent *
The approximate net payload of 2098 pounds at 11% of GVWR on this model is ○ deficient ○ excessive ○ cautionary ◉ good ○ excellent *
Total highway safety penalties are: 12 *   Value: 8 0   Durability: 7 8   Highway Control Rating: 3 0   Highway Safety: 1 8

Brand	Year	Type	Length	Model	Chassis	Engine	Fuel Type	Price	Wheelbase	Towing	GVWR	Curb Weight
Kountry Star	1994	MHA	35	34CBDS-sl	CH	7.4L	G	$2600	202 T	1,500	18,500	16,417

Livability Code: SB 30-90
Wheelbase-to-length ratio of 49% is considered ◉ dangerous ○ fatiguing ○ good ○ excellent *
The approximate net payload of 2083 pounds at 11% of GVWR on this model is ○ deficient ○ excessive ○ cautionary ◉ good ○ excellent *
Total highway safety penalties are: 12 *   Value: 8 0   Durability: 7 8   Highway Control Rating: 3 0   Highway Safety: 1 8

Brand	Year	Type	Length	Model	Chassis	Engine	Fuel Type	Price	Wheelbase	Towing	GVWR	Curb Weight
Kountry Star	1994	MHA	35	34WCB	CH	7.4L	G	$2500	202 T	1,500	18,500	15,452

Livability Code: SB 30-90
Wheelbase-to-length ratio of 49% is considered ◉ dangerous ○ fatiguing ○ good ○ excellent *
The approximate net payload of 3048 pounds at 16% of GVWR on this model is ○ deficient ○ excessive ○ cautionary ○ good ◉ excellent *
Total highway safety penalties are: 9 *   Value: 8 2   Durability: 7 8   Highway Control Rating: 4 0   Highway Safety: 3 1

Brand	Year	Type	Length	Model	Chassis	Engine	Fuel Type	Price	Wheelbase	Towing	GVWR	Curb Weight
Kountry Star	1994	MHA	35	34WCBS-sl	CH	7.4L	G	$2600	202 T	1,500	18,500	16,417

Livability Code: SB 30-90
Wheelbase-to-length ratio of 49% is considered ◉ dangerous ○ fatiguing ○ good ○ excellent *
The approximate net payload of 2083 pounds at 11% of GVWR on this model is ○ deficient ○ excessive ○ cautionary ◉ good ○ excellent *
Total highway safety penalties are: 12 *   Value: 8 0   Durability: 7 8   Highway Control Rating: 3 0   Highway Safety: 1 8

Brand	Year	Type	Length	Model	Chassis	Engine	Fuel Type	Price	Wheelbase	Towing	GVWR	Curb Weight
Kountry Star	1994	MHA	35	34CBD-sl	FO	7.5L	G	$2600	202 T	5,500	19,500	16,840

Livability Code: SB 30-90
Wheelbase-to-length ratio of 49% is considered ◉ dangerous ○ fatiguing ○ good ○ excellent *
The approximate net payload of 2660 pounds at 14% of GVWR on this model is ○ deficient ○ excessive ○ cautionary ◉ good ○ excellent *
Total highway safety penalties are: 7 *   Value: 8 3   Durability: 7 8   Highway Control Rating: 3 5   Highway Safety: 2 8

Brand	Year	Type	Length	Model	Chassis	Engine	Fuel Type	Price	Wheelbase	Towing	GVWR	Curb Weight
Kountry Star	1994	MHA	35	34CBDS-sl	FO	7.5L	G	$2600	202 T	5,500	19,500	16,852

Livability Code: SB 30-90
Wheelbase-to-length ratio of 49% is considered ◉ dangerous ○ fatiguing ○ good ○ excellent *
The approximate net payload of 2648 pounds at 14% of GVWR on this model is ○ deficient ○ excessive ○ cautionary ◉ good ○ excellent *
Total highway safety penalties are: 7 *   Value: 8 3   Durability: 7 8   Highway Control Rating: 3 5   Highway Safety: 2 8

Note: Safety ratings are based on the assumption that the engineering of the RV has allowed for proper balance by placing fresh, gray, and black holding tanks in a location so as not to change the balance of the RV when the tanks are empty or full. **Always double-check wheelbase, GVWR, and weights at front and rear axles.**

*See Section 1 for details on how conclusions are reached.

Brand	Year	Type	Length	Model	Chassis	Engine	Fuel Type	Average Price per Linear Foot When New	Adjusted Wheel-base	Approx. Towing Capacity	Gross Vehicle Weight Rating	Average Curb Weight
Kountry Star	1994	MHA	35	34WCBS-sl	FO	7.5L	G	$2600	202 T	5,500	19,500	16,852

Livability Code: SB 30-90

Wheelbase-to-length ratio of 49% is considered ◉ dangerous ○ fatiguing ○ good ○ excellent *

The approximate net payload of 2648 pounds at 14% of GVWR on this model is ○ deficient ○ excessive ○ cautionary ◉ good ○ excellent *

Total highway safety penalties are: 7 *   Value: **8 3**   Durability: **7 8**   Highway Control Rating: **3 5**   Highway Safety: **2 8**

| **Kountry Star** | 1994 | MHA | 35 | 34WCB | FO | 7.5L | G | $2500 | 202 T | 5,500 | 19,500 | 15,890 |

Livability Code: SB 30-90

Wheelbase-to-length ratio of 49% is considered ◉ dangerous ○ fatiguing ○ good ○ excellent *

The approximate net payload of 3610 pounds at 19% of GVWR on this model is ○ deficient ○ excessive ○ cautionary ○ good ◉ excellent *

Total highway safety penalties are: 4 *   Value: **8 4**   Durability: **7 8**   Highway Control Rating: **4 2**   Highway Safety: **3 8**

| **Kountry Star** | 1994 | MHA | 35 | 34CB-SL | SP | CU250 | D | $3300 | 212 | 5,000 | 26,000 | 20,671 |

Livability Code: SB 30-90

Wheelbase-to-length ratio of 51% is considered ○ dangerous ◉ fatiguing ○ good ○ excellent *

The approximate net payload of 5329 pounds at 20% of GVWR on this model is ○ deficient ○ excessive ○ cautionary ○ good ◉ excellent *

Total highway safety penalties are: 5 *   Value: **8 4**   Durability: **7 8**   Highway Control Rating: **5 1**   Highway Safety: **4 6**

| **Kountry Star** | 1994 | MHA | 38 | 37CBSA-sl | FO | 7.5L | G | $2400 | 224 T | 5,500 | 19,500 | 17,551 |

Livability Code: SB 30-90

Wheelbase-to-length ratio of 49% is considered ◉ dangerous ○ fatiguing ○ good ○ excellent *

The approximate net payload of 1949 pounds at 10% of GVWR on this model is ○ deficient ○ excessive ○ cautionary ◉ good ○ excellent *

Total highway safety penalties are: 7 *   Value: **8 3**   Durability: **7 8**   Highway Control Rating: **3 0**   Highway Safety: **2 3**

| **Kountry Star** | 1994 | MHA | 38 | 37WDSK-sl | FO | 7.5L | G | $2400 | 224 T | 5,500 | 19,500 | 17,694 |

Livability Code: SB 30-90

Wheelbase-to-length ratio of 49% is considered ◉ dangerous ○ fatiguing ○ good ○ excellent *

The approximate net payload of 1806 pounds at 9% of GVWR on this model is ○ deficient ○ excessive ◉ cautionary ○ good ○ excellent *

Total highway safety penalties are: 7 *   Value: **8 3**   Durability: **7 8**   Highway Control Rating: **2 5**   Highway Safety: **1 8**

| **Kountry Star** | 1994 | MHA | 38 | 38WDSK-sl | SP | CU250 | D | $3100 | 252 | 5,000 | 26,000 | 21,977 |

Livability Code: SB 30-90

Wheelbase-to-length ratio of 55% is considered ○ dangerous ○ fatiguing ◉ good ○ excellent *

The approximate net payload of 4023 pounds at 15% of GVWR on this model is ○ deficient ○ excessive ○ cautionary ◉ good ○ excellent *

Total highway safety penalties are: 5 *   Value: **8 4**   Durability: **7 8**   Highway Control Rating: **9 2**   Highway Safety: **8 7**   ★★★

| **Kountry Star** | 1994 | MHA | 38 | 38WDSL-sl | SP | CU250 | D | $3100 | 252 | 5,000 | 26,000 | 22,137 |

Livability Code: SB 30-90

Wheelbase-to-length ratio of 55% is considered ○ dangerous ○ fatiguing ◉ good ○ excellent *

The approximate net payload of 3863 pounds at 15% of GVWR on this model is ○ deficient ○ excessive ○ cautionary ◉ good ○ excellent *

Total highway safety penalties are: 6 *   Value: **8 3**   Durability: **7 8**   Highway Control Rating: **9 1**   Highway Safety: **8 5**   ★★★

| **Kountry Star** | 1994 | MHA | 38 | 38 CBSA-sl | SP | CU250 | D | $3100 | 252 | 5,000 | 26,000 | 21,907 |

Livability Code: SB 30-90

Wheelbase-to-length ratio of 55% is considered ○ dangerous ○ fatiguing ◉ good ○ excellent *

The approximate net payload of 4093 pounds at 16% of GVWR on this model is ○ deficient ○ excessive ○ cautionary ○ good ◉ excellent *

Total highway safety penalties are: 6 *   Value: **8 3**   Durability: **7 8**   Highway Control Rating: **9 3**   Highway Safety: **8 7**   ★★★

| **Kountry Star** | 1994 | MHA | 40 | 40CBSA-sl | SP | CU250 | D | $2900 | 276 | 5,000 | 26,000 | 22,440 |

Livability Code: SB 30-90

Wheelbase-to-length ratio of 58% is considered ○ dangerous ○ fatiguing ○ good ◉ excellent *

The approximate net payload of 3561 pounds at 14% of GVWR on this model is ○ deficient ○ excessive ○ cautionary ◉ good ○ excellent *

Total highway safety penalties are: 6 *   Value: **8 3**   Durability: **7 8**   Highway Control Rating: **9 7**   Highway Safety: **9 1**   ★★★

| **Kountry Star** | 1994 | MHA | 40 | 40WDSK-sl | SP | CU250 | D | $2900 | 276 | 5,000 | 26,000 | 22,590 |

Livability Code: SB 30-90

Wheelbase-to-length ratio of 58% is considered ○ dangerous ○ fatiguing ○ good ◉ excellent *

The approximate net payload of 3411 pounds at 13% of GVWR on this model is ○ deficient ○ excessive ○ cautionary ◉ good ○ excellent *

Total highway safety penalties are: 6 *   Value: **8 3**   Durability: **7 8**   Highway Control Rating: **9 6**   Highway Safety: **9 0**   ★★★

| **Kountry Star** | 1995 | MHA | 33 | SA 3200 | FO | 7.5L | G | $2500 | 200 | 8,000 | 17,000 | 14,964 |

Livability Code: SB 30-90

Wheelbase-to-length ratio of 51% is considered ○ dangerous ◉ fatiguing ○ good ○ excellent *

The approximate net payload of 2036 pounds at 12% of GVWR on this model is ○ deficient ○ excessive ○ cautionary ◉ good ○ excellent *

Total highway safety penalties are: 2 *   Value: **8 5**   Durability: **7 8**   Highway Control Rating: **4 0**   Highway Safety: **3 8**

| **Kountry Star** | 1995 | MHA | 35 | SA 3410 | FO | 7.5L | G | $2500 | 202 T | 5,500 | 19,500 | 16,369 |

Livability Code: SB 30-90

Wheelbase-to-length ratio of 49% is considered ◉ dangerous ○ fatiguing ○ good ○ excellent *

The approximate net payload of 3131 pounds at 16% of GVWR on this model is ○ deficient ○ excessive ○ cautionary ○ good ◉ excellent *

Total highway safety penalties are: 4 *   Value: **8 4**   Durability: **7 8**   Highway Control Rating: **3 9**   Highway Safety: **3 5**

Note: Safety ratings are based on the assumption that the engineering of the RV has allowed for proper balance by placing fresh, gray, and black holding tanks in a location so as not to change the balance of the RV when the tanks are empty or full. **Always double-check wheelbase, GVWR, and weights at front and rear axles.**

*See Section 1 for details on how conclusions are reached.

Brand	Year	Type	Length	Model	Chassis	Engine	Fuel Type	Average Price per Linear Foot When New	Adjusted Wheelbase	Approx. Towing Capacity	Gross Vehicle Weight Rating	Average Curb Weight

Kountry Star   1995   MHA   35   SA 3450-sl   FO   7.5L   G $2700   202 T   5,000   20,000   17,119
Livability Code: SB 30-90
Wheelbase-to-length ratio of 49% is considered ◉ dangerous ○ fatiguing ○ good ○ excellent *
The approximate net payload of 2881 pounds at 14% of GVWR on this model is ○ deficient ○ excessive ○ cautionary ◉ good ○ excellent *
Total highway safety penalties are: 7 *   Value: 83   Durability: 78   Highway Control Rating: 36   Highway Safety: 29

Kountry Star   1995   MHA   35   SA 3451-sl   FO   7.5L   G $2700   202 T   5,000   20,000   17,119
Livability Code: SB 30-90
Wheelbase-to-length ratio of 49% is considered ◉ dangerous ○ fatiguing ○ good ○ excellent *
The approximate net payload of 2881 pounds at 14% of GVWR on this model is ○ deficient ○ excessive ○ cautionary ◉ good ○ excellent *
Total highway safety penalties are: 7 *   Value: 83   Durability: 78   Highway Control Rating: 36   Highway Safety: 29

Kountry Star   1995   MHA   35   SA 3455-sl   FO   7.5L   G $2700   202 T   5,000   20,000   17,019
Livability Code: SB 30-90
Wheelbase-to-length ratio of 49% is considered ◉ dangerous ○ fatiguing ○ good ○ excellent *
The approximate net payload of 2981 pounds at 15% of GVWR on this model is ○ deficient ○ excessive ○ cautionary ◉ good ○ excellent *
Total highway safety penalties are: 7 *   Value: 83   Durability: 78   Highway Control Rating: 37   Highway Safety: 30

Kountry Star   1995   MHA   35   SP 3450-sl   SP   CU250   D $3400   212   5,000   26,000   20,998
Livability Code: SB 30-90
Wheelbase-to-length ratio of 51% is considered ○ dangerous ◉ fatiguing ○ good ○ excellent *
The approximate net payload of 5002 pounds at 19% of GVWR on this model is ○ deficient ○ excessive ○ cautionary ○ good ◉ excellent *
Total highway safety penalties are: 5 *   Value: 84   Durability: 78   Highway Control Rating: 51   Highway Safety: 46

Kountry Star   1995   MHA   35   SP 3455-sl   SP   CU250   D $3400   212   5,000   26,000   21,018
Livability Code: SB 30-90
Wheelbase-to-length ratio of 51% is considered ○ dangerous ◉ fatiguing ○ good ○ excellent *
The approximate net payload of 4982 pounds at 19% of GVWR on this model is ○ deficient ○ excessive ○ cautionary ○ good ◉ excellent *
Total highway safety penalties are: 5 *   Value: 84   Durability: 78   Highway Control Rating: 51   Highway Safety: 46

Kountry Star   1995   MHA   38   SA 3710   FO   7.5L   G $2500   224 T   5,500   19,500   17,096
Livability Code: SB 30-90
Wheelbase-to-length ratio of 49% is considered ◉ dangerous ○ fatiguing ○ good ○ excellent *
The approximate net payload of 2404 pounds at 12% of GVWR on this model is ○ deficient ○ excessive ○ cautionary ◉ good ○ excellent *
Total highway safety penalties are: 4 *   Value: 84   Durability: 78   Highway Control Rating: 34   Highway Safety: 30

Kountry Star   1995   MHA   38   SA 3755-sl   FO   7.5L   G $2500   224 T   5,000   20,000   17,876
Livability Code: SB 30-90
Wheelbase-to-length ratio of 49% is considered ◉ dangerous ○ fatiguing ○ good ○ excellent *
The approximate net payload of 2124 pounds at 11% of GVWR on this model is ○ deficient ○ excessive ○ cautionary ◉ good ○ excellent *
Total highway safety penalties are: 7 *   Value: 83   Durability: 78   Highway Control Rating: 31   Highway Safety: 24

Kountry Star   1995   MHA   38   SA 3756-sl   FO   7.5L   G $2500   224 T   5,000   20,000   17,876
Livability Code: SB 30-90
Wheelbase-to-length ratio of 49% is considered ◉ dangerous ○ fatiguing ○ good ○ excellent *
The approximate net payload of 2124 pounds at 11% of GVWR on this model is ○ deficient ○ excessive ○ cautionary ◉ good ○ excellent *
Total highway safety penalties are: 7 *   Value: 83   Durability: 78   Highway Control Rating: 31   Highway Safety: 24

Kountry Star   1995   MHA   38   SA 3760-sl   FO   7.5L   G $2500   224 T   5,000   20,000   17,876
Livability Code: SB 30-90
Wheelbase-to-length ratio of 49% is considered ◉ dangerous ○ fatiguing ○ good ○ excellent *
The approximate net payload of 2124 pounds at 11% of GVWR on this model is ○ deficient ○ excessive ○ cautionary ◉ good ○ excellent *
Total highway safety penalties are: 7 *   Value: 83   Durability: 78   Highway Control Rating: 31   Highway Safety: 24

Kountry Star   1995   MHA   38   SP 3855-sl   SP   CU250   D $3100   252   5,000   26,000   22,205
Livability Code: SB 30-90
Wheelbase-to-length ratio of 55% is considered ○ dangerous ○ fatiguing ◉ good ○ excellent *
The approximate net payload of 3795 pounds at 15% of GVWR on this model is ○ deficient ○ excessive ○ cautionary ◉ good ○ excellent *
Total highway safety penalties are: 5 *   Value: 84   Durability: 78   Highway Control Rating: 91   Highway Safety: 86   ★★★

Kountry Star   1995   MHA   38   SP 3856-sl   SP   CU250   D $3100   252   5,000   26,000   23,390
Livability Code: SB 30-90
Wheelbase-to-length ratio of 55% is considered ○ dangerous ○ fatiguing ◉ good ○ excellent *
The approximate net payload of 2610 pounds at 10% of GVWR on this model is ○ deficient ○ excessive ○ cautionary ◉ good ○ excellent *
Total highway safety penalties are: 5 *   Value: 84   Durability: 78   Highway Control Rating: 88   Highway Safety: 83   ★★★

Kountry Star   1995   MHA   38   SP 3860-sl   SP   CU250   D $3100   252   5,000   26,000   21,975
Livability Code: SB 30-90
Wheelbase-to-length ratio of 55% is considered ○ dangerous ○ fatiguing ◉ good ○ excellent *
The approximate net payload of 4025 pounds at 15% of GVWR on this model is ○ deficient ○ excessive ○ cautionary ◉ good ○ excellent *
Total highway safety penalties are: 5 *   Value: 84   Durability: 78   Highway Control Rating: 92   Highway Safety: 87   ★★★

Note: Safety ratings are based on the assumption that the engineering of the RV has allowed for proper balance by placing fresh, gray, and black holding tanks in a location so as not to change the balance of the RV when the tanks are empty or full. **Always double-check wheelbase, GVWR, and weights at front and rear axles.**

*See Section 1 for details on how conclusions are reached.

Brand	Year	Type	Length	Model	Chassis	Engine	Fuel Type	Average Price per Linear Foot When New	Adjusted Wheelbase	Approx. Towing Capacity	Gross Vehicle Weight Rating	Average Curb Weight

Kountry Star 1995 MHA 38 SP 4010 SP CU250 D $3100 276 1,600 29,400 22,107
Livability Code: SB 30-90
Wheelbase-to-length ratio of 61% is considered ○ dangerous ○ fatiguing ○ good ◉ excellent *
The approximate net payload of 7293 pounds at 25% of GVWR on this model is ○ deficient ○ excessive ○ cautionary ◉ good ○ excellent *
Total highway safety penalties are: 2 *   Value: 85   Durability: 78   Highway Control Rating: 100   Highway Safety: 98   ★★★

Kountry Star 1995 MHA 40 SP 4056-sl SP CU250 D $3000 276 1,600 29,400 24,024
Livability Code: SB 30-90
Wheelbase-to-length ratio of 58% is considered ○ dangerous ○ fatiguing ○ good ◉ excellent *
The approximate net payload of 5376 pounds at 18% of GVWR on this model is ○ deficient ○ excessive ○ cautionary ○ good ◉ excellent *
Total highway safety penalties are: 6 *   Value: 83   Durability: 78   Highway Control Rating: 100   Highway Safety: 94   ★★★

Kountry Star 1996 MHA 33 SA 3255-sl CH 7.4L G $2800 200 3,500 16,500 15,154
Livability Code: SB 30-90
Wheelbase-to-length ratio of 51% is considered ○ dangerous ◉ fatiguing ○ good ○ excellent *
The approximate net payload of 1346 pounds at 8% of GVWR on this model is ○ deficient ○ excessive ◉ cautionary ○ good ○ excellent *
Total highway safety penalties are: 9 *   Value: 82   Durability: 78   Highway Control Rating: 24   Highway Safety: 15

Kountry Star 1996 MHA 33 SA 3255 -sl FO 7.5L G $2800 200 8,000 17,000 15,554
Livability Code: SB 30-90
Wheelbase-to-length ratio of 51% is considered ○ dangerous ◉ fatiguing ○ good ○ excellent *
The approximate net payload of 1446 pounds at 9% of GVWR on this model is ○ deficient ○ excessive ◉ cautionary ○ good ○ excellent *
Total highway safety penalties are: 5 *   Value: 84   Durability: 78   Highway Control Rating: 29   Highway Safety: 24

Kountry Star 1996 MHA 35 SA 3410 CH 7.4L G $2600 202 T 1,500 18,500 15,572
Livability Code: SB 30-90
Wheelbase-to-length ratio of 48% is considered ◉ dangerous ○ fatiguing ○ good ○ excellent *
The approximate net payload of 2928 pounds at 16% of GVWR on this model is ○ deficient ○ excessive ○ cautionary ○ good ◉ excellent *
Total highway safety penalties are: 9 *   Value: 82   Durability: 78   Highway Control Rating: 38   Highway Safety: 29

Kountry Star 1996 MHA 35 SA 3450-sl CH 7.4L G $2800 202 T 1,500 18,500 16,472
Livability Code: SB 30-90
Wheelbase-to-length ratio of 48% is considered ◉ dangerous ○ fatiguing ○ good ○ excellent *
The approximate net payload of 2028 pounds at 11% of GVWR on this model is ○ deficient ○ excessive ○ cautionary ◉ good ○ excellent *
Total highway safety penalties are: 12 *   Value: 80   Durability: 78   Highway Control Rating: 28   Highway Safety: 16

Kountry Star 1996 MHA 35 SA 3451-sl CH 7.4L G $2800 202 T 1,500 18,500 16,472
Livability Code: SB 30-90
Wheelbase-to-length ratio of 48% is considered ◉ dangerous ○ fatiguing ○ good ○ excellent *
The approximate net payload of 2028 pounds at 11% of GVWR on this model is ○ deficient ○ excessive ○ cautionary ◉ good ○ excellent *
Total highway safety penalties are: 12 *   Value: 80   Durability: 78   Highway Control Rating: 28   Highway Safety: 16

Kountry Star 1996 MHA 35 SA 3455-sl CH 7.4L G $2800 202 T 1,500 18,500 16,472
Livability Code: SB 30-90
Wheelbase-to-length ratio of 48% is considered ◉ dangerous ○ fatiguing ○ good ○ excellent *
The approximate net payload of 2028 pounds at 11% of GVWR on this model is ○ deficient ○ excessive ○ cautionary ◉ good ○ excellent *
Total highway safety penalties are: 12 *   Value: 80   Durability: 78   Highway Control Rating: 28   Highway Safety: 16

Kountry Star 1996 MHA 35 SA 3458-sl CH 7.4L G $2800 202 T 1,500 18,500 16,472
Livability Code: SB 30-90
Wheelbase-to-length ratio of 48% is considered ◉ dangerous ○ fatiguing ○ good ○ excellent *
The approximate net payload of 2028 pounds at 11% of GVWR on this model is ○ deficient ○ excessive ○ cautionary ◉ good ○ excellent *
Total highway safety penalties are: 12 *   Value: 80   Durability: 78   Highway Control Rating: 28   Highway Safety: 16

Kountry Star 1996 MHA 35 SA 3410-sl FO 7.5L G $2600 202 T 5,000 20,000 16,972
Livability Code: SB 30-90
Wheelbase-to-length ratio of 48% is considered ◉ dangerous ○ fatiguing ○ good ○ excellent *
The approximate net payload of 3028 pounds at 15% of GVWR on this model is ○ deficient ○ excessive ○ cautionary ◉ good ○ excellent *
Total highway safety penalties are: 7 *   Value: 83   Durability: 78   Highway Control Rating: 36   Highway Safety: 29

Kountry Star 1996 MHA 35 SA 3450-sl FO 7.5L G $2800 202 T 5,000 20,000 16,972
Livability Code: SB 30-90
Wheelbase-to-length ratio of 48% is considered ◉ dangerous ○ fatiguing ○ good ○ excellent *
The approximate net payload of 3028 pounds at 15% of GVWR on this model is ○ deficient ○ excessive ○ cautionary ◉ good ○ excellent *
Total highway safety penalties are: 7 *   Value: 83   Durability: 78   Highway Control Rating: 36   Highway Safety: 29

Kountry Star 1996 MHA 35 SA 3451-sl FO 7.5L G $2800 202 T 5,000 20,000 16,972
Livability Code: SB 30-90
Wheelbase-to-length ratio of 48% is considered ◉ dangerous ○ fatiguing ○ good ○ excellent *
The approximate net payload of 3028 pounds at 15% of GVWR on this model is ○ deficient ○ excessive ○ cautionary ◉ good ○ excellent *
Total highway safety penalties are: 7 *   Value: 83   Durability: 78   Highway Control Rating: 36   Highway Safety: 29

Note: Safety ratings are based on the assumption that the engineering of the RV has allowed for proper balance by placing fresh, gray, and black holding tanks in a location so as not to change the balance of the RV when the tanks are empty or full. **Always double-check wheelbase, GVWR, and weights at front and rear axles.**

*See Section 1 for details on how conclusions are reached.

Brand	Year	Type	Length	Model	Chassis	Engine	Fuel Type	Average Price per Linear Foot When New	Adjusted Wheelbase	Approx. Towing Capacity	Gross Vehicle Weight Rating	Average Curb Weight
Kountry Star	1996	MHA	35	SA 3455-sl	FO	7.5L	G	$2800	202 T	5,000	20,000	16,972

Livability Code: SB 30-90   Wheelbase-to-length ratio of 48% is considered ⦿ dangerous ◯ fatiguing ◯ good ◯ excellent *

The approximate net payload of 3028 pounds at 15% of GVWR on this model is ◯ deficient ◯ excessive ◯ cautionary ⦿ good ◯ excellent *

Total highway safety penalties are: 7 *   Value: 83   Durability: 78   Highway Control Rating: 36   Highway Safety: 29

| Kountry Star | 1996 | MHA | 35 | SA 3458-sl | FO | 7.5L | G | $2800 | 202 T | 5,000 | 20,000 | 16,972 |

Livability Code: SB 30-90   Wheelbase-to-length ratio of 48% is considered ⦿ dangerous ◯ fatiguing ◯ good ◯ excellent *

The approximate net payload of 3028 pounds at 15% of GVWR on this model is ◯ deficient ◯ excessive ◯ cautionary ⦿ good ◯ excellent *

Total highway safety penalties are: 7 *   Value: 83   Durability: 78   Highway Control Rating: 36   Highway Safety: 29

| Kountry Star | 1996 | MHA | 35 | SP 3450-sl | SP | Cu300 | D | $3300 | 212 | 16,000 | 26,000 | 21,250 |

Livability Code: SB 30-90   Wheelbase-to-length ratio of 50% is considered ⦿ dangerous ◯ fatiguing ◯ good ◯ excellent *

The approximate net payload of 4750 pounds at 18% of GVWR on this model is ◯ deficient ◯ excessive ◯ cautionary ◯ good ⦿ excellent *

Total highway safety penalties are: 5 *   Value: 84   Durability: 78   Highway Control Rating: 47   Highway Safety: 42

| Kountry Star | 1996 | MHA | 35 | SP 3455-sl | SP | Cu300 | D | $3300 | 212 | 16,000 | 26,000 | 21,250 |

Livability Code: SB 30-90   Wheelbase-to-length ratio of 50% is considered ⦿ dangerous ◯ fatiguing ◯ good ◯ excellent *

The approximate net payload of 4750 pounds at 18% of GVWR on this model is ◯ deficient ◯ excessive ◯ cautionary ◯ good ⦿ excellent *

Total highway safety penalties are: 5 *   Value: 84   Durability: 78   Highway Control Rating: 47   Highway Safety: 42

| Kountry Star | 1996 | MHA | 38 | SA 3710 | FO | 7.5L | G | $2500 | 224 T | 5,000 | 20,000 | 16,850 |

Livability Code: SB 30-90   Wheelbase-to-length ratio of 49% is considered ⦿ dangerous ◯ fatiguing ◯ good ◯ excellent *

The approximate net payload of 3150 pounds at 16% of GVWR on this model is ◯ deficient ◯ excessive ◯ cautionary ◯ good ⦿ excellent *

Total highway safety penalties are: 4 *   Value: 84   Durability: 78   Highway Control Rating: 41   Highway Safety: 37

| Kountry Star | 1996 | MHA | 38 | SA 3755-sl | FO | 7.5L | G | $2500 | 224 T | 5,000 | 20,000 | 17,750 |

Livability Code: SB 30-90   Wheelbase-to-length ratio of 49% is considered ⦿ dangerous ◯ fatiguing ◯ good ◯ excellent *

The approximate net payload of 2250 pounds at 11% of GVWR on this model is ◯ deficient ◯ excessive ◯ cautionary ⦿ good ◯ excellent *

Total highway safety penalties are: 7 *   Value: 83   Durability: 78   Highway Control Rating: 32   Highway Safety: 25

| Kountry Star | 1996 | MHA | 38 | SA 3756-sl | FO | 7.5L | G | $2500 | 224 T | 5,000 | 20,000 | 17,750 |

Livability Code: SB 30-90   Wheelbase-to-length ratio of 49% is considered ⦿ dangerous ◯ fatiguing ◯ good ◯ excellent *

The approximate net payload of 2250 pounds at 11% of GVWR on this model is ◯ deficient ◯ excessive ◯ cautionary ⦿ good ◯ excellent *

Total highway safety penalties are: 7 *   Value: 83   Durability: 78   Highway Control Rating: 32   Highway Safety: 25

| Kountry Star | 1996 | MHA | 38 | SA 3757-sl | FO | 7.5L | G | $2500 | 224 T | 5,000 | 20,000 | 17,750 |

Livability Code: SB 30-90   Wheelbase-to-length ratio of 49% is considered ⦿ dangerous ◯ fatiguing ◯ good ◯ excellent *

The approximate net payload of 2250 pounds at 11% of GVWR on this model is ◯ deficient ◯ excessive ◯ cautionary ⦿ good ◯ excellent *

Total highway safety penalties are: 7 *   Value: 83   Durability: 78   Highway Control Rating: 32   Highway Safety: 25

| Kountry Star | 1996 | MHA | 38 | SA 3760-sl | FO | 7.5L | G | $2500 | 224 T | 5,000 | 20,000 | 17,750 |

Livability Code: SB 30-90   Wheelbase-to-length ratio of 49% is considered ⦿ dangerous ◯ fatiguing ◯ good ◯ excellent *

The approximate net payload of 2250 pounds at 11% of GVWR on this model is ◯ deficient ◯ excessive ◯ cautionary ⦿ good ◯ excellent *

Total highway safety penalties are: 7 *   Value: 83   Durability: 78   Highway Control Rating: 32   Highway Safety: 25

| Kountry Star | 1996 | MHA | 39 | SP 3855-sl | SP | Cu230 | D | $2900 | 252 | 16,000 | 26,000 | 22,157 |

Livability Code: SB 30-90   Wheelbase-to-length ratio of 54% is considered ◯ dangerous ◯ fatiguing ⦿ good ◯ excellent *

The approximate net payload of 3843 pounds at 15% of GVWR on this model is ◯ deficient ◯ excessive ◯ cautionary ⦿ good ◯ excellent *

Total highway safety penalties are: 5 *   Value: 84   Durability: 78   Highway Control Rating: 80   Highway Safety: 75   ★★★

| Kountry Star | 1996 | MHA | 39 | SP 3856-sl | SP | Cu230 | D | $2900 | 252 | 16,000 | 26,000 | 22,157 |

Livability Code: SB 30-90   Wheelbase-to-length ratio of 54% is considered ◯ dangerous ◯ fatiguing ⦿ good ◯ excellent *

The approximate net payload of 3843 pounds at 15% of GVWR on this model is ◯ deficient ◯ excessive ◯ cautionary ⦿ good ◯ excellent *

Total highway safety penalties are: 5 *   Value: 84   Durability: 78   Highway Control Rating: 80   Highway Safety: 75   ★★★

| Kountry Star | 1996 | MHA | 39 | SP 3857-sl | SP | Cu230 | D | $2900 | 252 | 16,000 | 26,000 | 22,157 |

Livability Code: SB 30-90   Wheelbase-to-length ratio of 54% is considered ◯ dangerous ◯ fatiguing ⦿ good ◯ excellent *

The approximate net payload of 3843 pounds at 15% of GVWR on this model is ◯ deficient ◯ excessive ◯ cautionary ⦿ good ◯ excellent *

Total highway safety penalties are: 5 *   Value: 84   Durability: 78   Highway Control Rating: 80   Highway Safety: 75   ★★★

Note: Safety ratings are based on the assumption that the engineering of the RV has allowed for proper balance by placing fresh, gray, and black holding tanks in a location so as not to change the balance of the RV when the tanks are empty or full. **Always double-check wheelbase, GVWR, and weights at front and rear axles.**

Section 2: The Ratings

Brand	Year	Type	Length	Model	Chassis	Engine	Fuel Type	Average Price per Linear Foot When New	Adjusted Wheelbase	Approx. Towing Capacity	Gross Vehicle Weight Rating	Average Curb Weight
Kountry Star	1996	MHA	39	SP 3860-sl	SP	Cu230	D	$2900	252	16,000	26,000	22,157

Livability Code: SB 30-90
Wheelbase-to-length ratio of 54% is considered ○ dangerous ○ fatiguing ◉ good ○ excellent *
The approximate net payload of 3843 pounds at 15% of GVWR on this model is ○ deficient ○ excessive ○ cautionary ◉ good ○ excellent *
Total highway safety penalties are: 5 *   Value: 8 4   Durability: 7 8   Highway Control Rating: 8 0   Highway Safety: 7 5   ★★★

Brand	Year	Type	Length	Model	Chassis	Engine	Fuel Type		Adjusted Wheelbase	Approx. Towing Capacity	GVWR	Curb Weight
Kountry Star	1996	MHA	41	SP 4010	SP	Cu230	D	$2800	276	12,600	29,400	22,375

Livability Code: SB 30-90
Wheelbase-to-length ratio of 56% is considered ○ dangerous ○ fatiguing ◉ good ○ excellent *
The approximate net payload of 7025 pounds at 24% of GVWR on this model is ○ deficient ○ excessive ○ cautionary ○ good ◉ excellent *
Total highway safety penalties are: 2 *   Value: 8 5   Durability: 7 8   Highway Control Rating: 9 8   Highway Safety: 9 6   ★★★

Kountry Star	1996	MHA	41	SP 4055-sl	SP	Cu230	D	$2800	276	12,600	29,400	23,275

Livability Code: SB 30-90
Wheelbase-to-length ratio of 56% is considered ○ dangerous ○ fatiguing ◉ good ○ excellent *
The approximate net payload of 6125 pounds at 21% of GVWR on this model is ○ deficient ○ excessive ○ cautionary ○ good ◉ excellent *
Total highway safety penalties are: 5 *   Value: 8 4   Durability: 7 8   Highway Control Rating: 1 0 0   Highway Safety: 9 5   ★★★

Kountry Star	1996	MHA	41	SP 4056-sl	SP	Cu230	D	$2800	276	12,600	29,400	23,275

Livability Code: SB 30-90
Wheelbase-to-length ratio of 56% is considered ○ dangerous ○ fatiguing ◉ good ○ excellent *
The approximate net payload of 6125 pounds at 21% of GVWR on this model is ○ deficient ○ excessive ○ cautionary ○ good ◉ excellent *
Total highway safety penalties are: 5 *   Value: 8 4   Durability: 7 8   Highway Control Rating: 1 0 0   Highway Safety: 9 5   ★★★

Kountry Star	1996	MHA	41	SP 4057-sl	SP	Cu230	D	$2800	276	12,600	29,400	23,275

Livability Code: SB 30-90
Wheelbase-to-length ratio of 56% is considered ○ dangerous ○ fatiguing ◉ good ○ excellent *
The approximate net payload of 6125 pounds at 21% of GVWR on this model is ○ deficient ○ excessive ○ cautionary ○ good ◉ excellent *
Total highway safety penalties are: 5 *   Value: 8 4   Durability: 7 8   Highway Control Rating: 1 0 0   Highway Safety: 9 5   ★★★

Kountry Star	1996	MHA	41	SP 4060-sl	SP	Cu230	D	$2800	276	12,600	29,400	23,275

Livability Code: SB 30-90
Wheelbase-to-length ratio of 56% is considered ○ dangerous ○ fatiguing ◉ good ○ excellent *
The approximate net payload of 6125 pounds at 21% of GVWR on this model is ○ deficient ○ excessive ○ cautionary ○ good ◉ excellent *
Total highway safety penalties are: 5 *   Value: 8 4   Durability: 7 8   Highway Control Rating: 1 0 0   Highway Safety: 9 5   ★★★

Kountry Star	1997	MHA	30	SA2959	CH	7.4L	G	$3100	178	4,500	16,500	14,971

Livability Code: SB 30-90
Wheelbase-to-length ratio of 50% is considered ◉ dangerous ○ fatiguing ○ good ○ excellent *
The approximate net payload of 1529 pounds at 9% of GVWR on this model is ○ deficient ○ excessive ◉ cautionary ○ good ○ excellent *
Total highway safety penalties are: 7 *   Value: 8 3   Durability: 7 8   Highway Control Rating: 2 8   Highway Safety: 2 1

Kountry Star	1997	MHA	30	SA2959	FO	7.5L	G	$3100	178	8,000	17,000	15,371

Livability Code: SB 30-90
Wheelbase-to-length ratio of 50% is considered ◉ dangerous ○ fatiguing ○ good ○ excellent *
The approximate net payload of 1629 pounds at 10% of GVWR on this model is ○ deficient ○ excessive ○ cautionary ◉ good ○ excellent *
Total highway safety penalties are: 5 *   Value: 8 4   Durability: 7 8   Highway Control Rating: 3 3   Highway Safety: 2 8

Kountry Star	1997	MHA	30	SA2959 fr.dsl	FR	CU210	D	$3800	178	5,000	20,500	16,471

Livability Code: SB 30-90
Wheelbase-to-length ratio of 50% is considered ◉ dangerous ○ fatiguing ○ good ○ excellent *
The approximate net payload of 4029 pounds at 20% of GVWR on this model is ○ deficient ○ excessive ○ cautionary ○ good ◉ excellent *
Total highway safety penalties are: 5 *   Value: 8 4   Durability: 7 8   Highway Control Rating: 4 9   Highway Safety: 4 4

Kountry Star	1997	MHA	34	SA3356 fr.dsl	FR	CU210	D	$3400	200	5,000	20,500	17,602

Livability Code: SB 30-90
Wheelbase-to-length ratio of 50% is considered ◉ dangerous ○ fatiguing ○ good ○ excellent *
The approximate net payload of 2898 pounds at 14% of GVWR on this model is ○ deficient ○ excessive ○ cautionary ○ good ◉ excellent *
Total highway safety penalties are: 5 *   Value: 8 4   Durability: 7 8   Highway Control Rating: 3 9   Highway Safety: 3 4

Kountry Star	1997	MHA	35	SA3410	CH	7.4L	G	$2700	214 T	2,000	19,000	16,285

Livability Code: SB 30-90
Wheelbase-to-length ratio of 52% is considered ○ dangerous ◉ fatiguing ○ good ○ excellent *
The approximate net payload of 2715 pounds at 14% of GVWR on this model is ○ deficient ○ excessive ○ cautionary ◉ good ○ excellent *
Total highway safety penalties are: 9 *   Value: 8 2   Durability: 7 8   Highway Control Rating: 5 4   Highway Safety: 4 5

Kountry Star	1997	MHA	35	SA3411	CH	7.4L	G	$2700	214 T	2,000	19,000	16,285

Livability Code: SB 30-90
Wheelbase-to-length ratio of 52% is considered ○ dangerous ◉ fatiguing ○ good ○ excellent *
The approximate net payload of 2715 pounds at 14% of GVWR on this model is ○ deficient ○ excessive ○ cautionary ◉ good ○ excellent *
Total highway safety penalties are: 9 *   Value: 8 2   Durability: 7 8   Highway Control Rating: 5 4   Highway Safety: 4 5

Note: Safety ratings are based on the assumption that the engineering of the RV has allowed for proper balance by placing fresh, gray, and black holding tanks in a location so as not to change the balance of the RV when the tanks are empty or full. **Always double-check wheelbase, GVWR, and weights at front and rear axles.**

*See Section 1 for details on how conclusions are reached.

Brand	Year	Type	Length	Model	Chassis	Engine	Fuel Type	Average Price per Linear Foot When New	Adjusted Wheelbase	Approx. Towing Capacity	Gross Vehicle Weight Rating	Average Curb Weight
Kountry Star	1997	MHA	35	SA3450	CH	7.4L	G	$2700	214 T	2,000	19,000	17,185

Livability Code: SB 30-90
Wheelbase-to-length ratio of 52% is considered ○ dangerous ● fatiguing ○ good ○ excellent *
The approximate net payload of 1815 pounds at 10% of GVWR on this model is ○ deficient ○ excessive ○ cautionary ● good ○ excellent *
Total highway safety penalties are: 12 *   Value: 8 0   Durability: 7 8   Highway Control Rating: 4 5   Highway Safety: 3 3

Brand	Year	Type	Length	Model	Chassis	Engine	Fuel Type		Adjusted Wheelbase	Approx. Towing Capacity	Gross Vehicle Weight Rating	Average Curb Weight
Kountry Star	1997	MHA	35	SA3481	CH	7.4L	G	$2700	214 T	2,000	19,000	17,185

Livability Code: SB 30-90
Wheelbase-to-length ratio of 52% is considered ○ dangerous ● fatiguing ○ good ○ excellent *
The approximate net payload of 1815 pounds at 10% of GVWR on this model is ○ deficient ○ excessive ○ cautionary ● good ○ excellent *
Total highway safety penalties are: 12 *   Value: 8 0   Durability: 7 8   Highway Control Rating: 4 5   Highway Safety: 3 3

Kountry Star	1997	MHA	35	SA3410	FO	7.5L	G	$2700	214 T	5,000	20,000	16,785

Livability Code: SB 30-90
Wheelbase-to-length ratio of 52% is considered ○ dangerous ● fatiguing ○ good ○ excellent *
The approximate net payload of 3215 pounds at 16% of GVWR on this model is ○ deficient ○ excessive ○ cautionary ○ good ● excellent *
Total highway safety penalties are: 4 *   Value: 8 4   Durability: 7 8   Highway Control Rating: 5 8   Highway Safety: 5 4   ★

Kountry Star	1997	MHA	35	SA3411	FO	7.5L	G	$2700	214 T	5,000	20,000	16,785

Livability Code: SB 30-90
Wheelbase-to-length ratio of 52% is considered ○ dangerous ● fatiguing ○ good ○ excellent *
The approximate net payload of 3215 pounds at 16% of GVWR on this model is ○ deficient ○ excessive ○ cautionary ○ good ● excellent *
Total highway safety penalties are: 4 *   Value: 8 4   Durability: 7 8   Highway Control Rating: 5 8   Highway Safety: 5 4   ★

Kountry Star	1997	MHA	35	SA3450	FO	7.5L	G	$2700	214 T	5,000	20,000	17,685

Livability Code: SB 30-90
Wheelbase-to-length ratio of 52% is considered ○ dangerous ● fatiguing ○ good ○ excellent *
The approximate net payload of 2315 pounds at 12% of GVWR on this model is ○ deficient ○ excessive ○ cautionary ● good ○ excellent *
Total highway safety penalties are: 7 *   Value: 8 3   Durability: 7 8   Highway Control Rating: 4 9   Highway Safety: 4 2

Kountry Star	1997	MHA	35	SA3481	FO	7.5L	G	$2700	214 T	5,000	20,000	17,685

Livability Code: SB 30-90
Wheelbase-to-length ratio of 52% is considered ○ dangerous ● fatiguing ○ good ○ excellent *
The approximate net payload of 2315 pounds at 12% of GVWR on this model is ○ deficient ○ excessive ○ cautionary ● good ○ excellent *
Total highway safety penalties are: 7 *   Value: 8 3   Durability: 7 8   Highway Control Rating: 4 9   Highway Safety: 4 2

Kountry Star	1997	MHA	35	SA3410 fr.dsl	FR	CU210	D	$3300	216	5,000	20,500	16,985

Livability Code: SB 30-90
Wheelbase-to-length ratio of 52% is considered ○ dangerous ● fatiguing ○ good ○ excellent *
The approximate net payload of 3515 pounds at 17% of GVWR on this model is ○ deficient ○ excessive ○ cautionary ○ good ● excellent *
Total highway safety penalties are: 2 *   Value: 8 5   Durability: 7 8   Highway Control Rating: 6 1   Highway Safety: 5 9   ★

Kountry Star	1997	MHA	35	SA3411 fr.dsl	FR	CU210	D	$3300	216	5,000	20,500	16,985

Livability Code: SB 30-90
Wheelbase-to-length ratio of 52% is considered ○ dangerous ● fatiguing ○ good ○ excellent *
The approximate net payload of 3515 pounds at 17% of GVWR on this model is ○ deficient ○ excessive ○ cautionary ○ good ● excellent *
Total highway safety penalties are: 2 *   Value: 8 5   Durability: 7 8   Highway Control Rating: 6 1   Highway Safety: 5 9   ★

Kountry Star	1997	MHA	35	SA3450 fr.dsl	FR	CU210	D	$3300	216	5,000	20,500	17,885

Livability Code: SB 30-90
Wheelbase-to-length ratio of 52% is considered ○ dangerous ● fatiguing ○ good ○ excellent *
The approximate net payload of 2615 pounds at 13% of GVWR on this model is ○ deficient ○ excessive ○ cautionary ● good ○ excellent *
Total highway safety penalties are: 5 *   Value: 8 4   Durability: 7 8   Highway Control Rating: 5 3   Highway Safety: 4 8

Kountry Star	1997	MHA	35	SA3481 fr.dsl	FR	CU210	D	$3300	216	5,000	20,500	17,885

Livability Code: SB 30-90
Wheelbase-to-length ratio of 52% is considered ○ dangerous ● fatiguing ○ good ○ excellent *
The approximate net payload of 2615 pounds at 13% of GVWR on this model is ○ deficient ○ excessive ○ cautionary ● good ○ excellent *
Total highway safety penalties are: 5 *   Value: 8 4   Durability: 7 8   Highway Control Rating: 5 3   Highway Safety: 4 8

Kountry Star	1997	MHA	36	SA3558	CH	7.4L	G	$2700	214 T	2,000	19,000	17,468

Livability Code: SB 30-90
Wheelbase-to-length ratio of 50% is considered ● dangerous ○ fatiguing ○ good ○ excellent *
The approximate net payload of 1532 pounds at 8% of GVWR on this model is ○ deficient ○ excessive ● cautionary ○ good ○ excellent *
Total highway safety penalties are: 13 *   Value: 8 0   Durability: 7 8   Highway Control Rating: 2 2   Highway Safety: 9

Kountry Star	1997	MHA	36	SA3558	FO	7.5L	G	$2700	214 T	5,000	20,000	17,968

Livability Code: SB 30-90
Wheelbase-to-length ratio of 50% is considered ● dangerous ○ fatiguing ○ good ○ excellent *
The approximate net payload of 2032 pounds at 10% of GVWR on this model is ○ deficient ○ excessive ○ cautionary ● good ○ excellent *
Total highway safety penalties are: 7 *   Value: 8 3   Durability: 7 8   Highway Control Rating: 3 3   Highway Safety: 2 6

Note: Safety ratings are based on the assumption that the engineering of the RV has allowed for proper balance by placing fresh, gray, and black holding tanks in a location so as not to change the balance of the RV when the tanks are empty or full. **Always double-check wheelbase, GVWR, and weights at front and rear axles.**

*See Section 1 for details on how conclusions are reached.

Brand	Year	Type	Length	Model	Chassis	Engine	Fuel Type	Average Price per Linear Foot When New	Adjusted Wheelbase	Approx. Towing Capacity	Gross Vehicle Weight Rating	Average Curb Weight
Kountry Star	1997	MHA	36	SA3558 fr.dsl	FR	CU210	D	$3200	216	5,000	20,500	18,168

Livability Code: SB 30-90

Wheelbase-to-length ratio of 51% is considered ○ dangerous ● fatiguing ○ good ○ excellent*

The approximate net payload of 2332 pounds at 11% of GVWR on this model is ○ deficient ○ excessive ○ cautionary ● good ○ excellent*

Total highway safety penalties are: 5*   Value: 8 4   Durability: 7 8   Highway Control Rating: 3 7   Highway Safety: 3 2

Brand	Year	Type	Length	Model	Chassis	Engine	Fuel Type	Avg Price/Linear Foot	Adj Wheelbase	Approx. Towing	GVWR	Avg Curb Weight
Kountry Star	1997	MHA	38	SA3710	FO	7.5L	G	$2600	236 T	5,000	20,000	17,662

Livability Code: SB 30-90

Wheelbase-to-length ratio of 52% is considered ○ dangerous ● fatiguing ○ good ○ excellent*

The approximate net payload of 2338 pounds at 12% of GVWR on this model is ○ deficient ○ excessive ○ cautionary ● good ○ excellent*

Total highway safety penalties are: 4*   Value: 8 4   Durability: 7 8   Highway Control Rating: 5 2   Highway Safety: 4 8

Kountry Star	1997	MHA	38	SA3757	FO	7.5L	G	$2600	236 T	5,000	20,000	18,562

Livability Code: SB 30-90

Wheelbase-to-length ratio of 52% is considered ○ dangerous ● fatiguing ○ good ○ excellent*

The approximate net payload of 1438 pounds at 7% of GVWR on this model is ○ deficient ○ excessive ● cautionary ○ good ○ excellent*

Total highway safety penalties are: 7*   Value: 8 3   Durability: 7 8   Highway Control Rating: 3 1   Highway Safety: 2 4

Kountry Star	1997	MHA	38	SA3758	FO	7.5L	G	$2600	236 T	5,000	20,000	18,562

Livability Code: SB 30-90

Wheelbase-to-length ratio of 52% is considered ○ dangerous ● fatiguing ○ good ○ excellent*

The approximate net payload of 1438 pounds at 7% of GVWR on this model is ○ deficient ○ excessive ● cautionary ○ good ○ excellent*

Total highway safety penalties are: 7*   Value: 8 3   Durability: 7 8   Highway Control Rating: 3 1   Highway Safety: 2 4

Kountry Star	1997	MHA	38	SA3760	FO	7.5L	G	$2600	236 T	5,000	20,000	18,562

Livability Code: SB 30-90

Wheelbase-to-length ratio of 52% is considered ○ dangerous ● fatiguing ○ good ○ excellent*

The approximate net payload of 1438 pounds at 7% of GVWR on this model is ○ deficient ○ excessive ● cautionary ○ good ○ excellent*

Total highway safety penalties are: 7*   Value: 8 3   Durability: 7 8   Highway Control Rating: 3 1   Highway Safety: 2 4

Kountry Star	1997	MHA	38	SA3780	FO	7.5L	G	$2600	236 T	5,000	20,000	18,562

Livability Code: SB 30-90

Wheelbase-to-length ratio of 52% is considered ○ dangerous ● fatiguing ○ good ○ excellent*

The approximate net payload of 1438 pounds at 7% of GVWR on this model is ○ deficient ○ excessive ● cautionary ○ good ○ excellent*

Total highway safety penalties are: 7*   Value: 8 3   Durability: 7 8   Highway Control Rating: 3 1   Highway Safety: 2 4

Kountry Star	1997	MHA	38	SA3710 fr.dsl	FR	CU210	D	$3000	228	5,000	20,500	17,862

Livability Code: SB 30-90

Wheelbase-to-length ratio of 50% is considered ● dangerous ○ fatiguing ○ good ○ excellent*

The approximate net payload of 2638 pounds at 13% of GVWR on this model is ○ deficient ○ excessive ○ cautionary ● good ○ excellent*

Total highway safety penalties are: 2*   Value: 8 5   Durability: 7 8   Highway Control Rating: 4 0   Highway Safety: 3 8

Kountry Star	1997	MHA	38	SA3757 fr.dsl	FR	CU210	D	$3000	228	5,000	20,500	18,762

Livability Code: SB 30-90

Wheelbase-to-length ratio of 50% is considered ● dangerous ○ fatiguing ○ good ○ excellent*

The approximate net payload of 1738 pounds at 8% of GVWR on this model is ○ deficient ○ excessive ● cautionary ○ good ○ excellent*

Total highway safety penalties are: 5*   Value: 8 4   Durability: 7 8   Highway Control Rating: 2 4   Highway Safety: 1 9

Kountry Star	1997	MHA	38	SA3758 fr.dsl	FR	CU210	D	$3000	228	5,000	20,500	18,762

Livability Code: SB 30-90

Wheelbase-to-length ratio of 50% is considered ● dangerous ○ fatiguing ○ good ○ excellent*

The approximate net payload of 1738 pounds at 8% of GVWR on this model is ○ deficient ○ excessive ● cautionary ○ good ○ excellent*

Total highway safety penalties are: 5*   Value: 8 4   Durability: 7 8   Highway Control Rating: 2 4   Highway Safety: 1 9

Kountry Star	1997	MHA	38	SA3760 fr.dsl	FR	CU210	D	$3000	228	5,000	20,500	18,762

Livability Code: SB 30-90

Wheelbase-to-length ratio of 50% is considered ● dangerous ○ fatiguing ○ good ○ excellent*

The approximate net payload of 1738 pounds at 8% of GVWR on this model is ○ deficient ○ excessive ● cautionary ○ good ○ excellent*

Total highway safety penalties are: 5*   Value: 8 4   Durability: 7 8   Highway Control Rating: 2 4   Highway Safety: 1 9

Kountry Star	1997	MHA	38	SA3780 fr.dsl	FR	CU210	D	$3000	228	5,000	20,500	18,762

Livability Code: SB 30-90

Wheelbase-to-length ratio of 50% is considered ● dangerous ○ fatiguing ○ good ○ excellent*

The approximate net payload of 1738 pounds at 8% of GVWR on this model is ○ deficient ○ excessive ● cautionary ○ good ○ excellent*

Total highway safety penalties are: 5*   Value: 8 4   Durability: 7 8   Highway Control Rating: 2 4   Highway Safety: 1 9

Kountry Star	1998	MHA	28	SA2707	FO	7.5L	G	$3500	170	8,000	17,000	13,905

Livability Code: SB 30-90

Wheelbase-to-length ratio of 51% is considered ○ dangerous ● fatiguing ○ good ○ excellent*

The approximate net payload of 3095 pounds at 18% of GVWR on this model is ○ deficient ○ excessive ○ cautionary ○ good ● excellent*

Total highway safety penalties are: 2*   Value: 8 5   Durability: 7 8   Highway Control Rating: 5 2   Highway Safety: 5 0   ★

Note: Safety ratings are based on the assumption that the engineering of the RV has allowed for proper balance by placing fresh, gray, and black holding tanks in a location so as not to change the balance of the RV when the tanks are empty or full. **Always double-check wheelbase, GVWR, and weights at front and rear axles.**

*See Section 1 for details on how conclusions are reached.

Brand	Year	Type	Length	Model	Chassis	Engine	Fuel Type	Average Price per Linear Foot When New	Adjusted Wheelbase	Approx. Towing Capacity	Gross Vehicle Weight Rating	Average Curb Weight
Kountry Star	1998	MHA	28	SA2707 opch fr.dsl	FR	210HP	D	$4500	172	5,000	20,500	15,005

Livability Code: SB 30-90 Wheelbase-to-length ratio of 52% is considered ○ dangerous ● fatiguing ○ good ○ excellent*

The approximate net payload of 5495 pounds at 27% of GVWR on this model is ○ deficient ○ excessive ○ cautionary ● good ○ excellent*

Total highway safety penalties are: 2* Value: 85 Durability: 78 Highway Control Rating: 56 Highway Safety: 54 ★

Brand	Year	Type	Length	Model	Chassis	Engine	Fuel Type	Price/Ft	Wheelbase	Towing	GVWR	Curb Weight
Kountry Star	1998	MHA	30	SA2903	FO	7.5L	G	$3300	178	8,000	17,000	14,471

Livability Code: SB 30-90 Wheelbase-to-length ratio of 50% is considered ● dangerous ○ fatiguing ○ good ○ excellent*

The approximate net payload of 2529 pounds at 15% of GVWR on this model is ○ deficient ○ excessive ○ cautionary ● good ○ excellent*

Total highway safety penalties are: 2* Value: 85 Durability: 78 Highway Control Rating: 43 Highway Safety: 41

Kountry Star	1998	MHA	30	SA2959	FO	7.5L	G	$3300	178	8,000	17,000	15,371

Livability Code: SB 30-90 Wheelbase-to-length ratio of 50% is considered ● dangerous ○ fatiguing ○ good ○ excellent*

The approximate net payload of 1629 pounds at 10% of GVWR on this model is ○ deficient ○ excessive ○ cautionary ● good ○ excellent*

Total highway safety penalties are: 5* Value: 84 Durability: 78 Highway Control Rating: 33 Highway Safety: 28

Kountry Star	1998	MHA	30	SA2903 opch	FR	210HP	D	$4200	178	5,000	20,500	15,571

Livability Code: SB 30-90 Wheelbase-to-length ratio of 50% is considered ● dangerous ○ fatiguing ○ good ○ excellent*

The approximate net payload of 4929 pounds at 24% of GVWR on this model is ○ deficient ○ excessive ○ cautionary ○ good ● excellent*

Total highway safety penalties are: 2* Value: 85 Durability: 78 Highway Control Rating: 45 Highway Safety: 43

Kountry Star	1998	MHA	30	SA2959 opch fr.dsl	FR	210HP	D	$4200	178	5,000	20,500	16,471

Livability Code: SB 30-90 Wheelbase-to-length ratio of 50% is considered ● dangerous ○ fatiguing ○ good ○ excellent*

The approximate net payload of 4029 pounds at 20% of GVWR on this model is ○ deficient ○ excessive ○ cautionary ○ good ● excellent*

Total highway safety penalties are: 5* Value: 84 Durability: 78 Highway Control Rating: 49 Highway Safety: 44

Kountry Star	1998	MHA	34	SA3305 fr.dsl	FR	210HP	D	$3700	200	5,000	20,500	16,702

Livability Code: SB 30-90 Wheelbase-to-length ratio of 50% is considered ● dangerous ○ fatiguing ○ good ○ excellent*

The approximate net payload of 3798 pounds at 19% of GVWR on this model is ○ deficient ○ excessive ○ cautionary ○ good ● excellent*

Total highway safety penalties are: 2* Value: 85 Durability: 78 Highway Control Rating: 46 Highway Safety: 44

Kountry Star	1998	MHA	34	SA3356 fr.dsl	FR	210HP	D	$3700	200	5,000	20,500	17,602

Livability Code: SB 30-90 Wheelbase-to-length ratio of 50% is considered ● dangerous ○ fatiguing ○ good ○ excellent*

The approximate net payload of 2898 pounds at 14% of GVWR on this model is ○ deficient ○ excessive ○ cautionary ● good ○ excellent*

Total highway safety penalties are: 5* Value: 84 Durability: 78 Highway Control Rating: 39 Highway Safety: 34

Kountry Star	1998	MHA	35	SA3413	FO	7.5L	G	$2800	214 T	5,000	20,000	16,785

Livability Code: SB 30-90 Wheelbase-to-length ratio of 52% is considered ○ dangerous ● fatiguing ○ good ○ excellent*

The approximate net payload of 3215 pounds at 16% of GVWR on this model is ○ deficient ○ excessive ○ cautionary ○ good ● excellent*

Total highway safety penalties are: 4* Value: 84 Durability: 78 Highway Control Rating: 58 Highway Safety: 54 ★

Kountry Star	1998	MHA	35	SA3451	FO	7.5L	G	$2800	214 T	5,000	20,000	17,685

Livability Code: SB 30-90 Wheelbase-to-length ratio of 52% is considered ○ dangerous ● fatiguing ○ good ○ excellent*

The approximate net payload of 2315 pounds at 12% of GVWR on this model is ○ deficient ○ excessive ○ cautionary ● good ○ excellent*

Total highway safety penalties are: 7* Value: 83 Durability: 78 Highway Control Rating: 49 Highway Safety: 42

Kountry Star	1998	MHA	35	SA3413 opch fr.dsl	FR	210HP	D	$3600	216	5,000	20,500	16,985

Livability Code: SB 30-90 Wheelbase-to-length ratio of 52% is considered ○ dangerous ● fatiguing ○ good ○ excellent*

The approximate net payload of 3515 pounds at 17% of GVWR on this model is ○ deficient ○ excessive ○ cautionary ○ good ● excellent*

Total highway safety penalties are: 2* Value: 85 Durability: 78 Highway Control Rating: 61 Highway Safety: 59 ★

Kountry Star	1998	MHA	35	SA3451 opch fr.dsl	FR	210HP	D	$3600	216	5,000	20,500	17,885

Livability Code: SB 30-90 Wheelbase-to-length ratio of 52% is considered ○ dangerous ● fatiguing ○ good ○ excellent*

The approximate net payload of 2615 pounds at 13% of GVWR on this model is ○ deficient ○ excessive ○ cautionary ● good ○ excellent*

Total highway safety penalties are: 5* Value: 84 Durability: 78 Highway Control Rating: 53 Highway Safety: 48

Kountry Star	1998	MHA	36	SA3535	FO	7.5L	G	$2800	214 T	5,000	20,000	17,068

Livability Code: SB 30-90 Wheelbase-to-length ratio of 50% is considered ● dangerous ○ fatiguing ○ good ○ excellent*

The approximate net payload of 2932 pounds at 15% of GVWR on this model is ○ deficient ○ excessive ○ cautionary ● good ○ excellent*

Total highway safety penalties are: 4* Value: 84 Durability: 78 Highway Control Rating: 43 Highway Safety: 39

Note: Safety ratings are based on the assumption that the engineering of the RV has allowed for proper balance by placing fresh, gray, and black holding tanks in a location so as not to change the balance of the RV when the tanks are empty or full. **Always double-check wheelbase, GVWR, and weights at front and rear axles.**

*See Section 1 for details on how conclusions are reached.

Brand	Year	Type	Length	Model	Chassis	Engine	Fuel Type	Average Price per Linear Foot When New	Adjusted Wheelbase	Approx. Towing Capacity	Gross Vehicle Weight Rating	Average Curb Weight
Kountry Star	1998	MHA	36	SA3558	FO	7.5L	G	$2800	214 T	5,000	20,000	17,968

Livability Code: SB 30-90
Wheelbase-to-length ratio of 50% is considered ● dangerous ○ fatiguing ○ good ○ excellent *
The approximate net payload of 2032 pounds at 10% of GVWR on this model is ○ deficient ○ excessive ○ cautionary ● good ○ excellent *
Total highway safety penalties are: 7 *   Value: 8 3   Durability: 7 8   Highway Control Rating: 3 3   Highway Safety: 2 6

Brand	Year	Type	Length	Model	Chassis	Engine	Fuel Type	Average Price per Linear Foot When New	Adjusted Wheelbase	Approx. Towing Capacity	Gross Vehicle Weight Rating	Average Curb Weight
Kountry Star	1998	MHA	36	SA3535 opch fr.dsl	FR	210HP	D	$3500	216	5,000	20,500	17,268

Livability Code: SB 30-90
Wheelbase-to-length ratio of 51% is considered ○ dangerous ● fatiguing ○ good ○ excellent *
The approximate net payload of 3232 pounds at 16% of GVWR on this model is ○ deficient ○ excessive ○ cautionary ○ good ● excellent *
Total highway safety penalties are: 2 *   Value: 8 5   Durability: 7 8   Highway Control Rating: 4 6   Highway Safety: 4 4

Brand	Year	Type	Length	Model	Chassis	Engine	Fuel Type	Average Price per Linear Foot When New	Adjusted Wheelbase	Approx. Towing Capacity	Gross Vehicle Weight Rating	Average Curb Weight
Kountry Star	1998	MHA	36	SA3558 opch fr.dsl	FR	210HP	D	$3500	228	5,000	20,500	18,168

Livability Code: SB 30-90
Wheelbase-to-length ratio of 53% is considered ○ dangerous ● fatiguing ○ good ○ excellent *
The approximate net payload of 2332 pounds at 11% of GVWR on this model is ○ deficient ○ excessive ○ cautionary ● good ○ excellent *
Total highway safety penalties are: 5 *   Value: 8 4   Durability: 7 8   Highway Control Rating: 6 2   Highway Safety: 5 7   ★

Brand	Year	Type	Length	Model	Chassis	Engine	Fuel Type	Average Price per Linear Foot When New	Adjusted Wheelbase	Approx. Towing Capacity	Gross Vehicle Weight Rating	Average Curb Weight
Kountry Star	1998	MHA	38	SA3758	FO	7.5L	G	$2600	236 T	5,000	20,000	18,562

Livability Code: SB 30-90
Wheelbase-to-length ratio of 52% is considered ○ dangerous ● fatiguing ○ good ○ excellent *
The approximate net payload of 1438 pounds at 7% of GVWR on this model is ○ deficient ○ excessive ● cautionary ○ good ○ excellent *
Total highway safety penalties are: 7 *   Value: 8 3   Durability: 7 8   Highway Control Rating: 3 1   Highway Safety: 2 4

Brand	Year	Type	Length	Model	Chassis	Engine	Fuel Type	Average Price per Linear Foot When New	Adjusted Wheelbase	Approx. Towing Capacity	Gross Vehicle Weight Rating	Average Curb Weight
Kountry Star	1998	MHA	38	SA3761	FO	7.5L	G	$2600	236 T	5,000	20,000	18,562

Livability Code: SB 30-90
Wheelbase-to-length ratio of 52% is considered ○ dangerous ● fatiguing ○ good ○ excellent *
The approximate net payload of 1438 pounds at 7% of GVWR on this model is ○ deficient ○ excessive ● cautionary ○ good ○ excellent *
Total highway safety penalties are: 7 *   Value: 8 3   Durability: 7 8   Highway Control Rating: 3 1   Highway Safety: 2 4

Brand	Year	Type	Length	Model	Chassis	Engine	Fuel Type	Average Price per Linear Foot When New	Adjusted Wheelbase	Approx. Towing Capacity	Gross Vehicle Weight Rating	Average Curb Weight
Kountry Star	1998	MHA	38	SA3766	FO	7.5L	G	$2600	236 T	5,000	20,000	18,562

Livability Code: SB 30-90
Wheelbase-to-length ratio of 52% is considered ○ dangerous ● fatiguing ○ good ○ excellent *
The approximate net payload of 1438 pounds at 7% of GVWR on this model is ○ deficient ○ excessive ● cautionary ○ good ○ excellent *
Total highway safety penalties are: 12 *   Value: 8 0   Durability: 7 8   Highway Control Rating: 3 1   Highway Safety: 1 9

Brand	Year	Type	Length	Model	Chassis	Engine	Fuel Type	Average Price per Linear Foot When New	Adjusted Wheelbase	Approx. Towing Capacity	Gross Vehicle Weight Rating	Average Curb Weight
Kountry Star	1998	MHA	38	SA3767	FO	7.5L	G	$2600	236 T	5,000	20,000	18,562

Livability Code: SB 30-90
Wheelbase-to-length ratio of 52% is considered ○ dangerous ● fatiguing ○ good ○ excellent *
The approximate net payload of 1438 pounds at 7% of GVWR on this model is ○ deficient ○ excessive ● cautionary ○ good ○ excellent *
Total highway safety penalties are: 12 *   Value: 8 0   Durability: 7 8   Highway Control Rating: 3 1   Highway Safety: 1 9

Brand	Year	Type	Length	Model	Chassis	Engine	Fuel Type	Average Price per Linear Foot When New	Adjusted Wheelbase	Approx. Towing Capacity	Gross Vehicle Weight Rating	Average Curb Weight
Kountry Star	1998	MHA	38	SA3780	FO	7.5L	G	$2600	236 T	5,000	20,000	18,562

Livability Code: SB 30-90
Wheelbase-to-length ratio of 52% is considered ○ dangerous ● fatiguing ○ good ○ excellent *
The approximate net payload of 1438 pounds at 7% of GVWR on this model is ○ deficient ○ excessive ● cautionary ○ good ○ excellent *
Total highway safety penalties are: 7 *   Value: 8 3   Durability: 7 8   Highway Control Rating: 3 1   Highway Safety: 2 4

Brand	Year	Type	Length	Model	Chassis	Engine	Fuel Type	Average Price per Linear Foot When New	Adjusted Wheelbase	Approx. Towing Capacity	Gross Vehicle Weight Rating	Average Curb Weight
Kountry Star	1998	MHA	38	SA3796	FO	7.5L	G	$2600	236 T	5,000	20,000	18,562

Livability Code: SB 30-90
Wheelbase-to-length ratio of 52% is considered ○ dangerous ● fatiguing ○ good ○ excellent *
The approximate net payload of 1438 pounds at 7% of GVWR on this model is ○ deficient ○ excessive ● cautionary ○ good ○ excellent *
Total highway safety penalties are: 7 *   Value: 8 3   Durability: 7 8   Highway Control Rating: 3 1   Highway Safety: 2 4

Brand	Year	Type	Length	Model	Chassis	Engine	Fuel Type	Average Price per Linear Foot When New	Adjusted Wheelbase	Approx. Towing Capacity	Gross Vehicle Weight Rating	Average Curb Weight
Kountry Star	1998	MHA	38	SA3797	FO	7.5L	G	$2600	236 T	5,000	20,000	18,562

Livability Code: SB 30-90
Wheelbase-to-length ratio of 52% is considered ○ dangerous ● fatiguing ○ good ○ excellent *
The approximate net payload of 1438 pounds at 7% of GVWR on this model is ○ deficient ○ excessive ● cautionary ○ good ○ excellent *
Total highway safety penalties are: 7 *   Value: 8 3   Durability: 7 8   Highway Control Rating: 3 1   Highway Safety: 2 4

Brand	Year	Type	Length	Model	Chassis	Engine	Fuel Type	Average Price per Linear Foot When New	Adjusted Wheelbase	Approx. Towing Capacity	Gross Vehicle Weight Rating	Average Curb Weight
Kountry Star	1998	MHA	38	SA3758 opch fr.dsl	FR	210HP	D	$3300	228	5,000	20,500	18,762

Livability Code: SB 30-90
Wheelbase-to-length ratio of 50% is considered ● dangerous ○ fatiguing ○ good ○ excellent *
The approximate net payload of 1738 pounds at 8% of GVWR on this model is ○ deficient ○ excessive ● cautionary ○ good ○ excellent *
Total highway safety penalties are: 5 *   Value: 8 4   Durability: 7 8   Highway Control Rating: 2 4   Highway Safety: 1 9

Brand	Year	Type	Length	Model	Chassis	Engine	Fuel Type	Average Price per Linear Foot When New	Adjusted Wheelbase	Approx. Towing Capacity	Gross Vehicle Weight Rating	Average Curb Weight
Kountry Star	1998	MHA	38	SA3761 opch fr.dsl	FR	210HP	D	$3300	228	5,000	20,500	18,762

Livability Code: SB 30-90
Wheelbase-to-length ratio of 50% is considered ● dangerous ○ fatiguing ○ good ○ excellent *
The approximate net payload of 1738 pounds at 8% of GVWR on this model is ○ deficient ○ excessive ● cautionary ○ good ○ excellent *
Total highway safety penalties are: 5 *   Value: 8 4   Durability: 7 8   Highway Control Rating: 2 4   Highway Safety: 1 9

Note: Safety ratings are based on the assumption that the engineering of the RV has allowed for proper balance by placing fresh, gray, and black holding tanks in a location so as not to change the balance of the RV when the tanks are empty or full. **Always double-check wheelbase, GVWR, and weights at front and rear axles.**

*See Section 1 for details on how conclusions are reached.

Brand	Year	Type	Length	Model	Chassis	Engine	Fuel Type	Average Price per Linear Foot When New	Adjusted Wheelbase	Approx. Towing Capacity	Gross Vehicle Weight Rating	Average Curb Weight
Kountry Star	1998	MHA	38	SA3766 opch fr.dsl	FR	210HP	D	$3300	228	5,000	20,500	18,762

Livability Code: SB 30-90   Wheelbase-to-length ratio of 50% is considered ● dangerous ○ fatiguing ○ good ○ excellent *

The approximate net payload of 1738 pounds at 8% of GVWR on this model is ○ deficient ○ excessive ● cautionary ○ good ○ excellent *

Total highway safety penalties are: 5 *   Value: 8 4   Durability: 7 8   Highway Control Rating: 2 4   Highway Safety: 1 9

Brand	Year	Type	Length	Model	Chassis	Engine	Fuel	Price/ft	Wheelbase	Towing	GVWR	Curb
Kountry Star	1998	MHA	38	SA3767 opch fr.dsl	FR	210HP	D	$3300	228	5,000	20,500	18,762

Livability Code: SB 30-90   Wheelbase-to-length ratio of 50% is considered ● dangerous ○ fatiguing ○ good ○ excellent *

The approximate net payload of 1738 pounds at 8% of GVWR on this model is ○ deficient ○ excessive ● cautionary ○ good ○ excellent *

Total highway safety penalties are: 5 *   Value: 8 4   Durability: 7 8   Highway Control Rating: 2 4   Highway Safety: 1 9

Kountry Star	1998	MHA	38	SA3780 opch fr.dsl	FR	210HP	D	$3300	228	5,000	20,500	18,762

Livability Code: SB 30-90   Wheelbase-to-length ratio of 50% is considered ● dangerous ○ fatiguing ○ good ○ excellent *

The approximate net payload of 1738 pounds at 8% of GVWR on this model is ○ deficient ○ excessive ● cautionary ○ good ○ excellent *

Total highway safety penalties are: 5 *   Value: 8 4   Durability: 7 8   Highway Control Rating: 2 4   Highway Safety: 1 9

Kountry Star	1998	MHA	38	SA3796 opch fr.dsl	FR	210HP	D	$3300	228	5,000	20,500	18,762

Livability Code: SB 30-90   Wheelbase-to-length ratio of 50% is considered ● dangerous ○ fatiguing ○ good ○ excellent *

The approximate net payload of 1738 pounds at 8% of GVWR on this model is ○ deficient ○ excessive ● cautionary ○ good ○ excellent *

Total highway safety penalties are: 5 *   Value: 8 4   Durability: 7 8   Highway Control Rating: 2 4   Highway Safety: 1 9

Kountry Star	1998	MHA	38	SA3797 opch fr.dsl	FR	210HP	D	$3300	228	5,000	20,500	18,762

Livability Code: SB 30-90   Wheelbase-to-length ratio of 50% is considered ● dangerous ○ fatiguing ○ good ○ excellent *

The approximate net payload of 1738 pounds at 8% of GVWR on this model is ○ deficient ○ excessive ● cautionary ○ good ○ excellent *

Total highway safety penalties are: 5 *   Value: 8 4   Durability: 7 8   Highway Control Rating: 2 4   Highway Safety: 1 9

Kountry Star	1999	MHA	28	SA2708	FO	6.8L	G	$3500	172	8,000	18,000	13,960

Livability Code: SB 30-90   Wheelbase-to-length ratio of 52% is considered ○ dangerous ● fatiguing ○ good ○ excellent *

The approximate net payload of 4040 pounds at 22% of GVWR on this model is ○ deficient ○ excessive ○ cautionary ○ good ● excellent *

Total highway safety penalties are: 2 *   Value: 8 5   Durability: 7 8   Highway Control Rating: 6 9   Highway Safety: 6 7   ★★

Kountry Star	1999	MHA	28	SA2708 fr.dsl	FR	CU210	D	$4500	172	5,000	20,500	14,422

Livability Code: SB 30-90   Wheelbase-to-length ratio of 52% is considered ● dangerous ● fatiguing ○ good ○ excellent *

The approximate net payload of 6079 pounds at 30% of GVWR on this model is ○ deficient ○ excessive ○ cautionary ● good ○ excellent *

Total highway safety penalties are: 2 *   Value: 8 5   Durability: 7 8   Highway Control Rating: 6 2   Highway Safety: 6 0   ★★

Kountry Star	1999	MHA	30	SA2956	CH	7.4L	G	$2200	172	5,000	21,000	16,970

Livability Code: SB 30-90   Wheelbase-to-length ratio of 49% is considered ● dangerous ○ fatiguing ○ good ○ excellent *

The approximate net payload of 4030 pounds at 19% of GVWR on this model is ○ deficient ○ excessive ○ cautionary ○ good ● excellent *

Total highway safety penalties are: 9 *   Value: 8 2   Durability: 7 8   Highway Control Rating: 5 3   Highway Safety: 4 4

Kountry Star	1999	MHA	30	SA2956	FO	6.8L	G	$3300	178	8,000	18,000	15,650

Livability Code: SB 30-90   Wheelbase-to-length ratio of 50% is considered ● dangerous ○ fatiguing ○ good ○ excellent *

The approximate net payload of 2350 pounds at 13% of GVWR on this model is ○ deficient ○ excessive ○ cautionary ● good ○ excellent *

Total highway safety penalties are: 7 *   Value: 8 3   Durability: 7 8   Highway Control Rating: 5 0   Highway Safety: 4 3

Kountry Star	1999	MHA	30	SA2956 fr.dsl	FR	CU210	D	$4200	178	5,000	20,500	16,372

Livability Code: SB 30-90   Wheelbase-to-length ratio of 50% is considered ● dangerous ○ fatiguing ○ good ○ excellent *

The approximate net payload of 4128 pounds at 20% of GVWR on this model is ○ deficient ○ excessive ○ cautionary ○ good ● excellent *

Total highway safety penalties are: 7 *   Value: 8 3   Durability: 7 8   Highway Control Rating: 6 0   Highway Safety: 5 3

Kountry Star	1999	MHA	34	SA3357	CH	7.4L	G	$1900	200	5,000	21,000	18,060

Livability Code: SB 30-90   Wheelbase-to-length ratio of 50% is considered ● dangerous ○ fatiguing ○ good ○ excellent *

The approximate net payload of 2940 pounds at 14% of GVWR on this model is ○ deficient ○ excessive ○ cautionary ● good ○ excellent *

Total highway safety penalties are: 11 *   Value: 8 1   Durability: 7 8   Highway Control Rating: 5 0   Highway Safety: 3 9

Kountry Star	1999	MHA	34	SA3357	FO	6.8L	G	$2900	200	5,500	20,500	17,370

Livability Code: SB 30-90   Wheelbase-to-length ratio of 50% is considered ● dangerous ○ fatiguing ○ good ○ excellent *

The approximate net payload of 3130 pounds at 15% of GVWR on this model is ○ deficient ○ excessive ○ cautionary ● good ○ excellent *

Total highway safety penalties are: 7 *   Value: 8 3   Durability: 7 8   Highway Control Rating: 5 2   Highway Safety: 4 5

Note: Safety ratings are based on the assumption that the engineering of the RV has allowed for proper balance by placing fresh, gray, and black holding tanks in a location so as not to change the balance of the RV when the tanks are empty or full. **Always double-check wheelbase, GVWR, and weights at front and rear axles.**

*See Section 1 for details on how conclusions are reached.

Brand	Year	Type	Length	Model	Chassis	Engine	Fuel Type	Average Price per Linear Foot When New	Adjusted Wheel-base	Approx. Towing Capacity	Gross Vehicle Weight Rating	Average Curb Weight
Kountry Star	1999	MHA	34	SA3357 fr.dsl	FR	CU210	D	$3700	200	5,000	20,500	17,422

Livability Code: SB 30-90
Wheelbase-to-length ratio of 50% is considered ● dangerous ○ fatiguing ○ good ○ excellent *
The approximate net payload of 3078 pounds at 15% of GVWR on this model is ○ deficient ○ excessive ○ cautionary ● good ○ excellent *
Total highway safety penalties are: 7 *   Value: 8 3   Durability: 7 8   Highway Control Rating: 5 2   Highway Safety: 4 5

Brand	Year	Type	Length	Model	Chassis	Engine	Fuel Type	Average Price per Linear Foot When New	Adjusted Wheel-base	Approx. Towing Capacity	Gross Vehicle Weight Rating	Average Curb Weight
Kountry Star	1999	MHA	38	SA3758	CH	7.4L	G	$1700	240	5,000	21,000	18,626

Livability Code: SB 30-90
Wheelbase-to-length ratio of 53% is considered ○ dangerous ● fatiguing ○ good ○ excellent *
The approximate net payload of 2374 pounds at 11% of GVWR on this model is ○ deficient ○ excessive ○ cautionary ● good ○ excellent *
Total highway safety penalties are: 11 *   Value: 8 1   Durability: 7 8   Highway Control Rating: 6 7   Highway Safety: 5 6   ★

Brand	Year	Type	Length	Model	Chassis	Engine	Fuel Type	Average Price per Linear Foot When New	Adjusted Wheel-base	Approx. Towing Capacity	Gross Vehicle Weight Rating	Average Curb Weight
Kountry Star	1999	MHA	38	SA3762	CH	7.4L	G	$1700	240	5,000	21,000	18,626

Livability Code: SB 30-90
Wheelbase-to-length ratio of 53% is considered ○ dangerous ● fatiguing ○ good ○ excellent *
The approximate net payload of 2374 pounds at 11% of GVWR on this model is ○ deficient ○ excessive ○ cautionary ● good ○ excellent *
Total highway safety penalties are: 11 *   Value: 8 1   Durability: 7 8   Highway Control Rating: 6 7   Highway Safety: 5 6   ★

Brand	Year	Type	Length	Model	Chassis	Engine	Fuel Type	Average Price per Linear Foot When New	Adjusted Wheel-base	Approx. Towing Capacity	Gross Vehicle Weight Rating	Average Curb Weight
Kountry Star	1999	MHA	38	SA3767	CH	7.4L	G	$1700	240	5,000	21,000	18,626

Livability Code: SB 30-90
Wheelbase-to-length ratio of 53% is considered ○ dangerous ● fatiguing ○ good ○ excellent *
The approximate net payload of 2374 pounds at 11% of GVWR on this model is ○ deficient ○ excessive ○ cautionary ● good ○ excellent *
Total highway safety penalties are: 16 *   Value: 7 8   Durability: 7 8   Highway Control Rating: 6 7   Highway Safety: 5 1   ★

Brand	Year	Type	Length	Model	Chassis	Engine	Fuel Type	Average Price per Linear Foot When New	Adjusted Wheel-base	Approx. Towing Capacity	Gross Vehicle Weight Rating	Average Curb Weight
Kountry Star	1999	MHA	38	SA3780	CH	7.4L	G	$1700	240	5,000	21,000	18,626

Livability Code: SB 30-90
Wheelbase-to-length ratio of 53% is considered ○ dangerous ● fatiguing ○ good ○ excellent *
The approximate net payload of 2374 pounds at 11% of GVWR on this model is ○ deficient ○ excessive ○ cautionary ● good ○ excellent *
Total highway safety penalties are: 11 *   Value: 8 1   Durability: 7 8   Highway Control Rating: 6 7   Highway Safety: 5 6   ★

Brand	Year	Type	Length	Model	Chassis	Engine	Fuel Type	Average Price per Linear Foot When New	Adjusted Wheel-base	Approx. Towing Capacity	Gross Vehicle Weight Rating	Average Curb Weight
Kountry Star	1999	MHA	38	SA3758	FO	6.8L	G	$2600	240	5,500	20,500	18,126

Livability Code: SB 30-90
Wheelbase-to-length ratio of 53% is considered ○ dangerous ● fatiguing ○ good ○ excellent *
The approximate net payload of 2374 pounds at 12% of GVWR on this model is ○ deficient ○ excessive ○ cautionary ● good ○ excellent *
Total highway safety penalties are: 5 *   Value: 8 4   Durability: 7 8   Highway Control Rating: 6 8   Highway Safety: 6 3   ★★

Brand	Year	Type	Length	Model	Chassis	Engine	Fuel Type	Average Price per Linear Foot When New	Adjusted Wheel-base	Approx. Towing Capacity	Gross Vehicle Weight Rating	Average Curb Weight
Kountry Star	1999	MHA	38	SA3762	FO	6.8L	G	$2600	240	5,500	20,500	18,126

Livability Code: SB 30-90
Wheelbase-to-length ratio of 53% is considered ○ dangerous ● fatiguing ○ good ○ excellent *
The approximate net payload of 2374 pounds at 12% of GVWR on this model is ○ deficient ○ excessive ○ cautionary ● good ○ excellent *
Total highway safety penalties are: 5 *   Value: 8 4   Durability: 7 8   Highway Control Rating: 6 8   Highway Safety: 6 3   ★★

Brand	Year	Type	Length	Model	Chassis	Engine	Fuel Type	Average Price per Linear Foot When New	Adjusted Wheel-base	Approx. Towing Capacity	Gross Vehicle Weight Rating	Average Curb Weight
Kountry Star	1999	MHA	38	SA3767	FO	6.8L	G	$2600	240	5,500	20,500	18,126

Livability Code: SB 30-90
Wheelbase-to-length ratio of 53% is considered ○ dangerous ● fatiguing ○ good ○ excellent *
The approximate net payload of 2374 pounds at 12% of GVWR on this model is ○ deficient ○ excessive ○ cautionary ● good ○ excellent *
Total highway safety penalties are: 10 *   Value: 8 1   Durability: 7 8   Highway Control Rating: 6 8   Highway Safety: 5 8   ★

Brand	Year	Type	Length	Model	Chassis	Engine	Fuel Type	Average Price per Linear Foot When New	Adjusted Wheel-base	Approx. Towing Capacity	Gross Vehicle Weight Rating	Average Curb Weight
Kountry Star	1999	MHA	38	SA3780	FO	6.8L	G	$2600	240	5,500	20,500	18,126

Livability Code: SB 30-90
Wheelbase-to-length ratio of 53% is considered ○ dangerous ● fatiguing ○ good ○ excellent *
The approximate net payload of 2374 pounds at 12% of GVWR on this model is ○ deficient ○ excessive ○ cautionary ● good ○ excellent *
Total highway safety penalties are: 5 *   Value: 8 4   Durability: 7 8   Highway Control Rating: 6 8   Highway Safety: 6 3   ★★

Brand	Year	Type	Length	Model	Chassis	Engine	Fuel Type	Average Price per Linear Foot When New	Adjusted Wheel-base	Approx. Towing Capacity	Gross Vehicle Weight Rating	Average Curb Weight
Kountry Star	1999	MHA	38	SA3758 fr.dsl	FR	CU210	D	$3300	228	5,000	20,500	17,948

Livability Code: SB 30-90
Wheelbase-to-length ratio of 51% is considered ○ dangerous ● fatiguing ○ good ○ excellent *
The approximate net payload of 2553 pounds at 12% of GVWR on this model is ○ deficient ○ excessive ○ cautionary ● good ○ excellent *
Total highway safety penalties are: 5 *   Value: 8 4   Durability: 7 8   Highway Control Rating: 5 0   Highway Safety: 4 5

Brand	Year	Type	Length	Model	Chassis	Engine	Fuel Type	Average Price per Linear Foot When New	Adjusted Wheel-base	Approx. Towing Capacity	Gross Vehicle Weight Rating	Average Curb Weight
Kountry Star	1999	MHA	38	SA3762 fr.dsl	FR	CU210	D	$3300	228	5,000	20,500	17,948

Livability Code: SB 30-90
Wheelbase-to-length ratio of 51% is considered ○ dangerous ● fatiguing ○ good ○ excellent *
The approximate net payload of 2553 pounds at 12% of GVWR on this model is ○ deficient ○ excessive ○ cautionary ● good ○ excellent *
Total highway safety penalties are: 5 *   Value: 8 4   Durability: 7 8   Highway Control Rating: 5 0   Highway Safety: 4 5

Brand	Year	Type	Length	Model	Chassis	Engine	Fuel Type	Average Price per Linear Foot When New	Adjusted Wheel-base	Approx. Towing Capacity	Gross Vehicle Weight Rating	Average Curb Weight
Kountry Star	1999	MHA	38	SA3767 fr.dsl	FR	CU210	D	$3300	228	5,000	20,500	17,948

Livability Code: SB 30-90
Wheelbase-to-length ratio of 51% is considered ○ dangerous ● fatiguing ○ good ○ excellent *
The approximate net payload of 2553 pounds at 12% of GVWR on this model is ○ deficient ○ excessive ○ cautionary ● good ○ excellent *
Total highway safety penalties are: 10 *   Value: 8 1   Durability: 7 8   Highway Control Rating: 5 0   Highway Safety: 4 0

Note: Safety ratings are based on the assumption that the engineering of the RV has allowed for proper balance by placing fresh, gray, and black holding tanks in a location so as not to change the balance of the RV when the tanks are empty or full. **Always double-check wheelbase, GVWR, and weights at front and rear axles.**

*See Section 1 for details on how conclusions are reached.

Brand	Year	Type	Length	Model	Chassis	Engine	Fuel Type	Average Price per Linear Foot When New	Adjusted Wheel-base	Approx. Towing Capacity	Gross Vehicle Weight Rating	Average Curb Weight
Kountry Star	1999	MHA	38	SA3780 fr.dsl	FR	CU210	D	$3300	228	5,000	20,500	17,948

Livability Code: SB 30-90 — Wheelbase-to-length ratio of 51% is considered ○ dangerous ◉ fatiguing ○ good ○ excellent *
The approximate net payload of 2553 pounds at 12% of GVWR on this model is ○ deficient ○ excessive ○ cautionary ◉ good ○ excellent *
Total highway safety penalties are: 5 * Value: 8 4 Durability: 7 8 Highway Control Rating: 5 0 Highway Safety: 4 5

Brand	Year	Type	Length	Model	Chassis	Engine	Fuel Type	Avg Price/ Linear Foot	Adj Wheelbase	Towing Cap	GVWR	Avg Curb Wt
Kustom Koach	1997	MHC	22	C200	FO	5.4L	G	$4000	138	1,500	10,500	9,578

Livability Code: VA 30-90 — Wheelbase-to-length ratio of 53% is considered ○ dangerous ◉ fatiguing ○ good ○ excellent *
The approximate net payload of 922 pounds at 9% of GVWR on this model is ○ deficient ○ excessive ◉ cautionary ○ good ○ excellent *
Total highway safety penalties are: 2 * Value: 8 0 Durability: 7 7 Highway Control Rating: 6 0 Highway Safety: 5 8 ★

Kustom Koach	1997	MHC	22	C220	FO	6.8L	G	$4000	158	1,500	11,500	9,586

Livability Code: VA 30-90 — Wheelbase-to-length ratio of 60% is considered ○ dangerous ○ fatiguing ○ good ◉ excellent *
The approximate net payload of 1914 pounds at 17% of GVWR on this model is ○ deficient ○ excessive ○ cautionary ○ good ◉ excellent *
Total highway safety penalties are: 2 * Value: 8 0 Durability: 7 7 Highway Control Rating: 1 0 0 Highway Safety: 9 8 ★★★

Kustom Koach	1997	MHC	25	C250	FO	6.8L	G	$3500	158	1,500	11,500	10,476

Livability Code: VA 30-90 — Wheelbase-to-length ratio of 53% is considered ○ dangerous ◉ fatiguing ○ good ○ excellent *
The approximate net payload of 1024 pounds at 9% of GVWR on this model is ○ deficient ○ excessive ◉ cautionary ○ good ○ excellent *
Total highway safety penalties are: 2 * Value: 8 0 Durability: 7 7 Highway Control Rating: 6 0 Highway Safety: 5 8 ★

Kustom Koach	1997	MHC	31	C300	FO	6.8L	G	$2800	208	1,500	14;050	12,734

Livability Code: VA 30-90 — Wheelbase-to-length ratio of 56% is considered ○ dangerous ○ fatiguing ◉ good ○ excellent *
The approximate net payload of 1316 pounds at 9% of GVWR on this model is ○ deficient ○ excessive ◉ cautionary ○ good ○ excellent *
Total highway safety penalties are: 2 * Value: 8 0 Durability: 7 7 Highway Control Rating: 7 9 Highway Safety: 7 7 ★★★

Kustom Koach	1998	MHC	22	C200	FO	5.4L	G	$4000	138	1,500	10,500	9,578

Livability Code: VA 30-90 — Wheelbase-to-length ratio of 53% is considered ○ dangerous ◉ fatiguing ○ good ○ excellent *
The approximate net payload of 922 pounds at 9% of GVWR on this model is ○ deficient ○ excessive ◉ cautionary ○ good ○ excellent *
Total highway safety penalties are: 2 * Value: 8 0 Durability: 7 7 Highway Control Rating: 6 0 Highway Safety: 5 8 ★

Kustom Koach	1998	MHC	22	C220	FO	6.8L	G	$4000	158	1,500	11,500	9,586

Livability Code: VA 30-90 — Wheelbase-to-length ratio of 60% is considered ○ dangerous ○ fatiguing ○ good ◉ excellent *
The approximate net payload of 1914 pounds at 17% of GVWR on this model is ○ deficient ○ excessive ○ cautionary ○ good ◉ excellent *
Total highway safety penalties are: 2 * Value: 8 0 Durability: 7 7 Highway Control Rating: 1 0 0 Highway Safety: 9 8 ★★★

Kustom Koach	1998	MHC	25	C250	FO	6.8L	G	$3500	158	1,500	11,500	10,476

Livability Code: VA 30-90 — Wheelbase-to-length ratio of 53% is considered ○ dangerous ◉ fatiguing ○ good ○ excellent *
The approximate net payload of 1024 pounds at 9% of GVWR on this model is ○ deficient ○ excessive ◉ cautionary ○ good ○ excellent *
Total highway safety penalties are: 2 * Value: 8 0 Durability: 7 7 Highway Control Rating: 6 0 Highway Safety: 5 8 ★

Kustom Koach	1998	MHC	31	C300	FO	6.8L	G	$2800	208	1,500	14,050	12,734

Livability Code: VA 30-90 — Wheelbase-to-length ratio of 56% is considered ○ dangerous ○ fatiguing ◉ good ○ excellent *
The approximate net payload of 1316 pounds at 9% of GVWR on this model is ○ deficient ○ excessive ◉ cautionary ○ good ○ excellent *
Total highway safety penalties are: 2 * Value: 8 0 Durability: 7 7 Highway Control Rating: 7 9 Highway Safety: 7 7 ★★★

La Palma	1999	MHA	30	29W	FO	6.8L	G	$2800	190	5,000	18,000	14,135

Livability Code: SB 30-90 — Wheelbase-to-length ratio of 53% is considered ○ dangerous ◉ fatiguing ○ good ○ excellent *
The approximate net payload of 3866 pounds at 21% of GVWR on this model is ○ deficient ○ excessive ○ cautionary ○ good ◉ excellent *
Total highway safety penalties are: 2 * Value: 7 7 Durability: 7 0 Highway Control Rating: 7 7 Highway Safety: 7 5 ★★★

La Palma	1999	MHA	33	32C	FO	6.8L	G	$2600	208	5,000	20,500	16,771

Livability Code: SB 30-90 — Wheelbase-to-length ratio of 53% is considered ○ dangerous ◉ fatiguing ○ good ○ excellent *
The approximate net payload of 3729 pounds at 18% of GVWR on this model is ○ deficient ○ excessive ○ cautionary ○ good ◉ excellent *
Total highway safety penalties are: 2 * Value: 7 7 Durability: 7 0 Highway Control Rating: 7 7 Highway Safety: 7 5 ★★★

La Palma	1999	MHA	33	32S	FO	6.8L	G	$2600	208	5,000	20,500	17,671

Livability Code: SB 30-90 — Wheelbase-to-length ratio of 53% is considered ○ dangerous ◉ fatiguing ○ good ○ excellent *
The approximate net payload of 2829 pounds at 14% of GVWR on this model is ○ deficient ○ excessive ○ cautionary ◉ good ○ excellent *
Total highway safety penalties are: 12 * Value: 7 2 Durability: 7 0 Highway Control Rating: 7 1 Highway Safety: 5 9 ★

Note: Safety ratings are based on the assumption that the engineering of the RV has allowed for proper balance by placing fresh, gray, and black holding tanks in a location so as not to change the balance of the RV when the tanks are empty or full. **Always double-check wheelbase, GVWR, and weights at front and rear axles.**

*See Section 1 for details on how conclusions are reached.

Brand	Year	Type	Length	Model	Chassis	Engine	Fuel Type	Average Price per Linear Foot When New	Adjusted Wheelbase	Approx. Towing Capacity	Gross Vehicle Weight Rating	Average Curb Weight
La Palma	**1999**	MHA	35	34S	FO	6.8L	G	$2400	228	5,000	20,500	18,246

Livability Code: SB 30-90
Wheelbase-to-length ratio of 54% is considered ○ dangerous ○ fatiguing ◉ good ○ excellent*
The approximate net payload of 2255 pounds at 11% of GVWR on this model is ○ deficient ○ excessive ○ cautionary ◉ good ○ excellent*
Total highway safety penalties are: 12*   Value: 72   Durability: 70   Highway Control Rating: 75   Highway Safety: 63   ★★

Brand	Year	Type	Length	Model	Chassis	Engine	Fuel Type	Avg Price/Linear Foot	Adj. Wheelbase	Towing Capacity	GVWR	Avg Curb Weight
La Palma	**1999**	MHA	35	34F	FO	6.8L	G	$2400	228	5,000	20,500	18,246

Livability Code: SB 30-90
Wheelbase-to-length ratio of 54% is considered ○ dangerous ○ fatiguing ◉ good ○ excellent*
The approximate net payload of 2255 pounds at 11% of GVWR on this model is ○ deficient ○ excessive ○ cautionary ◉ good ○ excellent*
Total highway safety penalties are: 12*   Value: 72   Durability: 70   Highway Control Rating: 75   Highway Safety: 63   ★★

Brand	Year	Type	Length	Model	Chassis	Engine	Fuel Type	Avg Price/Linear Foot	Adj. Wheelbase	Towing Capacity	GVWR	Avg Curb Weight
La Palma	**1999**	MHA	37	36G	FO	6.8L	G	$2300	228	5,000	20,500	18,664

Livability Code: SB 30-90
Wheelbase-to-length ratio of 52% is considered ○ dangerous ◉ fatiguing ○ good ○ excellent*
The approximate net payload of 1836 pounds at 9% of GVWR on this model is ○ deficient ○ excessive ◉ cautionary ○ good ○ excellent*
Total highway safety penalties are: 12*   Value: 72   Durability: 70   Highway Control Rating: 50   Highway Safety: 38

Brand	Year	Type	Length	Model	Chassis	Engine	Fuel Type	Avg Price/Linear Foot	Adj. Wheelbase	Towing Capacity	GVWR	Avg Curb Weight
La Salle	**1990**	MHA	32	LS 325 QB	CH	7.4L	G	$3500	190	1,500	14,500	12,609

Livability Code: SB 30-90
Wheelbase-to-length ratio of 49% is considered ◉ dangerous ○ fatiguing ○ good ○ excellent*
The approximate net payload of 1891 pounds at 13% of GVWR on this model is ○ deficient ○ excessive ○ cautionary ◉ good ○ excellent*
Total highway safety penalties are: 6*   Value: 75   Durability: 70   Highway Control Rating: 37   Highway Safety: 31

Brand	Year	Type	Length	Model	Chassis	Engine	Fuel Type	Avg Price/Linear Foot	Adj. Wheelbase	Towing Capacity	GVWR	Avg Curb Weight
La Salle	**1991**	MHA	32	LS 323 QB	CH	7.4L	G	$3600	190	2,500	14,500	14,168

Livability Code: SB 30-90
Wheelbase-to-length ratio of 49% is considered ◉ dangerous ○ fatiguing ○ good ○ excellent*
The approximate net payload of 332 pounds at 2% of GVWR on this model is ◉ deficient ○ excessive ○ cautionary ○ good ○ excellent*
Total highway safety penalties are: 6*   Value: 75   Durability: 70   Highway Control Rating: 3   Highway Safety: -3

Brand	Year	Type	Length	Model	Chassis	Engine	Fuel Type	Avg Price/Linear Foot	Adj. Wheelbase	Towing Capacity	GVWR	Avg Curb Weight
Landau	**1999**	MHA	30	2905	CH	7.4L	G	$2700	178	4,200	14,800	13,134

Livability Code: SB 30-90
Wheelbase-to-length ratio of 50% is considered ◉ dangerous ○ fatiguing ○ good ○ excellent*
The approximate net payload of 1666 pounds at 11% of GVWR on this model is ○ deficient ○ excessive ○ cautionary ◉ good ○ excellent*
Total highway safety penalties are: 4*   Value: 81   Durability: 70   Highway Control Rating: 45   Highway Safety: 41

Brand	Year	Type	Length	Model	Chassis	Engine	Fuel Type	Avg Price/Linear Foot	Adj. Wheelbase	Towing Capacity	GVWR	Avg Curb Weight
Landau	**1999**	MHA	30	2905	FO	6.8L	G	$2700	178	10,300	15,700	13,689

Livability Code: SB 30-90
Wheelbase-to-length ratio of 50% is considered ◉ dangerous ○ fatiguing ○ good ○ excellent*
The approximate net payload of 2011 pounds at 13% of GVWR on this model is ○ deficient ○ excessive ○ cautionary ◉ good ○ excellent*
Total highway safety penalties are: 2*   Value: 82   Durability: 70   Highway Control Rating: 48   Highway Safety: 46

Brand	Year	Type	Length	Model	Chassis	Engine	Fuel Type	Avg Price/Linear Foot	Adj. Wheelbase	Towing Capacity	GVWR	Avg Curb Weight
Landau	**1999**	MHA	33	3190	CH	7.4L	G	$2400	212	4,200	14,800	14,132

Livability Code: SB 30-90
Wheelbase-to-length ratio of 53% is considered ○ dangerous ◉ fatiguing ○ good ○ excellent*
The approximate net payload of 668 pounds at 5% of GVWR on this model is ◉ deficient ○ excessive ○ cautionary ○ good ○ excellent*
Total highway safety penalties are: 6*   Value: 80   Durability: 70   Highway Control Rating: 40   Highway Safety: 34

Brand	Year	Type	Length	Model	Chassis	Engine	Fuel Type	Avg Price/Linear Foot	Adj. Wheelbase	Towing Capacity	GVWR	Avg Curb Weight
Landau	**1999**	MHA	33	3190 so	CH	7.4L	G	$2400	212	4,500	16,500	14,782

Livability Code: SB 30-90
Wheelbase-to-length ratio of 53% is considered ○ dangerous ◉ fatiguing ○ good ○ excellent*
The approximate net payload of 1718 pounds at 10% of GVWR on this model is ○ deficient ○ excessive ○ cautionary ◉ good ○ excellent*
Total highway safety penalties are: 9*   Value: 79   Durability: 70   Highway Control Rating: 65   Highway Safety: 56   ★

Brand	Year	Type	Length	Model	Chassis	Engine	Fuel Type	Avg Price/Linear Foot	Adj. Wheelbase	Towing Capacity	GVWR	Avg Curb Weight
Landau	**1999**	MHA	33	3190	FO	6.8L	G	$2400	212	8,000	18,000	14,619

Livability Code: SB 30-90
Wheelbase-to-length ratio of 53% is considered ○ dangerous ◉ fatiguing ○ good ○ excellent*
The approximate net payload of 3381 pounds at 19% of GVWR on this model is ○ deficient ○ excessive ○ cautionary ○ good ◉ excellent*
Total highway safety penalties are: 2*   Value: 82   Durability: 70   Highway Control Rating: 79   Highway Safety: 77   ★★★

Brand	Year	Type	Length	Model	Chassis	Engine	Fuel Type	Avg Price/Linear Foot	Adj. Wheelbase	Towing Capacity	GVWR	Avg Curb Weight
Landau	**1999**	MHA	33	3190 Slide	FO	6.8L	G	$2400	212	8,000	18,000	15,582

Livability Code: SB 30-90
Wheelbase-to-length ratio of 53% is considered ○ dangerous ◉ fatiguing ○ good ○ excellent*
The approximate net payload of 2418 pounds at 13% of GVWR on this model is ○ deficient ○ excessive ○ cautionary ◉ good ○ excellent*
Total highway safety penalties are: 5*   Value: 81   Durability: 70   Highway Control Rating: 71   Highway Safety: 66   ★★

Brand	Year	Type	Length	Model	Chassis	Engine	Fuel Type	Avg Price/Linear Foot	Adj. Wheelbase	Towing Capacity	GVWR	Avg Curb Weight
Landau	**1999**	MHA	33	3301 Slide	FO	6.8L	G	$2400	220	8,000	18,000	16,032

Livability Code: SB 30-90
Wheelbase-to-length ratio of 55% is considered ○ dangerous ○ fatiguing ◉ good ○ excellent*
The approximate net payload of 1968 pounds at 11% of GVWR on this model is ○ deficient ○ excessive ○ cautionary ◉ good ○ excellent*
Total highway safety penalties are: 7*   Value: 79   Durability: 70   Highway Control Rating: 83   Highway Safety: 76   ★★★

Note: Safety ratings are based on the assumption that the engineering of the RV has allowed for proper balance by placing fresh, gray, and black holding tanks in a location so as not to change the balance of the RV when the tanks are empty or full. **Always double-check wheelbase, GVWR, and weights at front and rear axles.**

*See Section 1 for details on how conclusions are reached.

Brand	Year	Type	Length	Model	Chassis	Engine	Fuel Type	Average Price per Linear Foot When New	Adjusted Wheelbase	Approx. Towing Capacity	Gross Vehicle Weight Rating	Average Curb Weight
Landau	1999	MHA	35	3410 Slide	CH	7.4L	G	$2300	228	4,500	16,500	15,589

Livability Code: SB 30-90 Wheelbase-to-length ratio of 55% is considered ○ dangerous ○ fatiguing ● good ○ excellent*

The approximate net payload of 911 pounds at 6% of GVWR on this model is ● deficient ○ excessive ○ cautionary ○ good ○ excellent*

Total highway safety penalties are: 17* Value: 74 Durability: 70 Highway Control Rating: 56 Highway Safety: 39

Brand	Year	Type	Length	Model	Chassis	Engine	Fuel Type	Price/Ft	Wheelbase	Towing	GVWR	Curb Wt
Landau	1999	MHA	35	3410 Slide	FO	6.8L	G	$2300	220	8,000	18,000	15,889

Livability Code: SB 30-90 Wheelbase-to-length ratio of 53% is considered ○ dangerous ● fatiguing ○ good ○ excellent*

The approximate net payload of 2111 pounds at 12% of GVWR on this model is ○ deficient ○ excessive ○ cautionary ● good ○ excellent*

Total highway safety penalties are: 12* Value: 77 Durability: 70 Highway Control Rating: 67 Highway Safety: 55 ★

| Landau | 1999 | MHA | 36 | 3512 | CH | 7.4L | G | $2200 | 228 | 4,500 | 16,500 | 14,956 |

Livability Code: SB 30-90 Wheelbase-to-length ratio of 53% is considered ○ dangerous ● fatiguing ○ good ○ excellent*

The approximate net payload of 1544 pounds at 9% of GVWR on this model is ○ deficient ○ excessive ● cautionary ○ good ○ excellent*

Total highway safety penalties are: 7* Value: 79 Durability: 70 Highway Control Rating: 60 Highway Safety: 53 ★

| Landau | 1999 | MHA | 36 | 3512 | FO | 6.8L | G | $2200 | 228 | 8,000 | 18,000 | 15,756 |

Livability Code: SB 30-90 Wheelbase-to-length ratio of 53% is considered ○ dangerous ● fatiguing ○ good ○ excellent*

The approximate net payload of 2244 pounds at 12% of GVWR on this model is ○ deficient ○ excessive ○ cautionary ● good ○ excellent*

Total highway safety penalties are: 2* Value: 82 Durability: 70 Highway Control Rating: 69 Highway Safety: 67 ★★

| Landau | 1999 | MHA | 36 | 3512 Slide | FO | 6.8L | G | $2200 | 220 | 8,000 | 18,000 | 16,306 |

Livability Code: SB 30-90 Wheelbase-to-length ratio of 51% is considered ○ dangerous ● fatiguing ○ good ○ excellent*

The approximate net payload of 1694 pounds at 9% of GVWR on this model is ○ deficient ○ excessive ● cautionary ○ good ○ excellent*

Total highway safety penalties are: 7* Value: 79 Durability: 70 Highway Control Rating: 44 Highway Safety: 37

| Las Brisas | 1990 | MHA | 29 | 274 | CH | 7.4L | G | $1600 | 158 | 4,500 | 15,000 | 12,089 |

Livability Code: SB 30-90 Wheelbase-to-length ratio of 46% is considered ● dangerous ○ fatiguing ○ good ○ excellent*

The approximate net payload of 2911 pounds at 19% of GVWR on this model is ○ deficient ○ excessive ○ cautionary ○ good ● excellent*

Total highway safety penalties are: 4* Value: 89 Durability: 90 Highway Control Rating: 34 Highway Safety: 30

| Las Brisas | 1990 | MHA | 29 | 275 | CH | 7.4L | G | $1600 | 158 | 4,500 | 15,000 | 12,089 |

Livability Code: SB 30-90 Wheelbase-to-length ratio of 46% is considered ● dangerous ○ fatiguing ○ good ○ excellent*

The approximate net payload of 2911 pounds at 19% of GVWR on this model is ○ deficient ○ excessive ○ cautionary ○ good ● excellent*

Total highway safety penalties are: 4* Value: 89 Durability: 90 Highway Control Rating: 34 Highway Safety: 30

| Las Brisas | 1990 | MHA | 31 | 314 | CH | 7.4L | G | $1500 | 190 | 4,500 | 15,000 | 12,642 |

Livability Code: SB 30-90 Wheelbase-to-length ratio of 51% is considered ○ dangerous ● fatiguing ○ good ○ excellent*

The approximate net payload of 2358 pounds at 16% of GVWR on this model is ○ deficient ○ excessive ○ cautionary ○ good ● excellent*

Total highway safety penalties are: 5* Value: 89 Durability: 90 Highway Control Rating: 48 Highway Safety: 43

| Las Brisas | 1990 | MHA | 31 | 315 | CH | 7.4L | G | $1500 | 190 | 4,500 | 15,000 | 12,642 |

Livability Code: SB 30-90 Wheelbase-to-length ratio of 51% is considered ○ dangerous ● fatiguing ○ good ○ excellent*

The approximate net payload of 2358 pounds at 16% of GVWR on this model is ○ deficient ○ excessive ○ cautionary ○ good ● excellent*

Total highway safety penalties are: 5* Value: 89 Durability: 90 Highway Control Rating: 48 Highway Safety: 43

| Las Brisas | 1991 | MHA | 32 | 314 | CH | 7.4L | G | $1600 | 190 | 2,500 | 14,500 | 12,588 |

Livability Code: SB 30-90 Wheelbase-to-length ratio of 50% is considered ● dangerous ○ fatiguing ○ good ○ excellent*

The approximate net payload of 1912 pounds at 13% of GVWR on this model is ○ deficient ○ excessive ○ cautionary ● good ○ excellent*

Total highway safety penalties are: 5* Value: 88 Durability: 90 Highway Control Rating: 39 Highway Safety: 34

| Lazy Daze | 1990 | MHC | 26 | 26RB | FO | 7.5L | G | $1500 | 176 | 1,500 | 11,000 | 10,281 |

Livability Code: SB 20-90 Wheelbase-to-length ratio of 56% is considered ○ dangerous ○ fatiguing ● good ○ excellent*

The approximate net payload of 719 pounds at 7% of GVWR on this model is ○ deficient ○ excessive ● cautionary ○ good ○ excellent*

Total highway safety penalties are: 2* Value: 85 Durability: 90 Highway Control Rating: 68 Highway Safety: 66 ★★

| Lazy Daze | 1991 | MHC | 26 | 26 | FO | 7.5L | G | $1700 | 176 | 1,500 | 11,500 | 10,312 |

Livability Code: SB 20-90 Wheelbase-to-length ratio of 56% is considered ○ dangerous ○ fatiguing ● good ○ excellent*

The approximate net payload of 1188 pounds at 10% of GVWR on this model is ○ deficient ○ excessive ○ cautionary ● good ○ excellent*

Total highway safety penalties are: 2* Value: 85 Durability: 90 Highway Control Rating: 86 Highway Safety: 84 ★★★★

Note: Safety ratings are based on the assumption that the engineering of the RV has allowed for proper balance by placing fresh, gray, and black holding tanks in a location so as not to change the balance of the RV when the tanks are empty or full. **Always double-check wheelbase, GVWR, and weights at front and rear axles.**

*See Section 1 for details on how conclusions are reached.

Brand	Year	Type	Length	Model	Chassis	Engine	Fuel Type	Average Price per Linear Foot When New	Adjusted Wheelbase	Approx. Towing Capacity	Gross Vehicle Weight Rating	Average Curb Weight
Lazy Daze	1995	MHC	22	22 TB	CH	7.4L	G	$1900	146	1,500	10,500	9,442

Livability Code: SB 20-90
Wheelbase-to-length ratio of 55% is considered ○ dangerous ○ fatiguing ◉ good ○ excellent *
The approximate net payload of 1058 pounds at 10% of GVWR on this model is ○ deficient ○ excessive ○ cautionary ◉ good ○ excellent *
Total highway safety penalties are: 2 * — Value: 8 5 — Durability: 9 0 — Highway Control Rating: 8 2 — Highway Safety: 8 0 — ★★★★

Brand	Year	Type	Length	Model	Chassis	Engine	Fuel Type	Price/Ft	Wheelbase	Towing	GVWR	Curb Wt
Lazy Daze	1995	MHC	22	22 MP	CH	7.4L	G	$1900	146	1,500	10,500	9,468

Livability Code: SB 20-90
Wheelbase-to-length ratio of 55% is considered ○ dangerous ○ fatiguing ◉ good ○ excellent *
The approximate net payload of 1032 pounds at 10% of GVWR on this model is ○ deficient ○ excessive ○ cautionary ◉ good ○ excellent *
Total highway safety penalties are: 2 * — Value: 8 5 — Durability: 9 0 — Highway Control Rating: 8 2 — Highway Safety: 8 0 — ★★★★

Brand	Year	Type	Length	Model	Chassis	Engine	Fuel Type	Price/Ft	Wheelbase	Towing	GVWR	Curb Wt
Lazy Daze	1995	MHC	22	22 RL	CH	7.4L	G	$1900	146	1,500	10,500	9,445

Livability Code: SB 20-90
Wheelbase-to-length ratio of 55% is considered ○ dangerous ○ fatiguing ◉ good ○ excellent *
The approximate net payload of 1055 pounds at 10% of GVWR on this model is ○ deficient ○ excessive ○ cautionary ◉ good ○ excellent *
Total highway safety penalties are: 2 * — Value: 8 5 — Durability: 9 0 — Highway Control Rating: 8 2 — Highway Safety: 8 0 — ★★★★

Brand	Year	Type	Length	Model	Chassis	Engine	Fuel Type	Price/Ft	Wheelbase	Towing	GVWR	Curb Wt
Lazy Daze	1995	MHC	22	22 FL	CH	7.4L	G	$1900	146	1,500	10,500	9,533

Livability Code: SB 20-90
Wheelbase-to-length ratio of 55% is considered ○ dangerous ○ fatiguing ◉ good ○ excellent *
The approximate net payload of 967 pounds at 9% of GVWR on this model is ○ deficient ○ excessive ◉ cautionary ○ good ○ excellent *
Total highway safety penalties are: 2 * — Value: 8 5 — Durability: 9 0 — Highway Control Rating: 7 7 — Highway Safety: 7 5 — ★★★

Brand	Year	Type	Length	Model	Chassis	Engine	Fuel Type	Price/Ft	Wheelbase	Towing	GVWR	Curb Wt
Lazy Daze	1995	MHC	23	22 TB	FO	7.5L	G	$2600	158	1,500	10,500	9,527

Livability Code: SB 20-90
Wheelbase-to-length ratio of 58% is considered ○ dangerous ○ fatiguing ○ good ◉ excellent *
The approximate net payload of 973 pounds at 9% of GVWR on this model is ○ deficient ○ excessive ◉ cautionary ○ good ○ excellent *
Total highway safety penalties are: 2 * — Value: 8 5 — Durability: 9 0 — Highway Control Rating: 8 8 — Highway Safety: 8 6 — ★★★★

Brand	Year	Type	Length	Model	Chassis	Engine	Fuel Type	Price/Ft	Wheelbase	Towing	GVWR	Curb Wt
Lazy Daze	1995	MHC	23	22 MP	FO	7.5L	G	$2600	158	1,500	10,500	9,554

Livability Code: SB 20-90
Wheelbase-to-length ratio of 58% is considered ○ dangerous ○ fatiguing ○ good ◉ excellent *
The approximate net payload of 946 pounds at 9% of GVWR on this model is ○ deficient ○ excessive ◉ cautionary ○ good ○ excellent *
Total highway safety penalties are: 2 * — Value: 8 5 — Durability: 9 0 — Highway Control Rating: 8 7 — Highway Safety: 8 5 — ★★★★

Brand	Year	Type	Length	Model	Chassis	Engine	Fuel Type	Price/Ft	Wheelbase	Towing	GVWR	Curb Wt
Lazy Daze	1995	MHC	23	22 RL	FO	7.5L	G	$2600	158	1,500	10,500	9,531

Livability Code: SB 20-90
Wheelbase-to-length ratio of 58% is considered ○ dangerous ○ fatiguing ○ good ◉ excellent *
The approximate net payload of 969 pounds at 9% of GVWR on this model is ○ deficient ○ excessive ◉ cautionary ○ good ○ excellent *
Total highway safety penalties are: 2 * — Value: 8 5 — Durability: 9 0 — Highway Control Rating: 8 8 — Highway Safety: 8 6 — ★★★★

Brand	Year	Type	Length	Model	Chassis	Engine	Fuel Type	Price/Ft	Wheelbase	Towing	GVWR	Curb Wt
Lazy Daze	1995	MHC	23	22 FL	FO	7.5L	G	$2600	158	1,500	10,500	9,619

Livability Code: SB 20-90
Wheelbase-to-length ratio of 58% is considered ○ dangerous ○ fatiguing ○ good ◉ excellent *
The approximate net payload of 881 pounds at 8% of GVWR on this model is ○ deficient ○ excessive ◉ cautionary ○ good ○ excellent *
Total highway safety penalties are: 2 * — Value: 8 5 — Durability: 9 0 — Highway Control Rating: 8 2 — Highway Safety: 8 0 — ★★★★

Brand	Year	Type	Length	Model	Chassis	Engine	Fuel Type	Price/Ft	Wheelbase	Towing	GVWR	Curb Wt
Lazy Daze	1995	MHC	27	26 MB	FO	7.5L	G	$2200	176	1,500	11,500	10,877

Livability Code: SB 20-90
Wheelbase-to-length ratio of 55% is considered ○ dangerous ○ fatiguing ◉ good ○ excellent *
The approximate net payload of 623 pounds at 5% of GVWR on this model is ◉ deficient ○ excessive ○ cautionary ○ good ○ excellent *
Total highway safety penalties are: 2 * — Value: 8 5 — Durability: 9 0 — Highway Control Rating: 5 8 — Highway Safety: 5 6 — ★

Brand	Year	Type	Length	Model	Chassis	Engine	Fuel Type	Price/Ft	Wheelbase	Towing	GVWR	Curb Wt
Lazy Daze	1995	MHC	27	26 RB	FO	7.5L	G	$2200	176	1,500	11,500	10,840

Livability Code: SB 20-90
Wheelbase-to-length ratio of 55% is considered ○ dangerous ○ fatiguing ◉ good ○ excellent *
The approximate net payload of 660 pounds at 6% of GVWR on this model is ◉ deficient ○ excessive ○ cautionary ○ good ○ excellent *
Total highway safety penalties are: 2 * — Value: 8 5 — Durability: 9 0 — Highway Control Rating: 5 8 — Highway Safety: 5 6 — ★

Brand	Year	Type	Length	Model	Chassis	Engine	Fuel Type	Price/Ft	Wheelbase	Towing	GVWR	Curb Wt
Lazy Daze	1995	MHC	31	30	CH	7.4L	G	$1800	190	2,500	14,500	12,709

Livability Code: SB 20-90
Wheelbase-to-length ratio of 52% is considered ○ dangerous ◉ fatiguing ○ good ○ excellent *
The approximate net payload of 1791 pounds at 12% of GVWR on this model is ○ deficient ○ excessive ○ cautionary ◉ good ○ excellent *
Total highway safety penalties are: 2 * — Value: 8 5 — Durability: 9 0 — Highway Control Rating: 6 2 — Highway Safety: 6 0 — ★★

Brand	Year	Type	Length	Model	Chassis	Engine	Fuel Type	Price/Ft	Wheelbase	Towing	GVWR	Curb Wt
Lazy Daze	1998	MHC	22	22M-T	CH	5.7L	G	$2700	159	2,000	11,500	9,636

Livability Code: SB 20-90
Wheelbase-to-length ratio of 60% is considered ○ dangerous ○ fatiguing ○ good ◉ excellent *
The approximate net payload of 1864 pounds at 16% of GVWR on this model is ○ deficient ○ excessive ○ cautionary ○ good ◉ excellent *
Total highway safety penalties are: 2 * — Value: 9 0 — Durability: 9 0 — Highway Control Rating: 1 0 0 — Highway Safety: 9 8 — ★★★★★

Note: Safety ratings are based on the assumption that the engineering of the RV has allowed for proper balance by placing fresh, gray, and black holding tanks in a location so as not to change the balance of the RV when the tanks are empty or full. **Always double-check wheelbase, GVWR, and weights at front and rear axles.**

*See Section 1 for details on how conclusions are reached.

Brand	Year	Type	Length	Model	Chassis	Engine	Fuel Type	Average Price per Linear Foot When New	Adjusted Wheelbase	Approx. Towing Capacity	Gross Vehicle Weight Rating	Average Curb Weight
Lazy Daze	1998	MHC	22	22M-T op eng	CH	7.4L	G	$2700	159	5,500	11,500	9,636

Livability Code: SB 20-90   Wheelbase-to-length ratio of 60% is considered ○ dangerous ○ fatiguing ○ good ◉ excellent *
The approximate net payload of 1864 pounds at 16% of GVWR on this model is ○ deficient ○ excessive ○ cautionary ○ good ◉ excellent *
Total highway safety penalties are: 2 *   Value: 90   Durability: 90   Highway Control Rating: 100   Highway Safety: 98   ★★★★★

Lazy Daze	1998	MHC	24	23.5T-K	FO	6.8L	G	$2500	158	7,000	11,500	10,020

Livability Code: SB 20-90   Wheelbase-to-length ratio of 56% is considered ○ dangerous ○ fatiguing ◉ good ○ excellent *
The approximate net payload of 1480 pounds at 13% of GVWR on this model is ○ deficient ○ excessive ○ cautionary ◉ good ○ excellent *
Total highway safety penalties are: 2 *   Value: 90   Durability: 90   Highway Control Rating: 90   Highway Safety: 88   ★★★★

Lazy Daze	1998	MHC	24	23.5RL	FO	6.8L	G	$2500	158	7,000	11,500	10,018

Livability Code: SB 20-90   Wheelbase-to-length ratio of 56% is considered ○ dangerous ○ fatiguing ◉ good ○ excellent *
The approximate net payload of 1482 pounds at 13% of GVWR on this model is ○ deficient ○ excessive ○ cautionary ◉ good ○ excellent *
Total highway safety penalties are: 2 *   Value: 90   Durability: 90   Highway Control Rating: 90   Highway Safety: 88   ★★★★

Lazy Daze	1998	MHC	24	23.5FD	FO	6.8L	G	$2500	158	7,000	11,500	10,077

Livability Code: SB 20-90   Wheelbase-to-length ratio of 56% is considered ○ dangerous ○ fatiguing ◉ good ○ excellent *
The approximate net payload of 1423 pounds at 12% of GVWR on this model is ○ deficient ○ excessive ○ cautionary ◉ good ○ excellent *
Total highway safety penalties are: 2 *   Value: 90   Durability: 90   Highway Control Rating: 89   Highway Safety: 87   ★★★★

Lazy Daze	1998	MHC	27	26.5 M-B	FO	6.8L	G	$2200	176	5,950	14,050	11,606

Livability Code: SB 20-90   Wheelbase-to-length ratio of 55% is considered ○ dangerous ○ fatiguing ◉ good ○ excellent *
The approximate net payload of 2444 pounds at 17% of GVWR on this model is ○ deficient ○ excessive ○ cautionary ○ good ◉ excellent *
Total highway safety penalties are: 2 *   Value: 90   Durability: 90   Highway Control Rating: 95   Highway Safety: 93   ★★★★★

Lazy Daze	1998	MHC	27	26.5 RB	FO	6.8L	G	$2200	176	5,950	14,050	11,506

Livability Code: SB 20-90   Wheelbase-to-length ratio of 55% is considered ○ dangerous ○ fatiguing ◉ good ○ excellent *
The approximate net payload of 2544 pounds at 18% of GVWR on this model is ○ deficient ○ excessive ○ cautionary ○ good ◉ excellent *
Total highway safety penalties are: 2 *   Value: 90   Durability: 90   Highway Control Rating: 96   Highway Safety: 94   ★★★★★

Lazy Daze	1998	MHC	27	26.5 IB	FO	6.8L	G	$2200	176	5,950	14,050	11,578

Livability Code: SB 20-90   Wheelbase-to-length ratio of 55% is considered ○ dangerous ○ fatiguing ◉ good ○ excellent *
The approximate net payload of 2472 pounds at 18% of GVWR on this model is ○ deficient ○ excessive ○ cautionary ○ good ◉ excellent *
Total highway safety penalties are: 2 *   Value: 90   Durability: 90   Highway Control Rating: 95   Highway Safety: 93   ★★★★★

Lazy Daze	1998	MHC	30	30 IB	FO	6.8L	G	$2000	211	5,950	14,050	12,590

Livability Code: SB 20-90   Wheelbase-to-length ratio of 59% is considered ○ dangerous ○ fatiguing ○ good ◉ excellent *
The approximate net payload of 1460 pounds at 10% of GVWR on this model is ○ deficient ○ excessive ○ cautionary ◉ good ○ excellent *
Total highway safety penalties are: 2 *   Value: 90   Durability: 90   Highway Control Rating: 94   Highway Safety: 92   ★★★★★

Lazy Daze	1999	MHC	24	23.5 RL	FO	6.8L	G	$2700	158	7,000	11,500	9,909

Livability Code: SB 20-90   Wheelbase-to-length ratio of 56% is considered ○ dangerous ○ fatiguing ◉ good ○ excellent *
The approximate net payload of 1591 pounds at 14% of GVWR on this model is ○ deficient ○ excessive ○ cautionary ◉ good ○ excellent *
Total highway safety penalties are: 2 *   Value: 95   Durability: 90   Highway Control Rating: 92   Highway Safety: 90   ★★★★★

Lazy Daze	1999	MHC	24	23.5 T-KB	FO	6.8L	G	$2700	158	7,000	11,500	9,911

Livability Code: SB 20-90   Wheelbase-to-length ratio of 56% is considered ○ dangerous ○ fatiguing ◉ good ○ excellent *
The approximate net payload of 1589 pounds at 14% of GVWR on this model is ○ deficient ○ excessive ○ cautionary ◉ good ○ excellent *
Total highway safety penalties are: 2 *   Value: 95   Durability: 90   Highway Control Rating: 92   Highway Safety: 90   ★★★★★

Lazy Daze	1999	MHC	24	23.5 FD	FO	6.8L	G	$2700	158	7,000	11,500	9,974

Livability Code: SB 20-90   Wheelbase-to-length ratio of 56% is considered ○ dangerous ○ fatiguing ◉ good ○ excellent *
The approximate net payload of 1526 pounds at 13% of GVWR on this model is ○ deficient ○ excessive ○ cautionary ◉ good ○ excellent *
Total highway safety penalties are: 2 *   Value: 95   Durability: 90   Highway Control Rating: 91   Highway Safety: 89   ★★★★

Lazy Daze	1999	MHC	24	23.5 FL	FO	6.8L	G	$2700	158	7,000	11,500	9,981

Livability Code: SB 20-90   Wheelbase-to-length ratio of 56% is considered ○ dangerous ○ fatiguing ◉ good ○ excellent *
The approximate net payload of 1519 pounds at 13% of GVWR on this model is ○ deficient ○ excessive ○ cautionary ◉ good ○ excellent *
Total highway safety penalties are: 2 *   Value: 95   Durability: 90   Highway Control Rating: 90   Highway Safety: 88   ★★★★

Note: Safety ratings are based on the assumption that the engineering of the RV has allowed for proper balance by placing fresh, gray, and black holding tanks in a location so as not to change the balance of the RV when the tanks are empty or full. **Always double-check wheelbase, GVWR, and weights at front and rear axles.**

The RV Rating Book

*See Section 1 for details on how conclusions are reached.

Brand	Year	Type	Length	Model	Chassis	Engine	Fuel Type	Average Price per Linear Foot When New	Adjusted Wheelbase	Approx. Towing Capacity	Gross Vehicle Weight Rating	Average Curb Weight
Lazy Daze	1999	MHC	27	26.5 RK	FO	6.8L	G	$2400	176	5,950	14,050	11,503

Livability Code: SB 20-90
Wheelbase-to-length ratio of 55% is considered ○ dangerous ○ fatiguing ◉ good ○ excellent*
The approximate net payload of 2547 pounds at 18% of GVWR on this model is ○ deficient ○ excessive ○ cautionary ○ good ◉ excellent*
Total highway safety penalties are: 2*   Value: 95   Durability: 90   Highway Control Rating: 96   Highway Safety: 94   ★★★★★

Brand	Year	Type	Length	Model	Chassis	Engine	Fuel Type	Price/Ft	Wheelbase	Towing	GVWR	Curb Weight
Lazy Daze	1999	MHC	27	26.5 MB	FO	6.8L	G	$2400	176	5,950	14,050	11,505

Livability Code: SB 20-90
Wheelbase-to-length ratio of 55% is considered ○ dangerous ○ fatiguing ◉ good ○ excellent*
The approximate net payload of 2545 pounds at 18% of GVWR on this model is ○ deficient ○ excessive ○ cautionary ○ good ◉ excellent*
Total highway safety penalties are: 2*   Value: 95   Durability: 90   Highway Control Rating: 96   Highway Safety: 94   ★★★★★

Brand	Year	Type	Length	Model	Chassis	Engine	Fuel Type	Price/Ft	Wheelbase	Towing	GVWR	Curb Weight
Lazy Daze	1999	MHC	27	26.5 RB	FO	6.8L	G	$2400	176	5,950	14,050	11,423

Livability Code: SB 20-90
Wheelbase-to-length ratio of 55% is considered ○ dangerous ○ fatiguing ◉ good ○ excellent*
The approximate net payload of 2627 pounds at 19% of GVWR on this model is ○ deficient ○ excessive ○ cautionary ○ good ◉ excellent*
Total highway safety penalties are: 2*   Value: 95   Durability: 90   Highway Control Rating: 96   Highway Safety: 94   ★★★★★

Brand	Year	Type	Length	Model	Chassis	Engine	Fuel Type	Price/Ft	Wheelbase	Towing	GVWR	Curb Weight
Lazy Daze	1999	MHC	27	26.5 IB	FO	6.8L	G	$2400	176	5,950	14,050	11,473

Livability Code: SB 20-90
Wheelbase-to-length ratio of 55% is considered ○ dangerous ○ fatiguing ◉ good ○ excellent*
The approximate net payload of 2577 pounds at 18% of GVWR on this model is ○ deficient ○ excessive ○ cautionary ○ good ◉ excellent*
Total highway safety penalties are: 2*   Value: 95   Durability: 90   Highway Control Rating: 96   Highway Safety: 94   ★★★★★

Brand	Year	Type	Length	Model	Chassis	Engine	Fuel Type	Price/Ft	Wheelbase	Towing	GVWR	Curb Weight
Lazy Daze	1999	MHC	30	30 IB	FO	6.8L	G	$2200	211	5,950	14,050	12,547

Livability Code: SB 20-90
Wheelbase-to-length ratio of 59% is considered ○ dangerous ○ fatiguing ○ good ◉ excellent*
The approximate net payload of 1503 pounds at 11% of GVWR on this model is ○ deficient ○ excessive ○ cautionary ○ good ◉ excellent*
Total highway safety penalties are: 2*   Value: 95   Durability: 90   Highway Control Rating: 95   Highway Safety: 93   ★★★★★

Brand	Year	Type	Length	Model	Chassis	Engine	Fuel Type	Price/Ft	Wheelbase	Towing	GVWR	Curb Weight
Leisure Travel	1997	MHB	19.	19 std	DO	5.2L	G	$2900	128	1,500	8,500	7,200

Livability Code: VA 30-90
Wheelbase-to-length ratio of 56% is considered ○ dangerous ○ fatiguing ◉ good ○ excellent*
The approximate net payload of 1300 pounds at 15% of GVWR on this model is ○ deficient ○ excessive ○ cautionary ◉ good ○ excellent*
Total highway safety penalties are: 2*   Value: 80   Durability: 78   Highway Control Rating: 94   Highway Safety: 92   ★★★

Brand	Year	Type	Length	Model	Chassis	Engine	Fuel Type	Price/Ft	Wheelbase	Towing	GVWR	Curb Weight
Leisure Travel	1997	MHB	19	19 std op eng	DO	5.9L	G	$2900	128	1,500	8,500	7,200

Livability Code: VA 30-90
Wheelbase-to-length ratio of 56% is considered ○ dangerous ○ fatiguing ◉ good ○ excellent*
The approximate net payload of 1300 pounds at 15% of GVWR on this model is ○ deficient ○ excessive ○ cautionary ◉ good ○ excellent*
Total highway safety penalties are: 2*   Value: 80   Durability: 78   Highway Control Rating: 94   Highway Safety: 92   ★★★

Brand	Year	Type	Length	Model	Chassis	Engine	Fuel Type	Price/Ft	Wheelbase	Towing	GVWR	Curb Weight
Leisure Travel	1997	MHB	19	19 wide	DO	5.2L	G	$2900	128	1,500	8,500	7,343

Livability Code: VA 30-90
Wheelbase-to-length ratio of 56% is considered ○ dangerous ○ fatiguing ◉ good ○ excellent*
The approximate net payload of 1158 pounds at 14% of GVWR on this model is ○ deficient ○ excessive ○ cautionary ◉ good ○ excellent*
Total highway safety penalties are: 2*   Value: 80   Durability: 78   Highway Control Rating: 92   Highway Safety: 90   ★★★

Brand	Year	Type	Length	Model	Chassis	Engine	Fuel Type	Price/Ft	Wheelbase	Towing	GVWR	Curb Weight
Leisure Travel	1997	MHB	19	19 wide op eng	DO	5.9L	G	$2900	128	1,500	8,500	7,343

Livability Code: VA 30-90
Wheelbase-to-length ratio of 56% is considered ○ dangerous ○ fatiguing ◉ good ○ excellent*
The approximate net payload of 1158 pounds at 14% of GVWR on this model is ○ deficient ○ excessive ○ cautionary ◉ good ○ excellent*
Total highway safety penalties are: 2*   Value: 80   Durability: 78   Highway Control Rating: 92   Highway Safety: 90   ★★★

Brand	Year	Type	Length	Model	Chassis	Engine	Fuel Type	Price/Ft	Wheelbase	Towing	GVWR	Curb Weight
Leisure Travel	1998	MHB	19	Freedom	DO	5.2L	G	$2900	127	1,500	8,500	7,343

Livability Code: VA 30-90
Wheelbase-to-length ratio of 56% is considered ○ dangerous ○ fatiguing ◉ good ○ excellent*
The approximate net payload of 1158 pounds at 14% of GVWR on this model is ○ deficient ○ excessive ○ cautionary ◉ good ○ excellent*
Total highway safety penalties are: 2*   Value: 80   Durability: 78   Highway Control Rating: 91   Highway Safety: 89   ★★★

Brand	Year	Type	Length	Model	Chassis	Engine	Fuel Type	Price/Ft	Wheelbase	Towing	GVWR	Curb Weight
Leisure Travel	1998	MHB	19	Freedom op eng	DO	5.9L	G	$2900	127	1,500	8,500	7,343

Livability Code: VA 30-90
Wheelbase-to-length ratio of 56% is considered ○ dangerous ○ fatiguing ◉ good ○ excellent*
The approximate net payload of 1158 pounds at 14% of GVWR on this model is ○ deficient ○ excessive ○ cautionary ◉ good ○ excellent*
Total highway safety penalties are: 2*   Value: 80   Durability: 78   Highway Control Rating: 91   Highway Safety: 89   ★★★

Brand	Year	Type	Length	Model	Chassis	Engine	Fuel Type	Price/Ft	Wheelbase	Towing	GVWR	Curb Weight
Leisure Travel	1999	MHB	19	3S	DO	5.2L	G	$2900	127	1,500	8,500	7,343

Livability Code: VA 30-90
Wheelbase-to-length ratio of 56% is considered ○ dangerous ○ fatiguing ◉ good ○ excellent*
The approximate net payload of 1158 pounds at 14% of GVWR on this model is ○ deficient ○ excessive ○ cautionary ◉ good ○ excellent*
Total highway safety penalties are: 2*   Value: 80   Durability: 78   Highway Control Rating: 91   Highway Safety: 89   ★★★

Note: Safety ratings are based on the assumption that the engineering of the RV has allowed for proper balance by placing fresh, gray, and black holding tanks in a location so as not to change the balance of the RV when the tanks are empty or full. **Always double-check wheelbase, GVWR, and weights at front and rear axles.**

*See Section 1 for details on how conclusions are reached.

Brand	Year	Type	Length	Model	Chassis	Engine	Fuel Type	Average Price per Linear Foot When New	Adjusted Wheelbase	Approx. Towing Capacity	Gross Vehicle Weight Rating	Average Curb Weight
Leisure Travel	1999	MHB	19	2SA	DO	5.2L	G	$2900	127	1,500	8,500	7,343

Livability Code: VA 30-90   Wheelbase-to-length ratio of 56% is considered ○ dangerous ○ fatiguing ◉ good ○ excellent *

The approximate net payload of 1158 pounds at 14% of GVWR on this model is ○ deficient ○ excessive ○ cautionary ◉ good ○ excellent *

Total highway safety penalties are: 2 *   Value: **80** Durability: **78** Highway Control Rating: **91**   Highway Safety: **89**   ★★★

Brand	Year	Type	Length	Model	Chassis	Engine	Fuel Type	Price/Ft	Wheelbase	Towing	GVWR	Curb Weight
Leisure Travel	1999	MHB	19	2SB	DO	5.2L	G	$2900	127	1,500	8,500	7,343

Livability Code: VA 30-90   Wheelbase-to-length ratio of 56% is considered ○ dangerous ○ fatiguing ◉ good ○ excellent *

The approximate net payload of 1158 pounds at 14% of GVWR on this model is ○ deficient ○ excessive ○ cautionary ◉ good ○ excellent *

Total highway safety penalties are: 2 *   Value: **80** Durability: **78** Highway Control Rating: **91**   Highway Safety: **89**   ★★★

Leisure Travel	1999	MHB	19	4S op eng	DO	5.9L	G	$2900	127	1,500	8,500	7,343

Livability Code: VA 30-90   Wheelbase-to-length ratio of 56% is considered ○ dangerous ○ fatiguing ◉ good ○ excellent *

The approximate net payload of 1158 pounds at 14% of GVWR on this model is ○ deficient ○ excessive ○ cautionary ◉ good ○ excellent *

Total highway safety penalties are: 2 *   Value: **80** Durability: **78** Highway Control Rating: **91**   Highway Safety: **89**   ★★★

Leisure Travel	1999	MHB	19	3S op eng	DO	5.9L	G	$2900	127	1,500	8,500	7,343

Livability Code: VA 30-90   Wheelbase-to-length ratio of 56% is considered ○ dangerous ○ fatiguing ◉ good ○ excellent *

The approximate net payload of 1158 pounds at 14% of GVWR on this model is ○ deficient ○ excessive ○ cautionary ◉ good ○ excellent *

Total highway safety penalties are: 2 *   Value: **80** Durability: **78** Highway Control Rating: **91**   Highway Safety: **89**   ★★★

Leisure Travel	1999	MHB	19	2SA op eng	DO	5.9L	G	$2900	127	1,500	8,500	7,343

Livability Code: VA 30-90   Wheelbase-to-length ratio of 56% is considered ○ dangerous ○ fatiguing ◉ good ○ excellent *

The approximate net payload of 1158 pounds at 14% of GVWR on this model is ○ deficient ○ excessive ○ cautionary ◉ good ○ excellent *

Total highway safety penalties are: 2 *   Value: **80** Durability: **78** Highway Control Rating: **91**   Highway Safety: **89**   ★★★

Leisure Travel	1999	MHB	19	2SB op eng	DO	5.9L	G	$2900	127	1,500	8,500	7,343

Livability Code: VA 30-90   Wheelbase-to-length ratio of 56% is considered ○ dangerous ○ fatiguing ◉ good ○ excellent *

The approximate net payload of 1158 pounds at 14% of GVWR on this model is ○ deficient ○ excessive ○ cautionary ◉ good ○ excellent *

Total highway safety penalties are: 2 *   Value: **80** Durability: **78** Highway Control Rating: **91**   Highway Safety: **89**   ★★★

Leisure Travel	1999	MHB	19	4S	DO	5.2L	G	$2900	127	1,500	8,500	7,343

Livability Code: VA 30-90   Wheelbase-to-length ratio of 56% is considered ○ dangerous ○ fatiguing ◉ good ○ excellent *

The approximate net payload of 1158 pounds at 14% of GVWR on this model is ○ deficient ○ excessive ○ cautionary ◉ good ○ excellent *

Total highway safety penalties are: 2 *   Value: **80** Durability: **78** Highway Control Rating: **91**   Highway Safety: **89**   ★★★

Lextra	1991	MHA	25	25	LG	5.9L	G	$1600	158	1,500	10,400	9,738

Livability Code: 30-80   Wheelbase-to-length ratio of 53% is considered ○ dangerous ◉ fatiguing ○ good ○ excellent *

The approximate net payload of 662 pounds at 6% of GVWR on this model is ◉ deficient ○ excessive ○ cautionary ○ good ○ excellent *

Total highway safety penalties are: 2 *   Value: **77** Durability: **70** Highway Control Rating: **35**   Highway Safety: **33**

Limited	1990	MHA	36	XL 936	CH	7.4L	G	$2300	232 T	1,500	19,000	15,539

Livability Code: SB 30-90   Wheelbase-to-length ratio of 53% is considered ○ dangerous ◉ fatiguing ○ good ○ excellent *

The approximate net payload of 3461 pounds at 18% of GVWR on this model is ○ deficient ○ excessive ○ cautionary ○ good ◉ excellent *

Total highway safety penalties are: 10 *   Value: **81** Durability: **77** Highway Control Rating: **74**   Highway Safety: **64**   ★★

Limited XL	1991	MHA	34	340	FO	7.5L	G	$1900	208	8,000	17,000	15,808

Livability Code: SB 30-90   Wheelbase-to-length ratio of 50% is considered ◉ dangerous ○ fatiguing ○ good ○ excellent *

The approximate net payload of 1192 pounds at 7% of GVWR on this model is ○ deficient ○ excessive ◉ cautionary ○ good ○ excellent *

Total highway safety penalties are: 2 *   Value: **85** Durability: **77** Highway Control Rating: **17**   Highway Safety: **15**

London Aire	1990	MHA	29	28RBD	FO	7.5L	G	$2700	182 T	1,500	15,000	12,988

Livability Code: FT 30-90   Wheelbase-to-length ratio of 53% is considered ○ dangerous ◉ fatiguing ○ good ○ excellent *

The approximate net payload of 2012 pounds at 13% of GVWR on this model is ○ deficient ○ excessive ○ cautionary ◉ good ○ excellent *

Total highway safety penalties are: 4 *   Value: **79** Durability: **78** Highway Control Rating: **64**   Highway Safety: **60**   ★★

London Aire	1990	MHA	37	37 SA/SS	CH	7.4L	G	$3400	202 T	1,500	18,000	15,810

Livability Code: FT 30-90   Wheelbase-to-length ratio of 45% is considered ◉ dangerous ○ fatiguing ○ good ○ excellent *

The approximate net payload of 2190 pounds at 12% of GVWR on this model is ○ deficient ○ excessive ○ cautionary ◉ good ○ excellent *

Total highway safety penalties are: 11 *   Value: **76** Durability: **78** Highway Control Rating: **19**   Highway Safety: **8**

Note: Safety ratings are based on the assumption that the engineering of the RV has allowed for proper balance by placing fresh, gray, and black holding tanks in a location so as not to change the balance of the RV when the tanks are empty or full. **Always double-check wheelbase, GVWR, and weights at front and rear axles.**

*See Section 1 for details on how conclusions are reached.

Brand	Year	Type	Length	Model	Chassis	Engine	Fuel Type	Average Price per Linear Foot When New	Adjusted Wheelbase	Approx. Towing Capacity	Gross Vehicle Weight Rating	Average Curb Weight
London Aire	1991	MHA	29	28 WCB	FO	7.5L	G	$3400	182 T	4,500	15,000	13,667

Livability Code: VA 30-90   Wheelbase-to-length ratio of 53% is considered ○ dangerous ● fatiguing ○ good ○ excellent *

The approximate net payload of 1333 pounds at 9% of GVWR on this model is ○ deficient ○ excessive ● cautionary ○ good ○ excellent *

Total highway safety penalties are: 4 *   Value: **7 9**   Durability: **7 8**   Highway Control Rating: **5 2**   Highway Safety: **4 8**

Brand	Year	Type	Length	Model	Chassis	Engine	Fuel Type	Avg Price/Lin Ft	Adj Wheelbase	Approx Tow Cap	GVWR	Avg Curb Wt
London Aire	1991	MHA	38	37 WC/SA/SS	CH	7.4L	G	$3500	202 T	1,500	18,500	16,749

Livability Code: FT 30-90   Wheelbase-to-length ratio of 44% is considered ● dangerous ○ fatiguing ○ good ○ excellent *

The approximate net payload of 1751 pounds at 9% of GVWR on this model is ○ deficient ○ excessive ● cautionary ○ good ○ excellent *

Total highway safety penalties are: 11 *   Value: **7 6**   Durability: **7 8**   Highway Control Rating: **8**   Highway Safety: **- 3**

Brand	Year	Type	Length	Model	Chassis	Engine	Fuel Type	Avg Price/Lin Ft	Adj Wheelbase	Approx Tow Cap	GVWR	Avg Curb Wt
London Aire	1994	MHA	38	38 CBSA-sl	SP	CU300	D	$5400	252	5,000	26,000	24,620

Livability Code: FT 30-90   Wheelbase-to-length ratio of 55% is considered ○ dangerous ○ fatiguing ● good ○ excellent *

The approximate net payload of 1380 pounds at 5% of GVWR on this model is ● deficient ○ excessive ○ cautionary ○ good ○ excellent *

Total highway safety penalties are: 5 *   Value: **7 9**   Durability: **7 8**   Highway Control Rating: **5 8**   Highway Safety: **5 3**   ★

Brand	Year	Type	Length	Model	Chassis	Engine	Fuel Type	Avg Price/Lin Ft	Adj Wheelbase	Approx Tow Cap	GVWR	Avg Curb Wt
London Aire	1994	MHA	38	38 WDSK-sl	SP	CU300	D	$5400	252	5,000	26,000	24,910

Livability Code: FT 30-90   Wheelbase-to-length ratio of 55% is considered ○ dangerous ○ fatiguing ● good ○ excellent *

The approximate net payload of 1090 pounds at 4% of GVWR on this model is ● deficient ○ excessive ○ cautionary ○ good ○ excellent *

Total highway safety penalties are: 5 *   Value: **7 9**   Durability: **7 8**   Highway Control Rating: **5 7**   Highway Safety: **5 2**   ★

Brand	Year	Type	Length	Model	Chassis	Engine	Fuel Type	Avg Price/Lin Ft	Adj Wheelbase	Approx Tow Cap	GVWR	Avg Curb Wt
London Aire	1994	MHA	38	38 WDSL-sl	SP	CU300	D	$5400	252	5,000	26,000	25,070

Livability Code: FT 30-90   Wheelbase-to-length ratio of 55% is considered ○ dangerous ○ fatiguing ● good ○ excellent *

The approximate net payload of 930 pounds at 4% of GVWR on this model is ● deficient ○ excessive ○ cautionary ○ good ○ excellent *

Total highway safety penalties are: 6 *   Value: **7 8**   Durability: **7 8**   Highway Control Rating: **5 6**   Highway Safety: **5 0**   ★

Brand	Year	Type	Length	Model	Chassis	Engine	Fuel Type	Avg Price/Lin Ft	Adj Wheelbase	Approx Tow Cap	GVWR	Avg Curb Wt
London Aire	1994	MHA	40	40 CBSA-sl	SP	CU300	D	$5300	276	5,000	26,000	25,090

Livability Code: FT 30-90   Wheelbase-to-length ratio of 58% is considered ○ dangerous ○ fatiguing ○ good ● excellent *

The approximate net payload of 910 pounds at 4% of GVWR on this model is ● deficient ○ excessive ○ cautionary ○ good ○ excellent *

Total highway safety penalties are: 6 *   Value: **7 8**   Durability: **7 8**   Highway Control Rating: **6 4**   Highway Safety: **5 8**   ★

Brand	Year	Type	Length	Model	Chassis	Engine	Fuel Type	Avg Price/Lin Ft	Adj Wheelbase	Approx Tow Cap	GVWR	Avg Curb Wt
London Aire	1994	MHA	40	40 WDSK-sl	SP	CU300	D	$5300	276	5,000	26,000	25,390

Livability Code: FT 30-90   Wheelbase-to-length ratio of 58% is considered ○ dangerous ○ fatiguing ○ good ● excellent *

The approximate net payload of 610 pounds at 2% of GVWR on this model is ● deficient ○ excessive ○ cautionary ○ good ○ excellent *

Total highway safety penalties are: 6 *   Value: **7 8**   Durability: **7 8**   Highway Control Rating: **6 3**   Highway Safety: **5 7**   ★

Brand	Year	Type	Length	Model	Chassis	Engine	Fuel Type	Avg Price/Lin Ft	Adj Wheelbase	Approx Tow Cap	GVWR	Avg Curb Wt
London Aire	1995	MHA	37	LP 3655-sl	SP	CU300	D	$5600	236	1,600	29,400	24,322

Livability Code: FT 30-90   Wheelbase-to-length ratio of 53% is considered ○ dangerous ● fatiguing ○ good ○ excellent *

The approximate net payload of 5078 pounds at 17% of GVWR on this model is ○ deficient ○ excessive ○ cautionary ○ good ● excellent *

Total highway safety penalties are: 5 *   Value: **7 9**   Durability: **7 8**   Highway Control Rating: **7 2**   Highway Safety: **6 7**   ★★

Brand	Year	Type	Length	Model	Chassis	Engine	Fuel Type	Avg Price/Lin Ft	Adj Wheelbase	Approx Tow Cap	GVWR	Avg Curb Wt
London Aire	1995	MHA	40	LP 4010	SP	CU300	D	$5400	276	1,600	29,400	25,940

Livability Code: FT 30-90   Wheelbase-to-length ratio of 58% is considered ○ dangerous ○ fatiguing ○ good ● excellent *

The approximate net payload of 3460 pounds at 12% of GVWR on this model is ○ deficient ○ excessive ○ cautionary ○ good ● excellent *

Total highway safety penalties are: 2 *   Value: **8 0**   Durability: **7 8**   Highway Control Rating: **9 3**   Highway Safety: **9 1**   ★★★

Brand	Year	Type	Length	Model	Chassis	Engine	Fuel Type	Avg Price/Lin Ft	Adj Wheelbase	Approx Tow Cap	GVWR	Avg Curb Wt
London Aire	1995	MHA	40	LP 4055-sl	SP	CU300	D	$5500	276	1,600	29,400	26,990

Livability Code: FT 30-90   Wheelbase-to-length ratio of 58% is considered ○ dangerous ○ fatiguing ○ good ● excellent *

The approximate net payload of 2410 pounds at 8% of GVWR on this model is ○ deficient ○ excessive ● cautionary ○ good ○ excellent *

Total highway safety penalties are: 6 *   Value: **7 8**   Durability: **7 8**   Highway Control Rating: **7 9**   Highway Safety: **7 3**   ★★★

Brand	Year	Type	Length	Model	Chassis	Engine	Fuel Type	Avg Price/Lin Ft	Adj Wheelbase	Approx Tow Cap	GVWR	Avg Curb Wt
London Aire	1995	MHA	40	LP 4060-sl	SP	CU300	D	$5500	276	1,600	29,400	26,990

Livability Code: FT 30-90   Wheelbase-to-length ratio of 58% is considered ○ dangerous ○ fatiguing ○ good ● excellent *

The approximate net payload of 2410 pounds at 8% of GVWR on this model is ○ deficient ○ excessive ● cautionary ○ good ○ excellent *

Total highway safety penalties are: 6 *   Value: **7 8**   Durability: **7 8**   Highway Control Rating: **7 9**   Highway Safety: **7 3**   ★★★

Brand	Year	Type	Length	Model	Chassis	Engine	Fuel Type	Avg Price/Lin Ft	Adj Wheelbase	Approx Tow Cap	GVWR	Avg Curb Wt
London Aire	1995	MHA	40	LP 4056-sl	SP	CU300	D	$5500	276	1,600	29,400	26,990

Livability Code: FT 30-90   Wheelbase-to-length ratio of 58% is considered ○ dangerous ○ fatiguing ○ good ● excellent *

The approximate net payload of 2410 pounds at 8% of GVWR on this model is ○ deficient ○ excessive ● cautionary ○ good ○ excellent *

Total highway safety penalties are: 6 *   Value: **7 8**   Durability: **7 8**   Highway Control Rating: **7 9**   Highway Safety: **7 3**   ★★★

Note: Safety ratings are based on the assumption that the engineering of the RV has allowed for proper balance by placing fresh, gray, and black holding tanks in a location so as not to change the balance of the RV when the tanks are empty or full. **Always double-check wheelbase, GVWR, and weights at front and rear axles.**

*See Section 1 for details on how conclusions are reached.

Brand	Year	Type	Length	Model	Chassis	Engine	Fuel Type	Average Price per Linear Foot When New	Adjusted Wheelbase	Approx. Towing Capacity	Gross Vehicle Weight Rating	Average Curb Weight
London Aire	1996	MHA	39	LP3856	SP	CU300	D	$5600	252	12,600	29,400	26,416

London Aire — 1996 — MHA 39 — LP3856
Livability Code: FT 30-90
Wheelbase-to-length ratio of 54% is considered ○ dangerous ○ fatiguing ◉ good ○ excellent *
The approximate net payload of 2984 pounds at 10% of GVWR on this model is ○ deficient ○ excessive ○ cautionary ◉ good ○ excellent *
Total highway safety penalties are: 5 *　　Value: 7 9　Durability: 7 8　Highway Control Rating: 7 6　　Highway Safety: 7 1　　★★★

London Aire — 1996 — MHA 39 — LP4055 — SP — CU300 — D — $5600 — 276 — 12,600 — 29,400 — 26,416
Livability Code: FT 30-90
Wheelbase-to-length ratio of 59% is considered ○ dangerous ○ fatiguing ○ good ◉ excellent *
The approximate net payload of 2984 pounds at 10% of GVWR on this model is ○ deficient ○ excessive ○ cautionary ◉ good ○ excellent *
Total highway safety penalties are: 5 *　　Value: 7 9　Durability: 7 8　Highway Control Rating: 9 6　　Highway Safety: 9 1　　★★★

London Aire — 1996 — MHA 39 — LP4056 — SP — CU300 — D — $5600 — 276 — 12,600 — 29,400 — 26,416
Livability Code: FT 30-90
Wheelbase-to-length ratio of 59% is considered ○ dangerous ○ fatiguing ○ good ◉ excellent *
The approximate net payload of 2984 pounds at 10% of GVWR on this model is ○ deficient ○ excessive ○ cautionary ◉ good ○ excellent *
Total highway safety penalties are: 5 *　　Value: 7 9　Durability: 7 8　Highway Control Rating: 9 6　　Highway Safety: 9 1　　★★★

London Aire — 1996 — MHA 39 — LP4057 — SP — CU300 — D — $5600 — 276 — 12,600 — 29,400 — 26,416
Livability Code: FT 30-90
Wheelbase-to-length ratio of 59% is considered ○ dangerous ○ fatiguing ○ good ◉ excellent *
The approximate net payload of 2984 pounds at 10% of GVWR on this model is ○ deficient ○ excessive ○ cautionary ◉ good ○ excellent *
Total highway safety penalties are: 5 *　　Value: 7 9　Durability: 7 8　Highway Control Rating: 9 6　　Highway Safety: 9 1　　★★★

London Aire — 1996 — MHA 39 — LP4060 — SP — CU300 — D — $5600 — 276 — 12,600 — 29,400 — 26,416
Livability Code: FT 30-90
Wheelbase-to-length ratio of 59% is considered ○ dangerous ○ fatiguing ○ good ◉ excellent *
The approximate net payload of 2984 pounds at 10% of GVWR on this model is ○ deficient ○ excessive ○ cautionary ◉ good ○ excellent *
Total highway safety penalties are: 5 *　　Value: 7 9　Durability: 7 8　Highway Control Rating: 9 6　　Highway Safety: 9 1　　★★★

London Aire — 1996 — MHA 39 — LP4061 — SP — CU300 — D — $5600 — 276 — 12,600 — 29,400 — 26,416
Livability Code: FT 30-90
Wheelbase-to-length ratio of 59% is considered ○ dangerous ○ fatiguing ○ good ◉ excellent *
The approximate net payload of 2984 pounds at 10% of GVWR on this model is ○ deficient ○ excessive ○ cautionary ◉ good ○ excellent *
Total highway safety penalties are: 5 *　　Value: 7 9　Durability: 7 8　Highway Control Rating: 9 6　　Highway Safety: 9 1　　★★★

London Aire — 1997 — MHA 41 — LP 4057 — FR — CU300 — D — $6000 — 276 — 5,000 — 31,000 — 28,547
Livability Code: FT 30-90
Wheelbase-to-length ratio of 56% is considered ○ dangerous ○ fatiguing ◉ good ○ excellent *
The approximate net payload of 2453 pounds at 8% of GVWR on this model is ○ deficient ○ excessive ◉ cautionary ○ good ○ excellent *
Total highway safety penalties are: 5 *　　Value: 7 9　Durability: 7 8　Highway Control Rating: 7 4　　Highway Safety: 6 9　　★★

London Aire — 1997 — MHA 41 — LP 4059 — FR — CU300 — D — $6000 — 276 — 5,000 — 31,000 — 28,547
Livability Code: FT 30-90
Wheelbase-to-length ratio of 56% is considered ○ dangerous ○ fatiguing ◉ good ○ excellent *
The approximate net payload of 2453 pounds at 8% of GVWR on this model is ○ deficient ○ excessive ◉ cautionary ○ good ○ excellent *
Total highway safety penalties are: 5 *　　Value: 7 9　Durability: 7 8　Highway Control Rating: 7 4　　Highway Safety: 6 9　　★★

London Aire — 1997 — MHA 41 — LP 4060 — FR — CU300 — D — $6000 — 276 — 5,000 — 31,000 — 28,547
Livability Code: FT 30-90
Wheelbase-to-length ratio of 56% is considered ○ dangerous ○ fatiguing ◉ good ○ excellent *
The approximate net payload of 2453 pounds at 8% of GVWR on this model is ○ deficient ○ excessive ◉ cautionary ○ good ○ excellent *
Total highway safety penalties are: 5 *　　Value: 7 9　Durability: 7 8　Highway Control Rating: 7 4　　Highway Safety: 6 9　　★★

London Aire — 1997 — MHA 41 — LP 4080 — FR — CU300 — D — $6100 — 276 — 5,000 — 31,000 — 28,547
Livability Code: FT 30-90
Wheelbase-to-length ratio of 56% is considered ○ dangerous ○ fatiguing ◉ good ○ excellent *
The approximate net payload of 2453 pounds at 8% of GVWR on this model is ○ deficient ○ excessive ◉ cautionary ○ good ○ excellent *
Total highway safety penalties are: 5 *　　Value: 7 9　Durability: 7 8　Highway Control Rating: 7 4　　Highway Safety: 6 9　　★★

London Aire — 1997 — MHA 41 — LP 4057 — SP — CU300 — D — $6000 — 276 — 5,000 — 31,000 — 28,647
Livability Code: FT 30-90
Wheelbase-to-length ratio of 56% is considered ○ dangerous ○ fatiguing ◉ good ○ excellent *
The approximate net payload of 2353 pounds at 8% of GVWR on this model is ○ deficient ○ excessive ◉ cautionary ○ good ○ excellent *
Total highway safety penalties are: 5 *　　Value: 7 9　Durability: 7 8　Highway Control Rating: 7 4　　Highway Safety: 6 9　　★★

London Aire — 1997 — MHA 41 — LP 4059 — SP — CU300 — D — $6000 — 276 — 5,000 — 31,000 — 28,647
Livability Code: FT 30-90
Wheelbase-to-length ratio of 56% is considered ○ dangerous ○ fatiguing ◉ good ○ excellent *
The approximate net payload of 2353 pounds at 8% of GVWR on this model is ○ deficient ○ excessive ◉ cautionary ○ good ○ excellent *
Total highway safety penalties are: 5 *　　Value: 7 9　Durability: 7 8　Highway Control Rating: 7 4　　Highway Safety: 6 9　　★★

Note: Safety ratings are based on the assumption that the engineering of the RV has allowed for proper balance by placing fresh, gray, and black holding tanks in a location so as not to change the balance of the RV when the tanks are empty or full. **Always double-check wheelbase, GVWR, and weights at front and rear axles.**

*See Section 1 for details on how conclusions are reached.

Section 2: The Ratings

Brand	Year	Type	Length	Model	Chassis	Engine	Fuel Type	Average Price per Linear Foot When New	Adjusted Wheelbase	Approx. Towing Capacity	Gross Vehicle Weight Rating	Average Curb Weight
London Aire	1997	MHA	41	LP 4060	SP	CU300	D	$6000	276	5,000	31,000	28,647

Livability Code: FT 30-90

Wheelbase-to-length ratio of 56% is considered ○ dangerous ○ fatiguing ◉ good ○ excellent *

The approximate net payload of 2353 pounds at 8% of GVWR on this model is ○ deficient ○ excessive ◉ cautionary ○ good ○ excellent *

Total highway safety penalties are: 5 *   Value: **7 9**   Durability: **7 8**   Highway Control Rating: **7 4**   Highway Safety: **6 9**   ★★

Brand	Year	Type	Length	Model	Chassis	Engine	Fuel Type	Price	Wheelbase	Towing	GVWR	Curb Weight
London Aire	1997	MHA	41	LP 4080	SP	CU300	D	$6100	276	5,000	31,000	28,647

Livability Code: FT 30-90

Wheelbase-to-length ratio of 56% is considered ○ dangerous ○ fatiguing ◉ good ○ excellent *

The approximate net payload of 2353 pounds at 8% of GVWR on this model is ○ deficient ○ excessive ◉ cautionary ○ good ○ excellent *

Total highway safety penalties are: 5 *   Value: **7 9**   Durability: **7 8**   Highway Control Rating: **7 4**   Highway Safety: **6 9**   ★★

London Aire	1998	MHA	43	LB4257	SP	450 HP	D	$5800	286	10,000	36,200	34,509

Livability Code: FT 30-90

Wheelbase-to-length ratio of 55% is considered ○ dangerous ○ fatiguing ◉ good ○ excellent *

The approximate net payload of 1691 pounds at 5% of GVWR on this model is ◉ deficient ○ excessive ○ cautionary ○ good ○ excellent *

Total highway safety penalties are: 5 *   Value: **7 9**   Durability: **7 8**   Highway Control Rating: **5 8**   Highway Safety: **5 3**   ★

London Aire	1998	MHA	43	LB4258	SP	450 HP	D	$5800	286	10,000	36,200	34,509

Livability Code: FT 30-90

Wheelbase-to-length ratio of 55% is considered ○ dangerous ○ fatiguing ◉ good ○ excellent *

The approximate net payload of 1691 pounds at 5% of GVWR on this model is ◉ deficient ○ excessive ○ cautionary ○ good ○ excellent *

Total highway safety penalties are: 5 *   Value: **7 9**   Durability: **7 8**   Highway Control Rating: **5 8**   Highway Safety: **5 3**   ★

London Aire	1998	MHA	43	LB4259	SP	450 HP	D	$5800	286	10,000	36,200	34,509

Livability Code: FT 30-90

Wheelbase-to-length ratio of 55% is considered ○ dangerous ○ fatiguing ◉ good ○ excellent *

The approximate net payload of 1691 pounds at 5% of GVWR on this model is ◉ deficient ○ excessive ○ cautionary ○ good ○ excellent *

Total highway safety penalties are: 5 *   Value: **7 9**   Durability: **7 8**   Highway Control Rating: **5 8**   Highway Safety: **5 3**   ★

London Aire	1999	MHA	41	LP 4080	SP	CU350	D	$6100	276	9,800	32,200	30,804

Livability Code: FT 30-90

Wheelbase-to-length ratio of 56% is considered ○ dangerous ○ fatiguing ◉ good ○ excellent *

The approximate net payload of 1396 pounds at 4% of GVWR on this model is ◉ deficient ○ excessive ○ cautionary ○ good ○ excellent *

Total highway safety penalties are: 5 *   Value: **8 5**   Durability: **8 1**   Highway Control Rating: **6 1**   Highway Safety: **5 6**   ★

London Aire	1999	MHA	41	LP 4082	SP	CU350	D	$6100	276	9,800	32,200	30,804

Livability Code: FT 30-90

Wheelbase-to-length ratio of 56% is considered ○ dangerous ○ fatiguing ◉ good ○ excellent *

The approximate net payload of 1396 pounds at 4% of GVWR on this model is ◉ deficient ○ excessive ○ cautionary ○ good ○ excellent *

Total highway safety penalties are: 5 *   Value: **8 5**   Durability: **8 1**   Highway Control Rating: **6 1**   Highway Safety: **5 6**   ★

London Aire	1999	MHA	43	LB 4258	SP	450 HP	D	$5800	286	10,000	36,200	34,509

Livability Code: FT 30-90

Wheelbase-to-length ratio of 55% is considered ○ dangerous ○ fatiguing ◉ good ○ excellent *

The approximate net payload of 1691 pounds at 5% of GVWR on this model is ◉ deficient ○ excessive ○ cautionary ○ good ○ excellent *

Total highway safety penalties are: 5 *   Value: **8 5**   Durability: **8 1**   Highway Control Rating: **5 8**   Highway Safety: **5 3**   ★

London Aire	1999	MHA	43	LB 4259	SP	450 HP	D	$5800	286	10,000	36,200	34,509

Livability Code: FT 30-90

Wheelbase-to-length ratio of 55% is considered ○ dangerous ○ fatiguing ◉ good ○ excellent *

The approximate net payload of 1691 pounds at 5% of GVWR on this model is ◉ deficient ○ excessive ○ cautionary ○ good ○ excellent *

Total highway safety penalties are: 5 *   Value: **8 5**   Durability: **8 1**   Highway Control Rating: **5 8**   Highway Safety: **5 3**   ★

Luxor	1995	MHA	37	37WQ 300	OS	Cu8.3L	D	$4600	228	1,500	25,500	22,397

Livability Code: FT 30-90

Wheelbase-to-length ratio of 51% is considered ○ dangerous ◉ fatiguing ○ good ○ excellent *

The approximate net payload of 3103 pounds at 12% of GVWR on this model is ○ deficient ○ excessive ○ cautionary ◉ good ○ excellent *

Total highway safety penalties are: 2 *   Value: **8 6**   Durability: **7 9**   Highway Control Rating: **4 2**   Highway Safety: **4 0**

Luxor	1996	MHA	37	37WQ	FR	CU300	D	$5100	228	4,000	26,000	23,697

Livability Code: FT 30-90

Wheelbase-to-length ratio of 51% is considered ○ dangerous ◉ fatiguing ○ good ○ excellent *

The approximate net payload of 2303 pounds at 9% of GVWR on this model is ○ deficient ○ excessive ◉ cautionary ○ good ○ excellent *

Total highway safety penalties are: 2 *   Value: **8 6**   Durability: **7 9**   Highway Control Rating: **3 3**   Highway Safety: **3 1**

Luxor	1997	MHA	38	37WQ pusher	FR	Cu325	D	$5200	228	2,590	27,410	25,109

Livability Code: FT 30-90

Wheelbase-to-length ratio of 50% is considered ◉ dangerous ○ fatiguing ○ good ○ excellent *

The approximate net payload of 2301 pounds at 8% of GVWR on this model is ○ deficient ○ excessive ◉ cautionary ○ good ○ excellent *

Total highway safety penalties are: 2 *   Value: **8 6**   Durability: **7 9**   Highway Control Rating: **2 3**   Highway Safety: **2 1**

Note: Safety ratings are based on the assumption that the engineering of the RV has allowed for proper balance by placing fresh, gray, and black holding tanks in a location so as not to change the balance of the RV when the tanks are empty or full. **Always double-check wheelbase, GVWR, and weights at front and rear axles.**

*See Section 1 for details on how conclusions are reached.

Section 2: The Ratings

Brand	Year	Type	Length	Model	Chassis	Engine	Fuel Type	Average Price per Linear Foot When New	Adjusted Wheelbase	Approx. Towing Capacity	Gross Vehicle Weight Rating	Average Curb Weight
Luxor	1997	MHA	38	37WP pusher	FR	Cu325	D	$5200	228	2,590	27,410	25,109

Livability Code: FT 30-90
Wheelbase-to-length ratio of 50% is considered ● dangerous ○ fatiguing ○ good ○ excellent *
The approximate net payload of 2301 pounds at 8% of GVWR on this model is ○ deficient ○ excessive ● cautionary ○ good ○ excellent *
Total highway safety penalties are: 2 * Value: 8 6 Durability: 7 9 Highway Control Rating: 2 3 Highway Safety: 2 1

Brand	Year	Type	Length	Model	Chassis	Engine	Fuel Type	Price/LF	Adj. Wheelbase	Towing	GVWR	Curb Wt
Luxor	1998	MHA	38	37WQ	FR	CU325	D	$5400	228	5,000	27,410	25,190

Livability Code: FT 30-90
Wheelbase-to-length ratio of 50% is considered ● dangerous ○ fatiguing ○ good ○ excellent *
The approximate net payload of 2220 pounds at 8% of GVWR on this model is ○ deficient ○ excessive ● cautionary ○ good ○ excellent *
Total highway safety penalties are: 2 * Value: 8 6 Durability: 7 9 Highway Control Rating: 2 2 Highway Safety: 2 0

Brand	Year	Type	Length	Model	Chassis	Engine	Fuel Type	Price/LF	Adj. Wheelbase	Towing	GVWR	Curb Wt
Luxor	1998	MHA	38	37WP	FR	CU325	D	$5500	228	5,000	27,410	25,148

Livability Code: FT 30-90
Wheelbase-to-length ratio of 50% is considered ● dangerous ○ fatiguing ○ good ○ excellent *
The approximate net payload of 2262 pounds at 8% of GVWR on this model is ○ deficient ○ excessive ● cautionary ○ good ○ excellent *
Total highway safety penalties are: 2 * Value: 8 6 Durability: 7 9 Highway Control Rating: 2 2 Highway Safety: 2 0

Brand	Year	Type	Length	Model	Chassis	Engine	Fuel Type	Price/LF	Adj. Wheelbase	Towing	GVWR	Curb Wt
Magna	1992	MHA	36	36	GI	CU300	D	$6500	246	1,500	27,910	25,705

Livability Code: FT 30-90
Wheelbase-to-length ratio of 57% is considered ○ dangerous ○ fatiguing ● good ○ excellent *
The approximate net payload of 2205 pounds at 8% of GVWR on this model is ○ deficient ○ excessive ● cautionary ○ good ○ excellent *
Total highway safety penalties are: 2 * Value: 9 0 Durability: 9 0 Highway Control Rating: 7 6 Highway Safety: 7 4 ★★★

Brand	Year	Type	Length	Model	Chassis	Engine	Fuel Type	Price/LF	Adj. Wheelbase	Towing	GVWR	Curb Wt
Magna	1994	MHA	34	34	GI	CU250	D	$7300	222	1,500 e	27,910	25,053

Livability Code: FT 30-90
Wheelbase-to-length ratio of 54% is considered ○ dangerous ○ fatiguing ● good ○ excellent *
The approximate net payload of 2857 pounds at 10% of GVWR on this model is ○ deficient ○ excessive ○ cautionary ● good ○ excellent *
Total highway safety penalties are: 2 * Value: 9 0 Durability: 9 0 Highway Control Rating: 7 7 Highway Safety: 7 5 ★★★

Brand	Year	Type	Length	Model	Chassis	Engine	Fuel Type	Price/LF	Adj. Wheelbase	Towing	GVWR	Curb Wt
Magna	1994	MHA	36	36	GI	CU250	D	$7000	246	1,500 e	27,910	25,705

Livability Code: FT 30-90
Wheelbase-to-length ratio of 57% is considered ○ dangerous ○ fatiguing ● good ○ excellent *
The approximate net payload of 2205 pounds at 8% of GVWR on this model is ○ deficient ○ excessive ● cautionary ○ good ○ excellent *
Total highway safety penalties are: 2 * Value: 9 0 Durability: 9 0 Highway Control Rating: 7 6 Highway Safety: 7 4 ★★★

Brand	Year	Type	Length	Model	Chassis	Engine	Fuel Type	Price/LF	Adj. Wheelbase	Towing	GVWR	Curb Wt
Magna	1994	MHA	38	38	GI	CU250	D	$6800	270	1,500 e	31,680	28,243

Livability Code: FT 30-90
Wheelbase-to-length ratio of 59% is considered ○ dangerous ○ fatiguing ○ good ● excellent *
The approximate net payload of 3437 pounds at 11% of GVWR on this model is ○ deficient ○ excessive ○ cautionary ● good ○ excellent *
Total highway safety penalties are: 2 * Value: 9 0 Durability: 9 0 Highway Control Rating: 9 8 Highway Safety: 9 6 ★★★★★

Brand	Year	Type	Length	Model	Chassis	Engine	Fuel Type	Price/LF	Adj. Wheelbase	Towing	GVWR	Curb Wt
Magna	1995	MHA	34	34	GI	CU250	D	$7700	222	1,500	27,910	25,053

Livability Code: FT 30-90
Wheelbase-to-length ratio of 54% is considered ○ dangerous ○ fatiguing ● good ○ excellent *
The approximate net payload of 2857 pounds at 10% of GVWR on this model is ○ deficient ○ excessive ○ cautionary ● good ○ excellent *
Total highway safety penalties are: 2 * Value: 9 0 Durability: 9 0 Highway Control Rating: 7 7 Highway Safety: 7 5 ★★★

Brand	Year	Type	Length	Model	Chassis	Engine	Fuel Type	Price/LF	Adj. Wheelbase	Towing	GVWR	Curb Wt
Magna	1995	MHA	34	34 op eng	GI	CU300	D	$7900	222	1,500	27,910	25,553

Livability Code: FT 30-90
Wheelbase-to-length ratio of 54% is considered ○ dangerous ○ fatiguing ● good ○ excellent *
The approximate net payload of 2357 pounds at 8% of GVWR on this model is ○ deficient ○ excessive ● cautionary ○ good ○ excellent *
Total highway safety penalties are: 2 * Value: 9 0 Durability: 9 0 Highway Control Rating: 6 0 Highway Safety: 5 8 ★

Brand	Year	Type	Length	Model	Chassis	Engine	Fuel Type	Price/LF	Adj. Wheelbase	Towing	GVWR	Curb Wt
Magna	1995	MHA	36	36	GI	CU250	D	$7300	246	1,500	27,910	25,705

Livability Code: FT 30-90
Wheelbase-to-length ratio of 57% is considered ○ dangerous ○ fatiguing ● good ○ excellent *
The approximate net payload of 2205 pounds at 8% of GVWR on this model is ○ deficient ○ excessive ● cautionary ○ good ○ excellent *
Total highway safety penalties are: 2 * Value: 9 0 Durability: 9 0 Highway Control Rating: 7 6 Highway Safety: 7 4 ★★★

Brand	Year	Type	Length	Model	Chassis	Engine	Fuel Type	Price/LF	Adj. Wheelbase	Towing	GVWR	Curb Wt
Magna	1995	MHA	36	36 op eng	GI	CU300	D	$7500	246	1,500	27,910	26,205

Livability Code: FT 30-90
Wheelbase-to-length ratio of 57% is considered ○ dangerous ○ fatiguing ● good ○ excellent *
The approximate net payload of 1705 pounds at 6% of GVWR on this model is ● deficient ○ excessive ○ cautionary ○ good ○ excellent *
Total highway safety penalties are: 2 * Value: 9 0 Durability: 9 0 Highway Control Rating: 6 5 Highway Safety: 6 3 ★

Brand	Year	Type	Length	Model	Chassis	Engine	Fuel Type	Price/LF	Adj. Wheelbase	Towing	GVWR	Curb Wt
Magna	1995	MHA	38	38	GI	CU250	D	$7200	270	1,500	31,680	28,243

Livability Code: FT 30-90
Wheelbase-to-length ratio of 59% is considered ○ dangerous ○ fatiguing ○ good ● excellent *
The approximate net payload of 3437 pounds at 11% of GVWR on this model is ○ deficient ○ excessive ○ cautionary ● good ○ excellent *
Total highway safety penalties are: 2 * Value: 9 0 Durability: 9 0 Highway Control Rating: 9 8 Highway Safety: 9 6 ★★★★★

Note: Safety ratings are based on the assumption that the engineering of the RV has allowed for proper balance by placing fresh, gray, and black holding tanks in a location so as not to change the balance of the RV when the tanks are empty or full. **Always double-check wheelbase, GVWR, and weights at front and rear axles.**

The RV Rating Book

*See Section 1 for details on how conclusions are reached.

Brand	Year	Type	Length	Model	Chassis	Engine	Fuel Type	Average Price per Linear Foot When New	Adjusted Wheelbase	Approx. Towing Capacity	Gross Vehicle Weight Rating	Average Curb Weight
Magna	1995	MHA	38	38 op eng	Gl	CU300	D	$7300	270	1,500	31,680	28,743

Livability Code: FT 30-90

Wheelbase-to-length ratio of 59% is considered ○ dangerous ○ fatiguing ○ good ◉ excellent *

The approximate net payload of 2937 pounds at 9% of GVWR on this model is ○ deficient ○ excessive ◉ cautionary ○ good ○ excellent *

Total highway safety penalties are: 2 *   Value: 90   Durability: 90   Highway Control Rating: 91   Highway Safety: 89   ★★★★

Brand	Year	Type	Length	Model	Chassis	Engine	Fuel Type	Price/Ft	Wheelbase	Towing	GVWR	Curb Wt
Magna	1996	MHA	36	36 Side Door	Gl	CU300	D	$7500	246	1,500	29,410	26,455

Livability Code: FT 30-90

Wheelbase-to-length ratio of 57% is considered ○ dangerous ○ fatiguing ◉ good ○ excellent *

The approximate net payload of 2955 pounds at 10% of GVWR on this model is ○ deficient ○ excessive ○ cautionary ◉ good ○ excellent *

Total highway safety penalties are: 2 *   Value: 90   Durability: 90   Highway Control Rating: 88   Highway Safety: 86   ★★★★

Brand	Year	Type	Length	Model	Chassis	Engine	Fuel Type	Price/Ft	Wheelbase	Towing	GVWR	Curb Wt
Magna	1996	MHA	38	38 Side Door	Gl	CU300	D	$6900	270	5,000	32,360	28,583

Livability Code: FT 30-90

Wheelbase-to-length ratio of 59% is considered ○ dangerous ○ fatiguing ○ good ◉ excellent *

The approximate net payload of 3777 pounds at 12% of GVWR on this model is ○ deficient ○ excessive ○ cautionary ◉ good ○ excellent *

Total highway safety penalties are: 2 *   Value: 90   Durability: 90   Highway Control Rating: 99   Highway Safety: 97   ★★★★★

Brand	Year	Type	Length	Model	Chassis	Engine	Fuel Type	Price/Ft	Wheelbase	Towing	GVWR	Curb Wt
Magna	1997	MHA	36	36	Gl	CU300	D	$7200	240	1,500 e	29,410	26,455

Livability Code: FT 30-90

Wheelbase-to-length ratio of 56% is considered ○ dangerous ○ fatiguing ◉ good ○ excellent *

The approximate net payload of 2955 pounds at 10% of GVWR on this model is ○ deficient ○ excessive ○ cautionary ◉ good ○ excellent *

Total highway safety penalties are: 2 *   Value: 90   Durability: 90   Highway Control Rating: 89   Highway Safety: 87   ★★★★

Brand	Year	Type	Length	Model	Chassis	Engine	Fuel Type	Price/Ft	Wheelbase	Towing	GVWR	Curb Wt
Magna	1997	MHA	38	38	Gl	CU300	D	$6900	264	5,000	32,360	28,583

Livability Code: FT 30-90

Wheelbase-to-length ratio of 58% is considered ○ dangerous ○ fatiguing ○ good ◉ excellent *

The approximate net payload of 3777 pounds at 12% of GVWR on this model is ○ deficient ○ excessive ○ cautionary ◉ good ○ excellent *

Total highway safety penalties are: 2 *   Value: 90   Durability: 90   Highway Control Rating: 95   Highway Safety: 93   ★★★★★

Brand	Year	Type	Length	Model	Chassis	Engine	Fuel Type	Price/Ft	Wheelbase	Towing	GVWR	Curb Wt
Magna	1997	MHA	40	40	Gl	CU300	D	$6500	274	1,500 e	35,700	30,906

Livability Code: FT 30-90

Wheelbase-to-length ratio of 57% is considered ○ dangerous ○ fatiguing ◉ good ○ excellent *

The approximate net payload of 4794 pounds at 13% of GVWR on this model is ○ deficient ○ excessive ○ cautionary ◉ good ○ excellent *

Total highway safety penalties are: 2 *   Value: 90   Durability: 90   Highway Control Rating: 94   Highway Safety: 92   ★★★★★

Brand	Year	Type	Length	Model	Chassis	Engine	Fuel Type	Price/Ft	Wheelbase	Towing	GVWR	Curb Wt
Magna	1997	MHA	40	40 slide	Gl	CU300	D	$6500	274	1,500 e	35,700	31,806

Livability Code: FT 30-90

Wheelbase-to-length ratio of 57% is considered ○ dangerous ○ fatiguing ◉ good ○ excellent *

The approximate net payload of 3894 pounds at 11% of GVWR on this model is ○ deficient ○ excessive ○ cautionary ◉ good ○ excellent *

Total highway safety penalties are: 7 *   Value: 87   Durability: 90   Highway Control Rating: 90   Highway Safety: 83   ★★★★

Brand	Year	Type	Length	Model	Chassis	Engine	Fuel Type	Price/Ft	Wheelbase	Towing	GVWR	Curb Wt
Magna	1998	MHA	36	36	Gl	DE330	D	$7500	236	7,000	35,700	28,650

Livability Code: FT 30-90

Wheelbase-to-length ratio of 55% is considered ○ dangerous ○ fatiguing ◉ good ○ excellent *

The approximate net payload of 7050 pounds at 20% of GVWR on this model is ○ deficient ○ excessive ○ cautionary ○ good ◉ excellent *

Total highway safety penalties are: 2 *   Value: 90   Durability: 90   Highway Control Rating: 95   Highway Safety: 93   ★★★★★

Brand	Year	Type	Length	Model	Chassis	Engine	Fuel Type	Price/Ft	Wheelbase	Towing	GVWR	Curb Wt
Magna	1998	MHA	36	36 Galley Slide	Gl	DE330	D	$7900	236	7,000	35,700	30,150

Livability Code: FT 30-90

Wheelbase-to-length ratio of 55% is considered ○ dangerous ○ fatiguing ◉ good ○ excellent *

The approximate net payload of 5550 pounds at 16% of GVWR on this model is ○ deficient ○ excessive ○ cautionary ○ good ◉ excellent *

Total highway safety penalties are: 12 *   Value: 85   Durability: 90   Highway Control Rating: 91   Highway Safety: 79   ★★★

Brand	Year	Type	Length	Model	Chassis	Engine	Fuel Type	Price/Ft	Wheelbase	Towing	GVWR	Curb Wt
Magna	1998	MHA	38	38	Gl	DE330	D	$7300	260	7,000	35,700	29,677

Livability Code: FT 30-90

Wheelbase-to-length ratio of 57% is considered ○ dangerous ○ fatiguing ◉ good ○ excellent *

The approximate net payload of 6023 pounds at 17% of GVWR on this model is ○ deficient ○ excessive ○ cautionary ○ good ◉ excellent *

Total highway safety penalties are: 2 *   Value: 90   Durability: 90   Highway Control Rating: 100   Highway Safety: 98   ★★★★★

Brand	Year	Type	Length	Model	Chassis	Engine	Fuel Type	Price/Ft	Wheelbase	Towing	GVWR	Curb Wt
Magna	1998	MHA	40	40	Gl	DE330	D	$7100	274	7,000	35,700	30,153

Livability Code: FT 30-90

Wheelbase-to-length ratio of 57% is considered ○ dangerous ○ fatiguing ◉ good ○ excellent *

The approximate net payload of 5547 pounds at 16% of GVWR on this model is ○ deficient ○ excessive ○ cautionary ○ good ◉ excellent *

Total highway safety penalties are: 2 *   Value: 90   Durability: 90   Highway Control Rating: 100   Highway Safety: 98   ★★★★★

Brand	Year	Type	Length	Model	Chassis	Engine	Fuel Type	Price/Ft	Wheelbase	Towing	GVWR	Curb Wt
Magna	1998	MHA	40	40 Great Room	Gl	DE330	D	$7400	274	7,000	35,700	31,303

Livability Code: FT 30-90

Wheelbase-to-length ratio of 57% is considered ○ dangerous ○ fatiguing ◉ good ○ excellent *

The approximate net payload of 4397 pounds at 12% of GVWR on this model is ○ deficient ○ excessive ○ cautionary ◉ good ○ excellent *

Total highway safety penalties are: 7 *   Value: 87   Durability: 90   Highway Control Rating: 92   Highway Safety: 85   ★★★★

Note: Safety ratings are based on the assumption that the engineering of the RV has allowed for proper balance by placing fresh, gray, and black holding tanks in a location so as not to change the balance of the RV when the tanks are empty or full. **Always double-check wheelbase, GVWR, and weights at front and rear axles.**

*See Section 1 for details on how conclusions are reached.

Brand	Year	Type	Length	Model	Chassis	Engine	Fuel Type	Average Price per Linear Foot When New	Adjusted Wheelbase	Approx. Towing Capacity	Gross Vehicle Weight Rating	Average Curb Weight
Magna	1999	MHA	36	Tribute	DY	CU350	D	$8300	239	7,000	35,700	28,813

Livability Code: FT 30-90
Wheelbase-to-length ratio of 55% is considered ○ dangerous ○ fatiguing ◉ good ○ excellent *
The approximate net payload of 6887 pounds at 19% of GVWR on this model is ○ deficient ○ excessive ○ cautionary ○ good ◉ excellent *
Total highway safety penalties are: 2 *   Value: 9 6   Durability: 9 3   Highway Control Rating: 9 7   Highway Safety: 9 5   ★★★★★

| Magna | 1999 | MHA | 36 | Sentry | DY | CU350 | D | $8300 | 239 | 7,000 | 35,700 | 28,313 |

Livability Code: FT 30-90
Wheelbase-to-length ratio of 55% is considered ○ dangerous ○ fatiguing ◉ good ○ excellent *
The approximate net payload of 7387 pounds at 21% of GVWR on this model is ○ deficient ○ excessive ○ cautionary ○ good ◉ excellent *
Total highway safety penalties are: 2 *   Value: 9 6   Durability: 9 3   Highway Control Rating: 9 7   Highway Safety: 9 5   ★★★★★

| Magna | 1999 | MHA | 36 | Chef's Choice | DY | CU350 | D | $8300 | 239 | 7,000 | 35,700 | 30,628 |

Livability Code: FT 30-90
Wheelbase-to-length ratio of 55% is considered ○ dangerous ○ fatiguing ◉ good ○ excellent *
The approximate net payload of 5072 pounds at 14% of GVWR on this model is ○ deficient ○ excessive ○ cautionary ○ good ◉ excellent *
Total highway safety penalties are: 13 *   Value: 9 1   Durability: 9 3   Highway Control Rating: 9 0   Highway Safety: 7 7   ★★★

| Magna | 1999 | MHA | 38 | Aspire | DY | CU350 | D | $7900 | 263 | 7,000 | 35,700 | 29,709 |

Livability Code: FT 30-90
Wheelbase-to-length ratio of 58% is considered ○ dangerous ○ fatiguing ○ good ◉ excellent *
The approximate net payload of 5991 pounds at 17% of GVWR on this model is ○ deficient ○ excessive ○ cautionary ○ good ◉ excellent *
Total highway safety penalties are: 2 *   Value: 9 6   Durability: 9 3   Highway Control Rating: 1 0 0   Highway Safety: 9 8   ★★★★★

| Magna | 1999 | MHA | 38 | Olympia (discon.) | DY | CU350 | D | $7900 | 263 | 7,000 | 35,700 | 30,253 |

Livability Code: FT 30-90
Wheelbase-to-length ratio of 58% is considered ○ dangerous ○ fatiguing ○ good ◉ excellent *
The approximate net payload of 5447 pounds at 15% of GVWR on this model is ○ deficient ○ excessive ○ cautionary ◉ good ○ excellent *
Total highway safety penalties are: 2 *   Value: 9 6   Durability: 9 3   Highway Control Rating: 1 0 0   Highway Safety: 9 8   ★★★★★

| Magna | 1999 | MHA | 40 | Parade | DY | CU350 | D | $7500 | 277 | 7,000 | 35,700 | 29,789 |

Livability Code: FT 30-90
Wheelbase-to-length ratio of 58% is considered ○ dangerous ○ fatiguing ○ good ◉ excellent *
The approximate net payload of 5912 pounds at 17% of GVWR on this model is ○ deficient ○ excessive ○ cautionary ○ good ◉ excellent *
Total highway safety penalties are: 2 *   Value: 9 6   Durability: 9 3   Highway Control Rating: 1 0 0   Highway Safety: 9 8   ★★★★★

| Magna | 1999 | MHA | 40 | Fanfare | DY | CU350 | D | $7500 | 277 | 7,000 | 35,700 | 31,950 |

Livability Code: FT 30-90
Wheelbase-to-length ratio of 58% is considered ○ dangerous ○ fatiguing ○ good ◉ excellent *
The approximate net payload of 3751 pounds at 11% of GVWR on this model is ○ deficient ○ excessive ○ cautionary ◉ good ○ excellent *
Total highway safety penalties are: 7 *   Value: 9 4   Durability: 9 3   Highway Control Rating: 9 2   Highway Safety: 8 5   ★★★★

| Magna | 1999 | MHA | 40 | Indulgence | DY | CU350 | D | $7500 | 277 | 7,000 | 36,300 | 31,926 |

Livability Code: FT 30-90
Wheelbase-to-length ratio of 58% is considered ○ dangerous ○ fatiguing ○ good ◉ excellent *
The approximate net payload of 4374 pounds at 12% of GVWR on this model is ○ deficient ○ excessive ○ cautionary ◉ good ○ excellent *
Total highway safety penalties are: 13 *   Value: 9 1   Durability: 9 3   Highway Control Rating: 9 4   Highway Safety: 8 1   ★★★★

| Magna | 1999 | MHA | 40 | Fanfare myc | DY | CU350 | D | $7500 | 277 | 7,000 | 36,300 | 32,100 |

Livability Code: FT 30-90
Wheelbase-to-length ratio of 58% is considered ○ dangerous ○ fatiguing ○ good ◉ excellent *
The approximate net payload of 4201 pounds at 12% of GVWR on this model is ○ deficient ○ excessive ○ cautionary ◉ good ○ excellent *
Total highway safety penalties are: 7 *   Value: 9 4   Durability: 9 3   Highway Control Rating: 9 4   Highway Safety: 8 7   ★★★★

| Marquis | 1990 | MHA | 40 | Jubilee 40 | Gl | Cat | D | $7100 | 262 | 1,500 | 36,220 | 31,153 |

Livability Code: FT 30-90
Wheelbase-to-length ratio of 55% is considered ○ dangerous ○ fatiguing ◉ good ○ excellent *
The approximate net payload of 5067 pounds at 14% of GVWR on this model is ○ deficient ○ excessive ○ cautionary ◉ good ○ excellent *
Total highway safety penalties are: 2 *   Value: 8 2   Durability: 8 2   Highway Control Rating: 8 7   Highway Safety: 8 5   ★★★★

| Marquis | 1991 | MHA | 40 | Regent 40 | Gl | Cat | D | $7300 | 262 | 1,500 | 32,320 | 30,378 |

Livability Code: FT 30-90
Wheelbase-to-length ratio of 55% is considered ○ dangerous ○ fatiguing ◉ good ○ excellent *
The approximate net payload of 1942 pounds at 6% of GVWR on this model is ◉ deficient ○ excessive ○ cautionary ○ good ○ excellent *
Total highway safety penalties are: 2 *   Value: 8 2   Durability: 8 2   Highway Control Rating: 5 6   Highway Safety: 5 4   ★

| Marquis | 1992 | MHA | 40 | 40 | Gl | Cat | D | $8800 | 262 | 3,000 | 32,320 | 29,308 |

Livability Code: FT 30-90
Wheelbase-to-length ratio of 55% is considered ○ dangerous ○ fatiguing ◉ good ○ excellent *
The approximate net payload of 3012 pounds at 9% of GVWR on this model is ○ deficient ○ excessive ◉ cautionary ○ good ○ excellent *
Total highway safety penalties are: 2 *   Value: 8 2   Durability: 8 2   Highway Control Rating: 7 4   Highway Safety: 7 2   ★★★

Note: Safety ratings are based on the assumption that the engineering of the RV has allowed for proper balance by placing fresh, gray, and black holding tanks in a location so as not to change the balance of the RV when the tanks are empty or full. **Always double-check wheelbase, GVWR, and weights at front and rear axles.**

*See Section 1 for details on how conclusions are reached.

Brand	Year	Type	Length	Model	Chassis	Engine	Fuel Type	Average Price per Linear Foot When New	Adjusted Wheelbase	Approx. Towing Capacity	Gross Vehicle Weight Rating	Average Curb Weight
Marquis	1995	MHA	37	36 Topaz 300	GI	Cu8.3L	D	$7600	228	5,000	31,720	28,602

Livability Code: FT 30-90

Wheelbase-to-length ratio of 52% is considered ○ dangerous ● fatiguing ○ good ○ excellent *

The approximate net payload of 3118 pounds at 10% of GVWR on this model is ○ deficient ● excessive ○ cautionary ○ good ○ excellent *

Total highway safety penalties are: 2 *   Value: 82   Durability: 82   Highway Control Rating: 47   Highway Safety: 45

Brand	Year	Type	Length	Model	Chassis	Engine	Fuel Type	Average Price per Linear Foot When New	Adjusted Wheelbase	Approx. Towing Capacity	Gross Vehicle Weight Rating	Average Curb Weight
Marquis	1995	MHA	39	38 Pearl 300	GI	Cu8.3L	D	$7400	252	5,000	31,720	29,448

Livability Code: FT 30-90

Wheelbase-to-length ratio of 55% is considered ○ dangerous ○ fatiguing ● good ○ excellent *

The approximate net payload of 2272 pounds at 7% of GVWR on this model is ○ deficient ○ excessive ● cautionary ○ good ○ excellent *

Total highway safety penalties are: 2 *   Value: 82   Durability: 82   Highway Control Rating: 62   Highway Safety: 60   ★★

Brand	Year	Type	Length	Model	Chassis	Engine	Fuel Type	Average Price per Linear Foot When New	Adjusted Wheelbase	Approx. Towing Capacity	Gross Vehicle Weight Rating	Average Curb Weight
Marquis	1995	MHA	40	40 Diamond 300	GI	Cu8.3L	D	$7400	270	5,000	31,720	30,260

Livability Code: FT 30-90

Wheelbase-to-length ratio of 56% is considered ○ dangerous ○ fatiguing ● good ○ excellent *

The approximate net payload of 1460 pounds at 5% of GVWR on this model is ● deficient ○ excessive ○ cautionary ○ good ○ excellent *

Total highway safety penalties are: 2 *   Value: 82   Durability: 82   Highway Control Rating: 59   Highway Safety: 57   ★

Brand	Year	Type	Length	Model	Chassis	Engine	Fuel Type	Average Price per Linear Foot When New	Adjusted Wheelbase	Approx. Towing Capacity	Gross Vehicle Weight Rating	Average Curb Weight
Marquis	1997	MHA	38	Emerald	GI	CA330	D	$8200	252	5,000	31,720	28,263

Livability Code: FT 30-90

Wheelbase-to-length ratio of 55% is considered ○ dangerous ○ fatiguing ● good ○ excellent *

The approximate net payload of 3457 pounds at 11% of GVWR on this model is ○ deficient ○ excessive ○ cautionary ● good ○ excellent *

Total highway safety penalties are: 2 *   Value: 82   Durability: 82   Highway Control Rating: 88   Highway Safety: 86   ★★★★

Brand	Year	Type	Length	Model	Chassis	Engine	Fuel Type	Average Price per Linear Foot When New	Adjusted Wheelbase	Approx. Towing Capacity	Gross Vehicle Weight Rating	Average Curb Weight
Marquis	1997	MHA	40	Garnet	GI	Ca330	D	$7900	252	5,000	31,720	28,916

Livability Code: FT 30-90

Wheelbase-to-length ratio of 53% is considered ○ dangerous ● fatiguing ○ good ○ excellent *

The approximate net payload of 2804 pounds at 9% of GVWR on this model is ○ deficient ○ excessive ● cautionary ○ good ○ excellent *

Total highway safety penalties are: 2 *   Value: 82   Durability: 82   Highway Control Rating: 52   Highway Safety: 50   ★

Brand	Year	Type	Length	Model	Chassis	Engine	Fuel Type	Average Price per Linear Foot When New	Adjusted Wheelbase	Approx. Towing Capacity	Gross Vehicle Weight Rating	Average Curb Weight
Marquis	1997	MHA	40	Opal	GI	Ca330	D	$7900	252	5,000	31,720	28,916

Livability Code: FT 30-90

Wheelbase-to-length ratio of 53% is considered ○ dangerous ● fatiguing ○ good ○ excellent *

The approximate net payload of 2804 pounds at 9% of GVWR on this model is ○ deficient ○ excessive ● cautionary ○ good ○ excellent *

Total highway safety penalties are: 2 *   Value: 82   Durability: 82   Highway Control Rating: 52   Highway Safety: 50   ★

Brand	Year	Type	Length	Model	Chassis	Engine	Fuel Type	Average Price per Linear Foot When New	Adjusted Wheelbase	Approx. Towing Capacity	Gross Vehicle Weight Rating	Average Curb Weight
Marquis	1997	MHA	40	Ruby	GI	Ca330	D	$8200	252	5,000	31,720	28,916

Livability Code: FT 30-90

Wheelbase-to-length ratio of 53% is considered ○ dangerous ● fatiguing ○ good ○ excellent *

The approximate net payload of 2804 pounds at 9% of GVWR on this model is ○ deficient ○ excessive ● cautionary ○ good ○ excellent *

Total highway safety penalties are: 2 *   Value: 82   Durability: 82   Highway Control Rating: 52   Highway Safety: 50   ★

Brand	Year	Type	Length	Model	Chassis	Engine	Fuel Type	Average Price per Linear Foot When New	Adjusted Wheelbase	Approx. Towing Capacity	Gross Vehicle Weight Rating	Average Curb Weight
Marquis	1997	MHA	40	Saphire	GI	Ca330	D	$9300	252	5,000	31,720	28,916

Livability Code: FT 30-90

Wheelbase-to-length ratio of 53% is considered ○ dangerous ● fatiguing ○ good ○ excellent *

The approximate net payload of 2804 pounds at 9% of GVWR on this model is ○ deficient ○ excessive ● cautionary ○ good ○ excellent *

Total highway safety penalties are: 2 *   Value: 82   Durability: 82   Highway Control Rating: 52   Highway Safety: 50   ★

Brand	Year	Type	Length	Model	Chassis	Engine	Fuel Type	Average Price per Linear Foot When New	Adjusted Wheelbase	Approx. Towing Capacity	Gross Vehicle Weight Rating	Average Curb Weight
Marquis	1998	MHA	40	40 Garnet	GI	CA425	D	$8500	270	5,000	36,220	32,083

Livability Code: FT 30-90

Wheelbase-to-length ratio of 56% is considered ○ dangerous ○ fatiguing ● good ○ excellent *

The approximate net payload of 4137 pounds at 11% of GVWR on this model is ○ deficient ○ excessive ○ cautionary ● good ○ excellent *

Total highway safety penalties are: 2 *   Value: 87   Durability: 82   Highway Control Rating: 87   Highway Safety: 85   ★★★★

Brand	Year	Type	Length	Model	Chassis	Engine	Fuel Type	Average Price per Linear Foot When New	Adjusted Wheelbase	Approx. Towing Capacity	Gross Vehicle Weight Rating	Average Curb Weight
Marquis	1998	MHA	40	40 Tourmaline	GI	CA425	D	$8500	270	5,000	36,220	32,533

Livability Code: FT 30-90

Wheelbase-to-length ratio of 56% is considered ○ dangerous ○ fatiguing ● good ○ excellent *

The approximate net payload of 3687 pounds at 10% of GVWR on this model is ○ deficient ○ excessive ○ cautionary ● good ○ excellent *

Total highway safety penalties are: 12 *   Value: 77   Durability: 82   Highway Control Rating: 85   Highway Safety: 73   ★★★

Brand	Year	Type	Length	Model	Chassis	Engine	Fuel Type	Average Price per Linear Foot When New	Adjusted Wheelbase	Approx. Towing Capacity	Gross Vehicle Weight Rating	Average Curb Weight
Marquis	1998	MHA	40	40 Opal	GI	CA425	D	$8500	270	5,000	36,220	32,083

Livability Code: FT 30-90

Wheelbase-to-length ratio of 56% is considered ○ dangerous ○ fatiguing ● good ○ excellent *

The approximate net payload of 4137 pounds at 11% of GVWR on this model is ○ deficient ○ excessive ○ cautionary ● good ○ excellent *

Total highway safety penalties are: 2 *   Value: 87   Durability: 82   Highway Control Rating: 87   Highway Safety: 85   ★★★★

Brand	Year	Type	Length	Model	Chassis	Engine	Fuel Type	Average Price per Linear Foot When New	Adjusted Wheelbase	Approx. Towing Capacity	Gross Vehicle Weight Rating	Average Curb Weight
Marquis	1998	MHA	40	40 Jasper	GI	CA425	D	$8500	270	5,000	36,220	32,533

Livability Code: FT 30-90

Wheelbase-to-length ratio of 56% is considered ○ dangerous ○ fatiguing ● good ○ excellent *

The approximate net payload of 3687 pounds at 10% of GVWR on this model is ○ deficient ○ excessive ○ cautionary ● good ○ excellent *

Total highway safety penalties are: 12 *   Value: 77   Durability: 82   Highway Control Rating: 85   Highway Safety: 73   ★★★

Note: Safety ratings are based on the assumption that the engineering of the RV has allowed for proper balance by placing fresh, gray, and black holding tanks in a location so as not to change the balance of the RV when the tanks are empty or full. **Always double-check wheelbase, GVWR, and weights at front and rear axles.**

*See Section 1 for details on how conclusions are reached.

Section 2: The Ratings

Brand	Year	Type	Length	Model	Chassis	Engine	Fuel Type	Average Price per Linear Foot When New	Adjusted Wheelbase	Approx. Towing Capacity	Gross Vehicle Weight Rating	Average Curb Weight
Marquis	1998	MHA	40	40 Garnet	MA	CA425	D	$8500	270	5,000	36,220	32,053

Livability Code: FT 30-90   Wheelbase-to-length ratio of 56% is considered ○ dangerous ○ fatiguing ◉ good ○ excellent *

The approximate net payload of 4167 pounds at 12% of GVWR on this model is ○ deficient ○ excessive ○ cautionary ◉ good ○ excellent *

Total highway safety penalties are: 2 *   Value: 8 7   Durability: 8 2   Highway Control Rating: 8 9   Highway Safety: 8 7   ★★★★

Brand	Year	Type	Length	Model	Chassis	Engine	Fuel Type	Price/Ft	Adj. WB	Towing	GVWR	Curb Wt
Marquis	1998	MHA	40	40 Tourmaline	MA	CA425	D	$8500	270	5,000	36,220	32,503

Livability Code: FT 30-90   Wheelbase-to-length ratio of 56% is considered ○ dangerous ○ fatiguing ◉ good ○ excellent *

The approximate net payload of 3717 pounds at 10% of GVWR on this model is ○ deficient ○ excessive ○ cautionary ◉ good ○ excellent *

Total highway safety penalties are: 12 *   Value: 7 7   Durability: 8 2   Highway Control Rating: 8 5   Highway Safety: 7 3   ★★★

Marquis	1998	MHA	40	40 Opal	MA	CA425	D	$8500	270	5,000	36,220	32,053

Livability Code: FT 30-90   Wheelbase-to-length ratio of 56% is considered ○ dangerous ○ fatiguing ◉ good ○ excellent *

The approximate net payload of 4167 pounds at 12% of GVWR on this model is ○ deficient ○ excessive ○ cautionary ◉ good ○ excellent *

Total highway safety penalties are: 2 *   Value: 8 7   Durability: 8 2   Highway Control Rating: 8 9   Highway Safety: 8 7   ★★★★

Marquis	1998	MHA	40	40 Jasper	MA	CA425	D	$8500	270	5,000	36,220	32,503

Livability Code: FT 30-90   Wheelbase-to-length ratio of 56% is considered ○ dangerous ○ fatiguing ◉ good ○ excellent *

The approximate net payload of 3717 pounds at 10% of GVWR on this model is ○ deficient ○ excessive ○ cautionary ◉ good ○ excellent *

Total highway safety penalties are: 12 *   Value: 7 7   Durability: 8 2   Highway Control Rating: 8 5   Highway Safety: 7 3   ★★★

Marquis	1999	MHA	41	40 Garnet	MA	CA425	D	$8500	270	5,000	36,200	31,417

Livability Code: FT 30-90   Wheelbase-to-length ratio of 55% is considered ○ dangerous ○ fatiguing ◉ good ○ excellent *

The approximate net payload of 4783 pounds at 13% of GVWR on this model is ○ deficient ○ excessive ○ cautionary ◉ good ○ excellent *

Total highway safety penalties are: 2 *   Value: 8 6   Durability: 7 9   Highway Control Rating: 8 7   Highway Safety: 8 5   ★★★

Marquis	1999	MHA	41	40 Tourmaline	MA	CA425	D	$8500	270	5,000	36,200	32,317

Livability Code: FT 30-90   Wheelbase-to-length ratio of 55% is considered ○ dangerous ○ fatiguing ◉ good ○ excellent *

The approximate net payload of 3883 pounds at 11% of GVWR on this model is ○ deficient ○ excessive ○ cautionary ◉ good ○ excellent *

Total highway safety penalties are: 12 *   Value: 8 0   Durability: 7 9   Highway Control Rating: 8 3   Highway Safety: 7 1   ★★★

Marquis	1999	MHA	41	40 Opal	MA	CA425	D	$8500	270	5,000	36,200	31,417

Livability Code: FT 30-90   Wheelbase-to-length ratio of 55% is considered ○ dangerous ○ fatiguing ◉ good ○ excellent *

The approximate net payload of 4783 pounds at 13% of GVWR on this model is ○ deficient ○ excessive ○ cautionary ◉ good ○ excellent *

Total highway safety penalties are: 2 *   Value: 8 6   Durability: 7 9   Highway Control Rating: 8 7   Highway Safety: 8 5   ★★★

Marquis	1999	MHA	41	40 Jasper	MA	CA425	D	$8500	270	5,000	36,200	32,317

Livability Code: FT 30-90   Wheelbase-to-length ratio of 55% is considered ○ dangerous ○ fatiguing ◉ good ○ excellent *

The approximate net payload of 3883 pounds at 11% of GVWR on this model is ○ deficient ○ excessive ○ cautionary ◉ good ○ excellent *

Total highway safety penalties are: 12 *   Value: 8 0   Durability: 7 9   Highway Control Rating: 8 3   Highway Safety: 7 1   ★★★

Maverick	1996	MHC	23	23RK	CH	5.7L	G	$2200	166	1,500	10,500	9,447

Livability Code: VA 30-90   Wheelbase-to-length ratio of 60% is considered ○ dangerous ○ fatiguing ○ good ◉ excellent *

The approximate net payload of 1053 pounds at 10% of GVWR on this model is ○ deficient ○ excessive ○ cautionary ◉ good ○ excellent *

Total highway safety penalties are: 2 *   Value: 7 9   Durability: 7 4   Highway Control Rating: 9 8   Highway Safety: 9 6   ★★★

Maverick	1996	MHC	23	23RK	FO	7.5L	G	$2300	174	1,500 e	11,500	9,838

Livability Code: VA 30-90   Wheelbase-to-length ratio of 63% is considered ○ dangerous ○ fatiguing ○ good ◉ excellent *

The approximate net payload of 1662 pounds at 14% of GVWR on this model is ○ deficient ○ excessive ○ cautionary ◉ good ○ excellent *

Total highway safety penalties are: 2 *   Value: 7 9   Durability: 7 4   Highway Control Rating: 1 0 0   Highway Safety: 9 8   ★★★

Maverick	1996	MHC	30	28QB	FO	7.5L	G	$1800	206	6,600	12,400	11,266

Livability Code: VA 30-90   Wheelbase-to-length ratio of 57% is considered ○ dangerous ○ fatiguing ◉ good ○ excellent *

The approximate net payload of 1134 pounds at 9% of GVWR on this model is ○ deficient ○ excessive ◉ cautionary ○ good ○ excellent *

Total highway safety penalties are: 2 *   Value: 7 9   Durability: 7 4   Highway Control Rating: 8 4   Highway Safety: 8 2   ★★★

Maverick	1996	MHC	31	29MBW	FO	7.5L	G	$1800	218	4,950	14,050	11,847

Livability Code: VA 30-90   Wheelbase-to-length ratio of 58% is considered ○ dangerous ○ fatiguing ○ good ◉ excellent *

The approximate net payload of 2203 pounds at 16% of GVWR on this model is ○ deficient ○ excessive ○ cautionary ○ good ◉ excellent *

Total highway safety penalties are: 2 *   Value: 7 9   Durability: 7 4   Highway Control Rating: 1 0 0   Highway Safety: 9 8   ★★★

Note: Safety ratings are based on the assumption that the engineering of the RV has allowed for proper balance by placing fresh, gray, and black holding tanks in a location so as not to change the balance of the RV when the tanks are empty or full. **Always double-check wheelbase, GVWR, and weights at front and rear axles.**

The RV Rating Book

*See Section 1 for details on how conclusions are reached.

Brand	Year	Type	Length	Model	Chassis	Engine	Fuel Type	Average Price per Linear Foot When New	Adjusted Wheelbase	Approx. Towing Capacity	Gross Vehicle Weight Rating	Average Curb Weight
Maverick	1996	MHC	31	29GTW	FO	7.5L	G	$1800	218	4,950	14,050	11,872

Livability Code: VA 30-90
Wheelbase-to-length ratio of 58% is considered ○ dangerous ○ fatiguing ○ good ◉ excellent *
The approximate net payload of 2178 pounds at 16% of GVWR on this model is ○ deficient ○ excessive ○ cautionary ◉ good ◉ excellent *
Total highway safety penalties are: 2 *   Value: **79**   Durability: **74**   Highway Control Rating: **100**   Highway Safety: **98**   ★★★

Brand	Year	Type	Length	Model	Chassis	Engine	Fuel Type	Avg Price/Lin Ft	Adj Wheelbase	Towing	GVWR	Curb Weight
Maverick	1997	MHC	23	23RK	FO	7.5L	G	$2300	174	7,000	11,500	9,908

Livability Code: VA 30-90
Wheelbase-to-length ratio of 62% is considered ○ dangerous ○ fatiguing ○ good ◉ excellent *
The approximate net payload of 1592 pounds at 14% of GVWR on this model is ○ deficient ○ excessive ○ cautionary ◉ good ○ excellent *
Total highway safety penalties are: 2 *   Value: **79**   Durability: **74**   Highway Control Rating: **100**   Highway Safety: **98**   ★★★

Maverick	1997	MHC	30	28QB	FO	7.5L	G	$1900	206	5,950	14,050	11,627

Livability Code: VA 30-90
Wheelbase-to-length ratio of 57% is considered ○ dangerous ○ fatiguing ◉ good ○ excellent *
The approximate net payload of 2424 pounds at 17% of GVWR on this model is ○ deficient ○ excessive ○ cautionary ○ good ◉ excellent *
Total highway safety penalties are: 2 *   Value: **79**   Durability: **74**   Highway Control Rating: **100**   Highway Safety: **98**   ★★★

Maverick	1997	MHC	31	29MBW	FO	7.5L	G	$1800	218	5,950	14,050	12,265

Livability Code: VA 30-90
Wheelbase-to-length ratio of 58% is considered ○ dangerous ○ fatiguing ○ good ◉ excellent *
The approximate net payload of 1785 pounds at 13% of GVWR on this model is ○ deficient ○ excessive ○ cautionary ◉ good ○ excellent *
Total highway safety penalties are: 2 *   Value: **79**   Durability: **74**   Highway Control Rating: **98**   Highway Safety: **96**   ★★★

Maverick	1997	MHC	31	29GTW	FO	7.5L	G	$1800	218	5,950	14,050	12,213

Livability Code: VA 30-90
Wheelbase-to-length ratio of 58% is considered ○ dangerous ○ fatiguing ○ good ◉ excellent *
The approximate net payload of 1838 pounds at 13% of GVWR on this model is ○ deficient ○ excessive ○ cautionary ◉ good ○ excellent *
Total highway safety penalties are: 2 *   Value: **79**   Durability: **74**   Highway Control Rating: **98**   Highway Safety: **96**   ★★★

Maverick	1998	MHC	23	23RK	FO	6.8L	G	$2400	174	7,000	11,500	9,908

Livability Code: VA 30-90
Wheelbase-to-length ratio of 62% is considered ○ dangerous ○ fatiguing ○ good ◉ excellent *
The approximate net payload of 1592 pounds at 14% of GVWR on this model is ○ deficient ○ excessive ○ cautionary ◉ good ○ excellent *
Total highway safety penalties are: 2 *   Value: **79**   Durability: **74**   Highway Control Rating: **100**   Highway Safety: **98**   ★★★

Maverick	1998	MHC	26	26 FBW	FO	6.8L	G	$2100	176	5,950	14,050	11,253

Livability Code: VA 30-90
Wheelbase-to-length ratio of 56% is considered ○ dangerous ○ fatiguing ◉ good ○ excellent *
The approximate net payload of 2798 pounds at 20% of GVWR on this model is ○ deficient ○ excessive ○ cautionary ○ good ◉ excellent *
Total highway safety penalties are: 2 *   Value: **79**   Durability: **74**   Highway Control Rating: **100**   Highway Safety: **98**   ★★★

Maverick	1998	MHC	30	29QB	FO	6.8L	G	$1800	206	5,950	14,050	11,627

Livability Code: VA 30-90
Wheelbase-to-length ratio of 57% is considered ○ dangerous ○ fatiguing ◉ good ○ excellent *
The approximate net payload of 2424 pounds at 17% of GVWR on this model is ○ deficient ○ excessive ○ cautionary ○ good ◉ excellent *
Total highway safety penalties are: 2 *   Value: **79**   Durability: **74**   Highway Control Rating: **100**   Highway Safety: **98**   ★★★

Maverick	1998	MHC	31	30MBW	FO	6.8L	G	$1800	218	5,950	14,050	12,265

Livability Code: VA 30-90
Wheelbase-to-length ratio of 58% is considered ○ dangerous ○ fatiguing ○ good ◉ excellent *
The approximate net payload of 1786 pounds at 13% of GVWR on this model is ○ deficient ○ excessive ○ cautionary ◉ good ○ excellent *
Total highway safety penalties are: 2 *   Value: **79**   Durability: **74**   Highway Control Rating: **98**   Highway Safety: **96**   ★★★

Maverick	1998	MHC	31	30GTW	FO	6.8L	G	$1800	218	5,950	14,050	12,213

Livability Code: VA 30-90
Wheelbase-to-length ratio of 58% is considered ○ dangerous ○ fatiguing ○ good ◉ excellent *
The approximate net payload of 1838 pounds at 13% of GVWR on this model is ○ deficient ○ excessive ○ cautionary ◉ good ○ excellent *
Total highway safety penalties are: 2 *   Value: **79**   Durability: **74**   Highway Control Rating: **98**   Highway Safety: **96**   ★★★

Maverick	1999	MHC	24	23 RK SO	FO	6.8L	G	$2300	174	7,000	11,500	10,839

Livability Code: VA 30-90
Wheelbase-to-length ratio of 60% is considered ○ dangerous ○ fatiguing ○ good ◉ excellent *
The approximate net payload of 661 pounds at 6% of GVWR on this model is ◉ deficient ○ excessive ○ cautionary ○ good ○ excellent *
Total highway safety penalties are: 6 *   Value: **75**   Durability: **70**   Highway Control Rating: **75**   Highway Safety: **69**   ★

Maverick	1999	MHC	24	23 RK	FO	6.8L	G	$2300	174	7,000	11,500	10,337

Livability Code: VA 30-90
Wheelbase-to-length ratio of 60% is considered ○ dangerous ○ fatiguing ○ good ◉ excellent *
The approximate net payload of 1164 pounds at 10% of GVWR on this model is ○ deficient ○ excessive ○ cautionary ◉ good ○ excellent *
Total highway safety penalties are: 2 *   Value: **77**   Durability: **70**   Highway Control Rating: **98**   Highway Safety: **96**   ★★★

Note: Safety ratings are based on the assumption that the engineering of the RV has allowed for proper balance by placing fresh, gray, and black holding tanks in a location so as not to change the balance of the RV when the tanks are empty or full. **Always double-check wheelbase, GVWR, and weights at front and rear axles.**

*See Section 1 for details on how conclusions are reached.

Brand	Year	Type	Length	Model	Chassis	Engine	Fuel Type	Average Price per Linear Foot When New	Adjusted Wheelbase	Approx. Towing Capacity	Gross Vehicle Weight Rating	Average Curb Weight
Maverick	1999	MHC	26	26 FB	FO	6.8L	G	$2100	176	5,950	14,050	11,397

Livability Code: VA 30-90   Wheelbase-to-length ratio of 56% is considered ○ dangerous ○ fatiguing ◉ good ○ excellent *

The approximate net payload of 2653 pounds at 19% of GVWR on this model is ○ deficient ○ excessive ○ cautionary ○ good ◉ excellent *

Total highway safety penalties are: 2 *   Value: 7 7   Durability: 7 0   Highway Control Rating: 9 8   Highway Safety: 9 6   ★★★

Brand	Year	Type	Length	Model	Chassis	Engine	Fuel Type	Avg Price/Lin Ft	Adj Wheelbase	Approx Towing	GVWR	Avg Curb Wt
Maverick	1999	MHC	31	30 GT	FO	6.8L	G	$1800	214	5,950	14,050	12,409

Livability Code: VA 30-90   Wheelbase-to-length ratio of 57% is considered ○ dangerous ○ fatiguing ◉ good ○ excellent *

The approximate net payload of 1642 pounds at 12% of GVWR on this model is ○ deficient ○ excessive ○ cautionary ◉ good ○ excellent *

Total highway safety penalties are: 2 *   Value: 7 7   Durability: 7 0   Highway Control Rating: 9 3   Highway Safety: 9 1   ★★★

Maverick	1999	MHC	31	30 MB	FO	6.8L	G	$1800	215	5,950	14,050	12,321

Livability Code: VA 30-90   Wheelbase-to-length ratio of 58% is considered ○ dangerous ○ fatiguing ○ good ◉ excellent *

The approximate net payload of 1729 pounds at 12% of GVWR on this model is ○ deficient ○ excessive ○ cautionary ◉ good ○ excellent *

Total highway safety penalties are: 2 *   Value: 7 7   Durability: 7 0   Highway Control Rating: 9 5   Highway Safety: 9 3   ★★★

Maverick	1999	MHC	31	30 RQ SO	FO	6.8L	G	$1800	215	5,950	14,050	12,996

Livability Code: VA 30-90   Wheelbase-to-length ratio of 58% is considered ○ dangerous ○ fatiguing ○ good ◉ excellent *

The approximate net payload of 1054 pounds at 8% of GVWR on this model is ○ deficient ○ excessive ◉ cautionary ○ good ○ excellent *

Total highway safety penalties are: 12 *   Value: 7 2   Durability: 7 0   Highway Control Rating: 7 9   Highway Safety: 6 7   ★★

Max	1998	MHC	26	Journey 26	FO	6.8L	G	$3300	176	1,500	11,500	11,315

Livability Code: SB 30-80   Wheelbase-to-length ratio of 56% is considered ○ dangerous ○ fatiguing ◉ good ○ excellent *

The approximate net payload of 185 pounds at 2% of GVWR on this model is ◉ deficient ○ excessive ○ cautionary ○ good ○ excellent *

Total highway safety penalties are: 5 *   Value: 7 9   Durability: 7 9   Highway Control Rating: 5 8   Highway Safety: 5 3   ★

Max	1998	MHC	26	Venture 26	FO	6.8L	G	$3100	176	1,500	11,500	10,865

Livability Code: SB 30-80   Wheelbase-to-length ratio of 56% is considered ○ dangerous ○ fatiguing ◉ good ○ excellent *

The approximate net payload of 635 pounds at 6% of GVWR on this model is ◉ deficient ○ excessive ○ cautionary ○ good ○ excellent *

Total highway safety penalties are: 2 *   Value: 8 1   Durability: 7 9   Highway Control Rating: 6 2   Highway Safety: 6 0   ★

Max	1998	MHC	30	Getaway 30	FO	6.8L	G	$2800	202	1,500	14,050	12,544

Livability Code: SB 30-80   Wheelbase-to-length ratio of 56% is considered ○ dangerous ○ fatiguing ◉ good ○ excellent *

The approximate net payload of 1506 pounds at 11% of GVWR on this model is ○ deficient ○ excessive ○ cautionary ◉ good ○ excellent *

Total highway safety penalties are: 2 *   Value: 8 1   Durability: 7 9   Highway Control Rating: 8 6   Highway Safety: 8 4   ★★★

Max	1998	MHC	30	Quest 30	FO	6.8L	G	$2800	202	1,500	14,050	12,544

Livability Code: SB 30-80   Wheelbase-to-length ratio of 56% is considered ○ dangerous ○ fatiguing ◉ good ○ excellent *

The approximate net payload of 1506 pounds at 11% of GVWR on this model is ○ deficient ○ excessive ○ cautionary ◉ good ○ excellent *

Total highway safety penalties are: 2 *   Value: 8 1   Durability: 7 9   Highway Control Rating: 8 6   Highway Safety: 8 4   ★★★

Max	1998	MHC	30	Diversion 30	FO	6.8L	G	$3000	202	1,500	14,050	13,444

Livability Code: SB 30-80   Wheelbase-to-length ratio of 56% is considered ○ dangerous ○ fatiguing ◉ good ○ excellent *

The approximate net payload of 606 pounds at 4% of GVWR on this model is ◉ deficient ○ excessive ○ cautionary ○ good ○ excellent *

Total highway safety penalties are: 7 *   Value: 7 8   Durability: 7 9   Highway Control Rating: 6 0   Highway Safety: 5 3   ★

Max	1998	MHC	30	Haven 30	FO	6.8L	G	$3000	202	1,500	14,050	13,444

Livability Code: SB 30-80   Wheelbase-to-length ratio of 56% is considered ○ dangerous ○ fatiguing ◉ good ○ excellent *

The approximate net payload of 606 pounds at 4% of GVWR on this model is ◉ deficient ○ excessive ○ cautionary ○ good ○ excellent *

Total highway safety penalties are: 7 *   Value: 7 8   Durability: 7 9   Highway Control Rating: 6 0   Highway Safety: 5 3   ★

Micro Warrior	1991	MMH	22	321 RB	TO	3.0L	G	$1300	137	1,500	6,000	5,455

Livability Code: VA 30-90   Wheelbase-to-length ratio of 53% is considered ○ dangerous ◉ fatiguing ○ good ○ excellent *

The approximate net payload of 545 pounds at 9% of GVWR on this model is ○ deficient ○ excessive ◉ cautionary ○ good ○ excellent *

Total highway safety penalties are: 2 *   Value: 8 2   Durability: 7 0   Highway Control Rating: 6 9   Highway Safety: 6 7   ★★

Micro Warrior	1992	MMH	21	320 RB	TO	3.0L	G	$1300	137	1,500	6,000	5,319

Livability Code: VA 30-90   Wheelbase-to-length ratio of 55% is considered ○ dangerous ○ fatiguing ◉ good ○ excellent *

The approximate net payload of 681 pounds at 11% of GVWR on this model is ○ deficient ○ excessive ○ cautionary ◉ good ○ excellent *

Total highway safety penalties are: 2 *   Value: 8 2   Durability: 7 0   Highway Control Rating: 8 4   Highway Safety: 8 2   ★★★

Note: Safety ratings are based on the assumption that the engineering of the RV has allowed for proper balance by placing fresh, gray, and black holding tanks in a location so as not to change the balance of the RV when the tanks are empty or full. **Always double-check wheelbase, GVWR, and weights at front and rear axles.**

*See Section 1 for details on how conclusions are reached.

Brand	Year	Type	Length	Model	Chassis	Engine	Fuel Type	Average Price per Linear Foot When New	Adjusted Wheelbase	Approx. Towing Capacity	Gross Vehicle Weight Rating	Average Curb Weight

Micro Warrior 1992 MMH 22 321 RB TO 3.0L G $1300 137 1,500 6,000 5,455
Livability Code: VA 30-90
Wheelbase-to-length ratio of 53% is considered ○ dangerous ◉ fatiguing ○ good ○ excellent *
The approximate net payload of 545 pounds at 9% of GVWR on this model is ○ deficient ○ excessive ◉ cautionary ○ good ○ excellent *
Total highway safety penalties are: 2 * Value: 8 2 Durability: 7 0 Highway Control Rating: 6 9 Highway Safety: 6 7 ★★

Micro Warrior 1992 MMH 22 321 RL TO 3.0L G $1300 137 1,500 6,000 5,455
Livability Code: VA 30-90
Wheelbase-to-length ratio of 53% is considered ○ dangerous ◉ fatiguing ○ good ○ excellent *
The approximate net payload of 545 pounds at 9% of GVWR on this model is ○ deficient ○ excessive ◉ cautionary ○ good ○ excellent *
Total highway safety penalties are: 2 * Value: 8 2 Durability: 7 0 Highway Control Rating: 6 9 Highway Safety: 6 7 ★★

Micro Warrior 1993 MMH 22 321 RL TO 3.0L G $1400 137 1,500 6,000 5,455
Livability Code: VA 30-90
Wheelbase-to-length ratio of 53% is considered ○ dangerous ◉ fatiguing ○ good ○ excellent *
The approximate net payload of 545 pounds at 9% of GVWR on this model is ○ deficient ○ excessive ◉ cautionary ○ good ○ excellent *
Total highway safety penalties are: 2 * Value: 8 2 Durability: 7 0 Highway Control Rating: 6 9 Highway Safety: 6 7 ★★

Micro Warrior 1993 MMH 22 321 RB TO 3.0L G $1400 137 1,500 6,000 5,455
Livability Code: VA 30-90
Wheelbase-to-length ratio of 53% is considered ○ dangerous ◉ fatiguing ○ good ○ excellent *
The approximate net payload of 545 pounds at 9% of GVWR on this model is ○ deficient ○ excessive ◉ cautionary ○ good ○ excellent *
Total highway safety penalties are: 2 * Value: 8 2 Durability: 7 0 Highway Control Rating: 6 9 Highway Safety: 6 7 ★★

Micro Warrior 1994 MMH 22 321 RB TO 3.0L G $1400 137 1,500 6,000 5,455
Livability Code: VA 30-90
Wheelbase-to-length ratio of 53% is considered ○ dangerous ◉ fatiguing ○ good ○ excellent *
The approximate net payload of 545 pounds at 9% of GVWR on this model is ○ deficient ○ excessive ◉ cautionary ○ good ○ excellent *
Total highway safety penalties are: 2 * Value: 8 2 Durability: 7 0 Highway Control Rating: 6 9 Highway Safety: 6 7 ★★

Micro Warrior 1994 MMH 22 321 RD TO 3.0L G $1400 137 1,500 6,000 5,489
Livability Code: VA 30-90
Wheelbase-to-length ratio of 53% is considered ○ dangerous ◉ fatiguing ○ good ○ excellent *
The approximate net payload of 511 pounds at 9% of GVWR on this model is ○ deficient ○ excessive ◉ cautionary ○ good ○ excellent *
Total highway safety penalties are: 2 * Value: 8 2 Durability: 7 0 Highway Control Rating: 6 7 Highway Safety: 6 5 ★★

Minnie 1990 MHC 27 426RT FO 7.5L G $1600 176 1,500 11,000 10,101
Livability Code: VA 30-90
Wheelbase-to-length ratio of 55% is considered ○ dangerous ○ fatiguing ◉ good ○ excellent *
The approximate net payload of 899 pounds at 8% of GVWR on this model is ○ deficient ○ excessive ◉ cautionary ○ good ○ excellent *
Total highway safety penalties are: 2 * Value: 8 3 Durability: 7 2 Highway Control Rating: 6 9 Highway Safety: 6 7 ★★

Minnie 1996 MHC 21 21RK CH 5.7L G $2000 125 3,300 10,200 8,810
Livability Code: VA 30-90
Wheelbase-to-length ratio of 49% is considered ◉ dangerous ○ fatiguing ○ good ○ excellent *
The approximate net payload of 1390 pounds at 14% of GVWR on this model is ○ deficient ○ excessive ○ cautionary ◉ good ○ excellent *
Total highway safety penalties are: 2 * Value: 8 3 Durability: 7 2 Highway Control Rating: 5 3 Highway Safety: 5 1

Minnie 1996 MHC 21 21RB CH 5.7L G $1800 125 3,300 10,200 8,810
Livability Code: VA 30-90
Wheelbase-to-length ratio of 49% is considered ◉ dangerous ○ fatiguing ○ good ○ excellent *
The approximate net payload of 1390 pounds at 14% of GVWR on this model is ○ deficient ○ excessive ○ cautionary ◉ good ○ excellent *
Total highway safety penalties are: 2 * Value: 8 3 Durability: 7 2 Highway Control Rating: 5 3 Highway Safety: 5 1

Minnie 1996 MHC 21 21RK FO 7.5L G $2000 138 8,000 10,500 8,810
Livability Code: VA 30-90
Wheelbase-to-length ratio of 55% is considered ○ dangerous ○ fatiguing ◉ good ○ excellent *
The approximate net payload of 1690 pounds at 16% of GVWR on this model is ○ deficient ○ excessive ○ cautionary ○ good ◉ excellent *
Total highway safety penalties are: 2 * Value: 8 3 Durability: 7 2 Highway Control Rating: 9 1 Highway Safety: 8 9 ★★★

Minnie 1996 MHC 21 21RK op eng FO 7.3 L D $2100 138 8,500 11,500 9,410
Livability Code: VA 30-90
Wheelbase-to-length ratio of 55% is considered ○ dangerous ○ fatiguing ◉ good ○ excellent *
The approximate net payload of 2090 pounds at 18% of GVWR on this model is ○ deficient ○ excessive ○ cautionary ○ good ◉ excellent *
Total highway safety penalties are: 2 * Value: 8 3 Durability: 7 2 Highway Control Rating: 9 3 Highway Safety: 9 1 ★★★

Minnie 1996 MHC 21 21RB FO 7.5L G $1800 138 8,000 10,500 8,810
Livability Code: VA 30-90
Wheelbase-to-length ratio of 55% is considered ○ dangerous ○ fatiguing ◉ good ○ excellent *
The approximate net payload of 1690 pounds at 16% of GVWR on this model is ○ deficient ○ excessive ○ cautionary ○ good ◉ excellent *
Total highway safety penalties are: 2 * Value: 8 3 Durability: 7 2 Highway Control Rating: 9 1 Highway Safety: 8 9 ★★★

Note: Safety ratings are based on the assumption that the engineering of the RV has allowed for proper balance by placing fresh, gray, and black holding tanks in a location so as not to change the balance of the RV when the tanks are empty or full. **Always double-check wheelbase, GVWR, and weights at front and rear axles.**

*See Section 1 for details on how conclusions are reached.

Section 2: The Ratings

Brand	Year	Type	Length	Model	Chassis	Engine	Fuel Type	Average Price per Linear Foot When New	Adjusted Wheelbase	Approx. Towing Capacity	Gross Vehicle Weight Rating	Average Curb Weight
Minnie	1996	MHC	21	21RB op eng	FO	7.3 L	D	$2100	138	8,500	11,500	9,410

Livability Code: VA 30-90
Wheelbase-to-length ratio of 55% is considered ○ dangerous ○ fatiguing ◉ good ○ excellent *
The approximate net payload of 2090 pounds at 18% of GVWR on this model is ○ deficient ○ excessive ○ cautionary ○ good ◉ excellent *
Total highway safety penalties are: 2 * Value: 8 3 Durability: 7 2 Highway Control Rating: 9 3 Highway Safety: 9 1 ★★★

Minnie	1996	MHC	25	24RC	FO	7.5L	G	$1600	158	7,000	11,500	9,641

Livability Code: VA 30-90
Wheelbase-to-length ratio of 54% is considered ○ dangerous ○ fatiguing ◉ good ○ excellent *
The approximate net payload of 1859 pounds at 16% of GVWR on this model is ○ deficient ○ excessive ○ cautionary ○ good ◉ excellent *
Total highway safety penalties are: 2 * Value: 8 3 Durability: 7 2 Highway Control Rating: 8 4 Highway Safety: 8 2 ★★★

Minnie	1996	MHC	25	24RC op eng	FO	7.3L	D	$1800	158	7,800	12,200	10,341

Livability Code: VA 30-90
Wheelbase-to-length ratio of 54% is considered ○ dangerous ○ fatiguing ◉ good ○ excellent *
The approximate net payload of 1859 pounds at 15% of GVWR on this model is ○ deficient ○ excessive ○ cautionary ◉ good ○ excellent *
Total highway safety penalties are: 2 * Value: 8 3 Durability: 7 2 Highway Control Rating: 8 2 Highway Safety: 8 0 ★★★

Minnie	1996	MHC	28	27RC	FO	7.5L	G	$1500	188	6,100	12,400	10,510

Livability Code: VA 30-90
Wheelbase-to-length ratio of 56% is considered ○ dangerous ○ fatiguing ◉ good ○ excellent *
The approximate net payload of 1890 pounds at 15% of GVWR on this model is ○ deficient ○ excessive ○ cautionary ◉ good ○ excellent *
Total highway safety penalties are: 2 * Value: 8 3 Durability: 7 2 Highway Control Rating: 9 6 Highway Safety: 9 4 ★★★

Minnie	1996	MHC	28	27RC op eng	FO	7.3L	D	$1700	188	7,600	12,400	11,010

Livability Code: VA 30-90
Wheelbase-to-length ratio of 56% is considered ○ dangerous ○ fatiguing ◉ good ○ excellent *
The approximate net payload of 1390 pounds at 11% of GVWR on this model is ○ deficient ○ excessive ○ cautionary ◉ good ○ excellent *
Total highway safety penalties are: 2 * Value: 8 3 Durability: 7 2 Highway Control Rating: 8 8 Highway Safety: 8 6 ★★★

Minnie	1996	MHC	29	29RQ op eng	FO	7.3L	D	$1700	190	7,600	12,400	11,345

Livability Code: VA 30-90
Wheelbase-to-length ratio of 54% is considered ○ dangerous ○ fatiguing ◉ good ○ excellent *
The approximate net payload of 1055 pounds at 9% of GVWR on this model is ○ deficient ○ excessive ◉ cautionary ○ good ○ excellent *
Total highway safety penalties are: 2 * Value: 8 3 Durability: 7 2 Highway Control Rating: 6 7 Highway Safety: 6 5 ★★

Minnie	1996	MHC	29	29RQ	FO	7.5L	G	$1500	190	6,100	12,400	10,845

Livability Code: VA 30-90
Wheelbase-to-length ratio of 54% is considered ○ dangerous ○ fatiguing ◉ good ○ excellent *
The approximate net payload of 1555 pounds at 13% of GVWR on this model is ○ deficient ○ excessive ○ cautionary ◉ good ○ excellent *
Total highway safety penalties are: 2 * Value: 8 3 Durability: 7 2 Highway Control Rating: 7 8 Highway Safety: 7 6 ★★★

Minnie	1997	MHC	22	21RK	FO	7.5L	G	$1900	138	8,000	10,500	8,979

Livability Code: VA 30-90
Wheelbase-to-length ratio of 52% is considered ○ dangerous ◉ fatiguing ○ good ○ excellent *
The approximate net payload of 1521 pounds at 14% of GVWR on this model is ○ deficient ○ excessive ○ cautionary ◉ good ○ excellent *
Total highway safety penalties are: 2 * Value: 8 3 Durability: 7 2 Highway Control Rating: 6 7 Highway Safety: 6 5 ★★

Minnie	1997	MHC	22	21RK op eng	FO	7.3L	D	$2200	138	8,500	11,500	9,619

Livability Code: VA 30-90
Wheelbase-to-length ratio of 52% is considered ○ dangerous ◉ fatiguing ○ good ○ excellent *
The approximate net payload of 1881 pounds at 16% of GVWR on this model is ○ deficient ○ excessive ○ cautionary ○ good ◉ excellent *
Total highway safety penalties are: 2 * Value: 8 3 Durability: 7 2 Highway Control Rating: 7 1 Highway Safety: 6 9 ★★

Minnie	1997	MHC	22	21RB	FO	7.5L	G	$1900	138	8,000	10,500	8,971

Livability Code: VA 30-90
Wheelbase-to-length ratio of 52% is considered ○ dangerous ◉ fatiguing ○ good ○ excellent *
The approximate net payload of 1529 pounds at 15% of GVWR on this model is ○ deficient ○ excessive ○ cautionary ◉ good ○ excellent *
Total highway safety penalties are: 2 * Value: 8 3 Durability: 7 2 Highway Control Rating: 6 8 Highway Safety: 6 6 ★★

Minnie	1997	MHC	22	21RB op eng	FO	7.3L	D	$2100	138	8,500	11,500	9,303

Livability Code: VA 30-90
Wheelbase-to-length ratio of 52% is considered ○ dangerous ◉ fatiguing ○ good ○ excellent *
The approximate net payload of 2197 pounds at 19% of GVWR on this model is ○ deficient ○ excessive ○ cautionary ○ good ◉ excellent *
Total highway safety penalties are: 2 * Value: 8 3 Durability: 7 2 Highway Control Rating: 7 4 Highway Safety: 7 2 ★★★

Minnie	1997	MHC	23	21RK opch	CH	7.4L	G	$1900	139	1,500	11,500	9,223

Livability Code: VA 30-90
Wheelbase-to-length ratio of 51% is considered ○ dangerous ◉ fatiguing ○ good ○ excellent *
The approximate net payload of 2277 pounds at 20% of GVWR on this model is ○ deficient ○ excessive ○ cautionary ○ good ◉ excellent *
Total highway safety penalties are: 2 * Value: 8 3 Durability: 7 2 Highway Control Rating: 6 8 Highway Safety: 6 6 ★★

Note: Safety ratings are based on the assumption that the engineering of the RV has allowed for proper balance by placing fresh, gray, and black holding tanks in a location so as not to change the balance of the RV when the tanks are empty or full. **Always double-check wheelbase, GVWR, and weights at front and rear axles.**

The RV Rating Book

*See Section 1 for details on how conclusions are reached.

Brand	Year	Type	Length	Model	Chassis	Engine	Fuel Type	Average Price per Linear Foot When New	Adjusted Wheelbase	Approx. Towing Capacity	Gross Vehicle Weight Rating	Average Curb Weight
Minnie	1997	MHC	23	21RB opch	CH	7.4L	G	$1700	139	1,500	11,500	9,223

Livability Code: VA 30-90

Wheelbase-to-length ratio of 51% is considered ○ dangerous ◉ fatiguing ○ good ○ excellent*

The approximate net payload of 2277 pounds at 20% of GVWR on this model is ○ deficient ◉ excessive ○ cautionary ○ good ◉ excellent

Total highway safety penalties are: 2*   Value: **83**   Durability: **72**   Highway Control Rating: **68**   Highway Safety: **66**   ★★

Brand	Year	Type	Length	Model	Chassis	Engine	Fuel Type	Avg Price/Linear Foot	Adj Wheelbase	Approx Towing	GVWR	Avg Curb Weight
Minnie	1997	MHC	25	24RC	FO	7.5L	G	$1700	158	7,000	11,500	9,597

Livability Code: VA 30-90

Wheelbase-to-length ratio of 54% is considered ○ dangerous ○ fatiguing ◉ good ○ excellent*

The approximate net payload of 1903 pounds at 17% of GVWR on this model is ○ deficient ○ excessive ○ cautionary ○ good ◉ excellent

Total highway safety penalties are: 2*   Value: **83**   Durability: **72**   Highway Control Rating: **84**   Highway Safety: **82**   ★★★

Minnie	1997	MHC	25	24RC op eng	FO	7.3L	D	$1900	158	8,500	11,500	9,834

Livability Code: VA 30-90

Wheelbase-to-length ratio of 54% is considered ○ dangerous ○ fatiguing ◉ good ○ excellent*

The approximate net payload of 1666 pounds at 14% of GVWR on this model is ○ deficient ○ excessive ○ cautionary ◉ good ○ excellent*

Total highway safety penalties are: 2*   Value: **83**   Durability: **72**   Highway Control Rating: **80**   Highway Safety: **78**   ★★★

Minnie	1997	MHC	25	24RC opch	CH	7.4L	G	$1700	158	1,500	12,300	9,925

Livability Code: VA 30-90

Wheelbase-to-length ratio of 53% is considered ○ dangerous ◉ fatiguing ○ good ○ excellent*

The approximate net payload of 2375 pounds at 19% of GVWR on this model is ○ deficient ○ excessive ○ cautionary ○ good ◉ excellent*

Total highway safety penalties are: 2*   Value: **83**   Durability: **72**   Highway Control Rating: **80**   Highway Safety: **78**   ★★★

Minnie	1997	MHC	28	27RC	FO	7.5L	G	$1700	188	5,950	14,050	10,434

Livability Code: VA 30-90

Wheelbase-to-length ratio of 56% is considered ○ dangerous ○ fatiguing ◉ good ○ excellent*

The approximate net payload of 3616 pounds at 26% of GVWR on this model is ○ deficient ○ excessive ○ cautionary ◉ good ○ excellent*

Total highway safety penalties are: 2*   Value: **83**   Durability: **72**   Highway Control Rating: **96**   Highway Safety: **94**   ★★★

Minnie	1997	MHC	28	27RC op eng	FO	7.3L	D	$1700	188	5,950	14,050	11,510

Livability Code: VA 30-90

Wheelbase-to-length ratio of 56% is considered ○ dangerous ○ fatiguing ◉ good ○ excellent*

The approximate net payload of 2540 pounds at 18% of GVWR on this model is ○ deficient ○ excessive ○ cautionary ○ good ◉ excellent*

Total highway safety penalties are: 2*   Value: **83**   Durability: **72**   Highway Control Rating: **99**   Highway Safety: **97**   ★★★

Minnie	1997	MHC	28	27RC opch	CH	7.4L	G	$1500	189	1,500	12,300	10,573

Livability Code: VA 30-90

Wheelbase-to-length ratio of 56% is considered ○ dangerous ○ fatiguing ◉ good ○ excellent*

The approximate net payload of 1727 pounds at 14% of GVWR on this model is ○ deficient ○ excessive ○ cautionary ◉ good ○ excellent*

Total highway safety penalties are: 2*   Value: **83**   Durability: **72**   Highway Control Rating: **92**   Highway Safety: **90**   ★★★

Minnie	1997	MHC	29	29RQ	FO	7.5L	G	$1600	190	5,950	14,050	10,709

Livability Code: VA 30-90

Wheelbase-to-length ratio of 54% is considered ○ dangerous ○ fatiguing ◉ good ○ excellent*

The approximate net payload of 3341 pounds at 24% of GVWR on this model is ○ deficient ○ excessive ○ cautionary ○ good ◉ excellent*

Total highway safety penalties are: 2*   Value: **83**   Durability: **72**   Highway Control Rating: **85**   Highway Safety: **83**   ★★★

Minnie	1997	MHC	29	29RQ op eng	FO	7.3L	D	$1800	190	5,950	14,050	10,875

Livability Code: VA 30-90

Wheelbase-to-length ratio of 54% is considered ○ dangerous ○ fatiguing ◉ good ○ excellent*

The approximate net payload of 3175 pounds at 23% of GVWR on this model is ○ deficient ○ excessive ○ cautionary ○ good ◉ excellent*

Total highway safety penalties are: 2*   Value: **84**   Durability: **76**   Highway Control Rating: **86**   Highway Safety: **84**   ★★★

Minnie	1997	MHC	31	31WU	FO	7.5L	G	$1600	205	5,950	14,050	11,391

Livability Code: VA 30-90

Wheelbase-to-length ratio of 54% is considered ○ dangerous ○ fatiguing ◉ good ○ excellent*

The approximate net payload of 2659 pounds at 19% of GVWR on this model is ○ deficient ○ excessive ○ cautionary ○ good ◉ excellent*

Total highway safety penalties are: 2*   Value: **83**   Durability: **72**   Highway Control Rating: **90**   Highway Safety: **88**   ★★★

Minnie	1997	MHC	31	31WU op eng	FO	7.3L	D	$1800	205	5,950	14,050	12,608

Livability Code: VA 30-90

Wheelbase-to-length ratio of 54% is considered ○ dangerous ○ fatiguing ◉ good ○ excellent*

The approximate net payload of 1442 pounds at 10% of GVWR on this model is ○ deficient ○ excessive ○ cautionary ◉ good ○ excellent*

Total highway safety penalties are: 2*   Value: **83**   Durability: **72**   Highway Control Rating: **75**   Highway Safety: **73**   ★★★

Minnie	1998	MHC	22	22WK	FO	6.8L	G	$2000	138	8,000	10,500	9,079

Livability Code: VA 30-90

Wheelbase-to-length ratio of 52% is considered ○ dangerous ◉ fatiguing ○ good ○ excellent*

The approximate net payload of 1421 pounds at 14% of GVWR on this model is ○ deficient ○ excessive ○ cautionary ◉ good ○ excellent*

Total highway safety penalties are: 2*   Value: **83**   Durability: **72**   Highway Control Rating: **66**   Highway Safety: **64**   ★★

Note: Safety ratings are based on the assumption that the engineering of the RV has allowed for proper balance by placing fresh, gray, and black holding tanks in a location so as not to change the balance of the RV when the tanks are empty or full. **Always double-check wheelbase, GVWR, and weights at front and rear axles.**

*See Section 1 for details on how conclusions are reached.

Brand	Year	Type	Length	Model	Chassis	Engine	Fuel Type	Average Price per Linear Foot When New	Adjusted Wheelbase	Approx. Towing Capacity	Gross Vehicle Weight Rating	Average Curb Weight
Minnie	1998	MHC	22	22RB	FO	6.8L	G	$2000	138	8,000	10,500	8,899

Livability Code: VA 30-90 Wheelbase-to-length ratio of 52% is considered ○ dangerous ● fatiguing ○ good ○ excellent *
The approximate net payload of 1601 pounds at 15% of GVWR on this model is ○ deficient ○ excessive ○ cautionary ● good ○ excellent *
Total highway safety penalties are: 2 *   Value: 8 3   Durability: 7 2   Highway Control Rating: 6 9   Highway Safety: 6 7   ★★

Brand	Year	Type	Length	Model	Chassis	Engine	Fuel Type	Price/Ft	Adj Wheelbase	Towing	GVWR	Curb Weight
Minnie	1998	MHC	23	22WK opch	CH	7.4L	G	$1900	139	4,700	12,300	9,096

Livability Code: VA 30-90 Wheelbase-to-length ratio of 51% is considered ○ dangerous ● fatiguing ○ good ○ excellent *
The approximate net payload of 3204 pounds at 26% of GVWR on this model is ○ deficient ○ excessive ○ cautionary ● good ○ excellent *
Total highway safety penalties are: 2 *   Value: 8 3   Durability: 7 2   Highway Control Rating: 6 2   Highway Safety: 6 0   ★★

Minnie	1998	MHC	23	22RB opch	CH	7.4L	G	$1900	139	4,700	12,300	8,990

Livability Code: VA 30-90 Wheelbase-to-length ratio of 51% is considered ○ dangerous ● fatiguing ○ good ○ excellent *
The approximate net payload of 3310 pounds at 27% of GVWR on this model is ○ deficient ○ excessive ○ cautionary ● good ○ excellent *
Total highway safety penalties are: 2 *   Value: 8 3   Durability: 7 2   Highway Control Rating: 6 1   Highway Safety: 5 9   ★

Minnie	1998	MHC	25	24RC	FO	6.8L	G	$1800	158	7,000	11,500	9,455

Livability Code: VA 30-90 Wheelbase-to-length ratio of 54% is considered ○ dangerous ○ fatiguing ● good ○ excellent *
The approximate net payload of 2045 pounds at 18% of GVWR on this model is ○ deficient ○ excessive ○ cautionary ○ good ● excellent *
Total highway safety penalties are: 2 *   Value: 8 3   Durability: 7 2   Highway Control Rating: 8 5   Highway Safety: 8 3   ★★★

Minnie	1998	MHC	25	24RC opch	CH	7.4L	G	$1800	159	4,700	12,300	9,599

Livability Code: VA 30-90 Wheelbase-to-length ratio of 53% is considered ○ dangerous ● fatiguing ○ good ○ excellent *
The approximate net payload of 2701 pounds at 22% of GVWR on this model is ○ deficient ○ excessive ○ cautionary ○ good ● excellent *
Total highway safety penalties are: 2 *   Value: 8 3   Durability: 7 2   Highway Control Rating: 8 0   Highway Safety: 7 8   ★★★

Minnie	1998	MHC	27	27WU	CH	7.4L	G	$1700	188	4,700	12,300	10,361

Livability Code: VA 30-90 Wheelbase-to-length ratio of 58% is considered ○ dangerous ○ fatiguing ○ good ● excellent *
The approximate net payload of 1939 pounds at 16% of GVWR on this model is ○ deficient ○ excessive ○ cautionary ○ good ● excellent *
Total highway safety penalties are: 2 *   Value: 8 3   Durability: 7 2   Highway Control Rating: 1 0 0   Highway Safety: 9 8   ★★★

Minnie	1998	MHC	29	29WQ	FO	6.8L	G	$1700	190	5,950	14,050	10,981

Livability Code: VA 30-90 Wheelbase-to-length ratio of 54% is considered ○ dangerous ○ fatiguing ● good ○ excellent *
The approximate net payload of 3069 pounds at 22% of GVWR on this model is ○ deficient ○ excessive ○ cautionary ○ good ● excellent *
Total highway safety penalties are: 2 *   Value: 8 3   Durability: 7 2   Highway Control Rating: 8 7   Highway Safety: 8 5   ★★★

Minnie	1998	MHC	29	29WQ op eng	FO	7.3L	D	$1800	190	5,950	14,050	11,350

Livability Code: VA 30-90 Wheelbase-to-length ratio of 54% is considered ○ dangerous ○ fatiguing ● good ○ excellent *
The approximate net payload of 2700 pounds at 19% of GVWR on this model is ○ deficient ○ excessive ○ cautionary ○ good ● excellent *
Total highway safety penalties are: 2 *   Value: 8 3   Durability: 7 2   Highway Control Rating: 8 8   Highway Safety: 8 6   ★★★

Minnie	1998	MHC	31	31WU	FO	6.8L	G	$1600	205	5,950	14,050	11,536

Livability Code: VA 30-90 Wheelbase-to-length ratio of 54% is considered ○ dangerous ○ fatiguing ● good ○ excellent *
The approximate net payload of 2514 pounds at 18% of GVWR on this model is ○ deficient ○ excessive ○ cautionary ○ good ● excellent *
Total highway safety penalties are: 2 *   Value: 8 3   Durability: 7 2   Highway Control Rating: 8 9   Highway Safety: 8 7   ★★★

Minnie	1998	MHC	31	31 WM	FO	6.8L	G	$1700	220	5,950	14,050	12,180

Livability Code: VA 30-90 Wheelbase-to-length ratio of 58% is considered ○ dangerous ○ fatiguing ○ good ● excellent *
The approximate net payload of 1870 pounds at 13% of GVWR on this model is ○ deficient ○ excessive ○ cautionary ● good ○ excellent *
Total highway safety penalties are: 7 *   Value: 8 0   Durability: 7 2   Highway Control Rating: 9 9   Highway Safety: 9 2   ★★★

Minnie	1998	MHC	31	31WU op eng	FO	FO215	D	$1700	205	5,950	14,050	11,957

Livability Code: VA 30-90 Wheelbase-to-length ratio of 54% is considered ○ dangerous ○ fatiguing ● good ○ excellent *
The approximate net payload of 2093 pounds at 15% of GVWR on this model is ○ deficient ○ excessive ○ cautionary ○ good ● excellent *
Total highway safety penalties are: 2 *   Value: 8 3   Durability: 7 2   Highway Control Rating: 8 5   Highway Safety: 8 3   ★★★

Minnie	1999	MHC	22	22E	FO	6.8L	G	$2500	138	7,800	10,700	9,071

Livability Code: VA 30-90 Wheelbase-to-length ratio of 52% is considered ○ dangerous ● fatiguing ○ good ○ excellent *
The approximate net payload of 1629 pounds at 15% of GVWR on this model is ○ deficient ○ excessive ○ cautionary ● good ○ excellent *
Total highway safety penalties are: 2 *   Value: 8 4   Durability: 7 6   Highway Control Rating: 6 9   Highway Safety: 6 7   ★★

Note: Safety ratings are based on the assumption that the engineering of the RV has allowed for proper balance by placing fresh, gray, and black holding tanks in a location so as not to change the balance of the RV when the tanks are empty or full. **Always double-check wheelbase, GVWR, and weights at front and rear axles.**

*See Section 1 for details on how conclusions are reached.

Section 2: The Ratings

Brand	Year	Type	Length	Model	Chassis	Engine	Fuel Type	Average Price per Linear Foot When New	Adjusted Wheelbase	Approx. Towing Capacity	Gross Vehicle Weight Rating	Average Curb Weight
Minnie	1999	MHC	22	22R	FO	6.8L	G	$2500	138	7,800	10,700	9,343

Livability Code: VA 30-90

Wheelbase-to-length ratio of 52% is considered ○ dangerous ◉ fatiguing ○ good ○ excellent *

The approximate net payload of 1357 pounds at 13% of GVWR on this model is ○ deficient ○ excessive ○ cautionary ◉ good ○ excellent *

Total highway safety penalties are: 2 *   Value: 8 4   Durability: 7 6   Highway Control Rating: 6 4   Highway Safety: 6 2   ★★

Brand	Year	Type	Length	Model	Chassis	Engine	Fuel Type	Price/Ft	Wheelbase	Towing	GVWR	Curb Wt
Minnie	1999	MHC	23	22E	CH	7.4L	G	$2400	139	4,700	12,300	9,120

Livability Code: VA 30-90

Wheelbase-to-length ratio of 51% is considered ○ dangerous ◉ fatiguing ○ good ○ excellent *

The approximate net payload of 3180 pounds at 26% of GVWR on this model is ○ deficient ○ excessive ○ cautionary ◉ good ○ excellent *

Total highway safety penalties are: 2 *   Value: 8 4   Durability: 7 6   Highway Control Rating: 6 2   Highway Safety: 6 0   ★★

Brand	Year	Type	Length	Model	Chassis	Engine	Fuel Type	Price/Ft	Wheelbase	Towing	GVWR	Curb Wt
Minnie	1999	MHC	23	22R	CH	7.4L	G	$2400	139	4,700	12,300	8,963

Livability Code: VA 30-90

Wheelbase-to-length ratio of 51% is considered ○ dangerous ◉ fatiguing ○ good ○ excellent *

The approximate net payload of 3337 pounds at 27% of GVWR on this model is ○ deficient ○ excessive ○ cautionary ◉ good ○ excellent *

Total highway safety penalties are: 2 *   Value: 8 4   Durability: 7 6   Highway Control Rating: 6 1   Highway Safety: 5 9   ★

Brand	Year	Type	Length	Model	Chassis	Engine	Fuel Type	Price/Ft	Wheelbase	Towing	GVWR	Curb Wt
Minnie	1999	MHC	25	24W	FO	6.8L	G	$2200	158	7,000	11,500	9,609

Livability Code: VA 30-90

Wheelbase-to-length ratio of 54% is considered ○ dangerous ○ fatiguing ◉ good ○ excellent *

The approximate net payload of 1891 pounds at 16% of GVWR on this model is ○ deficient ○ excessive ○ cautionary ○ good ◉ excellent *

Total highway safety penalties are: 2 *   Value: 8 4   Durability: 7 6   Highway Control Rating: 8 4   Highway Safety: 8 2   ★★★

Brand	Year	Type	Length	Model	Chassis	Engine	Fuel Type	Price/Ft	Wheelbase	Towing	GVWR	Curb Wt
Minnie	1999	MHC	25	24W	CH	7.4L	G	$2200	159	4,700	12,300	9,685

Livability Code: VA 30-90

Wheelbase-to-length ratio of 53% is considered ○ dangerous ◉ fatiguing ○ good ○ excellent *

The approximate net payload of 2615 pounds at 21% of GVWR on this model is ○ deficient ○ excessive ○ cautionary ○ good ◉ excellent *

Total highway safety penalties are: 2 *   Value: 8 4   Durability: 7 6   Highway Control Rating: 8 1   Highway Safety: 7 9   ★★★

Brand	Year	Type	Length	Model	Chassis	Engine	Fuel Type	Price/Ft	Wheelbase	Towing	GVWR	Curb Wt
Minnie	1999	MHC	27	27U opch	FO	6.8L	G	$2000	188	5,950	14,050	11,140

Livability Code: VA 30-90

Wheelbase-to-length ratio of 58% is considered ○ dangerous ○ fatiguing ○ good ◉ excellent *

The approximate net payload of 2910 pounds at 21% of GVWR on this model is ○ deficient ○ excessive ○ cautionary ○ good ◉ excellent *

Total highway safety penalties are: 2 *   Value: 8 4   Durability: 7 6   Highway Control Rating: 1 0 0   Highway Safety: 9 8   ★★★

Brand	Year	Type	Length	Model	Chassis	Engine	Fuel Type	Price/Ft	Wheelbase	Towing	GVWR	Curb Wt
Minnie	1999	MHC	28	27U	CH	7.4L	G	$2000	189	4,700	12,300	10,750

Livability Code: VA 30-90

Wheelbase-to-length ratio of 57% is considered ○ dangerous ○ fatiguing ◉ good ○ excellent *

The approximate net payload of 1550 pounds at 13% of GVWR on this model is ○ deficient ○ excessive ○ cautionary ◉ good ○ excellent *

Total highway safety penalties are: 2 *   Value: 8 4   Durability: 7 6   Highway Control Rating: 9 4   Highway Safety: 9 2   ★★★

Brand	Year	Type	Length	Model	Chassis	Engine	Fuel Type	Price/Ft	Wheelbase	Towing	GVWR	Curb Wt
Minnie	1999	MHC	29	29N	FO	6.8L	G	$1900	190	5,950	14,050	11,011

Livability Code: VA 30-90

Wheelbase-to-length ratio of 54% is considered ○ dangerous ○ fatiguing ◉ good ○ excellent *

The approximate net payload of 3039 pounds at 22% of GVWR on this model is ○ deficient ○ excessive ○ cautionary ○ good ◉ excellent *

Total highway safety penalties are: 2 *   Value: 8 4   Durability: 7 6   Highway Control Rating: 8 7   Highway Safety: 8 5   ★★★

Brand	Year	Type	Length	Model	Chassis	Engine	Fuel Type	Price/Ft	Wheelbase	Towing	GVWR	Curb Wt
Minnie	1999	MHC	31	31G	FO	6.8L	G	$1800	205	5,950	14,050	11,578

Livability Code: VA 30-90

Wheelbase-to-length ratio of 54% is considered ○ dangerous ○ fatiguing ◉ good ○ excellent *

The approximate net payload of 2472 pounds at 18% of GVWR on this model is ○ deficient ○ excessive ○ cautionary ○ good ◉ excellent *

Total highway safety penalties are: 2 *   Value: 8 4   Durability: 7 6   Highway Control Rating: 8 8   Highway Safety: 8 6   ★★★

Brand	Year	Type	Length	Model	Chassis	Engine	Fuel Type	Price/Ft	Wheelbase	Towing	GVWR	Curb Wt
Minnie	1999	MHC	31	31C	FO	6.8L	G	$1800	220	5,950	14,050	11,987

Livability Code: VA 30-90

Wheelbase-to-length ratio of 58% is considered ○ dangerous ○ fatiguing ○ good ◉ excellent *

The approximate net payload of 2063 pounds at 15% of GVWR on this model is ○ deficient ○ excessive ○ cautionary ◉ good ○ excellent *

Total highway safety penalties are: 7 *   Value: 8 2   Durability: 7 6   Highway Control Rating: 1 0 0   Highway Safety: 9 3   ★★★

Brand	Year	Type	Length	Model	Chassis	Engine	Fuel Type	Price/Ft	Wheelbase	Towing	GVWR	Curb Wt
Minnie 300	1995	MHC	22	21RK	CH	5.7L	G	$1800	125	3,300	10,200	9,068

Livability Code: VA 30-90

Wheelbase-to-length ratio of 47% is considered ◉ dangerous ○ fatiguing ○ good ○ excellent *

The approximate net payload of 1132 pounds at 11% of GVWR on this model is ○ deficient ○ excessive ○ cautionary ◉ good ○ excellent *

Total highway safety penalties are: 2 *   Value: 8 3   Durability: 7 2   Highway Control Rating: 4 0   Highway Safety: 3 8

Brand	Year	Type	Length	Model	Chassis	Engine	Fuel Type	Price/Ft	Wheelbase	Towing	GVWR	Curb Wt
Minnie 300	1995	MHC	22	21RB	CH	5.7L	G	$1800	125	3,300	10,200	9,068

Livability Code: VA 30-90

Wheelbase-to-length ratio of 47% is considered ◉ dangerous ○ fatiguing ○ good ○ excellent *

The approximate net payload of 1132 pounds at 11% of GVWR on this model is ○ deficient ○ excessive ○ cautionary ◉ good ○ excellent *

Total highway safety penalties are: 2 *   Value: 8 3   Durability: 7 2   Highway Control Rating: 4 0   Highway Safety: 3 8

Note: Safety ratings are based on the assumption that the engineering of the RV has allowed for proper balance by placing fresh, gray, and black holding tanks in a location so as not to change the balance of the RV when the tanks are empty or full. **Always double-check wheelbase, GVWR, and weights at front and rear axles.**

*See Section 1 for details on how conclusions are reached.

Brand	Year	Type	Length	Model	Chassis	Engine	Fuel Type	Average Price per Linear Foot When New	Adjusted Wheelbase	Approx. Towing Capacity	Gross Vehicle Weight Rating	Average Curb Weight
Minnie 300	1995	MHC	22	21RK	FO	7.5L	G	$1800	138	3,500	10,500	9,068

Livability Code: VA 30-90
Wheelbase-to-length ratio of 52% is considered ○ dangerous ● fatiguing ○ good ○ excellent *
The approximate net payload of 1432 pounds at 14% of GVWR on this model is ○ deficient ○ excessive ○ cautionary ● good ○ excellent *
Total highway safety penalties are: 2 *   Value: 8 3   Durability: 7 2   Highway Control Rating: 6 6   Highway Safety: 6 4   ★★

Brand	Year	Type	Length	Model	Chassis	Engine	Fuel Type	Price/Ft	Wheelbase	Towing	GVWR	Curb Wt
Minnie 300	1995	MHC	22	21RB	FO	7.5L	G	$1800	138	3,500	10,500	9,068

Livability Code: VA 30-90
Wheelbase-to-length ratio of 52% is considered ○ dangerous ● fatiguing ○ good ○ excellent *
The approximate net payload of 1432 pounds at 14% of GVWR on this model is ○ deficient ○ excessive ○ cautionary ● good ○ excellent *
Total highway safety penalties are: 2 *   Value: 8 3   Durability: 7 2   Highway Control Rating: 6 6   Highway Safety: 6 4   ★★

Minnie 300	1995	MHC	25	24RC	FO	7.5L	G	$1600	158	2,500	11,500	9,696

Livability Code: VA 30-90
Wheelbase-to-length ratio of 54% is considered ○ dangerous ○ fatiguing ● good ○ excellent *
The approximate net payload of 1804 pounds at 16% of GVWR on this model is ○ deficient ○ excessive ○ cautionary ○ good ● excellent *
Total highway safety penalties are: 2 *   Value: 8 3   Durability: 7 2   Highway Control Rating: 8 3   Highway Safety: 8 1   ★★★

Minnie 300	1995	MHC	25	24RC-N	FO	7.3L	D	$1800	158	1,800	12,200	9,896

Livability Code: VA 30-90
Wheelbase-to-length ratio of 54% is considered ○ dangerous ○ fatiguing ● good ○ excellent *
The approximate net payload of 2304 pounds at 19% of GVWR on this model is ○ deficient ○ excessive ○ cautionary ○ good ● excellent *
Total highway safety penalties are: 2 *   Value: 8 3   Durability: 7 2   Highway Control Rating: 8 6   Highway Safety: 8 4   ★★★

Minnie 300	1995	MHC	28	27RC	FO	7.5L	G	$1500	188	3,500	12,400	10,571

Livability Code: VA 30-90
Wheelbase-to-length ratio of 56% is considered ○ dangerous ○ fatiguing ● good ○ excellent *
The approximate net payload of 1829 pounds at 15% of GVWR on this model is ○ deficient ○ excessive ○ cautionary ● good ○ excellent *
Total highway safety penalties are: 2 *   Value: 8 3   Durability: 7 2   Highway Control Rating: 9 5   Highway Safety: 9 3   ★★★

Minnie 300	1995	MHC	28	27RC-N	FO	7.3L	D	$1700	188	1,800	12,200	10,571

Livability Code: VA 30-90
Wheelbase-to-length ratio of 56% is considered ○ dangerous ○ fatiguing ● good ○ excellent *
The approximate net payload of 1629 pounds at 13% of GVWR on this model is ○ deficient ○ excessive ○ cautionary ● good ○ excellent *
Total highway safety penalties are: 2 *   Value: 8 3   Durability: 7 2   Highway Control Rating: 9 2   Highway Safety: 9 0   ★★★

Minnie 300	1995	MHC	29	28RQ	FO	7.5L	G	$1500	190	3,500	12,400	10,825

Livability Code: VA 30-90
Wheelbase-to-length ratio of 55% is considered ○ dangerous ○ fatiguing ● good ○ excellent *
The approximate net payload of 1575 pounds at 13% of GVWR on this model is ○ deficient ○ excessive ○ cautionary ● good ○ excellent *
Total highway safety penalties are: 2 *   Value: 8 3   Durability: 7 2   Highway Control Rating: 8 5   Highway Safety: 8 3   ★★★

Minnie 300	1995	MHC	29	28RQ-N	FO	7.3L	D	$1600	190	1,800	12,200	10,825

Livability Code: VA 30-90
Wheelbase-to-length ratio of 55% is considered ○ dangerous ○ fatiguing ● good ○ excellent *
The approximate net payload of 1375 pounds at 11% of GVWR on this model is ○ deficient ○ excessive ○ cautionary ● good ○ excellent *
Total highway safety penalties are: 2 *   Value: 8 3   Durability: 7 2   Highway Control Rating: 8 1   Highway Safety: 7 9   ★★★

Minnie Winnie	1991	MHC	25	424 RC	FO	7.5L	G	$1700	158	1,500	11,500	9,862

Livability Code: VA 30-90
Wheelbase-to-length ratio of 53% is considered ○ dangerous ● fatiguing ○ good ○ excellent *
The approximate net payload of 1638 pounds at 14% of GVWR on this model is ○ deficient ○ excessive ○ cautionary ● good ○ excellent *
Total highway safety penalties are: 2 *   Value: 8 3   Durability: 7 2   Highway Control Rating: 7 5   Highway Safety: 7 3   ★★★

Minnie Winnie	1992	MHC	23	22 RG	CH	5.7L	G	$1600	146	3,300	10,200	9,316

Livability Code: VA 30-90
Wheelbase-to-length ratio of 54% is considered ○ dangerous ○ fatiguing ● good ○ excellent *
The approximate net payload of 884 pounds at 9% of GVWR on this model is ○ deficient ○ excessive ● cautionary ○ good ○ excellent *
Total highway safety penalties are: 2 *   Value: 8 3   Durability: 7 2   Highway Control Rating: 6 8   Highway Safety: 6 6   ★★

Minnie Winnie	1992	MHC	24	22 RG	FO	7.5L	G	$1600	158	2,500	11,500	9,635

Livability Code: VA 30-90
Wheelbase-to-length ratio of 56% is considered ○ dangerous ○ fatiguing ● good ○ excellent *
The approximate net payload of 1865 pounds at 16% of GVWR on this model is ○ deficient ○ excessive ○ cautionary ○ good ● excellent *
Total highway safety penalties are: 2 *   Value: 8 3   Durability: 7 2   Highway Control Rating: 9 6   Highway Safety: 9 4   ★★★

Minnie Winnie	1992	MHC	24	24 RC	CH	5.7L	G	$1600	146	3,000	10,500	9,557

Livability Code: VA 30-90
Wheelbase-to-length ratio of 52% is considered ○ dangerous ● fatiguing ○ good ○ excellent *
The approximate net payload of 943 pounds at 9% of GVWR on this model is ○ deficient ○ excessive ● cautionary ○ good ○ excellent *
Total highway safety penalties are: 2 *   Value: 8 3   Durability: 7 2   Highway Control Rating: 5 2   Highway Safety: 5 0   ★

Note: Safety ratings are based on the assumption that the engineering of the RV has allowed for proper balance by placing fresh, gray, and black holding tanks in a location so as not to change the balance of the RV when the tanks are empty or full. **Always double-check wheelbase, GVWR, and weights at front and rear axles.**

*See Section 1 for details on how conclusions are reached.

Section 2: The Ratings

Brand	Year	Type	Length	Model	Chassis	Engine	Fuel Type	Average Price per Linear Foot When New	Adjusted Wheelbase	Approx. Towing Capacity	Gross Vehicle Weight Rating	Average Curb Weight
Minnie Winnie	1993	MHC	23	22 RG	CH	5.7L	G	$1500	146	3,000	10,500	9,316

Livability Code: VA 30-90
Wheelbase-to-length ratio of 54% is considered ○ dangerous ○ fatiguing ◉ good ○ excellent *
The approximate net payload of 1184 pounds at 11% of GVWR on this model is ○ deficient ○ excessive ○ cautionary ◉ good ○ excellent *
Total highway safety penalties are: 2 *   Value: 83   Durability: 72   Highway Control Rating: 76   Highway Safety: 74   ★★★

Brand	Year	Type	Length	Model	Chassis	Engine	Fuel Type	Price/Ft	Wheelbase	Towing	GVWR	Curb Weight
Minnie Winnie	1993	MHC	23	22 RG	CH	7.4L	G	$1600	146	3,000	10,500	9,316

Livability Code: VA 30-90
Wheelbase-to-length ratio of 54% is considered ○ dangerous ○ fatiguing ◉ good ○ excellent *
The approximate net payload of 1184 pounds at 11% of GVWR on this model is ○ deficient ○ excessive ○ cautionary ◉ good ○ excellent *
Total highway safety penalties are: 2 *   Value: 83   Durability: 72   Highway Control Rating: 76   Highway Safety: 74   ★★★

Brand	Year	Type	Length	Model	Chassis	Engine	Fuel Type	Price/Ft	Wheelbase	Towing	GVWR	Curb Weight
Minnie Winnie	1993	MHC	24	22 RG	FO	7.5L	G	$1500	158	2,500	11,500	9,635

Livability Code: VA 30-90
Wheelbase-to-length ratio of 56% is considered ○ dangerous ○ fatiguing ◉ good ○ excellent *
The approximate net payload of 1865 pounds at 16% of GVWR on this model is ○ deficient ○ excessive ○ cautionary ○ good ◉ excellent *
Total highway safety penalties are: 2 *   Value: 83   Durability: 72   Highway Control Rating: 96   Highway Safety: 94   ★★★

Brand	Year	Type	Length	Model	Chassis	Engine	Fuel Type	Price/Ft	Wheelbase	Towing	GVWR	Curb Weight
Minnie Winnie	1993	MHC	24	22 RG op eng	FO	7.3L	D	$1600	158	2,500	11,500	10,135

Livability Code: VA 30-90
Wheelbase-to-length ratio of 56% is considered ○ dangerous ○ fatiguing ◉ good ○ excellent *
The approximate net payload of 1365 pounds at 12% of GVWR on this model is ○ deficient ○ excessive ○ cautionary ◉ good ○ excellent *
Total highway safety penalties are: 2 *   Value: 83   Durability: 72   Highway Control Rating: 88   Highway Safety: 86   ★★★

Brand	Year	Type	Length	Model	Chassis	Engine	Fuel Type	Price/Ft	Wheelbase	Towing	GVWR	Curb Weight
Minnie Winnie	1993	MHC	24	24 RC	CH	5.7L	G	$1500	146	3,000	10,500	9,557

Livability Code: VA 30-90
Wheelbase-to-length ratio of 52% is considered ○ dangerous ◉ fatiguing ○ good ○ excellent *
The approximate net payload of 943 pounds at 9% of GVWR on this model is ○ deficient ○ excessive ◉ cautionary ○ good ○ excellent *
Total highway safety penalties are: 2 *   Value: 83   Durability: 72   Highway Control Rating: 52   Highway Safety: 50   ★

Brand	Year	Type	Length	Model	Chassis	Engine	Fuel Type	Price/Ft	Wheelbase	Towing	GVWR	Curb Weight
Minnie Winnie	1993	MHC	24	24 RC	CH	7.4L	G	$1500	146	3,000	10,500	9,557

Livability Code: VA 30-90
Wheelbase-to-length ratio of 52% is considered ○ dangerous ◉ fatiguing ○ good ○ excellent *
The approximate net payload of 943 pounds at 9% of GVWR on this model is ○ deficient ○ excessive ◉ cautionary ○ good ○ excellent *
Total highway safety penalties are: 2 *   Value: 83   Durability: 72   Highway Control Rating: 52   Highway Safety: 50   ★

Brand	Year	Type	Length	Model	Chassis	Engine	Fuel Type	Price/Ft	Wheelbase	Towing	GVWR	Curb Weight
Minnie Winnie	1993	MHC	25	24 RC	FO	7.5L	G	$1500	158	2,500	11,500	9,875

Livability Code: VA 30-90
Wheelbase-to-length ratio of 54% is considered ○ dangerous ○ fatiguing ◉ good ○ excellent *
The approximate net payload of 1625 pounds at 14% of GVWR on this model is ○ deficient ○ excessive ○ cautionary ◉ good ○ excellent *
Total highway safety penalties are: 2 *   Value: 83   Durability: 72   Highway Control Rating: 80   Highway Safety: 78   ★★★

Brand	Year	Type	Length	Model	Chassis	Engine	Fuel Type	Price/Ft	Wheelbase	Towing	GVWR	Curb Weight
Minnie Winnie	1993	MHC	25	24 RC op eng	FO	7.3L	D	$1500	158	2,500	11,500	10,375

Livability Code: VA 30-90
Wheelbase-to-length ratio of 54% is considered ○ dangerous ○ fatiguing ◉ good ○ excellent *
The approximate net payload of 1125 pounds at 10% of GVWR on this model is ○ deficient ○ excessive ○ cautionary ◉ good ○ excellent *
Total highway safety penalties are: 2 *   Value: 83   Durability: 72   Highway Control Rating: 77   Highway Safety: 75   ★★★

Brand	Year	Type	Length	Model	Chassis	Engine	Fuel Type	Price/Ft	Wheelbase	Towing	GVWR	Curb Weight
Minnie Winnie	1993	MHC	27	27 RQ	FO	7.5L	G	$1500	188	3,700	12,200	10,687

Livability Code: VA 30-90
Wheelbase-to-length ratio of 57% is considered ○ dangerous ○ fatiguing ◉ good ○ excellent *
The approximate net payload of 1513 pounds at 12% of GVWR on this model is ○ deficient ○ excessive ○ cautionary ◉ good ○ excellent *
Total highway safety penalties are: 2 *   Value: 83   Durability: 72   Highway Control Rating: 93   Highway Safety: 91   ★★★

Brand	Year	Type	Length	Model	Chassis	Engine	Fuel Type	Price/Ft	Wheelbase	Towing	GVWR	Curb Weight
Minnie Winnie	1993	MHC	27	27 RQ op eng	FO	7.3L	D	$1600	188	1,500	12,200	11,187

Livability Code: VA 30-90
Wheelbase-to-length ratio of 57% is considered ○ dangerous ○ fatiguing ◉ good ○ excellent *
The approximate net payload of 1013 pounds at 8% of GVWR on this model is ○ deficient ○ excessive ◉ cautionary ○ good ○ excellent *
Total highway safety penalties are: 2 *   Value: 83   Durability: 72   Highway Control Rating: 78   Highway Safety: 76   ★★★

Brand	Year	Type	Length	Model	Chassis	Engine	Fuel Type	Price/Ft	Wheelbase	Towing	GVWR	Curb Weight
Minnie Winnie	1993	MHC	28	27 RC	FO	7.5L	G	$1400	188	3,700	12,200	10,774

Livability Code: VA 30-90
Wheelbase-to-length ratio of 56% is considered ○ dangerous ○ fatiguing ◉ good ○ excellent *
The approximate net payload of 1426 pounds at 12% of GVWR on this model is ○ deficient ○ excessive ○ cautionary ◉ good ○ excellent *
Total highway safety penalties are: 2 *   Value: 83   Durability: 72   Highway Control Rating: 89   Highway Safety: 87   ★★★

Brand	Year	Type	Length	Model	Chassis	Engine	Fuel Type	Price/Ft	Wheelbase	Towing	GVWR	Curb Weight
Minnie Winnie	1993	MHC	28	27 RC op eng	FO	7.3L	D	$1700	188	1,500	12,200	11,274

Livability Code: VA 30-90
Wheelbase-to-length ratio of 56% is considered ○ dangerous ○ fatiguing ◉ good ○ excellent *
The approximate net payload of 926 pounds at 8% of GVWR on this model is ○ deficient ○ excessive ◉ cautionary ○ good ○ excellent *
Total highway safety penalties are: 2 *   Value: 83   Durability: 72   Highway Control Rating: 74   Highway Safety: 72   ★★★

Note: Safety ratings are based on the assumption that the engineering of the RV has allowed for proper balance by placing fresh, gray, and black holding tanks in a location so as not to change the balance of the RV when the tanks are empty or full. **Always double-check wheelbase, GVWR, and weights at front and rear axles.**

*See Section 1 for details on how conclusions are reached.

Brand	Year	Type	Length	Model	Chassis	Engine	Fuel Type	Average Price per Linear Foot When New	Adjusted Wheel-base	Approx. Towing Capacity	Gross Vehicle Weight Rating	Average Curb Weight
Minnie Winnie	1994	MHC	21	21 RB	CH	5.7L	G	$1800	125	1,500	10,200	9,010

Livability Code: VA 30-90

Wheelbase-to-length ratio of 49% is considered ● dangerous ○ fatiguing ○ good ○ excellent *

The approximate net payload of 1190 pounds at 12% of GVWR on this model is ○ deficient ○ excessive ○ cautionary ● good ○ excellent *

Total highway safety penalties are: 2 *   Value: 8 3   Durability: 7 2   Highway Control Rating: 4 9   Highway Safety: 4 7

Brand	Year	Type	Length	Model	Chassis	Engine	Fuel Type	Price/Ft	Wheelbase	Towing	GVWR	Curb Wt
Minnie Winnie	1994	MHC	22	21 RB	FO	7.5L	G	$1700	138	1,500	10,500	9,229

Livability Code: VA 30-90

Wheelbase-to-length ratio of 52% is considered ○ dangerous ● fatiguing ○ good ○ excellent *

The approximate net payload of 1271 pounds at 12% of GVWR on this model is ○ deficient ○ excessive ○ cautionary ● good ○ excellent *

Total highway safety penalties are: 2 *   Value: 8 3   Durability: 7 2   Highway Control Rating: 6 3   Highway Safety: 6 1   ★★

Brand	Year	Type	Length	Model	Chassis	Engine	Fuel Type	Price/Ft	Wheelbase	Towing	GVWR	Curb Wt
Minnie Winnie	1994	MHC	24	23 RD	FO	7.5L	G	$1600	158	1,500	11,500	9,635

Livability Code: VA 30-90

Wheelbase-to-length ratio of 56% is considered ○ dangerous ○ fatiguing ● good ○ excellent *

The approximate net payload of 1865 pounds at 16% of GVWR on this model is ○ deficient ○ excessive ○ cautionary ○ good ● excellent *

Total highway safety penalties are: 2 *   Value: 8 3   Durability: 7 2   Highway Control Rating: 9 6   Highway Safety: 9 4   ★★★

Brand	Year	Type	Length	Model	Chassis	Engine	Fuel Type	Price/Ft	Wheelbase	Towing	GVWR	Curb Wt
Minnie Winnie	1994	MHC	24	23 RD op eng	FO	7.3L	D	$1700	158	1,500	11,500	10,135

Livability Code: VA 30-90

Wheelbase-to-length ratio of 56% is considered ○ dangerous ○ fatiguing ● good ○ excellent *

The approximate net payload of 1365 pounds at 12% of GVWR on this model is ○ deficient ○ excessive ○ cautionary ● good ○ excellent *

Total highway safety penalties are: 2 *   Value: 8 3   Durability: 7 2   Highway Control Rating: 8 8   Highway Safety: 8 6   ★★★

Brand	Year	Type	Length	Model	Chassis	Engine	Fuel Type	Price/Ft	Wheelbase	Towing	GVWR	Curb Wt
Minnie Winnie	1994	MHC	25	24 RC	FO	7.5L	G	$1600	158	1,500	11,500	9,875

Livability Code: VA 30-90

Wheelbase-to-length ratio of 54% is considered ○ dangerous ○ fatiguing ● good ○ excellent *

The approximate net payload of 1625 pounds at 14% of GVWR on this model is ○ deficient ○ excessive ○ cautionary ● good ○ excellent *

Total highway safety penalties are: 2 *   Value: 8 3   Durability: 7 2   Highway Control Rating: 8 0   Highway Safety: 7 8   ★★★

Brand	Year	Type	Length	Model	Chassis	Engine	Fuel Type	Price/Ft	Wheelbase	Towing	GVWR	Curb Wt
Minnie Winnie	1994	MHC	25	24 RC op eng	FO	7.3L	D	$1700	158	1,500	11,500	10,375

Livability Code: VA 30-90

Wheelbase-to-length ratio of 54% is considered ○ dangerous ○ fatiguing ● good ○ excellent *

The approximate net payload of 1125 pounds at 10% of GVWR on this model is ○ deficient ○ excessive ○ cautionary ● good ○ excellent *

Total highway safety penalties are: 2 *   Value: 8 3   Durability: 7 2   Highway Control Rating: 7 7   Highway Safety: 7 5   ★★★

Brand	Year	Type	Length	Model	Chassis	Engine	Fuel Type	Price/Ft	Wheelbase	Towing	GVWR	Curb Wt
Minnie Winnie	1994	MHC	27	27 RQ	FO	7.5L	G	$1500	188	1,500	12,200	10,687

Livability Code: VA 30-90

Wheelbase-to-length ratio of 57% is considered ○ dangerous ○ fatiguing ● good ○ excellent *

The approximate net payload of 1513 pounds at 12% of GVWR on this model is ○ deficient ○ excessive ○ cautionary ● good ○ excellent *

Total highway safety penalties are: 2 *   Value: 8 3   Durability: 7 2   Highway Control Rating: 9 3   Highway Safety: 9 1   ★★★

Brand	Year	Type	Length	Model	Chassis	Engine	Fuel Type	Price/Ft	Wheelbase	Towing	GVWR	Curb Wt
Minnie Winnie	1994	MHC	27	27 RQ op eng	FO	7.3L	D	$1600	188	1,500	12,200	11,187

Livability Code: VA 30-90

Wheelbase-to-length ratio of 57% is considered ○ dangerous ○ fatiguing ● good ○ excellent *

The approximate net payload of 1013 pounds at 8% of GVWR on this model is ○ deficient ○ excessive ● cautionary ○ good ○ excellent *

Total highway safety penalties are: 2 *   Value: 8 3   Durability: 7 2   Highway Control Rating: 7 8   Highway Safety: 7 6   ★★★

Brand	Year	Type	Length	Model	Chassis	Engine	Fuel Type	Price/Ft	Wheelbase	Towing	GVWR	Curb Wt
Minnie Winnie	1994	MHC	28	27 RC	FO	7.5L	G	$1500	188	1,500	12,200	10,774

Livability Code: VA 30-90

Wheelbase-to-length ratio of 56% is considered ○ dangerous ○ fatiguing ● good ○ excellent *

The approximate net payload of 1426 pounds at 12% of GVWR on this model is ○ deficient ○ excessive ○ cautionary ● good ○ excellent *

Total highway safety penalties are: 2 *   Value: 8 3   Durability: 7 2   Highway Control Rating: 8 9   Highway Safety: 8 7   ★★★

Brand	Year	Type	Length	Model	Chassis	Engine	Fuel Type	Price/Ft	Wheelbase	Towing	GVWR	Curb Wt
Minnie Winnie	1994	MHC	28	27 RC op eng	FO	7.3L	D	$1600	188	1,500	12,200	11,274

Livability Code: VA 30-90

Wheelbase-to-length ratio of 56% is considered ○ dangerous ○ fatiguing ● good ○ excellent *

The approximate net payload of 926 pounds at 8% of GVWR on this model is ○ deficient ○ excessive ● cautionary ○ good ○ excellent *

Total highway safety penalties are: 2 *   Value: 8 3   Durability: 7 2   Highway Control Rating: 7 4   Highway Safety: 7 2   ★★★

Brand	Year	Type	Length	Model	Chassis	Engine	Fuel Type	Price/Ft	Wheelbase	Towing	GVWR	Curb Wt
Minnie Winnie	1994	MHC	29	28 RQ	FO	7.5L	G	$1400	190	1,500	12,200	11,037

Livability Code: VA 30-90

Wheelbase-to-length ratio of 55% is considered ○ dangerous ○ fatiguing ● good ○ excellent *

The approximate net payload of 1164 pounds at 10% of GVWR on this model is ○ deficient ○ excessive ○ cautionary ● good ○ excellent *

Total highway safety penalties are: 2 *   Value: 8 3   Durability: 7 2   Highway Control Rating: 7 9   Highway Safety: 7 7   ★★★

Brand	Year	Type	Length	Model	Chassis	Engine	Fuel Type	Price/Ft	Wheelbase	Towing	GVWR	Curb Wt
Minnie Winnie	1994	MHC	29	28 RQ op eng	FO	7.3L	D	$1500	190	1,500	12,200	11,537

Livability Code: VA 30-90

Wheelbase-to-length ratio of 55% is considered ○ dangerous ○ fatiguing ● good ○ excellent *

The approximate net payload of 664 pounds at 5% of GVWR on this model is ● deficient ○ excessive ○ cautionary ○ good ○ excellent *

Total highway safety penalties are: 2 *   Value: 8 3   Durability: 7 2   Highway Control Rating: 5 6   Highway Safety: 5 4   ★

Note: Safety ratings are based on the assumption that the engineering of the RV has allowed for proper balance by placing fresh, gray, and black holding tanks in a location so as not to change the balance of the RV when the tanks are empty or full. **Always double-check wheelbase, GVWR, and weights at front and rear axles.**

*See Section 1 for details on how conclusions are reached.

Brand	Year	Type	Length	Model	Chassis	Engine	Fuel Type	Average Price per Linear Foot When New	Adjusted Wheelbase	Approx. Towing Capacity	Gross Vehicle Weight Rating	Average Curb Weight

Minnie Winnie | 1995 | MHC | 29 | 28RQ | FO | 7.5L | G | $1400 | 190 | 3,500 | 12,400 | 11,037
Livability Code: VA 30-90
Wheelbase-to-length ratio of 55% is considered ○ dangerous ○ fatiguing ◉ good ○ excellent *
The approximate net payload of 1364 pounds at 11% of GVWR on this model is ○ deficient ○ excessive ○ cautionary ◉ good ○ excellent *
Total highway safety penalties are: 2 * Value: **8 3** Durability: **7 2** Highway Control Rating: **8 1** Highway Safety: **7 9** ★★★

Minnie Winnie | 1995 | MHC | 29 | 29WQ | FO | 7.5L | G | $1800 | 190 | 3,500 | 12,400 | 11,370
Livability Code: VA 30-90
Wheelbase-to-length ratio of 55% is considered ○ dangerous ○ fatiguing ◉ good ○ excellent *
The approximate net payload of 1030 pounds at 8% of GVWR on this model is ○ deficient ○ excessive ◉ cautionary ○ good ○ excellent *
Total highway safety penalties are: 2 * Value: **8 3** Durability: **7 2** Highway Control Rating: **6 9** Highway Safety: **6 7** ★★

Minnie Winnie | 1995 | MHC | 29 | 29WU | FO | 7.5L | G | $1800 | 190 | 3,500 | 12,400 | 11,370
Livability Code: VA 30-90
Wheelbase-to-length ratio of 55% is considered ○ dangerous ○ fatiguing ◉ good ○ excellent *
The approximate net payload of 1030 pounds at 8% of GVWR on this model is ○ deficient ○ excessive ◉ cautionary ○ good ○ excellent *
Total highway safety penalties are: 2 * Value: **8 3** Durability: **7 2** Highway Control Rating: **6 9** Highway Safety: **6 7** ★★

Minnie Winnie | 1995 | MHC | 29 | 28RQ-N | FO | 7.3L | D | $1600 | 190 | 1,600 | 12,400 | 11,037
Livability Code: VA 30-90
Wheelbase-to-length ratio of 55% is considered ○ dangerous ○ fatiguing ◉ good ○ excellent *
The approximate net payload of 1364 pounds at 11% of GVWR on this model is ○ deficient ○ excessive ○ cautionary ◉ good ○ excellent *
Total highway safety penalties are: 2 * Value: **8 3** Durability: **7 2** Highway Control Rating: **8 1** Highway Safety: **7 9** ★★★

Minnie Winnie | 1995 | MHC | 29 | 29WQ-N | FO | 7.3L | D | $1900 | 190 | 1,600 | 12,400 | 11,370
Livability Code: VA 30-90
Wheelbase-to-length ratio of 55% is considered ○ dangerous ○ fatiguing ◉ good ○ excellent *
The approximate net payload of 1030 pounds at 8% of GVWR on this model is ○ deficient ○ excessive ◉ cautionary ○ good ○ excellent *
Total highway safety penalties are: 2 * Value: **8 3** Durability: **7 2** Highway Control Rating: **6 9** Highway Safety: **6 7** ★★

Minnie Winnie | 1995 | MHC | 29 | 29WU-N | FO | 7.3L | D | $1900 | 190 | 1,600 | 12,400 | 11,370
Livability Code: VA 30-90
Wheelbase-to-length ratio of 55% is considered ○ dangerous ○ fatiguing ◉ good ○ excellent *
The approximate net payload of 1030 pounds at 8% of GVWR on this model is ○ deficient ○ excessive ◉ cautionary ○ good ○ excellent *
Total highway safety penalties are: 2 * Value: **8 3** Durability: **7 2** Highway Control Rating: **6 9** Highway Safety: **6 7** ★★

Minnie Winnie | 1996 | MHC | 29 | 29WQ | FO | 7.5L | G | $1700 | 190 | 6,100 | 12,400 | 11,462
Livability Code: VA 30-90
Wheelbase-to-length ratio of 54% is considered ○ dangerous ○ fatiguing ◉ good ○ excellent *
The approximate net payload of 938 pounds at 8% of GVWR on this model is ○ deficient ○ excessive ◉ cautionary ○ good ○ excellent *
Total highway safety penalties are: 2 * Value: **8 3** Durability: **7 2** Highway Control Rating: **6 1** Highway Safety: **5 9** ★

Minnie Winnie | 1996 | MHC | 29 | 29WU | FO | 7.5L | G | $1700 | 190 | 6,100 | 12,400 | 11,462
Livability Code: VA 30-90
Wheelbase-to-length ratio of 54% is considered ○ dangerous ○ fatiguing ◉ good ○ excellent *
The approximate net payload of 938 pounds at 8% of GVWR on this model is ○ deficient ○ excessive ◉ cautionary ○ good ○ excellent *
Total highway safety penalties are: 2 * Value: **8 3** Durability: **7 2** Highway Control Rating: **6 1** Highway Safety: **5 9** ★

Minnie Winnie | 1997 | MHC | 29 | 29WQ | FO | 6.8L | G | $1900 | 190 | 5,950 | 14,050 | 11,669
Livability Code: VA 30-90
Wheelbase-to-length ratio of 54% is considered ○ dangerous ○ fatiguing ◉ good ○ excellent *
The approximate net payload of 2381 pounds at 17% of GVWR on this model is ○ deficient ○ excessive ○ cautionary ○ good ◉ excellent *
Total highway safety penalties are: 2 * Value: **8 3** Durability: **7 2** Highway Control Rating: **8 6** Highway Safety: **8 4** ★★★

Minnie Winnie | 1997 | MHC | 29 | 29WU | FO | 6.8L | G | $1900 | 190 | 5,950 | 14,050 | 11,758
Livability Code: VA 30-90
Wheelbase-to-length ratio of 54% is considered ○ dangerous ○ fatiguing ◉ good ○ excellent *
The approximate net payload of 2292 pounds at 16% of GVWR on this model is ○ deficient ○ excessive ○ cautionary ○ good ◉ excellent *
Total highway safety penalties are: 2 * Value: **8 3** Durability: **7 2** Highway Control Rating: **8 5** Highway Safety: **8 3** ★★★

Minnie Winnie | 1997 | MHC | 29 | 29WQ op eng | FO | 7.3L | D | $2100 | 190 | 5,950 | 14,050 | 12,168
Livability Code: VA 30-90
Wheelbase-to-length ratio of 54% is considered ○ dangerous ○ fatiguing ◉ good ○ excellent *
The approximate net payload of 1882 pounds at 13% of GVWR on this model is ○ deficient ○ excessive ○ cautionary ◉ good ○ excellent *
Total highway safety penalties are: 2 * Value: **8 3** Durability: **7 2** Highway Control Rating: **7 9** Highway Safety: **7 7** ★★★

Minnie Winnie | 1997 | MHC | 29 | 29WU op eng | FO | 7.3L | D | $2100 | 190 | 5,950 | 14,050 | 12,330
Livability Code: VA 30-90
Wheelbase-to-length ratio of 54% is considered ○ dangerous ○ fatiguing ◉ good ○ excellent *
The approximate net payload of 1720 pounds at 12% of GVWR on this model is ○ deficient ○ excessive ○ cautionary ◉ good ○ excellent *
Total highway safety penalties are: 2 * Value: **8 3** Durability: **7 2** Highway Control Rating: **7 7** Highway Safety: **7 5** ★★★

Note: Safety ratings are based on the assumption that the engineering of the RV has allowed for proper balance by placing fresh, gray, and black holding tanks in a location so as not to change the balance of the RV when the tanks are empty or full. **Always double-check wheelbase, GVWR, and weights at front and rear axles.**

*See Section 1 for details on how conclusions are reached.

Section 2: The Ratings

Brand	Year	Type	Length	Model	Chassis	Engine	Fuel Type	Average Price per Linear Foot When New	Adjusted Wheelbase	Approx. Towing Capacity	Gross Vehicle Weight Rating	Average Curb Weight
Minnie Winnie	1997	MHC	31	31WQ	FO	6.8L	G	$1800	205	5,950	14,050	11,847

Livability Code: VA 30-90

Wheelbase-to-length ratio of 55% is considered ○ dangerous ○ fatiguing ◉ good ○ excellent*

The approximate net payload of 2203 pounds at 16% of GVWR on this model is ○ deficient ○ excessive ○ cautionary ○ good ◉ excellent*

Total highway safety penalties are: 2*   Value: 83   Durability: 72   Highway Control Rating: 93   Highway Safety: 91   ★★★

Brand	Year	Type	Length	Model	Chassis	Engine	Fuel Type	Price/LF	Wheelbase	Towing	GVWR	Curb Wt
Minnie Winnie	1997	MHC	31	31WQ op eng	FO	7.3L	D	$2000	205	5,950	14,050	12,345

Livability Code: VA 30-90

Wheelbase-to-length ratio of 55% is considered ○ dangerous ○ fatiguing ◉ good ○ excellent*

The approximate net payload of 1705 pounds at 12% of GVWR on this model is ○ deficient ○ excessive ○ cautionary ◉ good ○ excellent*

Total highway safety penalties are: 2*   Value: 83   Durability: 72   Highway Control Rating: 85   Highway Safety: 83   ★★★

Brand	Year	Type	Length	Model	Chassis	Engine	Fuel Type	Price/LF	Wheelbase	Towing	GVWR	Curb Wt
Minnie Winnie	1998	MHC	29	29WQ	FO	6.8L	G	$1900	190	5,950	14,050	11,543

Livability Code: VA 30-90

Wheelbase-to-length ratio of 54% is considered ○ dangerous ○ fatiguing ◉ good ○ excellent*

The approximate net payload of 2507 pounds at 18% of GVWR on this model is ○ deficient ○ excessive ○ cautionary ○ good ◉ excellent*

Total highway safety penalties are: 2*   Value: 83   Durability: 72   Highway Control Rating: 87   Highway Safety: 85   ★★★

Brand	Year	Type	Length	Model	Chassis	Engine	Fuel Type	Price/LF	Wheelbase	Towing	GVWR	Curb Wt
Minnie Winnie	1998	MHC	29	29WQ op eng	FO	7.3L	D	$2100	190	5,950	14,050	12,055

Livability Code: VA 30-90

Wheelbase-to-length ratio of 54% is considered ○ dangerous ○ fatiguing ◉ good ○ excellent*

The approximate net payload of 1995 pounds at 14% of GVWR on this model is ○ deficient ○ excessive ○ cautionary ◉ good ○ excellent*

Total highway safety penalties are: 2*   Value: 83   Durability: 72   Highway Control Rating: 81   Highway Safety: 79   ★★★

Brand	Year	Type	Length	Model	Chassis	Engine	Fuel Type	Price/LF	Wheelbase	Towing	GVWR	Curb Wt
Minnie Winnie	1998	MHC	29	29WU	FO	6.8L	G	$1900	190	5,950	14,050	11,850

Livability Code: VA 30-90

Wheelbase-to-length ratio of 54% is considered ○ dangerous ○ fatiguing ◉ good ○ excellent*

The approximate net payload of 2200 pounds at 16% of GVWR on this model is ○ deficient ○ excessive ○ cautionary ○ good ◉ excellent*

Total highway safety penalties are: 2*   Value: 83   Durability: 72   Highway Control Rating: 84   Highway Safety: 82   ★★★

Brand	Year	Type	Length	Model	Chassis	Engine	Fuel Type	Price/LF	Wheelbase	Towing	GVWR	Curb Wt
Minnie Winnie	1998	MHC	29	29WU op eng	FO	7.3L	D	$2100	190	5,950	14,050	12,070

Livability Code: VA 30-90

Wheelbase-to-length ratio of 54% is considered ○ dangerous ○ fatiguing ◉ good ○ excellent*

The approximate net payload of 1980 pounds at 14% of GVWR on this model is ○ deficient ○ excessive ○ cautionary ◉ good ○ excellent*

Total highway safety penalties are: 2*   Value: 83   Durability: 72   Highway Control Rating: 81   Highway Safety: 79   ★★★

Brand	Year	Type	Length	Model	Chassis	Engine	Fuel Type	Price/LF	Wheelbase	Towing	GVWR	Curb Wt
Minnie Winnie	1998	MHC	31	31WQ	FO	6.8L	G	$1800	205	5,950	14,050	11,934

Livability Code: VA 30-90

Wheelbase-to-length ratio of 55% is considered ○ dangerous ○ fatiguing ◉ good ○ excellent*

The approximate net payload of 2116 pounds at 15% of GVWR on this model is ○ deficient ○ excessive ○ cautionary ◉ good ○ excellent*

Total highway safety penalties are: 2*   Value: 83   Durability: 72   Highway Control Rating: 91   Highway Safety: 89   ★★★

Brand	Year	Type	Length	Model	Chassis	Engine	Fuel Type	Price/LF	Wheelbase	Towing	GVWR	Curb Wt
Minnie Winnie	1998	MHC	31	31WS	FO	6.8L	G	$1900	205	5,950	14,050	12,510

Livability Code: VA 30-90

Wheelbase-to-length ratio of 55% is considered ○ dangerous ○ fatiguing ◉ good ○ excellent*

The approximate net payload of 1540 pounds at 11% of GVWR on this model is ○ deficient ○ excessive ○ cautionary ◉ good ○ excellent*

Total highway safety penalties are: 7*   Value: 80   Durability: 72   Highway Control Rating: 83   Highway Safety: 76   ★★★

Brand	Year	Type	Length	Model	Chassis	Engine	Fuel Type	Price/LF	Wheelbase	Towing	GVWR	Curb Wt
Minnie Winnie	1999	MHC	29	29U	FO	6.8L	G	$2100	190	5,950	14,050	11,742

Livability Code: VA 30-90

Wheelbase-to-length ratio of 54% is considered ○ dangerous ○ fatiguing ◉ good ○ excellent*

The approximate net payload of 2308 pounds at 16% of GVWR on this model is ○ deficient ○ excessive ○ cautionary ○ good ◉ excellent*

Total highway safety penalties are: 2*   Value: 84   Durability: 76   Highway Control Rating: 85   Highway Safety: 83   ★★★

Brand	Year	Type	Length	Model	Chassis	Engine	Fuel Type	Price/LF	Wheelbase	Towing	GVWR	Curb Wt
Minnie Winnie	1999	MHC	30	30V	FO	6.8L	G	$2000	205	5,950	14,050	12,428

Livability Code: VA 30-90

Wheelbase-to-length ratio of 57% is considered ○ dangerous ○ fatiguing ◉ good ○ excellent*

The approximate net payload of 1622 pounds at 12% of GVWR on this model is ○ deficient ○ excessive ○ cautionary ◉ good ○ excellent*

Total highway safety penalties are: 12*   Value: 80   Durability: 76   Highway Control Rating: 90   Highway Safety: 78   ★★★

Brand	Year	Type	Length	Model	Chassis	Engine	Fuel Type	Price/LF	Wheelbase	Towing	GVWR	Curb Wt
Minnie Winnie	1999	MHC	31	31A	FO	6.8L	G	$1900	205	5,950	14,050	12,047

Livability Code: VA 30-90

Wheelbase-to-length ratio of 55% is considered ○ dangerous ○ fatiguing ◉ good ○ excellent*

The approximate net payload of 2003 pounds at 14% of GVWR on this model is ○ deficient ○ excessive ○ cautionary ◉ good ○ excellent*

Total highway safety penalties are: 2*   Value: 84   Durability: 76   Highway Control Rating: 89   Highway Safety: 87   ★★★

Brand	Year	Type	Length	Model	Chassis	Engine	Fuel Type	Price/LF	Wheelbase	Towing	GVWR	Curb Wt
Minnie Winnie DL	1992	MHC	24	22 RG	FO	7.5L	G	$1700	158	2,500	11,500	9,635

Livability Code: VA 30-90

Wheelbase-to-length ratio of 56% is considered ○ dangerous ○ fatiguing ◉ good ○ excellent*

The approximate net payload of 1865 pounds at 16% of GVWR on this model is ○ deficient ○ excessive ○ cautionary ○ good ◉ excellent*

Total highway safety penalties are: 2*   Value: 83   Durability: 72   Highway Control Rating: 96   Highway Safety: 94   ★★★

Note: Safety ratings are based on the assumption that the engineering of the RV has allowed for proper balance by placing fresh, gray, and black holding tanks in a location so as not to change the balance of the RV when the tanks are empty or full. **Always double-check wheelbase, GVWR, and weights at front and rear axles.**

*See Section 1 for details on how conclusions are reached.

Brand	Year	Type	Length	Model	Chassis	Engine	Fuel Type	Average Price per Linear Foot When New	Adjusted Wheel-base	Approx. Towing Capacity	Gross Vehicle Weight Rating	Average Curb Weight

Minnie Winnie DL 1992 MHC 25 24 RC FO 7.5L G $1700 158 2,500 11,500 9,875
Livability Code: VA 30-90
Wheelbase-to-length ratio of 54% is considered ○ dangerous ○ fatiguing ◉ good ○ excellent *
The approximate net payload of 1625 pounds at 14% of GVWR on this model is ○ deficient ○ excessive ○ cautionary ◉ good ○ excellent *
Total highway safety penalties are: 2 * Value: 8 3 Durability: 7 2 Highway Control Rating: 8 0 Highway Safety: 7 8 ★★★

Minnie Winnie DL 1992 MHC 25 24 RC FO 7.5L G $1600 158 2,500 11,500 9,875
Livability Code: VA 30-90
Wheelbase-to-length ratio of 54% is considered ○ dangerous ○ fatiguing ◉ good ○ excellent *
The approximate net payload of 1625 pounds at 14% of GVWR on this model is ○ deficient ○ excessive ○ cautionary ◉ good ○ excellent *
Total highway safety penalties are: 2 * Value: 8 3 Durability: 7 2 Highway Control Rating: 8 0 Highway Safety: 7 8 ★★★

Minnie Winnie DL 1992 MHC 27 27 RQ FO 7.5L G $1700 188 4,400 11,500 10,487
Livability Code: VA 30-90
Wheelbase-to-length ratio of 57% is considered ○ dangerous ○ fatiguing ◉ good ○ excellent *
The approximate net payload of 1013 pounds at 9% of GVWR on this model is ○ deficient ○ excessive ◉ cautionary ○ good ○ excellent *
Total highway safety penalties are: 2 * Value: 8 3 Durability: 7 2 Highway Control Rating: 8 3 Highway Safety: 8 1 ★★★

Minnie Winnie DL 1992 MHC 27 27 RQ FO 7.5L G $1600 188 4,400 11,500 10,487
Livability Code: VA 30-90
Wheelbase-to-length ratio of 57% is considered ○ dangerous ○ fatiguing ◉ good ○ excellent *
The approximate net payload of 1013 pounds at 9% of GVWR on this model is ○ deficient ○ excessive ◉ cautionary ○ good ○ excellent *
Total highway safety penalties are: 2 * Value: 8 3 Durability: 7 2 Highway Control Rating: 8 3 Highway Safety: 8 1 ★★★

Minnie Winnie DL 1992 MHC 28 27 RC FO 7.5L G $1600 188 2,500 11,500 10,596
Livability Code: VA 30-90
Wheelbase-to-length ratio of 56% is considered ○ dangerous ○ fatiguing ◉ good ○ excellent *
The approximate net payload of 904 pounds at 8% of GVWR on this model is ○ deficient ○ excessive ◉ cautionary ○ good ○ excellent *
Total highway safety penalties are: 2 * Value: 8 3 Durability: 7 2 Highway Control Rating: 7 4 Highway Safety: 7 2 ★★★

Minnie Winnie DL 1992 MHC 28 27 RC FO 7.5L G $1500 188 2,500 11,500 10,596
Livability Code: VA 30-90
Wheelbase-to-length ratio of 56% is considered ○ dangerous ○ fatiguing ◉ good ○ excellent *
The approximate net payload of 904 pounds at 8% of GVWR on this model is ○ deficient ○ excessive ◉ cautionary ○ good ○ excellent *
Total highway safety penalties are: 2 * Value: 8 3 Durability: 7 2 Highway Control Rating: 7 4 Highway Safety: 7 2 ★★★

Minnie Winnie DL 1992 MHC 28 27 RT FO 7.5L G $1500 176 2,500 11,500 10,596
Livability Code: VA 30-90
Wheelbase-to-length ratio of 53% is considered ○ dangerous ◉ fatiguing ○ good ○ excellent *
The approximate net payload of 904 pounds at 8% of GVWR on this model is ○ deficient ○ excessive ◉ cautionary ○ good ○ excellent *
Total highway safety penalties are: 2 * Value: 8 3 Durability: 7 2 Highway Control Rating: 5 3 Highway Safety: 5 1 ★

Minnie Winnie DL 1993 MHC 27 27 RQ FO 7.5L G $1700 188 3,700 12,200 10,687
Livability Code: VA 30-90
Wheelbase-to-length ratio of 57% is considered ○ dangerous ○ fatiguing ◉ good ○ excellent *
The approximate net payload of 1513 pounds at 12% of GVWR on this model is ○ deficient ○ excessive ○ cautionary ◉ good ○ excellent *
Total highway safety penalties are: 2 * Value: 8 3 Durability: 7 2 Highway Control Rating: 9 3 Highway Safety: 9 1 ★★★

Minnie Winnie DL 1993 MHC 27 27 RQ op eng FO 7.3L D $1800 188 1,500 12,200 11,187
Livability Code: VA 30-90
Wheelbase-to-length ratio of 57% is considered ○ dangerous ○ fatiguing ◉ good ○ excellent *
The approximate net payload of 1013 pounds at 8% of GVWR on this model is ○ deficient ○ excessive ◉ cautionary ○ good ○ excellent *
Total highway safety penalties are: 2 * Value: 8 3 Durability: 7 2 Highway Control Rating: 7 8 Highway Safety: 7 6 ★★★

Minnie Winnie DL 1993 MHC 28 27 RC FO 7.5L G $1600 188 3,700 12,200 10,774
Livability Code: VA 30-90
Wheelbase-to-length ratio of 56% is considered ○ dangerous ○ fatiguing ◉ good ○ excellent *
The approximate net payload of 1426 pounds at 12% of GVWR on this model is ○ deficient ○ excessive ○ cautionary ◉ good ○ excellent *
Total highway safety penalties are: 2 * Value: 8 3 Durability: 7 2 Highway Control Rating: 8 9 Highway Safety: 8 7 ★★★

Minnie Winnie DL 1993 MHC 28 27 RC op eng FO 7.3L D $1600 188 1,500 12,200 11,274
Livability Code: VA 30-90
Wheelbase-to-length ratio of 56% is considered ○ dangerous ○ fatiguing ◉ good ○ excellent *
The approximate net payload of 926 pounds at 8% of GVWR on this model is ○ deficient ○ excessive ◉ cautionary ○ good ○ excellent *
Total highway safety penalties are: 2 * Value: 8 3 Durability: 7 2 Highway Control Rating: 7 4 Highway Safety: 7 2 ★★★

Minnie Winnie DL 1994 MHC 27 27 RQ-DL FO 7.5L G $1700 188 1,500 12,200 10,687
Livability Code: VA 30-90
Wheelbase-to-length ratio of 57% is considered ○ dangerous ○ fatiguing ◉ good ○ excellent *
The approximate net payload of 1513 pounds at 12% of GVWR on this model is ○ deficient ○ excessive ○ cautionary ◉ good ○ excellent *
Total highway safety penalties are: 2 * Value: 8 3 Durability: 7 2 Highway Control Rating: 9 3 Highway Safety: 9 1 ★★★

Note: Safety ratings are based on the assumption that the engineering of the RV has allowed for proper balance by placing fresh, gray, and black holding tanks in a location so as not to change the balance of the RV when the tanks are empty or full. **Always double-check wheelbase, GVWR, and weights at front and rear axles.**

*See Section 1 for details on how conclusions are reached.

Brand	Year	Type	Length	Model	Chassis	Engine	Fuel Type	Average Price per Linear Foot When New	Adjusted Wheelbase	Approx. Towing Capacity	Gross Vehicle Weight Rating	Average Curb Weight
Minnie Winnie DL	**1994**	MHC	27	27 RQ-DL op eng	FO	7.3L	D	$1800	188	1,500	12,200	11,187

Livability Code: VA 30-90
Wheelbase-to-length ratio of 56% is considered ○ dangerous ○ fatiguing ● good ○ excellent*
The approximate net payload of 1013 pounds at 8% of GVWR on this model is ○ deficient ○ excessive ● cautionary ○ good ○ excellent*
Total highway safety penalties are: 2*   Value: **83**   Durability: **72**   Highway Control Rating: **78**   Highway Safety: **76**   ★★★

| **Minnie Winnie DL** | **1994** | MHC | 28 | 27 RC DL | FO | 7.5L | G | $1700 | 188 | 1,500 | 12,200 | 10,774 |

Livability Code: VA 30-90
Wheelbase-to-length ratio of 56% is considered ○ dangerous ○ fatiguing ● good ○ excellent*
The approximate net payload of 1426 pounds at 12% of GVWR on this model is ○ deficient ○ excessive ○ cautionary ● good ○ excellent*
Total highway safety penalties are: 2*   Value: **83**   Durability: **72**   Highway Control Rating: **89**   Highway Safety: **87**   ★★★

| **Minnie Winnie DL** | **1994** | MHC | 28 | 27 RC DL op eng | FO | 7.3L | D | $1800 | 188 | 1,500 | 12,200 | 11,274 |

Livability Code: VA 30-90
Wheelbase-to-length ratio of 56% is considered ○ dangerous ○ fatiguing ● good ○ excellent*
The approximate net payload of 926 pounds at 8% of GVWR on this model is ○ deficient ○ excessive ● cautionary ○ good ○ excellent*
Total highway safety penalties are: 2*   Value: **83**   Durability: **72**   Highway Control Rating: **74**   Highway Safety: **72**   ★★★

| **Minnie Winnie DL** | **1994** | MHC | 29 | 28 RQ DL | FO | 7.5L | G | $1600 | 190 | 1,500 | 12,400 | 11,037 |

Livability Code: VA 30-90
Wheelbase-to-length ratio of 55% is considered ○ dangerous ○ fatiguing ● good ○ excellent*
The approximate net payload of 1364 pounds at 11% of GVWR on this model is ○ deficient ○ excessive ○ cautionary ● good ○ excellent*
Total highway safety penalties are: 2*   Value: **83**   Durability: **72**   Highway Control Rating: **81**   Highway Safety: **79**   ★★★

| **Minnie Winnie DL** | **1994** | MHC | 29 | 28 RQ DL op eng | FO | 7.3L | D | $1700 | 190 | 1,500 | 12,400 | 11,537 |

Livability Code: VA 30-90
Wheelbase-to-length ratio of 55% is considered ○ dangerous ○ fatiguing ● good ○ excellent*
The approximate net payload of 864 pounds at 7% of GVWR on this model is ○ deficient ○ excessive ● cautionary ○ good ○ excellent*
Total highway safety penalties are: 2*   Value: **83**   Durability: **72**   Highway Control Rating: **62**   Highway Safety: **60**   ★★

| **Monitor** | **1990** | MHC | 27 | 26RB | FO | 7.5L | G | $1600 | 158 | 1,500 | 11,000 | 10,351 |

Livability Code: SB 30-90
Wheelbase-to-length ratio of 49% is considered ● dangerous ○ fatiguing ○ good ○ excellent*
The approximate net payload of 649 pounds at 6% of GVWR on this model is ● deficient ○ excessive ○ cautionary ○ good ○ excellent*
Total highway safety penalties are: 2*   Value: **81**   Durability: **80**   Highway Control Rating: **20**   Highway Safety: **18**

| **Monitor** | **1991** | MHA | 34 | 33 CSXS | CH | 7.4L | G | $1800 | 202 T | 1,500 | 17,200 | 14,122 |

Livability Code: SB 30-90
Wheelbase-to-length ratio of 50% is considered ● dangerous ○ fatiguing ○ good ○ excellent*
The approximate net payload of 3078 pounds at 18% of GVWR on this model is ○ deficient ○ excessive ○ cautionary ● excellent*
Total highway safety penalties are: 9*   Value: **78**   Durability: **80**   Highway Control Rating: **45**   Highway Safety: **36**

| **Mountain Aire** | **1994** | MHA | 30 | 29WCB | CH | 7.4L | G | $2600 | 178 | 4,000 | 16,000 | 13,694 |

Livability Code: FT 30-90
Wheelbase-to-length ratio of 49% is considered ● dangerous ○ fatiguing ○ good ○ excellent*
The approximate net payload of 2307 pounds at 14% of GVWR on this model is ○ deficient ○ excessive ○ cautionary ● good ○ excellent*
Total highway safety penalties are: 5*   Value: **79**   Durability: **78**   Highway Control Rating: **39**   Highway Safety: **34**

| **Mountain Aire** | **1994** | MHA | 30 | 29WCB | FO | 7.5L | G | $2600 | 178 | 8,000 | 17,000 | 14,129 |

Livability Code: FT 30-90
Wheelbase-to-length ratio of 49% is considered ● dangerous ○ fatiguing ○ good ○ excellent*
The approximate net payload of 2872 pounds at 17% of GVWR on this model is ○ deficient ○ excessive ○ cautionary ○ good ● excellent*
Total highway safety penalties are: 2*   Value: **80**   Durability: **78**   Highway Control Rating: **44**   Highway Safety: **42**

| **Mountain Aire** | **1994** | MHA | 33 | 32CBD-sl | FO | 7.5L | G | $2800 | 200 | 8,000 | 17,000 | 15,811 |

Livability Code: FT 30-90
Wheelbase-to-length ratio of 51% is considered ○ dangerous ● fatiguing ○ good ○ excellent*
The approximate net payload of 1189 pounds at 7% of GVWR on this model is ○ deficient ○ excessive ● cautionary ○ good ○ excellent*
Total highway safety penalties are: 5*   Value: **79**   Durability: **78**   Highway Control Rating: **19**   Highway Safety: **14**

| **Mountain Aire** | **1994** | MHA | 35 | 34CBD-sl | CH | 7.4L | G | $2900 | 202 T | 1,500 | 18,500 | 16,735 |

Livability Code: FT 30-90
Wheelbase-to-length ratio of 49% is considered ● dangerous ○ fatiguing ○ good ○ excellent*
The approximate net payload of 1765 pounds at 10% of GVWR on this model is ○ deficient ○ excessive ○ cautionary ● good ○ excellent*
Total highway safety penalties are: 12*   Value: **75**   Durability: **78**   Highway Control Rating: **27**   Highway Safety: **15**

| **Mountain Aire** | **1994** | MHA | 35 | 34CBDS-sl | CH | 7.4L | G | $2900 | 202 T | 1,500 | 18,500 | 16,750 |

Livability Code: FT 30-90
Wheelbase-to-length ratio of 49% is considered ● dangerous ○ fatiguing ○ good ○ excellent*
The approximate net payload of 1750 pounds at 9% of GVWR on this model is ○ deficient ○ excessive ● cautionary ○ good ○ excellent*
Total highway safety penalties are: 12*   Value: **75**   Durability: **78**   Highway Control Rating: **23**   Highway Safety: **11**

Note: Safety ratings are based on the assumption that the engineering of the RV has allowed for proper balance by placing fresh, gray, and black holding tanks in a location so as not to change the balance of the RV when the tanks are empty or full. **Always double-check wheelbase, GVWR, and weights at front and rear axles.**

The RV Rating Book

*See Section 1 for details on how conclusions are reached.

Section 2: The Ratings

Brand	Year	Type	Length	Model	Chassis	Engine	Fuel Type	Average Price per Linear Foot When New	Adjusted Wheelbase	Approx. Towing Capacity	Gross Vehicle Weight Rating	Average Curb Weight
Mountain Aire	1994	MHA	35	34WCB	CH	7.4L	G	$2700	202 T	1,500	18,500	15,785

Livability Code: FT 30-90

Wheelbase-to-length ratio of 49% is considered ◉ dangerous ○ fatiguing ○ good ○ excellent *

The approximate net payload of 2715 pounds at 15% of GVWR on this model is ○ deficient ○ excessive ○ cautionary ◉ good ○ excellent *

Total highway safety penalties are: 9 *   Value: 7 7   Durability: 7 8   Highway Control Rating: 3 7   Highway Safety: 2 8

Brand	Year	Type	Length	Model	Chassis	Engine	Fuel Type	Price/Ft	Wheelbase	Towing	GVWR	Curb Wt
Mountain Aire	1994	MHA	35	34WCBS-sl	CH	7.4L	G	$2900	202 T	1,500	18,500	16,750

Livability Code: FT 30-90

Wheelbase-to-length ratio of 49% is considered ◉ dangerous ○ fatiguing ○ good ○ excellent *

The approximate net payload of 1750 pounds at 9% of GVWR on this model is ○ deficient ○ excessive ◉ cautionary ○ good ○ excellent *

Total highway safety penalties are: 12 *   Value: 7 5   Durability: 7 8   Highway Control Rating: 2 3   Highway Safety: 1 1

Mountain Aire	1994	MHA	35	34CBD-sl	FO	7.5L	G	$2900	202 T	5,500	19,500	17,173

Livability Code: FT 30-90

Wheelbase-to-length ratio of 49% is considered ◉ dangerous ○ fatiguing ○ good ○ excellent *

The approximate net payload of 2327 pounds at 12% of GVWR on this model is ○ deficient ○ excessive ○ cautionary ◉ good ○ excellent *

Total highway safety penalties are: 7 *   Value: 7 8   Durability: 7 8   Highway Control Rating: 3 1   Highway Safety: 2 4

Mountain Aire	1994	MHA	35	34CBDS-sl	FO	7.5L	G	$2900	202 T	5,500	19,500	17,185

Livability Code: FT 30-90

Wheelbase-to-length ratio of 49% is considered ◉ dangerous ○ fatiguing ○ good ○ excellent *

The approximate net payload of 2315 pounds at 12% of GVWR on this model is ○ deficient ○ excessive ○ cautionary ◉ good ○ excellent *

Total highway safety penalties are: 7 *   Value: 7 8   Durability: 7 8   Highway Control Rating: 3 1   Highway Safety: 2 4

Mountain Aire	1994	MHA	35	34WCB	FO	7.5L	G	$2700	202 T	5,500	19,500	16,223

Livability Code: FT 30-90

Wheelbase-to-length ratio of 49% is considered ◉ dangerous ○ fatiguing ○ good ○ excellent *

The approximate net payload of 3277 pounds at 17% of GVWR on this model is ○ deficient ○ excessive ○ cautionary ○ good ◉ excellent *

Total highway safety penalties are: 4 *   Value: 7 9   Durability: 7 8   Highway Control Rating: 4 0   Highway Safety: 3 6

Mountain Aire	1994	MHA	35	34WCBS-sl	FO	7.5L	G	$2900	202 T	5,500	19,500	17,173

Livability Code: FT 30-90

Wheelbase-to-length ratio of 49% is considered ◉ dangerous ○ fatiguing ○ good ○ excellent *

The approximate net payload of 2327 pounds at 12% of GVWR on this model is ○ deficient ○ excessive ○ cautionary ◉ good ○ excellent *

Total highway safety penalties are: 7 *   Value: 7 8   Durability: 7 8   Highway Control Rating: 3 1   Highway Safety: 2 4

Mountain Aire	1994	MHA	38	37CBSA-sl	FO	7.5L	G	$2700	224 T	5,500	19,500	17,916

Livability Code: FT 30-90

Wheelbase-to-length ratio of 49% is considered ◉ dangerous ○ fatiguing ○ good ○ excellent *

The approximate net payload of 1584 pounds at 8% of GVWR on this model is ○ deficient ○ excessive ◉ cautionary ○ good ○ excellent *

Total highway safety penalties are: 7 *   Value: 7 8   Durability: 7 8   Highway Control Rating: 1 9   Highway Safety: 1 2

Mountain Aire	1994	MHA	38	37WDSK-sl	FO	7.5L	G	$2700	224 T	5,500	19,500	18,059

Livability Code: FT 30-90

Wheelbase-to-length ratio of 49% is considered ◉ dangerous ○ fatiguing ○ good ○ excellent *

The approximate net payload of 1441 pounds at 7% of GVWR on this model is ○ deficient ○ excessive ◉ cautionary ○ good ○ excellent *

Total highway safety penalties are: 7 *   Value: 7 8   Durability: 7 8   Highway Control Rating: 1 3   Highway Safety: 6

Mountain Aire	1995	MHA	33	MA 3200	FO	7.5L	G	$2400	200	8,000	17,000	15,348

Livability Code: FT 30-90

Wheelbase-to-length ratio of 51% is considered ○ dangerous ◉ fatiguing ○ good ○ excellent *

The approximate net payload of 1652 pounds at 10% of GVWR on this model is ○ deficient ○ excessive ○ cautionary ◉ good ○ excellent *

Total highway safety penalties are: 2 *   Value: 8 0   Durability: 7 8   Highway Control Rating: 3 6   Highway Safety: 3 4

Mountain Aire	1995	MHA	35	MA 3410	FO	7.5L	G	$2500	202 T	5,500	19,500	16,813

Livability Code: FT 30-90

Wheelbase-to-length ratio of 49% is considered ◉ dangerous ○ fatiguing ○ good ○ excellent *

The approximate net payload of 2687 pounds at 14% of GVWR on this model is ○ deficient ○ excessive ○ cautionary ◉ good ○ excellent *

Total highway safety penalties are: 4 *   Value: 7 9   Durability: 7 8   Highway Control Rating: 3 5   Highway Safety: 3 1

Mountain Aire	1995	MHA	35	MA 3450-sl	FO	7.5L	G	$2700	202 T	5,000	20,000	17,713

Livability Code: FT 30-90

Wheelbase-to-length ratio of 49% is considered ◉ dangerous ○ fatiguing ○ good ○ excellent *

The approximate net payload of 2287 pounds at 11% of GVWR on this model is ○ deficient ○ excessive ○ cautionary ◉ good ○ excellent *

Total highway safety penalties are: 7 *   Value: 7 8   Durability: 7 8   Highway Control Rating: 3 0   Highway Safety: 2 3

Mountain Aire	1995	MHA	35	MA 3451-sl	FO	7.5L	G	$2800	202 T	5,000	20,000	17,713

Livability Code: FT 30-90

Wheelbase-to-length ratio of 49% is considered ◉ dangerous ○ fatiguing ○ good ○ excellent *

The approximate net payload of 2287 pounds at 11% of GVWR on this model is ○ deficient ○ excessive ○ cautionary ◉ good ○ excellent *

Total highway safety penalties are: 7 *   Value: 7 8   Durability: 7 8   Highway Control Rating: 3 0   Highway Safety: 2 3

Note: Safety ratings are based on the assumption that the engineering of the RV has allowed for proper balance by placing fresh, gray, and black holding tanks in a location so as not to change the balance of the RV when the tanks are empty or full. **Always double-check wheelbase, GVWR, and weights at front and rear axles.**

*See Section 1 for details on how conclusions are reached.

Brand	Year	Type	Length	Model	Chassis	Engine	Fuel Type	Average Price per Linear Foot When New	Adjusted Wheelbase	Approx. Towing Capacity	Gross Vehicle Weight Rating	Average Curb Weight
Mountain Aire	1995	MHA	35	MA 3455-sl	FO	7.5L	G	$2700	202 T	5,000	20,000	17,713

Livability Code: FT 30-90
Wheelbase-to-length ratio of 49% is considered ● dangerous ○ fatiguing ○ good ○ excellent *
The approximate net payload of 2287 pounds at 11% of GVWR on this model is ○ deficient ○ excessive ○ cautionary ● good ○ excellent *
Total highway safety penalties are: 7 * Value: 7 8 Durability: 7 8 Highway Control Rating: 3 0 Highway Safety: 2 3

Brand	Year	Type	Length	Model	Chassis	Engine	Fuel Type	Avg Price/LF	Adj Wheelbase	Towing	GVWR	Curb Weight
Mountain Aire	1995	MHA	35	MP3450-sl	SP	CU250	D	$4700	212	5,000	26,000	21,941

Livability Code: FT 30-90
Wheelbase-to-length ratio of 51% is considered ○ dangerous ● fatiguing ○ good ○ excellent *
The approximate net payload of 4059 pounds at 16% of GVWR on this model is ○ deficient ○ excessive ○ cautionary ○ good ● excellent *
Total highway safety penalties are: 5 * Value: 7 9 Durability: 7 8 Highway Control Rating: 4 7 Highway Safety: 4 2

Mountain Aire	1995	MHA	35	MP3455-sl	SP	CU250	D	$4800	252	5,000	26,000	21,941

Livability Code: FT 30-90
Wheelbase-to-length ratio of 60% is considered ○ dangerous ○ fatiguing ○ good ● excellent *
The approximate net payload of 4059 pounds at 16% of GVWR on this model is ○ deficient ○ excessive ○ cautionary ○ good ● excellent *
Total highway safety penalties are: 5 * Value: 7 9 Durability: 7 8 Highway Control Rating: 1 0 0 Highway Safety: 9 5 ★★★

Mountain Aire	1995	MHA	38	MA 3710	FO	7.5L	G	$2600	224 T	5,500	19,500	17,746

Livability Code: FT 30-90
Wheelbase-to-length ratio of 49% is considered ● dangerous ○ fatiguing ○ good ○ excellent *
The approximate net payload of 1754 pounds at 9% of GVWR on this model is ○ deficient ○ excessive ● cautionary ○ good ○ excellent *
Total highway safety penalties are: 4 * Value: 7 9 Durability: 7 8 Highway Control Rating: 2 5 Highway Safety: 2 1

Mountain Aire	1995	MHA	38	MA 3755-sl	FO	7.5L	G	$2600	224 T	5,000	20,000	18,646

Livability Code: FT 30-90
Wheelbase-to-length ratio of 49% is considered ● dangerous ○ fatiguing ○ good ○ excellent *
The approximate net payload of 1354 pounds at 7% of GVWR on this model is ○ deficient ○ excessive ● cautionary ○ good ○ excellent *
Total highway safety penalties are: 7 * Value: 7 8 Durability: 7 8 Highway Control Rating: 1 2 Highway Safety: 5

Mountain Aire	1995	MHA	38	MA 3756-sl	FO	7.5L	G	$2600	224 T	5,000	20,000	18,646

Livability Code: FT 30-90
Wheelbase-to-length ratio of 49% is considered ● dangerous ○ fatiguing ○ good ○ excellent *
The approximate net payload of 1354 pounds at 7% of GVWR on this model is ○ deficient ○ excessive ● cautionary ○ good ○ excellent *
Total highway safety penalties are: 7 * Value: 7 8 Durability: 7 8 Highway Control Rating: 1 2 Highway Safety: 5

Mountain Aire	1995	MHA	38	MA 3760-sl	FO	7.5L	G	$2600	224 T	5,000	20,000	18,646

Livability Code: FT 30-90
Wheelbase-to-length ratio of 49% is considered ● dangerous ○ fatiguing ○ good ○ excellent *
The approximate net payload of 1354 pounds at 7% of GVWR on this model is ○ deficient ○ excessive ● cautionary ○ good ○ excellent *
Total highway safety penalties are: 7 * Value: 7 8 Durability: 7 8 Highway Control Rating: 1 2 Highway Safety: 5

Mountain Aire	1995	MHA	38	MP3855-sl	SP	CU250	D	$4400	252	5,000	26,000	22,846

Livability Code: FT 30-90
Wheelbase-to-length ratio of 55% is considered ○ dangerous ○ fatiguing ● good ○ excellent *
The approximate net payload of 3154 pounds at 12% of GVWR on this model is ○ deficient ○ excessive ○ cautionary ● good ○ excellent *
Total highway safety penalties are: 5 * Value: 7 9 Durability: 7 8 Highway Control Rating: 8 6 Highway Safety: 8 1 ★★★

Mountain Aire	1995	MHA	38	MP3856-sl	SP	CU250	D	$4400	252	5,000	26,000	22,846

Livability Code: FT 30-90
Wheelbase-to-length ratio of 55% is considered ○ dangerous ○ fatiguing ● good ○ excellent *
The approximate net payload of 3154 pounds at 12% of GVWR on this model is ○ deficient ○ excessive ○ cautionary ● good ○ excellent *
Total highway safety penalties are: 5 * Value: 7 9 Durability: 7 8 Highway Control Rating: 8 6 Highway Safety: 8 1 ★★★

Mountain Aire	1995	MHA	38	MP3860-sl	SP	CU250	D	$4400	252	5,000	26,000	22,846

Livability Code: FT 30-90
Wheelbase-to-length ratio of 55% is considered ○ dangerous ○ fatiguing ● good ○ excellent *
The approximate net payload of 3154 pounds at 12% of GVWR on this model is ○ deficient ○ excessive ○ cautionary ● good ○ excellent *
Total highway safety penalties are: 5 * Value: 7 9 Durability: 7 8 Highway Control Rating: 8 6 Highway Safety: 8 1 ★★★

Mountain Aire	1995	MHA	38	MP4010	SP	CU250	D	$4400	276	1,600	29,400	22,546

Livability Code: FT 30-90
Wheelbase-to-length ratio of 61% is considered ○ dangerous ○ fatiguing ○ good ● excellent *
The approximate net payload of 6854 pounds at 23% of GVWR on this model is ○ deficient ○ excessive ○ cautionary ○ good ● excellent *
Total highway safety penalties are: 2 * Value: 8 0 Durability: 7 8 Highway Control Rating: 1 0 0 Highway Safety: 9 8 ★★★

Mountain Aire	1995	MHA	40	MP4056-sl	SP	CU250	D	$4300	276	1,600	29,400	24,162

Livability Code: FT 30-90
Wheelbase-to-length ratio of 58% is considered ○ dangerous ○ fatiguing ○ good ● excellent *
The approximate net payload of 5238 pounds at 18% of GVWR on this model is ○ deficient ○ excessive ○ cautionary ○ good ● excellent *
Total highway safety penalties are: 6 * Value: 7 8 Durability: 7 8 Highway Control Rating: 1 0 0 Highway Safety: 9 4 ★★★

Note: Safety ratings are based on the assumption that the engineering of the RV has allowed for proper balance by placing fresh, gray, and black holding tanks in a location so as not to change the balance of the RV when the tanks are empty or full. **Always double-check wheelbase, GVWR, and weights at front and rear axles.**

Brand	Year	Type	Length	Model	Chassis	Engine	Fuel Type	Average Price per Linear Foot When New	Adjusted Wheelbase	Approx. Towing Capacity	Gross Vehicle Weight Rating	Average Curb Weight
Mountain Aire	1996	MHA	33	MA 3255-sl	FO	7.5L	G	$2900	200	8,000	17,000	16,191

Livability Code: FT 30-90
Wheelbase-to-length ratio of 51% is considered ○ dangerous ◉ fatiguing ○ good ○ excellent *
The approximate net payload of 809 pounds at 5% of GVWR on this model is ◉ deficient ○ excessive ○ cautionary ○ good ○ excellent *
Total highway safety penalties are: 5 *   Value: 7 9   Durability: 7 8   Highway Control Rating: 1 3   Highway Safety: 8

Brand	Year	Type	Length	Model	Chassis	Engine	Fuel Type	Price/Linear Foot	Adj. Wheelbase	Towing Cap.	GVWR	Avg. Curb Wt.
Mountain Aire	1996	MHA	33	MA 3255-sl	CH	7.4L	G	$2900	200	3,500	16,500	15,832

Livability Code: FT 30-90
Wheelbase-to-length ratio of 51% is considered ○ dangerous ◉ fatiguing ○ good ○ excellent *
The approximate net payload of 668 pounds at 4% of GVWR on this model is ◉ deficient ○ excessive ○ cautionary ○ good ○ excellent *
Total highway safety penalties are: 9 *   Value: 7 7   Durability: 7 8   Highway Control Rating: 1 0   Highway Safety: 1

Mountain Aire	1996	MHA	35	MA 3410	FO	7.5L	G	$2800	202 T	5,000	20,000	16,785

Livability Code: FT 30-90
Wheelbase-to-length ratio of 49% is considered ◉ dangerous ○ fatiguing ○ good ○ excellent *
The approximate net payload of 3215 pounds at 16% of GVWR on this model is ○ deficient ○ excessive ○ cautionary ○ good ◉ excellent *
Total highway safety penalties are: 4 *   Value: 7 9   Durability: 7 8   Highway Control Rating: 4 0   Highway Safety: 3 6

Mountain Aire	1996	MHA	35	MA 3450-sl	FO	7.5L	G	$2800	202 T	5,000	20,000	17,685

Livability Code: FT 30-90
Wheelbase-to-length ratio of 49% is considered ◉ dangerous ○ fatiguing ○ good ○ excellent *
The approximate net payload of 2315 pounds at 12% of GVWR on this model is ○ deficient ○ excessive ○ cautionary ◉ good ○ excellent *
Total highway safety penalties are: 7 *   Value: 7 8   Durability: 7 8   Highway Control Rating: 3 1   Highway Safety: 2 4

Mountain Aire	1996	MHA	35	MA 3451-sl	FO	7.5L	G	$2800	202 T	5,000	20,000	17,685

Livability Code: FT 30-90
Wheelbase-to-length ratio of 49% is considered ◉ dangerous ○ fatiguing ○ good ○ excellent *
The approximate net payload of 2315 pounds at 12% of GVWR on this model is ○ deficient ○ excessive ○ cautionary ◉ good ○ excellent *
Total highway safety penalties are: 7 *   Value: 7 8   Durability: 7 8   Highway Control Rating: 3 1   Highway Safety: 2 4

Mountain Aire	1996	MHA	35	MA 3455-sl	FO	7.5L	G	$2700	202 T	5,000	20,000	17,685

Livability Code: FT 30-90
Wheelbase-to-length ratio of 49% is considered ◉ dangerous ○ fatiguing ○ good ○ excellent *
The approximate net payload of 2315 pounds at 12% of GVWR on this model is ○ deficient ○ excessive ○ cautionary ◉ good ○ excellent *
Total highway safety penalties are: 7 *   Value: 7 8   Durability: 7 8   Highway Control Rating: 3 1   Highway Safety: 2 4

Mountain Aire	1996	MHA	35	MA 3458-sl	FO	7.5L	G	$2800	202 T	5,000	20,000	17,685

Livability Code: FT 30-90
Wheelbase-to-length ratio of 49% is considered ◉ dangerous ○ fatiguing ○ good ○ excellent *
The approximate net payload of 2315 pounds at 12% of GVWR on this model is ○ deficient ○ excessive ○ cautionary ◉ good ○ excellent *
Total highway safety penalties are: 7 *   Value: 7 8   Durability: 7 8   Highway Control Rating: 3 1   Highway Safety: 2 4

Mountain Aire	1996	MHA	35	MA 3410	CH	7.4L	G	$2800	202 T	1,500	18,500	16,398

Livability Code: FT 30-90
Wheelbase-to-length ratio of 48% is considered ◉ dangerous ○ fatiguing ○ good ○ excellent *
The approximate net payload of 2102 pounds at 11% of GVWR on this model is ○ deficient ○ excessive ○ cautionary ◉ good ○ excellent *
Total highway safety penalties are: 9 *   Value: 7 7   Durability: 7 8   Highway Control Rating: 2 8   Highway Safety: 1 9

Mountain Aire	1996	MHA	35	MA 3450-sl	CH	7.4L	G	$2800	202 T	1,500	18,500	17,298

Livability Code: FT 30-90
Wheelbase-to-length ratio of 48% is considered ◉ dangerous ○ fatiguing ○ good ○ excellent *
The approximate net payload of 1202 pounds at 6% of GVWR on this model is ◉ deficient ○ excessive ○ cautionary ○ good ○ excellent *
Total highway safety penalties are: 12 *   Value: 7 5   Durability: 7 8   Highway Control Rating: 3   Highway Safety: - 9

Mountain Aire	1996	MHA	35	MA 3451-sl	CH	7.4L	G	$2800	202 T	1,500	18,500	17,298

Livability Code: FT 30-90
Wheelbase-to-length ratio of 48% is considered ◉ dangerous ○ fatiguing ○ good ○ excellent *
The approximate net payload of 1202 pounds at 6% of GVWR on this model is ◉ deficient ○ excessive ○ cautionary ○ good ○ excellent *
Total highway safety penalties are: 12 *   Value: 7 5   Durability: 7 8   Highway Control Rating: 3   Highway Safety: - 9

Mountain Aire	1996	MHA	35	MA 3455-sl	CH	7.4L	G	$2800	202 T	1,500	18,500	17,298

Livability Code: FT 30-90
Wheelbase-to-length ratio of 48% is considered ◉ dangerous ○ fatiguing ○ good ○ excellent *
The approximate net payload of 1202 pounds at 6% of GVWR on this model is ◉ deficient ○ excessive ○ cautionary ○ good ○ excellent *
Total highway safety penalties are: 12 *   Value: 7 5   Durability: 7 8   Highway Control Rating: 3   Highway Safety: - 9

Mountain Aire	1996	MHA	35	MA 3458-sl	CH	7.4L	G	$2800	202 T	1,500	18,500	17,298

Livability Code: FT 30-90
Wheelbase-to-length ratio of 48% is considered ◉ dangerous ○ fatiguing ○ good ○ excellent *
The approximate net payload of 1202 pounds at 6% of GVWR on this model is ◉ deficient ○ excessive ○ cautionary ○ good ○ excellent *
Total highway safety penalties are: 12 *   Value: 7 5   Durability: 7 8   Highway Control Rating: 3   Highway Safety: - 9

Note: Safety ratings are based on the assumption that the engineering of the RV has allowed for proper balance by placing fresh, gray, and black holding tanks in a location so as not to change the balance of the RV when the tanks are empty or full. **Always double-check wheelbase, GVWR, and weights at front and rear axles.**

*See Section 1 for details on how conclusions are reached.

Brand	Year	Type	Length	Model	Chassis	Engine	Fuel Type	Average Price per Linear Foot When New	Adjusted Wheelbase	Approx. Towing Capacity	Gross Vehicle Weight Rating	Average Curb Weight
Mountain Aire	1996	MHA	38	MA 3755-sl	FO	7.5L	G	$2600	224 T	5,000	20,000	18,562

Livability Code: FT 30-90
Wheelbase-to-length ratio of 50% is considered ◉ dangerous ○ fatiguing ○ good ○ excellent *
The approximate net payload of 1438 pounds at 7% of GVWR on this model is ○ deficient ○ excessive ◉ cautionary ○ good ○ excellent *
Total highway safety penalties are: 7 *   Value: **7 8**   Durability: **7 8**   Highway Control Rating: **1 4**   Highway Safety: **7**

Brand	Year	Type	Length	Model	Chassis	Engine	Fuel Type	Avg Price/Linear Ft	Adj Wheelbase	Towing Cap	GVWR	Avg Curb Wt
Mountain Aire	1996	MHA	38	MA 3756-sl	FO	7.5L	G	$2600	224 T	5,000	20,000	18,562

Livability Code: FT 30-90
Wheelbase-to-length ratio of 50% is considered ◉ dangerous ○ fatiguing ○ good ○ excellent *
The approximate net payload of 1438 pounds at 7% of GVWR on this model is ○ deficient ○ excessive ◉ cautionary ○ good ○ excellent *
Total highway safety penalties are: 7 *   Value: **7 8**   Durability: **7 8**   Highway Control Rating: **1 4**   Highway Safety: **7**

Mountain Aire	1996	MHA	38	MA 3757-sl	FO	7.5L	G	$2600	224 T	5,000	20,000	18,562

Livability Code: FT 30-90
Wheelbase-to-length ratio of 50% is considered ◉ dangerous ○ fatiguing ○ good ○ excellent *
The approximate net payload of 1438 pounds at 7% of GVWR on this model is ○ deficient ○ excessive ◉ cautionary ○ good ○ excellent *
Total highway safety penalties are: 7 *   Value: **7 8**   Durability: **7 8**   Highway Control Rating: **1 4**   Highway Safety: **7**

Mountain Aire	1996	MHA	38	MA 3760-sl	FO	7.5L	G	$2600	224 T	5,000	20,000	18,562

Livability Code: FT 30-90
Wheelbase-to-length ratio of 50% is considered ◉ dangerous ○ fatiguing ○ good ○ excellent *
The approximate net payload of 1438 pounds at 7% of GVWR on this model is ○ deficient ○ excessive ◉ cautionary ○ good ○ excellent *
Total highway safety penalties are: 7 *   Value: **7 8**   Durability: **7 8**   Highway Control Rating: **1 4**   Highway Safety: **7**

Mountain Aire	1996	MHA	38	MP 3730	SP	CU250	D	$4300	240	16,000	26,000	21,946

Livability Code: FT 30-90
Wheelbase-to-length ratio of 53% is considered ○ dangerous ◉ fatiguing ○ good ○ excellent *
The approximate net payload of 4054 pounds at 16% of GVWR on this model is ○ deficient ○ excessive ○ cautionary ○ good ◉ excellent *
Total highway safety penalties are: 2 *   Value: **8 0**   Durability: **7 8**   Highway Control Rating: **6 9**   Highway Safety: **6 7**   ★★

Mountain Aire	1996	MHA	38	MP 3855-sl	SP	CU250	D	$4400	252	16,000	26,000	22,846

Livability Code: FT 30-90
Wheelbase-to-length ratio of 55% is considered ○ dangerous ○ fatiguing ◉ good ○ excellent *
The approximate net payload of 3154 pounds at 12% of GVWR on this model is ○ deficient ○ excessive ○ cautionary ◉ good ○ excellent *
Total highway safety penalties are: 5 *   Value: **7 9**   Durability: **7 8**   Highway Control Rating: **8 6**   Highway Safety: **8 1**   ★★★

Mountain Aire	1996	MHA	38	MP 3856-sl	SP	CU250	D	$4400	252	16,000	26,000	22,846

Livability Code: FT 30-90
Wheelbase-to-length ratio of 55% is considered ○ dangerous ○ fatiguing ◉ good ○ excellent *
The approximate net payload of 3154 pounds at 12% of GVWR on this model is ○ deficient ○ excessive ○ cautionary ◉ good ○ excellent *
Total highway safety penalties are: 5 *   Value: **7 9**   Durability: **7 8**   Highway Control Rating: **8 6**   Highway Safety: **8 1**   ★★★

Mountain Aire	1996	MHA	38	MP 3857-sl	SP	CU250	D	$4400	252	16,000	26,000	22,846

Livability Code: FT 30-90
Wheelbase-to-length ratio of 55% is considered ○ dangerous ○ fatiguing ◉ good ○ excellent *
The approximate net payload of 3154 pounds at 12% of GVWR on this model is ○ deficient ○ excessive ○ cautionary ◉ good ○ excellent *
Total highway safety penalties are: 5 *   Value: **7 9**   Durability: **7 8**   Highway Control Rating: **8 6**   Highway Safety: **8 1**   ★★★

Mountain Aire	1996	MHA	38	MP 3860-sl	SP	CU250	D	$4400	252	16,000	26,000	22,846

Livability Code: FT 30-90
Wheelbase-to-length ratio of 55% is considered ○ dangerous ○ fatiguing ◉ good ○ excellent *
The approximate net payload of 3154 pounds at 12% of GVWR on this model is ○ deficient ○ excessive ○ cautionary ◉ good ○ excellent *
Total highway safety penalties are: 5 *   Value: **7 9**   Durability: **7 8**   Highway Control Rating: **8 6**   Highway Safety: **8 1**   ★★★

Mountain Aire	1996	MHA	40	MP 4055-sl	SP	CU250	D	$4300	276	12,600	29,400	24,162

Livability Code: FT 30-90
Wheelbase-to-length ratio of 58% is considered ○ dangerous ○ fatiguing ○ good ◉ excellent *
The approximate net payload of 5238 pounds at 18% of GVWR on this model is ○ deficient ○ excessive ○ cautionary ○ good ◉ excellent *
Total highway safety penalties are: 6 *   Value: **7 8**   Durability: **7 8**   Highway Control Rating: **1 0 0**   Highway Safety: **9 4**   ★★★

Mountain Aire	1996	MHA	40	MP 4056-sl	SP	CU250	D	$4300	276	12,600	29,400	24,162

Livability Code: FT 30-90
Wheelbase-to-length ratio of 58% is considered ○ dangerous ○ fatiguing ○ good ◉ excellent *
The approximate net payload of 5238 pounds at 18% of GVWR on this model is ○ deficient ○ excessive ○ cautionary ○ good ◉ excellent *
Total highway safety penalties are: 6 *   Value: **7 8**   Durability: **7 8**   Highway Control Rating: **1 0 0**   Highway Safety: **9 4**   ★★★

Mountain Aire	1996	MHA	40	MP 4057-sl	SP	CU250	D	$4300	276	12,600	29,400	24,012

Livability Code: FT 30-90
Wheelbase-to-length ratio of 58% is considered ○ dangerous ○ fatiguing ○ good ◉ excellent *
The approximate net payload of 5388 pounds at 18% of GVWR on this model is ○ deficient ○ excessive ○ cautionary ○ good ◉ excellent *
Total highway safety penalties are: 5 *   Value: **7 9**   Durability: **7 8**   Highway Control Rating: **1 0 0**   Highway Safety: **9 5**   ★★★

Note: Safety ratings are based on the assumption that the engineering of the RV has allowed for proper balance by placing fresh, gray, and black holding tanks in a location so as not to change the balance of the RV when the tanks are empty or full. **Always double-check wheelbase, GVWR, and weights at front and rear axles.**

*See Section 1 for details on how conclusions are reached.

Brand	Year	Type	Length	Model	Chassis	Engine	Fuel Type	Average Price per Linear Foot When New	Adjusted Wheelbase	Approx. Towing Capacity	Gross Vehicle Weight Rating	Average Curb Weight
Mountain Aire	1996	MHA	40	MP 4059-sl	SP	CU250	D	$4300	276	12,600	29,400	24,012

Livability Code: FT 30-90

Wheelbase-to-length ratio of 58% is considered ○ dangerous ○ fatiguing ○ good ◉ excellent *

The approximate net payload of 5388 pounds at 18% of GVWR on this model is ○ deficient ○ excessive ○ cautionary ○ good ◉ excellent *

Total highway safety penalties are: 5 *   Value: 7 9   Durability: 7 8   Highway Control Rating: 1 0 0   Highway Safety: 9 5   ★★★

Brand	Year	Type	Length	Model	Chassis	Engine	Fuel Type	Price/Ft	Wheelbase	Towing	GVWR	Curb Weight
Mountain Aire	1996	MHA	40	MP 4060-sl	SP	CU250	D	$4300	276	12,600	29,400	24,162

Livability Code: FT 30-90

Wheelbase-to-length ratio of 58% is considered ○ dangerous ○ fatiguing ○ good ◉ excellent *

The approximate net payload of 5238 pounds at 18% of GVWR on this model is ○ deficient ○ excessive ○ cautionary ○ good ◉ excellent *

Total highway safety penalties are: 6 *   Value: 7 8   Durability: 7 8   Highway Control Rating: 1 0 0   Highway Safety: 9 4   ★★★

Brand	Year	Type	Length	Model	Chassis	Engine	Fuel Type	Price/Ft	Wheelbase	Towing	GVWR	Curb Weight
Mountain Aire	1996	MHA	40	MP 4062-sl	SP	CU250	D	$4300	276	12,600	29,400	24,162

Livability Code: FT 30-90

Wheelbase-to-length ratio of 58% is considered ○ dangerous ○ fatiguing ○ good ◉ excellent *

The approximate net payload of 5238 pounds at 18% of GVWR on this model is ○ deficient ○ excessive ○ cautionary ○ good ◉ excellent *

Total highway safety penalties are: 6 *   Value: 7 8   Durability: 7 8   Highway Control Rating: 1 0 0   Highway Safety: 9 4   ★★★

Brand	Year	Type	Length	Model	Chassis	Engine	Fuel Type	Price/Ft	Wheelbase	Towing	GVWR	Curb Weight
Mountain Aire	1997	MHA	30	MA 2959 opch	CH	7.4L	G	$3200	178	4,500	16,500	14,572

Livability Code: FT 30-90

Wheelbase-to-length ratio of 50% is considered ◉ dangerous ○ fatiguing ○ good ○ excellent *

The approximate net payload of 1928 pounds at 12% of GVWR on this model is ○ deficient ○ excessive ○ cautionary ◉ good ○ excellent *

Total highway safety penalties are: 7 *   Value: 7 8   Durability: 7 8   Highway Control Rating: 3 7   Highway Safety: 3 0

Brand	Year	Type	Length	Model	Chassis	Engine	Fuel Type	Price/Ft	Wheelbase	Towing	GVWR	Curb Weight
Mountain Aire	1997	MHA	30	MA 2959	FO	7.5L	G	$3200	178	8,000	17,000	15,072

Livability Code: FT 30-90

Wheelbase-to-length ratio of 50% is considered ◉ dangerous ○ fatiguing ○ good ○ excellent *

The approximate net payload of 1928 pounds at 11% of GVWR on this model is ○ deficient ○ excessive ○ cautionary ◉ good ○ excellent *

Total highway safety penalties are: 5 *   Value: 7 9   Durability: 7 8   Highway Control Rating: 3 5   Highway Safety: 3 0

Brand	Year	Type	Length	Model	Chassis	Engine	Fuel Type	Price/Ft	Wheelbase	Towing	GVWR	Curb Weight
Mountain Aire	1997	MHA	30	MA2959 fr.dsl	FR	Cu210	D	$6000	178	4,500	20,500	16,172

Livability Code: FT 30-90

Wheelbase-to-length ratio of 50% is considered ◉ dangerous ○ fatiguing ○ good ○ excellent *

The approximate net payload of 4328 pounds at 21% of GVWR on this model is ○ deficient ○ excessive ○ cautionary ○ good ◉ excellent *

Total highway safety penalties are: 5 *   Value: 7 9   Durability: 7 8   Highway Control Rating: 4 8   Highway Safety: 4 3

Brand	Year	Type	Length	Model	Chassis	Engine	Fuel Type	Price/Ft	Wheelbase	Towing	GVWR	Curb Weight
Mountain Aire	1997	MHA	34	MA 3556 fr.dsl	FR	Cu210	D	$5300	200	4,500	20,500	17,263

Livability Code: FT 30-90

Wheelbase-to-length ratio of 50% is considered ◉ dangerous ○ fatiguing ○ good ○ excellent *

The approximate net payload of 3237 pounds at 16% of GVWR on this model is ○ deficient ○ excessive ○ cautionary ○ good ◉ excellent *

Total highway safety penalties are: 5 *   Value: 7 9   Durability: 7 8   Highway Control Rating: 4 3   Highway Safety: 3 8

Brand	Year	Type	Length	Model	Chassis	Engine	Fuel Type	Price/Ft	Wheelbase	Towing	GVWR	Curb Weight
Mountain Aire	1997	MHA	35	MA 3410 opch	CH	7.4L	G	$2900	214 T	2,000	19,000	16,835

Livability Code: FT 30-90

Wheelbase-to-length ratio of 52% is considered ○ dangerous ◉ fatiguing ○ good ○ excellent *

The approximate net payload of 2165 pounds at 11% of GVWR on this model is ○ deficient ○ excessive ○ cautionary ◉ good ○ excellent *

Total highway safety penalties are: 12 *   Value: 7 5   Durability: 7 8   Highway Control Rating: 4 8   Highway Safety: 3 6

Brand	Year	Type	Length	Model	Chassis	Engine	Fuel Type	Price/Ft	Wheelbase	Towing	GVWR	Curb Weight
Mountain Aire	1997	MHA	35	MA 3481 opch	CH	7.4L	G	$2900	214 T	2,000	19,000	16,835

Livability Code: FT 30-90

Wheelbase-to-length ratio of 52% is considered ○ dangerous ◉ fatiguing ○ good ○ excellent *

The approximate net payload of 2165 pounds at 11% of GVWR on this model is ○ deficient ○ excessive ○ cautionary ◉ good ○ excellent *

Total highway safety penalties are: 12 *   Value: 7 5   Durability: 7 8   Highway Control Rating: 4 8   Highway Safety: 3 6

Brand	Year	Type	Length	Model	Chassis	Engine	Fuel Type	Price/Ft	Wheelbase	Towing	GVWR	Curb Weight
Mountain Aire	1997	MHA	35	MA 3410	FO	7.5L	G	$3000	214 T	5,000	20,000	17,335

Livability Code: FT 30-90

Wheelbase-to-length ratio of 52% is considered ○ dangerous ◉ fatiguing ○ good ○ excellent *

The approximate net payload of 2665 pounds at 13% of GVWR on this model is ○ deficient ○ excessive ○ cautionary ◉ good ○ excellent *

Total highway safety penalties are: 7 *   Value: 7 8   Durability: 7 8   Highway Control Rating: 5 2   Highway Safety: 4 5

Brand	Year	Type	Length	Model	Chassis	Engine	Fuel Type	Price/Ft	Wheelbase	Towing	GVWR	Curb Weight
Mountain Aire	1997	MHA	35	MA 3481	FO	7.5L	G	$3000	214 T	5,000	20,000	17,335

Livability Code: FT 30-90

Wheelbase-to-length ratio of 52% is considered ○ dangerous ◉ fatiguing ○ good ○ excellent *

The approximate net payload of 2665 pounds at 13% of GVWR on this model is ○ deficient ○ excessive ○ cautionary ◉ good ○ excellent *

Total highway safety penalties are: 7 *   Value: 7 8   Durability: 7 8   Highway Control Rating: 5 2   Highway Safety: 4 5

Brand	Year	Type	Length	Model	Chassis	Engine	Fuel Type	Price/Ft	Wheelbase	Towing	GVWR	Curb Weight
Mountain Aire	1997	MHA	35	MA 3410 fr.dsl	FR	Cu210	D	$5100	216	4,500	20,500	16,635

Livability Code: FT 30-90

Wheelbase-to-length ratio of 52% is considered ○ dangerous ◉ fatiguing ○ good ○ excellent *

The approximate net payload of 3865 pounds at 19% of GVWR on this model is ○ deficient ○ excessive ○ cautionary ○ good ◉ excellent *

Total highway safety penalties are: 2 *   Value: 8 0   Durability: 7 8   Highway Control Rating: 6 2   Highway Safety: 6 0   ★★

Note: Safety ratings are based on the assumption that the engineering of the RV has allowed for proper balance by placing fresh, gray, and black holding tanks in a location so as not to change the balance of the RV when the tanks are empty or full. **Always double-check wheelbase, GVWR, and weights at front and rear axles.**

*See Section 1 for details on how conclusions are reached.

Brand	Year	Type	Length	Model	Chassis	Engine	Fuel Type	Average Price per Linear Foot When New	Adjusted Wheelbase	Approx. Towing Capacity	Gross Vehicle Weight Rating	Average Curb Weight
Mountain Aire	1997	MHA	35	MA3481 fr.dsl	FR	Cu210	D	$5100	216	4,500	20,500	17,535

Livability Code: FT 30-90
Wheelbase-to-length ratio of 52% is considered ○ dangerous ◉ fatiguing ○ good ○ excellent *
The approximate net payload of 2965 pounds at 14% of GVWR on this model is ○ deficient ○ excessive ○ cautionary ◉ good ○ excellent *
Total highway safety penalties are: 5 * Value: 7 9 Durability: 7 8 Highway Control Rating: 5 6 Highway Safety: 5 1 ★

Mountain Aire	1997	MHA	35	MP 3481 opch	FR	250HP	D	$5100	212	5,000	26,000	21,290

Livability Code: FT 30-90
Wheelbase-to-length ratio of 51% is considered ○ dangerous ◉ fatiguing ○ good ○ excellent *
The approximate net payload of 4710 pounds at 18% of GVWR on this model is ○ deficient ○ excessive ○ cautionary ○ good ◉ excellent *
Total highway safety penalties are: 5 * Value: 7 9 Durability: 7 8 Highway Control Rating: 5 0 Highway Safety: 4 5

Mountain Aire	1997	MHA	35	MP 3481 opch	SP	250HP	D	$3400	212	5,000	26,000	21,590

Livability Code: FT 30-90
Wheelbase-to-length ratio of 51% is considered ○ dangerous ◉ fatiguing ○ good ○ excellent *
The approximate net payload of 4410 pounds at 17% of GVWR on this model is ○ deficient ○ excessive ○ cautionary ○ good ◉ excellent *
Total highway safety penalties are: 5 * Value: 7 9 Durability: 7 8 Highway Control Rating: 4 8 Highway Safety: 4 3

Mountain Aire	1997	MHA	36	MA 3558 opch	CH	7.4L	G	$2800	214 T	2,000	19,000	17,108

Livability Code: FT 30-90
Wheelbase-to-length ratio of 50% is considered ◉ dangerous ○ fatiguing ○ good ○ excellent *
The approximate net payload of 1892 pounds at 10% of GVWR on this model is ○ deficient ○ excessive ○ cautionary ◉ good ○ excellent *
Total highway safety penalties are: 13 * Value: 7 5 Durability: 7 8 Highway Control Rating: 3 3 Highway Safety: 2 0

Mountain Aire	1997	MHA	36	MA 3558 opch	FO	7.5L	G	$4200	214 T	5,000	20,000	17,608

Livability Code: FT 30-90
Wheelbase-to-length ratio of 50% is considered ◉ dangerous ○ fatiguing ○ good ○ excellent *
The approximate net payload of 2392 pounds at 12% of GVWR on this model is ○ deficient ○ excessive ○ cautionary ◉ good ○ excellent *
Total highway safety penalties are: 7 * Value: 7 8 Durability: 7 8 Highway Control Rating: 3 7 Highway Safety: 3 0

Mountain Aire	1997	MHA	36	MA3558 fr.dsl	FR	Cu210	D	$5000	216	4,500	20,500	17,808

Livability Code: FT 30-90
Wheelbase-to-length ratio of 51% is considered ○ dangerous ◉ fatiguing ○ good ○ excellent *
The approximate net payload of 2692 pounds at 13% of GVWR on this model is ○ deficient ○ excessive ○ cautionary ◉ good ○ excellent *
Total highway safety penalties are: 5 * Value: 7 9 Durability: 7 8 Highway Control Rating: 4 1 Highway Safety: 3 6

Mountain Aire	1997	MHA	38	MA 3757	FO	7.5L	G	$2800	236 T	5,000	20,000	18,181

Livability Code: FT 30-90
Wheelbase-to-length ratio of 52% is considered ○ dangerous ◉ fatiguing ○ good ○ excellent *
The approximate net payload of 1819 pounds at 9% of GVWR on this model is ○ deficient ○ excessive ◉ cautionary ○ good ○ excellent *
Total highway safety penalties are: 7 * Value: 7 8 Durability: 7 8 Highway Control Rating: 4 3 Highway Safety: 3 6

Mountain Aire	1997	MHA	38	MA 3758	FO	7.5L	G	$2800	236 T	5,000	20,000	18,181

Livability Code: FT 30-90
Wheelbase-to-length ratio of 52% is considered ○ dangerous ◉ fatiguing ○ good ○ excellent *
The approximate net payload of 1819 pounds at 9% of GVWR on this model is ○ deficient ○ excessive ◉ cautionary ○ good ○ excellent *
Total highway safety penalties are: 7 * Value: 7 8 Durability: 7 8 Highway Control Rating: 4 3 Highway Safety: 3 6

Mountain Aire	1997	MHA	38	MA 3760	FO	7.5L	G	$2800	236 T	5,000	20,000	18,181

Livability Code: FT 30-90
Wheelbase-to-length ratio of 52% is considered ○ dangerous ◉ fatiguing ○ good ○ excellent *
The approximate net payload of 1819 pounds at 9% of GVWR on this model is ○ deficient ○ excessive ◉ cautionary ○ good ○ excellent *
Total highway safety penalties are: 7 * Value: 7 8 Durability: 7 8 Highway Control Rating: 4 3 Highway Safety: 3 6

Mountain Aire	1997	MHA	38	MA 3780	FO	7.5L	G	$2800	236 T	5,000	20,000	18,181

Livability Code: FT 30-90
Wheelbase-to-length ratio of 52% is considered ○ dangerous ◉ fatiguing ○ good ○ excellent *
The approximate net payload of 1819 pounds at 9% of GVWR on this model is ○ deficient ○ excessive ◉ cautionary ○ good ○ excellent *
Total highway safety penalties are: 7 * Value: 7 8 Durability: 7 8 Highway Control Rating: 4 3 Highway Safety: 3 6

Mountain Aire	1997	MHA	38	MA 3757 fr.dsl	FR	Cu210	D	$4700	228	4,500	20,500	18,381

Livability Code: FT 30-90
Wheelbase-to-length ratio of 50% is considered ◉ dangerous ○ fatiguing ○ good ○ excellent *
The approximate net payload of 2119 pounds at 10% of GVWR on this model is ○ deficient ○ excessive ○ cautionary ◉ good ○ excellent *
Total highway safety penalties are: 5 * Value: 7 9 Durability: 7 8 Highway Control Rating: 3 5 Highway Safety: 3 0

Mountain Aire	1997	MHA	38	MA3758 fr.dsl	FR	Cu210	D	$4700	228	4,500	20,500	18,381

Livability Code: FT 30-90
Wheelbase-to-length ratio of 50% is considered ◉ dangerous ○ fatiguing ○ good ○ excellent *
The approximate net payload of 2119 pounds at 10% of GVWR on this model is ○ deficient ○ excessive ○ cautionary ◉ good ○ excellent *
Total highway safety penalties are: 5 * Value: 7 9 Durability: 7 8 Highway Control Rating: 3 5 Highway Safety: 3 0

Note: Safety ratings are based on the assumption that the engineering of the RV has allowed for proper balance by placing fresh, gray, and black holding tanks in a location so as not to change the balance of the RV when the tanks are empty or full. **Always double-check wheelbase, GVWR, and weights at front and rear axles.**

Brand	Year	Type	Length	Model	Chassis	Engine	Fuel Type	Average Price per Linear Foot When New	Adjusted Wheelbase	Approx. Towing Capacity	Gross Vehicle Weight Rating	Average Curb Weight
Mountain Aire	**1997**	MHA	38	MA3760 fr.dsl	FR	Cu210	D	$4700	228	4,500	20,500	18,381

Livability Code: FT 30-90   Wheelbase-to-length ratio of 50% is considered ◉ dangerous ○ fatiguing ○ good ○ excellent *

The approximate net payload of 2119 pounds at 10% of GVWR on this model is ○ deficient ○ excessive ○ cautionary ◉ good ○ excellent *

Total highway safety penalties are: 5 *   Value: **79**   Durability: **78**   Highway Control Rating: **35**   Highway Safety: **30**

Brand	Year	Type	Length	Model	Chassis	Engine	Fuel Type	Average Price per Linear Foot When New	Adjusted Wheelbase	Approx. Towing Capacity	Gross Vehicle Weight Rating	Average Curb Weight
Mountain Aire	**1997**	MHA	38	MA3780 fr.dsl	FR	Cu210	D	$4700	228	4,500	20,500	18,381

Livability Code: FT 30-90   Wheelbase-to-length ratio of 50% is considered ◉ dangerous ○ fatiguing ○ good ○ excellent *

The approximate net payload of 2119 pounds at 10% of GVWR on this model is ○ deficient ○ excessive ○ cautionary ◉ good ○ excellent *

Total highway safety penalties are: 5 *   Value: **79**   Durability: **78**   Highway Control Rating: **35**   Highway Safety: **30**

Brand	Year	Type	Length	Model	Chassis	Engine	Fuel Type	Average Price per Linear Foot When New	Adjusted Wheelbase	Approx. Towing Capacity	Gross Vehicle Weight Rating	Average Curb Weight
Mountain Aire	**1997**	MHA	38	MP 3860 opch	FR	250HP	D	$4700	252	5,000	27,400	23,363

Livability Code: FT 30-90   Wheelbase-to-length ratio of 55% is considered ○ dangerous ○ fatiguing ◉ good ○ excellent *

The approximate net payload of 4037 pounds at 15% of GVWR on this model is ○ deficient ○ excessive ○ cautionary ◉ good ○ excellent *

Total highway safety penalties are: 5 *   Value: **79**   Durability: **78**   Highway Control Rating: **91**   Highway Safety: **86**   ★★★

Brand	Year	Type	Length	Model	Chassis	Engine	Fuel Type	Average Price per Linear Foot When New	Adjusted Wheelbase	Approx. Towing Capacity	Gross Vehicle Weight Rating	Average Curb Weight
Mountain Aire	**1997**	MHA	38	MP 3880 opch	FR	250HP	D	$4700	252	5,000	27,400	23,363

Livability Code: FT 30-90   Wheelbase-to-length ratio of 55% is considered ○ dangerous ○ fatiguing ◉ good ○ excellent *

The approximate net payload of 4037 pounds at 15% of GVWR on this model is ○ deficient ○ excessive ○ cautionary ◉ good ○ excellent *

Total highway safety penalties are: 5 *   Value: **79**   Durability: **78**   Highway Control Rating: **91**   Highway Safety: **86**   ★★★

Brand	Year	Type	Length	Model	Chassis	Engine	Fuel Type	Average Price per Linear Foot When New	Adjusted Wheelbase	Approx. Towing Capacity	Gross Vehicle Weight Rating	Average Curb Weight
Mountain Aire	**1997**	MHA	38	MP 3860 pusher	SP	250HP	D	$4700	252	5,000	27,400	23,463

Livability Code: FT 30-90   Wheelbase-to-length ratio of 55% is considered ○ dangerous ○ fatiguing ◉ good ○ excellent *

The approximate net payload of 3937 pounds at 14% of GVWR on this model is ○ deficient ○ excessive ○ cautionary ◉ good ○ excellent *

Total highway safety penalties are: 5 *   Value: **79**   Durability: **78**   Highway Control Rating: **90**   Highway Safety: **85**   ★★★

Brand	Year	Type	Length	Model	Chassis	Engine	Fuel Type	Average Price per Linear Foot When New	Adjusted Wheelbase	Approx. Towing Capacity	Gross Vehicle Weight Rating	Average Curb Weight
Mountain Aire	**1997**	MHA	38	MP 3880 pusher	SP	250HP	D	$4700	252	5,000	27,400	23,463

Livability Code: FT 30-90   Wheelbase-to-length ratio of 55% is considered ○ dangerous ○ fatiguing ◉ good ○ excellent *

The approximate net payload of 3937 pounds at 14% of GVWR on this model is ○ deficient ○ excessive ○ cautionary ◉ good ○ excellent *

Total highway safety penalties are: 5 *   Value: **79**   Durability: **78**   Highway Control Rating: **90**   Highway Safety: **85**   ★★★

Brand	Year	Type	Length	Model	Chassis	Engine	Fuel Type	Average Price per Linear Foot When New	Adjusted Wheelbase	Approx. Towing Capacity	Gross Vehicle Weight Rating	Average Curb Weight
Mountain Aire	**1997**	MHA	40	MP 4057 opch	FR	250HP	D	$4500	276	5,000	31,000	24,208

Livability Code: FT 30-90   Wheelbase-to-length ratio of 58% is considered ○ dangerous ○ fatiguing ○ good ◉ excellent *

The approximate net payload of 6792 pounds at 22% of GVWR on this model is ○ deficient ○ excessive ○ cautionary ○ good ◉ excellent *

Total highway safety penalties are: 5 *   Value: **79**   Durability: **78**   Highway Control Rating: **100**   Highway Safety: **95**   ★★★

Brand	Year	Type	Length	Model	Chassis	Engine	Fuel Type	Average Price per Linear Foot When New	Adjusted Wheelbase	Approx. Towing Capacity	Gross Vehicle Weight Rating	Average Curb Weight
Mountain Aire	**1997**	MHA	40	MP 4059 opch	FR	250HP	D	$4500	276	5,000	31,000	24,208

Livability Code: FT 30-90   Wheelbase-to-length ratio of 58% is considered ○ dangerous ○ fatiguing ○ good ◉ excellent *

The approximate net payload of 6792 pounds at 22% of GVWR on this model is ○ deficient ○ excessive ○ cautionary ○ good ◉ excellent *

Total highway safety penalties are: 5 *   Value: **79**   Durability: **78**   Highway Control Rating: **100**   Highway Safety: **95**   ★★★

Brand	Year	Type	Length	Model	Chassis	Engine	Fuel Type	Average Price per Linear Foot When New	Adjusted Wheelbase	Approx. Towing Capacity	Gross Vehicle Weight Rating	Average Curb Weight
Mountain Aire	**1997**	MHA	40	MP 4060 opch	FR	250HP	D	$4500	276	5,000	31,000	24,208

Livability Code: FT 30-90   Wheelbase-to-length ratio of 58% is considered ○ dangerous ○ fatiguing ○ good ◉ excellent *

The approximate net payload of 6792 pounds at 22% of GVWR on this model is ○ deficient ○ excessive ○ cautionary ○ good ◉ excellent *

Total highway safety penalties are: 5 *   Value: **79**   Durability: **78**   Highway Control Rating: **100**   Highway Safety: **95**   ★★★

Brand	Year	Type	Length	Model	Chassis	Engine	Fuel Type	Average Price per Linear Foot When New	Adjusted Wheelbase	Approx. Towing Capacity	Gross Vehicle Weight Rating	Average Curb Weight
Mountain Aire	**1997**	MHA	40	MP 4065 opch	FR	250HP	D	$4500	276	5,000	31,000	24,208

Livability Code: FT 30-90   Wheelbase-to-length ratio of 58% is considered ○ dangerous ○ fatiguing ○ good ◉ excellent *

The approximate net payload of 6792 pounds at 22% of GVWR on this model is ○ deficient ○ excessive ○ cautionary ○ good ◉ excellent *

Total highway safety penalties are: 5 *   Value: **79**   Durability: **78**   Highway Control Rating: **100**   Highway Safety: **95**   ★★★

Brand	Year	Type	Length	Model	Chassis	Engine	Fuel Type	Average Price per Linear Foot When New	Adjusted Wheelbase	Approx. Towing Capacity	Gross Vehicle Weight Rating	Average Curb Weight
Mountain Aire	**1997**	MHA	40	MP 4080 opch	FR	250HP	D	$4500	276	5,000	31,000	24,208

Livability Code: FT 30-90   Wheelbase-to-length ratio of 58% is considered ○ dangerous ○ fatiguing ○ good ◉ excellent *

The approximate net payload of 6792 pounds at 22% of GVWR on this model is ○ deficient ○ excessive ○ cautionary ○ good ◉ excellent *

Total highway safety penalties are: 5 *   Value: **79**   Durability: **78**   Highway Control Rating: **100**   Highway Safety: **95**   ★★★

Brand	Year	Type	Length	Model	Chassis	Engine	Fuel Type	Average Price per Linear Foot When New	Adjusted Wheelbase	Approx. Towing Capacity	Gross Vehicle Weight Rating	Average Curb Weight
Mountain Aire	**1997**	MHA	40	MP 4057 pusher	SP	250HP	D	$4500	276	5,000	31,000	24,308

Livability Code: FT 30-90   Wheelbase-to-length ratio of 58% is considered ○ dangerous ○ fatiguing ○ good ◉ excellent *

The approximate net payload of 6692 pounds at 22% of GVWR on this model is ○ deficient ○ excessive ○ cautionary ○ good ◉ excellent *

Total highway safety penalties are: 5 *   Value: **79**   Durability: **78**   Highway Control Rating: **100**   Highway Safety: **95**   ★★★

Note: Safety ratings are based on the assumption that the engineering of the RV has allowed for proper balance by placing fresh, gray, and black holding tanks in a location so as not to change the balance of the RV when the tanks are empty or full. **Always double-check wheelbase, GVWR, and weights at front and rear axles.**

*See Section 1 for details on how conclusions are reached.

Brand	Year	Type	Length	Model	Chassis	Engine	Fuel Type	Average Price per Linear Foot When New	Adjusted Wheelbase	Approx. Towing Capacity	Gross Vehicle Weight Rating	Average Curb Weight

Mountain Aire   **1997**   MHA   40   MP 4059 pusher   SP   250HP   D $4500   276   5,000   31,000   24,308

Livability Code: FT 30-90   Wheelbase-to-length ratio of 58% is considered ○ dangerous ○ fatiguing ○ good ◉ excellent *

The approximate net payload of 6692 pounds at 22% of GVWR on this model is ○ deficient ○ excessive ○ cautionary ○ good ◉ excellent *

Total highway safety penalties are: 5 *   Value: **79**   Durability: **78**   Highway Control Rating: **100**   Highway Safety: **95**   ★★★

Mountain Aire   **1997**   MHA   40   MP 4060 pusher   SP   250HP   D $4500   276   5,000   31,000   24,308

Livability Code: FT 30-90   Wheelbase-to-length ratio of 58% is considered ○ dangerous ○ fatiguing ○ good ◉ excellent *

The approximate net payload of 6692 pounds at 22% of GVWR on this model is ○ deficient ○ excessive ○ cautionary ○ good ◉ excellent *

Total highway safety penalties are: 5 *   Value: **79**   Durability: **78**   Highway Control Rating: **100**   Highway Safety: **95**   ★★★

Mountain Aire   **1997**   MHA   40   MP 4065 pusher   SP   250HP   D $4500   276   5,000   31,000   24,308

Livability Code: FT 30-90   Wheelbase-to-length ratio of 58% is considered ○ dangerous ○ fatiguing ○ good ◉ excellent *

The approximate net payload of 6692 pounds at 22% of GVWR on this model is ○ deficient ○ excessive ○ cautionary ○ good ◉ excellent *

Total highway safety penalties are: 5 *   Value: **79**   Durability: **78**   Highway Control Rating: **100**   Highway Safety: **95**   ★★★

Mountain Aire   **1997**   MHA   40   MP 4080 pusher   SP   250HP   D $4500   276   5,000   31,000   24,308

Livability Code: FT 30-90   Wheelbase-to-length ratio of 58% is considered ○ dangerous ○ fatiguing ○ good ◉ excellent *

The approximate net payload of 6692 pounds at 22% of GVWR on this model is ○ deficient ○ excessive ○ cautionary ○ good ◉ excellent *

Total highway safety penalties are: 5 *   Value: **79**   Durability: **78**   Highway Control Rating: **100**   Highway Safety: **95**   ★★★

Mountain Aire   **1998**   MHA   34   MA3356 fr.dsl   FR   CU210   D $5900   200   1,500   20,500   18,281

Livability Code: FT 30-90   Wheelbase-to-length ratio of 50% is considered ◉ dangerous ○ fatiguing ○ good ○ excellent *

The approximate net payload of 2219 pounds at 11% of GVWR on this model is ○ deficient ○ excessive ○ cautionary ◉ good ○ excellent *

Total highway safety penalties are: 5 *   Value: **79**   Durability: **78**   Highway Control Rating: **33**   Highway Safety: **28**

Mountain Aire   **1998**   MHA   35   MA3413   FO   7.5L   G $3700   214 T   5,000   20,000   17,484

Livability Code: FT 30-90   Wheelbase-to-length ratio of 52% is considered ○ dangerous ◉ fatiguing ○ good ○ excellent *

The approximate net payload of 2516 pounds at 13% of GVWR on this model is ○ deficient ○ excessive ○ cautionary ◉ good ○ excellent *

Total highway safety penalties are: 4 *   Value: **79**   Durability: **78**   Highway Control Rating: **51**   Highway Safety: **47**

Mountain Aire   **1998**   MHA   35   MA3451   FO   7.5L   G $3700   214 T   5,000   20,000   18,384

Livability Code: FT 30-90   Wheelbase-to-length ratio of 52% is considered ○ dangerous ◉ fatiguing ○ good ○ excellent *

The approximate net payload of 1616 pounds at 8% of GVWR on this model is ○ deficient ○ excessive ◉ cautionary ○ good ○ excellent *

Total highway safety penalties are: 7 *   Value: **78**   Durability: **78**   Highway Control Rating: **35**   Highway Safety: **28**

Mountain Aire   **1998**   MHA   35   MA3413 opch fr.dsl   FR   CU210   D $5700   216   1,500   20,500   17,684

Livability Code: FT 30-90   Wheelbase-to-length ratio of 52% is considered ○ dangerous ◉ fatiguing ○ good ○ excellent *

The approximate net payload of 2816 pounds at 14% of GVWR on this model is ○ deficient ○ excessive ○ cautionary ◉ good ○ excellent *

Total highway safety penalties are: 2 *   Value: **80**   Durability: **78**   Highway Control Rating: **55**   Highway Safety: **53**   ★

Mountain Aire   **1998**   MHA   35   MA3451 opch fr.dsl   FR   CU210   D $5700   216   1,500   20,500   18,584

Livability Code: FT 30-90   Wheelbase-to-length ratio of 52% is considered ○ dangerous ◉ fatiguing ○ good ○ excellent *

The approximate net payload of 1916 pounds at 9% of GVWR on this model is ○ deficient ○ excessive ◉ cautionary ○ good ○ excellent *

Total highway safety penalties are: 5 *   Value: **79**   Durability: **78**   Highway Control Rating: **43**   Highway Safety: **38**

Mountain Aire   **1998**   MHA   36   MA3535   FO   7.5L   G $3600   214 T   5,000   20,000   17,787

Livability Code: FT 30-90   Wheelbase-to-length ratio of 50% is considered ◉ dangerous ○ fatiguing ○ good ○ excellent *

The approximate net payload of 2213 pounds at 11% of GVWR on this model is ○ deficient ○ excessive ○ cautionary ◉ good ○ excellent *

Total highway safety penalties are: 4 *   Value: **79**   Durability: **78**   Highway Control Rating: **35**   Highway Safety: **31**

Mountain Aire   **1998**   MHA   36   MA3558   FO   7.5L   G $3600   214 T   5,000   20,000   18,687

Livability Code: FT 30-90   Wheelbase-to-length ratio of 50% is considered ◉ dangerous ○ fatiguing ○ good ○ excellent *

The approximate net payload of 1313 pounds at 7% of GVWR on this model is ○ deficient ○ excessive ◉ cautionary ○ good ○ excellent *

Total highway safety penalties are: 7 *   Value: **78**   Durability: **78**   Highway Control Rating: **16**   Highway Safety: **9**

Mountain Aire   **1998**   MHA   36   MA3535 opch fr.dsl   FR   CU210   D $5600   216   1,500   20,500   17,987

Livability Code: FT 30-90   Wheelbase-to-length ratio of 51% is considered ○ dangerous ◉ fatiguing ○ good ○ excellent *

The approximate net payload of 2513 pounds at 12% of GVWR on this model is ○ deficient ○ excessive ○ cautionary ◉ good ○ excellent *

Total highway safety penalties are: 2 *   Value: **80**   Durability: **78**   Highway Control Rating: **39**   Highway Safety: **37**

Note: Safety ratings are based on the assumption that the engineering of the RV has allowed for proper balance by placing fresh, gray, and black holding tanks in a location so as not to change the balance of the RV when the tanks are empty or full. **Always double-check wheelbase, GVWR, and weights at front and rear axles.**

*See Section 1 for details on how conclusions are reached.

Section 2: The Ratings

Brand	Year	Type	Length	Model	Chassis	Engine	Fuel Type	Average Price per Linear Foot When New	Adjusted Wheelbase	Approx. Towing Capacity	Gross Vehicle Weight Rating	Average Curb Weight
Mountain Aire	1998	MHA	36	MA3558 opch fr.dsl	FR	CU210	D	$5600	216	1,500	20,500	18,887

Livability Code: FT 30-90
Wheelbase-to-length ratio of 51% is considered ○ dangerous ◉ fatiguing ○ good ○ excellent *
The approximate net payload of 1613 pounds at 8% of GVWR on this model is ○ deficient ○ excessive ◉ cautionary ○ good ○ excellent *
Total highway safety penalties are: 5 *   Value: 79   Durability: 78   Highway Control Rating: 24   Highway Safety: 19

Mountain Aire	1998	MHA	38	MA3707	FO	7.5L	G	$3400	236 T	5,000	20,000	18,393

Livability Code: FT 30-90
Wheelbase-to-length ratio of 52% is considered ○ dangerous ◉ fatiguing ○ good ○ excellent *
The approximate net payload of 1607 pounds at 8% of GVWR on this model is ○ deficient ○ excessive ◉ cautionary ○ good ○ excellent *
Total highway safety penalties are: 4 *   Value: 79   Durability: 78   Highway Control Rating: 38   Highway Safety: 34

Mountain Aire	1998	MHA	38	MA3758	FO	7.5L	G	$3400	236 T	5,000	20,000	19,293

Livability Code: FT 30-90
Wheelbase-to-length ratio of 52% is considered ○ dangerous ◉ fatiguing ○ good ○ excellent *
The approximate net payload of 707 pounds at 4% of GVWR on this model is ◉ deficient ○ excessive ○ cautionary ○ good ○ excellent *
Total highway safety penalties are: 7 *   Value: 78   Durability: 78   Highway Control Rating: 23   Highway Safety: 16

Mountain Aire	1998	MHA	38	MA3761	FO	7.5L	G	$3400	236 T	5,000	20,000	19,293

Livability Code: FT 30-90
Wheelbase-to-length ratio of 52% is considered ○ dangerous ◉ fatiguing ○ good ○ excellent *
The approximate net payload of 707 pounds at 4% of GVWR on this model is ◉ deficient ○ excessive ○ cautionary ○ good ○ excellent *
Total highway safety penalties are: 7 *   Value: 78   Durability: 78   Highway Control Rating: 23   Highway Safety: 16

Mountain Aire	1998	MHA	38	MA3766	FO	7.5L	G	$3400	236 T	5,000	20,000	19,293

Livability Code: FT 30-90
Wheelbase-to-length ratio of 52% is considered ○ dangerous ◉ fatiguing ○ good ○ excellent *
The approximate net payload of 707 pounds at 4% of GVWR on this model is ◉ deficient ○ excessive ○ cautionary ○ good ○ excellent *
Total highway safety penalties are: 12 *   Value: 75   Durability: 78   Highway Control Rating: 23   Highway Safety: 11

Mountain Aire	1998	MHA	38	MA3767	FO	7.5L	G	$3400	236 T	5,000	20,000	19,293

Livability Code: FT 30-90
Wheelbase-to-length ratio of 52% is considered ○ dangerous ◉ fatiguing ○ good ○ excellent *
The approximate net payload of 707 pounds at 4% of GVWR on this model is ◉ deficient ○ excessive ○ cautionary ○ good ○ excellent *
Total highway safety penalties are: 7 *   Value: 78   Durability: 78   Highway Control Rating: 23   Highway Safety: 16

Mountain Aire	1998	MHA	38	MA3780	FO	7.5L	G	$3400	236 T	5,000	20,000	19,293

Livability Code: FT 30-90
Wheelbase-to-length ratio of 52% is considered ○ dangerous ◉ fatiguing ○ good ○ excellent *
The approximate net payload of 707 pounds at 4% of GVWR on this model is ◉ deficient ○ excessive ○ cautionary ○ good ○ excellent *
Total highway safety penalties are: 7 *   Value: 78   Durability: 78   Highway Control Rating: 23   Highway Safety: 16

Mountain Aire	1998	MHA	38	MA3796	FO	7.5L	G	$3400	236 T	5,000	20,000	19,293

Livability Code: FT 30-90
Wheelbase-to-length ratio of 52% is considered ○ dangerous ◉ fatiguing ○ good ○ excellent *
The approximate net payload of 707 pounds at 4% of GVWR on this model is ◉ deficient ○ excessive ○ cautionary ○ good ○ excellent *
Total highway safety penalties are: 7 *   Value: 78   Durability: 78   Highway Control Rating: 23   Highway Safety: 16

Mountain Aire	1998	MHA	38	MA3797	FO	7.5L	G	$3400	236 T	5,000	20,000	19,293

Livability Code: FT 30-90
Wheelbase-to-length ratio of 52% is considered ○ dangerous ◉ fatiguing ○ good ○ excellent *
The approximate net payload of 707 pounds at 4% of GVWR on this model is ◉ deficient ○ excessive ○ cautionary ○ good ○ excellent *
Total highway safety penalties are: 7 *   Value: 78   Durability: 78   Highway Control Rating: 23   Highway Safety: 16

Mountain Aire	1998	MHA	38	MA3707 opch fr.dsl	FR	CU210	D	$5300	228	1,500	20,500	18,593

Livability Code: FT 30-90
Wheelbase-to-length ratio of 51% is considered ○ dangerous ◉ fatiguing ○ good ○ excellent *
The approximate net payload of 1907 pounds at 9% of GVWR on this model is ○ deficient ○ excessive ◉ cautionary ○ good ○ excellent *
Total highway safety penalties are: 2 *   Value: 80   Durability: 78   Highway Control Rating: 30   Highway Safety: 28

Mountain Aire	1998	MHA	38	MA3758 opch fr.dsl	FR	CU210	D	$5300	228	1,500	20,500	19,493

Livability Code: FT 30-90
Wheelbase-to-length ratio of 51% is considered ○ dangerous ◉ fatiguing ○ good ○ excellent *
The approximate net payload of 1007 pounds at 5% of GVWR on this model is ◉ deficient ○ excessive ○ cautionary ○ good ○ excellent *
Total highway safety penalties are: 5 *   Value: 79   Durability: 78   Highway Control Rating: 11   Highway Safety: 6

Mountain Aire	1998	MHA	38	MA3761 opch fr.dsl	FR	CU210	D	$5300	228	1,500	20,500	19,493

Livability Code: FT 30-90
Wheelbase-to-length ratio of 51% is considered ○ dangerous ◉ fatiguing ○ good ○ excellent *
The approximate net payload of 1007 pounds at 5% of GVWR on this model is ◉ deficient ○ excessive ○ cautionary ○ good ○ excellent *
Total highway safety penalties are: 5 *   Value: 79   Durability: 78   Highway Control Rating: 11   Highway Safety: 6

Note: Safety ratings are based on the assumption that the engineering of the RV has allowed for proper balance by placing fresh, gray, and black holding tanks in a location so as not to change the balance of the RV when the tanks are empty or full. **Always double-check wheelbase, GVWR, and weights at front and rear axles.**

*See Section 1 for details on how conclusions are reached.

Section 2: The Ratings

Brand	Year	Type	Length	Model	Chassis	Engine	Fuel Type	Average Price per Linear Foot When New	Adjusted Wheelbase	Approx. Towing Capacity	Gross Vehicle Weight Rating	Average Curb Weight
Mountain Aire	1998	MHA	38	MA3766 opch fr.dsl	FR	CU210	D	$5300	228	1,500	20,500	19,493

Livability Code: FT 30-90　Wheelbase-to-length ratio of 51% is considered ○ dangerous ◉ fatiguing ○ good ○ excellent *

The approximate net payload of 1007 pounds at 5% of GVWR on this model is ◉ deficient ○ excessive ○ cautionary ○ good ○ excellent *

Total highway safety penalties are: 10 *　Value: 7 6　Durability: 7 8　Highway Control Rating: 1 1　Highway Safety: 1

| Mountain Aire | 1998 | MHA | 38 | MA3767 opch fr.dsl | FR | CU210 | D | $5300 | 228 | 1,500 | 20,500 | 19,493 |

Livability Code: FT 30-90　Wheelbase-to-length ratio of 51% is considered ○ dangerous ◉ fatiguing ○ good ○ excellent *

The approximate net payload of 1007 pounds at 5% of GVWR on this model is ◉ deficient ○ excessive ○ cautionary ○ good ○ excellent *

Total highway safety penalties are: 10 *　Value: 7 6　Durability: 7 8　Highway Control Rating: 1 1　Highway Safety: 1

| Mountain Aire | 1998 | MHA | 38 | MA3780 opch fr.dsl | FR | CU210 | D | $5300 | 228 | 1,500 | 20,500 | 19,493 |

Livability Code: FT 30-90　Wheelbase-to-length ratio of 51% is considered ○ dangerous ◉ fatiguing ○ good ○ excellent *

The approximate net payload of 1007 pounds at 5% of GVWR on this model is ◉ deficient ○ excessive ○ cautionary ○ good ○ excellent *

Total highway safety penalties are: 5 *　Value: 7 9　Durability: 7 8　Highway Control Rating: 1 1　Highway Safety: 6

| Mountain Aire | 1998 | MHA | 38 | MA3796 opch fr.dsl | FR | CU210 | D | $5300 | 228 | 1,500 | 20,500 | 19,493 |

Livability Code: FT 30-90　Wheelbase-to-length ratio of 51% is considered ○ dangerous ◉ fatiguing ○ good ○ excellent *

The approximate net payload of 1007 pounds at 5% of GVWR on this model is ◉ deficient ○ excessive ○ cautionary ○ good ○ excellent *

Total highway safety penalties are: 5 *　Value: 7 9　Durability: 7 8　Highway Control Rating: 1 1　Highway Safety: 6

| Mountain Aire | 1998 | MHA | 38 | MA3797 opch fr.dsl | FR | CU210 | D | $5300 | 228 | 1,500 | 20,500 | 19,493 |

Livability Code: FT 30-90　Wheelbase-to-length ratio of 51% is considered ○ dangerous ◉ fatiguing ○ good ○ excellent *

The approximate net payload of 1007 pounds at 5% of GVWR on this model is ◉ deficient ○ excessive ○ cautionary ○ good ○ excellent *

Total highway safety penalties are: 5 *　Value: 7 9　Durability: 7 8　Highway Control Rating: 1 1　Highway Safety: 6

| Mountain Aire | 1998 | MHA | 38 | MP3866 opch | FR | CA330 | D | $5300 | 252 | 5,000 | 27,400 | 24,514 |

Livability Code: FT 30-90　Wheelbase-to-length ratio of 55% is considered ○ dangerous ○ fatiguing ◉ good ○ excellent *

The approximate net payload of 2886 pounds at 11% of GVWR on this model is ○ deficient ○ excessive ○ cautionary ◉ good ○ excellent *

Total highway safety penalties are: 10 *　Value: 7 6　Durability: 7 8　Highway Control Rating: 8 8　Highway Safety: 7 8　★★★

| Mountain Aire | 1998 | MHA | 38 | MP3883 opch | FR | CA330 | D | $5300 | 252 | 5,000 | 27,400 | 24,514 |

Livability Code: FT 30-90　Wheelbase-to-length ratio of 55% is considered ○ dangerous ○ fatiguing ◉ good ○ excellent *

The approximate net payload of 2886 pounds at 11% of GVWR on this model is ○ deficient ○ excessive ○ cautionary ◉ good ○ excellent *

Total highway safety penalties are: 5 *　Value: 7 9　Durability: 7 8　Highway Control Rating: 8 8　Highway Safety: 8 3　★★★

| Mountain Aire | 1998 | MHA | 38 | MP3866 | SP | CU325 | D | $5300 | 252 | 10,000 | 27,400 | 24,614 |

Livability Code: FT 30-90　Wheelbase-to-length ratio of 55% is considered ○ dangerous ○ fatiguing ◉ good ○ excellent *

The approximate net payload of 2786 pounds at 10% of GVWR on this model is ○ deficient ○ excessive ○ cautionary ◉ good ○ excellent *

Total highway safety penalties are: 10 *　Value: 7 6　Durability: 7 8　Highway Control Rating: 8 8　Highway Safety: 7 8　★★★

| Mountain Aire | 1998 | MHA | 38 | MP3883 | SP | CU325 | D | $5300 | 252 | 10,000 | 27,400 | 24,614 |

Livability Code: FT 30-90　Wheelbase-to-length ratio of 55% is considered ○ dangerous ○ fatiguing ◉ good ○ excellent *

The approximate net payload of 2786 pounds at 10% of GVWR on this model is ○ deficient ○ excessive ○ cautionary ◉ good ○ excellent *

Total highway safety penalties are: 5 *　Value: 7 9　Durability: 7 8　Highway Control Rating: 8 8　Highway Safety: 8 3　★★★

| Mountain Aire | 1998 | MHA | 40 | MP4030 opch | FR | CA330 | D | $5000 | 276 | 5,000 | 31,000 | 24,520 |

Livability Code: FT 30-90　Wheelbase-to-length ratio of 58% is considered ○ dangerous ○ fatiguing ○ good ◉ excellent *

The approximate net payload of 6480 pounds at 21% of GVWR on this model is ○ deficient ○ excessive ○ cautionary ○ good ◉ excellent *

Total highway safety penalties are: 2 *　Value: 8 0　Durability: 7 8　Highway Control Rating: 1 0 0　Highway Safety: 9 8　★★★

| Mountain Aire | 1998 | MHA | 40 | MP4057 opch | FR | CA330 | D | $5000 | 276 | 5,000 | 31,000 | 25,420 |

Livability Code: FT 30-90　Wheelbase-to-length ratio of 58% is considered ○ dangerous ○ fatiguing ○ good ◉ excellent *

The approximate net payload of 5580 pounds at 18% of GVWR on this model is ○ deficient ○ excessive ○ cautionary ○ good ◉ excellent *

Total highway safety penalties are: 5 *　Value: 7 9　Durability: 7 8　Highway Control Rating: 1 0 0　Highway Safety: 9 5　★★★

| Mountain Aire | 1998 | MHA | 40 | MP4059 opch | FR | CA330 | D | $5000 | 276 | 5,000 | 31,000 | 25,420 |

Livability Code: FT 30-90　Wheelbase-to-length ratio of 58% is considered ○ dangerous ○ fatiguing ○ good ◉ excellent *

The approximate net payload of 5580 pounds at 18% of GVWR on this model is ○ deficient ○ excessive ○ cautionary ○ good ◉ excellent *

Total highway safety penalties are: 5 *　Value: 7 9　Durability: 7 8　Highway Control Rating: 1 0 0　Highway Safety: 9 5　★★★

Note: Safety ratings are based on the assumption that the engineering of the RV has allowed for proper balance by placing fresh, gray, and black holding tanks in a location so as not to change the balance of the RV when the tanks are empty or full. **Always double-check wheelbase, GVWR, and weights at front and rear axles.**

*See Section 1 for details on how conclusions are reached.

Brand	Year	Type	Length	Model	Chassis	Engine	Fuel Type	Average Price per Linear Foot When New	Adjusted Wheelbase	Approx. Towing Capacity	Gross Vehicle Weight Rating	Average Curb Weight
Mountain Aire	1998	MHA	40	MP4060 opch	FR	CA330	D	$5000	276	5,000	31,000	25,420

Livability Code: FT 30-90
Wheelbase-to-length ratio of 58% is considered ○ dangerous ○ fatiguing ○ good ◉ excellent *
The approximate net payload of 5580 pounds at 18% of GVWR on this model is ○ deficient ○ excessive ○ cautionary ○ good ◉ excellent *
Total highway safety penalties are: 5 * Value: 79 Durability: 78 Highway Control Rating: 100 Highway Safety: 95 ★★★

Brand	Year	Type	Length	Model	Chassis	Engine	Fuel Type	Avg Price/Lin Ft	Adj Wheelbase	Approx Towing Cap	GVWR	Avg Curb Weight
Mountain Aire	1998	MHA	40	MP4065 opch	FR	CA330	D	$5000	276	5,000	31,000	25,420

Livability Code: FT 30-90
Wheelbase-to-length ratio of 58% is considered ○ dangerous ○ fatiguing ○ good ◉ excellent *
The approximate net payload of 5580 pounds at 18% of GVWR on this model is ○ deficient ○ excessive ○ cautionary ○ good ◉ excellent *
Total highway safety penalties are: 10 * Value: 76 Durability: 78 Highway Control Rating: 100 Highway Safety: 90 ★★★

Mountain Aire	1998	MHA	40	MP4068 opch	FR	CA330	D	$5000	276	5,000	31,000	25,420

Livability Code: FT 30-90
Wheelbase-to-length ratio of 58% is considered ○ dangerous ○ fatiguing ○ good ◉ excellent *
The approximate net payload of 5580 pounds at 18% of GVWR on this model is ○ deficient ○ excessive ○ cautionary ○ good ◉ excellent *
Total highway safety penalties are: 10 * Value: 76 Durability: 78 Highway Control Rating: 100 Highway Safety: 90 ★★★

Mountain Aire	1998	MHA	40	MP4080 opch	FR	CA330	D	$5000	276	5,000	31,000	25,420

Livability Code: FT 30-90
Wheelbase-to-length ratio of 58% is considered ○ dangerous ○ fatiguing ○ good ◉ excellent *
The approximate net payload of 5580 pounds at 18% of GVWR on this model is ○ deficient ○ excessive ○ cautionary ○ good ◉ excellent *
Total highway safety penalties are: 5 * Value: 79 Durability: 78 Highway Control Rating: 100 Highway Safety: 95 ★★★

Mountain Aire	1998	MHA	40	MP4081 opch	FR	CA330	D	$5000	276	5,000	31,000	25,420

Livability Code: FT 30-90
Wheelbase-to-length ratio of 58% is considered ○ dangerous ○ fatiguing ○ good ◉ excellent *
The approximate net payload of 5580 pounds at 18% of GVWR on this model is ○ deficient ○ excessive ○ cautionary ○ good ◉ excellent *
Total highway safety penalties are: 5 * Value: 79 Durability: 78 Highway Control Rating: 100 Highway Safety: 95 ★★★

Mountain Aire	1998	MHA	40	MP4087 opch	FR	CA330	D	$5000	276	5,000	31,000	25,420

Livability Code: FT 30-90
Wheelbase-to-length ratio of 58% is considered ○ dangerous ○ fatiguing ○ good ◉ excellent *
The approximate net payload of 5580 pounds at 18% of GVWR on this model is ○ deficient ○ excessive ○ cautionary ○ good ◉ excellent *
Total highway safety penalties are: 5 * Value: 79 Durability: 78 Highway Control Rating: 100 Highway Safety: 95 ★★★

Mountain Aire	1998	MHA	40	MP4030	SP	CU325	D	$5000	276	10,000	31,000	24,620

Livability Code: FT 30-90
Wheelbase-to-length ratio of 58% is considered ○ dangerous ○ fatiguing ○ good ◉ excellent *
The approximate net payload of 6380 pounds at 21% of GVWR on this model is ○ deficient ○ excessive ○ cautionary ○ good ◉ excellent *
Total highway safety penalties are: 2 * Value: 80 Durability: 78 Highway Control Rating: 100 Highway Safety: 98 ★★★

Mountain Aire	1998	MHA	40	MP4057	SP	CU325	D	$5000	276	10,000	31,000	25,520

Livability Code: FT 30-90
Wheelbase-to-length ratio of 58% is considered ○ dangerous ○ fatiguing ○ good ◉ excellent *
The approximate net payload of 5480 pounds at 18% of GVWR on this model is ○ deficient ○ excessive ○ cautionary ○ good ◉ excellent *
Total highway safety penalties are: 5 * Value: 79 Durability: 78 Highway Control Rating: 100 Highway Safety: 95 ★★★

Mountain Aire	1998	MHA	40	MP4059	SP	CU325	D	$5000	276	10,000	31,000	25,520

Livability Code: FT 30-90
Wheelbase-to-length ratio of 58% is considered ○ dangerous ○ fatiguing ○ good ◉ excellent *
The approximate net payload of 5480 pounds at 18% of GVWR on this model is ○ deficient ○ excessive ○ cautionary ○ good ◉ excellent *
Total highway safety penalties are: 5 * Value: 79 Durability: 78 Highway Control Rating: 100 Highway Safety: 95 ★★★

Mountain Aire	1998	MHA	40	MP4060	SP	CU325	D	$5000	276	10,000	31,000	25,520

Livability Code: FT 30-90
Wheelbase-to-length ratio of 58% is considered ○ dangerous ○ fatiguing ○ good ◉ excellent *
The approximate net payload of 5480 pounds at 18% of GVWR on this model is ○ deficient ○ excessive ○ cautionary ○ good ◉ excellent *
Total highway safety penalties are: 5 * Value: 79 Durability: 78 Highway Control Rating: 100 Highway Safety: 95 ★★★

Mountain Aire	1998	MHA	40	MP4065	SP	CU325	D	$5000	276	10,000	31,000	25,520

Livability Code: FT 30-90
Wheelbase-to-length ratio of 58% is considered ○ dangerous ○ fatiguing ○ good ◉ excellent *
The approximate net payload of 5480 pounds at 18% of GVWR on this model is ○ deficient ○ excessive ○ cautionary ○ good ◉ excellent *
Total highway safety penalties are: 10 * Value: 76 Durability: 78 Highway Control Rating: 100 Highway Safety: 90 ★★★

Mountain Aire	1998	MHA	40	MP4068	SP	CU325	D	$5000	276	10,000	31,000	25,520

Livability Code: FT 30-90
Wheelbase-to-length ratio of 58% is considered ○ dangerous ○ fatiguing ○ good ◉ excellent *
The approximate net payload of 5480 pounds at 18% of GVWR on this model is ○ deficient ○ excessive ○ cautionary ○ good ◉ excellent *
Total highway safety penalties are: 10 * Value: 76 Durability: 78 Highway Control Rating: 100 Highway Safety: 90 ★★★

Note: Safety ratings are based on the assumption that the engineering of the RV has allowed for proper balance by placing fresh, gray, and black holding tanks in a location so as not to change the balance of the RV when the tanks are empty or full. **Always double-check wheelbase, GVWR, and weights at front and rear axles.**

*See Section 1 for details on how conclusions are reached.

Brand	Year	Type	Length	Model	Chassis	Engine	Fuel Type	Average Price per Linear Foot When New	Adjusted Wheelbase	Approx. Towing Capacity	Gross Vehicle Weight Rating	Average Curb Weight
Mountain Aire	1998	MHA	40	MP4080	SP	CU325	D	$5000	276	10,000	31,000	25,520

Livability Code: FT 30-90 — Wheelbase-to-length ratio of 58% is considered ○ dangerous ○ fatiguing ○ good ◉ excellent *
The approximate net payload of 5480 pounds at 18% of GVWR on this model is ○ deficient ○ excessive ○ cautionary ○ good ◉ excellent *
Total highway safety penalties are: 5 * — Value: 7 9 — Durability: 7 8 — Highway Control Rating: 1 0 0 — Highway Safety: 9 5 — ★★★

Brand	Year	Type	Length	Model	Chassis	Engine	Fuel Type	Avg Price/Linear Foot	Adj Wheelbase	Towing Capacity	GVWR	Avg Curb Weight
Mountain Aire	1998	MHA	40	MP4081	SP	CU325	D	$5000	276	10,000	31,000	25,520

Livability Code: FT 30-90 — Wheelbase-to-length ratio of 58% is considered ○ dangerous ○ fatiguing ○ good ◉ excellent *
The approximate net payload of 5480 pounds at 18% of GVWR on this model is ○ deficient ○ excessive ○ cautionary ○ good ◉ excellent *
Total highway safety penalties are: 5 * — Value: 7 9 — Durability: 7 8 — Highway Control Rating: 1 0 0 — Highway Safety: 9 5 — ★★★

Mountain Aire	1998	MHA	40	MP4087	SP	CU325	D	$5000	276	10,000	31,000	25,520

Livability Code: FT 30-90 — Wheelbase-to-length ratio of 58% is considered ○ dangerous ○ fatiguing ○ good ◉ excellent *
The approximate net payload of 5480 pounds at 18% of GVWR on this model is ○ deficient ○ excessive ○ cautionary ○ good ◉ excellent *
Total highway safety penalties are: 5 * — Value: 7 9 — Durability: 7 8 — Highway Control Rating: 1 0 0 — Highway Safety: 9 5 — ★★★

Mountain Aire	1999	MHA	34	MA3356	FO	6.8L	G	$3500	200	5,500	20,500	18,420

Livability Code: FT 30-90 — Wheelbase-to-length ratio of 50% is considered ◉ dangerous ○ fatiguing ○ good ○ excellent *
The approximate net payload of 2080 pounds at 10% of GVWR on this model is ○ deficient ○ excessive ○ cautionary ◉ good ○ excellent *
Total highway safety penalties are: 5 * — Value: 7 9 — Durability: 7 8 — Highway Control Rating: 4 1 — Highway Safety: 3 6

Mountain Aire	1999	MHA	34	MA3356 fr.dsl	FR	CU210	D	$5900	200	1,500	20,500	18,620

Livability Code: FT 30-90 — Wheelbase-to-length ratio of 50% is considered ◉ dangerous ○ fatiguing ○ good ○ excellent *
The approximate net payload of 1880 pounds at 9% of GVWR on this model is ○ deficient ○ excessive ◉ cautionary ○ good ○ excellent *
Total highway safety penalties are: 5 * — Value: 7 9 — Durability: 7 8 — Highway Control Rating: 3 7 — Highway Safety: 3 2

Mountain Aire	1999	MHA	34	MA3356	CH	7.4L	G	$3500	200	5,000	21,000	19,077

Livability Code: FT 30-90 — Wheelbase-to-length ratio of 49% is considered ◉ dangerous ○ fatiguing ○ good ○ excellent *
The approximate net payload of 1923 pounds at 9% of GVWR on this model is ○ deficient ○ excessive ◉ cautionary ○ good ○ excellent *
Total highway safety penalties are: 10 * — Value: 7 6 — Durability: 7 8 — Highway Control Rating: 3 4 — Highway Safety: 2 4

Mountain Aire	1999	MHA	36	MA3559	FO	6.8L	G	$3300	216	5,500	20,500	19,046

Livability Code: FT 30-90 — Wheelbase-to-length ratio of 51% is considered ○ dangerous ◉ fatiguing ○ good ○ excellent *
The approximate net payload of 1454 pounds at 7% of GVWR on this model is ○ deficient ○ excessive ◉ cautionary ○ good ○ excellent *
Total highway safety penalties are: 5 * — Value: 7 9 — Durability: 7 8 — Highway Control Rating: 2 8 — Highway Safety: 2 3

Mountain Aire	1999	MHA	36	MA3559 fr.dsl	FR	CU210	D	$5600	216	1,500	20,500	19,246

Livability Code: FT 30-90 — Wheelbase-to-length ratio of 51% is considered ○ dangerous ◉ fatiguing ○ good ○ excellent *
The approximate net payload of 1254 pounds at 6% of GVWR on this model is ◉ deficient ○ excessive ○ cautionary ○ good ○ excellent *
Total highway safety penalties are: 5 * — Value: 7 9 — Durability: 7 8 — Highway Control Rating: 2 2 — Highway Safety: 1 7

Mountain Aire	1999	MHA	36	MA3559	CH	7.4L	G	$3300	216	5,000	21,000	19,703

Livability Code: FT 30-90 — Wheelbase-to-length ratio of 50% is considered ◉ dangerous ○ fatiguing ○ good ○ excellent *
The approximate net payload of 1297 pounds at 6% of GVWR on this model is ◉ deficient ○ excessive ○ cautionary ○ good ○ excellent *
Total highway safety penalties are: 11 * — Value: 7 6 — Durability: 7 8 — Highway Control Rating: 1 9 — Highway Safety: 8

Mountain Aire	1999	MHA	38	MA3758	FO	6.8L	G	$3200	240	5,500	20,500	19,673

Livability Code: FT 30-90 — Wheelbase-to-length ratio of 53% is considered ○ dangerous ◉ fatiguing ○ good ○ excellent *
The approximate net payload of 827 pounds at 4% of GVWR on this model is ◉ deficient ○ excessive ○ cautionary ○ good ○ excellent *
Total highway safety penalties are: 5 * — Value: 7 9 — Durability: 7 8 — Highway Control Rating: 3 9 — Highway Safety: 3 4

Mountain Aire	1999	MHA	38	MA3762	FO	6.8L	G	$3200	240	5,500	20,500	19,673

Livability Code: FT 30-90 — Wheelbase-to-length ratio of 53% is considered ○ dangerous ◉ fatiguing ○ good ○ excellent *
The approximate net payload of 827 pounds at 4% of GVWR on this model is ◉ deficient ○ excessive ○ cautionary ○ good ○ excellent *
Total highway safety penalties are: 5 * — Value: 7 9 — Durability: 7 8 — Highway Control Rating: 3 9 — Highway Safety: 3 4

Mountain Aire	1999	MHA	38	MA3767	FO	6.8L	G	$3200	240	5,500	20,500	19,673

Livability Code: FT 30-90 — Wheelbase-to-length ratio of 53% is considered ○ dangerous ◉ fatiguing ○ good ○ excellent *
The approximate net payload of 827 pounds at 4% of GVWR on this model is ◉ deficient ○ excessive ○ cautionary ○ good ○ excellent *
Total highway safety penalties are: 10 * — Value: 7 6 — Durability: 7 8 — Highway Control Rating: 3 9 — Highway Safety: 2 9

Note: Safety ratings are based on the assumption that the engineering of the RV has allowed for proper balance by placing fresh, gray, and black holding tanks in a location so as not to change the balance of the RV when the tanks are empty or full. **Always double-check wheelbase, GVWR, and weights at front and rear axles.**

*See Section 1 for details on how conclusions are reached.

Brand	Year	Type	Length	Model	Chassis	Engine	Fuel Type	Average Price per Linear Foot When New	Adjusted Wheelbase	Approx. Towing Capacity	Gross Vehicle Weight Rating	Average Curb Weight
Mountain Aire	1999	MHA	38	MA3780	FO	6.8L	G	$3200	240	5,500	20,500	19,673

Livability Code: FT 30-90
Wheelbase-to-length ratio of 53% is considered ○ dangerous ⊙ fatiguing ○ good ○ excellent *
The approximate net payload of 827 pounds at 4% of GVWR on this model is ⊙ deficient ○ excessive ○ cautionary ○ good ○ excellent *
Total highway safety penalties are: 5 *   Value: 7 9   Durability: 7 8   Highway Control Rating: 3 9   Highway Safety: 3 4

Brand	Year	Type	Length	Model	Chassis	Engine	Fuel Type	Average Price per Linear Foot When New	Adjusted Wheelbase	Approx. Towing Capacity	Gross Vehicle Weight Rating	Average Curb Weight
Mountain Aire	1999	MHA	38	MA3796	FO	6.8L	G	$3200	240	5,500	20,500	19,673

Livability Code: FT 30-90
Wheelbase-to-length ratio of 53% is considered ○ dangerous ⊙ fatiguing ○ good ○ excellent *
The approximate net payload of 827 pounds at 4% of GVWR on this model is ⊙ deficient ○ excessive ○ cautionary ○ good ○ excellent *
Total highway safety penalties are: 5 *   Value: 7 9   Durability: 7 8   Highway Control Rating: 3 9   Highway Safety: 3 4

Brand	Year	Type	Length	Model	Chassis	Engine	Fuel Type	Average Price per Linear Foot When New	Adjusted Wheelbase	Approx. Towing Capacity	Gross Vehicle Weight Rating	Average Curb Weight
Mountain Aire	1999	MHA	38	MA3797	FO	6.8L	G	$3200	240	5,500	20,500	19,673

Livability Code: FT 30-90
Wheelbase-to-length ratio of 53% is considered ○ dangerous ⊙ fatiguing ○ good ○ excellent *
The approximate net payload of 827 pounds at 4% of GVWR on this model is ⊙ deficient ○ excessive ○ cautionary ○ good ○ excellent *
Total highway safety penalties are: 5 *   Value: 7 9   Durability: 7 8   Highway Control Rating: 3 9   Highway Safety: 3 4

Brand	Year	Type	Length	Model	Chassis	Engine	Fuel Type	Average Price per Linear Foot When New	Adjusted Wheelbase	Approx. Towing Capacity	Gross Vehicle Weight Rating	Average Curb Weight
Mountain Aire	1999	MHA	38	MA3758	CH	7.4L	G	$3200	240	5,000	21,000	20,329

Livability Code: FT 30-90
Wheelbase-to-length ratio of 52% is considered ○ dangerous ⊙ fatiguing ○ good ○ excellent *
The approximate net payload of 671 pounds at 3% of GVWR on this model is ⊙ deficient ○ excessive ○ cautionary ○ good ○ excellent *
Total highway safety penalties are: 12 *   Value: 7 5   Durability: 7 8   Highway Control Rating: 3 1   Highway Safety: 1 9

Brand	Year	Type	Length	Model	Chassis	Engine	Fuel Type	Average Price per Linear Foot When New	Adjusted Wheelbase	Approx. Towing Capacity	Gross Vehicle Weight Rating	Average Curb Weight
Mountain Aire	1999	MHA	38	MA3762	CH	7.4L	G	$3200	240	5,000	21,000	20,329

Livability Code: FT 30-90
Wheelbase-to-length ratio of 52% is considered ○ dangerous ⊙ fatiguing ○ good ○ excellent *
The approximate net payload of 671 pounds at 3% of GVWR on this model is ⊙ deficient ○ excessive ○ cautionary ○ good ○ excellent *
Total highway safety penalties are: 12 *   Value: 7 5   Durability: 7 8   Highway Control Rating: 3 1   Highway Safety: 1 9

Brand	Year	Type	Length	Model	Chassis	Engine	Fuel Type	Average Price per Linear Foot When New	Adjusted Wheelbase	Approx. Towing Capacity	Gross Vehicle Weight Rating	Average Curb Weight
Mountain Aire	1999	MHA	38	MA3767	CH	7.4L	G	$3200	240	5,000	21,000	20,329

Livability Code: FT 30-90
Wheelbase-to-length ratio of 52% is considered ○ dangerous ⊙ fatiguing ○ good ○ excellent *
The approximate net payload of 671 pounds at 3% of GVWR on this model is ⊙ deficient ○ excessive ○ cautionary ○ good ○ excellent *
Total highway safety penalties are: 17 *   Value: 7 3   Durability: 7 8   Highway Control Rating: 3 1   Highway Safety: 1 4

Brand	Year	Type	Length	Model	Chassis	Engine	Fuel Type	Average Price per Linear Foot When New	Adjusted Wheelbase	Approx. Towing Capacity	Gross Vehicle Weight Rating	Average Curb Weight
Mountain Aire	1999	MHA	38	MA3780	CH	7.4L	G	$3200	240	5,000	21,000	20,329

Livability Code: FT 30-90
Wheelbase-to-length ratio of 52% is considered ○ dangerous ⊙ fatiguing ○ good ○ excellent *
The approximate net payload of 671 pounds at 3% of GVWR on this model is ⊙ deficient ○ excessive ○ cautionary ○ good ○ excellent *
Total highway safety penalties are: 12 *   Value: 7 5   Durability: 7 8   Highway Control Rating: 3 1   Highway Safety: 1 9

Brand	Year	Type	Length	Model	Chassis	Engine	Fuel Type	Average Price per Linear Foot When New	Adjusted Wheelbase	Approx. Towing Capacity	Gross Vehicle Weight Rating	Average Curb Weight
Mountain Aire	1999	MHA	38	MA3796	CH	7.4L	G	$3200	240	5,000	21,000	20,329

Livability Code: FT 30-90
Wheelbase-to-length ratio of 52% is considered ○ dangerous ⊙ fatiguing ○ good ○ excellent *
The approximate net payload of 671 pounds at 3% of GVWR on this model is ⊙ deficient ○ excessive ○ cautionary ○ good ○ excellent *
Total highway safety penalties are: 12 *   Value: 7 5   Durability: 7 8   Highway Control Rating: 3 1   Highway Safety: 1 9

Brand	Year	Type	Length	Model	Chassis	Engine	Fuel Type	Average Price per Linear Foot When New	Adjusted Wheelbase	Approx. Towing Capacity	Gross Vehicle Weight Rating	Average Curb Weight
Mountain Aire	1999	MHA	38	MA3797	CH	7.4L	G	$3200	240	5,000	21,000	20,329

Livability Code: FT 30-90
Wheelbase-to-length ratio of 52% is considered ○ dangerous ⊙ fatiguing ○ good ○ excellent *
The approximate net payload of 671 pounds at 3% of GVWR on this model is ⊙ deficient ○ excessive ○ cautionary ○ good ○ excellent *
Total highway safety penalties are: 12 *   Value: 7 5   Durability: 7 8   Highway Control Rating: 3 1   Highway Safety: 1 9

Brand	Year	Type	Length	Model	Chassis	Engine	Fuel Type	Average Price per Linear Foot When New	Adjusted Wheelbase	Approx. Towing Capacity	Gross Vehicle Weight Rating	Average Curb Weight
Mountain Aire	1999	MHA	40	MP4060	SP	CU325	D	$5000	276	1,500	31,000	25,924

Livability Code: FT 30-90
Wheelbase-to-length ratio of 58% is considered ○ dangerous ○ fatiguing ○ good ⊙ excellent *
The approximate net payload of 5076 pounds at 16% of GVWR on this model is ○ deficient ○ excessive ○ cautionary ○ good ⊙ excellent *
Total highway safety penalties are: 5 *   Value: 8 4   Durability: 7 8   Highway Control Rating: 1 0 0   Highway Safety: 9 5   ★★★

Brand	Year	Type	Length	Model	Chassis	Engine	Fuel Type	Average Price per Linear Foot When New	Adjusted Wheelbase	Approx. Towing Capacity	Gross Vehicle Weight Rating	Average Curb Weight
Mountain Aire	1999	MHA	40	MP4064	SP	CU325	D	$5000	276	1,500	31,000	25,924

Livability Code: FT 30-90
Wheelbase-to-length ratio of 58% is considered ○ dangerous ○ fatiguing ○ good ⊙ excellent *
The approximate net payload of 5076 pounds at 16% of GVWR on this model is ○ deficient ○ excessive ○ cautionary ○ good ⊙ excellent *
Total highway safety penalties are: 10 *   Value: 8 1   Durability: 7 8   Highway Control Rating: 1 0 0   Highway Safety: 9 0   ★★★

Brand	Year	Type	Length	Model	Chassis	Engine	Fuel Type	Average Price per Linear Foot When New	Adjusted Wheelbase	Approx. Towing Capacity	Gross Vehicle Weight Rating	Average Curb Weight
Mountain Aire	1999	MHA	40	MP4080	SP	CU325	D	$5000	276	1,500	31,000	25,924

Livability Code: FT 30-90
Wheelbase-to-length ratio of 58% is considered ○ dangerous ○ fatiguing ○ good ⊙ excellent *
The approximate net payload of 5076 pounds at 16% of GVWR on this model is ○ deficient ○ excessive ○ cautionary ○ good ⊙ excellent *
Total highway safety penalties are: 5 *   Value: 8 4   Durability: 7 8   Highway Control Rating: 1 0 0   Highway Safety: 9 5   ★★★

Note: Safety ratings are based on the assumption that the engineering of the RV has allowed for proper balance by placing fresh, gray, and black holding tanks in a location so as not to change the balance of the RV when the tanks are empty or full. **Always double-check wheelbase, GVWR, and weights at front and rear axles.**

*See Section 1 for details on how conclusions are reached.

Brand	Year	Type	Length	Model	Chassis	Engine	Fuel Type	Average Price per Linear Foot When New	Adjusted Wheelbase	Approx. Towing Capacity	Gross Vehicle Weight Rating	Average Curb Weight
Mountain Aire	1999	MHA	40	MP4081	SP	CU325	D	$5000	276	1,500	31,000	25,924

Mountain Aire — 1999 — MHA 40 — MP4081
Livability Code: FT 30-90
Wheelbase-to-length ratio of 58% is considered ○ dangerous ○ fatiguing ○ good ◉ excellent *
The approximate net payload of 5076 pounds at 16% of GVWR on this model is ○ deficient ○ excessive ○ cautionary ○ good ◉ excellent *
Total highway safety penalties are: 5 *   Value: 8 4   Durability: 7 8   Highway Control Rating: 1 0 0   Highway Safety: 9 5   ★★★

Mountain Aire — 1999 — MHA 40 — MP4059 — SP — CU325 — D — $5000 — 276 — 1,500 — 31,000 — 25,924
Livability Code: FT 30-90
Wheelbase-to-length ratio of 58% is considered ○ dangerous ○ fatiguing ○ good ◉ excellent *
The approximate net payload of 5076 pounds at 16% of GVWR on this model is ○ deficient ○ excessive ○ cautionary ○ good ◉ excellent *
Total highway safety penalties are: 5 *   Value: 8 4   Durability: 7 8   Highway Control Rating: 1 0 0   Highway Safety: 9 5   ★★★

Navigator — 1995 — MHA 39 — 38WD — SP — CU400 — D — $5900 — 246 — 4,000 — 33,200 — 27,245
Livability Code: FT 30-90
Wheelbase-to-length ratio of 53% is considered ○ dangerous ◉ fatiguing ○ good ○ excellent *
The approximate net payload of 5956 pounds at 18% of GVWR on this model is ○ deficient ○ excessive ○ cautionary ○ good ◉ excellent *
Total highway safety penalties are: 2 *   Value: 8 1   Durability: 8 0   Highway Control Rating: 7 3   Highway Safety: 7 1   ★★★

Navigator — 1995 — MHA 39 — 38WB — SP — CU300 — D — $5600 — 246 — 4,000 — 29,410 — 25,717
Livability Code: FT 30-90
Wheelbase-to-length ratio of 53% is considered ○ dangerous ◉ fatiguing ○ good ○ excellent *
The approximate net payload of 3693 pounds at 13% of GVWR on this model is ○ deficient ◉ excessive ○ cautionary ○ good ○ excellent *
Total highway safety penalties are: 2 *   Value: 8 1   Durability: 8 0   Highway Control Rating: 6 5   Highway Safety: 6 3   ★★

Navigator — 1996 — MHA 39 — 38WD — SP — CU300 — D — $4100 — 246 — 2,410 — 31,000 — 27,167
Livability Code: FT 30-90
Wheelbase-to-length ratio of 53% is considered ○ dangerous ◉ fatiguing ○ good ○ excellent *
The approximate net payload of 3833 pounds at 12% of GVWR on this model is ○ deficient ○ excessive ○ cautionary ○ good ○ excellent *
Total highway safety penalties are: 2 *   Value: 8 1   Durability: 8 0   Highway Control Rating: 6 4   Highway Safety: 6 2   ★★

Navigator — 1996 — MHA 39 — 38WD — SP — CU400 — D — $4300 — 246 — 4,000 — 33,200 — 29,167
Livability Code: FT 30-90
Wheelbase-to-length ratio of 53% is considered ○ dangerous ◉ fatiguing ○ good ○ excellent *
The approximate net payload of 4033 pounds at 12% of GVWR on this model is ○ deficient ○ excessive ○ cautionary ○ good ○ excellent *
Total highway safety penalties are: 2 *   Value: 8 1   Durability: 8 0   Highway Control Rating: 6 3   Highway Safety: 6 1   ★★

Navigator — 1996 — MHA 40 — 40CD — SP — CU300 — D — $4200 — 262 — 2,410 — 31,000 — 27,550
Livability Code: FT 30-90
Wheelbase-to-length ratio of 55% is considered ○ dangerous ○ fatiguing ◉ good ○ excellent *
The approximate net payload of 3450 pounds at 11% of GVWR on this model is ○ deficient ○ excessive ○ cautionary ○ good ○ excellent *
Total highway safety penalties are: 2 *   Value: 8 1   Durability: 8 0   Highway Control Rating: 8 6   Highway Safety: 8 4   ★★★★

Navigator — 1996 — MHA 40 — 40WD — SP — CU300 — D — $4200 — 262 — 2,410 — 31,000 — 27,550
Livability Code: FT 30-90
Wheelbase-to-length ratio of 55% is considered ○ dangerous ○ fatiguing ◉ good ○ excellent *
The approximate net payload of 3450 pounds at 11% of GVWR on this model is ○ deficient ○ excessive ○ cautionary ◉ good ○ excellent *
Total highway safety penalties are: 2 *   Value: 8 1   Durability: 8 0   Highway Control Rating: 8 6   Highway Safety: 8 4   ★★★★

Navigator — 1996 — MHA 40 — 40WDS-sl — SP — CU300 — D — $4300 — 262 — 2,410 — 31,000 — 28,600
Livability Code: FT 30-90
Wheelbase-to-length ratio of 55% is considered ○ dangerous ○ fatiguing ◉ good ○ excellent *
The approximate net payload of 2400 pounds at 8% of GVWR on this model is ○ deficient ○ excessive ◉ cautionary ○ good ○ excellent *
Total highway safety penalties are: 7 *   Value: 7 8   Durability: 8 0   Highway Control Rating: 6 8   Highway Safety: 6 1   ★★

Navigator — 1996 — MHA 40 — 40CD — SP — CU400 — D — $4400 — 262 — 4,000 — 33,200 — 29,500
Livability Code: FT 30-90
Wheelbase-to-length ratio of 55% is considered ○ dangerous ○ fatiguing ◉ good ○ excellent *
The approximate net payload of 3700 pounds at 11% of GVWR on this model is ○ deficient ○ excessive ○ cautionary ○ good ○ excellent *
Total highway safety penalties are: 2 *   Value: 8 1   Durability: 8 0   Highway Control Rating: 8 6   Highway Safety: 8 4   ★★★★

Navigator — 1996 — MHA 40 — 40WD — SP — CU400 — D — $4400 — 262 — 4,000 — 33,200 — 29,500
Livability Code: FT 30-90
Wheelbase-to-length ratio of 55% is considered ○ dangerous ○ fatiguing ◉ good ○ excellent *
The approximate net payload of 3700 pounds at 11% of GVWR on this model is ○ deficient ○ excessive ○ cautionary ○ good ○ excellent *
Total highway safety penalties are: 2 *   Value: 8 1   Durability: 8 0   Highway Control Rating: 8 6   Highway Safety: 8 4   ★★★★

Navigator — 1996 — MHA 40 — 40WDS-sl — SP — CU400 — D — $4500 — 262 — 4,000 — 33,200 — 30,600
Livability Code: FT 30-90
Wheelbase-to-length ratio of 55% is considered ○ dangerous ○ fatiguing ◉ good ○ excellent *
The approximate net payload of 2600 pounds at 8% of GVWR on this model is ○ deficient ○ excessive ◉ cautionary ○ good ○ excellent *
Total highway safety penalties are: 7 *   Value: 7 8   Durability: 8 0   Highway Control Rating: 6 8   Highway Safety: 6 1   ★★

Note: Safety ratings are based on the assumption that the engineering of the RV has allowed for proper balance by placing fresh, gray, and black holding tanks in a location so as not to change the balance of the RV when the tanks are empty or full. **Always double-check wheelbase, GVWR, and weights at front and rear axles.**

See Section 1 for details on how conclusions are reached.

Section 2: The Ratings

Brand	Year	Type	Length	Model	Chassis	Engine	Fuel Type	Average Price per Linear Foot When New	Adjusted Wheelbase	Approx. Towing Capacity	Gross Vehicle Weight Rating	Average Curb Weight
Navigator	1997	MHA	39	38 WD	RO	CU325	D	$4400	246	4,500	34,700	30,702

Livability Code: FT 30-90

Wheelbase-to-length ratio of 53% is considered ○ dangerous ◉ fatiguing ○ good ○ excellent *

The approximate net payload of 3998 pounds at 12% of GVWR on this model is ○ deficient ○ excessive ○ cautionary ◉ good ○ excellent *

Total highway safety penalties are: 2 *   Value: 8 1   Durability: 8 0   Highway Control Rating: 6 3   Highway Safety: 6 1   ★★

Brand	Year	Type	Length	Model	Chassis	Engine	Fuel Type	Price/Lin.Ft	Wheelbase	Towing	GVWR	Curb Wt
Navigator	1997	MHA	39	38 WDS	RO	CU325	D	$4400	246	4,500	34,700	31,602

Livability Code: FT 30-90

Wheelbase-to-length ratio of 53% is considered ○ dangerous ◉ fatiguing ○ good ○ excellent *

The approximate net payload of 3098 pounds at 9% of GVWR on this model is ○ deficient ○ excessive ◉ cautionary ○ good ○ excellent *

Total highway safety penalties are: 7 *   Value: 7 8   Durability: 8 0   Highway Control Rating: 5 4   Highway Safety: 4 7

Brand	Year	Type	Length	Model	Chassis	Engine	Fuel Type	Price/Lin.Ft	Wheelbase	Towing	GVWR	Curb Wt
Navigator	1997	MHA	40	40 WD	RO	CU325	D	$4300	262	4,500	34,700	31,222

Livability Code: FT 30-90

Wheelbase-to-length ratio of 55% is considered ○ dangerous ○ fatiguing ◉ good ○ excellent *

The approximate net payload of 3478 pounds at 10% of GVWR on this model is ○ deficient ○ excessive ○ cautionary ◉ good ○ excellent *

Total highway safety penalties are: 2 *   Value: 8 1   Durability: 8 0   Highway Control Rating: 8 5   Highway Safety: 8 3   ★★★★

Brand	Year	Type	Length	Model	Chassis	Engine	Fuel Type	Price/Lin.Ft	Wheelbase	Towing	GVWR	Curb Wt
Navigator	1997	MHA	40	40 WDS2	RO	CU325	D	$5400	262	4,500	34,700	32,122

Livability Code: FT 30-90

Wheelbase-to-length ratio of 55% is considered ○ dangerous ○ fatiguing ◉ good ○ excellent *

The approximate net payload of 2578 pounds at 7% of GVWR on this model is ○ deficient ○ excessive ◉ cautionary ○ good ○ excellent *

Total highway safety penalties are: 7 *   Value: 7 8   Durability: 8 0   Highway Control Rating: 6 3   Highway Safety: 5 6   ★

Brand	Year	Type	Length	Model	Chassis	Engine	Fuel Type	Price/Lin.Ft	Wheelbase	Towing	GVWR	Curb Wt
Navigator	1997	MHA	40	40 CD	RO	CU325	D	$4500	262	4,500	34,700	31,222

Livability Code: FT 30-90

Wheelbase-to-length ratio of 55% is considered ○ dangerous ○ fatiguing ◉ good ○ excellent *

The approximate net payload of 3478 pounds at 10% of GVWR on this model is ○ deficient ○ excessive ○ cautionary ◉ good ○ excellent *

Total highway safety penalties are: 2 *   Value: 8 1   Durability: 8 0   Highway Control Rating: 8 5   Highway Safety: 8 3   ★★★★

Brand	Year	Type	Length	Model	Chassis	Engine	Fuel Type	Price/Lin.Ft	Wheelbase	Towing	GVWR	Curb Wt
Navigator	1997	MHA	40	40 WDS	RO	CU325	D	$4500	262	4,500	34,700	32,122

Livability Code: FT 30-90

Wheelbase-to-length ratio of 55% is considered ○ dangerous ○ fatiguing ◉ good ○ excellent *

The approximate net payload of 2578 pounds at 7% of GVWR on this model is ○ deficient ○ excessive ◉ cautionary ○ good ○ excellent *

Total highway safety penalties are: 7 *   Value: 7 8   Durability: 8 0   Highway Control Rating: 6 3   Highway Safety: 5 6   ★

Brand	Year	Type	Length	Model	Chassis	Engine	Fuel Type	Price/Lin.Ft	Wheelbase	Towing	GVWR	Curb Wt
Navigator	1998	MHA	39	38WD	RO	CU325	D	$4900	246	4,500	34,700	30,702

Livability Code: FT 30-90

Wheelbase-to-length ratio of 53% is considered ○ dangerous ◉ fatiguing ○ good ○ excellent *

The approximate net payload of 3998 pounds at 12% of GVWR on this model is ○ deficient ○ excessive ○ cautionary ◉ good ○ excellent *

Total highway safety penalties are: 2 *   Value: 8 1   Durability: 8 0   Highway Control Rating: 6 3   Highway Safety: 6 1   ★★

Brand	Year	Type	Length	Model	Chassis	Engine	Fuel Type	Price/Lin.Ft	Wheelbase	Towing	GVWR	Curb Wt
Navigator	1998	MHA	39	38WDS	RO	CU325	D	$4900	246	4,500	34,700	31,602

Livability Code: FT 30-90

Wheelbase-to-length ratio of 53% is considered ○ dangerous ◉ fatiguing ○ good ○ excellent *

The approximate net payload of 3098 pounds at 9% of GVWR on this model is ○ deficient ○ excessive ◉ cautionary ○ good ○ excellent *

Total highway safety penalties are: 12 *   Value: 7 6   Durability: 8 0   Highway Control Rating: 5 4   Highway Safety: 4 2

Brand	Year	Type	Length	Model	Chassis	Engine	Fuel Type	Price/Lin.Ft	Wheelbase	Towing	GVWR	Curb Wt
Navigator	1998	MHA	40	40CD	RO	CU325	D	$4800	262	4,500	34,700	31,222

Livability Code: FT 30-90

Wheelbase-to-length ratio of 55% is considered ○ dangerous ○ fatiguing ◉ good ○ excellent *

The approximate net payload of 3478 pounds at 10% of GVWR on this model is ○ deficient ○ excessive ○ cautionary ◉ good ○ excellent *

Total highway safety penalties are: 2 *   Value: 8 1   Durability: 8 0   Highway Control Rating: 8 5   Highway Safety: 8 3   ★★★★

Brand	Year	Type	Length	Model	Chassis	Engine	Fuel Type	Price/Lin.Ft	Wheelbase	Towing	GVWR	Curb Wt
Navigator	1998	MHA	40	40WD	RO	CU325	D	$4800	262	4,500	34,700	31,851

Livability Code: FT 30-90

Wheelbase-to-length ratio of 55% is considered ○ dangerous ○ fatiguing ◉ good ○ excellent *

The approximate net payload of 2849 pounds at 8% of GVWR on this model is ○ deficient ○ excessive ◉ cautionary ○ good ○ excellent *

Total highway safety penalties are: 2 *   Value: 8 1   Durability: 8 0   Highway Control Rating: 6 8   Highway Safety: 6 6   ★★

Brand	Year	Type	Length	Model	Chassis	Engine	Fuel Type	Price/Lin.Ft	Wheelbase	Towing	GVWR	Curb Wt
Navigator	1998	MHA	40	40WDS	RO	CU325	D	$4800	262	4,500	34,700	32,122

Livability Code: FT 30-90

Wheelbase-to-length ratio of 55% is considered ○ dangerous ○ fatiguing ◉ good ○ excellent *

The approximate net payload of 2578 pounds at 7% of GVWR on this model is ○ deficient ○ excessive ◉ cautionary ○ good ○ excellent *

Total highway safety penalties are: 12 *   Value: 7 6   Durability: 8 0   Highway Control Rating: 6 3   Highway Safety: 5 1   ★

Brand	Year	Type	Length	Model	Chassis	Engine	Fuel Type	Price/Lin.Ft	Wheelbase	Towing	GVWR	Curb Wt
Navigator	1998	MHA	40	40WDS2	RO	CU325	D	$4800	262	4,500	34,700	32,122

Livability Code: FT 30-90

Wheelbase-to-length ratio of 55% is considered ○ dangerous ○ fatiguing ◉ good ○ excellent *

The approximate net payload of 2578 pounds at 7% of GVWR on this model is ○ deficient ○ excessive ◉ cautionary ○ good ○ excellent *

Total highway safety penalties are: 12 *   Value: 7 6   Durability: 8 0   Highway Control Rating: 6 3   Highway Safety: 5 1   ★

Note: Safety ratings are based on the assumption that the engineering of the RV has allowed for proper balance by placing fresh, gray, and black holding tanks in a location so as not to change the balance of the RV when the tanks are empty or full. **Always double-check wheelbase, GVWR, and weights at front and rear axles.**

*See Section 1 for details on how conclusions are reached.

Section 2: The Ratings

Brand	Year	Type	Length	Model	Chassis	Engine	Fuel Type	Average Price per Linear Foot When New	Adjusted Wheelbase	Approx. Towing Capacity	Gross Vehicle Weight Rating	Average Curb Weight

Navigator 1998 MHA 40 40WDS2 RO CU325 D $4800 262 4,500 34,700 32,122
Livability Code: FT 30-90
Wheelbase-to-length ratio of 55% is considered ○ dangerous ○ fatiguing ● good ○ excellent *
The approximate net payload of 2578 pounds at 7% of GVWR on this model is ○ deficient ○ excessive ● cautionary ○ good ○ excellent *
Total highway safety penalties are: 12* Value: 7 6 Durability: 8 0 Highway Control Rating: 6 3 Highway Safety: 5 1 ★

Navigator 1999 MHA 39 38WDS op eng RO CU450 D $4900 246 10,000 35,300 30,984
Livability Code: FT 30-90
Wheelbase-to-length ratio of 53% is considered ○ dangerous ● fatiguing ○ good ○ excellent *
The approximate net payload of 4316 pounds at 12% of GVWR on this model is ○ deficient ○ excessive ○ cautionary ● good ○ excellent *
Total highway safety penalties are: 12* Value: 8 1 Durability: 8 0 Highway Control Rating: 6 6 Highway Safety: 5 4 ★

Navigator 1999 MHA 39 38WDS RO CU350 D $4900 246 10,000 35,300 30,484
Livability Code: FT 30-90
Wheelbase-to-length ratio of 53% is considered ○ dangerous ● fatiguing ○ good ○ excellent *
The approximate net payload of 4816 pounds at 14% of GVWR on this model is ○ deficient ○ excessive ○ cautionary ● good ○ excellent *
Total highway safety penalties are: 12* Value: 8 1 Durability: 8 0 Highway Control Rating: 7 0 Highway Safety: 5 8 ★

Navigator 1999 MHA 41 40PBS RO CU350 D $4600 262 10,000 35,300 31,096
Livability Code: FT 30-90
Wheelbase-to-length ratio of 53% is considered ○ dangerous ● fatiguing ○ good ○ excellent *
The approximate net payload of 4204 pounds at 12% of GVWR on this model is ○ deficient ○ excessive ○ cautionary ● good ○ excellent *
Total highway safety penalties are: 12* Value: 8 1 Durability: 8 0 Highway Control Rating: 6 8 Highway Safety: 5 6 ★

Navigator 1999 MHA 41 40WDS RO CU350 D $4600 262 10,000 35,300 31,096
Livability Code: FT 30-90
Wheelbase-to-length ratio of 53% is considered ○ dangerous ● fatiguing ○ good ○ excellent *
The approximate net payload of 4204 pounds at 12% of GVWR on this model is ○ deficient ○ excessive ○ cautionary ● good ○ excellent *
Total highway safety penalties are: 12* Value: 8 1 Durability: 8 0 Highway Control Rating: 6 8 Highway Safety: 5 6 ★

Navigator 1999 MHA 41 40PBS op eng RO CU450 D $4600 262 10,000 35,300 31,596
Livability Code: FT 30-90
Wheelbase-to-length ratio of 53% is considered ○ dangerous ● fatiguing ○ good ○ excellent *
The approximate net payload of 3704 pounds at 10% of GVWR on this model is ○ deficient ○ excessive ○ cautionary ● good ○ excellent *
Total highway safety penalties are: 12* Value: 8 1 Durability: 8 0 Highway Control Rating: 6 5 Highway Safety: 5 3 ★

Navigator 1999 MHA 41 40WDS op eng RO CU450 D $4600 262 10,000 35,300 31,596
Livability Code: FT 30-90
Wheelbase-to-length ratio of 53% is considered ○ dangerous ● fatiguing ○ good ○ excellent *
The approximate net payload of 3704 pounds at 10% of GVWR on this model is ○ deficient ○ excessive ○ cautionary ● good ○ excellent *
Total highway safety penalties are: 12* Value: 8 1 Durability: 8 0 Highway Control Rating: 6 5 Highway Safety: 5 3 ★

Navigator 1999 MHA 42 42CDS RO CU350 D $4500 260 1,500 e 45,300 36,524
Livability Code: FT 30-90
Wheelbase-to-length ratio of 51% is considered ○ dangerous ● fatiguing ○ good ○ excellent *
The approximate net payload of 8776 pounds at 19% of GVWR on this model is ○ deficient ○ excessive ○ cautionary ○ good ● excellent *
Total highway safety penalties are: 12* Value: 8 1 Durability: 8 0 Highway Control Rating: 6 2 Highway Safety: 5 0 ★

Navigator 1999 MHA 42 42DSS RO CU350 D $4500 260 10,000 45,300 36,524
Livability Code: FT 30-90
Wheelbase-to-length ratio of 51% is considered ○ dangerous ● fatiguing ○ good ○ excellent *
The approximate net payload of 8776 pounds at 19% of GVWR on this model is ○ deficient ○ excessive ○ cautionary ○ good ● excellent *
Total highway safety penalties are: 12* Value: 8 1 Durability: 8 0 Highway Control Rating: 6 2 Highway Safety: 5 0 ★

Navigator 1999 MHA 42 42CDS op eng RO CU450 D $4500 260 1,500 e 45,300 37,024
Livability Code: FT 30-90
Wheelbase-to-length ratio of 51% is considered ○ dangerous ● fatiguing ○ good ○ excellent *
The approximate net payload of 8276 pounds at 18% of GVWR on this model is ○ deficient ○ excessive ○ cautionary ○ good ● excellent *
Total highway safety penalties are: 12* Value: 8 1 Durability: 8 0 Highway Control Rating: 6 1 Highway Safety: 4 9

Navigator 1999 MHA 42 42DSS op eng RO CU450 D $4500 260 10,000 45,300 37,024
Livability Code: FT 30-90
Wheelbase-to-length ratio of 51% is considered ○ dangerous ● fatiguing ○ good ○ excellent *
The approximate net payload of 8276 pounds at 18% of GVWR on this model is ○ deficient ○ excessive ○ cautionary ○ good ● excellent *
Total highway safety penalties are: 12* Value: 8 1 Durability: 8 0 Highway Control Rating: 6 1 Highway Safety: 4 9

Newell 1997 MHA all models custom ? ?
Livability Code: FT 30-90
Wheelbase-to-length ratio of ? is considered ○ dangerous ○ fatiguing ○ good ○ excellent *
The approximate net payload of pounds at of GVWR on this model is ○ deficient ○ excessive ○ cautionary ○ good ○ excellent *
Total highway safety penalties are: 0* Value: 0 Durability: 9 0 Highway Control Rating: 0 Highway Safety: 0

Note: Safety ratings are based on the assumption that the engineering of the RV has allowed for proper balance by placing fresh, gray, and black holding tanks in a location so as not to change the balance of the RV when the tanks are empty or full. **Always double-check wheelbase, GVWR, and weights at front and rear axles.**

*See Section 1 for details on how conclusions are reached.

Section 2: The Ratings

Brand	Year	Type	Length	Model	Chassis	Engine	Fuel Type	Average Price per Linear Foot When New	Adjusted Wheelbase	Approx. Towing Capacity	Gross Vehicle Weight Rating	Average Curb Weight
Newell	1998	MHA		all models custom								?

Livability Code: FT 30-90 — Wheelbase-to-length ratio of ? is considered ○ dangerous ○ fatiguing ○ good ○ excellent *
The approximate net payload of __ pounds at __ of GVWR on this model is ○ deficient ○ excessive ○ cautionary ○ good ○ excellent *
Total highway safety penalties are: 0 * — Value: 0 — Durability: 9 0 — Highway Control Rating: 0 — Highway Safety: 0

Brand	Year	Type	Length	Model	Chassis	Engine	Fuel Type	Price/LF	Adj. Wheelbase	Towing	GVWR	Curb Wt
Newell	1999	MHA		all models custom								?

Livability Code: FT 30-90 — Wheelbase-to-length ratio of ? is considered ○ dangerous ○ fatiguing ○ good ○ excellent *
The approximate net payload of __ pounds at __ of GVWR on this model is ○ deficient ○ excessive ○ cautionary ○ good ○ excellent *
Total highway safety penalties are: 0 * — Value: 0 — Durability: 9 0 — Highway Control Rating: 0 — Highway Safety: 0

Brand	Year	Type	Length	Model	Chassis	Engine	Fuel Type	Price/LF	Adj. Wheelbase	Towing	GVWR	Curb Wt
Newell 2000	1990	MHA	43	42-102	NW	De	D	$8200	306 T	1,500	45,200	39,981

Livability Code: FT 30-90 — Wheelbase-to-length ratio of 60% is considered ○ dangerous ○ fatiguing ○ good ◉ excellent *
The approximate net payload of 5219 pounds at 12% of GVWR on this model is ○ deficient ○ excessive ○ cautionary ◉ good ○ excellent *
Total highway safety penalties are: 4 * — Value: 9 4 — Durability: 9 0 — Highway Control Rating: 1 0 0 — Highway Safety: 9 6 — ★★★★★

Brand	Year	Type	Length	Model	Chassis	Engine	Fuel Type	Price/LF	Adj. Wheelbase	Towing	GVWR	Curb Wt
Newell 2000	1991	MHA	44	43-102	NW	De	D	$8000	318 T	1,500	45,200	40,408

Livability Code: FT 30-90 — Wheelbase-to-length ratio of 61% is considered ○ dangerous ○ fatiguing ○ good ◉ excellent *
The approximate net payload of 4792 pounds at 11% of GVWR on this model is ○ deficient ○ excessive ○ cautionary ◉ good ○ excellent *
Total highway safety penalties are: 4 * — Value: 9 4 — Durability: 9 0 — Highway Control Rating: 1 0 0 — Highway Safety: 9 6 — ★★★★★

Brand	Year	Type	Length	Model	Chassis	Engine	Fuel Type	Price/LF	Adj. Wheelbase	Towing	GVWR	Curb Wt
Olympic	1996	MHC	22	OL-22B	FO	7.5L	G	$2100	158	3,500	12,400	9,980

Livability Code: VA 30-90 — Wheelbase-to-length ratio of 60% is considered ○ dangerous ○ fatiguing ○ good ◉ excellent *
The approximate net payload of 2420 pounds at 20% of GVWR on this model is ○ deficient ○ excessive ○ cautionary ○ good ◉ excellent *
Total highway safety penalties are: 2 * — Value: 7 7 — Durability: 7 0 — Highway Control Rating: 1 0 0 — Highway Safety: 9 8 — ★★★

Brand	Year	Type	Length	Model	Chassis	Engine	Fuel Type	Price/LF	Adj. Wheelbase	Towing	GVWR	Curb Wt
Olympic	1996	MHC	23	OL-23D	FO	7.5L	G	$2000	158	3,500	12,400	10,220

Livability Code: VA 30-90 — Wheelbase-to-length ratio of 57% is considered ○ dangerous ○ fatiguing ◉ good ○ excellent *
The approximate net payload of 2180 pounds at 18% of GVWR on this model is ○ deficient ○ excessive ○ cautionary ○ good ◉ excellent *
Total highway safety penalties are: 2 * — Value: 7 7 — Durability: 7 0 — Highway Control Rating: 1 0 0 — Highway Safety: 9 8 — ★★★

Brand	Year	Type	Length	Model	Chassis	Engine	Fuel Type	Price/LF	Adj. Wheelbase	Towing	GVWR	Curb Wt
Olympic	1996	MHC	29	OL-29M	FO	7.5L	G	$1700	190	3,500	12,400	11,660

Livability Code: VA 30-90 — Wheelbase-to-length ratio of 55% is considered ○ dangerous ○ fatiguing ◉ good ○ excellent *
The approximate net payload of 740 pounds at 6% of GVWR on this model is ◉ deficient ○ excessive ○ cautionary ○ good ○ excellent *
Total highway safety penalties are: 2 * — Value: 7 7 — Durability: 7 0 — Highway Control Rating: 5 6 — Highway Safety: 5 4 — ★

Brand	Year	Type	Length	Model	Chassis	Engine	Fuel Type	Price/LF	Adj. Wheelbase	Towing	GVWR	Curb Wt
Olympic	1996	MHC	29	OL-29K	FO	7.5L	G	$1700	190	3,500	12,400	11,660

Livability Code: VA 30-90 — Wheelbase-to-length ratio of 55% is considered ○ dangerous ○ fatiguing ◉ good ○ excellent *
The approximate net payload of 740 pounds at 6% of GVWR on this model is ◉ deficient ○ excessive ○ cautionary ○ good ○ excellent *
Total highway safety penalties are: 2 * — Value: 7 7 — Durability: 7 0 — Highway Control Rating: 5 6 — Highway Safety: 5 4 — ★

Brand	Year	Type	Length	Model	Chassis	Engine	Fuel Type	Price/LF	Adj. Wheelbase	Towing	GVWR	Curb Wt
Overland	1996	MHA	32	32	FR		D	$3700	190	5,000	23,000	18,776

Livability Code:
Wheelbase-to-length ratio of 49% is considered ◉ dangerous ○ fatiguing ○ good ○ excellent *
The approximate net payload of 4224 pounds at 18% of GVWR on this model is ○ deficient ○ excessive ○ cautionary ○ good ◉ excellent *
Total highway safety penalties are: 2 * — Value: 7 9 — Durability: 7 5 — Highway Control Rating: 4 5 — Highway Safety: 4 3

Brand	Year	Type	Length	Model	Chassis	Engine	Fuel Type	Price/LF	Adj. Wheelbase	Towing	GVWR	Curb Wt
Overland	1996	MHA	34	34	FR		D	$3600	208	5,000	23,000	19,917

Livability Code:
Wheelbase-to-length ratio of 51% is considered ○ dangerous ◉ fatiguing ○ good ○ excellent *
The approximate net payload of 3083 pounds at 13% of GVWR on this model is ○ deficient ○ excessive ○ cautionary ◉ good ○ excellent *
Total highway safety penalties are: 2 * — Value: 7 9 — Durability: 7 5 — Highway Control Rating: 4 3 — Highway Safety: 4 1

Brand	Year	Type	Length	Model	Chassis	Engine	Fuel Type	Price/LF	Adj. Wheelbase	Towing	GVWR	Curb Wt
Overland	1996	MHA	36	36	FR		D	$3500	228	5,000	23,000	20,783

Livability Code:
Wheelbase-to-length ratio of 53% is considered ○ dangerous ◉ fatiguing ○ good ○ excellent *
The approximate net payload of 2217 pounds at 10% of GVWR on this model is ○ deficient ○ excessive ○ cautionary ◉ good ○ excellent *
Total highway safety penalties are: 2 * — Value: 7 9 — Durability: 7 5 — Highway Control Rating: 5 7 — Highway Safety: 5 5 — ★

Brand	Year	Type	Length	Model	Chassis	Engine	Fuel Type	Price/LF	Adj. Wheelbase	Towing	GVWR	Curb Wt
Overland	1996	MHA	39	39	FR		D	$4000	252	5,000	29,000	24,212

Livability Code:
Wheelbase-to-length ratio of 54% is considered ○ dangerous ○ fatiguing ◉ good ○ excellent *
The approximate net payload of 4788 pounds at 17% of GVWR on this model is ○ deficient ○ excessive ○ cautionary ○ good ◉ excellent *
Total highway safety penalties are: 2 * — Value: 7 9 — Durability: 7 5 — Highway Control Rating: 8 1 — Highway Safety: 7 9 — ★★★

Note: Safety ratings are based on the assumption that the engineering of the RV has allowed for proper balance by placing fresh, gray, and black holding tanks in a location so as not to change the balance of the RV when the tanks are empty or full. **Always double-check wheelbase, GVWR, and weights at front and rear axles.**

*See Section 1 for details on how conclusions are reached.

Section 2: The Ratings

Brand	Year	Type	Length	Model	Chassis	Engine	Fuel Type	Average Price per Linear Foot When New	Adjusted Wheelbase	Approx. Towing Capacity	Gross Vehicle Weight Rating	Average Curb Weight
Overland	1996	MHA	43	43	SP		D	$5700	292	2,500	36,000	29,639

Livability Code:
Wheelbase-to-length ratio of 57% is considered ○ dangerous ○ fatiguing ● good ○ excellent *
The approximate net payload of 6361 pounds at 18% of GVWR on this model is ○ deficient ○ excessive ○ cautionary ○ good ● excellent *
Total highway safety penalties are: 2 *   Value: **7 9**   Durability: **7 5**   Highway Control Rating: **1 0 0**   Highway Safety: **9 8**   ★★★

Brand	Year	Type	Length	Model	Chassis	Engine	Fuel Type		Adj. Wheelbase	Towing	GVWR	Curb Wt
Overland Lorado	1997	MHA	37	LO 3741 - SO	FR	CA275	D	$4400	228	5,000	24,850	23,527

Livability Code: SB 30-90
Wheelbase-to-length ratio of 51% is considered ○ dangerous ● fatiguing ○ good ○ excellent *
The approximate net payload of 1323 pounds at 5% of GVWR on this model is ● deficient ○ excessive ○ cautionary ○ good ○ excellent *
Total highway safety penalties are: 7 *   Value: **7 6**   Durability: **7 5**   Highway Control Rating: **1 2**   Highway Safety: **5**

Overland Lorado	1997	MHA	37	LO 3742	FR	CA275	D	$4400	228	5,000	24,850	22,627

Livability Code: SB 30-90
Wheelbase-to-length ratio of 51% is considered ○ dangerous ● fatiguing ○ good ○ excellent *
The approximate net payload of 2223 pounds at 9% of GVWR on this model is ○ deficient ○ excessive ● cautionary ○ good ○ excellent *
Total highway safety penalties are: 2 *   Value: **7 9**   Durability: **7 5**   Highway Control Rating: **3 1**   Highway Safety: **2 9**

Overland Lorado	1997	MHA	41	LO 4140 FL	FR	CU300	D	$4000	276	5,000	29,410	25,075

Livability Code: SB 30-90
Wheelbase-to-length ratio of 56% is considered ○ dangerous ○ fatiguing ● good ○ excellent *
The approximate net payload of 4335 pounds at 15% of GVWR on this model is ○ deficient ○ excessive ○ cautionary ● good ○ excellent *
Total highway safety penalties are: 2 *   Value: **7 9**   Durability: **7 5**   Highway Control Rating: **9 2**   Highway Safety: **9 0**   ★★★

Overland Lorado	1997	MHA	41	LO 4141-SO FL	FR	CU300	D	$4000	276	5,000	29,410	25,925

Livability Code: SB 30-90
Wheelbase-to-length ratio of 56% is considered ○ dangerous ○ fatiguing ● good ○ excellent *
The approximate net payload of 3485 pounds at 12% of GVWR on this model is ○ deficient ○ excessive ○ cautionary ● good ○ excellent *
Total highway safety penalties are: 7 *   Value: **7 6**   Durability: **7 5**   Highway Control Rating: **8 6**   Highway Safety: **7 9**   ★★★

Overland Lorado	1997	MHA	41	LO 4143-SO FL	FR	CU300	D	$4000	276	5,000	29,410	25,910

Livability Code: SB 30-90
Wheelbase-to-length ratio of 56% is considered ○ dangerous ○ fatiguing ● good ○ excellent *
The approximate net payload of 3500 pounds at 12% of GVWR on this model is ○ deficient ○ excessive ○ cautionary ● good ○ excellent *
Total highway safety penalties are: 8 *   Value: **7 6**   Durability: **7 5**   Highway Control Rating: **8 6**   Highway Safety: **7 8**   ★★★

Overland Lorado	1999	MHA	35	LO 3540 FL	FR	CU275	D	$4900	208	5,000	26,350	23,839

Livability Code: SB 30-90
Wheelbase-to-length ratio of 49% is considered ● dangerous ○ fatiguing ○ good ○ excellent *
The approximate net payload of 2511 pounds at 10% of GVWR on this model is ○ deficient ○ excessive ○ cautionary ● good ○ excellent *
Total highway safety penalties are: 7 *   Value: **7 6**   Durability: **7 5**   Highway Control Rating: **3 9**   Highway Safety: **3 2**

Overland Lorado	1999	MHA	37	LO 3741-SO FL	FR	CU275	D	$4600	228	5,000	26,350	24,331

Livability Code: SB 30-90
Wheelbase-to-length ratio of 51% is considered ○ dangerous ● fatiguing ○ good ○ excellent *
The approximate net payload of 2019 pounds at 8% of GVWR on this model is ○ deficient ○ excessive ● cautionary ○ good ○ excellent *
Total highway safety penalties are: 7 *   Value: **7 6**   Durability: **7 5**   Highway Control Rating: **3 4**   Highway Safety: **2 7**

Overland Lorado	1999	MHA	37	LO 3742 FL	FR	CU275	D	$4600	228	5,000	26,350	24,619

Livability Code: SB 30-90
Wheelbase-to-length ratio of 51% is considered ○ dangerous ● fatiguing ○ good ○ excellent *
The approximate net payload of 1731 pounds at 7% of GVWR on this model is ○ deficient ○ excessive ● cautionary ○ good ○ excellent *
Total highway safety penalties are: 2 *   Value: **7 9**   Durability: **7 5**   Highway Control Rating: **2 8**   Highway Safety: **2 6**

Overland Lorado	1999	MHA	41	LO 4140 FL	FR	CU300	D	$4100	276	5,000	29,410	25,549

Livability Code: SB 30-90
Wheelbase-to-length ratio of 56% is considered ○ dangerous ○ fatiguing ● good ○ excellent *
The approximate net payload of 3861 pounds at 13% of GVWR on this model is ○ deficient ○ excessive ○ cautionary ● good ○ excellent *
Total highway safety penalties are: 2 *   Value: **7 9**   Durability: **7 5**   Highway Control Rating: **8 9**   Highway Safety: **8 7**   ★★★

Overland Lorado	1999	MHA	41	LO 4141-SO FL	FR	CU300	D	$4100	276	5,000	29,410	26,960

Livability Code: SB 30-90
Wheelbase-to-length ratio of 56% is considered ○ dangerous ○ fatiguing ● good ○ excellent *
The approximate net payload of 2450 pounds at 8% of GVWR on this model is ○ deficient ○ excessive ● cautionary ○ good ○ excellent *
Total highway safety penalties are: 8 *   Value: **7 6**   Durability: **7 5**   Highway Control Rating: **7 2**   Highway Safety: **6 4**   ★★

Overland Lorado	1999	MHA	41	LO 4145-SO FL	FR	CU300	D	$4100	276	5,000	29,410	27,254

Livability Code: SB 30-90
Wheelbase-to-length ratio of 56% is considered ○ dangerous ○ fatiguing ● good ○ excellent *
The approximate net payload of 2156 pounds at 7% of GVWR on this model is ○ deficient ○ excessive ● cautionary ○ good ○ excellent *
Total highway safety penalties are: 8 *   Value: **7 6**   Durability: **7 5**   Highway Control Rating: **6 6**   Highway Safety: **5 8**   ★

Note: Safety ratings are based on the assumption that the engineering of the RV has allowed for proper balance by placing fresh, gray, and black holding tanks in a location so as not to change the balance of the RV when the tanks are empty or full. **Always double-check wheelbase, GVWR, and weights at front and rear axles.**

*See Section 1 for details on how conclusions are reached.

Brand	Year	Type	Length	Model	Chassis	Engine	Fuel Type	Average Price per Linear Foot When New	Adjusted Wheel-base	Approx. Towing Capacity	Gross Vehicle Weight Rating	Average Curb Weight
Overland Lorado	1999	MHA	41	LO 4144-SO FL	FR	CU300	D	$4100	276	5,000	29,410	26,817

Livability Code: SB 30-90
Wheelbase-to-length ratio of 56% is considered ○ dangerous ○ fatiguing ◉ good ○ excellent *
The approximate net payload of 2593 pounds at 9% of GVWR on this model is ○ deficient ○ excessive ◉ cautionary ○ good ○ excellent *
Total highway safety penalties are: 7 * Value: 7 6 Durability: 7 5 Highway Control Rating: 7 7 Highway Safety: 7 0 ★★★

Brand	Year	Type	Length	Model	Chassis	Engine	Fuel Type	Price/Ft	Wheelbase	Towing	GVWR	Curb Wt
Overland Lorado	1999	MHA	41	Spartan 41	SP	CU325	D	$4100	276	9,000	31,000	28,168

Livability Code: SB 30-90
Wheelbase-to-length ratio of 56% is considered ○ dangerous ○ fatiguing ◉ good ○ excellent *
The approximate net payload of 2832 pounds at 9% of GVWR on this model is ○ deficient ○ excessive ◉ cautionary ○ good ○ excellent *
Total highway safety penalties are: 2 * Value: 7 9 Durability: 7 5 Highway Control Rating: 7 8 Highway Safety: 7 6 ★★★

Brand	Year	Type	Length	Model	Chassis	Engine	Fuel Type	Price/Ft	Wheelbase	Towing	GVWR	Curb Wt
Overland Osprey	1997	MHA	41	4012-SO FL	FR	CU300	D	$4000	276	5,000	29,410	28,273

Livability Code:
Wheelbase-to-length ratio of 56% is considered ○ dangerous ○ fatiguing ◉ good ○ excellent *
The approximate net payload of 1137 pounds at 4% of GVWR on this model is ◉ deficient ○ excessive ○ cautionary ○ good ○ excellent *
Total highway safety penalties are: 7 * Value: 7 6 Durability: 7 5 Highway Control Rating: 5 8 Highway Safety: 5 1 ★

Brand	Year	Type	Length	Model	Chassis	Engine	Fuel Type	Price/Ft	Wheelbase	Towing	GVWR	Curb Wt
Overland Osprey	1997	MHA	41	4020 FL	FR	CU300	D	$4100	276	5,000	29,410	27,373

Livability Code:
Wheelbase-to-length ratio of 56% is considered ○ dangerous ○ fatiguing ◉ good ○ excellent *
The approximate net payload of 2037 pounds at 7% of GVWR on this model is ○ deficient ○ excessive ◉ cautionary ○ good ○ excellent *
Total highway safety penalties are: 2 * Value: 7 9 Durability: 7 5 Highway Control Rating: 6 6 Highway Safety: 6 4 ★★

Brand	Year	Type	Length	Model	Chassis	Engine	Fuel Type	Price/Ft	Wheelbase	Towing	GVWR	Curb Wt
Overland Osprey	1997	MHA	41	4021-SO FL	FR	CU300	D	$4100	276	5,000	29,410	28,273

Livability Code:
Wheelbase-to-length ratio of 56% is considered ○ dangerous ○ fatiguing ◉ good ○ excellent *
The approximate net payload of 1137 pounds at 4% of GVWR on this model is ◉ deficient ○ excessive ○ cautionary ○ good ○ excellent *
Total highway safety penalties are: 7 * Value: 7 6 Durability: 7 5 Highway Control Rating: 5 8 Highway Safety: 5 1 ★

Brand	Year	Type	Length	Model	Chassis	Engine	Fuel Type	Price/Ft	Wheelbase	Towing	GVWR	Curb Wt
Overland Osprey	1997	MHA	41	4012-SO SP	SP	CU400	D	$4100	276	5,000	33,000	30,068

Livability Code:
Wheelbase-to-length ratio of 56% is considered ○ dangerous ○ fatiguing ◉ good ○ excellent *
The approximate net payload of 2932 pounds at 9% of GVWR on this model is ○ deficient ○ excessive ◉ cautionary ○ good ○ excellent *
Total highway safety penalties are: 7 * Value: 7 6 Durability: 7 5 Highway Control Rating: 7 7 Highway Safety: 7 0 ★★★

Brand	Year	Type	Length	Model	Chassis	Engine	Fuel Type	Price/Ft	Wheelbase	Towing	GVWR	Curb Wt
Overland Osprey	1997	MHA	41	4020 SP	SP	CU400	D	$4100	276	5,000	33,000	29,168

Livability Code:
Wheelbase-to-length ratio of 56% is considered ○ dangerous ○ fatiguing ◉ good ○ excellent *
The approximate net payload of 3832 pounds at 12% of GVWR on this model is ○ deficient ○ excessive ○ cautionary ◉ good ○ excellent *
Total highway safety penalties are: 2 * Value: 7 9 Durability: 7 5 Highway Control Rating: 8 6 Highway Safety: 8 4 ★★★

Brand	Year	Type	Length	Model	Chassis	Engine	Fuel Type	Price/Ft	Wheelbase	Towing	GVWR	Curb Wt
Overland Osprey	1997	MHA	41	4021-SO SP	SP	CU400	D	$4100	276	5,000	33,000	30,068

Livability Code:
Wheelbase-to-length ratio of 56% is considered ○ dangerous ○ fatiguing ◉ good ○ excellent *
The approximate net payload of 2932 pounds at 9% of GVWR on this model is ○ deficient ○ excessive ◉ cautionary ○ good ○ excellent *
Total highway safety penalties are: 7 * Value: 7 6 Durability: 7 5 Highway Control Rating: 7 7 Highway Safety: 7 0 ★★★

Brand	Year	Type	Length	Model	Chassis	Engine	Fuel Type	Price/Ft	Wheelbase	Towing	GVWR	Curb Wt
Pace Arrow Vision	1996	MHA	34	33L	CH	7.4L	G	$1900	208	3,000	16,500	14,611

Livability Code: FT 30-90
Wheelbase-to-length ratio of 52% is considered ○ dangerous ◉ fatiguing ○ good ○ excellent *
The approximate net payload of 1889 pounds at 11% of GVWR on this model is ○ deficient ○ excessive ○ cautionary ◉ good ○ excellent *
Total highway safety penalties are: 6 * Value: 7 6 Durability: 7 3 Highway Control Rating: 4 8 Highway Safety: 4 2

Brand	Year	Type	Length	Model	Chassis	Engine	Fuel Type	Price/Ft	Wheelbase	Towing	GVWR	Curb Wt
Pace Arrow Vision	1996	MHA	34	33P	CH	7.4L	G	$2300	208	3,000	16,500	14,611

Livability Code: FT 30-90
Wheelbase-to-length ratio of 52% is considered ○ dangerous ◉ fatiguing ○ good ○ excellent *
The approximate net payload of 1889 pounds at 11% of GVWR on this model is ○ deficient ○ excessive ○ cautionary ◉ good ○ excellent *
Total highway safety penalties are: 6 * Value: 7 6 Durability: 7 3 Highway Control Rating: 4 8 Highway Safety: 4 2

Brand	Year	Type	Length	Model	Chassis	Engine	Fuel Type	Price/Ft	Wheelbase	Towing	GVWR	Curb Wt
Pace Arrow Vision	1996	MHA	34	33L	FO	7.5L	G	$2300	208	3,500	17,000	15,011

Livability Code: FT 30-90
Wheelbase-to-length ratio of 52% is considered ○ dangerous ◉ fatiguing ○ good ○ excellent *
The approximate net payload of 1989 pounds at 12% of GVWR on this model is ○ deficient ○ excessive ○ cautionary ◉ good ○ excellent *
Total highway safety penalties are: 2 * Value: 7 8 Durability: 7 3 Highway Control Rating: 5 0 Highway Safety: 4 8

Brand	Year	Type	Length	Model	Chassis	Engine	Fuel Type	Price/Ft	Wheelbase	Towing	GVWR	Curb Wt
Pace Arrow Vision	1996	MHA	34	33P	FO	7.5L	G	$2300	208	3,500	17,000	15,011

Livability Code: FT 30-90
Wheelbase-to-length ratio of 52% is considered ○ dangerous ◉ fatiguing ○ good ○ excellent *
The approximate net payload of 1989 pounds at 12% of GVWR on this model is ○ deficient ○ excessive ○ cautionary ◉ good ○ excellent *
Total highway safety penalties are: 2 * Value: 7 8 Durability: 7 3 Highway Control Rating: 5 0 Highway Safety: 4 8

Note: Safety ratings are based on the assumption that the engineering of the RV has allowed for proper balance by placing fresh, gray, and black holding tanks in a location so as not to change the balance of the RV when the tanks are empty or full. **Always double-check wheelbase, GVWR, and weights at front and rear axles.**

*See Section 1 for details on how conclusions are reached.

Brand	Year	Type	Length	Model	Chassis	Engine	Fuel Type	Average Price per Linear Foot When New	Adjusted Wheelbase	Approx. Towing Capacity	Gross Vehicle Weight Rating	Average Curb Weight
Pace Arrow Vision	1996	MHA	35	35D	FO	7.5L	G	$2300	228	3,500	17,000	15,435

Livability Code: FT 30-90
Wheelbase-to-length ratio of 54% is considered ○ dangerous ○ fatiguing ◉ good ○ excellent *
The approximate net payload of 1565 pounds at 9% of GVWR on this model is ○ deficient ○ excessive ◉ cautionary ○ good ○ excellent *
Total highway safety penalties are: 2 *   Value: **7 8**   Durability: **7 3**   Highway Control Rating: **6 5**   Highway Safety: **6 3**   ★★

Pace Arrow Vision	1996	MHA	35	35W	FO	7.5L	G	$2300	228	3,500	17,000	15,435

Livability Code: FT 30-90
Wheelbase-to-length ratio of 54% is considered ○ dangerous ○ fatiguing ◉ good ○ excellent *
The approximate net payload of 1565 pounds at 9% of GVWR on this model is ○ deficient ○ excessive ◉ cautionary ○ good ○ excellent *
Total highway safety penalties are: 2 *   Value: **7 8**   Durability: **7 3**   Highway Control Rating: **6 5**   Highway Safety: **6 3**   ★★

Pace Arrow Vision	1996	MHA	38	37J	CH	7.4L	G	$2200	232 T	1,300	18,700	16,498

Livability Code: FT 30-90
Wheelbase-to-length ratio of 51% is considered ○ dangerous ◉ fatiguing ○ good ○ excellent *
The approximate net payload of 2202 pounds at 12% of GVWR on this model is ○ deficient ○ excessive ○ cautionary ◉ good ○ excellent *
Total highway safety penalties are: 11 *   Value: **7 4**   Durability: **7 3**   Highway Control Rating: **4 1**   Highway Safety: **3 0**

Pace Arrow Vision	1996	MHA	38	37J	FO	7.5L	G	$2200	232 T	3,500	20,000	16,998

Livability Code: FT 30-90
Wheelbase-to-length ratio of 51% is considered ○ dangerous ◉ fatiguing ○ good ○ excellent *
The approximate net payload of 3002 pounds at 15% of GVWR on this model is ○ deficient ○ excessive ○ cautionary ◉ good ○ excellent *
Total highway safety penalties are: 4 *   Value: **7 7**   Durability: **7 3**   Highway Control Rating: **4 7**   Highway Safety: **4 3**

Pace Arrow Vision	1997	MHA	34	33 L	CH	7.4L	G	$2600	208	3,500	16,500	14,611

Livability Code: FT 30-90
Wheelbase-to-length ratio of 52% is considered ○ dangerous ◉ fatiguing ○ good ○ excellent *
The approximate net payload of 1889 pounds at 11% of GVWR on this model is ○ deficient ○ excessive ○ cautionary ◉ good ○ excellent *
Total highway safety penalties are: 6 *   Value: **7 6**   Durability: **7 3**   Highway Control Rating: **4 8**   Highway Safety: **4 2**

Pace Arrow Vision	1997	MHA	34	33 P	CH	7.4L	G	$2600	208	3,500	16,500	14,611

Livability Code: FT 30-90
Wheelbase-to-length ratio of 52% is considered ○ dangerous ◉ fatiguing ○ good ○ excellent *
The approximate net payload of 1889 pounds at 11% of GVWR on this model is ○ deficient ○ excessive ○ cautionary ◉ good ○ excellent *
Total highway safety penalties are: 6 *   Value: **7 6**   Durability: **7 3**   Highway Control Rating: **4 8**   Highway Safety: **4 2**

Pace Arrow Vision	1997	MHA	34	33 L	FO	7.5L	G	$2600	208	3,500	17,000	15,011

Livability Code: FT 30-90
Wheelbase-to-length ratio of 52% is considered ○ dangerous ◉ fatiguing ○ good ○ excellent *
The approximate net payload of 1989 pounds at 12% of GVWR on this model is ○ deficient ○ excessive ○ cautionary ◉ good ○ excellent *
Total highway safety penalties are: 2 *   Value: **7 8**   Durability: **7 3**   Highway Control Rating: **5 0**   Highway Safety: **4 8**

Pace Arrow Vision	1997	MHA	34	33 P	FO	7.5L	G	$2600	208	3,500	17,000	15,011

Livability Code: FT 30-90
Wheelbase-to-length ratio of 52% is considered ○ dangerous ◉ fatiguing ○ good ○ excellent *
The approximate net payload of 1989 pounds at 12% of GVWR on this model is ○ deficient ○ excessive ○ cautionary ◉ good ○ excellent *
Total highway safety penalties are: 2 *   Value: **7 8**   Durability: **7 3**   Highway Control Rating: **5 0**   Highway Safety: **4 8**

Pace Arrow Vision	1997	MHA	35	35 D	CH	7.4L	G	$2500	228	3,500	16,500	15,035

Livability Code: FT 30-90
Wheelbase-to-length ratio of 54% is considered ○ dangerous ○ fatiguing ◉ good ○ excellent *
The approximate net payload of 1465 pounds at 9% of GVWR on this model is ○ deficient ○ excessive ◉ cautionary ○ good ○ excellent *
Total highway safety penalties are: 7 *   Value: **7 6**   Durability: **7 3**   Highway Control Rating: **6 4**   Highway Safety: **5 7**   ★

Pace Arrow Vision	1997	MHA	35	35 W	CH	7.4L	G	$2800	228	3,500	16,500	15,035

Livability Code: FT 30-90
Wheelbase-to-length ratio of 54% is considered ○ dangerous ○ fatiguing ◉ good ○ excellent *
The approximate net payload of 1465 pounds at 9% of GVWR on this model is ○ deficient ○ excessive ◉ cautionary ○ good ○ excellent *
Total highway safety penalties are: 7 *   Value: **7 6**   Durability: **7 3**   Highway Control Rating: **6 4**   Highway Safety: **5 7**   ★

Pace Arrow Vision	1997	MHA	35	35 D	FO	7.5L	G	$2800	228	3,500	17,000	15,435

Livability Code: FT 30-90
Wheelbase-to-length ratio of 54% is considered ○ dangerous ○ fatiguing ◉ good ○ excellent *
The approximate net payload of 1565 pounds at 9% of GVWR on this model is ○ deficient ○ excessive ◉ cautionary ○ good ○ excellent *
Total highway safety penalties are: 2 *   Value: **7 8**   Durability: **7 3**   Highway Control Rating: **6 5**   Highway Safety: **6 3**   ★★

Pace Arrow Vision	1997	MHA	35	35 W	FO	7.5L	G	$2800	228	3,500	17,000	15,435

Livability Code: FT 30-90
Wheelbase-to-length ratio of 54% is considered ○ dangerous ○ fatiguing ◉ good ○ excellent *
The approximate net payload of 1565 pounds at 9% of GVWR on this model is ○ deficient ○ excessive ◉ cautionary ○ good ○ excellent *
Total highway safety penalties are: 2 *   Value: **7 8**   Durability: **7 3**   Highway Control Rating: **6 5**   Highway Safety: **6 3**   ★★

Note: Safety ratings are based on the assumption that the engineering of the RV has allowed for proper balance by placing fresh, gray, and black holding tanks in a location so as not to change the balance of the RV when the tanks are empty or full. **Always double-check wheelbase, GVWR, and weights at front and rear axles.**

The RV Rating Book

*See Section 1 for details on how conclusions are reached.

Section 2: The Ratings

Brand	Year	Type	Length	Model	Chassis	Engine	Fuel Type	Average Price per Linear Foot When New	Adjusted Wheelbase	Approx. Towing Capacity	Gross Vehicle Weight Rating	Average Curb Weight
Pace Arrow Vision	1997	MHA	37	36 B	CH	7.4L	G	$2600	214 T	1,500	19,500	17,206

Livability Code: FT 30-90
Wheelbase-to-length ratio of 49% is considered ⦿ dangerous ◯ fatiguing ◯ good ◯ excellent *
The approximate net payload of 2294 pounds at 12% of GVWR on this model is ◯ deficient ◯ excessive ◯ cautionary ⦿ good ◯ excellent *
Total highway safety penalties are: 16 *   Value: 7 1   Durability: 7 3   Highway Control Rating: 3 2   Highway Safety: 1 6

Brand	Year	Type	Length	Model	Chassis	Engine	Fuel Type	Price/Ft	Wheelbase	Towing	GVWR	Curb Weight
Pace Arrow Vision	1997	MHA	37	36 B ops rear BR	CH	7.4L	G	$2700	214 T	1,500	19,500	17,956

Livability Code: FT 30-90
Wheelbase-to-length ratio of 49% is considered ⦿ dangerous ◯ fatiguing ◯ good ◯ excellent *
The approximate net payload of 1544 pounds at 8% of GVWR on this model is ◯ deficient ◯ excessive ⦿ cautionary ◯ good ◯ excellent *
Total highway safety penalties are: 20 *   Value: 6 9   Durability: 7 3   Highway Control Rating: 1 7   Highway Safety: - 3

Brand	Year	Type	Length	Model	Chassis	Engine	Fuel Type	Price/Ft	Wheelbase	Towing	GVWR	Curb Weight
Pace Arrow Vision	1997	MHA	37	36 B	FO	7.5L	G	$2600	214 T	3,500	20,000	17,606

Livability Code: FT 30-90
Wheelbase-to-length ratio of 49% is considered ⦿ dangerous ◯ fatiguing ◯ good ◯ excellent *
The approximate net payload of 2394 pounds at 12% of GVWR on this model is ◯ deficient ◯ excessive ◯ cautionary ⦿ good ◯ excellent *
Total highway safety penalties are: 10 *   Value: 7 4   Durability: 7 3   Highway Control Rating: 3 2   Highway Safety: 2 2

Brand	Year	Type	Length	Model	Chassis	Engine	Fuel Type	Price/Ft	Wheelbase	Towing	GVWR	Curb Weight
Pace Arrow Vision	1997	MHA	37	36 B ops rearBR	FO	7.5L	G	$2700	214 T	3,500	20,000	18,356

Livability Code: FT 30-90
Wheelbase-to-length ratio of 49% is considered ⦿ dangerous ◯ fatiguing ◯ good ◯ excellent *
The approximate net payload of 1644 pounds at 8% of GVWR on this model is ◯ deficient ◯ excessive ⦿ cautionary ◯ good ◯ excellent *
Total highway safety penalties are: 14 *   Value: 7 2   Durability: 7 3   Highway Control Rating: 1 7   Highway Safety: 3

Brand	Year	Type	Length	Model	Chassis	Engine	Fuel Type	Price/Ft	Wheelbase	Towing	GVWR	Curb Weight
Pace Arrow Vision	1997	MHA	38	37 A	CH	7.4L	G	$2600	232 T	1,500	19,500	16,651

Livability Code: FT 30-90
Wheelbase-to-length ratio of 51% is considered ◯ dangerous ⦿ fatiguing ◯ good ◯ excellent *
The approximate net payload of 2849 pounds at 15% of GVWR on this model is ◯ deficient ◯ excessive ◯ cautionary ⦿ good ◯ excellent *
Total highway safety penalties are: 11 *   Value: 7 4   Durability: 7 3   Highway Control Rating: 4 6   Highway Safety: 3 5

Brand	Year	Type	Length	Model	Chassis	Engine	Fuel Type	Price/Ft	Wheelbase	Towing	GVWR	Curb Weight
Pace Arrow Vision	1997	MHA	38	37 A	FO	7.5L	G	$2600	232 T	3,500	20,000	17,051

Livability Code: FT 30-90
Wheelbase-to-length ratio of 51% is considered ◯ dangerous ⦿ fatiguing ◯ good ◯ excellent *
The approximate net payload of 2949 pounds at 15% of GVWR on this model is ◯ deficient ◯ excessive ◯ cautionary ⦿ good ◯ excellent *
Total highway safety penalties are: 4 *   Value: 7 7   Durability: 7 3   Highway Control Rating: 4 6   Highway Safety: 4 2

Brand	Year	Type	Length	Model	Chassis	Engine	Fuel Type	Price/Ft	Wheelbase	Towing	GVWR	Curb Weight
Pace Arrow Vision	1998	MHA	34	34C	CH	7.4L	G	$2900	202 T	1,500	19,500	16,384

Livability Code: FT 30-90
Wheelbase-to-length ratio of 50% is considered ⦿ dangerous ◯ fatiguing ◯ good ◯ excellent *
The approximate net payload of 3116 pounds at 16% of GVWR on this model is ◯ deficient ◯ excessive ◯ cautionary ◯ good ⦿ excellent *
Total highway safety penalties are: 19 *   Value: 7 0   Durability: 7 3   Highway Control Rating: 4 6   Highway Safety: 2 7

Brand	Year	Type	Length	Model	Chassis	Engine	Fuel Type	Price/Ft	Wheelbase	Towing	GVWR	Curb Weight
Pace Arrow Vision	1998	MHA	34	34C	FO	7.5L	G	$2900	202 T	3,500	20,000	16,784

Livability Code: FT 30-90
Wheelbase-to-length ratio of 50% is considered ⦿ dangerous ◯ fatiguing ◯ good ◯ excellent *
The approximate net payload of 3216 pounds at 16% of GVWR on this model is ◯ deficient ◯ excessive ◯ cautionary ◯ good ⦿ excellent *
Total highway safety penalties are: 15 *   Value: 7 2   Durability: 7 3   Highway Control Rating: 4 6   Highway Safety: 3 1

Brand	Year	Type	Length	Model	Chassis	Engine	Fuel Type	Price/Ft	Wheelbase	Towing	GVWR	Curb Weight
Pace Arrow Vision	1998	MHA	34	33L	CH	7.4L	G	$2900	208	3,500	16,500	14,611

Livability Code: FT 30-90
Wheelbase-to-length ratio of 52% is considered ◯ dangerous ⦿ fatiguing ◯ good ◯ excellent *
The approximate net payload of 1889 pounds at 11% of GVWR on this model is ◯ deficient ◯ excessive ◯ cautionary ⦿ good ◯ excellent *
Total highway safety penalties are: 6 *   Value: 7 6   Durability: 7 3   Highway Control Rating: 4 8   Highway Safety: 4 2

Brand	Year	Type	Length	Model	Chassis	Engine	Fuel Type	Price/Ft	Wheelbase	Towing	GVWR	Curb Weight
Pace Arrow Vision	1998	MHA	34	33P	CH	7.4L	G	$2900	208	3,500	16,500	14,611

Livability Code: FT 30-90
Wheelbase-to-length ratio of 52% is considered ◯ dangerous ⦿ fatiguing ◯ good ◯ excellent *
The approximate net payload of 1889 pounds at 11% of GVWR on this model is ◯ deficient ◯ excessive ◯ cautionary ⦿ good ◯ excellent *
Total highway safety penalties are: 6 *   Value: 7 6   Durability: 7 3   Highway Control Rating: 4 8   Highway Safety: 4 2

Brand	Year	Type	Length	Model	Chassis	Engine	Fuel Type	Price/Ft	Wheelbase	Towing	GVWR	Curb Weight
Pace Arrow Vision	1998	MHA	34	33L	FO	7.5L	G	$2900	208	3,500	17,000	15,011

Livability Code: FT 30-90
Wheelbase-to-length ratio of 52% is considered ◯ dangerous ⦿ fatiguing ◯ good ◯ excellent *
The approximate net payload of 1989 pounds at 12% of GVWR on this model is ◯ deficient ◯ excessive ◯ cautionary ⦿ good ◯ excellent *
Total highway safety penalties are: 2 *   Value: 7 8   Durability: 7 3   Highway Control Rating: 5 0   Highway Safety: 4 8

Brand	Year	Type	Length	Model	Chassis	Engine	Fuel Type	Price/Ft	Wheelbase	Towing	GVWR	Curb Weight
Pace Arrow Vision	1998	MHA	34	33P	FO	7.5L	G	$2900	208	3,500	17,000	15,011

Livability Code: FT 30-90
Wheelbase-to-length ratio of 52% is considered ◯ dangerous ⦿ fatiguing ◯ good ◯ excellent *
The approximate net payload of 1989 pounds at 12% of GVWR on this model is ◯ deficient ◯ excessive ◯ cautionary ⦿ good ◯ excellent *
Total highway safety penalties are: 2 *   Value: 7 8   Durability: 7 3   Highway Control Rating: 5 0   Highway Safety: 4 8

Note: Safety ratings are based on the assumption that the engineering of the RV has allowed for proper balance by placing fresh, gray, and black holding tanks in a location so as not to change the balance of the RV when the tanks are empty or full. **Always double-check wheelbase, GVWR, and weights at front and rear axles.**

*See Section 1 for details on how conclusions are reached.

Brand	Year	Type	Length	Model	Chassis	Engine	Fuel Type	Average Price per Linear Foot When New	Adjusted Wheelbase	Approx. Towing Capacity	Gross Vehicle Weight Rating	Average Curb Weight

Pace Arrow Vision — 1998 — MHA — 35 — 35W — CH — 7.4L — G — $2900 — 228 — 3,500 — 16,500 — 15,035
Livability Code: FT 30-90
Wheelbase-to-length ratio of 54% is considered ○ dangerous ○ fatiguing ◉ good ○ excellent *
The approximate net payload of 1465 pounds at 9% of GVWR on this model is ○ deficient ○ excessive ◉ cautionary ○ good ○ excellent *
Total highway safety penalties are: 7 *   Value: 7 6   Durability: 7 3   Highway Control Rating: 6 4   Highway Safety: 5 7   ★

Pace Arrow Vision — 1998 — MHA — 35 — 35W — FO — 7.5L — G — $2900 — 228 — 3,500 — 17,000 — 15,435
Livability Code: FT 30-90
Wheelbase-to-length ratio of 54% is considered ○ dangerous ○ fatiguing ◉ good ○ excellent *
The approximate net payload of 1565 pounds at 9% of GVWR on this model is ○ deficient ○ excessive ◉ cautionary ○ good ○ excellent *
Total highway safety penalties are: 2 *   Value: 7 8   Durability: 7 3   Highway Control Rating: 6 5   Highway Safety: 6 3   ★★

Pace Arrow Vision — 1998 — MHA — 37 — 36B — CH — 7.4L — G — $2700 — 214 T — 1,500 — 19,500 — 17,206
Livability Code: FT 30-90
Wheelbase-to-length ratio of 49% is considered ◉ dangerous ○ fatiguing ○ good ○ excellent *
The approximate net payload of 2294 pounds at 12% of GVWR on this model is ○ deficient ○ excessive ○ cautionary ○ good ○ excellent *
Total highway safety penalties are: 16 *   Value: 7 1   Durability: 7 3   Highway Control Rating: 3 2   Highway Safety: 1 6

Pace Arrow Vision — 1998 — MHA — 37 — 36B sl, opsl bedroom — CH — 7.4L — G — $2700 — 214 T — 1,500 — 19,500 — 17,731
Livability Code: FT 30-90
Wheelbase-to-length ratio of 49% is considered ◉ dangerous ○ fatiguing ○ good ○ excellent *
The approximate net payload of 1769 pounds at 9% of GVWR on this model is ○ deficient ○ excessive ◉ cautionary ○ good ○ excellent *
Total highway safety penalties are: 19 *   Value: 7 0   Durability: 7 3   Highway Control Rating: 2 3   Highway Safety: 4

Pace Arrow Vision — 1998 — MHA — 37 — 36B — FO — 7.5L — G — $2700 — 214 T — 3,500 — 20,000 — 17,606
Livability Code: FT 30-90
Wheelbase-to-length ratio of 49% is considered ◉ dangerous ○ fatiguing ○ good ○ excellent *
The approximate net payload of 2394 pounds at 12% of GVWR on this model is ○ deficient ○ excessive ○ cautionary ◉ good ○ excellent *
Total highway safety penalties are: 10 *   Value: 7 4   Durability: 7 3   Highway Control Rating: 3 2   Highway Safety: 2 2

Pace Arrow Vision — 1998 — MHA — 37 — 36B sl, opsl bedroom — FO — 7.5L — G — $2700 — 214 T — 3,500 — 20,000 — 18,131
Livability Code: FT 30-90
Wheelbase-to-length ratio of 49% is considered ◉ dangerous ○ fatiguing ○ good ○ excellent *
The approximate net payload of 1869 pounds at 9% of GVWR on this model is ○ deficient ○ excessive ◉ cautionary ○ good ○ excellent *
Total highway safety penalties are: 13 *   Value: 7 3   Durability: 7 3   Highway Control Rating: 2 4   Highway Safety: 1 1

Pace Arrow Vision — 1998 — MHA — 38 — 37A — CH — 7.4L — G — $2600 — 232 T — 1,500 — 19,500 — 16,651
Livability Code: FT 30-90
Wheelbase-to-length ratio of 51% is considered ○ dangerous ◉ fatiguing ○ good ○ excellent *
The approximate net payload of 2849 pounds at 15% of GVWR on this model is ○ deficient ○ excessive ○ cautionary ◉ good ○ excellent *
Total highway safety penalties are: 11 *   Value: 7 4   Durability: 7 3   Highway Control Rating: 4 6   Highway Safety: 3 5

Pace Arrow Vision — 1998 — MHA — 38 — 37A — FO — 7.5L — G — $2600 — 232 T — 3,500 — 20,000 — 17,051
Livability Code: FT 30-90
Wheelbase-to-length ratio of 51% is considered ○ dangerous ◉ fatiguing ○ good ○ excellent *
The approximate net payload of 2949 pounds at 15% of GVWR on this model is ○ deficient ○ excessive ○ cautionary ◉ good ○ excellent *
Total highway safety penalties are: 4 *   Value: 7 7   Durability: 7 3   Highway Control Rating: 4 6   Highway Safety: 4 2

Pace Arrow Vision — 1999 — MHA — 34 — 33L — CH — 7.4L — G — $2900 — 208 — 3,500 — 16,500 — 14,611
Livability Code: FT 30-90
Wheelbase-to-length ratio of 52% is considered ○ dangerous ◉ fatiguing ○ good ○ excellent *
The approximate net payload of 1889 pounds at 11% of GVWR on this model is ○ deficient ○ excessive ○ cautionary ◉ good ○ excellent *
Total highway safety penalties are: 6 *   Value: 7 6   Durability: 7 3   Highway Control Rating: 5 6   Highway Safety: 5 0   ★

Pace Arrow Vision — 1999 — MHA — 34 — 33L — FO — 6.8L — G — $2900 — 208 — 5,000 — 20,500 — 15,911
Livability Code: FT 30-90
Wheelbase-to-length ratio of 52% is considered ○ dangerous ◉ fatiguing ○ good ○ excellent *
The approximate net payload of 4589 pounds at 22% of GVWR on this model is ○ deficient ○ excessive ○ cautionary ○ good ◉ excellent *
Total highway safety penalties are: 2 *   Value: 7 8   Durability: 7 3   Highway Control Rating: 6 7   Highway Safety: 6 5   ★★

Pace Arrow Vision — 1999 — MHA — 35 — 34C — CH — 7.4L — G — $2900 — 202 T — 1,500 e — 20,000 — 16,649
Livability Code: FT 30-90
Wheelbase-to-length ratio of 49% is considered ◉ dangerous ○ fatiguing ○ good ○ excellent *
The approximate net payload of 3351 pounds at 17% of GVWR on this model is ○ deficient ○ excessive ○ cautionary ○ good ◉ excellent *
Total highway safety penalties are: 20 *   Value: 6 9   Durability: 7 3   Highway Control Rating: 5 1   Highway Safety: 3 1

Pace Arrow Vision — 1999 — MHA — 35 — 34C — FO — 6.8L — G — $2900 — 208 — 5,000 — 20,500 — 17,049
Livability Code: FT 30-90
Wheelbase-to-length ratio of 50% is considered ◉ dangerous ○ fatiguing ○ good ○ excellent *
The approximate net payload of 3451 pounds at 17% of GVWR on this model is ○ deficient ○ excessive ○ cautionary ○ good ◉ excellent *
Total highway safety penalties are: 12 *   Value: 7 3   Durability: 7 3   Highway Control Rating: 5 6   Highway Safety: 4 4

Note: Safety ratings are based on the assumption that the engineering of the RV has allowed for proper balance by placing fresh, gray, and black holding tanks in a location so as not to change the balance of the RV when the tanks are empty or full. **Always double-check wheelbase, GVWR, and weights at front and rear axles.**

Section 2: The Ratings

Brand	Year	Type	Length	Model	Chassis	Engine	Fuel Type	Average Price per Linear Foot When New	Adjusted Wheelbase	Approx. Towing Capacity	Gross Vehicle Weight Rating	Average Curb Weight
Pace Arrow Vision	1999	MHA	35	35W	FO	6.8L	G	$2900	228	5,000	20,500	16,335

Livability Code: FT 30-90 — Wheelbase-to-length ratio of 54% is considered ○ dangerous ○ fatiguing ◉ good ○ excellent *

The approximate net payload of 4165 pounds at 20% of GVWR on this model is ○ deficient ○ excessive ○ cautionary ○ good ◉ excellent *

Total highway safety penalties are: 2 *   Value: **7 8**   Durability: **7 3**   Highway Control Rating: **8 8**   Highway Safety: **8 6**   ★★★

Brand	Year	Type	Length	Model	Chassis	Engine	Fuel Type	Price/Ft	Wheelbase	Towing	GVWR	Curb Weight
Pace Arrow Vision	1999	MHA	37	36B opsl	CH	7.4L	G	$2700	214 T	1,500 e	20,000	17,656

Livability Code: FT 30-90 — Wheelbase-to-length ratio of 49% is considered ◉ dangerous ○ fatiguing ○ good ○ excellent *

The approximate net payload of 2344 pounds at 12% of GVWR on this model is ○ deficient ○ excessive ○ cautionary ◉ good ○ excellent *

Total highway safety penalties are: 18 *   Value: **7 0**   Durability: **7 3**   Highway Control Rating: **4 2**   Highway Safety: **2 4**

Pace Arrow Vision	1999	MHA	37	36B	CH	7.4L	G	$2700	214 T	1,500 e	20,000	17,206

Livability Code: FT 30-90 — Wheelbase-to-length ratio of 49% is considered ◉ dangerous ○ fatiguing ○ good ○ excellent *

The approximate net payload of 2794 pounds at 14% of GVWR on this model is ○ deficient ○ excessive ○ cautionary ◉ good ○ excellent *

Total highway safety penalties are: 16 *   Value: **7 1**   Durability: **7 3**   Highway Control Rating: **4 6**   Highway Safety: **3 0**

Pace Arrow Vision	1999	MHA	37	36B opsl	FO	6.8L	G	$2700	228	5,000	20,500	18,056

Livability Code: FT 30-90 — Wheelbase-to-length ratio of 52% is considered ○ dangerous ◉ fatiguing ○ good ○ excellent *

The approximate net payload of 2444 pounds at 12% of GVWR on this model is ○ deficient ○ excessive ○ cautionary ◉ good ○ excellent *

Total highway safety penalties are: 10 *   Value: **7 4**   Durability: **7 3**   Highway Control Rating: **5 8**   Highway Safety: **4 8**

Pace Arrow Vision	1999	MHA	37	36B	FO	6.8L	G	$2700	228	5,000	20,500	17,606

Livability Code: FT 30-90 — Wheelbase-to-length ratio of 52% is considered ○ dangerous ◉ fatiguing ○ good ○ excellent *

The approximate net payload of 2894 pounds at 14% of GVWR on this model is ○ deficient ○ excessive ○ cautionary ◉ good ○ excellent *

Total highway safety penalties are: 7 *   Value: **7 6**   Durability: **7 3**   Highway Control Rating: **6 3**   Highway Safety: **5 6**   ★

Pace Arrow Vision	1999	MHA	37	36Z opsl	CH	7.4L	G	$2700	228	3,500	22,500	19,162

Livability Code: FT 30-90 — Wheelbase-to-length ratio of 51% is considered ○ dangerous ◉ fatiguing ○ good ○ excellent *

The approximate net payload of 3338 pounds at 15% of GVWR on this model is ○ deficient ◉ excessive ○ cautionary ○ good ○ excellent *

Total highway safety penalties are: 21 *   Value: **6 9**   Durability: **7 3**   Highway Control Rating: **5 7**   Highway Safety: **3 6**

Pace Arrow Vision	1999	MHA	37	36Z	CH	7.4L	G	$2700	228	3,500	22,500	18,712

Livability Code: FT 30-90 — Wheelbase-to-length ratio of 51% is considered ○ dangerous ◉ fatiguing ○ good ○ excellent *

The approximate net payload of 3788 pounds at 17% of GVWR on this model is ○ deficient ○ excessive ○ cautionary ○ good ◉ excellent *

Total highway safety penalties are: 18 *   Value: **7 0**   Durability: **7 3**   Highway Control Rating: **6 0**   Highway Safety: **4 2**

Patriot	1993	MHA	32	Charleston 31	SP	Cu5.9L	D	$5100	174	4,000	18,000	16,828

Livability Code: FT 30-90 — Wheelbase-to-length ratio of 46% is considered ◉ dangerous ○ fatiguing ○ good ○ excellent *

The approximate net payload of 1172 pounds at 7% of GVWR on this model is ○ deficient ○ excessive ◉ cautionary ○ good ○ excellent *

Total highway safety penalties are: 2 *   Value: **8 1**   Durability: **8 0**   Highway Control Rating: **1**   Highway Safety: **- 1**

Patriot	1993	MHA	34	Savannah 33	SP	CU300	D	$5000	198	5,000	26,000	21,555

Livability Code: FT 30-90 — Wheelbase-to-length ratio of 49% is considered ◉ dangerous ○ fatiguing ○ good ○ excellent *

The approximate net payload of 4445 pounds at 17% of GVWR on this model is ○ deficient ○ excessive ○ cautionary ○ good ◉ excellent *

Total highway safety penalties are: 2 *   Value: **8 1**   Durability: **8 0**   Highway Control Rating: **4 3**   Highway Safety: **4 1**

Patriot	1993	MHA	36	Saratoga 36	SP	CU300	D	$5100	228	5,000	26,000	22,459

Livability Code: FT 30-90 — Wheelbase-to-length ratio of 53% is considered ○ dangerous ◉ fatiguing ○ good ○ excellent *

The approximate net payload of 3541 pounds at 14% of GVWR on this model is ○ deficient ○ excessive ○ cautionary ◉ good ○ excellent *

Total highway safety penalties are: 2 *   Value: **8 1**   Durability: **8 0**   Highway Control Rating: **6 5**   Highway Safety: **6 3**   ★★

Patriot	1993	MHA	36	Concord 36	SP	CU300	D	$5100	228	5,000	26,000	22,459

Livability Code: FT 30-90 — Wheelbase-to-length ratio of 53% is considered ○ dangerous ◉ fatiguing ○ good ○ excellent *

The approximate net payload of 3541 pounds at 14% of GVWR on this model is ○ deficient ○ excessive ○ cautionary ◉ good ○ excellent *

Total highway safety penalties are: 2 *   Value: **8 1**   Durability: **8 0**   Highway Control Rating: **6 5**   Highway Safety: **6 3**   ★★

Patriot	1993	MHA	38	Lexington 38	SP	CU300	D	$5100	252	5,000	26,000	22,645

Livability Code: FT 30-90 — Wheelbase-to-length ratio of 55% is considered ○ dangerous ○ fatiguing ◉ good ○ excellent *

The approximate net payload of 3355 pounds at 13% of GVWR on this model is ○ deficient ○ excessive ○ cautionary ◉ good ○ excellent *

Total highway safety penalties are: 2 *   Value: **8 1**   Durability: **8 0**   Highway Control Rating: **8 7**   Highway Safety: **8 5**   ★★★★

Note: Safety ratings are based on the assumption that the engineering of the RV has allowed for proper balance by placing fresh, gray, and black holding tanks in a location so as not to change the balance of the RV when the tanks are empty or full. **Always double-check wheelbase, GVWR, and weights at front and rear axles.**

*See Section 1 for details on how conclusions are reached.

Brand	Year	Type	Length	Model	Chassis	Engine	Fuel Type	Average Price per Linear Foot When New	Adjusted Wheelbase	Approx. Towing Capacity	Gross Vehicle Weight Rating	Average Curb Weight
Patriot	1995	MHA	34	Savannah 33	SP	CU300	D	$5000	198	2,000	29,000	22,177

Livability Code: FT 30-90

Wheelbase-to-length ratio of 49% is considered ● dangerous ○ fatiguing ○ good ○ excellent *

The approximate net payload of 6823 pounds at 24% of GVWR on this model is ○ deficient ○ excessive ○ cautionary ○ good ● excellent *

Total highway safety penalties are: 2 *   Value: **8 1**   Durability: **8 0**   Highway Control Rating: **4 2**   Highway Safety: **4 0**

| Patriot | 1995 | MHA | 37 | Trenton 37 | SP | CU300 | D | $5300 | 240 | 5,000 | 29,000 | 23,044 |

Livability Code: FT 30-90

Wheelbase-to-length ratio of 54% is considered ○ dangerous ○ fatiguing ● good ○ excellent *

The approximate net payload of 5956 pounds at 21% of GVWR on this model is ○ deficient ○ excessive ○ cautionary ○ good ● excellent *

Total highway safety penalties are: 2 *   Value: **8 1**   Durability: **8 0**   Highway Control Rating: **8 5**   Highway Safety: **8 3**   ★★★★

| Patriot | 1995 | MHA | 40 | Camden 40 | SP | CU300 | D | $5200 | 270 | 5,000 | 29,000 | 24,782 |

Livability Code: FT 30-90

Wheelbase-to-length ratio of 56% is considered ○ dangerous ○ fatiguing ● good ○ excellent *

The approximate net payload of 4218 pounds at 15% of GVWR on this model is ○ deficient ○ excessive ○ cautionary ○ good ● excellent *

Total highway safety penalties are: 2 *   Value: **8 1**   Durability: **8 0**   Highway Control Rating: **9 6**   Highway Safety: **9 4**   ★★★★

| Patriot | 1995 | MHA | 40 | Yorktown 40 | SP | CU300 | D | $5200 | 270 | 5,000 | 29,000 | 24,782 |

Livability Code: FT 30-90

Wheelbase-to-length ratio of 56% is considered ○ dangerous ○ fatiguing ● good ○ excellent *

The approximate net payload of 4218 pounds at 15% of GVWR on this model is ○ deficient ○ excessive ○ cautionary ○ good ● excellent *

Total highway safety penalties are: 2 *   Value: **8 1**   Durability: **8 0**   Highway Control Rating: **9 5**   Highway Safety: **9 3**   ★★★★

| Patriot | 1996 | MHA | 33 | Savannah 33 | MA | CA300 | D | $5700 | 195 | 6,000 | 30,000 | 24,088 |

Livability Code: FT 30-90

Wheelbase-to-length ratio of 49% is considered ● dangerous ○ fatiguing ○ good ○ excellent *

The approximate net payload of 5912 pounds at 20% of GVWR on this model is ○ deficient ○ excessive ○ cautionary ○ good ● excellent *

Total highway safety penalties are: 2 *   Value: **8 1**   Durability: **8 0**   Highway Control Rating: **4 6**   Highway Safety: **4 4**

| Patriot | 1996 | MHA | 37 | Trenton 37 | MA | CA300 | D | $5400 | 237 | 6,000 | 30,000 | 25,190 |

Livability Code: FT 30-90

Wheelbase-to-length ratio of 53% is considered ○ dangerous ● fatiguing ○ good ○ excellent *

The approximate net payload of 4810 pounds at 16% of GVWR on this model is ○ deficient ○ excessive ○ cautionary ○ good ● excellent *

Total highway safety penalties are: 2 *   Value: **8 1**   Durability: **8 0**   Highway Control Rating: **7 2**   Highway Safety: **7 0**   ★★★

| Patriot | 1996 | MHA | 40 | Camden 40 | MA | CA300 | D | $5300 | 272 | 6,000 | 30,000 | 26,016 |

Livability Code: FT 30-90

Wheelbase-to-length ratio of 57% is considered ○ dangerous ○ fatiguing ● good ○ excellent *

The approximate net payload of 3984 pounds at 13% of GVWR on this model is ○ deficient ○ excessive ○ cautionary ● good ○ excellent *

Total highway safety penalties are: 2 *   Value: **8 1**   Durability: **8 0**   Highway Control Rating: **9 3**   Highway Safety: **9 1**   ★★★★

| Patriot | 1996 | MHA | 40 | Yorktown 40 | MA | CA300 | D | $5300 | 272 | 6,000 | 30,000 | 26,016 |

Livability Code: FT 30-90

Wheelbase-to-length ratio of 57% is considered ○ dangerous ○ fatiguing ● good ○ excellent *

The approximate net payload of 3984 pounds at 13% of GVWR on this model is ○ deficient ○ excessive ○ cautionary ● good ○ excellent *

Total highway safety penalties are: 2 *   Value: **8 1**   Durability: **8 0**   Highway Control Rating: **9 3**   Highway Safety: **9 1**   ★★★★

| Patriot | 1997 | MHA | 33 | 33 Savannah | MA | CA300 | D | $5700 | 195 | 5,000 | 30,000 | 24,088 |

Livability Code: FT 30-90

Wheelbase-to-length ratio of 49% is considered ● dangerous ○ fatiguing ○ good ○ excellent *

The approximate net payload of 5912 pounds at 20% of GVWR on this model is ○ deficient ○ excessive ○ cautionary ○ good ● excellent *

Total highway safety penalties are: 2 *   Value: **8 1**   Durability: **8 0**   Highway Control Rating: **4 6**   Highway Safety: **4 4**

| Patriot | 1997 | MHA | 37 | 37 Saratoga | MA | CA300 | D | $5400 | 237 | 5,000 | 30,000 | 25,190 |

Livability Code: FT 30-90

Wheelbase-to-length ratio of 53% is considered ○ dangerous ● fatiguing ○ good ○ excellent *

The approximate net payload of 4810 pounds at 16% of GVWR on this model is ○ deficient ○ excessive ○ cautionary ○ good ● excellent *

Total highway safety penalties are: 2 *   Value: **8 1**   Durability: **8 0**   Highway Control Rating: **7 2**   Highway Safety: **7 0**   ★★★

| Patriot | 1997 | MHA | 37 | 37 Trenton | MA | CA300 | D | $5400 | 237 | 5,000 | 30,000 | 25,190 |

Livability Code: FT 30-90

Wheelbase-to-length ratio of 53% is considered ○ dangerous ● fatiguing ○ good ○ excellent *

The approximate net payload of 4810 pounds at 16% of GVWR on this model is ○ deficient ○ excessive ○ cautionary ○ good ● excellent *

Total highway safety penalties are: 2 *   Value: **8 1**   Durability: **8 0**   Highway Control Rating: **7 2**   Highway Safety: **7 0**   ★★★

| Patriot | 1997 | MHA | 40 | 40 Yorktown | MA | CA300 | D | $5300 | 272 | 5,000 | 30,000 | 26,016 |

Livability Code: FT 30-90

Wheelbase-to-length ratio of 57% is considered ○ dangerous ○ fatiguing ● good ○ excellent *

The approximate net payload of 3984 pounds at 13% of GVWR on this model is ○ deficient ○ excessive ○ cautionary ● good ○ excellent *

Total highway safety penalties are: 2 *   Value: **8 1**   Durability: **8 0**   Highway Control Rating: **9 3**   Highway Safety: **9 1**   ★★★★

Note: Safety ratings are based on the assumption that the engineering of the RV has allowed for proper balance by placing fresh, gray, and black holding tanks in a location so as not to change the balance of the RV when the tanks are empty or full. **Always double-check wheelbase, GVWR, and weights at front and rear axles.**

Brand	Year	Type	Length	Model	Chassis	Engine	Fuel Type	Average Price per Linear Foot When New	Adjusted Wheelbase	Approx. Towing Capacity	Gross Vehicle Weight Rating	Average Curb Weight
Patriot	**1997**	MHA	40	40 Camden	MA	CA300	D	$5300	272	5,000	30,000	26,016

Livability Code: FT 30-90
Wheelbase-to-length ratio of 57% is considered ○ dangerous ○ fatiguing ● good ○ excellent *
The approximate net payload of 3984 pounds at 13% of GVWR on this model is ○ deficient ○ excessive ○ cautionary ● good ○ excellent *
Total highway safety penalties are: 2 *   Value: **8 1**   Durability: **8 0**   Highway Control Rating: **9 3**   Highway Safety: **9 1**   ★★★★

| **Patriot** | **1998** | MHA | 33 | 33 Concord | MA | CA300 | D | $6100 | 195 | 5,000 | 31,000 | 25,788 |

Livability Code: FT 30-90
Wheelbase-to-length ratio of 49% is considered ● dangerous ○ fatiguing ○ good ○ excellent *
The approximate net payload of 5212 pounds at 17% of GVWR on this model is ○ deficient ○ excessive ○ cautionary ○ good ● excellent *
Total highway safety penalties are: 14 *   Value: **6 9**   Durability: **7 8**   Highway Control Rating: **4 3**   Highway Safety: **2 9**

| **Patriot** | **1998** | MHA | 33 | 33 Savannah | MA | CA300 | D | $6100 | 195 | 5,000 | 31,000 | 24,588 |

Livability Code: FT 30-90
Wheelbase-to-length ratio of 49% is considered ● dangerous ○ fatiguing ○ good ○ excellent *
The approximate net payload of 6412 pounds at 21% of GVWR on this model is ○ deficient ○ excessive ○ cautionary ○ good ● excellent *
Total highway safety penalties are: 2 *   Value: **7 5**   Durability: **7 8**   Highway Control Rating: **4 5**   Highway Safety: **4 3**

| **Patriot** | **1998** | MHA | 37 | 37 Ticonderoga | MA | CA300 | D | $5400 | 237 | 5,000 | 31,000 | 26,890 |

Livability Code: FT 30-90
Wheelbase-to-length ratio of 53% is considered ○ dangerous ● fatiguing ○ good ○ excellent *
The approximate net payload of 4110 pounds at 13% of GVWR on this model is ○ deficient ○ excessive ○ cautionary ● good ○ excellent *
Total highway safety penalties are: 14 *   Value: **6 9**   Durability: **7 8**   Highway Control Rating: **6 6**   Highway Safety: **5 2**   ★

| **Patriot** | **1998** | MHA | 37 | 37 Trenton | MA | CA300 | D | $5400 | 237 | 5,000 | 31,000 | 25,690 |

Livability Code: FT 30-90
Wheelbase-to-length ratio of 53% is considered ○ dangerous ● fatiguing ○ good ○ excellent *
The approximate net payload of 5310 pounds at 17% of GVWR on this model is ○ deficient ○ excessive ○ cautionary ○ good ● excellent *
Total highway safety penalties are: 2 *   Value: **7 5**   Durability: **7 8**   Highway Control Rating: **7 3**   Highway Safety: **7 1**   ★★★

| **Patriot** | **1998** | MHA | 40 | 40 Brandywine | MA | CA300 | D | $5000 | 272 | 5,000 | 31,000 | 27,716 |

Livability Code: FT 30-90
Wheelbase-to-length ratio of 57% is considered ○ dangerous ○ fatiguing ● good ○ excellent *
The approximate net payload of 3284 pounds at 11% of GVWR on this model is ○ deficient ○ excessive ○ cautionary ● good ○ excellent *
Total highway safety penalties are: 14 *   Value: **6 9**   Durability: **7 8**   Highway Control Rating: **8 8**   Highway Safety: **7 4**   ★★

| **Patriot** | **1998** | MHA | 40 | 40 Monticello | MA | CA300 | D | $5000 | 272 | 5,000 | 31,000 | 27,716 |

Livability Code: FT 30-90
Wheelbase-to-length ratio of 57% is considered ○ dangerous ○ fatiguing ● good ○ excellent *
The approximate net payload of 3284 pounds at 11% of GVWR on this model is ○ deficient ○ excessive ○ cautionary ● good ○ excellent *
Total highway safety penalties are: 14 *   Value: **6 9**   Durability: **7 8**   Highway Control Rating: **8 8**   Highway Safety: **7 4**   ★★

| **Patriot** | **1998** | MHA | 40 | 40 Yorktown | MA | CA300 | D | $5000 | 272 | 5,000 | 31,000 | 27,716 |

Livability Code: FT 30-90
Wheelbase-to-length ratio of 57% is considered ○ dangerous ○ fatiguing ● good ○ excellent *
The approximate net payload of 3284 pounds at 11% of GVWR on this model is ○ deficient ○ excessive ○ cautionary ● good ○ excellent *
Total highway safety penalties are: 14 *   Value: **6 9**   Durability: **7 8**   Highway Control Rating: **8 8**   Highway Safety: **7 4**   ★★

| **Patriot** | **1999** | MHA | 35 | Concord | MA | CA330 | D | $5700 | 195 | 5,000 | 31,000 | 26,011 |

Livability Code: FT 30-90
Wheelbase-to-length ratio of 47% is considered ● dangerous ○ fatiguing ○ good ○ excellent *
The approximate net payload of 4989 pounds at 16% of GVWR on this model is ○ deficient ○ excessive ○ cautionary ○ good ● excellent *
Total highway safety penalties are: 12 *   Value: **7 3**   Durability: **7 4**   Highway Control Rating: **4 2**   Highway Safety: **3 0**

| **Patriot** | **1999** | MHA | 37 | Trenton | MA | CA330 | D | $5400 | 231 | 5,000 | 31,000 | 25,772 |

Livability Code: FT 30-90
Wheelbase-to-length ratio of 52% is considered ○ dangerous ● fatiguing ○ good ○ excellent *
The approximate net payload of 5228 pounds at 17% of GVWR on this model is ○ deficient ○ excessive ○ cautionary ○ good ● excellent *
Total highway safety penalties are: 2 *   Value: **7 9**   Durability: **7 4**   Highway Control Rating: **6 6**   Highway Safety: **6 4**   ★★

| **Patriot** | **1999** | MHA | 37 | Ticonderoga | MA | CA330 | D | $5400 | 231 | 5,000 | 31,000 | 26,822 |

Livability Code: FT 30-90
Wheelbase-to-length ratio of 52% is considered ○ dangerous ● fatiguing ○ good ○ excellent *
The approximate net payload of 4178 pounds at 13% of GVWR on this model is ○ deficient ○ excessive ○ cautionary ● good ○ excellent *
Total highway safety penalties are: 13 *   Value: **7 3**   Durability: **7 4**   Highway Control Rating: **6 0**   Highway Safety: **4 7**

| **Patriot** | **1999** | MHA | 41 | Brandywine | MA | CA330 | D | $4900 | 266 | 5,000 | 31,000 | 27,834 |

Livability Code: FT 30-90
Wheelbase-to-length ratio of 54% is considered ○ dangerous ○ fatiguing ● good ○ excellent *
The approximate net payload of 3166 pounds at 10% of GVWR on this model is ○ deficient ○ excessive ○ cautionary ● good ○ excellent *
Total highway safety penalties are: 14 *   Value: **7 3**   Durability: **7 4**   Highway Control Rating: **8 0**   Highway Safety: **6 6**   ★★

Note: Safety ratings are based on the assumption that the engineering of the RV has allowed for proper balance by placing fresh, gray, and black holding tanks in a location so as not to change the balance of the RV when the tanks are empty or full. **Always double-check wheelbase, GVWR, and weights at front and rear axles.**

*See Section 1 for details on how conclusions are reached.

Brand	Year	Type	Length	Model	Chassis	Engine	Fuel Type	Average Price per Linear Foot When New	Adjusted Wheelbase	Approx. Towing Capacity	Gross Vehicle Weight Rating	Average Curb Weight

Patriot 1999 MHA 41 Monticello MA CA330 D $4900 266 5,000 31,000 27,834
Livability Code: FT 30-90
Wheelbase-to-length ratio of 54% is considered ○ dangerous ○ fatiguing ● good ○ excellent *
The approximate net payload of 3166 pounds at 10% of GVWR on this model is ○ deficient ○ excessive ○ cautionary ● good ○ excellent *
Total highway safety penalties are: 14 *   Value: 7 3   Durability: 7 4   Highway Control Rating: 8 0   Highway Safety: 6 6   ★★

Phoenix Camper Van 1999 MHB 18 170 SL FO 5.4L G $3900 138 1,500 7,500 6,604
Livability Code: VA 30-90
Wheelbase-to-length ratio of 65% is considered ○ dangerous ○ fatiguing ○ good ● excellent *
The approximate net payload of 896 pounds at 12% of GVWR on this model is ○ deficient ○ excessive ○ cautionary ● good ○ excellent *
Total highway safety penalties are: 2 *   Value: 7 7   Durability: 7 0   Highway Control Rating: 1 0 0   Highway Safety: 9 8   ★★★

Phoenix Camper Van 1999 MHB 19 190SL FO 5.4L G $3700 138 1,500 8,600 7,245
Livability Code: VA 30-90
Wheelbase-to-length ratio of 59% is considered ○ dangerous ○ fatiguing ○ good ● excellent *
The approximate net payload of 1355 pounds at 16% of GVWR on this model is ○ deficient ○ excessive ○ cautionary ○ good ● excellent *
Total highway safety penalties are: 2 *   Value: 7 7   Durability: 7 0   Highway Control Rating: 1 0 0   Highway Safety: 9 8   ★★★

Phoenix Camper Van 1999 MHB 19 190TB FO 5.4L G $3700 138 1,500 8,600 7,237
Livability Code: VA 30-90
Wheelbase-to-length ratio of 59% is considered ○ dangerous ○ fatiguing ○ good ● excellent *
The approximate net payload of 1363 pounds at 16% of GVWR on this model is ○ deficient ○ excessive ○ cautionary ○ good ● excellent *
Total highway safety penalties are: 2 *   Value: 7 7   Durability: 7 0   Highway Control Rating: 1 0 0   Highway Safety: 9 8   ★★★

Phoenix Camper Van 1999 MHB 19 190SB FO 5.4L G $3700 138 1,500 8,600 7,241
Livability Code: VA 30-90
Wheelbase-to-length ratio of 59% is considered ○ dangerous ○ fatiguing ○ good ● excellent *
The approximate net payload of 1359 pounds at 16% of GVWR on this model is ○ deficient ○ excessive ○ cautionary ○ good ● excellent *
Total highway safety penalties are: 2 *   Value: 7 7   Durability: 7 0   Highway Control Rating: 1 0 0   Highway Safety: 9 8   ★★★

Phoenix Cruiser 1999 MHC 23 23 PC FO 5.4L G $3500 158 1,500 11,500 9,522
Livability Code: VA 30-90
Wheelbase-to-length ratio of 57% is considered ○ dangerous ○ fatiguing ● good ○ excellent *
The approximate net payload of 1978 pounds at 17% of GVWR on this model is ○ deficient ○ excessive ○ cautionary ○ good ● excellent *
Total highway safety penalties are: 2 *   Value: 7 9   Durability: 7 5   Highway Control Rating: 1 0 0   Highway Safety: 9 8   ★★★

Pinnacle 1990 MHA 33 340 Q CH 7.4L G $2600 208 4,500 15,000 13,830
Livability Code: SB 30-90
Wheelbase-to-length ratio of 53% is considered ○ dangerous ● fatiguing ○ good ○ excellent *
The approximate net payload of 1170 pounds at 8% of GVWR on this model is ○ deficient ○ excessive ● cautionary ○ good ○ excellent *
Total highway safety penalties are: 6 *   Value: 7 8   Durability: 7 7   Highway Control Rating: 4 6   Highway Safety: 4 0

Pinnacle 1991 MHA 34 340QB CH 7.4L G $1400 208 1,500 15,000 13,873
Livability Code: SB 30-90
Wheelbase-to-length ratio of 51% is considered ○ dangerous ● fatiguing ○ good ○ excellent *
The approximate net payload of 1127 pounds at 8% of GVWR on this model is ○ deficient ○ excessive ● cautionary ○ good ○ excellent *
Total highway safety penalties are: 6 *   Value: 7 8   Durability: 7 7   Highway Control Rating: 2 6   Highway Safety: 2 0

Pinnacle 1992 MHA 26 265 CH 7.4L G $2200 158 1,500 12,500 11,843
Livability Code: SB 30-90
Wheelbase-to-length ratio of 50% is considered ● dangerous ○ fatiguing ○ good ○ excellent *
The approximate net payload of 657 pounds at 5% of GVWR on this model is ● deficient ○ excessive ○ cautionary ○ good ○ excellent *
Total highway safety penalties are: 3 *   Value: 7 9   Durability: 7 7   Highway Control Rating: 9   Highway Safety: 6

Pinnacle 1992 MHA 28 270 CH 7.4L G $2100 158 4,500 15,000 12,706
Livability Code: SB 30-90
Wheelbase-to-length ratio of 47% is considered ● dangerous ○ fatiguing ○ good ○ excellent *
The approximate net payload of 2294 pounds at 15% of GVWR on this model is ○ deficient ○ excessive ○ cautionary ● good ○ excellent *
Total highway safety penalties are: 3 *   Value: 7 9   Durability: 7 7   Highway Control Rating: 3 4   Highway Safety: 3 1

Pinnacle 1992 MHA 29 285 CH 7.4L G $2100 158 4,500 15,000 13,017
Livability Code: SB 30-90
Wheelbase-to-length ratio of 45% is considered ● dangerous ○ fatiguing ○ good ○ excellent *
The approximate net payload of 1983 pounds at 13% of GVWR on this model is ○ deficient ○ excessive ○ cautionary ● good ○ excellent *
Total highway safety penalties are: 4 *   Value: 7 9   Durability: 7 7   Highway Control Rating: 2 3   Highway Safety: 1 9

Pinnacle 1992 MHA 31 300 CH 7.4L G $2100 178 4,500 15,000 13,457
Livability Code: SB 30-90
Wheelbase-to-length ratio of 48% is considered ● dangerous ○ fatiguing ○ good ○ excellent *
The approximate net payload of 1543 pounds at 10% of GVWR on this model is ○ deficient ○ excessive ○ cautionary ● good ○ excellent *
Total highway safety penalties are: 5 *   Value: 7 8   Durability: 7 7   Highway Control Rating: 2 7   Highway Safety: 2 2

Note: Safety ratings are based on the assumption that the engineering of the RV has allowed for proper balance by placing fresh, gray, and black holding tanks in a location so as not to change the balance of the RV when the tanks are empty or full. **Always double-check wheelbase, GVWR, and weights at front and rear axles.**

The RV Rating Book

*See Section 1 for details on how conclusions are reached.

Section 2: The Ratings

Brand	Year	Type	Length	Model	Chassis	Engine	Fuel Type	Average Price per Linear Foot When New	Adjusted Wheelbase	Approx. Towing Capacity	Gross Vehicle Weight Rating	Average Curb Weight
Pinnacle	1992	MHA	31	305	CH	7.4L	G	$2100	178	4,500	15,000	13,457

Livability Code: SB 30-90
Wheelbase-to-length ratio of 48% is considered ●dangerous ○fatiguing ○good ○excellent *
The approximate net payload of 1543 pounds at 10% of GVWR on this model is ○deficient ○excessive ○cautionary ●good ○excellent *
Total highway safety penalties are: 5 *   Value: **78**   Durability: **77**   Highway Control Rating: **27**   Highway Safety: **22**

Brand	Year	Type	Length	Model	Chassis	Engine	Fuel Type	Average Price per Linear Foot When New	Adjusted Wheelbase	Approx. Towing Capacity	Gross Vehicle Weight Rating	Average Curb Weight
Pinnacle	1992	MHA	31	300	FO	7.5L	G	$2100	178	8,000	17,000	14,057

Livability Code: SB 30-90
Wheelbase-to-length ratio of 48% is considered ●dangerous ○fatiguing ○good ○excellent *
The approximate net payload of 2943 pounds at 17% of GVWR on this model is ○deficient ○excessive ○cautionary ○good ●excellent *
Total highway safety penalties are: 2 *   Value: **80**   Durability: **77**   Highway Control Rating: **40**   Highway Safety: **38**

Brand	Year	Type	Length	Model	Chassis	Engine	Fuel Type	Average Price per Linear Foot When New	Adjusted Wheelbase	Approx. Towing Capacity	Gross Vehicle Weight Rating	Average Curb Weight
Pinnacle	1992	MHA	31	305	FO	7.5L	G	$2100	178	8,000	17,000	14,057

Livability Code: SB 30-90
Wheelbase-to-length ratio of 48% is considered ●dangerous ○fatiguing ○good ○excellent *
The approximate net payload of 2943 pounds at 17% of GVWR on this model is ○deficient ○excessive ○cautionary ○good ●excellent *
Total highway safety penalties are: 2 *   Value: **80**   Durability: **77**   Highway Control Rating: **40**   Highway Safety: **38**

Brand	Year	Type	Length	Model	Chassis	Engine	Fuel Type	Average Price per Linear Foot When New	Adjusted Wheelbase	Approx. Towing Capacity	Gross Vehicle Weight Rating	Average Curb Weight
Pinnacle	1992	MHA	32	320	CH	7.4L	G	$2100	190	4,500	15,000	13,794

Livability Code: SB 30-90
Wheelbase-to-length ratio of 49% is considered ●dangerous ○fatiguing ○good ○excellent *
The approximate net payload of 1206 pounds at 8% of GVWR on this model is ○deficient ○excessive ●cautionary ○good ○excellent *
Total highway safety penalties are: 6 *   Value: **78**   Durability: **77**   Highway Control Rating: **20**   Highway Safety: **14**

Brand	Year	Type	Length	Model	Chassis	Engine	Fuel Type	Average Price per Linear Foot When New	Adjusted Wheelbase	Approx. Towing Capacity	Gross Vehicle Weight Rating	Average Curb Weight
Pinnacle	1992	MHA	32	320	FO	7.5L	G	$2100	190	8,000	17,000	14,394

Livability Code: SB 30-90
Wheelbase-to-length ratio of 49% is considered ●dangerous ○fatiguing ○good ○excellent *
The approximate net payload of 2606 pounds at 15% of GVWR on this model is ○deficient ○excessive ○cautionary ●good ○excellent *
Total highway safety penalties are: 2 *   Value: **80**   Durability: **77**   Highway Control Rating: **41**   Highway Safety: **39**

Brand	Year	Type	Length	Model	Chassis	Engine	Fuel Type	Average Price per Linear Foot When New	Adjusted Wheelbase	Approx. Towing Capacity	Gross Vehicle Weight Rating	Average Curb Weight
Pinnacle	1992	MHA	34	340	CH	7.4L	G	$2100	208	4,500	15,000	14,261

Livability Code: SB 30-90
Wheelbase-to-length ratio of 51% is considered ○dangerous ●fatiguing ○good ○excellent *
The approximate net payload of 739 pounds at 5% of GVWR on this model is ●deficient ○excessive ○cautionary ○good ○excellent *
Total highway safety penalties are: 6 *   Value: **78**   Durability: **77**   Highway Control Rating: **13**   Highway Safety: **7**

Brand	Year	Type	Length	Model	Chassis	Engine	Fuel Type	Average Price per Linear Foot When New	Adjusted Wheelbase	Approx. Towing Capacity	Gross Vehicle Weight Rating	Average Curb Weight
Pinnacle	1992	MHA	34	340	FO	7.5L	G	$2100	208	8,000	17,000	14,861

Livability Code: SB 30-90
Wheelbase-to-length ratio of 51% is considered ○dangerous ●fatiguing ○good ○excellent *
The approximate net payload of 2139 pounds at 13% of GVWR on this model is ○deficient ○excessive ○cautionary ●good ○excellent *
Total highway safety penalties are: 2 *   Value: **80**   Durability: **77**   Highway Control Rating: **43**   Highway Safety: **41**

Brand	Year	Type	Length	Model	Chassis	Engine	Fuel Type	Average Price per Linear Foot When New	Adjusted Wheelbase	Approx. Towing Capacity	Gross Vehicle Weight Rating	Average Curb Weight
Pinnacle	1993	MHA	29	285	CH	7.4L	G	$2100	178	4,500	15,000	13,017

Livability Code: SB 30-90
Wheelbase-to-length ratio of 51% is considered ○dangerous ●fatiguing ○good ○excellent *
The approximate net payload of 1983 pounds at 13% of GVWR on this model is ○deficient ○excessive ○cautionary ●good ○excellent *
Total highway safety penalties are: 4 *   Value: **79**   Durability: **77**   Highway Control Rating: **43**   Highway Safety: **39**

Brand	Year	Type	Length	Model	Chassis	Engine	Fuel Type	Average Price per Linear Foot When New	Adjusted Wheelbase	Approx. Towing Capacity	Gross Vehicle Weight Rating	Average Curb Weight
Pinnacle	1993	MHA	29	285	FO	7.5L	G	$2100	178	8,000	17,000	13,617

Livability Code: SB 30-90
Wheelbase-to-length ratio of 51% is considered ○dangerous ●fatiguing ○good ○excellent *
The approximate net payload of 3383 pounds at 20% of GVWR on this model is ○deficient ○excessive ○cautionary ○good ●excellent *
Total highway safety penalties are: 2 *   Value: **80**   Durability: **77**   Highway Control Rating: **53**   Highway Safety: **51**   ★

Brand	Year	Type	Length	Model	Chassis	Engine	Fuel Type	Average Price per Linear Foot When New	Adjusted Wheelbase	Approx. Towing Capacity	Gross Vehicle Weight Rating	Average Curb Weight
Pinnacle	1993	MHA	31	300	CH	7.4L	G	$2100	178	4,500	15,000	13,457

Livability Code: SB 30-90
Wheelbase-to-length ratio of 48% is considered ●dangerous ○fatiguing ○good ○excellent *
The approximate net payload of 1543 pounds at 10% of GVWR on this model is ○deficient ○excessive ○cautionary ●good ○excellent *
Total highway safety penalties are: 5 *   Value: **78**   Durability: **77**   Highway Control Rating: **27**   Highway Safety: **22**

Brand	Year	Type	Length	Model	Chassis	Engine	Fuel Type	Average Price per Linear Foot When New	Adjusted Wheelbase	Approx. Towing Capacity	Gross Vehicle Weight Rating	Average Curb Weight
Pinnacle	1993	MHA	31	305	CH	7.4L	G	$2100	178	4,500	15,000	13,457

Livability Code: SB 30-90
Wheelbase-to-length ratio of 48% is considered ●dangerous ○fatiguing ○good ○excellent *
The approximate net payload of 1543 pounds at 10% of GVWR on this model is ○deficient ○excessive ○cautionary ●good ○excellent *
Total highway safety penalties are: 5 *   Value: **78**   Durability: **77**   Highway Control Rating: **27**   Highway Safety: **22**

Brand	Year	Type	Length	Model	Chassis	Engine	Fuel Type	Average Price per Linear Foot When New	Adjusted Wheelbase	Approx. Towing Capacity	Gross Vehicle Weight Rating	Average Curb Weight
Pinnacle	1993	MHA	31	300	FO	7.5L	G	$2100	178	8,000	17,000	14,057

Livability Code: SB 30-90
Wheelbase-to-length ratio of 48% is considered ●dangerous ○fatiguing ○good ○excellent *
The approximate net payload of 2943 pounds at 17% of GVWR on this model is ○deficient ○excessive ○cautionary ○good ●excellent *
Total highway safety penalties are: 2 *   Value: **80**   Durability: **77**   Highway Control Rating: **40**   Highway Safety: **38**

Note: Safety ratings are based on the assumption that the engineering of the RV has allowed for proper balance by placing fresh, gray, and black holding tanks in a location so as not to change the balance of the RV when the tanks are empty or full. **Always double-check wheelbase, GVWR, and weights at front and rear axles.**

*See Section 1 for details on how conclusions are reached.

Brand	Year	Type	Length	Model	Chassis	Engine	Fuel Type	Average Price per Linear Foot When New	Adjusted Wheelbase	Approx. Towing Capacity	Gross Vehicle Weight Rating	Average Curb Weight

Pinnacle 1993 MHA 31 305 FO 7.5L G $2100 178 8,000 17,000 14,057
Livability Code: SB 30-90
Wheelbase-to-length ratio of 48% is considered ◉ dangerous ○ fatiguing ○ good ○ excellent *
The approximate net payload of 2943 pounds at 17% of GVWR on this model is ○ deficient ○ excessive ○ cautionary ○ good ◉ excellent *
Total highway safety penalties are: 2 *   Value: **80**   Durability: **77**   Highway Control Rating: **40**   Highway Safety: **38**

Pinnacle 1993 MHA 32 320 CH 7.4L G $2100 190 4,500 15,000 13,794
Livability Code: SB 30-90
Wheelbase-to-length ratio of 49% is considered ◉ dangerous ○ fatiguing ○ good ○ excellent *
The approximate net payload of 1206 pounds at 8% of GVWR on this model is ○ deficient ○ excessive ◉ cautionary ○ good ○ excellent *
Total highway safety penalties are: 6 *   Value: **78**   Durability: **77**   Highway Control Rating: **20**   Highway Safety: **14**

Pinnacle 1993 MHA 32 320 FO 7.5L G $2100 190 8,000 17,000 14,394
Livability Code: SB 30-90
Wheelbase-to-length ratio of 49% is considered ◉ dangerous ○ fatiguing ○ good ○ excellent *
The approximate net payload of 2606 pounds at 15% of GVWR on this model is ○ deficient ○ excessive ○ cautionary ◉ good ○ excellent *
Total highway safety penalties are: 2 *   Value: **80**   Durability: **77**   Highway Control Rating: **41**   Highway Safety: **39**

Pinnacle 1993 MHA 34 340 CH 7.4L G $2100 208 4,500 15,000 14,261
Livability Code: SB 30-90
Wheelbase-to-length ratio of 51% is considered ○ dangerous ◉ fatiguing ○ good ○ excellent *
The approximate net payload of 739 pounds at 5% of GVWR on this model is ◉ deficient ○ excessive ○ cautionary ○ good ○ excellent *
Total highway safety penalties are: 6 *   Value: **78**   Durability: **77**   Highway Control Rating: **13**   Highway Safety: **7**

Pinnacle 1993 MHA 34 340 FO 7.5L G $2100 208 8,000 17,000 14,861
Livability Code: SB 30-90
Wheelbase-to-length ratio of 51% is considered ○ dangerous ◉ fatiguing ○ good ○ excellent *
The approximate net payload of 2139 pounds at 13% of GVWR on this model is ○ deficient ○ excessive ○ cautionary ◉ good ○ excellent *
Total highway safety penalties are: 2 *   Value: **80**   Durability: **77**   Highway Control Rating: **43**   Highway Safety: **41**

Pinnacle 1994 MHA 31 305 FO 7.5L G $2100 178 8,000 17,000 14,032
Livability Code: SB 30-90
Wheelbase-to-length ratio of 48% is considered ◉ dangerous ○ fatiguing ○ good ○ excellent *
The approximate net payload of 2968 pounds at 17% of GVWR on this model is ○ deficient ○ excessive ○ cautionary ○ good ◉ excellent *
Total highway safety penalties are: 2 *   Value: **80**   Durability: **77**   Highway Control Rating: **41**   Highway Safety: **39**

Pinnacle 1994 MHA 31 300 CH 7.4L G $2100 178 4,500 15,000 13,457
Livability Code: SB 30-90
Wheelbase-to-length ratio of 48% is considered ◉ dangerous ○ fatiguing ○ good ○ excellent *
The approximate net payload of 1543 pounds at 10% of GVWR on this model is ○ deficient ○ excessive ○ cautionary ◉ good ○ excellent *
Total highway safety penalties are: 5 *   Value: **78**   Durability: **77**   Highway Control Rating: **27**   Highway Safety: **22**

Pinnacle 1994 MHA 31 305 CH 7.4L G $2100 178 4,500 15,000 13,457
Livability Code: SB 30-90
Wheelbase-to-length ratio of 48% is considered ◉ dangerous ○ fatiguing ○ good ○ excellent *
The approximate net payload of 1543 pounds at 10% of GVWR on this model is ○ deficient ○ excessive ○ cautionary ◉ good ○ excellent *
Total highway safety penalties are: 5 *   Value: **78**   Durability: **77**   Highway Control Rating: **27**   Highway Safety: **22**

Pinnacle 1994 MHA 31 300 FO 7.5L G $2100 178 8,000 17,000 14,057
Livability Code: SB 30-90
Wheelbase-to-length ratio of 48% is considered ◉ dangerous ○ fatiguing ○ good ○ excellent *
The approximate net payload of 2943 pounds at 17% of GVWR on this model is ○ deficient ○ excessive ○ cautionary ○ good ◉ excellent *
Total highway safety penalties are: 2 *   Value: **80**   Durability: **77**   Highway Control Rating: **40**   Highway Safety: **38**

Pinnacle 1994 MHA 32 320 CH 7.4L G $2200 190 4,500 15,000 13,794
Livability Code: SB 30-90
Wheelbase-to-length ratio of 49% is considered ◉ dangerous ○ fatiguing ○ good ○ excellent *
The approximate net payload of 1206 pounds at 8% of GVWR on this model is ○ deficient ○ excessive ◉ cautionary ○ good ○ excellent *
Total highway safety penalties are: 6 *   Value: **78**   Durability: **77**   Highway Control Rating: **20**   Highway Safety: **14**

Pinnacle 1994 MHA 32 320 FO 7.5L G $2200 190 8,000 17,000 14,394
Livability Code: SB 30-90
Wheelbase-to-length ratio of 49% is considered ◉ dangerous ○ fatiguing ○ good ○ excellent *
The approximate net payload of 2606 pounds at 15% of GVWR on this model is ○ deficient ○ excessive ○ cautionary ◉ good ○ excellent *
Total highway safety penalties are: 2 *   Value: **80**   Durability: **77**   Highway Control Rating: **41**   Highway Safety: **39**

Pinnacle 1994 MHA 34 340 CH 7.4L G $2100 208 1,500 16,000 14,361
Livability Code: SB 30-90
Wheelbase-to-length ratio of 51% is considered ○ dangerous ◉ fatiguing ○ good ○ excellent *
The approximate net payload of 1639 pounds at 10% of GVWR on this model is ○ deficient ○ excessive ○ cautionary ◉ good ○ excellent *
Total highway safety penalties are: 6 *   Value: **78**   Durability: **77**   Highway Control Rating: **38**   Highway Safety: **32**

Note: Safety ratings are based on the assumption that the engineering of the RV has allowed for proper balance by placing fresh, gray, and black holding tanks in a location so as not to change the balance of the RV when the tanks are empty or full. **Always double-check wheelbase, GVWR, and weights at front and rear axles.**

The RV Rating Book

*See Section 1 for details on how conclusions are reached.

Brand	Year	Type	Length	Model	Chassis	Engine	Fuel Type	Average Price per Linear Foot When New	Adjusted Wheelbase	Approx. Towing Capacity	Gross Vehicle Weight Rating	Average Curb Weight
Pinnacle	**1994**	MHA	34	340	FO	7.5L	G	$2100	208	8,000	17,000	14,861

Livability Code: SB 30-90
Wheelbase-to-length ratio of 51% is considered ○ dangerous ◉ fatiguing ○ good ○ excellent *
The approximate net payload of 2139 pounds at 13% of GVWR on this model is ○ deficient ○ excessive ○ cautionary ◉ good ○ excellent *
Total highway safety penalties are: 2 *   Value: 80   Durability: 77   Highway Control Rating: 43   Highway Safety: 41

Pinnacle	**1995**	MHA	31	305	FO	7.5L	G	$2100	178	8,000	17,000	14,032

Livability Code: SB 30-90
Wheelbase-to-length ratio of 48% is considered ◉ dangerous ○ fatiguing ○ good ○ excellent *
The approximate net payload of 2968 pounds at 17% of GVWR on this model is ○ deficient ○ excessive ○ cautionary ○ good ◉ excellent *
Total highway safety penalties are: 2 *   Value: 80   Durability: 77   Highway Control Rating: 41   Highway Safety: 39

Pinnacle	**1995**	MHA	31	300	CH	7.4L	G	$2100	178	4,500	15,000	13,457

Livability Code: SB 30-90
Wheelbase-to-length ratio of 48% is considered ◉ dangerous ○ fatiguing ○ good ○ excellent *
The approximate net payload of 1543 pounds at 10% of GVWR on this model is ○ deficient ○ excessive ○ cautionary ◉ good ○ excellent *
Total highway safety penalties are: 5 *   Value: 78   Durability: 77   Highway Control Rating: 27   Highway Safety: 22

Pinnacle	**1995**	MHA	31	305	CH	7.4L	G	$2100	178	4,500	15,000	13,457

Livability Code: SB 30-90
Wheelbase-to-length ratio of 48% is considered ◉ dangerous ○ fatiguing ○ good ○ excellent *
The approximate net payload of 1543 pounds at 10% of GVWR on this model is ○ deficient ○ excessive ○ cautionary ◉ good ○ excellent *
Total highway safety penalties are: 5 *   Value: 78   Durability: 77   Highway Control Rating: 27   Highway Safety: 22

Pinnacle	**1995**	MHA	31	300	FO	7.5L	G	$2100	178	8,000	17,000	14,057

Livability Code: SB 30-90
Wheelbase-to-length ratio of 48% is considered ◉ dangerous ○ fatiguing ○ good ○ excellent *
The approximate net payload of 2943 pounds at 17% of GVWR on this model is ○ deficient ○ excessive ○ cautionary ○ good ◉ excellent *
Total highway safety penalties are: 2 *   Value: 80   Durability: 77   Highway Control Rating: 40   Highway Safety: 38

Pinnacle	**1995**	MHA	32	320	CH	7.4L	G	$2200	190	4,500	15,000	13,794

Livability Code: SB 30-90
Wheelbase-to-length ratio of 49% is considered ◉ dangerous ○ fatiguing ○ good ○ excellent *
The approximate net payload of 1206 pounds at 8% of GVWR on this model is ○ deficient ○ excessive ◉ cautionary ○ good ○ excellent *
Total highway safety penalties are: 6 *   Value: 78   Durability: 77   Highway Control Rating: 20   Highway Safety: 14

Pinnacle	**1995**	MHA	32	320	FO	7.5L	G	$2200	190	8,000	17,000	14,394

Livability Code: SB 30-90
Wheelbase-to-length ratio of 49% is considered ◉ dangerous ○ fatiguing ○ good ○ excellent *
The approximate net payload of 2606 pounds at 15% of GVWR on this model is ○ deficient ○ excessive ○ cautionary ◉ good ○ excellent *
Total highway safety penalties are: 2 *   Value: 80   Durability: 77   Highway Control Rating: 41   Highway Safety: 39

Pinnacle	**1995**	MHA	34	340	CH	7.4L	G	$2100	208	1,500	16,000	14,361

Livability Code: SB 30-90
Wheelbase-to-length ratio of 51% is considered ○ dangerous ◉ fatiguing ○ good ○ excellent *
The approximate net payload of 1639 pounds at 10% of GVWR on this model is ○ deficient ○ excessive ○ cautionary ◉ good ○ excellent *
Total highway safety penalties are: 6 *   Value: 78   Durability: 77   Highway Control Rating: 38   Highway Safety: 32

Pinnacle	**1995**	MHA	34	340LX	CH	7.4L	G	$2100	208	1,500	16,000	14,361

Livability Code: SB 30-90
Wheelbase-to-length ratio of 51% is considered ○ dangerous ◉ fatiguing ○ good ○ excellent *
The approximate net payload of 1639 pounds at 10% of GVWR on this model is ○ deficient ○ excessive ○ cautionary ◉ good ○ excellent *
Total highway safety penalties are: 6 *   Value: 78   Durability: 77   Highway Control Rating: 38   Highway Safety: 32

Pinnacle	**1995**	MHA	34	340	FO	7.5L	G	$2100	208	8,000	17,000	14,861

Livability Code: SB 30-90
Wheelbase-to-length ratio of 51% is considered ○ dangerous ◉ fatiguing ○ good ○ excellent *
The approximate net payload of 2139 pounds at 13% of GVWR on this model is ○ deficient ○ excessive ○ cautionary ◉ good ○ excellent *
Total highway safety penalties are: 2 *   Value: 80   Durability: 77   Highway Control Rating: 43   Highway Safety: 41

Pinnacle	**1995**	MHA	34	340LX	FO	7.5L	G	$2100	208	8,000	17,000	14,861

Livability Code: SB 30-90
Wheelbase-to-length ratio of 51% is considered ○ dangerous ◉ fatiguing ○ good ○ excellent *
The approximate net payload of 2139 pounds at 13% of GVWR on this model is ○ deficient ○ excessive ○ cautionary ◉ good ○ excellent *
Total highway safety penalties are: 2 *   Value: 80   Durability: 77   Highway Control Rating: 43   Highway Safety: 41

Pinnacle	**1997**	MHA	30	2955	FO	7.5L	G	$2300	190	8,000	17,000	14,065

Livability Code: SB 30-90
Wheelbase-to-length ratio of 53% is considered ○ dangerous ◉ fatiguing ○ good ○ excellent *
The approximate net payload of 2935 pounds at 17% of GVWR on this model is ○ deficient ○ excessive ○ cautionary ○ good ◉ excellent *
Total highway safety penalties are: 2 *   Value: 80   Durability: 77   Highway Control Rating: 71   Highway Safety: 69   ★★

Note: Safety ratings are based on the assumption that the engineering of the RV has allowed for proper balance by placing fresh, gray, and black holding tanks in a location so as not to change the balance of the RV when the tanks are empty or full. **Always double-check wheelbase, GVWR, and weights at front and rear axles.**

*See Section 1 for details on how conclusions are reached.

Brand	Year	Type	Length	Model	Chassis	Engine	Fuel Type	Average Price per Linear Foot When New	Adjusted Wheelbase	Approx. Towing Capacity	Gross Vehicle Weight Rating	Average Curb Weight
Pinnacle	1997	MHA	31	3050	FO	7.5L	G	$2300	190	8,000	17,000	15,205

Livability Code: SB 30-90
Wheelbase-to-length ratio of 51% is considered ○ dangerous ● fatiguing ○ good ○ excellent *
The approximate net payload of 1795 pounds at 11% of GVWR on this model is ○ deficient ● excessive ○ cautionary ● good ○ excellent *
Total highway safety penalties are: 7 * Value: 7 7 Durability: 7 7 Highway Control Rating: 3 8 Highway Safety: 3 1

Brand	Year	Type	Length	Model	Chassis	Engine	Fuel Type	Price/Lin Ft	Wheelbase	Towing	GVWR	Curb Weight
Pinnacle	1997	MHA	33	3390	FO	7.5L	G	$2200	232 T	5,000	20,000	17,173

Livability Code: SB 30-90
Wheelbase-to-length ratio of 59% is considered ○ dangerous ○ fatiguing ○ good ● excellent *
The approximate net payload of 2828 pounds at 14% of GVWR on this model is ○ deficient ○ excessive ○ cautionary ● good ○ excellent *
Total highway safety penalties are: 10 * Value: 7 6 Durability: 7 7 Highway Control Rating: 1 0 0 Highway Safety: 9 0 ★★★

Pinnacle	1997	MHA	35	3480	FO	7.5L	G	$2100	232 T	5,000	20,000	17,521

Livability Code: SB 30-90
Wheelbase-to-length ratio of 55% is considered ○ dangerous ○ fatiguing ● good ○ excellent *
The approximate net payload of 2480 pounds at 12% of GVWR on this model is ○ deficient ○ excessive ○ cautionary ● good ○ excellent *
Total highway safety penalties are: 10 * Value: 7 6 Durability: 7 7 Highway Control Rating: 8 5 Highway Safety: 7 5 ★★★

Pinnacle	1997	MHA	35	3485	FO	7.5L	G	$2100	228	8,000	17,000	15,433

Livability Code: SB 30-90
Wheelbase-to-length ratio of 54% is considered ○ dangerous ○ fatiguing ● good ○ excellent *
The approximate net payload of 1567 pounds at 9% of GVWR on this model is ○ deficient ○ excessive ● cautionary ○ good ○ excellent *
Total highway safety penalties are: 2 * Value: 8 0 Durability: 7 7 Highway Control Rating: 6 5 Highway Safety: 6 3 ★★

Pinnacle	1998	MHA	30	P2955	FO	7.5L	G	$2400	190	8,000	17,000	14,025

Livability Code: SB 30-90
Wheelbase-to-length ratio of 53% is considered ○ dangerous ● fatiguing ○ good ○ excellent *
The approximate net payload of 2975 pounds at 18% of GVWR on this model is ○ deficient ○ excessive ○ cautionary ● good ○ excellent *
Total highway safety penalties are: 2 * Value: 8 0 Durability: 7 7 Highway Control Rating: 7 1 Highway Safety: 6 9 ★★

Pinnacle	1998	MHA	31	P3050	FO	7.5L	G	$2400	190	8,000	17,000	14,483

Livability Code: SB 30-90
Wheelbase-to-length ratio of 51% is considered ○ dangerous ● fatiguing ○ good ○ excellent *
The approximate net payload of 2518 pounds at 15% of GVWR on this model is ○ deficient ○ excessive ○ cautionary ● good ○ excellent *
Total highway safety penalties are: 5 * Value: 7 8 Durability: 7 7 Highway Control Rating: 4 6 Highway Safety: 4 1

Pinnacle	1998	MHA	34	P3390	FO	7.5L	G	$2600	232 T	5,000	20,000	17,228

Livability Code: SB 30-90
Wheelbase-to-length ratio of 57% is considered ○ dangerous ○ fatiguing ● good ○ excellent *
The approximate net payload of 2772 pounds at 14% of GVWR on this model is ○ deficient ○ excessive ○ cautionary ● good ○ excellent *
Total highway safety penalties are: 11 * Value: 7 5 Durability: 7 7 Highway Control Rating: 9 4 Highway Safety: 8 3 ★★★

Pinnacle	1998	MHA	35	P3480	FO	7.5L	G	$2500	232 T	5,000	20,000	17,296

Livability Code: SB 30-90
Wheelbase-to-length ratio of 55% is considered ○ dangerous ○ fatiguing ● good ○ excellent *
The approximate net payload of 2705 pounds at 14% of GVWR on this model is ○ deficient ○ excessive ○ cautionary ● good ○ excellent *
Total highway safety penalties are: 10 * Value: 7 6 Durability: 7 7 Highway Control Rating: 8 8 Highway Safety: 7 8 ★★★

Pinnacle	1998	MHA	35	P3485	FO	7.5L	G	$2200	228	8,000	17,000	15,208

Livability Code: SB 30-90
Wheelbase-to-length ratio of 54% is considered ○ dangerous ○ fatiguing ● good ○ excellent *
The approximate net payload of 1792 pounds at 11% of GVWR on this model is ○ deficient ○ excessive ○ cautionary ● good ○ excellent *
Total highway safety penalties are: 2 * Value: 8 0 Durability: 7 7 Highway Control Rating: 7 6 Highway Safety: 7 4 ★★★

Pinnacle	1998	MHA	36	P3505	FO	7.5L	G	$2100	228	8,000	17,000	15,845

Livability Code: SB 30-90
Wheelbase-to-length ratio of 53% is considered ○ dangerous ● fatiguing ○ good ○ excellent *
The approximate net payload of 1155 pounds at 7% of GVWR on this model is ○ deficient ○ excessive ● cautionary ○ good ○ excellent *
Total highway safety penalties are: 2 * Value: 8 0 Durability: 7 7 Highway Control Rating: 4 1 Highway Safety: 3 9

Pinnacle by Establish.	1989	MHA	31	310	CH	7.4L	G	$1600	178	2,500	14,500	12,888

Livability Code: SB 30-90
Wheelbase-to-length ratio of 48% is considered ● dangerous ○ fatiguing ○ good ○ excellent *
The approximate net payload of 1612 pounds at 11% of GVWR on this model is ○ deficient ○ excessive ○ cautionary ● good ○ excellent *
Total highway safety penalties are: 5 * Value: 7 8 Durability: 7 7 Highway Control Rating: 2 6 Highway Safety: 2 1

Pinnacle by Thor	1999	MHA	31	2955	FO	6.8L	G	$2400	190	7,000	18,000	15,124

Livability Code: SB 30-90
Wheelbase-to-length ratio of 51% is considered ○ dangerous ● fatiguing ○ good ○ excellent *
The approximate net payload of 2876 pounds at 16% of GVWR on this model is ○ deficient ○ excessive ○ cautionary ○ good ● excellent *
Total highway safety penalties are: 2 * Value: 8 0 Durability: 7 7 Highway Control Rating: 6 0 Highway Safety: 5 8 ★

Note: Safety ratings are based on the assumption that the engineering of the RV has allowed for proper balance by placing fresh, gray, and black holding tanks in a location so as not to change the balance of the RV when the tanks are empty or full. **Always double-check wheelbase, GVWR, and weights at front and rear axles.**

Brand	Year	Type	Length	Model	Chassis	Engine	Fuel Type	Average Price per Linear Foot When New	Adjusted Wheelbase	Approx. Towing Capacity	Gross Vehicle Weight Rating	Average Curb Weight

Pinnacle by Thor — 1999 — MHA — 32 — 3050 — FO — 6.8L — G — $2300 — 190 — 7,000 — 18,000 — 15,873

Livability Code: SB 30-90
Wheelbase-to-length ratio of 50% is considered ◉ dangerous ○ fatiguing ○ good ○ excellent *
The approximate net payload of 2127 pounds at 12% of GVWR on this model is ○ deficient ○ excessive ○ cautionary ◉ good ○ excellent *
Total highway safety penalties are: 5 *   Value: 7 8   Durability: 7 7   Highway Control Rating: 4 7   Highway Safety: 4 2

Pinnacle by Thor — 1999 — MHA — 35 — 3390 — FO — 6.8L — G — $2100 — 228 — 4,500 — 20,500 — 18,085

Livability Code: SB 30-90
Wheelbase-to-length ratio of 55% is considered ○ dangerous ○ fatiguing ◉ good ○ excellent *
The approximate net payload of 2415 pounds at 12% of GVWR on this model is ○ deficient ○ excessive ○ cautionary ◉ good ○ excellent *
Total highway safety penalties are: 16 *   Value: 7 3   Durability: 7 7   Highway Control Rating: 8 5   Highway Safety: 6 9   ★★

Pinnacle by Thor — 1999 — MHA — 36 — 3480 — FO — 6.8L — G — $2100 — 232 T — 4,500 — 20,500 — 18,324

Livability Code: SB 30-90
Wheelbase-to-length ratio of 54% is considered ○ dangerous ○ fatiguing ◉ good ○ excellent *
The approximate net payload of 2176 pounds at 11% of GVWR on this model is ○ deficient ○ excessive ○ cautionary ◉ good ○ excellent *
Total highway safety penalties are: 10 *   Value: 7 6   Durability: 7 7   Highway Control Rating: 7 9   Highway Safety: 6 9   ★★

Pinnacle by Thor — 1999 — MHA — 36 — 3490 — FO — 6.8L — G — $2100 — 232 T — 4,500 — 20,500 — 18,849

Livability Code: SB 30-90
Wheelbase-to-length ratio of 54% is considered ○ dangerous ○ fatiguing ◉ good ○ excellent *
The approximate net payload of 1651 pounds at 8% of GVWR on this model is ○ deficient ○ excessive ◉ cautionary ○ good ○ excellent *
Total highway safety penalties are: 13 *   Value: 7 4   Durability: 7 7   Highway Control Rating: 6 1   Highway Safety: 4 8

Pinnacle by Thor — 1999 — MHA — 37 — 3505 — FO — 6.8L — G — $2000 — 228 — 7,000 — 18,000 — 16,748

Livability Code: SB 30-90
Wheelbase-to-length ratio of 52% is considered ○ dangerous ◉ fatiguing ○ good ○ excellent *
The approximate net payload of 1252 pounds at 7% of GVWR on this model is ○ deficient ○ excessive ◉ cautionary ○ good ○ excellent *
Total highway safety penalties are: 2 *   Value: 8 0   Durability: 7 7   Highway Control Rating: 3 8   Highway Safety: 3 6

Pleasure-Way — 1997 — MHB — 19 — SRL — DO — 5.2L — G — $2600 — 127 — 1,500 — 8,510 — 7,146

Livability Code: VA 30-90
Wheelbase-to-length ratio of 55% is considered ○ dangerous ○ fatiguing ◉ good ○ excellent *
The approximate net payload of 1364 pounds at 16% of GVWR on this model is ○ deficient ○ excessive ○ cautionary ○ good ◉ excellent *
Total highway safety penalties are: 2 *   Value: 8 5   Durability: 7 8   Highway Control Rating: 9 3   Highway Safety: 9 1   ★★★

Pleasure-Way — 1997 — MHB — 19 — STW — DO — 5.2L — G — $2600 — 127 — 1,500 — 8,510 — 7,146

Livability Code: VA 30-90
Wheelbase-to-length ratio of 55% is considered ○ dangerous ○ fatiguing ◉ good ○ excellent *
The approximate net payload of 1364 pounds at 16% of GVWR on this model is ○ deficient ○ excessive ○ cautionary ○ good ◉ excellent *
Total highway safety penalties are: 2 *   Value: 8 5   Durability: 7 8   Highway Control Rating: 9 3   Highway Safety: 9 1   ★★★

Pleasure-Way — 1997 — MHB — 19 — MPL — DO — 5.2L — G — $2600 — 127 — 1,500 — 8,510 — 7,146

Livability Code: VA 30-90
Wheelbase-to-length ratio of 55% is considered ○ dangerous ○ fatiguing ◉ good ○ excellent *
The approximate net payload of 1364 pounds at 16% of GVWR on this model is ○ deficient ○ excessive ○ cautionary ○ good ◉ excellent *
Total highway safety penalties are: 2 *   Value: 8 5   Durability: 7 8   Highway Control Rating: 9 3   Highway Safety: 9 1   ★★★

Pleasure-Way — 1997 — MHB — 19 — EXCELL-RL — DO — 5.2L — G — $2800 — 127 — 1,500 — 8,510 — 7,106

Livability Code: VA 30-90
Wheelbase-to-length ratio of 55% is considered ○ dangerous ○ fatiguing ◉ good ○ excellent *
The approximate net payload of 1404 pounds at 16% of GVWR on this model is ○ deficient ○ excessive ○ cautionary ○ good ◉ excellent *
Total highway safety penalties are: 2 *   Value: 8 5   Durability: 7 8   Highway Control Rating: 9 3   Highway Safety: 9 1   ★★★

Pleasure-Way — 1997 — MHB — 19 — EXCELL-TW — DO — 5.2L — G — $2800 — 127 — 1,500 — 8,510 — 7,106

Livability Code: VA 30-90
Wheelbase-to-length ratio of 55% is considered ○ dangerous ○ fatiguing ◉ good ○ excellent *
The approximate net payload of 1404 pounds at 16% of GVWR on this model is ○ deficient ○ excessive ○ cautionary ○ good ◉ excellent *
Total highway safety penalties are: 2 *   Value: 8 5   Durability: 7 8   Highway Control Rating: 9 3   Highway Safety: 9 1   ★★★

Pleasure-Way — 1997 — MHB — 19 — EXCELL-MP — DO — 5.2L — G — $2800 — 127 — 1,500 — 8,510 — 7,106

Livability Code: VA 30-90
Wheelbase-to-length ratio of 55% is considered ○ dangerous ○ fatiguing ◉ good ○ excellent *
The approximate net payload of 1404 pounds at 16% of GVWR on this model is ○ deficient ○ excessive ○ cautionary ○ good ◉ excellent *
Total highway safety penalties are: 2 *   Value: 8 5   Durability: 7 8   Highway Control Rating: 9 3   Highway Safety: 9 1   ★★★

Pleasure-Way — 1998 — MHB — accurate specs n/a — ?

Livability Code: VA 30-90
Wheelbase-to-length ratio of ? is considered ○ dangerous ○ fatiguing ○ good ○ excellent *
The approximate net payload of pounds at of GVWR on this model is ○ deficient ○ excessive ○ cautionary ○ good ○ excellent *
Total highway safety penalties are: 0 *   Value: 0   Durability: 7 8   Highway Control Rating: 0   Highway Safety: 0

Note: Safety ratings are based on the assumption that the engineering of the RV has allowed for proper balance by placing fresh, gray, and black holding tanks in a location so as not to change the balance of the RV when the tanks are empty or full. **Always double-check wheelbase, GVWR, and weights at front and rear axles.**

*See Section 1 for details on how conclusions are reached.

Brand	Year	Type	Length	Model	Chassis	Engine	Fuel Type	Average Price per Linear Foot When New	Adjusted Wheelbase	Approx. Towing Capacity	Gross Vehicle Weight Rating	Average Curb Weight
Pleasure-Way	1999	MHB	20	Excel RL	DO	5.9L	G	$2800	127	1,500	9,200	7,866

Livability Code: VA 30-90
Wheelbase-to-length ratio of 54% is considered ○ dangerous ○ fatiguing ◉ good ○ excellent *
The approximate net payload of 1334 pounds at 14% of GVWR on this model is ○ deficient ○ excessive ○ cautionary ◉ good ○ excellent *
Total highway safety penalties are: 2 * Value: 86 Durability: 80 Highway Control Rating: 82 Highway Safety: 80 ★★★★

Brand	Year	Type	Length	Model	Chassis	Engine	Fuel Type	Price/Ft	Wheelbase	Towing	GVWR	Curb Wt
Pleasure-Way	1999	MHB	20	Excel TW	DO	5.9L	G	$2800	127	1,500	9,200	7,866

Livability Code: VA 30-90
Wheelbase-to-length ratio of 54% is considered ○ dangerous ○ fatiguing ◉ good ○ excellent *
The approximate net payload of 1334 pounds at 14% of GVWR on this model is ○ deficient ○ excessive ○ cautionary ◉ good ○ excellent *
Total highway safety penalties are: 2 * Value: 86 Durability: 80 Highway Control Rating: 82 Highway Safety: 80 ★★★★

Pleasure-Way	1999	MHB	20	Excel MP	DO	5.9L	G	$2800	127	1,500	9,200	7,866

Livability Code: VA 30-90
Wheelbase-to-length ratio of 54% is considered ○ dangerous ○ fatiguing ◉ good ○ excellent *
The approximate net payload of 1334 pounds at 14% of GVWR on this model is ○ deficient ○ excessive ○ cautionary ◉ good ○ excellent *
Total highway safety penalties are: 2 * Value: 86 Durability: 80 Highway Control Rating: 82 Highway Safety: 80 ★★★★

Pleasure-Way	1999	MHB	20	Excel SRL	DO	5.9L	G	$2800	127	1,500	8,700	7,322

Livability Code: VA 30-90
Wheelbase-to-length ratio of 54% is considered ○ dangerous ○ fatiguing ◉ good ○ excellent *
The approximate net payload of 1379 pounds at 16% of GVWR on this model is ○ deficient ○ excessive ○ cautionary ○ good ◉ excellent *
Total highway safety penalties are: 2 * Value: 86 Durability: 80 Highway Control Rating: 85 Highway Safety: 83 ★★★★

Pleasure-Way	1999	MHB	20	Excel STW	DO	5.9L	G	$2800	127	1,500	8,700	7,322

Livability Code: VA 30-90
Wheelbase-to-length ratio of 54% is considered ○ dangerous ○ fatiguing ◉ good ○ excellent *
The approximate net payload of 1379 pounds at 16% of GVWR on this model is ○ deficient ○ excessive ○ cautionary ○ good ◉ excellent *
Total highway safety penalties are: 2 * Value: 86 Durability: 80 Highway Control Rating: 85 Highway Safety: 83 ★★★★

Pleasure-Way	1999	MHB	20	Excel MPL	DO	5.9L	G	$2800	127	1,500	8,700	7,322

Livability Code: VA 30-90
Wheelbase-to-length ratio of 54% is considered ○ dangerous ○ fatiguing ◉ good ○ excellent *
The approximate net payload of 1379 pounds at 16% of GVWR on this model is ○ deficient ○ excessive ○ cautionary ◉ good ○ excellent *
Total highway safety penalties are: 2 * Value: 86 Durability: 80 Highway Control Rating: 85 Highway Safety: 83 ★★★★

Premier	1990	MHA	37	36	RO	Cum	D	$4300	228	1,500	25,300	23,894

Livability Code: FT 30-90
Wheelbase-to-length ratio of 52% is considered ○ dangerous ◉ fatiguing ○ good ○ excellent *
The approximate net payload of 1406 pounds at 6% of GVWR on this model is ◉ deficient ○ excessive ○ cautionary ○ good ○ excellent *
Total highway safety penalties are: 2 * Value: 79 Durability: 75 Highway Control Rating: 24 Highway Safety: 22

Pursuit	1995	MHA	26	2500	CH	7.4L	G	$1800	158	1,500	12,300	10,423

Livability Code: SB 30-90
Wheelbase-to-length ratio of 51% is considered ○ dangerous ◉ fatiguing ○ good ○ excellent *
The approximate net payload of 1877 pounds at 15% of GVWR on this model is ○ deficient ○ excessive ○ cautionary ◉ good ○ excellent *
Total highway safety penalties are: 2 * Value: 77 Durability: 71 Highway Control Rating: 46 Highway Safety: 44

Pursuit	1995	MHA	29	2805	CH	7.4L	G	$1700	178	4,200	14,800	11,693

Livability Code: SB 30-90
Wheelbase-to-length ratio of 51% is considered ○ dangerous ◉ fatiguing ○ good ○ excellent *
The approximate net payload of 3107 pounds at 21% of GVWR on this model is ○ deficient ○ excessive ○ cautionary ○ good ◉ excellent *
Total highway safety penalties are: 4 * Value: 76 Durability: 71 Highway Control Rating: 52 Highway Safety: 48

Pursuit	1995	MHA	29	2805	FO	7.5L	G	$1700	178	3,800	15,200	12,237

Livability Code: SB 30-90
Wheelbase-to-length ratio of 51% is considered ○ dangerous ◉ fatiguing ○ good ○ excellent *
The approximate net payload of 2964 pounds at 19% of GVWR on this model is ○ deficient ○ excessive ○ cautionary ○ good ◉ excellent *
Total highway safety penalties are: 2 * Value: 77 Durability: 71 Highway Control Rating: 52 Highway Safety: 50 ★

Pursuit	1995	MHA	30	2900	CH	7.4L	G	$1700	190	4,200	14,800	11,882

Livability Code: SB 30-90
Wheelbase-to-length ratio of 53% is considered ○ dangerous ◉ fatiguing ○ good ○ excellent *
The approximate net payload of 2919 pounds at 20% of GVWR on this model is ○ deficient ○ excessive ○ cautionary ○ good ◉ excellent *
Total highway safety penalties are: 5 * Value: 76 Durability: 71 Highway Control Rating: 73 Highway Safety: 68 ★★

Pursuit	1995	MHA	30	2900	FO	7.5L	G	$1700	190	8,000	17,000	12,655

Livability Code: SB 30-90
Wheelbase-to-length ratio of 53% is considered ○ dangerous ◉ fatiguing ○ good ○ excellent *
The approximate net payload of 4345 pounds at 26% of GVWR on this model is ○ deficient ○ excessive ○ cautionary ◉ good ○ excellent *
Total highway safety penalties are: 2 * Value: 77 Durability: 71 Highway Control Rating: 68 Highway Safety: 66 ★★

Note: Safety ratings are based on the assumption that the engineering of the RV has allowed for proper balance by placing fresh, gray, and black holding tanks in a location so as not to change the balance of the RV when the tanks are empty or full. **Always double-check wheelbase, GVWR, and weights at front and rear axles.**

*See Section 1 for details on how conclusions are reached.

Section 2: The Ratings

Brand	Year	Type	Length	Model	Chassis	Engine	Fuel Type	Average Price per Linear Foot When New	Adjusted Wheelbase	Approx. Towing Capacity	Gross Vehicle Weight Rating	Average Curb Weight
Pursuit	1995	MHA	33	3200	CH	7.4L	G	$1500	208	4,200	14,800	12,246

Livability Code: SB 30-90 Wheelbase-to-length ratio of 53% is considered ○ dangerous ◉ fatiguing ○ good ○ excellent *

The approximate net payload of 2554 pounds at 17% of GVWR on this model is ○ deficient ○ excessive ○ cautionary ○ good ◉ excellent *

Total highway safety penalties are: 6 * Value: 7 5 Durability: 7 1 Highway Control Rating: 7 2 Highway Safety: 6 6 ★★

Brand	Year	Type	Length	Model	Chassis	Engine	Fuel Type	Avg Price/Lin Ft	Adj Wheelbase	Tow Cap	GVWR	Avg Curb Wt
Pursuit	1995	MHA	33	3200	FO	7.5L	G	$1500	208	3,800	15,200	13,045

Livability Code: SB 30-90 Wheelbase-to-length ratio of 53% is considered ○ dangerous ◉ fatiguing ○ good ○ excellent *

The approximate net payload of 2155 pounds at 14% of GVWR on this model is ○ deficient ○ excessive ○ cautionary ◉ good ○ excellent *

Total highway safety penalties are: 2 * Value: 7 7 Durability: 7 1 Highway Control Rating: 6 7 Highway Safety: 6 5 ★★

Brand	Year	Type	Length	Model	Chassis	Engine	Fuel Type	Avg Price/Lin Ft	Adj Wheelbase	Tow Cap	GVWR	Avg Curb Wt
Pursuit	1996	MHA	26	2501	CH	7.4L	G	$1800	158	1,500	12,300	10,577

Livability Code: SB 30-90 Wheelbase-to-length ratio of 51% is considered ○ dangerous ◉ fatiguing ○ good ○ excellent *

The approximate net payload of 1723 pounds at 14% of GVWR on this model is ○ deficient ○ excessive ○ cautionary ◉ good ○ excellent *

Total highway safety penalties are: 2 * Value: 7 7 Durability: 7 1 Highway Control Rating: 4 4 Highway Safety: 4 2

Brand	Year	Type	Length	Model	Chassis	Engine	Fuel Type	Avg Price/Lin Ft	Adj Wheelbase	Tow Cap	GVWR	Avg Curb Wt
Pursuit	1996	MHA	29	2808	CH	7.4L	G	$1700	178	1,500	14,800	11,678

Livability Code: SB 30-90 Wheelbase-to-length ratio of 51% is considered ○ dangerous ◉ fatiguing ○ good ○ excellent *

The approximate net payload of 3122 pounds at 21% of GVWR on this model is ○ deficient ○ excessive ○ cautionary ○ good ◉ excellent *

Total highway safety penalties are: 4 * Value: 7 6 Durability: 7 1 Highway Control Rating: 5 2 Highway Safety: 4 8

Brand	Year	Type	Length	Model	Chassis	Engine	Fuel Type	Avg Price/Lin Ft	Adj Wheelbase	Tow Cap	GVWR	Avg Curb Wt
Pursuit	1996	MHA	29	2808	FO	7.5	G	$1700	178	1,500	15,200	12,237

Livability Code: SB 30-90 Wheelbase-to-length ratio of 51% is considered ○ dangerous ◉ fatiguing ○ good ○ excellent *

The approximate net payload of 2964 pounds at 19% of GVWR on this model is ○ deficient ○ excessive ○ cautionary ○ good ◉ excellent *

Total highway safety penalties are: 2 * Value: 7 7 Durability: 7 1 Highway Control Rating: 5 2 Highway Safety: 5 0 ★

Brand	Year	Type	Length	Model	Chassis	Engine	Fuel Type	Avg Price/Lin Ft	Adj Wheelbase	Tow Cap	GVWR	Avg Curb Wt
Pursuit	1996	MHA	31	2901	CH	7.4L	G	$1600	190	1,500	14,800	12,256

Livability Code: SB 30-90 Wheelbase-to-length ratio of 51% is considered ○ dangerous ◉ fatiguing ○ good ○ excellent *

The approximate net payload of 2544 pounds at 17% of GVWR on this model is ○ deficient ○ excessive ○ cautionary ○ good ◉ excellent *

Total highway safety penalties are: 5 * Value: 7 6 Durability: 7 1 Highway Control Rating: 5 0 Highway Safety: 4 5

Brand	Year	Type	Length	Model	Chassis	Engine	Fuel Type	Avg Price/Lin Ft	Adj Wheelbase	Tow Cap	GVWR	Avg Curb Wt
Pursuit	1996	MHA	31	2901	FO	7.5L	G	$1600	190	1,500	15,200	12,674

Livability Code: SB 30-90 Wheelbase-to-length ratio of 51% is considered ○ dangerous ◉ fatiguing ○ good ○ excellent *

The approximate net payload of 2527 pounds at 17% of GVWR on this model is ○ deficient ○ excessive ○ cautionary ○ good ◉ excellent *

Total highway safety penalties are: 2 * Value: 7 7 Durability: 7 1 Highway Control Rating: 4 9 Highway Safety: 4 7

Brand	Year	Type	Length	Model	Chassis	Engine	Fuel Type	Avg Price/Lin Ft	Adj Wheelbase	Tow Cap	GVWR	Avg Curb Wt
Pursuit	1996	MHA	33	3200	CH	7.4L	G	$1600	208	1,500	14,800	12,474

Livability Code: SB 30-90 Wheelbase-to-length ratio of 53% is considered ○ dangerous ◉ fatiguing ○ good ○ excellent *

The approximate net payload of 2326 pounds at 16% of GVWR on this model is ○ deficient ○ excessive ○ cautionary ○ good ◉ excellent *

Total highway safety penalties are: 6 * Value: 7 5 Durability: 7 1 Highway Control Rating: 7 0 Highway Safety: 6 4 ★★

Brand	Year	Type	Length	Model	Chassis	Engine	Fuel Type	Avg Price/Lin Ft	Adj Wheelbase	Tow Cap	GVWR	Avg Curb Wt
Pursuit	1996	MHA	33	3200	FO	7.5L	G	$1600	208	1,500	15,200	13,045

Livability Code: SB 30-90 Wheelbase-to-length ratio of 53% is considered ○ dangerous ◉ fatiguing ○ good ○ excellent *

The approximate net payload of 2155 pounds at 14% of GVWR on this model is ○ deficient ○ excessive ○ cautionary ◉ good ○ excellent *

Total highway safety penalties are: 2 * Value: 7 7 Durability: 7 1 Highway Control Rating: 6 7 Highway Safety: 6 5 ★★

Brand	Year	Type	Length	Model	Chassis	Engine	Fuel Type	Avg Price/Lin Ft	Adj Wheelbase	Tow Cap	GVWR	Avg Curb Wt
Pursuit	1997	MHA	26	2501	CH	7.4L	G	$1800	158	4,700	12,300	10,786

Livability Code: SB 30-90 Wheelbase-to-length ratio of 51% is considered ○ dangerous ◉ fatiguing ○ good ○ excellent *

The approximate net payload of 1514 pounds at 12% of GVWR on this model is ○ deficient ○ excessive ○ cautionary ◉ good ○ excellent *

Total highway safety penalties are: 3 * Value: 7 7 Durability: 7 1 Highway Control Rating: 3 9 Highway Safety: 3 6

Brand	Year	Type	Length	Model	Chassis	Engine	Fuel Type	Avg Price/Lin Ft	Adj Wheelbase	Tow Cap	GVWR	Avg Curb Wt
Pursuit	1997	MHA	29	2808	CH	7.4L	G	$1700	178	4,200	14,800	11,983

Livability Code: SB 30-90 Wheelbase-to-length ratio of 51% is considered ○ dangerous ◉ fatiguing ○ good ○ excellent *

The approximate net payload of 2817 pounds at 19% of GVWR on this model is ○ deficient ○ excessive ○ cautionary ○ good ◉ excellent *

Total highway safety penalties are: 4 * Value: 7 6 Durability: 7 1 Highway Control Rating: 5 1 Highway Safety: 4 7

Brand	Year	Type	Length	Model	Chassis	Engine	Fuel Type	Avg Price/Lin Ft	Adj Wheelbase	Tow Cap	GVWR	Avg Curb Wt
Pursuit	1997	MHA	29	2808	FO	7.5L	G	$1700	178	9,800	15,200	12,395

Livability Code: SB 30-90 Wheelbase-to-length ratio of 51% is considered ○ dangerous ◉ fatiguing ○ good ○ excellent *

The approximate net payload of 2805 pounds at 18% of GVWR on this model is ○ deficient ○ excessive ○ cautionary ○ good ◉ excellent *

Total highway safety penalties are: 2 * Value: 7 7 Durability: 7 1 Highway Control Rating: 5 1 Highway Safety: 4 9

Note: Safety ratings are based on the assumption that the engineering of the RV has allowed for proper balance by placing fresh, gray, and black holding tanks in a location so as not to change the balance of the RV when the tanks are empty or full. **Always double-check wheelbase, GVWR, and weights at front and rear axles.**

*See Section 1 for details on how conclusions are reached.

Brand	Year	Type	Length	Model	Chassis	Engine	Fuel Type	Average Price per Linear Foot When New	Adjusted Wheelbase	Approx. Towing Capacity	Gross Vehicle Weight Rating	Average Curb Weight

Pursuit 1997 MHA 31 2901 CH 7.4L G $1600 190 4,200 14,800 12,393
Livability Code: SB 30-90   Wheelbase-to-length ratio of 51% is considered ○ dangerous ◉ fatiguing ○ good ○ excellent *
The approximate net payload of 2407 pounds at 16% of GVWR on this model is ○ deficient ○ excessive ○ cautionary ○ good ◉ excellent *
Total highway safety penalties are: 5 *   Value: 7 6   Durability: 7 1   Highway Control Rating: 4 9   Highway Safety: 4 4

Pursuit 1997 MHA 31 2901 FO 7.5L G $1600 190 9,800 15,200 12,967
Livability Code: SB 30-90   Wheelbase-to-length ratio of 51% is considered ○ dangerous ◉ fatiguing ○ good ○ excellent *
The approximate net payload of 2233 pounds at 15% of GVWR on this model is ○ deficient ○ excessive ○ cautionary ◉ good ○ excellent *
Total highway safety penalties are: 2 *   Value: 7 7   Durability: 7 1   Highway Control Rating: 4 6   Highway Safety: 4 4

Pursuit 1997 MHA 32 3150 CH 7.4L G $1600 212 4,200 14,800 12,736
Livability Code: SB 30-90   Wheelbase-to-length ratio of 55% is considered ○ dangerous ○ fatiguing ◉ good ○ excellent *
The approximate net payload of 2064 pounds at 14% of GVWR on this model is ○ deficient ○ excessive ○ cautionary ◉ good ○ excellent *
Total highway safety penalties are: 6 *   Value: 7 6   Durability: 7 1   Highway Control Rating: 8 7   Highway Safety: 8 1   ★★★

Pursuit 1997 MHA 32 3150 FO 7.5L G $1600 212 9,800 15,200 13,375
Livability Code: SB 30-90   Wheelbase-to-length ratio of 55% is considered ○ dangerous ○ fatiguing ◉ good ○ excellent *
The approximate net payload of 1825 pounds at 12% of GVWR on this model is ○ deficient ○ excessive ○ cautionary ◉ good ○ excellent *
Total highway safety penalties are: 2 *   Value: 7 7   Durability: 7 1   Highway Control Rating: 8 7   Highway Safety: 8 5   ★★★

Pursuit 1997 MHA 33 3200 CH 7.4L G $1600 208 4,200 14,800 12,629
Livability Code: SB 30-90   Wheelbase-to-length ratio of 53% is considered ○ dangerous ◉ fatiguing ○ good ○ excellent *
The approximate net payload of 2171 pounds at 15% of GVWR on this model is ○ deficient ○ excessive ○ cautionary ◉ good ○ excellent *
Total highway safety penalties are: 6 *   Value: 7 5   Durability: 7 1   Highway Control Rating: 6 8   Highway Safety: 6 2   ★★

Pursuit 1997 MHA 33 3200 FO 7.5L G $1600 208 9,800 15,200 13,252
Livability Code: SB 30-90   Wheelbase-to-length ratio of 53% is considered ○ dangerous ◉ fatiguing ○ good ○ excellent *
The approximate net payload of 1948 pounds at 13% of GVWR on this model is ○ deficient ○ excessive ○ cautionary ◉ good ○ excellent *
Total highway safety penalties are: 2 *   Value: 7 7   Durability: 7 1   Highway Control Rating: 6 4   Highway Safety: 6 2   ★★

Pursuit 1998 MHA 26 2601 FO 7.5L G $2100 158 9,800 15,200 11,431
Livability Code: SB 30-90   Wheelbase-to-length ratio of 51% is considered ○ dangerous ◉ fatiguing ○ good ○ excellent *
The approximate net payload of 3769 pounds at 25% of GVWR on this model is ○ deficient ◉ excessive ○ cautionary ○ good ○ excellent *
Total highway safety penalties are: 2 *   Value: 7 7   Durability: 7 1   Highway Control Rating: 4 6   Highway Safety: 4 4

Pursuit 1998 MHA 29 2908 CH 7.4L G $1900 178 4,200 14,800 12,105
Livability Code: SB 30-90   Wheelbase-to-length ratio of 51% is considered ○ dangerous ◉ fatiguing ○ good ○ excellent *
The approximate net payload of 2695 pounds at 18% of GVWR on this model is ○ deficient ○ excessive ○ cautionary ○ good ◉ excellent *
Total highway safety penalties are: 4 *   Value: 7 6   Durability: 7 1   Highway Control Rating: 5 0   Highway Safety: 4 6

Pursuit 1998 MHA 29 2908 FO 7.5L G $1900 178 9,800 15,200 12,542
Livability Code: SB 30-90   Wheelbase-to-length ratio of 51% is considered ○ dangerous ◉ fatiguing ○ good ○ excellent *
The approximate net payload of 2658 pounds at 17% of GVWR on this model is ○ deficient ○ excessive ○ cautionary ○ good ◉ excellent *
Total highway safety penalties are: 2 *   Value: 7 7   Durability: 7 1   Highway Control Rating: 4 9   Highway Safety: 4 7

Pursuit 1998 MHA 31 3101 CH 7.4L G $1800 190 4,200 14,800 12,618
Livability Code: SB 30-90   Wheelbase-to-length ratio of 51% is considered ○ dangerous ◉ fatiguing ○ good ○ excellent *
The approximate net payload of 2182 pounds at 15% of GVWR on this model is ○ deficient ○ excessive ○ cautionary ◉ good ○ excellent *
Total highway safety penalties are: 5 *   Value: 7 6   Durability: 7 1   Highway Control Rating: 4 7   Highway Safety: 4 2

Pursuit 1998 MHA 31 3101 FO 7.5L G $1800 190 9,800 15,200 13,080
Livability Code: SB 30-90   Wheelbase-to-length ratio of 51% is considered ○ dangerous ◉ fatiguing ○ good ○ excellent *
The approximate net payload of 2120 pounds at 14% of GVWR on this model is ○ deficient ○ excessive ○ cautionary ◉ good ○ excellent *
Total highway safety penalties are: 2 *   Value: 7 7   Durability: 7 1   Highway Control Rating: 4 5   Highway Safety: 4 3

Pursuit 1998 MHA 33 3300 CH 7.4L G $1700 208 4,200 14,800 12,693
Livability Code: SB 30-90   Wheelbase-to-length ratio of 53% is considered ○ dangerous ◉ fatiguing ○ good ○ excellent *
The approximate net payload of 2107 pounds at 14% of GVWR on this model is ○ deficient ○ excessive ○ cautionary ◉ good ○ excellent *
Total highway safety penalties are: 6 *   Value: 7 5   Durability: 7 1   Highway Control Rating: 6 7   Highway Safety: 6 1   ★★

Note: Safety ratings are based on the assumption that the engineering of the RV has allowed for proper balance by placing fresh, gray, and black holding tanks in a location so as not to change the balance of the RV when the tanks are empty or full. **Always double-check wheelbase, GVWR, and weights at front and rear axles.**

See Section 1 for details on how conclusions are reached.

Brand	Year	Type	Length	Model	Chassis	Engine	Fuel Type	Average Price per Linear Foot When New	Adjusted Wheelbase	Approx. Towing Capacity	Gross Vehicle Weight Rating	Average Curb Weight
Pursuit	1998	MHA	33	3300	FO	7.5L	G	$1700	208	9,800	15,200	13,316

Livability Code: SB 30-90
Wheelbase-to-length ratio of 53% is considered ○ dangerous ◉ fatiguing ○ good ○ excellent *
The approximate net payload of 1884 pounds at 12% of GVWR on this model is ○ deficient ○ excessive ○ cautionary ◉ good ○ excellent *
Total highway safety penalties are: 2 *   Value: 7 7   Durability: 7 1   Highway Control Rating: 6 3   Highway Safety: 6 1   ★★

Brand	Year	Type	Length	Model	Chassis	Engine	Fuel Type	Average Price per Linear Foot When New	Adjusted Wheelbase	Approx. Towing Capacity	Gross Vehicle Weight Rating	Average Curb Weight
Pursuit	1998	MHA	33	3350	CH	7.4L	G	$1700	212	4,200	14,800	12,949

Livability Code: SB 30-90
Wheelbase-to-length ratio of 54% is considered ○ dangerous ○ fatiguing ◉ good ○ excellent *
The approximate net payload of 1851 pounds at 13% of GVWR on this model is ○ deficient ○ excessive ○ cautionary ◉ good ○ excellent *
Total highway safety penalties are: 6 *   Value: 7 5   Durability: 7 1   Highway Control Rating: 7 6   Highway Safety: 7 0   ★★★

Brand	Year	Type	Length	Model	Chassis	Engine	Fuel Type	Average Price per Linear Foot When New	Adjusted Wheelbase	Approx. Towing Capacity	Gross Vehicle Weight Rating	Average Curb Weight
Pursuit	1998	MHA	33	3350	FO	7.5L	G	$1700	212	9,800	15,200	13,519

Livability Code: SB 30-90
Wheelbase-to-length ratio of 54% is considered ○ dangerous ○ fatiguing ◉ good ○ excellent *
The approximate net payload of 1681 pounds at 11% of GVWR on this model is ○ deficient ○ excessive ○ cautionary ◉ good ○ excellent *
Total highway safety penalties are: 2 *   Value: 7 7   Durability: 7 1   Highway Control Rating: 7 5   Highway Safety: 7 3   ★★★

Brand	Year	Type	Length	Model	Chassis	Engine	Fuel Type	Average Price per Linear Foot When New	Adjusted Wheelbase	Approx. Towing Capacity	Gross Vehicle Weight Rating	Average Curb Weight
Pursuit	1998	MHA	35	3512	CH	7.4L	G	$1600	228	4,500	16,500	14,896

Livability Code: SB 30-90
Wheelbase-to-length ratio of 54% is considered ○ dangerous ○ fatiguing ◉ good ○ excellent *
The approximate net payload of 1604 pounds at 10% of GVWR on this model is ○ deficient ○ excessive ○ cautionary ◉ good ○ excellent *
Total highway safety penalties are: 13 *   Value: 7 2   Durability: 7 1   Highway Control Rating: 7 5   Highway Safety: 6 2   ★★

Brand	Year	Type	Length	Model	Chassis	Engine	Fuel Type	Average Price per Linear Foot When New	Adjusted Wheelbase	Approx. Towing Capacity	Gross Vehicle Weight Rating	Average Curb Weight
Pursuit	1998	MHA	35	3512	FO	7.5L	G	$1600	228	8,000	17,000	15,352

Livability Code: SB 30-90
Wheelbase-to-length ratio of 54% is considered ○ dangerous ○ fatiguing ◉ good ○ excellent *
The approximate net payload of 1648 pounds at 10% of GVWR on this model is ○ deficient ○ excessive ○ cautionary ◉ good ○ excellent *
Total highway safety penalties are: 7 *   Value: 7 5   Durability: 7 1   Highway Control Rating: 7 5   Highway Safety: 6 8   ★★

Brand	Year	Type	Length	Model	Chassis	Engine	Fuel Type	Average Price per Linear Foot When New	Adjusted Wheelbase	Approx. Towing Capacity	Gross Vehicle Weight Rating	Average Curb Weight
Pursuit	1999	MHA	27	2601	CH	7.4L	G	$2000	159	4,700	12,300	11,166

Livability Code: SB 30-90
Wheelbase-to-length ratio of 49% is considered ◉ dangerous ○ fatiguing ○ good ○ excellent *
The approximate net payload of 1134 pounds at 9% of GVWR on this model is ○ deficient ○ excessive ◉ cautionary ○ good ○ excellent *
Total highway safety penalties are: 3 *   Value: 7 7   Durability: 7 1   Highway Control Rating: 3 5   Highway Safety: 3 2

Brand	Year	Type	Length	Model	Chassis	Engine	Fuel Type	Average Price per Linear Foot When New	Adjusted Wheelbase	Approx. Towing Capacity	Gross Vehicle Weight Rating	Average Curb Weight
Pursuit	1999	MHA	31	2905	CH	7.4L	G	$1800	178	4,200	14,800	12,436

Livability Code: SB 30-90
Wheelbase-to-length ratio of 49% is considered ◉ dangerous ○ fatiguing ○ good ○ excellent *
The approximate net payload of 2364 pounds at 16% of GVWR on this model is ○ deficient ○ excessive ○ cautionary ○ good ◉ excellent *
Total highway safety penalties are: 5 *   Value: 7 6   Durability: 7 1   Highway Control Rating: 5 0   Highway Safety: 4 5

Brand	Year	Type	Length	Model	Chassis	Engine	Fuel Type	Average Price per Linear Foot When New	Adjusted Wheelbase	Approx. Towing Capacity	Gross Vehicle Weight Rating	Average Curb Weight
Pursuit	1999	MHA	31	2905	FO	6.8L	G	$1800	178	10,300	15,700	13,225

Livability Code: SB 30-90
Wheelbase-to-length ratio of 49% is considered ◉ dangerous ○ fatiguing ○ good ○ excellent *
The approximate net payload of 2475 pounds at 16% of GVWR on this model is ○ deficient ○ excessive ○ cautionary ○ good ◉ excellent *
Total highway safety penalties are: 2 *   Value: 7 7   Durability: 7 1   Highway Control Rating: 5 0   Highway Safety: 4 8

Brand	Year	Type	Length	Model	Chassis	Engine	Fuel Type	Average Price per Linear Foot When New	Adjusted Wheelbase	Approx. Towing Capacity	Gross Vehicle Weight Rating	Average Curb Weight
Pursuit	1999	MHA	32	3101	CH	7.4L	G	$1700	190	4,200	14,800	12,640

Livability Code: SB 30-90
Wheelbase-to-length ratio of 50% is considered ◉ dangerous ○ fatiguing ○ good ○ excellent *
The approximate net payload of 2160 pounds at 15% of GVWR on this model is ○ deficient ○ excessive ○ cautionary ◉ good ○ excellent *
Total highway safety penalties are: 5 *   Value: 7 6   Durability: 7 1   Highway Control Rating: 5 2   Highway Safety: 4 7

Brand	Year	Type	Length	Model	Chassis	Engine	Fuel Type	Average Price per Linear Foot When New	Adjusted Wheelbase	Approx. Towing Capacity	Gross Vehicle Weight Rating	Average Curb Weight
Pursuit	1999	MHA	32	3101	FO	6.8L	G	$1700	190	10,300	15,700	13,705

Livability Code: SB 30-90
Wheelbase-to-length ratio of 50% is considered ◉ dangerous ○ fatiguing ○ good ○ excellent *
The approximate net payload of 1995 pounds at 13% of GVWR on this model is ○ deficient ○ excessive ○ cautionary ◉ good ○ excellent *
Total highway safety penalties are: 2 *   Value: 7 7   Durability: 7 1   Highway Control Rating: 4 8   Highway Safety: 4 6

Brand	Year	Type	Length	Model	Chassis	Engine	Fuel Type	Average Price per Linear Foot When New	Adjusted Wheelbase	Approx. Towing Capacity	Gross Vehicle Weight Rating	Average Curb Weight
Pursuit	1999	MHA	34	3205	CH	7.4L	G	$1600	212	4,200	14,800	13,256

Livability Code: SB 30-90
Wheelbase-to-length ratio of 53% is considered ○ dangerous ◉ fatiguing ○ good ○ excellent *
The approximate net payload of 1544 pounds at 10% of GVWR on this model is ○ deficient ○ excessive ○ cautionary ◉ good ○ excellent *
Total highway safety penalties are: 6 *   Value: 7 5   Durability: 7 1   Highway Control Rating: 6 3   Highway Safety: 5 7   ★

Brand	Year	Type	Length	Model	Chassis	Engine	Fuel Type	Average Price per Linear Foot When New	Adjusted Wheelbase	Approx. Towing Capacity	Gross Vehicle Weight Rating	Average Curb Weight
Pursuit	1999	MHA	34	3250	CH	7.4L	G	$1600	212	4,500	16,500	13,197

Livability Code: SB 30-90
Wheelbase-to-length ratio of 53% is considered ○ dangerous ◉ fatiguing ○ good ○ excellent *
The approximate net payload of 3303 pounds at 20% of GVWR on this model is ○ deficient ○ excessive ○ cautionary ○ good ◉ excellent *
Total highway safety penalties are: 6 *   Value: 7 5   Durability: 7 1   Highway Control Rating: 7 8   Highway Safety: 7 2   ★★★

Note: Safety ratings are based on the assumption that the engineering of the RV has allowed for proper balance by placing fresh, gray, and black holding tanks in a location so as not to change the balance of the RV when the tanks are empty or full. **Always double-check wheelbase, GVWR, and weights at front and rear axles.**

*See Section 1 for details on how conclusions are reached.

Brand	Year	Type	Length	Model	Chassis	Engine	Fuel Type	Average Price per Linear Foot When New	Adjusted Wheelbase	Approx. Towing Capacity	Gross Vehicle Weight Rating	Average Curb Weight
Pursuit	1999	MHA	34	3250 sl	CH	7.4L	G	$1600	212	4,500	16,500	13,806

Livability Code: SB 30-90   Wheelbase-to-length ratio of 53% is considered ○ dangerous ◉ fatiguing ○ good ○ excellent *

The approximate net payload of 2694 pounds at 16% of GVWR on this model is ○ deficient ○ excessive ○ cautionary ○ good ◉ excellent *

Total highway safety penalties are: 9 *   Value: **74**   Durability: **71**   Highway Control Rating: **75**   Highway Safety: **66**   ★★

Brand	Year	Type	Length	Model	Chassis	Engine	Fuel Type	Avg Price/Linear Foot	Wheelbase	Towing	GVWR	Curb Weight
Pursuit	1999	MHA	34	3205	FO	6.8L	G	$1600	212	10,300	15,700	14,506

Livability Code: SB 30-90   Wheelbase-to-length ratio of 53% is considered ○ dangerous ◉ fatiguing ○ good ○ excellent *

The approximate net payload of 1194 pounds at 8% of GVWR on this model is ○ deficient ○ excessive ◉ cautionary ○ good ○ excellent *

Total highway safety penalties are: 2 *   Value: **77**   Durability: **71**   Highway Control Rating: **51**   Highway Safety: **49**

Pursuit	1999	MHA	34	3250	FO	6.8L	G	$1600	212	10,300	15,700	14,445

Livability Code: SB 30-90   Wheelbase-to-length ratio of 53% is considered ○ dangerous ◉ fatiguing ○ good ○ excellent *

The approximate net payload of 1255 pounds at 8% of GVWR on this model is ○ deficient ○ excessive ◉ cautionary ○ good ○ excellent *

Total highway safety penalties are: 2 *   Value: **77**   Durability: **71**   Highway Control Rating: **52**   Highway Safety: **50**   ★

Pursuit	1999	MHA	34	3250 sl	FO	6.8L	G	$1600	212	8,000	18,000	14,910

Livability Code: SB 30-90   Wheelbase-to-length ratio of 53% is considered ○ dangerous ◉ fatiguing ○ good ○ excellent *

The approximate net payload of 3090 pounds at 17% of GVWR on this model is ○ deficient ○ excessive ○ cautionary ○ good ◉ excellent *

Total highway safety penalties are: 5 *   Value: **76**   Durability: **71**   Highway Control Rating: **76**   Highway Safety: **71**   ★★★

Pursuit	1999	MHA	36	3512 sl	FO	6.8L	G	$1500	220	8,000	18,000	15,898

Livability Code: SB 30-90   Wheelbase-to-length ratio of 51% is considered ○ dangerous ◉ fatiguing ○ good ○ excellent *

The approximate net payload of 2102 pounds at 12% of GVWR on this model is ○ deficient ○ excessive ○ cautionary ◉ good ○ excellent *

Total highway safety penalties are: 7 *   Value: **75**   Durability: **71**   Highway Control Rating: **52**   Highway Safety: **45**

Pursuit	1999	MHA	36	3512 sl myc	FO	6.8L	G	$1500	220	5,500	20,500	16,498

Livability Code: SB 30-90   Wheelbase-to-length ratio of 51% is considered ○ dangerous ◉ fatiguing ○ good ○ excellent *

The approximate net payload of 4002 pounds at 20% of GVWR on this model is ○ deficient ○ excessive ○ cautionary ○ good ◉ excellent *

Total highway safety penalties are: 7 *   Value: **75**   Durability: **71**   Highway Control Rating: **64**   Highway Safety: **57**   ★

Renegade	1999	MHA	37	Durango opch	MA	CA275	D	$3900	228	5,000	28,000	21,417

Livability Code: SB 30-90   Wheelbase-to-length ratio of 51% is considered ○ dangerous ◉ fatiguing ○ good ○ excellent *

The approximate net payload of 6583 pounds at 24% of GVWR on this model is ○ deficient ○ excessive ○ cautionary ○ good ◉ excellent *

Total highway safety penalties are: 12 *   Value: **77**   Durability: **70**   Highway Control Rating: **59**   Highway Safety: **47**

Renegade	1999	MHA	37	Mesa opch	MA	CA275	D	$3900	228	5,000	28,000	21,492

Livability Code: SB 30-90   Wheelbase-to-length ratio of 51% is considered ○ dangerous ◉ fatiguing ○ good ○ excellent *

The approximate net payload of 6508 pounds at 23% of GVWR on this model is ○ deficient ○ excessive ○ cautionary ○ good ◉ excellent *

Total highway safety penalties are: 13 *   Value: **76**   Durability: **70**   Highway Control Rating: **59**   Highway Safety: **46**

Renegade	1999	MHA	37	Casa Grande opch	MA	CA275	D	$3900	228	5,000	28,000	21,417

Livability Code: SB 30-90   Wheelbase-to-length ratio of 51% is considered ○ dangerous ◉ fatiguing ○ good ○ excellent *

The approximate net payload of 6583 pounds at 24% of GVWR on this model is ○ deficient ○ excessive ○ cautionary ○ good ◉ excellent *

Total highway safety penalties are: 12 *   Value: **77**   Durability: **70**   Highway Control Rating: **59**   Highway Safety: **47**

Renegade	1999	MHA	37	Mesa	SP	CA275	D	$3900	228	5,000	28,000	21,492

Livability Code: SB 30-90   Wheelbase-to-length ratio of 51% is considered ○ dangerous ◉ fatiguing ○ good ○ excellent *

The approximate net payload of 6508 pounds at 23% of GVWR on this model is ○ deficient ○ excessive ○ cautionary ○ good ◉ excellent *

Total highway safety penalties are: 13 *   Value: **76**   Durability: **70**   Highway Control Rating: **59**   Highway Safety: **46**

Renegade	1999	MHA	37	Casa Grande	SP	CA275	D	$3900	228	5,000	28,000	21,417

Livability Code: SB 30-90   Wheelbase-to-length ratio of 51% is considered ○ dangerous ◉ fatiguing ○ good ○ excellent *

The approximate net payload of 6583 pounds at 24% of GVWR on this model is ○ deficient ○ excessive ○ cautionary ○ good ◉ excellent *

Total highway safety penalties are: 12 *   Value: **77**   Durability: **70**   Highway Control Rating: **59**   Highway Safety: **47**

Renegade	1999	MHA	37	Durango	SP	CA275	D	$3900	228	5,000	28,000	21,417

Livability Code: SB 30-90   Wheelbase-to-length ratio of 51% is considered ○ dangerous ◉ fatiguing ○ good ○ excellent *

The approximate net payload of 6583 pounds at 24% of GVWR on this model is ○ deficient ○ excessive ○ cautionary ○ good ◉ excellent *

Total highway safety penalties are: 12 *   Value: **77**   Durability: **70**   Highway Control Rating: **59**   Highway Safety: **47**

Note: Safety ratings are based on the assumption that the engineering of the RV has allowed for proper balance by placing fresh, gray, and black holding tanks in a location so as not to change the balance of the RV when the tanks are empty or full. **Always double-check wheelbase, GVWR, and weights at front and rear axles.**

*See Section 1 for details on how conclusions are reached.

Brand	Year	Type	Length	Model	Chassis	Engine	Fuel Type	Average Price per Linear Foot When New	Adjusted Wheelbase	Approx. Towing Capacity	Gross Vehicle Weight Rating	Average Curb Weight
Residency	1995	MHA	33	3275	FO	7.5L	G	$2200	208	8,000	17,000	15,188

Livability Code: SB 30-90
Wheelbase-to-length ratio of 53% is considered ○ dangerous ● fatiguing ○ good ○ excellent *
The approximate net payload of 1812 pounds at 11% of GVWR on this model is ○ deficient ○ excessive ○ cautionary ● good ○ excellent *
Total highway safety penalties are: 2 *   Value: **7 9**   Durability: **7 6**   Highway Control Rating: **5 8**   Highway Safety: **5 6**   ★

Brand	Year	Type	Length	Model	Chassis	Engine	Fuel Type	Price	Wheelbase	Towing	GVWR	Curb Weight
Residency	1995	MHA	33	3295	FO	7.5L	G	$2200	228	8,000	17,000	15,188

Livability Code: SB 30-90
Wheelbase-to-length ratio of 58% is considered ○ dangerous ○ fatiguing ○ good ● excellent *
The approximate net payload of 1812 pounds at 11% of GVWR on this model is ○ deficient ○ excessive ○ cautionary ● good ○ excellent *
Total highway safety penalties are: 2 *   Value: **7 9**   Durability: **7 6**   Highway Control Rating: **9 1**   Highway Safety: **8 9**   ★★★

Brand	Year	Type	Length	Model	Chassis	Engine	Fuel Type	Price	Wheelbase	Towing	GVWR	Curb Weight
Residency	1995	MHA	33	3300	FO	7.5L	G	$2200	228	8,000	17,000	15,188

Livability Code: SB 30-90
Wheelbase-to-length ratio of 58% is considered ○ dangerous ○ fatiguing ○ good ● excellent *
The approximate net payload of 1812 pounds at 11% of GVWR on this model is ○ deficient ○ excessive ○ cautionary ● good ○ excellent *
Total highway safety penalties are: 2 *   Value: **7 9**   Durability: **7 6**   Highway Control Rating: **9 1**   Highway Safety: **8 9**   ★★★

Brand	Year	Type	Length	Model	Chassis	Engine	Fuel Type	Price	Wheelbase	Towing	GVWR	Curb Weight
Residency	1995	MHA	35	3450	FO	7.5L	G	$2100	228	8,000	17,000	15,629

Livability Code: SB 30-90
Wheelbase-to-length ratio of 55% is considered ○ dangerous ○ fatiguing ● good ○ excellent *
The approximate net payload of 1371 pounds at 8% of GVWR on this model is ○ deficient ○ excessive ● cautionary ○ good ○ excellent *
Total highway safety penalties are: 2 *   Value: **7 9**   Durability: **7 6**   Highway Control Rating: **6 9**   Highway Safety: **6 7**   ★★

Brand	Year	Type	Length	Model	Chassis	Engine	Fuel Type	Price	Wheelbase	Towing	GVWR	Curb Weight
Residency	1995	MHA	35	3500	FO	7.5L	G	$2100	228	8,000	17,000	15,794

Livability Code: SB 30-90
Wheelbase-to-length ratio of 54% is considered ○ dangerous ○ fatiguing ● good ○ excellent *
The approximate net payload of 1206 pounds at 7% of GVWR on this model is ○ deficient ○ excessive ● cautionary ○ good ○ excellent *
Total highway safety penalties are: 2 *   Value: **7 9**   Durability: **7 6**   Highway Control Rating: **5 3**   Highway Safety: **5 1**   ★

Brand	Year	Type	Length	Model	Chassis	Engine	Fuel Type	Price	Wheelbase	Towing	GVWR	Curb Weight
Residency	1995	MHA	36	3600	OS	CU230	D	$3200	228	4,000	20,500	18,114

Livability Code: SB 30-90
Wheelbase-to-length ratio of 53% is considered ○ dangerous ● fatiguing ○ good ○ excellent *
The approximate net payload of 2386 pounds at 12% of GVWR on this model is ○ deficient ○ excessive ○ cautionary ● good ○ excellent *
Total highway safety penalties are: 2 *   Value: **7 9**   Durability: **7 6**   Highway Control Rating: **6 1**   Highway Safety: **5 9**   ★

Brand	Year	Type	Length	Model	Chassis	Engine	Fuel Type	Price	Wheelbase	Towing	GVWR	Curb Weight
Residency	1996	MHA	32	3195	FO	7.5L	G	$2300	208	8,000	17,000	14,885

Livability Code: SB 30-90
Wheelbase-to-length ratio of 54% is considered ○ dangerous ○ fatiguing ● good ○ excellent *
The approximate net payload of 2115 pounds at 12% of GVWR on this model is ○ deficient ○ excessive ○ cautionary ● good ○ excellent *
Total highway safety penalties are: 2 *   Value: **7 9**   Durability: **7 6**   Highway Control Rating: **7 9**   Highway Safety: **7 7**   ★★★

Brand	Year	Type	Length	Model	Chassis	Engine	Fuel Type	Price	Wheelbase	Towing	GVWR	Curb Weight
Residency	1996	MHA	33	3275	FO	7.5L	G	$2300	208	8,000	17,000	14,984

Livability Code: SB 30-90
Wheelbase-to-length ratio of 53% is considered ○ dangerous ● fatiguing ○ good ○ excellent *
The approximate net payload of 2016 pounds at 12% of GVWR on this model is ○ deficient ○ excessive ○ cautionary ● good ○ excellent *
Total highway safety penalties are: 2 *   Value: **7 9**   Durability: **7 6**   Highway Control Rating: **6 1**   Highway Safety: **5 9**   ★

Brand	Year	Type	Length	Model	Chassis	Engine	Fuel Type	Price	Wheelbase	Towing	GVWR	Curb Weight
Residency	1996	MHA	35	3450	FO	7.5L	G	$2200	228	8,000	17,000	15,304

Livability Code: SB 30-90
Wheelbase-to-length ratio of 55% is considered ○ dangerous ○ fatiguing ● good ○ excellent *
The approximate net payload of 1696 pounds at 10% of GVWR on this model is ○ deficient ○ excessive ○ cautionary ● good ○ excellent *
Total highway safety penalties are: 2 *   Value: **7 9**   Durability: **7 6**   Highway Control Rating: **8 6**   Highway Safety: **8 4**   ★★★

Brand	Year	Type	Length	Model	Chassis	Engine	Fuel Type	Price	Wheelbase	Towing	GVWR	Curb Weight
Residency	1996	MHA	35	3480	FO	7.5L	G	$2300	228	8,000	17,000	15,477

Livability Code: SB 30-90
Wheelbase-to-length ratio of 54% is considered ○ dangerous ○ fatiguing ● good ○ excellent *
The approximate net payload of 1523 pounds at 9% of GVWR on this model is ○ deficient ○ excessive ● cautionary ○ good ○ excellent *
Total highway safety penalties are: 2 *   Value: **7 9**   Durability: **7 6**   Highway Control Rating: **6 4**   Highway Safety: **6 2**   ★★

Brand	Year	Type	Length	Model	Chassis	Engine	Fuel Type	Price	Wheelbase	Towing	GVWR	Curb Weight
Residency	1996	MHA	35	3485	FO	7.5L	G	$2300	232 T	5,000	20,000	17,594

Livability Code: SB 30-90
Wheelbase-to-length ratio of 55% is considered ○ dangerous ○ fatiguing ● good ○ excellent *
The approximate net payload of 2406 pounds at 12% of GVWR on this model is ○ deficient ○ excessive ○ cautionary ● good ○ excellent *
Total highway safety penalties are: 10 *   Value: **7 6**   Durability: **7 6**   Highway Control Rating: **8 8**   Highway Safety: **7 8**   ★★★

Brand	Year	Type	Length	Model	Chassis	Engine	Fuel Type	Price	Wheelbase	Towing	GVWR	Curb Weight
Residency	1996	MHA	35	3500	FO	7.5L	G	$2300	228	8,000	17,000	15,402

Livability Code: SB 30-90
Wheelbase-to-length ratio of 54% is considered ○ dangerous ○ fatiguing ● good ○ excellent *
The approximate net payload of 1598 pounds at 9% of GVWR on this model is ○ deficient ○ excessive ● cautionary ○ good ○ excellent *
Total highway safety penalties are: 2 *   Value: **7 9**   Durability: **7 6**   Highway Control Rating: **6 5**   Highway Safety: **6 3**   ★★

Note: Safety ratings are based on the assumption that the engineering of the RV has allowed for proper balance by placing fresh, gray, and black holding tanks in a location so as not to change the balance of the RV when the tanks are empty or full. **Always double-check wheelbase, GVWR, and weights at front and rear axles.**

*See Section 1 for details on how conclusions are reached.

Section 2: The Ratings

Brand	Year	Type	Length	Model	Chassis	Engine	Fuel Type	Average Price per Linear Foot When New	Adjusted Wheelbase	Approx. Towing Capacity	Gross Vehicle Weight Rating	Average Curb Weight
Residency	1996	MHA	37	3650	FO	7.5L	G	$2200	232 T	5,000	20,000	18,035

Livability Code: SB 30-90
Wheelbase-to-length ratio of 53% is considered ○ dangerous ◉ fatiguing ○ good ○ excellent *
The approximate net payload of 1965 pounds at 10% of GVWR on this model is ○ deficient ○ excessive ○ cautionary ◉ good ○ excellent *
Total highway safety penalties are: 10 *   Value: 7 6   Durability: 7 6   Highway Control Rating: 5 7   Highway Safety: 4 7

Brand	Year	Type	Length	Model	Chassis	Engine	Fuel Type	Average Price per Linear Foot When New	Adjusted Wheelbase	Approx. Towing Capacity	Gross Vehicle Weight Rating	Average Curb Weight
Residency	1997	MHA	33	3390	FO	7.5L	G	$2800	232 T	5,000	20,000	17,338

Livability Code: SB 30-90
Wheelbase-to-length ratio of 59% is considered ○ dangerous ○ fatiguing ○ good ◉ excellent *
The approximate net payload of 2663 pounds at 13% of GVWR on this model is ○ deficient ○ excessive ○ cautionary ◉ good ○ excellent *
Total highway safety penalties are: 10 *   Value: 7 6   Durability: 7 6   Highway Control Rating: 1 0 0   Highway Safety: 9 0   ★★★

Brand	Year	Type	Length	Model	Chassis	Engine	Fuel Type	Average Price per Linear Foot When New	Adjusted Wheelbase	Approx. Towing Capacity	Gross Vehicle Weight Rating	Average Curb Weight
Residency	1997	MHA	35	3480	FO	7.5L	G	$2600	232 T	5,000	20,000	17,697

Livability Code: SB 30-90
Wheelbase-to-length ratio of 55% is considered ○ dangerous ○ fatiguing ◉ good ○ excellent *
The approximate net payload of 2304 pounds at 12% of GVWR on this model is ○ deficient ○ excessive ○ cautionary ◉ good ○ excellent *
Total highway safety penalties are: 10 *   Value: 7 6   Durability: 7 6   Highway Control Rating: 8 8   Highway Safety: 7 8   ★★★

Brand	Year	Type	Length	Model	Chassis	Engine	Fuel Type	Average Price per Linear Foot When New	Adjusted Wheelbase	Approx. Towing Capacity	Gross Vehicle Weight Rating	Average Curb Weight
Residency	1997	MHA	35	3485	FO	7.5L	G	$2300	228	8,000	17,000	15,609

Livability Code: SB 30-90
Wheelbase-to-length ratio of 54% is considered ○ dangerous ○ fatiguing ◉ good ○ excellent *
The approximate net payload of 1391 pounds at 8% of GVWR on this model is ○ deficient ○ excessive ◉ cautionary ○ good ○ excellent *
Total highway safety penalties are: 2 *   Value: 7 9   Durability: 7 6   Highway Control Rating: 5 9   Highway Safety: 5 7   ★

Brand	Year	Type	Length	Model	Chassis	Engine	Fuel Type	Average Price per Linear Foot When New	Adjusted Wheelbase	Approx. Towing Capacity	Gross Vehicle Weight Rating	Average Curb Weight
Residency	1997	MHA	35	3505	FO	7.5L	G	$2300	228	8,000	17,000	15,869

Livability Code: SB 30-90
Wheelbase-to-length ratio of 54% is considered ○ dangerous ○ fatiguing ◉ good ○ excellent *
The approximate net payload of 1131 pounds at 7% of GVWR on this model is ○ deficient ○ excessive ◉ cautionary ○ good ○ excellent *
Total highway safety penalties are: 2 *   Value: 7 9   Durability: 7 6   Highway Control Rating: 5 2   Highway Safety: 5 0   ★

Brand	Year	Type	Length	Model	Chassis	Engine	Fuel Type	Average Price per Linear Foot When New	Adjusted Wheelbase	Approx. Towing Capacity	Gross Vehicle Weight Rating	Average Curb Weight
Residency	1997	MHA	37	3650	FO	7.5L	G	$2500	252 T	5,000	20,000	18,051

Livability Code: SB 30-90
Wheelbase-to-length ratio of 57% is considered ○ dangerous ○ fatiguing ◉ good ○ excellent *
The approximate net payload of 1949 pounds at 10% of GVWR on this model is ○ deficient ○ excessive ○ cautionary ◉ good ○ excellent *
Total highway safety penalties are: 10 *   Value: 7 6   Durability: 7 6   Highway Control Rating: 8 8   Highway Safety: 7 8   ★★★

Brand	Year	Type	Length	Model	Chassis	Engine	Fuel Type	Average Price per Linear Foot When New	Adjusted Wheelbase	Approx. Towing Capacity	Gross Vehicle Weight Rating	Average Curb Weight
Residency	1998	MHA	34	R3390	FO	7.5L	G	$2800	232 T	5,000	20,000	17,818

Livability Code: SB 30-90
Wheelbase-to-length ratio of 57% is considered ○ dangerous ○ fatiguing ◉ good ○ excellent *
The approximate net payload of 2182 pounds at 11% of GVWR on this model is ○ deficient ○ excessive ○ cautionary ◉ good ○ excellent *
Total highway safety penalties are: 10 *   Value: 7 6   Durability: 7 6   Highway Control Rating: 8 8   Highway Safety: 7 8   ★★★

Brand	Year	Type	Length	Model	Chassis	Engine	Fuel Type	Average Price per Linear Foot When New	Adjusted Wheelbase	Approx. Towing Capacity	Gross Vehicle Weight Rating	Average Curb Weight
Residency	1998	MHA	35	R3490	FO	7.5L	G	$2800	232 T	5,000	20,000	18,575

Livability Code: SB 30-90
Wheelbase-to-length ratio of 55% is considered ○ dangerous ○ fatiguing ◉ good ○ excellent *
The approximate net payload of 1425 pounds at 7% of GVWR on this model is ○ deficient ○ excessive ◉ cautionary ○ good ○ excellent *
Total highway safety penalties are: 13 *   Value: 7 4   Durability: 7 6   Highway Control Rating: 6 5   Highway Safety: 5 2   ★

Brand	Year	Type	Length	Model	Chassis	Engine	Fuel Type	Average Price per Linear Foot When New	Adjusted Wheelbase	Approx. Towing Capacity	Gross Vehicle Weight Rating	Average Curb Weight
Residency	1998	MHA	35	R3480	FO	7.5L	G	$2700	232 T	5,000	20,000	18,108

Livability Code: SB 30-90
Wheelbase-to-length ratio of 55% is considered ○ dangerous ○ fatiguing ◉ good ○ excellent *
The approximate net payload of 1892 pounds at 9% of GVWR on this model is ○ deficient ○ excessive ◉ cautionary ○ good ○ excellent *
Total highway safety penalties are: 10 *   Value: 7 6   Durability: 7 6   Highway Control Rating: 7 6   Highway Safety: 6 6   ★★

Brand	Year	Type	Length	Model	Chassis	Engine	Fuel Type	Average Price per Linear Foot When New	Adjusted Wheelbase	Approx. Towing Capacity	Gross Vehicle Weight Rating	Average Curb Weight
Residency	1998	MHA	36	R3580	FO	7.5L	G	$2600	232 T	5,000	20,000	18,282

Livability Code: SB 30-90
Wheelbase-to-length ratio of 54% is considered ○ dangerous ○ fatiguing ◉ good ○ excellent *
The approximate net payload of 1718 pounds at 9% of GVWR on this model is ○ deficient ○ excessive ◉ cautionary ○ good ○ excellent *
Total highway safety penalties are: 10 *   Value: 7 6   Durability: 7 6   Highway Control Rating: 6 4   Highway Safety: 5 4   ★

Brand	Year	Type	Length	Model	Chassis	Engine	Fuel Type	Average Price per Linear Foot When New	Adjusted Wheelbase	Approx. Towing Capacity	Gross Vehicle Weight Rating	Average Curb Weight
Residency	1998	MHA	37	R3650	FO	7.5L	G	$2600	232 T	5,000	20,000	18,722

Livability Code: SB 30-90
Wheelbase-to-length ratio of 53% is considered ○ dangerous ◉ fatiguing ○ good ○ excellent *
The approximate net payload of 1278 pounds at 6% of GVWR on this model is ◉ deficient ○ excessive ○ cautionary ○ good ○ excellent *
Total highway safety penalties are: 11 *   Value: 7 5   Durability: 7 6   Highway Control Rating: 3 4   Highway Safety: 2 3

Brand	Year	Type	Length	Model	Chassis	Engine	Fuel Type	Average Price per Linear Foot When New	Adjusted Wheelbase	Approx. Towing Capacity	Gross Vehicle Weight Rating	Average Curb Weight
Residency by Thor	1999	MHA	35	3390	FO	6.8L	G	$2900	228	4,500	20,500	19,265

Livability Code: SB 30-90
Wheelbase-to-length ratio of 55% is considered ○ dangerous ○ fatiguing ◉ good ○ excellent *
The approximate net payload of 1235 pounds at 6% of GVWR on this model is ◉ deficient ○ excessive ○ cautionary ○ good ○ excellent *
Total highway safety penalties are: 20 *   Value: 7 0   Durability: 7 6   Highway Control Rating: 5 6   Highway Safety: 3 6

Note: Safety ratings are based on the assumption that the engineering of the RV has allowed for proper balance by placing fresh, gray, and black holding tanks in a location so as not to change the balance of the RV when the tanks are empty or full. **Always double-check wheelbase, GVWR, and weights at front and rear axles.**

*See Section 1 for details on how conclusions are reached.

Brand	Year	Type	Length	Model	Chassis	Engine	Fuel Type	Average Price per Linear Foot When New	Adjusted Wheelbase	Approx. Towing Capacity	Gross Vehicle Weight Rating	Average Curb Weight
Residency by Thor	1999	MHA	36	3480	FO	6.8L	G	$2800	232 T	4,500	20,500	19,040

Livability Code: SB 30-90 — Wheelbase-to-length ratio of 54% is considered ○ dangerous ○ fatiguing ● good ○ excellent *

The approximate net payload of 1460 pounds at 7% of GVWR on this model is ○ deficient ○ excessive ● cautionary ○ good ○ excellent *

Total highway safety penalties are: 15 * — Value: 7 3 — Durability: 7 6 — Highway Control Rating: 5 5 — Highway Safety: 4 0

Brand	Year	Type	Length	Model	Chassis	Engine	Fuel Type	Price/Lin.Ft	Wheelbase	Towing	GVWR	Curb Wt
Residency by Thor	1999	MHA	36	3580	FO	6.8L	G	$2800	232 T	4,500	20,500	19,040

Livability Code: SB 30-90 — Wheelbase-to-length ratio of 54% is considered ○ dangerous ○ fatiguing ● good ○ excellent *

The approximate net payload of 1460 pounds at 7% of GVWR on this model is ○ deficient ○ excessive ● cautionary ○ good ○ excellent *

Total highway safety penalties are: 15 * — Value: 7 3 — Durability: 7 6 — Highway Control Rating: 5 5 — Highway Safety: 4 0

Brand	Year	Type	Length	Model	Chassis	Engine	Fuel Type	Price/Lin.Ft	Wheelbase	Towing	GVWR	Curb Wt
Residency by Thor	1999	MHA	37	3490	FO	6.8L	G	$2700	252 T	4,500	20,500	19,805

Livability Code: SB 30-90 — Wheelbase-to-length ratio of 57% is considered ○ dangerous ○ fatiguing ● good ○ excellent *

The approximate net payload of 695 pounds at 3% of GVWR on this model is ● deficient ○ excessive ○ cautionary ○ good ○ excellent *

Total highway safety penalties are: 19 * — Value: 7 1 — Durability: 7 6 — Highway Control Rating: 6 4 — Highway Safety: 4 5

Brand	Year	Type	Length	Model	Chassis	Engine	Fuel Type	Price/Lin.Ft	Wheelbase	Towing	GVWR	Curb Wt
Residency by Thor	1999	MHA	37	3650	FO	6.8L	G	$2700	252 T	4,500	20,500	19,940

Livability Code: SB 30-90 — Wheelbase-to-length ratio of 56% is considered ○ dangerous ○ fatiguing ● good ○ excellent *

The approximate net payload of 560 pounds at 3% of GVWR on this model is ● deficient ○ excessive ○ cautionary ○ good ○ excellent *

Total highway safety penalties are: 19 * — Value: 7 1 — Durability: 7 6 — Highway Control Rating: 5 9 — Highway Safety: 4 0

Brand	Year	Type	Length	Model	Chassis	Engine	Fuel Type	Price/Lin.Ft	Wheelbase	Towing	GVWR	Curb Wt
Residential Suite	1991	MHA	39	39	CH	7.4L	G	$1800	232 T	1,500	20,200	17,142

Livability Code: SB 30-90 — Wheelbase-to-length ratio of 50% is considered ● dangerous ○ fatiguing ○ good ○ excellent *

The approximate net payload of 3058 pounds at 15% of GVWR on this model is ○ deficient ○ excessive ○ cautionary ● good ○ excellent *

Total highway safety penalties are: 11 * — Value: 7 6 — Durability: 8 0 — Highway Control Rating: 4 1 — Highway Safety: 3 0

Brand	Year	Type	Length	Model	Chassis	Engine	Fuel Type	Price/Lin.Ft	Wheelbase	Towing	GVWR	Curb Wt
RexAir	1995	MHA	29	SL2800	CH	7.4L	G	$2200	190	3,500	16,500	14,097

Livability Code: SB 30-90 — Wheelbase-to-length ratio of 54% is considered ○ dangerous ○ fatiguing ● good ○ excellent *

The approximate net payload of 2403 pounds at 15% of GVWR on this model is ○ deficient ○ excessive ○ cautionary ● good ○ excellent *

Total highway safety penalties are: 4 * — Value: 8 4 — Durability: 7 7 — Highway Control Rating: 8 0 — Highway Safety: 7 6 — ★★★

Brand	Year	Type	Length	Model	Chassis	Engine	Fuel Type	Price/Lin.Ft	Wheelbase	Towing	GVWR	Curb Wt
RexAir	1995	MHA	29	SL2800	FO	7.5L	G	$2200	190	8,000	17,000	14,518

Livability Code: SB 30-90 — Wheelbase-to-length ratio of 54% is considered ○ dangerous ○ fatiguing ● good ○ excellent *

The approximate net payload of 2482 pounds at 15% of GVWR on this model is ○ deficient ○ excessive ○ cautionary ● good ○ excellent *

Total highway safety penalties are: 2 * — Value: 8 5 — Durability: 7 7 — Highway Control Rating: 8 0 — Highway Safety: 7 8 — ★★★

Brand	Year	Type	Length	Model	Chassis	Engine	Fuel Type	Price/Lin.Ft	Wheelbase	Towing	GVWR	Curb Wt
RexAir	1995	MHA	31	SL2900	CH	7.4L	G	$2100	208	3,500	16,500	14,345

Livability Code: SB 30-90 — Wheelbase-to-length ratio of 56% is considered ○ dangerous ○ fatiguing ● good ○ excellent *

The approximate net payload of 2155 pounds at 13% of GVWR on this model is ○ deficient ○ excessive ○ cautionary ● good ○ excellent *

Total highway safety penalties are: 5 * — Value: 8 3 — Durability: 7 7 — Highway Control Rating: 9 3 — Highway Safety: 8 8 — ★★★

Brand	Year	Type	Length	Model	Chassis	Engine	Fuel Type	Price/Lin.Ft	Wheelbase	Towing	GVWR	Curb Wt
RexAir	1995	MHA	31	SL2900	FO	7.5L	G	$2100	208	8,000	17,000	14,945

Livability Code: SB 30-90 — Wheelbase-to-length ratio of 56% is considered ○ dangerous ○ fatiguing ● good ○ excellent *

The approximate net payload of 2055 pounds at 12% of GVWR on this model is ○ deficient ○ excessive ○ cautionary ● good ○ excellent *

Total highway safety penalties are: 2 * — Value: 8 5 — Durability: 7 7 — Highway Control Rating: 9 2 — Highway Safety: 9 0 — ★★★

Brand	Year	Type	Length	Model	Chassis	Engine	Fuel Type	Price/Lin.Ft	Wheelbase	Towing	GVWR	Curb Wt
RexAir	1995	MHA	32	SL3000	CH	7.4L	G	$2000	208	3,500	16,500	14,782

Livability Code: SB 30-90 — Wheelbase-to-length ratio of 55% is considered ○ dangerous ○ fatiguing ● good ○ excellent *

The approximate net payload of 1718 pounds at 10% of GVWR on this model is ○ deficient ○ excessive ○ cautionary ● good ○ excellent *

Total highway safety penalties are: 5 * — Value: 8 3 — Durability: 7 7 — Highway Control Rating: 8 5 — Highway Safety: 8 0 — ★★★

Brand	Year	Type	Length	Model	Chassis	Engine	Fuel Type	Price/Lin.Ft	Wheelbase	Towing	GVWR	Curb Wt
RexAir	1995	MHA	32	SL3000	FO	7.5L	G	$2000	208	8,000	17,000	15,178

Livability Code: SB 30-90 — Wheelbase-to-length ratio of 55% is considered ○ dangerous ○ fatiguing ● good ○ excellent *

The approximate net payload of 1822 pounds at 11% of GVWR on this model is ○ deficient ○ excessive ○ cautionary ● good ○ excellent *

Total highway safety penalties are: 2 * — Value: 8 5 — Durability: 7 7 — Highway Control Rating: 8 6 — Highway Safety: 8 4 — ★★★

Brand	Year	Type	Length	Model	Chassis	Engine	Fuel Type	Price/Lin.Ft	Wheelbase	Towing	GVWR	Curb Wt
RexAir	1995	MHA	32	SL3200	OS	CU230	D	$3100	190	4,500	20,500	18,038

Livability Code: SB 30-90 — Wheelbase-to-length ratio of 49% is considered ● dangerous ○ fatiguing ○ good ○ excellent *

The approximate net payload of 2462 pounds at 12% of GVWR on this model is ○ deficient ○ excessive ○ cautionary ● good ○ excellent *

Total highway safety penalties are: 2 * — Value: 8 5 — Durability: 7 7 — Highway Control Rating: 3 5 — Highway Safety: 3 3

Note: Safety ratings are based on the assumption that the engineering of the RV has allowed for proper balance by placing fresh, gray, and black holding tanks in a location so as not to change the balance of the RV when the tanks are empty or full. **Always double-check wheelbase, GVWR, and weights at front and rear axles.**

*See Section 1 for details on how conclusions are reached.

Brand	Year	Type	Length	Model	Chassis	Engine	Fuel Type	Average Price per Linear Foot When New	Adjusted Wheelbase	Approx. Towing Capacity	Gross Vehicle Weight Rating	Average Curb Weight
RexAir	**1995**	MHA	32	SL3100	CH	7.4L	G	$2200	208	3,500	16,500	14,896

Livability Code: SB 30-90
Wheelbase-to-length ratio of 54% is considered ○ dangerous ○ fatiguing ◉ good ○ excellent *
The approximate net payload of 1604 pounds at 10% of GVWR on this model is ○ deficient ○ excessive ○ cautionary ◉ good ○ excellent *
Total highway safety penalties are: 6 * Value: **83** Durability: **77** Highway Control Rating: **75** Highway Safety: **69** ★★

Brand	Year	Type	Length	Model	Chassis	Engine	Fuel Type	Avg Price/Ft	Wheelbase	Towing	GVWR	Curb Weight
RexAir	**1995**	MHA	32	SL3250 sl	CH	7.4L	G	$2300	208	3,500	16,500	15,796

Livability Code: SB 30-90
Wheelbase-to-length ratio of 54% is considered ○ dangerous ○ fatiguing ◉ good ○ excellent *
The approximate net payload of 704 pounds at 4% of GVWR on this model is ◉ deficient ○ excessive ○ cautionary ○ good ○ excellent *
Total highway safety penalties are: 11 * Value: **80** Durability: **77** Highway Control Rating: **44** Highway Safety: **33**

Brand	Year	Type	Length	Model	Chassis	Engine	Fuel Type	Avg Price/Ft	Wheelbase	Towing	GVWR	Curb Weight
RexAir	**1995**	MHA	32	SL3100	FO	7.5L	G	$2200	208	8,000	17,000	15,296

Livability Code: SB 30-90
Wheelbase-to-length ratio of 54% is considered ○ dangerous ○ fatiguing ◉ good ○ excellent *
The approximate net payload of 1704 pounds at 10% of GVWR on this model is ○ deficient ○ excessive ○ cautionary ◉ good ○ excellent *
Total highway safety penalties are: 2 * Value: **85** Durability: **77** Highway Control Rating: **75** Highway Safety: **73** ★★★

Brand	Year	Type	Length	Model	Chassis	Engine	Fuel Type	Avg Price/Ft	Wheelbase	Towing	GVWR	Curb Weight
RexAir	**1995**	MHA	32	SL3250 sl	FO	7.5L	G	$2300	208	8,000	17,000	16,196

Livability Code: SB 30-90
Wheelbase-to-length ratio of 54% is considered ○ dangerous ○ fatiguing ◉ good ○ excellent *
The approximate net payload of 804 pounds at 5% of GVWR on this model is ◉ deficient ○ excessive ○ cautionary ○ good ○ excellent *
Total highway safety penalties are: 7 * Value: **82** Durability: **77** Highway Control Rating: **45** Highway Safety: **38**

Brand	Year	Type	Length	Model	Chassis	Engine	Fuel Type	Avg Price/Ft	Wheelbase	Towing	GVWR	Curb Weight
RexAir	**1995**	MHA	33	SL3200	CH	7.4L	G	$2000	208	3,500	16,500	14,982

Livability Code: SB 30-90
Wheelbase-to-length ratio of 53% is considered ○ dangerous ◉ fatiguing ○ good ○ excellent *
The approximate net payload of 1518 pounds at 9% of GVWR on this model is ○ deficient ○ excessive ◉ cautionary ○ good ○ excellent *
Total highway safety penalties are: 6 * Value: **83** Durability: **77** Highway Control Rating: **55** Highway Safety: **49**

Brand	Year	Type	Length	Model	Chassis	Engine	Fuel Type	Avg Price/Ft	Wheelbase	Towing	GVWR	Curb Weight
RexAir	**1995**	MHA	33	SL3200	FO	7.5L	G	$2000	208	8,000	17,000	15,362

Livability Code: SB 30-90
Wheelbase-to-length ratio of 53% is considered ○ dangerous ◉ fatiguing ○ good ○ excellent *
The approximate net payload of 1639 pounds at 10% of GVWR on this model is ○ deficient ○ excessive ○ cautionary ◉ good ○ excellent *
Total highway safety penalties are: 2 * Value: **85** Durability: **77** Highway Control Rating: **65** Highway Safety: **63** ★★

Brand	Year	Type	Length	Model	Chassis	Engine	Fuel Type	Avg Price/Ft	Wheelbase	Towing	GVWR	Curb Weight
RexAir	**1995**	MHA	34	SL3300	OS	CU230	D	$2900	208	4,500	20,500	18,451

Livability Code: SB 30-90
Wheelbase-to-length ratio of 52% is considered ○ dangerous ◉ fatiguing ○ good ○ excellent *
The approximate net payload of 2049 pounds at 10% of GVWR on this model is ○ deficient ○ excessive ○ cautionary ◉ good ○ excellent *
Total highway safety penalties are: 2 * Value: **85** Durability: **77** Highway Control Rating: **46** Highway Safety: **44**

Brand	Year	Type	Length	Model	Chassis	Engine	Fuel Type	Avg Price/Ft	Wheelbase	Towing	GVWR	Curb Weight
RexAir	**1995**	MHA	34	SL3300	CH	7.4L	G	$2100	228	3,500	16,500	15,143

Livability Code: SB 30-90
Wheelbase-to-length ratio of 56% is considered ○ dangerous ○ fatiguing ◉ good ○ excellent *
The approximate net payload of 1357 pounds at 8% of GVWR on this model is ○ deficient ○ excessive ◉ cautionary ○ good ○ excellent *
Total highway safety penalties are: 7 * Value: **83** Durability: **77** Highway Control Rating: **73** Highway Safety: **66** ★★

Brand	Year	Type	Length	Model	Chassis	Engine	Fuel Type	Avg Price/Ft	Wheelbase	Towing	GVWR	Curb Weight
RexAir	**1995**	MHA	34	SL3300	FO	7.5L	G	$2100	228	8,000	17,000	15,718

Livability Code: SB 30-90
Wheelbase-to-length ratio of 56% is considered ○ dangerous ○ fatiguing ◉ good ○ excellent *
The approximate net payload of 1282 pounds at 8% of GVWR on this model is ○ deficient ○ excessive ◉ cautionary ○ good ○ excellent *
Total highway safety penalties are: 2 * Value: **85** Durability: **77** Highway Control Rating: **72** Highway Safety: **70** ★★★

Brand	Year	Type	Length	Model	Chassis	Engine	Fuel Type	Avg Price/Ft	Wheelbase	Towing	GVWR	Curb Weight
RexAir	**1995**	MHA	34	SL3400	OS	CU230	D	$2900	208	4,500	20,500	18,589

Livability Code: SB 30-90
Wheelbase-to-length ratio of 51% is considered ○ dangerous ◉ fatiguing ○ good ○ excellent *
The approximate net payload of 1911 pounds at 9% of GVWR on this model is ○ deficient ○ excessive ◉ cautionary ○ good ○ excellent *
Total highway safety penalties are: 2 * Value: **85** Durability: **77** Highway Control Rating: **32** Highway Safety: **30**

Brand	Year	Type	Length	Model	Chassis	Engine	Fuel Type	Avg Price/Ft	Wheelbase	Towing	GVWR	Curb Weight
RexAir	**1995**	MHA	35	SL3400	CH	7.4L	G	$2000	232 T	2,500	19,500	16,127

Livability Code: SB 30-90
Wheelbase-to-length ratio of 56% is considered ○ dangerous ○ fatiguing ◉ good ○ excellent *
The approximate net payload of 3373 pounds at 17% of GVWR on this model is ○ deficient ○ excessive ○ cautionary ○ good ◉ excellent *
Total highway safety penalties are: 9 * Value: **81** Durability: **77** Highway Control Rating: **98** Highway Safety: **89** ★★★

Brand	Year	Type	Length	Model	Chassis	Engine	Fuel Type	Avg Price/Ft	Wheelbase	Towing	GVWR	Curb Weight
RexAir	**1995**	MHA	35	SL3400	FO	7.5L	G	$2000	232 T	5,000	20,000	16,672

Livability Code: SB 30-90
Wheelbase-to-length ratio of 56% is considered ○ dangerous ○ fatiguing ◉ good ○ excellent *
The approximate net payload of 3328 pounds at 17% of GVWR on this model is ○ deficient ○ excessive ○ cautionary ○ good ◉ excellent *
Total highway safety penalties are: 4 * Value: **84** Durability: **77** Highway Control Rating: **97** Highway Safety: **93** ★★★

Note: Safety ratings are based on the assumption that the engineering of the RV has allowed for proper balance by placing fresh, gray, and black holding tanks in a location so as not to change the balance of the RV when the tanks are empty or full. **Always double-check wheelbase, GVWR, and weights at front and rear axles.**

*See Section 1 for details on how conclusions are reached.

Section 2: The Ratings

Brand	Year	Type	Length	Model	Chassis	Engine	Fuel Type	Average Price per Linear Foot When New	Adjusted Wheelbase	Approx. Towing Capacity	Gross Vehicle Weight Rating	Average Curb Weight
RexAir	1995	MHA	36	SL3550 sl	CH	7.4L	G	$2200	252 T	500	19,500	17,546
RexAir	1995	MHA	36	SL3550 sl	FO	7.5L	G	$2200	252 T	5,000	20,000	17,946
RexAir	1995	MHA	36	SL3500	OS	CU230	D	$2800	228	4,500	20,500	19,139
RexAir	1995	MHA	36	SL3600	OS	CU230	D	$2800	228	4,500	20,500	19,139
RexAir	1995	MHA	36	SL3550 sl	OS	CU230	D	$2800	228	4,500	20,500	19,889
RexAir	1995	MHA	36	SL3650 sl	OS	CU230	D	$2800	228	4,500	20,500	20,189
RexAir	1995	MHA	36	SL3650 sl	CH	7.4L	G	$2200	252 T	500	19,500	17,989
RexAir	1995	MHA	36	SL3650 sl	FO	7.5L	G	$2200	252 T	5,000	20,000	18,389
RexAir	1995	MHA	37	SL3600	CH	7.4L	G	$2000	252 T	500	19,500	17,024
RexAir	1995	MHA	37	SL3500	CH	7.4L	G	$1900	252 T	2,500	19,500	17,024
RexAir	1995	MHA	37	SL3600	FO	7.5L	G	$2000	252 T	5,000	20,000	17,118
RexAir	1995	MHA	37	SL3500	FO	7.5L	G	$1900	252 T	5,000	20,000	16,948

RexAir — 1995 MHA 36 SL3550 sl (CH)
Livability Code: SB 30-90
Wheelbase-to-length ratio of 59% is considered ○ dangerous ○ fatiguing ○ good ◉ excellent*
The approximate net payload of 1954 pounds at 10% of GVWR on this model is ○ deficient ○ excessive ○ cautionary ◉ good ○ excellent*
Total highway safety penalties are: 14*   Value: 7 9   Durability: 7 7   Highway Control Rating: 9 4   Highway Safety: 8 0   ★★★

RexAir — 1995 MHA 36 SL3550 sl (FO)
Livability Code: SB 30-90
Wheelbase-to-length ratio of 59% is considered ○ dangerous ○ fatiguing ○ good ◉ excellent*
The approximate net payload of 2054 pounds at 10% of GVWR on this model is ○ deficient ○ excessive ○ cautionary ◉ good ○ excellent*
Total highway safety penalties are: 9*   Value: 8 1   Durability: 7 7   Highway Control Rating: 9 5   Highway Safety: 8 6   ★★★

RexAir — 1995 MHA 36 SL3500 (OS)
Livability Code: SB 30-90
Wheelbase-to-length ratio of 53% is considered ○ dangerous ◉ fatiguing ○ good ○ excellent*
The approximate net payload of 1361 pounds at 7% of GVWR on this model is ○ deficient ○ excessive ◉ cautionary ○ good ○ excellent*
Total highway safety penalties are: 2*   Value: 8 5   Durability: 7 7   Highway Control Rating: 4 0   Highway Safety: 3 8

RexAir — 1995 MHA 36 SL3600 (OS)
Livability Code: SB 30-90
Wheelbase-to-length ratio of 53% is considered ○ dangerous ◉ fatiguing ○ good ○ excellent*
The approximate net payload of 1361 pounds at 7% of GVWR on this model is ○ deficient ○ excessive ◉ cautionary ○ good ○ excellent*
Total highway safety penalties are: 2*   Value: 8 5   Durability: 7 7   Highway Control Rating: 4 0   Highway Safety: 3 8

RexAir — 1995 MHA 36 SL3550 sl (OS)
Livability Code: SB 30-90
Wheelbase-to-length ratio of 53% is considered ○ dangerous ◉ fatiguing ○ good ○ excellent*
The approximate net payload of 611 pounds at 3% of GVWR on this model is ◉ deficient ○ excessive ○ cautionary ○ good ○ excellent*
Total highway safety penalties are: 7*   Value: 8 3   Durability: 7 7   Highway Control Rating: 3 2   Highway Safety: 2 5

RexAir — 1995 MHA 36 SL3650 sl (OS)
Livability Code: SB 30-90
Wheelbase-to-length ratio of 53% is considered ○ dangerous ◉ fatiguing ○ good ○ excellent*
The approximate net payload of 311 pounds at 2% of GVWR on this model is ◉ deficient ○ excessive ○ cautionary ○ good ○ excellent*
Total highway safety penalties are: 8*   Value: 8 2   Durability: 7 7   Highway Control Rating: 3 0   Highway Safety: 2 2

RexAir — 1995 MHA 36 SL3650 sl (CH)
Livability Code: SB 30-90
Wheelbase-to-length ratio of 58% is considered ○ dangerous ○ fatiguing ○ good ◉ excellent*
The approximate net payload of 1511 pounds at 8% of GVWR on this model is ○ deficient ○ excessive ◉ cautionary ○ good ○ excellent*
Total highway safety penalties are: 16*   Value: 7 8   Durability: 7 7   Highway Control Rating: 8 0   Highway Safety: 6 4   ★★

RexAir — 1995 MHA 36 SL3650 sl (FO)
Livability Code: SB 30-90
Wheelbase-to-length ratio of 58% is considered ○ dangerous ○ fatiguing ○ good ◉ excellent*
The approximate net payload of 1611 pounds at 8% of GVWR on this model is ○ deficient ○ excessive ◉ cautionary ○ good ○ excellent*
Total highway safety penalties are: 11*   Value: 8 0   Durability: 7 7   Highway Control Rating: 8 0   Highway Safety: 6 9   ★★

RexAir — 1995 MHA 37 SL3600 (CH)
Livability Code: SB 30-90
Wheelbase-to-length ratio of 58% is considered ○ dangerous ○ fatiguing ○ good ◉ excellent*
The approximate net payload of 2476 pounds at 13% of GVWR on this model is ○ deficient ○ excessive ○ cautionary ◉ good ○ excellent*
Total highway safety penalties are: 10*   Value: 8 1   Durability: 7 7   Highway Control Rating: 9 8   Highway Safety: 8 8   ★★★

RexAir — 1995 MHA 37 SL3500 (CH)
Livability Code: SB 30-90
Wheelbase-to-length ratio of 58% is considered ○ dangerous ○ fatiguing ○ good ◉ excellent*
The approximate net payload of 2476 pounds at 13% of GVWR on this model is ○ deficient ○ excessive ○ cautionary ◉ good ○ excellent*
Total highway safety penalties are: 10*   Value: 8 1   Durability: 7 7   Highway Control Rating: 9 5   Highway Safety: 8 5   ★★★

RexAir — 1995 MHA 37 SL3600 (FO)
Livability Code: SB 30-90
Wheelbase-to-length ratio of 58% is considered ○ dangerous ○ fatiguing ○ good ◉ excellent*
The approximate net payload of 2882 pounds at 14% of GVWR on this model is ○ deficient ○ excessive ○ cautionary ◉ good ○ excellent*
Total highway safety penalties are: 4*   Value: 8 4   Durability: 7 7   Highway Control Rating: 1 0 0   Highway Safety: 9 6   ★★★

RexAir — 1995 MHA 37 SL3500 (FO)
Livability Code: SB 30-90
Wheelbase-to-length ratio of 58% is considered ○ dangerous ○ fatiguing ○ good ◉ excellent*
The approximate net payload of 3052 pounds at 15% of GVWR on this model is ○ deficient ○ excessive ○ cautionary ◉ good ○ excellent*
Total highway safety penalties are: 4*   Value: 8 4   Durability: 7 7   Highway Control Rating: 1 0 0   Highway Safety: 9 6   ★★★

Note: Safety ratings are based on the assumption that the engineering of the RV has allowed for proper balance by placing fresh, gray, and black holding tanks in a location so as not to change the balance of the RV when the tanks are empty or full. **Always double-check wheelbase, GVWR, and weights at front and rear axles.**

*See Section 1 for details on how conclusions are reached.

Brand	Year	Type	Length	Model	Chassis	Engine	Fuel Type	Average Price per Linear Foot When New	Adjusted Wheelbase	Approx. Towing Capacity	Gross Vehicle Weight Rating	Average Curb Weight
RexAir	1995	MHA	39	SL3800	FO	7.5L	G	$1900	252 T	5,000	20,000	18,193

Livability Code: SB 30-90

Wheelbase-to-length ratio of 54% is considered ○ dangerous ○ fatiguing ◉ good ○ excellent *

The approximate net payload of 1807 pounds at 9% of GVWR on this model is ○ deficient ○ excessive ◉ cautionary ○ good ○ excellent *

Total highway safety penalties are 4 *   Value: 8 4   Durability: 7 7   Highway Control Rating: 6 6   Highway Safety: 6 2   ★★

Brand	Year	Type	Length	Model	Chassis	Engine	Fuel Type	Avg Price/ft	Adj. Wheelbase	Towing	GVWR	Curb Wt
RexAir	1996	MHA	29	SL2800	CH	7.4L	G	$2200	190	3,500	16,500	14,011

Livability Code: SB 30-90

Wheelbase-to-length ratio of 54% is considered ○ dangerous ○ fatiguing ◉ good ○ excellent *

The approximate net payload of 2489 pounds at 15% of GVWR on this model is ○ deficient ○ excessive ○ cautionary ◉ good ○ excellent *

Total highway safety penalties are 4 *   Value: 8 4   Durability: 7 7   Highway Control Rating: 8 1   Highway Safety: 7 7   ★★★

RexAir	1996	MHA	29	SL2800	FO	7.5L	G	$2200	190	8,000	17,000	14,497

Livability Code: SB 30-90

Wheelbase-to-length ratio of 54% is considered ○ dangerous ○ fatiguing ◉ good ○ excellent *

The approximate net payload of 2503 pounds at 15% of GVWR on this model is ○ deficient ○ excessive ○ cautionary ◉ good ○ excellent *

Total highway safety penalties are: 2 *   Value: 8 5   Durability: 7 7   Highway Control Rating: 7 9   Highway Safety: 7 7   ★★★

RexAir	1996	MHA	31	SL2900	FO	7.5L	G	$2000	208 T	8,000	17,000	14,954

Livability Code: SB 30-90

Wheelbase-to-length ratio of 56% is considered ○ dangerous ○ fatiguing ◉ good ○ excellent *

The approximate net payload of 2046 pounds at 12% of GVWR on this model is ○ deficient ○ excessive ○ cautionary ◉ good ○ excellent *

Total highway safety penalties are: 2 *   Value: 8 5   Durability: 7 7   Highway Control Rating: 8 8   Highway Safety: 8 6   ★★★

RexAir	1996	MHA	32	SL3000	CH	7.4L	G	$2000	208	3,500	16,500	14,696

Livability Code: SB 30-90

Wheelbase-to-length ratio of 55% is considered ○ dangerous ○ fatiguing ◉ good ○ excellent *

The approximate net payload of 1804 pounds at 11% of GVWR on this model is ○ deficient ○ excessive ○ cautionary ◉ good ○ excellent *

Total highway safety penalties are: 5 *   Value: 8 3   Durability: 7 7   Highway Control Rating: 8 8   Highway Safety: 8 3   ★★★

RexAir	1996	MHA	32	SL2900	CH	7.4L	G	$2000	208	3,500	16,500	14,754

Livability Code: SB 30-90

Wheelbase-to-length ratio of 55% is considered ○ dangerous ○ fatiguing ◉ good ○ excellent *

The approximate net payload of 1746 pounds at 11% of GVWR on this model is ○ deficient ○ excessive ○ cautionary ◉ good ○ excellent *

Total highway safety penalties are: 5 *   Value: 8 3   Durability: 7 7   Highway Control Rating: 8 6   Highway Safety: 8 1   ★★★

RexAir	1996	MHA	32	SL3000	FO	7.5L	G	$2000	208	8,000	17,000	15,182

Livability Code: SB 30-90

Wheelbase-to-length ratio of 55% is considered ○ dangerous ○ fatiguing ◉ good ○ excellent *

The approximate net payload of 1818 pounds at 11% of GVWR on this model is ○ deficient ○ excessive ○ cautionary ◉ good ○ excellent *

Total highway safety penalties are: 2 *   Value: 8 5   Durability: 7 7   Highway Control Rating: 8 6   Highway Safety: 8 4   ★★★

RexAir	1996	MHA	32	SL3100	CH	7.4L	G	$2200	208	3,500	16,500	14,896

Livability Code: SB 30-90

Wheelbase-to-length ratio of 54% is considered ○ dangerous ○ fatiguing ◉ good ○ excellent *

The approximate net payload of 1604 pounds at 10% of GVWR on this model is ○ deficient ○ excessive ○ cautionary ◉ good ○ excellent *

Total highway safety penalties are: 6 *   Value: 8 3   Durability: 7 7   Highway Control Rating: 7 5   Highway Safety: 6 9   ★★

RexAir	1996	MHA	32	SL3250 sl	CH	7.4L	G	$2300	208	3,500	16,500	15,796

Livability Code: SB 30-90

Wheelbase-to-length ratio of 54% is considered ○ dangerous ○ fatiguing ◉ good ○ excellent *

The approximate net payload of 704 pounds at 4% of GVWR on this model is ◉ deficient ○ excessive ○ cautionary ○ good ○ excellent *

Total highway safety penalties are: 11 *   Value: 8 0   Durability: 7 7   Highway Control Rating: 4 4   Highway Safety: 3 3

RexAir	1996	MHA	32	SL3100	FO	7.5L	G	$2200	208	8,000	17,000	15,296

Livability Code: SB 30-90

Wheelbase-to-length ratio of 54% is considered ○ dangerous ○ fatiguing ◉ good ○ excellent *

The approximate net payload of 1704 pounds at 10% of GVWR on this model is ○ deficient ○ excessive ○ cautionary ◉ good ○ excellent *

Total highway safety penalties are: 2 *   Value: 8 5   Durability: 7 7   Highway Control Rating: 7 5   Highway Safety: 7 3   ★★★

RexAir	1996	MHA	32	SL3250 sl	FO	7.5L	G	$2300	208	8,000	17,000	16,196

Livability Code: SB 30-90

Wheelbase-to-length ratio of 54% is considered ○ dangerous ○ fatiguing ◉ good ○ excellent *

The approximate net payload of 804 pounds at 5% of GVWR on this model is ◉ deficient ○ excessive ○ cautionary ○ good ○ excellent *

Total highway safety penalties are: 7 *   Value: 8 2   Durability: 7 7   Highway Control Rating: 4 5   Highway Safety: 3 8

RexAir	1996	MHA	33	SL3200	CH	7.4L	G	$2000	208	3,500	16,500	14,982

Livability Code: SB 30-90

Wheelbase-to-length ratio of 53% is considered ○ dangerous ◉ fatiguing ○ good ○ excellent *

The approximate net payload of 1518 pounds at 9% of GVWR on this model is ○ deficient ○ excessive ◉ cautionary ○ good ○ excellent *

Total highway safety penalties are: 6 *   Value: 8 3   Durability: 7 7   Highway Control Rating: 5 5   Highway Safety: 4 9

Note: Safety ratings are based on the assumption that the engineering of the RV has allowed for proper balance by placing fresh, gray, and black holding tanks in a location so as not to change the balance of the RV when the tanks are empty or full. **Always double-check wheelbase, GVWR, and weights at front and rear axles.**

Section 2: The Ratings

Brand	Year	Type	Length	Model	Chassis	Engine	Fuel Type	Average Price per Linear Foot When New	Adjusted Wheelbase	Approx. Towing Capacity	Gross Vehicle Weight Rating	Average Curb Weight
RexAir	1996	MHA	33	SL3200	FO	7.5L	G	$2000	208	8,000	17,000	15,382

Livability Code: SB 30-90
Wheelbase-to-length ratio of 53% is considered ○ dangerous ◉ fatiguing ○ good ○ excellent *
The approximate net payload of 1618 pounds at 10% of GVWR on this model is ○ deficient ○ excessive ○ cautionary ◉ good ○ excellent *
Total highway safety penalties are: 2 *   Value: 8 5   Durability: 7 7   Highway Control Rating: 5 9   Highway Safety: 5 7   ★

Brand	Year	Type	Length	Model	Chassis	Engine	Fuel Type	Avg Price/Linear Foot	Adj. Wheelbase	Approx. Towing Capacity	GVWR	Avg Curb Weight
RexAir	1996	MHA	34	SL3300	CH	7.4L	G	$2000	228	3,500	16,500	15,382

Livability Code: SB 30-90
Wheelbase-to-length ratio of 56% is considered ○ dangerous ○ fatiguing ◉ good ○ excellent *
The approximate net payload of 1118 pounds at 7% of GVWR on this model is ○ deficient ○ excessive ◉ cautionary ○ good ○ excellent *
Total highway safety penalties are: 6 *   Value: 8 3   Durability: 7 7   Highway Control Rating: 6 7   Highway Safety: 6 1   ★★

Brand	Year	Type	Length	Model	Chassis	Engine	Fuel Type	Avg Price/Linear Foot	Adj. Wheelbase	Approx. Towing Capacity	GVWR	Avg Curb Weight
RexAir	1996	MHA	34	SL3300	FO	7.5L	G	$2100	228	8,000	17,000	15,810

Livability Code: SB 30-90
Wheelbase-to-length ratio of 56% is considered ○ dangerous ○ fatiguing ◉ good ○ excellent *
The approximate net payload of 1190 pounds at 7% of GVWR on this model is ○ deficient ○ excessive ◉ cautionary ○ good ○ excellent *
Total highway safety penalties are: 2 *   Value: 8 5   Durability: 7 7   Highway Control Rating: 6 7   Highway Safety: 6 5   ★★

Brand	Year	Type	Length	Model	Chassis	Engine	Fuel Type	Avg Price/Linear Foot	Adj. Wheelbase	Approx. Towing Capacity	GVWR	Avg Curb Weight
RexAir	1996	MHA	34	SL3400	CH	7.4L	G	$2100	232 T	1,500	19,500	16,083

Livability Code: SB 30-90
Wheelbase-to-length ratio of 57% is considered ○ dangerous ○ fatiguing ◉ good ○ excellent *
The approximate net payload of 3417 pounds at 18% of GVWR on this model is ○ deficient ○ excessive ○ cautionary ○ good ◉ excellent *
Total highway safety penalties are: 9 *   Value: 8 1   Durability: 7 7   Highway Control Rating: 1 0 0   Highway Safety: 9 1   ★★★

Brand	Year	Type	Length	Model	Chassis	Engine	Fuel Type	Avg Price/Linear Foot	Adj. Wheelbase	Approx. Towing Capacity	GVWR	Avg Curb Weight
RexAir	1996	MHA	35	SL3400	FO	7.5L	G	$2000	232 T	5,000	20,000	16,692

Livability Code: SB 30-90
Wheelbase-to-length ratio of 56% is considered ○ dangerous ○ fatiguing ◉ good ○ excellent *
The approximate net payload of 3308 pounds at 17% of GVWR on this model is ○ deficient ○ excessive ○ cautionary ○ good ◉ excellent *
Total highway safety penalties are: 4 *   Value: 8 4   Durability: 7 7   Highway Control Rating: 9 7   Highway Safety: 9 3   ★★★

Brand	Year	Type	Length	Model	Chassis	Engine	Fuel Type	Avg Price/Linear Foot	Adj. Wheelbase	Approx. Towing Capacity	GVWR	Avg Curb Weight
RexAir	1996	MHA	36	SL3550 sl	CH	7.4L	G	$2200	252 T	1,500	19,500	17,546

Livability Code: SB 30-90
Wheelbase-to-length ratio of 59% is considered ○ dangerous ○ fatiguing ○ good ◉ excellent *
The approximate net payload of 1954 pounds at 10% of GVWR on this model is ○ deficient ○ excessive ○ cautionary ◉ good ○ excellent *
Total highway safety penalties are: 14 *   Value: 7 9   Durability: 7 7   Highway Control Rating: 9 4   Highway Safety: 8 0   ★★★

Brand	Year	Type	Length	Model	Chassis	Engine	Fuel Type	Avg Price/Linear Foot	Adj. Wheelbase	Approx. Towing Capacity	GVWR	Avg Curb Weight
RexAir	1996	MHA	36	SL3500	CH	7.4L	G	$2000	252 T	1,500	19,500	16,796

Livability Code: SB 30-90
Wheelbase-to-length ratio of 59% is considered ○ dangerous ○ fatiguing ○ good ◉ excellent *
The approximate net payload of 2704 pounds at 14% of GVWR on this model is ○ deficient ○ excessive ○ cautionary ◉ good ○ excellent *
Total highway safety penalties are: 10 *   Value: 8 1   Durability: 7 7   Highway Control Rating: 1 0 0   Highway Safety: 9 0   ★★★

Brand	Year	Type	Length	Model	Chassis	Engine	Fuel Type	Avg Price/Linear Foot	Adj. Wheelbase	Approx. Towing Capacity	GVWR	Avg Curb Weight
RexAir	1996	MHA	36	SL3550 sl	FO	7.5L	G	$2200	252 T	5,000	20,000	17,946

Livability Code: SB 30-90
Wheelbase-to-length ratio of 59% is considered ○ dangerous ○ fatiguing ○ good ◉ excellent *
The approximate net payload of 2054 pounds at 10% of GVWR on this model is ○ deficient ○ excessive ○ cautionary ◉ good ○ excellent *
Total highway safety penalties are: 9 *   Value: 8 1   Durability: 7 7   Highway Control Rating: 9 5   Highway Safety: 8 6   ★★★

Brand	Year	Type	Length	Model	Chassis	Engine	Fuel Type	Avg Price/Linear Foot	Adj. Wheelbase	Approx. Towing Capacity	GVWR	Avg Curb Weight
RexAir	1996	MHA	36	SL3650 sl	CH	7.4L	G	$2200	252 T	1,500	19,500	17,989

Livability Code: SB 30-90
Wheelbase-to-length ratio of 58% is considered ○ dangerous ○ fatiguing ○ good ◉ excellent *
The approximate net payload of 1511 pounds at 8% of GVWR on this model is ○ deficient ○ excessive ◉ cautionary ○ good ○ excellent *
Total highway safety penalties are: 16 *   Value: 7 8   Durability: 7 7   Highway Control Rating: 8 0   Highway Safety: 6 4   ★★

Brand	Year	Type	Length	Model	Chassis	Engine	Fuel Type	Avg Price/Linear Foot	Adj. Wheelbase	Approx. Towing Capacity	GVWR	Avg Curb Weight
RexAir	1996	MHA	36	SL3650 sl	FO	7.5L	G	$2200	252 T	5,000	20,000	18,389

Livability Code: SB 30-90
Wheelbase-to-length ratio of 58% is considered ○ dangerous ○ fatiguing ○ good ◉ excellent *
The approximate net payload of 1611 pounds at 8% of GVWR on this model is ○ deficient ○ excessive ◉ cautionary ○ good ○ excellent *
Total highway safety penalties are: 11 *   Value: 8 0   Durability: 7 7   Highway Control Rating: 8 0   Highway Safety: 6 9   ★★

Brand	Year	Type	Length	Model	Chassis	Engine	Fuel Type	Avg Price/Linear Foot	Adj. Wheelbase	Approx. Towing Capacity	GVWR	Avg Curb Weight
RexAir	1996	MHA	37	SL3600	CH	7.4L	G	$2000	252 T	1,500	19,500	17,024

Livability Code: SB 30-90
Wheelbase-to-length ratio of 58% is considered ○ dangerous ○ fatiguing ○ good ◉ excellent *
The approximate net payload of 2476 pounds at 13% of GVWR on this model is ○ deficient ○ excessive ○ cautionary ◉ good ○ excellent *
Total highway safety penalties are: 10 *   Value: 8 1   Durability: 7 7   Highway Control Rating: 9 5   Highway Safety: 8 5   ★★★

Brand	Year	Type	Length	Model	Chassis	Engine	Fuel Type	Avg Price/Linear Foot	Adj. Wheelbase	Approx. Towing Capacity	GVWR	Avg Curb Weight
RexAir	1996	MHA	37	SL3500	FO	7.5L	G	$1900	252 T	5,000	20,000	17,424

Livability Code: SB 30-90
Wheelbase-to-length ratio of 58% is considered ○ dangerous ○ fatiguing ○ good ◉ excellent *
The approximate net payload of 2576 pounds at 13% of GVWR on this model is ○ deficient ○ excessive ○ cautionary ◉ good ○ excellent *
Total highway safety penalties are: 4 *   Value: 8 4   Durability: 7 7   Highway Control Rating: 9 6   Highway Safety: 9 2   ★★★

Note: Safety ratings are based on the assumption that the engineering of the RV has allowed for proper balance by placing fresh, gray, and black holding tanks in a location so as not to change the balance of the RV when the tanks are empty or full. **Always double-check wheelbase, GVWR, and weights at front and rear axles.**

*See Section 1 for details on how conclusions are reached.

Brand	Year	Type	Length	Model	Chassis	Engine	Fuel Type	Average Price per Linear Foot When New	Adjusted Wheelbase	Approx. Towing Capacity	Gross Vehicle Weight Rating	Average Curb Weight
RexAir	**1996**	MHA	37	SL3600	FO	7.5L	G	$2000	252 T	5,000	20,000	17,424

Livability Code: SB 30-90   Wheelbase-to-length ratio of 58% is considered ◯ dangerous ◯ fatiguing ◯ good ◉ excellent *

The approximate net payload of 2576 pounds at 13% of GVWR on this model is ◯ deficient ◯ excessive ◯ cautionary ◉ good ◯ excellent *

Total highway safety penalties are: 4 *   Value: **8 4**   Durability: **7 7**   Highway Control Rating: **9 6**   Highway Safety: **9 2**   ★★★

Brand	Year	Type	Length	Model	Chassis	Engine	Fuel Type	Price/Ft	Wheelbase	Towing	GVWR	Curb Weight
RexAir	**1996**	MHA	39	SL3800	FO	7.5L	G	$1900	252 T	5,000	20,000	18,053

Livability Code: SB 30-90   Wheelbase-to-length ratio of 54% is considered ◯ dangerous ◯ fatiguing ◉ good ◯ excellent *

The approximate net payload of 1947 pounds at 10% of GVWR on this model is ◯ deficient ◯ excessive ◯ cautionary ◯ good ◯ excellent *

Total highway safety penalties are: 4 *   Value: **8 4**   Durability: **7 7**   Highway Control Rating: **7 6**   Highway Safety: **7 2**   ★★★

Brand	Year	Type	Length	Model	Chassis	Engine	Fuel Type	Price/Ft	Wheelbase	Towing	GVWR	Curb Weight
RexAir	**1997**	MHA	29	SL2800	CH	7.4L	G	$2200	190	3,500	16,500	14,011

Livability Code: SB 30-90   Wheelbase-to-length ratio of 54% is considered ◯ dangerous ◯ fatiguing ◉ good ◯ excellent *

The approximate net payload of 2489 pounds at 15% of GVWR on this model is ◯ deficient ◯ excessive ◯ cautionary ◉ good ◯ excellent *

Total highway safety penalties are: 4 *   Value: **8 4**   Durability: **7 7**   Highway Control Rating: **8 1**   Highway Safety: **7 7**   ★★★

Brand	Year	Type	Length	Model	Chassis	Engine	Fuel Type	Price/Ft	Wheelbase	Towing	GVWR	Curb Weight
RexAir	**1997**	MHA	29	SL2800	FO	7.5L	G	$2200	190	8,000	17,000	14,411

Livability Code: SB 30-90   Wheelbase-to-length ratio of 54% is considered ◯ dangerous ◯ fatiguing ◉ good ◯ excellent *

The approximate net payload of 2589 pounds at 15% of GVWR on this model is ◯ deficient ◯ excessive ◯ cautionary ◉ good ◯ excellent *

Total highway safety penalties are: 2 *   Value: **8 5**   Durability: **7 7**   Highway Control Rating: **8 1**   Highway Safety: **7 9**   ★★★

Brand	Year	Type	Length	Model	Chassis	Engine	Fuel Type	Price/Ft	Wheelbase	Towing	GVWR	Curb Weight
RexAir	**1997**	MHA	31	SL2900	CH	7.4L	G	$2000	208	3,500	16,500	14,468

Livability Code: SB 30-90   Wheelbase-to-length ratio of 56% is considered ◯ dangerous ◯ fatiguing ◉ good ◯ excellent *

The approximate net payload of 2032 pounds at 12% of GVWR on this model is ◯ deficient ◯ excessive ◯ cautionary ◉ good ◯ excellent *

Total highway safety penalties are: 5 *   Value: **8 3**   Durability: **7 7**   Highway Control Rating: **9 0**   Highway Safety: **8 5**   ★★★

Brand	Year	Type	Length	Model	Chassis	Engine	Fuel Type	Price/Ft	Wheelbase	Towing	GVWR	Curb Weight
RexAir	**1997**	MHA	31	SL2900	FO	7.5L	G	$2000	208	8,000	17,000	14,868

Livability Code: SB 30-90   Wheelbase-to-length ratio of 56% is considered ◯ dangerous ◯ fatiguing ◉ good ◯ excellent *

The approximate net payload of 2132 pounds at 13% of GVWR on this model is ◯ deficient ◯ excessive ◯ cautionary ◉ good ◯ excellent *

Total highway safety penalties are: 2 *   Value: **8 5**   Durability: **7 7**   Highway Control Rating: **9 1**   Highway Safety: **8 9**   ★★★

Brand	Year	Type	Length	Model	Chassis	Engine	Fuel Type	Price/Ft	Wheelbase	Towing	GVWR	Curb Weight
RexAir	**1997**	MHA	32	SL3000	CH	7.4L	G	$2000	208	3,500	16,500	14,696

Livability Code: SB 30-90   Wheelbase-to-length ratio of 55% is considered ◯ dangerous ◯ fatiguing ◉ good ◯ excellent *

The approximate net payload of 1804 pounds at 11% of GVWR on this model is ◯ deficient ◯ excessive ◯ cautionary ◉ good ◯ excellent *

Total highway safety penalties are: 5 *   Value: **8 3**   Durability: **7 7**   Highway Control Rating: **8 8**   Highway Safety: **8 3**   ★★★

Brand	Year	Type	Length	Model	Chassis	Engine	Fuel Type	Price/Ft	Wheelbase	Towing	GVWR	Curb Weight
RexAir	**1997**	MHA	32	SL3000	FO	7.5L	G	$2200	208	8,000	17,000	15,096

Livability Code: SB 30-90   Wheelbase-to-length ratio of 55% is considered ◯ dangerous ◯ fatiguing ◉ good ◯ excellent *

The approximate net payload of 1904 pounds at 11% of GVWR on this model is ◯ deficient ◯ excessive ◯ cautionary ◉ good ◯ excellent *

Total highway safety penalties are: 2 *   Value: **8 5**   Durability: **7 7**   Highway Control Rating: **8 8**   Highway Safety: **8 6**   ★★★

Brand	Year	Type	Length	Model	Chassis	Engine	Fuel Type	Price/Ft	Wheelbase	Towing	GVWR	Curb Weight
RexAir	**1997**	MHA	32	SL3100	CH	7.4L	G	$2200	208	3,500	16,500	14,896

Livability Code: SB 30-90   Wheelbase-to-length ratio of 54% is considered ◯ dangerous ◯ fatiguing ◉ good ◯ excellent *

The approximate net payload of 1604 pounds at 10% of GVWR on this model is ◯ deficient ◯ excessive ◯ cautionary ◉ good ◯ excellent *

Total highway safety penalties are: 6 *   Value: **8 3**   Durability: **7 7**   Highway Control Rating: **7 5**   Highway Safety: **6 9**   ★★

Brand	Year	Type	Length	Model	Chassis	Engine	Fuel Type	Price/Ft	Wheelbase	Towing	GVWR	Curb Weight
RexAir	**1997**	MHA	32	SL3200	CH	7.4L	G	$2100	208	3,500	16,500	14,896

Livability Code: SB 30-90   Wheelbase-to-length ratio of 54% is considered ◯ dangerous ◯ fatiguing ◉ good ◯ excellent *

The approximate net payload of 1604 pounds at 10% of GVWR on this model is ◯ deficient ◯ excessive ◯ cautionary ◉ good ◯ excellent *

Total highway safety penalties are: 6 *   Value: **8 3**   Durability: **7 7**   Highway Control Rating: **7 5**   Highway Safety: **6 9**   ★★

Brand	Year	Type	Length	Model	Chassis	Engine	Fuel Type	Price/Ft	Wheelbase	Towing	GVWR	Curb Weight
RexAir	**1997**	MHA	32	SL3250	CH	7.4L	G	$2300	208	3,500	16,500	15,796

Livability Code: SB 30-90   Wheelbase-to-length ratio of 54% is considered ◯ dangerous ◯ fatiguing ◉ good ◯ excellent *

The approximate net payload of 704 pounds at 4% of GVWR on this model is ◉ deficient ◯ excessive ◯ cautionary ◯ good ◯ excellent *

Total highway safety penalties are: 11 *   Value: **8 0**   Durability: **7 7**   Highway Control Rating: **4 4**   Highway Safety: **3 3**

Brand	Year	Type	Length	Model	Chassis	Engine	Fuel Type	Price/Ft	Wheelbase	Towing	GVWR	Curb Weight
RexAir	**1997**	MHA	32	SL3100	FO	7.5L	G	$2200	208	8,000	17,000	15,296

Livability Code: SB 30-90   Wheelbase-to-length ratio of 54% is considered ◯ dangerous ◯ fatiguing ◉ good ◯ excellent *

The approximate net payload of 1704 pounds at 10% of GVWR on this model is ◯ deficient ◯ excessive ◯ cautionary ◉ good ◯ excellent *

Total highway safety penalties are: 2 *   Value: **8 5**   Durability: **7 7**   Highway Control Rating: **7 5**   Highway Safety: **7 3**   ★★★

Note: Safety ratings are based on the assumption that the engineering of the RV has allowed for proper balance by placing fresh, gray, and black holding tanks in a location so as not to change the balance of the RV when the tanks are empty or full. **Always double-check wheelbase, GVWR, and weights at front and rear axles.**

Section 2: The Ratings

Brand	Year	Type	Length	Model	Chassis	Engine	Fuel Type	Average Price per Linear Foot When New	Adjusted Wheelbase	Approx. Towing Capacity	Gross Vehicle Weight Rating	Average Curb Weight
RexAir	1997	MHA	32	SL3200	FO	7.5L	G	$2100	208	8,000	17,000	15,296

Livability Code: SB 30-90
Wheelbase-to-length ratio of 54% is considered ○ dangerous ○ fatiguing ◉ good ○ excellent *
The approximate net payload of 1704 pounds at 10% of GVWR on this model is ○ deficient ○ excessive ○ cautionary ◉ good ○ excellent *
Total highway safety penalties are: 2 *   Value: 85   Durability: 77   Highway Control Rating: 75   Highway Safety: 73   ★★★

Brand	Year	Type	Length	Model	Chassis	Engine	Fuel Type	Price/Ft	Wheelbase	Towing	GVWR	Curb Wt
RexAir	1997	MHA	32	SL3250	FO	7.5L	G	$2100	208	8,000	17,000	16,196

Livability Code: SB 30-90
Wheelbase-to-length ratio of 54% is considered ○ dangerous ○ fatiguing ◉ good ○ excellent *
The approximate net payload of 804 pounds at 5% of GVWR on this model is ◉ deficient ○ excessive ○ cautionary ○ good ○ excellent *
Total highway safety penalties are: 7 *   Value: 82   Durability: 77   Highway Control Rating: 45   Highway Safety: 38

Brand	Year	Type	Length	Model	Chassis	Engine	Fuel Type	Price/Ft	Wheelbase	Towing	GVWR	Curb Wt
RexAir	1997	MHA	32	SL3100	FR	Cu230	D	$3400	190	4,500	20,500	17,396

Livability Code: SB 30-90
Wheelbase-to-length ratio of 49% is considered ◉ dangerous ○ fatiguing ○ good ○ excellent *
The approximate net payload of 3104 pounds at 15% of GVWR on this model is ○ deficient ○ excessive ○ cautionary ◉ good ○ excellent *
Total highway safety penalties are: 2 *   Value: 85   Durability: 77   Highway Control Rating: 40   Highway Safety: 38

Brand	Year	Type	Length	Model	Chassis	Engine	Fuel Type	Price/Ft	Wheelbase	Towing	GVWR	Curb Wt
RexAir	1997	MHA	32	SL3200	FR	Cu230	D	$3400	190	4,500	20,500	17,396

Livability Code: SB 30-90
Wheelbase-to-length ratio of 49% is considered ◉ dangerous ○ fatiguing ○ good ○ excellent *
The approximate net payload of 3104 pounds at 15% of GVWR on this model is ○ deficient ○ excessive ○ cautionary ◉ good ○ excellent *
Total highway safety penalties are: 2 *   Value: 85   Durability: 77   Highway Control Rating: 40   Highway Safety: 38

Brand	Year	Type	Length	Model	Chassis	Engine	Fuel Type	Price/Ft	Wheelbase	Towing	GVWR	Curb Wt
RexAir	1997	MHA	32	SL3250	FR	Cu230	D	$3400	190	4,500	20,500	18,296

Livability Code: SB 30-90
Wheelbase-to-length ratio of 49% is considered ◉ dangerous ○ fatiguing ○ good ○ excellent *
The approximate net payload of 2204 pounds at 11% of GVWR on this model is ○ deficient ○ excessive ○ cautionary ◉ good ○ excellent *
Total highway safety penalties are: 7 *   Value: 82   Durability: 77   Highway Control Rating: 32   Highway Safety: 25

Brand	Year	Type	Length	Model	Chassis	Engine	Fuel Type	Price/Ft	Wheelbase	Towing	GVWR	Curb Wt
RexAir	1997	MHA	32	SL3100	SP	Cu230	D	$3400	190	2,000	24,000	20,539

Livability Code: SB 30-90
Wheelbase-to-length ratio of 49% is considered ◉ dangerous ○ fatiguing ○ good ○ excellent *
The approximate net payload of 3461 pounds at 14% of GVWR on this model is ○ deficient ○ excessive ○ cautionary ◉ good ○ excellent *
Total highway safety penalties are: 2 *   Value: 85   Durability: 77   Highway Control Rating: 38   Highway Safety: 36

Brand	Year	Type	Length	Model	Chassis	Engine	Fuel Type	Price/Ft	Wheelbase	Towing	GVWR	Curb Wt
RexAir	1997	MHA	32	SL3200	SP	Cu230	D	$3400	190	2,000	24,000	20,539

Livability Code: SB 30-90
Wheelbase-to-length ratio of 49% is considered ◉ dangerous ○ fatiguing ○ good ○ excellent *
The approximate net payload of 3461 pounds at 14% of GVWR on this model is ○ deficient ○ excessive ○ cautionary ◉ good ○ excellent *
Total highway safety penalties are: 2 *   Value: 85   Durability: 77   Highway Control Rating: 38   Highway Safety: 36

Brand	Year	Type	Length	Model	Chassis	Engine	Fuel Type	Price/Ft	Wheelbase	Towing	GVWR	Curb Wt
RexAir	1997	MHA	32	SL3250	SP	Cu230	D	$3400	190	2,000	24,000	21,439

Livability Code: SB 30-90
Wheelbase-to-length ratio of 49% is considered ◉ dangerous ○ fatiguing ○ good ○ excellent *
The approximate net payload of 2561 pounds at 11% of GVWR on this model is ○ deficient ○ excessive ○ cautionary ◉ good ○ excellent *
Total highway safety penalties are: 7 *   Value: 82   Durability: 77   Highway Control Rating: 31   Highway Safety: 24

Brand	Year	Type	Length	Model	Chassis	Engine	Fuel Type	Price/Ft	Wheelbase	Towing	GVWR	Curb Wt
RexAir	1997	MHA	34	SL3300	CH	7.4L	G	$2000	228	3,500	16,500	15,382

Livability Code: SB 30-90
Wheelbase-to-length ratio of 56% is considered ○ dangerous ○ fatiguing ◉ good ○ excellent *
The approximate net payload of 1118 pounds at 7% of GVWR on this model is ○ deficient ○ excessive ◉ cautionary ○ good ○ excellent *
Total highway safety penalties are: 6 *   Value: 83   Durability: 77   Highway Control Rating: 67   Highway Safety: 61   ★★

Brand	Year	Type	Length	Model	Chassis	Engine	Fuel Type	Price/Ft	Wheelbase	Towing	GVWR	Curb Wt
RexAir	1997	MHA	34	SL3300	FO	7.5L	G	$2100	228	8,000	17,000	15,782

Livability Code: SB 30-90
Wheelbase-to-length ratio of 56% is considered ○ dangerous ○ fatiguing ◉ good ○ excellent *
The approximate net payload of 1218 pounds at 7% of GVWR on this model is ○ deficient ○ excessive ◉ cautionary ○ good ○ excellent *
Total highway safety penalties are: 2 *   Value: 85   Durability: 77   Highway Control Rating: 68   Highway Safety: 66   ★★

Brand	Year	Type	Length	Model	Chassis	Engine	Fuel Type	Price/Ft	Wheelbase	Towing	GVWR	Curb Wt
RexAir	1997	MHA	34	SL3300	FR	Cu230	D	$3200	208	4,500	20,500	17,882

Livability Code: SB 30-90
Wheelbase-to-length ratio of 51% is considered ○ dangerous ◉ fatiguing ○ good ○ excellent *
The approximate net payload of 2618 pounds at 13% of GVWR on this model is ○ deficient ○ excessive ○ cautionary ◉ good ○ excellent *
Total highway safety penalties are: 2 *   Value: 85   Durability: 77   Highway Control Rating: 43   Highway Safety: 41

Brand	Year	Type	Length	Model	Chassis	Engine	Fuel Type	Price/Ft	Wheelbase	Towing	GVWR	Curb Wt
RexAir	1997	MHA	34	SL3300	SP	Cu230	D	$3200	208	2,000	24,000	20,990

Livability Code: SB 30-90
Wheelbase-to-length ratio of 51% is considered ○ dangerous ◉ fatiguing ○ good ○ excellent *
The approximate net payload of 3010 pounds at 13% of GVWR on this model is ○ deficient ○ excessive ○ cautionary ◉ good ○ excellent *
Total highway safety penalties are: 2 *   Value: 85   Durability: 77   Highway Control Rating: 42   Highway Safety: 40

Note: Safety ratings are based on the assumption that the engineering of the RV has allowed for proper balance by placing fresh, gray, and black holding tanks in a location so as not to change the balance of the RV when the tanks are empty or full. **Always double-check wheelbase, GVWR, and weights at front and rear axles.**

*See Section 1 for details on how conclusions are reached.

Brand	Year	Type	Length	Model	Chassis	Engine	Fuel Type	Average Price per Linear Foot When New	Adjusted Wheel-base	Approx. Towing Capacity	Gross Vehicle Weight Rating	Average Curb Weight
RexAir	1997	MHA	34	SL3400	CH	7.4L	G	$2000	232 T	1,500	19,500	16,368

Livability Code: SB 30-90 — Wheelbase-to-length ratio of 57% is considered ○ dangerous ○ fatiguing ◉ good ○ excellent *

The approximate net payload of 3132 pounds at 16% of GVWR on this model is ○ deficient ○ excessive ○ cautionary ○ good ◉ excellent *

Total highway safety penalties are: 9 * — Value: 8 1 — Durability: 7 7 — Highway Control Rating: 9 8 — Highway Safety: 8 9 — ★★★

Brand	Year	Type	Length	Model	Chassis	Engine	Fuel Type	Price/LF	Wheelbase	Towing	GVWR	Curb Weight
RexAir	1997	MHA	34	SL3400	FO	7.5L	G	$2100	232 T	5,000	20,000	16,768

Livability Code: SB 30-90 — Wheelbase-to-length ratio of 57% is considered ○ dangerous ○ fatiguing ◉ good ○ excellent *

The approximate net payload of 3232 pounds at 16% of GVWR on this model is ○ deficient ○ excessive ○ cautionary ○ good ◉ excellent *

Total highway safety penalties are: 4 * — Value: 8 4 — Durability: 7 7 — Highway Control Rating: 9 8 — Highway Safety: 9 4 — ★★★

RexAir	1997	MHA	34	SL3400	FR	Cu230	D	$3200	208	4,500	20,500	17,968

Livability Code: SB 30-90 — Wheelbase-to-length ratio of 51% is considered ○ dangerous ◉ fatiguing ○ good ○ excellent *

The approximate net payload of 2532 pounds at 12% of GVWR on this model is ○ deficient ○ excessive ○ cautionary ◉ good ○ excellent *

Total highway safety penalties are: 2 * — Value: 8 5 — Durability: 7 7 — Highway Control Rating: 4 0 — Highway Safety: 3 8

RexAir	1997	MHA	34	SL3400	SP	Cu230	D	$3200	208	2,000	24,000	21,070

Livability Code: SB 30-90 — Wheelbase-to-length ratio of 51% is considered ○ dangerous ◉ fatiguing ○ good ○ excellent *

The approximate net payload of 2930 pounds at 12% of GVWR on this model is ○ deficient ○ excessive ○ cautionary ◉ good ○ excellent *

Total highway safety penalties are: 2 * — Value: 8 5 — Durability: 7 7 — Highway Control Rating: 3 9 — Highway Safety: 3 7

RexAir	1997	MHA	36	SL3500	CH	7.4L	G	$2000	252 T	1,500	19,500	16,796

Livability Code: SB 30-90 — Wheelbase-to-length ratio of 59% is considered ○ dangerous ○ fatiguing ○ good ◉ excellent *

The approximate net payload of 2704 pounds at 14% of GVWR on this model is ○ deficient ○ excessive ○ cautionary ◉ good ○ excellent *

Total highway safety penalties are: 10 * — Value: 8 1 — Durability: 7 7 — Highway Control Rating: 1 0 0 — Highway Safety: 9 0 — ★★★

RexAir	1997	MHA	36	SL3550	CH	7.4L	G	$2200	252 T	1,500	19,500	17,546

Livability Code: SB 30-90 — Wheelbase-to-length ratio of 59% is considered ○ dangerous ○ fatiguing ○ good ◉ excellent *

The approximate net payload of 1954 pounds at 10% of GVWR on this model is ○ deficient ○ excessive ○ cautionary ○ good ○ excellent *

Total highway safety penalties are: 14 * — Value: 7 9 — Durability: 7 7 — Highway Control Rating: 9 4 — Highway Safety: 8 0 — ★★★

RexAir	1997	MHA	36	SL3500	FO	7.5L	G	$2000	252 T	5,000	20,000	17,196

Livability Code: SB 30-90 — Wheelbase-to-length ratio of 59% is considered ○ dangerous ○ fatiguing ○ good ◉ excellent *

The approximate net payload of 2804 pounds at 14% of GVWR on this model is ○ deficient ○ excessive ○ cautionary ◉ good ○ excellent *

Total highway safety penalties are: 4 * — Value: 8 4 — Durability: 7 7 — Highway Control Rating: 1 0 0 — Highway Safety: 9 6 — ★★★

RexAir	1997	MHA	36	SL3550	FO	7.5L	G	$2300	252 T	5,000	20,000	17,946

Livability Code: SB 30-90 — Wheelbase-to-length ratio of 59% is considered ○ dangerous ○ fatiguing ○ good ◉ excellent *

The approximate net payload of 2054 pounds at 10% of GVWR on this model is ○ deficient ○ excessive ○ cautionary ◉ good ○ excellent *

Total highway safety penalties are: 9 * — Value: 8 1 — Durability: 7 7 — Highway Control Rating: 9 5 — Highway Safety: 8 6 — ★★★

RexAir	1997	MHA	36	SL3500	FR	Cu230	D	$3100	228	4,500	20,500	18,396

Livability Code: SB 30-90 — Wheelbase-to-length ratio of 53% is considered ○ dangerous ◉ fatiguing ○ good ○ excellent *

The approximate net payload of 2104 pounds at 10% of GVWR on this model is ○ deficient ○ excessive ○ cautionary ◉ good ○ excellent *

Total highway safety penalties are: 2 * — Value: 8 5 — Durability: 7 7 — Highway Control Rating: 6 0 — Highway Safety: 5 8 — ★

RexAir	1997	MHA	36	SL3550	FR	Cu230	D	$3100	228	4,500	20,500	19,146

Livability Code: SB 30-90 — Wheelbase-to-length ratio of 53% is considered ○ dangerous ◉ fatiguing ○ good ○ excellent *

The approximate net payload of 1354 pounds at 7% of GVWR on this model is ○ deficient ○ excessive ◉ cautionary ○ good ○ excellent *

Total highway safety penalties are: 7 * — Value: 8 3 — Durability: 7 7 — Highway Control Rating: 4 2 — Highway Safety: 3 5

RexAir	1997	MHA	36	SL3500	SP	Cu230	D	$3100	228	2,000	24,000	21,468

Livability Code: SB 30-90 — Wheelbase-to-length ratio of 53% is considered ○ dangerous ◉ fatiguing ○ good ○ excellent *

The approximate net payload of 2532 pounds at 11% of GVWR on this model is ○ deficient ○ excessive ○ cautionary ◉ good ○ excellent *

Total highway safety penalties are: 2 * — Value: 8 5 — Durability: 7 7 — Highway Control Rating: 6 1 — Highway Safety: 5 9 — ★

RexAir	1997	MHA	36	SL3550	SP	Cu230	D	$3100	228	2,000	24,000	22,218

Livability Code: SB 30-90 — Wheelbase-to-length ratio of 53% is considered ○ dangerous ◉ fatiguing ○ good ○ excellent *

The approximate net payload of 1782 pounds at 7% of GVWR on this model is ○ deficient ○ excessive ◉ cautionary ○ good ○ excellent *

Total highway safety penalties are: 7 * — Value: 8 3 — Durability: 7 7 — Highway Control Rating: 4 3 — Highway Safety: 3 6

Note: Safety ratings are based on the assumption that the engineering of the RV has allowed for proper balance by placing fresh, gray, and black holding tanks in a location so as not to change the balance of the RV when the tanks are empty or full. **Always double-check wheelbase, GVWR, and weights at front and rear axles.**

*See Section 1 for details on how conclusions are reached.

Section 2: The Ratings

Brand	Year	Type	Length	Model	Chassis	Engine	Fuel Type	Average Price per Linear Foot When New	Adjusted Wheelbase	Approx. Towing Capacity	Gross Vehicle Weight Rating	Average Curb Weight
RexAir	1997	MHA	36	SL3600	CH	7.4L	G	$2000	252 T	1,500	19,500	16,939

Livability Code: SB 30-90
Wheelbase-to-length ratio of 58% is considered ○ dangerous ○ fatiguing ○ good ◉ excellent *
The approximate net payload of 2561 pounds at 13% of GVWR on this model is ○ deficient ○ excessive ○ cautionary ◉ good ○ excellent *
Total highway safety penalties are: 10 *   Value: **8 1**   Durability: **7 7**   Highway Control Rating: **9 7**   Highway Safety: **8 7**   ★★★

Brand	Year	Type	Length	Model	Chassis	Engine	Fuel Type	Price/Ft	Wheelbase	Towing	GVWR	Curb Weight
RexAir	1997	MHA	36	SL3650	CH	7.4L	G	$2200	252 T	1,500	19,500	17,989

Livability Code: SB 30-90
Wheelbase-to-length ratio of 58% is considered ○ dangerous ○ fatiguing ○ good ◉ excellent *
The approximate net payload of 1511 pounds at 8% of GVWR on this model is ○ deficient ○ excessive ◉ cautionary ○ good ○ excellent *
Total highway safety penalties are: 16 *   Value: **7 8**   Durability: **7 7**   Highway Control Rating: **8 0**   Highway Safety: **6 4**   ★★

Brand	Year	Type	Length	Model	Chassis	Engine	Fuel Type	Price/Ft	Wheelbase	Towing	GVWR	Curb Weight
RexAir	1997	MHA	36	SL3600	FO	7.5L	G	$2000	252 T	5,000	20,000	17,339

Livability Code: SB 30-90
Wheelbase-to-length ratio of 58% is considered ○ dangerous ○ fatiguing ○ good ◉ excellent *
The approximate net payload of 2661 pounds at 13% of GVWR on this model is ○ deficient ○ excessive ○ cautionary ◉ good ○ excellent *
Total highway safety penalties are: 4 *   Value: **8 4**   Durability: **7 7**   Highway Control Rating: **9 8**   Highway Safety: **9 4**   ★★★

Brand	Year	Type	Length	Model	Chassis	Engine	Fuel Type	Price/Ft	Wheelbase	Towing	GVWR	Curb Weight
RexAir	1997	MHA	36	SL3650	FO	7.5L	G	$2200	252 T	5,000	20,000	18,389

Livability Code: SB 30-90
Wheelbase-to-length ratio of 58% is considered ○ dangerous ○ fatiguing ○ good ◉ excellent *
The approximate net payload of 1611 pounds at 8% of GVWR on this model is ○ deficient ○ excessive ◉ cautionary ○ good ○ excellent *
Total highway safety penalties are: 11 *   Value: **8 0**   Durability: **7 7**   Highway Control Rating: **8 0**   Highway Safety: **6 9**   ★★

Brand	Year	Type	Length	Model	Chassis	Engine	Fuel Type	Price/Ft	Wheelbase	Towing	GVWR	Curb Weight
RexAir	1997	MHA	36	SL3600	FR	Cu230	D	$3100	228	4,500	20,500	18,539

Livability Code: SB 30-90
Wheelbase-to-length ratio of 52% is considered ○ dangerous ◉ fatiguing ○ good ○ excellent *
The approximate net payload of 1961 pounds at 10% of GVWR on this model is ○ deficient ○ excessive ○ cautionary ◉ good ○ excellent *
Total highway safety penalties are: 2 *   Value: **8 5**   Durability: **7 7**   Highway Control Rating: **4 9**   Highway Safety: **4 7**

Brand	Year	Type	Length	Model	Chassis	Engine	Fuel Type	Price/Ft	Wheelbase	Towing	GVWR	Curb Weight
RexAir	1997	MHA	36	SL3650	FR	Cu230	D	$3100	228	4,500	20,500	19,589

Livability Code: SB 30-90
Wheelbase-to-length ratio of 52% is considered ○ dangerous ◉ fatiguing ○ good ○ excellent *
The approximate net payload of 911 pounds at 4% of GVWR on this model is ◉ deficient ○ excessive ○ cautionary ○ good ○ excellent *
Total highway safety penalties are: 8 *   Value: **8 2**   Durability: **7 7**   Highway Control Rating: **2 5**   Highway Safety: **1 7**

Brand	Year	Type	Length	Model	Chassis	Engine	Fuel Type	Price/Ft	Wheelbase	Towing	GVWR	Curb Weight
RexAir	1997	MHA	36	SL3600	SP	Cu230	D	$3100	228	2,000	24,000	21,600

Livability Code: SB 30-90
Wheelbase-to-length ratio of 52% is considered ○ dangerous ◉ fatiguing ○ good ○ excellent *
The approximate net payload of 2400 pounds at 10% of GVWR on this model is ○ deficient ○ excessive ○ cautionary ◉ good ○ excellent *
Total highway safety penalties are: 2 *   Value: **8 5**   Durability: **7 7**   Highway Control Rating: **4 9**   Highway Safety: **4 7**

Brand	Year	Type	Length	Model	Chassis	Engine	Fuel Type	Price/Ft	Wheelbase	Towing	GVWR	Curb Weight
RexAir	1997	MHA	36	SL3650	SP	Cu230	D	$3100	228	2,000	24,000	22,650

Livability Code: SB 30-90
Wheelbase-to-length ratio of 52% is considered ○ dangerous ◉ fatiguing ○ good ○ excellent *
The approximate net payload of 1350 pounds at 6% of GVWR on this model is ◉ deficient ○ excessive ○ cautionary ○ good ○ excellent *
Total highway safety penalties are: 8 *   Value: **8 2**   Durability: **7 7**   Highway Control Rating: **2 6**   Highway Safety: **1 8**

Brand	Year	Type	Length	Model	Chassis	Engine	Fuel Type	Price/Ft	Wheelbase	Towing	GVWR	Curb Weight
RexAir	1997	MHA	39	SL3800	FO	7.5L	G	$1900	252 T	5,000	20,000	18,053

Livability Code: SB 30-90
Wheelbase-to-length ratio of 54% is considered ○ dangerous ○ fatiguing ◉ good ○ excellent *
The approximate net payload of 1947 pounds at 10% of GVWR on this model is ○ deficient ○ excessive ○ cautionary ◉ good ○ excellent *
Total highway safety penalties are: 4 *   Value: **8 4**   Durability: **7 7**   Highway Control Rating: **7 6**   Highway Safety: **7 2**   ★★★

Brand	Year	Type	Length	Model	Chassis	Engine	Fuel Type	Price/Ft	Wheelbase	Towing	GVWR	Curb Weight
RexAir	1998	MHA	29	SL2800	CH	7.4L	G	$3300	190	1,500	16,500	14,011

Livability Code: SB 30-90
Wheelbase-to-length ratio of 54% is considered ○ dangerous ○ fatiguing ◉ good ○ excellent *
The approximate net payload of 2489 pounds at 15% of GVWR on this model is ○ deficient ○ excessive ○ cautionary ◉ good ○ excellent *
Total highway safety penalties are: 4 *   Value: **8 4**   Durability: **7 7**   Highway Control Rating: **8 1**   Highway Safety: **7 7**   ★★★

Brand	Year	Type	Length	Model	Chassis	Engine	Fuel Type	Price/Ft	Wheelbase	Towing	GVWR	Curb Weight
RexAir	1998	MHA	29	SL2800	FO	7.5L	G	$3300	190	1,500	17,000	14,411

Livability Code: SB 30-90
Wheelbase-to-length ratio of 54% is considered ○ dangerous ○ fatiguing ◉ good ○ excellent *
The approximate net payload of 2589 pounds at 15% of GVWR on this model is ○ deficient ○ excessive ○ cautionary ◉ good ○ excellent *
Total highway safety penalties are: 2 *   Value: **8 5**   Durability: **7 7**   Highway Control Rating: **8 1**   Highway Safety: **7 9**   ★★★

Brand	Year	Type	Length	Model	Chassis	Engine	Fuel Type	Price/Ft	Wheelbase	Towing	GVWR	Curb Weight
RexAir	1998	MHA	31	SL2900DS	CH	7.4L	G	$3100	190	1,500	16,500	14,411

Livability Code: SB 30-90
Wheelbase-to-length ratio of 52% is considered ○ dangerous ◉ fatiguing ○ good ○ excellent *
The approximate net payload of 2089 pounds at 13% of GVWR on this model is ○ deficient ○ excessive ○ cautionary ◉ good ○ excellent *
Total highway safety penalties are: 5 *   Value: **8 3**   Durability: **7 7**   Highway Control Rating: **5 3**   Highway Safety: **4 8**

Note: Safety ratings are based on the assumption that the engineering of the RV has allowed for proper balance by placing fresh, gray, and black holding tanks in a location so as not to change the balance of the RV when the tanks are empty or full. **Always double-check wheelbase, GVWR, and weights at front and rear axles.**

*See Section 1 for details on how conclusions are reached.

Section 2: The Ratings

Brand	Year	Type	Length	Model	Chassis	Engine	Fuel Type	Average Price per Linear Foot When New	Adjusted Wheelbase	Approx. Towing Capacity	Gross Vehicle Weight Rating	Average Curb Weight
RexAir	1998	MHA	31	SL2900DS	FO	7.5L	G	$3100	190	1,500	17,000	14,811

Livability Code: SB 30-90
Wheelbase-to-length ratio of 52% is considered: ○ dangerous ● fatiguing ○ good ○ excellent *
The approximate net payload of 2189 pounds at 13% of GVWR on this model is ○ deficient ○ excessive ○ cautionary ● good ○ excellent *
Total highway safety penalties are: 2 *   Value: 8 5   Durability: 7 7   Highway Control Rating: 5 3   Highway Safety: 5 1   ★

Brand	Year	Type	Length	Model	Chassis	Engine	Fuel Type	Avg Price/Linear Foot	Adj Wheelbase	Towing Cap	GVWR	Avg Curb Wt
RexAir	1998	MHA	31	SL2900	CH	7.4L	G	$3100	208	1,500	16,500	14,468

Livability Code: SB 30-90
Wheelbase-to-length ratio of 56% is considered: ○ dangerous ○ fatiguing ● good ○ excellent *
The approximate net payload of 2032 pounds at 12% of GVWR on this model is ○ deficient ○ excessive ○ cautionary ● good ○ excellent *
Total highway safety penalties are: 5 *   Value: 8 3   Durability: 7 7   Highway Control Rating: 9 0   Highway Safety: 8 5   ★★★

Brand	Year	Type	Length	Model	Chassis	Engine	Fuel Type	Avg Price/Linear Foot	Adj Wheelbase	Towing Cap	GVWR	Avg Curb Wt
RexAir	1998	MHA	31	SL2900	FO	7.5L	G	$3100	208	1,500	17,000	14,868

Livability Code: SB 30-90
Wheelbase-to-length ratio of 56% is considered: ○ dangerous ○ fatiguing ● good ○ excellent *
The approximate net payload of 2132 pounds at 13% of GVWR on this model is ○ deficient ○ excessive ○ cautionary ● good ○ excellent *
Total highway safety penalties are: 2 *   Value: 8 5   Durability: 7 7   Highway Control Rating: 9 1   Highway Safety: 8 9   ★★★

Brand	Year	Type	Length	Model	Chassis	Engine	Fuel Type	Avg Price/Linear Foot	Adj Wheelbase	Towing Cap	GVWR	Avg Curb Wt
RexAir	1998	MHA	31	SL2900FB	CH	7.4L	G	$3100	208	1,500	16,500	14,554

Livability Code: SB 30-90
Wheelbase-to-length ratio of 56% is considered: ○ dangerous ○ fatiguing ● good ○ excellent *
The approximate net payload of 1946 pounds at 12% of GVWR on this model is ○ deficient ○ excessive ○ cautionary ● good ○ excellent *
Total highway safety penalties are: 5 *   Value: 8 3   Durability: 7 7   Highway Control Rating: 8 8   Highway Safety: 8 3   ★★★

Brand	Year	Type	Length	Model	Chassis	Engine	Fuel Type	Avg Price/Linear Foot	Adj Wheelbase	Towing Cap	GVWR	Avg Curb Wt
RexAir	1998	MHA	31	SL2900FB	FO	7.5L	G	$3100	208	1,500	17,000	14,954

Livability Code: SB 30-90
Wheelbase-to-length ratio of 56% is considered: ○ dangerous ○ fatiguing ● good ○ excellent *
The approximate net payload of 2046 pounds at 12% of GVWR on this model is ○ deficient ○ excessive ○ cautionary ● good ○ excellent *
Total highway safety penalties are: 2 *   Value: 8 5   Durability: 7 7   Highway Control Rating: 8 8   Highway Safety: 8 6   ★★★

Brand	Year	Type	Length	Model	Chassis	Engine	Fuel Type	Avg Price/Linear Foot	Adj Wheelbase	Towing Cap	GVWR	Avg Curb Wt
RexAir	1998	MHA	32	SL3000	CH	7.4L	G	$3000	208	1,500	16,500	14,696

Livability Code: SB 30-90
Wheelbase-to-length ratio of 55% is considered: ○ dangerous ○ fatiguing ● good ○ excellent *
The approximate net payload of 1804 pounds at 11% of GVWR on this model is ○ deficient ○ excessive ○ cautionary ● good ○ excellent *
Total highway safety penalties are: 5 *   Value: 8 3   Durability: 7 7   Highway Control Rating: 8 8   Highway Safety: 8 3   ★★★

Brand	Year	Type	Length	Model	Chassis	Engine	Fuel Type	Avg Price/Linear Foot	Adj Wheelbase	Towing Cap	GVWR	Avg Curb Wt
RexAir	1998	MHA	32	SL3000	FO	7.5L	G	$3000	208	1,500	17,000	15,096

Livability Code: SB 30-90
Wheelbase-to-length ratio of 55% is considered: ○ dangerous ○ fatiguing ● good ○ excellent *
The approximate net payload of 1904 pounds at 11% of GVWR on this model is ○ deficient ○ excessive ○ cautionary ● good ○ excellent *
Total highway safety penalties are: 2 *   Value: 8 5   Durability: 7 7   Highway Control Rating: 8 8   Highway Safety: 8 6   ★★★

Brand	Year	Type	Length	Model	Chassis	Engine	Fuel Type	Avg Price/Linear Foot	Adj Wheelbase	Towing Cap	GVWR	Avg Curb Wt
RexAir	1998	MHA	32	SL3100	CH	7.4L	G	$3000	208	1,500	16,500	14,896

Livability Code: SB 30-90
Wheelbase-to-length ratio of 54% is considered: ○ dangerous ○ fatiguing ● good ○ excellent *
The approximate net payload of 1604 pounds at 10% of GVWR on this model is ○ deficient ○ excessive ○ cautionary ● good ○ excellent *
Total highway safety penalties are: 6 *   Value: 8 3   Durability: 7 7   Highway Control Rating: 7 5   Highway Safety: 6 9   ★★

Brand	Year	Type	Length	Model	Chassis	Engine	Fuel Type	Avg Price/Linear Foot	Adj Wheelbase	Towing Cap	GVWR	Avg Curb Wt
RexAir	1998	MHA	32	SL3200	CH	7.4L	G	$3000	208	1,500	16,500	14,896

Livability Code: SB 30-90
Wheelbase-to-length ratio of 54% is considered: ○ dangerous ○ fatiguing ● good ○ excellent *
The approximate net payload of 1604 pounds at 10% of GVWR on this model is ○ deficient ○ excessive ○ cautionary ● good ○ excellent *
Total highway safety penalties are: 6 *   Value: 8 3   Durability: 7 7   Highway Control Rating: 7 5   Highway Safety: 6 9   ★★

Brand	Year	Type	Length	Model	Chassis	Engine	Fuel Type	Avg Price/Linear Foot	Adj Wheelbase	Towing Cap	GVWR	Avg Curb Wt
RexAir	1998	MHA	32	SL3250	CH	7.4L	G	$3000	208	1,500	16,500	15,796

Livability Code: SB 30-90
Wheelbase-to-length ratio of 54% is considered: ○ dangerous ○ fatiguing ● good ○ excellent *
The approximate net payload of 704 pounds at 4% of GVWR on this model is ● deficient ○ excessive ○ cautionary ○ good ○ excellent *
Total highway safety penalties are: 11 *   Value: 8 0   Durability: 7 7   Highway Control Rating: 4 4   Highway Safety: 3 3

Brand	Year	Type	Length	Model	Chassis	Engine	Fuel Type	Avg Price/Linear Foot	Adj Wheelbase	Towing Cap	GVWR	Avg Curb Wt
RexAir	1998	MHA	32	SL3100	FO	7.5L	G	$3000	208	1,500	17,000	15,296

Livability Code: SB 30-90
Wheelbase-to-length ratio of 54% is considered: ○ dangerous ○ fatiguing ● good ○ excellent *
The approximate net payload of 1704 pounds at 10% of GVWR on this model is ○ deficient ○ excessive ○ cautionary ● good ○ excellent *
Total highway safety penalties are: 2 *   Value: 8 5   Durability: 7 7   Highway Control Rating: 7 5   Highway Safety: 7 3   ★★★

Brand	Year	Type	Length	Model	Chassis	Engine	Fuel Type	Avg Price/Linear Foot	Adj Wheelbase	Towing Cap	GVWR	Avg Curb Wt
RexAir	1998	MHA	32	SL3200	FO	7.5L	G	$3000	208	1,500	17,000	15,296

Livability Code: SB 30-90
Wheelbase-to-length ratio of 54% is considered: ○ dangerous ○ fatiguing ● good ○ excellent *
The approximate net payload of 1704 pounds at 10% of GVWR on this model is ○ deficient ○ excessive ○ cautionary ● good ○ excellent *
Total highway safety penalties are: 2 *   Value: 8 5   Durability: 7 7   Highway Control Rating: 7 5   Highway Safety: 7 3   ★★★

Note: Safety ratings are based on the assumption that the engineering of the RV has allowed for proper balance by placing fresh, gray, and black holding tanks in a location so as not to change the balance of the RV when the tanks are empty or full. **Always double-check wheelbase, GVWR, and weights at front and rear axles.**

*See Section 1 for details on how conclusions are reached.

Brand	Year	Type	Length	Model	Chassis	Engine	Fuel Type	Average Price per Linear Foot When New	Adjusted Wheelbase	Approx. Towing Capacity	Gross Vehicle Weight Rating	Average Curb Weight
RexAir	1998	MHA	32	SL3250	FO	7.5L	G	$3000	208	1,500	17,000	16,196

Livability Code: SB 30-90
Wheelbase-to-length ratio of 54% is considered ○ dangerous ○ fatiguing ◉ good ○ excellent *
The approximate net payload of 804 pounds at 5% of GVWR on this model is ◉ deficient ○ excessive ○ cautionary ○ good ○ excellent *
Total highway safety penalties are: 7 *   Value: 82   Durability: 77   Highway Control Rating: 45   Highway Safety: 38

Brand	Year	Type	Length	Model	Chassis	Engine	Fuel Type	Avg Price/Ft	Adj Wheelbase	Towing	GVWR	Curb Weight
RexAir	1998	MHA	34	SL3300	CH	7.4L	G	$2800	228	1,500	16,500	15,382

Livability Code: SB 30-90
Wheelbase-to-length ratio of 56% is considered ○ dangerous ○ fatiguing ◉ good ○ excellent *
The approximate net payload of 1118 pounds at 7% of GVWR on this model is ○ deficient ○ excessive ◉ cautionary ○ good ○ excellent *
Total highway safety penalties are: 6 *   Value: 83   Durability: 77   Highway Control Rating: 67   Highway Safety: 61   ★★

| RexAir | 1998 | MHA | 34 | SL3300S | CH | 7.4L | G | $2800 | 228 | 1,500 | 16,500 | 15,382 |

Livability Code: SB 30-90
Wheelbase-to-length ratio of 56% is considered ○ dangerous ○ fatiguing ◉ good ○ excellent *
The approximate net payload of 1118 pounds at 7% of GVWR on this model is ○ deficient ○ excessive ◉ cautionary ○ good ○ excellent *
Total highway safety penalties are: 6 *   Value: 83   Durability: 77   Highway Control Rating: 67   Highway Safety: 61   ★★

| RexAir | 1998 | MHA | 34 | SL3300 | FO | 7.5L | G | $2800 | 228 | 1,500 | 17,000 | 15,782 |

Livability Code: SB 30-90
Wheelbase-to-length ratio of 56% is considered ○ dangerous ○ fatiguing ◉ good ○ excellent *
The approximate net payload of 1218 pounds at 7% of GVWR on this model is ○ deficient ○ excessive ◉ cautionary ○ good ○ excellent *
Total highway safety penalties are: 2 *   Value: 85   Durability: 77   Highway Control Rating: 68   Highway Safety: 66   ★★

| RexAir | 1998 | MHA | 34 | SL3300S | FO | 7.5L | G | $2800 | 228 | 1,500 | 17,000 | 15,782 |

Livability Code: SB 30-90
Wheelbase-to-length ratio of 56% is considered ○ dangerous ○ fatiguing ◉ good ○ excellent *
The approximate net payload of 1218 pounds at 7% of GVWR on this model is ○ deficient ○ excessive ◉ cautionary ○ good ○ excellent *
Total highway safety penalties are: 2 *   Value: 85   Durability: 77   Highway Control Rating: 68   Highway Safety: 66   ★★

| RexAir | 1998 | MHA | 34 | SL3400 | CH | 7.4L | G | $2800 | 232 T | 1,500 | 19,500 | 16,368 |

Livability Code: SB 30-90
Wheelbase-to-length ratio of 57% is considered ○ dangerous ○ fatiguing ◉ good ○ excellent *
The approximate net payload of 3132 pounds at 16% of GVWR on this model is ○ deficient ○ excessive ○ cautionary ○ good ◉ excellent *
Total highway safety penalties are: 9 *   Value: 81   Durability: 77   Highway Control Rating: 98   Highway Safety: 89   ★★★

| RexAir | 1998 | MHA | 34 | SL3450 | CH | 7.4L | G | $2800 | 232 T | 1,500 | 19,500 | 17,268 |

Livability Code: SB 30-90
Wheelbase-to-length ratio of 57% is considered ○ dangerous ○ fatiguing ◉ good ○ excellent *
The approximate net payload of 2232 pounds at 11% of GVWR on this model is ○ deficient ○ excessive ○ cautionary ◉ good ○ excellent *
Total highway safety penalties are: 14 *   Value: 79   Durability: 77   Highway Control Rating: 89   Highway Safety: 75   ★★★

| RexAir | 1998 | MHA | 34 | SL3400 | FO | 7.5L | G | $2800 | 232 T | 1,500 | 20,000 | 16,768 |

Livability Code: SB 30-90
Wheelbase-to-length ratio of 57% is considered ○ dangerous ○ fatiguing ◉ good ○ excellent *
The approximate net payload of 3232 pounds at 16% of GVWR on this model is ○ deficient ○ excessive ○ cautionary ○ good ◉ excellent *
Total highway safety penalties are: 4 *   Value: 84   Durability: 77   Highway Control Rating: 98   Highway Safety: 94   ★★★

| RexAir | 1998 | MHA | 34 | SL3450 | FO | 7.5L | G | $2800 | 232 T | 1,500 | 20,000 | 17,668 |

Livability Code: SB 30-90
Wheelbase-to-length ratio of 57% is considered ○ dangerous ○ fatiguing ◉ good ○ excellent *
The approximate net payload of 2332 pounds at 12% of GVWR on this model is ○ deficient ○ excessive ○ cautionary ◉ good ○ excellent *
Total highway safety penalties are: 10 *   Value: 81   Durability: 77   Highway Control Rating: 90   Highway Safety: 80   ★★★

| RexAir | 1998 | MHA | 36 | SL3500 | CH | 7.4L | G | $2700 | 252 T | 1,500 | 19,500 | 16,796 |

Livability Code: SB 30-90
Wheelbase-to-length ratio of 59% is considered ○ dangerous ○ fatiguing ○ good ◉ excellent *
The approximate net payload of 2704 pounds at 14% of GVWR on this model is ○ deficient ○ excessive ○ cautionary ◉ good ○ excellent *
Total highway safety penalties are: 10 *   Value: 81   Durability: 77   Highway Control Rating: 100   Highway Safety: 90   ★★★

| RexAir | 1998 | MHA | 36 | SL3550D | CH | 7.4L | G | $2700 | 252 T | 1,500 | 19,500 | 17,546 |

Livability Code: SB 30-90
Wheelbase-to-length ratio of 59% is considered ○ dangerous ○ fatiguing ○ good ◉ excellent *
The approximate net payload of 1954 pounds at 10% of GVWR on this model is ○ deficient ○ excessive ○ cautionary ◉ good ○ excellent *
Total highway safety penalties are: 14 *   Value: 79   Durability: 77   Highway Control Rating: 94   Highway Safety: 80   ★★★

| RexAir | 1998 | MHA | 36 | SL3500 | FO | 7.5L | G | $2700 | 252 T | 1,500 | 20,000 | 17,196 |

Livability Code: SB 30-90
Wheelbase-to-length ratio of 59% is considered ○ dangerous ○ fatiguing ○ good ◉ excellent *
The approximate net payload of 2804 pounds at 14% of GVWR on this model is ○ deficient ○ excessive ○ cautionary ◉ good ○ excellent *
Total highway safety penalties are: 4 *   Value: 84   Durability: 77   Highway Control Rating: 100   Highway Safety: 96   ★★★

Note: Safety ratings are based on the assumption that the engineering of the RV has allowed for proper balance by placing fresh, gray, and black holding tanks in a location so as not to change the balance of the RV when the tanks are empty or full. **Always double-check wheelbase, GVWR, and weights at front and rear axles.**

*See Section 1 for details on how conclusions are reached.

Section 2: The Ratings

Brand	Year	Type	Length	Model	Chassis	Engine	Fuel Type	Average Price per Linear Foot When New	Adjusted Wheelbase	Approx. Towing Capacity	Gross Vehicle Weight Rating	Average Curb Weight
RexAir	1998	MHA	36	SL3550D	FO	7.5L	G	$2700	252 T	1,500	20,000	17,946

Livability Code: SB 30-90
Wheelbase-to-length ratio of 59% is considered ○ dangerous ○ fatiguing ○ good ● excellent *
The approximate net payload of 2054 pounds at 10% of GVWR on this model is ○ deficient ○ excessive ○ cautionary ● good ○ excellent *
Total highway safety penalties are: 9 * Value: 81 Durability: 77 Highway Control Rating: 95 Highway Safety: 86 ★★★

Brand	Year	Type	Length	Model	Chassis	Engine	Fuel Type	Avg Price/Linear Foot	Adjusted Wheelbase	Towing Capacity	GVWR	Curb Weight
RexAir	1998	MHA	36	SL3550D myc	FO	6.8L	G	$2700	242	1,500	20,500	17,892

Livability Code: SB 30-90
Wheelbase-to-length ratio of 56% is considered ○ dangerous ○ fatiguing ● good ○ excellent *
The approximate net payload of 2608 pounds at 13% of GVWR on this model is ○ deficient ○ excessive ○ cautionary ● good ○ excellent *
Total highway safety penalties are: 7 * Value: 82 Durability: 77 Highway Control Rating: 92 Highway Safety: 85 ★★★

RexAir	1998	MHA	36	SL3600S	FO	7.5L	G	$2700	252 T	1,500	20,000	17,339

Livability Code: SB 30-90
Wheelbase-to-length ratio of 58% is considered ○ dangerous ○ fatiguing ○ good ● excellent *
The approximate net payload of 2661 pounds at 13% of GVWR on this model is ○ deficient ○ excessive ○ cautionary ● good ○ excellent *
Total highway safety penalties are: 4 * Value: 84 Durability: 77 Highway Control Rating: 98 Highway Safety: 94 ★★★

RexAir	1998	MHA	36	SL3650	FO	7.5L	G	$2700	252 T	1,500	20,000	18,389

Livability Code: SB 30-90
Wheelbase-to-length ratio of 58% is considered ○ dangerous ○ fatiguing ○ good ● excellent *
The approximate net payload of 1611 pounds at 8% of GVWR on this model is ○ deficient ○ excessive ● cautionary ○ good ○ excellent *
Total highway safety penalties are: 11 * Value: 80 Durability: 77 Highway Control Rating: 80 Highway Safety: 69 ★★

RexAir	1998	MHA	39	SL3800	FO	7.5L	G	$2500	252 T	1,500	20,000	18,953

Livability Code: SB 30-90
Wheelbase-to-length ratio of 54% is considered ○ dangerous ○ fatiguing ● good ○ excellent *
The approximate net payload of 1047 pounds at 5% of GVWR on this model is ● deficient ○ excessive ○ cautionary ○ good ○ excellent *
Total highway safety penalties are: 10 * Value: 81 Durability: 77 Highway Control Rating: 47 Highway Safety: 37

RexAir	1999	MHA	26	SL2500	CH	7.4L	G	$3100	158	4,200	14,800	12,987

Livability Code: SB 30-90
Wheelbase-to-length ratio of 51% is considered ○ dangerous ● fatiguing ○ good ○ excellent *
The approximate net payload of 1813 pounds at 12% of GVWR on this model is ○ deficient ○ excessive ○ cautionary ● good ○ excellent *
Total highway safety penalties are: 3 * Value: 85 Durability: 77 Highway Control Rating: 49 Highway Safety: 46

RexAir	1999	MHA	31	SL2900-FB	CH	7.4L	G	$3100	208	4,500	16,500	14,768

Livability Code: SB 30-90
Wheelbase-to-length ratio of 55% is considered ○ dangerous ○ fatiguing ● good ○ excellent *
The approximate net payload of 1732 pounds at 10% of GVWR on this model is ○ deficient ○ excessive ○ cautionary ● good ○ excellent *
Total highway safety penalties are: 5 * Value: 83 Durability: 77 Highway Control Rating: 82 Highway Safety: 77 ★★★

RexAir	1999	MHA	31	SL2900-FB	FO	6.8L	G	$3100	208	8,000	18,000	15,208

Livability Code: SB 30-90
Wheelbase-to-length ratio of 55% is considered ○ dangerous ○ fatiguing ● good ○ excellent *
The approximate net payload of 2792 pounds at 16% of GVWR on this model is ○ deficient ○ excessive ○ cautionary ○ good ● excellent *
Total highway safety penalties are: 2 * Value: 85 Durability: 77 Highway Control Rating: 93 Highway Safety: 91 ★★★

RexAir	1999	MHA	32	SL3100	FO	6.8L	G	$3000	208	8,000	18,000	15,568

Livability Code: SB 30-90
Wheelbase-to-length ratio of 54% is considered ○ dangerous ○ fatiguing ● good ○ excellent *
The approximate net payload of 2432 pounds at 14% of GVWR on this model is ○ deficient ○ excessive ○ cautionary ● good ○ excellent *
Total highway safety penalties are: 2 * Value: 85 Durability: 77 Highway Control Rating: 79 Highway Safety: 77 ★★★

RexAir	1999	MHA	32	SL3200	FO	6.8L	G	$3000	208	8,000	18,000	15,928

Livability Code: SB 30-90
Wheelbase-to-length ratio of 54% is considered ○ dangerous ○ fatiguing ● good ○ excellent *
The approximate net payload of 2072 pounds at 12% of GVWR on this model is ○ deficient ○ excessive ○ cautionary ● good ○ excellent *
Total highway safety penalties are: 2 * Value: 85 Durability: 77 Highway Control Rating: 75 Highway Safety: 73 ★★★

RexAir	1999	MHA	32	SL3250BSL	FO	6.8L	G	$3000	208	5,500	20,500	17,828

Livability Code: SB 30-90
Wheelbase-to-length ratio of 54% is considered ○ dangerous ○ fatiguing ● good ○ excellent *
The approximate net payload of 2672 pounds at 13% of GVWR on this model is ○ deficient ○ excessive ○ cautionary ● good ○ excellent *
Total highway safety penalties are: 10 * Value: 81 Durability: 77 Highway Control Rating: 77 Highway Safety: 67 ★★

RexAir	1999	MHA	32	SL3250	FO	6.8L	G	$3000	208	8,000	18,000	16,708

Livability Code: SB 30-90
Wheelbase-to-length ratio of 54% is considered ○ dangerous ○ fatiguing ● good ○ excellent *
The approximate net payload of 1292 pounds at 7% of GVWR on this model is ○ deficient ○ excessive ● cautionary ○ good ○ excellent *
Total highway safety penalties are: 7 * Value: 82 Durability: 77 Highway Control Rating: 55 Highway Safety: 48

Note: Safety ratings are based on the assumption that the engineering of the RV has allowed for proper balance by placing fresh, gray, and black holding tanks in a location so as not to change the balance of the RV when the tanks are empty or full. **Always double-check wheelbase, GVWR, and weights at front and rear axles.**

Brand	Year	Type	Length	Model	Chassis	Engine	Fuel Type	Average Price per Linear Foot When New	Adjusted Wheelbase	Approx. Towing Capacity	Gross Vehicle Weight Rating	Average Curb Weight
RexAir	1999	MHA	32	SL3250GT	FO	6.8L	G	$3000	208	8,000	18,000	17,168

Livability Code: SB 30-90

Wheelbase-to-length ratio of 54% is considered ○ dangerous ○ fatiguing ● good ○ excellent *

The approximate net payload of 832 pounds at 5% of GVWR on this model is ● deficient ○ excessive ○ cautionary ○ good ○ excellent *

Total highway safety penalties are: 13 *   Value: **7 9**   Durability: **7 7**   Highway Control Rating: **4 7**   Highway Safety: **3 4**

| **RexAir** | 1999 | MHA | 34 | SL3300 | FO | 6.8L | G | $2800 | 228 | 5,500 | 20,500 | 15,968 |

Livability Code: SB 30-90

Wheelbase-to-length ratio of 56% is considered ○ dangerous ○ fatiguing ● good ○ excellent *

The approximate net payload of 4532 pounds at 22% of GVWR on this model is ○ deficient ○ excessive ○ cautionary ○ good ● excellent *

Total highway safety penalties are: 2 *   Value: **8 5**   Durability: **7 7**   Highway Control Rating: **9 8**   Highway Safety: **9 6**   ★★★

| **RexAir** | 1999 | MHA | 34 | SL3400 | FO | 6.8L | G | $2800 | 228 | 5,500 | 20,500 | 16,848 |

Livability Code: SB 30-90

Wheelbase-to-length ratio of 56% is considered ○ dangerous ○ fatiguing ● good ○ excellent *

The approximate net payload of 3652 pounds at 18% of GVWR on this model is ○ deficient ○ excessive ○ cautionary ○ good ● excellent *

Total highway safety penalties are: 2 *   Value: **8 5**   Durability: **7 7**   Highway Control Rating: **9 6**   Highway Safety: **9 4**   ★★★

| **RexAir** | 1999 | MHA | 35 | SL3450-GT | FO | 6.8L | G | $2700 | 228 | 8,000 | 18,000 | 17,628 |

Livability Code: SB 30-90

Wheelbase-to-length ratio of 54% is considered ○ dangerous ○ fatiguing ● good ○ excellent *

The approximate net payload of 372 pounds at 2% of GVWR on this model is ● deficient ○ excessive ○ cautionary ○ good ○ excellent *

Total highway safety penalties are: 15 *   Value: **7 8**   Durability: **7 7**   Highway Control Rating: **4 6**   Highway Safety: **3 1**

| **RexAir** | 1999 | MHA | 36 | SL3550BSL | FO | 6.8L | G | $2700 | 242 | 5,500 | 20,500 | 18,548 |

Livability Code: SB 30-90

Wheelbase-to-length ratio of 56% is considered ○ dangerous ○ fatiguing ● good ○ excellent *

The approximate net payload of 1952 pounds at 10% of GVWR on this model is ○ deficient ○ excessive ○ cautionary ● good ○ excellent *

Total highway safety penalties are: 10 *   Value: **8 1**   Durability: **7 7**   Highway Control Rating: **8 5**   Highway Safety: **7 5**   ★★★

| **RexAir** | 1999 | MHA | 36 | SL3550-D | FO | 6.8L | G | $2700 | 242 | 5,500 | 20,500 | 17,688 |

Livability Code: SB 30-90

Wheelbase-to-length ratio of 56% is considered ○ dangerous ○ fatiguing ● good ○ excellent *

The approximate net payload of 2812 pounds at 14% of GVWR on this model is ○ deficient ○ excessive ○ cautionary ● good ○ excellent *

Total highway safety penalties are: 7 *   Value: **8 3**   Durability: **7 7**   Highway Control Rating: **9 4**   Highway Safety: **8 7**   ★★★

| **RexAir** | 1999 | MHA | 36 | SL3550GT | FO | 6.8L | G | $2700 | 242 | 5,500 | 20,500 | 17,768 |

Livability Code: SB 30-90

Wheelbase-to-length ratio of 56% is considered ○ dangerous ○ fatiguing ● good ○ excellent *

The approximate net payload of 2732 pounds at 13% of GVWR on this model is ○ deficient ○ excessive ○ cautionary ● good ○ excellent *

Total highway safety penalties are: 12 *   Value: **8 0**   Durability: **7 7**   Highway Control Rating: **9 2**   Highway Safety: **8 0**   ★★★

| **RexAir** | 1999 | MHA | 36 | SL3650-LG | FO | 6.8L | G | $2700 | 242 | 5,500 | 20,500 | 17,968 |

Livability Code: SB 30-90

Wheelbase-to-length ratio of 56% is considered ○ dangerous ○ fatiguing ● good ○ excellent *

The approximate net payload of 2532 pounds at 12% of GVWR on this model is ○ deficient ○ excessive ○ cautionary ● good ○ excellent *

Total highway safety penalties are: 13 *   Value: **7 9**   Durability: **7 7**   Highway Control Rating: **8 7**   Highway Safety: **7 4**   ★★★

| **RexAir** | 1999 | MHA | 36 | SL3650BSL | FO | 6.8L | G | $2700 | 242 | 5,500 | 20,500 | 18,828 |

Livability Code: SB 30-90

Wheelbase-to-length ratio of 56% is considered ○ dangerous ○ fatiguing ● good ○ excellent *

The approximate net payload of 1672 pounds at 8% of GVWR on this model is ○ deficient ○ excessive ● cautionary ○ good ○ excellent *

Total highway safety penalties are: 10 *   Value: **8 1**   Durability: **7 7**   Highway Control Rating: **7 2**   Highway Safety: **6 2**   ★★

| **RexAir** | 1999 | MHA | 37 | SL3550DGT | SP | CU8.3L | D | $3500 | 228 | 10,000 | 24,000 | 22,560 |

Livability Code: SB 30-90

Wheelbase-to-length ratio of 51% is considered ○ dangerous ● fatiguing ○ good ○ excellent *

The approximate net payload of 1440 pounds at 6% of GVWR on this model is ● deficient ○ excessive ○ cautionary ○ good ○ excellent *

Total highway safety penalties are: 12 *   Value: **8 0**   Durability: **7 7**   Highway Control Rating: **2 5**   Highway Safety: **1 3**

| **RexAir** | 1999 | MHA | 37 | SL3550D | SP | CU8.3L | D | $3500 | 228 | 10,000 | 24,000 | 22,175 |

Livability Code: SB 30-90

Wheelbase-to-length ratio of 51% is considered ○ dangerous ● fatiguing ○ good ○ excellent *

The approximate net payload of 1825 pounds at 8% of GVWR on this model is ○ deficient ○ excessive ● cautionary ○ good ○ excellent *

Total highway safety penalties are: 7 *   Value: **8 3**   Durability: **7 7**   Highway Control Rating: **3 6**   Highway Safety: **2 9**

| **Rialta** | 1995 | MHC | 21 | 21RD | VW | 2.5L | G | $2000 | 152 | 2,000 | 7,000 | 6,118 |

Livability Code: VA 40-80

Wheelbase-to-length ratio of 61% is considered ○ dangerous ○ fatiguing ○ good ● excellent *

The approximate net payload of 882 pounds at 13% of GVWR on this model is ○ deficient ○ excessive ○ cautionary ● good ○ excellent *

Total highway safety penalties are: 2 *   Value: **8 6**   Durability: **8 0**   Highway Control Rating: **1 0 0**   Highway Safety: **9 8**   ★★★★

Note: Safety ratings are based on the assumption that the engineering of the RV has allowed for proper balance by placing fresh, gray, and black holding tanks in a location so as not to change the balance of the RV when the tanks are empty or full. **Always double-check wheelbase, GVWR, and weights at front and rear axles.**

*See Section 1 for details on how conclusions are reached.

Brand	Year	Type	Length	Model	Chassis	Engine	Fuel Type	Average Price per Linear Foot When New	Adjusted Wheelbase	Approx. Towing Capacity	Gross Vehicle Weight Rating	Average Curb Weight
Rialta	1996	MHC	21	21RD	VW	2.5L	G	$2100	152	2,000	7,000	6,118

Livability Code: VA 40-80

Wheelbase-to-length ratio of 61% is considered ○ dangerous ○ fatiguing ○ good ◉ excellent *

The approximate net payload of 882 pounds at 13% of GVWR on this model is ○ deficient ○ excessive ○ cautionary ◉ good ○ excellent *

Total highway safety penalties are: 2 *   Value: **86** Durability: **80** Highway Control Rating: **100** Highway Safety: **98**   ★★★★

Brand	Year	Type	Length	Model	Chassis	Engine	Fuel Type	Price/ft	Wheelbase	Towing	GVWR	Curb Wt
Rialta	1996	MHC	21	21RC	VW	2.5L	G	$2100	152	2,000	7,000	6,118

Livability Code: VA 40-80

Wheelbase-to-length ratio of 61% is considered ○ dangerous ○ fatiguing ○ good ◉ excellent *

The approximate net payload of 882 pounds at 13% of GVWR on this model is ○ deficient ○ excessive ○ cautionary ◉ good ○ excellent *

Total highway safety penalties are: 2 *   Value: **86** Durability: **80** Highway Control Rating: **100** Highway Safety: **98**   ★★★★

Brand	Year	Type	Length	Model	Chassis	Engine	Fuel Type	Price/ft	Wheelbase	Towing	GVWR	Curb Wt
Rialta	1997	MHC	22	22RC	VW	2.8L	G	$2300	152	1,975	7,275	6,311

Livability Code: VA 40-80

Wheelbase-to-length ratio of 58% is considered ○ dangerous ○ fatiguing ○ good ◉ excellent *

The approximate net payload of 964 pounds at 13% of GVWR on this model is ○ deficient ○ excessive ○ cautionary ◉ good ○ excellent *

Total highway safety penalties are: 2 *   Value: **86** Durability: **80** Highway Control Rating: **98** Highway Safety: **96**   ★★★★

Brand	Year	Type	Length	Model	Chassis	Engine	Fuel Type	Price/ft	Wheelbase	Towing	GVWR	Curb Wt
Rialta	1997	MHC	22	22RD	VW	2.8L	G	$2300	152	1,975	7,275	6,339

Livability Code: VA 40-80

Wheelbase-to-length ratio of 58% is considered ○ dangerous ○ fatiguing ○ good ◉ excellent *

The approximate net payload of 936 pounds at 13% of GVWR on this model is ○ deficient ○ excessive ○ cautionary ◉ good ○ excellent *

Total highway safety penalties are: 2 *   Value: **86** Durability: **80** Highway Control Rating: **98** Highway Safety: **96**   ★★★★

Brand	Year	Type	Length	Model	Chassis	Engine	Fuel Type	Price/ft	Wheelbase	Towing	GVWR	Curb Wt
Rialta	1998	MHC	22	22RC	VW	2.8L	G	$2300	152	2,000	7,275	6,181

Livability Code: VA 40-80

Wheelbase-to-length ratio of 58% is considered ○ dangerous ○ fatiguing ○ good ◉ excellent *

The approximate net payload of 1094 pounds at 15% of GVWR on this model is ○ deficient ○ excessive ○ cautionary ◉ good ○ excellent *

Total highway safety penalties are: 2 *   Value: **86** Durability: **80** Highway Control Rating: **100** Highway Safety: **98**   ★★★★

Brand	Year	Type	Length	Model	Chassis	Engine	Fuel Type	Price/ft	Wheelbase	Towing	GVWR	Curb Wt
Rialta	1998	MHC	22	22RD	VW	2.8L	G	$2300	152	2,000	7,275	6,344

Livability Code: VA 40-80

Wheelbase-to-length ratio of 58% is considered ○ dangerous ○ fatiguing ○ good ◉ excellent *

The approximate net payload of 931 pounds at 13% of GVWR on this model is ○ deficient ○ excessive ○ cautionary ◉ good ○ excellent *

Total highway safety penalties are: 2 *   Value: **86** Durability: **80** Highway Control Rating: **97** Highway Safety: **95**   ★★★★

Brand	Year	Type	Length	Model	Chassis	Engine	Fuel Type	Price/ft	Wheelbase	Towing	GVWR	Curb Wt
Rialta	1999	MHC	22	22Q	VW	2.8L	G	$2400	152	2,000	7,275	6,380

Livability Code: VA 40-80

Wheelbase-to-length ratio of 58% is considered ○ dangerous ○ fatiguing ○ good ◉ excellent *

The approximate net payload of 895 pounds at 12% of GVWR on this model is ○ deficient ○ excessive ○ cautionary ◉ good ○ excellent *

Total highway safety penalties are: 2 *   Value: **86** Durability: **80** Highway Control Rating: **96** Highway Safety: **94**   ★★★★

Brand	Year	Type	Length	Model	Chassis	Engine	Fuel Type	Price/ft	Wheelbase	Towing	GVWR	Curb Wt
Rialta	1999	MHC	22	22F	VW	2.8L	G	$2400	152	2,000	7,275	6,342

Livability Code: VA 40-80

Wheelbase-to-length ratio of 58% is considered ○ dangerous ○ fatiguing ○ good ◉ excellent *

The approximate net payload of 933 pounds at 13% of GVWR on this model is ○ deficient ○ excessive ○ cautionary ◉ good ○ excellent *

Total highway safety penalties are: 2 *   Value: **86** Durability: **80** Highway Control Rating: **98** Highway Safety: **96**   ★★★★

Brand	Year	Type	Length	Model	Chassis	Engine	Fuel Type	Price/ft	Wheelbase	Towing	GVWR	Curb Wt
Rialta	1999	MHC	22	22HD	VW	2.8L	G	$2400	152	2,000	7,275	6,448

Livability Code: VA 40-80

Wheelbase-to-length ratio of 58% is considered ○ dangerous ○ fatiguing ○ good ◉ excellent *

The approximate net payload of 827 pounds at 11% of GVWR on this model is ○ deficient ○ excessive ○ cautionary ◉ good ○ excellent *

Total highway safety penalties are: 2 *   Value: **86** Durability: **80** Highway Control Rating: **94** Highway Safety: **92**   ★★★★

Brand	Year	Type	Length	Model	Chassis	Engine	Fuel Type	Price/ft	Wheelbase	Towing	GVWR	Curb Wt
Rialta	1999	MHC	22	22QD	VW	2.8L	G	$2400	152	2,000	7,275	6,431

Livability Code: VA 40-80

Wheelbase-to-length ratio of 58% is considered ○ dangerous ○ fatiguing ○ good ◉ excellent *

The approximate net payload of 844 pounds at 12% of GVWR on this model is ○ deficient ○ excessive ○ cautionary ◉ good ○ excellent *

Total highway safety penalties are: 2 *   Value: **86** Durability: **80** Highway Control Rating: **95** Highway Safety: **93**   ★★★★

Brand	Year	Type	Length	Model	Chassis	Engine	Fuel Type	Price/ft	Wheelbase	Towing	GVWR	Curb Wt
Rialta	1999	MHC	22	22FD	VW	2.8L	G	$2400	152	2,000	7,275	6,376

Livability Code: VA 40-80

Wheelbase-to-length ratio of 58% is considered ○ dangerous ○ fatiguing ○ good ◉ excellent *

The approximate net payload of 899 pounds at 12% of GVWR on this model is ○ deficient ○ excessive ○ cautionary ◉ good ○ excellent *

Total highway safety penalties are: 2 *   Value: **86** Durability: **80** Highway Control Rating: **96** Highway Safety: **94**   ★★★★

Brand	Year	Type	Length	Model	Chassis	Engine	Fuel Type	Price/ft	Wheelbase	Towing	GVWR	Curb Wt
Roadtrek	1990	MHB	19	Popular	DO	5.2L	G	$1800	127	1,500	6,400	5,699

Livability Code: WE 40-80

Wheelbase-to-length ratio of 56% is considered ○ dangerous ○ fatiguing ◉ good ○ excellent *

The approximate net payload of 702 pounds at 11% of GVWR on this model is ○ deficient ○ excessive ○ cautionary ◉ good ○ excellent *

Total highway safety penalties are: 2 *   Value: **86** Durability: **79** Highway Control Rating: **86** Highway Safety: **84**   ★★★

Note: Safety ratings are based on the assumption that the engineering of the RV has allowed for proper balance by placing fresh, gray, and black holding tanks in a location so as not to change the balance of the RV when the tanks are empty or full. **Always double-check wheelbase, GVWR, and weights at front and rear axles.**

Brand	Year	Type	Length	Model	Chassis	Engine	Fuel Type	Average Price per Linear Foot When New	Adjusted Wheelbase	Approx. Towing Capacity	Gross Vehicle Weight Rating	Average Curb Weight
Roadtrek	1991	MHB	19	Versatile	DO	5.9L	G	$1800	127	1,500	6,400	5,749

Livability Code: WE 40-80   Wheelbase-to-length ratio of 56% is considered ○ dangerous ○ fatiguing ◉ good ○ excellent *

The approximate net payload of 652 pounds at 10% of GVWR on this model is ○ deficient ○ excessive ○ cautionary ○ good ○ excellent *

Total highway safety penalties are: 2 *   Value: 8 6   Durability: 7 9   Highway Control Rating: 8 4   Highway Safety: 8 2   ★★★

Brand	Year	Type	Length	Model	Chassis	Engine	Fuel Type	Price/Ft	Wheelbase	Towing	GVWR	Curb Weight
Roadtrek	1991	MHB	21	Independent	CH	5.7L	G	$1900	146	1,500	8,600	6,952

Livability Code: WE 40-80   Wheelbase-to-length ratio of 59% is considered ○ dangerous ○ fatiguing ○ good ◉ excellent *

The approximate net payload of 1649 pounds at 19% of GVWR on this model is ○ deficient ○ excessive ○ cautionary ○ good ◉ excellent *

Total highway safety penalties are: 2 *   Value: 8 6   Durability: 7 9   Highway Control Rating: 1 0 0   Highway Safety: 9 8   ★★★

Brand	Year	Type	Length	Model	Chassis	Engine	Fuel Type	Price/Ft	Wheelbase	Towing	GVWR	Curb Weight
Roadtrek	1995	MHB	18	170 - G20	CH	5.7L	G	$2400	125	4,125	6,875	5,729

Livability Code: WE 40-80   Wheelbase-to-length ratio of 58% is considered ○ dangerous ○ fatiguing ○ good ◉ excellent *

The approximate net payload of 1147 pounds at 17% of GVWR on this model is ○ deficient ○ excessive ○ cautionary ○ good ◉ excellent *

Total highway safety penalties are: 2 *   Value: 8 6   Durability: 7 9   Highway Control Rating: 1 0 0   Highway Safety: 9 8   ★★★

Brand	Year	Type	Length	Model	Chassis	Engine	Fuel Type	Price/Ft	Wheelbase	Towing	GVWR	Curb Weight
Roadtrek	1995	MHB	19	190 -318	DO	5.2L	G	$2400	128	5,000	7,500	6,381

Livability Code: WE 40-80   Wheelbase-to-length ratio of 55% is considered ○ dangerous ○ fatiguing ◉ good ○ excellent *

The approximate net payload of 1119 pounds at 15% of GVWR on this model is ○ deficient ○ excessive ○ cautionary ◉ good ○ excellent *

Total highway safety penalties are: 2 *   Value: 8 6   Durability: 7 9   Highway Control Rating: 9 1   Highway Safety: 8 9   ★★★

Brand	Year	Type	Length	Model	Chassis	Engine	Fuel Type	Price/Ft	Wheelbase	Towing	GVWR	Curb Weight
Roadtrek	1995	MHB	19	190 -350	DO	5.9L	G	$2400	128	5,500	7,500	6,381

Livability Code: WE 40-80   Wheelbase-to-length ratio of 55% is considered ○ dangerous ○ fatiguing ◉ good ○ excellent *

The approximate net payload of 1119 pounds at 15% of GVWR on this model is ○ deficient ○ excessive ○ cautionary ◉ good ○ excellent *

Total highway safety penalties are: 2 *   Value: 8 6   Durability: 7 9   Highway Control Rating: 9 1   Highway Safety: 8 9   ★★★

Brand	Year	Type	Length	Model	Chassis	Engine	Fuel Type	Price/Ft	Wheelbase	Towing	GVWR	Curb Weight
Roadtrek	1995	MHB	20	190 -350	CH	5.7L	G	$2300	146	4,900	8,600	6,658

Livability Code: WE 40-80   Wheelbase-to-length ratio of 62% is considered ○ dangerous ○ fatiguing ○ good ◉ excellent *

The approximate net payload of 1942 pounds at 23% of GVWR on this model is ○ deficient ○ excessive ○ cautionary ○ good ◉ excellent *

Total highway safety penalties are: 2 *   Value: 8 6   Durability: 7 9   Highway Control Rating: 1 0 0   Highway Safety: 9 8   ★★★

Brand	Year	Type	Length	Model	Chassis	Engine	Fuel Type	Price/Ft	Wheelbase	Towing	GVWR	Curb Weight
Roadtrek	1995	MHB	20	190 -454	CH	7.4L	G	$2300	146	8,400	8,600	6,658

Livability Code: WE 40-80   Wheelbase-to-length ratio of 62% is considered ○ dangerous ○ fatiguing ○ good ◉ excellent *

The approximate net payload of 1942 pounds at 23% of GVWR on this model is ○ deficient ○ excessive ○ cautionary ○ good ◉ excellent *

Total highway safety penalties are: 2 *   Value: 8 6   Durability: 7 9   Highway Control Rating: 1 0 0   Highway Safety: 9 8   ★★★

Brand	Year	Type	Length	Model	Chassis	Engine	Fuel Type	Price/Ft	Wheelbase	Towing	GVWR	Curb Weight
Roadtrek	1995	MHB	21	210 -350	CH	5.7L	G	$2200	146	8,400	8,600	6,902

Livability Code: WE 40-80   Wheelbase-to-length ratio of 59% is considered ○ dangerous ○ fatiguing ○ good ◉ excellent *

The approximate net payload of 1699 pounds at 20% of GVWR on this model is ○ deficient ○ excessive ○ cautionary ○ good ◉ excellent *

Total highway safety penalties are: 2 *   Value: 8 6   Durability: 7 9   Highway Control Rating: 1 0 0   Highway Safety: 9 8   ★★★

Brand	Year	Type	Length	Model	Chassis	Engine	Fuel Type	Price/Ft	Wheelbase	Towing	GVWR	Curb Weight
Roadtrek	1995	MHB	21	210 -350	CH	5.7L	G	$2200	125	2,125	6,875	5,967

Livability Code: WE 40-80   Wheelbase-to-length ratio of 50% is considered ◉ dangerous ○ fatiguing ○ good ○ excellent *

The approximate net payload of 909 pounds at 13% of GVWR on this model is ○ deficient ○ excessive ○ cautionary ◉ good ○ excellent *

Total highway safety penalties are: 2 *   Value: 8 6   Durability: 7 9   Highway Control Rating: 6 0   Highway Safety: 5 8

Brand	Year	Type	Length	Model	Chassis	Engine	Fuel Type	Price/Ft	Wheelbase	Towing	GVWR	Curb Weight
Roadtrek	1996	MHB	18	170 - G20	CH	5.7L	G	$2400	125	4,125	6,875	5,729

Livability Code: WE 40-80   Wheelbase-to-length ratio of 58% is considered ○ dangerous ○ fatiguing ○ good ◉ excellent *

The approximate net payload of 1147 pounds at 17% of GVWR on this model is ○ deficient ○ excessive ○ cautionary ○ good ◉ excellent *

Total highway safety penalties are: 2 *   Value: 8 6   Durability: 7 9   Highway Control Rating: 1 0 0   Highway Safety: 9 8   ★★★

Brand	Year	Type	Length	Model	Chassis	Engine	Fuel Type	Price/Ft	Wheelbase	Towing	GVWR	Curb Weight
Roadtrek	1996	MHB	19	190 -318	DO	5.2L	G	$2400	128	5,000	7,500	6,381

Livability Code: WE 40-80   Wheelbase-to-length ratio of 55% is considered ○ dangerous ○ fatiguing ◉ good ○ excellent *

The approximate net payload of 1119 pounds at 15% of GVWR on this model is ○ deficient ○ excessive ○ cautionary ◉ good ○ excellent *

Total highway safety penalties are: 2 *   Value: 8 6   Durability: 7 9   Highway Control Rating: 9 1   Highway Safety: 8 9   ★★★

Brand	Year	Type	Length	Model	Chassis	Engine	Fuel Type	Price/Ft	Wheelbase	Towing	GVWR	Curb Weight
Roadtrek	1996	MHB	19	190 -350	DO	5.9L	G	$2400	128	5,500	7,500	6,381

Livability Code: WE 40-80   Wheelbase-to-length ratio of 55% is considered ○ dangerous ○ fatiguing ◉ good ○ excellent *

The approximate net payload of 1119 pounds at 15% of GVWR on this model is ○ deficient ○ excessive ○ cautionary ◉ good ○ excellent *

Total highway safety penalties are: 2 *   Value: 8 6   Durability: 7 9   Highway Control Rating: 9 1   Highway Safety: 8 9   ★★★

Note: Safety ratings are based on the assumption that the engineering of the RV has allowed for proper balance by placing fresh, gray, and black holding tanks in a location so as not to change the balance of the RV when the tanks are empty or full. **Always double-check wheelbase, GVWR, and weights at front and rear axles.**

*See Section 1 for details on how conclusions are reached.

Brand	Year	Type	Length	Model	Chassis	Engine	Fuel Type	Average Price per Linear Foot When New	Adjusted Wheelbase	Approx. Towing Capacity	Gross Vehicle Weight Rating	Average Curb Weight
Roadtrek	1996	MHB	20	190 -350	CH	5.7L	G	$2300	146	4,900	8,600	6,658

Livability Code: WE 40-80

Wheelbase-to-length ratio of 62% is considered ○ dangerous ○ fatiguing ○ good ◉ excellent *

The approximate net payload of 1942 pounds at 23% of GVWR on this model is ○ deficient ○ excessive ○ cautionary ○ good ◉ excellent *

Total highway safety penalties are: 2 *　　Value: 86　Durability: 79　Highway Control Rating: 100　Highway Safety: 98　★★★

Brand	Year	Type	Length	Model	Chassis	Engine	Fuel Type					
Roadtrek	1996	MHB	20	190 -454	CH	7.4L	G	$2300	146	8,400	8,600	6,658

Livability Code: WE 40-80

Wheelbase-to-length ratio of 62% is considered ○ dangerous ○ fatiguing ○ good ◉ excellent *

The approximate net payload of 1942 pounds at 23% of GVWR on this model is ○ deficient ○ excessive ○ cautionary ○ good ◉ excellent *

Total highway safety penalties are: 2 *　　Value: 86　Durability: 79　Highway Control Rating: 100　Highway Safety: 98　★★★

Roadtrek	1996	MHB	21	210 -454	CH	7.4L	G	$2200	146	8,400	8,600	6,902

Livability Code: WE 40-80

Wheelbase-to-length ratio of 59% is considered ○ dangerous ○ fatiguing ○ good ◉ excellent *

The approximate net payload of 1699 pounds at 20% of GVWR on this model is ○ deficient ○ excessive ○ cautionary ○ good ◉ excellent *

Total highway safety penalties are: 2 *　　Value: 86　Durability: 79　Highway Control Rating: 100　Highway Safety: 98　★★★

Roadtrek	1996	MHB	21	210 -350	CH	5.7L	G	$2200	125	2,125	6,875	5,967

Livability Code: WE 40-80

Wheelbase-to-length ratio of 50% is considered ◉ dangerous ○ fatiguing ○ good ○ excellent *

The approximate net payload of 909 pounds at 13% of GVWR on this model is ○ deficient ○ excessive ○ cautionary ◉ good ○ excellent *

Total highway safety penalties are: 2 *　　Value: 86　Durability: 79　Highway Control Rating: 60　Highway Safety: 58

Roadtrek	1997	MHB	18	170	DO	5.2L	G	$2400	128	3,200	6,800	5,861

Livability Code: WE 40-80

Wheelbase-to-length ratio of 60% is considered ○ dangerous ○ fatiguing ○ good ◉ excellent *

The approximate net payload of 939 pounds at 14% of GVWR on this model is ○ deficient ○ excessive ○ cautionary ○ good ◉ excellent *

Total highway safety penalties are: 2 *　　Value: 86　Durability: 79　Highway Control Rating: 100　Highway Safety: 98　★★★

Roadtrek	1997	MHB	19	190	DO	5.2L	G	$2500	128	3,990	8,510	6,537

Livability Code: WE 40-80

Wheelbase-to-length ratio of 55% is considered ○ dangerous ○ fatiguing ◉ good ○ excellent *

The approximate net payload of 1973 pounds at 23% of GVWR on this model is ○ deficient ○ excessive ○ cautionary ○ good ◉ excellent *

Total highway safety penalties are: 2 *　　Value: 86　Durability: 79　Highway Control Rating: 94　Highway Safety: 92　★★★

Roadtrek	1997	MHB	19	190 op eng	DO	5.9L	G	$2500	128	4,490	8,510	6,537

Livability Code: WE 40-80

Wheelbase-to-length ratio of 55% is considered ○ dangerous ○ fatiguing ◉ good ○ excellent *

The approximate net payload of 1973 pounds at 23% of GVWR on this model is ○ deficient ○ excessive ○ cautionary ○ good ◉ excellent *

Total highway safety penalties are: 2 *　　Value: 86　Durability: 79　Highway Control Rating: 94　Highway Safety: 92　★★★

Roadtrek	1997	MHB	21	200 Versatile	CH	5.7L	G	$2300	139	4,000	9,500	7,610

Livability Code: WE 40-80

Wheelbase-to-length ratio of 56% is considered ○ dangerous ○ fatiguing ◉ good ○ excellent *

The approximate net payload of 1890 pounds at 20% of GVWR on this model is ○ deficient ○ excessive ○ cautionary ○ good ◉ excellent *

Total highway safety penalties are: 2 *　　Value: 86　Durability: 79　Highway Control Rating: 100　Highway Safety: 98　★★★

Roadtrek	1997	MHB	21	200 Vers. op eng	CH	7.4L	G	$2300	139	7,500	9,500	7,610

Livability Code: WE 40-80

Wheelbase-to-length ratio of 56% is considered ○ dangerous ○ fatiguing ◉ good ○ excellent *

The approximate net payload of 1890 pounds at 20% of GVWR on this model is ○ deficient ○ excessive ○ cautionary ○ good ◉ excellent *

Total highway safety penalties are: 2 *　　Value: 86　Durability: 79　Highway Control Rating: 100　Highway Safety: 98　★★★

Roadtrek	1997	MHB	21	200 Vers. op eng	CH	GM6.5	D	$2200	139	5,000	9,500	8,110

Livability Code: WE 40-80

Wheelbase-to-length ratio of 56% is considered ○ dangerous ○ fatiguing ◉ good ○ excellent *

The approximate net payload of 1390 pounds at 15% of GVWR on this model is ○ deficient ○ excessive ○ cautionary ◉ good ○ excellent *

Total highway safety penalties are: 2 *　　Value: 86　Durability: 79　Highway Control Rating: 95　Highway Safety: 93　★★★

Roadtrek	1998	MHB	17	170-Popular	DO	5.2L	G	$2600	128	3,200	6,800	5,824

Livability Code: WE 40-80

Wheelbase-to-length ratio of 62% is considered ○ dangerous ○ fatiguing ○ good ◉ excellent *

The approximate net payload of 976 pounds at 14% of GVWR on this model is ○ deficient ○ excessive ○ cautionary ◉ good ○ excellent *

Total highway safety penalties are: 2 *　　Value: 86　Durability: 79　Highway Control Rating: 100　Highway Safety: 98　★★★

Roadtrek	1998	MHB	17	170-Popular op eng	DO	5.9L	G	$2600	128	5,200	6,800	5,824

Livability Code: WE 40-80

Wheelbase-to-length ratio of 62% is considered ○ dangerous ○ fatiguing ○ good ◉ excellent *

The approximate net payload of 976 pounds at 14% of GVWR on this model is ○ deficient ○ excessive ○ cautionary ◉ good ○ excellent *

Total highway safety penalties are: 2 *　　Value: 86　Durability: 79　Highway Control Rating: 100　Highway Safety: 98　★★★

Note: Safety ratings are based on the assumption that the engineering of the RV has allowed for proper balance by placing fresh, gray, and black holding tanks in a location so as not to change the balance of the RV when the tanks are empty or full. **Always double-check wheelbase, GVWR, and weights at front and rear axles.**

*See Section 1 for details on how conclusions are reached.

Brand	Year	Type	Length	Model	Chassis	Engine	Fuel Type	Average Price per Linear Foot When New	Adjusted Wheelbase	Approx. Towing Capacity	Gross Vehicle Weight Rating	Average Curb Weight
Roadtrek	1998	MHB	19	190-Versatile	DO	5.2L	G	$2500	128	3,990	8,510	6,551

Livability Code: WE 40-80
Wheelbase-to-length ratio of 55% is considered ○ dangerous ○ fatiguing ◉ good ○ excellent*
The approximate net payload of 1959 pounds at 23% of GVWR on this model is ○ deficient ○ excessive ○ cautionary ○ good ◉ excellent*
Total highway safety penalties are: 2*   Value: 8 6   Durability: 7 9   Highway Control Rating: 9 4   Highway Safety: 9 2   ★★★

| Roadtrek | 1998 | MHB | 19 | 190-Versatile op eng | DO | 5.9L | G | $2500 | 128 | 4,490 | 8,510 | 6,551 |

Livability Code: WE 40-80
Wheelbase-to-length ratio of 55% is considered ○ dangerous ○ fatiguing ◉ good ○ excellent*
The approximate net payload of 1959 pounds at 23% of GVWR on this model is ○ deficient ○ excessive ○ cautionary ○ good ◉ excellent*
Total highway safety penalties are: 2*   Value: 8 6   Durability: 7 9   Highway Control Rating: 9 4   Highway Safety: 9 2   ★★★

| Roadtrek | 1998 | MHB | 19 | 190-Popular | DO | 5.2L | G | $2500 | 128 | 3,990 | 8,510 | 6,551 |

Livability Code: WE 40-80
Wheelbase-to-length ratio of 55% is considered ○ dangerous ○ fatiguing ◉ good ○ excellent*
The approximate net payload of 1959 pounds at 23% of GVWR on this model is ○ deficient ○ excessive ○ cautionary ○ good ◉ excellent*
Total highway safety penalties are: 2*   Value: 8 6   Durability: 7 9   Highway Control Rating: 9 4   Highway Safety: 9 2   ★★★

| Roadtrek | 1998 | MHB | 19 | 190-Popular op eng | DO | 5.9L | G | $2500 | 128 | 4,490 | 8,510 | 6,551 |

Livability Code: WE 40-80
Wheelbase-to-length ratio of 55% is considered ○ dangerous ○ fatiguing ◉ good ○ excellent*
The approximate net payload of 1959 pounds at 23% of GVWR on this model is ○ deficient ○ excessive ○ cautionary ○ good ◉ excellent*
Total highway safety penalties are: 2*   Value: 8 6   Durability: 7 9   Highway Control Rating: 9 4   Highway Safety: 9 2   ★★★

| Roadtrek | 1998 | MHB | 21 | 200-Versatile | CH | 5.7L | G | $2600 | 139 | 4,000 | 9,500 | 7,597 |

Livability Code: WE 40-80
Wheelbase-to-length ratio of 56% is considered ○ dangerous ○ fatiguing ◉ good ○ excellent*
The approximate net payload of 1903 pounds at 20% of GVWR on this model is ○ deficient ○ excessive ○ cautionary ○ good ◉ excellent*
Total highway safety penalties are: 2*   Value: 8 6   Durability: 7 9   Highway Control Rating: 1 0 0   Highway Safety: 9 8   ★★★

| Roadtrek | 1998 | MHB | 21 | 200-Versatile op eng | CH | 7.4L | G | $2700 | 139 | 7,500 | 9,500 | 7,597 |

Livability Code: WE 40-80
Wheelbase-to-length ratio of 56% is considered ○ dangerous ○ fatiguing ◉ good ○ excellent*
The approximate net payload of 1903 pounds at 20% of GVWR on this model is ○ deficient ○ excessive ○ cautionary ○ good ◉ excellent*
Total highway safety penalties are: 2*   Value: 8 6   Durability: 7 9   Highway Control Rating: 1 0 0   Highway Safety: 9 8   ★★★

| Roadtrek | 1998 | MHB | 21 | 200-Versatile op eng | CH | 6.5L | D | $2800 | 139 | 5,000 | 9,500 | 8,097 |

Livability Code: WE 40-80
Wheelbase-to-length ratio of 56% is considered ○ dangerous ○ fatiguing ◉ good ○ excellent*
The approximate net payload of 1403 pounds at 15% of GVWR on this model is ○ deficient ○ excessive ○ cautionary ◉ good ○ excellent*
Total highway safety penalties are: 2*   Value: 8 6   Durability: 7 9   Highway Control Rating: 9 5   Highway Safety: 9 3   ★★★

| Roadtrek | 1999 | MHB | 18 | 170 Popular | DO | 5.2L | G | $2800 | 128 | 4,500 | 7,000 | 5,696 |

Livability Code: WE 40-80
Wheelbase-to-length ratio of 59% is considered ○ dangerous ○ fatiguing ○ good ◉ excellent*
The approximate net payload of 1304 pounds at 19% of GVWR on this model is ○ deficient ○ excessive ○ cautionary ○ good ◉ excellent*
Total highway safety penalties are: 2*   Value: 8 6   Durability: 7 9   Highway Control Rating: 1 0 0   Highway Safety: 9 8   ★★★

| Roadtrek | 1999 | MHB | 18 | 170 Popular op eng | DO | 5.9L | G | $2800 | 128 | 4,800 | 7,700 | 5,976 |

Livability Code: WE 40-80
Wheelbase-to-length ratio of 59% is considered ○ dangerous ○ fatiguing ○ good ◉ excellent*
The approximate net payload of 1724 pounds at 22% of GVWR on this model is ○ deficient ○ excessive ○ cautionary ○ good ◉ excellent*
Total highway safety penalties are: 2*   Value: 8 6   Durability: 7 9   Highway Control Rating: 1 0 0   Highway Safety: 9 8   ★★★

| Roadtrek | 1999 | MHB | 20 | 190 Popular | DO | 5.2L | G | $2500 | 128 | 3,800 | 8,700 | 6,664 |

Livability Code: WE 40-80
Wheelbase-to-length ratio of 54% is considered ○ dangerous ○ fatiguing ◉ good ○ excellent*
The approximate net payload of 2036 pounds at 23% of GVWR on this model is ○ deficient ○ excessive ○ cautionary ○ good ◉ excellent*
Total highway safety penalties are: 2*   Value: 8 6   Durability: 7 9   Highway Control Rating: 8 6   Highway Safety: 8 4   ★★★

| Roadtrek | 1999 | MHB | 20 | 190 Popular op eng | DO | 5.9L | G | $2500 | 128 | 4,300 | 8,700 | 6,664 |

Livability Code: WE 40-80
Wheelbase-to-length ratio of 54% is considered ○ dangerous ○ fatiguing ◉ good ○ excellent*
The approximate net payload of 2036 pounds at 23% of GVWR on this model is ○ deficient ○ excessive ○ cautionary ○ good ◉ excellent*
Total highway safety penalties are: 2*   Value: 8 6   Durability: 7 9   Highway Control Rating: 8 6   Highway Safety: 8 4   ★★★

| Roadtrek | 1999 | MHB | 20 | 190 Versatile | DO | 5.2L | G | $2500 | 128 | 3,800 | 8,700 | 6,664 |

Livability Code: WE 40-80
Wheelbase-to-length ratio of 54% is considered ○ dangerous ○ fatiguing ◉ good ○ excellent*
The approximate net payload of 2036 pounds at 23% of GVWR on this model is ○ deficient ○ excessive ○ cautionary ○ good ◉ excellent*
Total highway safety penalties are: 2*   Value: 8 6   Durability: 7 9   Highway Control Rating: 8 6   Highway Safety: 8 4   ★★★

Note: Safety ratings are based on the assumption that the engineering of the RV has allowed for proper balance by placing fresh, gray, and black holding tanks in a location so as not to change the balance of the RV when the tanks are empty or full. **Always double-check wheelbase, GVWR, and weights at front and rear axles.**

*See Section 1 for details on how conclusions are reached.

Brand	Year	Type	Length	Model	Chassis	Engine	Fuel Type	Average Price per Linear Foot When New	Adjusted Wheelbase	Approx. Towing Capacity	Gross Vehicle Weight Rating	Average Curb Weight
Roadtrek	1999	MHB	20 190	Versatile op eng DO		5.9L	G	$2500	128	4,300	8,700	6,664

Livability Code: WE 40-80   Wheelbase-to-length ratio of 54% is considered ○ dangerous ○ fatiguing ◉ good ○ excellent *

The approximate net payload of 2036 pounds at 23% of GVWR on this model is ○ deficient ○ excessive ○ cautionary ○ good ◉ excellent *

Total highway safety penalties are: 2 *   Value: 8 6   Durability: 7 9   Highway Control Rating: 8 6   Highway Safety: 8 4   ★★★

| Roadtrek | 1999 | MHB | 21 | 200 Versatile | CH | 5.7L | G | $2400 | 139 | 4,000 | 9,500 | 7,384 |

Livability Code: WE 40-80   Wheelbase-to-length ratio of 56% is considered ○ dangerous ○ fatiguing ◉ good ○ excellent *

The approximate net payload of 2116 pounds at 22% of GVWR on this model is ○ deficient ○ excessive ○ cautionary ○ good ◉ excellent *

Total highway safety penalties are: 2 *   Value: 8 6   Durability: 7 9   Highway Control Rating: 9 9   Highway Safety: 9 7   ★★★

| Roadtrek | 1999 | MHB | 21 | 200 Versatile op eng | CH | 7.4L | G | $2400 | 139 | 7,500 | 9,500 | 7,384 |

Livability Code: WE 40-80   Wheelbase-to-length ratio of 56% is considered ○ dangerous ○ fatiguing ◉ good ○ excellent *

The approximate net payload of 2116 pounds at 22% of GVWR on this model is ○ deficient ○ excessive ○ cautionary ○ good ◉ excellent *

Total highway safety penalties are: 2 *   Value: 8 6   Durability: 7 9   Highway Control Rating: 9 9   Highway Safety: 9 7   ★★★

| Roadtrek | 1999 | MHB | 21 | 200 Versatile op eng | CH | 6.5L | D | $2400 | 139 | 5,000 | 9,500 | 7,884 |

Livability Code: WE 40-80   Wheelbase-to-length ratio of 56% is considered ○ dangerous ○ fatiguing ◉ good ○ excellent *

The approximate net payload of 1616 pounds at 17% of GVWR on this model is ○ deficient ○ excessive ○ cautionary ○ good ◉ excellent *

Total highway safety penalties are: 2 *   Value: 8 6   Durability: 7 9   Highway Control Rating: 9 8   Highway Safety: 9 6   ★★★

| Rolls Air | 1996 | MHA | 29 | 2800 | CH | 7.4L | G | $2700 | 190 | 3,500 | 16,500 | 14,249 |

Livability Code: FT 30-90   Wheelbase-to-length ratio of 55% is considered ○ dangerous ○ fatiguing ◉ good ○ excellent *

The approximate net payload of 2251 pounds at 14% of GVWR on this model is ○ deficient ○ excessive ○ cautionary ◉ good ○ excellent *

Total highway safety penalties are: 4 *   Value: 8 4   Durability: 7 7   Highway Control Rating: 8 7   Highway Safety: 8 3   ★★★

| Rolls Air | 1996 | MHA | 29 | 2800 | FO | 7.5L | G | $2700 | 190 | 8,000 | 17,000 | 14,649 |

Livability Code: FT 30-90   Wheelbase-to-length ratio of 55% is considered ○ dangerous ○ fatiguing ◉ good ○ excellent *

The approximate net payload of 2351 pounds at 14% of GVWR on this model is ○ deficient ○ excessive ○ cautionary ◉ good ○ excellent *

Total highway safety penalties are: 2 *   Value: 8 5   Durability: 7 7   Highway Control Rating: 8 8   Highway Safety: 8 6   ★★★

| Rolls Air | 1996 | MHA | 30 | 2900 | CH | 7.4L | G | $2600 | 208 | 3,500 | 16,500 | 14,663 |

Livability Code: FT 30-90   Wheelbase-to-length ratio of 57% is considered ○ dangerous ○ fatiguing ◉ good ○ excellent *

The approximate net payload of 1837 pounds at 11% of GVWR on this model is ○ deficient ○ excessive ○ cautionary ◉ good ○ excellent *

Total highway safety penalties are: 5 *   Value: 8 3   Durability: 7 7   Highway Control Rating: 9 1   Highway Safety: 8 6   ★★★

| Rolls Air | 1996 | MHA | 30 | 2900 | FO | 7.5L | G | $2600 | 208 | 8,000 | 17,000 | 15,063 |

Livability Code: FT 30-90   Wheelbase-to-length ratio of 57% is considered ○ dangerous ○ fatiguing ◉ good ○ excellent *

The approximate net payload of 1937 pounds at 11% of GVWR on this model is ○ deficient ○ excessive ○ cautionary ◉ good ○ excellent *

Total highway safety penalties are: 2 *   Value: 8 5   Durability: 7 7   Highway Control Rating: 9 1   Highway Safety: 8 9   ★★★

| Rolls Air | 1996 | MHA | 31 | 3000 | CH | 7.4L | G | $2500 | 208 | 3,500 | 16,500 | 14,899 |

Livability Code: FT 30-90   Wheelbase-to-length ratio of 56% is considered ○ dangerous ○ fatiguing ◉ good ○ excellent *

The approximate net payload of 1601 pounds at 10% of GVWR on this model is ○ deficient ○ excessive ○ cautionary ◉ good ○ excellent *

Total highway safety penalties are: 5 *   Value: 8 3   Durability: 7 7   Highway Control Rating: 8 9   Highway Safety: 8 4   ★★★

| Rolls Air | 1996 | MHA | 31 | 3000 | FO | 7.5L | G | $2500 | 208 | 8,000 | 17,000 | 15,299 |

Livability Code: FT 30-90   Wheelbase-to-length ratio of 56% is considered ○ dangerous ○ fatiguing ◉ good ○ excellent *

The approximate net payload of 1701 pounds at 10% of GVWR on this model is ○ deficient ○ excessive ○ cautionary ◉ good ○ excellent *

Total highway safety penalties are: 2 *   Value: 8 5   Durability: 7 7   Highway Control Rating: 8 9   Highway Safety: 8 7   ★★★

| Rolls Air | 1996 | MHA | 32 | 3100 | CH | 7.4L | G | $2500 | 208 | 3,500 | 16,500 | 15,136 |

Livability Code: FT 30-90   Wheelbase-to-length ratio of 54% is considered ○ dangerous ○ fatiguing ◉ good ○ excellent *

The approximate net payload of 1364 pounds at 8% of GVWR on this model is ○ deficient ○ excessive ◉ cautionary ○ good ○ excellent *

Total highway safety penalties are: 5 *   Value: 8 3   Durability: 7 7   Highway Control Rating: 6 0   Highway Safety: 5 5   ★

| Rolls Air | 1996 | MHA | 32 | 3200 | CH | 7.4L | G | $2500 | 208 | 3,500 | 16,500 | 15,136 |

Livability Code: FT 30-90   Wheelbase-to-length ratio of 54% is considered ○ dangerous ○ fatiguing ◉ good ○ excellent *

The approximate net payload of 1364 pounds at 8% of GVWR on this model is ○ deficient ○ excessive ◉ cautionary ○ good ○ excellent *

Total highway safety penalties are: 5 *   Value: 8 3   Durability: 7 7   Highway Control Rating: 6 0   Highway Safety: 5 5   ★

Note: Safety ratings are based on the assumption that the engineering of the RV has allowed for proper balance by placing fresh, gray, and black holding tanks in a location so as not to change the balance of the RV when the tanks are empty or full. **Always double-check wheelbase, GVWR, and weights at front and rear axles.**

The RV Rating Book

*See Section 1 for details on how conclusions are reached.

Section 2: The Ratings

Brand	Year	Type	Length	Model	Chassis	Engine	Fuel Type	Average Price per Linear Foot When New	Adjusted Wheelbase	Approx. Towing Capacity	Gross Vehicle Weight Rating	Average Curb Weight
Rolls Air	1996	MHA	32	3250	CH	7.4L	G	$2700	208	3,500	16,500	16,036

Livability Code: FT 30-90
Wheelbase-to-length ratio of 54% is considered ○ dangerous ○ fatiguing ◉ good ○ excellent *
The approximate net payload of 464 pounds at 3% of GVWR on this model is ◉ deficient ○ excessive ○ cautionary ○ good ○ excellent *
Total highway safety penalties are: 11 *   Value: 80   Durability: 77   Highway Control Rating: 45   Highway Safety: 34

Brand	Year	Type	Length	Model	Chassis	Engine	Fuel Type	Avg Price/Lin Ft	Adj Wheelbase	Towing Cap	GVWR	Avg Curb Wt
Rolls Air	1996	MHA	32	3100	FO	7.5L	G	$2500	208	8,000	17,000	15,536

Livability Code: FT 30-90
Wheelbase-to-length ratio of 54% is considered ○ dangerous ○ fatiguing ◉ good ○ excellent *
The approximate net payload of 1464 pounds at 9% of GVWR on this model is ○ deficient ○ excessive ◉ cautionary ○ good ○ excellent *
Total highway safety penalties are: 2 *   Value: 85   Durability: 77   Highway Control Rating: 65   Highway Safety: 63   ★★

Brand	Year	Type	Length	Model	Chassis	Engine	Fuel Type	Avg Price/Lin Ft	Adj Wheelbase	Towing Cap	GVWR	Avg Curb Wt
Rolls Air	1996	MHA	32	3200	FO	7.5L	G	$2500	208	8,000	17,000	15,536

Livability Code: FT 30-90
Wheelbase-to-length ratio of 54% is considered ○ dangerous ○ fatiguing ◉ good ○ excellent *
The approximate net payload of 1464 pounds at 9% of GVWR on this model is ○ deficient ○ excessive ◉ cautionary ○ good ○ excellent *
Total highway safety penalties are: 2 *   Value: 85   Durability: 77   Highway Control Rating: 65   Highway Safety: 63   ★★

Brand	Year	Type	Length	Model	Chassis	Engine	Fuel Type	Avg Price/Lin Ft	Adj Wheelbase	Towing Cap	GVWR	Avg Curb Wt
Rolls Air	1996	MHA	32	3250	FO	7.5L	G	$2700	208	8,000	17,000	16,436

Livability Code: FT 30-90
Wheelbase-to-length ratio of 54% is considered ○ dangerous ○ fatiguing ◉ good ○ excellent *
The approximate net payload of 564 pounds at 3% of GVWR on this model is ◉ deficient ○ excessive ○ cautionary ○ good ○ excellent *
Total highway safety penalties are: 7 *   Value: 82   Durability: 77   Highway Control Rating: 45   Highway Safety: 38

Brand	Year	Type	Length	Model	Chassis	Engine	Fuel Type	Avg Price/Lin Ft	Adj Wheelbase	Towing Cap	GVWR	Avg Curb Wt
Rolls Air	1996	MHA	34	3300	CH	7.4L	G	$2400	208	3,500	16,500	15,609

Livability Code: FT 30-90
Wheelbase-to-length ratio of 52% is considered ○ dangerous ◉ fatiguing ○ good ○ excellent *
The approximate net payload of 891 pounds at 5% of GVWR on this model is ◉ deficient ○ excessive ○ cautionary ○ good ○ excellent *
Total highway safety penalties are: 6 *   Value: 83   Durability: 77   Highway Control Rating: 23   Highway Safety: 17

Brand	Year	Type	Length	Model	Chassis	Engine	Fuel Type	Avg Price/Lin Ft	Adj Wheelbase	Towing Cap	GVWR	Avg Curb Wt
Rolls Air	1996	MHA	34	3400	CH	7.4L	G	$2400	232 T	1,500	19,500	16,509

Livability Code: FT 30-90
Wheelbase-to-length ratio of 58% is considered ○ dangerous ○ fatiguing ○ good ◉ excellent *
The approximate net payload of 2991 pounds at 15% of GVWR on this model is ○ deficient ○ excessive ○ cautionary ◉ good ○ excellent *
Total highway safety penalties are: 9 *   Value: 81   Durability: 77   Highway Control Rating: 100   Highway Safety: 91   ★★★

Brand	Year	Type	Length	Model	Chassis	Engine	Fuel Type	Avg Price/Lin Ft	Adj Wheelbase	Towing Cap	GVWR	Avg Curb Wt
Rolls Air	1996	MHA	34	3300	FO	7.5L	G	$2400	228	8,000	17,000	16,009

Livability Code: FT 30-90
Wheelbase-to-length ratio of 57% is considered ○ dangerous ○ fatiguing ◉ good ○ excellent *
The approximate net payload of 991 pounds at 6% of GVWR on this model is ◉ deficient ○ excessive ○ cautionary ○ good ○ excellent *
Total highway safety penalties are: 2 *   Value: 85   Durability: 77   Highway Control Rating: 64   Highway Safety: 62   ★

Brand	Year	Type	Length	Model	Chassis	Engine	Fuel Type	Avg Price/Lin Ft	Adj Wheelbase	Towing Cap	GVWR	Avg Curb Wt
Rolls Air	1996	MHA	34	3400	FO	7.5L	G	$2400	232 T	5,000	20,000	16,909

Livability Code: FT 30-90
Wheelbase-to-length ratio of 58% is considered ○ dangerous ○ fatiguing ○ good ◉ excellent *
The approximate net payload of 3091 pounds at 15% of GVWR on this model is ○ deficient ○ excessive ○ cautionary ◉ good ○ excellent *
Total highway safety penalties are: 4 *   Value: 84   Durability: 77   Highway Control Rating: 100   Highway Safety: 96   ★★★

Brand	Year	Type	Length	Model	Chassis	Engine	Fuel Type	Avg Price/Lin Ft	Adj Wheelbase	Towing Cap	GVWR	Avg Curb Wt
Rolls Air	1996	MHA	34	3300	SP	CU275	D	$4000	208	3,000	23,000	20,009

Livability Code: FT 30-90
Wheelbase-to-length ratio of 52% is considered ○ dangerous ◉ fatiguing ○ good ○ excellent *
The approximate net payload of 2991 pounds at 13% of GVWR on this model is ○ deficient ○ excessive ○ cautionary ◉ good ○ excellent *
Total highway safety penalties are: 2 *   Value: 85   Durability: 77   Highway Control Rating: 52   Highway Safety: 50   ★

Brand	Year	Type	Length	Model	Chassis	Engine	Fuel Type	Avg Price/Lin Ft	Adj Wheelbase	Towing Cap	GVWR	Avg Curb Wt
Rolls Air	1996	MHA	34	3400	SP	CU275	D	$4000	208	3,000	23,000	20,009

Livability Code: FT 30-90
Wheelbase-to-length ratio of 52% is considered ○ dangerous ◉ fatiguing ○ good ○ excellent *
The approximate net payload of 2991 pounds at 13% of GVWR on this model is ○ deficient ○ excessive ○ cautionary ◉ good ○ excellent *
Total highway safety penalties are: 2 *   Value: 85   Durability: 77   Highway Control Rating: 52   Highway Safety: 50   ★

Brand	Year	Type	Length	Model	Chassis	Engine	Fuel Type	Avg Price/Lin Ft	Adj Wheelbase	Towing Cap	GVWR	Avg Curb Wt
Rolls Air	1996	MHA	35	3500	CH	7.4L	G	$2300	252 T	1,500	19,500	17,042

Livability Code: FT 30-90
Wheelbase-to-length ratio of 59% is considered ○ dangerous ○ fatiguing ○ good ◉ excellent *
The approximate net payload of 2458 pounds at 13% of GVWR on this model is ○ deficient ○ excessive ○ cautionary ◉ good ○ excellent *
Total highway safety penalties are: 10 *   Value: 81   Durability: 77   Highway Control Rating: 100   Highway Safety: 90   ★★★

Brand	Year	Type	Length	Model	Chassis	Engine	Fuel Type	Avg Price/Lin Ft	Adj Wheelbase	Towing Cap	GVWR	Avg Curb Wt
Rolls Air	1996	MHA	35	3550	CH	7.4L	G	$2500	252 T	500	19,500	17,792

Livability Code: FT 30-90
Wheelbase-to-length ratio of 59% is considered ○ dangerous ○ fatiguing ○ good ◉ excellent *
The approximate net payload of 1708 pounds at 9% of GVWR on this model is ○ deficient ○ excessive ◉ cautionary ○ good ○ excellent *
Total highway safety penalties are: 14 *   Value: 79   Durability: 77   Highway Control Rating: 91   Highway Safety: 77   ★★★

Note: Safety ratings are based on the assumption that the engineering of the RV has allowed for proper balance by placing fresh, gray, and black holding tanks in a location so as not to change the balance of the RV when the tanks are empty or full. **Always double-check wheelbase, GVWR, and weights at front and rear axles.**

*See Section 1 for details on how conclusions are reached.

Section 2: The Ratings

Brand	Year	Type	Length	Model	Chassis	Engine	Fuel Type	Average Price per Linear Foot When New	Adjusted Wheelbase	Approx. Towing Capacity	Gross Vehicle Weight Rating	Average Curb Weight
Rolls Air	1996	MHA	35	3500	FO	7.5L	G	$2300	252 T	5,000	20,000	17,442

Livability Code: FT 30-90
Wheelbase-to-length ratio of 59% is considered ○ dangerous ○ fatiguing ○ good ● excellent *
The approximate net payload of 2558 pounds at 13% of GVWR on this model is ○ deficient ○ excessive ○ cautionary ● good ○ excellent *
Total highway safety penalties are: 4 *   Value: **8 4**   Durability: **7 7**   Highway Control Rating: **1 0 0**   Highway Safety: **9 6**   ★★★

Brand	Year	Type	Length	Model	Chassis	Engine	Fuel Type	Price/Ft	Wheelbase	Towing	GVWR	Curb Wt
Rolls Air	1996	MHA	35	3550	FO	7.5L	G	$2500	252 T	5,000	20,000	18,192

Livability Code: FT 30-90
Wheelbase-to-length ratio of 59% is considered ○ dangerous ○ fatiguing ○ good ● excellent *
The approximate net payload of 1808 pounds at 9% of GVWR on this model is ○ deficient ○ excessive ● cautionary ○ good ○ excellent *
Total highway safety penalties are: 9 *   Value: **8 1**   Durability: **7 7**   Highway Control Rating: **9 2**   Highway Safety: **8 3**   ★★★

Brand	Year	Type	Length	Model	Chassis	Engine	Fuel Type	Price/Ft	Wheelbase	Towing	GVWR	Curb Wt
Rolls Air	1996	MHA	35	3500	SP	CU275	D	$4000	208	3,000	23,000	20,542

Livability Code: FT 30-90
Wheelbase-to-length ratio of 49% is considered ● dangerous ○ fatiguing ○ good ○ excellent *
The approximate net payload of 2458 pounds at 11% of GVWR on this model is ○ deficient ○ excessive ○ cautionary ● good ○ excellent *
Total highway safety penalties are: 2 *   Value: **8 5**   Durability: **7 7**   Highway Control Rating: **3 1**   Highway Safety: **2 9**

Brand	Year	Type	Length	Model	Chassis	Engine	Fuel Type	Price/Ft	Wheelbase	Towing	GVWR	Curb Wt
Rolls Air	1996	MHA	35	3550	SP	CU275	D	$4100	208	3,000	23,000	21,292

Livability Code: FT 30-90
Wheelbase-to-length ratio of 49% is considered ● dangerous ○ fatiguing ○ good ○ excellent *
The approximate net payload of 1708 pounds at 7% of GVWR on this model is ○ deficient ○ excessive ● cautionary ○ good ○ excellent *
Total highway safety penalties are: 7 *   Value: **8 3**   Durability: **7 7**   Highway Control Rating: **1 3**   Highway Safety: **6**

Brand	Year	Type	Length	Model	Chassis	Engine	Fuel Type	Price/Ft	Wheelbase	Towing	GVWR	Curb Wt
Rolls Air	1996	MHA	36	3600	CH	7.4L	G	$2300	252 T	1,500	19,500	17,219

Livability Code: FT 30-90
Wheelbase-to-length ratio of 58% is considered ○ dangerous ○ fatiguing ○ good ● excellent *
The approximate net payload of 2281 pounds at 12% of GVWR on this model is ○ deficient ○ excessive ○ cautionary ● good ○ excellent *
Total highway safety penalties are: 10 *   Value: **8 1**   Durability: **7 7**   Highway Control Rating: **9 7**   Highway Safety: **8 7**   ★★★

Brand	Year	Type	Length	Model	Chassis	Engine	Fuel Type	Price/Ft	Wheelbase	Towing	GVWR	Curb Wt
Rolls Air	1996	MHA	36	3600	FO	7.5L	G	$2300	252 T	5,000	20,000	17,619

Livability Code: FT 30-90
Wheelbase-to-length ratio of 58% is considered ○ dangerous ○ fatiguing ○ good ● excellent *
The approximate net payload of 2381 pounds at 12% of GVWR on this model is ○ deficient ○ excessive ○ cautionary ● good ○ excellent *
Total highway safety penalties are: 4 *   Value: **8 4**   Durability: **7 7**   Highway Control Rating: **9 7**   Highway Safety: **9 3**   ★★★

Brand	Year	Type	Length	Model	Chassis	Engine	Fuel Type	Price/Ft	Wheelbase	Towing	GVWR	Curb Wt
Rolls Air	1996	MHA	36	3650	FO	7.5L	G	$2400	252 T	5,000	20,000	18,669

Livability Code: FT 30-90
Wheelbase-to-length ratio of 58% is considered ○ dangerous ○ fatiguing ○ good ● excellent *
The approximate net payload of 1331 pounds at 7% of GVWR on this model is ○ deficient ○ excessive ● cautionary ○ good ○ excellent *
Total highway safety penalties are: 11 *   Value: **8 0**   Durability: **7 7**   Highway Control Rating: **7 6**   Highway Safety: **6 5**   ★★

Brand	Year	Type	Length	Model	Chassis	Engine	Fuel Type	Price/Ft	Wheelbase	Towing	GVWR	Curb Wt
Rolls Air	1996	MHA	36	3600	SP	CU275	D	$3900	228	3,000	23,000	20,719

Livability Code: FT 30-90
Wheelbase-to-length ratio of 53% is considered ○ dangerous ● fatiguing ○ good ○ excellent *
The approximate net payload of 2281 pounds at 10% of GVWR on this model is ○ deficient ○ excessive ○ cautionary ● good ○ excellent *
Total highway safety penalties are: 2 *   Value: **8 5**   Durability: **7 7**   Highway Control Rating: **5 8**   Highway Safety: **5 6**   ★

Brand	Year	Type	Length	Model	Chassis	Engine	Fuel Type	Price/Ft	Wheelbase	Towing	GVWR	Curb Wt
Rolls Air	1996	MHA	36	3650	SP	CU275	D	$3900	228	3,000	23,000	21,769

Livability Code: FT 30-90
Wheelbase-to-length ratio of 53% is considered ○ dangerous ● fatiguing ○ good ○ excellent *
The approximate net payload of 1231 pounds at 5% of GVWR on this model is ● deficient ○ excessive ○ cautionary ○ good ○ excellent *
Total highway safety penalties are: 8 *   Value: **8 2**   Durability: **7 7**   Highway Control Rating: **3 5**   Highway Safety: **2 7**

Brand	Year	Type	Length	Model	Chassis	Engine	Fuel Type	Price/Ft	Wheelbase	Towing	GVWR	Curb Wt
Rolls Air	1996	MHA	38	3800	FO	7.5L	G	$2300	252	5,000	20,000	18,329

Livability Code: FT 30-90
Wheelbase-to-length ratio of 55% is considered ○ dangerous ○ fatiguing ● good ○ excellent *
The approximate net payload of 1671 pounds at 8% of GVWR on this model is ○ deficient ○ excessive ● cautionary ○ good ○ excellent *
Total highway safety penalties are: 4 *   Value: **8 4**   Durability: **7 7**   Highway Control Rating: **6 9**   Highway Safety: **6 5**   ★★

Brand	Year	Type	Length	Model	Chassis	Engine	Fuel Type	Price/Ft	Wheelbase	Towing	GVWR	Curb Wt
Rolls Air	1997	MHA	29	2800	CH	7.4L	G	$2700	190	3,500	16,500	14,249

Livability Code: FT 30-90
Wheelbase-to-length ratio of 55% is considered ○ dangerous ○ fatiguing ● good ○ excellent *
The approximate net payload of 2251 pounds at 14% of GVWR on this model is ○ deficient ○ excessive ○ cautionary ● good ○ excellent *
Total highway safety penalties are: 4 *   Value: **8 4**   Durability: **7 7**   Highway Control Rating: **8 7**   Highway Safety: **8 3**   ★★★

Brand	Year	Type	Length	Model	Chassis	Engine	Fuel Type	Price/Ft	Wheelbase	Towing	GVWR	Curb Wt
Rolls Air	1997	MHA	29	2800	FO	7.5L	G	$2700	190	8,000	17,000	14,649

Livability Code: FT 30-90
Wheelbase-to-length ratio of 55% is considered ○ dangerous ○ fatiguing ● good ○ excellent *
The approximate net payload of 2351 pounds at 14% of GVWR on this model is ○ deficient ○ excessive ○ cautionary ● good ○ excellent *
Total highway safety penalties are: 2 *   Value: **8 5**   Durability: **7 7**   Highway Control Rating: **8 8**   Highway Safety: **8 6**   ★★★

Note: Safety ratings are based on the assumption that the engineering of the RV has allowed for proper balance by placing fresh, gray, and black holding tanks in a location so as not to change the balance of the RV when the tanks are empty or full. **Always double-check wheelbase, GVWR, and weights at front and rear axles.**

*See Section 1 for details on how conclusions are reached.

Brand	Year	Type	Length	Model	Chassis	Engine	Fuel Type	Average Price per Linear Foot When New	Adjusted Wheelbase	Approx. Towing Capacity	Gross Vehicle Weight Rating	Average Curb Weight
Rolls Air	**1997**	MHA	30	2900	CH	7.4L	G	$2600	208	3,500	16,500	14,663

Livability Code: FT 30-90
Wheelbase-to-length ratio of 57% is considered ○ dangerous ○ fatiguing ● good ○ excellent *
The approximate net payload of 1837 pounds at 11% of GVWR on this model is ○ deficient ○ excessive ○ cautionary ● good ○ excellent *
Total highway safety penalties are: 5 *   Value: **8 3**   Durability: **7 7**   Highway Control Rating: **9 1**   Highway Safety: **8 6**   ★★★

Brand	Year	Type	Length	Model	Chassis	Engine	Fuel Type	Price/Ft	Wheelbase	Towing	GVWR	Curb Weight
Rolls Air	**1997**	MHA	30	2900	FO	7.5L	G	$2600	208	8,000	17,000	15,063

Livability Code: FT 30-90
Wheelbase-to-length ratio of 57% is considered ○ dangerous ○ fatiguing ● good ○ excellent *
The approximate net payload of 1937 pounds at 11% of GVWR on this model is ○ deficient ○ excessive ○ cautionary ● good ○ excellent *
Total highway safety penalties are: 2 *   Value: **8 5**   Durability: **7 7**   Highway Control Rating: **9 1**   Highway Safety: **8 9**   ★★★

Rolls Air	**1997**	MHA	31	3000	CH	7.4L	G	$2500	208	3,500	16,500	14,899

Livability Code: FT 30-90
Wheelbase-to-length ratio of 56% is considered ○ dangerous ○ fatiguing ● good ○ excellent *
The approximate net payload of 1601 pounds at 10% of GVWR on this model is ○ deficient ○ excessive ○ cautionary ● good ○ excellent *
Total highway safety penalties are: 5 *   Value: **8 3**   Durability: **7 7**   Highway Control Rating: **8 9**   Highway Safety: **8 4**   ★★★

Rolls Air	**1997**	MHA	31	3000	FO	7.5L	G	$2500	208	3,000	17,000	15,299

Livability Code: FT 30-90
Wheelbase-to-length ratio of 56% is considered ○ dangerous ○ fatiguing ● good ○ excellent *
The approximate net payload of 1701 pounds at 10% of GVWR on this model is ○ deficient ○ excessive ○ cautionary ● good ○ excellent *
Total highway safety penalties are: 2 *   Value: **8 5**   Durability: **7 7**   Highway Control Rating: **8 9**   Highway Safety: **8 7**   ★★★

Rolls Air	**1997**	MHA	32	3100	CH	7.4L	G	$2500	208	3,500	16,500	15,166

Livability Code: FT 30-90
Wheelbase-to-length ratio of 54% is considered ○ dangerous ○ fatiguing ● good ○ excellent *
The approximate net payload of 1334 pounds at 8% of GVWR on this model is ○ deficient ○ excessive ● cautionary ○ good ○ excellent *
Total highway safety penalties are: 6 *   Value: **8 3**   Durability: **7 7**   Highway Control Rating: **5 9**   Highway Safety: **5 3**   ★

Rolls Air	**1997**	MHA	32	3200	CH	7.4L	G	$2500	208	8,500	16,500	15,166

Livability Code: FT 30-90
Wheelbase-to-length ratio of 54% is considered ○ dangerous ○ fatiguing ● good ○ excellent *
The approximate net payload of 1334 pounds at 8% of GVWR on this model is ○ deficient ○ excessive ● cautionary ○ good ○ excellent *
Total highway safety penalties are: 6 *   Value: **8 3**   Durability: **7 7**   Highway Control Rating: **5 9**   Highway Safety: **5 3**   ★

Rolls Air	**1997**	MHA	32	3250	CH	7.4L	G	$2700	208	8,500	16,500	16,066

Livability Code: FT 30-90
Wheelbase-to-length ratio of 54% is considered ○ dangerous ○ fatiguing ● good ○ excellent *
The approximate net payload of 434 pounds at 3% of GVWR on this model is ● deficient ○ excessive ○ cautionary ○ good ○ excellent *
Total highway safety penalties are: 11 *   Value: **8 0**   Durability: **7 7**   Highway Control Rating: **4 4**   Highway Safety: **3 3**

Rolls Air	**1997**	MHA	32	3100	FO	7.5L	G	$2500	208	8,000	17,000	15,566

Livability Code: FT 30-90
Wheelbase-to-length ratio of 54% is considered ○ dangerous ○ fatiguing ● good ○ excellent *
The approximate net payload of 1434 pounds at 8% of GVWR on this model is ○ deficient ○ excessive ● cautionary ○ good ○ excellent *
Total highway safety penalties are: 2 *   Value: **8 5**   Durability: **7 7**   Highway Control Rating: **6 0**   Highway Safety: **5 8**   ★

Rolls Air	**1997**	MHA	32	3200	FO	7.5L	G	$2500	208	3,000	17,000	15,566

Livability Code: FT 30-90
Wheelbase-to-length ratio of 54% is considered ○ dangerous ○ fatiguing ● good ○ excellent *
The approximate net payload of 1434 pounds at 8% of GVWR on this model is ○ deficient ○ excessive ● cautionary ○ good ○ excellent *
Total highway safety penalties are: 2 *   Value: **8 5**   Durability: **7 7**   Highway Control Rating: **6 0**   Highway Safety: **5 8**   ★

Rolls Air	**1997**	MHA	32	3250	FO	7.5L	G	$2700	208	3,000	17,000	16,466

Livability Code: FT 30-90
Wheelbase-to-length ratio of 54% is considered ○ dangerous ○ fatiguing ● good ○ excellent *
The approximate net payload of 534 pounds at 3% of GVWR on this model is ● deficient ○ excessive ○ cautionary ○ good ○ excellent *
Total highway safety penalties are: 7 *   Value: **8 2**   Durability: **7 7**   Highway Control Rating: **4 4**   Highway Safety: **3 7**   ★

Rolls Air	**1997**	MHA	34	3300	CH	7.4L	G	$2400	228	3,500	16,500	15,609

Livability Code: FT 30-90
Wheelbase-to-length ratio of 57% is considered ○ dangerous ○ fatiguing ● good ○ excellent *
The approximate net payload of 891 pounds at 5% of GVWR on this model is ● deficient ○ excessive ○ cautionary ○ good ○ excellent *
Total highway safety penalties are: 6 *   Value: **8 3**   Durability: **7 7**   Highway Control Rating: **6 3**   Highway Safety: **5 7**   ★

Rolls Air	**1997**	MHA	34	3400 opch	CH	7.4L	G	$2500	232 T	5,500	19,500	16,509

Livability Code: FT 30-90
Wheelbase-to-length ratio of 58% is considered ○ dangerous ○ fatiguing ○ good ● excellent *
The approximate net payload of 2991 pounds at 15% of GVWR on this model is ○ deficient ○ excessive ○ cautionary ● good ○ excellent *
Total highway safety penalties are: 9 *   Value: **8 1**   Durability: **7 7**   Highway Control Rating: **1 0 0**   Highway Safety: **9 1**   ★★★

Note: Safety ratings are based on the assumption that the engineering of the RV has allowed for proper balance by placing fresh, gray, and black holding tanks in a location so as not to change the balance of the RV when the tanks are empty or full. **Always double-check wheelbase, GVWR, and weights at front and rear axles.**

*See Section 1 for details on how conclusions are reached.

Brand	Year	Type	Length	Model	Chassis	Engine	Fuel Type	Average Price per Linear Foot When New	Adjusted Wheelbase	Approx. Towing Capacity	Gross Vehicle Weight Rating	Average Curb Weight
Rolls Air	1997	MHA	34	3400	CH	7.4L	G	$2400	208	8,500	16,500	15,609

Livability Code: FT 30-90   Wheelbase-to-length ratio of 52% is considered ○ dangerous ◉ fatiguing ○ good ○ excellent *

The approximate net payload of 891 pounds at 5% of GVWR on this model is ◉ deficient ○ excessive ○ cautionary ○ good ○ excellent *

Total highway safety penalties are: 6 *   Value: 8 3   Durability: 7 7   Highway Control Rating: 2 3   Highway Safety: 1 7

Brand	Year	Type	Length	Model	Chassis	Engine	Fuel Type	Price/Ft	Wheelbase	Towing	GVWR	Curb Wt
Rolls Air	1997	MHA	34	3300	FO	7.5L	G	$2400	228	8,000	17,000	16,009

Livability Code: FT 30-90   Wheelbase-to-length ratio of 57% is considered ○ dangerous ○ fatiguing ◉ good ○ excellent *

The approximate net payload of 991 pounds at 6% of GVWR on this model is ◉ deficient ○ excessive ○ cautionary ○ good ○ excellent *

Total highway safety penalties are: 2 *   Value: 8 5   Durability: 7 7   Highway Control Rating: 6 4   Highway Safety: 6 2   ★

Rolls Air	1997	MHA	34	3400 opch	FO	7.5L	G	$2500	232 T	5,000	20,000	16,909

Livability Code: FT 30-90   Wheelbase-to-length ratio of 58% is considered ○ dangerous ○ fatiguing ○ good ◉ excellent *

The approximate net payload of 3091 pounds at 15% of GVWR on this model is ○ deficient ○ excessive ○ cautionary ◉ good ○ excellent *

Total highway safety penalties are: 4 *   Value: 8 4   Durability: 7 7   Highway Control Rating: 1 0 0   Highway Safety: 9 6   ★★★

Rolls Air	1997	MHA	34	3400	FO	7.5L	G	$2400	208	8,000	17,000	16,009

Livability Code: FT 30-90   Wheelbase-to-length ratio of 52% is considered ○ dangerous ◉ fatiguing ○ good ○ excellent *

The approximate net payload of 991 pounds at 6% of GVWR on this model is ◉ deficient ○ excessive ○ cautionary ○ good ○ excellent *

Total highway safety penalties are: 2 *   Value: 8 5   Durability: 7 7   Highway Control Rating: 2 3   Highway Safety: 2 1

Rolls Air	1997	MHA	34	3400	SP	CU275	D	$4000	208	3,000	23,000	20,276

Livability Code: FT 30-90   Wheelbase-to-length ratio of 50% is considered ◉ dangerous ○ fatiguing ○ good ○ excellent *

The approximate net payload of 2724 pounds at 12% of GVWR on this model is ○ deficient ○ excessive ○ cautionary ◉ good ○ excellent *

Total highway safety penalties are: 2 *   Value: 8 5   Durability: 7 7   Highway Control Rating: 3 8   Highway Safety: 3 6

Rolls Air	1997	MHA	34	3450	SP	CU275	D	$3900	208	1,500	23,000	21,176

Livability Code: FT 30-90   Wheelbase-to-length ratio of 50% is considered ◉ dangerous ○ fatiguing ○ good ○ excellent *

The approximate net payload of 1824 pounds at 8% of GVWR on this model is ○ deficient ○ excessive ◉ cautionary ○ good ○ excellent *

Total highway safety penalties are: 7 *   Value: 8 2   Durability: 7 7   Highway Control Rating: 2 3   Highway Safety: 1 6

Rolls Air	1997	MHA	34	3300	SP	CU275	D	$3900	208	1,500	23,000	20,276

Livability Code: FT 30-90   Wheelbase-to-length ratio of 50% is considered ◉ dangerous ○ fatiguing ○ good ○ excellent *

The approximate net payload of 2724 pounds at 12% of GVWR on this model is ○ deficient ○ excessive ○ cautionary ◉ good ○ excellent *

Total highway safety penalties are: 2 *   Value: 8 5   Durability: 7 7   Highway Control Rating: 3 8   Highway Safety: 3 6

Rolls Air	1997	MHA	35	3500 opch	CH	7.4L	G	$2400	252 T	1,500	19,500	17,042

Livability Code: FT 30-90   Wheelbase-to-length ratio of 59% is considered ○ dangerous ○ fatiguing ○ good ◉ excellent *

The approximate net payload of 2458 pounds at 13% of GVWR on this model is ○ deficient ○ excessive ○ cautionary ○ good ○ excellent *

Total highway safety penalties are: 10 *   Value: 8 1   Durability: 7 7   Highway Control Rating: 1 0 0   Highway Safety: 9 0   ★★★

Rolls Air	1997	MHA	35	3550 opch	CH	7.4L	G	$2500	252 T	1,500	19,500	17,792

Livability Code: FT 30-90   Wheelbase-to-length ratio of 59% is considered ○ dangerous ○ fatiguing ○ good ◉ excellent *

The approximate net payload of 1708 pounds at 9% of GVWR on this model is ○ deficient ○ excessive ◉ cautionary ○ good ○ excellent *

Total highway safety penalties are: 14 *   Value: 7 9   Durability: 7 7   Highway Control Rating: 9 1   Highway Safety: 7 7   ★★★

Rolls Air	1997	MHA	35	3500	CH	7.4L	G	$2500	228	3,500	16,500	16,142

Livability Code: FT 30-90   Wheelbase-to-length ratio of 54% is considered ○ dangerous ○ fatiguing ◉ good ○ excellent *

The approximate net payload of 358 pounds at 2% of GVWR on this model is ◉ deficient ○ excessive ○ cautionary ○ good ○ excellent *

Total highway safety penalties are: 7 *   Value: 8 2   Durability: 7 7   Highway Control Rating: 4 2   Highway Safety: 3 5

Rolls Air	1997	MHA	35	3550	CH	7.4L	G	$2500	228	3,500	16,500	16,142

Livability Code: FT 30-90   Wheelbase-to-length ratio of 54% is considered ○ dangerous ○ fatiguing ◉ good ○ excellent *

The approximate net payload of 358 pounds at 2% of GVWR on this model is ◉ deficient ○ excessive ○ cautionary ○ good ○ excellent *

Total highway safety penalties are: 7 *   Value: 8 2   Durability: 7 7   Highway Control Rating: 4 2   Highway Safety: 3 5

Rolls Air	1997	MHA	35	3500 opch	FO	7.5L	G	$2500	252 T	5,000	20,000	17,442

Livability Code: FT 30-90   Wheelbase-to-length ratio of 59% is considered ○ dangerous ○ fatiguing ○ good ◉ excellent *

The approximate net payload of 2558 pounds at 13% of GVWR on this model is ○ deficient ○ excessive ○ cautionary ○ good ○ excellent *

Total highway safety penalties are: 4 *   Value: 8 4   Durability: 7 7   Highway Control Rating: 1 0 0   Highway Safety: 9 6   ★★★

Note: Safety ratings are based on the assumption that the engineering of the RV has allowed for proper balance by placing fresh, gray, and black holding tanks in a location so as not to change the balance of the RV when the tanks are empty or full. **Always double-check wheelbase, GVWR, and weights at front and rear axles.**

*See Section 1 for details on how conclusions are reached.

Section 2: The Ratings

Brand	Year	Type	Length	Model	Chassis	Engine	Fuel Type	Average Price per Linear Foot When New	Adjusted Wheelbase	Approx. Towing Capacity	Gross Vehicle Weight Rating	Average Curb Weight
Rolls Air	1997	MHA	35	3550 opch	FO	7.5L	G	$2500	252 T	5,000	20,000	18,192

Livability Code: FT 30-90
Wheelbase-to-length ratio of 59% is considered ○ dangerous ○ fatiguing ○ good ● excellent *
The approximate net payload of 1808 pounds at 9% of GVWR on this model is ○ deficient ○ excessive ● cautionary ○ good ○ excellent *
Total highway safety penalties are: 9 *   Value: 8 1   Durability: 7 7   Highway Control Rating: 9 2   Highway Safety: 8 3   ★★★

Brand	Year	Type	Length	Model	Chassis	Engine	Fuel Type	Price/Linear Foot	Adjusted Wheelbase	Towing Capacity	GVWR	Curb Weight
Rolls Air	1997	MHA	35	3500	FO	7.5L	G	$2300	228	8,000	17,000	16,542

Livability Code: FT 30-90
Wheelbase-to-length ratio of 54% is considered ○ dangerous ○ fatiguing ● good ○ excellent *
The approximate net payload of 458 pounds at 3% of GVWR on this model is ● deficient ○ excessive ○ cautionary ○ good ○ excellent *
Total highway safety penalties are: 2 *   Value: 8 5   Durability: 7 7   Highway Control Rating: 4 3   Highway Safety: 4 1

Brand	Year	Type	Length	Model	Chassis	Engine	Fuel Type	Price/Linear Foot	Adjusted Wheelbase	Towing Capacity	GVWR	Curb Weight
Rolls Air	1997	MHA	35	3550	FO	7.5L	G	$2300	228	8,000	17,000	16,542

Livability Code: FT 30-90
Wheelbase-to-length ratio of 54% is considered ○ dangerous ○ fatiguing ● good ○ excellent *
The approximate net payload of 458 pounds at 3% of GVWR on this model is ● deficient ○ excessive ○ cautionary ○ good ○ excellent *
Total highway safety penalties are: 2 *   Value: 8 5   Durability: 7 7   Highway Control Rating: 4 3   Highway Safety: 4 1

Brand	Year	Type	Length	Model	Chassis	Engine	Fuel Type	Price/Linear Foot	Adjusted Wheelbase	Towing Capacity	GVWR	Curb Weight
Rolls Air	1997	MHA	36	3600	CH	7.4L	G	$2300	252 T	1,500	19,500	17,249

Livability Code: FT 30-90
Wheelbase-to-length ratio of 58% is considered ○ dangerous ○ fatiguing ○ good ● excellent *
The approximate net payload of 2251 pounds at 12% of GVWR on this model is ○ deficient ○ excessive ○ cautionary ● good ○ excellent *
Total highway safety penalties are: 10 *   Value: 8 1   Durability: 7 7   Highway Control Rating: 9 6   Highway Safety: 8 6   ★★★

Brand	Year	Type	Length	Model	Chassis	Engine	Fuel Type	Price/Linear Foot	Adjusted Wheelbase	Towing Capacity	GVWR	Curb Weight
Rolls Air	1997	MHA	36	3650	CH	7.4L	G	$2400	252 T	1,500	19,500	18,299

Livability Code: FT 30-90
Wheelbase-to-length ratio of 58% is considered ○ dangerous ○ fatiguing ○ good ● excellent *
The approximate net payload of 1201 pounds at 6% of GVWR on this model is ● deficient ○ excessive ○ cautionary ○ good ○ excellent *
Total highway safety penalties are: 16 *   Value: 7 8   Durability: 7 7   Highway Control Rating: 7 0   Highway Safety: 5 4   ★

Brand	Year	Type	Length	Model	Chassis	Engine	Fuel Type	Price/Linear Foot	Adjusted Wheelbase	Towing Capacity	GVWR	Curb Weight
Rolls Air	1997	MHA	36	3600	FO	7.5L	G	$2300	252 T	5,000	20,000	17,649

Livability Code: FT 30-90
Wheelbase-to-length ratio of 58% is considered ○ dangerous ○ fatiguing ○ good ● excellent *
The approximate net payload of 2351 pounds at 12% of GVWR on this model is ○ deficient ○ excessive ○ cautionary ● good ○ excellent *
Total highway safety penalties are: 4 *   Value: 8 4   Durability: 7 7   Highway Control Rating: 9 6   Highway Safety: 9 2   ★★★

Brand	Year	Type	Length	Model	Chassis	Engine	Fuel Type	Price/Linear Foot	Adjusted Wheelbase	Towing Capacity	GVWR	Curb Weight
Rolls Air	1997	MHA	36	3650	FO	7.5L	G	$2400	252 T	5,000	20,000	18,699

Livability Code: FT 30-90
Wheelbase-to-length ratio of 58% is considered ○ dangerous ○ fatiguing ○ good ● excellent *
The approximate net payload of 1301 pounds at 7% of GVWR on this model is ○ deficient ○ excessive ● cautionary ○ good ○ excellent *
Total highway safety penalties are: 11 *   Value: 8 0   Durability: 7 7   Highway Control Rating: 7 5   Highway Safety: 6 4   ★★

Brand	Year	Type	Length	Model	Chassis	Engine	Fuel Type	Price/Linear Foot	Adjusted Wheelbase	Towing Capacity	GVWR	Curb Weight
Rolls Air	1997	MHA	36	3500	FR	CU300	D	$3800	228	3,000	26,000	21,549

Livability Code: FT 30-90
Wheelbase-to-length ratio of 53% is considered ○ dangerous ● fatiguing ○ good ○ excellent *
The approximate net payload of 4451 pounds at 17% of GVWR on this model is ○ deficient ○ excessive ○ cautionary ○ good ● excellent *
Total highway safety penalties are: 2 *   Value: 8 5   Durability: 7 7   Highway Control Rating: 7 1   Highway Safety: 6 9   ★★

Brand	Year	Type	Length	Model	Chassis	Engine	Fuel Type	Price/Linear Foot	Adjusted Wheelbase	Towing Capacity	GVWR	Curb Weight
Rolls Air	1997	MHA	36	3550	FR	CU300	D	$4000	228	3,000	26,000	22,299

Livability Code: FT 30-90
Wheelbase-to-length ratio of 53% is considered ○ dangerous ● fatiguing ○ good ○ excellent *
The approximate net payload of 3701 pounds at 14% of GVWR on this model is ○ deficient ○ excessive ○ cautionary ● good ○ excellent *
Total highway safety penalties are: 7 *   Value: 8 3   Durability: 7 7   Highway Control Rating: 6 6   Highway Safety: 5 9   ★

Brand	Year	Type	Length	Model	Chassis	Engine	Fuel Type	Price/Linear Foot	Adjusted Wheelbase	Towing Capacity	GVWR	Curb Weight
Rolls Air	1997	MHA	36	3600	FR	CU300	D	$3900	228	3,000	26,000	21,549

Livability Code: FT 30-90
Wheelbase-to-length ratio of 53% is considered ○ dangerous ● fatiguing ○ good ○ excellent *
The approximate net payload of 4451 pounds at 17% of GVWR on this model is ○ deficient ○ excessive ○ cautionary ○ good ● excellent *
Total highway safety penalties are: 2 *   Value: 8 5   Durability: 7 7   Highway Control Rating: 7 1   Highway Safety: 6 9   ★★

Brand	Year	Type	Length	Model	Chassis	Engine	Fuel Type	Price/Linear Foot	Adjusted Wheelbase	Towing Capacity	GVWR	Curb Weight
Rolls Air	1997	MHA	36	3650	FR	CU300	D	$4000	228	3,000	26,000	22,599

Livability Code: FT 30-90
Wheelbase-to-length ratio of 53% is considered ○ dangerous ● fatiguing ○ good ○ excellent *
The approximate net payload of 3401 pounds at 13% of GVWR on this model is ○ deficient ○ excessive ○ cautionary ● good ○ excellent *
Total highway safety penalties are: 8 *   Value: 8 2   Durability: 7 7   Highway Control Rating: 6 4   Highway Safety: 5 6   ★

Brand	Year	Type	Length	Model	Chassis	Engine	Fuel Type	Price/Linear Foot	Adjusted Wheelbase	Towing Capacity	GVWR	Curb Weight
Rolls Air	1997	MHA	36	3500	SP	CU275	D	$3900	228	3,000	23,000	20,749

Livability Code: FT 30-90
Wheelbase-to-length ratio of 53% is considered ○ dangerous ● fatiguing ○ good ○ excellent *
The approximate net payload of 2251 pounds at 10% of GVWR on this model is ○ deficient ○ excessive ○ cautionary ● good ○ excellent *
Total highway safety penalties are: 2 *   Value: 8 5   Durability: 7 7   Highway Control Rating: 5 7   Highway Safety: 5 5   ★

Note: Safety ratings are based on the assumption that the engineering of the RV has allowed for proper balance by placing fresh, gray, and black holding tanks in a location so as not to change the balance of the RV when the tanks are empty or full. **Always double-check wheelbase, GVWR, and weights at front and rear axles.**

*See Section 1 for details on how conclusions are reached.

Section 2: The Ratings

Brand	Year	Type	Length	Model	Chassis	Engine	Fuel Type	Average Price per Linear Foot When New	Adjusted Wheelbase	Approx. Towing Capacity	Gross Vehicle Weight Rating	Average Curb Weight
Rolls Air	1997	MHA	36	3550	SP	CU275	D	$4000	228	3,000	23,000	21,499

Livability Code: FT 30-90   Wheelbase-to-length ratio of 53% is considered ○ dangerous ◉ fatiguing ○ good ○ excellent *

The approximate net payload of 1501 pounds at 7% of GVWR on this model is ○ deficient ○ excessive ◉ cautionary ○ good ○ excellent *

Total highway safety penalties are: 7 *   Value: 8 3   Durability: 7 7   Highway Control Rating: 4 0   Highway Safety: 3 3

Brand	Year	Type	Length	Model	Chassis	Engine	Fuel Type	Avg Price/Ft	Adj. Wheelbase	Tow Cap	GVWR	Curb Wt
Rolls Air	1997	MHA	36	3600	SP	CU275	D	$3900	228	3,000	23,000	20,749

Livability Code: FT 30-90   Wheelbase-to-length ratio of 53% is considered ○ dangerous ◉ fatiguing ○ good ○ excellent *

The approximate net payload of 2251 pounds at 10% of GVWR on this model is ○ deficient ○ excessive ○ cautionary ◉ good ○ excellent *

Total highway safety penalties are: 2 *   Value: 8 5   Durability: 7 7   Highway Control Rating: 5 7   Highway Safety: 5 5   ★

Rolls Air	1997	MHA	36	3650	SP	CU275	D	$3900	228	3,000	23,000	21,799

Livability Code: FT 30-90   Wheelbase-to-length ratio of 53% is considered ○ dangerous ◉ fatiguing ○ good ○ excellent *

The approximate net payload of 1201 pounds at 5% of GVWR on this model is ◉ deficient ○ excessive ○ cautionary ○ good ○ excellent *

Total highway safety penalties are: 8 *   Value: 8 2   Durability: 7 7   Highway Control Rating: 3 4   Highway Safety: 2 6

Rolls Air	1997	MHA	38	3800	FO	7.5L	G	$2300	252 T	5,000	20,000	18,329

Livability Code: FT 30-90   Wheelbase-to-length ratio of 55% is considered ○ dangerous ○ fatiguing ◉ good ○ excellent *

The approximate net payload of 1671 pounds at 8% of GVWR on this model is ○ deficient ○ excessive ◉ cautionary ○ good ○ excellent *

Total highway safety penalties are: 4 *   Value: 8 4   Durability: 7 7   Highway Control Rating: 6 9   Highway Safety: 6 5   ★★

Rose Air	1998	MHA	29	2800	CH	7.4L	G	$2700	190	3,500	16,500	14,249

Livability Code: FT 30-90   Wheelbase-to-length ratio of 55% is considered ○ dangerous ○ fatiguing ◉ good ○ excellent *

The approximate net payload of 2251 pounds at 14% of GVWR on this model is ○ deficient ○ excessive ○ cautionary ◉ good ○ excellent *

Total highway safety penalties are: 4 *   Value: 8 4   Durability: 7 7   Highway Control Rating: 8 7   Highway Safety: 8 3   ★★★

Rose Air	1998	MHA	29	2800	FO	7.5L	G	$2700	190	8,000	17,000	14,649

Livability Code: FT 30-90   Wheelbase-to-length ratio of 55% is considered ○ dangerous ○ fatiguing ◉ good ○ excellent *

The approximate net payload of 2351 pounds at 14% of GVWR on this model is ○ deficient ○ excessive ○ cautionary ◉ good ○ excellent *

Total highway safety penalties are: 2 *   Value: 8 5   Durability: 7 7   Highway Control Rating: 8 8   Highway Safety: 8 6   ★★★

Rose Air	1998	MHA	30	2900	CH	7.4L	G	$2600	208	3,500	16,500	14,663

Livability Code: FT 30-90   Wheelbase-to-length ratio of 57% is considered ○ dangerous ○ fatiguing ◉ good ○ excellent *

The approximate net payload of 1837 pounds at 11% of GVWR on this model is ○ deficient ○ excessive ○ cautionary ◉ good ○ excellent *

Total highway safety penalties are: 5 *   Value: 8 3   Durability: 7 7   Highway Control Rating: 9 1   Highway Safety: 8 6   ★★★

Rose Air	1998	MHA	30	2900	FO	7.5L	G	$2600	208	8,000	17,000	15,063

Livability Code: FT 30-90   Wheelbase-to-length ratio of 57% is considered ○ dangerous ○ fatiguing ◉ good ○ excellent *

The approximate net payload of 1937 pounds at 11% of GVWR on this model is ○ deficient ○ excessive ○ cautionary ◉ good ○ excellent *

Total highway safety penalties are: 2 *   Value: 8 5   Durability: 7 7   Highway Control Rating: 9 1   Highway Safety: 8 9   ★★★

Rose Air	1998	MHA	31	3000	CH	7.4L	G	$2500	208	3,500	16,500	14,899

Livability Code: FT 30-90   Wheelbase-to-length ratio of 56% is considered ○ dangerous ○ fatiguing ◉ good ○ excellent *

The approximate net payload of 1601 pounds at 10% of GVWR on this model is ○ deficient ○ excessive ○ cautionary ◉ good ○ excellent *

Total highway safety penalties are: 5 *   Value: 8 3   Durability: 7 7   Highway Control Rating: 8 9   Highway Safety: 8 4   ★★★

Rose Air	1998	MHA	31	3000	FO	7.5L	G	$2500	208	3,000	17,000	15,299

Livability Code: FT 30-90   Wheelbase-to-length ratio of 56% is considered ○ dangerous ○ fatiguing ◉ good ○ excellent *

The approximate net payload of 1701 pounds at 10% of GVWR on this model is ○ deficient ○ excessive ○ cautionary ◉ good ○ excellent *

Total highway safety penalties are: 2 *   Value: 8 5   Durability: 7 7   Highway Control Rating: 8 9   Highway Safety: 8 7   ★★★

Rose Air	1998	MHA	32	3100	CH	7.4L	G	$2500	208	3,500	16,500	15,166

Livability Code: FT 30-90   Wheelbase-to-length ratio of 54% is considered ○ dangerous ○ fatiguing ◉ good ○ excellent *

The approximate net payload of 1334 pounds at 8% of GVWR on this model is ○ deficient ○ excessive ◉ cautionary ○ good ○ excellent *

Total highway safety penalties are: 6 *   Value: 8 3   Durability: 7 7   Highway Control Rating: 5 9   Highway Safety: 5 3   ★

Rose Air	1998	MHA	32	3200	CH	7.4L	G	$2500	208	8,500	16,500	15,166

Livability Code: FT 30-90   Wheelbase-to-length ratio of 54% is considered ○ dangerous ○ fatiguing ◉ good ○ excellent *

The approximate net payload of 1334 pounds at 8% of GVWR on this model is ○ deficient ○ excessive ◉ cautionary ○ good ○ excellent *

Total highway safety penalties are: 6 *   Value: 8 3   Durability: 7 7   Highway Control Rating: 5 9   Highway Safety: 5 3   ★

Note: Safety ratings are based on the assumption that the engineering of the RV has allowed for proper balance by placing fresh, gray, and black holding tanks in a location so as not to change the balance of the RV when the tanks are empty or full. **Always double-check wheelbase, GVWR, and weights at front and rear axles.**

*See Section 1 for details on how conclusions are reached.

Section 2: The Ratings

Brand	Year	Type	Length	Model	Chassis	Engine	Fuel Type	Average Price per Linear Foot When New	Adjusted Wheelbase	Approx. Towing Capacity	Gross Vehicle Weight Rating	Average Curb Weight
Rose Air	1998	MHA	32	3250	CH	7.4L	G	$2700	208	8,500	16,500	16,066

Livability Code: FT 30-90
Wheelbase-to-length ratio of 54% is considered ○ dangerous ○ fatiguing ◉ good ○ excellent*
The approximate net payload of 434 pounds at 3% of GVWR on this model is ◉ deficient ○ excessive ○ cautionary ○ good ○ excellent*
Total highway safety penalties are: 11*   Value: **80**   Durability: **77**   Highway Control Rating: **44**   Highway Safety: **33**

Brand	Year	Type	Length	Model	Chassis	Engine	Fuel Type	Price/Linear Foot	Wheelbase	Towing Cap.	GVWR	Curb Weight
Rose Air	1998	MHA	32	3100	FO	7.5L	G	$2500	208	8,000	17,000	15,566

Livability Code: FT 30-90
Wheelbase-to-length ratio of 54% is considered ○ dangerous ○ fatiguing ◉ good ○ excellent*
The approximate net payload of 1434 pounds at 8% of GVWR on this model is ○ deficient ○ excessive ◉ cautionary ○ good ○ excellent*
Total highway safety penalties are: 2*   Value: **85**   Durability: **77**   Highway Control Rating: **60**   Highway Safety: **58**   ★

Brand	Year	Type	Length	Model	Chassis	Engine	Fuel Type	Price/Linear Foot	Wheelbase	Towing Cap.	GVWR	Curb Weight
Rose Air	1998	MHA	32	3200	FO	7.5L	G	$2500	208	3,000	17,000	15,566

Livability Code: FT 30-90
Wheelbase-to-length ratio of 54% is considered ○ dangerous ○ fatiguing ◉ good ○ excellent*
The approximate net payload of 1434 pounds at 8% of GVWR on this model is ○ deficient ○ excessive ◉ cautionary ○ good ○ excellent*
Total highway safety penalties are: 2*   Value: **85**   Durability: **77**   Highway Control Rating: **60**   Highway Safety: **58**   ★

Brand	Year	Type	Length	Model	Chassis	Engine	Fuel Type	Price/Linear Foot	Wheelbase	Towing Cap.	GVWR	Curb Weight
Rose Air	1998	MHA	32	3250	FO	7.5L	G	$2700	208	3,000	17,000	16,466

Livability Code: FT 30-90
Wheelbase-to-length ratio of 54% is considered ○ dangerous ○ fatiguing ◉ good ○ excellent*
The approximate net payload of 534 pounds at 3% of GVWR on this model is ◉ deficient ○ excessive ○ cautionary ○ good ○ excellent*
Total highway safety penalties are: 7*   Value: **82**   Durability: **77**   Highway Control Rating: **44**   Highway Safety: **37**

Brand	Year	Type	Length	Model	Chassis	Engine	Fuel Type	Price/Linear Foot	Wheelbase	Towing Cap.	GVWR	Curb Weight
Rose Air	1998	MHA	34	3300	CH	7.4L	G	$2400	228	3,500	16,500	15,609

Livability Code: FT 30-90
Wheelbase-to-length ratio of 57% is considered ○ dangerous ○ fatiguing ◉ good ○ excellent*
The approximate net payload of 891 pounds at 5% of GVWR on this model is ◉ deficient ○ excessive ○ cautionary ○ good ○ excellent*
Total highway safety penalties are: 6*   Value: **83**   Durability: **77**   Highway Control Rating: **63**   Highway Safety: **57**   ★

Brand	Year	Type	Length	Model	Chassis	Engine	Fuel Type	Price/Linear Foot	Wheelbase	Towing Cap.	GVWR	Curb Weight
Rose Air	1998	MHA	34	3400 opch	CH	7.4L	G	$2500	232 T	5,500	19,500	16,509

Livability Code: FT 30-90
Wheelbase-to-length ratio of 58% is considered ○ dangerous ○ fatiguing ○ good ◉ excellent*
The approximate net payload of 2991 pounds at 15% of GVWR on this model is ○ deficient ○ excessive ○ cautionary ◉ good ○ excellent*
Total highway safety penalties are: 9*   Value: **81**   Durability: **77**   Highway Control Rating: **100**   Highway Safety: **91**   ★★★

Brand	Year	Type	Length	Model	Chassis	Engine	Fuel Type	Price/Linear Foot	Wheelbase	Towing Cap.	GVWR	Curb Weight
Rose Air	1998	MHA	34	3400	CH	7.4L	G	$2400	208	8,500	16,500	15,609

Livability Code: FT 30-90
Wheelbase-to-length ratio of 52% is considered ○ dangerous ◉ fatiguing ○ good ○ excellent*
The approximate net payload of 891 pounds at 5% of GVWR on this model is ◉ deficient ○ excessive ○ cautionary ○ good ○ excellent*
Total highway safety penalties are: 6*   Value: **83**   Durability: **77**   Highway Control Rating: **23**   Highway Safety: **17**

Brand	Year	Type	Length	Model	Chassis	Engine	Fuel Type	Price/Linear Foot	Wheelbase	Towing Cap.	GVWR	Curb Weight
Rose Air	1998	MHA	34	3300	FO	7.5L	G	$2400	228	8,000	17,000	16,009

Livability Code: FT 30-90
Wheelbase-to-length ratio of 57% is considered ○ dangerous ○ fatiguing ◉ good ○ excellent*
The approximate net payload of 991 pounds at 6% of GVWR on this model is ◉ deficient ○ excessive ○ cautionary ○ good ○ excellent*
Total highway safety penalties are: 2*   Value: **85**   Durability: **77**   Highway Control Rating: **64**   Highway Safety: **62**   ★

Brand	Year	Type	Length	Model	Chassis	Engine	Fuel Type	Price/Linear Foot	Wheelbase	Towing Cap.	GVWR	Curb Weight
Rose Air	1998	MHA	34	3400 opch	FO	7.5L	G	$2500	232 T	5,000	20,000	16,909

Livability Code: FT 30-90
Wheelbase-to-length ratio of 58% is considered ○ dangerous ○ fatiguing ○ good ◉ excellent*
The approximate net payload of 3091 pounds at 15% of GVWR on this model is ○ deficient ○ excessive ○ cautionary ◉ good ○ excellent*
Total highway safety penalties are: 4*   Value: **84**   Durability: **77**   Highway Control Rating: **100**   Highway Safety: **96**   ★★★

Brand	Year	Type	Length	Model	Chassis	Engine	Fuel Type	Price/Linear Foot	Wheelbase	Towing Cap.	GVWR	Curb Weight
Rose Air	1998	MHA	34	3400	FO	7.5L	G	$2400	208	8,000	17,000	16,009

Livability Code: FT 30-90
Wheelbase-to-length ratio of 52% is considered ○ dangerous ◉ fatiguing ○ good ○ excellent*
The approximate net payload of 991 pounds at 6% of GVWR on this model is ◉ deficient ○ excessive ○ cautionary ○ good ○ excellent*
Total highway safety penalties are: 2*   Value: **85**   Durability: **77**   Highway Control Rating: **23**   Highway Safety: **21**

Brand	Year	Type	Length	Model	Chassis	Engine	Fuel Type	Price/Linear Foot	Wheelbase	Towing Cap.	GVWR	Curb Weight
Rose Air	1998	MHA	34	3400	SP	CU275	D	$4000	208	3,000	23,000	20,276

Livability Code: FT 30-90
Wheelbase-to-length ratio of 50% is considered ◉ dangerous ○ fatiguing ○ good ○ excellent*
The approximate net payload of 2724 pounds at 12% of GVWR on this model is ○ deficient ○ excessive ○ cautionary ◉ good ○ excellent*
Total highway safety penalties are: 2*   Value: **85**   Durability: **77**   Highway Control Rating: **38**   Highway Safety: **36**

Brand	Year	Type	Length	Model	Chassis	Engine	Fuel Type	Price/Linear Foot	Wheelbase	Towing Cap.	GVWR	Curb Weight
Rose Air	1998	MHA	34	3450	SP	CU275	D	$3900	208	1,500	23,000	21,176

Livability Code: FT 30-90
Wheelbase-to-length ratio of 50% is considered ◉ dangerous ○ fatiguing ○ good ○ excellent*
The approximate net payload of 1824 pounds at 8% of GVWR on this model is ○ deficient ○ excessive ◉ cautionary ○ good ○ excellent*
Total highway safety penalties are: 7*   Value: **82**   Durability: **77**   Highway Control Rating: **23**   Highway Safety: **16**

Note: Safety ratings are based on the assumption that the engineering of the RV has allowed for proper balance by placing fresh, gray, and black holding tanks in a location so as not to change the balance of the RV when the tanks are empty or full. **Always double-check wheelbase, GVWR, and weights at front and rear axles.**

*See Section 1 for details on how conclusions are reached.

Brand	Year	Type	Length	Model	Chassis	Engine	Fuel Type	Average Price per Linear Foot When New	Adjusted Wheelbase	Approx. Towing Capacity	Gross Vehicle Weight Rating	Average Curb Weight

Rose Air — 1998 — MHA — 34 — 3300 — SP — CU275 — D — $3900 — 208 — 1,500 — 23,000 — 20,408
Livability Code: FT 30-90
Wheelbase-to-length ratio of 50% is considered ◉ dangerous ○ fatiguing ○ good ○ excellent *
The approximate net payload of 2592 pounds at 11% of GVWR on this model is ○ deficient ○ excessive ○ cautionary ◉ good ○ excellent *
Total highway safety penalties are: 2 *   Value: 8 5   Durability: 7 7   Highway Control Rating: 3 6   Highway Safety: 3 4

Rose Air — 1998 — MHA — 35 — 3500 opch — CH — 7.4L — G — $2400 — 252 T — 1,500 — 19,500 — 17,042
Livability Code: FT 30-90
Wheelbase-to-length ratio of 59% is considered ○ dangerous ○ fatiguing ○ good ◉ excellent *
The approximate net payload of 2458 pounds at 13% of GVWR on this model is ○ deficient ○ excessive ○ cautionary ◉ good ○ excellent *
Total highway safety penalties are: 10 *   Value: 8 1   Durability: 7 7   Highway Control Rating: 1 0 0   Highway Safety: 9 0   ★★★

Rose Air — 1998 — MHA — 35 — 3550 opch — CH — 7.4L — G — $2500 — 252 T — 1,500 — 19,500 — 17,792
Livability Code: FT 30-90
Wheelbase-to-length ratio of 59% is considered ○ dangerous ○ fatiguing ○ good ◉ excellent *
The approximate net payload of 1708 pounds at 9% of GVWR on this model is ○ deficient ○ excessive ◉ cautionary ○ good ○ excellent *
Total highway safety penalties are: 14 *   Value: 7 9   Durability: 7 7   Highway Control Rating: 9 1   Highway Safety: 7 7   ★★★

Rose Air — 1998 — MHA — 35 — 3500 — CH — 7.4L — G — $2500 — 228 — 3,500 — 16,500 — 16,142
Livability Code: FT 30-90
Wheelbase-to-length ratio of 54% is considered ○ dangerous ○ fatiguing ◉ good ○ excellent *
The approximate net payload of 358 pounds at 2% of GVWR on this model is ◉ deficient ○ excessive ○ cautionary ○ good ○ excellent *
Total highway safety penalties are: 7 *   Value: 8 2   Durability: 7 7   Highway Control Rating: 4 2   Highway Safety: 3 5

Rose Air — 1998 — MHA — 35 — 3550 — CH — 7.4L — G — $2500 — 228 — 3,500 — 16,500 — 16,172
Livability Code: FT 30-90
Wheelbase-to-length ratio of 54% is considered ○ dangerous ○ fatiguing ◉ good ○ excellent *
The approximate net payload of 328 pounds at 2% of GVWR on this model is ◉ deficient ○ excessive ○ cautionary ○ good ○ excellent *
Total highway safety penalties are: 12 *   Value: 8 0   Durability: 7 7   Highway Control Rating: 4 2   Highway Safety: 3 0

Rose Air — 1998 — MHA — 35 — 3500 opch — FO — 7.5L — G — $2500 — 252 T — 5,000 — 20,000 — 17,442
Livability Code: FT 30-90
Wheelbase-to-length ratio of 59% is considered ○ dangerous ○ fatiguing ○ good ◉ excellent *
The approximate net payload of 2558 pounds at 13% of GVWR on this model is ○ deficient ○ excessive ○ cautionary ◉ good ○ excellent *
Total highway safety penalties are: 4 *   Value: 8 4   Durability: 7 7   Highway Control Rating: 1 0 0   Highway Safety: 9 6   ★★★

Rose Air — 1998 — MHA — 35 — 3550 opch — FO — 7.5L — G — $2500 — 252 T — 5,000 — 20,000 — 18,192
Livability Code: FT 30-90
Wheelbase-to-length ratio of 59% is considered ○ dangerous ○ fatiguing ○ good ◉ excellent *
The approximate net payload of 1808 pounds at 9% of GVWR on this model is ○ deficient ○ excessive ◉ cautionary ○ good ○ excellent *
Total highway safety penalties are: 9 *   Value: 8 1   Durability: 7 7   Highway Control Rating: 9 2   Highway Safety: 8 3   ★★★

Rose Air — 1998 — MHA — 35 — 3500 — FO — 7.5L — G — $2300 — 228 — 8,000 — 17,000 — 16,542
Livability Code: FT 30-90
Wheelbase-to-length ratio of 54% is considered ○ dangerous ○ fatiguing ◉ good ○ excellent *
The approximate net payload of 458 pounds at 3% of GVWR on this model is ◉ deficient ○ excessive ○ cautionary ○ good ○ excellent *
Total highway safety penalties are: 2 *   Value: 8 5   Durability: 7 7   Highway Control Rating: 4 3   Highway Safety: 4 1

Rose Air — 1998 — MHA — 35 — 3550 — FO — 7.5L — G — $2300 — 228 — 8,000 — 17,000 — 16,572
Livability Code: FT 30-90
Wheelbase-to-length ratio of 54% is considered ○ dangerous ○ fatiguing ◉ good ○ excellent *
The approximate net payload of 428 pounds at 3% of GVWR on this model is ◉ deficient ○ excessive ○ cautionary ○ good ○ excellent *
Total highway safety penalties are: 7 *   Value: 8 3   Durability: 7 7   Highway Control Rating: 4 3   Highway Safety: 3 6

Rose Air — 1998 — MHA — 36 — 3600 — CH — 7.4L — G — $2300 — 252 T — 1,500 — 19,500 — 17,249
Livability Code: FT 30-90
Wheelbase-to-length ratio of 58% is considered ○ dangerous ○ fatiguing ○ good ◉ excellent *
The approximate net payload of 2251 pounds at 12% of GVWR on this model is ○ deficient ○ excessive ○ cautionary ◉ good ○ excellent *
Total highway safety penalties are: 10 *   Value: 8 1   Durability: 7 7   Highway Control Rating: 9 6   Highway Safety: 8 6   ★★★

Rose Air — 1998 — MHA — 36 — 3650 — CH — 7.4L — G — $2400 — 252 T — 1,500 — 19,500 — 18,299
Livability Code: FT 30-90
Wheelbase-to-length ratio of 58% is considered ○ dangerous ○ fatiguing ○ good ◉ excellent *
The approximate net payload of 1201 pounds at 6% of GVWR on this model is ◉ deficient ○ excessive ○ cautionary ○ good ○ excellent *
Total highway safety penalties are: 16 *   Value: 7 8   Durability: 7 7   Highway Control Rating: 7 0   Highway Safety: 5 4   ★

Rose Air — 1998 — MHA — 36 — 3600 — FO — 7.5L — G — $2300 — 252 T — 5,000 — 20,000 — 17,649
Livability Code: FT 30-90
Wheelbase-to-length ratio of 58% is considered ○ dangerous ○ fatiguing ○ good ◉ excellent *
The approximate net payload of 2351 pounds at 12% of GVWR on this model is ○ deficient ○ excessive ○ cautionary ◉ good ○ excellent *
Total highway safety penalties are: 4 *   Value: 8 4   Durability: 7 7   Highway Control Rating: 9 6   Highway Safety: 9 2   ★★★

Note: Safety ratings are based on the assumption that the engineering of the RV has allowed for proper balance by placing fresh, gray, and black holding tanks in a location so as not to change the balance of the RV when the tanks are empty or full. **Always double-check wheelbase, GVWR, and weights at front and rear axles.**

*See Section 1 for details on how conclusions are reached.

Section 2: The Ratings

Brand	Year	Type	Length	Model	Chassis	Engine	Fuel Type	Average Price per Linear Foot When New	Adjusted Wheelbase	Approx. Towing Capacity	Gross Vehicle Weight Rating	Average Curb Weight
Rose Air	1998	MHA	36	3650	FO	7.5L	G	$2400	252 T	5,000	20,000	18,699

Livability Code: FT 30-90
Wheelbase-to-length ratio of 58% is considered ○ dangerous ○ fatiguing ○ good ● excellent *
The approximate net payload of 1301 pounds at 7% of GVWR on this model is ○ deficient ○ excessive ● cautionary ○ good ○ excellent *
Total highway safety penalties are: 11 *   Value: 8 0   Durability: 7 7   Highway Control Rating: 7 5   Highway Safety: 6 4   ★★

Brand	Year	Type	Length	Model	Chassis	Engine	Fuel Type	Price/LF	Wheelbase	Towing	GVWR	Curb Weight
Rose Air	1998	MHA	36	3500	FR	CU300	D	$3800	228	3,000	26,000	21,549

Livability Code: FT 30-90
Wheelbase-to-length ratio of 53% is considered ○ dangerous ● fatiguing ○ good ○ excellent *
The approximate net payload of 4451 pounds at 17% of GVWR on this model is ○ deficient ○ excessive ○ cautionary ○ good ● excellent *
Total highway safety penalties are: 2 *   Value: 8 5   Durability: 7 7   Highway Control Rating: 7 1   Highway Safety: 6 9   ★★

Rose Air	1998	MHA	36	3550	FR	CU300	D	$4000	228	3,000	26,000	22,299

Livability Code: FT 30-90
Wheelbase-to-length ratio of 53% is considered ○ dangerous ● fatiguing ○ good ○ excellent *
The approximate net payload of 3701 pounds at 14% of GVWR on this model is ○ deficient ○ excessive ○ cautionary ● good ○ excellent *
Total highway safety penalties are: 7 *   Value: 8 3   Durability: 7 7   Highway Control Rating: 6 6   Highway Safety: 5 9   ★

Rose Air	1998	MHA	36	3600	FR	CU300	D	$3900	228	3,000	26,000	21,549

Livability Code: FT 30-90
Wheelbase-to-length ratio of 53% is considered ○ dangerous ● fatiguing ○ good ○ excellent *
The approximate net payload of 4451 pounds at 17% of GVWR on this model is ○ deficient ○ excessive ○ cautionary ○ good ● excellent *
Total highway safety penalties are: 2 *   Value: 8 5   Durability: 7 7   Highway Control Rating: 7 1   Highway Safety: 6 9   ★★

Rose Air	1998	MHA	36	3650	FR	CU300	D	$4000	228	3,000	26,000	22,599

Livability Code: FT 30-90
Wheelbase-to-length ratio of 53% is considered ○ dangerous ● fatiguing ○ good ○ excellent *
The approximate net payload of 3401 pounds at 13% of GVWR on this model is ○ deficient ○ excessive ○ cautionary ● good ○ excellent *
Total highway safety penalties are: 8 *   Value: 8 2   Durability: 7 7   Highway Control Rating: 6 4   Highway Safety: 5 6   ★

Rose Air	1998	MHA	36	3500	SP	CU275	D	$3900	228	3,000	23,000	20,744

Livability Code: FT 30-90
Wheelbase-to-length ratio of 53% is considered ○ dangerous ● fatiguing ○ good ○ excellent *
The approximate net payload of 2256 pounds at 10% of GVWR on this model is ○ deficient ○ excessive ○ cautionary ● good ○ excellent *
Total highway safety penalties are: 2 *   Value: 8 5   Durability: 7 7   Highway Control Rating: 5 7   Highway Safety: 5 5   ★

Rose Air	1998	MHA	36	3550	SP	CU275	D	$4000	228	3,000	23,000	21,499

Livability Code: FT 30-90
Wheelbase-to-length ratio of 53% is considered ○ dangerous ● fatiguing ○ good ○ excellent *
The approximate net payload of 1501 pounds at 7% of GVWR on this model is ○ deficient ○ excessive ● cautionary ○ good ○ excellent *
Total highway safety penalties are: 7 *   Value: 8 3   Durability: 7 7   Highway Control Rating: 4 0   Highway Safety: 3 3

Rose Air	1998	MHA	36	3600	SP	CU275	D	$3900	228	3,000	23,000	20,749

Livability Code: FT 30-90
Wheelbase-to-length ratio of 53% is considered ○ dangerous ● fatiguing ○ good ○ excellent *
The approximate net payload of 2251 pounds at 10% of GVWR on this model is ○ deficient ○ excessive ○ cautionary ● good ○ excellent *
Total highway safety penalties are: 2 *   Value: 8 5   Durability: 7 7   Highway Control Rating: 5 7   Highway Safety: 5 5   ★

Rose Air	1998	MHA	36	3650	SP	CU275	D	$3900	228	3,000	23,000	21,799

Livability Code: FT 30-90
Wheelbase-to-length ratio of 53% is considered ○ dangerous ● fatiguing ○ good ○ excellent *
The approximate net payload of 1201 pounds at 5% of GVWR on this model is ● deficient ○ excessive ○ cautionary ○ good ○ excellent *
Total highway safety penalties are: 8 *   Value: 8 2   Durability: 7 7   Highway Control Rating: 3 4   Highway Safety: 2 6

Rose Air	1998	MHA	38	3800	FO	7.5L	G	$2400	252 T	5,000	20,000	18,329

Livability Code: FT 30-90
Wheelbase-to-length ratio of 55% is considered ○ dangerous ○ fatiguing ● good ○ excellent *
The approximate net payload of 1671 pounds at 8% of GVWR on this model is ○ deficient ○ excessive ● cautionary ○ good ○ excellent *
Total highway safety penalties are: 4 *   Value: 8 4   Durability: 7 7   Highway Control Rating: 6 9   Highway Safety: 6 5   ★★

Rose Air	1999	MHA	32	3100	FO	6.8L	G	$3100	208	8,000	18,000	16,433

Livability Code: FT 30-90
Wheelbase-to-length ratio of 54% is considered ○ dangerous ○ fatiguing ● good ○ excellent *
The approximate net payload of 1567 pounds at 9% of GVWR on this model is ○ deficient ○ excessive ● cautionary ○ good ○ excellent *
Total highway safety penalties are: 2 *   Value: 8 5   Durability: 7 7   Highway Control Rating: 6 7   Highway Safety: 6 5   ★★

Rose Air	1999	MHA	32	3250	FO	6.8L	G	$3100	208	8,000	18,000	17,053

Livability Code: FT 30-90
Wheelbase-to-length ratio of 54% is considered ○ dangerous ○ fatiguing ● good ○ excellent *
The approximate net payload of 947 pounds at 5% of GVWR on this model is ● deficient ○ excessive ○ cautionary ○ good ○ excellent *
Total highway safety penalties are: 7 *   Value: 8 2   Durability: 7 7   Highway Control Rating: 4 9   Highway Safety: 4 2

Note: Safety ratings are based on the assumption that the engineering of the RV has allowed for proper balance by placing fresh, gray, and black holding tanks in a location so as not to change the balance of the RV when the tanks are empty or full. **Always double-check wheelbase, GVWR, and weights at front and rear axles.**

*See Section 1 for details on how conclusions are reached.

Brand	Year	Type	Length	Model	Chassis	Engine	Fuel Type	Average Price per Linear Foot When New	Adjusted Wheelbase	Approx. Towing Capacity	Gross Vehicle Weight Rating	Average Curb Weight
Rose Air	1999	MHA	32	3250BSL	FO	6.8L	G	$3100	208	5,500	20,500	17,808

Livability Code: FT 30-90
Wheelbase-to-length ratio of 54% is considered ○ dangerous ○ fatiguing ◉ good ○ excellent *
The approximate net payload of 2692 pounds at 13% of GVWR on this model is ○ deficient ○ excessive ○ cautionary ◉ good ○ excellent *
Total highway safety penalties are: 10 * Value: 81 Durability: 77 Highway Control Rating: 79 Highway Safety: 69 ★★

Brand	Year	Type	Length	Model	Chassis	Engine	Fuel Type	Average Price per Linear Foot When New	Adjusted Wheelbase	Approx. Towing Capacity	Gross Vehicle Weight Rating	Average Curb Weight
Rose Air	1999	MHA	32	3250BSL opcap	FO	6.8L	G	$3100	208	5,500	20,500	18,068

Livability Code: FT 30-90
Wheelbase-to-length ratio of 54% is considered ○ dangerous ○ fatiguing ◉ good ○ excellent *
The approximate net payload of 2432 pounds at 12% of GVWR on this model is ○ deficient ○ excessive ○ cautionary ◉ good ○ excellent *
Total highway safety penalties are: 10 * Value: 81 Durability: 77 Highway Control Rating: 76 Highway Safety: 66 ★★

Brand	Year	Type	Length	Model	Chassis	Engine	Fuel Type	Average Price per Linear Foot When New	Adjusted Wheelbase	Approx. Towing Capacity	Gross Vehicle Weight Rating	Average Curb Weight
Rose Air	1999	MHA	32	3250 opch	FO	6.8L	G	$3100	208	5,500	20,500	17,303

Livability Code: FT 30-90
Wheelbase-to-length ratio of 54% is considered ○ dangerous ○ fatiguing ◉ good ○ excellent *
The approximate net payload of 3197 pounds at 16% of GVWR on this model is ○ deficient ○ excessive ○ cautionary ○ good ◉ excellent *
Total highway safety penalties are: 7 * Value: 82 Durability: 77 Highway Control Rating: 84 Highway Safety: 77 ★★★

Brand	Year	Type	Length	Model	Chassis	Engine	Fuel Type	Average Price per Linear Foot When New	Adjusted Wheelbase	Approx. Towing Capacity	Gross Vehicle Weight Rating	Average Curb Weight
Rose Air	1999	MHA	34	3300S	FO	6.8L	G	$2900	228	8,000	18,000	16,285

Livability Code: FT 30-90
Wheelbase-to-length ratio of 57% is considered ○ dangerous ○ fatiguing ◉ good ○ excellent *
The approximate net payload of 1715 pounds at 10% of GVWR on this model is ○ deficient ○ excessive ○ cautionary ◉ good ○ excellent *
Total highway safety penalties are: 2 * Value: 85 Durability: 77 Highway Control Rating: 86 Highway Safety: 84 ★★★

Brand	Year	Type	Length	Model	Chassis	Engine	Fuel Type	Average Price per Linear Foot When New	Adjusted Wheelbase	Approx. Towing Capacity	Gross Vehicle Weight Rating	Average Curb Weight
Rose Air	1999	MHA	34	3400	FO	6.8L	G	$2900	228	5,500	20,500	17,005

Livability Code: FT 30-90
Wheelbase-to-length ratio of 57% is considered ○ dangerous ○ fatiguing ◉ good ○ excellent *
The approximate net payload of 3495 pounds at 17% of GVWR on this model is ○ deficient ○ excessive ○ cautionary ○ good ◉ excellent *
Total highway safety penalties are: 2 * Value: 85 Durability: 77 Highway Control Rating: 100 Highway Safety: 98 ★★★

Brand	Year	Type	Length	Model	Chassis	Engine	Fuel Type	Average Price per Linear Foot When New	Adjusted Wheelbase	Approx. Towing Capacity	Gross Vehicle Weight Rating	Average Curb Weight
Rose Air	1999	MHA	35	3400	SP	CU8.3L	D	$3900	208	11,000	23,000	20,526

Livability Code: FT 30-90
Wheelbase-to-length ratio of 49% is considered ◉ dangerous ○ fatiguing ○ good ○ excellent *
The approximate net payload of 2474 pounds at 11% of GVWR on this model is ○ deficient ○ excessive ○ cautionary ◉ good ○ excellent *
Total highway safety penalties are: 2 * Value: 85 Durability: 77 Highway Control Rating: 42 Highway Safety: 40

Brand	Year	Type	Length	Model	Chassis	Engine	Fuel Type	Average Price per Linear Foot When New	Adjusted Wheelbase	Approx. Towing Capacity	Gross Vehicle Weight Rating	Average Curb Weight
Rose Air	1999	MHA	35	3450	SP	CU8.3L	D	$3900	208	11,000	23,000	21,106

Livability Code: FT 30-90
Wheelbase-to-length ratio of 49% is considered ◉ dangerous ○ fatiguing ○ good ○ excellent *
The approximate net payload of 1894 pounds at 8% of GVWR on this model is ○ deficient ○ excessive ◉ cautionary ○ good ○ excellent *
Total highway safety penalties are: 2 * Value: 85 Durability: 77 Highway Control Rating: 29 Highway Safety: 27

Brand	Year	Type	Length	Model	Chassis	Engine	Fuel Type	Average Price per Linear Foot When New	Adjusted Wheelbase	Approx. Towing Capacity	Gross Vehicle Weight Rating	Average Curb Weight
Rose Air	1999	MHA	35	3500	FO	6.8L	G	$2900	242	5,500	20,500	17,296

Livability Code: FT 30-90
Wheelbase-to-length ratio of 57% is considered ○ dangerous ○ fatiguing ◉ good ○ excellent *
The approximate net payload of 3204 pounds at 16% of GVWR on this model is ○ deficient ○ excessive ○ cautionary ○ good ◉ excellent *
Total highway safety penalties are: 2 * Value: 85 Durability: 77 Highway Control Rating: 100 Highway Safety: 98 ★★★

Brand	Year	Type	Length	Model	Chassis	Engine	Fuel Type	Average Price per Linear Foot When New	Adjusted Wheelbase	Approx. Towing Capacity	Gross Vehicle Weight Rating	Average Curb Weight
Rose Air	1999	MHA	35	3550BSL	FO	6.8L	G	$2900	242	5,500	20,500	18,666

Livability Code: FT 30-90
Wheelbase-to-length ratio of 57% is considered ○ dangerous ○ fatiguing ◉ good ○ excellent *
The approximate net payload of 1834 pounds at 9% of GVWR on this model is ○ deficient ○ excessive ◉ cautionary ○ good ○ excellent *
Total highway safety penalties are: 10 * Value: 81 Durability: 77 Highway Control Rating: 83 Highway Safety: 73 ★★★

Brand	Year	Type	Length	Model	Chassis	Engine	Fuel Type	Average Price per Linear Foot When New	Adjusted Wheelbase	Approx. Towing Capacity	Gross Vehicle Weight Rating	Average Curb Weight
Rose Air	1999	MHA	35	3550BSL opcap	FO	6.8L	G	$2900	242	5,500	20,500	18,856

Livability Code: FT 30-90
Wheelbase-to-length ratio of 57% is considered ○ dangerous ○ fatiguing ◉ good ○ excellent *
The approximate net payload of 1644 pounds at 8% of GVWR on this model is ○ deficient ○ excessive ◉ cautionary ○ good ○ excellent *
Total highway safety penalties are: 10 * Value: 81 Durability: 77 Highway Control Rating: 77 Highway Safety: 67 ★★

Brand	Year	Type	Length	Model	Chassis	Engine	Fuel Type	Average Price per Linear Foot When New	Adjusted Wheelbase	Approx. Towing Capacity	Gross Vehicle Weight Rating	Average Curb Weight
Rose Air	1999	MHA	35	3550-D	FO	6.8L	G	$2900	242	5,500	20,500	17,966

Livability Code: FT 30-90
Wheelbase-to-length ratio of 57% is considered ○ dangerous ○ fatiguing ◉ good ○ excellent *
The approximate net payload of 2534 pounds at 12% of GVWR on this model is ○ deficient ○ excessive ○ cautionary ◉ good ○ excellent *
Total highway safety penalties are: 7 * Value: 83 Durability: 77 Highway Control Rating: 93 Highway Safety: 86 ★★★

Brand	Year	Type	Length	Model	Chassis	Engine	Fuel Type	Average Price per Linear Foot When New	Adjusted Wheelbase	Approx. Towing Capacity	Gross Vehicle Weight Rating	Average Curb Weight
Rose Air	1999	MHA	36	3450GT	FO	6.8L	G	$2800	228	5,500	20,500	18,160

Livability Code: FT 30-90
Wheelbase-to-length ratio of 54% is considered ○ dangerous ○ fatiguing ◉ good ○ excellent *
The approximate net payload of 2340 pounds at 11% of GVWR on this model is ○ deficient ○ excessive ○ cautionary ◉ good ○ excellent *
Total highway safety penalties are: 12 * Value: 80 Durability: 77 Highway Control Rating: 78 Highway Safety: 66 ★★

Note: Safety ratings are based on the assumption that the engineering of the RV has allowed for proper balance by placing fresh, gray, and black holding tanks in a location so as not to change the balance of the RV when the tanks are empty or full. **Always double-check wheelbase, GVWR, and weights at front and rear axles.**

*See Section 1 for details on how conclusions are reached.

Brand	Year	Type	Length	Model	Chassis	Engine	Fuel Type	Average Price per Linear Foot When New	Adjusted Wheelbase	Approx. Towing Capacity	Gross Vehicle Weight Rating	Average Curb Weight
Rose Air	**1999**	MHA	36	3650-BSL	FO	6.8L	G	$2800	242	5,500	20,500	19,049

Livability Code: FT 30-90   Wheelbase-to-length ratio of 56% is considered ○ dangerous ○ fatiguing ◉ good ○ excellent *

The approximate net payload of 1451 pounds at 7% of GVWR on this model is ○ deficient ○ excessive ◉ cautionary ○ good ○ excellent *

Total highway safety penalties are: 10 *   Value: **8 1**   Durability: **7 7**   Highway Control Rating: **6 7**   Highway Safety: **5 7**   ★

Brand	Year	Type	Length	Model	Chassis	Engine	Fuel Type	Price	Wheelbase	Towing	GVWR	Curb Weight
Rose Air	**1999**	MHA	36	3650BSL	FO	6.8L	G	$2800	242	5,500	20,500	19,089

Livability Code: FT 30-90   Wheelbase-to-length ratio of 56% is considered ○ dangerous ○ fatiguing ◉ good ○ excellent *

The approximate net payload of 1411 pounds at 7% of GVWR on this model is ○ deficient ○ excessive ◉ cautionary ○ good ○ excellent *

Total highway safety penalties are: 10 *   Value: **8 1**   Durability: **7 7**   Highway Control Rating: **6 7**   Highway Safety: **5 7**   ★

Brand	Year	Type	Length	Model	Chassis	Engine	Fuel Type	Price	Wheelbase	Towing	GVWR	Curb Weight
Rose Air	**1999**	MHA	36	3650LG	FO	6.8L	G	$2800	242	5,500	20,500	18,374

Livability Code: FT 30-90   Wheelbase-to-length ratio of 56% is considered ○ dangerous ○ fatiguing ◉ good ○ excellent *

The approximate net payload of 2126 pounds at 10% of GVWR on this model is ○ deficient ○ excessive ○ cautionary ◉ good ○ excellent *

Total highway safety penalties are: 12 *   Value: **8 0**   Durability: **7 7**   Highway Control Rating: **8 5**   Highway Safety: **7 3**   ★★★

Brand	Year	Type	Length	Model	Chassis	Engine	Fuel Type	Price	Wheelbase	Towing	GVWR	Curb Weight
Rose Air	**1999**	MHA	36	3650-GT	FO	6.8L	G	$2800	242	5,500	20,500	18,314

Livability Code: FT 30-90   Wheelbase-to-length ratio of 56% is considered ○ dangerous ○ fatiguing ◉ good ○ excellent *

The approximate net payload of 2186 pounds at 11% of GVWR on this model is ○ deficient ○ excessive ○ cautionary ◉ good ○ excellent *

Total highway safety penalties are: 12 *   Value: **8 0**   Durability: **7 7**   Highway Control Rating: **8 6**   Highway Safety: **7 4**   ★★★

Brand	Year	Type	Length	Model	Chassis	Engine	Fuel Type	Price	Wheelbase	Towing	GVWR	Curb Weight
Rose Air	**1999**	MHA	37	3500	SP	CU8.3L	D	$3600	228	11,000	23,000	20,892

Livability Code: FT 30-90   Wheelbase-to-length ratio of 51% is considered ○ dangerous ◉ fatiguing ○ good ○ excellent *

The approximate net payload of 2108 pounds at 9% of GVWR on this model is ○ deficient ○ excessive ◉ cautionary ○ good ○ excellent *

Total highway safety penalties are: 2 *   Value: **8 5**   Durability: **7 7**   Highway Control Rating: **4 3**   Highway Safety: **4 1**

Brand	Year	Type	Length	Model	Chassis	Engine	Fuel Type	Price	Wheelbase	Towing	GVWR	Curb Weight
Rose Air	**1999**	MHA	37	3550D	SP	CU8.3L	D	$3600	228	10,000	24,000	21,917

Livability Code: FT 30-90   Wheelbase-to-length ratio of 51% is considered ○ dangerous ◉ fatiguing ○ good ○ excellent *

The approximate net payload of 2083 pounds at 9% of GVWR on this model is ○ deficient ○ excessive ◉ cautionary ○ good ○ excellent *

Total highway safety penalties are: 7 *   Value: **8 3**   Durability: **7 7**   Highway Control Rating: **4 2**   Highway Safety: **3 5**

Brand	Year	Type	Length	Model	Chassis	Engine	Fuel Type	Price	Wheelbase	Towing	GVWR	Curb Weight
Rose Air	**1999**	MHA	37	3550D opcap	SP	CU8.3L	D	$3600	228	10,000	24,000	22,237

Livability Code: FT 30-90   Wheelbase-to-length ratio of 51% is considered ○ dangerous ◉ fatiguing ○ good ○ excellent *

The approximate net payload of 1763 pounds at 7% of GVWR on this model is ○ deficient ○ excessive ◉ cautionary ○ good ○ excellent *

Total highway safety penalties are: 7 *   Value: **8 3**   Durability: **7 7**   Highway Control Rating: **3 1**   Highway Safety: **2 4**

Brand	Year	Type	Length	Model	Chassis	Engine	Fuel Type	Price	Wheelbase	Towing	GVWR	Curb Weight
Rose Air	**1999**	MHA	37	3650	SP	CU8.3L	D	$3600	228	10,000	24,000	22,187

Livability Code: FT 30-90   Wheelbase-to-length ratio of 51% is considered ○ dangerous ◉ fatiguing ○ good ○ excellent *

The approximate net payload of 1813 pounds at 8% of GVWR on this model is ○ deficient ○ excessive ◉ cautionary ○ good ○ excellent *

Total highway safety penalties are: 8 *   Value: **8 2**   Durability: **7 7**   Highway Control Rating: **3 6**   Highway Safety: **2 8**

Brand	Year	Type	Length	Model	Chassis	Engine	Fuel Type	Price	Wheelbase	Towing	GVWR	Curb Weight
Rose Air	**1999**	MHA	37	3650GT	SP	CU8.3L	D	$3600	228	10,000	24,000	22,012

Livability Code: FT 30-90   Wheelbase-to-length ratio of 51% is considered ○ dangerous ◉ fatiguing ○ good ○ excellent *

The approximate net payload of 1988 pounds at 8% of GVWR on this model is ○ deficient ○ excessive ◉ cautionary ○ good ○ excellent *

Total highway safety penalties are: 12 *   Value: **8 0**   Durability: **7 7**   Highway Control Rating: **3 7**   Highway Safety: **2 5**

Brand	Year	Type	Length	Model	Chassis	Engine	Fuel Type	Price	Wheelbase	Towing	GVWR	Curb Weight
Royal Classic	**1998**	MHC	30	30RBSS	FO	6.8L	G	$3000	214	1,500	14,050	13,402

Livability Code: VA 30-90   Wheelbase-to-length ratio of 60% is considered ○ dangerous ○ fatiguing ○ good ◉ excellent *

The approximate net payload of 648 pounds at 5% of GVWR on this model is ◉ deficient ○ excessive ○ cautionary ○ good ○ excellent *

Total highway safety penalties are: 8 *   Value: **7 6**   Durability: **7 5**   Highway Control Rating: **7 4**   Highway Safety: **6 6**   ★

Brand	Year	Type	Length	Model	Chassis	Engine	Fuel Type	Price	Wheelbase	Towing	GVWR	Curb Weight
Royal Classic	**1998**	MHC	32	310RC	FO	6.8L	G	$2800	214	1,500	14,050	12,856

Livability Code: VA 30-90   Wheelbase-to-length ratio of 56% is considered ○ dangerous ○ fatiguing ◉ good ○ excellent *

The approximate net payload of 1194 pounds at 8% of GVWR on this model is ○ deficient ○ excessive ◉ cautionary ○ good ○ excellent *

Total highway safety penalties are: 2 *   Value: **7 9**   Durability: **7 5**   Highway Control Rating: **7 3**   Highway Safety: **7 1**   ★★★

Brand	Year	Type	Length	Model	Chassis	Engine	Fuel Type	Price	Wheelbase	Towing	GVWR	Curb Weight
Royal Classic	**1999**	MHC	30	30RBSS	FO	6.8L	G	$3000	214	1,500	14,050	13,402

Livability Code: VA 30-90   Wheelbase-to-length ratio of 60% is considered ○ dangerous ○ fatiguing ○ good ◉ excellent *

The approximate net payload of 648 pounds at 5% of GVWR on this model is ◉ deficient ○ excessive ○ cautionary ○ good ○ excellent *

Total highway safety penalties are: 8 *   Value: **7 6**   Durability: **7 5**   Highway Control Rating: **7 4**   Highway Safety: **6 6**   ★

Note: Safety ratings are based on the assumption that the engineering of the RV has allowed for proper balance by placing fresh, gray, and black holding tanks in a location so as not to change the balance of the RV when the tanks are empty or full. **Always double-check wheelbase, GVWR, and weights at front and rear axles.**

*See Section 1 for details on how conclusions are reached.

Section 2: The Ratings

Brand	Year	Type	Length	Model	Chassis	Engine	Fuel Type	Average Price per Linear Foot When New	Adjusted Wheelbase	Approx. Towing Capacity	Gross Vehicle Weight Rating	Average Curb Weight
Royal Classic	1999	MHC	32	310RC	FO	6.8L	G	$2800	214	1,500	14,050	12,856

Livability Code: VA 30-90 — Wheelbase-to-length ratio of 56% is considered ○ dangerous ○ fatiguing ● good ○ excellent*

The approximate net payload of 1194 pounds at 8% of GVWR on this model is ○ deficient ○ excessive ● cautionary ○ good ○ excellent*

Total highway safety penalties are: 2* — Value: 79 Durability: 75 Highway Control Rating: 73 Highway Safety: 71 ★★★

| Safari | 1999 | MHC | 24 | 2400 | CH | 7.4L | G | $2900 | 179 | 6,700 | 12,300 | 10,948 |

Livability Code: SB 30-90 — Wheelbase-to-length ratio of 62% is considered ○ dangerous ○ fatiguing ○ good ● excellent*

The approximate net payload of 1352 pounds at 11% of GVWR on this model is ○ deficient ○ excessive ○ cautionary ● good ○ excellent*

Total highway safety penalties are: 2* — Value: 79 Durability: 75 Highway Control Rating: 100 Highway Safety: 98 ★★★

| Safari | 1999 | MHC | 24 | 2400 | FO | 6.8L | G | $2900 | 178 | 5,950 | 14,050 | 11,148 |

Livability Code: SB 30-90 — Wheelbase-to-length ratio of 62% is considered ○ dangerous ○ fatiguing ○ good ● excellent*

The approximate net payload of 2902 pounds at 21% of GVWR on this model is ○ deficient ○ excessive ○ cautionary ○ good ● excellent*

Total highway safety penalties are: 2* — Value: 79 Durability: 75 Highway Control Rating: 100 Highway Safety: 98 ★★★

| Safari | 1999 | MHC | 24 | 2400 op eng | FO | 7.3L | D | $2900 | 178 | 5,950 | 14,050 | 11,578 |

Livability Code: SB 30-90 — Wheelbase-to-length ratio of 62% is considered ○ dangerous ○ fatiguing ○ good ● excellent*

The approximate net payload of 2472 pounds at 18% of GVWR on this model is ○ deficient ○ excessive ○ cautionary ○ good ● excellent*

Total highway safety penalties are: 2* — Value: 79 Durability: 75 Highway Control Rating: 100 Highway Safety: 98 ★★★

| Safari | 1999 | MHC | 26 | 2620 | CH | 7.4L | G | $2700 | 179 | 6,700 | 12,300 | 11,868 |

Livability Code: SB 30-90 — Wheelbase-to-length ratio of 57% is considered ○ dangerous ○ fatiguing ● good ○ excellent*

The approximate net payload of 432 pounds at 4% of GVWR on this model is ● deficient ○ excessive ○ cautionary ○ good ○ excellent*

Total highway safety penalties are: 2* — Value: 79 Durability: 75 Highway Control Rating: 64 Highway Safety: 62 ★

| Safari | 1999 | MHC | 26 | 2620 | FO | 6.8L | G | $2700 | 178 | 5,950 | 14,050 | 12,268 |

Livability Code: SB 30-90 — Wheelbase-to-length ratio of 57% is considered ○ dangerous ○ fatiguing ● good ○ excellent*

The approximate net payload of 1782 pounds at 13% of GVWR on this model is ○ deficient ○ excessive ○ cautionary ● good ○ excellent*

Total highway safety penalties are: 2* — Value: 79 Durability: 75 Highway Control Rating: 94 Highway Safety: 92 ★★★

| Safari | 1999 | MHC | 26 | 2620 op eng | FO | 7.3L | D | $2700 | 178 | 5,950 | 14,050 | 12,698 |

Livability Code: SB 30-90 — Wheelbase-to-length ratio of 57% is considered ○ dangerous ○ fatiguing ● good ○ excellent*

The approximate net payload of 1352 pounds at 10% of GVWR on this model is ○ deficient ○ excessive ○ cautionary ● good ○ excellent*

Total highway safety penalties are: 2* — Value: 79 Durability: 75 Highway Control Rating: 88 Highway Safety: 86 ★★★

| Safari | 1999 | MHC | 30 | 3000 | CH | 7.4L | G | $2300 | 197 | 6,700 | 12,300 | 12,108 |

Livability Code: SB 30-90 — Wheelbase-to-length ratio of 55% is considered ○ dangerous ○ fatiguing ● good ○ excellent*

The approximate net payload of 192 pounds at 2% of GVWR on this model is ● deficient ○ excessive ○ cautionary ○ good ○ excellent*

Total highway safety penalties are: 2* — Value: 79 Durability: 75 Highway Control Rating: 52 Highway Safety: 50 ★

| Safari | 1999 | MHC | 30 | 3010 | CH | 7.4L | G | $2300 | 197 | 6,700 | 12,300 | 12,183 |

Livability Code: SB 30-90 — Wheelbase-to-length ratio of 55% is considered ○ dangerous ○ fatiguing ● good ○ excellent*

The approximate net payload of 117 pounds at 1% of GVWR on this model is ● deficient ○ excessive ○ cautionary ○ good ○ excellent*

Total highway safety penalties are: 2* — Value: 79 Durability: 75 Highway Control Rating: 52 Highway Safety: 50 ★

| Safari | 1999 | MHC | 30 | 3000 | FO | 6.8L | G | $2300 | 196 | 5,950 | 14,050 | 12,508 |

Livability Code: SB 30-90 — Wheelbase-to-length ratio of 54% is considered ○ dangerous ○ fatiguing ● good ○ excellent*

The approximate net payload of 1542 pounds at 11% of GVWR on this model is ○ deficient ○ excessive ○ cautionary ● good ○ excellent*

Total highway safety penalties are: 2* — Value: 79 Durability: 75 Highway Control Rating: 77 Highway Safety: 75 ★★★

| Safari | 1999 | MHC | 30 | 3010 | FO | 6.8L | G | $2300 | 196 | 5,950 | 14,050 | 12,658 |

Livability Code: SB 30-90 — Wheelbase-to-length ratio of 54% is considered ○ dangerous ○ fatiguing ● good ○ excellent*

The approximate net payload of 1392 pounds at 10% of GVWR on this model is ○ deficient ○ excessive ○ cautionary ● good ○ excellent*

Total highway safety penalties are: 2* — Value: 79 Durability: 75 Highway Control Rating: 75 Highway Safety: 73 ★★★

| Safari | 1999 | MHC | 30 | 3000 op eng | FO | 7.3L | D | $2300 | 196 | 5,950 | 14,050 | 12,938 |

Livability Code: SB 30-90 — Wheelbase-to-length ratio of 54% is considered ○ dangerous ○ fatiguing ● good ○ excellent*

The approximate net payload of 1112 pounds at 8% of GVWR on this model is ○ deficient ○ excessive ● cautionary ○ good ○ excellent*

Total highway safety penalties are: 2* — Value: 79 Durability: 75 Highway Control Rating: 64 Highway Safety: 62 ★★

Note: Safety ratings are based on the assumption that the engineering of the RV has allowed for proper balance by placing fresh, gray, and black holding tanks in a location so as not to change the balance of the RV when the tanks are empty or full. **Always double-check wheelbase, GVWR, and weights at front and rear axles.**

*See Section 1 for details on how conclusions are reached.

Section 2: The Ratings

Brand	Year	Type	Length	Model	Chassis	Engine	Fuel Type	Average Price per Linear Foot When New	Adjusted Wheelbase	Approx. Towing Capacity	Gross Vehicle Weight Rating	Average Curb Weight
Safari	1999	MHC	30	3010 op eng	FO	7.3L	D	$2300	196	5,950	14,050	13,088

Livability Code: SB 30-90
Wheelbase-to-length ratio of 54% is considered ○ dangerous ○ fatiguing ● good ○ excellent *
The approximate net payload of 962 pounds at 7% of GVWR on this model is ○ deficient ○ excessive ● cautionary ○ good ○ excellent *
Total highway safety penalties are: 2 *   Value: 79   Durability: 75   Highway Control Rating: 58   Highway Safety: 56   ★

Brand	Year	Type	Length	Model	Chassis	Engine	Fuel Type	Price/Ft	Wheelbase	Towing	GVWR	Curb Wt
Safari	1999	MHC	31	3100	FO	6.8L	G	$2300	196	5,950	14,050	13,368

Livability Code: SB 30-90
Wheelbase-to-length ratio of 53% is considered ○ dangerous ● fatiguing ○ good ○ excellent *
The approximate net payload of 682 pounds at 5% of GVWR on this model is ● deficient ○ excessive ○ cautionary ○ good ○ excellent *
Total highway safety penalties are: 12 *   Value: 74   Durability: 75   Highway Control Rating: 41   Highway Safety: 29

Brand	Year	Type	Length	Model	Chassis	Engine	Fuel Type	Price/Ft	Wheelbase	Towing	GVWR	Curb Wt
Safari	1999	MHC	31	3100 op eng	FO	7.3L	D	$2300	196	5,950	14,050	13,798

Livability Code: SB 30-90
Wheelbase-to-length ratio of 53% is considered ○ dangerous ● fatiguing ○ good ○ excellent *
The approximate net payload of 252 pounds at 2% of GVWR on this model is ● deficient ○ excessive ○ cautionary ○ good ○ excellent *
Total highway safety penalties are: 12 *   Value: 74   Durability: 75   Highway Control Rating: 38   Highway Safety: 26

Brand	Year	Type	Length	Model	Chassis	Engine	Fuel Type	Price/Ft	Wheelbase	Towing	GVWR	Curb Wt
Sahara	1995	MHA	31	3044	MA	Cu5.9L	D	$3800	178	4,000	22,500	19,364

Livability Code: SB 30-90
Wheelbase-to-length ratio of 48% is considered ● dangerous ○ fatiguing ○ good ○ excellent *
The approximate net payload of 3136 pounds at 14% of GVWR on this model is ○ deficient ○ excessive ○ cautionary ● good ○ excellent *
Total highway safety penalties are: 2 *   Value: 73   Durability: 72   Highway Control Rating: 34   Highway Safety: 32

Brand	Year	Type	Length	Model	Chassis	Engine	Fuel Type	Price/Ft	Wheelbase	Towing	GVWR	Curb Wt
Sahara	1995	MHA	34	3334	MA	Cu5.9L	D	$3600	208	4,000	22,500	20,014

Livability Code: SB 30-90
Wheelbase-to-length ratio of 51% is considered ○ dangerous ● fatiguing ○ good ○ excellent *
The approximate net payload of 2486 pounds at 11% of GVWR on this model is ○ deficient ○ excessive ○ cautionary ● good ○ excellent *
Total highway safety penalties are: 2 *   Value: 73   Durability: 72   Highway Control Rating: 40   Highway Safety: 38

Brand	Year	Type	Length	Model	Chassis	Engine	Fuel Type	Price/Ft	Wheelbase	Towing	GVWR	Curb Wt
Sahara	1995	MHA	34	3354	MA	Cu5.9L	D	$3600	208	4,000	22,500	20,014

Livability Code: SB 30-90
Wheelbase-to-length ratio of 51% is considered ○ dangerous ● fatiguing ○ good ○ excellent *
The approximate net payload of 2486 pounds at 11% of GVWR on this model is ○ deficient ○ excessive ○ cautionary ● good ○ excellent *
Total highway safety penalties are: 2 *   Value: 73   Durability: 72   Highway Control Rating: 40   Highway Safety: 38

Brand	Year	Type	Length	Model	Chassis	Engine	Fuel Type	Price/Ft	Wheelbase	Towing	GVWR	Curb Wt
Sahara	1995	MHA	34	3390	MA	Cu5.9L	D	$3600	208	4,000	22,500	20,014

Livability Code: SB 30-90
Wheelbase-to-length ratio of 51% is considered ○ dangerous ● fatiguing ○ good ○ excellent *
The approximate net payload of 2486 pounds at 11% of GVWR on this model is ○ deficient ○ excessive ○ cautionary ● good ○ excellent *
Total highway safety penalties are: 2 *   Value: 73   Durability: 72   Highway Control Rating: 40   Highway Safety: 38

Brand	Year	Type	Length	Model	Chassis	Engine	Fuel Type	Price/Ft	Wheelbase	Towing	GVWR	Curb Wt
Sahara	1995	MHA	36	3530	MA	Cu5.9L	D	$3500	228	4,000	22,500	20,521

Livability Code: SB 30-90
Wheelbase-to-length ratio of 54% is considered ○ dangerous ○ fatiguing ● good ○ excellent *
The approximate net payload of 1979 pounds at 9% of GVWR on this model is ○ deficient ○ excessive ● cautionary ○ good ○ excellent *
Total highway safety penalties are: 2 *   Value: 73   Durability: 72   Highway Control Rating: 63   Highway Safety: 61   ★★

Brand	Year	Type	Length	Model	Chassis	Engine	Fuel Type	Price/Ft	Wheelbase	Towing	GVWR	Curb Wt
Sahara	1995	MHA	36	3550	MA	Cu5.9L	D	$3500	228	4,000	22,500	20,521

Livability Code: SB 30-90
Wheelbase-to-length ratio of 54% is considered ○ dangerous ○ fatiguing ● good ○ excellent *
The approximate net payload of 1979 pounds at 9% of GVWR on this model is ○ deficient ○ excessive ● cautionary ○ good ○ excellent *
Total highway safety penalties are: 2 *   Value: 73   Durability: 72   Highway Control Rating: 63   Highway Safety: 61   ★★

Brand	Year	Type	Length	Model	Chassis	Engine	Fuel Type	Price/Ft	Wheelbase	Towing	GVWR	Curb Wt
Sahara	1995	MHA	36	3560	MA	Cu5.9L	D	$3500	228	4,000	22,500	20,521

Livability Code: SB 30-90
Wheelbase-to-length ratio of 54% is considered ○ dangerous ○ fatiguing ● good ○ excellent *
The approximate net payload of 1979 pounds at 9% of GVWR on this model is ○ deficient ○ excessive ● cautionary ○ good ○ excellent *
Total highway safety penalties are: 2 *   Value: 73   Durability: 72   Highway Control Rating: 63   Highway Safety: 61   ★★

Brand	Year	Type	Length	Model	Chassis	Engine	Fuel Type	Price/Ft	Wheelbase	Towing	GVWR	Curb Wt
Sahara	1996	MHA	30	3044	MA	Ca250	D	$4100	178	4,000	24,000	20,262

Livability Code: SB 30-90
Wheelbase-to-length ratio of 49% is considered ● dangerous ○ fatiguing ○ good ○ excellent *
The approximate net payload of 3738 pounds at 16% of GVWR on this model is ○ deficient ○ excessive ○ cautionary ○ good ● excellent *
Total highway safety penalties are: 2 *   Value: 73   Durability: 72   Highway Control Rating: 42   Highway Safety: 40

Brand	Year	Type	Length	Model	Chassis	Engine	Fuel Type	Price/Ft	Wheelbase	Towing	GVWR	Curb Wt
Sahara	1996	MHA	34	3334	MA	Ca250	D	$3700	208	4,000	24,000	21,281

Livability Code: SB 30-90
Wheelbase-to-length ratio of 51% is considered ○ dangerous ● fatiguing ○ good ○ excellent *
The approximate net payload of 2719 pounds at 11% of GVWR on this model is ○ deficient ○ excessive ○ cautionary ● good ○ excellent *
Total highway safety penalties are: 2 *   Value: 73   Durability: 72   Highway Control Rating: 40   Highway Safety: 38

Note: Safety ratings are based on the assumption that the engineering of the RV has allowed for proper balance by placing fresh, gray, and black holding tanks in a location so as not to change the balance of the RV when the tanks are empty or full. **Always double-check wheelbase, GVWR, and weights at front and rear axles.**

*See Section 1 for details on how conclusions are reached.

Section 2: The Ratings

Brand	Year	Type	Length	Model	Chassis	Engine	Fuel Type	Average Price per Linear Foot When New	Adjusted Wheelbase	Approx. Towing Capacity	Gross Vehicle Weight Rating	Average Curb Weight

Sahara 1996 MHA 34 3352 MA Ca250 D $3700 208 4,000 24,000 21,281
Livability Code: SB 30-90
Wheelbase-to-length ratio of 51% is considered ○ dangerous ◉ fatiguing ○ good ○ excellent *
The approximate net payload of 2719 pounds at 11% of GVWR on this model is ○ deficient ○ excessive ○ cautionary ◉ good ○ excellent *
Total highway safety penalties are: 2 * Value: **7 3** Durability: **7 2** Highway Control Rating: **4 0** Highway Safety: **3 8**

Sahara 1996 MHA 34 3390 MA Ca250 D $3700 208 4,000 24,000 21,281
Livability Code: SB 30-90
Wheelbase-to-length ratio of 51% is considered ○ dangerous ◉ fatiguing ○ good ○ excellent *
The approximate net payload of 2719 pounds at 11% of GVWR on this model is ○ deficient ○ excessive ○ cautionary ◉ good ○ excellent *
Total highway safety penalties are: 2 * Value: **7 3** Durability: **7 2** Highway Control Rating: **4 0** Highway Safety: **3 8**

Sahara 1996 MHA 36 3530 MA Ca250 D $3600 228 4,000 24,000 21,777
Livability Code: SB 30-90
Wheelbase-to-length ratio of 54% is considered ○ dangerous ○ fatiguing ◉ good ○ excellent *
The approximate net payload of 2223 pounds at 9% of GVWR on this model is ○ deficient ○ excessive ◉ cautionary ○ good ○ excellent *
Total highway safety penalties are: 2 * Value: **7 3** Durability: **7 2** Highway Control Rating: **6 3** Highway Safety: **6 1** ★★

Sahara 1996 MHA 36 3550 MA Ca250 D $3600 228 4,000 24,000 21,777
Livability Code: SB 30-90
Wheelbase-to-length ratio of 54% is considered ○ dangerous ○ fatiguing ◉ good ○ excellent *
The approximate net payload of 2223 pounds at 9% of GVWR on this model is ○ deficient ○ excessive ◉ cautionary ○ good ○ excellent *
Total highway safety penalties are: 2 * Value: **7 3** Durability: **7 2** Highway Control Rating: **6 3** Highway Safety: **6 1** ★★

Sahara 1996 MHA 36 3590 MA Ca250 D $3600 228 4,000 24,000 21,777
Livability Code: SB 30-90
Wheelbase-to-length ratio of 54% is considered ○ dangerous ○ fatiguing ◉ good ○ excellent *
The approximate net payload of 2223 pounds at 9% of GVWR on this model is ○ deficient ○ excessive ◉ cautionary ○ good ○ excellent *
Total highway safety penalties are: 2 * Value: **7 3** Durability: **7 2** Highway Control Rating: **6 3** Highway Safety: **6 1** ★★

Sahara 1996 MHA 38 3730 MA Ca250 D $3400 252 4,000 24,000 22,465
Livability Code: SB 30-90
Wheelbase-to-length ratio of 55% is considered ○ dangerous ○ fatiguing ◉ good ○ excellent *
The approximate net payload of 1535 pounds at 6% of GVWR on this model is ◉ deficient ○ excessive ○ cautionary ○ good ○ excellent *
Total highway safety penalties are: 2 * Value: **7 3** Durability: **7 2** Highway Control Rating: **5 9** Highway Safety: **5 7** ★

Sahara 1996 MHA 38 3740 MA Ca250 D $3400 252 4,000 24,000 22,465
Livability Code: SB 30-90
Wheelbase-to-length ratio of 55% is considered ○ dangerous ○ fatiguing ◉ good ○ excellent *
The approximate net payload of 1535 pounds at 6% of GVWR on this model is ◉ deficient ○ excessive ○ cautionary ○ good ○ excellent *
Total highway safety penalties are: 2 * Value: **7 3** Durability: **7 2** Highway Control Rating: **5 9** Highway Safety: **5 7** ★

Sahara 1996 MHA 38 3750 MA Ca250 D $3400 252 4,000 24,000 22,465
Livability Code: SB 30-90
Wheelbase-to-length ratio of 55% is considered ○ dangerous ○ fatiguing ◉ good ○ excellent *
The approximate net payload of 1535 pounds at 6% of GVWR on this model is ◉ deficient ○ excessive ○ cautionary ○ good ○ excellent *
Total highway safety penalties are: 2 * Value: **7 3** Durability: **7 2** Highway Control Rating: **5 9** Highway Safety: **5 7** ★

Sahara 1996 MHA 38 3790 MA Ca250 D $3400 252 4,000 24,000 22,465
Livability Code: SB 30-90
Wheelbase-to-length ratio of 55% is considered ○ dangerous ○ fatiguing ◉ good ○ excellent *
The approximate net payload of 1535 pounds at 6% of GVWR on this model is ◉ deficient ○ excessive ○ cautionary ○ good ○ excellent *
Total highway safety penalties are: 2 * Value: **7 3** Durability: **7 2** Highway Control Rating: **5 9** Highway Safety: **5 7** ★

Sahara 1996 MHA 40 4030 MA Ca250 D $3300 278 4,000 24,000 23,099
Livability Code: SB 30-90
Wheelbase-to-length ratio of 57% is considered ○ dangerous ○ fatiguing ◉ good ○ excellent *
The approximate net payload of 901 pounds at 4% of GVWR on this model is ◉ deficient ○ excessive ○ cautionary ○ good ○ excellent *
Total highway safety penalties are: 2 * Value: **7 3** Durability: **7 2** Highway Control Rating: **6 4** Highway Safety: **6 2** ★

Sahara 1996 MHA 40 4050 MA Ca250 D $3300 278 4,000 24,000 23,099
Livability Code: SB 30-90
Wheelbase-to-length ratio of 57% is considered ○ dangerous ○ fatiguing ◉ good ○ excellent *
The approximate net payload of 901 pounds at 4% of GVWR on this model is ◉ deficient ○ excessive ○ cautionary ○ good ○ excellent *
Total highway safety penalties are: 2 * Value: **7 3** Durability: **7 2** Highway Control Rating: **6 4** Highway Safety: **6 2** ★

Sahara 1996 MHA 40 4088 MA Ca250 D $3300 278 4,000 24,000 23,099
Livability Code: SB 30-90
Wheelbase-to-length ratio of 57% is considered ○ dangerous ○ fatiguing ◉ good ○ excellent *
The approximate net payload of 901 pounds at 4% of GVWR on this model is ◉ deficient ○ excessive ○ cautionary ○ good ○ excellent *
Total highway safety penalties are: 2 * Value: **7 3** Durability: **7 2** Highway Control Rating: **6 4** Highway Safety: **6 2** ★

Note: Safety ratings are based on the assumption that the engineering of the RV has allowed for proper balance by placing fresh, gray, and black holding tanks in a location so as not to change the balance of the RV when the tanks are empty or full. **Always double-check wheelbase, GVWR, and weights at front and rear axles.**

*See Section 1 for details on how conclusions are reached.

Section 2: The Ratings

Brand	Year	Type	Length	Model	Chassis	Engine	Fuel Type	Average Price per Linear Foot When New	Adjusted Wheelbase	Approx. Towing Capacity	Gross Vehicle Weight Rating	Average Curb Weight
Sahara	1996	MHA	40	4090	MA	Ca250	D	$3300	278	4,000	24,000	23,099

Livability Code: SB 30-90
Wheelbase-to-length ratio of 57% is considered ○ dangerous ○ fatiguing ● good ○ excellent *
The approximate net payload of 901 pounds at 4% of GVWR on this model is ● deficient ○ excessive ○ cautionary ○ good ○ excellent *
Total highway safety penalties are: 2 * Value: **7 3** Durability: **7 2** Highway Control Rating: **6 4** Highway Safety: **6 2** ★

Brand	Year	Type	Length	Model	Chassis	Engine	Fuel Type	Average Price per Linear Foot When New	Adjusted Wheelbase	Approx. Towing Capacity	Gross Vehicle Weight Rating	Average Curb Weight
Sahara	1997	MHA	30	3044	MA	Ca250	D	$4100	178	5,000	24,000	19,861

Livability Code: SB 30-90
Wheelbase-to-length ratio of 49% is considered ● dangerous ○ fatiguing ○ good ○ excellent *
The approximate net payload of 4139 pounds at 17% of GVWR on this model is ○ deficient ○ excessive ○ cautionary ○ good ● excellent *
Total highway safety penalties are: 2 * Value: **7 3** Durability: **7 2** Highway Control Rating: **4 4** Highway Safety: **4 2**

Brand	Year	Type	Length	Model	Chassis	Engine	Fuel Type	Average Price per Linear Foot When New	Adjusted Wheelbase	Approx. Towing Capacity	Gross Vehicle Weight Rating	Average Curb Weight
Sahara	1997	MHA	33	3344	MA	Ca250	D	$3800	208	5,000	24,000	20,539

Livability Code: SB 30-90
Wheelbase-to-length ratio of 53% is considered ○ dangerous ● fatiguing ○ good ○ excellent *
The approximate net payload of 3461 pounds at 14% of GVWR on this model is ○ deficient ○ excessive ○ cautionary ● good ○ excellent *
Total highway safety penalties are: 2 * Value: **7 3** Durability: **7 2** Highway Control Rating: **6 5** Highway Safety: **6 3** ★★

Brand	Year	Type	Length	Model	Chassis	Engine	Fuel Type	Average Price per Linear Foot When New	Adjusted Wheelbase	Approx. Towing Capacity	Gross Vehicle Weight Rating	Average Curb Weight
Sahara	1997	MHA	33	3354	MA	Ca250	D	$3800	208	5,000	24,000	20,539

Livability Code: SB 30-90
Wheelbase-to-length ratio of 53% is considered ○ dangerous ● fatiguing ○ good ○ excellent *
The approximate net payload of 3461 pounds at 14% of GVWR on this model is ○ deficient ○ excessive ○ cautionary ● good ○ excellent *
Total highway safety penalties are: 2 * Value: **7 3** Durability: **7 2** Highway Control Rating: **6 5** Highway Safety: **6 3** ★★

Brand	Year	Type	Length	Model	Chassis	Engine	Fuel Type	Average Price per Linear Foot When New	Adjusted Wheelbase	Approx. Towing Capacity	Gross Vehicle Weight Rating	Average Curb Weight
Sahara	1997	MHA	35	3530	MA	Ca250	D	$3700	228	5,000	24,000	21,075

Livability Code: SB 30-90
Wheelbase-to-length ratio of 54% is considered ○ dangerous ○ fatiguing ● good ○ excellent *
The approximate net payload of 2926 pounds at 12% of GVWR on this model is ○ deficient ○ excessive ○ cautionary ● good ○ excellent *
Total highway safety penalties are: 2 * Value: **7 3** Durability: **7 2** Highway Control Rating: **7 9** Highway Safety: **7 7** ★★★

Brand	Year	Type	Length	Model	Chassis	Engine	Fuel Type	Average Price per Linear Foot When New	Adjusted Wheelbase	Approx. Towing Capacity	Gross Vehicle Weight Rating	Average Curb Weight
Sahara	1997	MHA	35	3550	MA	Ca250	D	$3700	228	5,000	24,000	21,075

Livability Code: SB 30-90
Wheelbase-to-length ratio of 54% is considered ○ dangerous ○ fatiguing ● good ○ excellent *
The approximate net payload of 2926 pounds at 12% of GVWR on this model is ○ deficient ○ excessive ○ cautionary ● good ○ excellent *
Total highway safety penalties are: 2 * Value: **7 3** Durability: **7 2** Highway Control Rating: **7 9** Highway Safety: **7 7** ★★★

Brand	Year	Type	Length	Model	Chassis	Engine	Fuel Type	Average Price per Linear Foot When New	Adjusted Wheelbase	Approx. Towing Capacity	Gross Vehicle Weight Rating	Average Curb Weight
Sahara	1997	MHA	35	3540	MA	Ca250	D	$3700	228	5,000	24,000	21,075

Livability Code: SB 30-90
Wheelbase-to-length ratio of 54% is considered ○ dangerous ○ fatiguing ● good ○ excellent *
The approximate net payload of 2926 pounds at 12% of GVWR on this model is ○ deficient ○ excessive ○ cautionary ● good ○ excellent *
Total highway safety penalties are: 2 * Value: **7 3** Durability: **7 2** Highway Control Rating: **7 9** Highway Safety: **7 7** ★★★

Brand	Year	Type	Length	Model	Chassis	Engine	Fuel Type	Average Price per Linear Foot When New	Adjusted Wheelbase	Approx. Towing Capacity	Gross Vehicle Weight Rating	Average Curb Weight
Sahara	1998	MHA	31	3006	MA	CA250	D	$4200	178	5,000	24,000	20,934

Livability Code: SB 30-90
Wheelbase-to-length ratio of 48% is considered ● dangerous ○ fatiguing ○ good ○ excellent *
The approximate net payload of 3066 pounds at 13% of GVWR on this model is ○ deficient ○ excessive ○ cautionary ● good ○ excellent *
Total highway safety penalties are: 7 * Value: **6 9** Durability: **7 0** Highway Control Rating: **3 1** Highway Safety: **2 4**

Brand	Year	Type	Length	Model	Chassis	Engine	Fuel Type	Average Price per Linear Foot When New	Adjusted Wheelbase	Approx. Towing Capacity	Gross Vehicle Weight Rating	Average Curb Weight
Sahara	1998	MHA	31	3044	MA	CA250	D	$4200	178	5,000	24,000	20,484

Livability Code: SB 30-90
Wheelbase-to-length ratio of 48% is considered ● dangerous ○ fatiguing ○ good ○ excellent *
The approximate net payload of 3516 pounds at 15% of GVWR on this model is ○ deficient ○ excessive ○ cautionary ● good ○ excellent *
Total highway safety penalties are: 2 * Value: **7 2** Durability: **7 0** Highway Control Rating: **3 5** Highway Safety: **3 3**

Brand	Year	Type	Length	Model	Chassis	Engine	Fuel Type	Average Price per Linear Foot When New	Adjusted Wheelbase	Approx. Towing Capacity	Gross Vehicle Weight Rating	Average Curb Weight
Sahara	1998	MHA	34	3334	MA	CA250	D	$3800	208	5,000	24,000	21,062

Livability Code: SB 30-90
Wheelbase-to-length ratio of 51% is considered ○ dangerous ● fatiguing ○ good ○ excellent *
The approximate net payload of 2938 pounds at 12% of GVWR on this model is ○ deficient ○ excessive ○ cautionary ● good ○ excellent *
Total highway safety penalties are: 2 * Value: **7 2** Durability: **7 0** Highway Control Rating: **4 0** Highway Safety: **3 8**

Brand	Year	Type	Length	Model	Chassis	Engine	Fuel Type	Average Price per Linear Foot When New	Adjusted Wheelbase	Approx. Towing Capacity	Gross Vehicle Weight Rating	Average Curb Weight
Sahara	1998	MHA	36	3506	MA	CA250	D	$3600	228	5,000	24,000	22,885

Livability Code: SB 30-90
Wheelbase-to-length ratio of 53% is considered ○ dangerous ● fatiguing ○ good ○ excellent *
The approximate net payload of 1115 pounds at 5% of GVWR on this model is ● deficient ○ excessive ○ cautionary ○ good ○ excellent *
Total highway safety penalties are: 13 * Value: **6 7** Durability: **7 0** Highway Control Rating: **3 3** Highway Safety: **2 0**

Brand	Year	Type	Length	Model	Chassis	Engine	Fuel Type	Average Price per Linear Foot When New	Adjusted Wheelbase	Approx. Towing Capacity	Gross Vehicle Weight Rating	Average Curb Weight
Sahara	1998	MHA	36	3540	MA	CA250	D	$3600	228	5,000	24,000	21,997

Livability Code: SB 30-90
Wheelbase-to-length ratio of 53% is considered ○ dangerous ● fatiguing ○ good ○ excellent *
The approximate net payload of 2003 pounds at 8% of GVWR on this model is ○ deficient ○ excessive ● cautionary ○ good ○ excellent *
Total highway safety penalties are: 2 * Value: **7 2** Durability: **7 0** Highway Control Rating: **4 7** Highway Safety: **4 5**

Note: Safety ratings are based on the assumption that the engineering of the RV has allowed for proper balance by placing fresh, gray, and black holding tanks in a location so as not to change the balance of the RV when the tanks are empty or full. **Always double-check wheelbase, GVWR, and weights at front and rear axles.**

*See Section 1 for details on how conclusions are reached.

Brand	Year	Type	Length	Model	Chassis	Engine	Fuel Type	Average Price per Linear Foot When New	Adjusted Wheelbase	Approx. Towing Capacity	Gross Vehicle Weight Rating	Average Curb Weight
Sahara	**1998**	MHA	36	3550	MA	CA250	D	$3600	228	5,000	24,000	21,997

Livability Code: SB 30-90 Wheelbase-to-length ratio of 53% is considered ○ dangerous ◉ fatiguing ○ good ○ excellent *
The approximate net payload of 2003 pounds at 8% of GVWR on this model is ○ deficient ○ excessive ◉ cautionary ○ good ○ excellent *
Total highway safety penalties are: 2 * Value: **7 2** Durability: **7 0** Highway Control Rating: **4 7** Highway Safety: **4 5**

Brand	Year	Type	Length	Model	Chassis	Engine	Fuel Type	Avg Price/Ft	Wheelbase	Towing	GVWR	Curb Wt
Sahara	**1999**	MHA	33	3044	MA	CA300	D	$3900	178	5,000	26,000	21,198

Livability Code: SB 30-90 Wheelbase-to-length ratio of 46% is considered ◉ dangerous ○ fatiguing ○ good ○ excellent *
The approximate net payload of 4802 pounds at 18% of GVWR on this model is ○ deficient ○ excessive ○ cautionary ○ good ◉ excellent *
Total highway safety penalties are: 2 * Value: **7 7** Durability: **7 1** Highway Control Rating: **4 2** Highway Safety: **4 0**

Brand	Year	Type	Length	Model	Chassis	Engine	Fuel Type	Avg Price/Ft	Wheelbase	Towing	GVWR	Curb Wt
Sahara	**1999**	MHA	33	3006	MA	CA300	D	$3900	178	5,000	26,000	21,898

Livability Code: SB 30-90 Wheelbase-to-length ratio of 46% is considered ◉ dangerous ○ fatiguing ○ good ○ excellent *
The approximate net payload of 4102 pounds at 16% of GVWR on this model is ○ deficient ○ excessive ○ cautionary ○ good ◉ excellent *
Total highway safety penalties are: 12 * Value: **7 3** Durability: **7 1** Highway Control Rating: **3 9** Highway Safety: **2 7**

Brand	Year	Type	Length	Model	Chassis	Engine	Fuel Type	Avg Price/Ft	Wheelbase	Towing	GVWR	Curb Wt
Sahara	**1999**	MHA	35	3334	MA	CA300	D	$3700	208	5,000	26,000	21,705

Livability Code: SB 30-90 Wheelbase-to-length ratio of 50% is considered ◉ dangerous ○ fatiguing ○ good ○ excellent *
The approximate net payload of 4296 pounds at 17% of GVWR on this model is ○ deficient ○ excessive ○ cautionary ○ good ◉ excellent *
Total highway safety penalties are: 2 * Value: **7 7** Durability: **7 1** Highway Control Rating: **5 3** Highway Safety: **5 1**

Brand	Year	Type	Length	Model	Chassis	Engine	Fuel Type	Avg Price/Ft	Wheelbase	Towing	GVWR	Curb Wt
Sahara	**1999**	MHA	37	3506	MA	CA300	D	$3500	228	5,000	26,000	23,422

Livability Code: SB 30-90 Wheelbase-to-length ratio of 52% is considered ○ dangerous ◉ fatiguing ○ good ○ excellent *
The approximate net payload of 2578 pounds at 10% of GVWR on this model is ○ deficient ○ excessive ○ cautionary ◉ good ○ excellent *
Total highway safety penalties are: 12 * Value: **7 2** Durability: **7 1** Highway Control Rating: **5 4** Highway Safety: **4 2**

Brand	Year	Type	Length	Model	Chassis	Engine	Fuel Type	Avg Price/Ft	Wheelbase	Towing	GVWR	Curb Wt
Sahara	**1999**	MHA	37	3540	MA	CA300	D	$3500	228	5,000	26,000	22,597

Livability Code: SB 30-90 Wheelbase-to-length ratio of 52% is considered ○ dangerous ◉ fatiguing ○ good ○ excellent *
The approximate net payload of 3403 pounds at 13% of GVWR on this model is ○ deficient ○ excessive ○ cautionary ◉ good ○ excellent *
Total highway safety penalties are: 2 * Value: **7 7** Durability: **7 1** Highway Control Rating: **6 0** Highway Safety: **5 8** ★

Brand	Year	Type	Length	Model	Chassis	Engine	Fuel Type	Avg Price/Ft	Wheelbase	Towing	GVWR	Curb Wt
Sahara	**1999**	MHA	37	3550	MA	CA300	D	$3500	228	5,000	26,000	22,597

Livability Code: SB 30-90 Wheelbase-to-length ratio of 52% is considered ○ dangerous ◉ fatiguing ○ good ○ excellent *
The approximate net payload of 3403 pounds at 13% of GVWR on this model is ○ deficient ○ excessive ○ cautionary ◉ good ○ excellent *
Total highway safety penalties are: 2 * Value: **7 7** Durability: **7 1** Highway Control Rating: **6 0** Highway Safety: **5 8** ★

Brand	Year	Type	Length	Model	Chassis	Engine	Fuel Type	Avg Price/Ft	Wheelbase	Towing	GVWR	Curb Wt
Sea Breeze	**1990**	MMH	22	800	TO	3.0L	G	$4300	137	1,500	6,000	5,374

Livability Code: SB 30-90 Wheelbase-to-length ratio of 53% is considered ○ dangerous ◉ fatiguing ○ good ○ excellent *
The approximate net payload of 626 pounds at 10% of GVWR on this model is ○ deficient ○ excessive ○ cautionary ◉ good ○ excellent *
Total highway safety penalties are: 2 * Value: **9 5** Durability: **9 0** Highway Control Rating: **5 8** Highway Safety: **5 6** ★

Brand	Year	Type	Length	Model	Chassis	Engine	Fuel Type	Avg Price/Ft	Wheelbase	Towing	GVWR	Curb Wt
Sea Breeze	**1991**	MMH	22	21	TO	3.0L	G	$4300	137	1,500	6,000	5,336

Livability Code: SB 30-90 Wheelbase-to-length ratio of 52% is considered ○ dangerous ◉ fatiguing ○ good ○ excellent *
The approximate net payload of 664 pounds at 11% of GVWR on this model is ○ deficient ○ excessive ○ cautionary ◉ good ○ excellent *
Total highway safety penalties are: 2 * Value: **9 0** Durability: **9 0** Highway Control Rating: **4 8** Highway Safety: **4 6**

Brand	Year	Type	Length	Model	Chassis	Engine	Fuel Type	Avg Price/Ft	Wheelbase	Towing	GVWR	Curb Wt
Sea Breeze	**1993**	MHA	29	SB129	CH	7.4L	G	$1600	190	4,200	14,800	11,941

Livability Code: SB 30-90 Wheelbase-to-length ratio of 55% is considered ○ dangerous ○ fatiguing ◉ good ○ excellent *
The approximate net payload of 2860 pounds at 19% of GVWR on this model is ○ deficient ○ excessive ○ cautionary ○ good ◉ excellent *
Total highway safety penalties are: 4 * Value: **8 9** Durability: **9 0** Highway Control Rating: **9 4** Highway Safety: **9 0** ★★★★

Brand	Year	Type	Length	Model	Chassis	Engine	Fuel Type	Avg Price/Ft	Wheelbase	Towing	GVWR	Curb Wt
Sea Breeze	**1993**	MHA	31	SB131	CH	7.4L	G	$1900	208	4,200	14,800	13,005

Livability Code: SB 30-90 Wheelbase-to-length ratio of 56% is considered ○ dangerous ○ fatiguing ◉ good ○ excellent *
The approximate net payload of 1795 pounds at 12% of GVWR on this model is ○ deficient ○ excessive ○ cautionary ◉ good ○ excellent *
Total highway safety penalties are: 5 * Value: **8 9** Durability: **9 0** Highway Control Rating: **8 8** Highway Safety: **8 3** ★★★★

Brand	Year	Type	Length	Model	Chassis	Engine	Fuel Type	Avg Price/Ft	Wheelbase	Towing	GVWR	Curb Wt
Sea Breeze	**1993**	MHA	31	SB131	FO	7.5L	G	$1600	208	1,500 e	15,200	13,335

Livability Code: SB 30-90 Wheelbase-to-length ratio of 56% is considered ○ dangerous ○ fatiguing ◉ good ○ excellent *
The approximate net payload of 1865 pounds at 12% of GVWR on this model is ○ deficient ○ excessive ○ cautionary ◉ good ○ excellent *
Total highway safety penalties are: 2 * Value: **9 0** Durability: **9 0** Highway Control Rating: **8 8** Highway Safety: **8 6** ★★★★

Note: Safety ratings are based on the assumption that the engineering of the RV has allowed for proper balance by placing fresh, gray, and black holding tanks in a location so as not to change the balance of the RV when the tanks are empty or full. **Always double-check wheelbase, GVWR, and weights at front and rear axles.**

Section 2: The Ratings

Brand	Year	Type	Length	Model	Chassis	Engine	Fuel Type	Average Price per Linear Foot When New	Adjusted Wheelbase	Approx. Towing Capacity	Gross Vehicle Weight Rating	Average Curb Weight
Sea Breeze	1993	MHA	33	SB133	CH	7.4L	G	$1500	228	4,200	14,800	13,530

Livability Code: SB 30-90
Wheelbase-to-length ratio of 58% is considered ○ dangerous ○ fatiguing ○ good ◉ excellent *
The approximate net payload of 1270 pounds at 9% of GVWR on this model is ○ deficient ○ excessive ◉ cautionary ○ good ○ excellent *
Total highway safety penalties are: 6 *   Value: **8 8**   Durability: **9 0**   Highway Control Rating: **8 7**   Highway Safety: **8 1**   ★★★★

Brand	Year	Type	Length	Model	Chassis	Engine	Fuel Type	Avg Price/Lin Ft	Adj Wheelbase	Approx Towing	GVWR	Avg Curb Wt
Sea Breeze	1993	MHA	33	SB133	FO	7.5L	G	$1500	228	1,500 e	15,200	13,875

Livability Code: SB 30-90
Wheelbase-to-length ratio of 58% is considered ○ dangerous ○ fatiguing ○ good ◉ excellent *
The approximate net payload of 1325 pounds at 9% of GVWR on this model is ○ deficient ○ excessive ◉ cautionary ○ good ○ excellent *
Total highway safety penalties are: 2 *   Value: **9 0**   Durability: **9 0**   Highway Control Rating: **8 7**   Highway Safety: **8 5**   ★★★★

Sea Breeze	1994	MHA	29	SB129	CH	7.4L	G	$1900	190	2,200	14,800	12,557

Livability Code: SB 30-90
Wheelbase-to-length ratio of 55% is considered ○ dangerous ○ fatiguing ◉ good ○ excellent *
The approximate net payload of 2243 pounds at 15% of GVWR on this model is ○ deficient ○ excessive ○ cautionary ◉ good ○ excellent *
Total highway safety penalties are: 4 *   Value: **8 9**   Durability: **9 0**   Highway Control Rating: **9 0**   Highway Safety: **8 6**   ★★★★

Sea Breeze	1994	MHA	32	SB131	CH	7.4L	G	$1800	208	2,200	14,800	13,480

Livability Code: SB 30-90
Wheelbase-to-length ratio of 55% is considered ○ dangerous ○ fatiguing ◉ good ○ excellent *
The approximate net payload of 1320 pounds at 9% of GVWR on this model is ○ deficient ○ excessive ◉ cautionary ○ good ○ excellent *
Total highway safety penalties are: 5 *   Value: **8 8**   Durability: **9 0**   Highway Control Rating: **7 5**   Highway Safety: **7 0**   ★★★

Sea Breeze	1994	MHA	32	SB131	FO	7.5L	G	$1800	208	8,000	17,000	14,010

Livability Code: SB 30-90
Wheelbase-to-length ratio of 55% is considered ○ dangerous ○ fatiguing ○ good ◉ excellent *
The approximate net payload of 2990 pounds at 18% of GVWR on this model is ○ deficient ○ excessive ○ cautionary ○ good ◉ excellent *
Total highway safety penalties are: 2 *   Value: **9 0**   Durability: **9 0**   Highway Control Rating: **9 4**   Highway Safety: **9 2**   ★★★★★

Sea Breeze	1994	MHA	33	SB133	CH	7.4L	G	$1800	228	3,000	16,000	13,875

Livability Code: SB 30-90
Wheelbase-to-length ratio of 58% is considered ○ dangerous ○ fatiguing ○ good ◉ excellent *
The approximate net payload of 2125 pounds at 13% of GVWR on this model is ○ deficient ○ excessive ○ cautionary ◉ good ○ excellent *
Total highway safety penalties are: 6 *   Value: **8 8**   Durability: **9 0**   Highway Control Rating: **1 0 0**   Highway Safety: **9 4**   ★★★★

Sea Breeze	1994	MHA	33	SB133	FO	7.5L	G	$1800	228	8,000	17,000	14,410

Livability Code: SB 30-90
Wheelbase-to-length ratio of 58% is considered ○ dangerous ○ fatiguing ○ good ◉ excellent *
The approximate net payload of 2590 pounds at 15% of GVWR on this model is ○ deficient ○ excessive ○ cautionary ◉ good ○ excellent *
Total highway safety penalties are: 2 *   Value: **9 0**   Durability: **9 0**   Highway Control Rating: **1 0 0**   Highway Safety: **9 8**   ★★★★★

Sea Breeze	1995	MHA	29	SB129	CH	7.4L	G	$1900	190	4,200	14,800	12,525

Livability Code: SB 30-90
Wheelbase-to-length ratio of 55% is considered ○ dangerous ○ fatiguing ◉ good ○ excellent *
The approximate net payload of 2275 pounds at 15% of GVWR on this model is ○ deficient ○ excessive ○ cautionary ◉ good ○ excellent *
Total highway safety penalties are: 4 *   Value: **8 9**   Durability: **9 0**   Highway Control Rating: **8 9**   Highway Safety: **8 5**   ★★★★

Sea Breeze	1995	MHA	32	SB131	CH	7.4L	G	$1800	208	4,200	14,800	12,990

Livability Code: SB 30-90
Wheelbase-to-length ratio of 55% is considered ○ dangerous ○ fatiguing ◉ good ○ excellent *
The approximate net payload of 1811 pounds at 12% of GVWR on this model is ○ deficient ○ excessive ○ cautionary ◉ good ○ excellent *
Total highway safety penalties are: 5 *   Value: **8 8**   Durability: **9 0**   Highway Control Rating: **8 8**   Highway Safety: **8 3**   ★★★★

Sea Breeze	1995	MHA	32	SB131	FO	7.5L	G	$1800	208	8,000	17,000	13,550

Livability Code: SB 30-90
Wheelbase-to-length ratio of 55% is considered ○ dangerous ○ fatiguing ○ good ◉ excellent *
The approximate net payload of 3451 pounds at 20% of GVWR on this model is ○ deficient ○ excessive ○ cautionary ○ good ◉ excellent *
Total highway safety penalties are: 2 *   Value: **9 0**   Durability: **9 0**   Highway Control Rating: **9 6**   Highway Safety: **9 4**   ★★★★★

Sea Breeze	1995	MHA	33	SB133	CH	7.4L	G	$1800	228	3,500	16,500	13,609

Livability Code: SB 30-90
Wheelbase-to-length ratio of 58% is considered ○ dangerous ○ fatiguing ○ good ◉ excellent *
The approximate net payload of 2892 pounds at 18% of GVWR on this model is ○ deficient ○ excessive ○ cautionary ○ good ◉ excellent *
Total highway safety penalties are: 6 *   Value: **8 8**   Durability: **9 0**   Highway Control Rating: **1 0 0**   Highway Safety: **9 4**   ★★★★

Sea Breeze	1995	MHA	33	SB133	FO	7.5L	G	$1800	228	8,000	17,000	13,924

Livability Code: SB 30-90
Wheelbase-to-length ratio of 58% is considered ○ dangerous ○ fatiguing ○ good ◉ excellent *
The approximate net payload of 3077 pounds at 18% of GVWR on this model is ○ deficient ○ excessive ○ cautionary ○ good ◉ excellent *
Total highway safety penalties are: 2 *   Value: **9 0**   Durability: **9 0**   Highway Control Rating: **1 0 0**   Highway Safety: **9 8**   ★★★★★

Note: Safety ratings are based on the assumption that the engineering of the RV has allowed for proper balance by placing fresh, gray, and black holding tanks in a location so as not to change the balance of the RV when the tanks are empty or full. **Always double-check wheelbase, GVWR, and weights at front and rear axles.**

*See Section 1 for details on how conclusions are reached.

Section 2: The Ratings

Brand	Year	Type	Length	Model	Chassis	Engine	Fuel Type	Average Price per Linear Foot When New	Adjusted Wheelbase	Approx. Towing Capacity	Gross Vehicle Weight Rating	Average Curb Weight
Sea Breeze	1996	MHA	29	SB129	CH	7.4L	G	$1800	190	4,200	14,800	12,430

Livability Code: SB 30-90 — Wheelbase-to-length ratio of 55% is considered ○ dangerous ○ fatiguing ● good ○ excellent *

The approximate net payload of 2370 pounds at 16% of GVWR on this model is ○ deficient ○ excessive ○ cautionary ○ good ● excellent *

Total highway safety penalties are: 4 * — Value: 8 9 — Durability: 9 0 — Highway Control Rating: 9 1 — Highway Safety: 8 7 — ★★★★

| Sea Breeze | 1996 | MHA | 32 | SB131 | CH | 7.4L | G | $1700 | 208 | 4,200 | 14,800 | 13,122 |

Livability Code: SB 30-90 — Wheelbase-to-length ratio of 55% is considered ○ dangerous ○ fatiguing ● good ○ excellent *

The approximate net payload of 1678 pounds at 11% of GVWR on this model is ○ deficient ○ excessive ○ cautionary ● good ○ excellent *

Total highway safety penalties are: 5 * — Value: 8 8 — Durability: 9 0 — Highway Control Rating: 8 7 — Highway Safety: 8 2 — ★★★★

| Sea Breeze | 1996 | MHA | 32 | SB131 | FO | 7.5L | G | $1700 | 208 | 8,000 | 17,000 | 13,507 |

Livability Code: SB 30-90 — Wheelbase-to-length ratio of 55% is considered ○ dangerous ○ fatiguing ● good ○ excellent *

The approximate net payload of 3493 pounds at 21% of GVWR on this model is ○ deficient ○ excessive ○ cautionary ○ good ● excellent *

Total highway safety penalties are: 2 * — Value: 9 0 — Durability: 9 0 — Highway Control Rating: 9 5 — Highway Safety: 9 3 — ★★★★★

| Sea Breeze | 1996 | MHA | 33 | SB133 | CH | 7.4L | G | $1700 | 228 | 4,000 | 16,000 | 13,346 |

Livability Code: SB 30-90 — Wheelbase-to-length ratio of 58% is considered ○ dangerous ○ fatiguing ○ good ● excellent *

The approximate net payload of 2654 pounds at 17% of GVWR on this model is ○ deficient ○ excessive ○ cautionary ○ good ● excellent *

Total highway safety penalties are: 6 * — Value: 8 8 — Durability: 9 0 — Highway Control Rating: 1 0 0 — Highway Safety: 9 4 — ★★★★

| Sea Breeze | 1996 | MHA | 33 | SB133 | FO | 7.5L | G | $1700 | 228 | 8,000 | 17,000 | 13,966 |

Livability Code: SB 30-90 — Wheelbase-to-length ratio of 58% is considered ○ dangerous ○ fatiguing ○ good ● excellent *

The approximate net payload of 3034 pounds at 18% of GVWR on this model is ○ deficient ○ excessive ○ cautionary ○ good ● excellent *

Total highway safety penalties are: 2 * — Value: 9 0 — Durability: 9 0 — Highway Control Rating: 1 0 0 — Highway Safety: 9 8 — ★★★★★

| Sea Breeze | 1997 | MHA | 29 | 129 | CH | 7.4L | G | $2100 | 190 | 1,500 | 14,800 | 12,406 |

Livability Code: SB 30-90 — Wheelbase-to-length ratio of 54% is considered ○ dangerous ○ fatiguing ● good ○ excellent *

The approximate net payload of 2394 pounds at 16% of GVWR on this model is ○ deficient ○ excessive ○ cautionary ○ good ● excellent *

Total highway safety penalties are: 4 * — Value: 8 9 — Durability: 9 0 — Highway Control Rating: 8 2 — Highway Safety: 7 8 — ★★★

| Sea Breeze | 1997 | MHA | 31 | 131 | CH | 7.4L | G | $2100 | 208 | 1,500 | 14,800 | 12,938 |

Livability Code: SB 30-90 — Wheelbase-to-length ratio of 55% is considered ○ dangerous ○ fatiguing ● good ○ excellent *

The approximate net payload of 1862 pounds at 13% of GVWR on this model is ○ deficient ○ excessive ○ cautionary ● good ○ excellent *

Total highway safety penalties are: 5 * — Value: 8 8 — Durability: 9 0 — Highway Control Rating: 8 7 — Highway Safety: 8 2 — ★★★★

| Sea Breeze | 1997 | MHA | 31 | 131 opch | FO | 7.5L | G | $2000 | 208 | 1,500 | 17,000 | 13,553 |

Livability Code: SB 30-90 — Wheelbase-to-length ratio of 55% is considered ○ dangerous ○ fatiguing ● good ○ excellent *

The approximate net payload of 3447 pounds at 20% of GVWR on this model is ○ deficient ○ excessive ○ cautionary ○ good ● excellent *

Total highway safety penalties are: 2 * — Value: 9 0 — Durability: 9 0 — Highway Control Rating: 9 7 — Highway Safety: 9 5 — ★★★★★

| Sea Breeze | 1997 | MHA | 33 | 133 | CH | 7.4L | G | $2000 | 228 | 1,500 | 16,500 | 13,700 |

Livability Code: SB 30-90 — Wheelbase-to-length ratio of 58% is considered ○ dangerous ○ fatiguing ○ good ● excellent *

The approximate net payload of 2800 pounds at 17% of GVWR on this model is ○ deficient ○ excessive ○ cautionary ○ good ● excellent *

Total highway safety penalties are: 6 * — Value: 8 8 — Durability: 9 0 — Highway Control Rating: 1 0 0 — Highway Safety: 9 4 — ★★★★

| Sea Breeze | 1997 | MHA | 33 | 133 opch | FO | 7.5L | G | $2100 | 228 | 1,500 | 17,000 | 13,780 |

Livability Code: SB 30-90 — Wheelbase-to-length ratio of 58% is considered ○ dangerous ○ fatiguing ○ good ● excellent *

The approximate net payload of 3220 pounds at 19% of GVWR on this model is ○ deficient ○ excessive ○ cautionary ○ good ● excellent *

Total highway safety penalties are: 2 * — Value: 9 0 — Durability: 9 0 — Highway Control Rating: 1 0 0 — Highway Safety: 9 8 — ★★★★★

| Sea Breeze | 1998 | MHA | 29 | 1290 | CH | 7.4L | G | $2100 | 190 | 4,200 | 14,800 | 12,406 |

Livability Code: SB 30-90 — Wheelbase-to-length ratio of 54% is considered ○ dangerous ○ fatiguing ● good ○ excellent *

The approximate net payload of 2394 pounds at 16% of GVWR on this model is ○ deficient ○ excessive ○ cautionary ○ good ● excellent *

Total highway safety penalties are: 4 * — Value: 9 4 — Durability: 9 0 — Highway Control Rating: 8 2 — Highway Safety: 7 8 — ★★★

| Sea Breeze | 1998 | MHA | 31 | 1310 | CH | 7.4L | G | $1900 | 208 | 4,200 | 14,800 | 12,938 |

Livability Code: SB 30-90 — Wheelbase-to-length ratio of 55% is considered ○ dangerous ○ fatiguing ● good ○ excellent *

The approximate net payload of 1862 pounds at 13% of GVWR on this model is ○ deficient ○ excessive ○ cautionary ● good ○ excellent *

Total highway safety penalties are: 5 * — Value: 9 3 — Durability: 9 0 — Highway Control Rating: 8 7 — Highway Safety: 8 2 — ★★★★

Note: Safety ratings are based on the assumption that the engineering of the RV has allowed for proper balance by placing fresh, gray, and black holding tanks in a location so as not to change the balance of the RV when the tanks are empty or full. **Always double-check wheelbase, GVWR, and weights at front and rear axles.**

*See Section 1 for details on how conclusions are reached.

Section 2: The Ratings

Brand	Year	Type	Length	Model	Chassis	Engine	Fuel Type	Average Price per Linear Foot When New	Adjusted Wheelbase	Approx. Towing Capacity	Gross Vehicle Weight Rating	Average Curb Weight
Sea Breeze	1998	MHA	31	1310	FO	7.5L	G	$2100	208	5,000	17,000	13,553

Livability Code: SB 30-90
Wheelbase-to-length ratio of 55% is considered ○ dangerous ○ fatiguing ◉ good ○ excellent*
The approximate net payload of 3447 pounds at 20% of GVWR on this model is ○ deficient ○ excessive ○ cautionary ○ good ◉ excellent*
Total highway safety penalties are: 2* Value: **95** Durability: **90** Highway Control Rating: **97** Highway Safety: **95** ★★★★★

Brand	Year	Type	Length	Model	Chassis	Engine	Fuel Type	Average Price per Linear Foot When New	Adjusted Wheelbase	Approx. Towing Capacity	Gross Vehicle Weight Rating	Average Curb Weight
Sea Breeze	1998	MHA	31	1310 myc	FO	7.5L	G	$2100	208	4,000	18,000	14,063

Livability Code: SB 30-90
Wheelbase-to-length ratio of 55% is considered ○ dangerous ○ fatiguing ◉ good ○ excellent*
The approximate net payload of 3937 pounds at 22% of GVWR on this model is ○ deficient ○ excessive ○ cautionary ○ good ◉ excellent*
Total highway safety penalties are: 2* Value: **95** Durability: **90** Highway Control Rating: **95** Highway Safety: **93** ★★★★★

Brand	Year	Type	Length	Model	Chassis	Engine	Fuel Type	Average Price per Linear Foot When New	Adjusted Wheelbase	Approx. Towing Capacity	Gross Vehicle Weight Rating	Average Curb Weight
Sea Breeze	1998	MHA	33	1330	CH	7.4L	G	$1800	228	4,500	16,500	13,700

Livability Code: SB 30-90
Wheelbase-to-length ratio of 58% is considered ○ dangerous ○ fatiguing ○ good ◉ excellent*
The approximate net payload of 2800 pounds at 17% of GVWR on this model is ○ deficient ○ excessive ○ cautionary ○ good ◉ excellent*
Total highway safety penalties are: 6* Value: **93** Durability: **90** Highway Control Rating: **100** Highway Safety: **94** ★★★★★

Brand	Year	Type	Length	Model	Chassis	Engine	Fuel Type	Average Price per Linear Foot When New	Adjusted Wheelbase	Approx. Towing Capacity	Gross Vehicle Weight Rating	Average Curb Weight
Sea Breeze	1998	MHA	33	1330	FO	7.5L	G	$2000	228	5,000	17,000	14,020

Livability Code: SB 30-90
Wheelbase-to-length ratio of 58% is considered ○ dangerous ○ fatiguing ○ good ◉ excellent*
The approximate net payload of 2980 pounds at 18% of GVWR on this model is ○ deficient ○ excessive ○ cautionary ○ good ◉ excellent*
Total highway safety penalties are: 2* Value: **95** Durability: **90** Highway Control Rating: **100** Highway Safety: **98** ★★★★★

Brand	Year	Type	Length	Model	Chassis	Engine	Fuel Type	Average Price per Linear Foot When New	Adjusted Wheelbase	Approx. Towing Capacity	Gross Vehicle Weight Rating	Average Curb Weight
Sea Breeze	1998	MHA	33	1330 myc	FO	7.5L	G	$2000	228	4,000	18,000	14,420

Livability Code: SB 30-90
Wheelbase-to-length ratio of 58% is considered ○ dangerous ○ fatiguing ○ good ◉ excellent*
The approximate net payload of 3580 pounds at 20% of GVWR on this model is ○ deficient ○ excessive ○ cautionary ○ good ◉ excellent*
Total highway safety penalties are: 2* Value: **95** Durability: **90** Highway Control Rating: **100** Highway Safety: **98** ★★★★★

Brand	Year	Type	Length	Model	Chassis	Engine	Fuel Type	Average Price per Linear Foot When New	Adjusted Wheelbase	Approx. Towing Capacity	Gross Vehicle Weight Rating	Average Curb Weight
Sea Breeze	1999	MHA	29	1290	CH	7.4L	G	$2100	190	4,200	14,800	12,280

Livability Code: SB 30-90
Wheelbase-to-length ratio of 54% is considered ○ dangerous ○ fatiguing ◉ good ○ excellent*
The approximate net payload of 2520 pounds at 17% of GVWR on this model is ○ deficient ○ excessive ○ cautionary ○ good ◉ excellent*
Total highway safety penalties are: 4* Value: **94** Durability: **90** Highway Control Rating: **85** Highway Safety: **81** ★★★★

Brand	Year	Type	Length	Model	Chassis	Engine	Fuel Type	Average Price per Linear Foot When New	Adjusted Wheelbase	Approx. Towing Capacity	Gross Vehicle Weight Rating	Average Curb Weight
Sea Breeze	1999	MHA	31	1310	CH	7.4L	G	$1900	208	4,200	14,800	12,840

Livability Code: SB 30-90
Wheelbase-to-length ratio of 55% is considered ○ dangerous ○ fatiguing ◉ good ○ excellent*
The approximate net payload of 1960 pounds at 13% of GVWR on this model is ○ deficient ○ excessive ○ cautionary ○ good ◉ excellent*
Total highway safety penalties are: 5* Value: **93** Durability: **90** Highway Control Rating: **88** Highway Safety: **83** ★★★★

Brand	Year	Type	Length	Model	Chassis	Engine	Fuel Type	Average Price per Linear Foot When New	Adjusted Wheelbase	Approx. Towing Capacity	Gross Vehicle Weight Rating	Average Curb Weight
Sea Breeze	1999	MHA	31	1310	FO	6.8L	G	$2100	208	5,000	18,000	14,090

Livability Code: SB 30-90
Wheelbase-to-length ratio of 55% is considered ○ dangerous ○ fatiguing ◉ good ○ excellent*
The approximate net payload of 3910 pounds at 22% of GVWR on this model is ○ deficient ○ excessive ○ cautionary ○ good ◉ excellent*
Total highway safety penalties are: 2* Value: **95** Durability: **90** Highway Control Rating: **96** Highway Safety: **94** ★★★★★

Brand	Year	Type	Length	Model	Chassis	Engine	Fuel Type	Average Price per Linear Foot When New	Adjusted Wheelbase	Approx. Towing Capacity	Gross Vehicle Weight Rating	Average Curb Weight
Sea Breeze	1999	MHA	33	1330	FO	6.8L	G	$2000	228	5,000	18,000	14,590

Livability Code: SB 30-90
Wheelbase-to-length ratio of 58% is considered ○ dangerous ○ fatiguing ○ good ◉ excellent*
The approximate net payload of 3410 pounds at 19% of GVWR on this model is ○ deficient ○ excessive ○ cautionary ○ good ◉ excellent*
Total highway safety penalties are: 2* Value: **95** Durability: **90** Highway Control Rating: **100** Highway Safety: **98** ★★★★★

Brand	Year	Type	Length	Model	Chassis	Engine	Fuel Type	Average Price per Linear Foot When New	Adjusted Wheelbase	Approx. Towing Capacity	Gross Vehicle Weight Rating	Average Curb Weight
Sea View	1998	MHA	31	8310	FO	7.5L	G	$2300	208	5,000	17,000	15,031

Livability Code: SB 30-90
Wheelbase-to-length ratio of 55% is considered ○ dangerous ○ fatiguing ◉ good ○ excellent*
The approximate net payload of 1969 pounds at 12% of GVWR on this model is ○ deficient ○ excessive ○ cautionary ○ good ○ excellent*
Total highway safety penalties are: 12* Value: **90** Durability: **90** Highway Control Rating: **86** Highway Safety: **74** ★★★

Brand	Year	Type	Length	Model	Chassis	Engine	Fuel Type	Average Price per Linear Foot When New	Adjusted Wheelbase	Approx. Towing Capacity	Gross Vehicle Weight Rating	Average Curb Weight
Sea View	1998	MHA	31	8310 myc	FO	6.8L	G	$2300	208	5,000	18,000	15,343

Livability Code: SB 30-90
Wheelbase-to-length ratio of 55% is considered ○ dangerous ○ fatiguing ◉ good ○ excellent*
The approximate net payload of 2657 pounds at 15% of GVWR on this model is ○ deficient ○ excessive ○ cautionary ○ good ○ excellent*
Total highway safety penalties are: 12* Value: **90** Durability: **90** Highway Control Rating: **92** Highway Safety: **80** ★★★★

Brand	Year	Type	Length	Model	Chassis	Engine	Fuel Type	Average Price per Linear Foot When New	Adjusted Wheelbase	Approx. Towing Capacity	Gross Vehicle Weight Rating	Average Curb Weight
Sea View	1998	MHA	33	8330	FO	7.5L	G	$2100	208	5,000	17,000	15,612

Livability Code: SB 30-90
Wheelbase-to-length ratio of 53% is considered ○ dangerous ◉ fatiguing ○ good ○ excellent*
The approximate net payload of 1388 pounds at 8% of GVWR on this model is ○ deficient ○ excessive ◉ cautionary ○ good ○ excellent*
Total highway safety penalties are: 7* Value: **92** Durability: **90** Highway Control Rating: **47** Highway Safety: **40**

Note: Safety ratings are based on the assumption that the engineering of the RV has allowed for proper balance by placing fresh, gray, and black holding tanks in a location so as not to change the balance of the RV when the tanks are empty or full. **Always double-check wheelbase, GVWR, and weights at front and rear axles.**

*See Section 1 for details on how conclusions are reached.

Brand	Year	Type	Length	Model	Chassis	Engine	Fuel Type	Average Price per Linear Foot When New	Adjusted Wheel-base	Approx. Towing Capacity	Gross Vehicle Weight Rating	Average Curb Weight
Sea View	**1998**	MHA	33	8331	FO	7.5L	G	$2100	208	5,000	17,000	15,410

Livability Code: SB 30-90   Wheelbase-to-length ratio of 53% is considered ○ dangerous ● fatiguing ○ good ○ excellent *

The approximate net payload of 1590 pounds at 9% of GVWR on this model is ○ deficient ○ excessive ● cautionary ○ good ○ excellent *

Total highway safety penalties are: 12 *   Value: 9 0   Durability: 9 0   Highway Control Rating: 5 3   Highway Safety: 4 1

Brand	Year	Type	Length	Model	Chassis	Engine	Fuel Type	Average Price per Linear Foot When New	Adjusted Wheel-base	Approx. Towing Capacity	Gross Vehicle Weight Rating	Average Curb Weight
Sea View	**1998**	MHA	33	8330 myc	FO	6.8L	G	$2100	208	5,000	18,000	15,925

Livability Code: SB 30-90   Wheelbase-to-length ratio of 53% is considered ○ dangerous ● fatiguing ○ good ○ excellent *

The approximate net payload of 2075 pounds at 12% of GVWR on this model is ○ deficient ○ excessive ○ cautionary ● good ○ excellent *

Total highway safety penalties are: 7 *   Value: 9 2   Durability: 9 0   Highway Control Rating: 6 1   Highway Safety: 5 4   ★

Brand	Year	Type	Length	Model	Chassis	Engine	Fuel Type	Average Price per Linear Foot When New	Adjusted Wheel-base	Approx. Towing Capacity	Gross Vehicle Weight Rating	Average Curb Weight
Sea View	**1998**	MHA	33	8331 myc	FO	6.8L	G	$2100	208	5,000	18,000	15,722

Livability Code: SB 30-90   Wheelbase-to-length ratio of 53% is considered ○ dangerous ● fatiguing ○ good ○ excellent *

The approximate net payload of 2278 pounds at 13% of GVWR on this model is ○ deficient ○ excessive ○ cautionary ● good ○ excellent *

Total highway safety penalties are: 12 *   Value: 9 0   Durability: 9 0   Highway Control Rating: 6 3   Highway Safety: 5 1   ★

Brand	Year	Type	Length	Model	Chassis	Engine	Fuel Type	Average Price per Linear Foot When New	Adjusted Wheel-base	Approx. Towing Capacity	Gross Vehicle Weight Rating	Average Curb Weight
Sea View	**1999**	MHA	31	8310	FO	6.8L	G	$2300	208	5,000	18,000	15,353

Livability Code: SB 30-90   Wheelbase-to-length ratio of 55% is considered ○ dangerous ○ fatiguing ● good ○ excellent *

The approximate net payload of 2647 pounds at 15% of GVWR on this model is ○ deficient ○ excessive ○ cautionary ● good ○ excellent *

Total highway safety penalties are: 12 *   Value: 9 0   Durability: 9 0   Highway Control Rating: 9 2   Highway Safety: 8 0   ★★★★

Brand	Year	Type	Length	Model	Chassis	Engine	Fuel Type	Average Price per Linear Foot When New	Adjusted Wheel-base	Approx. Towing Capacity	Gross Vehicle Weight Rating	Average Curb Weight
Sea View	**1999**	MHA	33	8330	FO	6.8L	G	$2100	208	5,000	18,000	16,108

Livability Code: SB 30-90   Wheelbase-to-length ratio of 53% is considered ○ dangerous ● fatiguing ○ good ○ excellent *

The approximate net payload of 1892 pounds at 11% of GVWR on this model is ○ deficient ○ excessive ○ cautionary ● good ○ excellent *

Total highway safety penalties are: 7 *   Value: 9 2   Durability: 9 0   Highway Control Rating: 6 4   Highway Safety: 5 7   ★

Brand	Year	Type	Length	Model	Chassis	Engine	Fuel Type	Average Price per Linear Foot When New	Adjusted Wheel-base	Approx. Towing Capacity	Gross Vehicle Weight Rating	Average Curb Weight
Sea View	**1999**	MHA	33	8331	FO	6.8L	G	$2100	208	5,000	18,000	15,703

Livability Code: SB 30-90   Wheelbase-to-length ratio of 53% is considered ○ dangerous ● fatiguing ○ good ○ excellent *

The approximate net payload of 2297 pounds at 13% of GVWR on this model is ○ deficient ○ excessive ○ cautionary ● good ○ excellent *

Total highway safety penalties are: 12 *   Value: 9 0   Durability: 9 0   Highway Control Rating: 6 8   Highway Safety: 5 6   ★

Brand	Year	Type	Length	Model	Chassis	Engine	Fuel Type	Average Price per Linear Foot When New	Adjusted Wheel-base	Approx. Towing Capacity	Gross Vehicle Weight Rating	Average Curb Weight
Sea View	**1999**	MHA	35	8340	FO	6.8L	G	$2000	228	2,500	20,500	16,700

Livability Code: SB 30-90   Wheelbase-to-length ratio of 55% is considered ○ dangerous ○ fatiguing ● good ○ excellent *

The approximate net payload of 3800 pounds at 19% of GVWR on this model is ○ deficient ○ excessive ○ cautionary ○ good ● excellent *

Total highway safety penalties are: 7 *   Value: 9 2   Durability: 9 0   Highway Control Rating: 9 5   Highway Safety: 8 8   ★★★★

Brand	Year	Type	Length	Model	Chassis	Engine	Fuel Type	Average Price per Linear Foot When New	Adjusted Wheel-base	Approx. Towing Capacity	Gross Vehicle Weight Rating	Average Curb Weight
Serengeti	**1996**	MHA	34	3334	MA	Ca300	D	$4400	208	5,000	28,000	23,281

Livability Code: SB 30-90   Wheelbase-to-length ratio of 51% is considered ○ dangerous ● fatiguing ○ good ○ excellent *

The approximate net payload of 4719 pounds at 17% of GVWR on this model is ○ deficient ○ excessive ○ cautionary ○ good ● excellent *

Total highway safety penalties are: 2 *   Value: 7 7   Durability: 7 0   Highway Control Rating: 5 1   Highway Safety: 4 9

Brand	Year	Type	Length	Model	Chassis	Engine	Fuel Type	Average Price per Linear Foot When New	Adjusted Wheel-base	Approx. Towing Capacity	Gross Vehicle Weight Rating	Average Curb Weight
Serengeti	**1996**	MHA	34	3354	MA	Ca300	D	$4400	208	5,000	28,000	23,281

Livability Code: SB 30-90   Wheelbase-to-length ratio of 51% is considered ○ dangerous ● fatiguing ○ good ○ excellent *

The approximate net payload of 4719 pounds at 17% of GVWR on this model is ○ deficient ○ excessive ○ cautionary ○ good ● excellent *

Total highway safety penalties are: 2 *   Value: 7 7   Durability: 7 0   Highway Control Rating: 5 1   Highway Safety: 4 9

Brand	Year	Type	Length	Model	Chassis	Engine	Fuel Type	Average Price per Linear Foot When New	Adjusted Wheel-base	Approx. Towing Capacity	Gross Vehicle Weight Rating	Average Curb Weight
Serengeti	**1996**	MHA	34	3390	MA	Ca300	D	$4400	208	5,000	28,000	23,281

Livability Code: SB 30-90   Wheelbase-to-length ratio of 51% is considered ○ dangerous ● fatiguing ○ good ○ excellent *

The approximate net payload of 4719 pounds at 17% of GVWR on this model is ○ deficient ○ excessive ○ cautionary ○ good ● excellent *

Total highway safety penalties are: 2 *   Value: 7 7   Durability: 7 0   Highway Control Rating: 5 1   Highway Safety: 4 9

Brand	Year	Type	Length	Model	Chassis	Engine	Fuel Type	Average Price per Linear Foot When New	Adjusted Wheel-base	Approx. Towing Capacity	Gross Vehicle Weight Rating	Average Curb Weight
Serengeti	**1996**	MHA	36	3530	MA	Ca300	D	$4300	228	5,000	28,000	23,777

Livability Code: SB 30-90   Wheelbase-to-length ratio of 54% is considered ○ dangerous ○ fatiguing ● good ○ excellent *

The approximate net payload of 4223 pounds at 15% of GVWR on this model is ○ deficient ○ excessive ○ cautionary ● good ○ excellent *

Total highway safety penalties are: 2 *   Value: 7 7   Durability: 7 0   Highway Control Rating: 7 8   Highway Safety: 7 6   ★★★

Brand	Year	Type	Length	Model	Chassis	Engine	Fuel Type	Average Price per Linear Foot When New	Adjusted Wheel-base	Approx. Towing Capacity	Gross Vehicle Weight Rating	Average Curb Weight
Serengeti	**1996**	MHA	36	3550	MA	Ca300	D	$4300	228	5,000	28,000	23,777

Livability Code: SB 30-90   Wheelbase-to-length ratio of 54% is considered ○ dangerous ○ fatiguing ● good ○ excellent *

The approximate net payload of 4223 pounds at 15% of GVWR on this model is ○ deficient ○ excessive ○ cautionary ● good ○ excellent *

Total highway safety penalties are: 2 *   Value: 7 7   Durability: 7 0   Highway Control Rating: 7 8   Highway Safety: 7 6   ★★★

Note: Safety ratings are based on the assumption that the engineering of the RV has allowed for proper balance by placing fresh, gray, and black holding tanks in a location so as not to change the balance of the RV when the tanks are empty or full. **Always double-check wheelbase, GVWR, and weights at front and rear axles.**

*See Section 1 for details on how conclusions are reached.

Brand	Year	Type	Length	Model	Chassis	Engine	Fuel Type	Average Price per Linear Foot When New	Adjusted Wheelbase	Approx. Towing Capacity	Gross Vehicle Weight Rating	Average Curb Weight
Serengeti	1996	MHA	36	3590	MA	Ca300	D	$4300	228	5,000	28,000	23,777

Livability Code: SB 30-90
Wheelbase-to-length ratio of 54% is considered ○ dangerous ○ fatiguing ◉ good ○ excellent *
The approximate net payload of 4223 pounds at 15% of GVWR on this model is ○ deficient ○ excessive ○ cautionary ◉ good ○ excellent *
Total highway safety penalties are: 2 *   Value: 7 7   Durability: 7 0   Highway Control Rating: 7 8   Highway Safety: 7 6   ★★★

Serengeti	1996	MHA	38	3740	MA	Ca300	D	$4300	252	5,000	28,000	24,465

Livability Code: SB 30-90
Wheelbase-to-length ratio of 55% is considered ○ dangerous ○ fatiguing ◉ good ○ excellent *
The approximate net payload of 3535 pounds at 13% of GVWR on this model is ○ deficient ○ excessive ○ cautionary ◉ good ○ excellent *
Total highway safety penalties are: 2 *   Value: 7 7   Durability: 7 0   Highway Control Rating: 8 7   Highway Safety: 8 5   ★★★

Serengeti	1996	MHA	38	3750	MA	Ca300	D	$4300	252	5,000	28,000	24,465

Livability Code: SB 30-90
Wheelbase-to-length ratio of 55% is considered ○ dangerous ○ fatiguing ◉ good ○ excellent *
The approximate net payload of 3535 pounds at 13% of GVWR on this model is ○ deficient ○ excessive ○ cautionary ◉ good ○ excellent *
Total highway safety penalties are: 2 *   Value: 7 7   Durability: 7 0   Highway Control Rating: 8 7   Highway Safety: 8 5   ★★★

Serengeti	1996	MHA	38	3790	MA	Ca300	D	$4100	252	5,000	28,000	24,465

Livability Code: SB 30-90
Wheelbase-to-length ratio of 55% is considered ○ dangerous ○ fatiguing ◉ good ○ excellent *
The approximate net payload of 3535 pounds at 13% of GVWR on this model is ○ deficient ○ excessive ○ cautionary ◉ good ○ excellent *
Total highway safety penalties are: 2 *   Value: 7 7   Durability: 7 0   Highway Control Rating: 8 7   Highway Safety: 8 5   ★★★

Serengeti	1996	MHA	39	3730	MA	Ca300	D	$4200	252	5,000	28,000	24,741

Livability Code: SB 30-90
Wheelbase-to-length ratio of 54% is considered ○ dangerous ○ fatiguing ◉ good ○ excellent *
The approximate net payload of 3259 pounds at 12% of GVWR on this model is ○ deficient ○ excessive ○ cautionary ◉ good ○ excellent *
Total highway safety penalties are: 2 *   Value: 7 7   Durability: 7 0   Highway Control Rating: 7 7   Highway Safety: 7 5   ★★★

Serengeti	1996	MHA	40	4030	MA	Ca300	D	$4300	278	5,000	28,000	25,099

Livability Code: SB 30-90
Wheelbase-to-length ratio of 57% is considered ○ dangerous ○ fatiguing ◉ good ○ excellent *
The approximate net payload of 2901 pounds at 10% of GVWR on this model is ○ deficient ○ excessive ○ cautionary ◉ good ○ excellent *
Total highway safety penalties are: 2 *   Value: 7 7   Durability: 7 0   Highway Control Rating: 9 0   Highway Safety: 8 8   ★★★

Serengeti	1996	MHA	40	4050	MA	Ca300	D	$4300	278	5,000	28,000	25,099

Livability Code: SB 30-90
Wheelbase-to-length ratio of 57% is considered ○ dangerous ○ fatiguing ◉ good ○ excellent *
The approximate net payload of 2901 pounds at 10% of GVWR on this model is ○ deficient ○ excessive ○ cautionary ◉ good ○ excellent *
Total highway safety penalties are: 2 *   Value: 7 7   Durability: 7 0   Highway Control Rating: 9 0   Highway Safety: 8 8   ★★★

Serengeti	1996	MHA	40	4088	MA	Ca300	D	$4300	278	5,000	28,000	25,099

Livability Code: SB 30-90
Wheelbase-to-length ratio of 57% is considered ○ dangerous ○ fatiguing ◉ good ○ excellent *
The approximate net payload of 2901 pounds at 10% of GVWR on this model is ○ deficient ○ excessive ○ cautionary ◉ good ○ excellent *
Total highway safety penalties are: 2 *   Value: 7 7   Durability: 7 0   Highway Control Rating: 9 0   Highway Safety: 8 8   ★★★

Serengeti	1996	MHA	40	4090	MA	Ca300	D	$4300	278	5,000	28,000	25,099

Livability Code: SB 30-90
Wheelbase-to-length ratio of 57% is considered ○ dangerous ○ fatiguing ◉ good ○ excellent *
The approximate net payload of 2901 pounds at 10% of GVWR on this model is ○ deficient ○ excessive ○ cautionary ◉ good ○ excellent *
Total highway safety penalties are: 2 *   Value: 7 7   Durability: 7 0   Highway Control Rating: 9 0   Highway Safety: 8 8   ★★★

Serengeti	1997	MHA	33	3334	MA	Ca300	D	$4800	208	5,000	28,000	23,088

Livability Code: SB 30-90
Wheelbase-to-length ratio of 53% is considered ○ dangerous ◉ fatiguing ○ good ○ excellent *
The approximate net payload of 4912 pounds at 18% of GVWR on this model is ○ deficient ○ excessive ○ cautionary ○ good ◉ excellent *
Total highway safety penalties are: 2 *   Value: 7 7   Durability: 7 0   Highway Control Rating: 7 0   Highway Safety: 6 8   ★★

Serengeti	1997	MHA	33	3354	MA	Ca300	D	$4800	208	5,000	28,000	23,088

Livability Code: SB 30-90
Wheelbase-to-length ratio of 53% is considered ○ dangerous ◉ fatiguing ○ good ○ excellent *
The approximate net payload of 4912 pounds at 18% of GVWR on this model is ○ deficient ○ excessive ○ cautionary ○ good ◉ excellent *
Total highway safety penalties are: 2 *   Value: 7 7   Durability: 7 0   Highway Control Rating: 7 0   Highway Safety: 6 8   ★★

Serengeti	1997	MHA	35	3530	MA	Ca300	D	$4500	228	5,000	28,000	23,639

Livability Code: SB 30-90
Wheelbase-to-length ratio of 54% is considered ○ dangerous ○ fatiguing ◉ good ○ excellent *
The approximate net payload of 4361 pounds at 16% of GVWR on this model is ○ deficient ○ excessive ○ cautionary ○ good ◉ excellent *
Total highway safety penalties are: 2 *   Value: 7 7   Durability: 7 0   Highway Control Rating: 8 2   Highway Safety: 8 0   ★★★

Note: Safety ratings are based on the assumption that the engineering of the RV has allowed for proper balance by placing fresh, gray, and black holding tanks in a location so as not to change the balance of the RV when the tanks are empty or full. **Always double-check wheelbase, GVWR, and weights at front and rear axles.**

*See Section 1 for details on how conclusions are reached.

Section 2: The Ratings

Brand	Year	Type	Length	Model	Chassis	Engine	Fuel Type	Average Price per Linear Foot When New	Adjusted Wheelbase	Approx. Towing Capacity	Gross Vehicle Weight Rating	Average Curb Weight
Serengeti	1997	MHA	35	3540	MA	Ca300	D	$4500	228	5,000	28,000	23,639

Livability Code: SB 30-90   Wheelbase-to-length ratio of 54% is considered ○ dangerous ○ fatiguing ◉ good ○ excellent*

The approximate net payload of 4361 pounds at 16% of GVWR on this model is ○ deficient ○ excessive ○ cautionary ○ good ◉ excellent*

Total highway safety penalties are: 2*   Value: 7 7   Durability: 7 0   Highway Control Rating: 8 2   Highway Safety: 8 0   ★★★

Brand	Year	Type	Length	Model	Chassis	Engine	Fuel Type	Avg Price/Linear Foot	Adj. Wheelbase	Approx. Towing	GVWR	Avg Curb Weight
Serengeti	1997	MHA	35	3550	MA	Ca300	D	$4500	228	5,000	28,000	23,639

Livability Code: SB 30-90   Wheelbase-to-length ratio of 54% is considered ○ dangerous ○ fatiguing ◉ good ○ excellent*

The approximate net payload of 4361 pounds at 16% of GVWR on this model is ○ deficient ○ excessive ○ cautionary ○ good ◉ excellent*

Total highway safety penalties are: 2*   Value: 7 7   Durability: 7 0   Highway Control Rating: 8 2   Highway Safety: 8 0   ★★★

Serengeti	1997	MHA	37	3730	MA	Ca300	D	$4600	252	5,000	28,000	24,190

Livability Code: SB 30-90   Wheelbase-to-length ratio of 57% is considered ○ dangerous ○ fatiguing ◉ good ○ excellent*

The approximate net payload of 3810 pounds at 14% of GVWR on this model is ○ deficient ○ excessive ○ cautionary ◉ good ○ excellent*

Total highway safety penalties are: 2*   Value: 7 7   Durability: 7 0   Highway Control Rating: 9 4   Highway Safety: 9 2   ★★★

Serengeti	1997	MHA	37	3740	MA	Ca300	D	$4600	252	5,000	28,000	24,190

Livability Code: SB 30-90   Wheelbase-to-length ratio of 57% is considered ○ dangerous ○ fatiguing ◉ good ○ excellent*

The approximate net payload of 3810 pounds at 14% of GVWR on this model is ○ deficient ○ excessive ○ cautionary ◉ good ○ excellent*

Total highway safety penalties are: 2*   Value: 7 7   Durability: 7 0   Highway Control Rating: 9 4   Highway Safety: 9 2   ★★★

Serengeti	1997	MHA	37	3750	MA	Ca300	D	$4600	252	5,000	28,000	24,190

Livability Code: SB 30-90   Wheelbase-to-length ratio of 57% is considered ○ dangerous ○ fatiguing ◉ good ○ excellent*

The approximate net payload of 3810 pounds at 14% of GVWR on this model is ○ deficient ○ excessive ○ cautionary ◉ good ○ excellent*

Total highway safety penalties are: 2*   Value: 7 7   Durability: 7 0   Highway Control Rating: 9 4   Highway Safety: 9 2   ★★★

Serengeti	1997	MHA	40	4030	MA	Ca300	D	$4300	276	5,000	28,000	25,016

Livability Code: SB 30-90   Wheelbase-to-length ratio of 58% is considered ○ dangerous ○ fatiguing ○ good ◉ excellent*

The approximate net payload of 2984 pounds at 11% of GVWR on this model is ○ deficient ○ excessive ○ cautionary ◉ good ○ excellent*

Total highway safety penalties are: 2*   Value: 7 7   Durability: 7 0   Highway Control Rating: 9 1   Highway Safety: 8 9   ★★★

Serengeti	1997	MHA	40	4050	MA	Ca300	D	$4300	276	5,000	28,000	25,016

Livability Code: SB 30-90   Wheelbase-to-length ratio of 58% is considered ○ dangerous ○ fatiguing ○ good ◉ excellent*

The approximate net payload of 2984 pounds at 11% of GVWR on this model is ○ deficient ○ excessive ○ cautionary ◉ good ○ excellent*

Total highway safety penalties are: 2*   Value: 7 7   Durability: 7 0   Highway Control Rating: 9 1   Highway Safety: 8 9   ★★★

Serengeti	1997	MHA	40	4040	MA	Ca300	D	$4300	276	5,000	28,000	25,016

Livability Code: SB 30-90   Wheelbase-to-length ratio of 58% is considered ○ dangerous ○ fatiguing ○ good ◉ excellent*

The approximate net payload of 2984 pounds at 11% of GVWR on this model is ○ deficient ○ excessive ○ cautionary ◉ good ○ excellent*

Total highway safety penalties are: 2*   Value: 7 7   Durability: 7 0   Highway Control Rating: 9 1   Highway Safety: 8 9   ★★★

Signature	1990	MHA	40	Monarch 40	RO	Cum	D	$6600	270	1,500	34,700	31,737

Livability Code: FT 30-90   Wheelbase-to-length ratio of 56% is considered ○ dangerous ○ fatiguing ◉ good ○ excellent*

The approximate net payload of 2963 pounds at 9% of GVWR on this model is ○ deficient ○ excessive ◉ cautionary ○ good ○ excellent*

Total highway safety penalties are: 2*   Value: 7 9   Durability: 7 5   Highway Control Rating: 7 8   Highway Safety: 7 6   ★★★

Signature	1991	MHA	40	Monarch 40	RO	Cum	D	$6700	270	1,500	34,700	32,432

Livability Code: FT 30-90   Wheelbase-to-length ratio of 56% is considered ○ dangerous ○ fatiguing ◉ good ○ excellent*

The approximate net payload of 2268 pounds at 7% of GVWR on this model is ○ deficient ○ excessive ◉ cautionary ○ good ○ excellent*

Total highway safety penalties are: 2*   Value: 7 9   Durability: 7 5   Highway Control Rating: 6 6   Highway Safety: 6 4   ★★

Signature	1992	MHA	36	36 Baron 250	RO	Cu8.3L	D	$6800	222	1,500	34,700	30,202

Livability Code: FT 30-90   Wheelbase-to-length ratio of 51% is considered ○ dangerous ◉ fatiguing ○ good ○ excellent*

The approximate net payload of 4498 pounds at 13% of GVWR on this model is ○ deficient ○ excessive ○ cautionary ◉ good ○ excellent*

Total highway safety penalties are: 2*   Value: 7 9   Durability: 7 5   Highway Control Rating: 4 4   Highway Safety: 4 2

Signature	1992	MHA	36	36 Commodore 250	RO	Cu8.3L	D	$6800	222	1,500	34,700	30,202

Livability Code: FT 30-90   Wheelbase-to-length ratio of 51% is considered ○ dangerous ◉ fatiguing ○ good ○ excellent*

The approximate net payload of 4498 pounds at 13% of GVWR on this model is ○ deficient ○ excessive ○ cautionary ◉ good ○ excellent*

Total highway safety penalties are: 2*   Value: 7 9   Durability: 7 5   Highway Control Rating: 4 4   Highway Safety: 4 2

Note: Safety ratings are based on the assumption that the engineering of the RV has allowed for proper balance by placing fresh, gray, and black holding tanks in a location so as not to change the balance of the RV when the tanks are empty or full. **Always double-check wheelbase, GVWR, and weights at front and rear axles.**

*See Section 1 for details on how conclusions are reached.

Brand	Year	Type	Length	Model	Chassis	Engine	Fuel Type	Average Price per Linear Foot When New	Adjusted Wheelbase	Approx. Towing Capacity	Gross Vehicle Weight Rating	Average Curb Weight
Signature	1992	MHA	36	36 Tycoon 250	RO	Cu8.3L	D	$6800	222	1,500	34,700	30,202

Livability Code: FT 30-90
Wheelbase-to-length ratio of 51% is considered ◯ dangerous ◉ fatiguing ◯ good ◯ excellent *
The approximate net payload of 4498 pounds at 13% of GVWR on this model is ◯ deficient ◯ excessive ◯ cautionary ◉ good ◯ excellent *
Total highway safety penalties are: 2 *   Value: 7 9   Durability: 7 5   Highway Control Rating: 4 4   Highway Safety: 4 2

Brand	Year	Type	Length	Model	Chassis	Engine	Fuel Type	Price/ft	Wheelbase	Towing	GVWR	Curb Wt
Signature	1992	MHA	36	36 Baron 300	RO	Cu8.3L	D	$7100	222	1,500	34,700	30,202

Livability Code: FT 30-90
Wheelbase-to-length ratio of 51% is considered ◯ dangerous ◉ fatiguing ◯ good ◯ excellent *
The approximate net payload of 4498 pounds at 13% of GVWR on this model is ◯ deficient ◯ excessive ◯ cautionary ◉ good ◯ excellent *
Total highway safety penalties are: 2 *   Value: 7 9   Durability: 7 5   Highway Control Rating: 4 4   Highway Safety: 4 2

Signature	1992	MHA	36	36 Commodore 300	RO	Cu8.3L	D	$7100	222	1,500	34,700	30,202

Livability Code: FT 30-90
Wheelbase-to-length ratio of 51% is considered ◯ dangerous ◉ fatiguing ◯ good ◯ excellent *
The approximate net payload of 4498 pounds at 13% of GVWR on this model is ◯ deficient ◯ excessive ◯ cautionary ◉ good ◯ excellent *
Total highway safety penalties are: 2 *   Value: 7 9   Durability: 7 5   Highway Control Rating: 4 4   Highway Safety: 4 2

Signature	1992	MHA	36	36 Tycoon 300	RO	Cu8.3L	D	$7100	222	1,500	34,700	30,202

Livability Code: FT 30-90
Wheelbase-to-length ratio of 51% is considered ◯ dangerous ◉ fatiguing ◯ good ◯ excellent *
The approximate net payload of 4498 pounds at 13% of GVWR on this model is ◯ deficient ◯ excessive ◯ cautionary ◉ good ◯ excellent *
Total highway safety penalties are: 2 *   Value: 7 9   Durability: 7 5   Highway Control Rating: 4 4   Highway Safety: 4 2

Signature	1992	MHA	38	38 Duke 300	RO	Cu8.3L	D	$6900	246	1,500	34,700	30,916

Livability Code: FT 30-90
Wheelbase-to-length ratio of 54% is considered ◯ dangerous ◯ fatiguing ◉ good ◯ excellent *
The approximate net payload of 3784 pounds at 11% of GVWR on this model is ◯ deficient ◯ excessive ◯ cautionary ◉ good ◯ excellent *
Total highway safety penalties are: 2 *   Value: 7 9   Durability: 7 5   Highway Control Rating: 7 6   Highway Safety: 7 4   ★★★

Signature	1992	MHA	38	38 Commodore 300	RO	Cu8.3L	D	$6900	246	1,500	34,700	30,916

Livability Code: FT 30-90
Wheelbase-to-length ratio of 54% is considered ◯ dangerous ◯ fatiguing ◉ good ◯ excellent *
The approximate net payload of 3784 pounds at 11% of GVWR on this model is ◯ deficient ◯ excessive ◯ cautionary ◉ good ◯ excellent *
Total highway safety penalties are: 2 *   Value: 7 9   Durability: 7 5   Highway Control Rating: 7 6   Highway Safety: 7 4   ★★★

Signature	1992	MHA	38	38 Tycoon 300	RO	Cu8.3L	D	$6900	246	1,500	34,700	30,916

Livability Code: FT 30-90
Wheelbase-to-length ratio of 54% is considered ◯ dangerous ◯ fatiguing ◉ good ◯ excellent *
The approximate net payload of 3784 pounds at 11% of GVWR on this model is ◯ deficient ◯ excessive ◯ cautionary ◉ good ◯ excellent *
Total highway safety penalties are: 2 *   Value: 7 9   Durability: 7 5   Highway Control Rating: 7 6   Highway Safety: 7 4   ★★★

Signature	1992	MHA	38	38 Duke 330	RO	Cu8.3L	D	$7500	246	1,500	34,700	30,916

Livability Code: FT 30-90
Wheelbase-to-length ratio of 54% is considered ◯ dangerous ◯ fatiguing ◉ good ◯ excellent *
The approximate net payload of 3784 pounds at 11% of GVWR on this model is ◯ deficient ◯ excessive ◯ cautionary ◉ good ◯ excellent *
Total highway safety penalties are: 2 *   Value: 7 9   Durability: 7 5   Highway Control Rating: 7 6   Highway Safety: 7 4   ★★★

Signature	1992	MHA	38	38 Commodore 330	RO	Cu8.3L	D	$7500	246	1,500	34,700	30,916

Livability Code: FT 30-90
Wheelbase-to-length ratio of 54% is considered ◯ dangerous ◯ fatiguing ◉ good ◯ excellent *
The approximate net payload of 3784 pounds at 11% of GVWR on this model is ◯ deficient ◯ excessive ◯ cautionary ◉ good ◯ excellent *
Total highway safety penalties are: 2 *   Value: 7 9   Durability: 7 5   Highway Control Rating: 7 6   Highway Safety: 7 4   ★★★

Signature	1992	MHA	38	38 Tycoon 330	RO	Cu8.3L	D	$7500	246	1,500	34,700	30,916

Livability Code: FT 30-90
Wheelbase-to-length ratio of 54% is considered ◯ dangerous ◯ fatiguing ◉ good ◯ excellent *
The approximate net payload of 3784 pounds at 11% of GVWR on this model is ◯ deficient ◯ excessive ◯ cautionary ◉ good ◯ excellent *
Total highway safety penalties are: 2 *   Value: 7 9   Durability: 7 5   Highway Control Rating: 7 6   Highway Safety: 7 4   ★★★

Signature	1992	MHA	40	40 Monarch 300	RO	Cu8.3L	D	$6900	270	1,500	34,700	31,630

Livability Code: FT 30-90
Wheelbase-to-length ratio of 56% is considered ◯ dangerous ◯ fatiguing ◉ good ◯ excellent *
The approximate net payload of 3070 pounds at 9% of GVWR on this model is ◯ deficient ◯ excessive ◉ cautionary ◯ good ◯ excellent *
Total highway safety penalties are: 2 *   Value: 7 9   Durability: 7 5   Highway Control Rating: 8 0   Highway Safety: 7 8   ★★★

Signature	1992	MHA	40	40 Senator 300	RO	Cu8.3L	D	$6900	270	1,500	34,700	31,630

Livability Code: FT 30-90
Wheelbase-to-length ratio of 56% is considered ◯ dangerous ◯ fatiguing ◉ good ◯ excellent *
The approximate net payload of 3070 pounds at 9% of GVWR on this model is ◯ deficient ◯ excessive ◉ cautionary ◯ good ◯ excellent *
Total highway safety penalties are: 2 *   Value: 7 9   Durability: 7 5   Highway Control Rating: 8 0   Highway Safety: 7 8   ★★★

Note: Safety ratings are based on the assumption that the engineering of the RV has allowed for proper balance by placing fresh, gray, and black holding tanks in a location so as not to change the balance of the RV when the tanks are empty or full. **Always double-check wheelbase, GVWR, and weights at front and rear axles.**

*See Section 1 for details on how conclusions are reached.

Section 2: The Ratings

Brand	Year	Type	Length	Model	Chassis	Engine	Fuel Type	Average Price per Linear Foot When New	Adjusted Wheelbase	Approx. Towing Capacity	Gross Vehicle Weight Rating	Average Curb Weight
Signature	1992	MHA	40	40 Ambassador 300	RO	Cu8.3L	D	$6900	270	1,500	34,700	31,630

Livability Code: FT 30-90   Wheelbase-to-length ratio of 56% is considered ○ dangerous ○ fatiguing ◉ good ○ excellent *

The approximate net payload of 3070 pounds at 9% of GVWR on this model is ○ deficient ○ excessive ◉ cautionary ○ good ○ excellent *

Total highway safety penalties are: 2 *   Value: **7 9** Durability: **7 5** Highway Control Rating: **8 0** Highway Safety: **7 8** ★★★

Brand	Year	Type	Length	Model	Chassis	Engine	Fuel Type	Average Price per Linear Foot When New	Adjusted Wheelbase	Approx. Towing Capacity	Gross Vehicle Weight Rating	Average Curb Weight
Signature	1992	MHA	40	40 Monarch 330	RO	Cu8.3L	D	$7400	270	1,500	34,700	31,630

Livability Code: FT 30-90   Wheelbase-to-length ratio of 56% is considered ○ dangerous ○ fatiguing ◉ good ○ excellent *

The approximate net payload of 3070 pounds at 9% of GVWR on this model is ○ deficient ○ excessive ◉ cautionary ○ good ○ excellent *

Total highway safety penalties are: 2 *   Value: **7 9** Durability: **7 5** Highway Control Rating: **8 0** Highway Safety: **7 8** ★★★

Brand	Year	Type	Length	Model	Chassis	Engine	Fuel Type	Average Price per Linear Foot When New	Adjusted Wheelbase	Approx. Towing Capacity	Gross Vehicle Weight Rating	Average Curb Weight
Signature	1992	MHA	40	40 Senator 330	RO	Cu8.3L	D	$7400	270	1,500	34,700	31,630

Livability Code: FT 30-90   Wheelbase-to-length ratio of 56% is considered ○ dangerous ○ fatiguing ◉ good ○ excellent *

The approximate net payload of 3070 pounds at 9% of GVWR on this model is ○ deficient ○ excessive ◉ cautionary ○ good ○ excellent *

Total highway safety penalties are: 2 *   Value: **7 9** Durability: **7 5** Highway Control Rating: **8 0** Highway Safety: **7 8** ★★★

Brand	Year	Type	Length	Model	Chassis	Engine	Fuel Type	Average Price per Linear Foot When New	Adjusted Wheelbase	Approx. Towing Capacity	Gross Vehicle Weight Rating	Average Curb Weight
Signature	1992	MHA	40	40 Ambassador 330	RO	Cu8.3L	D	$7400	270	1,500	34,700	31,630

Livability Code: FT 30-90   Wheelbase-to-length ratio of 56% is considered ○ dangerous ○ fatiguing ◉ good ○ excellent *

The approximate net payload of 3070 pounds at 9% of GVWR on this model is ○ deficient ○ excessive ◉ cautionary ○ good ○ excellent *

Total highway safety penalties are: 2 *   Value: **7 9** Durability: **7 5** Highway Control Rating: **8 0** Highway Safety: **7 8** ★★★

Brand	Year	Type	Length	Model	Chassis	Engine	Fuel Type	Average Price per Linear Foot When New	Adjusted Wheelbase	Approx. Towing Capacity	Gross Vehicle Weight Rating	Average Curb Weight
Signature	1995	MHA	38	38-300	RO	Cu8.3L	D	$7800	246	1,500	35,000	31,066

Livability Code: FT 30-90   Wheelbase-to-length ratio of 54% is considered ○ dangerous ○ fatiguing ◉ good ○ excellent *

The approximate net payload of 3934 pounds at 11% of GVWR on this model is ○ deficient ○ excessive ○ cautionary ○ good ○ excellent *

Total highway safety penalties are: 2 *   Value: **7 9** Durability: **7 5** Highway Control Rating: **7 7** Highway Safety: **7 5** ★★★

Brand	Year	Type	Length	Model	Chassis	Engine	Fuel Type	Average Price per Linear Foot When New	Adjusted Wheelbase	Approx. Towing Capacity	Gross Vehicle Weight Rating	Average Curb Weight
Signature	1995	MHA	38	38-400	RO	Cu8.3L	D	$8400	246	1,500	35,000	31,066

Livability Code: FT 30-90   Wheelbase-to-length ratio of 54% is considered ○ dangerous ○ fatiguing ◉ good ○ excellent *

The approximate net payload of 3934 pounds at 11% of GVWR on this model is ○ deficient ○ excessive ○ cautionary ○ good ○ excellent *

Total highway safety penalties are: 2 *   Value: **7 9** Durability: **7 5** Highway Control Rating: **7 7** Highway Safety: **7 5** ★★★

Brand	Year	Type	Length	Model	Chassis	Engine	Fuel Type	Average Price per Linear Foot When New	Adjusted Wheelbase	Approx. Towing Capacity	Gross Vehicle Weight Rating	Average Curb Weight
Signature	1995	MHA	40	40-300	RO	Cu8.3L	D	$7600	270	1,500	35,000	31,780

Livability Code: FT 30-90   Wheelbase-to-length ratio of 56% is considered ○ dangerous ○ fatiguing ◉ good ○ excellent *

The approximate net payload of 3220 pounds at 9% of GVWR on this model is ○ deficient ○ excessive ◉ cautionary ○ good ○ excellent *

Total highway safety penalties are: 2 *   Value: **7 9** Durability: **7 5** Highway Control Rating: **8 0** Highway Safety: **7 8** ★★★

Brand	Year	Type	Length	Model	Chassis	Engine	Fuel Type	Average Price per Linear Foot When New	Adjusted Wheelbase	Approx. Towing Capacity	Gross Vehicle Weight Rating	Average Curb Weight
Signature	1995	MHA	40	40-400	RO	Cu8.3L	D	$8200	270	1,500	35,000	31,780

Livability Code: FT 30-90   Wheelbase-to-length ratio of 56% is considered ○ dangerous ○ fatiguing ◉ good ○ excellent *

The approximate net payload of 3220 pounds at 9% of GVWR on this model is ○ deficient ○ excessive ◉ cautionary ○ good ○ excellent *

Total highway safety penalties are: 2 *   Value: **7 9** Durability: **7 5** Highway Control Rating: **8 0** Highway Safety: **7 8** ★★★

Brand	Year	Type	Length	Model	Chassis	Engine	Fuel Type	Average Price per Linear Foot When New	Adjusted Wheelbase	Approx. Towing Capacity	Gross Vehicle Weight Rating	Average Curb Weight
Signature	1995	MHA	45	45-300	RO	Cu8.3L	D	$8100	321 T	1,500	48,000	40,065

Livability Code: FT 30-90   Wheelbase-to-length ratio of 59% is considered ○ dangerous ○ fatiguing ○ good ◉ excellent *

The approximate net payload of 7935 pounds at 17% of GVWR on this model is ○ deficient ○ excessive ○ cautionary ○ good ◉ excellent *

Total highway safety penalties are: 4 *   Value: **7 8** Durability: **7 5** Highway Control Rating: **1 0 0** Highway Safety: **9 6** ★★★

Brand	Year	Type	Length	Model	Chassis	Engine	Fuel Type	Average Price per Linear Foot When New	Adjusted Wheelbase	Approx. Towing Capacity	Gross Vehicle Weight Rating	Average Curb Weight
Signature	1996	MHA	40	40 Admiral -300	RO	Cu8.3L	D	$7700	270	1,500	35,000	31,780

Livability Code: FT 30-90   Wheelbase-to-length ratio of 56% is considered ○ dangerous ○ fatiguing ◉ good ○ excellent *

The approximate net payload of 3220 pounds at 9% of GVWR on this model is ○ deficient ○ excessive ◉ cautionary ○ good ○ excellent *

Total highway safety penalties are: 2 *   Value: **7 9** Durability: **7 5** Highway Control Rating: **8 0** Highway Safety: **7 8** ★★★

Brand	Year	Type	Length	Model	Chassis	Engine	Fuel Type	Average Price per Linear Foot When New	Adjusted Wheelbase	Approx. Towing Capacity	Gross Vehicle Weight Rating	Average Curb Weight
Signature	1996	MHA	40	40 Admiral -400	RO	Cu8.3L	D	$8300	270	1,500	35,000	31,780

Livability Code: FT 30-90   Wheelbase-to-length ratio of 56% is considered ○ dangerous ○ fatiguing ◉ good ○ excellent *

The approximate net payload of 3220 pounds at 9% of GVWR on this model is ○ deficient ○ excessive ◉ cautionary ○ good ○ excellent *

Total highway safety penalties are: 2 *   Value: **7 9** Durability: **7 5** Highway Control Rating: **8 0** Highway Safety: **7 8** ★★★

Brand	Year	Type	Length	Model	Chassis	Engine	Fuel Type	Average Price per Linear Foot When New	Adjusted Wheelbase	Approx. Towing Capacity	Gross Vehicle Weight Rating	Average Curb Weight
Signature	1996	MHA	45	45 Senator -400	RO	Cu8.3L	D	$8100	321 T	1,500	45,000	38,565

Livability Code: FT 30-90   Wheelbase-to-length ratio of 59% is considered ○ dangerous ○ fatiguing ○ good ◉ excellent *

The approximate net payload of 6435 pounds at 14% of GVWR on this model is ○ deficient ○ excessive ○ cautionary ◉ good ○ excellent *

Total highway safety penalties are: 4 *   Value: **7 8** Durability: **7 5** Highway Control Rating: **1 0 0** Highway Safety: **9 6** ★★★

Note: Safety ratings are based on the assumption that the engineering of the RV has allowed for proper balance by placing fresh, gray, and black holding tanks in a location so as not to change the balance of the RV when the tanks are empty or full. **Always double-check wheelbase, GVWR, and weights at front and rear axles.**

Brand	Year	Type	Length	Model	Chassis	Engine	Fuel Type	Average Price per Linear Foot When New	Adjusted Wheelbase	Approx. Towing Capacity	Gross Vehicle Weight Rating	Average Curb Weight
Signature	1996	MHA	45	45 Senator -500	RO	Cu8.3L	D	$8500	321 T	1,500	45,000	38,565

Livability Code: FT 30-90
Wheelbase-to-length ratio of 59% is considered ○ dangerous ○ fatiguing ○ good ● excellent *
The approximate net payload of 6435 pounds at 14% of GVWR on this model is ○ deficient ○ excessive ○ cautionary ● good ○ excellent *
Total highway safety penalties are: 4 *   Value: **7 8**   Durability: **7 5**   Highway Control Rating: **1 0 0**   Highway Safety: **9 6**   ★★★

| **Signature** | 1997 | MHA | 40 | Admiral FD | RO | Cu325 | D | $8100 | 270 | 10,000 | 35,000 | 31,780 |

Livability Code: FT 30-90
Wheelbase-to-length ratio of 56% is considered ○ dangerous ○ fatiguing ● good ○ excellent *
The approximate net payload of 3220 pounds at 9% of GVWR on this model is ○ deficient ○ excessive ● cautionary ○ good ○ excellent *
Total highway safety penalties are: 2 *   Value: **7 9**   Durability: **7 5**   Highway Control Rating: **8 0**   Highway Safety: **7 8**   ★★★

| **Signature** | 1997 | MHA | 40 | Cambridge FD | RO | Cu325 | D | $8100 | 270 | 10,000 | 35,000 | 31,780 |

Livability Code: FT 30-90
Wheelbase-to-length ratio of 56% is considered ○ dangerous ○ fatiguing ● good ○ excellent *
The approximate net payload of 3220 pounds at 9% of GVWR on this model is ○ deficient ○ excessive ● cautionary ○ good ○ excellent *
Total highway safety penalties are: 2 *   Value: **7 9**   Durability: **7 5**   Highway Control Rating: **8 0**   Highway Safety: **7 8**   ★★★

| **Signature** | 1997 | MHA | 40 | Empress SD | RO | Cu325 | D | $8100 | 270 | 10,000 | 35,000 | 31,780 |

Livability Code: FT 30-90
Wheelbase-to-length ratio of 56% is considered ○ dangerous ○ fatiguing ● good ○ excellent *
The approximate net payload of 3220 pounds at 9% of GVWR on this model is ○ deficient ○ excessive ● cautionary ○ good ○ excellent *
Total highway safety penalties are: 2 *   Value: **7 9**   Durability: **7 5**   Highway Control Rating: **8 0**   Highway Safety: **7 8**   ★★★

| **Signature** | 1997 | MHA | 40 | Monarch FD | RO | Cu325 | D | $8800 | 270 | 10,000 | 35,000 | 31,780 |

Livability Code: FT 30-90
Wheelbase-to-length ratio of 56% is considered ○ dangerous ○ fatiguing ● good ○ excellent *
The approximate net payload of 3220 pounds at 9% of GVWR on this model is ○ deficient ○ excessive ● cautionary ○ good ○ excellent *
Total highway safety penalties are: 2 *   Value: **7 9**   Durability: **7 5**   Highway Control Rating: **8 0**   Highway Safety: **7 8**   ★★★

| **Signature** | 1997 | MHA | 40 | Monarch SD | RO | Cu325 | D | $8800 | 270 | 10,000 | 35,000 | 31,780 |

Livability Code: FT 30-90
Wheelbase-to-length ratio of 56% is considered ○ dangerous ○ fatiguing ● good ○ excellent *
The approximate net payload of 3220 pounds at 9% of GVWR on this model is ○ deficient ○ excessive ● cautionary ○ good ○ excellent *
Total highway safety penalties are: 2 *   Value: **7 9**   Durability: **7 5**   Highway Control Rating: **8 0**   Highway Safety: **7 8**   ★★★

| **Signature** | 1997 | MHA | 40 | Premier FD | RO | Cu325 | D | $8800 | 270 | 10,000 | 35,000 | 31,780 |

Livability Code: FT 30-90
Wheelbase-to-length ratio of 56% is considered ○ dangerous ○ fatiguing ● good ○ excellent *
The approximate net payload of 3220 pounds at 9% of GVWR on this model is ○ deficient ○ excessive ● cautionary ○ good ○ excellent *
Total highway safety penalties are: 2 *   Value: **7 9**   Durability: **7 5**   Highway Control Rating: **8 0**   Highway Safety: **7 8**   ★★★

| **Signature** | 1997 | MHA | 40 | President FD | RO | Cu325 | D | $8800 | 270 | 10,000 | 35,000 | 31,780 |

Livability Code: FT 30-90
Wheelbase-to-length ratio of 56% is considered ○ dangerous ○ fatiguing ● good ○ excellent *
The approximate net payload of 3220 pounds at 9% of GVWR on this model is ○ deficient ○ excessive ● cautionary ○ good ○ excellent *
Total highway safety penalties are: 2 *   Value: **7 9**   Durability: **7 5**   Highway Control Rating: **8 0**   Highway Safety: **7 8**   ★★★

| **Signature** | 1997 | MHA | 40 | Suite Slide | RO | Cu325 | D | $8800 | 270 | 10,000 | 35,000 | 32,680 |

Livability Code: FT 30-90
Wheelbase-to-length ratio of 56% is considered ○ dangerous ○ fatiguing ● good ○ excellent *
The approximate net payload of 2320 pounds at 7% of GVWR on this model is ○ deficient ○ excessive ● cautionary ○ good ○ excellent *
Total highway safety penalties are: 7 *   Value: **7 6**   Durability: **7 5**   Highway Control Rating: **6 8**   Highway Safety: **6 1**   ★★

| **Signature** | 1997 | MHA | 45 | Senator SD FD | RO | CU450 | D | $8000 | 290 | 10,000 | 45,000 | 38,565 |

Livability Code: FT 30-90
Wheelbase-to-length ratio of 54% is considered ○ dangerous ○ fatiguing ● good ○ excellent *
The approximate net payload of 6435 pounds at 14% of GVWR on this model is ○ deficient ○ excessive ○ cautionary ● good ○ excellent *
Total highway safety penalties are: 2 *   Value: **7 9**   Durability: **7 5**   Highway Control Rating: **7 9**   Highway Safety: **7 7**   ★★★

| **Signature** | 1997 | MHA | 45 | Senator XLFD | RO | CU450 | D | $8000 | 290 | 10,000 | 45,000 | 38,565 |

Livability Code: FT 30-90
Wheelbase-to-length ratio of 54% is considered ○ dangerous ○ fatiguing ● good ○ excellent *
The approximate net payload of 6435 pounds at 14% of GVWR on this model is ○ deficient ○ excessive ○ cautionary ● good ○ excellent *
Total highway safety penalties are: 2 *   Value: **7 9**   Durability: **7 5**   Highway Control Rating: **7 9**   Highway Safety: **7 7**   ★★★

| **Signature** | 1998 | MHA | 40 | 40 No Slide | RO | CU325 | D | $8200 | 270 | 10,000 | 35,000 | 31,780 |

Livability Code: FT 30-90
Wheelbase-to-length ratio of 56% is considered ○ dangerous ○ fatiguing ● good ○ excellent *
The approximate net payload of 3220 pounds at 9% of GVWR on this model is ○ deficient ○ excessive ● cautionary ○ good ○ excellent *
Total highway safety penalties are: 2 *   Value: **7 9**   Durability: **7 5**   Highway Control Rating: **8 0**   Highway Safety: **7 8**   ★★★

Note: Safety ratings are based on the assumption that the engineering of the RV has allowed for proper balance by placing fresh, gray, and black holding tanks in a location so as not to change the balance of the RV when the tanks are empty or full. **Always double-check wheelbase, GVWR, and weights at front and rear axles.**

*See Section 1 for details on how conclusions are reached.

Section 2: The Ratings

Brand	Year	Type	Length	Model	Chassis	Engine	Fuel Type	Average Price per Linear Foot When New	Adjusted Wheelbase	Approx. Towing Capacity	Gross Vehicle Weight Rating	Average Curb Weight
Signature	1998	MHA	40	40 Slide	RO	CU325	D	$8400	270	10,000	35,000	32,680

Livability Code: FT 30-90
Wheelbase-to-length ratio of 56% is considered ○ dangerous ○ fatiguing ◉ good ○ excellent *
The approximate net payload of 2320 pounds at 7% of GVWR on this model is ○ deficient ○ excessive ◉ cautionary ○ good ○ excellent *
Total highway safety penalties are: 12 *   Value: 7 4   Durability: 7 5   Highway Control Rating: 6 8   Highway Safety: 5 6   ★

Signature	1998	MHA	42	42 No Slide	RO	CU450	D	$9000	270	10,000	35,000	32,494

Livability Code: FT 30-90
Wheelbase-to-length ratio of 54% is considered ○ dangerous ○ fatiguing ◉ good ○ excellent *
The approximate net payload of 2506 pounds at 7% of GVWR on this model is ○ deficient ○ excessive ◉ cautionary ○ good ○ excellent *
Total highway safety penalties are: 2 *   Value: 7 9   Durability: 7 5   Highway Control Rating: 5 1   Highway Safety: 4 9

Signature	1998	MHA	42	42 Slide	RO	CU450	D	$9200	270	10,000	35,000	33,394

Livability Code: FT 30-90
Wheelbase-to-length ratio of 54% is considered ○ dangerous ○ fatiguing ◉ good ○ excellent *
The approximate net payload of 1606 pounds at 5% of GVWR on this model is ◉ deficient ○ excessive ○ cautionary ○ good ○ excellent *
Total highway safety penalties are: 12 *   Value: 7 4   Durability: 7 5   Highway Control Rating: 4 4   Highway Safety: 3 2

Signature	1998	MHA	45	45 No Slide	RO	CU450	D	$8600	270	10,000	35,000	33,565

Livability Code: FT 30-90
Wheelbase-to-length ratio of 50% is considered ◉ dangerous ○ fatiguing ○ good ○ excellent *
The approximate net payload of 1435 pounds at 4% of GVWR on this model is ◉ deficient ○ excessive ○ cautionary ○ good ○ excellent *
Total highway safety penalties are: 2 *   Value: 7 9   Durability: 7 5   Highway Control Rating: 8   Highway Safety: 6

Signature	1998	MHA	45	45 Slide	RO	CU450	D	$8700	270	10,000	35,000	34,465

Livability Code: FT 30-90
Wheelbase-to-length ratio of 50% is considered ◉ dangerous ○ fatiguing ○ good ○ excellent *
The approximate net payload of 535 pounds at 2% of GVWR on this model is ◉ deficient ○ excessive ○ cautionary ○ good ○ excellent *
Total highway safety penalties are: 12 *   Value: 7 4   Durability: 7 5   Highway Control Rating: 5   Highway Safety: - 7

Signature	1999	MHA	40	Admiral FD	RO	CU450	D	$10000	270	10,000	35,800	32,180

Livability Code: FT 30-90
Wheelbase-to-length ratio of 56% is considered ○ dangerous ○ fatiguing ◉ good ○ excellent *
The approximate net payload of 3620 pounds at 10% of GVWR on this model is ○ deficient ○ excessive ○ cautionary ◉ good ○ excellent *
Total highway safety penalties are: 2 *   Value: 7 9   Durability: 7 5   Highway Control Rating: 8 5   Highway Safety: 8 3   ★★★

Signature	1999	MHA	40	Suite Slide	RO	CU450	D	$10000	270	10,000	35,800	33,230

Livability Code: FT 30-90
Wheelbase-to-length ratio of 56% is considered ○ dangerous ○ fatiguing ◉ good ○ excellent *
The approximate net payload of 2570 pounds at 7% of GVWR on this model is ○ deficient ○ excessive ◉ cautionary ○ good ○ excellent *
Total highway safety penalties are: 13 *   Value: 7 3   Durability: 7 5   Highway Control Rating: 6 8   Highway Safety: 5 5   ★

Signature	1999	MHA	40	Premier FD	RO	CU450	D	$10000	270	10,000	35,800	32,180

Livability Code: FT 30-90
Wheelbase-to-length ratio of 56% is considered ○ dangerous ○ fatiguing ◉ good ○ excellent *
The approximate net payload of 3620 pounds at 10% of GVWR on this model is ○ deficient ○ excessive ○ cautionary ◉ good ○ excellent *
Total highway safety penalties are: 2 *   Value: 7 9   Durability: 7 5   Highway Control Rating: 8 5   Highway Safety: 8 3   ★★★

Signature	1999	MHA	42	SD Suite Slide	RO	CU450	D	$9500	270	10,000	45,800	39,094

Livability Code: FT 30-90
Wheelbase-to-length ratio of 54% is considered ○ dangerous ○ fatiguing ◉ good ○ excellent *
The approximate net payload of 6706 pounds at 15% of GVWR on this model is ○ deficient ○ excessive ○ cautionary ◉ good ○ excellent *
Total highway safety penalties are: 14 *   Value: 7 3   Durability: 7 5   Highway Control Rating: 8 0   Highway Safety: 6 6   ★★

Signature	1999	MHA	42	Classic FD	RO	CU450	D	$9500	270	10,000	45,800	37,894

Livability Code: FT 30-90
Wheelbase-to-length ratio of 54% is considered ○ dangerous ○ fatiguing ◉ good ○ excellent *
The approximate net payload of 7906 pounds at 17% of GVWR on this model is ○ deficient ○ excessive ○ cautionary ○ good ◉ excellent *
Total highway safety penalties are: 2 *   Value: 7 9   Durability: 7 5   Highway Control Rating: 8 4   Highway Safety: 8 2   ★★★

Signature	1999	MHA	42	Classic Suite Slide FD	RO	CU450	D	$9500	270	10,000	45,800	39,094

Livability Code: FT 30-90
Wheelbase-to-length ratio of 54% is considered ○ dangerous ○ fatiguing ◉ good ○ excellent *
The approximate net payload of 6706 pounds at 15% of GVWR on this model is ○ deficient ○ excessive ○ cautionary ◉ good ○ excellent *
Total highway safety penalties are: 14 *   Value: 7 3   Durability: 7 5   Highway Control Rating: 8 0   Highway Safety: 6 6   ★★

Signature	1999	MHA	45	Classic FD 45	RO	CU450	D	$8900	294 T	10,000	45,800	38,965

Livability Code: FT 30-90
Wheelbase-to-length ratio of 54% is considered ○ dangerous ○ fatiguing ◉ good ○ excellent *
The approximate net payload of 6835 pounds at 15% of GVWR on this model is ○ deficient ○ excessive ○ cautionary ◉ good ○ excellent *
Total highway safety penalties are: 4 *   Value: 7 8   Durability: 7 5   Highway Control Rating: 8 4   Highway Safety: 8 0   ★★★

Note: Safety ratings are based on the assumption that the engineering of the RV has allowed for proper balance by placing fresh, gray, and black holding tanks in a location so as not to change the balance of the RV when the tanks are empty or full. **Always double-check wheelbase, GVWR, and weights at front and rear axles.**

See Section 1 for details on how conclusions are reached.

Section 2: The Ratings

Brand	Year	Type	Length	Model	Chassis	Engine	Fuel Type	Average Price per Linear Foot When New	Adjusted Wheelbase	Approx. Towing Capacity	Gross Vehicle Weight Rating	Average Curb Weight
Signature	1999	MHA	45	Classic Suite Slide FD	RO	CU450	D	$8900	294 T	10,000	45,800	40,165

Livability Code: FT 30-90
Wheelbase-to-length ratio of 54% is considered ○ dangerous ○ fatiguing ◉ good ○ excellent *
The approximate net payload of 5635 pounds at 12% of GVWR on this model is ○ deficient ○ excessive ○ cautionary ◉ good ○ excellent *
Total highway safety penalties are: 17 *   Value: **72** Durability: **75** Highway Control Rating: **78**   Highway Safety: **61**   ★★

Brand	Year	Type	Length	Model	Chassis	Engine	Fuel Type	Average Price per Linear Foot When New	Adjusted Wheelbase	Approx. Towing Capacity	Gross Vehicle Weight Rating	Average Curb Weight
Signature	1999	MHA	45	Senator XLFD	RO	CU450	D	$8900	294 T	10,000	45,800	38,965

Livability Code: FT 30-90
Wheelbase-to-length ratio of 54% is considered ○ dangerous ○ fatiguing ◉ good ○ excellent *
The approximate net payload of 6835 pounds at 15% of GVWR on this model is ○ deficient ○ excessive ○ cautionary ◉ good ○ excellent *
Total highway safety penalties are: 4 *   Value: **78** Durability: **75** Highway Control Rating: **84**   Highway Safety: **80**   ★★★

Brand	Year	Type	Length	Model	Chassis	Engine	Fuel Type	Average Price per Linear Foot When New	Adjusted Wheelbase	Approx. Towing Capacity	Gross Vehicle Weight Rating	Average Curb Weight
Silver Eagle	1990	MHA	33	32	CH	7.4L	G	$1700	208	2,500	14,500	14,178

Livability Code: SB 30-90
Wheelbase-to-length ratio of 53% is considered ○ dangerous ◉ fatiguing ○ good ○ excellent *
The approximate net payload of 322 pounds at 2% of GVWR on this model is ◉ deficient ○ excessive ○ cautionary ○ good ○ excellent *
Total highway safety penalties are: 6 *   Value: **75** Durability: **70** Highway Control Rating: **30**   Highway Safety: **24**

Brand	Year	Type	Length	Model	Chassis	Engine	Fuel Type	Average Price per Linear Foot When New	Adjusted Wheelbase	Approx. Towing Capacity	Gross Vehicle Weight Rating	Average Curb Weight
Silver Eagle	1991	MHA	32	32	OS	CuMC1	D	$1900	190	1,500	16,000	14,493

Livability Code: SB 30-90
Wheelbase-to-length ratio of 50% is considered ◉ dangerous ○ fatiguing ○ good ○ excellent *
The approximate net payload of 1507 pounds at 9% of GVWR on this model is ○ deficient ○ excessive ◉ cautionary ○ good ○ excellent *
Total highway safety penalties are: 2 *   Value: **77** Durability: **70** Highway Control Rating: **28**   Highway Safety: **26**

Brand	Year	Type	Length	Model	Chassis	Engine	Fuel Type	Average Price per Linear Foot When New	Adjusted Wheelbase	Approx. Towing Capacity	Gross Vehicle Weight Rating	Average Curb Weight
Space Craft	1990	MHA	34	S-33ER	CH	7.4L	G	$2300	232 T	1,500	18,500	16,212

Livability Code: SB 30-90
Wheelbase-to-length ratio of 58% is considered ○ dangerous ○ fatiguing ○ good ◉ excellent *
The approximate net payload of 2288 pounds at 12% of GVWR on this model is ○ deficient ○ excessive ○ cautionary ◉ good ○ excellent *
Total highway safety penalties are: 9 *   Value: **74** Durability: **70** Highway Control Rating: **94**   Highway Safety: **85**   ★★★

Brand	Year	Type	Length	Model	Chassis	Engine	Fuel Type	Average Price per Linear Foot When New	Adjusted Wheelbase	Approx. Towing Capacity	Gross Vehicle Weight Rating	Average Curb Weight
Space Craft	1997	MHA	32	31 SB	CH	7.4L	G	$2200	178	1,500	14,500	12,848

Livability Code: SB 30-90
Wheelbase-to-length ratio of 46% is considered ◉ dangerous ○ fatiguing ○ good ○ excellent *
The approximate net payload of 1652 pounds at 11% of GVWR on this model is ○ deficient ○ excessive ○ cautionary ◉ good ○ excellent *
Total highway safety penalties are: 6 *   Value: **75** Durability: **70** Highway Control Rating: **22**   Highway Safety: **16**

Brand	Year	Type	Length	Model	Chassis	Engine	Fuel Type	Average Price per Linear Foot When New	Adjusted Wheelbase	Approx. Towing Capacity	Gross Vehicle Weight Rating	Average Curb Weight
Space Craft	1997	MHA	32	31 SB ops	CH	7.4L	G	$2200	178	1,500	14,500	13,548

Livability Code: SB 30-90
Wheelbase-to-length ratio of 46% is considered ◉ dangerous ○ fatiguing ○ good ○ excellent *
The approximate net payload of 952 pounds at 7% of GVWR on this model is ○ deficient ○ excessive ◉ cautionary ○ good ○ excellent *
Total highway safety penalties are: 10 *   Value: **73** Durability: **70** Highway Control Rating: **2**   Highway Safety: **-8**

Brand	Year	Type	Length	Model	Chassis	Engine	Fuel Type	Average Price per Linear Foot When New	Adjusted Wheelbase	Approx. Towing Capacity	Gross Vehicle Weight Rating	Average Curb Weight
Space Craft	1997	MHA	32	31 SB	FO	7.5L	G	$2200	178	1,500	14,500	13,128

Livability Code: SB 30-90
Wheelbase-to-length ratio of 46% is considered ◉ dangerous ○ fatiguing ○ good ○ excellent *
The approximate net payload of 1372 pounds at 9% of GVWR on this model is ○ deficient ○ excessive ◉ cautionary ○ good ○ excellent *
Total highway safety penalties are: 2 *   Value: **77** Durability: **70** Highway Control Rating: **15**   Highway Safety: **13**

Brand	Year	Type	Length	Model	Chassis	Engine	Fuel Type	Average Price per Linear Foot When New	Adjusted Wheelbase	Approx. Towing Capacity	Gross Vehicle Weight Rating	Average Curb Weight
Space Craft	1997	MHA	32	31SB ops	FO	7.5L	G	$2200	178	1,500	14,500	13,828

Livability Code: SB 30-90
Wheelbase-to-length ratio of 46% is considered ◉ dangerous ○ fatiguing ○ good ○ excellent *
The approximate net payload of 672 pounds at 5% of GVWR on this model is ◉ deficient ○ excessive ○ cautionary ○ good ○ excellent *
Total highway safety penalties are: 7 *   Value: **75** Durability: **70** Highway Control Rating: **1**   Highway Safety: **-6**

Brand	Year	Type	Length	Model	Chassis	Engine	Fuel Type	Average Price per Linear Foot When New	Adjusted Wheelbase	Approx. Towing Capacity	Gross Vehicle Weight Rating	Average Curb Weight
Space Craft	1997	MHA	35	34 SB	FO	7.5L	G	$2200	208	1,500	17,000	14,208

Livability Code: SB 30-90
Wheelbase-to-length ratio of 50% is considered ◉ dangerous ○ fatiguing ○ good ○ excellent *
The approximate net payload of 2792 pounds at 16% of GVWR on this model is ○ deficient ○ excessive ○ cautionary ○ good ◉ excellent *
Total highway safety penalties are: 12 *   Value: **72** Durability: **70** Highway Control Rating: **43**   Highway Safety: **31**

Brand	Year	Type	Length	Model	Chassis	Engine	Fuel Type	Average Price per Linear Foot When New	Adjusted Wheelbase	Approx. Towing Capacity	Gross Vehicle Weight Rating	Average Curb Weight
Space Craft	1997	MHA	35	34 SB	FO	7.5L	G	$2200	208	1,500	17,000	14,488

Livability Code: SB 30-90
Wheelbase-to-length ratio of 50% is considered ◉ dangerous ○ fatiguing ○ good ○ excellent *
The approximate net payload of 2512 pounds at 15% of GVWR on this model is ○ deficient ○ excessive ○ cautionary ◉ good ○ excellent *
Total highway safety penalties are: 7 *   Value: **74** Durability: **70** Highway Control Rating: **41**   Highway Safety: **34**

Brand	Year	Type	Length	Model	Chassis	Engine	Fuel Type	Average Price per Linear Foot When New	Adjusted Wheelbase	Approx. Towing Capacity	Gross Vehicle Weight Rating	Average Curb Weight
Space Craft	1997	MHA	38	Residential G37	CH	7.4L	G	$2700	249 T	1,500	19,500	18,560

Livability Code: SB 30-90
Wheelbase-to-length ratio of 55% is considered ○ dangerous ○ fatiguing ◉ good ○ excellent *
The approximate net payload of 940 pounds at 5% of GVWR on this model is ◉ deficient ○ excessive ○ cautionary ○ good ○ excellent *
Total highway safety penalties are: 16 *   Value: **70** Durability: **70** Highway Control Rating: **57**   Highway Safety: **41**

Note: Safety ratings are based on the assumption that the engineering of the RV has allowed for proper balance by placing fresh, gray, and black holding tanks in a location so as not to change the balance of the RV when the tanks are empty or full. **Always double-check wheelbase, GVWR, and weights at front and rear axles.**

*See Section 1 for details on how conclusions are reached.

Section 2: The Ratings

Brand	Year	Type	Length	Model	Chassis	Engine	Fuel Type	Average Price per Linear Foot When New	Adjusted Wheelbase	Approx. Towing Capacity	Gross Vehicle Weight Rating	Average Curb Weight
Space Craft	1997	MHA	38	Residential G37	FO	7.5L	G	$2700	249 T	1,500	20,000	18,840

Livability Code: SB 30-90 — Wheelbase-to-length ratio of 55% is considered ○ dangerous ○ fatiguing ● good ○ excellent *

The approximate net payload of 1160 pounds at 6% of GVWR on this model is ● deficient ○ excessive ○ cautionary ○ good ○ excellent *

Total highway safety penalties are: 10 * — Value: 7 3   Durability: 7 0   Highway Control Rating: 5 8   Highway Safety: 4 8

Brand	Year	Type	Length	Model	Chassis	Engine	Fuel Type	Price/Ft	Wheelbase	Towing	GVWR	Curb Wt
Space Craft	1998	MHA		accurate specs n/a								?

Livability Code: SB 30-90 — Wheelbase-to-length ratio of ? is considered ○ dangerous ○ fatiguing ○ good ○ excellent *

The approximate net payload of pounds at of GVWR on this model is ○ deficient ○ excessive ○ cautionary ○ good ○ excellent *

Total highway safety penalties are: 0 * — Value: 0   Durability: 7 0   Highway Control Rating: 0   Highway Safety: 0

Brand	Year	Type	Model	Curb Wt
Space Craft	1999	MHA	accurate specs n/a	?

Livability Code: SB 30-90 — Wheelbase-to-length ratio of ? is considered ○ dangerous ○ fatiguing ○ good ○ excellent *

The approximate net payload of pounds at of GVWR on this model is ○ deficient ○ excessive ○ cautionary ○ good ○ excellent *

Total highway safety penalties are: 0 * — Value: 0   Durability: 7 0   Highway Control Rating: 0   Highway Safety: 0

Brand	Year	Type	Length	Model	Chassis	Engine	Fuel Type	Price/Ft	Wheelbase	Towing	GVWR	Curb Wt
Spirit	1990	MHA	28	27 EU	CH	7.4L	G	$1400	158	1,500	12,300	10,614

Livability Code: VA 30-90 — Wheelbase-to-length ratio of 47% is considered ● dangerous ○ fatiguing ○ good ○ excellent *

The approximate net payload of 1686 pounds at 14% of GVWR on this model is ○ deficient ○ excessive ○ cautionary ● good ○ excellent *

Total highway safety penalties are: 4 * — Value: 8 4   Durability: 7 6   Highway Control Rating: 3 0   Highway Safety: 2 6

| Spirit | 1990 | MHC | 27 | 327RT | FO | 7.5L | G | $1500 | 176 | 1,500 | 11,000 | 10,143 |

Livability Code: VA 30-90 — Wheelbase-to-length ratio of 54% is considered ○ dangerous ○ fatiguing ● good ○ excellent *

The approximate net payload of 857 pounds at 8% of GVWR on this model is ○ deficient ○ excessive ● cautionary ○ good ○ excellent *

Total highway safety penalties are: 2 * — Value: 8 4   Durability: 7 6   Highway Control Rating: 6 3   Highway Safety: 6 1   ★★

| Spirit | 1990 | MMH | 21 | 319RB | TO | 3.0L | G | $1300 | 137 | 1,500 | 6,000 | 5,319 |

Livability Code: VA 30-90 — Wheelbase-to-length ratio of 55% is considered ○ dangerous ○ fatiguing ● good ○ excellent *

The approximate net payload of 681 pounds at 11% of GVWR on this model is ○ deficient ○ excessive ○ cautionary ● good ○ excellent *

Total highway safety penalties are: 2 * — Value: 8 4   Durability: 7 6   Highway Control Rating: 8 4   Highway Safety: 8 2   ★★★

| Spirit | 1991 | MHA | 23 | WCF 23 EC | CH | 7.4L | G | $1600 | 137 | 4,200 | 11,800 | 9,458 |

Livability Code: VA 30-90 — Wheelbase-to-length ratio of 50% is considered ● dangerous ○ fatiguing ○ good ○ excellent *

The approximate net payload of 2342 pounds at 20% of GVWR on this model is ○ deficient ○ excessive ○ cautionary ○ good ● excellent *

Total highway safety penalties are: 1 * — Value: 8 5   Durability: 7 6   Highway Control Rating: 4 7   Highway Safety: 4 6

| Spirit | 1991 | MHC | 21 | 321 RG | CH | 5.7L | G | $1700 | 125 | 3,300 | 10,200 | 8,899 |

Livability Code: VA 30-90 — Wheelbase-to-length ratio of 49% is considered ● dangerous ○ fatiguing ○ good ○ excellent *

The approximate net payload of 1301 pounds at 13% of GVWR on this model is ○ deficient ○ excessive ○ cautionary ● good ○ excellent *

Total highway safety penalties are: 2 * — Value: 8 4   Durability: 7 6   Highway Control Rating: 5 0   Highway Safety: 4 8

| Spirit | 1991 | MHC | 22 | 321 RL | TO | 3.0L | G | $1300 | 137 | 1,500 | 6,000 | 5,455 |

Livability Code: VA 30-90 — Wheelbase-to-length ratio of 53% is considered ○ dangerous ● fatiguing ○ good ○ excellent *

The approximate net payload of 545 pounds at 9% of GVWR on this model is ○ deficient ○ excessive ● cautionary ○ good ○ excellent *

Total highway safety penalties are: 2 * — Value: 8 4   Durability: 7 6   Highway Control Rating: 6 1   Highway Safety: 5 9   ★

| Spirit | 1991 | MHC | 22 | 321 RG | FO | 7.5L | G | $2400 | 138 | 2,800 | 10,200 | 9,046 |

Livability Code: VA 30-90 — Wheelbase-to-length ratio of 52% is considered ○ dangerous ● fatiguing ○ good ○ excellent *

The approximate net payload of 1154 pounds at 11% of GVWR on this model is ○ deficient ○ excessive ○ cautionary ● good ○ excellent *

Total highway safety penalties are: 2 * — Value: 8 4   Durability: 7 6   Highway Control Rating: 6 2   Highway Safety: 6 0   ★★

| Spirit | 1991 | MHC | 23 | 324 RC | CH | 5.7L | G | $1600 | 146 | 3,000 | 10,500 | 9,321 |

Livability Code: VA 30-90 — Wheelbase-to-length ratio of 52% is considered ○ dangerous ● fatiguing ○ good ○ excellent *

The approximate net payload of 1179 pounds at 11% of GVWR on this model is ○ deficient ○ excessive ○ cautionary ● good ○ excellent *

Total highway safety penalties are: 2 * — Value: 8 4   Durability: 7 6   Highway Control Rating: 6 2   Highway Safety: 6 0   ★★

| Spirit | 1991 | MHC | 24 | 324 RC | FO | 7.5L | G | $1600 | 158 | 1,500 | 11,500 | 9,548 |

Livability Code: VA 30-90 — Wheelbase-to-length ratio of 55% is considered ○ dangerous ○ fatiguing ● good ○ excellent *

The approximate net payload of 1952 pounds at 17% of GVWR on this model is ○ deficient ○ excessive ○ cautionary ○ good ● excellent *

Total highway safety penalties are: 2 * — Value: 8 4   Durability: 7 6   Highway Control Rating: 9 4   Highway Safety: 9 2   ★★★

Note: Safety ratings are based on the assumption that the engineering of the RV has allowed for proper balance by placing fresh, gray, and black holding tanks in a location so as not to change the balance of the RV when the tanks are empty or full. **Always double-check wheelbase, GVWR, and weights at front and rear axles.**

*See Section 1 for details on how conclusions are reached.

Section 2: The Ratings

Brand	Year	Type	Length	Model	Chassis	Engine	Fuel Type	Average Price per Linear Foot When New	Adjusted Wheelbase	Approx. Towing Capacity	Gross Vehicle Weight Rating	Average Curb Weight
Spirit	1991	MHC	27	327 RB	FO	7.5L	G	$1500	176	1,500	11,500	10,202

Livability Code: VA 30-90
Wheelbase-to-length ratio of 54% is considered ○ dangerous ○ fatiguing ◉ good ○ excellent *
The approximate net payload of 1298 pounds at 11% of GVWR on this model is ○ deficient ○ excessive ○ cautionary ◉ good ○ excellent *
Total highway safety penalties are: 2 *   Value: 8 4   Durability: 7 6   Highway Control Rating: 7 7   Highway Safety: 7 5   ★★★

Brand	Year	Type	Length	Model	Chassis	Engine	Fuel Type	Avg Price/Lin Ft	Adj Wheelbase	Towing	GVWR	Curb Wt
Spirit	1994	MHC	22	321 RB	TO	3.0L	G	$1400	137	1,500	6,000	5,455

Livability Code: VA 30-90
Wheelbase-to-length ratio of 53% is considered ○ dangerous ◉ fatiguing ○ good ○ excellent *
The approximate net payload of 545 pounds at 9% of GVWR on this model is ◉ deficient ○ excessive ◉ cautionary ○ good ○ excellent *
Total highway safety penalties are: 2 *   Value: 8 4   Durability: 7 6   Highway Control Rating: 6 1   Highway Safety: 5 9   ★

Spirit	1994	MHC	22	321 RD	TO	3.0L	G	$1400	137	1,500	6,000	5,489

Livability Code: VA 30-90
Wheelbase-to-length ratio of 53% is considered ○ dangerous ◉ fatiguing ○ good ○ excellent *
The approximate net payload of 511 pounds at 9% of GVWR on this model is ○ deficient ○ excessive ◉ cautionary ○ good ○ excellent *
Total highway safety penalties are: 2 *   Value: 8 4   Durability: 7 6   Highway Control Rating: 5 9   Highway Safety: 5 7   ★

Spirit	1995	MHC	21	21RK	CH	5.7L	G	$1900	125	2,800	10,200	8,810

Livability Code: VA 30-90
Wheelbase-to-length ratio of 49% is considered ◉ dangerous ○ fatiguing ○ good ○ excellent *
The approximate net payload of 1390 pounds at 14% of GVWR on this model is ○ deficient ○ excessive ○ cautionary ◉ good ○ excellent *
Total highway safety penalties are: 2 *   Value: 8 4   Durability: 7 6   Highway Control Rating: 5 3   Highway Safety: 5 1

Spirit	1995	MHC	21	21RB	CH	5.7L	G	$1400	125	2,800	10,200	8,810

Livability Code: VA 30-90
Wheelbase-to-length ratio of 49% is considered ◉ dangerous ○ fatiguing ○ good ○ excellent *
The approximate net payload of 1390 pounds at 14% of GVWR on this model is ○ deficient ○ excessive ○ cautionary ◉ good ○ excellent *
Total highway safety penalties are: 2 *   Value: 8 4   Durability: 7 6   Highway Control Rating: 5 3   Highway Safety: 5 1

Spirit	1995	MHC	22	21RK	FO	7.5L	G	$1800	138	1,500	10,500	8,995

Livability Code: VA 30-90
Wheelbase-to-length ratio of 52% is considered ○ dangerous ◉ fatiguing ○ good ○ excellent *
The approximate net payload of 1505 pounds at 14% of GVWR on this model is ○ deficient ○ excessive ○ cautionary ◉ good ○ excellent *
Total highway safety penalties are: 2 *   Value: 8 4   Durability: 7 6   Highway Control Rating: 6 7   Highway Safety: 6 5   ★★

Spirit	1995	MHC	22	21RB	FO	7.5L	G	$1800	138	1,500	10,500	8,995

Livability Code: VA 30-90
Wheelbase-to-length ratio of 52% is considered ○ dangerous ◉ fatiguing ○ good ○ excellent *
The approximate net payload of 1505 pounds at 14% of GVWR on this model is ○ deficient ○ excessive ○ cautionary ◉ good ○ excellent *
Total highway safety penalties are: 2 *   Value: 8 4   Durability: 7 6   Highway Control Rating: 6 7   Highway Safety: 6 5   ★★

Spirit	1995	MHC	25	24RC	FO	7.5L	G	$1600	158	2,500	11,500	9,614

Livability Code: VA 30-90
Wheelbase-to-length ratio of 54% is considered ○ dangerous ○ fatiguing ◉ good ○ excellent *
The approximate net payload of 1886 pounds at 16% of GVWR on this model is ○ deficient ○ excessive ○ cautionary ○ good ◉ excellent *
Total highway safety penalties are: 2 *   Value: 8 4   Durability: 7 6   Highway Control Rating: 8 4   Highway Safety: 8 2   ★★★

Spirit	1995	MHC	28	27RC	FO	7.5L	G	$1500	188	1,600	12,400	10,480

Livability Code: VA 30-90
Wheelbase-to-length ratio of 56% is considered ○ dangerous ○ fatiguing ◉ good ○ excellent *
The approximate net payload of 1920 pounds at 15% of GVWR on this model is ○ deficient ○ excessive ○ cautionary ◉ good ○ excellent *
Total highway safety penalties are: 2 *   Value: 8 4   Durability: 7 6   Highway Control Rating: 9 6   Highway Safety: 9 4   ★★★

Spirit	1995	MHC	29	28RQ	FO	7.5L	G	$1500	190	1,600	12,400	10,729

Livability Code: VA 30-90
Wheelbase-to-length ratio of 55% is considered ○ dangerous ○ fatiguing ◉ good ○ excellent *
The approximate net payload of 1671 pounds at 13% of GVWR on this model is ○ deficient ○ excessive ○ cautionary ◉ good ○ excellent *
Total highway safety penalties are: 2 *   Value: 8 4   Durability: 7 6   Highway Control Rating: 8 6   Highway Safety: 8 4   ★★★

Spirit	1996	MHC	21	21RK	CH	5.7L	G	$1900	125	3,300	10,200	8,810

Livability Code: VA 30-90
Wheelbase-to-length ratio of 49% is considered ◉ dangerous ○ fatiguing ○ good ○ excellent *
The approximate net payload of 1390 pounds at 14% of GVWR on this model is ○ deficient ○ excessive ○ cautionary ◉ good ○ excellent *
Total highway safety penalties are: 2 *   Value: 8 4   Durability: 7 6   Highway Control Rating: 5 3   Highway Safety: 5 1

Spirit	1996	MHC	21	21RB	CH	5.7L	G	$1800	125	3,300	10,200	8,810

Livability Code: VA 30-90
Wheelbase-to-length ratio of 49% is considered ◉ dangerous ○ fatiguing ○ good ○ excellent *
The approximate net payload of 1390 pounds at 14% of GVWR on this model is ○ deficient ○ excessive ○ cautionary ◉ good ○ excellent *
Total highway safety penalties are: 2 *   Value: 8 4   Durability: 7 6   Highway Control Rating: 5 3   Highway Safety: 5 1

Note: Safety ratings are based on the assumption that the engineering of the RV has allowed for proper balance by placing fresh, gray, and black holding tanks in a location so as not to change the balance of the RV when the tanks are empty or full. **Always double-check wheelbase, GVWR, and weights at front and rear axles.**

*See Section 1 for details on how conclusions are reached.

Brand	Year	Type	Length	Model	Chassis	Engine	Fuel Type	Average Price per Linear Foot When New	Adjusted Wheelbase	Approx. Towing Capacity	Gross Vehicle Weight Rating	Average Curb Weight
Spirit	1996	MHC	21	21RB	FO	7.3L	D	$2100	138	8,500	11,500	8,910

Livability Code: VA 30-90
Wheelbase-to-length ratio of 55% is considered ○ dangerous ○ fatiguing ◉ good ○ excellent *
The approximate net payload of 2590 pounds at 23% of GVWR on this model is ○ deficient ○ excessive ○ cautionary ○ good ◉ excellent *
Total highway safety penalties are: 2 *   Value: 84   Durability: 76   Highway Control Rating: 92   Highway Safety: 90   ★★★

Brand	Year	Type	Length	Model	Chassis	Engine	Fuel Type	Price/Ft	Wheelbase	Towing	GVWR	Curb Weight
Spirit	1996	MHC	22	21RK	FO	7.5L	G	$1800	138	8,000	10,500	9,019

Livability Code: VA 30-90
Wheelbase-to-length ratio of 52% is considered ○ dangerous ◉ fatiguing ○ good ○ excellent *
The approximate net payload of 1481 pounds at 14% of GVWR on this model is ○ deficient ○ excessive ○ cautionary ◉ good ○ excellent *
Total highway safety penalties are: 2 *   Value: 84   Durability: 76   Highway Control Rating: 67   Highway Safety: 65   ★★

Brand	Year	Type	Length	Model	Chassis	Engine	Fuel Type	Price/Ft	Wheelbase	Towing	GVWR	Curb Weight
Spirit	1996	MHC	22	21RK	FO	7.3L	D	$2000	138	8,500	11,500	9,119

Livability Code: VA 30-90
Wheelbase-to-length ratio of 52% is considered ○ dangerous ◉ fatiguing ○ good ○ excellent *
The approximate net payload of 2381 pounds at 21% of GVWR on this model is ○ deficient ○ excessive ○ cautionary ○ good ◉ excellent *
Total highway safety penalties are: 2 *   Value: 84   Durability: 76   Highway Control Rating: 74   Highway Safety: 72   ★★★

Brand	Year	Type	Length	Model	Chassis	Engine	Fuel Type	Price/Ft	Wheelbase	Towing	GVWR	Curb Weight
Spirit	1996	MHC	22	21RB	FO	7.5L	G	$1700	138	8,000	10,500	9,019

Livability Code: VA 30-90
Wheelbase-to-length ratio of 52% is considered ○ dangerous ◉ fatiguing ○ good ○ excellent *
The approximate net payload of 1481 pounds at 14% of GVWR on this model is ○ deficient ○ excessive ○ cautionary ◉ good ○ excellent *
Total highway safety penalties are: 2 *   Value: 84   Durability: 76   Highway Control Rating: 67   Highway Safety: 65   ★★

Brand	Year	Type	Length	Model	Chassis	Engine	Fuel Type	Price/Ft	Wheelbase	Towing	GVWR	Curb Weight
Spirit	1996	MHC	25	24RC	FO	7.5L	G	$1600	158	7,000	11,500	9,641

Livability Code: VA 30-90
Wheelbase-to-length ratio of 54% is considered ○ dangerous ○ fatiguing ◉ good ○ excellent *
The approximate net payload of 1859 pounds at 16% of GVWR on this model is ○ deficient ○ excessive ○ cautionary ○ good ◉ excellent *
Total highway safety penalties are: 2 *   Value: 84   Durability: 76   Highway Control Rating: 84   Highway Safety: 82   ★★★

Brand	Year	Type	Length	Model	Chassis	Engine	Fuel Type	Price/Ft	Wheelbase	Towing	GVWR	Curb Weight
Spirit	1996	MHC	25	24RC	FO	7.3L	D	$1800	158	8,500	11,500	9,641

Livability Code: VA 30-90
Wheelbase-to-length ratio of 54% is considered ○ dangerous ○ fatiguing ◉ good ○ excellent *
The approximate net payload of 1859 pounds at 16% of GVWR on this model is ○ deficient ○ excessive ○ cautionary ○ good ◉ excellent *
Total highway safety penalties are: 2 *   Value: 84   Durability: 76   Highway Control Rating: 84   Highway Safety: 82   ★★★

Brand	Year	Type	Length	Model	Chassis	Engine	Fuel Type	Price/Ft	Wheelbase	Towing	GVWR	Curb Weight
Spirit	1996	MHC	28	27RC	FO	7.5L	G	$1500	188	6,100	12,400	10,510

Livability Code: VA 30-90
Wheelbase-to-length ratio of 56% is considered ○ dangerous ○ fatiguing ◉ good ○ excellent *
The approximate net payload of 1890 pounds at 15% of GVWR on this model is ○ deficient ○ excessive ○ cautionary ◉ good ○ excellent *
Total highway safety penalties are: 2 *   Value: 84   Durability: 76   Highway Control Rating: 96   Highway Safety: 94   ★★★

Brand	Year	Type	Length	Model	Chassis	Engine	Fuel Type	Price/Ft	Wheelbase	Towing	GVWR	Curb Weight
Spirit	1996	MHC	28	27RC	FO	7.3L	D	$1700	188	7,600	12,400	10,510

Livability Code: VA 30-90
Wheelbase-to-length ratio of 56% is considered ○ dangerous ○ fatiguing ◉ good ○ excellent *
The approximate net payload of 1890 pounds at 15% of GVWR on this model is ○ deficient ○ excessive ○ cautionary ◉ good ○ excellent *
Total highway safety penalties are: 2 *   Value: 84   Durability: 76   Highway Control Rating: 96   Highway Safety: 94   ★★★

Brand	Year	Type	Length	Model	Chassis	Engine	Fuel Type	Price/Ft	Wheelbase	Towing	GVWR	Curb Weight
Spirit	1996	MHC	29	29RC	FO	7.5L	G	$1500	190	6,100	12,400	10,845

Livability Code: VA 30-90
Wheelbase-to-length ratio of 54% is considered ○ dangerous ○ fatiguing ◉ good ○ excellent *
The approximate net payload of 1555 pounds at 13% of GVWR on this model is ○ deficient ○ excessive ○ cautionary ◉ good ○ excellent *
Total highway safety penalties are: 2 *   Value: 84   Durability: 76   Highway Control Rating: 78   Highway Safety: 76   ★★★

Brand	Year	Type	Length	Model	Chassis	Engine	Fuel Type	Price/Ft	Wheelbase	Towing	GVWR	Curb Weight
Spirit	1996	MHC	29	29RC	FO	7.3L	D	$1700	190	7,600	12,400	10,845

Livability Code: VA 30-90
Wheelbase-to-length ratio of 54% is considered ○ dangerous ○ fatiguing ◉ good ○ excellent *
The approximate net payload of 1555 pounds at 13% of GVWR on this model is ○ deficient ○ excessive ○ cautionary ◉ good ○ excellent *
Total highway safety penalties are: 2 *   Value: 84   Durability: 76   Highway Control Rating: 78   Highway Safety: 76   ★★★

Brand	Year	Type	Length	Model	Chassis	Engine	Fuel Type	Price/Ft	Wheelbase	Towing	GVWR	Curb Weight
Spirit	1997	MHC	22	21RK	FO	7.5L	G	$1900	138	8,000	10,500	8,979

Livability Code: VA 30-90
Wheelbase-to-length ratio of 52% is considered ○ dangerous ◉ fatiguing ○ good ○ excellent *
The approximate net payload of 1521 pounds at 14% of GVWR on this model is ○ deficient ○ excessive ○ cautionary ◉ good ○ excellent *
Total highway safety penalties are: 2 *   Value: 84   Durability: 76   Highway Control Rating: 67   Highway Safety: 65   ★★

Brand	Year	Type	Length	Model	Chassis	Engine	Fuel Type	Price/Ft	Wheelbase	Towing	GVWR	Curb Weight
Spirit	1997	MHC	22	21RB	FO	7.5L	G	$1900	138	8,000	10,500	9,019

Livability Code: VA 30-90
Wheelbase-to-length ratio of 52% is considered ○ dangerous ◉ fatiguing ○ good ○ excellent *
The approximate net payload of 1481 pounds at 14% of GVWR on this model is ○ deficient ○ excessive ○ cautionary ◉ good ○ excellent *
Total highway safety penalties are: 2 *   Value: 84   Durability: 76   Highway Control Rating: 67   Highway Safety: 65   ★★

Note: Safety ratings are based on the assumption that the engineering of the RV has allowed for proper balance by placing fresh, gray, and black holding tanks in a location so as not to change the balance of the RV when the tanks are empty or full. **Always double-check wheelbase, GVWR, and weights at front and rear axles.**

*See Section 1 for details on how conclusions are reached.

Section 2: The Ratings

Brand	Year	Type	Length	Model	Chassis	Engine	Fuel Type	Average Price per Linear Foot When New	Adjusted Wheelbase	Approx. Towing Capacity	Gross Vehicle Weight Rating	Average Curb Weight
Spirit	1997	MHC	22	21RK op eng	FO	7.3L	D	$2000	138	1,500	11,500	9,619

Livability Code: VA 30-90

Wheelbase-to-length ratio of 52% is considered ○ dangerous ● fatiguing ○ good ○ excellent *

The approximate net payload of 1881 pounds at 16% of GVWR on this model is ○ deficient ○ excessive ○ cautionary ○ good ● excellent *

Total highway safety penalties are: 2 *   Value: **8 4**   Durability: **7 6**   Highway Control Rating: **7 1**   Highway Safety: **6 9**   ★★

Brand	Year	Type	Length	Model	Chassis	Engine	Fuel Type	Price/LF	Wheelbase	Towing	GVWR	Curb Weight
Spirit	1997	MHC	22	21RB op eng	FO	7.3L	D	$2100	138	8,500	11,500	9,303

Livability Code: VA 30-90

Wheelbase-to-length ratio of 52% is considered ○ dangerous ● fatiguing ○ good ○ excellent *

The approximate net payload of 2197 pounds at 19% of GVWR on this model is ○ deficient ○ excessive ○ cautionary ○ good ● excellent *

Total highway safety penalties are: 2 *   Value: **8 4**   Durability: **7 6**   Highway Control Rating: **7 4**   Highway Safety: **7 2**   ★★★

Brand	Year	Type	Length	Model	Chassis	Engine	Fuel Type	Price/LF	Wheelbase	Towing	GVWR	Curb Weight
Spirit	1997	MHC	23	21RK op eng	CH	7.4L	G	$1700	139	1,500	11,500	9,223

Livability Code: VA 30-90

Wheelbase-to-length ratio of 51% is considered ○ dangerous ● fatiguing ○ good ○ excellent *

The approximate net payload of 2277 pounds at 20% of GVWR on this model is ○ deficient ○ excessive ○ cautionary ○ good ● excellent *

Total highway safety penalties are: 2 *   Value: **8 4**   Durability: **7 6**   Highway Control Rating: **6 8**   Highway Safety: **6 6**   ★★

Brand	Year	Type	Length	Model	Chassis	Engine	Fuel Type	Price/LF	Wheelbase	Towing	GVWR	Curb Weight
Spirit	1997	MHC	23	21RB op eng	CH	7.4L	G	$1700	139	1,500	11,500	9,223

Livability Code: VA 30-90

Wheelbase-to-length ratio of 51% is considered ○ dangerous ● fatiguing ○ good ○ excellent *

The approximate net payload of 2277 pounds at 20% of GVWR on this model is ○ deficient ○ excessive ○ cautionary ○ good ● excellent *

Total highway safety penalties are: 2 *   Value: **8 4**   Durability: **7 6**   Highway Control Rating: **6 8**   Highway Safety: **6 6**   ★★

Brand	Year	Type	Length	Model	Chassis	Engine	Fuel Type	Price/LF	Wheelbase	Towing	GVWR	Curb Weight
Spirit	1997	MHC	25	24RC	FO	7.5L	G	$1700	158	7,000	11,500	9,597

Livability Code: VA 30-90

Wheelbase-to-length ratio of 54% is considered ○ dangerous ○ fatiguing ● good ○ excellent *

The approximate net payload of 1903 pounds at 17% of GVWR on this model is ○ deficient ○ excessive ○ cautionary ○ good ● excellent *

Total highway safety penalties are: 2 *   Value: **8 4**   Durability: **7 6**   Highway Control Rating: **8 4**   Highway Safety: **8 2**   ★★★

Brand	Year	Type	Length	Model	Chassis	Engine	Fuel Type	Price/LF	Wheelbase	Towing	GVWR	Curb Weight
Spirit	1997	MHC	25	24RC op eng	FO	7.3L	D	$1900	158	8,500	11,500	9,834

Livability Code: VA 30-90

Wheelbase-to-length ratio of 54% is considered ○ dangerous ○ fatiguing ● good ○ excellent *

The approximate net payload of 1666 pounds at 14% of GVWR on this model is ○ deficient ○ excessive ○ cautionary ● good ○ excellent *

Total highway safety penalties are: 2 *   Value: **8 4**   Durability: **7 6**   Highway Control Rating: **8 0**   Highway Safety: **7 8**   ★★★

Brand	Year	Type	Length	Model	Chassis	Engine	Fuel Type	Price/LF	Wheelbase	Towing	GVWR	Curb Weight
Spirit	1997	MHC	25	24RC op eng	CH	7.4L	G	$1800	158	1,500	12,300	9,925

Livability Code: VA 30-90

Wheelbase-to-length ratio of 53% is considered ○ dangerous ● fatiguing ○ good ○ excellent *

The approximate net payload of 2375 pounds at 19% of GVWR on this model is ○ deficient ○ excessive ○ cautionary ○ good ● excellent *

Total highway safety penalties are: 2 *   Value: **8 4**   Durability: **7 6**   Highway Control Rating: **8 0**   Highway Safety: **7 8**   ★★★

Brand	Year	Type	Length	Model	Chassis	Engine	Fuel Type	Price/LF	Wheelbase	Towing	GVWR	Curb Weight
Spirit	1997	MHC	28	27RC op eng	FO	7.3L	D	$1600	188	1,500	14,050	11,510

Livability Code: VA 30-90

Wheelbase-to-length ratio of 56% is considered ○ dangerous ○ fatiguing ● good ○ excellent *

The approximate net payload of 2540 pounds at 18% of GVWR on this model is ○ deficient ○ excessive ○ cautionary ○ good ● excellent *

Total highway safety penalties are: 2 *   Value: **8 4**   Durability: **7 6**   Highway Control Rating: **9 9**   Highway Safety: **9 7**   ★★★

Brand	Year	Type	Length	Model	Chassis	Engine	Fuel Type	Price/LF	Wheelbase	Towing	GVWR	Curb Weight
Spirit	1997	MHC	28	27RC	FO	7.5L	G	$1600	188	5,950	14,050	10,434

Livability Code: VA 30-90

Wheelbase-to-length ratio of 56% is considered ○ dangerous ○ fatiguing ● good ○ excellent *

The approximate net payload of 3616 pounds at 26% of GVWR on this model is ○ deficient ○ excessive ○ cautionary ○ good ● excellent *

Total highway safety penalties are: 2 *   Value: **8 4**   Durability: **7 6**   Highway Control Rating: **9 6**   Highway Safety: **9 4**   ★★★

Brand	Year	Type	Length	Model	Chassis	Engine	Fuel Type	Price/LF	Wheelbase	Towing	GVWR	Curb Weight
Spirit	1997	MHC	28	27RC op eng	CH	7.4L	G	$1800	189	1,500	12,300	10,573

Livability Code: VA 30-90

Wheelbase-to-length ratio of 56% is considered ○ dangerous ○ fatiguing ● good ○ excellent *

The approximate net payload of 1727 pounds at 14% of GVWR on this model is ○ deficient ○ excessive ○ cautionary ● good ○ excellent *

Total highway safety penalties are: 2 *   Value: **8 4**   Durability: **7 6**   Highway Control Rating: **9 2**   Highway Safety: **9 0**   ★★★

Brand	Year	Type	Length	Model	Chassis	Engine	Fuel Type	Price/LF	Wheelbase	Towing	GVWR	Curb Weight
Spirit	1997	MHC	29	29RQ op eng	FO	7.3L	D	$1800	190	5,950	14,050	10,875

Livability Code: VA 30-90

Wheelbase-to-length ratio of 54% is considered ○ dangerous ○ fatiguing ● good ○ excellent *

The approximate net payload of 3175 pounds at 23% of GVWR on this model is ○ deficient ○ excessive ○ cautionary ○ good ● excellent *

Total highway safety penalties are: 2 *   Value: **8 4**   Durability: **7 6**   Highway Control Rating: **8 6**   Highway Safety: **8 4**   ★★★

Brand	Year	Type	Length	Model	Chassis	Engine	Fuel Type	Price/LF	Wheelbase	Towing	GVWR	Curb Weight
Spirit	1997	MHC	29	29RQ	FO	7.5L	G	$1600	190	5,950	14,050	10,709

Livability Code: VA 30-90

Wheelbase-to-length ratio of 54% is considered ○ dangerous ○ fatiguing ● good ○ excellent *

The approximate net payload of 3341 pounds at 24% of GVWR on this model is ○ deficient ○ excessive ○ cautionary ○ good ● excellent *

Total highway safety penalties are: 2 *   Value: **8 4**   Durability: **7 6**   Highway Control Rating: **8 5**   Highway Safety: **8 3**   ★★★

Note: Safety ratings are based on the assumption that the engineering of the RV has allowed for proper balance by placing fresh, gray, and black holding tanks in a location so as not to change the balance of the RV when the tanks are empty or full. **Always double-check wheelbase, GVWR, and weights at front and rear axles.**

*See Section 1 for details on how conclusions are reached.

Brand	Year	Type	Length	Model	Chassis	Engine	Fuel Type	Average Price per Linear Foot When New	Adjusted Wheelbase	Approx. Towing Capacity	Gross Vehicle Weight Rating	Average Curb Weight
Spirit	1997	MHC	31	31WU op eng	FO	7.3L	D	$1700	205	1,500	14,050	12,608

Livability Code: VA 30-90
Wheelbase-to-length ratio of 54% is considered ○ dangerous ○ fatiguing ◉ good ○ excellent *
The approximate net payload of 1442 pounds at 10% of GVWR on this model is ○ deficient ○ excessive ○ cautionary ◉ good ○ excellent *
Total highway safety penalties are: 2 * Value: 84 Durability: 76 Highway Control Rating: 75 Highway Safety: 73 ★★★

Brand	Year	Type	Length	Model	Chassis	Engine	Fuel Type	Price/Ft	Wheelbase	Towing	GVWR	Curb Weight
Spirit	1997	MHC	31	31WU	FO	7.5L	G	$1600	205	5,950	14,050	11,391

Livability Code: VA 30-90
Wheelbase-to-length ratio of 54% is considered ○ dangerous ○ fatiguing ◉ good ○ excellent *
The approximate net payload of 2659 pounds at 19% of GVWR on this model is ○ deficient ○ excessive ○ cautionary ○ good ◉ excellent *
Total highway safety penalties are: 2 * Value: 84 Durability: 76 Highway Control Rating: 90 Highway Safety: 88 ★★★

Spirit	1998	MHC	22	22WK	FO	6.8L	G	$2000	138	8,000	10,500	9,079

Livability Code: VA 30-90
Wheelbase-to-length ratio of 52% is considered ○ dangerous ◉ fatiguing ○ good ○ excellent *
The approximate net payload of 1421 pounds at 14% of GVWR on this model is ○ deficient ○ excessive ○ cautionary ◉ good ○ excellent *
Total highway safety penalties are: 2 * Value: 84 Durability: 76 Highway Control Rating: 66 Highway Safety: 64 ★★

Spirit	1998	MHC	23	22WK opch	CH	7.4L	G	$1900	139	4,700	12,300	9,384

Livability Code: VA 30-90
Wheelbase-to-length ratio of 51% is considered ○ dangerous ◉ fatiguing ○ good ○ excellent *
The approximate net payload of 2916 pounds at 24% of GVWR on this model is ○ deficient ○ excessive ○ cautionary ○ good ◉ excellent *
Total highway safety penalties are: 2 * Value: 84 Durability: 76 Highway Control Rating: 64 Highway Safety: 62 ★★

Spirit	1998	MHC	25	24WD	FO	6.8L	G	$1800	158	7,000	11,500	9,547

Livability Code: VA 30-90
Wheelbase-to-length ratio of 54% is considered ○ dangerous ○ fatiguing ◉ good ○ excellent *
The approximate net payload of 1953 pounds at 17% of GVWR on this model is ○ deficient ○ excessive ○ cautionary ○ good ◉ excellent *
Total highway safety penalties are: 2 * Value: 84 Durability: 76 Highway Control Rating: 84 Highway Safety: 82 ★★★

Spirit	1998	MHC	25	24WD opch	CH	7.4L	G	$1800	159	4,700	12,300	9,825

Livability Code: VA 30-90
Wheelbase-to-length ratio of 53% is considered ○ dangerous ◉ fatiguing ○ good ○ excellent *
The approximate net payload of 2475 pounds at 20% of GVWR on this model is ○ deficient ○ excessive ○ cautionary ○ good ◉ excellent *
Total highway safety penalties are: 2 * Value: 84 Durability: 76 Highway Control Rating: 82 Highway Safety: 80 ★★★

Spirit	1998	MHC	28	27WP myc	CH	7.4L	G	$1700	189	4,700	12,300	10,597

Livability Code: VA 30-90
Wheelbase-to-length ratio of 57% is considered ○ dangerous ○ fatiguing ◉ good ○ excellent *
The approximate net payload of 1704 pounds at 14% of GVWR on this model is ○ deficient ○ excessive ○ cautionary ◉ good ○ excellent *
Total highway safety penalties are: 2 * Value: 84 Durability: 76 Highway Control Rating: 97 Highway Safety: 95 ★★★

Spirit	1998	MHC	29	29WQ	FO	6.8L	G	$1700	190	5,950	14,050	10,981

Livability Code: VA 30-90
Wheelbase-to-length ratio of 54% is considered ○ dangerous ○ fatiguing ◉ good ○ excellent *
The approximate net payload of 3069 pounds at 22% of GVWR on this model is ○ deficient ○ excessive ○ cautionary ○ good ◉ excellent *
Total highway safety penalties are: 2 * Value: 84 Durability: 76 Highway Control Rating: 87 Highway Safety: 85 ★★★

Spirit	1998	MHC	29	29WQ op eng	FO	7.3L	D	$1800	190	5,950	14,050	11,350

Livability Code: VA 30-90
Wheelbase-to-length ratio of 54% is considered ○ dangerous ○ fatiguing ◉ good ○ excellent *
The approximate net payload of 2700 pounds at 19% of GVWR on this model is ○ deficient ○ excessive ○ cautionary ○ good ◉ excellent *
Total highway safety penalties are: 2 * Value: 84 Durability: 76 Highway Control Rating: 88 Highway Safety: 86 ★★★

Spirit	1998	MHC	31	31WU	FO	6.8L	G	$1600	205	5,950	14,050	11,536

Livability Code: VA 30-90
Wheelbase-to-length ratio of 54% is considered ○ dangerous ○ fatiguing ◉ good ○ excellent *
The approximate net payload of 2514 pounds at 18% of GVWR on this model is ○ deficient ○ excessive ○ cautionary ○ good ◉ excellent *
Total highway safety penalties are: 2 * Value: 84 Durability: 76 Highway Control Rating: 89 Highway Safety: 87 ★★★

Spirit	1998	MHC	31	31WT	FO	6.8L	G	$1700	220	5,950	14,050	12,043

Livability Code: VA 30-90
Wheelbase-to-length ratio of 58% is considered ○ dangerous ○ fatiguing ○ good ◉ excellent *
The approximate net payload of 2007 pounds at 14% of GVWR on this model is ○ deficient ○ excessive ○ cautionary ◉ good ○ excellent *
Total highway safety penalties are: 7 * Value: 82 Durability: 76 Highway Control Rating: 100 Highway Safety: 93 ★★★

Spirit	1998	MHC	31	31WU op eng	FO	FO215	D	$1700	205	5,950	14,050	11,957

Livability Code: VA 30-90
Wheelbase-to-length ratio of 54% is considered ○ dangerous ○ fatiguing ◉ good ○ excellent *
The approximate net payload of 2093 pounds at 15% of GVWR on this model is ○ deficient ○ excessive ○ cautionary ◉ good ○ excellent *
Total highway safety penalties are: 2 * Value: 84 Durability: 76 Highway Control Rating: 85 Highway Safety: 83 ★★★

Note: Safety ratings are based on the assumption that the engineering of the RV has allowed for proper balance by placing fresh, gray, and black holding tanks in a location so as not to change the balance of the RV when the tanks are empty or full. **Always double-check wheelbase, GVWR, and weights at front and rear axles.**

*See Section 1 for details on how conclusions are reached.

Section 2: The Ratings

Brand	Year	Type	Length	Model	Chassis	Engine	Fuel Type	Average Price per Linear Foot When New	Adjusted Wheelbase	Approx. Towing Capacity	Gross Vehicle Weight Rating	Average Curb Weight
Spirit	1999	MHC	22	22E	FO	6.8L	G	$2500	138	7,800	10,700	9,071

Livability Code: VA 30-90
Wheelbase-to-length ratio of 52% is considered ○ dangerous ● fatiguing ○ good ○ excellent *
The approximate net payload of 1629 pounds at 15% of GVWR on this model is ○ deficient ○ excessive ○ cautionary ● good ○ excellent *
Total highway safety penalties are: 2 * Value: 84 Durability: 76 Highway Control Rating: 69 Highway Safety: 67 ★★

Brand	Year	Type	Length	Model	Chassis	Engine	Fuel Type	Average Price per Linear Foot When New	Adjusted Wheelbase	Approx. Towing Capacity	Gross Vehicle Weight Rating	Average Curb Weight
Spirit	1999	MHC	22	22R	FO	6.8L	G	$2500	138	7,800	10,700	9,343

Livability Code: VA 30-90
Wheelbase-to-length ratio of 52% is considered ○ dangerous ● fatiguing ○ good ○ excellent *
The approximate net payload of 1357 pounds at 13% of GVWR on this model is ○ deficient ○ excessive ○ cautionary ● good ○ excellent *
Total highway safety penalties are: 2 * Value: 84 Durability: 76 Highway Control Rating: 64 Highway Safety: 62 ★★

Spirit	1999	MHC	23	22E	CH	7.4L	G	$2400	139	4,700	12,300	9,120

Livability Code: VA 30-90
Wheelbase-to-length ratio of 51% is considered ○ dangerous ● fatiguing ○ good ○ excellent *
The approximate net payload of 3180 pounds at 26% of GVWR on this model is ○ deficient ○ excessive ○ cautionary ● good ○ excellent *
Total highway safety penalties are: 2 * Value: 84 Durability: 76 Highway Control Rating: 62 Highway Safety: 60 ★★

Spirit	1999	MHC	23	22R	CH	7.4L	G	$2400	139	4,700	12,300	8,963

Livability Code: VA 30-90
Wheelbase-to-length ratio of 51% is considered ○ dangerous ● fatiguing ○ good ○ excellent *
The approximate net payload of 3337 pounds at 27% of GVWR on this model is ○ deficient ○ excessive ○ cautionary ● good ○ excellent *
Total highway safety penalties are: 2 * Value: 84 Durability: 76 Highway Control Rating: 61 Highway Safety: 59 ★

Spirit	1999	MHC	25	24V	FO	6.8L	G	$2200	158	7,000	11,500	9,559

Livability Code: VA 30-90
Wheelbase-to-length ratio of 54% is considered ○ dangerous ○ fatiguing ● good ○ excellent *
The approximate net payload of 1941 pounds at 17% of GVWR on this model is ○ deficient ○ excessive ○ cautionary ○ good ● excellent *
Total highway safety penalties are: 2 * Value: 84 Durability: 76 Highway Control Rating: 84 Highway Safety: 82 ★★★

Spirit	1999	MHC	25	24V	CH	7.4L	G	$2200	159	4,700	12,300	9,742

Livability Code: VA 30-90
Wheelbase-to-length ratio of 53% is considered ○ dangerous ● fatiguing ○ good ○ excellent *
The approximate net payload of 2558 pounds at 21% of GVWR on this model is ○ deficient ○ excessive ○ cautionary ○ good ● excellent *
Total highway safety penalties are: 2 * Value: 84 Durability: 76 Highway Control Rating: 81 Highway Safety: 79 ★★★

Spirit	1999	MHC	27	27P	FO	6.8L	G	$2000	188	5,950	14,050	10,716

Livability Code: VA 30-90
Wheelbase-to-length ratio of 58% is considered ○ dangerous ○ fatiguing ○ good ● excellent *
The approximate net payload of 3334 pounds at 24% of GVWR on this model is ○ deficient ○ excessive ○ cautionary ○ good ● excellent *
Total highway safety penalties are: 2 * Value: 84 Durability: 76 Highway Control Rating: 100 Highway Safety: 98 ★★★

Spirit	1999	MHC	28	27P	CH	7.4L	G	$2000	189	4,700	12,300	10,565

Livability Code: VA 30-90
Wheelbase-to-length ratio of 57% is considered ○ dangerous ○ fatiguing ● good ○ excellent *
The approximate net payload of 1735 pounds at 14% of GVWR on this model is ○ deficient ○ excessive ○ cautionary ● good ○ excellent *
Total highway safety penalties are: 2 * Value: 84 Durability: 76 Highway Control Rating: 97 Highway Safety: 95 ★★★

Spirit	1999	MHC	29	29N	FO	6.8L	G	$1900	190	5,950	14,050	11,011

Livability Code: VA 30-90
Wheelbase-to-length ratio of 54% is considered ○ dangerous ○ fatiguing ● good ○ excellent *
The approximate net payload of 3039 pounds at 22% of GVWR on this model is ○ deficient ○ excessive ○ cautionary ○ good ● excellent *
Total highway safety penalties are: 2 * Value: 84 Durability: 76 Highway Control Rating: 87 Highway Safety: 85 ★★★

Spirit	1999	MHC	31	31G	FO	6.8L	G	$1800	205	5,950	14,050	11,578

Livability Code: VA 30-90
Wheelbase-to-length ratio of 54% is considered ○ dangerous ○ fatiguing ● good ○ excellent *
The approximate net payload of 2472 pounds at 18% of GVWR on this model is ○ deficient ○ excessive ○ cautionary ○ good ● excellent *
Total highway safety penalties are: 2 * Value: 84 Durability: 76 Highway Control Rating: 88 Highway Safety: 86 ★★★

Spirit	1999	MHC	31	31T	FO	6.8L	G	$1800	220	5,950	14,050	12,020

Livability Code: VA 30-90
Wheelbase-to-length ratio of 58% is considered ○ dangerous ○ fatiguing ○ good ● excellent *
The approximate net payload of 2030 pounds at 14% of GVWR on this model is ○ deficient ○ excessive ○ cautionary ● good ○ excellent *
Total highway safety penalties are: 7 * Value: 82 Durability: 76 Highway Control Rating: 100 Highway Safety: 93 ★★★

Sportsmobile	1991	MHB	17	RB-12Travel	FO	5.8L	G	$1500	127	1,500	6,400	6,109

Livability Code: VA 30-90
Wheelbase-to-length ratio of 61% is considered ○ dangerous ○ fatiguing ○ good ● excellent *
The approximate net payload of 292 pounds at 5% of GVWR on this model is ● deficient ○ excessive ○ cautionary ○ good ○ excellent *
Total highway safety penalties are: 2 * Value: 80 Durability: 78 Highway Control Rating: 78 Highway Safety: 76 ★★

Note: Safety ratings are based on the assumption that the engineering of the RV has allowed for proper balance by placing fresh, gray, and black holding tanks in a location so as not to change the balance of the RV when the tanks are empty or full. **Always double-check wheelbase, GVWR, and weights at front and rear axles.**

*See Section 1 for details on how conclusions are reached.

Brand	Year	Type	Length	Model	Chassis	Engine	Fuel Type	Average Price per Linear Foot When New	Adjusted Wheelbase	Approx. Towing Capacity	Gross Vehicle Weight Rating	Average Curb Weight
Sportsmobile	1991	MHB	20	Cruiser EB-17	FO	5.8L	G	$1400	138	1,500	8,100	7,136

Livability Code: VA 30-90
Wheelbase-to-length ratio of 58% is considered ○ dangerous ○ fatiguing ○ good ◉ excellent *
The approximate net payload of 964 pounds at 12% of GVWR on this model is ○ deficient ○ excessive ○ cautionary ◉ good ○ excellent *
Total highway safety penalties are: 2 * Value: 80 Durability: 78 Highway Control Rating: 94 Highway Safety: 92 ★★★

| Sportsmobile | 1997 | MHB | 18 | VAN RB | DO | 5.2L | G | $2300 | 128 | 1,500 | 7,500 | 6,531 |

Livability Code: VA 30-90
Wheelbase-to-length ratio of 60% is considered ○ dangerous ○ fatiguing ○ good ◉ excellent *
The approximate net payload of 969 pounds at 13% of GVWR on this model is ○ deficient ○ excessive ○ cautionary ◉ good ○ excellent *
Total highway safety penalties are: 2 * Value: 80 Durability: 78 Highway Control Rating: 100 Highway Safety: 98 ★★★

| Sportsmobile | 1997 | MHB | 19 | VAN RB | FO | 5.4L | G | $2200 | 138 | 1,500 | 7,500 | 6,711 |

Livability Code: VA 30-90
Wheelbase-to-length ratio of 62% is considered ○ dangerous ○ fatiguing ○ good ◉ excellent *
The approximate net payload of 789 pounds at 11% of GVWR on this model is ○ deficient ○ excessive ○ cautionary ◉ good ○ excellent *
Total highway safety penalties are: 2 * Value: 80 Durability: 78 Highway Control Rating: 100 Highway Safety: 98 ★★★

| Sportsmobile | 1997 | MHB | 19 | VAN RB | FO | 5.4L | G | $2200 | 138 | 1,500 | 9,500 | 7,511 |

Livability Code: VA 30-90
Wheelbase-to-length ratio of 62% is considered ○ dangerous ○ fatiguing ○ good ◉ excellent *
The approximate net payload of 1989 pounds at 21% of GVWR on this model is ○ deficient ○ excessive ○ cautionary ◉ good ○ excellent *
Total highway safety penalties are: 2 * Value: 80 Durability: 78 Highway Control Rating: 100 Highway Safety: 98 ★★★

| Sportsmobile | 1997 | MHB | 19 | VAN RB | GM | 5.7L | G | $2200 | 138 | 1,500 | 8,600 | 7,231 |

Livability Code: VA 30-90
Wheelbase-to-length ratio of 61% is considered ○ dangerous ○ fatiguing ○ good ◉ excellent *
The approximate net payload of 1370 pounds at 16% of GVWR on this model is ○ deficient ○ excessive ○ cautionary ◉ good ○ excellent *
Total highway safety penalties are: 2 * Value: 80 Durability: 78 Highway Control Rating: 100 Highway Safety: 98 ★★★

| Sportsmobile | 1997 | MHB | 20 | VAN EB | DO | 5.9L | G | $2000 | 128 | 1,500 | 8,510 | 7,374 |

Livability Code: VA 30-90
Wheelbase-to-length ratio of 54% is considered ○ dangerous ○ fatiguing ◉ good ○ excellent *
The approximate net payload of 1136 pounds at 13% of GVWR on this model is ○ deficient ○ excessive ○ cautionary ◉ good ○ excellent *
Total highway safety penalties are: 2 * Value: 80 Durability: 78 Highway Control Rating: 79 Highway Safety: 77 ★★★

| Sportsmobile | 1997 | MHB | 20 | VAN EB | FO | 5.4L | G | $2000 | 138 | 1,500 | 8,600 | 7,470 |

Livability Code: VA 30-90
Wheelbase-to-length ratio of 57% is considered ○ dangerous ○ fatiguing ◉ good ○ excellent *
The approximate net payload of 1130 pounds at 13% of GVWR on this model is ○ deficient ○ excessive ○ cautionary ◉ good ○ excellent *
Total highway safety penalties are: 2 * Value: 80 Durability: 78 Highway Control Rating: 94 Highway Safety: 92 ★★★

| Sportsmobile | 1997 | MHB | 20 | VAN EB | FO | 5.4L | G | $2000 | 138 | 1,500 | 9,400 | 7,790 |

Livability Code: VA 30-90
Wheelbase-to-length ratio of 57% is considered ○ dangerous ○ fatiguing ◉ good ○ excellent *
The approximate net payload of 1610 pounds at 17% of GVWR on this model is ○ deficient ○ excessive ○ cautionary ○ good ◉ excellent *
Total highway safety penalties are: 2 * Value: 80 Durability: 78 Highway Control Rating: 100 Highway Safety: 98 ★★★

| Sportsmobile | 1997 | MHB | 21 | VAN EB | GM | 5.7L | G | $1900 | 155 | 1,500 | 9,510 | 7,954 |

Livability Code: VA 30-90
Wheelbase-to-length ratio of 62% is considered ○ dangerous ○ fatiguing ○ good ◉ excellent *
The approximate net payload of 1556 pounds at 16% of GVWR on this model is ○ deficient ○ excessive ○ cautionary ○ good ◉ excellent *
Total highway safety penalties are: 2 * Value: 80 Durability: 78 Highway Control Rating: 100 Highway Safety: 98 ★★★

| Sportsmobile | 1998 | MHB | 18 | RB B-3500 | DO | 5.2L | G | $2300 | 128 | 1,500 | 7,500 | 6,540 |

Livability Code: VA 30-90
Wheelbase-to-length ratio of 60% is considered ○ dangerous ○ fatiguing ○ good ◉ excellent *
The approximate net payload of 960 pounds at 13% of GVWR on this model is ○ deficient ○ excessive ○ cautionary ◉ good ○ excellent *
Total highway safety penalties are: 2 * Value: 80 Durability: 78 Highway Control Rating: 100 Highway Safety: 98 ★★★

| Sportsmobile | 1998 | MHB | 18 | RB E-250 | FO | 5.4L | G | $2300 | 138 | 1,500 | 8,600 | 7,020 |

Livability Code: VA 30-90
Wheelbase-to-length ratio of 64% is considered ○ dangerous ○ fatiguing ○ good ◉ excellent *
The approximate net payload of 1580 pounds at 18% of GVWR on this model is ○ deficient ○ excessive ○ cautionary ○ good ◉ excellent *
Total highway safety penalties are: 2 * Value: 80 Durability: 78 Highway Control Rating: 100 Highway Safety: 98 ★★★

| Sportsmobile | 1998 | MHB | 18 | RB E-350 | FO | 5.4L | G | $2300 | 138 | 1,500 | 9,500 | 7,380 |

Livability Code: VA 30-90
Wheelbase-to-length ratio of 64% is considered ○ dangerous ○ fatiguing ○ good ◉ excellent *
The approximate net payload of 2120 pounds at 22% of GVWR on this model is ○ deficient ○ excessive ○ cautionary ○ good ◉ excellent *
Total highway safety penalties are: 2 * Value: 80 Durability: 78 Highway Control Rating: 100 Highway Safety: 98 ★★★

Note: Safety ratings are based on the assumption that the engineering of the RV has allowed for proper balance by placing fresh, gray, and black holding tanks in a location so as not to change the balance of the RV when the tanks are empty or full. **Always double-check wheelbase, GVWR, and weights at front and rear axles.**

*See Section 1 for details on how conclusions are reached.

Brand	Year	Type	Length	Model	Chassis	Engine	Fuel Type	Average Price per Linear Foot When New	Adjusted Wheel-base	Approx. Towing Capacity	Gross Vehicle Weight Rating	Average Curb Weight
Sportsmobile	1998	MHB	18	RB2500	GM	5.7L	G	$2300	135	1,500	8,600	7,100

Livability Code: VA 30-90   Wheelbase-to-length ratio of 61% is considered ○ dangerous ○ fatiguing ○ good ◉ excellent *

The approximate net payload of 1500 pounds at 17% of GVWR on this model is ○ deficient ○ excessive ○ cautionary ○ good ◉ excellent *

Total highway safety penalties are: 2 *   Value: 80   Durability: 78   Highway Control Rating: 100   Highway Safety: 98   ★★★

| Sportsmobile | 1998 | MHB | 20 | EB E-250 | FO | 5.4L | G | $2100 | 138 | 1,500 | 8,600 | 7,340 |

Livability Code: VA 30-90   Wheelbase-to-length ratio of 59% is considered ○ dangerous ○ fatiguing ○ good ◉ excellent *

The approximate net payload of 1260 pounds at 15% of GVWR on this model is ○ deficient ○ excessive ○ cautionary ◉ good ○ excellent *

Total highway safety penalties are: 2 *   Value: 80   Durability: 78   Highway Control Rating: 100   Highway Safety: 98   ★★★

| Sportsmobile | 1998 | MHB | 20 | EB E-350 | FO | 5.4L | G | $2100 | 138 | 1,500 | 9,400 | 7,660 |

Livability Code: VA 30-90   Wheelbase-to-length ratio of 59% is considered ○ dangerous ○ fatiguing ○ good ◉ excellent *

The approximate net payload of 1740 pounds at 19% of GVWR on this model is ○ deficient ○ excessive ○ cautionary ○ good ◉ excellent *

Total highway safety penalties are: 2 *   Value: 80   Durability: 78   Highway Control Rating: 100   Highway Safety: 98   ★★★

| Sportsmobile | 1998 | MHB | 20 | EB B-3500 | DO | 5.9L | G | $2100 | 128 | 1,500 | 8,510 | 7,384 |

Livability Code: VA 30-90   Wheelbase-to-length ratio of 54% is considered ○ dangerous ○ fatiguing ◉ good ○ excellent *

The approximate net payload of 1126 pounds at 13% of GVWR on this model is ○ deficient ○ excessive ○ cautionary ◉ good ○ excellent *

Total highway safety penalties are: 2 *   Value: 80   Durability: 78   Highway Control Rating: 79   Highway Safety: 77   ★★★

| Sportsmobile | 1998 | MHB | 20 | EB3500 | GM | 5.7L | G | $2100 | 155 | 1,500 | 9,500 | 7,800 |

Livability Code: VA 30-90   Wheelbase-to-length ratio of 65% is considered ○ dangerous ○ fatiguing ○ good ◉ excellent *

The approximate net payload of 1700 pounds at 18% of GVWR on this model is ○ deficient ○ excessive ○ cautionary ○ good ◉ excellent *

Total highway safety penalties are: 2 *   Value: 80   Durability: 78   Highway Control Rating: 100   Highway Safety: 98   ★★★

| Sportsmobile | 1999 | MHB | 18 | RB B2500 | DO | 5.2L | G | $2300 | 128 | 1,500 | 7,700 | 6,620 |

Livability Code: VA 30-90   Wheelbase-to-length ratio of 60% is considered ○ dangerous ○ fatiguing ○ good ◉ excellent *

The approximate net payload of 1080 pounds at 14% of GVWR on this model is ○ deficient ○ excessive ○ cautionary ◉ good ○ excellent *

Total highway safety penalties are: 2 *   Value: 80   Durability: 78   Highway Control Rating: 100   Highway Safety: 98   ★★★

| Sportsmobile | 1999 | MHB | 18 | RB B3500 | DO | 5.2L | G | $2300 | 128 | 1,500 | 8,700 | 7,020 |

Livability Code: VA 30-90   Wheelbase-to-length ratio of 60% is considered ○ dangerous ○ fatiguing ○ good ◉ excellent *

The approximate net payload of 1680 pounds at 19% of GVWR on this model is ○ deficient ○ excessive ○ cautionary ○ good ◉ excellent *

Total highway safety penalties are: 2 *   Value: 80   Durability: 78   Highway Control Rating: 100   Highway Safety: 98   ★★★

| Sportsmobile | 1999 | MHB | 18 | RB E-250 | FO | 5.4L | G | $2300 | 138 | 1,500 | 8,600 | 7,000 |

Livability Code: VA 30-90   Wheelbase-to-length ratio of 65% is considered ○ dangerous ○ fatiguing ○ good ◉ excellent *

The approximate net payload of 1600 pounds at 19% of GVWR on this model is ○ deficient ○ excessive ○ cautionary ○ good ◉ excellent *

Total highway safety penalties are: 2 *   Value: 80   Durability: 78   Highway Control Rating: 100   Highway Safety: 98   ★★★

| Sportsmobile | 1999 | MHB | 18 | RB E-350 | FO | 5.4L | G | $2300 | 138 | 1,500 | 9,500 | 7,360 |

Livability Code: VA 30-90   Wheelbase-to-length ratio of 65% is considered ○ dangerous ○ fatiguing ○ good ◉ excellent *

The approximate net payload of 2140 pounds at 23% of GVWR on this model is ○ deficient ○ excessive ○ cautionary ○ good ◉ excellent *

Total highway safety penalties are: 2 *   Value: 80   Durability: 78   Highway Control Rating: 100   Highway Safety: 98   ★★★

| Sportsmobile | 1999 | MHB | 18 | RB 3500 | GM | 5.7L | G | $2300 | 135 | 1,500 | 9,500 | 7,460 |

Livability Code: VA 30-90   Wheelbase-to-length ratio of 61% is considered ○ dangerous ○ fatiguing ○ good ◉ excellent *

The approximate net payload of 2040 pounds at 21% of GVWR on this model is ○ deficient ○ excessive ○ cautionary ○ good ◉ excellent *

Total highway safety penalties are: 2 *   Value: 80   Durability: 78   Highway Control Rating: 100   Highway Safety: 98   ★★★

| Sportsmobile | 1999 | MHB | 18 | RB 2500 | GM | 5.7L | G | $2300 | 135 | 1,500 | 8,600 | 7,100 |

Livability Code: VA 30-90   Wheelbase-to-length ratio of 61% is considered ○ dangerous ○ fatiguing ○ good ◉ excellent *

The approximate net payload of 1500 pounds at 17% of GVWR on this model is ○ deficient ○ excessive ○ cautionary ○ good ◉ excellent *

Total highway safety penalties are: 2 *   Value: 80   Durability: 78   Highway Control Rating: 100   Highway Safety: 98   ★★★

| Sportsmobile | 1999 | MHB | 19 | EB E-250 | FO | 5.4L | G | $2200 | 138 | 1,500 | 8,600 | 7,320 |

Livability Code: VA 30-90   Wheelbase-to-length ratio of 59% is considered ○ dangerous ○ fatiguing ○ good ◉ excellent *

The approximate net payload of 1280 pounds at 15% of GVWR on this model is ○ deficient ○ excessive ○ cautionary ◉ good ○ excellent *

Total highway safety penalties are: 2 *   Value: 80   Durability: 78   Highway Control Rating: 100   Highway Safety: 98   ★★★

Note: Safety ratings are based on the assumption that the engineering of the RV has allowed for proper balance by placing fresh, gray, and black holding tanks in a location so as not to change the balance of the RV when the tanks are empty or full. **Always double-check wheelbase, GVWR, and weights at front and rear axles.**

*See Section 1 for details on how conclusions are reached.

Section 2: The Ratings

Brand	Year	Type	Length	Model	Chassis	Engine	Fuel Type	Average Price per Linear Foot When New	Adjusted Wheelbase	Approx. Towing Capacity	Gross Vehicle Weight Rating	Average Curb Weight
Sportsmobile	1999	MHB	19	EB E-350	FO	5.4L	G	$2200	138	1,500	9,400	7,640

Livability Code: VA 30-90
Wheelbase-to-length ratio of 59% is considered ○ dangerous ○ fatiguing ○ good ◉ excellent *
The approximate net payload of 1760 pounds at 19% of GVWR on this model is ○ deficient ○ excessive ○ cautionary ○ good ◉ excellent *
Total highway safety penalties are: 2 *   Value: 8 0   Durability: 7 8   Highway Control Rating: 1 0 0   Highway Safety: 9 8   ★★★

Brand	Year	Type	Length	Model	Chassis	Engine	Fuel Type	Price/Foot	Wheelbase	Towing	GVWR	Curb Weight
Sportsmobile	1999	MHB	20	EB B3500	DO	5.9L	G	$2100	128	1,500	9,200	7,660

Livability Code: VA 30-90
Wheelbase-to-length ratio of 54% is considered ○ dangerous ○ fatiguing ◉ good ○ excellent *
The approximate net payload of 1540 pounds at 17% of GVWR on this model is ○ deficient ○ excessive ○ cautionary ○ good ◉ excellent *
Total highway safety penalties are: 2 *   Value: 8 0   Durability: 7 8   Highway Control Rating: 8 6   Highway Safety: 8 4   ★★★

Sportsmobile	1999	MHB	20	EB 3500	GM	5.7L	G	$2100	155	1,500	9,500	7,800

Livability Code: VA 30-90
Wheelbase-to-length ratio of 65% is considered ○ dangerous ○ fatiguing ○ good ◉ excellent *
The approximate net payload of 1700 pounds at 18% of GVWR on this model is ○ deficient ○ excessive ○ cautionary ○ good ◉ excellent *
Total highway safety penalties are: 2 *   Value: 8 0   Durability: 7 8   Highway Control Rating: 1 0 0   Highway Safety: 9 8   ★★★

Suncruiser	1990	MHA	28	27RQ	CH	7.4L	G	$1700	158	2,500	14,500	12,314

Livability Code: SB 30-90
Wheelbase-to-length ratio of 48% is considered ◉ dangerous ○ fatiguing ○ good ○ excellent *
The approximate net payload of 2186 pounds at 15% of GVWR on this model is ○ deficient ○ excessive ○ cautionary ◉ good ○ excellent *
Total highway safety penalties are: 3 *   Value: 8 5   Durability: 7 8   Highway Control Rating: 3 4   Highway Safety: 3 1

Suncruiser	1990	MHA	32	31 RQ	CH	7.4L	G	$1700	190	4,500	15,000	13,487

Livability Code: SB 30-90
Wheelbase-to-length ratio of 49% is considered ◉ dangerous ○ fatiguing ○ good ○ excellent *
The approximate net payload of 1513 pounds at 10% of GVWR on this model is ○ deficient ○ excessive ○ cautionary ◉ good ○ excellent *
Total highway safety penalties are: 6 *   Value: 8 3   Durability: 7 8   Highway Control Rating: 3 1   Highway Safety: 2 5

Suncruiser	1990	MHA	32	31 RQ	FO	7.5L	G	$1700	190	5,000	16,000	13,987

Livability Code: SB 30-90
Wheelbase-to-length ratio of 49% is considered ◉ dangerous ○ fatiguing ○ good ○ excellent *
The approximate net payload of 2013 pounds at 13% of GVWR on this model is ○ deficient ○ excessive ○ cautionary ◉ good ○ excellent *
Total highway safety penalties are: 2 *   Value: 8 5   Durability: 7 8   Highway Control Rating: 3 6   Highway Safety: 3 4

Suncruiser	1990	MHA	34	34 RA	CH	7.4L	G	$1600	190	4,500	15,000	13,936

Livability Code: SB 30-90
Wheelbase-to-length ratio of 47% is considered ◉ dangerous ○ fatiguing ○ good ○ excellent *
The approximate net payload of 1064 pounds at 7% of GVWR on this model is ○ deficient ○ excessive ◉ cautionary ○ good ○ excellent *
Total highway safety penalties are: 6 *   Value: 8 3   Durability: 7 8   Highway Control Rating: 5   Highway Safety: - 1

Suncruiser	1990	MHA	34	34 RA	FO	7.5L	G	$1600	228	5,000	16,000	14,436

Livability Code: SB 30-90
Wheelbase-to-length ratio of 56% is considered ○ dangerous ○ fatiguing ◉ good ○ excellent *
The approximate net payload of 1564 pounds at 10% of GVWR on this model is ○ deficient ○ excessive ○ cautionary ◉ good ○ excellent *
Total highway safety penalties are: 2 *   Value: 8 5   Durability: 7 8   Highway Control Rating: 8 5   Highway Safety: 8 3   ★★★

Suncruiser	1990	MHA	40	40 RQ	OS	7.5L	G	$2000	236 T	6,500	18,500	17,584

Livability Code: SB 30-90
Wheelbase-to-length ratio of 49% is considered ◉ dangerous ○ fatiguing ○ good ○ excellent *
The approximate net payload of 916 pounds at 5% of GVWR on this model is ◉ deficient ○ excessive ○ cautionary ○ good ○ excellent *
Total highway safety penalties are: 4 *   Value: 8 4   Durability: 7 8   Highway Control Rating: 6   Highway Safety: 2

Suncruiser	1990	MHA	40	40 DXL	OS	7.5L	G	$2000	236 T	1,500	18,500	17,584

Livability Code: SB 30-90
Wheelbase-to-length ratio of 49% is considered ◉ dangerous ○ fatiguing ○ good ○ excellent *
The approximate net payload of 916 pounds at 5% of GVWR on this model is ◉ deficient ○ excessive ○ cautionary ○ good ○ excellent *
Total highway safety penalties are: 4 *   Value: 8 4   Durability: 7 8   Highway Control Rating: 6   Highway Safety: 2

Suncruiser	1991	MHA	32	ICM 32RQ	CH	7.4L	G	$1700	190	1,500	16,000	13,587

Livability Code: SB 30-90
Wheelbase-to-length ratio of 49% is considered ◉ dangerous ○ fatiguing ○ good ○ excellent *
The approximate net payload of 2413 pounds at 15% of GVWR on this model is ○ deficient ○ excessive ○ cautionary ◉ good ○ excellent *
Total highway safety penalties are: 6 *   Value: 8 3   Durability: 7 8   Highway Control Rating: 4 1   Highway Safety: 3 5

Suncruiser	1992	MHA	32	32RQ	CH	7.4L	G	$1700	208	1,500	16,000	13,587

Livability Code: SB 30-90
Wheelbase-to-length ratio of 54% is considered ○ dangerous ○ fatiguing ◉ good ○ excellent *
The approximate net payload of 2413 pounds at 15% of GVWR on this model is ○ deficient ○ excessive ○ cautionary ◉ good ○ excellent *
Total highway safety penalties are: 6 *   Value: 8 3   Durability: 7 8   Highway Control Rating: 8 0   Highway Safety: 7 4   ★★★

Note: Safety ratings are based on the assumption that the engineering of the RV has allowed for proper balance by placing fresh, gray, and black holding tanks in a location so as not to change the balance of the RV when the tanks are empty or full. **Always double-check wheelbase, GVWR, and weights at front and rear axles.**

The RV Rating Book

*See Section 1 for details on how conclusions are reached.

Section 2: The Ratings

Brand	Year	Type	Length	Model	Chassis	Engine	Fuel Type	Average Price per Linear Foot When New	Adjusted Wheelbase	Approx. Towing Capacity	Gross Vehicle Weight Rating	Average Curb Weight
Suncruiser	1992	MHA	32	32RQ	FO	7.5L	G	$1800	208	8,000	17,000	14,087

Livability Code: SB 30-90
Wheelbase-to-length ratio of 54% is considered ○ dangerous ○ fatiguing ● good ○ excellent *
The approximate net payload of 2913 pounds at 17% of GVWR on this model is ○ deficient ○ excessive ○ cautionary ○ good ● excellent *
Total highway safety penalties are: 2 * Value: 8 5 Durability: 7 8 Highway Control Rating: 8 3 Highway Safety: 8 1 ★★★

Brand	Year	Type	Length	Model	Chassis	Engine	Fuel	Price/Ft	WB	Tow	GVWR	Curb
Suncruiser	1992	MHA	34	34RQ	CH	7.4L	G	$1700	228	1,500	16,000	14,086

Livability Code: SB 30-90
Wheelbase-to-length ratio of 56% is considered ○ dangerous ○ fatiguing ● good ○ excellent *
The approximate net payload of 1914 pounds at 12% of GVWR on this model is ○ deficient ○ excessive ○ cautionary ● good ○ excellent *
Total highway safety penalties are: 7 * Value: 8 3 Durability: 7 8 Highway Control Rating: 8 8 Highway Safety: 8 1 ★★★

Suncruiser	1992	MHA	34	34RA	CH	7.4L	G	$1700	228	1,500	16,000	14,086

Livability Code: SB 30-90
Wheelbase-to-length ratio of 56% is considered ○ dangerous ○ fatiguing ● good ○ excellent *
The approximate net payload of 1914 pounds at 12% of GVWR on this model is ○ deficient ○ excessive ○ cautionary ● good ○ excellent *
Total highway safety penalties are: 7 * Value: 8 3 Durability: 7 8 Highway Control Rating: 8 8 Highway Safety: 8 1 ★★★

Suncruiser	1992	MHA	34	34RQ	FO	7.5L	G	$1700	228	8,000	17,000	14,586

Livability Code: SB 30-90
Wheelbase-to-length ratio of 56% is considered ○ dangerous ○ fatiguing ● good ○ excellent *
The approximate net payload of 2414 pounds at 14% of GVWR on this model is ○ deficient ○ excessive ○ cautionary ● good ○ excellent *
Total highway safety penalties are: 2 * Value: 8 5 Durability: 7 8 Highway Control Rating: 9 2 Highway Safety: 9 0 ★★★

Suncruiser	1992	MHA	34	34RA	FO	7.5L	G	$1700	228	8,000	17,000	14,586

Livability Code: SB 30-90
Wheelbase-to-length ratio of 56% is considered ○ dangerous ○ fatiguing ● good ○ excellent *
The approximate net payload of 2414 pounds at 14% of GVWR on this model is ○ deficient ○ excessive ○ cautionary ● good ○ excellent *
Total highway safety penalties are: 2 * Value: 8 5 Durability: 7 8 Highway Control Rating: 9 2 Highway Safety: 9 0 ★★★

Suncruiser	1994	MHA	30	29RQ	CH	7.4L	G	$2000	178	2,200	14,800	12,988

Livability Code: SB 30-90
Wheelbase-to-length ratio of 49% is considered ● dangerous ○ fatiguing ○ good ○ excellent *
The approximate net payload of 1812 pounds at 12% of GVWR on this model is ○ deficient ○ excessive ○ cautionary ● good ○ excellent *
Total highway safety penalties are: 5 * Value: 8 4 Durability: 7 8 Highway Control Rating: 3 5 Highway Safety: 3 0

Suncruiser	1994	MHA	30	29RQ	FO	7.5L	G	$2000	178	3,800	15,200	13,388

Livability Code: SB 30-90
Wheelbase-to-length ratio of 49% is considered ● dangerous ○ fatiguing ○ good ○ excellent *
The approximate net payload of 1812 pounds at 12% of GVWR on this model is ○ deficient ○ excessive ○ cautionary ● good ○ excellent *
Total highway safety penalties are: 2 * Value: 8 5 Durability: 7 8 Highway Control Rating: 3 5 Highway Safety: 3 3

Suncruiser	1994	MHA	32	32RQ	CH	7.4L	G	$1900	208	1,500	16,000	13,587

Livability Code: SB 30-90
Wheelbase-to-length ratio of 54% is considered ○ dangerous ○ fatiguing ● good ○ excellent *
The approximate net payload of 2413 pounds at 15% of GVWR on this model is ○ deficient ○ excessive ○ cautionary ● good ○ excellent *
Total highway safety penalties are: 6 * Value: 8 3 Durability: 7 8 Highway Control Rating: 8 0 Highway Safety: 7 4 ★★★

Suncruiser	1994	MHA	32	32RQ	FO	7.5L	G	$1900	208	8,000	17,000	14,087

Livability Code: SB 30-90
Wheelbase-to-length ratio of 54% is considered ○ dangerous ○ fatiguing ● good ○ excellent *
The approximate net payload of 2913 pounds at 17% of GVWR on this model is ○ deficient ○ excessive ○ cautionary ○ good ● excellent *
Total highway safety penalties are: 2 * Value: 8 5 Durability: 7 8 Highway Control Rating: 8 3 Highway Safety: 8 1 ★★★

Suncruiser	1994	MHA	34	34RQ	CH	7.4L	G	$1900	228	1,500	16,000	14,086

Livability Code: SB 30-90
Wheelbase-to-length ratio of 56% is considered ○ dangerous ○ fatiguing ● good ○ excellent *
The approximate net payload of 1914 pounds at 12% of GVWR on this model is ○ deficient ○ excessive ○ cautionary ● good ○ excellent *
Total highway safety penalties are: 7 * Value: 8 3 Durability: 7 8 Highway Control Rating: 8 8 Highway Safety: 8 1 ★★★

Suncruiser	1994	MHA	34	34RA	CH	7.4L	G	$1900	228	1,500	16,000	14,086

Livability Code: SB 30-90
Wheelbase-to-length ratio of 56% is considered ○ dangerous ○ fatiguing ● good ○ excellent *
The approximate net payload of 1914 pounds at 12% of GVWR on this model is ○ deficient ○ excessive ○ cautionary ● good ○ excellent *
Total highway safety penalties are: 7 * Value: 8 3 Durability: 7 8 Highway Control Rating: 8 8 Highway Safety: 8 1 ★★★

Suncruiser	1994	MHA	34	34RQ	FO	7.5L	G	$1900	228	8,000	17,000	14,586

Livability Code: SB 30-90
Wheelbase-to-length ratio of 56% is considered ○ dangerous ○ fatiguing ● good ○ excellent *
The approximate net payload of 2414 pounds at 14% of GVWR on this model is ○ deficient ○ excessive ○ cautionary ● good ○ excellent *
Total highway safety penalties are: 2 * Value: 8 5 Durability: 7 8 Highway Control Rating: 9 2 Highway Safety: 9 0 ★★★

Note: Safety ratings are based on the assumption that the engineering of the RV has allowed for proper balance by placing fresh, gray, and black holding tanks in a location so as not to change the balance of the RV when the tanks are empty or full. **Always double-check wheelbase, GVWR, and weights at front and rear axles.**

*See Section 1 for details on how conclusions are reached.

Brand	Year	Type	Length	Model	Chassis	Engine	Fuel Type	Average Price per Linear Foot When New	Adjusted Wheelbase	Approx. Towing Capacity	Gross Vehicle Weight Rating	Average Curb Weight
Suncruiser	1994	MHA	34	34RA	FO	7.5L	G	$1900	228	8,000	17,000	14,586

Livability Code: SB 30-90
Wheelbase-to-length ratio of 56% is considered ○ dangerous ○ fatiguing ◉ good ○ excellent *
The approximate net payload of 2414 pounds at 14% of GVWR on this model is ○ deficient ○ excessive ○ cautionary ◉ good ○ excellent *
Total highway safety penalties are: 2 * Value: 8 5 Durability: 7 8 Highway Control Rating: 9 2 Highway Safety: 9 0 ★★★

Brand	Year	Type	Length	Model	Chassis	Engine	Fuel Type	Avg Price/LF When New	Adj Wheelbase	Approx Towing	GVWR	Avg Curb Weight
Suncruiser	1994	MHA	34	34 RQ-P	OS	CU190	D	$2900	228	1,500	18,340	15,786

Livability Code: SB 30-90
Wheelbase-to-length ratio of 56% is considered ○ dangerous ○ fatiguing ◉ good ○ excellent *
The approximate net payload of 2554 pounds at 14% of GVWR on this model is ○ deficient ○ excessive ○ cautionary ◉ good ○ excellent *
Total highway safety penalties are: 2 * Value: 8 5 Durability: 7 8 Highway Control Rating: 9 2 Highway Safety: 9 0 ★★★

Brand	Year	Type	Length	Model	Chassis	Engine	Fuel Type	Avg Price/LF When New	Adj Wheelbase	Approx Towing	GVWR	Avg Curb Weight
Suncruiser	1994	MHA	34	34 RQ-P	OS	CU230	D	$2900	228	1,500	19,840	16,086

Livability Code: SB 30-90
Wheelbase-to-length ratio of 56% is considered ○ dangerous ○ fatiguing ○ good ◉ excellent *
The approximate net payload of 3754 pounds at 19% of GVWR on this model is ○ deficient ○ excessive ○ cautionary ○ good ◉ excellent *
Total highway safety penalties are: 2 * Value: 8 5 Durability: 7 8 Highway Control Rating: 9 9 Highway Safety: 9 7 ★★★

Brand	Year	Type	Length	Model	Chassis	Engine	Fuel Type	Avg Price/LF When New	Adj Wheelbase	Approx Towing	GVWR	Avg Curb Weight
Suncruiser	1994	MHA	37	37RW	CH	7.4L	G	$1900	252 T	1,500	18,000	15,835

Livability Code: SB 30-90
Wheelbase-to-length ratio of 56% is considered ○ dangerous ○ fatiguing ◉ good ○ excellent *
The approximate net payload of 2165 pounds at 12% of GVWR on this model is ○ deficient ○ excessive ○ cautionary ◉ good ○ excellent *
Total highway safety penalties are: 11 * Value: 8 1 Durability: 7 8 Highway Control Rating: 8 9 Highway Safety: 7 8 ★★★

Brand	Year	Type	Length	Model	Chassis	Engine	Fuel Type	Avg Price/LF When New	Adj Wheelbase	Approx Towing	GVWR	Avg Curb Weight
Suncruiser	1994	MHA	37	37RW	FO	7.5L	G	$1900	252 T	6,000	19,000	16,135

Livability Code: SB 30-90
Wheelbase-to-length ratio of 56% is considered ○ dangerous ○ fatiguing ◉ good ○ excellent *
The approximate net payload of 2865 pounds at 15% of GVWR on this model is ○ deficient ○ excessive ○ cautionary ◉ good ○ excellent *
Total highway safety penalties are: 4 * Value: 8 4 Durability: 7 8 Highway Control Rating: 9 5 Highway Safety: 9 1 ★★★

Brand	Year	Type	Length	Model	Chassis	Engine	Fuel Type	Avg Price/LF When New	Adj Wheelbase	Approx Towing	GVWR	Avg Curb Weight
Suncruiser	1995	MHA	30	29RQ	CH	7.4L	G	$2100	178	4,200	14,800	12,988

Livability Code: SB 30-90
Wheelbase-to-length ratio of 49% is considered ◉ dangerous ○ fatiguing ○ good ○ excellent *
The approximate net payload of 1812 pounds at 12% of GVWR on this model is ○ deficient ○ excessive ○ cautionary ◉ good ○ excellent *
Total highway safety penalties are: 5 * Value: 8 4 Durability: 7 8 Highway Control Rating: 3 5 Highway Safety: 3 0

Brand	Year	Type	Length	Model	Chassis	Engine	Fuel Type	Avg Price/LF When New	Adj Wheelbase	Approx Towing	GVWR	Avg Curb Weight
Suncruiser	1995	MHA	30	29RQ-D	CH	GM6.5	D	$2200	178	4,200	14,800	12,988

Livability Code: SB 30-90
Wheelbase-to-length ratio of 49% is considered ◉ dangerous ○ fatiguing ○ good ○ excellent *
The approximate net payload of 1812 pounds at 12% of GVWR on this model is ○ deficient ○ excessive ○ cautionary ◉ good ○ excellent *
Total highway safety penalties are: 5 * Value: 8 4 Durability: 7 8 Highway Control Rating: 3 5 Highway Safety: 3 0

Brand	Year	Type	Length	Model	Chassis	Engine	Fuel Type	Avg Price/LF When New	Adj Wheelbase	Approx Towing	GVWR	Avg Curb Weight
Suncruiser	1995	MHA	30	29RQ	FO	7.5L	G	$2100	178	3,800	15,200	13,388

Livability Code: SB 30-90
Wheelbase-to-length ratio of 49% is considered ◉ dangerous ○ fatiguing ○ good ○ excellent *
The approximate net payload of 1812 pounds at 12% of GVWR on this model is ○ deficient ○ excessive ○ cautionary ◉ good ○ excellent *
Total highway safety penalties are: 2 * Value: 8 5 Durability: 7 8 Highway Control Rating: 3 5 Highway Safety: 3 3

Brand	Year	Type	Length	Model	Chassis	Engine	Fuel Type	Avg Price/LF When New	Adj Wheelbase	Approx Towing	GVWR	Avg Curb Weight
Suncruiser	1995	MHA	32	32RQ	CH	7.4L	G	$2100	208	1,500	16,000	13,587

Livability Code: SB 30-90
Wheelbase-to-length ratio of 54% is considered ○ dangerous ○ fatiguing ◉ good ○ excellent *
The approximate net payload of 2413 pounds at 15% of GVWR on this model is ○ deficient ○ excessive ○ cautionary ◉ good ○ excellent *
Total highway safety penalties are: 6 * Value: 8 3 Durability: 7 8 Highway Control Rating: 8 0 Highway Safety: 7 4 ★★★

Brand	Year	Type	Length	Model	Chassis	Engine	Fuel Type	Avg Price/LF When New	Adj Wheelbase	Approx Towing	GVWR	Avg Curb Weight
Suncruiser	1995	MHA	32	32RQ	FO	7.5L	G	$2100	208	8,000	17,000	14,087

Livability Code: SB 30-90
Wheelbase-to-length ratio of 54% is considered ○ dangerous ○ fatiguing ◉ good ○ excellent *
The approximate net payload of 2913 pounds at 17% of GVWR on this model is ○ deficient ○ excessive ○ cautionary ○ good ◉ excellent *
Total highway safety penalties are: 2 * Value: 8 5 Durability: 7 8 Highway Control Rating: 8 3 Highway Safety: 8 1 ★★★

Brand	Year	Type	Length	Model	Chassis	Engine	Fuel Type	Avg Price/LF When New	Adj Wheelbase	Approx Towing	GVWR	Avg Curb Weight
Suncruiser	1995	MHA	34	34RQ	CH	7.4L	G	$2100	228	1,500	16,000	14,086

Livability Code: SB 30-90
Wheelbase-to-length ratio of 56% is considered ○ dangerous ○ fatiguing ◉ good ○ excellent *
The approximate net payload of 1914 pounds at 12% of GVWR on this model is ○ deficient ○ excessive ○ cautionary ◉ good ○ excellent *
Total highway safety penalties are: 7 * Value: 8 3 Durability: 7 8 Highway Control Rating: 8 8 Highway Safety: 8 1 ★★★

Brand	Year	Type	Length	Model	Chassis	Engine	Fuel Type	Avg Price/LF When New	Adj Wheelbase	Approx Towing	GVWR	Avg Curb Weight
Suncruiser	1995	MHA	34	34RA	CH	7.4L	G	$2100	228	1,500	16,000	14,086

Livability Code: SB 30-90
Wheelbase-to-length ratio of 56% is considered ○ dangerous ○ fatiguing ◉ good ○ excellent *
The approximate net payload of 1914 pounds at 12% of GVWR on this model is ○ deficient ○ excessive ○ cautionary ◉ good ○ excellent *
Total highway safety penalties are: 7 * Value: 8 3 Durability: 7 8 Highway Control Rating: 8 8 Highway Safety: 8 1 ★★★

Note: Safety ratings are based on the assumption that the engineering of the RV has allowed for proper balance by placing fresh, gray, and black holding tanks in a location so as not to change the balance of the RV when the tanks are empty or full. **Always double-check wheelbase, GVWR, and weights at front and rear axles.**

*See Section 1 for details on how conclusions are reached.

Section 2: The Ratings

Brand	Year	Type	Length	Model	Chassis	Engine	Fuel Type	Average Price per Linear Foot When New	Adjusted Wheelbase	Approx. Towing Capacity	Gross Vehicle Weight Rating	Average Curb Weight
Suncruiser	1995	MHA	34	34RQ opsl	CH	7.4L	G	$2200	228	8,000	16,000	14,836

Livability Code: SB 30-90
Wheelbase-to-length ratio of 56% is considered ○ dangerous ○ fatiguing ◉ good ○ excellent *
The approximate net payload of 1164 pounds at 7% of GVWR on this model is ○ deficient ○ excessive ◉ cautionary ○ good ○ excellent *
Total highway safety penalties are: 11 *   Value: 8 1   Durability: 7 8   Highway Control Rating: 6 7   Highway Safety: 5 6   ★

Brand	Year	Type	Length	Model	Chassis	Engine	Fuel Type	Avg Price/Ft	Adj Wheelbase	Towing	GVWR	Curb Weight
Suncruiser	1995	MHA	34	34RQ	FO	7.5L	G	$2100	228	8,000	17,000	14,586

Livability Code: SB 30-90
Wheelbase-to-length ratio of 56% is considered ○ dangerous ○ fatiguing ◉ good ○ excellent *
The approximate net payload of 2414 pounds at 14% of GVWR on this model is ○ deficient ○ excessive ○ cautionary ◉ good ○ excellent *
Total highway safety penalties are: 2 *   Value: 8 5   Durability: 7 8   Highway Control Rating: 9 2   Highway Safety: 9 0   ★★★

Brand	Year	Type	Length	Model	Chassis	Engine	Fuel Type	Avg Price/Ft	Adj Wheelbase	Towing	GVWR	Curb Weight
Suncruiser	1995	MHA	34	34RA	FO	7.5L	G	$2100	228	8,000	17,000	14,586

Livability Code: SB 30-90
Wheelbase-to-length ratio of 56% is considered ○ dangerous ○ fatiguing ◉ good ○ excellent *
The approximate net payload of 2414 pounds at 14% of GVWR on this model is ○ deficient ○ excessive ○ cautionary ◉ good ○ excellent *
Total highway safety penalties are: 2 *   Value: 8 5   Durability: 7 8   Highway Control Rating: 9 2   Highway Safety: 9 0   ★★★

Brand	Year	Type	Length	Model	Chassis	Engine	Fuel Type	Avg Price/Ft	Adj Wheelbase	Towing	GVWR	Curb Weight
Suncruiser	1995	MHA	34	34RQ opsl	FO	7.5L	G	$2200	228	8,000	17,000	15,336

Livability Code: SB 30-90
Wheelbase-to-length ratio of 56% is considered ○ dangerous ○ fatiguing ◉ good ○ excellent *
The approximate net payload of 1664 pounds at 10% of GVWR on this model is ○ deficient ○ excessive ○ cautionary ◉ good ○ excellent *
Total highway safety penalties are: 7 *   Value: 8 3   Durability: 7 8   Highway Control Rating: 9 0   Highway Safety: 8 3   ★★★

Brand	Year	Type	Length	Model	Chassis	Engine	Fuel Type	Avg Price/Ft	Adj Wheelbase	Towing	GVWR	Curb Weight
Suncruiser	1995	MHA	34	34RQ	OS	CU230	D	$3000	228	1,500	19,840	16,086

Livability Code: SB 30-90
Wheelbase-to-length ratio of 56% is considered ○ dangerous ○ fatiguing ◉ good ○ excellent *
The approximate net payload of 3754 pounds at 19% of GVWR on this model is ○ deficient ○ excessive ○ cautionary ○ good ◉ excellent *
Total highway safety penalties are: 2 *   Value: 8 5   Durability: 7 8   Highway Control Rating: 9 9   Highway Safety: 9 7   ★★★

Brand	Year	Type	Length	Model	Chassis	Engine	Fuel Type	Avg Price/Ft	Adj Wheelbase	Towing	GVWR	Curb Weight
Suncruiser	1995	MHA	34	34RQ opsl	OS	CU230	D	$3000	228	1,500	19,840	16,836

Livability Code: SB 30-90
Wheelbase-to-length ratio of 56% is considered ○ dangerous ○ fatiguing ◉ good ○ excellent *
The approximate net payload of 3004 pounds at 15% of GVWR on this model is ○ deficient ○ excessive ○ cautionary ◉ good ○ excellent *
Total highway safety penalties are: 7 *   Value: 8 3   Durability: 7 8   Highway Control Rating: 9 4   Highway Safety: 8 7   ★★★

Brand	Year	Type	Length	Model	Chassis	Engine	Fuel Type	Avg Price/Ft	Adj Wheelbase	Towing	GVWR	Curb Weight
Suncruiser	1995	MHA	37	37RW	FO	7.5L	G	$2300	252 T	6,000	19,000	16,135

Livability Code: SB 30-90
Wheelbase-to-length ratio of 56% is considered ○ dangerous ○ fatiguing ◉ good ○ excellent *
The approximate net payload of 2865 pounds at 15% of GVWR on this model is ○ deficient ○ excessive ○ cautionary ◉ good ○ excellent *
Total highway safety penalties are: 4 *   Value: 8 4   Durability: 7 8   Highway Control Rating: 9 5   Highway Safety: 9 1   ★★★

Brand	Year	Type	Length	Model	Chassis	Engine	Fuel Type	Avg Price/Ft	Adj Wheelbase	Towing	GVWR	Curb Weight
Suncruiser	1996	MHA	30	29RQ	CH	7.4L	G	$1900	178	6,200	14,800	12,988

Livability Code: SB 30-90
Wheelbase-to-length ratio of 49% is considered ◉ dangerous ○ fatiguing ○ good ○ excellent *
The approximate net payload of 1812 pounds at 12% of GVWR on this model is ○ deficient ○ excessive ○ cautionary ◉ good ○ excellent *
Total highway safety penalties are: 5 *   Value: 8 4   Durability: 7 8   Highway Control Rating: 3 5   Highway Safety: 3 0

Brand	Year	Type	Length	Model	Chassis	Engine	Fuel Type	Avg Price/Ft	Adj Wheelbase	Towing	GVWR	Curb Weight
Suncruiser	1996	MHA	32	29RQ	CH	GM6.5	D	$1900	178	4,200	14,800	13,537

Livability Code: SB 30-90
Wheelbase-to-length ratio of 46% is considered ◉ dangerous ○ fatiguing ○ good ○ excellent *
The approximate net payload of 1263 pounds at 9% of GVWR on this model is ○ deficient ○ excessive ◉ cautionary ○ good ○ excellent *
Total highway safety penalties are: 6 *   Value: 8 3   Durability: 7 8   Highway Control Rating: 1 3   Highway Safety: 7

Brand	Year	Type	Length	Model	Chassis	Engine	Fuel Type	Avg Price/Ft	Adj Wheelbase	Towing	GVWR	Curb Weight
Suncruiser	1996	MHA	32	32RQ	CH	7.4L	G	$1900	208	4,500	16,500	13,737

Livability Code: SB 30-90
Wheelbase-to-length ratio of 54% is considered ○ dangerous ○ fatiguing ◉ good ○ excellent *
The approximate net payload of 2763 pounds at 17% of GVWR on this model is ○ deficient ○ excessive ○ cautionary ○ good ◉ excellent *
Total highway safety penalties are: 6 *   Value: 8 3   Durability: 7 8   Highway Control Rating: 8 2   Highway Safety: 7 6   ★★★

Brand	Year	Type	Length	Model	Chassis	Engine	Fuel Type	Avg Price/Ft	Adj Wheelbase	Towing	GVWR	Curb Weight
Suncruiser	1996	MHA	32	29RQ	FO	7.5L	G	$1800	178	9,800	15,200	13,937

Livability Code: SB 30-90
Wheelbase-to-length ratio of 46% is considered ◉ dangerous ○ fatiguing ○ good ○ excellent *
The approximate net payload of 1263 pounds at 8% of GVWR on this model is ○ deficient ○ excessive ◉ cautionary ○ good ○ excellent *
Total highway safety penalties are: 2 *   Value: 8 5   Durability: 7 8   Highway Control Rating: 8   Highway Safety: 6

Brand	Year	Type	Length	Model	Chassis	Engine	Fuel Type	Avg Price/Ft	Adj Wheelbase	Towing	GVWR	Curb Weight
Suncruiser	1996	MHA	32	32RQ	FO	7.5L	G	$1900	208	8,000	17,000	14,137

Livability Code: SB 30-90
Wheelbase-to-length ratio of 54% is considered ○ dangerous ○ fatiguing ◉ good ○ excellent *
The approximate net payload of 2863 pounds at 17% of GVWR on this model is ○ deficient ○ excessive ○ cautionary ○ good ◉ excellent *
Total highway safety penalties are: 2 *   Value: 8 5   Durability: 7 8   Highway Control Rating: 8 2   Highway Safety: 8 0   ★★★

Note: Safety ratings are based on the assumption that the engineering of the RV has allowed for proper balance by placing fresh, gray, and black holding tanks in a location so as not to change the balance of the RV when the tanks are empty or full. **Always double-check wheelbase, GVWR, and weights at front and rear axles.**

*See Section 1 for details on how conclusions are reached.

Brand	Year	Type	Length	Model	Chassis	Engine	Fuel Type	Average Price per Linear Foot When New	Adjusted Wheelbase	Approx. Towing Capacity	Gross Vehicle Weight Rating	Average Curb Weight
Suncruiser	1996	MHA	34	34RQ	CH	7.4L	G	$1900	228	4,500	16,500	14,236

Livability Code: SB 30-90
Wheelbase-to-length ratio of 56% is considered ○ dangerous ○ fatiguing ◉ good ○ excellent *
The approximate net payload of 2264 pounds at 14% of GVWR on this model is ○ deficient ○ excessive ○ cautionary ◉ good ○ excellent *
Total highway safety penalties are: 7 *　Value: **8 3**　Durability: **7 8**　Highway Control Rating: **9 0**　Highway Safety: **8 3**　★★★

Brand	Year	Type	Length	Model	Chassis	Engine	Fuel Type	Price/LF	Wheelbase	Towing	GVWR	Curb Wt
Suncruiser	1996	MHA	34	34RA	CH	7.4L	G	$1900	228	4,500	16,500	14,236

Livability Code: SB 30-90
Wheelbase-to-length ratio of 56% is considered ○ dangerous ○ fatiguing ◉ good ○ excellent *
The approximate net payload of 2264 pounds at 14% of GVWR on this model is ○ deficient ○ excessive ○ cautionary ◉ good ○ excellent *
Total highway safety penalties are: 7 *　Value: **8 3**　Durability: **7 8**　Highway Control Rating: **9 0**　Highway Safety: **8 3**　★★★

Suncruiser	1996	MHA	34	34WK	CH	7.4L	G	$1900	228	4,500	16,500	14,770

Livability Code: SB 30-90
Wheelbase-to-length ratio of 56% is considered ○ dangerous ○ fatiguing ◉ good ○ excellent *
The approximate net payload of 1730 pounds at 10% of GVWR on this model is ○ deficient ○ excessive ○ cautionary ◉ good ○ excellent *
Total highway safety penalties are: 7 *　Value: **8 3**　Durability: **7 8**　Highway Control Rating: **8 9**　Highway Safety: **8 2**　★★★

Suncruiser	1996	MHA	34	34RQ	FO	7.5L	G	$1900	228	8,000	17,000	14,636

Livability Code: SB 30-90
Wheelbase-to-length ratio of 56% is considered ○ dangerous ○ fatiguing ◉ good ○ excellent *
The approximate net payload of 2364 pounds at 14% of GVWR on this model is ○ deficient ○ excessive ○ cautionary ◉ good ○ excellent *
Total highway safety penalties are: 2 *　Value: **8 5**　Durability: **7 8**　Highway Control Rating: **9 0**　Highway Safety: **8 8**　★★★

Suncruiser	1996	MHA	34	34RA	FO	7.5L	G	$1900	228	8,000	17,000	14,636

Livability Code: SB 30-90
Wheelbase-to-length ratio of 56% is considered ○ dangerous ○ fatiguing ◉ good ○ excellent *
The approximate net payload of 2364 pounds at 14% of GVWR on this model is ○ deficient ○ excessive ○ cautionary ◉ good ○ excellent *
Total highway safety penalties are: 2 *　Value: **8 5**　Durability: **7 8**　Highway Control Rating: **9 0**　Highway Safety: **8 8**　★★★

Suncruiser	1996	MHA	34	34WK	FO	7.5L	G	$2900	228	8,000	17,000	14,636

Livability Code: SB 30-90
Wheelbase-to-length ratio of 56% is considered ○ dangerous ○ fatiguing ◉ good ○ excellent *
The approximate net payload of 2364 pounds at 14% of GVWR on this model is ○ deficient ○ excessive ○ cautionary ◉ good ○ excellent *
Total highway safety penalties are: 2 *　Value: **8 5**　Durability: **7 8**　Highway Control Rating: **9 0**　Highway Safety: **8 8**　★★★

Suncruiser	1996	MHA	34	34RQ-P	FR	Cu5.9L	D	$2900	228	1,500	19,840	17,136

Livability Code: SB 30-90
Wheelbase-to-length ratio of 56% is considered ○ dangerous ○ fatiguing ◉ good ○ excellent *
The approximate net payload of 2704 pounds at 14% of GVWR on this model is ○ deficient ○ excessive ○ cautionary ◉ good ○ excellent *
Total highway safety penalties are: 7 *　Value: **8 3**　Durability: **7 8**　Highway Control Rating: **9 0**　Highway Safety: **8 3**　★★★

Suncruiser	1996	MHA	37	36WQ-P	FR	Cu5.9L	D	$2800	252	1,500	19,840	17,406

Livability Code: SB 30-90
Wheelbase-to-length ratio of 57% is considered ○ dangerous ○ fatiguing ◉ good ○ excellent *
The approximate net payload of 2434 pounds at 12% of GVWR on this model is ○ deficient ○ excessive ○ cautionary ◉ good ○ excellent *
Total highway safety penalties are: 2 *　Value: **8 5**　Durability: **7 8**　Highway Control Rating: **9 3**　Highway Safety: **9 1**　★★★

Suncruiser	1996	MHA	38	37RW	FO	7.5L	G	$2000	252 T	5,000	20,000	17,285

Livability Code: SB 30-90
Wheelbase-to-length ratio of 56% is considered ○ dangerous ○ fatiguing ◉ good ○ excellent *
The approximate net payload of 2715 pounds at 14% of GVWR on this model is ○ deficient ○ excessive ○ cautionary ◉ good ○ excellent *
Total highway safety penalties are: 10 *　Value: **8 1**　Durability: **7 8**　Highway Control Rating: **9 1**　Highway Safety: **8 1**　★★★

Suncruiser	1997	MHA	30	30 WQ	CH	7.4L	G	$2100	178	4,200	14,800	13,283

Livability Code: SB 30-90
Wheelbase-to-length ratio of 49% is considered ◉ dangerous ○ fatiguing ○ good ○ excellent *
The approximate net payload of 1517 pounds at 10% of GVWR on this model is ○ deficient ○ excessive ○ cautionary ◉ good ○ excellent *
Total highway safety penalties are: 5 *　Value: **8 4**　Durability: **7 8**　Highway Control Rating: **3 0**　Highway Safety: **2 5**

Suncruiser	1997	MHA	30	30 WQ op eng	CH	GM6.5	D	$2100	178	1,500	14,800	13,983

Livability Code: SB 30-90
Wheelbase-to-length ratio of 49% is considered ◉ dangerous ○ fatiguing ○ good ○ excellent *
The approximate net payload of 817 pounds at 6% of GVWR on this model is ◉ deficient ○ excessive ○ cautionary ○ good ○ excellent *
Total highway safety penalties are: 5 *　Value: **8 4**　Durability: **7 8**　Highway Control Rating: **7**　Highway Safety: **2**

Suncruiser	1997	MHA	30	30 WQ op eng	FO	7.5L	G	$2100	178	9,800	15,200	13,696

Livability Code: SB 30-90
Wheelbase-to-length ratio of 49% is considered ◉ dangerous ○ fatiguing ○ good ○ excellent *
The approximate net payload of 1504 pounds at 10% of GVWR on this model is ○ deficient ○ excessive ○ cautionary ◉ good ○ excellent *
Total highway safety penalties are: 2 *　Value: **8 5**　Durability: **7 8**　Highway Control Rating: **3 0**　Highway Safety: **2 8**

Note: Safety ratings are based on the assumption that the engineering of the RV has allowed for proper balance by placing fresh, gray, and black holding tanks in a location so as not to change the balance of the RV when the tanks are empty or full. **Always double-check wheelbase, GVWR, and weights at front and rear axles.**

*See Section 1 for details on how conclusions are reached.

Brand	Year	Type	Length	Model	Chassis	Engine	Fuel Type	Average Price per Linear Foot When New	Adjusted Wheelbase	Approx. Towing Capacity	Gross Vehicle Weight Rating	Average Curb Weight
Suncruiser	1997	MHA	32	32 WQ	CH	7.4L	G	$2100	208	3,500	16,500	14,240

Livability Code: SB 30-90   Wheelbase-to-length ratio of 54% is considered ○ dangerous ○ fatiguing ◉ good ○ excellent *
The approximate net payload of 2260 pounds at 14% of GVWR on this model is ○ deficient ○ excessive ○ cautionary ◉ good ○ excellent *
Total highway safety penalties are: 6 *   Value: 83   Durability: 78   Highway Control Rating: 78   Highway Safety: 72   ★★★

| Suncruiser | 1997 | MHA | 32 | 32 WQ op eng | FO | 7.5L | G | $2100 | 208 | 8,000 | 17,000 | 14,427 |

Livability Code: SB 30-90   Wheelbase-to-length ratio of 54% is considered ○ dangerous ○ fatiguing ◉ good ○ excellent *
The approximate net payload of 2573 pounds at 15% of GVWR on this model is ○ deficient ○ excessive ○ cautionary ◉ good ○ excellent *
Total highway safety penalties are: 2 *   Value: 85   Durability: 78   Highway Control Rating: 78   Highway Safety: 76   ★★★

| Suncruiser | 1997 | MHA | 34 | 34 RQ | CH | 7.4L | G | $2200 | 216 | 3,500 | 16,500 | 15,005 |

Livability Code: SB 30-90   Wheelbase-to-length ratio of 53% is considered ○ dangerous ◉ fatiguing ○ good ○ excellent *
The approximate net payload of 1495 pounds at 9% of GVWR on this model is ○ deficient ○ excessive ◉ cautionary ○ good ○ excellent *
Total highway safety penalties are: 12 *   Value: 80   Durability: 78   Highway Control Rating: 52   Highway Safety: 40

| Suncruiser | 1997 | MHA | 34 | 34 RQ op eng | FO | 7.5L | G | $2200 | 216 | 8,000 | 17,000 | 15,386 |

Livability Code: SB 30-90   Wheelbase-to-length ratio of 53% is considered ○ dangerous ◉ fatiguing ○ good ○ excellent *
The approximate net payload of 1614 pounds at 9% of GVWR on this model is ○ deficient ○ excessive ◉ cautionary ○ good ○ excellent *
Total highway safety penalties are: 7 *   Value: 83   Durability: 78   Highway Control Rating: 53   Highway Safety: 46

| Suncruiser | 1997 | MHA | 34 | 34 WK | CH | 7.4L | G | $2000 | 228 | 3,500 | 16,500 | 14,439 |

Livability Code: SB 30-90   Wheelbase-to-length ratio of 55% is considered ○ dangerous ○ fatiguing ◉ good ○ excellent *
The approximate net payload of 2061 pounds at 12% of GVWR on this model is ○ deficient ○ excessive ○ cautionary ◉ good ○ excellent *
Total highway safety penalties are: 7 *   Value: 83   Durability: 78   Highway Control Rating: 86   Highway Safety: 79   ★★★

| Suncruiser | 1997 | MHA | 34 | 34 WA | CH | 7.4L | G | $2000 | 228 | 3,500 | 16,500 | 14,411 |

Livability Code: SB 30-90   Wheelbase-to-length ratio of 55% is considered ○ dangerous ○ fatiguing ◉ good ○ excellent *
The approximate net payload of 2089 pounds at 13% of GVWR on this model is ○ deficient ○ excessive ○ cautionary ◉ good ○ excellent *
Total highway safety penalties are: 7 *   Value: 83   Durability: 78   Highway Control Rating: 88   Highway Safety: 81   ★★★

| Suncruiser | 1997 | MHA | 34 | 34 WK op eng | FO | 7.5L | G | $2000 | 228 | 8,000 | 17,000 | 14,980 |

Livability Code: SB 30-90   Wheelbase-to-length ratio of 55% is considered ○ dangerous ○ fatiguing ◉ good ○ excellent *
The approximate net payload of 2020 pounds at 12% of GVWR on this model is ○ deficient ○ excessive ○ cautionary ◉ good ○ excellent *
Total highway safety penalties are: 2 *   Value: 85   Durability: 78   Highway Control Rating: 86   Highway Safety: 84   ★★★

| Suncruiser | 1997 | MHA | 34 | 34 WA op eng | FO | 7.5L | G | $2000 | 228 | 8,000 | 17,000 | 14,924 |

Livability Code: SB 30-90   Wheelbase-to-length ratio of 55% is considered ○ dangerous ○ fatiguing ◉ good ○ excellent *
The approximate net payload of 2076 pounds at 12% of GVWR on this model is ○ deficient ○ excessive ○ cautionary ◉ good ○ excellent *
Total highway safety penalties are: 2 *   Value: 85   Durability: 78   Highway Control Rating: 86   Highway Safety: 84   ★★★

| Suncruiser | 1997 | MHA | 34 | 34WK-P | FR | Cu5.9L | D | $3200 | 228 | 5,000 | 20,700 | 18,793 |

Livability Code: SB 30-90   Wheelbase-to-length ratio of 55% is considered ○ dangerous ○ fatiguing ◉ good ○ excellent *
The approximate net payload of 1907 pounds at 9% of GVWR on this model is ○ deficient ○ excessive ◉ cautionary ○ good ○ excellent *
Total highway safety penalties are: 7 *   Value: 83   Durability: 78   Highway Control Rating: 77   Highway Safety: 70   ★★★

| Suncruiser | 1997 | MHA | 36 | 35 WQ | CH | 7.4L | G | $1900 | 228 | 1,500 | 16,500 | 15,247 |

Livability Code: SB 30-90   Wheelbase-to-length ratio of 53% is considered ○ dangerous ◉ fatiguing ○ good ○ excellent *
The approximate net payload of 1253 pounds at 8% of GVWR on this model is ○ deficient ○ excessive ◉ cautionary ○ good ○ excellent *
Total highway safety penalties are: 8 *   Value: 82   Durability: 78   Highway Control Rating: 46   Highway Safety: 38

| Suncruiser | 1997 | MHA | 36 | 35 WQ | FO | 7.5L | G | $2000 | 228 | 8,000 | 17,000 | 15,227 |

Livability Code: SB 30-90   Wheelbase-to-length ratio of 53% is considered ○ dangerous ◉ fatiguing ○ good ○ excellent *
The approximate net payload of 1773 pounds at 10% of GVWR on this model is ○ deficient ○ excessive ○ cautionary ◉ good ○ excellent *
Total highway safety penalties are: 2 *   Value: 85   Durability: 78   Highway Control Rating: 58   Highway Safety: 56   ★

| Suncruiser | 1997 | MHA | 36 | 35 WQ slide | FO | 7.5L | G | $2100 | 228 | 8,000 | 17,000 | 16,547 |

Livability Code: SB 30-90   Wheelbase-to-length ratio of 53% is considered ○ dangerous ◉ fatiguing ○ good ○ excellent *
The approximate net payload of 453 pounds at 3% of GVWR on this model is ◉ deficient ○ excessive ○ cautionary ○ good ○ excellent *
Total highway safety penalties are: 13 *   Value: 80   Durability: 78   Highway Control Rating: 36   Highway Safety: 23

Note: Safety ratings are based on the assumption that the engineering of the RV has allowed for proper balance by placing fresh, gray, and black holding tanks in a location so as not to change the balance of the RV when the tanks are empty or full. **Always double-check wheelbase, GVWR, and weights at front and rear axles.**

*See Section 1 for details on how conclusions are reached.

Brand	Year	Type	Length	Model	Chassis	Engine	Fuel Type	Average Price per Linear Foot When New	Adjusted Wheelbase	Approx. Towing Capacity	Gross Vehicle Weight Rating	Average Curb Weight
Suncruiser	1997	MHA	38	37RW	FO	7.5L	G	$2200	252 T	5,000	20,000	17,189

Livability Code: SB 30-90   Wheelbase-to-length ratio of 56% is considered ○ dangerous ○ fatiguing ◉ good ○ excellent *

The approximate net payload of 2811 pounds at 14% of GVWR on this model is ○ deficient ○ excessive ○ cautionary ◉ good ○ excellent *

Total highway safety penalties are: 10 *   Value: 8 1   Durability: 7 8   Highway Control Rating: 9 2   Highway Safety: 8 2   ★★★

Brand	Year	Type	Length	Model	Chassis	Engine	Fuel Type	Average Price per Linear Foot When New	Adjusted Wheelbase	Approx. Towing Capacity	Gross Vehicle Weight Rating	Average Curb Weight
Suncruiser	1998	MHA	31	30WQ	CH	7.4L	G	$2100	190	4,500	16,500	13,786

Livability Code: SB 30-90   Wheelbase-to-length ratio of 51% is considered ○ dangerous ◉ fatiguing ○ good ○ excellent *

The approximate net payload of 2714 pounds at 16% of GVWR on this model is ○ deficient ○ excessive ○ cautionary ○ good ◉ excellent *

Total highway safety penalties are: 5 *   Value: 8 4   Durability: 7 8   Highway Control Rating: 4 9   Highway Safety: 4 4

Suncruiser	1998	MHA	31	30WQ opch	FO	7.5L	G	$2100	190	8,000	17,000	14,183

Livability Code: SB 30-90   Wheelbase-to-length ratio of 51% is considered ○ dangerous ◉ fatiguing ○ good ○ excellent *

The approximate net payload of 2817 pounds at 17% of GVWR on this model is ○ deficient ○ excessive ○ cautionary ○ good ◉ excellent *

Total highway safety penalties are: 2 *   Value: 8 5   Durability: 7 8   Highway Control Rating: 4 9   Highway Safety: 4 7

Suncruiser	1998	MHA	33	32WQ	CH	7.4L	G	$2100	208	4,500	16,500	14,131

Livability Code: SB 30-90   Wheelbase-to-length ratio of 53% is considered ○ dangerous ◉ fatiguing ○ good ○ excellent *

The approximate net payload of 2369 pounds at 14% of GVWR on this model is ○ deficient ○ excessive ○ cautionary ◉ good ○ excellent *

Total highway safety penalties are: 6 *   Value: 8 3   Durability: 7 8   Highway Control Rating: 6 7   Highway Safety: 6 1   ★★

Suncruiser	1998	MHA	33	32WQ opch	FO	7.5L	G	$2000	208	8,000	17,000	14,532

Livability Code: SB 30-90   Wheelbase-to-length ratio of 53% is considered ○ dangerous ◉ fatiguing ○ good ○ excellent *

The approximate net payload of 2468 pounds at 15% of GVWR on this model is ○ deficient ○ excessive ○ cautionary ◉ good ○ excellent *

Total highway safety penalties are: 2 *   Value: 8 5   Durability: 7 8   Highway Control Rating: 6 8   Highway Safety: 6 6   ★★

Suncruiser	1998	MHA	34	33WQ	FO	7.5L	G	$2200	216	8,000	17,000	15,659

Livability Code: SB 30-90   Wheelbase-to-length ratio of 53% is considered ○ dangerous ◉ fatiguing ○ good ○ excellent *

The approximate net payload of 1341 pounds at 8% of GVWR on this model is ○ deficient ○ excessive ◉ cautionary ○ good ○ excellent *

Total highway safety penalties are: 12 *   Value: 8 0   Durability: 7 8   Highway Control Rating: 4 8   Highway Safety: 3 6

Suncruiser	1998	MHA	35	34WQ-P	FR	CU230	D	$2900	228	5,000	20,700	18,821

Livability Code: SB 30-90   Wheelbase-to-length ratio of 55% is considered ○ dangerous ○ fatiguing ◉ good ○ excellent *

The approximate net payload of 1879 pounds at 9% of GVWR on this model is ○ deficient ○ excessive ◉ cautionary ○ good ○ excellent *

Total highway safety penalties are: 7 *   Value: 8 3   Durability: 7 8   Highway Control Rating: 7 5   Highway Safety: 6 8   ★★

Suncruiser	1998	MHA	35	34WA	CH	7.4L	G	$2000	228	4,500	16,500	14,659

Livability Code: SB 30-90   Wheelbase-to-length ratio of 54% is considered ○ dangerous ○ fatiguing ◉ good ○ excellent *

The approximate net payload of 1841 pounds at 11% of GVWR on this model is ○ deficient ○ excessive ○ cautionary ◉ good ○ excellent *

Total highway safety penalties are: 7 *   Value: 8 3   Durability: 7 8   Highway Control Rating: 7 7   Highway Safety: 7 0   ★★★

Suncruiser	1998	MHA	35	34WA opch	FO	7.5L	G	$2000	228	8,000	17,000	15,089

Livability Code: SB 30-90   Wheelbase-to-length ratio of 54% is considered ○ dangerous ○ fatiguing ◉ good ○ excellent *

The approximate net payload of 1911 pounds at 11% of GVWR on this model is ○ deficient ○ excessive ○ cautionary ◉ good ○ excellent *

Total highway safety penalties are: 2 *   Value: 8 5   Durability: 7 8   Highway Control Rating: 7 7   Highway Safety: 7 5   ★★★

Suncruiser	1998	MHA	35	35WP	CH	7.4L	G	$2000	216	4,500	16,500	14,736

Livability Code: SB 30-90   Wheelbase-to-length ratio of 51% is considered ○ dangerous ◉ fatiguing ○ good ○ excellent *

The approximate net payload of 1764 pounds at 11% of GVWR on this model is ○ deficient ○ excessive ○ cautionary ◉ good ○ excellent *

Total highway safety penalties are: 7 *   Value: 8 3   Durability: 7 8   Highway Control Rating: 3 8   Highway Safety: 3 1

Suncruiser	1998	MHA	35	35WP opch	FO	7.5L	G	$2000	216	8,000	17,000	15,102

Livability Code: SB 30-90   Wheelbase-to-length ratio of 51% is considered ○ dangerous ◉ fatiguing ○ good ○ excellent *

The approximate net payload of 1898 pounds at 11% of GVWR on this model is ○ deficient ○ excessive ○ cautionary ◉ good ○ excellent *

Total highway safety penalties are: 2 *   Value: 8 5   Durability: 7 8   Highway Control Rating: 3 8   Highway Safety: 3 6

Suncruiser	1998	MHA	35	35WP slide	FO	7.5L	G	$2200	216	8,000	17,000	15,847

Livability Code: SB 30-90   Wheelbase-to-length ratio of 51% is considered ○ dangerous ◉ fatiguing ○ good ○ excellent *

The approximate net payload of 1153 pounds at 7% of GVWR on this model is ○ deficient ○ excessive ◉ cautionary ○ good ○ excellent *

Total highway safety penalties are: 7 *   Value: 8 3   Durability: 7 8   Highway Control Rating: 1 9   Highway Safety: 1 2

Note: Safety ratings are based on the assumption that the engineering of the RV has allowed for proper balance by placing fresh, gray, and black holding tanks in a location so as not to change the balance of the RV when the tanks are empty or full. **Always double-check wheelbase, GVWR, and weights at front and rear axles.**

Section 2: The Ratings

Brand	Year	Type	Length	Model	Chassis	Engine	Fuel Type	Average Price per Linear Foot When New	Adjusted Wheelbase	Approx. Towing Capacity	Gross Vehicle Weight Rating	Average Curb Weight
Suncruiser	1998	MHA	38	37WW	FO	7.5L	G	$2100	252 T	5,000	20,000	17,480

Livability Code: SB 30-90   Wheelbase-to-length ratio of 55% is considered ○ dangerous ○ fatiguing ◉ good ○ excellent*

The approximate net payload of 2520 pounds at 13% of GVWR on this model is ○ deficient ○ excessive ○ cautionary ◉ good ○ excellent*

Total highway safety penalties are: 10*   Value: **8 1**   Durability: **7 8**   Highway Control Rating: **8 7**   Highway Safety: **7 7**   ★★★

Brand	Year	Type	Length	Model	Chassis	Engine	Fuel Type	Price	Wheelbase	Towing	GVWR	Curb Weight
Suncruiser	1999	MHA	31	30A	CH	7.4L	G	$2600	190	4,500	16,500	13,946

Livability Code: SB 30-90   Wheelbase-to-length ratio of 51% is considered ○ dangerous ◉ fatiguing ○ good ○ excellent*

The approximate net payload of 2554 pounds at 15% of GVWR on this model is ○ deficient ○ excessive ○ cautionary ◉ good ○ excellent*

Total highway safety penalties are: 5*   Value: **8 4**   Durability: **7 8**   Highway Control Rating: **5 7**   Highway Safety: **5 2**   ★

Suncruiser	1999	MHA	31	30A	FO	6.8L	G	$2600	190	8,000	18,000	14,742

Livability Code: SB 30-90   Wheelbase-to-length ratio of 51% is considered ○ dangerous ◉ fatiguing ○ good ○ excellent*

The approximate net payload of 3258 pounds at 18% of GVWR on this model is ○ deficient ○ excessive ○ cautionary ○ good ◉ excellent*

Total highway safety penalties are: 2*   Value: **8 5**   Durability: **7 8**   Highway Control Rating: **6 1**   Highway Safety: **5 9**   ★

Suncruiser	1999	MHA	33	32T	CH	7.4L	G	$2400	208	4,500	16,500	14,492

Livability Code: SB 30-90   Wheelbase-to-length ratio of 53% is considered ○ dangerous ◉ fatiguing ○ good ○ excellent*

The approximate net payload of 2008 pounds at 12% of GVWR on this model is ○ deficient ○ excessive ○ cautionary ◉ good ○ excellent*

Total highway safety penalties are: 6*   Value: **8 3**   Durability: **7 8**   Highway Control Rating: **6 8**   Highway Safety: **6 2**   ★★

Suncruiser	1999	MHA	33	32T	FO	6.8L	G	$2400	208	8,000	18,000	15,346

Livability Code: SB 30-90   Wheelbase-to-length ratio of 53% is considered ○ dangerous ◉ fatiguing ○ good ○ excellent*

The approximate net payload of 2654 pounds at 15% of GVWR on this model is ○ deficient ○ excessive ○ cautionary ◉ good ○ excellent*

Total highway safety penalties are: 2*   Value: **8 5**   Durability: **7 8**   Highway Control Rating: **7 3**   Highway Safety: **7 1**   ★★★

Suncruiser	1999	MHA	34	33B	CH	7.4L	G	$2400	216	4,500	16,500	15,564

Livability Code: SB 30-90   Wheelbase-to-length ratio of 53% is considered ○ dangerous ◉ fatiguing ○ good ○ excellent*

The approximate net payload of 936 pounds at 6% of GVWR on this model is ◉ deficient ○ excessive ○ cautionary ○ good ○ excellent*

Total highway safety penalties are: 16*   Value: **7 8**   Durability: **7 8**   Highway Control Rating: **4 1**   Highway Safety: **2 5**

Suncruiser	1999	MHA	34	33B	FO	6.8L	G	$2400	216	5,500	20,500	16,328

Livability Code: SB 30-90   Wheelbase-to-length ratio of 53% is considered ○ dangerous ◉ fatiguing ○ good ○ excellent*

The approximate net payload of 4172 pounds at 20% of GVWR on this model is ○ deficient ○ excessive ○ cautionary ○ good ◉ excellent*

Total highway safety penalties are: 12*   Value: **8 0**   Durability: **7 8**   Highway Control Rating: **7 9**   Highway Safety: **6 7**   ★★

Suncruiser	1999	MHA	34	34V-P	FR	CU275	D	$3500	228	5,000	23,600	19,350

Livability Code: SB 30-90   Wheelbase-to-length ratio of 55% is considered ○ dangerous ○ fatiguing ◉ good ○ excellent*

The approximate net payload of 4250 pounds at 18% of GVWR on this model is ○ deficient ○ excessive ○ cautionary ○ good ◉ excellent*

Total highway safety penalties are: 7*   Value: **8 3**   Durability: **7 8**   Highway Control Rating: **9 6**   Highway Safety: **8 9**   ★★★

Suncruiser	1999	MHA	35	34H	CH	7.4L	G	$2300	228	4,500	16,500	15,088

Livability Code: SB 30-90   Wheelbase-to-length ratio of 54% is considered ○ dangerous ○ fatiguing ◉ good ○ excellent*

The approximate net payload of 1412 pounds at 9% of GVWR on this model is ○ deficient ○ excessive ◉ cautionary ○ good ○ excellent*

Total highway safety penalties are: 7*   Value: **8 3**   Durability: **7 8**   Highway Control Rating: **6 7**   Highway Safety: **6 0**   ★★

Suncruiser	1999	MHA	35	34H	FO	6.8L	G	$2300	228	5,500	20,500	15,862

Livability Code: SB 30-90   Wheelbase-to-length ratio of 54% is considered ○ dangerous ○ fatiguing ◉ good ○ excellent*

The approximate net payload of 4638 pounds at 23% of GVWR on this model is ○ deficient ○ excessive ○ cautionary ○ good ◉ excellent*

Total highway safety penalties are: 2*   Value: **8 5**   Durability: **7 8**   Highway Control Rating: **8 6**   Highway Safety: **8 4**   ★★★

Suncruiser	1999	MHA	35	35C	CH	7.4L	G	$2300	220	4,500	16,500	15,187

Livability Code: SB 30-90   Wheelbase-to-length ratio of 52% is considered ○ dangerous ◉ fatiguing ○ good ○ excellent*

The approximate net payload of 1313 pounds at 8% of GVWR on this model is ○ deficient ○ excessive ◉ cautionary ○ good ○ excellent*

Total highway safety penalties are: 13*   Value: **8 0**   Durability: **7 8**   Highway Control Rating: **4 4**   Highway Safety: **3 1**

Suncruiser	1999	MHA	35	35C	FO	6.8L	G	$2300	228	5,500	20,500	16,111

Livability Code: SB 30-90   Wheelbase-to-length ratio of 54% is considered ○ dangerous ○ fatiguing ◉ good ○ excellent*

The approximate net payload of 4389 pounds at 21% of GVWR on this model is ○ deficient ○ excessive ○ cautionary ○ good ◉ excellent*

Total highway safety penalties are: 7*   Value: **8 3**   Durability: **7 8**   Highway Control Rating: **8 6**   Highway Safety: **7 9**   ★★★

Note: Safety ratings are based on the assumption that the engineering of the RV has allowed for proper balance by placing fresh, gray, and black holding tanks in a location so as not to change the balance of the RV when the tanks are empty or full. **Always double-check wheelbase, GVWR, and weights at front and rear axles.**

*See Section 1 for details on how conclusions are reached.

Section 2: The Ratings

Brand	Year	Type	Length	Model	Chassis	Engine	Fuel Type	Average Price per Linear Foot When New	Adjusted Wheelbase	Approx. Towing Capacity	Gross Vehicle Weight Rating	Average Curb Weight
Suncruiser	1999	MHA	38	37G	FO	6.8L	G	$2100	248	5,500	20,500	17,658

Livability Code: SB 30-90 — Wheelbase-to-length ratio of 54% is considered ○ dangerous ○ fatiguing ◉ good ○ excellent*
The approximate net payload of 2842 pounds at 14% of GVWR on this model is ○ deficient ○ excessive ○ cautionary ◉ good ○ excellent*
Total highway safety penalties are: 7* — Value: 83 Durability: 78 Highway Control Rating: 81 Highway Safety: 74 ★★★

Brand	Year	Type	Length	Model	Chassis	Engine	Fuel	$/ft	Wheelbase	Towing	GVWR	Curb
Sundancer	1990	MHC	25	424RC	FO	7.5L	G	$1600	158	1,500	11,000	9,683

Livability Code: VA 30-90 — Wheelbase-to-length ratio of 53% is considered ○ dangerous ◉ fatiguing ○ good ○ excellent*
The approximate net payload of 1317 pounds at 12% of GVWR on this model is ○ deficient ○ excessive ○ cautionary ◉ good ○ excellent*
Total highway safety penalties are: 2* — Value: 84 Durability: 74 Highway Control Rating: 70 Highway Safety: 68 ★★

Sundancer	1991	MHC	25	424 RC	FO	7.5L	G	$1600	158	1,500	11,500	9,738

Livability Code: VA 30-90 — ratio of 53% ○ dangerous ◉ fatiguing ○ good ○ excellent*
The approximate net payload of 1762 pounds at 15% ○ deficient ○ excessive ○ cautionary ◉ good ○ excellent*
Total highway safety penalties are: 2* — Value: 84 Durability: 74 Highway Control Rating: 77 Highway Safety: 75 ★★★

Sundancer	1991	MHC	28	427 RT	FO	7.5L	G	$1600	176	1,500	11,500	10,350

Livability Code: VA 30-90 — ratio of 53% ○ dangerous ◉ fatiguing ○ good ○ excellent*
The approximate net payload of 1150 pounds at 10% ○ deficient ○ excessive ○ cautionary ◉ good ○ excellent*
Total highway safety penalties are: 2* — Value: 84 Durability: 74 Highway Control Rating: 66 Highway Safety: 64 ★★

Sundancer	1995	MHC	29	28RQ	FO	7.5L	G	$1700	190	1,600	12,400	10,761

Livability Code: VA 30-90 — ratio of 55% ○ dangerous ○ fatiguing ◉ good ○ excellent*
The approximate net payload of 1639 pounds at 13% ○ deficient ○ excessive ○ cautionary ◉ good ○ excellent*
Total highway safety penalties are: 2* — Value: 84 Durability: 74 Highway Control Rating: 85 Highway Safety: 83 ★★★

Sundancer	1995	MHC	29	29WQ	FO	7.5L	G	$1800	190	1,600	12,400	11,080

Livability Code: VA 30-90 — ratio of 55% ○ dangerous ○ fatiguing ◉ good ○ excellent*
The approximate net payload of 1320 pounds at 11% ○ deficient ○ excessive ○ cautionary ◉ good ○ excellent*
Total highway safety penalties are: 2* — Value: 84 Durability: 74 Highway Control Rating: 81 Highway Safety: 79 ★★★

Sundancer	1995	MHC	29	29WU	FO	7.5L	G	$1800	190	1,600	12,400	11,080

Livability Code: VA 30-90 — ratio of 55% ○ dangerous ○ fatiguing ◉ good ○ excellent*
The approximate net payload of 1320 pounds at 11% ○ deficient ○ excessive ○ cautionary ◉ good ○ excellent*
Total highway safety penalties are: 2* — Value: 84 Durability: 74 Highway Control Rating: 81 Highway Safety: 79 ★★★

Sundancer	1996	MHC	29	29WQ	FO	7.5L	G	$1700	190	6,100	12,400	11,168

Livability Code: VA 30-90 — ratio of 54% ○ dangerous ○ fatiguing ◉ good ○ excellent*
The approximate net payload of 1232 pounds at 10% ○ deficient ○ excessive ○ cautionary ◉ good ○ excellent*
Total highway safety penalties are: 2* — Value: 84 Durability: 74 Highway Control Rating: 79 Highway Safety: 77 ★★★

Sundancer	1996	MHC	29	29WU	FO	7.5L	G	$1700	190	6,100	12,400	11,168

Livability Code: VA 30-90 — ratio of 54% ○ dangerous ○ fatiguing ◉ good ○ excellent*
The approximate net payload of 1232 pounds at 10% ○ deficient ○ excessive ○ cautionary ◉ good ○ excellent*
Total highway safety penalties are: 2* — Value: 84 Durability: 74 Highway Control Rating: 79 Highway Safety: 77 ★★★

Sundancer	1997	MHC	29	29 WQ	FO	7.5L	G	$1900	190	5,950	14,050	11,669

Livability Code: VA 30-90 — ratio of 54% ○ dangerous ○ fatiguing ◉ good ○ excellent*
The approximate net payload of 2381 pounds at 17% ○ deficient ○ excessive ○ cautionary ○ good ◉ excellent*
Total highway safety penalties are: 2* — Value: 84 Durability: 74 Highway Control Rating: 86 Highway Safety: 84 ★★★

Sundancer	1997	MHC	29	29 WU	FO	7.5L	G	$1900	190	5,950	14,050	11,758

Livability Code: VA 30-90 — ratio of 54% ○ dangerous ○ fatiguing ◉ good ○ excellent*
The approximate net payload of 2292 pounds at 16% ○ deficient ○ excessive ○ cautionary ○ good ◉ excellent*
Total highway safety penalties are: 2* — Value: 84 Durability: 74 Highway Control Rating: 85 Highway Safety: 83 ★★★

Sundancer	1997	MHC	29	29 WQ op eng	FO	7.3L	D	$1900	190	1,500	14,050	12,168

Livability Code: VA 30-90 — ratio of 54% ○ dangerous ○ fatiguing ◉ good ○ excellent*
The approximate net payload of 1882 pounds at 13% ○ deficient ○ excessive ○ cautionary ◉ good ○ excellent*
Total highway safety penalties are: 2* — Value: 84 Durability: 74 Highway Control Rating: 79 Highway Safety: 77 ★★★

Note: Safety ratings are based on the assumption that the engineering of the RV has allowed for proper balance by placing fresh, gray, and black holding tanks in a location so as not to change the balance of the RV when the tanks are empty or full. **Always double-check wheelbase, GVWR, and weights at front and rear axles.**

*See Section 1 for details on how conclusions are reached.

Brand	Year	Type	Length	Model	Chassis	Engine	Fuel Type	Average Price per Linear Foot When New	Adjusted Wheelbase	Approx. Towing Capacity	Gross Vehicle Weight Rating	Average Curb Weight
Sundancer	1997	MHC	29	29 WU op eng	FO	7.3L	D	$2100	190	5,950	14,050	12,168

Livability Code: VA 30-90 Wheelbase-to-length ratio of 54% is considered ○ dangerous ○ fatiguing ◉ good ○ excellent *

The approximate net payload of 1882 pounds at 13% of GVWR on this model is ○ deficient ○ excessive ○ cautionary ◉ good ○ excellent *

Total highway safety penalties are: 2 * Value: 8 4 Durability: 7 4 Highway Control Rating: 7 9 Highway Safety: 7 7 ★★★

Brand	Year	Type	Length	Model	Chassis	Engine	Fuel Type	Average Price per Linear Foot When New	Adjusted Wheelbase	Approx. Towing Capacity	Gross Vehicle Weight Rating	Average Curb Weight
Sundancer	1997	MHC	31	31 WQ	FO	7.5L	G	$1800	205	5,950	14,050	11,847

Livability Code: VA 30-90 Wheelbase-to-length ratio of 55% is considered ○ dangerous ○ fatiguing ◉ good ○ excellent *

The approximate net payload of 2203 pounds at 16% of GVWR on this model is ○ deficient ○ excessive ○ cautionary ○ good ◉ excellent *

Total highway safety penalties are: 2 * Value: 8 4 Durability: 7 4 Highway Control Rating: 9 3 Highway Safety: 9 1 ★★★

Brand	Year	Type	Length	Model	Chassis	Engine	Fuel Type	Average Price per Linear Foot When New	Adjusted Wheelbase	Approx. Towing Capacity	Gross Vehicle Weight Rating	Average Curb Weight
Sundancer	1997	MHC	31	31 WQ op eng	FO	7.3L	D	$1800	205	5,950	14,050	12,345

Livability Code: VA 30-90 Wheelbase-to-length ratio of 55% is considered ○ dangerous ○ fatiguing ◉ good ○ excellent *

The approximate net payload of 1705 pounds at 12% of GVWR on this model is ○ deficient ○ excessive ○ cautionary ◉ good ○ excellent *

Total highway safety penalties are: 2 * Value: 8 4 Durability: 7 4 Highway Control Rating: 8 5 Highway Safety: 8 3 ★★★

Brand	Year	Type	Length	Model	Chassis	Engine	Fuel Type	Average Price per Linear Foot When New	Adjusted Wheelbase	Approx. Towing Capacity	Gross Vehicle Weight Rating	Average Curb Weight
Sundancer	1998	MHC	29	29WQ	FO	6.8L	G	$1900	190	5,950	14,050	11,543

Livability Code: VA 30-90 Wheelbase-to-length ratio of 54% is considered ○ dangerous ○ fatiguing ◉ good ○ excellent *

The approximate net payload of 2507 pounds at 18% of GVWR on this model is ○ deficient ○ excessive ○ cautionary ○ good ◉ excellent *

Total highway safety penalties are: 2 * Value: 8 4 Durability: 7 4 Highway Control Rating: 8 7 Highway Safety: 8 5 ★★★

Brand	Year	Type	Length	Model	Chassis	Engine	Fuel Type	Average Price per Linear Foot When New	Adjusted Wheelbase	Approx. Towing Capacity	Gross Vehicle Weight Rating	Average Curb Weight
Sundancer	1998	MHC	29	29WQ op eng	FO	7.3L	D	$2100	190	5,950	14,050	12,055

Livability Code: VA 30-90 Wheelbase-to-length ratio of 54% is considered ○ dangerous ○ fatiguing ◉ good ○ excellent *

The approximate net payload of 1995 pounds at 14% of GVWR on this model is ○ deficient ○ excessive ○ cautionary ◉ good ○ excellent *

Total highway safety penalties are: 2 * Value: 8 4 Durability: 7 4 Highway Control Rating: 8 1 Highway Safety: 7 9 ★★★

Brand	Year	Type	Length	Model	Chassis	Engine	Fuel Type	Average Price per Linear Foot When New	Adjusted Wheelbase	Approx. Towing Capacity	Gross Vehicle Weight Rating	Average Curb Weight
Sundancer	1998	MHC	29	29WU	FO	6.8L	G	$1900	190	5,950	14,050	11,850

Livability Code: VA 30-90 Wheelbase-to-length ratio of 54% is considered ○ dangerous ○ fatiguing ◉ good ○ excellent *

The approximate net payload of 2200 pounds at 16% of GVWR on this model is ○ deficient ○ excessive ○ cautionary ○ good ◉ excellent *

Total highway safety penalties are: 2 * Value: 8 4 Durability: 7 4 Highway Control Rating: 8 4 Highway Safety: 8 2 ★★★

Brand	Year	Type	Length	Model	Chassis	Engine	Fuel Type	Average Price per Linear Foot When New	Adjusted Wheelbase	Approx. Towing Capacity	Gross Vehicle Weight Rating	Average Curb Weight
Sundancer	1998	MHC	29	29WU op eng	FO	7.3L	D	$2100	190	5,950	14,050	12,070

Livability Code: VA 30-90 Wheelbase-to-length ratio of 54% is considered ○ dangerous ○ fatiguing ◉ good ○ excellent *

The approximate net payload of 1980 pounds at 14% of GVWR on this model is ○ deficient ○ excessive ○ cautionary ◉ good ○ excellent *

Total highway safety penalties are: 2 * Value: 8 4 Durability: 7 4 Highway Control Rating: 8 1 Highway Safety: 7 9 ★★★

Brand	Year	Type	Length	Model	Chassis	Engine	Fuel Type	Average Price per Linear Foot When New	Adjusted Wheelbase	Approx. Towing Capacity	Gross Vehicle Weight Rating	Average Curb Weight
Sundancer	1998	MHC	31	31WQ	FO	6.8L	G	$1800	205	5,950	14,050	11,934

Livability Code: VA 30-90 Wheelbase-to-length ratio of 55% is considered ○ dangerous ○ fatiguing ◉ good ○ excellent *

The approximate net payload of 2116 pounds at 15% of GVWR on this model is ○ deficient ○ excessive ○ cautionary ◉ good ○ excellent *

Total highway safety penalties are: 2 * Value: 8 4 Durability: 7 4 Highway Control Rating: 9 1 Highway Safety: 8 9 ★★★

Brand	Year	Type	Length	Model	Chassis	Engine	Fuel Type	Average Price per Linear Foot When New	Adjusted Wheelbase	Approx. Towing Capacity	Gross Vehicle Weight Rating	Average Curb Weight
Sundancer	1998	MHC	31	31WS	FO	6.8L	G	$1900	205	5,950	14,050	12,510

Livability Code: VA 30-90 Wheelbase-to-length ratio of 55% is considered ○ dangerous ○ fatiguing ◉ good ○ excellent *

The approximate net payload of 1540 pounds at 11% of GVWR on this model is ○ deficient ○ excessive ○ cautionary ◉ good ○ excellent *

Total highway safety penalties are: 7 * Value: 8 1 Durability: 7 4 Highway Control Rating: 8 3 Highway Safety: 7 6 ★★★

Brand	Year	Type	Length	Model	Chassis	Engine	Fuel Type	Average Price per Linear Foot When New	Adjusted Wheelbase	Approx. Towing Capacity	Gross Vehicle Weight Rating	Average Curb Weight
Sundancer	1999	MHC	29	29U	FO	6.8L	G	$2100	190	5,950	14,050	11,742

Livability Code: VA 30-90 Wheelbase-to-length ratio of 54% is considered ○ dangerous ○ fatiguing ◉ good ○ excellent *

The approximate net payload of 2308 pounds at 16% of GVWR on this model is ○ deficient ○ excessive ○ cautionary ○ good ◉ excellent *

Total highway safety penalties are: 2 * Value: 8 4 Durability: 7 6 Highway Control Rating: 8 5 Highway Safety: 8 3 ★★★

Brand	Year	Type	Length	Model	Chassis	Engine	Fuel Type	Average Price per Linear Foot When New	Adjusted Wheelbase	Approx. Towing Capacity	Gross Vehicle Weight Rating	Average Curb Weight
Sundancer	1999	MHC	30	30V	FO	6.8L	G	$2000	205	5,950	14,050	12,428

Livability Code: VA 30-90 Wheelbase-to-length ratio of 57% is considered ○ dangerous ○ fatiguing ◉ good ○ excellent *

The approximate net payload of 1622 pounds at 12% of GVWR on this model is ○ deficient ○ excessive ○ cautionary ◉ good ○ excellent *

Total highway safety penalties are: 12 * Value: 7 9 Durability: 7 6 Highway Control Rating: 9 0 Highway Safety: 7 8 ★★★

Brand	Year	Type	Length	Model	Chassis	Engine	Fuel Type	Average Price per Linear Foot When New	Adjusted Wheelbase	Approx. Towing Capacity	Gross Vehicle Weight Rating	Average Curb Weight
Sundancer	1999	MHC	31	31A	FO	6.8L	G	$1900	205	5,950	14,050	12,047

Livability Code: VA 30-90 Wheelbase-to-length ratio of 55% is considered ○ dangerous ○ fatiguing ◉ good ○ excellent *

The approximate net payload of 2003 pounds at 14% of GVWR on this model is ○ deficient ○ excessive ○ cautionary ◉ good ○ excellent *

Total highway safety penalties are: 2 * Value: 8 4 Durability: 7 6 Highway Control Rating: 8 9 Highway Safety: 8 7 ★★★

Note: Safety ratings are based on the assumption that the engineering of the RV has allowed for proper balance by placing fresh, gray, and black holding tanks in a location so as not to change the balance of the RV when the tanks are empty or full. **Always double-check wheelbase, GVWR, and weights at front and rear axles.**

*See Section 1 for details on how conclusions are reached.

Brand	Year	Type	Length	Model	Chassis	Engine	Fuel Type	Average Price per Linear Foot When New	Adjusted Wheelbase	Approx. Towing Capacity	Gross Vehicle Weight Rating	Average Curb Weight
Sunflyer	1990	MHA	25	25RC	CH	7.4L	G	$1700	137	1,500	12,300	10,820

Livability Code: 30-80
Wheelbase-to-length ratio of 46% is considered ● dangerous ○ fatiguing ○ good ○ excellent *
The approximate net payload of 1480 pounds at 12% of GVWR on this model is ○ deficient ○ excessive ○ cautionary ● good ○ excellent *
Total highway safety penalties are: 2 *   Value: 84   Durability: 74   Highway Control Rating: 21   Highway Safety: 19

Brand	Year	Type	Length	Model	Chassis	Engine	Fuel Type		Adjusted Wheelbase	Approx. Towing Capacity	Gross Vehicle Weight Rating	Average Curb Weight
Sunflyer	1990	MHA	28	27RT	CH	7.4L	G	$1800	168	2,500	14,500	12,254

Livability Code: 30-80
Wheelbase-to-length ratio of 50% is considered ● dangerous ○ fatiguing ○ good ○ excellent *
The approximate net payload of 2246 pounds at 15% of GVWR on this model is ○ deficient ○ excessive ○ cautionary ● good ○ excellent *
Total highway safety penalties are: 4 *   Value: 83   Durability: 74   Highway Control Rating: 43   Highway Safety: 39

Sunflyer	1990	MHA	33	31RQ	CH	7.4L	G	$1600	200	4,500	15,000	13,529

Livability Code: 30-80
Wheelbase-to-length ratio of 51% is considered ○ dangerous ● fatiguing ○ good ○ excellent *
The approximate net payload of 1471 pounds at 10% of GVWR on this model is ○ deficient ○ excessive ○ cautionary ● good ○ excellent *
Total highway safety penalties are: 6 *   Value: 82   Durability: 74   Highway Control Rating: 35   Highway Safety: 29

Sunflyer	1990	MHA	33	31RQ	FO	7.5L	G	$1600	200	5,000	16,000	13,629

Livability Code: 30-80
Wheelbase-to-length ratio of 51% is considered ○ dangerous ● fatiguing ○ good ○ excellent *
The approximate net payload of 2371 pounds at 15% of GVWR on this model is ○ deficient ○ excessive ○ cautionary ● good ○ excellent *
Total highway safety penalties are: 2 *   Value: 84   Durability: 74   Highway Control Rating: 45   Highway Safety: 43

Sunflyer	1990	MHA	35	33 RQ	CH	7.4L	G	$1600	228	4,500	15,000	13,765

Livability Code: 30-80
Wheelbase-to-length ratio of 54% is considered ○ dangerous ○ fatiguing ● good ○ excellent *
The approximate net payload of 1236 pounds at 8% of GVWR on this model is ○ deficient ○ excessive ● cautionary ○ good ○ excellent *
Total highway safety penalties are: 7 *   Value: 81   Durability: 74   Highway Control Rating: 60   Highway Safety: 53   ★

Sunflyer	1990	MHA	35	33 RQ	FO	7.5L	G	$1600	228	5,000	16,000	14,168

Livability Code: 30-80
Wheelbase-to-length ratio of 54% is considered ○ dangerous ○ fatiguing ● good ○ excellent *
The approximate net payload of 1832 pounds at 11% of GVWR on this model is ○ deficient ○ excessive ○ cautionary ● good ○ excellent *
Total highway safety penalties are: 2 *   Value: 84   Durability: 74   Highway Control Rating: 78   Highway Safety: 76   ★★★

Sunflyer	1990	MHA	36	36RQ	CH	7.4L	G	$1800	224 T	1,500	17,000	15,113

Livability Code: 30-80
Wheelbase-to-length ratio of 52% is considered ○ dangerous ● fatiguing ○ good ○ excellent *
The approximate net payload of 1887 pounds at 11% of GVWR on this model is ○ deficient ○ excessive ○ cautionary ● good ○ excellent *
Total highway safety penalties are: 10 *   Value: 80   Durability: 74   Highway Control Rating: 49   Highway Safety: 39

Sunflyer	1990	MHA	36	36RQ	FO	7.5L	G	$1800	224 T	7,000	18,000	15,313

Livability Code: 30-80
Wheelbase-to-length ratio of 52% is considered ○ dangerous ● fatiguing ○ good ○ excellent *
The approximate net payload of 2687 pounds at 15% of GVWR on this model is ○ deficient ○ excessive ○ cautionary ● good ○ excellent *
Total highway safety penalties are: 4 *   Value: 82   Durability: 74   Highway Control Rating: 57   Highway Safety: 53   ★

Sunflyer	1991	MHA	36	36 RA	FO	7.5L	G	$1800	224 T	7,000	18,000	15,265

Livability Code: 30-80
Wheelbase-to-length ratio of 52% is considered ○ dangerous ● fatiguing ○ good ○ excellent *
The approximate net payload of 2735 pounds at 15% of GVWR on this model is ○ deficient ○ excessive ○ cautionary ● good ○ excellent *
Total highway safety penalties are: 4 *   Value: 82   Durability: 74   Highway Control Rating: 57   Highway Safety: 53   ★

Sunflyer	1992	MHA	28	28 RT	CH	7.4L	G	$2100	168	2,200	14,800	12,379

Livability Code: 30-80
Wheelbase-to-length ratio of 50% is considered ● dangerous ○ fatiguing ○ good ○ excellent *
The approximate net payload of 2421 pounds at 16% of GVWR on this model is ○ deficient ○ excessive ○ cautionary ○ good ● excellent *
Total highway safety penalties are: 4 *   Value: 83   Durability: 74   Highway Control Rating: 44   Highway Safety: 40

Sunflyer	1992	MHA	28	30 RU	CH	7.4L	G	$2200	178	1,500	16,000	12,479

Livability Code: 30-80
Wheelbase-to-length ratio of 53% is considered ○ dangerous ● fatiguing ○ good ○ excellent *
The approximate net payload of 3521 pounds at 22% of GVWR on this model is ○ deficient ○ excessive ○ cautionary ○ good ● excellent *
Total highway safety penalties are: 4 *   Value: 83   Durability: 74   Highway Control Rating: 72   Highway Safety: 68   ★★

Sunflyer	1992	MHA	31	30 RU	FO	7.5L	G	$2000	178	8,000	17,000	13,689

Livability Code: 30-80
Wheelbase-to-length ratio of 48% is considered ● dangerous ○ fatiguing ○ good ○ excellent *
The approximate net payload of 3311 pounds at 19% of GVWR on this model is ○ deficient ○ excessive ○ cautionary ○ good ● excellent *
Total highway safety penalties are: 2 *   Value: 84   Durability: 74   Highway Control Rating: 40   Highway Safety: 38

Note: Safety ratings are based on the assumption that the engineering of the RV has allowed for proper balance by placing fresh, gray, and black holding tanks in a location so as not to change the balance of the RV when the tanks are empty or full. **Always double-check wheelbase, GVWR, and weights at front and rear axles.**

*See Section 1 for details on how conclusions are reached.

Brand	Year	Type	Length	Model	Chassis	Engine	Fuel Type	Average Price per Linear Foot When New	Adjusted Wheelbase	Approx. Towing Capacity	Gross Vehicle Weight Rating	Average Curb Weight
Sunflyer	1992	MHA	33	32 RQ	CH	7.4L	G	$1900	200	1,500	16,000	13,629

Livability Code: 30-80   Wheelbase-to-length ratio of 51% is considered ○ dangerous ● fatiguing ○ good ○ excellent *

The approximate net payload of 2371 pounds at 15% of GVWR on this model is ○ deficient ○ excessive ○ cautionary ● good ○ excellent *

Total highway safety penalties are: 6 *   Value: 8 2   Durability: 7 4   Highway Control Rating: 4 5   Highway Safety: 3 9

Brand	Year	Type	Length	Model	Chassis	Engine	Fuel Type	Price/Ft	Wheelbase	Towing	GVWR	Curb Weight
Sunflyer	1992	MHA	33	32 RQ	FO	7.5L	G	$1900	200	8,000	17,000	14,129

Livability Code: 30-80   Wheelbase-to-length ratio of 51% is considered ○ dangerous ● fatiguing ○ good ○ excellent *

The approximate net payload of 2871 pounds at 17% of GVWR on this model is ○ deficient ○ excessive ○ cautionary ○ good ● excellent *

Total highway safety penalties are: 2 *   Value: 8 4   Durability: 7 4   Highway Control Rating: 4 8   Highway Safety: 4 6

Sunflyer	1992	MHA	35	34 RQ	CH	7.4L	G	$1900	228	1,500	16,000	14,192

Livability Code: 30-80   Wheelbase-to-length ratio of 54% is considered ○ dangerous ○ fatiguing ● good ○ excellent *

The approximate net payload of 1808 pounds at 11% of GVWR on this model is ○ deficient ○ excessive ○ cautionary ● good ○ excellent *

Total highway safety penalties are: 7 *   Value: 8 1   Durability: 7 4   Highway Control Rating: 7 7   Highway Safety: 7 0   ★★★

Sunflyer	1992	MHA	35	34 RQ	FO	7.5L	G	$1900	228	8,000	17,000	14,692

Livability Code: 30-80   Wheelbase-to-length ratio of 54% is considered ○ dangerous ○ fatiguing ● good ○ excellent *

The approximate net payload of 2308 pounds at 14% of GVWR on this model is ○ deficient ○ excessive ○ cautionary ● good ○ excellent *

Total highway safety penalties are: 2 *   Value: 8 4   Durability: 7 4   Highway Control Rating: 7 8   Highway Safety: 7 6   ★★★

Sunflyer	1998	MHA	34	33WB	FO	7.5L	G	$2600	216	8,000	17,000	15,926

Livability Code: SB 30-90   Wheelbase-to-length ratio of 53% is considered ○ dangerous ● fatiguing ○ good ○ excellent *

The approximate net payload of 1074 pounds at 6% of GVWR on this model is ● deficient ○ excessive ○ cautionary ○ good ○ excellent *

Total highway safety penalties are: 12 *   Value: 8 1   Durability: 8 0   Highway Control Rating: 3 6   Highway Safety: 2 4

Sunflyer	1998	MHA	34	33WB myc	FO	6.8L	G	$2700	216	5,500	20,500	16,376

Livability Code: SB 30-90   Wheelbase-to-length ratio of 53% is considered ○ dangerous ● fatiguing ○ good ○ excellent *

The approximate net payload of 4124 pounds at 20% of GVWR on this model is ○ deficient ○ excessive ○ cautionary ○ good ● excellent *

Total highway safety penalties are: 12 *   Value: 8 1   Durability: 8 0   Highway Control Rating: 7 9   Highway Safety: 6 7   ★★

Sunflyer	1998	MHA	35	34WY	CH	7.4L	G	$2900	219	5,000	21,000	17,550

Livability Code: SB 30-90   Wheelbase-to-length ratio of 52% is considered ○ dangerous ● fatiguing ○ good ○ excellent *

The approximate net payload of 3450 pounds at 16% of GVWR on this model is ○ deficient ○ excessive ○ cautionary ○ good ● excellent *

Total highway safety penalties are: 21 *   Value: 7 7   Durability: 8 0   Highway Control Rating: 6 1   Highway Safety: 4 0

Sunflyer	1998	MHA	35	34WY myc	FO	6.8L	G	$2700	228	5,500	20,500	17,197

Livability Code: SB 30-90   Wheelbase-to-length ratio of 55% is considered ○ dangerous ○ fatiguing ● good ○ excellent *

The approximate net payload of 3303 pounds at 16% of GVWR on this model is ○ deficient ○ excessive ○ cautionary ○ good ● excellent *

Total highway safety penalties are: 16 *   Value: 7 9   Durability: 8 0   Highway Control Rating: 9 1   Highway Safety: 7 5   ★★★

Sunflyer	1998	MHA	36	35WH	CH	7.4L	G	$2300	228	4,500	16,500	14,910

Livability Code: SB 30-90   Wheelbase-to-length ratio of 53% is considered ○ dangerous ● fatiguing ○ good ○ excellent *

The approximate net payload of 1590 pounds at 10% of GVWR on this model is ○ deficient ○ excessive ○ cautionary ● good ○ excellent *

Total highway safety penalties are: 8 *   Value: 8 3   Durability: 8 0   Highway Control Rating: 5 7   Highway Safety: 4 9

Sunflyer	1998	MHA	36	36WL myc	CH	7.4L	G	$2700	233	5,000	21,000	17,916

Livability Code: SB 30-90   Wheelbase-to-length ratio of 54% is considered ○ dangerous ○ fatiguing ● good ○ excellent *

The approximate net payload of 3084 pounds at 15% of GVWR on this model is ○ deficient ○ excessive ○ cautionary ○ good ● excellent *

Total highway safety penalties are: 19 *   Value: 7 8   Durability: 8 0   Highway Control Rating: 7 9   Highway Safety: 6 0   ★★

Sunflyer	1998	MHA	36	35WH opch	FO	7.5L	G	$2300	228	8,000	17,000	15,295

Livability Code: SB 30-90   Wheelbase-to-length ratio of 53% is considered ○ dangerous ● fatiguing ○ good ○ excellent *

The approximate net payload of 1705 pounds at 10% of GVWR on this model is ○ deficient ○ excessive ○ cautionary ● good ○ excellent *

Total highway safety penalties are: 2 *   Value: 8 6   Durability: 8 0   Highway Control Rating: 5 8   Highway Safety: 5 6   ★

Sunflyer	1998	MHA	36	36WL-P	FR	CU275	D	$3500	242	5,000	24,850	19,966

Livability Code: SB 30-90   Wheelbase-to-length ratio of 56% is considered ○ dangerous ○ fatiguing ● good ○ excellent *

The approximate net payload of 4884 pounds at 20% of GVWR on this model is ○ deficient ○ excessive ○ cautionary ○ good ● excellent *

Total highway safety penalties are: 13 *   Value: 8 0   Durability: 8 0   Highway Control Rating: 9 9   Highway Safety: 8 6   ★★★★

Note: Safety ratings are based on the assumption that the engineering of the RV has allowed for proper balance by placing fresh, gray, and black holding tanks in a location so as not to change the balance of the RV when the tanks are empty or full. **Always double-check wheelbase, GVWR, and weights at front and rear axles.**

*See Section 1 for details on how conclusions are reached.

Section 2: The Ratings

Brand	Year	Type	Length	Model	Chassis	Engine	Fuel Type	Average Price per Linear Foot When New	Adjusted Wheelbase	Approx. Towing Capacity	Gross Vehicle Weight Rating	Average Curb Weight
Sunflyer	1998	MHA	36	36WL-P myc	FR	CU275	D	$3500	242	5,000	24,850	20,173

Livability Code: SB 30-90 Wheelbase-to-length ratio of 56% is considered ○ dangerous ○ fatiguing ◉ good ○ excellent *
The approximate net payload of 4677 pounds at 19% of GVWR on this model is ○ deficient ○ excessive ○ cautionary ○ good ◉ excellent *
Total highway safety penalties are: 13 * Value: **8 0** Durability: **8 0** Highway Control Rating: **9 8** Highway Safety: **8 5** ★★★★

Brand	Year	Type	Length	Model	Chassis	Engine	Fuel Type	Price/Ft	Wheelbase	Towing	GVWR	Curb Weight
Sunflyer	1999	MHA	34	33B	FO	6.8L	G	$2800	216	5,500	20,500	16,770

Livability Code: SB 30-90 Wheelbase-to-length ratio of 53% is considered ○ dangerous ◉ fatiguing ○ good ○ excellent *
The approximate net payload of 3730 pounds at 18% of GVWR on this model is ○ deficient ○ excessive ○ cautionary ○ good ◉ excellent *
Total highway safety penalties are: 12 * Value: **8 1** Durability: **8 0** Highway Control Rating: **7 7** Highway Safety: **6 5** ★★

Sunflyer	1999	MHA	35	34Y	CH	7.4L	G	$2700	219	5,000	21,000	18,029

Livability Code: SB 30-90 Wheelbase-to-length ratio of 52% is considered ○ dangerous ◉ fatiguing ○ good ○ excellent *
The approximate net payload of 2971 pounds at 14% of GVWR on this model is ○ deficient ○ excessive ○ cautionary ◉ good ○ excellent *
Total highway safety penalties are: 20 * Value: **7 7** Durability: **8 0** Highway Control Rating: **6 4** Highway Safety: **4 4**

Sunflyer	1999	MHA	35	34Y	FO	6.8L	G	$2700	228	5,500	20,500	17,422

Livability Code: SB 30-90 Wheelbase-to-length ratio of 54% is considered ○ dangerous ○ fatiguing ◉ good ○ excellent *
The approximate net payload of 3078 pounds at 15% of GVWR on this model is ○ deficient ○ excessive ○ cautionary ◉ good ○ excellent *
Total highway safety penalties are: 15 * Value: **7 9** Durability: **8 0** Highway Control Rating: **8 3** Highway Safety: **6 8** ★★

Sunflyer	1999	MHA	35	35U	CH	7.4L	G	$2700	233	5,000	21,000	18,239

Livability Code: SB 30-90 Wheelbase-to-length ratio of 55% is considered ○ dangerous ○ fatiguing ◉ good ○ excellent *
The approximate net payload of 2761 pounds at 13% of GVWR on this model is ○ deficient ○ excessive ○ cautionary ◉ good ○ excellent *
Total highway safety penalties are: 18 * Value: **7 8** Durability: **8 0** Highway Control Rating: **8 6** Highway Safety: **6 8** ★★

Sunflyer	1999	MHA	35	35U	FO	6.8L	G	$2700	228	5,500	20,500	17,855

Livability Code: SB 30-90 Wheelbase-to-length ratio of 54% is considered ○ dangerous ○ fatiguing ◉ good ○ excellent *
The approximate net payload of 2645 pounds at 13% of GVWR on this model is ○ deficient ○ excessive ○ cautionary ◉ good ○ excellent *
Total highway safety penalties are: 13 * Value: **8 1** Durability: **8 0** Highway Control Rating: **7 7** Highway Safety: **6 4** ★★

Sunflyer	1999	MHA	36	35C myc	CH	7.4L	G	$2600	219	5,000	21,000	17,648

Livability Code: SB 30-90 Wheelbase-to-length ratio of 51% is considered ○ dangerous ◉ fatiguing ○ good ○ excellent *
The approximate net payload of 3352 pounds at 16% of GVWR on this model is ○ deficient ○ excessive ○ cautionary ○ good ◉ excellent *
Total highway safety penalties are: 13 * Value: **8 1** Durability: **8 0** Highway Control Rating: **5 9** Highway Safety: **4 6**

Sunflyer	1999	MHA	36	35C	FO	6.8L	G	$2600	228	5,500	20,500	17,155

Livability Code: SB 30-90 Wheelbase-to-length ratio of 53% is considered ○ dangerous ◉ fatiguing ○ good ○ excellent *
The approximate net payload of 3345 pounds at 16% of GVWR on this model is ○ deficient ○ excessive ○ cautionary ○ good ◉ excellent *
Total highway safety penalties are: 7 * Value: **8 3** Durability: **8 0** Highway Control Rating: **7 5** Highway Safety: **6 8** ★★

Sunflyer	1999	MHA	36	36L	CH	7.4L	G	$2600	233	5,000	21,000	17,950

Livability Code: SB 30-90 Wheelbase-to-length ratio of 54% is considered ○ dangerous ○ fatiguing ◉ good ○ excellent *
The approximate net payload of 3050 pounds at 15% of GVWR on this model is ○ deficient ○ excessive ○ cautionary ○ good ○ excellent *
Total highway safety penalties are: 18 * Value: **7 8** Durability: **8 0** Highway Control Rating: **8 1** Highway Safety: **6 3** ★★

Sunflyer	1999	MHA	36	36L	FO	6.8L	G	$2600	242	5,500	20,500	17,672

Livability Code: SB 30-90 Wheelbase-to-length ratio of 56% is considered ○ dangerous ○ fatiguing ◉ good ○ excellent *
The approximate net payload of 2828 pounds at 14% of GVWR on this model is ○ deficient ○ excessive ○ cautionary ◉ good ○ excellent *
Total highway safety penalties are: 12 * Value: **8 1** Durability: **8 0** Highway Control Rating: **9 1** Highway Safety: **7 9** ★★★

Sunflyer	1999	MHA	36	36L-P	FR	CU275	D	$3300	242	5,000	24,850	20,210

Livability Code: SB 30-90 Wheelbase-to-length ratio of 56% is considered ○ dangerous ○ fatiguing ◉ good ○ excellent *
The approximate net payload of 4640 pounds at 19% of GVWR on this model is ○ deficient ○ excessive ○ cautionary ○ good ◉ excellent *
Total highway safety penalties are: 12 * Value: **8 1** Durability: **8 0** Highway Control Rating: **9 8** Highway Safety: **8 6** ★★★★

Sunrise	1994	MHA	23	23RC-CH	CH	7.4L	G	$1900	137	4,200	11,800	9,849

Livability Code: SB 30-90 Wheelbase-to-length ratio of 50% is considered ◉ dangerous ○ fatiguing ○ good ○ excellent *
The approximate net payload of 1951 pounds at 17% of GVWR on this model is ○ deficient ○ excessive ○ cautionary ○ good ◉ excellent *
Total highway safety penalties are: 1 * Value: **8 4** Durability: **7 4** Highway Control Rating: **4 4** Highway Safety: **4 3**

Note: Safety ratings are based on the assumption that the engineering of the RV has allowed for proper balance by placing fresh, gray, and black holding tanks in a location so as not to change the balance of the RV when the tanks are empty or full. **Always double-check wheelbase, GVWR, and weights at front and rear axles.**

*See Section 1 for details on how conclusions are reached.

Brand	Year	Type	Length	Model	Chassis	Engine	Fuel Type	Average Price per Linear Foot When New	Adjusted Wheelbase	Approx. Towing Capacity	Gross Vehicle Weight Rating	Average Curb Weight
Sunrise	1994	MHA	23	23RC-Dsl	CH	GM6.5	D	$2000	137	1,500	12,300	9,999

Livability Code: SB 30-90   Wheelbase-to-length ratio of 50% is considered ●dangerous ○fatiguing ○good ○excellent *

The approximate net payload of 2301 pounds at 19% of GVWR on this model is ○deficient ○excessive ○cautionary ○good ●excellent *

Total highway safety penalties are: 1 *   Value: 8 4   Durability: 7 4   Highway Control Rating: 4 6   Highway Safety: 4 5

Brand	Year	Type	Length	Model	Chassis	Engine	Fuel Type	Price/Ft	Adj. WB	Tow Cap.	GVWR	Curb Wt.
Sunrise	1994	MHA	27	27RC-CH	CH	7.4L	G	$1800	158	1,500	12,300	10,901

Livability Code: SB 30-90   Wheelbase-to-length ratio of 49% is considered ●dangerous ○fatiguing ○good ○excellent *

The approximate net payload of 1399 pounds at 11% of GVWR on this model is ○deficient ○excessive ○cautionary ●good ○excellent *

Total highway safety penalties are: 3 *   Value: 8 3   Durability: 7 4   Highway Control Rating: 3 1   Highway Safety: 2 8

Brand	Year	Type	Length	Model	Chassis	Engine	Fuel Type	Price/Ft	Adj. WB	Tow Cap.	GVWR	Curb Wt.
Sunrise	1994	MHA	27	27RQ-CH	CH	7.4L	G	$1900	158	1,500	12,300	10,901

Livability Code: SB 30-90   Wheelbase-to-length ratio of 49% is considered ●dangerous ○fatiguing ○good ○excellent *

The approximate net payload of 1399 pounds at 11% of GVWR on this model is ○deficient ○excessive ○cautionary ●good ○excellent *

Total highway safety penalties are: 3 *   Value: 8 3   Durability: 7 4   Highway Control Rating: 3 1   Highway Safety: 2 8

Brand	Year	Type	Length	Model	Chassis	Engine	Fuel Type	Price/Ft	Adj. WB	Tow Cap.	GVWR	Curb Wt.
Sunrise	1994	MHA	27	27RC-Dsl	CH	GM6.5	D	$1900	158	2,200	14,800	11,801

Livability Code: SB 30-90   Wheelbase-to-length ratio of 49% is considered ●dangerous ○fatiguing ○good ○excellent *

The approximate net payload of 2999 pounds at 20% of GVWR on this model is ○deficient ○excessive ○cautionary ○good ●excellent *

Total highway safety penalties are: 3 *   Value: 8 3   Durability: 7 4   Highway Control Rating: 4 4   Highway Safety: 4 1

Brand	Year	Type	Length	Model	Chassis	Engine	Fuel Type	Price/Ft	Adj. WB	Tow Cap.	GVWR	Curb Wt.
Sunrise	1994	MHA	27	27RQ-Dsl	CH	GM6.5	D	$2000	158	2,200	14,800	11,801

Livability Code: SB 30-90   Wheelbase-to-length ratio of 49% is considered ●dangerous ○fatiguing ○good ○excellent *

The approximate net payload of 2999 pounds at 20% of GVWR on this model is ○deficient ○excessive ○cautionary ○good ●excellent *

Total highway safety penalties are: 3 *   Value: 8 3   Durability: 7 4   Highway Control Rating: 4 4   Highway Safety: 4 1

Brand	Year	Type	Length	Model	Chassis	Engine	Fuel Type	Price/Ft	Adj. WB	Tow Cap.	GVWR	Curb Wt.
Sunrise	1994	MHA	30	29RQ-CH	CH	7.4L	G	$1800	178	2,200	14,800	12,410

Livability Code: SB 30-90   Wheelbase-to-length ratio of 50% is considered ●dangerous ○fatiguing ○good ○excellent *

The approximate net payload of 2390 pounds at 16% of GVWR on this model is ○deficient ○excessive ○cautionary ○good ●excellent *

Total highway safety penalties are: 4 *   Value: 8 2   Durability: 7 4   Highway Control Rating: 4 5   Highway Safety: 4 1

Brand	Year	Type	Length	Model	Chassis	Engine	Fuel Type	Price/Ft	Adj. WB	Tow Cap.	GVWR	Curb Wt.
Sunrise	1994	MHA	30	29RQ-Dsl	CH	GM6.5	D	$1900	178	2,200	14,800	12,410

Livability Code: SB 30-90   Wheelbase-to-length ratio of 50% is considered ●dangerous ○fatiguing ○good ○excellent *

The approximate net payload of 2390 pounds at 16% of GVWR on this model is ○deficient ○excessive ○cautionary ○good ●excellent *

Total highway safety penalties are: 4 *   Value: 8 2   Durability: 7 4   Highway Control Rating: 4 5   Highway Safety: 4 1

Brand	Year	Type	Length	Model	Chassis	Engine	Fuel Type	Price/Ft	Adj. WB	Tow Cap.	GVWR	Curb Wt.
Sunrise	1994	MHA	30	29RQ-FO	FO	7.5L	G	$1800	178	3,800	15,200	12,690

Livability Code: SB 30-90   Wheelbase-to-length ratio of 50% is considered ●dangerous ○fatiguing ○good ○excellent *

The approximate net payload of 2510 pounds at 17% of GVWR on this model is ○deficient ○excessive ○cautionary ○good ●excellent *

Total highway safety penalties are: 2 *   Value: 8 4   Durability: 7 4   Highway Control Rating: 4 5   Highway Safety: 4 3

Brand	Year	Type	Length	Model	Chassis	Engine	Fuel Type	Price/Ft	Adj. WB	Tow Cap.	GVWR	Curb Wt.
Sunrise	1994	MHA	32	31RQ-CH	CH	7.4L	G	$1800	190	2,200	14,800	12,816

Livability Code: SB 30-90   Wheelbase-to-length ratio of 50% is considered ●dangerous ○fatiguing ○good ○excellent *

The approximate net payload of 1984 pounds at 13% of GVWR on this model is ○deficient ○excessive ○cautionary ●good ○excellent *

Total highway safety penalties are: 5 *   Value: 8 2   Durability: 7 4   Highway Control Rating: 4 0   Highway Safety: 3 5

Brand	Year	Type	Length	Model	Chassis	Engine	Fuel Type	Price/Ft	Adj. WB	Tow Cap.	GVWR	Curb Wt.
Sunrise	1994	MHA	32	31RQ-Dsl	CH	GM6.5	D	$1800	190	2,200	14,800	12,816

Livability Code: SB 30-90   Wheelbase-to-length ratio of 50% is considered ●dangerous ○fatiguing ○good ○excellent *

The approximate net payload of 1984 pounds at 13% of GVWR on this model is ○deficient ○excessive ○cautionary ●good ○excellent *

Total highway safety penalties are: 5 *   Value: 8 2   Durability: 7 4   Highway Control Rating: 4 0   Highway Safety: 3 5

Brand	Year	Type	Length	Model	Chassis	Engine	Fuel Type	Price/Ft	Adj. WB	Tow Cap.	GVWR	Curb Wt.
Sunrise	1994	MHA	32	31RQ-FO	FO	7.5L	G	$1800	190	3,800	15,200	13,096

Livability Code: SB 30-90   Wheelbase-to-length ratio of 50% is considered ●dangerous ○fatiguing ○good ○excellent *

The approximate net payload of 2104 pounds at 14% of GVWR on this model is ○deficient ○excessive ○cautionary ●good ○excellent *

Total highway safety penalties are: 2 *   Value: 8 4   Durability: 7 4   Highway Control Rating: 4 1   Highway Safety: 3 9

Brand	Year	Type	Length	Model	Chassis	Engine	Fuel Type	Price/Ft	Adj. WB	Tow Cap.	GVWR	Curb Wt.
Sunrise	1994	MHA	34	33RQ-CH	CH	7.4L	G	$1700	208	2,200	14,800	13,380

Livability Code: SB 30-90   Wheelbase-to-length ratio of 51% is considered ○dangerous ●fatiguing ○good ○excellent *

The approximate net payload of 1420 pounds at 10% of GVWR on this model is ○deficient ○excessive ○cautionary ●good ○excellent *

Total highway safety penalties are: 7 *   Value: 8 1   Durability: 7 4   Highway Control Rating: 3 6   Highway Safety: 2 9

Note: Safety ratings are based on the assumption that the engineering of the RV has allowed for proper balance by placing fresh, gray, and black holding tanks in a location so as not to change the balance of the RV when the tanks are empty or full. **Always double-check wheelbase, GVWR, and weights at front and rear axles.**

*See Section 1 for details on how conclusions are reached.

Brand	Year	Type	Length	Model	Chassis	Engine	Fuel Type	Average Price per Linear Foot When New	Adjusted Wheel-base	Approx. Towing Capacity	Gross Vehicle Weight Rating	Average Curb Weight
Sunrise	**1994**	MHA	34	33RQ-FO	FO	7.5L	G	$1700	208	8,000	17,000	14,120

Livability Code: SB 30-90
Wheelbase-to-length ratio of 51% is considered ○ dangerous ● fatiguing ○ good ○ excellent *
The approximate net payload of 2880 pounds at 17% of GVWR on this model is ○ deficient ○ excessive ○ cautionary ○ good ● excellent *
Total highway safety penalties are: 2 *   Value: **8 4**   Durability: **7 4**   Highway Control Rating: **4 9**   Highway Safety: **4 7**

Brand	Year	Type	Length	Model	Chassis	Engine	Fuel Type	Avg Price/Linear Ft	Wheelbase	Towing	GVWR	Curb Wt
Sunrise	**1995**	MHA	23	23RC	CH	7.4L	G	$2000	137	4,700	12,300	9,999

Livability Code: SB 30-90
Wheelbase-to-length ratio of 50% is considered ● dangerous ○ fatiguing ○ good ○ excellent *
The approximate net payload of 2301 pounds at 19% of GVWR on this model is ○ deficient ○ excessive ○ cautionary ○ good ● excellent *
Total highway safety penalties are: 1 *   Value: **8 4**   Durability: **7 4**   Highway Control Rating: **4 6**   Highway Safety: **4 5**

Sunrise	**1995**	MHA	23	23RC	CH	GM6.5	D	$2200	137	4,700	12,300	9,999

Livability Code: SB 30-90
Wheelbase-to-length ratio of 50% is considered ● dangerous ○ fatiguing ○ good ○ excellent *
The approximate net payload of 2301 pounds at 19% of GVWR on this model is ○ deficient ○ excessive ○ cautionary ○ good ● excellent *
Total highway safety penalties are: 1 *   Value: **8 4**   Durability: **7 4**   Highway Control Rating: **4 6**   Highway Safety: **4 5**

Sunrise	**1995**	MHA	27	27RQ	CH	7.4L	G	$2000	158	4,700	12,300	10,901

Livability Code: SB 30-90
Wheelbase-to-length ratio of 49% is considered ● dangerous ○ fatiguing ○ good ○ excellent *
The approximate net payload of 1399 pounds at 11% of GVWR on this model is ○ deficient ○ excessive ○ cautionary ● good ○ excellent *
Total highway safety penalties are: 3 *   Value: **8 3**   Durability: **7 4**   Highway Control Rating: **3 1**   Highway Safety: **2 8**

Sunrise	**1995**	MHA	27	27RQ op eng	CH	GM6.5	D	$2200	158	4,700	12,300	11,401

Livability Code: SB 30-90
Wheelbase-to-length ratio of 49% is considered ● dangerous ○ fatiguing ○ good ○ excellent *
The approximate net payload of 899 pounds at 7% of GVWR on this model is ○ deficient ○ excessive ● cautionary ○ good ○ excellent *
Total highway safety penalties are: 3 *   Value: **8 3**   Durability: **7 4**   Highway Control Rating: **1 2**   Highway Safety: **9**

Sunrise	**1995**	MHA	28	28RC	CH	7.4L	G	$2000	158	4,200	14,800	12,027

Livability Code: SB 30-90
Wheelbase-to-length ratio of 47% is considered ● dangerous ○ fatiguing ○ good ○ excellent *
The approximate net payload of 2773 pounds at 19% of GVWR on this model is ○ deficient ○ excessive ○ cautionary ○ good ● excellent *
Total highway safety penalties are: 4 *   Value: **8 3**   Durability: **7 4**   Highway Control Rating: **3 7**   Highway Safety: **3 3**

Sunrise	**1995**	MHA	28	28RC Dsl	CH	GM6.5	D	$2100	158	4,200	14,800	12,027

Livability Code: SB 30-90
Wheelbase-to-length ratio of 47% is considered ● dangerous ○ fatiguing ○ good ○ excellent *
The approximate net payload of 2773 pounds at 19% of GVWR on this model is ○ deficient ○ excessive ○ cautionary ○ good ● excellent *
Total highway safety penalties are: 4 *   Value: **8 3**   Durability: **7 4**   Highway Control Rating: **3 7**   Highway Safety: **3 3**

Sunrise	**1995**	MHA	30	29RQ	CH	7.4L	G	$1900	178	4,200	14,800	12,410

Livability Code: SB 30-90
Wheelbase-to-length ratio of 50% is considered ● dangerous ○ fatiguing ○ good ○ excellent *
The approximate net payload of 2390 pounds at 16% of GVWR on this model is ○ deficient ○ excessive ○ cautionary ○ good ● excellent *
Total highway safety penalties are: 4 *   Value: **8 2**   Durability: **7 4**   Highway Control Rating: **4 5**   Highway Safety: **4 1**

Sunrise	**1995**	MHA	30	29RQ	CH	GM6.5	D	$2000	178	4,200	14,800	12,410

Livability Code: SB 30-90
Wheelbase-to-length ratio of 50% is considered ● dangerous ○ fatiguing ○ good ○ excellent *
The approximate net payload of 2390 pounds at 16% of GVWR on this model is ○ deficient ○ excessive ○ cautionary ○ good ● excellent *
Total highway safety penalties are: 4 *   Value: **8 2**   Durability: **7 4**   Highway Control Rating: **4 5**   Highway Safety: **4 1**

Sunrise	**1995**	MHA	30	29RQ	FO	7.5L	G	$1900	178	3,800	15,200	12,690

Livability Code: SB 30-90
Wheelbase-to-length ratio of 50% is considered ● dangerous ○ fatiguing ○ good ○ excellent *
The approximate net payload of 2510 pounds at 17% of GVWR on this model is ○ deficient ○ excessive ○ cautionary ○ good ● excellent *
Total highway safety penalties are: 2 *   Value: **8 4**   Durability: **7 4**   Highway Control Rating: **4 5**   Highway Safety: **4 3**

Sunrise	**1995**	MHA	32	31RQ	CH	7.4L	G	$1800	190	4,200	14,800	12,816

Livability Code: SB 30-90
Wheelbase-to-length ratio of 50% is considered ● dangerous ○ fatiguing ○ good ○ excellent *
The approximate net payload of 1984 pounds at 13% of GVWR on this model is ○ deficient ○ excessive ○ cautionary ● good ○ excellent *
Total highway safety penalties are: 5 *   Value: **8 2**   Durability: **7 4**   Highway Control Rating: **4 0**   Highway Safety: **3 5**

Sunrise	**1995**	MHA	32	31RQ	CH	GM6.5	D	$1900	190	4,200	14,800	12,816

Livability Code: SB 30-90
Wheelbase-to-length ratio of 50% is considered ● dangerous ○ fatiguing ○ good ○ excellent *
The approximate net payload of 1984 pounds at 13% of GVWR on this model is ○ deficient ○ excessive ○ cautionary ● good ○ excellent *
Total highway safety penalties are: 5 *   Value: **8 2**   Durability: **7 4**   Highway Control Rating: **4 0**   Highway Safety: **3 5**

Note: Safety ratings are based on the assumption that the engineering of the RV has allowed for proper balance by placing fresh, gray, and black holding tanks in a location so as not to change the balance of the RV when the tanks are empty or full. **Always double-check wheelbase, GVWR, and weights at front and rear axles.**

*See Section 1 for details on how conclusions are reached.

Brand	Year	Type	Length	Model	Chassis	Engine	Fuel Type	Average Price per Linear Foot When New	Adjusted Wheelbase	Approx. Towing Capacity	Gross Vehicle Weight Rating	Average Curb Weight
Sunrise	1995	MHA	32	31RQ	FO	7.5L	G	$1800	190	3,800	15,200	13,096

Livability Code: SB 30-90   Wheelbase-to-length ratio of 50% is considered ◉ dangerous ○ fatiguing ○ good ○ excellent *

The approximate net payload of 2104 pounds at 14% of GVWR on this model is ○ deficient ○ excessive ○ cautionary ◉ good ○ excellent *

Total highway safety penalties are: 2 *   Value: 8 4   Durability: 7 4   Highway Control Rating: 4 1   Highway Safety: 3 9

Brand	Year	Type	Length	Model	Chassis	Engine	Fuel Type	Price/Ft	Wheelbase	Towing	GVWR	Curb Weight
Sunrise	1995	MHA	32	31RQ	OS	Cu5.9L	D	$2500	178	1,500	17,000	13,453

Livability Code: SB 30-90   Wheelbase-to-length ratio of 47% is considered ◉ dangerous ○ fatiguing ○ good ○ excellent *

The approximate net payload of 3547 pounds at 21% of GVWR on this model is ○ deficient ◉ excessive ○ cautionary ○ good ○ excellent *

Total highway safety penalties are: 2 *   Value: 8 4   Durability: 7 4   Highway Control Rating: 3 7   Highway Safety: 3 5

Brand	Year	Type	Length	Model	Chassis	Engine	Fuel Type	Price/Ft	Wheelbase	Towing	GVWR	Curb Weight
Sunrise	1995	MHA	34	33RQ	CH	7.4L	G	$1800	208	4,200	14,800	13,380

Livability Code: SB 30-90   Wheelbase-to-length ratio of 51% is considered ○ dangerous ◉ fatiguing ○ good ○ excellent *

The approximate net payload of 1420 pounds at 10% of GVWR on this model is ○ deficient ◉ excessive ○ cautionary ○ good ○ excellent *

Total highway safety penalties are: 7 *   Value: 8 1   Durability: 7 4   Highway Control Rating: 3 6   Highway Safety: 2 9

Brand	Year	Type	Length	Model	Chassis	Engine	Fuel Type	Price/Ft	Wheelbase	Towing	GVWR	Curb Weight
Sunrise	1995	MHA	34	33RQ	FO	7.5L	G	$1800	208	8,000	17,000	14,120

Livability Code: SB 30-90   Wheelbase-to-length ratio of 51% is considered ○ dangerous ◉ fatiguing ○ good ○ excellent *

The approximate net payload of 2880 pounds at 17% of GVWR on this model is ○ deficient ○ excessive ○ cautionary ○ good ◉ excellent *

Total highway safety penalties are: 2 *   Value: 8 4   Durability: 7 4   Highway Control Rating: 4 9   Highway Safety: 4 7

Brand	Year	Type	Length	Model	Chassis	Engine	Fuel Type	Price/Ft	Wheelbase	Towing	GVWR	Curb Weight
Sunrise	1996	MHA	25	25RC	CH	7.4L	G	$1900	158	3,700	12,300	10,540

Livability Code: SB 30-90   Wheelbase-to-length ratio of 52% is considered ○ dangerous ◉ fatiguing ○ good ○ excellent *

The approximate net payload of 1760 pounds at 14% of GVWR on this model is ○ deficient ○ excessive ○ cautionary ◉ good ○ excellent *

Total highway safety penalties are: 2 *   Value: 8 4   Durability: 7 4   Highway Control Rating: 5 5   Highway Safety: 5 3   ★

Brand	Year	Type	Length	Model	Chassis	Engine	Fuel Type	Price/Ft	Wheelbase	Towing	GVWR	Curb Weight
Sunrise	1996	MHA	25	25RC opch	CH	7.4L	G	$2100	158	4,200	14,800	11,440

Livability Code: SB 30-90   Wheelbase-to-length ratio of 52% is considered ○ dangerous ◉ fatiguing ○ good ○ excellent *

The approximate net payload of 3360 pounds at 23% of GVWR on this model is ○ deficient ○ excessive ○ cautionary ○ good ◉ excellent *

Total highway safety penalties are: 2 *   Value: 8 4   Durability: 7 4   Highway Control Rating: 6 0   Highway Safety: 5 8   ★

Brand	Year	Type	Length	Model	Chassis	Engine	Fuel Type	Price/Ft	Wheelbase	Towing	GVWR	Curb Weight
Sunrise	1996	MHA	25	25RC -D	CH	GM6.5	D	$2100	158	3,700	12,300	10,540

Livability Code: SB 30-90   Wheelbase-to-length ratio of 52% is considered ○ dangerous ◉ fatiguing ○ good ○ excellent *

The approximate net payload of 1760 pounds at 14% of GVWR on this model is ○ deficient ○ excessive ○ cautionary ◉ good ○ excellent *

Total highway safety penalties are: 2 *   Value: 8 4   Durability: 7 4   Highway Control Rating: 5 5   Highway Safety: 5 3   ★

Brand	Year	Type	Length	Model	Chassis	Engine	Fuel Type	Price/Ft	Wheelbase	Towing	GVWR	Curb Weight
Sunrise	1996	MHA	25	25RC opch	CH	7.4L	G	$2000	158	1,200	14,800	11,440

Livability Code: SB 30-90   Wheelbase-to-length ratio of 52% is considered ○ dangerous ◉ fatiguing ○ good ○ excellent *

The approximate net payload of 3360 pounds at 23% of GVWR on this model is ○ deficient ○ excessive ○ cautionary ○ good ◉ excellent *

Total highway safety penalties are: 2 *   Value: 8 4   Durability: 7 4   Highway Control Rating: 6 0   Highway Safety: 5 8   ★

Brand	Year	Type	Length	Model	Chassis	Engine	Fuel Type	Price/Ft	Wheelbase	Towing	GVWR	Curb Weight
Sunrise	1996	MHA	28	28RC	CH	7.4L	G	$1900	158	4,200	14,800	12,027

Livability Code: SB 30-90   Wheelbase-to-length ratio of 47% is considered ◉ dangerous ○ fatiguing ○ good ○ excellent *

The approximate net payload of 2773 pounds at 19% of GVWR on this model is ○ deficient ○ excessive ○ cautionary ○ good ◉ excellent *

Total highway safety penalties are: 4 *   Value: 8 3   Durability: 7 4   Highway Control Rating: 3 7   Highway Safety: 3 3

Brand	Year	Type	Length	Model	Chassis	Engine	Fuel Type	Price/Ft	Wheelbase	Towing	GVWR	Curb Weight
Sunrise	1996	MHA	28	28RC-D	CH	GM6.5	D	$2000	158	4,200	14,800	12,027

Livability Code: SB 30-90   Wheelbase-to-length ratio of 47% is considered ◉ dangerous ○ fatiguing ○ good ○ excellent *

The approximate net payload of 2773 pounds at 19% of GVWR on this model is ○ deficient ○ excessive ○ cautionary ○ good ◉ excellent *

Total highway safety penalties are: 4 *   Value: 8 3   Durability: 7 4   Highway Control Rating: 3 7   Highway Safety: 3 3

Brand	Year	Type	Length	Model	Chassis	Engine	Fuel Type	Price/Ft	Wheelbase	Towing	GVWR	Curb Weight
Sunrise	1996	MHA	30	29RQ	CH	7.4L	G	$1800	178	4,200	14,800	12,433

Livability Code: SB 30-90   Wheelbase-to-length ratio of 50% is considered ◉ dangerous ○ fatiguing ○ good ○ excellent *

The approximate net payload of 2367 pounds at 16% of GVWR on this model is ○ deficient ○ excessive ○ cautionary ○ good ◉ excellent *

Total highway safety penalties are: 4 *   Value: 8 2   Durability: 7 4   Highway Control Rating: 4 4   Highway Safety: 4 0

Brand	Year	Type	Length	Model	Chassis	Engine	Fuel Type	Price/Ft	Wheelbase	Towing	GVWR	Curb Weight
Sunrise	1996	MHA	30	29RQ D	CH	GM6.5	D	$1900	178	4,200	14,800	12,433

Livability Code: SB 30-90   Wheelbase-to-length ratio of 50% is considered ◉ dangerous ○ fatiguing ○ good ○ excellent *

The approximate net payload of 2367 pounds at 16% of GVWR on this model is ○ deficient ○ excessive ○ cautionary ○ good ◉ excellent *

Total highway safety penalties are: 4 *   Value: 8 2   Durability: 7 4   Highway Control Rating: 4 4   Highway Safety: 4 0

Note: Safety ratings are based on the assumption that the engineering of the RV has allowed for proper balance by placing fresh, gray, and black holding tanks in a location so as not to change the balance of the RV when the tanks are empty or full. **Always double-check wheelbase, GVWR, and weights at front and rear axles.**

*See Section 1 for details on how conclusions are reached.

Brand	Year	Type	Length	Model	Chassis	Engine	Fuel Type	Average Price per Linear Foot When New	Adjusted Wheelbase	Approx. Towing Capacity	Gross Vehicle Weight Rating	Average Curb Weight
Sunrise	1996	MHA	30	29RQ	FO	7.5L	G	$1800	178	9,800	15,200	12,713

Livability Code: SB 30-90   Wheelbase-to-length ratio of 50% is considered ◉ dangerous ○ fatiguing ○ good ○ excellent *
The approximate net payload of 2487 pounds at 16% of GVWR on this model is ○ deficient ○ excessive ○ cautionary ○ good ◉ excellent *
Total highway safety penalties are: 2 *   Value: **8 4**   Durability: **7 4**   Highway Control Rating: **4 4**   Highway Safety: **4 2**

Brand	Year	Type	Length	Model	Chassis	Engine	Fuel Type	Price/Ft	Wheelbase	Towing	GVWR	Curb Wt
Sunrise	1996	MHA	32	31RQ	CH	7.4L	G	$1700	190	4,200	14,800	12,839

Livability Code: SB 30-90   Wheelbase-to-length ratio of 50% is considered ◉ dangerous ○ fatiguing ○ good ○ excellent *
The approximate net payload of 1961 pounds at 13% of GVWR on this model is ○ deficient ○ excessive ○ cautionary ◉ good ○ excellent *
Total highway safety penalties are: 5 *   Value: **8 2**   Durability: **7 4**   Highway Control Rating: **3 9**   Highway Safety: **3 4**

Brand	Year	Type	Length	Model	Chassis	Engine	Fuel Type	Price/Ft	Wheelbase	Towing	GVWR	Curb Wt
Sunrise	1996	MHA	32	31RQ D	CH	GM6.5	D	$1800	190	4,200	14,800	12,839

Livability Code: SB 30-90   Wheelbase-to-length ratio of 50% is considered ◉ dangerous ○ fatiguing ○ good ○ excellent *
The approximate net payload of 1961 pounds at 13% of GVWR on this model is ○ deficient ○ excessive ○ cautionary ◉ good ○ excellent *
Total highway safety penalties are: 5 *   Value: **8 2**   Durability: **7 4**   Highway Control Rating: **3 9**   Highway Safety: **3 4**

Brand	Year	Type	Length	Model	Chassis	Engine	Fuel Type	Price/Ft	Wheelbase	Towing	GVWR	Curb Wt
Sunrise	1996	MHA	32	31RQ	FO	7.5L	G	$1700	190	9,800	15,200	13,119

Livability Code: SB 30-90   Wheelbase-to-length ratio of 50% is considered ◉ dangerous ○ fatiguing ○ good ○ excellent *
The approximate net payload of 2081 pounds at 14% of GVWR on this model is ○ deficient ○ excessive ○ cautionary ○ good ○ excellent *
Total highway safety penalties are: 2 *   Value: **8 4**   Durability: **7 4**   Highway Control Rating: **4 1**   Highway Safety: **3 9**

Brand	Year	Type	Length	Model	Chassis	Engine	Fuel Type	Price/Ft	Wheelbase	Towing	GVWR	Curb Wt
Sunrise	1996	MHA	32	32RQ	FO	CU5.9L	G	$2800	178	8,000	17,000	13,323

Livability Code: SB 30-90   Wheelbase-to-length ratio of 46% is considered ◉ dangerous ○ fatiguing ○ good ○ excellent *
The approximate net payload of 3677 pounds at 22% of GVWR on this model is ○ deficient ○ excessive ○ cautionary ○ good ◉ excellent *
Total highway safety penalties are: 2 *   Value: **8 4**   Durability: **7 4**   Highway Control Rating: **3 4**   Highway Safety: **3 2**

Brand	Year	Type	Length	Model	Chassis	Engine	Fuel Type	Price/Ft	Wheelbase	Towing	GVWR	Curb Wt
Sunrise	1996	MHA	33	32RQ-190	FR	Cu5.9L	D	$2700	178	2,000	18,000	14,103

Livability Code: SB 30-90   Wheelbase-to-length ratio of 45% is considered ◉ dangerous ○ fatiguing ○ good ○ excellent *
The approximate net payload of 3897 pounds at 22% of GVWR on this model is ○ deficient ○ excessive ○ cautionary ○ good ◉ excellent *
Total highway safety penalties are: 2 *   Value: **8 4**   Durability: **7 4**   Highway Control Rating: **2 9**   Highway Safety: **2 7**

Brand	Year	Type	Length	Model	Chassis	Engine	Fuel Type	Price/Ft	Wheelbase	Towing	GVWR	Curb Wt
Sunrise	1996	MHA	34	33RQ	CH	7.4L	G	$1700	208	4,200	14,800	13,335

Livability Code: SB 30-90   Wheelbase-to-length ratio of 51% is considered ○ dangerous ◉ fatiguing ○ good ○ excellent *
The approximate net payload of 1465 pounds at 10% of GVWR on this model is ○ deficient ○ excessive ○ cautionary ◉ good ○ excellent *
Total highway safety penalties are: 6 *   Value: **8 1**   Durability: **7 4**   Highway Control Rating: **3 7**   Highway Safety: **3 1**

Brand	Year	Type	Length	Model	Chassis	Engine	Fuel Type	Price/Ft	Wheelbase	Towing	GVWR	Curb Wt
Sunrise	1996	MHA	34	33RQ opch	CH	7.4L	G	$1700	208	2,500	16,500	13,775

Livability Code: SB 30-90   Wheelbase-to-length ratio of 51% is considered ○ dangerous ◉ fatiguing ○ good ○ excellent *
The approximate net payload of 2725 pounds at 17% of GVWR on this model is ○ deficient ○ excessive ○ cautionary ○ good ◉ excellent *
Total highway safety penalties are: 6 *   Value: **8 1**   Durability: **7 4**   Highway Control Rating: **5 0**   Highway Safety: **4 4**

Brand	Year	Type	Length	Model	Chassis	Engine	Fuel Type	Price/Ft	Wheelbase	Towing	GVWR	Curb Wt
Sunrise	1996	MHA	34	33RQ	FO	7.5L	G	$1700	208	8,000	17,000	14,075

Livability Code: SB 30-90   Wheelbase-to-length ratio of 51% is considered ○ dangerous ◉ fatiguing ○ good ○ excellent *
The approximate net payload of 2925 pounds at 17% of GVWR on this model is ○ deficient ○ excessive ○ cautionary ○ good ◉ excellent *
Total highway safety penalties are: 2 *   Value: **8 4**   Durability: **7 4**   Highway Control Rating: **5 0**   Highway Safety: **4 8**

Brand	Year	Type	Length	Model	Chassis	Engine	Fuel Type	Price/Ft	Wheelbase	Towing	GVWR	Curb Wt
Sunrise	1997	MHA	25	25 RC	CH	7.4L	G	$2100	158	3,700	12,300	10,650

Livability Code: SB 30-90   Wheelbase-to-length ratio of 52% is considered ○ dangerous ◉ fatiguing ○ good ○ excellent *
The approximate net payload of 1650 pounds at 13% of GVWR on this model is ○ deficient ○ excessive ○ cautionary ◉ good ○ excellent *
Total highway safety penalties are: 2 *   Value: **8 4**   Durability: **7 4**   Highway Control Rating: **5 3**   Highway Safety: **5 1**   ★

Brand	Year	Type	Length	Model	Chassis	Engine	Fuel Type	Price/Ft	Wheelbase	Towing	GVWR	Curb Wt
Sunrise	1997	MHA	25	25 RC opch (Ca)	CH	7.4L	G	$2100	158	4,200	14,800	11,304

Livability Code: SB 30-90   Wheelbase-to-length ratio of 52% is considered ○ dangerous ◉ fatiguing ○ good ○ excellent *
The approximate net payload of 3496 pounds at 24% of GVWR on this model is ○ deficient ○ excessive ○ cautionary ○ good ◉ excellent *
Total highway safety penalties are: 2 *   Value: **8 4**   Durability: **7 4**   Highway Control Rating: **5 9**   Highway Safety: **5 7**   ★

Brand	Year	Type	Length	Model	Chassis	Engine	Fuel Type	Price/Ft	Wheelbase	Towing	GVWR	Curb Wt
Sunrise	1997	MHA	25	25 RC op eng	CH	GM6.5	D	$2300	158	1,500	12,300	11,028

Livability Code: SB 30-90   Wheelbase-to-length ratio of 52% is considered ○ dangerous ◉ fatiguing ○ good ○ excellent *
The approximate net payload of 1272 pounds at 10% of GVWR on this model is ○ deficient ○ excessive ○ cautionary ◉ good ○ excellent *
Total highway safety penalties are: 2 *   Value: **8 4**   Durability: **7 4**   Highway Control Rating: **4 7**   Highway Safety: **4 5**

Note: Safety ratings are based on the assumption that the engineering of the RV has allowed for proper balance by placing fresh, gray, and black holding tanks in a location so as not to change the balance of the RV when the tanks are empty or full. **Always double-check wheelbase, GVWR, and weights at front and rear axles.**

*See Section 1 for details on how conclusions are reached.

Section 2: The Ratings

Brand	Year	Type	Length	Model	Chassis	Engine	Fuel Type	Average Price per Linear Foot When New	Adjusted Wheelbase	Approx. Towing Capacity	Gross Vehicle Weight Rating	Average Curb Weight
Sunrise	1997	MHA	25	25 RC	CH	7.4L	G	$2200	158	1,500	12,300	10,528

Livability Code: SB 30-90
Wheelbase-to-length ratio of 52% is considered ○ dangerous ◉ fatiguing ○ good ○ excellent *
The approximate net payload of 1772 pounds at 14% of GVWR on this model is ○ deficient ○ excessive ○ cautionary ◉ good ○ excellent *
Total highway safety penalties are: 2 * Value: 8 4 Durability: 7 4 Highway Control Rating: 5 5 Highway Safety: 5 3 ★

Brand	Year	Type	Length	Model	Chassis	Engine	Fuel Type	Price	Wheelbase	Towing	GVWR	Curb Wt
Sunrise	1997	MHA	29	28 RQ-BSMT	CH	7.4L	G	$2000	158	4,200	14,800	12,084

Livability Code: SB 30-90
Wheelbase-to-length ratio of 46% is considered ◉ dangerous ○ fatiguing ○ good ○ excellent *
The approximate net payload of 2716 pounds at 18% of GVWR on this model is ○ deficient ○ excessive ○ cautionary ○ good ◉ excellent *
Total highway safety penalties are: 4 * Value: 8 3 Durability: 7 4 Highway Control Rating: 3 3 Highway Safety: 2 9

Sunrise	1997	MHA	29	28RQ-BSMT op eng	CH	GM6.5	D	$2100	158	1,500	14,800	12,713

Livability Code: SB 30-90
Wheelbase-to-length ratio of 46% is considered ◉ dangerous ○ fatiguing ○ good ○ excellent *
The approximate net payload of 2087 pounds at 14% of GVWR on this model is ○ deficient ○ excessive ○ cautionary ◉ good ○ excellent *
Total highway safety penalties are: 4 * Value: 8 3 Durability: 7 4 Highway Control Rating: 2 7 Highway Safety: 2 3

Sunrise	1997	MHA	30	29 RQ	CH	7.4L	G	$1900	178	4,200	14,800	12,295

Livability Code: SB 30-90
Wheelbase-to-length ratio of 50% is considered ◉ dangerous ○ fatiguing ○ good ○ excellent *
The approximate net payload of 2505 pounds at 17% of GVWR on this model is ○ deficient ○ excessive ○ cautionary ◉ good ○ excellent *
Total highway safety penalties are: 4 * Value: 8 2 Durability: 7 4 Highway Control Rating: 4 5 Highway Safety: 4 1

Sunrise	1997	MHA	30	29 RQ op eng	CH	GM6.5	D	$1900	178	1,500	14,800	12,978

Livability Code: SB 30-90
Wheelbase-to-length ratio of 50% is considered ◉ dangerous ○ fatiguing ○ good ○ excellent *
The approximate net payload of 1822 pounds at 12% of GVWR on this model is ○ deficient ○ excessive ○ cautionary ◉ good ○ excellent *
Total highway safety penalties are: 4 * Value: 8 2 Durability: 7 4 Highway Control Rating: 3 7 Highway Safety: 3 3

Sunrise	1997	MHA	30	29 RQ opch	FO	7.5L	G	$1900	178	9,800	15,200	12,667

Livability Code: SB 30-90
Wheelbase-to-length ratio of 50% is considered ◉ dangerous ○ fatiguing ○ good ○ excellent *
The approximate net payload of 2533 pounds at 17% of GVWR on this model is ○ deficient ○ excessive ○ cautionary ◉ good ○ excellent *
Total highway safety penalties are: 2 * Value: 8 4 Durability: 7 4 Highway Control Rating: 4 5 Highway Safety: 4 3

Sunrise	1997	MHA	31	30 RQ-BSMT	CH	7.4L	G	$1900	190	4,200	14,800	12,564

Livability Code: SB 30-90
Wheelbase-to-length ratio of 52% is considered ○ dangerous ◉ fatiguing ○ good ○ excellent *
The approximate net payload of 2236 pounds at 15% of GVWR on this model is ○ deficient ○ excessive ○ cautionary ◉ good ○ excellent *
Total highway safety penalties are: 5 * Value: 8 2 Durability: 7 4 Highway Control Rating: 5 7 Highway Safety: 5 2 ★

Sunrise	1997	MHA	31	30 RQ-BSMTop eng	CH	GM6.5	D	$1900	190	1,500	14,800	12,676

Livability Code: SB 30-90
Wheelbase-to-length ratio of 52% is considered ○ dangerous ◉ fatiguing ○ good ○ excellent *
The approximate net payload of 2124 pounds at 14% of GVWR on this model is ○ deficient ○ excessive ○ cautionary ◉ good ○ excellent *
Total highway safety penalties are: 5 * Value: 8 2 Durability: 7 4 Highway Control Rating: 5 5 Highway Safety: 5 0 ★

Sunrise	1997	MHA	31	30 RQ-BSMTopch	FO	7.5L	G	$1900	190	9,800	15,200	13,000

Livability Code: SB 30-90
Wheelbase-to-length ratio of 52% is considered ○ dangerous ◉ fatiguing ○ good ○ excellent *
The approximate net payload of 2200 pounds at 14% of GVWR on this model is ○ deficient ○ excessive ○ cautionary ◉ good ○ excellent *
Total highway safety penalties are: 2 * Value: 8 4 Durability: 7 4 Highway Control Rating: 5 5 Highway Safety: 5 3 ★

Sunrise	1997	MHA	32	31 RQ	CH	7.4L	G	$1900	190	4,200	14,800	12,700

Livability Code: SB 30-90
Wheelbase-to-length ratio of 50% is considered ◉ dangerous ○ fatiguing ○ good ○ excellent *
The approximate net payload of 2100 pounds at 14% of GVWR on this model is ○ deficient ○ excessive ○ cautionary ◉ good ○ excellent *
Total highway safety penalties are: 5 * Value: 8 2 Durability: 7 4 Highway Control Rating: 4 1 Highway Safety: 3 6

Sunrise	1997	MHA	32	31 RQ op eng	CH	GM6.5	D	$1800	190	1,500	14,800	13,397

Livability Code: SB 30-90
Wheelbase-to-length ratio of 50% is considered ◉ dangerous ○ fatiguing ○ good ○ excellent *
The approximate net payload of 1403 pounds at 9% of GVWR on this model is ○ deficient ○ excessive ◉ cautionary ○ good ○ excellent *
Total highway safety penalties are: 5 * Value: 8 2 Durability: 7 4 Highway Control Rating: 2 9 Highway Safety: 2 4

Sunrise	1997	MHA	32	31 RQ opch	FO	7.5L	G	$1900	190	9,800	15,200	13,118

Livability Code: SB 30-90
Wheelbase-to-length ratio of 50% is considered ◉ dangerous ○ fatiguing ○ good ○ excellent *
The approximate net payload of 2082 pounds at 14% of GVWR on this model is ○ deficient ○ excessive ○ cautionary ◉ good ○ excellent *
Total highway safety penalties are: 2 * Value: 8 4 Durability: 7 4 Highway Control Rating: 4 1 Highway Safety: 3 9

Note: Safety ratings are based on the assumption that the engineering of the RV has allowed for proper balance by placing fresh, gray, and black holding tanks in a location so as not to change the balance of the RV when the tanks are empty or full. **Always double-check wheelbase, GVWR, and weights at front and rear axles.**

*See Section 1 for details on how conclusions are reached.

Brand	Year	Type	Length	Model	Chassis	Engine	Fuel Type	Average Price per Linear Foot When New	Adjusted Wheelbase	Approx. Towing Capacity	Gross Vehicle Weight Rating	Average Curb Weight
Sunrise	1997	MHA	32	32 RQ-BSMT	CH	7.4L	G	$1900	208	4,200	14,800	12,922

Livability Code: SB 30-90
Wheelbase-to-length ratio of 54% is considered ○ dangerous ○ fatiguing ◉ good ○ excellent *
The approximate net payload of 1878 pounds at 13% of GVWR on this model is ○ deficient ○ excessive ○ cautionary ◉ good ○ excellent *
Total highway safety penalties are: 5 *   Value: 82   Durability: 74   Highway Control Rating: 79   Highway Safety: 74   ★★★

| Sunrise | 1997 | MHA | 32 | 32 RQ-BSMT opch | CH | 7.4L | G | $1900 | 208 | 1,500 | 16,500 | 13,644 |

Livability Code: SB 30-90
Wheelbase-to-length ratio of 54% is considered ○ dangerous ○ fatiguing ◉ good ○ excellent *
The approximate net payload of 2856 pounds at 17% of GVWR on this model is ○ deficient ○ excessive ○ cautionary ○ good ◉ excellent *
Total highway safety penalties are: 5 *   Value: 82   Durability: 74   Highway Control Rating: 84   Highway Safety: 79   ★★★

| Sunrise | 1997 | MHA | 32 | 32 RQ-BSMT opch | FO | 7.5L | G | $1900 | 208 | 8,000 | 17,000 | 13,742 |

Livability Code: SB 30-90
Wheelbase-to-length ratio of 54% is considered ○ dangerous ○ fatiguing ◉ good ○ excellent *
The approximate net payload of 3258 pounds at 19% of GVWR on this model is ○ deficient ○ excessive ○ cautionary ○ good ◉ excellent *
Total highway safety penalties are: 2 *   Value: 84   Durability: 74   Highway Control Rating: 86   Highway Safety: 84   ★★★

| Sunrise | 1997 | MHA | 33 | 33 RQ | CH | 7.4L | G | $1900 | 216 | 4,200 | 14,800 | 13,149 |

Livability Code: SB 30-90
Wheelbase-to-length ratio of 55% is considered ○ dangerous ○ fatiguing ◉ good ○ excellent *
The approximate net payload of 1651 pounds at 11% of GVWR on this model is ○ deficient ○ excessive ○ cautionary ◉ good ○ excellent *
Total highway safety penalties are: 6 *   Value: 82   Durability: 74   Highway Control Rating: 86   Highway Safety: 80   ★★★

| Sunrise | 1997 | MHA | 33 | 33 RQ opch vortec | CH | 7.4L | G | $1900 | 216 | 3,500 | 16,500 | 13,494 |

Livability Code: SB 30-90
Wheelbase-to-length ratio of 55% is considered ○ dangerous ○ fatiguing ◉ good ○ excellent *
The approximate net payload of 3006 pounds at 18% of GVWR on this model is ○ deficient ○ excessive ○ cautionary ○ good ◉ excellent *
Total highway safety penalties are: 6 *   Value: 82   Durability: 74   Highway Control Rating: 93   Highway Safety: 87   ★★★

| Sunrise | 1997 | MHA | 33 | 33 RQ opch | FO | 7.5L | G | $1900 | 216 | 8,000 | 17,000 | 13,795 |

Livability Code: SB 30-90
Wheelbase-to-length ratio of 55% is considered ○ dangerous ○ fatiguing ◉ good ○ excellent *
The approximate net payload of 3205 pounds at 19% of GVWR on this model is ○ deficient ○ excessive ○ cautionary ○ good ◉ excellent *
Total highway safety penalties are: 2 *   Value: 84   Durability: 74   Highway Control Rating: 94   Highway Safety: 92   ★★★

| Sunrise | 1998 | MHA | 27 | SE26WU opch | CH | 7.4L | G | $1900 | 159 | 3,700 | 12,300 | 11,066 |

Livability Code: SB 30-90
Wheelbase-to-length ratio of 50% is considered ◉ dangerous ○ fatiguing ○ good ○ excellent *
The approximate net payload of 1234 pounds at 10% of GVWR on this model is ○ deficient ○ excessive ○ cautionary ◉ good ○ excellent *
Total highway safety penalties are: 3 *   Value: 83   Durability: 74   Highway Control Rating: 33   Highway Safety: 30

| Sunrise | 1998 | MHA | 27 | SE26WU opch | CH | 7.4L | G | $2000 | 159 | 4,200 | 14,800 | 11,765 |

Livability Code: SB 30-90
Wheelbase-to-length ratio of 50% is considered ◉ dangerous ○ fatiguing ○ good ○ excellent *
The approximate net payload of 3035 pounds at 21% of GVWR on this model is ○ deficient ○ excessive ○ cautionary ○ good ◉ excellent *
Total highway safety penalties are: 3 *   Value: 83   Durability: 74   Highway Control Rating: 48   Highway Safety: 45

| Sunrise | 1998 | MHA | 30 | SE29WQ | CH | 7.4L | G | $2000 | 178 | 4,500 | 16,500 | 13,284 |

Livability Code: SB 30-90
Wheelbase-to-length ratio of 49% is considered ◉ dangerous ○ fatiguing ○ good ○ excellent *
The approximate net payload of 3217 pounds at 19% of GVWR on this model is ○ deficient ○ excessive ○ cautionary ○ good ◉ excellent *
Total highway safety penalties are: 5 *   Value: 82   Durability: 74   Highway Control Rating: 46   Highway Safety: 41

| Sunrise | 1998 | MHA | 30 | SE29WQ | FO | 7.5L | G | $1900 | 178 | 9,800 | 15,200 | 13,171 |

Livability Code: SB 30-90
Wheelbase-to-length ratio of 49% is considered ◉ dangerous ○ fatiguing ○ good ○ excellent *
The approximate net payload of 2030 pounds at 13% of GVWR on this model is ○ deficient ○ excessive ○ cautionary ◉ good ○ excellent *
Total highway safety penalties are: 2 *   Value: 84   Durability: 74   Highway Control Rating: 37   Highway Safety: 35

| Sunrise | 1998 | MHA | 30 | SE29WQ myc | FO | 6.8L | G | $2000 | 178 | 10,500 | 15,500 | 13,231 |

Livability Code: SB 30-90
Wheelbase-to-length ratio of 49% is considered ◉ dangerous ○ fatiguing ○ good ○ excellent *
The approximate net payload of 2270 pounds at 15% of GVWR on this model is ○ deficient ○ excessive ○ cautionary ◉ good ○ excellent *
Total highway safety penalties are: 2 *   Value: 84   Durability: 74   Highway Control Rating: 50   Highway Safety: 48

| Sunrise | 1998 | MHA | 31 | 30WQ opch | CH | 7.4L | G | $2000 | 190 | 4,500 | 16,500 | 13,674 |

Livability Code: SB 30-90
Wheelbase-to-length ratio of 51% is considered ○ dangerous ◉ fatiguing ○ good ○ excellent *
The approximate net payload of 2826 pounds at 17% of GVWR on this model is ○ deficient ○ excessive ○ cautionary ○ good ◉ excellent *
Total highway safety penalties are: 5 *   Value: 82   Durability: 74   Highway Control Rating: 50   Highway Safety: 45

Note: Safety ratings are based on the assumption that the engineering of the RV has allowed for proper balance by placing fresh, gray, and black holding tanks in a location so as not to change the balance of the RV when the tanks are empty or full. **Always double-check wheelbase, GVWR, and weights at front and rear axles.**

*See Section 1 for details on how conclusions are reached.

Brand	Year	Type	Length	Model	Chassis	Engine	Fuel Type	Average Price per Linear Foot When New	Adjusted Wheelbase	Approx. Towing Capacity	Gross Vehicle Weight Rating	Average Curb Weight
Sunrise	1998	MHA	31	30WQ	FO	7.5L	G	$1900	190	9,800	15,200	13,534

Livability Code: SB 30-90
Wheelbase-to-length ratio of 51% is considered ○ dangerous ● fatiguing ○ good ○ excellent *
The approximate net payload of 1666 pounds at 11% of GVWR on this model is ○ deficient ● excessive ○ cautionary ● good ○ excellent *
Total highway safety penalties are: 2 *   Value: 8 4   Durability: 7 4   Highway Control Rating: 3 9   Highway Safety: 3 7

Sunrise	1998	MHA	31	30WQ opch	FO	7.5L	G	$1900	190	8,000	17,000	14,186

Livability Code: SB 30-90
Wheelbase-to-length ratio of 51% is considered ○ dangerous ● fatiguing ○ good ○ excellent *
The approximate net payload of 2814 pounds at 17% of GVWR on this model is ○ deficient ● excessive ○ cautionary ○ good ● excellent *
Total highway safety penalties are: 2 *   Value: 8 4   Durability: 7 4   Highway Control Rating: 4 9   Highway Safety: 4 7

Sunrise	1998	MHA	31	30WQ myc	FO	6.8L	G	$2000	190	10,500	15,500	13,594

Livability Code: SB 30-90
Wheelbase-to-length ratio of 51% is considered ○ dangerous ● fatiguing ○ good ○ excellent *
The approximate net payload of 1906 pounds at 12% of GVWR on this model is ○ deficient ● excessive ○ cautionary ● good ○ excellent *
Total highway safety penalties are: 2 *   Value: 8 4   Durability: 7 4   Highway Control Rating: 5 1   Highway Safety: 4 9

Sunrise	1998	MHA	31	30WQ opch myc	FO	6.8L	G	$2000	190	8,000	18,000	14,386

Livability Code: SB 30-90
Wheelbase-to-length ratio of 51% is considered ○ dangerous ● fatiguing ○ good ○ excellent *
The approximate net payload of 3614 pounds at 20% of GVWR on this model is ○ deficient ● excessive ○ cautionary ○ good ● excellent *
Total highway safety penalties are: 2 *   Value: 8 4   Durability: 7 4   Highway Control Rating: 6 2   Highway Safety: 6 0   ★★

Sunrise	1998	MHA	32	SE31WQ opch	CH	7.4L	G	$1900	190	4,500	16,500	13,679

Livability Code: SB 30-90
Wheelbase-to-length ratio of 49% is considered ● dangerous ○ fatiguing ○ good ○ excellent *
The approximate net payload of 2821 pounds at 17% of GVWR on this model is ○ deficient ● excessive ○ cautionary ○ good ● excellent *
Total highway safety penalties are: 6 *   Value: 8 2   Durability: 7 4   Highway Control Rating: 4 4   Highway Safety: 3 8

Sunrise	1998	MHA	32	DL31DQ	CH	7.4L	G	$2000	190	4,500	16,500	13,539

Livability Code: SB 30-90
Wheelbase-to-length ratio of 49% is considered ● dangerous ○ fatiguing ○ good ○ excellent *
The approximate net payload of 2961 pounds at 18% of GVWR on this model is ○ deficient ○ excessive ○ cautionary ○ good ● excellent *
Total highway safety penalties are: 6 *   Value: 8 2   Durability: 7 4   Highway Control Rating: 4 5   Highway Safety: 3 9

Sunrise	1998	MHA	32	SE31WQ	FO	7.5L	G	$1800	190	9,800	15,200	13,499

Livability Code: SB 30-90
Wheelbase-to-length ratio of 49% is considered ● dangerous ○ fatiguing ○ good ○ excellent *
The approximate net payload of 1701 pounds at 11% of GVWR on this model is ○ deficient ○ excessive ○ cautionary ● good ○ excellent *
Total highway safety penalties are: 2 *   Value: 8 4   Durability: 7 4   Highway Control Rating: 3 3   Highway Safety: 3 1

Sunrise	1998	MHA	32	SE31WQ opch	FO	7.5L	G	$1800	190	8,000	17,000	13,969

Livability Code: SB 30-90
Wheelbase-to-length ratio of 49% is considered ● dangerous ○ fatiguing ○ good ○ excellent *
The approximate net payload of 3031 pounds at 18% of GVWR on this model is ○ deficient ● excessive ○ cautionary ○ good ● excellent *
Total highway safety penalties are: 2 *   Value: 8 4   Durability: 7 4   Highway Control Rating: 4 5   Highway Safety: 4 3

Sunrise	1998	MHA	32	DL31DQ opch	FO	7.5L	G	$2000	190	8,000	17,000	14,050

Livability Code: SB 30-90
Wheelbase-to-length ratio of 49% is considered ● dangerous ○ fatiguing ○ good ○ excellent *
The approximate net payload of 2950 pounds at 17% of GVWR on this model is ○ deficient ● excessive ○ cautionary ○ good ● excellent *
Total highway safety penalties are: 2 *   Value: 8 4   Durability: 7 4   Highway Control Rating: 4 4   Highway Safety: 4 2

Sunrise	1998	MHA	32	SE31WQ myc	FO	6.8L	G	$1900	190	10,500	15,500	13,559

Livability Code: SB 30-90
Wheelbase-to-length ratio of 49% is considered ● dangerous ○ fatiguing ○ good ○ excellent *
The approximate net payload of 1941 pounds at 13% of GVWR on this model is ○ deficient ○ excessive ○ cautionary ● good ○ excellent *
Total highway safety penalties are: 2 *   Value: 8 4   Durability: 7 4   Highway Control Rating: 4 6   Highway Safety: 4 4

Sunrise	1998	MHA	32	SE31WQ opch myc	FO	6.8L	G	$1900	190	8,000	18,000	14,169

Livability Code: SB 30-90
Wheelbase-to-length ratio of 49% is considered ● dangerous ○ fatiguing ○ good ○ excellent *
The approximate net payload of 3831 pounds at 21% of GVWR on this model is ○ deficient ○ excessive ○ cautionary ○ good ● excellent *
Total highway safety penalties are: 2 *   Value: 8 4   Durability: 7 4   Highway Control Rating: 5 6   Highway Safety: 5 4

Sunrise	1998	MHA	32	DL31DQ opch myc	FO	6.8L	G	$2100	190	8,000	18,000	14,250

Livability Code: SB 30-90
Wheelbase-to-length ratio of 49% is considered ● dangerous ○ fatiguing ○ good ○ excellent *
The approximate net payload of 3750 pounds at 21% of GVWR on this model is ○ deficient ○ excessive ○ cautionary ○ good ● excellent *
Total highway safety penalties are: 2 *   Value: 8 4   Durability: 7 4   Highway Control Rating: 5 6   Highway Safety: 5 4

Note: Safety ratings are based on the assumption that the engineering of the RV has allowed for proper balance by placing fresh, gray, and black holding tanks in a location so as not to change the balance of the RV when the tanks are empty or full. **Always double-check wheelbase, GVWR, and weights at front and rear axles.**

*See Section 1 for details on how conclusions are reached.

Brand	Year	Type	Length	Model	Chassis	Engine	Fuel Type	Average Price per Linear Foot When New	Adjusted Wheelbase	Approx. Towing Capacity	Gross Vehicle Weight Rating	Average Curb Weight
Sunrise	1998	MHA	33	32WQ	CH	7.4L	G	$1900	208	4,500	16,500	14,065

Livability Code: SB 30-90
Wheelbase-to-length ratio of 53% is considered ○ dangerous ◉ fatiguing ○ good ○ excellent *
The approximate net payload of 2435 pounds at 15% of GVWR on this model is ○ deficient ○ excessive ○ cautionary ◉ good ○ excellent *
Total highway safety penalties are: 6 *   Value: 82   Durability: 74   Highway Control Rating: 69   Highway Safety: 63   ★★

| Sunrise | 1998 | MHA | 33 | 32WQ opch | FO | 7.5L | G | $1900 | 208 | 8,000 | 17,000 | 14,333 |

Livability Code: SB 30-90
Wheelbase-to-length ratio of 53% is considered ○ dangerous ◉ fatiguing ○ good ○ excellent *
The approximate net payload of 2667 pounds at 16% of GVWR on this model is ○ deficient ○ excessive ○ cautionary ○ good ◉ excellent *
Total highway safety penalties are: 2 *   Value: 84   Durability: 74   Highway Control Rating: 71   Highway Safety: 69   ★★

| Sunrise | 1998 | MHA | 33 | 32WQ opch myc | FO | 6.8L | G | $1900 | 208 | 8,000 | 18,000 | 14,533 |

Livability Code: SB 30-90
Wheelbase-to-length ratio of 53% is considered ○ dangerous ◉ fatiguing ○ good ○ excellent *
The approximate net payload of 3467 pounds at 19% of GVWR on this model is ○ deficient ○ excessive ○ cautionary ○ good ◉ excellent *
Total highway safety penalties are: 2 *   Value: 84   Durability: 74   Highway Control Rating: 79   Highway Safety: 77   ★★★

| Sunrise | 1998 | MHA | 33 | DL33DQ | FO | 7.5L | G | $2000 | 216 | 8,000 | 17,000 | 14,371 |

Livability Code: SB 30-90
Wheelbase-to-length ratio of 54% is considered ○ dangerous ○ fatiguing ◉ good ○ excellent *
The approximate net payload of 2629 pounds at 15% of GVWR on this model is ○ deficient ○ excessive ○ cautionary ◉ good ○ excellent *
Total highway safety penalties are: 2 *   Value: 84   Durability: 74   Highway Control Rating: 80   Highway Safety: 78   ★★★

| Sunrise | 1998 | MHA | 33 | DL33DQ slide | FO | 7.5L | G | $2100 | 216 | 8,000 | 17,000 | 14,811 |

Livability Code: SB 30-90
Wheelbase-to-length ratio of 54% is considered ○ dangerous ○ fatiguing ◉ good ○ excellent *
The approximate net payload of 2189 pounds at 13% of GVWR on this model is ○ deficient ○ excessive ○ cautionary ◉ good ○ excellent *
Total highway safety penalties are: 5 *   Value: 82   Durability: 74   Highway Control Rating: 79   Highway Safety: 74   ★★★

| Sunrise | 1998 | MHA | 35 | 34WA myc | CH | 7.4L | G | $1900 | 228 | 4,500 | 16,500 | 14,811 |

Livability Code: SB 30-90
Wheelbase-to-length ratio of 54% is considered ○ dangerous ○ fatiguing ◉ good ○ excellent *
The approximate net payload of 1689 pounds at 10% of GVWR on this model is ○ deficient ○ excessive ○ cautionary ◉ good ○ excellent *
Total highway safety penalties are: 7 *   Value: 81   Durability: 74   Highway Control Rating: 79   Highway Safety: 72   ★★★

| Sunrise | 1998 | MHA | 35 | 34WA myc | FO | 7.5L | G | $1900 | 228 | 8,000 | 17,000 | 15,011 |

Livability Code: SB 30-90
Wheelbase-to-length ratio of 54% is considered ○ dangerous ○ fatiguing ◉ good ○ excellent *
The approximate net payload of 1989 pounds at 12% of GVWR on this model is ○ deficient ○ excessive ○ cautionary ◉ good ○ excellent *
Total highway safety penalties are: 2 *   Value: 84   Durability: 74   Highway Control Rating: 77   Highway Safety: 75   ★★★

| Sunrise | 1998 | MHA | 35 | 34WA myc | FO | 6.8L | G | $1900 | 228 | 5,500 | 20,500 | 16,411 |

Livability Code: SB 30-90
Wheelbase-to-length ratio of 54% is considered ○ dangerous ○ fatiguing ◉ good ○ excellent *
The approximate net payload of 4089 pounds at 20% of GVWR on this model is ○ deficient ○ excessive ○ cautionary ○ good ◉ excellent *
Total highway safety penalties are: 2 *   Value: 84   Durability: 74   Highway Control Rating: 89   Highway Safety: 87   ★★★

| Sunrise | 1998 | MHA | 35 | 35WP | CH | 7.4L | G | $1900 | 216 | 4,500 | 16,500 | 14,598 |

Livability Code: SB 30-90
Wheelbase-to-length ratio of 51% is considered ○ dangerous ◉ fatiguing ○ good ○ excellent *
The approximate net payload of 1902 pounds at 12% of GVWR on this model is ○ deficient ○ excessive ○ cautionary ◉ good ○ excellent *
Total highway safety penalties are: 7 *   Value: 81   Durability: 74   Highway Control Rating: 50   Highway Safety: 43

| Sunrise | 1998 | MHA | 35 | 35WP opch | FO | 7.5L | G | $1900 | 216 | 8,000 | 17,000 | 14,931 |

Livability Code: SB 30-90
Wheelbase-to-length ratio of 51% is considered ○ dangerous ◉ fatiguing ○ good ○ excellent *
The approximate net payload of 2069 pounds at 12% of GVWR on this model is ○ deficient ○ excessive ○ cautionary ◉ good ○ excellent *
Total highway safety penalties are: 2 *   Value: 84   Durability: 74   Highway Control Rating: 40   Highway Safety: 38

| Sunrise | 1998 | MHA | 35 | 35WP slide opch | FO | 7.5L | G | $2100 | 216 | 8,000 | 17,000 | 15,676 |

Livability Code: SB 30-90
Wheelbase-to-length ratio of 51% is considered ○ dangerous ◉ fatiguing ○ good ○ excellent *
The approximate net payload of 1324 pounds at 8% of GVWR on this model is ○ deficient ○ excessive ◉ cautionary ○ good ○ excellent *
Total highway safety penalties are: 7 *   Value: 81   Durability: 74   Highway Control Rating: 25   Highway Safety: 18

| Sunrise | 1998 | MHA | 35 | 35WP opch myc | FO | 6.8L | G | $1900 | 216 | 5,500 | 20,500 | 15,631 |

Livability Code: SB 30-90
Wheelbase-to-length ratio of 51% is considered ○ dangerous ◉ fatiguing ○ good ○ excellent *
The approximate net payload of 4869 pounds at 24% of GVWR on this model is ○ deficient ○ excessive ○ cautionary ○ good ◉ excellent *
Total highway safety penalties are: 2 *   Value: 84   Durability: 74   Highway Control Rating: 58   Highway Safety: 56   ★

Note: Safety ratings are based on the assumption that the engineering of the RV has allowed for proper balance by placing fresh, gray, and black holding tanks in a location so as not to change the balance of the RV when the tanks are empty or full. **Always double-check wheelbase, GVWR, and weights at front and rear axles.**

*See Section 1 for details on how conclusions are reached.

Brand	Year	Type	Length	Model	Chassis	Engine	Fuel Type	Average Price per Linear Foot When New	Adjusted Wheelbase	Approx. Towing Capacity	Gross Vehicle Weight Rating	Average Curb Weight
Sunrise	1998	MHA	35	35WP slide opch myc	FO	6.8L	G	$2000	216	5,500	20,500	16,376

Livability Code: SB 30-90

Wheelbase-to-length ratio of 51% is considered ○ dangerous ◉ fatiguing ○ good ○ excellent *

The approximate net payload of 4124 pounds at 20% of GVWR on this model is ○ deficient ○ excessive ○ cautionary ○ good ◉ excellent *

Total highway safety penalties are: 7 *   Value: **8 1**   Durability: **7 4**   Highway Control Rating: **6 2**   Highway Safety: **5 5**   ★

Brand	Year	Type	Length	Model	Chassis	Engine	Fuel Type	Avg Price/Lin Ft	Adj Wheelbase	Towing Cap	GVWR	Curb Wt
Sunrise	1999	MHA	27	26P	CH	7.4L	G	$2600	159	3,700	12,300	11,175

Livability Code: SB 30-90

Wheelbase-to-length ratio of 50% is considered ◉ dangerous ○ fatiguing ○ good ○ excellent *

The approximate net payload of 1125 pounds at 9% of GVWR on this model is ○ deficient ○ excessive ◉ cautionary ○ good ○ excellent *

Total highway safety penalties are: 3 *   Value: **8 4**   Durability: **7 5**   Highway Control Rating: **3 7**   Highway Safety: **3 4**

Brand	Year	Type	Length	Model	Chassis	Engine	Fuel Type	Avg Price/Lin Ft	Adj Wheelbase	Towing Cap	GVWR	Curb Wt
Sunrise	1999	MHA	27	26P opch	CH	7.4L	G	$2600	159	4,200	14,800	11,846

Livability Code: SB 30-90

Wheelbase-to-length ratio of 50% is considered ◉ dangerous ○ fatiguing ○ good ○ excellent *

The approximate net payload of 2954 pounds at 20% of GVWR on this model is ○ deficient ○ excessive ○ cautionary ◉ good ○ excellent *

Total highway safety penalties are: 3 *   Value: **8 4**   Durability: **7 5**   Highway Control Rating: **5 8**   Highway Safety: **5 5**

Brand	Year	Type	Length	Model	Chassis	Engine	Fuel Type	Avg Price/Lin Ft	Adj Wheelbase	Towing Cap	GVWR	Curb Wt
Sunrise	1999	MHA	30	29A	CH	7.4L	G	$2300	178	4,200	14,800	12,976

Livability Code: SB 30-90

Wheelbase-to-length ratio of 49% is considered ◉ dangerous ○ fatiguing ○ good ○ excellent *

The approximate net payload of 1824 pounds at 12% of GVWR on this model is ○ deficient ○ excessive ○ cautionary ◉ good ○ excellent *

Total highway safety penalties are: 5 *   Value: **8 3**   Durability: **7 5**   Highway Control Rating: **4 5**   Highway Safety: **4 0**

Brand	Year	Type	Length	Model	Chassis	Engine	Fuel Type	Avg Price/Lin Ft	Adj Wheelbase	Towing Cap	GVWR	Curb Wt
Sunrise	1999	MHA	30	29A	FO	6.8L	G	$2300	178	10,300	15,700	13,486

Livability Code: SB 30-90

Wheelbase-to-length ratio of 49% is considered ◉ dangerous ○ fatiguing ○ good ○ excellent *

The approximate net payload of 2215 pounds at 14% of GVWR on this model is ○ deficient ○ excessive ○ cautionary ◉ good ○ excellent *

Total highway safety penalties are: 2 *   Value: **8 4**   Durability: **7 5**   Highway Control Rating: **4 9**   Highway Safety: **4 7**

Brand	Year	Type	Length	Model	Chassis	Engine	Fuel Type	Avg Price/Lin Ft	Adj Wheelbase	Towing Cap	GVWR	Curb Wt
Sunrise	1999	MHA	31	30A	CH	7.4L	G	$2200	190	4,200	14,800	13,284

Livability Code: SB 30-90

Wheelbase-to-length ratio of 51% is considered ○ dangerous ◉ fatiguing ○ good ○ excellent *

The approximate net payload of 1516 pounds at 10% of GVWR on this model is ○ deficient ○ excessive ○ cautionary ◉ good ○ excellent *

Total highway safety penalties are: 5 *   Value: **8 3**   Durability: **7 5**   Highway Control Rating: **4 7**   Highway Safety: **4 2**

Brand	Year	Type	Length	Model	Chassis	Engine	Fuel Type	Avg Price/Lin Ft	Adj Wheelbase	Towing Cap	GVWR	Curb Wt
Sunrise	1999	MHA	31	30A	FO	6.8L	G	$2200	190	10,300	15,700	13,831

Livability Code: SB 30-90

Wheelbase-to-length ratio of 51% is considered ○ dangerous ◉ fatiguing ○ good ○ excellent *

The approximate net payload of 1869 pounds at 12% of GVWR on this model is ○ deficient ○ excessive ○ cautionary ◉ good ○ excellent *

Total highway safety penalties are: 2 *   Value: **8 4**   Durability: **7 5**   Highway Control Rating: **5 0**   Highway Safety: **4 8**

Brand	Year	Type	Length	Model	Chassis	Engine	Fuel Type	Avg Price/Lin Ft	Adj Wheelbase	Towing Cap	GVWR	Curb Wt
Sunrise	1999	MHA	31	30A opch	FO	6.8L	G	$2200	190	8,000	18,000	14,352

Livability Code: SB 30-90

Wheelbase-to-length ratio of 51% is considered ○ dangerous ◉ fatiguing ○ good ○ excellent *

The approximate net payload of 3648 pounds at 20% of GVWR on this model is ○ deficient ○ excessive ○ cautionary ○ good ◉ excellent *

Total highway safety penalties are: 2 *   Value: **8 4**   Durability: **7 5**   Highway Control Rating: **6 2**   Highway Safety: **6 0**   ★★

Brand	Year	Type	Length	Model	Chassis	Engine	Fuel Type	Avg Price/Lin Ft	Adj Wheelbase	Towing Cap	GVWR	Curb Wt
Sunrise	1999	MHA	32	31B	FO	6.8L	G	$2200	190	10,300	15,700	13,903

Livability Code: SB 30-90

Wheelbase-to-length ratio of 49% is considered ◉ dangerous ○ fatiguing ○ good ○ excellent *

The approximate net payload of 1797 pounds at 11% of GVWR on this model is ○ deficient ○ excessive ○ cautionary ◉ good ○ excellent *

Total highway safety penalties are: 2 *   Value: **8 4**   Durability: **7 5**   Highway Control Rating: **4 3**   Highway Safety: **4 1**

Brand	Year	Type	Length	Model	Chassis	Engine	Fuel Type	Avg Price/Lin Ft	Adj Wheelbase	Towing Cap	GVWR	Curb Wt
Sunrise	1999	MHA	32	31B opch	FO	6.8L	G	$2200	190	8,000	18,000	14,389

Livability Code: SB 30-90

Wheelbase-to-length ratio of 49% is considered ◉ dangerous ○ fatiguing ○ good ○ excellent *

The approximate net payload of 3611 pounds at 20% of GVWR on this model is ○ deficient ○ excessive ○ cautionary ○ good ◉ excellent *

Total highway safety penalties are: 2 *   Value: **8 4**   Durability: **7 5**   Highway Control Rating: **5 7**   Highway Safety: **5 5**

Brand	Year	Type	Length	Model	Chassis	Engine	Fuel Type	Avg Price/Lin Ft	Adj Wheelbase	Towing Cap	GVWR	Curb Wt
Sunrise	1999	MHA	33	32T	CH	7.4L	G	$2100	208	4,500	16,500	13,966

Livability Code: SB 30-90

Wheelbase-to-length ratio of 53% is considered ○ dangerous ◉ fatiguing ○ good ○ excellent *

The approximate net payload of 2534 pounds at 15% of GVWR on this model is ○ deficient ○ excessive ○ cautionary ◉ good ○ excellent *

Total highway safety penalties are: 6 *   Value: **8 2**   Durability: **7 5**   Highway Control Rating: **7 4**   Highway Safety: **6 8**   ★★

Brand	Year	Type	Length	Model	Chassis	Engine	Fuel Type	Avg Price/Lin Ft	Adj Wheelbase	Towing Cap	GVWR	Curb Wt
Sunrise	1999	MHA	33	32T	FO	6.8L	G	$2100	208	8,000	18,000	14,649

Livability Code: SB 30-90

Wheelbase-to-length ratio of 53% is considered ○ dangerous ◉ fatiguing ○ good ○ excellent *

The approximate net payload of 3351 pounds at 19% of GVWR on this model is ○ deficient ○ excessive ○ cautionary ○ good ◉ excellent *

Total highway safety penalties are: 2 *   Value: **8 4**   Durability: **7 5**   Highway Control Rating: **7 9**   Highway Safety: **7 7**   ★★★

Note: Safety ratings are based on the assumption that the engineering of the RV has allowed for proper balance by placing fresh, gray, and black holding tanks in a location so as not to change the balance of the RV when the tanks are empty or full. **Always double-check wheelbase, GVWR, and weights at front and rear axles.**

*See Section 1 for details on how conclusions are reached.

Brand	Year	Type	Length	Model	Chassis	Engine	Fuel Type	Average Price per Linear Foot When New	Adjusted Wheelbase	Approx. Towing Capacity	Gross Vehicle Weight Rating	Average Curb Weight

Sunrise   1999   MHA   35   35C   CH   7.4L   G $2000   220   4,500   16,500   14,696
Livability Code: SB 30-90   Wheelbase-to-length ratio of 52% is considered ○ dangerous ● fatiguing ○ good ○ excellent *
The approximate net payload of 1804 pounds at 11% of GVWR on this model is ○ deficient ○ excessive ○ cautionary ● good ○ excellent *
Total highway safety penalties are: 7 *   Value: 81   Durability: 75   Highway Control Rating: 57   Highway Safety: 50   ★

Sunrise   1999   MHA   35   35C slide   CH   7.4L   G $2000   220   4,500   16,500   15,546
Livability Code: SB 30-90   Wheelbase-to-length ratio of 52% is considered ○ dangerous ● fatiguing ○ good ○ excellent *
The approximate net payload of 954 pounds at 6% of GVWR on this model is ● deficient ○ excessive ○ cautionary ○ good ○ excellent *
Total highway safety penalties are: 13 *   Value: 79   Durability: 75   Highway Control Rating: 31   Highway Safety: 18

Sunrise   1999   MHA   35   35C   FO   6.8L   G $2000   228   5,500   20,500   15,939
Livability Code: SB 30-90   Wheelbase-to-length ratio of 54% is considered ○ dangerous ○ fatiguing ● good ○ excellent *
The approximate net payload of 4561 pounds at 22% of GVWR on this model is ○ deficient ○ excessive ○ cautionary ○ good ● excellent *
Total highway safety penalties are: 2 *   Value: 84   Durability: 75   Highway Control Rating: 85   Highway Safety: 83   ★★★

Sunrise   1999   MHA   35   35C slide   FO   6.8L   G $2000   228   5,500   20,500   16,789
Livability Code: SB 30-90   Wheelbase-to-length ratio of 54% is considered ○ dangerous ○ fatiguing ● good ○ excellent *
The approximate net payload of 3711 pounds at 18% of GVWR on this model is ○ deficient ○ excessive ○ cautionary ○ good ● excellent *
Total highway safety penalties are: 7 *   Value: 81   Durability: 75   Highway Control Rating: 85   Highway Safety: 78   ★★★

Swinger   1992   MHA   28   Bus 2708   CH   7.4L   G $1700   178   1,500   12,300   11,350
Livability Code: SB 30-90   Wheelbase-to-length ratio of 53% is considered ○ dangerous ● fatiguing ○ good ○ excellent *
The approximate net payload of 950 pounds at 8% of GVWR on this model is ○ deficient ○ excessive ● cautionary ○ good ○ excellent *
Total highway safety penalties are: 4 *   Value: 78   Durability: 75   Highway Control Rating: 47   Highway Safety: 43

Swinger   1992   MHA   30   Bus 2995   CH   7.4L   G $1700   190   2,200   14,800   12,625
Livability Code: SB 30-90   Wheelbase-to-length ratio of 53% is considered ○ dangerous ● fatiguing ○ good ○ excellent *
The approximate net payload of 2175 pounds at 15% of GVWR on this model is ○ deficient ○ excessive ○ cautionary ● good ○ excellent *
Total highway safety penalties are: 5 *   Value: 78   Durability: 75   Highway Control Rating: 67   Highway Safety: 62   ★★

Swinger   1992   MHA   32   Bus 3190   CH   7.4L   G $1600   218   2,200   14,800   13,005
Livability Code: SB 30-90   Wheelbase-to-length ratio of 57% is considered ○ dangerous ○ fatiguing ● good ○ excellent *
The approximate net payload of 1795 pounds at 12% of GVWR on this model is ○ deficient ○ excessive ○ cautionary ● good ○ excellent *
Total highway safety penalties are: 5 *   Value: 77   Durability: 75   Highway Control Rating: 94   Highway Safety: 89   ★★★

Swinger   1993   MHA   28   Bus 2708   CH   7.4L   G $1700   178   1,500   12,300   11,350
Livability Code: SB 30-90   Wheelbase-to-length ratio of 53% is considered ○ dangerous ● fatiguing ○ good ○ excellent *
The approximate net payload of 950 pounds at 8% of GVWR on this model is ○ deficient ○ excessive ● cautionary ○ good ○ excellent *
Total highway safety penalties are: 4 *   Value: 78   Durability: 75   Highway Control Rating: 47   Highway Safety: 43

Swinger   1993   MHA   30   Bus 2995   CH   7.4L   G $1500   190   2,200   14,800   12,625
Livability Code: SB 30-90   Wheelbase-to-length ratio of 53% is considered ○ dangerous ● fatiguing ○ good ○ excellent *
The approximate net payload of 2175 pounds at 15% of GVWR on this model is ○ deficient ○ excessive ○ cautionary ● good ○ excellent *
Total highway safety penalties are: 5 *   Value: 78   Durability: 75   Highway Control Rating: 67   Highway Safety: 62   ★★

Swinger   1993   MHA   30   Bus 2995   FO   7.5L   G $1500   190   3,800   15,200   13,025
Livability Code: SB 30-90   Wheelbase-to-length ratio of 53% is considered ○ dangerous ● fatiguing ○ good ○ excellent *
The approximate net payload of 2175 pounds at 14% of GVWR on this model is ○ deficient ○ excessive ○ cautionary ● good ○ excellent *
Total highway safety penalties are: 2 *   Value: 79   Durability: 75   Highway Control Rating: 66   Highway Safety: 64   ★★

Swinger   1993   MHA   32   Bus 3190   CH   7.4L   G $1500   218   2,200   14,800   13,005
Livability Code: SB 30-90   Wheelbase-to-length ratio of 57% is considered ○ dangerous ○ fatiguing ● good ○ excellent *
The approximate net payload of 1795 pounds at 12% of GVWR on this model is ○ deficient ○ excessive ○ cautionary ● good ○ excellent *
Total highway safety penalties are: 5 *   Value: 77   Durability: 75   Highway Control Rating: 94   Highway Safety: 89   ★★★

Swinger   1993   MHA   32   Bus 3190   FO   7.5L   G $1500   218   3,800   15,200   13,405
Livability Code: SB 30-90   Wheelbase-to-length ratio of 57% is considered ○ dangerous ○ fatiguing ● good ○ excellent *
The approximate net payload of 1795 pounds at 12% of GVWR on this model is ○ deficient ○ excessive ○ cautionary ● good ○ excellent *
Total highway safety penalties are: 2 *   Value: 79   Durability: 75   Highway Control Rating: 93   Highway Safety: 91   ★★★

Note: Safety ratings are based on the assumption that the engineering of the RV has allowed for proper balance by placing fresh, gray, and black holding tanks in a location so as not to change the balance of the RV when the tanks are empty or full. **Always double-check wheelbase, GVWR, and weights at front and rear axles.**

The RV Rating Book

*See Section 1 for details on how conclusions are reached.

Section 2: The Ratings

Brand	Year	Type	Length	Model	Chassis	Engine	Fuel Type	Average Price per Linear Foot When New	Adjusted Wheelbase	Approx. Towing Capacity	Gross Vehicle Weight Rating	Average Curb Weight

Swinger — 1994 — MHA — 26 — Custom 2701 — CH — 7.4L — G — $1500 — 158 — 1,500 — 12,300 — 10,923
Livability Code: SB 30-90
Wheelbase-to-length ratio of 50% is considered ⦿ dangerous ◯ fatiguing ◯ good ◯ excellent *
The approximate net payload of 1378 pounds at 11% of GVWR on this model is ◯ deficient ◯ excessive ◯ cautionary ⦿ good ◯ excellent *
Total highway safety penalties are: 3 * Value: **7 9** Durability: **7 5** Highway Control Rating: **3 6** Highway Safety: **3 3**

Swinger — 1994 — MHA — 28 — 2708 — CH — 7.4L — G — $1600 — 178 — 2,200 — 14,800 — 12,150
Livability Code: SB 30-90
Wheelbase-to-length ratio of 53% is considered ◯ dangerous ⦿ fatiguing ◯ good ◯ excellent *
The approximate net payload of 2650 pounds at 18% of GVWR on this model is ◯ deficient ◯ excessive ◯ cautionary ◯ good ⦿ excellent *
Total highway safety penalties are: 4 * Value: **7 8** Durability: **7 5** Highway Control Rating: **7 2** Highway Safety: **6 8** ★★

Swinger — 1994 — MHA — 29 — Custom 2900 — CH — 7.4L — G — $1400 — 190 — 2,200 — 14,800 — 12,388
Livability Code: SB 30-90
Wheelbase-to-length ratio of 55% is considered ◯ dangerous ◯ fatiguing ⦿ good ◯ excellent *
The approximate net payload of 2413 pounds at 16% of GVWR on this model is ◯ deficient ◯ excessive ◯ cautionary ◯ good ⦿ excellent *
Total highway safety penalties are: 4 * Value: **7 8** Durability: **7 5** Highway Control Rating: **9 1** Highway Safety: **8 7** ★★★

Swinger — 1994 — MHA — 30 — 2995 — FO — 7.5L — G — $1600 — 190 — 3,800 — 15,200 — 12,930
Livability Code: SB 30-90
Wheelbase-to-length ratio of 53% is considered ◯ dangerous ⦿ fatiguing ◯ good ◯ excellent *
The approximate net payload of 2270 pounds at 15% of GVWR on this model is ◯ deficient ◯ excessive ◯ cautionary ⦿ good ◯ excellent *
Total highway safety penalties are: 2 * Value: **7 9** Durability: **7 5** Highway Control Rating: **7 0** Highway Safety: **6 8** ★★

Swinger — 1994 — MHA — 30 — 2995 — CH — 7.4L — G — $1600 — 190 — 2,200 — 14,800 — 12,625
Livability Code: SB 30-90
Wheelbase-to-length ratio of 53% is considered ◯ dangerous ⦿ fatiguing ◯ good ◯ excellent *
The approximate net payload of 2175 pounds at 15% of GVWR on this model is ◯ deficient ◯ excessive ◯ cautionary ◯ good ◯ excellent *
Total highway safety penalties are: 5 * Value: **7 8** Durability: **7 5** Highway Control Rating: **6 7** Highway Safety: **6 2** ★★

Swinger — 1994 — MHA — 31 — 3190 — FO — 7.5L — G — $1600 — 218 — 8,000 — 17,000 — 13,463
Livability Code: SB 30-90
Wheelbase-to-length ratio of 59% is considered ◯ dangerous ◯ fatiguing ◯ good ⦿ excellent *
The approximate net payload of 3538 pounds at 21% of GVWR on this model is ◯ deficient ◯ excessive ◯ cautionary ◯ good ⦿ excellent *
Total highway safety penalties are: 2 * Value: **7 9** Durability: **7 5** Highway Control Rating: **1 0 0** Highway Safety: **9 8** ★★★

Swinger — 1994 — MHA — 32 — Custom 3200 — CH — 7.4L — G — $1300 — 208 — 2,200 — 14,800 — 13,053
Livability Code: SB 30-90
Wheelbase-to-length ratio of 55% is considered ◯ dangerous ◯ fatiguing ⦿ good ◯ excellent *
The approximate net payload of 1748 pounds at 12% of GVWR on this model is ◯ deficient ◯ excessive ◯ cautionary ◯ good ◯ excellent *
Total highway safety penalties are: 5 * Value: **7 7** Durability: **7 5** Highway Control Rating: **8 7** Highway Safety: **8 2** ★★★

Swinger — 1994 — MHA — 32 — Custom 3200 — FO — 7.5L — G — $1400 — 208 — 3,800 — 15,200 — 13,453
Livability Code: SB 30-90
Wheelbase-to-length ratio of 55% is considered ◯ dangerous ◯ fatiguing ⦿ good ◯ excellent *
The approximate net payload of 1748 pounds at 11% of GVWR on this model is ◯ deficient ◯ excessive ◯ cautionary ⦿ good ◯ excellent *
Total highway safety penalties are: 2 * Value: **7 9** Durability: **7 5** Highway Control Rating: **8 6** Highway Safety: **8 4** ★★★

Swinger — 1994 — MHA — 32 — 3190 — CH — 7.4L — G — $1500 — 218 — 2,200 — 14,800 — 13,100
Livability Code: SB 30-90
Wheelbase-to-length ratio of 57% is considered ◯ dangerous ◯ fatiguing ⦿ good ◯ excellent *
The approximate net payload of 1700 pounds at 11% of GVWR on this model is ◯ deficient ◯ excessive ◯ cautionary ⦿ good ◯ excellent *
Total highway safety penalties are: 6 * Value: **7 7** Durability: **7 5** Highway Control Rating: **8 9** Highway Safety: **8 3** ★★★

Swinger — 1994 — MHA — 34 — 3406 — FO — 7.5L — G — $1500 — 228 — 8,000 — 17,000 — 14,080
Livability Code: SB 30-90
Wheelbase-to-length ratio of 57% is considered ◯ dangerous ◯ fatiguing ⦿ good ◯ excellent *
The approximate net payload of 2920 pounds at 17% of GVWR on this model is ◯ deficient ◯ excessive ◯ cautionary ◯ good ⦿ excellent *
Total highway safety penalties are: 2 * Value: **7 9** Durability: **7 5** Highway Control Rating: **9 9** Highway Safety: **9 7** ★★★

Swinger — 1994 — MHA — 34 — 3406 — CH — 7.4L — G — $1500 — 228 — 2,200 — 14,800 — 13,551
Livability Code: SB 30-90
Wheelbase-to-length ratio of 56% is considered ◯ dangerous ◯ fatiguing ⦿ good ◯ excellent *
The approximate net payload of 1249 pounds at 8% of GVWR on this model is ◯ deficient ◯ excessive ⦿ cautionary ◯ good ◯ excellent *
Total highway safety penalties are: 6 * Value: **7 7** Durability: **7 5** Highway Control Rating: **7 4** Highway Safety: **6 8** ★★

Swinger — 1994 — MHA — 34 — 3410 — FO — 7.5L — G — $1500 — 228 — 8,000 — 17,000 — 14,175
Livability Code: SB 30-90
Wheelbase-to-length ratio of 56% is considered ◯ dangerous ◯ fatiguing ⦿ good ◯ excellent *
The approximate net payload of 2825 pounds at 17% of GVWR on this model is ◯ deficient ◯ excessive ◯ cautionary ◯ good ⦿ excellent *
Total highway safety penalties are: 2 * Value: **7 9** Durability: **7 5** Highway Control Rating: **9 6** Highway Safety: **9 4** ★★★

Note: Safety ratings are based on the assumption that the engineering of the RV has allowed for proper balance by placing fresh, gray, and black holding tanks in a location so as not to change the balance of the RV when the tanks are empty or full. **Always double-check wheelbase, GVWR, and weights at front and rear axles.**

*See Section 1 for details on how conclusions are reached.

Brand	Year	Type	Length	Model	Chassis	Engine	Fuel Type	Average Price per Linear Foot When New	Adjusted Wheelbase	Approx. Towing Capacity	Gross Vehicle Weight Rating	Average Curb Weight
Swinger	1994	MHA	35	3410	CH	7.4L	G	$1400	228	2,200	14,800	13,718

Livability Code: SB 30-90
Wheelbase-to-length ratio of 55% is considered ○ dangerous ○ fatiguing ● good ○ excellent *
The approximate net payload of 1083 pounds at 7% of GVWR on this model is ○ deficient ○ excessive ● cautionary ○ good ○ excellent *
Total highway safety penalties are: 7 *   Value: 77   Durability: 75   Highway Control Rating: 64   Highway Safety: 57   ★

Brand	Year	Type	Length	Model	Chassis	Engine	Fuel Type	Price/ft	Wheelbase	Towing	GVWR	Curb Weight
Swinger	1995	MHA	28	2708	CH	7.4L	G	$2000	178	4,200	14,800	11,992

Livability Code: SB 30-90
Wheelbase-to-length ratio of 53% is considered ○ dangerous ● fatiguing ○ good ○ excellent *
The approximate net payload of 2809 pounds at 19% of GVWR on this model is ○ deficient ○ excessive ○ cautionary ○ good ● excellent *
Total highway safety penalties are: 4 *   Value: 78   Durability: 75   Highway Control Rating: 73   Highway Safety: 69   ★★

Swinger	1995	MHA	28	2708	FO	7.5L	G	$2000	178	3,800	15,200	12,550

Livability Code: SB 30-90
Wheelbase-to-length ratio of 53% is considered ○ dangerous ● fatiguing ○ good ○ excellent *
The approximate net payload of 2650 pounds at 17% of GVWR on this model is ○ deficient ○ excessive ○ cautionary ○ good ● excellent *
Total highway safety penalties are: 2 *   Value: 79   Durability: 75   Highway Control Rating: 72   Highway Safety: 70   ★★★

Swinger	1995	MHA	30	2995	CH	7.4L	G	$1900	190	4,200	14,800	12,605

Livability Code: SB 30-90
Wheelbase-to-length ratio of 53% is considered ○ dangerous ● fatiguing ○ good ○ excellent *
The approximate net payload of 2195 pounds at 15% of GVWR on this model is ○ deficient ○ excessive ○ cautionary ● good ○ excellent *
Total highway safety penalties are: 5 *   Value: 78   Durability: 75   Highway Control Rating: 67   Highway Safety: 62   ★★

Swinger	1995	MHA	30	2995	FO	7.5L	G	$1900	190	3,800	15,200	13,025

Livability Code: SB 30-90
Wheelbase-to-length ratio of 53% is considered ○ dangerous ● fatiguing ○ good ○ excellent *
The approximate net payload of 2175 pounds at 14% of GVWR on this model is ○ deficient ○ excessive ○ cautionary ● good ○ excellent *
Total highway safety penalties are: 2 *   Value: 79   Durability: 75   Highway Control Rating: 66   Highway Safety: 64   ★★

Swinger	1995	MHA	32	3190	CH	7.4L	G	$1800	218	4,200	14,800	13,125

Livability Code: SB 30-90
Wheelbase-to-length ratio of 57% is considered ○ dangerous ○ fatiguing ● good ○ excellent *
The approximate net payload of 1676 pounds at 11% of GVWR on this model is ○ deficient ○ excessive ○ cautionary ● good ○ excellent *
Total highway safety penalties are: 6 *   Value: 77   Durability: 75   Highway Control Rating: 89   Highway Safety: 83   ★★★

Swinger	1995	MHA	32	3190	FO	7.5L	G	$1900	218	8,000	17,000	13,700

Livability Code: SB 30-90
Wheelbase-to-length ratio of 57% is considered ○ dangerous ○ fatiguing ● good ○ excellent *
The approximate net payload of 3300 pounds at 19% of GVWR on this model is ○ deficient ○ excessive ○ cautionary ○ good ● excellent *
Total highway safety penalties are: 2 *   Value: 79   Durability: 75   Highway Control Rating: 100   Highway Safety: 98   ★★★

Swinger	1995	MHA	33	3295	CH	7.4L	G	$1800	218	4,200	14,800	13,198

Livability Code: SB 30-90
Wheelbase-to-length ratio of 56% is considered ○ dangerous ○ fatiguing ● good ○ excellent *
The approximate net payload of 1602 pounds at 11% of GVWR on this model is ○ deficient ○ excessive ○ cautionary ● good ○ excellent *
Total highway safety penalties are: 6 *   Value: 77   Durability: 75   Highway Control Rating: 85   Highway Safety: 79   ★★★

Swinger	1995	MHA	33	3295	FO	7.5L	G	$1800	218	8,000	17,000	13,843

Livability Code: SB 30-90
Wheelbase-to-length ratio of 56% is considered ○ dangerous ○ fatiguing ● good ○ excellent *
The approximate net payload of 3158 pounds at 19% of GVWR on this model is ○ deficient ○ excessive ○ cautionary ○ good ● excellent *
Total highway safety penalties are: 2 *   Value: 79   Durability: 75   Highway Control Rating: 98   Highway Safety: 96   ★★★

Swinger	1995	MHA	35	3411	CH	7.4L	G	$1700	228	3,000	16,000	13,620

Livability Code: SB 30-90
Wheelbase-to-length ratio of 55% is considered ○ dangerous ○ fatiguing ● good ○ excellent *
The approximate net payload of 2380 pounds at 15% of GVWR on this model is ○ deficient ○ excessive ○ cautionary ○ good ● excellent *
Total highway safety penalties are: 7 *   Value: 77   Durability: 75   Highway Control Rating: 90   Highway Safety: 83   ★★★

Swinger	1995	MHA	35	3412	CH	7.4L	G	$1700	228	3,000	16,000	13,685

Livability Code: SB 30-90
Wheelbase-to-length ratio of 55% is considered ○ dangerous ○ fatiguing ● good ○ excellent *
The approximate net payload of 2315 pounds at 14% of GVWR on this model is ○ deficient ○ excessive ○ cautionary ● good ○ excellent *
Total highway safety penalties are: 7 *   Value: 77   Durability: 75   Highway Control Rating: 89   Highway Safety: 82   ★★★

Swinger	1995	MHA	35	3411	FO	7.5L	G	$1700	228	8,000	17,000	14,318

Livability Code: SB 30-90
Wheelbase-to-length ratio of 55% is considered ○ dangerous ○ fatiguing ● good ○ excellent *
The approximate net payload of 2683 pounds at 16% of GVWR on this model is ○ deficient ○ excessive ○ cautionary ○ good ● excellent *
Total highway safety penalties are: 2 *   Value: 79   Durability: 75   Highway Control Rating: 92   Highway Safety: 90   ★★★

Note: Safety ratings are based on the assumption that the engineering of the RV has allowed for proper balance by placing fresh, gray, and black holding tanks in a location so as not to change the balance of the RV when the tanks are empty or full. **Always double-check wheelbase, GVWR, and weights at front and rear axles.**

*See Section 1 for details on how conclusions are reached.

Brand	Year	Type	Length	Model	Chassis	Engine	Fuel Type	Average Price per Linear Foot When New	Adjusted Wheel-base	Approx. Towing Capacity	Gross Vehicle Weight Rating	Average Curb Weight
Swinger	**1995**	MHA	35	3412	FO	7.5L	G	$1700	228	8,000	17,000	14,318

Livability Code: SB 30-90
Wheelbase-to-length ratio of 55% is considered ○ dangerous ○ fatiguing ◉ good ○ excellent *
The approximate net payload of 2683 pounds at 16% of GVWR on this model is ○ deficient ○ excessive ○ cautionary ○ good ◉ excellent *
Total highway safety penalties are: 2 * Value: **7 9** Durability: **7 5** Highway Control Rating: **9 2** Highway Safety: **9 0** ★★★

| **Swinger** | **1995** | MHA | 35 | 3595 | CH | 7.4L | G | $1700 | 228 | 3,000 | 16,000 | 13,815 |

Livability Code: SB 30-90
Wheelbase-to-length ratio of 54% is considered ○ dangerous ○ fatiguing ◉ good ○ excellent *
The approximate net payload of 2185 pounds at 14% of GVWR on this model is ○ deficient ○ excessive ○ cautionary ◉ good ○ excellent *
Total highway safety penalties are: 7 * Value: **7 6** Durability: **7 5** Highway Control Rating: **7 8** Highway Safety: **7 1** ★★★

| **Swinger** | **1995** | MHA | 35 | 3595 | FO | 7.5L | G | $1700 | 228 | 8,000 | 17,000 | 14,508 |

Livability Code: SB 30-90
Wheelbase-to-length ratio of 54% is considered ○ dangerous ○ fatiguing ◉ good ○ excellent *
The approximate net payload of 2493 pounds at 15% of GVWR on this model is ○ deficient ○ excessive ○ cautionary ◉ good ○ excellent *
Total highway safety penalties are: 2 * Value: **7 9** Durability: **7 5** Highway Control Rating: **7 8** Highway Safety: **7 6** ★★★

| **Swinger** | **1996** | MHA | 25 | Custom 2501 | CH | 7.4L | G | $2000 | 158 | 1,500 | 12,300 | 10,750 |

Livability Code: SB 30-90
Wheelbase-to-length ratio of 53% is considered ○ dangerous ◉ fatiguing ○ good ○ excellent *
The approximate net payload of 1550 pounds at 13% of GVWR on this model is ○ deficient ○ excessive ○ cautionary ○ good ◉ excellent *
Total highway safety penalties are: 2 * Value: **7 9** Durability: **7 5** Highway Control Rating: **6 3** Highway Safety: **6 1** ★★

| **Swinger** | **1996** | MHA | 28 | Custom 2808 | CH | 7.4L | G | $2100 | 178 | 2,200 | 14,800 | 11,821 |

Livability Code: SB 30-90
Wheelbase-to-length ratio of 53% is considered ○ dangerous ◉ fatiguing ○ good ○ excellent *
The approximate net payload of 2979 pounds at 20% of GVWR on this model is ○ deficient ○ excessive ○ cautionary ○ good ◉ excellent *
Total highway safety penalties are: 4 * Value: **7 8** Durability: **7 5** Highway Control Rating: **7 4** Highway Safety: **7 0** ★★★

| **Swinger** | **1996** | MHA | 28 | Custom 2808 | FO | 7.5L | G | $2100 | 178 | 3,800 | 15,200 | 12,550 |

Livability Code: SB 30-90
Wheelbase-to-length ratio of 53% is considered ○ dangerous ◉ fatiguing ○ good ○ excellent *
The approximate net payload of 2650 pounds at 17% of GVWR on this model is ○ deficient ○ excessive ○ cautionary ○ good ◉ excellent *
Total highway safety penalties are: 2 * Value: **7 9** Durability: **7 5** Highway Control Rating: **7 2** Highway Safety: **7 0** ★★★

| **Swinger** | **1996** | MHA | 29 | Custom 2901 | CH | 7.4L | G | $1900 | 190 | 2,200 | 14,800 | 12,213 |

Livability Code: SB 30-90
Wheelbase-to-length ratio of 55% is considered ○ dangerous ○ fatiguing ◉ good ○ excellent *
The approximate net payload of 2587 pounds at 17% of GVWR on this model is ○ deficient ○ excessive ○ cautionary ○ good ◉ excellent *
Total highway safety penalties are: 4 * Value: **7 8** Durability: **7 5** Highway Control Rating: **9 3** Highway Safety: **8 9** ★★★

| **Swinger** | **1996** | MHA | 29 | Custom 2901 | FO | 7.5L | G | $1900 | 190 | 3,800 | 15,200 | 12,788 |

Livability Code: SB 30-90
Wheelbase-to-length ratio of 55% is considered ○ dangerous ○ fatiguing ◉ good ○ excellent *
The approximate net payload of 2413 pounds at 16% of GVWR on this model is ○ deficient ○ excessive ○ cautionary ○ good ◉ excellent *
Total highway safety penalties are: 2 * Value: **7 9** Durability: **7 5** Highway Control Rating: **9 1** Highway Safety: **8 9** ★★★

| **Swinger** | **1996** | MHA | 30 | 2808 | CH | 7.4L | G | $1900 | 178 | 2,200 | 14,800 | 12,662 |

Livability Code: SB 30-90
Wheelbase-to-length ratio of 50% is considered ◉ dangerous ○ fatiguing ○ good ○ excellent *
The approximate net payload of 2139 pounds at 14% of GVWR on this model is ○ deficient ○ excessive ○ cautionary ◉ good ○ excellent *
Total highway safety penalties are: 4 * Value: **7 8** Durability: **7 5** Highway Control Rating: **4 1** Highway Safety: **3 7**

| **Swinger** | **1996** | MHA | 30 | 2808 slide | CH | 7.4L | G | $1900 | 178 | 500 | 16,500 | 13,278 |

Livability Code: SB 30-90
Wheelbase-to-length ratio of 50% is considered ◉ dangerous ○ fatiguing ○ good ○ excellent *
The approximate net payload of 3222 pounds at 20% of GVWR on this model is ○ deficient ○ excessive ○ cautionary ○ good ◉ excellent *
Total highway safety penalties are: 7 * Value: **7 6** Durability: **7 5** Highway Control Rating: **4 8** Highway Safety: **4 1**

| **Swinger** | **1996** | MHA | 30 | 2808 | FO | 7.5L | G | $1900 | 178 | 3,800 | 15,200 | 13,028 |

Livability Code: SB 30-90
Wheelbase-to-length ratio of 50% is considered ◉ dangerous ○ fatiguing ○ good ○ excellent *
The approximate net payload of 2172 pounds at 14% of GVWR on this model is ○ deficient ○ excessive ○ cautionary ◉ good ○ excellent *
Total highway safety penalties are: 2 * Value: **7 9** Durability: **7 5** Highway Control Rating: **4 1** Highway Safety: **3 9**

| **Swinger** | **1996** | MHA | 30 | 2808 slide | FO | 7.5L | G | $1900 | 178 | 8,000 | 17,000 | 13,678 |

Livability Code: SB 30-90
Wheelbase-to-length ratio of 50% is considered ◉ dangerous ○ fatiguing ○ good ○ excellent *
The approximate net payload of 3322 pounds at 20% of GVWR on this model is ○ deficient ○ excessive ○ cautionary ○ good ◉ excellent *
Total highway safety penalties are: 5 * Value: **7 8** Durability: **7 5** Highway Control Rating: **4 8** Highway Safety: **4 3**

Note: Safety ratings are based on the assumption that the engineering of the RV has allowed for proper balance by placing fresh, gray, and black holding tanks in a location so as not to change the balance of the RV when the tanks are empty or full. **Always double-check wheelbase, GVWR, and weights at front and rear axles.**

*See Section 1 for details on how conclusions are reached.

Brand	Year	Type	Length	Model	Chassis	Engine	Fuel Type	Average Price per Linear Foot When New	Adjusted Wheelbase	Approx. Towing Capacity	Gross Vehicle Weight Rating	Average Curb Weight
Swinger	1996	MHA	32	2995	CH	7.4L	G	$1800	190	2,200	14,800	12,999

Livability Code: SB 30-90
Wheelbase-to-length ratio of 50% is considered ⦿ dangerous ○ fatiguing ○ good ○ excellent *
The approximate net payload of 1801 pounds at 12% of GVWR on this model is ○ deficient ○ excessive ○ cautionary ⦿ good ○ excellent *
Total highway safety penalties are: 5 *   Value: 7 7   Durability: 7 5   Highway Control Rating: 3 7   Highway Safety: 3 2

Swinger	1996	MHA	32	2995 slide	CH	7.4L	G	$1800	190	500	16,500	13,758

Livability Code: SB 30-90
Wheelbase-to-length ratio of 50% is considered ⦿ dangerous ○ fatiguing ○ good ○ excellent *
The approximate net payload of 2742 pounds at 17% of GVWR on this model is ○ deficient ○ excessive ○ cautionary ○ good ⦿ excellent *
Total highway safety penalties are: 8 *   Value: 7 6   Durability: 7 5   Highway Control Rating: 4 5   Highway Safety: 3 7

Swinger	1996	MHA	32	2995	FO	7.5L	G	$1800	190	3,800	15,200	13,508

Livability Code: SB 30-90
Wheelbase-to-length ratio of 50% is considered ⦿ dangerous ○ fatiguing ○ good ○ excellent *
The approximate net payload of 1692 pounds at 11% of GVWR on this model is ○ deficient ○ excessive ○ cautionary ⦿ good ○ excellent *
Total highway safety penalties are: 2 *   Value: 7 9   Durability: 7 5   Highway Control Rating: 3 5   Highway Safety: 3 3

Swinger	1996	MHA	32	2995 slide	FO	7.5L	G	$1800	190	8,000	17,000	14,158

Livability Code: SB 30-90
Wheelbase-to-length ratio of 50% is considered ⦿ dangerous ○ fatiguing ○ good ○ excellent *
The approximate net payload of 2842 pounds at 17% of GVWR on this model is ○ deficient ○ excessive ○ cautionary ○ good ⦿ excellent *
Total highway safety penalties are: 5 *   Value: 7 8   Durability: 7 5   Highway Control Rating: 4 5   Highway Safety: 4 0

Swinger	1996	MHA	32	Custom 3200	CH	7.4L	G	$1800	208	2,200	14,800	12,920

Livability Code: SB 30-90
Wheelbase-to-length ratio of 55% is considered ○ dangerous ○ fatiguing ⦿ good ○ excellent *
The approximate net payload of 1880 pounds at 13% of GVWR on this model is ○ deficient ○ excessive ○ cautionary ⦿ good ○ excellent *
Total highway safety penalties are: 5 *   Value: 7 7   Durability: 7 5   Highway Control Rating: 8 5   Highway Safety: 8 0   ★★★

Swinger	1996	MHA	32	Custom 3200	FO	7.5L	G	$1800	208	3,800	15,200	13,453

Livability Code: SB 30-90
Wheelbase-to-length ratio of 55% is considered ○ dangerous ○ fatiguing ⦿ good ○ excellent *
The approximate net payload of 1748 pounds at 11% of GVWR on this model is ○ deficient ○ excessive ○ cautionary ⦿ good ○ excellent *
Total highway safety penalties are: 2 *   Value: 7 9   Durability: 7 5   Highway Control Rating: 8 6   Highway Safety: 8 4   ★★★

Swinger	1996	MHA	34	3190	CH	7.4L	G	$1700	212	2,200	14,800	13,564

Livability Code: SB 30-90
Wheelbase-to-length ratio of 52% is considered ○ dangerous ⦿ fatiguing ○ good ○ excellent *
The approximate net payload of 1236 pounds at 8% of GVWR on this model is ○ deficient ○ excessive ⦿ cautionary ○ good ○ excellent *
Total highway safety penalties are: 6 *   Value: 7 7   Durability: 7 5   Highway Control Rating: 3 8   Highway Safety: 3 2

Swinger	1996	MHA	34	3190 slide	CH	7.4L	G	$1800	212	500	16,500	14,238

Livability Code: SB 30-90
Wheelbase-to-length ratio of 52% is considered ○ dangerous ⦿ fatiguing ○ good ○ excellent *
The approximate net payload of 2262 pounds at 14% of GVWR on this model is ○ deficient ○ excessive ○ cautionary ⦿ good ○ excellent *
Total highway safety penalties are: 9 *   Value: 7 5   Durability: 7 5   Highway Control Rating: 5 7   Highway Safety: 4 8

Swinger	1996	MHA	34	3190	FO	7.5L	G	$1700	212	8,000	17,000	14,188

Livability Code: SB 30-90
Wheelbase-to-length ratio of 52% is considered ○ dangerous ⦿ fatiguing ○ good ○ excellent *
The approximate net payload of 2812 pounds at 17% of GVWR on this model is ○ deficient ○ excessive ○ cautionary ○ good ⦿ excellent *
Total highway safety penalties are: 2 *   Value: 7 9   Durability: 7 5   Highway Control Rating: 6 1   Highway Safety: 5 9   ★

Swinger	1996	MHA	34	3190 slide	FO	7.5L	G	$1800	212	8,000	17,000	14,638

Livability Code: SB 30-90
Wheelbase-to-length ratio of 52% is considered ○ dangerous ⦿ fatiguing ○ good ○ excellent *
The approximate net payload of 2362 pounds at 14% of GVWR on this model is ○ deficient ○ excessive ○ cautionary ⦿ good ○ excellent *
Total highway safety penalties are: 5 *   Value: 7 8   Durability: 7 5   Highway Control Rating: 5 7   Highway Safety: 5 2   ★

Swinger	1996	MHA	34	3190	SP	CU210	D	$4500	190	1,500	18,000	14,588

Livability Code: SB 30-90
Wheelbase-to-length ratio of 47% is considered ⦿ dangerous ○ fatiguing ○ good ○ excellent *
The approximate net payload of 3412 pounds at 19% of GVWR on this model is ○ deficient ○ excessive ○ cautionary ○ good ⦿ excellent *
Total highway safety penalties are: 2 *   Value: 7 9   Durability: 7 5   Highway Control Rating: 3 7   Highway Safety: 3 5

Swinger	1996	MHA	34	3190 slide	SP	CU210	D	$2700	190	1,500 e	18,000	15,038

Livability Code: SB 30-90
Wheelbase-to-length ratio of 47% is considered ⦿ dangerous ○ fatiguing ○ good ○ excellent *
The approximate net payload of 2962 pounds at 16% of GVWR on this model is ○ deficient ○ excessive ○ cautionary ○ good ⦿ excellent *
Total highway safety penalties are: 5 *   Value: 7 8   Durability: 7 5   Highway Control Rating: 3 4   Highway Safety: 2 9

Note: Safety ratings are based on the assumption that the engineering of the RV has allowed for proper balance by placing fresh, gray, and black holding tanks in a location so as not to change the balance of the RV when the tanks are empty or full. **Always double-check wheelbase, GVWR, and weights at front and rear axles.**

Section 2: The Ratings

Brand	Year	Type	Length	Model	Chassis	Engine	Fuel Type	Average Price per Linear Foot When New	Adjusted Wheelbase	Approx. Towing Capacity	Gross Vehicle Weight Rating	Average Curb Weight
Swinger	1996	MHA	35	3412	CH	7.4L	G	$1700	220	1,500	16,500	14,241

Livability Code: SB 30-90
Wheelbase-to-length ratio of 52% is considered ○ dangerous ● fatiguing ○ good ○ excellent *
The approximate net payload of 2259 pounds at 14% of GVWR on this model is ○ deficient ○ excessive ○ cautionary ● good ○ excellent *
Total highway safety penalties are: 7 *   Value: 7 6   Durability: 7 5   Highway Control Rating: 5 5   Highway Safety: 4 8

Brand	Year	Type	Length	Model	Chassis	Engine	Fuel Type	Price/Ft	Wheelbase	Towing	GVWR	Curb Wt
Swinger	1996	MHA	35	3412	CH	7.4L	G	$1900	228	1,500	16,500	15,072

Livability Code: SB 30-90
Wheelbase-to-length ratio of 54% is considered ○ dangerous ○ fatiguing ● good ○ excellent *
The approximate net payload of 1428 pounds at 9% of GVWR on this model is ○ deficient ○ excessive ● cautionary ○ good ○ excellent *
Total highway safety penalties are: 13 *   Value: 7 4   Durability: 7 5   Highway Control Rating: 6 4   Highway Safety: 5 1   ★

Brand	Year	Type	Length	Model	Chassis	Engine	Fuel Type	Price/Ft	Wheelbase	Towing	GVWR	Curb Wt
Swinger	1996	MHA	35	3412	FO	7.5L	G	$1700	220	8,000	17,000	14,572

Livability Code: SB 30-90
Wheelbase-to-length ratio of 52% is considered ○ dangerous ● fatiguing ○ good ○ excellent *
The approximate net payload of 2428 pounds at 14% of GVWR on this model is ○ deficient ○ excessive ○ cautionary ● good ○ excellent *
Total highway safety penalties are: 2 *   Value: 7 9   Durability: 7 5   Highway Control Rating: 5 5   Highway Safety: 5 3   ★

Brand	Year	Type	Length	Model	Chassis	Engine	Fuel Type	Price/Ft	Wheelbase	Towing	GVWR	Curb Wt
Swinger	1996	MHA	35	3412	FO	7.5L	G	$1900	228	8,000	17,000	15,472

Livability Code: SB 30-90
Wheelbase-to-length ratio of 54% is considered ○ dangerous ○ fatiguing ● good ○ excellent *
The approximate net payload of 1528 pounds at 9% of GVWR on this model is ○ deficient ○ excessive ● cautionary ○ good ○ excellent *
Total highway safety penalties are: 7 *   Value: 7 6   Durability: 7 5   Highway Control Rating: 6 4   Highway Safety: 5 7   ★

Brand	Year	Type	Length	Model	Chassis	Engine	Fuel Type	Price/Ft	Wheelbase	Towing	GVWR	Curb Wt
Swinger	1996	MHA	35	3412	SP	CU210	D	$2700	208	1,500	18,000	14,972

Livability Code: SB 30-90
Wheelbase-to-length ratio of 49% is considered ● dangerous ○ fatiguing ○ good ○ excellent *
The approximate net payload of 3028 pounds at 17% of GVWR on this model is ○ deficient ○ excessive ○ cautionary ○ good ● excellent *
Total highway safety penalties are: 2 *   Value: 7 9   Durability: 7 5   Highway Control Rating: 4 2   Highway Safety: 4 0

Brand	Year	Type	Length	Model	Chassis	Engine	Fuel Type	Price/Ft	Wheelbase	Towing	GVWR	Curb Wt
Swinger	1996	MHA	35	3412	SP	CU210	D	$2700	208	1,500 e	18,000	15,872

Livability Code: SB 30-90
Wheelbase-to-length ratio of 49% is considered ● dangerous ○ fatiguing ○ good ○ excellent *
The approximate net payload of 2128 pounds at 12% of GVWR on this model is ○ deficient ○ excessive ○ cautionary ● good ○ excellent *
Total highway safety penalties are: 7 *   Value: 7 6   Durability: 7 5   Highway Control Rating: 3 3   Highway Safety: 2 6

Brand	Year	Type	Length	Model	Chassis	Engine	Fuel Type	Price/Ft	Wheelbase	Towing	GVWR	Curb Wt
Swinger	1996	MHA	36	3411	CH	7.4L	G	$1700	228	1,500	16,500	14,227

Livability Code: SB 30-90
Wheelbase-to-length ratio of 53% is considered ○ dangerous ● fatiguing ○ good ○ excellent *
The approximate net payload of 2273 pounds at 14% of GVWR on this model is ○ deficient ○ excessive ○ cautionary ● good ○ excellent *
Total highway safety penalties are: 7 *   Value: 7 6   Durability: 7 5   Highway Control Rating: 6 8   Highway Safety: 6 1   ★★

Brand	Year	Type	Length	Model	Chassis	Engine	Fuel Type	Price/Ft	Wheelbase	Towing	GVWR	Curb Wt
Swinger	1996	MHA	36	3411 slide	CH	7.4L	G	$1700	228	1,500	16,500	14,694

Livability Code: SB 30-90
Wheelbase-to-length ratio of 53% is considered ○ dangerous ● fatiguing ○ good ○ excellent *
The approximate net payload of 1806 pounds at 11% of GVWR on this model is ○ deficient ○ excessive ○ cautionary ● good ○ excellent *
Total highway safety penalties are: 10 *   Value: 7 5   Durability: 7 5   Highway Control Rating: 6 2   Highway Safety: 5 2   ★

Brand	Year	Type	Length	Model	Chassis	Engine	Fuel Type	Price/Ft	Wheelbase	Towing	GVWR	Curb Wt
Swinger	1996	MHA	36	3411	FO	7.5L	G	$1700	228	8,000	17,000	14,644

Livability Code: SB 30-90
Wheelbase-to-length ratio of 53% is considered ○ dangerous ● fatiguing ○ good ○ excellent *
The approximate net payload of 2356 pounds at 14% of GVWR on this model is ○ deficient ○ excessive ○ cautionary ● good ○ excellent *
Total highway safety penalties are: 2 *   Value: 7 9   Durability: 7 5   Highway Control Rating: 6 8   Highway Safety: 6 6   ★★

Brand	Year	Type	Length	Model	Chassis	Engine	Fuel Type	Price/Ft	Wheelbase	Towing	GVWR	Curb Wt
Swinger	1996	MHA	36	3411 slide	FO	7.5L	G	$1700	228	8,000	17,000	15,094

Livability Code: SB 30-90
Wheelbase-to-length ratio of 53% is considered ○ dangerous ● fatiguing ○ good ○ excellent *
The approximate net payload of 1906 pounds at 11% of GVWR on this model is ○ deficient ○ excessive ○ cautionary ● good ○ excellent *
Total highway safety penalties are: 5 *   Value: 7 8   Durability: 7 5   Highway Control Rating: 6 2   Highway Safety: 5 7   ★

Brand	Year	Type	Length	Model	Chassis	Engine	Fuel Type	Price/Ft	Wheelbase	Towing	GVWR	Curb Wt
Swinger	1996	MHA	36	3595	CH	7.4L	G	$1700	228	1,500	16,500	14,387

Livability Code: SB 30-90
Wheelbase-to-length ratio of 53% is considered ○ dangerous ● fatiguing ○ good ○ excellent *
The approximate net payload of 2113 pounds at 13% of GVWR on this model is ○ deficient ○ excessive ○ cautionary ● good ○ excellent *
Total highway safety penalties are: 8 *   Value: 7 6   Durability: 7 5   Highway Control Rating: 6 3   Highway Safety: 5 5   ★

Brand	Year	Type	Length	Model	Chassis	Engine	Fuel Type	Price/Ft	Wheelbase	Towing	GVWR	Curb Wt
Swinger	1996	MHA	36	3595 slide	CH	7.4L	G	$1700	228	1,500	16,500	14,814

Livability Code: SB 30-90
Wheelbase-to-length ratio of 53% is considered ○ dangerous ● fatiguing ○ good ○ excellent *
The approximate net payload of 1686 pounds at 10% of GVWR on this model is ○ deficient ○ excessive ○ cautionary ● good ○ excellent *
Total highway safety penalties are: 10 *   Value: 7 5   Durability: 7 5   Highway Control Rating: 5 7   Highway Safety: 4 7

Note: Safety ratings are based on the assumption that the engineering of the RV has allowed for proper balance by placing fresh, gray, and black holding tanks in a location so as not to change the balance of the RV when the tanks are empty or full. **Always double-check wheelbase, GVWR, and weights at front and rear axles.**

*See Section 1 for details on how conclusions are reached.

Brand	Year	Type	Length	Model	Chassis	Engine	Fuel Type	Average Price per Linear Foot When New	Adjusted Wheelbase	Approx. Towing Capacity	Gross Vehicle Weight Rating	Average Curb Weight
Swinger	1996	MHA	36	3595	FO	7.5L	G	$1700	228	8,000	17,000	14,764

Livability Code: SB 30-90   Wheelbase-to-length ratio of 53% is considered ○ dangerous ● fatiguing ○ good ○ excellent *
The approximate net payload of 2236 pounds at 13% of GVWR on this model is ○ deficient ○ excessive ○ cautionary ● good ○ excellent *
Total highway safety penalties are: 2 *   Value: 7 9   Durability: 7 5   Highway Control Rating: 6 3   Highway Safety: 6 1   ★★

Brand	Year	Type	Length	Model	Chassis	Engine	Fuel Type	Price/Ft	Wheelbase	Towing	GVWR	Curb Wt
Swinger	1996	MHA	36	3595 slide	FO	7.5L	G	$1700	228	8,000	17,000	15,214

Livability Code: SB 30-90   Wheelbase-to-length ratio of 53% is considered ○ dangerous ● fatiguing ○ good ○ excellent *
The approximate net payload of 1786 pounds at 11% of GVWR on this model is ○ deficient ○ excessive ○ cautionary ● good ○ excellent *
Total highway safety penalties are: 5 *   Value: 7 8   Durability: 7 5   Highway Control Rating: 5 9   Highway Safety: 5 4   ★

Brand	Year	Type	Length	Model	Chassis	Engine	Fuel Type	Price/Ft	Wheelbase	Towing	GVWR	Curb Wt
Swinger	1997	MHA	30	2808	CH	7.4L	G	$2000	178	1,500	14,800	12,804

Livability Code: SB 30-90   Wheelbase-to-length ratio of 50% is considered ● dangerous ○ fatiguing ○ good ○ excellent *
The approximate net payload of 1996 pounds at 13% of GVWR on this model is ○ deficient ○ excessive ○ cautionary ● good ○ excellent *
Total highway safety penalties are: 4 *   Value: 7 8   Durability: 7 5   Highway Control Rating: 3 9   Highway Safety: 3 5

Brand	Year	Type	Length	Model	Chassis	Engine	Fuel Type	Price/Ft	Wheelbase	Towing	GVWR	Curb Wt
Swinger	1997	MHA	30	2808 slide	CH	7.4L	G	$2000	178	1,500	16,500	13,563

Livability Code: SB 30-90   Wheelbase-to-length ratio of 50% is considered ● dangerous ○ fatiguing ○ good ○ excellent *
The approximate net payload of 2937 pounds at 18% of GVWR on this model is ○ deficient ○ excessive ○ cautionary ○ good ● excellent *
Total highway safety penalties are: 7 *   Value: 7 6   Durability: 7 5   Highway Control Rating: 4 6   Highway Safety: 3 9

Brand	Year	Type	Length	Model	Chassis	Engine	Fuel Type	Price/Ft	Wheelbase	Towing	GVWR	Curb Wt
Swinger	1997	MHA	30	2808	FO	7.5L	G	$2000	178	1,500	15,200	13,313

Livability Code: SB 30-90   Wheelbase-to-length ratio of 50% is considered ● dangerous ○ fatiguing ○ good ○ excellent *
The approximate net payload of 1887 pounds at 12% of GVWR on this model is ○ deficient ○ excessive ○ cautionary ● good ○ excellent *
Total highway safety penalties are: 2 *   Value: 7 9   Durability: 7 5   Highway Control Rating: 3 7   Highway Safety: 3 5

Brand	Year	Type	Length	Model	Chassis	Engine	Fuel Type	Price/Ft	Wheelbase	Towing	GVWR	Curb Wt
Swinger	1997	MHA	30	2808 slide	FO	7.5L	G	$2000	178	1,500	17,000	13,963

Livability Code: SB 30-90   Wheelbase-to-length ratio of 50% is considered ● dangerous ○ fatiguing ○ good ○ excellent *
The approximate net payload of 3037 pounds at 18% of GVWR on this model is ○ deficient ○ excessive ○ cautionary ○ good ● excellent *
Total highway safety penalties are: 5 *   Value: 7 8   Durability: 7 5   Highway Control Rating: 4 6   Highway Safety: 4 1

Brand	Year	Type	Length	Model	Chassis	Engine	Fuel Type	Price/Ft	Wheelbase	Towing	GVWR	Curb Wt
Swinger	1997	MHA	32	2995	CH	7.4L	G	$1900	190	1,500	14,800	13,151

Livability Code: SB 30-90   Wheelbase-to-length ratio of 50% is considered ● dangerous ○ fatiguing ○ good ○ excellent *
The approximate net payload of 1649 pounds at 11% of GVWR on this model is ○ deficient ○ excessive ○ cautionary ● good ○ excellent *
Total highway safety penalties are: 5 *   Value: 7 7   Durability: 7 5   Highway Control Rating: 3 5   Highway Safety: 3 0

Brand	Year	Type	Length	Model	Chassis	Engine	Fuel Type	Price/Ft	Wheelbase	Towing	GVWR	Curb Wt
Swinger	1997	MHA	32	2995 slide	CH	7.4L	G	$1900	190	1,500	16,500	14,062

Livability Code: SB 30-90   Wheelbase-to-length ratio of 50% is considered ● dangerous ○ fatiguing ○ good ○ excellent *
The approximate net payload of 2438 pounds at 15% of GVWR on this model is ○ deficient ○ excessive ○ cautionary ● good ○ excellent *
Total highway safety penalties are: 8 *   Value: 7 6   Durability: 7 5   Highway Control Rating: 4 2   Highway Safety: 3 4

Brand	Year	Type	Length	Model	Chassis	Engine	Fuel Type	Price/Ft	Wheelbase	Towing	GVWR	Curb Wt
Swinger	1997	MHA	32	2995	FO	7.5L	G	$1900	190	1,500	15,200	13,812

Livability Code: SB 30-90   Wheelbase-to-length ratio of 50% is considered ● dangerous ○ fatiguing ○ good ○ excellent *
The approximate net payload of 1388 pounds at 9% of GVWR on this model is ○ deficient ○ excessive ● cautionary ○ good ○ excellent *
Total highway safety penalties are: 2 *   Value: 7 9   Durability: 7 5   Highway Control Rating: 2 8   Highway Safety: 2 6

Brand	Year	Type	Length	Model	Chassis	Engine	Fuel Type	Price/Ft	Wheelbase	Towing	GVWR	Curb Wt
Swinger	1997	MHA	32	2995 slide	FO	7.5L	G	$1900	190	1,500	17,000	14,462

Livability Code: SB 30-90   Wheelbase-to-length ratio of 50% is considered ● dangerous ○ fatiguing ○ good ○ excellent *
The approximate net payload of 2538 pounds at 15% of GVWR on this model is ○ deficient ○ excessive ○ cautionary ● good ○ excellent *
Total highway safety penalties are: 5 *   Value: 7 8   Durability: 7 5   Highway Control Rating: 4 2   Highway Safety: 3 7

Brand	Year	Type	Length	Model	Chassis	Engine	Fuel Type	Price/Ft	Wheelbase	Towing	GVWR	Curb Wt
Swinger	1997	MHA	34	3190	CH	7.4L	G	$1800	212	1,500	14,800	13,726

Livability Code: SB 30-90   Wheelbase-to-length ratio of 52% is considered ○ dangerous ● fatiguing ○ good ○ excellent *
The approximate net payload of 1074 pounds at 7% of GVWR on this model is ○ deficient ○ excessive ● cautionary ○ good ○ excellent *
Total highway safety penalties are: 6 *   Value: 7 7   Durability: 7 5   Highway Control Rating: 3 2   Highway Safety: 2 6

Brand	Year	Type	Length	Model	Chassis	Engine	Fuel Type	Price/Ft	Wheelbase	Towing	GVWR	Curb Wt
Swinger	1997	MHA	34	3190 slide	CH	7.4L	G	$1900	212	1,500	16,500	14,562

Livability Code: SB 30-90   Wheelbase-to-length ratio of 52% is considered ○ dangerous ● fatiguing ○ good ○ excellent *
The approximate net payload of 1938 pounds at 12% of GVWR on this model is ○ deficient ○ excessive ○ cautionary ● good ○ excellent *
Total highway safety penalties are: 9 *   Value: 7 5   Durability: 7 5   Highway Control Rating: 5 3   Highway Safety: 4 4

Note: Safety ratings are based on the assumption that the engineering of the RV has allowed for proper balance by placing fresh, gray, and black holding tanks in a location so as not to change the balance of the RV when the tanks are empty or full. **Always double-check wheelbase, GVWR, and weights at front and rear axles.**

*See Section 1 for details on how conclusions are reached.

Brand	Year	Type	Length	Model	Chassis	Engine	Fuel Type	Average Price per Linear Foot When New	Adjusted Wheel-base	Approx. Towing Capacity	Gross Vehicle Weight Rating	Average Curb Weight

Swinger — 1997 — MHA — 34 — 3190 — FO — 7.5L — G — $1900 — 212 — 1,500 — 17,000 — 14,512
Livability Code: SB 30-90
Wheelbase-to-length ratio of 52% is considered ○ dangerous ● fatiguing ○ good ○ excellent *
The approximate net payload of 2488 pounds at 15% of GVWR on this model is ○ deficient ○ excessive ○ cautionary ● good ○ excellent *
Total highway safety penalties are: 2 *   Value: 7 9   Durability: 7 5   Highway Control Rating: 5 9   Highway Safety: 5 7   ★

Swinger — 1997 — MHA — 34 — 3190 slide — FO — 7.5L — G — $1900 — 212 — 1,500 — 17,000 — 14,512
Livability Code: SB 30-90
Wheelbase-to-length ratio of 52% is considered ○ dangerous ● fatiguing ○ good ○ excellent *
The approximate net payload of 2488 pounds at 15% of GVWR on this model is ○ deficient ○ excessive ○ cautionary ● good ○ excellent *
Total highway safety penalties are: 2 *   Value: 7 9   Durability: 7 5   Highway Control Rating: 5 9   Highway Safety: 5 7   ★

Swinger — 1997 — MHA — 34 — 3190 slide — SP — CU210 — D — $2700 — 190 — 1,500 — 18,000 — 15,486
Livability Code: SB 30-90
Wheelbase-to-length ratio of 46% is considered ● dangerous ○ fatiguing ○ good ○ excellent *
The approximate net payload of 2514 pounds at 14% of GVWR on this model is ○ deficient ○ excessive ○ cautionary ● good ○ excellent *
Total highway safety penalties are: 5 *   Value: 7 8   Durability: 7 5   Highway Control Rating: 2 7   Highway Safety: 2 2

Swinger — 1997 — MHA — 35 — 3412 — CH — 7.4L — G — $1800 — 228 — 1,500 — 16,500 — 14,410
Livability Code: SB 30-90
Wheelbase-to-length ratio of 54% is considered ○ dangerous ○ fatiguing ● good ○ excellent *
The approximate net payload of 2090 pounds at 13% of GVWR on this model is ○ deficient ○ excessive ○ cautionary ● good ○ excellent *
Total highway safety penalties are: 7 *   Value: 7 6   Durability: 7 5   Highway Control Rating: 7 8   Highway Safety: 7 1   ★★★

Swinger — 1997 — MHA — 35 — 3412 slide — CH — 7.4L — G — $1900 — 220 — 1,500 — 16,500 — 15,411
Livability Code: SB 30-90
Wheelbase-to-length ratio of 52% is considered ○ dangerous ● fatiguing ○ good ○ excellent *
The approximate net payload of 1089 pounds at 7% of GVWR on this model is ○ deficient ○ excessive ● cautionary ○ good ○ excellent *
Total highway safety penalties are: 13 *   Value: 7 4   Durability: 7 5   Highway Control Rating: 3 0   Highway Safety: 1 7

Swinger — 1997 — MHA — 35 — 3412 — FO — 7.5L — G — $1900 — 228 — 1,500 — 17,000 — 14,911
Livability Code: SB 30-90
Wheelbase-to-length ratio of 54% is considered ○ dangerous ○ fatiguing ● good ○ excellent *
The approximate net payload of 2089 pounds at 12% of GVWR on this model is ○ deficient ○ excessive ○ cautionary ● good ○ excellent *
Total highway safety penalties are: 2 *   Value: 7 9   Durability: 7 5   Highway Control Rating: 7 7   Highway Safety: 7 5   ★★★

Swinger — 1997 — MHA — 35 — 3412 slide — FO — 7.5L — G — $1900 — 220 — 1,500 — 17,000 — 15,811
Livability Code: SB 30-90
Wheelbase-to-length ratio of 52% is considered ○ dangerous ● fatiguing ○ good ○ excellent *
The approximate net payload of 1189 pounds at 7% of GVWR on this model is ○ deficient ○ excessive ● cautionary ○ good ○ excellent *
Total highway safety penalties are: 7 *   Value: 7 6   Durability: 7 5   Highway Control Rating: 3 0   Highway Safety: 2 3

Swinger — 1997 — MHA — 36 — 3595 — CH — 7.4L — G — $1800 — 228 — 1,500 — 16,500 — 14,560
Livability Code: SB 30-90
Wheelbase-to-length ratio of 53% is considered ○ dangerous ● fatiguing ○ good ○ excellent *
The approximate net payload of 1940 pounds at 12% of GVWR on this model is ○ deficient ○ excessive ○ cautionary ● good ○ excellent *
Total highway safety penalties are: 8 *   Value: 7 6   Durability: 7 5   Highway Control Rating: 6 1   Highway Safety: 5 3   ★

Swinger — 1997 — MHA — 36 — 3595 slide — CH — 7.4L — G — $1800 — 228 — 1,500 — 16,500 — 15,611
Livability Code: SB 30-90
Wheelbase-to-length ratio of 53% is considered ○ dangerous ● fatiguing ○ good ○ excellent *
The approximate net payload of 889 pounds at 5% of GVWR on this model is ● deficient ○ excessive ○ cautionary ○ good ○ excellent *
Total highway safety penalties are: 13 *   Value: 7 4   Durability: 7 5   Highway Control Rating: 3 4   Highway Safety: 2 1

Swinger — 1997 — MHA — 36 — 3595 — FO — 7.5L — G — $1800 — 228 — 1,500 — 17,000 — 15,111
Livability Code: SB 30-90
Wheelbase-to-length ratio of 53% is considered ○ dangerous ● fatiguing ○ good ○ excellent *
The approximate net payload of 1889 pounds at 11% of GVWR on this model is ○ deficient ○ excessive ○ cautionary ● good ○ excellent *
Total highway safety penalties are: 2 *   Value: 7 9   Durability: 7 5   Highway Control Rating: 5 9   Highway Safety: 5 7   ★

Swinger — 1997 — MHA — 36 — 3595 slide — FO — 7.5L — G — $1800 — 228 — 1,500 — 17,000 — 16,011
Livability Code: SB 30-90
Wheelbase-to-length ratio of 53% is considered ○ dangerous ● fatiguing ○ good ○ excellent *
The approximate net payload of 989 pounds at 6% of GVWR on this model is ● deficient ○ excessive ○ cautionary ○ good ○ excellent *
Total highway safety penalties are: 7 *   Value: 7 6   Durability: 7 5   Highway Control Rating: 3 4   Highway Safety: 2 7

Swinger — 1998 — MHA — 30 — 2908 — CH — 7.4L — G — $2200 — 178 — 4,200 — 14,800 — 12,610
Livability Code: SB 30-90
Wheelbase-to-length ratio of 50% is considered ● dangerous ○ fatiguing ○ good ○ excellent *
The approximate net payload of 2190 pounds at 15% of GVWR on this model is ○ deficient ○ excessive ○ cautionary ● good ○ excellent *
Total highway safety penalties are: 4 *   Value: 7 8   Durability: 7 5   Highway Control Rating: 4 2   Highway Safety: 3 8

Note: Safety ratings are based on the assumption that the engineering of the RV has allowed for proper balance by placing fresh, gray, and black holding tanks in a location so as not to change the balance of the RV when the tanks are empty or full. **Always double-check wheelbase, GVWR, and weights at front and rear axles.**

*See Section 1 for details on how conclusions are reached.

Brand	Year	Type	Length	Model	Chassis	Engine	Fuel Type	Average Price per Linear Foot When New	Adjusted Wheelbase	Approx. Towing Capacity	Gross Vehicle Weight Rating	Average Curb Weight
Swinger	1998	MHA	30	2908 slide	CH	7.4L	G	$2200	178	4,500	16,500	13,470

Livability Code: SB 30-90   Wheelbase-to-length ratio of 50% is considered ◉ dangerous ○ fatiguing ○ good ○ excellent *

The approximate net payload of 3030 pounds at 18% of GVWR on this model is ○ deficient ○ excessive ○ cautionary ○ good ◉ excellent *

Total highway safety penalties are: 7 *   Value: 7 6   Durability: 7 5   Highway Control Rating: 4 7   Highway Safety: 4 0

| Swinger | 1998 | MHA | 30 | 2908 | FO | 7.5L | G | $2200 | 178 | 9,800 | 15,200 | 13,165 |

Livability Code: SB 30-90   Wheelbase-to-length ratio of 50% is considered ◉ dangerous ○ fatiguing ○ good ○ excellent *

The approximate net payload of 2035 pounds at 13% of GVWR on this model is ○ deficient ○ excessive ○ cautionary ◉ good ○ excellent *

Total highway safety penalties are: 2 *   Value: 7 9   Durability: 7 5   Highway Control Rating: 3 9   Highway Safety: 3 7

| Swinger | 1998 | MHA | 30 | 2908 slide | FO | 7.5L | G | $2200 | 178 | 8,000 | 17,000 | 13,785 |

Livability Code: SB 30-90   Wheelbase-to-length ratio of 50% is considered ◉ dangerous ○ fatiguing ○ good ○ excellent *

The approximate net payload of 3215 pounds at 19% of GVWR on this model is ○ deficient ○ excessive ○ cautionary ○ good ◉ excellent *

Total highway safety penalties are: 5 *   Value: 7 8   Durability: 7 5   Highway Control Rating: 4 7   Highway Safety: 4 2

| Swinger | 1998 | MHA | 32 | 3195 | CH | 7.4L | G | $2100 | 190 | 4,200 | 14,800 | 13,154 |

Livability Code: SB 30-90   Wheelbase-to-length ratio of 50% is considered ◉ dangerous ○ fatiguing ○ good ○ excellent *

The approximate net payload of 1646 pounds at 11% of GVWR on this model is ○ deficient ○ excessive ○ cautionary ◉ good ○ excellent *

Total highway safety penalties are: 5 *   Value: 7 7   Durability: 7 5   Highway Control Rating: 3 5   Highway Safety: 3 0

| Swinger | 1998 | MHA | 32 | 3195 slide | CH | 7.4L | G | $2100 | 190 | 4,500 | 16,500 | 13,822 |

Livability Code: SB 30-90   Wheelbase-to-length ratio of 50% is considered ◉ dangerous ○ fatiguing ○ good ○ excellent *

The approximate net payload of 2678 pounds at 16% of GVWR on this model is ○ deficient ○ excessive ○ cautionary ○ good ◉ excellent *

Total highway safety penalties are: 8 *   Value: 7 6   Durability: 7 5   Highway Control Rating: 4 5   Highway Safety: 3 7

| Swinger | 1998 | MHA | 32 | 3195 | FO | 7.5L | G | $2100 | 190 | 9,800 | 15,200 | 13,609 |

Livability Code: SB 30-90   Wheelbase-to-length ratio of 50% is considered ◉ dangerous ○ fatiguing ○ good ○ excellent *

The approximate net payload of 1591 pounds at 10% of GVWR on this model is ○ deficient ○ excessive ○ cautionary ◉ good ○ excellent *

Total highway safety penalties are: 2 *   Value: 7 9   Durability: 7 5   Highway Control Rating: 3 3   Highway Safety: 3 1

| Swinger | 1998 | MHA | 32 | 3195 slide | FO | 7.5L | G | $2100 | 190 | 8,000 | 17,000 | 14,364 |

Livability Code: SB 30-90   Wheelbase-to-length ratio of 50% is considered ◉ dangerous ○ fatiguing ○ good ○ excellent *

The approximate net payload of 2636 pounds at 16% of GVWR on this model is ○ deficient ○ excessive ○ cautionary ○ good ◉ excellent *

Total highway safety penalties are: 5 *   Value: 7 8   Durability: 7 5   Highway Control Rating: 4 4   Highway Safety: 3 9

| Swinger | 1998 | MHA | 34 | 3390 | CH | 7.4L | G | $1900 | 212 | 4,200 | 14,800 | 13,596 |

Livability Code: SB 30-90   Wheelbase-to-length ratio of 52% is considered ○ dangerous ◉ fatiguing ○ good ○ excellent *

The approximate net payload of 1204 pounds at 8% of GVWR on this model is ○ deficient ○ excessive ◉ cautionary ○ good ○ excellent *

Total highway safety penalties are: 6 *   Value: 7 7   Durability: 7 5   Highway Control Rating: 3 8   Highway Safety: 3 2

| Swinger | 1998 | MHA | 34 | 3390 slide | CH | 7.4L | G | $1900 | 212 | 4,500 | 16,500 | 14,459 |

Livability Code: SB 30-90   Wheelbase-to-length ratio of 52% is considered ○ dangerous ◉ fatiguing ○ good ○ excellent *

The approximate net payload of 2041 pounds at 12% of GVWR on this model is ○ deficient ○ excessive ○ cautionary ◉ good ○ excellent *

Total highway safety penalties are: 9 *   Value: 7 5   Durability: 7 5   Highway Control Rating: 5 3   Highway Safety: 4 4

| Swinger | 1998 | MHA | 34 | 3390 | FO | 7.5L | G | $1900 | 212 | 8,000 | 17,000 | 14,344 |

Livability Code: SB 30-90   Wheelbase-to-length ratio of 52% is considered ○ dangerous ◉ fatiguing ○ good ○ excellent *

The approximate net payload of 2656 pounds at 16% of GVWR on this model is ○ deficient ○ excessive ○ cautionary ○ good ◉ excellent *

Total highway safety penalties are: 2 *   Value: 7 9   Durability: 7 5   Highway Control Rating: 6 0   Highway Safety: 5 8   ★

| Swinger | 1998 | MHA | 34 | 3390 slide | FO | 7.5L | G | $1900 | 212 | 8,000 | 17,000 | 14,569 |

Livability Code: SB 30-90   Wheelbase-to-length ratio of 52% is considered ○ dangerous ◉ fatiguing ○ good ○ excellent *

The approximate net payload of 2431 pounds at 14% of GVWR on this model is ○ deficient ○ excessive ○ cautionary ◉ good ○ excellent *

Total highway safety penalties are: 5 *   Value: 7 8   Durability: 7 5   Highway Control Rating: 5 7   Highway Safety: 5 2   ★

| Swinger | 1998 | MHA | 35 | 3512 | CH | 7.4L | G | $1900 | 228 | 4,500 | 16,500 | 14,828 |

Livability Code: SB 30-90   Wheelbase-to-length ratio of 54% is considered ○ dangerous ○ fatiguing ◉ good ○ excellent *

The approximate net payload of 1672 pounds at 10% of GVWR on this model is ○ deficient ○ excessive ○ cautionary ◉ good ○ excellent *

Total highway safety penalties are: 7 *   Value: 7 6   Durability: 7 5   Highway Control Rating: 7 4   Highway Safety: 6 7   ★★

Note: Safety ratings are based on the assumption that the engineering of the RV has allowed for proper balance by placing fresh, gray, and black holding tanks in a location so as not to change the balance of the RV when the tanks are empty or full. **Always double-check wheelbase, GVWR, and weights at front and rear axles.**

Brand	Year	Type	Length	Model	Chassis	Engine	Fuel Type	Average Price per Linear Foot When New	Adjusted Wheelbase	Approx. Towing Capacity	Gross Vehicle Weight Rating	Average Curb Weight
Swinger	1998	MHA	35	3512 slide	CH	7.4L	G	$1900	220	4,500	16,500	15,436

Livability Code: SB 30-90
Wheelbase-to-length ratio of 52% is considered ○ dangerous ● fatiguing ○ good ○ excellent*
The approximate net payload of 1064 pounds at 6% of GVWR on this model is ● deficient ○ excessive ○ cautionary ○ good ○ excellent*
Total highway safety penalties are: 13*   Value: 74   Durability: 75   Highway Control Rating: 24   Highway Safety: 11

Brand	Year	Type	Length	Model	Chassis	Engine	Fuel Type	Price/Ft	Wheelbase	Towing	GVWR	Curb Weight
Swinger	1998	MHA	35	3512	FO	7.5L	G	?	228	8,000	17,000	15,158

Livability Code: SB 30-90
Wheelbase-to-length ratio of 54% is considered ○ dangerous ○ fatiguing ● good ○ excellent*
The approximate net payload of 1842 pounds at 11% of GVWR on this model is ○ deficient ○ excessive ○ cautionary ● good ○ excellent*
Total highway safety penalties are: 2*   Value: 79   Durability: 75   Highway Control Rating: 75   Highway Safety: 73   ★★★

Swinger	1998	MHA	35	3512 slide	FO	7.5L	G	$0	220	4,000	17,000	15,836

Livability Code: SB 30-90
Wheelbase-to-length ratio of 52% is considered ○ dangerous ● fatiguing ○ good ○ excellent*
The approximate net payload of 1164 pounds at 7% of GVWR on this model is ○ deficient ○ excessive ● cautionary ○ good ○ excellent*
Total highway safety penalties are: 7*   Value: 76   Durability: 75   Highway Control Rating: 30   Highway Safety: 23

Telstar	1986	MHC	23	4231	CH	5.7L	G	$3100	146	3,000	10,500	9,320

Livability Code: VA 30-90
Wheelbase-to-length ratio of 53% is considered ○ dangerous ● fatiguing ○ good ○ excellent*
The approximate net payload of 1180 pounds at 11% of GVWR on this model is ○ deficient ○ excessive ○ cautionary ● good ○ excellent*
Total highway safety penalties are: 2*   Value: 78   Durability: 73   Highway Control Rating: 68   Highway Safety: 66   ★★

Telstar	1990	MHC	25	TS 257 DB	FO	7.5L	G	$2000	176	1,500	11,550	9,994

Livability Code: VA 30-90
Wheelbase-to-length ratio of 58% is considered ○ dangerous ○ fatiguing ○ good ● excellent*
The approximate net payload of 1556 pounds at 13% of GVWR on this model is ○ deficient ○ excessive ○ cautionary ● good ○ excellent*
Total highway safety penalties are: 2*   Value: 78   Durability: 73   Highway Control Rating: 99   Highway Safety: 97   ★★★

Telstar	1991	MHC	23	TS 237 DB	FO	7.5L	G	$1800	158	1,500	11,550	9,907

Livability Code: VA 30-90
Wheelbase-to-length ratio of 56% is considered ○ dangerous ○ fatiguing ● good ○ excellent*
The approximate net payload of 1643 pounds at 14% of GVWR on this model is ○ deficient ○ excessive ○ cautionary ● good ○ excellent*
Total highway safety penalties are: 2*   Value: 78   Durability: 73   Highway Control Rating: 93   Highway Safety: 91   ★★★

Telstar	1993	MHC	24	TS 247	FO	7.5L	G	$2000	158	1,500	11,000	10,040

Livability Code: VA 30-90
Wheelbase-to-length ratio of 54% is considered ○ dangerous ○ fatiguing ● good ○ excellent*
The approximate net payload of 960 pounds at 9% of GVWR on this model is ○ deficient ○ excessive ● cautionary ○ good ○ excellent*
Total highway safety penalties are: 2*   Value: 78   Durability: 73   Highway Control Rating: 69   Highway Safety: 67   ★★

Telstar	1993	MHC	24	TS 247 Dsl	FO	7.5L	D	$2100	158	1,500	11,000	10,040

Livability Code: VA 30-90
Wheelbase-to-length ratio of 54% is considered ○ dangerous ○ fatiguing ● good ○ excellent*
The approximate net payload of 960 pounds at 9% of GVWR on this model is ○ deficient ○ excessive ● cautionary ○ good ○ excellent*
Total highway safety penalties are: 2*   Value: 78   Durability: 73   Highway Control Rating: 69   Highway Safety: 67   ★★

Telstar	1993	MHC	28	TS 272	FO	7.5L	G	$1800	200	1,500	12,400	11,061

Livability Code: VA 30-90
Wheelbase-to-length ratio of 60% is considered ○ dangerous ○ fatiguing ○ good ● excellent*
The approximate net payload of 1339 pounds at 11% of GVWR on this model is ○ deficient ○ excessive ○ cautionary ● good ○ excellent*
Total highway safety penalties are: 2*   Value: 78   Durability: 73   Highway Control Rating: 99   Highway Safety: 97   ★★★

Telstar	1993	MHC	28	TS 272 Dsl	FO	7.5L	D	$1900	200	1,500	12,400	11,061

Livability Code: VA 30-90
Wheelbase-to-length ratio of 60% is considered ○ dangerous ○ fatiguing ○ good ● excellent*
The approximate net payload of 1339 pounds at 11% of GVWR on this model is ○ deficient ○ excessive ○ cautionary ● good ○ excellent*
Total highway safety penalties are: 2*   Value: 78   Durability: 73   Highway Control Rating: 99   Highway Safety: 97   ★★★

Telstar	1993	MHC	28	TS 273	FO	7.5L	G	$1800	200	1,500	12,400	11,061

Livability Code: VA 30-90
Wheelbase-to-length ratio of 60% is considered ○ dangerous ○ fatiguing ○ good ● excellent*
The approximate net payload of 1339 pounds at 11% of GVWR on this model is ○ deficient ○ excessive ○ cautionary ● good ○ excellent*
Total highway safety penalties are: 2*   Value: 78   Durability: 73   Highway Control Rating: 99   Highway Safety: 97   ★★★

Telstar	1993	MHC	28	TS 273 Dsl	FO	7.5L	D	$1900	200	1,500	12,400	11,061

Livability Code: VA 30-90
Wheelbase-to-length ratio of 60% is considered ○ dangerous ○ fatiguing ○ good ● excellent*
The approximate net payload of 1339 pounds at 11% of GVWR on this model is ○ deficient ○ excessive ○ cautionary ● good ○ excellent*
Total highway safety penalties are: 2*   Value: 78   Durability: 73   Highway Control Rating: 99   Highway Safety: 97   ★★★

Note: Safety ratings are based on the assumption that the engineering of the RV has allowed for proper balance by placing fresh, gray, and black holding tanks in a location so as not to change the balance of the RV when the tanks are empty or full. **Always double-check wheelbase, GVWR, and weights at front and rear axles.**

*See Section 1 for details on how conclusions are reached.

Brand	Year	Type	Length	Model	Chassis	Engine	Fuel Type	Average Price per Linear Foot When New	Adjusted Wheelbase	Approx. Towing Capacity	Gross Vehicle Weight Rating	Average Curb Weight
Telstar	1993	MHC	28	TS 274	FO	7.5L	G	$1800	200	1,500	12,400	11,061

Livability Code: VA 30-90   Wheelbase-to-length ratio of 60% is considered ○ dangerous ○ fatiguing ○ good ● excellent *

The approximate net payload of 1339 pounds at 11% of GVWR on this model is ○ deficient ○ excessive ○ cautionary ● good ○ excellent *

Total highway safety penalties are: 2 *   Value: 7 8   Durability: 7 3   Highway Control Rating: 9 9   Highway Safety: 9 7   ★★★

| Telstar | 1993 | MHC | 28 | TS 274 Dsl | FO | 7.3L | D | $1900 | 200 | 1,500 | 12,400 | 11,061 |

Livability Code: VA 30-90   Wheelbase-to-length ratio of 60% is considered ○ dangerous ○ fatiguing ○ good ● excellent *

The approximate net payload of 1339 pounds at 11% of GVWR on this model is ○ deficient ○ excessive ○ cautionary ● good ○ excellent *

Total highway safety penalties are: 2 *   Value: 7 8   Durability: 7 3   Highway Control Rating: 9 9   Highway Safety: 9 7   ★★★

| Telstar | 1994 | MHC | 24 | TS 247 RD | FO | 7.5L | G | $2000 | 158 | 1,500 | 11,000 | 10,040 |

Livability Code: VA 30-90   Wheelbase-to-length ratio of 54% is considered ○ dangerous ○ fatiguing ● good ○ excellent *

The approximate net payload of 960 pounds at 9% of GVWR on this model is ○ deficient ○ excessive ● cautionary ○ good ○ excellent *

Total highway safety penalties are: 2 *   Value: 7 8   Durability: 7 3   Highway Control Rating: 6 9   Highway Safety: 6 7   ★★

| Telstar | 1994 | MHC | 24 | TS 247 CB | FO | 7.5L | G | $2000 | 158 | 1,500 | 11,000 | 10,040 |

Livability Code: VA 30-90   Wheelbase-to-length ratio of 54% is considered ○ dangerous ○ fatiguing ● good ○ excellent *

The approximate net payload of 960 pounds at 9% of GVWR on this model is ○ deficient ○ excessive ● cautionary ○ good ○ excellent *

Total highway safety penalties are: 2 *   Value: 7 8   Durability: 7 3   Highway Control Rating: 6 9   Highway Safety: 6 7   ★★

| Telstar | 1994 | MHC | 24 | 247 RD Dsl | FO | 7.3L | D | $2100 | 158 | 1,500 | 11,000 | 10,040 |

Livability Code: VA 30-90   Wheelbase-to-length ratio of 54% is considered ○ dangerous ○ fatiguing ● good ○ excellent *

The approximate net payload of 960 pounds at 9% of GVWR on this model is ○ deficient ○ excessive ● cautionary ○ good ○ excellent *

Total highway safety penalties are: 2 *   Value: 7 8   Durability: 7 3   Highway Control Rating: 6 9   Highway Safety: 6 7   ★★

| Telstar | 1994 | MHC | 24 | 247 CB Dsl | FO | 7.3L | D | $2100 | 158 | 1,500 | 11,000 | 10,040 |

Livability Code: VA 30-90   Wheelbase-to-length ratio of 54% is considered ○ dangerous ○ fatiguing ● good ○ excellent *

The approximate net payload of 960 pounds at 9% of GVWR on this model is ○ deficient ○ excessive ● cautionary ○ good ○ excellent *

Total highway safety penalties are: 2 *   Value: 7 8   Durability: 7 3   Highway Control Rating: 6 9   Highway Safety: 6 7   ★★

| Telstar | 1994 | MHC | 28 | TS 272 QB | FO | 7.5L | G | $1800 | 200 | 1,500 | 12,400 | 11,061 |

Livability Code: VA 30-90   Wheelbase-to-length ratio of 60% is considered ○ dangerous ○ fatiguing ○ good ● excellent *

The approximate net payload of 1339 pounds at 11% of GVWR on this model is ○ deficient ○ excessive ○ cautionary ● good ○ excellent *

Total highway safety penalties are: 2 *   Value: 7 8   Durability: 7 3   Highway Control Rating: 9 9   Highway Safety: 9 7   ★★★

| Telstar | 1994 | MHC | 28 | TS 273 QB | FO | 7.5L | G | $1800 | 200 | 1,500 | 12,400 | 11,061 |

Livability Code: VA 30-90   Wheelbase-to-length ratio of 60% is considered ○ dangerous ○ fatiguing ○ good ● excellent *

The approximate net payload of 1339 pounds at 11% of GVWR on this model is ○ deficient ○ excessive ○ cautionary ● good ○ excellent *

Total highway safety penalties are: 2 *   Value: 7 8   Durability: 7 3   Highway Control Rating: 9 9   Highway Safety: 9 7   ★★★

| Telstar | 1994 | MHC | 28 | TS 274 QB | FO | 7.5L | G | $1800 | 200 | 1,500 | 12,400 | 11,061 |

Livability Code: VA 30-90   Wheelbase-to-length ratio of 60% is considered ○ dangerous ○ fatiguing ○ good ● excellent *

The approximate net payload of 1339 pounds at 11% of GVWR on this model is ○ deficient ○ excessive ○ cautionary ● good ○ excellent *

Total highway safety penalties are: 2 *   Value: 7 8   Durability: 7 3   Highway Control Rating: 9 9   Highway Safety: 9 7   ★★★

| Telstar | 1994 | MHC | 28 | 272 QB Dsl | FO | 7.3L | D | $1900 | 200 | 1,500 | 12,400 | 11,061 |

Livability Code: VA 30-90   Wheelbase-to-length ratio of 60% is considered ○ dangerous ○ fatiguing ○ good ● excellent *

The approximate net payload of 1339 pounds at 11% of GVWR on this model is ○ deficient ○ excessive ○ cautionary ● good ○ excellent *

Total highway safety penalties are: 2 *   Value: 7 8   Durability: 7 3   Highway Control Rating: 9 9   Highway Safety: 9 7   ★★★

| Telstar | 1994 | MHC | 28 | 273 QB Dsl | FO | 7.3L | D | $1900 | 200 | 1,500 | 12,400 | 11,061 |

Livability Code: VA 30-90   Wheelbase-to-length ratio of 60% is considered ○ dangerous ○ fatiguing ○ good ● excellent *

The approximate net payload of 1339 pounds at 11% of GVWR on this model is ○ deficient ○ excessive ○ cautionary ● good ○ excellent *

Total highway safety penalties are: 2 *   Value: 7 8   Durability: 7 3   Highway Control Rating: 9 9   Highway Safety: 9 7   ★★★

| Telstar | 1994 | MHC | 28 | 274 QB Dsl | FO | 7.3L | D | $1900 | 200 | 1,500 | 12,400 | 11,061 |

Livability Code: VA 30-90   Wheelbase-to-length ratio of 60% is considered ○ dangerous ○ fatiguing ○ good ● excellent *

The approximate net payload of 1339 pounds at 11% of GVWR on this model is ○ deficient ○ excessive ○ cautionary ● good ○ excellent *

Total highway safety penalties are: 2 *   Value: 7 8   Durability: 7 3   Highway Control Rating: 9 9   Highway Safety: 9 7   ★★★

Note: Safety ratings are based on the assumption that the engineering of the RV has allowed for proper balance by placing fresh, gray, and black holding tanks in a location so as not to change the balance of the RV when the tanks are empty or full. **Always double-check wheelbase, GVWR, and weights at front and rear axles.**

Section 2: The Ratings

Brand	Year	Type	Length	Model	Chassis	Engine	Fuel Type	Average Price per Linear Foot When New	Adjusted Wheelbase	Approx. Towing Capacity	Gross Vehicle Weight Rating	Average Curb Weight
Telstar	1995	MHC	24	247 RD	FO	7.5L	G	$2200	158	1,500	11,000	10,040

Livability Code: VA 30-90
Wheelbase-to-length ratio of 54% is considered ○ dangerous ○ fatiguing ◉ good ○ excellent *
The approximate net payload of 960 pounds at 9% of GVWR on this model is ○ deficient ○ excessive ◉ cautionary ○ good ○ excellent *
Total highway safety penalties are: 2 *   Value: 7 8   Durability: 7 3   Highway Control Rating: 6 9   Highway Safety: 6 7   ★★

Brand	Year	Type	Length	Model	Chassis	Engine	Fuel Type	Avg Price/Ft	Wheelbase	Towing	GVWR	Curb Weight
Telstar	1995	MHC	24	247 CB	FO	7.5L	G	$2200	158	1,500	11,000	10,040

Livability Code: VA 30-90
Wheelbase-to-length ratio of 54% is considered ○ dangerous ○ fatiguing ◉ good ○ excellent *
The approximate net payload of 960 pounds at 9% of GVWR on this model is ○ deficient ○ excessive ◉ cautionary ○ good ○ excellent *
Total highway safety penalties are: 2 *   Value: 7 8   Durability: 7 3   Highway Control Rating: 6 9   Highway Safety: 6 7   ★★

| Telstar | 1995 | MHC | 28 | TS272 QB | FO | 7.5L | G | $1900 | 200 | 1,500 | 12,400 | 11,061 |

Livability Code: VA 30-90
Wheelbase-to-length ratio of 60% is considered ○ dangerous ○ fatiguing ○ good ◉ excellent *
The approximate net payload of 1339 pounds at 11% of GVWR on this model is ○ deficient ○ excessive ○ cautionary ◉ good ○ excellent *
Total highway safety penalties are: 2 *   Value: 7 8   Durability: 7 3   Highway Control Rating: 9 9   Highway Safety: 9 7   ★★★

| Telstar | 1995 | MHC | 28 | 274 QB | FO | 7.5L | G | $1900 | 200 | 1,500 | 12,400 | 11,061 |

Livability Code: VA 30-90
Wheelbase-to-length ratio of 60% is considered ○ dangerous ○ fatiguing ○ good ◉ excellent *
The approximate net payload of 1339 pounds at 11% of GVWR on this model is ○ deficient ○ excessive ○ cautionary ◉ good ○ excellent *
Total highway safety penalties are: 2 *   Value: 7 8   Durability: 7 3   Highway Control Rating: 9 9   Highway Safety: 9 7   ★★★

| Telstar | 1995 | MHC | 28 | 273 QB | FO | 7.5L | G | $2000 | 200 | 1,500 | 12,400 | 11,061 |

Livability Code: VA 30-90
Wheelbase-to-length ratio of 60% is considered ○ dangerous ○ fatiguing ○ good ◉ excellent *
The approximate net payload of 1339 pounds at 11% of GVWR on this model is ○ deficient ○ excessive ○ cautionary ◉ good ○ excellent *
Total highway safety penalties are: 2 *   Value: 7 8   Durability: 7 3   Highway Control Rating: 9 9   Highway Safety: 9 7   ★★★

| Telstar | 1996 | MHC | 24 | TS 247 RD | FO | 7.5L | G | $2300 | 158 | 1,500 | 11,500 | 10,040 |

Livability Code: VA 30-90
Wheelbase-to-length ratio of 54% is considered ○ dangerous ○ fatiguing ◉ good ○ excellent *
The approximate net payload of 1460 pounds at 13% of GVWR on this model is ○ deficient ○ excessive ○ cautionary ◉ good ○ excellent *
Total highway safety penalties are: 2 *   Value: 7 8   Durability: 7 3   Highway Control Rating: 8 0   Highway Safety: 7 8   ★★★

| Telstar | 1996 | MHC | 24 | TS 247 CB | FO | 7.5L | G | $2100 | 158 | 1,500 | 11,500 | 10,040 |

Livability Code: VA 30-90
Wheelbase-to-length ratio of 54% is considered ○ dangerous ○ fatiguing ◉ good ○ excellent *
The approximate net payload of 1460 pounds at 13% of GVWR on this model is ○ deficient ○ excessive ○ cautionary ◉ good ○ excellent *
Total highway safety penalties are: 2 *   Value: 7 8   Durability: 7 3   Highway Control Rating: 8 0   Highway Safety: 7 8   ★★★

| Telstar | 1996 | MHC | 27 | TS 272 QB | FO | 7.5L | G | $2100 | 200 | 1,500 | 12,410 | 10,924 |

Livability Code: VA 30-90
Wheelbase-to-length ratio of 61% is considered ○ dangerous ○ fatiguing ○ good ◉ excellent *
The approximate net payload of 1486 pounds at 12% of GVWR on this model is ○ deficient ○ excessive ○ cautionary ◉ good ○ excellent *
Total highway safety penalties are: 2 *   Value: 7 8   Durability: 7 3   Highway Control Rating: 1 0 0   Highway Safety: 9 8   ★★★

| Telstar | 1996 | MHC | 27 | TS 273 QB | FO | 7.5L | G | $2100 | 200 | 1,500 | 12,410 | 10,924 |

Livability Code: VA 30-90
Wheelbase-to-length ratio of 61% is considered ○ dangerous ○ fatiguing ○ good ◉ excellent *
The approximate net payload of 1486 pounds at 12% of GVWR on this model is ○ deficient ○ excessive ○ cautionary ◉ good ○ excellent *
Total highway safety penalties are: 2 *   Value: 7 8   Durability: 7 3   Highway Control Rating: 1 0 0   Highway Safety: 9 8   ★★★

| Telstar | 1996 | MHC | 27 | TS 274 QB | FO | 7.5L | G | $2000 | 200 | 1,500 | 12,410 | 10,924 |

Livability Code: VA 30-90
Wheelbase-to-length ratio of 61% is considered ○ dangerous ○ fatiguing ○ good ◉ excellent *
The approximate net payload of 1486 pounds at 12% of GVWR on this model is ○ deficient ○ excessive ○ cautionary ◉ good ○ excellent *
Total highway safety penalties are: 2 *   Value: 7 8   Durability: 7 3   Highway Control Rating: 1 0 0   Highway Safety: 9 8   ★★★

| Tioga | 1990 | MHC | 27 | T26 | FO | 7.5L | G | $1700 | 176 | 1,500 | 11,200 | 10,501 |

Livability Code: SB 30-80
Wheelbase-to-length ratio of 54% is considered ○ dangerous ○ fatiguing ◉ good ○ excellent *
The approximate net payload of 699 pounds at 6% of GVWR on this model is ◉ deficient ○ excessive ○ cautionary ○ good ○ excellent *
Total highway safety penalties are: 2 *   Value: 7 9   Durability: 7 6   Highway Control Rating: 5 2   Highway Safety: 5 0   ★

| Tioga | 1991 | MHC | 27 | F26 | FO | 7.5L | G | $1700 | 176 | 3,500 | 11,500 | 10,545 |

Livability Code: SB 30-80
Wheelbase-to-length ratio of 54% is considered ○ dangerous ○ fatiguing ◉ good ○ excellent *
The approximate net payload of 955 pounds at 8% of GVWR on this model is ○ deficient ○ excessive ◉ cautionary ○ good ○ excellent *
Total highway safety penalties are: 2 *   Value: 7 9   Durability: 7 6   Highway Control Rating: 6 4   Highway Safety: 6 2   ★★

Note: Safety ratings are based on the assumption that the engineering of the RV has allowed for proper balance by placing fresh, gray, and black holding tanks in a location so as not to change the balance of the RV when the tanks are empty or full. **Always double-check wheelbase, GVWR, and weights at front and rear axles.**

*See Section 1 for details on how conclusions are reached.

Brand	Year	Type	Length	Model	Chassis	Engine	Fuel Type	Average Price per Linear Foot When New	Adjusted Wheelbase	Approx. Towing Capacity	Gross Vehicle Weight Rating	Average Curb Weight
Tioga	1991	MHC	27	S26	FO	7.5L	G	$1700	176	3,500	11,500	10,558

Livability Code: SB 30-80
Wheelbase-to-length ratio of 54% is considered ○ dangerous ○ fatiguing ◉ good ○ excellent *
The approximate net payload of 942 pounds at 8% of GVWR on this model is ○ deficient ○ excessive ◉ cautionary ○ good ○ excellent *
Total highway safety penalties are: 2 *   Value: **7 9**   Durability: **7 6**   Highway Control Rating: **6 4**   Highway Safety: **6 2**   ★★

Brand	Year	Type	Length	Model	Chassis	Engine	Fuel Type		Wheelbase	Towing	GVWR	Curb Weight
Tioga	1991	MHC	27	T26	FO	7.5L	G	$1700	176	3,500	11,500	10,623

Livability Code: SB 30-80
Wheelbase-to-length ratio of 54% is considered ○ dangerous ○ fatiguing ◉ good ○ excellent *
The approximate net payload of 877 pounds at 8% of GVWR on this model is ○ deficient ○ excessive ◉ cautionary ○ good ○ excellent *
Total highway safety penalties are: 2 *   Value: **7 9**   Durability: **7 6**   Highway Control Rating: **6 3**   Highway Safety: **6 1**   ★★

Tioga	1992	MHC	27	S 26	FO	7.5L	G	$1500	176	3,500	11,500	10,590

Livability Code: SB 30-80
Wheelbase-to-length ratio of 54% is considered ○ dangerous ○ fatiguing ◉ good ○ excellent *
The approximate net payload of 910 pounds at 8% of GVWR on this model is ○ deficient ○ excessive ◉ cautionary ○ good ○ excellent *
Total highway safety penalties are: 2 *   Value: **7 9**   Durability: **7 6**   Highway Control Rating: **6 3**   Highway Safety: **6 1**   ★★

Tioga	1992	MHC	28	F 28	FO	7.5L	G	$1500	176	3,500	11,500	10,679

Livability Code: SB 30-80
Wheelbase-to-length ratio of 52% is considered ○ dangerous ◉ fatiguing ○ good ○ excellent *
The approximate net payload of 821 pounds at 7% of GVWR on this model is ○ deficient ○ excessive ◉ cautionary ○ good ○ excellent *
Total highway safety penalties are: 2 *   Value: **7 9**   Durability: **7 6**   Highway Control Rating: **4 2**   Highway Safety: **4 0**

Tioga	1992	MHC	28	Y 28	FO	7.5L	G	$1500	176	3,500	11,500	10,800

Livability Code: SB 30-80
Wheelbase-to-length ratio of 52% is considered ○ dangerous ◉ fatiguing ○ good ○ excellent *
The approximate net payload of 700 pounds at 6% of GVWR on this model is ◉ deficient ○ excessive ○ cautionary ○ good ○ excellent *
Total highway safety penalties are: 2 *   Value: **7 9**   Durability: **7 6**   Highway Control Rating: **3 6**   Highway Safety: **3 4**

Tioga	1993	MHC	27	26 S	FO	7.5L	G	$1800	176	3,000	12,000	10,630

Livability Code: SB 30-80
Wheelbase-to-length ratio of 54% is considered ○ dangerous ○ fatiguing ◉ good ○ excellent *
The approximate net payload of 1370 pounds at 11% of GVWR on this model is ○ deficient ○ excessive ○ cautionary ◉ good ○ excellent *
Total highway safety penalties are: 2 *   Value: **7 9**   Durability: **7 6**   Highway Control Rating: **7 7**   Highway Safety: **7 5**   ★★★

Tioga	1993	MHC	28	28 F	FO	7.5L	G	$1800	176	3,000	12,000	10,709

Livability Code: SB 30-80
Wheelbase-to-length ratio of 52% is considered ○ dangerous ◉ fatiguing ○ good ○ excellent *
The approximate net payload of 1291 pounds at 11% of GVWR on this model is ○ deficient ○ excessive ○ cautionary ◉ good ○ excellent *
Total highway safety penalties are: 2 *   Value: **7 9**   Durability: **7 6**   Highway Control Rating: **6 0**   Highway Safety: **5 8**   ★

Tioga	1993	MHC	28	28 Y	FO	7.5L	G	$1800	176	3,000	12,000	10,840

Livability Code: SB 30-80
Wheelbase-to-length ratio of 52% is considered ○ dangerous ◉ fatiguing ○ good ○ excellent *
The approximate net payload of 1160 pounds at 10% of GVWR on this model is ○ deficient ○ excessive ○ cautionary ◉ good ○ excellent *
Total highway safety penalties are: 2 *   Value: **7 9**   Durability: **7 6**   Highway Control Rating: **5 8**   Highway Safety: **5 6**   ★

Tioga	1994	MHC	24	23D	FO	7.5L	G	$1600	158	3,500	12,400	10,114

Livability Code: SB 30-80
Wheelbase-to-length ratio of 55% is considered ○ dangerous ○ fatiguing ◉ good ○ excellent *
The approximate net payload of 2286 pounds at 18% of GVWR on this model is ○ deficient ○ excessive ○ cautionary ○ good ◉ excellent *
Total highway safety penalties are: 2 *   Value: **7 9**   Durability: **7 6**   Highway Control Rating: **9 4**   Highway Safety: **9 2**   ★★★

Tioga	1994	MHC	27	27J	FO	7.5L	G	$1900	190	3,500	12,400	10,836

Livability Code: SB 30-80
Wheelbase-to-length ratio of 58% is considered ○ dangerous ○ fatiguing ○ good ◉ excellent *
The approximate net payload of 1564 pounds at 13% of GVWR on this model is ○ deficient ○ excessive ○ cautionary ◉ good ○ excellent *
Total highway safety penalties are: 2 *   Value: **7 9**   Durability: **7 6**   Highway Control Rating: **9 8**   Highway Safety: **9 6**   ★★★

Tioga	1994	MHC	27	28V	FO	7.5L	G	$1900	190	3,500	12,400	10,836

Livability Code: SB 30-80
Wheelbase-to-length ratio of 58% is considered ○ dangerous ○ fatiguing ○ good ◉ excellent *
The approximate net payload of 1564 pounds at 13% of GVWR on this model is ○ deficient ○ excessive ○ cautionary ◉ good ○ excellent *
Total highway safety penalties are: 2 *   Value: **7 9**   Durability: **7 6**   Highway Control Rating: **9 8**   Highway Safety: **9 6**   ★★★

Tioga	1994	MHC	29	29Z	FO	7.5L	G	$1800	190	3,500	12,400	11,242

Livability Code: SB 30-80
Wheelbase-to-length ratio of 55% is considered ○ dangerous ○ fatiguing ◉ good ○ excellent *
The approximate net payload of 1158 pounds at 9% of GVWR on this model is ○ deficient ○ excessive ◉ cautionary ○ good ○ excellent *
Total highway safety penalties are: 2 *   Value: **7 9**   Durability: **7 6**   Highway Control Rating: **7 5**   Highway Safety: **7 3**   ★★★

Note: Safety ratings are based on the assumption that the engineering of the RV has allowed for proper balance by placing fresh, gray, and black holding tanks in a location so as not to change the balance of the RV when the tanks are empty or full. **Always double-check wheelbase, GVWR, and weights at front and rear axles.**

*See Section 1 for details on how conclusions are reached.

Section 2: The Ratings

Brand	Year	Type	Length	Model	Chassis	Engine	Fuel Type	Average Price per Linear Foot When New	Adjusted Wheelbase	Approx. Towing Capacity	Gross Vehicle Weight Rating	Average Curb Weight
Tioga	1995	MHC	30	29H	FO	7.5L	G	$1600	214	3,500	12,400	11,900

Livability Code: SB 30-80
Wheelbase-to-length ratio of 59% is considered ○ dangerous ○ fatiguing ○ good ◉ excellent *
The approximate net payload of 500 pounds at 4% of GVWR on this model is ◉ deficient ○ excessive ○ cautionary ○ good ○ excellent *
Total highway safety penalties are: 2 *   Value: 7 9   Durability: 7 6   Highway Control Rating: 7 2   Highway Safety: 7 0   ★★

Brand	Year	Type	Length	Model	Chassis	Engine	Fuel Type	Price/Ft	Wheelbase	Towing	GVWR	Curb Weight
Tioga	1995	MHC	31	31N	FO	7.5L	G	$1600	214	3,500	12,400	12,236

Livability Code: SB 30-80
Wheelbase-to-length ratio of 57% is considered ○ dangerous ○ fatiguing ◉ good ○ excellent *
The approximate net payload of 164 pounds at 1% of GVWR on this model is ◉ deficient ○ excessive ○ cautionary ○ good ○ excellent *
Total highway safety penalties are: 2 *   Value: 7 9   Durability: 7 6   Highway Control Rating: 5 9   Highway Safety: 5 7   ★

Brand	Year	Type	Length	Model	Chassis	Engine	Fuel Type	Price/Ft	Wheelbase	Towing	GVWR	Curb Weight
Tioga	1995	MHC	31	31T	FO	7.5L	G	$1600	214	3,500	12,400	12,236

Livability Code: SB 30-80
Wheelbase-to-length ratio of 57% is considered ○ dangerous ○ fatiguing ◉ good ○ excellent *
The approximate net payload of 164 pounds at 1% of GVWR on this model is ◉ deficient ○ excessive ○ cautionary ○ good ○ excellent *
Total highway safety penalties are: 2 *   Value: 7 9   Durability: 7 6   Highway Control Rating: 5 9   Highway Safety: 5 7   ★

Brand	Year	Type	Length	Model	Chassis	Engine	Fuel Type	Price/Ft	Wheelbase	Towing	GVWR	Curb Weight
Tioga	1996	MHC	30	29G	FO	350	G	$1600	214	3,500	12,400	11,900

Livability Code: SB 30-80
Wheelbase-to-length ratio of 59% is considered ○ dangerous ○ fatiguing ○ good ◉ excellent *
The approximate net payload of 500 pounds at 4% of GVWR on this model is ◉ deficient ○ excessive ○ cautionary ○ good ○ excellent *
Total highway safety penalties are: 2 *   Value: 7 9   Durability: 7 6   Highway Control Rating: 7 2   Highway Safety: 7 0   ★★

Brand	Year	Type	Length	Model	Chassis	Engine	Fuel Type	Price/Ft	Wheelbase	Towing	GVWR	Curb Weight
Tioga	1996	MHC	30	29H	FO	350	G	$1600	214	3,500	12,400	11,900

Livability Code: SB 30-80
Wheelbase-to-length ratio of 59% is considered ○ dangerous ○ fatiguing ○ good ◉ excellent *
The approximate net payload of 500 pounds at 4% of GVWR on this model is ◉ deficient ○ excessive ○ cautionary ○ good ○ excellent *
Total highway safety penalties are: 2 *   Value: 7 9   Durability: 7 6   Highway Control Rating: 7 2   Highway Safety: 7 0   ★★

Brand	Year	Type	Length	Model	Chassis	Engine	Fuel Type	Price/Ft	Wheelbase	Towing	GVWR	Curb Weight
Tioga	1996	MHC	30	29K	FO	350	G	$1600	214	3,500	12,400	11,900

Livability Code: SB 30-80
Wheelbase-to-length ratio of 59% is considered ○ dangerous ○ fatiguing ○ good ◉ excellent *
The approximate net payload of 500 pounds at 4% of GVWR on this model is ◉ deficient ○ excessive ○ cautionary ○ good ○ excellent *
Total highway safety penalties are: 2 *   Value: 7 9   Durability: 7 6   Highway Control Rating: 7 2   Highway Safety: 7 0   ★★

Brand	Year	Type	Length	Model	Chassis	Engine	Fuel Type	Price/Ft	Wheelbase	Towing	GVWR	Curb Weight
Tioga	1996	MHC	31	31N	CH	P 30	G	$1600	208	4,500	14,500	13,536

Livability Code: SB 30-80
Wheelbase-to-length ratio of 55% is considered ○ dangerous ○ fatiguing ◉ good ○ excellent *
The approximate net payload of 964 pounds at 7% of GVWR on this model is ○ deficient ○ excessive ◉ cautionary ○ good ○ excellent *
Total highway safety penalties are: 2 *   Value: 7 9   Durability: 7 6   Highway Control Rating: 6 4   Highway Safety: 6 2   ★★

Brand	Year	Type	Length	Model	Chassis	Engine	Fuel Type	Price/Ft	Wheelbase	Towing	GVWR	Curb Weight
Tioga	1996	MHC	31	31T	CH	P 30	G	$1600	208	4,500	14,500	13,536

Livability Code: SB 30-80
Wheelbase-to-length ratio of 55% is considered ○ dangerous ○ fatiguing ◉ good ○ excellent *
The approximate net payload of 964 pounds at 7% of GVWR on this model is ○ deficient ○ excessive ◉ cautionary ○ good ○ excellent *
Total highway safety penalties are: 2 *   Value: 7 9   Durability: 7 6   Highway Control Rating: 6 4   Highway Safety: 6 2   ★★

Brand	Year	Type	Length	Model	Chassis	Engine	Fuel Type	Price/Ft	Wheelbase	Towing	GVWR	Curb Weight
Tioga	1997	MHC	30	29H	FO	6.8L	G	$1700	214	3,500	14,050	11,975

Livability Code: SB 30-80
Wheelbase-to-length ratio of 59% is considered ○ dangerous ○ fatiguing ○ good ◉ excellent *
The approximate net payload of 2076 pounds at 15% of GVWR on this model is ○ deficient ○ excessive ○ cautionary ◉ good ○ excellent *
Total highway safety penalties are: 2 *   Value: 7 9   Durability: 7 6   Highway Control Rating: 1 0 0   Highway Safety: 9 8   ★★★

Brand	Year	Type	Length	Model	Chassis	Engine	Fuel Type	Price/Ft	Wheelbase	Towing	GVWR	Curb Weight
Tioga	1997	MHC	31	31K	FO	6.8L	G	$1700	214	3,500	14,050	12,159

Livability Code: SB 30-80
Wheelbase-to-length ratio of 57% is considered ○ dangerous ○ fatiguing ◉ good ○ excellent *
The approximate net payload of 1891 pounds at 13% of GVWR on this model is ○ deficient ○ excessive ○ cautionary ◉ good ○ excellent *
Total highway safety penalties are: 2 *   Value: 7 9   Durability: 7 6   Highway Control Rating: 9 3   Highway Safety: 9 1   ★★★

Brand	Year	Type	Length	Model	Chassis	Engine	Fuel Type	Price/Ft	Wheelbase	Towing	GVWR	Curb Weight
Tioga	1997	MHC	31	31N	FO	6.8L	G	$1700	214	3,500	14,050	12,121

Livability Code: SB 30-80
Wheelbase-to-length ratio of 57% is considered ○ dangerous ○ fatiguing ◉ good ○ excellent *
The approximate net payload of 1929 pounds at 14% of GVWR on this model is ○ deficient ○ excessive ○ cautionary ◉ good ○ excellent *
Total highway safety penalties are: 2 *   Value: 7 9   Durability: 7 6   Highway Control Rating: 9 5   Highway Safety: 9 3   ★★★

Brand	Year	Type	Length	Model	Chassis	Engine	Fuel Type	Price/Ft	Wheelbase	Towing	GVWR	Curb Weight
Tioga	1997	MHC	31	31T	FO	6.8L	G	$1600	214	3,500	14,050	12,121

Livability Code: SB 30-80
Wheelbase-to-length ratio of 57% is considered ○ dangerous ○ fatiguing ◉ good ○ excellent *
The approximate net payload of 1929 pounds at 14% of GVWR on this model is ○ deficient ○ excessive ○ cautionary ◉ good ○ excellent *
Total highway safety penalties are: 2 *   Value: 7 9   Durability: 7 6   Highway Control Rating: 9 5   Highway Safety: 9 3   ★★★

Note: Safety ratings are based on the assumption that the engineering of the RV has allowed for proper balance by placing fresh, gray, and black holding tanks in a location so as not to change the balance of the RV when the tanks are empty or full. **Always double-check wheelbase, GVWR, and weights at front and rear axles.**

*See Section 1 for details on how conclusions are reached.

Section 2: The Ratings

Brand	Year	Type	Length	Model	Chassis	Engine	Fuel Type	Average Price per Linear Foot When New	Adjusted Wheel-base	Approx. Towing Capacity	Gross Vehicle Weight Rating	Average Curb Weight
Tioga	1998	MHC	20	19A	FO	6.8L	G	$2600	138	3,500	10,500	8,724

Livability Code: VA 30-90   Wheelbase-to-length ratio of 58% is considered ○ dangerous ○ fatiguing ○ good ◉ excellent *
The approximate net payload of 1776 pounds at 17% of GVWR on this model is ○ deficient ○ excessive ○ cautionary ○ good ◉ excellent *
Total highway safety penalties are: 2 *   Value: 7 8   Durability: 7 3   Highway Control Rating: 1 0 0   Highway Safety: 9 8   ★★★

Brand	Year	Type	Length	Model	Chassis	Engine	Fuel Type	Price/ft	Wheelbase	Towing	GVWR	Curb Weight
Tioga	1998	MHC	23	22C	FO	6.8L	G	$2300	138	3,500	10,500	9,265

Livability Code: VA 30-90   Wheelbase-to-length ratio of 51% is considered ○ dangerous ◉ fatiguing ○ good ○ excellent *
The approximate net payload of 1236 pounds at 12% of GVWR on this model is ○ deficient ○ excessive ○ cautionary ◉ good ○ excellent *
Total highway safety penalties are: 2 *   Value: 7 8   Durability: 7 3   Highway Control Rating: 5 5   Highway Safety: 5 3   ★

Tioga	1998	MHC	23	22E	FO	6.8L	G	$2300	138	3,500	10,500	9,373

Livability Code: VA 30-90   Wheelbase-to-length ratio of 50% is considered ◉ dangerous ○ fatiguing ○ good ○ excellent *
The approximate net payload of 1127 pounds at 11% of GVWR on this model is ○ deficient ○ excessive ○ cautionary ◉ good ○ excellent *
Total highway safety penalties are: 2 *   Value: 7 8   Durability: 7 3   Highway Control Rating: 4 9   Highway Safety: 4 7

Tioga	1998	MHC	25	24D	FO	6.8L	G	$2100	158	3,500	11,500	10,101

Livability Code: VA 30-90   Wheelbase-to-length ratio of 54% is considered ○ dangerous ○ fatiguing ◉ good ○ excellent *
The approximate net payload of 1399 pounds at 12% of GVWR on this model is ○ deficient ○ excessive ○ cautionary ◉ good ○ excellent *
Total highway safety penalties are: 2 *   Value: 7 8   Durability: 7 3   Highway Control Rating: 7 6   Highway Safety: 7 4   ★★★

Tioga	1998	MHC	25	24D	CH	7.4L	G	$2100	159	2,700	12,300	10,393

Livability Code: VA 30-90   Wheelbase-to-length ratio of 53% is considered ○ dangerous ◉ fatiguing ○ good ○ excellent *
The approximate net payload of 1908 pounds at 16% of GVWR on this model is ○ deficient ○ excessive ○ cautionary ○ good ◉ excellent *
Total highway safety penalties are: 2 *   Value: 7 8   Durability: 7 3   Highway Control Rating: 7 7   Highway Safety: 7 5   ★★★

Tioga	1998	MHC	27	26F	FO	6.8L	G	$1900	176	3,500	14,050	11,280

Livability Code: VA 30-90   Wheelbase-to-length ratio of 55% is considered ○ dangerous ○ fatiguing ◉ good ○ excellent *
The approximate net payload of 2770 pounds at 20% of GVWR on this model is ○ deficient ○ excessive ○ cautionary ○ good ◉ excellent *
Total highway safety penalties are: 2 *   Value: 7 8   Durability: 7 3   Highway Control Rating: 9 6   Highway Safety: 9 4   ★★★

Tioga	1998	MHC	29	29Z	FO	6.8L	G	$1800	190	3,500	14,050	11,872

Livability Code: VA 30-90   Wheelbase-to-length ratio of 54% is considered ○ dangerous ○ fatiguing ◉ good ○ excellent *
The approximate net payload of 2178 pounds at 16% of GVWR on this model is ○ deficient ○ excessive ○ cautionary ○ good ◉ excellent *
Total highway safety penalties are: 2 *   Value: 7 8   Durability: 7 3   Highway Control Rating: 8 5   Highway Safety: 8 3   ★★★

Tioga	1999	MHC	23	22C	FO	6.8L	G	$2300	138	3,500	10,500	9,523

Livability Code: VA 30-90   Wheelbase-to-length ratio of 51% is considered ○ dangerous ◉ fatiguing ○ good ○ excellent *
The approximate net payload of 977 pounds at 9% of GVWR on this model is ○ deficient ○ excessive ◉ cautionary ○ good ○ excellent *
Total highway safety penalties are: 2 *   Value: 7 8   Durability: 7 3   Highway Control Rating: 4 7   Highway Safety: 4 5

Tioga	1999	MHC	23	22C	CH	7.4L	G	$2300	139	3,500	12,300	9,937

Livability Code: VA 30-90   Wheelbase-to-length ratio of 50% is considered ◉ dangerous ○ fatiguing ○ good ○ excellent *
The approximate net payload of 2363 pounds at 19% of GVWR on this model is ○ deficient ○ excessive ○ cautionary ○ good ◉ excellent *
Total highway safety penalties are: 2 *   Value: 7 8   Durability: 7 3   Highway Control Rating: 6 4   Highway Safety: 6 2

Tioga	1999	MHC	24	23B	FO	6.8L	G	$2200	158	3,500	11,500	9,919

Livability Code: VA 30-90   Wheelbase-to-length ratio of 55% is considered ○ dangerous ○ fatiguing ◉ good ○ excellent *
The approximate net payload of 1581 pounds at 14% of GVWR on this model is ○ deficient ○ excessive ○ cautionary ◉ good ○ excellent *
Total highway safety penalties are: 2 *   Value: 7 8   Durability: 7 3   Highway Control Rating: 8 9   Highway Safety: 8 7   ★★★

Tioga	1999	MHC	24	23B	CH	7.4L	G	$2200	159	3,500	12,300	10,188

Livability Code: VA 30-90   Wheelbase-to-length ratio of 55% is considered ○ dangerous ○ fatiguing ◉ good ○ excellent *
The approximate net payload of 2112 pounds at 17% of GVWR on this model is ○ deficient ○ excessive ○ cautionary ○ good ◉ excellent *
Total highway safety penalties are: 2 *   Value: 7 8   Durability: 7 3   Highway Control Rating: 9 4   Highway Safety: 9 2   ★★★

Tioga	1999	MHC	25	24D.	FO	6.8L	G	$2100	158	3,500	11,500	10,101

Livability Code: VA 30-90   Wheelbase-to-length ratio of 54% is considered ○ dangerous ○ fatiguing ◉ good ○ excellent *
The approximate net payload of 1399 pounds at 12% of GVWR on this model is ○ deficient ○ excessive ○ cautionary ◉ good ○ excellent *
Total highway safety penalties are: 2 *   Value: 7 8   Durability: 7 3   Highway Control Rating: 7 6   Highway Safety: 7 4   ★★★

Note: Safety ratings are based on the assumption that the engineering of the RV has allowed for proper balance by placing fresh, gray, and black holding tanks in a location so as not to change the balance of the RV when the tanks are empty or full. **Always double-check wheelbase, GVWR, and weights at front and rear axles.**

*See Section 1 for details on how conclusions are reached.

Section 2: The Ratings

Brand	Year	Type	Length	Model	Chassis	Engine	Fuel Type	Average Price per Linear Foot When New	Adjusted Wheelbase	Approx. Towing Capacity	Gross Vehicle Weight Rating	Average Curb Weight
Tioga	1999	MHC	25	24D	CH	7.4L	G	$2100	159	3,500	12,300	10,393

Livability Code: VA 30-90 Wheelbase-to-length ratio of 53% is considered ○ dangerous ◉ fatiguing ○ good ○ excellent *
The approximate net payload of 1908 pounds at 16% of GVWR on this model is ○ deficient ○ excessive ○ cautionary ○ good ◉ excellent *
Total highway safety penalties are: 2 *   Value: 78   Durability: 73   Highway Control Rating: 77   Highway Safety: 75   ★★★

Brand	Year	Type	Length	Model	Chassis	Engine	Fuel Type	Price/LF	Wheelbase	Towing	GVWR	Curb Weight
Tioga	1999	MHC	27	26F	FO	6.8L	G	$1900	176	3,500	14,050	11,082

Livability Code: VA 30-90 Wheelbase-to-length ratio of 55% is considered ○ dangerous ○ fatiguing ◉ good ○ excellent *
The approximate net payload of 2968 pounds at 21% of GVWR on this model is ○ deficient ○ excessive ○ cautionary ○ good ◉ excellent *
Total highway safety penalties are: 2 *   Value: 78   Durability: 73   Highway Control Rating: 95   Highway Safety: 93   ★★★

Tioga	1999	MHC	29	29L	FO	6.8L	G	$1800	190	3,500	14,050	12,772

Livability Code: VA 30-90 Wheelbase-to-length ratio of 54% is considered ○ dangerous ○ fatiguing ◉ good ○ excellent *
The approximate net payload of 1278 pounds at 9% of GVWR on this model is ○ deficient ○ excessive ◉ cautionary ○ good ○ excellent *
Total highway safety penalties are: 12 *   Value: 73   Durability: 73   Highway Control Rating: 69   Highway Safety: 57   ★

Tioga	1999	MHC	29	29Z	FO	6.8L	G	$1800	190	3,500	14,050	11,872

Livability Code: VA 30-90 Wheelbase-to-length ratio of 54% is considered ○ dangerous ○ fatiguing ◉ good ○ excellent *
The approximate net payload of 2178 pounds at 16% of GVWR on this model is ○ deficient ○ excessive ○ cautionary ○ good ◉ excellent *
Total highway safety penalties are: 2 *   Value: 78   Durability: 73   Highway Control Rating: 85   Highway Safety: 83   ★★★

Tioga	1999	MHC	30	29H	FO	6.8L	G	$1700	214	3,500	14,050	12,031

Livability Code: VA 30-90 Wheelbase-to-length ratio of 59% is considered ○ dangerous ○ fatiguing ○ good ◉ excellent *
The approximate net payload of 2019 pounds at 14% of GVWR on this model is ○ deficient ○ excessive ○ cautionary ◉ good ○ excellent *
Total highway safety penalties are: 2 *   Value: 78   Durability: 73   Highway Control Rating: 100   Highway Safety: 98   ★★★

Tioga	1999	MHC	31	31T	FO	6.8L	G	$1700	214	3,500	14,050	12,350

Livability Code: VA 30-90 Wheelbase-to-length ratio of 57% is considered ○ dangerous ○ fatiguing ◉ good ○ excellent *
The approximate net payload of 1700 pounds at 12% of GVWR on this model is ○ deficient ○ excessive ○ cautionary ◉ good ○ excellent *
Total highway safety penalties are: 2 *   Value: 78   Durability: 73   Highway Control Rating: 91   Highway Safety: 89   ★★★

Tioga	1999	MHC	31	31W	FO	6.8L	G	$1700	214	3,500	14,050	13,250

Livability Code: VA 30-90 Wheelbase-to-length ratio of 57% is considered ○ dangerous ○ fatiguing ◉ good ○ excellent *
The approximate net payload of 800 pounds at 6% of GVWR on this model is ◉ deficient ○ excessive ○ cautionary ○ good ○ excellent *
Total highway safety penalties are: 7 *   Value: 76   Durability: 73   Highway Control Rating: 64   Highway Safety: 57   ★

Tioga Arrow	1990	MHC	26	26S	FO	7.5L	G	$1600	176	3,800	11,200	10,433

Livability Code: SB 30-80 Wheelbase-to-length ratio of 56% is considered ○ dangerous ○ fatiguing ○ good ◉ excellent *
The approximate net payload of 767 pounds at 7% of GVWR on this model is ○ deficient ○ excessive ◉ cautionary ○ good ○ excellent *
Total highway safety penalties are: 2 *   Value: 79   Durability: 76   Highway Control Rating: 66   Highway Safety: 64   ★★

Tioga Arrow	1991	MHC	24	P23	CH	7.4L	G	$1600	146	3,500	10,500	9,665

Livability Code: SB 30-80 Wheelbase-to-length ratio of 51% is considered ○ dangerous ◉ fatiguing ○ good ○ excellent *
The approximate net payload of 835 pounds at 8% of GVWR on this model is ○ deficient ○ excessive ◉ cautionary ○ good ○ excellent *
Total highway safety penalties are: 2 *   Value: 79   Durability: 76   Highway Control Rating: 39   Highway Safety: 37

Tioga Arrow	1991	MHC	24	P23	FO	7.5L	G	$1600	158	3,500	11,500	9,894

Livability Code: SB 30-80 Wheelbase-to-length ratio of 55% is considered ○ dangerous ○ fatiguing ◉ good ○ excellent *
The approximate net payload of 1606 pounds at 14% of GVWR on this model is ○ deficient ○ excessive ○ cautionary ◉ good ○ excellent *
Total highway safety penalties are: 2 *   Value: 79   Durability: 76   Highway Control Rating: 88   Highway Safety: 86   ★★★

Tioga Arrow	1991	MHC	26	S26	FO	7.5L	G	$1500	176	3,500	11,500	10,365

Livability Code: SB 30-80 Wheelbase-to-length ratio of 56% is considered ○ dangerous ○ fatiguing ◉ good ○ excellent *
The approximate net payload of 1135 pounds at 10% of GVWR on this model is ○ deficient ○ excessive ○ cautionary ◉ good ○ excellent *
Total highway safety penalties are: 2 *   Value: 79   Durability: 76   Highway Control Rating: 83   Highway Safety: 81   ★★★

Tioga Arrow	1991	MHC	27	Y27	FO	7.5L	G	$1500	176	3,500	11,500	10,633

Livability Code: SB 30-80 Wheelbase-to-length ratio of 54% is considered ○ dangerous ○ fatiguing ◉ good ○ excellent *
The approximate net payload of 867 pounds at 8% of GVWR on this model is ○ deficient ○ excessive ◉ cautionary ○ good ○ excellent *
Total highway safety penalties are: 2 *   Value: 79   Durability: 76   Highway Control Rating: 60   Highway Safety: 58   ★

Note: Safety ratings are based on the assumption that the engineering of the RV has allowed for proper balance by placing fresh, gray, and black holding tanks in a location so as not to change the balance of the RV when the tanks are empty or full. **Always double-check wheelbase, GVWR, and weights at front and rear axles.**

*See Section 1 for details on how conclusions are reached.

Brand	Year	Type	Length	Model	Chassis	Engine	Fuel Type	Average Price per Linear Foot When New	Adjusted Wheelbase	Approx. Towing Capacity	Gross Vehicle Weight Rating	Average Curb Weight
Tioga Arrow	1992	MHC	24	P23	CH	7.4L	G	$1700	146	3,500	10,500	9,735

Livability Code: SB 30-80   Wheelbase-to-length ratio of 51% is considered ○ dangerous ◉ fatiguing ○ good ○ excellent *

The approximate net payload of 765 pounds at 7% of GVWR on this model is ○ deficient ○ excessive ◉ cautionary ○ good ○ excellent *

Total highway safety penalties are: 2 *   Value: 7 9   Durability: 7 6   Highway Control Rating: 3 4   Highway Safety: 3 2

Brand	Year	Type	Length	Model	Chassis	Engine	Fuel Type	Price	Wheelbase	Towing	GVWR	Curb Weight
Tioga Arrow	1992	MHC	25	P23	FO	7.5L	G	$1600	158	3,500	11,500	9,961

Livability Code: SB 30-80   Wheelbase-to-length ratio of 53% is considered ○ dangerous ◉ fatiguing ○ good ○ excellent *

The approximate net payload of 1539 pounds at 13% of GVWR on this model is ○ deficient ○ excessive ○ cautionary ◉ good ○ excellent *

Total highway safety penalties are: 2 *   Value: 7 9   Durability: 7 6   Highway Control Rating: 7 3   Highway Safety: 7 1   ★★★

Brand	Year	Type	Length	Model	Chassis	Engine	Fuel Type	Price	Wheelbase	Towing	GVWR	Curb Weight
Tioga Arrow	1992	MHC	26	S26	FO	7.5L	G	$1600	176	3,500	11,500	10,415

Livability Code: SB 30-80   Wheelbase-to-length ratio of 56% is considered ○ dangerous ○ fatiguing ◉ good ○ excellent *

The approximate net payload of 1085 pounds at 9% of GVWR on this model is ○ deficient ○ excessive ◉ cautionary ○ good ○ excellent *

Total highway safety penalties are: 2 *   Value: 7 9   Durability: 7 6   Highway Control Rating: 7 9   Highway Safety: 7 7   ★★★

Brand	Year	Type	Length	Model	Chassis	Engine	Fuel Type	Price	Wheelbase	Towing	GVWR	Curb Weight
Tioga Arrow	1992	MHC	27	Y 27	FO	7.5L	G	$1600	176	3,500	11,500	10,677

Livability Code: SB 30-80   Wheelbase-to-length ratio of 54% is considered ○ dangerous ○ fatiguing ◉ good ○ excellent *

The approximate net payload of 823 pounds at 7% of GVWR on this model is ○ deficient ○ excessive ◉ cautionary ○ good ○ excellent *

Total highway safety penalties are: 2 *   Value: 7 9   Durability: 7 6   Highway Control Rating: 5 5   Highway Safety: 5 3   ★

Brand	Year	Type	Length	Model	Chassis	Engine	Fuel Type	Price	Wheelbase	Towing	GVWR	Curb Weight
Tioga Arrow	1992	MHC	27	F 27	FO	7.5L	G	$1600	176	3,500	11,500	10,550

Livability Code: SB 30-80   Wheelbase-to-length ratio of 54% is considered ○ dangerous ○ fatiguing ◉ good ○ excellent *

The approximate net payload of 950 pounds at 8% of GVWR on this model is ○ deficient ○ excessive ◉ cautionary ○ good ○ excellent *

Total highway safety penalties are: 2 *   Value: 7 9   Durability: 7 6   Highway Control Rating: 6 1   Highway Safety: 5 9   ★

Brand	Year	Type	Length	Model	Chassis	Engine	Fuel Type	Price	Wheelbase	Towing	GVWR	Curb Weight
Tioga Arrow	1993	MHC	22	21 C	CH	7.4L	G	$1800	125	3,500	10,200	9,152

Livability Code: SB 30-80   Wheelbase-to-length ratio of 48% is considered ◉ dangerous ○ fatiguing ○ good ○ excellent *

The approximate net payload of 1048 pounds at 10% of GVWR on this model is ○ deficient ○ excessive ○ cautionary ◉ good ○ excellent *

Total highway safety penalties are: 2 *   Value: 7 9   Durability: 7 6   Highway Control Rating: 4 2   Highway Safety: 4 0

Brand	Year	Type	Length	Model	Chassis	Engine	Fuel Type	Price	Wheelbase	Towing	GVWR	Curb Weight
Tioga Arrow	1993	MHC	22	21C	FO	7.5L	G	$1900	138	3,500	10,500	9,234

Livability Code: SB 30-80   Wheelbase-to-length ratio of 53% is considered ○ dangerous ◉ fatiguing ○ good ○ excellent *

The approximate net payload of 1266 pounds at 12% of GVWR on this model is ○ deficient ○ excessive ○ cautionary ◉ good ○ excellent *

Total highway safety penalties are: 2 *   Value: 7 9   Durability: 7 6   Highway Control Rating: 7 2   Highway Safety: 7 0   ★★★

Brand	Year	Type	Length	Model	Chassis	Engine	Fuel Type	Price	Wheelbase	Towing	GVWR	Curb Weight
Tioga Arrow	1993	MHC	24	23D	CH	7.4L	G	$1800	146	3,500	10,500	9,815

Livability Code: SB 30-80   Wheelbase-to-length ratio of 51% is considered ○ dangerous ◉ fatiguing ○ good ○ excellent *

The approximate net payload of 685 pounds at 7% of GVWR on this model is ○ deficient ○ excessive ◉ cautionary ○ good ○ excellent *

Total highway safety penalties are: 2 *   Value: 7 9   Durability: 7 6   Highway Control Rating: 3 3   Highway Safety: 3 1

Brand	Year	Type	Length	Model	Chassis	Engine	Fuel Type	Price	Wheelbase	Towing	GVWR	Curb Weight
Tioga Arrow	1993	MHC	24	23P	CH	7.4L	G	$1700	146	3,500	10,500	9,763

Livability Code: SB 30-80   Wheelbase-to-length ratio of 51% is considered ○ dangerous ◉ fatiguing ○ good ○ excellent *

The approximate net payload of 737 pounds at 7% of GVWR on this model is ○ deficient ○ excessive ◉ cautionary ○ good ○ excellent *

Total highway safety penalties are: 2 *   Value: 7 9   Durability: 7 6   Highway Control Rating: 3 3   Highway Safety: 3 1

Brand	Year	Type	Length	Model	Chassis	Engine	Fuel Type	Price	Wheelbase	Towing	GVWR	Curb Weight
Tioga Arrow	1993	MHC	24	23D	FO	7.5L	G	$1800	158	3,500	11,500	9,947

Livability Code: SB 30-80   Wheelbase-to-length ratio of 55% is considered ○ dangerous ○ fatiguing ◉ good ○ excellent *

The approximate net payload of 1553 pounds at 14% of GVWR on this model is ○ deficient ○ excessive ○ cautionary ◉ good ○ excellent *

Total highway safety penalties are: 2 *   Value: 7 9   Durability: 7 6   Highway Control Rating: 8 8   Highway Safety: 8 6   ★★★

Brand	Year	Type	Length	Model	Chassis	Engine	Fuel Type	Price	Wheelbase	Towing	GVWR	Curb Weight
Tioga Arrow	1993	MHC	24	23P	FO	7.5L	G	$1800	158	3,500	11,500	9,867

Livability Code: SB 30-80   Wheelbase-to-length ratio of 55% is considered ○ dangerous ○ fatiguing ◉ good ○ excellent *

The approximate net payload of 1633 pounds at 14% of GVWR on this model is ○ deficient ○ excessive ○ cautionary ◉ good ○ excellent *

Total highway safety penalties are: 2 *   Value: 7 9   Durability: 7 6   Highway Control Rating: 8 8   Highway Safety: 8 6   ★★★

Brand	Year	Type	Length	Model	Chassis	Engine	Fuel Type	Price	Wheelbase	Towing	GVWR	Curb Weight
Tioga Arrow	1993	MHC	26	26S	FO	7.5L	G	$1700	176	3,500	11,500	10,415

Livability Code: SB 30-80   Wheelbase-to-length ratio of 56% is considered ○ dangerous ○ fatiguing ◉ good ○ excellent *

The approximate net payload of 1085 pounds at 9% of GVWR on this model is ○ deficient ○ excessive ◉ cautionary ○ good ○ excellent *

Total highway safety penalties are: 2 *   Value: 7 9   Durability: 7 6   Highway Control Rating: 7 9   Highway Safety: 7 7   ★★★

Note: Safety ratings are based on the assumption that the engineering of the RV has allowed for proper balance by placing fresh, gray, and black holding tanks in a location so as not to change the balance of the RV when the tanks are empty or full. **Always double-check wheelbase, GVWR, and weights at front and rear axles.**

*See Section 1 for details on how conclusions are reached.

Brand	Year	Type	Length	Model	Chassis	Engine	Fuel Type	Average Price per Linear Foot When New	Adjusted Wheelbase	Approx. Towing Capacity	Gross Vehicle Weight Rating	Average Curb Weight
Tioga Arrow	1993	MHC	27	27F	FO	7.5L	G	$1600	176	3,500	11,500	10,550

Livability Code: SB 30-80

Wheelbase-to-length ratio of 54% is considered ○ dangerous ○ fatiguing ◉ good ○ excellent *

The approximate net payload of 950 pounds at 8% of GVWR on this model is ○ deficient ○ excessive ◉ cautionary ○ good ○ excellent *

Total highway safety penalties are: 2 *   Value: 7 9   Durability: 7 6   Highway Control Rating: 6 1   Highway Safety: 5 9   ★

Brand	Year	Type	Length	Model	Chassis	Engine	Fuel Type	Price/LF	Wheelbase	Towing	GVWR	Curb Weight
Tioga Arrow	1993	MHC	27	27Y	FO	7.5L	G	$1600	176	3,500	11,500	10,677

Livability Code: SB 30-80

Wheelbase-to-length ratio of 54% is considered ○ dangerous ○ fatiguing ◉ good ○ excellent *

The approximate net payload of 823 pounds at 7% of GVWR on this model is ○ deficient ○ excessive ◉ cautionary ○ good ○ excellent *

Total highway safety penalties are: 2 *   Value: 7 9   Durability: 7 6   Highway Control Rating: 5 5   Highway Safety: 5 3   ★

Brand	Year	Type	Length	Model	Chassis	Engine	Fuel Type	Price/LF	Wheelbase	Towing	GVWR	Curb Weight
Tioga Arrow	1994	MHC	30	29H	FO	7.5L	G	$1600	214	3,500	12,400	11,900

Livability Code: SB 30-80

Wheelbase-to-length ratio of 59% is considered ○ dangerous ○ fatiguing ○ good ◉ excellent *

The approximate net payload of 500 pounds at 4% of GVWR on this model is ◉ deficient ○ excessive ○ cautionary ○ good ○ excellent *

Total highway safety penalties are: 2 *   Value: 7 9   Durability: 7 6   Highway Control Rating: 7 2   Highway Safety: 7 0   ★★

Brand	Year	Type	Length	Model	Chassis	Engine	Fuel Type	Price/LF	Wheelbase	Towing	GVWR	Curb Weight
Tioga Arrow	1994	MHC	31	31N	FO	7.5L	G	$1500	214	3,500	12,400	12,236

Livability Code: SB 30-80

Wheelbase-to-length ratio of 57% is considered ○ dangerous ○ fatiguing ◉ good ○ excellent *

The approximate net payload of 164 pounds at 1% of GVWR on this model is ◉ deficient ○ excessive ○ cautionary ○ good ○ excellent *

Total highway safety penalties are: 2 *   Value: 7 9   Durability: 7 6   Highway Control Rating: 5 9   Highway Safety: 5 7   ★

Brand	Year	Type	Length	Model	Chassis	Engine	Fuel Type	Price/LF	Wheelbase	Towing	GVWR	Curb Weight
Tioga Arrow	1994	MHC	31	31T	FO	7.5L	G	$1500	214	3,500	12,400	12,236

Livability Code: SB 30-80

Wheelbase-to-length ratio of 57% is considered ○ dangerous ○ fatiguing ◉ good ○ excellent *

The approximate net payload of 164 pounds at 1% of GVWR on this model is ◉ deficient ○ excessive ○ cautionary ○ good ○ excellent *

Total highway safety penalties are: 2 *   Value: 7 9   Durability: 7 6   Highway Control Rating: 5 9   Highway Safety: 5 7   ★

Brand	Year	Type	Length	Model	Chassis	Engine	Fuel Type	Price/LF	Wheelbase	Towing	GVWR	Curb Weight
Tioga Montara	1990	MHC	22	21C	CH	5.7L	G	$1400	125	1,500	10,200	8,925

Livability Code: VA 30-90

Wheelbase-to-length ratio of 48% is considered ◉ dangerous ○ fatiguing ○ good ○ excellent *

The approximate net payload of 1275 pounds at 12% of GVWR on this model is ○ deficient ○ excessive ○ cautionary ○ good ○ excellent *

Total highway safety penalties are: 2 *   Value: 7 8   Durability: 7 2   Highway Control Rating: 4 7   Highway Safety: 4 5

Brand	Year	Type	Length	Model	Chassis	Engine	Fuel Type	Price/LF	Wheelbase	Towing	GVWR	Curb Weight
Tioga Montara	1991	MHC	19	A18	CH	7.4L	G	$1600	125	3,500	10,200	8,785

Livability Code: VA 30-90

Wheelbase-to-length ratio of 55% is considered ○ dangerous ○ fatiguing ◉ good ○ excellent *

The approximate net payload of 1415 pounds at 14% of GVWR on this model is ○ deficient ○ excessive ○ cautionary ◉ good ○ excellent *

Total highway safety penalties are: 2 *   Value: 7 8   Durability: 7 2   Highway Control Rating: 8 9   Highway Safety: 8 7   ★★★

Brand	Year	Type	Length	Model	Chassis	Engine	Fuel Type	Price/LF	Wheelbase	Towing	GVWR	Curb Weight
Tioga Montara	1991	MHC	20	A18	FO	7.5L	G	$1600	138	3,500	10,500	9,087

Livability Code: VA 30-90

Wheelbase-to-length ratio of 58% is considered ○ dangerous ○ fatiguing ○ good ◉ excellent *

The approximate net payload of 1413 pounds at 13% of GVWR on this model is ○ deficient ○ excessive ○ cautionary ◉ good ○ excellent *

Total highway safety penalties are: 2 *   Value: 7 8   Durability: 7 2   Highway Control Rating: 9 6   Highway Safety: 9 4   ★★★

Brand	Year	Type	Length	Model	Chassis	Engine	Fuel Type	Price/LF	Wheelbase	Towing	GVWR	Curb Weight
Tioga Montara	1991	MHC	22	21C	CH	7.4L	G	$1400	125	3,500	10,200	9,100

Livability Code: VA 30-90

Wheelbase-to-length ratio of 48% is considered ◉ dangerous ○ fatiguing ○ good ○ excellent *

The approximate net payload of 1100 pounds at 11% of GVWR on this model is ○ deficient ○ excessive ○ cautionary ◉ good ○ excellent *

Total highway safety penalties are: 2 *   Value: 7 8   Durability: 7 2   Highway Control Rating: 4 4   Highway Safety: 4 2

Brand	Year	Type	Length	Model	Chassis	Engine	Fuel Type	Price/LF	Wheelbase	Towing	GVWR	Curb Weight
Tioga Montara	1991	MHC	22	21C	FO	7.5L	G	$1400	138	3,500	10,500	9,336

Livability Code: VA 30-90

Wheelbase-to-length ratio of 52% is considered ○ dangerous ◉ fatiguing ○ good ○ excellent *

The approximate net payload of 1164 pounds at 11% of GVWR on this model is ○ deficient ○ excessive ○ cautionary ◉ good ○ excellent *

Total highway safety penalties are: 2 *   Value: 7 8   Durability: 7 2   Highway Control Rating: 6 2   Highway Safety: 6 0   ★★

Brand	Year	Type	Length	Model	Chassis	Engine	Fuel Type	Price/LF	Wheelbase	Towing	GVWR	Curb Weight
Tioga Montara	1991	MHC	24	23D	CH	7.4L	G	$1400	146	3,500	10,500	9,715

Livability Code: VA 30-90

Wheelbase-to-length ratio of 51% is considered ○ dangerous ◉ fatiguing ○ good ○ excellent *

The approximate net payload of 785 pounds at 7% of GVWR on this model is ○ deficient ○ excessive ◉ cautionary ○ good ○ excellent *

Total highway safety penalties are: 2 *   Value: 7 8   Durability: 7 2   Highway Control Rating: 3 4   Highway Safety: 3 2

Brand	Year	Type	Length	Model	Chassis	Engine	Fuel Type	Price/LF	Wheelbase	Towing	GVWR	Curb Weight
Tioga Montara	1991	MHC	25	D23	FO	7.5L	G	$1400	158	3,500	11,500	9,945

Livability Code: VA 30-90

Wheelbase-to-length ratio of 54% is considered ○ dangerous ○ fatiguing ◉ good ○ excellent *

The approximate net payload of 1555 pounds at 14% of GVWR on this model is ○ deficient ○ excessive ○ cautionary ◉ good ○ excellent *

Total highway safety penalties are: 2 *   Value: 7 8   Durability: 7 2   Highway Control Rating: 7 9   Highway Safety: 7 7   ★★★

Note: Safety ratings are based on the assumption that the engineering of the RV has allowed for proper balance by placing fresh, gray, and black holding tanks in a location so as not to change the balance of the RV when the tanks are empty or full. **Always double-check wheelbase, GVWR, and weights at front and rear axles.**

*See Section 1 for details on how conclusions are reached.

Section 2: The Ratings

Brand	Year	Type	Length	Model	Chassis	Engine	Fuel Type	Average Price per Linear Foot When New	Adjusted Wheelbase	Approx. Towing Capacity	Gross Vehicle Weight Rating	Average Curb Weight
Tioga Montara	1992	MHC	19	A18	CH	7.4L	G	$1700	125	3,500	10,200	8,668

Livability Code: VA 30-90
Wheelbase-to-length ratio of 55% is considered ○ dangerous ○ fatiguing ● good ○ excellent *
The approximate net payload of 1532 pounds at 15% of GVWR on this model is ○ deficient ○ excessive ○ cautionary ● good ○ excellent *
Total highway safety penalties are: 2 * Value: 78 Durability: 72 Highway Control Rating: 91 Highway Safety: 89 ★★★

Brand	Year	Type	Length	Model	Chassis	Engine	Fuel Type	Price/Ft	Wheelbase	Towing	GVWR	Curb Wt
Tioga Montara	1992	MHC	19	A18	FO	7.5L	G	$1700	138	3,500	10,500	8,750

Livability Code: VA 30-90
Wheelbase-to-length ratio of 61% is considered ○ dangerous ○ fatiguing ○ good ● excellent *
The approximate net payload of 1750 pounds at 17% of GVWR on this model is ○ deficient ○ excessive ○ cautionary ○ good ● excellent *
Total highway safety penalties are: 2 * Value: 78 Durability: 72 Highway Control Rating: 100 Highway Safety: 98 ★★★

Brand	Year	Type	Length	Model	Chassis	Engine	Fuel Type	Price/Ft	Wheelbase	Towing	GVWR	Curb Wt
Tioga Montara	1992	MHC	22	21C	CH	7.4L	G	$1500	125	3,500	10,200	9,168

Livability Code: VA 30-90
Wheelbase-to-length ratio of 48% is considered ● dangerous ○ fatiguing ○ good ○ excellent *
The approximate net payload of 1032 pounds at 10% of GVWR on this model is ○ deficient ○ excessive ○ cautionary ● good ○ excellent *
Total highway safety penalties are: 2 * Value: 78 Durability: 72 Highway Control Rating: 42 Highway Safety: 40

Brand	Year	Type	Length	Model	Chassis	Engine	Fuel Type	Price/Ft	Wheelbase	Towing	GVWR	Curb Wt
Tioga Montara	1992	MHC	22	21C	FO	7.5L	G	$1500	138	3,500	10,500	9,240

Livability Code: VA 30-90
Wheelbase-to-length ratio of 53% is considered ○ dangerous ● fatiguing ○ good ○ excellent *
The approximate net payload of 1260 pounds at 12% of GVWR on this model is ○ deficient ○ excessive ○ cautionary ● good ○ excellent *
Total highway safety penalties are: 2 * Value: 78 Durability: 72 Highway Control Rating: 72 Highway Safety: 70 ★★★

Brand	Year	Type	Length	Model	Chassis	Engine	Fuel Type	Price/Ft	Wheelbase	Towing	GVWR	Curb Wt
Tioga Montara	1992	MHC	24	23D	CH	7.4L	G	$1500	146	3,500	10,500	9,815

Livability Code: VA 30-90
Wheelbase-to-length ratio of 51% is considered ○ dangerous ● fatiguing ○ good ○ excellent *
The approximate net payload of 685 pounds at 7% of GVWR on this model is ○ deficient ○ excessive ● cautionary ○ good ○ excellent *
Total highway safety penalties are: 2 * Value: 78 Durability: 72 Highway Control Rating: 33 Highway Safety: 31

Brand	Year	Type	Length	Model	Chassis	Engine	Fuel Type	Price/Ft	Wheelbase	Towing	GVWR	Curb Wt
Tioga Montara	1992	MHC	25	23D	FO	7.5L	G	$1500	158	3,500	11,500	9,998

Livability Code: VA 30-90
Wheelbase-to-length ratio of 54% is considered ○ dangerous ○ fatiguing ● good ○ excellent *
The approximate net payload of 1502 pounds at 13% of GVWR on this model is ○ deficient ○ excessive ○ cautionary ● good ○ excellent *
Total highway safety penalties are: 2 * Value: 78 Durability: 72 Highway Control Rating: 78 Highway Safety: 76 ★★★

Brand	Year	Type	Length	Model	Chassis	Engine	Fuel Type	Price/Ft	Wheelbase	Towing	GVWR	Curb Wt
Tioga Montara	1992	MHC	27	F 27	FO	7.5L	G	$1400	176	3,500	11,500	10,550

Livability Code: VA 30-90
Wheelbase-to-length ratio of 54% is considered ○ dangerous ○ fatiguing ● good ○ excellent *
The approximate net payload of 950 pounds at 8% of GVWR on this model is ○ deficient ○ excessive ● cautionary ○ good ○ excellent *
Total highway safety penalties are: 2 * Value: 78 Durability: 72 Highway Control Rating: 61 Highway Safety: 59 ★

Brand	Year	Type	Length	Model	Chassis	Engine	Fuel Type	Price/Ft	Wheelbase	Towing	GVWR	Curb Wt
Tioga Montara	1992	MHC	27	Y 27	FO	7.5L	G	$1400	176	3,500	11,500	10,677

Livability Code: VA 30-90
Wheelbase-to-length ratio of 54% is considered ○ dangerous ○ fatiguing ● good ○ excellent *
The approximate net payload of 823 pounds at 7% of GVWR on this model is ○ deficient ○ excessive ● cautionary ○ good ○ excellent *
Total highway safety penalties are: 2 * Value: 78 Durability: 72 Highway Control Rating: 55 Highway Safety: 53 ★

Brand	Year	Type	Length	Model	Chassis	Engine	Fuel Type	Price/Ft	Wheelbase	Towing	GVWR	Curb Wt
Tioga Montara	1993	MHC	19	18A	FO	7.5L	G	$1900	138	3,500	10,500	8,751

Livability Code: VA 30-90
Wheelbase-to-length ratio of 59% is considered ○ dangerous ○ fatiguing ○ good ● excellent *
The approximate net payload of 1749 pounds at 17% of GVWR on this model is ○ deficient ○ excessive ○ cautionary ○ good ● excellent *
Total highway safety penalties are: 2 * Value: 78 Durability: 72 Highway Control Rating: 100 Highway Safety: 98 ★★★

Brand	Year	Type	Length	Model	Chassis	Engine	Fuel Type	Price/Ft	Wheelbase	Towing	GVWR	Curb Wt
Tioga Montara	1993	MHC	22	21C	CH	7.4L	G	$1600	125	3,500	10,200	9,168

Livability Code: VA 30-90
Wheelbase-to-length ratio of 48% is considered ● dangerous ○ fatiguing ○ good ○ excellent *
The approximate net payload of 1032 pounds at 10% of GVWR on this model is ○ deficient ○ excessive ○ cautionary ● good ○ excellent *
Total highway safety penalties are: 2 * Value: 78 Durability: 72 Highway Control Rating: 42 Highway Safety: 40

Brand	Year	Type	Length	Model	Chassis	Engine	Fuel Type	Price/Ft	Wheelbase	Towing	GVWR	Curb Wt
Tioga Montara	1993	MHC	22	21C	FO	7.5L	G	$1600	138	3,500	10,500	9,259

Livability Code: VA 30-90
Wheelbase-to-length ratio of 52% is considered ○ dangerous ● fatiguing ○ good ○ excellent *
The approximate net payload of 1241 pounds at 12% of GVWR on this model is ○ deficient ○ excessive ○ cautionary ● good ○ excellent *
Total highway safety penalties are: 2 * Value: 78 Durability: 72 Highway Control Rating: 63 Highway Safety: 61 ★★

Brand	Year	Type	Length	Model	Chassis	Engine	Fuel Type	Price/Ft	Wheelbase	Towing	GVWR	Curb Wt
Tioga Montara	1993	MHC	24	23D	CH	7.4L	G	$1600	146	3,500	10,500	9,815

Livability Code: VA 30-90
Wheelbase-to-length ratio of 51% is considered ○ dangerous ● fatiguing ○ good ○ excellent *
The approximate net payload of 685 pounds at 7% of GVWR on this model is ○ deficient ○ excessive ● cautionary ○ good ○ excellent *
Total highway safety penalties are: 2 * Value: 78 Durability: 72 Highway Control Rating: 33 Highway Safety: 31

Note: Safety ratings are based on the assumption that the engineering of the RV has allowed for proper balance by placing fresh, gray, and black holding tanks in a location so as not to change the balance of the RV when the tanks are empty or full. **Always double-check wheelbase, GVWR, and weights at front and rear axles.**

*See Section 1 for details on how conclusions are reached.

Section 2: The Ratings

Brand	Year	Type	Length	Model	Chassis	Engine	Fuel Type	Average Price per Linear Foot When New	Adjusted Wheelbase	Approx. Towing Capacity	Gross Vehicle Weight Rating	Average Curb Weight
Tioga Montara	1993	MHC	25	23D	FO	7.5L	G	$1600	158	3,000	12,000	10,018

Livability Code: VA 30-90   Wheelbase-to-length ratio of 54% is considered ○ dangerous ○ fatiguing ● good ○ excellent*

The approximate net payload of 1982 pounds at 17% of GVWR on this model is ○ deficient ○ excessive ○ cautionary ○ good ● excellent*

Total highway safety penalties are: 2*   Value: **7 8**   Durability: **7 2**   Highway Control Rating: **8 4**   Highway Safety: **8 2**   ★★★

Brand	Year	Type	Length	Model	Chassis	Engine	Fuel Type	Price	Wheelbase	Towing	GVWR	Curb Weight
Tioga Montara	1993	MHC	28	27F	FO	7.5L	G	$1400	176	3,000	12,000	10,585

Livability Code: VA 30-90   Wheelbase-to-length ratio of 53% is considered ○ dangerous ● fatiguing ○ good ○ excellent*

The approximate net payload of 1415 pounds at 12% of GVWR on this model is ○ deficient ○ excessive ○ cautionary ● good ○ excellent*

Total highway safety penalties are: 2*   Value: **7 8**   Durability: **7 2**   Highway Control Rating: **7 0**   Highway Safety: **6 8**   ★★

Brand	Year	Type	Length	Model	Chassis	Engine	Fuel Type	Price	Wheelbase	Towing	GVWR	Curb Weight
Tioga Montara	1993	MHC	28	27Y	FO	7.5L	G	$1400	176	3,000	12,000	10,713

Livability Code: VA 30-90   Wheelbase-to-length ratio of 53% is considered ○ dangerous ● fatiguing ○ good ○ excellent*

The approximate net payload of 1287 pounds at 11% of GVWR on this model is ○ deficient ○ excessive ○ cautionary ● good ○ excellent*

Total highway safety penalties are: 2*   Value: **7 8**   Durability: **7 2**   Highway Control Rating: **6 8**   Highway Safety: **6 6**   ★★

Brand	Year	Type	Length	Model	Chassis	Engine	Fuel Type	Price	Wheelbase	Towing	GVWR	Curb Weight
Tioga Montara	1994	MHC	19	18A	FO	7.5L	G	$1900	138	3,500	10,500	8,777

Livability Code: VA 30-90   Wheelbase-to-length ratio of 59% is considered ○ dangerous ○ fatiguing ○ good ● excellent*

The approximate net payload of 1723 pounds at 16% of GVWR on this model is ○ deficient ○ excessive ○ cautionary ○ good ● excellent*

Total highway safety penalties are: 2*   Value: **7 8**   Durability: **7 2**   Highway Control Rating: **1 0 0**   Highway Safety: **9 8**   ★★★

Brand	Year	Type	Length	Model	Chassis	Engine	Fuel Type	Price	Wheelbase	Towing	GVWR	Curb Weight
Tioga Montara	1994	MHC	22	21C	CH	7.4L	G	$1600	125	3,500	10,200	9,250

Livability Code: VA 30-90   Wheelbase-to-length ratio of 48% is considered ● dangerous ○ fatiguing ○ good ○ excellent*

The approximate net payload of 950 pounds at 9% of GVWR on this model is ○ deficient ○ excessive ● cautionary ○ good ○ excellent*

Total highway safety penalties are: 2*   Value: **7 8**   Durability: **7 2**   Highway Control Rating: **3 8**   Highway Safety: **3 6**

Brand	Year	Type	Length	Model	Chassis	Engine	Fuel Type	Price	Wheelbase	Towing	GVWR	Curb Weight
Tioga Montara	1994	MHC	22	21C	FO	7.5L	G	$1700	138	3,500	10,500	9,363

Livability Code: VA 30-90   Wheelbase-to-length ratio of 52% is considered ○ dangerous ● fatiguing ○ good ○ excellent*

The approximate net payload of 1137 pounds at 11% of GVWR on this model is ○ deficient ○ excessive ○ cautionary ● good ○ excellent*

Total highway safety penalties are: 2*   Value: **7 8**   Durability: **7 2**   Highway Control Rating: **6 1**   Highway Safety: **5 9**   ★

Brand	Year	Type	Length	Model	Chassis	Engine	Fuel Type	Price	Wheelbase	Towing	GVWR	Curb Weight
Tioga Montara	1994	MHC	25	23D	CH	7.4L	G	$1600	146	3,500	10,500	9,950

Livability Code: VA 30-90   Wheelbase-to-length ratio of 49% is considered ● dangerous ○ fatiguing ○ good ○ excellent*

The approximate net payload of 550 pounds at 5% of GVWR on this model is ● deficient ○ excessive ○ cautionary ○ good ○ excellent*

Total highway safety penalties are: 2*   Value: **7 8**   Durability: **7 2**   Highway Control Rating: **2 2**   Highway Safety: **2 0**

Brand	Year	Type	Length	Model	Chassis	Engine	Fuel Type	Price	Wheelbase	Towing	GVWR	Curb Weight
Tioga Montara	1994	MHC	25	23D	FO	7.5L	G	$1600	158	3,500	12,400	10,250

Livability Code: VA 30-90   Wheelbase-to-length ratio of 54% is considered ○ dangerous ○ fatiguing ● good ○ excellent*

The approximate net payload of 2150 pounds at 17% of GVWR on this model is ○ deficient ○ excessive ○ cautionary ○ good ● excellent*

Total highway safety penalties are: 2*   Value: **7 8**   Durability: **7 2**   Highway Control Rating: **8 5**   Highway Safety: **8 3**   ★★★

Brand	Year	Type	Length	Model	Chassis	Engine	Fuel Type	Price	Wheelbase	Towing	GVWR	Curb Weight
Tioga Montara	1994	MHC	25	23P	FO	7.5L	G	$1600	158	3,500	12,400	10,250

Livability Code: VA 30-90   Wheelbase-to-length ratio of 54% is considered ○ dangerous ○ fatiguing ● good ○ excellent*

The approximate net payload of 2150 pounds at 17% of GVWR on this model is ○ deficient ○ excessive ○ cautionary ○ good ● excellent*

Total highway safety penalties are: 2*   Value: **7 8**   Durability: **7 2**   Highway Control Rating: **8 5**   Highway Safety: **8 3**   ★★★

Brand	Year	Type	Length	Model	Chassis	Engine	Fuel Type	Price	Wheelbase	Towing	GVWR	Curb Weight
Tioga Montara	1994	MHC	26	26J	FO	7.5L	G	$1600	190	3,500	12,400	10,633

Livability Code: VA 30-90   Wheelbase-to-length ratio of 60% is considered ○ dangerous ○ fatiguing ○ good ● excellent*

The approximate net payload of 1767 pounds at 14% of GVWR on this model is ○ deficient ○ excessive ○ cautionary ● good ○ excellent*

Total highway safety penalties are: 2*   Value: **7 8**   Durability: **7 2**   Highway Control Rating: **1 0 0**   Highway Safety: **9 8**   ★★★

Brand	Year	Type	Length	Model	Chassis	Engine	Fuel Type	Price	Wheelbase	Towing	GVWR	Curb Weight
Tioga Montara	1994	MHC	28	27V	FO	7.5L	G	$1500	190	3,500	12,400	10,994

Livability Code: VA 30-90   Wheelbase-to-length ratio of 57% is considered ○ dangerous ○ fatiguing ● good ○ excellent*

The approximate net payload of 1406 pounds at 11% of GVWR on this model is ○ deficient ○ excessive ○ cautionary ● good ○ excellent*

Total highway safety penalties are: 2*   Value: **7 8**   Durability: **7 2**   Highway Control Rating: **8 9**   Highway Safety: **8 7**   ★★★

Brand	Year	Type	Length	Model	Chassis	Engine	Fuel Type	Price	Wheelbase	Towing	GVWR	Curb Weight
Tioga Montara	1994	MHC	29	29Z	FO	7.5L	G	$1500	190	3,500	12,400	11,242

Livability Code: VA 30-90   Wheelbase-to-length ratio of 55% is considered ○ dangerous ○ fatiguing ● good ○ excellent*

The approximate net payload of 1158 pounds at 9% of GVWR on this model is ○ deficient ○ excessive ● cautionary ○ good ○ excellent*

Total highway safety penalties are: 2*   Value: **7 8**   Durability: **7 2**   Highway Control Rating: **7 5**   Highway Safety: **7 3**   ★★★

Note: Safety ratings are based on the assumption that the engineering of the RV has allowed for proper balance by placing fresh, gray, and black holding tanks in a location so as not to change the balance of the RV when the tanks are empty or full. **Always double-check wheelbase, GVWR, and weights at front and rear axles.**

*See Section 1 for details on how conclusions are reached.

Brand	Year	Type	Length	Model	Chassis	Engine	Fuel Type	Average Price per Linear Foot When New	Adjusted Wheelbase	Approx. Towing Capacity	Gross Vehicle Weight Rating	Average Curb Weight
Tioga Montara	1995	MHC	22	21C	FO	7.5L	G	$1800	138	3,500	10,500	9,431

Livability Code: VA 30-90
Wheelbase-to-length ratio of 52% is considered ○ dangerous ● fatiguing ○ good ○ excellent *
The approximate net payload of 1069 pounds at 10% of GVWR on this model is ○ deficient ○ excessive ○ cautionary ● good ○ excellent *
Total highway safety penalties are: 2 *   Value: **7 8**   Durability: **7 2**   Highway Control Rating: **6 3**   Highway Safety: **6 1**   ★★

Tioga Montara	1995	MHC	24	22B	FO	7.5L	G	$1700	138	3,500	10,500	9,702

Livability Code: VA 30-90
Wheelbase-to-length ratio of 49% is considered ● dangerous ○ fatiguing ○ good ○ excellent *
The approximate net payload of 798 pounds at 8% of GVWR on this model is ○ deficient ○ excessive ● cautionary ○ good ○ excellent *
Total highway safety penalties are: 2 *   Value: **7 8**   Durability: **7 2**   Highway Control Rating: **3 3**   Highway Safety: **3 1**

Tioga Montara	1995	MHC	25	23D	FO	7.5L	G	$1700	158	3,500	12,400	10,317

Livability Code: VA 30-90
Wheelbase-to-length ratio of 53% is considered ○ dangerous ○ fatiguing ○ good ○ excellent *
The approximate net payload of 2083 pounds at 17% of GVWR on this model is ○ deficient ○ excessive ○ cautionary ○ good ● excellent *
Total highway safety penalties are: 2 *   Value: **7 8**   Durability: **7 2**   Highway Control Rating: **7 8**   Highway Safety: **7 6**   ★★★

Tioga Montara	1995	MHC	25	23P	FO	7.5L	G	$1700	158	3,500	12,400	10,430

Livability Code: VA 30-90
Wheelbase-to-length ratio of 52% is considered ○ dangerous ● fatiguing ○ good ○ excellent *
The approximate net payload of 1970 pounds at 16% of GVWR on this model is ○ deficient ○ excessive ○ cautionary ○ good ● excellent *
Total highway safety penalties are: 2 *   Value: **7 8**   Durability: **7 2**   Highway Control Rating: **7 0**   Highway Safety: **6 8**   ★★

Tioga Montara	1995	MHC	29	27V	FO	7.5L	G	$1600	190	3,500	12,400	11,175

Livability Code: VA 30-90
Wheelbase-to-length ratio of 55% is considered ○ dangerous ○ fatiguing ● good ○ excellent *
The approximate net payload of 1225 pounds at 10% of GVWR on this model is ○ deficient ○ excessive ○ cautionary ● good ○ excellent *
Total highway safety penalties are: 2 *   Value: **7 8**   Durability: **7 2**   Highway Control Rating: **8 7**   Highway Safety: **8 5**   ★★★

Tioga Montara	1995	MHC	30	29Z	FO	7.5L	G	$1400	190	3,500	12,400	11,468

Livability Code: VA 30-90
Wheelbase-to-length ratio of 53% is considered ○ dangerous ● fatiguing ○ good ○ excellent *
The approximate net payload of 932 pounds at 8% of GVWR on this model is ○ deficient ○ excessive ● cautionary ○ good ○ excellent *
Total highway safety penalties are: 2 *   Value: **7 8**   Durability: **7 2**   Highway Control Rating: **5 4**   Highway Safety: **5 2**   ★

Tioga Montara	1996	MHC	22	21C -460	FO	7.5L	G	$2000	138	3,500	10,500	9,680

Livability Code: VA 30-90
Wheelbase-to-length ratio of 52% is considered ○ dangerous ● fatiguing ○ good ○ excellent *
The approximate net payload of 820 pounds at 8% of GVWR on this model is ○ deficient ○ excessive ● cautionary ○ good ○ excellent *
Total highway safety penalties are: 2 *   Value: **7 8**   Durability: **7 2**   Highway Control Rating: **4 8**   Highway Safety: **4 6**

Tioga Montara	1996	MHC	22	21C -351	FO	5.8L	G	$1800	138	1,000	10,500	9,680

Livability Code: VA 30-90
Wheelbase-to-length ratio of 52% is considered ○ dangerous ● fatiguing ○ good ○ excellent *
The approximate net payload of 820 pounds at 8% of GVWR on this model is ○ deficient ○ excessive ● cautionary ○ good ○ excellent *
Total highway safety penalties are: 2 *   Value: **7 8**   Durability: **7 2**   Highway Control Rating: **4 8**   Highway Safety: **4 6**

Tioga Montara	1996	MHC	23	22B -460	FO	7.5L	G	$1900	138	3,500	10,500	9,848

Livability Code: VA 30-90
Wheelbase-to-length ratio of 51% is considered ○ dangerous ● fatiguing ○ good ○ excellent *
The approximate net payload of 652 pounds at 6% of GVWR on this model is ● deficient ○ excessive ○ cautionary ○ good ○ excellent *
Total highway safety penalties are: 2 *   Value: **7 8**   Durability: **7 2**   Highway Control Rating: **2 7**   Highway Safety: **2 5**

Tioga Montara	1996	MHC	23	22B -351	FO	5.8L	G	$1800	138	1,000	10,500	9,848

Livability Code: VA 30-90
Wheelbase-to-length ratio of 51% is considered ○ dangerous ● fatiguing ○ good ○ excellent *
The approximate net payload of 652 pounds at 6% of GVWR on this model is ● deficient ○ excessive ○ cautionary ○ good ○ excellent *
Total highway safety penalties are: 2 *   Value: **7 8**   Durability: **7 2**   Highway Control Rating: **2 7**   Highway Safety: **2 5**

Tioga Montara	1996	MHC	25	23D op eng	FO	7.5L	G	$1900	158	3,500	12,400	10,604

Livability Code: VA 30-90
Wheelbase-to-length ratio of 54% is considered ○ dangerous ○ fatiguing ● good ○ excellent *
The approximate net payload of 1796 pounds at 14% of GVWR on this model is ○ deficient ○ excessive ○ cautionary ● good ○ excellent *
Total highway safety penalties are: 2 *   Value: **7 8**   Durability: **7 2**   Highway Control Rating: **8 0**   Highway Safety: **7 8**   ★★★

Tioga Montara	1996	MHC	25	23P op eng	FO	7.5L	G	$1800	158	3,500	12,400	10,604

Livability Code: VA 30-90
Wheelbase-to-length ratio of 54% is considered ○ dangerous ○ fatiguing ● good ○ excellent *
The approximate net payload of 1796 pounds at 14% of GVWR on this model is ○ deficient ○ excessive ○ cautionary ● good ○ excellent *
Total highway safety penalties are: 2 *   Value: **7 8**   Durability: **7 2**   Highway Control Rating: **8 0**   Highway Safety: **7 8**   ★★★

Note: Safety ratings are based on the assumption that the engineering of the RV has allowed for proper balance by placing fresh, gray, and black holding tanks in a location so as not to change the balance of the RV when the tanks are empty or full. **Always double-check wheelbase, GVWR, and weights at front and rear axles.**

*See Section 1 for details on how conclusions are reached.

Section 2: The Ratings

Brand	Year	Type	Length	Model	Chassis	Engine	Fuel Type	Average Price per Linear Foot When New	Adjusted Wheelbase	Approx. Towing Capacity	Gross Vehicle Weight Rating	Average Curb Weight
Tioga Montara	1996	MHC	25	23D	FO	5.8L	G	$1700	158	1,000	12,400	10,604

Livability Code: VA 30-90
Wheelbase-to-length ratio of 54% is considered ○ dangerous ○ fatiguing ◉ good ○ excellent *
The approximate net payload of 1796 pounds at 14% of GVWR on this model is ○ deficient ○ excessive ○ cautionary ◉ good ○ excellent *
Total highway safety penalties are: 2 *   Value: **7 8**   Durability: **7 2**   Highway Control Rating: **8 0**   Highway Safety: **7 8**   ★★★

Brand	Year	Type	Length	Model	Chassis	Engine	Fuel Type	Price/Ft	Wheelbase	Towing	GVWR	Curb Weight
Tioga Montara	1996	MHC	25	23P	FO	5.8L	G	$1700	158	1,000	12,400	10,604

Livability Code: VA 30-90
Wheelbase-to-length ratio of 54% is considered ○ dangerous ○ fatiguing ◉ good ○ excellent *
The approximate net payload of 1796 pounds at 14% of GVWR on this model is ○ deficient ○ excessive ○ cautionary ◉ good ○ excellent *
Total highway safety penalties are: 2 *   Value: **7 8**   Durability: **7 2**   Highway Control Rating: **8 0**   Highway Safety: **7 8**   ★★★

Tioga Montara	1996	MHC	29	29M -460	FO	7.5L	G	$1600	190	3,500	12,400	11,738

Livability Code: VA 30-90
Wheelbase-to-length ratio of 55% is considered ○ dangerous ○ fatiguing ◉ good ○ excellent *
The approximate net payload of 662 pounds at 5% of GVWR on this model is ◉ deficient ○ excessive ○ cautionary ○ good ○ excellent *
Total highway safety penalties are: 2 *   Value: **7 8**   Durability: **7 2**   Highway Control Rating: **5 6**   Highway Safety: **5 4**   ★

Tioga Montara	1996	MHC	29	29Z -460	FO	7.5L	G	$1600	190	3,500	12,400	11,660

Livability Code: VA 30-90
Wheelbase-to-length ratio of 55% is considered ○ dangerous ○ fatiguing ◉ good ○ excellent *
The approximate net payload of 740 pounds at 6% of GVWR on this model is ◉ deficient ○ excessive ○ cautionary ○ good ○ excellent *
Total highway safety penalties are: 2 *   Value: **7 8**   Durability: **7 2**   Highway Control Rating: **5 6**   Highway Safety: **5 4**   ★

Tioga Montara	1996	MHC	29	29M -351	FO	5.8L	G	$1600	190	1,000	12,400	11,660

Livability Code: VA 30-90
Wheelbase-to-length ratio of 55% is considered ○ dangerous ○ fatiguing ◉ good ○ excellent *
The approximate net payload of 740 pounds at 6% of GVWR on this model is ◉ deficient ○ excessive ○ cautionary ○ good ○ excellent *
Total highway safety penalties are: 2 *   Value: **7 8**   Durability: **7 2**   Highway Control Rating: **5 6**   Highway Safety: **5 4**   ★

Tioga Montara	1996	MHC	29	29Z -351	FO	5.8L	G	$1600	190	1,000	12,400	11,660

Livability Code: VA 30-90
Wheelbase-to-length ratio of 55% is considered ○ dangerous ○ fatiguing ◉ good ○ excellent *
The approximate net payload of 740 pounds at 6% of GVWR on this model is ◉ deficient ○ excessive ○ cautionary ○ good ○ excellent *
Total highway safety penalties are: 2 *   Value: **7 8**   Durability: **7 2**   Highway Control Rating: **5 6**   Highway Safety: **5 4**   ★

Tioga Montara	1997	MHC	23	22C	FO	6.8L	G	$2000	138	3,500	10,500	9,477

Livability Code: VA 30-90
Wheelbase-to-length ratio of 51% is considered ○ dangerous ◉ fatiguing ○ good ○ excellent *
The approximate net payload of 1023 pounds at 10% of GVWR on this model is ○ deficient ○ excessive ○ cautionary ◉ good ○ excellent *
Total highway safety penalties are: 2 *   Value: **7 8**   Durability: **7 2**   Highway Control Rating: **5 1**   Highway Safety: **4 9**

Tioga Montara	1997	MHC	23	22B	FO	6.8L	G	$2000	138	3,500	10,500	9,543

Livability Code: VA 30-90
Wheelbase-to-length ratio of 50% is considered ◉ dangerous ○ fatiguing ○ good ○ excellent *
The approximate net payload of 957 pounds at 9% of GVWR on this model is ○ deficient ○ excessive ◉ cautionary ○ good ○ excellent *
Total highway safety penalties are: 2 *   Value: **7 8**   Durability: **7 2**   Highway Control Rating: **4 3**   Highway Safety: **4 1**

Tioga Montara	1997	MHC	25	24D	FO	7.3L	D	$1800	158	3,500	11,500	10,446

Livability Code: VA 30-90
Wheelbase-to-length ratio of 53% is considered ○ dangerous ◉ fatiguing ○ good ○ excellent *
The approximate net payload of 1054 pounds at 9% of GVWR on this model is ○ deficient ○ excessive ◉ cautionary ○ good ○ excellent *
Total highway safety penalties are: 2 *   Value: **7 8**   Durability: **7 2**   Highway Control Rating: **6 0**   Highway Safety: **5 8**   ★

Tioga Montara	1997	MHC	25	24D	FO	6.8L	G	$1800	158	3,500	11,500	10,132

Livability Code: VA 30-90
Wheelbase-to-length ratio of 53% is considered ○ dangerous ◉ fatiguing ○ good ○ excellent *
The approximate net payload of 1368 pounds at 12% of GVWR on this model is ○ deficient ○ excessive ○ cautionary ◉ good ○ excellent *
Total highway safety penalties are: 2 *   Value: **7 8**   Durability: **7 2**   Highway Control Rating: **6 9**   Highway Safety: **6 7**   ★★

Tioga Montara	1997	MHC	25	24P	FO	6.8L	G	$1800	158	3,500	11,500	10,149

Livability Code: VA 30-90
Wheelbase-to-length ratio of 53% is considered ○ dangerous ◉ fatiguing ○ good ○ excellent *
The approximate net payload of 1351 pounds at 12% of GVWR on this model is ○ deficient ○ excessive ○ cautionary ◉ good ○ excellent *
Total highway safety penalties are: 2 *   Value: **7 8**   Durability: **7 2**   Highway Control Rating: **6 9**   Highway Safety: **6 7**   ★★

Tioga Montara	1997	MHC	27	26F	FO	6.8L	G	$1700	176	3,500	14,050	11,280

Livability Code: VA 30-90
Wheelbase-to-length ratio of 55% is considered ○ dangerous ○ fatiguing ◉ good ○ excellent *
The approximate net payload of 2770 pounds at 20% of GVWR on this model is ○ deficient ○ excessive ○ cautionary ○ good ◉ excellent *
Total highway safety penalties are: 2 *   Value: **7 8**   Durability: **7 2**   Highway Control Rating: **9 6**   Highway Safety: **9 4**   ★★★

Note: Safety ratings are based on the assumption that the engineering of the RV has allowed for proper balance by placing fresh, gray, and black holding tanks in a location so as not to change the balance of the RV when the tanks are empty or full. **Always double-check wheelbase, GVWR, and weights at front and rear axles.**

*See Section 1 for details on how conclusions are reached.

Brand	Year	Type	Length	Model	Chassis	Engine	Fuel Type	Average Price per Linear Foot When New	Adjusted Wheelbase	Approx. Towing Capacity	Gross Vehicle Weight Rating	Average Curb Weight
Tioga Montara	1997	MHC	29	29Z	FO	6.8L	G	$1600	190	3,500	14,050	11,618

Livability Code: VA 30-90 — Wheelbase-to-length ratio of 54% is considered ○ dangerous ○ fatiguing ◉ good ○ excellent *

The approximate net payload of 2432 pounds at 17% of GVWR on this model is ○ deficient ○ excessive ○ cautionary ○ good ◉ excellent *

Total highway safety penalties are: 2 * — Value: 7 8 — Durability: 7 2 — Highway Control Rating: 8 7 — Highway Safety: 8 5 — ★★★

Brand	Year	Type	Length	Model	Chassis	Engine	Fuel Type	Price/Ft	Wheelbase	Towing	GVWR	Curb Weight
Tioga SL	1998	MHC	30	29H	FO	6.8L	G	$1700	214	3,500	14,050	12,031

Livability Code: VA 30-90 — Wheelbase-to-length ratio of 59% is considered ○ dangerous ○ fatiguing ○ good ◉ excellent *

The approximate net payload of 2019 pounds at 14% of GVWR on this model is ○ deficient ○ excessive ○ cautionary ◉ good ○ excellent *

Total highway safety penalties are: 2 * — Value: 7 8 — Durability: 7 3 — Highway Control Rating: 1 0 0 — Highway Safety: 9 8 — ★★★

Brand	Year	Type	Length	Model	Chassis	Engine	Fuel Type	Price/Ft	Wheelbase	Towing	GVWR	Curb Weight
Tioga SL	1998	MHC	31	31T	FO	6.8L	G	$1600	214	3,500	14,050	12,350

Livability Code: VA 30-90 — Wheelbase-to-length ratio of 57% is considered ○ dangerous ○ fatiguing ◉ good ○ excellent *

The approximate net payload of 1700 pounds at 12% of GVWR on this model is ○ deficient ○ excessive ○ cautionary ◉ good ○ excellent *

Total highway safety penalties are: 2 * — Value: 7 8 — Durability: 7 3 — Highway Control Rating: 9 1 — Highway Safety: 8 9 — ★★★

Brand	Year	Type	Length	Model	Chassis	Engine	Fuel Type	Price/Ft	Wheelbase	Towing	GVWR	Curb Weight
Tioga SL	1998	MHC	31	31W	FO	6.8L	G	$1600	214	3,500	14,050	13,250

Livability Code: VA 30-90 — Wheelbase-to-length ratio of 57% is considered ○ dangerous ○ fatiguing ◉ good ○ excellent *

The approximate net payload of 800 pounds at 6% of GVWR on this model is ◉ deficient ○ excessive ○ cautionary ○ good ○ excellent *

Total highway safety penalties are: 7 * — Value: 7 6 — Durability: 7 3 — Highway Control Rating: 6 4 — Highway Safety: 5 7 — ★

Brand	Year	Type	Length	Model	Chassis	Engine	Fuel Type	Price/Ft	Wheelbase	Towing	GVWR	Curb Weight
Tioga Walkabout	1996	MHC	20	19A	FO	7.5L	G	$2200	138	3,500	10,500	8,453

Livability Code: VA 30-90 — Wheelbase-to-length ratio of 59% is considered ○ dangerous ○ fatiguing ○ good ◉ excellent *

The approximate net payload of 2047 pounds at 19% of GVWR on this model is ○ deficient ○ excessive ○ cautionary ○ good ◉ excellent *

Total highway safety penalties are: 2 * — Value: 7 9 — Durability: 7 5 — Highway Control Rating: 1 0 0 — Highway Safety: 9 8 — ★★★

Brand	Year	Type	Length	Model	Chassis	Engine	Fuel Type	Price/Ft	Wheelbase	Towing	GVWR	Curb Weight
Tioga Walkabout	1996	MHC	22	21C	FO	7.5L	G	$2000	138	3,500	10,500	8,950

Livability Code: VA 30-90 — Wheelbase-to-length ratio of 52% is considered ○ dangerous ◉ fatiguing ○ good ○ excellent *

The approximate net payload of 1550 pounds at 15% of GVWR on this model is ○ deficient ○ excessive ○ cautionary ◉ good ○ excellent *

Total highway safety penalties are: 2 * — Value: 7 9 — Durability: 7 5 — Highway Control Rating: 6 9 — Highway Safety: 6 7 — ★★

Brand	Year	Type	Length	Model	Chassis	Engine	Fuel Type	Price/Ft	Wheelbase	Towing	GVWR	Curb Weight
Tioga Walkabout	1996	MHC	25	23D	FO	7.5L	G	$1900	158	3,500	12,400	9,787

Livability Code: VA 30-90 — Wheelbase-to-length ratio of 54% is considered ○ dangerous ○ fatiguing ◉ good ○ excellent *

The approximate net payload of 2613 pounds at 21% of GVWR on this model is ○ deficient ○ excessive ○ cautionary ○ good ◉ excellent *

Total highway safety penalties are: 2 * — Value: 7 9 — Durability: 7 5 — Highway Control Rating: 8 6 — Highway Safety: 8 4 — ★★★

Brand	Year	Type	Length	Model	Chassis	Engine	Fuel Type	Price/Ft	Wheelbase	Towing	GVWR	Curb Weight
Tioga Walkabout	1996	MHC	29	29Z	FO	7.5L	G	$1700	190	3,500	12,400	10,697

Livability Code: VA 30-90 — Wheelbase-to-length ratio of 55% is considered ○ dangerous ○ fatiguing ◉ good ○ excellent *

The approximate net payload of 1703 pounds at 14% of GVWR on this model is ○ deficient ○ excessive ○ cautionary ◉ good ○ excellent *

Total highway safety penalties are: 2 * — Value: 7 9 — Durability: 7 5 — Highway Control Rating: 8 7 — Highway Safety: 8 5 — ★★★

Brand	Year	Type	Length	Model	Chassis	Engine	Fuel Type	Price/Ft	Wheelbase	Towing	GVWR	Curb Weight
Tioga Walkabout	1997	MHC	20	19A	FO	6.8L	G	$2300	138	3,500	10,500	8,536

Livability Code: VA 30-90 — Wheelbase-to-length ratio of 58% is considered ○ dangerous ○ fatiguing ○ good ◉ excellent *

The approximate net payload of 1964 pounds at 19% of GVWR on this model is ○ deficient ○ excessive ○ cautionary ○ good ◉ excellent *

Total highway safety penalties are: 2 * — Value: 7 9 — Durability: 7 5 — Highway Control Rating: 1 0 0 — Highway Safety: 9 8 — ★★★

Brand	Year	Type	Length	Model	Chassis	Engine	Fuel Type	Price/Ft	Wheelbase	Towing	GVWR	Curb Weight
Tioga Walkabout	1997	MHC	23	22C	FO	6.8L	G	$2000	138	3,500	10,500	9,053

Livability Code: VA 30-90 — Wheelbase-to-length ratio of 51% is considered ○ dangerous ◉ fatiguing ○ good ○ excellent *

The approximate net payload of 1447 pounds at 14% of GVWR on this model is ○ deficient ○ excessive ○ cautionary ◉ good ○ excellent *

Total highway safety penalties are: 2 * — Value: 7 9 — Durability: 7 5 — Highway Control Rating: 5 9 — Highway Safety: 5 7 — ★

Brand	Year	Type	Length	Model	Chassis	Engine	Fuel Type	Price/Ft	Wheelbase	Towing	GVWR	Curb Weight
Tioga Walkabout	1997	MHC	23	22E	FO	6.8L	G	$2000	138	3,500	10,500	9,156

Livability Code: VA 30-90 — Wheelbase-to-length ratio of 50% is considered ◉ dangerous ○ fatiguing ○ good ○ excellent *

The approximate net payload of 1344 pounds at 13% of GVWR on this model is ○ deficient ○ excessive ○ cautionary ◉ good ○ excellent *

Total highway safety penalties are: 2 * — Value: 7 9 — Durability: 7 5 — Highway Control Rating: 5 4 — Highway Safety: 5 2

Brand	Year	Type	Length	Model	Chassis	Engine	Fuel Type	Price/Ft	Wheelbase	Towing	GVWR	Curb Weight
Tioga Walkabout	1997	MHC	25	24D	FO	6.8L	G	$1900	158	3,500	11,500	9,670

Livability Code: VA 30-90 — Wheelbase-to-length ratio of 53% is considered ○ dangerous ◉ fatiguing ○ good ○ excellent *

The approximate net payload of 1830 pounds at 16% of GVWR on this model is ○ deficient ○ excessive ○ cautionary ○ good ◉ excellent *

Total highway safety penalties are: 2 * — Value: 7 9 — Durability: 7 5 — Highway Control Rating: 7 7 — Highway Safety: 7 5 — ★★★

Note: Safety ratings are based on the assumption that the engineering of the RV has allowed for proper balance by placing fresh, gray, and black holding tanks in a location so as not to change the balance of the RV when the tanks are empty or full. **Always double-check wheelbase, GVWR, and weights at front and rear axles.**

*See Section 1 for details on how conclusions are reached.

Brand	Year	Type	Length	Model	Chassis	Engine	Fuel Type	Average Price per Linear Foot When New	Adjusted Wheel-base	Approx. Towing Capacity	Gross Vehicle Weight Rating	Average Curb Weight
Tioga Walkabout	**1997**	MHC	27	26F	FO	6.8L	G	$1800	176	3,500	14,050	10,722

Livability Code: VA 30-90   Wheelbase-to-length ratio of 55% is considered ○ dangerous ○ fatiguing ◉ good ○ excellent*

The approximate net payload of 3328 pounds at 24% of GVWR on this model is ○ deficient ○ excessive ○ cautionary ○ good ◉ excellent*

Total highway safety penalties are: 2*   Value: 79 Durability: 75 Highway Control Rating: 93   Highway Safety: 91 ★★★

Brand	Year	Type	Length	Model	Chassis	Engine	Fuel Type	Avg Price/Linear Foot	Adjusted Wheelbase	Approx. Towing Capacity	GVWR	Avg Curb Weight
Tioga Walkabout	**1997**	MHC	29	29Z	FO	6.8L	G	$1700	190	3,500	14,050	11,259

Livability Code: VA 30-90   Wheelbase-to-length ratio of 54% is considered ○ dangerous ○ fatiguing ◉ good ○ excellent*

The approximate net payload of 2791 pounds at 20% of GVWR on this model is ○ deficient ○ excessive ○ cautionary ○ good ◉ excellent*

Total highway safety penalties are: 2*   Value: 79 Durability: 75 Highway Control Rating: 89   Highway Safety: 87 ★★★

| **Titan** | **1992** | MHA | 29 | 287 QB | CH | 7.4L | G | $1700 | 178 | 2,200 | 14,800 | 12,904 |

Livability Code: SB 30-90   Wheelbase-to-length ratio of 51% is considered ○ dangerous ◉ fatiguing ○ good ○ excellent*

The approximate net payload of 1896 pounds at 13% of GVWR on this model is ○ deficient ○ excessive ○ cautionary ◉ good ○ excellent*

Total highway safety penalties are: 4*   Value: 76 Durability: 70 Highway Control Rating: 42   Highway Safety: 38

| **Titan** | **1992** | MHA | 29 | 287 TB | CH | 7.4L | G | $1700 | 178 | 2,200 | 14,800 | 12,904 |

Livability Code: SB 30-90   Wheelbase-to-length ratio of 51% is considered ○ dangerous ◉ fatiguing ○ good ○ excellent*

The approximate net payload of 1896 pounds at 13% of GVWR on this model is ○ deficient ○ excessive ○ cautionary ◉ good ○ excellent*

Total highway safety penalties are: 4*   Value: 76 Durability: 70 Highway Control Rating: 42   Highway Safety: 38

| **Titan** | **1992** | MHA | 31 | 303 QB | CH | 7.4L | G | $1700 | 190 | 2,200 | 14,800 | 13,384 |

Livability Code: SB 30-90   Wheelbase-to-length ratio of 51% is considered ○ dangerous ◉ fatiguing ○ good ○ excellent*

The approximate net payload of 1416 pounds at 10% of GVWR on this model is ○ deficient ○ excessive ○ cautionary ◉ good ○ excellent*

Total highway safety penalties are: 5*   Value: 75 Durability: 70 Highway Control Rating: 36   Highway Safety: 31

| **Titan** | **1992** | MHA | 31 | 303 TB | CH | 7.4L | G | $1700 | 190 | 2,200 | 14,800 | 13,384 |

Livability Code: SB 30-90   Wheelbase-to-length ratio of 51% is considered ○ dangerous ◉ fatiguing ○ good ○ excellent*

The approximate net payload of 1416 pounds at 10% of GVWR on this model is ○ deficient ○ excessive ○ cautionary ◉ good ○ excellent*

Total highway safety penalties are: 5*   Value: 75 Durability: 70 Highway Control Rating: 36   Highway Safety: 31

| **Titan** | **1992** | MHA | 32 | 323 QB | CH | 7.4L | G | $1600 | 190 | 1,500 | 16,000 | 14,080 |

Livability Code: SB 30-90   Wheelbase-to-length ratio of 49% is considered ◉ dangerous ○ fatiguing ○ good ○ excellent*

The approximate net payload of 1920 pounds at 12% of GVWR on this model is ○ deficient ○ excessive ○ cautionary ◉ good ○ excellent*

Total highway safety penalties are: 6*   Value: 75 Durability: 70 Highway Control Rating: 35   Highway Safety: 29

| **Titan** | **1992** | MHA | 32 | 323 TB | CH | 7.4L | G | $1600 | 190 | 1,500 | 16,000 | 14,080 |

Livability Code: SB 30-90   Wheelbase-to-length ratio of 49% is considered ◉ dangerous ○ fatiguing ○ good ○ excellent*

The approximate net payload of 1920 pounds at 12% of GVWR on this model is ○ deficient ○ excessive ○ cautionary ◉ good ○ excellent*

Total highway safety penalties are: 6*   Value: 75 Durability: 70 Highway Control Rating: 35   Highway Safety: 29

| **Titan** | **1992** | MHA | 34 | 341 QB | CH | 7.4L | G | $1600 | 208 | 1,500 | 16,000 | 14,560 |

Livability Code: SB 30-90   Wheelbase-to-length ratio of 51% is considered ○ dangerous ◉ fatiguing ○ good ○ excellent*

The approximate net payload of 1440 pounds at 9% of GVWR on this model is ○ deficient ○ excessive ◉ cautionary ○ good ○ excellent*

Total highway safety penalties are: 7*   Value: 75 Durability: 70 Highway Control Rating: 31   Highway Safety: 24

| **Titan** | **1992** | MHA | 34 | 347 QB | CH | 7.4L | G | $1600 | 208 | 1,500 | 16,000 | 14,560 |

Livability Code: SB 30-90   Wheelbase-to-length ratio of 51% is considered ○ dangerous ◉ fatiguing ○ good ○ excellent*

The approximate net payload of 1440 pounds at 9% of GVWR on this model is ○ deficient ○ excessive ◉ cautionary ○ good ○ excellent*

Total highway safety penalties are: 7*   Value: 75 Durability: 70 Highway Control Rating: 31   Highway Safety: 24

| **Titan** | **1992** | MHA | 34 | 347 TB | CH | 7.4L | G | $1600 | 208 | 1,500 | 16,000 | 14,560 |

Livability Code: SB 30-90   Wheelbase-to-length ratio of 51% is considered ○ dangerous ◉ fatiguing ○ good ○ excellent*

The approximate net payload of 1440 pounds at 9% of GVWR on this model is ○ deficient ○ excessive ◉ cautionary ○ good ○ excellent*

Total highway safety penalties are: 7*   Value: 75 Durability: 70 Highway Control Rating: 31   Highway Safety: 24

| **Titan** | **1992** | MHA | 36 | 363 QB | OS | Cu5.9L | D | $1700 | 228 | 1,500 | 18,000 | 15,816 |

Livability Code: SB 30-90   Wheelbase-to-length ratio of 53% is considered ○ dangerous ◉ fatiguing ○ good ○ excellent*

The approximate net payload of 2184 pounds at 12% of GVWR on this model is ○ deficient ○ excessive ○ cautionary ◉ good ○ excellent*

Total highway safety penalties are: 2*   Value: 77 Durability: 70 Highway Control Rating: 62   Highway Safety: 60 ★★

Note: Safety ratings are based on the assumption that the engineering of the RV has allowed for proper balance by placing fresh, gray, and black holding tanks in a location so as not to change the balance of the RV when the tanks are empty or full. **Always double-check wheelbase, GVWR, and weights at front and rear axles.**

*See Section 1 for details on how conclusions are reached.

Brand	Year	Type	Length	Model	Chassis	Engine	Fuel Type	Average Price per Linear Foot When New	Adjusted Wheel-base	Approx. Towing Capacity	Gross Vehicle Weight Rating	Average Curb Weight
Titan	1992	MHA	36	363 TB	OS	Cu5.9L	D	$1700	228	1,500	18,000	15,816

Livability Code: SB 30-90   Wheelbase-to-length ratio of 53% is considered ○ dangerous ◉ fatiguing ○ good ○ excellent *

The approximate net payload of 2184 pounds at 12% of GVWR on this model is ○ deficient ○ excessive ○ cautionary ◉ good ○ excellent *

Total highway safety penalties are: 2 *   Value: 7 7   Durability: 7 0   Highway Control Rating: 6 2   Highway Safety: 6 0   ★★

Brand	Year	Type	Length	Model	Chassis	Engine	Fuel Type	Price/LF	Wheelbase	Towing	GVWR	Curb Wt
Tradewinds	1997	MHA	37	737	FR	Ca 7.2L	D	$3700	228	5,000	24,850	22,180

Livability Code: SB 30-90   Wheelbase-to-length ratio of 52% is considered ○ dangerous ◉ fatiguing ○ good ○ excellent *

The approximate net payload of 2670 pounds at 11% of GVWR on this model is ○ deficient ○ excessive ○ cautionary ◉ good ○ excellent *

Total highway safety penalties are: 7 *   Value: 8 7   Durability: 9 0   Highway Control Rating: 4 9   Highway Safety: 4 2

Tradewinds	1998	MHA	37	7370	FR	CA300	D	$3800	228	5,000	24,850	22,005

Livability Code: SB 30-90   Wheelbase-to-length ratio of 52% is considered ○ dangerous ◉ fatiguing ○ good ○ excellent *

The approximate net payload of 2845 pounds at 11% of GVWR on this model is ○ deficient ○ excessive ○ cautionary ◉ good ○ excellent *

Total highway safety penalties are: 7 *   Value: 9 2   Durability: 9 0   Highway Control Rating: 5 0   Highway Safety: 4 3

Tradewinds	1999	MHA	37	7370	FR	CA300	D	$3800	228	5,000	26,350	21,720

Livability Code: SB 30-90   Wheelbase-to-length ratio of 52% is considered ○ dangerous ◉ fatiguing ○ good ○ excellent *

The approximate net payload of 4630 pounds at 18% of GVWR on this model is ○ deficient ○ excessive ○ cautionary ○ good ◉ excellent *

Total highway safety penalties are: 7 *   Value: 9 2   Durability: 9 0   Highway Control Rating: 6 8   Highway Safety: 6 1   ★★

Tradewinds	1999	MHA	37	7371	FR	CA300	D	$3800	228	5,000	26,350	21,040

Livability Code: SB 30-90   Wheelbase-to-length ratio of 52% is considered ○ dangerous ◉ fatiguing ○ good ○ excellent *

The approximate net payload of 5310 pounds at 20% of GVWR on this model is ○ deficient ○ excessive ○ cautionary ◉ good ○ excellent *

Total highway safety penalties are: 12 *   Value: 9 0   Durability: 9 0   Highway Control Rating: 7 0   Highway Safety: 5 8   ★

Tradewinds	1999	MHA	37	7372	FR	CA300	D	$3800	228	5,000	26,350	21,040

Livability Code: SB 30-90   Wheelbase-to-length ratio of 52% is considered ○ dangerous ◉ fatiguing ○ good ○ excellent *

The approximate net payload of 5310 pounds at 20% of GVWR on this model is ○ deficient ○ excessive ○ cautionary ○ good ◉ excellent *

Total highway safety penalties are: 12 *   Value: 9 0   Durability: 9 0   Highway Control Rating: 7 0   Highway Safety: 5 8   ★

TransVan	1990	MHC	21	202 SD	FO	5.8L	G	$1900	138	1,500	10,500	8,919

Livability Code: VA 30-90   Wheelbase-to-length ratio of 55% is considered ○ dangerous ○ fatiguing ◉ good ○ excellent *

The approximate net payload of 1581 pounds at 15% of GVWR on this model is ○ deficient ○ excessive ○ cautionary ◉ good ○ excellent *

Total highway safety penalties are: 2 *   Value: 7 7   Durability: 7 0   Highway Control Rating: 9 1   Highway Safety: 8 9   ★★★

TransVan	1990	MHC	21	206 RD	FO	5.8L	G	$1900	138	1,500	10,500	8,983

Livability Code: VA 30-90   Wheelbase-to-length ratio of 54% is considered ○ dangerous ○ fatiguing ◉ good ○ excellent *

The approximate net payload of 1517 pounds at 14% of GVWR on this model is ○ deficient ○ excessive ○ cautionary ◉ good ○ excellent *

Total highway safety penalties are: 2 *   Value: 7 7   Durability: 7 0   Highway Control Rating: 8 3   Highway Safety: 8 1   ★★★

TransVan	1990	MHC	21	207 SD	FO	5.8L	G	$1900	138	1,500	10,500	8,614

Livability Code: VA 30-90   Wheelbase-to-length ratio of 54% is considered ○ dangerous ○ fatiguing ◉ good ○ excellent *

The approximate net payload of 1886 pounds at 18% of GVWR on this model is ○ deficient ○ excessive ○ cautionary ○ good ◉ excellent *

Total highway safety penalties are: 2 *   Value: 7 7   Durability: 7 0   Highway Control Rating: 8 8   Highway Safety: 8 6   ★★★

TransVan	1991	MHC	21	202 SD	FO	5.8L	G	$1900	138	1,500	10,500	8,919

Livability Code: VA 30-90   Wheelbase-to-length ratio of 55% is considered ○ dangerous ○ fatiguing ◉ good ○ excellent *

The approximate net payload of 1581 pounds at 15% of GVWR on this model is ○ deficient ○ excessive ○ cautionary ◉ good ○ excellent *

Total highway safety penalties are: 2 *   Value: 7 7   Durability: 7 0   Highway Control Rating: 9 1   Highway Safety: 8 9   ★★★

TransVan	1991	MHC	21	207 SD	FO	5.8L	G	$1900	138	1,500	10,500	8,983

Livability Code: VA 30-90   Wheelbase-to-length ratio of 54% is considered ○ dangerous ○ fatiguing ◉ good ○ excellent *

The approximate net payload of 1517 pounds at 14% of GVWR on this model is ○ deficient ○ excessive ○ cautionary ◉ good ○ excellent *

Total highway safety penalties are: 2 *   Value: 7 7   Durability: 7 0   Highway Control Rating: 8 3   Highway Safety: 8 1   ★★★

TransVan	1991	MHC	21	206 RD	FO	5.8L	G	$1900	138	1,500	10,500	8,983

Livability Code: VA 30-90   Wheelbase-to-length ratio of 54% is considered ○ dangerous ○ fatiguing ◉ good ○ excellent *

The approximate net payload of 1517 pounds at 14% of GVWR on this model is ○ deficient ○ excessive ○ cautionary ◉ good ○ excellent *

Total highway safety penalties are: 2 *   Value: 7 7   Durability: 7 0   Highway Control Rating: 8 3   Highway Safety: 8 1   ★★★

Note: Safety ratings are based on the assumption that the engineering of the RV has allowed for proper balance by placing fresh, gray, and black holding tanks in a location so as not to change the balance of the RV when the tanks are empty or full. **Always double-check wheelbase, GVWR, and weights at front and rear axles.**

See Section 1 for details on how conclusions are reached.

Section 2: The Ratings

Brand	Year	Type	Length	Model	Chassis	Engine	Fuel Type	Average Price per Linear Foot When New	Adjusted Wheelbase	Approx. Towing Capacity	Gross Vehicle Weight Rating	Average Curb Weight
Travel Home	1998	MHB	17	Country Club 17	DO	5.2L	G	$2700	127	1,500	7,700	6,438

Livability Code: WE 30-80   Wheelbase-to-length ratio of 62% is considered ○ dangerous ○ fatiguing ○ good ◉ excellent *

The approximate net payload of 1263 pounds at 16% of GVWR on this model is ○ deficient ○ excessive ○ cautionary ○ good ◉ excellent *

Total highway safety penalties are: 2 *   Value: 7 7   Durability: 7 0   Highway Control Rating: 1 0 0   Highway Safety: 9 8   ★★★

Brand	Year	Type	Length	Model	Chassis	Engine	Fuel Type					
Travel Home	1998	MHB	19	Country Cruiser	FO	5.4L	G	$3200	138	1,500	9,400	7,803

Livability Code: WE 30-80   Wheelbase-to-length ratio of 61% is considered ○ dangerous ○ fatiguing ○ good ◉ excellent *

The approximate net payload of 1597 pounds at 17% of GVWR on this model is ○ deficient ○ excessive ○ cautionary ○ good ◉ excellent *

Total highway safety penalties are: 2 *   Value: 7 7   Durability: 7 0   Highway Control Rating: 1 0 0   Highway Safety: 9 8   ★★★

Travel Home	1998	MHB	19	Country Villa	FO	5.4L	G	$3200	138	1,500	9,400	7,803

Livability Code: WE 30-80   Wheelbase-to-length ratio of 61% is considered ○ dangerous ○ fatiguing ○ good ◉ excellent *

The approximate net payload of 1597 pounds at 17% of GVWR on this model is ○ deficient ○ excessive ○ cautionary ○ good ◉ excellent *

Total highway safety penalties are: 2 *   Value: 7 7   Durability: 7 0   Highway Control Rating: 1 0 0   Highway Safety: 9 8   ★★★

Travel Home	1999	MHB	17	Country Club	DO	5.2L	G	$2700	127	1,500	6,400	5,918

Livability Code: WE 30-80   Wheelbase-to-length ratio of 62% is considered ○ dangerous ○ fatiguing ○ good ◉ excellent *

The approximate net payload of 483 pounds at 8% of GVWR on this model is ○ deficient ○ excessive ◉ cautionary ○ good ○ excellent *

Total highway safety penalties are: 2 *   Value: 7 7   Durability: 7 0   Highway Control Rating: 9 5   Highway Safety: 9 3   ★★★

Travel Home	1999	MHB	19	Country Cruiser	FO	5.4L	G	$3200	138	1,500	9,400	7,513

Livability Code: WE 30-80   Wheelbase-to-length ratio of 61% is considered ○ dangerous ○ fatiguing ○ good ◉ excellent *

The approximate net payload of 1888 pounds at 20% of GVWR on this model is ○ deficient ○ excessive ○ cautionary ○ good ◉ excellent *

Total highway safety penalties are: 2 *   Value: 7 7   Durability: 7 0   Highway Control Rating: 1 0 0   Highway Safety: 9 8   ★★★

Travel Home	1999	MHB	19	Country Villa	FO	5.4L	G	$3200	138	1,500	9,400	7,513

Livability Code: WE 30-80   Wheelbase-to-length ratio of 61% is considered ○ dangerous ○ fatiguing ○ good ◉ excellent *

The approximate net payload of 1888 pounds at 20% of GVWR on this model is ○ deficient ○ excessive ○ cautionary ○ good ◉ excellent *

Total highway safety penalties are: 2 *   Value: 7 7   Durability: 7 0   Highway Control Rating: 1 0 0   Highway Safety: 9 8   ★★★

Trek	1992	MHA	24	2400 RB	IS	3.9L	D	$2300	150	4,350	13,250	11,488

Livability Code: SB 30-90   Wheelbase-to-length ratio of 52% is considered ○ dangerous ◉ fatiguing ○ good ○ excellent *

The approximate net payload of 1762 pounds at 13% of GVWR on this model is ○ deficient ○ excessive ○ cautionary ◉ good ○ excellent *

Total highway safety penalties are: 2 *   Value: 8 0   Durability: 7 8   Highway Control Rating: 5 4   Highway Safety: 5 2   ★

Trek	1992	MHA	26	2600 DB	IS	3.9L	D	$2200	178	4,350	13,250	11,866

Livability Code: SB 30-90   Wheelbase-to-length ratio of 57% is considered ○ dangerous ○ fatiguing ◉ good ○ excellent *

The approximate net payload of 1384 pounds at 10% of GVWR on this model is ○ deficient ○ excessive ○ cautionary ◉ good ○ excellent *

Total highway safety penalties are: 2 *   Value: 8 0   Durability: 7 8   Highway Control Rating: 8 8   Highway Safety: 8 6   ★★★

Trek	1992	MHA	28	2830 QB	IS	3.9L	D	$2200	178	4,350	13,250	12,244

Livability Code: SB 30-90   Wheelbase-to-length ratio of 53% is considered ○ dangerous ◉ fatiguing ○ good ○ excellent *

The approximate net payload of 1006 pounds at 8% of GVWR on this model is ○ deficient ○ excessive ◉ cautionary ○ good ○ excellent *

Total highway safety penalties are: 2 *   Value: 8 0   Durability: 7 8   Highway Control Rating: 4 7   Highway Safety: 4 5

Trek	1992	MHA	28	2840 RB	IS	3.9L	D	$2200	178	4,350	13,250	12,244

Livability Code: SB 30-90   Wheelbase-to-length ratio of 53% is considered ○ dangerous ◉ fatiguing ○ good ○ excellent *

The approximate net payload of 1006 pounds at 8% of GVWR on this model is ○ deficient ○ excessive ◉ cautionary ○ good ○ excellent *

Total highway safety penalties are: 2 *   Value: 8 0   Durability: 7 8   Highway Control Rating: 4 7   Highway Safety: 4 5

Trek	1993	MHA	24	2400 RB	IS	3.9L	D	$2500	150	4,350	13,250	11,488

Livability Code: SB 30-90   Wheelbase-to-length ratio of 52% is considered ○ dangerous ◉ fatiguing ○ good ○ excellent *

The approximate net payload of 1762 pounds at 13% of GVWR on this model is ○ deficient ○ excessive ○ cautionary ◉ good ○ excellent *

Total highway safety penalties are: 2 *   Value: 8 0   Durability: 7 8   Highway Control Rating: 5 4   Highway Safety: 5 2   ★

Trek	1993	MHA	26	2600 DB	IS	3.9L	D	$2400	178	4,350	13,250	11,866

Livability Code: SB 30-90   Wheelbase-to-length ratio of 57% is considered ○ dangerous ○ fatiguing ◉ good ○ excellent *

The approximate net payload of 1384 pounds at 10% of GVWR on this model is ○ deficient ○ excessive ○ cautionary ◉ good ○ excellent *

Total highway safety penalties are: 2 *   Value: 8 0   Durability: 7 8   Highway Control Rating: 8 8   Highway Safety: 8 6   ★★★

Note: Safety ratings are based on the assumption that the engineering of the RV has allowed for proper balance by placing fresh, gray, and black holding tanks in a location so as not to change the balance of the RV when the tanks are empty or full. **Always double-check wheelbase, GVWR, and weights at front and rear axles.**

*See Section 1 for details on how conclusions are reached.

Section 2: The Ratings

Brand	Year	Type	Length	Model	Chassis	Engine	Fuel Type	Average Price per Linear Foot When New	Adjusted Wheelbase	Approx. Towing Capacity	Gross Vehicle Weight Rating	Average Curb Weight
Trek	1993	MHA	28	2830 QB	IS	3.9L	D	$2400	178	4,350	13,250	12,244

Livability Code: SB 30-90 — Wheelbase-to-length ratio of 53% is considered ○ dangerous ● fatiguing ○ good ○ excellent*
The approximate net payload of 1006 pounds at 8% of GVWR on this model is ○ deficient ○ excessive ● cautionary ○ good ○ excellent*
Total highway safety penalties are: 2* — Value: 80 — Durability: 78 — Highway Control Rating: 47 — Highway Safety: 45

Brand	Year	Type	Length	Model	Chassis	Engine	Fuel Type	Price	Wheelbase	Towing	GVWR	Curb Weight
Trek	1993	MHA	28	2840 RB	IS	3.9L	D	$2400	178	4,350	13,250	12,244

Livability Code: SB 30-90 — Wheelbase-to-length ratio of 53% is considered ○ dangerous ● fatiguing ○ good ○ excellent*
The approximate net payload of 1006 pounds at 8% of GVWR on this model is ○ deficient ○ excessive ● cautionary ○ good ○ excellent*
Total highway safety penalties are: 2* — Value: 80 — Durability: 78 — Highway Control Rating: 47 — Highway Safety: 45

Trek	1994	MHA	24	2400 RB	IS	3.9L	D	$2600	150	4,350	13,250	11,488

Livability Code: SB 30-90 — Wheelbase-to-length ratio of 52% is considered ○ dangerous ● fatiguing ○ good ○ excellent*
The approximate net payload of 1762 pounds at 13% of GVWR on this model is ○ deficient ○ excessive ○ cautionary ● good ○ excellent*
Total highway safety penalties are: 2* — Value: 80 — Durability: 78 — Highway Control Rating: 54 — Highway Safety: 52 — ★

Trek	1994	MHA	26	2600 DB	IS	3.9L	D	$2500	178	4,350	13,250	11,866

Livability Code: SB 30-90 — Wheelbase-to-length ratio of 57% is considered ○ dangerous ○ fatiguing ● good ○ excellent*
The approximate net payload of 1384 pounds at 10% of GVWR on this model is ○ deficient ○ excessive ○ cautionary ● good ○ excellent*
Total highway safety penalties are: 2* — Value: 80 — Durability: 78 — Highway Control Rating: 88 — Highway Safety: 86 — ★★★

Trek	1994	MHA	28	2830 QB	IS	3.9L	D	$2500	178	4,350	13,250	12,244

Livability Code: SB 30-90 — Wheelbase-to-length ratio of 53% is considered ○ dangerous ● fatiguing ○ good ○ excellent*
The approximate net payload of 1006 pounds at 8% of GVWR on this model is ○ deficient ○ excessive ● cautionary ○ good ○ excellent*
Total highway safety penalties are: 2* — Value: 80 — Durability: 78 — Highway Control Rating: 47 — Highway Safety: 45

Trek	1994	MHA	28	2840 RB	IS	3.9L	D	$2500	178	4,350	13,250	12,244

Livability Code: SB 30-90 — Wheelbase-to-length ratio of 53% is considered ○ dangerous ● fatiguing ○ good ○ excellent*
The approximate net payload of 1006 pounds at 8% of GVWR on this model is ○ deficient ○ excessive ● cautionary ○ good ○ excellent*
Total highway safety penalties are: 2* — Value: 80 — Durability: 78 — Highway Control Rating: 47 — Highway Safety: 45

Trek	1995	MHA	26	2420	CH	7.4L	G	$2500	158	4,200	14,800	12,179

Livability Code: SB 30-90 — Wheelbase-to-length ratio of 51% is considered ○ dangerous ● fatiguing ○ good ○ excellent*
The approximate net payload of 2621 pounds at 18% of GVWR on this model is ○ deficient ○ excessive ○ cautionary ○ good ● excellent*
Total highway safety penalties are: 2* — Value: 80 — Durability: 78 — Highway Control Rating: 51 — Highway Safety: 49

Trek	1995	MHA	26	2430	CH	7.4L	G	$2500	158	4,200	14,800	12,179

Livability Code: SB 30-90 — Wheelbase-to-length ratio of 51% is considered ○ dangerous ● fatiguing ○ good ○ excellent*
The approximate net payload of 2621 pounds at 18% of GVWR on this model is ○ deficient ○ excessive ○ cautionary ○ good ● excellent*
Total highway safety penalties are: 2* — Value: 79 — Durability: 76 — Highway Control Rating: 51 — Highway Safety: 49

Trek	1995	MHA	26	2460	CH	7.4L	G	$2700	158	4,200	14,800	12,179

Livability Code: SB 30-90 — Wheelbase-to-length ratio of 51% is considered ○ dangerous ● fatiguing ○ good ○ excellent*
The approximate net payload of 2621 pounds at 18% of GVWR on this model is ○ deficient ○ excessive ○ cautionary ○ good ● excellent*
Total highway safety penalties are: 2* — Value: 80 — Durability: 78 — Highway Control Rating: 51 — Highway Safety: 49

Trek	1995	MHA	29	2820	CH	7.4L	G	$2500	178	4,000	16,000	13,133

Livability Code: SB 30-90 — Wheelbase-to-length ratio of 52% is considered ○ dangerous ● fatiguing ○ good ○ excellent*
The approximate net payload of 2867 pounds at 18% of GVWR on this model is ○ deficient ○ excessive ○ cautionary ○ good ● excellent*
Total highway safety penalties are: 4* — Value: 79 — Durability: 78 — Highway Control Rating: 60 — Highway Safety: 56 — ★

Trek	1995	MHA	29	2830	CH	7.4L	G	$2500	178	4,000	16,000	13,133

Livability Code: SB 30-90 — Wheelbase-to-length ratio of 52% is considered ○ dangerous ● fatiguing ○ good ○ excellent*
The approximate net payload of 2867 pounds at 18% of GVWR on this model is ○ deficient ○ excessive ○ cautionary ○ good ● excellent*
Total highway safety penalties are: 4* — Value: 79 — Durability: 78 — Highway Control Rating: 60 — Highway Safety: 56 — ★

Trek	1995	MHA	31	3060	CH	7.4L	G	$2400	190	4,000	16,000	13,785

Livability Code: SB 30-90 — Wheelbase-to-length ratio of 52% is considered ○ dangerous ● fatiguing ○ good ○ excellent*
The approximate net payload of 2215 pounds at 14% of GVWR on this model is ○ deficient ○ excessive ○ cautionary ● good ○ excellent*
Total highway safety penalties are: 5* — Value: 79 — Durability: 78 — Highway Control Rating: 55 — Highway Safety: 50 — ★

Note: Safety ratings are based on the assumption that the engineering of the RV has allowed for proper balance by placing fresh, gray, and black holding tanks in a location so as not to change the balance of the RV when the tanks are empty or full. **Always double-check wheelbase, GVWR, and weights at front and rear axles.**

*See Section 1 for details on how conclusions are reached.

Brand	Year	Type	Length	Model	Chassis	Engine	Fuel Type	Average Price per Linear Foot When New	Adjusted Wheel-base	Approx. Towing Capacity	Gross Vehicle Weight Rating	Average Curb Weight
Trek	**1995**	MHA	31	3040 pusher	CH	GM190	D	$3100	178	5,000	18,000	14,385

Livability Code: SB 30-90
Wheelbase-to-length ratio of 49% is considered ◉ dangerous ○ fatiguing ○ good ○ excellent *
The approximate net payload of 3615 pounds at 20% of GVWR on this model is ○ deficient ○ excessive ○ cautionary ○ good ◉ excellent *
Total highway safety penalties are: 5 * Value: 7 9 Durability: 7 8 Highway Control Rating: 4 4 Highway Safety: 3 9

Brand	Year	Type	Length	Model	Chassis	Engine	Fuel Type	Price/Linear Ft	Wheelbase	Towing	GVWR	Curb Wt
Trek	**1995**	MHA	31	3060 pusher	CH	GM190	D	$3100	178	5,000	18,000	14,385

Livability Code: SB 30-90
Wheelbase-to-length ratio of 49% is considered ◉ dangerous ○ fatiguing ○ good ○ excellent *
The approximate net payload of 3615 pounds at 20% of GVWR on this model is ○ deficient ○ excessive ○ cautionary ○ good ◉ excellent *
Total highway safety penalties are: 5 * Value: 7 9 Durability: 7 8 Highway Control Rating: 4 4 Highway Safety: 3 9

Brand	Year	Type	Length	Model	Chassis	Engine	Fuel Type	Price/Linear Ft	Wheelbase	Towing	GVWR	Curb Wt
Trek	**1995**	MHA	31	3030	CH	7.4L	G	$2200	190	4,000	16,000	13,785

Livability Code: SB 30-90
Wheelbase-to-length ratio of 52% is considered ○ dangerous ◉ fatiguing ○ good ○ excellent *
The approximate net payload of 2215 pounds at 14% of GVWR on this model is ○ deficient ○ excessive ○ cautionary ◉ good ○ excellent *
Total highway safety penalties are: 5 * Value: 7 8 Durability: 7 6 Highway Control Rating: 5 5 Highway Safety: 5 0 ★

Brand	Year	Type	Length	Model	Chassis	Engine	Fuel Type	Price/Linear Ft	Wheelbase	Towing	GVWR	Curb Wt
Trek	**1995**	MHA	33	3330 pusher	CH	GM190	D	$2900	208	5,000	18,000	15,112

Livability Code: SB 30-90
Wheelbase-to-length ratio of 52% is considered ○ dangerous ◉ fatiguing ○ good ○ excellent *
The approximate net payload of 2888 pounds at 16% of GVWR on this model is ○ deficient ○ excessive ○ cautionary ○ good ◉ excellent *
Total highway safety penalties are: 6 * Value: 7 8 Durability: 7 8 Highway Control Rating: 6 0 Highway Safety: 5 4 ★

Brand	Year	Type	Length	Model	Chassis	Engine	Fuel Type	Price/Linear Ft	Wheelbase	Towing	GVWR	Curb Wt
Trek	**1995**	MHA	33	3352 pusher	CH	GM190	D	$2900	208	5,000	18,000	15,112

Livability Code: SB 30-90
Wheelbase-to-length ratio of 52% is considered ○ dangerous ◉ fatiguing ○ good ○ excellent *
The approximate net payload of 2888 pounds at 16% of GVWR on this model is ○ deficient ○ excessive ○ cautionary ○ good ◉ excellent *
Total highway safety penalties are: 6 * Value: 7 8 Durability: 7 8 Highway Control Rating: 6 0 Highway Safety: 5 4 ★

Brand	Year	Type	Length	Model	Chassis	Engine	Fuel Type	Price/Linear Ft	Wheelbase	Towing	GVWR	Curb Wt
Trek	**1996**	MHA	26	2420	CH	7.4L	G	$2600	158	4,200	14,800	13,148

Livability Code: SB 30-90
Wheelbase-to-length ratio of 51% is considered ○ dangerous ◉ fatiguing ○ good ○ excellent *
The approximate net payload of 1652 pounds at 11% of GVWR on this model is ○ deficient ○ excessive ○ cautionary ◉ good ○ excellent *
Total highway safety penalties are: 2 * Value: 8 0 Durability: 7 8 Highway Control Rating: 3 9 Highway Safety: 3 7

Brand	Year	Type	Length	Model	Chassis	Engine	Fuel Type	Price/Linear Ft	Wheelbase	Towing	GVWR	Curb Wt
Trek	**1996**	MHA	26	2430	CH	7.4L	G	$2600	158	4,200	14,800	13,148

Livability Code: SB 30-90
Wheelbase-to-length ratio of 51% is considered ○ dangerous ◉ fatiguing ○ good ○ excellent *
The approximate net payload of 1652 pounds at 11% of GVWR on this model is ○ deficient ○ excessive ○ cautionary ◉ good ○ excellent *
Total highway safety penalties are: 2 * Value: 8 0 Durability: 7 8 Highway Control Rating: 3 9 Highway Safety: 3 7

Brand	Year	Type	Length	Model	Chassis	Engine	Fuel Type	Price/Linear Ft	Wheelbase	Towing	GVWR	Curb Wt
Trek	**1996**	MHA	26	2420 fr dsl	CH	GM6.5	D	$2700	158	4,200	14,800	13,148

Livability Code: SB 30-90
Wheelbase-to-length ratio of 51% is considered ○ dangerous ◉ fatiguing ○ good ○ excellent *
The approximate net payload of 1652 pounds at 11% of GVWR on this model is ○ deficient ○ excessive ○ cautionary ◉ good ○ excellent *
Total highway safety penalties are: 2 * Value: 8 0 Durability: 7 8 Highway Control Rating: 3 9 Highway Safety: 3 7

Brand	Year	Type	Length	Model	Chassis	Engine	Fuel Type	Price/Linear Ft	Wheelbase	Towing	GVWR	Curb Wt
Trek	**1996**	MHA	26	2430 fr dsl	CH	GM6.5	D	$2700	158	4,200	14,800	13,148

Livability Code: SB 30-90
Wheelbase-to-length ratio of 51% is considered ○ dangerous ◉ fatiguing ○ good ○ excellent *
The approximate net payload of 1652 pounds at 11% of GVWR on this model is ○ deficient ○ excessive ○ cautionary ◉ good ○ excellent *
Total highway safety penalties are: 2 * Value: 8 0 Durability: 7 8 Highway Control Rating: 3 9 Highway Safety: 3 7

Brand	Year	Type	Length	Model	Chassis	Engine	Fuel Type	Price/Linear Ft	Wheelbase	Towing	GVWR	Curb Wt
Trek	**1996**	MHA	29	2820	CH	7.4L	G	$2400	178	3,500	16,500	14,241

Livability Code: SB 30-90
Wheelbase-to-length ratio of 52% is considered ○ dangerous ◉ fatiguing ○ good ○ excellent *
The approximate net payload of 2259 pounds at 14% of GVWR on this model is ○ deficient ○ excessive ○ cautionary ◉ good ○ excellent *
Total highway safety penalties are: 4 * Value: 7 9 Durability: 7 8 Highway Control Rating: 5 4 Highway Safety: 5 0 ★

Brand	Year	Type	Length	Model	Chassis	Engine	Fuel Type	Price/Linear Ft	Wheelbase	Towing	GVWR	Curb Wt
Trek	**1996**	MHA	29	2830	CH	7.4L	G	$2400	178	3,500	16,500	14,241

Livability Code: SB 30-90
Wheelbase-to-length ratio of 52% is considered ○ dangerous ◉ fatiguing ○ good ○ excellent *
The approximate net payload of 2259 pounds at 14% of GVWR on this model is ○ deficient ○ excessive ○ cautionary ◉ good ○ excellent *
Total highway safety penalties are: 4 * Value: 7 9 Durability: 7 8 Highway Control Rating: 5 4 Highway Safety: 5 0 ★

Brand	Year	Type	Length	Model	Chassis	Engine	Fuel Type	Price/Linear Ft	Wheelbase	Towing	GVWR	Curb Wt
Trek	**1996**	MHA	29	2820 fr dsl	CH	GM6.5	D	$2400	178	3,500	16,500	14,241

Livability Code: SB 30-90
Wheelbase-to-length ratio of 52% is considered ○ dangerous ◉ fatiguing ○ good ○ excellent *
The approximate net payload of 2259 pounds at 14% of GVWR on this model is ○ deficient ○ excessive ○ cautionary ◉ good ○ excellent *
Total highway safety penalties are: 4 * Value: 7 9 Durability: 7 8 Highway Control Rating: 5 4 Highway Safety: 5 0 ★

Note: Safety ratings are based on the assumption that the engineering of the RV has allowed for proper balance by placing fresh, gray, and black holding tanks in a location so as not to change the balance of the RV when the tanks are empty or full. **Always double-check wheelbase, GVWR, and weights at front and rear axles.**

*See Section 1 for details on how conclusions are reached.

Brand	Year	Type	Length	Model	Chassis	Engine	Fuel Type	Average Price per Linear Foot When New	Adjusted Wheelbase	Approx. Towing Capacity	Gross Vehicle Weight Rating	Average Curb Weight

Trek 1996 MHA 29 2830 fr dsl CH GM6.5 D $2400 178 3,500 16,500 14,241
Livability Code: SB 30-90   Wheelbase-to-length ratio of 52% is considered ○ dangerous ● fatiguing ○ good ○ excellent*
The approximate net payload of 2259 pounds at 14% of GVWR on this model is ○ deficient ○ excessive ○ cautionary ● good ○ excellent*
Total highway safety penalties are: 4*   Value: 79 Durability: 78 Highway Control Rating: 54   Highway Safety: 50   ★

Trek 1996 MHA 31 3030 CH 7.4L G $2400 190 3,500 16,500 14,777
Livability Code: SB 30-90   Wheelbase-to-length ratio of 52% is considered ○ dangerous ● fatiguing ○ good ○ excellent*
The approximate net payload of 1723 pounds at 10% of GVWR on this model is ○ deficient ○ excessive ○ cautionary ● good ○ excellent*
Total highway safety penalties are: 5*   Value: 79 Durability: 78 Highway Control Rating: 48   Highway Safety: 43

Trek 1996 MHA 31 3060 CH 7.4L G $2500 190 3,500 16,500 14,777
Livability Code: SB 30-90   Wheelbase-to-length ratio of 52% is considered ○ dangerous ● fatiguing ○ good ○ excellent*
The approximate net payload of 1723 pounds at 10% of GVWR on this model is ○ deficient ○ excessive ○ cautionary ● good ○ excellent*
Total highway safety penalties are: 5*   Value: 79 Durability: 78 Highway Control Rating: 48   Highway Safety: 43

Trek 1996 MHA 31 3060 pusher CH GM6.5 D $2700 190 5,000 18,000 15,577
Livability Code: SB 30-90   Wheelbase-to-length ratio of 52% is considered ○ dangerous ● fatiguing ○ good ○ excellent*
The approximate net payload of 2423 pounds at 13% of GVWR on this model is ○ deficient ○ excessive ○ cautionary ● good ○ excellent*
Total highway safety penalties are: 5*   Value: 79 Durability: 78 Highway Control Rating: 54   Highway Safety: 49

Trek 1996 MHA 31 3030 fr dsl CH GM6.5 D $2700 190 3,500 16,500 14,777
Livability Code: SB 30-90   Wheelbase-to-length ratio of 52% is considered ○ dangerous ● fatiguing ○ good ○ excellent*
The approximate net payload of 1723 pounds at 10% of GVWR on this model is ○ deficient ○ excessive ○ cautionary ● good ○ excellent*
Total highway safety penalties are: 5*   Value: 79 Durability: 78 Highway Control Rating: 48   Highway Safety: 43

Trek 1996 MHA 31 3060 fr dsl CH GM6.5 D $2400 190 3,500 16,500 14,777
Livability Code: SB 30-90   Wheelbase-to-length ratio of 52% is considered ○ dangerous ● fatiguing ○ good ○ excellent*
The approximate net payload of 1723 pounds at 10% of GVWR on this model is ○ deficient ○ excessive ○ cautionary ● good ○ excellent*
Total highway safety penalties are: 5*   Value: 79 Durability: 78 Highway Control Rating: 48   Highway Safety: 43

Trek 1996 MHA 33 3330 pusher CH GM6.5 D $2900 208 5,000 18,000 16,410
Livability Code: SB 30-90   Wheelbase-to-length ratio of 52% is considered ○ dangerous ● fatiguing ○ good ○ excellent*
The approximate net payload of 1590 pounds at 9% of GVWR on this model is ○ deficient ○ excessive ● cautionary ○ good ○ excellent*
Total highway safety penalties are: 6*   Value: 78 Durability: 78 Highway Control Rating: 42   Highway Safety: 36

Trek 1996 MHA 33 3352 pusher CH GM6.5 D $2900 208 5,000 18,000 16,410
Livability Code: SB 30-90   Wheelbase-to-length ratio of 52% is considered ○ dangerous ● fatiguing ○ good ○ excellent*
The approximate net payload of 1590 pounds at 9% of GVWR on this model is ○ deficient ○ excessive ● cautionary ○ good ○ excellent*
Total highway safety penalties are: 6*   Value: 78 Durability: 78 Highway Control Rating: 42   Highway Safety: 36

Trek 1997 MHA 26 2420 CH 7.4L G $2500 158 4,200 14,800 13,148
Livability Code: SB 30-90   Wheelbase-to-length ratio of 51% is considered ○ dangerous ● fatiguing ○ good ○ excellent*
The approximate net payload of 1652 pounds at 11% of GVWR on this model is ○ deficient ○ excessive ○ cautionary ● good ○ excellent*
Total highway safety penalties are: 2*   Value: 80 Durability: 78 Highway Control Rating: 39   Highway Safety: 37

Trek 1997 MHA 26 2430 CH 7.4L G $2500 158 4,200 14,800 13,148
Livability Code: SB 30-90   Wheelbase-to-length ratio of 51% is considered ○ dangerous ● fatiguing ○ good ○ excellent*
The approximate net payload of 1652 pounds at 11% of GVWR on this model is ○ deficient ○ excessive ○ cautionary ● good ○ excellent*
Total highway safety penalties are: 2*   Value: 80 Durability: 78 Highway Control Rating: 39   Highway Safety: 37

Trek 1997 MHA 26 2420 op eng CH GM6.5 D $2700 158 4,200 14,800 13,148
Livability Code: SB 30-90   Wheelbase-to-length ratio of 51% is considered ○ dangerous ● fatiguing ○ good ○ excellent*
The approximate net payload of 1652 pounds at 11% of GVWR on this model is ○ deficient ○ excessive ○ cautionary ● good ○ excellent*
Total highway safety penalties are: 2*   Value: 80 Durability: 78 Highway Control Rating: 39   Highway Safety: 37

Trek 1997 MHA 26 2430 op eng CH GM6.5 D $2700 158 4,200 14,800 13,148
Livability Code: SB 30-90   Wheelbase-to-length ratio of 51% is considered ○ dangerous ● fatiguing ○ good ○ excellent*
The approximate net payload of 1652 pounds at 11% of GVWR on this model is ○ deficient ○ excessive ○ cautionary ● good ○ excellent*
Total highway safety penalties are: 2*   Value: 80 Durability: 78 Highway Control Rating: 39   Highway Safety: 37

Note: Safety ratings are based on the assumption that the engineering of the RV has allowed for proper balance by placing fresh, gray, and black holding tanks in a location so as not to change the balance of the RV when the tanks are empty or full. **Always double-check wheelbase, GVWR, and weights at front and rear axles.**

*See Section 1 for details on how conclusions are reached.

Section 2: The Ratings

Brand	Year	Type	Length	Model	Chassis	Engine	Fuel Type	Average Price per Linear Foot When New	Adjusted Wheelbase	Approx. Towing Capacity	Gross Vehicle Weight Rating	Average Curb Weight
Trek	1997	MHA	29	2820	CH	7.4L	G	$2400	178	4,500	16,500	14,330

Livability Code: SB 30-90   Wheelbase-to-length ratio of 51% is considered ○ dangerous ● fatiguing ○ good ○ excellent*

The approximate net payload of 2170 pounds at 13% of GVWR on this model is ○ deficient ○ excessive ○ cautionary ● good ○ excellent*

Total highway safety penalties are: 4*   Value: 7 9   Durability: 7 8   Highway Control Rating: 4 3   Highway Safety: 3 9

Brand	Year	Type	Length	Model	Chassis	Engine	Fuel Type	Price/Ft	Wheelbase	Towing	GVWR	Curb Wt
Trek	1997	MHA	29	2830	CH	7.4L	G	$2400	178	4,500	16,500	14,330

Livability Code: SB 30-90   Wheelbase-to-length ratio of 51% is considered ○ dangerous ● fatiguing ○ good ○ excellent*

The approximate net payload of 2170 pounds at 13% of GVWR on this model is ○ deficient ○ excessive ○ cautionary ● good ○ excellent*

Total highway safety penalties are: 4*   Value: 7 9   Durability: 7 8   Highway Control Rating: 4 3   Highway Safety: 3 9

Brand	Year	Type	Length	Model	Chassis	Engine	Fuel Type	Price/Ft	Wheelbase	Towing	GVWR	Curb Wt
Trek	1997	MHA	29	2820 op eng	CH	GM6.5	D	$2500	178	4,500	16,500	14,330

Livability Code: SB 30-90   Wheelbase-to-length ratio of 51% is considered ○ dangerous ● fatiguing ○ good ○ excellent*

The approximate net payload of 2170 pounds at 13% of GVWR on this model is ○ deficient ○ excessive ○ cautionary ● good ○ excellent*

Total highway safety penalties are: 4*   Value: 7 9   Durability: 7 8   Highway Control Rating: 4 3   Highway Safety: 3 9

Brand	Year	Type	Length	Model	Chassis	Engine	Fuel Type	Price/Ft	Wheelbase	Towing	GVWR	Curb Wt
Trek	1997	MHA	29	2830 op eng	CH	GM6.5	D	$2500	178	4,500	16,500	14,330

Livability Code: SB 30-90   Wheelbase-to-length ratio of 51% is considered ○ dangerous ● fatiguing ○ good ○ excellent*

The approximate net payload of 2170 pounds at 13% of GVWR on this model is ○ deficient ○ excessive ○ cautionary ● good ○ excellent*

Total highway safety penalties are: 4*   Value: 7 9   Durability: 7 8   Highway Control Rating: 4 3   Highway Safety: 3 9

Brand	Year	Type	Length	Model	Chassis	Engine	Fuel Type	Price/Ft	Wheelbase	Towing	GVWR	Curb Wt
Trek	1997	MHA	31	3060	CH	7.4L	G	$2400	190	4,500	16,500	14,926

Livability Code: SB 30-90   Wheelbase-to-length ratio of 51% is considered ○ dangerous ● fatiguing ○ good ○ excellent*

The approximate net payload of 1574 pounds at 10% of GVWR on this model is ○ deficient ○ excessive ○ cautionary ● good ○ excellent*

Total highway safety penalties are: 5*   Value: 7 9   Durability: 7 8   Highway Control Rating: 3 6   Highway Safety: 3 1

Brand	Year	Type	Length	Model	Chassis	Engine	Fuel Type	Price/Ft	Wheelbase	Towing	GVWR	Curb Wt
Trek	1997	MHA	31	3060 pusher	CH	GM6.5	D	$3100	190	5,000	18,000	15,726

Livability Code: SB 30-90   Wheelbase-to-length ratio of 51% is considered ○ dangerous ● fatiguing ○ good ○ excellent*

The approximate net payload of 2274 pounds at 13% of GVWR on this model is ○ deficient ○ excessive ○ cautionary ● good ○ excellent*

Total highway safety penalties are: 5*   Value: 7 9   Durability: 7 8   Highway Control Rating: 4 2   Highway Safety: 3 7

Brand	Year	Type	Length	Model	Chassis	Engine	Fuel Type	Price/Ft	Wheelbase	Towing	GVWR	Curb Wt
Trek	1997	MHA	31	3060 op eng	CH	GM6.5	D	$2500	190	4,500	16,500	14,926

Livability Code: SB 30-90   Wheelbase-to-length ratio of 51% is considered ○ dangerous ● fatiguing ○ good ○ excellent*

The approximate net payload of 1574 pounds at 10% of GVWR on this model is ○ deficient ○ excessive ○ cautionary ● good ○ excellent*

Total highway safety penalties are: 5*   Value: 7 9   Durability: 7 8   Highway Control Rating: 3 6   Highway Safety: 3 1

Brand	Year	Type	Length	Model	Chassis	Engine	Fuel Type	Price/Ft	Wheelbase	Towing	GVWR	Curb Wt
Trek	1997	MHA	34	3330 pusher	CH	GM6.5	D	$2800	208	5,000	18,000	16,618

Livability Code: SB 30-90   Wheelbase-to-length ratio of 51% is considered ○ dangerous ● fatiguing ○ good ○ excellent*

The approximate net payload of 1382 pounds at 8% of GVWR on this model is ○ deficient ○ excessive ● cautionary ○ good ○ excellent*

Total highway safety penalties are: 7*   Value: 7 8   Durability: 7 8   Highway Control Rating: 2 5   Highway Safety: 1 8

Brand	Year	Type	Length	Model	Chassis	Engine	Fuel Type	Price/Ft	Wheelbase	Towing	GVWR	Curb Wt
Trek	1997	MHA	34	3352 pusher	CH	GM6.5	D	$2800	208	5,000	18,000	16,618

Livability Code: SB 30-90   Wheelbase-to-length ratio of 51% is considered ○ dangerous ● fatiguing ○ good ○ excellent*

The approximate net payload of 1382 pounds at 8% of GVWR on this model is ○ deficient ○ excessive ● cautionary ○ good ○ excellent*

Total highway safety penalties are: 7*   Value: 7 8   Durability: 7 8   Highway Control Rating: 2 5   Highway Safety: 1 8

Brand	Year	Type	Length	Model	Chassis	Engine	Fuel Type	Price/Ft	Wheelbase	Towing	GVWR	Curb Wt
Trek	1998	MHA	25	2480	CH	GM6.5	D	$3200	158	4,200	14,800	12,940

Livability Code: SB 30-90   Wheelbase-to-length ratio of 53% is considered ○ dangerous ● fatiguing ○ good ○ excellent*

The approximate net payload of 1860 pounds at 13% of GVWR on this model is ○ deficient ○ excessive ○ cautionary ● good ○ excellent*

Total highway safety penalties are: 2*   Value: 8 0   Durability: 7 8   Highway Control Rating: 6 3   Highway Safety: 6 1   ★★

Brand	Year	Type	Length	Model	Chassis	Engine	Fuel Type	Price/Ft	Wheelbase	Towing	GVWR	Curb Wt
Trek	1998	MHA	25	2480 op eng	CH	7.4L	G	$3200	158	4,200	14,800	12,940

Livability Code: SB 30-90   Wheelbase-to-length ratio of 53% is considered ○ dangerous ● fatiguing ○ good ○ excellent*

The approximate net payload of 1860 pounds at 13% of GVWR on this model is ○ deficient ○ excessive ○ cautionary ● good ○ excellent*

Total highway safety penalties are: 2*   Value: 8 0   Durability: 7 8   Highway Control Rating: 6 3   Highway Safety: 6 1   ★★

Brand	Year	Type	Length	Model	Chassis	Engine	Fuel Type	Price/Ft	Wheelbase	Towing	GVWR	Curb Wt
Trek	1998	MHA	26	2430	CH	GM6.5	D	$3100	158	4,200	14,800	13,148

Livability Code: SB 30-90   Wheelbase-to-length ratio of 51% is considered ○ dangerous ● fatiguing ○ good ○ excellent*

The approximate net payload of 1652 pounds at 11% of GVWR on this model is ○ deficient ○ excessive ○ cautionary ● good ○ excellent*

Total highway safety penalties are: 2*   Value: 8 0   Durability: 7 8   Highway Control Rating: 3 9   Highway Safety: 3 7

Note: Safety ratings are based on the assumption that the engineering of the RV has allowed for proper balance by placing fresh, gray, and black holding tanks in a location so as not to change the balance of the RV when the tanks are empty or full. **Always double-check wheelbase, GVWR, and weights at front and rear axles.**

*See Section 1 for details on how conclusions are reached.

Section 2: The Ratings

Brand	Year	Type	Length	Model	Chassis	Engine	Fuel Type	Average Price per Linear Foot When New	Adjusted Wheelbase	Approx. Towing Capacity	Gross Vehicle Weight Rating	Average Curb Weight
Trek	**1998**	MHA	26	2430 op eng	CH	7.4L	G	$3100	158	4,200	14,800	13,148

Livability Code: SB 30-90 Wheelbase-to-length ratio of 51% is considered ○ dangerous ◉ fatiguing ○ good ○ excellent *
The approximate net payload of 1652 pounds at 11% of GVWR on this model is ○ deficient ○ excessive ○ cautionary ◉ good ○ excellent *
Total highway safety penalties are: 2 * Value: 80 Durability: 78 Highway Control Rating: 39 Highway Safety: 37

Brand	Year	Type	Length	Model	Chassis	Engine	Fuel Type	Avg Price/LF	Wheelbase	Towing	GVWR	Curb Wt
Trek	**1998**	MHA	29	2830	CH	GM6.5	D	$2800	178	4,500	16,500	14,241

Livability Code: SB 30-90 Wheelbase-to-length ratio of 52% is considered ○ dangerous ◉ fatiguing ○ good ○ excellent *
The approximate net payload of 2259 pounds at 14% of GVWR on this model is ○ deficient ○ excessive ○ cautionary ◉ good ○ excellent *
Total highway safety penalties are: 4 * Value: 79 Durability: 78 Highway Control Rating: 54 Highway Safety: 50 ★

Brand	Year	Type	Length	Model	Chassis	Engine	Fuel Type	Avg Price/LF	Wheelbase	Towing	GVWR	Curb Wt
Trek	**1998**	MHA	29	2830 op eng	CH	7.4L	G	$2800	178	4,500	16,500	14,241

Livability Code: SB 30-90 Wheelbase-to-length ratio of 52% is considered ○ dangerous ◉ fatiguing ○ good ○ excellent *
The approximate net payload of 2259 pounds at 14% of GVWR on this model is ○ deficient ○ excessive ○ cautionary ◉ good ○ excellent *
Total highway safety penalties are: 4 * Value: 79 Durability: 78 Highway Control Rating: 54 Highway Safety: 50 ★

Brand	Year	Type	Length	Model	Chassis	Engine	Fuel Type	Avg Price/LF	Wheelbase	Towing	GVWR	Curb Wt
Trek	**1999**	MHA	25	2480	CH	7.4L	G	$3200	158	4,200	14,800	13,175

Livability Code: SB 30-90 Wheelbase-to-length ratio of 53% is considered ○ dangerous ◉ fatiguing ○ good ○ excellent *
The approximate net payload of 1625 pounds at 11% of GVWR on this model is ○ deficient ○ excessive ○ cautionary ◉ good ○ excellent *
Total highway safety penalties are: 2 * Value: 79 Durability: 76 Highway Control Rating: 64 Highway Safety: 62 ★★

Brand	Year	Type	Length	Model	Chassis	Engine	Fuel Type	Avg Price/LF	Wheelbase	Towing	GVWR	Curb Wt
Trek	**1999**	MHA	26	2430	CH	7.4L	G	$3100	158	4,200	14,800	13,360

Livability Code: SB 30-90 Wheelbase-to-length ratio of 50% is considered ◉ dangerous ○ fatiguing ○ good ○ excellent *
The approximate net payload of 1440 pounds at 10% of GVWR on this model is ○ deficient ○ excessive ○ cautionary ◉ good ○ excellent *
Total highway safety penalties are: 3 * Value: 79 Durability: 76 Highway Control Rating: 43 Highway Safety: 40

Brand	Year	Type	Length	Model	Chassis	Engine	Fuel Type	Avg Price/LF	Wheelbase	Towing	GVWR	Curb Wt
Trek	**1999**	MHA	29	2830	CH	7.4L	G	$2800	178	4,500	16,500	14,236

Livability Code: SB 30-90 Wheelbase-to-length ratio of 51% is considered ○ dangerous ◉ fatiguing ○ good ○ excellent *
The approximate net payload of 2264 pounds at 14% of GVWR on this model is ○ deficient ○ excessive ○ cautionary ◉ good ○ excellent *
Total highway safety penalties are: 4 * Value: 78 Durability: 76 Highway Control Rating: 53 Highway Safety: 49

Brand	Year	Type	Length	Model	Chassis	Engine	Fuel Type	Avg Price/LF	Wheelbase	Towing	GVWR	Curb Wt
Triple E Commander	**1995**	MHA	30	A 2901	CH	7.4L	G	$1900	190	1,500	16,000	13,421

Livability Code: SB 30-90 Wheelbase-to-length ratio of 53% is considered ○ dangerous ◉ fatiguing ○ good ○ excellent *
The approximate net payload of 2580 pounds at 16% of GVWR on this model is ○ deficient ○ excessive ○ cautionary ○ good ◉ excellent *
Total highway safety penalties are: 5 * Value: 77 Durability: 73 Highway Control Rating: 70 Highway Safety: 65 ★★

Brand	Year	Type	Length	Model	Chassis	Engine	Fuel Type	Avg Price/LF	Wheelbase	Towing	GVWR	Curb Wt
Triple E Commander	**1995**	MHA	30	A 2901	FO	7.5L	G	$1900	190	8,000	17,000	14,035

Livability Code: SB 30-90 Wheelbase-to-length ratio of 53% is considered ○ dangerous ◉ fatiguing ○ good ○ excellent *
The approximate net payload of 2965 pounds at 17% of GVWR on this model is ○ deficient ○ excessive ○ cautionary ○ good ◉ excellent *
Total highway safety penalties are: 2 * Value: 78 Durability: 73 Highway Control Rating: 71 Highway Safety: 69 ★★

Brand	Year	Type	Length	Model	Chassis	Engine	Fuel Type	Avg Price/LF	Wheelbase	Towing	GVWR	Curb Wt
Triple E Commander	**1995**	MHA	33	A 3201	CH	7.4L	G	$1900	208	1,500	16,000	14,138

Livability Code: SB 30-90 Wheelbase-to-length ratio of 53% is considered ○ dangerous ◉ fatiguing ○ good ○ excellent *
The approximate net payload of 1862 pounds at 12% of GVWR on this model is ○ deficient ○ excessive ○ cautionary ◉ good ○ excellent *
Total highway safety penalties are: 6 * Value: 76 Durability: 73 Highway Control Rating: 61 Highway Safety: 55 ★

Brand	Year	Type	Length	Model	Chassis	Engine	Fuel Type	Avg Price/LF	Wheelbase	Towing	GVWR	Curb Wt
Triple E Commander	**1995**	MHA	33	A 3201	FO	7.5L	G	$1900	208	8,000	17,000	14,588

Livability Code: SB 30-90 Wheelbase-to-length ratio of 53% is considered ○ dangerous ◉ fatiguing ○ good ○ excellent *
The approximate net payload of 2412 pounds at 14% of GVWR on this model is ○ deficient ○ excessive ○ cautionary ◉ good ○ excellent *
Total highway safety penalties are: 2 * Value: 78 Durability: 73 Highway Control Rating: 65 Highway Safety: 63 ★★

Brand	Year	Type	Length	Model	Chassis	Engine	Fuel Type	Avg Price/LF	Wheelbase	Towing	GVWR	Curb Wt
Triple E Commander	**1995**	MHA	33	A 3201 pusher	OS	CU190	D	$3300	208	1,500	18,000	15,736

Livability Code: SB 30-90 Wheelbase-to-length ratio of 53% is considered ○ dangerous ◉ fatiguing ○ good ○ excellent *
The approximate net payload of 2264 pounds at 13% of GVWR on this model is ○ deficient ○ excessive ○ cautionary ◉ good ○ excellent *
Total highway safety penalties are: 2 * Value: 78 Durability: 73 Highway Control Rating: 63 Highway Safety: 61 ★★

Brand	Year	Type	Length	Model	Chassis	Engine	Fuel Type	Avg Price/LF	Wheelbase	Towing	GVWR	Curb Wt
Triple E Commander	**1995**	MHA	33	A 3201 pusher	OS	CU230	D	$3300	208	1,500	19,840	16,373

Livability Code: SB 30-90 Wheelbase-to-length ratio of 53% is considered ○ dangerous ◉ fatiguing ○ good ○ excellent *
The approximate net payload of 3467 pounds at 17% of GVWR on this model is ○ deficient ○ excessive ○ cautionary ○ good ◉ excellent *
Total highway safety penalties are: 2 * Value: 78 Durability: 73 Highway Control Rating: 71 Highway Safety: 69 ★★

Note: Safety ratings are based on the assumption that the engineering of the RV has allowed for proper balance by placing fresh, gray, and black holding tanks in a location so as not to change the balance of the RV when the tanks are empty or full. **Always double-check wheelbase, GVWR, and weights at front and rear axles.**

*See Section 1 for details on how conclusions are reached.

Brand	Year	Type	Length	Model	Chassis	Engine	Fuel Type	Average Price per Linear Foot When New	Adjusted Wheelbase	Approx. Towing Capacity	Gross Vehicle Weight Rating	Average Curb Weight

Triple E Commander 1995 MHA 34 A 3402 FO 7.5L G $1900 228 8,000 17,000 14,885
Livability Code: SB 30-90
Wheelbase-to-length ratio of 56% is considered ○ dangerous ○ fatiguing ◉ good ○ excellent *
The approximate net payload of 2115 pounds at 12% of GVWR on this model is ○ deficient ○ excessive ○ cautionary ◉ good ○ excellent *
Total highway safety penalties are: 2 *   Value: **7 8**   Durability: **7 3**   Highway Control Rating: **8 8**   Highway Safety: **8 6**   ★★★

Triple E Commander 1995 MHA 34 A 3403 FO 7.5L G $1900 228 8,000 17,000 14,885
Livability Code: SB 30-90
Wheelbase-to-length ratio of 56% is considered ○ dangerous ○ fatiguing ◉ good ○ excellent *
The approximate net payload of 2115 pounds at 12% of GVWR on this model is ○ deficient ○ excessive ○ cautionary ◉ good ○ excellent *
Total highway safety penalties are: 2 *   Value: **7 8**   Durability: **7 3**   Highway Control Rating: **8 8**   Highway Safety: **8 6**   ★★★

Triple E Commander 1995 MHA 34 A 3402 pusher OS CU190 D $3500 228 1,500 18,000 16,062
Livability Code: SB 30-90
Wheelbase-to-length ratio of 56% is considered ○ dangerous ○ fatiguing ◉ good ○ excellent *
The approximate net payload of 1938 pounds at 11% of GVWR on this model is ○ deficient ○ excessive ○ cautionary ◉ good ○ excellent *
Total highway safety penalties are: 2 *   Value: **7 8**   Durability: **7 3**   Highway Control Rating: **8 5**   Highway Safety: **8 3**   ★★★

Triple E Commander 1995 MHA 34 A 3402 pusher OS CU230 D $3500 228 1,500 19,840 16,841
Livability Code: SB 30-90
Wheelbase-to-length ratio of 56% is considered ○ dangerous ○ fatiguing ◉ good ○ excellent *
The approximate net payload of 2999 pounds at 15% of GVWR on this model is ○ deficient ○ excessive ○ cautionary ◉ good ○ excellent *
Total highway safety penalties are: 2 *   Value: **7 8**   Durability: **7 3**   Highway Control Rating: **9 3**   Highway Safety: **9 1**   ★★★

Triple E Commander 1996 MHA 30 A-2901 CH 7.4L G $2000 190 1,500 16,000 13,566
Livability Code: SB 30-90
Wheelbase-to-length ratio of 53% is considered ○ dangerous ◉ fatiguing ○ good ○ excellent *
The approximate net payload of 2434 pounds at 15% of GVWR on this model is ○ deficient ○ excessive ○ cautionary ◉ good ○ excellent *
Total highway safety penalties are: 5 *   Value: **7 7**   Durability: **7 3**   Highway Control Rating: **6 8**   Highway Safety: **6 3**   ★★

Triple E Commander 1996 MHA 30 A-2901 FO 7.5L G $2000 190 8,000 17,000 14,148
Livability Code: SB 30-90
Wheelbase-to-length ratio of 53% is considered ○ dangerous ◉ fatiguing ○ good ○ excellent *
The approximate net payload of 2852 pounds at 17% of GVWR on this model is ○ deficient ○ excessive ○ cautionary ○ good ◉ excellent *
Total highway safety penalties are: 2 *   Value: **7 8**   Durability: **7 3**   Highway Control Rating: **7 0**   Highway Safety: **6 8**   ★★

Triple E Commander 1996 MHA 33 A-3201 CH 7.4L G $1800 208 1,500 16,000 14,297
Livability Code: SB 30-90
Wheelbase-to-length ratio of 53% is considered ○ dangerous ◉ fatiguing ○ good ○ excellent *
The approximate net payload of 1703 pounds at 11% of GVWR on this model is ○ deficient ○ excessive ○ cautionary ◉ good ○ excellent *
Total highway safety penalties are: 6 *   Value: **7 6**   Durability: **7 3**   Highway Control Rating: **5 9**   Highway Safety: **5 3**   ★

Triple E Commander 1996 MHA 33 A-3201 FO 7.5L G $1800 208 8,000 17,000 14,909
Livability Code: SB 30-90
Wheelbase-to-length ratio of 53% is considered ○ dangerous ◉ fatiguing ○ good ○ excellent *
The approximate net payload of 2091 pounds at 12% of GVWR on this model is ○ deficient ○ excessive ○ cautionary ◉ good ○ excellent *
Total highway safety penalties are: 2 *   Value: **7 8**   Durability: **7 3**   Highway Control Rating: **6 2**   Highway Safety: **6 0**   ★★

Triple E Commander 1996 MHA 34 A-3402 FO 7.5L G $1800 228 8,000 17,000 15,210
Livability Code: SB 30-90
Wheelbase-to-length ratio of 56% is considered ○ dangerous ○ fatiguing ◉ good ○ excellent *
The approximate net payload of 1790 pounds at 11% of GVWR on this model is ○ deficient ○ excessive ○ cautionary ◉ good ○ excellent *
Total highway safety penalties are: 2 *   Value: **7 8**   Durability: **7 3**   Highway Control Rating: **8 5**   Highway Safety: **8 3**   ★★★

Triple E Commander 1996 MHA 34 A-3403 FO 7.5L G $1800 228 8,000 17,000 15,254
Livability Code: SB 30-90
Wheelbase-to-length ratio of 56% is considered ○ dangerous ○ fatiguing ◉ good ○ excellent *
The approximate net payload of 1746 pounds at 10% of GVWR on this model is ○ deficient ○ excessive ○ cautionary ◉ good ○ excellent *
Total highway safety penalties are: 2 *   Value: **7 8**   Durability: **7 3**   Highway Control Rating: **8 9**   Highway Safety: **8 7**   ★★★

Triple E Commander 1996 MHA 34 A-3404 FO 7.5L G $1800 228 8,000 17,000 15,254
Livability Code: SB 30-90
Wheelbase-to-length ratio of 56% is considered ○ dangerous ○ fatiguing ◉ good ○ excellent *
The approximate net payload of 1746 pounds at 10% of GVWR on this model is ○ deficient ○ excessive ○ cautionary ◉ good ○ excellent *
Total highway safety penalties are: 2 *   Value: **7 8**   Durability: **7 3**   Highway Control Rating: **8 9**   Highway Safety: **8 7**   ★★★

Triple E Commander 1996 MHA 34 A-3503FS FO 7.5L G $1800 228 8,000 17,000 15,993
Livability Code: SB 30-90
Wheelbase-to-length ratio of 56% is considered ○ dangerous ○ fatiguing ◉ good ○ excellent *
The approximate net payload of 1007 pounds at 6% of GVWR on this model is ◉ deficient ○ excessive ○ cautionary ○ good ○ excellent *
Total highway safety penalties are: 7 *   Value: **7 6**   Durability: **7 3**   Highway Control Rating: **6 0**   Highway Safety: **5 3**   ★

Note: Safety ratings are based on the assumption that the engineering of the RV has allowed for proper balance by placing fresh, gray, and black holding tanks in a location so as not to change the balance of the RV when the tanks are empty or full. **Always double-check wheelbase, GVWR, and weights at front and rear axles.**

*See Section 1 for details on how conclusions are reached.

Brand	Year	Type	Length	Model	Chassis	Engine	Fuel Type	Average Price per Linear Foot When New	Adjusted Wheel-base	Approx. Towing Capacity	Gross Vehicle Weight Rating	Average Curb Weight

Triple E Commander 1996 MHA 34 A-3402 pusher FR D $2600 208 5,200 19,800 17,092
Livability Code: SB 30-90
Wheelbase-to-length ratio of 51% is considered ○ dangerous ◉ fatiguing ○ good ○ excellent *
The approximate net payload of 2708 pounds at 14% of GVWR on this model is ○ deficient ○ excessive ○ cautionary ◉ good ○ excellent *
Total highway safety penalties are: 2 *   Value: **7 8**   Durability: **7 3**   Highway Control Rating: **4 3**   Highway Safety: **4 1**

Triple E Commander 1997 MHA 30 A-2901 FO 7.5L G $2000 190 1,500 17,000 14,568
Livability Code: SB 30-90
Wheelbase-to-length ratio of 53% is considered ○ dangerous ◉ fatiguing ○ good ○ excellent *
The approximate net payload of 2432 pounds at 14% of GVWR on this model is ○ deficient ○ excessive ○ cautionary ◉ good ○ excellent *
Total highway safety penalties are: 2 *   Value: **7 8**   Durability: **7 3**   Highway Control Rating: **6 6**   Highway Safety: **6 4**   ★★

Triple E Commander 1997 MHA 33 A-3201 FO 7.5L G $1800 208 1,500 17,000 15,197
Livability Code: SB 30-90
Wheelbase-to-length ratio of 53% is considered ○ dangerous ◉ fatiguing ○ good ○ excellent *
The approximate net payload of 1803 pounds at 11% of GVWR on this model is ○ deficient ○ excessive ○ cautionary ◉ good ○ excellent *
Total highway safety penalties are: 2 *   Value: **7 8**   Durability: **7 3**   Highway Control Rating: **5 9**   Highway Safety: **5 7**   ★

Triple E Commander 1997 MHA 34 A-3301 FO 7.5L G $1800 228 1,500 17,000 15,471
Livability Code: SB 30-90
Wheelbase-to-length ratio of 57% is considered ○ dangerous ○ fatiguing ◉ good ○ excellent *
The approximate net payload of 1529 pounds at 9% of GVWR on this model is ○ deficient ○ excessive ◉ cautionary ○ good ○ excellent *
Total highway safety penalties are: 2 *   Value: **7 8**   Durability: **7 3**   Highway Control Rating: **8 1**   Highway Safety: **7 9**   ★★★

Triple E Commander 1997 MHA 34 A-3402 FO 7.5L G $1800 228 1,500 17,000 15,598
Livability Code: SB 30-90
Wheelbase-to-length ratio of 56% is considered ○ dangerous ○ fatiguing ◉ good ○ excellent *
The approximate net payload of 1402 pounds at 8% of GVWR on this model is ○ deficient ○ excessive ◉ cautionary ○ good ○ excellent *
Total highway safety penalties are: 2 *   Value: **7 8**   Durability: **7 3**   Highway Control Rating: **7 2**   Highway Safety: **7 0**   ★★★

Triple E Commander 1997 MHA 34 A-3503 FO 7.5L G $1800 228 1,500 17,000 16,418
Livability Code: SB 30-90
Wheelbase-to-length ratio of 56% is considered ○ dangerous ○ fatiguing ◉ good ○ excellent *
The approximate net payload of 582 pounds at 3% of GVWR on this model is ◉ deficient ○ excessive ○ cautionary ○ good ○ excellent *
Total highway safety penalties are: 7 *   Value: **7 6**   Durability: **7 3**   Highway Control Rating: **5 8**   Highway Safety: **5 1**   ★

Triple E Commander 1998 MHA 30 A2901 FO 7.5L G $2300 190 1,500 17,000 14,615
Livability Code: SB 30-90
Wheelbase-to-length ratio of 53% is considered ○ dangerous ◉ fatiguing ○ good ○ excellent *
The approximate net payload of 2385 pounds at 14% of GVWR on this model is ○ deficient ○ excessive ○ cautionary ◉ good ○ excellent *
Total highway safety penalties are: 2 *   Value: **8 0**   Durability: **7 7**   Highway Control Rating: **6 6**   Highway Safety: **6 4**   ★★

Triple E Commander 1998 MHA 33 A3201 FO 7.5L G $2200 208 1,500 17,000 15,424
Livability Code: SB 30-90
Wheelbase-to-length ratio of 53% is considered ○ dangerous ◉ fatiguing ○ good ○ excellent *
The approximate net payload of 1576 pounds at 9% of GVWR on this model is ○ deficient ○ excessive ◉ cautionary ○ good ○ excellent *
Total highway safety penalties are: 2 *   Value: **8 0**   Durability: **7 7**   Highway Control Rating: **5 3**   Highway Safety: **5 1**   ★

Triple E Commander 1998 MHA 34 A3402 FO 7.5L G $2300 228 1,500 17,000 15,713
Livability Code: SB 30-90
Wheelbase-to-length ratio of 56% is considered ○ dangerous ○ fatiguing ◉ good ○ excellent *
The approximate net payload of 1287 pounds at 8% of GVWR on this model is ○ deficient ○ excessive ◉ cautionary ○ good ○ excellent *
Total highway safety penalties are: 2 *   Value: **8 0**   Durability: **7 7**   Highway Control Rating: **7 2**   Highway Safety: **7 0**   ★★★

Triple E Commander 1998 MHA 34 A3504 FO 7.5L G $2300 228 1,500 17,000 15,736
Livability Code: SB 30-90
Wheelbase-to-length ratio of 56% is considered ○ dangerous ○ fatiguing ◉ good ○ excellent *
The approximate net payload of 1264 pounds at 7% of GVWR on this model is ○ deficient ○ excessive ◉ cautionary ○ good ○ excellent *
Total highway safety penalties are: 2 *   Value: **8 0**   Durability: **7 7**   Highway Control Rating: **6 7**   Highway Safety: **6 5**   ★★

Triple E Commander 1998 MHA 34 A3503FS FO 7.5L G $2700 228 1,500 17,000 16,644
Livability Code: SB 30-90
Wheelbase-to-length ratio of 56% is considered ○ dangerous ○ fatiguing ◉ good ○ excellent *
The approximate net payload of 356 pounds at 2% of GVWR on this model is ◉ deficient ○ excessive ○ cautionary ○ good ○ excellent *
Total highway safety penalties are: 7 *   Value: **7 7**   Durability: **7 7**   Highway Control Rating: **5 6**   Highway Safety: **4 9**

Triple E Commander 1999 MHA 30 A2901 FO 6.8L G $2300 190 1,500 18,000 14,881
Livability Code: SB 30-90
Wheelbase-to-length ratio of 53% is considered ○ dangerous ◉ fatiguing ○ good ○ excellent *
The approximate net payload of 3119 pounds at 17% of GVWR on this model is ○ deficient ○ excessive ○ cautionary ○ good ◉ excellent *
Total highway safety penalties are: 2 *   Value: **8 0**   Durability: **7 7**   Highway Control Rating: **7 7**   Highway Safety: **7 5**   ★★★

Note: Safety ratings are based on the assumption that the engineering of the RV has allowed for proper balance by placing fresh, gray, and black holding tanks in a location so as not to change the balance of the RV when the tanks are empty or full. **Always double-check wheelbase, GVWR, and weights at front and rear axles.**

The RV Rating Book

*See Section 1 for details on how conclusions are reached.

Section 2: The Ratings

Brand	Year	Type	Length	Model	Chassis	Engine	Fuel Type	Average Price per Linear Foot When New	Adjusted Wheelbase	Approx. Towing Capacity	Gross Vehicle Weight Rating	Average Curb Weight
Triple E Commander	1999	MHA	33	A3201	FO	6.8L	G	$2200	208	1,500	18,000	15,634

Livability Code: SB 30-90
Wheelbase-to-length ratio of 53% is considered ○ dangerous ◉ fatiguing ○ good ○ excellent *
The approximate net payload of 2367 pounds at 13% of GVWR on this model is ○ deficient ○ excessive ○ cautionary ◉ good ○ excellent *
Total highway safety penalties are: 2 *   Value: 80   Durability: 77   Highway Control Rating: 71   Highway Safety: 69   ★★

Brand	Year	Type	Length	Model	Chassis	Engine	Fuel Type	Price/LF	Adj Wheelbase	Towing	GVWR	Curb Weight
Triple E Commander	1999	MHA	33	A3302GS	FO	6.8L	G	$2800	228	1,500	20,500	17,205

Livability Code: SB 30-90
Wheelbase-to-length ratio of 58% is considered ○ dangerous ○ fatiguing ○ good ◉ excellent *
The approximate net payload of 3295 pounds at 16% of GVWR on this model is ○ deficient ○ excessive ○ cautionary ○ good ◉ excellent *
Total highway safety penalties are: 12 *   Value: 75   Durability: 77   Highway Control Rating: 100   Highway Safety: 88   ★★★

Triple E Commander	1999	MHA	34	A3402	FO	6.8L	G	$2300	228	1,500	18,000	16,089

Livability Code: SB 30-90
Wheelbase-to-length ratio of 56% is considered ○ dangerous ○ fatiguing ◉ good ○ excellent *
The approximate net payload of 1912 pounds at 11% of GVWR on this model is ○ deficient ○ excessive ○ cautionary ◉ good ○ excellent *
Total highway safety penalties are: 2 *   Value: 80   Durability: 77   Highway Control Rating: 86   Highway Safety: 84   ★★★

Triple E Commander	1999	MHA	34	A3504	FO	6.8L	G	$2300	228	1,500	18,000	16,122

Livability Code: SB 30-90
Wheelbase-to-length ratio of 56% is considered ○ dangerous ○ fatiguing ◉ good ○ excellent *
The approximate net payload of 1878 pounds at 10% of GVWR on this model is ○ deficient ○ excessive ○ cautionary ◉ good ○ excellent *
Total highway safety penalties are: 2 *   Value: 80   Durability: 77   Highway Control Rating: 85   Highway Safety: 83   ★★★

Triple E Commander	1999	MHA	34	A3503FS	FO	6.8L	G	$2700	228	1,500	20,500	17,628

Livability Code: SB 30-90
Wheelbase-to-length ratio of 56% is considered ○ dangerous ○ fatiguing ◉ good ○ excellent *
The approximate net payload of 2872 pounds at 14% of GVWR on this model is ○ deficient ○ excessive ○ cautionary ◉ good ○ excellent *
Total highway safety penalties are: 7 *   Value: 77   Durability: 77   Highway Control Rating: 92   Highway Safety: 85   ★★★

Triple E Commander	1999	MHA	34	A3505GS	FO	6.8L	G	$2700	228	1,500	20,500	16,897

Livability Code: SB 30-90
Wheelbase-to-length ratio of 56% is considered ○ dangerous ○ fatiguing ◉ good ○ excellent *
The approximate net payload of 3603 pounds at 18% of GVWR on this model is ○ deficient ○ excessive ○ cautionary ○ good ◉ excellent *
Total highway safety penalties are: 12 *   Value: 75   Durability: 77   Highway Control Rating: 98   Highway Safety: 86   ★★★

Triple E Commander	1999	MHA	34	A-3505GS DP	FR	CA300	D	$3500	208	1,500	26,350	21,675

Livability Code: SB 30-90
Wheelbase-to-length ratio of 51% is considered ○ dangerous ◉ fatiguing ○ good ○ excellent *
The approximate net payload of 4675 pounds at 18% of GVWR on this model is ○ deficient ○ excessive ○ cautionary ○ good ◉ excellent *
Total highway safety penalties are: 5 *   Value: 78   Durability: 77   Highway Control Rating: 60   Highway Safety: 55   ★

Triple E Commander	1999	MHA	34	A-3506 DP	FR	CA300	D	$3500	208	1,500	26,350	22,575

Livability Code: SB 30-90
Wheelbase-to-length ratio of 51% is considered ○ dangerous ◉ fatiguing ○ good ○ excellent *
The approximate net payload of 3775 pounds at 14% of GVWR on this model is ○ deficient ○ excessive ○ cautionary ◉ good ○ excellent
Total highway safety penalties are: 15 *   Value: 73   Durability: 77   Highway Control Rating: 55   Highway Safety: 40

Triple E Embassy	1995	MHA	27	A 26	CH	7.4L	G	$1900	158	1,500	12,300	11,060

Livability Code: SB 30-90
Wheelbase-to-length ratio of 49% is considered ◉ dangerous ○ fatiguing ○ good ○ excellent *
The approximate net payload of 1240 pounds at 10% of GVWR on this model is ○ deficient ○ excessive ○ cautionary ◉ good ○ excellent *
Total highway safety penalties are: 3 *   Value: 78   Durability: 73   Highway Control Rating: 31   Highway Safety: 28

Triple E Embassy	1995	MHA	30	A 29	CH	7.4L	G	$1800	190	1,500	16,000	12,984

Livability Code: SB 30-90
Wheelbase-to-length ratio of 53% is considered ○ dangerous ◉ fatiguing ○ good ○ excellent *
The approximate net payload of 3016 pounds at 19% of GVWR on this model is ○ deficient ○ excessive ○ cautionary ○ good ◉ excellent *
Total highway safety penalties are: 5 *   Value: 77   Durability: 73   Highway Control Rating: 72   Highway Safety: 67   ★★

Triple E Embassy	1995	MHA	30	A 29	FO	7.5L	G	$1800	190	8,000	17,000	13,313

Livability Code: SB 30-90
Wheelbase-to-length ratio of 53% is considered ○ dangerous ◉ fatiguing ○ good ○ excellent *
The approximate net payload of 3687 pounds at 22% of GVWR on this model is ○ deficient ○ excessive ○ cautionary ○ good ◉ excellent *
Total highway safety penalties are: 2 *   Value: 78   Durability: 73   Highway Control Rating: 72   Highway Safety: 70   ★★★

Triple E Embassy	1995	MHA	32	A 31	CH	7.4L	G	$1700	190	1,500	16,000	13,450

Livability Code: SB 30-90
Wheelbase-to-length ratio of 49% is considered ◉ dangerous ○ fatiguing ○ good ○ excellent *
The approximate net payload of 2550 pounds at 16% of GVWR on this model is ○ deficient ○ excessive ○ cautionary ○ good ◉ excellent *
Total highway safety penalties are: 6 *   Value: 76   Durability: 73   Highway Control Rating: 43   Highway Safety: 37

Note: Safety ratings are based on the assumption that the engineering of the RV has allowed for proper balance by placing fresh, gray, and black holding tanks in a location so as not to change the balance of the RV when the tanks are empty or full. **Always double-check wheelbase, GVWR, and weights at front and rear axles.**

*See Section 1 for details on how conclusions are reached.

Brand	Year	Type	Length	Model	Chassis	Engine	Fuel Type	Average Price per Linear Foot When New	Adjusted Wheelbase	Approx. Towing Capacity	Gross Vehicle Weight Rating	Average Curb Weight
Triple E Embassy	1995	MHA	32	A 31	FO	7.5L	G	$1700	190	8,000	17,000	13,744

Livability Code: SB 30-90 — Wheelbase-to-length ratio of 49% is considered ◉ dangerous ○ fatiguing ○ good ○ excellent *

The approximate net payload of 3256 pounds at 19% of GVWR on this model is ○ deficient ○ excessive ○ cautionary ○ good ◉ excellent *

Total highway safety penalties are: 2 * — Value: 7 8 — Durability: 7 3 — Highway Control Rating: 4 6 — Highway Safety: 4 4

Brand	Year	Type	Length	Model	Chassis	Engine	Fuel Type	Avg Price/Linear Foot	Adjusted Wheelbase	Approx. Towing Capacity	GVWR	Avg Curb Weight
Triple E Embassy	1995	MHA	34	A 33 pusher	OS	CU190	D	$2600	190	1,500	16,000	14,248

Livability Code: SB 30-90 — Wheelbase-to-length ratio of 47% is considered ◉ dangerous ○ fatiguing ○ good ○ excellent *

The approximate net payload of 1752 pounds at 11% of GVWR on this model is ○ deficient ○ excessive ○ cautionary ◉ good ○ excellent *

Total highway safety penalties are: 2 * — Value: 7 8 — Durability: 7 3 — Highway Control Rating: 2 4 — Highway Safety: 2 2

Triple E Embassy	1996	MHA	28	A27	CH	7.4L	G	$2000	178	2,200	14,800	12,322

Livability Code: SB 30-90 — Wheelbase-to-length ratio of 52% is considered ○ dangerous ◉ fatiguing ○ good ○ excellent *

The approximate net payload of 2478 pounds at 17% of GVWR on this model is ○ deficient ○ excessive ○ cautionary ◉ good ◉ excellent *

Total highway safety penalties are: 4 * — Value: 7 7 — Durability: 7 3 — Highway Control Rating: 6 1 — Highway Safety: 5 7 — ★

Triple E Embassy	1996	MHA	28	A27	FO	7.5L	G	$2000	178	3,800	15,200	12,486

Livability Code: SB 30-90 — Wheelbase-to-length ratio of 52% is considered ○ dangerous ◉ fatiguing ○ good ○ excellent *

The approximate net payload of 2714 pounds at 18% of GVWR on this model is ○ deficient ○ excessive ○ cautionary ○ good ◉ excellent *

Total highway safety penalties are: 2 * — Value: 7 8 — Durability: 7 3 — Highway Control Rating: 6 2 — Highway Safety: 6 0 — ★★

Triple E Embassy	1996	MHA	30	A 29	CH	7.4L	G	$1900	190	1,500	16,000	12,984

Livability Code: SB 30-90 — Wheelbase-to-length ratio of 53% is considered ○ dangerous ◉ fatiguing ○ good ○ excellent *

The approximate net payload of 3016 pounds at 19% of GVWR on this model is ○ deficient ○ excessive ○ cautionary ○ good ◉ excellent *

Total highway safety penalties are: 5 * — Value: 7 7 — Durability: 7 3 — Highway Control Rating: 7 2 — Highway Safety: 6 7 — ★★

Triple E Embassy	1996	MHA	30	A 29	FO	7.5L	G	$1900	190	8,000	17,000	13,313

Livability Code: SB 30-90 — Wheelbase-to-length ratio of 53% is considered ○ dangerous ◉ fatiguing ○ good ○ excellent *

The approximate net payload of 3687 pounds at 22% of GVWR on this model is ○ deficient ○ excessive ○ cautionary ○ good ◉ excellent *

Total highway safety penalties are: 2 * — Value: 7 8 — Durability: 7 3 — Highway Control Rating: 7 2 — Highway Safety: 7 0 — ★★★

Triple E Embassy	1996	MHA	32	A 31	CH	7.4L	G	$2200	190	1,500	16,000	13,450

Livability Code: SB 30-90 — Wheelbase-to-length ratio of 49% is considered ◉ dangerous ○ fatiguing ○ good ○ excellent *

The approximate net payload of 2550 pounds at 16% of GVWR on this model is ○ deficient ○ excessive ○ cautionary ○ good ◉ excellent *

Total highway safety penalties are: 6 * — Value: 7 6 — Durability: 7 3 — Highway Control Rating: 4 3 — Highway Safety: 3 7

Triple E Embassy	1996	MHA	32	A 31	FO	7.5L	G	$2200	190	8,000	17,000	13,744

Livability Code: SB 30-90 — Wheelbase-to-length ratio of 49% is considered ◉ dangerous ○ fatiguing ○ good ○ excellent *

The approximate net payload of 3256 pounds at 19% of GVWR on this model is ○ deficient ○ excessive ○ cautionary ○ good ◉ excellent *

Total highway safety penalties are: 2 * — Value: 7 8 — Durability: 7 3 — Highway Control Rating: 4 6 — Highway Safety: 4 4

Triple E Embassy	1997	MHA	28	A-27	FO	7.5L	G	$2000	178	1,500	15,200	12,512

Livability Code: SB 30-90 — Wheelbase-to-length ratio of 52% is considered ○ dangerous ◉ fatiguing ○ good ○ excellent *

The approximate net payload of 2688 pounds at 18% of GVWR on this model is ○ deficient ○ excessive ○ cautionary ○ good ◉ excellent *

Total highway safety penalties are: 2 * — Value: 7 8 — Durability: 7 3 — Highway Control Rating: 6 2 — Highway Safety: 6 0 — ★★

Triple E Embassy	1997	MHA	30	A-29	FO	7.5L	G	$2000	190	1,500	17,000	13,351

Livability Code: SB 30-90 — Wheelbase-to-length ratio of 53% is considered ○ dangerous ◉ fatiguing ○ good ○ excellent *

The approximate net payload of 3649 pounds at 21% of GVWR on this model is ○ deficient ○ excessive ○ cautionary ○ good ◉ excellent *

Total highway safety penalties are: 2 * — Value: 7 8 — Durability: 7 3 — Highway Control Rating: 7 2 — Highway Safety: 7 0 — ★★★

Triple E Embassy	1997	MHA	32	A-31	FO	7.5L	G	$2200	190	1,500	17,000	13,775

Livability Code: SB 30-90 — Wheelbase-to-length ratio of 49% is considered ◉ dangerous ○ fatiguing ○ good ○ excellent *

The approximate net payload of 3225 pounds at 19% of GVWR on this model is ○ deficient ○ excessive ○ cautionary ○ good ◉ excellent *

Total highway safety penalties are: 2 * — Value: 7 8 — Durability: 7 3 — Highway Control Rating: 4 6 — Highway Safety: 4 4

Triple E Embassy	1998	MHA	29	A27	FO	7.5L	G	$1800	178	1,500	15,200	12,701

Livability Code: SB 30-90 — Wheelbase-to-length ratio of 52% is considered ○ dangerous ◉ fatiguing ○ good ○ excellent *

The approximate net payload of 2499 pounds at 16% of GVWR on this model is ○ deficient ○ excessive ○ cautionary ○ good ◉ excellent *

Total highway safety penalties are: 2 * — Value: 7 8 — Durability: 7 3 — Highway Control Rating: 5 8 — Highway Safety: 5 6 — ★

Note: Safety ratings are based on the assumption that the engineering of the RV has allowed for proper balance by placing fresh, gray, and black holding tanks in a location so as not to change the balance of the RV when the tanks are empty or full. **Always double-check wheelbase, GVWR, and weights at front and rear axles.**

*See Section 1 for details on how conclusions are reached.

Section 2: The Ratings

Brand	Year	Type	Length	Model	Chassis	Engine	Fuel Type	Average Price per Linear Foot When New	Adjusted Wheel-base	Approx. Towing Capacity	Gross Vehicle Weight Rating	Average Curb Weight
Triple E Embassy	1998	MHA	30	A29	FO	7.5L	G	$1900	190	1,500	17,000	13,367

Livability Code: SB 30-90
Wheelbase-to-length ratio of 53% is considered ○ dangerous ◉ fatiguing ○ good ○ excellent *
The approximate net payload of 3633 pounds at 21% of GVWR on this model is ○ deficient ○ excessive ○ cautionary ○ good ◉ excellent *
Total highway safety penalties are: 2 * Value: **7 8** Durability: **7 3** Highway Control Rating: **7 2** Highway Safety: **7 0** ★★★

Brand	Year	Type	Length	Model	Chassis	Engine	Fuel Type	Avg Price/Linear Ft	Wheelbase	Towing	GVWR	Curb Weight
Triple E Embassy	1998	MHA	32	A31	FO	7.5L	G	$1900	190	1,500	17,000	13,791

Livability Code: SB 30-90
Wheelbase-to-length ratio of 49% is considered ◉ dangerous ○ fatiguing ○ good ○ excellent *
The approximate net payload of 3209 pounds at 19% of GVWR on this model is ○ deficient ○ excessive ○ cautionary ○ good ◉ excellent *
Total highway safety penalties are: 2 * Value: **7 8** Durability: **7 3** Highway Control Rating: **4 6** Highway Safety: **4 4**

Triple E Embassy	1999	MHA	28	A27	FO	6.8L	G	$2300	178	1,500	15,500	12,801

Livability Code: SB 30-90
Wheelbase-to-length ratio of 53% is considered ○ dangerous ◉ fatiguing ○ good ○ excellent *
The approximate net payload of 2699 pounds at 17% of GVWR on this model is ○ deficient ○ excessive ○ cautionary ○ good ◉ excellent *
Total highway safety penalties are: 5 * Value: **7 7** Durability: **7 3** Highway Control Rating: **7 7** Highway Safety: **7 2** ★★★

Triple E Embassy	1999	MHA	29	A-29	FO	6.8L	G	$2200	190	1,500	18,000	13,601

Livability Code: SB 30-90
Wheelbase-to-length ratio of 54% is considered ○ dangerous ○ fatiguing ◉ good ○ excellent *
The approximate net payload of 4399 pounds at 24% of GVWR on this model is ○ deficient ○ excessive ○ cautionary ○ good ◉ excellent *
Total highway safety penalties are: 5 * Value: **7 7** Durability: **7 3** Highway Control Rating: **8 4** Highway Safety: **7 9** ★★★

Triple E Embassy	1999	MHA	31	A31	FO	6.8L	G	$2100	190	1,500	18,000	13,992

Livability Code: SB 30-90
Wheelbase-to-length ratio of 51% is considered ○ dangerous ◉ fatiguing ○ good ○ excellent *
The approximate net payload of 4008 pounds at 22% of GVWR on this model is ○ deficient ○ excessive ○ cautionary ○ good ◉ excellent *
Total highway safety penalties are: 5 * Value: **7 7** Durability: **7 3** Highway Control Rating: **6 0** Highway Safety: **5 5** ★

Triple E Embassy	1999	MHA	33	A-32SS	FO	6.8L	G	$2000	208	1,500	18,000	14,811

Livability Code: SB 30-90
Wheelbase-to-length ratio of 53% is considered ○ dangerous ◉ fatiguing ○ good ○ excellent *
The approximate net payload of 3189 pounds at 18% of GVWR on this model is ○ deficient ○ excessive ○ cautionary ○ good ◉ excellent *
Total highway safety penalties are: 8 * Value: **7 5** Durability: **7 3** Highway Control Rating: **7 8** Highway Safety: **7 0** ★★★

Triple E Empress	1992	MHA	34	992	CH	7.4L	G	$2300	190	1,500	16,000	13,810

Livability Code: SB 30-90
Wheelbase-to-length ratio of 47% is considered ◉ dangerous ○ fatiguing ○ good ○ excellent *
The approximate net payload of 2190 pounds at 14% of GVWR on this model is ○ deficient ○ excessive ○ cautionary ◉ good ○ excellent *
Total highway safety penalties are: 9 * Value: **7 6** Durability: **7 7** Highway Control Rating: **3 0** Highway Safety: **2 1**

Triple E Empress	1992	MHA	34	992	FO	7.5L	G	$2300	190	8,000	17,000	14,376

Livability Code: SB 30-90
Wheelbase-to-length ratio of 47% is considered ◉ dangerous ○ fatiguing ○ good ○ excellent *
The approximate net payload of 2624 pounds at 15% of GVWR on this model is ○ deficient ○ excessive ○ cautionary ◉ good ○ excellent *
Total highway safety penalties are: 5 * Value: **7 8** Durability: **7 7** Highway Control Rating: **3 2** Highway Safety: **2 7**

Triple E Empress	1992	MHA	34	992	OS	Cu5.9L	D	$2900	190	1,500	18,000	15,212

Livability Code: SB 30-90
Wheelbase-to-length ratio of 47% is considered ◉ dangerous ○ fatiguing ○ good ○ excellent *
The approximate net payload of 2788 pounds at 15% of GVWR on this model is ○ deficient ○ excessive ○ cautionary ◉ good ○ excellent *
Total highway safety penalties are: 5 * Value: **7 8** Durability: **7 7** Highway Control Rating: **3 2** Highway Safety: **2 7**

Triple E Empress	1992	MHA	35	1061	CH	7.4L	G	$2300	208	1,500	16,000	14,232

Livability Code: SB 30-90
Wheelbase-to-length ratio of 50% is considered ◉ dangerous ○ fatiguing ○ good ○ excellent *
The approximate net payload of 1768 pounds at 11% of GVWR on this model is ○ deficient ○ excessive ○ cautionary ◉ good ○ excellent *
Total highway safety penalties are: 10 * Value: **7 6** Durability: **7 7** Highway Control Rating: **3 3** Highway Safety: **2 3**

Triple E Empress	1992	MHA	35	1062	CH	7.4L	G	$2300	208	1,500	16,000	14,232

Livability Code: SB 30-90
Wheelbase-to-length ratio of 50% is considered ◉ dangerous ○ fatiguing ○ good ○ excellent *
The approximate net payload of 1768 pounds at 11% of GVWR on this model is ○ deficient ○ excessive ○ cautionary ◉ good ○ excellent *
Total highway safety penalties are: 10 * Value: **7 6** Durability: **7 7** Highway Control Rating: **3 3** Highway Safety: **2 3**

Triple E Empress	1992	MHA	35	1061	FO	7.5L	G	$2300	208	8,000	17,000	14,519

Livability Code: SB 30-90
Wheelbase-to-length ratio of 50% is considered ◉ dangerous ○ fatiguing ○ good ○ excellent *
The approximate net payload of 2481 pounds at 15% of GVWR on this model is ○ deficient ○ excessive ○ cautionary ◉ good ○ excellent *
Total highway safety penalties are: 5 * Value: **7 8** Durability: **7 7** Highway Control Rating: **4 1** Highway Safety: **3 6**

Note: Safety ratings are based on the assumption that the engineering of the RV has allowed for proper balance by placing fresh, gray, and black holding tanks in a location so as not to change the balance of the RV when the tanks are empty or full. **Always double-check wheelbase, GVWR, and weights at front and rear axles.**

*See Section 1 for details on how conclusions are reached.

Brand	Year	Type	Length	Model	Chassis	Engine	Fuel Type	Average Price per Linear Foot When New	Adjusted Wheel-base	Approx. Towing Capacity	Gross Vehicle Weight Rating	Average Curb Weight

Triple E Empress — 1992 — MHA — 35 — 1062 — FO — 7.5L — G — $2300 — 208 — 8,000 — 17,000 — 14,674
Livability Code: SB 30-90   Wheelbase-to-length ratio of 50% is considered ◉ dangerous ○ fatiguing ○ good ○ excellent *
The approximate net payload of 2326 pounds at 14% of GVWR on this model is ○ deficient ○ excessive ○ cautionary ◉ good ○ excellent *
Total highway safety penalties are: 5 *   Value: 7 8   Durability: 7 7   Highway Control Rating: 3 9   Highway Safety: 3 4

Triple E Empress — 1992 — MHA — 35 — 1061 — OS — Cu5.9L — D — $2900 — 208 — 1,500 — 18,000 — 15,536
Livability Code: SB 30-90   Wheelbase-to-length ratio of 50% is considered ◉ dangerous ○ fatiguing ○ good ○ excellent *
The approximate net payload of 2464 pounds at 14% of GVWR on this model is ○ deficient ○ excessive ○ cautionary ◉ good ○ excellent *
Total highway safety penalties are: 5 *   Value: 7 8   Durability: 7 7   Highway Control Rating: 3 9   Highway Safety: 3 4

Triple E Empress — 1992 — MHA — 35 — 1062 — OS — Cu5.9L — D — $2900 — 208 — 1,500 — 18,000 — 15,536
Livability Code: SB 30-90   Wheelbase-to-length ratio of 50% is considered ◉ dangerous ○ fatiguing ○ good ○ excellent *
The approximate net payload of 2464 pounds at 14% of GVWR on this model is ○ deficient ○ excessive ○ cautionary ◉ good ○ excellent *
Total highway safety penalties are: 5 *   Value: 7 8   Durability: 7 7   Highway Control Rating: 3 9   Highway Safety: 3 4

Triple E Empress — 1992 — MHA — 36 — 1081 DP — OS — Cu5.9L — D — $2800 — 208 — 1,500 — 18,000 — 15,686
Livability Code: SB 30-90   Wheelbase-to-length ratio of 49% is considered ◉ dangerous ○ fatiguing ○ good ○ excellent *
The approximate net payload of 2314 pounds at 13% of GVWR on this model is ○ deficient ○ excessive ○ cautionary ◉ good ○ excellent *
Total highway safety penalties are: 5 *   Value: 7 8   Durability: 7 7   Highway Control Rating: 3 4   Highway Safety: 2 9

Triple E Empress — 1992 — MHA — 38 — 1203 — FO — 7.5L — G — $2400 — 232 T — 6,000 — 19,000 — 16,646
Livability Code: SB 30-90   Wheelbase-to-length ratio of 51% is considered ○ dangerous ◉ fatiguing ○ good ○ excellent *
The approximate net payload of 2354 pounds at 12% of GVWR on this model is ○ deficient ○ excessive ○ cautionary ◉ good ○ excellent *
Total highway safety penalties are: 7 *   Value: 7 7   Durability: 7 7   Highway Control Rating: 4 0   Highway Safety: 3 3

Triple E Empress — 1992 — MHA — 38 — 1203 — OS — Cu5.9L — D — $2600 — 208 ? — 1,500 — 18,000 — 16,285
Livability Code: SB 30-90   Wheelbase-to-length ratio of 46% is considered ◉ dangerous ○ fatiguing ○ good ○ excellent *
The approximate net payload of 1715 pounds at 10% of GVWR on this model is ○ deficient ○ excessive ○ cautionary ◉ good ○ excellent *
Total highway safety penalties are: 5 *   Value: 7 8   Durability: 7 7   Highway Control Rating: 1 7   Highway Safety: 1 2

Triple E Empress — 1994 — MHA — 36 — 35 — OS — Cu5.9L — D — $2800 — 228 — 1,500 — 19,840 — 16,578
Livability Code: SB 30-90   Wheelbase-to-length ratio of 53% is considered ○ dangerous ◉ fatiguing ○ good ○ excellent *
The approximate net payload of 3262 pounds at 16% of GVWR on this model is ○ deficient ○ excessive ○ cautionary ○ good ◉ excellent *
Total highway safety penalties are: 5 *   Value: 7 8   Durability: 7 7   Highway Control Rating: 7 2   Highway Safety: 6 7   ★★

Triple E Empress — 1995 — MHA — 35 — A 3501 — FO — 7.5L — G — $2200 — 208 — 8,000 — 17,000 — 14,695
Livability Code: SB 30-90   Wheelbase-to-length ratio of 50% is considered ◉ dangerous ○ fatiguing ○ good ○ excellent *
The approximate net payload of 2305 pounds at 14% of GVWR on this model is ○ deficient ○ excessive ○ cautionary ◉ good ○ excellent *
Total highway safety penalties are: 5 *   Value: 7 8   Durability: 7 7   Highway Control Rating: 3 9   Highway Safety: 3 4

Triple E Empress — 1995 — MHA — 36 — A 3602 — FO — 7.5L — G — $2100 — 228 — 8,000 — 17,000 — 15,304
Livability Code: SB 30-90   Wheelbase-to-length ratio of 53% is considered ○ dangerous ◉ fatiguing ○ good ○ excellent *
The approximate net payload of 1696 pounds at 10% of GVWR on this model is ○ deficient ○ excessive ○ cautionary ◉ good ○ excellent *
Total highway safety penalties are: 5 *   Value: 7 8   Durability: 7 7   Highway Control Rating: 6 0   Highway Safety: 5 5   ★

Triple E Empress — 1995 — MHA — 36 — A 3601 — OS — CU230 — D — $3200 — 228 — 1,500 — 19,840 — 17,422
Livability Code: SB 30-90   Wheelbase-to-length ratio of 53% is considered ○ dangerous ◉ fatiguing ○ good ○ excellent *
The approximate net payload of 2418 pounds at 12% of GVWR on this model is ○ deficient ○ excessive ○ cautionary ◉ good ○ excellent *
Total highway safety penalties are: 5 *   Value: 7 8   Durability: 7 7   Highway Control Rating: 6 4   Highway Safety: 5 9   ★

Triple E Empress — 1995 — MHA — 36 — A 3602 — OS — CU230 — D — $3200 — 228 — 1,500 — 19,840 — 17,960
Livability Code: SB 30-90   Wheelbase-to-length ratio of 53% is considered ○ dangerous ◉ fatiguing ○ good ○ excellent *
The approximate net payload of 1880 pounds at 9% of GVWR on this model is ○ deficient ○ excessive ◉ cautionary ○ good ○ excellent *
Total highway safety penalties are: 5 *   Value: 7 8   Durability: 7 7   Highway Control Rating: 5 5   Highway Safety: 5 0   ★

Triple E Empress — 1996 — MHA — 37 — A3601 — FR — Cu5.9L — D — $3200 — 228 — 1,500 — 23,000 — 20,640
Livability Code: SB 30-90   Wheelbase-to-length ratio of 52% is considered ○ dangerous ◉ fatiguing ○ good ○ excellent *
The approximate net payload of 2360 pounds at 10% of GVWR on this model is ○ deficient ○ excessive ○ cautionary ◉ good ○ excellent *
Total highway safety penalties are: 5 *   Value: 7 8   Durability: 7 7   Highway Control Rating: 4 6   Highway Safety: 4 1

Note: Safety ratings are based on the assumption that the engineering of the RV has allowed for proper balance by placing fresh, gray, and black holding tanks in a location so as not to change the balance of the RV when the tanks are empty or full. **Always double-check wheelbase, GVWR, and weights at front and rear axles.**

*See Section 1 for details on how conclusions are reached.

Section 2: The Ratings

Brand	Year	Type	Length	Model	Chassis	Engine	Fuel Type	Average Price per Linear Foot When New	Adjusted Wheelbase	Approx. Towing Capacity	Gross Vehicle Weight Rating	Average Curb Weight
Triple E Empress	1996	MHA	37	A3603	FR	Cu5.9L	D	$3200	228	1,500	23,000	20,640

Livability Code: SB 30-90
Wheelbase-to-length ratio of 52% is considered ○ dangerous ◉ fatiguing ○ good ○ excellent *
The approximate net payload of 2360 pounds at 10% of GVWR on this model is ○ deficient ○ excessive ○ cautionary ◉ good ○ excellent *
Total highway safety penalties are: 5 *   Value: 7 8   Durability: 7 7   Highway Control Rating: 4 6   Highway Safety: 4 1

Brand	Year	Type	Length	Model	Chassis	Engine	Fuel Type	Price/ft	Wheelbase	Towing	GVWR	Curb Wt
Triple E Empress	1997	MHA	36	A 3601	FR	Ca275	D	$3300	228	1,500	24,850	21,234

Livability Code: SB 30-90
Wheelbase-to-length ratio of 52% is considered ○ dangerous ◉ fatiguing ○ good ○ excellent *
The approximate net payload of 3616 pounds at 15% of GVWR on this model is ○ deficient ○ excessive ○ cautionary ◉ good ○ excellent *
Total highway safety penalties are: 5 *   Value: 7 8   Durability: 7 7   Highway Control Rating: 5 8   Highway Safety: 5 3   ★

| Triple E Empress | 1997 | MHA | 36 | A 3603FS | FR | Ca275 | D | $3300 | 228 | 1,500 | 24,850 | 22,283 |

Livability Code: SB 30-90
Wheelbase-to-length ratio of 52% is considered ○ dangerous ◉ fatiguing ○ good ○ excellent *
The approximate net payload of 2567 pounds at 10% of GVWR on this model is ○ deficient ○ excessive ○ cautionary ◉ good ○ excellent *
Total highway safety penalties are: 10 *   Value: 7 6   Durability: 7 7   Highway Control Rating: 4 8   Highway Safety: 3 8

| Triple E Empress | 1998 | MHA | 36 | A3601 | FR | CA300 | D | $4100 | 228 | 1,500 | 26,350 | 22,242 |

Livability Code: SB 30-90
Wheelbase-to-length ratio of 52% is considered ○ dangerous ◉ fatiguing ○ good ○ excellent *
The approximate net payload of 4109 pounds at 16% of GVWR on this model is ○ deficient ○ excessive ○ cautionary ○ good ◉ excellent *
Total highway safety penalties are: 5 *   Value: 7 8   Durability: 7 7   Highway Control Rating: 6 0   Highway Safety: 5 5   ★

| Triple E Empress | 1998 | MHA | 36 | A3603FS | FR | CA300 | D | $4300 | 228 | 1,500 | 26,350 | 23,249 |

Livability Code: SB 30-90
Wheelbase-to-length ratio of 52% is considered ○ dangerous ◉ fatiguing ○ good ○ excellent *
The approximate net payload of 3101 pounds at 12% of GVWR on this model is ○ deficient ○ excessive ○ cautionary ◉ good ○ excellent *
Total highway safety penalties are: 10 *   Value: 7 6   Durability: 7 7   Highway Control Rating: 5 2   Highway Safety: 4 2

| Triple E Empress | 1998 | MHA | 36 | A3604FS | FR | CA300 | D | $4300 | 228 | 1,500 | 26,350 | 23,122 |

Livability Code: SB 30-90
Wheelbase-to-length ratio of 52% is considered ○ dangerous ◉ fatiguing ○ good ○ excellent *
The approximate net payload of 3229 pounds at 12% of GVWR on this model is ○ deficient ○ excessive ○ cautionary ◉ good ○ excellent *
Total highway safety penalties are: 10 *   Value: 7 6   Durability: 7 7   Highway Control Rating: 5 2   Highway Safety: 4 2

| Triple E Empress | 1999 | MHA | 36 | A 3601 | FR | CA300 | D | $4200 | 228 | 1,500 | 26,350 | 22,242 |

Livability Code: SB 30-90
Wheelbase-to-length ratio of 52% is considered ○ dangerous ◉ fatiguing ○ good ○ excellent *
The approximate net payload of 4109 pounds at 16% of GVWR on this model is ○ deficient ○ excessive ○ cautionary ○ good ◉ excellent *
Total highway safety penalties are: 5 *   Value: 7 8   Durability: 7 7   Highway Control Rating: 6 7   Highway Safety: 6 2   ★★

| Triple E Empress | 1999 | MHA | 36 | A3603FS | FR | CA300 | D | $4200 | 228 | 1,500 | 26,350 | 22,799 |

Livability Code: SB 30-90
Wheelbase-to-length ratio of 52% is considered ○ dangerous ◉ fatiguing ○ good ○ excellent *
The approximate net payload of 3551 pounds at 13% of GVWR on this model is ○ deficient ○ excessive ○ cautionary ◉ good ○ excellent *
Total highway safety penalties are: 5 *   Value: 7 8   Durability: 7 7   Highway Control Rating: 6 2   Highway Safety: 5 7   ★

| Triple E Empress | 1999 | MHA | 36 | A3604FS | FR | CA300 | D | $4200 | 228 | 1,500 | 26,350 | 22,672 |

Livability Code: SB 30-90
Wheelbase-to-length ratio of 52% is considered ○ dangerous ◉ fatiguing ○ good ○ excellent *
The approximate net payload of 3679 pounds at 14% of GVWR on this model is ○ deficient ○ excessive ○ cautionary ◉ good ○ excellent *
Total highway safety penalties are: 5 *   Value: 7 8   Durability: 7 7   Highway Control Rating: 6 4   Highway Safety: 5 9   ★

| Triple E Invitation | 1990 | MHA | 38 | A - 1202 SE | CH | 7.4L | G | $2800 | 232 T | 1,500 | 18,000 | 16,011 |

Livability Code: SB 30-90
Wheelbase-to-length ratio of 51% is considered ○ dangerous ◉ fatiguing ○ good ○ excellent *
The approximate net payload of 1989 pounds at 11% of GVWR on this model is ○ deficient ○ excessive ○ cautionary ◉ good ○ excellent *
Total highway safety penalties are: 11 *   Value: 7 3   Durability: 7 0   Highway Control Rating: 3 8   Highway Safety: 2 7

| Triple E Invitation | 1991 | MHA | 38 | 38 | FO | 7.5L | G | $2900 | 232 T | 6,000 | 19,000 | 16,890 |

Livability Code: SB 30-90
Wheelbase-to-length ratio of 51% is considered ○ dangerous ◉ fatiguing ○ good ○ excellent *
The approximate net payload of 2110 pounds at 11% of GVWR on this model is ○ deficient ○ excessive ○ cautionary ◉ good ○ excellent *
Total highway safety penalties are: 4 *   Value: 7 6   Durability: 7 0   Highway Control Rating: 3 8   Highway Safety: 3 4

| Triple E Regency | 1990 | MHC | 31 | C941XL | FO | 7.5L | G | $1700 | 176 | 1,500 | 14,000 | 13,139 |

Livability Code: SB 30-90
Wheelbase-to-length ratio of 47% is considered ◉ dangerous ○ fatiguing ○ good ○ excellent *
The approximate net payload of 861 pounds at 6% of GVWR on this model is ◉ deficient ○ excessive ○ cautionary ○ good ○ excellent *
Total highway safety penalties are: 2 *   Value: 7 8   Durability: 7 3   Highway Control Rating: 1 4   Highway Safety: 1 2

Note: Safety ratings are based on the assumption that the engineering of the RV has allowed for proper balance by placing fresh, gray, and black holding tanks in a location so as not to change the balance of the RV when the tanks are empty or full. **Always double-check wheelbase, GVWR, and weights at front and rear axles.**

*See Section 1 for details on how conclusions are reached.

Brand	Year	Type	Length	Model	Chassis	Engine	Fuel Type	Average Price per Linear Foot When New	Adjusted Wheelbase	Approx. Towing Capacity	Gross Vehicle Weight Rating	Average Curb Weight

Triple E Regency 1991 MHC 28 822 FO 7.5L G $1800 176 1,500 11,500 10,921
Livability Code: SB 30-90
Wheelbase-to-length ratio of 52% is considered ○ dangerous ● fatiguing ○ good ○ excellent *
The approximate net payload of 579 pounds at 5% of GVWR on this model is ● deficient ○ excessive ○ cautionary ○ good ○ excellent *
Total highway safety penalties are: 2 *   Value: **7 8** Durability: **7 3** Highway Control Rating: **3 5**   Highway Safety: **3 3**

Triple E Regency 1992 MHC 24 734 FO 7.5L G $2000 158 2,500 11,500 9,417
Livability Code: SB 30-90
Wheelbase-to-length ratio of 55% is considered ○ dangerous ○ fatiguing ● good ○ excellent *
The approximate net payload of 2083 pounds at 18% of GVWR on this model is ○ deficient ○ excessive ○ cautionary ○ good ● excellent *
Total highway safety penalties are: 2 *   Value: **7 8** Durability: **7 3** Highway Control Rating: **9 4**   Highway Safety: **9 2**   ★★★

Triple E Regency 1992 MHC 24 734 Dsl FO 7.3L D $2100 158 1,500 11,500 9,965
Livability Code: SB 30-90
Wheelbase-to-length ratio of 55% is considered ○ dangerous ○ fatiguing ● good ○ excellent *
The approximate net payload of 1535 pounds at 13% of GVWR on this model is ○ deficient ○ excessive ○ cautionary ● good ○ excellent *
Total highway safety penalties are: 2 *   Value: **7 8** Durability: **7 3** Highway Control Rating: **8 6**   Highway Safety: **8 4**   ★★★

Triple E Regency 1992 MHC 27 797 FO 7.5L G $1900 176 1,500 11,500 10,527
Livability Code: SB 30-90
Wheelbase-to-length ratio of 54% is considered ○ dangerous ○ fatiguing ● good ○ excellent *
The approximate net payload of 973 pounds at 8% of GVWR on this model is ○ deficient ○ excessive ● cautionary ○ good ○ excellent *
Total highway safety penalties are: 2 *   Value: **7 8** Durability: **7 3** Highway Control Rating: **6 1**   Highway Safety: **5 9**   ★

Triple E Regency 1992 MHC 27 797 Dsl FO 7.3L D $2000 176 1,500 11,500 10,739
Livability Code: SB 30-90
Wheelbase-to-length ratio of 54% is considered ○ dangerous ○ fatiguing ● good ○ excellent *
The approximate net payload of 761 pounds at 7% of GVWR on this model is ○ deficient ○ excessive ● cautionary ○ good ○ excellent *
Total highway safety penalties are: 2 *   Value: **7 8** Durability: **7 3** Highway Control Rating: **5 4**   Highway Safety: **5 2**   ★

Triple E Regency 1992 MHC 28 822 FO 7.5L G $1900 176 1,500 11,500 10,601
Livability Code: SB 30-90
Wheelbase-to-length ratio of 52% is considered ○ dangerous ● fatiguing ○ good ○ excellent *
The approximate net payload of 899 pounds at 8% of GVWR on this model is ○ deficient ○ excessive ● cautionary ○ good ○ excellent *
Total highway safety penalties are: 2 *   Value: **7 8** Durability: **7 3** Highway Control Rating: **4 8**   Highway Safety: **4 6**

Triple E Regency 1992 MHC 28 822 Dsl FO 7.3L D $2000 176 1,500 11,500 10,921
Livability Code: SB 30-90
Wheelbase-to-length ratio of 52% is considered ○ dangerous ● fatiguing ○ good ○ excellent *
The approximate net payload of 579 pounds at 5% of GVWR on this model is ● deficient ○ excessive ○ cautionary ○ good ○ excellent *
Total highway safety penalties are: 2 *   Value: **7 8** Durability: **7 3** Highway Control Rating: **3 5**   Highway Safety: **3 3**

Triple E Regency 1992 MHC 31 941 FO 7.5L G $2000 200 T 2,500 14,500 12,368
Livability Code: SB 30-90
Wheelbase-to-length ratio of 53% is considered ○ dangerous ● fatiguing ○ good ○ excellent *
The approximate net payload of 2132 pounds at 15% of GVWR on this model is ○ deficient ○ excessive ○ cautionary ● good ○ excellent *
Total highway safety penalties are: 4 *   Value: **7 7** Durability: **7 3** Highway Control Rating: **7 7**   Highway Safety: **7 3**   ★★★

Triple E Regency 1992 MHC 31 941 Dsl FO 7.3L D $2100 200 T 2,500 14,500 12,527
Livability Code: SB 30-90
Wheelbase-to-length ratio of 53% is considered ○ dangerous ● fatiguing ○ good ○ excellent *
The approximate net payload of 1973 pounds at 14% of GVWR on this model is ○ deficient ○ excessive ○ cautionary ● good ○ excellent *
Total highway safety penalties are: 4 *   Value: **7 7** Durability: **7 3** Highway Control Rating: **7 4**   Highway Safety: **7 0**   ★★★

Triple E Senator 1996 MHC 23 C-21 FO 7.5L G $1800 138 1,500 11,500 9,667
Livability Code: SB 30-90
Wheelbase-to-length ratio of 51% is considered ○ dangerous ● fatiguing ○ good ○ excellent *
The approximate net payload of 1833 pounds at 16% of GVWR on this model is ○ deficient ○ excessive ○ cautionary ○ good ● excellent *
Total highway safety penalties are: 2 *   Value: **7 8** Durability: **7 3** Highway Control Rating: **6 4**   Highway Safety: **6 2**   ★★

Triple E Senator 1996 MHC 24 C-24 FO 7.5L G $1900 158 1,500 11,500 10,015
Livability Code: SB 30-90
Wheelbase-to-length ratio of 54% is considered ○ dangerous ○ fatiguing ● good ○ excellent *
The approximate net payload of 1485 pounds at 13% of GVWR on this model is ○ deficient ○ excessive ○ cautionary ● good ○ excellent *
Total highway safety penalties are: 2 *   Value: **7 8** Durability: **7 3** Highway Control Rating: **8 0**   Highway Safety: **7 8**   ★★★

Triple E Senator 1996 MHC 29 C-28 FO 7.5L G $1600 190 1,500 11,500 10,938
Livability Code: SB 30-90
Wheelbase-to-length ratio of 55% is considered ○ dangerous ○ fatiguing ● good ○ excellent *
The approximate net payload of 562 pounds at 5% of GVWR on this model is ● deficient ○ excessive ○ cautionary ○ good ○ excellent *
Total highway safety penalties are: 2 *   Value: **7 8** Durability: **7 3** Highway Control Rating: **5 7**   Highway Safety: **5 5**   ★

Note: Safety ratings are based on the assumption that the engineering of the RV has allowed for proper balance by placing fresh, gray, and black holding tanks in a location so as not to change the balance of the RV when the tanks are empty or full. **Always double-check wheelbase, GVWR, and weights at front and rear axles.**

*See Section 1 for details on how conclusions are reached.

Brand	Year	Type	Length	Model	Chassis	Engine	Fuel Type	Average Price per Linear Foot When New	Adjusted Wheelbase	Approx. Towing Capacity	Gross Vehicle Weight Rating	Average Curb Weight

Triple E Senator — 1997 — MHC — 23 — C-22 — FO — 6.8L — G — $1800 — 138 — 1,500 — 10,500 — 9,777
Livability Code: SB 30-90
Wheelbase-to-length ratio of 50% is considered ● dangerous ○ fatiguing ○ good ○ excellent *
The approximate net payload of 723 pounds at 7% of GVWR on this model is ○ deficient ○ excessive ● cautionary ○ good ○ excellent *
Total highway safety penalties are: 2 *   Value: 7 8   Durability: 7 3   Highway Control Rating: 3 1   Highway Safety: 2 9

Triple E Senator — 1997 — MHC — 24 — C-24 — FO — 6.8L — G — $1900 — 158 — 1,500 — 11,500 — 9,964
Livability Code: SB 30-90
Wheelbase-to-length ratio of 54% is considered ○ dangerous ○ fatiguing ● good ○ excellent *
The approximate net payload of 1536 pounds at 13% of GVWR on this model is ○ deficient ○ excessive ○ cautionary ● good ○ excellent *
Total highway safety penalties are: 2 *   Value: 7 8   Durability: 7 3   Highway Control Rating: 8 0   Highway Safety: 7 8   ★★★

Triple E Senator — 1997 — MHC — 29 — C-28 — FO — 6.8L — G — $1600 — 190 — 1,500 — 11,500 — 10,912
Livability Code: SB 30-90
Wheelbase-to-length ratio of 55% is considered ○ dangerous ○ fatiguing ● good ○ excellent *
The approximate net payload of 588 pounds at 5% of GVWR on this model is ● deficient ○ excessive ○ cautionary ○ good ○ excellent *
Total highway safety penalties are: 2 *   Value: 7 8   Durability: 7 3   Highway Control Rating: 5 7   Highway Safety: 5 5   ★

Triple E Senator — 1998 — MHC — 23 — C22 — FO — 6.8L — G — $1900 — 138 — 1,500 — 11,500 — 9,778
Livability Code: SB 30-90
Wheelbase-to-length ratio of 50% is considered ● dangerous ○ fatiguing ○ good ○ excellent *
The approximate net payload of 1722 pounds at 15% of GVWR on this model is ○ deficient ● excessive ○ cautionary ● good ○ excellent *
Total highway safety penalties are: 2 *   Value: 8 0   Durability: 7 7   Highway Control Rating: 5 8   Highway Safety: 5 6

Triple E Senator — 1998 — MHC — 24 — C24 — FO — 6.8L — G — $1900 — 158 — 1,500 — 11,500 — 10,318
Livability Code: SB 30-90
Wheelbase-to-length ratio of 54% is considered ○ dangerous ○ fatiguing ● good ○ excellent *
The approximate net payload of 1182 pounds at 10% of GVWR on this model is ○ deficient ○ excessive ○ cautionary ● good ○ excellent *
Total highway safety penalties are: 2 *   Value: 8 0   Durability: 7 7   Highway Control Rating: 7 4   Highway Safety: 7 2   ★★★

Triple E Senator — 1998 — MHC — 24 — C24XL — FO — 6.8L — G — $1900 — 158 — 1,500 — 14,000 — 10,818
Livability Code: SB 30-90
Wheelbase-to-length ratio of 54% is considered ○ dangerous ○ fatiguing ○ good ● excellent *
The approximate net payload of 3182 pounds at 23% of GVWR on this model is ○ deficient ○ excessive ○ cautionary ○ good ● excellent *
Total highway safety penalties are: 2 *   Value: 8 0   Durability: 7 7   Highway Control Rating: 8 7   Highway Safety: 8 5   ★★★

Triple E Senator — 1998 — MHC — 29 — C28 — FO — 6.8L — G — $1700 — 190 — 1,500 — 11,500 — 10,939
Livability Code: SB 30-90
Wheelbase-to-length ratio of 55% is considered ○ dangerous ○ fatiguing ● good ○ excellent *
The approximate net payload of 561 pounds at 5% of GVWR on this model is ● deficient ○ excessive ○ cautionary ○ good ○ excellent *
Total highway safety penalties are: 2 *   Value: 8 0   Durability: 7 7   Highway Control Rating: 5 7   Highway Safety: 5 5   ★

Triple E Senator — 1998 — MHC — 29 — C28XL — FO — 6.8L — G — $1900 — 190 — 1,500 — 14,000 — 11,439
Livability Code: SB 30-90
Wheelbase-to-length ratio of 55% is considered ○ dangerous ○ fatiguing ● good ○ excellent *
The approximate net payload of 2561 pounds at 18% of GVWR on this model is ○ deficient ○ excessive ○ cautionary ○ good ● excellent *
Total highway safety penalties are: 2 *   Value: 8 0   Durability: 7 7   Highway Control Rating: 9 5   Highway Safety: 9 3   ★★★

Triple E Senator — 1999 — MHC — 23 — C22 — FO — 6.8L — G — $1900 — 138 — 1,500 — 10,500 — 9,778
Livability Code: SB 30-90
Wheelbase-to-length ratio of 50% is considered ● dangerous ○ fatiguing ○ good ○ excellent *
The approximate net payload of 722 pounds at 7% of GVWR on this model is ○ deficient ○ excessive ● cautionary ○ good ○ excellent *
Total highway safety penalties are: 2 *   Value: 8 0   Durability: 7 7   Highway Control Rating: 3 1   Highway Safety: 2 9

Triple E Senator — 1999 — MHC — 24 — C24 — FO — 6.8L — G — $1900 — 158 — 1,500 — 11,500 — 10,318
Livability Code: SB 30-90
Wheelbase-to-length ratio of 54% is considered ○ dangerous ○ fatiguing ● good ○ excellent *
The approximate net payload of 1182 pounds at 10% of GVWR on this model is ○ deficient ○ excessive ○ cautionary ● good ○ excellent *
Total highway safety penalties are: 2 *   Value: 8 0   Durability: 7 7   Highway Control Rating: 7 4   Highway Safety: 7 2   ★★★

Triple E Senator — 1999 — MHC — 29 — C28 — FO — 6.8L — G — $1700 — 190 — 1,500 — 11,500 — 10,939
Livability Code: SB 30-90
Wheelbase-to-length ratio of 55% is considered ○ dangerous ○ fatiguing ● good ○ excellent *
The approximate net payload of 561 pounds at 5% of GVWR on this model is ● deficient ○ excessive ○ cautionary ○ good ○ excellent *
Total highway safety penalties are: 2 *   Value: 8 0   Durability: 7 7   Highway Control Rating: 5 7   Highway Safety: 5 5   ★

Triple E Senator — 1999 — MHC — 29 — C28XL — FO — 6.8L — G — $1900 — 190 — 1,500 — 14,050 — 11,467
Livability Code: SB 30-90
Wheelbase-to-length ratio of 55% is considered ○ dangerous ○ fatiguing ● good ○ excellent *
The approximate net payload of 2583 pounds at 18% of GVWR on this model is ○ deficient ○ excessive ○ cautionary ○ good ● excellent *
Total highway safety penalties are: 2 *   Value: 8 0   Durability: 7 7   Highway Control Rating: 9 6   Highway Safety: 9 4   ★★★

Note: Safety ratings are based on the assumption that the engineering of the RV has allowed for proper balance by placing fresh, gray, and black holding tanks in a location so as not to change the balance of the RV when the tanks are empty or full. **Always double-check wheelbase, GVWR, and weights at front and rear axles.**

*See Section 1 for details on how conclusions are reached.

Brand	Year	Type	Length	Model	Chassis	Engine	Fuel Type	Average Price per Linear Foot When New	Adjusted Wheelbase	Approx. Towing Capacity	Gross Vehicle Weight Rating	Average Curb Weight

Tropi-Cal 1991 MHA 28 274 FO 7.5L G $1500 176 1,500 11,500 10,616
Livability Code: SB 30-90
Wheelbase-to-length ratio of 53% is considered ○ dangerous ● fatiguing ○ good ○ excellent *
The approximate net payload of 884 pounds at 8% of GVWR on this model is ○ deficient ● excessive ● cautionary ○ good ○ excellent *
Total highway safety penalties are: 2 *   Value: **90** Durability: **90** Highway Control Rating: **46** Highway Safety: **44**

Tropi-Cal 1992 MHA 28 274 FO 7.5L G $1700 176 7,500 11,500 10,746
Livability Code: SB 30-90
Wheelbase-to-length ratio of 53% is considered ○ dangerous ● fatiguing ○ good ○ excellent *
The approximate net payload of 754 pounds at 7% of GVWR on this model is ○ deficient ● excessive ● cautionary ○ good ○ excellent *
Total highway safety penalties are: 2 *   Value: **90** Durability: **90** Highway Control Rating: **40** Highway Safety: **38**

Tropi-Cal 1992 MHA 28 270 FO 7.5L G $1700 176 7,500 11,500 10,746
Livability Code: SB 30-90
Wheelbase-to-length ratio of 53% is considered ○ dangerous ● fatiguing ○ good ○ excellent *
The approximate net payload of 754 pounds at 7% of GVWR on this model is ○ deficient ● excessive ● cautionary ○ good ○ excellent *
Total highway safety penalties are: 2 *   Value: **90** Durability: **90** Highway Control Rating: **40** Highway Safety: **38**

Tropi-Cal 1992 MHA 28 275 FO 7.5L G $1700 176 7,500 11,500 10,746
Livability Code: SB 30-90
Wheelbase-to-length ratio of 53% is considered ○ dangerous ● fatiguing ○ good ○ excellent *
The approximate net payload of 754 pounds at 7% of GVWR on this model is ○ deficient ● excessive ● cautionary ○ good ○ excellent *
Total highway safety penalties are: 2 *   Value: **90** Durability: **90** Highway Control Rating: **40** Highway Safety: **38**

Tropi-Cal 1992 MHA 30 290 CH 7.4L G $1700 178 4,700 12,300 11,154
Livability Code: SB 30-90
Wheelbase-to-length ratio of 50% is considered ● dangerous ○ fatiguing ○ good ○ excellent *
The approximate net payload of 1146 pounds at 9% of GVWR on this model is ○ deficient ● excessive ● cautionary ○ good ○ excellent *
Total highway safety penalties are: 4 *   Value: **89** Durability: **90** Highway Control Rating: **28** Highway Safety: **24**

Tropi-Cal 1992 MHA 33 320 CH 7.4L G $1600 208 4,200 14,800 11,744
Livability Code: SB 30-90
Wheelbase-to-length ratio of 53% is considered ○ dangerous ● fatiguing ○ good ○ excellent *
The approximate net payload of 3056 pounds at 21% of GVWR on this model is ○ deficient ○ excessive ○ cautionary ○ good ● excellent *
Total highway safety penalties are: 6 *   Value: **88** Durability: **90** Highway Control Rating: **74** Highway Safety: **68**   ★★

Tropi-Cal 1992 MHA 33 320 CH 7.4L G $1600 208 4,200 14,800 11,824
Livability Code: SB 30-90
Wheelbase-to-length ratio of 53% is considered ○ dangerous ● fatiguing ○ good ○ excellent *
The approximate net payload of 2976 pounds at 20% of GVWR on this model is ○ deficient ○ excessive ○ cautionary ○ good ● excellent *
Total highway safety penalties are: 6 *   Value: **88** Durability: **90** Highway Control Rating: **75** Highway Safety: **69**   ★★

Tropi-Cal 1993 MHA 34 340 CH 7.4L G $1700 208 4,200 14,800 13,007
Livability Code: SB 30-90
Wheelbase-to-length ratio of 51% is considered ○ dangerous ● fatiguing ○ good ○ excellent *
The approximate net payload of 1793 pounds at 12% of GVWR on this model is ○ deficient ○ excessive ○ cautionary ● good ○ excellent *
Total highway safety penalties are: 7 *   Value: **88** Durability: **90** Highway Control Rating: **40** Highway Safety: **33**

Tropi-Cal 1993 MHA 34 340 FO 7.5L G $1700 208 3,800 15,200 13,202
Livability Code: SB 30-90
Wheelbase-to-length ratio of 51% is considered ○ dangerous ● fatiguing ○ good ○ excellent *
The approximate net payload of 1998 pounds at 13% of GVWR on this model is ○ deficient ○ excessive ○ cautionary ● good ○ excellent *
Total highway safety penalties are: 2 *   Value: **90** Durability: **90** Highway Control Rating: **42** Highway Safety: **40**

Tropi-Cal 1994 MHA 28 270 CH 7.4L G $2000 176 6,700 12,300 10,968
Livability Code: SB 30-90
Wheelbase-to-length ratio of 53% is considered ○ dangerous ● fatiguing ○ good ○ excellent *
The approximate net payload of 1332 pounds at 11% of GVWR on this model is ○ deficient ○ excessive ○ cautionary ● good ○ excellent *
Total highway safety penalties are: 3 *   Value: **89** Durability: **90** Highway Control Rating: **59** Highway Safety: **56**   ★

Tropi-Cal 1994 MHA 28 270 FO 7.5L G $1900 176 7,500 11,500 10,666
Livability Code: SB 30-90
Wheelbase-to-length ratio of 53% is considered ○ dangerous ● fatiguing ○ good ○ excellent *
The approximate net payload of 834 pounds at 7% of GVWR on this model is ○ deficient ○ excessive ● cautionary ○ good ○ excellent *
Total highway safety penalties are: 2 *   Value: **90** Durability: **90** Highway Control Rating: **41** Highway Safety: **39**

Tropi-Cal 1994 MHA 33 320 CH 7.4L G $1800 208 4,200 14,800 11,912
Livability Code: SB 30-90
Wheelbase-to-length ratio of 53% is considered ○ dangerous ● fatiguing ○ good ○ excellent *
The approximate net payload of 2888 pounds at 20% of GVWR on this model is ○ deficient ○ excessive ○ cautionary ○ good ● excellent *
Total highway safety penalties are: 6 *   Value: **88** Durability: **90** Highway Control Rating: **74** Highway Safety: **68**   ★★

Note: Safety ratings are based on the assumption that the engineering of the RV has allowed for proper balance by placing fresh, gray, and black holding tanks in a location so as not to change the balance of the RV when the tanks are empty or full. **Always double-check wheelbase, GVWR, and weights at front and rear axles.**

*See Section 1 for details on how conclusions are reached.

Brand	Year	Type	Length	Model	Chassis	Engine	Fuel Type	Average Price per Linear Foot When New	Adjusted Wheelbase	Approx. Towing Capacity	Gross Vehicle Weight Rating	Average Curb Weight
Tropi-Cal	1994	MHA	33	320	FO	7.5L	G	$1800	208	3,800	15,200	13,722

Livability Code: SB 30-90
Wheelbase-to-length ratio of 53% is considered ○ dangerous ● fatiguing ○ good ○ excellent *
The approximate net payload of 1478 pounds at 10% of GVWR on this model is ○ deficient ○ excessive ○ cautionary ● good ○ excellent *
Total highway safety penalties are: 2 *   Value: 9 0   Durability: 9 0   Highway Control Rating: 5 9   Highway Safety: 5 7   ★

Brand	Year	Type	Length	Model	Chassis	Engine	Fuel Type	Avg Price/Lin Ft	Adj Wheelbase	Towing Cap	GVWR	Curb Wt
Tropi-Cal	1994	MHA	34	340	CH	7.4L	G	$1800	228	4,200	14,800	13,007

Livability Code: SB 30-90
Wheelbase-to-length ratio of 56% is considered ○ dangerous ○ fatiguing ● good ○ excellent *
The approximate net payload of 1793 pounds at 12% of GVWR on this model is ○ deficient ○ excessive ○ cautionary ● good ○ excellent *
Total highway safety penalties are: 7 *   Value: 8 8   Durability: 9 0   Highway Control Rating: 8 8   Highway Safety: 8 1   ★★★★

Tropi-Cal	1994	MHA	34	340	FO	7.5L	G	$1800	228	3,800	15,200	13,202

Livability Code: SB 30-90
Wheelbase-to-length ratio of 56% is considered ○ dangerous ○ fatiguing ● good ○ excellent *
The approximate net payload of 1998 pounds at 13% of GVWR on this model is ○ deficient ○ excessive ○ cautionary ● good ○ excellent *
Total highway safety penalties are: 2 *   Value: 9 0   Durability: 9 0   Highway Control Rating: 9 0   Highway Safety: 8 8   ★★★★

Tropi-Cal	1996	MHA	36	234	FO	7.5L	G	$2100	228	8,000	17,000	16,190

Livability Code: SB 30-90
Wheelbase-to-length ratio of 53% is considered ○ dangerous ● fatiguing ○ good ○ excellent *
The approximate net payload of 810 pounds at 5% of GVWR on this model is ● deficient ○ excessive ○ cautionary ○ good ○ excellent *
Total highway safety penalties are: 2 *   Value: 9 0   Durability: 9 0   Highway Control Rating: 3 5   Highway Safety: 3 3

Tropi-Cal	1996	MHA	36	235	CH	7.4L	G	$2400	232 T	1,500	19,500	17,350

Livability Code: SB 30-90
Wheelbase-to-length ratio of 54% is considered ○ dangerous ○ fatiguing ● good ○ excellent *
The approximate net payload of 2150 pounds at 11% of GVWR on this model is ○ deficient ○ excessive ○ cautionary ● good ○ excellent *
Total highway safety penalties are: 15 *   Value: 8 3   Durability: 9 0   Highway Control Rating: 7 5   Highway Safety: 6 0   ★★

Tropi-Cal	1996	MHA	36	235 myc	CH	7.4L	G	$2400	252 T	1,500	19,500	16,900

Livability Code: SB 30-90
Wheelbase-to-length ratio of 58% is considered ○ dangerous ○ fatiguing ○ good ● excellent *
The approximate net payload of 2600 pounds at 13% of GVWR on this model is ○ deficient ○ excessive ○ cautionary ● good ○ excellent *
Total highway safety penalties are: 15 *   Value: 8 3   Durability: 9 0   Highway Control Rating: 9 9   Highway Safety: 8 4   ★★★★

Tropi-Cal	1996	MHA	36	235	FO	7.5L	G	$2400	232 T	5,000	20,000	17,950

Livability Code: SB 30-90
Wheelbase-to-length ratio of 54% is considered ○ dangerous ○ fatiguing ● good ○ excellent *
The approximate net payload of 2050 pounds at 10% of GVWR on this model is ○ deficient ○ excessive ○ cautionary ● good ○ excellent *
Total highway safety penalties are: 10 *   Value: 8 6   Durability: 9 0   Highway Control Rating: 7 5   Highway Safety: 6 5   ★★

Tropi-Cal	1996	MHA	36	235 myc	FO	7.5L	G	$2400	252 T	5,000	20,000	17,500

Livability Code: SB 30-90
Wheelbase-to-length ratio of 58% is considered ○ dangerous ○ fatiguing ○ good ● excellent *
The approximate net payload of 2500 pounds at 13% of GVWR on this model is ○ deficient ○ excessive ○ cautionary ● good ○ excellent *
Total highway safety penalties are: 10 *   Value: 8 6   Durability: 9 0   Highway Control Rating: 9 8   Highway Safety: 8 8   ★★★★

Tropi-Cal	1996	MHA	37	236	FO	7.5L	G	$2200	252 T	5,000	20,000	17,790

Livability Code: SB 30-90
Wheelbase-to-length ratio of 57% is considered ○ dangerous ○ fatiguing ● good ○ excellent *
The approximate net payload of 2210 pounds at 11% of GVWR on this model is ○ deficient ○ excessive ○ cautionary ● good ○ excellent *
Total highway safety penalties are: 10 *   Value: 8 6   Durability: 9 0   Highway Control Rating: 8 9   Highway Safety: 7 9   ★★★

Tropi-Cal	1996	MHA	37	236L	FO	7.5L	G	$2200	252 T	5,000	20,000	17,340

Livability Code: SB 30-90
Wheelbase-to-length ratio of 57% is considered ○ dangerous ○ fatiguing ● good ○ excellent *
The approximate net payload of 2660 pounds at 13% of GVWR on this model is ○ deficient ○ excessive ○ cautionary ● good ○ excellent *
Total highway safety penalties are: 10 *   Value: 8 6   Durability: 9 0   Highway Control Rating: 9 4   Highway Safety: 8 4   ★★★★

Tropi-Cal	1997	MHA	36	234	FO	7.5L	G	$2200	228	8,000	17,000	16,250

Livability Code: SB 30-90
Wheelbase-to-length ratio of 53% is considered ○ dangerous ● fatiguing ○ good ○ excellent *
The approximate net payload of 750 pounds at 4% of GVWR on this model is ● deficient ○ excessive ○ cautionary ○ good ○ excellent *
Total highway safety penalties are: 2 *   Value: 9 0   Durability: 9 0   Highway Control Rating: 3 4   Highway Safety: 3 2

Tropi-Cal	1997	MHA	36	235	CH	7.4L	G	$2500	232 T	0	19,500	17,350

Livability Code: SB 30-90
Wheelbase-to-length ratio of 54% is considered ○ dangerous ○ fatiguing ● good ○ excellent *
The approximate net payload of 2150 pounds at 11% of GVWR on this model is ○ deficient ○ excessive ○ cautionary ● good ○ excellent *
Total highway safety penalties are: 15 *   Value: 8 3   Durability: 9 0   Highway Control Rating: 7 5   Highway Safety: 6 0   ★★

Note: Safety ratings are based on the assumption that the engineering of the RV has allowed for proper balance by placing fresh, gray, and black holding tanks in a location so as not to change the balance of the RV when the tanks are empty or full. **Always double-check wheelbase, GVWR, and weights at front and rear axles.**

*See Section 1 for details on how conclusions are reached.

Brand	Year	Type	Length	Model	Chassis	Engine	Fuel Type	Average Price per Linear Foot When New	Adjusted Wheel-base	Approx. Towing Capacity	Gross Vehicle Weight Rating	Average Curb Weight

Tropi-Cal | **1997** | MHA | 36 | 235 | FO | 7.5L | G | $2500 | 232 T | 5,000 | 20,000 | 17,950

Livability Code: SB 30-90
Wheelbase-to-length ratio of 54% is considered ○ dangerous ○ fatiguing ◉ good ○ excellent *
The approximate net payload of 2050 pounds at 10% of GVWR on this model is ○ deficient ○ excessive ○ cautionary ◉ good ○ excellent *
Total highway safety penalties are: 10 * Value: **86** Durability: **90** Highway Control Rating: **75** Highway Safety: **65** ★★

Tropi-Cal | **1997** | MHA | 37 | 236 | FO | 7.5L | G | $2200 | 252 T | 5,000 | 20,000 | 17,810

Livability Code: SB 30-90
Wheelbase-to-length ratio of 57% is considered ○ dangerous ○ fatiguing ◉ good ○ excellent *
The approximate net payload of 2190 pounds at 11% of GVWR on this model is ○ deficient ○ excessive ○ cautionary ◉ good ○ excellent *
Total highway safety penalties are: 4 * Value: **89** Durability: **90** Highway Control Rating: **89** Highway Safety: **85** ★★★★

Tropi-Cal | **1998** | MHA | 34 | 6330 | FO | 7.5L | G | $2500 | 208 | 5,000 | 17,000 | 16,060

Livability Code: SB 30-90
Wheelbase-to-length ratio of 52% is considered ○ dangerous ◉ fatiguing ○ good ○ excellent *
The approximate net payload of 940 pounds at 6% of GVWR on this model is ◉ deficient ○ excessive ○ cautionary ○ good ○ excellent *
Total highway safety penalties are: 7 * Value: **92** Durability: **90** Highway Control Rating: **22** Highway Safety: **15**

Tropi-Cal | **1998** | MHA | 36 | 6340 | FO | 7.5L | G | $2400 | 228 | 5,000 | 17,000 | 16,250

Livability Code: SB 30-90
Wheelbase-to-length ratio of 53% is considered ○ dangerous ◉ fatiguing ○ good ○ excellent *
The approximate net payload of 750 pounds at 4% of GVWR on this model is ◉ deficient ○ excessive ○ cautionary ○ good ○ excellent *
Total highway safety penalties are: 2 * Value: **95** Durability: **90** Highway Control Rating: **34** Highway Safety: **32**

Tropi-Cal | **1998** | MHA | 36 | 6350 | CH | 7.4L | G | $2400 | 232 T | 1,500 | 19,500 | 17,350

Livability Code: SB 30-90
Wheelbase-to-length ratio of 54% is considered ○ dangerous ○ fatiguing ◉ good ○ excellent *
The approximate net payload of 2150 pounds at 11% of GVWR on this model is ○ deficient ○ excessive ○ cautionary ◉ good ○ excellent *
Total highway safety penalties are: 15 * Value: **88** Durability: **90** Highway Control Rating: **75** Highway Safety: **60** ★★

Tropi-Cal | **1998** | MHA | 36 | 6351 | CH | 7.4L | G | $2400 | 232 T | 1,500 | 19,500 | 17,810

Livability Code: SB 30-90
Wheelbase-to-length ratio of 54% is considered ○ dangerous ○ fatiguing ◉ good ○ excellent *
The approximate net payload of 1690 pounds at 9% of GVWR on this model is ○ deficient ○ excessive ◉ cautionary ○ good ○ excellent *
Total highway safety penalties are: 15 * Value: **88** Durability: **90** Highway Control Rating: **63** Highway Safety: **48**

Tropi-Cal | **1998** | MHA | 36 | 6350 | FO | 7.5L | G | $2400 | 232 T | 5,000 | 20,000 | 18,160

Livability Code: SB 30-90
Wheelbase-to-length ratio of 54% is considered ○ dangerous ○ fatiguing ◉ good ○ excellent *
The approximate net payload of 1840 pounds at 9% of GVWR on this model is ○ deficient ○ excessive ◉ cautionary ○ good ○ excellent *
Total highway safety penalties are: 10 * Value: **91** Durability: **90** Highway Control Rating: **64** Highway Safety: **54** ★

Tropi-Cal | **1998** | MHA | 36 | 6351 | FO | 7.5L | G | $2400 | 232 T | 5,000 | 20,000 | 18,010

Livability Code: SB 30-90
Wheelbase-to-length ratio of 54% is considered ○ dangerous ○ fatiguing ◉ good ○ excellent *
The approximate net payload of 1990 pounds at 10% of GVWR on this model is ○ deficient ○ excessive ○ cautionary ◉ good ○ excellent *
Total highway safety penalties are: 10 * Value: **91** Durability: **90** Highway Control Rating: **74** Highway Safety: **64** ★★

Tropi-Cal | **1998** | MHA | 37 | 6360 | FO | 7.5L | G | $2300 | 232 T | 5,000 | 20,000 | 17,810

Livability Code: SB 30-90
Wheelbase-to-length ratio of 52% is considered ○ dangerous ◉ fatiguing ○ good ○ excellent *
The approximate net payload of 2190 pounds at 11% of GVWR on this model is ○ deficient ○ excessive ○ cautionary ◉ good ○ excellent *
Total highway safety penalties are: 4 * Value: **94** Durability: **90** Highway Control Rating: **50** Highway Safety: **46**

Tropi-Cal | **1998** | MHA | 37 | 6361 | FO | 7.5L | G | $2300 | 232 T | 5,000 | 20,000 | 17,810

Livability Code: SB 30-90
Wheelbase-to-length ratio of 52% is considered ○ dangerous ◉ fatiguing ○ good ○ excellent *
The approximate net payload of 2190 pounds at 11% of GVWR on this model is ○ deficient ○ excessive ○ cautionary ◉ good ○ excellent *
Total highway safety penalties are: 4 * Value: **94** Durability: **90** Highway Control Rating: **50** Highway Safety: **46**

Tropi-Cal | **1999** | MHA | 34 | 6330 | FO | 6.8L | G | $2500 | 208 | 5,000 | 18,000 | 16,560

Livability Code: SB 30-90
Wheelbase-to-length ratio of 52% is considered ○ dangerous ◉ fatiguing ○ good ○ excellent *
The approximate net payload of 1440 pounds at 8% of GVWR on this model is ○ deficient ○ excessive ◉ cautionary ○ good ○ excellent *
Total highway safety penalties are: 7 * Value: **92** Durability: **90** Highway Control Rating: **42** Highway Safety: **35**

Tropi-Cal | **1999** | MHA | 34 | 6331 myc | FO | 6.8L | G | $2500 | 208 | 2,500 | 20,500 | 16,857

Livability Code: SB 30-90
Wheelbase-to-length ratio of 52% is considered ○ dangerous ◉ fatiguing ○ good ○ excellent *
The approximate net payload of 3643 pounds at 18% of GVWR on this model is ○ deficient ○ excessive ○ cautionary ○ good ◉ excellent *
Total highway safety penalties are: 12 * Value: **90** Durability: **90** Highway Control Rating: **67** Highway Safety: **55** ★

Note: Safety ratings are based on the assumption that the engineering of the RV has allowed for proper balance by placing fresh, gray, and black holding tanks in a location so as not to change the balance of the RV when the tanks are empty or full. **Always double-check wheelbase, GVWR, and weights at front and rear axles.**

*See Section 1 for details on how conclusions are reached.

Brand	Year	Type	Length	Model	Chassis	Engine	Fuel Type	Average Price per Linear Foot When New	Adjusted Wheelbase	Approx. Towing Capacity	Gross Vehicle Weight Rating	Average Curb Weight
Tropi-Cal	1999	MHA	34	6331	FO	6.8L	G	$2500	208	5,000	18,000	16,360

Livability Code: SB 30-90
Wheelbase-to-length ratio of 52% is considered ○ dangerous ● fatiguing ○ good ○ excellent*
The approximate net payload of 1640 pounds at 9% of GVWR on this model is ○ deficient ○ excessive ● cautionary ○ good ○ excellent*
Total highway safety penalties are: 7* Value: 9 2 Durability: 9 0 Highway Control Rating: 4 9 Highway Safety: 4 2

Brand	Year	Type	Length	Model	Chassis	Engine	Fuel Type	Price/ft	Wheelbase	Towing	GVWR	Curb Weight
Tropi-Cal	1999	MHA	36	6340	FO	6.8L	G	$2400	228	5,000	18,000	15,825

Livability Code: SB 30-90
Wheelbase-to-length ratio of 53% is considered ○ dangerous ● fatiguing ○ good ○ excellent*
The approximate net payload of 2175 pounds at 12% of GVWR on this model is ○ deficient ○ excessive ○ cautionary ● good ○ excellent*
Total highway safety penalties are: 2* Value: 9 5 Durability: 9 0 Highway Control Rating: 6 7 Highway Safety: 6 5 ★★

Brand	Year	Type	Length	Model	Chassis	Engine	Fuel Type	Price/ft	Wheelbase	Towing	GVWR	Curb Weight
Tropi-Cal	1999	MHA	36	6350	CH	7.4L	G	$2400	232 T	1,500	19,500	17,270

Livability Code: SB 30-90
Wheelbase-to-length ratio of 54% is considered ○ dangerous ○ fatiguing ● good ○ excellent*
The approximate net payload of 2230 pounds at 11% of GVWR on this model is ○ deficient ○ excessive ○ cautionary ● good ○ excellent*
Total highway safety penalties are: 15* Value: 8 8 Durability: 9 0 Highway Control Rating: 7 8 Highway Safety: 6 3 ★★

Brand	Year	Type	Length	Model	Chassis	Engine	Fuel Type	Price/ft	Wheelbase	Towing	GVWR	Curb Weight
Tropi-Cal	1999	MHA	36	6351	CH	7.4L	G	$2400	232 T	2,000	19,500	17,730

Livability Code: SB 30-90
Wheelbase-to-length ratio of 54% is considered ○ dangerous ○ fatiguing ● good ○ excellent*
The approximate net payload of 1770 pounds at 9% of GVWR on this model is ○ deficient ○ excessive ● cautionary ○ good ○ excellent*
Total highway safety penalties are: 15* Value: 8 8 Durability: 9 0 Highway Control Rating: 6 6 Highway Safety: 5 1 ★

Brand	Year	Type	Length	Model	Chassis	Engine	Fuel Type	Price/ft	Wheelbase	Towing	GVWR	Curb Weight
Tropi-Cal	1999	MHA	36	6350	FO	6.8L	G	$2400	232 T	5,000	21,000	18,520

Livability Code: SB 30-90
Wheelbase-to-length ratio of 54% is considered ○ dangerous ○ fatiguing ● good ○ excellent*
The approximate net payload of 2480 pounds at 12% of GVWR on this model is ○ deficient ○ excessive ○ cautionary ● good ○ excellent*
Total highway safety penalties are: 10* Value: 9 1 Durability: 9 0 Highway Control Rating: 7 5 Highway Safety: 6 5 ★★

Brand	Year	Type	Length	Model	Chassis	Engine	Fuel Type	Price/ft	Wheelbase	Towing	GVWR	Curb Weight
Tropi-Cal	1999	MHA	36	6351	FO	6.8L	G	$2400	232 T	5,000	21,000	18,370

Livability Code: SB 30-90
Wheelbase-to-length ratio of 54% is considered ○ dangerous ○ fatiguing ● good ○ excellent*
The approximate net payload of 2630 pounds at 13% of GVWR on this model is ○ deficient ○ excessive ○ cautionary ● good ○ excellent*
Total highway safety penalties are: 10* Value: 9 1 Durability: 9 0 Highway Control Rating: 7 6 Highway Safety: 6 6 ★★

Brand	Year	Type	Length	Model	Chassis	Engine	Fuel Type	Price/ft	Wheelbase	Towing	GVWR	Curb Weight
Tropi-Cal	1999	MHA	37	6370	FO	6.8L	G	$2300	252 T	5,000	21,000	18,490

Livability Code: SB 30-90
Wheelbase-to-length ratio of 57% is considered ○ dangerous ○ fatiguing ● good ○ excellent*
The approximate net payload of 2510 pounds at 12% of GVWR on this model is ○ deficient ○ excessive ○ cautionary ● good ○ excellent*
Total highway safety penalties are: 15* Value: 8 9 Durability: 9 0 Highway Control Rating: 9 1 Highway Safety: 7 6 ★★★

Brand	Year	Type	Length	Model	Chassis	Engine	Fuel Type	Price/ft	Wheelbase	Towing	GVWR	Curb Weight
Tropi-Cal	1999	MHA	37	6371	FO	6.8L	G	$2300	252 T	5,000	21,000	18,940

Livability Code: SB 30-90
Wheelbase-to-length ratio of 57% is considered ○ dangerous ○ fatiguing ● good ○ excellent*
The approximate net payload of 2060 pounds at 10% of GVWR on this model is ○ deficient ○ excessive ○ cautionary ● good ○ excellent*
Total highway safety penalties are: 18* Value: 8 7 Durability: 9 0 Highway Control Rating: 8 7 Highway Safety: 6 9 ★★

Brand	Year	Type	Length	Model	Chassis	Engine	Fuel Type	Price/ft	Wheelbase	Towing	GVWR	Curb Weight
Ultimate Advantage	1999	MHA	38	38K	FR	CA275	D	$3400	243	5,000	27,410	24,841

Livability Code: SB 30-90
Wheelbase-to-length ratio of 53% is considered ○ dangerous ● fatiguing ○ good ○ excellent*
The approximate net payload of 2569 pounds at 9% of GVWR on this model is ○ deficient ○ excessive ● cautionary ○ good ○ excellent*
Total highway safety penalties are: 12* Value: 8 0 Durability: 7 8 Highway Control Rating: 6 0 Highway Safety: 4 8

Brand	Year	Type	Length	Model	Chassis	Engine	Fuel Type	Price/ft	Wheelbase	Towing	GVWR	Curb Weight
Ultimate Advantage	1999	MHA	40	40J myc	FR	CA275	D	$3300	267	5,000	29,410	25,365

Livability Code: SB 30-90
Wheelbase-to-length ratio of 56% is considered ○ dangerous ○ fatiguing ● good ○ excellent*
The approximate net payload of 4045 pounds at 14% of GVWR on this model is ○ deficient ○ excessive ○ cautionary ● good ○ excellent*
Total highway safety penalties are: 13* Value: 8 0 Durability: 7 8 Highway Control Rating: 9 1 Highway Safety: 7 8 ★★★

Brand	Year	Type	Length	Model	Chassis	Engine	Fuel Type	Price/ft	Wheelbase	Towing	GVWR	Curb Weight
Ultimate Freedom	1999	MHA	38	38KD	FR	CA300	D	$3400	243	5,000	31,000	26,672

Livability Code: SB 30-90
Wheelbase-to-length ratio of 53% is considered ○ dangerous ● fatiguing ○ good ○ excellent*
The approximate net payload of 4328 pounds at 14% of GVWR on this model is ○ deficient ○ excessive ○ cautionary ● good ○ excellent*
Total highway safety penalties are: 12* Value: 8 0 Durability: 7 8 Highway Control Rating: 7 2 Highway Safety: 6 0 ★★

Brand	Year	Type	Length	Model	Chassis	Engine	Fuel Type	Price/ft	Wheelbase	Towing	GVWR	Curb Weight
Ultimate Freedom	1999	MHA	40	40JD	FR	CA300	D	$3300	267	5,000	31,000	27,727

Livability Code: SB 30-90
Wheelbase-to-length ratio of 56% is considered ○ dangerous ○ fatiguing ● good ○ excellent*
The approximate net payload of 3273 pounds at 11% of GVWR on this model is ○ deficient ○ excessive ○ cautionary ● good ○ excellent*
Total highway safety penalties are: 13* Value: 8 0 Durability: 7 8 Highway Control Rating: 8 4 Highway Safety: 7 1 ★★★

Note: Safety ratings are based on the assumption that the engineering of the RV has allowed for proper balance by placing fresh, gray, and black holding tanks in a location so as not to change the balance of the RV when the tanks are empty or full. **Always double-check wheelbase, GVWR, and weights at front and rear axles.**

*See Section 1 for details on how conclusions are reached.

Section 2: The Ratings

Brand	Year	Type	Length	Model	Chassis	Engine	Fuel Type	Average Price per Linear Foot When New	Adjusted Wheelbase	Approx. Towing Capacity	Gross Vehicle Weight Rating	Average Curb Weight
Ultrastar	1990	MHA	27	264 QB	CH	7.4L	G	$2100	158	1,500	12,300	10,793

Livability Code: SB 30-90
Wheelbase-to-length ratio of 49% is considered ◉ dangerous ○ fatiguing ○ good ○ excellent *
The approximate net payload of 1507 pounds at 12% of GVWR on this model is ○ deficient ○ excessive ○ cautionary ◉ good ○ excellent *
Total highway safety penalties are: 3 *   Value: 7 7   Durability: 7 0   Highway Control Rating: 3 5   Highway Safety: 3 2

Brand	Year	Type	Length	Model	Chassis	Engine	Fuel Type	Avg. Price/Ft	Wheelbase	Towing	GVWR	Curb Wt
Ultrastar	1990	MHA	27	273 QB	CH	7.4L	G	$2100	158	1,500	12,300	10,926

Livability Code: SB 30-90
Wheelbase-to-length ratio of 48% is considered ◉ dangerous ○ fatiguing ○ good ○ excellent *
The approximate net payload of 1374 pounds at 11% of GVWR on this model is ○ deficient ○ excessive ○ cautionary ◉ good ○ excellent *
Total highway safety penalties are: 3 *   Value: 7 6   Durability: 7 0   Highway Control Rating: 2 9   Highway Safety: 2 6

Brand	Year	Type	Length	Model	Chassis	Engine	Fuel Type	Avg. Price/Ft	Wheelbase	Towing	GVWR	Curb Wt
Ultrastar	1990	MHA	27	273 TB	CH	7.4L	G	$2100	178	1,500	12,300	10,926

Livability Code: SB 30-90
Wheelbase-to-length ratio of 55% is considered ○ dangerous ○ fatiguing ◉ good ○ excellent *
The approximate net payload of 1374 pounds at 11% of GVWR on this model is ○ deficient ○ excessive ○ cautionary ◉ good ○ excellent *
Total highway safety penalties are: 3 *   Value: 7 6   Durability: 7 0   Highway Control Rating: 8 6   Highway Safety: 8 3   ★★★

Brand	Year	Type	Length	Model	Chassis	Engine	Fuel Type	Avg. Price/Ft	Wheelbase	Towing	GVWR	Curb Wt
Ultrastar	1990	MHA	29	283 QB	CH	7.4L	G	$2000	178	1,200	14,800	12,235

Livability Code: SB 30-90
Wheelbase-to-length ratio of 52% is considered ○ dangerous ◉ fatiguing ○ good ○ excellent *
The approximate net payload of 2565 pounds at 17% of GVWR on this model is ○ deficient ○ excessive ○ cautionary ○ good ◉ excellent *
Total highway safety penalties are: 4 *   Value: 7 6   Durability: 7 0   Highway Control Rating: 6 0   Highway Safety: 5 6   ★

Brand	Year	Type	Length	Model	Chassis	Engine	Fuel Type	Avg. Price/Ft	Wheelbase	Towing	GVWR	Curb Wt
Ultrastar	1990	MHA	29	283 TB	CH	7.4L	G	$2000	178	1,200	14,800	12,235

Livability Code: SB 30-90
Wheelbase-to-length ratio of 52% is considered ○ dangerous ◉ fatiguing ○ good ○ excellent *
The approximate net payload of 2565 pounds at 17% of GVWR on this model is ○ deficient ○ excessive ○ cautionary ○ good ◉ excellent *
Total highway safety penalties are: 4 *   Value: 7 6   Durability: 7 0   Highway Control Rating: 6 0   Highway Safety: 5 6   ★

Brand	Year	Type	Length	Model	Chassis	Engine	Fuel Type	Avg. Price/Ft	Wheelbase	Towing	GVWR	Curb Wt
Ultrastar	1990	MHA	30	293 QB	CH	7.4L	G	$2000	178	1,200	14,800	12,456

Livability Code: SB 30-90
Wheelbase-to-length ratio of 50% is considered ◉ dangerous ○ fatiguing ○ good ○ excellent *
The approximate net payload of 2344 pounds at 16% of GVWR on this model is ○ deficient ○ excessive ○ cautionary ○ good ◉ excellent *
Total highway safety penalties are: 4 *   Value: 7 6   Durability: 7 0   Highway Control Rating: 4 5   Highway Safety: 4 1

Brand	Year	Type	Length	Model	Chassis	Engine	Fuel Type	Avg. Price/Ft	Wheelbase	Towing	GVWR	Curb Wt
Ultrastar	1990	MHA	30	293 TB	CH	7.4L	G	$2000	178	1,200	14,800	12,456

Livability Code: SB 30-90
Wheelbase-to-length ratio of 50% is considered ◉ dangerous ○ fatiguing ○ good ○ excellent *
The approximate net payload of 2344 pounds at 16% of GVWR on this model is ○ deficient ○ excessive ○ cautionary ○ good ◉ excellent *
Total highway safety penalties are: 4 *   Value: 7 6   Durability: 7 0   Highway Control Rating: 4 5   Highway Safety: 4 1

Brand	Year	Type	Length	Model	Chassis	Engine	Fuel Type	Avg. Price/Ft	Wheelbase	Towing	GVWR	Curb Wt
Ultrastar	1990	MHA	32	313 QB	CH	7.4L	G	$1900	208	1,500	16,000	13,377

Livability Code: SB 30-90
Wheelbase-to-length ratio of 55% is considered ○ dangerous ○ fatiguing ◉ good ○ excellent *
The approximate net payload of 2623 pounds at 16% of GVWR on this model is ○ deficient ○ excessive ○ cautionary ○ good ◉ excellent *
Total highway safety penalties are: 5 *   Value: 7 5   Durability: 7 0   Highway Control Rating: 9 2   Highway Safety: 8 7   ★★★

Brand	Year	Type	Length	Model	Chassis	Engine	Fuel Type	Avg. Price/Ft	Wheelbase	Towing	GVWR	Curb Wt
Ultrastar	1990	MHA	32	313 TB	CH	7.4L	G	$1900	208	1,500	16,000	13,377

Livability Code: SB 30-90
Wheelbase-to-length ratio of 55% is considered ○ dangerous ○ fatiguing ◉ good ○ excellent *
The approximate net payload of 2623 pounds at 16% of GVWR on this model is ○ deficient ○ excessive ○ cautionary ○ good ◉ excellent *
Total highway safety penalties are: 5 *   Value: 7 5   Durability: 7 0   Highway Control Rating: 9 2   Highway Safety: 8 7   ★★★

Brand	Year	Type	Length	Model	Chassis	Engine	Fuel Type	Avg. Price/Ft	Wheelbase	Towing	GVWR	Curb Wt
Ultrastar	1990	MHA	34	333 QB	CH	7.4L	G	$1800	228	1,500	16,000	13,819

Livability Code: SB 30-90
Wheelbase-to-length ratio of 57% is considered ○ dangerous ○ fatiguing ◉ good ○ excellent *
The approximate net payload of 2181 pounds at 14% of GVWR on this model is ○ deficient ○ excessive ○ cautionary ◉ good ○ excellent *
Total highway safety penalties are: 6 *   Value: 7 5   Durability: 7 0   Highway Control Rating: 9 4   Highway Safety: 8 8   ★★★

Brand	Year	Type	Length	Model	Chassis	Engine	Fuel Type	Avg. Price/Ft	Wheelbase	Towing	GVWR	Curb Wt
Ultrastar	1990	MHA	34	339 QB	CH	7.4L	G	$1900	228	1,500	16,000	13,819

Livability Code: SB 30-90
Wheelbase-to-length ratio of 57% is considered ○ dangerous ○ fatiguing ◉ good ○ excellent *
The approximate net payload of 2181 pounds at 14% of GVWR on this model is ○ deficient ○ excessive ○ cautionary ◉ good ○ excellent *
Total highway safety penalties are: 6 *   Value: 7 5   Durability: 7 0   Highway Control Rating: 9 4   Highway Safety: 8 8   ★★★

Brand	Year	Type	Length	Model	Chassis	Engine	Fuel Type	Avg. Price/Ft	Wheelbase	Towing	GVWR	Curb Wt
Ultrastar	1990	MHA	34	339 TB	CH	7.4L	G	$1900	228	1,500	16,000	13,819

Livability Code: SB 30-90
Wheelbase-to-length ratio of 57% is considered ○ dangerous ○ fatiguing ◉ good ○ excellent *
The approximate net payload of 2181 pounds at 14% of GVWR on this model is ○ deficient ○ excessive ○ cautionary ◉ good ○ excellent *
Total highway safety penalties are: 6 *   Value: 7 5   Durability: 7 0   Highway Control Rating: 9 4   Highway Safety: 8 8   ★★★

Note: Safety ratings are based on the assumption that the engineering of the RV has allowed for proper balance by placing fresh, gray, and black holding tanks in a location so as not to change the balance of the RV when the tanks are empty or full. **Always double-check wheelbase, GVWR, and weights at front and rear axles.**

*See Section 1 for details on how conclusions are reached.

Brand	Year	Type	Length	Model	Chassis	Engine	Fuel Type	Average Price per Linear Foot When New	Adjusted Wheelbase	Approx. Towing Capacity	Gross Vehicle Weight Rating	Average Curb Weight
Ultrastar	1990	MHA	34	US333 TB	CH	7.4L	G	$1900	228	1,500	16,000	13,963

Livability Code: SB 30-90 Wheelbase-to-length ratio of 56% is considered ○ dangerous ○ fatiguing ◉ good ○ excellent*
The approximate net payload of 2037 pounds at 13% of GVWR on this model is ○ deficient ○ excessive ○ cautionary ◉ good ○ excellent*
Total highway safety penalties are: 6* Value: 75 Durability: 70 Highway Control Rating: 90 Highway Safety: 84 ★★★

Brand	Year	Type	Length	Model	Chassis	Engine	Fuel Type	Price	Adjusted Wheelbase	Towing	GVWR	Curb Weight
Ultrastar	1991	MHA	27	US-264	CH	7.4L	G	$2000	158	1,500	12,300	10,882

Livability Code: SB 30-90 Wheelbase-to-length ratio of 49% is considered ◉ dangerous ○ fatiguing ○ good ○ excellent*
The approximate net payload of 1418 pounds at 12% of GVWR on this model is ○ deficient ○ excessive ○ cautionary ◉ good ○ excellent*
Total highway safety penalties are: 3* Value: 77 Durability: 70 Highway Control Rating: 32 Highway Safety: 29

Ultrastar	1991	MHA	29	US-283	CH	7.4L	G	$1900	178	2,500	14,500	12,203

Livability Code: SB 30-90 Wheelbase-to-length ratio of 51% is considered ○ dangerous ◉ fatiguing ○ good ○ excellent*
The approximate net payload of 2297 pounds at 16% of GVWR on this model is ○ deficient ○ excessive ○ cautionary ○ good ◉ excellent*
Total highway safety penalties are: 4* Value: 76 Durability: 70 Highway Control Rating: 49 Highway Safety: 45

Ultrastar	1991	MHA	32	US-313	CH	7.4L	G	$1800	208	2,500	14,500	12,866

Livability Code: SB 30-90 Wheelbase-to-length ratio of 54% is considered ○ dangerous ○ fatiguing ◉ good ○ excellent*
The approximate net payload of 1634 pounds at 11% of GVWR on this model is ○ deficient ○ excessive ○ cautionary ◉ good ○ excellent*
Total highway safety penalties are: 6* Value: 75 Durability: 70 Highway Control Rating: 77 Highway Safety: 71 ★★★

Ultrastar	1991	MHA	34	US-333-QB	CH	7.4L	G	$1800	228	1,500	16,000	13,907

Livability Code: SB 30-90 Wheelbase-to-length ratio of 56% is considered ○ dangerous ○ fatiguing ◉ good ○ excellent*
The approximate net payload of 2093 pounds at 13% of GVWR on this model is ○ deficient ○ excessive ○ cautionary ◉ good ○ excellent*
Total highway safety penalties are: 7* Value: 75 Durability: 70 Highway Control Rating: 90 Highway Safety: 83 ★★★

Ultrastar	1994	MHA	29	US 283 QB	FO	7.5L	G	$2300	178	3,800	15,200	12,813

Livability Code: SB 30-90 Wheelbase-to-length ratio of 52% is considered ○ dangerous ◉ fatiguing ○ good ○ excellent*
The approximate net payload of 2387 pounds at 16% of GVWR on this model is ○ deficient ○ excessive ○ cautionary ○ good ◉ excellent*
Total highway safety penalties are: 2* Value: 77 Durability: 70 Highway Control Rating: 58 Highway Safety: 56 ★

Ultrastar	1994	MHA	30	US 293 QB	FO	7.5L	G	$2200	178	3,800	15,200	13,048

Livability Code: SB 30-90 Wheelbase-to-length ratio of 50% is considered ◉ dangerous ○ fatiguing ○ good ○ excellent*
The approximate net payload of 2152 pounds at 14% of GVWR on this model is ○ deficient ○ excessive ○ cautionary ◉ good ○ excellent*
Total highway safety penalties are: 2* Value: 77 Durability: 70 Highway Control Rating: 41 Highway Safety: 39

Ultrastar	1994	MHA	32	US 313 QB	FO	7.5L	G	$2100	208	8,000	17,000	14,237

Livability Code: SB 30-90 Wheelbase-to-length ratio of 55% is considered ○ dangerous ○ fatiguing ◉ good ○ excellent*
The approximate net payload of 2763 pounds at 16% of GVWR on this model is ○ deficient ○ excessive ○ cautionary ○ good ◉ excellent*
Total highway safety penalties are: 2* Value: 77 Durability: 70 Highway Control Rating: 92 Highway Safety: 90 ★★★

Ultrastar	1994	MHA	34	US 336 QB	FO	7.5L	G	$2100	228	8,000	17,000	14,706

Livability Code: SB 30-90 Wheelbase-to-length ratio of 56% is considered ○ dangerous ○ fatiguing ◉ good ○ excellent*
The approximate net payload of 2294 pounds at 13% of GVWR on this model is ○ deficient ○ excessive ○ cautionary ◉ good ○ excellent*
Total highway safety penalties are: 2* Value: 77 Durability: 70 Highway Control Rating: 92 Highway Safety: 90 ★★★

Ultrastar	1994	MHA	34	US 339 QB	FO	7.5L	G	$2100	228	8,000	17,000	14,706

Livability Code: SB 30-90 Wheelbase-to-length ratio of 56% is considered ○ dangerous ○ fatiguing ◉ good ○ excellent*
The approximate net payload of 2294 pounds at 13% of GVWR on this model is ○ deficient ○ excessive ○ cautionary ◉ good ○ excellent*
Total highway safety penalties are: 2* Value: 77 Durability: 70 Highway Control Rating: 92 Highway Safety: 90 ★★★

Ultrastar	1995	MHA	29	283 QB	FO	7.5L	G	$2200	178	3,800	15,200	12,813

Livability Code: SB 30-90 Wheelbase-to-length ratio of 52% is considered ○ dangerous ◉ fatiguing ○ good ○ excellent*
The approximate net payload of 2387 pounds at 16% of GVWR on this model is ○ deficient ○ excessive ○ cautionary ○ good ◉ excellent*
Total highway safety penalties are: 2* Value: 77 Durability: 70 Highway Control Rating: 58 Highway Safety: 56 ★

Ultrastar	1995	MHA	34	339 QB	FO	7.5L	G	$2100	228	8,000	17,000	14,706

Livability Code: SB 30-90 Wheelbase-to-length ratio of 56% is considered ○ dangerous ○ fatiguing ◉ good ○ excellent*
The approximate net payload of 2294 pounds at 13% of GVWR on this model is ○ deficient ○ excessive ○ cautionary ◉ good ○ excellent*
Total highway safety penalties are: 2* Value: 77 Durability: 70 Highway Control Rating: 92 Highway Safety: 90 ★★★

Note: Safety ratings are based on the assumption that the engineering of the RV has allowed for proper balance by placing fresh, gray, and black holding tanks in a location so as not to change the balance of the RV when the tanks are empty or full. **Always double-check wheelbase, GVWR, and weights at front and rear axles.**

*See Section 1 for details on how conclusions are reached.

Brand	Year	Type	Length	Model	Chassis	Engine	Fuel Type	Average Price per Linear Foot When New	Adjusted Wheel-base	Approx. Towing Capacity	Gross Vehicle Weight Rating	Average Curb Weight
Vacationer	1994	MHA	28	27WB	CH	7.4L	G	$1800	158	4,200	14,800	12,485

Livability Code: SB 30-90   Wheelbase-to-length ratio of 47% is considered ◉ dangerous ○ fatiguing ○ good ○ excellent *

The approximate net payload of 2315 pounds at 16% of GVWR on this model is ○ deficient ○ excessive ○ cautionary ○ good ◉ excellent *

Total highway safety penalties are: 4 *   Value: 7 9   Durability: 7 7   Highway Control Rating: 3 4   Highway Safety: 3 0

Brand	Year	Type	Length	Model	Chassis	Engine	Fuel Type	Price/ft	Wheelbase	Towing	GVWR	Curb Wt
Vacationer	1994	MHA	32	31CB	CH	7.4L	G	$1700	190	3,000	16,000	13,685

Livability Code: SB 30-90   Wheelbase-to-length ratio of 49% is considered ◉ dangerous ○ fatiguing ○ good ○ excellent *

The approximate net payload of 2315 pounds at 14% of GVWR on this model is ○ deficient ○ excessive ○ cautionary ◉ good ○ excellent *

Total highway safety penalties are: 6 *   Value: 7 8   Durability: 7 7   Highway Control Rating: 3 9   Highway Safety: 3 3

Brand	Year	Type	Length	Model	Chassis	Engine	Fuel Type	Price/ft	Wheelbase	Towing	GVWR	Curb Wt
Vacationer	1994	MHA	32	R31CB	FO	7.5L	G	$1700	190	8,000	17,000	14,392

Livability Code: SB 30-90   Wheelbase-to-length ratio of 49% is considered ◉ dangerous ○ fatiguing ○ good ○ excellent *

The approximate net payload of 2608 pounds at 15% of GVWR on this model is ○ deficient ○ excessive ○ cautionary ◉ good ○ excellent *

Total highway safety penalties are: 2 *   Value: 8 0   Durability: 7 7   Highway Control Rating: 4 1   Highway Safety: 3 9

Brand	Year	Type	Length	Model	Chassis	Engine	Fuel Type	Price/ft	Wheelbase	Towing	GVWR	Curb Wt
Vacationer	1994	MHA	34	33CS	FO	7.5L	G	$1600	208	8,000	17,000	14,584

Livability Code: SB 30-90   Wheelbase-to-length ratio of 51% is considered ○ dangerous ◉ fatiguing ○ good ○ excellent *

The approximate net payload of 2416 pounds at 14% of GVWR on this model is ○ deficient ○ excessive ○ cautionary ◉ good ○ excellent *

Total highway safety penalties are: 2 *   Value: 8 0   Durability: 7 7   Highway Control Rating: 4 5   Highway Safety: 4 3

Brand	Year	Type	Length	Model	Chassis	Engine	Fuel Type	Price/ft	Wheelbase	Towing	GVWR	Curb Wt
Vacationer	1995	MHA	28	27WB	CH	7.4L	G	$1900	158	4,200	14,800	12,322

Livability Code: SB 30-90   Wheelbase-to-length ratio of 47% is considered ◉ dangerous ○ fatiguing ○ good ○ excellent *

The approximate net payload of 2478 pounds at 17% of GVWR on this model is ○ deficient ○ excessive ○ cautionary ○ good ◉ excellent *

Total highway safety penalties are: 4 *   Value: 7 9   Durability: 7 7   Highway Control Rating: 3 5   Highway Safety: 3 1

Brand	Year	Type	Length	Model	Chassis	Engine	Fuel Type	Price/ft	Wheelbase	Towing	GVWR	Curb Wt
Vacationer	1995	MHA	32	31CB	CH	7.4L	G	$1800	190	3,000	16,000	13,714

Livability Code: SB 30-90   Wheelbase-to-length ratio of 49% is considered ◉ dangerous ○ fatiguing ○ good ○ excellent *

The approximate net payload of 2286 pounds at 14% of GVWR on this model is ○ deficient ○ excessive ○ cautionary ◉ good ○ excellent *

Total highway safety penalties are: 6 *   Value: 7 8   Durability: 7 7   Highway Control Rating: 3 9   Highway Safety: 3 3

Brand	Year	Type	Length	Model	Chassis	Engine	Fuel Type	Price/ft	Wheelbase	Towing	GVWR	Curb Wt
Vacationer	1995	MHA	32	31CB	FO	7.5L	G	$1800	190	8,000	17,000	14,123

Livability Code: SB 30-90   Wheelbase-to-length ratio of 49% is considered ◉ dangerous ○ fatiguing ○ good ○ excellent *

The approximate net payload of 2877 pounds at 17% of GVWR on this model is ○ deficient ○ excessive ○ cautionary ○ good ◉ excellent *

Total highway safety penalties are: 2 *   Value: 8 0   Durability: 7 7   Highway Control Rating: 4 3   Highway Safety: 4 1

Brand	Year	Type	Length	Model	Chassis	Engine	Fuel Type	Price/ft	Wheelbase	Towing	GVWR	Curb Wt
Vacationer	1995	MHA	34	33CS	FO	7.5L	G	$1700	208	8,000	17,000	14,561

Livability Code: SB 30-90   Wheelbase-to-length ratio of 51% is considered ○ dangerous ◉ fatiguing ○ good ○ excellent *

The approximate net payload of 2439 pounds at 14% of GVWR on this model is ○ deficient ○ excessive ○ cautionary ◉ good ○ excellent *

Total highway safety penalties are: 2 *   Value: 8 0   Durability: 7 7   Highway Control Rating: 4 5   Highway Safety: 4 3

Brand	Year	Type	Length	Model	Chassis	Engine	Fuel Type	Price/ft	Wheelbase	Towing	GVWR	Curb Wt
Vacationer	1996	MHA	32	SE 31CB	CH	7.4L	G	$1800	190	3,000	16,500	14,303

Livability Code: SB 30-90   Wheelbase-to-length ratio of 49% is considered ◉ dangerous ○ fatiguing ○ good ○ excellent *

The approximate net payload of 2197 pounds at 13% of GVWR on this model is ○ deficient ○ excessive ○ cautionary ◉ good ○ excellent *

Total highway safety penalties are: 6 *   Value: 7 8   Durability: 7 7   Highway Control Rating: 3 7   Highway Safety: 3 1

Brand	Year	Type	Length	Model	Chassis	Engine	Fuel Type	Price/ft	Wheelbase	Towing	GVWR	Curb Wt
Vacationer	1996	MHA	32	SE 31CB	FO	7.5L	G	$1800	190	8,000	17,000	14,811

Livability Code: SB 30-90   Wheelbase-to-length ratio of 49% is considered ◉ dangerous ○ fatiguing ○ good ○ excellent *

The approximate net payload of 2189 pounds at 13% of GVWR on this model is ○ deficient ○ excessive ○ cautionary ◉ good ○ excellent *

Total highway safety penalties are: 2 *   Value: 8 0   Durability: 7 7   Highway Control Rating: 3 6   Highway Safety: 3 4

Brand	Year	Type	Length	Model	Chassis	Engine	Fuel Type	Price/ft	Wheelbase	Towing	GVWR	Curb Wt
Vacationer	1996	MHA	34	SE 33CS	FO	7.5L	G	$1700	208	8,000	17,000	15,147

Livability Code: SB 30-90   Wheelbase-to-length ratio of 51% is considered ○ dangerous ◉ fatiguing ○ good ○ excellent *

The approximate net payload of 1853 pounds at 11% of GVWR on this model is ○ deficient ○ excessive ○ cautionary ◉ good ○ excellent *

Total highway safety penalties are: 2 *   Value: 8 0   Durability: 7 7   Highway Control Rating: 3 9   Highway Safety: 3 7

Brand	Year	Type	Length	Model	Chassis	Engine	Fuel Type	Price/ft	Wheelbase	Towing	GVWR	Curb Wt
Vacationer	1997	MHA	32	31CG	CH	7.4L	G	$2100	208	3,500	16,500	14,075

Livability Code: SB 30-90   Wheelbase-to-length ratio of 55% is considered ○ dangerous ○ fatiguing ◉ good ○ excellent *

The approximate net payload of 2425 pounds at 15% of GVWR on this model is ○ deficient ○ excessive ○ cautionary ◉ good ○ excellent *

Total highway safety penalties are: 5 *   Value: 7 8   Durability: 7 7   Highway Control Rating: 8 8   Highway Safety: 8 3   ★★★

Note: Safety ratings are based on the assumption that the engineering of the RV has allowed for proper balance by placing fresh, gray, and black holding tanks in a location so as not to change the balance of the RV when the tanks are empty or full. **Always double-check wheelbase, GVWR, and weights at front and rear axles.**

*See Section 1 for details on how conclusions are reached.

Section 2: The Ratings

Brand	Year	Type	Length	Model	Chassis	Engine	Fuel Type	Average Price per Linear Foot When New	Adjusted Wheelbase	Approx. Towing Capacity	Gross Vehicle Weight Rating	Average Curb Weight
Vacationer	1997	MHA	32	31CG	FO	7.5L	G	$2100	208	3,500	17,000	14,705

Livability Code: SB 30-90

Wheelbase-to-length ratio of 55% is considered ○ dangerous ○ fatiguing ◉ good ○ excellent *

The approximate net payload of 2295 pounds at 14% of GVWR on this model is ○ deficient ○ excessive ○ cautionary ◉ good ○ excellent *

Total highway safety penalties are: 2 *   Value: **80** Durability: **77** Highway Control Rating: **86**   Highway Safety: **84**   ★★★

| **Vacationer** | 1997 | MHA | 33 | 32CG | CH | 7.4L | G | $2100 | 208 | 3,500 | 16,500 | 14,884 |

Livability Code: SB 30-90

Wheelbase-to-length ratio of 53% is considered ○ dangerous ◉ fatiguing ○ good ○ excellent *

The approximate net payload of 1616 pounds at 10% of GVWR on this model is ○ deficient ○ excessive ○ cautionary ◉ good ○ excellent *

Total highway safety penalties are: 6 *   Value: **78** Durability: **77** Highway Control Rating: **58**   Highway Safety: **52**   ★

| **Vacationer** | 1997 | MHA | 33 | 32CG | FO | 7.5L | G | $2100 | 208 | 3,500 | 17,000 | 15,195 |

Livability Code: SB 30-90

Wheelbase-to-length ratio of 53% is considered ○ dangerous ◉ fatiguing ○ good ○ excellent *

The approximate net payload of 1805 pounds at 11% of GVWR on this model is ○ deficient ○ excessive ○ cautionary ◉ good ○ excellent *

Total highway safety penalties are: 2 *   Value: **80** Durability: **77** Highway Control Rating: **60**   Highway Safety: **58**   ★

| **Vacationer** | 1997 | MHA | 35 | 34CG | CH | 7.4L | G | $2000 | 228 | 3,500 | 16,500 | 15,444 |

Livability Code: SB 30-90

Wheelbase-to-length ratio of 55% is considered ○ dangerous ○ fatiguing ◉ good ○ excellent *

The approximate net payload of 1056 pounds at 6% of GVWR on this model is ◉ deficient ○ excessive ○ cautionary ○ good ○ excellent *

Total highway safety penalties are: 7 *   Value: **77** Durability: **77** Highway Control Rating: **57**   Highway Safety: **50**   ★

| **Vacationer** | 1997 | MHA | 35 | 34CG | FO | 7.5L | G | $2000 | 228 | 3,500 | 17,000 | 15,844 |

Livability Code: SB 30-90

Wheelbase-to-length ratio of 55% is considered ○ dangerous ○ fatiguing ◉ good ○ excellent *

The approximate net payload of 1156 pounds at 7% of GVWR on this model is ○ deficient ○ excessive ◉ cautionary ○ good ○ excellent *

Total highway safety penalties are: 2 *   Value: **80** Durability: **77** Highway Control Rating: **62**   Highway Safety: **60**   ★★

| **Vacationer** | 1997 | MHA | 35 | 35SG | CH | 7.4L | G | $2000 | 228 | 3,500 | 16,500 | 15,523 |

Livability Code: SB 30-90

Wheelbase-to-length ratio of 54% is considered ○ dangerous ○ fatiguing ◉ good ○ excellent *

The approximate net payload of 978 pounds at 6% of GVWR on this model is ◉ deficient ○ excessive ○ cautionary ○ good ○ excellent *

Total highway safety penalties are: 7 *   Value: **77** Durability: **77** Highway Control Rating: **46**   Highway Safety: **39**

| **Vacationer** | 1997 | MHA | 35 | 35KS | CH | 7.4L | G | $2000 | 228 | 3,500 | 16,500 | 16,131 |

Livability Code: SB 30-90

Wheelbase-to-length ratio of 54% is considered ○ dangerous ○ fatiguing ◉ good ○ excellent *

The approximate net payload of 369 pounds at 2% of GVWR on this model is ◉ deficient ○ excessive ○ cautionary ○ good ○ excellent *

Total highway safety penalties are: 13 *   Value: **75** Durability: **77** Highway Control Rating: **42**   Highway Safety: **29**

| **Vacationer** | 1997 | MHA | 35 | 35SG | FO | 7.5L | G | $2000 | 228 | 3,500 | 17,000 | 15,984 |

Livability Code: SB 30-90

Wheelbase-to-length ratio of 54% is considered ○ dangerous ○ fatiguing ◉ good ○ excellent *

The approximate net payload of 1016 pounds at 6% of GVWR on this model is ◉ deficient ○ excessive ○ cautionary ○ good ○ excellent *

Total highway safety penalties are: 2 *   Value: **80** Durability: **77** Highway Control Rating: **46**   Highway Safety: **44**

| **Vacationer** | 1997 | MHA | 35 | 35KS | FO | 7.5L | G | $2000 | 228 | 3,500 | 17,000 | 16,884 |

Livability Code: SB 30-90

Wheelbase-to-length ratio of 54% is considered ○ dangerous ○ fatiguing ◉ good ○ excellent *

The approximate net payload of 116 pounds at 1% of GVWR on this model is ◉ deficient ○ excessive ○ cautionary ○ good ○ excellent *

Total highway safety penalties are: 7 *   Value: **77** Durability: **77** Highway Control Rating: **41**   Highway Safety: **34**

| **Vacationer** | 1998 | MHA | 32 | 31CG | CH | 7.4L | G | $2300 | 208 | 3,500 | 16,500 | 15,054 |

Livability Code: SB 30-90

Wheelbase-to-length ratio of 55% is considered ○ dangerous ○ fatiguing ◉ good ○ excellent *

The approximate net payload of 1446 pounds at 9% of GVWR on this model is ○ deficient ○ excessive ◉ cautionary ○ good ○ excellent *

Total highway safety penalties are: 8 *   Value: **77** Durability: **77** Highway Control Rating: **74**   Highway Safety: **66**   ★★

| **Vacationer** | 1998 | MHA | 32 | 31CG | FO | 7.5L | G | $2300 | 208 | 3,500 | 17,000 | 15,454 |

Livability Code: SB 30-90

Wheelbase-to-length ratio of 55% is considered ○ dangerous ○ fatiguing ◉ good ○ excellent *

The approximate net payload of 1546 pounds at 9% of GVWR on this model is ○ deficient ○ excessive ◉ cautionary ○ good ○ excellent *

Total highway safety penalties are: 5 *   Value: **78** Durability: **77** Highway Control Rating: **74**   Highway Safety: **69**   ★★

| **Vacationer** | 1998 | MHA | 33 | 32CG | CH | 7.4L | G | $2300 | 208 | 3,500 | 16,500 | 14,884 |

Livability Code: SB 30-90

Wheelbase-to-length ratio of 53% is considered ○ dangerous ◉ fatiguing ○ good ○ excellent *

The approximate net payload of 1616 pounds at 10% of GVWR on this model is ○ deficient ○ excessive ○ cautionary ◉ good ○ excellent *

Total highway safety penalties are: 6 *   Value: **78** Durability: **77** Highway Control Rating: **58**   Highway Safety: **52**   ★

Note: Safety ratings are based on the assumption that the engineering of the RV has allowed for proper balance by placing fresh, gray, and black holding tanks in a location so as not to change the balance of the RV when the tanks are empty or full. **Always double-check wheelbase, GVWR, and weights at front and rear axles.**

*See Section 1 for details on how conclusions are reached.

Section 2: The Ratings

Brand	Year	Type	Length	Model	Chassis	Engine	Fuel Type	Average Price per Linear Foot When New	Adjusted Wheelbase	Approx. Towing Capacity	Gross Vehicle Weight Rating	Average Curb Weight
Vacationer	1998	MHA	33	32CG	FO	7.5L	G	$2300	208	3,500	17,000	15,427

Livability Code: SB 30-90
Wheelbase-to-length ratio of 53% is considered ○ dangerous ● fatiguing ○ good ○ excellent *
The approximate net payload of 1573 pounds at 9% of GVWR on this model is ○ deficient ○ excessive ● cautionary ○ good ○ excellent *
Total highway safety penalties are: 2 * Value: 80 Durability: 77 Highway Control Rating: 53 Highway Safety: 51 ★

Brand	Year	Type	Length	Model	Chassis	Engine	Fuel Type	Average Price per Linear Foot When New	Adjusted Wheelbase	Approx. Towing Capacity	Gross Vehicle Weight Rating	Average Curb Weight
Vacationer	1998	MHA	35	34CG	FO	7.5L	G	$2100	228	3,500	17,000	15,788

Livability Code: SB 30-90
Wheelbase-to-length ratio of 55% is considered ○ dangerous ○ fatiguing ● good ○ excellent *
The approximate net payload of 1212 pounds at 7% of GVWR on this model is ○ deficient ○ excessive ● cautionary ○ good ○ excellent *
Total highway safety penalties are: 2 * Value: 80 Durability: 77 Highway Control Rating: 63 Highway Safety: 61 ★★

Brand	Year	Type	Length	Model	Chassis	Engine	Fuel Type	Average Price per Linear Foot When New	Adjusted Wheelbase	Approx. Towing Capacity	Gross Vehicle Weight Rating	Average Curb Weight
Vacationer	1998	MHA	35	35WGS	FO	7.5L	G	$2100	232 T	3,500	19,400	17,784

Livability Code: SB 30-90
Wheelbase-to-length ratio of 55% is considered ○ dangerous ○ fatiguing ● good ○ excellent *
The approximate net payload of 1616 pounds at 8% of GVWR on this model is ○ deficient ○ excessive ● cautionary ○ good ○ excellent *
Total highway safety penalties are: 15 * Value: 73 Durability: 77 Highway Control Rating: 69 Highway Safety: 54 ★

Brand	Year	Type	Length	Model	Chassis	Engine	Fuel Type	Average Price per Linear Foot When New	Adjusted Wheelbase	Approx. Towing Capacity	Gross Vehicle Weight Rating	Average Curb Weight
Vacationer	1998	MHA	36	36SG	FO	7.5L	G	$2100	232 T	3,500	19,400	17,080

Livability Code: SB 30-90
Wheelbase-to-length ratio of 54% is considered ○ dangerous ○ fatiguing ● good ○ excellent *
The approximate net payload of 2320 pounds at 12% of GVWR on this model is ○ deficient ○ excessive ○ cautionary ● good ○ excellent *
Total highway safety penalties are: 4 * Value: 79 Durability: 77 Highway Control Rating: 76 Highway Safety: 72 ★★★

Brand	Year	Type	Length	Model	Chassis	Engine	Fuel Type	Average Price per Linear Foot When New	Adjusted Wheelbase	Approx. Towing Capacity	Gross Vehicle Weight Rating	Average Curb Weight
Vacationer	1998	MHA	36	36SGS	FO	7.5L	G	$2100	232 T	3,500	19,400	17,980

Livability Code: SB 30-90
Wheelbase-to-length ratio of 54% is considered ○ dangerous ○ fatiguing ● good ○ excellent *
The approximate net payload of 1420 pounds at 7% of GVWR on this model is ○ deficient ○ excessive ● cautionary ○ good ○ excellent *
Total highway safety penalties are: 15 * Value: 73 Durability: 77 Highway Control Rating: 52 Highway Safety: 37

Brand	Year	Type	Length	Model	Chassis	Engine	Fuel Type	Average Price per Linear Foot When New	Adjusted Wheelbase	Approx. Towing Capacity	Gross Vehicle Weight Rating	Average Curb Weight
Vacationer	1998	MHA	36	36WGS	FO	7.5L	G	$2100	232 T	3,500	19,400	17,980

Livability Code: SB 30-90
Wheelbase-to-length ratio of 54% is considered ○ dangerous ○ fatiguing ● good ○ excellent *
The approximate net payload of 1420 pounds at 7% of GVWR on this model is ○ deficient ○ excessive ● cautionary ○ good ○ excellent *
Total highway safety penalties are: 15 * Value: 73 Durability: 77 Highway Control Rating: 52 Highway Safety: 37

Brand	Year	Type	Length	Model	Chassis	Engine	Fuel Type	Average Price per Linear Foot When New	Adjusted Wheelbase	Approx. Towing Capacity	Gross Vehicle Weight Rating	Average Curb Weight
Vacationer	1999	MHA	32	31CG	CH	7.4L	G	$2300	208	3,500	16,500	14,649

Livability Code: SB 30-90
Wheelbase-to-length ratio of 55% is considered ○ dangerous ○ fatiguing ● good ○ excellent *
The approximate net payload of 1851 pounds at 11% of GVWR on this model is ○ deficient ○ excessive ○ cautionary ● good ○ excellent *
Total highway safety penalties are: 5 * Value: 78 Durability: 77 Highway Control Rating: 81 Highway Safety: 76 ★★★

Brand	Year	Type	Length	Model	Chassis	Engine	Fuel Type	Average Price per Linear Foot When New	Adjusted Wheelbase	Approx. Towing Capacity	Gross Vehicle Weight Rating	Average Curb Weight
Vacationer	1999	MHA	32	31CG	FO	6.8L	G	$2300	208	5,000	18,000	15,449

Livability Code: SB 30-90
Wheelbase-to-length ratio of 55% is considered ○ dangerous ○ fatiguing ● good ○ excellent *
The approximate net payload of 2551 pounds at 14% of GVWR on this model is ○ deficient ○ excessive ○ cautionary ● good ○ excellent *
Total highway safety penalties are: 2 * Value: 80 Durability: 77 Highway Control Rating: 87 Highway Safety: 85 ★★★

Brand	Year	Type	Length	Model	Chassis	Engine	Fuel Type	Average Price per Linear Foot When New	Adjusted Wheelbase	Approx. Towing Capacity	Gross Vehicle Weight Rating	Average Curb Weight
Vacationer	1999	MHA	33	32CG	CH	7.4L	G	$2300	208	3,500	16,500	14,930

Livability Code: SB 30-90
Wheelbase-to-length ratio of 53% is considered ○ dangerous ● fatiguing ○ good ○ excellent *
The approximate net payload of 1570 pounds at 10% of GVWR on this model is ○ deficient ○ excessive ○ cautionary ● good ○ excellent *
Total highway safety penalties are: 6 * Value: 78 Durability: 77 Highway Control Rating: 62 Highway Safety: 56 ★

Brand	Year	Type	Length	Model	Chassis	Engine	Fuel Type	Average Price per Linear Foot When New	Adjusted Wheelbase	Approx. Towing Capacity	Gross Vehicle Weight Rating	Average Curb Weight
Vacationer	1999	MHA	33	32CG	FO	6.8L	G	$2300	208	5,000	18,000	15,730

Livability Code: SB 30-90
Wheelbase-to-length ratio of 53% is considered ○ dangerous ● fatiguing ○ good ○ excellent *
The approximate net payload of 2270 pounds at 13% of GVWR on this model is ○ deficient ○ excessive ○ cautionary ● good ○ excellent *
Total highway safety penalties are: 2 * Value: 80 Durability: 77 Highway Control Rating: 69 Highway Safety: 67 ★★

Brand	Year	Type	Length	Model	Chassis	Engine	Fuel Type	Average Price per Linear Foot When New	Adjusted Wheelbase	Approx. Towing Capacity	Gross Vehicle Weight Rating	Average Curb Weight
Vacationer	1999	MHA	33	33PS	FO	6.8L	G	$2300	208	5,000	20,500	17,242

Livability Code: SB 30-90
Wheelbase-to-length ratio of 52% is considered ○ dangerous ● fatiguing ○ good ○ excellent *
The approximate net payload of 3258 pounds at 16% of GVWR on this model is ○ deficient ○ excessive ○ cautionary ○ good ● excellent *
Total highway safety penalties are: 12 * Value: 75 Durability: 77 Highway Control Rating: 67 Highway Safety: 55 ★

Brand	Year	Type	Length	Model	Chassis	Engine	Fuel Type	Average Price per Linear Foot When New	Adjusted Wheelbase	Approx. Towing Capacity	Gross Vehicle Weight Rating	Average Curb Weight
Vacationer	1999	MHA	35	34CG	FO	6.8L	G	$2100	228	5,000	20,500	16,648

Livability Code: SB 30-90
Wheelbase-to-length ratio of 55% is considered ○ dangerous ○ fatiguing ● good ○ excellent *
The approximate net payload of 3852 pounds at 19% of GVWR on this model is ○ deficient ○ excessive ○ cautionary ○ good ● excellent *
Total highway safety penalties are: 2 * Value: 80 Durability: 77 Highway Control Rating: 95 Highway Safety: 93 ★★★

Note: Safety ratings are based on the assumption that the engineering of the RV has allowed for proper balance by placing fresh, gray, and black holding tanks in a location so as not to change the balance of the RV when the tanks are empty or full. **Always double-check wheelbase, GVWR, and weights at front and rear axles.**

*See Section 1 for details on how conclusions are reached.

Section 2: The Ratings

Brand	Year	Type	Length	Model	Chassis	Engine	Fuel Type	Average Price per Linear Foot When New	Adjusted Wheelbase	Approx. Towing Capacity	Gross Vehicle Weight Rating	Average Curb Weight
Vacationer	1999	MHA	35	35WGS	FO	6.8L	G	$2100	228	5,000	20,500	17,747

Livability Code: SB 30-90   Wheelbase-to-length ratio of 54% is considered ○ dangerous ○ fatiguing ◉ good ○ excellent *

The approximate net payload of 2753 pounds at 13% of GVWR on this model is ○ deficient ○ excessive ○ cautionary ◉ good ○ excellent *

Total highway safety penalties are: 12 *   Value: **7 5**   Durability: **7 7**   Highway Control Rating: **7 8**   Highway Safety: **6 6**   ★★

Brand	Year	Type	Length	Model	Chassis	Engine	Fuel	Avg Price/LF	Adj WB	Tow Cap	GVWR	Avg Curb Wt
Vacationer	1999	MHA	36	36SGS	FO	6.8L	G	$2100	228	5,000	20,500	18,030

Livability Code: SB 30-90   Wheelbase-to-length ratio of 53% is considered ○ dangerous ◉ fatiguing ○ good ○ excellent *

The approximate net payload of 2470 pounds at 12% of GVWR on this model is ○ deficient ○ excessive ○ cautionary ◉ good ○ excellent *

Total highway safety penalties are: 12 *   Value: **7 5**   Durability: **7 7**   Highway Control Rating: **6 7**   Highway Safety: **5 5**   ★

Vacationer	1999	MHA	36	36WGS	FO	6.8L	G	$2100	228	5,000	20,500	18,030

Livability Code: SB 30-90   Wheelbase-to-length ratio of 53% is considered ○ dangerous ◉ fatiguing ○ good ○ excellent *

The approximate net payload of 2470 pounds at 12% of GVWR on this model is ○ deficient ○ excessive ○ cautionary ◉ good ○ excellent *

Total highway safety penalties are: 12 *   Value: **7 5**   Durability: **7 7**   Highway Control Rating: **6 7**   Highway Safety: **5 5**   ★

Vectra	1993	MHA	34	33RQ	CH	7.4L	G	$2000	228	5,000	16,000	14,335

Livability Code: SB 30-90   Wheelbase-to-length ratio of 56% is considered ○ dangerous ○ fatiguing ◉ good ○ excellent *

The approximate net payload of 1665 pounds at 10% of GVWR on this model is ○ deficient ○ excessive ○ cautionary ◉ good ○ excellent *

Total highway safety penalties are: 6 *   Value: **8 3**   Durability: **7 9**   Highway Control Rating: **8 6**   Highway Safety: **8 0**   ★★★

Vectra	1993	MHA	36	35 RQ-P	SP	CU230	D	$2800	228	5,000	20,000	16,802

Livability Code: SB 30-90   Wheelbase-to-length ratio of 54% is considered ○ dangerous ○ fatiguing ◉ good ○ excellent *

The approximate net payload of 3198 pounds at 16% of GVWR on this model is ○ deficient ○ excessive ○ cautionary ○ good ◉ excellent *

Total highway safety penalties are: 2 *   Value: **8 6**   Durability: **7 9**   Highway Control Rating: **8 0**   Highway Safety: **7 8**   ★★★

Vectra	1993	MHA	37	37RW	FO	7.5L	G	$2100	252 T	7,000	18,000	16,090

Livability Code: SB 30-90   Wheelbase-to-length ratio of 57% is considered ○ dangerous ○ fatiguing ◉ good ○ excellent *

The approximate net payload of 1910 pounds at 11% of GVWR on this model is ○ deficient ○ excessive ○ cautionary ◉ good ○ excellent *

Total highway safety penalties are: 4 *   Value: **8 4**   Durability: **7 9**   Highway Control Rating: **8 8**   Highway Safety: **8 4**   ★★★

Vectra	1994	MHA	32	31RQ	CH	7.4L	G	$2400	208	5,000	16,000	13,817

Livability Code: SB 30-90   Wheelbase-to-length ratio of 55% is considered ○ dangerous ○ fatiguing ◉ good ○ excellent *

The approximate net payload of 2183 pounds at 14% of GVWR on this model is ○ deficient ○ excessive ○ cautionary ◉ good ○ excellent *

Total highway safety penalties are: 5 *   Value: **8 4**   Durability: **7 9**   Highway Control Rating: **8 7**   Highway Safety: **8 2**   ★★★

Vectra	1994	MHA	34	33RQ	CH	7.4L	G	$2300	228	5,000	16,000	14,335

Livability Code: SB 30-90   Wheelbase-to-length ratio of 56% is considered ○ dangerous ○ fatiguing ◉ good ○ excellent *

The approximate net payload of 1665 pounds at 10% of GVWR on this model is ○ deficient ○ excessive ○ cautionary ◉ good ○ excellent *

Total highway safety penalties are: 6 *   Value: **8 3**   Durability: **7 9**   Highway Control Rating: **8 6**   Highway Safety: **8 0**   ★★★

Vectra	1994	MHA	34	33RQ	FO	7.5L	G	$2300	228	8,000	17,000	14,835

Livability Code: SB 30-90   Wheelbase-to-length ratio of 56% is considered ○ dangerous ○ fatiguing ◉ good ○ excellent *

The approximate net payload of 2165 pounds at 13% of GVWR on this model is ○ deficient ○ excessive ○ cautionary ◉ good ○ excellent *

Total highway safety penalties are: 2 *   Value: **8 6**   Durability: **7 9**   Highway Control Rating: **9 1**   Highway Safety: **8 9**   ★★★

Vectra	1994	MHA	36	35RQ-P	SP	CU230	D	$3100	228	5,000	20,000	16,802

Livability Code: SB 30-90   Wheelbase-to-length ratio of 54% is considered ○ dangerous ○ fatiguing ◉ good ○ excellent *

The approximate net payload of 3198 pounds at 16% of GVWR on this model is ○ deficient ○ excessive ○ cautionary ○ good ◉ excellent *

Total highway safety penalties are: 2 *   Value: **8 6**   Durability: **7 9**   Highway Control Rating: **8 0**   Highway Safety: **7 8**   ★★★

Vectra	1994	MHA	37	37RW	FO	7.5L	G	$2400	252 T	6,000	19,000	16,390

Livability Code: SB 30-90   Wheelbase-to-length ratio of 57% is considered ○ dangerous ○ fatiguing ◉ good ○ excellent *

The approximate net payload of 2610 pounds at 14% of GVWR on this model is ○ deficient ○ excessive ○ cautionary ◉ good ○ excellent *

Total highway safety penalties are: 4 *   Value: **8 4**   Durability: **7 9**   Highway Control Rating: **9 5**   Highway Safety: **9 1**   ★★★

Vectra	1995	MHA	32	31RQ	FO	7.5L	G	$2500	208	8,000	17,000	14,317

Livability Code: SB 30-90   Wheelbase-to-length ratio of 55% is considered ○ dangerous ○ fatiguing ◉ good ○ excellent *

The approximate net payload of 2683 pounds at 16% of GVWR on this model is ○ deficient ○ excessive ○ cautionary ○ good ◉ excellent *

Total highway safety penalties are: 2 *   Value: **8 6**   Durability: **7 9**   Highway Control Rating: **9 1**   Highway Safety: **8 9**   ★★★

Note: Safety ratings are based on the assumption that the engineering of the RV has allowed for proper balance by placing fresh, gray, and black holding tanks in a location so as not to change the balance of the RV when the tanks are empty or full. **Always double-check wheelbase, GVWR, and weights at front and rear axles.**

*See Section 1 for details on how conclusions are reached.

Section 2: The Ratings

Brand	Year	Type	Length	Model	Chassis	Engine	Fuel Type	Average Price per Linear Foot When New	Adjusted Wheel-base	Approx. Towing Capacity	Gross Vehicle Weight Rating	Average Curb Weight
Vectra	1995	MHA	32	31RQ	CH	7.4L	G	$2500	208	5,000	16,000	13,894

Livability Code: SB 30-90
Wheelbase-to-length ratio of 54% is considered ○ dangerous ○ fatiguing ◉ good ○ excellent *
The approximate net payload of 2106 pounds at 13% of GVWR on this model is ○ deficient ○ excessive ○ cautionary ◉ good ○ excellent *
Total highway safety penalties are: 6 * Value: 8 4 Durability: 7 9 Highway Control Rating: 7 9 Highway Safety: 7 3 ★★★

Brand	Year	Type	Length	Model	Chassis	Engine	Fuel	Price	Wheelbase	Towing	GVWR	Curb
Vectra	1995	MHA	34	33RQ	CH	7.4L	G	$2400	228	5,000	16,000	14,335

Livability Code: SB 30-90
Wheelbase-to-length ratio of 56% is considered ○ dangerous ○ fatiguing ◉ good ○ excellent *
The approximate net payload of 1665 pounds at 10% of GVWR on this model is ○ deficient ○ excessive ○ cautionary ◉ good ○ excellent *
Total highway safety penalties are: 6 * Value: 8 3 Durability: 7 9 Highway Control Rating: 8 6 Highway Safety: 8 0 ★★★

Vectra	1995	MHA	34	33RQ	FO	7.5L	G	$2400	228	8,000	17,000	14,835

Livability Code: SB 30-90
Wheelbase-to-length ratio of 56% is considered ○ dangerous ○ fatiguing ◉ good ○ excellent *
The approximate net payload of 2165 pounds at 13% of GVWR on this model is ○ deficient ○ excessive ○ cautionary ◉ good ○ excellent *
Total highway safety penalties are: 2 * Value: 8 6 Durability: 7 9 Highway Control Rating: 9 1 Highway Safety: 8 9 ★★★

Vectra	1995	MHA	35	34RA	FO	7.5L	G	$2400	228	8,000	17,000	15,120

Livability Code: SB 30-90
Wheelbase-to-length ratio of 55% is considered ○ dangerous ○ fatiguing ◉ good ○ excellent *
The approximate net payload of 1880 pounds at 11% of GVWR on this model is ○ deficient ○ excessive ○ cautionary ◉ good ○ excellent *
Total highway safety penalties are: 2 * Value: 8 6 Durability: 7 9 Highway Control Rating: 8 6 Highway Safety: 8 4 ★★★

Vectra	1995	MHA	35	34RA	CH	7.4L	G	$2400	228	5,000	16,000	14,646

Livability Code: SB 30-90
Wheelbase-to-length ratio of 54% is considered ○ dangerous ○ fatiguing ◉ good ○ excellent *
The approximate net payload of 1354 pounds at 8% of GVWR on this model is ○ deficient ○ excessive ◉ cautionary ○ good ○ excellent *
Total highway safety penalties are: 7 * Value: 8 3 Durability: 7 9 Highway Control Rating: 6 1 Highway Safety: 5 4 ★

Vectra	1995	MHA	36	35RQ-P	OS	CU230	D	$3300	228	3,500	21,500	18,102

Livability Code: SB 30-90
Wheelbase-to-length ratio of 54% is considered ○ dangerous ○ fatiguing ◉ good ○ excellent *
The approximate net payload of 3398 pounds at 16% of GVWR on this model is ○ deficient ○ excessive ○ cautionary ○ good ◉ excellent *
Total highway safety penalties are: 2 * Value: 8 6 Durability: 7 9 Highway Control Rating: 8 0 Highway Safety: 7 8 ★★★

Vectra	1995	MHA	36	35RQ-P opch	SP	CU230	D	$3300	228	3,500	21,500	18,102

Livability Code: SB 30-90
Wheelbase-to-length ratio of 54% is considered ○ dangerous ○ fatiguing ◉ good ○ excellent *
The approximate net payload of 3398 pounds at 16% of GVWR on this model is ○ deficient ○ excessive ○ cautionary ○ good ◉ excellent *
Total highway safety penalties are: 2 * Value: 8 6 Durability: 7 9 Highway Control Rating: 8 0 Highway Safety: 7 8 ★★★

Vectra	1995	MHA	37	37RW	CH	7.4L	G	$2500	252 T	3,000	18,000	16,090

Livability Code: SB 30-90
Wheelbase-to-length ratio of 57% is considered ○ dangerous ○ fatiguing ◉ good ○ excellent *
The approximate net payload of 1910 pounds at 11% of GVWR on this model is ○ deficient ○ excessive ○ cautionary ◉ good ○ excellent *
Total highway safety penalties are: 10 * Value: 8 1 Durability: 7 9 Highway Control Rating: 8 8 Highway Safety: 7 8 ★★★

Vectra	1995	MHA	37	37RW	FO	7.5L	G	$2500	252 T	6,000	19,000	16,390

Livability Code: SB 30-90
Wheelbase-to-length ratio of 57% is considered ○ dangerous ○ fatiguing ◉ good ○ excellent *
The approximate net payload of 2610 pounds at 14% of GVWR on this model is ○ deficient ○ excessive ○ cautionary ◉ good ○ excellent *
Total highway safety penalties are: 4 * Value: 8 4 Durability: 7 9 Highway Control Rating: 9 5 Highway Safety: 9 1 ★★★

Vectra	1996	MHA	32	31RQ	CH	7.4L	G	$2300	208	4,500	16,500	13,917

Livability Code: SB 30-90
Wheelbase-to-length ratio of 55% is considered ○ dangerous ○ fatiguing ◉ good ○ excellent *
The approximate net payload of 2583 pounds at 16% of GVWR on this model is ○ deficient ○ excessive ○ cautionary ○ good ◉ excellent *
Total highway safety penalties are: 5 * Value: 8 4 Durability: 7 9 Highway Control Rating: 9 1 Highway Safety: 8 6 ★★★

Vectra	1996	MHA	32	31RQ	FO	7.5L	G	$2300	208	8,000	17,000	14,317

Livability Code: SB 30-90
Wheelbase-to-length ratio of 55% is considered ○ dangerous ○ fatiguing ◉ good ○ excellent *
The approximate net payload of 2683 pounds at 16% of GVWR on this model is ○ deficient ○ excessive ○ cautionary ○ good ◉ excellent *
Total highway safety penalties are: 2 * Value: 8 6 Durability: 7 9 Highway Control Rating: 9 1 Highway Safety: 8 9 ★★★

Vectra	1996	MHA	34	33RQ	CH	7.4L	G	$2300	228	4,500	16,500	14,435

Livability Code: SB 30-90
Wheelbase-to-length ratio of 56% is considered ○ dangerous ○ fatiguing ◉ good ○ excellent *
The approximate net payload of 2065 pounds at 13% of GVWR on this model is ○ deficient ○ excessive ○ cautionary ◉ good ○ excellent *
Total highway safety penalties are: 6 * Value: 8 3 Durability: 7 9 Highway Control Rating: 9 1 Highway Safety: 8 5 ★★★

Note: Safety ratings are based on the assumption that the engineering of the RV has allowed for proper balance by placing fresh, gray, and black holding tanks in a location so as not to change the balance of the RV when the tanks are empty or full. **Always double-check wheelbase, GVWR, and weights at front and rear axles.**

*See Section 1 for details on how conclusions are reached.

Brand	Year	Type	Length	Model	Chassis	Engine	Fuel Type	Average Price per Linear Foot When New	Adjusted Wheelbase	Approx. Towing Capacity	Gross Vehicle Weight Rating	Average Curb Weight
Vectra	1996	MHA	34	34RQ	CH	7.4L	G	$2500	228	4,500	16,500	15,410

Livability Code: SB 30-90
Wheelbase-to-length ratio of 56% is considered ○ dangerous ○ fatiguing ● good ○ excellent *
The approximate net payload of 1090 pounds at 7% of GVWR on this model is ● deficient ○ excessive ● cautionary ○ good ○ excellent *
Total highway safety penalties are: 12 *   Value: 8 1   Durability: 7 9   Highway Control Rating: 6 8   Highway Safety: 5 6   ★

Brand	Year	Type	Length	Model	Chassis	Engine	Fuel Type	Price/Ft	Wheelbase	Towing	GVWR	Curb Wt
Vectra	1996	MHA	34	33RQ	FO	7.5L	G	$2300	228	8,000	17,000	14,835

Livability Code: SB 30-90
Wheelbase-to-length ratio of 56% is considered ○ dangerous ○ fatiguing ● good ○ excellent *
The approximate net payload of 2165 pounds at 13% of GVWR on this model is ○ deficient ○ excessive ○ cautionary ● good ○ excellent *
Total highway safety penalties are: 2 *   Value: 8 6   Durability: 7 9   Highway Control Rating: 9 1   Highway Safety: 8 9   ★★★

Brand	Year	Type	Length	Model	Chassis	Engine	Fuel Type	Price/Ft	Wheelbase	Towing	GVWR	Curb Wt
Vectra	1996	MHA	34	34RQ-P sl	FR	CU230	D	$3400	228	4,300	20,700	18,610

Livability Code: SB 30-90
Wheelbase-to-length ratio of 56% is considered ○ dangerous ○ fatiguing ● good ○ excellent *
The approximate net payload of 2090 pounds at 10% of GVWR on this model is ○ deficient ○ excessive ○ cautionary ● good ○ excellent *
Total highway safety penalties are: 8 *   Value: 8 3   Durability: 7 9   Highway Control Rating: 8 6   Highway Safety: 7 8   ★★★

Brand	Year	Type	Length	Model	Chassis	Engine	Fuel Type	Price/Ft	Wheelbase	Towing	GVWR	Curb Wt
Vectra	1996	MHA	35	34RA	CH	7.4L	G	$2400	228	4,500	16,500	14,746

Livability Code: SB 30-90
Wheelbase-to-length ratio of 54% is considered ○ dangerous ○ fatiguing ● good ○ excellent *
The approximate net payload of 1754 pounds at 11% of GVWR on this model is ○ deficient ○ excessive ○ cautionary ● good ○ excellent *
Total highway safety penalties are: 7 *   Value: 8 3   Durability: 7 9   Highway Control Rating: 7 8   Highway Safety: 7 1   ★★★

Brand	Year	Type	Length	Model	Chassis	Engine	Fuel Type	Price/Ft	Wheelbase	Towing	GVWR	Curb Wt
Vectra	1996	MHA	35	34RA	FO	7.5L	G	$2400	228	8,000	17,000	15,146

Livability Code: SB 30-90
Wheelbase-to-length ratio of 54% is considered ○ dangerous ○ fatiguing ● good ○ excellent *
The approximate net payload of 1854 pounds at 11% of GVWR on this model is ○ deficient ○ excessive ○ cautionary ● good ○ excellent *
Total highway safety penalties are: 2 *   Value: 8 6   Durability: 7 9   Highway Control Rating: 7 8   Highway Safety: 7 6   ★★★

Brand	Year	Type	Length	Model	Chassis	Engine	Fuel Type	Price/Ft	Wheelbase	Towing	GVWR	Curb Wt
Vectra	1996	MHA	36	35RQ-P	FR	CU230	D	$3100	228	3,500	21,500	18,102

Livability Code: SB 30-90
Wheelbase-to-length ratio of 54% is considered ○ dangerous ○ fatiguing ● good ○ excellent *
The approximate net payload of 3398 pounds at 16% of GVWR on this model is ○ deficient ○ excessive ○ cautionary ○ good ● excellent *
Total highway safety penalties are: 2 *   Value: 8 6   Durability: 7 9   Highway Control Rating: 8 0   Highway Safety: 7 8   ★★★

Brand	Year	Type	Length	Model	Chassis	Engine	Fuel Type	Price/Ft	Wheelbase	Towing	GVWR	Curb Wt
Vectra	1996	MHA	36	35RQ-P opch	SP	CU230	D	$3100	228	2,000	23,000	19,302

Livability Code: SB 30-90
Wheelbase-to-length ratio of 54% is considered ○ dangerous ○ fatiguing ● good ○ excellent *
The approximate net payload of 3698 pounds at 16% of GVWR on this model is ○ deficient ○ excessive ○ cautionary ○ good ● excellent *
Total highway safety penalties are: 2 *   Value: 8 6   Durability: 7 9   Highway Control Rating: 8 0   Highway Safety: 7 8   ★★★

Brand	Year	Type	Length	Model	Chassis	Engine	Fuel Type	Price/Ft	Wheelbase	Towing	GVWR	Curb Wt
Vectra	1996	MHA	37	37RW	CH	7.4L	G	$2500	252 T	3,000	18,000	16,090

Livability Code: SB 30-90
Wheelbase-to-length ratio of 57% is considered ○ dangerous ○ fatiguing ● good ○ excellent *
The approximate net payload of 1910 pounds at 11% of GVWR on this model is ○ deficient ○ excessive ○ cautionary ● good ○ excellent *
Total highway safety penalties are: 10 *   Value: 8 1   Durability: 7 9   Highway Control Rating: 8 8   Highway Safety: 7 8   ★★★

Brand	Year	Type	Length	Model	Chassis	Engine	Fuel Type	Price/Ft	Wheelbase	Towing	GVWR	Curb Wt
Vectra	1996	MHA	37	37RW	FO	7.5L	G	$2500	252 T	6,000	19,000	16,390

Livability Code: SB 30-90
Wheelbase-to-length ratio of 57% is considered ○ dangerous ○ fatiguing ● good ○ excellent *
The approximate net payload of 2610 pounds at 14% of GVWR on this model is ○ deficient ○ excessive ○ cautionary ● good ○ excellent *
Total highway safety penalties are: 4 *   Value: 8 4   Durability: 7 9   Highway Control Rating: 9 5   Highway Safety: 9 1   ★★★

Brand	Year	Type	Length	Model	Chassis	Engine	Fuel Type	Price/Ft	Wheelbase	Towing	GVWR	Curb Wt
Vectra	1997	MHA	32	31RQ	CH	7.4L	G	$2500	208	3,500	16,500	14,469

Livability Code: SB 30-90
Wheelbase-to-length ratio of 55% is considered ○ dangerous ○ fatiguing ● good ○ excellent *
The approximate net payload of 2031 pounds at 12% of GVWR on this model is ○ deficient ○ excessive ○ cautionary ● good ○ excellent *
Total highway safety penalties are: 5 *   Value: 8 4   Durability: 7 9   Highway Control Rating: 8 8   Highway Safety: 8 3   ★★★

Brand	Year	Type	Length	Model	Chassis	Engine	Fuel Type	Price/Ft	Wheelbase	Towing	GVWR	Curb Wt
Vectra	1997	MHA	32	31RQ	FO	7.5L	G	$2500	208	8,000	17,000	15,043

Livability Code: SB 30-90
Wheelbase-to-length ratio of 55% is considered ○ dangerous ○ fatiguing ● good ○ excellent *
The approximate net payload of 1957 pounds at 12% of GVWR on this model is ○ deficient ○ excessive ○ cautionary ● good ○ excellent *
Total highway safety penalties are: 2 *   Value: 8 6   Durability: 7 9   Highway Control Rating: 8 7   Highway Safety: 8 5   ★★★

Brand	Year	Type	Length	Model	Chassis	Engine	Fuel Type	Price/Ft	Wheelbase	Towing	GVWR	Curb Wt
Vectra	1997	MHA	34	34RQ	CH	7.4L	G	$2600	228	3,000	16,500	15,492

Livability Code: SB 30-90
Wheelbase-to-length ratio of 56% is considered ○ dangerous ○ fatiguing ● good ○ excellent *
The approximate net payload of 1008 pounds at 6% of GVWR on this model is ● deficient ○ excessive ○ cautionary ○ good ○ excellent *
Total highway safety penalties are: 12 *   Value: 8 1   Durability: 7 9   Highway Control Rating: 6 3   Highway Safety: 5 1   ★

Note: Safety ratings are based on the assumption that the engineering of the RV has allowed for proper balance by placing fresh, gray, and black holding tanks in a location so as not to change the balance of the RV when the tanks are empty or full. **Always double-check wheelbase, GVWR, and weights at front and rear axles.**

*See Section 1 for details on how conclusions are reached.

Brand	Year	Type	Length	Model	Chassis	Engine	Fuel Type	Average Price per Linear Foot When New	Adjusted Wheel-base	Approx. Towing Capacity	Gross Vehicle Weight Rating	Average Curb Weight

Vectra — 1997 — MHA — 34 — 34RQ-P — FR — CU230 — D — $3600 — 228 — 5,000 — 20,700 — 18,968
Livability Code: SB 30-90
Wheelbase-to-length ratio of 56% is considered ○ dangerous ○ fatiguing ◉ good ○ excellent *
The approximate net payload of 1732 pounds at 8% of GVWR on this model is ○ deficient ○ excessive ◉ cautionary ○ good ○ excellent *
Total highway safety penalties are: 8 *   Value: 8 3   Durability: 7 9   Highway Control Rating: 7 5   Highway Safety: 6 7   ★★

Vectra Grand Tour — 1996 — MHA — 35 — 34WQ — CH — 7.4L — G — $2400 — 228 — 4,500 — 16,500 — 15,284
Livability Code: SB 30-90
Wheelbase-to-length ratio of 55% is considered ○ dangerous ○ fatiguing ◉ good ○ excellent *
The approximate net payload of 1216 pounds at 7% of GVWR on this model is ○ deficient ○ excessive ◉ cautionary ○ good ○ excellent *
Total highway safety penalties are: 7 *   Value: 8 3   Durability: 7 9   Highway Control Rating: 6 3   Highway Safety: 5 6   ★

Vectra Grand Tour — 1996 — MHA — 35 — 34WQ — FO — 7.5L — G — $2400 — 228 — 8,000 — 17,000 — 15,684
Livability Code: SB 30-90
Wheelbase-to-length ratio of 55% is considered ○ dangerous ○ fatiguing ◉ good ○ excellent *
The approximate net payload of 1316 pounds at 8% of GVWR on this model is ○ deficient ○ excessive ◉ cautionary ○ good ○ excellent *
Total highway safety penalties are: 2 *   Value: 8 6   Durability: 7 9   Highway Control Rating: 6 8   Highway Safety: 6 6   ★★

Vectra Grand Tour — 1996 — MHA — 36 — 35WQ-P — FR — CU230 — D — $3400 — 228 — 2,000 — 23,000 — 19,487
Livability Code: SB 30-90
Wheelbase-to-length ratio of 53% is considered ○ dangerous ◉ fatiguing ○ good ○ excellent *
The approximate net payload of 3513 pounds at 15% of GVWR on this model is ○ deficient ○ excessive ○ cautionary ◉ good ○ excellent *
Total highway safety penalties are: 2 *   Value: 8 6   Durability: 7 9   Highway Control Rating: 6 8   Highway Safety: 6 6   ★★

Vectra Grand Tour — 1996 — MHA — 37 — 36WA — CH — 7.4L — G — $2400 — 252 T — 3,000 — 18,000 — 16,635
Livability Code: SB 30-90
Wheelbase-to-length ratio of 57% is considered ○ dangerous ○ fatiguing ◉ good ○ excellent *
The approximate net payload of 1365 pounds at 8% of GVWR on this model is ○ deficient ○ excessive ◉ cautionary ○ good ○ excellent *
Total highway safety penalties are: 10 *   Value: 8 1   Durability: 7 9   Highway Control Rating: 7 7   Highway Safety: 6 7   ★★

Vectra Grand Tour — 1996 — MHA — 37 — 36WA — FO — 7.5L — G — $2400 — 252 T — 5,000 — 20,000 — 17,135
Livability Code: SB 30-90
Wheelbase-to-length ratio of 57% is considered ○ dangerous ○ fatiguing ◉ good ○ excellent *
The approximate net payload of 2865 pounds at 14% of GVWR on this model is ○ deficient ○ excessive ○ cautionary ◉ good ○ excellent *
Total highway safety penalties are: 4 *   Value: 8 4   Durability: 7 9   Highway Control Rating: 9 6   Highway Safety: 9 2   ★★★

Vectra Grand Tour — 1997 — MHA — 35 — 34WQ — CH — 7.4L — G — $2500 — 228 — 3,500 — 16,500 — 15,133
Livability Code: SB 30-90
Wheelbase-to-length ratio of 55% is considered ○ dangerous ○ fatiguing ◉ good ○ excellent *
The approximate net payload of 1367 pounds at 8% of GVWR on this model is ○ deficient ○ excessive ◉ cautionary ○ good ○ excellent *
Total highway safety penalties are: 7 *   Value: 8 3   Durability: 7 9   Highway Control Rating: 6 8   Highway Safety: 6 1   ★★

Vectra Grand Tour — 1997 — MHA — 35 — 34WQ — FO — 7.5L — G — $2500 — 228 — 8,000 — 17,000 — 15,489
Livability Code: SB 30-90
Wheelbase-to-length ratio of 55% is considered ○ dangerous ○ fatiguing ◉ good ○ excellent *
The approximate net payload of 1511 pounds at 9% of GVWR on this model is ○ deficient ○ excessive ◉ cautionary ○ good ○ excellent *
Total highway safety penalties are: 2 *   Value: 8 6   Durability: 7 9   Highway Control Rating: 7 4   Highway Safety: 7 2   ★★★

Vectra Grand Tour — 1997 — MHA — 36 — 35WQ-P — FR — Ca7.2L — D — $3700 — 228 — 5,000 — 24,850 — 20,055
Livability Code: SB 30-90
Wheelbase-to-length ratio of 53% is considered ○ dangerous ◉ fatiguing ○ good ○ excellent *
The approximate net payload of 4795 pounds at 19% of GVWR on this model is ○ deficient ○ excessive ○ cautionary ○ good ◉ excellent *
Total highway safety penalties are: 2 *   Value: 8 6   Durability: 7 9   Highway Control Rating: 7 3   Highway Safety: 7 1   ★★★

Vectra Grand Tour — 1997 — MHA — 37 — 36WA — CH — 7.4L — G — $2600 — 252 T — 2,000 — 18,000 — 16,202
Livability Code: SB 30-90
Wheelbase-to-length ratio of 57% is considered ○ dangerous ○ fatiguing ◉ good ○ excellent *
The approximate net payload of 1798 pounds at 10% of GVWR on this model is ○ deficient ○ excessive ○ cautionary ◉ good ○ excellent *
Total highway safety penalties are: 10 *   Value: 8 1   Durability: 7 9   Highway Control Rating: 8 8   Highway Safety: 7 8   ★★★

Vectra Grand Tour — 1997 — MHA — 37 — 36WQ — CH — 7.4L — G — $2600 — 252 T — 500 — 19,500 — 16,822
Livability Code: SB 30-90
Wheelbase-to-length ratio of 57% is considered ○ dangerous ○ fatiguing ◉ good ○ excellent *
The approximate net payload of 2678 pounds at 14% of GVWR on this model is ○ deficient ○ excessive ○ cautionary ◉ good ○ excellent *
Total highway safety penalties are: 13 *   Value: 8 0   Durability: 7 9   Highway Control Rating: 9 6   Highway Safety: 8 3   ★★★

Vectra Grand Tour — 1997 — MHA — 37 — 36WA — FO — 7.5L — G — $2600 — 252 T — 5,000 — 20,000 — 16,813
Livability Code: SB 30-90
Wheelbase-to-length ratio of 57% is considered ○ dangerous ○ fatiguing ◉ good ○ excellent *
The approximate net payload of 3187 pounds at 16% of GVWR on this model is ○ deficient ○ excessive ○ cautionary ○ good ◉ excellent *
Total highway safety penalties are: 4 *   Value: 8 4   Durability: 7 9   Highway Control Rating: 1 0 0   Highway Safety: 9 6   ★★★

Note: Safety ratings are based on the assumption that the engineering of the RV has allowed for proper balance by placing fresh, gray, and black holding tanks in a location so as not to change the balance of the RV when the tanks are empty or full. **Always double-check wheelbase, GVWR, and weights at front and rear axles.**

*See Section 1 for details on how conclusions are reached.

Brand	Year	Type	Length	Model	Chassis	Engine	Fuel Type	Average Price per Linear Foot When New	Adjusted Wheel-base	Approx. Towing Capacity	Gross Vehicle Weight Rating	Average Curb Weight
Vectra Grand Tour	1997	MHA	37	36WQ	FO	7.5L	G	$2600	252 T	5,000	20,000	16,877

Livability Code: SB 30-90

Wheelbase-to-length ratio of 57% is considered ○ dangerous ○ fatiguing ◉ good ○ excellent *

The approximate net payload of 3123 pounds at 16% of GVWR on this model is ○ deficient ○ excessive ○ cautionary ○ good ◉ excellent *

Total highway safety penalties are: 4 *   Value: 8 4   Durability: 7 9   Highway Control Rating: 1 0 0   Highway Safety: 9 6   ★★★

Brand	Year	Type	Length	Model	Chassis	Engine	Fuel Type	Price/Lin Ft	Wheelbase	Towing	GVWR	Curb Weight
Vectra Grand Tour	1997	MHA	37	36WQ slide	FO	7.5L	G	$2700	252 T	5,000	20,000	17,735

Livability Code: SB 30-90

Wheelbase-to-length ratio of 57% is considered ○ dangerous ○ fatiguing ◉ good ○ excellent *

The approximate net payload of 2265 pounds at 11% of GVWR on this model is ○ deficient ○ excessive ○ cautionary ◉ good ○ excellent *

Total highway safety penalties are: 8 *   Value: 8 3   Durability: 7 9   Highway Control Rating: 9 0   Highway Safety: 8 2   ★★★

Vectra Grand Tour	1998	MHA	35	34WQ	CH	7.4L	G	$2600	228	4,500	16,500	15,324

Livability Code: SB 30-90

Wheelbase-to-length ratio of 55% is considered ○ dangerous ○ fatiguing ◉ good ○ excellent *

The approximate net payload of 1176 pounds at 7% of GVWR on this model is ○ deficient ○ excessive ◉ cautionary ○ good ○ excellent *

Total highway safety penalties are: 7 *   Value: 8 3   Durability: 7 9   Highway Control Rating: 6 2   Highway Safety: 5 5   ★

Vectra Grand Tour	1998	MHA	35	34WQ opch	FO	7.5L	G	$2500	228	8,000	17,000	15,616

Livability Code: SB 30-90

Wheelbase-to-length ratio of 55% is considered ○ dangerous ○ fatiguing ◉ good ○ excellent *

The approximate net payload of 1384 pounds at 8% of GVWR on this model is ○ deficient ○ excessive ◉ cautionary ○ good ○ excellent *

Total highway safety penalties are: 2 *   Value: 8 6   Durability: 7 9   Highway Control Rating: 6 8   Highway Safety: 6 6   ★★

Vectra Grand Tour	1998	MHA	36	35WQ-P	FR	CA300	D	$3700	228	5,000	26,350	20,433

Livability Code: SB 30-90

Wheelbase-to-length ratio of 53% is considered ○ dangerous ◉ fatiguing ○ good ○ excellent *

The approximate net payload of 5917 pounds at 22% of GVWR on this model is ○ deficient ○ excessive ○ cautionary ○ good ◉ excellent *

Total highway safety penalties are: 2 *   Value: 8 6   Durability: 7 9   Highway Control Rating: 7 2   Highway Safety: 7 0   ★★★

Vectra Grand Tour	1998	MHA	37	36WA	CH	7.4L	G	$2600	252 T	3,000	18,000	16,588

Livability Code: SB 30-90

Wheelbase-to-length ratio of 57% is considered ○ dangerous ○ fatiguing ◉ good ○ excellent *

The approximate net payload of 1412 pounds at 8% of GVWR on this model is ○ deficient ○ excessive ◉ cautionary ○ good ○ excellent *

Total highway safety penalties are: 10 *   Value: 8 1   Durability: 7 9   Highway Control Rating: 7 7   Highway Safety: 6 7   ★★

Vectra Grand Tour	1998	MHA	37	36WQ	FO	7.5L	G	$2600	252 T	5,000	20,000	17,018

Livability Code: SB 30-90

Wheelbase-to-length ratio of 57% is considered ○ dangerous ○ fatiguing ◉ good ○ excellent *

The approximate net payload of 2982 pounds at 15% of GVWR on this model is ○ deficient ○ excessive ○ cautionary ◉ good ○ excellent *

Total highway safety penalties are: 4 *   Value: 8 4   Durability: 7 9   Highway Control Rating: 9 8   Highway Safety: 9 4   ★★★

Vectra Grand Tour	1998	MHA	37	36WQ slide	FO	7.5L	G	$2800	252 T	5,000	20,000	17,608

Livability Code: SB 30-90

Wheelbase-to-length ratio of 57% is considered ○ dangerous ○ fatiguing ◉ good ○ excellent *

The approximate net payload of 2392 pounds at 12% of GVWR on this model is ○ deficient ○ excessive ○ cautionary ◉ good ○ excellent *

Total highway safety penalties are: 8 *   Value: 8 3   Durability: 7 9   Highway Control Rating: 9 2   Highway Safety: 8 4   ★★★

Vectra Grand Tour	1999	MHA	38	37B	CH	7.4L	G	$2600	252	3,500	22,500	20,302

Livability Code: SB 30-90

Wheelbase-to-length ratio of 55% is considered ○ dangerous ○ fatiguing ◉ good ○ excellent *

The approximate net payload of 2198 pounds at 10% of GVWR on this model is ○ deficient ○ excessive ○ cautionary ◉ good ○ excellent *

Total highway safety penalties are: 16 *   Value: 7 9   Durability: 7 9   Highway Control Rating: 8 1   Highway Safety: 6 5   ★★

Vectra Grand Tour	1999	MHA	40	39Y	CH	7.4L	G	$2500	272	3,500	22,500	20,629

Livability Code: SB 30-90

Wheelbase-to-length ratio of 57% is considered ○ dangerous ○ fatiguing ◉ good ○ excellent *

The approximate net payload of 1871 pounds at 8% of GVWR on this model is ○ deficient ○ excessive ◉ cautionary ○ good ○ excellent *

Total highway safety penalties are: 16 *   Value: 7 9   Durability: 7 9   Highway Control Rating: 7 8   Highway Safety: 6 2   ★★

Vision	1990	MHA	22	SB22	FO	7.5L	G	$1300	158	7,500	11,500	9,340

Livability Code: 30-80

Wheelbase-to-length ratio of 60% is considered ○ dangerous ○ fatiguing ○ good ◉ excellent *

The approximate net payload of 2160 pounds at 19% of GVWR on this model is ○ deficient ○ excessive ○ cautionary ○ good ◉ excellent *

Total highway safety penalties are: 2 *   Value: 8 5   Durability: 7 7   Highway Control Rating: 1 0 0   Highway Safety: 9 8   ★★★

Vision	1991	MHA	24	TB 24	FO	7.5L	G	$1500	158	7,500	11,500	9,284

Livability Code: SB 30-90

Wheelbase-to-length ratio of 54% is considered ○ dangerous ○ fatiguing ◉ good ○ excellent *

The approximate net payload of 2216 pounds at 19% of GVWR on this model is ○ deficient ○ excessive ○ cautionary ○ good ◉ excellent *

Total highway safety penalties are: 2 *   Value: 8 5   Durability: 7 7   Highway Control Rating: 8 5   Highway Safety: 8 3   ★★★

Note: Safety ratings are based on the assumption that the engineering of the RV has allowed for proper balance by placing fresh, gray, and black holding tanks in a location so as not to change the balance of the RV when the tanks are empty or full. **Always double-check wheelbase, GVWR, and weights at front and rear axles.**

*See Section 1 for details on how conclusions are reached.

Section 2: The Ratings

Brand	Year	Type	Length	Model	Chassis	Engine	Fuel Type	Average Price per Linear Foot When New	Adjusted Wheelbase	Approx. Towing Capacity	Gross Vehicle Weight Rating	Average Curb Weight
Vision	1997	MHA	24	V-23	CH	7.4L	G	$2000	158	1,500	14,800	11,569

Livability Code: SB 30-90 — Wheelbase-to-length ratio of 55% is considered ○ dangerous ○ fatiguing ◉ good ○ excellent *

The approximate net payload of 3231 pounds at 22% of GVWR on this model is ○ deficient ○ excessive ○ cautionary ○ good ◉ excellent *

Total highway safety penalties are: 1 * — Value: 8 4 Durability: 7 4 Highway Control Rating: 9 6 Highway Safety: 9 5 ★★★

Brand	Year	Type	Length	Model	Chassis	Engine	Fuel Type	Price/Ft	Wheelbase	Towing	GVWR	Curb Wt
Vision	1997	MHA	26	V-25	FO	7.5L	G	$1900	158	1,500	15,200	12,479

Livability Code: SB 30-90 — Wheelbase-to-length ratio of 51% is considered ○ dangerous ◉ fatiguing ○ good ○ excellent *

The approximate net payload of 2721 pounds at 18% of GVWR on this model is ○ deficient ○ excessive ○ cautionary ○ good ◉ excellent *

Total highway safety penalties are: 2 * — Value: 8 4 Durability: 7 4 Highway Control Rating: 5 0 Highway Safety: 4 8

Vision	1997	MHA	28	V-27	FO	7.5L	G	$1800	178	1,500	15,200	12,989

Livability Code: SB 30-90 — Wheelbase-to-length ratio of 53% is considered ○ dangerous ◉ fatiguing ○ good ○ excellent *

The approximate net payload of 2211 pounds at 15% of GVWR on this model is ○ deficient ○ excessive ○ cautionary ◉ good ○ excellent *

Total highway safety penalties are: 2 * — Value: 8 4 Durability: 7 4 Highway Control Rating: 6 9 Highway Safety: 6 7 ★★

Vision	1997	MHA	30	V-29	FO	7.5L	G	$1700	190	1,500	15,200	13,550

Livability Code: SB 30-90 — Wheelbase-to-length ratio of 53% is considered ○ dangerous ◉ fatiguing ○ good ○ excellent *

The approximate net payload of 1650 pounds at 11% of GVWR on this model is ○ deficient ○ excessive ○ cautionary ◉ good ○ excellent *

Total highway safety penalties are: 2 * — Value: 8 4 Durability: 7 4 Highway Control Rating: 6 0 Highway Safety: 5 8 ★

Vision	1998	MHA	24	V-23	CH	7.4L	G	$2300	158	1,500	14,800	11,569

Livability Code: SB 30-90 — Wheelbase-to-length ratio of 55% is considered ○ dangerous ○ fatiguing ◉ good ○ excellent *

The approximate net payload of 3231 pounds at 22% of GVWR on this model is ○ deficient ○ excessive ○ cautionary ○ good ◉ excellent *

Total highway safety penalties are: 1 * — Value: 8 5 Durability: 7 6 Highway Control Rating: 9 6 Highway Safety: 9 5 ★★★

Vision	1998	MHA	26	V-25	FO	7.5L	G	$2100	158	1,500	15,200	12,479

Livability Code: SB 30-90 — Wheelbase-to-length ratio of 51% is considered ○ dangerous ◉ fatiguing ○ good ○ excellent *

The approximate net payload of 2721 pounds at 18% of GVWR on this model is ○ deficient ○ excessive ○ cautionary ○ good ◉ excellent *

Total highway safety penalties are: 2 * — Value: 8 4 Durability: 7 6 Highway Control Rating: 5 0 Highway Safety: 4 8

Vision	1998	MHA	26	V-25 myc	FO	6.8L	G	$2100	158	1,500	15,500	13,079

Livability Code: SB 30-90 — Wheelbase-to-length ratio of 51% is considered ○ dangerous ◉ fatiguing ○ good ○ excellent *

The approximate net payload of 2421 pounds at 16% of GVWR on this model is ○ deficient ○ excessive ○ cautionary ○ good ◉ excellent *

Total highway safety penalties are: 2 * — Value: 8 4 Durability: 7 6 Highway Control Rating: 5 8 Highway Safety: 5 6 ★

Vision	1998	MHA	28	V-27	FO	7.5L	G	$2000	178	1,500	15,200	12,989

Livability Code: SB 30-90 — Wheelbase-to-length ratio of 53% is considered ○ dangerous ◉ fatiguing ○ good ○ excellent *

The approximate net payload of 2211 pounds at 15% of GVWR on this model is ○ deficient ○ excessive ○ cautionary ◉ good ○ excellent *

Total highway safety penalties are: 2 * — Value: 8 4 Durability: 7 6 Highway Control Rating: 6 9 Highway Safety: 6 7 ★★

Vision	1998	MHA	28	V-27 myc	FO	6.8L	G	$2000	178	1,500	15,500	13,589

Livability Code: SB 30-90 — Wheelbase-to-length ratio of 53% is considered ○ dangerous ◉ fatiguing ○ good ○ excellent *

The approximate net payload of 1911 pounds at 12% of GVWR on this model is ○ deficient ○ excessive ○ cautionary ◉ good ○ excellent *

Total highway safety penalties are: 2 * — Value: 8 4 Durability: 7 6 Highway Control Rating: 6 9 Highway Safety: 6 7 ★★

Vision	1998	MHA	30	V-29	FO	7.5L	G	$1800	190	1,500	15,200	13,550

Livability Code: SB 30-90 — Wheelbase-to-length ratio of 53% is considered ○ dangerous ◉ fatiguing ○ good ○ excellent *

The approximate net payload of 1650 pounds at 11% of GVWR on this model is ○ deficient ○ excessive ○ cautionary ◉ good ○ excellent *

Total highway safety penalties are: 2 * — Value: 8 4 Durability: 7 6 Highway Control Rating: 6 0 Highway Safety: 5 8 ★

Vision	1998	MHA	30	V-29 myc	FO	6.8L	G	$1800	190	1,500	15,500	14,150

Livability Code: SB 30-90 — Wheelbase-to-length ratio of 53% is considered ○ dangerous ◉ fatiguing ○ good ○ excellent *

The approximate net payload of 1350 pounds at 9% of GVWR on this model is ○ deficient ○ excessive ◉ cautionary ○ good ○ excellent *

Total highway safety penalties are: 2 * — Value: 8 4 Durability: 7 6 Highway Control Rating: 5 7 Highway Safety: 5 5 ★

Vision	1999	MHA	24	V-23	CH	7.4L	G	$2300	158	1,500	14,800	11,679

Livability Code: SB 30-90 — Wheelbase-to-length ratio of 55% is considered ○ dangerous ○ fatiguing ◉ good ○ excellent *

The approximate net payload of 3122 pounds at 21% of GVWR on this model is ○ deficient ○ excessive ○ cautionary ○ good ◉ excellent *

Total highway safety penalties are: 1 * — Value: 8 5 Durability: 7 7 Highway Control Rating: 9 7 Highway Safety: 9 6 ★★★

Note: Safety ratings are based on the assumption that the engineering of the RV has allowed for proper balance by placing fresh, gray, and black holding tanks in a location so as not to change the balance of the RV when the tanks are empty or full. **Always double-check wheelbase, GVWR, and weights at front and rear axles.**

*See Section 1 for details on how conclusions are reached.

Section 2: The Ratings

Brand	Year	Type	Length	Model	Chassis	Engine	Fuel Type	Average Price per Linear Foot When New	Adjusted Wheelbase	Approx. Towing Capacity	Gross Vehicle Weight Rating	Average Curb Weight
Vision	1999	MHA	26	V-25	FO	6.8L	G	$2100	158	10,300	15,700	13,104

Livability Code: SB 30-90
Wheelbase-to-length ratio of 51% is considered ○ dangerous ● fatiguing ○ good ○ excellent *
The approximate net payload of 2597 pounds at 17% of GVWR on this model is ○ deficient ○ excessive ○ cautionary ○ good ● excellent *
Total highway safety penalties are: 2 *   Value: 8 5   Durability: 7 7   Highway Control Rating: 5 9   Highway Safety: 5 7   ★

Brand	Year	Type	Length	Model	Chassis	Engine	Fuel Type	Price/ft	Wheelbase	Towing	GVWR	Curb Wt
Vision	1999	MHA	28	V-27	FO	6.8L	G	$2000	178	10,300	15,700	13,429

Livability Code: SB 30-90
Wheelbase-to-length ratio of 53% is considered ○ dangerous ● fatiguing ○ good ○ excellent *
The approximate net payload of 2272 pounds at 14% of GVWR on this model is ○ deficient ○ excessive ○ cautionary ● good ○ excellent *
Total highway safety penalties are: 2 *   Value: 8 5   Durability: 7 7   Highway Control Rating: 7 3   Highway Safety: 7 1   ★★★

Brand	Year	Type	Length	Model	Chassis	Engine	Fuel Type	Price/ft	Wheelbase	Towing	GVWR	Curb Wt
Vision	1999	MHA	30	V-29	CH	7.4L	G	$1800	190	4,500	16,500	13,119

Livability Code: SB 30-90
Wheelbase-to-length ratio of 53% is considered ○ dangerous ● fatiguing ○ good ○ excellent *
The approximate net payload of 3381 pounds at 20% of GVWR on this model is ○ deficient ○ excessive ○ cautionary ○ good ● excellent *
Total highway safety penalties are: 5 *   Value: 8 4   Durability: 7 7   Highway Control Rating: 7 8   Highway Safety: 7 3   ★★★

Brand	Year	Type	Length	Model	Chassis	Engine	Fuel Type	Price/ft	Wheelbase	Towing	GVWR	Curb Wt
Vision	1999	MHA	30	V-29	FO	6.8L	G	$1800	190	10,300	15,700	14,159

Livability Code: SB 30-90
Wheelbase-to-length ratio of 53% is considered ○ dangerous ● fatiguing ○ good ○ excellent *
The approximate net payload of 1541 pounds at 10% of GVWR on this model is ○ deficient ○ excessive ○ cautionary ● good ○ excellent *
Total highway safety penalties are: 2 *   Value: 8 5   Durability: 7 7   Highway Control Rating: 6 2   Highway Safety: 6 0   ★★

Brand	Year	Type	Length	Model	Chassis	Engine	Fuel Type	Price/ft	Wheelbase	Towing	GVWR	Curb Wt
Vision	1999	MHA	34	V-34	FO	6.8L	G	$1600	228	8,000	18,000	15,149

Livability Code: SB 30-90
Wheelbase-to-length ratio of 56% is considered ○ dangerous ○ fatiguing ● good ○ excellent *
The approximate net payload of 2851 pounds at 16% of GVWR on this model is ○ deficient ○ excessive ○ cautionary ○ good ● excellent *
Total highway safety penalties are: 2 *   Value: 8 5   Durability: 7 7   Highway Control Rating: 9 6   Highway Safety: 9 4   ★★★

Brand	Year	Type	Length	Model	Chassis	Engine	Fuel Type	Price/ft	Wheelbase	Towing	GVWR	Curb Wt
Vogue	1997	MHA	38	Vogue 38	VO	Ca350	D	$9600	250	1,500	34,000	29,436

Livability Code: FT 30-90
Wheelbase-to-length ratio of 55% is considered ○ dangerous ○ fatiguing ● good ○ excellent *
The approximate net payload of 4564 pounds at 13% of GVWR on this model is ○ deficient ○ excessive ○ cautionary ● good ○ excellent *
Total highway safety penalties are: 2 *   Value: 8 6   Durability: 8 0   Highway Control Rating: 8 6   Highway Safety: 8 4   ★★★★

Brand	Year	Type	Length	Model	Chassis	Engine	Fuel Type	Price/ft	Wheelbase	Towing	GVWR	Curb Wt
Vogue	1997	MHA	40	Prevost 40	PR	12.7L	D	$13800	280	1,500	45,000	35,556

Livability Code: FT 30-90
Wheelbase-to-length ratio of 58% is considered ○ dangerous ○ fatiguing ○ good ● excellent *
The approximate net payload of 9444 pounds at 21% of GVWR on this model is ○ deficient ○ excessive ○ cautionary ○ good ● excellent *
Total highway safety penalties are: 2 *   Value: 8 6   Durability: 8 0   Highway Control Rating: 1 0 0   Highway Safety: 9 8   ★★★★

Brand	Year	Type	Length	Model	Chassis	Engine	Fuel Type	Price/ft	Wheelbase	Towing	GVWR	Curb Wt
Vogue	1997	MHA	40	Vogue 40	VO	Ca350	D	$9500	274	1,500	34,000	30,089

Livability Code: FT 30-90
Wheelbase-to-length ratio of 57% is considered ○ dangerous ○ fatiguing ● good ○ excellent *
The approximate net payload of 3911 pounds at 12% of GVWR on this model is ○ deficient ○ excessive ○ cautionary ● good ○ excellent *
Total highway safety penalties are: 2 *   Value: 8 6   Durability: 8 0   Highway Control Rating: 9 1   Highway Safety: 8 9   ★★★★

Brand	Year	Type	Length	Model	Chassis	Engine	Fuel Type	Price/ft	Wheelbase	Towing	GVWR	Curb Wt
Vogue	1997	MHA	45	Prevost 45	PR	12.7L	D	$14400	315	1,500	45,000	37,188

Livability Code: FT 30-90
Wheelbase-to-length ratio of 58% is considered ○ dangerous ● fatiguing ○ good ○ excellent *
The approximate net payload of 7812 pounds at 17% of GVWR on this model is ○ deficient ○ excessive ○ cautionary ○ good ● excellent *
Total highway safety penalties are: 2 *   Value: 8 6   Durability: 8 0   Highway Control Rating: 1 0 0   Highway Safety: 9 8   ★★★★

Brand	Year	Type	Length	Model	Chassis	Engine	Fuel Type	Price/ft	Wheelbase	Towing	GVWR	Curb Wt
Vogue	1998	MHA	38	Vogue 38	VO	CA305	D	$10000	250	1,500	34,350	29,611

Livability Code: FT 30-90
Wheelbase-to-length ratio of 55% is considered ○ dangerous ○ fatiguing ● good ○ excellent *
The approximate net payload of 4739 pounds at 14% of GVWR on this model is ○ deficient ○ excessive ○ cautionary ● good ○ excellent *
Total highway safety penalties are: 2 *   Value: 8 6   Durability: 8 0   Highway Control Rating: 8 7   Highway Safety: 8 5   ★★★★

Brand	Year	Type	Length	Model	Chassis	Engine	Fuel Type	Price/ft	Wheelbase	Towing	GVWR	Curb Wt
Vogue	1998	MHA	40	Prevost 40	PR	12.7L	D	$9500	304 T	1,500	47,000	36,556

Livability Code: FT 30-90
Wheelbase-to-length ratio of 63% is considered ○ dangerous ○ fatiguing ○ good ● excellent *
The approximate net payload of 10444 pounds at 22% of GVWR on this model is ○ deficient ○ excessive ○ cautionary ○ good ● excellent *
Total highway safety penalties are: 4 *   Value: 8 5   Durability: 8 0   Highway Control Rating: 1 0 0   Highway Safety: 9 6   ★★★★

Brand	Year	Type	Length	Model	Chassis	Engine	Fuel Type	Price/ft	Wheelbase	Towing	GVWR	Curb Wt
Vogue	1998	MHA	40	Vogue 40	VO	CA305	D	$9500	274	1,500	34,350	30,264

Livability Code: FT 30-90
Wheelbase-to-length ratio of 57% is considered ○ dangerous ○ fatiguing ● good ○ excellent *
The approximate net payload of 4086 pounds at 12% of GVWR on this model is ○ deficient ○ excessive ○ cautionary ● good ○ excellent *
Total highway safety penalties are: 2 *   Value: 8 6   Durability: 8 0   Highway Control Rating: 9 1   Highway Safety: 8 9   ★★★★

Note: Safety ratings are based on the assumption that the engineering of the RV has allowed for proper balance by placing fresh, gray, and black holding tanks in a location so as not to change the balance of the RV when the tanks are empty or full. **Always double-check wheelbase, GVWR, and weights at front and rear axles.**

*See Section 1 for details on how conclusions are reached.

Brand	Year	Type	Length	Model	Chassis	Engine	Fuel Type	Average Price per Linear Foot When New	Adjusted Wheelbase	Approx. Towing Capacity	Gross Vehicle Weight Rating	Average Curb Weight
Vogue	1998	MHA	44	Vogue 45	VO	CA500	D	$8600	311 T	1,500	46,000	37,460

Livability Code: FT 30-90
Wheelbase-to-length ratio of 59% is considered ○ dangerous ○ fatiguing ○ good ◉ excellent *
The approximate net payload of 8540 pounds at 19% of GVWR on this model is ○ deficient ○ excessive ○ cautionary ○ good ◉ excellent *
Total highway safety penalties are: 4 *   Value: 85   Durability: 80   Highway Control Rating: 100   Highway Safety: 96   ★★★★

Brand	Year	Type	Length	Model	Chassis	Engine	Fuel Type	Avg	Adjusted Wheelbase	Towing	GVWR	Curb
Vogue	1998	MHA	45	Prevost 45	PR	12.7L	D	$8400	339 T	1,500	47,000	38,188

Livability Code: FT 30-90
Wheelbase-to-length ratio of 63% is considered ○ dangerous ○ fatiguing ○ good ◉ excellent *
The approximate net payload of 8812 pounds at 19% of GVWR on this model is ○ deficient ○ excessive ○ cautionary ○ good ◉ excellent *
Total highway safety penalties are: 4 *   Value: 85   Durability: 80   Highway Control Rating: 100   Highway Safety: 96   ★★★★

Brand	Year	Type	Length	Model	Chassis	Engine	Fuel Type	Avg	Adjusted Wheelbase	Towing	GVWR	Curb
Vogue	1999	MHA	39	5000/38	VO	CA455	D	$9700	274	1,500	34,000	29,730

Livability Code: FT 30-90
Wheelbase-to-length ratio of 59% is considered ○ dangerous ○ fatiguing ○ good ◉ excellent *
The approximate net payload of 4270 pounds at 13% of GVWR on this model is ○ deficient ○ excessive ○ cautionary ◉ good ○ excellent *
Total highway safety penalties are: 4 *   Value: 85   Durability: 80   Highway Control Rating: 99   Highway Safety: 95   ★★★★

Brand	Year	Type	Length	Model	Chassis	Engine	Fuel Type	Avg	Adjusted Wheelbase	Towing	GVWR	Curb
Vogue	1999	MHA	39	5000/38 opsl	VO	CA455	D	$9700	274	1,500	34,000	30,780

Livability Code: FT 30-90
Wheelbase-to-length ratio of 59% is considered ○ dangerous ○ fatiguing ○ good ◉ excellent *
The approximate net payload of 3220 pounds at 9% of GVWR on this model is ○ deficient ○ excessive ◉ cautionary ○ good ○ excellent *
Total highway safety penalties are: 16 *   Value: 79   Durability: 80   Highway Control Rating: 89   Highway Safety: 73   ★★★

Brand	Year	Type	Length	Model	Chassis	Engine	Fuel Type	Avg	Adjusted Wheelbase	Towing	GVWR	Curb
Vogue	1999	MHA	40	XL 40	PR	DE500	D	$9500	304 T	1,500	48,900	37,506

Livability Code: FT 30-90
Wheelbase-to-length ratio of 63% is considered ○ dangerous ○ fatiguing ○ good ◉ excellent *
The approximate net payload of 11394 pounds at 23% of GVWR on this model is ○ deficient ○ excessive ○ cautionary ○ good ◉ excellent *
Total highway safety penalties are: 4 *   Value: 85   Durability: 80   Highway Control Rating: 100   Highway Safety: 96   ★★★★

Brand	Year	Type	Length	Model	Chassis	Engine	Fuel Type	Avg	Adjusted Wheelbase	Towing	GVWR	Curb
Vogue	1999	MHA	40	XL 40 opsl	PR	DE500	D	$9500	304 T	1,500	48,900	38,556

Livability Code: FT 30-90
Wheelbase-to-length ratio of 63% is considered ○ dangerous ○ fatiguing ○ good ◉ excellent *
The approximate net payload of 10344 pounds at 21% of GVWR on this model is ○ deficient ○ excessive ○ cautionary ○ good ◉ excellent *
Total highway safety penalties are: 16 *   Value: 79   Durability: 80   Highway Control Rating: 100   Highway Safety: 84   ★★★

Brand	Year	Type	Length	Model	Chassis	Engine	Fuel Type	Avg	Adjusted Wheelbase	Towing	GVWR	Curb
Vogue	1999	MHA	40	5000/40	VO	CA455	D	$9500	262 T	1,500	46,350	36,362

Livability Code: FT 30-90
Wheelbase-to-length ratio of 54% is considered ○ dangerous ○ fatiguing ◉ good ○ excellent *
The approximate net payload of 9988 pounds at 22% of GVWR on this model is ○ deficient ○ excessive ○ cautionary ○ good ◉ excellent *
Total highway safety penalties are: 4 *   Value: 85   Durability: 80   Highway Control Rating: 87   Highway Safety: 83   ★★★★

Brand	Year	Type	Length	Model	Chassis	Engine	Fuel Type	Avg	Adjusted Wheelbase	Towing	GVWR	Curb
Vogue	1999	MHA	40	5000/40 opsl	VO	CA455	D	$9500	262 T	1,500	46,350	37,412

Livability Code: FT 30-90
Wheelbase-to-length ratio of 54% is considered ○ dangerous ○ fatiguing ○ good ◉ excellent *
The approximate net payload of 8938 pounds at 19% of GVWR on this model is ○ deficient ○ excessive ○ cautionary ◉ good ○ excellent *
Total highway safety penalties are: 16 *   Value: 79   Durability: 80   Highway Control Rating: 87   Highway Safety: 71   ★★★

Brand	Year	Type	Length	Model	Chassis	Engine	Fuel Type	Avg	Adjusted Wheelbase	Towing	GVWR	Curb
Vogue	1999	MHA	44	5000/45	VO	CA455	D	$8600	311 T	1,500	46,350	37,635

Livability Code: FT 30-90
Wheelbase-to-length ratio of 59% is considered ○ dangerous ○ fatiguing ○ good ◉ excellent *
The approximate net payload of 8715 pounds at 19% of GVWR on this model is ○ deficient ○ excessive ○ cautionary ○ good ◉ excellent *
Total highway safety penalties are: 4 *   Value: 85   Durability: 80   Highway Control Rating: 100   Highway Safety: 96   ★★★★

Brand	Year	Type	Length	Model	Chassis	Engine	Fuel Type	Avg	Adjusted Wheelbase	Towing	GVWR	Curb
Vogue	1999	MHA	44	5000/45 opsl	VO	CA455	D	$8600	311 T	1,500	46,350	38,685

Livability Code: FT 30-90
Wheelbase-to-length ratio of 59% is considered ○ dangerous ○ fatiguing ○ good ◉ excellent *
The approximate net payload of 7665 pounds at 17% of GVWR on this model is ○ deficient ○ excessive ○ cautionary ○ good ◉ excellent *
Total highway safety penalties are: 16 *   Value: 79   Durability: 80   Highway Control Rating: 100   Highway Safety: 84   ★★★

Brand	Year	Type	Length	Model	Chassis	Engine	Fuel Type	Avg	Adjusted Wheelbase	Towing	GVWR	Curb
Vogue	1999	MHA	45	XL 45	PR	DE500	D	$8400	339 T	1,500	49,000	39,188

Livability Code: FT 30-90
Wheelbase-to-length ratio of 63% is considered ○ dangerous ○ fatiguing ○ good ◉ excellent *
The approximate net payload of 9812 pounds at 20% of GVWR on this model is ○ deficient ○ excessive ○ cautionary ○ good ◉ excellent *
Total highway safety penalties are: 4 *   Value: 85   Durability: 80   Highway Control Rating: 100   Highway Safety: 96   ★★★★

Brand	Year	Type	Length	Model	Chassis	Engine	Fuel Type	Avg	Adjusted Wheelbase	Towing	GVWR	Curb
Vogue	1999	MHA	45	XL 45 opsl	PR	DE500	D	$8400	339 T	1,500	49,000	40,238

Livability Code: FT 30-90
Wheelbase-to-length ratio of 63% is considered ○ dangerous ○ fatiguing ○ good ◉ excellent *
The approximate net payload of 8762 pounds at 18% of GVWR on this model is ○ deficient ○ excessive ○ cautionary ○ good ◉ excellent *
Total highway safety penalties are: 16 *   Value: 79   Durability: 80   Highway Control Rating: 100   Highway Safety: 84   ★★★

Note: Safety ratings are based on the assumption that the engineering of the RV has allowed for proper balance by placing fresh, gray, and black holding tanks in a location so as not to change the balance of the RV when the tanks are empty or full. **Always double-check wheelbase, GVWR, and weights at front and rear axles.**

*See Section 1 for details on how conclusions are reached.

Brand	Year	Type	Length	Model	Chassis	Engine	Fuel Type	Average Price per Linear Foot When New	Adjusted Wheel-base	Approx. Towing Capacity	Gross Vehicle Weight Rating	Average Curb Weight
Vogue IV	1990	MHA	34	34	OS	7.5L	G	$4000	228	7,000	18,000	17,780

Livability Code: FT 30-90   Wheelbase-to-length ratio of 56% is considered ○ dangerous ○ fatiguing ◉ good ○ excellent*

The approximate net payload of 220 pounds at 1% of GVWR on this model is ◉ deficient ○ excessive ○ cautionary ○ good ○ excellent*

Total highway safety penalties are: 2*   Value: 86   Durability: 80   Highway Control Rating: 56   Highway Safety: 54   ★

Brand	Year	Type	Length	Model	Chassis	Engine	Fuel Type		Wheelbase	Towing	GVWR	Curb Weight
Vogue Prima Vista	1990	MHA	40	40	CR	Det	D	$8200	264	1,500	32,040	29,076

Livability Code: FT 30-90   Wheelbase-to-length ratio of 55% is considered ○ dangerous ○ fatiguing ◉ good ○ excellent*

The approximate net payload of 2964 pounds at 9% of GVWR on this model is ○ deficient ○ excessive ◉ cautionary ○ good ○ excellent*

Total highway safety penalties are: 2*   Value: 86   Durability: 80   Highway Control Rating: 76   Highway Safety: 74   ★★★

Vogue V	1996	MHA	38	38H	PR	Ca317	D	$8900	250	1,500	34,000	29,403

Livability Code: FT 30-90   Wheelbase-to-length ratio of 55% is considered ○ dangerous ○ fatiguing ◉ good ○ excellent*

The approximate net payload of 4597 pounds at 14% of GVWR on this model is ○ deficient ○ excessive ○ cautionary ◉ good ○ excellent*

Total highway safety penalties are: 2*   Value: 86   Durability: 80   Highway Control Rating: 87   Highway Safety: 85   ★★★★

Vogue V	1996	MHA	40	40	PR	Ca317	D	$8800	274	1,500	34,000	30,089

Livability Code: FT 30-90   Wheelbase-to-length ratio of 57% is considered ○ dangerous ○ fatiguing ◉ good ○ excellent*

The approximate net payload of 3911 pounds at 12% of GVWR on this model is ○ deficient ○ excessive ○ cautionary ◉ good ○ excellent*

Total highway safety penalties are: 2*   Value: 86   Durability: 80   Highway Control Rating: 91   Highway Safety: 89   ★★★★

Wanderlodge	1990	MHA	40	WLWB3907	BL	De8V9	D	$9800	271 T	1,500	45,200	41,882

Livability Code: FT 30-90   Wheelbase-to-length ratio of 57% is considered ○ dangerous ○ fatiguing ◉ good ○ excellent*

The approximate net payload of 3318 pounds at 7% of GVWR on this model is ○ deficient ○ excessive ◉ cautionary ○ good ○ excellent*

Total highway safety penalties are: 4*   Value: 87   Durability: 85   Highway Control Rating: 71   Highway Safety: 67   ★★

Wanderlodge	1991	MHA	37	WLSP3608	BL	Ca320	D	$8000	236	1,500	37,400	34,407

Livability Code: FT 30-90   Wheelbase-to-length ratio of 53% is considered ○ dangerous ◉ fatiguing ○ good ○ excellent*

The approximate net payload of 2993 pounds at 8% of GVWR on this model is ○ deficient ○ excessive ◉ cautionary ○ good ○ excellent*

Total highway safety penalties are: 2*   Value: 88   Durability: 85   Highway Control Rating: 49   Highway Safety: 47

Wanderlodge	1991	MHA	40	WB 3907	BL	De	D	$10100	271 T	1,500	47,400	43,421

Livability Code: FT 30-90   Wheelbase-to-length ratio of 57% is considered ○ dangerous ○ fatiguing ◉ good ○ excellent*

The approximate net payload of 3979 pounds at 8% of GVWR on this model is ○ deficient ○ excessive ◉ cautionary ○ good ○ excellent*

Total highway safety penalties are: 4*   Value: 87   Durability: 85   Highway Control Rating: 77   Highway Safety: 73   ★★★

Wanderlodge	1991	MHA	40	WB3907	BL	De8V9	D	$10100	271 T	1,500	47,400	42,721

Livability Code: FT 30-90   Wheelbase-to-length ratio of 57% is considered ○ dangerous ○ fatiguing ◉ good ○ excellent*

The approximate net payload of 4679 pounds at 10% of GVWR on this model is ○ deficient ○ excessive ○ cautionary ◉ good ○ excellent*

Total highway safety penalties are: 4*   Value: 87   Durability: 85   Highway Control Rating: 78   Highway Safety: 74   ★★★

Wanderlodge	1993	MHA	40	WL 40	BL	De8V9	D	$11000	271 T	10,000	47,400	43,494

Livability Code: FT 30-90   Wheelbase-to-length ratio of 56% is considered ○ dangerous ○ fatiguing ◉ good ○ excellent*

The approximate net payload of 3906 pounds at 8% of GVWR on this model is ○ deficient ○ excessive ◉ cautionary ○ good ○ excellent*

Total highway safety penalties are: 4*   Value: 87   Durability: 85   Highway Control Rating: 75   Highway Safety: 71   ★★★

Wanderlodge	1994	MHA	40	WL 40	BL	De8V9	D	$11800	271 T	10,000	47,400	43,494

Livability Code: FT 30-90   Wheelbase-to-length ratio of 56% is considered ○ dangerous ○ fatiguing ◉ good ○ excellent*

The approximate net payload of 3906 pounds at 8% of GVWR on this model is ○ deficient ○ excessive ◉ cautionary ○ good ○ excellent*

Total highway safety penalties are: 4*   Value: 87   Durability: 85   Highway Control Rating: 75   Highway Safety: 71   ★★★

Wanderlodge	1996	MHA		accurate specs n/a								?

Livability Code: FT 30-90   Wheelbase-to-length ratio of ? is considered ○ dangerous ○ fatiguing ○ good ○ excellent*

The approximate net payload of pounds at of GVWR on this model is ○ deficient ○ excessive ○ cautionary ○ good ○ excellent*

Total highway safety penalties are: 0*   Value: 0   Durability: 85   Highway Control Rating: 0   Highway Safety: 0

Wanderlodge	1997	MHA	41	41	BL	De500	D	$10500	271 T	1,500	48,600	43,119

Livability Code: FT 30-90   Wheelbase-to-length ratio of 55% is considered ○ dangerous ○ fatiguing ◉ good ○ excellent*

The approximate net payload of 5481 pounds at 11% of GVWR on this model is ○ deficient ○ excessive ○ cautionary ◉ good ○ excellent*

Total highway safety penalties are: 4*   Value: 87   Durability: 85   Highway Control Rating: 68   Highway Safety: 64   ★★

Note: Safety ratings are based on the assumption that the engineering of the RV has allowed for proper balance by placing fresh, gray, and black holding tanks in a location so as not to change the balance of the RV when the tanks are empty or full. **Always double-check wheelbase, GVWR, and weights at front and rear axles.**

*See Section 1 for details on how conclusions are reached.

Brand	Year	Type	Length	Model	Chassis	Engine	Fuel Type	Average Price per Linear Foot When New	Adjusted Wheelbase	Approx. Towing Capacity	Gross Vehicle Weight Rating	Average Curb Weight
Wanderlodge	1997	MHA	43	43	BL	De500	D	$12800	283 T	1,500	50,600	45,037

Livability Code: FT 30-90   Wheelbase-to-length ratio of 55% is considered ○ dangerous ○ fatiguing ◉ good ○ excellent *
The approximate net payload of 5563 pounds at 11% of GVWR on this model is ○ deficient ○ excessive ○ cautionary ◉ good ○ excellent *
Total highway safety penalties are: 4 *   Value: 8 7   Durability: 8 5   Highway Control Rating: 6 7   Highway Safety: 6 3   ★★

Brand	Year	Type	Length	Model	Chassis	Engine	Fuel Type	Avg Price/Ft	Wheelbase	Towing	GVWR	Curb Weight
Wanderlodge	1998	MHA	41	41LXi	BL	DE500	D	$12200	271 T	1,500	48,600	43,119

Livability Code: FT 30-90   Wheelbase-to-length ratio of 55% is considered ○ dangerous ○ fatiguing ◉ good ○ excellent *
The approximate net payload of 5481 pounds at 11% of GVWR on this model is ○ deficient ○ excessive ○ cautionary ◉ good ○ excellent *
Total highway safety penalties are: 4 *   Value: 8 7   Durability: 8 5   Highway Control Rating: 6 8   Highway Safety: 6 4   ★★

Wanderlodge	1998	MHA	41	41LXi slide	BL	DE500	D	$12200	271 T	1,500	48,600	44,769

Livability Code: FT 30-90   Wheelbase-to-length ratio of 55% is considered ○ dangerous ○ fatiguing ◉ good ○ excellent *
The approximate net payload of 3831 pounds at 8% of GVWR on this model is ○ deficient ○ excessive ◉ cautionary ○ good ○ excellent *
Total highway safety penalties are: 19 *   Value: 7 9   Durability: 8 5   Highway Control Rating: 7 0   Highway Safety: 5 1   ★

Wanderlodge	1998	MHA	43	43LXi	BL	DE500	D	$11600	283 T	1,500	50,600	45,037

Livability Code: FT 30-90   Wheelbase-to-length ratio of 55% is considered ○ dangerous ○ fatiguing ◉ good ○ excellent *
The approximate net payload of 5563 pounds at 11% of GVWR on this model is ○ deficient ○ excessive ○ cautionary ◉ good ○ excellent *
Total highway safety penalties are: 4 *   Value: 8 7   Durability: 8 5   Highway Control Rating: 6 7   Highway Safety: 6 3   ★★

Wanderlodge	1998	MHA	43	43LXi slide	BL	DE500	D	$11600	283 T	1,500	50,600	46,687

Livability Code: FT 30-90   Wheelbase-to-length ratio of 55% is considered ○ dangerous ○ fatiguing ◉ good ○ excellent *
The approximate net payload of 3913 pounds at 8% of GVWR on this model is ○ deficient ○ excessive ◉ cautionary ○ good ○ excellent *
Total highway safety penalties are: 19 *   Value: 7 9   Durability: 8 5   Highway Control Rating: 6 9   Highway Safety: 5 0   ★

Wanderlodge	1999	MHA	40	40 LX	BL	CU450	D	$12500	271 T	1,500 e	48,900	42,810

Livability Code: FT 30-90   Wheelbase-to-length ratio of 56% is considered ○ dangerous ○ fatiguing ◉ good ○ excellent *
The approximate net payload of 6090 pounds at 12% of GVWR on this model is ○ deficient ○ excessive ○ cautionary ◉ good ○ excellent *
Total highway safety penalties are: 4 *   Value: 8 7   Durability: 8 5   Highway Control Rating: 7 9   Highway Safety: 7 5   ★★★

Wanderlodge	1999	MHA	41	41 LXi	BL	CU500	D	$12200	271 T	1,500 e	48,900	43,269

Livability Code: FT 30-90   Wheelbase-to-length ratio of 55% is considered ○ dangerous ○ fatiguing ◉ good ○ excellent *
The approximate net payload of 5631 pounds at 12% of GVWR on this model is ○ deficient ○ excessive ○ cautionary ◉ good ○ excellent *
Total highway safety penalties are: 4 *   Value: 8 7   Durability: 8 5   Highway Control Rating: 6 8   Highway Safety: 6 4   ★★

Wanderlodge	1999	MHA	41	41 LXi slide	BL	CU500	D	$12200	271 T	1,500 e	48,900	44,694

Livability Code: FT 30-90   Wheelbase-to-length ratio of 55% is considered ○ dangerous ○ fatiguing ◉ good ○ excellent *
The approximate net payload of 4206 pounds at 9% of GVWR on this model is ○ deficient ○ excessive ◉ cautionary ○ good ○ excellent *
Total highway safety penalties are: 18 *   Value: 8 0   Durability: 8 5   Highway Control Rating: 7 6   Highway Safety: 5 8   ★

Wanderlodge	1999	MHA	43	43 LXi	BL	CU500	D	$11600	283 T	1,500 e	48,900	44,187

Livability Code: FT 30-90   Wheelbase-to-length ratio of 55% is considered ○ dangerous ○ fatiguing ◉ good ○ excellent *
The approximate net payload of 4713 pounds at 10% of GVWR on this model is ○ deficient ○ excessive ○ cautionary ◉ good ○ excellent *
Total highway safety penalties are: 4 *   Value: 8 7   Durability: 8 5   Highway Control Rating: 6 1   Highway Safety: 5 7   ★

Wanderlodge	1999	MHA	43	43 LXi slide	BL	CU500	D	$11600	283 T	1,500 e	48,900	45,612

Livability Code: FT 30-90   Wheelbase-to-length ratio of 55% is considered ○ dangerous ○ fatiguing ◉ good ○ excellent *
The approximate net payload of 3288 pounds at 7% of GVWR on this model is ○ deficient ○ excessive ◉ cautionary ○ good ○ excellent *
Total highway safety penalties are: 18 *   Value: 8 0   Durability: 8 5   Highway Control Rating: 6 3   Highway Safety: 4 5

Windcruiser	1990	MHA	34	32 RQ	CH	7.4L	G	$1700	190	4,500	15,000	13,161

Livability Code: 30-80   Wheelbase-to-length ratio of 47% is considered ◉ dangerous ○ fatiguing ○ good ○ excellent *
The approximate net payload of 1839 pounds at 12% of GVWR on this model is ○ deficient ○ excessive ○ cautionary ◉ good ○ excellent *
Total highway safety penalties are: 6 *   Value: 8 1   Durability: 7 4   Highway Control Rating: 2 7   Highway Safety: 2 1

Windcruiser	1991	MHA	34	33 RQ	CH	7.4L	G	$1900	200	1,500	16,000	13,914

Livability Code: 30-80   Wheelbase-to-length ratio of 49% is considered ◉ dangerous ○ fatiguing ○ good ○ excellent *
The approximate net payload of 2086 pounds at 13% of GVWR on this model is ○ deficient ○ excessive ○ cautionary ◉ good ○ excellent *
Total highway safety penalties are: 7 *   Value: 8 1   Durability: 7 4   Highway Control Rating: 3 5   Highway Safety: 2 8

Note: Safety ratings are based on the assumption that the engineering of the RV has allowed for proper balance by placing fresh, gray, and black holding tanks in a location so as not to change the balance of the RV when the tanks are empty or full. **Always double-check wheelbase, GVWR, and weights at front and rear axles.**

*See Section 1 for details on how conclusions are reached.

Section 2: The Ratings

Brand	Year	Type	Length	Model	Chassis	Engine	Fuel Type	Average Price per Linear Foot When New	Adjusted Wheelbase	Approx. Towing Capacity	Gross Vehicle Weight Rating	Average Curb Weight
Windsor	1995	MHA	32	32SB 230	RO	Cu5.9L	D	$3900	198	5,000	23,500	21,149

Livability Code: SB 30-90 — Wheelbase-to-length ratio of 51% is considered ○ dangerous ◉ fatiguing ○ good ○ excellent *
The approximate net payload of 2351 pounds at 10% of GVWR on this model is ○ deficient ○ excessive ○ cautionary ◉ good ○ excellent *
Total highway safety penalties are: 2 * — Value: 7 9 — Durability: 7 5 — Highway Control Rating: 3 6 — Highway Safety: 3 4

Brand	Year	Type	Length	Model	Chassis	Engine	Fuel Type	Avg Price/Linear Foot	Adj. Wheelbase	Towing Cap.	GVWR	Avg Curb Wt
Windsor	1995	MHA	34	34FL-230	RO	Cu5.9L	D	$3800	213	5,000	23,500	21,720

Livability Code: SB 30-90 — Wheelbase-to-length ratio of 52% is considered ○ dangerous ◉ fatiguing ○ good ○ excellent *
The approximate net payload of 1780 pounds at 8% of GVWR on this model is ○ deficient ○ excessive ◉ cautionary ○ good ○ excellent *
Total highway safety penalties are: 2 * — Value: 7 9 — Durability: 7 5 — Highway Control Rating: 3 7 — Highway Safety: 3 5

Brand	Year	Type	Length	Model	Chassis	Engine	Fuel Type	Avg Price/Linear Foot	Adj. Wheelbase	Towing Cap.	GVWR	Avg Curb Wt
Windsor	1995	MHA	36	36SB 230	RO	Cu5.9L	D	$3800	218	5,000	23,500	22,147

Livability Code: SB 30-90 — Wheelbase-to-length ratio of 50% is considered ◉ dangerous ○ fatiguing ○ good ○ excellent *
The approximate net payload of 1353 pounds at 6% of GVWR on this model is ◉ deficient ○ excessive ○ cautionary ○ good ○ excellent *
Total highway safety penalties are: 2 * — Value: 7 9 — Durability: 7 5 — Highway Control Rating: 1 1 — Highway Safety: 9

Brand	Year	Type	Length	Model	Chassis	Engine	Fuel Type	Avg Price/Linear Foot	Adj. Wheelbase	Towing Cap.	GVWR	Avg Curb Wt
Windsor	1995	MHA	36	36PB 230	RO	Cu5.9L	D	$3800	218	5,000	23,500	22,477

Livability Code: SB 30-90 — Wheelbase-to-length ratio of 50% is considered ◉ dangerous ○ fatiguing ○ good ○ excellent *
The approximate net payload of 1023 pounds at 4% of GVWR on this model is ◉ deficient ○ excessive ○ cautionary ○ good ○ excellent *
Total highway safety penalties are: 2 * — Value: 7 9 — Durability: 7 5 — Highway Control Rating: 1 0 — Highway Safety: 8

Brand	Year	Type	Length	Model	Chassis	Engine	Fuel Type	Avg Price/Linear Foot	Adj. Wheelbase	Towing Cap.	GVWR	Avg Curb Wt
Windsor	1996	MHA	32	32SBFD 230	RO	Cu5.9L	D	$4200	198	2,500	26,000	21,774

Livability Code: SB 30-90 — Wheelbase-to-length ratio of 51% is considered ○ dangerous ◉ fatiguing ○ good ○ excellent *
The approximate net payload of 4226 pounds at 16% of GVWR on this model is ○ deficient ○ excessive ○ cautionary ○ good ◉ excellent *
Total highway safety penalties are: 2 * — Value: 7 9 — Durability: 7 5 — Highway Control Rating: 4 8 — Highway Safety: 4 6

Brand	Year	Type	Length	Model	Chassis	Engine	Fuel Type	Avg Price/Linear Foot	Adj. Wheelbase	Towing Cap.	GVWR	Avg Curb Wt
Windsor	1996	MHA	32	32SBFD 250	RO	Cu8.3L	D	$4300	198	2,500	26,000	21,774

Livability Code: SB 30-90 — Wheelbase-to-length ratio of 51% is considered ○ dangerous ◉ fatiguing ○ good ○ excellent *
The approximate net payload of 4226 pounds at 16% of GVWR on this model is ○ deficient ○ excessive ○ cautionary ○ good ◉ excellent *
Total highway safety penalties are: 2 * — Value: 7 9 — Durability: 7 5 — Highway Control Rating: 4 8 — Highway Safety: 4 6

Brand	Year	Type	Length	Model	Chassis	Engine	Fuel Type	Avg Price/Linear Foot	Adj. Wheelbase	Towing Cap.	GVWR	Avg Curb Wt
Windsor	1996	MHA	32	32SBFD 230 myc	RO	Cu5.9L	D	$4400	198	500	28,000	24,245

Livability Code: SB 30-90 — Wheelbase-to-length ratio of 51% is considered ○ dangerous ◉ fatiguing ○ good ○ excellent *
The approximate net payload of 3755 pounds at 13% of GVWR on this model is ○ deficient ○ excessive ○ cautionary ◉ good ○ excellent *
Total highway safety penalties are: 2 * — Value: 7 9 — Durability: 7 5 — Highway Control Rating: 4 2 — Highway Safety: 4 0

Brand	Year	Type	Length	Model	Chassis	Engine	Fuel Type	Avg Price/Linear Foot	Adj. Wheelbase	Towing Cap.	GVWR	Avg Curb Wt
Windsor	1996	MHA	32	32SBFD 250 myc	RO	Cu8.3L	D	$4300	198	500	28,000	24,245

Livability Code: SB 30-90 — Wheelbase-to-length ratio of 51% is considered ○ dangerous ◉ fatiguing ○ good ○ excellent *
The approximate net payload of 3755 pounds at 13% of GVWR on this model is ○ deficient ○ excessive ○ cautionary ◉ good ○ excellent *
Total highway safety penalties are: 2 * — Value: 7 9 — Durability: 7 5 — Highway Control Rating: 4 2 — Highway Safety: 4 0

Brand	Year	Type	Length	Model	Chassis	Engine	Fuel Type	Avg Price/Linear Foot	Adj. Wheelbase	Towing Cap.	GVWR	Avg Curb Wt
Windsor	1996	MHA	34	34FL-230	RO	Cu5.9L	D	$4100	213	2,500	26,000	22,345

Livability Code: SB 30-90 — Wheelbase-to-length ratio of 52% is considered ○ dangerous ◉ fatiguing ○ good ○ excellent *
The approximate net payload of 3655 pounds at 14% of GVWR on this model is ○ deficient ○ excessive ○ cautionary ◉ good ○ excellent *
Total highway safety penalties are: 2 * — Value: 7 9 — Durability: 7 5 — Highway Control Rating: 5 6 — Highway Safety: 5 4 ★

Brand	Year	Type	Length	Model	Chassis	Engine	Fuel Type	Avg Price/Linear Foot	Adj. Wheelbase	Towing Cap.	GVWR	Avg Curb Wt
Windsor	1996	MHA	34	34FL-250	RO	Cu8.3L	D	$4200	213	2,500	26,000	22,345

Livability Code: SB 30-90 — Wheelbase-to-length ratio of 52% is considered ○ dangerous ◉ fatiguing ○ good ○ excellent *
The approximate net payload of 3655 pounds at 14% of GVWR on this model is ○ deficient ○ excessive ○ cautionary ◉ good ○ excellent *
Total highway safety penalties are: 2 * — Value: 7 9 — Durability: 7 5 — Highway Control Rating: 5 6 — Highway Safety: 5 4 ★

Brand	Year	Type	Length	Model	Chassis	Engine	Fuel Type	Avg Price/Linear Foot	Adj. Wheelbase	Towing Cap.	GVWR	Avg Curb Wt
Windsor	1996	MHA	34	34FL-275 myc	RO	Cu8.3L	D	$4200	213	500	28,000	24,751

Livability Code: SB 30-90 — Wheelbase-to-length ratio of 52% is considered ○ dangerous ◉ fatiguing ○ good ○ excellent *
The approximate net payload of 3249 pounds at 12% of GVWR on this model is ○ deficient ○ excessive ○ cautionary ◉ good ○ excellent *
Total highway safety penalties are: 2 * — Value: 7 9 — Durability: 7 5 — Highway Control Rating: 5 2 — Highway Safety: 5 0 ★

Brand	Year	Type	Length	Model	Chassis	Engine	Fuel Type	Avg Price/Linear Foot	Adj. Wheelbase	Towing Cap.	GVWR	Avg Curb Wt
Windsor	1996	MHA	36	36SB 230	RO	Cu5.9L	D	$4000	218	2,500	26,000	22,772

Livability Code: SB 30-90 — Wheelbase-to-length ratio of 50% is considered ◉ dangerous ○ fatiguing ○ good ○ excellent *
The approximate net payload of 3228 pounds at 12% of GVWR on this model is ○ deficient ○ excessive ○ cautionary ◉ good ○ excellent *
Total highway safety penalties are: 2 * — Value: 7 9 — Durability: 7 5 — Highway Control Rating: 3 9 — Highway Safety: 3 7

Note: Safety ratings are based on the assumption that the engineering of the RV has allowed for proper balance by placing fresh, gray, and black holding tanks in a location so as not to change the balance of the RV when the tanks are empty or full. **Always double-check wheelbase, GVWR, and weights at front and rear axles.**

*See Section 1 for details on how conclusions are reached.

Brand	Year	Type	Length	Model	Chassis	Engine	Fuel Type	Average Price per Linear Foot When New	Adjusted Wheelbase	Approx. Towing Capacity	Gross Vehicle Weight Rating	Average Curb Weight
Windsor	1996	MHA	36	36PB 230	RO	Cu5.9L	D	$4000	218	2,500	26,000	23,102

Livability Code: SB 30-90
Wheelbase-to-length ratio of 50% is considered ◉ dangerous ○ fatiguing ○ good ○ excellent *
The approximate net payload of 2898 pounds at 11% of GVWR on this model is ○ deficient ○ excessive ○ cautionary ◉ good ○ excellent *
Total highway safety penalties are: 2 *   Value: 7 9   Durability: 7 5   Highway Control Rating: 3 7   Highway Safety: 3 5

Brand	Year	Type	Length	Model	Chassis	Engine	Fuel Type	Price/Linear Ft	Wheelbase	Towing	GVWR	Curb Weight
Windsor	1996	MHA	36	36SB 250	RO	Cu8.3L	D	$4000	218	2,500	26,000	22,772

Livability Code: SB 30-90
Wheelbase-to-length ratio of 50% is considered ◉ dangerous ○ fatiguing ○ good ○ excellent *
The approximate net payload of 3228 pounds at 12% of GVWR on this model is ○ deficient ◉ excessive ○ cautionary ◉ good ○ excellent *
Total highway safety penalties are: 2 *   Value: 7 9   Durability: 7 5   Highway Control Rating: 3 9   Highway Safety: 3 7

Brand	Year	Type	Length	Model	Chassis	Engine	Fuel Type	Price/Linear Ft	Wheelbase	Towing	GVWR	Curb Weight
Windsor	1996	MHA	36	36PB 250	RO	Cu8.3L	D	$4000	218	2,500	26,000	23,102

Livability Code: SB 30-90
Wheelbase-to-length ratio of 50% is considered ◉ dangerous ○ fatiguing ○ good ○ excellent *
The approximate net payload of 2898 pounds at 11% of GVWR on this model is ○ deficient ○ excessive ○ cautionary ◉ good ○ excellent *
Total highway safety penalties are: 2 *   Value: 7 9   Durability: 7 5   Highway Control Rating: 3 7   Highway Safety: 3 5

Brand	Year	Type	Length	Model	Chassis	Engine	Fuel Type	Price/Linear Ft	Wheelbase	Towing	GVWR	Curb Weight
Windsor	1996	MHA	36	36SB 275 myc	RO	Cu8.3L	D	$4000	218	500	28,000	25,383

Livability Code: SB 30-90
Wheelbase-to-length ratio of 50% is considered ◉ dangerous ○ fatiguing ○ good ○ excellent *
The approximate net payload of 2617 pounds at 9% of GVWR on this model is ○ deficient ○ excessive ◉ cautionary ○ good ○ excellent *
Total highway safety penalties are: 2 *   Value: 7 9   Durability: 7 5   Highway Control Rating: 3 0   Highway Safety: 2 8

Brand	Year	Type	Length	Model	Chassis	Engine	Fuel Type	Price/Linear Ft	Wheelbase	Towing	GVWR	Curb Weight
Windsor	1996	MHA	36	36PB 275 myc	RO	Cu8.3L	D	$4000	218	500	28,000	25,383

Livability Code: SB 30-90
Wheelbase-to-length ratio of 50% is considered ◉ dangerous ○ fatiguing ○ good ○ excellent *
The approximate net payload of 2617 pounds at 9% of GVWR on this model is ○ deficient ○ excessive ◉ cautionary ○ good ○ excellent *
Total highway safety penalties are: 2 *   Value: 7 9   Durability: 7 5   Highway Control Rating: 3 0   Highway Safety: 2 8

Brand	Year	Type	Length	Model	Chassis	Engine	Fuel Type	Price/Linear Ft	Wheelbase	Towing	GVWR	Curb Weight
Windsor	1996	MHA	38	38 myc	RO	Cu8.3L	D	$3900	242	500	28,000	26,016

Livability Code: SB 30-90
Wheelbase-to-length ratio of 53% is considered ○ dangerous ◉ fatiguing ○ good ○ excellent *
The approximate net payload of 1984 pounds at 7% of GVWR on this model is ○ deficient ○ excessive ◉ cautionary ○ good ○ excellent *
Total highway safety penalties are: 2 *   Value: 7 9   Durability: 7 5   Highway Control Rating: 4 2   Highway Safety: 4 0

Brand	Year	Type	Length	Model	Chassis	Engine	Fuel Type	Price/Linear Ft	Wheelbase	Towing	GVWR	Curb Weight
Windsor	1997	MHA	32	32 SB FD	RO	Cu275	D	$4300	191	1,500	28,000	24,118

Livability Code: SB 30-90
Wheelbase-to-length ratio of 50% is considered ◉ dangerous ○ fatiguing ○ good ○ excellent *
The approximate net payload of 3882 pounds at 14% of GVWR on this model is ○ deficient ○ excessive ○ cautionary ◉ good ○ excellent *
Total highway safety penalties are: 2 *   Value: 7 9   Durability: 7 5   Highway Control Rating: 4 0   Highway Safety: 3 8

Brand	Year	Type	Length	Model	Chassis	Engine	Fuel Type	Price/Linear Ft	Wheelbase	Towing	GVWR	Curb Weight
Windsor	1997	MHA	34	34 PB FB	RO	Cu275	D	$4100	217	1,500	28,000	24,751

Livability Code: SB 30-90
Wheelbase-to-length ratio of 53% is considered ○ dangerous ◉ fatiguing ○ good ○ excellent *
The approximate net payload of 3249 pounds at 12% of GVWR on this model is ○ deficient ○ excessive ○ cautionary ◉ good ○ excellent *
Total highway safety penalties are: 2 *   Value: 7 9   Durability: 7 5   Highway Control Rating: 6 3   Highway Safety: 6 1   ★★

Brand	Year	Type	Length	Model	Chassis	Engine	Fuel Type	Price/Linear Ft	Wheelbase	Towing	GVWR	Curb Weight
Windsor	1997	MHA	36	36 SB FB	RO	Cu275	D	$3900	228	1,500	28,000	25,383

Livability Code: SB 30-90
Wheelbase-to-length ratio of 53% is considered ○ dangerous ◉ fatiguing ○ good ○ excellent *
The approximate net payload of 2617 pounds at 9% of GVWR on this model is ○ deficient ○ excessive ◉ cautionary ○ good ○ excellent *
Total highway safety penalties are: 2 *   Value: 7 9   Durability: 7 5   Highway Control Rating: 5 3   Highway Safety: 5 1   ★

Brand	Year	Type	Length	Model	Chassis	Engine	Fuel Type	Price/Linear Ft	Wheelbase	Towing	GVWR	Curb Weight
Windsor	1997	MHA	36	36 PB FD	RO	Cu275	D	$3900	228	1,500	28,000	25,383

Livability Code: SB 30-90
Wheelbase-to-length ratio of 53% is considered ○ dangerous ◉ fatiguing ○ good ○ excellent *
The approximate net payload of 2617 pounds at 9% of GVWR on this model is ○ deficient ○ excessive ◉ cautionary ○ good ○ excellent *
Total highway safety penalties are: 2 *   Value: 7 9   Durability: 7 5   Highway Control Rating: 5 3   Highway Safety: 5 1   ★

Brand	Year	Type	Length	Model	Chassis	Engine	Fuel Type	Price/Linear Ft	Wheelbase	Towing	GVWR	Curb Weight
Windsor	1997	MHA	36	36 Slide	RO	Cu275	D	$4100	228	1,500	28,000	26,283

Livability Code: SB 30-90
Wheelbase-to-length ratio of 53% is considered ○ dangerous ◉ fatiguing ○ good ○ excellent *
The approximate net payload of 1717 pounds at 6% of GVWR on this model is ◉ deficient ○ excessive ○ cautionary ○ good ○ excellent *
Total highway safety penalties are: 7 *   Value: 7 6   Durability: 7 5   Highway Control Rating: 3 5   Highway Safety: 2 8

Brand	Year	Type	Length	Model	Chassis	Engine	Fuel Type	Price/Linear Ft	Wheelbase	Towing	GVWR	Curb Weight
Windsor	1997	MHA	38	38 PB FD	RO	Cu275	D	$4000	242	1,500	28,000	25,558

Livability Code: SB 30-90
Wheelbase-to-length ratio of 53% is considered ○ dangerous ◉ fatiguing ○ good ○ excellent *
The approximate net payload of 2442 pounds at 9% of GVWR on this model is ○ deficient ○ excessive ◉ cautionary ○ good ○ excellent *
Total highway safety penalties are: 2 *   Value: 7 9   Durability: 7 5   Highway Control Rating: 5 3   Highway Safety: 5 1   ★

Note: Safety ratings are based on the assumption that the engineering of the RV has allowed for proper balance by placing fresh, gray, and black holding tanks in a location so as not to change the balance of the RV when the tanks are empty or full. **Always double-check wheelbase, GVWR, and weights at front and rear axles.**

*See Section 1 for details on how conclusions are reached.

Brand	Year	Type	Length	Model	Chassis	Engine	Fuel Type	Average Price per Linear Foot When New	Adjusted Wheelbase	Approx. Towing Capacity	Gross Vehicle Weight Rating	Average Curb Weight
Windsor	1997	MHA	38	38 Slide	RO	Cu275	D	$4100	242	1,500	28,000	26,916

Livability Code: SB 30-90
Wheelbase-to-length ratio of 53% is considered ○ dangerous ◉ fatiguing ○ good ○ excellent *
The approximate net payload of 1084 pounds at 4% of GVWR on this model is ◉ deficient ○ excessive ○ cautionary ○ good ○ excellent *
Total highway safety penalties are: 7 *   Value: **7 6**   Durability: **7 5**   Highway Control Rating: **3 4**   Highway Safety: **2 7**

Brand	Year	Type	Length	Model	Chassis	Engine	Fuel Type	Average Price per Linear Foot When New	Adjusted Wheelbase	Approx. Towing Capacity	Gross Vehicle Weight Rating	Average Curb Weight
Windsor	1998	MHA	32	32SB	RO	CU300	D	$4900	191	10,000	29,000	24,420

Livability Code: SB 30-90
Wheelbase-to-length ratio of 50% is considered ◉ dangerous ○ fatiguing ○ good ○ excellent *
The approximate net payload of 4580 pounds at 16% of GVWR on this model is ○ deficient ○ excessive ○ cautionary ○ good ◉ excellent *
Total highway safety penalties are: 2 *   Value: **7 9**   Durability: **7 5**   Highway Control Rating: **4 4**   Highway Safety: **4 2**

Brand	Year	Type	Length	Model	Chassis	Engine	Fuel Type	Average Price per Linear Foot When New	Adjusted Wheelbase	Approx. Towing Capacity	Gross Vehicle Weight Rating	Average Curb Weight
Windsor	1998	MHA	34	34PB	RO	CU300	D	$4800	217	10,000	29,000	25,040

Livability Code: SB 30-90
Wheelbase-to-length ratio of 53% is considered ○ dangerous ◉ fatiguing ○ good ○ excellent *
The approximate net payload of 3960 pounds at 14% of GVWR on this model is ○ deficient ○ excessive ○ cautionary ◉ good ○ excellent *
Total highway safety penalties are: 2 *   Value: **7 9**   Durability: **7 5**   Highway Control Rating: **6 7**   Highway Safety: **6 5**   ★★

Brand	Year	Type	Length	Model	Chassis	Engine	Fuel Type	Average Price per Linear Foot When New	Adjusted Wheelbase	Approx. Towing Capacity	Gross Vehicle Weight Rating	Average Curb Weight
Windsor	1998	MHA	36	36PB	RO	CU300	D	$4600	228	10,000	29,000	25,660

Livability Code: SB 30-90
Wheelbase-to-length ratio of 53% is considered ○ dangerous ◉ fatiguing ○ good ○ excellent *
The approximate net payload of 3340 pounds at 12% of GVWR on this model is ○ deficient ○ excessive ○ cautionary ◉ good ○ excellent *
Total highway safety penalties are: 2 *   Value: **7 9**   Durability: **7 5**   Highway Control Rating: **6 1**   Highway Safety: **5 9**   ★

Brand	Year	Type	Length	Model	Chassis	Engine	Fuel Type	Average Price per Linear Foot When New	Adjusted Wheelbase	Approx. Towing Capacity	Gross Vehicle Weight Rating	Average Curb Weight
Windsor	1998	MHA	36	36SB	RO	CU300	D	$4600	228	10,000	29,000	25,660

Livability Code: SB 30-90
Wheelbase-to-length ratio of 53% is considered ○ dangerous ◉ fatiguing ○ good ○ excellent *
The approximate net payload of 3340 pounds at 12% of GVWR on this model is ○ deficient ○ excessive ○ cautionary ◉ good ○ excellent *
Total highway safety penalties are: 2 *   Value: **7 9**   Durability: **7 5**   Highway Control Rating: **6 1**   Highway Safety: **5 9**   ★

Brand	Year	Type	Length	Model	Chassis	Engine	Fuel Type	Average Price per Linear Foot When New	Adjusted Wheelbase	Approx. Towing Capacity	Gross Vehicle Weight Rating	Average Curb Weight
Windsor	1998	MHA	36	36 Suite Slide	RO	CU300	D	$4800	228	10,000	29,000	26,560

Livability Code: SB 30-90
Wheelbase-to-length ratio of 53% is considered ○ dangerous ◉ fatiguing ○ good ○ excellent *
The approximate net payload of 2440 pounds at 8% of GVWR on this model is ○ deficient ○ excessive ◉ cautionary ○ good ○ excellent *
Total highway safety penalties are: 12 *   Value: **7 4**   Durability: **7 5**   Highway Control Rating: **4 7**   Highway Safety: **3 5**

Brand	Year	Type	Length	Model	Chassis	Engine	Fuel Type	Average Price per Linear Foot When New	Adjusted Wheelbase	Approx. Towing Capacity	Gross Vehicle Weight Rating	Average Curb Weight
Windsor	1998	MHA	36	36 Suite Slide PB	RO	CU300	D	$4800	228	10,000	29,000	26,625

Livability Code: SB 30-90
Wheelbase-to-length ratio of 53% is considered ○ dangerous ◉ fatiguing ○ good ○ excellent *
The approximate net payload of 2375 pounds at 8% of GVWR on this model is ○ deficient ○ excessive ◉ cautionary ○ good ○ excellent *
Total highway safety penalties are: 12 *   Value: **7 4**   Durability: **7 5**   Highway Control Rating: **4 7**   Highway Safety: **3 5**

Brand	Year	Type	Length	Model	Chassis	Engine	Fuel Type	Average Price per Linear Foot When New	Adjusted Wheelbase	Approx. Towing Capacity	Gross Vehicle Weight Rating	Average Curb Weight
Windsor	1998	MHA	38	38PB	RO	CU300	D	$4500	242	10,000	29,000	26,280

Livability Code: SB 30-90
Wheelbase-to-length ratio of 53% is considered ○ dangerous ◉ fatiguing ○ good ○ excellent *
The approximate net payload of 2720 pounds at 9% of GVWR on this model is ○ deficient ○ excessive ◉ cautionary ○ good ○ excellent *
Total highway safety penalties are: 2 *   Value: **7 9**   Durability: **7 5**   Highway Control Rating: **5 4**   Highway Safety: **5 2**   ★

Brand	Year	Type	Length	Model	Chassis	Engine	Fuel Type	Average Price per Linear Foot When New	Adjusted Wheelbase	Approx. Towing Capacity	Gross Vehicle Weight Rating	Average Curb Weight
Windsor	1998	MHA	38	38 Suite Slide	RO	CU300	D	$4700	242	10,000	29,000	27,180

Livability Code: SB 30-90
Wheelbase-to-length ratio of 53% is considered ○ dangerous ◉ fatiguing ○ good ○ excellent *
The approximate net payload of 1820 pounds at 6% of GVWR on this model is ◉ deficient ○ excessive ○ cautionary ○ good ○ excellent *
Total highway safety penalties are: 12 *   Value: **7 4**   Durability: **7 5**   Highway Control Rating: **3 6**   Highway Safety: **2 4**

Brand	Year	Type	Length	Model	Chassis	Engine	Fuel Type	Average Price per Linear Foot When New	Adjusted Wheelbase	Approx. Towing Capacity	Gross Vehicle Weight Rating	Average Curb Weight
Windsor	1999	MHA	32	32 SB FD	RO	CU330	D	$5500	191	10,000	29,000	24,470

Livability Code: SB 30-90
Wheelbase-to-length ratio of 50% is considered ◉ dangerous ○ fatiguing ○ good ○ excellent *
The approximate net payload of 4530 pounds at 16% of GVWR on this model is ○ deficient ○ excessive ○ cautionary ○ good ◉ excellent *
Total highway safety penalties are: 2 *   Value: **7 9**   Durability: **7 5**   Highway Control Rating: **5 3**   Highway Safety: **5 1**

Brand	Year	Type	Length	Model	Chassis	Engine	Fuel Type	Average Price per Linear Foot When New	Adjusted Wheelbase	Approx. Towing Capacity	Gross Vehicle Weight Rating	Average Curb Weight
Windsor	1999	MHA	34	34 PB FD	RO	CU330	D	$5100	217	10,000	29,000	25,093

Livability Code: SB 30-90
Wheelbase-to-length ratio of 53% is considered ○ dangerous ◉ fatiguing ○ good ○ excellent *
The approximate net payload of 3907 pounds at 13% of GVWR on this model is ○ deficient ○ excessive ○ cautionary ◉ good ○ excellent *
Total highway safety penalties are: 2 *   Value: **7 9**   Durability: **7 5**   Highway Control Rating: **7 1**   Highway Safety: **6 9**   ★★

Brand	Year	Type	Length	Model	Chassis	Engine	Fuel Type	Average Price per Linear Foot When New	Adjusted Wheelbase	Approx. Towing Capacity	Gross Vehicle Weight Rating	Average Curb Weight
Windsor	1999	MHA	34	34 PB FD myc	RO	CU330	D	$5100	217	10,000	31,300	26,243

Livability Code: SB 30-90
Wheelbase-to-length ratio of 53% is considered ○ dangerous ◉ fatiguing ○ good ○ excellent *
The approximate net payload of 5057 pounds at 16% of GVWR on this model is ○ deficient ○ excessive ○ cautionary ○ good ◉ excellent *
Total highway safety penalties are: 2 *   Value: **7 9**   Durability: **7 5**   Highway Control Rating: **7 6**   Highway Safety: **7 4**   ★★★

Note: Safety ratings are based on the assumption that the engineering of the RV has allowed for proper balance by placing fresh, gray, and black holding tanks in a location so as not to change the balance of the RV when the tanks are empty or full. **Always double-check wheelbase, GVWR, and weights at front and rear axles.**

*See Section 1 for details on how conclusions are reached.

Brand	Year	Type	Length	Model	Chassis	Engine	Fuel Type	Average Price per Linear Foot When New	Adjusted Wheelbase	Approx. Towing Capacity	Gross Vehicle Weight Rating	Average Curb Weight
Windsor	1999	MHA	36	36 PB FD	RO	CU330	D	$4900	228	10,000	29,000	25,716

Livability Code: SB 30-90
Wheelbase-to-length ratio of 53% is considered ○ dangerous ◉ fatiguing ○ good ○ excellent *
The approximate net payload of 3284 pounds at 11% of GVWR on this model is ○ deficient ○ excessive ○ cautionary ◉ good ○ excellent *
Total highway safety penalties are: 2 * Value: 79 Durability: 75 Highway Control Rating: 65 Highway Safety: 63 ★★

Brand	Year	Type	Length	Model	Chassis	Engine	Fuel Type	Price/Ft	Wheelbase	Towing	GVWR	Curb Weight
Windsor	1999	MHA	36	36 SB FD	RO	CU330	D	$4900	228	10,000	29,000	25,716

Livability Code: SB 30-90
Wheelbase-to-length ratio of 53% is considered ○ dangerous ◉ fatiguing ○ good ○ excellent *
The approximate net payload of 3284 pounds at 11% of GVWR on this model is ○ deficient ○ excessive ○ cautionary ◉ good ○ excellent *
Total highway safety penalties are: 2 * Value: 79 Durability: 75 Highway Control Rating: 65 Highway Safety: 63 ★★

Windsor	1999	MHA	36	36 Suite Slide FD	RO	CU330	D	$4900	228	10,000	29,000	26,691

Livability Code: SB 30-90
Wheelbase-to-length ratio of 53% is considered ○ dangerous ◉ fatiguing ○ good ○ excellent *
The approximate net payload of 2309 pounds at 8% of GVWR on this model is ○ deficient ○ excessive ◉ cautionary ○ good ○ excellent *
Total highway safety penalties are: 13 * Value: 74 Durability: 75 Highway Control Rating: 52 Highway Safety: 39

Windsor	1999	MHA	36	36 Suite Slide PB FD	RO	CU330	D	$4900	228	10,000	29,000	26,691

Livability Code: SB 30-90
Wheelbase-to-length ratio of 53% is considered ○ dangerous ◉ fatiguing ○ good ○ excellent *
The approximate net payload of 2309 pounds at 8% of GVWR on this model is ○ deficient ○ excessive ◉ cautionary ○ good ○ excellent *
Total highway safety penalties are: 13 * Value: 74 Durability: 75 Highway Control Rating: 52 Highway Safety: 39

Windsor	1999	MHA	36	36 PB FD myc	RO	CU330	D	$4900	228	10,000	31,300	26,504

Livability Code: SB 30-90
Wheelbase-to-length ratio of 53% is considered ○ dangerous ◉ fatiguing ○ good ○ excellent *
The approximate net payload of 4796 pounds at 15% of GVWR on this model is ○ deficient ○ excessive ○ cautionary ◉ good ○ excellent *
Total highway safety penalties are: 2 * Value: 79 Durability: 75 Highway Control Rating: 74 Highway Safety: 72 ★★★

Windsor	1999	MHA	36	36 SB FD myc	RO	CU330	D	$4900	228	10,000	31,300	26,504

Livability Code: SB 30-90
Wheelbase-to-length ratio of 53% is considered ○ dangerous ◉ fatiguing ○ good ○ excellent *
The approximate net payload of 4796 pounds at 15% of GVWR on this model is ○ deficient ○ excessive ○ cautionary ◉ good ○ excellent *
Total highway safety penalties are: 2 * Value: 79 Durability: 75 Highway Control Rating: 74 Highway Safety: 72 ★★★

Windsor	1999	MHA	38	38 PB FD	RO	CU330	D	$4600	242	10,000	31,300	27,489

Livability Code: SB 30-90
Wheelbase-to-length ratio of 53% is considered ○ dangerous ◉ fatiguing ○ good ○ excellent *
The approximate net payload of 3811 pounds at 12% of GVWR on this model is ○ deficient ○ excessive ○ cautionary ◉ good ○ excellent *
Total highway safety penalties are: 2 * Value: 79 Durability: 75 Highway Control Rating: 68 Highway Safety: 66 ★★

Windsor	1999	MHA	38	38 Suite Slide FD	RO	CU330	D	$4600	242	10,000	31,300	28,464

Livability Code: SB 30-90
Wheelbase-to-length ratio of 53% is considered ○ dangerous ◉ fatiguing ○ good ○ excellent *
The approximate net payload of 2836 pounds at 9% of GVWR on this model is ○ deficient ○ excessive ◉ cautionary ○ good ○ excellent *
Total highway safety penalties are: 13 * Value: 74 Durability: 75 Highway Control Rating: 59 Highway Safety: 46

Windsor	1999	MHA	40	40 Suite Slide FD	RO	CU330	D	$4400	242	10,000	31,300	29,178

Livability Code: SB 30-90
Wheelbase-to-length ratio of 50% is considered ◉ dangerous ○ fatiguing ○ good ○ excellent *
The approximate net payload of 2123 pounds at 7% of GVWR on this model is ○ deficient ○ excessive ◉ cautionary ○ good ○ excellent *
Total highway safety penalties are: 13 * Value: 74 Durability: 75 Highway Control Rating: 27 Highway Safety: 14

Windsor	1999	MHA	40	40 Slide FD opch	RO	CU330	D	$4400	270	10,000	31,300	29,178

Livability Code: SB 30-90
Wheelbase-to-length ratio of 56% is considered ○ dangerous ○ fatiguing ◉ good ○ excellent *
The approximate net payload of 2123 pounds at 7% of GVWR on this model is ○ deficient ○ excessive ◉ cautionary ○ good ○ excellent *
Total highway safety penalties are: 13 * Value: 74 Durability: 75 Highway Control Rating: 68 Highway Safety: 55 ★

Xplorer	1990	MHA	36	SP 440	SP	Cu6BT	D	$4500	243	1,500	25,750	20,270

Livability Code: SB 30-90
Wheelbase-to-length ratio of 56% is considered ○ dangerous ○ fatiguing ◉ good ○ excellent *
The approximate net payload of 5480 pounds at 21% of GVWR on this model is ○ deficient ○ excessive ○ cautionary ○ good ◉ excellent *
Total highway safety penalties are: 2 * Value: 81 Durability: 80 Highway Control Rating: 100 Highway Safety: 98 ★★★★

Xplorer	1990	MHB	19	230XL	DO	5.9L	G	$1900	127	1,500	7,500	6,621

Livability Code: SB 30-90
Wheelbase-to-length ratio of 55% is considered ○ dangerous ○ fatiguing ◉ good ○ excellent *
The approximate net payload of 879 pounds at 12% of GVWR on this model is ○ deficient ○ excessive ○ cautionary ◉ good ○ excellent *
Total highway safety penalties are: 2 * Value: 81 Durability: 80 Highway Control Rating: 84 Highway Safety: 82 ★★★★

Note: Safety ratings are based on the assumption that the engineering of the RV has allowed for proper balance by placing fresh, gray, and black holding tanks in a location so as not to change the balance of the RV when the tanks are empty or full. **Always double-check wheelbase, GVWR, and weights at front and rear axles.**

The RV Rating Book

*See Section 1 for details on how conclusions are reached.

Brand	Year	Type	Length	Model	Chassis	Engine	Fuel Type	Average Price per Linear Foot When New	Adjusted Wheelbase	Approx. Towing Capacity	Gross Vehicle Weight Rating	Average Curb Weight
Xplorer	1991	MHA	36	SP 36	SP	Cum	D	$5100	243	1,500	25,750	20,270

Livability Code: SB 30-90
Wheelbase-to-length ratio of 56% is considered ○ dangerous ○ fatiguing ◉ good ○ excellent *
The approximate net payload of 5480 pounds at 21% of GVWR on this model is ○ deficient ○ excessive ○ cautionary ○ good ◉ excellent *
Total highway safety penalties are: 2 * Value: 81 Durability: 80 Highway Control Rating: 100 Highway Safety: 98 ★★★★

Brand	Year	Type	Length	Model	Chassis	Engine	Fuel Type	Price/Lin Ft	Wheelbase	Towing	GVWR	Curb Wt
Xplorer	1991	MHB	19	230XL	DO	5.9L	G	$1900	127	1,500	7,500	6,088

Livability Code: VA 30-90
Wheelbase-to-length ratio of 55% is considered ○ dangerous ○ fatiguing ◉ good ○ excellent *
The approximate net payload of 1412 pounds at 19% of GVWR on this model is ○ deficient ○ excessive ○ cautionary ○ good ◉ excellent *
Total highway safety penalties are: 2 * Value: 81 Durability: 80 Highway Control Rating: 95 Highway Safety: 93 ★★★★

Xplorer	1993	MHB	18	197 STD	DO	5.9L	G	$1800	128	1,500	8,510	6,613

Livability Code: WE 40-80
Wheelbase-to-length ratio of 59% is considered ○ dangerous ○ fatiguing ○ good ◉ excellent *
The approximate net payload of 1897 pounds at 22% of GVWR on this model is ○ deficient ○ excessive ○ cautionary ○ good ◉ excellent *
Total highway safety penalties are: 2 * Value: 81 Durability: 80 Highway Control Rating: 100 Highway Safety: 98 ★★★★

Xplorer	1993	MHB	19	XTRA VAN	DO	5.9L	G	$1900	128	1,500	8,510	7,056

Livability Code: WE 40-80
Wheelbase-to-length ratio of 55% is considered ○ dangerous ○ fatiguing ◉ good ○ excellent *
The approximate net payload of 1455 pounds at 17% of GVWR on this model is ○ deficient ○ excessive ○ cautionary ○ good ◉ excellent *
Total highway safety penalties are: 2 * Value: 81 Durability: 80 Highway Control Rating: 95 Highway Safety: 93 ★★★★

Xplorer	1993	MHB	19	XTRA VAN TB	DO	5.9L	G	$1900	128	1,500	8,510	7,056

Livability Code: WE 40-80
Wheelbase-to-length ratio of 55% is considered ○ dangerous ○ fatiguing ◉ good ○ excellent *
The approximate net payload of 1455 pounds at 17% of GVWR on this model is ○ deficient ○ excessive ○ cautionary ○ good ◉ excellent *
Total highway safety penalties are: 2 * Value: 81 Durability: 80 Highway Control Rating: 95 Highway Safety: 93 ★★★★

Xplorer	1993	MHB	19	XTRA VAN SB	DO	5.9L	G	$2000	128	1,500	8,510	7,156

Livability Code: WE 40-80
Wheelbase-to-length ratio of 55% is considered ○ dangerous ○ fatiguing ◉ good ○ excellent *
The approximate net payload of 1355 pounds at 16% of GVWR on this model is ○ deficient ○ excessive ○ cautionary ○ good ◉ excellent *
Total highway safety penalties are: 2 * Value: 81 Durability: 80 Highway Control Rating: 94 Highway Safety: 92 ★★★★

Xplorer	1993	MHB	19	197 MAX	DO	5.9L	G	$1800	128	1,500	8,510	6,850

Livability Code: WE 40-80
Wheelbase-to-length ratio of 55% is considered ○ dangerous ○ fatiguing ◉ good ○ excellent *
The approximate net payload of 1661 pounds at 20% of GVWR on this model is ○ deficient ○ excessive ○ cautionary ○ good ◉ excellent *
Total highway safety penalties are: 2 * Value: 81 Durability: 80 Highway Control Rating: 97 Highway Safety: 95 ★★★★

Xplorer	1993	MHB	20	230XL	DO	5.9L	G	$2100	128	1,500	8,510	7,268

Livability Code: WE 40-80
Wheelbase-to-length ratio of 53% is considered ○ dangerous ◉ fatiguing ○ good ○ excellent *
The approximate net payload of 1243 pounds at 15% of GVWR on this model is ○ deficient ○ excessive ○ cautionary ◉ good ○ excellent *
Total highway safety penalties are: 2 * Value: 81 Durability: 80 Highway Control Rating: 79 Highway Safety: 77 ★★★

Xplorer	1994	MHB	18	197 STD	DO	5.9L	G	$2000	128	1,500	8,510	6,613

Livability Code: WE 40-80
Wheelbase-to-length ratio of 59% is considered ○ dangerous ○ fatiguing ○ good ◉ excellent *
The approximate net payload of 1897 pounds at 22% of GVWR on this model is ○ deficient ○ excessive ○ cautionary ○ good ◉ excellent *
Total highway safety penalties are: 2 * Value: 81 Durability: 80 Highway Control Rating: 100 Highway Safety: 98 ★★★★

Xplorer	1994	MHB	19	XTRA VAN 222	DO	5.9L	G	$2200	128	1,500	8,510	7,056

Livability Code: WE 40-80
Wheelbase-to-length ratio of 55% is considered ○ dangerous ○ fatiguing ◉ good ○ excellent *
The approximate net payload of 1455 pounds at 17% of GVWR on this model is ○ deficient ○ excessive ○ cautionary ○ good ◉ excellent *
Total highway safety penalties are: 2 * Value: 81 Durability: 80 Highway Control Rating: 95 Highway Safety: 93 ★★★★

Xplorer	1994	MHB	19	XTRA VAN SB	DO	5.9L	G	$2200	128	1,500	8,510	7,156

Livability Code: WE 40-80
Wheelbase-to-length ratio of 55% is considered ○ dangerous ○ fatiguing ◉ good ○ excellent *
The approximate net payload of 1355 pounds at 16% of GVWR on this model is ○ deficient ○ excessive ○ cautionary ○ good ◉ excellent *
Total highway safety penalties are: 2 * Value: 81 Durability: 80 Highway Control Rating: 94 Highway Safety: 92 ★★★★

Xplorer	1994	MHB	19	197 MAX	DO	5.9L	G	$2000	128	1,500	8,510	6,850

Livability Code: WE 40-80
Wheelbase-to-length ratio of 55% is considered ○ dangerous ○ fatiguing ◉ good ○ excellent *
The approximate net payload of 1661 pounds at 20% of GVWR on this model is ○ deficient ○ excessive ○ cautionary ○ good ◉ excellent *
Total highway safety penalties are: 2 * Value: 81 Durability: 80 Highway Control Rating: 97 Highway Safety: 95 ★★★★

Note: Safety ratings are based on the assumption that the engineering of the RV has allowed for proper balance by placing fresh, gray, and black holding tanks in a location so as not to change the balance of the RV when the tanks are empty or full. **Always double-check wheelbase, GVWR, and weights at front and rear axles.**

*See Section 1 for details on how conclusions are reached.

Brand	Year	Type	Length	Model	Chassis	Engine	Fuel Type	Average Price per Linear Foot When New	Adjusted Wheelbase	Approx. Towing Capacity	Gross Vehicle Weight Rating	Average Curb Weight
Xplorer	1994	MHB	19	XTRA VAN TB	DO	5.9L	G	$2200	128	1,500	8,510	7,056

Livability Code: WE 40-80
Wheelbase-to-length ratio of 55% is considered ○ dangerous ○ fatiguing ◉ good ○ excellent *
The approximate net payload of 1455 pounds at 17% of GVWR on this model is ○ deficient ○ excessive ○ cautionary ○ good ◉ excellent *
Total highway safety penalties are: 2 *   Value: 8 1   Durability: 8 0   Highway Control Rating: 9 5   Highway Safety: 9 3   ★★★★

Brand	Year	Type	Length	Model	Chassis	Engine	Fuel Type	Price/LF	Wheelbase	Towing	GVWR	Curb Weight
Xplorer	1994	MHB	20	230XL	DO	5.9L	G	$2300	128	1,500	8,510	7,268

Livability Code: WE 40-80
Wheelbase-to-length ratio of 53% is considered ○ dangerous ◉ fatiguing ○ good ○ excellent *
The approximate net payload of 1243 pounds at 15% of GVWR on this model is ○ deficient ○ excessive ○ cautionary ◉ good ○ excellent *
Total highway safety penalties are: 2 *   Value: 8 1   Durability: 8 0   Highway Control Rating: 7 9   Highway Safety: 7 7   ★★★

Xplorer	1994	MHB	21	236XL	DO	5.9L	G	$2200	128	1,500	8,510	7,374

Livability Code: WE 40-80
Wheelbase-to-length ratio of 51% is considered ○ dangerous ◉ fatiguing ○ good ○ excellent *
The approximate net payload of 1137 pounds at 13% of GVWR on this model is ○ deficient ○ excessive ○ cautionary ◉ good ○ excellent *
Total highway safety penalties are: 2 *   Value: 8 1   Durability: 8 0   Highway Control Rating: 6 3   Highway Safety: 6 1   ★★

Xplorer	1996	MHB	18	197S	DO	5.9L	G	$2300	128	1,500	8,510	6,647

Livability Code: WE 40-80
Wheelbase-to-length ratio of 60% is considered ○ dangerous ○ fatiguing ○ good ◉ excellent *
The approximate net payload of 1863 pounds at 22% of GVWR on this model is ○ deficient ○ excessive ○ cautionary ○ good ◉ excellent *
Total highway safety penalties are: 2 *   Value: 8 1   Durability: 8 0   Highway Control Rating: 1 0 0   Highway Safety: 9 8   ★★★★

Xplorer	1996	MHB	20	197M	DO	5.9L	G	$2300	128	1,500	8,510	6,957

Livability Code: WE 40-80
Wheelbase-to-length ratio of 54% is considered ○ dangerous ○ fatiguing ◉ good ○ excellent *
The approximate net payload of 1553 pounds at 18% of GVWR on this model is ○ deficient ○ excessive ○ cautionary ○ good ◉ excellent *
Total highway safety penalties are: 2 *   Value: 8 1   Durability: 8 0   Highway Control Rating: 8 7   Highway Safety: 8 5   ★★★★

Xplorer	1996	MHB	21	230XL	DO	5.9L	G	$2400	128	1,500	8,510	7,320

Livability Code: WE 40-80
Wheelbase-to-length ratio of 52% is considered ○ dangerous ◉ fatiguing ○ good ○ excellent *
The approximate net payload of 1190 pounds at 14% of GVWR on this model is ○ deficient ○ excessive ○ cautionary ○ good ○ excellent *
Total highway safety penalties are: 2 *   Value: 8 1   Durability: 8 0   Highway Control Rating: 7 0   Highway Safety: 6 8   ★★

Xplorer	1996	MHB	21	236XL	DO	5.9L	G	$2400	128	1,500	8,510	7,444

Livability Code: WE 40-80
Wheelbase-to-length ratio of 50% is considered ◉ dangerous ○ fatiguing ○ good ○ excellent *
The approximate net payload of 1067 pounds at 13% of GVWR on this model is ○ deficient ○ excessive ○ cautionary ◉ good ○ excellent *
Total highway safety penalties are: 2 *   Value: 8 1   Durability: 8 0   Highway Control Rating: 5 9   Highway Safety: 5 7

Xplorer	1997	MHB	17	197 Standard	DO	5.2L	G	$2500	128	1,500	6,400	5,898

Livability Code: VA 30-90
Wheelbase-to-length ratio of 63% is considered ○ dangerous ○ fatiguing ○ good ◉ excellent *
The approximate net payload of 502 pounds at 8% of GVWR on this model is ○ deficient ○ excessive ◉ cautionary ○ good ○ excellent *
Total highway safety penalties are: 2 *   Value: 8 1   Durability: 8 0   Highway Control Rating: 9 8   Highway Safety: 9 6   ★★★★

Xplorer	1997	MHB	18	MUR-VAN	DO	5.2L	G	$2300	128	1,500	6,400	6,095

Livability Code: VA 30-90
Wheelbase-to-length ratio of 59% is considered ○ dangerous ○ fatiguing ○ good ◉ excellent *
The approximate net payload of 305 pounds at 5% of GVWR on this model is ◉ deficient ○ excessive ○ cautionary ○ good ○ excellent *
Total highway safety penalties are: 2 *   Value: 8 1   Durability: 8 0   Highway Control Rating: 7 2   Highway Safety: 7 0   ★★

Xplorer	1997	MHB	19	197 MAXI	DO	5.2L	G	$2300	128	1,500	6,400	6,253

Livability Code: VA 30-90
Wheelbase-to-length ratio of 57% is considered ○ dangerous ○ fatiguing ◉ good ○ excellent *
The approximate net payload of 147 pounds at 2% of GVWR on this model is ◉ deficient ○ excessive ○ cautionary ○ good ○ excellent *
Total highway safety penalties are: 2 *   Value: 8 1   Durability: 8 0   Highway Control Rating: 6 1   Highway Safety: 5 9   ★

Xplorer	1997	MHB	19	230XL	DO	5.9L	G	$2700	128	1,500	8,510	7,216

Livability Code: VA 30-90
Wheelbase-to-length ratio of 55% is considered ○ dangerous ○ fatiguing ◉ good ○ excellent *
The approximate net payload of 1294 pounds at 15% of GVWR on this model is ○ deficient ○ excessive ○ cautionary ◉ good ○ excellent *
Total highway safety penalties are: 2 *   Value: 8 1   Durability: 8 0   Highway Control Rating: 9 1   Highway Safety: 8 9   ★★★★

Xplorer	1997	MHB	21	236XL	DO	5.9L	G	$2400	128	1,500	8,510	7,644

Livability Code: VA 30-90
Wheelbase-to-length ratio of 50% is considered ◉ dangerous ○ fatiguing ○ good ○ excellent *
The approximate net payload of 866 pounds at 10% of GVWR on this model is ○ deficient ○ excessive ○ cautionary ◉ good ○ excellent *
Total highway safety penalties are: 2 *   Value: 8 1   Durability: 8 0   Highway Control Rating: 5 3   Highway Safety: 5 1

Note: Safety ratings are based on the assumption that the engineering of the RV has allowed for proper balance by placing fresh, gray, and black holding tanks in a location so as not to change the balance of the RV when the tanks are empty or full. **Always double-check wheelbase, GVWR, and weights at front and rear axles.**

Brand	Year	Type	Length	Model	Chassis	Engine	Fuel Type	Average Price per Linear Foot When New	Adjusted Wheel-base	Approx. Towing Capacity	Gross Vehicle Weight Rating	Average Curb Weight
Xplorer	1998	MHB	19	230XLW	DO	5.9L	G	$2700	128	1,500	8,510	7,264

Livability Code: VA 30-90

Wheelbase-to-length ratio of 55% is considered ○ dangerous ○ fatiguing ◉ good ○ excellent *

The approximate net payload of 1246 pounds at 15% of GVWR on this model is ○ deficient ○ excessive ○ cautionary ◉ good ○ excellent *

Total highway safety penalties are: 2 *   Value: 8 1   Durability: 8 0   Highway Control Rating: 9 1   Highway Safety: 8 9   ★★★★

Brand	Year	Type	Length	Model	Chassis	Engine	Fuel Type	Price/LF	Wheelbase	Towing	GVWR	Curb Wt
Xplorer	1998	MHB	21	236XLW	DO	5.9L	G	$2500	128	1,500	8,510	7,437

Livability Code: VA 30-90

Wheelbase-to-length ratio of 51% is considered ○ dangerous ◉ fatiguing ○ good ○ excellent *

The approximate net payload of 1073 pounds at 13% of GVWR on this model is ○ deficient ○ excessive ○ cautionary ◉ good ○ excellent *

Total highway safety penalties are: 2 *   Value: 8 1   Durability: 8 0   Highway Control Rating: 6 3   Highway Safety: 6 1   ★★

Brand	Year	Type	Length	Model	Chassis	Engine	Fuel Type	Price/LF	Wheelbase	Towing	GVWR	Curb Wt
Xplorer	1999	MHB	20	TBM SP	DO	5.2L	G	$2700	127	1,500	8,700	6,934

Livability Code: VA 30-90

Wheelbase-to-length ratio of 54% is considered ○ dangerous ○ fatiguing ◉ good ○ excellent *

The approximate net payload of 1766 pounds at 20% of GVWR on this model is ○ deficient ○ excessive ○ cautionary ○ good ◉ excellent *

Total highway safety penalties are: 2 *   Value: 8 1   Durability: 8 0   Highway Control Rating: 9 0   Highway Safety: 8 8   ★★★★

Brand	Year	Type	Length	Model	Chassis	Engine	Fuel Type	Price/LF	Wheelbase	Towing	GVWR	Curb Wt
Xplorer	1999	MHB	20	TBM SU	DO	5.2L	G	$2700	127	1,500	8,700	7,184

Livability Code: VA 30-90

Wheelbase-to-length ratio of 54% is considered ○ dangerous ○ fatiguing ◉ good ○ excellent *

The approximate net payload of 1516 pounds at 17% of GVWR on this model is ○ deficient ○ excessive ○ cautionary ○ good ◉ excellent *

Total highway safety penalties are: 2 *   Value: 8 1   Durability: 8 0   Highway Control Rating: 8 8   Highway Safety: 8 6   ★★★★

Brand	Year	Type	Length	Model	Chassis	Engine	Fuel Type	Price/LF	Wheelbase	Towing	GVWR	Curb Wt
Xplorer XMC	1991	MHA	25	25	CH	7.4L	G	$2100	145	1,500	10,400	9,810

Livability Code: 30-80

Wheelbase-to-length ratio of 48% is considered ◉ dangerous ○ fatiguing ○ good ○ excellent *

The approximate net payload of 590 pounds at 6% of GVWR on this model is ◉ deficient ○ excessive ○ cautionary ○ good ○ excellent *

Total highway safety penalties are: 2 *   Value: 8 1   Durability: 8 0   Highway Control Rating: 4   Highway Safety: 2

Brand	Year	Type	Length	Model	Chassis	Engine	Fuel Type	Price/LF	Wheelbase	Towing	GVWR	Curb Wt
Xplorer XMC TB	1990	MHA	25	25	DO	5.9L	G	$2000	145	1,500	10,400	9,558

Livability Code: 30-80

Wheelbase-to-length ratio of 48% is considered ◉ dangerous ○ fatiguing ○ good ○ excellent *

The approximate net payload of 842 pounds at 8% of GVWR on this model is ○ deficient ○ excessive ◉ cautionary ○ good ○ excellent *

Total highway safety penalties are: 2 *   Value: 8 1   Durability: 8 0   Highway Control Rating: 1 6   Highway Safety: 1 4

Brand	Year	Type	Length	Model	Chassis	Engine	Fuel Type	Price/LF	Wheelbase	Towing	GVWR	Curb Wt
Zanzibar	1999	MHA	39	3876	MA	CA275	D	$3800	252	4,000	29,000	23,931

Livability Code: SB 30-90

Wheelbase-to-length ratio of 54% is considered ○ dangerous ○ fatiguing ◉ good ○ excellent *

The approximate net payload of 5069 pounds at 17% of GVWR on this model is ○ deficient ○ excessive ○ cautionary ○ good ◉ excellent *

Total highway safety penalties are: 13 *   Value: 7 2   Durability: 7 0   Highway Control Rating: 8 4   Highway Safety: 7 1   ★★★

Brand	Year	Type	Length	Model	Chassis	Engine	Fuel Type	Price/LF	Wheelbase	Towing	GVWR	Curb Wt
Zanzibar	1999	MHA	39	3886	MA	CA275	D	$3800	252	4,000	29,000	24,006

Livability Code: SB 30-90

Wheelbase-to-length ratio of 54% is considered ○ dangerous ○ fatiguing ◉ good ○ excellent *

The approximate net payload of 4994 pounds at 17% of GVWR on this model is ○ deficient ○ excessive ○ cautionary ○ good ◉ excellent *

Total highway safety penalties are: 14 *   Value: 7 1   Durability: 7 0   Highway Control Rating: 8 4   Highway Safety: 7 0   ★★★

Note: Safety ratings are based on the assumption that the engineering of the RV has allowed for proper balance by placing fresh, gray, and black holding tanks in a location so as not to change the balance of the RV when the tanks are empty or full. **Always double-check wheelbase, GVWR, and weights at front and rear axles.**

*See Section 1 for details on how conclusions are reached.

Motor Homes Glossary

from

The Language of RVing

by JD Gallant

AC:

When you talk about AC (alternating current), you should be thinking about household electricity — the 110 to 120 volt current that makes modern living so pleasurable. Alternating current is produced by generators and alternators. (Even Hoover Dam and nuclear power plants are nothing more than big generators.) In alternating current, the electrons function much like snowbirds — they spend their lives moving back and forth between point A and point B. (Direct current electrons are like RV trekkers — they just keep going.) It's important to remember that AC is dangerous whether it's coming from a 600 watt portable generator or from a million watt turbine. Work with AC only if you know what you are doing.

actual cash value:

The real value of any RV to a dealership is its actual cash value (ACV). The salesperson may talk wholesale or retail value, but in the back of his or her mind there's a figure of the real worth that must be used to calculate the trade. Normally, ACV is the book wholesale value plus or minus condition, options, size, floor plan, interior colors, and other factors that influence salability.

For example, if a 1985 motor home 30 feet long that has twin beds, orange interior, and a small dent on the side is being considered as a trade-in, the wholesale value might be $10,000 but because of the condition and the unpopularity of the length, floor plan, and color, the salesperson might give it an ACV of $8,600. The salesperson will also consider the length of time the RV might sit on the lot. Of course, if the RV is in exceptional condition, the positives could give the unit an ACV above the book wholesale figure. The ACV will be the same amount the dealership would pay in cash.

Having been both RV buyer and salesperson, I know how hard it is to find out if a trade-in allowance is fair. The easiest way to do this is to: 1) get a quote from three RV dealers who are receptive towards buying your RV outright, and 2) get wholesale figures from at least two RV appraisal books. Average the two highest bids and the two appraisal book figures and you will have a fair ACV value. Add the normal no-trade discount of the RV you are buying and you'll have a good basis for a trade-in allowance.

Most of us think our RVs are worth more than they actually are, but I've also found too many who have practically given their RVs away. Knowing the real value of your RV will help make you a happy camper.

aluminum roof:

If you were an RV manufacturer and you wanted to put the cheapest roof you could on the RVs you were building, you would probably choose the flat, one-piece, thin-aluminum roof. The one-piece, thin-aluminum roof is nothing more than a single sheet of aluminum of approximately .020-inch thickness that you lay over the roof rafters (you might opt for plywood or chipboard backing if you wanted to push it) and then peen it over the sides (you might opt to leave the front and rear cuts out of sight), and cut holes so you can install your vents and accessories.

Salespeople can now easily tell prospective buyers that the roof cannot leak because it's a solid, one-piece, metal roof. They fail to tell you (probably because they don't know) that the one-piece, thin-aluminum roof has the worst record of all types of roofs for leaking around vents and along the edge of the roof. This roof is very subject to expansion and contraction from heat and cold. This expansion and contraction creates stress at all points of fastening which causes a loosening of fasteners and sealants. Because this type of roof is not forgiving to poor manufacturing practices, a prospective buyer should look carefully at the manufacturer who installs it.

altitude performance:

Many motor homes with carbureted engines that perform well at altitudes near sea level may lose performance at higher altitudes. Diesel and gas injected engines are normally not affected. If you have a problem of this nature, you should find a good "mountain" mechanic and a service bulletin from the engine's builder that tells how to make corrections.

ammeter:

A device for measuring the amount of flow of current in an electrical circuit, the ammeter can be very helpful to the RVer. By watching an ammeter, you will get an idea of how much electricity is being used by the various lights and accessories as they are turned on. Of course, this might not be important if you always have full hookups; but should you go RV trekking or boon-docking, you might find that the amount of electricity used becomes very important.

Since an ammeter hooks directly into the main DC circuit, you must use extreme care in connecting wires for the extension, in soldering the connectors and terminal ends, and in fastening the terminal ends to the meter. Sloppy work at installing an ammeter will cause more trouble than it will cure. If you have the work done by a mechanic, always double check to be sure that the connections do not add resistance to the circuit.

ampere:

Amperage is a measurement of electron flow in the electrical circuit and is called "amps" (not juice!). The exact amount of electrons flowing to make one amp is 6,250,000,000,000,000,000 in one second. While the amount of electron flow through a circuit is variable, the voltage should be a constant. For example, a 4 kW RV generator may put out 110 to 120 volts, but amperes could vary from 1 to almost 40 depending upon the demand. The electron flow (amperes) is determined by the amount of electrical pressure (voltage) produced by the battery or the generator.

Let's think of the wire as a community of very tiny beings (we call them electrons) that spend their lives sleeping. In order to get these little guys out of bed and working for you, you need an electron alarm clock. A generator or battery is perfect for the job because either one is capable of building enough pressure (voltage) to pull and push the electrons out of their resting place and move them back and forth along the wire just as soon as you flip the light switch. The electrons are so angry at being rudely awakened that they create heat energy (electricity) in the process. If by turning on one small light you have upset 6,250,000,000,000,000,000 of these tiny beings, just think of the riot you cause every time you start the coffee pot.

I understand how easy it is to get lost in the technical aspects of electricity. Even though we live in a world of atomic energy and computers, fathoming the power and movements of this itsy bitsy teeny weeny thing can make our brains spin.

Another way to consider voltage and amperage is to think of your generator or battery as a dammed lake. Think of the power of the water behind the dam as voltage. Now, think of every drop of water that flows through the dam as an electron. When you take a shower, think about it. It won't take long for you to get a good picture of water drops (electrons) being moved by pressure (voltage) from a dam or pump (generator or battery) to give you a good washing. Think of it just enough to help you understand what keeps your RV going. Leave the theory to the scientists.

ANSI:

The only construction code to which the RV industry somewhat adheres is known simply as ANSI. Somewhere in the past, I believe, this stood for American National Standards Institute which eventually became American Standards Association. The standards for the RV industry are now under the combined control of the National Fire Protection Association (NFPA) and Recreational Vehicle Industry Association (RVIA). There is no legal enforcement power attached to ANSI. It is strictly a guide designed for any governing bodies and various associations who wish to use it.

ASME:

Permanently mounted on an RV, the ASME tank is built to specifications approved by the American Society of Mechanical Engineers. ASME tanks are used on motor homes and vehicles that use LPG (liquid petroleum gas) as motor fuel.

axle dry weight:

If you were to pull your brand new RV onto a scale before you loaded it with fuel, LPG, fresh water and your personal gear, you would be getting the axle dry weight.

axle ratio:

To acquire more power at the rear wheels, all engine-driven vehicles have a system of gears for the driving wheels. These gear sets come with varying ratios needed to acquire either power or efficiency. As an example, a 4 to 1 axle ratio will allow for power while a 3 to 1 axle ratio will allow for fuel efficiency when cruising.

Every RVer needs to understand that axle ratio is a very important part of the lifestyle. The relationships of power, speed, fuel efficiency, and engine life are intricately tied to axle ratios. You cannot avoid the subject. Decisions about axle ratios should be made in conjunction with RV weight, driving habits, and budget. A major consideration should be the amount of miles you expect to travel with a load and the amount of miles you travel empty.

For those of you who want to know some of the technical aspects of getting power to the drive wheels, you'll need to focus on the following:

1) torque represents the amount of power at the drive wheels,
2) to develop torque you'll need horsepower at the engine and gearing at the wheels,
3) torque is directly relative to RPM and horsepower,
4) a 1 to 1 axle ratio represents a turn of the drive wheel for every revolution of the drive shaft, and
5) you should be able to get most of the information required about axle ratios from your operator's manual.

Something to consider about your driving habits is that too low gears will cause more engine wear because the engine turns more RPMs per mile. Too high gears will cause premature failure by keeping combustion chamber temperatures too high. I've known RVers who wear out their engines well under 50,000 miles just because they pushed low-geared motor homes too hard on hills. Big motor homes with little engines need to be low geared to get them to move. If you have this type of combination, be careful about pushing the pedal to the metal. Get the right information and think about your driving habits. Don't learn the hard way.

back-end:

The "back-end" is a term used to refer to the selling of services after the sale of the vehicle. Back-end selling is usually conducted by an F&I (finance and insurance) officer, business manager, or finance manager. In small dealerships, the salesperson or sales manager may sell back-end services.

Back-end gross profits to the dealership usually equal or exceed the gross profit on the vehicle purchase. These services include financing, payment protection, life insurance, extended service coverage, and various vehicle coatings. A buyer should be aware that he or she will be exposed to high-pressure selling of these services.

balance:

Balance is a critical factor for a motor home's handling characteristics. If the balance of an RV is off, the unit will sway and handle poorly. Although storage compartments are important to the RVing lifestyle, simply filling these compartments can be very dangerous. A typical RVer will fill every empty space out of a sense of efficiency — which, of course, is destroyed in the process. The secret of good handling is keeping everything in balance. When you load, be careful not to get carried away with putting all your heavy tools and equipment in the wrong storage compartments. All RVs should travel level from front-to-rear and side-to-side under all load conditions.

base camp:

Those RVers who have truly made RVing a lifestyle have found that establishing an acceptable base camp is always a challenge. Since a base camp is a sojournment site where you might stay for a month or a year, selection has to be made carefully. You may want to establish a base camp for a variety of reasons, including a place to rest from travel until the mood to move on returns. Whatever the reason, you will want to look carefully at the location of the site and its occupants. Try to find at least three sites to choose from and then study the situation for a day or so before making one of them your temporary home. Even paying on a daily basis is better than putting out a month's rent and then wishing you were somewhere else. It's just another habit that makes RVing the pleasure it can be.

This is as good a time as any to mention RVing with dogs. I love a good dog, and I think dogs can be a great asset to the RVer if the animal is disciplined and not too large. The biggest problem with dogs is the rules of humans and the carelessness of dog owners. Dogs can be great companions and the best security device available. And don't underrate the many short walks around the trees or into the bushes that will keep you fit. A dog can be a great RV buddy — especially if you're a genuine RV trekker.

battery:

A battery is a grouping of voltaic cells, each of which produces approximately two volts of electricity by chemical action. Modern automotive and RV batteries contain six of these cells in series, thus producing a bit more than 12 volts of direct current. This type of battery is known as a lead-acid storage battery because positive and negative plates are made of a lead composition, and the liquid (or gel) electrolyte that starts the chemical action consists of sulfuric acid and water. The chemical action takes place whenever the two posts on top of the battery are connected. The amount of current flowing between the two posts is determined by the amount of resistance in the circuit from lights, motors, and other accessories as they do their jobs. Current in excess of 12 volts must be applied to the posts to recharge the battery. Alternators, generators, and converters with built-in battery chargers serve this purpose.

battery capacity:

It's confusing to try to determine how long a new or in-use battery will produce power to satisfy self-contained needs. Most deep-cycle battery manufacturers rate their batteries with a chart that will tell you how long they'll last if you discharge the battery at 5, 10, 15, 20, 25, etc., amps. I'm not sure whether the system was designed to make life miserable for RVers or simply to confuse the matter. Because of these inconsistencies, I've developed a system that I think will work for most RVers. The following system will tell you how much a new or in-use battery will produce for that trip to the countryside.

Begin with the premise that a maximum load put onto your batteries during the peak of the evening when dinner is being prepared is 10 amps. If you use more than that, your stay will probably be limited to a brisk walk before and after dinner — because your battery is going to die. If you use the 10-amp discharge rate to check your batteries, you can easily determine if there is enough capacity to serve your needs. Another reason I like to use this discharge rate is that 10 amps is approximately the amount of draw I get when I leave my headlights on — which you already know will kill the battery in a very short time.

Now that you've paid many thousands of dollars for an RV, why not spend a few bucks and install a voltmeter that will measure between 9 and 15 volts and an ammeter that will measure up to a 30 amp charge and discharge rate? (Good sets are available in most auto stores for less than $50.)

To use these meters correctly, check your battery voltage with everything off and your AC electrical cord disconnected. Note your battery voltage — which should be slightly over 12 volts. Turn on enough lights and accessories to show a 10 amp discharge on your ammeter. Set some sort of alarm for every 15 minutes and note the voltage each time it goes off until the battery voltage falls to 11.5 volts.

You now have a chart from which you can compare the battery discharge rate of your battery pack (or an individual battery) at any point in its life cycle. If you do this two or three times a year, you'll get a good picture of how long your battery power will last when you are in the desert or wilderness.

battery half-life:

Because batteries wear with use just like tires and engines, there is a time when it is practical to replace the batteries even though they can still produce some electricity. If you have two batteries in your RV that together are producing what one new battery should produce, these batteries have reached the half-life point. Instead of carrying two heavy batteries that may not serve your needs, you should consider replacing them.

battery hydrometer:

A hydrometer measures the specific gravity of liquids. It is used primarily to measure the concentration of sulfuric acid in the battery's electrolyte to tell us the state of charge of the individual cells. (Fully charged, specific gravity should be about 1.250.) Because many modern batteries are sealed, hydrometer checks are not always possible. It is, however, the only accurate way to check the condition of the electrolyte. If you do use a hydrometer, follow manufacturer's instructions closely. Remember that sulfuric acid is dangerous to eyes, skin, clothing, and paint. Always use eye protection and rubber gloves! If you can't use a hydrometer, perform a battery capacity test.

battery isolator:

When the generating system of the motor home is hooked up to an RV battery, it is advisable to separate the starting battery from the RV battery with an isolator. An isolator will prevent the discharge of the vehicle's starting battery when using lights and accessories in the RV. An isolator can be of the solenoid type or can function electronically. The solenoid type isolator is inexpensive and easy to install. It might, however, have to be replaced every few years because the mechanical part of the device wears every time it's used. The more expensive electronic isolators assist in regulating current to the RV battery and can last the life of the RV.

battery sulfation:

Because the electrical power produced by batteries is created by chemical action, there are certain processes that depreciate the energy output. Primary among these battery problems is a condition known as sulfation. Sulfation is the hardening of chemicals on the battery plates caused by being in a discharged state. RV and marine batteries are particularly subject to this condition because they are often left discharged for long periods or are not fully recharged.

As a battery discharges, the chemicals (primarily sulfuric acid) in the liquid (electrolyte) settle on the plates. A high charging rate of 14 to 16 volts will force the chemicals back into the water to give the battery a charged condition. If the voltage is not high enough to cause the chemicals to leave the plates, they will harden on the plates and reduce the ability of the battery to produce electrical power. Although deep cycle batteries are not as prone to sulfation as starting batteries, this condition is still the primary cause of premature battery failure. Always return your battery to a fully charged state as soon as possible.

Gel batteries may be another advancement for the RVing lifestyle. Claims are that these batteries withstand longer periods of discharge without damage to the battery and are less susceptible to overcharge than liquid electrolyte. If it works out this way, gel batteries can be a great improvement.

black water:

The water that comes from the RV toilet is called black water. The only place to dump black water is into a sewer system. Use a good biodegradable chemical to keep toilet odors out of the RV and help keep our environment clean.

blue book: See Kelley Blue Book.

bow wave:

Like the turbulence of water created by the bow of a boat, a bow wave is turbulence of air created by a moving vehicle. Example: When you're sitting in a small fishing boat and the bow wave of a larger boat hits your boat, you can easily feel the effect. The same thing can happen when moving air hits your RV.

If your motor home is not designed or balanced correctly, the bow wave of a passing truck can set up a swaying motion that is technically called "yaw". Sway has probably caused more accidents to RVs than any other single cause. I know of many cases when the

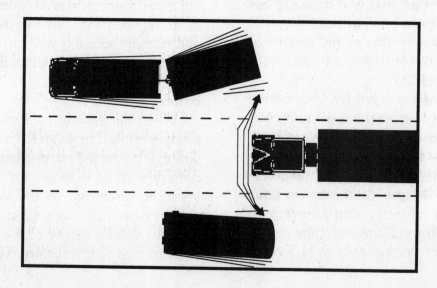

entire episode took less than a minute — ending with the RV on its side or in the ditch or both.

You cannot blame the bow wave for an accident anymore than you can blame eating for food poisoning. It should be obvious that a roadworthy RV will be designed, maintained, and loaded to negate the action of a bow wave.

Of course, the effects of a bow wave will be more noticeable with a short-wheelbase motor home. Motor homes having wheelbases 50 percent or shorter of the total length are greatly affected by bow waves. The higher the profile the greater the effect. I do not consider motor homes with such wheelbases as safe for highway travel. However, if you have a well balanced, long-wheelbase motor home, you should have little problem with bow waves.

brand name:

Whenever you go into an electronics store you probably notice that big promotions begin with the name. The name is almost everything in electronics equipment. This emphasis on brand name is the result of good promotions and public demand for good electronics products. We all know there are some names in stereos, televisions, and video recorders that are considered a safe buy. Because of this, those of us who are habitual shoppers choose the brand name and then shop for a price.

In the RV industry, name identification has a long ways to go. It is unfortunate that three out of every four RV shoppers can't connect the brand name with an RV manufacturer. The proliferation of new brand names from major manufacturers who want to capture a larger share of the market keeps complicating the problem. Still another reason for the problem has been the ease of getting into the RV manufacturing business. Small companies can emerge, build a good looking product, and the uninformed RV public will gobble it up. The process may be healthy for the free enterprise system, but it can be very costly to the RV consumer.

The major motor home manufacturers — Fleetwood, Winnebago, Holiday Rambler, National, Rexhall, Tiffin, Country Coach, Monaco, Coachmen, and others — are eager to capture you as a customer. Once you know the reputation of the manufacturer of any brand, you will be able to make better choices. Like most consumer products, RVs can be rated. Due to the lack of regulation, the consistency of the RV industry to produce a good product is much worse than quality consistency in the automobile industry. For this reason you must be more diligent in your consideration of brand name.

Brand names are so important to your investment factor that you should never invest in an RV without investigating the manufacturer. The philosophy of the parent corporation in regard to providing a good product will show up with a minimum of research. A good manufacturer will build a good product at a good value. Quality of workmanship will never be cut by good RV manufacturers, because they have reputations to protect. Good manufacturers hire good workers at all their plants and back their products with good warranties. Good RV manufacturers will produce RVs that will protect your investment.

As you begin your search for an RV, look at the brand name before you look at anything else. Look the salesperson straight in the eye as you ask about the manufacturer. Watch for answers without hesitation. As you go about the unit, compare quality in workmanship and materials with the statements the salesperson makes about the manufacturer. Always check with RV Consumer Group. If you begin to think this way, you might consider buying only from established manufacturers who have been around long enough to have a history. When you realize that all brands are not created equal, you'll have learned that RV value begins with the name.

Btu:

This designation of change in temperature stands for British thermal unit. A Btu is the amount of heat energy required to change the temperature of one pound of water by one degree of Fahrenheit at a specific temperature. A common RV furnace rating would be 25,000 Btu and an RV roof air conditioner would be 13,500 Btu.

buy-rate:

RV dealers can make money during buyer financing by getting a share of the interest money. They do this by getting a buy-rate from financial institutions then adding a profit to that rate. Some dealers will hold that profit to a fraction of a percentage point to cover costs of the financing office, but some get greedy and tack-on as many full percentage points as the unwary buyer will tolerate. Check my book *How to Buy an RV Without Getting Ripped Off* for more tips on financing.

buyer's agreement:

When you approve the basic price of an RV with options, sales tax, license, and trade-in value subject to other terms and conditions, you have concluded a buyer's agreement. When you tell the salesperson that you want the RV to be taken off the market and be prepared to your specifications, the buyer's agreement becomes a buyer's order. The buyer's order is a legal and binding contract between you and the dealership. The terms written across the face of the buyer's agreement must be explicit enough to allow you an opportunity to cancel the order if something goes awry.

cash conversion:

The term "cash conversion" describes the salesperson's approach to persuade the cash buyer that it is better to finance than to pay cash. The advantages stressed will be that the buyer will be able to get cheap payment protection, will have cash available for other needs, may be able to get income tax credits for interest paid, and might be able to invest cash in programs that will allow for more income through interest or dividends than expenses in interest paid

on the loan. The primary purpose of the cash conversion is to open more doors for insurance and other back-end services. Each buyer should study this proposal with the same care as used for the purchase price of the RV. If you are resigned to writing a check for your RV, I recommend that you hold the course when approached with the cash conversion angle.

cash value: See actual cash value (ACV).

catalytic heater:

Because the standard forced-air furnace that comes with most RVs consumes a huge quantity of battery power and is basically fuel inefficient, many RVers install radiant heat catalytic furnaces. Because radiant heat warms the objects before it heats the air, radiant heaters are extremely pleasant when it's cold outside. I have heated 35-foot RVs with catalytic heaters and have found them quite effective at heating corners and sitting areas. I think that every RV trekker should have a power-vented catalytic heater installed in the dining area to warm the feet and legs. It'll save on propane and battery power.

Not all catalytic furnaces are power-vented. If they are not power-vented, they are dangerous to use because they consume air and produce substantial moisture. If you must use a non-vented catalytic furnace in your motor home, use it in conjunction with the forced air furnace and always lock a window open so you have a minimum of 12 square inches of venting to the outside. (This is in addition to normal venting.)

CB Radio:

A CB (citizen's band) radio is an inexpensive communication device for emergency transmissions. There's almost always a listening ear within range of a good CB antenna. A CB radio is extremely helpful when RVers are traveling in convoy. With an additional handset, it can be used for directional backing or to maintain contact with base camp when on short excursions. Many RVers are now using cellular phones.

chassis:

A chassis is generally considered the frame structure of a vehicle, appliance, instrument, or any equipment to which other pieces of equipment are attached. A chassis in a motor home is the unit as it comes from the auto manufacturer to which is attached floor, walls, roof, and whatever else it takes to make it into an RV.

When you buy an RV, you should consider the chassis as carefully as the house. Some chassis have poor reputations while others have superb reputations. On most motor homes you'll find a Ford or General Motors chassis. For bus-type class A's you'll probably find that most are built on an Oshkosh (Freightliner) or Spartan chassis.

The chassis manufacturer has very little control over construction techniques used by the RV manufacturer, many of whom are building poorly designed houses on reputable chassis.

chassis capacity:

Capacity and measurement terms have been used by chassis and RV manufacturers for years to tell us how much payload an RV can safely carry. Most of the terms we'll be using have been handed down to us by the commercial sector of the transportation industry — primarily commercial trucking. Prior to the early nineties these terms were generally accepted definitions. Now, however, that has changed somewhat.

The big change is how the Recreational Vehicle Industry Association (RVIA) has determined to tell you how much your RV will weigh when it arrives at the sales lot if it were somewhat operational. This means that if it's a motor home, the fuel tank will be full. The weight is either an estimation of the average weight of a particular model when it leaves the factory without dealer-installed options and fresh water, or it could be an exact weight of that particular RV as determined by its scale weight. Because the program is voluntary, the choice is left to the manufacturer.

Estimation for Unloaded Vehicle Weight (UVW) should not be allowed. UVW means the weight of the vehicle after you unload the payload or prior to loading the payload. It literally means "unloaded vehicle weight." This cannot be "estimated" in the broad sense because UVW is a scale weight. But RVIA can't call the "average-estimated weight" by the term "wet weight" because wet weight implies that water tanks are full. Because full water tanks mean that many of the RVs may exceed their gross vehicle weight rating before they reach the dealership, RVIA dropped the weight of the fresh water and gave it some authenticity by calling it UVW. Although we, at RV Consumer Group, appreciate the effort to give the consumer some pertinent information in an arena where any information is appreciated, we think RVIA could have done much better.

We must, however, live with the term established. We will take whatever information the manufacturer gives us, add the water, add an estimated dealer-installed option figure from size and category, and determine an estimated curb weight. We urge you to take the time to weigh your motor home and get us the verified weights. This is the only way that RV consumers can protect themselves from those manufacturers who tend to lean more to marketing than to real and honest numbers. To help you understand the process, I will now define terms relating to RV weights:

dry base weight: Dry base weight is the total weight of a manufactured RV without any optional equipment, modifications, or liquids. It's a basic figure needed for those who want to customize their RV with optional equipment and optional holding tanks. This weight should be published in every brochure because every manufacturer should have this weight. On the MSRP (manufacturer's suggested retail price) sheet, it is dry weight of the standard built RV. It will not have any options or liquids.

wet base weight: Wet base weight is easy to figure because it is the dry base weight plus liquids needed to make it functional. This should include propane, engine fuel, and drinking water tank full. This does not include optional factory-installed equipment unless specified. The wet base weight is an ideal figure for determining payload.

The difference between the dry base weight and the wet base weight measured at the front axle for motor homes will tell the user how the RV was engineered for balance. If there is a dramatic difference at the front axle between the dry base weight and the wet base weight, there may be a problem with the location of fuel or fresh water tanks. The secret of good balance is to weigh the RV at the front, rear, and each side with fresh water tanks full.

It has been my dream to see all RV manufacturers post accurate weight labels on each RV. If a manufacturer puts the wet base weight and the weight of each option in the optional equipment column of the MSRP sheet, any consumer could use the information to calculate very close finished weights. A manufacturer who does this would truly be a consumer-friendly RV manufacturer. If such figures were accurate, the manufacturer would deserve our praise.

UVW: UVW stands for "unloaded vehicle weight." The RV industry converted this term to its use in the early nineties. RVIA defines UVW as the weight of the RV with manufacturer-installed optional equipment and fuel — but without any drinking water. An industry-wide labeling program wants all manufacturers to show the RV's UVW when it's ready to leave the factory. You should keep in mind, however, that this program does not require the weights to be accurate. Some manufacturers have chosen to weigh each model with standard-run equipment—that is, equipment normally ordered by dealers — and then list this number as an average.

Many brochures confuse dry weight and wet weight with UVW. We cannot be sure if this is intentional or due to ignorance. Because of the sheer numbers of RV brochures, posted weight figures are extremely difficult to monitor. Although the changing of definitions has made it difficult for everyone in the industry, it is the responsibility of manufactures to produce brochures with clear and accurate information.

curb weight: Curb weight is the actual weight of the RV when it sits at your curb and is ready to take on you, your passengers, and your personal payload. Fresh water holding tanks, fuel tank, and propane containers must be full. Even though you do not normally fill your fresh water tank to start your trip, a true curb weight would include water. The only way you can find the curb weight is to have it weighed without any persons or personal equipment and supplies. GVWR minus curb weight should give you a true personal payload figure.

payload: Payload is the total weight of people and their personal gear and supplies you can load into an RV that is ready to "hit the road" without exceeding its capacity rating. You get maximum available payload by subtracting the curb weight from the GVWR. If the RV's specifications include only the dry weight, you will need to add the weight of liquids, batteries, propane, and optional equipment to arrive at an estimated curb weight. If you have the manufacturer's unloaded vehicle weight, you'll need to add the weight of water (8 pounds per gallon) to that figure before you subtract from the GVWR. It still remains that the best way to find your payload, and how close you are to the GVWR once you load, is to get the RV weighed on a commercial scale. (Go to www.basecamps.org for instructions.)

GAWR: Each axle assembly on your RV will have a GAWR (gross axle weight rating). GAWR is the most important RV capacity rating. It tells how many pounds each axle assembly — which includes axles, springs, brakes, wheels, tires, and other suspension components—can sustain. Although the chassis or axle assembly manufacturer gives us the GAWR, it is important to understand that downgrading wheels and/or tires will downgrade the GAWR.

GCWR: GCWR (gross combined weight rating) is a manufacturer's specification of the towing vehicle's capacity for pulling itself and another vehicle. This is generally an economic factor because of limitation of engines and transmissions to pull without destroying themselves in the process. Many RVers who pull more than the manufacturer recommends face serious maintenance and repair costs. Exceeding the GCWR can be a serious safety issue if the towed vehicle does not have adequate brakes or if the brakes lose their

effectiveness. A good rule is to never exceed the GCWR.

Matching two vehicles when using the GCWR specification requires weighing both vehicles fully loaded (including fuels, liquids, options, driver, passengers, and miscellaneous gear), but never allowing the trailer or dinghy weight to exceed the towing vehicle's GCWR specifications — which always includes the weight of both vehicles. Because RV dealerships do not generally weigh RVs, it is common for RV salespeople to use the dinghy's (sometimes called "toad") dry weight as a guide for matching towed vehicle to the towing vehicle. You must include all items that are loaded into the dinghy.

Even though a motor home's engine and drive train have a standard GCWR from the chassis manufacturer, the RV manufacturer may have modified the chassis in a manner that effectively reduces its towing capacity. If you are planning to tow an auto or trailer with a motor home, you should check directly with the RV manufacturer to see if the chassis has been extended behind the rear wheels or stretched between the wheels or has had other modifications that will affect the towing capacity for that particular model.

GVWR: The GVWR (gross vehicle weight rating) is the maximum load carrying capacity of the RV's axles, tires, wheels, and other components of the suspension. In motor homes it is the total of each axle's GAWR unless the chassis or RV manufacturer determines to limit the carrying

capacity because some components such as brakes have limitations below the suspension's carrying capacity. The GVWR is the most an RV should ever weigh when its axles are on a scale.

class A motor home:

If you take a stripped truck chassis, set a trailer on it, and fix the front so you can drive it down the road, you'll have a crude class A motor home. A bus with living accommodations is also considered a class A motor home. Most manufacturers of class A motor homes

buy chassis with drive trains from an automobile manufacturer then build the structure according to their design. Because of proliferation of motor home manufacturers, it's important that new RVers choose a unit that has a name with a good reputation.

The class A is popular because of its easy access to living quarters from the driver's and passenger's seat. Because a bus chassis can be used for a class A, it can be built to any length that is legal to drive on the highway. A well-built class A is a pleasure to drive on straight roads; but, for some people, motor homes over 27 feet long can be a problem to back up and turn in close places. Because of the width at the driving compartment, many RVers have problems with judging right side clearance. A good rule for driving a class A is to hug to the left and let the right take care of itself when in a tight predicament.

Any motor home should be judged by reputation and value. When considering the purchase of a motor home, you should review your budget very carefully because this mode of RVing has the highest cost per mile factor. If you can afford an overall cost of $.50 to $1 per mile over a five year period (including depreciation), you probably can afford a class A motor home.

In 1997, RV Consumer Group began investigating the crashworthiness of class A motor homes. We have determined that class A motor homes are generally incapable of sustaining reasonable integrity in an accident where the vehicle rolls over on its side or completely tumbles. For complete details of this investigation you should visit our website at www.rv.org.

class B motor home:

If you take a small van, modify the roof so you can walk and stand inside, cut some holes for doors, windows and vents, put in a toilet area, install appliances for  cooking, and figure some place where you can sleep, you might have yourself a class B motor home. Specifically, a class B motor home is a factory-produced altered van.

class C motor home:

Also called a mini motor home, the class C motor home is like putting a large truck camper on a van chassis. The class C has an overhead  bed area that extends over the windshield and, like a van or truck, has an all-steel cab. Almost anyone can safely drive a class C because it handles much like a large car or truck. Caution should always be used when purchasing a class C over 24 feet because a large overhang behind the rear wheels could make balance critical and affect the steering characteristics of the unit. Look for the longest wheelbase you can get. Because many small manufacturers are building class C motor homes, close attention must be given to workmanship, design, and materials used. It all gets back to brand name.

combustion chamber temperature:

Since the burning of any kind of fuel creates

heat in direct proportion to the amount of fuel consumed, it should be clear to every RVer that the more your foot pushes the accelerator the more heat will be produced by the engine. The purpose of the heat gauge or warning light is to let us know when the temperature gets close to the boiling point of the coolant which is normally between 212 and 260 degrees Fahrenheit at sea level.

The cooling process is quite simple. The engine heat is carried away from the engine by air and the radiator coolant. The temperatures in the engine vary greatly. Although the heat of the combustion could reach over 5000 degrees (Fahrenheit), the metal surrounding the combustion chamber generally stays in the 500 to 1000 degree range. This heat is transferred to the coolant and then to the air for dissipation. The coolant temperatures should stay somewhere between 180 and 200 degrees under normal operating conditions.

The coolant temperature gauge reflects the coolant temperature very slowly. If you had a temperature gauge inserted near the combustion chamber of your motor home or trailer towing vehicle, you would probably be surprised to see temperatures rise close to 1000 degrees every time you climb a hill. These high temperatures are what slowly (but most assuredly) destroy cylinder walls, piston rings, valves, valve seats, and valve guides. Having an efficient radiator and cooling system will help keep the temperature down, but driving habits that take all of this into consideration will improve the life of your engine considerably.

Allowing the engine to climb a hill at its own pace is guaranteed to save you thousands of dollars in engine repairs. When you drive through the hills and mountains, you'll be putting more work on your engine while driving at higher altitudes. More engine work means more heat and higher altitudes means a lower boiling point for the coolant. Unless the cooling system is properly maintained, your motor home or tow vehicle may look like a teapot blowing its top and your checking account may suddenly get much thinner. I'm sure when you think about this, you will realize that pushing hard on the accelerator while climbing hills could be very costly.

Here are a few ways that helped me break the habit of accelerating on hills:

1) Every time I find myself accelerating on a hill, I picture myself throwing away a $20 bill.
2) As the gas pedal goes down, I imagine what smoking three packs of cigarettes in one hour would do to my lungs. (And I don't smoke!)
3) When I catch myself really pushing it, I force myself to remember my Army days — and having to run with a full backpack. I broke the habit in short order!

composition wood:

Composition wood is a by-product of natural wood assembled to be used in place of natural wood. Plywood, chipboard (OSB), and sawdust (particle) board are three types of composition wood used extensively in all types and brands of recreational vehicles.

Because plywood is made by laminating thin strips of natural wood together to give it strength as a large sheet, the ability of plywood to resist buckling and rotting will depend on the types of wood and glue used in the process. Some RV manufacturers use high-quality plywood in floors, roofs, and cabinetry with success because of the care used in the selection process.

Called by many brand names, chipboard is nothing more than chips of wood pressed and glued together in large sheets. Because the reputation of an RV takes at least 10 years to establish, we may not know for years how chipboard will hold up when compared to plywood for floor and roof sheeting. Chipboard advocates say that it is superior in strength to plywood and that the glue, layering process, and trees used for the manufacture of chipboard products are very important. It gets down to quality of the manufacturing process once again.

A disconcerting tendency has been to cut the cost of RV construction by using materials composed of sawdust in cabinets and the house structure. Sawdust board has not had a good reputation for resisting rot, distortion, or stress. Although all sawdust board is not of equal quality, you should consider all sawdust board as quality cutting to the bare bone. Consider this: Low-quality material in the cabinets means that you're probably walking on low quality.

Because RVs are naturally subject to many stresses, the three factors needed to keep your RV together for many years are workmanship, design, and materials. As you consider an RV for purchase, don't forget to check the materials — particularly wood materials.

condensation:

A major problem with RVing in temperate climates is the moisture that develops inside of the RV. The cause of this moisture is the result of a natural process of perspiring and cooking. Care when cooking (such as keeping the lids on pans) can eliminate much of the latter, but most people find it difficult to give up breathing and perspiring. Because living in a home with a very high humidity is unhealthy and usually uncomfortable, you need to get the moist air out of the RV and bring in some drier air.

A way to keep the RV dry is to keep a fan moving the inside air to the outside. In a cold climate, however, care must be taken that a balance is maintained between eliminating moisture and losing heat. If the problem becomes so severe that moisture is collecting in closets, showing on walls, and dripping heavily off windows onto paneling and floor, something has to be done immediately to prevent mildew and rot. If the RV's furnace exhausts to the outside and some windows are opened slightly, the problem should not be severe. If you have storm windows on the inside, remove some of the storms to allow the heavy air to

condense on the glass where it will usually drip through small holes in the window frames. Very small electric heaters or dryers placed in corners and closets will expand air molecules so they won't hold moisture and thus keep those areas dry. Make it a habit to open all drawers and cabinet doors when you leave your RV for an extended time. There are also chemicals on the market that are helpful in absorbing moisture.

consignment:

RVers are very prone to changing their minds and wanting a different RV type, floor plan, size, or brand. It doesn't mean that RVers are fickle (although I think that most of us are), but RVers often outgrow the unit they thought would last them for 10 to 20 years after only 3 or 4 years. Because getting another RV isn't as simple as it may seem at first, you might want to consign your old RV to an RV dealer to get cash instead of trading it in on a new unit. If this choice is made, there are two basic consignment programs that you will need to understand.

The first and most common consignment program is one where the dealer keeps a specific percentage of the selling price. This usually varies between 10 and 15 percent to cover advertising costs, space, and delivery preparations. If you go for the percentage basis, you will need to know the selling price and immediately deduct the percentage and any payoff to the bank to find out what you'll realize in your pocket.

The other way to enter the consignment program is to demand a specific amount for the unit and let the dealership keep what it can get over that amount. This works well with a dealership that takes in many trades because trading requires high figures at both ends of the deal. I personally like this program because it's always difficult to explain the real value of a trade-in to the RV owner who is scrutinizing the whole deal to be sure he gets his share.

Consigning has some good advantages that

should be considered unless you are a natural salesperson and have a readily salable unit.

converter:

An RV converter changes 120 volt alternating current to 12 volt direct current to supply the 12 volt system of lighting and accessories. Most modern converters also have a built-in battery charger for low-rate charging. The capacity and the quality of the converter are important to the snowbird and the fulltimer because cheaper converters can be troublesome and noisy.

Corian:

A marble-like material, Corian® is a trademark product of DuPont. Because it is extremely hard and heat resistant, it makes an ideal surface for the multipurpose uses associated with RV countertops. The nonporous material is very stain resistant — even the worst of stains can be removed with fine sandpaper. Corian® is generally an option except on high-line RVs.

DC:

The current you get from your RV battery is DC (direct current); i.e., the electrons flow in one direction. The difference between DC and AC (alternating current) is important because most of your RV equipment will operate only on DC. To get DC when connected to AC you need a converter.

deep cycle battery:

Designed specifically for the marine and RV industries, the deep cycle battery is made of plates that resist deterioration when in a partially discharged state. Although they are not as powerful at putting out high current rates for engine starting, deep cycle batteries perform the same basic function as the automotive starting battery. Even though deep cycle batteries can recover quite easily from being discharged, severe discharging will always have a deteriorating effect on your RV battery. If at all possible, keep your battery voltage above 11 volts and you'll find that its half-life will extend quite easily to two or three years. Also keep in mind that operating on low voltage has a damaging effect on fans and motors.

demand system:

The three primary systems used to bring water from the RV's fresh water tank to the faucets are hand pump, pressure tank, and demand. The demand system is practically the only system used today, although very small RVs still use the hand pump. The demand pump keeps water pressure in the lines so you get immediate flow whenever you turn on the faucet.

deposit:

When you have agreed to specific terms of purchase on an RV that you want, you should put a deposit of good faith on the order. The deposit should be given with the condition that specific terms — such as the time required to arrange financing — are written on the order. The deposit usually takes the unit off the market for a specific number of days, but deposits by themselves should not authorize a get-ready order.

down payment:

The down payment is a percentage of the total amount required by the loaning institution. If the terms are cash, the down payment may be any amount required by the dealership to conclude the terms of purchase and begin the order or get-ready process. If a deposit has been made, this amount will become part of the down payment.

dry rot:

Dry rot is a deterioration of wood caused by contact with fresh water. It's called dry rot because it takes so little moisture to cause rotting that it often gives the impression of being dry even as it falls apart. The condition can almost always be traced to poor workmanship or poor maintenance. Any wood that is kept even slightly moist for a few months is subject to dry rot. Dry rot is common in many types and brands of RVs regardless of the frame structure.

You can see and smell dry rot. Look carefully in corners, around windows, behind cushions, and in storage compartments. Look for drooping ceilings and soft floors. If there's any question, poke carefully with a very fine and sharp ice pick or knife blade. An RV with a lot of dry rot is almost impossible to fix.

dry weight: See chassis capacity.

DSI:

DSI stands for direct start ignition. DSI is used for water heaters that can be started from inside the RV. The switch for the DSI water heater is usually located near the galley area and allows the occupant to turn it on and off at will. Although this device eliminates going outside to light and turn off the water heater, some models can be troublesome if water gets into the heater area from passing trucks, rain blown by wind, or careless washing. A serious RV trekker should consider the manually controlled water heater or carry spare parts and a how-to book.

electrolysis:

A condition common to older motor homes, electrolysis is a complicated chemical reaction that takes place between metals or metal and some other element. Electrolysis is a reaction caused between unfriendly elements in the skin of the RV. Its effect is a deterioration of the skin from inside out. Little (and sometimes not so little) holes will show in the skin, and poking will show that the metal has been eaten away from the inside. Sometimes the problem has been traced to poor grounding of the skin, frame, generator, and other current-carrying components. When you discover electrolysis in an RV before you buy it, you can be glad that it doesn't belong to you. Electrolysis is a condition that won't cure itself, is expensive to correct,

and usually causes other problems.

EPDM: See rubber roofing.

equalizing hitch: See weight distributing hitch.

extended service contract:

When you buy a new or a pre-owned RV, the dealership may offer you an extended service contract. (Because salespeople rarely call anything a contract, it might be called an extended service agreement.) For a new RV, the service contract begins at the end of the manufacturer's warranty term. Price of an extended service contract can vary from about $1500 to $3,000 for a motor home. Motor homes usually have mileage limitations between 60,000 and 100,000 miles.

Major considerations when buying an extended service contract should be the policy underwriters and the deductible. If the underwriter is known to be financially stable and the deductible is reasonable for the annual fee, ponder it as you would the RV price and the terms for financing. If you plan on living in the unit, it is especially important that you consider it seriously since fulltiming maintenance costs can be extensive. In some cases, it might be a good idea to give up an accessory for the service contract.

fair-market value:

Fair-market value is a figure used by the insurance industry and the IRS to compute a realistic value on the item. For example, if you wrecked your RV and didn't want it repaired, you would try to convince the insurance company of the fair-market value so they would cash you out with enough to buy a comparable unit. The IRS might try to determine fair-market value for an item donated to a charitable organization.

The fair-market value of an RV is the amount you should be able to realize after exerting reasonable effort and advertising. When using a value appraisal book, fair-market value could be anywhere between wholesale and retail.

fiberglass-capped roof:

The fiberglass-capped roof has been quite successful when attached to a quality RV. Although fiberglass has a limited life expectancy, its use as a roof covering has not been a problem for the normal 20-year life of a good RV. Cutting into a fiberglass roof to mount accessories requires careful sealing against the hard surface. Although fiberglass might become brittle after years of bombardment by the sun's rays, a good fiberglass-capped roof should not be a detriment to years of happy RVing.

forced air furnace:

Most modern RVs have furnaces that start automatically, are thermostatically controlled, and have a blower that forces the air into the various living areas. Although forced air furnaces are reasonably efficient, they put almost as much hot air outside as they do inside. This air movement to the outside is designed to assist in purging the RV of unwanted pollutants and moisture. A major problem with RV furnaces is that the amount of current used to operate the fan motor (somewhere between 5 and 10 amps) can completely discharge a battery overnight if the weather is anywhere near freezing and you want to stay reasonably warm. Thus, cold weather camping will usually require that you be hooked up to some sort of recharging system.

The amount of propane consumed will, of course, depend on the outside temperature and your thermostat setting. Generally you can figure that a 30 foot well-insulated RV will consume about one gallon of propane per day at temperatures around freezing.

Because propane furnaces are usually designed to operate strictly on DC, the life of the fan assembly depends much on operating the furnace on full voltage. If you are connected to an external source, I recommend that you consider a combination of electric and propane for heating.

formaldehyde:

Because our society is conscious of elements that could be dangerous to our health, good RV manufacturers limit the amount of formaldehyde used in their products. Formaldehyde is described as being a colorless, pungent, irritating gas used chiefly as a disinfectant and preservative and in synthesizing other compounds and resins. There is debate at this time as to the lasting effects of its fumes on humans.

We know that formaldehyde irritates some people's eyes and is suspected of causing headaches. Although some of the items used in the process of putting an RV together do contain formaldehyde, the EPA has stated that any adverse effects should be easily eliminated by a good airing. If, however, the agent is buried deep in the walls and around the sleeping area, the effects may continue for some time. Good RV manufacturers try to minimize the amount of formaldehyde used in their units. I still recommend that every RVer get into the habit of checking for sufficient air flow through vents and windows.

freeze-up:

If you ever live in your RV in temperatures around freezing, you'll probably get to know what freeze-up means. This term is used to describe a restriction of LPG flowing through the regulator. Although it generally refers to tank moisture freezing in the regulator, it can also allude to anything that causes a malfunction at the regulator. If you restore LPG pressure by pouring warm water on the regulator, you can bet that you have moisture in the tank (cylinder). Mention this to your LPG service center and they'll probably add a touch of methyl alcohol to take care of the problem. Oh yes, it doesn't have to be freezing outside to get freeze-up. It usually happens, however, somewhere below 40 degrees Fahrenheit (5 degrees Celsius).

fuel fungus:

Fuel fungus applies only to diesel fuel. This small living organism loves to grow wherever moisture and diesel fuel mix. It is, fortunately, not a common ailment; but you should prepare for it. Get yourself a can of fungicide and store it in your vehicle in case you suspect there's moisture in your fuel. Those little rascals can make a mess of your entire fuel system if you let them breed.

fulltiming:

RVers who live in their RVs on a full-time basis are called fulltimers. Fulltiming is a rather new phenomenon to our society, and because of its complexities, it is as controversial as it is new. I went fulltiming for about ten years in the '70s and '80s and found out the adventures were tantamount to what sailboat cruisers have been facing for years. Ending up in unfamiliar places, solving mechanical difficulties, meeting different and interesting people, overcoming communication problems with family left behind, and always trying to understand why personal philosophies change so often make fulltiming an adventure and a half.

Fulltiming requires an RV designed for fulltiming if the adventure is going to extend beyond a couple of years. Many fulltimers who have become disillusioned with the lifestyle may have made wrong choices at the very beginning. Choosing the right RV for fulltiming must not be a haphazard venture. Design, workmanship, and materials used must be a prerequisite, but then so should the price and the manufacturer's workmanship reputation. Although motor homes can serve as fulltiming rigs for the years when extensive travel is involved, they are not usually satisfactory for retired persons who are planning on spending most of the rest of their lives in an RV.

Manufacturers who specialize in RVs for fulltimers and snowbirds are in actuality building travel homes. Because travel homes are designed for the long stay, they are usually over 30 feet and have plenty of storage. They must have excellent galley design, appliances, and upgraded equipment. They should be constructed to withstand cold and warm temperatures while keeping the occupants in a comfort zone comparable to normal home life. Travel homes are designed for sojournments from three months to five years.

Try to keep emotions out of your choice for the type of RV you'll be buying for fulltiming or snowbirding. Don't buy a motor home for a travel home just because you always wanted to be a truck driver or an airplane pilot. A motor home is a wonderful traveler; but as you check it out as a travel home, consider those long stays where you won't be moving it for months or years . Keep in mind that a motor home is the most expensive way to full-time or snowbird. Depreciation is high, and the power train is an integral part of your home. A motor home might be right for you — but think about it.

There is no reason for age to be a limiting factor for fulltiming. As long as a person can climb into an RV, it can work as well as being at home. There are, naturally, limitations on driving a motor home. Anyone over 70 should realize that reaction time and vision have diminished somewhat; so a smaller vehicle or bringing along a guest driver might be the prudent thing to do. Because I am fast approaching the age when RVing is my escape to quiet places, I am more than willing to leave some of the driving to others. Maybe you should do the same?

I am an advocate of fulltiming for those retired people who are looking for adventure, warm places, and the luxury of being untethered. To those who are considering such a lifestyle, I can only say that finding out if fulltiming is for you means getting your feet wet.

You can full-time on a shoestring, but don't expect it to be easy. I've met many people who are still fulltiming with only their social security checks as guaranteed income. Most of these were lucky or skilled enough to begin with the right unit, to start off with the right friends and connections, and to avoid the pitfalls that discourage many beginning fulltimers.

Plainly speaking, you need to exercise extreme care at matching your future lifestyle with the type of RV you are contemplating. Choosing an RV for fulltiming is an adventure in itself. If you're a new RVer, however, you might find out too late that being an RV neophyte can be as costly as it is frustrating. However, if you stick to common-sense rules as outlined in this book and other resources, the odds are that you'll make the right choice and find a lifestyle that will be full of beautiful adventures.

galley:

The galley is the kitchen area in ships, airplanes, and RVs. To those of us who have spent extensive time in these mobile vehicles, the design, materials, and workmanship used to build the galley can never be taken lightly. The galley of an RV is critical to fulltimers and snowbirds. I use the galley to judge overall quality of the motor home. I have long felt that if the galley is not put together right, the quality of the rest of the RV must be given serious scrutiny.

Upon entering an RV, my first inspection is invariably of all the drawers. I look at the materials first. If sawdust board is evident, I might not look any further. If the drawers are built with high-quality composition board, I will look to see if the material is treated to resist moisture and put together securely. I am always turned off by plywood drawer faceboards that become food-particle catchers unless the plywood is well finished or capped. I like lightweight natural wood all around with good quality paneling for the bottom. Depending on the projected use of the RV, you'll need to determine whether the fastening method used to attach the sideboards to the faceboard and backboard is adequate. The expense of tongue and groove fastening is probably an overbuild for a vacation RV but would give a fulltiming unit some good longevity factors.

I always study the slide mechanism on the drawers. Although I look at practicality relative to use, I like well-mounted side-guides for snowbirding and fulltiming use. If the drawers are made well, however, the plastic bottom guides will work for vacation and RV trekking use. Of course, very sloppy drawers are not acceptable for any use. A drawer that will not stay in the cabinet when traveling down the highway or over country lanes will mean disaster sooner or later.

I must admit that I don't like vinyl wrap in the galley. For vacation use, however, I do accept it. I am particularly against cabinet facings and support pieces wrapped in vinyl where pots and pans are normally stored. Unless the vinyl is of high quality and superbly attached to good natural wood, wear and tear will show with a small amount of use.

The quality of the sink and the faucet is paramount. If both of these items are not of home quality, you won't be happy with the galley for long. Counter tops are almost always made of composition board — some of high quality and some of low quality. I've seen counters on some RVs warp before they get sold. High-quality compo wood could work if the top covering keeps moisture from contacting the material. I've seen too many problems with tile covering on the galley counters to accept this material for serious RVing. For homes it may be okay — but not for RVs. Corian® countertops are excellent.

I am generally thumbs down on cabinet doors that are designed like a picture frame (angle cuts at corners) and stapled in the back to hold the door together. This is generally the cheapest form of cabinet door building. Two or three years down the road these cuts will open to become large gaps. If picture-frame doors are backed with thin plywood glued to the hardwood, the longevity should be adequate. High-quality tongue-and-groove cabinet hardwood doors should be installed on all good RVs.

I do not like vinyl-wrapped paneling even if it does give the RV interior a consistent 'clean' look. High-quality photo-finish paneling with a superb protective coating applied during the manufacturing process costs only a bit more and will give the RV that fresh look for at least 20 years. Don't accept less in a snowbirding or fulltiming RV.

Take whatever time you need to check the galley on every RV you consider. If you start with the galley, you'll quickly eliminate many RVs before you waste hours of valuable searching time.

GAWR: See chassis capacity.

GCWR: See chassis capacity.

generator:

A generator is a mechanical device for producing electricity. Although most modern generators produce alternating current, generators can be designed to produce direct current for special situations where alternating current is not desired. Rotating generators can be powered by wind, water flow, engine, or almost anything that can turn a pulley. The common RV generator is permanently mounted in the RV and can be fueled by gasoline, LPG, or diesel. Portable generators are also common to the RVing lifestyle.

A big problem new RVers face is trying to decide what size generator they need to supply basic needs when hookups are not available. The 400 to 1000 watt portables are only good for battery charging and light AC use. Portables from 1000 to 2000 watts will supply enough electricity to do almost anything except operate an air conditioning unit. A 2000 watt (2 kW) generator will operate a 13,000 Btu air conditioner (so they say) only with a struggle. A 4000 to 6000 watt generator will run a small household.

gray water:

The waste water from the kitchen sink and the shower is gray water. Allowing gray water to flow onto the ground surface might be acceptable in remote campgrounds providing it doesn't puddle and biodegradable detergents are used, but you must always check with campground authorities. It is generally best to plan on disposing of gray water with the black water at a proper dump station. Hint: Whenever you dump your holding tanks, be sure that you dump your gray water last to wash out the sewer hose.

gross dry weight: See chassis capacity, dry base weight.

gross wet weight: See chassis capacity, wet base weight.

ground fault interrupter:

To save lives, ground fault interrupter (GFI) circuits are installed in bathrooms and outside electrical outlets. Because this device is sensitive to grounding, it will shut the circuit off if any grounding occurs. Most homes and good RVs will have GFI circuit breakers in the bathroom. You can readily tell a GFI by the two buttons — one for test (T) and one for reset (R).

In good RVs, the GFI in the bathroom is also connected to the outside receptacle. If you picked up a wet drill motor connected to a GFI circuit, you would probably get a tingle instead of the shock of your life. Always use the GFI receptacle when working outside with electrical tools.

guarantee:

When you assure someone that nothing will go wrong and back up that assurance with a bond for damages resulting from the malfunction, you have created a guarantee. A guarantee usually implies a specific remuneration whereas a warranty is less specific in its terms.

GVWR: See chassis capacity.

high book:

High book is a term used by the auto and RV dealers. It means the same as retail price.

hold:

Salespeople will generally accept a certain amount of money to hold or keep a unit reserved for the customer for a specific period. When the terms of the purchase are established, a customer may leave a check or cash to allow enough time to arrange for financing or other requirements. A hold should be refundable and should be so written on the buyer's agreement.

home base:

Keeping a home base is something that many full-time RVers do for as many reasons as there are people. I've known many fulltimers who could never survive the uncertainties of being a nomad unless they knew they could return home if they wanted or had to. Some fulltimers keep a home base for financial security. There are, or course, always those who cannot tear away from the homestead without suffering from guilt at deserting their roots. If it takes the keeping of a home base to make RVing pleasurable — do it.

RVing, like life itself, is a compromise. You can cut the size of the home base down if you need the money; you can get rid of the big homestead and buy a smaller one that accomplishes the same purpose; or if you want to do what most of us have done, you can stick some money aside to buy another home base whenever you get the urge and find a place that meets your fancy. There is nothing wrong with the keeping of a home base as long as you keep it simple.

insulation:

Whether you live in warm or cold climate, your RV will need to be insulated to keep the inside temperature different from the outside temperature. The amount of insulation that you have between the walls is determined by an R-value. If an RV does not have a good R-value, you'll be spending too much money on electricity and fuel while wasting precious natural resources.

Think of the R-value as the ability of your RV's walls to resist the transfer of heat or cold from outside to inside or inside to outside. The higher the R-value the lower the impact on your comfort zone by nature. Because your RV's walls are approximately two inches thick, you should have approximately two inches of insulation. If you have a wood structure, the two-inch insulation will probably be two-inch fiberglass matting which has an R-value of about R7. If the construction is of aluminum framing, the R-value of the insulation will depend upon the type, quality, density, thickness of the foam material used — which should be somewhere between R8 and R12 in normal RV walls.

The entire picture of insulation rating, however, is not as simple as it might appear on the surface. If the structure is metal, the cold and heat transfer through metal will readily diminish the overall ability of the unit to resist temperature change. A wood structure will be easier to keep warm or cold. If, however, a metal framed unit is carefully insulated and foam sheeting is placed under the exterior skin, the penetration by excessive heat or cold should be minimal. Also keep in mind that openings in the walls for slideouts, windows, doors, and vents have a big influence on temperature control. In cold-wet climates you have the additional problem of condensation. If the walls are not as well insulated as the windows, condensation will form on the inside walls and cause serious problems.

Good RV manufacturers attempt to build a unit with an insulating material that has an R-value commensurate with the use for which the RV was designed. A weekender, for example, should do well with R5 insulation for wood built RVs and standard foam between the studs of metal framed RVs. A larger unit that might be used for longer term live-in use should have foam sheeting (at least 1/4 inch) over the entire frame structure to give it additional resistance to temperature transfer. Personally, I would prefer foam sheeting over the frame structure of any RV in which I plan on spending time in temperatures above 80 degrees Fahrenheit (26 degrees Celsius) or below 40 degrees Fahrenheit (5 degrees Celsius). Because foam sheeting is expensive to install, most RVers who use their units for normal camping can do well with standard fiberglass matting or foam insulation.

Take time to study any samples, demonstrations of insulation material, and installation techniques. When shopping for an RV, remember that the difference is not as much in quoted insulation figures as in the overall performance history of the unit.

interest rate:

Because RVs, unlike homes and autos, are considered luxury items, some banks consider the risks of repossession higher and impose higher interest rates for financing these purchases. If you take the time to study the financing figures, you'll find that half a percent can make a big difference in the monthly payment — and thus the overall cost of the RV. It's easy to get on the phone and call the various banks and RV dealerships to determine the best rate available.

inverter:

An inverter is a device for converting direct current to 115 volt alternating current. Inverters are not used very much by RVers because efficient ones are expensive (about $1 per watt output) and most RV accessories are designed to operate on DC. An excellent use for an inverter is to operate computers and other electronic equipment that are not available in 12 volts. If you decide for a good inverter, be sure that you get one that requires very little amperage draw to operate the inverter without anything connected.

investment factor:

If you want to figure on getting a monetary return in addition to pleasure from your RV, you will need to determine an investment factor based on the monetary cost of owning an RV. The investment factor can thus be considered the percentage of return you will get for your original investment. Try to think of investment factor as the amount you'll get in cash value when you sell or trade your RV in relation to the amount you spent. If your investment factor is 40 percent after owning an RV for 10 years, you are about average. If your return is 50 percent of the original cost, you have done very well.

Figuring an investment factor is one way of determining how your new RV will hold its value. We all know that as soon as you leave the dealership, the value of your new unit will drop to or below the wholesale price. This means that you'll probably need to keep the RV from 5 to 10 years at an average inflation rate of about 6 percent to get 60 or 70 percent of your original outlay returned.

Because the investment factor is based upon salability at some time in the future, the price you pay and the quality of the RV will be the two most important factors. By buying a lower priced unit that has a good reputation for holding together, you can increase the investment factor. On the other hand, if you invest in a unit that will fall apart, your investment factor will be low. Of course, buying the unit below the manufacturer's suggested retail price will always improve the investment factor.

Size can also hurt the investment factor. Most RVs over 30 feet will suffer more depreciation than shorter RVs. The investment factor will change as the demand for length, floor plan, and interior design changes. Some lower quality RVs will suffer major depreciation  no matter how long they are kept. Anyone looking seriously towards a high investment factor will study RV trends as an investor in the stock market would study trends in the national economy.

Good maintenance is always a requirement for keeping a high resale value. Because most of us put off doing maintenance, we should look at RV characteristics that minimize maintenance. Better appliances, superb workmanship, quality materials, and good design all help to keep an RV in good condition for 20 years or longer.

Although size, colors, floor plan, design, and price affect the investment factor, nothing affects it like the name. A brand that is reasonably priced and has a reputation for holding together will always have the highest return on the original cost.

I found out that where you live can also influence the investment factor. Because acid rain contains sulfur, sulfur dioxide, and nitric oxide, it is important that you flush and wash your RV as often as possible. These chemicals can cause damage to the RV's surface. An etching and a dulling of the surface is bound to happen if you get into an area where acid rain is common; but it can be minimized with a mild soap washing. Special cleansers are required if etching does occur. Paying attention to the outside of the RV will give you a higher investment factor and not cost you the $1000 in depreciation that it cost me.

Budgets, of course, limit us to an amount we can spend. It means being careful about spending more than what is needed. When RV shopping, we often find that we can put off getting many of the options until a later date. By not buying options with the RV, you can take a step upward in quality to increase the investment factor. Awning, TV antenna, air conditioning, and microwave are important only if you need them and can afford them. First consider that the flexibility allowed by a good investment might be what you'll need down the road.

invoice:

When you talk about invoice while dealing for an RV, you are actually referring to dealer cost. A good dealership will not show you the invoice under any conditions because they know that such practice could open up price wars and questionable promotion tactics that have long been associated with the auto industry. The auto and the RV industries are distinctly different in the way they must serve the needs of the public, and I hope it will stay that way. If the RV dealer, however, says that he'll give you dealer invoice plus some other figure, you should be shown the invoice from the RV manufacturer then add the figure that was negotiated. A price negotiated from invoice doesn't mean much if you don't see the invoice once earnest money is presented and all other terms are met.

Kelley Blue Book:

The Kelley Blue Book (copyrighted by Kelley Blue Book Co., Irvine, California 92718) is distributed to automotive and RV dealerships to estimate the value of used vehicles. The Kelley Blue Book lists all RVs in alphabetical order and gives the models, weight, manufacturer's suggested retail price when new, the current average wholesale value, and the current average retail value. The values are for the base unit and do not include add-on options. There is a list of options with values in the front of the book. The book must be current and should be considered only as an estimate of value since condition is a big factor in the actual cash value. Because banks often use appraisal books as guides for lending money, the wholesale value is often called loan value.

kW:

kW stands for kilowatt (1000 watts). Most RV generators produce between 2 and 6.5 kilowatts.

lemon laws:

Almost every state has a lemon law to protect new motor vehicle buyers, and a few states have laws that protect used motor vehicle buyers. This protection varies greatly from state to state. It generally protects the consumer when a vehicle fails sufficiently to warrant repeated returns to the dealership with subsequent loss of the use of the vehicle. To win a lemon law case, it is imperative that the vehicle owner keeps accurate records to substantiate losses in time and money due to the failure. If there is any question about your vehicle being eligible for lemon law protection, call your state attorney general.

leveling:

A most important word in RVing, leveling is too often neglected. Leveling your RV will keep your refrigerator operating more efficiently for years to come. The life of a refrigerator is proportional to the amount of time spent at conscientious leveling. Also keep in mind that a leveled RV is much more pleasurable to stay in. There are literally hundreds of ideas and aids to assist you in leveling your RV. Check with your local RV supply store or at www.basecamps.org.

license estimate:

When the amount of license is included in the buyer's agreement, it is usually an estimated figure. Although most salespeople know the license costs within 20 percent, some states have formulas so complex that it might require a call to the licensing department to get the exact license figure. If the figure is approximate, the salesperson should write 'license estimate' to let you know that you will either get a refund or need to pay more.

limited warranty:

All warranties are somewhat limited, but good manufacturers guarantee all components of the RV for at least one year. What this means to you is that the local dealership will assist you in handling claims against any component that fails during the RV's warranty term. Limited warranties may have exclusions for transfer of ownership, use as a residence, travel out of the country, and components not built by the RV manufacturer. If the brochure even mentions 'limited' when it explains its warranty coverage, send for a copy of warranty terms from the manufacturer.

load ratings:

The only way you can get load ratings is through the chassis or vehicle manufacturer. It might not always be good information, but it's the only practical source of information. Every vehicle manufacturer has a trailering guide and a GVWR rating for the vehicle. It will include information about the engine, the drive train, the suspension, and the tires. Get all this information for your chassis and keep it handy.

low book:

The wholesale price of a vehicle in a value appraisal book is also known as low book.

LPG:

LPG (liquid petroleum gas) applies to propane and butane. The primary difference between the two is that butane freezes readily (about the same temperature as water) and propane resists freezing until it gets to about minus 50 degrees Fahrenheit. RVers in cold country will be using propane. Although butane is heavier than propane, both are heavier than air. Because LPG can pool in low spots, the smallest leak can be a safety hazard. LPG is colorless and odorless, but a chemical with a pungent odor is added to assist in detecting leaks. Although LPG is basically safe for RVing (not for boating), care must always be taken to avoid explosion and fire.

LPG leak detector:

This device emits an audible beeping in the presence of propane or heavy fumes from fluids and aerosol dispensers. It is located near the floor of the RV or in the bilge of a boat. LPG leak detectors are available with shut-off valves to close the flow of propane. (For safety, most LPG leak detectors will emit a warning sound if the voltage lowers below 12 volts.) Some LPG leak detectors are also sensitive to carbon monoxide.

LPG regulator:

Because propane tanks contain pressures from 100 to 200 pounds per square inch and your RV's appliances are designed to operate on about one-half pound per square inch, a regulator must be used to reduce the pressure. Most LPG regulators, and all LPG RV regulators, are of the two-stage type. RVs that have two propane cylinders usually have an automatic changeover as part of the regulator so that when one bottle runs out it automatically allows you to continue using the propane. Propane regulators are durable but should be shielded from adverse weather conditions whenever possible. Other than carefully cleaning the diaphragm vent, regulator checks should be performed by a certified RV mechanic. If in question, replace the regulator with a new one and keep the questionable one as a spare until you can get it checked.

manufacturer's suggested retail price:

At the bottom of the pricing structure we have invoice and at the top we have manufacturer's suggested retail price (MSRP). The invoice is the wholesale price and the MSRP is the retail price. The retail price can be any figure the dealer wants it to be. The MSRP can be ignored by the dealer who can ask any amount he wants for the unit. Here lies the danger: Unless you know the MSRP you can't know what the builder thinks the RV is worth. Unless you know the MSRP, you must rely upon your experiences and the word of the salesperson to determine the value of any RV. Unless you know the MSRP, you won't have a basis by which to compare values with other RVs. Very simply, you must know the MSRP to begin establishing a value for the unit.

An MSRP sheet should be sent with each RV from the plant at which it was built. The MSRP sheet will tell you:

1) the model,
2) the serial number,
3) where it was built,
4) all the items normally included in the build of that model,
5) optional items included in the build,
6) the basic retail price of the unit,
7) the retail price of the options, and
8) the total manufacturer's suggested retail price.

Sometimes freight and dealer preparation costs will be included in the MSRP total figure. Some manufacturers send a color-banded MSRP

MANUFACTURER'S SUGGESTED RETAIL PRICE

DEALER   MANUFACTURING PLANT   INVOICE #

ADDRESS   BRAND   MODEL   COLOR   YEAR

VEHICLE SERIAL NUMBER   DATE OF MANUFACTURE

THE FOLLOWING ITEMS ARE STANDARD ON THIS MODEL AT NO EXTRA CHARGE

MANUFACTURER'S SUGGESTED RETAIL PRICE OF THIS MODEL: $

OPTIONAL EQUIPMENT INSTALLED ON THIS VEHICLE BY MANUFACTURER
OPTION #   DESCRIPTION

OPTIONS SUBTOTAL
VEHICLE TOTAL
DESTINATION CHARGE
DEALER PREP
OTHER
TOTAL AMOUNT $

sheet with each new unit. This computer print-out will reflect what the manufacturer thinks is a fair retail value for that particular unit based upon the building cost. As you compare one RV with another, MSRP sheets will give you a good beginning for establishing values of the various brands. As you compare manufacturers, however, keep in mind that the MSRP does not guarantee value.

All manufacturers should furnish MSRP sheets with each new RV. A color-banded MSRP sheet will keep those retail figures honest. It will let you, the consumer, make choices based on those figures. All RV buyers should ask to see the manufacturer's suggested retail price sheet. The original MSRP sheets should be kept in a book in the dealership office while unaltered copies are placed in the RV. These color-banded MSRP sheets should be readily shown to you upon request. The manufacturer allows the dealer a very generous profit. The dealer can hold that profit or drop it — that will be his choice. For you to make an intelligent choice, you need to know the MSRP. Remember, it's your savings that are being spent.

marine toilets:

For years the RV industry used toilets that were designed for marine use. Because RV toilets and marine toilets have similar features, this terminology continues even though it shouldn't. RV toilets open directly into a tank while marine toilets usually incorporate a pump for pumping the waste into a tank or into the ocean (tsk, tsk).

mildew:

A very unhealthy condition when prevalent in an RV, mildew must be avoided. Mildew spores are the cause of many allergies. Because mildew spores thrive on moisture, keep the inside of the RV as dry as possible. A heating system that circulates air to the outside should be used in wet climates, and cooking with covered pots should become a habit. Keeping the overhead fan on during showering is an abso-lute necessity. There are chemicals available to hang in the RV that will destroy mildew, but it's possible that these chemicals are as harmful as the mildew itself if used during a live-in situation.

motor home: See class A motor home.

multi-viscosity oil:

Although most of you have been driving autos for years, the internal operation of an engine might still be a mystery to many of you. But, because RVing puts a heavy burden upon the engine, you need to have an understanding of what oil does and how it prevents wear.

Oil is simply a lubricating film that reduces the friction between two moving pieces of machinery. It flows well and acts like millions of little ball bearings to keep metals from touching each other and to act as a sealant between piston rings and cylinder walls. If we used oils only on slow-moving, cool-operating equipment, life would be easy for the stuff; but because we put oil in truck, auto, and motor home engines to climb hills at high speeds at almost intolerable temperatures, oil becomes a hard-working slave.

You might think of oil as a commodity that, like fuel, you just put into the engine and all will be well. This is not so! Every RVer must consider the viscosity of the oil. The viscosity (ability of the oil to flow) should change as the temperature changes and as the engine gets older. (Just like our diets!) If you use a good brand of oil, you can mix the viscosity anytime you want; but you should stay with one brand. In the old days (ahem!), we used oils designated by the Society of Automotive Engineers (SAE) simply as 10, 20, 30, and 40 viscosity. These numbers only mean that 10 oil flows 4 times faster at a specific temperature than 40. Because oil gets thicker when cold and thinner when hot, we need to use the lower numbers in the winter and the higher numbers in the summer. The 'W' designation on some oils means that the oil will flow or stay fluid over a wider range of temperatures. The problem comes with engine use, because the engine temperature changes drastically from the time of cold starting to climbing a mountain pass.

Multi-viscosity oil came into the picture to help overcome the temperature changes within the engine. These oils have a two number designation on the container. Ratings of 10w-30, 10w-40, 20w-50, etc., are all common designations used by oil companies to tell us the flow capabilities of the oil as related by the single number designation of 10, 20, 30, 40, and 50. What multi-viscosity oil does is hold its viscosity as the temperature increases. Thus, the 20w-50 oil will have the cold starting viscosity of a 20 oil but will be able to have a viscosity of a 50 oil at a higher operating temperature. Simply, a 20w-50 oil would not thin out at higher temperatures at the same rate as does the 20 oils. The 50 designation in this case will show its ability to retain body. Keep in mind this does not mean that the 50 viscosity is the same viscosity at high temperatures as at starting. Under operating conditions, the 20w-50 will still thin out when hot, but it will flow at the rate of straight 50 viscosity when hot. Thus, when cold a 20w-50 oil will flow like a straight 20 oil and when hot it will flow like a straight 50 oil. It works the same way for 10w-30 or any other multi-viscosity rating.

A problem with using straight 40 or 50 oil is that it's so thick when cold that the oil will stick to the cylinder walls until the engine warms up. If the piston rings are not perfect this could create a severe smoke condition. Oils with such designations as 20w-30, 20w-40, or 20w-50 will eliminate this problem while maintaining good viscosity when the engine is hot.

I carry a few containers of 10w-30 in case I get into cold country and want to thin my oil down a bit for smooth starting and cool engine operation, but I normally operate my RV pulling engines on 20w-40 or 20w-50. I've learned that hard working engines sound better and last longer with this oil. All of my autos get 20w-40 for summer use as soon as they reach 10,000 miles on the odometer. Any engine that uses any amount of oil should use a higher multi-viscosity oil to keep engine fuel from passing the rings during compression and polluting the engine oil. The less oil and fuel you burn, the healthier the trees and shrubberies will stay. Everything will benefit from conscientious oil use.

N.A.D.A. Appraisal Guide:
The N.A.D.A. Appraisal Guide is an estimating guide for values on used automobiles and RVs. Published periodically by the National Automobile Dealer's Association.

odometer:
It's a fact that the odometer reading on a motor home will usually be the determining factor of its value. Don't drive your motor home on trips that are frivolous unless you can afford the depreciation caused by excessive mileage. Enjoy your motor home — but use it for the adventures for which it was built.

ohmmeter:
Because most RVers keep a multimeter around to measure voltage, you should also know that one part of that meter measures ohms. Ohms is a measurement of resistance in a circuit. (Specifically: for each volt at the battery terminals, one ohm resistance will allow one ampere to flow.) Although most RVers never use an ohmmeter, it's a handy instrument to find out if there's a break in an electrical circuit. A small amount of study of ohmmeter principles and use might help the RV trekker do some good diagnostic work on electrical systems that are getting more complicated every day.

optional equipment:
On some RVs the optional equipment list is quite long. The difference between standard equipment, standard options, and optional equipment is often confusing to new RVers. Standard equipment is automatically included

in the construction of the RV and usually cannot be deleted. Standard-run options are put on stock RVs for sale to dealers, and these options will usually show on the MSRP sheet to the right of the standard equipment. Standard-run options can be deleted by special order. With some manufacturers, special build options are available during time of build by special order. Of course, many options are available at the dealership that may not be available from the manufacturer. Although options at the dealership may not be as negotiable as the completed unit, a buyer should be aware that dealer-installed options can become part of the negotiated package.

out-the-door:

If a salesperson tells you that you can have the unit for a certain out-the-door price, they are usually referring to the price of the unit with appropriate sales tax and license. Never assume, however, that an out-the-door figure means anything that is not written on the buyer's order.

When you sit down with the RV salesperson, be friendly. If you're going to get the deal you want, you're going to get it because of firmness — not from being cantankerous. If you become an adversary and the salesperson finds out that you don't know what you think you know, the facts will be twisted to his or her advantage. Be friendly, be firm, be fair, and be quick to leave if you don't think you're being treated right. Remember, you can't go wheeling until you've done your dealing.

overheating:

Engine overheating usually becomes a problem when the vehicle is between five and ten years old or when a newer vehicle is overburdened. The most important thing to remember is that the more fuel you consume the more heat will need to be carried away — thus high fuel consumption creates a greater potential for overheating.

Heat is created in the engine and carried in coolant to the radiator where it is transferred to the surrounding air. Every year that passes will

A slight amount of overheating may result in little or no coolant loss. However, when the condition causing the overheating becomes more extreme, coolant loss will result. The list of causes follows:

✓ Manifold heat control valve sticking.
✓ Fan belt slipping.
✓ Thermostat stuck.
✓ Radiator fins obstructed.
✓ External leak at cylinder head gasket.
✓ Internal leak at cylinder head gasket.
✓ Internal leak into combustion chamber.
✓ Radiator cap valve leaks.
✓ Radiator cap valve stuck.
✓ Faulty fan drive clutch.
✓ Worn pulleys.
✓ Defective water pump.
✓ Radiator hose collapsing.
✓ Blocked or restricted water manifold.
✓ Cooling system clogged with rust and scale.

✓ Radiator frontal area obstructed.
✓ Air pocket in cooling system.
✓ Leaking radiator.
✓ Leaking cooling system hoses.
✓ Leaking engine water jacket.
✓ Leaking car heater.
✓ Leaking radiator supply tank.
✓ Cylinder core hole plugs leaking.
✓ Excessive engine friction.
✓ Thermostat defective.
✓ Ignition timing retarded.
✓ Brakes dragging.
✓ Cooling system capacity inadequate for load being carried or towed.
✓ Excessive use of air conditioner while vehicle is parked.

List referenced from Goodheart-Willcox's *Automotive Encyclopedia,* © 1975. (If you would like to learn more about automotive fundamentals, we highly recommend this publication. It is clearly written and well illustrated.)

reflect some eroding of the efficiency of the radiator. This is a result of internal coating or corrosion of the radiator core or restriction of air flow through the radiator due to inefficiency at the water pump, fan, or radiator fins. Any coating, corrosion, or sludge buildup will prevent efficient heat transfer or coolant circulation thought the radiator. Every RV will eventually get to a point where the slightest burden will cause a rise of the temperature within the engine.

Since maintaining a coolant temperature of about 200 degrees Fahrenheit (90 degrees Celsius) is important for efficient engine operation, every RVer should be cognizant of the rate of temperature increase when hill climbing. If the engine temperature gets too high, engine metal (heads, blocks, pistons, rings, valves) will expand to a point where loss of power, excessive wear, or malfunction will take place. Most of this can be prevented by a complete check of cooling system components annually or every 12,000 miles — whichever comes first.

If, when hill climbing or overburdened, the temperature increases above the normal operating range, the first thing to do is to decrease fuel consumption by letting up on the gas pedal. When climbing, shift to a lower gear (reduces the burden), keep the RPMs up a bit (increases pump and fan efficiency), turn on the internal heater (will get you hot but cool the engine), and let your gas pedal foot act like it's a feather instead of a lead ball. Do not stop on a hill unless you are losing coolant. If your coolant and pressure system is adequate, you should be able to maintain temperatures well above the boiling point of water for a short time without appreciable damage. When you do stop to check or cool the system, notice if steam or coolant vapors are evident. If coolant losses are limited to heat expansion, allow the engine to cool by idling as you watch the temperature gauge closely. (Every RV should have a temperature gauge.) If at any time the engine temperature drops precipitously, suspect a coolant loss because a temperature sensor will not register steam or vapor. If the engine becomes noisy or suffers serious power loss, there is probably no coolant left in the engine. In this case, you should always shut the engine down immediately to avoid further damage.

payment protection:

An item that every RV buyer should consider is payment protection due to death or disability. This is an insurance program that is especially valuable to persons getting close to retirement age. Because payment protection does not usually take the age of the applicant into consideration (to the maximum limit) for rate setting, it can be very affordable insurance for those over 50.

When you consider life payment protection, you should realize that there are two types: gross and net. With gross coverage you build a sort of equity into the policy — but only during the policy term. Net is simply decreasing term insurance, gives you coverage for the payment only, is obviously cheaper, and is adequate for most people. Disability coverage should be looked at by those still in the work force with heavy financial obligations. What I am stressing here is that you investigate payment protection as part of the financing program. Don't automatically rule it out!

payment term:

Too many people look only at the payment when they're considering an RV purchase. If you aren't careful about the term, you might find out that the RV depreciates much faster than the loan balance disappears. The term should be based upon the practical life of the unit being purchased. If you are buying a brand that has a questionable reputation, you should probably consider a 24 to 60 month term. On a new unit from a quality manufacturer, a 10 year term is not unreasonable if you plan on keeping it for a while. I personally do not advocate over 10 years on motor homes. Quality fulltiming RVs could be financed to 12 years if necessary.

polarity tester:

Because electrical current can be dangerous to the RVer, RV equipment, and the RV itself, simple precautions should include checking the polarity of the 110 or 220 volt outlet before you plug in your RV's extension cord. Incorrect polarity and grounding can create havoc with some electronic and electrical equipment and possibly zap you when you step from or into your RV. Polarity testers are cheap and easy to use. Get one today!

qualifying:

A salesperson qualifies a prospective buyer to determine capability of buying a product or sincere interest in buying a product. By using good qualifying techniques, a salesperson will quickly determine how much time to spend with the prospect and what manipulative techniques will work best.

We all know that the best qualifying techniques often backfire, but the process is so ingrained in most salespeople that it's as automatic as eating.

A good RV salesperson will discreetly ask a few basic what, when, where, why, and how questions to determine what kind of assistance is needed and then get into a good presentation and allow the customer to make the choices.

Quartzsite:

If you want to be a snowbird among snowbirds for a couple of months each winter, wait until after Christmas and go west of Phoenix, Arizona, by about 80 miles or east of Blythe, California, by about 20 miles and find the small town of Quartzsite, Arizona. You will find thousands of RVers camped for a couple of months in this desert community. If, however, you became an RVer to get away from crowds and commotion, you probably won't stay long. All I can say is that it'll be an experience — even if it's a once-is-enough experience.

radiused windows:

When the windows are curved at the cor-ners, we consider them radiused. Radiused windows are considered more attractive and seal better. Since good radiused windows are more expensive, they are sometimes not used on low-line RVs. It should be clear, though, that a good brand of windows with 90 degree corners is better than a cheap brand of radiused windows. The quality of RV windows is usually comparable to the quality of the unit.

receiver:

A hitch receiver is usually fastened to the tow vehicle's frame by welding or bolting. The receiver is the receptacle for the hitch shank upon which the ball mount is fastened. Receivers are used for heavy duty towing. Standard receivers usually cost from $150 to $200. Bolt-on receivers are available for most motor homes.

reflexive move:

When you hit the road with your RV, you should be prepared for circumstances that will require action without thought. A car approaching you head-on while passing another car would require a reflexive move on your part. The smell of propane would signal you to shut off the main valve and open doors and windows immediately. The sound of someone outside might cause you to turn on an outside light and remain quiet. The smell of heavy smoke in a wilderness would encourage you to prepare to leave camp on a moment's notice. There are a lot of emergency situations you should think about before they happen. Reflexive moves are as important in RVing as they are to a soldier in the field.

There are many examples of reflexive moves that should be practiced. When driving your RV in an unexpected and questionable situation, practice keeping hard to the left and let the right take care of itself. You can judge the left side clearance easier than you can the right. A good example is an unexpected approach to a narrow bridge with a logging truck entering from the other end. Stay on your side of the road — but barely! A clipped mirror is better than a crunched right side.

When the question of self-defense comes up, the subject of guns soon follows. I have a prejudice against handguns that come from many sources, but I'm sure the statistics of accidental injuries with these weapons have influenced me the most. RVers who think they need a weapon for self-protection should consider a small-bore shotgun; but go to a certified gun-handling class, tuck it out of sight, and keep it locked with a trigger guard. Communicate with your traveling companion on where to keep the key, when the lock is to be removed, and how the weapon is to be handled. Since RVing is extremely safe, chances are you'll never need to use any kind of weapon for self-defense. Attending self-defense/awareness workshops is a good idea.

refrigerator leveling:

When an RV refrigerator is off level, the gases that produce the cooling will overheat. It is extremely important that whenever an RV is stopped, the refrigerator is either shut off or the unit is leveled as quickly and perfectly as possible. Although modern RV refrigerators are not as subject to damage from being off level as they used to be, leveling is still very important.

R factor or R value: See insulation.

rubber roofing:

Rubber roofing has been installed on RVs since 1983 and has become a standard for RV roofing since 1990. With the technical name of ethylene propylene diene monomer (EPDM), rubber roofing has taken strides toward replacing aluminum as an RV covering. RV manufacturers who install rubber roofing say this type of roof offers low maintenance, ease of repair, clean appearance, noise insulation, and better insulation from temperature. Disadvantages of this type of roofing are that it is possible to tear with sharp objects and might suffer from deterioration in very hot climates. There is a possibility that fungus might attack rubber roof-

ing and cause problems in hot-wet climates. These limitations are minor when compared to the advantages. All EPDM manufacturers offer a 10-year limited warranty. The limited part usually means that they'll do something for you if the roof leaks because of manufacturing (material) defects. It is not guaranteed against leaking since most leakages are caused by defects originating with the RV builder.

I think that EPDM is the possible answer to many problems that have caused too short of a life span for the average RV. Leaking of the roof has been a major problem for the last 30 years during which rotted beams, floors, and roofs have taken a big toll.

If EPDM is applied and maintained correctly, I believe that it will decrease the high structure failure rate with which RVing has been plagued. Because some RV manufacturers will learn how to cut costs while taking advantage of the promotional aspects of rubber roofing, we cannot automatically consider rubber roofing as a sign of quality. You should also be aware that rubber sheeting is available to RV builders in varying thicknesses from .040 to .060 inches. Because of demand for EPDM material, the quality is already beginning to vary from good to superb. I'm afraid that in the near future that quality may vary from bad to superb. Looking at brand reputation will still be the order of the day.

RV trekking:

When an RVer leaves the city and freeways behind for the countryside and wilderness, we call it RV trekking. A trek is usually considered a journey involving organization and a sense of adventure. Thus, RV trekking is an intent to leave behind the mainstream of civilization by using an RV, a boat, or other type of vehicle. A true RV trekker will have a self-contained unit and be somewhat self-reliant because mechanics, RV supply centers, and medical support facilities may be quite a distance from the camp site.

If you want to be a serious RV trekker, you must first find yourself an RV that will serve the purpose. Before you choose, you need to look at the venture and your demands for the unit. You need to be sure that you and your companion(s) will be satisfied with the accommodations to last the duration. The floor plan and size will usually be determined by common sense when you look at the type of terrain you plan to travel over, the power required to move the unit with its cargo, and the accommodations required by the occupants.

A trekking RV must be established as a good traveler. Curvy roads, gravel, bumps, rain, snow, and wind tend to weed out the bad travelers. Small camp sites, stumps, big rocks, and rough ground will make you start thinking more about size. Uneven tire wear, broken suspension pieces, leaking windows, and the softening of floors and walls after a few seasons of use will start you thinking about quality. Frozen pipes, sweating walls, LPG guzzling, power shortages, cramped sleeping, and inefficient storage will force you to dream of better features. RV trekking will take you to the most beautiful parts of the country and allow you pleasurable stays in nature if you plan correctly. Listening to a salesperson or a friend who has never done it won't work!

RV trekking does not mean you have to go small — it means you have to be selective. You've probably done your homework on RV types and realize that the mini motor home is the easiest to control and park. This is not to say that a class A motor home would be unsafe — it has more to do with the conditions under which you will be traveling and your capabilities in handling the unit. What you need to remember is that some RV types have a more forgiving nature to road conditions and your driving habits. If you choose a unit that is difficult to handle under bad road conditions, you'll need to drive accordingly.

One of my own personal experiences while RV trekking took place in the late seventies when Connie and I arrived on top of the Sierra Nevada Mountains just east of Fresno, California to seek a base camp site for future excursions into the wilderness. Because of some engine difficulties with the old motor home, we decided to stop at a 7500 foot elevation campground just off the main highway. As we pulled into the camping area, we noticed a group of RVers who appeared to be settling in for the night. Being tired by the long and slow climb from 1000 to 7500 feet, we decided to quickly settle in ourselves.

We woke to discover it had snowed during the night. When I tried to open the motor home door, I was surprised to find it blocked. I finally pushed the door open to find the snow to be about five feet deep. After getting outside to look around, I found the campground deserted. It seemed that Connie and I were the only ones unaware of the impending storm.

We spent two months snowbound in the campground before a snowplow could get close enough to help us. During those two months we lived very uncomfortably because we were not well prepared. Heating was poor, propane had to be carried for 1/2 mile — much of it through deep snow, we had to lower ourselves by a long rope to a river below to get water (before finding out that a few feet behind us there was a creek under all that snow), we had

Our dog, Alcazar, outside our motor home's front door.

to make leggings from old Levis, and we had to trek two miles to a resort store to get supplies. It was an adventure that we now are glad we had — but not one we'd ever want to repeat.

Had we realized the importance of communicating with other campers, the forced stay would have been avoided. We now talk to other campers as soon as we enter a strange campground. We learned. But then, RVing is learning!

secret warranty:

This term is often used to describe notifying vehicle owners of defects found in their RVs (or autos) by public notice. Although not applicable in every case, RV owners should be aware that recall notices are not always mailed. If you hear of a recall through any source, check with the vehicle manufacturer to see if it applies to you.

self-contained:

An RV that gives you basic housing accommodations of a kitchen (galley) with gray water tank, toilet with holding tank, shower with hot water, a sleeping area even if it is a sofa, battery operated lighting, and a built-in water supply system is considered self-contained. Anything less than this is not considered self-contained. Under today's standards an ice box instead of a gas-electric refrigerator will keep the unit from being self-contained. If a shower and hot running water are not included, it is not self-contained. The question of self-containment usually comes into play when looking at older and smaller units.

shank:

The shank is the part of the hitch that inserts into the hitch receiver. On heavy duty towing systems a ball mount is either welded or bolted to the shank. If bolted to the shank, most ball mounts are adjustable.

signature:

If you "okay" or "approve" a buyer's agreement with your name, you have made a legal commitment by affixing your signature. If, however, you have not taken possession of the vehicle, you may only be obligated for costs of preparations you have ordered.

size:

Because North Americans like big homes, we are emotionally inclined to buy big RVs. The bigger the RV, however, the more initial cost, the more wear, and the less safety. Before you decide to go big, think about the pros and cons of extending height, length, and width beyond your first inclination.

height: Height influences stability on the road. Like a sailboat with lots of sail, a big side can catch lots of wind — especially winds created by passing vehicles. You should also consider height if you expect to boondock or do some serious RV trekking. Tree limbs love to grab 10 to 12 foot high RVs.

length: Like height, length is major consideration. An RV that is too long will have reduced highway stability and limited access to campgrounds. An RV that is too short may make for crowded living conditions. Length should be one of the top items on your list of priorities when choosing any type of RV.

width: The normal maximum width of an RV is 96 inches. Anything over 96 inches is considered a widebody. Some states (under the pressure of RV manufacturing lobbyists) have approved RV widths to 102 inches. Keep in mind that widebody RVs with an awning attached are illegal for highway travel because federal standards establish that only "safety devices" can allow the vehicle width to exceed 102 inches.

Before you consider a widebody RV, you should look carefully at where you'll be going, what you'll be doing, and how your driving habits and reaction time might influence the safety factor of RV driving. Although widebody RVs appeal to snowbirds and fulltimers, I can assure you that the extra width makes a big difference when you get off the wide highways and into the countryside. Long and wide can also be a problem for many when traveling city streets. Think about it before you jump into something big.

skirting:

If you're going to spend the winter in your RV, keeping the cold and snow away from your floor is essential. You do this with skirting.

There are many ways of skirting your RV. Much will depend upon the duration of the stay. If you are in for only a few months, build yourself a canvas covered lightweight frame structure in small sections that will lay against the RV at about the floor line. Let the snow hold the skirting, or you can put some dirt to hold it in place. Lightweight skirting of 2 feet by 6 feet can be stored almost anywhere. Skirting will help to keep you and the RV in some comfort, but comfort and snow don't seem to go together well.

slideout room:

A slideout room is an addition that can be mechanically moved outward to expand a specific area of the RV. Commonly used in travel homes, slideout rooms have been growing in popularity since the mid-eighties. Because the slideout requires that a piece of the natural wall be cut away and reinforced, one can readily see that many problems can surface. Not only does the

structure of the RV have to be superb to support the added weight of the room; but there is always the problem of sealing against rain, dust, and water from passing trucks.

Although RV manufacturers have produced a few excellent RVs with slideout rooms, there is the inherent problem with balance and structural integrity. A wise buyer will investigate and compare design, material, workmanship, and reputation of the manufacturer. The controversy over electric, hydraulic, and air as power to move the slideout is still with us. I personally believe that 12 volt motor-driven slideouts will give better and longer service if operated on full voltage.

Not all slideout rooms are destined to hold up under the stress of travel or live-in situations. Some of the good manufacturers are even now having structural problems with larger slideouts. I must caution you to consider the lifestyle you are entering as you consider a slideout room. For fulltimers the slideout room appears to be a blessing, but for those who travel extensively, consider a smaller slideout room — if at all. I do not consider a galley slideout as a safe addition to a motor home. One needs only to think about the consequences of an accident where the motor home lays on its side or flips over to realize the risk of such an addition.

slider windows:

Because slider windows open wide in either an up-and-down or side-to-side motion, they allow for good view and excellent air flow. They can, however, cause problems when there is rain accompanied by wind. When considering an RV, try to balance the window design with the lifestyle you are choosing. See torque windows.

snowbird:

If you hate the cold and have made the commitment to buy an RV to head for warmer places when the snow flies at home, you are about to become a snowbird. Snowbirding is not new to our society. For years lucky people have been going south to spend winters in Florida, Arizona, and Southern California. Since the early fifties, however, people have been making these trips with their RVs rather than staying in second homes or hotels.

Snowbirding is a philosophy. As a snowbird, you'll do everything in your power to be in the warm and balmy weather while your northern neighbors are buried in snow. You like the greenery of the north, but you need to be up and away before the wind is cold enough to tingle the nose. As a snowbird, you don't need to apologize for no longer loving the four seasons. Three are enough for you!

Snowbirding with an RV is an adventure. Every time you head south you can go to a different place with the same home that you've had for the last ten trips. You can meet new friends, or you can meet old friends at designated places. You can snowbird on almost any budget — and age is no limit. The RV has opened up America from the state of Washington to Maine. The RV has given warmth to more toes, fingers, and noses than has the Benjamin Franklin stove. The RV has opened a world of adventure to us.

Smart snowbirds choose quality RVs for the three or four months they spend in the South. Unlike fulltimers, snowbirds allow their RVs to rest during the summer months; therefore, the demand on the unit is not as heavy. If, however, you are considering a fulltiming venture, take care to consider a rig that will satisfy both snowbirding and fulltiming needs.

I cannot overemphasize the need for quality in a snowbird unit because I've been there. I have seen the problems. I've seen too many snowbird RVs that look like they've been on a jungle safari after only three or four trips south. I've seen snowbirding RVs that have depreciated to a third of their original cost after less than five years and 5,000 miles on the trail. This is unnecessary. A good RV will serve the snowbird for 10 years without substantial failure. When you choose a snowbird RV, you must

look for quality. The highest upgrade in appliances and fixtures is essential. Upholstery should have name tags that you recognize as quality. You'll need proven air conditioners and furnaces in case you get there early or get caught there late. You'll want superior tires and suspension in case you get the urge to extend your travel by three or four thousand miles. And, of course, you'll want a good looking unit because you're going to be proud to be a snowbird.

solar panel:

RVers might use light collecting cells (solar panels) for converting sunlight into electricity for charging batteries. Most good solar panels will charge from 2.5 to 4 amps. An RVer can put as many solar panels on the roof as needed, but they are expensive. Figure on about $500 initial cost for a good panel that will supply 4 amps at the peak of a sunny day. Although this will assist in keeping a battery charged, solar charging systems are not yet designed to replace the generator or converter for the average RVer.

Batteries require at least 14 volts to reach a full charge, and it takes a good set of solar panels to maintain this voltage for sufficient time to keep the batteries from sulfating under moderate use. Solar panels work very well for the RV trekker in sun country, but sometimes the expense is difficult to justify for the occasional RV user. I think the time isn't far off when every quality RV will be wired for solar panels.

We know that particulates in the air restrict sunlight from reaching the earth. You should also realize that all smoke is dangerous to you, your spouse, your family, and your friends. If the smoke comes from burning ink or plastics, it's deadly. I cannot emphasize enough that limiting what goes into bonfires is the only way to prevent the government from stopping all outside burning. When recreational bonfires become a thing of the past, we'll all be to blame. Think of the importance of clear skies every time you think of solar panels.

stabilizing jacks:

When you walk inside your RV and it rocks like a boat, you know you need stabilizing jacks. Stabilizing jacks are usually welded to the frame and are operated by hand or 12 volt motors. Some stabilizing jacks can actually give a lifting effect to help level the unit, but most are used strictly for stabilizing.

standard equipment:

Every RV comes new with standard equipment. Standard equipment is usually listed in the brochure and on the left side of the MSRP (manufacturer's suggested retail price) sheet. Standard equipment is included in the unit price and usually cannot be deleted from the build. There are, however, optional upgrades that can replace many items on the standard equipment list. A buyer should always check the standard equipment list to find out exactly what is included with the unit. The brand and specifications of standard equipment are important.

storm windows:

Storm windows have their place in RVing, but that place is limited. If you use storm or double pane windows in a wet climate, you could be subjecting yourself to an unhealthy home environment. I have seen many cases where RVers have put storm windows on their units to eliminate the fogging only to allow the condensation to settle on interior walls. The settling of condensation in closets and cabinets will cause mildew, which is in itself very unhealthy. If the moisture cannot condense, the humidity will increase until it virtually rains inside the RV.

Try putting storm windows on no more than 50 percent of your window space if condensation is a problem. This will allow moisture to condense on the colder windows instead of the walls. It will also act as a gauge by which you call tell how much moisture your living conditions are putting into the air. Trying to save heat while ignoring health is tantamount to living on macaroni to save money.

subject to...:

You should never enter into RV buying negotiations without an understanding of how to control the buying terms. Although most RV dealerships are basically honest, the terms written on the buyer's agreement by the salesperson will be considered a contract once the order is signed by the buyer. To avoid unpleasant misunderstandings, simply write any questionable terms after the statement "subject to..." on the face of the buyer's agreement. "Subject to a financing rate of 10 percent," is an example. "Subject to approval of road test by buyers," is a good one for motor home buyers. "Subject to acceptable financing terms," will give you an easy out if you need it. Whatever you do, be sure the 'subject to' statement is clearly written on the buyer's agreement if there is any question about the purchase terms.

tag axles:

A tag axle is a non-driving single wheel assembly added by a motor home builder to increase the wheelbase or boost the GVWR rating—or both. It is essentially an inexpensive method of modifying a chassis to meet demands for an increase in length and weight without a major increase in price. See wheelbase.

three-way refrigerator:

Three-way refrigerators operate on 110 volt electricity, propane, and 12 volt (battery) power. Because of the heavy current draw needed for operating on 12 volts, most motor homes are equipped with two-way refrigerators operating only 110 volts and propane. Motor homes don't have a problem with generating 12 volt current, so they should be equipped with three-way refrigerators.

It is not safe to travel with propane container valves open. If you wish to avoid doing so with a two-way refrigerator, you should be sure the refrigerator is full and cold before the beginning of each trip or travel day. Do not open the refrigerator unless you have time to level the RV, turn on the propane, and light it. It might take some planning, but it's a good habit.

I personally think that it's time to consider more three-way refrigerators in RVs. By keeping the refrigerator smaller than a warehouse, by being sure that the wiring is correctly installed, and by building more efficient refrigerators, there is no reason you can't have the three choices for varying needs.

It is always hard to believe that RV refrigerators should cost as much as they do. But since we all have to live with the price until competition gets into the arena, you'll have to do everything just right to make your adventures safe and enjoyable. This means thinking of an RV refrigerator as a machine instead of a household appliance.

tire load range:

Quality RV manufacturers install tires of a load range commensurate with the suspension and frame load capabilities of the unit. If you decide to change the tire load range for any reason, be sure to check with the RV manufacturer and the tire manufacturer. Increasing tire load range so you can carry heavier loads just won't do!

torque:

If you are seriously into towing power, you'll need to understand the basics about horsepower and torque. Actually what RVers need to know is how the vehicle will perform for their particular needs. If we get into horsepower and torque too much, we might lose sight of practical performance — which takes other factors, such as transmission and type of fuel, into consideration.

Torque is the twisting force at the engine's output shaft or the rear wheels. We can get more practical pulling power (PPP) at the rear wheels by changing transmission or rear axle configuration, but engine torque is pretty much tied into the engine by its relationship to horsepower and RPM. To avoid getting too technical, let's try to make it simple.

First of all, you cannot get more power from the vehicle than what is being developed in the engine. If you want power, you need a powerful engine. Since horsepower is directly related to torque and RPM, you might want to consider the horsepower and then work the rest of it through gearing.

Second, you should consider your driving habits relating to hill climbing. If you go a little crazy every time you have to slow to 40 MPH when climbing a hill, you'll need to look at the torque curve and adjust it to an axle ratio that will work for you without sending engine RPMs into the ozone.

Third, all of this will require some consideration of the load you'll be carrying. If that load is constant, you shouldn't have too great of a problem getting something that will be efficient while keeping you happy; but if you are not sure what the load will be, it's all guesswork.

You cannot manufacture power at the driving wheels, you can only adjust it.

torque windows:

Much like jalousie windows in application, RV torque windows are closed by turning a knob or crank. Torque windows are advantageous in rainy weather because they can be adjusted to keep out the blowing rain while controlling air flow. Torque windows are helpful in cold climates because condensation is easier to control when it can drip through a slightly opened torque window. However, torque windows do not provide as good a picture view as do slider windows. A combination of torque and slider windows work well for most RV lifestyles.

tow dolly:

A tow dolly is hitched behind a motor home to support the front wheels of a small car or truck for what is called dinghy towing. Tow dollies have become popular since the proliferation of front-wheel drive automobiles. Although the tow dolly is quick and easy to use, backing the unit is difficult at best. A tow dolly is another vehicle to be maintained — and licensed. A tow dolly might work for a snowbird but rarely works well for a fulltimer or RV trekker.

trade-in allowance:

The allowance given for a trade-in will reflect the actual cash value of the RV plus any given cash discount from the retail or asking price of the unit being purchased.

trial close:

When an RV salesperson starts leading you to the sales office before you indicate a desire to buy, he is using a trial close technique. The trial close will be a test of your resistance to his or her methods of selling. Statements like, "Let's see

what the payments are on this model," will indicate that you are being tested.

The best way to avoid getting trial closes will be to leave your emotions at home. Since this is almost impossible to do when buying an RV, at least keep them under control. Try not to give buying signals like, "Wow! This is just perfect for my needs."

All good salespeople look for buying signals and are ready with a trial close. Control of the buying process is always yours. Don't give it away.

turn:

"Turn" is a term used at dealerships to indicate a process of bouncing a prospect from salesperson to salesperson to sales manager. The idea is to give other salespeople a chance at closing the prospective buyer. The term comes from the auto industry where turns are common and often mandatory. If you feel yourself being bounced like a yo-yo during the buying process, you'll know that you have been "turned."

upside down:

Being upside down is the unhappy condition of owing more for a vehicle than it's worth. The causes for being upside down can be paying too much for the vehicle, trying to trade it or sell it too soon after the purchase, or getting involved in a bad financing program. In the RV world, the problem is serious because many RVers want to trade or sell before half the financing term has been reached.

UVW: See chassis capacity.

vacation RV:

A vacation RV is designed for weekends and vacations. Because of this limited use, size and accommodations can be somewhat downgraded. It is important, however, that workmanship and structural materials are not also downgraded.

A vacation RV should fit a variety of needs with the first being the ability to hold value. Most RVers who buy RVs strictly for vacations change their minds about the size and floor plan in less than three years because families grow or leave home, tow vehicle capacities change, or the RVer feels that another type of floor plan might be better. Whatever the reason, a change is bound to happen. When the desire to change enters the picture, the main barrier to that change will probably be trade-in value.

For good trade-in value, a vacation RV should sleep four or more people. It should have bathroom facilities that can be private because occupants may vary from one year to the next. Storage is important although hanging closets may be minimized. Living room features are not as important as is comfortable sitting while eating. Beds can be made up at the sofa and dinette, but they should be comfortable. It should have a good heating system because vacations do not always take place in comfort zones.

If there is a possibility that you will change your mind in three to five years, look at the RV as others might see it. New or used, the value of any RV is based upon marketable features which include brand name, floor plan, and size. Buy your vacation RV with thoughts of trade-in and you'll probably do okay.

Although the vacation RV need not be as tough as a motorized trekking RV or as livable as a snowbird RV—it must be a good traveler. Since vacationers often get in a hurry, care must be given to avoid RVs that do not handle well when forced into an unexpected stop or turn. Many vacation-class RV buyers compromise safety for size and accommodations.

vacuum gauge:

Every RVer should have a vacuum gauge connected to the manifold of the engine. Watching the vacuum gauge will help you understand what is happening and what is changing inside the engine. A properly installed vacuum gauge will help indicate the volumetric efficiency of the engine at idle and air flow efficiency at partial and full throttle. By getting used to watching the gauge, you will become conscious of throttle operation. This alone will keep the combustion chamber temperatures down and allow you to put more miles between fuel stops.

vinyl wrapped wood:

To cut costs of manufacturing, some RV builders are wrapping vinyl around composition board and cheap wood to imitate hardwood in cabinetry. Although composition material can be acceptable if it's of high density, its use should be questioned. Composition wood made of sawdust has not had a good reputation for holding cabinet hinges and other hardware. I am also cautious about using vinyl wrapped wood around the galley. Wear and tear on vinyl from putting pots and pans under the sink can make the cabinetry look pretty bad. A study of RV cabinet facings should be part of the first inspection.

Once again the buyer should be looking at the manufacturer's reputation for putting together a unit that will travel many bumpy roads without falling apart. High-priced motor homes should have hardwood cabinetry.

volt:

A volt is a measurement of electrical power. It is the most important electrical measurement factor because voltage is what makes it all work. Voltage is the electrical pressure across the generator terminals or the battery posts that pushes the electrons through the circuit. As an example, the high power lines that bring power to your city might carry thousands of volts of electrical power while the battery in your car produces only 12 volts. The amount of power it takes to move electrons along a circuit (amperage) depends upon the resistance of the circuit. Because your RV demands less electrical power than your home, less voltage is required. Direct current circuits are also safer to diagnose and repair.

voltmeter:

A voltmeter measures the electrical pressure impressed across the two posts of a battery or generator. Most voltmeters will measure both AC and DC. A voltmeter is handy in an RV because you can watch what's happening to the battery when using lights, furnace motors, and accessories. Because a voltmeter consumes very little current, it can be connected anywhere in the circuit.

Many of my RVing friends have not yet grasped the fact that operating on 12 volt power means needing 12 volts. Operating on much less than 12 volts can cause many problems with the system. It is important to keep in mind that discharging your RV batteries below 10.5 volts will cause electric motors to overheat and fail.

A good voltmeter can be invaluable to understanding and diagnosing 12 volt power. I urge each of you to budget $50 to $100 for a built-in voltmeter. This small investment will probably save you three times that much money in batteries and furnace motors alone.

warranty:

A warranty stipulates in writing the terms for covering any malfunction in your RV. Although you will always receive some sort of warranty from a manufacturer, warranties may also be issued by a dealership to cover specific repairs or components for used units. You must be sure that the warranty is explicit. Always ask to see a copy of the terms of the warranty since it is difficult to enforce performance of an implied warranty.

Good RV manufacturers issue a warranty to cover all aspects of their product for a specific length of time. Be sure that the word "limited" is not incorporated into the warranty without knowing where it is limited. You should study the warranty as you would study the buyer's agreement and financing contract.

watt:

A measuring unit of electrical power, a watt is determined by multiplying the voltage times the amperage. Using this formula you can easily understand that to get 40 amps of 110 to 120 volts of electrical power you need a 4000 watt generator. When you consider that most homes have a minimum of 200 amp electrical service (20,000 watts), you can see that you can't put everything electrical from your home into your RV. The same formula applies to direct current.

wheel alignment:

There are four settings for wheel alignment with RVs: caster, camber, toe-in, and tracking. Since wheel alignment causes much grief for RVers, you should have at least a basic understanding of causes, effects, and cures.

Caster is a tilting of the front wheel spindles to give more control to the steering. Caster usually has a rearward tilt (positive) but a slightly forward tilt (negative) is often used. The degree of tilting, whether forward of rearward, will depend on the type of steering mechanism and the general design of the vehicle. Borderline negative caster on a motor home loaded heavy in the rear, for example, could give a wandering effect. Too much positive caster with a heavily front-loaded vehicle could make steering more difficult. Incorrect caster setting will not wear tires.

Camber can be considered an adjustment of anything off of a straight line. Camber on a vehicle wheel is the tilting of the wheel inward or outward. To compensate for load, a vehicle's wheels on a particular axle may be set closer at the bottom than at the top (positive camber). To assist in high-speed turning, however, a vehicle's wheels may be set closer at the top than at the bottom (negative camber). A wheel-alignment expert will often adjust camber according to vehicle use and front end tolerances. The easiest way to check for proper camber setting is to watch the tires for wear. If camber setting is not almost perfect, you'll find your RV's tires wearing on one edge more than

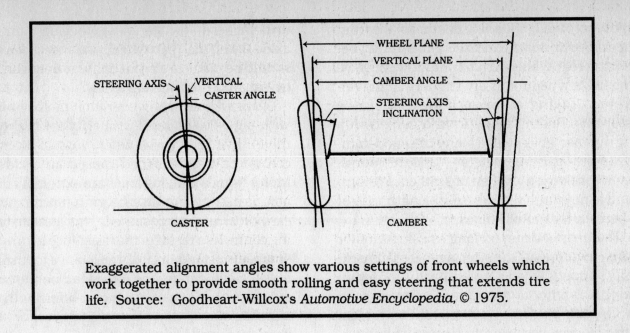

Exaggerated alignment angles show various settings of front wheels which work together to provide smooth rolling and easy steering that extends tire life. Source: Goodheart-Willcox's *Automotive Encyclopedia*, © 1975.

the other. Of course, handling and braking will not be up to par if the camber is way off.

Toe-in is another setting you should be conscious of in motor homes. Motor home rear wheels are set straight ahead whereas the front wheels have a slight toe-in to adjust for tolerances built into the steering system. A bad toe-in setting (whether too much in or too much out) causes a buffing of the tread instead of just rolling on the tread as your vehicle goes down the road. If toe-in is off, the steering wheel may be off center or the front wheels may pull hard to the left or right. Toe-in is easily checked and often easily adjusted. The easiest way to check toe-in is by rubbing your fingers across the tread to feel for a feathering or roughness. On rough-use RVs, I often do my own toe-in setting with a steel tape measure—which requires being careful about level and points of reference. The secret of good toe-in maintenance is close monitoring of buffing and steering. All road vehicles should have the alignment checked by an expert with the proper equipment.

wheelbase:

The wheelbase of a vehicle is the distance between the center of the front axle to the center of the rear axle. This measurement is important to RVers because it will be an indication of the unit's stability and maneuverability.

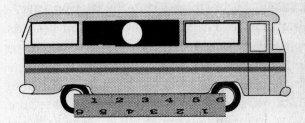

Wheelbase is especially important to motor homers because it will be an indication of the motor home's stability and maneuverability. Motor homes have many problems related to wheelbase. Too many manufacturers are building class A's and C's that have a wheelbase-to-length ratio of close to or under 50 percent. An RV with a short wheelbase may be hard to handle when not loaded for balance or when it's subjected to wind or passing trucks. Any motor home with a wheelbase-to-length ratio of under 54 percent will be fatiguing to drive under normal highway conditions.

Motor homes with low wheelbase-to-length ratios are very sensitive to loading. Although a low wheelbase-to-length ratio motor home might drive well unloaded, floating of the front wheels might occur when weight is added behind the rear wheels. This condition could be dangerous when roads are slippery or gravel-covered. Taking a curve too fast could be disastrous. Pulling away from a curb with a long overhang has peeled many trees and damaged many parking meters — and, of course, the motor home didn't go unscathed. I recommend a minimum wheelbase-to-length ratio of 54 percent for motor homes.

There is a tendency for long wheelbase motor homes to overload the steering axle. This generally happens when RV manufacturers design floor plans without regard for the steering axles' GAWR. The best way to avoid a problem with steering because of steering axle overloading is to weigh the motor home and make sure that you have a minimum payload capacity of at least 10 percent of the front axles' GAWR with driver and passenger in place.

Adding tag axles is a common method of increasing wheelbase while increasing carrying capacity. Although this solution sounds wonderful at first, there are disadvantages to tag axles. A tag axle is a non-driving single wheel axle assembly added by a motor home builder to increase the wheelbase or boost the GVWR rating — or both. It is essentially an inexpensive method of modifying a chassis to meet demands for an increase in length and weight without a major increase in price. Tag axles, in fact, have been known to hinder turning ability — and for that reason RV Consumer Group does not consider tag axles a good solution to short wheelbase motor homes.

Because of the demands placed on RV manufacturers by consumers for wider and longer motor homes, the standard 16,000 to 18,000 GVWR chassis is often overburdened. The addition of a tag axle increases the GVWR by 2000 to 3000 pounds. This, of course, allows the manufacturer to add more options — and a slideout room. Even though the manufacturer often claims that the effective wheelbase is increased by up to 48 inches, I add a maximum of 24 inches to the standard wheelbase for tag axles. I believe that wheelbase measurement should be made to a point halfway between the driving axle and the tag axle.

I am adamant, however, that motor homes with tag axles be used primarily for highway travel. I've seen cases where loss of steering control on a gravel road caused an accident. Motor homes with tag axles are extremely dangerous in snow because steering control can be easily lost and not regained. This loss of steering control is a result of the resistance to turning of wheels in tandem. This resistance to turning is especially dangerous if the load on the front axle is light. If you own a motor home with tag axles, be sure to slow down on gravel or slippery roads and keep monitoring the weight on your steering axle.

On the other side of the picture, a motor home with too long a wheelbase has a long turning radius and does not make an ideal utility vehicle. If a compromise is made, it should be done with an understanding of the consequences of that compromise. We have, unfortunately, learned about the handling characteristics of vehicles from accident reports.

widebody:

The normal maximum width of an RV is 96 inches. Anything over 96 inches is considered a widebody. Some states (under the pressure of RV manufacturing lobbyists) have approved RV widths to 102 inches for secondary roads — but not all. Keep in mind that widebody RVs with an awning attached are, at this time, illegal for highway travel.

Before you consider a widebody, you should look carefully at where you'll be going, what you'll be doing, and how your driving habits and reaction time might influence the safety factor of RV driving. Although widebody RVs appeal to snowbirds and fulltimers, I can assure you that the extra width makes a big difference when you get off the wide highways and into the countryside. Long and wide can also be a problem for many when traveling city streets. Think about it before you jump into something big.

wholesale:

Every RV dealership must make a profit on the RVs they sell. To make a profit, they buy or take in trades at a wholesale value and sell them at a retail value. Although the difference between wholesale and retail could usually reflect approximately 30% gross profit, daily interest charges on inventory (flooring) and other costs of keeping an RV on the sales lot can easily consume much of this. The wholesale value of a new RV is often called invoice. The wholesale value of a used RV is usually determined by using the Kelley Blue Book or the N.A.D.A. Appraisal Guide.

Zzzz:

RVers: Don't sleep on the job! Entering the RVing lifestyle is a challenging affair. If you take it as anything else, you are most probably going to be disappointed and disillusioned very shortly. ✦

A poem for all snowbirds and fulltiming RVers

As a boy I climbed a tree
as a teen the girls I'd see,
as a man I strolled so bold,
as a parent I was getting old;
but now the years are getting on
and I look back on all that's gone,
I shed no tear
I must confess
for I'm having fun
with much, much less.

jd gallant

Brand Directory

To help you locate RV manufacturers, we have included a brand directory in this section. Please recognize that some manufacturers have gone out of business or sold out to another manufacturer. Thus, the directory may not contain information for all manufacturers.

The directory is sorted in alphabetical order by brand name, followed by manufacturer name and telephone number. When available, we have furnished the manufacturer's toll free number.

Directory by Type, Brand, and Manufacturer

Type	Brand	Manufacturer	Telephone #
MHA	Admiral	Holiday Rambler / Monaco	800-650-7337
MHA	Adventurer	Winnebago	515-582-3535
MHA	Aerbus	Rexhall	805-726-0565
MHA	Affinity	Country Coach	800-654-0223
MHA	Allegro	Tiffin	256-356-8661
MHA	Allure	Country Coach	800-654-0223
MHA	Alpine Coach	Western RV	509-457-4133
MHA	American Clipper	Rexhall	805-726-0565
MHA	American Dream	Fleetwood	800-648-6582
MHA	American Eagle	Fleetwood	800-648-6582
MHA	American Tradition	Fleetwood	800-648-6582
MHA	Anthem	Rexhall	805-726-0565
MHA	Brave	Winnebago	515-582-3535
MHA	Chieftain	Winnebago	515-582-3535
MHA	Concept	Country Coach	800-654-0223
MHA	Continental	Safari	541-995-8214
MHA	Cruise Air	Georgie Boy	800-521-8733
MHA	Cruise Master	Georgie Boy	800-521-8733
MHA	Diplomat	Monaco	800-634-0855
MHA	Discovery	Fleetwood	800-444-4905
MHA	Dolphin	National RV	909-943-6007
MHA	Dutch Star	Newmar	219-773-7791
MHA	Dynasty	Monaco	800-634-0855
MHA	Encounter	Georgie Boy	800-521-8733
MHA	Endeavor	Holiday Rambler / Monaco	800-650-7337
MHA	Executive	Monaco	800-634-0855
MHA	Foretravel	Foretravel	800-955-6226
MHA	Imperial	Holiday Rambler / Monaco	800-650-7337
MHA	Intrigue	Country Coach	800-654-0223
MHA	Isata	Dynamax	888-295-7859
MHA	Ivory	Safari	541-995-8214
MHA	Kountry Aire	Newmar	219-773-7791
MHA	Kountry Star	Newmar	219-773-7791
MHA	La Palma	Monaco	800-634-0855
MHA	Landau	Georgie Boy	800-521-8733
MHA	London Aire	Newmar	219-773-7791
MHA	Luxor	Winnebago	515--582-3535

Directory by Type, Brand, and Manufacturer

Type	Brand	Manufacturer	Telephone #
MHA	Magna	Country Coach	800-654-0223
MHA	Marquis	Beaver / Safari	800-423-2837
MHA	Mountain Aire	Newmar	219-773-7791
MHA	Navigator	Holiday Rambler / Monaco	800-650-7337
MHA	Newell	Newell Coach	888-363-9355
MHA	Overland Lorado	Overland / Odessa	219-293-0595
MHA	Pace Arrow Vision	Fleetwood	909-351-3500
MHA	Patriot	Beaver / Safari	800-423-2837
MHA	Pinnacle	Thor West	909-390-0300
MHA	Pursuit	Georgie Boy	800-521-8733
MHA	Renegade	Harney Coach / Safari	541-573-8800
MHA	Residency	Thor West	909-390-0300
MHA	RexAir	Rexhall	805-726-0565
MHA	Rose Air	Rexhall	805-726-0565
MHA	Sahara	Safari	541-995-8214
MHA	Sea Breeze	National RV	909-943-6007
MHA	Sea View	National RV	909-943-6007
MHA	Serengeti	Safari	541-995-8214
MHA	Signature	Monaco	800-634-0855
MHA	Suncruiser	Winnebago	515-582-3535
MHA	Sunflyer	Winnebago	515-582-3535
MHA	Sunrise	Winnebago	515-582-3535
MHA	Swinger	Georgie Boy	616-663-3415
MHA	Tradewinds	National RV	909-943-6007
MHA	Trek	Safari	541-995-8214
MHA	Triple E	Triple E - Canada	204-325-4361
MHA	Tropi-Cal	National RV	909-943-6007
MHA	Ultimate Advantage	Winnebago	515-582-3535
MHA	Ultimate Freedom	Winnebago	515-582-3535
MHA	Vacationer	Holiday Rambler / Monaco	800-650-7337
MHA	Vectra Grand Tour	Winnebago	515-582-3535
MHA	Vision	Rexhall	805-726-0565
MHA	Vogue	Featherlite	800-468-6483
MHA	Wanderlodge	Blue Bird	912-825-2021
MHA	Windsor	Monaco	800-634-0855
MHA	Zanzibar	Safari	541-995-8214
MHB	Coach House	Coach House	941-485-0984

Directory by Type, Brand, and Manufacturer

Type	Brand	Manufacturer	Telephone #
MHB	Leisure Travel	Leisure Travel Vans	204-822-3009
MHB	Phoenix Camper Van	Phoenix USA	219-848-0207
MHB	Pleasure-Way	Pleasure-Way	306-934-6578
MHB	Roadtrek	Home & Park Canada	800-663-0066
MHB	Sportsmobile	Sportsmobile	800-828-8506
MHB	Travel Home	Knighthill Leisure Group	604-273-1800
MHB	Xplorer	Xplorer	800-343-2771
MHC	Bigfoot	Bigfoot Ind. - Canada	250-546-2155
MHC	Born Free	Born Free Motorcoach	800-247-1835
MHC	Chinook	Trail Wagons	800-552-8886
MHC	Jamboree	Fleetwood	800-444-4905
MHC	Jayco	Jayco	800-785-2926
MHC	Kustom Koach	Kustom Koach / Travelaire	403-347-6641
MHC	Lazy Daze	Lazy Daze	909-627-1103
MHC	Maverick	Georgie Boy	800-521-8733
MHC	Max	Country Coach	800-654-0223
MHC	Minnie Winnie	Winnebago	515-582-3535
MHC	Phoenix Cruiser	Phoenix USA	219-848-0207
MHC	Rialta	Winnebago	515-582-3535
MHC	Royal Classic	Glendale RV	519-245-1600
MHC	Safari	Safari	541-995-8214
MHC	Spirit	Winnebago	515-582-3535
MHC	Sundancer	Winnebago	515-582-3535
MHC	Tioga	Fleetwood	800-444-4905

Get these other books to complete your research:

How to Buy an RV
Without Getting Ripped Off

JD Gallant, author of several RV consumer books, candidly shows you how to save thousands of dollars with 10 simple rules and hundreds of secrets. This book is guaranteed to put *you* in control of the buying process.

Find out:

- ❖ How to avoid getting trapped into the wrong RV.
- ❖ How to work a trade into a deal.
- ❖ How to figure a fair retail price.
- ❖ How to work a discount to within 2%.
- ❖ How to know when you're getting the best deal possible.

Here's what consumers are saying about this book:

"After reading this book we visited some dealerships and managed to escape with our plan and our money — it was easy to recognize the methods employed by the Smoothies we encountered. Thank you!"
Sharon & Elwood Leonard, Wisconsin

"Putting this book into action opened my eyes and made me an informed consumer who won't get ripped off. It is invaluable."
Gunter Leonhard, California

"Following the book's rules we let the salespersons talk their talk, but we were looking through the eyes of your experience and advice. We were armed with more information than many people who have been RVing for years."
Gene Rusco, California

How to Outwit any Auto, Truck, or RV Dealer *Every Time*

JD Gallant, author of several RV consumer books, now brings you this tongue-in-cheek review of the auto and RV sales arena to put you in control of the buying process.

How to Outwit any Auto, Truck, or RV Dealer Every Time is a powerful auto and recreational vehicle buying guide. Once you know the secrets in this book, your buying habits will never be the same.

Every day consumers pay too much money for overpriced vehicles and needless services. If you want to keep from being manipulated, this book is for you!

To order call 1-800-405-3325.

JOIN
RV CONSUMER GROUP
AND HELP SAFEGUARD
THE RVING LIFESTYLE.

CALL 1-800-405-3325
OR VISIT OUR WEBSITE AT
WWW.RV.ORG